A DICTIONARY
OF
NORTH AMERICAN AUTHORS

A DICTIONARY

OF

NORTH AMERICAN AUTHORS

DECEASED BEFORE 1950

Compiled by

W. STEWART WALLACE, M.A., LL.D.
LIBRARIAN OF THE UNIVERSITY OF TORONTO

THE RYERSON PRESS
TORONTO   CANADA

REPUBLISHED BY GALE RESEARCH COMPANY, BOOK TOWER, DETROIT, 1968

Reprinted with permission of the
original publisher

Library of Congress Catalog Card Number: 68-19955

PREFACE

THIS *Dictionary* will, it is hoped, prove useful to students of North American literature and, indeed, to students of all those subjects on which North Americans have written. It is a key to information about North Americans who have written on subjects ranging from agriculture to zymology. But this is not its chief object. It is primarily a tool for librarians, and especially for library cataloguers. Its object is to provide, where possible, those details about North American authors—such as the full name of the author and the date and place of his or her birth and death—for which librarians have often to make a prolonged and sometimes unsuccessful search.

When I first embarked, some ten or twelve years ago, on the preparation of this *Dictionary,* I intended to make it a biobibliography, giving not only the full name of the author and the details of birth and death, but also a list of each author's works. But the recent publication of the *Printed Catalogue of Library of Congress Cards,* with its *Supplement,* containing a high percentage of all publications of North American authors, has rendered the addition of bibliographical data hardly necessary; and in any case the greatly increased cost of printing has made the inclusion of bibliographies a prohibitive luxury. Instead, it has been decided to add to each entry, in square brackets, numerals indicating some sources of bibliographical, as well as further biographical, information. A key to these symbols will be found immediately following this preface. Where no numerals have been added, it must be understood that the information included in the entries has been derived from obituary notices, from private enquiry, or from the *Printed Catalogue of Library of Congress Cards.* For the dates of birth and death in some of the entries in the Library of Congress cards, I have not ventured to inflict on the Library of Congress enquiries in regard to its authorities. To do so would have been an imposition. On the other hand, I have no hesitation in saying that there will be found in this *Dictionary* many dates of birth and death not to be found in the Library of Congress cards.

Considerations of space have limited in several ways the scope of the present work. In the first place, it has been found necessary to exclude those authors who have published only pamphlets, articles in periodicals, or reprints. In the second place, those authors have been excluded whose works, published posthumously, have contained the necessary biographical information. In the third place, authors have been omitted about whom no useful information could be ascertained.

That the *Dictionary* contains only notices of authors no longer living requires perhaps a word of explanation and justification. There are in existence so many periodical sources of information with regard to living North American authors —such as *Who's who in America, Who's who among North American authors, Current biography, Who's who in Canada,* and the *Canadian who's who*—that

v

to include living authors would have meant the duplication of material already easily accessible, and soon out-of-date. If the present work is essentially a necrology, it follows at least the august example set by the *Dictionary of national biography* and the *Dictionary of American biography*.

In a work which is mainly a compilation, and in which there is a multiplicity of detail, it is not to be expected that errors will not be found, both factual and typographical. I shall be grateful if those who find such errors will be good enough to call my attention to them.

I have been indebted to a great many people who have answered my enquiries about the date of death of North American authors (which is always a guide to valuable obituary notices), and among these I should like to mention especially my colleagues in libraries across the length and breadth of North America; but they are so numerous that I cannot acknowledge my debt to each of them individually. I can only hope that, if they see these lines, they will accept the general assurance of my thanks. I should, however, fail in my duty if I did not here express my gratitude to my secretary, Miss Julia Jarvis, who has collaborated with me in preparing the manuscript for the printer and in seeing the proofs through the press.

W. S. W.

University of Toronto Library.

KEY TO REFERENCE SYMBOLS

1. A Johnson and D. Malone (eds.), *Dictionary of American biography*, 21 vols. and index (New York, 1929-37).
1a. H. E. Starr (ed.), *Dictionary of American biography*, supplement I (New York, 1944).
2. *The Encyclopedia Americana*, revised ed., 30 vols. (New York, 1937).
2a. *The Americana annual* (New York, 1923—).
3. J. G. Wilson and J. Fiske (eds.), *Appleton's cyclopaedia of American biography*, 6 vols. (New York, 1887-89).
3a. J. G. Wilson, *Appleton's cyclopaedia of American biography*, vol. vii (New York, 1900).
3b. *Appleton's annual cyclopaedia*, 1861-1903.
4. *National cyclopaedia of American biography*, 23 vols. (New York, 1892-1947).
5. R. Johnson (ed.), *Biographical dictionary of America*, 10 vols. (Boston, 1906).
6. S. A. Allibone, *A critical dictionary of English literature*, 3 vols. (Philadelphia, 1863-71).
6a. J. F. Kirk, *A supplement to Allibone's critical dictionary of English literature*, 2 vols. (Philadelphia, 1891).
7. W. J. Burke and W. D. Howe, *American authors and books* (New York, 1943).
8. O. F. Adams, *A dictionary of American authors*, 5th ed., revised and enlarged (Boston, 1904).
9. S. J. Kunitz and H. Haycroft (eds.), *American authors, 1600-1900* (New York, 1938).
10. A. N. Marquis (ed.), *Who's who in America*, vol. 1—(Chicago, 1900—).
11. *Who's who among North American authors*, vol. 1—(Los Angeles, 1921—).
12. M. Block, *Current biography* (New York, 1940—).
13. J. McK. Cattell and J. Cattell, *American men of science*, 6 vols. (New York, 1906—).
14. J. Cattell, *Directory of American scholars* (Lancaster, Pa., 1942).
15. S. J. Kunitz and H. Haycroft, *The junior book of authors* (New York, 1935).
16. D. Howes (ed.), *American women* (Los Angeles, 1935).
17. B. M. Fullerton, *Selective bibliography of American literature* (New York, 1932).
18. E. C. Stedman, *An American anthology, 1787-1900* (Boston, 1901).
19. J. C. Stockbridge (comp.), *The Anthony memorial* (Providence, R.I., 1886).
20. O. Thompson, *The international cyclopedia of music and musicians* (New York, 1939).
21. *The guide to Catholic literature*, 2 vols. (Detroit, 1940-44).
22. M. Hoehn, *Catholic authors* (Newark, 1948).
23. *The American Catholic who's who* (Detroit, Mich., 1935—).
24. W. E. McIntyre, *Baptist authors*, 3 parts (Montreal, 1914).
25. E. C. Starr, *A Baptist bibliography*, section A (Philadelphia, 1947).
26. W. Cathcart, *The Baptist encyclopaedia*, 2 vols. (Philadelphia, 1881).
27. W. S. Wallace, *The dictionary of Canadian biography*, 2 vols. (Toronto, 1945).
28. Sir C. G. D. Roberts and A. L. Tunnell (eds.) *A standard dictionary of Canadian who was who*, 2 vols. (Toronto, 1934-38).
29. H. J. Morgan, *Bibliotheca canadensis* (Ottawa, 1867).
30. *Canadian who's who*, vols. 1-4 (Toronto, 1910-48).
31. H. J. Morgan (ed.), *The Canadian men and women of the time* (Toronto, 1898).
31a. H. J. Morgan (ed.), *The Canadian men and women of the time* (Toronto, 1912).
32. J. B. Allaire, *Dictionnaire biographique du clergé canadien-français*, 6 vols. (St. Hyacinthe, Que., 1908-34).
33. R. J. Long, *Nova Scotia authors and their work* (East Orange, N.J., 1918).
34. E. A. Alderman and C. A. Smith (eds.), *Library of Southern literature*, 17 vols., (Atlanta, Ga., 1929).
35. E. J. Hinkel (ed.), *Biographies of California authors*, 2 vols. (Oakland, Calif., 1942).
36. N. Bateman and others, *Historical encyclopedia of Illinois*, 2 vols. (Chicago, 1929).
37. A. Marple, *Iowa authors and their works* (Des Moines, Ia., 1918).
38. J. Williamson, *A bibliography of the state of Maine*, 2 vols. (Portland, Me., 1876).
39. Madge V. K. Goodrich, *A bibliography of Michigan authors* (Richmond, Va., 1928).
40. Bernice M. Foster, *Michigan novelists* (Ann Arbor, Mich., 1928).
41. A. Powers, *History of Oregon literature* (Portland, Ore., 1935).
42. G. A. Wauchope, *The writers of South Carolina* (Columbia, S.C., 1910).

43. M. D. Gilman, *The bibliography of Vermont* (Burlington, Vt., 1897).
44. Mary E. Hazeltine, *One hundred years of Wisconsin authorship* (Madison, Wis., 1937).
45. *Amherst College biographical record of the graduates and non-graduates, 1821-1939* (Amherst, Mass., 1939).
46. *General catalogue of Bowdoin College and the Medical School of Maine, 1794-1912* (Brunswick, Me., 1912).
47. *The historical catalogue of Brown University, 1764-1934* (Providence, R.I., 1936).
48. *Columbia University alumni register, 1754-1931* (New York, 1932).
49. *Dartmouth College and Associated Schools general catalogue* (Hanover, N.H., 1940).
50. *Alumni catalogue of Davidson College, 1837-1924* (Charlotte, N.C., 1924).
51. *Harvard University quinquennial catalogue of the officers and graduates, 1636-1930* (Cambridge, Mass., 1930), supplemented by J. L. Sibley, *Biographical sketches of graduates of Harvard University,* 6 vols. (Cambridge, Mass., 1873-1942) and the class books of the various years.
52. *The semi-centennial alumni record of the University of Illinois* (Chicago, 1918).
53. *University of Michigan catalogue of graduates, non-graduates, officers, and members of the faculties, 1837-1921* (Ann Arbor, Mich., 1923).
54. *Alumni history of the University of North Carolina,* 2nd ed. (Durham, N.C., 1924).
55. *General alumni catalogue of the University of Pennsylvania* (Philadelphia, 1922).
56. *General catalogue of Princeton University, 1746-1906* (Princeton, N.J., 1908), supplemented by *Biographical catalogue of the Princeton Theological Seminary, 1815-1932* (Princeton, N.J., 1933).
57. *Stanford University alumni directory, 1891-1931* (Stanford University, Calif., 1932).
58. *Vassar College alumnae biographical register* (Poughkeepsie, N.Y., 1939).
59. *General catalogue of the University of Vermont and State Agricultural College, 1791-1900* (Burlington, Vt., 1901).
60. *Alumni record of Wesleyan University, Middletown, Conn.,* 4th ed. (New Haven, Conn., 1911).
61. *General catalogue of the officers and graduates of Williams College* (Williamstown, Mass., 1910).
62. *Catalogue of the officers and graduates of Yale University, 1701-1924* (New Haven, Conn., 1924). supplemented by F. B. Dexter, *Biographical sketches of the graduates of Yale College,* 6 vols. (New York, 1885-1912), and *Obituary record of graduates of Yale College* (New Haven, Conn., 1860—).
63. *General biographical catalogue of Auburn Theological Seminary, 1818-1918* (Auburn, N.Y., 1918).
64. *Alphabetic biographical catalog, The Crozer Theological Seminary, 1855-1933* (Chester, Pa., 1933).
65. *Drew Theological Seminary alumni record, 1869-1895* (New York, 1895).
66. *McCormick Theological Seminary general catalogue, 1830-1912* (Chicago, 1912).
67. *General catalogue of the Colgate-Rochester Divinity School, 1819-1930* (Rochester, N.Y., 1930).
68. *Alumni catalogue of Union Theological Seminary, 1836-1926* (New York, 1926).
69. *Kappa Alpha record, 1825-1940* (n.p., 1941).
70. W. Upham and Mrs. Rose B. Dunlap, *Minnesota biographies, 1655-1912* (Collections of the Minnesota Historical Society, vol. xiv, St. Paul, Minn., 1912).
71. P.K. Foley, *American authors* (Boston, 1897).
72. M. Johnson, *American first editions,* 4th ed. (New York, 1942).
73. W. J. Coates, *A bibliography of Vermont poetry,* vol. I (Montpelier, Vt., 1942).
74. J. W. Townsend, *Kentucky in American letters, 1784-1912,* 2 vols. (Cedar Rapids, Ia., 1912).
75. M. H. Marable and E. Boylan, *A handbook of Oklahoma writers* (Norman, Okla., 1939).
76. H. H. Kelly, *A cyclopedia of American medical biography,* 2 vols. (Philadelphia, 1912).
77. W. T. Wynn, *Southern literature* (New York, 1932).
78. H. E. Shepherd, *The representative authors of Maryland* (New York, 1911).

A DICTIONARY
OF
NORTH AMERICAN AUTHORS

A

Aaron, Samuel, clergyman and educationist, b. New Britain, Pa., 1800; d. Mount Holly, N.J., April 11, 1865. [3]

Abarbanell, Jacob Ralph, lawyer, novelist, and playwright, b. New York, N.Y., 1852; d. New York, N.Y., Nov. 9, 1922. [10]

Abbatt, William, historian, b. New York, N.Y., 1851; d. New York, N.Y., Sept. 14, 1934. [7; 10; 11]

Abbe, Cleveland, meteorologist, b. New York, N.Y., 1838; d. Washington, D.C., Oct. 28, 1916. [1; 3; 4; 6; 10]

Abbe, Frederick Randolph, poet, b. Litchfield, Conn., 1827; d. Dorchester, Mass., March 31, 1889. [62]

Abbey, Everett Lucius, educationist, b. 1855; d. Cleveland, O., Jan. 21, 1945.

Abbey, Henry, poet, b. Rondout, N.Y., 1842; d. Tenafly, N.J., June 7, 1911. [1; 4; 10]

Abbey, Richard, clergyman, b. Genesee county, N.Y., 1805; d. 1901. [3]

Abbot, Abiel, clergyman, b. Wilton, N. H., 1765; d. Cambridge, Mass., Jan. 31, 1859. [3; 51]

Abbot, Abiel, clergyman, b. Andover, Mass., 1770; d. Staten Island, N.Y., June 7, 1828. [3; 51]

Abbot, Everett Vergnies, lawyer, b. Meadville, Pa., 1862; d. Milton, N.Y., Aug. 19, 1925. [4; 10]

Abbot, Ezra, biblical critic, b. Jackson, Me., 1819; d. Cambridge, Mass., March 21, 1884. [1; 3; 46]

Abbot, Francis Ellingwood, clergyman and philosopher, b. Boston, Mass., 1836; d. Oct. 23, 1903. [1; 3; 10]

Abbot, Gorham Dummer, clergyman and educationist, b. Brunswick, Me., 1807; d. South Natick, Mass., Aug. 3, 1874. [1; 46]

Abbot, Henry Larcom, military engineer, b. Beverly, Mass., 1831; d. Cambridge, Mass., Oct. 1, 1927. [1; 3; 10]

Abbot, Joel, physician, b. Fairfield, Conn., 1766; d. Washington, Ga., Nov. 19, 1826. [3]

Abbot, William Ebenezer, clergyman, b. Beverly, Mass., 1810; d. Dorchester, Mass., May 4, 1888. [46]

Abbot, Willis John, journalist, b. New Haven, Conn., March 16, 1863; d. Brookline, Mass., May 19, 1934. [2; 10; 46]

Abbott, Alexander Crever, physician, b. Baltimore, Md., 1860; d. Cape Cod, Mass., Sept. 11, 1935. [10]

Abbott, Arletta Maria, educationist, b. Watertown, Conn., 1856; d. Coconut Grove, Fla., Feb. 22, 1933. [53; 58]

Abbott, Arthur Vaughan, civil engineer, b. New York, N.Y., 1854; d. 1906. [10]

Abbott, Augustus Levi, lawyer, b. Weymouth, Mass., 1858; d. St. Louis, Mo., Oct. 15, 1934. [10; 47]

Abbott, Austin, lawyer, b. Boston, Mass., 1831; d. New York, N.Y., April 19, 1869. [1; 3]

Abbott, Benjamin Vaughan, lawyer, b. Boston, Mass., 1830; d. Brooklyn, N.Y., Feb. 17, 1890. [1; 4; 8]

Abbott, Byrdine Akers, clergyman, b. Abbott, Va., 1866; d. St. Louis, Mo., June 24, 1936. [10]

Abbott, Charles Conrad, naturalist and archaeologist, b. Trenton, N.J., 1843; d. Bristol, Pa., July 27, 1919. [1; 4; 8; 10]

Abbott, Charles Edward, novelist, b. Hallowell, Me., 1811; d. Hartford, Conn., July 25, 1880. [45; 46]

Abbott, Edward, clergyman, b. Farmington, Me., 1841; d. Boston, Mass., April 5, 1908. [1; 2; 8; 10]

Abbott, Edwin Milton, lawyer and poet, b. Philadelphia, Pa., 1877; d. Philadelphia, Pa., Nov. 8, 1940. [10]

Abbott, Ernest Hamlin, clergyman, b. Cornwall-on-Hudson, N.Y., 1870; d. Aug. 8, 1931. [8; 10; 51; 68]

Abbott, Frances Matilda, naturalist, b. Concord, N. H., 1857; d. Concord, N.H., Sept. 21, 1939. [10]

Abbott, Frank Frost, classical scholar, b. Reading, Conn., 1860; d. Switzerland, July 23, 1924. [1; 2; 4; 10]

Abbott, Frederick Wallace, physician, b. Dover, N.H., 1851; d. Taunton, Mass., June 19, 1919. [10]

Abbott, Grace, social worker, b. Grand Island, Neb., 1878; d. Chicago, Ill., June 19, 1939. [10]

Abbott, Harry, lawyer, b. Montreal, Que., 1857; d. St. Augustine, Fla., March 5, 1898. [31]

Abbott, Henry Pryor Almon, bishop, b. Halifax, N.S., 1881; d. Lexington, Ky., April 4, 1945. [10]

Abbott, Herbert Vaughan, educationist, b. Terre Haute, Ind., 1865; d. Northampton, Mass., March 24, 1929. [10;45]

Abbott, Jacob, clergyman, educationist, and writer of books for children, b. Hallowell, Me., 1803; d. Farmington, Me., Aug. 8, 1879. [1; 2; 3; 4; 8]

Abbott, James Francis, biologist, b. Greeley, Colo., 1876; d. July 3, 1926. [10; 57]

Abbott, Sir John Joseph Caldwell, lawyer and politician, b. St. Andrews, Lower Canada, 1820; d. Montreal, Que., Oct., 31, 1893. [27]

1

Abbott, John Stevens Cabot, clergyman and historian, b. Brunswick, Me., 1805; d. Fair Haven, Conn., June 17, 1877. [1; 2; 3; 4; 6]

Abbott, Joseph, b. Cumberland, England, 1789; d. Montreal, Que., Jan., 1863. [27]

Abbott, Keene, journalist and novelist, b. Fremont, Neb., 1876; d. Omaha, Neb., July 5, 1941. [10]

Abbott, Lawrence Fraser, journalist, b. Brooklyn, N.Y., 1859; d. New York, N.Y., Feb 6, 1933. [10]

Abbott, Lemuel Abijah, soldier and genealogist, b. 1842; d. 1911.

Abbott, Luther Jewett, educationist, b. 1872; d. Edmond, Okla., March 9, 1914. [10]

Abbott, Lyman, clergyman and editor, b. Roxbury, Mass., 1835; d. New York, N.Y., Oct. 22, 1922. [1; 2; 3; 8; 10]

Abbott, Mrs. Mary Perkins, née Ives, novelist, b. Salem, Mass., 1851; d. 1904. [10]

Abbott, Mather Almon, educationist, b. Halifax, N.S., 1874; d. Lawrenceville, N.J., May 17, 1934. [10]

Abbott, Maude Elizabeth Seymour, physician, b. St. Andrews, Que., 1867; d. Montreal, Que., Sept. 2, 1940. [30]

Abbott, Nathan, educationist, b. Norridgewock, Me., 1854; d. San Diego, Calif., Jan. 29, 1941. [10; 62]

Abbott, Russell Bigelow, educationist, b. Brookville, Ind., 1823; d. Albert Lea, Minn., Jan. 14, 1917. [8; 10; 70]

Abbott, Samuel Warren, physician, b. Woburn, Mass., 1837; d. Oct. 22, 1904. [1; 10]

Abbott, Twyman Osmand, lawyer, d. 1937.

Abbott, Wallace Calvin, lawyer, b. Bridgewater, Vt., 1857; d. Chicago, Ill., July 4, 1921. [10; 49]

Abbott, Walter Scott, journalist and local historian, b. Pomfret, Vt., 1830; d. ?

Abdullah, Achmed, novelist, b. Yalta, Russia, 1881; d. New York, N. Y., May 12, 1945. [7; 10; 11; 12]

Abeel, David, missionary, b. New Brunswick, N.J., 1804; d. Albany, N.Y., Sept 4, 1846. [1; 2; 3; 4]

Abel, Mrs. Mary W., née Hinman, dietitian, b. Montour Falls, N.Y., 1850; d. Baltimore, Md., Jan 20, 1938. [11]

Abelow, Samuel Philip, educationist, d. New York, N.Y., Nov. 14, 1948.

Abercrombie, James, clergyman and educationist, b. Philadelphia, Pa., 1758; d. Philadelphia, Pa., June 26, 1841. [3]

Abercrombie, John William, educationist, b. St. Clair county, Ala., 1866; d. Anniston, Ala., July 2, 1940. [10; 34]

Abernethy, Alonzo, educationist, b. Sandusky county, O., 1836; d. Des Moines, Ia., Feb. 20, 1915. [10; 37]

Abert, Sylvanus Thayer, civil engineer, b. Philadelphia, Pa., 1828; d. 1903. [3; 10; 56]

Abraham, Robert, journalist, b. Cumberlandshire, England; d. Montreal, Que., Nov. 10, 1854. [27]

Abrams, Albert, physician, b. San Francisco, Calif., 1863; d. San Francisco, Calif., Jan 13, 1924. [1; 2; 10; 35]

Absinthe, Père (pseud.), See Kelly, George C.

Acheson, Alexander Wilson, physician, b. Washington, Pa., 1842; d. Denison, Tex., Sept. 7, 1934. [10]

Acheson, Arthur, Shakespearian scholar, b. Kent, England, 1864; d. New York, N.Y., Sept. 5, 1930.

Acheson, Edward Goodrich, inventor, b. Washington, Pa., 1856; d. New York, N.Y., July 6, 1931. [10]

Achintre, Auguste, journalist, b. Besançon, France, 1834; d. Montreal, Que., June 25, 1886. [27]

Achorn, Edgar Oakes, lawyer, b. Newcastle, Me., 1859; d. 1935. [46]

Achorn, John Warren, physician, b. Newcastle, Me., 1857; d. Annisquam, Mass., Aug. 5, 1926. [46]

Ackerman, William K., railway president, b. New York., N.Y., 1832; d. Feb. 7, 1905. [36]

Ackley, Mrs. Mary Ellen, née Medley, pioneer, b. Missouri, 1842; d. California, about 1929. [35]

Adair, Mrs. Bethenia Angelina, née Owens, physician, b. 1840; d. Astoria, Ore., Sept. 11, 1926.

Adair, Robert, clergyman b. Belfast, Ireland, 1802; d. Philadelphia, Pa., June 20, 1890. [56]

Adam, George, physicist, b. 1846; d. ?

Adam, Graeme Mercer, journalist, b. Loanhead, Midlothian, Scotland, 1839; d. New York, N.Y., Oct. 30, 1912. [27]

Adam, Robert Borthwick, merchant and book-collector, b. 1863; d. Buffalo, N.Y., April 11, 1940.

Adams, Abigail, letter-writer, b. Weymouth, Mass., 1744; d. Quincy, Mass., Oct. 28, 1818. [1; 3]

Adams, Alice Dana, religious writer, b. 1864; d. March, 1934.

Adams, Alva, politician, b. Iowa county, Wis.; d. Battle Creek, Mich., Nov. 1, 1922. [10]

Adams, Amos, clergyman and historian, b. Medfield, Mass., 1728; d. Dorchester, Mass., Oct. 5, 1775. [3; 51]

Adams, Andy, cowboy, b. Whitley county, Ind., 1859; d. Sept. 26, 1935. [7; 10; 11]

Adams, Braman Blanchard, journalist, b. 1851; d. Mount Vernon, N.Y., June 27, 1944.

Adams, Brooks, lawyer and historian, b. Quincy, Mass., 1848; d. Boston Mass., Feb. 13, 1927. [1; 10; 51]

Adams, Charles, clergyman and educationist, b. Stratham, N.H., 1808; d. Washington, D.C., Jan. 18, 1890. [8; 46]

Adams, Charles Abel, novelist, b. 1854; d. ?

Adams, Charles Baker, naturalist, b. Dorchester, Mass., 1814; d. St. Thomas, West Indies, Jan. 19, 1853. [1; 3; 4]

Adams, Charles Clarence, educationist, b. West Sunbury, Pa., 1883; d. Cairo, Egypt, March 9, 1948.

Adams, Charles Coffin, clergyman, b. Newburyport, Mass., 1810; d. New York, N.Y., Feb. 24, 1888. [3]

Adams, Charles Collard, genealogist, b. 1836; d. Middletown, Conn., May 4, 1925. [60]

Adams, Charles Darwin, educationist, b. Keene, N,H.. 1856; d. New Milford, Conn., May. 28, 1938. [10]

Adams, Charles Follen, b. Dorchester, Mass., 1842; d. Roxbury, Mass., March. 8, 1918. [1; 3; 4; 10; 17]

Adams, Charles Francis, diplomat and publicist, b. Boston Mass., 1807; d. Boston, Mass., Nov. 21, 1886. [1; 2; 3; 4; 7; 51]

Adams, Charles Francis, historian and publicist, b. Boston, Mass., 1835; d. Washington, D.C., March. 20, 1915. [1; 2; 7; 10; 51]

Adams, Charles Francis, physicist, b. Pike, Wyoming county, N.Y., 1854; d. Detroit, Mich., Oct. 29, 1914. [13; 45]

Adams, Charles Josiah, clergyman, b. New Lisbon, O., 1850; d. July 4, 1924. [8; 10]

Adams, Charles Kendall, educationist and historian, b. Derby, Vt., 1835; d. Redlands, Calif., July 26, 1902. [1; 2; 3; 10; 53]

Adams, Charles Laban, educationist, b. 1856; d. 1914.

Adams, Charles True, lawyer and bridge expert, b. Chicago, Ill., 1900; d. Chicago, Ill., Dec. 15, 1942. [51]

Adams, Cyrus Cornelius, geographer, b. Naperville, Ill., 1849; d. New York, N.Y., May 4, 1928. [10]

Adams, Daniel, physician and educationist, b. Townsend, Mass., 1773; d. Keene, N.H., June 8, 1864. [1; 49]

Adams, Edward Dean, engineer and financier, b. Boston, Mass., 1846; d. New York, N.Y., May 20, 1931. [10]

Adams, Edward Francis, journalist, b. Augusta, Me., 1839; d. San Francisco, Calif., Nov. 19, 1929. [10]

Adams, Eliashib, autobiographer, b. Canterbury, Conn., 1773; d. Bangor, Me., Aug. 28, 1855. [30]

Adams, Mrs. Emma Hildreth, née Drake, writer of religious books for young people, b. Perry, N.Y., 1827; d. probably in Los Angeles, Calif, about 1900. [35]

Adams, Ephraim, clergyman, b. 1818; d. 1907. [37]

Adams, Ephraim Douglass, educationist, b. Decorah, Ia., 1865; d. Stanford University, Calif., Sept. 1, 1930. [1a; 10]

Adams, Ernest Kempton, electrical engineer, b. Boston, Mass., 1873; d. Watkins, N.Y., July 21, 1904. [62]

Adams, Evangeline Smith, astrologer, b. Jersey City, N.J.; d. New York, N.Y., Nov. 10, 1932. [11]

Adams, Francis Colburn, miscellaneous writer, b. South Carolina; d. probably Washington, D.C., soon after 1890. [6; 34]

Adams, Frank Dawson, geologist, b. Montreal, Que., 1859; d. Montreal, Que., Dec. 26, 1942. [30]

Adams, Frederick Upham, inventor and journalist, b. Boston, Mass., 1859; d. Larchmont, N.Y., Aug. 28, 1921. [1; 10]

Adams, Frederick W., physician, b. Pawlet, Vt., 1786; d. Montpelier, Vt., Dec. 17, 1858. [3; 4; 43]

Adams, George Burton, historian, b. Fairfield, Vt., 1851; d. New Haven, Conn., May 26, 1925. [1; 10]

Adams, George Moulton, clergyman, b. Castine, Me., 1824; d. Auburndale, Mass., Jan. 11, 1906. [10; 46]

Adams, Hannah, compiler, b. Medfield, Mass., 1755; d. Boston, Mass., Dec. 15, 1831. [1; 4]

Adams, Harrison (pseud.). See Rathborne, St. George Henry.

Adams, Henry, historian, b. Boston, Mass., 1838; d. Washington, D.C., March 27, 1918. [1; 2; 10]

Adams, Henry Austin, journalist, b. Santiago, Cuba, 1861; d. Coronado, Calif., 1931. [10; 21; 35]

Adams, Henry Carter, economist, b. Davenport, Ia., 1851; d. Ann Arbor, Mich., Aug. 11, 1921. [1; 2; 10]

Adams, Henry Kingman, local historian, b. 1828; d. 1903.

Adams, Henry Wright, clergyman, b. 1818; d. 1881.

Adams, Herbert Baxter, educationist and historian, b. Shuterburg, Mass., 1850; d. Baltimore, Md., July 30, 1901. [1; 2; 3; 10; 45]

Adams, James Alonzo, clergyman, b. Ashland county, O., 1842; d. Chicago, Ill,. June 4, 1925. [10; 68]

Adams, James Barton, journalist, b. Somerset, O., 1843; d. Vancouver, Wash., Oct. 22, 1918. [4]

Adams, James McKee, biblical scholar, b. 1886; d. 1945. [25]

Adams, James Truslow, historian, b. Brooklyn, N.Y., 1878; d. Westport, Conn., May 18, 1949. [10; 11; 12]

Adams, Jasper, educationist, b. Medway, Mass.; d. Charleston, S.C., Oct. 25, 1941. [1; 3]

Adams, Jedidiah Howe, physician and biographer, b. 1866; d. Paoli, Pa., May 25, 1919. [55]

Adams, Jesse Earl, educationist, b. Monroe county, Ind., 1888; d. Lexington, Ky., March 9, 1945. [10]

Adams, John, clergyman and poet, b. 1704; d. Cambridge, Mass., Jan, 23, 1740. [3; 51]

Adams, John, second president of the United States, b. Braintree, Mass., 1735; d. Quincy, Mass., July 4, 1826. [1; 2; 3; 5; 6; 7; 8]

Adams, John, school-teacher, b. Canterbury, Conn., 1772; d. Jacksonville, Ill., April 24, 1863. [62]

Adams, John Coleman, clergyman, b. Malden, Mass., 1849; d. Hartford, Conn., June 22, 1922. [1; 8; 10]

Adams, John Greenleaf, clergyman, b. Portsmouth, N.H., 1810; d. 1887. [6; 8]

Adams, John Quincy, sixth president of the United States, b. Braintree, Mass., 1767; d. Washington, D.C., Feb. 23, 1848. [1; 2; 3; 4; 5; 6; 7]

Adams, John Quincy, clergyman, b. Philadelphia, Pa., 1825; d. New York, N.Y., July 27, 1881. [6; 24; 25]

Adams, John Quincy, clergyman, b. Ogden, N.Y., 1849; d. Waterloo, N.Y., Jan. 1, 1940. [63]

Adams, John Stowell, spiritualist and musician, d. 1893.

Adams, John Turvill, lawyer and novelist, b. Demerara, S. America, 1805; d. Norwich, Conn., March 30, 1882. [8; 62]

Adams, John William, veterinary surgeon, b. Middleton, Miss., 1862; d. Swarthmore, Pa., Oct. 22, 1926. [10]

Adams, Joseph Henry, writer of books for boys, b. Brooklyn, N.Y., 1867; d. Brooklyn, N.Y., Feb. 8, 1941.

Adams, Josiah Quincy, librarian and educationist, b. Greenville, S.C., 1881; d. Washington, D.C., Nov. 10, 1946. [10; 11]

Adams, Julius Walker, civil engineer, b. Boston, Mass., 1812; d. 1899. [4; 8; 10]

Adams, Mary (pseud.). See Ward, Mrs Elizabeth Stuart, née Phelps.

Adams, Mrs. Mary Jane, née **Mathews,** poet and educationist, b. Granard, Ireland, 1840; d. Redlands, Calif., Dec. 10, 1902. [7; 10]

Adams, Moses (pseud.). See Bagby, George William.

Adams, Myron, clergyman, b. East Bloomfield, N. Y., 1841; d. Dec. 29, 1895. [8]

Adams, Myron Howell, physician, b. 1846; d. Bronxville, N.Y., June 6, 1929.

Adams, Myron Winslow, educationist, b. Gilsum, N.H,. 1860; d. West Townsend, Mass., May 26, 1939. [10; 49]

Adams, Nathaniel, local historian, b. Portsmouth, N.H., 1856; d. Exeter, N.H., Aug. 5, 1929. [49]

Adams, Nehemiah, clergyman, b. Salem, Mass., 1806; d. Boston, Mass., Oct. 6, 1878. [4; 51]

Adams, Oscar Fay, littérateur, b. Worcester, Mass., 1855; d. North Truro, Mass., April 30, 1919. [10]

Adams, Robert Chamblet, soldier and miscellaneous writer, b. Boston, Mass., 1839; d. Sedgwick, Me., Aug. 10, 1892.. [6; 8]

Adams, Robert Morrill, educationist and journalist, b. Hill, N.H., 1882; d. Philadelphia, Pa., Dec. 12, 1931. [62]

Adams, Romanzo, sociologist, b. Bloomingdale, Wis., 1868; d. Sept. 10, 1942. [10]

Adams, Samuel, revolutionary politician, b. Boston, Mass., 1722; d. Boston, Mass., Oct. 2, 1803. [1; 2 ; 3; 4; 5; 6; 7]

Adams, Seymour Webster, clergyman, b. Vernon, N.Y., 1815; d. Cleveland, O., Sept. 24, 1864. [67]

Adams, Sherman Wolcott, jurist and local historian, b. 1836; d. 1898. [51]

Adams, Silas, local historian, b. Bowdoinham, Me., 1841; d. Waterville, Me., March 12, 1926. [38]

Adams, Thomas Albert Smith, clergyman and poet, b. Noxubee county, Miss., 1839; d. Jackson, Miss., Dec. 21, 1888. [34]

Adams, Thomas Sewell, political economist, b. Baltimore, Md., 1873; d. New Haven, Conn., Feb. 8, 1933. [10]

Adams, William, clergyman, b. Colchester, Conn., 1807; d. Orange Mountain, N.J., Aug. 31, 1880. [1; 3; 6]

Adams, William, educationist, b. Monaghan, Ireland, 1813; d. Nashotah, Wis., Jan. 2, 1897. [3]

Adams, William Forbes, historian, b. Lawrence, Kans., 1898; d. Los Angeles, Calif., July 27, 1935. [57; 62]

Adams, William Frederick, genealogist, b. 1848; d. ?

Adams, William Lysander, journalist and physician, b. Ohio, 1821; d. Hood River, Ore., April 26, 1906. [6; 41]

Adams, William Taylor, writer of stories for young people, b. Bellingham, Mass., 1832; d. Boston, Mass., March 27, 1897. [1; 3; 7]

Adams, Zabdiel, clergyman, b. 1736; d. 1801. [6; 51]

Adamson, William Agar, clergyman, b. Dublin, Ireland, 1800; d. Ottawa, Ont., Aug. 7, 1868. [27]

Addams, George Stanton, lawyer, b. 1869; d. April 14, 1933.

Addams, Jane, philanthropist, b. Cedarvale, Ill., 1860; d. Chicago. Ill., May 21, 1935. [la; 10; 11]

Addington, Sarah, journalist, novelist, and writer of books for children, b. Cincinnati, O., 1891; d. New York, N.Y., Nov. 7, 1940. [10; 11]

Addison, Daniel Dulany, clergyman, b. Wheeling, W. Va., 1863; d. Brookline, Mass., March 27, 1863. [10]

Addison, Mrs. Elinor, née **Adams,** poet, b. Toronto, Ont.; d. Mount Vernon, N.Y., Dec., 1948.

Ade, George, humorist, b. Kentland, Ind., 1866; d. Kentland, Ind., May 16, 1944. [4; 7; 9; 10; 11]

Ade, John, local historian, b. 1828; d. Valparaiso, Ind., April 28, 1914.

Adeler, Max (pseud.). See Clark, Charles Heber.

Adger, John B., theologian, b. Charleston, S. C., 1810; d. Charleston, S.C., 1899. [34]

Adidnac (pseud.). See Whitaker, Lily C.

Adler, Cyrus, educationist, b. Van Buren, Ark., 1863; d. Philadelphia, Pa., April 7, 1940. [10]

Adler, Felix, philosopher and reformer, b. Germany, 1851; d. New York, N.Y., April 24, 1933. [la; 10; 11]

Adler, George J., philologist, b. Leipzig, Germany, 1821; d. New York, N.Y., Aug. 24, 1868. [1; 3; 6]

Adlum, John, pioneer in viticulture, b. York, Pa., 1759; d. March 1, 1836. [1]

Aesop, G. Washington (pseud.) See Lanigan, George Thomas.

Affleck, Thomas, agricultural writer, b. Dumfries, Scotland, 1812; d. near Huston, Tex., Dec. 30, 1868. [1]

Afterem, George (pseud.). See Williams, Harold.

Agassiz, Alexander Emmanuel, zoologist and oceanographer, b. Neuchâtel, Switzerland, 1835; d. at sea, March 27, 1910. [1; 2; 3; 4; 6; 10]

Agassiz, Mrs Elizabeth Cabot, née Cary, educationist, b. Boston , Mass., 1822; d. Arlington Heights, Mass., June 27, 1907. [1; 10]

Agassiz, Jean Louis Rodolphe, naturalist, b. Switzerland, 1807; d. Cambridge, Mass., Dec. 14, 1873. [1; 2; 3; 4; 6;]

Ager, Waldemar Theodore, novelist, b. Norway, 1869; d. Eau Claire, Wis., Aug. 1, 1941. [10; 44]

Agnew, Daniel, jurist and historian, b. Trenton, N.J., 1809; d. 1902. [4; 10]

Agnew, David Hayes, surgeon, b. Lancaster county, Pa., 1818; d. Philadelphia, Pa., March 22, 1892. [1]

Ah-Chin-Le (pseud.). See Swasey, John B.

Ahern, George Patrick, soldier and forester, b. New York, N.Y., 1859; d. Washington, D.C., May 13, 1942. [62]

Ahern, Michael Joseph, physician, b. Quebec, Que., 1844; d. Quebec, Que., April 18, 1914. [27]

Aiken, Charles Francis, educationist, b. Boston, Mass., 1863; d. Boston Mass., July 8, 1925. [10; 21; 51]

Aiken, George L., actor, playwright, and novelist, b. Boston, Mass., 1830; d. Jersey City, N.J., April 27, 1876. [1]

Aiken, Solomon, clergyman, b. Hardwick, Mass., 1758; d. Hardwick, Vt., June 1, 1833. [43]

Aikins, Herbert Austin, philosopher, b. Toronto, Ont., 1867; d. Cleveland, O., Nov. 13, 1946. [62]

Aikman, William, clergyman, b. New York, N.Y., 1824; d. Atlantic City, N.J., May 25, 1909. [10]

Aimwell, Walter (pseud.). See Simonds, William.

Ainslie, Hew, poet, b. Ayrshire, Scotland, 1792; d. Louisville, Ky., March 11, 1878. [1; 3; 34]

Ainslie, Peter, clergyman, b. Dunnsville, Va., 1867; d. Baltimore, Md., Feb. 23, 1934. [10]

Aitken, Robert, publisher, b. Dalkeith, Scotland, 1734; d. Philadelphia, Pa., July, 1802. [3]

Aix (pseud.). See Bausman, Frederick.

Aked, Charles Frederic, clergyman, b. Nottingham, England, 1864; d. Los Angeles, Calif., Aug. 12, 1941. [10]

Akeley, Carl Ethan, naturalist and explorer, b, Orleans county, N.Y., 1864; d. on safari, Africa, Nov. 17, 1926. [1; 10]

Akers, Mrs. Elizabeth, née Chase, poet and journalist, b. Franklin county, Me., 1832; d. Tuckahoe, N.Y., Aug. 7, 1911. [1; 10]

Akers, Floyd (pseud). See Baum, Lyman Frank.

Akins, Thomas Beamish. lawyer and historian, b. Liverpool, N.S., 1809; d. Halifax, N.S., May 6, 1891. [27; 33]

Albaugh, Benjamin Franklin, gardener, b. 1836; d. after 1912.

Albee, Ernest, philosopher, b. Langdon, N.H., 1865; d. Ithaca, N. Y. May 25, 1927. [1; 10]

Albee, John, clergyman, b. Bellingham, Mass., 1833; d. March 24, 1915. [4; 8; 10; 71]

Albert, Thomas, priest and historian, b. Madawaska, N.B., 1879; d. Grand Sault, N.B., Nov. 16, 1924. [27]

Alberton, Edwin (pseud.). See Philips, Albert Edwin.

Albree, John, historian, b. Boston Mass., 1859; d. Concord, Mass., Feb. 2, 1938. [45]

Albright, Jacob Dissinger, physician, b. Lancaster county, Pa., 1870; d. Philadelphia, Pa., Feb. 12, 1926. [4]

Albro, Addis, clergyman, b. Middleburgh, N.Y., 1855; d. Columbus, N.M., Oct. 15, 1911. [10]

Albro, John Adams, clergyman, b. Newport, R.I., 1799; d. West Roxbury, Mass., Dec. 20, 1866. [46]

Alchin, Carolyn Alden, musician, b. 1857; d. 1926.

Alcott, Abigail May. See Nierker, Mrs. Abigail May, née Alcott.

Alcott, Amos Bronson, educationist, b. near Wolcott, Conn., 1799; d. Boston, Mass., March 4, 1888. [1; 2; 3; 5; 6; 71]

Alcott, Louisa May, novelist, b. Germantown, Pa., 1832; d. Boston, Mass., March 6, 1888. [1; 2; 3; 7; 8; 9; 71; 72]

Alcott, Ten (pseud.). See Totten, Charles Adiel Lewis.

Alcott, William Andrus, educationist, b. Wolcott, Conn., 1798; d. Newton, Mass., March 29, 1859. [1; 3; 4; 6]

Alden, Augustus Ephraim, genealogist and biographer, b. 1837; d. 1914.

Alden, Charles Henry, soldier, b. Philadelphia, Pa., 1836; d. 1906. [10]

Alden, Mrs. Cynthia May, née Westover, journalist, b. Afton, Ia., 1861; d. Brooklyn, N.Y., Jan. 8, 1931. [4; 10; 11; 37]

Alden, Cyrus, lawyer, b. 1785; d. 1855.

Alden, Ebenezer, physician and historian, b. Randolph, Mass., 1788; d. Randolph, Mass., Jan. 26, 1881. [1; 3; 6]

Alden, George Ira, mechanical engineer, b. Templeton, Mass., 1843; d. Princeton, Mass. Sept. 13, 1926. [4; 51]

Alden, Mrs. George R. See Alden, Mrs. Isabella, née Macdonald.

Alden, Henry Mills, editor, b. Mount Tabor, Vt., 1836; d. New York, N.Y., Oct. 17, 1919. [1; 7; 10; 61]

Alden, Mrs. Isabella, née Macdonald ("Pansy"), writer of books for girls, b. Rochester, N.Y., Nov. 3, 1841; d. Palo Alto, Calif., Aug. 5, 1930. [3; 4; 6; 7; 8; 10; 15]

Alden, John, clergyman, b. Ashfield, Mass,. 1810; d. Providence, R.I., March 13, 1894. [45]

Alden, John Berry, editor and publisher, b. Henry county, Ia., 1847; d. Neshanic, N.J., Dec. 4, 1924. [10]

Alden, Joseph, educationist, b. Cairo, N.Y., 1807; d. New York, N.Y., Aug. 30, 1885. [1; 3; 6]

Alden, Raymond Macdonald, educationist, b. New Hartford, N.Y., 1873; d. Philadelphia, Pa., Sept. 24, 1924. [1; 4; 10; 35]

Alden, Timothy, clergyman and antiquarian, b. Yarmouth, Mass., 1771; d. Pittsburg, Pa., July 5, 1839. [3; 4; 6]

Alden, William Livingston, journalist, b. Williamstown, Mass., 1837; d. Buffalo, N.Y., Jan. 14, 1908. [1; 10; 71]

Alderman, Edwin Anderson, educationist, b. Wilmington, N.C., 1861; d. Cornellsville, Pa., April 29, 1931. [10; 11; 34]

Alderson, William Atkinson, lawyer, b. St. Charles, Mo., 1856; d. Feb. 6, 1938. [35]

Aldrich, Anne Reeve, poet and novelist, b. New York, N.Y., 1866; d. New York, N.Y., June 28, 1892. [4; 7; 8; 71]

Aldrich, Mrs. Auretta, née **Roys,** educationist, b. Fletcher, Vt., 1829; d. Springfield, Mass., Oct. 29, 1920. [10]

Aldrich, Charles, biographer, b. Ellington, N.Y., 1828; d. 1908. [10; 37]

Aldrich, Charles Roberts, lawyer, b. Fort Wayne, Ind., 1877; d. Carmel, Calif., March 31, 1933. [62]

Aldrich, Mrs. Flora L., née **Southard,** physician, b. Westford, N.Y., 1859; d. Anoka, Minn., March 19, 1921. [70]

Aldrich, George, local historian, b. Westmoreland, N.H., 1816; d. Walpole, N.H., April 24, 1888.

Aldrich, James, poet, b. Mattituck, N.Y., 1810; d. New York, N.Y., Sept 9, 1866 [4]

Aldrich, Jeremiah Knight, clergyman, b. 1826; d. 1905.

Aldrich, Mrs. Lillian, née **Woodman,** wife of Thomas Bailey Aldrich (q.v.), d. Rockland, Me., May 22, 1927.

Aldrich, Mildred, war commentator, b. Providence, R.I., 1853; d. France, Feb. 19, 1928. [10]

Aldrich, Peleg Emery, lawyer, b. 1813; d. 1895. [51]

Aldrich, Perley Dunn, musician, b. Blackstone, Mass., 1863; d. Philadelphia, Pa., Nov. 20, 1933. [10; 20]

Aldrich, Richard, music critic, b. Providence, R.I., 1863; d, Rome, Italy, June 2, 1937. [10; 11; 20]

Aldrich, Thomas Bailey, poet, novelist, and editor, b. Portsmouth, N.H., 1836; d. Boston, Mass., March 19, 1907. [1; 2; 3; 4; 5; 6; 7; 8; 9; 10; 71; 72]

Aldrich, Mrs. Thomas Bailey. See Aldrich, Mrs. Lillian, née Woodman.

Aldrich, Wilbur, lawyer, d. Jan. 13, 1922. [48]

Alemany, José Sadoc, archbishop, b. Spain, 1814; d. Valencia, Spain, April 14, 1888. [1; 3]

Alerding, Herman Joseph, bishop, b. Westphalia, Germany, 1845; d. Dec. 6, 1924. [10; 21]

Alethitheras (pseud.). See Osborn, Laughton.

Alexander, Alexander Septimus, veterinary surgeon, b. 1860; d. Madison, Wis., July 12, 1935. [2a]

Alexander, Archibald, clergyman and educationist, b. Rockbridge county, Va., 1772; d. Princeton, N.J., Oct. 22, 1851. [1; 3; 4; 6]

Alexander, Archibald, educationist, b. 1855; d. 1917. [56]

Alexander, Caleb, clergyman and educationist, b. Northfield, Mass., 1775; d. Onondaga, N.Y., April 12, 1828. [3; 8]

Alexander, Charles Beatty, lawyer, b. New York, N.Y., 1849; d. Feb. 7, 1927. [4; 10]

Alexander, Charles Wesley, miscellaneous writer, b. 1837; d. 1927.

Alexander, De Alva Stanwood, politician and historian, b. Richmond, Me., 1845; d. Buffalo, N.Y., Jan. 30, 1925. [1; 10]

Alexander, Edward Porter, soldier, b. Washington, Ga., 1835; d. Savanna, Ga., April 28, 1910. [1; 10; 34]

Alexander, Francesca, artist, b. Boston, Mass., about 1834; d. Florence, Italy, Jan. 22, 1917. [6; 7; 10]

Alexander, Gross, clergyman, b. Scottsville, Ky., 1852; d. Long Beach, Calif., Sept. 6, 1915. [1; 10; 34]

Alexander, Hartley Burr, educationist, b. Lincoln, Neb., 1873; d. Claremont, Calif., July 27. 1939. [7; 10]

Alexander, Henry Carrington, clergyman, b. Princeton. N.J., 1835; d. New York, N.Y., June 17, 1894. [56]

Alexander, James McKinney, missionary, b. Hawaiian Islands, 1835; d. Oakland, Calif., April 11, 1911. [61]

Alexander, James Lynne, clergyman and poet, b. Glenhead, Antrim, Ireland, 1800; d. Grimsby, Ont., Aug. 22, 1879. [27]

Alexander, James Waddel, clergyman, b. near Gordonsville, Va., 1804; d. Red Sweet Spring, Va., July 31, 1859. [2; 8; 34; 56]

Alexander, James Waddel, financier, b. Princeton, N.J., 1839; d. Sept. 21, 1915. [3a; 10; 56]

Alexander, John Brevard, physician, b. Mecklenburg county, N.C., 1834; d. Cowan's Ford, N.C., 1911. [10; 34]

Alexander, John Edminston, clergyman and educationist, b. near Lewiston, Pa., 1815; d. 1901. [4]

Alexander, John Henry, scientist and poet, b. Annapolis, Md., 1812; d. Baltimore, Md., March 2, 1867. [1; 3; 34]

Alexander, John Henry, soldier, b. Virginia, 1846; d. ? [34]

Alexander, John L., clergyman, b. Scotland, 1875; d. Webster Groves, Mo., May 28, 1932. [10]

Alexander, Joseph Addison, educationist, b. Philadelphia, Pa., 1804; d. Princeton, N.J., Jan. 28, 1860. [1; 6; 7; 56]

Alexander, Mrs. Lillie, née **McMakin,** novelist, d. Baldwin, Kans., Oct. 17, 1943.

Alexander, Magnus Washington, engineer, b. New York, N.Y., 1870; d. New York, N.Y., Sept. 10, 1932. [10]

Alexander, Maitland, clergyman, b. New York, N.Y., 1867; d. Sewickley, Pa., Jan. 3, 1940. [10]

Alexander, Rev. Richard W. (pseud.). See Mercedes, Sister.

Alexander, Robert, soldier, b. Baltimore, Md., 1863; d. New York, N.Y., Aug, 26, 1941. [10]

Alexander, Samuel Davies, clergyman, b. Princeton, N.J., 1819; d. New York, N.Y., Oct. 26, 1894. [1; 8; 56]

Alexander, Stephen, astronomer, b. Schenectady, N.Y., 1806; d. Princeton, N.J., June 25, 1883. [1; 3; 6; 56]

Alexander, William, poet, b. 1808; d. Harrisburg, Pa., Oct. 8, 1875. [55]

Alexander, William, insurance executive, b. 1848; d. Winter Park, Fla., March 25, 1937.

Alexander, William De Witt, historian, b. Honolulu, Hawaii, 1833; d. Honolulu, Hawaii, Feb. 22, 1913. [1; 10]

Alexander, William John, educationist, b. Hamilton, Ont., 1855; d. Halifax., N.S., June 28, 1944. [27]

Aley, Robert Judson, educationist, b. Coal City, Ind., 1863; d. New York, N.Y., Nov. 18, 1935. [10; 11]

Alford, Leon Pratt, industrial engineer, b. Simsbury, Conn., 1877; d. New York, N.Y., Jan. 2, 1942. [10]

Alford, Loyal Adolphus, clergyman and poet, b. 1814; d. 1883. [6]

Alfriend, Frank H., journalist, fl. 1868-70. [34]

Alger, Horatio, writer of books for boys, b. Revere, Mass., 1834; d. Natick, Mass., July 18, 1899. [1; 2; 3; 6; 7; 8; 9; 15]

Alger, Philip Rounseville, soldier, b. Boston, Mass., 1859; d. Annapolis, Md., Feb. 23, 1912. [4; 10]

Alger, Russell Alexander, politician, b. Lafayette, O., 1836; d. Washington, D.C., Jan. 24, 1907. [1; 10]

Alger, William Rounseville, clergyman, b. Freetown, Mass., 1822; d. Boston, Mass., Feb. 7, 1905. [1; 2; 3; 6; 10; 51]

Algie, James, physician and novelist, b. Ayr, Ont., 1857; d. St. Petersburg, Fla., Jan. 16, 1928. [27]

Alguno, Señor (pseud.). See Ames, Nathan.

Alien (pseud.). See Baker, Mrs. Louis Alien.

Allaben, Frank, genealogist, b. 1867; d. New York, N.Y., Feb. 15, 1927.

Allan, Mrs. Elizabeth, née Preston, writer of books for young people, b. Lexington, Va., 1848; d. April 29, 1933. [7; 34]

Allan, William, soldier, b. Winchester, Va., 1837; d. McDonough, Md., Sept. 17, 1889. [34]

Allan, William, clergyman and broadcaster, b. Scotland; d. in the sinking of the Athenia off the Hebrides, Sept. 3, 1939, [27]

Allee, Mrs. Marjorie, née Hill, writer of books for children, b. Carthage, Ind., 1890; d. Chicago, Ill., April 30, 1945. [10]

Allen, Abel Leighton, lawyer, b. Kenton, O., 1850; d. Dec. 8, 1927. [10]

Allen, Alexander Viets Griswold, clergyman and educationist, b. Otis, Mass., 1841; d. Boston, Mass., July 1, 1908. [1; 4; 10]

Allen, Andrew Hussey, archivist, b. New York, N.Y., 1855; d. Washington, D.C,. Nov. 15, 1921. [10; 51]

Allen, Benjamin, clergyman, b. Hudson, N.Y., 1789; d. at sea, Jan. 13, 1829 [3; 6]

Allen, Beverly Sprague, educationist, b. San Franscisco, Calif., 1881; d. Berkeley, Calif., March 29, 1935. [10; 35]

Allen, Charles, jurist, b. Greenfield, Mass., 1827; d. Boston, Mass., Jan. 13, 1913. [1; 4; 10; 51]

Allen, Charles Dexter, authority on book-plates, b. Windsor Locks, Conn., 1865; d. Bellport, Long Island, N.Y., Sept 10, 1926. [10]

Allen, Charles Linnaeus, horticulturist, b. 1828; d. 1909.

Allen, Charles Warrenne, physician, b. Flemington, N.J., 1854; d. 1906. [10]

Allen, Mrs. Cynthia M., née Fairchild, humanitarian, b. 1839; d. 1901.

Allen, David Oliver, missionary, b. Barre, Mass., 1799; d. Lowell, Mass., July 19, 1863. [1]

Allen, Diarca Howe, clergyman and educationist, b. Lebanon, N.H., 1808; d. Granville, O., Nov. 9, 1870. [49]

Allen, Don (pseud.). See True, Hiram L.

Allen, Edgar, anatomist, b. Canon City, Colo., 1892; d. New Haven, Conn., Feb. 3, 1943. [10; 47]

Allen, Edward Archibald, educationist, b. Suffolk, Va., 1843; d. Columbia, Mo., Sept. 22, 1922. [34]

Allen, Elizabeth, poet, b. Craftsbury, Vt., 1796; d. Coventry, Vt., Nov. 14, 1849. [73]

Allen, Mrs. Elizabeth, née Chase. See Akers, Mrs. Elizabeth, née Chase.

Allen, Mrs. Emma Sarah, née Gage, novelist, b. Mount Vernon, Ind., 1859; d. ? [35]

Allen, Emory Adams, historian, 1853; reported to have died in Prague, Czechoslovakia, al.out 1933.

Allen, Eric William, journalist and educationist, b. Appleton, Wis., 1879; d. Eugene, Ore., March 5, 1944. [10; 11]

Allen, Ethan, soldier, b. Litchfield, Conn., 1737; d. Burlington, Vt., Feb. 12, 1789. [1; 2; 3; 4; 6; 27]

Allen, Ethan, clergyman, b. 1796; d. May 19, 1867. [47]

Allen, Ethan, lawyer and playwright, b. Monmouth county, N.J., 1831; d. New York, N.Y., Dec. 11, 1911. [10; 47]

Allen, Mrs. Fairchild. See Allen, Mrs. Cynthia M., née Fairchild.

Allen, Fred Hooey, clergyman and writer on art, b. Lyme, N.H., 1845; d. New York, N.Y., Dec. 24, 1926. [4; 10]

Allen, Frederic DeForest, educationist, b. Oberlin, O., 1844; d. near Cambridge, Mass., Aug. 4, 1897. [1; 4]

Allen, Frederic Sturges, lexicographer, b. Norwalk, Conn., 1861; d. Springfield, Mass., Aug. 8, 1920. [10; 62]

Allen, Frederic James, educationist, b. Limerick, Me., 1864; d. Cambridge, Mass., Feb. 17, 1927. [10; 49]

Allen, George, clergyman, b. Worcester, Mass., 1792; d. Worcester, Mass., March 31, 1883. [62]

Allen, George, clergyman and educationist, b. Milton, Vt., 1808; d. Worcester, Mass., May 28, 1876. [1; 4; 43; 59]

Allen, Harrison, physician and anatomist, b. Philadelphia, Pa., 1841; d. Philadelphia, Pa., Nov. 14, 1897. [1; 4; 55]

Allen, Henry Clay, physician, b. 1836; d. Chicago, Ill., Jan. 22, 1909. [61]

Allen, Henry Tureman, soldier, b. Sharpsburg, Ky., 1859; d. Buena Vista Spring, Pa., Aug. 30, 1930. [10]

Allen, Henry Watkins, soldier, b. Prince Edward county, Va., 1820; d. Mexico City, Mexico, April 22, 1866. [1; 3; 4; 34]

Allen, Hervey, novelist, b. Pittsburg, Pa., 1889; d. Miami, Fla., Dec. 28, 1949. [10; 11; 12]

Allen, Horace Newton, missionary, b. Delaware, O., 1858; d. Toledo, O., Dec. 11, 1932. [10]

Allen, Horatio, civil engineer, b. Schenectady, N. Y., 1802; d. South Orange, N.J., Jan. 1. 1890. [1; 4]

Allen, Hugh (pseud.). See Rathborne, St. George Henry.

Allen, Ira, soldier and politician, b. Cornwall, Conn., 1751; d. Philadelphia, Pa., Jan. 15, 1814. [1; 2; 3; 6; 43]

Allen, Ira Wilder, educationist, b. 1827; d. Chicago, Ill., Dec. 1896.

Allen, James Lane, novelist, b. Lexington, Ky., 1849; d. New York, N.Y., Feb. 18, 1925. [1; 10; 11; 34; 72]

Allen, Jerome, educationist, b. Westminster, Vt., 1830; d. Brooklyn, N.Y., May 26, 1894. [8]

Allen, Joel Asaph, zoologist, b. Springfield, Mass., 1838; d. Cornwall-on-the- Hudson, N.Y., Aug. 29, 1921. [1; 6; 13]

Allen, John (pseud.). See Clute, Oscar.

Allen, John Alpheus, chemist and botanist, b. Hebron, Me., 1863; d. Manzanita, Ore., June 5, 1916. [62]

Allen, Sir John Campbell, jurist, b. Kingsclear, N.B., 1817; d. Sept. 27, 1898. [27]

Allen, John Edward, journalist, b. Des Moines, Ia., 1889; d. Garden City, N.Y., July 12, 1947. [11]

Allen, John Henry, mariner, b. St. Andrews, West Indies, 1836; d. at sea, 1890. [3a]

Allen, John Harden, evangelist, b. 1847; d. ?

Allen, John Robert, clergyman and educationist, b. Iredell county, N.C., 1851; d. Dallas, Tex., Feb. 6, 1937. [34]

Allen, John Robins, engineer, b. Milwaukee, Wis., 1869; d. Pittsburg, Pa., Oct. 26. 1920. [4]

Allen, John S., clergyman, b. Burlington, N.S., 1841; d. Nakusp, B.C., Dec. 9, 1923. [33]

Allen, John Taylor, pioneer, b. Honey Grove, Tex., 1848; d. after 1918.

Allen, Jonathan Adams, physician, b. Holliston, Mass., 1787; d. Middlebury, Vt., 1848. [43]

Allen, Jonathan Adams, physician, ˙ b. Middlebury, Vt., 1826; d. Chicago, Ill., 1890. [43]

Allen, Joseph, clergyman, b. Medfield, Mass., 1790; d. Northboro, Mass., 1873. [6; 51]

Allen, Joseph Antisell, clergyman, b. Tipperary, Ireland, 1814; d. Kingston, Ont., Oct. 6, 1900. [27]

Allen, Joseph Henry, clergyman and editor, b. Northboro, Mass., 1820; d. Cambridge, Mass., March 20, 1898. [1; 4; 6; 51]

Allen, Lewis Falley, agriculturist and stock-breeder, b. Westfield, Mass., 1800; d. May 2, 1890. [1]

Allen, Luman, novelist, fl. 1881-1893.

Allen, Lyman Whitney, clergyman and poet, b. St. Louis. Mo., 1854; d. Newark, N.J., Jan. 27, 1930. [10; 11]

Allen, Mrs. Martha, née Meir, temperance advocate. b. Owen Sound, Ont., 1854; d. Long Beach, Long Island, N.Y., June 19, 1926. [10]

Allen, Mrs. Mary, née Wood, physician, b. 1841; d. Washington, D.C., Jan 21, 1908.

Allen, Mrs. Maryland, née Riley, journalist, b. Montgomery county, Md.; d. Portland, Ore., Jan. 31, 1927. [10]

Allen, Myron Oliver, physician and local historian, b. Bombay, India, 1832; d. Lowell, Mass., Aug. 1, 1861. [62]

Allen, Nathan, physician, b. Princeton, Mass., 1813; d. Lowell, Mass., Jan. 1, 1889. [1; 6]

Allen, Otis, lawyer, b. 1804; d. 1865.

Allen, Paul, poet and historian, b. Providence, R.I., 1775; d. Baltimore, Md., Aug. 18, 1826. [1; 34; 47]

Allen, Philip Loring, journalist, b. Madison, Wis., 1878; d. New York, N.Y., May 26, 1908. [10]

Allen, Philip Schuyler, educationist, b. Lake Forest, Ill., 1871; d. Chicago, Ill., April 27, 1937. [10]

Allen, Richard Hinckley, astronomer, b. 1838; d. 1908.

Allen, Richard Lamb, agriculturist and editor, b. Westfield, Mass., 1803; d. Stockholm, Sweden, Sept. 22, 1869. [1; 3; 5]

Allen, Rowland Hussey, clergyman, b. Norton, Mass., 1840; d. Boston, Mass., Sept. 12, 1872. [45]

Allen, Stanton P., soldier, b. 1849; d. 1901.

Allen, Stephen, clergyman, b. Industry, Me., 1810; d. Winthrop, Me., July 3, 1888. [46]

Allen, Stephen Haley, lawyer, b. Sinclairville, N.Y., 1847; d. Topeka, Kans., Oct. 26, 1931. [10; 11]

Allen, Stephen Merrill, banker and merchant, b. Albany, N.Y., 1819; d. Jan. 19, 1894. [6; 8]

Allen, Thornton Whitney, song-writer, b. Newark, N.J., 1890; d. Hyannis, Mass., July 30, 1944.

Allen, Timothy Field, physician and botanist, b. Westminster, Vt., 1837; d. New York, N.Y., Dec. 5, 1902. [1; 5; 10]

Allen, Walter, journalist, b. Boston, Mass., 1840; d. Newton Highlands, Mass., Feb. 7, 1907. [10; 62]

Allen, Wilkes, clergyman, b. 1775; d. 1845. [51]

Allen, William, local historian, b. 1780; d. 1873. [38]

Allen, William, clergyman and educationist, b. Pittsfield, Mass., 1784; d. Northampton, Mass., July 16, 1868. [1; 3; 4; 5; 8]

Allen, William Francis, educationist, b. Northboro, Mass., 1830; d. Madison, Wis., Dec. 9, 1889. [1; 2; 44;]

Allen, William Frederick, railway expert, b. Bordentown, N.J., 1846; d. South Orange, N.J., Nov. 9, 1915. [1]

Allen, Willis Boyd, writer of books for boys, b. Kittery Point, Me., 1855; d. Crawford Notch, N.H., Sept. 11, 1938. [4; 7; 10; 11]

Allen, Zachariah, scientist and inventor, b. Providence, R.I., 1795; d. Providence, R.I., March 17, 1882. [1; 3; 47]

Allerton, Mrs. Ellen, née **Palmer,** poet, b. 1835; d. 1893.

Allerton, Samuel Waters, capitalist and agriculturist, b. Dutchess county, N.Y., 1828; d. Chicago, Ill., Feb. 22, 1914. [4; 10]

Alley, Henry, apiarist, b. Newburyport, Mass., 1835; d. Wenham, Mass., Feb. 10, 1908.

Alley, James Pinckney, cartoonist, b. near Benton, Ark., 1885; d. Memphis, Tenn., April 16, 1934. [10]

Allibone, Samuel Austin, literary lexicographer and librarian, b. Philadelphia, Pa., 1816; d. Lucerne, Switzerland, Sept. 2, 1889. [1; 2; 3; 4; 7]

Allin, Cephas Daniel, educationist, b. Clinton, Ont., 1874; d. Minneapolis, Minn., Oct. 23, 1927. [27]

Allin, John, clergyman, b. England, 1596; d. Dedham, Mass., Aug. 26, 1671. [3; 51]

Alline, Henry, clergyman, b. Rhode Island, 1748; d. North Hampton, N.H., 1784 [27]

Alling, Arthur Nathaniel, ophthalmologist, b. New Haven, Conn., 1862; d. New Haven, Conn., March 15, 1949. [10; 62]

Allinson, Mrs. Anne Crosby, née **Emery,** educationist, b. Ellsworth, Me., 1871; d. near Ellsworth, Me., Aug. 16, 1932. [10; 47]

Allinson, David, publisher, b. Woodbury, N.J., 1774; d. Burlington, N.J., 1858. [3a]

Allinson, Edward Pease, lawyer and local historian, b. 1852; d. 1901.

Allinson, Francis Greenleaf, educationist, b. Burlington, N.J., 1856; d. Hancock Point, Me., June 23, 1931. [4; 10; 51]

Alliot, Hector, archaeologist and bibliographer, b. France, 1862; d. Feb. 15, 1919. [10]

Allison, Burgiss, clergyman, b. 1753; d. 1827.

Allison, Charles Elmer, clergyman, b. Florida, N.Y., 1847; d. Yonkers, N.Y., Jan. 2, 1908. [68]

Allison, David, educationist and historian, b. Newport, N.S., 1836; d. Halifax, N.S., Feb. 13, 1924. [27]

Allison, John, jurist, b. 1845; d. 1920. [34]

Allison, John Maudgridge Snowden, historian, b. Pittsburg, Pa., 1888; d. New Haven, Conn., April 6, 1944. [7; 10; 62]

Allison, Nathaniel, surgeon, b. St. Louis, Mo., 1876; d. Chicago, Ill., Aug. 30, 1931. [10; 51]

Allison, Thomas Jefferson, poet, b. 1850; d. ?

Allison, William Henry, clergyman, b. Somerville, Mass., 1870; d. Sept. 20, 1941. [10; 11; 52]

Allison, William Talbot, educationist, b. Unionville, Ont., 1874; d. Winnipeg, Man., Feb. 4, 1941. [27]

Allison, Young Ewing, editor and librettist, b. Henderson, Ky., 1853; d. Louisville, Ky., July 7, 1932. [74]

Allmond, Marcus Blakey, educationist and poet, b. Stanardsville, Va., 1851; d. Louisville, Ky., Sept 1, 1909. [10; 34]

Alloway, Mrs. Mary, née **Wilson,** historian and novelist, b. Montreal, Canada, 1848; d. while on a visit to California, Jan. 11, 1919. [27]

Allport, Frank, ophthalmologist, b. Watertown, N.Y., 1856; d. Nice, France, Aug. 2, 1935. [10]

Allston, Robert Francis Withers, planter and politician, b. All Saints parish, S.C., 1808; d. near Georgetown, S.C., April 7, 1864. [1; 34; 42]

Allston, Washington, painter and poet, b. Brook Green Domain, S.C., 1779; d. Cambridge, Mass., July 9, 1843. [1; 3; 5; 6; 7; 34; 42; 71]

Allyn, Lewis Benajah, chemist, b. 1874; d. Westfield, Mass., May 7, 1940.

Almore, Caspar (pseud.). See Beasley, Frederick Williamson.

Alpers, William Charles, chemist, b. Harburg, Germany, 1851; d. Cleveland, O., Feb. 20, 1917. [4; 10]

Alphonse, Mother. See Lathrop, Mrs. Rose, née Hawthorne.

Alsop, Richard, poet and satirist, b. Middletown, Conn., 1761; d. Flatbush, Long Island, N.Y., Aug. 20, 1815. [1; 4; 7]

Alsop, Samuel, surveyor, fl. 1837-1860. [6]

Altgelt, John Peter, politician, b. Nassau, Germany, 1847; d. Joliet, Ill., March 12, 1902. [1; 2; 4; 5; 36]

Altschul, Charles, banker, b. 1857; d. New York, N.Y., April 26, 1927.

Altsheler, Joseph Alexander, writer of stories for boys, b. Three Springs, Hart county, Ky., 1862; d. New York, N.Y., June 5, 1919. [1; 4; 10; 15]

Alum, Hardly (pseud.). See Sullivan, Edward Dean.

Alves, Juliet, See Hoyt, Mrs. Juliet, née Alves.

Alvord, Benjamin, soldier, b. Rutland, Vt., 1813; d. Washington, D.C., Oct. 16, 1884. [1; 3; 4]

Alvord, Clarence Walworth, historian, b. Greenfield, Mass., 1868; d. Italy, Jan. 24, 1928. [1; 10]

Alvord, Samuel Morgan, educationist, b. Bolton, Conn., 1869; d. Bolton, Conn., Dec. 1, 1943. [62]

Ambauen, Andrew Joseph, priest, b. Unterwalden, Switzerland, 1847; d. ? [4; 10; 21]

Ambrose, Brother (pseud.). See Noyes, Charles.

Ambrose, Daniel Leib, journalist, b. 1843; d. Canton, Ill., Feb. 15, 1922. [6; 36]

Ambrose, Paul (pseud.). See Kennedy, John Pendleton.

Amelia (pseud.). See Welby, Mrs. Amelia Ball, née Coppuck.

Ameringer, Oscar, socialist, b. Lanpheim, Germany, 1870; d. Oklahoma City, Okla., Nov. 5, 1942. [12]

Ames, Azel, physician, b. 1845; d. Danvers, Mass., Nov. 12, 1908. [52]

Ames, Charles Gordon, clergyman and editor, b. Dorchester, Mass., 1828; d. Boston, Mass., April 15, 1912. [1; 4; 10]

Ames, Mrs. Eleanor Maria, née **Easterbrook,** editor and novelist, b. Warren, R.I., 1831; d. Weekapong, R.I., Jan. 24, 1908. [10]

Ames, Fisher, politician, b. Dedham, Mass., 1758; d. Dedham, Mass., July 4, 1808. [1]

Ames, Fisher, lawyer, b. Lowell, Mass., 1838; d. 1918. [10; 51]

Ames, Herman Vandenburg, historian, b. Lancaster, Mass., 1865; d. Philadelphia, Pa., Feb. 7, 1935. [10; 45]

Ames, James Barr, lawyer and educationist, b. Boston, Mass., 1846; d. Cambridge, Mass., Jan. 8, 1910. [1; 10; 52]

Ames, Joseph Bushnell, novelist, b. Titusville, Pa., 1878; d. Morristown, N.J., June 20, 1928. [10]

Ames, Joseph Sweetman, physicist, b. Manchester, Vt., 1864; d. Baltimore, Md., June 24, 1943. [10; 13]

Ames, Mrs. Mary, née **Clemmer,** journalist and novelist,b. Utica, N.Y., 1839; d. Washington, D.C., May 18, 1884. [1; 2; 3; 6; 70]

Ames, Mrs. Mary, née **Lesley,** librarian, b. Philadelphia, Pa., 1853; d. St. Paul, Minn., Feb. 22, 1929. [10; 70]

Ames, Nathan, lawyer and poet, b. New Hampshire, 1825; d. Saugus, Mass., Aug. 17, 1865. [19; 51]

Ames, Nathaniel, physician and almanac-maker, b. Bridgewater, Mass., 1708; d. Dedham, Mass., July 11, 1764. [1]

Ames, Nathaniel, sailor, d. Jan. 18, 1835. [7]

Ami, Henry Marc, geologist, b. Belle Rivière, Que., 1858; d. Mentone, France, Jan. 4, 1931. [27]

Ammen, Daniel, naval officer, b. Brown county, O., 1819; d. Washington, D.C., July 11, 1898. [1; 3; 6]

Amory, Mrs. Martha Babcock, née **Greene,** biographer, b. 1812; d. 1880. [6]

Amory, Robert, physician, b. Boston, Mass., 1842; d. Boston, Mass., Aug. 28, 1910. [10; 52]

Amory, Thomas Coffin, lawyer and historian, b. Boston, Mass., 1812; d. Aug. 20, 1889. [3; 5; 7]

Amram, David Werner, lawyer, b. Philadelphia, Pa., 1866; d. Beach Haven, N.J., June 27, 1939. [55]

Amsden, Charles Avery, archaeologist, b. 1899; d. Moravia, Calif., March 3, 1941.

Anagnos, Mrs. Julia Romana, née **Howe,** poet, b. Rome, Italy, 1844; d. Boston, Mass., Mar. 10, 1886. [4]

Anagnos, Michael, educator of the blind, b. Papengo, Epirus, Turkey, 1837; d. Turn Severin, Roumania, June 29, 1906. [4]

Anderegg, Frederick, mathematician, b. Meiringen, Switzerland, 1852; d. Oberlin, O., Oct. 9, 1922. [10]

Anders, James Meschter, physician, b. Fairview, Pa., 1854; d. Philadelphia, Pa., Aug. 29, 1936. [10]

Anderson, Abraham Archibald, artist, b. New Jersey, 1847; d. New York, N.Y., April 27, 1940. [10]

Anderson, Alexander, physician and wood-engraver, b. New York, N.Y., 1775; d. Jersey City, N.Y. Jan. 17, 1870. [3; 7]

Anderson, Alexander Caulfield, fur-trader, b. Calcutta, India, 1814; d. Victoria, B.C., May 9, 1884. [27]

Anderson, Alexander Dwight, lawyer, b. Mansfield, Conn., 1843; d. Mount Vernon, Va., Nov. 21, 1901. [6; 62]

Anderson, Charles Palmerston, bishop, b. Kemptville, Ont., 1864; d. Chicago. Ill., Jan. 30, 1930. [10]

Anderson, David, journalist, b. Scotland, 1875; d. Oakland, Calif., Dec. 21, 1947.

Anderson, Dice Robins, historian, b. Charlottesville, Va., 1880; d. Fredericksburg, Va., Oct. 23, 1942. [10; 11]

Anderson, Duncan, clergyman and poet, b. Scotland, 1828; d. Canada, April 3, 1903. [27]

Anderson, Edward Lowell, lawyer, b. Cincinatti, O., 1842; d. Cincinnati, O., March 29, 1916. [10]

Anderson, Edward Pretot, traveller, b. Dutchess county, N.Y., 1855; d. Block Island, R.I., Aug. 23, 1887, [55]

Anderson, Elam Jonathan, educationist, b. Chicago, Ill., 1890; d. Redlands, Calif., Aug. 17, 1944. [10]

Anderson, Frederick Irving, journalist, b. Aurora, Ill., 1877; d. Pittsfield, Mass., Dec. 24, 1947. [11]

Anderson, Galusha, clergyman and educationist, b. Clarendon, N.Y., 1832; d. Newton Centre, Mass., July 20, 1918. [1; 10; 25]

Anderson, Mrs. Galusha. See Anderson, Mrs. Mary Eleanor, née Roberts.

Anderson, Garland, playwright and lecturer, b. Wichita, Kans., 1886; d. New York, N.Y., June 1, 1939. [35]

Anderson, George Washington, clergyman, b. Philadelphia, Pa., 1816; d. Rosemont, Pa., July 3, 1903. [24; 25]

Anderson, Henry Tompkins, clergyman, b. 1812; d. Washington, D.C., Sept. 19, 1872. [1; 4]

Anderson, James Thomas Milton, educationist and politician, b. Fairbank, Ont., 1878; d. Saskatoon, Sask., Dec. 28, 1946. [30]

Anderson, Jerome A., physician, b. Randolph county, Ind., 1847; d. San Francisco, Calif., Dec. 6, 1903. [35]

Anderson, John, drama critic, b. Pensacola, Fla., 1896; d. New York, N.Y., July 16, 1943. [7]

Anderson, John Jacob, educationist, b. New York, N.Y., 1821; d. 1906. [3; 10]

Anderson, Joseph, clergyman, b. Rossshire, Scotland, 1836; d. Waterbury, Conn., Aug. 18. 1916. [10; 68]

Anderson, Lewis Flint, educationist, b. Waterford, Ont., 1866; d. Columbus, O., Nov. 17, 1932. [10; 11]

Anderson, Margaret Steele, poet, b. Louisville, Ky., 1875; d. Louisville, Ky., Jan. 16, 1921. [74]

Anderson, Martin Brewer, educationist, b. Brunswick, Me., 1815; d. Lake Helen, Fla., Feb. 20, 1890. [2; 8]

Anderson, Mrs. Mary Eleanor, née **Roberts,** poet, b. 1840; d. 1916.

Anderson, Melville Best, educationist, b. Kalamazoo, Mich., 1851; d. La Jolla, Calif., June 22, 1933. [10; 35]

Anderson, Neal Larkin, clergyman, b. York, S.C., 1865; d. Savannah, Ga., May 19, 1931. [10]

Anderson, Olive San Louie, educationist, b. Lexington, O., 1842; drowned in the Sacramento river, Calif., June 5, 1886. [35]

Anderson, Rasmus Bjorn, educationist, b. Albion, Wis., 1846; d. Madison, Wis., March 2, 1936. [6; 10; 11; 44]

Anderson, Richard Clough, naturalist, b. Cincinnati, O., 1872; d. Cincinnati, O., Oct. 20, 1916.

Anderson, Robert, soldier, b. near Louisville, Ky., 1805; d. 1871.

Anderson, Rufus, clergyman, b. North Yarmouth, Me., 1796; d. Boston, Mass., May 30, 1880. [3; 46; 49]

Anderson, Sherwood, journalist, poet, and novelist, b. Camden, O., 1876; d. Cristobal, Canal Zone, Panama, March 8, 1941. [1a; 7; 9; 10; 11; 12]

Anderson, Thomas McArthur, soldier, b. Chillicothe, O., 1836; d. Vancouver, Wash., May 8, 1917. [10]

Anderson, Troyer Steele, historian, b. Minneapolis, Minn., 1900; d. Swarthmore, Pa., April 3, 1948. [14]

Anderson, Wilbert Lee, clergyman, b. East Berkshire, Vt., 1859; d. Methuen, Mass., March 25, 1915. [62]

Anderson, William Brennan, clergyman, .b Monmouth, Ill., 1868; d. Germantown, Pa., Jan. 6, 1940. [10]

Anderson, William Caldwell, lawyer, b. Youngstown, Pa., 1852; d. Pittsburg, Pa., Nov. 25, 1910. [62]

Anderson, William Gilbert, educationist, b. St. Joseph, Mich., 1860; d. New Haven, Conn., July 7, 1947. [10; 62]

Anderson, William James, physician and journalist, b. Scotland, about 1813; d. Quebec, Que., May 17, 1873. [27]

Anderson, Winslow, physician, b. about 1861; d. New York, N.Y., May 7, 1917. [10]

Andreas, Alfred Theodore, publisher, b. 1839; d. 1900.

Andreen, Gustav Albert, educationist, b. Porter, Ind., 1864; d. Moline, Ill., Oct. 1, 1940. [10; 62]

Andress, James Mace, educationist, b. Chesaning, Mich., 1881; d. Newtonville, Mass., Feb. 5, 1942. [10]

Andrew, Abram Piatt, soldier and politician, b. La Porte, Ind., 1873; d. Gloucester, Mass., June 2, 1936. [10]

Andrew, James Osgood, bishop, b. Wilkes county, Ga., 1794; d. Mobile, Ala., March 2, 1871. [1; 5; 6; 34]

Andrew, John Albion, lawyer, b. Windham, Me., 1818; d. Boston, Mass., Oct. 30. 1867. [5; 6]

Andrews, Alfred, genealogist, b. 1797; d. 1876. [4]

Andrews, Annulet. See Ohl, Mrs. Maude Annulet, née Andrews.

Andrews, Byron, journalist, b. 1852; d. ?

Andrews, Charles McLean, historian, b. Wethersfield, Conn., 1863; d. New Haven, Conn., Sept. 9, 1943. [7; 10; 11]

Andrews, Charlton, playwright and novelist, b. Connersville, Ind., 1878; d. Boothbay Harbor, Me., Aug. 13, 1939. [7; 11]

Andrews, Christopher Columbus, lawyer, b. Hillsborough, N.Y., 1829; d. Rochester, Minn., Sept. 21, [1; 5; 6; 10; 70]

Andrews, Clarence Edward, educationist, b. New York, N.Y., 1883; d. Columbus, O., Dec. 12, 1932. [10; 62]

Andrews, Ebenezer Baldwin, clergyman and geologist, b. Danbury, Conn., 1821; d. 1880. [6]

Andrews, Edmund, surgeon, b. Putney, Vt., 1824; d. Chicago, Ill., Jan. 2, 1904. [6; 10; 53]

Andrews, Elisha Benjamin, educationist, b. Hinsdale, N.H., 1844; d. Interlachen, Fla., Oct. 30, 1917. [1; 2; 6; 47]

Andrews, Eliza Frances, educationist and novelist, b. Washington, Ga., 1840; d. Rome, Ga., Jan. 20, 1939. [4; 10; 34]

Andrews, Emerson, evangelist, b. 1806; d. ? [6]

Andrews, Ethan Allen, lexicographer and grammarian, b. New Britain, Conn., 1787; d. New Britain, Conn., March 4, 1858. [2; 4; 6; 62]

Andrews, Fanny. See Andrews, Eliza Frances.

Andrews, Garnett, jurist, b. near Washington, Ga., 1798; d. Washington, Ga., Aug. 14, 1873. [34]

Andrews, George Gordon, historian, b. Illinois, 1887; d. Iowa City, Ia., March 29, 1938.

Andrews, Mrs. Gwendolen, née Foulke, poet, b. 1863; d. 1936.

Andrews, Henry Franklin, genealogist, b. 1844; d. Exira, Ia., May 20, 1919. [37]

Andrews, Israel Ward, educationist, b. Danbury, Conn., 1815; d. Hartford, Conn., April 18, 1888. [1; 2; 3; 6]

Andrews, James DeWitt, lawyer and educationist, b. Sterling, Ill., 1856; d. Brooklyn, N.Y., April 11, 1928. [10]

Andrews, Jane educationist, b. Newburyport, Mass., 1833; d. Newburyport, Mass., July 15, 1887. [7; 8; 17]

Andrews, John, clergyman and educationist, b. Cecil county, Md., 1746; d. Philadelphia, Pa., March 29, 1813. [1; 3; 4]

Andrews, John Bertram, economist, b. South Wayne, Wis., 1780; d. New York, N. Y., Jan. 4, 1943. [10; 11]

Andrews, Launcelot Winchester, chemist, b. London, Ont., 1856; d. Belmont, Mass., April 14, 1938. [10; 11; 62]

Andrews, Lorenzo Frank, journalist, b. 1828; d. Des Moines, Ia., July 5, 1915. [37]

Andrews, Lorrin, missionary, b. East Windsor, Conn., 1795; d. Honolulu, Hawaii, Sept. 22, 1868. [4]

Andrews, Mrs. Marietta, née Minnegerode, painter, b. Richmond Va., 1869; d. near Alexandria, Va., Aug. 7, 1931. [10]

Andrews, Martin Register, local historian, b. Meigs, O., 1842; d. Marietta, O., April 20, 1913. [10]

Andrews, Mrs. Mary Raymond, née Shipman, novelist, b. Mobile, Ala., about 1865; d. Syracuse, N.Y. Aug 2, 1936. [7; 10; 11]

Andrews, Matthew Page, historian, b. Shepherdstown, W. Va., 1879; d. Baltimore, Md., June 20, 1947. [10; 11; 34]

Andrews, Matthew Thomas, clergyman, b. near McComb City, Miss., 1869; d. Texarcana, Tex., 1939. [10]

• Andrews, Samuel James, clergyman, b. Danbury, Conn., 1817; d. Oct. 11, 1906. [1; 3; 10]

Andrews, Sidney, journalist, b. Massachusetts, 1835; d. April 10, 1880. [1; 6]

Andrews, Stephen Pearl, reformer and philosopher, b. Templeton, Mass., 1812; d. New York, N.Y., May 21, 1886. [1; 3; 6; 8]

Andrews, Thomas Sheldon, genealogist, b. 1829; d. 1891.

Andrews, William D., life-guard, b. 1853; d. Toronto, Ont., 1903.

Andrews, William Given, clergyman, b. Kent, Conn., 1835; d. Guildford, Conn., Dec. 23, 1912. [10]

Andrews, William Loring, bibliophile, b. New York, N.Y., 1837; d. New York N.Y., March 9, 1920. [1; 10]

Andrews, William Page, editor, b. Framingham, Mass., 1848; d. Sept 22, 1916. [10]

Andrews, William Symes, electrical engineer, b. Saltford, Somersetshire, England, 1847; d. Schenectady, N.Y., July 1, 1929. [10]

Andros, Richard Salter Storrs, poet, b. 1817; d. 1868. [19]

Andros, Thomas, clergyman, b. 1759; d. Dec. 30, 1845. [46]

Angel, Myron, local historian, b. Oneonta, N.Y., 1827; d. San Luis Obispo, Calif., June 27, 1911. [35]

Angel, Rosa Evangeline, poet. d. 1895.

Angell, George Thorndike, reformer, b. Southridge, Mass., 1823; d. Boston, Mass., March 16, 1909. [1; 10]

Angell, Henry Clay, oculist, b. Providence, R.I., 1829; d. Boston, Mass., May 27, 1911. [8; 10]

Angell, Hildegarde (pseud.). See Smith, Hildegarde Angell.

Angell, James Burrill, journalist and educationist, b. near Scituate, R.I., 1829; d. Ann Arbor, Mich., April, 1916. [1; 7; 10; 47]

Angell, James Rowland, educationist, b. Burlington, Vt., 1869; d. New Haven, Conn., March 4, 1949. [4; 7; 10; 11; 14]

Angell, Joseph Kinnicutt, lawyer, b. Providence, R.I., 1794; d. Boston, Mass., May 1, 1857. [1; 3; 4; 5; 6]

Angell, Oliver, educationist, b. 1787; d. Providence, R.I., Nov. 11, 1858. [47]

Anger, Joseph Humfrey, musician, b. Berkshire, England, 1862; d. Toronto, Ont., June 11, 1913. [27]

Angers, Charles, biographer, b. Murray Bay, Que., 1854; d. 1929. [27]

Angers, Félicité, novelist, b. Murray Bay, Que., 1845; d. Quebec, Que., 1924. [27]

Angers, François Réal, lawyer, b. 1813; d. Quebec, Que., April, 1860. [27]

Angle, Edward Hartley, orthodontist, b. Herrick, Bradford county, Pa., 1855; d. Pasadena, Calif., Aug. 11 1930. [4; 10]

Angus (pseud.). See Williams, Ephie Augustus.

Anicetus (pseud.). See Clark, William Adolphus.

Annand, William, politician, b. Halifax, N. S., 1808; d. London, England, Oct. 12, 1887. [3; 27]

Anshutz, Edward Pollock, editor, b. Clarington, O., 1846; d. Jan. 31, 1918. [10]

Ansley, Clarke Fisher, encyclopaedist, b. Swedona, Ill., 1869; d. Soleburg, Pa., Feb. 14, 1939. [7; 10]

Anspach, Frederick Rinehart, clergyman, b. Pennsylvania, 1815; d. Baltimore, Md., Sept. 16, 1867. [3; 34] •

Anspacher, Louis Kaufman, poet and playwright, b. Cincinnati, O., 1878; d. Nashville, Tenn., May 10, 1947. [7; 10; 11]

Anstice, Henry, clergyman, b. New York, N.Y., 1841; d. Dec. 18, 1922. [10; 61]

Anthon, Charles, classical scholar, b. New York, N.Y., 1797; d. New York, N.Y., July 29, 1867. [1; 2; 3; 4; 5; 6]

Anthon, Charles Edward, educationist and numismatist, b. New York, N.Y., 1823; d. Bremen, Germany, June 7, 1883. [1; 2; 3; 4; 6]

Anthon, John, lawyer, b. Detroit, Mich., 1784; d. New York, N.Y., March 5, 1863. [1; 3; 4; 8]

Anthony, Alfred Williams, clergyman and educationist, b. Providence, R.I., 1860; d. Waltham, Mass., Jan. 20, 1939. [10; 11; 47]

Anthony, Elliott, jurist, b. Spafford, N.Y., 1827; d. Evanston, Ill., Feb. 24, 1898. [36]

Anthony Gardner Chace, educationist, b. Providence, R.I., 1856; d. New Rochelle, N.Y., Nov. 28, 1937. [10; 11]

Anthony, Geraldine, novelist, d. New York, N.Y., Oct. 20, 1912.

Anthony, Henry Bowen, journalist and politician, b. Coventry, R.I., 1815; d. Providence, R.I., Sept. 2, 1884. [4; 6; 47]

Anthony, Mary Borden, suffragist, b. 1864; d. Providence, R.I., May 21, 1947.

Anthony, Susan Brownell, suffragist, b. South Adams, Mass., 1820; d. Rochester, N.Y., March 13, 1906. [1; 2; 3; 10]

Anthony, Susanna, religious writer, b. 1726; d. Newport, R.I., June 23, 1791. [3]

Anthony, William Arnold, physicist, b. Coventry, R. I., 1835; d. New York, N.Y., 1908. [10; 47]

Anthrops (pseud.). See Storrs, George.

Antin, Mary, sociologist, d. Suffern, N.Y., May 15, 1949.

Antisell, Thomas, physician and chemist, b. Dublin, Ireland, 1817; d. near Washington, D.C., June 14, 1893. [4; 6]

Antrobus, Augustus M., local historian, b. 1839; d. ? [37]

Apes, William, missionary, b. near Colrain, Mass., 1798; d. ? [1; 34]

Apgar, Austin Craig, naturalist, b. Peapack, N. J., 1838; d. Trenton, N.J., March 4, 1908. [8; 10]

Apgar, Ellis A., botanist, d. 1905.

Appel, Theodore, clergyman, b. Easton, Pa., 1823; d. 1907. [3; 8; 10]

Appel, Theodore Burton, physician, b. Lancaster, Pa., 1871; d. July 31, 1937. [10; 55]

Applegate, Frank Guy, artist, b. Atlanta, Ill., 1882; d. Santa Fé, N.M., Feb. 13, 1931. [10]

Applegate, Jesse, surveyor and publicist, b. Kentucky, 1811; d. near Drain, Ore., April 22, 1888. [1; 4; 41]

Applegate, John Stilwell, lawyer, b. Middletown, N.J., 1837; d. Red Bank, N.J., Nov. 10, 1916. [10]

Appleton, Elizabeth Haven, chronicler, b. 1815; d. 1890.

Appleton, Everard Jack, poet, b. 1872; d. 1931.

Appleton, Jesse, educationist, b. New Ipswich, N.H., 1772; d. Brunswick, Me., Nov. 12, 1819. [3; 4; 49]

Appleton, John, lawyer, b. New Ipswich, N.H., 1804; d. Bangor, Me., Feb. 7, 1891. [3a]

Appleton, John Howard, chemist, b. Portland, Me., 1844; d. Providence, R.I., Feb. 19, 1930. [6; 8; 10]

Appleton, Lilla Estelle, psychologist, b. Victory, Vt., 1858; d. May 8, 1937. [10]

Appleton, Nathan, manufacturer, banker, and politician, b. Ipswich, Mass., 1779; d. Boston, Mass., July 14, 1861. [1; 4; 6]

Appleton, Nathan, soldier, b. 1843; d. 1906.

Appleton, Nathaniel, clergyman. b. Ipswich, Mass., 1693; d. Boston, Mass., Feb. 9, 1784. [4; 51]

Appleton, Thomas Gold, essayist, poet, and artist, b. Boston, Mass., 1812; d. New York, N.Y., April 17, 1884. [1; 3; 7; 71]

Appleton, William Hyde, classical scholar, b. Portland, Me., 1842; d. Philadelphia, Pa., April 3, 1926. [51]

Appleton, William Sumner, genealogist, b. Boston, Mass., 1840; d. Boston, Mass., April 28, 1903. [51]

Apthorp, William Foster, drama and music critic, b. Boston, Mass., 1848; d. Vevey, Switzerland, Feb. 19, 1913. [4]

Archambault, Joseph Louis, lawyer and playwright, b. Varennes, Que., 1849; d. Montreal, Que., May 27, 1925. [27]

Archambault, Louis Misaël, priest, b. Chambly, Lower Canada, 1812; d. St. Hugues, Que., July 10, 1894. [32]

Archer, George Washington, physician, d. Belair, Md., 1907. [55]

Archer, Lane (pseud.). See Hauck, Mrs. Louise, née Platt.

Archibald, Andrew Webster, clergyman, b. Kingston, N.Y., 1851; d. Los Angeles, Calif., Nov. 15, 1926. [10; 62]

Archibald, Mrs. Edith Jessie, née Archibald, biographer and novelist, b. 1854; d. 1934. [11]

Archibald, James Francis Jewell, war correspondent, b. New York, N.Y., 1871; d. Hollywood, Calif., May 28, 1934.

Archibald, William Charles, genealogist, b. Musquodoboit, N.S., 1824; d. Virginia, Sept. 29, 1924.

Arctander, John William, lawyer, b. Stockholm, Sweden, 1849; d. 1920. [70]

Arey, Mrs. Harriet Ellen, née Grannis, poet and educationist, b. Cavendish, Vt., 1819; d. Brooklyn, N.Y., April 26, 1901. [8; 43]

Aristides (pseud.). See Hanson, Alexander Contee.

Aristides (pseud.). See McKenney, Thomas Loraine.

Arkell, William J., publisher, b. Canajoharie, N.Y., 1856; d. Los Angeles, Calif., Dec. 30, 1930. [10]

Armes, Ellen Elizabeth, novelist, b. 1847; d. 1904.

Armes, George Augustus, soldier, b. 1844; d. Ventnor, N. J., Dec. 18, 1919.

Armitage, Thomas, clergyman, b. Pontefract, England, 1819; d. Yonkers, N.Y., Jan. 20, 1896. [4; 6; 8; 24; 25]

Armitage, William James, clergyman, b. near London, Ont., 1860; d. Halifax, N.S., Sept. 10, 1929. (27)

Armor, William Crawford, historian, fl. 1872-1897.

Armour, Edward Douglas, lawyer and poet, b. Port Hope, Ont., 1851; d. Toronto, Ont., Oct. 3, 1922. [27]

Armour, Jonathan Ogden, capitalist, b. Milwaukee, Wis., 1863; d. London, England, Aug. 16, 1927. [4; 10]

Arms, Goodsil Filley, clergyman, b. Sutton, Que., 1854; d. Tarpon Springs, Fla., Dec. 9, 1932. [60]

Arms, Mrs. Mary L., née **Day,** blind woman, b. 1836; d.   ?

Armsby, Henry Prentiss, agricultural chemist, b. Northbridge, Mass., 1853; d. State College, Pa., Oct. 19, 1921. [1; 4; 10; 62]

Armstrong, Andrew Campbell, philosopher, b. New York, N.Y., 1860; d. Cromwell, Conn., Feb. 21, 1935. [10]

Armstrong, David Maitland, painter, b. near Newburgh, N.Y., 1836; d. May 26, 1918.   [1; 10]

Armstrong, Edward Cooke, educationist, b. Winchester, Va., 1871; d. Princeton, N.J., March 5, 1948.   [10]

Armstrong, George Dodd, clergyman, b. Mendham, Morris county, N.J., 1813; d. Norfolk, Va., May 11, 1899.   [1; 3; 6]

Armstrong, George Henry, educationist, b. Yonge, Leeds county, Ont., 1858; d. Kingston, Ont., April 14, 1938.   [27]

Armstrong, James, jurist, b. Berthier, Lower Canada, 1821; d. 1888.

Armstrong, James Clayton, clergyman, b. 1847; d.   ?

Armstrong, James Edward, clergyman, b. 1830; d. after 1907.

Armstrong, James Elder, biographer, b. 1855; d. Sept. 13, 1936.

Armstrong, John, soldier and diplomat, b. Carlisle, Pa., 1758; d. Red Hook, N.Y., April 1, 1843.   [1; 4; 8]

Armstrong, Joseph, Christian scientist, b. 1848; d. 1907.

Armstrong, Lebbeus, clergyman, b. 1775; d. 1860.

Armstrong, Le Roy, journalist, b. Plymouth, Ind., 1854; d. Lankershim, Calif., March 29, 1927.   [10]

Armstrong, Mrs. Margaret, née **Neilson,** artist and novelist, b. New York, N.Y., 1867; d. New York, N.Y., July 18, 1944. [7; 10; 11]

Armstrong, Mrs. Mary Frances, née **Morgan,** educationist, d. 1903.

Armstrong, Moses Kimball, journalist, politician, and banker, b. Milan, O., 1832; d. Albert Lea, Minn., Jan. 11, 1906. [3; 70]

Armstrong, Paul, playwright, b. Kidder, Mo., 1869; d. New York, N.Y., Aug. 30, 1915.   [4; 7; 10]

Armstrong, Perry A., pioneer, b. near Newark, O., 1823; d.   ?

Armstrong, Robert Allen, educationist, b. Frenchton, Va., 1860; d. Morgantown, W. Va,. Sept. 15, 1936. [7; 10]

Armstrong, Samuel Chapman, educationist, b. Maui, Hawaiian Islands, 1839; d. Hampton, Va., May 11, 1893.   [1; 4]

Armstrong, William, novelist, b. Frederick county, Md., 1856; d. ?

Armstrong, William Jackson, lecturer, b. Warren county, O., 1841; d. Los Angeles, Calif., 1913.   [10]

Armstrong, William Nevins, lawyer, b. Honolulu, Hawaii, 1835; d. Washington, D.C., Oct. 15, 1905.

Arndt, Walter Tallmadge, journalist, b. Depere, Wis., 1872; d. Trenton, N.J., Jan. 1, 1932. [10; 51]

Arnett, Alexander Mathews, historian, b. near Sylvania, Ga., 1888; d. Greensboro, N.C., Aug. 7, 1945.   [10]

Arnold, Abraham B., physician, b. Germany, 1820; d. San Francisco, Calif., March 28, 1904. [5]

Arnold, Abraham Kerns, soldier, b. Bedford, Pa., 1837; d. Coldsprings, Ont., Nov. 23, 1901.   [3a; 10]

Arnold, Albert Nicholas, clergyman, b. Cranston, R.I., 1814; d. Pawtucket, R.I., Oct. 11, 1883. [6;   8; 47]

Arnold, Alexander Streeter, novelist and playwright, b. 1829; d.   ?

Arnold, Anthony Brown, poet, b. Providence, R.I., 1791; d. 1885.

Arnold, Mrs. Augusta, née **Foote,** compiler, b. Seneca Falls, N.Y., 1844; d. 1903. [8]

Arnold, Birch (pseud.).   See Bartlett, Mrs. Alice Elinor, née Bowen.

Arnold, Edmund Samuel Foster, physician, b. London, England, 1820; d. Jacksonville, Fla., Nov. 22, 1907. [10]

Arnold, Felix, educationist, b. New York, N.Y., 1879; d. about 1927. [10]

Arnold, George, poet, b. New York, N.Y., 1834; d. Strawberry Farms, N.J., Nov. 9, 1865. [3; 4; 19; 71]

Arnold, Henry Lucian, engineer, d. 1915.

Arnold, Henry Vernon, publisher and local historian, b. 1848; d.   ?

Arnold, Howard Payson, lawyer, b. Boston, Mass., 1831; d. 1910. [8; 10; 51]

Arnold, Isaac Newton, lawyer and politican, b. Hartwick, N.Y., 1815; d. Chicago, Ill., April 24, 1884.   [1; 4; 6]

Arnold, James Loring, electrical engineer, b. Brooklyn, N. Y., 1868; d. Orlando, Fla., April 23, 1935.   [10]

Arnold, James Newell, genealogist, b. 1844; d. 1927.

Arnold, John Paul, brewer, b. 1854; d. Dec. 6, 1931.

Arnold, Josias Lyndon, poet, b. Providence, R.I., 1768; d. St. Johnsbury, Vt., June 7, 1796. [43; 49]

Arnold, Lauren Briggs, dairy husbandman, b. Fairfield, N.Y., 1814; d. March 7, 1888. [1]

Arnold, Levi McKeen, spiritualist, b. 1813; d. 1864.   [6]

Arnold, Samuel George, journalist, b. near Utica, N.Y., 1806; d. Washington, D.C., May 3, 1891.   [4]

Arnold, Samuel Greene, historian, b. Providence, R.I., 1821; d. Providence, R.I., Feb. 13, 1880. [1; 3; 47]

Arnold, Thomas Jackson, lawyer and biographer, b. Beverly, Va., 1845; d. Jan. 10, 1933.   [10; 11]

Arnold, William Harris, bibliophile, b. 1854; d. Jan. 2. 1923. [7]

Arnold, William Rosenzweig, educationist, b. Beirut, Syria, 1872; d. Cambridge, Mass., Dec. 11, 1929. [10; 68]

Arnoux, William Henry, lawyer, b. New York, N.Y., 1831; d. 1907. [10]

Arny, Henry Vinecome, pharmaceutical chemist, b. New Orleans, La., 1868; d. Montclair, N.J., Nov. 3, 1943. [10; 13]

Arny, William Frederick Milton, politician, b. 1813; d. New Mexico, 1881.

Aron, Albert William, educationist, b. Atkins, Ia., 1886; d. Urbana, Ill., Oct. 31, 1945. [10]

Aronson, Rudolph, musical composer, b. New York, N.Y., 1856; d. New York, N.Y., Feb. 5, 1919. [10; 20]

Arp, Bill (pseud.). See Smith, Charles Henry (1826-1903).

Arr, E. H. (pseud.). See Rollins, Mrs. Ellen Chapman, née Hobbs.

Arrington, Alfred W., lawyer and poet, b. Iredell county, N.C., 1810; d. Chicago, Ill., Dec. 31, 1867. [1; 7; 34]

Arthur, Joseph Charles, botanist, b. Lowville, N.Y., 1850; d. Lafayette, Ind., April 30, 1942. [10]

Arthur, Robert, dentist, b. 1819; d. 1880.

Arthur, Timothy Shay, novelist, b. near Newburg, N.Y., 1809; d. Philadelphia, Pa., March 6, 1885. [1; 2; 3; 5; 9]

Arthur, William, clergyman, b. near Ballymena, Ireland, 1797; d. Newtonville, N.Y., Oct. 27, 1875. [1; 24; 25]

Arvine, Kazlitt, clergyman, b. Centerville, N.Y., 1819; d. Worcester, Mass., July 15, 1851. [6; 24; 26; 60]

Asakawa, Kwan-Ichi, historian, b. Japan, 1873; d. West Wardsboro, Vt., Aug. 10, 1948. [10]

Asbury, Francis, bishop, b. near Birmingham, England, 1745; d. Spottsylvania, Va., March 31, 1816. [1; 2; 3; 4; 5; 7; 34]

Asbury, Henry, lawyer, b. Harrison county, Ky., 1810; d. Chicago, Ill., Nov. 19, 1896.

Ash, Peter (pseud.). See Hauck, Mrs. Louise, née Platt.

Ashbrook, Harriette, novelist, b. 1898; d. Scotts Bluffs, Neb., June 6, 1946.

Ashburn, Percy Moreau, physician and soldier, b. Batavia, O., 1872; d. Washington, D.C., Aug. 20, 1940. [10]

Ashby, Thomas Almond, historian, b. 1848; d. 1916.

Ashe, Robert Pickering, clergyman, b. 1875; d. ?

Ashe, Samuel A'Court, lawyer, b. near Wilmington, N.C., 1840; d. Raleigh, N.C., Aug. 31, 1938. [7; 10; 34]

Asher, Georg Michael, historian, b. Germany; d. Brooklyn, N.Y., 1905. [6]

Asher, Philip, chemist, b. 1876; d. 1920. [13]

Ashford, Bailey Kelly, medical officer, b. Washington, D.C., 1873; d. San Juan, Puerto Rico, Nov. 1, 1934. [10]

Ashhurst, John, surgeon, b. Philadelphia, Pa., Aug. 23, 1839; d. Philadelphia, Pa., July 7, 1900. [10]

Ashhurst, Richard Lewis, lawyer, b. Naples, Italy, 1838; d. 1911. [10]

Ashley, Barnas Freeman, clergyman, b. Milton, Queen's county, N.S., 1833; d. ? [33]

Ashley, Clarence Degrand, lawyer and educationist, b. Boston, Mass., 1851; d. New York, N.Y., Jan. 26, 1916. [62]

Ashley, Clifford Warren, marine painter, b. New Bedford, Mass., 1881; d. New Bedford, Mass., Sept. 18, 1947. [10; 11]

Ashley, Ossian Doolittle, railway president, b. Townsend, Vt., 1821; d. 1904. [10]

Ashley, Schuyler, essayist and poet, b. 1897; d. 1927.

Ashmead, Albert Sydney, physician, d. Philadelphia, Pa., Feb. 20, 1911.

Ashmead, Henry Graham, local historian, b. Philadelphia, Pa., 1838; d. Chester, Pa., 1920. [4]

Ashmead, William Harris, entomologist, b. Philadelphia, Pa., 1858; d. Washington, D.C., Oct. 17, 1908. [1; 10]

Ashmont (pseud.). See Perry, Joseph Franklin.

Ashmore, Otis, educationist, b. Lincoln county, Ga., 1853; d. ? [34]

Ashmore, Ruth (pseud.). See Mallon, Mrs. Isabel Allderdice, née Sloan.

Ashmore, Sidney Gillespie, educationist, b. London, England, 1852; d. Schenectady, N.Y., May 22, 1911. [10]

Ashmore, William, clergyman, b. Zanesville, O., 1824; d. Toledo, O., April 21, 1909. [25]

Ashmun, Jehudi, missionary and colonial agent, b. Champlain, N.Y., 1794; d. Boston, Mass., Aug. 25, 1828. [1; 3]

Ashmun, Margaret Eliza, educationist and novelist, b. Rural Waupaca county, Wis.; d. Springfield, Mass., March 15, 1940. [7; 10; 11; 44]

Ashton, Charles Hamilton, mathematician, b. 1866; d. Lawrence, Kans., Aug. 2, 1936. [11]

Ashton, Joseph Nickerson, musician, b. Salem, Mass., 1868; d. Andover, Mass., Aug. 2, 1946. [20; 47]

Ashton, Mrs. Sophia, née **Goodrich,** religious writer, b. 1819; d. ? [6]

Ashton, Warren T. (pseud.). See Adams, William Taylor.

Ashton, William Easterly, physician, b. Philadelphia, Pa., 1859; d. Philadelphia, Pa., May 30, 1933. [10; 55]

Aspinwall, Thomas, soldier, b. Brookline, Mass., 1786; d. Aug. 11, 1876.

Asplund, John, clergyman, b. Sweden; d. Fishing Creek, Va., 1807. [24; 25]

Asquith, Mary, actress, b. 1873; d. Brooklyn, N.Y., Dec. 22, 1942. [2a]

Asselin, Joseph François Olivar, journalist, b. St. Hilarion, Que., 1874; d. Montreal, Que., April 18, 1937. [30]

Astor, John Jacob, inventor, b. Rineback, N.Y., 1864; d. at sea, in the **Titanic** disaster, April 15, 1912. [1; 10]

Astor, William Waldorf, capitalist and journalist, b. New York, N.Y., 1848; d. Brighton, England, Oct. 18, 1919. [1; 3; 10]

Athearn, Walter Scott, educationist, b. Marengo, Ia., 1872; d. St. Louis, Mo., Nov. 13, 1934. [10; 37]

Athern, Anna (pseud.). See Pike, Mrs. Frances West, née Atherton.

Atherton, Mrs. Gertrude Franklin, née Horn, novelist, b. San Francisco, Calif., 1857; d. San Francisco, Calif., June 14, 1948. [4; 7; 9; 10; 11; 12; 35]

Atkeson, Thomas Clark, agriculturist, b. Buffalo, W. Va., 1852; d. 1935. [10]

Atkeson, William Oscar, lawyer, b. Buffalo, W. Va., 1854; d. ? [11]

Atkins, Dudley, physician, b. Newburyport, Mass., 1898; d. Brooklyn, N.Y., April 7, 1945. [46]

Atkins, Edwin Farnsworth, manufacturer, b. Boston, Mass., 1850; d. Belmont, Mass., May 20, 1926. [10]

Atkins, Thomas Astley, lawyer, b. 1839; d. 1916. [51]

Atkinson, Edward, industrialist and economist, b. Brookline, Mass., 1827; d. Boston, Mass., Dec. 11, 1905. [1; 2; 3; 4; 5; 6; 10]

Atkinson, Mrs. Eleanor, née Stackhouse, journalist and novelist, b. Rensselaer, Ind., 1863; d. Orangeburg, N.Y., Nov. 5, 1942. [10]

Atkinson, Francis Blake, journalist and naturalist, d. New York, N.Y., April, 1930.

Atkinson, Fred Washington, educationist, b. Reading, Mass., 1865; d. Tuscon, Ariz., Oct. 21, 1945. [51]

Atkinson, George Francis, botanist, b. Raisinville, Mich., 1854; d. Tacoma, Wash., Nov. 15, 1918. [1; 10]

Atkinson, George Henry, clergyman, b. Newburyport, Mass., 1819; d. Feb. 25, 1889. [1]

Atkinson, George Wesley, lawyer, b. Kanawha county, Va., 1845; d. Charleston, W. Va., April 14, 1925. [1; 7; 8; 10; 34]

Atkinson, John, clergyman and historian, b. Deerfield, N.J., 1835; d. Haverstraw, N.Y., Dec. 8, 1897. [3; 6]

Atkinson, Joseph, journalist and local historian, b. near Belfast, Ireland, 1846; d. Newark, N.J., Dec. 17, 1924.

Atkinson, William Biddle, physician, b. 1832; d 1909. [6]

Atkinson, William Davis, lawyer, b. 1850; d. ? [34]

Atkinson, William Parsons, educationist, b. Boston, Mass., 1820; d. Boston, Mass., March 10, 1890. [8; 51]

Atkinson, William Walker, writer on psychology and New Thought, b. Baltimore, Md., 1862; d. Arcadia, Calif., Nov. 22, 1932. [10]

Atkinson, Wilmer, journalist, b. Bucks county, Pa., 1840; d. Philadelphia, Pa., May 10, 1920. [1; 7; 10]

Atlee, Edwin Augustus, physician and poet, b. 1776; d. Philadelphia, Pa., March 8, 1852. [55]

Atterbury, Anson Phelps, clergyman, b. New York, N.Y., 1854; d. New York, N.Y., Jan. 4, 1931. [10]

Atterley, Joseph (pseud.). See Tucker, George.

Atwater, Caleb, pioneer, b. North Adams, Mass., 1778; d. Circleville, O., March 13, 1867. [1; 3; 6]

Atwater, Edward Elias, clergyman, b. New Haven, Conn., 1816; d. Hawthorn, Fla., Dec. 2, 1887. [6; 62]

Atwater, Francis, local historian, b. Plymouth, Conn., 1858; d. Nov. 25, 1935. [10; 62]

Atwater, George Parkin, clergyman, b. Lisbon, O., 1874; d. Brooklyn, N.Y., Oct. 21, 1935. [10]

Atwater, Horace Cowles, clergyman, b. Homer, N.Y., 1819; d. 1879. [6]

Atwater, Isaac, jurist, b. Homer, N.Y., 1818; d. Minneapolis, Minn., Dec. 22, 1906. [70]

Atwater, John Birdseye, clergyman, b. Minneapolis, Minn., 1855; d. Minneapolis, Minn., May 20, 1921. [62]

Atwater, Lyman Hotchkiss, clergyman and educationist, b. New Haven, Conn., 1813; d. Princeton, N.J., Feb. 17, 1883. [1; 3; 4; 56; 62]

Atwater, Wilbur Olin, agricultural chemist, b. Johnsburg, N.Y., 1844; d. Middletown, Conn., Sept. 22, 1907. [1; 3; 4; 10]

Atwood, Anthony, clergyman, b. Burlington, N.J., 1801; d. 1888. [6]

Atwood, David, journalist and politician, b. Bedford, N.H., 1815; d. Madison, Wis., Dec. 11, 1889. [1; 44]

Atwood, Harry Fuller, publicist, b. near Morgan Park, Ill., 1870; d. Chicago, Ill., Dec. 13, 1930. [10]

Atwood, Henry Dean, poet, b. Taunton, Mass., 1839; d. 1921. [51]

Atwood, Isaac Morgan, clergyman and educationist, b. Pembroke, N.Y., 1838; d. Washington, D.C., Oct. 26, 1917. [3a; 10]

Atwood, Millard Van Marter, journalist, b. Groton, N.Y., 1886; d. Rochester, N.Y., Nov. 3, 1941. [7; 11]

Atwood, Nora, educationist, b. Portland, Me., 1866; d. Washington, D.C., Jan. 10, 1948.

Atwood, Wallace Walter, geographer, b. Chicago, Ill., 1872; d. Annisquam, Mass, July 24, 1949. [10; 11]

Aubert de Gaspé, Philippe, social historian, b. Quebec, Canada, 1786; d. Quebec, Que., Jan. 29, 1871. [27]

Aubert de Gaspé, Philippe, novelist, b. 1814; d. Halifax, N.S. March 7, 1841. [27]

Aubin, Napoléon, journalist, b. near Geneva, Switzerland, 1812; d. Montreal, Que., June 12, 1890. [27]

Auchincloss, William Stuart, civil engineer and religious writer, b. New York, N.Y., 1842; d. April 11, 1928. [10]

Auclair, Joseph, priest, b. Jeune Lorette, Lower Canada, 1813; d. Quebec, Que., Nov. 29, 1887. [32]

Auden, William Henry, educationist, b. England, 1867; d. London, Ont., Jan. 26, 1940. [30]

Audet, François Joseph, archivist, b. Detroit, Mich., 1867; d. Ottawa, Ont., Sept. 13, 1943. [30]

Audsley, George Ashdown, architect and organ designer, b. Elgin, Scotland, 1838; d. Bloomfield, N.J., June 21, 1925. [1]

Audubon, John James, artist and ornithologist, b. Bahamas, 1785; d. near New York, N.Y., Jan. 27, 1851. [1; 2; 3; 4; 5; 6; 7; 8; 9]

Audubon, Maria R., biographer, d. Salem, N.Y., Dec. 22, 1925. [34]

Auerbach, Joseph Smith, lawyer, b. Rockville Centre, Long Island, N.Y., 1855; d. New York, N.Y., Sept. 16, 1944. [10]

Auger, Joseph Cyrille, notary public, b. Terrebonne, Lower Canada, 1836; d. Montreal, Que., Jan. 18, 1891.

Aughey, John Hill, clergyman, b. 1828; d. ?

Aughey, Samuel, clergyman, b. 1831; d. 1912.

Aughinbaugh, William Edmund, physician, lawyer, and explorer, b. Westmoreland county, Va., 1871; d. New York, N.Y., Dec. 18, 1940. [10; 11]

Augur, Herbert Bassett, educationist, b. Hartford, Conn., 1874; d. Portland, Ore., Nov. 19, 1938. [62]

Augustin, John Alcée, journalist and poet, b. New Orleans, La., 1838; d. New Orleans, La., Feb. 5, 1888. [34]

Augustus, John, philanthropist, b. 1785; d. 1859.

Auld, Alexander, music teacher, b. near Harrisburg, Pa., 1816; d. about 1889. [7]

Auld, Robert Campbell MacCombie, cattle-breeder and journalist, b. London, England, 1857; d. New York, N.Y., April 21, 1937.

Aultman, Dwight Edward, soldier, b. Allegheny, Pa., 1872; d. Washington, D.C., Dec. 12, 1929. [10]

Aunt Carrie (pseud.). See Smith, Mrs. Caroline L.

Aunt Elmina (pseud.). See Slenker, Mrs. Elmina, née Drake.

Aurelia (pseud.). See Mace, Aurelia Gay.

Auringer, Obadiah Cyrus, clergyman and poet, b. Glens Falls, N.Y., 1849; d. Glens Falls, N.Y., Oct. 2, 1937. [4; 7; 10; 11]

Austen, Peter Townsend, chemist, b. Clifton, Staten Island, N.Y., 1852; d. Dec. 30, 1907. [1; 3; 10]

Austin, Arthur Williams, lawyer and poet, b. Charlestown, Mass., 1807; d. July 26, 1884. [8; 51]

Austin, Benjamin, merchant and politician, b. Boston, Mass., 1752; d. Boston, Mass., May 4, 1820. [1; 3]

Austin, Benjamin Fish, clergyman and educationist, b. near Brighton, Ont., 1850; d. Los Angeles, Calif., 1932. [27; 35]

Austin, Coe Finch, botanist, b. Orange county, N.Y., 1831; d. Closter, N.J., March 18, 1880. [3; 8]

Austin, David, clergyman, b. New Haven, Conn., 1759; d. Norwich, Conn., Feb. 5, 1831. [1; 62]

Austin, Francis Marion, educationist, b. Wilmington, O., 1862; d. Feb. 4, 1922. [10]

Austin, George Lowell, physician, b. Lawrence, Mass., 1849; d. Melrose, Mass., June 5, 1893. [6; 8]

Austin, Mrs. Grace, née **Jewitt,** playwright, novelist, and poet, b. Laconia, N.H., 1872; d. Dallas, Tex., Sept. 27, 1948. [11]

Austin, Henry, lawyer, b. Boston, Mass., 1858; d. June 22, 1918. [10; 51]

Austin, Henry Willard, editor and poet, b. West Roxbury, Mass., 1858; d. Boston, Mass., Oct. 16, 1912. [51]

Austin, James Trecothick, politician, b. Boston, Mass., 1874; d. Boston Mass., May 8, 1870. [1; 3; 8]

Austin, Mrs. Jane, née **Goodwin,** novelist, b. Worcester, Mass., 1831; d. Boston, Mass., March 30, 1894. [1; 3a; 7; 8; 17; 71]

Austin, John Mather, clergyman, b. 1805; d. 1880. [8]

Austin, John Osborne, merchant and genealogist, b. Providence, R.I., 1849; d. Oct. 27, 1918. [7; 8; 10]

Austin, Leonard Strong, mining engineer, b. Stratford, Conn., 1846; d. Los Angeles, Calif., Oct. 29, 1929. [10; 62]

Austin, Louis Winslow, physicist, b. Orwell, Vt., 1867; d. June 27, 1932. [10; 11; 13]

Austin, Mrs. Mary, née **Hunter,** essayist, novelist, and playwright, b. Carlinville, Ill., 1868; d. Santa Fé, N.M., Aug. 13, 1934. [7; 8; 10; 35]

Austin, Oscar Phelps, journalist and statistician, b. Newark, Ill., 1848; d. New York, N.Y., 1933. [10; 11]

Austin, Richard Wilson, politician, b. Decatur, Ala., 1857; d. Washington, D.C., April 20, 1919. [10]

Austin, Samuel, clergyman and educationist, b. New Haven, Conn., 1760; d. Glastonbury, Conn., Dec. 4, 1830. [62]

Austin, Walter, lawyer, b. Sandwich Islands, 1864; d. Dedham, Mass., Jan. 22, 1929. [51]

Austin, William, lawyer and littérateur, b. Lunenburg, Mass., 1778; d. Charlestown, Mass., June 27, 1841. [1; 7; 17]

Auton, C. (pseud.). See Hoppin, Augustus.

Averill, Charles E., novelist, fl. 1848-1857. [7]

Avery, Benjamin Parke, journalist and diplomat, b. New York, N.Y., 1828; d. Peiping, China, Nov. 8, 1875. [1; 2; 3; 7; 35]

Avery, Elroy McKendrie, educationist, b. Erie, Mich., 1844; d. Dec. 1, 1935. [3; 10; 39]

Avery, Isaac Erwin, journalist, b. near Morgantown, N.C., 1871; d. Charlotte, N.C., April 2, 1904. [34]

Avery, Isaac Wheeler, lawyer and journalist, b. St. Augustine, Fla., 1837; d. Sept. 8, 1897. [1; 34]

Avery, John, clergyman, b. Preston, Conn., 1819; d. Norwich, Conn., April 23, 1902. [62]

Avery, Samuel, lawyer, b. 1731; d. 1806.

Avery, Samuel Putnam, art connoisseur, b, New York, N.Y., 1822; d. New York, N. Y., Aug. 11, 1904 [1; 7; 10]

Avery, Samuel Putnam, genealogist, b. 1847; d. 1890.

Avirett, James Battle, clergyman, b. Onslow county, Md., about 1837; d. 1912. [34]

Aydelott, Benjamin Parkham, clergyman, b. 1795; d. 1880. [6a]

Ayer, Frederick, manufacturer, b. Ledyard, Conn., 1822; d. March 14, 1918. [4; 10]

Ayer, Frederick Fannin, lawyer and poet, b. Lowell, Mass., d. Boston, Mass., June 9, 1942. [10; 52]

Ayer, Mrs. Harriet, née Hubbard, journalist, b. Chicago, Ill., 1854; d. New York, N.Y., Nov. 25, 1903. [8]

Ayer, Isaac Winslow, physician, fl. 1865-1895.

Ayer, James Cook, physician and manufacturer of medical supplies, b. Ledyard, Conn., 1818; d. Winchendon, Mass., July 3, 1878. [1]

Ayer, Joseph Cullen, clergyman and educationist, b. Newton, Mass., 1866; d. Philadelphia, Pa., April 15, 1944. [10]

Ayers, Edward Augustus, physician, b. 1855; d. Franklin, N.J., Dec. 3, 1917.

Ayers, John H., police offiicer, b. Rome, N.Y., about 1868; d. Brunswick, Ga., March 27, 1943.

Ayers, Mrs. Minnie Maud, née Hanff, poet, b. Baltimore, Md., 1880; d. New York, N.Y., Dec. 23, 1942.

Ayres, Alfred (pseud.). See Osmun, Thomas Embly.

Ayres, Anne, Protestant sister, b. London, England, 1816; d. New York, N.Y., Feb. 9, 1896. [1; 6; 8]

Ayres, Eugene Edmond, educationist, b. Russelville, Ky., 1859; d. Philadelphia, Pa., Aug. 5, 1920. [10]

Ayres, Harry Morgan, educationist, b. Montclair Heights, N.J., 1881; d. New York, N.Y., Nov. 20, 1948. [7; 10; 11]

Ayres, Jared Augustus, poet, b. 1814; d. 1886.

Ayres, Leonard Porter, economist, b. Niantic, Conn., 1879; d. Cleveland, O., Oct. 29, 1946. [10]

Ayres, Milan Church, clergyman, b. Lewiston, Ill., 1850; d. Washington, D.C., May 21, 1920. [62]

Ayres, Steven Beckwith, politician, b. Fort Dodge, Ia., 1861; d. New York, N.Y., June 1, 1929. [10]

Ayrinhac, Henry Amans, priest, b. St. Grégoire, France, 1867; d. California, 1930. [21]

Azarias, Brother (pseud.). See Mullany, Patrick Francis.

B

Babb, Clement Edwin, clergyman, b. Pittston, Pa., 1821; d. San José, Calif., Jan. 7, 1906. [10]

Babbitt, Charles Jacob, lawyer, b .1856; d. 1913.

Babbitt, Edwin Dwight, physician, b. Hamden, N.Y., 1828; d. 1905. [6; 10]

Babbitt, Eugene Howard, educationist, b. Bridgewater, Conn., 1859; d. Hartford, Conn., Nov. 19, 1927. [10; 51]

Babbitt, Frank Cole, educationist, b. Bridgewater, Conn., 1867; d. Hartford, Conn., Sept. 22, 1935. [10; 51]

Babbitt, Irving, educationist, b. Dayton, O., 1865; d. Cambridge, Mass., July 15, 1933. [la; 4; 7; 10; 11]

Babbitt, James Bradford, geologist, b. 1827; d. ?

Babcock, Charles Alamanzo, local historian, b. 1847; d. 1922.

Babcock, George DeAlbert, industrial engineer, b. Corinne, Utah, 1875; d. Washington, D.C., Jan. 12, 1942.

Babcock, Harmon Seeley, lawyer and poet, b. 1849; d. East Providence, R.I., Jan. 3, 1937. [47]

Babcock, James Staunton, poet, b. South Coventry, Conn., 1815; d. April 13, 1947. [7; 62]

Babcock, John Martin Luther, novelist, b. 1822; d. 1894.

Babcock, Kendric Charles, educationist, b. South Brookfield, N.Y., 1864; d. Urbana, Ill., March 11, 1932. [10; 11]

Babcock, Maltbie Davenport, clergyman, b. Syracuse, N.Y., 1858; d. Naples, Italy, May 18, 1901. [1; 4; 10]

Babcock, Robert Hall, physician, b. Watertown, N.Y., 1851; d. Chicago, Ill., June 27, 1930. [10]

Babcock, Rufus, clergyman, b. North Colebrook, Conn., 1798; d. Salem, Mass., May 4, 1875. [3; 6]

Babcock, Stephen, genealogist, b. 1832; d. 1916.

Babcock, William Henry, lawyer, poet, and historian, b. St. Louis, Mo., 1849; d. July 20, 1922.

Babenroth, Adolph Charles, educationist, b. Wilson, Minn., 1882; d. Feb. 20, 1928. [11]

Babson, John James, local historian, b. 1809; d. April 13, 1886.

Bâby, William Lewis, local historian, b. Sandwich, Upper Canada, 1812; d. Windsor, Ont., 1897. [27]

Bache, Alexander Dallas, physicist and philosopher, b. Philadelphia, Pa., 1806; d. Newport, R.I., Feb. 17, 1867. [1; 4; 51]

Bache, Franklin, physician and chemist, b. Philadelphia, Pa., 1792; d. Philadelphia, Pa., March 19, 1864. [1; 3; 4]

Bacheler, John Badger, writer of guide books, b. 1825; d. Hyde Park, Mass., Dec. 31, 1894. [6]

Bacher, Otto Henry, artist, b. Cleveland, O., 1856; d. Bronxville, N.Y., Aug. 16, 1909. [1; 4; 10]

Bachi, Pietro, educationist, b. Sicily, 1787; d. Boston, Mass., Aug. 22, 1853. [3]

Bachman, Frank Puterbaugh, educationist, b. Mackinaw, Ill., 1871; d. Nashville, Tenn., Feb. 17, 1934. [10; 11]

Bachman, John, clergyman and naturalist, b. Rinebeck, N.Y., 1790; d. Columbia, S.C., Feb. 24, 1874. [1; 3; 6; 34]

Bachner, Louis, musician, b. New York, N.Y., 1882; d. New York, N.Y., Dec. 26, 1946.

Backus, Azel, clergyman and educationist, b. Norwich, Conn., 1765; d. Clinton, N.Y., Dec. 9, 1817. [1; 62]

Backus, Charles, theologian, b. Franklin, Conn., 1749; d. Somers, Conn., Dec. 30, 1803. [3; 6; 62]

Backus, Isaac, clergyman and historian, b. Norwich, Conn., 1724; d. Middleboro, Mass., Nov. 20, 1806. [1; 2; 3; 4]

Backus, Joseph, lawyer, b. Granby, Mass., 1764; d. Bridgeport, Conn., Jan. 17, 1838. [49]

Backus, Truman Jay, educationist, b. Milan, N.Y., 1842; d. Brooklyn, N.Y., March 25, 1908. [1; 7; 10]

Backus, William Woodbridge, genealogist, b. Norwich, Conn., 1803; d. Norwich, Conn., July 13, 1892. [5]

Bacon, Albert Montreville, clergyman, b. Lockport, N.Y., 1827; d. Chicago, Ill., Oct. 31, 1898. [24]

Bacon, Mrs. Albion, née Fellows, poet and social reformer, b. Evansville, Ind., 1865; d. Evansville, Ind., Dec. 10, 1933. [7; 10; 11]

Bacon, Alexander Samuel, lawyer, b. Jackson, Mich., 1853; d. Brooklyn, N.Y., May 29, 1920. [10]

Bacon, Alice Mabel, educationist, b. New Haven, Conn., 1858; d. May 1, 1918. [1; 7; 10]

Bacon, Augustus Octavius, lawyer, b. Bryan county, Ga., 1839; d. Washington, D.C., Feb. 14, 1914. [5; 10]

Bacon, Benjamin Wisner, historian and theologian, b. Litchfield, Conn., 1860; d. New Haven, Conn., Feb. 1, 1932. [la; 10; 11; 62]

Bacon, Charles David, priest, b. Rivière-du-Sud, Lower Canada, 1840; d. L'Islet, Que., Sept 21, 1905. [32]

Bacon, Charles Sumner, physician, b. Spring Prairie, Wis., 1858; d. Chicago, Ill., July 10, 1947. [10]

Bacon, Charles William, b. Natick, Mass., 1856; d. Mount Vernon, N.Y., Nov. 9, 1938. [51]

Bacon, David Francis, physician, b. Prospect, Conn., 1813; d. New York, N.Y., Jan. 23, 1865. [3; 62]

Bacon, Delia Salter, originator of the Baconian theory of Shakespeare's plays, b. Tallmadge, O., 1811; d. Sept. 2, 1859. [1; 7]

Bacon, Dolores Marbourg (pseud.). See Bacon, Mrs. Mary Schell, née Hoke.

Bacon, Edgar Mayhew, historian, b. Nassau, Bahamas, 1855; d. Tarrytown, N.Y., Dec. 14, 1935. [7; 10]

Bacon, Edward, soldier and lawyer, b. Rochester, N.Y., 1830; d. Niles, Mich., 1901. [39]

Bacon, Edwin Faxon, educationist, b. Lockport, N.Y., 1832; d. Oneonta, N.Y., Dec. 17, 1910. [62]

Bacon, Edwin Munroe, journalist, b. Providence, R.I., 1844; d. Cambridge, Mass., Feb. 24, 1916. [1; 2; 3; 4; 7; 10]

Bacon, Mrs. Eugenia, née Jones, novelist and artist, b. Liberty county, Ga., 1840; d. ? [34]

Bacon, Ezekiel, jurist, b. Boston, Mass., 1776; d. Utica, N.Y., Oct. 18, 1870. [3; 4]

Bacon, Frank, actor and playwright, b. Marysville, Calif., 1864; d. Chicago, Ill., Nov. 19, 1922. [1; 7; 10; 35]

Bacon, Frederick Hampden, lawyer, b. Niles, Mich., 1849; d. St. Louis, Mo., Aug. 10, 1928. [4]

Bacon, Gaspar Griswold, educationist, b. Jamaica Plains, Mass., 1886; d. Dunham, Mass., Dec. 24, 1947. [51]

Bacon, George Blagden, clergyman, b. New Haven, Conn., 1836; d. Orange Valley, N. J., Sept. 15, 1876. [62]

Bacon, Gorham, physician, b. 1855; d. Yarmouth Port, Mass., March 5, 1940. [51]

Bacon, Henry, artist, b. Haverhill, Mass., 1839; d. Cairo, Egypt, March 13, 1912. [3]

Bacon, Leonard, clergyman, b. Detroit, Mich., 1802; d. New Haven, Conn., Dec. 24, 1881. [1; 3; 6; 7; 62]

Bacon, Leonard Woolsey, clergyman, b. New Haven, Conn., 1830; d. Assonet, Mass., May 12, 1907. [1; 7; 10; 62]

Bacon, Mrs. Mary Schell, née Hoke, novelist and playwright, b. Atchison, Kans., 1870; d. New York, N. Y., June 2, 1934. [7; 10]

Bacon, Robert, diplomat, b. Boston, Mass., 1860; d. New York, N.Y., May 29, 1919. [1; 2; 4; 10; 51]

Bacon, Selden, lawyer, b. New Haven, Conn., 1861; d. Mount Kisco, N.Y., June 25, 1946.

Bacon, Theodore, lawyer, b. New Haven, Conn., 1834; d. Rochester, N.Y., Jan. 23, 1900. [62]

Bacon, Theodore Davenport, clergyman, b. Stamford, Conn., 1863; d. Hamden, Conn., Oct. 7, 1930. [62]

Bacon, Thomas, clergyman, b. Isle of Man, about 1700; d. Frederick, Md., May 24, 1768. [3]

Bacon, Thomas Scott, clergyman, b. Saratoga Springs, N.Y., 1825; d. 1904. [4]

Bacon, William, clergyman, b. 1789; d. 1863. [6]

Bacon, William Plumb, broker and genealogist, b. Middletown, Conn., 1837; d. Hartford, Conn., Aug. 6, 1918. [62]

Bacon, William Thompson, clergyman and poet, b. Woodbury, Conn., 1814; d. Derby, Conn., May 18, 1881. [3; 62]

Badè, William Frederic, educationist, b. Carver, Minn., 1871; d. Berkeley, Calif., March 4, 1936. [10]

Badeau, Adam, soldier and diplomat, b. New York, N.Y., 1831; d. Ridgewood, N.J., March 20, 1895. [1; 4; 5; 7]

Badgley, Jonathan, grammarian, fl. 1837-1876. [6]

Badin, Stephen Theodore, missionary, b. Orléans, France, 1768; d. Cincinnati, O., April 19, 1853. [1; 74]

Badlam, Anna B., educationist, fl. 1887-1906.

Badley, Brenton Thoburn, bishop, b. Gonda, U.P., India, 1876; d. Delhi, India, Feb. 1, 1949. [10; 11]

Bagby, Albert Morris, musician and novelist, b. Rushville, Ill., 1859; d. New York, N.Y., Feb. 26, 1941. [10]

Bagby, Alfred, clergyman and local historian, b. King and Queen county, Va., 1828; d. ? [34]

Bagby, David Young, clergyman, b. Kenton county, Ky., 1849; d. ? [24; 34]

Bagby, George William, b. Buckingham county, Va., 1828; d. Richmond, Va., Nov. 29, 1883. [1; 3; 7; 34]

Bagg, Lyman Hotchkiss, journalist, b. West Springfield, Mass., 1846; d. Springfield, Mass., Oct. 23, 1911. [10; 62]

Bagg, Moses Mears, physician, b. Utica, N.Y., 1816; d. Utica, N.Y., May 2, 1900. [62]

Baggs, Mrs. Mae, née Lacy, traveller, b. Independence, Mo.; d. Toledo, O., Sept. 11, 1922. [10]

Bagioli, Antonio, musician, b. Bologna, Italy, 1795; d. New York, N.Y., Feb. 11, 1871.

Bagley, Clarence Booth, historian, b. De Kalb county, Ill., 1843; d. Seattle, Wash., Feb. 17, 1932. [10]

Bagley, William Chandler, educationist, b. Detroit, Mich., 1874; d. New York, N.Y., July 1, 1946. [39]

Bagnall, William Rhodes, clergyman and manufacturer, b. Boston, Mass., 1819; d. Middletown, Conn., Aug. 3, 1892. [60]

Bailey, Mrs. Abigail, née Abbott, soldier's wife, b. 1746; d. 1815. [43]

Bailey, Albert Hopson, clergyman, b. Poultney, Vt., 1821; d. Sheldon, Vt., Feb. 14, 1891. [60]

Bailey, Mrs. Alice, née Wood, novelist, b. Amherst, Mass., 1857; d. ? [7]

Bailey, Arthur Low, librarian, b. Methuen, Mass., 1867; d. Wilmington, Del., Feb. 17, 1940. [10]

Bailey, Arthur Scott, writer of books for children, b. St. Albans, Vt., 1877; d. Upper Montclair, N.J., Oct. 17, 1949. [11]

Bailey, Bert Heald, ornithologist, b. Fairley, Ia., 1875; d. Cedar Rapids, Ia., June 23, 1917. [10; 37]

Bailey, Ebenezer, educationist, b. Westbury, Mass., 1795; d. Lynn, Mass., Aug. 5, 1839. [1; 3; 6; 62]

Bailey, Edgar Henry Summerfield, chemist, b. Middlefield, Conn., 1848; d. Lawrence, Kans., June 1, 1933. [10; 11; 13; 62]

Bailey, Edward Lucas, clergyman, b. Lawsville, Pa., 1823; d. Carbondale, Pa., May 9, 1869. [24]

Bailey, Eli Stillman, physician, b. Little Genesee, N.Y., 1851; d. Chicago, Ill., April 26, 1926. [10]

Bailey, Frederic William, genealogist, d. 1918.

Bailey, Frederick Randolph, physician, b. Elizabeth, N.J., 1871; d. Sept. 16, 1923. [10]

Bailey, Gilbert Ellis, geologist, b. Pekin, Ill., 1852; d. Los Angeles, Calif., Dec. 6, 1924. [4; 10; 35]

Bailey, Gilbert Stephen, clergyman, b. Dalton, Pa., 1822; d. Pomona, Calif., Sept. 28, 1891. [3; 6; 24]

Bailey, Henry Turner, art teacher, b. Scituate, Mass., 1865; d. Chicago, Ill., Nov. 26, 1931. [10]

Bailey, Hollis Russell, lawyer, b. North Andover, Mass., 1852; d. Cambridge, Mass., Nov. 29, 1934. [10; 51]

Bailey, Isaac, lawyer, d. Providence, R.I., 1824. [47]

Bailey, Jacob Whitman, botanist, chemist, and geologist, b. Auburn, Mass., 1811; d. West Point, N.Y., Feb. 27, 1857. [1; 3; 4; 6; 49]

Bailey, James Montgomery, journalist and humorist, b. Albany, N.Y., 1841; d. Danbury, Conn., March 4, 1894. [1; 2; 3; 4; 7]

Bailey, John J., playwright, d. 1873.

Bailey, John Jay, librarian, b. 1833; d. Monroe, La., June 11, 1913.

Bailey, John Read, physician, b. New York, N.Y., 1833; d. Fort Smith, Ark., Jan. 18, 1910. [39]

Bailey, Joseph Whitman, lawyer, b. Fredericton, N.B., 1865; d. Fredericton, N.B., July 12, 1932.

Bailey, Loring Woart, chemist and geologist, b. West Point, N.Y., 1839; d. Fredericton, N.B., Jan. 10, 1925. [10; 27; 51]

Bailey, Margaret Emerson, novelist, b. Providence, R.I., 1880; d. New Canaan, Conn., Oct. 28, 1949. [7; 11]

Bailey, Mrs. Margaret Jewett, née Smith, novelist, fl. 1837-1854. [41]

Bailey, Mark, educationist, b. Dunbarton, N.H., 1827; d. New Haven, Conn., June 3, 1911. [49]

Bailey, Middlesex Alfred, educationist, b. 1856; d. Yonkers, N.Y., Nov. 25, 1923.

Bailey, Pearce, physician, b. 1865; d. New York, N.Y., Feb. 11, 1922. [48; 56]

Bailey, Prentiss, publisher, b. Utica, N.Y., 1873; d. Utica, N.Y., June 25, 1939. [11]

Bailey, Rufus William, clergyman, b. North Yarmouth, Me., 1793; d. Huntsville, Tex., April 25, 1863. [1; 5; 6; 49]

Bailey, Sarah Loring, local historian, b. 1834; d. 1896.

Bailey, Solon Irving, astronomer, b. Lisbon, N.H., 1854; d. Hanover, Mass., June 5, 1931. [10; 13]

Bailey, Thomas Pearce, psychologist, b. Georgetown, S.C., 1867; d. Winter Park, Fla., Feb. 8, 1949. [10; 11]

Bailey, Mrs. Urania Locke, née Stoughton, novelist and poet, b. Franklin county, Mass., 1820; d. 1882. [6]

Bailey, Vernon, biologist, b. Manchester, Mich., 1864; d. Washington, D.C., April 20, 1942. [10; 11]

Bailey, Warren Worth, journalist, b. New Winchester, Ind., 1855; d. Johnstown, Pa., Nov. 9, 1928. [10; 11]

Bailey, William Francis, lawyer, b. 1842; d. 1915.

Bailey, William Henry, lawyer, b. Pasquotank county, N. C., 1831; d. Seabrook, Tex., Aug. 27, 1908. [5; 10; 34]

Bailey, William Theodore, physician, b. 1828; d. 1896.

Bailey, William Whitman, b. West Point, N.Y., 1843; d. Providence, R.I., Feb. 20, 1914. [10; 47]

Baillargé, Charles, architect, b. Quebec, Lower Canada, 1825; d. Quebec, Que., May 10, 1906. [27]

Baillargé, Frédéric Alexandre, priest and educationist,, b. near Morrisburg, Ont., 1854; d. Verchères, Que., March 12, 1928. [27; 32]

Baillargeon, Charles François, archbishop, b. Ile aux Grues, Lower Canada, 1798; d. Quebec, Que., Oct. 13, 1870. [32]

Baily, Thomas Loyd, clergyman and novelist, b. Philadelphia, Pa., 1824; d. Atlantic City, N.J., 1914. [7; 24]

Bain, Charles Wesley, educationist, b. Portsmouth, Va., 1864; d. March 15, 1915. [10; 34]

Bain, Francis, naturalist, b. North River, P.E.I., 1842; d. North River, P.E.I., Nov. 20, 1894. [27]

Bain, James, librarian, b. London, England, 1842; d. Toronto, Ont., May 22, 1908. [27]

Bain, John Wallace, clergyman, b. 1833; d. 1910.

Bainbridge, Mrs. Lucy, née Seaman, social worker, b. Cleveland, O., 1842; d. New York, N.Y., Nov. 19, 1928. [10]

Bainbridge-Hoff, William. See Hoff, William Bainbridge.

Baines, Minnie Willis (pseud.). See Miller, Mrs. Minnie, née Willis.

Baird, Andrew J., clergyman, d. 1884.

Baird, Charles Washington, clergyman, b. Princeton, N.J., 1828; d. Rye, N.Y., Feb. 10, 1887. [1; 3; 5; 6; 7; 68]

Baird, George Washington, naval officer and free-mason, b. Washington, D.C., 1843; d. Washington, D.C., Oct. 4, 1930. [10]

Baird, Henry Martyn, clergyman and historian, b. Philadelphia, Pa., 1832; d. Yonkers, N.Y., Nov. 11, 1906. [1; 5; 7; 10; 68]

Baird, Jean Katherine, writer of books for girls, b. Renovo, Pa., 1872; d. Beaver, Pa., April 20, 1918. [10]

Baird, Robert, clergyman, b. near Pittsburg, Pa., 1793; d. Yonkers, N.Y., March 15, 1863. [1; 3; 5; 6]

Baird, Samuel John, clergyman, b. Newark, O., 1817; d. Clinton Forge, Va., April 10, 1893. [1; 3; 6; 34]

Baird, Spencer Fullerton, biologist, b. Reading, Pa., 1823; d. Wood's Hole, Mass., Aug. 10, 1888. [1; 3; 4; 5; 6]

Baird, Thomas Dickson, clergyman, b. 1773; d. 1839.

Baird, William Raimond, lawyer, b. Philadelphia, Pa., 1858; d. New York, N.Y., March 15, 1917. [10]

Baird, William Thomas, soldier, b. Fredericton, N.B., about 1819; d. Woodstock, N.B., Feb. 23, 1897. [27]

Baker, Mrs. Abigail, née **Gunn,** political scientist, d. 1923.

Baker, Abijah Richardson, clergyman, b. Franklin, Mass., 1805; d. Dorchester, Mass., April 30, 1876. [6; 45]

Baker, Alfred, mathematician, b. Toronto, Ont., 1848; d. Toronto, Ont., Oct. 28, 1942. [30]

Baker, Mrs. Alice, née **Griswold,** genealogist, b. 1849; d. 1913.

Baker, Andrew Jackson, lawyer, b. 1832; d. ?

Baker, Arthur Latham, mathematician, b. Cincinnati, O., 1853; d. Aug. 13, 1934. [10]

Baker, Arthur Mulford, clergyman, b. Wapakoneta, O., 1880; d. Philadelphia, Pa., Sept. 22, 1941. [10]

Baker, Benjamin Franklin, musician, b. Wenham, Mass., 1811; d. Boston, Mass., March 11, 1889. [4; 20]

Baker, Charles Richard, clergyman, b. Medford, Mass., 1842; d. Gratz, Austria, Aug. 8, 1898. [26]

Baker, Charles Whiting, civil engineer, b. Johnson, Vt., 1865; d. Montclair, N.J., June 6, 1941. [10]

Baker, Charlotte Alice, educationist, b. 1833; d. 1909.

Baker, Chauncey Brooke, soldier, b. Lancaster, O., 1860; d. Washington, D.C., Oct. 18, 1936. [10]

Baker, Mrs. Cornelia, née **McGee,** editor, b. Jackson county, O., 1855; d. Chicago, Ill., March 12, 1930. [10]

Baker, Daniel, clergyman and educationist, b. Midway, Ga., 1791; d. Austin, Tex., Dec. 10, 1857. [2; 6; 24; 34]

Baker, DeWitt Clinton, chemist and journalist, b. Portland, Me., 1832; d. Austin, Tex., April 17, 1881. [34]

Baker, Frank, jurist, b. Melmore, O., 1840; d. Chicago, Ill., July 9, 1916. [10]

Baker, Franklin Thomas, educationist, b. near Hagerstown, Md., 1864; d. Yonkers, N.Y., Feb. 3, 1949. [14]

Baker, Fred Abbott, lawyer, b. Holly, Oakland county, Mich., 1846; d. ?

Baker, George Augustus, lawyer and poet, b. 1849; d. New York, N.Y., Sept. 18, 1906. [10]

Baker, George Hall, librarian, bibliographer and artist, b. Ashfield, Mass., 1850; d. New York, N.Y., March 27, 1911. [10]

Baker, George Melville, playwright, b. Maine, 1832; d. Oct., 1890. [6; 7; 38]

Baker, George Pierce, educationist, b. Providence, R.I., 1866; d. New York, N.Y., Jan. 12, 1935. [7; 10; 51]

Baker, Mrs. Harriette Newell, née **Woods,** writer of juvenile fiction, b. Andover, Mass., 1818; d. Brooklyn, N.Y., April 27, 1893. [5; 6]

Baker, Henry Felt, economist, b. 1797; d. 1857. [51]

Baker, Henry Moore, lawyer and politician, b. Bow, N.H., 1841; d. Washington, D.C., May 30, 1912. [10]

Baker, Ira Osborn, civil engineer, b. Linton, Ind., 1853; d. Rochester, Minn., Nov, 7, 1925. [10]

Baker, James Hutchins, educationist, b. Harmony, Me., 1848; d. Denver, Colo., Sept. 10, 1925. [10]

Baker, James Loring, journalist, d. 1886. [51]

Baker, John Clapp, clergyman, b. 1828; d. Bellevue, Wash., Jan. 12, 1912. [24]

Baker, Joseph Eugene, local historian, b. 1847; d. 1914.

Baker, La Fayette Curry, detective, b. Stafford, N.Y., 1826; d. Philadelphia, Pa., July 3, 1868. [1; 3; 5; 6]

Baker, Lewis Carter, clergyman, b. Matawan, N.J., 1831; d. Princeton, N.J., April 6, 1915. [69]

Baker, Loren Lynn, economist, b. Kansas, 1884; d. Los Angeles, Calif., March 9, 1934.

Baker, Mrs. Louie Alien, novelist, b. 1858; d. ?

Baker, Louise Southard, poet and novelist, b. 1846; d. Nantucket, Mass., 1896.

Baker, Marcus, cartographer, b. Kalamazoo, Mich., 1849; d. Washington, D.C., Dec. 12, 1903. [10]

Baker, Myron Eugene, poet, d. 1901. [44]

Baker, Newton Diehl, United States secretary of state for war, b. Martinsburg, W. Va., 1871; d. Cleveland, O., Dec. 25, 1937. [2a; 7; 10; 47]

Baker, Osmon Cleander, bishop, b. Marlow, N.H., 1812; d. Concord, N.H., Dec. 20, 1871. [1; 3; 5; 6]

Baker, Ray Stannard, journalist and biographer, b. Lansing, Mich., 1870; d. Amherst, Mass., July 12, 1946. [7; 10; 11; 12]

Baker, Mrs. Sarah Schoonmaker, née **Tuthill,** writer of books for children, b. New Haven, Conn., 1824; d. 1906. [6; 10]

Baker, Sheridan, clergyman, b. 1824; d. 1890.

Baker, Smith, clergyman, b. Bowdoin, Me., 1836; d. Lowell, Mass., Nov. 10, 1917. [10]

Baker, Tarkington, journalist, b. Vincennes, Ind., 1878; d. New York, N.Y., Jan. 1, 1924. [10]

Baker, Theodore, musicologist, b. 1851; d. Dresden, Germany, Oct. 13, 1934. [20]

Baker, Thomas Rakestraw, educationist, b. Chester county, Pa., 1837; d. Winter Park, Fla., 1930. [10]

Baker, Thomas Stockham, educationist, b. Aberdeen, Md., 1871; d. Pittsburg, Pa., April 7, 1939. [10]

Baker, Walter, clergyman, b. Medford, Mass., 1849; d. Baltimore, Md., March 19, 1897. [51]

Baker, William Deal, satirist, b. 1812; d. Philadelphia, Pa., Sept. 17, 1876. [55]

Baker, William Mumford, clergyman, b. Washington, D.C., 1825; d. Boston, Mass., Aug. 20, 1883. [1; 3; 6; 7; 34]

Baker, William Spohn, antiquarian, b. Philadelphia, Pa., 1824; d. Philadelphia, Pa., April 8, 1897. [5; 6]

Baketel, Oliver Sherman, clergyman, b. Greentown, O., 1849; d. Maplewood, N.J., Feb. 4, 1937. [10]

Bakewell, William J., clergyman, fl. 1823-1842.

Balch, Edwin Swift, lawyer, b. Philadelphia, Pa., 1856; d. New York, N.Y., March 15, 1927. [10; 11; 51]

Balch, Elizabeth, novelist, b. 1843; d. 1890. [6; 8]

Balch, Frederick Homer, novelist, b. Lebanon, Ore., 1861; d. Portland, Ore., June 3, 1891. [41]

Balch, George Thacher, soldier, b. 1828; d. 1894.

Balch, Lewis, physician, b. 1847; d. New York, N.Y., Aug. 9, 1909.

Balch, Thomas, lawyer, b. Leesburg, Va., 1821; d. Philadelphia, Pa. March 29, 1877. [5; 55]

Balch, Thomas Bloomer, clergyman, b. Georgetown, D.C., 1793; d. Greenwich, Va., Feb. 14, 1878. [56]

Balch, Thomas Willing, lawyer and publicist, b. 1866; d. Atlantic City, N.J., June 7, 1927. [1; 10; 51]

Balch, William Ralston, journalist, b. 1852; d. Boston, Mass., March 7, 1923. [4; 6]

Balch, William Stevens, clergyman, b. Andover, Vt., 1806; d. Elgin, Ill., Dec. 1887. [43]

Baldridge, Samuel Coulter, clergyman, b. 1829; d. 1898.

Baldwin, Aaron Dwight, lawyer, b. 1850; d. Chicago, Ill., Oct. 28, 1912. [53]

Baldwin, Bird Thomas, psychologist, b. Marshallton, Pa., 1875; d. 1928. [10]

Baldwin, Caleb C., missionary, b. Bloomfield, N.J., 1820; d. East Orange, N.J., July 20, 1911. [6; 56]

Baldwin, Charles Candee, jurist and genealogist, b. 1834; d. 1895.

Baldwin, Charles Jacobs, clergyman, b. Charleston, N.Y., 1841; d. Granville, O., April 13, 1921. [10]

Baldwin, Charles Sears, educationist, b. New York, N.Y., 1867; d. New York, N.Y., Oct. 23, 1935. [7; 10; 48]

Baldwin, Cyrus, educationist, d. Dayton, O., Jan 19, 1909.

Baldwin, Daniel Pratt, lawyer, b. Lenox, N.Y., 1837; d. 1908. [10]

Baldwin, David Dwight, conchologist, b. Honolulu, Hawaii, 1831; d. Honolulu, Hawaii, June 16, 1912.

Baldwin, Ebenezer, clergyman and educationist, b. Norwich, Conn., 1745; d. Danbury, Conn., Oct. 1, 1776. [62]

Baldwin, Ebenezer, lawyer, b. New Haven, Conn., 1790; d. New Haven, Conn., Jan. 26, 1837. [62]

Baldwin, Edward Chauncey, educationist, b. West Cornwall, Conn., 1870; d. Urbana, Ill., July 9, 1940. [7; 10]

Baldwin, Elbert Francis, journalist, b. Cleveland, O., 1857; d. Geneva, Switzerland, Sept. 26, 1927. [10]

Baldwin, Elihu Whittlesey, clergyman and educationist, b. Durham, N.Y., 1789; d. Crawfordsville, Ind., Oct. 15, 1840. [1; 62]

Baldwin, Ernest Hickok, educationist, b. Branford, Conn., 1869; d. Saranac Lake, N.Y., Dec. 1, 1922. [62]

Baldwin, Eugene Francis, journalist, b. Watertown, Conn., 1840; d. Peoria, Ill., 1937. [4]

Baldwin, Evelyn Briggs, explorer, b. Springfield, Mo., 1862; d. Washington, D.C., Oct. 25, 1933. [1a; 10]

Baldwin, Frances Elizabeth, historian, b. 1899; d. July 4, 1931. [11]

Baldwin, Fred Clare, clergyman, b. Towaco, N.J., 1861; d. East Orange, N.J., April 30, 1939.

Baldwin, George Colfax, clergyman, b. Pompton, N.J., 1817; d. Philadelphia, Pa., April 21, 1899. [3; 6; 10; 24]

Baldwin, Harmon Allen, clergyman, b. Pierpont, O., 1869; d. Pittsburg, Pa., March 11, 1936. [10]

Baldwin, Henry, jurist, b. New Haven, Conn., 1780; d. Philadelphia, Pa., April 21, 1844. [1; 5]

Baldwin, Henry, historian, b. New York, N.Y., 1832; d. 1905. [10]

Baldwin, Henry, artist, b. Newark, N.J., 1846; d. New York, N.Y., May 30, 1911.

Baldwin, James, editor and writer of books for children, b. Hamilton county, Ind., 1841; d. South Orange, N.J., Aug. 30, 1925. [1; 5; 7; 10]

Baldwin, James Fairchild, surgeon, b. Orangeville, N.Y., 1850; d. Columbus, O., Jan. 20, 1936. [10]

Baldwin, James Mark, psychologist, b. Columbia, S.C., 1861; d. Paris, France, Nov. 8, 1934. [1a; 5; 7; 10; 11]

Baldwin, John Cook, physician, b. 1887; d. Baltimore, Md., July 3, 1939.

Baldwin, John Denison, journalist and politician, b. North Stonington, Conn., 1809; d. Worcester, Mass., July 18, 1883. [1; 2; 3; 5; 6; 7; 51]

Baldwin, Joseph, educationist, b. Newcastle, Pa., 1827; d. Austin, Tex., Jan. 13, 1899. [1]

Baldwin, Joseph Glover, jurist, b. near Winchester, Va., 1815; d. San Francisco, Calif., Sept. 30, 1864. [1; 3; 34]

Baldwin, Loammi, civil engineer and soldier, b. Woburn, Mass., 1780; d. Charlestown, Mass., June 30, 1838. [1; 3; 5; 6]

Baldwin, Mrs. Lydia Wood, novelist, b. Massachusetts, 1836; d. ? [8]

Baldwin, Maurice Scollard, bishop, b. Toronto, Upper Canada, 1836; d. London, Ont., Oct. 19, 1904. [27]

Baldwin, Simeon Eben, jurist, b. New Haven, Conn., 1840; d. New Haven, Conn., Jan. 30, 1927. [1; 10; 62]

Baldwin, Stephen Livingstone, missionary, b. Somerville, N.J., 1835; d. Brooklyn, N.Y., 1902. [60]

Baldwin, Thomas, clergyman, b. Bozrah, Conn., 1753; d. Waterville, Me., Aug. 29, 1825. [3; 24]

Baldwin, Thomas Williams, engineer and genealogist, b. Bangor, Me., 1849; d. Hardwick, Mass., 1926. [51]

Baldwin, William Henry, industrialist and sociologist, b. Youngstown, O., 1851; d. Sept. 26, 1923. [10]

Baldwin, William James St. John, mechanical engineer, b. at sea, 1844; d. May 7, 1924. [10]

Baldwin, Willis, lawyer, b. 1860; d. Monroe, Mich., March 19, 1926. [53]

Baldwyn, Augusta, poet, b. about 1821; d. St. Johns, Que., May 9, 1884. [27]

Balestier, Charles Wolcott, publisher and journalist, b. Rochester, N.Y., 1861; d. Dresden, Germany, Dec. 6, 1891. [1; 5; 7; 9]

Balestier, Joseph Nerée, lawyer and journalist, fl. 1840-1878.

Balfour, Grant (pseud.). See Grant, James Miller.

Balfour, Walter, clergyman, b. St. Ninians, Scotland, 1776; d. Charlestown, Mass., Jan. 3, 1852. [3]

Ball, Alice Eliza, educationist and ornithologist, b. Cincinnati, O., 1867; d. New York, N.Y., April 25, 1948.

Ball, Benjamin West, lawyer and poet, b. Concord, Mass., 1823; d. Rochester, N;H., July 13, 1896. [49]

Ball, Mrs. Caroline Augusta, née Rutledge, poet, b. Charlestown, S.C., 1823; d. ? [34; 42]

Ball, Charles Backus, civil engineer, b. New Haven, Conn., 1854; d. Chicago, Ill., Oct. 18, 1928. [10; 62]

Ball, Eustace Hale, novelist, painter, and musician, b. about 1882; d. Laguna Beach, Calif., April 20, 1931. [2a]

Ball, Farlin Quigley, jurist, b. Ohio, 1838; d. Aug. 29, 1917. [10]

Ball, Francis Kingsley, educationist, b. Mercer county, Pa., 1863; d. Brookline, Mass., June 8, 1940. [7; 11]

Ball, Frank Clayton, manufacturer, b. Greensburg, O., 1857; d. Muncie, Ind., March 19, 1943. [10]

Ball, George Harvey, clergyman, b. near Sherbrooke, Lower Canada, 1819; d. Clifton Springs, N.Y., Feb. 20, 1907. [10; 24]

Ball, James Moores, ophthalmologist, b. West Union, Ia., 1863; d. St. Louis, Mo., March, 1929. [10]

Ball, John, lawyer, b. Hebron, N.H., 1794; d. Grand Rapids, Mich., Feb. 5, 1884. [39]

Ball, Nicholas, pioneer, b. 1828; d. 1896.

Ball, Thomas, sculptor, b. Charlestown, Mass., 1819; d. Montclair, N.J., Dec. 11, 1911. [3; 10]

Ball, Timothy Horton, clergyman, b. Agawam, Mass., 1826; d. Sheffield, Ala., Nov. 8, 1913. [24]

Ball, Wayland Dalrymple, lecturer, b. 1858; d. 1893.

Ballagh, James Curtis, educationist, b. Brownsburg, Va., 1867; d. Philadelphia, Pa., Sept. 28, 1944. [7; 10; 34]

Ballance, Charles, local historian, b. 1800; d. ?

Ballantine, Elisha, clergyman, b. 1810; d. 1886.

Ballantine, Henry, merchant, b. India, 1846; d. Seattle, Wash., Oct. 30, 1914. [45]

Ballantine, Stuart, radio engineer, b. Germantown, Pa., 1898; d. Morristown, N.J., May 7, 1944. [10]

Ballantine, William Gay, clergyman and educationist, b. Washington, D.C., 1848; d. Springfield, Mass., Jan. 10, 1937. [4; 7; 10; 11; 68]

Ballard, Addison, clergyman, b. Farmington, Mass., 1822; d. Pittsfield, Mass., Dec. 2, 1914. [5; 10]

Ballard, Charles Rollin, educationist, b. Tinmouth, Vt., 1828; d. 1906. [49]

Ballard, Edward, clergyman, b. Hopkinton, N.H., 1804; d. Brunswick, Me., Nov. 14, 1870. [49]

Ballard, Ellis Ames, book-collector, b. Athens, O., 1861; d. Roxborough, Pa., June 13, 1938. [10]

Ballard, Harlan Hoge, librarian, b. Athens, O., 1853; d. Pittsfield, Mass., Feb. 8, 1934. [7; 10; 61]

Ballard, Mrs. Julia Perkins, née Pratt, writer of books for children, b. 1828; d. 1894. [6; 8]

Ballard, William, local historian, b. 1780; d. 1827. [51]

Ballenger, William Lincoln, physician, b. Economy, Ind., 1861; d. Hubbard Woods, Ill., Dec. 21, 1915. [10]

Ballinger, Richard Achilles, lawyer, b. Boonesboro, Ia., 1858; d. Seattle, Wash., June 6, 1922. [1; 10]

Ballou, Mrs. Addie Lucia, poet, b. Chagrin Falls, Idaho, 1837; d. San Francisco. Calif., Aug. 11, 1916. [35]

Ballou, Adin, clergyman and reformer, b. Cumberland, R.I., 1803; d. Milford, Mass., Aug. 5, 1890. [1; 4; 6]

Ballou, Hosea, clergyman, b. Richmond, N.H., 1771; d. Boston, Mass., June 7, 1852. [1; 2; 3; 4; 5; 6; 43]

Ballou, Hosea, clergyman, b. Guilford, Vt., 1796; d. Somerville, Mass., May 27, 1861. [1; 3; 5; 6]

Ballou, Luman A., poet, b. Danby, Vt., 1844; d. Ohio, after 1918. [73]

Ballou, Maturin Murray, journalist, b. Boston, Mass., 1820; d. Cairo, Egypt, March 27, 1895. [1; 2; 3; 5; 6; 71]

Ballou, Moses, clergyman, b. Monroe, Mass., 1811; d. Atco, N.J., May 19, 1879. [3; 5; 6]

Ballou, William Hosea, biologist and novelist, b. Hannibal, N.Y., 1857; d. Closter, N.J., Nov. 30, 1937. [7; 11]

Ballou, William Rice, veterinary surgeon, b. 1864; d. 1893.

Baltes, Peter Joseph, bishop, b. Bavaria, 1827; d. Alton, Ill., Feb. 15, 1886. [3; 36]

Baltzell, Winton James, musician, b. Shiremanstown, Pa., 1864; d. New York, N.Y., Jan. 10, 1928. [10; 20]

Bamford, Mary Ellen, novelist, b. Healdsburg, Calif., 1857; d. ? [7; 35]

Bancroft, Aaron, clergyman, b. Reading, Mass., 1755; d. Worcester, Mass., Aug. 19, 1839. [1; 3; 6]

Bancroft, Edgar Addison, lawyer and diplomat, b. Galesburg, Ill., 1857; d. Karuizawa, Japan, July 28, 1925. [1; 10]

Bancroft, Edward, physician, b. Westfield, Mass., 1744; d. Margate, England, Sept. 8, 1821. [1; 3; 5; 6]

Bancroft, Frederic, historian, b. Galesburg, Ill., 1860; d. Washington, D.C., Feb. 22, 1945. [7; 10; 45]

Bancroft, George, historian and diplomat, b. Worcester, Mass., 1800; d. Washington, D.C., Jan. 17, 1891. [1; 2; 3; 4; 5; 6; 71]

Bancroft, Hubert Howe, publisher and historian, b. Granville, O., 1832; d. Walnut Creek, Calif., March 2, 1918. [1; 2; 3; 4; 5; 6; 9]

Bancroft, Hugh, lawyer, b. Cambridge, Mass., 1879; d. Cohasset, Mass., Oct. 17, 1933. [10; 51]

Bancroft, Margaret, educationist, b. 1854; d. 1912.

Bancroft, Timothy Whiting, educationist, b. 1837; d. Providence, R.I., Dec. 8, 1890. [46]

Bancroft, William Henry, clergyman and poet, b. Philadelphia, Pa., 1858; d. Chester, Pa., Jan. 15, 1921. [56]

Bancroft, William Wallace, educationist, b. Chester, Pa., 1893; d. Norristown, Pa., March 17, 1947. [14; 55]

Bandelier, Adolph Francis Alphonse, historian, anthropologist, and explorer, b. Berne, Switzerland, 1840; d. Seville, Spain, March 18, 1914. [1; 10]

Bandler, Samuel Wyllis, physician, b. 1869; d. Scarsdale, N.Y., July 31, 1932.

Bandmann, Daniel Edward, actor, b. Hesse Cassel, Germany, 1840; d. Missoula, Mont., 1905. [10]

Banes, Charles Henry, soldier, b. Philadelphia, Pa., 1831; d. Jan. 15, 1897. [4]

Banfield, Edith Colby, poet, b. 1870; d. 1903. [7; 58]

Bangs, Mrs. Bleecker. See Bangs, Mrs. Charlotte Rebecca, née Woglom.

Bangs, Mrs. Charlotte Rebecca, née Woglom, historian, b. 1867; d. Brooklyn, N.Y., March 26, 1920.

Bangs, Heman, clergyman, b. Fairfield, Conn., 1790; d. 1869. [6]

Bangs, John, clergyman, b. 1781; d. 1849.

Bangs, John Kendrick, humorist, b. Yonkers, N.Y., 1862; d. Atlantic City, N.J., Jan, 21, 1922. [1; 2; 5; 7; 9; 10; 71; 72]

Bangs, Lemuel Bolton, physician, b. New York, N.Y., 1842; d. New York, N.Y., Oct. 4, 1914. [10]

Bangs, Nathan, clergyman, b. Stratford, Conn., 1778; d. New York, N.Y., May 3, 1862. [1; 3; 6; 7]

Bangs, Outram, ornithologist, b. Watertown, Mass., 1863; d. Wareham, Mass., Sept. 22, 1932. [10]

Banks, Charles Edward, physician and historian, b. 1854; d. Hartford, Conn., Oct. 22, 1931. [1a; 4; 7; 49]

Banks, Charles Eugene, poet, novelist, and publisher, b. Clinton county, Ia., 1852; d. Honolulu, Hawaii, April 29, 1932. [7; 10]

Banks, Edgar James, archaeologist, b. Sunderland, Mass., 1866; d. May 4, 1945. [7; 51]

Banks, Elizabeth, journalist and novelist, b. Taunton, N.J., 1870; d. London, England, July 18, 1938. [7; 10]

Banks, Louis Albert, clergyman, b. Corvallis, Ore., 1855; d. Roseburg, Ore., June 17, 1933. [2a; 10; 11; 41]

Banks, Mary Ross, historian, b. 1846; d. ? [34]

Banks, Mrs. Nancy, née Huston, novelist, b. Morganfield, Ky., about 1850; d. ? [34; 74]

Banks, William, journalist, d. Toronto, Ont., March 15, 1920. [27]

Banning, Edmund Prior, physician, b. 1810; d. ?

Banning, Kendall, soldier and editor, b. New York, N.Y., 1879; d. Baltimore, Md., Dec. 27, 1944. [7; 10; 11; 49]

Banning, Pierson Worrall, sociologist, b. Chicago, Ill., 1879; d. Los Angeles, Calif., July 7, 1927. [4; 10]

Bannister, Nathaniel Harrington, actor and playwright, b. 1813; d. New York, N.Y., Nov. 2, 1847. [1; 7]

Banta, David Demaree, local historian, b. Johnson county, Ind., 1833; d. Bloomington, Ind., April 9, 1896.

Banta, Mrs. Melissa Elizabeth, née Riddle,, poet, b. 1834; d. 1907.

Banta, Nathaniel Moore, publisher, b. Rensselaer, Ind., 1867; d. Arlington Heights, Ill., Feb. 5, 1932. [10; 11]

Bantock, Miles (pseud.). See Reddall, Henry Frederic.

Banvard, John, painter, b. New York, 1815; d. Watertown, S.D., May 26, 1891. [1; 3; 5; 6]

Banvard, Joseph, clergyman, b. New York, N.Y, 1810; d. Neponset, Mass., Sept. 28, 1887. [1; 3; 5; 6; 7]

Baraga, Irenaeus Friedrich, missionary, b. near Dobernig, Prussia, 1797; d. Marquette, Mich., Jan. 19, 1868. [1; 3; 5; 6]

Barbara (pseud.). See Wright, Mrs. Mabel, née Osgood.

Barbarossa (pseud.). See Scott, John (1820-1907).

Barbe, Waitman, educationist, b. Monongalia county, W. Va., 1864; d. Baltimore, Md., Oct. 30, 1925. [7; 10; 34]

Barbee, William J., physician, educationist, and preacher, b. Winchester, Ky., 1816; d. Winchester, Ky., Oct. 27, 1892. [3; 6; 34]

Barber, Daniel, priest, b. Simsbury, Conn., 1756; d. St. Inigoes, Md., 1834.

Barber, Edwin, poet, b. 1878; d. 1914.

Barber, Edwin Atlee, archaeologist, b. Baltimore, Md., 1851; d. West Chester, Pa., Dec. 12, 1916. [1; 10]

Barber, Elmer de Vergne, physician, b. 1858; d. about 1900.

Barber, Gershom Morse, jurist, b. 1823; d. 1903. [4]

Barber, John Warner, historian and engraver, b. East Windsor, Conn., 1798; d. New Haven, Conn., June 22, 1885. [1; 3; 5; 6; 7]

Barber, Jonathan, teacher of elocution, b. 1784; d. 1864. [6]

Barber, Joseph, ex-soldier, fl. 1864-1871. [6]

Barber, Lucius Israel, physician and local historian, b. 1806; d. 1889.

Barber, Samuel, local historian, b. Brooklyn, N.Y., 1848; d. Mendham, N.J., July 9, 1918.

Barbour, A. Maynard (pseud.). See Barbour, Anna May.

Barbour, Mrs. Anna May, novelist and deaconess, b. Mansfield, N.Y.; d. St. Paul, Minn., May 10, 1941. [7; 10]

Barbour, Clarence Augustus, educationist, b. Hartford, Conn., 1867; d. Providence, R.I., Jan. 16, 1937. [10; 47]

Barbour, Heman Humphrey, genealogist, b. 1820; d. 1875.

Barbour, Henry Gray, physiologist, b. Hartford, Conn., 1886; d. New Haven, Conn., Sept. 23, 1943. [10; 13]

Barbour, Lewis Green, clergyman and poet, b .Danville, Ky., 1829; d. Louisville, Ky., July 17, 1907. [56]

Barbour, Oliver Lorenzo, lawyer, b. Cambridge, N.Y., 1811; d. Saratoga Springs, N. Y., 1889. [1; 3]

Barbour, Ralph Henry, writer of books for young people, b. Cambridge, Mass., 1870; d. Pass Christian, Miss., Feb. 11, 1944. [7; 10; 11; 15]

Barbour, Thomas, naturalist, b. Martha's Vineyard, Mass., 1884; d. Boston, Mass., Jan. 7, 1946. [10]

Barclay, George Lippard, publisher, fl. 1868-1884.

Barclay, James Turner, physician and missionary, b. Hanover county, Va., 1807; d. 1874. [8; 34]

Barclay, Thomas, loyalist, b. New York, N.Y., 1753; d. New York, N.Y., April 21, 1830. [1; 3; 27]

Bard, Samuel, physician, b. Philadelphia, Pa., 1742; d. Hyde Park, N. Y., May 24, 1824. [1; 3; 5; 6]

Bard, Samuel A. (pseud.). See Squier, Ephraim George.

Barde, Frederick Samuel, journalist, b. Hannibal, Mo., 1869; d. Guthrie, Okla., July 23, 1916. [75]

Bardeen, Charles William, educationist, b. Groton, Mass., 1847; d. Syracuse, N.Y., Aug. 19, 1924. [1; 7; 10; 62]

Barker, Albert Smith, naval officer, b. Hanson, Mass., 1843; d. Washington. D.C., Jan. 29, 1916. [10]

Barker, Benjamin, novelist, fl. 1845-1847. [7]

Barker, Benjamin Fordyce, physician, b. Wilton, Me., 1818; d. New York, N.Y., May 30, 1891. [1; 3; 46]

Barker, David, lawyer and poet, b. 1816; d. 1874. [38]

Barker, Mrs. Ellen, née Blackmar. See Maxwell, Mrs. Ellen, née Blackmar.

Barker, Fordyce. See Barker, Benjamin Fordyce.

Barker, George Frederick, physicist, b. Charlestown, Mass., 1835; d. Philadelphia, Pa., May 24, 1910. [1; 3; 5; 62]

Barker, Henry Ames, city planner, b. Providence, R.I., 1868; d. Feb. 27, 1929. [10; 47]

Barker, Jacob, financier, b. Kennebec county, Me., 1779; d. Philadelphia, Pa., Dec. 26, 1871. [3; 5; 6; 34]

Barker, James Nelson, playwright and poet, b. Philadelphia, Pa., 1784; d. Washington, D.C., March 9, 1854. [1; 3; 4; 7]

Barker, John Marshall, educationist, b. Fredericktown, O., 1849; d. Newton Centre, Mass., May 2, 1930. [10; 11]

Barker, Lewellys Franklin, physician and educationist, b. Norwich, Ont., 1867; d. Baltimore, Md., July 13, 1943. [10; 11]

Barker, Reginald Charles, novelist, b. Brighton, England, 1881; d. Los Angeles, Calif., Oct. 21, 1937. [7; 10; 35]

Barker, Wharton, financier and publicist, b. Philadelphia, Pa., 1846; d. Philadelphia, Pa., April 9, 1921. [1; 3; 5; 6; 10]

Barkley, Archibald Henry, surgeon, b. 1872; d. Lexington, Ky., June 1, 1937. [11]

Barksdale, George, physician and novelist, b. 1882; d. Charleston, W. Va., Oct. 8, 1939. [34]

Barlow, Columbus, physician, b. 1847; d. Robinson, Ill., Oct. 8, 1907.

Barlow, Joel, poet and politician, b. Reading, Conn., 1754; d. Zarnowiec, Poland, Dec. 24, 1812. [1; 2; 3; 4; 6; 71]

Barlow, John Richard, poet, b. 1846; d. ?

Barlow, Joseph Lorenzo, clergyman, b. Kent, Conn., 1818; d. Bemus Heights, N.Y., Nov., 1896. [24]

Barlow, Nathan Pratt, clergyman, b. Camden, N.J., 1834; d. Long Beach, Calif., Sept. 7, 1920.

Barlow, Samuel Latham Mitchell, lawyer, b. Granville, Mass., 1826; d. Glen Cove, Long Island, N.Y., July 10, 1889. [1; 3; 4]

Barlow, Warren Sumner, poet, fl. 1868-1885.

Barnard, Charles, journalist and playwright, b. Boston, Mass., 1838; d. Pasadena, Calif., April 11, 1920. [1; 2; 3; 4; 5; 6; 7; 10]

Barnard, Charles Inman, journalist and war correspondent, b. Boston, Mass., 1850; d. Nice, France, May 11, 1942. [51]

Barnard, Daniel Dewey, lawyer and politician, b. East Hartford, Conn., 1796; d. Albany, N.Y., April 24, 1861. [1; 47; 61]

Barnard, Edouard André, agriculturist, b. Three Rivers, Lower Canada, 1834; d. L'Ange Gardien, Que., Aug. 19, 1898. [27]

Barnard, Edward Emerson, astronomer, b. Nashville, Tenn., 1857; d. Nashville, Tenn., Feb. 6, 1923. [1; 10; 13]

Barnard, Frederick Augustus Porter, educationist, b. Sheffield, Mass., 1809; d. New York, N.Y., April 27, 1889. [1; 2; 3; 4; 5; 6; 7; 62]

Barnard, Henry, educationist, b. Hartford, Conn., 1811; d, Hartford, Conn., July 5, 1900. [1; 2; 3; 4; 5; 6; 62]

Barnard, James Lynn, educationist, b. Milford, N.Y., 1867; d. Binghampton, N.Y., Aug. 10, 1941. [10]

Barnard, James Underwood, educationist, b. 1849; d. ?

Barnard, Job, jurist, b. Porter county, Ind., 1844; d. 1923.

Barnard, John, clergyman, b. Boston, Mass., 1681; d. Marblehead, Mass., Jan. 24, 1770. [1; 3; 6; 52]

Barnard, John Gross, soldier, b. Sheffield, Mass., 1815; d. Detroit, Mich., May 14, 1882. [1; 3; 5; 6]

Barnard, Oliver W., poet, b. 1828; d. ?

Barnard, William Nichols, educationist, b. 1875; d. Ithaca, N.Y., April 3, 1947. [10; 11]

Barnes, Albert, clergyman, b. Rome, N.Y., 1798; d. Philadelphia, Pa., Dec. 24, 1870. [1; 3; 5; 6; 7]

Barnes, Almont, civil servant, d. 1918.

Barnes, Annie Marie, novelist, b. Columbia, S.C., 1857, d. ? [7; 34]

Barnes, Charles Cicero, sociologist, b. Noble county, O., 1882; d. Detroit, Mich., Sept. 3, 1946. [62]

Barnes, Charles Reid, botanist, b. Madison, Ind., 1858; d. Chicago, Ill., Feb. 24, 1910. [1; 4; 5; 10]

Barnes, Charlotte Mary Sanford, actress and playwright, b. New York, N.Y., 1818; d. Philadelphia, Pa., April 14, 1863. [1; 7]

Barnes, Demas, merchant, b. Canandaigua, N.Y., 1827; d. New York, N.Y., May 1, 1888. [3]

Barnes, Mrs. Diantha, née Mills, poet, b. Nashville, Tenn; d. New York, N.Y., July 13, 1939.

Barnes, Earl, educationist, b. Martville, N.Y., 1861; d. New Hartford, Conn., May 29, 1935. [10]

Barnes, Mrs. Emily, née Ripley, local historian, b. 1800; d. ?

Barnes, Everett, educationist, d. Oct. 24, 1930. [48]

Barnes, Frank Coe, educationist, b. 1867; d. Schenectady, N.Y., Nov. 30, 1934.

Barnes, George Owen, evangelist, b. 1827; d. 1908.

Barnes, Gilbert Hobbs, economist, b. Lincoln, Neb., 1889; d. Delaware, O., Aug. 12, 1945. [10]

Barnes, Howard McKent, playwright, b. Baltimore, Md., 1884; d. Chicago, Ill., Oct. 19, 1945.

Barnes, James, journalist and writer of books for boys, b. Annapolis, Md., 1866; d. Princeton, N.J., April 30, 1936. [2; 4; 5; 7; 10; 34]

Barnes, Jasper Converse, psychologist, b. Meigsville, O., 1861; d. Maryville, Tenn., Sept. 13, 1931. [10; 11]

Barnes, John Sanford, naval officer, b. 1836; d. 1911.

Barnes, Lemuel Call, clergyman, b. Kirtland, O., 1854; d. Yonkers, N.Y., July 18, 1938. [10; 11; 24]

Barnes, Mrs. Mary Downing, née Sheldon, educationist, b. Oswego, N.Y., 1850; d. London, England, Aug. 27, 1898. [1]

Barnes, Orlando Mack, writer on Shakespeare, b. 1825; d. Lansing, Mich., Nov. 11, 1899. [53]

Barnes, Stephen Goodyear, clergyman and educationist, b. Perth Amboy, N.J., 1853; d. Essex Junction, Vt., Jan. 5, 1931. [10; 37; 73]

Barnes, William, lawyer, b. Pompey, N.Y., 1824; d. Feb. 23, 1913. [10]

Barnes, William Croft, cattle man, b. 1858; d. Phoenix, Ariz., Dec. 17, 1936. [10; 11]

Barnes, William Horatio, biographer, fl. 1866-1880.

Barnes, William Robbins, publisher, b. Hinsdale, Ill., 1866; d. Greenwich, Conn., Feb. 8, 1945. [7]

Barnett, Mrs. Evelyn Scott, née Snead, novelist, b. Louisville, Ky.; d. Louisville, Ky., Nov. 10, 1921. [10; 34; 74]

Barnett, George Ernest, economist, b. Cambridge, Md., 1873; d. Baltimore, Md., June, 1938.

Barney, John Stewart, architect and painter, b. 1868; d. New York, N.Y., Nov. 22, 1925. [2a]

Barnhill, John Finch, surgeon, b. Flora, Ill., 1865; d. Miami Beach, Fla., March 10, 1943. [10; 11]

Barns, William Eddy, journalist, b. Vevay, Ind., 1853; d. 1915. [10]

Barnum, Mrs. Frances Courtney, née Baylor. See Baylor, Frances Courtney.

Barnum, Francis Aloysius, priest, b. 1849; d. 1921. [21]

Barnum, Phineas Taylor, showman, b. Bethel, Conn., 1810; d. Bridgeport, Conn., April 7, 1891. [1; 2; 3; 4; 5; 6; 7; 8; 9]

Barnum, Samuel Weed, clergyman, b. North Salem, N.Y., 1820; d. New Haven, Conn., Nov. 18, 1891. [4; 62]

Barnwell (pseud.) See Roosevelt, Robert Barnwell.

Barnwell, Robert Woodward, clergyman, b. Beaufort, S.C., 1849; d. 1902. [10; 34]

Barr, Mrs. Amelia Edith, née Huddleston, novelist, b. Ulverston, Lancashire, England, 1831; d. Richmond Hill, Long Island, N.Y., March 10, 1919. [1; 2; 6; 7; 10]

Barr, James, journalist, b. Wallacetown, Ont., 1862; d. Putney, England, March 21, 1923. [31a]

Barr, John Henry, mechanical engineer, b. Terre Haute, Ind., 1861; d. Ithaca, N.Y., March 29, 1937. [10; 11]

Barr, Martin W., psychiatrist, b. Wilmington, Del., 1860; d. Middletown, Del., Dec. 25, 1938.

Barr, William Miller, industrial engineer, fl. 1879-1918.

Barrass, Edward, clergyman, b. Durham, England, 1821; d. Toronto, Ont., 1898. [27]

Barratt, Norris Stanley, jurist, b. Philadelphia, Pa., 1862; d. Philadelphia, Pa., April 26, 1924. [10]

Barré, Raoul, caricaturist, b. Montreal, Que., 1874; d. Montreal, Que., May 22, 1932. [27]

Barre, W. L., biographer, b. Warren county, Ky., 1830; d. ? [6]

Barrell, George, seaman, b. 1809; d. ?

Barrell, Joseph, geologist, b. New Providence, N.J., 1869; d. New Haven, Conn., May 4, 1919. [1; 10; 62]

Barrell, Sarah Sayward. See Wood, Mrs. Sarah Sayward, née Barrell.

Barrett, Albert Reed, banker, b. 1841; d. 1936.

Barrett, Benjamin Fiske, clergyman, b. Dresden, Me., 1808; d. Philadelphia, Pa., Aug. 6, 1892. [1; 6; 46]

Barrett, Charles Simon, agriculturist, b. Pike county, Ga., 1866; d. Union City, Ga., April 4, 1935. [1a; 10]

Barrett, Don Carlos, educationist, b. Spring Valley, O., 1868; d. Indianapolis, Ind., Jan. 19, 1943. [10]

Barrett, Edward, naval officer, b. Louisiana, 1828; d. March 31, 1881. [4; 6]

Barrett, Harrison Delivan, spiritualist, b. Canaan, Me., 1863; d. about 1911. [10]

Barrett, James Francis, priest, b. Bridgeport, Conn., 1888; d. Farmington, Conn., May 29, 1934. [21; 22]

Barrett, Jay Amos, educationist, b. 1865; d. Berkeley, Calif., Dec. 2, 1936.

Barrett, John, diplomat, b. Grafton, Vt., 1866; d. Bellows Falls, Vt., Oct. 17, 1938. [10; 49]

Barrett, John Presley, clergyman, b. 1852; d. ?

Barrett, John Erigena, journalist and poet, b. Ireland, 1849; d. ? [4]

Barrett, Joseph Hartwell, journalist, b. Ludlow, Vt., 1824; d. 1907. [4; 10]

Barrett, Joseph Osgood, sociologist, b. Canaan, Me.; d. Brown's Valley, Minn., Feb. 8, 1898. [70]

Barrett, Mrs. Kate. née **Waller,** philanthropist, b. Clifton, Stafford county, Va., 1858; d. Alexandria, Va., Feb. 23, 1925. [1; 10]

Barrett, Lawrence, actor, b. Paterson, N.J., 1838; d. New York, N.Y., March 20, 1891. [1; 3; 4]

Barrett, Leonard Andrew, clergyman, b. Covington, Ky., 1874; d. Wooster, O., Feb. 27, 1945. [10; 11]

Barrett, Mary (pseud.). See Nutting, Mary Olivia.

Barrett, Monte (pseud.). See Barrett, Montgomery.

Barrett, Montgomery, novelist, b. 1897; d. Oct., 8, 1949. [11]

Barrett, Robert South, clergyman, b. 1851; d. 1896. [34]

Barrett, Selah Hibbard, clergyman, b. 1822; d. 1883. [6]

Barrett, Solomon, educationist, fl. 1847-1876.

Barrett, Walter (pseud.). See Scoville, Joseph Alfred.

Barrett, William, genealogist, b. Wilton, N.H., 1836; d. St. Paul, Minn., Sept. 14, 1888. [52]

Barrett, Wilson, playwright and novelist, b. England, 1848; d. 1904. [10]

Barrett, Wilton Agnew, motion picture executive, b. Philadelphia, Pa., 1886; d. New York, N.Y., Feb. 18, 1940.

Barringer, Daniel Moreau, mining engineer, b. Raleigh, N.C., 1860; d. Haverford, Pa., Nov. 30, 1929. [4; 10]

Barringer, Paul Brandon, educationist, b. Concord, N.C., 1857; d. Charlottesville, Va., Jan. 19, 1941. [4; 10]

Barrington, E. (pseud.). See Beck, Mrs. Lily Adams. née Moresby.

Barritt, Mrs. Frances, née **Fuller.** See Victor, Mrs. Frances, née Fuller.

Barroll, Benjamin Crockett, lawyer, b. 1819; d. 1908.

Barron, Clarence Walker, journalist, b. Boston, Mass., 1855; d. Battle Creek, Mich., Oct. 2, 1928. [1a; 10]

Barron, Elwyn Alfred, playwright and novelist, b. Lima, N.Y., 1855; d. Sept. 28, 1929. [7; 10]

Barron, Hannah Eayrs, poet, b. 1809; d. ?

Barron, John Augustus, jurist, b. Toronto, Ont., 1850; d. Stratford, Ont., Jan. 8, 1936. [27]

Barron, Joseph Thomas, priest and educationist, b. Minneapolis, Minn., 1889; d. Washington, D.C., 1939. [21]

Barron, Leonard, horticulturist, b. Chiswick, England, 1868; d. East Hempstead, Long Island, N.Y., April 9, 1938. [10; 11]

Barron, Samuel Benton, soldier, b. 1834; d. 1912. [34]

Barrow, Mrs. Frances Elizabeth, née **Mease,** writer of juvenile fiction, b. Charleston, S.C., 1822; d. New York, N.Y., May 7, 1894. [6; 7; 34]

Barrow, Mrs. Kate, née **Trader,** poet, b. 1860; d. 1939.

Barrows, Charles Henry, lawyer, b. Springfield, Mass., 1853; d. Springfield, Mass., Oct. 13, 1918. [10; 51]

Barrows, Edward Morley, sociologist, b. Columbus, O., 1887; d. Alexandria, Va., Dec. 14, 1940.

Barrows, Elijah Porter, clergyman and educationist, b. Mansfield, Conn., 1807; d. Oberlin, O., Sept. 14, 1888. [2; 3; 62]

Barrows, Henry Robbins, biologist, b. 1880; d. New York, N.Y., July 16, 1935. [13]

Barrows, Mrs. Isabel Chapin. See Barrows, Mrs. Katherine Isabel, née Hayes.

Barrows, John Henry, clergyman and educationist, b. near Medina, Mich., 1847; d. Oberlin, O., June 3, 1902. [1; 2; 7]

Barrows, John Otis, educationist, b. Mansfield, Conn., 1833; d. Norwichtown, Conn., Jan. 26, 1918. [10; 45]

Barrows, Mrs. Katherine Isabel, née Hayes, penologist, b. Irasburg, Vt., 1845; d. Oct. 25, 1912. [2; 8; 10]

Barrows, Nathaniel A., journalist, b. 1900; d. near Bombay, India, July 12, 1949.

Barrows, Samuel June, clergyman, editor, and reformer, b. New York, N.Y., 1845; d. New York, N.Y., April 21, 1909. [1; 2; 6; 10]

Barrows, Walter Bradford, ornithologist, b. Wellesley Hills, Mass., 1855; d. 1923. [39]

Barrows, William, clergyman, b. New Braintree, Mass., 1815; d. Cataumet, Mass., Sept. 9, 1891. [6; 45]

Barrus, Clara, physician and biographer, b. Port Byron, N.Y., 1864; d. Scarsdale, N.Y., April 4, 1931. [10; 11]

Barrus, George Hale, steam engineer, b. Goshen, Mass., 1854; d. Brookline, Mass., April, 1929. [10]

Barrus, Hiram, local historian, b. 1822; d. 1883.

Barry, David Sheldon, journalist, b. Detroit, Mich., 1859; d. Washington, D.C., Feb. 10, 1936. [10]

Barry, Henry Aloysius, priest, d. 1907. [21]

Barry, John Stetson, historian, b. Boston, Mass., 1819; d. St. Louis, Mo., Dec. 11, 1872. [3; 6]

Barry, Joseph, historian, b. about 1828; d. 1905.

Barry, Joseph Gayle Hurd, clergyman, b. Middle Haddam, Conn., 1858; d. New Canaan, Conn., May 28, 1931. [10; 11; 60]

Barry, Patrick, horticulturist, b. near Belfast, Ireland, 1816; d. Rochester, N.Y., June 23, 1890. [1; 4]

Barry, Philip, playwright, b. Rochester, N.Y., 1896; d. New York, N.Y., Dec. 3, 1949. [10; 51]

Barry, Robertine, journalist, b. Trois Pistoles, Que., 1866; d. 1910. [27]

Barry, Theodore Augustus, pioneer, b. 1825; d. 1881.

Barry, William, clergyman and local historian, b. Boston, Mass., 1805; d. Chicago, Ill., Jan. 17, 1885. [3; 6]

Barry, William Edward, local historian, b. 1846; d. 1932.

Barry, William Farquhar, soldier, b. New York, N.Y., 1818; d. Fort McHenry, Baltimore, Md., July 18, 1879. [1; 3; 4]

Barstow, George, lawyer and historian, b. Haverhill, N.Y., 1812; d. San Francisco, Calif., Sept. 9, 1883. [49]

Barthe, Georges Isidore, journalist, b. Restigouche, N.B., 1834; d. Ottawa, Ont., Aug. 11, 1900. [27]

Barthe, Joseph Guillaume, journalist, b. at sea, 1818; d. Montreal, Que., Aug. 4, 1893. [27]

Barthe, Ulric, journalist, b. Quebec, Que., 1853; d. Quebec, Aug. 3, 1921. [27]

Bartholomew, Edward Fry, educationist, b. Sunbury, Pa., 1846; d. Rock Island, Ill., June 10, 1946. [14]

Bartholomew, George Kellam, educationist, b. Hartford, Vt., 1835; d. Cincinnati, O., Oct. 3, 1917. [4; 49]

Bartholomew, Wallace Edgar, educationist, b. 1877; d. 1920.

Bartholow, Roberts, physician, b. New Windsor, Md., 1831; d. Philadelphia, Pa., May 10, 1904. [1; 3; 4; 6; 10]

Bartlet, William Stoodley, clergyman, b. Newburyport, Mass., 1809; d. 1883. [6]

Bartlett, Albert Leroy, educationist, b. Haverhill, Mass., 1852; d. Haverhill, Mass., May 14, 1934. [7; 10]

Bartlett, Mrs. Alice, née Hunt, poet, b. Bennington, Vt., 1870; d. New York, N.Y., Sept. 14, 1949. [10]

Bartlett, Mrs. Alice Elinor, née Bowen, journalist, b. Delavan, Wis., 1848; d. Detroit, Mich., 1920. [7; 10; 39]

Bartlett, Charles Henry, historian, b. 1853; d. ?

Bartlett, Clarence, physician, b. 1858; d. Philadelphia, Pa., Aug. 27, 1935. [4]

Bartlett, Dana Prescott, mathematician, b. Boston, Mass., 1863; d. Boston, Mass., Sept. 9, 1936. [11; 13]

Bartlett, David Vandewater Golden, journalist, b. 1828; d. 1912. [6]

Bartlett, David W. (pseud.). See Bartlett, David Vandewater Golden.

Bartlett, Edward Everett, printer, b. Brooklyn, N.Y., 1863; d. Greenwich, Conn., Sept. 24, 1942.

Bartlett, Edwin Julius, educationist, b. Hudson, O., 1851; d. Hanover, N.H., June 10, 1932. [10; 49]

Bartlett, Elisha, physician, b. Smithfield, R.I., 1805; d. Smithfield, R. I., July 19, 1855. [1; 3; 6; 47]

Bartlett, Frank W., sailor, b. Boston, Mass., 1856; d. Aug. 1, 1932. [11]

Bartlett, Frederic Huntington, physician, b. 1872; d. New York, N.Y., Oct. 20, 1948. [48; 50]

Bartlett, George Bradford, writer of books on games, b. Concord, Mass., 1832; d. Bristol, R.I., June 21, 1896.

Bartlett, George Miller, mechanical engineer, b. Chicago, Ill., 1873; d. Indianapolis, Ind., Sept. 16, 1936. [11; 45]

Bartlett, Gertrude. See Taylor, Mrs. Gertrude, née Bartlett.

Bartlett, Mrs. Helen, née Birch, poet, b. 1884; d. 1925.

Bartlett, John, editor, compiler, and publisher, b. Plymouth, Mass., 1820; d. Cambridge, Mass., Dec. 3, 1905. [1; 2; 3; 4; 5; 7; 10; 21]

Bartlett, John Russell, antiquarian and bibliographer, b. Providence, R.I., 1805; d. Providence, R.I., May 28, 1886. [1; 2; 3; 4; 7; 47; 71]

Bartlett, John Thomas, efficiency expert, b. Raymond, N.H., 1892; d. Boulder, Colo., Jan. 23, 1947. [10]

Bartlett, Joseph, politician and adventurer, b. Plymouth, Mass., 1762; d. Boston, Mass., Oct. 27, 1827. [1; 2; 3; 4; 6; 7; 51]

Bartlett, Joseph Gardner, genealogist, b. 1872; d. 1927. [10]

Bartlett, Maro Loomis, musician, b. Brownhelm, O., 1847; d. Des Moines, Ia.. 1919. [20]

Bartlett, Napier, journalist, b. Georgia, 1836; d. 1877. [34]

Bartlett, Robert Abram, Arctic explorer, b. Brigus, Newfoundland, 1875; d. New York, N.Y., April 28, 1946. [7; 10]

Bartlett, Samuel Colcord, clergyman and educationist, b. Salisbury, N.H., 1817; d. Hanover, N.H., Nov. 16, 1898. [1; 2; 3; 6]

Bartlett, Stanley Foss, journalist, b. 1902; d. Lewiston, Me., July 13, 1937.

Bartlett, Truman Howe, sculptor, b. Vermont, 1835; d. 1923.

Bartlett, William Chambers, soldier, b. 1839; d. 1908.

Bartlett, William Chauncey, essayist, b. Haddam, Conn., 1818; d. Oakland, Calif., Dec. 7, 1907. [35]

Bartlett, William Henry, educationist, d. Worcester, Mass., 1904. [10]

Bartlett, William Holms Chambers, educationist, b. Lancaster county, Pa., 1809; d. Yonkers, N.Y., Feb. 10, 1893. [1a; 2; 3; 6]

Bartlett, William Warren, journalist and local historian, b. 1861; d. 1893. [44]

Bartley, Elias Hudson, physician, b. Bartley, N.J., 1849; d. Brooklyn, N.Y., Jan. 12, 1937. [10; 11]

Bartley, Jámes Avis, poet, b. Louisa county, Va., 1830; d. ? [34]

Bartol, Cyrus Augustus, clergyman, b. Freeport, Me., 1813; d. Boston, Mass., Dec. 16, 1900. [1; 3; 6; 10]

Bartol, William Cyrus, mathematician, b. Huntington, Pa., 1847; d. Lewisburgh, Pa., Oct. 31, 1940. [10; 13]

Barton, Albert Olaus, historian, b. 1871; d. Madison, Wis., Oct. 22, 1947. [10; 44]

Barton, Mrs. Ardelia Maria, née Cotton, poet, b. Nobleboro, Me., 1843; d. ? [35]

Barton, Benjamin Smith, physician and naturalist, b. Lancaster, Pa., 1766; d. Philadelphia, Pa., Dec. 19, 1815. [1; 2; 3; 4; 6]

Barton, Clara Harlowe, humanitarian, b. Oxford, Mass., 1821; d. Glen Echo, Md., April 12, 1912. [1; 2; 7; 10]

Barton, George, novelist and historian, b. Philadelphia, Pa., 1866; d. Philadelphia, Pa., March 16, 1940. [10; 22]

Barton, George Aaron, clergyman and educationist, b. Farnham, Que., 1859; d. Weston, Mass., June 28, 1942. [7; 10]

Barton, James Levi, clergyman, b. Charlotte, Vt., 1855; d. Boston, Mass., July 21, 1936. [10; 11]

Barton, John Kennedy, naval engineer, b. Philadelphia, Pa., 1853; d. Philadelphia, Pa., Dec. 23, 1921. [10]

Barton, Ralph, caricaturist, b. Kansas City, Mo., 1891; d. New York, N.Y., May 20, 1931. [7; 10]

Barton, Robert Thomas, lawyer, b. Winchester, Va., 1842; d. Winchester, Va., Jan. 17, 1917. [4; 10]

Barton, Samuel Marx, educationist, b. near Winchester, Va., 1859; d. Sewanee, Tenn., Jan. 5, 1926. [10; 34]

Barton, Wilfred Mason, physician, b. Washington, D.C., 1871; d. Rochester, Minn., April 3, 1930. [10; 11]

Barton, William, political economist, d. Philadelphia, Pa., 1817. [6]

Barton, William Eleazar, clergyman, b. Sublette, Ill., 1861; d. Brooklyn, N.Y., Dec. 7, 1930. [1a; 2; 4; 7; 10]

Barton, William Henry, educationist, b. Baltimore, Md., 1893; d. New York, N.Y., July 7, 1944. [10; 11]

Barton, William Paul Crillon, naval surgeon and botanist, b. Philadelphia, Pa., 1786; d. Philadelphia, Pa., Feb. 29, 1856. [1; 2; 3; 4; 5; 6]

Bartow, Evelyn Pierrepont, genealogist, b. about 1846; d. 1902. [48]

Bartram, John, botanist, b. near Darby, Pa., 1699; d. Kingsessing, Pa., Sept. 22, 1777. [1; 3; 4; 6; 7]

Bartram, William, traveller and naturalist, b. Kingsessing, Pa., 1739; d. Kingsessing, Pa., July 22, 1823. [1; 3; 4; 6; 7]

Baruch, Simon, physician, b. Poland, 1840; d. New York, N.Y., June 3, 1921. [1; 10]

Barus, Carl, physicist, b. Cincinatti, O., 1856; d. Providence, R.I., Sept. 20, 1935. [1a; 4; 10; 47]

Barwick, Walter, lawyer, b. Woodstock, Ont.; d. Salisbury, England, July 1, 1906. [31]

Bascom, Florence, genealogist, b. Williamstown, Mass., 1862; d. Williamstown, Mass., June 18, 1945. [10; 11]

Bascom, Henry Bidleman, bishop, b. Hancock, N.Y., 1796; d. Louisville, Ky., Sept. 8, 1850. [1; 3; 34]

Bascom, John, philosopher, b. Genoa, N.Y., 1827; d. Williamstown, Mass., Oct. 2, 1911. [1; 2; 3; 4; 6; 7; 10]

Bascom, Robert O., historian, b. 1855; d. 1909.

Base, Daniel, chemist, b. Baltimore, Md., 1869; d. Baltimore, Md., June 17, 1926. [10; 13]

Bashford, Herbert, playwright and poet, b. Sioux City, Ia., 1871; d. Piedmont, Calif., July 13, 1928. [10; 35]

Bashford, James Whitford, missionary and educationist, b. Fayette, Wis., 1842; d. Pasadena, Calif., March 8, 1919. [1; 4; 10]

Bashore, Harvey Brown, physician, b. West Fairview, Pa., 1864; d. West Fairview, Pa., Nov. 28, 1934. [62]

Baskervill, Charles Read, educationist, b. Covington, Tenn., 1872; d. Chicago, Ill., July 22, 1935. [7; 10; 11]

Baskervill, William Malone, educationist, b. Fayette county, Tenn., 1850; d. Nashville, Tenn., Sept. 6, 1899. [34]

Baskerville, Charles, chemist, b. Deer Brook, Miss., 1870; d. New York, N.Y., Jan. 28, 1922. [1; 10]

·Baskett, James Newton, zoologist and novelist, b. Nicholas county, Ky., 1849; d. Mexico, Mo., June 14, 1925. [2; 4; 7; 10; 11; 34; 74]

Baskin, Robert Newton, pioneer, b. 1835; d. ?

Bass, Edgar Wales, soldier and mathematician, b. Prairie du Chien, Wis., 1843; d. Bar Harbor, Me., Nov. 6, 1918. [10]

Bass, Henry Royce, local historian, b. 1848; d. 1884.

Bass, John Foster, war correspondent, b. Chicago, Ill, 1866; d. Tucson, Ariz., April 16, 1931. [10]

Bassett, Mrs. Adelaide Florence, née **Samuels,** writer of books for children, b. Boston, Mass., 1845; d. ? [10]

Bassett, James, missionary, b. near Hamilton, Upper Canada, 1834; d. Los Angeles, Calif., March 11, 1906. [1; 2; 6]

Bassett, John Spencer, historian, b. Tarboro, N.C., 1867; d. Washington, D.C., Jan. 27, 1928. [1; 2; 7; 10; 11]

Bassett, Mrs. Mary E., née **Stone,** novelist and poet, b. 1857; d. 1924.

Bassett, Samuel Clay, local historian, b. 1844; d. ?

Bassett, Samuel Eliot, educationist, b. Wilton, Conn, 1873; d. Burlington, Vt., Dec. 2, 1936. [10]

Basshe, Emanuel Jo, playwright, b. Vilna, Russia, 1900; d. New York, N.Y., Oct. 29, 1939.

Bassnett, Thomas, meteorologist, b. 1808; d. ? [6]

Bastian, George Conrad, journalist, b. 1875; d. Evanston, Ill., Jan 4, 1925.

Bastin, Edson Sewell, botanist, b. Ozaukee county, Wis., 1843; d. Chicago, Ill., April 6, 1897. [4]

Batchelder, Eugene, lawyer and poet, b. 1822; d. 1878. [51]

Batchelder, Ira Kendrick, local historian, b. 1811; d. ?

Batchelder, James, locomotive engineer, b. 1828; d. ?

Batchelder, James Locke, journalist, b. Newburyport, Mass., 1816; d. Chicago, Ill., April 4, 1909. [45]

Batchelder, John Putnam, physician, b. Wilton, N.H., 1784; d. New York, N.Y., April 8, 1868. [1; 4; 49]

Batchelder, Roger, journalist, b. Washington, D.C., 1897; d. Evansville, Ind., Dec. 13, 1947. [7; 10]

Batchelder, Samuel, manufacturer, b. Jaffrey, N.H., 1784; d. Cambridge, Mass., Feb. 5, 1879. [1; 4]

Batchelder, Samuel, lawyer, b. 1830; d. 1888. [51]

Batchelder, Samuel Francis, lawyer and historian, b. Cambridge, Mass., 1870; d. Boston, Mass., June 10, 1927. [51]

Batchellor, Albert Stillman, lawyer and historian, b. Bethlehem, N.H., 1850; d. Littleton, N.H., June 15, 1913. [49]

Batchelor, George, clergyman, b. Southbury, Conn., 1836; d. Cambridge, Mass., June 21, 1923. [1; 10]

Batdorf, John William, economist, b. 1852; d. ?

Bateman, Harry, mathematical physicist, b. Manchester, England, 1882; d. on a train in Utah, Jan. 23, 1946. [10; 11; 13]

Bateman, Newton, educationist, b. Cumberland county, N.J., 1822; d. Galesburg, Ill., Oct. 21, 1897. [1; 36]

Bateman, Mrs. Sidney Frances, née **Cowell,** playwright, b. probably in New Jersey, 1823; d. London, England, Jan. 13, 1881. [1; 7]

Bateman, William O., lawyer, fl. 1858-1876. [6]

Baten, Anderson Monroe, publisher, b. Brenham, Tex., 1888; d. May, 1943. [7; 10]

Bates, Arlo, educationist, novelist, and poet, b. East Machias, Me., 1850; d. Boston, Mass., Aug. 24, 1918. [1; 2; 3; 4; 6; 7; 71]

Bates, Charlotte Fiske, poet, b. New York, N.Y., 1838; d. Cambridge, Mass., Sept. 1, 1916. [2; 3; 7; 10]

Bates, Mrs. Clara, née **Doty,** writer of books for children, b. Ann Arbor, Mich., 1838; d. Chicago, Ill., Oct. 14, 1895. [7; 8; 39]

Bates, Clement, lawyer, b. Cincinnati, O., 1845; d. Cincinnati, O., Jan. 16, 1931. [10; 11]

Bates, David, poet, b. Hamilton county, O., 1809; d. Philadelphia, Pa., Jan. 25, 1870. [3; 4; 7]

Bates, David Homer, telegraph operator, b. 1843; d. New York, N.Y., June 15, 1926.

Bates, Ernest Sutherland, literary critic, b. Gambier, O., 1879; d. New York, N.Y., Dec. 4, 1939. [7; 10]

Bates, Frank Amasa, sportsman and naturalist, b. 1858; d. Braintree, Mass., Dec. 20, 1915.

Bates, Mrs. Harriet Leonora, née **Vose,** novelist, b. Quincy, Ill., 1856; d. Boston, Mass., March, 1886. [4; 7]

Bates, Herbert, educationist, b. Hyde Park, Mass., 1868; d. Bellmore, Long Island, N.Y., April 16, 1929. [7; 10; 51]

Bates, James Hale, traveller, b. 1826; d. 1901.

Bates, Jerome Paine, journalist, b. Dudley, Mass., 1837; d. Los Angeles, Calif., June 17, 1915.

Bates, Joseph, Seventh-day adventist, b. 1792; d. 1872.

Bates, Joseph Clement, lawyer, b. 1836; d. 1913.

Bates, Katherine Lee, poet and educationist, b. Falmouth, Mass., 1859; d. Wellesley, Mass., March 28, 1929. [1a; 7; 10]

Bates, Lindell Theodore, lawyer, b. Tacoma, Wash., 1890; d. London, England, April 13, 1937. [62]

Bates, Lindon Wallace, civil engineer, b. Marshfield, Vt., 1858; d. Paris, France, April 22, 1924. [10]

Bates, Lindon Wallace, civil engineer, b. Portland, Ore., 1883; d. at sea, May 7, 1915. [10; 62]

Bates, Mrs. Margret Holmes, née **Ernsperger,** poet and novelist, b. Fremont, O., 1844; d. New York, N.Y., 1927. [4; 7; 10]

Bates, Morgan, novelist, b. Albany, N.Y., 1847; d. Traverse City, Mich., 1902. [39]

Bates, Oric, archaeologist, b. 1883; d. Camp Zachary Taylor, Louisville, Ky., Oct 8, 1918. [51]

Bates, Robert Chapman, educationist, b. New York, N.Y., 1901; d. New Haven, Conn., Dec. 1, 1942. [62]

Bates, Samuel Austin, genealogist, b. 1822; d. 1897.

Bates, Samuel Penniman, educationist, b. Mendon, Mass., 1827; d. Meadville, Pa., July 17, 1902. [1; 6; 10; 47]

Bates, Walter, loyalist, b. Darien, Conn., 1760; d. Kings county, N.B., Feb. 11, 1842. [1; 7; 27]

Bates, William Henry, clergyman, b. Champion, N.Y., 1840; d. Greeley, Colo., Aug. 1, 1924. [63]

Bates, William Horatio, physician, b. 1860; d. New York, N.Y., July 10, 1931.

Bates, William Nickerson, educationist, b. Cambridge, Mass., 1867; d. Cambridge, Mass., June 10, 1949. [7; 10; 51]

Bates, William Oscar, journalist and playwright, b. Harrisburg, Ind., 1852; d. Indianapolis, Ind., Oct. 29, 1924. [10]

Bates, William Wallace, shipbuilder, b. Shubenacadie, N.S., 1827; d. Denver, Colo., Nov., 1912. [10]

Battell, Joseph, editor and publisher, b. Middlebury, Vt., 1839; d. Feb. 22, 1915. [10]

Batten, John Mullin, physician, b. Chester county, Pa., 1837; d. Downington, Pa., Jan. 23, 1916. [4]

Batten, Loring Woart, clergyman, b. Gloucester county, N.J., 1859; d. Swarthmore, Pa., Jan. 6, 1946. [7; 11; 51]

Batten, Samuel Zane, clergyman, b. Swedesboro, N.J., 1859; d. Philadelphia, Pa., June 26, 1925. [10]

Battershall, Fletcher Williams, lawyer, b. 1866; d. 1929. [4; 8]

Battershall, Jesse Park, chemist, b. Troy, N.Y., 1851; d. Poughkeepsie, N.Y., Jan. 12, 1891. [3]

Battershall, Walton Wesley, clergyman, b. Troy, N.Y., 1840; d. Albany, N.Y., March 19, 1920. [4; 10; 62]

Batterson, Hermon Griswold, clergyman, b. Marbledale, Conn., 1827; d. 1903. [4; 7; 10]

Batterson, James Goodwin, industrialist, b. Bloomingfield, N.Y., 1823; d. Hartford, Conn., Sept. 18, 1901. [1; 2; 10]

Battey, Thomas C., Quaker, fl. 1871-1903. [6]

Battin, William, jurist and local historian, b. 1832; d. ?]37]

Battle, Archibald John, clergyman, b. Powelton, Ga., 1826; d. Macon, Ga., Sept. 28, 1907. [10; 34]

Battle, Kemp Plummer, educationist and historian, b. Franklin county, N.C., 1831; d. Raleigh, N.C., Feb. 14, 1919. [1; 4; 10; 34; 54]

Battle, William Horn, jurist, b. Edgecombe county, N.C., 1803; d. Chapel Hill, N.C., March 14, 1879. [1; 54]

Batts, Robert Lynn, jurist, b. Bastrop, Tex., 1864; d. Austin, Tex., May 19, 1935. [1a; 10]

Batty, Joseph H., sportsman, d. 1906. [6]

Bauer, Wright (pseud.). See Hobart, George Vere.

Baughman, Abraham J., local historian, b. 1838; d. 1913.

Baughman, Theodore, scout, b. 1845; d. ?

Baum, Frank George, electrical engineer, b. Ste. Genevieve, Mo., 1870; d. March 14, 1932. [10; 57]

Baum, Lyman Frank, writer of books for children, b. Chittenango, N.Y., 1856; d. Hollywood, Calif., May 6, 1919. [1; 4; 7; 10]

Bausch, Edward, optician, b. Rochester, N. Y., 1854; d. Rochester, N.Y., July 30, 1944.

Bauslin, David Henry, theologian, b. Winchester, Va., 1854; d. Springfield, O., March 3, 1922. [10]

Bausman, Benjamin, clergyman, b. near Lancaster, Pa., 1824; d. Reading, Pa., May 8, 1909. [1; 10]

Bausman, Frederick, lawyer and novelist, b. Pittsburgh, Pa., 1861; d. Seattle, Wash., June 19, 1931. [10]

Bax, Emily, private secretary, b. England, 1882; d. New York, N.Y., Jan. 3, 1943.

Baxley, Henry Willis, physician, b. Baltimore, Md., 1803; d. Baltimore, Md., March 13, 1876. [1; 76]

Baxley, Isaac Rieman, poet, b. Baltimore, Md., 1850; d. Montecito, Calif., Aug. 30, 1920. [35]

Baxter, Albert, local historian, b. Washington county, Vt., 1823; d. 1905. [39]

Baxter, Edmund Dillahunty, lawyer, b. Nashville, Tenn., 1838; d. Nashville, Tenn., 1910. [10]

Baxter, James Phinney, historian, b. Gorham, Me., 1831; d. Portland, Me., May 8, 1921. [2; 6; 10; 37]

Baxter, Jedidiah Hyde, medical officer, b. Strafford, Vt., 1837; d. Dec. 4, 1890. [3; 43]

Baxter, Jere, b. Nashville, Tenn., 1852; d. 1904. [10]

Baxter, John Babington Macaulay, soldier, politician, and jurist, b. Saint John, N.B., 1868; d. Saint John, N.B., Dec. 27, 1946. [30]

Baxter, Katharine Schuyler, traveller, b. 1845; d. ?

Baxter, Katherine, journalist, d. Kansas City, Mo., 1924.

Baxter, Lydia, poet and hymn-writer, b. Petersburg, N.Y., 1809; d. New York, N.Y., Jan. 23, 1874. [3; 7]

Baxter, Sylvester, journalist, b. West Yarmouth, Mass., 1850; d. San Juan, Porto Rico, Jan. 28, 1927. [2; 7; 10]

Baxter, William, clergyman, b. Leeds, England, 1820; d. Newcastle, Pa., Feb. 11, 1880. [1; 3; 6; 7]

Baxter, William, engineer, b. 1854; d. ?

Bay, James (pseud.). See Clark, James Bayard.

Bayard, Samuel, lawyer, b. Philadelphia, Pa., 1767; d. Princeton, N.J., May 12, 1840. [1; 3; 56]

Bayard, Samuel John, poet and biographer, d. 1879. [6; 56]

Bayles, George James, lawyer, b. Irvington-on-Hudson, N.Y., 1869; d. Nov. 20, 1914. [10]

Bayles, James Copper, engineer, b. New York., N.Y., 1845; d. New York, N.Y., May 7, 1913. [1; 4;]

Bayles, Richard Mather, local historian, fl. 1874-1891.

Bayles, William Harrison, historian, b. 1841; d. ?

Bayley, James Roosevelt, archbishop, b. Boston, Mass., 1846; d. Denver, Colo., Oct. 28, 1917. [10; 46]

Bayley, Frank William, writer on art, b. 1863; d. Newburyport, Mass., July 24, 1932.

Bayley, James Roosevelt, archibishop, b. Rye, N.Y., 1814; d. Newark, N.J., Oct. 3, 1877. [1; 2; 4; 21]

Bayley, John, clergyman, b. England, 1814; d. 1880.

Bayley, Richard, physician, b. Fairfield, Conn., 1745; d. Staten Island, N.Y., Aug. 17, 1801. [1; 2; 3; 4]

Bayley, William Shirley, geologist, b. Baltimore, Md., 1861; d. Glen Rock, N.J., Feb. 14, 1943. [13]

Baylies, Edwin, lawyer, b. Clinton, N.Y., 1840; d. Johnstown, N.Y., May 18, 1925. [10]

Baylies, Francis, historian, b. Taunton, Mass., 1783; d. Taunton, Mass., Oct. 28, 1852. [1; 4]

Baylies, Nicholas, jurist, b. Uxbridge, Mass., about 1772; d. Lyndon, Vt., Aug. 17, 1847. [43]

Baylies, Nicholas, historian, d. 1893. [37]

Baylis, Samuel Mathewson, merchant, b. Montreal, Que., 1854; d. Montreal, Que., July 12, 1941. [27]

Bayliss, Alfred, educationist, b. Gloucestershire, Engalnd, 1847; d. Macomb, Ill., 1911. [10]

Bayliss, Mrs. Clara, née **Kern,** writer of books for young people, b. near Kalamozoo, Mich., 1848; d. ? [7; 10]

Baylor, Adelaide Steele, home economist, b. Wabash, Ind., about 1865; d. Washington, D.C., Dec. 18, 1935. [10]

Baylor, Frances Courtney, novelist, b. Fort Smith, Ark., 1848; d. Winchester, Va., Oct. 19, 1920. [1; 2; 3; 4; 7; 34]

Bayne, Samuel Gamble, banker and traveller, b. Ulster, Ireland, 1844; d. New York, N.Y., April 20, 1924. [10] ·

Baynes, Ernest Harold, naturalist, b. Calcutta, India, 1868; d. Meriden, N.H., Jan. 21, 1925. [10]

Beach, Abel, poet, b. 1829; d. Iowa City, Ia., June 19, 1899. [37]

Beach, Alfred Eli, journalist, b. Springfield, Mass., 1826; d. New York, N.Y., Jan. 1, 1896. [4; 6]

Beach, Arthur Granville, educationist, b. Marietta, O., 1870; d. Marietta, O., Jan. 28, 1934. [10; 62]

Beach, Chandler Belden, editor, b. 1839; d. 1928.

Beach, Charles Fisk, clergyman, b. Jewett, N.Y., 1827; d. Philadelphia, Pa., May 25, 1908. [2; 10; 62]

Beach, Charles Fisk, lawyer, b. Kentucky, 1854; d. June 6, 1934. [2; 10; 34]

Beach, David Nelson, clergyman, b. South Orange, N.J., 1848; d. Southington, Conn., Oct. 18, 1926. [10; 62]

Beach, Edward Latimer, naval officer, b. Toledo, O., 1867; d. Palo Alto, Calif., Dec. 20, 1943. [10]

Beach, Harlan Page, missionary, b. South Orange, N.J., 1854; d. Winter Park, Fla., March 4, 1933. [1a; 2a; 4; 62]

Beach, John Sheldon, lawyer, b. New Haven, Conn., 1819; d. New Haven, Conn., Sept. 12, 1887. [62]

Beach, Lewis, lawyer and local historian, b. New York, N.Y., 1835; d. Cornwall, N.Y., Aug. 10, 1886. [62]

Beach, Moses Yale, journalist, b. Wallingford, Conn., 1800; d. Wallingford, Conn., Jan. 19, 1868. [2; 4]

Beach, Mrs. Rebecca, née **Gibbons,** novelist, b. 1823; d. 1893. [6]

Beach, Rex, novelist, b. Atwood, Mich. 1877; d. near Sebring, Fla., Dec. 7, 1949. [7; 10; 11; 12]

Beach, Samuel Bellamy, lawyer and poet, b. Whitestown, N.Y., about 1780; d. Oneonta, Otsego county, N.Y., July 31, 1866.

Beach, Seth Curtis, clergyman, b. 1837; d. 1925. [51]

Beach, William Dorrance, soldier, b. Brooklyn, N.Y., 1856; d. Mount Vernon, N.Y., June 18, 1932. [10]

Beach, Wooster, physician, b. Trumbull, Conn., 1794; d. New York, N.Y., Jan. 28, 1868. [1; 4]

Beadle, Delos White, lawyer and horticulturist, b. St. Catherines, Upper Canada, 1823; d. Toronto, Ont., Aug. 30, 1905. [27; 62]

Beadle, Erastus Flavel, publisher, b. Cooperstown, N.Y., 1821; d. Cooperstown, N.Y., Dec. 18, 1894. [1a; 7]

Beadle, John Hanson, journalist, b. Parke county, Ind., 1840; d. Washington, D.C., Jan. 15, 1897. [4]

Beadle, William Henry Harrison, civil engineer and educationist, b. Parke county, Ind., 1838; d. San Francisco, Calif., Nov. 13, 1915. [1; 10; 53]

Beakes, Samuel Willard, local historian, b. Burlingham, N.Y., 1861; d. Washington, D.C., Feb. 9, 1927. [10]

Beal, William James, botanist, b. Adrian, Mich, 1833; d. Amherst, Mass., May 12, 1924. [1; 3; 4; 10; 39]

Beale, Charles Willing, novelist, b. Washington, D.C., 1845; d. Arden, N.C., Aug. 13, 1932. [34]

Beale, George William, soldier b. 1842; d. ?

Beale, Joseph Henry, lawyer, b. Dorchester, Mass., 1861; d. Cambridge, Mass., Jan. 20, 1943. [10; 51]

Beale, Mrs. Maria, née **Taylor,** novelist, b. Richmond, Va., 1849; d. ? [34]

Beale, Richard Lee Turberville, soldier, b. Westmoreland county, Va., 1819; d. Hague, Westmoreland county, Va., April 21, 1893. [1]

Beale, Truxtun, diplomat, b. San Francisco, Calif., 1856; d. near Annapolis, Md., June 2, 1936. [2; 4; 10]

Beall, John Bramblett, soldier, b. Tennessee, 1833; d. 1917. [34]

Beaman, Alexander Gaylord, insurance executive, b. West Hartford, Conn., 1885; d. Los Angeles, Calif., Oct, 22, 1943. [10]

Beaman, Charles Cotesworth, lawyer, b. Houlton, Me., 1840; d. New York, N.Y., Dec. 15, 1900. [1; 10]

Beaman, Edmond Addison, clergyman, b. Wendell, Mass., 1811; d. ? [45]

Beamish, Richard Joseph, lawyer and journalist, b. Scranton, Pa., 1869; d. Harrisburg, Pa., Oct. 1, 1945. [10; 11]

Bean, Fannie, novelist, b. Vinalhaven, Me.; d. after 1893. [6]

Bean, Tarleton Hoffman, ichthyologist, b. Bainbridge, Pa., 1846; d. Albany, N.Y., Dec. 28, 1916. [1; .10]

Bean, Theodore Weber, local historian, b. 1833; d. 1891.

Beard, Adelia Belle, illustrator, b. Painesville, O.; d. Flushing, N.Y., Feb. 16, 1920. [10]

Beard, Annie E. S., journalist, b. London, England; d. Minneapolis, Minn., 1930.

Beard, Augustus Field, clergyman, b. Norwalk, Conn., 1833; d. Norwalk, Conn., Dec. 22, 1934. [10; 62]

Beard, Charles Austin, historian, b. near Knightstown, Ind., 1874; d. New Haven, Conn., Sept. 1, 1948. [7; 10; 12]

Beard, Charles Heady, physician, b. Spencer county, Ky., 1855; d. Chicago, Ill., June 3, 1916. [10]

Beard, Daniel Carter, illustrator and writer of books for boys, b. Cincinnati, O., 1850; d. Suffern, N.Y., June 11, 1941. [7; 10; 11; 15]

Beard, Frank. See Beard, Thomas Francis.

Beard, George Miller, physician, b. Montville, Conn., 1839; d. New York, N.Y., Jan. 23, 1883. [1; 2; 3; 4; 6]

Beard, James Carter, illustrator, b. Cincinnati, O., 1837; d. New Orleans, La., Nov. 15, 1913. [1; 7; 10]

Beard, James Thom, mining engineer, b. Brooklyn, N.Y., 1855; d. Danbury, Conn., Dec. 26, 1941. [10]

Beard, Lina, illustrator, b. Cincinnati, O.; d. Flushing, N.Y., Jan. 8, 1933. [10; 11]

Beard, Mary, nurse, b. Dover, N.H., 1876; d. New York, N.Y., Dec. 4, 1946.

Beard, Oliver Thomas, novelist, b. 1832; d. ? [39]

Beard, Richard, clergyman, b. Sumner county, Tenn., 1799; d. Lebanon, Tenn., Dec. 2, 1880. [1; 2; 6; 34]

Beard, Thomas Francis, illustrator, b. Cincinnati, O., 1842; d. Chicago, Ill., Sept. 28, 1905. [1; 7; 10]

Beard, William Holbrook, painter, b. Painesville, O., 1825; d. New York, N.Y., Feb. 20, 1900. [1; 3; 10]

Beardshear, William Miller, educationist, b. Dayton, O., 1850; d. 1902. [10; 37]

Beardslee, Clark Smith, clergyman, b. Coventry, N.Y., 1850; d. Hartford, Conn., April 14, 1914. [10; 45]

Beardslee, John Walter, clergyman, b. Ottawa county, O., 1837; d. New Brunswick, N.J., March 31, 1921.

Beardsley, Eben Edwards, clergyman, b. Stepney, Conn., 1808; d. New Haven, Conn., Dec. 2, 1891. [1; 3]

Beardsley, Isaac Haight, genealogist, b. 1831; d. 1902.

Beardsley, Levi, lawyer, b. Hoosic, N.Y., 1785; d. New York, N.Y., March 19, 1857. [3]

Beardsley, William Agur, clergyman, b. Monroe, Conn., 1865; d. New Haven, Conn., Dec. 28, 1946. [10]

Beasley, Frederick, clergyman, b. near Edenton, N.C., 1777; d. Elizabethtown, N.J., Nov. 1, 1845. [1; 3; 6; 34]

Beasley, Frederick Williamson, clergyman. b. 1808; d. Philadelphia, Pa., Dec. 28, 1878. [19]

Beasley, Thomas Dykes, descriptive writer, b. England, 1850; d. ? [35]

Beath, Robert Bruns, military historian, b. Philadelphia, Pa., 1839; d. Philadelphia, Pa., Nov. 25, 1914. [10]

Beatley, Mrs. Clara, née Bancroft, educationist, b. Shirley, Mass., 1858; d. Boston, Mass., Oct. 20, 1923. [10]

Beaton, David, clergyman, b. Scotland, 1848; d. Janesville, Wis., Feb. 11, 1920. [10]

Beattie, Francis Robert, clergyman and educationist, b. near Guelph, Ont., 1848; d. Louisville, Ky., Sept. 6, 1906. [1; 4; 10; 34]

Beatty, Adam, lawyer and agricultural writer, b. Hagerstown, Md., 1777; d. Mason county, Ky., June 9, 1858. [1; 4]

Beatty, Arthur, educationist, b. St. Mary's, Ont., 1869; d. Madison, Wis., Feb. 27, 1943. [7; 10; 11]

Beatty, Bessie, journalist, b. Los Angeles, Calif., 1886; d. Nyack, N.Y., April 6, 1947. [7; 10; 11]

Beatty, John, soldier and novelist, b. Sandusky, O., 1828; d. Columbus, O., Dec. 21, 1914. [1; 7; 10]

Beatty, John Wesley, art director, b. Pittsburgh, Pa., 1851; d. Clifton Springs, N.Y., Sept. 29, 1924. [10]

Beattys, Harry Harvey, clergyman, b. Poughkeepsie, N.Y., 1860; d. March 10, 1939. [60]

Beaubien, Charles Philippe, priest, b. Montreal, Que., 1843; d. Sault-au-Recollet, Que., July 2, 1914. [32]

Beaubien, Henry Des Rivières, lawyer, b. about 1800; d. Montreal, Lower Canada, Oct. 6, 1834.

Beauchamp, Jean Joseph, lawyer, b. Montreal, Que., 1852; d. Montreal, Que., 1923.

Beauchamp, Lou Jenks, lecturer, b. Cincinnati, O., 1851; d. Hamilton, O., June 4, 1920. [10]

Beauchamp, William, clergyman, b. Kent county, Del., 1772; d. Paoli, Orange county, Ind., Oct. 7, 1824. [1; 6]

Beauchamp, William Martin, archaeologist, b. Coldenham, N.Y., 1830; d. Syracuse, N.Y., Dec. 13, 1925. [1; 7; 10]

Beauchemin, Nérée, poet, b. Yamachiche, Que., 1850; d. Three Rivers, Que., June 29, 1931. [27]

Beaudé, Henri, priest and littérateur, b. Arthabaskaville, Que., 1870; d. Rome, Italy, July 11, 1930. [27]

Beaudouin, Joseph Damase, priest and historian, b. St. Isidore, Que., 1856; d. Quebec, Que., March 5, 1917. [32]

Beaudry, David Hercule, priest, b. Quebec, Lower Canada, 1822; d. Napierville, Que., Jan. 2, 1876. [32]

Beaudry, Louis Napoléon, clergyman. b. Highgate, Vt., 1833; d. 1892. [6]

Beaugrand, Honoré, journalist, b. Lanoraie, Que., 1849; d. Westmount, Que., Oct. 7, 1906. [27]

Beaujeu, Monongahéla de, historian, b. Coteau-du-Lac, Que., 1870; d. at sea, March 19, 1928. [27]

Beaumont, Mrs. Betty, née **Bentley,** business woman, b. 1828; d. ?

Beaumont, Charles, priest, b. Charlesbourg, Lower Canada, 1820; d. L'Ange Gardien, Que., Sept. 2, 1889. [32]

Beaumont, Henry, psychologist, b. The Hague, Netherlands, 1902; d. Lexington, Ky., Feb 21, 1947.

Beaumont, William, surgeon, b. Lebanon, Conn., 1785; d. St. Louis, Mo., April 25, 1853. [1; 3; 4]

Beauregard, Alphonse, poet, b. St. Hyacinthe, Que., 1885; d. Montreal, Que., Jan. 15, 1924. [27]

Beauregard, Pierre Gustave Toutant, soldier, b. near New Orleans, La., 1818; d. New Orleans, La., Feb. 20, 1893. [1; 2; 3; 4; 5; 6; 34]

Beaven, James, clergyman and educationist, b. England, 1801; d. Niagara, Ont., Nov. 8, 1875. [27]

Beazley, Mrs. Rosalind R., writer of short stories, d. Berea, Ky., April 22, 1924. [2a]

Béchard, Auguste, biographer and historian, b. Longueuil, Lower Canada, 1828; d. Danville, Que., Aug. 30, 1893. [27]

Bechtel, John Hendricks, compiler, b. 1841; d. after 1911.

Beck, Amanda Kathryn, nurse, b. 1870; d. 1937.

Beck, Bodag Felix, physician, b. Budapesth, Hungary, 1868; d. Kingston, N.Y., Jan. 1, 1942.

Beck, Carl, surgeon, b. Germany, 1856; d. Pelham, N.Y., June 9, 1911. [1; 10; 11]

Beck, Charles, educationist, b. Heidelberg, Germany, 1798; d. Cambridge, Mass., March 19, 1866. [1; 3; 6; 51]

Beck, James Montgomery, lawyer, b. Philadelphia, Pa., 1861; d. Washington, D. C., April 12, 1936. [2a; 10]

Beck, John Brodhead, physician, b. Schenectady, N.Y., 1794; d. Rinebeck, N.Y., April 9, 1851. [1; 3; 4; 6]

Beck, Lewis Caleb, physician and scientist, b. Schenectady, N.Y., 1798; d. Albany, N.Y., April 20, 1853. [1; 3; 6]

Beck, Mrs. Lily Adams, née **Moresby,** novelist, d. Kyoto, Japan, Jan. 3, 1931. [27]

Beck, Theodric Romeyn, physician, b. Schenectady, N.Y., 1791; d. Utica, N.Y., Nov. 19, 1855. [1; 3; 4; 6]

Becker, Alexander Christian, physician, b. 1815; d. 1849.

Becker, Carl Lotus, historian, b. Lincoln township, Iowa, 1873; d. Ithaca, N.Y., April 10, 1945. [7; 10; 11]

Becker, John P., revolutionist, b. 1765; d. 1837.

Beckett, James Beach, lawyer, b. Chicago, Ill., 1871; d. Pasadena, Calif., April 8, 1947. [62]

Beckett, Sylvester Breakmore, publisher and poet, b. 1812; d. 1882. [38]

Beckley, Hosea, clergyman, b. Berlin, Conn., 1779; d. Chesterfield, N.H., Oct. 15, 1843. [62]

Beckman, Mrs. Nellie, née **Sims,** writer of reminiscences, b. Jacksonville, Ill.; d. Oakland, Calif., Nov. 2, 1936. [35]

Beckman, Mrs. William. See Beckman, Mrs. Nellie, née Sims.

Beckmeyer, Clement, clergyman, d. 1921.

Beckwith, Albert Clayton, local historian, b. 1836; d. Whitewater, Wis., 1915. [44]

Beckwith, Charles Minnigerode, bishop, b. Prince George county, Va., 1851; Montgomery, Ala., April 18, 1928. [10; 34]

Beckwith, Clarence Augustine, theologian, b. Charlemont, Mass., 1849; d. Bangor, Me., April 2, 1931. [1a; 10]

Beckwith, George Cone, clergyman, b. 1800; d. Boston, Mass., May 12, 1870. [3]

Beckwith, Hiram Williams, historian, b. Danville, Ill., 1832; d. Chicago, Ill., Dec. 22, 1903. [36]

Beckwith, Isbon Thaddeus, educationist, b. Old Lyme, Conn., 1843; d. Atlantic City, N.J., Sept. 9, 1936. [10; 62]

Beckwith, Paul Edmond, anthropologist, b. St. Louis, Mo., 1848; d. 1907. [10; 34]

Bédard, Joseph Edouard, lawyer, b. Beauport, Que., 1845; d. Beauport, Que., Jan. 30, 1927. [27]

Bédard, Pierre Joseph, physician, b. Montreal, Que., 1869; d. July 5, 1905. [27]

Bédard, Théophile Pierre, historian, b. Quebec, Lower Canada, 1837; d. Lynn, Mass., Jan. 16, 1900. [27]

Bede, Brother, educationist, b. 1874; d. 1939. [21]

Bedell, Edwin Augustus, lawyer, b. 1853; d. 1908.

Bedell, Gregory Thurston, bishop, b. Hudson, N.Y., 1817; d. New York, N.Y., March 11, 1892. [3; 4; 6]

Bedell, Gregory Townsend,clergyman, b. Staten Island, N.Y., 1793; d. Baltimore, Md., Aug. 30, 1834. [3; 4; 6]

Bedford, Gunning S., physician, b. Baltimore, Md., 1806; d. New York, N.Y., Sept. 5, 1870. [3]

Bedford-Jones, Henry, novelist, b. Napanee, Ont., 1887; d. Beverly Hills, Calif., May 6, 1949. [11]

Bedlow, Henry, poet, b. New York N.Y., 1821; d. Monte Carlo, May 25, 1914. [4]

Beebe, James Albert, clergyman, b. Mound Valley, Kans., 1878; d. Meadville, Pa., May 7, 1934. [10]

Beebe, Katherine, educationist, b. 1860; d. ?

Beecher, Catherine Esther, educationist and reformer, b. East Hampton, Long Island, N.Y., 1800; d. Elmira, N.Y., May 12, 1878. [1; 3; 6; 7]

Beecher, Charles, clergyman, b. Litchfield, Conn., 1815; d. Haverhill, Mass., April 20, 1900. [1; 3; 6; 7; 10; 62]

Beecher, Edward, clergyman, b. East Hampton, Long Island, N.Y., 1803; d. Brooklyn, N.Y., July 28, 1895. [1; 3; 6; 7; 62]

Beecher, Mrs. Eunice White, née Bullard, clergyman's wife, b. West Sutton, Mass., 1812; d. Stamford, Conn., March 8, 1897. [2; 3; 6]

Beecher, Henry Ward, clergyman, b. Litchfield, Conn., 1813; d. Brooklyn, N.Y., March 8, 1887. [1; 2; 3; 4; 5; 6; 7]

Beecher, Mrs. Henry Ward. See Beecher, Mrs. Eunice White, née Bullard.

Beecher, Lyman, clergyman, b. New Haven, Conn., 1775; d. Brooklyn, N.Y., Jan. 10, 1863. [1; 3; 6; 7]

Beecher, Mrs. Mary Howell, novelist and poet, b. 1854; d. Brooklyn, N.Y., May 22, 1923.

Beecher, May Howell (pseud.). See Beecher, Mrs. Mary Howell.

Beecher, Thomas Kinnicut, clergyman, b. Litchfield, Conn., 1824; d. Elmira, N.Y., March 14, 1900. [1; 4; 10]

Beecher, William Constantine, lawyer, b. 1849; d. Whitefield, N.H., Sept. 18, 1928. [2a]

Beecher, Willis Judson, clergyman, b. Hampden, O., 1838; d. Auburn, N.Y., May 10, 1912. [4; 10; 63]

Beede, Charles Gould, poet, d. Ames, Ia., 1906. [37]

Beede, Ivan, novelist, b. 1897; d. New York, N.Y., Aug. 18, 1946.

Beehler, William Henry, naval officer, b. Baltimore, Md., 1848; d. Annapolis, Md., June 23, 1915. [10]

Beekman, James Spencer Cannon, poet, d. 1906.

Beekman, Ross (pseud.). See Dey, Frederick Van Rensselaer.

Beer, Edwin, urologist, b. New York, N. Y., 1876., d. New York, N.Y., Aug. 13, 1938. [13]

Beer, George Louis, historian, b. Staten Island, N.Y., 1872; d. New York, N.Y., March 15, 1920. [1; 4; 10]

Beer, Thomas, novelist and biographer, b. Council 'Bluffs, Ia., 1889; d. New York, N.Y., April 18, 1940. [7; 10; 12]

Beers, Clifford Whittingham, pioneer in mental hygiene, b. New Haven, Conn., 1876; d. Providence, R.I., July 9, 1943. [10; 62]

Beers, Eli, economist, b. Bridgewater, Conn., 1856; d. Pasadena, Calif., April 24, 1946. [62]

Beers, Mrs. Ethelinda, née Elliot, poet, b. Goshen, N.Y., 1827; d. Orange, N.Y., Oct. 11, 1879. [1; 4; 9]

Beers, Mrs. Fannie A., writer of reminiscences, fl. 1860-1888. [34]

Beers, Henry Augustin, educationist, b. Buffalo, N.Y., 1847; d. New Haven, Conn., Sept. 7, 1926. [1; 2; 7; 10; 62]

Beers, William George, sportsman, b. Montreal, Que., 1843; d. Montreal, Que., Dec. 26, 1900. [27]

Beeson, John, humanitarian, b. 1803; d. ?

Begg, Alexander, historian, b. Caithness, Scotland, 1825; d. Victoria, B.C., 1904. [27]

Begg, Alexander, historian, b. Quebec, Lower Canada, 1840; d. Toronto, Ont., 1898. [27]

Beggs, George Erle, educationist, b. Springfield, Ill., 1883; d. Princeton, N.J., Nov. 23, 1939. [10]

Beggs, Stephen R., clergyman, b. 1801; d. 1895. [36]

Bégin, Louis Nazaire, cardinal, b. Lévis, Lower Canada, 1840; d. Quebec, Que., July 20, 1925. [27; 32]

Behr, Hans Herman, physician and naturalist, b. Germany, 1818; d. San Francisco, Calif., March 13, 1904.

Behrend, Bernard Arthur, electrical engineer, b. Villeneuve, Switzerland, 1875; d. March 25, 1932. [1a; 10]

Behrends, Adolphus Julius Frederick, clergyman, b. Nijmegen, Holland, 1839; d. Brooklyn, N.Y., May 22, 1900. [1; 4; 10]

Behrendt, Walter Curt, educationist, b. Metz, France, 1884; d. Norwich, Vt., April 26, 1945.

Beighle, Mrs. Nellie, née Craib, poet, b. Sorel, Que., 1851; d. Sacramento, Calif., 1916. [35]

Beland, Henri Séverin, physician and politician, b. Louiseville, Que., 1869; d. near Kingston, Ont., April 22, 1935. [27]

Bélanger, Jean Amable, poet, b. Rivière-Ouelle, Lower Canada, 1832; d. Ottawa, Ont., March 16, 1913. [27]

Belasco, David, playwright and producer of plays, b. San Francisco, Calif., 1853; d. New York, N.Y., May 14, 1931. [1a; 7; 10]

Belcher, Alexander Emerson, commercial traveller, b. near Toronto, Ont., 1844; d. Toronto, Ont., Nov. 26, 1926. [31a]

Belcher, Joseph, clergyman, b. Birmingham, England, 1794; d. Philadelphia, Pa., July 10, 1859. [3; 6]

Belcourt, Georges Antoine, missionary, b. Baie-du-Fèbvre, Lower Canada, 1803; d. Shediac, N.B., May 11, 1874. [1; 27]

Belden, A. Russell, clergyman, fl. 1851. [24]

Belden, Ezekiel Porter, lawyer, b. Wethersfield, Conn., 1823; d. Harlem, N.Y., March 6, 1911. [62]

Belden, Mrs. Jessie Perry, née Van Zile, novelist, b. Troy, N.Y., 1857; d. New York, N.Y., Feb. 2, 1910. [10]

Belden, Lemuel W., physician, b. 1801; d. 1839.

Belfield, Henry Holmes, educationist, b. Philadelphia, Pa., Nov. 17, 1837; d. Ann Arbor, Mich., June 5, 1912. [10]

Belfield, William Thomas, physician, b. St. Louis, Mo., 1856; d. Chicago, Ill., Oct. 14, 1929. [10]

Belisle, David W., miscellaneous writer, fl. 1849-1859. [6]

Belknap, Charles Eugene, soldier, politician, and local historian, b. Massena, N.Y., 1846; d. Grand Rapids, Mich., Jan. 16, 1929. [39]

Belknap, Jeremy, clergyman, b. Boston, Mass., 1774; d. Boston, Mass., June 20, 1798. [1; 2; 3; 4; 6; 51]

Belknap, William Worth, soldier, b. Newburg, N.Y., 1829; d. Washington, D.C., Oct. 12, 1890. [1; 3]

Bell, Agrippa Nelson, physician, b. Northampton county, Va., 1820; d. Brooklyn, N.Y., Oct. 15, 1911. [4; 10]

Bell, Alexander Graham, inventor, b. Edinburgh, Scotland, 1847; d. Baddeck, N.S., Aug. 2, 1922. [1; 2; 3; 4; 10; 27]

Bell, Alexander Melville, educationist, b. Edinburgh, Scotland, 1819; d. Washington, D.C., Aug. 7, 1905. [1; 2; 3; 6; 10]

Bell, Andrew James, educationist, b. Ottawa, Ont., 1856; d. Toronto, Ont., Dec. 24, 1932. [27]

Bell, Arthur Wellington, investment banker, b. Allegheny, Pa., 1875; d. Boston, Mass., July 9, 1945. [62]

Bell, Benjamin, clergyman, b. Dutchess county, N.Y., 1752; d. West Amesbury, Mass., Dec. 31, 1836. [62]

Bell, Charles Henry, lawyer and politician. b. Chester, N.H., 1823; d. Exeter, N.H., Nov. 11, 1893. [1; 4; 7]

Bell, Charles Napier, historian, b. Perth, Ont., 1854; d. Winnipeg, Man., Aug. 29, 1936. [27]

Bell, Charles William, lawyer, b. Hamilton, Ont., 1876; d. Hamilton, Ont., Feb. 8, 1938. [27]

Bell, Clark, lawyer, b. Whitesville, N.Y., 1832; d. New York, N.Y., Feb. 22, 1918. [1; 10]

Bell, Edwin, lawyer, b. Chatham, Ont., 1860; d. Toronto. Ont., Dec. 6, 1921. [31a]

Bell, Edwin C., journalist, b. 1848; d. Titusville, Pa., July 18, 1923.

Bell, Edward Price, journalist, b. Parke county, Ind., 1869; d. Gulfport, Miss., Sept. 23, 1943. [10]

Bell, Ernest (pseud.). See Swales, Mrs. Susan Matilda, née Bradshaw.

Bell, Frederick McKelvey, physician, b. Kingston, Ont., 1878; d. New York, N.Y., Jan. 6, 1931, [27]

Bell, George W., economist, b. 1832; d. 1907. [37]

Bell, George William, clergyman and educationist, b. Buffalo, N.Y., 1873; d. Stoneham, Mass., Nov. 5, 1920. [4]

Bell, Goodloe Harper, educationist, b. 1832; d. 1899.

Bell, Hiram Parks, lawyer and politician, b. Jackson county, Ga., 1827; d. Atlanta, Ga., Aug. 17, 1907. [10]

Bell, Hill McClelland, educationist, b. Licking county, O., 1860; d. Los Angeles, Calif., Jan. 9, 1927. [4; 10; 37]

Bell, J. Cawdor (pseud.). See Campbell, John.

Bell, James Mackintosh, geologist, b. St. Andrews, Que., 1877; d. Almonte, Ont., March 31, 1934. [27]

Bell, James Madison, poet, b. Gallipolis, O., 1826; d. 1902. [1; 7]

Bell, John, physician, b. Ireland, 1796; d. 1872. [3]

Bell, John Calhoun, lawyer and politician, b. Franklin county, Tenn., 1851; d. Grand Junction, Colo., Aug. 12, 1933. [10]

Bell, John Thomas, local historian, b. 1842; d. ?

Bell, Lilian Lida, novelist, b. Chicago, Ill., 1867; d. Los Angeles, Calif., July 18, 1929. [7; 10]

Bell, Louis, physicist and engineer, b. Chester, N. H., 1864; d. West Newton, Mass., June 14, 1923. [1; 10]

Bell, Lura (pseud.). See Williamson, Julia May.

Bell, Luther Vose, physician, b. Chester, N.H., 1806; d. near Budd's Ferry, Md., Feb. 11, 1862. [3]

Bell, Ralcy Husted, physician, b. New York, N.Y., 1869; d. Kingston, N.Y., May 29, 1931. [10]

Bell, Roscoe Rutherford, veterinary surgeon, b. Augusta county, Va., 1858; d. ? [10]

Bell, Vereen McNeill, novelist and naval officer, b. 1911; d. on active service in the Philippines, Oct. 25, 1944.

Bell, Walter Nehemiah, educationist, d. Paris, Ont., Nov. 22, 1921.

Bell, Wilbur Cosby, clergyman, b. Augusta county, Va., 1881; d. April 6, 1933. [10]

Bell, William Hemphill, soldier, b. West Chester, Pa., 1834; d. Arvada, Colo., Oct. 18, 1906. [10]

Bell, William Melvin, bishop, b. Whitley county, Ind., Nov. 12, 1860; d. Oct. 6, 1933. [10]

Bellamann, Henry, musician, poet, and novelist, b. Fulton, Mo., 1882; d. New York, N.Y., June 16, 1945. [7; 10; 11; 20]

Bellamy, Mrs. Blanche, née **Wilder,** journalist, b. Albany, N.Y., 1852; d. Brooklyn, N.Y., April 4, 1919. [10]

Bellamy, Charles Joseph, publisher and novelist, b. Chicopee Falls, Mass., 1852; d. Springfield, Mass.; Dec. 12, 1910. [7; 10]

Bellamy, Edward, journalist, b. Chicopee Falls, Mass., 1850; d. Chicopee Falls, Mass., May 22, 1898. [1; 2; 3; 4; 6; 7; 71]

Bellamy, Mrs. Elizabeth Whitfield, née **Croom,** novelist, b. near Quincy, Fla., 1837; d. Mobile, Ala., April 13, 1900. [1; 4; 7; 10; 34]

Bellamy, Joseph, theologian, b. Wallingford, Conn., 1719; d. Bethlehem, Conn., March 6, 1790. [1; 3; 4; 62]

Bellefeuille, Joseph Edouard Lefèbvre de, lawyer, b. St. Eustache, Lower Canada, 1840; d. Montreal, Que., Jan. 12, 1926. [27]

Bellemare, Joseph Elzéar, priest and local historian, b. Yamachiche, Que., 1849; d. Nicolet, Que., Feb. 29, 1924. [27]

Bellemare, Raphaël, local historian, b. Yamachiche, Lower Canada, 1821; d. Montreal, Que., 1906. [31]

Bellerive, Georges, lawyer and biographer, b. Lévis, Que., 1859; d. Quebec, Que., May 23, 1935. [11]

Bellew, Frank Henry Temple, caricaturist, b. Cawnpore, India, 1820; d. New York, N.Y., June 29, 1888. [1; 36; 7]

Bellew, Frank W., illustrator, b. 1862; d. 1894. [7]

Bellew, Harold Kyrle Money, actor and short-story writer, b. Calcutta, India, 1857; d. Salt Lake City, Utah, Nov. 1, 1911. [10]

Belling, John, geneticist, b. 1866; d. Berkeley, Calif., Feb. 28, 1933. [11; 35]

Bellows, Albert Finch, painter, b. Milford, Mass., 1829; d. Auburndale, Mass., Nov. 24, 1883. [1; 3; 4;]

Bellows, Albert Jones, physician, b. 1804; d. 1869. [52]

Bellows, Charles Fitzroy, mathematician, b. 1832; d. Ypsilanti, Mich., April 16, 1907. [53]

Bellows, Henry Adams, publicity director and poet, b. Portland, Me., 1885; d. Minneapolis, Minn., Dec. 29, 1939. [7; 10]

Bellows, Henry Whitney, clergyman, b. Boston, Mass., 1814; d. New York, N.Y., Jan. 30, 1882. [1; 3; 6; 7]

Bellows, Russell Nevins, clergyman, b. New York, N.Y., 1842; d. Belmont, N.Y., March 13, 1914. [51]

Belmont, August, banker and diplomat, b. Alzei, Prussia, 1816; d. New York, N.Y., Nov. 24, 1890. [1; 4]

Belmont, Perry, lawyer, politician, and diplomat, b. New York, N.Y., 1850; d. Newport, R. I., May 25, 1947. [10; 52]

Belrose, Louis, poet, b. Pennsylvania, 1845; d. 1894. [8]

Beman, Nathan Sidney Smith, clergyman and educationist, b. New Lebanon, N.Y., 1785; d. Carbondale, Ill., Aug. 6, 1871. [1; 3; 6]

Beman, Wooster Woodruff, mathematician, b. Southington, Conn., 1850; d. Ann Arbor, Mich., Jan 8, 1922. [2; 10; 53]

Bement, Caleb N., agriculturist, b. 1790; d. Poughkeepsie, N.Y., Dec. 22, 1868. [1; 6]

Bement, Douglas, educationist, b. Lansing, Mich., 1898; d. Seattle, Wash., May 15, 1943. [62]

Bemis, Albert Farwell, merchant, b. Boston, Mass., 1870; d. Chestnut Hill, Mass., April 12, 1936. [10]

Bemis, Edward Webster, economist, b. Springfield, Mass., 1860; d. Sept. 25, 1930. [10]

Bemis, George, lawyer and publicist, b. Waltham, Mass., 1816; d. Nice, France, June 5, 1876. [1; 3; 6]

Bemis, Harold Edward, veterinary surgeon, b. Cawker City, Kans., 1883; d. Bywood Manor, Pa., April 4, 1931. [1a]

Benbow, John Glen, publisher, b. Fort Madison, Ia., 1884; d. New York, N.Y., Feb. 21, 1944.

Benchley, Robert Charles, humorist, b. Worcester, Mass., 1889; d. New York, N.Y., Nov. 21, 1945. [7; 10; 52]

Bendbow, Hesper (pseud.). See Archer, George Washington.

Bender, Henry Richard, clergyman, b. 1847; d. ?

Bender, Horace (pseud.). See Greenough, Horatio.

Bender, Ida Catherine, educationist, b. Buffalo, N.Y., 1858; d. Buffalo, N.Y., June 11, 1916. [4].

Bender, Louis Prosper, physician, b. Quebec, Que., 1844; d. Quebec, Que., Jan. 24, 1917. [27]

Bender, Wilbur H., educationist, b. Williams Centre, O., 1860; d. Des Moines, Ia., Sept. 20, 1927. [37]

Bendire, Charles Emil, ornithologist, b. near Darmstadt, Germany, 1836; d. 1897.

Benedict, Mrs. Anne Elizabeth, née Kendrick, novelist, b. Rochester, N.Y., 1851; d. ? [24]

Benedict, David, clergyman and historian, b. Norwalk, Conn., 1779; d. Pawtucket, R.I., Dec. 5, 1874. [1; 3; 6; 24]

Benedict, Erastus Cornelius, lawyer and educationist, b. Branford, Conn., 1800; d. New York, N.Y., Oct. 22, 1880. [1; 3; 4; 6]

Benedict, Frank Lee, novelist, b. Alexandria, N.Y., 1834; d. Philadelphia, Pa., Dec. 17, 1910. [6; 7; 10; 34]

Benedict, George Grenville, journalist, b. Burlington, Vt., 1826; d. 1907. [10; 43]

Benedict, Harry Yandell, educationist, b. Louisville, Ky., 1869; d. Austin, Tex., May 10, 1937. [10]

Benedict, Henry Marvin, genealogist, b. Albany, N.Y., 1827; d. Saratoga Springs, N.Y., July 5, 1875. [69]

Benedict, Joel Tyler, educationist, b. Mentz, N.Y., 1821; d. Parsippany, N.Y., March 16, 1892.

Benedict, Mrs. Lovina B. (otherwise Mother Benedict), b. 1826; d. 1899. [37]

Benedict, Roswell Alphonzo, poet and economist, b. 1855; d. ?

Benedict, Ruth Fulton, anthropologist, b. New York, N.Y., 1887; d. New York, N.Y., Sept. 17, 1948. [14; 58]

Benedict, Suzan Rose, educationist, b. 1873; d. Northampton, Mass., April 9, 1942. [13; 48]

Benedict, Wayland Richardson, educationist, b. Rochester, N.Y., 1848; d. Arlington Heights, Mass., July 21, 1915. [10]

Benedict, William H., local historian, b. 1845; d. New Brunswick, N.J., Feb. 22, 1929.

Benét, Stephen Vincent, soldier b. St. Augustine, Fla., 1827; d. 1895. [3; 6; 34]

Benét, Stephen Vincent, poet and novelist, b. Bethlehem, Pa., 1898; d. New York, N.Y., March 13, 1943. [7; 10; 11]

Benezet, Anthony, philanthropist, b. St. Quentin, France, 1713; d. Philadelphia, Pa., May 3, 1784. [1; 2; 3; 4; 5; 6]

Bengough, Mrs. Elisa, née Armstrong, novelist, fl. 1897-1902. [10]

Bengough, John Wilson, cartoonist and poet, b. Toronto, Ont., 1851; d. Toronto, Ont., Oct. 2, 1923. [27]

Benjamin, Asher, architect, b. Greenfield, Mass., 1773; d. Springfield, Mass., July 26, 1845. [1]

Benjamin, Charles Henry, educationist, b. Patten, Me., 1856; d. Washington, D.C., Aug. 2, 1937. [10; 11]

Benjamin, DeWitt Clinton, clergyman, b. 1820; d. 1871.

Benjamin, Mrs. Elizabeth Dundas, née **Bedell,** novelist and religious writer, b. Philadelphia, Pa.; d. Stratford, Conn., 1890. [6]

Benjamin, Judah Philip, lawyer and politician, b. British West Indies, 1811; d. Paris, France, May 6, 1884. [1; 2; 3; 4; 5; 6]

Benjamin, Louis Nathan, lawyer, b. Belleville, Ont., about 1842; d. Montreal, Que., April 10, 1887. [27]

Benjamin, Marcus, editor, b. San Francisco, Calif., 1857; d. Oct. 22, 1932. [4; 10; 11]

Benjamin, Mrs. Mary Gladding, née **Wheeler,** biographer, b. Providence, R.I., 1814; d. 1871. [6]

Benjamin, Park, journalist and poet, b. Demerara, British Guiana, 1809; d. New York, N.Y., Sept. 12, 1864. [1; 2; 3; 4; 6; 71]

Benjamin, Park, lawyer, b. New York, N.Y., 1849; d. Stamford, Conn., Aug. 21, 1922. [2; 10]

Benjamin, Reuben Moore, lawyer, b. Chatham Centre, N.Y., 1833; d. Bloomington, Ill., Aug. 4, 1917. [10]

Benjamin, Samuel Greene Wheeler, painter and diplomat, b. Argos, Greece, 1837; d. Burlington, Vt., July 19, 1914. [1; 7; 10; 71]

Bennet, Sanford Fillmore, physician and song-writer, b. Eden, N.Y., 1836; d. Elkhorn, Wis., June 11, 1898. [1; 7; 44]

Bennett, Alfred Allen, chemist, b. Milford, N.H., 1850; d. Orange, Calif., June 23, 1922. [13]

Bennett, Charles Alpheus, publisher, b. Holden, Mass., 1864; d. Peoria, Ill., June 18, 1942. [11]

Bennett, Charles Andrew Armstrong, educationist, b. Ireland, 1885; d. New Haven, Conn., May 1, 1930. [10; 62]

Bennett, Charles Edwin, educationist, b. Providence, R.I., 1858; d. Ithaca, N.Y., May 2, 1921. [1; 2; 7; 10; 47]

Bennett, Charles Wesley, archaeologist, b. East Bethany, N.Y., 1828; d. Evanston, Ill., April 17, 1891. [3]

Bennett, Daniel K., clergyman, b. 1830; d. 1897. [34]

Bennett, De Robigne Mortimer, freethinker, b. near Otsego Lake, N.Y., 1818; d. New York, N.Y., Dec. 6, 1882. [1; 3; 6]

Bennett, Edmund Hatch, jurist, b. Manchester, Vt., 1824; d. Boston, Mass., Jan. 2, 1898. [1; 4; 43]

Bennett, Emerson, poet and novelist, b. Monson, Mass., 1822; d. Philadelphia, Pa., May 11, 1905. [1; 2; 3; 7; 10]

Bennett, Emily Thacher, poet, fl. 1865-1900.

Bennett, Estelline, journalist, b. Deadwood, S.D.; d. Chicago, Ill., Jan. 22, 1948.

Bennett, Frank Marion, sailor, b. Marcellus, Mich., 1857; d. Cassopolis, Mich., Feb. 11, 1924. [4]

Bennett, Henry Holcomb, local historian, b. Chillecothe, O., 1863; d. April 30, 1924. [10]

Bennett, Horace Wilson, novelist, b. Hamburg, Mich., 1862; d. Denver, Colo., June 9, 1941. [7; 10]

Bennett, Ida Dandridge, gardener, b. Coldwater, Mich., 1860; d. 1925. [10; 39]

Bennett, James O'Donnell, journalist, b. Jackson, Mich., 1870, d. Chicago, Ill., Feb. 27, 1940. [7; 10]

Bennett, Jesse Lee, educationist, b. Baltimore county, Md., 1885; d. near Baltimore, Md., April 21, 1931. [10]

Bennett, Mrs. Mary E., poet and novelist, fl. 1824-1872. [6]

Bennett, Mary E., novelist, b. Connecticut, 1841; d. ? [8]

Bennett, Milo Lyman, jurist, b. Sharon, Conn., 1789; d. Taunton, Mass., July 7, 1868. [43]

Bennett, Sanford Fillmore, physician and poet, b. 1836; d. 1898.

Bennett, William Harper, historian, b. 1860; d. April 18, 1931. [21]

Bennett, William Wallace, clergyman, b. 1821; d. 1887. [6; 34]

Benoit, Joseph Paul Augustine, priest and biographer, b. France, 1850; d. Lyon, France, Nov. 20, 1915. [32]

Benrimo, Joseph Henry, actor and playwright, b. San Francisco, Calif., 1871; d. New York, N.Y., March 26, 1942. [10; 12]

Bensell, James Berry, poet, b. New York, N.Y., 1856; d. New York, N.Y., Feb. 3, 1886. [3]

Bensley, Benjamin Arthur, biologist, b. Barton, Ont., 1875; d. Toronto, Ont., Jan. 20, 1934. [27]

Benson, Allan Louis, journalist, b. Plainwell, Mich., 1871; d. Yonkers, N.Y., Aug. 19, 1940. [7; 10]

Benson, Blackwood Ketchum, educationist and novelist, b. Edgefield district, S.C., 1845; d. ? [10; 34]

Benson, Carl (pseud.). See Bristed, Charles Astor.

Benson, Egbert, jurist, b. New York, N.Y., 1746; d. Jamaica, N.Y., Aug. 24, 1933. [1; 3; 4; 6]

Benson, Eugene, painter, b. Hyde Park, N.Y., 1839; d. Venice, Italy, Feb. 28, 1908. [1; 2; 3; 4; 7]

Benson, George Willard, art collector, b. 1859; d. Buffalo, N.Y., Aug. 29, 1944.

Benson, Henry Clark, missionary, b. near Zenia, O., 1815; d. ? [6]

Benson, John Alfred, physician, d. Chicago, Ill., March 9, 1899. [48]

Benson, Louis Fitzgerald, clergyman and hymnologist, b. Philadelphia, Pa., 1855; d. Philadelphia, Pa., Oct. 10, 1930. [10]

Benson, Lawrence Sluter, mathematician, fl. 1864-1885. [6]

Benson, William Shepherd, naval officer, b. Macon, Ga., 1855; d. Washington, D.C., May 20, 1932. [1a; 10]

Bent, Allen Herbert, genealogist and bibliographer, b. 1867; d. 1926,

Bent, Samuel Arthur, educationist, b. Boston, Mass., 1841; d. Boston, Mass., Nov. 22, 1912. [10]

Bent, Silas, naval officer and oceanographer, b. St. Louis, Mo., 1820; d. Shelter Island, Long Island, N.Y., Aug. 26, 1887. [1; 4]

Bent, Silas, journalist, b. Millersburg, Ky., 1882; d. Stamford, Conn., July 30, 1945. [7; 10]

Bentley, William, clergyman, b. Boston, Mass., 1759; d. Salem, Mass., Dec. 29, 1819. [1; 7]

Bentley, Wilson Alwyn, meteorologist, b. Jericho, Vt., 1865; d. Jericho, Vt., Dec. 23, 1931. [1a; 10; 11]

Benton, Angelo Ames, clergyman, b. Canea, Crete, 1837; d. Grafton, Pa., Sept. 29, 1912. [10]

Benton, Charles William, educationist, b. Tolland, Conn., 1852; d. Minneapolis, Minn., Nov. 11, 1913. [62]

Benton, Elbert Jay, educationist, b. Dubuque, Ia., 1871; d. Cleveland, O., March 28, 1946. [10; 11]

Benton, Frank, apiculturist, b. 1852; d. 1919.

Benton, Guy Potter, educationist, b. Kenton, O., 1865; d. Minneapolis, Minn., June 29, 1927. [2; 4; 10]

Benton, James Gilchrist, ordnance expert, b. Lebanon, N.Y., 1820; d. Springfield, Mass., Aug. 23, 1881. [1; 4]

Benton, Joel, journalist and poet, b. Amenia, N.Y., 1832; d. Poughkeepsie, N.Y., Sept. 15, 1911. [1; 2; 3; 4; 7; 10]

Benton, Joseph Augustine, clergyman, b. Guilford, Conn., 1818; d. Oakland, Calif., April 8, 1892. [35; 62]

Benton, Josiah Henry, lawyer, b. Addison, Vt., 1843; d. Boston, Mass., Feb. 6, 1917. [1; 10]

Benton, Reuben Clark, lawyer, b. Waterford, Vt., 1830; d. Minneapolis, Minn., Jan. 8, 1895. [59; 70]

Benton, Thomas Hart, politician, b. Hillsboro, N.H., 1782; d. Washington, D.C., April 10, 1858. [1; 2; 3; 4; 6; 34]

Berard, Augusta Blanche, educationist, b. West Point, N.Y., 1824; d. 1901. [3]

Berard, Claudius, educationist, b. Bordeaux, France, 1786; d. West Point, N.Y., May 6, 1848. [3]

Berdan, John Milton, educationist, b. Toledo, O., 1873; d. New Haven, Conn., April 3, 1949. [14; 62]

Berg, Ernst Julius, educationist, b. Sweden, 1871; d. Schenectady, N.Y., Sept. 9, 1941. [10; 11; 13]

Berg, Joseph Frederick, clergyman, b. Antigua, B.W.I., 1812; d. New Brunswick, N.J., July 20, 1871. [1; 3; 6]

Berg, Walter Gilman, civil engineer, b. New York, N.Y., 1858; d. 1908. [10]

Bergen, Mrs. Fanny, née **Dickerson,** naturalist, b. Mansfield, O., 1846; d. ? [10]

Bergen, Frank, lawyer, b. 1851; d. Elizabeth, N.J., Nov. 12, 1934.

Bergen, Joseph Young, educationist, b. Red Beach, Me., 1851; d. Cambridge, Mass., Oct. 10, 1917. [3; 10]

Bergen, Teunis Garret, genealogist, b. Brooklyn, N.Y., 1806; d. Brooklyn, N.Y., April 24, 1881. [4]

Berger, Victor Louis, socialist, b. Austria Hungary, 1860; d. Milwaukee, Wis., Aug. 7, 1929. [1a; 10]

Bergey, David Hendricks, bacteriologist, b. Montgomery county, Pa., 1860; d. Philadelphia, Pa., Sept. 5, 1937. [10; 11; 13]

Bergh, Henry, philanthropist, b. New York, N.Y., 1820; d. New York N.Y., March 12, 1888. [1; 2; 3; 4; 7]

Bergh. Louis de Coppet, architect, b. New York, N.Y., 1856; d. Montclair, N.J., Jan. 28, 1913. [10]

Berghold, Alexander, priest, b. Austria, 1838; d. ? [70]

Berglund, Abraham, economist, b. San Francisco, Calif., 1875; d. Charlottesville, Va., May 28, 1942. [10]

Bergtold, William Harry, physician and ornithologist, b. Buffalo, N.Y., 1865; d. Denver, Colo., March 20, 1936. [10; 11; 13]

Berkeley, William Nathaniel, physician, b. Chestertown, Md., 1868; d. New York, N.Y., Oct., 23, 1928. [10]

Berkeley, William Noland, chemist, b. 1867; d. Lynchburg, Va., Nov. 25, 1945. [11; 13]

Berkey, William Augustus, economist, b. Perry county, O., 1823; d. Grand Rapids, Mich., 1902. [39]

Berkley, Henry Johns, neurologist, b. Baltimore, Md., 1860; d. Baltimore, Md., April 6, 1940. [10]

Berkman, Alexander, anarchist, b. Vilna, Russia, 1870; d. Nice, France, June 28, 1936. [2a]

Berkowitz, Henry, rabbi, b. Pittsburg, Pa., 1857; d. Atlantic City, N.J., Feb. 7, 1924. [1; 10]

Berkowitz, Hyman Chonon, educationist, b. Russia, 1895; d. Madison, Wis., Jan. 17, 1945. [14]

Berliner, Emile, inventor, b. Hanover, Germany, 1851; d. Washington, D.C., Aug. 3, 1929. [1a; 3; 4; 10]

Berman, Edward, economist, b. Quincy, Mass., 1897; d. Washington, D.C., May 31, 1938. [10]

Bermingham, Edward John, physician, b. 1853; d. New York, N.Y., July 15, 1922. [48]

Bernadou, John Baptiste, naval officer, b. Philadelphia, Pa., 1858; d. New York, N.Y., Oct. 12, 1908. [4; 10]

Bernard, Alexis Xyste, bishop, b. Beloeil, Que., 1847; d. St. Hyacinthe, Que., June 18, 1923. [27]

Bernard, David, clergyman, b. 1798; d. 1876. [24]

Bernard, George S., journalist, b. Virginia, 1837; d. 1912. [34]

Bernard, John, actor and theatrical manager, b. Portsmouth, England, 1756; d. London, England, Nov. 29, 1828. [1]

Bernard, Pierre (pseud.). See Gonthier, Pierre Théophile.

Bernays, Augustus Charles, surgeon, b. Highland, Ill., 1854; d. St. Louis, Mo., May 22, 1907. [1; 4]

Berney, Saffold, publicist, fl. 1878-1893. [34]

Bernfeld, Lupescu Morris, engineer, b. 1885; d. New York, N.Y., Nov. 14, 1943.

Bernhardt, Wilhelm, educationist, b. Halle, Germany; d. Washington, D.C., 1909. [10]

Bernheim, Abraham Charles, lawyer, b. about 1866; d. 1895. [48]

Bernheim, Gotthardt Dellmann, clergyman, b. Prussia, 1827; d. 1916. [4; 34]

Bernier, Joseph Elzéar, navigator and explorer, b. L'Islet, Que., 1852; d. Lévis, Que., Dec. 26, 1934. [27]

Bernier, Thomas Alfred, civil servant, b. Henriville, Que., 1844; d. St. Boniface, Man., Dec. 30, 1908. [27]

Bernstein, Herman, journalist, b. Russia, 1876; d. Sheffield, Mass., Aug. 31, 1935. [1a; 7; 10]

Berrian, William, clergyman, b. New York, N.Y., 1787; d. New York, N.Y., Nov. 7, 1862. [3; 6; 7]

Berry, Edward Wilber, palaeontologist, b. Newark, N.J., 1875; d. Stonington, Conn., Sept. 20, 1945. [10; 11; 13]

Berry, Erick, (pseud.). See Allee, Mrs. Marjorie, née Hill.

Berry, George Ricker, theologian, b. West Sumner, Me., 1865; d. Cambridge, Mass., May 24, 1935. [10; 11]

Berry, Stephen, printer and freemason, b. Augusta, Me., 1833; d. ? [38]

Berryhill, S. Newton, poet, b. 1830; d. 1888. [7; 34]

Berryman, John R., lawyer, b. 1849; d. 1914.

Berthelot, Amable, lawyer and politician, b. Quebec, Canada, 1777; d. Quebec, Que., Nov. 24, 1847. [27]

Berthold, Victor Maximilian, historian, b. 1856; d. Dec. 30, 1932.

Beshoar, Michael, physician, b. Mifflintown, Pa., 1833; d. Trinidad, Colo., Sept. 5, 1907. [4]

Bessey, Charles Edwin, botanist, b. Mayne county, O., 1845; d. Lincoln, Neb., Feb. 25; 1915. [1; 10]

Best, Mary Agnes, biographer, b. about 1867; d. New York, N.Y., Oct. 13, 1942.

Best, Nolan Rice, religious writer, b. Rich Hill, O., 1871; d. Baltimore, Md., July 20, 1930. [10]

Best, William Newton, engineer, b. Clayton, Ill., 1860; d. Brooklyn, N.Y., April 11, 1922. [4]

Bethea, Jack, journalist and novelist, b. 1892; d. Birmingham, Ala., July 2, 1928. [10]

Bethune, Alexander Neil, bishop, b. Williamstown, Upper Canada, 1800; d. Toronto, Ont., Feb. 3, 1879. [27]

Bethune, George Washington, clergyman and poet, b. New York, N.Y., 1805; d. Florence, Italy, April 28, 1862. [1; 3; 6; 7; 19]

Betten, Francis Sales, priest and historian, b. Germany, 1863; d. Milwaukee, Wis., Dec. 8, 1942. [10; 21]

Bettner, George Shonnard, physician, b. 1801; d. 1860. [54]

Bettridge, William Craddock, soldier and clergyman, b. Warwickshire, England, 1791; d. Strathroy, Ont., Nov. 21, 1879. [27]

Betts, Charles Wyllys, historian, b. 1845; d. 1887.

Betts, Craven Langstroth, poet, b. Saint John, N.B., 1853; d. Santa Cruz, Calif., July 30, 1941. [7; 10; 11]

Betts, Frederick William, clergyman, b. Winnebago county, Ill., 1858; d. Syracuse, N.Y., March 4, 1932 .[10]

Betts, George Herbert, psychologist, b. Clarksville, Ia., 1868; d. Evanston, Ill., Dec. 8, 1934. [10; 13]

Betts, Samuel Rossiter, jurist, b. Richmond, Mass., 1787; d. New Haven, Conn., Nov. 3, 1868. [1; 3; 4; 6]

Bevan, Wilson Lloyd, clergyman and educationist, b. Baltimore, Md., 1866; d. Sewanee, Tenn., April 8, 1935. [10]

Bevans, Neile (pseud.). See Van Slingerland, Mrs. Nellie Bingham.

Beveridge, Albert Jeremiah, politician and historian, b. Highland county, O., 1862; d. Indianapolis, Ind., April 27, 1927. [1; 2; 7; 10; 11]

Beveridge, John, educationist, b. Scotland; d. Philadelphia, Pa., June 30, 1767. [3; 4; 18]

Beveridge, John Harrie, educationist, b. Highland county, O., 1869; d. Omaha, Neb., Oct. 12, 1932. [10]

Beverley, Robert, historian, b. Middlesex county, Va., about 1673; d. Beverley Park, Va., about 1722. [1; 2; 3; 4; 5; 6; 7; 34]

Bevier, Abraham Garret, local historian, b. 1812; d. 1861.

Bevier, Isabel, home economist, b. Plymouth, O., 1860; d. Urbana, Ill., March 17, 1942. [10; 11]

Bevier, Louis, educationist, b. Marbletown, N.Y., 1857; d. New Brunswick, N.J., May 5, 1925. [10]

Bey, Ali (pseud.). See Knapp, Samuel Lorenzo.

Bianchi, Mrs. Martha Gilbert, née Dickinson, poet and biographer, b. Amherst, Mass., 1866; d. New York, N.Y., Dec. 22, 1943. [7; 10; 11]

Bianco, Mrs. Margery, née Williams, writer of books for children, b. London, England, 1881; d. New York, N.Y., Sept. 4, 1944. [7; 10]

Bibaud, François Marie Uncas Maximilien, biographer and historian, b. Montreal, Lower Canada, 1824; d. Montreal, Que., July 9, 1887. [27]

Bibaud, Michel, journalist and historian, b. near Montreal, Canada, 1782; d. Montreal, Que., July 3, 1857. [27]

Bibb, William Wyatt, physician, b. Amelia county, Va., 1781; d. Fort Jackson, Ala., July 9, 1820. [4]

Bickley, Lloyd Wharton, novelist, b. 1801; d. 1855.

Bickmore, Albert Smith, naturalist, b. Tenant's Harbor, Me., 1839; d. Nonquitt, Mass., Aug. 12, 1914. [1; 4; 7; 10]

Bicknell, Anna Louise, historian, b. France, about 1835; d. ? [8]

Bicknell, Edward, lawyer, b. Boston, Mass., 1855; d. Portland, Me., Sept. 12, 1922. [52]

Bicknell, Ernest Percy, humanitarian, b. near Vincennes, Ind., 1862; d. Washington, D.C., Sept. 29, 1935. [10]

Bicknell, Frank Martin, writer of fiction for young people, b. Melrose, Mass., 1854; d. Malden, Mass., Aug. 21, 1916. [10]

Bicknell, George Augustus, lawyer, b. 1815; d. New Albany, Ind., April 11, 1891. [6]

Bicknell, James, lawyer, b. London, England, 1862; d. Toronto, Ont., Oct. 11, 1914. [31a]

Bicknell, Thomas Williams, educationist, b. Barrington, R.I., 1834; d. Providence, R.I., Oct. 6, 1925. [3; 4; 7; 10; 47]

Biddle, Anthony Joseph Drexel, soldier, b. Philadelphia, Pa., 1874; d. Ludlow, Long Island, N.Y., May 27, 1948. [4; 7; 10]

Biddle, Arthur, lawyer, b. Philadelphia, Pa., 1852; d. Philadelphia, Pa., March 8, 1897. [2]

Biddle, Clement, poet, d. Philadelphia, Pa., March 16, 1879. [55]

Biddle, Clinton Poston, educationist, b. 1897; d. Weston, Mass., April 11, 1939. [51]

Biddle, George Washington, lawyer, b. Philadelphia, Pa., 1843; d. Philadelphia, Pa., April 9, 1886.

Biddle, Horace Peters, jurist and poet, b. Hocking county, O., 1811; d. Logansport, Ind., March 13, 1900. [1; 4; 7; 10]

Biddle, Jacob Albert, clergyman, b. Rochester, O., 1845; d. South Manchester, Conn., Sept. 24, 1914. [62]

Biddle, John Barclay, physician, b. 1815; d. Philadelphia, Pa., Jan. 19. 1879. [55]

Biddle, Nicholas, financier, b. Philadelphia, Pa., 1778; d. Philadelphia, Pa., Feb. 27, 1844. [1; 2; 3; 4; 5; 6; 7]

Biddle, Richard, lawyer, b. Philadelphia, Pa., 1796; d. Pittsburg, Pa., June 7, 1847. [3; 6]

Bidwell, Barnabas, lawyer and politician, b. Tyringham, Mass., 1763; d. Kingston, Upper Canada, July 27, 1833. [4; 7; 27]

Bidwell, Daniel Doane, journalist, b. East Hartford, Conn., 1866; d. Hartford, Conn., April 24, 1937. [7; 10; 11; 62]

Bidwell, Frederic David, historian, b. New York, N.Y., 1873. d. Albany, N.Y., Dec. 21. 1947.

Biederwolf, William Edward, evangelist, b. Monticello, Ind., 1867; d. Palm Beach, Fla., Sept. 10, 1939. [10; 11]

Bien, Herman M., rabbi, b. Germany, 1831; d. Vicksburg, Miss., 1895. [34; 35]

Bierbower, Austin, lawyer and philosopher, b. Shelly's Island, Pa., 1844; d. Chicago, Ill., Sept. 28, 1913. [6; 10]

Bierce, Ambrose, journalist and novelist, b. Meigs county, O., June 24, 1842; disappeared mysteriously in Mexico about 1914. [1; 2; 4; 7; 10; 35]

Bierce, Lucius Verus, soldier and local historian, b. Summit county, O., 1801; d. 1876.

Bierly, Willis Reed, lawyer, fl. 1877-1908.

Bierwirth, Heinrich Conrad, educationist, b. Germany, 1853; d. Cambridge, Mass., Feb. 3, 1940. [52]

Biery, James Solomon, lawyer and politician, b. Venango county, Pa., 1839; d. Allentown, Pa., Dec. 3, 1904.

Bigelow, Abijah, poet, b. Westminster, Mass., 1775; d. Worcester, Mass., April 5, 1860. [49]

Bigelow, Andrew, clergyman, b. 1795; d. 1877. [6; 51]

Bigelow, Mrs. Edith Evelyn, née Jaffray, novelist, b. 1861; d. Dec. 1, 1932. [8]

Bigelow, Edward Fuller, naturalist, b. Colchester, Conn., 1860; d. Greenwich, Conn,. July 13, 1938. [2; 10]

Bigelow, Edwin Victor, clergyman, b. Kingsport, N.S., 1866; d. Boston Mass., Oct. 26, 1929. [62]

Bigelow, Erastus Brigham, inventor and economist, b. West Boyleston, Mass., 1814; d. Boston, Mass., Dec. 6, 1879. [1; 3; 4; 6]

Bigelow, Francis Hill, antiquarian, b. Cambridge, Mass., 1859; d. Cambridge, Mass., June 17, 1933. [10]

Bigelow, Frank Hagar, meteorologist, b. Concord, Mass., 1851; d. Vienna, Austria, March 2, 1924. [1; 10]

Bigelow, Henry Jacob, surgeon, b. Boston, Mass., 1818; d. Boston, Mass., Oct. 30, 1890. [1; 3; 6]

Bigelow, Jacob, physician and botanist, b. Sudbury, Mass., 1786; d. Boston, Mass., Jan. 10, 1879. [1; 2; 3; 4; 5; 6]

Bigelow, John, lawyer, journalist, and diplomat, b. Malden, N.Y., 1817; d. New York, N.Y., Dec. 19, 1911. [1; 2; 7; 10]

Bigelow, John, soldier, b. New York, N.Y., 1854; d. Washington, D.C., Feb. 29, 1939. [10; 11]

Bigelow, Lafayette Jotham, lawyer, b. 1835; d. 1870. [6]

Bigelow, Lewis, lawyer and politician, b. Petersham, Mass., 1785; d. Peoria, Ill., Oct. 3, 1838. [3; 4]

Bigelow, Marshall Train, printer, b. South Natick, Mass., 1822; d. Cambridge, Mass., Dec. 28, 1902. [2; 10]

Bigelow, Mrs. Mary Ann Hubbard, née Townsend, poet, d. 1870.

Bigelow, Melville Madison, lawyer, b. near Eaton Rapids,. Mich., 1846; d. Boston, Mass., May 4, 1921. [1; 10]

Bigelow, Mrs. Poultney, See Bigelow, Mrs. Edith Evelyn, née Jaffray.

Bigelow, Samuel Fowler, biographer, b. 1837; d .1915.

Bigelow, Samuel Lawrence, educationist, b. Boston, Mass., 1870; d. West Hartford, Conn., Dec. 3, 1947. [10; 52]

Bigelow, William Sturgis, physician and orientalist, b. Boston, Mass., 1850; d. Boston, Mass., Oct. 6, 1926. [1; 10; 52]

Biggar, Charles Robert Webster, lawyer and biographer, b. Murray, Ont., 1847; d. Toronto, Ont., Oct. 16, 1909. [27]

Biggar, Emerson Bristol, journalist, b. Winona, Ont., 1853; d. Toronto, Ont., May 31, 1921. [27]

Biggar, Henry Percival, historian and archivist, b. Carrying Place, Ont., 1872; d. Worplesdon, Surrey, England, July 25, 1938. [27]

Biggar, Oliver Mowat, lawyer, b. Toronto, Ont., 1876; d. Ottawa, Ont., Sept. 5, 1948. [30]

Biggers, Earl Derr, novelist and playwright, b. Warren, O., 1884; d. Pasadena, Calif., April 5, 1933. [1a; 7; 9; 10; 11; 51]

Biggs, Asa, jurist, b. Williamston, N.C., 1811; d. Norfolk, Va., March 6, 1878. [1; 4]

Biggs, Joseph, historian, b. 1776; d. 1844. [34]

Bigham, Robert Williams, clergyman, b. near Milledgeville, Ga., 1824; d. Demorest, Ga., Oct. 11, 1900. [34]

Bigler, David, bishop and poet, b. Hagerstown, Md., 1806; d. Lancaster, Pa., July 2, 1875. [4]

Bigler, William H., physician, b. Philadelphia, Pa., 1840; d. 1904. [10]

Biglow, William, educationist, b. Natick, Mass., 1773; d. Boston, Mass., Jan. 12, 1844. [3; 7; 51]

Bigly, Cantell A. (pseud.). See Peck, George Washington.

Bignell, Mrs. Effie, née Molt, naturalist, b. Vermont, 1855; d. ? [10]

Bigney, Mark Frederick, journalist and poet, b. Pugwash, N.S., 1817; d. New Orleans, La., 1886. [7; 34]

Bilgram, Hugo, machinist, b. Germany, 1847; d. Aug. 29, 1933. [10]

Bill, Edward Lyman, editor and novelist, b. Lyme, Conn., 1862; d. New Rochelle, N.Y., Jan. 1, 1916. [10]

Bill, Ingraham E., clergyman, b. Billtown, N.S., 1805; d. St. Martins, N.B., 1891. [27]

Bill, Ledyard, publisher, b. Ledyard, Conn., 1836; d. Paxton, Mass., 1907. [10]

Billings, Anna Hunt, educationist, b. Hatfield, Mass., 1861; d. Los Angeles, Calif., Aug. 5, 1944. [62]

Billings, Edward Everett, civil engineer and novelist, b. New York, N.Y., 1855; d. ? [10]

Billings, Frank, physician, b. Highland, Iowa county, Wis., 1854; d. Chicago, Ill., Sept. 20, 1932. [1a; 4; 10]

Billings, Frank Seaver, veterinary surgeon, b. Boston, Mass., 1845; d. Sharon, Mass., Oct. 14, 1912.

Billings, John Davis, soldier, b. 1842; d. ?

Billings, John Shaw, surgeon and librarian, b. Switzerland county, Ind., 1839; d. New York, N.Y., March 11, 1913. [1; 2; 3; 4; 5; 6; 7]

Billings, Josh (pseud.). See Shaw, Henry Wheeler.

Billings, William, musician, b. Boston, Mass., 1746; d. Boston, Mass., Sept. 26, 1800. [1; 3; 4; 7]

Billingsley, Amos Stevens, clergyman, b. 1818; d. 1897. [6]

Billon, Frederic Louis, local historian, b. Philadelphia, Pa., 1801; d. St. Louis, Mo., Oct. 20, 1895. [34]

Billson, William Weldon, lawyer, b. Springfield, Ill., 1847; d. Duluth, Minn., Sept. 2, 1923. [10]

Bingham, Caleb, writer of schoolbooks, b. Salisbury, Conn., 1757; d. Boston, Mass., April 6, 1817. [1; 3; 6; 7]

Bingham, Hiram, missionary, b. Bennington, Vt., 1789; d. New Haven, Conn., Nov. 11, 1869. [1; 3; 6; 7]

Bingham, Hiram, missionary, b. Honolulu, Hawaii, 1831; d. Baltimore, Md., Oct. 25, 1908. [1; 10]

Bingham, Jennie Maria, religious writer, b. 1859; d. ?

Bingham, Joel Foote, clergyman, b. Andover, Conn., 1827; d. Hartford, Conn., Oct. 18, 1914. [10; 62]

Bingham, Luther Goodyear, religious writer, b. 1798; d. 1877. [6]

Bingham, Rowland V., missionary, d. Toronto, Ont., Dec. 8, 1942.

Bingham, Stephen D., historian, b. 1828; d. ? [39]

Bingham, Theodore Alfred, soldier and genealogist, b. Andover, Conn., 1858; d. Chester, N.S., Sept. 6, 1934. [10]

Bingham, William, banker and politician, b. Philadelphia, Pa., 1752; d. Bath, England, Feb. 6, 1804. [1; 4]

Bingham, William, grammarian, b. Mebanesville, N.C., 1835; d. Mebanesville, N.C., Feb. 18, 1873. [1; 3; 6; 34]

Binion, Samuel Augustus, Egyptologist, b. 1853; d. New York, N.Y., Jan. 8, 1914.

Binkley, Robert Cedric, educationist, b. Mannheim, Pa., 1897; d. Cleveland, O., April 11, 1940. [7; 10]

Binmore, Henry, lawyer, fl. 1880-1899. [6]

Binney, Amos, merchant and naturalist, b. Boston, Mass., 1800; d. Rome, Italy, Oct. 18, 1847. [1; 4]

Binney, Amos, clergyman, b. 1802; d. 1878.

Binney, Amos, physician, b. 1803; d. Boston, Mass., Feb. 18, 1847. [47]

Binney, Charles Chauncey, lawyer, b. Philadelphia, Pa., 1855; d. Little Boar's Head, N.H., July 10, 1913. [10; 51]

Binney, Charles James Fox, genealogist, b. 1806; d. 1888.

Binney, Horace, lawyer, b. Northern Liberties, Pa., 1780; d. Philadelphia, Pa., Aug. 12, 1875. [1; 3; 4; 6]

Binnie, John Fairbairn, surgeon, b. Scotland, 1863; d. San Diego, Calif., Nov. 28, 1936.

Binns, Charles Fergus, ceramic expert, b. Worcester, England, 1857; d. New York, N.Y., Dec. 4, 1934. [2a; 10]

Binns, John, journalist and politician, b. Dublin, Ireland, 1772; d. Philadelphia, Pa., June 16, 1860. [1; 3; 6; 7]

Binns, John Alexander, agriculturist, b. Loudoun county, Va., about 1761; d. 1813. [1]

Birch, Thomas Erskine, elocutionist, b. 1760; d. 1820.

Birchmore, John Woodbridge, clergyman, b. Charlestown, Mass., 1822; d. Cambridge, Mass., March 21, 1900. [62]

Bird, Frederic Mayer, clergyman and educationist, b. Philadelphia, Pa., 1838; d. South Bethlehem, Pa., April 2, 1908. [1; 7; 10]

Bird, Joseph, music-master, fl. 1850-1852.

Bird, Robert Montgomery, novelist and playwright, b. Newcastle county, Del., 1806; d. Philadelphia, Pa., Jan. 23, 1854. [1; 2; 3; 4; 5; 6; 70; 71]

Bird, Robert Montgomery, chemist, b. Petersburg, Va., 1867; d. University, Va., June 4, 1938. [10; 13]

Birdsall, Ralph, clergyman, b. Stockton, Calif., 1871; d. Cooperstown, N.Y., Sept. 23, 1918.

Birdsall, William Wilfred, educationist, b. Richmond, Ind., 1854; d. Philadelphia, Pa., March 17, 1909. [4; 10]

Birdseye, Clarence Frank, lawyer, b. Brooklyn, N.Y., 1854; d. Atlantic City, N.J., Aug. 20, 1927. [45]

Birge, Julius Charles, pioneer, b. Whitewater, Wis., 1839; d. St. Louis, Mo., Dec. 8, 1923. [4]

Birge, William Spoford, physician, b. 1857; d. Provincetown, Mass., March 26, 1925.

Birkbeck, Morris, pioneer and publicist, b. Settle, England, 1764; drowned in the Fox river, Wis., June 4, 1825. [1; 2; 3; 4; 6]

Birkhimer, William Edward, soldier, b. Somerset, O., 1848; d. Washington, D.C., June 10, 1914. [10]

Birkhoff, George David, mathematician, b. Overisel, Mich., 1884; d. Cambridge, Mass., Nov. 12, 1944. [10; 11]

Birkmire, William Harvey, engineer, b. Schuylkill Falls, Pa., 1860; d. New York, N.Y., Feb. 9, 1924. [10]

Birney, James Gillespie, abolitionist, b. Danville, Ky., Feb. 4, 1792; d. Perth Amboy, N.J., Nov. 25, 1857. [1; 2; 34]

Birney, William, lawyer and biographer, b. Madison county, Ala., 1819; d. Washington, D.C., Aug. 14, 1901. [1; 2; 34]

Birnie, Rogers, soldier, b. 1851; d. Sept. 26, 1939.

Bisbee, Frederick Adelbert, clergyman, b. Nunda, N.Y., 1855; d. Arlington Heights, Mass., Nov. 15, 1923. [10]

Bisbee, Lewis H., lawyer, b. 1839; d. 1898.

Bisbee, Marvin Davis, librarian, b. Chester, Vt., 1845; d. Sebago Lake, Me., Aug. 28, 1913. [4; 49]

Bisbee, William Henry, soldier, b. Rhode Island, 1840; d. Brookline, Mass., June 11, 1942. [10]

Biser, Benjamin Franklin, glass-maker, b. 1868; d. 1928.

Bishop, Abraham, politician, b. New Haven, Conn., 1763; d. New Haven, Conn., April 28, 1844. [1; 62]

Bishop, Albert Webb, soldier, fl. 1863-1894.

Bishop, Avord Longley, educationist, b. Williamston, N.S., 1875; d. New Haven, Conn., May 8, 1932. [10; 11; 62]

Bishop, Cortlandt Field, historian, b. New York, N.Y., 1870; d. Lenox, Mass., March 30, 1935. [7]

Bishop, Mrs. Emily Montague, née Mulkin, lecturer, b. Forestville, N.Y., 1858; d. 1916. [10]

Bishop, Ernest Simons, physician, b. Pawtucket, R.I., 1876; d .New York, N.Y., Nov. 16, 1927. [47]

Bishop, Farnham, educationist, b. New York, N.Y., 1886; d. San Rafael, Calif., Feb. 16, 1930. [10; 35]

Bishop, George Riker, educationist, b. 1841; d. 1931.

Bishop, George Sayles, clergyman, b. Rochester, N.Y., 1836; d. East Orange, N.J., March 12, 1914. [10; 45]

Bishop, Giles, marine, d. San Diego, Calif., April 10, 1925.

Bishop, Mrs. Harriet E., school-teacher, b. Vergennes, Vt., 1817; d. St. Paul, Minn., Aug. 8, 1883. [70]

Bishop, Harry Gore, soldier, b. Grand Rapids, Mich., 1874; d. Washington, D.C., Aug. 31, 1934. [10]

Bishop, Henry Fitch, local historian, b. 1820; d. 1910.

Bishop, Jesse Phelps, lawyer, b. New Haven, Vt., 1815; d. Cleveland, O., 1881. [24]

Bishop, Joel Prentiss, lawyer, b. Volney, N.Y., 1814; d. Cambridge, Mass., Nov. 4, 1901. [1; 3; 5; 6]

Bishop, John Leander, physician and statistician, b. Kings county, N.S., 1820; d. Newark, N.J., Sept. 23, 1868. [24]

Bishop, John Peale, poet and novelist, b. 1892; d. Hyannis, Mass., April 4, 1944. [7; 10]

Bishop, Joseph Bucklin, journalist, b. Seekonk, Mass., 1847; d. New York, N.Y., Dec. 13, 1928. [10; 11; 21]

Bishop, Judson Wade, soldier, b. Evansville, N.Y., 1831; d. St. Paul, Minn., 1917. [70]

Bishop, Levi, lawyer and poet, b. Russell, Mass., 1815; d. Detroit, Mich., Dec. 23, 1881. [3; 39]

Bishop, Louis Faugères, physician, b. New Brunswick, N.J., 1864; d. New York, N.Y., Oct. 6, 1941. [10; 11]

Bishop, Nathaniel Holmes, traveller, b. Medford, Mass., 1837; d. 1902. [6; 7]

Bishop, Putnam Peter, clergyman, b. Vermont, 1823; d. Citra, Fla., Dec. 11, 1896. [24; 34]

Bishop, Robert Hamilton, clergyman, b. near Edinburgh, Scotland, 1777; d. College Hill, O., April 29, 1855. [1a; 3; 6]

Bishop, Robert Roberts, jurist, b. Medfield, Mass., 1834; d. Newton, Mass., Oct. 7, 1909. [1; 51]

Bishop, Seth Scott, laryngologist, b. Fond du Lac, Wis., 1852; d. Chicago, Ill., Sept. 6. 1923. [1; 2; 10]

Bishop, William Henry, novelist, b. Hartford, Conn., 1847; d. Brooklyn, Conn., Sept. 26, 1928. [3; 6; 7; 10; 62]

Bishop, William Samuel, clergyman, b. Northampton, Mass., 1865; d. Washington, D.C., March 15, 1944. [10; 11]

Bisland, Elizabeth. See Wetmore, Mrs. Elizabeth, née Bisland.

Bispham, David Scull, opera singer, b. Philadelphia, Pa., 1857; d. New York, N.Y., Oct. 2, 1921. [1; 10]

Bispham, George Tucker, lawyer, b. Philadelphia, Pa., 1838; d. Newport, R.I., June 28, 1906. [10; 55]

Bissell, Allen Page, clergyman and educationist, b. Rome Mills, N.Y., 1835; d. Nyack, N.Y., Feb. 18, 1914.

Bissell, Arthur Dart, clergyman and poet, b. India, 1858; d. Claremont, Calif., May 24, 1925. [62]

Bissell, Champion, poet, b. Rochester, N.Y., 1830; d. New York, N.Y., Jan. 1, 1899. [62]

Bissell, Edwin Cone, clergyman, b. Schoharie, N.Y., 1832; d. Chicago, Ill., April 10, 1894. [4]

Bissell, Mary Taylor, physician, b. 1854; d. Brooklyn, N.Y., April 1, 1936.

Bissell, Richard Mervin, insurance executive, b. Chicago, Ill., 1862; d. Farmington, Conn., July 18, 1941. [10; 62]

Bissett, Clark Prescott, lawyer and educationist, b. Alameda, Calif., 1875; d. Seattle, Wash., Jan. 9, 1932. [10]

Bittenbender, Mrs. Ada Matilda, née Cole, prohibitionist, b. 1848; d. ?

Bitting, William Coleman, clergyman, b. Hanover county, Va., 1857; d. Jan. 10, 1931. [10]

Bittinger, John Quincy, clergyman, b. Berwick, Pa., 1831; d. Haverhill, N.H., April 5, 1895. [49]

Bittinger, Lucy Forney, historian, b. Cleveland, O., 1859; d. 1907. [2]

Bixby, Ammi Leander, journalist and poet, b. Potsdam, N.Y., 1856; d. Lincoln, Neb., Dec. 24, 1934. [10; 11]

Bixby, George Stephenson, journalist, b. Chelsea, Vt., 1861; d. Plattsburg, N.Y., April 21, 1937.

Bixby, James Thompson, clergyman, b. Barré, Mass., 1843; d. Yonkers, N.Y., Dec. 26, 1921. [1; 2; 4; 7; 10; 51]

Bixby, John Munson, lawyer, b. Fairfield, Conn., 1800; d. New York, N.Y., Nov. 22, 1876. [3]

Bizzell, William Bennett, educationist, b. Independence, Tex., 1876; d. Norman, Okla., May 13, 1944. [10; 11; 75]

Bjerregaard, Carl Hendrick Andreas, librarian and philosopher, b. Denmark, 1845; d. New York, N.Y., Jan. 28, 1922. [1; 2; 7; 10]

Black, Alexander, journalist, novelist, and photographer, b. New York, N.Y., 1859; d. New York, N.Y., May 8, 1940. [7; 10]

Black, Chauncey Forward, lawyer, b. Somerset, Pa.; d. York, Pa., 1904. [10]

Black, Cyrus, genealogist, b. Amherst, N.S., 1809; d. Amherst, N.S., 1898. [24]

Black, Ebenezer Charlton, educationist, b. Liddlesdale, Scotland, 1861; d. Cambridge, Mass., July 11, 1927. [10]

Black, George Fraser, librarian and historian, b. Stirling, Scotland, 1865; d. Lyndhurst, N.J., Sept. 7, 1948. [7]

Black, Greene Vardiman, dentist, b. Scott county, Ill., 1836; d. Chicago, Ill., Aug. 31, 1915. [10]

Black, Henry Campbell, lawyer, b. Ossining, N.Y., 1860; d. Washington, D.C., March 19, 1927. [10]

Black, James William, historian, b. Baltimore, Md., 1866; d. Schenectady, N.Y., Sept. 3, 1934. [10]

Black, Jeremiah Sullivan, lawyer, b. Somerset county, Pa., 1810; d. York, Pa., Aug. 19, 1883. [1; 4]

Black, John Janvier, physician, b. Delaware City, Del., 1837; d. New Castle, Del., Sept, 27, 1909. [10; 55]

Black, McKnight, poet, d. Philadelphia, Pa., Aug. 21, 1931.

Black, Mrs. Margaret Horton, née Potter. See Potter, Margaret Horton.

Black, Samuel Charles, clergyman, b. Monticello, Ia., 1869; d. Denver, Colo., July 25, 1921. [10]

Black, Warren Columbus, clergyman, b. near Crystal Springs, Miss., 1848; d. Meridian, Miss., 1915. [34]

Black, William Leslie, industrialist, b. 1843; d. Fort McKavett, Tex., May 11, 1931.

Black, William Murray, military engineer, b. Lancaster, Pa., 1855; d. Washington, D.C., Sept. 24, 1933. [1a; 2; 10]

Blackadder, Edward, physician and poet, b. Wolfville, N.S., 1869; d. Bedford, N.S., Oct. 22, 1922. [27; 33]

Blackall, Christopher Rubey, clergyman, b. Albany, N.Y., 1830; d. Philadelphia, Pa., Jan. 25, 1924. [24]

Blackall, Mrs. Emily, née Lucas, novelist, b. Louisville, Ky., 1836; d. New York, N.Y., 1900. [24]

Blackbird, Andrew J., Indian historian, b. Grand Traverse region, Mich., about 1820; d. ? [39]

Blackburn, Charles S., poet, b. Minden, La., 1850; d. Little Rock, Ark., 1929.

Blackburn, George Andrew, clergyman, b. Green county, Tenn., 1861; d. Columbia, S.C., May, 1918. [10; 34]

Blackburn, Laura (pseud.). See Blanden, Charles Granger.

Blackburn, Mrs. Margaret Elizabeth, novelist, b. Macomb, Ill., 1847; d. Portland, Ore., Feb. 20, 1902. [24]

Blackburn, William Maxwell, clergyman, b. Carlisle, Ind., 1828; d. East Pierre, S.D., Dec. 29, 1898. [1; 2; 3; 4; 5; 6; 7; 10]

Blackford, Charles Minor, lawyer, b. Fredericksburg, Va., 1833; d. Lynchburg, Va., March 10, 1903. [1; 4]

Black Hawk, Indian chief, b. Kaskaskia, Ill., 1767; d. at his camp on the Des Moines river, Oct. 3, 1838. [3]

Blackledge, Mrs. Katherine, née **Treat,** novelist, fl. 1866-1924. (35]

Blackman, William Fremont, clergyman and educationist, b. North Pitcher, N.Y., 1855; d. Winter Park, Fla., Aug. 9, 1932. [10; 34]

Blackmar, Frank Wilson, educationist, b. West Springfield, Pa., 1854; d. Lawrence, Kans., March 30, 1931. [2; 10; 11]

Blackmore, Simon Augustine, priest, b. Milwaukee, Wis., 1849; d. Cleveland, O., Sept. 25, 1926. [10; 21]

Blackwell, Mrs. Antoinette Louisa, née **Brown,** Unitarian minister, b. Henrietta, N.Y., 1825; d. Elizabeth, N.J., Nov. 5, 1921. [2; 10]

Blackwell, Elizabeth, physician, b. Bristol, England, 1821; d. Hastings, England, May 31, 1911. [1; 4; 10]

Blackwell, Robert S., lawyer, b. 1823; d. 1863.

Blackwell, Sarah Ellen, artist, b. Bristol, England, 1828; d. ? [4]

Blackwood, Alexander Leslie, surgeon, b. Huntingdon county, Que., 1862; d. Chicago, Ill., Dec. 30, 1924. [10]

Blagden, Silliman, clergyman and poet, b. Washington, D.C., 1846; d. Boston, Mass., Nov. 20, 1907. [62]

Blaikie, William, lawyer and athlete, b. New York, N.Y., 1843; d. New York, N.Y., Dec. 6, 1904. [1; 10; 51]

Blaine, James Gillespie, politician, b. West Brownsville, Pa., 1830; d. Washington, D.C., Jan. 27, 1893. [1; 2; 3; 4; 5; 6; 7]

Blair, Andrew Alexander, chemist, b. Woodford county, Ky., 1848; d. Chestnut Hil, Pa., Jan. 26, 1932. [3; 10]

Blair, Duncan B., clergyman, b. Scotland, 1815; d. Laggan, N.S., 1891. [33]

Blair, Edward Tyler, manufacturer, b. Chicago, Ill., 1857; d. Chicago, Ill., Jan. 18, 1939. [62]

Blair, Mrs. Eliza, née **Nelson,** novelist, b. Plymouth, N.H., 1859; d. Manchester, N.H., 1907. [10]

Blair, Emma Helen, historian, b. Menasha, Wis.; d. Madison, Wis., Sept. 25, 1911. [10; 44]

Blair, Henry William, politician, b. Campton, N.H., 1834; d. Washington, D.C., March 14, 1920. [10]

Blair, Samuel, clergyman, b. Ulster, Ireland, 1712; d. Chester county, Pa., July 5, 1751. [1; 3]

Blair, Thomas Stewart, physician, b. 1867; d. Santa Ana, Calif., April 12, 1939.

Blair, Walter, educationist, b. Richmond, Va., 1835; d. Atlantic City, N.J., Sept. 12, 1909. [4]

Blair, Walter Acheson, river pilot, b. Galena, Ill., 1856; d. after 1930.

Blair, William, lawyer, b. 1782; d. about 1852.

Blaisdell, Albert Franklin, physician and historical writer, b. South Hampton, N.H., 1847; d. Winchester, Mass., March 17, 1927. [10; 49]

Blaisdell, Elijah Whittier, novelist, b. 1825; d. 1900.

Blake, Clarence John, physician, b. Boston, Mass., 1843; d. Boston, Mass., Jan. 29, 1919. [10]

Blake, Dominick T., lawyer, d. 1839.

Blake, Eli Whitney, manufacturer and inventor, b. Westborough, Mass., 1795; d. New Haven, Conn., Aug. 18, 1886. [1; 4; 62]

Blake, Mrs. Euphemia, née **Vale,** historian, b. 1817; d. 1904. [8]

Blake, Francis Everett, local historian, b. 1839; d. 1916.

Blake, Henry Nichols, lawyer and soldier, b. Boston, Mass., 1838; d. Boston, Mass., Nov. 29, 1933. [4; 10; 51]

Blake, Henry Taylor, lawyer, b. New Haven, Conn., 1828; d. New Haven, Conn., April 6, 1922. [62]

Blake, Henry William, electrical engineer, b. New Haven, Conn., 1865; d. Englewood, N.J., May 20, 1929. [1; 4; 10; 62]

Blake, James Vila, clergyman and poet, b. Brooklyn, N.Y., Jan. 21, 1842; d. Chicago, Ill., April 28, 1925. [4; 10; 51]

Blake, John Lauris, educationist, b. Northwood, N.H., 1788; d. Orange, N.J., July 6, 1857. [1; 2; 3; 4; 6; 7; 8; 47]

Blake, John Y. Fillmore, soldier, b. 1856; d. New York, N.Y., Jan. 24, 1907.

Blake, Jonathan, local historian, b. 1780; d. 1864.

Blake, Joseph Augustus, surgeon, b. San Francisco, Calif., 1864; d. Litchfield, Conn., Aug. 12, 1937. [10; 62]

Blake, Mrs. Katherine, née **Evans,** novelist, b. Rockport, Ind., 1859; d. ? [70]

Blake, Mrs. Lillie, née **Devereux,** novelist and feminist, b. Raleigh, N.C., 1835; d. New York, N.Y., Dec. 30, 1913. [1; 4; 7; 10]

Blake, Lucien Ira, physicist, b. Mansfield, Mass., 1852; d. Boston, Mass., May 4, 1916. [4; 10; 45]

Blake, Margaret (pseud.). See Schem, Lida Clara.

Blake, Mrs. Mary Elizabeth, née **McGrath,** poet, b. Dungarven, Ireland, 1840; d. Boston, Mass., Feb. 26, 1907. [1; 7; 10]

Blake, Mortimer, clergyman, b. 1813; d. 1884. [6]

Blake, Rodney (pseud.). See Clemens, William Montgomery.

Blake, Silas Leroy, clergyman, b. 1834; d. 1902.

Blake, Thaddeus, C., clergyman, fl. 1879-1882. [34]

Blake, William Hume, lawyer and fisherman, b. Toronto, Ont., 1861; d. Victoria, B.C., Feb. 5, 1924. [27]

Blake, William J., local historian, fl. 1820-1849.

Blake, William O., compiler, fl. 1857-1863.

Blake, William Phipps, geologist and mining engineer, b. New York, N.Y., 1826; d. Berkeley, Calif., May 21, 1910. [1; 3; 4; 6; 10]

Blake, Wilson Wilberforce, archaeologist, b. 1850; d. 1918.

Blakely, Paul Lendrum, priest, b. Covington, Ky., 1880; d. New York, N.Y., Feb. 26, 1943. [21; 22]

Blakeman, Phineas, clergyman, b. Stratford, Conn., 1813; d. South Wales, Erie county, N.Y., Feb. 17, 1870. [62]

Blakeman, Rufus, physician, d. 1848. [62]

Blakeslee, Erastus, soldier and clergyman, b. Plymouth, Conn., 1838; d. Brookline, Mass., 1908. [10; 62]

Blakeslee, Victor Franklin, naval officer, b. 1898; d. April 4, 1947.

Blanchard, Amos, clergyman, b. Peacham, Vt., 1800; d. Barnet, Vt., Jan. 6, 1869. [43]

Blanchard, Amy Ella, writer of books for children, b. Baltimore, Md., 1856; d. Bailey Island, Me., July 5, 1926. [2a; 10]

Blanchard, Calvin, publicist, fl. 1857-1877.

Blanchard, Charles Albert, educationist, b. Galesburg, Ill., 1814; d. Wheaton, Ill. Dec. 20, 1925. [10]

Blanchard, Frank LeRoy, journalist and advertising expert, b. Lewiston, Me., 1858; d. Lewiston, Me., May 30, 1936. [10]

Blanchard, Frank Nelson, zoologist, b. Stoneham, Mass., 1888; d. Ann Arbor, Mich., Sept., 1937. [11; 13]

Blanchard, Frederic Thomas, educationist, b. Harvard, Mass., 1878; d. Hollywood, Calif., Feb. 3, 1947. [10; 11; 52]

Blanchard, Grace, librarian, b. Dunleith, Ill.; d. Concord, N.Y., Jan. 9, 1944. [10; 11]

Blanchard, Henry Percy, lawyer, b. Windsor, N.S., 1862; d. Windsor, N.S., June 11, 1939.

Blanchard, Jonathan, clergyman and educationist, b. Rockingham, Vt., 1811; d. Wheaton, Ill., May 14, 1892. [1; 3; 5; 6; 36]

Blanchard, Mrs. Lucy, née **Mansfield,** novelist, b. Boston, Mass., 1869; d. Salt Lake City, Utah, April 23, 1927. [10]

Blanchard, Orlando, educationist, b. Cazenovia, N.Y., 1801; d. ? [60]

Blanchard, Rufus, cartographer and historian, b. Lyndeboro, N.H., 1821; d. Wheaton, Ill., Jan 3, 1904. [10]

Blanchard, William Martin, chemist, b. Perguimans county, N.C., 1874; d. Greencastle, Ind., Dec. 21, 1942. [10; 11; 13]

Blanchard, William Stinson, clergyman and poet, b. Wilton, Me., 1813; d. Winthrop, Me., May 10, 1896. [46]

Blanchet, François Norbert, archbishop, b. St. Pierre, Rivière-du-Sud, Lower Canada, 1795; d. Portland, Ore., June 18, 1883. [27]

Blanchet, François Xavier, physician and politician, b. St. Pierre, Rivière-du-Sud, Canada, 1776; d. Quebec, Lower Canada, June 24, 1830. [27]

Blanchet, François Xavier, missionary, b. St. Charles de Bellechasse, Lower Canada, 1835; d. Portland, Ore., May 22, 1906. [32]

Bland, Henry Meade, poet and educationist, b. Fairfield, Calif., 1863; d. San José, Calif., April 29, 1931. [10; 35]

Bland, Miles Carlisle, engineer, b. 1875; d. 1926.

Bland, Pascal Brooke, physician, b. Monocacy, Pa., 1875; d. Bryn Mawr, Pa., Oct. 31, 1940. [10]

Bland, Thomas Augustus, physician, b. 1830; d. ?

Blanden, Charles Granger, poet, b. Marengo. Ill., 1857; d. San Diego, Calif., Dec. 20, 1933. [10; 35; 37]

Blaney, Henry Robertson, artist, b. Dedham, Mass., 1855; d. about 1913.

Blankenburg, Mrs. Lucretia M., née **Longshore,** biographer, b. 1845; d. Philadelphia, Pa., March 28, 1937. [4]

Blanton, Annie Webb, educationist, b. Houston, Tex.; d. Austin, Tex., Oct. 1945. [10; 11]

Blashfield, Edwin Howland, painter, b. New York, N.Y., 1848; d. South Dennis, Cape Cod, Mass., Oct. 12, 1936. [3; 7; 10; 11]

Blashfield, Mrs. Evangeline, née **Wilbour,** painter's wife, d. New York, N.Y., Nov. 15, 1918. [7]

Blatch, Mrs. Harriot, née **Stanton,** feminist, b. Seneca Falls, N.Y., 1856; d. Greenwich, Conn., Nov. 20, 1940. [10; 11]

Blatchford, Eliphalet Wickes, manufacturer, b. Stillwater, N.Y., 1826; d. Chicago, Ill., Jan. 25, 1914. [10]

Blatchford, Samuel, jurist, b. New York, N. Y., 1820; d. Newport, R.I., July 7, 1893. [1; 3; 4; 6]

Blatchford, Thomas Windeatt, physician, b. Devonshire, England, 1794; d. Troy, N.Y., Jan. 7, 1866. [48]

Blatchley, Willis Stanley, geologist, b. North Madison, Conn., 1859; d. Indianapolis, Ind., May 28, 1940. [7; 10]

Blauvelt, Augustus, clergyman, b. Covert, Seneca county, N.Y., 1832; d. 1900. [6]

Bledsoe, Albert Taylor, educationist, b. Frankfort, Ky., 1809; d. Alexandria, Va., Dec. 8, 1877. [1; 2; 3; 4; 5; 6; 7; 75]

Bledsoe, Samuel Thomas, lawyer and railway president, b. Kentucky, 1868; d. Chicago, Ill., March 8, 1939. [10]

Bleecker, Mrs. Ann Eliza, née **Schuyler,** poet, b. New York, N.Y., 1752; d. near Schaghtichope, N.Y., Nov. 23, 1783. [1; 4; 7]

Bleecker, Anthony, mariner, b. 1770; d. 1827. [7]

Blennerhasset, Mrs. Margaret, née **Agnew,** poet, b. New York, N.Y., about 1778; d. New York, N.Y., June 16, 1842. [2; 3]

Blessing, George Frederick, educationist, b. Carrollton, Ky., 1875; d. Swarthmore, Pa., June 25, 1921. [10]

Blethen, Joseph, publisher and playwright, b. Farmington, Me., 1870; d. Oct. 7, 1937. [7]

Blewett, George John, clergyman, b. near St. Thomas, Ont., 1873; d. Go-Home Bay, Ont., Aug. 15, 1912. [27]

Blewett, Mrs. Jean, née **McKishnie,** poet and journalist, b. Scotia, Kent county, Ont., 1862; d. Chatham, Ont., Aug. 19, 1934. [27]

Bleyer, Willard Grosvenor, educationist, b. Milwaukee, Wis., 1873; d. Madison, Wis., Oct., 31, 1935. [1a; 10; 11; 44]

Bligh, Harris Harding, lawyer, b. Cornwallis, N.S., 1842; d. Ottawa, Ont., Aug. 21, 1918. [27]

Blinn, Henry Clay, Shaker elder, b. 1824; d. East Canterbury, N.H., 1905.

Bliss, Daniel, missionary, b. Georgia, Vt., 1823; d. Beirut, Syria, July 27, 1916. [1; 3; 10]

Bliss, Edwin Munsell, missionary, b. Erzerum, Turkey, 1848; d. Washington, D.C,. Aug. 7, 1919. [1; 2; 10]

Bliss, Eugene Frederick, educationist, b. Granville, N.Y., 1836; d. 1918. [51]

Bliss, Frank Chapman, publisher, fl. 1872-1888.

Bliss, Frederick Jones, archaeologist, b. Mount Lebanon, Syria, 1859; d. White Plains, N.Y., June 3, 1937. [4; 10; 68]

Bliss, George, lawyer, b. Springfield, Mass., 1793; d. Springfield, Mass., April 19, 1873.

Bliss, George, lawyer, b. 1830; d. Wakefield, R.I., Sept. 2, 1897.

Bliss, Henry, lawyer, b. Saint John, N.B., 1797; d. London, England, July 31, 1873. [27]

Bliss, Leonard, educationist and local historian, b. 1811; d. about Oct. 8, 1842.

Bliss, Orville Justus, traveller, b. 1848; d. Chicago, Ill., 1875. [62]

Bliss, Philemon, jurist, b. North Canton, Conn., 1813; d. St. Paul, Minn., Aug. 24, 1889. [1]

Bliss, Sylvester, educationist, d. 1863.

Bliss, William Dwight Porter, clergyman, b. Constantinople, Turkey, 1856; d. New York, N.Y., Oct. 8, 1926. [1; 10; 45]

Bliss, William Root, historian, b. Jewett City, Conn., 1825; d. Short Hills, N.J., April 9, 1906. [10]

Blitz, Antonio, magician, b. Deal, England, 1810; d. Philadelphia, Pa., Jan. 28, 1877. [1; 3; 6]

Blochin, Mrs. Anne Elizabeth, née Wilson, poet and dog-fancier, b. Kentucky; d. Toronto, Ont., Oct. 17, 1946.

Block, Louis James, poet, playwright, and educationist, b. Austria, 1851; d. Chicago, Ill., Dec. 8, 1927. [10]

Block, Rudolph, journalist, b. New York, N.Y., 1870; d. Tucson, Ariz., April 29, 1940. [10]

Blodget, Lorin, statistician and climatologist, b. near Jamestown, N.Y., 1823; d. Philadelphia, Pa., March 24, 1901. [1; 2; 3; 4]

Blodget, Samuel, merchant and economist, b. Goffstown, N.H., 1757; d. Baltimore, Md., April 11, 1814. [4]

Blodgett, Samuel Haskell, physician, b. 1863; d. Batavia, N.Y., Sept. 3, 1940.

Bloede, Gertrude, poet, b. Dresden, Germany, 1845; d. Baldwin, Long Island, N.Y., Aug. 14, 1905. [1; 7; 71]

Blomgren, Carl August, clergyman, b. Sweden, 1865; d. Sparta, Mich., June 29, 1926. [62]

Blood, Benjamin Paul, philosopher and poet, b. Amsterdam, N.Y., 1832; d. near Amsterdam, N.Y., Jan. 5, 1919. [1; 7; 10]

Blood, Henry Ames, poet and playwright, b. Temple, N.H., 1836; d. Washington, D.C., Dec. 3, 1900. [49]

Bloodgood, John D., clergyman, d. 1915.

Bloodgood, Simeon De Witt, merchant, b. Utica, N.Y., 1799; d. New York, N.Y., July 14, 1866. [3]

Bloom, Sol, politician, b. Pekin, Ill., 1870; d. Washington, D.C., March 7, 1949. [10]

Bloomer, Arthur Finley, freemason, b. 1853; d. 1908.

Bloomfield, Leonard, educationist, b. Chicago, Ill., 1887; d. New Haven, Conn., April 18, 1949. [10; 51]

Bloomfield, Maurice, Orientalist, b. Austria, 1855; d. San Francisco, Calif., June 13, 1928. [1; 4; 10]

Bloomfield, Meyer, lawyer, b. Roumania, 1878; d. New York, N.Y., March 14, 1938. [10; 11]

Bloomfield-Moore, Mrs. Clara Sophia, née Jessup, poet and novelist, b. 1824; d. Philadelphia, Pa., 1899. [8]

Bloomgarden, Solomon, Yiddish writer, b. Lithuania, 1870; d. New York, N.Y., Jan. 10, 1927. [1; 7]

Bloomingdale, Charles, novelist, b. Philadelphia, Pa., 1868; d. Philadelphia, Pa., Feb. 24, 1942.

Blossom, Henry Martyn, playwright, b. St. Louis, Md., 1866; d. New York, N.Y., March 23, 1919. [10]

Blot, Pierre, dietician, b. France, 1818; d. New York, N.Y., 1874 [6]

Blount, James Henderson, lawyer, b. Clinton, Ga., 1869; d. Oct. 7, 1918. [10]

Blow, Susan Elizabeth, educationist, b. St. Louis, Mo., 1843; d. New York, N.Y., March 26, 1916. [1; 2; 7]

Blumenstiel, Alexander, lawyer, d. 1905.

Blumenthal, George, theatrical producer, b. New York, N. Y., 1862; d. Monsey, N.Y., July 23, 1943. [12]

Blumgarten, Solomon. See Bloomgarten, Solomon.

Blunt, George William, hydrographer, b. Newburyport, Mass., 1802; d. New York, N.Y., April 19, 1878. [1; 4]

Blunt, Joseph, lawyer, b. Newburyport, Mass., 1792: d. New York, N.Y., June 16, 1860. [3]

Blunt, Stanhope English, soldier, b. Boston, Mass., 1850; d. Palm Beach, Fla., March 22, 1926. [2; 4]

Bly, Nellie (pseud.). See Seaman, Mrs. Elizabeth, née Cochrane.

Blythe, Samuel George, journalist, b. Geneseo, N.Y., 1868; d. Monterey, Calif., July 17, 1947. [7; 10; 11]

Blythe, Vernon, See Castle, Vernon Blythe.

Boardman, George Dana, clergyman, b. Tavoy, Burma, 1828; d. Atlantic City, N.J., April 28, 1903. [3; 6; 24]

Boardman, George Nye, theologian, b. Pittsford, Vt., 1825; d. Chicago, Ill., Nov. 9, 1917. [4; 10]

Boardman, Henry Augustus, clergyman, b. Troy, N.Y., 1808; d. Philadelphia, Pa., June 15, 1880. [3a; 4]

Boardman, Samuel Lane, journalist, b. Bloomfield, Me., 1836; d. Bangor, Me., Oct. 15, 1914. [10]

Boardman, William Edwin, clergyman, b. 1810; d. 1886.

Boardman, William Henry, publisher, b. Dixon, Ill., 1846; d. Ridgefield, Conn., Feb. 16, 1914. [10; 53]

Boas, Franz, anthopologist, b. Minden, Germany, 1858; d. New York, N.Y., Dec. 21, 1942. [4; 7; 10; 11]

Boas, Ralph Philip, educationist, b. Providence, R.I., 1887; d. Attleboro, Mass., Dec. 5, 1945. [13; 47]

Bôcher, Maxime, mathematician, b. Boston, Mass., 1867; d. Cambridge, Mass., Sept. 12, 1918. [1; 10; 51]

Bocock, John Holmes, clergyman, b. Buckingham county, Va., 1813; d. Lexington, Va., July 17, 1872. [34]

Bocock, John Paul, poet, b. Harrisburg, Va., 1856; d. 1903. [34]

Bodansky, Meyer, biochemist, b. Russia, 1896; d. Galveston, Tex., June 14, 1941. [10; 13]

Bodenhamer, William, physician, b. East Berlin, Pa., 1808; d. New Rochelle, N.Y., March 31, 1905. [76]

Bodge, George Madison, clergyman, b. Windham, Me., 1841; d. 1914. [46]

Bodine, George Imlay, banker and poet, b. Philadelphia, Pa., 1882; d. Philadelphia, Pa., July 9, 1947.

Bodine, William Budd, clergyman, b. near Mount Holly, N.J., 1841; d. Philadelphia, Pa., Sept. 28, 1907. [4; 56]

Bodley, Temple, lawyer and historian, b. Louisville, Ky., 1852; d. Louisville, Ky., Nov. 23, 1940. [7; 10; 11]

Body, Charles William Edmund, clergyman, b. Clapham, England, 1851; d. New York, N.Y., Sept. 20, 1912. [10]

Boehm, Henry, clergyman, b. Conestoga, Pa., 1775; d. Lancaster county, Pa., Dec. 28, 1875. [1; 2; 3; 4; 6]

Boericke, Felix Oriel, physician, b. 1857; d. Bryn Athyn, Pa., Feb. 23, 1929.

Boericke, William, physician, b. 1849; d. San Francisco, Calif, April 1, 1929.

Boezinger, Bruno, educationist, b. Switzerland, 1859; d. Palo Alto, Calif., April 11, 1939.

Bogart, William Henry, journalist, b. Albany, N.Y., 1810; d. Aurora, N.Y., Aug. 21, 1888. [4; 7; 10]

Bogen, Boris D., educationist, b. 1869; d. June 20, 1929.

Boggs, William Bambrick, missionary, b. Lower Stewiacke, N.S., 1842; d. India, July 25, 1913. [33]

Boggs, William Robertson, soldier, b. Augusta, Ga., 1829; d. Winston, N.C., 1911. [10]

Bogue, Mrs. A. H. See Bell, Lillian Lida.

Bohan, Mrs. Elizabeth, née **Baker,** reformer, b. Birmingham, England, 1849; d. Los Angeles, Calif., about 1942. [11; 35]

Bohn, Eric (pseud.). See Brown, John Price.

Boies, Henry Lamson, local historian, b. 1830; d. 1887.

Boies, Henry Martyn, philanthropist, b. Lee, Mass., 1837; d. Wilkesbarre, Pa., Dec. 12, 1903. [1; 10; 62]

Boies, Lura Anna, poet, b. 1835; d. 1859.

Bois, Louis Edouard, priest and historian, b. Quebec, Lower Canada, 1813; d. Maskinongé, Que., Sept. 1889. [27]

Boise, James Robinson, educationist, b. Blandford, Mass., 1815; d. Chicago, Ill., Feb. 9, 1895. [3; 4]

Boise, Otis Bardwell, musician, b. Oberlin, O., 1844; d. Baltimore, Md., Dec. 2, 1912. [10; 20]

Boisot, Louis, lawyer, b. Dubuque, Ia., 1856; d. La Grange, Ill., July 21, 1933. [10]

Boit, Robert Apthorp, novelist and genealogist, b. Boston, Mass., 1846; d. 1919. [51]

Bok, Edward William, editor and philanthropist, b. Helder, Netherlands, 1863; d. near Lake Wales, Fla., Jan. 9, 1930. [1a; 2; 7; 10; 11]

Boker, George Henry, poet and playwright, b. Philadelphia, Pa., 1823; d. Philadelphia, Pa., Jan. 2, 1890. [1; 2; 3; 4; 5; 6; 71]

Bokum, Hermann, clergyman, b. 1807; d. 1878. [6]

Bolduc, Jean Baptiste Zacharie, missionary, b. St. Joachim, Lower Canada, 1818; d. near Quebec, Que., May 8, 1889. [27]

Boley, William Henry, bookseller and local historian, b. Lexington, Va., 1883; d. Lexington, Va., Feb. 27, 1939.

Boller, Alfred Pancoast, civil engineer, b. Philadelphia, Pa., 1840; d. Orange, N.J., Dec. 9, 1912. [4; 10]

Boller, Henry Augustus, pioneer, b. about 1838; d. Denver, Colo., Oct. 30, 1902.

Bolles, Albert Sidney, jurist and educationist, b. Montville, Conn., 1846; d. Williamstown, Mass., May 8, 1939. [10]

Bolles, Frank, naturalist, b. Winchester, Mass., 1856; d. Cambridge, Mass., Jan. 10, 1894. [1; 7; 51]

Bolles, James Aaron, clergyman, b. 1810; d. 1894.

Bolles, John Augustus, lawyer, b. Eastford, Conn., 1809; d. Washington, D.C., May 25, 1878. [3; 6; 47]

Bolles, John Rogers, poet, b. 1810; d. 1895.

Bolles, Simeon, clergyman, b. Bethlehem, N.H., 1830; d. ?

Bolles, William, educationist, b. Marlboro, Conn., 1800; d. Marlboro, Conn., March 20, 1883. [45]

Bollman, Justus Erick, physician and adventurer, b. Hanover, Germany, 1769; d. Jamaica, British West Indies, Dec. 9, 1821. [1; 3]

Bolmar, Antoine, educationist, b. France, 1797; d. West Chester, Pa., Feb. 27, 1861. [4]

Bolster, William Wheeler, lawyer, b. Auburn, Me., 1823; d. 1907. [38]

Bolte, John Willard, miscellaneous writer, b. San Francisco, Calif., 1884; d. Hollywood, Calif., Aug. 31, 1942.

Bolton, Charles Edward, traveller and lecturer, b. South Hadley Falls, Mass., 1841; d. Cleveland, O., Oct. 23, 1901. [4; 10]

Bolton, Mrs. Henrietta, née Irving, wife of H. C. Bolton (q. v.), d. 1930.

Bolton, Henry Carrington, chemist and bibliographer, b. New York, N.Y., 1843; d. Washington, D.C., Nov. 19, 1903. [1; 4; 10]

Bolton, Horace Wilbert, clergyman, b. 1839; d. ?

Bolton, Mother Margaret, religious teacher, b. Richfield Springs, N.Y., 1873; d. New York, N.Y., Feb. 27, 1943.]10; 21[

Bolton, Reginald Pelham, engineer, historian, and poet, b. London, England, 1856; d. New York, N.Y., Feb. 18, 1942. [4; 10; 11]

Bolton, Robert, clergyman, local historian, and genealogist, b. 1814; d. 1877. [6]

Bolton, Mrs. Sarah, née Knowles, biographer and poet, b. Farmington, Conn., 1840; d. Cleveland, O., Feb. 21, 1916. [1; 2; 3; 4; 6; 7; 10]

Bolton, Mrs. Sarah Tittle, née Barrett, poet, b. Newport, Ky., 1814; d. Indianapolis, Ind., Aug. 4, 1893. [1; 3; 6; 7; 34]

Boltwood, Edward, journalist and local historian, b. Pittsfield, Mass., 1870; d. Lebanon Springs, N.Y., Sept. 6, 1924. [10; 62]

Boltwood, Henry Leonidas, educationist, b. Amherst, Mass., 1831; d. Evanston, Ill., Jan. 23, 1906. [45]

Boltwood, Lucius Manlius, genealogist, b. Amherst, Mass., 1825; d. Grand Rapids, Mich., Feb. 28, 1905. [45]

Bombaugh, Charles Carroll, physician and editor, b. Harrisburg, Pa., 1828; d. Baltimore, Md., May 24, 1906. [4]

Bomberger, John Henry Augustus, clergyman, b. Lancaster, Pa., 1817; d. Collegeville, Pa., Aug. 19, 1890. [1; 3; 6]

Bompas, William Carpenter, missionary bishop, b. London, England, 1834; d. Cariboo Crossing, Yukon, June 9, 1906. [27]

Boncoeur, L. (pseud.). See Urbine, Mrs. Levina, née Buoncuora.

Bond, Alexander Russell, editor and patent attorney, b. Bulgaria, 1876; d. Plainfield, N.J., June 3, 1937. [10]

Bond, Beverly Waugh, clergyman, b. 1843; d. 1920. [34]

Bond, Mrs. Carrie, née Jacobs, poet and musician, b. Janesville, Wis., 1862; d. Hollywood, Calif., Dec. 28, 1946. [7; 11; 35]

Bond, Mrs. Elizabeth, née Powell, educationist, b. Dutchess county, N.Y., 1841; d. Germantown, Pa., March 29, 1926. [1; 4]

Bond, Henry, physician and genealogist, b. Watertown, Mass., 1790; d. Philadelphia, Pa., May 4, 1859. [3]

Bond, John Wesley, druggist, b. Pennsylvania, 1825; d. Pine Bluff, Ark., March 13, 1903. [70]

Bond, Mrs. Octavia Louise, née Zollicoffer, genealogist, b. 1846; d. ?

Bond, Oliver James, soldier and educationist, b. Marion, S.C., 1865; d. Charleston, S.C., Oct. 1, 1933. [10]

Bond, Thomas Emerson, physician and journalist; b. Baltimore, Md., 1782; d. New York, N.Y., March 14, 1856. [4; 34]

Bone, Scott Cardelle, journalist, b. Shelby county, Ind., 1860; d. Santa Barbara, Calif., Jan. 27, 1936. [10; 35]

Bone, Winstead Paine, educationist, b. Douglas, Tex., 1861; d. Lebanon, Tex., Feb. 12, 1942. [10]

Bonehill, Capt, Ralph (pseud.). See Stratemeyer, Edward.

Boner, John Henry, poet, b. Salem, N.C., 1845; d. Washington, D.C., March 6, 1903. [1; 4; 7; 10; 34]

Bonesteel, Mrs. Mary, née Greene, writer of books for children, b .1864; d. ? [21]

Bonham, John Milton, lawyer, b. York, Pa., 1835; d. Atlantic City, N.J., June 17, 1897. [60]

Bonham, Milledge Louis, historian, b. Barnwell, S.C., 1880; d. Clinton, N.Y., Jan. 22, 1941. [7; 10; 11]

Bonin, Joseph, priest, b. Lanoraie, Que., 1845; d. Berthier-en-haut, Que., Dec. 26, 1917. [32]

Bonnell, Henry Houston, educationist, b. Philadelphia, Pa., 1859; d. Chestnut Hill, Pa., Nov. 7, 1926. [10; 55]

Bonnell, John Mitchell, educationist, b. Bucks county, Pa., 1820; d. Macon, Ga., Sept. 1871. [4; 34]

Bonner, Geraldine, novelist, b. Staten Island, N.Y., 1870; d. New York, N.Y., July 17, 1930. [10; 35]

Bonner, John, journalist and writer of history books for children, b. Quebec, Lower Canada, 1828; d. San Francisco, Calif., May 7, 1899. [4]

Bonner, Sherwood (pseud.). See McDowell, Mrs. Katherine Sherwood, née Bonner.

Bonnet, Theodore F., journalist, b. San Francisco, Calif., 1865; d. San Francisco, Calif., Aug. 5, 1920. [35]

Bonney, Charles Carroll, lawyer, b. Hamilton, N.Y., 1831; d. Chicago, Ill., Aug. 23, 1903. [1; 10; 36]

Bonney, Edward, novelist, b. 1807; d. 1864. [7]

Bonnycastle, Charles, mathematician, b. Woolwich, England, 1792; d. Charlottesville, Va., Oct., 1840. [3; 4]

Bonnycastle, Sir Richard Henry, soldier, b. England ,1791; d. Kingston, Ont., Nov. 3, 1847. [27]

Bonsall, Mrs. Elizabeth, née Hubbard, editor, b. Cambridge, Mass., 1890; d. Swarthmore, Pa., Feb. 14, 1937. [10; 11]

Bonser, Frederick Gordon, educationist, b. Tower Hill, Ill., 1875; d. Pompton Lakes, N.J., June 8, 1931. [10]

Bonte, George Willard, illustrator and designer, b. Cincinnati, O., 1873; d. New York, N.Y., March 13, 1946. [10]

Bonynge, Robert William, lawyer, b. New York, N.Y., 1863; d. New York, N.Y., Sept. 29, 1939. [10]

Book, John William, priest, b. near Starlight, Ind., 1850; d. ? [4; 21]

Book, William Frederick, psychologist, b. Princeton, Ind., 1873; d. Long Beach, Calif., May 22, 1940. [10]

Book, William Henry, clergyman, b. Craig county, Va., 1863; d. Orlando, Fla., July 10, 1946. [10; 11]

Bookwalter, John Wesley, manufacturer, b. 1837; d. 1915.

Boone, Charles Theodore, lawyer, b. Chester county, Pa., 1838; d. San Francisco, Calif., 1903. [10]

Boone, Richard Gause, educationist, b. Spiceland, Ind., 1849; d. Berkeley, Calif., April 8, 1923. [10]

Booraem, John Van Vorst, engineer, b. Jersey City, N.J., 1838; d. Brooklyn, N.Y., May 24, 1923. [10]

Boos, William Frederick, toxicologist, b. Longwood, Mass., 1870; d. Fall River, Mass., Aug. 11, 1949. [10; 13]

Booth, Charles Douglas Greaves, educationist, b. 1887; d. New York, N.Y., Feb. 22, 1944.

Booth, Charles Octavius, clergyman, b. Mobile county, Ala., 1845; d. ? [24]

Booth, Edwin Gillam, soldier, b. 1810; d. 1886.

Booth, George Wilson, soldier, b. 1844; d. 1914.

Booth, Henry Kendall, clergyman, b. Peru, Ill., 1876; d. Long Beach, Calif., Oct. 16, 1942. [10]

Booth, Henry Matthias, clergyman and educationist, b. New York, N.Y., 1843; d. Auburn, N.Y., March 18, 1899. [4; 10; 61]

Booth, Herbert, religious writer, b. 1862; d. Yonkers, N.Y., Sept. 25, 1926.

Booth, James Curtis, chemist, b. Philadelphia, Pa., 1810; d. West Haverford, Pa., March 21, 1888. [1; 2; 3; 4; 6]

Booth, Mrs. Mary H.C., poet, b. Connecticut, 1831; d. New York, N.Y., April 11, 1865. [3]

Booth, Mary Louise, historian, b. Yaphank, Long Island, N.Y., 1831; d. New York, N.Y., March 5, 1899. [1; 7]

Booth, Walter Sherman, publisher, b. Bridgewater, Conn., 1827; d. Minneapolis, Minn., June 2, 1901. [70]

Booth, William Stone, littérateur, b. Gloucester, England, 1864; d. Cambridge, Mass., Oct. 14, 1926. [4; 10]

Booy, Theodoor de. See De Booy, Theodoor.

Borah, William Edgar, politician, b. Fairfield, Ill., 1865; d. Boise, Ida., Jan. 19, 1940. [2; 4; 10; 12]

Borden, John, lawyer, b. 1825; d. 1918. [51]

Borden, Sir Robert Laird, Canadian prime minister, b. Grand Pré, N.S., 1854; d. Ottawa, Ont., June 10, 1937. [27]

Borden, Simeon, civil engineer, b. Fall River, Mass., 1798; d. Fall River, Mass., Oct. 28, 1856. [1]

Bordley, John Beale, lawyer and agriculturist, b. Annapolis, Md., 1727; d. Philadelphia, Pa., Jan. 26, 1804. [1; 2; 3; 4; 6]

Borland, James Brown, publisher, b. Harlansburg, Pa., 1861; d. Franklin, Pa., May 19, 1939.

Borland, John, clergyman, b. 1809; d. Canada, March 31, 1888. [27]

Borland, William Patterson, lawyer and politician, b. Leavenworth, Kans., 1867; d. New York, N.Y., Feb. 21, 1919. [10; 53]

Born, Wolfgang, art expert, b. Breslau, Germany, 1893; d. New York, N.Y., June 15, 1949.

Borthwick, John Douglas, clergyman and historian, b. near Edinburgh, Scotland, 1832; d. Montreal, Que., Jan. 14, 1912. [27]

Borup, George, explorer, b. 1884; d. 1912.

Bosher, Mrs. Kate Lee, née **Langley,** novelist, b. Norfolk, Va., 1865; d. Norfolk, Va., July 27, 1932. [2; 10; 34]

Boston, Leonard Napoleon, physician, b. Town Hill, Va., 1871; d. Philadelphia, Pa., July 4, 1931. [10]

Bostwick, Arthur Elmore, librarian, b. Litchfield, Conn., 1860; d. St. Louis, Mo., Feb. 13, 1942. [4; 7; 10; 11]

Bostwick, Charles Francis, lawyer, b. Tuckahoe, N.Y., 1866; d. New York, N.Y., June 28, 1923. [10; 48]

Bostwick, Mrs. Helen Louise, née **Barron,** poet, b. Charlestown, N.H., 1826; d. 1907. [3; 8]

Bostwick, Homer, physician, fl. 1830-1851.

Bosworth, Edward Increase, clergyman, b. Elgin, Ill., 1861; d. Oberlin, O., July 1, 1927. [1; 10; 62]

Bosworth, Francke Huntington, laryngologist, b. Marietta, O., 1843; d. New York, N.Y., Oct. 17, 1925. [1; 10]

Bosworth, Newton, clergyman, b. England, about 1776; d. Paris, Ont., July 14, 1848. [24; 27]

Botsford, Edmund, clergyman, d. Georgetown, S.C., Dec. 26, 1819. [24]

Botsford, George Willis, historian, b. West Union, Ia., 1862; d. New York, N.Y., Dec. 13, 1917. [1; 7; 10]

Botsford, Jay Barrett, historian, b. 1896; d. Providence, R.I., June 1, 1938. [47]

Botsford, Mrs. Margaret, poet and novelist, fl. 1812-1828.

Botta, Mrs. Anne Charlotte, née **Lynch,** poet, b. Bennington, Vt., 1820; d. New York, N.Y., March 23, 1891. [1; 3; 4; 43]

Botta, Vincenzo, educationist, b. Piedmont, Italy, 1818; d. New York, N.Y., Oct. 5, 1894. [1; 2; 3; 4; 7]

Bottome, Francis, clergyman, b. 1823; d. 1894.

Bottome, Mrs. Margaret, née **McDonald,** religious writer, b. New York, N.Y., 1827; d. New York, N.Y., Nov. 14, 1906. [1; 4; 7; 10]

Botts, John Minor, lawyer and politician, b. Dumfries, Va., 1802; d. Culpepper, Va., Jan. 7, 1869. [1; 4; 34]

Botume, John Franklin, musician, b. Boston, Mass., 1855; d. Boston, Mass., Oct. 17, 1907. [51]

Boucher, Jonathan, clergyman, b. Cumberland, England, 1734; d. Epsom, England, April 27, 1804. [1; 2; 3; 4]

Boucher, Pierre, historian, b. France, 1622; d. Boucherville, New France (Canada), April 19, 1717. [27]

Boucher de la Bruère, politician, b. St. Hyacinthe, Lower Canada, 1837; d. Quebec, Que., March 17, 1917. [27]

Boucher-Belleville, Jean Baptiste, priest,, b. Quebec, Canada, 1763; d. Laprairie, Lower Canada, Sept. 6, 1839. [32]

Bouchette, Joseph, surveyor, b. Quebec, Canada, 1774; d. Montreal, Que., April 9, 1841. [27]

Bouchette, Robert Errol, civil servant and economist, b. Quebec, Que., 1863; d. Ottawa, Ont., Aug. 13, 1912. [27]

Boucke, Oswald Fred, economist, b. Germany, 1881; d. State College, Pa., March 12, 1935. [10]

Boudinot, Elias, revolutionary politician, b. Philadelphia, Pa., 1740; d. Burlington, N.J., Oct. 24, 1821. [1; 2; 3; 4; 5; 6; 7]

Bouffard, Jean, lawyer and educationist, d. St. Laurent, Island of Orleans, Que., July 9, 1920.

Boughton, Mrs. **Martha Elizabeth,** née **Arnold,** poet, b. Corunna, Mich.; d. Brooklyn, N.Y., May 18, 1928. [10; 11]

Boughton, Willis, educationist, b. Victor, N.Y., 1854; d. Brooklyn, N.Y., June 16, 1942. [7; 14]

Bouldin, Powhatan, historian, b. Virginia, 1830; d. 1907. [34]

Boulton, Charles Arkoll, soldier, b. Cobourg, Ont., 1841; d. Shellmouth, Man., May 18, 1899. [27]

Bounds, Edward McKendree, clergyman, b. 1835; d. 1913.

Bourassa, Gustave, priest, b. Montebello, Que., 1860; d. Montreal, Que., Nov. 20, 1904. [27]

Bourassa, Napoléon, architect and painter, b. L'Acadie, Lower Canada, 1827; d. Lachenaie, Que., Aug. 27, 1916. [27]

Bourgeois, Philéas Frédéric, priest, b. Memramcook, N.B., 1855; d. Moncton, N.B., April 3, 1913. [27; 32]

Bourget, Ignace, bishop, b. Point Levy, Lower Canada, 1799; d. Sault-aux-Récollets, near Montreal, Que., June 8, 1885. [27; 32]

Bourinot, Sir John George, historian, b. Sydney, N.S., 1837; d. Ottawa, Ont., Oct. 13, 1902. [27]

Bourke, John Gregory, soldier and ethnologist, b. Philadelphia, Pa., 1846; d. Philadelphia, Pa., June 8, 1896. [1; 3; 4; 6]

Bourne, Benjamin Franklin, mariner, fl. 1853-1876. [6]

Bourne, Edward Emerson, jurist and local historian, b. Kennebunk, Me., 1797; d. Kennebunk, Me., Sept. 23, 1873. [3; 38]

Bourne, Edward Gaylord, historian, b. Strykersville, N.Y., 1860; d. New Haven, Conn., Feb. 24, 1908. [1; 2; 10; 62]

Bourne, Ella, educationist, b. Greenfield, Ind., 1869; d. Oakland, Calif., July 2, 1947. [14]

Bourne, George, clergyman and abolitionist, b. Westbury, England, 1780; d. New York, N.Y., Nov. 20, 1845. [1; 3; 6]

Bourne, Randolph Silliman, essayist, b. Bloomfield, N.J., 1886; d. New York, N.Y., Dec. 22, 1918. [1; 7; 10]

Bourne, William Oland, poet and educationist, fl. 1845-1888.

Boutell, Henry Sherman, bibliographer, b. 1905; d. London, England, March 23, 1931.

Boutell, Lewis Henry, lawyer and biographer, b. 1826; d. Chicago, Ill., Jan. 16, 1899. [51]

Bouton, Archibald Lewis, educationist, b. Cortland, N.Y., 1872; d. Pasadena, Calif., April 18, 1941. [7; 10]

Bouton, John Bell, journalist, b. Concord, N.H., 1830; d. Cambridge, Mass., Nov. 18, 1902. [1; 3; 4; 7]

Bouton, Nathaniel, clergyman, b. Norwalk, Conn., 1797; d. Concord, N.H., June 6, 1878. [1; 3; 4; 6]

Boutwell, George Sewall, politician, b. Brookline, Mass., 1818; d. Groton, Mass., Feb. 27, 1905. [1; 2; 10]

Bouvé, Mrs. **Pauline Carrington,** née Rust, journalist, b. Little Rock, Ark.; d. 1928. [10]

Bouvé, Thomas Tracy, merchant and naturalist, b. Boston, Mass., 1815; d. Hingham, Mass., June 3, 1896. [3; 4; 6]

Bouvet, Marie Marguerite, writer of books for children, b. New Orleans, La., 1865; d. Reading, Pa., May 27, 1915. [1; 7; 10]

Bouvier, John, jurist, b. France, 1787; d. Philadelphia, Pa., Nov. 18, 1851. [1; 2; 3; 4]

Bovard, William Sherman, clergyman, b. Alpha, Ind., 1864; d. Evanston, Ill., Sept. 6, 1936. [10]

Bovee, Christian Nestell, lawyer, b. New York, N.Y., 1820; d. Philadelphia, Pa., 1904. [3; 10]

Bovee, John Wesley, gynaecologist, b. Clayton, N.Y., 1861; d. Washington, D.C., Sept. 3, 1927. [10]

Bovell, James, clergyman and physician, b. Barbados, 1817; d. Nevis, West Indies, Jan. 6, 1880. [27]

Bovey, Henry Taylor, educationist, b. Devonshire, England, 1852; d. Eastbourne, England, Feb. 2, 1912. [27]

Bow, Jonathan Gaines, clergyman. b. Burkesville, Ky., about 1850; d. ? [24]

Bowden, John, clergyman, b. Ireland, 1751; d. Ballston Spa, N.Y., July 3, 1817. [1; 3; 4; 6]

Bowditch, Charles Pickering, archaeologist, b. Boston, Mass., 1842; d. Boston, Mass., June 1, 1921. [1; 10; 51]

Bowditch, Henry Ingersoll, physician, b. Salem, Mass., 1808; d. Boston, Mass., Jan. 14, 1892. [1; 3; 4; 6]

Bowditch, Henry Pickering, physiologist, b. Boston, Mass., 1840; d. Jamaica plain, Mass., March 13, 1911. [1; 10; 51]

Bowditch, Nathaniel, mathematician and astronomer, b. Salem, Mass., 1773; d. Boston, Mass., March 16, 1838. [1; 2; 3; 4]

Bowditch, Nathaniel Ingersoll, lawyer, b. Salem, Mass., 1805; d. Brookline, Mass., April 16, 1861. [3; 6; 51]

Bowditch, Vincent Yardley, physician, b. Weston, Mass., 1852; d. Boston, Mass., Dec. 20, 1929. [10]

Bowditch, William Ingersoll, lawyer, b. Salem, Mass., 1819; d. Boston, Mass., 1909. [51]

Bowdoin, William Goodrich, art critic, b. South Hadley Falls, Mass., 1860; d. Brooklyn, N.Y., March 22, 1947. [7; 10; 11]

Bowen, Abel, publisher, b. Greenbush, N.Y., 1790; d. Boston, Mass., March 11, 1850. [1; 3; 6; 7]

Bowen, Benjamin Lester, educationist, b. Chili, N.Y., 1860; d. July 28, 1920. [10]

Bowen, Clarence Winthrop, historian, b. Brooklyn, N.Y., 1852; d. Hartford, Conn., Nov. 2, 1935. [10; 62]

Bowen, Clayton Raymond, clergyman, b. Wellsboro, Pa., 1877; d. Oct. 17, 1934. [10]

Bowen, Eli, descriptive writer, b. Lancaster, Pa., 1824; d. before 1886. [3; 6]

Bowen, Eliza A., educationist, b. 1828; d. 1898. [34]

Bowen, Ezra, educationist, b. Bethlehem, Pa., 1891; d. New York, N.Y., Dec. 26, 1945. [48]

Bowen, Francis, philosopher, b. Charlestown, Mass., 1811; d. Boston, Mass., Jan. 14, 1890. [1; 2; 3; 4; 6; 7; 51]

Bowen, George, missionary. b. Middlebury, Vt., 1816; d. Bombay, India, Feb. 5, 1888. [1]

Bowen, Herbert Wolcott, poet and diplomat, b. Brooklyn, N.Y., 1856; d. Woodstock, Conn., May 29, 1927. [1; 2; 7; 10]

Bowen, John Eliot, journalist, b. Brooklyn, N.Y., 1858; d. Brooklyn, N.Y., Jan. 3, 1890. [62]

Bowen, Littleton Purnell, clergyman, b. 1833; d. Berlin, Md., April 8, 1933.

Bowen, Nathaniel, bishop, b. 1779; d. 1839. [4]

Bowen, Mrs. Sue, née **Petigru.** See King, Mrs. Susan, née Petigru.

Bowen, Thomas Jefferson, missionary and explorer, b. Georgia, 1814; d. Georgia, Nov. 24, 1875. [6; 24; 34]

Bowen, Wilbur Pardon, educationist, b. Lima, Mich., 1864; d. Ypsilanti, Mich., Sept. 5, 1928. [10; 11]

Bowen, William Abraham, journalist, b. Santa Rosa, Fla., 1856; d. April 15, 1921. [10]

Bowen, William Alvin, lawyer and writer of fairy tales, b. Baltimore, Md., 1877; d. Los Angeles, Calif., Sept. 18, 1937. [10; 35]

Bowen, William Henry, clergyman, b. Johnston, R.I., 1836; d. Providence, R.I., Feb. 13, 1915. [24; 47]

Bower, B. M. (pseud.). See Sinclair, Mrs. Bertha, née Muzzy.

Bowers, John Hugh, educationist, b. near Franklin, W. Va., 1875; d. Pittsburg, Kans., April 6, 1923. [10]

Bowie, William, geodesist, b. Annapolis Junction, Md., 1872; d. 1941. [10; 11]

Bowker, Richard Rogers, publisher, b. Salem, Mass., 1848; d. near Stockbridge, Mass., Nov. 12, 1933 [1a; 4; 7; 10]

Bowler, Metcalf, agriculturist, b. London, England, 1726; d. Rhode Island, Sept. 24, 1789. [3; 4]

Bowles, John, novelist, b. 1833; d. 1900.

Bowles, Joseph Moore, designer, b. 1860; d. New York, N.Y., Jan. 7, 1934.

Bowles, Ralph Hartt, educationist, b. Cherryfield, Me., 1870; d. near Caldwell, N.J., Aug. 31, 1919. [51]

Bowles, Samuel, journalist, b. Springfield, Mass., 1826; d. Springfield, Mass., Jan. 16, 1878. [1; 2; 3; 6; 7]

Bowles, William Augustus, Indian chief, b. Frederick, Md., 1744; d. 1805. [4; 34]

Bowman, Edward Morris, musician, b. Barnard, Vt., 1848; d. Brooklyn, N.Y., Aug. 27, 1913. [4; 10; 20]

Bowman, Harold Martin, lawyer, b. Des Moines, Ia., 1876; d. Boston, Mass., Nov. 21, 1949. [10]

Bowman, Mrs. Louise, née **Morey.** poet, b. Sherbrooke, Que., 1882; d. Montreal, Que., Sept. 28, 1944. [11; 27]

Bowman, Samuel Millard, soldier, b. Briar Creek, Va., 1815; d. Kansas City, Mo., June 4, 1885. [49]

Bowman, Shadrach Laycock, clergyman, b. Plains, Pa., 1829; d. Ocean Grove, N.J., Sept. 16, 1906. [4]

Bowman, Thomas, bishop, b. Berwick, Pa., 1817; d. Orange, N.J., March 3, 1914. [1; 4]

Bowne, Borden Parker, philosopher and theologian, b. Leonardville, N.J., 1847; d. Boston, Mass., April 1, 1910. [1; 7; 10]

Bowser, Edward Albert, mathematician, b. Sackville, N.B., 1837; d. Honolulu, Hawaii, Feb. 22, 1910. [2; 10]

Bowsfield, Colvin Cullen, journalist, b. Orangeville, Ont., 1855; d. Jan. 28, 1940. [10]

Boyce, Augustus Anson, lawyer, b. Cortland, N.Y., 1813; d. Santa Barbara, Calif., Sept. 11, 1909. [69]

Boyce, Ella Ruth, educationist, b. Oil City, Pa., 1875; d. Los Angeles, Calif., July 16, 1943.

Boyce, James Petigru, clergyman, b. Charleston, S.C., 1827; d. Pau, France, Dec. 28, 1888. [24]

Boyce, John, priest and novelist, b. Donegal, Ireland, 1810; d. Worcester, Mass., Jan. 2, 1864. [21]

Boyce, William Dickson, publisher, b. 1848; d. 1929.

Boyd, Belle, spy, b. Martinsburg, Va., 1843; d. Kilbourne, Wis., June 11, 1900. [1; 7]

Boyd, Charles Newell, organist, b. Pleasant Unity, Pa., 1875; d. Pittsburg, Pa., April 24, 1937. [20]

Boyd, Ernest Augustus, literary critic, b. Dublin, Ireland, 1887; d. New York, N.Y., Dec. 30, 1946. [7; 10]

Boyd, Jackson, poet, b. 1861; d. 1920.

Boyd, James, horticulturist, b. Boston, Mass., 1858; d. Haverford, Pa., Dec. 2, 1929. [10]

Boyd, James, novelist, b. Dauphin county, Pa., 1888; d. Princeton, N.J., Feb. 25, 1944. [7; 10; 11]

Boyd, James Penny, historian, b. Lancaster county, Pa., 1836; d. Philadelphia, Pa., 1910. [10]

Boyd, James Robert, clergyman and educationist, b. Hunter, N.Y., 1804; d. Geneva, N.Y., Feb. 19, 1890. [3]

Boyd, John, journalist and biographer, b. Montreal, Que., 1864; d. near St. Jovite, Que., Jan. 31, 1933. [27]

Boyd, Sir John Alexander, jurist, b. Toronto, Upper Canada, 1837; d. Toronto, Ont., Nov. 23, 1916. [27]

Boyd, John Edward, humorist, b. Center Moriches, N.Y., 1843; d. Berkeley, Calif., Jan. 26, 1912. [35]

Boyd, Richard Henry, clergyman, b. Noxubee county, Miss., 1843; d. Nashville, Tenn., Aug. 23, 1922. [1; 24]

Boyd, Robert, clergyman, b. Girvan, Scotland, 1816; d. Waukesha, Wis., Aug. 1, 1879. [24]

Boyd, Thomas Alexander, journalist, b. Defiance, O., 1898; d. Ridgefield, Conn., Jan. 27, 1935. [1a; 7; 10; 11]

Boyd, William Kenneth, historian, b. Curryville, Mo., 1879; d. Durham, N.C., Jan. 19, 1938. [10]

Boyden, Albert Gardner, educationist, b. South Walpole, Mass., 1827; d. Bridgewater, Mass., May 30, 1915. [10]

Boyden, Arthur Clarke, educationist, b. Bridgewater, Mass., 1852; d. Bridgewater, Mass., March 15, 1933. [10; 11; 45]

Boyé, Martin Hans, chemist, b. Copenhagen, Denmark, 1812; d. Coopersburg, Pa., March 5, 1909. [1; 10]

Boyer, Charles Clinton, clergyman and educationist, b. 1860; d. Aug. 20, 1932.

Boyer, Charles Shimer, local historian, b. Bethlehem, Pa., 1869; d. Moorestown, N.J., Nov. 10, 1936. [55]

Boyer, Charles Sumner, educationist, b. 1856; d. Philadelphia, Pa., March 27, 1928. [4; 13; 47]

Boyer, Emanuel Roth, biologist, b. York, Pa., 1857; d. Chicago, Ill., 1900. [10; 51]

Boyer, Mrs. Nathalie, née **Robinson,** biographer, b. 1861; d. Philadelphia, Pa., Dec. 18, 1940.

Boyesen, Hjalmar Hjorth, educationist and novelist, b. Norway, 1848; d. New York, N.Y., Oct. 4, 1895. [1; 2; 3; 4; 6; 71]

Boykin, Samuel, clergyman, b. Milledgeville, Ga., 1829; d. Nashville, Tenn., Nov. 3, 1899. [24; 34]

Boylan, Mrs. Grace, née **Duffie,** poet and novelist, b. Kalamazoo, Mich., 1861; d. Memphis, Tenn., March 24, 1935. [7; 10]

Boylan, William Aloysius, educationist, b. New York, N.Y., 1869; d. New York, N.Y., July 8, 1940. [10; 21]

Boyle, Charles Cumberson, ophthalmologist, b. 1854; d. New York, N.Y., June 19, 1931.

Boyle, David, ethnologist and archaeologist, b. Greenock, Scotland, 1842; d. Toronto, Ont., Feb. 14, 1911. [27]

Boyle, Esmeralda, poet, b. 1840; d. ?

Boyle, James, journalist, b. Essex, England, 1853; d. Columbus, O., June 11, 1939. [10]

Boyle, James Ernest, economist, b. Boyle, Kans., 1873; d. Ithaca, N.Y., Sept. 18, 1938. [10]

Boyle, Mrs. Virginia, née **Frazer,** poet and novelist, b. near Chattanooga, Tenn., 1863; d. Memphis, Tenn., Dec. 13, 1938. [4; 7; 10; 34]

Boylston, Peter (pseud.). See Curtis, George Ticknor.

Boynton, Charles Brandon, clergyman, b. Stockbridge, Mass., 1806; d. Cincinnati, O., April 27, 1883. [1; 3; 6]

Boynton, Frank David, educationist, b. Potsdam, N.Y., 1863; d. Ithaca, N.Y., June 17, 1930. [10]

Boynton, George Mills, clergyman, b. Brooklyn, N.Y., 1837; d. Boston, Mass., May 17, 1908. [10; 62; 68]

Boynton, Henry Van Ness, soldier, b. West Stockbridge, Mass., 1835; d. Atlantic City, N.J., June 3, 1905. [3; 10]

Boynton, Henry Walcott, littérateur, b. Guilford, Conn., 1869; d. Providence, R.I., May 11, 1947. [7; 10; 11]

Boynton, Jeremy, clergyman, b. 1824; d. 1883.

Boynton, Nehemiah, clergyman, b. Medford, Mass., 1856; d. Medford, Mass., Nov. 8, 1933. [10; 45]

Boynton, Percy Holmes, educationist, b. Newark, N.J., 1875; d. New London, Conn., July 8, 1946. [7; 10; 11]

Boys, William Fuller Alves, jurist, b. New York, N.Y., 1833; d. Barrie, Ont., Nov. 29, 1914. [27]

Boyton, Paul, adventurer, b. Kildare county, Ireland, 1848; d. Brooklyn, N.Y., April 18, 1924.

Bozman, John Leeds, jurist and historian, b. Talbot county, Md., 1757; d. Talbot county, Md. ,April 23, 1823. [1; 2; 3; 7; 34]

Brabant, Auguste Joseph, missionary, b. Courtray, Belgium, 1845; d. Victoria, B.C., July 4, 1912. [27]

Brace, Benjamin (pseud.). See McCutcheon, Ben Frederick.

Brace, Charles Loring, philanthropist, b. Litchfield, Conn., 1826; d. Campfer, Switzerland, Aug. 11, 1890. [1; 2; 3; 4; 5; 6; 7]

Brace, De Witt Bristol, educationist, b. Wilson, N.Y., 1859; d. Lincoln, Neb., Oct. 2, 1905. [1; 10]

Brace, John Pierce, educationist and novelist, b. Litchfield, Conn., 1793; d. Litchfield, Conn., Oct. 18, 1872. [1; 3; 6; 7]

Brace, Johathan, clergyman, b. Hartford, Conn., 1810; d. Hartford, Conn., Oct. 1, 1877. [45]

Brace, Maria Porter. See Kimball, Mrs. Maria Porter, née Brace.

Bracken, Henry Martyn, physician, b. Noblestown, Pa., 1854; d. Claremont, Calif., Sept. 25, 1938. [10; 70]

Brackenridge, Henry Marie, lawyer, b. Pittsburg, Pa., 1786; d. Pittsburg, Pa., Jan. 18, 1871. [1; 2; 6; 7]

Brackenridge, Hugh Henry, jurist, b. Scotland, 1748; d. Carlisle, Pa., June 25, 1816. [1; 3; 6; 7; 72]

Brackett, Albert Gallatin, soldier, b. Cherry Valley, N.Y., 1829; d. Washington, D.C., June 25, 1896. [3]

Brackett, Anna Callender, educationist, b. Boston, Mass., 1836; d. Stowe, Vt., March 9, 1911. [1; 2; 10]

Brackett, Charles Albert, dentist, b. Lampster, N.H., 1856; d. Newport, R.I., March 20, 1927. [10]

Brackett, Edward Augustus, sculptor and poet, b. Vassalboro, Me., 1818; d. Boston, Mass., March 5, 1905. [1; 3; 7]

Brackett, Jeffrey Richardson, sociologist, b. Quincy, Mass., 1860; d. Charleston, S.C., Dec. 4, 1949. [14; 51]

Bracq, Jean Charlemagne, historian, b. Cambrai, France, 1853; d. Keene, N.H., Dec. 18, 1934. [2a; 10]

Bradbury, Ammi Ruhamah, clergyman, b. Minot, Me., 1810; d. Providence, R.I., Sept. 15, 1899. [46]

Bradbury, Charles, local historian, b. 1798; d. 1864. [38]

Bradbury, Harry Bower, lawyer, b. 1863; d. 1923.

Bradbury, Osgood, novelist, fl. 1844-1865. [7; 38]

Bradbury, Samuel, physician, b. Germantown, Pa., 1883; d. Bangor, Me., Aug. 29, 1947. [11]

Bradbury, William Batchelder, musician and song writer, b. York, Me., 1816; d. Montclair, N.J., Jan. 7, 1868. [1; 3; 7; 20]

Bradbury, William Frothingham, mathematician, b. Westminster, Mass., 1829; d. Cambridge, Mass., Oct. 22, 1914. [3; 45]

Bradford, Alden, historian, b. Duxbury, Mass., 1765; d. Boston, Mass., Oct., 26, 1843. [1; 2; 3; 4; 6; 7; 51]

Bradford, Alexander Warfield, lawyer and ethnologist, b. Albany, N.Y., 1815; d. New York, N.Y., Nov. 5, 1867. [1; 3; 6;]

Bradford, Amory Howe, clergyman, b. Granby, N.Y., 1846; d. Montclair, N.J., Feb. 18, 1911. [1; 2; 7; 10]

Bradford, Charles Barker, journalist and sportsman, b. Detroit, Mich., 1862; d. Richmond Hill, Long Island, N.Y., Nov. 12, 1917. [10]

Bradford, Duncan, astronomer, d. 1887. [51]

Bradford, Ebenezer, clergyman, b. 1746; d. 1801. [38]

Bradford, Edward Hickling, surgeon, b. Boston, Mass., 1848; d. Boston, Mass., May 7, 1926. [1; 10]

Bradford, Gamaliel, physician and essayist, b. 1795; d. Boston, Mass., Oct., 22, 1839. [51]

Bradford, Gamaliel, politician, b. Boston, Mass., 1831; d. Boston, Mass., Aug. 20, 1911. [1; 51]

Bradford, Gamaliel, biographer, critic, poet, and playwright, b. Boston, Mass., 1863; d. Wellesley Hills, Mass., April 11, 1932. [1a; 2a; 7; 10; 11]

Bradford, John, journalist, b. near Warrenton, Va., 1749; d. Lexington, Ky., March 31, 1830. [74]

Bradford, Joseph, poet and playwright, b. Nashville, Tenn., 1843; d. Boston, Mass., April 13 ,1886. [7; 34]

Bradford, Roark, humorist, b. Lauderdale county, Tenn., 1896; d. New Orleans, La., Nov. 13, 1948. [7; 10]

Bradford, Mrs. Sarah Elizabeth, née Hopkins, writer of books for children, b. 1818; d. ? [6; 7]

Bradford, Thomas Lindsley, physician, b. Francestown, N.H., 1849; d. Philadelphia, Pa., Dec. 3, 1918. [4; 10]

Bradford, William, historian, b. Yorkshire, England, 1589-90; d. Plymouth, Mass., May 9-19, 1657. [1; 2; 3; 4; 7]

Bradford, William, jurist, b. Philadelphia, Pa., 1755; d. Philadelphia, Pa., Aug. 23, 1795. [1; 3; 4; 6]

Bradford, William John Alden, lawyer and traveller, b. Wiscasset, Me., 1797; d. at sea, Nov. 28, 1858. [51]

Bradlee, Caleb Davis, clergyman and poet, b. Boston, Mass., 1831; d. Brookline, Mass., May 1, 1897. [3; 4]

Bradley, Cornelius Beach, clergyman and educationist, b. Bangkok, Siam, 1843; d. Berkeley, Calif., Feb. 17, 1936. [62]

Bradley, Cyrus Parker, biographer, b. Canterbury, N.H., 1818; d. Concord, N.H., July 6, 1838. [50]

Bradley, Glenn Danford, historian, b. Kinderhook, Mich., 1884; d. Toledo, O., Jan. 4, 1930. [10; 53]

Bradley, Isaac Samuel, librarian and bibliographer, b. Albany, N.Y., 1853; d. Madison, Wis., April 22, 1912. [44]

Bradley, John Edwin, educationist, b. Lee, Mass., 1839; d. Randolph, Mass., Oct. 7, 1912. [1; 2; 10]

Bradley, Joseph P., jurist, b. Berne, N.Y., 1813; d. Washington, D.C., Jan. 22, 1892. [1; 2; 4]

Bradley, Joshua, clergyman, b. Randolph, Mass., 1773; d. St. Paul, Minn., Nov. 22, 1855. [24; 70]

Bradley, Mrs. Mary Emily, née Neely, poet and writer of books for girls, b. Easton, Md., 1835; d. Washington, D.C., 1898. [6; 7]

Bradley, Milton, manufacturer, b. Vienna, Me., 1836; d. Springfield, Mass., May 30, 1911. [1; 7; 10]

Bradley, Samuel Carlyle, clergyman, b. 1842; d. ?

Bradley, Stephen Row, politician, b. Cheshire, Conn., 1754; d. Walpole, N.H., Dec. 16, 1830. [1; 3; 6; 43]

Bradley, Theodore James, chemist, b. Albany, N.Y., 1874; d. Brookline, Mass., Dec. 12, 1936. [10; 13]

Bradley, Thomas Bibb, poet, b. 1830; d. 1855. [34]

Bradley, Walter Parke, educationist, b. Lee, Mass., 1862; d. Southampton, Long Island, N.Y., Sept. 14, 1947.

Bradley, Warren Ives, writer of stories for boys, b. Bristol, Conn., 1847; d. Bristol, Conn., June 15, 1868. [3; 4; 7]

Bradley, William Aspenwall, literary and artistic critic, b. Hartford, Conn., 1878; d. Paris, France, Jan. 9, 1939. [7; 10]

Bradley, William O'Connell, politician, b. Garrard county, Ky., 1847; d. Washington, D.C., May 23, 1914. [1; 4; 10]

Bradner, Lester, clergyman, b. Chicago, Ill., 1867; d. Saunderstown, R.I., Sept. 21, 1929. [10]

Bradshaw, Sidney Ernest, educationist, b. near Covington, Tenn., 1869; d. Greenville, S.C., Aug. 31, 1938. [10; 34]

Bradshaw, Thomas, financier, b. Manchester, England, 1868; d. Toronto, Ont., Nov. 10, 1939. [27]

Bradshaw, Wellesley (pseud.). See Alexander, Charles Wesley.

Bradshaw, William Richard, lecturer, b. 1852; d. Flushing, Long Island, N.Y., July 19, 1927.

Bradstreet, Mrs. Anne, née Dudley, poet, b. Northampton, England, 1613; d. Andover, Mass., Sept. 16, 1672. [1; 2; 3; 4; 5; 6; 7]

Bradt, Charles Edwin, clergyman, b. Laporte, Ind., 1863; d. Evanston, Ill., Sept. 5, 1922. [10]

Brady, Cyrus Townsend, clergyman, novelist and historian, b. Allegheny, Pa., 1861; d. Yonkers, N.Y., Jan. 24, 1920. [1; 2; 4; 7; 10]

Brady, James Boyd, clergyman, b. county Antrim, Ireland, 1845; d. Boston, Mass., 1912. [10]

Brady, James Topham, lawyer, b. New York, N.Y., 1815; d. New York, N.Y., Feb. 9, 1869. [3]

Brady, John Everett, educationist, b. Davidson, N.C., 1860; d. Franklinton, N.C., Jan. 20, 1941. [10]

Brady, William N., mariner, d. 1887. [6]

Bragdon, Claude Fayette, architect, b. Oberlin, O., 1866; d. New York, N.Y., Sept. 17, 1946. [7; 10; 4]

Bragdon, Mrs. Olive Evelyth, née Hurd, novelist, b. York county, Me., 1858; d. Boston, Mass., March 14, 1915. [10]

Brain, Belle Marvel, missionary, b. Springfield, O., 1859; d. Schenectady, N.Y., May 25, 1933. [10; 11]

Brainard, David Legge, soldier and explorer, b. 1856; d. Washington, D.C., March 22, 1946. [7; 10]

Brainard, John Gardiner Calkins, poet, b. New London, Conn., 1796; d. New London, Conn., Sept. 26, 1828. [1; 2; 3; 4; 6; 71]

Brainerd, Cephas, lawyer, b. Haddam, Conn., 1831 d. New York, N.Y., 1910. [10]

Brainerd, Chauncey Corey, journalist and novelist, b. New York, N.Y., April 16, 1874; d. Jan. 28, 1922. [10]

Brainerd, Mrs. Edith Rathbone, née Jacobs, novelist, d. 1922. [10]

Brainerd, David, missionary, b. Haddam, Conn., 1718; d. Northampton, Mass., Oct. 9, 1747. [1; 2; 3; 4; 7]

Brainerd, Mrs. Eleanor, née Hoyt, novelist, b. 1868; d. Pasadena, Calif., March 18, 1942. [7; 10]

Brainerd, Erastus, journalist, b. Middletown, Conn., 1855; d. Seattle, Wash., Dec. 25, 1922. [1; 4; 7]

Brainerd, Ezra, botanist, b. St. Andrews, Vt., 1844; d. Middlebury, Vt., Dec. 8, 1924. [1; 4; 10]

Brainerd, Henry Clark, physician, b. 1845; d. Cleveland, O., Dec. 1, 1930.

Brainerd, Ira Hutchinson, lawyer, b. 1861; d. New York, N.Y., May 1, 1935.

Brainerd, Thomas, clergyman, b. Leyden, N.Y., 1804; d. Philadelphia, Pa., Aug. 21, 1866. [1]

Branagan, Thomas, poet and abolitionist, b. Dublin, Ireland, 1774; d. ? [19]

Branch, Anna Hempstead, poet, b. New London, Conn., 1875; d. New London, Conn., Sept. 8, 1937. [7; 10; 11]

Branch, Mrs. Mary Lydia, née Bolles, writer of stories for children, b. New London, Conn., 1840; d. New London, Conn., April 17, 1922. [3; 4; 10]

Branch, Oliver Ernesto, lawyer, b. Madison, O., 1847; d. Manchester, N.H., June 23, 1916. [10; 49]

Brand, Albert Rich, ornithologist, b. New York, N.Y., 1889; d. Ithaca, N.Y., March 28, 1940.

Brand, James, clergyman, b. Three Rivers, Lower Canada, 1834; d. Oberlin, O., April 11, 1899. [62]

Brand, Max. (pseud.). See Faust, Frederick.

Brand, William Francis, clergyman and biographer, b. 1814; d. 1907.

Brande, Dorothea, See Collins, Mrs. Dorothea, née Brande.

Brandeis, Louis Dembitz, jurist, b. Louisville, Ky., 1856; d. Washington, D.C., Oct. 5, 1941. [4; 10]

Brandeis, Mrs. Madeline, née Frank, writer of children's stories, b. San Francisco, Calif., 1890; d. Gallup, N.M., June 28, 1937. [7; 16]

Brandenburg, Edwin Charles, lawyer, b. Washington, D.C., 1865; d. Montrose, Md., 1935. [10]

Brandow, John Henry, clergyman, b. Windham, N.Y., 1853; d. Schoharie, N.Y., Oct. 14, 1921.

Brandreth, Benjamin, physician, b. 1807; d. 1880.

Brandreth, Paulina, poet, b. Ossining, N.Y., d. Newton, Conn., April 18, 1946.

Brands, Orestes M., writer on hygiene, b. 1843; d. ?

Brandt, Francis Burke, educationist, b. Philadelphia, Pa., 1865; d. at sea, Aug. 31, 1939. [51]

Brandt, Hermann Carl George, educationist, b. Vilson, Germany, 1850; d. Clinton, N.Y., Dec. 20, 1920. [10]

Brandt, Olaf Elias, educationist, b. near Oconomowac, Wis. 1862; d. Minneapolis, Minn., Feb. 20, 1940. [10; 70]

Brann, Henry Athanasius, priest, b. Parkstown, Ireland, 1837; d. New York, N.Y., Dec. 28, 1921. [2; 10; 21]

Brann, William Cowper, journalist, b. Coles county, Ill., 1855; d. Waco, Tex., April 2, 1898. [7]

Brannan, Joseph Doddridge, lawyer and educationist, b. Circleville, O., 1848; d. Cambridge, Mass., July 26, 1930. [10; 51]

Brannan, William Penn, painter, b. 1825; d. Cincinnati, O., Aug. 9, 1866. [3]

Branner, John Casper, geologist and genealogist, b. Jefferson county, Tenn., 1850; d. Stanford University, Calif., March 1, 1922, [1; 4; 10]

Brannon, Henry, jurist, b. Winchester, Va., 1837; d. Weston, W. Va., Nov. 24, 1914. [1; 2; 10]

Branson, Edward Regnier, lawyer, b. 1875; d. 1937.

Branson, Eugene Cuningham, educationist, b. Morehead City, N.C., 1861; d. Chapel Hill, N.C., March 13, 1933. [10; 11; 34]

Brantly, William Theophilus, lawyer, b. 1852; d. Baltimore, Md., April 21, 1945.

Brashear, John Alfred, manufacturer, b. Brownsville, Pa., 1840; d. Pittsburg, Pa., April 8, 1920. [10]

Brashears, Noah, poet, fl. 1814-1832.

Brastow, Lewis Orsmond, clergyman and educationist, b. Brewer, Me., 1834; d. Woodmont, Conn., Aug. 10, 1912. [10; 62]

Brattle, William, clergyman, b. Boston, Mass., 1662; d. Cambridge, Mass., Feb. 15, 1716-17. [1; 3; 51]

Bratton, Samuel Tilden, geographer, b. Johnson county, Mo., 1878; d. Columbia, Mo., Oct. 18, 1940. [10]

Braun, Antoine Nicolas, priest, b. France, 1815; d. Montreal, Que., Feb. 1, 1885. [32]

Brawley, Benjamin Griffith, educationist, b. Columbia, S.C., 1882; d. Washington, D.C., Feb. 1, 1939. [7; 10; 11]

Braxton, Allen Caperton, lawyer, b. Monroe county, W. Va., 1862; d. Richmond, Va., March, 1941. [10]

Bray, Frank Chapin, journalist, b. Salineville, O., 1866; d. New York, N.Y., March 24, 1949. [10]

Bray, Henry Truro, clergyman, b. Truro, England, 1846; d. Chicago, Ill., Oct. 23, 1922. [10]

Bray, Mrs. Mary, née Matthews, poet and novelist, b. 1837; d. ?

Bray, Thomas Wells, clergyman, b. 1738; d. 1808.

Brayley, Arthur Wellington, historian, b. 1863; d. Boston, Mass., Dec. 13, 1919.

Brayman, Mason, journalist and poet, b. Buffalo, N.Y., 1813; d. Kansas City, Mo., Feb. 27, 1895. [1; 4]

Braymer, Daniel Harvey, electrical engineer, b. Hebron, N.Y., 1883; d. Omaha, Neb., Oct. 29, 1932. [10; 11]

Brayton, Alembert Winthrop, physician and ornithologist, b. Avon, N.Y., 1848; d. Indianapolis, Ind., Sept. 23, 1926. [10; 11]

Brazer, John, clergyman, b. Worcester, Mass., 1789; d. Charleston, S.C., Feb. 25, 1846. [1; 51]

Brazier, Marion Howard, journalist, b. Boston, Mass., 1850; d. Boston, Mass., about 1925. [10; 11]

Breakenridge, John, poet, b. Niagara, Upper Canada, 1820; d. 1854. [27]

Brearley, Harry Chase, journalist, b. Detroit, Mich., 1870; d. San Diego, Calif., Feb. 11, 1940.

Brearley, William Henry, journalist, b. Plymouth, Mich., 1846; d. New York, N.Y.. March 26, 1909. [10; 39]

Breasted, James Henry, orientalist and historian, b. Rockford, Ill., 1865; d. New York, N.Y., Dec. 2, 1935. [1a; 2; 7; 10; 11]

Breaux, Daisy (pseud.). See Calhoun, Mrs. Cornelia Donovan, née O'Donovan.

Breaux, Joseph A., jurist, b. Iberville parish, La., 1838; d. Iberia, La., July 23, 1926. [4; 10]

Breck, Edward, naval officer, b. San Francisco, Calif., 1861; d. South Milford, N.S., May 14, 1929. [10]

Breck, James Lloyd, clergyman, b. Philadelphia, Pa., 1818; d. Benicia, Calif., March 30, 1876. [2; 70]

Breck, Joseph, horticulturist, b. 1794; d. 1873.

Breck, Samuel, merchant and politician, b. Boston, Mass., 1771; d. Philadelphia, Pa., Aug. 31, 1862. [1; 2; 3]

Breck, Samuel, soldier and genealogist, b. Middleborough, Mass., 1834; d. Brookline, Mass., Feb. 23, 1918. [4; 10]

Breckenridge, James, clergyman and poet, b. Argyleshire, Scotland; d. Streetsville, Ont., Dec. 10, 1879. [27]

Breckenridge, Roeliff Morton, economist, b. Plymouth, O., 1870; d. May 5, 1914. [48]

Breckinridge, John, clergyman, b. Cabell's Dale, Ky., 1797; d. Cabell's Dale, Ky., Aug. 4, 1841. [2; 3; 34; 74]

Breckinridge, Robert Jefferson, clergyman, b. Cabell's Dale, Ky., 1800; d. Danville, Ky., Dec. 27, 1871. [1; 2; 3; 34; 74]

Breckinridge, Scott Dudley, physician, b. San Francisco, Calif., 1882; d. Lexington, Ky., Aug. 1, 1941.

Breckinridge, Sophonisba Preston, social worker, b. Lexington, Ky., 1866; d. Chicago, Ill., July 30, 1948. [10]

Breed, David Riddle, clergyman, b. Pittsburg, Pa., 1848; d. Pittsburg, Pa., Dec. 11, 1931. [10; 11]

Breed, William Denison, investment banker, b. Lake Forest, Ill., 1876; d. Indianapolis, Ind., March 25, 1931. [62]

Breed, William Pratt, clergyman, b. Greenbush, N.Y., 1816; d. Philadelphia, Pa., 1889. [6]

Breede, Adam, journalist and hunter of big game, b. Plattsmouth, Neb., 1879; d. Kansas City, Mo., March 1, 1928.

Breen, Andrew Edward, priest and educationist, b. Amitz, N.Y., 1863; d. St. Francis, Wis., Sept. 10, 1938. [21]

Breese, Burtis Burr, psychologist, b. Horseheads, N.Y., 1867; d. Cincinnati, O., July 31, 1939. [10]

Breese, Sidney, jurist, b. Whitesboro, N.Y., 1800; d. Pinckney, Ill., June 27, 1878. [1; 10]

Breese, Mrs. Zona, née Gale. See Gale, Zona.

Breidenbaugh, Edward Swayer, chemist, b. Newville, Pa., 1849; d. Gettysburg, Pa., Sept. 5, 1926. [10]

Breitman, Hans (pseud.). See Leland, Charles Godfrey.

Bremner, Archibald, journalist, b. Newfoundland, 1849; d. London, Ont., June 29, 1901.

Bremner, Benjamin, historian, b. 1851; d. Charlottetown, P.E.I., Dec. 29, 1938.

Brennan, Martin Stanislaus, priest, b. 1845; d. St. Louis, Mo., Oct. 4, 1927. [21]

Brennan, Richard, priest, b. about 1833; d. 1893.

Brent, Charles Henry, bishop, b. Newcastle, Ont., 1862; d. Lausanne, Switzerland, March 27, 1929. [1a; 2; 4; 10]

Brent, Henry Johnson, painter and editor, b. Washington, D.C., 1811; d. New York, N.Y., Aug. 3, 1880. [3; 4; 7]

Brent, Joseph Lancaster, soldier, b. Charles county, Md., 1826; d. Baltimore, Md., 1905. [10]

Brentford, Burke (pseud.). See Urner, Nathan D.

Breslich, Arthur Louis, educationist, b. Insterburg, Germany, 1873; d. Milwaukee, Wis., June 17, 1924. [10]

Breton, Pierre Napoléon, numismatist, b. Montreal, Que., 1858; d. Varennes, Que., Nov. 1917. [31]

Brett, George Sidney, philosopher, b. England, 1879; d. Toronto, Ont., Oct. 27, 1944. [30]

Brevard, Caroline Mays, educationist, b. Tallahassee, Fla., 1860; d. 1920. [34]

Brevoort, James Carson, civil engineer, b. New York, N.Y., 1818; d. Brooklyn, N.Y., Dec. 7, 1887. [3; 4]

Brewer, Abraham Titus, lawyer, b. Monroe county, O., 1841; d. Cleveland, O., April 17, 1933. [10]

Brewer, Clifton Hartwell, clergyman, b. Fitzwilliam, N.H., 1876; d. New Haven, Conn., Sept. 28, 1947. [51]

Brewer, Daniel Chauncey, lawyer, b. Boston, Mass., 1861; d. Boston, Mass., July 30, 1932. [10; 11]

Brewer, David Josiah, jurist, b. Smyrna, Asia Minor, 1837; d. Washington, D.C., March 28, 1910. [1; 2; 3; 4]

Brewer, George Emerson, surgeon, b. Westfield, N.Y., 1861; d. New York, N.Y., Dec. 24, 1939. [10]

Brewer, Josiah, missionary, b .Berkshire county, Mass., 1796; d. Stockbridge, Mass., Nov. 19, 1872. [3; 4]

Brewer, Luther Albertus, publisher and local historian, b. Welsh Run, Pa., 1858; d. Cedar Rapids, Ia., May 6, 1933. [7; 10; 11; 37]

Brewer, Nicholas Richard, painter, b. High Forest, Minn., 1857; d. St. Paul, Minn., Feb. 15, 1949. [4; 70]

Brewer, Thomas Mayo, ornithologist, b. Boston, Mass., 1814; d. Boston Mass., Jan. 24, 1880. [1; 2; 3; 4; 6]

Brewer, William Henry, botanist, b. Poughkeepsie, N.Y., 1828; d. New Haven, Conn., Nov. 2, 1910. [1; 3; 62]

Brewer, Willis, lawyer and politician, b. Sumter county, Ala., 1844; d. Montgomery, Ala., Oct. 30, 1912. [34]

Brewerton, George Douglas, soldier, b. Rhode Island, 1820; d. New York, N.Y., Jan. 31, 1901. [3; 6]

Brewster, Anne Maria Hampton, novelist, b. Philadelphia, Pa., 1818; d. 1892. [6]

Brewster, Charles Warren, journalist, b. Portsmouth, N.H., 1812; d. Portsmouth, N.H., Aug. 3, 1868. [3]

Brewster, Chauncey Bunce, bishop, b. Windham, Conn., 1848; d. Hartford, Conn., April 1, 1941. [4; 10; 62]

Brewster, Edward, playwright, b. Chicago, Ill., 1886; d. New York, N.Y., April 1, [10]

Brewster, Eugene Valentine, journalist and motion-picture director, b. Bay Shore, N.Y., 1871; d. Brooklyn, N.Y., Jan. 1, 1939. [7; 10; 11]

Brewster, Frederick Carroll, lawyer, b. Philadelphia, Pa., 1825; d. Charlotte, N.C., Dec. 30, 1898. [1; 2; 4]

Brewster, George, educationist, b. 1800; d. 1865.

Brewster, Harold Pomeroy, journalist, b. Ravenna, O., 1831; d. Rochester, N.Y., 1906. [4]

Brewster, James Henry, lawyer, b. New Haven, Conn., 1856; d. Denver, Colo., Oct. 7, 1920. [10; 62]

Brewster, Jonathan McDuffee, clergyman, b. Alton, N.H., 1835; d. Providence, R.I., June 2, 1882. [24]

Brewster, William, ornithologist, b. Wakefield, Mass., 1851; d. Cambridge, Mass., July 11, 1919. [1; 4; 10]

Brewster, William Nesbitt, missionary, b. Highland, O., 1862; d. Springfield, O., Nov. 22, 1916. [10]

Brick, Abraham Lincoln, politician, b. St. Joseph's county, Ind., 1860; d. Indianapolis, Ind., April 7, 1908. [10]

Brickner, Walter Max, surgeon, b. New York, N.Y., 1875; d. Atlantic Beach, Long Island, N.Y., July 22, 1930. [10; 11]

Bricktop (pseud.). See Small, George G.

Bridge, Horatio, naval officer, b. Augusta, Me., 1806; d. Athens, Pa., March 18, 1893. [2; 3]

Bridge, James Howard, secretary and journalist, b. Manchester, England, 1856; d. New York, N.Y., May 28, 1939. [7; 10]

Bridge, Norman, physician, b. Windsor, Vt., 1844; d. Los Angeles, Calif., Jan. 10, 1925. [10]

Bridge, Thomas, clergyman, b. near London, England, 1657; d. Boston, Mass., Sept. 26, 1715. [51]

Bridgeman, Thomas, horticulturist, d. 1850. [6]

Bridges, Calvin Blackman, geneticist, b. Schuyler Falls, N.Y., 1889; d. Dec. 27, 1938. [10; 13]

Bridges, Milton Arlanden, physician, b. New York, N.Y., 1894; d. New York, N.Y., Aug. 19, 1939. [10]

Bridges, Robert, poet and essayist, b. Shippensburg, Pa., 1858; d. Sept. 2, 1941. [7; 10; 11; 12]

Bridgman, Frederic Arthur, painter, b. Tuskegee, Ala., 1847; d. Rouen, France, Jan. 13, 1928. [1; 2; 3]

Bridgman, Mrs. Helen, née **Bartlett,** miscellaneous writer, b. Milwaukee, Wis., 1855; d. Oct. 17, 1935. [7; 11]

Bridgman, Herbert Lawrence, journalist and explorer, b. Amherst, Mass., 1844; d. at sea, Sept. 24, 1924. [1; 2; 4; 10]

Bridgman, Howard Allen, clergyman, b. Northampton, Mass., 1860; d. Shirley Centre, Mass., March 16, 1929. [10; 62]

Bridgman, Lewis Jesse, illustrator, b. Lawrence, Mass., 1857; d. Salem, Mass., May 2, 1931. [10; 11]

Bridgman, Marcus Fayette, poet, b. Windsor, Vt., 1824; d. Boston, Mass., Jan. 20, 1899. [49]

Bridgman, Raymond Landon, journalist, b. Amherst, Mass., 1848; d. Auburndale, Mass., Feb. 20, 1925. [10]

Bridgman, Thomas, historian, b. 1795; d. ?

Briggs, Charles Augustus, clergyman, b. New York, N.Y., 1841; d. New York, N.Y., June 8, 1913. [1; 7; 10]

Briggs, Charles Frederick, journalist, b. Nantucket, Mass., 1804; d. Brooklyn, N.Y., June 20, 1877. [1; 2; 3; 4; 7]

Briggs, Clara A., cartoonist, b. Reedsburg, Wis., 1875; d. New York, N.Y., Jan. 31, 1930. [1a; 7; 10]

Briggs, Mrs. Emily, née **Edson,** novelist, b. 1831; d. 1910.

Briggs, Erasmus, local historian, b. 1818; d. ?

Briggs, Jimuel (pseud.). See Thompson, Thomas Phillips.

Briggs, Le Baron Russell, educationist, b. Salem, Mass., 1855; d. Milwaukee, Wis., April 24, 1934. [1a; 2; 7; 10; 51]

Briggs, Lloyd Vernon, psychiatrist, b. Boston, Mass., 1863; d. Tucson, Ariz., Feb. 28, 1941. [7; 10; 11]

Brigham, Albert Perry, geographer, b. Perry, N.Y., 1855; d. Washington, D.C., March 31, 1932. [1a; 2; 10; 11]

Brigham, Amariah, physician, b. New Marlborough, Mass., 1798; d. Utica, N.Y., Sept. 8, 1849. [1; 2; 3; 4]

Brigham, Carl Campbell, psychologist, b. Marlborough, Mass., 1890; d. Princeton, N.J., Jan. 24, 1943. [10; 11]

Brigham, Charles Henry, clergyman, b. Boston, Mass., 1820; d. Brooklyn, N.Y., Feb. 19, 1879. [3; 51]

Brigham, Gershom Nelson, physician and poet, b. Fayston, Vt., 1820; d. Chicago, Ill., June 21, 1886. [39; 43]

Brigham, Johnson, journalist and librarian, b. Cherry Valley, N.Y., 1846; d. Des Moines, Ia., Oct. 8, 1936. [10; 11]

Brigham, Mrs. Sarah Jeanette, née **Lathbury,** illustrator and writer of books for young people, b. Manchester, N.Y., 1835; d. Oct. 18, 1929. [10]

Brigham, Willard Irving Tyler, genealogist, b. 1859; d. 1904.

Brigham, William Tufts, ethnologist, b. Boston, Mass., 1841; d. Honolulu, Hawaii, Jan, 30, 1926. [2; 10; 51]

Bright, James Wilson, philologist, b. Aaronsburg, Pa., 1852; d. Baltimore, Md., Nov. 29. 1926. [1; 2; 7; 10]

Bright, Jonathan Brown, genealogist, b. Waltham, Mass., 1800; d. Waltham, Mass., Dec. 17, 1879. [3]

Brightly, Frank Frederick, lawyer, b. 1845; d. Philadelphia, Pa., Feb. 12, 1920. [55]

Brightly, Frederick Charles, lawyer, b. Bungay, England, 1812; d. Germantown, Pa., Jan. 24, 1888. [1; 2; 4]

Brill, Abraham Arden, psychiatrist, b. Austria, 1874; d. New York, N.Y., March 2, 1948. [10; 11; 13]

Brill, George Reiter, illustrator and poet, b. Allegheny City, Pa., 1867; d. March 6, 1918. [10]

Brimmer, Martin, traveller, b. Boston, Mass., 1829; d. Boston, Mass., Jan. 14, 1896. [51]

Brinckerhoff, Isaac W., clergyman, b. Ithaca, N.Y., 1821; d. New York, N.Y., Feb. 24, 1910. [24]

Brincklé, Joshua Gordon, poet, d. Philadelphia, Pa., April 28, 1880. [55]

Brinckloe, William Draper, architect, b. 1872; d. 1933.

Brine, Mrs. Mary Dow, née **Northam,** writer of books for children, b. New York, N.Y., 1838; d. New York, N.Y., July 20, 1925. [7; 8]

Briney, John Benton, clergyman, b. 1839; d. ?

Brinkerhoff, Roeliff, banker and lawyer, b. Cayuga County, N.Y., 1828; d. Mansfield, O., June 4, 1911. [1; 10]

Brinley, Charles Augustus, manufacturer, b. Hartford, Conn., 1847; d. Philadelphia, Pa., March 2, 1919. [62]

Brinley, Francis, lawyer, b. Boston, Mass., 1800; d. 1889. [3; 51]

Brinsmade, Robert Bruce, mining engineer, b. Elmira, N.Y., 1873; d. Mexico, Sept. 28, 1936. [10; 11]

Brinton, Christian, art critic, b. West Chester, Pa., 1870; d. West Chester, Pa., July 14, 1942. [7; 10]

Brinton, Daniel Garrison, anthropologist, b. Thornbury, Pa. ,1837; d. Atlantic City, N.J., July 31, 1899. [1; 2; 3; 4; 7; 10; 62]

Brinton, John Hill, surgeon, b. Philadelphia, Pa., 1832; d. Philadelphia, Pa., March 18, 1907. [1; 2; 10]

Brisbane, Albert, reformer, b. Batavia, N.Y., 1809; d. Richmond, Va., May 1, 1890. [1; 3; 7]

Brisbane, Albert Hall, novelist, b. Charleston, S.C., about 1800; d. Summerville, S.C., Sept. 28, 1861. [3; 34]

Brisbane, Arthur, journalist, b. Buffalo, N.Y., 1864; d. New York, N.Y., Dec. 25, 1936. [4; 7; 10]

Brisbane, William Henry, clergyman, b. near Charleston, S.C., about 1803; d. Arena, Wis., April 5, 1878. [26]

Brisbin, James Sanks, soldier, b. Boalsburg, Pa., 1837; d. Philadelphia, Pa., Jan. 14, 1892. [3]

Brisco, Norris Arthur, economist, b. Napanee, Ont., 1875; d. Summit, N.J., May 9, 1944. [10]

Bristed, Charles Astor, educationist, b. New York, N.Y., 1820; d. Washington, D.C., Jan. 15, 1874. [1; 2; 3; 4; 5; 6; 7]

Bristed, John, clergyman, b. Sherborne, England, 1778; d. Bristol, R.I., Feb. 23, 1855. [1; 2; 3; 4; 7]

Bristol, Mrs. Augusta, née **Cooper,** poet and lecturer, b. Corydon, N.H., 1835; d. Vineland, N.J., May 9, 1910. [3]

Bristol, Elias Leroy Macomb, physician and poet, b. about 1852; d. Detroit, Mich., May 15, 1929.

Bristol, Frank Milton, bishop, b. Orleans county, N.Y., 1851; d. Upper Montclair, N.J., April 24, 1932. [2; 10]

Bristol, John Isaac Devoe, life insurance expert, b. Springwells, Mich., 1845; d. April 30, 1932. [10]

Bristol, Sherlock, clergyman, b. 1815; d. 1906.

Britan, Halbert Hains, psychologist, b. Bethlehem, Ind., 1874; d. Lewiston, Me., Aug. 5, 1945. [62]

Brittain, Alfred, clergyman, b. London, England, 1867; d. New Canaan, Conn., July 1, 1943.

Brittain, Carlo Bonaparte, naval officer, b. Pineville, Ky., 1867; d. Richmond, Ky., April 22, 1920. [10]

Brittain, John, naturalist, b. near Sussex, N.B., 1849; d. Ste. Anne de Bellevue, Que., March 17, 1913. [31a]

Brittan, Belle (pseud.). See Fuller, Hiram.

Brittan, Harriette G., missionary, b. England, about 1823; d. San Francisco, Calif., April 30, 1897. [6]

Brittan, Samuel Byron, physician, d. 1883.

Britton, Nathaniel Lord, botanist, b. Staten Island, N.Y., 1858; d. New York, N.Y., June 5, 1934. [1a; 2; 3; 4; 10; 13]

Britton, Wilton Everett, entomologist, b. Marlboro, Mass., 1868; d. New Haven, Conn., Feb. 15, 1939. [10; 13; 62]

Britts, Mrs. Mattie, née **Dyer,** writer of books for children, b. New York, N.Y., 1842; d. ? [6; 24]

Broaddus, Andrew, clergyman, b. Caroline county, Va., 1770; d. Salem, Va., Dec. 1, 1848. [2; 3; 24; 34]

Broaddus, Andrew, clergyman and genealogist, b. Caroline county, Va., 1818; d. Caroline county, Va., April 19, 1900. [24]

Broadhurst, George Howells, playwright, b. England, 1866; d. New York, N.Y., Jan. 4, 1937. [7]

Broadhurst, Thomas William, playwright and novelist, b. England, 1857; d. New York, N.Y., May 1, 1936. [2a]

Broadus, Edmund Kemper, educationist, b. Alexandria, Va., 1876; d. Edmonton, Alta., Dec. 17, 1936. [11; 27]

Broadus, John Albert, clergyman, b. Culpepper county, Va., 1827; d. Louisville, Ky., March 16, 1895. [24; 34]

Brock, Isaac, clergyman, b. near Winchester, England, 1829; d. Jan. 1, 1911. [27]

Brock, Robert Alonzo, historian, b. Richmond, Va., 1839. d; Richmond, Va., July 12, 1914. [7; 34]

Brockett, Linus Pierpont, physician, b. Canton, Conn., 1820; d. Brooklyn, N.Y., Jan. 13, 1893. [1; 3; 7; 24]

Brocklesby, John, educationist, b. West Bromwich, England, 1811; d. Hartford, Conn., June 21, 1889. [4; 6]

Brockway, Mrs. Alice, née **Pickford.** See Evans, Mrs. Alice, née Pickford.

Brockway, Beman, journalist, b. 1815; d. about 1892.

Brockway, Fred John, anatomist, b. South Sutton, N.H., 1860; d. Brattleboro, Vt., April 21, 1901. [10; 62]

Brockway, Thomas, clergyman, b. Lyme, Conn., 1744-5; d. Lyme, Conn., July 4, 1807. [62]

Brockway, Zebulon Reed, penologist, b. Lyme, Conn., 1827; d. Elmira, N.Y., Oct. 21, 1920. [1; 10]

Brodhead, Mrs. Eva Wilder, née **McGlasson,** novelist, b. 1870; d. Denver, Colo., Aug. 5, 1915. [7]

Brodhead, John Romeyn, historian, b. Philadelphia, Pa., 1814; d. New York, N.Y., May 6, 1873. [1; 3; 7]

Brokaw, Irving, artist, b. New York, 1869; d. West Palm Beach, Fla., March 19, 1939.

Brokmeyer, Henry Conrad, philosopher, b. near Minden, Prussia, 1828; d. St. Louis, Mo., July 26, 1906. [1; 7]

Bromwell, Henry Pelham Holmes, lawyer, poet, and freemason, b. Baltimore, Md., 1823; d. Denver, Colo., Jan. 7, 1903.

Bronfenbrenner, Mrs. Martha, née **Ornstein,** educationist, b. Vienna, Austria, 1878; d. Pittsburg, Pa., April, 1915.

Bronk, Isabelle, educationist, b. Duanesburg, N.Y., 1858; d. Media, Pa., Jan. 10, 1934. [10]

Bronson, Asa, clergyman, b. Saratoga county, N.Y., 1798; d. Fall River, Mass., Nov. 29, 1866. [24]

Bronson, Edgar Beecher, rancher, b. 1856; d. Feb. 4, 1917.

Bronson, Henry, physician and historian, b. Waterbury, Conn., 1804; d. New Haven, Conn., Nov. 26, 1893. [1; 4; 62]

Bronson, Sherlock Anson, clergyman and biographer, b. Waterbury, Conn., 1807; d. Mansfield, O., May 7, 1890. [4]

Bronson, Walter Cochrane, educationist, b. Roxbury, Mass., 1862; d. Oxford, England, June 2, 1928. [1; 7; 10; 24]

Bronson, William White, clergyman, b. 1816; d. Philadelphia, Pa., Oct. 9, 1900. [55]

Bronson-Howard, George Fitzalan. See Howard, George Fitzalan Bronson.

Brooke, Charles Frederick Tucker, educationist, b. Morgantown, W. Va., 1883; d. New Haven, Conn., June 22, 1946. [7; 10; 62]

Brooke, Francis Taliaferro, soldier, b. near Fredericksburg, Va., 1763; d. Fredericksburg, Va., March 3, 1851. [1; 3; 6]

Brooke, Mrs. Mary, née **Coffin,** octogenarian, b. 1833; d. after 1916.

Brooke, St. George Tucker, lawyer, b. University of Virginia, Va., 1844; d. Charles Town, W. Va., May 16, 1914. [10; 34]

Brooke, Wesley (pseud.). See Lunt, George.

Brookes, James Hall, clergyman, b. Pulaski, Tenn., 1830; d. 1897. [4]

Brookings, Robert Somers, manufacturer, b. Cecil county, Md., 1850; d. Washington, D.C., Nov., 15, 1932. [1a; 4; 10]

Brooks, Alfred Hulse, geologist and explorer, b. Ann Arbor, Mich., 1871; d. Washington, D.C., Nov. 21, 1924. [1; 2; 10]

Brooks, Amy, writer of stories for girls, d. 1931. [7]

Brooks, Arthur, clergyman, b. Boston, Mass., 1845; d. at sea, July 10, 1895. [4; 51]

Brooks, Bryant Butler, politician, b. Bernardston, Mass., 1861; d. Casper, Wyo., Dec. 8, 1944. [4; 10]

Brooks, Byron Alden, educationist, b. Jefferson county, N.Y., 1845; d. Brooklyn, N.Y., Sept. 28, 1911. [1; 4]

Brooks, Charles, clergyman, b. Medford, Mass., 1795; d. Medford, Mass., July 7, 1872. [1; 3; 4]

Brooks, Charles Alvin, clergyman, b. Watkins, N.Y., 1871; d. Chicago, Ill., Dec. 15, 1936. [10; 11]

Brooks, Charles Stephen, essayist and playwright, b. Cleveland, O., 1878; d. Cleveland, O., June 29, 1934. [7; 10; 11; 62]

Brooks, Charles Timothy, clergyman and poet, b. Salem, Mass., 1813; d. Newport, R.I., June 14, 1883. [1; 3; 4; 7]

Brooks, Charles Wesley, clergyman, b. Solon, N.Y., 1836; d. Watkins, N.Y., Sept. 21, 1911. [24]

Brooks, Christopher Parkinson, economist, b. England, 1866; d. New Bedford, Mass., Aug. 4, 1909. [10]

Brooks, Edward, mathematician, b. Rockland county, N.Y., 1831; d. Philadelphia, Pa., June 29, 1912. [3; 10]

Brooks, Elbridge Streeter, writer of books for young people, b. Lowell, Mass., 1846; d. Somerville, Mass., Jan. 7, 1902. [1; 2; 7; 10]

Brooks, Elisabeth Willard. See Kellner, Mrs. Elizabeth Willard, née Brooks.

Brooks, Erastus, journalist, b. Portland, Me., 1815; d. Staten Island, N.Y., Nov. 25, 1886. [1; 3]

Brooks, Eugene Clyde, educationist, b. Green county, N.C., 1871; d. Raleigh, N.C., Oct. 18, 1947. [7]

Brooks, Francis, poet, b. 1867; d. 1898.

Brooks, Fred Emerson, poet and playwright, b. Waverley, N.Y., 1850; d. Berkeley, Calif., June 1, 1923. [7; 10; 35]

Brooks, Harlow, physician, b. Medo, Minn., 1871; d. New York, N.Y., April 13, 1936. [10; 11; 13]

Brooks, Henry S., journalist, b. London, England; d. Dobbs Ferry, N.Y., 1910. [10]

Brooks, Henry Turner, pathologist, b. Baltimore, Md., 1861; d. New Rochelle, N.Y., Jan. 1, 1946. [13]

Brooks Jabez, educationist, b. Stockport, England, 1823; d. San José, Calif., Jan. 26, 1910. [10]

Brooks, James, journalist and politician, b. Portland, Me., 1810; d. Washington, D.C., April 30, 1873. [1; 3; 7]

Brooks, James Gordon, journalist and poet, b. Claverack, N.Y., 1801; d. Albany, N.Y., Feb. 20, 1841. [1; 2; 7]

Brooks, James Wilton, lawyer, b. New York, N.Y., 1853; d. Atlantic City, N.J., July 6, 1916. [10]

Brooks, Jennie, ornithologist, b. 1853; d. ? [10]

Brooks, John Graham, economist, b. Acworth, N.H., 1846; d. Cambridge, Mass., Feb. 8, 1938. [10]

Brooks, Mrs. Maria, née **Gowen,** poet, b. Medford, Mass., 1795; d. Matanzas, Cuba, Nov. 11, 1845. [1; 6; 7; 71]

Brooks, Nathan Covington, educationist, b. Cecil county, Md., 1819; d. Philadelphia, Pa., Oct. 6, 1898. [3; 4]

Brooks, Noah, journalist, b. Castine, Me., 1830; d. Pasadena, Calif., Aug. 16, 1903. [1; 2; 3; 4; 7]

Brooks, Phillips, bishop, b. Boston, Mass., 1835; d. Boston, Mass., Jan. 23, 1893. [1; 2; 3; 4; 5; 6; 7]

Brooks, Robert Clarkson, educationist, b. Piqua, O., 1874; d. Chester, Pa., Feb. 2, 1941. [7; 10]

Brooks, Mrs. Sarah, née **Warner,** poet and writer of short stories, d. Medford, Mass., 1906. [7; 10]

Brooks, Ulysses Robert, lawyer, b. Barnwell, S.C., 1846; d. 1917. [34]

Brooks, Walter, stockbroker, b. New York, N.Y., 1856; d. New York, N.Y., March 26, 1933. [62]

Brooks, William Keith, naturalist, b. Cleveland, O., 1848; d. Baltimore, Md., Nov. 12, 1908 [1; 10; 61]

Brooks, William Penn, educationist, b. South Scituate, Mass., 1851; d. Springfield, Mass., March 8, 1938. [10; 11]

Brookshire, Elijah Voorhees, lawyer and politician, b. Montgomery county, Ind., 1856; d. Springfield, Mass., April 17, 1936. [10]

Broome, Isaac, sculptor, b. Valcartier, Lower Canada, 1835; d. Trenton, N.J., May 4, 1922. [10]

Broomell, Isaac Norman, dental surgeon, b. Chester county, Pa., 1858; d. Philadelphia, Pa., March 23, 1941. [10; 11]

Brophy, Mrs. Loire, businesswoman, b. 1898; d. New York, N.Y., March 4, 1947.

Brophy, Truman William, oral surgeon, b. Will county, Ill., 1848; d. Chicago, Ill., Feb. 4, 1928. [1; 10]

Brosnahan, Katherine Mary. See Eleanore, Sister Mary.

Brosnahan, Timothy, priest, b. Alexandria, Va., 1856; d. Baltimore, Md., June 4, 1915. [10; 21]

Bross, William, journalist, b. Sussex county, N.J., 1813; d. Chicago, Ill., Jan. 27, 1890. [1; 7]

Brotherhead, William, bookseller, fl. 1849-1894. [7]

Brothers, Abram, physician, b. 1861; d. New York, N.Y., Oct. 13, 1910. [48]

Brotherston, Bruce Wallace, educationist, b. Cobourg, Ont., 1877; d. Holliston, Mass., April 17, 1947. [61]

Brotherton, Mrs. Alice, née **Williams,** poet, b. Cambridge, Ind.; d. Cincinnati, O., Feb. 9, 1930. [7; 10]

Brotherton, Theodore Widney, lawyer, b. Piqua, O., 1847; d. Los Angeles, Calif., Dec. 6, 1915.

Brougham, John, actor and playwright, b. Dublin, Ireland, 1810; d. New York, N.Y., June 7, 1880. [1; 2; 3; 7; 71]

Broughton, Leonard Gaston, clergyman, b. Wake county, N.C., 1864; d. Atlanta, Ga., Feb. 22, 1936. [10]

Broun, Heywood, journalist, b. Brooklyn, N.Y., 1888; d. New York, N.Y., Dec. 18, 1939. [7; 10; 11]

Brousseau, Kate, psychologist, b. Ypsilanti, Mich., 1862; d. Los Angeles, Calif., July 8, 1938. [10]

Broussard, James Francis, educationist, b. St. Martinville, La., 1881; d. Baton Rouge, La., Nov. 2, 1942. [10; 21]

Brower, Daniel Roberts, physician, b. Philadelphia, Pa., 1839; d. Chicago, Ill., March 1, 1909. [4; 10]

Brower, Harriette Moore, musician, b. Albany, N.Y., 1869; d. New York, N.Y., March 10, 1928. [10]

Brower, Jacob Vrandenberg, explorer and archaeologist, b. York, Mich., 1844; d. St. Cloud, Minn., June 1, 1905. [1; 2; 7; 70]

Brower, William Leverich, church historian, b. New York, N.Y., 1846; d. New York, N.Y., May 9, 1940. [10]

Brown, Aaron Venable, politician, b. Brunswick county Va., 1795; d. Washington, D.C., March 8, 1859. [1; 4; 34]

Brown, Abbie Farwell, poet and writer of books for children, b. Boston, Mass., 1875; d. Boston, Mass., March 5, 1927. [2; 7; 10]

Brown, Abram English, historian, b. Bedford, Mass., 1849; d. Bedford, Mass., Feb. 25, 1909. [10]

Brown, Addison, jurist and botanist, b. West Newbury, Mass., 1830; d. New York, N.Y., April 9, 1930. [1; 10; 51]

Brown, Albert Gallatin, politician, b. Chester district, S.C., 1813; d. near Terry, Hinds county, Miss., June 12, 1880. [1; 4; 34]

Brown, Alexander, historian, b. Nelson county, Va., 1843; d. Nelson county, Va., Aug. 29, 1906. [1; 2; 4; 7; 34]

Brown, Alonzo Leighton, soldier, b. Auburn, N.Y., 1838; d. Brownton, Minn., Oct. 11, 1904. [70]

Brown, Arthur Charles Lewis, educationist, b. Avon, N.Y., 1869; d. Evanston, Ill., June 28, 1946. [7; 10]

Brown, Bolton Coit, artist, b. Dresden, N.Y., 1864; d. New York, N.Y., Sept. 15, 1936. [7; 10]

Brown, Burdette Boardman, clergyman, b. Andover, N.Y., 1871; d. Los Angeles, Calif., April 24, 1942. [10; 62]

Brown, Calvin Smith, educationist, b. Obion county, Tenn., 1866; d. University, Miss., Sept. 10, 1945. [7; 11]

Brown, Carleton Fairchild, educationist, b. Oberlin, O., 1869; d. Montclair, N.J., June 25, 1941. [7; 10; 11]

Brown, Caroline (pseud.) See Krout, Caroline Virginia.

Brown, Carroll Neidé, lexicographer, b. Abingdon, Mass., 1869; d. New York, N.Y., Dec. 15, 1938. [51]

Brown, Charles Brockden, novelist, b. Philadelphia, Pa., 1771; d. Philadelphia, Pa., Feb. 22, 1810. [1; 2; 4; 7]

Brown, Charles Rufus, clergyman, b. Kingston, N.H., 1849; d. Stoneham, Mass., Feb. 2, 1914. [1; 2; 10]

Brown, Charles Walter, educationist, b. St. Louis, Mo., 1866; d. Chicago, Ill., Oct. 9, 1934. [10]

Brown, Charles William, sailor, b .Newburyport, Mass., 1858; d. Sewickley, Pa., March 6, 1928. [10]

Brown, Christian Henry, oculist, b. Lancaster, Pa., 1857; d. Philadelphia, Pa., Dec. 11, 1933. [10; 11]

Brown, Cyril, journalist, b. Rochester, N.Y., 1887; d. Oceanside, Long Island, N.Y., Oct. 7, 1949.

Brown, David Arthur, local historian, b. Attleboro, Mass., 1839; d. Concord, N.H., Sept. 9, 1903.

Brown, David Paul, lawyer and playwright, b. Philadelphia, Pa., 1795; d. Philadelphia, Pa., July 11, 1872. [1; 3; 4; 6; 7]

Brown, David Walter, lawyer, b. Ogdensburg, N.Y., 1852; d. New York, N.Y., May 5, 1920. [62]

Brown, Mrs. Demetra, née **Vaka,** novelist and historian, b. Constantinople, Turkey, 1877; d. Chicago, Ill., Dec. 17, 1946. [7]

Brown, Edmund Woodward, clergyman, b. Schuyler county, N.Y., 1831; d. San Francisco, Calif., May 29, 1902. [62]

Brown, Edna Adelaide, librarian and writer of books for children, b. Providence, R.I., 1875; d. Andover, Mass., June 23, 1944. [7; 10; 11]

Brown, Edward Osgood, lawyer, b. Salem, Mass., 1847; d. Chicago, Ill., Dec. 8, 1923. [10]

Brown, Elizabeth Virginia, writer of books for children, b. 1866; d. 1915.

Brown, Elmer Ellsworth, educationist, b. Klantone, N.Y., 1861; d. New York, N.Y., Nov. 3, 1934. [1a; 4; 7; 10]

Brown, Ernest William, mathematician ,b. Hull, England, 1866; d. New Haven, Conn., July 22, 1938. [10; 11]

Brown, Fortune Charles, clergyman, b. about 1813; d. 1888.

Brown, Francis, theologian, b. Hanover, N.H., 1849; d. New York, N.Y., Oct. 15, 1916. [1; 2; 4; 49]

Brown, Francis Henry, physician, b. Boston, Mass., 1835; d. Boston, Mass., May 16, 1917. [10; 51]

Brown, Frank Clyde, educationist, b. Harrisonburg, Va., 1870; d. Durham, N.C., June 2, 1943. [10]

Brown, Frank Llewellyn, writer on religious education, b. Brooklyn, N.Y., 1862; d. Brooklyn, N.Y., March 23, 1922. [10]

Brown, Frederic Kenyon, clergyman, b. Oldham, England, 1882; d. Lancaster, Mass., Dec. 7, 1935. [10]

Brown, George, clergyman, b. 1792; d. ?

Brown, George Pliny, educationist, b. Lenox, O., 1836; d. Bloomington, Ill., Feb. 1, 1910. [1; 10]

Brown, George Washington, physician, b. 1820; d. Rockford, Ill., Feb. 5, 1915.

Brown, George Washington, oil operator, b. 1828; d. ?

Brown, George William, jurist, b. Baltimore, Md., 1812; d. Lake Mohonk, N.Y., Sept. 6, 1840. [1; 34]

Brown, George William, missionary, b. 1870; d. Hartford, Conn., Dec. 4, 1932. [2a]

Brown, Glenn, architect, b. Fauquier county, Va., 1854; d. Washington, D.C., April 22, 1932. [10; 11]

Brown, Goodwin, nutritionist, b. 1852; d. 1912.

Brown, Goold, grammarian, b. Providence, R.I., 1791; d. Lyme, Mass., March 31, 1857. [1; 3; 4; 7]

Brown, Harold Haven, artist, b. Malden, Mass., 1869; d. Provincetown, Mass., April 7, 1932. [10]

Brown, Helen Dawes, educationist and writer of books for girls, b. Concord, Mass., 1857; d. Chicago, Ill., Sept. 6, 1941. [7; 10; 11]

Brown, Henry, lawyer and historian, b. Hebron, Conn., 1789; d. Chicago, Ill., May 16, 1849. [36]

Brown, Henry Billings, jurist, b. South Lee, Mass., 1836; d. Bronxville, N.Y., Sept. 4, 1913. [1; 10; 62]

Brown, Henry Harrison, lecturer, b. Uxbridge, Mass., 1840; d. Glenwood, Calif., May 8, 1918. [10]

Brown, Howard Nicholson, clergyman, b. Columbia, N.Y., 1849; d. Framingham Centre, Mass., Dec. 13, 1932. [10]

Brown, Hubert William, missionary, b. 1858; d. 1906.

Brown, Irving (pseud.). See Adams, William Taylor.

Brown, Irving, legal writer, b. Oneida county, N.Y., 1835; d. Feb. 6, 1899. [3]

Brown, Irving Henry, educationist, b. Madison, Wis., 1888; d. Tucson, Ariz., Dec. 28, 1940. [7; 10; 11]

Brown, Isaac Hinton, publisher, b. 1842; d. 1889.

Brown, Isaac Van Arsdale, clergyman, b. Somerset county, N.J., 1784; d. Trenton, N.J., April 19, 1861. [1; 3; 56]

Brown, James, poet, b. Forfarshire, Scotland, 1790; d. near St. Andrews, N.B., 1870. [27]

Brown, James, grammarian, fl. 1815-1854. [3]

Brown, James Fuller, clergyman, b. Scotch Plains, N.J., 1819; d. Mullica Hill, N.J., April 26, 1901. [24]

Brown, James Moore, frontiersman, b. 1799; d. 1862.

Brown, James Stephens, pioneer, b. 1828; d. ?

Brown, Jefferson Beale, jurist, b. Key West, Fla., 1857; d. Key West, Fla., May 4, 1937.

Brown, John Augustus, local historian, b. Exeter, N.H., 1857; d. Exeter, N.H., Sept. 12, 1910.

Brown, John Crosby, banker, b. New York, N.Y., 1838; d. West Orange, N.J., June 25, 1909. [10]

Brown, John Franklin, educationist and editor, b. Springboro, O., 1865; d. New Rochelle, N.Y., Feb. 15, 1940. [10; 11]

Brown, John Henry, pioneer, b. 1810; d. 1905.

Brown, John Henry, historian, b. 1820; d. 1895. [4; 34]

Brown, John Henry, poet, b. Ottawa, Ont,. 1859; d. Ottawa, Ont., Nov. 30, 1946. [31a]

Brown, John Howard, editor, b. Rinebeck, N.Y., 1840; d. Brooklyn, N.Y., April 22, 1917. [10]

Brown, John Mason, historian, b. 1837; d. 1890. [34]

Brown, John Newton, clergyman, b. New London, Conn., 1803; d. Germantown, Pa., May 15, 1868. [3]

Brown, John Patrick, educationist, b. Philadelphia, Pa., 1839; d. Boston, Mass., May 13, 1896. [52]

Brown, John Pinkney, forester, b. Rising Sun, Ind., 1842; d. Connersville, Ind., 1915. [10]

Brown, John Porter, orientalist, b. Chillicothe, O., 1814; d. Constantinople, Turkey, April 28, 1872. [1; 3]

Brown, John Price, physician and novelist, b. Manchester, England, 1844; d. Toronto, Ont., April 3, 1938. [27]

Brown, John Richard, clergyman and educationist, b. Brooklyn, N.Y., 1870; d. St. Louis, Mo., Oct. 30, 1926. [10]

Brown, John Walker, clergyman, b. 1814; d. 1849.

Brown, Jonathan, physician, b. Kensington, N.H., 1805; d. Kensington, N.H., Feb. 13, 1864. [49]

Brown, Joseph, clergyman, b. 1837; d. 1918.

Brown, Joseph Clinton, educationist, b. Piqua, O., 1879; d. New York, N.Y., Jan. 16, 1945. [10; 11]

Brown, Joseph Epes, educationist, d. Ashville, N.C., May 5, 1937.

Brown, Joseph Henry, historian, b. Illinois, 1831; d. Portland, Ore., Aug. 15, 1898. [41]

Brown, Joseph M., politician, b. Canton, Ga., 1851; d. Marietta, Ga., March 3, 1932. [10; 34]

Brown, Kate Louise, educationist, b. Adams, Mass., 1857; d. Dorchester, Mass., Dec. 31, 1921. [10]

Brown, Katherine Holland, novelist, b. Alton, Ill.; d. Orlando, Fla., June 2, 1931. [10]

Brown, Lawrason, physician, b. Baltimore, Md., 1871; d. Saranac Lake, N.Y., Dec. 26, 1938. [10; 11; 49]

Brown, Leonard, poet and school-teacher, b. 1837; d. Des Moines, Ia., 1914. [37]

Brown, Mrs. Letitia J., née Shaw, biographer, b. 1829; d. 1887.

Brown, Lewis, local historian, b. 1858; d. Simcoe, Ont., Nov. 26, 1930.

Brown, Marie Adelaide. See Shipley, Mrs. Mary Adelaide, née Brown.

Brown, Marshall Stewart, historian, b. Keene, N.H., 1875; d. New York, N.Y., Sept. 18, 1948. [10; 14; 47]

Brown, Mrs. Mary Elizabeth, née Adams, genealogist and compiler, b. 1842; d. 1917.

Brown, Mrs. Mary, née Hosmer, local historian, b. Detroit, Mich., 1856; d. 1931. [11]

Brown, Mary Josephine, writer of books for children, b. New York, N.Y., 1875; d. 1912. [21]

Brown, Mary Willcox. See Glenn, Mrs. Mary Willcox, née Brown.

Brown, Matthew, educationist, b. Northumberland county, Pa., 1776; d. Pittsburg, Pa., July 29, 1853. [4]

Brown, Moses True, elocutionist, b. Deerfield, N.H., 1827; d. Sandusky, O., 1900. [36; 10]

Brown, Neal, lawyer, b. Hebron, Wis., 1856; d. Watkins, N.Y., Sept. 8, 1917. [10; 44]

Brown, Olympia, feminist, b. Kalamazoo county, Mich., 1835; d. Baltimore, Md., Oct. 23, 1926. [1; 4; 6; 44]

Brown, Oswald Eugene, clergyman and educationist, b. Canton, Mo., 1861; d. Nashville, Tenn., Oct. 22, 1939. [10]

Brown, Peter, journalist, b. Scotland, about 1784; d. Toronto, Ont., 1863. [27]

Brown, Peter Arrell, lawyer, b. Philadelphia, Pa., 1782; d. 1860. [6]

Brown, Mrs. Phoebe Allen, née Hinsdale, hymn-writer, b. Canaan, N.Y., 1783; d. Marshall, Ill., Oct. 10, 1861. [1; 2; 6; 7]

Brown, Ray, illustrator, b. Groton, Conn., 1865; d. New York, N.Y., April 30, 1944. [10]

Brown, Robert Elliott, clergyman, b. Middleville, Ont., 1873; d. Oberlin, O., Nov. 25, 1938. [10; 62]

Brown, Rome Green, lawyer, b. Montpelier, Vt., 1862; d. Minneapolis, Minn., May 22, 1926. [10; 51]

Brown, Samuel Boardman, geologist, b. Preston county, W. Va., 1860; d. Sept. 18, 1926. [11]

Brown, Samuel Gilman, biographer, b. North Yarmouth, Me., 1813; d. Utica, N.Y., Nov. 4, 1885. [1; 3; 49]

Brown, Samuel Horton, physician, b. Philadelphia, Pa., 1878; d. Philadelphia, Pa., June 12, 1940. [10]

Brown, Samuel R., historian, b. 1775; d. Cherry Valley, N.Y., Sept. 15, 1817. [3]

Brown, Samuel Robbins, missionary, b. East Windsor, Conn., 1810; d. Munson, Mass., June, 1880. [2; 4; 6; 62]

Brown, Sanford Miller, clergyman, b. Yodkin county, N.C., 1855; d. Kansas City, Mo., Sept. 21, 1938. [10]

Brown, Solyman, dentist and educationist, b. Litchfield, Conn., 1790; d. Dodge Center, Minn., Feb. 13, 1876. [1; 7; 62]

Brown, Stinson Joseph, naval officer, b. Penn Yan, N.Y., 1854; d. Nice, France, Dec. 20, 1923. [10]

Brown, Tarleton, soldier, b. Barnwell district, S.C., 1754; d. 1846. [3]

Brown, Theron, clergyman, b. Willimantic, Conn., 1832; d. Newtonville, Mass., Feb. 14, 1914. [7; 10; 62]

Brown, Thomas Allston, historian, b. Newburyport, Mass., 1836; d. New York, N.Y., April 2, 1918. [7; 10]

Brown, Thomas Edwin, clergyman, b. Washington, D.C., 1841; d. Independence, Kans., Jan. 27, 1924. [10]

Brown, Thomas Kite, lexicographer, b. Westown, Pa., 1885; d. Philadelphia, Pa., June 5, 1944. [11]

Brown, Thomas Storrow, journalist, b. St. Andrews, N.B., 1803; d. Montreal, Que., December, 1888. [27]

Brown, Thurlow Weed, journalist, d. Fort Atkinson, Wis., May 4, 1866. [3]

Brown, Valentine, poet, b. Portland, Ore., 1862; d. ? [41]

Brown, Vandyke (pseud.). See Cook, Marc.

Brown, W. Kennedy, clergyman, b. Fayette county, Pa., 1834; d. Oct., 1915. [10]

Brown, Waldo Franklin, agriculturist, b. 1832; d. ?

Brown, Walter Lee, mining engineer, b. 1853; d. Evanston, Ill., 1904.

Brown, William Adams, clergyman and educationist, b. New York, N.Y., 1865; d. New York, N.Y., Dec. 15, 1943. [7; 10; 11; 62]

Brown, William Carlos, railway president, b. 1853; d. Pasadena, Calif., Dec. 6, 1924. [4; 10]

Brown, William Garrott, historian, b. Marion, Ala., 1868; d. New Canaan, Conn., Oct. 19, 1913. [3; 4; 7; 51]

Brown, William Harvey, traveller, b. 1862; d. 1913.

Brown, William Henry, biographer, b. 1808; d. 1883.

Brown, William Henry, botanist, b. Richmond, Va., 1884; d. Baltimore, Md., Nov. 9, 1939. [10; 11; 13]

Brown, William Hill, novelist, b. Boston, Mass., 1765; d. Boston, Mass., Sept. 2, 1793. [1a; 5; 4; 7]

Brown, William Horace, novelist, b. near Logansport, Ind., 1855; d. Chicago, Ill., March 19, 1917. [4; 10]

Brown, William Montgomery, bishop, b. near Orrville, O., 1855; d. Galion, O., Oct. 31, 1937. [10; 11]

Brown, William Perry, writer of books for boys. b. Indian territory, U.S.A., 1847; d. Sept. 4, 1923. [7; 34]

Brown, William Wells, negro reformer, b. Lexington, Ky., about 1816; d. Chelsea, Mass., Nov. 6, 1884. [7; 9]

Brown, William Young, clergyman, b. 1827; d. 1914.

Brown-Buck, Mrs. **Lillie,** née **West,** actress and drama critic, b. West Burlington, Ia., 1860; d. Chicago, Ill., July 30, 1939. [10]

Browne, Albert Gallatin, lawyer, b. Salem, Mass., 1835; d. Boston, Mass., June 25, 1891. [4; 6]

Browne, Mrs. **Alice,** née **Harriman,** novelist and poet, b. 1861; d. 1925.

Browne, Causten, lawyer, b. Washington, D.C., 1828; d. Boston, Mass., 1909. [4; 10]

Browne, Charles, physician, b. Philadelphia, Pa., 1875; d. Princeton, N.Y., Aug. 16, 1947. [55]

Browne, Charles Farrar, humorist, b. near Waterford, Me., 1834; d. Southampton, England, March 6, 1867. [1; 2; 3; 4; 5; 6; 7; 71]

Browne, Daniel Jay, agricultural and scientific writer, b. Freemont, N.H., 1804; d. ? [1]

Browne, Dunn (pseud.). See Fisk, Samuel.

Browne, Francis Fisher, editor, b. South Halifax, Vt., 1843; d. Santa Barbara, Calif., May 11, 1913. [1; 2; 7; 10]

Browne, George Henry, educationist, b. Natick, Mass., 1857; d. Cambridge, Mass., Jan. 20, 1931. [10; 51]

Browne, George Waldo, journalist, b. Deerfield, N.H., 1851; d. Manchester, N.H., Aug, 13, 1930. [2; 7; 10; 11]

Browne, Irving, lawyer, b. Marshall, N.Y., 1835; d. Buffalo, N.Y., Feb. 6, 1899. [1; 4; 7]

Browne, Mrs. **J. D. H.** See Browne, Mrs. Tryphena Matilda, née Archer.

Browne, John Ross, traveller, b. Dublin, Ireland, 1821; d. Oakland, Calif., Dec. 8, 1875. [1; 2; 3; 4; 6; 7]

Browne, Junius Henri, journalist, b. Seneca Falls, N.Y., 1833; d. New York, N.Y., April 2, 1902 [1; 4; 6; 7]

Browne, Lewis, religious writer, b. London, England, 1897; d. Santa Monica, Calif., Jan. 3, 1949. [10; 35]

Browne, Lewis Allen, playwright, b. North Sandwich, N.H., 1876; d. West Englewood, N.J., May 24, 1937. [7; 10]

Browne, Patrick William, priest, b. Carbonear, Newfoundland, 1864; d. Washington, D.C., 1937. [21]

Browne, Porter Emerson, playwright and novelist, b. Beverley, Mass., 1879; d. Norwalk, Conn., Sept. 20, 1934. [7; 10]

Browne, Mrs. **Tryphena Matilda,** née **Archer,** poet and novelist, b. 1837; d. 1933.

Browne, Walter, playwright, b. 1856; d. 1911.

Browne, William Hand, educaticnist, b. Baltimore, Md., 1828; d. Baltimore, Md., Dec. 13, 1912. [2; 7; 10]

Browne, William Hardcastle, lawyer, b. Philadelphia, Pa., 1840; d. Philadelphia, Pa., Feb. 14, 1906. [10]

Brownell, Atherton, journalist and playwright, b. Lynn, Mass., 1866; d. New York, N.Y., April 22, 1924. [10]

Brownell, Charles De Wolf, anthropologist, b. 1822; d. ?

Brownell, Clarence Ludlow, educationist, b. Hartford, Conn., 1864; d. Jacksonville, Fla., Feb. 2, 1927. [2; 10]

Brownell, George Griffin, educationist, b. Fairfield, N.Y., 1869; d. Tuscaloosa, Ala., Aug. 31, 1931. [10]

Brownell, Henry Howard, poet and historian, b. Providence, R.I., 1820; d. East Hartford, Conn., Oct. 31, 1872. [1; 2; 3; 4; 6; 7]

Brownell, Thomas Church, bishop, b. Westport, Mass., 1778; d. Hartford, Conn., Jan. 13, 1865. [2; 4; 6]

Brownell, William Crary, literary critic, b. New York, N.Y., 1851; d. Williamstown, Mass., July 22, 1928. [1; 2; 4; 7; 10]

Browning, Charles Clifton, physician, b. Denver, Ill., 1861; d. San Marino, Calif., Sept. 28, 1939. [35]

Browning, Charles Henry, genealogist, b. Cincinnati, O.; d. Ardmore, Pa., June, 1926. [10]

Browning, Henry C. (pseud.). See Ritchie, Mrs. Anna Cora, née Ogden.

Browning, Philip Embury, chemist, b. Rhinebeck, N.Y., 1866; d. New Haven, Conn., Jan. 2, 1937. [10; 13; 62]

Browning, Webster E., missionary, b. Brownsville, Mo., 1869; d. Cleveland, O., April 16, 1942. [7; 56]

Browning, William, neurologist, b. New London county, Conn., 1855; d. Brooklyn, N.Y., Jan. 5, 1941. [10]

Browning, William Garritson, clergyman, b. 1825; d. 1910.

Browning, William Webb, physician, b. Metuchen, N.J., 1852; d. Brooklyn, N.Y., Oct. 3, 1900.

Brownjohn, John (pseud.). See Talbot, Charles Remington.

Brownlee, William Craig, clergyman, b. Scotland, 1784; d. New York, N.Y., Feb. 10, 1860. [1; 2; 3; 5]

Brownlow, William Gannaway, clergyman, b. Wythe county, Va., 1805; d. Knoxville, Tenn., April 29, 1877. [1; 2; 6; 34]

Brown-Potter, Mrs. **Cora.** See Potter, Mrs. Cora, née Urquhart.

Brownson, Carleton Lewis, educationist, b. New Canaan, Conn., 1866; d. Goshen, N.Y., Sept, 26, 1948. [7; 10]

Brownson, Henry Francis, priest, b. Canton, Mass., 1835; d. Detroit, Mich., Dec. 17, 1913. [4; 21]

Brownson, Josephine Van Dyke, educationist, b. Detroit, Mich.; d. Detroit, Mich., Nov. 10, 1942. [11; 21]

Brownson, Orestes Augustus, publicist, b. Stockbridge, Vt., 1803; d. Detroit, Mich., April 17, 1876. [1; 2; 3; 4; 6; 7]

Brownson, Sarah M. See Tenney, Mrs. Sarah M., née Brownson.

Brubacher, Abram Roger, educationist, b. Lebanon, Pa., 1870; d. Albany, N.Y., Aug. 23, 1939. [10; 11]

Brubaker, Albert Philson, physiologist, b. Somerset, Pa., 1852; d. Philadelphia, Pa., April 29, 1943. [13]

Bruce, Andrew Alexander, jurist, b. India, 1866; d. Chicago, Ill., Dec. 6, 1934. [1a; 10]

Bruce, Arthur Loring (pseud.). See Crowninshield, Francis Welch.

Bruce, Dwight Hall, historian, b. Lenox, N.Y., 1834; d. Syracuse, N.Y., 1908. [10]

Bruce, Harold Lawton, educationist, b. Belchertown, Mass., 1887; d. Berkeley, Calif., April 6, 1934. [10; 62]

Bruce, Helm, lawyer, b. Louisville, Ky., 1860; d. Louisville, Ky. Aug. 10, 1927. [4; 10]

Bruce, James Douglas, educationist, b. Charlotte county, Va., 1862; d. Knoxville, Tenn., Feb. 19, 1923. [4; 10]

Bruce, Kenneth, publisher, b. Poughkeepsie, N.Y., 1876; d. Hot Springs, Va., Sept. 3, 1916.

Bruce, Philip Alexander, historian and biographer, b. Staunton Hill, Va., 1856; d. Charlottesville, Va., Aug. 16, 1933. [1a; 7; 10; 11]

Bruce, Wallace, lecturer, b. Hillsdale, N.Y., 1844; d. De Funiak Springs, Fla., Jan. 2, 1914. [3; 7; 10]

Bruce, William Cabell, lawyer, politician and biographer, b. Staunton Hill, Va., 1860; d. Baltimore, Md., May 9, 1946. [4; 7; 10; 11]

Bruchési, Louis Joseph Paul Napoléon, archbishop, b. Montreal, Que., 1855; d. Montreal, Que., Sept. 20, 1939. [27; 32]

Bruen, Edward Tunis, physician, b. 1851; d. Philadelphia, Pa., 1889. [55]

Bruen, Matthias, clergyman, b. Newark, N.J., 1793; d. New York N.Y., Sept. 6. 1829. [3]

Brumbaugh, Martin Grove, educationist, b. Huntingdon county, Pa., 1862; d. Pinehurst, N.C., March 14, 1930. [10; 11]

Brummitt, Dan Brearley, clergyman, b. Batley, England, 1867; d. Kansas City, Mo., April 5, 1939. [10]

Brun, Samuel Jacques, chronicler, b. France, 1857; d. San José, Calif., after 1907. [35]

Brundage, Albert Harrison, toxicologist, b. Candor, N.Y., 1862; d. Central Islip, Long Island, N.Y., March 12, 1936. [10]

Brundage, William Milton, clergyman, b. Stone Ridge, N.Y., 1857; d. Westfield, N.Y., Aug. 14, 1921. [10]

Bruneau, Joseph, priest, b. Lyons, France, 1866; d. Baltimore, Md., Aug. 17, 1933. [21]

Bruner, Jane Woodworth, novelist, b. California, about 1850; d. Long Beach, Calif., about 1925. [35]

Bruner, Lawrence, entomologist, b. Catasauqua, Pa., 1856; d. Lincoln, Neb., Jan. 30, 1937. [10]

Brunet, Louis Ovide, priest and botanist, b. Quebec, Lower Canada, 1826; d. Quebec, Que., Oct. 2, 1877. [32]

Brunner, Arnold William, architect, b. New York, N.Y., 1857; d. New York, N.Y., Feb. 12, 1925. [10]

Brunner, David B., educationist, b. Amity, Pa., 1835; d. 1903.

Brunowe, Marion, J. (pseud.). See Brown, Mary Josephine.

Brunson, Alfred, clergyman, b. Danbury, Conn., 1793; d. Prairie du Chien, Wis., Aug. 3, 1882.

Brunton, David William, mining engineer, b. Ayr, Ont., 1849; d. Denver, Colo., Dec. 20, 1927. [1; 10]

Brush, Mrs. Christine, née Chaplin, artist and novelist, b. 1842; d. Brooklyn, N.Y., Feb. 3, 1892. [7]

Brush, George Jarvis, mineralogist, b. Brooklyn, N.Y., 1831; d. New Haven, Conn., Feb. 6, 1912. [1; 2; 3; 4; 62]

Brush, Mrs. Mary Elizabeth, née Quackenbush, novelist, b. 1857; d. ?

Brushingham, John Patrick, clergyman, b. Cuba, N.Y., 1855; d. Chicago, Ill., April 7, 1927. [4; 10]

Brutus (pseud.). See Turnbull, Robert James.

Bryan, Clark W., advertiser, b. 1824; d. 1899.

Bryan, Daniel, poet, b. 1795; d. 1866. [19; 34]

Bryan, Elmer Burritt, educationist, b. Van Wert, O., 1865; d. Detroit, Mich., Oct. 15, 1934. [10]

Bryan, Enoch Albert, educationist, b. Bloomington, Ind., 1855; d. Pullman, Wash., Nov. 6, 1941. [10]

Bryan, George, lawyer, b. Allegheny, Pa., 1860; d. Richmond, Va., Feb. 26, 1930. [10; 11]

Bryan, George Sands, poet and biographer, b. Matteawan, N.Y., 1879; d. Mount Vernon, N.Y., Dec. 22, 1943. [7; 10; 11]

Bryan, James, physician, b. 1810; d. Elizabeth, N.J., Nov. 5, 1881. [56]

Bryan, Mary Edwards, journalist and novelist, b. Jefferson county, Fla., 1842; d. Atlanta, Ga., June 15, 1913. [1; 3; 7; 10]

Bryan, William Jennings, politician, b. Salem, Ill., 1860; d. Dayton, Tenn., July 26, 1925. [1; 2; 3; 4; 5; 6; 7]

Bryan, William Swan Plumer, clergyman, b. Alleghenv City, Pa., 1856; d. Chicago, Ill., May 28, 1925. [10]

Bryan, Worcester Allen, surgeon, b. Alexandria, Tenn., 1873; d. Nashville, Tenn., April 30, 1940. [10; 11]

Bryant, Alfred, clergyman, b. Springfield, N.Y., 1807; d. Lansing, Mich., June 2, 1881. [30]

Bryant, Arthur, forester, b. 1803; d. 1883. [6]

Bryant, Charles S., lawyer, b. Ontario county, N.Y., 1808; d. St Paul, Minn., May 1, 1885. [70]

Bryant, Edwin, pioneer, b. Massachusetts, 1805; d. Louisville, Ky., 1869. [3; 7; 34]

Bryant, Edwin Eustace, lawyer, b. Milton, Vt., 1835; d. Madison, Wis., 1903. [10]

Bryant, Frank Augustus, physician, b. North Jackson, Pa., 1851; d. White Plains, N.Y., April, 1921. [4]

Bryant, Henry Grier, explorer, b. Allegheny City, Pa., 1859; d. Philadelphia, Pa., Dec. 7, 1932. [2; 10]

Bryant, Joel, physician, b. Suffolk county, N.Y., 1813; d. Brooklyn, N.Y., Nov. 20, 1868. [3]

Bryant, John Delavan, physician, b. 1811; d. Philadelphia, Pa., Aug. 2, 1877. [6]

Bryant, John Howard, poet, b. Cummington, Mass., 1807; d. Princeton, Ill., Jan. 14, 1902. [1; 2; 10]

Bryant, Joseph Decatur, surgeon, b. East Troy, Wis., 1845; d. New York, N.Y., April 7, 1914. [1; 10]

Bryant, Mrs. Lorinda, née **Munson,** writer of books for children, b. Granville, O., 1855; d. New York, N.Y., Dec. 13, 1933. [2a; 10; 11]

Bryant, Louise, journalist, b. 1890; d. Paris, France, Jan. 9, 1936. [2a]

Bryant, Ralph Clement, educationist, b. Princeton, Ill., 1877; d. New Haven, Conn., Feb. 1, 1939. [10]

Bryant, William Cullen, poet, b. Cummington, Mass., 1794; d. New York, N.Y., June 12, 1878. [1; 2; 3; 4; 5; 6; 7; 71; 72]

Bryant, William McKendree, educationist, b. Lake county, Ind., 1843; d. Waynesville, N.C., 1919. [10]

Bryce, Clarence Archibald, physician, b. 1849; d. Richmond, Va., Sept. 1, 1928.

Bryce, George, clergyman and historian, b. Mount Pleasant, Ont., 1844; d. Ottawa, Ont., Aug. 5, 1931. [27]

Bryce, Lloyd Stephens, novelist, b. Flushing, Long Island, N.Y., 1851; d. Talbot county, Md., April 2, 1917. [1; 7; 10]

Bryce, Ronald (pseud.). See Rockey, Howard.

Brydges, Harold (pseud.). See Bridge, James Howard.

Bryson, Thomas H., priest, b. 1880; d. Pittsburg, Pa., March 23, 1943. [21]

Bubier, Edward Trevert, electrical engineer, b. 1858; d. 1904.

Buchanan, Andrew Hays, mathematician, b. Washington county, Ark., 1828; d. 1914. [10]

Buchanan, Arthur William Patrick, lawyer, b. Montreal, Que., 1870; d. Montreal, Que., Oct. 31, 1939. [27]

Buchanan, Charles Milton, physician, b. 1868; d. Seattle, Wash., Jan. 18, 1920.

Buchanan, Isaac, merchant and politician, b. Glasgow, Scotland, 1810; d. Hamilton, Ont., Oct. 1, 1883. [27]

Buchanan, James Shannon, educationist, b. Franklin, Tenn., 1864; d. Norman, Okla., March 20, 1930. [10; 75]

Buchanan, John Jenkins, surgeon, b. Wellsville, O., 1855; d. Pittsburg, Pa., Aug. 24, 1937. [10]

Buchanan, Joseph, philosopher, b. Washington county, Va., 1785; d. Louisville, Ky., Sept. 29, 1829. [1; 34]

Buchanan, Joseph Ray, journalist, b. Hannibal, Mo., 1851; d. Montclair, N.J., Sept. 13, 1924. [10]

Buchanan, Joseph Rodes, physician, b. Frankford, Ky., 1814; d. San José, Calif., Dec. 26, 1899. [1; 2; 3; 4; 6]

Buchanan, Mrs. Madeleine, née **Sharps,** novelist, d. Philadelphia, Pa., Sept. 4, 1940.

Buchanan, Roberdeau, astronomer, b. Philadelphia, Pa., 1839; d. Dec. 18, 1916. [10]

Buchanan, Thompson, playwright, b. New York, N.Y., 1877; d. New York, N.Y., Oct. 15, 1938. [7; 10]

Buchner, Edward Franklin, educationist, b. Paxton, Ill., 1868; d. Munich, Germany, Sept. 22, 1929. [1; 62]

Buck, Albert Henry, otologist and medical historian, b. New York, N.Y., 1842; d. Cornwall, N.Y., Nov. 16, 1922. [1; 2; 3; 4; 10; 62]

Buck, Charles William, lawyer and novelist, b. Vicksburg, Miss., 1849; d. Louisville, Ky., Nov. 30, 1930. [10; 34]

Buck, Daniel, jurist, b. Boonville, N.Y., 1829; d. Mankato, Minn., May 21, 1905. [70]

Buck, Daniel Dana, clergyman, b. 1814; d. 1895.

Buck, Dudley, organist, b. Hartford, Conn., 1839; d. Orange, N.J., Oct. 6, 1909. [1; 2; 3; 6; 10; 20]

Buck, Edward, lawyer, b. New York, N.Y., 1814; d. Andover, Mass., July 16, 1876 [62]

Buck, Gertrude, educationist, b. Kalamazoo, Mich., 1871; d. Poughkeepsie, N.Y., Jan. 8, 1922. [10; 39]

Buck, Gurdon, surgeon, b. New York, N.Y., 1807; d. New York, N.Y., March 6, 1877. [1; 3; 4]

Buck, James Smith, historian, b. Lyme, N.H., 1812; d. Milwaukee, Wis., Sept. 20, 1852. [43]

Buck, Jirah Dewey, physician, b. Fredonia, N.Y., 1838; d. Cincinnati, O., Dec. 13, 1916. [2; 10]

Buck, Mrs. Lillie, née **West.** actress and drama critic, b. West Burlington, Ia., 1860; d. July 3, 1939.

Buck, Oscar MacMillan, educationist, b. Cawnpore, India, 1885; d. Madison, N.J., Feb. 10, 1941. [10]

Buck, William Joseph, historian, b. 1825; d. ?

Buckalew, Charles Rollin, politician, b. Columbia county, Pa., 1821; d. Bloomsburg, Pa., May 19, 1899. [1; 4; 10]

Bucke, Richard Maurice, physician, b. Norfolk, England, 1837; d. London, Ont., Feb. 19, 1902. [27]

Buckham, James, poet, b. Burlington, Vt., 1858; d. Melrose, Mass., Jan. 8, 1908. [4; 10]

Buckham, John Wright, theologian, b. Burlington, Vt., 1864; d. Berkeley, Calif., March 29, 1945. [7; 10]

Buckham, Matthew Henry, educationist, b. Hinckley, England, 1832; d. Burlington, Vt., 1910. [10]

Buckhout, Mrs. Byron M., traveller, b. 1836; d. 1914. [39]

Buckingham, Catherine Putnam, educationist, b. 1808; d. 1888.

Buckingham, Edgar, physicist, b. Philadelphia, Pa., 1867; d. Chevy Chase, Md., April 29, 1940. [10; 11; 13]

Buckingham, Emma May, poet and novelist, fl. 1873-1906.

Buckingham, Joseph Tinker, journalist, b. Windham, Conn., 1779; d. Cambridge, Mass., April 11, 1861. [2; 4; 7]

Buckingham, Samuel Giles, clergyman, b. Lebanon, Conn., 1812; d. Springfield, Mass., July 12, 1898. [62]

Buckingham, William, journalist, b. Devonshire, England, 1832; d. Stratford, Ont., June 11, 1915. [27]

Buckler, Thomas Hepburn, physician, b. near Baltimore, Md., 1812; d. Baltimore, Md., April 20, 1901. [1]

Buckley, Albert Coulson, neurologist, b. Philadelphia, Pa., 1873; d. Philadelphia, Pa., Aug. 17, 1939. [10]

Buckley, James Monroe, clergyman, b. Rahway, N.J., 1836; d. Morristown, N.J., Feb. 8, 1920. [1; 2; 6; 7; 60]

Buckminster, Joseph, clergyman, b. Rutland, Mass., 1751; d. Reedsboro, Vt., June 10, 1812. [1; 3; 4; 7]

Buckner, Elijah D., physician, b. 1843; d. 1907.

Budd, Henry, lawyer, b. 1849; d. Philadelphia, Pa., May 28, 1921. [55]

Budd, Joseph Lancaster, horticulturist, b. near Peekskill, N.Y., 1835; d. Phoenix, Ariz., Dec. 20, 1904. [1]

Budgett, Mrs. Elizabeth, née **Janes.** See Dejeans, Elizabeth.

Budington, William Ives, clergyman, b. New Haven, Conn., 1815; d. Brooklyn, N.Y., Nov. 29, 1879. [3; 4]

Buehler, Huber Gray, educationist, b. Gettysburg, Pa., 1864; d. Lakeville, Conn., June 20, 1924. [1; 10]

Buel, James William, journalist, b. Golconda, Ill., 1849; d. San Diego, Calif., Nov. 16, 1920. [4; 7; 10]

Buel, Jesse, agriculturist, b. Coventry, Conn., 1778; d. Danbury, Conn., Oct. 6, 1839. [1; 3; 4]

Buel, Richard Hooker, civil engineer, b. Cumberland, Md., 1842; d. ? [6; 34]

Buel, Samuel, clergyman, b. Troy, N.Y., 1815; d. New York, N.Y., Feb. 2, 1892. [2; 6]

Buell, Augustus C., civil engineer, b. Norwich, N.Y., 1847; d. Philadelphia, Pa., May 23, 1904. [10]

Buell, Colin Sherman, educationist, b. Kellingworth, Conn., 1861; d. New London, Conn., Jan. 30, 1938. [11; 62]

Buell, Marcus Darius, theologian, b. Wayland, N.J., 1851; d. Winter Park, Fla., Nov. 24, 1933. [10]

Buell, Raymond Leslie, publicist, b. Chicago, Ill., 1896; d. Montreal, Que., Feb. 20, 1946. [7; 10]

Buell, Seth Herbert, clergyman, b. Plymouth, Conn., 1875; d. St. Louis, Mo., Jan. 1, 1943. [62]

Buffalo Bill (pseud.). See Cody, William Frederick.

Buffalo Child Long Lance, Blackfoot chief, b. Montana; d. March 20, 1932. [10; 27]

Buffett, Edward Payson, physician and novelist, b. Smithtown, Long Island, N.Y., 1833; d. Jersey City, N.J., Sept. 9, 1904. [62]

Buffington, Joseph, jurist, b. Kittanning, Pa., 1855; d. Pittsburg, Pa., Oct. 21, 1947. [10]

Buffinton, Arthur Howland, educationist, b. Somerset, Mass., 1887; d. Williamstown, Mass., June 5, 1945. [14]

Buffum, Charles Albert, educationist, b. 1853; d. Newton, Mass., July 19, 1941.

Buffum, Edward Gould, journalist, b. Rhode Island, 1820; d. Paris, France, Oct. 24, 1867. [3; 6; 7]

Buffum, George Tower, merchant, b. Winchester, N.H., 1846; d. Winchester, N.H., March 9, 1926. [7; 10]

Buffum, Joseph Howard, physician, b. 1849; d. San Francisco, Calif., Sept. 15, 1925.

Buies, Arthur, journalist, b. near Montreal, Lower Canada, 1840; d. Quebec, Que., Jan. 26, 1901. [27]

Buist, Robert, horticulturist, b. Scotland, 1805; d. 1880. [6]

Bulfinch, Stephen Greenleaf, clergyman, b. Boston, Mass., 1809; d. Cambridge, Mass., Oct. 12, 1890. [3; 6; 7]

Bulfinch, Thomas, banker, b. Boston, Mass., 1797; d. Boston, Mass., May 27, 1867. [1; 3; 6; 7]

Bulkley, Charles Henry Augustus, clergyman, b. Charleston, S.C., 1819; d. Washington, D.C., Feb. 2, 1893. [68]

Bulkley, John, clergyman, b. Wethersfield, Conn., 1679; d. Colchester, Conn., June 10, 1731. [51]

Bulkley, Lucius Duncan, physician, b. New York, N.Y., 1845; d. Englewood, N.J., July 20, 1928. [1; 62]

Bull, Charles Livingston, illustrator, b. New York state, 1874; d. Oradell, N.J., March 22, 1932. [7; 10]

Bull, Mrs. Sara Chapman, née **Thorp,** biographer, b. Oxford, N.Y., 1850; d. Cambridge, Mass., 1911. [10]

Bull, Sidney Augustus, local historian, b. 1847; d. Billerica, Mass., June 22, 1944.

Bull, William Perkins, lawyer, financier, and historian, b. York county, Ont., 1870; d. Niagara-on-the-Lake, Ont., June 30, 1948.

Bulla, Charles Dehaven, clergyman, b. Albany, Mo., 1862; d. Nashville, Tenn., Feb. 2, 1932. [10]

Bullard, Arthur, journalist, b. St. Joseph, Mo., 1879; d. Geneva, Switzerland, Sept. 10, 1929. [10]

Bullard, Asa, clergyman, b. Northbridge, Mass., 1804; d. Cambridge, Mass., April 5, 1888. [3; 45]

Bullard, Frank Dearborn, surgeon, b. Lincoln Center. Me., 1860; d. Los Angeles, Calif., Sept. 8, 1936. [10; 35]

Bullard, Robert Lee, soldier, b. Youngsboro, Ala., 1861; d. Governor's Island, N.Y., Sept. 11, 1947. [10; 11]

Bullard, William Hannum Grubb, naval officer, b. Media, Pa., 1866; d. Media, Pa., Nov. 24, 1927. [1; 10]

Bullard, William Norton, neurologist, b. Newport, R.I., 1853; d. Lenox, Mass., April 13, 1931. [10; 51]

Bullen, Henry Lewis, type-founder, b. Ballarat, Australia, 1857; d. Elmhurst, N.J., April 27, 1938.

Buller, Arthur Henry Reginald, botanist, b. Birmingham, England, 1874; d. Winnipeg, Mann., July 3, 1944. [27]

Bullions, Peter, philologist, b. Moss Side, Scotland, 1791; d. Troy, N.Y., Feb. 13, 1864. [3; 6]

Bulloch, James Dunwody, naval officer, b. Georgia, 1824; d. Liverpool, England, 1901. [1; 6; 34]

Bullock, Alexander Hamilton, politician, b. Royalston, Mass., 1816; d. Worcester, Mass., Jan. 11, 1882. [3; 4]

Bullock, Charles Jesse, economist, b. Boston, Mass., 1869; d. Hingham, Mass., March 17, 1941. [10]

Bullock, Cynthia, poet, b. Wayne county, N.Y., 1821; d. ? [19]

Bullock, William, clergyman, b. Essex, England, 1797; d. Halifax, N.S., March 7, 1874. [27]

Bullowa, Ferdinand Ezra M., lawyer, d. Cleveland, O., Feb. 28, 1919. [48]

Bullowa, Jesse Godfrey Moritz, physician, b. New York, N.Y., 1879; d. New York, N.Y., Nov. 9, 1943. [48]

Bulmer. Mrs. **Agnes,** née **Collinson,** poet, b. 1775; d. 1836. [6; 19]

Bump, Charles Weathers, journalist, b. Baltimore, Md., 1872; d. 1908. [10]

Bump, Orlando Franklin, lawyer, b. Afton, N.Y., 1841; d. Baltimore, Md., Jan. 29, 1884. [3; 5; 6; 62]

Bumpus, Herman Carey, biologist, b. Buckfield, Me., 1862; d. Pasadena, Calif., June 21, 1943. [10; 14]

Bumstead, Freeman Josiah, physician, b. Boston, Mass., 1826; d. New York, N.Y., Nov. 28, 1879. [1; 3; 51]

Bunce, Oliver Bell, publisher, b. New York, N.Y., 1828; d. New York, N.Y., May 15, 1890. [1; 2; 3; 4; 6; 7]

Bundy, Elizabeth Roxana, physician, b. 1850; d. Philadelphia, Pa., July 2, 1919.

Bundy, Jonas Mills, journalist, b. Colebrook, N.H., 1835; d. Paris, France, Sept. 8, 1891. [1; 4; 6; 7]

Bungay, George Washington, journalist, b. Suffolk, England, 1826; d. 1892. [6; 7]

Bunker, Alonzo, missionary, b. Atkinson, Me., 1837; d. Groton, Mass., March 8, 1912. [10]

Bunker, Robert Emmet, lawyer, b. 1848; d. Muskegon, Mich., Jan. 11, 1931. [53]

Bunn, Charles Wilson, lawyer b. Galesville Wis., 1855; d. St. Paul., Min., Jan. 2, 1941. [10]

Bunnell, Lafayette Houghton, physician, b. Rochester, N.Y., 1824; d. Winona, Minn., July, 1903. [70]

Bunner, Henry Cuyler, poet and short-story writer, b. Oswego, N.Y., 1855; d. Nutley, N.J., May 11, 1896. [1; 2; 4; 6; 7; 71]

Bunny (pseud.). See Schultze, Carl Emil.

Bunting, Henry Stanhope, publisher and advertising expert, b. Galveston, Tex., 1869; d. Stamford, Conn., Dec. 2, 1948.

Buntline, Ned (pseud.). See Judson, Edward Zane Carroll.

Bunts, Frank Emory, surgeon, b. Youngstown, O., 1861; d. Cleveland, O., Nov. 28, 1928. [4; 10]

Bunyanus (pseud.). See Weeks, William Raymond.

Buoy, Charles Wesley, clergyman, b. 1841; d. 1887.

Burbank, Luther, naturalist, b. Lancaster, Mass., 1849; d. Santa Rosa, Calif., April 11, 1926. [1; 2; 4; 7; 10]

Burbidge, George Wheelock, b. 1847; d. Ottawa, Ont., Feb. 18, 1908.

Burch, Ernest Ward, theologian, b. New London, Conn., 1875; d. Evanston, Ill., Nov. 8, 1933. [10]

Burchard, Samuel Dickinson, clergyman, b. Steuben, N.Y., 1812; d. Saratoga, N.Y., Sept. 25, 1891. [4]

Burdett, Charles, novelist, b. New York, N.Y., 1815; d. ? [7]

Burdett, Everett Watson, lawyer, b. Olive Branch, Miss., 1854; d. Boston, Mass., Jan. 18, 1925. [10]

Burdette, Robert Jones, humorist, b. Greensboro, Pa., 1844; d. Pasadena, Calif., Nov. 19, 1914. [2; 3; 4; 7; 10; 71]

Burdick, Austin C. (pseud.). See Cobb, Sylvanus.

Burdick, Charles Kellogg, lawyer, b. Utica, N.Y., 1883; d. Ithaca, N.Y., June 22, 1940. [10]

Burdick, Charles Rollin, clergyman, b. 1826; d. 1897.

Burdick, Francis Marion, lawyer, b. De Ruyter, N.Y., 1845; d. De Ruyter, N.Y., June 30, 1920. [4; 10]

Burdick, Joel Wakeman, manufacturer, b. Almond, N.Y., 1853; d. Pittsburg, Pa., May 12, 1925. [10]

Burdick, William Livesey, lawyer, b. East Greenwich, R.I., 1860; d. Lawrence, Kans., June 11, 1946. [62]

Burges, Tristram, politician, b. Rochester, Mass., 1770; d. Providence, R.I., Oct. 13, 1853. [2; 6]

Burgess, Alexander, bishop, b. Providence, R.I., 1819; d. St. Albans, Vt., Oct. 31, 1901. [2; 10]

Burgess, Ebenezer, clergyman, b. Wareham, Mass., 1790; d. Dedham, Mass., Dec. 5, 1870. [3; 47]

Burgess, Edward Sanford, botanist, b. Little Valley, N.Y., 1855; d. New York, N.Y., Feb. 23, 1928. [10]

Burgess, George, bishop, b. Providence, R.I., 1809; d. Haiti, April 23, 1866. [4; 7; 47]

Burgess, George Kimball, physicist, b. Newton, Mass., 1874; d. Washington, D.C., July 2, 1932. [1a; 2; 10; 11]

Burgess, Isaac Bronson, educationist, b. 1858; d. Nov. 10, 1933.

Burgess, John William, educationist, b. Cornersville, Tenn., 1844; d. Brookline, Mass., Jan. 13, 1931. [1a; 2; 4]

Burgess, Theodore Chalon, educationist, b. Little Valley, N.Y., 1859; d. Peoria, Ill., Feb. 26, 1925. [10]

Burgess, William, clergyman, b. Norwich, England, 1843; d. Des Plaines, Ill., July 31, 1922. [10]

Burghardt, Henry Dwight, educationist, b. Curtisville, Mass., d. Pasadena, Calif., July 8, 1949.

Burgoyne, Arthur Gordon, journalist, d. 1914.

Burgwyn, Collinson Pierrepont Edwards, novelist, b. Jackson, N.C., 1852; d. Richmond, Va., Feb. 23, 1915. [51]

Burk, Frederic Lister, educationist, b. Blenheim, Ont., 1862; d. Kentfield, Calif., June 12, 1924. [1; 10]

Burk, John Daly, playwright, b. Ireland, about 1775; d. near Campbell's Bridge, Va., April 11, 1808. [1; 4; 7]

Burk, William Herbert, clergyman, b. Philadelphia, Pa., 1867; d. Valley Forge, Pa., June 30, 1933. [10]

Burke, AEdanus, jurist, b. Galway, Ireland, 1743; d. Charleston, S.C., March 30, 1802. [1; 3; 4]

Burke, Edmund, priest, b. Kildare, Ireland, 1753; d. Halifax, N.S., Nov. 29, 1820. [27]

Burke, Edmund J., priest and educationist, b. New York, N.Y., 1858; d. New York, N.Y., Jan. 1, 1941. [21]

Burke, Finley, lawyer, b. 1855; d. 1903. [37]

Burke, John, poet d. 1873.

Burke, John Joseph, priest, b. 1875; d. Washington, D.C., Oct. 30, 1936. [10; 21]

Burke, Robert Belle, educationist, b. Pittsburg, Pa., 1868; d. Philadelphia, Pa., July 1, 1944. [10]

Burkitt, Lemuel, clergyman, b. 1850; d. near Windsor, N.C., about 1806. [24; 34]

Burkley, Francis Joseph, business executive, b. Omaha, Neb., 1857; d, Omaha, Neb., Sept., 1940. [21]

Burks, Martin Parks, jurist, b. Liberty, Va., 1851; d. Lexington, Va., April 30, 1928. [10]

Burleigh (pseud.). See Smith, Matthew Hale.

Burleigh, Charles Calistus, abolitionist, b. Plainfield, Conn., 1810; d. Florence, Mass., June 14, 1878. [1; 3; 4]

Burleigh, Clarence Blendon, journalist and writer of books for boys, b. Linneus, Me., 1864; d. Augusta, Me., May 2, 1910. [10]

Burleigh, George Shepard, poet, b. Plainfield, Conn., 1821; d. Providence, R.I., July 21, 1903. [7; 10]

Burleigh, William Henry, poet and journalist, b. Woodstock, Conn., 1812; d. Brooklyn, N.Y., March 18, 1871.[1; 3; 7; 71]

Burleson, Hugh Latimer, bishop, b. Northfield, Minn., 1865; d. New York, N.Y., Aug. 1, 1933. [1a; 10]

Burlin, Mrs. Natalie, née Curtis, musician, b. New York, N.Y., 1875; d. Paris, France, Oct. 23, 1921. [1; 7; 10]

Burlingame, Edward Livermore, editor, b. Boston, Mass., 1848; d. New York, N.Y., Nov. 15, 1922. [1; 2; 7; 10]

Burlingame, Eugene Watson, Orientalist, b. Albany, N.Y., 1876; d. Albany, N.Y., Aug. 3, 1932. [62]

Burnam, John Miller, educationist, b. Irvine, Ky., 1864; d. Pomona, Calif., Nov. 19, 1921. [1; 62]

Burnap, George Washington, clergyman, b. Merrimack, N.H., 1802; d. Philadelphia, Pa., Sept. 8, 1859. [1; 3; 4; 6]

Burnap, Uzziah Cicero, clergyman, b. Windham, Vt., 1794; d, Lowell, Mass., 1854. [43]

Burnet, Jacob, jurist, b. Newark, N.Y., 1770; d. Cincinnati, O., May 10, 1853. [1; 3; 4; 6]

Burnett, Charles Theodore, educationist, b. Springfield, Mass., 1873; d. Brunswick, Me., Jan. 31, 1946. [10; 11; 46]

Burnett, Chester Henry, otologist, b. Philadelphia, Pa., 1842; d. Bryn Mawr, Pa., Jan. 30, 1902. [1; 62]

Burnett, Edmund Cody, historian, b. Henry county, Ala., 1864; d. Washington, D.C., Jan. 10, 1949. [10]

Burnett, Mrs. Frances, née **Hodgson,** novelist, b. Manchester, England, 1849; d. Plandome, Long Island, N.Y., Oct. 29, 1924. [1; 2; 3; 4; 5; 6; 7; 10; 11]

Burnett, John Franklin, clergyman, b. 1851 d. 1929.

Burnett, Peter Hardeman, pioneer, b. Nashville, Tenn., 1807; d. San Francisco, Calif., May 10, 1895. [1; 2; 21; 35]

Burnett, Swan Moses, physician, b. New Market, Tenn., 1847; d. Washington, D.C., Jan. 18, 1906. [1; 10]

Burnett, Vivian, biographer, b. Paris, France, 1876; d, Manhasset Bay, Long Island, N.Y., July 25, 1937. [7]

Burnham, Benjamin Franklin, jurist, b. Groton, Vt., 1830; d. Boston, Mass., May 21, 1898. [4; 60]

Burnham, Charles Guilford, educationist, b. Dunbarton, N.H., 1803; d. Montgomery, Ala., June 29, 1866. [49]

Burnham, Mrs. Clara Louise, née **Root,** novelist, b. Newton, Mass., 1854; d. Casco Bay, Me., June 20, 1927. [1; 7; 10]

Burnham, Frederick Russell, soldier, b. Tivoli, Minn., 1861; d. Santa Barbara, Calif., Sept. 1, 1947. [7; 10]

Burnham, George Pickering, poultryman and secret service agent, b. 1814; d. 1902.

Burnham, John Bird, explorer and naturalist, b. New Castle, Del., 1869; d. near Willsboro, N.Y., Sept. 23, 1939. [7; 10]

Burnham, John Hampden, lawyer and novelist, b. Peterborough, Ont., 1860; d. Peterborough, Ont., April 25, 1940. [27; 30]

Burnham, Sarah Maria, educationist, b. 1818; d. Cambridge, Mass., Aug. 24, 1901.

Burnham, Smith, educationist, b. Jackson county, Mich., 1866; d. Kalamazoo, Mich., Dec. 13, 1947. [7; 39]

Burnham, William Henry, educationist, b. Dunbarton, N. H., 1855; d. Dunbarton, N.H., June 25, 1941. [10; 11]

Burnham, William Power, soldier, b. Scranton, Pa., 1860; d. San Francisco, Calif., Sept. 27, 1930. [10]

Burns, Jabez, clergyman, b. Oldham, Lancashire, England, 1805; d. 1876. [6; 7]

Burns, James Aloysius, priest and educationist, b. Michigan City, Ind., 1867; d. Notre Dame, Ind., Sept. 9, 1940. [10; 21]

Burns, James Jesse, educationist, b. Brownsville, O., 1838; d. Defiance, O., 1911. [10]

Burns, Robert Ferrier, clergyman, b. Paisley, Scotland, 1826; d. near Dundee, Scotland, April 5, 1896. [27]

Burns, Walter Noble, journalist, b. Lebanon, Ky., 1872; d. Chicago, Ill., April 15, 1932. [7; 10]

Burns, William Henry, clergyman, b. New Glasgow, N.S., 1840; d. Evanston, Ill., April 4, 1916. [10]

Burns, William John, detective, b. Baltimore, Md., 1861; d. Sarasota, Fla., April 14, 1932. [1a; 4; 10]

Burpee, Charles Winslow, soldier and historian, b. Rockville, Conn., 1859; d. Hartford, Conn., May 13, 1945. [7; 11; 62]

Burpee, Lawrence Johnston, historian, b. Halifax, N.S., 1873; d. Oxford, England, Oct. 13, 1946. [30]

Burque, François Xavier, priest, b. St. Hyacinthe, Que., 1851; d. Quebec, Que., Oct. 22, 1923. [27]

Burr, Aaron, clergyman, b. Fairfield Conn,. 1716; d. Princeton, N. J., Sept. 24, 1757. [1; 3; 4]

Burr, Aaron, politician, b. Newark, N.J., 1756; d. Port Richmond, Staten Island, N.Y., Sept. 14, 1836. [1; 2; 3; 4; 5; 6; 7]

Burr, Aaron Ainsworth (pseud.). See Dey, Frederick Van Rensselaer.

Burr, Mrs. Anna Robeson, née **Brown,** novelist, b. Philadelphia, Pa., 1873; d. Bryn Mawr, Pa., Sept. 10, 1941. [7; 10; 11]

Burr, Charles Chauncey, journalist, b. 1817; d. 1883. [7]

Burr, Colonel Bell, physician, b. Lansing, Mich., 1856; d. April 11, 1931. [10; 39]

Burr, Enoch Fitch, clergyman, b. Westport, Conn., 1818; d. Lyme, Conn., May 8, 1907. 1; 3; 10; 62]

Burr, Frank A., biographer, b. 1843; d. 1894.

Burr, George Lincoln, historian, b. Oramel, N.Y., 1857; d. Ithaca, N.Y., June 27, 1938. [7; 10; 11]

Burr, Hanford Montrose, clergyman and educationist, b. Lyme, Conn., 1864; d. Springfield, Mass., Oct. 5, 1941. [11; 45]

Burr, Mrs. Katherine Douglas, née **King,** novelist, d. 1901.

Burr, William Henry, reporter, b. Stump City, N.Y., 1819; d. Washington, D.C., 1908. [10]

Burr, William Hubert, civil engineer, b. Watertown, Conn., 1851; d. New York, N.Y., Dec. 13, 1934 [1a; 2; 10]

Burrage, Henry Sweetser, clergyman, b. Finchburg, Mass., 1837; d. Kennebunkport, Me., March 9, 1926. [1; 10; 47]

Burrage, Walter Lincoln, physician, b. Boston, Mass., 1860; d. Brookline, Mass., Jan. 26, 1935. [1a; 10; 51]

Burrell, David James, clergyman, b. Mount Pleasant, Pa., 1844; d. Madison, N.J., Dec. 5, 1926. [1; 10]

Burrell, Herbert Leslie, surgeon, b. Boston, Mass., 1856; d. Boston, Mass., April 27, 1910. [4; 10; 51]

Burrell, Joseph Dunn, clergyman, b. Freeport, Ill., 1858; d. Barcelona, Spain, April 13, 1930. [10; 62]

Burrell, Martin, politician and librarian, b. Faringdon, England, 1858; d. Ottawa, Ont., March 20, 1938. [27]

Burrill, Alexander Mansfield, lawyer, b. 1807; d. Kearney, N.J., Feb. 7, 1869. [1]

Burrill, Thomas Jonathan, botanist, b. near Pittsfield, Mass., 1839; d. Urbana, Ill., April 14, 1916. [1; 10; 13]

Burris, William Paxton, educationist, b. Indiana, 1865; d. Los Angeles, Calif., Nov. 8, 1946.

Burritt, Eldon Grant, educationist, b. Hilton, N.Y., 1868; d. Greenville, Ill., Aug. 15, 1927. [10]

Burritt, Elihu, reformer, b. New Britain, Conn., 1811; d. New Britain, Conn., March 7, 1879. [1; 2; 3; 4; 7]

Burritt, Elijah Hinsdale, educationist, b. 1794; d. 1838.

Burroughs, Charles, clergyman and poet, b. Boston Mass., 1787; d. Portsmouth, N.H., March 5, 1868. [19; 51]

Burroughs, John, naturalist, b. Roxbury, N.Y., 1837; d. on the train from California, March 29, 1921. [1; 2; 3; 4; 5; 6; 7; 71]

Burroughs, Stephen, adventurer, b. Killingly, Conn., 1766; d. Three Rivers, Lower Canada, Jan. 28, 1840. [3; 49]

Burrowes, George, poet, b. Trenton, N.J., 1811; d. 1894. [3]

Burrowes, Katherine, music teacher, b. Kingston, Ont.; d. Detroit, Mich., Nov. 5, 1939. [10]

Burrowes, Peter Edward, socialist, b. Dublin, Ireland, 1844; d. ? [10]

Burrows, Mrs. Angie M. H., poet, b. 1860; d. North Tonawanda, N.Y., March 6, 1944.

Burrows, Lansing, clergyman, b. Philadelphia, Pa., 1843; d. Americus, Ga., Oct. 17, 1919. [4; 10]

Burt, Armistead, lawyer and poet, b. Abbeville district, Sc., 1802; d. 1883. [34]

Burt, Benjamin Chapman, educationist, b. 1852; d. Jan. 10, 1915. [53]

Burt, Henry Jackson, civil engineer, b. Urbana, Ill., 1873; d. Wheaton, Ill., July 28, 1928. [10]

Burt, Mary Elizabeth, educationist, b. Lake Geneva, Wis., 1850; d. Cotesville, N.J., Oct. 17, 1918. [1; 7; 10]

Burt, Nathaniel Clark, clergyman, b. Fairton, N.J., 1825; d. Rome, Italy, March 4, 1874. [3]

Burt, Pitts Harrison, stockbroker and novelist, b. Cincinnati, O., 1837; d. Cincinnati, O., Aug. 16, 1906. [62]

Burt, Stephen Smith, physician, b. Oneida, N.Y., 1850; d, New York, N.Y., March 26, 1932. [10]

Burt, William, bishop, b. Padstow, Cornwall, England, 1852; d. Clifton Springs, N.Y., April 9, 1936. [10]

Burt, William Austin, surveyor, b. Worcester, Mass., 1792; d. Detroit, Mich., Aug. 18, 1858. [2; 3]

Burtchaell, Mrs. **Clara Grace,** née Dolliver, poet, b. Milwaukee, Wis.; d. Oakland, Calif., Nov. 11, 1940. [35]

Burtin, Nicholas Victor, priest, b. Metz, France, 1828; d. Quebec, Que., Dec. 30, 1902. [32]

Burton, Asa, clergyman, b. Stonington, Conn., 1752; d. Thetford, Vt., May 1, 1836. [1; 3; 49]

Burton, Charles Emerson, clergyman, b. Iowa, 1869; d. Georges Mills, N.H., Aug. 27, 1940. [10]

Burton, Charles Pierce, writer of books for boys, b. Anderson, Ind., 1862; d. Aurora, Ill., March 31, 1947. [7; 10; 11]

Burton, Clarence Monroe, historian, b. 1853; d. Detroit, Mich., Oct. 23, 1932. [1a; 7; 10]

Burton, Eli Franklin, physicist, b. Green River, Ont., 1879; d. Toronto, Ont., July 6, 1948. [30]

Burton, Ernest DeWitt, educationist, b Granville, O., 1856; d. Chicago, Ill., May 26, 1925. [1; 2; 4; 10]

Burton, Frederick Russell, student of Indian music, b. Jonesville, Mich., 1861; d. Lake Hoptacong, N.J., Sept. 30, 1909. [1; 7; 10; 51]

Burton, Harry Edwin, educationist, b. Boston, Mass., 1868; d. Hanover, N.H., March 20, 1945. [10; 11; 51]

Burton, John, clergyman, b. England, 1834; d. Gravenhurst, Ont., July 6, 1897. [27]

Burton, Marion Le Roy, clergyman and educationist, b. Brooklyn, Ia., 1874; d. Ann Arbor, Mich., Feb. 18, 1925. [1; 2; 7; 10]

Burton, Nathan Smith, clergyman, b. Manlius, N.Y., 1821; d. Oak Park, Ill., April 20, 1909. [24]

Burton, Nathaniel Judson, clergyman, b. Trumbull, Conn., 1824; d. Hartford, Conn., Oct. 13, 1887. [1; 3; 6; 62]

Burton, Richard, poet, b. Hartford, Conn., 1861; d. Winter Park, Fla., April 7, 1940. [7; 10; 11]

Burton, Theodore Elijah, politician, b. Jefferson, O., 1851; d. Cleveland, O., Oct. 28, 1929. [1a; 4; 10]

Burton, Warren, clergyman, b. Wilton, N.H., 1800; d. Salem, Mass., June 6, 1866. [1; 3; 4; 6; 7]

Burton, William Evans, actor, b. London, England, 1804; d. New York, N.Y., Feb. 10, 1860. [1; 3; 7]

Burtt, John, poet, b. Scotland, 1789; d. Salem, N.J., March 24, 1866. [3]

Burwash, Nathanael, educationist, b. near St. Andrews, Lower Canada, 1839; d. Toronto, Ont., March 30, 1918. [27]

Burwell, Adam Hood, clergyman, b. England, about 1790; d. Kingston, Ont., Nov. 2, 1849. [27]

Burwell, Letitia MacCreary, social historian, fl. 1860-1900. [34]

Burwell, William MacCreary, journalist, b. 1809; d. 1888. [34]

Busbee, Charles Manly, lawyer, b. Raleigh, N.C., 1845; d. Raleigh, N.C., 1909. [10]

Busbee, Fabius Hayward, lawyer, b. Raleigh, N.C., 1848; d. 1908. [10]

Busbey, Hamilton, horseman, b. Clark county, O., 1840; d. Hampton Roads, Va., Aug. 1, 1924. [10]

Busbey, L. White, journalist, b. Vienna, O., 1852; d. Washington, D.C., Oct. 31, 1925. [10]

Busch, Frederick Carl, physiologist, b. Buffalo, N.Y., 1873; d. 1914. [13]

Busey, Samuel Clagett, physician, b. Maryland, 1828; d. Washington, D.C., Feb. 12, 1901. [10]

Bush, Charles Peck, clergyman, b. Brighton, N.Y., 1813; d. Albany, N.Y., Feb. 22, 1880. [62]

Bush, George, clergyman, b. Norwich, Vt., 1796; d. Rochester, N.Y., Sept. 19, 1859. [1; 3; 4; 49]

Bush, George Gary, educationist, b. 1843; d. Washington, D.C., 1898. [34]

Bush, Irving T., writer on transportation, b. Ridgeway, Mich., 1869; d. New York, N.Y., Oct. 21, 1948. [10]

Bush, Richard James, explorer, fl. 1865-1899. [6]

Bushnell, Charles Ira, antiquary, b. New York, N.Y., 1826; d. New York, N.Y., 1883. [3]

Bushnell, Curtis Clark, educationist, b. New Haven, Conn., 1870; d. New Hartford, N.Y., Sept. 27, 1936. [62]

Bushnell, George Ensign, physician, b. Worcester, Mass., 1853; d. Pasadena, Calif., July 19, 1924. [1; 10]

Bushnell, Horace, clergyman, b. Litchfield, Conn., 1802; d. Hartford. Conn., Feb. 17, 1876. [1; 2; 3; 4; 5; 6; 7]

Bushnell, John Edward, clergyman, b. 1858; d. ?

Bushnell, Joseph Platt, immigration agent, b. 1842; d. about 1922. [37]

Buskirk, Samuel Hamilton, lawyer, b. 1820; d. 1879.

Busser, Samuel Edwin, clergyman, b. York, Pa., 1850; d. Los Angeles, Calif., Sept. 17, 1926. [62]

Buswell, Henry Foster, lawyer, b. Bradford, N.H., 1842; d. Stoughton, Mass., Sept. 13, 1919. [10; 51]

Butin, Romain François, priest and educationist, b. Loire, France, 1871; d. Washington, D.C., Dec. 8, 1937. [10; 21]

Butler, Alford Augustus, clergyman, b. Portland Me., 1845; d. May 25, 1920. [10]

Butler, Benjamin Franklin, lawyer and politician, b. Kinderhook Landing, N.Y., 1795; d. Paris, France, Nov. 8, 1858. [1; 3; 4; 6]

Butler, Benjamin Franklin, lawyer, soldier, and politician, b. Deerfield, N.H., 1818; d. Washington, D.C., Jan. 11, 1893. [1; 2; 3; 4]

Butler, Bion H., local historian, b. 1857; d. Feb. 21, 1935.

Butler, Caleb, educationist, b. Pelham, N.H., 1776; d. Groton, Mass., Oct. 7, 1854. [3; 49]

Butler, Charles Henry, lawyer, b. New York, N.Y., 1859; d. Washington, D.C., Feb. 9, 1940. [10]

Butler, Clement Moore, clergyman, b. Troy, N.Y., 1810; d .Philadelphia, Pa., Nov. 12, 1890. [3; 4]

Butler, Ellis Parker, humorist, b. Muscatine, Ia., 1869; d. Housatonic, Mass., Sept. 13, 1937. [7; 10; 11]

Butler, Francis, dog-trainer, b. England, 1810; d. Brooklyn, N.Y., June 17, 1874. [3]

Butler, Frederick, educationist, b. Wethersfield, Conn., 1766; d. Wethersfield, Conn., April 4, 1843. [3; 62]

Butler, George Frank, physician and poet, b. Moravia, N.Y., 1857; d. Wilmette, Ill., June 22, 1931. [10]

Butler, Glentworth Reeve, physician, b. Philadelphia, Pa., 1855; d. Brooklyn, N.Y., Dec. 6, 1926. [10]

Butler, Hiram Erastus, writer on occult science, b. 1841; d. 1916.

Butler, Howard Crosbv, archaeologist, b. Croton Falls, N.Y., 1872; d. Neuilly, France, Aug. 15, 1922. [1; 4; 7; 10]

Butler, Howard Russell, painter, b. New York, N.Y., 1856; d. Princeton, N.J., May 22, 1934. [4; 10]

Butler, James Davie, educationist, b. Rutland, Vt., 1815; d. Madison, Wis., Nov. 20, 1905. [10; 44]

Butler, James Glentworth, clergyman, b. Brooklyn, N.Y., 1821; d. Boonton, N.J., Dec. 28, 1916. [2; 4]

Butler, John Jay, clergyman, b. Berwick, Me., 1814; d. Hillsdale, Mich., June 16, 1891. [4; 39]

Butler, John Simpkins, physician, b. Northampton, Mass., 1803; d. Hartford, Conn., May 21, 1890. [62]

Butler, John Wesley, missionary, b. Shelburn Falls, Mass., 1851; d. Mexico City, Mexico, March 17, 1918. [10]

Butler, Joseph Green, manufacturer, b. Mercer county, Pa., 1840; d. Youngstown, O., Dec. 19, 1927. [10]

Butler, Lucius Castle, physician, b. Essex, Vt., 1820; d. Essex, Vt., May 25, 1888. [43]

Butler, Mann., historian, b. Baltimore, Md., 1784; d. Missouri, 1852. [74]

Butler, Nathaniel, educationist, b. Eastport, Me., 1853; d. Chicago, Ill., March 3, 1927. [4; 10]

Butler, Nicholas Murray, educationist, b. Elizabeth, N.J., 1862; d. New York, N.Y., Dec. 7, 1947. [4; 7; 10; 11; 12]

Butler, Noble, educationist, b. Washington county, Pa., 1819; d. Louisville, Ky., 1882. [3; 34]

Butler, Smedley Darlington, soldier, b. West Chester, Pa., 1881; d. Philadelphia, Pa., June 21, 1940. [2a; 10; 12]

Butler, Thomas Belden, jurist, b. Wethersfield, Conn., 1806; d. Norwalk, Conn., June 8, 1873. [1; 3; 4]

Butler, William, missionary, b. Dublin, Ireland, 1818; d. Old Orchard, Me., Aug. 18, 1899. [1; 3; 4; 6]

Butler, William Allen, lawyer, b. Albany, N.Y., 1825; d. Yonkers, N.Y., Sept. 9, 1902. [1; 4; 7; 10; 71]

Butler, William Allen, lawyer, b. New York, N.Y., 1853; d. New York, N.Y., July 1, 1923. [10]

Butler, William Frederick, publisher, b. Cincinnati, O.; d. Milwaukee, Wis., March 28, 1926. [10]

Butler, William Mill, journalist, b. Rochester, N.Y., 1857; d. Maplewood, N.J., May 13, 1946. [7; 10]

Butler, Willis Howard, clergyman, b. Bangor, Me., 1873; d. Hartford, Conn., Oct. 22, 1930. [10; 68]

Butler, Wilson Ryder, political scientist, b. Hancock, Me., 1855; d. Hancock, Me., May 16, 1910. [46]

Butsch, Russell Lewis Carl, educationist, b. Tacoma, Wash., 1897; d. Milwaukee, Wis., Feb. 7, 1946. [62]

Butt, Archibald Willingham, soldier, b. Augusta, Ga., 1866; d. Washington, D.C., April 15, 1912. [10]

Buttenwieser, Moses, educationist, b. Germany, 1862; d. Palo Alta, Calif., March 12, 1939. [10; 11]

Butterfield, Consul Willshire, historian, b. Mexico, N.Y., 1824; d. South Omaha, Neb., Sept. 25, 1899. [3; 6; 10]

Butterfield, Daniel, soldier, b. Utica, N.Y., 1831; d. Cold Spring, N.C., July 17, 1901. [2; 4; 10]

Butterfield, Kenyon Leech, educationist, b. Lapeer, Mich., 1868; d. Amherst, Mass., Nov. 25, 1935. [1a; 10; 11]

Butterworth, Hezekiah, journalist, b. Warren, R.I., 1839; d. Warren, R.I., Sept. 5, 1905. [1; 7; 10]

Button, Clayton Adelbert, physician, b. 1853; d. Holland, N.Y., Feb. 24, 1915.

Butts, Isaac, journalist, b. Washington, N.Y., 1816; d. Rochester, N.Y., Nov. 20, 1874. [1; 3; 4; 6]

Butts, Mrs. Sarah Harriet, biographer, b. Columbus, Ga., 1845; d. Brunswick, Ga., June 16, 1905. [34]

Buxton, Henry James, journalist, b. Warren, Mass., 1882; d. Stockton Springs, Me., Aug. 30, 1939.

Byars, William Vincent, journalist, b. Covington, Tenn., 1857; d. Kirkwood, Mo., June 21, 1938. [17; 10; 34]

Byas, Hugh, journalist, b. Scotland, 1875; d. New Haven, Conn., March 6, 1945.

Byerly, William Elwood, mathematician, b. Philadelphia, Pa., 1849; d. Swarthmore, Pa., Dec. 20, 1935. [1a; 10; 51]

Byers, Samuel Hawkins Marshall, soldier and poet, b. Pulaski, Pa., 1838; d. Los Angeles, Calif., May 24, 1933. [2; 7; 10; 11]

Byers, William Newton, journalist and politician, b. Madison county, O., 1831; d. Denver, Colo., 1903. [10]

Byford, Henry Turman, gynaecologist, b. Evansville, Ind., 1853; d. Chicago, Ill., June 5, 1938. [10; 11]

Byford, William Heath, physician, b. Eaton, O., 1817; d. Chicago, Ill., May 21, 1891. [1; 3; 4; 6]

Byington, Edwin Hallock, clergyman, b. Adrianople, Turkey, 1860; d. Needham, Mass., Jan. 25, 1944. [45]

Byington, Ezra Hoyt, clergyman, b. Hinesborough, Vt., 1828; d. Newton, Mass., May 16, 1901. [10; 59]

Byles, Mather, clergyman, b. Boston, Mass., 1706; d. Boston, Mass., July 5, 1788. [1; 2; 3; 4; 5; 6; 7; 51]

Byne, Arthur, architect, b. Philadelphia, Pa., Sept. 25, 1883; d. Madrid, Spain, July 15, 1935. [10]

Byne, Mrs. Mildred, née Stapley, writer on art and architecture, b .New York, N.Y., 1875; d. Madrid, Spain, Dec. 24, 1941. [10]

Bynner, Edwin Lassetter, lawyer and novelist, b. Brooklyn, N.Y., 1842; d. Boston, Mass., Aug. 5, 1893. [4; 7]

Byrd, Mary Emma, astronomer, b. Le Roy, Mich., 1899; d. near Lawrence, Kans., 1934. [13]

Byrd, William, lawyer, b. Westover, Va., 1674; d. Westover, Va., Aug. 26, 1744. [1; 2; 3; 4; 7; 34]

Byrn, Edward Wright, historian, b. 1849; d. 1921.

Byrne, Austin Thomas, civil engineer, b. Belfast, Me., 1859; d. Ardonia, N.Y., May 24, 1934. [10]

Byrne, Bernard Myles, physician, b. 1813; d. 1860.

Byrne, Charles Alfred, journalist, b. London, England, 1848; d. Jersey City, N.J., Aug. 23, 1909. [10]

Byrne, Joseph Grandson, physician, b. Ireland, 1870; d. New York, N.Y., May 13, 1945. [10; 11]

Byrnes, Thomas F., police official, b. Ireland, 1842; d. New York, N.Y., May 7, 1910. [1; 4]

C

Cabell, James Lawrence, physician, b. Nelson county, Va., 1813; d. Albemarle county, Va., Aug. 13, 1889. [1; 4; 34]

Cabell, Nathaniel Francis, historian, b. Nelson county, Va., 1807; d. Bedford, Va., Sept. 1, 1891. [1; 7]

Cable, George Washington, novelist, b. New Orleans, La., 1844; d. St. Petersburg, Fla., Jan. 31, 1925. [1; 2; 3; 4; 5; 6; 34; 72]

Cabot, Mrs. Carolyn Sturgis, née **Channing,** writer of books for children, b. Concord, Mass., 1846; d. Jan. 26, 1917. [10]

Cabot, Mrs. Ella, née **Lyman,** educationist, b. Boston, Mass., 1866; d. Cambridge, Mass., Sept. 20, 1934. [10; 11]

Cabot, Hugh, surgeon, b. Beverly Farms, Mass., 1872; d. near Ellsworth, Me., Aug. 14, 1945. [10; 51]

Cabot, James Elliot, biographer, b. Boston, Mass., 1821; d. Brookline, Mass., Jan. 6, 1903. [2; 5; 51]

Cabot, Philip, educationist, b. Beverly Farms, Mass., 1872; d. Cambridge, Mass., Dec. 25, 1941. [10; 51]

Cabot, Richard Clarke, physician, b. Brookline, Mass., 1868; d. Boston, Mass., May 8, 1939. [1; 10; 11; 51]

Cabot, William Brooks, engineer and explorer, b. Brattleboro, Vt., 1858; d. Boston, Mass., Jan. 31, 1949. [62]

Cadieux, Louis Marie, priest, b. Montreal, Canada, 1783; d. Rivière Ouelle, Lower Canada, June 13, 1838. [27]

Cadman, Paul Fletcher, economist, b. 1889; d. near Oakland, Calif., Nov .11, 1946. [10]

Cadman, Samuel Parkes, clergyman, b. Wellington, England, 1864; d. Plattsburg, N.Y., July 12, 1936. [4; 7; 10; 11]

Cadwalader, John, soldier, b. Philadelphia, Pa., 1742; d. Shrewsbury, Pa., Feb. 10, 1786. [1; 4]

Cadwalader, Thomas, physician, b. Philadelphia, Pa., 1708; d. Trenton, N.J., Nov. 14, 1799. [1]

Cady, Daniel Leavens, lawyer and poet, b. West Windsor, Vt., 1861; d. April 1, 1934. [7]

Cady, Edwin Welling, lawyer and educationist, b. Lyons, N.Y., 1873; d. Skaneateles, N.Y., April 18, 1939. [2a]

Cady, H. Emilie, physician, b. 1848; d. New York, N.Y., Jan. 3, 1941.

Caffin, Charles Henry, art critic, b. Kent, England, 1854; d. New York, N.Y., Jan. 14, 1918. [1; 4; 7; 10]

Cagiati, Mrs. Gaetano. See Van Vorst, Marie.

Cain, William, civil engineer, b. Hillsboro, N.C., 1847; d. Chapel Hill, N.C., Dec. 6, 1930. [1a; 10]

Caines, George, lawyer, b. 1771; d. Catskill, N.Y., July 10, 1825. [1]

Cairns, Kate (pseud.). See Bosher, Mrs. Kate Lee, née Langley.

Cairns, William B., educationist, b. Ellsworth, Wis., 1867; d. Madison, Wis., Aug. 3, 1932. [7; 10; 11]

Cajori, Florian, historian of mathematics, b. Switzerland, 1859; d, San Francisco, Cal., Aug. 14, 1930. [1a; 10; 13]

Calderon de la Barca, Mrs. **Frances Erskine,** née **Inglis,** diplomat's wife, b. Scotland. 1804; d. 1882. [3]

Caldwell, Charles, physician, b. Caswell county, N.C., 1772; d. Louisville Ky., July 9, 1853. [1; 3; 4; 34]

Caldwell, George Chapman, chemist, b. Framingham, Mass., 1834; d. Canandaigua, N.Y., Sept. 3, 1907. [3; 4]

Caldwell, George Walter, physician, b. Lincoln, Vt., 1866; d. Hollywood, Calif., March 11, 1946. [35]

Caldwell, Howard Hayne, poet, b. Newberry, S.C, 1831; d. 1858. [34; 42]

Caldwell, Howard Walter, educationist, b. Bryan, O., 1853; d. Lincoln, Neb., March 2, 1927. [7; 10]

Caldwell, Joseph, mathematician, b. Lamington, N.J., 1773; d. Chapel Hill, N.C., Jan. 24, 1835. [1; 3; 4; 5]

Caldwell, Joshua William, lawyer, b. Athens, Tenn., 1856; d. 1909. [4; 5; 10; 34]

Caldwell, Lisle Boues, clergyman, b. Wilna, N.Y., 1834; d. ? [3; 5; 34]

Caldwell, Merritt, educationist, b. Hebron, Me., 1806; d. Portland, Me., June 6, 1848. [3; 38]

Caldwell, Samuel Lunt, educationist, b. Newburyport, Mass., 1820; d. Providence, R.I., Sept. 26, 1889. [3; 4; 5]

Caldwell, William Warner, poet, b. Newburyport, Mass., 1823; d. Newburyport, Mass., Oct. 23, 1908. [3; 46]

Calef, Robert, merchant, b. England, 1648; d. Roxbury, Mass., April 13, 1719. [1; 7]

Calfee, John Edward, educationist, b. Arcola, Mo., 1875; d. Asheville, N.C., Nov. 28, 1940. [10]

Calhoun, Mrs. Cornelia Donovan, née **O'Donovan,** hostess at the White House, b. 1864; d. Charleston, S.C., March 21, 1949.

Calhoun, Joseph Gilbert, lawyer, b. Manchester, Conn., 1856; d. Hartford, Conn., Feb. 3, 1932. [62]

Calhoun, Newell Meeker, clergyman b. Warren, Conn., 1847; d. Orange, Conn., Aug. 5, 1932. [62]

Calisch, Edmund Nathaniel, rabbi, b. Toledo, O., 1865; d. Richmond, Va., Jan. 7, 1946. [10; 21]

Calkin, John Burgess, educationist, b. Cornwallis, N.S., 1829; d. Truro, N.S., Sept. 14, 1918. [27]

Calkins, Franklin Wells, novelist, b. Iowa county, Wis., 1857; d. Dec. 20, 1928. [7; 10; 11; 44]

Calkins, Gary Nathan, biologist, b. Valparaiso, Ind., 1869; d. Scarsdale, N.Y., Jan. 4, 1943. [10; 11; 13]

Calkins, Harvey Reeves, clergyman, b. Valparaiso, Ind., 1866; d. Evanston, Ill., Feb. 16, 1941. [10]

Calkins, Mary Whiton, philosopher, b. Hartford, Conn., 1863; d. Newton, Mass., Feb. 26, 1930. [1a; 4; 10]

Calkins, Norman Allison, educationist, b. Gainesville, N.Y., 1822; d. New York N.Y., Dec. 22, 1895. [1; 3; 4]

Calkins, Phineas Wolcott, clergyman, b. Painted Post, N.Y., 1831; d. Newton, Mass., Dec. 31, 1924. [1; 10]

Call, Annie Payson, educationist, b. Arlington, Mass., 1853; d. after 1918. [10]

Call, William Timothy, writer of books for young people, b. Bangor, Me., 1856; d. New York, N.Y., Nov. 13, 1917.

Callaway, Frances Bennett, educationist, d. 1905.

Callaway, Morgan, educationist, b. Cuthbert, Ga., 1862; d. Austin, Tex., April 3, 1936. [10; 11; 34]

Callender, Edward Belcher, lawyer, b. Boston, Mass., 1851; d. Dorchester, Mass., Feb. 5, 1917. [8; 10]

Callender, Guy Stevens, economic historian, b. Harts Grove, O., 1865; d. Indian Neck, Conn., Aug. 8, 1915. [1; 4; 10]

Callender, James Thomson, publicist, b. Scotland, 1758; d. near Richmond, Va., July 1, 1803. [1; 34]

Callender, John, clergyman, b. Boston, Mass., 1706; d. Newport, R.I., Jan. 26, 1748. [1; 4; 7]

Callender, Romaine, musician and novelist, b. England, 1857; d. Philadelphia, Pa., July 1, 1930. [10; 11]

Calnek, William Arthur, local historian, b. Granville, N.S., 1822; d. Bridgewater, N.S., June 11, 1892. [27]

Calthrop, Samuel Robert, clergyman, b. Lincolnshire, England, 1829; d. 1917. [8; 10]

Calvert, Bruce, T., editor, b. 1866; d. New York, N.Y., May 31, 1940.

Calvert, George Henry, poet, playwright, and essayist, b. near Bladensburg, Md., 1803; d. Newport, R.I., May 24, 1889. [1; 2; 3; 4; 7; 71]

Calverton, Victor Francis, literary critic, b. Baltimore, Md., 1900. d. New York, N.Y., Nov. 20, 1940. [7; 10]

Calvin, Delano Dexter, architect and historian, b. Kingston, Ont., 1881; d. Toronto, Ont., Nov. 3, 1948.

Camac, Charles Nicoll Bancker, physician, b. Philadelphia, Pa., 1868; d. Altadena, Calif., Sept. 27, 1940. [10; 11; 12]

Cambreleng, Churchill Caldom, politician and diplomat, b. Washington, D.C., 1786; d. West Neck, Long Island, N.Y., April 30, 1863. [1; 4]

Cameron, Archibald, clergyman, b. Lochaber, Scotland, about 1771; d. Shelbyville, Ky., Dec. 4, 1936. [1]

Cameron, Arnold Guyot, educationist, b. Princeton, N.J., 1864; d. Princeton, N.J., July 29, 1947. [10; 11]

Cameron, Charles Innes, poet, b. Scotland, 1837; d. New Edinburgh, Ont., 1879. [27]

Cameron, Edward Herbert, psychologist, b. Yarmouth, N.S., 1875; d. Chicago, Ill., Dec. 20, 1938. [62]

Cameron, Edward Robert, lawyer, b. London, Ont., 1857; d. Ottawa, Ont., March 18, 1931. [27]

Cameron, George Frederick, poet, b. New Glasgow, N.S., 1854; d. Kingston, Ont., Sept. 17, 1885. [27]

Cameron, Malcolm Graeme, jurist, b. Goderich, Ont., 1857; d. Cobourg, Ont., Aug. 10, 1925. [27]

Cameron, Margaret, novelist and playwright, b. Ottawa, Ill., 1867; d. Winter Park, Fla., Feb. 4, 1947. [7; 10; 11]

Cameron, William Evelyn, journalist, b. Petersburg, Va., 1842; d. Louisa, Va., Jan. 25, 1927. [1; 4; 10; 34]

Camp, Charles Wadsworth, journalist and playwright, b. Philadelphia, Pa., 1879; d. Jacksonville, Fla., Oct. 31, 1936. [10]

Camp, David Nelson, educationist, b. Durham, Conn., 1820; d. New Britain, Conn., Oct. 19, 1916. [4; 10; 62]

Camp, Wadsworth. See Camp, Charles Wadsworth.

Camp, Walter Chauncey, football coach and bridge expert, b. New Britain, Conn., 1859; d. New York N.Y., March 14, 1925. [1; 7; 10]

Campbell, Alexander, clergyman, b. county Antrim, Ireland, 1788; d. Bethany, Va., March 4, 1866. [1; 4; 7; 34]

Campbell, Alexander Augustus, clergyman, b. Amherst county, Va., 1789; d. Jackson, Tenn., May 27, 1846. [3; 34]

Campbell, Alexander James, clergyman, fl. 1859-1878. [8]

Campbell, Bartley, journalist and playwright, b. Pittsburg, Pa., 1843; d. Middletown, N.J., July 30, 1888. [1; 4]

Campbell, Charles, historian, b. Petersburg, Va., 1807; d .Staunton, Va., July 11, 1876. [1; 3; 4; 7; 34]

Campbell, Charles Milton, journalist, b. Middletown, O., 1852; d. New York N.Y., Aug. 11, 1940. [10]

Campbell, Douglas, lawyer, b. Cherry Valley, N.Y., 1839; d. Schenectady, N.Y., March 7, 1893. [8; 51]

Campbell, Duncan, historian, b. Scotland, about 1819; d. Halifax, N.S., Aug. 26, 1866. [27]

Campbell, Erving (pseud.). See Pratt, Jacob Loring.

Campbell, George Alexander, clergyman, b. Morpeth, Ont., 1869; d. St. Louis, Mo., Aug. 17, 1943. [10]

Campbell, Mrs. Helen, née Stuart, novelist, b. Lockport, N.Y., 1839; d. 1918. [3; 4; 7; 8]

Campbell, Henry Colin, historian, b. 1862; d. Milwaukee, Wis., Jan. 2, 1923. [10; 44]

Campbell, James Mann, clergyman b. Scotland, 1840; d. Claremont, Calif.; May 7, 1926. [2]

Campbell, James Valentine, jurist, b. Buffalo, N.Y., 1823; d. Detroit, Mich., March 26, 1890. [1; 3; 4; 8]

Campbell, Jesse H., clergyman, b. McIntosh county, Ga., 1807; d. Columbus, Ga., April 8, 1881. [24; 26; 34]

Campbell, John, publisher and bookseller, b. Ireland, 1810; d. Philadelphia, Pa., April 29, 1874. [7]

Campbell, John, clergyman, b. Edinburgh, Scotland, 1840; d. Go-Home Bay, Ont., July 30, 1904. [27]

Campbell, John Archibald, jurist, b. Washington, Ga., 1811; d. Baltimore, Md., March 12, 1889. [1; 2; 3; 4]

Campbell, John Lyle, chemist, b. Rockbridge county, Va., 1818; d. Lexington, Va., Feb. 2, 1886. [3; 8]

Campbell, John Lyle, physicist, b. Salem, Ind., 1827; d. Crawfordsville, Ind., 1904. [10]

Campbell, John Poage, clergyman, b. Augusta county, Va., 1767; d. near Chillicothe, O., Nov. 4, 1814. [3; 34]

Campbell, John Ten Brook, civil engineer, b. near Montezuma, Ind., 1833; d. 1911. [4; 10]

Campbell, Killis, educationist, b. King William county, Va., 1872; d. Austin, Tex., Aug. 8, 1937. [7; 10]

Campbell, Lachlan (pseud.). See Campbell, Mrs. Minnie Spence, née Eakin.

Campbell, Loomis Joseph, philologist, b. 1831; d. Oneonta, N.Y., Nov. 6, 1896. [62]

Campbell, Mrs. Minnie Spence, née Eakin, poet, b. Marshall, Mo.; d. Marshall, Mo., June 10, 1940.

Campbell, Robert, clergyman, b. Lanark county, Upper Canada, 1835; d. Montreal, Que., March 13, 1921. [27]

Campbell, Robert Fishburne, clergyman, b. Lexington, Va., 1858; d. Asheville, N.C., April 3, 1947. [10; 11]

Campbell, Robert Granville, historian, b. Glenwood, Va., 1879; d. Baltimore, Md., Oct. 19, 1932. [10]

Campbell, Rollo, publisher, b. Perthshire, Scotland, 1803; d. Montreal, Que., Jan. 2, 1871. [27]

Campbell, Samuel Miner, clergyman, b. Steuben county, N.Y., 1823; d. Minneapolis, Minn., Nov. 17, 1892. [70]

Campbell, Scott (pseud.). See Davis, Frederick William.

Campbell, Thomas Joseph, priest and historian, b. New York, N.Y., 1848; d. Monroe, N.Y., Dec. 14, 1925. [1; 10; 21]

Campbell, William Henry, clergyman and educationist, b. Baltimore, Md., 1808; d. New Brunswick, N.J., Dec. 7, 1890. [1; 3; 4]

Campbell, William W., jurist and historian, b. Cherry Valley, N.Y., 1806; d. Cherry Valley, N.Y., Sept. 7, 1881. [1; 3; 4]

Campbell, William Wallace, astronomer, b. Hancock county, O., 1862; d. San Francisco, Calif., June 14, 1938. [4; 10; 11]

Campbell, William Wilfred, poet, dramatist, and novelist, b. Berlin (Kitchener), Ont., 1861; d. Ottawa, Ont., Jan. 1, 1918. [27]

Candler, Allen Daniel, politician, b. Lumpkin county, Ga., 1834; d. Atlanta, Ga., Oct. 26, 1910. [1; 3]

Candler, Warren Akin, bishop, b. Carrol county, Ga., 1857; d. Atlanta, Ga., Sept. 25, 1941. [10; 34]

Candee, Mrs. Helen, née Churchill, miscellaneous writer, b. New York, N.Y., 1858; d. York Harbor, Me., Aug. 23, 1949. [11]

Candy, Albert Luther, mathematician, b. Grant county, Ind., 1857; d. Lincoln, Neb., before 1948. [10]

Canfield, Arthur Graves, educationist, b. Sunderland, Vt., 1859; d. Dec. 5, 1947. [10; 14]

Canfield, Mrs. Flavia A., née Camp, artist and novelist, b. 1844; d. Arlington, Vt., Aug. 13, 1930. [2a]

Canfield, Mrs. George Edwin, née Gordon. See Gordon, Elizabeth.

Canfield, Henry Judson, agriculturist, b. Connecticut, 1789; d. 1856. [3; 8]

Canfield, James Hulme, educationist, b. Delaware, O., 1847; d. New York, N.Y., March 29, 1909. [1; 4; 10]

Canfield, William Walker, journalist and novelist, b. Ellicottville, N.Y., 1857; d. Utica, N.Y., Aug. 28, 1937. [7]

Canniff, William, physician and historian, b. Thurlow, Ont., 1830; d. Belleville, Ont., Oct. 18, 1910. [27]

Canning, Josiah Dean, poet, b. 1816; d. Gill, Mass., March 25, 1892. [7]

Cannon, Charles James, poet and playwright, b. New York, N.Y., 1800; d. New York, N.Y., Nov. 9, 1860. [1; 2; 3; 4; 7; 8]

Cannon, George Lyman, geologist, b. New York, N.Y., 1860; d. Colorado, before 1918. [8]

Cannon, Henry Lewin, historian, b. Cleveland, O., 1871; d. Palo Alto, Calif., Jan. 5, 1919. [51; 55; 62]

Cannon, James Graham, financier, b. Delhi, N.Y., 1858; d. Golden's Bridge, N.Y., July 5, 1916. [2; 10]

Cannon, James Spencer, clergyman, b. Curaçoa, 1776; d. New Brunswick, N.J., July 25, 1852. [3]

Cannon, Walter Bradford, physiologist, b. Prairie du Chien, Wis., 1871; d. Franklin, N.H., Oct. 1, 1945. [4; 10; 11]

Canonge, Louis Placide, journalist and playwright, b. New Orleans, La., 1822; d. Jan. 22, 1893. [7]

Canontas, Seraphim George, lawyer, b. Greece, 1874; d. New York, N.Y., April 2, 1944.

Canright, Dudley Marion, clergyman, b. Kinderhook, Mich., 1840; d. Grand Rapids, Mich., May 12, 1919. [10; 39]

Canuck, Janey (pseud.). See Murphy, Mrs. Emily Cowan, née Ferguson.

Caouette, Jean Baptiste, poet and novelist, b. Quebec, Que., 1864; d. Beauport, Que., Aug. 2, 1922. [27]

Capen, Elmer Hewitt, clergyman, b. Stoughton, Mass., 1838; d. Stoughton, Mass., March 22, 1905. [1; 3; 4]

Capen, Nahum, historian, b. Canton, Mass., 1804; d. Dorchester, Mass., Jan. 8, 1886. [1; 3]

Capers, William, clergyman, b. St. Thomas parish, S.C., 1790; d. Anderson, S.C., Jan. 29, 1855. [1; 3; 4; 34]

Capon, William Albert, dental surgeon, b. 1860; d. Philadelphia, Pa., Jan. 9, 1947.

Cappon, James, educationist, b. Dundee, Scotland, 1855; d. Kingston, Ont., Sept. 19, 1939. [27]

Capps, Stephen Reid, geologist, b. Jacksonville, Ill., 1881; d. Washington, D.C., Jan. 19, 1949. [10; 13]

Capsadell, Louisa (pseud.). See Hammond, Mrs. Henrietta, née Hardy.

Cardozo, Benjamin Nathan, jurist, b. New York, N.Y., 1870; d. Port Chester, N.Y., July 9, 1938. [7; 10; 11]

Cardozo, Jacob Newton, economist and journalist, b. Savannah, Ga., 1786; d. Savannah, Ga., Aug. 30, 1873. [1; 34]

Carey, Charles Henry, jurist and historian, b. Cincinnati, O., 1857; d. Portland, Ore., Aug. 26, 1941. [10; 11]

Carey, Eben James, anatomist, b. Chicago, Ill., 1889; d. Milwaukee, Wis., June 6, 1947. [10; 11]

Carey, Harry Wardwell, pathologist, b. Stamford, Conn., 1875; d. Troy, N.Y., Aug. 14, 1935. [62]

Carey, Henry Charles, publisher and economist, b. Philadelphia, Pa., 1793; d. Philadelphia, Pa., Oct. 13, 1879. [1; 3; 4; 8]

Carey, Matthew, publisher and economist, b. Dublin, Ireland, 1760; d. Philadelphia, Pa., Sept. 16, 1839. [1; 2; 3; 4; 5; 6; 7; 17]

Carey, Thomas Joseph, publisher, b. 1853; d. ?

Carhart, Daniel, civil engineer, b. Clinton, N.J., 1839; d. Pittsburgh, Pa., Dec. 8, 1926. [10]

Carhart, Henry Smith, physicist, b. Coeymans, N.Y., 1844; d. Pasadena, Calif., Feb. 13, 1920. [3; 10]

Carleton (pseud.). See Coffin, Charles Carleton.

Carleton, Bukk G., surgeon, b. Whitefield, N.H., 1856; d. New York, N.Y., Oct. 21, 1914. [4; 10]

Carleton, Cousin May (pseud.). See Fleming, Mrs. May Agnes, née Early.

Carleton, George Washington, traveller, b. New York, N.Y., 1822; d. Saratoga, N.Y., Oct. 11, 1902. [6]

Carleton, Henry, lawyer, b. Virginia, 1786; d. Philadelphia, Pa., March 28, 1863. [1; 3; 62]

Carleton, Henry Guy, journalist and playwright, b. Fort Union, N.M., 1856; d. Hot Springs, Ark., Dec. 10, 1910. [7; 10]

Carleton, James Henry, soldier, b. Maine, 1814; d. San Antonio, Tex., Jan. 7, 1873. [3]

Carleton, Monroe Guy, journalist, b. Genesee county, N.Y., 1833; d. Grass Lake, Mich., Feb. 22, 1918. [4]

Carleton, Osgood, mathematician, b. 1742; d. Litchfield, N.H., June, 1816. [3]

Carleton, Will, poet, b. near Hudson, Mich., 1845; d. Brooklyn, N.Y., Dec. 18, 1912. [1; 2; 3; 4; 5; 6; 7; 71]

Carlin, Francis (pseud.). See MacDonnell, James Francis Carlin.

Carlson, Evans Fordyce, soldier, b. Sydney, N.Y., 1896; d. near Portland, Ore., May 27, 1947. [10]

Carlton, Robert (pseud.) See Hall, Baynard Rush.

Carlton, William Newnham Chattin, librarian, b. Kent, England, 1873; d. New York, N.Y., Feb. 3, 1943. [7; 10]

Carmack, Edward Ward, politician, b. near Castalian Springs, Tenn., 1858; d. Nashville, Tenn., Nov. 9, 1908. [1; 2; 10]

Carman, Albert Richardson, journalist and novelist, b. Belleville, Ont., 1865; d. Montreal, Que., Oct. 16, 1939. [27]

Carman, Bliss, poet and essayist, b. Fredericton, N.B., 1861; d. New Canaan, Conn., June 8, 1929. [1; 2; 4; 7; 10; 27; 28; 72]

Carnegie, Andrew, financier and philanthropist, b. Dunfermline, Scotland, 1835; d. Shadowbrook, Mass., Aug. 11, 1919. [1; 2; 3; 4; 7]

Carnochan, Janet, historian, b. Stamford, Upper Canada, 1839; d. Niagara-on-the Lake, Ont., March 31, 1926. [27]

Carnochan, John Murray, surgeon, b. Savannah, Ga., 1817; d. New York, N.Y., Oct. 28, 1887. [1; 3; 4]

Caron, Joseph William Ivanhoë, priest and historian, b. L'Islet, Que., 1875; d. Quebec, Que.. Oct. 1, 1941. [27; 32]

Carpenter, Anna May, poet, b. Chambersburg, Pa.; d. Chester, Pa., March 26, 1900.

Carpenter, Chapin Howard, missionary, b. Milford, N.H., 1835; d. Nemuro, Japan, Feb. 2, 1887. [6]

Carpenter, Edmund Janes, journalist and historian, b. North Attleboro, Mass., 1845; d. Milton, Mass., Feb. 21, 1924. [1; 2; 4; 7; 8; 47]

Carpenter, Ernest Charles, clergyman, b. 1865; d. Brooklyn, N.Y., April 21, 1942.

Carpenter, Esther Bernon, historian, b. Wakefield, R.I., 1848; d. Wakefield, R.I., Oct. 22, 1893. [8]

Carpenter, Francis Bicknell, portrait-painter, b. Homer, N.Y., 1830; d. New York, N.Y., May 23, 1900. [1; 3; 4; 10]

Carpenter, Frank George, journalist and traveller, b. Mansfield, O., 1855; d. Nanking, China, June 18, 1924. [1; 10]

Carpenter, Frank Oliver, educationist, b. Milford, Mass., 1858; d. Boston, Mass., June 15, 1913. [8; 10]

Carpenter, George Rice, educationist, b. Labrador, 1863; d. New York, N.Y., April 8, 1909. [1; 2; 7; 10]

Carpenter, George Washington, scientist, b. Germantown, Pa., 1802; d. Germantown, Pa., June 7, 1860. [3; 4]

Carpenter, Henry Bernard, clergyman and poet, b. Dublin, Ireland, 1840; d. Sorrento, Me., July 17, 1890. [8]

Carpenter, Rolla Clinton, civil engineer, b. Orion, Mich., 1852; d. Ithaca, N.Y., Jan. 19, 1919. [2; 7; 10]

Carpenter, Stephen Cullen, journalist, b. Ireland; d. Washington ,D.C., about 1820. [1; 3; 7; 8]

Carpenter, Stephen Haskins, educationist, b. Little Falls, N.Y., 1831; d. Geneva, N.Y., Dec. 7, 1878. [1; 3; 4]

Carpenter, William Henry, novelist and historian, b. London, England, 1814; d. Baltimore, Md., 1899. [7; 8]

Carr, Benjamin, musical composer, b. England, 1769; d. Philadelphia, Pa., May 24, 1831. [1; 20]

Carr, Clark Ezra, lawyer, b. Boston Corners, N.Y., 1836; d. near Peoria, Ill., Feb. 28, 1919. [10]

Carr, Edwin Hamlin, clergyman and compiler, b. Rushville, Ind., 1865; d. Ossining, N.Y., June 7, 1945.

Carr, Emily, painter, b. Victoria, B.C., 1871; d. Victoria, B.C., March 2, 1945. [30]

Carr, Harry, journalist, b. Tipton, Ia., 1877; d. Los Angeles, Calif., Jan. 18, 1936. [10; 35]

Carr, Lucien, archaeologist, b. Troy, Mo., 1829; d. Cambridge, Mass., Jan. 27, 1915. [2; 8]

Carr, Mrs. Sarah, née **Pratt,** writer of books for boys, b. Freeport, Me., 1850; d. San Diego, Calif., after 1942. [7; 35]

Carré, Henry Beach, clergyman, b. New Orleans, La., 1871; d. Birmingham, Ala., Jan. 31, 1928. [10]

Carrel, Frank, journalist, b. Quebec, Que., 1870; d. Quebec, Que., July 30, 1940. [27]

Carrère, John Merven, architect, b. Rio de Janeiro, Brazil, 1858; d. New York, N.Y., March 1, 1911. [1; 10]

Carr-Harris, Mrs. Bertha, née **Wright,** biographer, b. 1863; d. Ottawa, Ont., Nov. 22, 1949.

Carrier, Augustus Stiles, clergyman, b. Ripley, N.Y., 1857; d. Miami, Fla., Sept. 4, 1923. [1; 10; 52]

Carrier, Louis Napoléon, historian, b. St. Henri de Lévis, Lower Canada, 1837; d. Lévis, Que., July 19, 1912. [27]

Carrington, Henry Beebee, lawyer and soldier, b. Wallingford, Conn., 1824; d. Hyde Park, Mass., Oct. 26, 1912. [1; 3; 7; 10; 62]

Carrington, Mrs. Margaret Irvine, née **Sullivant,** soldier's wife, b. Cleveland, O.; d. Crawfordsville, Ind., 1870. [6]

Carrington, William John, physician, b. Jefferson City, Mo., 1884; d. Clinton, Ia., July 24, 1947.

Carrington, William Thomas, educationist, b. Callaway county, Mo., 1854; d. Jefferson City, Mo., Jan. 21, 1937. [10]

Carroll, Alexander Mitchell, educationist, b. Wake Forest, N.C., 1870; d. March 3, 1925. [7; 24]

Carroll, Anna Ella, political writer, b. Somerset county, Md., 1815; d. Washington, D.C., Feb. 19, 1894. [8]

Carroll, Benajah Harvey, clergyman, b. near Carrollton, Miss., 1843; d. Waco, Tex., Nov. 11, 1914. [10; 24]

Carroll, Charles, lawyer and educationist, b. Providence, R:I:, 1876; d. Providence, R.I., Feb. 4, 1936. [10; 11; 21]

Carroll, Dixie (pseud.). See Cook, Carrol Blaine.

Carroll, Henry King, clergyman, b. Dennisville, N.Y., 1848; d. North Plainfield, N.J., Jan. 21, 1931. [2; 10]

Carroll, Howard, journalist and politician, b. Albany, N.Y., 1854; d. New York, N.Y., Dec. 30, 1916. [1; 7; 10]

Carroll, James Milton, clergyman and educationist, b. Monticello, Ark., 1852; d. Fort Worth, Tex., Jan. 10, 1931. [10]

Carroll, John, archbishop, b. Upper Marlborough, Md., 1735; d. Georgetown, D.C., Dec. 3, 1815. [1; 2; 3; 4; 5; 6; 7]

Carroll, John, clergyman, b. 1807; d. Toronto, Ont., Dec. 13, 1884. [27]

Carroll, John Charles, journalist, b. 1885; d. Chicago, Ill., Jan. 5, 1939.

Carroll, John Joseph, priest, b. county Sligo, Ireland, 1856; d. 1917. [2; 8; 10]

Carroll, Teresa Austin, nun, b. Clonmel, Ireland, 1829; d. 1909. [21]

Carruth, Frances Weston. See Prindle, Mrs. Frances Weston, née Carruth.

Carruth, Fred Hayden, journalist, b. near Lake City, Minn., 1862; d. Briarcliff Manor. N.Y., Jan. 3, 1932. [1a; 2; 7; 8]

Carruth, William Herbert, educationist, b. Osawatomie, Kans., 1859; d. Grand Rapids, Mich., Dec. 15, 1924. [4; 7; 10]

Carruthers, George, industrialist, b. Avening, Ont., 1869; d. Toronto, Ont., March 31, 1947. [30]

Carruthers, John, missionary, b. Scotland; d. Hamilton, Ont., 1866. [27]

Carruthers, William Alexander. See Caruthers, William Alexander.

Carryl, Charles Edward, broker and story-writer, b. New York, N.Y., 1841; d. 1920. [7; 10]

Carryl, Guy Wetmore, poet and novelist, b. New York, N.Y., 1873; d. New York, N.Y., April 1, 1904. [1; 4; 7]

Carson, Hampton Lawrence, lawyer and historian, b. Philadelphia, Pa., 1852; d. Bryn Mawr, Pa., July 18, 1929. [1a; 8; 10]

Carson, John Renshaw, electrical engineer, b. Pittsburg, Pa., 1887; d. New Hope, Va., Oct. 31, 1940. [10]

Carson, Joseph, physician and botanist, b. Philadelphia, Pa., 1808; d. Philadelphia, Pa., Dec. 30, 1876. [1; 4]

Carson, William Henry, novelist, b. New York., 1859; d. ? [8]

Carter, Mrs. Anna Alice, née **Hoppin.** See Chapin, Mrs. Alice, née Hoppin.

Carter, Boake, radio commentator, b. Baku, Russia, 1898; d. Los. Angeles, Calif., Nov. 17, 1944. [10]

Carter, Mrs. Emma, née **Smuller,** poet. b, Oakfield, N.Y.; d. Oct. 18, 1928. [10]

Carter, Franklin, educationist, b. Waterbury, Conn., 1837; d. Williamstown, Mass., Nov. 22, 1919. [1; 4; 10]

Carter, George William, clergyman ,b. Rosario, Argentina, 1867; d. New York, N.Y., March 19, 1930. [62]

Carter, James, clergyman and educationist, b. New York, N.Y., 1853; d. Oxford, Pa., April 8, 1944. [7; 10; 11]

Carter, James Coolidge, lawyer, b. Lancaster, Mass., 1827; d. New York, N.Y., Feb. 14, 1905. [1; 3; 8; 10]

Carter, James Gordon, educationist, b. Leominster, Mass., 1795; d. Chicago, Ill., July 21, 1849. [1; 3; 4]

Carter, James Madison Gore, physician, b. Johnson county, Ill., 1843; d. Los Angeles, Calif., March 3, 1919. [2; 10]

Carter, Jesse Benedict, educationist, b. New York, N.Y., 1872; d. Cervignano, Italy, July 20, 1917. [1; 7; 10]

Carter, John Henton, journalist, poet, and novelist, d. Marietta, O., May 4, 1882.

Carter, Mary Elizabeth, housekeeper, b. Albany, N.Y., 1836; d. ? [10]

Carter, Nathaniel Franklin, clergyman and poet, b. 1830; d. Concord, N.H., Oct. 30, 1915. [8; 49]

Carter, Nathaniel Hazeltine, journalist and poet, b. Concord, N.H., 1787; d. Marseilles, France, Jan. 3, 1830. [3; 49]

Carter, Nicholas (pseud.). See Davis, Frederick William.

Carter, Nick (pseud.). See Coryell, John Russell.

Carter, Peter, publisher, b. Scotland, 1825; d. New York, N.Y., 1900. [3; 8]

Carter, Robert, journalist and novelist, b. Albany, N.Y., 1819; d. Cambridge, Mass., Feb. 15, 1879. [1; 3; 7]

Carter, Russell Kelso, educationist, b. Baltimore, Md., 1849; d. Baltimore, Md., Aug. 23, 1928. [3; 8; 34]

Carter, Ruth (pseud.). See Robertson, Mrs. Sarah Franklin, née Davis.

Carter, William, clergyman, b. Pittington, England, 1868; d. Montclair, N.J., July 26, 1949. [10]

Carter, William Giles Harding, soldier, b. Nashville, Tenn., 1851; d. Washington, D.C. May 25, 1925. [2; 10]

Carter, William Spencer, educationist, b. Warren county, N.J., 1869; d. Newton, Mass., May 12, 1944. [10]

Cartwright, Conway Edward, clergyman, b. Kingston, Upper Canada, 1837; d. Vancouver, B.C., Jan. 26, 1920. [27]

Cartwright, Otho Grandford, accountant, b. Belmont, N.Y., 1869; d. New York, N.Y., Nov. 29, 1943. [62]

Cartwright, Peter, clergyman, b. Amherst county, Va., 1785; d. near Pleasant Plains, Ill., Sept. 25, 1872. [1; 3; 4; 6; 7; 34]

Cartwright, Sir Richard John, politician, b. Kingston, Upper Canada, 1835; d. Kingston, Ont., Sept. 24, 1912. [27]

Carus, Paul, philosopher, b. Germany, 1852; d. La Salle, Ill., Feb. 11, 1919. [1; 7; 8; 10]

Caruthers, Eli Washington, clergyman, b. Rowan county, N.C., 1793; d. Guilford county, N.C., Nov. 14, 1865. [4; 34]

Caruthers, William Alexander, physician and novelist, b. Virginia, about 1800; d. Marietta, Ga., Aug. 29, 1846. [1; 3; 7; 8; 34]

Carver, George, educationist, b. Cincinnati, O., 1888; d. Pittsburg, Pa., Oct., 29, 1949. [14]

Carver, John (pseud.). See Dodge, Nathaniel Shatswell.

Cary, Alice, poet and novelist, b. near Cincinnati, O., 1820; d. New York, N.Y., Feb. 12, 1871. [1; 2; 3; 4; 6; 7; 71]

Cary, Edward, journalist, b. Albany, N.Y., 1840; d. Brooklyn, N.Y., May 23, 1917. [1; 7]

Cary, Edward Richard, engineer, b. Troy, N.Y., 1865; d. Columbia, S.C., July 17, 1941. [10]

Cary, Elisabeth Luther, biographer, b. Brooklyn, N.Y., 1867; d. Brooklyn, N.Y., July 13, 1936. [7; 10]

Cary, George Lovell, theologian, b. Medway, Mass., 1830; d. Calgary, Alta., June 25, 1910. [10; 51]

Cary, Melbert Brinckerhoff, printer, b. New York, N.Y., 1892; d. New York, N.Y., May 27, 1941. [10]

Cary, Otis, missionary, b. Foxboro, Mass., 1851; d. Bradford, Mass., July 23, 1932. [45]

Cary, Phoebe, poet, b. near Cincinnati, O., 1824; d. Newport, R.I., July 31, 1871. [1; 2; 3; 4; 7; 71]

Cary, Thomas, journalist, b. Bristol, England, 1751; d. Quebec, Lower Canada, 1823. [27]

Casanowicz, Immanuel Moses, archaeologist, b. Russia, 1853; d. Washington, D.C., Sept. 26, 1927. [10]

Case. Adelaide Teague, educationist, b. St. Louis, Mo., 1887; d. Boston, Mass., June 19, 1948. [11]

Case, Alden Buell, missionary, b. Gustavus, O., 1851; d. Pomona, Calif., Oct. 27, 1932. [62]

Case, Arthur Ellicott, educationist, b. Trenton, N.J., 1894; d. Evanston, Ill., Jan. 19, 1946. [10; 62]

Case, Erastus Ely, physician, b. Canton, Conn., 1847; d. Windsor, Conn., Oct. 27, 1918. [62]

Case, Frank, hotel-keeper, b. Buffalo, N.Y., 1870; d. New York, N.Y., June 7, 1946.

Case, Mary Emily, educationist, b. New York, N.Y., 1857; d. Bratenahl, O., Sept. 2, 1941. [10]

Case, Shirley Jackson, educationist, b. Hatfield Point, N.B., 1872; d. Lakeland, Fla., Dec. 5, 1947. [10; 11; 30]

Case, Theodore Spencer, physician and journalist, b. Butts county, Ga., 1832; d. Kansas City, Mo., Feb. 10, 1900. [10]

Case, William Scoville, jurist and novelist, b. Tariffville, Conn., 1863; d. West Hartford, Conn., Feb. 28, 1928. [1; 10]

Casey, Silas, soldier, b. East Greenwich, R.I., 1807; d. Brooklyn, N.Y., Jan. 22, 1882. [1; 3; 4]

Casgrain, Henri Raymond, priest, poet, and historian, b. Rivière-Ouelle, Lower Canada, 1831; d. Quebec, Que., Feb. 12, 1904. [27]

Casgrain, Philippe Baby, historian, b. Quebec, Lower Canada, 1826; d. Quebec, Que., May 23, 1917. [27]

Casgrain, René Edouard, priest, b. Rivière-Ouelle, Lower Canada, 1839; d. Quebec, Que., April 25, 1917. [32]

Cash, Wilbur Joseph, editor, b. 1901; d. Mexico City, Mexico, June 26, 1941.

Caskey, Lacey Davis, museum curator, b. Honesdale, Pa., 1880; d. Boston, Mass., May 20, 1944. [62]

Caskoden, Edwin (pseud.). See Major, Charles.

Casler, John Overton, soldier, b. Frederick county, Va., 1838; d. ? [34]

Cass, Lewis, soldier and politician, b. Exeter, N.H., 1782; d. Detroit Mich., June 17, 1866. [1; 3; 4; 7]

Cassegrain, Arthur, poet, b. L'Islet, Lower Canada, 1835; d. Feb. 9, 1868. [27]

Cassel, Daniel Kalb, genealogist, b. Montgomery county, Pa., 1820; d. Philadelphia, Pa., March ,1898.

Casselman, Alexander Clark, educationist, b. Finch, Ont., 1852; d. North Bay, Ont., Feb. 10, 1940. [27]

Cassels, Samuel Jones, poet, b. 1806; d. 1853. [7]

Cassin, John, ornithologist, b. Delaware county, Pa., 1813; d. Philadelphia, Pa., Jan. 10, 1869. [1; 2; 3; 4]

Cassirer, Ernst, philosopher, b. Breslau, Germany, 1874; d. New York, N.Y., April 13, 1945.

Castle, Henry Anson, lawyer, b. near Quincy, Ill., 1841; d. Silver Lake, Minn., Aug. 16, 1916. [1; 10; 70]

Castle, Vernon Blythe, dancer, b. Norwich, England, 1887; d. Fort Worth, Tex., Feb. 15, 1918. [1]

Castleberry, John Jackson, clergyman, b. Savannah, Tenn., 1877; d. Cincinatti, O., Aug. 7, 1937. [62]

Castlemon, Harry (pseud.). See Fosdick, Charles Austin.

Caswall, Henry, clergyman, b. Hampshire, England, 1810; d. Franklin, Pa., Dec. 17, 1870. [3; 8]

Caswell, Alexis, clergyman and mathematician, b. Taunton, Mass., 1799; d. Providence, R.I., Jan. 8, 1877. [1; 3; 4; 8]

Cate, Eliza Jane, novelist, b. 1812; d. Poughkeepsie, N.Y., Jan. 9, 1883. [8]

Cathcart, William, clergyman and historian, b. Londonderry county, Ireland, 1826; d. Philadelphia, Pa., July 8, 1908. [1; 3; 10; 24]

Cathell, Daniel Webster, physician, b. Worcester county, Md., 1839; d. Baltimore, Md., May 1, 1925. [10]

Cather, Mrs. Katherine, née Dunlap, writer of books for children, b. Navarre, O.; d. California, Feb. 6, 1926. [2a]

Cather, Willa Sibert, novelist, b. near Winchester, Va., 1876; d. New York, N.Y., April 24, 1947. [7; 10; 11; 12]

Catherwood, Mrs. Mary, née Hartwell, novelist, b. Luray, O., 1847; d. Chicago, Ill., Dec. 26, 1902. [1; 4; 7; 10]

Cathrall, Isaac, physician, b. Philadelphia, Pa., 1764; d. Feb. 22, 1819. [3]

Catlin, George, painter and ethnologist, b. Wilkesbarre, Pa., 1798; d. Jersey City, N.J., Dec. 23, 1872. [1; 2; 3; 4; 5; 6; 7]

Catlin, George Byron, journalist and historian, b. Rushville, N.Y., 1857; d. Detroit, Mich., March 15, 1934. [39]

Catlin, George Lynde, journalist and poet, b. Staten Island, N.Y., 1840; d. New York, N.Y., Jan. 14, 1896. [8]

Cato (pseud.). See Livingston, Robert R.

Caton, John Dean, jurist, b. Monroe, N.Y., 1812; d. Chicago, Ill., July 30, 1895. [1; 3; 4]

Cattell, Edward James, novelist and statistician, b. Philadelphia, Pa., 1856; d. Philadelphia, Pa., Jan. 6, 1938. [10]

Cattell, James McKeen, educationist, b. Easton, Pa., 1860; d. Lancaster, Pa., Jan. 20, 1944. [7; 10; 13]

Catterall, Ralph Charles Henry, educationist, b. Bolton, England, 1866; d. Huron, Mich., Aug. 3, 1914. [10]

Cauchon, Joseph Edouard, politician, b. Quebec, Lower Canada, 1816; d. near Qu'Appelle, N.W.T., Canada, Feb. 23, 1885. [27]

Cauffman, Stanley Hart, novelist, b. Philadelphia, Pa., 1880; d. Philadelphia, Pa.. Feb. 11, 1947. [11]

Caughey, James, clergyman, b. Ireland, 1810; d. 1892. [8]

Caulkins, Frances Mainwaring, local historian, b. New London, Conn., 1796; d. New London, Conn., Feb. 3, 1869. [3; 8]

Caustic, Christopher (pseud.). See Fessenden, Thomas Green.

Caverly, Abiel Moore, physician, b. Canterbury, N.H., 1817; d. Pittsford, Vt., 1879. [8; 49]

Caverly, Robert Boodey, lawyer, b. Barrington, N.H., 1806; d. 1887. [8; 51]

Caverno, Charles, clergyman, b. Strafford, N.Y., 1832; d. Lombard, Ill., Sept. 29, 1916. [10; 49]

Cavins, Lorimer Victor, educationist, b. near Mattoon, Ill., 1880; d. Charleston, W. Va., Jan. 28, 1945. [10]

Cawein, Madison Julius, poet, b. Louisville, Ky., 1865; d. Louisville, Ky., Dec. 7, 1914. [1; 2; 4; 7; 10; 34; 72]

Cazes, Paul de, educationist, b. France, 1841; d. Neuilly-sur-Seine, France, May 28, 1913. [27]

Cecil (pseud.). See Fisher, Sidney George.

Centz, P.C. (pseud.). See Sage, Bernard Janin.

Cervus, G. I. (pseud.). See Roe, William James.

Cesare, Oscar, cartoonist, b. Sweden, 1885; d. Stamford, Conn., July 24, 1948.

Cesnola, Luigi Palma di, soldier and archaeologist, b. Rivarola, Italy, 1832; d. New York, N.Y., Nov. 20, 1904. [1; 2; 4]

Chadbourne, Paul Ansel, educationist, b. North Berwick, Me., 1823; d. New York, N.Y., Feb. 23, 1883. [1; 3; 4; 8]

Chaddock, Robert Emmet, statistician, b. 1879; d. New York, N.Y., Oct. 21, 1940. [10]

Chadsey, Charles Ernest, educationist, b. 1870; d. Urbana, Ill., April 9, 1930. [2; 10]

Chadwick, Edward Marion, genealogist, b. Ancaster, Upper Canada, 1840; d. Toronto, Ont., Dec. 15, 1921. [27]

Chadwick, French Ensor, naval officer, b. Morgantown, W. Va., 1844; d. New York, N.Y., Jan. 27, 1919. [1; 2; 4; 10]

Chadwick, Henry, sportsman, b. Exeter, England, 1824; d. Brooklyn, N.Y., April 20, 1908. [1; 7; 8]

Chadwick, John White, clergyman and poet, b. Marblehead, Mass., 1840; d. Brooklyn., Dec. 11, 1904. [1; 3; 4; 7; 8; 10]

Chaffin, Lucien Gates, musician, b. Worcester, Mass., 1846; d. New York, N.Y., May 26, 1927. [10; 20]

Chaffin, William Ladd, clergyman, b. 1837; d. 1922. [8]

Chafin, Eugene Wilder, prohibitionist, b. East Troy, Wis., 1852; d. Long Branch, Calif., Nov. 30, 1920. [1; 2]

Chaillé, Stanford Emerson, physician, b. Natchez, Miss., 1830; d. New Orleans, La., May 27, 1911. [2; 3; 34]

Chaillé-Long, Charles, explorer, b. Princess Anne, Md., 1842; d. Virginia Beach, Va., March 26, 1917. [1; 2; 7; 10]

Chalkley, Thomas, clergyman, b. Southwark, England, 1675; d. Tortola, Virgin Islands, Nov. 4, 1741. [1; 4]

Challen, James, clergyman and poet, b. Hackensack, N.J., 1802; d. ? [6]

Chalmers, Lionel, physician, b. Scotland, about 1815; d. Charleston, S.C., 1777. [3]

Chalmers, Stephen, poet and novelist, b. Dunoon, Scotland, 1880; d. Laguna Beach, Calif., Dec. 14, 1935. [7; 10; 11]

Chamberlain, Alexander Francis, anthropologist, b. Norfolk, England, 1865; d. Worcester, Mass., April 8, 1914. [7; 10; 27]

Chamberlain, Daniel Henry, politician, b. West Brookfield, Mass., 1835; d. Charlottesville, Va., April 13, 1907. [2; 3; 4; 10]

Chamberlain, Henry Richardson, journalist, b. Peoria, Ill., 1859; d. London, England, Feb. 15, 1911. [1; 10]

Chamberlain, Jacob, clergyman, b. Sharon, Conn., 1835; d. Madanapalle, India, March 2, 1908. [1; 2]

Chamberlain, Joshua Lawrence, soldier and educationist, b. Brewer, Me., 1828; d. Portland, Me., Feb. 24, 1914. [1; 3; 4; 10]

Chamberlain, Leander Trowbridge, clergyman, b. West Brookfield, Mass., 1837; d. Pasadena, Calif., May 10, 1913. [10; 62]

Chamberlain, Mellen, historian, b. Pembroke, N.H., 1821; d. Chelsea, Mass., June 25, 1900. [1; 2; 7; 10]

Chamberlain, Montague, ornithologist, b. Saint John, N.B., 1844; d. Boston, Mass., Feb. 10, 1924. [2; 10]

Chamberlain, Nathan Henry, clergyman and novelist, b. Bourne, Mass., 1828; d. Bourne, Mass., April 1, 1901. [1; 51]

Chamberlain, William Isaac, missionary, b. Madras, India, 1862; d. New York, N.Y., Sept. 28, 1937. [10]

Chamberlin, Georgia Louise, educationist, b. Grand Bend, Pa., 1862; d. Montclair, N.J., Sept. 6, 1943.

Chamberlin, Joseph Edgar, journalist, b. Newbury, Vt., 1851; d. South Hanson, Mass., July 6, 1935. [2; 7; 10]

Chamberlin, Thomas Chrowder, geologist, b. Mattoon, Ill., 1843; d. Chicago, Ill., Nov. 15, 1928. [1; 3; 7; 10]

Chambers, Edward Thomas Davies, journalist and civil servant, b. Essex, England, 1852; d. Quebec, Que., Oct. 5, 1931. [27]

Chambers, Ernest John, soldier and civil servant, b. Staffordshire, England, 1862; d. Ottawa, Ont., May 11, 1925. 27]

Chambers, George, lawyer, b. Chambersburg, Pa., 1786; d. Chambersburg, Pa., March 25, 1866. [1; 4]

Chambers, James Julius, journalist and novelist, b. Bellefontaine, O., 1850; d. New York, N.Y., Feb. 12, 1920. [1; 3; 10]

Chambers, Robert William, artist and novelist, b. Brooklyn, N.Y., 1865; d. New York, N.Y., Dec. 16, 1933. [1a; 7; 10; 72]

Chambers, Talbot Wilson, clergyman, b. Carlisle, Pa., 1819; d. New York, N.Y., Feb. 3, 1896. [1; 3; 4]

Chambliss, Alexander Wilds, clergyman, b. 1812; d. Montgomery, Mo., Dec. 18, 1893. [24]

Champion, John Benjamin, clergyman and educationist, b. Greenvale, P.E.I., 1868; d. Philadelphia, Pa., Jan. 18, 1948. [10; 24]

Champion, Roland (pseud.). See Corning, James Leonard.

Champlin, Edwin Ross, journalist and poet, b. East Westerly, R.I., 1854; d. Gloucester, Mass., Sept. 8, 1928. [7; 10]

Champlin, James Tift, educationist, b. Colchester, Conn., 1811; d. Portland, Me., March 15, 1882; [2; 3; 4; 24]

Champlin, John Denison, editor, b. Stonington, Conn., 1834; d. New York, N.Y., Jan. 8, 1915. [1; 2; 4; 7; 10; 62]

Champlin, Virginia (pseud.). See Lord, Grace Virginia.

Champney, Mrs. Elizabeth J., née Williams, novelist, b. Springfield, O., 1850; d. Seattle, Wash., Oct. 13, 1922. [2; 3; 7; 10]

Chance, Mrs. Julie Grinnell. See Cruger. Mrs. Julie Grinnell, née Storrow.

Chancellor, Charles William, physician, b. Spottsylvania county, Va., 1833; d. Washington, D.C., Jan. 31, 1915. [2; 3; 4; 10]

Chandler, Charles de Forest, soldier, b. Cleveland, O., 1878; d. Washington, D.C., May 18, 1939. [10]

Chandler, Charles Henry, journalist, b. Prescott, Mass., 1840; d. Boston, Mass., Jan. 4, 1885. [3]

Chandler, Elizabeth Margaret, poet, b. Centre, Del., 1807; d. Sewanee county, Mich., Nov. 22, 1834. [1; 3; 7; 8]

Chandler, Francis Ward, architect, b. Boston, Mass., 1844; d. North Haven, Me., Sept. 8, 1926. [2; 10]

Chandler, Frank Wadleigh, educationist, b. Brooklyn, N.Y., 1873; d. Prout's Neck, Me., June 13, 1947. [7; 10]

Chandler, Mrs. G. W. See Chandler, Mrs. Izora Cecilia.

Chandler, George, physician and genealogist, b. Pomfret, Conn., 1806; d. Worcester, Mass., May 17, 1893. [69]

Chandler, Mrs. Izora Cecilia, artist and writer of books for young people, d. Kingston, N.Y., Aug. 25, 1906. [10]

Chandler, John Scudder, missionary, b. Madura, South India, 1849; d. Kodaikanal, South India, June 19, 1934. [1a; 62]

Chandler, Joseph Ripley, journalist and politician, b. Kingston, Mass., 1792; d. Philadelphia, Pa., July 10, 1890. [1; 3; 4; 7]

Chandler, Julian Alvin Carroll, educationist, b. Guineys, Va., 1872; d. Norfolk, Va., May 31, 1934. [1a; 10; 11]

Chandler, Katherine, naturalist, b. San. Francisco, Calif.; d. San Francisco, June 25, 1930. [10; 35]

Chandler, Mary Greene. See Ware, Mrs. Mary Greene, née Chandler.

Chandler, Peleg Whitman, lawyer, b. New Gloucester, Me., 1816; d. Boston, Mass., May 28, 1889. [1; 4]

Chandler, Thomas Bradbury, clergyman, b. Woodstock, Conn., 1728; d. Elizabethtown, N.J., June 17, 1790. [1; 3; 62]

Chandler, William Henry, traffic expert, b. 1878; d. Upper Montclair, N.J., Dec. 2, 1939. [10]

Chaney, George Leonard, clergyman, b. Salem, Mass., 1836; d. Salem, Mass., April 10, 1922. [8; 51]

Chaney, Lucian West, naturalist, b. Hauvelton, N.Y., 1857; d. Washington, D.C., May 6, 1935. [3; 10]

Chanler, William Astor, traveller, b. Newport, R. I., 1867; d. Mentone, France, March 4, 1934. [8; 10]

Channing, Blanche Mary, writer of books for children, b. 1863; d. 1902. [8]

Channing, C. G. Fairfax (pseud.). See Gross, Christian Channing.

Channing, Edward, historian, b. Dorchester, Mass., 1856; d. Cambridge, Mass., Jan. 7, 1931. [1a; 2; 3; 4; 7; 10; 51]

Channing, Edward Tyrrell, educationist, b. Newport, R.I., 1790; d. Cambridge, Mass., Feb. 8, 1856. [1; 3; 4; 7]

Channing, Grace Ellery, poet and essayist, b. Providence, R.I., 1862; d. New York, N.Y., April 3, 1937. [7; 10]

Channing, Walter, physician, b. Newport, R.I., 1786; d. Boston, Mass., July 27, 1876. [1; 3; 4; 51]

Channing, William Ellery, clergyman, b. Newport, R.I., 1780; d. Bennington, Vt., Oct. 2, 1842. [1; 2; 3; 4; 5; 6; 7; 10]

Channing, William Ellery, poet, b. Boston, Mass., 1818; d. Concord, Mass., Dec. 23, 1901. [1; 3; 7; 10]

Channing, William Francis, physician and inventor, b. Boston, Mass., 1820; d. Boston, Mass., March 19, 1901. [1; 3; 4; 8]

Channing, William Henry, clergyman, b. Boston, Mass., 1810; d. London, England, Dec. 23, 1884. [1; 3; 4; 7; 8]

Chanute, Octave, aeronautical pioneer, b. Paris, France, 1832; d. Chicago, Ill., Nov. 23, 1910. [1; 4; 10]

Chapais, John Charles, civil servant, b. St. Denis de Kamouraska, Que., 1850; d. St. Denis de Kamouraska, Que., July 23. 1926. [27]

Chapais, Sir Thomas, politician and historian, b. St. Denis de Kamouraska, Que., 1858; d. St. Denis de Kamouraska, July 15, 1948. [28]

Chapeau, Mrs. Ellen, née Chazal, short-story writer, b. Charleston, S.C., 1844; d. ? [34]

Chapin, Aaron Lucius, educationist, b. Hartford, Conn., 1817; d. Beloit, Wis., July 22, 1892. [1; 3; 4; 7]

Chapin, Alonzo Bowen, clergyman, b. Somers, Conn., 1808; d. Hartford, Conn., July 9 ,1858. [1; 3]

Chapin, Anna Alice, novelist and short-story writer, b. New York, N.Y., 1880; d. New York, N.Y., Feb. 26, 1920. [2; 7; 10]

Chapin, Carl Mattison, journalist, b. Waterbury, Conn., 1879; d. West Hartford, Conn., Feb. 22, 1938. [62]

Chapin, Charles E., journalist, b. 1858; d. Sing Sing, N.Y., Dec. 13, 1930. [7]

Chapin, Edward Whitman, essayist, b. Chicopee, Mass., 1840; d. Holyoke, Mass., May 7, 1924. [45]

Chapin, Edwin Hubbell, clergyman, b. Union Village, N.Y., 1814; d. New York, N.Y., Dec. 27, 1880. [1; 2; 3; 4; 7]

Chapin, Henry Dwight, physician, b. Steubenville, O., 1857; d. Bronxville, N.Y., June 27, 1942. [10; 11]

Chapin, Howard Miller, librarian and historian, b. Providence, R.I., 1887; d. Providence, R.I., Sept. 18, 1940. [7; 10; 11]

Chapin, James Henry, clergyman and educationist, b. Leavenworth, Ind., 1832; d. South Norwalk, Conn., March 14, 1892. [8]

Chapin, Stephen, clergyman, b. Milford, Mass., 1778; d. Washington, D.C., Oct. 1, 1845. [3; 4]

Chapin, Will E., cartoonist, b. Rahway, N.J., 1857; d. Hollywood, Calif., Oct. 15, 1937.

Chaplin, Mrs. Ada C., writer of religious books for young people, b. Falmouth, Mass., 1842; d. Mansfield, Conn., Dec. 9, 1883. [3; 7; 8]

Chaplin, Heman White, lawyer, b. Providence, R.I., 1847; d. Washington, D.C., Dec. 26, 1924. [8; 51]

Chaplin, Mrs. Jane, née **Dunbar,** writer of religious books for young people, b. Scotland, 1819; d. Boston, Mass., April 17, 1884. [3; 7]

Chaplin, Jeremiah, clergyman and educationist, b. Rowley, Mass., 1776; d. Hamilton, N.Y., May 7, 1841. [1; 47]

Chaplin, Jeremiah, clergyman and educationist, b. Danvers, Mass., 1813; d. New Utrecht, N.Y., March 5, 1886. [3; 6; 7; 8]

Chaplin, Stewart, lawyer and educationist, b. 1858; d. Woodstock, N.Y., Sept. 6, 1940. [47; 48]

Chapman, Alvan Whitworth, botanist and physician, b. Southampton, Mass., 1809; d. Apalachicola, Fla., April 6, 1899. [1; 4]

Chapman, Arthur, journalist, b. Rockford, Ill., 1873; d. New York, N.Y., Dec. 4, 1935. [7; 10; 11]

Chapman, Charles Edward, historian, b. Franklin, N.H., June 3, 1880; d. Oakland, Calif., Nov. 18, 1941. [7; 10; 11]

Chapman, Edward, geologist and poet, b. Kent, England, 1821; d. near London, England, Jan. 28, 1904. [27]

Chapman, Francis, lawyer, b. Burlington, N.J., 1869; d. Philadelphia, Pa., May 2, 1939. [10]

Chapman, Frank Michler, ornithologist, b. Englewood, N.J., 1864; d. New York, N.Y., Nov. 15, 1945. [4; 7; 10]

Chapman, George Thomas, clergyman, b. Pilton, Devonshire, England, 1786; d. Newburyport, Mass., Oct. 18, 1872. [3; 6]

Chapman, Harvey Wood, educationist, b. West Stratford, Conn., 1875; d. Bridgeport, Conn., Aug. 15, 1941. [62]

Chapman, Henry Cadwalader, physician and biologist, b. Philadelphia, Pa., 1845; d. Bar Harbor, Me., Sept. 7, 1909. [1; 3; 4; 10]

Chapman, Henry Smith, journalist, b. Gorham, Me., 1871; d. Salem, Mass., Nov. 22, 1936. [46]

Chapman, James Crosby, psychologist, b. Nottingham, England, 1889; d. Chatauqua, N.Y., July 15, 1925. [10]

Chapman, John Abney, educationist and poet, b. Edgefield county, N.C., 1821; d. 1906. [8; 34; 42]

Chapman, John Jay, lawyer and essayist, b. New York, N.Y., 1862; d. Poughkeepsie, N.Y., Nov. 3, 1933. [1a; 2; 7; 10; 11]

Chapman, John Wilbur, evangelist, b. Richmond, Ind., 1859; d. New York, N.Y., Dec. 25, 1918. [1]

Chapman, Mrs. Maria, née **Weston,** reformer, b. Weymouth, Mass., 1806; d. Weymouth, Mass., July 12, 1885. [1; 2; 4]

Chapman, Nathaniel, physician, b. Sumner Hill, Va., 1780; d. Philadelphia, Pa., July 1, 1853. [1; 3; 4]

Chapman, Mrs. Rose Woodallen, née **Allen,** writer on social hygiene, b. Lakeside, O., 1875; d. New York, N.Y., Oct. 27, 1923. [10]

Chapman, Royal Norton, educationist, b. Morristown, Minn., 1889; d. Minneapolis, Minn., Dec. 2, 1939. [13]

Chapman, William, poet, b. St. François de la Beauce, Que., 1850; d. Ottawa, Ont., Feb. 23, 1917. [27]

Chapman, William Gerard, literary agent, b. Peekskill, N.Y., 1877; d. Chicago Ill., June 11, 1945. [10; 11]

Chappell, Absalom Harris, lawyer and historian, b. Hancock county, Ga., 1801; d. Columbus, Ga., Dec. 11, 1878. [1; 4]

Chappell, George Shepard, architect and humorist, b. 1877; d. West Bantam, Conn., Nov. 25, 1946. [7; 62]

Charland, Paul Victor, priest and historian, b. St. Roch, Que., 1858; d. Quebec, Que., Dec. 24, 1939. [27]

Charles, Mrs. Emily, née **Thornton,** poet, b. Indiana, 1845; d. ? [8]

Charlesworth, Hector Willoughby, journalist, b. Hamilton, Ont., 1873; d. Toronto, Ont., Dec. 29, 1945. [27]

Charlton, Robert Milledge, poet, b. Savannah, Ga., 1807; d. Savannah, Ga., Jan. 18, 1854. [7; 34]

Chartrand, Joseph Demers, soldier, b. St. Vincent de Paul, Que., 1852; d. Kingston, Ont., April, 1905. [27]

Chase, Alvin Wood, physician, b. Cayuga county, N.Y., 1817; d. Ann Arbor, Mich., 1885. [39]

Chase, Arthur Minturn, novelist, b. New York, N.Y., 1873; d. South Salem, N.Y., Sept. 7, 1947. [7; 10]

Chase, Frank Eugene, playwright, b. 1857; d. 1920. [51]

Chase, Frank Herbert, librarian, b. Portland, Me., 1870; d. Hingham, Mass., Dec. 12, 1930. [62]

Chase, Franklin Henry, journalist, b. Syracuse, N.Y., 1864; d. Syracuse, N.Y., May 24, 1940.

Chase, George, lawyer and educationist, b. Portland, Me., 1849; d. New York, N.Y., Jan. 8, 1924. [1; 10; 62]

Chase, George Millet, educationist, b. Lewiston, Me., 1873; d. Lewiston, Me., Nov. 14, 1938. [11; 62]

Chase, George Wingate, local historian, b. Haverhill, Mass., 1826; d. 1867. [8]

Chase, Irah, clergyman, b. Stratton, Vt., 1793; d. Newton, Mass., Nov. 1, 1864. [1; 3; 43]

Chase, Isaac McKim, mechanical engineer, b. Baltimore, Md., 1837; d. 1903. [10]

Chase, Jason Franklin, clergyman, b. Boston, Mass., 1872; d. West Roxbury, Mass., Nov. 3, 1926. [10; 60]

Chase, Lewis Nathaniel, educationist, b. Sidney, Me., 1873; d. Washington, D.C., Sept. 23, 1937. [7; 10]

Chase, Lucien B., politician, b. Vermont, 1817; d. Clarksville, Tenn., Dec. 14, 1864. [3; 8]

Chase, Philander, bishop, b. Cornish, N.H., 1775; d. Jubilee College, Ill., Sept. 20, 1852. [1; 3; 4]

Chase, Pliny Earle, meteorologist, b. Worcester, Mass., 1820; d. Haverford, Pa., Dec. 17, 1886. [1; 3; 4]

Chase, Salmon Portland, jurist, b. Cornish, N.Y., 1808; d. New York, N.Y., May 7, 1873. [1; 4; 7]

Chase, Squire, missionary, b. Scipio, N.Y., 1802; d. Syracuse, N.Y., July 26, 1843. [3]

Chase, Thomas, educationist, b. Worcester, Mass., 1827; d. Providence, R.I., Oct. 5, 1892. [1; 3; 4]

Chase, Warren, spiritualist, b. 1813; d. 1891. [6]

Chase, William Ingraham, educationist, b. 1852; d. 1889.

Chase, William Sheafe, clergyman, b. Amboy, Ill., 1858; d. Kings Park, N.Y., 1940. [10]

Chatard, Francis Silas Marean, bishop, b. Baltimore, Md., 1834; d. Indianapolis, Ind., Sept. 7, 1918. [1; 4; 10]

Chatburn, George Richard, civil engineer, b. near Magnolia, Ia., 1863; d. Lincoln, Neb., Jan. 30, 1940. [10; 11]

Chatfield-Taylor, Hobart Chatfield, novelist and biographer, b. Chicago, Ill., 1865; d. Santa Barbara, Calif., Jan. 16, 1945. [4; 7; 10; 11]

Chatterton, Mason Daniel, lawyer, b. Mount Holly, Vt., 1833; d. Lansing, Mich., Oct. 28, 1903. [39]

Chauncey, Charles, clergyman and educationist, b. Hertfordshire, England, 1592; d. Cambridge, Mass., Feb. 19, 1672. [1; 3; 4]

Chauncey, Charles, clergyman, b. Boston, Mass., 1705; d. Boston, Mass., Feb. 10, 1787. [1; 3; 4]

Chauncey, Shelton (pseud.). See Nicholls, Charles Wilbur de Lyon.

Chauveau, Charles Auguste, lawyer, b. Quebec, Que., 1877; d. Quebec, Que., Dec. 17, 1940. [27]

Chauveau, Pierre Joseph Olivier, politician, b. Quebec, Lower Canada, 1820; d. Quebec, Que., April 4, 1890. [27]

Chauvenet, Regis, mining engineer, b. Philadelphia, Pa., 1842; d. Denver, Colo., Dec. 6, 1920. [4; 10]

Chauvenet, William, mathematician and astronomer, b. Milford, Pa., 1820; d. St Paul, Minn., Dec. 13, 1870. [1; 3; 4]

Checkley, John, clergyman, b. Boston, Mass., 1680; d. Providence, R.I., Feb. 15, 1754. [1; 3; 4; 43]

Cheetham, James, journalist, b. Manchester, England, 1772; d. New York, N.Y., Sept. 19, 1810. [1; 3]

Cheever, David Williams, surgeon, b. Portsmouth, N.H., 1831; d. 1915. [4; 51]

Cheever, Ezekiel, educationist, b. London, England, 1614; d. Boston, Mass., Aug. 21, 1708. [1; 3; 4; 7]

Cheever, George Barrell, clergyman, b. Hallowell, Me., 1807; d. Englewood, N.J., Oct. 1, 1890. [1; 3; 4; 7]

Cheever, Mrs. Harriet Anna, writer of books for children, fl. 1890-1911. [10]

Cheever, Henry Theodore, clergyman, b. Hallowell, Me., 1814; d. Worcester, Mass., Feb. 13, 1897. [1; 3; 4; 7]

Cheever, Noah Wood, lawyer, b. Mohawk, N.Y., 1839; d. Ann Arbor, Mich., July 20, 1905. [39]

Cheney, Annie Elizabeth, poet, b. Worcester, Mass., 1847; d. Los Angeles, Calif., April 26, 1916. [35]

Cheney, Charles Edward, bishop, b. Canandaigua, N.Y., 1836; d. Chicago, Ill., Nov. 15, 1916. [1; 2; 10]

Cheney, Mrs. Ednah Dow, née Littlehale, novelist and social reformer, b. Boston, Mass., 1824; d. Jamaica Plains, Mass., Nov. 19, 1904. [1; 7; 10]

Cheney, Mrs. Harriet Vaughan, née Foster, novelist, b. Massachusetts, 1815; d. ? [3; 7; 29]

Cheney, John Vance, poet and librarian, b. Groveland, N.Y., 1848; d. San Diego, Calif., May 1, 1922. [1; 7; 10; 35]

Cheney, Orion Howard, banker and lawyer, b. Bloomington, Ill., 1869; d. Paterson, N.Y., Jan. 17, 1939. [10]

Cheney, Simeon Pease, singer, b. Meredith, N.H., 1818; d. Franklin, Mass., May 10, 1890. [8; 43]

Cheney, Theseon Apoleon, historian, b. Leon, N.Y., 1830; d. Starkey, N.Y., Aug. 2, 1878. [3]

Cheney, Warren, poet and novelist, b. Canandaigua, N.Y., 1858; d. Berkeley, Calif., March 27, 1921. [10; 35]

Chesebro, Caroline, novelist, b. Canandaigua, N.Y., 1825; d. near Piedmont, N.Y., Feb. 16, 1873. [1; 3; 4; 7]

Cheshire, Joseph Blount, bishop, b. Tarborough, N.C., 1850; d. Charlotte, N.C., Dec. 27, 1932. [1a; 10; 11]

Chesnutt, Charles Waddell, novelist, b. Cleveland, O., 1858; d. Cleveland, O., Nov. 15, 1932. [2; 7; 8; 10; 11]

Chester, Albert Huntington, mineralogist, b. Saratoga Springs, N.Y., 1843; d. New Brunswick, N.J., 1903. [3; 10]

Chester, Alden, lawyer, b. Westford, N.Y., 1848; d. Albany, N.Y., Feb. 12, 1934. [10]

Chester, George Randolph, novelist, b. Cincinnati, O., 1869; d. New York, N.Y., Feb. 26, 1924. [1; 2; 7; 10]

Chester, John (pseud.). See Mitchell, John [1794-1870].

Chester, Joseph Lemuel, genealogist and antiquarian, b. Norwich, Conn., 1821; d. London, England, May 26, 1882. [1; 3; 4]

Chester, Samuel Hall, clergyman, b. Mount Holly, Ark., 1851; d. Montreat, N.C., April 27, 1940. [10; 11]

Chetlain, Augustus Louis, soldier and banker, b. St. Louis, Mo., 1824; d. Chicago, Ill., March 15, 1914. [1; 3; 4; 10]

Chevalier, Emile, journalist and novelist, b. Chatillon, France, 1828; d. Paris, France, Aug. 25, 1879. [27]

Chevalier, H. E. (pseud.). See Sears, Edward Isidore.

Cheyney, Edward Potts, historian, b. Wallingford, Pa., 1861; d. Chester, Pa., Feb. 1, 1947. [10]

Chickering, Jesse, political economist, b. Dover, N.H., 1797; d. West Roxbury, Mass.. May 29, 1855. [3; 8]

Chickering, John White, clergyman, b. Woburn, Mass., 1808; d. Brooklyn, N.Y., Dec. 9, 1888. [8; 10]

Chickering, William Henry, journalist, b. Piedmont, Calif., 1916; d. Lingayen Gulf, Philippine Islands, Jan. 6, 1945. [62]

Chidester, Floyd Earle, biologist, b. Chicago, Ill., 1884; d. Newark Valley, N.Y., June 20, 1947. [13]

Chiera, Edward, orientalist, b. Rome, Italy, 1885; d. Chicago, Ill., June 20, 1933. [1a; 10]

Child, Asaph Bemis, physician, b. 1813; d. 1879. [49]

Child, Clement Dexter, physicist, b. Madison, O., 1868; d. Rochester, N.Y., July 15, 1933. [10; 11; 13]

Child, David Lee, journalist, b. West Boylston, Mass., 1794; d. Wayland, Mass., Sept. 18, 1874. [1; 3; 4]

Child, Francis James, philologist, b. Boston, Mass., 1825; d. Cambridge, Mass., Sept. 11, 1896. [1; 3; 4; 7]

Child, Frank Samuel, clergyman, b. Exeter, N.Y., 1854; d. Bridgeport, Conn., May 3, 1922. [1; 7; 10; 68]

Child, James Erwin, local historian, b. Jefferson county, N. Y., 1833; d. Waseca, Minn., Jan. 25, 1912. [70]

Child, Mrs. Lydia Maria, née Francis, novelist, b. Medford, Mass., 1802; d. Wayland, Mass., Oct. 20, 1880. [1; 3; 4;ι7]

Child, Richard Washburn, diplomat and novelist, b. Worcester, Mass., 1881; d. New York, N.Y., Jan. 31, 1935. [1a; 7; 10; 11]

Childs, George William, publisher, b. Baltimore, Md., 1829; d. Philadelphia, Pa., Feb. 3, 1894. [1; 4; 7]

Childs, Thomas Spencer, clergyman, b. Springfield, Mass., 1825; d. Chevy Chase, Md.. March 21, 1914. [2; 8; 10]

Chilton, Eleanor Carroll, novelist, playwright, and poet, b. Charleston, W. Va., 1898; d. New York, N.Y., Feb. 19, 1949. [7]

Chiniquy, Charles Paschal Télesphore, clergyman, b. Kamouraska, Lower Canada, 1809; d. Montreal, Que., Jan. 16, 1899. [27]

Chipman, Daniel, lawyer, b. Salisbury, Conn., 1765; d. Ripton, Vt., April 23, 1850. [1; 3; 4; 7]

Chipman, George Ernest, lawyer, b. Tupperville, N.S., 1868; d. Chicago, Ill., June 4, 1916. [51]

Chipman, Nathaniel, jurist, b. Salisbury, Conn., 1752; d. Tinmouth, Vt., Feb. 15; 1843. [1; 3; 4]

Chipman, Ward, jurist, b. Saint John, N.B., 1787; d. Saint John, N.B., Nov. 26, 1851. [27]

Chipman, William Pendleton, clergyman and writer of books for boys, b. Old Mystic, Conn., 1854; d. Hartford, Conn., Feb. 28, 1937. [7; 10; 47]

Chipperfield, Robert Orr (pseud.). See Ostrander, Isabel Egenton.

Chisholm, Adam Stuart Muir, physician, b. Boston, Mass., 1855; d. Albany, N.Y., Oct. 19, 1931. [51]

Chisholme, David, journalist, b. Scotland, about 1796; d. Montreal, Que., Sept. 24, 1842. [27]

Chittenden, Ezra Porter, clergyman and poet, b. Westbrook, Conn., 1851; d. Waterville, Minn., Oct. 10, 1917. [62]

Chittenden, Hiram Martin, military engineer and historian, b. Yorkshire, N.Y., 1858; d. Seattle, Wash., Oct. 9, 1917. [7; 10]

Chittenden, Larry. See Chittenden, William Lawrence.

Chittenden, Lucius Eugene, lawyer, b. Williston, Vt., 1824; d. Burlington, Vt., July 22, 1902. [4; 8; 43]

Chittenden, Richard Handy, novelist and poet, b. Westbrook, Conn., 1836; d. New York, N.Y., Nov. 15, 1911. [62]

Chittenden, Russell Henry, biochemist, b. New Haven, Conn., 1856; d. New Haven, Conn., Dec. 26, 1943. [10; 62]

Chittenden, William Lawrence, poet, b. Montclair, N.J., 1862; d. New York, N.Y., Sept. 24, 1934. [4; 7; 8]

Chivers, Thomas Holley, physician and poet, b. near Washington, Ga., 1809; d. Decatur, Ga., Dec. 18, 1858. [1; 4; 7; 71; 74]

Choate, Isaac Bassett, educationist and journalist, b. Naples, Me., 1833; d. Westbrooke, Me., Oct. 7, 1917. [8; 10; 46]

Choate, Joseph Hodges, lawyer and diplomat, b. Salem, Mass., 1832; d. New York, N.Y., May 14, 1917. [1; 3; 7; 10]

Choate, Rufus, lawyer and politician, b. Essex, Mass., 1799; d. Halifax, N.S., July 13. 1859. [1: 4; 7]

Chopin, Mrs. Kate, née O'Flaherty, novelist b. St. Louis, Mo., 1851; d. St. Louis, Mo.. Aug. 22. 1904. [1; 3: 7; 10]

Choquette, Ernest, physician and novelist, b. Beloeil, Que., 1862; d. Montreal, Que., March 29, 1941. [27]

Chordal (pseud.). See Lee, James Waring.

Chorley, Edward Clowes, clergyman, b. Manchester, England, 1865; d. Cold Spring, N.Y., Nov. 2, 1949.

Chouinard, Ephrem, civil servant, b. Lévis, Que., 1854; d. Quebec, Que., Nov. 29, 1918. [27]

Chouinard, Ernest, journalist, b. Lévis, Que., 1856; d. Quebec, Que., Nov. 23, 1924. [27]

Chouinard, Honoré Julien Jean Baptiste, historian, b. Quebec, Que., 1850; d. Quebec, Que., Nov. 27, 1928. [27]

Choules, John Overton, clergyman, b. Bristol, England, 1801; d. New York, N.Y., Jan. 5, 1856. [3; 4; 8]

Chown, Alice Amelia, feminist, b. Kingston, Ont., 1866; d. Toronto, Ont., March 2, 1949. [30]

Chown, Samuel Dwight, clergyman, b. Kingston, Ont., 1853; d. Toronto, Ont., Jan. 30, 1933. [27]

Christianson, Theodore, politician and historian, b. Lac qui Parle, Minn., 1883; d. Dawson, Minn., Dec. 10, 1948. [10]

Christie, Alexander James, journalist, b. Scotland; d. Ottawa, Ont., 1843. [27]

Christie, Mrs. Annie Rothwell, née Fowler, novelist, b. London, England, 1837; d. New Liskeard, Ont., July 2, 1927. [27]

Christie, Robert, historian, b. Windsor, N.S., 1788; d. Quebec, Que., Oct. 13, 1856. [27]

Christman, William Weaver, farmer and poet, d. Delanson, N.Y., Feb. 26, 1937. [7; 10]

Christy, David, geologist and publisher, b. Cadiz, O., 1802; d. ? [1; 7]

Chroniqueuse (pseud.). See Logan, Mrs. Olive, née Logan.

Chrystal, James, clergyman, b. New York, N.Y., 1832; d. Jersey City, N.J., Nov. 11, 1908. [67]

Church, Albert Ensign, mathematician, b. Salisbury, Conn., 1807; d. West Point, N.Y., March 30, 1878. [3; 8]

Church, Benjamin, soldier, b. Plymouth, Mass., 1639; d. near Little Compton, R.I., Jan. 17, 1718. [1; 3; 4]

Church, Benjamin, physician and poet, b. Newport, R.I., 1734; d. at sea, 1776. [1; 7; 8]

Church, Mrs. Ella Rodman, née MacIlvane, writer of books for children, b. New York, 1831; d. ? [6]

Church, Francis Pharcellus, journalist, b. Rochester, N.Y., 1839; d. New York, N.Y., April 11, 1906. [1; 7; 10]

Church, George Earl, civil engineer and explorer, b. New Bedford, Mass., 1835; d. London, England, Jan. 5, 1910. [1; 4]

Church, Irving Porter, civil engineer and educationist, b. Ansonia, Conn., 1851; d. Ithaca, N.Y., May 8, 1931. [1a; 10]

Church, John Adams, metallurgist, b. Rochester, N.Y., 1843; d. New York, N.Y., Feb. 12, 1917. [1; 3; 10]

Church, Pharcellus, clergyman, b. Seneca, N.Y., 1801; d. Tarrytown, N.Y., June 5, 1886. [1; 3; 4]

Church, Samuel Harden, educationist, b. Caldwell county, Mo., 1858; d. Pittsburg, Pa., Oct. 11, 1943. [7; 10]

Church, William Conant, journalist, b. Rochester, N.Y., 1836; d. New York, N.Y., May 23, 1917. [1; 3; 7; 10]

Churchill, William, ethnologist, b. Brooklyn, N.Y., 1859; d. Washington, D.C., June 9, 1920. [1; 7; 10; 62]

Churchill, Winston, novelist, b. St. Louis, Mo., 1871; d. Winter Park, Fla., March 12, 1947. [7; 10; 11]

Churchward, James, soldier, b. England, 1852; d. Los Angeles, Calif., Jan. 4, 1936. [7]

Churton, Henry (pseud.). See Tourgée, Albion Winegar.

Chute, Horatio Nelson, physicist, b. Grovesend, Ont., 1847; d. Ann Arbor, Mich., March 11, 1928. [3; 10]

Cilley, Gordon Harper, journalist, b. Lenoir, N.C., 1874; d. Paoli, Pa., Jan. 18, 1938. [10]

Cilley, Jonathan Prince, soldier, b. Thomaston, Me., 1835; d. Rockland, Me., April 7, 1920. [3; 4; 10; 46]

Cimon, Henri, priest, b. Murray Bay, Que., 1855; d. Quebec, Que., April, 1927. [32]

Cincinnatus (pseud.). See Wheat, Marvin.

Cirkel, Fritz, civil engineer, b. 1863; d. Ottawa, Ont., Aug. 23, 1914. [13]

Cist, Charles, editor, b. Philadelphia, Pa., 1792; d. Cincinnati, O., Sept. 5, 1868. [1; 3; 4; 7]

Cist, Henry Martyn, soldier and historian, b. Cincinnati, O., 1839; d. Rome, Italy, Dec. 17, 1902. [1; 3; 7]

Cist, Lewis Jacob, poet, b. Harmony, Pa., 1818; d. Cincinnati, O., March 30, 1885. [3; 8]

Claflin, Mrs. Mary Bucklin, née Davenport, novelist, b. 1825; d. Whitinsville, Mass., June 13, 1896. [7; 8]

Claghorn, Kate Holladay, social worker, b. Aurora, Ill., 1864; d. Greenwich, Conn., March 22, 1938. [7; 62]

Claiborne, John Francis Hamtranck, lawyer, b. Natchez, Miss., 1809; d. Natchez, Miss., May 17, 1884. [1; 3; 7; 34]

Claiborne, John Herbert, physician, b. Brunswick county, Va., 1828; d. Petersburg, Va., Feb. 24, 1905. [3; 10; 34]

Claiborne, Nathaniel Herbert, politician, b. Sussex county, Va., 1777; d. Franklin county, Va., Aug. 15, 1859. [1; 3; 7; 34]

Clap, Nathaniel, clergyman, b. Dorchester, Mass., 1669; d. Newport, R.I., Oct. 30, 1745. [3; 4]

Clap, Roger, colonist, b. Devonshire, England, 1609; d. Boston, Mass., Feb. 2, 1691. [3; 4; 8]

Clap, Thomas, educationist, b. Scituate, Mass., 1703; d. New Haven, Conn., Jan. 7, 1767. [1; 3; 4]

Clapin, Sylva, lexicographer, b. St. Hyacinthe, Que., 1853; d. Ottawa, Ont., Feb. 17, 1928. [27]

88   DICTIONARY OF NORTH AMERICAN AUTHORS

Clapp, Edwin Jones, journalist and educationist, b. Hudson, Wis., 1881; d. New York, N.Y., Aug. 7, 1930. [62]

Clapp, Henry Austin, drama critic, b. Dorchester, Mass., 1841; d. Dorchester, Mass., Feb. 19, 1904. [2; 7; 10; 51]

Clapp, Theodore, clergyman, b. Easthampton, Mass., 1792; d. Louisville, Ky., May 17, 1866. [3; 8; 62]

Clapp, William Warland, journalist, b. Boston, Mass., 1826; d. Boston, Mass., Dec. 8, 1891. [1; 4; 7]

Clara Augusta (pseud.). See Jones, Clara Augusta.

Clare, Israel Smith, historian, b. Lancaster county, Pa., 1847; d. Lancaster, Pa., March 1, 1924. [7; 10]

Clark, Alexander, clergyman, b. Jefferson county, O., 1834; d. Georgia, July 6, 1879. [3; 7; 8]

Clark, Allen Culling, lawyer, b. Philadelphia, Pa., 1858; d. Washington, D.C., May 16, 1943. [7; 10]

Clark, Alonzo Howard, naturalist, b. Boston, Mass., 1850; d. Washington, D.C., Dec. 31, 1918. [3; 10]

Clark, Mrs. Annie Maria, née **Lawrence,** poet,, b. Still River Village, Mass., 1835; d. 1912. [7; 10]

Clark, Arthur Hamilton, mariner and historian, b. Boston, Mass., 1841; d. Newburyport, Mass., July 5, 1922. [1; 7]

Clark, Calvin Montague, clergyman, b. Hartford, Wis., 1862; d. Bangor, Me., March 1, 1947. [10; 11]

Clark, Mrs. Catherine Pickens, née **Upson.** See Clark, Mrs Kate, née Upson.

Clark, Champ, politician, b. Lawrenceburg, Ky., 1850; d. Washington, D.C., March 1, 1921. [1; 4; 10]

Clark, Charles Cotesworth Pinckney, physician, b. Tinmouth, Vt., 1822; d. Oswego, N.Y., Jan. 12, 1899. [3; 8]

Clark, Charles Dunning, dime novelist, d. 1892. [7]

Clark, Charles Heber, journalist and humorist, b. Berlin, Md., 1847; d. Eaglesmere, Pa., Aug. 10, 1915. [1; 4; 7; 10]

Clark, Mrs. Charlotte, née **Moon,** novelist, b. 1829; d. 1895. [7]

Clark, Daniel, merchant, b. Sligo, Ireland, 1766; d. New Orleans, La., Aug. 16, 1813. [1; 34]

Clark, Daniel, physician, b. Grantown, Scotland, 1835; d. Toronto, Ont., June 4, 1912. [27]

Clark, Daniel Atkinson, clergyman, b. Rahway, N.J., 1779; d. New York, N.Y., March 3, 1840. [3]

Clark, Davis Wasgatt, bishop, b. Mount Desert Island, Me., 1812; d. Cincinnati, O., May 23, 1871. [3; 4; 8]

Clark, Edgar Frederick, clergyman, b. South Windsor, Conn., 1835; d. Providence, R.I., 1914. [60]

Clark, Edson Lyman, clergyman, b. Easthampton, Mass., 1827; d. Dalton, Mass., March 2, 1913. [6; 10; 62]

Clark, Edward Lord, clergyman, b. Nashua., N.H., 1834; d. Boston, Mass., Feb. 5, 1910. [10; 47]

Clark, Mrs. Eva Lee, née **Turner,** genealogist and Shakespearean student, b. Colusa, Calif., 1871; d. San Francisco, Calif., April 1, 1947.

Clark, Mrs. Felicia, née **Buttz,** novelist, b. New York, N.Y., 1862; d. Pasadena, Calif., Feb. 23, 1931. [7; 10]

Clark, Francis Edward, clergyman, b. Aylmer, Que., 1851; d. Newton, Mass., May 26, 1927. [1; 2; 10]

Clark, Fred Emerson, economist, b. Jackson county, Mich., 1890; d. Williamsburg, Va., Nov. 26, 1948. [10]

Clark, George Henry, clergyman, b. Newburyport, Mass., 1819; d. Hartford, Conn., March 31, 1906. [62]

Clark, George Hunt, poet, b. Northampton, Mass., 1809; d. Hartford, Conn., Aug. 20, 1881. [3; 6; 7]

Clark, George Huntington, geologist, b. Providence, R.I., 1859; d. Birmingham, Ala., Nov. 30, 1941. [62]

Clark, George Larkin, clergyman, b. Tewkesbury, Mass., 1849; d. Buffalo, N.Y., Oct. 28, 1919. [45]

Clark, George Thomas, librarian, b. San Francisco, Calif., 1862; d. Palo Alto, Calif., Oct. 19, 1940. [10]

Clark, George Whitfield, clergyman, b. South Orange, N.J., 1831; d. Hightstown, N.J., Nov. 10, 1911. [1; 3; 7; 8]

Clark, Grover, journalist and educationist, b. Osaka, Japan, 1891; d. New York, N.Y., July 17, 1938. [10]

Clark, Henry James, naturalist, b. Easton, Mass., 1826; d. Amherst, Mass., July 1, 1873. [1; 3; 4]

Clark, Henry Scott (pseud.). See Cox, Millard.

Clark, Imogen, novelist, b. New York, N.Y.; d. New York, N.Y., Jan. 2, 1936. [3; 7; 8; 10; 11]

Clark, James Bayard, physician, b. Elizabeth, N.J., 1869; d. New York, N.Y., May 21, 1947. [11]

Clark, James Beauchamp. See Clark, Champ.

Clark, James Gowdy, poet, b. Constantia, N.Y., 1830; d. 1897. [6; 8]

Clark, James Henry, physician, b. Livingston, N.Y., 1814; d. Montclair, N.J., 1869. [3; 8]

Clark, John Alonzo, clergyman, b. Pittsfield, Mass., 1801; d. Philadelphia, Pa., Nov. 27, 1843. [3; 8]

Clark, John Bates, political economist, b. Providence, R.I., 1847; d. New York, N.Y., March 21, 1938. [7; 10; 11]

Clark, John Jesse, educationist, b. Corning, N.Y., 1866; d. Lachine, Que., Jan. 17, 1939. [10; 11]

Clark, John Scott, educationist, b. Copenhagen, N.Y., 1854; d. Evanston, Ill., 1911. [8; 10]

Clark, Jonas, clergyman, b. Newton, Mass., 1730; d. Lexington, Mass., Nov. 15, 1805. [3; 7; 8]

Clark, Joseph Bourne, clergyman, b. Sturbridge, Mass., 1836; d. Brooklyn, N.Y., July 10, 1923. [10]

Clark, Joseph Sylvester, clergyman, b. South Plymouth, Mass., 1800; d. Newton, Mass., Aug. 17, 1861. [1; 45]

Clark, Mrs. Kate, née Upson, journalist and lecturer, b. Camden, Ala., 1851; d. Brooklyn, N.Y., Feb. 17, 1935. [2; 7; 10; 11]

Clark, Kenneth Sherman, musician, b. Pittsburg, Pa., 1882; d. Princeton, N.J., Jan. 22, 1945. [56]

Clark, Lewis Gaylord, editor, b. Otisco, N.Y., 1808; d. Piermont, N.Y., Nov. 3, 1873. [1; 4; 7]

Clark, Lydia Ann, educationist, b. Andover, Mass.; d. Columbus, O., Feb. 26, 1933. [11]

Clark, Nathaniel George, clergyman, b. Calais, Vt., 1835; d. West Roxbury, Mass., Jan. 3, 1896. [8; 43]

Clark, Olynthus Burroughs, historian, b. near Bloomington, Ill., 1864; d. Kalamazoo, Mich., Sept. 8, 1936. [10; 37]

Clark, Peter, clergyman, b. Watertown, Conn., 1693-4; d. Danvers, Mass., June 10, 1768. [51]

Clark, Robert Carlton, historian, b. 1877; d. Eugene, Ore., Dec. 4, 1939. [7; 10]

Clark, Rufus Wheelwright, clergyman, b. Newburyport, Mass., 1813; d. Nantucket, Mass., Aug. 9, 1886. [3; 4; 8]

Clark, Salter Storrs, lawyer, b. Brooklyn, N.Y., 1854; d. Westfield, N.J., April 4, 1935. [62]

Clark, Samuel Adams, clergyman, b. Newburyport, Mass., 1822; d. Elizabeth, N.J., Jan. 28, 1875. [3]

Clark, Simeon Tucker, physician and poet, b. Canton, Mass., 1836; d. Lockport, N.Y., Dec. 24, 1891. [8]

Clark, Stephen Watkins, educationist, b. Naples, N.Y., 1810; d. Spencerport, N.Y.. March 13, 1910. [45]

Clark, Mrs. Susanna Rebecca, née Graham, writer of books for young people, b. Nova Scotia, 1848; d. ? [6]

Clark, Theodore Minot, architect, b. Boston, Mass., 1845; d. Boston, Mass., April 30, 1909. [10]

Clark, Thomas, historian, b. Lancaster, Pa., 1787; d. Philadelphia, Pa., April 28, 1860. [3; 4; 8]

Clark, Thomas March, bishop, b. Newburyport, Mass., 1812; d. Newport, R.I., Sept. 7, 1903. [1; 3; 4]

Clark, Walter, jurist, b. Halifax county, N.C., 1846; d. Raleigh, N.C., May 19, 1924. [1; 2; 4; 34]

Clark, William Adolphus, poet, b. Boston, Mass., 1825; d. Malden, Mass., Nov. 26, 1906. [6]

Clark, William Robinson, clergyman and educationist, b. Inverurie, Scotland, 1829; d. Toronto, Ont., Nov. 12, 1912. [27]

Clark, William Smith, educationist, b. Ashfield, Mass., 1826; d. Amherst, Mass., March 9, 1886. [1; 3; 45]

Clark, Willis Gaylord, journalist and poet, b. Otisco, N.Y., 1808; d. Philadelphia, Pa., June 12, 1841. [1; 3; 4; 7]

Clarke, Charles, politician, b. Lincoln, England, 1826; d. Elora, Ont., April 6, 1909. [27]

Clarke, Charles Cameron, educationist, b. New York, N.Y., 1861; d. New Haven, Conn., Jan. 28, 1935. [62]

Clarke, Dorus, clergyman, b.. Westhampton, Mass., 1797; d. Boston, Mass., March 8, 1884. [3; 8; 61]

Clarke, Edith Emily, librarian, b. Syracuse, N.Y., 1859; d. New York, N.Y., Nov. 21, 1932. [2; 10]

Clarke, Edward Hammond, physician, b. Norton, Mass., 1820; d. Boston, Mass., Nov. 30, 1877. [3; 4; 8]

Clarke, Edwin Leavitt, sociologist, b. Westboro, Mass., 1888; d. Winter Park, Fla., Sept. 15, 1948. [10]

Clarke, Francis Devereux, educationist, b. Raleigh, N.C., 1849; d. Flint, Mich., Sept. 7, 1913. [1; 4]

Clarke, Frank Wigglesworth, chemist, b. Boston, Mass., 1847; d. Washington, D.C., May 23, 1931. [3; 10]

Clarke, Helen Archibald, editor and musician, b. Philadelphia, Pa., 1860; d. Boston, Mass., Feb. 8, 1926. [1; 7; 10]

Clarke, Hermann Frederick, investment banker and historian, b. Newton, Mass., 1882; d. Boston, Mass., Oct. 29, 1947. [10; 51]

Clarke, Hugh Archibald, musician, b. Toronto, Upper Canada, 1839; d. Bryn Athyn, Pa., Dec. 16, 1926. [10]

Clarke, Isaac Edwards, civil servant, b. Deerfield, Mass., 1830; d. Washington, D.C., Jan. 9, 1907. [8]

Clarke, James Freeman, clergyman, b. Hanover, N.H., 1810; d. Boston, Mass., June 8, 1888. [1; 3; 4; 7]

Clarke, Jean (pseud.). See Tuttle, Charles Richard.

Clarke, John Caldwell Calhoun, clergyman, b. Providence, R.I., 1833; d. Upper Alton, Ill., Sept. 15, 1915.

Clarke, John Mason, geologist, b. Canandaigua, N.Y., 1857; d. Albany, N.Y., May 29, 1925. [3; 10; 13]

Clarke, Joseph Ignatius Constantine, journalist and playwright, b. Kingstown, Ireland, 1846; d. New York, N.Y., Feb. 27, 1925. [1; 7; 10]

Clarke, Joseph Morison, clergyman, b. 1829; d. 1899. [8]

Clarke, McDonald, poet, b. Bath, Me., 1798; d. New York, N.Y., March 5, 1842. [3; 7; 8]

Clarke, Mrs. Mary Bayard, née Devereux, poet, b. Raleigh, N.C., 1827; d. New Bern, N.C., March 30, 1886. [1; 3; 7; 34]

Clarke, Rebecca Sophia, writer of books for children, b. Norridgewock, Me., 1833; d. Norridgewock, Me., Aug. 16, 1906. [1; 4; 7; 10]

Clarke, Richard Henry, lawyer, b. Washington, D.C., 1827; d. New York, N.Y., May 24, 1911. [3; 8]

Clarke, Robert, publisher, b. Annan, Scotland, 1829; d. Cincinnati, O., Aug. 26, 1899. [1; 3; 7; 10]

Clarke, Samuel A., poet and historian, b. Cuba, 1827; d. Salem, Ore., Aug. 20, 1909.

Clarke, Samuel Fessenden, naturalist, b. Geneva, Ill., 1851; d. Williamstown, Mass., Aug. 1, 1928. [3; 4]

Clarke, Sarah J., writer of books for boys, b. Norridgewock, Me., 1840; d. Norridgewock, Me., June, 1929. [7; 38]

Clarke, William Barker, clergyman, b. Cuba, 1829; d. Durham, Conn., Sept. 18, 1905. [62]

Clarke, William Hawes Crichton, lawyer, b. Washington, D.C., 1882; d. Jan. 2, 1942. [10]

Clarke, William Newton, clergyman, b. Cazenovia, N.Y., 1841; d. Deland, Fla., Jan. 14, 1912. [1; 4]

Clason, Isaac Starr, actor, b. New York, N.Y., 1789; d. London, England, 1834. [3; 8]

Clauson, James Earl, journalist, b. Troy, N.Y., 1873; d. Wickford, R.I., June 24, 1937. [7; 11; 45]

Clavers, Mrs. Mary (pseud.). See Kirkland, Mrs. Caroline Matilda, née Stansbury.

Claxton, Mrs. Norah Mary, née Holland. See Holland, Norah Mary.

Clay, Albert Tobias, orientalist, b. Hanover, Pa., 1866; d. New Haven, Conn., Sept. 14, 1925. [1; 7; 10; 62]

Clay, Cassius Marcellus, abolitionist, b. Madison county, Ky., 1810; d. Madison county, Ky., July 22, 1903. [1; 3; 4; 34]

Clay, Charles M. (pseud.). See Clark, Mrs. Charlotte, née Moon.

Clay, Henry, politician, b. Hanover county, Va., 1777; d. Washington, D.C., June 29, 1852. [1; 2; 3; 4; 5; 6; 7; 34; 74]

Clay, John Cecil, illustrator, b. Ronceverte, W. Va., 1875; d. Mamaroneck, N.Y., May 24, 1930. [7]

Clayton, Augustin Smith, lawyer, b. Fredericksburg, Va., 1783; d. Athens, Ga., June 21, 1939. [1; 3]

Clayton, Edward Hyers, missionary, b. 1886; d. Dayton, O., Nov. 18, 1946.

Clayton. Mrs. Victoria Virginia, novelist, b. near Charleston, S.C., 1832; d. 1908. [10]

Clearwater, Alphonse Trumpbour, jurist, b. West Point, N.Y., 1848; d. Kingston, N.Y., Sept. 23, 1933. [4; 10]

Cleaveland, Aaron. See Cleveland, Aaron.

Cleaveland, George Aaron, clergyman, b. Clarence, N.S., 1853; d. Hermosa Beach, Calif., Nov. 2, 1922. [24]

Cleaveland, John, clergyman, b. Canterbury, Conn., 1722; d. Ipswich, Mass., April 22, 1799. [3; 7; 62]

Cleaveland, Nehemiah, educationist, b. Topsfield, Mass., 1796; d. Westport, Mass., April 17, 1877. [3; 8]

Cleaveland, Parker, geologist, b. Rowley, Mass., 1780; d. Brunswick, Me., Oct. 15, 1858. [3; 4; 8; 51]

Cleland, Herdman Fitzgerald, geologist, b. Milan, Ill., 1869; d. off the coast of New Jersey, Jan. 24, 1935. [10; 11; 62]

Cleland, Thomas, clergyman, b. Fairfax county, Va., 1778; d. Jan. 31, 1858. [3; 34]

Clemens, Jeremiah, novelist, b. Huntsville, Ala., 1814; d. Huntsville, Ala., May 21, 1865. [1; 3; 7; 34]

Clemens, Samuel Langhorne, humorist, b. Florida, Mo., 1835; d. Redding, Conn., April 21, 1910. [1; 2; 3; 4; 5; 6; 7; 8; 71; 72]

Clemens, William Montgomery, genealogist, b. Paris, O., 1860; d. Asbury Park, N.J., Nov. 24, 1931. [8; 10; 11]

Clement, Mrs. Clara, née Erskine, writer on art, b. St. Louis, Mo., 1834; d. Feb. 20, 1916. [3; 10; 34]

Clement, Ernest Wilson, educationist, b. Dubuque, Ia., 1860; d. Floral Park, Long Island, N.Y., March 11, 1941. [10; 11]

Clement, William Henry Pope, jurist and historian, b. Vienna, Ont., 1858; d. Vancouver, B.C., May 3, 1922. [27]

Clements, Colin Campbell, playwright, b. Omaha, Neb., 1894; d. Philadelphia, Pa., Jan. 29, 1948. [7; 10; 11]

Clements, Frederic Edward, ecologist, b. Lincoln, Neb., 1874; d. Santa Barbara, Calif., July 26, 1945. [10; 11]

Clemmer, Mary. See Ames, Mrs. Mary, née Clemmer.

Clemo, Ebenezer, novelist, b. London, England, about 1831; d. Morristown, N.J., 1860. [27]

Clendenin, Frank Montrose, clergyman, b. Washington, D.C., 1853; d. Chappaqua, N.Y., Aug. 19, 1930. [10; 11]

Clendening, Logan, physician, b. Kansas City, Mo., 1884; d. Kansas City, Mo., Jan. 31, 1945. [7; 10]

Clergue, Helen, historian, b. Bangor, Me.; d. London, England, May 28, 1938.

Cleveland, Aaron, clergyman and poet, b. Haddam, Conn., 1744; d. New Haven, Conn., Sept. 21, 1815. [3; 4; 7]

Cleveland, Charles Dexter, educationist, b. Salem, Mass., 1802; d. Philadelphia, Pa., Aug. 18, 1869. [3; 7; 8]

Cleveland, Cynthia Eloise, lawyer, b. Canton, N.Y., 1845; d. ? [36; 10]

Cleveland, Frederick Albert, political economist, b. Stirling, Ill., 1865; d. Norwood, Mass., Jan. 26, 1946. [11]

Cleveland, Helen M., educationist, b. Sheffield, Mass.; d. Boston, Mass., 1909. [10]

Cleveland, Henry Russell, educationist, b. 1809; d. St. Louis, Mo., June 12, 1843. [3; 8]

Cleveland, Horace William Shaler, landscape architect, b. Lancaster, Mass., 1814; d. Hinsdale, Ill., Dec. 5, 1900. [1; 3; 4; 7]

Cleveland, Richard Jeffrey, navigator, b. Salem, Mass., 1773; d. Danvers, Mass., Nov. 23, 1860. [1]

Cleveland, Rose Elizabeth, essayist, b. Fayetteville, N.Y., 1846; d. Lucca, Italy, Nov., 1918. [3; 4; 10]

Clevenger, Shobal Vail, psychiatrist, b. Florence, Italy, 1843; d. Park Ridge, Ill., March 24, 1920. [1; 3; 4]

Clewell, John Henry, clergyman, b. Salem, N.C., 1855; d. Philadelphia, Pa., Feb. 20, 1922. [1; 10; 34]

Clews, Henry, banker, b. Staffordshire, England, 1836; d. New York, N.Y., Jan. 31, 1923. [2; 7; 8; 10]

Clifford, Cornelius Cyprian, priest, b. New York, N.Y., 1859; d. Whippany, N.J., Dec. 4, 1938. [21]

Clifford, Ella (pseud.). See Paull, Mrs. Minnie E., née Kenney.

Clifford, Philip Henry, clergyman, b. Brooklyn, N.Y., 1878; d. Brookline, Pa., Nov. 4, 1942.

Cliffton, William, poet, b. Philadelphia, Pa., 1772; d. Philadelphia, Pa., Dec., 1799. [1; 3; 7]

Clifton, Oliver Lee (pseud.). See Rathborne, St. George Henry.

Clifton, William. See Cliffton, William.

Clinch, Charles Powell, poet and playwright, b. New York, N.Y., 1797; d. New York N.Y., Dec. 16, 1880. [1; 4; 7]

Cline, Leonard Lanson, playwright, b. 1893; d. New York, N.Y., Jan. 15, 1929.

Clingman,, Thomas Lanier, politician, b. Huntersville, N.C., 1812; d. Raleigh, N.C., Nov. 4, 1897. [1; 3; 34]

Clinkscales, John George, educationist, b. Abbeville county, S.C., 1855; d. Spartansburg, S.C., Jan. 1, 1942. [10]

Clint, Mabel B., nursing sister, b. Quebec, Que.; d. Ste. Anne de Bellevue, Que., March 17, 1939.

Clinton, DeWitt, politician, b. Little Britain, N.Y., 1769; d. Albany, N.Y., Feb. 11, 1828. [1; 3; 4; 6; 7]

Clinton, George, soldier and politician, b. Little Britain, N.Y., 1739; d. Washington, D.C., April 20, 1812. [1; 3; 4]

Clinton, George Wylie, bishop, b. Cedar Creek township, S.C., 1859; d. Charlotte, N.C., May 12, 1921. [10]

Clinton, Henry Laurens, lawyer, b. 1820; d. New York, N.Y., June 7, 1899.

Clippinger, Walter Gillan, educationist, b. Lurgan, Pa., 1873; d. Dayton, O., Sept. 30, 1948. [10]

Close, Charles William, mental healer, b. Bangor, Me., 1859; d. 1915. [10]

Clover, Samuel Travers, journalist, b. London, England, 1859; d. Los Angeles, Calif., May 28, 1934. [7; 10]

Cluff, Walter, life insurance official, b. 1878; d. Hartford, Conn., April 26, 1943.

Clum, Franklin D., physician, b. Saugerties, N.Y., 1853; d. Cheviot, N.Y., July 8, 1925. [62]

Clute, Oscar, agriculturist, b. 1873; d. 1902. [39]

Clyde, John Cunningham, clergyman, b. White Deer Valley, Pa., 1841; d. Easton, Pa., Jan 28, 1915. [10]

Clymer, Mrs. Ella Maria, née Dietz, actress and poet, b. New York, N.Y., 1847; d. ? [2; 4]

Clymer, Meredith, physician, b. Philadelphia, Pa., 1817; d. New York, N.Y., April 20, 1902. [3; 8; 10]

Clymer, William Branford Shubrick, educationist, b. Washington, D.C., 1855; d. Cambridge, Mass., May 9, 1903. [51]

Coakley, Cornelius Godfrey, laryngologist, b. Brooklyn, N.Y., 1862; d. New York, N.Y., Nov. 22, 1934. [1a; 10]

Coan, Titus, missionary, b. Killingworth, Conn., 1801; d. Hilo, Hawaii, Dec. 1, 1882. [1; 3; 4]

Coan, Titus Munson, physician, b. Hilo, Hawaii, 1836; d. New York, N.Y., May 8, 1921. [3; 4; 10]

Coar, John Firman, educationist, b. Berlin, Germany, 1863; d. Boston, Mass., June 26, 1939. [10; 11]

Coates, Mrs. Florence Van Leer, née Earle, poet, b. Philadelphia, Pa., 1850; d. Philadelphia, Pa., April 6, 1927. [1; 4; 7; 10]

Coates, Henry Troth, publisher, b. Philadelphia, Pa., 1843; d. Philadelphia, Pa., Jan. 22, 1910. [7; 10]

Coates, Joseph Hornor, journalist, b. Philadelphia, Pa., 1849; d. Berwyn, Pa., Dec. 13, 1930. [10]

Cobb, Cyrus, artist, b. Malden, Mass., 1834; d. Allston, Mass., 1903. [3; 8; 10]

Cobb, Howell, politician, b. Cherry Hill, Ga., 1815; d. New York, N.Y., Oct. 9, 1868. [1; 3; 4; 34]

Cobb, Humphrey, novelist, b. Siena, Italy, 1899; d. Port Washington, Long Island, N.Y., April 25, 1944.

Cobb, Irvin Shrewsbury, humorist, b. Paducah, Ky., 1876; d. New York, N.Y., March 10, 1944. [4; 7; 10; 11]

Cobb, Jonathan Holmes, lawyer and manufacturer, b. Sharon, Mass., 1799; d. Dedham, Mass., March 12, 1882. [1; 3; 51]

Cobb, Joseph Beckham, novelist, b. Oglethorpe county, Ga., 1819; d. Columbus, Ga., Sept. 15, 1858. [3; 4; 7; 8]

Cobb, Lyman, educationist, b. Lenox, Mass., 1800; d. Colesburg, Pa., Oct. 26, 1864. [1; 3; 4; 8]

Cobb, Nathan Augustus, botanist, b. Spencer, Mass., 1859; d. Baltimore, Md., June 4, 1932. [1a; 10; 11; 13]

Cobb, Sanford Hoadley, clergyman, b. New York, N.Y., 1838; d. Kansas City, Mo., April 27, 1910. [10; 62]

Cobb, Sylvanus, clergyman, b. Norway, Me., 1799; d. Boston, Mass., Oct. 31, 1866. [1; 3]

Cobb, Sylvanus, clergyman, b. Waterville, Me., 1823; d. Hyde Park, Mass., July 20, 1887. [1; 3; 7]

Cobb, Thomas Read Rootes, lawyer and soldier, b. Cherry Hill, Ga., 1823; d. Fredericksburg, Va., Dec. 13, 1862. [1; 2; 4; 8; 34]

Cobb, William Henry, clergyman, b. Rochester, Mass., 1846; d. Boston, Mass., May 1, 1923. [1; 10]

Cobbett, Thomas, clergyman, b. Newbury, England, 1608; d. Ipswich, Mass., Nov. 5, 1685. [3]

Coblentz, Virgil, chemist, b. Springfield, O., 1862; d. Philadelphia, Pa., June 7, 1932. [8; 10; 11]

Coburn, Foster Dwight, writer on agriculture, b. Cold Springs, Wis., 1846; d. Topeka, Kans., May 11, 1924. [1; 10]

Coburn, Frank Warren, historian, b. Thetford, Vt., 1853; d. Lexington, Mass., 1923. [43]

Cochrane, Charles Henry, journalist, b. Lacon, Ill., 1856; d. West Hoboken, N.J., Sept. 14, 1940. [10]

Cochrane, Charles Norris, educationist, b. Omemee, Ont., 1889; d. Toronto, Ont., Nov. 23, 1945. [30]

Cochrane, Elizabeth. See Seaman, Mrs. Elizabeth, née Cochrane.

Cochrane, William, clergyman, b. Paisley, Scotland, 1831; d. Brantford, Ont., 1898. [27]

Cockburn, Alexander Peter, politician, b. Stormont county, Upper Canada, 1837; d. 1905. [27]

Cocke, James Richard, physician, b. 1863; d. 1900. [8]

Cocke, Philip St. George, planter, b. Fluvanna county, Va., 1809; d. Powhatan county, Va., Dec. 26, 1861. [1; 3; 4; 34]

Cocke, Zitella, poet and essayist, b. Perry county, Ala., 1831; d. 1929. [7; 10; 34]

Cocker, Benjamin Franklin, philosopher, b. 1821; d. Ann Arbor, Mich., April 8, 1883. [8; 53]

Cocker, William Johnson, educationist, b. 1846; d. Ann Arbor, Mich., May 19, 1901. [6; 8; 53]

Cockin, Hereward Kirby, poet, b. Yorkshire, England, 1854; d. Guelph, Ont., June 22, 1917. [27]

Cockran, William Bourke, lawyer and politician, b. county Sligo, Ireland, 1854; d. Washington, D.C., March 1, 1923. [1; 10; 21]

Coddington, William, colonist, b. Boston, England, 1601; d. Newport, R.I., Nov. 1, 1679. [1; 3; 8]

Codman, John, sea-captain, b. Dorchester, Mass., 1814; d. Boston, Mass., April 6, 1900. [1; 3; 7; 8]

Codman, John, clergyman, b. Boston, Mass., 1782; d. Dorchester, Mass., Dec. 23, 1847. [3; 8]

Cody, Hiram Alfred, clergyman and novelist, b. Cody's, N.B., 1872; d. Saint John, N.B., Feb. 9, 1948. [30]

Cody, William Frederick, hunter, scout, and showman, b. Scott county, Ia., 1846; d. Denver, Colo., Feb. 26, 1917. [1; 2; 4; 6; 7; 37]

Coe, Edward Benton, clergyman, b. Milford, Conn., 1842; d. New York, N.Y., March 19, 1914. [2; 10; 62]

Coerne, Louis Adolphe, musician, b. Newark, N.J., 1870; d. Boston, Mass., Sept. 11, 1922. [1; 10; 20]

Coffin, Charles Carleton, novelist and historian, b. Boscawen, N.H., 1823; d. Brookline, Mass., March 2, 1896. [1; 2; 3; 4; 5; 6; 7]

Coffin, Isaac Foster, educationist, b. Portland, Me., 1787; d. Jan. 24, 1861. [8]

Coffin, James Henry, mathematician and meteorologist, b. Williamsburg, Mass., 1806; d. Easton, Pa., Feb. 6, 1873. [1; 3; 4]

Coffin, John Huntington Crane, mathematician, b. Wiscasset, Me., 1815; d. Washington, D.C., Jan. 8, 1890. [2; 3; 4]

Coffin, Joshua, antiquarian, b. Newbury, Mass., 1792; d. Newbury, Mass., June 24, 1864. [3; 4; 8]

Coffin, Levi, philanthropist, b. near New Garden, N.C., 1798; d. Avondale, O., Sept. 16, 1877. [1; 3; 4]

Coffin, Robert Allen, educationist, b. Williamsburg, Mass., 1801; d. Conway, Mass., Sept. 4, 1878. [3; 8]

Coffin, Robert Barry, novelist, b. Hudson, N.Y., July 21, 1826; d. Fordham, N.Y., June 10, 1886. [3; 4; 7; 8]

Coffin, Robert Stevenson, poet, b. Brunswick, Me., 1797; d. Rowley, Mass., May 7, 1827. [3; 7; 8; 71]

Coffin, Roland Folger, sailor, b. Brooklyn, N.Y., 1826; d. Shelter Island, N.Y., July 17, 1888. [3; 4; 8]

Coffin, Selden Jennings, educationist, b. Ogdensburg, N.Y., 1838; d. Easton, Pa., March 15, 1915. [3; 10]

Coffin, William Foster, civil servant and historian, b. Bath, England, 1808; d. Ottawa, Ont., Jan. 28, 1878. [27]

Coggeshall, George, sailor, b. Milford, Conn., 1784; d. Milford, Conn., Aug. 6, 1861. [1; 3; 4; 7; 8]

Coggeshall, William Turner, journalist, b. Lewistown, Pa., Sept. 6, 1824; d. near Quito, Ecuador, Aug. 2, 1867. [1; 3; 4; 7; 8]

Coggins, Paschal Heston, lawyer and novelist, b. Philadelphia, Pa., 1852; d. Germantown, Pa., Nov. 14, 1917. [10]

Coggshall, William Turner. See Coggeshall, William Turner.

Coghill, George Ellet, anatomist, b. Beaucoup, Ill., 1872; d. Gainesville, Fla., July 23, 1941. [10]

Cogswell, Elliott Colby, clergyman, b. Tamworth, N.H., 1814; d. Rye Beach, N.H., Aug. 31, 1887. [49]

Cogswell, Frederick Hull, court reporter and historian, b. New Preston, Conn., 1859; d. New Haven, Conn., May 16, 1907. [10]

Cogswell, Jonathan, clergyman, b. Rowley, Mass., 1782; d. New Brunswick, N.J., Aug. 1, 1864. [3; 8; 51]

Cogswell, Joseph Green, bibliographer, b. Ipswich, Mass., 1786; d. Cambridge, Mass., Nov. 26, 1871. [1; 3; 4; 7; 51]

Cogswell, William, clergyman, b. Atkinson, N.H., 1787; d. Gilmanton, N.H., April 18, 1850. [3; 8; 49]

Cohen, Alfred J., drama critic, b. Birmingham, England, 1861; d. England, May 21, 1928. [7; 10]

Cohen, Jacob da Silva Solis, physician, b. New York, N.Y., 1839; d. Philadelphia, Pa., Dec. 21, 1927. [1; 10]

Cohen, Morris Raphael, educationist, b. Minsk, Russia, 1880; d. Washington, D.C., Jan. 28, 1947. [7; 10]

Coit, Henry Augustus, clergyman, b. Wilmington, Del., 1830; d. Concord, N.H., Feb. 5, 1895. [1]

Coit, James Milnor, educationist, b. Harrisburg, Pa., 1845; d. Munich, Germany, Jan. 5, 1922. [2; 3; 10]

Coit, Joseph Howland, clergyman, b. Wilmington, Del., 1831; d. Concord, N.H., 1906. [8; 10]

Coit, Thomas Winthrop, clergyman, b. New London, Conn., 1803; d. Middletown, Conn., June 21, 1885. [1; 3; 4; 62]

Coke, Thomas, clergyman, b. Brecon, Wales, 1747; d. at sea, May 3, 1814. [2; 3; 4]

Colburn, Dana Pond, educationist, b. West Dedham, Mass., 1823; d. Bristol, R.I., Dec. 15, 1859. [1; 4]

Colburn, Mrs. Frona Eunice Wait, née **Smith,** journalist and novelist, b. Woodland, Calif., 1859; d. Washington, D.C., Nov. 17, 1946. [35]

Colburn, Warren, educationist, b. Dedham, Mass., 1793; d. Lowell, Mass., Sept. 13, 1833. [1; 3; 4]

Colburn, Zerah, mathematician, b. Cabot, Vt., 1804; d. Norwich, Vt., March 2, 1840. [1; 3; 43]

Colburn, Zerah, engineer, b. Saratoga, N.Y., 1832; d. Massachusetts, May 4, 1870. [3; 4; 6; 8]

Colby, Charles Carroll, politician, b. Derby, Vt., 1827; d. Stanstead, Que., Jan. 10, 1907. [27]

Colby, Frank Moore, educationist, b. Washington, D.C., 1865; d. New York, N.Y., March 3, 1925. [1; 7; 10]

Colby, Frederick Myron, journalist, b. Warner, N.H., 1848; d. ? [6; 8]

Colby, James Fairbanks, educationist, b. St. Johnsbury, Vt., 1850; d. Hanover, N.H., Oct. 21, 1939. [10; 49]

Colby, John, revivalist, b. Sandwich, N.Y., 1787; d. Norfolk, Va., Nov. 28, 1817. [43]

Colby, John Stark, clergyman, b. 1851; d. 1898. [8]

Colby, June Rose, educationist, b. Cherry Valley, O., 1856; d. Normal, Ill., May 11, 1941. [10; 11]

Colby, Mrs. Nathalie, née **Sedgwick,** novelist, b. New York, N.Y., 1875; d. New York, N.Y., June 10, 1942. [7; 10; 11]

Colcord, Lincoln, novelist, b. at sea, 1883; d. Searsport, Me., Nov. 16, 1947. [7; 10; 11]

Colden, Cadwallader, physician, b. Dunse, Scotland, 1688; d. Long Island, N.Y., Sept. 28, 1776. [1; 2; 3; 4; 5; 6; 7]

Colden, Cadwallader David, lawyer, b. Flushing, N.Y., 1769; d. Jersey City, N.J., Feb. 7, 1834. [1; 3; 4]

Coldwell, Albert Edward, educationist, b. Gaspereau, N.S., 1841; d. Wolfville, N.S., Nov. 30, 1916. [33]

Cole, Cyrenus, journalist, b. Pella, Ia., 1863; d. Washington, D.C., Nov. 14, 1939. [7; 10]

Cole, George Watson, librarian and bibliographer, b. Warren, Conn., 1850; d. San Marino, Calif., Oct. 10, 1939. [7; 10; 11]

Cole, Samuel Valentine, educationist and poet, b. Machiasport, Me., 1851; d. Norton, Mass., May 6, 1925. [2; 10; 46]

Coleman, Algernon, educationist, b. News Ferry, Va., 1876; d. Chicago, Ill., Aug. 8, 1939. [10; 11]

Coleman, Arthur Philemon, geologist, b. Lachute, Que., 1852; d. Toronto, Ont., Feb. 26, 1939. [27]

Coleman, Caryl, painter, b. Buffalo, N.Y., 1847; d. Capri, Italy, Dec. 5, 1928. [10; 21]

Coleman, Christopher Bush, educationist, b. Springfield, Ill., 1875; d. Indianapolis, Ind., June 25, 1944. [7; 10; 11]

Coleman, Edward Davidson, librarian, b. Lithuania, 1891; d. Miami Beach, Fla., Sept. 3, 1939. [7]

Coleman, John, clergyman, b. Baltimore, Md., 1803; d. St. Louis, Mo., Sept. 16, 1869. [3]

Coleman, Mrs. Kathleen Blake, née **Watkins,** journalist, b. Ireland, 1864; d. Hamilton, Ont., May 16, 1915. [27]

Coleman, Leighton, bishop, b. Philadelphia, Pa., 1837; d. Wilmington, Del., Dec. 14, 1907. [1; 2; 10]

Coleman, Lyman, clergyman and educationist, b. Middlefield, Mass., 1796; d. Easton, Pa., March 16, 1882. [1; 3; 4; 6]

Coleman, William, journalist, b. Boston, Mass., 1766; d. New York, N.Y., July 14, 1829. [1; 3; 4; 7]

Coles, Abraham, physician and poet, b. Scotch Plains, N.J., 1813; d. Monterey, Calif., May 3, 1891. [3; 4; 7; 8]

Coles, George, clergyman, b. England, 1792; d. New York, N.Y., 1858. [8]

Colesworthy, Daniel Clement, publisher, b. Portland, Me., 1810; d. Chelsea, Mass., April 1, 1893. [3; 8]

Colgrove, Chauncey Peter, educationist, b. Bath, N.Y., Aug. 11, 1855; d. Pasadena, Calif., June 7, 1936. [37]

Collar, William Coe, educationist, b. Westford, Conn., 1833; d. Newton, Mass., Feb. 27, 1916. [10]

Collens, Thomas Wharton, jurist, b. New Orleans, La., 1812; d. New Orleans, La., Nov. 3, 1879. [1; 7; 8; 34]

Colles, Christopher, engineer and inventor, b. Ireland, about 1738; d. New York, N.Y., Oct. 4, 1816. [1; 2; 4]

Collier, Mrs. Ada, née **Langworthy,** poet, b. 1843; d. ? [8]

Collier, Frank Wilbur, clergyman, b. Ellicott's Mills, Md., 1870; d. Washington, D.C., Aug. 31, 1845. [10]

Collier, Hiram Price, essayist, b. Davenport, Ia., 1860; d. Fünen Island, Denmark, Nov. 3, 1913. [1; 4; 10]

Collier, Joseph Avery, clergyman, b. Plymouth, Mass., 1828; d. Kinderhook, N.Y., Aug. 13, 1864. [3; 8]

Collier, Peter, chemist, b. Chittenango, N.Y., Aug. 17, 1835; d. Ann Arbor, Mich., June 29, 1896. [1; 3; 4; 8]

Collier, Price. See Collier, Hiram Price.

Collier, Robert Laird, clergyman, b. Salisbury, Md., 1837; d. near Salisbury, Md., July 26, 1890. [4]

Collier, Thomas Stephens, poet and historian, b. 1843; d. New London, Conn., Sept., 1893. [4; 7; 8]

Collings, Harry Thomas, economist, b. Troy, N.Y., 1880; d. Philadelphia, Pa., Aug. 28, 1934. [62]

Collins, Charles, educationist, b. North Yarmouth, Me., 1813; d. Memphis, Tenn., July 10, 1875. [3; 4; 8]

Collins, Mrs. Dorothea, née **Brande,** novelist, b. Chicago, Ill., 1893; d. Boston, Mass., Dec. 17, 1948.

Collins, Frank Shipley, botanist, b. Charlestown, Mass., 1848; d. New Haven, Conn., May 25, 1920. [1; 10]

Collins, James, airman, b. 1904; d. near Farmingdale, Long Island, N.Y., March 22, 1935.

Collins, Joseph Edmund, journalist, b. Placentia, Newfoundland, 1855; d. New York, N.Y., 1892. [27]

Collins, Mrs. Laura J., née **Case,** poet, b. Maysville, Ky., 1826; d. Maysville, Ky., 1912. [10; 34]

Collins, Lewis, historian, b. Lexington, Ky., 1797; d. Lexington, Ky., Jan. 29, 1870. [74]

Collins, Percy (pseud.). See Collier, Hiram Price.

Collins, Thomas Wharton. See Collens, Thomas Wharton.

Collins, Treve, novelist, b. 1894; d. Teaneck, N.J., July 7, 1939.

Collins, Varnum Lansing, educationist, b. Hong Kong, China, 1870; d. Princeton, N.J., Oct. 9, 1936. [7; 10]

Collins, Winfield Hazlitt, educationist, b. Brookview, Md., 1870; d. Harrogate, Tenn., June 5, 1927. [62]

Collison, Wilson, playwright and novelist, b. Gloucester, O., 1893; d. Beverly Hills, Calif., May 25, 1941. [7; 10]

Collyer, Robert, clergyman, b. Yorkshire, England, 1823; d. New York, N.Y., Nov. 30, 1912. [1; 7; 8; 10]

Colman, Benjamin, clergyman, b. Boston, Mass., 1673; d. Boston, Mass., Aug. 29, 1747. [1; 3; 4; 51]

Colman, Henry, writer on agriculture, b. Boston, Mass., 1785; d. Islington, England, Aug. 14, 1849. [1; 3; 4]

Colman, John, merchant, b. 1670; d. 1753. [1]

Colman, Julia, writer on temperance and hygiene, b. 1828; d. Jan. 10, 1909.

Colman, Samuel, artist, b. Portland, Me., 1832; d. New York, N.Y., March 27, 1920. [1; 4]

Colquhoun, Arthur Hugh Urquhart, historian, b. Montreal, Que., 1861; d. Toronto, Ont., Feb. 9, 1936. [30]

Colton, Aaron Merrick, clergyman, b. Georgia, Vt., 1809; d. Easthampton, Mass., April 30, 1895. [62]

Colton, Arthur Willis, poet and novelist, b. Washington, Conn., 1868; d. Rockland county, N.Y., Dec. 28, 1943. [7; 10; 62]

Colton, Buel Preston, biologist, b. Princeton, Ill., 1852; d. Battle Creek, Mich., Sept. 7, 1906. [45]

Colton, Calvin, journalist, b. Longmeadow, Mass., 1789; d. Savannah, Ga., March 13, 1857. [1; 3; 4; 7]

Colton, Charles Henry, bishop, b. New York, N.Y., 1848; d. Buffalo, N.Y., May 9, 1915. [2; 10; 21]

Colton, Gardner Quincy, anaesthetist, b. Georgia, Vt., 1814; d. Rotterdam, Holland, Aug. 9, 1898. [1; 3; 4]

Colton, George Hooker, poet, b. Westford, N.Y., 1818; d. New York, N.Y., Dec 1, 1847. [3; 7; 8]

Coltor, John, playwright, b. Minnesota, 1889; d. Gainesville, Tex., Dec. 28, 1946. [11]

Colton, Walter, journalist, b. Rutland, Vt., 1797; d. Philadelphia, Pa., Jan. 22. 1851. [1; 3; 7; 43]

Colvil, Edward (pseud.). See Putnam, Mrs. Mary Traill Spence, née Lowell.

Colvin, Stephen Sheldon, educationist, b. Phenix, R.I., 1869; d. New York, N.Y., July 15, 1923. [1; 10]

Colvocoresses, George Musalas, naval officer, b. Chios, Greece, 1816; d. Bridgeport, Conn., June 3, 1872. [1; 3; 4]

Colwell, Stephen, politician economist, b. Brooke county, W. Va., 1800; d. Philadelphia, Pa., Jan. 15, 1871. [1; 3; 4; 34]

Coman, Katherine, historian, b. Newark, O., 1857; d. Wellesley, Mass., Jan. 11, 1915. [2; 8; 10]

Comegys, Benjamin Bartis, banker, b. Dover, Del., 1819; d. Philadelphia, Pa., March 29, 1900. [4]

Comer, Mrs. Cornelia Atwood, née **Pratt,** journalist, d. Seattle, Wash., 1929. [70]

Comes (pseud.) See Redlich, Marcellus Donald Alexander von.

Comfort, Mrs. Anna, née **Manning,** physician, b. Trenton, N.J., 1845; d. New York, N.Y., Jan. 11, 1931. [8; 10]

Comfort, George Fisk, educationist, b. Berkshire, N.Y., 1833; d. Montclair, N.J., May 5, 1910. [2; 8; 10]

Comfort, Will Levington, novelist, b. Kalamazoo, Mich., 1878; d. Los Angeles, Calif., Nov. 2. 1932. [1a; 7; 10; 11]

Comings, Benjamin Newton, physician, b. Cornish, N.H., 1819; d. New Britain, Conn., Dec. 4, 1899. [49]

Comly, John, educationist, b. 1774; d. Ryberry, Pa., Aug. 17, 1850. [3]

Commons, John Rogers, economist, b. Hollandsburg. O., 1862; d. Raleigh, N.C., May 11, 1945. [10; 11]

Compton, Alfred Donaldson, educationist, b. New York, N.Y., 1876; d. New York, N.Y., Jan. 28, 1949.

Compton, Margaret (pseud.). See Harrison, Mrs. Amelia, née Williams.

Comstock, Andrew, elocutionist, b. New, York, N.Y., 1795; d. 1864. [3]

Comstock, Anthony, reformer, b. New Canaan, Conn., 1844; d. New York, N.Y., Sept. 21, 1915. [1; 7; 10]

Comstock, Cyrus Ballou, genealogist, b. West Wrentham, Mass., 1831; d. New York, N.Y., 1910. [10]

Comstock, Enos Benjamin, illustrator and writer of books for children, b. Milwaukee, Wis., 1879; d. Leonia, N.J., March 19, 1945.

Comstock, George Cary, astronomer, b. Madison, Wis., 1855; d. Beloit, Wis., May 11, 1934. [1a; 10; 11; 44]

Comstock, Howard Warren, playwright, b. 1900; d. Fall River, Mass., May 28, 1938.

Comstock, John Henry, entomoligist, b. Janesville, Wis., 1849; d. Ithaca, N.Y., March 20, 1931. [1a; 3; 4; 10; 13]

Comstock, John Lee, scientist, b. Lyme, Conn., 1789; d. Hartford, Conn., Nov. 21, 1858. [2; 3; 8]

Comstock, Theodore Bryant, geologist, b. Cuyahoga Falls, O., 1849; d. Los Angeles, Calif., July 26, 1915. [2; 3; 4; 10]

Conan, Laure (pseud.). See Angers, Félicité.

Conant, Alban Jasper, archaelogist, b. Chelsea, Vt., 1821; d. New York, N.Y., Feb. 3, 1915. [1; 2; 10]

Conant, Carlos Everett, philologist, b. Cabot, Vt., 1870; d. Boston Mass., Jan. 27, 1925. [10]

Conant, Charles Arthur, journalist, b. Winchester, Mass,. 1861; d. Havana, Cuba, July 5, 1915. [1; 7; 10]

Conant, Edward, educationist, b. Pomfret, Vt., 1829; d. 1903. [43]

Conant, Mrs. Hannah O'Brien, née Chaplin, religious writer, b. Danvers, Mass., 1809; d. Brooklyn, N.Y., Feb. 18 ,1865. [1; 3; 4]

Conant, Mrs. Helen Peters, née Stevens, linguist, b. Methuen, Mass., 1839; d. Brooklyn, N.Y., April 17, 1899. [3; 8; 10]

Conant, Levi Leonard, mathematician, b. Littleton, Mass., 1857; d. Worcester, Mass., Oct. 11, 1916. [10; 49]

Conant, Robert Warren, educationist, b. Brooklvn, N.Y., 1852; d. Chicago, Ill., July 10, 1930. [62]

Conant, Thomas, pioneer, b. Oshawa, Ont., 1842; d. Oshawa, Ont., March 14, 1905. [27]

Conant, Thomas Jefferson, theologian and philologist, b. Brandon, Vt., 1802; d. Brooklyn, N.Y., April 30, 1891. [1; 2; 7]

Conaty, Thomas James, bishop, b. Ireland, 1847; d. Coronado Beach, Calif., Sept. 18, 1915. [1; 2;. 4; 10]

Concilio, Gennaro Luigi Vincenzo, clergyman, b. Naples, Italy, 1835; d. Jersey City, N.J., March 22, 1898. [3]

Condie, David Francis, physician, b. Philadelphia, Pa., 1796; d. Delaware county, Pa., March 31, 1875. [2; 8]

Condit, Blackford, clergyman, b. Sullivan county, Ind., 1829; d. 1906. [10]

Condit, Ebenezer, genealogist, b. 1837; d. 1913.

Condit, Jotham Halsey, genealogist, b. 1823; d. 1909.

Condon, Frank, journalist and humorist, b. Toledo, O., 1882; d. Beverly Hills, Calif., Dec. 19, 1940.

Condon, Thomas, clergyman and geologist, b .Ireland, 1822; d. Portland, Ore., Feb. 11, 1907. [1; 4]

Cone, Edward Payson, genealogist, b. 1835; d. 1905.

Cone, Edward Winfield, biographer, b. 1814; d. 1871.

Cone, Helen Gray, poet, b. New York, N.Y., 1859; d. New York, N.Y., Jan. 31, 1934. [7; 11]

Cone, Orello, b. Linclean, N.Y., 1835; d. Canton, N.Y., June 23, 1905. [1; 8; 10]

Cone, Spencer Houghton, clergyman, b. Princeton, N.J., 1785; d. New York, N.Y., Aug. 28, 1855. [1; 4]

Cone, Spencer Wallace, lawyer, b. Alexandria, Va., 1819; d. New York, N.Y., Jan. 21, 1888.

Congdon, Charles Taber, journalist and poet, b. New Bedford, Mass., 1821; d. New York, N.Y., Jan. 18, 1891. [1; 3; 4; 7]

Coningsby, Christopher (pseud.). See Harris, Samuel Smith.

Conklin, Edmund Smith, psychologist, b. New Britain, Conn., 1884; d. Bloomington, Ind., Oct. 6, 1942. [7; 10]

Conklin, Mrs. Jennie Maria, née Drinkwater, writer of books for girls, b. Portland, Me., 1841; d. New Vernon, N.J., April 28, 1900. [1; 7]

Conklin, Mrs. Nathaniel, See Conklin, Mrs. Jennie Maria, née Drinkwater.

Conklin, Mrs. Viola A., née Peckham, historian, b. New York, N.Y., 1849; d. ? [10]

Conkling, Alfred, jurist, b. Long Island, N.Y., 1789; d. Utica, N.Y., Feb. 5, 1874. [1; 3; 4]

Conkling, Alfred Ronalds, lawyer, b. New York, N.Y., b. 1850; d. New York, N.Y., Sept. 18, 1917. [3; 62]

Conkling, Margaret Cockburn, biographer, b. 1814; d. Jersey City, N.J., July 28, 1890. [3]

Conlin, Bernard, actor, b. Albany, N.Y., 1831; d. Philadelphia, Pa., 1891. [2]

Conn, Herbert William, biologist, b. Fitchburg, Mass., 1859; d. Middletown, Conn., April 18, 1917. [2; 10; 13]

Connell, Richard, novelist and short-story writer, b. Poughkeepsie, N.Y., 1893; d. Beverly Hills, Calif., Nov. 22, 1949. [10; 11]

Connelley, William Elsey, ethnologist and local historian, b. Johnson county, Ky., 1855; d. Topeka, Kans., July 15, 1930. [2; 10]

Connelly, Mrs. Celia, née **Logan Kellogg,** journalist, b. Philadelphia, Pa., 1837; d. New York, N.Y., June 18, 1904. [7; 8]

Connelly, Emma Mary, historian, b. near Louisville, Ky., d. about 1900. [7; 34]

Connelly, James H., novelist, b. Pittsburg, Pa., 1840; d. New York, N.Y., March 15, 1903. [7; 10]

Conner, Mrs. Charlotte Mary Sanford, née **Barnes.** See Barnes, Charlotte Mary Sanford.

Conning, John Stuart, clergyman, b. Whithorn, Scotland, 1862; d. Upper Montclair, N.J., June 20, 1946. [10]

Connolly, Alonzo Putnam, publisher, b. Sheffield, N.B., 1836; d. Nov. 13, 1915.

Connolly, Louise, educationist, b. 1862; d. Portland, Me., July 16, 1927. [2]

Connor, Henry Groves, jurist, b. Wilmington, D.C., 1852; d. Wilson, N.C., Nov. 23, 1924. [1; 4]

Connor, Ralph (pseud.). See Gordon, Charles William.

Conquest, Pleasanton Laws, poet, b. Fredericksburg, Va., 1882; d. Richmond, Va., Nov. 4, 1938.

Conrad, Arcturus A., clergyman, b. Shiloh, Ind., 1855; d. Cambridge, Mass., June 8, 1932. [10; 68]

Conrad, Carl Nicholas, clergyman, b. Rochester, N.Y., 1858; d. Rochester, N.Y., June 9, 1932. [10; 11]

Conrad, Frederick William, clergyman, b. Pine Grove, Pa., 1816; d. 1898. [8]

Conrad, Henry Clay, jurist and historian, b. Bridesburg, Pa., 1852; d. Georgetown, Del., Oct. 24, 1930. [4; 10]

Conrad, Robert Taylor, jurist and poet, b. Philadelphia, Pa., 1810; d. Philadelphia, Pa., June 10, 1858. [1; 3; 4; 7]

Conrad, Stephen (pseud.). See Stimtz, Stephen Conrad.

Conrad, Timothy Abbott, palaeontologist, b. Philadelphia, Pa., 1803; d. Philadelphia, Pa., Aug. 9, 1877. [3; 4]

Conroy, Joseph Patrick, priest and educationist, b. Chicago, Ill., 1869; d. Evanston, Ill., June 12, 1941. [21]

Considine, Daniel, priest, b. 1849; d. 1923. [21]

Converse, Charles Crozat, lawyer and musician, b. Warren, Mass., 1832; d. Highwood, N.J., Oct. 18, 1918. [1; 4]

Converse, Mrs. Harriet, née **Maxwell,** writer on Indian folklore, b. Elmira, N.Y., 1836; d. New York, N.Y., Nov. 18, 1903. [7; 10]

Converse, James Booth, clergyman, b. Philadelphia, Pa., 1844; d. Morristown, Tenn., Oct. 31, 1914. [1; 10]

Conway, Katherine Eleanor, journalist, b. Rochester, N.Y., 1853; d. Boston, Mass., Jan. 2, 1927. [7; 8; 10; 21]

Conway, Moncure Daniel, clergyman, b. Stafford county, Va., 1832; d. Paris, France, Nov. 15, 1907. [1; 3; 7; 10]

Conwell, Russell Herman, clergyman, b. South Worthington, Mass., 1843; d. Philadelphia, Pa., Dec. 6, 1925. [1; 4; 7; 8; 10]

Conybeare, Charles Frederick Pringle, poet, b. Middlesex, England, 1860; d. Lethbridge, Alta., July 31, 1927. [27]

Conyngham, David Power, journalist, b. 1840; d. 1883. [7; 8; 21]

Cook, Albert John, naturalist, b. Owosso, Mich., 1842; d. Owosso, Mich., Sept. 29, 1916. [3; 8; 10]

Cook, Albert Stanburrough, educationist, b. Montville, N.J., 1853; d. New Haven, Conn., Sept. 1, 1927. [1; 2; 4; 7; 10]

Cook, Carroll Blaine, fisherman, b. Grand Bend, Pa., 1883; d. Chicago, Ill., June 11, 1922. [10]

Cook, Clarence Chatham, art critic, b. Dorchester, Mass., 1828; d. Fishkill, N.Y., June 2, 1900. [1; 3; 4; 7]

Cook, David Caleb, publisher, b. East Wooster, N.Y., 1850; d. Elgin, Ill., July 29, 1927. [10]

Cook, Elizabeth Christine, educationist, b. Northampton, Mass., 1876; d. New York, N.Y., March 1, 1938. [48]

Cook, Mrs. Fannie, née **Frank,** novelist, b. St. Charles, Mo.; d. St. Louis, Mo., Aug. 25, 1949.

Cook, Flavius Josephus, clergyman and lecturer, b. Ticonderoga, N.Y., 1838; d. Ticonderoga, N.Y., June 24, 1901. [1; 10]

Cook, Frederick Albert, explorer, b. Sullivan county, N.Y., 1865; d. New Rochelle, N.Y., Aug. 5, 1940. [2; 4; 10]

Cook, George Cram, playwright, b. Davenport, Ia., 1873; d. Delphi, Greece, Jan. 14, 1924. [1; 4; 7; 10]

Cook, George Hammell, geologist, b. Hanover, N.J., 1818; d. New Brunswick, N.J., Sept. 22, 1889. [1; 3; 4]

Cook, James Henry, naturalist, b. Kalamazoo, Mich., 1858; d. near Agate, Neb., Jan. 26, 1942. [7; 10]

Cook, Joel, journalist, b. Philadelphia, Pa., 1842; d. Philadelphia, Pa., Dec. 15, 1910. [8; 10]

Cook, John Williston, educationist, b. near Oneida, N.Y., 1844; d. Chicago, Ill., July 16, 1922. [1; 4]

Cook, Joseph. See Cook, Flavius Josephus.

Cook, Marc, journalist, b. Providence, R.I., 1854; d. Utica, N.Y., Oct. 4, 1882. [3; 4]

Cook, Richard Briscoe, clergyman, b. Baltimore, Md., 1838; d. Wilmington, Del., May, 1916. [3; 10; 24]

Cook, Theodore Pease, journalist, b. Boston, Mass., 1844; d. July 17, 1916. [3; 48]

Cook, Walter Wheeler, lawyer and educationist, b. Columbus, O., 1873; d. Tupper Lake, N.Y., Nov. 7, 1943. [10]

Cook, Webster, educationist, b. Urania, Mich., 1854; d. Saginaw, Mich., June 30, 1908. [39]

Cook, William Henry, physician, b. 1832; d. 1899. [8]

Cook, William Wallace, writer of books for boys, b. Marshall, Mich., 1867; d. Marshall, Mich., July 20, 1933. [7; 10]

Cook, William Wilson, lawyer b. Hillsdale, Mich., 1858; d. Port Chester, N.Y., June 4, 1930. [8; 10]

Cooke, Edmund Vance, poet and lecturer, b,. Port Dover, Ont., 1866; d. Cleveland, O., Dec. 18, 1932. [4; 10; 11]

Cooke, Frederick Hale, lawyer, b. Woonsocket, R.I., 1859; d. Brooklyn, N.Y., Jan. 11, 1912.

Cooke, George Willis, clergyman, b. Comstock, Mich., 1848; d. Revere, Mass., April 30, 1923. [1; 7; 10]

Cooke, John Esten, physician, b. Bermuda, 1783; d. near the Ohio River, Oct. 19, 1853. [1; 4; 34]

Cooke, John Esten, novelist, b. Winchester, Va., 1830; d. near Boyce, Va., Sept. 27, 1886. [1; 2; 3; 4; 7; 8; 72]

Cooke, Josiah Parsons, chemist, b. Boston, Mass., 1827; d. Newport, R.I., Sept. 3, 1894. [1; 3; 4]

Cooke, Marjorie Benton, novelist and monologist, b. Richmond, Ind., 1876; d. Manila, Philippine Islands, April 26, 1920. [10]

Cooke, Martin Warren, lawyer, b. Whitehall, N.Y., 1840; d. 1898. [4; 8]

Cooke, Nicholas Francis, physician, b. Providence, R.I., 1829; d. Chicago, Ill., Feb. 1, 1885. [3; 8]

Cooke, Parsons, clergyman, b. Hadley, Mass., 1800; d. Lynn, Mass., Feb. 12, 1864. [3; 8]

Cooke, Philip Pendleton, poet, b. Martinsburg, Va., 1816; d. near Millwood, Va., Jan. 20, 1850. [1; 3; 4; 7; 34]

Cooke, Philip St. George, soldier, b. Leesburg, Va., 1809; d. Detroit, Mich., March 20, 1895. [1; 3: 4; 7; 34]

Cooke, Mrs. Rose, née Terry, poet and short-story writer, b. near Hartford, Conn., 1827; d. Pittsfield, Mass., July 18, 1892. [1; 3; 4; 7]

Cookman, Alfred, clergyman, b. Columbia, Pa., 1828; d. Newark, N.J., Nov. 13, 1871. [4; 8]

Coolbrith, Ina Donna, poet, b. near Springfield, Ill., 1842; d. Berkeley, Calif., Feb. 29, 1928. [1; 4; 7; 10; 35]

Cooley, LeRoy Clark, physicist, b. Point Peninsula, N.Y., 1833; d. Poughkeepsie, N.Y., Sept. 21, 1916. [3; 4; 10]

Cooley, Lyman Edgar, civil engineer, b. Canandaigua, N.Y., 1850; d. Chicago, Ill., Feb. 3, 1917. [1; 4; 10]

Cooley, Thomas McIntyre, jurist, b. near Attica, N.Y., 1824; d. Ann Arbor, Mich., Sept. 12, 1898. [1; 3; 4]

Coolidge, Archibald Cary, historian, b. Boston, Mass., 1866; d. Boston, Mass.. Jan. 14, 1928. [1; 7; 10; 51]

Coolidge, Calvin, president of the United States, b. Plymouth, Vt., 1872; d. Northampton, Mass. Jan, 5, 1933. [1a; 4; 7; 10]

Coolidge, Clarence Edwin, mechanical engineer, b. Willimantic, Conn., 1870; d. Atlanta, Ga., Sept. 25, 1946. [62]

Coolidge, Dane, naturalist and novelist, b. Natick, Mass., 1873; d. Berkeley, Calif., Aug. 8, 1940. [7; 10, 11; 35]

Coolidge, Emelyn Lincoln, pediatrician, b. Boston, Mass., 1873; d. New York, N.Y., April 14, 1949. [10]

Coolidge, John Gardner, diplomat, b Boston, Mass., 1863; d. Boston, Mass., Feb 28, 1936. [7; 10; 11; 51]

Coolidge, Louis Arthur, biographer, b. Natick, Mass., 1861; d. Milton, Mass., May 31, 1925. [4; 10; 51]

Coolidge, Mrs. Mary, née Roberts, sociologist, b. Kingsbury, Ind., 1860; d. ? [7; 10; 11]

Coolidge, Susan (pseud.). See Woolsey, Sarah Chauncey.

Coom, Charles Sleeman, novelist, b. England, 1853; d. after 1929. [10]

Coomaraswamy, Ananda Kentish, art expert and orientalist, b. Colombo, Ceylon, 1877; d. Needham, Mass., Sept. 9, 1947. [10]

Coombe, Thomas, clergyman and poet, b. Philadelphia, Pa., 1747; d. London, England, Aug. 15, 1822. [1; 4; 7; 8]

Coombs, Mrs. Anne, née Sheldon, novelist, b. Albany, N.Y., 1858; d. 1890. [7; 8]

Coombs, Mrs. Sarah, née Hall, horticulturist, b. 1868; d. White Plains, N.Y., Nov. 29, 1949.

Cooney, John Michael, novelist, b. Louisville, Ky., 1874; d. South Bend, Ind., Oct. 15, 1945. [21]

Cooney, Percival John, novelist, b. Peterborough, Ont., 1871; d. Los Angeles, Calif., May 17, 1932. [10; 35]

Cooney, Robert, historian, b. Dublin, Ireland, 1800; d. Toronto, Ont., March 17, 1870. [27]

Coonley, Mrs. Lydia, née Avery. See Ward, Mrs. Lydia, née Avery.

Coontz, Robert Edward, naval officer, b. Hannibal, Mo., 1864; d. Bremerton, Wash., Jan. 26, 1935. [1a; 10]

Cooper, Clayton Sedgewick, editor and lecturer, b. Henderson, N.Y., 1869; d. Rochester, Minn., Oct. 13, 1936. [7; 10; 11]

Cooper, Courtney Ryley, novelist and free-lance journalist, b. Kansas City, Mo., 1886; d. New York, N.Y., Sept. 28, 1940. [7; 10]

Cooper, Ellwood, horticulturist, b. Sadsbury, Pa., 1829; d. Santa Barbara, Calif., ? [3; 10]

Cooper, Frank (pseud.). See Simms, William Gilmore.

Cooper, Frederic Taber, educationist, b New York, N.Y., 1864; d. New London, Conn., May 19, 1937. [1; 10]

Cooper, Jacob, educationist, b. near Somerville, O., 1830; d. New Brunswick, N.J., Jan. 31, 1904. [1; 4; 10]

Cooper, James Fenimore, novelist, b. Burlington, N.J., 1789; d. Cooperstown, N.Y., Sept. 14, 1851. [1; 2; 3; 4; 5; 6; 7; 72]

Cooper, James Fenimore, poet, b. Albany, N.Y., 1897; d. Wrightstown, N.J., Feb. 17, 1918. [62]

Cooper, Myles, clergyman and educationist, b. Cumberland, England, 1737; d. Edinburg, Scotland, May 1, 1785. [1; 2; 3; 4]

Cooper, Oscar Henry, educationist, b. Carthage, Tex., 1852; d. Abilene, Tex., Aug. 22, 1932. [10; 34]

Cooper, Peter, inventor and philanthropist, b. New York, N.Y., 1791; d. New York, N.Y., April 4, 1883. [1; 3; 4; 7]

Cooper, Samuel, clergyman, b. Boston, Mass., 1725; d. Boston, Mass., Dec. 23, 1783. [1; 3; 51]

Cooper, Samuel, soldier, b. Hackensack, N.J., 1798; d. Cameron, Va., Dec. 3, 1876. [1; 3; 4]

Cooper, Samuel Williams, novelist, b. Philadelphia, Pa., 1860; d. Philadelphia, Pa., Jan. 13, 1939. [10]

Cooper. Susan Fenimore, writer of rural sketches, b. Scarsdale, N.Y., 1813; d. Cooperstown, N.Y., Dec. 31, 1894. [1; 3; 4; 7]

Cooper, Thomas, scientist and politician, b. London, England, 1759; d. Columbia, S.C., May 11, 1840. [1; 3; 4; 34]

Cooper, William, clergyman, b. Boston, Mass., 1694; d. Boston, Mass., Dec. 13, 1743. [3; 4; 8; 51]

Cooper, William John, educationist, b. Sacramento, Calif.. 1882; d. Kearney, Neb., Sept. 19, 1935. [1a; 10]

Cooperrider, George T., clergyman, b. Licking county, O., 1852; d. Columbus, O., Aug. 1916. [10]

Coover, John Edgar, psychologist, b. Remington, Ind., 1872; d. Palo Alto, Calif., Feb. 19, 1938. [10; 11]

Cope, Edward Drinker, zoologist and palaeontologist, b. Philadelphia, Pa., 1840; d. Philadelphia, Pa., April 12, 1897. [1; 3; 4]

Cope, Gilbert, genealogist, b. near West Chester, Pa., 1840; d. West Chester, Pa., Dec. 18, 1928. [3; 10]

Copeland, Benjamin, clergyman and poet, b. Clarendon, N.Y., 1855; d. Buffalo, N.Y., Dec. 1, 1940. [7]

Copeland, Royal Samuel, physician, b. Dexter, Mich., 1868; d. Washington, D.C., June 17, 1938. [4; 10]

Copp, Theodore Bayard Fletcher, writer of adventure stories, b. Brookline, Mass., 1902; d. Hastings-on-Hudson, N.Y., Jan. 1, 1945.

Coppée, Henry, educationist, b. Savannah, Ga., 1821; d. Bethlehem, Pa., March 21, 1895. [1; 2; 3; 4; 5; 6; 7; 34]

Copway, George, Indian missionary, b. Upper Canada, 1818; d. Pontiac, Mich., 1863. [1; 3; 7; 27]

Coquina (pseud.). See Shields, George Oliver.

Corbin, Mrs. Caroline Elizabeth, née Fairfield, novelist, b. Pomfret, Conn., 1835; d. ?

Corby, William, priest and educationist, b. Detroit, Mich., 1833; d. Dec. 28, 1897. [1; 7; 21]

Corey, Charles Henry, clergyman and educationist, b. New Canaan, N.B., 1834; d. Seabrook, N.H., Sept. 5, 1899. [10; 33]

Corinne (pseud.). See Dahlgren, Mrs. Sarah Madeline, née Vinton.

Corkey, Alexander, clergyman, b. Londonderry, Ireland, 1871; d. Wayne, Neb., Oct. 28, 1914. [10]

Cormack, Bartlett, playwright, b. Hammond, Ind., 1898; d. Phoenix, Ariz., Sept. 16, 1942.

Cornelius, Elias, educationist, b. Somers, N.Y., 1794; d. Hartford, Conn., Feb. 12, 1832. [3; 4]

Cornelius, Mrs. Mary Ann, née Mann, novelist, b. Pontiac, Mich., 1829; d. April 18, 1918. [10]

Cornell, Alonzo Barton, politician, b. Ithaca, N.Y., 1832; d. Ithaca, N.Y., Oct. 15, 1904. [1; 3; 4]

Cornell, John Henry, musician, b. New York, N.Y., 1828; d. New York, N.Y., March 1, 1894. [3; 20]

Cornell, William Mason, physician, b. Berkeley, Mass., 1802; d. Boston, Mass., April 14, 1895. [3; 8]

Corning, James Leonard, clergyman, b. 1828; d. 1903.

Corning, James Leonard, neurologist, b. Stamford, Conn., 1855; d. Morristown, N.J., Aug. 25, 1923. [4; 10]

Cornish, George Henry, clergyman, b. Exeter, England, 1834; d. Toronto, Ont., Aug. 25, 1912. [27]

Cornman, Oliver Perry, educationist, b. Philadelphia, Pa., 1866; d. Germantown, Pa., Sept. 6, 1930. [10]

Cornwall, C. M. (pseud.). See Roe, Mary Abigail.

Cornwall, Edward Everett, physician, b. Buenos Aires, Argentina, 1866; d. Brooklyn, N.Y., Oct. 6, 1940. [10]

Cornwall, Henry Bedinger, chemist, b. Southport, Conn., 1844; d. Southport, Conn., April 1, 1917. [2; 10]

Cornwallis, Kinahan, lawyer and novelist, b. London, England, 1839; d. New York, N.Y., Aug. 15, 1917. [1; 4; 7; 10]

Cornwall, Henry Sylvester, physician and poet, b. New London, Conn., 1831; d. New London, Conn., June 15, 1886. [62]

Corrothers, James David, clergyman and poet, b. Calvin, Mich., 1869; d. West Chester, Pa., Feb. 12, 1917. [1; 4; 7]

Corser, Harry Prosper, clergyman, b. Portageville, N.Y., 1864; d. Wrangell, Alaska, Feb. 3, 1936. [7; 10]

Corson, Hiram, educationist, b. Philadelphia, Pa., 1828; d. Ithaca, N.Y., June 15, 1911. [1; 2; 3; 4; 7; 10]

Corson, Juliet, dietician, b. Boston, Mass., 1842; d. New York, N.Y., June 18, 1897. [1; 3; 4]

Cortambert, Louis Richard, journalist, b. Paris, France, 1808; d. New York, N.Y., March 28, 1881. [1; 7]

Corthell, Elmer Lawrence, civil engineer, b. South Abington, Mass., Sept. 30, 1840; d. Albany, N.Y., May 16, 1916. [1; 10]

Cortissoz, Mrs. Ellen Mackay, née Hutchinson, journalist and poet, b. New York, N.Y.; d. New York, N.Y., Aug. 13, 1933. [7; 10]

Cortissoz, Royal, art critic, b. Brooklyn, N.Y., 1869; d. New York, N.Y., Oct. 17, 1948. [7; 10]

Corwin, Edward Tanjore, clergyman, b. New York, N.Y., 1834; d. North Branch, N.J., June 22, 1914. [1; 2]

Corwin, Thomas, politician, b. Bourbon county, Ky., 1794; d. Washington, D.C., Dec. 18, 1865. [3; 4]

Cory, Charles Barney, ornithologist, b. Boston, Mass., 1857; d. Ashland, Wis., July 29, 1921. [1; 7; 8; 10]

Cory, Charles Henry, clergyman, b. 1834; d. 1899. [8]

Cory, Herbert Ellsworth, educationist, b. Providence, R.I., 1883; d. Seattle, Wash., Feb. 1, 1947. [10; 22]

Coryell, John Russell, writer of books for boys, b. 1848; d. Readfield, Me., July 15, 1924. [4; 7]

Cosgrave, Mrs. Jessica, née Garretson, educationist, b. New York., N.Y., 1871; d. New York, N.Y., Nov. 1, 1949. [10]

Cosgrave, John O'Hara, journalist, b. Australia, 1866; d. New York, N.Y., Sept. 19, 1947. [10]

Cossett, Franceway Ranna, clergyman, b. Claremont, N.H., 1790; d. Lebanon, Tenn., July 3, 1863. [3; 34]

Costello, Frederick Hankerson, novelist, b. Bangor, Me., 1851; d. Bangor, Me., Aug. 2, 1921. [10]

Costigan, George Purcell, lawyer and educationist, b. Chicago, Ill., 1870; d. Berkeley, Calif., Nov. 18, 1934. [1a; 10; 11]

Coston, William, chaplain, b. Providence, R.I., 1858; d. Washington, D.C., June 27, 1942. [62]

Coté, Joseph Olivier, civil servant, b. Quebec, Lower Canada, 1820; d. Ottawa, Ont., April 24, 1882. [27]

Coté, Thomas, journalist, b. Trois Pistoles, Que., 1869; d. Montreal, Que., Jan. 16, 1918. [27]

Cotes, Mrs. Everard, née Duncan. See Duncan, Sara Jeanette.

Cotes, Hornor (pseud.). See Coates, Joseph Hornor.

Cothren, William, lawyer and genealogist, b. Farmington, Me., 1819; d. Sharon Springs, N.Y., July 11, 1888. [8; 46; 62]

Cotillo, Salvatore Albert, jurist, b. Italy, 1886; d. New York, N.Y., July 27, 1939. [21]

Cotting, Benjamin Eddy, physician, b. Arlington, Mass., 1812; d. 1897. [51]

Cotting, John Ruggles, chemist, b. Acton, Mass., 1783; d. Milledgeville, Ga., Oct. 13, 1867. [3; 4; 8]

Cotton, John, clergyman, b. Derby, England, 1585; d. Boston, Mass., Dec. 23, 1652. [1; 2; 3; 4; 7]

Coudert, Frederic René, lawyer, b. New York, N.Y., 1832; d. Washington, D.C., Dec. 20, 1903. [1; 2; 4; 10]

Coues, Elliott, naturalist and historian, b. Portsmouth, N.H., 1842; d. Baltimore, Md., Dec. 26, 1899. [1; 2; 3; 4; 7; 10]

Couët, Thomas Cyrille, priest, b. Quebec, Que., 1861; d. Portage des Roches, Chicoutimi River, Que., Sept. 17, 1931. [27; 32]

Coughlan, Mrs. Maria, née Moravsky, novelist, b. Russia, 1895; d. Miami, Fla., June 26, 1947.

Coulter, John Merle, botanist, b. China, 1851; d. Yonkers, N.Y., Dec. 23, 1928. [1; 3; 4; 10]

Coulter, Stanley, biologist, b. China, 1853; d. Lafayette, Ind., June 26, 1943. [10; 11]

Councilman, William Thomas, pathologist, b. Pikesville, Md., 1854; d. York Village, Me., May 26, 1933. [10; 2; 4; 10]

Courtemanche, Joseph Israel, priest, b. St. Jude, Que., 1847; d. St. Roch-sur-Richelieu, Que., Dec. 5, 1900. [27; 32]

Courtenay, Edward Henry, mathematician, b. Maryland, 1803; d. Charlottesville, Va., Dec. 21, 1853. [3; 4; 34]

Courtney, Joseph William, neurologist, b. Cambridge, Mass., 1868; d. Boston, Mass., June 6, 1928. [10; 51]

Cousin Alice (pseud.). See Haven, Mrs. Alice, née Bradley.

Cousin Kate (pseud.). See McIntosh, Maria Jane.

Cousins, Robert Bartow, educationist, b. Fayetteville, Ga., 1861; d. Kingsville, Tex., March 3, 1932. [10]

Covell, James, clergyman, b. Marblehead, Mass., 1796; d. Troy, N.Y., May 15, 1845. [3]

Coventry, John (pseud.). See Palmer, John Williamson.

Covert, William Chalmers, clergyman, b. Franklin, Ind., 1864; d. Philadelphia, Pa., Feb. 4, 1942. [7; 10; 11]

Cowan, Mrs. Bertha, née Muzzy. See Sinclair, Mrs. Bertha, née Muzzy.

Cowan, Frank, physician and poet, b. Greensburg, Pa., 1844; d. Greensburg, Pa., Feb. 12, 1905. [3; 7; 10]

Cowan, John Franklin, clergyman, b. Griffinshire, N.Y., 1854; d. San Diego, Calif., Dec. 19, 1942. [35]

Cowan, Robert Ernest, librarian and bibliographer, b. Toronto, Ont., 1862; d. Los Angeles, Calif., May 29, 1942. [7; 10]

Coward, Edward Fales, playwright, b. New York, N.Y., 1862; d. Onteora Park, N.Y., Aug. 29, 1933. [10]

Cowdery, Jonathan, surgeon, b. Sandisfield, Mass., 1767; d. Norfolk, Va., Nov. 20, 1852. [3]

Cowdin, Jasper Barnett, poet, fl. 1886. [8]

Cowell, Benjamin, jurist, b. Wrentham, Mass., 1781; d. Providence, R.I., May 6, 1860. [3; 47]

Cowell, Joseph, comedian, b. Kent, England, 1792; d. London, England, Nov. 14, 1863. [3]

Cowen, Benjamin Rush, legal official, b. Moorfield, O., 1831; d. Cincinatti, O., Jan. 29, 1908. [10]

Cowen, Esek, jurist, b. Rhode Island, 1787; d. Albany, N.Y., Feb. 11, 1844. [3]

Cowie, Isaac, fur-trader, b. Shetland Islands, Scotland, 1848; d. Winnipeg, Man., May 18, 1917. [27]

Cowles, Alfred Abernethy, poet, b. Torrington, Conn., 1845; d. New York, N.Y., Dec. 8, 1916. [2; 4]

Cowles, Mrs. Francis Dana. See Cowles, Mrs. Julia, née Darrow.

Cowles, Henry, clergyman, b. Norfolk, Conn., 1803; d. Janesville, Wis., Sept. 6, 1881. [3; 62]

Cowles, Henry Chandler, botanist, b. Kensington, Conn., 1869; d. Chicago, Ill., Sept. 12, 1939. [10]

Cowles, James Lewis, economist, b. Farmington, Conn., 1843; d. Richmond, Va., Oct. 22, 1922. [4; 10; 62]

Cowles, Mrs. Julia, née Darrow, writer of books for children, b. Norwalk, O., 1862; d. Toronto, Ont., Sept. 6, 1919. [10]

Cowles, William Lyman, educationist, b. Belchertown, Mass., 1856; d. Atlantic City, N.J., May 12, 1926. [2; 10; 45]

Cowley, Charles, lawyer and historian, b. Gloucestershire, England, 1832; d. Lowell, Mass., Feb. 6, 1908. [1; 4; 7; 8; 10]

Cox, Arthur Cleveland. See Coxe, Arthur Cleveland.

Cox, Coleman, philosopher, b. 1873; d. San Francisco, Calif., Nov. 26, 1940.

Cox, Eleanor Rogers, poet, b. Enniskillen, Ireland, 1867; d. New York, N.Y., Jan. 17, 1931. [10; 21]

Cox, Florence Tinsley, journalist, b. 1877; d. Brooklyn, N.Y., May 8, 1940.

Cox, George Clarke, political economist, b. Columbus, O., 1865; d. New York, N.Y., Dec. 17, 1943. [10; 11]

Cox, Henry Hamilton, poet, b. Ireland, about 1769; d. Ireland, 1821. [1; 7]

Cox, Mrs. J.J. See Cox, Mrs. Maria, née McIntosh.

Cox, Jacob Dolson, politician, b. Montreal, Lower Canada, 1828; d. Magnolia, Mass., Aug. 8, 1900. [1; 3; 4; 10]

Cox, James, advertising agent, d. St. Louis, Mo., 1902.

Cox, John Harrington, educationist, b. Illinois, 1863; d. Morgantown, W. Va., Nov. 21, 1945. [7; 11]

Cox, Kenyon, painter, b. Warren, O., 1856; d. New York, N.Y., March 17, 1919. [1; 4; 7; 10]

Cox, Mrs. Maria, née McIntosh, novelist, b. 1832; d. 1910.

Cox, Palmer, writer and illustrator of books for children, b. Granby, Lower Canada, 1840; d. Granby, Que., July 24, 1924. [1; 2; 3; 4; 7; 35]

Cox, Samuel Hanson, clergyman, b. Rahway, N.J., 1793; d. Bronxville, N.Y., Oct. 2, 1880. [1; 3; 4]

Cox, Samuel Sullivan, politician and diplomat, b. Zanesville, O., 1824; d. New York, N.Y., Sept. 10, 1889. [1; 3; 4; 7]

Cox, William, journalist, b. England; d. England, 1851. [3]

Cox, William J., educationist, b. 1851; d. 1913. [39]

Cox, William Van Zandt, banker and biographer, b. near Zanesville, O., 1852; Washington, D.C., July 24, 1923. [4; 10]

Coxe, Arthur Cleveland, bishop, b. Mendham, N.J., 1818; d. Clifton Springs, N.Y., July 20, 1896. [1; 3; 4; 7]

Coxe, Brinton, lawyer, b. Philadelphia, Pa., 1833; d. Drifton, Pa., Sept. 15, 1892. [55]

Coxe, John Redman, physician, b. Trenton, N.J., 1773; d. Philadelphia, Pa., March 22, 1864. [1; 3; 4]

Coxe, Macgrane, lawyer, b. Huntsville, Ala., 1859; d. New York, N.Y., April 20, 1923. [4; 10]

Coxe, Margaret, feminist, b. Burlington, N.J., about 1800; d. ? [3]

Coxe, Richard Smith, lawyer, b. Burlington, N.J., 1792; d. Washington, D.C., April 28, 1865. [1; 4]

Coxe, Tench, economist, b. Philadelphia, Pa., 1755; d. Philadelphia, Pa., July 17, 1824. [1; 3; 4]

Coxe, William, pomologist, b. Philadelphia, Pa., 1762; d. near Burlington, N.J., Feb. 25, 1831. [1]

Coxey, Willard Douglas, journalist and poet, b. Philadelphia, Pa., 1861; d. Great Barrington, Mass., Aug. 9, 1943.

Coyle, John Patterson, clergyman, b. 1852; d. 1895. [8]

Coyle, Robert Francis, clergyman, b. Roseneath, Ont., 1850; d. Fullerton, Calif., Feb. 5, 1917. [10; 63]

Coyle, Robert McCurdy, insurance broker, b. Cincinatti, O., 1860; d. Philadelphia, Pa., Feb. 24, 1936. [10]

Coyne, James Henry, lawyer and historian, St. Thomas, Ont., 1849; d. St. Thomas, Ont., Jan. 5, 1942. [11; 27]

Coyner, Charles Luther, lawyer, b. Long Glade, Va., 1853; d. ? [10; 34]

Cozzens, Frederick Swartwout, humorist, b. New York, N.Y., 1818; d. Brooklyn, N.Y., Dec. 23, 1869. [1; 3; 7]

Cozzens, Issachar, geologist, b. Newport, R.I., 1781; d. 1865. [3]

Cozzens, Samuel Woodwarth, lawyer and novelist, b. Marblehead, Mass., 1834; d. Thomaston, Ga., Nov. 4, 1878. [3; 7; 8; 35]

Crabitès, Pierre, jurist, b. New Orleans, La., 1877; d. Baghdad, Iraq, Oct. 9, 1943. [10; 22]

Crabtree, James William, educationist, b. Crabtree, Scioto county, O., 1864; d. Washington, D.C., June 9, 1945. [10]

Craddock, Charles Egbert (pseud.). See Murfree, Mary Noailles.

Crafts, James Mason, chemist, b. Boston, Mass., 1839; d. Ridgefield, Conn., June 20, 1917. [1; 3; 4]

Crafts, William, lawyer and poet, b. Charleston, S.C., 1787; d. Lebanon Springs, N.Y., Sept. 23, 1826. [1; 3; 7; 34]

Crafts, William Augustus, historian, b. 1819; d. 1906. [51]

Crafts, Wilbur Fisk, clergyman, b. Fryeburg, Me., 1850; d. Washington, D.C., Dec. 27, 1922. [2; 3; 4; 10]

Cragg, Kenneth C., journalist, b. near Drayton, Ont., 1904; d. Ottawa, Ont., Feb. 16, 1948.

Craig, James Alexander, orientalist, b. Fitzroy Harbour, Ont., 1855; d. Toronto, Ont. May 15, 1932.

Craig, John, missionary, b. near Toronto, Ont., 1852; d. Cocanada, India, July 20, 1923. [27]

Craig, Joseph Edgar, naval officer, b. Medina, N.Y., 1845; d. Washington, D.C., June 21, 1925. [10]

Craig, Mrs. Laura, née Gerould, religious writer, b. East Smithville, Pa., 1860; d. Buffalo, N.Y., Oct. 12, 1946.

Craig, Neville B., civil engineer, b. Pittsburg, Pa., 1847; d. Germantown, Pa., Aug. 8, 1926. [62]

Craig, Thomas, mathematician, b. Pittston, Pa., 1855; d. Baltimore, Md., May 8, 1900. [1]

Craighead, Erwin, journalist, b. Nashville, Tenn., 1852; d. Mobile, Ala., Feb. 3, 1932. [10; 11]

Craighead, Erwin, journalist, b. Nashville, Tenn., 1852; d. Mobile, Ala., Feb. 3, 1932. [10; 11]

Craighead, James Geddes, clergyman, b. near Carlisle, Pa., 1823; d. New York, N.Y., April 28, 1895. [68]

Craighill, William Price, military engineer, b. Charlestown, Va., 1833; d. Charlestown, Va., Jan. 18, 1909. [2; 3; 4; 10]

Crain, Thomas Crowell Taylor, jurist, b. New York, N.Y., 1860; d. New York, N.Y., May 29, 1942.

Cram, George Franklin, publisher, b. Lowell, Mass., 1842; d. Chicago, Ill., May 24, 1928. [10]

Cram, Ralph Adams, architect, b. Hampton Falls, N.H., 1863; d. Boston, Mass., Sept. 22, 1942. [4; 7; 10; 11]

Cramer, Julian (pseud.). See Chester, Joseph Lemuel.

Cramer, Michael John, clergyman, b. Switzerland, 1835; d. Carlisle, Pa., Jan. 23, 1898. [1; 4]

Cramer, Stuart Warren, textile manufacturer, b. Thomasville, N.C., 1868; d. Charlotte, N.C., July 2, 1940. [10]

Cramer, William, pathologist b. Brandenburg, Germany, 1878; d. Denver, Colo., Aug. 10, 1945.

Cramer, William Stuart, clergyman, b. Frederick county, Md., 1873; d. ? [10; 11]

Cramer, Zadok, navigator, b. 1773; d. 1813.

Cramp, John Mockett, educationist, b. Isle of Thanet, England, 1796; d. Wolfville, N.S., Dec. 6, 1881. [27]

Cranch, Christopher Pearse, artist and poet, b. Alexandria, Va., 1813; d. Cambridge, Mass., Jan. 20, 1892. [1; 2; 3; 4; 7; 34; 71]

Cranch, William, jurist, b. Weymouth, Mass., 1769; d. Washington, D.C., Sept. 1, 1855. [1; 2; 4; 51]

Crandall, Bruce Verne, journalist, b. Hillsdale, Mich., 1873; d. Three Lakes, Wis., Nov. 19, 1945. [7; 10]

Crandall, Charles Henry, poet, b. Greenwich, N.Y., 1858; d. Stamford, Conn., March 23, 1923. [1; 7; 10]

Crandall, Charles Lee, civil engineer, b. Bridgewater, N.Y., 1850; d. Ithaca, N.Y., Aug. 25, 1917. [2; 4; 10]

Crandall, Floyd Milford, physician, b. Belfast, N.Y., 1858; d. New York, N.Y., Nov. 19, 1919. [10]

Crandall, Irving Bardshar, sound engineer, b. Chattanooga, Tenn., 1890; d. New York, N.Y., April 23, 1927. [2; 4]

Crandall, Lathan Augustus, clergyman, b. Plymouth, Mass., 1850; d. Chicago, Ill., July 20, 1923. [10; 67]

Crandon, Le Roi Goddard, surgeon, b. Chelsea, Mass., 1873; d. Boston, Mass., Dec. 28, 1939. [10; 51]

Crane, Aaron Martin, lecturer, b. Glover, Vt., 1839; d. 1914. [10]

Crane, Anne Moncure. See Seemüler, Mrs. Anne Moncure, née Crane.

Crane, Mrs. Bathsheba H., née Morse, clergyman's wife, b. 1811; d. ?

Crane, Mrs. Caroline, née Bartlett, sanitarian, b. Hudson, Wis., 1858; d. Kalamazoo, Mich., March 24, 1935. [10; 39]

Crane, Cephas Bennett clergyman, b. Marion, N.Y., 1833; d. Cambridge, Mass., Jan. 4, 1917. [10]

Crane, Ellery Bicknell, genealogist, b. 1836; d. 1925.

Crane, Frank, clergyman and journalist, b. Urbana, Ill., 1861; d. Nice, France, Nov. 5, 1928. [1; 4; 7; 10]

Crane, Hart, poet, b. Garretsville, O., 1899; d. at sea, April 27, 1932. [1a; 7; 10; 72]

Crane, Ichabod (pseud.). See Thomas, John Daniel.

Crane, Jonathan Townley, clergyman, b. Connecticut Farms, N.J., 1819; d. Port Jervis, N.Y., Feb. 16, 1880. [1; 3; 4]

Crane, Oliver, clergyman, b. West Bloomfield, N.J., 1822; d. Boston, Mass., Nov. 29, 1896. [4; 8; 62]

Crane, Richard Teller, manufacturer, b. Patterson, N.J., 1832; d. 1912. [10]

Crane, Mrs. Sibylla, née Bailey, traveller, b. Boston, Mass., 1851; d. 1902. [4; 8]

Crane, Stephen, novelist and poet, b. Newark, N.J., 1871; d. Badenweiler, Germany, June 5, 1900. [1; 2; 4; 7; 10; 72]

Crane, Thomas Frederick, educationist, b. New York, N.Y., 1844; d. Deland, Fla., Dec. 9, 1927. [1; 2; 4; 7; 10]

Crane, William Carey, clergyman b. Richmond, Va., 1816; d. Independence, Tex., Feb. 27, 1885. [3; 34]

Crane, William Iler, educationist, b. Delaware county, O., 1866; d. Cass Lake, Minn., April 3, 1924. [10; 70]

Crankshaw, James, lawyer, b. Manchester, England, 1844; d. Montreal, Que., Dec. 16, 1921. [27]

Cranmer, Gibson Lamb, lawyer, b. Cincinatti, O., 1826; d. 1903. [10]

Cranston, Claudia, novelist, b. Denton, Tex., 1892; d. Winnsboro, Tex., June 26, 1947. [7; 10; 11]

Cranston, Earl, bishop, b. Athens, O., 1840; d. New Richmond, O., Aug. 18, 1932. [1a; 4; 10]

Crapsey, Adelaide, poet, b. New York, N.Y., 1878; d. Saranac Lake, N.Y., Oct. 8, 1914. [1; 7]

Crapsey, Algernon Sidney, clergyman, b. Fairmount, O., 1847; d. Rochester, N.Y., Dec. 31, 1927. [1; 4; 7; 10]

Craven, Braxton, educationist, b. Randolph county, N.C., 1822; d. Durham, N.C., Nov. 7, 1882. [4; 7]

Crawford, Alexander Wellington, educationist, b. Branchton, Ont., 1866; d. Hamilton, Ont., May 3, 1933. [11; 27]

Crawford, Mrs. Alice, née **Arnold,** poet, b. Fond du Lac, Wis., 1850; d. Traverse City, Mich., 1874. [44]

Crawford, Charles, poet and pamphleteer, fl. 1783-1801.

Crawford, Francis Marion, novelist, b. Italy, 1854; d. Sorrento, Italy, April 9, 1909. [1; 2; 4; 5; 7; 9; 71]

Crawford, Mrs. Hannah Louise, née MacNair, genealogist, b. Seymour, Ind., 1879; d. New York, N.Y., Sept. 24, 1943.

Crawford, Isabella Valancy, poet, b. Dublin, Ireland, 1850; d. Toronto, Ont., Feb. 12, 1887. [27]

Crawford, Captain Jack. See Crawford, John Wallace.

Crawford, James Pyle Wickersham, educationist, b. Lancaster, Pa., 1882; d. Philadelphia, Pa., Sept. 22, 1939. [10]

Crawford, John Wallace, poet and scout, b. Ireland, 1847; d. Brooklyn, N.Y., Feb. 28, 1917. [1; 4; 7; 10]

Crawford, Mary Caroline, journalist, b. Boston, Mass., 1874; d. Boston, Mass., Nov. 15, 1932. [7; 8; 10; 11]

Crawford, Nathaniel Macon, educationist, b. Oglethorpe county, Ga., 1811; d. Tunnel Hill, Ga., Oct. 27, 1871. [3; 8; 34]

Crawford, Oswald (pseud.). See Harris, William Richard.

Crawford, Samuel Johnson, politician, b. near Bedford, Ind., 1835; d. Topeka, Kans., Oct. 21, 1914. [1; 4]

Crawford, Samuel Wylie, physician, b. Franklin county, Pa., 1829; d. Philadelphia, Pa., Nov. 3, 1892. [2; 4; 8]

Crawford, William Henry, educationist, b. Wilton Center, Ill., 1855; d. Meadville, Pa., March 6, 1944. [10]

Crawford-Frost, William Albert, clergyman, b. Owen Sound, Ont., 1863; d. Calgary, Alta., March 3, 1936. [10; 11]

Crawley, Edwin Schofield, mathematician, b. Philadelphia, Pa., 1862; d. Chestnut Hill, Pa., Oct. 18, 1933. [10; 11]

Crawshaw, William Henry, educationist, b. Newburgh, N.Y., 1861; d. Hamilton, N.Y., July 3, 1940. [7; 10; 11]

Creamer, David, hymnologist, b. Baltimore, Md., 1812; d. Baltimore, Md., April 8, 1887. [1; 7]

Creange, Henry, economist, b. Alsace, Germany, 1877; d. Centerville, Mass., Aug. 13, 1945.

Creegan, Charles Cole, missionary, b. Brighton, Ia., 1850; d. Brooklyn, N.Y., Jan. 3, 1939. [10]

Creelman, James, journalist, b. Montreal, Que., 1859; d. Berlin, Germany, Feb. 12, 1915. [1; 4; 7; 10]

Creery, William Rufus, educationist, b. Baltimore, Md., 1824; d. Baltimore, Md., May 1, 1875. [3; 34]

Creevey, Mrs. Caroline Alathea, née Stickney, naturalist, b. Union City, Mich., 1843; d. 1920. [10]

Crehore, William Williams, civil engineer, b. Cleveland, O., 1864; d. Los Angeles, Calif., Sept. 13, 1918. [10]

Creighton, James Edwin, philosopher, b. Pictou, N.S., 1861; d. Ithaca, N.Y., Oct. 8, 1924. [1; 2; 4; 7; 10]

Creighton, William Black, clergyman, b. Dorchester, Ont., 1864; d. Toronto, Ont., Oct. 30, 1946. [30]

Creighton, William Henry Paul, engineer, b. Cincinnati, O., 1859; d. New Orleans, La., Jan. 24, 1933. [10; 11]

Crémazie, Joseph Jacques, lawyer, b. Quebec, Lower Canada, 1810; d. Quebec, Que., July 11, 1872. [27]

Crémazie, Joseph Octave, poet, b. Quebec, Lower Canada, 1827; d. Havre, France, Jan. 16, 1879. [27]

Cresson, William Penn, diplomat, b. Claymount, Del., 1873; d. Stockbridge, Mass., May 12, 1932. [10]

Creswell, Mrs. Julia, née **Pleasants,** poet and novelist, b. Huntsville, Ala., 1827; d. near Shreveport, La., June 9, 1886 [3; 8; 34]

Crèvecoeur, Michael Guillaume Jean de, essayist, b. near Caën, France, 1735; d. Sarcelles, France, Nov. 12, 1813. [1; 2; 3; 4; 7]

Crèvecoeur, St. John de. See Crèvecoeur, Michel Guillaume Jean de.

Creyton, Paul (pseud.). See Trowbridge, John Townsend.

Crichton, John (pseud.). See Guthrie, Norman Gregor.

Crile, George Washington, surgeon, b. Chile, O., 1864; d. Cleveland, O., Jan. 7, 1943. [10; 11]

Crimmins, John Daniel, philanthropist, b. New York, N.Y., 1844; d. New York, N.Y., Nov. 9, 1917. [1; 4; 10]

Crinkle, Nym (pseud.). See Wheeler, Andrew Carpenter.

Crissey, Forrest, journalist, b. Stockton, N.Y., 1864; d. Geneva, Ill., Nov. 5, 1943. [7; 10]

Crittenton, Charles Nelson, evangelist, b. Henderson, N.Y., 1833; d. San Francisco, Calif., Nov. 16, 1909. [1]

Crocker, Bosworth (pseud.). See Lewisohn, Mrs. Mary Arnold, née Crocker.

Crocker, Francis Bacon, electrical engineer, b. New York, N.Y., 1861; d. New York, N.Y., July 9, 1921. [2; 4; 10]

Crocker, George Glover, lawyer, b. Boston, Mass., 1843; d. Cohasset, Mass., May 26, 1913. [10; 51]

Crocker, Mrs. Hannah, née **Mather,** feminist, b. Boston, Mass., 1752; d. Roxbury, Mass., July 11, 1829. [1; 3]

Crocker, Henry, clergyman, b. Brewster, Mass., 1845; d. Chester, Vt., March 22, 1929. [11; 24]

Crocker, Henry Graham, lawyer, b. Milwaukee, Wis., 1868; d. Washington, D.C., May 6, 1930. [4]

Crocker, Uriah, publisher, b. Marblehead, Mass., 1796; d. Cohasset, Mass., July 19, 1887. [1; 3; 4; 7]

Crocker, Uriah Haskell, lawyer, b. Boston, Mass., 1832; d. Boston, Mass., March 8, 1902. [8; 51]

Crockett, Charles Winthrop, mathematician, b. Macon, Ga., 1862; d. Troy, N.Y., Dec. 30, 1936. [10]

Crockett, David, pioneer, b. Limestone, Tenn., 1786; d. Alamo, Tex., March 6, 1836. [1; 2; 3; 4; 7; 34]

Crockett, Ingram, poet and novelist, b. Henderson, Ky., 1856; d. ? [7; 34; 74]

Crockett, Walter Hill, local historian, b. Colchester, Vt., 1870; d. Burlington, Vt., Dec. 8, 1931. [10; 11]

Crockett, William Day, educationist, b. Sterling, N.Y., 1869; d. State College, Pa., Oct. 19, 1930. [10; 63]

Croffut, William Augustus, journalist, b. Redding, Conn., 1835; d. Washington, D.C., July 31, 1915. [7; 10]

Crofton, Francis Blake, journalist and librarian, b. Mayo county, Ireland, 1841; d. 1912. [27]

Crofton, Walter Cavendish, civil servant, b. about 1806; d. Toronto, Ont., July 26, 1870. [27]

Crogman, William Henry, educationist, b. St. Martins, B.W.I., 1841; d. Kansas City, Mo., Oct. 16, 1931. [4; 10]

Croil, James, historian, b. Glasgow, Scotland, 1821; d. Montreal, Que., Nov. 28, 1916. [27]

Croke, J. Greenbag (pseud.). See Hasbrouck, Joseph.

Croll, Philip Columbus, clergyman, b. Kutztown, Pa., 1852; d. Germantown, Pa., March 14, 1949. [11]

Croly, David Goodman, journalist, b. county Cork, Ireland, 1829; d. New York, N.Y., April 29, 1889. [1; 4; 7; 8]

Croly, Herbert David, editor, b. New York, N.Y., 1869; d. Santa Barbara, Calif., May 17, 1930. [1a; 7; 10]

Croly, Mrs. Jane, née **Cunningham,** journalist, b. Leicestershire, England, 1829; d. New York, N.Y., Dec. 23, 1901. [1; 4; 7; 8; 10]

Cromwell, Gladys Louise Husted, poet, b. Brooklyn, N.Y., 1885; d. at sea, Jan. 24, 1919. [1; 7]

Cromwell John Howard mechanical engineer, b. Cornwall, N.Y., 1857; d. Allenhurst, N.J., Nov. 28, 1937. [62]

Cronau, Rudolf, artist, b. Germany, 1855; d. North Tarrytown, N.Y., Oct. 27, 1939. [7; 10; 11]

Cronholm, Neander Nicholas, lawyer and historian, b. Sweden, 1843; d. Wilmette, Ill., Dec. 18, 1922.

Crook, Isaac, clergyman, b. Crossenville, O., 1833; d. Spokane, Wash., Feb. 20, 1916. [2; 4; 10]

Crook, James Walter, educationist, b. Bewdley, Ont., 1858; d. Springfield, Mass., Oct. 22, 1933. [10; 11]

Crooker, Joseph Henry, clergyman, b. Foxcroft, Me., 1850; d. Kansas City, Mo., May 29, 1931. [8; 10]

Crooks, George Richard, clergyman, b. Philadelphia, Pa., 1822; d. Madison, N.J., Feb. 20, 1897. [1; 3; 4; 8]

Crosby, Alpheus, educationist, b. Sandwich, N.H., 1810; d. Salem, Mass., April 17, 1874. [3; 4; 49]

Crosby, Ernest Howard, social reformer and poet, b. New York. N.Y., 1856; d. Baltimore, Md., Jan. 3, 1907. [1; 4; 7; 10]

Crosby, Fanny, poet and hymn-writer, b. Southeast, N.Y., 1820; d. Bridgeport, Conn., Feb. 12, 1915. [1; 2; 7; 10]

Crosby, Franklin, lawyer, b. Ware, Mass., 1829; d. Chicago, Ill., May, 1898. [45]

Crosby, Harry. See Crosby. Henry Grew.

Crosby, Henry Grew, poet, b. Boston, Mass., 1898; d. New York, N.Y., Dec. 10, 1929. [7; 11]

Crosby, Howard, clergyman, b. New York., N.Y., 1826; d. New York, N.Y., March 29, 1891. [1; 3; 4]

Crosby, Nathan, lawyer, b. Sandwich, N.H., 1798; d. Lowell, Mass., Feb. 9, 1885. [3; 49]

Crosby, Sylvester Sage, numismatist, d. 1914.

Crosby, Thomas, missionary, b. Yorkshire, England, 1840; d. Vancouver, B.C., Jan. 13, 1914. [27]

Crosby, William Otis, geologist, b. Decatur, O., 1850; d. Boston, Mass., Dec. 31, 1925. [1; 4; 13]

Croskill, John H., journalist, b. Halifax, N.S., 1810; d. 1855. [27]

Cross, Andrew Jay, optometrist, b. Antwerp, N.Y., 1855; d. White Plains, N.Y., April 9, 1925.

Cross, Arthur Lyon, historian, b. Portland, Me., 1873; d. Ann Arbor, Mich., June 21, 1940. [7; 10; 11]

Cross, Charles Robert, physicist, b. Troy, N.Y., 1848; d. Brookline, Mass., Nov. 16, 1921. [2; 3; 4; 10; 13]

Cross, Charles Whitman, geologist, b. Amherst, Mass., 1854; d. Washington, D.C., April 20, 1949. [13]

Cross, David Wallace, lawyer, b. Richland, N.Y., 1814; d. Cleveland, O., April 9, 1891. [3]

Cross, Earle Bennett, educationist, b. Burma, 1883; d. Rochester, N.Y., Nov. 30, 1946. [10]

Cross, George, clergyman, b. Bewdley, Ont., 1862; d. Rochester, N.Y., Jan. 19, 1929. [10; 24]

Cross, Mrs. Jane Tandy, née Chinn, novelist, b. Harrodsburg, Ky., 1817; d. Elizabethtown, Ky., Oct., 1870. [3; 34]

Cross, Jesse George, teacher of shorthand, b. 1835; d. 1914.

Cross, Joseph, clergyman, b. Somersetshire, England, 1813; d. 1893. [3]

Cross, Mrs. Lucy Rogers, née Hill, genealogist, b. 1834; d. ?

Cross, Roselle Theodore, clergyman, b. Richville, N.Y., 1844; d. Twinsburg, O., Nov. 18, 1924. [10]

Cross, Samuel Hazzard, educationist, b. Westerly, R.I., 1891; d. Cambridge, Mass., Oct. 14, 1946. [10; 51]

Cross, Trueman, soldier, b. Maryland; d. near Fort Brown, Tex., April 21, 1846. [3; 34]

Cross, Wilbur Lucius, educationist and politician, b. Mansfield, Conn., 1862; d. New Haven, Conn., Oct. 5, 1948. [10; 62]

Crosswell, Andrew. See Croswell, Andrew.

Croswell, Andrew, clergyman, b. Charlestown, Mass., 1709; d. Boston, Mass., April 12, 1785. [3]

Croswell, Harry, clergyman, b. Hartford, Conn., 1778; d. New Haven, Conn., March 13, 1858. [1; 3; 62]

Croswell, William, astronomer, d. 1834. [51]

Croswell, William, clergyman, b. Hudson, N.Y., 1804; d. Boston, Mass., Nov. 9, 1851. [3; 7]

Crothers, Mrs. Elizabeth, née Mills, poet, b. Sacramento, Calif., 1882; d. Palo Alto, Calif., Aug. 18, 1920. [35]

Crothers, Samuel McChord, clergyman and essayist, b. Oswego, Ill., 1857; d. Cambridge, Mass., Nov. 9, 1927. [1; 2; 4; 7; 10]

Crothers, Thomas Davison, physician, b. West Charlton, N.Y., 1842; d. Hartford, Conn., Jan. 12, 1918. [4; 10]

Crouch, Frederick William Nicholls, musician, b. London, England, 1808; d. Portland, Me., Aug. 18, 1896. [2; 20]

Crow, Carl, journalist, b. Highland, Mo., 1883; d. New York, N.Y., June 8, 1945. [7; 10; 11]

Crow, Mrs. Martha, née Foote, educationist, b. Sacketts Harbor, N.Y., 1854; d. Chicago, Ill., Jan. 1, 1924. [4; 10]

Crowell, Chester Theodore, journalist, b. Cleveland, O., 1888; d. Washington, D.C., Dec. 26, 1941. [10]

Crowell, Edward Payson, educationist, b. Essex, Mass., 1830; d. Amherst, Mass., March 26, 1911. [2; 10; 45]

Crowell, Eugene, spiritualist, b. 1817; d. New York, N.Y., 1894. [8]

Crowell, James R., journalist, b. Bryn Mawr, Pa., 1893; d. New York, N.Y., Jan. 18, 1948.

Crowell, John, clergyman, b. Philadelphia, Pa., 1814; d. East Orange, N.J., March 29, 1909. [10]

Crowell, John Franklin, economist, b. York, Pa., 1857; d. East Orange, N.J., Aug. 6, 1931. [4; 10; 62]

Crowell, Robert, clergyman and local historian, b. 1787; d. Essex, Mass., 1855. [6]

Crowell, Thomas Young, publisher, b. West Dennis, Mass., 1836; d. July 29, 1915. [7]

Crowell, William, clergyman, b. Middlefield, Mass., 1806; d. Flanders, N.J., Aug. 19, 1871. [3; 47]

Crowfield, Christopher (pseud.). See Stowe, Mrs. Harriet Elizabeth, née Beecher.

Crowley, Mary Catherine, novelist, b. Boston, Mass.; d. New York, N.Y., May 14, 1920. [8; 10]

Crownfield, Gertrude, writer of books for children, b. Baltimore, Md., 1867; d. New York, N.Y., June 2, 1945. [7; 10; 11]

Crowninshield, Bowdoin Bradlee, naval architect, b. New York, N.Y., 1867; d. Marblehead, Mass., Aug. 12, 1948. [10; 51]

Crowninshield, Francis Welch, journalist, b. 1872; d. New York, N.Y., Dec. 28, 1947. [7; 10]

Crowninshield, Frederic, painter and poet, b. Boston, Mass., 1845; d. Capri, Italy, Sept. 13, 1918. [1; 4; 7; 51]

Crowninshield, Mrs. Mary, née Bradford, novelist, b. 1854; d. Melrose, Mass., Oct. 14, 1913. [7; 8; 10]

Crowninshield, Mrs. Schuyler. See Crowninshield, Mrs. Mary, née Bradford.

Crowther, Samuel, journalist, b. Philadelphia, Pa., 1880; d. Boston, Mass., Oct. 27, 1947. [7; 10; 11]

Crozier, Arthur Alger, botanist, b. 1856; d. Ann Arbor, Mich., Jan. 29, 1899. [53]

Crozier, William Armstrong, genealogist, b. 1864; d. 1913.

Cru, Albert Louis, educationist, b. France, 1881; d. Berlin, N.H., Sept. 11, 1949. [14]

Cruger, Eliza, poet, fl. 1868. [6]

Cruger, Mrs. Julia Grinnell, née Storrow, novelist and poet, b. Paris, France; d. New York, N.Y., July 12, 1920. [4; 8; 10]

Cruger, Mary, novelist, b. near Oscawana, N.Y., 1834; d. near Montrose, N.Y., Nov. 15, 1908. [7; 8; 10]

Crummell, Alexander, clergyman, b. New York, N.Y., 1819; d. Point Pleasant, N.J., Sept. 9, 1898. [2; 7; 8]

Crumpton, M. Nataline, playwright and novelist, b. 1857; d. 1911.

Crumpton, Washington Bryan, clergyman, b. Camden, Ala., 1842; d. Montgomery, Ala., 1926. [10; 24]

Cruttenden, Daniel Henry, educationist, b. Galway, N.Y., 1816; d. Castleton, N.Y., June 21, 1874. [3]

Cryer, Matthew Henry, oral surgeon, b. Manchester, England, 1840; d. Lansdowne, Pa., Aug. 12, 1921. [10; 55]

Cubberley, Ellwood Patterson, educationist, b. Andrews, Ind., 1868; d. Stanford University, Calif., Sept. 14, 1941. [7; 10; 11]

Cuckson, John, clergyman, b. Lincolnshire, England, 1846; d. Plymouth, Mass., 1907. [10]

Cudahy, John, diplomat, b. Milwaukee, Wis., 1887; d. near Milwaukee, Wis., Sept. 6, 1943. [10; 21]

Cudahy, Patrick, meat-packer, b. county Kilkenny, Ireland, 1849; d. Milwaukee, Wis., July 25, 1919. [10]

Cugnet, François Joseph, lawyer, b. Quebec, Canada, 1720; d. Quebec, Canada, Sept. 16, 1789. [27]

Culbertson, Matthew Simpson, clergyman b. Chambersburg, Pa., 1818; d. China, Aug., 1862. [3]

Culbertson, Michael Simpson. See Culbertson, Matthew Simpson.

Cullen, Clarence Louis, short-story writer, d. West Deal, N.J., June 29, 1922.

Cullen, Countee, poet, b. New York, N.Y., 1903; d. New York, N.Y., Jan. 9, 1946. [7; 11]

Cullen, Thomas Francis, priest, b. Berkeley, R.I., 1877; d. Providence, R.I., July 26, 1945. [21]

Cullom, Shelby Moore, politician, b. Wayne county, Ky., 1829; d. Washington, D.C., Jan. 28, 1914. [1; 2; 4; 36]

Cullum, George Washington, soldier, b. New York, N.Y., 1809; d. New York, N.Y., Feb. 28, 1892. [1; 3; 4]

Culver, Henry Brundage, lawyer, b. 1869; d. St. Augustine, Fla., Nov. 28, 1946.

Culver, Raymond Benjamin, clergyman, b. Alagansee township, Mich., 1887; d. Beaumont, Calif., June 7, 1938. [10; 62]

Cumback, Will, lecturer, b. Franklin county, Ind., 1829; d. 1905.

Cumberland, Frederic Barlow, historian, b. Portsmouth, Eng., 1846; d. Port Hope, Ont., Sept. 1, 1913. [27]

Cuming, Fortescue, traveller, b. county Tyrone, Ireland, 1762; d. Vermilionville, La., 1828. [1; 7]

Cumming, Alexander, clergyman, b. Freehold, N.J., 1726; d. Boston, Mass., Aug. 25, 1763. [3]

Cumming, Alexander, horticulturist, b. 1883; d. Jan. 26, 1948.

Cumming, Henry Harford, educationist and soldier, b. Augusta, Ga., 1905; d. on active service, July 10, 1945.

Cumming, Kate, army nurse, b. 1835; d. ? [3; 6; 34]

Cummings, Amos Jay, journalist, b. Conklin, N.Y., 1841; d. Baltimore, Md., May 2, 1902. [1; 3; 4]

Cummings, Ariel Ivers, physician, b. Ashburnham, Mass., 1823; d. Hempstead, Tex., Sept. 9, 1863. [49]

Cummings, Asa, clergyman, b. Andover, Mass., 1791; d. at sea, June 5, 1856. [3; 38; 51]

Cummings, Charles Amos, architect, b. Boston, Mass., 1833; d. Boston, Mass., Aug. 11, 1905. [1; 2; 4]

Cummings, Jacob Abbot, educationist, b. 1773; d. 1820. [51]

Cummings, Jeremiah Williams, clergyman, b. Washington, D.C., 1823; d. New York, N.Y., Jan. 4, 1866. [3; 8]

Cummings, John, statistician, b. Colebrook, N.H., 1868; d. Washington, D.C., June 26, 1936. [10; 51]

Cummings, Joseph, clergyman and educationist, b. Falmouth, Me., 1817; d. Evanston, Ill., May 7, 1890. [1; 3; 4]

Cummings, Preston, clergyman, b. 1800; d. April 8, 1875. [47]

Cummings, St. James, educationist and poet, b. Topsfield, Mass., 1858; d. 1913. [34]

Cummings, Thomas Seir, miniature painter, b. Bath, England, 1804; d. Hackensack, N.J., Sept. 24, 1894. [1; 3; 4]

Cummings, Uriah, inventor and historian, b. Akron, N.Y.; d. Stamford, Conn., Nov. 12, 1910.

Cummins, Earl Everett, economist, b. Scranton, Pa., 1896; d. Schenectady, N.Y., June 7, 1938. [62]

Cummins, Ebenezer Harlow, clergyman, b. North Carolina, about 1790; d. Washington, D.C., Jan. 17, 1835. [3; 34]

Cummins, Mrs. Ella Sterling, née Clark. See Mighels, Mrs. Ella Sterling née Clark.

Cummins, George David, clergyman, b. Kent county, Del., 1822; d. Lutherville, Md., June 26, 1876. [1; 3; 4]

Cummins, George Wyckoff, physician and local historian, b. Vienna, N.J., 1865; d. Easton, Pa., April 17, 1942.

Cummins, Maria Susanna, novelist, b. Salem, Mass., 1827; d. Boston, Mass., Oct. 1, 1866. [1; 2; 3; 4; 7]

Cummins, Scott, poet, b. Iowa, 1846; d. Alva, Okla, 1928. [75]

Cundall, Frank, historian, b. 1858; d. Kingston, Jamaica, Nov. 15, 1937.

Cuney-Hare, Mrs. Maud. See Hare, Mrs. Maud, née Cuney.

Cunliffe, John William, educationist, b. Bolton, England, 1865; d. Ogunquit, Me., March 18, 1946. [7; 10; 11]

Cunliffe-Owen, Mrs. Marguerite de Godart, biographer and novelist, b. Brittany, France, 1861; d. New York, N.Y., Aug. 28, 1927. [2a]

Cunliffe-Owen, Philip Frederick, journalist, b. London, England, 1855; d. New York, N.Y., June 30, 1926. [10]

Cunningham, Francis Aloysius, priest; b. Boston, 1862; d. Dorchester, Mass., 1935. [21]

Cuoq, Jean André, priest and philologist, b. France, 1821; d. Oka, Que., July 21, 1898. [27]

Cuore, L. B. (pseud.). See Urbino, Mrs. Levina, née Buoncuore.

Cuppy, Hazlett Alva, editor, b. Shelburne, Ind., 1863; d. ? [10]

Cuppy, William Jacob, humorist, b. Auburn, Ind., 1884; d. New York, N.Y., Sept. 19, 1949. [7; 10]

Curator (pseud.). See Benson, Egbert.

Curran, John Elliott, novelist, b. 1818; d. 1890. [8; 48]

Curran, John Joseph, novelist, b. Elmira, N.Y., 1856; d. ? [35]

Currey, Josiah Seymour, historian, b. Peekskill, N.Y., 1844; d. Evanston, Ill., Dec. 25, 1928. [10]

Currie, George Graham, lawyer and poet, b. near Montreal, Que., 1867; d. Palm Beach, Fla., Sept, 5, 1926. [10]

Currie, John Allister, soldier and politician, b. Nottawa, Ont. 1868; d. Miami, Fla., June 28, 1931. [27]

Currier, Charles Gilman, physician, b. Boston, Mass., 1855; d. Greenwich, Conn., Jan. 3, 1945. [51]

Currier, Charles Warren, bishop, b. St. Thomas, B.W.I., 1857; d. near Baltimore, Md., Sept. 23, 1918. [1; 7; 10; 21]

Currier, Clinton Harvey, educationist, b. Manchester, N.H., 1876; d. Providence, R.I., Jan. 5, 1943. [47]

Currier, Thomas Franklin, librarian, b. Roxbury, Mass., 1873; d. Cambridge, Mass., Sept. 14, 1946. [7]

Curry, Albert Bruce, clergyman, b. Decatur county, Ga., 1852; d. Memphis, Tenn., Dec. 3, 1939. [10]

Curry, Daniel, clergyman, b. near Peekskill, N.Y., 1809; d. New York, N.Y., Aug. 17, 1887. [3; 4]

Curry, Jabez Lamar Monroe, educationist and politician, b. Lincoln county, Ga., 1825; d. near Asheville, N.C., Feb. 12, 1903. [1; 4; 7; 10; 34]

Curry, James Bernard, priest, b. New York, N.Y., 1856; d. New York, N.Y., June 26, 1932. [10; 21]

Curry, Otway, journalist and poet, b. Greenfield, O., 1804; d. Marysville, O., Feb. 17, 1855. [3; 4; 7]

Curry, Samuel Silas, educationist, b. Chatata, Tenn., 1847; d. Boston, Mass., Dec. 24, 1921. [4; 10]

Curry, William Melville, clergyman, b. Bloomington, Ind., 1867; d. Philadelphia, Pa., Dec. 18, 1935. [10; 11]

Curtin, Jeremiah, linguist, b. Greenfield, Wis., 1840; d. Burlington, Vt., Dec. 14, 1906. [1; 7; 10]

Curtis, Abel, grammarian, b. Lebanon, Conn., 1755; d. Norwich, Vt., Oct. 1, 1783. [43]

Curtis, Alva, physician; b. Columbia, N.H., 1797; d. Ohio, 1881. [3]

Curtis, Mrs. Ariana, née **Wormeley,** playwright, b. 1833; d. 1922.

Curtis, Benjamin Robbins, jurist, b. Watertown, Mass., 1809; d. Newport, R.I., Sept. 15, 1874. [2; 4; 8]

Curtis, Mrs. Caroline Gardiner, née **Cary,** novelist, b. 1827; d. ? [8]

Curtis, Charles Albert, soldier, b. Hallowell, Me., 1835; d. 1907. [10]

Curtis, Charles Boyd, lawyer, b. Penn Yan, N.Y., 1827; d. New York, N.Y., March 26, 1905. [8; 10]

Curtis, David A., journalist, b. Norwich, Conn., 1846; d. New York, N.Y., May 23, 1923. [10]

Curtis, Edward, physician, b. Providence, R.I., 1838; d. New York, N.Y., Nov. 28, 1912. [4; 7; 10]

Curtis, Edward Lewis, clergyman, b. Ann Arbor, Mich., 1853; d. near Rockland, Me., Aug. 26, 1911. [1; 10; 62]

Curtis, Mrs. Elizabeth, née **Gibbon,** antiquary, b. Charleston, S.C.; d. near Red Bank, N.J., Feb. 11. 1946.

Curtis, Eugene Newton, historian, b. White Plains, N.Y., 1880; d. Baltimore, Md., April 20, 1944. [10; 62]

Curtis, George Ticknor, lawyer and historian, b. Watertown, Mass., 1812; d. New York, N.Y., March 28, 1894. [1; 2; 3; 4; 7; 8]

Curtis, George William, editor, essayist, and biographer, b. Providence, R.I., 1824; d. New Brighton, Staten Island, N.Y., Aug. 31, 1892. [1; 2; 3; 4; 7; 72]

Curtis, Georgina Pell, novelist, b. New York, N.Y., 1859; d. Elizabeth, N.J., April 25, 1922. [10; 21]

Curtis, Henry Holbrook, physician, b. New York, N.Y., 1856; d. New York, N.Y., May 14, 1920. [4; 10; 62]

Curtis, Mrs. Isabel, née **Gordon,** editor, b. Huntly, Scotland, 1863; d. Washington, D.C., Dec. 23, 1915. [10]

Curtis, Moses Ashley, clergyman and botanist, b. Stockbridge, Mass., 1808; d. Hillsboro, N.C., April 10, 1872. [1; 4; 34]

Curtis, Newton Martin, soldier, b. De Peyster, N.Y., 1835; d. New York, N.Y., Jan. 8, 1910. [1; 4; 10]

Curtis, Olin Alfred, theologian, b. Frankfort, Me., 1850; d. Leonia, N.J., Jan. 8, 1918. [1; 10]

Curtis, Orson Blair, soldier, b. 1841; d. Detroit, Mich., Jan. 11, 1901. [53]

Curtis, Otis Freeman, plant physiologist, b. Sendia, Japan, 1888; d. Chatham, Mass., July 4, 1949. [10; 13]

Curtis, Thomas Fenner, clergyman, b. England, 1815; d. Cambridge, Mass., Aug. 9, 1872. [3; 24]

Curtis, Wardon Allan, novelist, b. New Mexico, 1867; d. Ashland, N.H., Jan. 20, 1940. [10]

Curtis, William Eleroy, journalist and traveller, b. Akron, O., 1850; d. Philadelphia, Pa., Oct. 5, 1911. [1; 4; 7; 8; 10]

Curtiss, Mrs. Abby, née **Allin,** poet, b. Pomfret, Conn., 1820; d. ? [3; 8]

Curtiss, George Boughton, lawyer and economist, b. Livingston county, N.Y., 1852; d. Binghampton, N.Y., June 20, 1920. [4]

Curtiss, Mrs. Harriette Augusta, née **Brown,** spiritualist, b. Philadelphia, Pa., about 1856; d. Washington, D.C., Sept. 22, 1932. [11]

Curtiss, Samuel Ives, theologian, b. Union, Conn., 1844; d. London, England, Sept. 22, 1904. [1; 3; 4; 8; 10]

Curtius (pseud.). See Taylor, John [1753-1824]

Curwood, James Oliver, novelist, b. Owosso, Mich., 1878; d. Owosso, Mich., Aug. 13, 1927. [1; 4; 7; 10]

Curzon, Mrs. Sarah Anne, poet, b. Birmingham, England, 1833; d. Toronto, Ont., 1898. [27]

Cushing, Caleb, politician, b. Essex county, Mass., 1800; d. Newburyport, Mass., Jan. 2, 1879. [1; 3; 4; 7; 8]

Cushing, Mrs. Caroline Elizabeth, née **Wilde,** traveller, b. Hallowell, Mass., 1802; d. Newburyport, Mass., Aug. 28, 1832.

Cushing, Charles Cyprian Strong, playwright, b. New Haven, Conn., 1879; d. Boston, Mass., March 6, 1941. [7; 10; 62]

Cushing, Mrs. Eliza Lanesford, née **Foster,** poet, and playwright, b. Massachusetts, 1794; d. ·? [6; 7]

Cushing, Frank Hamilton, ethnologist, b. Northeast, Pa., 1857; d. Washington, D.C., April 10, 1900, [1; 4; 7]

Cushing, Harry Cooke, electrical engineer, b. Fort Foote, Md., 1869; d. New Rochelle, N.Y., May 29, 1933. [69]

Cushing, Harvey Williams, surgeon, b. Cleveland, O., 1869; d. New Haven, Conn., Oct. 7, 1939. [7; 10; 11; 62]

Cushing, Josiah Nelson, missionary, b. Attleboro, Mass., 1840; d. St. Louis, Mo., May 17, 1905. [4]

Cushing, Luther Stearns, jurist, b. Lunenburg, Mass., 1803; d. Boston, Mass., June 22, 1856. [1; 3; 4]

Cushing, Marshall Henry, journalist, b. Higham, Mass., 1860; d. New York, N.Y., May 11, 1915. [51]

Cushing, Mary Gertrude, educationist, b. Montreal, Que., 1870; d. Holyoke, Mass., March 7, 1945.

Cushing, Paul (pseud.). See Wood-Seys, Roland Alexander.

Cushing, Thomas, physician and local historian, b. 1821; d. ?

Cushing, Tom (pseud.). See Cushing, Charles Cyprian Strong.

Cushing, William, clergyman, b. Lunenburg, Mass., 1811; d. Cambridge, Mass., Aug. 27, 1895. [6; 8; 51]

Cushman, Allerton Seward, chemist, b. Rome, Italy, 1867; d. New York, N.Y., May 1, 1930. [10; 13]

Cushman, David Quimby, clergyman, b. Wiscasset, Me., 1806; d. Warren, Me., Oct. 13, 1889. [38; 46]

Cushman, Henry Wyles, genealogist, b. Barnardston, Mass., 1805; d. Greenfield, Mass., Nov. 21, 1863. [4]

Cushman, Horatio Bardwell, historian, b. 1822; d. ?

Cushny, Arthur Robertson, physician, b. Morayshire, Scotland; d. near Edinburgh, Scotland, Feb. 25, 1926. [1]

Cusick, David, Indian scout, d. about 1840. [3]

Cussons, John, historian, b. 1838; d. 1912.

Custer, Edgar A., journalist and engineer, b. 1861; d. Philadelphia, Pa., Sept. 25, 1937.

Custer, Mrs. Elizabeth, née **Bacon,** frontierswoman, b. Bacon, Mich., about 1844; d. New York, N.Y., April 4, 1933. [3; 7; 8; 10]

Custer, George Armstrong, soldier, b. New Rumley, O., 1839; d. Wyoming, June 25, 1876. [1; 2; 3; 4]

Custis, George Washington Parke, playwright, b. Mount Airy, Md., 1781; d. Arlington, Va., Oct. 10, 1857. [1; 3; 4; 7; 34]

Cutbush, Edward, physician, b. Philadelphia, Pa., 1772; d. Geneva, N.Y., June 23, 1843. [4; 55]

Cutbush, James, chemist, b. Philadelphia, Pa., 1788; d. West Point, N.Y., Dec. 13, 1823. [1; 3]

Cutcheon, Byron Mac, soldier and politician, b. Londonderry, N.H., 1836; d. Ypsilanti, Mich., April 12, 1908. [10; 39]

Cuthbert, James Hazzard, clergyman, b. Beaufort, S.C., 1823; d. Aiken, S.C., May 6, 1893. [3; 8; 34]

Cuthbert, John A., jurist, b. Savannah, Ga., June 3, 1788; d. near Mobile, Ala., Sept. 22, 1881. [3; 34]

Cuthbert, Ross, lawyer, b. Canada, 1776; d. Quebec, Que., Aug. 28, 1861. [27]

Cutler, Benjamin Clarke, clergyman, b. Roxbury, Mass., 1798; d. Brooklyn, N.Y., Feb. 10, 1863. [3]

Cutler, Carroll, clergyman and educationist, b. Windham, N.H., 1829; d. Talladega, Ala., Jan. 24, 1894. [1; 4; 62]

Cutler, Elbridge Jefferson, educationist, b. Holliston, Mass., 1831; d. Cambridge, Mass., Dec. 27, 1870. [3; 4; 7; 8; 51]

Cutler, Mrs. Hannah Maria, née **Conant Tracy,** physician, b. Becket, Mass., 1815; d. 1896. [3; 8]

Cutler, Henry Stephen, musician, b. Boston, Mass., 1824; d. Boston, Mass., 1902. [3]

Cutler, Jervis, pioneer, b. Edgarton, Mass., 1768; d. Evansville, Ind., June 25, 1844. [3; 8]

Cutler, Joseph, lawyer, b. Sudbury, Mass., 1815; d. Cambridge, Mass., June 29, 1885. [45]

Cutler, Julia Perkins, biographer, b. 1815; d. ?

Cutler, Mrs. Lizzie, née **Petit,** novelist, b. Milton, Va., 1831; d. Richmond, Va., Jan. 16, 1902. [1; 3; 7; 8; 34]

Cutler, Nahum Sawin, genealogist, b. 1837; d. ?

Cutler, Samuel, clergyman, b. 1805; d. 1880. [67]

Cutler, William Parker, politician, b. Marietta, O., 1813; d. Marietta, O., April 11, 1889.

Cutter, Benjamin, physician, b. 1803; d. 1864. [51]

Cutter, Benjamin, musician, b. Woburn, Mass., 1857; d. Boston, Mass., 1910. [10]

Cutter, Bloodgood Haviland, poet, b. Great Neck, Long Island, N.Y., 1817; d. Sept. 26 ,1906. [7]

Cutter, Charles Ammi, librarian, b. Boston, Mass., 1837; d. Walpole, N.H., Sept. 6, 1903. [1; 4; 7; 10]

Cutter, Daniel Bateman, physician and local historian, b. Jaffrey, N.H., 1808; d. Peterborough, N.H., Dec. 7, 1889. [49; 62]

Cutter, Ephraim, physician, b. Woburn, Mass., 1832; d. West Falmouth, Mass., April 25, 1917. [1; 4]

Cutter, George Washington, poet, b. Quebec, Lower Canada, 1801; d. Washington, D.C., Dec. 25, 1865. [1; 3; 4; 7; 8; 74]

Cutter, William, journalist, b. North Yarmouth, Me., 1801; d. Brooklyn, N.Y., Feb. 8, 1867.

Cutter, William Parker, librarian, b. Washington, D.C., 1867; d. Boston, Mass., May 20, 1935. [10]

Cutter, William Richard, genealogist and historian, b. Woburn, Mass., 1847; d. Woburn, Mass., June 6, 1918.

Cutting, Elisabeth Brown, journalist, b. Brooklyn, N.Y., 1871; d. Bedford Hills, N.Y., Aug. 13, 1946. [7; 10]

Cutting, Hiram Adolphus, geologist, b. Concord, Vt., 1832; d. Lunenburg, Vt., April 18, 1892. [3; 4]

Cutting, Mrs. Mary Stewart, née Doubleday, short-story writer, b. New York, N.Y., 1851; d. Orange, N.J., Aug. 11, 1924. [7; 8; 10]

Cutting, Mary Stewart, suffragist, d. New York, N.Y., Feb. 11, 1928.

Cutting, Robert Fulton, financier and philanthropist, b. New York, N.Y., Sept. 21, 1934. [1a; 4; 10]

Cutting, Sewall Sylvester, educationist, b. Windsor, Vt., 1813; d. Brooklyn, N.Y., Feb. 7, 1882. [3; 8]

Cutting, Starr Willard, educationist, b. West Brattleboro, Vt., 1858; d. Brattleboro, Vt., Oct. 19, 1935. [10]

Cutts, James Madison, historian, b. 1805; d. 1863;

Cutts, Mary, poet, b. 1801; d. 1882. [6; 43]

Cutts, Mrs. Mary Pepperrell Sparhawk, née Jarvis, biographer, b. 1809; d. Jersey City, N.J., April 12, 1879. [43]

Cuyler, Cornelius C., clergyman and physician, b. Albany, N.Y., 1783; d. Philadelphia, Pa., Aug. 31, 1850. [3]

Cuyler, Theodore Ledyard, clergyman, b. Aurora, N.Y., 1822; d. Brooklyn, N.Y., Feb. 26, 1909. [1; 3; 4; 7; 8; 10]

Cymon (pseud.). See Somerby, Frederic Thomas.

Cypress, J., jr. (pseud.). See Hawes, William Post.

Cyr, Ellen M. See Smith, Mrs. Ellen M., née Cyr.

Cyr, Narcisse, clergyman, b. 1823; d. Springfield, Mass., March 18, 1894.

D

Dabney, Charles William, educationist, b. Hampden-Sydney, Va., 1855; d. Ashville, N.C., June 15, 1945. [10]

Dabney, Richard, poet, b. Louisa county, Va., 1787; d. Louisa county, Va., Nov. 25, 1825. [1; 3; 7; 34]

Dabney, Richard Heath, historian, b. Memphis, Tenn., 1860; d. Charlottesville, Va., May 16, 1947. [7; 10; 34]

Dabney, Robert Lewis, clergyman, b. Louisa county, Va., 1820; d. Victoria, Tex.,, Jan. 3, 1898. [1; 7; 34]

Dabney, Virginius, novelist, b. Elmington, Va., 1835; d. New York, N.Y., June 2, 1894. [1; 3; 7; 34]

Dabney, Walter Davis, lawyer and educationist, b. 1853; d. 1899.

Dabney, William Henry, genealogist, b. 1817; d. 1888.

Daboll, Nathan, educationist, b. Groton, Conn., 1750; d. Groton, Conn., March 9, 1818. [1; 3; 4; 7]

Daboll, Sherman B., local historian, b. 1844; d. 1910.

Da Costa, Jacob Mendez, physician, b. St. Thomas, West Indies, 1833; d. Villanova, Pa., Sept. 11, 1900. [1; 3; 4]

Da Costa, John Chalmers, physician, b. Philadelphia, Pa., 1863; d. Philadelphia, Pa., Dec. 6, 1910. [1a; 4; 10]

Dadd, George H., veterinary surgeon, b. England, 1813; d. ? [3]

Dafoe, John Wesley, journalist, b. Bangor, Ont., 1866; d. Winnipeg, Man., Jan. 9, 1944. [27; 30]

Dagg, John Leadley, clergyman and educationist, b. Middleburg, Va., 1794; d. Haynesville, Ala., June 11, 1884. [1; 3; 4; 34]

Daggett, Mrs. Charles Stewart. See Daggett, Mrs. Mary, née Stewart.

Daggett, John, local historian, b. 1805; d. Attleboro, Mass., Dec. 13, 1885. [47]

Daggett, Mrs. Mabel, née Potter, sociologist, b. Syracuse, N.Y., 1871; d. New York, N.Y., Nov. 14, 1927. [10; 11]

Daggett, Mrs. Mary née Stewart, novelist and playwright, b. Morristown, O., 1856; d. Pasadena, Calif., March 9, 1922. [4; 10; 35]

Daggett, Oliver Ellsworth, clergyman, b. New Haven, Conn., 1810; d. Hartford, Conn., Sept. 1, 1880. [3; 4; 62]

Daggett, Rollin Mallory, journalist and novelist, b. Richville, N.Y., 1831; d. San Francisco, Calif., Nov. 12, 1901. [4; 35]

Dagnall, John Malone, humorist, b. England, 1818; d. Brooklyn, N.Y., July 5, 1917.

Dahl, Joseph Oliver, expert in hotel management, b. 1893; d. Stamford, Conn., Aug. 4, 1942.

Dahlgren, John Adolphus Bernard, naval officer, b. Philadelphia, Pa., 1809; d. Washington, D.C., July 12, 1870. [1; 4]

Dahlgren, Mrs. Sarah Madeleine, née Vinton, poet and novelist, b. Gallipolis, O., 1825; d. Washington, D.C., May 28, 1898. [1; 4; 7]

Dahlgren, Ulric, biologist, b. Brooklyn, N.Y., 1870; d. Princeton, N.J., May 30, 1946. [10; 13]

Daingerfield, Elliott, artist, b. Harper's Ferry, Va., 1859; d. New York, N.Y., Oct. 22, 1932. [4; 10; 11]

Daingerfield, Foxhall Alexander, novelist, b. Harrisonburg, Va., 1887; d. near Lexington, Va., Oct. 17, 1933. [10]

Daish, John Broughton, lawyer, b. Quincy, Mich., 1867; d. Washington, D.C., 1918. [10]

Dalcho, Frederick, clergyman and physician, b. London, England, 1770; d. Charleston, S.C., Nov. 24, 1836. [1; 4; 34]

Dale, Alan (pseud.). See Cohen, Alfred J.

Dale, Annan (pseud.). See Johnston, James Wesley.

Dale, James Wilkinson, clergyman, b. Cantwell's Bridge, Del., 1812; d. Media, Pa., April 19, 1881. [3; 4]

Dale, Thomas Nelson, geologist, b. New York, N.Y., 1845; d. Pittsfield, Mass., Nov. 16, 1937. [4; 10; 11; 13]

Dales, John Blakely, clergyman, b. Kortright, N.Y., 1815; d. Chatauqua, N.Y., Aug. 28, 1893. [3]

Dall, Mrs. Caroline Wells, née Healey, reformer, b. Boston, Mass., 1822; d. Washington, D.C., Dec. 17, 1912. [1; 4; 7]

Dall, Charles Henry Appleton, clergyman, b. Baltimore, Md., 1816; d. Calcutta, India, July 18, 1886. [3]

Dall, William Healey, naturalist, b. Boston, Mass., 1845; d. Washington, D.C., March 27, 1927. [1; 4; 10]

Dallam, James Wilmer, lawyer and novelist, b. 1818; d. 1847. [7]

Dallas, Alexander James, lawyer, b. Jamaica, 1759; d. Trenton, N.J., Jan. 16, 1817. [1; 4]

Dallas, George Mifflin, politician, b. Philadelphia, Pa., 1792; d. Philadelphia, Pa., Dec. 31, 1864. [1; 4]

Dallas, Mrs. Mary, née Kyle, novelist, b. 1830; d. Philadelphia, Pa., 1897. [8]

Dallas, Richard (pseud.). See Williams, Nathan Winslow.

Dalton, Mrs. Annie Charlotte, née **Stoney,** poet, b. Huddersfield, England, 1865; d. Vancouver, B.C., Jan. 12, 1938. [11; 27]

Dalton, John Call, physiologist, b. Chelmsford, Mass., 1825; d. New York, N.Y., Feb. 12, 1889. [1; 4]

Dalton, Test, playwright and novelist, b. Chicago, Ill., 1875; d. New York, N.Y., Dec. 10, 1945. [7; 10; 11]

Daly, Augustin. See Daly, John Augustin.

Daly, Charles Patrick, jurist, b. New York, N.Y., 1816; d. Sag Harbor, Long Island, N.Y., Sept. 19, 1899. [1; 4; 7]

Daly, John Augustin, playwright, b. Plymouth, N.C., 1838; d. Paris, France, June 7, 1899. [1; 4; 7; 10; 34]

Daly, Joseph Francis, biographer, b. Plymouth, N.C., 1840; d. Aug. 6, 1916. [10; 21]

Daly, Thomas Augustine, journalist, b. Philadelphia, Pa., 1871; d. Philadelphia, Pa., Oct. 14, 1948. [10; 11]

Damon, Howard Franklin, physician, b. Scituate, Mass., 1833; d. Boston, Mass., Sept. 17, 1884. [3; 4]

Damon, Lindsay Todd, educationist, b. Brookline, Mass., 1871; d. New York, N.Y., May 6, 1940. [10; 11; 51]

Damon, Samuel Chenery, clergyman, b. Holden, Mass., 1815; d. Honolulu, Hawaii, Feb. 7, 1885. [45]

Damon, Mrs. Sophia M., née **Buckman,** novelist, b. Woodstock, Vt., 1836; d. Woodstock, Vt., March 8, 1888. [43]

Damon, William Emerson, naturalist, b. Windsor, Vt., 1838; d. Windsor, Vt., Dec. 1, 1911. [4; 8]

Dana, Alexander Hamilton, lawyer, b. Oswego, N.Y., 1807; d. Montclair, N.J., April 27, 1887. [8]

Dana, Arnold Guyot, journalist, b. New Haven, Conn., 1862; d. New Haven, Conn., Aug. 23, 1947. [62]

Dana, Charles Anderson, journalist, b. Hinsdale, N.H., 1819; d. Glen Cove, Long Island, N.Y., Oct. 17, 1897. [1; 3; 7]

Dana, Charles Edmund, art critic, b. Wilkesbarre, Pa., 1843; d. Philadelphia, Pa., Feb. 1, 1914. [10]

Dana, Charles Loomis, neurologist, b. Woodstock, Vt., 1852; d. Harmon, N.Y., Dec. 12, 1935. [1a; 4; 10; 49]

Dana, Edward Salisbury, mineralogist, b. New Haven, Conn., 1849; d. New Haven, Conn., June 16, 1935. [1a; 4; 10; 11; 62]

Dana, Harvey Eugene, clergyman, b. near Vicksburg, Miss., 1888; d. Kansas City, Kans., May 17, 1945. [7; 10; 11]

Dana, James, clergyman, b. Cambridge, Mass., 1735; d. New Haven, Conn., Aug. 18, 1812. [1; 4; 51]

Dana, James Dwight, mineralogist, b. Utica, N.Y., 1813; d. New Haven, Conn., April 14 ,1895. [1; 4]

Dana, James Freeman, chemist, b. Amherst, N.H., 1793; d. New York., April 14, 1827. [1; 4]

Dana, John Cotton, librarian, b. Woodstock, Vt., 1856; d. New York, N.Y., July 21, 1929. [1; 4; 7; 10]

Dana, Katharine Floyd, short-story writer, b. 1835; d. 1886. [8]

Dana, Malcolm McGregor, clergyman, b. Brooklyn, N.Y., 1838; d. Brooklyn, N.Y., July 26, 1897. [3; 70]

Dana, Mrs. Mary Stanley Bunce, née **Palmer.** See Shindler, Mrs. Mary Stanley Bunce, née Palmer.

Dana, Richard Henry, poet and essayist, b. Cambridge, Mass., 1787; d. Boston, Mass., Feb. 2, 1879. [1; 4; 7; 71]

Dana, Richard Henry, lawyer and traveller, b. Cambridge, Mass., 1815; d. Rome, Italy, Jan. 7, 1882. [1; 3; 4; 7; 71; 72]

Dana, Richard Henry, lawyer, b. Cambridge, Mass., 1851; d. Cambridge, Mass., Dec. 16, 1931. [4; 10; 11; 51]

Dana, Samuel Luther, chemist, b. Amherst, N.H., 1795; d. Lowell, Mass., March 11, 1868. [1; 4]

Dana, Samuel Worcester, lawyer, b. Amherst, Mass., 1828; d. New Castle, Pa., Jan. 1, 1921. [45]

Dana, Stephen Winchester, clergyman, b. Canaan, N.Y., 1840; d. Philadelphia, Pa., Jan. 8, 1910. [10; 61; 68]

Dana, William Coombs, clergyman, b. Massachusetts, 1810; d. Charleston, S.C., 1873. [8; 34]

Dana, William Henry, musician, b. Warren, O., 1846; d. Warren, O., Feb. 18, 1916. [4; 10; 20]

Dandy, Walter Edward, surgeon, b. Sedalia, Mo., 1886; d. Baltimore, Md., April 19, 1946. [10; 11]

Danenhower, John Wilson, explorer, b. Chicago, Ill., 1849; d. Annapolis, Md., April 20, 1887. [1; 4]

Danforth, Henry Gold, lawyer, b. Gates, N.Y., 1854; d. Rochester, N.Y., April 8, 1918. [10]

Danforth, John, clergyman, b. Roxbury, Mass., 1660; d. Dorchester, Mass., May 26, 1730. [3; 51]

Danforth, Joshua Noble, clergyman, b. Pittsfield, Mass., 1798; d. New Castle, Del., Nov. 14, 1861. [3; 4]

Danforth, Keyes, jurist, b. 1822; d. 1897.

Danforth, Samuel, clergyman, b. Suffolk, England, 1626; d. Roxbury, Mass., Nov. 19, 1674. [3; 51]

Danforth, Samuel, clergyman, b. Roxbury, Mass., 1666; d. Taunton, Mass., Nov. 14, 1727. [3; 51]

Daniel, Ferdinand Eugene, surgeon, b. Greenville county, Va., 1839; d. Austin, Tex., May 14, 1914. [10; 34]

Daniel, François, priest, b. Normandy, France, 1820; d. Montreal, Que., Feb. 20, 1908. [27]

Daniel, James Walter, clergyman, b. Laurens county, S.C., 1856; d. ? [34]

Daniel, John Franklin, biologist, b. O'Fallon, Mo., 1873; d. Berkeley, Calif., Nov. 2, 1942. [10; 11]

Daniel, John Moncure, journalist, b. Stafford county, Va. 1825; d. Richmond, Va., March 30, 1865. [1; 4; 34]

Daniel, John Warwick, lawyer, b. Lynchburg, Va., 1842; d. Lynchburg, Va., 1910. [10]

Daniell, Moses Grant, educationist, b. Boston, Mass., 1836; d. Boston, Mass., Oct. 18, 1909. [10; 51]

Daniels, Josephus, journalist and politician, b. Washington, N.C., 1862; d. Raleigh, N.C., Jan. 15, 1948. [7; 10; 34]

Daniels, Winthrop More, educationist, b. Dayton, O., 1867; d. Saybrook Point, Conn., Jan. 3, 1943. [10]

Danks, Heart Pease, musical composer, b. New Haven, Conn., 1834; d. Philadelphia, Pa., Nov. 20, 1903. [3; 4; 20]

Dann, Hollis Ellsworth, musician, b. Canton, Pa., May 1, 1861; d. New York, N.Y., Jan. 4, 1939. [10; 11; 20]

Dannelly, Mrs. Elizabeth Otis, née Marshall, poet, b. Georgia, 1836; d. 1896. [8]

Daoust, Charles Roger, journalist, b. Montreal, Que., 1865; d. Manchester, Que., Nov. 17, 1924. [27]

D'Apery, Mrs. Ellen, née Burrell, novelist, b. Wyoming Valley, Pa., 1842; d. New York, N.Y., May 3, 1915. [35]

Da Ponte, Lorenzo, poet and librettist, b. Ceneda, Italy, 1749; d. New York, N.Y., Aug. 17, 1838. [1; 20]

Darby, John, botanist, b. North Adams, Mass., 1804; d. New York, N.Y., Sept. 1, 1877. [1; 61]

Darby, John (pseud.). See Garretson, James Edmund.

Darby, William, geographer, b. Lancaster county, Pa., 1775; d. Washington, D.C., Oct. 9, 1854. [1; 4; 7]

Darby, William Dermot, editor, b. Ireland, 1885; d. New York, N.Y., Oct. 20, 1947.

Dare, Shirley (pseud.). See Power, Mrs. Susan C., née Manning.

Dargan, Edwin Charles, clergyman, b. Springville, S.C., 1852; d. Macon, Ga., Oct. 26, 1930. [10; 24; 34]

Dargan, Edwin Preston, educationist, b. Barboursville, Va., 1879; d. Chicaga, Ill., Dec. 13, 1940. [7; 10; 11]

D'Arles, Henri (pseud.). See Beaudé, Henri.

Darley, Felix Octavious Carr, illustrator, b. Philadelphia, Pa., 1822; d. Claymont, Del., March 27, 1888. [1; 4; 7]

Darling, Charles William, soldier, b. New Haven, Conn., 1830; d. Utica, N.Y., 1905. [10]

Darling, Henry, clergyman, b. Reading, Pa., 1823; d. Clinton, N.Y., April 20, 1891. [1; 4]

Darling, Mrs. Flora, née Adams, novelist and organizer, b. Lancaster, N.H., 1840; d. New York, N.Y., Jan. 6, 1910. [1; 4; 7; 10]

Darling, Mary Greenleaf, writer of books for girls, b. Boston, Mass., 1848; d. ? [7; 8]

Darling, Samuel Boyd, lawyer, b. Marlborough, Mass., 1873; d. Mount Kisko, N.Y., June 1, 1948. [62]

Darling, William, physician, b. Berwickshire, Scotland, 1815; d. New York, N.Y., Dec. 25, 1884. [3]

Darling, William Stewart, clergyman, b. Scotland, 1818; d. Alassio, Italy, Jan. 19, 1886. [27]

Darlington, James Henry, bishop, b. Brooklyn, N.Y., 1856; d. Kingston, N.Y., Aug. 14, 1930. [4; 10]

Darlington, Thomas, physician, b. Brooklyn, N.Y., 1858; d. near Port Jervis, N.Y., Aug. 23, 1945. [10]

Darlington, William, botanist, b. Dilworthtown, Pa., 1782; d. West Chester, Pa., April 23, 1863. [1; 4]

Darnell, Henry Faulkner, clergyman, b. London, England, 1831; d. Easton, Pa., 1915. [27]

Darrow, Clarence Seward, lawyer, b. Kinsman, O., 1857; d. Chicago, Ill., March 13, 1938. [7; 10; 11]

Darsie, Charles, clergyman, b. Warren, O., 1872; d. Cleveland, O., Sept. 23, 1948.

Darton, Nelson Horatio, geologist, b. New York, N.Y., 1865; d. Chevy Chase, Md., Feb. 28, 1948. [10; 11]

Darveau, Louis Michel, journalist, b. Quebec, Lower Canada, 1833; d. Quebec, Que., Aug. 24, 1875. [27]

Dash, Paul R. (pseud.). See Browne, Lewis Allen.

Dau, William Herman Theodore, clergyman, b. Pomerania, Germany, 1864; d. Berkeley, Calif., April 21, 1944. [10]

Daugé, Henri (pseud.). See Hammond, Mrs. Henrietta, née Hardy.

Daulton, Mrs. Agnes Warner, née McClelland, illustrator and lecturer, b. New Philadelphia, O., 1867; d. Woodstock, N.Y., June 5, 1944. [7; 10; 11]

Daulton, George, novelist, b. Knox county, Mo., 1861; d. New Brighton, N.Y., Jan. 29, 1913. [10]

Daveiss, Joseph Hamilton, lawyer, b. Bedford county, Va., 1774; d. Tippecanoe county, Ind., Nov. 8, 1811. [1; 4]

Davenport, Charles Benedict, biologist, b. Stamford, Conn., 1866; d. Huntington, Long Island, N.Y., Feb. 18, 1944. [10; 11; 13]

Davenport, Eugene, educationist, b. Woodland, Mich., 1856; d. Woodland, Mich., March 31, 1941. [7; 10; 11]

Davenport, Frances Gardiner, historian, b. Stamford, Conn., 1870; d. Washington, D.C., Nov. 11, 1927. [10]

Davenport, Herbert Joseph, economist, b. Wilmington, Vt., 1861; d. New York, N.Y., June 17, 1931. [1a; 10]

Davenport, Homer Calvin, cartoonist, b. near Silverton, Ore., 1867; d. New York, N.Y., May 2, 1912. [1; 7; 10; 41]

Davenport, James, clergyman, b. Stamford, Conn., 1716; d. Hopewell, N.J., 1757. [1]

Davenport, John, clergyman, b. Coventry, England, 1597; d. Boston, Mass., March 15, 1670. [1; 4]

Davenport, John Gaylord, clergyman, b. Wilton, Conn., 1840; d. Waterbury, Conn., June 9, 1922. [10; 68]

Davenport, Reuben Briggs, journalist, b. New York, N.Y.; d. Montpelier, France, March 11, 1932. [10]

Davenport, Walter Rice, clergyman, b. Williamstown, Vt., 1855; d. Montpelier, Vt., ? [10; 11]

Davenport, William Edwards, clergyman, b. North Stamford, Conn., 1862; d. Brooklyn, N.Y., April 28, 1944. [10]

Davey, John, tree-surgeon, b. Somerset, England, 1846; d. Akron, O., Nov. 8, 1923. [1; 4]

David, Jean Baptiste Marie, bishop, b. near Nantel, France, 1761; d. Bardstown, Ky., July 12, 1841. [1; 3; 4; 8; 21]

David, Laurent Olivier, historian, b. Sault-au-Recollet, Lower Canada, 1840; d. Montreal, Que., Aug. 24, 1926. [27]

Davidge, John Beale, surgeon, b. Annapolis, Md., 1768; d. Baltimore, Md., Aug. 23, 1829. [1; 4]

Davidge, William Pleater, actor, b. London, England, 1814; d. Cheyenne, Wyo., Aug. 7, 1888. [1; 4]

Davidson, Anstruther, physician, b. Scotland, 1860; d. Los Angeles, Calif., April 3, 1932. [4; 10]

Davidson, Charles, educationist, b. Streetboro, O., 1852; d. Claremont, Calif., Nov. 24, 1919. [10; 62]

Davidson, Sir Charles Peers, jurist, b. Huntingdon, Que., 1841; d. New York, N.Y., Jan. 29, 1929. [27]

Davidson, Gordon Charles, historian, b. 1884; d. Vancouver, B.C., May, 1922. [27]

Davidson, Mrs. Hannah Amelia, née Noyes, educationist, b. Campello, Mass., 1852; d. Claremont, Calif., Nov. 28, 1932. [4; 10; 11]

Davidson, Israel, educationist, b. Yanova, Russia, 1870; d. Great Neck, Long Island, N.Y., June 27, 1939. [7; 10; 11]

Davidson, James Wheeler, journalist and consular agent, b. Austin, Minn., 1872; d. Calgary, Alta., July 18, 1933. [10; 11]

Davidson, James Wood, journalist, b. Newberry county, S.C., 1829; d. June 15, 1905. [1; 3; 4; 7; 8; 34]

Davidson, John, political economist, b. Edinburgh, Scotland, 1869; d. Edinburgh, Scotland, July 31, 1905. [27]

Davidson, Lucretia Maria, poet, b. Plattsburg, N.Y., 1808; d. Plattsburg, N.Y., Aug. 27, 1825. [1; 4; 7]

Davidson, Robert, clergyman, b. Elkton, Md., 1750; d. Carlisle, Pa., Dec. 13, 1812. [1; 4; 34]

Davidson, Robert, clergyman, b. Carlisle, Pa., 1808; d. Philadelphia, Pa., April 6, 1876. [2; 4]

Davidson, Thomas, philosopher, b. Aberdeenshire Scotland; d. Montreal, Que., Sept. 14, 1900. [1; 4; 7]

Davidson, William Mehard, educationist, b. Jamestown. Pa., 1863; d. Pittsburg, Pa., July 27, 1930. [10]

Davies, Acton, drama critic, b. St. Johns, Que., 1870; d. Chicago, Ill., June 12, 1916. [10]

Davies, Charles, mathematician, b. Washington, Conn., 1798; d. Fishkill Landing, N.Y., Sept. 17, 1876. [3; 4]

Davies, Henry William, clergyman and grammarian, b. Cleveland, O., 1834; d. Toronto, Ont., March 19, 1895. [27]

Davies, Samuel, clergyman and educationist, b. New Castle county, Del., 1723; d. Princeton, N.J., Feb. 4, 1761. [1; 4]

Davies, Thomas Alfred, soldier, b. St. Lawrence county, N.Y., 1809; d. near Ogdensburg, N.Y., Aug. 19, 1899. [3; 4]

Davies, Thomas Frederick, bishop, b. Philadelphia, Pa., 1872; d. Lenox, Mass., Aug. 25, 1936. [4; 10; 62]

Davies William Walter, educationist, b. Cardiganshire, Wales, 1848; d. Delaware, O., May 5, 1922. [10]

Daviess, Joseph Hamilton, See Daveiss, Joseph Hamilton.

Daviess, Mrs. Maria, nee **Thompson,** novelist and poet, b. Harrodsburg, Ky., 1814; d. Harrodsburg, Ky., Dec. 19, 1896. [4; 34]

Daviess, Maria Thompson, artist and novelist, b. Harrodsburg, Ky., 1872; d. New York, N.Y., Sept. 3, 1924. [7; 10; 34; 74]

Davin, Nicholas Flood, lawyer and politician, b. county Limerick, Ireland, 1843; d. Winnipeg, Man., Oct. 18, 1901. [27]

Davis, Alexander Jackson, architect, b. New York, N.Y., 1803; d. West Orange, N.J., Jan. 24, 1892. [1; 4]

Davis, Andrew Jackson, spiritualist, b. Blooming Grove, N.Y., 1826; d. Jan. 13, 1910. [1; 4]

Davis, Andrew McFarland, antiquary, b. Worcester, Mass., 1833; d. Cambridge, Mass., March 29, 1920. [1; 10]

Davis, Arthur Powell, hydraulic engineer, b. Decatur, Ill., 1861; d. Oakland, Calif., Aug. 7, 1933. [1a; 10; 11]

Davis, Asahel, historian, b. 1791; d. ? [6]

Davis, Beale, novelist, b. Petersburg, Va., 1886; d. Hopewell, Va., Nov. 1, 1929. [10]

Davis, Boothe Colwell, educationist, b. Lewis county, W. Va., 1863; d. Holly Hill, Fla., Jan. 16, 1942. [10; 62]

Davis, Charles Augustus, merchant, b. New York, N.Y., 1795; d. New York, N.Y., Jan. 27, 1867. [3; 4]

Davis, Charles Belmont, novelist, b. Philadelphia, Pa., 1866; d. near Asheville, N.C., Dec. 9, 1926. [2; 10]

Davis, Charles Gilbert, physician, b. Clay county, Mo., 1849; d. Chicago, Ill., Oct. 31, 1928. [10]

Davis, Charles Henry, naval officer, b. Cambridge, Mass., 1845; d. Washington, D.C., Dec. 27, 1921. [1; 4; 10]

Davis, Charles Henry Stanley, physician and philologist, b. Goshen, Conn., 1840; d. Middletown, Conn., Nov. 7, 1917. [1; 10]

Davis, Cushman Kellogg, lawyer and politician, b. Henderson, N.Y., 1838; d. St. Paul, Minn., Nov. 27, 1900. [1; 4; 10; 70]

Davis, Daniel, lawyer, b. Barnstable, Mass., 1762; d. Cambridge, Mass., Oct. 27, 1835. [3; 51]

Davis, Dudley Hughes, poet, b. 1834; d. ? [34]

Davis, Mrs. Edith, née Smith, temperance worker, b. Milwaukee, Wis., 1859; d. Milwaukee, Wis., March 19, 1917. [10]

Davis, Edward Parker, physician, b. 1856; d. Philadelphia, Pa., Oct. 2, 1937.

Davis, Ellery Williams, mathematician, b. Oconowomoc, Wis., 1857; d. Lincoln, Neb., Feb. 2, 1918. [10]

Davis, Emerson, clergyman, b. Ware, Mass., 1798; d. Westfield, Mass., June 8, 1866. [3; 4; 61]

Davis, Frederick William, dime novelist, b. 1858; d. New Bedford, Mass., Jan. 4, 1933. [7]

Davis, Garrett Morrow, novelist, b. Kentucky, 1851; d. ? [34]

Davis, George Breckenridge, soldier and jurist, b. Ware, Mass., 1847; d. Washington, D.C., Dec. 15, 1914. [3; 4; 10]

Davis, George Theron, educationist, b. Boston, Mass., 1899; d. New Haven, Conn., June 27, 1944. [62]

Davis, George Thomas, lawyer, b. Sandwich, Mass., 1810; d. Portland, Me., June 17, 1877. [3; 4]

Davis, Gilbert Asa, local historian, b. Chester, Vt., 1835; d. ? [43]

Davis, Mrs. Grace Emeline, née Tinker, clergyman's wife, b. 1876; d. Chicago, Ill., Sept. 23, 1945.

Davis, Henry, clergyman, b. East Hampton, Long Island, N.Y., 1771; d. Clinton, N.Y., March 8, 1852. [1; 4]

Davis, Henry Winter, politician, b. Annapolis, Md., 1817; d. Baltimore, Md., Dec. 30, 1865. [1; 4; 34]

Davis, Herman Stearns, astronomer, b. Milford, Me., 1868; d. Pittsburg, Pa., May 23, 1933. [10; 13]

Davis, Horace, manufacturer, b. Worcester, Mass., 1831; d. San Francisco, Calif., July 12, 1916. [1; 4; 10]

Davis, J. Frank. See Davis, James Francis.

Davis, Jackson, educationist, b. Virginia, 1882; d. Cartersville, Va., April 15, 1947.

Davis, James Francis, journalist, novelist, and playwright, b. New Bedford, Mass., 1870; d. San Antonio, Tex., April 6, 1942. [7; 10; 11]

Davis, Jefferson, politician, b. Christian county, Ky., 1808; d. New Orleans, La., Dec. 6, 1899. [1; 4; 7; 34; 74]

Davis, Jerome Dean, missionary, b. Groton, N.Y., 1838; d. Oberlin, O., Nov. 4, 1910. [11]

Davis, John, jurist, b. Plymouth, Mass., 1761; d. Boston, Mass., Jan. 14, 1847. [1; 4]

Davis, John, traveller and bookseller, b. Salisbury, England, 1774; d. London, England, April 24, 1854. [7]

Davis, John A., clergyman, d. 1897.

Davis, John Anthony Gardner, jurist, b. Middlesex county, Va., 1801; d. Williamsburg, Va., Nov. 14, 1840. [3; 4; 34]

Davis, John Chandler Bancroft, diplomat, b. Worcester, Mass., 1822; d. Washington, D.C., Dec. 27, 1907. [1; 4; 10]

Davis, John D., theologian, b. Pittsburg, Pa., 1854; d. Philadelphia, Pa., June 21, 1926. [10; 56]

Davis, John McCan, lawyer, b. Fulton county, Ill., 1866; d. Springfield, Ill., May 11, 1916. [10]

Davis, John Patterson, lawyer, b. Niles, Mich., 1862; d. Asheville, N.C., Dec. 28, 1903. 10]

Davis, John Staige, surgeon, b. 1872; d. Baltimore, Md., Dec. 23, 1946. [10; 62]

Davis, John Woodbridge, civil engineer, b. New York, N.Y., 1854; d. New York, N.Y., Nov. 7, 1902. [3; 4]

Davis, Joseph Baker, engineer, b. Westport, Mass., 1845; d. Dexter, Mich., March 9, 1920. [10]

Davis, Kary Cadmus, agricultural educationist, b. Decatur, Ill., 1867; d. May 4, 1936. [10; 11]

Davis, Katharine Bement, sociologist, b. Buffalo, N.Y., 1860; d. Pacific Grove, Calif., Dec. 10, 1935. [1a; 10; 58]

Davis, Lemuel Clarke, journalist, b. near Sandusky, O., 1835; d. 1904. [3; 7; 10]

Davis, Lucius Daniel, clergyman, b. Jerusalem, N.Y., 1826; d. Newport, R.I., Oct. 31, 1900. [6]

Davis, Lyman Edwyn, clergyman, b. near Toledo, O., 1854; d. Baltimore, Md., Aug. 13, 1930. [10]

Davis, Mrs. Mary A., née Perkins, clergyman's wife, b. Centre Harbor, N.H., 1836; d. ? [24]

Davis, Mrs. Mary Evelyn, née Moore, playwright and novelist, b. Talladega, Ala., 1852; d. New Orleans, La., Jan. 1, 1909. [1; 4; 7; 34]

Davis, Matthew Livingston, journalist, b. New York, N.Y., 1773; d. Manhattanville, N.Y., June 21, 1850. [1; 4]

Davis, Minnie S., novelist, b. 1835; d. ? [34]

Davis, Nathan Smith, physician, b. Greene, N.Y., 1817; d. Chicago, Ill., June 16, 1904. [1; 3; 10]

Davis, Nathan Smith, physician, b. Chicago, Ill., 1858; d. Chicago, Ill., Dec. 21, 1920. [10]

Davis, Noah, jurist, b. Haverhill, N.H., 1818; d. New York, N.Y., March 20, 1902. [1; 4]

Davis, Noah Knowles, educationist, b. Philadelphia, Pa., 1830; d. Charlottesville, Va., May 3, 1910. [1; 4; 7; 10]

Davis, Oscar King, journalist, b. Baldwinsville, N.Y., 1866; d. Bronxville, N.Y., June 3, 1932. [1a; 10; 11]

Davis, Ozora Stearns, theologian, b. Wheelock, Vt., 1866; d. near Topeka, Kans., March 15, 1931. [10; 11; 49]

Davis, Mrs. Paulina, née Kellogg Wright, suffragist, b. Bloomfield, N.Y., Aug 7, 1813; d. Providence, R.I., Aug. 24, 1876. [1; 4]

Davis, Peter Seibert, clergyman, b. Funkstown, Md., 1828; d. 1892. [6]

Davis, Raymond Cazallis, librarian, b. Cushing, Me., 1836; d. Ann Arbor, Mich., June 10, 1919. [1; 10]

Davis, Mrs. Rebecca Blaine, née Harding, novelist, b. Washington, Pa., 1831; d. Mount Kisco, N.Y., Sept. 29, 1910. [1; 4; 7; 10]

Davis, Rebecca Ingersoll, essayist and poet, b. 1828; d. ? [38]

Davis, Reuben, lawyer, b. near Winchester, Tenn., 1813; d. Huntsville, Ala., Oct. 14. 1890. [1; 34]

Davis, Richard Harding, journalist and novelist, b. Philadelphia, Pa., 1864; d. Mount Kisco, N.Y., April 11, 1916. [1; 4; 10; 72]

Davis, Robert, writer of books for children, b. Beverly, Mass., 1881; d. Sept. 25, 1949. [7; 10]

Davis, Robert Hobart, journalist, b. Brownsville, Neb. 1869; d. Montreal, Que., Oct. 11, 1942. [7; 10; 11]

Davis, Royal Jenkins, journalist, b. Ridgefarm, Ill., 1878; d. New York, N.Y., Oct. 20, 1934. [10; 11]

Davis, Samuel Post, historian, b. Branford, Conn., 1850; d. Carson City, Nev., March 17, 1918. [35]

Davis, Samuel T., physician and sportsman, b. Huntington county, Pa., 1838; d. Lancaster, Pa., 1908. [10]

Davis, Stephen Brooks, lawyer, b. Middletown, Conn., 1874; d. New York, N.Y., Feb. 24, 1933. [10; 60]

Davis, Thomas Kirby, clergyman, b. 1826; d. Wooster, O., Dec. 24, 1918. [62]

Davis, Mrs. Varina, née Howell, biographer, b. Natchez, Miss., 1826; d. New York, N.Y., Oct. 16, 1906. [1; 4; 7; 10; 34]

Davis, Varina Anne Jefferson, novelist, b. Richmond, Va., 1864; d. Narragansett Pier, R.I., Sept. 18, 1898. [1; 7; 34]

Davis, William Bramwell, physician, b. Cincinnati, O., 1832; d. 1893. [3]

Davis, William Heath, pioneer, b. 1822; d. 1909. [7]

Davis, William Morris, whaler, b. about 1815; d. about 1890.

Davis, William Morris, geographer and geologist, b. Philadelphia, Pa., 1850; d. Pasadena, Calif., Feb. 6, 1934. [1a; 10; 11]

Davis, William Stearns, historian and novelist, b. Amherst, Mass., 1877; d. Exeter, N.H., Feb. 15, 1930. [7; 10]

Davis, William Thomas, historian and lawyer, b. Plymouth, Mass., 1822; d. Plymouth, Mass., Dec. 3, 1907. [1; 7; 10; 51]

Davis, William Watts Hart, journalist and historian, b. Bucks county, Pa., 1820; d. Doylestown, Pa., 1910. [7; 10]

Davis, Winnie. See Davis, Varina Anne Jefferson.

Davis, Woodbury, jurist, b. Standish, Me., 1818; d. Portland, Me., Aug. 15, 1871. [3]

Davison, Alvin, biologist, b. Hainesburg, N.J., 1868; d. Cincinnati, O., Aug. 31, 1915. [4; 56]

Davison, Charles Stewart, lawyer, b. New York, N.Y., 1855; d. New York, N.Y., Nov. 24, 1942. [10; 11]

Davison, Gideon Miner, journalist, b. about 1791; d. 1869.

Davison, Henry Pomeroy, banker, b. Troy, Pa., 1867; d. Locust Valley, N.Y., May 6, 1922. [10]

Dawe, George Grosvenor, editor and organizer, b. Horsham, Surrey, England, 1863; d. Washington, D.C., Sept. 13, 1948. [10]

Dawes, Anna Laurens, journalist, b. North Adams, Mass., 1851; d. Pittsfield, Mass., Sept. 25, 1938. [7; 10; 11]

Dawes, Rufus, poet and novelist, b. Boston, Mass., 1803; d. Washington, D.C., Nov. 30, 1859. [3; 4; 7; 71]

Dawes, Rufus Cutler, industralist, b. Marietta, O., 1867; d. Evanston, Ill., Jan. 8, 1940. [10]

Dawley, Thomas Robinson, biographer, 1832; d. 1904.

Dawley, Thomas Robinson, journalist, b. New York, N.Y., 1862; d. New York, N.Y., June 1, 1930. [10]

Dawson, Aeneas McDonell, priest and poet, b. Banffshire, Scotland, 1810; d. Ottawa, Ont., Dec. 29, 1894. [27]

Dawson, Benjamin Elisha, surgeon, b. Madison, Mo., 1852; d. Kansas City, Mo., Feb. 13, 1922. [4; 10]

Dawson, Daniel Lewis, poet, b. Lewistown, Pa., 1855; d. Philadelphia, Pa., Nov. 1, 1893. [4]

Dawson, Edgar, educationist, b. Scottsville, Va., 1872; d. New York, N.Y., April 30, 1946. [10]

Dawson, Emma Frances, poet and short-story writer, b. Massachusetts, 1851; d. Palo Alto, Calif., Feb. 6, 1926. [35]

Dawson, George, journalist, b. Falkirk, Scotland, 1813; d. Albany, N.Y., Feb. 17, 1883. [3; 4]

Dawson, George Ellsworth, educationist, b. Berkeley Springs, W. Va., 1861; d. Springfield, Mass., April 22, 1936. [4; 10]

Dawson, George Mercer, geologist, b. Pictou, N.S., 1849; d. Ottawa, Ont., March 2, 1901. [27]

Dawson, Henry Barton, historian, b. Lincolnshire, England, 1821; d. Tarrytown, N.Y., May 23, 1889. [1; 7]

Dawson, Sir John William, educationist and naturalist, b. Pictou, N.S., 1820; d. Montreal, Que., Nov. 19, 1899. [27]

Dawson, Lemuel Orah, clergyman, b. Chambers county, Ala., 1865; d. Birmingham, Ala., Jan. 14, 1938. [10]

Dawson, Mary, journalist, b. Philadelphia, Pa.; d. Long Island, N.Y., 1922. [10]

Dawson, Miles Menander, lawyer and actuary, b. Viroqua, Wis., 1863; d. Orlando, Fla., March 27, 1942. [10; 11]

Dawson, Mrs. Nell, née Perkins, literary critic, b. Chicago, Ill., 1870; d. New York, N.Y., April 23, 1923. [2]

Dawson, Samuel Edward, literary critic and historian, b. Halifax, N.S., 1833; d. Westmount, Que., Feb. 9, 1916. [27]

Dawson, Simon James, civil engineer, b. Banffshire, Scotland, 1820; d. Ottawa, Ont., Nov. 20, 1902. [27]

Dawson, Thomas Cleland, diplomat, b. Hudson, Wis., 1865; d. Washington, D.C., May 1, 1912. [10]

Dawson, Thomas Fulton, historian, b. 1853; d. Denver, Colo., June 25, 1923.

Dawson, William James, clergyman, b. Towcaster, England, 1854; d. Nelson, B.C., Aug. 23, 1928. [7; 10]

Dawson, William Leon, ornithologist, b. Leon, Ia., 1873; d. Santa Barbara, Calif., April 30, 1928. [10]

Day, Benjamin Henry, journalist, b. West Springfield, Mass., 1810; d. New York, N.Y. Dec. 21, 1889. [1; 4; 7]

Day, Mrs. Catherine Matilda, née Townsend, historian, b. Farnham, Lower Canada, 1815; d. South Stukeley, Que., Aug. 24, 1899. [27]

Day, Clarence, humorist, b. New York, N.Y., 1874; d. New York, N.Y., Dec. 28, 1935. [1a; 7; 10; 62]

Day, David Talbot, chemist and geologist, b. East Rockport, O., 1859; d. Washington, D.C., April 15, 1925. [1; 10]

Day, Frank Miles, architect, b. Philadelphia, Pa., 1861; d. Mount Airy, Pa., June 15, 1918. [1; 4; 10]

Day, George Edward, clergyman and educationist, b. Pittsfield, Mass., 1815; d. New Haven, Conn., July 2, 1905. [3; 4; 10]

Day, George Edward, social worker, b. North Dana, Mass., 1864; d. Somerville, Mass., Oct. 31, 1919. [10]

Day, Henry, lawyer, b. South Hadley, Mass., 1820; d. New York, N.Y., Jan. 9, 1893. [3; 4]

Day, Henry Noble, clergyman and educationist, b. West Preston, Conn., 1808; d. New Haven, Conn., Jan. 12, 1890. [1; 4; 7]

Day, Holman Francis, novelist and poet, b. Vassalboro, Me., 1865; d. Mill Valley, Calif., Feb. 19, 1935. [1a; 7; 10; 35]

Day, James Roscoe, clergyman and educationist, b. Whitneyville, Me., 1845; d. Atlantic City, N.J., March 13, 1923. [1; 4; 10]

Day, Jeremiah, educationist, b. New Preston, Conn., 1773; d. New Haven, Conn., Aug. 22, 1867. [1; 4; 62]

Day, Martha, poet, b. New Haven, Conn., 1813; d. New Haven, Conn., Dec. 2, 1833. [3]

Day, Mary L. See Arms, Mrs. Mary L., née Day.

Day, Richard Edwin, poet, journalist, and historian, b. Granby, N.Y., 1852; d. Albany, N.Y., Dec. 14, 1936. [4; 7; 10; 11]

Day, Sarah J., poet, b. Cincinnati, O., 1860; d. Englewood, N.J., May 11, 1940. [7; 10]

Day, Sherman, historian, b. 1806; d. 1884. [6]

Day, Thomas Fleming, editor and yachtsman, b. Weston-super-Mare, England, 1861; d. New York, N.Y., Aug. 18, 1927. [7; 10]

Day, William Baker, botanist, b. Peru, Ill., 1871; d. Oak Park, Ill., Dec. 10, 1938. [10; 13]

Dayton, Amos Cooper, clergyman and physician, b. Plainfield, N.J., 1813; d. Perry, Ga., June 11, 1865. [3; 4; 34]

Dayton, Katharine, journalist and playwright, b. Philadelphia, Pa.; d. New York, N.Y., March 4, 1945.

Dayton, Laura, See Fessenden, Mrs. Laura, née Dayton.

Dazey, Charles Turner, playwright, b. Lima, Ill., 1855; d. Quincy, Ill., Feb. 9, 1938. [7; 10; 11]

Dealey, James Quayle, journalist and sociologist, b. Manchester, England, 1861; d. Dallas, Tex., Jan. 22, 1937. [10; 11]

Dean, Alexander, play director, b .Newburyport, Mass., 1893; d. Cohasset, Mass., July 29, 1939. [10; 11]

Dean, Amos, lawyer and educationist, b. Barnard, Vt., 1803; d. Albany, N.Y., Jan. 26, 1868. [1; 3; 4; 43]

Dean, Arthur Davis, educationist, b. Cambridge, Mass., 1872; d. Danbury, Conn., Nov. 19, 1949. [10; 11]

Dean, Bashford, biologist, b. 1867; d. Battle Creek, Mich., Dec. 6, 1928. [1; 4; 10; 13]

Dean, James, educationist, b. Windsor, Vt., 1776; d. Burlington, Vt., Jan. 20, 1849. [3; 43]

Dean, John Marvin, clergyman, b. Cobleskill, N.Y., 1875; d. Greensburg, Pa., Nov. 10, 1935. [10]

Dean, John Ward, biographer, b. Wiscasset, Me., 1815; d. Medford, Mass., Jan. 22, 1902. [3; 8; 10]

Dean, Paul, clergyman, b. Barnard, Vt., 1789; d. Framingham, Mass., Oct. 1, 1860. [3; 8; 43]

Dean, Sidney, clergyman and politician, b. Glastonbury, Conn., 1818; d. Brookline, Mass., Oct. 29, 1901. [1]

Deane, Charles, historian, b. Biddeford, Me., 1813; d. Cambridge, Mass., Nov. 13, 1880. [1; 3; 7; 8]

Deane, Richard Burton, soldier, b. India, 1848; d. Diano, Mariana, Italy, Dec. 13, 1930. [27]

Deane, Samuel, clergyman and agriculturist, b. Dedham, Mass., 1733; d. Portland, Me., Nov. 12, 1814. [1; 4; 51]

Deane, Samuel, clergyman and local historian, b. Mansfield, Mass., 1784; d. Scituate, Mass., Aug. 9, 1834. [49]

Deane, Silas, diplomat, b. Groton, Conn., 1737; d. Deal, England, Aug. 23, 1789. [1; 3; 4]

Deane, William Reed, genealogist, b. Mansfield, Mass., 1809; d. Mansfield, Mass., June 16, 1871. [3; 8]

De Angelis, Thomas Jefferson, actor, b. San Francisco, Calif., 1859; d. Orange, N.J., March 20, 1933. [1a; 2; 10]

Dearborn, George Van Ness, psychiatrist, b. Nashua, N.H., 1869; d. New York, N.Y., Dec. 12, 1938. [10; 11]

Dearborn, Henry Alexander Scammell, politician, b. Exeter, N.H., 1783; d. Portland, Me., July 29, 1851. [1; 4]

Dearborn, Nathaniel, engraver, b. 1786; d. South Reading, Mass., Nov. 7, 1852. [3]

Deaver, John Blair, surgeon, b. Lancaster county, Pa., 1855; d. Wyncote, Pa., Sept. 25, 1931. [1a; 4; 10]

De Bekker, Leander Jan, journalist, b. 1872; d. Rome, Italy, Jan. 26, 1931. [11]

De Blois, Austen Kennedy, clergyman, b. Wolfville, N.S., 1866; d. Philadelphia, Pa., Aug. 10, 1945. [7; 10]

De Booy, Theodoor, archaeologist and explorer, b. Holland, 1882; d. Yonkers, N.Y., Feb. 18, 1919. [10]

De Bow, James Dunwoody Brownson, statistician, b. Charleston, S.C., 1820; d. Elizabeth, N.J., Feb. 27, 1867. [1; 3; 4; 34]

De Bower, Herbert Francis, educationist, b. Dane, Wis., 1874; d. Long Beach, N.Y., March 16, 1940. [10]

De Brahm, William Gerard, surveyor, b. 1717; d. Philadelphia, Pa., 1799. [1]

Debs, Eugene Victor, socialist, b. Terre Haute, Ind., 1855; d. Elmhurst, near Chicago, Ill., Oct. 20, 1926. [1; 4; 10]

De Casseres, Benjamin, journalist, b. Philadelphia, Pa., 1873; d. New York, N.Y., Dec. 6, 1945. [7; 10; 11]

De Celles, Alfred Duclos, librarian, b. St. Laurent, Que., 1843; d. Ottawa, Ont., Oct. 5, 1925. [27]

De Charms, Richard, clergyman, b. Philadelphia, Pa., 1796; d. Philadelphia, Pa., March 20, 1864. [62]

Decies, Elizabeth Wharton, Baroness, née Drexel, social leader, b. 1868; d. New York, N.Y., June 13, 1944. [10]

De Costa, Benjamin Franklin, clergyman and historian, b. Charlestown, Mass., 1831; d. New York, N.Y., Nov. 4, 1904. [1; 3; 4; 7; 8]

Decrow, William Emery, journalist, b. Bangor, Me., 1853; d. Boston, Mass., Nov. 25, 1905. [62]

Dee, Mrs. Minnie, née **Roof,** biographer, b. 1866; d. Portland, Ore., June 24, 1940. [11]

Deemer, Horace Emerson, jurist, b. Bourbon, Ind., 1858; d. 1917. [4; 10]

Deems, Charles Force, clergyman, b. Baltimore, Md., 1820; d. New York, N.Y., Nov. 18, 1893. [1; 3; 4; 34]

Deems, Edward Mark, clergyman, b. Greensboro, N.C.. 1852; d. New Brighton, N.Y., Aug. 7, 1929. [10; 34]

Deems, James Harry, musician, b. Baltimore, Md., 1848; d. Baltimore, Md., April 24, 1931. [10; 11; 20]

Deering, Fremont B. (pseud.). See Goldfrap, John Henry.

Deering, Nathaniel, playwright, b. Portland, Me., 1791; d. near Portland, Me., March 25, 1881. [1; 3; 4; 7; 8]

Defensor (pseud.). See Thomas, William.

De Fontaine, Felix Gregory, journalist, b. Boston, Mass., 1834; d. Columbia, S.C., Dec. 11, 1896. [1; 7]

De Forest, Charles Mills, economist, b. Waterloo, Ia. ,1878; d. St. Petersburg, Fla., April 12, 1947. [10; 62]

De Forest, Henry Pelouze, surgeon, b. Fulton, N.Y., 1864; d. New York, N.Y., June 13, 1948. [7; 10]

De Forest, John Kinne Hyde, missionary, b. Westbrook, Conn., 1844; d. Tokyo, Japan, May 8, 1911. [10]

De Forest, John William, novelist and poet, b. Seymour, Conn., 1826; d. New Haven, Conn., July 17, 1906. [1; 3; 7; 10; 62]

De Forest, Marian, playwright, b. Buffalo, N.Y.; d. Buffalo, N.Y., Feb. 17, 1935. [10]

De Garmo, Charles, educationist, b. Mukwanago, Wis., 1849; d. Miami, Fla., May 14, 1934. [10]

De Garmo, William Burton, physician, b. 1849; d. Coral Gables, Fla., Jan. 3, 1936. [11]

De Goesbriand, Louis, bishop, b. St. Urbain, France, 1816; d. Burlington, Vt., Nov. 3, 1899. [36; 4; 21]

De Gouy, Louis Pullig, chef, b. France, 1875; d. New York, N.Y., Nov. 14, 1947.

De Graff, Lawrence, jurist, b. Apple River, Ill., 1871; d. Des Moines, Ia., July 7, 1934. [10]

De Groot, Henry, pioneer, b. near Schenectady, N.Y., 1815; d. Alameda, Calif., March 28, 1893. [35]

De Hart, William Chetwood, soldier, b. New York, N.Y., 1800; d. 1848.

Dejeans, Elizabeth, novelist, b. New Philadelphia, O.: d. Dover, O., about Feb. 5, 1928. [7; 10; 11]

De Kay, Charles Augustus, journalist and poet, b. Washington, D.C.. 1848; d. New York, N.Y., May 23, 1935. [4; 7; 10]

De Kay, James Ellsworth, naturalist, b. Lisbon, Portugal, 1792; d. Oyster Bay, Long Island, N.Y., Nov. 21, 1851, [1; 3; 4; 8]

De Kay, John Wesley, financier and playwright, b. near New Hampton, Ia.. 1872; d. Takoma Park, Md., Oct. 4, 1938. [4]

De Koven, James, clergyman, b. Middletown, Conn., 1831; d. Racine, Wis., March 19, 1879. [1; 3; 4; 8]

De Kroyft, Mrs. Susan Helen, née **Aldrich,** novelist, b. Rochester, N.Y., 1818; d. Dansville, N.Y., Oct. 25, 1915. [3; 4; 7; 8; 10]

Delabarre, Edmund Burke, educationist, b. Dover, Me., 1863; d. Providence, R.I., March 16, 1945. [10; 11]

Delafield, Francis, physician, b. New York, N.Y.. 1841; d. near Stamford, Conn., July 17, 1915. [1; 4; 10]

Delafield, John, historical writer, b. England, 1812; d. probably in Ohio, about 1866.

De Laguna, Theodore de Leo, educationist, b. Oakland, Calif., 1876; d. Sept. 22, 1930. [1; 11]

Delamare, Henriette Eugénie, writer of books for children, b. Etrepagny, France; d. Pasadena, Calif., 1937. [11; 21]

Delamarre, Elzéar, priest, b. Laval, Que., 1854; d. Chicoutimi, Que., April 21, 1925. [32]

De Lancey, Edward Floyd, lawyer, b. Mamaroneck, N.Y., 1821; d. 1905. [10]

Deland, Ellen Douglas, novelist, b. Lake Mahopac, N.Y., 1860; d. Dedham, Mass., Feb. 21, 1923. [10]

Deland, Mrs. Margaretta Wade, née Campbell, novelist, b. Allegheny, Pa., 1857; d. Boston, Mass., Jan. 13, 1945. [7; 10; 11; 72]

Delano, Alonzo, pioneer, b. Aurora, N.Y., 1806; d. Grass Valley, Calif., Sept. 8, 1874. [7; 35]

Delano, Amasa, sea-captain; b. Duxbury, Mass., 1763; d. Boston, Mass., April 21, 1823. [1; 3; 4; 7; 8]

Delano, Mrs. Edith, née Barnard, novelist and playwright, b. Washington, D.C., 1875; d. Old Deerfield, Mass., Sept. 8, 1946. [7; 11]

Delano, Jane Arminda, nurse, b. Townsend, N.Y., 1862; d. Savenay Hospital Centre, France, April 15, 1919. [1; 4]

Delany, Martin Robison, politician, b. Charlestown, Va., 1812; d. Xenia, O., Jan. 24, 1885. [1]

Delany, Selden Peabody, clergyman, b. Fond du Lac, Wis., 1874; d. New York, N.Y., July 5, 1935. [10; 11; 21; 22]

Delavan, David Bryson, physician, b. New York, N.Y., 1850; d. New York, N.Y., May 23, 1942. [10; 62]

Delavan, Edward Cornelius, temperance advocate, b. Westchester county, N.Y., 1793; d. Schenectady, N.Y., Jan. 15, 1871. [1; 4; 8]

De Lee, Joseph Bolivar, obstetrician, b. Cold Springs, N.Y., 1869; d. Chicago, Ill., April 2, 1942. [10; 11]

De Leon, Daniel, socialist, b. Curaçao, 1852; d. New York, N.Y., May 11, 1914. [1; 10]

De Leon, Edwin, journalist and diplomat, b. Columbia, S.C., 1828; d. 1891. [4; 6; 8; 34]

De Leon, Edwin Warren, insurance executive, b. Charleston, S.C., 1868; d. New York, N.Y., 1918. [10]

De Leon, Thomas Cooper, soldier and journalist, b. Columbia, S.C., 1839; d. Mobile, Ala., March 19, 1914. [1; 4; 7; 34]

Deléry, François Charles, physician, b. St. Charles parish, La., 1815; d. Bay St. Louis, La., June 12, 1880. [1; 3; 34]

De Lestry, Edmond Louis, journalist, b. Lake Charles, La., 1860; d. St. Paul, Minn., Dec. 18, 1933. [10; 11]

Dellenbaugh, Frederick Samuel, artist and explorer, b. McConnelsville, O., 1853; d. New York, N.Y., Jan. 29, 1935. [1a; 7; 10; 11]

Del Mar, Alexander, political economist, b. New York, N.Y., 1836; d. Little Falls, N.J., July 1, 1926. [1; 3; 4; 10]

Del Mar, Walter, banker, b. New York, N.Y., 1862; d. New York, N.Y., April 10, 1944.

Delmas, Delphin Michael, lawyer, b. France, 1844; d. Santa Monica, Calif., Aug. 1, 1928. [1; 10]

De Long, Mrs. Emma J., née Wotton, explorer's wife, b. New York, N.Y., 1851; d. New York, N.Y., Nov. 24, 1940. [7]

De Long, George Washington, Arctic explorer, b. New York, N.Y., 1844; d. Siberia, Russia, Oct. 30, 1881. [1; 4; 7; 8]

Demarest, David D., clergyman, b. New Jersey, 1819; d. 1898. [3; 6; 8]

Demarest, John Terhune, clergyman, b. Teaneck, N.J., 1813; d. 1897. [6; 8]

Demarest, Mrs. Mary Augusta, née Lee, poet, b. New York, N.Y., 1836; d. Los Angeles, Calif., Jan. 8, 1888. [4; 6; 8]

De Menil, Alexander Nicolas, lawyer, b. St. Louis, Mo., 1849; d. St. Louis, Mo., Nov. 29, 1928. [4; 10; 11]

Demers, Albert Fox, journalist, b. Troy, N.Y., 1863; d. Troy, N.Y., Jan. 23, 1943. [7; 10]

Demers, Benjamin, priest, b. St. Romuald d'Etchemin, Que., Oct. 9, 1848; d. Quebec, Que., July 31, 1919. [27; 32]

Demers, Hector, poet, b. 1878; d. 1917. [27]

Demers, Jérôme, priest and educationist, b. St. Nicholas, Que., about 1774; d. Quebec, Que., May 17, 1853. [3; 27]

De Mille, Henry Churchill, playwright, b. Washington, N.C., 1853; d. Pompton, N.J., Feb. 10, 1893. [1; 7; 34]

De Mille, James, novelist and educationist, b. Saint John, N.B., 1836; d. Halifax, N.S., Jan. 28, 1880. [27]

Deming, Henry Champion, lawyer and politician, b. Colchester, Conn., 1815; d. Hartford, Conn., Oct. 9, 1872. [1; 3; 4; 8]

Deming, Horace Edward, lawyer, b. Palmyra, N.Y., 1850; d. New York, N.Y., June 11, 1930. [10]

Deming, Leonard, compiler, b. Canaan, Conn., 1787; d. Aug. 20, 1853. [43]

Deming, Philander, lawyer and court reporter, b. Carlisle, N.Y., 1829; d. Albany, N.Y., Feb. 9, 1915. [1; 4; 7; 8;]

Deming, Mrs. Therese, née Osterheld, writer of books for children, b. Bavaria, Germany, 1874; d. New York, N.Y., July 14, 1945. [7; 10; 11]

Dempster, John, theologian, b. Florida, N.Y., 1794; d. Evanston, Ill., Nov. 28, 1863. [1; 3; 4; 8]

De Muldor, Carl (pseud.). See Miller, Charles Henry.

Denby, Charles, diplomat, b. Mount Joy, Va., 1830; d. Jamestown, N.Y., Jan. 13, 1904. [1; 4; 10]

Denison, Charles, physician, b. Royalton, Vt., 1845; d. Denver, Colo., Jan. 10, 1909. [4; 43]

Denison, Charles Wheeler, clergyman, poet, and biographer, b. New London, Conn., 1809; d. Nov. 14, 1881. [3; 6; 7; 8]

Denison, Daniel, soldier, b. England, 1613; d. Ipswich, Mass., Sept. 20, 1682. [3]

Denison, Frederic, clergyman, b. Stonington, Conn., 1819; d. Providence, R.I., Aug. 16, 1901. [10; 47]

Denison, Frederick Charles, soldier, b. Toronto, Ont., 1846; d. Toronto, Ont., April 15, 1896. [27]

Denison, George Taylor, soldier and police magistrate, b. Toronto, Upper Canada, 1839; d. Toronto, Ont., June 6, 1925. [27]

Denison, Mrs. Grace Elizabeth, née **Sandys,** journalist, b. Chatham, Ont.; d. Toronto, Ont., Feb. 1, 1914. [27]

Denison, John Henry, clergyman, b. Boston, Mass., 1841; d. Denver, Colo., April 22, 1924. [10]

Denison, John Hopkins, clergyman, b. Westfield, Mass., 1870; d. New York, N.Y., Jan. 18, 1936. [10]

Denison, John Ledyard, publisher, b. Stonington, Conn., 1826; d. 1906. [3; 6; 10]

Denison, Mrs. Mary, née Andrews, novelist, b. Cambridge, Mass., 1826; d. Cambridge, Mass., Oct. 15, 1911. [3; 4; 7; 8; 10]

Denison, Septimus Julius Augustus, soldier, b. Toronto, Ont., 1859; d. Toronto, Ont., Nov. 8, 1937. [27]

Denison, Thomas Stewart, poet, b. Marshall county, Va., 1848; d. Chicago, Ill., 1911. [7; 10]

Dennen, Ernest Joseph, clergyman, b. Naugatuck, Conn., 1866; d. Cambridge, Mass., Jan. 22, 1937. [10; 11]

Dennen, Grace Atherton, journalist and poet, b. Woburn, Mass.; d. Los Angeles, Calif., June, 1927. [11]

Dennett, Roger Herbert, physician, b. Boston, Mass., 1876; d. New York, N.Y., Feb. 3, 1935. [10]

Denney, Joseph Villiers, educationist, b. Aurora, Ill., 1862; d. Columbus, O., June 19, 1935. [10]

Dennis, Alfred Lewis Pinneo, historian, b. Beirut, Syria, 1874; d. Worcester, Mass., Nov. 14, 1930. [1a; 10]

Dennis, Alfred Pearce, economist, b. Beverly, Md., 1869; d. Washington, D.C., Aug. 29, 1931. [10]

Dennis, Charles Henry, journalist, b. Decatur, Ill., 1860; d. Evanston, Ill., Sept. 25, 1943. [7; 10]

Dennis, David Worth, botanist, b. Economy, Ind., 1849; d. Richmond, Ind., May 13, 1916. [10]

Dennis, Frederic Shepard, surgeon, b. Newark, N.J., 1850; d. New York, N.Y., March 8, 1934. [1a; 4; 10]

Dennis, James Shepard, missionary, b. Newark, N.J., 1842; d. Montclair, N.J., March 21, 1914. [1; 4; 10]

Dennis, James Teakle, archaeologist, b. Baltimore, Md., 1865; d. Woodbrook, Md., April 1, 1918. [10]

Dennis, Louis Munroe, chemist, b. Chicago, Ill., 1863; d. Ithaca, N.Y., Dec. 9, 1936. [10; 13]

Denny, Sir Cecil Edward, Bart., historian, b. 1850; d. Edmonton, Alta., July 24, 1928. [27]

Denny, Collins, bishop, b. Winchester, Va., 1854; d. Richmond, Va., May 12, 1943. [10; 11]

Denny, Harold Norman, war correspondent, b. Des Moines, Ia., 1889; d. Des Moines, Ia., July 3, 1945. [7; 10]

Denny, Walter Bell, clergyman, b. Newark, N.J., 1882; d. London, England, June 23, 1937. [62]

Denslow, Van Buren, economist, b. Yonkers, N.Y., 1833; d. New York, N.Y., July 17, 1902. [6]

Denslow, William Wallace, illustrator, b. Philadelphia, Pa., 1856; d. New York, N.Y., March 27, 1915. [7; 10]

Densmore, Hiram Delos, botanist, b. Richmond, Wis., 1862; d. Beloit, Wis., July 18, 1940. [10; 11]

Dent, John Charles, journalist and historian, b. Kendal, England, 1841; d. Toronto, Ont., Sept. 27, 1888. [27]

Denton, Vernon Llewllyn, educationist, b. Shediac, N.B., 1881; d. Victoria, B.C., May 24, 1944.

Depew, Chauncey Mitchell, lawyer, politician, and after-dinner speaker, b. Peekskill, N.Y., 1834; d. New York, N.Y., April 5, 1928. [1; 2; 3; 4; 7; 8; 10]

De Peyster, John Watts, soldier and historian, b. New York, N.Y., 1821; d. New York, N.Y., May 4, 1907. [1; 2; 3; 4; 5; 6; 7; 8; 10]

De Puy, Henry Walter, historian, b. Pompey Hill, N.Y., 1820, d. Feb. 2, 1876. [1; 8]

De Puy, William Harrison, clergyman, b. Penn Yan, N.Y., 1821; d. Canaan, Conn., Sept. 4, 1901. [10]

De Quille, Dan (pseud.). See Wright, William [1829-1898]

Derby, Elias Hasket, lawyer, b. Salem, Mass., 1803; d. Boston, Mass., March 31, 1880. [1; 3; 4; 8]

Derby, George, sanitarian, b. Salem, Mass., 1819; d. Boston, Mass., June 20, 1874. [3; 51]

Derby, George Horatio, humorist, b. Dedham, Mass., 1823; d. New York, N.Y., May 15, 1861. [1; 3; 4; 7; 8]

Derby, James Cephas, publisher, b. Little Falls, N.Y., 1818; d. Brooklyn, N.Y., Sept. 20, 1892. [3; 4; 7]

Derby, John Barton, lawyer and poet, b. Salem, Mass., 1792; d. Boston, Mass., 1867. [3; 4; 8]

De Roo, Peter, priest and historian, b. 1839; d. Sept. 7, 1926. [21]

De Roussy de Sales, Raoul Jean Jacques François journalist, b. 1896; d. New York, N.Y., Dec. 3, 1942.

Derr, Louis, physicist, b. Pottsville, Pa., 1868; d. Brookline, Mass., May 12, 1923. [10; 13]

Dery, Desiderius George, manufacturer, b. Austria, 1867; d. Bethlehem, Pa., March 5, 1942. [10]

Desaulniers, François Sévère Lesieur, genealogist, b. Yamachiche, Que., 1850; d. Montreal, Que., Jan. 28, 1913. [27]

Desautels, Joseph, priest, b. Chambly, Lower Canada, 1814; d. Salem, Mass., Aug. 4, 1881. [27]

De Schweinitz, Edmund Alexander, bishop and historian, b. Bethlehem, Pa., 1825; d. Bethlehem, Pa., Dec. 18, 1887. [1; 3; 5; 6]

Des Ecorres, Charles (pseud.). See Chartrand, Joseph Demers.

Deshler, Charles Dunham, scientist, b. 1863; d. New Brunswick, N.J., April 14, 1943.

Deshon, George, priest, b. New London, Conn., 1823; d. New York, N.Y., Dec. 30, 1903. [6; 10; 21]

Desjardins, Louis Georges, civil servant, b. St. Jean Port Joli, Que., 1849; d. Montreal, Que., June 8, 1928. [27]

De Sloovere, Frederick Joseph, lawyer and educationist, b. Salem, Mass., 1887; d. Yonkers, N.Y., June 16, 1945.

Desmazures, Adam Charles Gustave, priest, b. Nogent-sur-Seine, France, 1818; d. Montreal, Que., Sept. 29, 1891. [27; 32]

De Smet, Pierre Jean, missionary, b. Termonde, Belgium, 1801; d. St. Louis, Mo., May 23, 1873. [1; 3; 4; 6]

Desmond, Humphrey Joseph, lawyer, b. Ozaukee county, Wis., 1858; d. Milwaukee, Wis., Feb. 16, 1932. [10; 44]

De Sola, Abraham, rabbi, b. London, England, 1825; d. New York, N.Y., June 5, 1882. [3; 29]

Desroches, J. Israel, physician, b. St. Esprit, Que., 1850; d. Montreal, Que., Nov. 25, 1922. [27]

Dessaulles, Louis Antoine, politician, b. St. Hyacinthe, Lower Canada, 1819; d. Paris, France, Aug. 5, 1895. [27]

Desti, Mrs. Mary, biographer, d. New York, N.Y., April 12 ,1931.

Des Voignes, Jules Verne, novelist, b. Marcellus, Mich., 1886; d. 1911. [39]

Deutsch, Gotthard, educationist, b. Austria, 1859; d. Cincinnati, O., Oct. 14, 1921. [1; 10]

De Veaux, Richard (pseud.). See Andrews, Mrs. Gwendolyn, née Foulke.

Develin, Mrs. Dora, née Harvey, local historian, d. Bryn Mawr, Pa., Nov. 11, 1940.

Devere, Mary Ainge, poet, fl. 1870-1915. [4]

Devereux, Mary, poet and novelist, b. Marblehead, Mass., d. Englewood, N.J., Feb. 19, 1914. [10]

Deville, Edouard Gaston, surveyor, b. France, 1849; d. Ottawa, Ont., Sept. 21, 1924. [27]

Devine, Edward James, priest, b. near Ottawa, Ont., 1860; d. Toronto, Ont., Nov. 5, 1927. [27]

Devine, Edward Thomas, educationist and social worker, b. Union, Ia., 1867; d. Chicago, Ill., Feb. 27, 1948. [4; 10; 11]

De Vinne, Daniel, clergyman, b. Londonderry, Ireland, 1793; d. Morrisania, N.Y., Feb. 10, 1883. [3; 8]

De Vinne, Theodore Low, printer, b. Stamford, Conn., 1828; d. New York, N.Y., Feb. 16, 1914. [1; 2; 3; 4; 6; 7; 8; 10]

Devins, John Bancroft, editor, b. New York, N.Y., 1856; d. 1911. [10]

Devoy, John, journalist, b. county Kildare, Ireland, 1842; d. Atlantic City, N.J., Sept. 29, 1928. [1]

De Vries, John Hendrik, clergyman, b. 1859; d. Old Saybrook, Conn., Feb. 3, 1939. [11]

De Vries, William Levering, clergyman, b. Baltimore, Md., 1865; d. Washington, D.C., March 14, 1937. [10]

Dew, Thomas Roderick, political economist, b. King and Queen county, Va., 1802; d. Paris, France, Aug. 6, 1846. [1; 3; 4; 8]

Dewart, Edward Hartley, clergyman and poet, b. county Cavan, Ireland, 1828; d. Toronto, Ont., June 17, 1903. [27]

Dewe, Joseph Adelbert, priest and historian, b. Ramsgate, England, 1866; d. San Antonio, Tex., 1935. [10; 21]

Dewees, William Potts, physician, b. Pottsgrove, Pa., 1768; d. Philadelphia, Pa., May 18, 1841. [1; 3; 8]

Dewey, Albert Peter, intelligence officer, b. Chicago, Ill., 1916; d. Saigon, Indo-China, Sept. 26, 1945. [62]

Dewey, Davis Rich, economist, b. Burlington, Vt., 1858; d. Cambridge, Mass., Dec. 13, 1942. [10]

Dewey, George, admiral, b. Montpelier, Vt., 1837; d. Washington, D.C., Jan. 16, 1917. [1; 2; 4; 10]

Dewey, Mary Elizabeth, biographer, b. Gloucester, Mass., 1821; d. Boston, Mass., June 4, 1910. [10]

Dewey, Melvil, librarian, b. Adams Centre, N.Y., 1851; d. Lake Placid, Fla., Dec. 26, 1931. [1a; 2; 4; 7; 10; 11]

Dewey, Orville, clergyman, b. Sheffield, Mass., 1794; d. Sheffield, Mass., March 21, 1882. [1; 3; 4; 7; 8]

Dewey, Willis Alonzo, physician, b. Middlebury, Vt., 1858; d. Middlebury, Vt., April 2, 1938. [10; 11]

Dewhurst, Edward Bury, dentist and tennis-player, b. Sydney, Australia, 1870; d. Philadelphia, Pa., Feb. 25, 1941.

Dewhurst, Frederic Eli, clergyman, b. Bradford, Me., 1855; d. Chicago, Ill., 1906. [10]

Dewing, Mrs. Maria Richards, née Oakey, artist, b. New York, N.Y., 1845; d. New York, N.Y., Dec. 13, 1927. [1; 10]

De Witt, Benjamin, physician, b. 1774; d. New York, N.Y., 1819. [8]

De Witt, John, clergyman, b. Albany, N.Y., 1821; d. Irvington, N.Y., Oct. 19, 1906. [3; 8; 10]

De Witt, Julia A. Woodhull, novelist and biographer, b. Harrisburg, Pa.; d. Carlisle, Pa., 1906. [10]

De Witt, Simeon, surveyor, b. Ulster county, N.Y., 1756; d. Ithaca, N.Y., Dec. 3, 1834. [1; 3; 4; 8]

De Wolf, Philip, chemist, b. 1880; d. Jan. 2, 1934. [47]

Dexter, Edwin Grant, educationist, b. Calais, Me., 1868; d. Lorton, Va., Dec. 5, 1938. [10; 47]

Dexter, Franklin Bowditch, librarian and historian, b. Fairhaven, Mass., 1842; d. New Haven, Conn., Aug. 13, 1920. [1; 4; 7; 10; 62]

Dexter, Henry Martyn, clergyman, b. Plympton, Mass., 1821; d. New Bedford, Mass., Nov. 13, 1890. [1; 3; 4; 8]

Dexter, Henry Morton, clergyman, b. Manchester, N.H., 1846; d. Edgartown, Martha's Vineyard, Mass., Oct. 29, 1910. [2; 10; 62]

Dexter, Samuel, merchant, b. Dedham, Mass., 1726; d. Mendon, Mass., June 10, 1810. [1; 3]

Dexter, Samuel, lawyer, b. Boston, Mass., 1761; d. Athens, N.Y., May 4, 1816. [1; 3; 4; 8]

Dexter, Seymour, lawyer and banker, b. Independence, N.Y., 1841; d. Elmira, N.Y., 1904. [10]

Dexter, Timothy, merchant, b. Malden, Mass., 1747; d. Newburyport, Mass., Oct. 23, 1806. [1; 3; 4; 7]

Dey, Frederick Van Rensselaer, novelist, b. 1865; d. New York, N.Y., April 26, 1922. [2a; 7]

Diaz, Mrs. Abby née Morton, novelist and feminist, b. Plymouth, Mass., 1821; d. Belmont, Mass., April 1, 1904. [1; 4; 7; 8; 10]

Dibble, Roy Floyd, biographer, b. Portland, N.Y., 1887; d. New York, N.Y., Dec. 3, 1929. [7; 10]

Dibble, Sheldon, missionary, b. Skaneateles, N.Y., 1809; d. Hawaiian Islands, Jan. 22, 1845. [3; 8]

Dick, William Brisbane, entertainer, b. 1827; d. 1901.

Dickerman, Edward Dwight, genealogist, b. 1827; d. 1907.

Dickerman, George Sherwood, clergyman, b. Mount Carmel, Conn., 1843; d. New Haven, Conn., Aug. 3, 1937. [10; 62]

Dickerson, Mary Cynthia, naturalist, b. Hastings, Mich., 1866; d. April 8, 1923. [10; 39]

Dickerson, Philemon, jurist and local historian, b. Succasunna, N.J., 1788; d. Paterson, N.J., Dec. 10, 1862. [1; 3; 4]

Dickerson, Roy Ernest, geologist, b. 1877; d. Kansas City, Mo., Feb. 24, 1944. [11; 12]

Dickey, Adam Herbert, Christian scientist, b. Toronto, Ont., 1864; d. Cohasset, Mass., Feb. 8, 1925. [10]

Dickey, John McElroy, clergyman, b. York district, S.C., 1789; d. near New Washington, Ind., Nov. 21, 1849. [3]

Dickey, Paul, playwright, b. 1885; d. New York, N.Y., Jan. 8, 1933. [2a]

Dickie, George William, naval architect, b. Arbroath, Scotland, 1844; d. San Mateo, Calif., Aug. 16, 1918. [2; 4; 10]

Dickie, James Francis, clergyman, b. Kilmarnock, Scotland, 1851; d. Detroit, Mich., May 28, 1933. [10]

Dickinson, Andrew, poet, b. 1801; d. 1883.

Dickinson, Anna Elizabeth, lecturer, b. Philadelphia, Pa., 1842; d. Goshen, N.Y., Oct. 22, 1932. [3; 4; 6; 7; 10]

Dickinson, Charles Henry, clergyman, b. West Springfield, Mass., 1857; d. Pleasantville, N.Y., April 14, 1938. [10; 11; 62]

Dickinson, Charles Monroe, lawyer, journalist, and diplomat, b. near Lowville, N.Y., 1842; d. Binghampton, N.Y., July 3, 1924. [1; 4; 7; 10]

Dickinson, Clinton Roy, journalist and soldier, b. Newark, N.J., 1888; d. Washington, D.C., Feb. 23, 1943. [7; 10]

Dickinson, Cornelius Evarts, clergyman, b. Heath, Mass., 1835; d. Marietta, O., March 7, 1925. [45]

Dickinson, Edward, musician, b. West Springfield, O., 1853; d. 1935. [7; 20; 45]

Dickinson, Emily, poet, b. Amherst, Mass., 1830; d. Amherst, Mass., May 15, 1886. [1; 4; 7; 72]

Dickinson, James Taylor, clergyman, b. Richmond, Va., 1861; d. Rochester, N.Y., April 20, 1929. [10]

Dickinson, John, publicist, b. Talbot county, Md., 1732; d. Wilmington, Del., Feb. 14, 1808. [1; 3; 4; 7; 8]

Dickinson, John Woodbridge, educationist, b. Chester, Mass., 1825; d. Newton, Mass., Feb. 16, 1901. [1; 61]

Dickinson, Jonathan, jurist, b. England; d. Philadelphia, Pa., 1722. [4; 8]

Dickinson, Jonathan, clergyman, b. Hatfield, Mass., 1688; d. Elizabethtown, N.J., Oct. 7, 1747. [1; 4; 62]

Dickinson, Marquis Fayette, lawyer, b. Amherst, Mass., 1840; d. North Amherst, Mass., Sept. 18, 1915. [10; 45]

Dickinson, Mrs. Mary, née Lowe, educationist, b. Fitchburg, Mass., 1839; d. June, 1914. [10]

Dickinson, Richard William, clergyman, b. New York, N.Y., 1804; d. Fordham, N.Y., Aug. 16, 1874. [3; 8; 62]

Dickinson, Rodolphus, clergyman, b. Deerfield, Mass., 1787; d. Deerfield, Mass., 1863, [62]

Dickinson, Roy, See Dickinson, Clinton Roy.

Dickman, Joseph Theodore, soldier, b. Dayton, O., 1857; d. Washington, D.C., Oct. 23, 1927. [1; 2; 4]

Dickson, Andrew Flinn, clergyman, b. Charleston, S.C., 1825; d. Tuscaloosa, Ala., Jan. 8, 1879. [3; 8; 34]

Dickson, David, agriculturist, b. Hancock county, Ga., 1809; d. Hancock county, Ga., Feb. 18, 1885. [1]

Dickson, Ernest Charles, educationist, b. Newmarket, Ont., 1881; d. near Eureka, Calif., Aug. 23, 1939.

Dickson, Frederick Stoever, lawyer and industrialist, b. Utica, N.Y., 1850; d. Philadelphia, Pa., Dec. 1, 1925. [10]

Dickson, John, lawyer and politician, b. Keene, N.H., 1783; d. West Bloomfield, N.Y., Feb. 22, 1852. [3; 4; 8]

Dickson, Samuel Henry, physician, b. Charleston, S.C., 1798; d. Philadelphia, Pa., March 31, 1872. [1; 3; 4; 8]

Didcoct, John Joseph, educationist, b. Danville, Ill., 1882; d. Nashville, Tenn., Oct. 19, 1927. [10]

Didier, Eugene Le Moine, littérateur, b. Baltimore, Md., 1838; d. Baltimore, Md., Sept. 8, 1913. [1; 3; 4; 7; 10]

Didier, Franklin James, physician, b. Baltimore, Md., 1784; d. Baltimore, Md., 1840. [3; 4; 8]

Didwin, Isaac (pseud.). See Sturdy, Wilfiam Allen.

Diehl, Samuel Willauer Black, naval officer, b. Reading, Pa., 1851; d. 1909. [10]

Diemer, Hugo, industrial engineer, b. Cincinnati, O., 1870; d. Chicago, Ill., March 3, 1937. [10; 11]

Dienst, George Elias, physician, b. Hamilton county, Ind., 1858; d. Aurora, Ill., April 10, 1932. [10]

Dieserud, Juul, library cataloguer, b. Norway, 1861; d. Montclair, N.J., Nov. 11, 1947.

Dietz, Ella. See Clymer, Mrs. Ella Maria. née Dietz.

Diggs, Mrs. Annie, née Le Porte, journalist, b. London, Ont., 1853; d. Sept. 7, 1916. [10]

Dill, James Brooks, jurist, b. Spencerport, N.Y., 1854; d. East Orange, N.J., Dec. 2, 1910. [4; 10; 62]

Dillard, James Hardy, educationist, b. Nansemond, Va., 1856; d. Charlottesville, Va., Aug. 2, 1940. [7; 10; 11]

Dillaway, Charles Knapp, educationist, b. 1804; d. 1889. [51]

Dillaye, Stephen Devalson, lawyer, b. Plymouth, N.Y., 1820; d. 1884. [3; 8]

Diller, Joseph Silas, geologist, b. Plainfield, Pa., 1850; d. Washington, D.C., Nov. 13, 1928. [1a; 4; 10]

Dillingham, Frances Bent, novelist, b. Chelsea, Mass.; d. ? [7]

Dillingham, John Hoag, educationist, b. West Falmouth, Mass., 1839; d. Philadelphia, Pa., March 15, 1910. [10; 51]

Dillon, John Brown, librarian and historian, b. Wellsburgh, W. Va., 1808; d. Indianapolis, Ind., Feb. 27, 1879. [7]

Dillon, John Forrest, jurist, b. Montgomery county, N.Y., 1831; d. New York, N.Y., May 6, 1914. [1; 4; 10]

Dillon, John Milton, lawyer, b. Davenport, Ia., 1868; d. Far Hills, N.J., Feb. 16, 1911. [37]

Dillon, Mrs. Mary C., née Johnson, novelist, b. Carlisle, Pa.; d. St Louis, Mo., 1923. [10; 34]

Diman, Jeremiah Lewis, clergyman and educationist, b. Bristol, R.I., 1831; d. Providence, R.I., Feb. 3, 1881. [1; 3; 4; 8]

Dimitry, Charles Patton, novelist, b. Washington, D.C., 1837; d. New Orleans, La., Nov. 10, 1910. [1; 3; 4; 7; 8; 10; 34]

Dimitry, John Bull Smith, journalist, b. Washington, D.C., 1835; d. 1901. [3; 8; 10; 34

Dimmick, Luther F., clergyman, b. Shaftsbury, Vt., 1790; d. Newburyport, Mass., May 16, 1860. [43]

Dimmock, George, biologist, b. Springfield, Mass., 1852; d. Springfield, Mass., May 17, 1930. [10; 13; 51]

Dimock, Anthony Weston, broker and novelist, b. Yarmouth, N.S., 1842; d. Happy Valley, N.Y., Sept. 12, 1918. [10]

Dimock, Julian Anthony, photographer, b. Elizabeth, N.J., 1873; d. East Corinth, Vt., Sept. 21, 1945. [11]

Dingley, Edward Nelson, journalist and politician, b. Auburn, Me., 1862; d. Washington, D.C., March 18, 1930. [4; 10]

Dinkins, James, soldier and banker, b. Madison county, Miss., 1845; d. New Orleans, La., July 19, 1939. [10; 34]

Dinnies, Mrs. Anna Peyre, née Shackleford, poet, b. Georgetown, S.C., 1816; d. New Orleans, La., Aug. 8, 1886. [3; 4; 8; 34]

Dinsmoor, Robert, poet, b. Windham, N.H., 1757; d. Windham, N.H., March 16, 1836. [1; 3; 4; 7]

Dinsmore, Charles Allen, clergyman, b. New York, N.Y., 1860; d. New Haven, Conn., Aug. 14, 1941. [7; 10; 11; 49; 62]

Dinsmore, John Walker, clergyman, b. Washington county, Pa., 1839; d. Los Gatos, Calif., April 2, 1922. [10]

Dinwiddie, Courtenay, sociologist, b. Alexandria, Va., 1882; d. New York, N.Y., Sept., 13, 1943. [10]

Dinwiddle, William, journalist, b. Charlottesville, Va., 1867; d. Washington, D.C., June 17, 1934. [10]

Dionne, Charles Eusèbe, naturalist, b. St. Denis de la Bouteillerie, Que., 1846; d. Quebec, Que., Jan. 25, 1925. [27]

Dionne, Narcisse Eutrope, historian and bibliographer, b. St. Denis de la Bouteillerie, Que., 1848; d. Quebec, Que., March 30, 1917. [27]

Disosway, Gabriel Poillon, antiquary, b. New York, N.Y., 1799; d. Staten Island, N.Y., July 9, 1868. [3; 8]

Disturnell, John, compiler of guide-books, b. Lansingburg, N.Y., 1801; d. New York, N.Y., Oct. 1, 1877. [1; 3; 4; 7; 8]

Dithmar, Edward Augustus, journalist, b. New York, N.Y., 1854; d. New York, N.Y., Oct. 16, 1917. [7; 10]

Ditman, Norman Edward, physician, b. Brooklyn, N.Y., 1877; d. Palm Beach, Fla., Dec. 15, 1944. [62]

Ditmars, Raymond Lee, naturalist, b. Newark, N.J., 1876; d. New York, N.Y., May 12, 1942. [7; 10; 11]

Ditrichstein, Leo, actor and playwright, b. Austria, 1865; d. Austria, June 28, 1928. [1; 4; 7; 10]

Ditson, George Leighton, traveller and novelist, b. Westford, Mass., 1812; d. New York, N.Y., Jan. 29, 1895. [1; 3; 4; 7; 8]

Dix, Dorothea Lynde, humanitarian and writer of books for children, b. Hampden, Me., 1802; d. Trenton, N.J., July 17, 1887. [1; 3; 4; 7; 8]

Dix, Edwin Asa, novelist and historian, b. Newark, N.Y., 1860; d. New York, N.Y., Aug. 25, 1911. [7; 10]

Dix, John Adams, soldier and politician, b. Boscawen, N.H., 1798; d. New York, N.Y., April 21, 1879. [1; 3; 4; 8]

Dix, John Homer, ophthalmologist, b. Boston, Mass., 1811; d. Boston, Mass., Aug. 25, 1884. [1; 3; 4; 8]

Dix, Morgan, clergyman, b. New York, N.Y., 1827; d. New York, N.Y., April 29, 1908. [1; 3; 4; 6; 7; 8; 10]

Dixon, Amzi Clarence, clergyman, b. Shelby, N.C., 1854; d. June 15, 1925. [2; 10; 34]

Dixon, Benjamin Homer, genealogist and religious writer, b. Amsterdam, Holland, 1819; d. Toronto, Ont., 1899. [31]

Dixon, Clarice Madeleine, educationist, b. Middleville, N.Y., 1889; d. New York, N.Y., Dec. 22, 1945.

Dixon, Frederick Augustus, playwright, b. England, 1843; d. Ottawa, Ont., 1919. [27]

Dixon, James Main, educationist, b. Paisley, Scotland, 1856; d. Los Angeles, Calif., Sept. 27, 1933. [2; 7; 10; 11]

Dixon, Joseph Kossuth, clergyman, b. Hemlock Lake, N.Y., 1856; d. Philadelphia, Pa., Aug. 24, 1926.

Dixon, Roland Burrage, anthropologist, b. Worcester, Mass., 1875; d. Cambridge, Mass., Dec. 20, 1934. [1a; 2; 4; 7 ;10; 51]

Dixon, Mrs. Susan, née **Bullitt,** historian, b. Oxmoor, Ky., 1829; d. Henderson, Ky., 1907. [4; 10]

Dixon, Thomas, clergyman and novelist, b. Shelby, N.C., 1864; d. Raleigh, N.C., April 3, 1946. [7; 10; 11]

Dixson, Zella Allen, librarian, b. Zanesville, O., 1858; d. Chicago, Ill., Jan. 12, 1924. [7; 10]

Doan, Frank Carleton, clergyman, b. Nelsonville, O., 1877; d. Rochester, N.Y., May 14, 1927. [10]

Doane, George Hobart, priest, b. Boston, Mass., 1830; d. Newark, N.J., Jan. 22, 1905. [3; 4; 8; 10]

Doane, George Washington, bishop, b. Trenton, N.J., 1799; d. April 27, 1859. [1; 3; 4; 7; 8]

Doane, William Croswell, bishop, b. Boston, Mass., 1832; d. Albany, N.Y., May 17, 1913. [1; 2; 3; 4; 7; 8; 10]

Dobbins, Frank Stockton, clergyman, b. Philadelphia, Pa., 1855; d. Philadelphia, Pa., July 22, 1916; [47]

Dobie, Charles Caldwell, novelist and playwright, b. San Francisco, Calif., 1881; d. San Francisco, Calif., Jan. 11, 1943. [7; 10; 11; 35]

Dobyns, William Ray, clergyman, b. Columbus, Mo., 1861; d. Birmingham, Ala., Jan. 26, 1932. [10]

Dock, Lavinia L., nurse, b. 1858; d. ?

Docking, James Tippet, clergyman, b. Cornwall, England, 1861; d. Holly Springs, Miss., March 23, 1916. [10]

Dod, Albert Baldwin, clergyman and educationist, b. 1805; d. Princeton, N.J., 1845. [56]

Dodd, Mrs. Anna Bowman, née **Blake,** journalist and traveller, b. Long Island, N.Y., 1855; d. Paris, France, Jan. 29, 1929. [8]

Dodd, Derrick (pseud.). See Gassaway, Franklin Harrison.

Dodd, Ira Seymour, clergyman, b. Bloomfield, N.J., 1842; d. Matunuck, R.I., Aug. 3, 1922. [10; 62]

Dodd, Lee Wilson, novelist, poet, and playwright, b. Franklin, Pa., 1879; d. New York, N.Y., May 16, 1933. [1a; 2; 7; 10; 11]

Dodd, Stephen, clergyman, b. Bloomfield, N.J., 1777; d. Morristown, N.J., Feb. 5, 1856. [3; 7; 62]

Dodd, William Edward, historian and diplomat, b. Clayton, N.C., 1869; d. near Round Hill, Va., Feb. 9, 1940. [7; 10; 12; 34]

Doddridge, Joseph, clergyman, b. near Bedford, Pa., 1769; d. Morristown, N.J., Feb. 5, 1856. [1; 3; 7; 8]

Dodds, Samuel, educationist, b. Prospect, Pa., 1858; d. Princeton, N.J., Dec. 26, 1947.

Dodge, Charles Wright, biologist, b. Cape Vincent, N.Y., 1863; d. Rochester, N. Y., April 16, 1934. [10; 11]

Dodge, Daniel Kilham, educationist, b. Brooklyn, N.Y., 1863; d. Pasadena, Calif., Oct. 13, 1933. [10]

Dodge, David Low, pacifist, b. Brooklyn, Conn., 1774; d. New York, N.Y., April 23, 1852. [1; 3; 4; 8]

Dodge, Ebenezer, theologian, b. Salem, Mass., 1819; d. Hamilton, N.Y., Jan. 4, 1890. [1; 3; 4; 8]

Dodge, Grenville Mellen, civil engineer, b. Danvers, Mass., 1831; d. Council Bluffs, Ia., Jan. 3, 1916. [10; 37]

Dodge, Henry Irving, novelist and playwright, b. Oswego county, N.Y., 1861; d. New York, N.Y., July 28, 1934. [7; 10]

Dodge, Henry Nehemiah, poet, b. New York, N.Y., 1843; d. Morristown, N.J., July 24, 1937. [7; 10]

Dodge, Louise Preston, educationist, b. Salem, Mass., 1869; d. Keene, N.H., Jan. 11, 1920. [62]

Dodge, Mary Abigail, miscellaneous writer, b. Hamilton, Mass., 1833; d. Hamilton, Mass., Aug. 17, 1896. [1; 2; 3; 4; 6; 7; 8]

DICTIONARY OF NORTH AMERICAN AUTHORS

123

Dodge, Mrs. Mary Elizabeth, née Mapes, story-writer and poet, b. New York, N.Y., 1831; d. Onteora Park, in the Catskills, N.Y., Aug. 21, 1905. [1; 2; 3; 4; 6; 7; 8; 72]

Dodge, Nathaniel Shatswell, journalist, b. Haverhill, Mass., 1810; d. Boston, Mass., Feb. 2, 1874. [3; 4; 8]

Dodge, Raymond, psychologist, b. Woburn, Mass., 1871; d. Tryon, N.C., April 8, 1942. [10; 11]

Dodge, Richard Irving, soldier, b. Huntsville, N.C., 1827; d. June 16, 1895. [4; 7]

Dodge, Theodore Ayrault, military historian, b. Pittsfield, Mass., 1842; d. near Nanteuil-le-Haudouin, France, Oct. 25, 1909. [1; 3; 7; 8]

Dods, John Bovee, spiritualist, b. New York, N.Y., 1795; d. Brooklyn, N.Y., March 21, 1872. [1; 3; 4; 8]

Doe, Charles Henry, journalist and novelist, b. Charlestown, Mass., 1838; d. Saint John, N.B., Aug. 15, 1900. [3; 8]

Doerflinger, Mrs. Helen Joy, née Homer. See Homer, Joy.

Doermann, Henry John, educationist, b. Hickory, N.C., 1890; d. Toledo, O., Nov. 20, 1932. [10]

Doesticks, Q. K. Philander (pseud.). See Thomson, Mortimer Neal.

Doggett, Daniel Seth, clergyman, b. Virginia, 1810; d. Richmond, Va., Oct. 27, 1880. [3; 8; 34]

Dohan, Mrs. Edith, née Hall, archaeologist, b. New Haven, Conn., 1877; d. Philadelphia, Pa., July 14, 1943.

Doherty, Patrick, priest, b. Quebec, Lower Canada, 1838; d. Quebec, Que., 1872. [3; 27]

Doherty, Philip Joseph, lawyer, b. Charlestown, Mass., 1856; d. Washington, D.C., April 15, 1928. [10]

Doin, Ernest, playwright, b. Bourges, France, 1809; d. Montreal, Que., Sept. 26, 1891. [27]

Dolbear, Amos Emerson, educationist and inventor, b. Norwich, Conn., 1837; d. Medford, Mass., Feb. 23, 1910. [10]

Dole, Charles Fletcher, clergyman, b. Brewer, Me., 1845; d. Boston, Mass., Nov. 27, 1927. [1; 2; 4; 7; 10; 11]

Dole, Edmund Pearson, lawyer, b. Skowhegan, Me., 1850; d. Jamaica Plains, Mass., Dec. 31, 1928. [10]

Dole, George Henry, clergyman, b. 1857; d. Wilmington, Del., Oct. 17, 1942.

Dole, Nathan Haskell, littérateur, b. Chelsea, Mass., 1852; d. Yonkers, N.Y., May 9, 1935. [1a; 2; 4; 7; 10; 11]

Dollar, Robert, shipowner, b. Falkirk, Scotland, 1844; d. San Rafael, Calif., May 16, 1932. [1a; 10; 27]

Dollard, James Bernard, priest and poet, b. Kilkenny county, Ireland, 1872; d. Toronto, Ont., April 28, 1946. [21; 30]

Donaghey, George W., politician, b. Oakland, La., 1856; d. Little Rock, Ark., Dec. 15, 1937. [10]

Donahoe, Daniel Joseph, lawyer and poet, b. Brimfield, Mass., 1853; d. Middletown, Conn., 1930. [10; 21]

Donahue, Lester Bernard, lawyer, b. Portland, Me., 1880; d. Upper Montclair, N.J., Oct. 31, 1941.

Donald, Elijah Winchester, clergyman, b. Andover, Mass., 1848; d. Ipswich, Mass., Aug. 6, 1904. [10; 45]

Donaldson, Alfred Lee, historian, b. 1866; d. Saranac Lake, N.Y., Nov. 6, 1923. [4]

Donaldson, Francis, physician, b. Baltimore, Md., 1823; d. Baltimore, Md., Dec. 9, 1891. [3; 8; 76]

Donaldson, Henry Herbert, neurologist, b. Yonkers, N.Y., 1857; d. West Philadelphia, Pa., Jan. 23, 1938. [4; 10; 62]

Donaldson, James Lowry, soldier, b. Baltimore, Md., 1814; d. Baltimore, Md., Nov. 4, 1885. [3; 4; 8; 34]

Donaldson, Thomas Corwin, lawyer, b. Columbus, O., 1843; d. Philadelphia, Pa., Nov. 18, 1898. [36]

Donehoo, George Patterson, clergyman and historian, b. Connellsville, Pa., 1862; d. Harrisburg, Pa., Jan. 11, 1934. [10]

Donlevy, Mrs. Harriet, née Farley, journalist, b. Claremount, N.H., 1817; d. New York, N.Y., Nov. 15, 1907. [1; 3; 6; 8; 10]

Donnell, Mrs. Annie, née Hamilton, novelist, b. Kents Hill, Me., 1862; d. ? [7; 11]

Donnell, Robert, clergyman, b. Guilford, N.C., 1784; d. Athens, Ala., May 24, 1855. [1]

Donnelly, Charles Francis, lawyer and poet, b. Athlone, Ireland, 1836; d. Boston, Mass., Jan. 31, 1909. [1; 4]

Donnelly, Eleanor Cecilia, poet, b. Philadelphia, Pa., 1838; d. West Chester, Pa., April 30, 1917. [4; 7; 10]

Donnelly, Harold Irvin, religious educationist, b. Salt Lake City, Utah, 1892; d. Auburn, N.Y., July 10, 1937. [10; 11]

Donnelly, Ignatius, politician and littérateur, b. Philadelphia, Pa., 1831; d. Nininger, Minn., Jan. 1, 1900. [1; 3; 4; 7; 10; 21]

Donnelly, Joseph Gordon, novelist, b. Milwaukee, Wis., 1856; d. May 10, 1915. [10]

Donovan, Joseph Wesley, jurist, b. Toledo, O., 1839; d. Detroit, Mich., June 17, 1933. [39]

D'Ooge, Benjamin Leonard, educationist, b. Grand Rapids, Mich., 1860; d. Allentown, Pa., March 7, 1940. [7; 11]

D'Ooge, Martin Luther, educationist, b. Holland, 1839; d. Ann Arbor, Mich., Sept. 12, 1915. [1; 4; 7; 10]

Dooley, John Henry, priest, b. 1866; d. New York, N.Y., Dec. 3, 1934. [21]

Doolittle, Benjamin, clergyman and physician, b. Wallingford, Conn., 1695; d. Northfield, Mass., Jan. 9, 1748-9. [3; 8; 62]

Doolittle, Charles Leander, astronomer, b. Ontario, Ind., 1843; d. Philadelphia, Pa., March 3, 1919. [1; 4; 10]

Doolittle, Eric, astronomer, b. Ontario, Ind., 1869; d. Philadelphia, Pa., Sept. 21, 1920. [10]

Doolittle, Justus, missionary, b. Rutland, N.Y., 1824; d. Clinton, N.Y., June 15, 1880. [6]

Doolittle, Mary Antoinette, religious enthusiast, b. New Lebanon, N.Y., 1810; d. Mount Lebanon, N.Y., Dec. 31, 1886. [3]

Doolittle, Theodore Sandford, educationist, b. Ovid, N.Y., 1836; d. New Brunswick, N.J., April 18, 1893. [3; 4]

Dopp, Katharine Elizabeth, educationist, b. Belmont, Wis., 1863; d. Chicago, Ill., May 14, 1944. [7; 10; 11]

Doran, James, novelist, b. county Mayo, Ireland, 1837; d. California, Oct. 8, 1917. [35]

Dorchester, Daniel, clergyman, b. Duxbury, Mass., 1827; d. Boston, Mass., March 13, 1907. [1; 8; 10]

Dorchester, Daniel, clergyman, b. Dudley, Mass., 1851; d. Lexington, Mass., Jan. 10, 1944. [4]

Dorgan, John Aylmer, poet, b. Philadelphia, Pa., 1836; d. Philadelphia, Pa., Jan. 1, 1867. [3; 4; 6; 8]

Dorr, Benjamin, clergyman, b. Salisbury, Mass., 1796; d. Germantown, Pa., Sept. 18, 1869. [3; 4; 6; 8]

Dorr, Mrs. Julia Caroline, née **Ripley,** novelist and poet, b. Charlestown, S.C., 1825; d. Rutland, Vt., Jan. 18, 1913. [1; 3; 4; 7; 10; 34]

Dorr, Mrs. Rheta Louise, née **Childe,** feminist, b. 1872; d. New Britain, Pa., Aug. 8, 1948. [11]

Dorrance, Gordon, clergyman, b. Stirling, Conn., 1765; d. Attica, N.Y., 1846. [3; 7]

Dorsey, Mrs. Anna Harrison, née **McKenney,** novelist and poet, b. Georgetown, D.C., 1815; d. Washington, D.C., Dec. 25, 1896. [1; 3; 4; 7; 21; 34]

Dorsey, Anna Vernon. See Williams, Mrs. Anna Vernon, née Dorsey.

Dorsey, Ella Loraine, novelist, b. Washington, D.C., 1853; d. Georgetown, D.C., 1935. [10; 21]

Dorsey, George Amos, anthropologist, b. Hebron, O., Feb. 8, 1868; d. New York, N.Y., March 29, 1931. [1a; 4; 7; 10]

Dorsey, John Syng, surgeon, b. Philadelphia, Pa., 1783; d. Philadelphia, Pa., Nov. 12, 1818. [1; 3]

Dorsey, Mrs. Sarah Anne, née **Ellis,** novelist, b. near Natchez, Miss., 1829; d. New Orleans, La., July 4, 1879. [1; 3; 4; 7; 8; 34]

Dorsheimer, William Edward, politician, b. Lyons, N.Y., 1832; d. Savannah, Ga., March 26, 1888. [1; 3; 4; 8]

Dosker, Henry Elias, ecclesiastical historian, b. Bunschoten, Netherlands, 1855; d. Louisville, Ky., Dec. 23, 1926. [2a; 10]

Dos Passos, John Randolph, lawyer, b. Philadelphia, Pa., 1844; d. New York, N.Y., Jan. 27, 1917. [1; 10]

Dos Passos, Mrs. Katherine, née **Smith,,** novelist, b. about 1897; d. Wareham, Mass., Sept. 12, 1947.

Doster, William Emile, lawyer, b. Bethlehem, Pa., 1837; d. Bethlehem, Pa., July 2, 1919.

Doty, Douglas Zabriskie, editor, b. New York, N.Y., 1874; d. Hollywood, Calif., Jan. 20, 1935. [7; 10]

Double, Luke (pseud.). See Hyde, Thomas Alexander.

Doubleday, Abner, soldier, b. Ballston Spa. N.Y., 1819; d. Mendham, N.J., Jan. 26, 1893. [1; 4; 8]

Doubleday, Mrs. Neltje, née **De Graff,** naturalist, b. Chicago, Ill., 1865; d. Canton, China, Feb. 21, 1918. [1; 4; 10]

Doubleday, Roman (pseud.). See Long, Lily Augusta.

Doubleday, Russell, publisher and writer of books for boys, b. Brooklyn, N.Y., 1872; d. Glen Cove, Long Island, N.Y., June 14, 1949. [7; 10]

Dougall, Lily, novelist, b. Montreal, Que., 1858; d. England, Oct., 1923. [27]

Dougherty, John Hampden, lawyer, b. New York, N.Y., 1849; d. New York, N.Y., Sept. 6, 1918. [4; 10]

Dougherty Raymond Philip, archaeologist, b. Lebanon, Pa., 1877; d. New Haven, Conn., July 13, 1933. [1a; 10; 62]

Doughty, Sir Arthur George, archivist and historian, b. Maidenhead, England, 1860; d. Ottawa, Ont., Dec. 1, 1936. [27]

Douglas, Alice May, poet, b. Bath, Me., 1865; d. Bath, Me., Jan. 6, 1943. [10; 11]

Douglas, Amanda Minnie, writer of books for young people, b. New York, N.Y., 1831; d. Newark, N.J., July 18, 1916. [1; 3; 4; 7; 8]

Douglas, Charles Henry James, educationist, b. 1856; d. New York, N.Y., June 11, 1931. [47]

Douglas, Charles Winfred, clergyman and musician, b. Oswego, N.Y., 1867; d. Santa Rosa, Calif., Jan. 18, 1944. [7; 10]

Douglas, Edith (pseud.). See Burnham, Mrs. Clara Louise, née Root.

Douglas, George William, journalist, b. Liberty, N.Y., 1863; d. Philadelphia, Pa., Feb. 15, 1945. [7; 10]

Douglas, James, engineer and historian, b. Quebec, Que., 1837; d. New York, N.Y., June 25, 1918. [10; 27]

Douglas, Katharine Waldo. See Fedden, Mrs. Katharine Waldo, née Douglas.

Douglas, Marian (pseud.). See Robinson, Mrs. Annie Douglas, née Green.

Douglas, Silas Hamilton, chemist, b. Fredonia, N.Y., 1816; d. Ann Arbor, Mich., Aug. 26, 1890. [4; 6]

Douglass, Benjamin Wallace, entomologist, b. Indianapolis, Ind., 1882; d. Morgantown, Ind., Dec. 6, 1939. [10]

Douglass, Frederick, orator and journalist, b. Talbot county, Md., about 1817; d. Washington, D.C., Feb. 20, 1895. [1; 2; 3; 4; 5; 6; 7; 8; 34]

Douglass, Truman Orville, clergyman, b. Bethel, Ill., 1842; d. Claremont, Calif., Sept. 11, 1925 [10; 37]

Douglass, William, physician, b. Scotland, about 1691; d. Boston, Mass., Oct. 21, 1752. [1; 3; 4]

Doutre, Gonzalve, lawyer, b. Montreal, Que., 1842; d. Montreal, Que., Feb. 28, 1880. [27]

Doutre, Joseph, lawyer, b. Beauharnois, Lower Canada, 1825; d. Montreal, Que., Feb. 3, 1886. [27]

Dove, David James, educationist, b. Portsmouth, England, about 1696; d. Philadelphia, Pa., April 1769. [1; 7]

Dow, jr. (pseud.). See Paige, Elbridge Gerry.

Dow, Charles Mason, banker and historian, b. Randolph, N.Y., 1854; d. Jamestown, N.Y., Dec. 10, 1920. [10]

Dow, Daniel, clergyman, b. Ashford, Conn., 1772; d. Thompson, Conn., July 19, 1849. [3; 4; 8]

Dow, Ethel C. (pseud.). See Kohon, Mrs. Ethel, née Chadowski.

Dow, George Francis, antiquary, b. Wakefield, N.H., 1868; d. Topsfield, Mass., June 5, 1936. [7; 10]

Dow, Lorenzo, evangelist, b. Coventry, Conn., 1777; d. Georgetown, Md., Feb. 2, 1834. [1; 3; 4; 7; 8]

Dow, Louis Henry, educationist, b. Lowell, Mass., 1872; d. Hanover, N.H., March 8, 1944. [10]

Dow, Neal, temperance reformer, b. Portland, Me., 1804; d. Portland, Me., Oct. 2, 1897. [4]

Dowd, Clement, biographer, b. near Carthage,, N.C., 1832; d. Charlotte, N.C., April 15, 1898. [34]

Dowd, Emma C., novelist, b. Meriden, Conn.; d. Meriden, Conn., Dec. 21, 1938. [7; 10; .11]

Dowd, Jane Luella, See Smith, Mrs. Jane Luella, née Dowd.

Dowd, Quincy Lamartine, clergyman, b. Seville, O., 1848; d. Lombard, Ill., April 15, 1936. [11; 62]

Dowe, Jennie Elizabeth Tupper, poet, b. Wilbraham, Mass., 1845; d. Boston, Mass., March 6, 1919. [7; 10]

Dowkontt, George D., medical missionary, b. about 1842; d. 1909.

Dowling, George Thomas, clergyman, b. New York, N.Y., 1849; d. 1928. [4]

Dowling, John, clergyman, b. Pevensey, England, 1807; d. Middletown, N.Y., July 4, 1878. [3; 4; 6; 8]

Dowling, Linnaeus Wayland, mathematician, b. 1867; d. 1928. [13]

Dowling, Morgan E., miscellaneous writer, b. Hull, England, 1845; d. Detroit, Mich., 1896. [39]

Downer, Charles Alfred, educationist, b. Jersey City, N.J., 1866; d. Samåden, Switzerland, Aug. 14, 1930. [10]

Downer, James Walker, educationist, b. Orange county, Va., 1864; d. Waco., Tex., March 19, 1932. [10]

Downes, Alfred Michael, journalist, b. New Haven, Conn., 1862; d. New York, N.Y., Dec. 10, 1907. [62]

Downes, John, mathematician, b. Brooklyn, N.Y., 1799; d. Washington, D.C., Sept. 30, 1882. [3]

Downes, Mrs. Louise, née Corson, political writer, b. Plainfield, N.J., 1857; d. New York, N.Y., Aug. 29, 1940.

Downes, William Howe, journalist and art critic, b. Derby, Conn. 1854; d. Brookline, Mass., Feb. 19, 1941. [7; 10; 11]

Downey, David George, clergyman, b. county Leitrim, Ireland, 1858; d. Mount Vernon, N.Y., March 7, 1935. [10; 60]

Downey, John Florian, educationist, b. Hiramsburg, O., 1846; d. Pasadena, Calif., April 28, 1939. [10]

Downey, June Etta, psychologist, b. Laramie, Wyo., 1872; d. Laramie, Wyo., Oct. 11, 1932. [1a; 10; 11]

Downie, David, missionary, b. 1838; d. India, July 19, 1927. [7; 47]

Downing, Andrew Jackson, landscape gardener and. architect, b. Newburgh, N.Y.. 1815; d. near Yonkers, N.Y., July 28, 1852. [1; 3; 4; 8]

Downing, Charles, horticulturist, b. Newburgh, N.Y., 1802; d. Jan. 18, 1885. [1; 4]

Downing, Fanny Murdaugh. See Downing, Mrs. Frances, née Murdaugh.

Downing, Mrs. Frances, née Murdaugh, poet and novelist, b. Portsmouth, Va., 1835; d. Portsmouth, Va., May 6, 1894. [3; 4; 7; 8; 34]

Downing, Jack (pseud.). See Davis, Charles Augustus.

Downing, Major Jack (pseud.). See Smith, Seba.

Downs, Charles Algernon, clergyman, b. Norwalk, Conn., 1823; d. Lebanon, N.Y., Sept. 20, 1906. [49; 68]

Downs, Mrs. Georgie, See Downs, Mrs. Sarah Elizabeth, née Forbush.

Downs, Mrs. Sarah Elizabeth, née Forbush, novelist, b. Wrentham, Mass., 1843; d. ? [7; 10]

Dowst, Henry Payson, novelist, b. 1876; d. 1921. [51]

Doxtater, Lee Walter, dentist, b. Harold, S.D., 1885; d. New York, N.Y., June 17, 1935. [10]

Doyle, Charles William, physician, b. India, 1852; d. Santa Cruz, Calif., May 2, 1903. [10; 35]

Doyle, Edward, poet, b. 1854; d. ? [7; 21]

Doyle, Francis Xavier, priest and educationist, b. 1886; d. Washington, D.C., Jan. 14, 1928. [21]

Doyle, John M., priest, b. Detroit, Mich., 1884; d. July 14, 1940. [21]

Doyle, Joseph Beatty, historian, b. 1849; d. ?

Doyle, Michael Joseph, poet, b. 1850; d. ? [21; 35]

Doyon, Constant, priest, b. Yamaska, Que.. 1875; d. St. Michel des Saints, Que., Oct. 18, 1927. [27]

Dozier, Orion Theophilus, poet, b. Marion county, Ga., 1848; d. Birmingham,' Ala., Feb. 10, 1925. [4; 34; 77]

Drachman, Bernard, rabbi, b. New York, N.Y., 1861; d. New York, N.Y., March 12, 1945. [7; 10]

Drachsler, Julius, sociologist, b. Czechoslovakia, 1889; d. New York, N.Y., July 22, 1927. [10]

Drake, Alexander Wilson, art director, b. Westfield, N.J., 1843; d. New York, N.Y., Feb. 4, 1916. [1; 4; 10]

Drake, Benjamin, journalist and biographer, b. Mayo Lick, Ky., 1795; d. Cincinnati, O., April 1, 1841. [1; 3; 4; 7; 8]

Drake, Charles Daniel, lawyer, b. Cincinnati, O., 1811; d. Washington, D.C., April 1, 1892. [1; 4; 6; 8]

Drake, Daniel, physician, b. Plainfield, N.J., 1785; d. Cincinnati, O., Nov. 6, 1852. [1; 3; 4; 7; 8]

Drake, Durant, philosopher, b. Hartford, Conn., 1878; d. Poughkeepsie, N.Y., Nov. 25, 1933. [10; 11]

Drake, Mrs. Emma Frances, née **Angell,** physician, b. 1849; d. ?

Drake, Francis Samuel, historian, b. Northwood, N.H., 1828; d. Washington, D.C., Feb. 22, 1885. [1; 3; 4; 7; 8]

Drake, James Madison, military historian, b. Somerset county, N.J., 1837; d. Elizabeth, N.J., Nov. 28, 1913. [10]

Drake, Joseph Rodman, poet, b. New York, N.Y., 1795; d. New York, N.Y., Sept. 21, 1820. [1; 3; 4; 7; 8]

Drake, Samuel Adams, historian, b. Boston, Mass., 1833; d. Kennebunkport, Me., Dec. 4, 1905. [1; 2; 3; 4; 6; 7; 10]

Drake, Samuel Gardner, historian, b. Pittsfield, N.H., 1789; d. Boston, Mass., June 14, 1875. [1; 2; 3; 4; 6; 7; 8]

Drapeau, Stanislaus, journalist, b. St. Roch, Que., 1821; d. Point Gatineau, Que., Feb. 21, 1893. [27]

Draper, Andrew Sloan, educationist, b. Otsego county, N.Y., 1848; d. Albany, N.Y., April 27, 1913. [4; 7; 10]

Draper, Henry, astronomer, b. Prince Edward county, Va., 1837; d. New York, N.Y., Nov. 20, 1882. [1; 3; 4; 7; 8; 34]

Draper, John Christopher, physician, b. Mecklenburg, Va., 1835; d. New York, N.Y., Dec. 20, 1885. [3; 4; 6; 7; 8; 34]

Draper, John William, chemist and historian, b. near Liverpool, England, 1811; d. Hastings-on-Hudson, N.Y., Jan. 4, 1882. [1; 3; 4; 7; 8]

Draper, Lyman Copeland, archivist and historian, b. Hamburg, N.Y., 1815; d. Madison, Wis., Aug. 26, 1891. [1; 3; 4; 7; 8]

Draper, William Franklin, diplomat, b. Lowell, Mass., 1842; d. Boston, Mass., Jan. 28, 1910. [1; 4; 10]

Draper, William George, jurist, b. about 1825; d. Kingston, Ont., Dec. 17, 1868. [27]

Drayton, Henry Shipman, physician, b. Jersey City, N.J., 1840; d. New York, N.Y., April 9, 1923. [10]

Drayton, John, jurist, b. near Charleston, S.C., 1766; d. Charleston, S.C., Nov. 27, 1822. [1; 3; 4; 8]

Drayton, Lillian R. (pseud.). See Coryell. John Russell.

Drayton, William Henry, revolutionary leader, b. near Charleston, Mass., 1742; d. Philadelphia, Pa., Sept. 3, 1779. [1; 3; 4; 8]

Dreiser, Theodore, novelist, b. Terre Haute, Ind., 1871; d. Hollywood, Calif., Dec. 28, 1945. [4; 7; 10; 11; 12; 72]

Dresser, Horace, lawyer, b. 1803; d. Jan. 27, 1877. [3]

Dresslar, Fletcher Bascom, educationist, b. Banta, Ind., 1858; d. Nashville, Tenn., Jan. 19, 1930. [10]

Dressler, Marie, actress, b. Cobourg, Ont., 1873; d. Santa Barbara, Calif., July 28, 1934. [7; 27]

Drew, Benjamin, educationist and civil servant, b. Massachusetts, 1812; d. July 19, 1903. [70]

Drew, Gilman Arthur, biologist, b. Newton, Ia., 1868; d. Oct. 26, 1934. [10; 37]

Drew, Dwight Chandler, Y.M.C.A. secretary, b. Preston, Minn., 1878; d. Boulder, Colo., July 22, 1932. [62]

Drew, John, actor, b. Philadelphia, Pa., Nov. 13, 1853; d. San Francisco, Calif., July 9, 1927. [1; 4; 7]

Dreyspring, Adolphe, educationist, b. Strasburg, Alsace, 1835; d. New York, N.Y., 1907. [10]

Driggs, Laurence La Tourette, aviation expert, b. Saginaw, Mich., 1876; d. Oxford, Md., May 26, 1945. [7; 10; 11]

Drinker, Anne, poet, b. Philadelphia, Pa., 1827; d. ? [4; 7]

Drinker, Henry Sturgis, engineer, lawyer, and educationist, b. Hongkong, China, 1850;' d. Beach Haven, N.J., July 26, 1937. [7; 10; 11]

Drinkwater, Jennie Maria. See Conklin, Mrs. Jennie Maria, née Drinkwater.

Driscoll, Clara, novelist, b. St. Marys, Tex., 1881; d. San Antonio, Tex., July 17, 1945. [7; 10]

Driscoll, Frederick, journalist, b. Montreal, Lower Canada, 1830; d. ? [27; 29]

Drisler, Henry, lexicographer, b. Staten Island, N.Y., 1818; d. New York, N.Y., Nov. 30, 1897. [1; 4; 6; 8]

Drolet, Gustave Adolphe, lawyer, b. St. Pie, Que., 1844; d. Montreal, Que., Oct. 17, 1904. [27]

Dromgoole, Will Allen, novelist and journalist, b. Murfreesboro, Tenn., 1860; d. Nashville, Tenn., Sept. 1, 1934. [1a; 3; 7; 10; 34]

Drone, Eaton Sylvester, journalist, b. Zanesville, O., 1842; d. Zanesville, O., Feb. 2, 1917. [3; 8; 10]

Droppers, Garrett, economic historian, b. Milwaukee, Wis., 1860; d. Williamstown, Mass., July 7, 1927. [2; 4; 10; 51]

Dropsie, Moses Aaron, lawyer, b. Philadelphia, Pa., 1821; d. Philadelphia, Pa., July 8, 1905. [1]

Drouet, Mrs. Bessie, née **Clarke,** artist and psychic researcher, b. about 1879; d. New York, N.Y., Aug. 27, 1940.

Drown, Daniel Augustus, poet, b. Portsmouth, N.H., 1823; d. Peabody, Mass., April 6, 1900. [49]

Drown, Edward Staples, theologian, b. New Haven, Conn., 1861; d. Cambridge, Mass., Jan. 24, 1936. [10; 51]

Drummond, Josiah Hayden, lawyer, b. Maine, 1827; d. Portland, Me., 1902. [10; 58]

Drummond, Lewis Henry, priest, b. Montreal, Que., 1848; d. Guelph, Ont., July 29, 1929. [27]

Drummond, Mrs. Sara King, née **Wiley,** poet, b. East Orange, N.J., 1871; d. East Orange, N.J., March 7, 1909. [10]

Drummond, William Henry, physician and poet, b. county Leitrim, Ireland, 1854; d. Cobalt, Ont., April 6, 1907. [27]

Drury, Augustus Waldo, clergyman and educationist, b. Madison county, Ind., 1851; d. Dayton, O., Feb. 18, 1935. [10; 11]

Drury, John Benjamin, clergyman, b. Rhinebeck, N.Y., 1838; d. March 21, 1909. [1; 4; 10]

Drury, Wells, journalist, b. New Boston, Ill., 1851; d. Berkeley, Calif., May 4, 1932. [10; 11; 35]

Dryden, John Fairfield, underwriter, b. near Farmington, Me., 1839; d. Newark, N.J., Nov. 24, 1911. [1; 4; 10]

Dryer, Charles Redway Wilmarth, geographer, b. Victor, N.Y., 1850; d. Fort Wayne, Ind., March 21, 1927. [4; 10]

Drysdale, William, journalist and novelist, b. Lancaster, Pa., 1852; d. Cranford, N.J., Sept. 20, 1901. [10]

Duane, Alexander, physician, b. Malone, N.Y., 1858; d. New York, N.Y., June 10, 1926. [10]

Duane, William, journalist, b. near Lake Champlain, N.Y., 1760; d. Philadelphia, Pa., Nov. 24, 1835. [1; 3; 4; 7; 8]

Duane, William, lawyer, b. Philadelphia, Pa., 1808; d. Nov. 4, 1882. [3]

Duane, William John, lawyer and politician, b. Clonmel, Ireland, 1780; d. Philadelphia, Pa., Sept. 27, 1865. [1; 3; 4]

Dubbs, Joseph Henry, clergyman and historian, b. North Whitehall, Pa., 1838; d. Lancaster, Pa., April 1, 1910. [1; 3; 4]

Dubois, Augustus Jay, civil engineer, b. Newton Falls, O., 1849; d. New Haven, Conn., Oct. 19, 1915. [1; 3; 4; 62]

Dubois, James T., diplomat, b. Hallstead, Pa., 1851; d. Hallstead, Pa., May 27, 1920. [4; 10]

Du Bois, Patterson, religious journalist and literary adviser, b. Philadelphia, Pa., 1847; d. Aug. 3, 1917. [10]

Du Bois, William Ewing, numismatist, b. Doylestown, Pa., 1810; d. Philadelphia, Pa., July 14, 1881. [1; 3; 6]

Du Bose, Horace Mellard, bishop, b. Choctaw county, Ala., 1858; d. Nashville, Tenn., Jan. 15, 1941. [4; 7; 10; 34]

Du Bose, William Porcher, theologian, b. Winnsboro, S.C., 1836; d. Sewanee, Tenn., Aug. 18, 1918. [1; 4; 7; 10; 34]

Ducatel, Julius Timoleon, chemist, b. Baltimore, Md., 1796; d. Baltimore, Md., April 23, 1849. [3; 4; 8]

Du Chaillu, Paul Belloni, explorer, b. France, 1835; d. St. Petersburg, Russia, April 30, 1903. [1; 7; 10; 34]

Duchaussois, Pierre Jean Baptiste, priest, b. Wallincourt, France, 1878; d. Marseilles, France, 1940. [27]

Duché, Jacob, clergyman, b. Philadelphia, Pa., 1737-8; d. Jan. 3, 1798. [1; 4; 7; 8]

Ducoudray-Holstein, H. Lafayette Villaume, soldier, b. Germany, 1763; d. Albany, N.Y., April 23, 1839. [3]

Dudley, Dean, antiquary b. Kingsfield, Me., 1823; d. 1906. [3; 8]

Dudley, Edgar Swartwout, soldier, b. Oppenheim, N.Y., 1845; d. Johnstown, N.Y., 1911. [10]

Dudley, Emelius Clark, physician, b. Westfield, Mass., 1850; d. Chicago, Ill., Dec. 1, 1928. [4; 10; 49]

Dudley, Mrs. Lucy, née **Bronson,** miscellaneous writer, b. Peninsula, O., 1848; d. May, 1920. [10]

Dudley, Myron Samuel, clergyman, b. 1837; d. 1905. [61]

Dudley, Thomas Underwood, bishop, b. Richmond, Va., 1837; d. New York, N.Y., Jan. 22, 1904. [3; 4; 6; 7; 10]

Dudley, William Russel, botanist, b. Guilford, Conn., 1849; d. Palo Alto, Calif., June 4, 1911. [1; 3; 4; 10]

Duell, Holland Sackett, lawyer and soldier, b. Syracuse, N.Y., 1881; d. Larchmont, N.Y., Nov. 25, 1942. [62]

Duer, John, jurist, b. Albany, N.Y., 1782; d. Staten Island, N.Y., Aug. 8, 1858. [1; 4]

Duer, William Alexander, jurist, b. Rhinebeck, N.Y., 1780; d. New York, N.Y., May 30, 1858. [1; 3; 4; 7; 8]

Duerr, Alvan Emile, educationist, b. Cleveland, O., 1872; d. New York, N.Y., Nov. 18, 1947. [10]

Duff, Emma Lorne, educationist, d. Toronto, Ont., March 31, 1935. [27]

Duff, Peter, educationist, b. New Brunswick, 1802; d. Pittsburgh, Pa., Sept. 13, 1869. [3; 8]

Duffey, Mrs. Eliza Bisbee, feminist, d. 1898.

Duffield, Divie Bethune, lawyer and poet, b. Carlisle, Pa., 1821; d. Detroit, Mich., March 12, 1891. [39; 62]

Duffield, George, clergyman, b. Strasburg, N.Y., 1794; d. Detroit, Mich., June 26, 1868. [1; 3; 4; 8]

Duffield, John Thomas, clergyman, b. McConnellsburg, Pa., 1823; d. Princeton, N.J., 1901. [10]

Duffield, Samuel Augustus Willoughby, clergyman and poet, b. Brooklyn, N.Y., 1843; d. Bloomfield, N.J., May 12, 1887. [1; 3; 4; 7; 8]

Duffield, William Ward, soldier, b. Carlisle, Pa., 1823; d. 1907. [10]

Duffy, Francis Patrick, priest and army chaplain, b. Cobourg, Ont., 1871; d. New York, N.Y., June 26, 1932. [1a; 2; 21]

Duffy, James Oscar Greeley, novelist and playwright, b. Strabane, Ireland, 1864; d. Wilmington, Del., Jan. 9, 1933. [10]

Duffy, Richard, journalist, b. New York, N.Y., 1873; d. New York, N.Y., March 5, 1949.

Dugan, Raymond Smith, astronomer, b. Montague, Mass., 1878; d. Bryn Mawr, Pa., Aug. 31, 1940. [10]

Duganne, Augustine Joseph Hickey, poet and journalist, b. Boston, Mass., 1823; d. New York, N.Y., Oct. 20, 1884. [1; 3; 4; 6; 7]

Dugas, Alphonse Chartes, priest, b. St. Liguori, Que., 1858; d. St. Polycarpe, Que., Oct. 21, 1924. [27]

Dugas, Georges, priest, b. St. Jacques de l'Achigan, Lower Canada, 1833; d. Ste. Anne des Plaines, Que., Dec. 14, 1928. [27]

Dugas, Marcel, archivist, b. 1883; d. Montreal, Que., Jan. 7, 1946.

Dugdale, Richard Louis, social economist, b. Paris, France, 1841; d. New York, N.Y., July 23, 1883. [1; 3; 4; 8]

Duggan, Thomas Stephen, priest, b. Deep River, Conn., 1850; d. Hartford, Conn., Nov. 2, 1945. [21]

Dugué, Charles Oscar, poet and playwright, b. New Orleans, La., 1821; d. Paris, France, Aug. 29, 1872. [1; 3; 4; 7; 34]

Duhring, Julia, essayist, b. Philadelphia, Pa., 1836; d. 1892. [3; 8]

Duhring, Louis Adolphus, dermatologist, b. Philadelphia, Pa., 1845; d. Philadelphia, Pa., May 8, 1913. [1; 4; 8; 10]

Duke, Basil Wilson, soldier and historian, b. Scott county, Ky., 1838; d. New York, N.Y., Sept. 16, 1916. [1; 10; 34; 74]

Duke, William, clergyman, b. Patapasco Neck, Md., 1757; d. Elkton, Md., 1840. [3; 34]

Duke, William Waddell, educationist, b. Lexington, Mo., 1882; d. Kansas City, Mo., April 11, 1946. [10; 62]

Dulaney, Benjamin Lewis, financier, b. Blountville, Tenn., 1857; d. Washington, D.C., March 4, 1930. [10]

Dulany, Daniel, lawyer, b. Queen's county, Ireland, 1685; d. Annapolis, Md., Dec. 5, 1753. [1]

Dulany, Daniel, lawyer, b. Annapolis, Md., 1722; d. Baltimore, Md., March 17, 1797. [1; 3; 4; 34]

Dull, Charles Elwood, educationist, b. Wood county, O., 1878; d. East Orange, N.J., Dec. 19, 1947.

Dulles, Allen Macy, theologian, b. Philadelphia, Pa., 1854; d. Auburn, N.Y., Nov. 13, 1930. [10]

Dulles, Charles Winslow, physician, b. Madras, India, 1850; d. Philadelphia, Pa., May 6, 1921. [10]

Dulles, John Welsh, missionary, b. Philadelphia, Pa., 1823; d. Philadelphia, Pa., April 13, 1887. [3; 4; 8]

Dumont, Mrs. Julia Louisa, née Carey, educationist, b. Waterford, O., 1794; d. Vevay, Ind., Jan. 2, 1857. [3]

Dunaway, Maude Edwin, poet, b. Vilonia, Ark., 1882; d. Little Rock, Ark., Feb. 7, 1934. [62]

Dunaway, Thomas Sanford, clergyman, b. 1872; d. 1932.

Dunbar, Charles Franklin, economist, b. Abington, Mass., 1830; d. Chicago, Ill., Jan. 29, 1900. [1; 4; 8; 10]

Dunbar, Newell, editor, b. Trenton, N.J., 1845; d. Newark, N.J., March 7, 1925. [10]

Dunbar, Paul Laurence, poet and novelist, b. Dayton, O., 1872; d. Dayton, O., Feb. 9, 1906. [1; 2; 4; 7; 10; 72]

Dunbar, Seymour, historian, b. Cincinnati, O., 1866; d. Hackensack, N.J., April 18, 1947.

Duncan, Duke (pseud.). See Rathborne, St. George Henry.

Duncan, James, labour official, b. Kincardine, Scotland, 1857; d. Quincy, Mass., Sept. 14, 1928. [1a; 10]

Duncan, Norman, novelist, b. Brantford, Ont., 1871; d. Buffalo, N.Y., Oct. 18, 1916. [7; 10; 27]

Duncan, Robert Kennedy, chemist, b. Brantford, Ont., 1868; d. Pittsburgh, Pa., Feb. 18, 1914. [1; 4; 10]

Duncan, Robert Moore, educationist, b. 1900; d. by drowning in the Atlantic Ocean, east of New York, N.Y., July 31, 1938.

Duncan, Sara Jeannette, novelist, b. Brantford, Ont., 1862; d. Ashmead, England, July 22, 1922. [27]

Duncan, Walter Wofford Tucker, clergyman, b. Moncton, N.B., 1869; d. Cleveland, O., Aug. 2, 1945. [10]

Duncan, Watson Boone, clergyman, b. Blacksburg, S.C., 1867; d. Lake City, S.C., March 16, 1930. [10; 11]

Duncan, Wiliam Cary, librettist, b. North Brookfield, Mass., 1874; d. North Brookfield, Mass., Nov. 21, 1945. [7; 10; 11]

Duncan, William Cecil, clergyman, b. New York, N.Y., 1824; d. New Orleans, La., May 1, 1864. [3; 6; 8]

Duncan, William Stevens, physician, b. Brownsville, Pa., 1834; d. Brownsville, Pa., May 16, 1892. [3; 8]

Duncan-Clark, Samuel John, journalist, b. Toronto, Ont., 1875; d. Toronto, Ont., June, 1938. [10]

Duncombe, Charles, physician and reformer, b. Connecticut, 1794; d. Hicksville, Calif., Oct. 1, 1875. [27]

Dungan, David Roberts, clergyman and educationist, b. Noble county, Ind., 1837; d. Glendale, Calif., Dec. 9, 1920. [10; 37]

Dunglison, Richard James, physician, b. Baltimore, Md., 1834; d. Philadelphia, Pa., March 5, 1901. [3; 10]

Dunglison, Robley, physician, b. Keswick, England, 1798; d. Philadelphia, Pa., April 1, 1869. [1; 3; 4; 6; 8]

Dunham, Carroll, physician, b. New York, N.Y., 1828; d. Irvington-on-Hudson, N.Y., Feb. 18, 1877. [3; 4]

Dunham, Henry Morton, musician, b. Brockton, Mass., 1853; d. Brookline, Mass., May 4, 1929. [1; 4; 10; 20]

Dunham, Samuel, clergyman, b. Southington, Conn., 1835; d. Binghampton, N.Y., Dec. 4, 1936. [62]

Dunham, Samuel Clarke, journalist, b. Woodford county, Ill., 1855; d. 1920. [10]

Dunham, William Russell, physician, b. 1833; d. Boston, Mass., 1911. [51]

Duniway, Mrs. Abigail Jane, née Scott, novelist and feminist, b. near Groveland, Tazewell county, Ill., 1834; d. Portland, Ore., Oct. 11, 1915. [1; 7; 41]

Duniway, Clyde Augustus, educationist, b. Albany, Ore., 1866; d. Palo Alto, Calif., Dec. 24, 1944. [4; 10; 11]

Dunlap, Mrs. Laura, née Comstock, journalist, b. 1855; d. New York, N.Y., July 16, 1947.

Dunlap, Samuel Fales, lawyer, b. Boston, Mass., 1835; d. 1905. [6; 51]

Dunlap, Colonel Walter B. (pseud.). See Cobb, Sylvanus [1823-1877]

Dunlap, William, artist, playwright, and historian, b. Perth Amboy, N.J., 1766; d. New York, N.Y., Sept. 28, 1839. [1; 2; 3; 4; 6; 7; 71]

Dunlop, James, lawyer, b. Chambersburg, Pa., 1795; d. Baltimore, Md., April 9, 1856. [1; 4]

Dunn, Arthur Wallace, journalist, b. Meeker county, Minn., 1859; d. Washington, D.C., Nov. 2, 1926. [10]

Dunn, Arthur William, educationist, b. Galesburg, Ill., 1868; d. Washington, D.C., Nov. 15, 1927. [10]

Dunn, Ballard S., clergyman, b. 1829; d. 1897. [6; 34]

Dunn, Byron Archibald, writer of books for boys, b. Hillsdale county, Mich., 1842; d. about 1923. [7; 10; 39]

Dunn, Eliza (pseud.). See Norton, Mrs. Edith Eliza, née Ames.

Dunn, Fannie Wyche, educationist, b. Petersburg, Va., 1879; d. New York, N.Y., Jan. 17, 1946. [10]

Dunn, Jacob Piatt, librarian and historian, b. Lawrenceburg, Ind., 1855; d. Indianapolis, Ind., June 6, 1924. [4; 8; 10]

Dunn, Joseph Allan Elphinstone, explorer and novelist, b. London, England, 1872; d. San Francisco, Calif., March 25, 1941. [7; 10; 35]

Dunn, Lewis Romaine, clergyman, b. New Brunswick, N.J., 1822; d. 1876. [6; 8]

Dunn, Mrs. Martha, née Baker, essayist, b. Hallowell, Me., 1848; d. Waterville, Me., July 22, 1915. [10; 38]

Dunn, Nathaniel, educationist and poet, b. Poland, Me., 1800; d. New York, N.Y., Oct. 17, 1889. [46]

Dunn, Oscar, journalist, b. Côteau du Lac, Que., 1844; d. Quebec, Que., April 15, 1885. [27]

Dunne, Edward Fitzsimons, politician and historian, b. Waterville, Conn., 1853; d. Chicago, Ill., May 24, 1937. [10]

Dunne, Finley Peter, humorist, b. Chicago, Ill., 1867; d. New York, N.Y., April 24, 1936. [2; 4; 7; 10; 72]

Dunning, Albert Elijah, clergyman, b. Brookfield, Conn., 1844; d. Boston, Mass., Nov. 14, 1923. [1; 4; 7; 10]

Dunning, Annie Ketchum, writer of books for girls, b. New York, N.Y., 1831; d. ? [7]

Dunning, Charlotte (pseud.). See Wood, Charlotte Dunning.

Dunning, Edwin James, dentist and littérateur, b. Camillus, N.Y., 1821; d. Cambridge, Mass., 1901. [10]

Dunning, William Archibald, political scientist, b. Plainfield, N.J., 1857; d. New York, N.Y., Aug. 25, 1922. [1; 4; 7; 10]

Dunton, John, bookseller, b. Huntingdonshire, England, 1659; d. New England, 1733. [3]

Du Ponceau, Pierre Etienne, lawyer, b. St. Martin, Ile de Ré, France, 1760; d. Philadelphia, Pa., April 1, 1844. [1; 4; 7; 8]

Du Pont, Mrs. Bessie, née Gardner, biographer, b. Trenton, N.J., 1864; d. near Greenville, Del., Dec. 12, 1949.

Du Pont, Henry Algernon, soldier, industrialist, and politician, b. near Wilmington, Del., 1838; d. Wilmington, Del., Dec. 31, 1926. [1; 4; 10]

Dupuis, Nathan Fellowes, mathematician, b. Portland, Frontenac county, Upper Canada, 1836; d. Long Beach, Calif., July 20, 1917. [27]

Dupuy, Eliza Ann, novelist, b. Petersburg, Va., 1814; d. New Orleans, La., Jan. 1881. [1; 3; 4; 6; 7; 8; 34]

Du Puy, William Atherton, journalist, b. Palestine, Tex., 1876; d. Fort Collins, Colo., Aug. 11, 1941. [7; 10; 11]

Duquet, Joseph Norbert, journalist, b. St. Charles de Bellechasse, Lower Canada, 1828; d. Quebec, Que., Aug. 10, 1891. [27]

Durand, Charles, lawyer and politician, b. near Hamilton, Upper Canada, 1811; d. Toronto, Ont., Aug. 16, 1905. [27]

Durand, Evelyn, poet, b. Toronto, Ont., 1870; d. Boulder, Colo., Dec. 5, 1900. [27]

Durand, John, art critic and translator, b. New York, N.Y., 1822; d. 1908. [3; 6]

Durant, Charles Ferson, aeronaut and scientist, b. New York, N.Y., 1805; d. Jersey City, N.J., March 2, 1873. [1; 3]

Durbin, John Price, clergyman and educationist, b. Bourbon county, Ky., 1800; d. New York, N.Y., Oct. 19, 1876. [1; 3; 4; 6; 7; 8]

Durell, Fletcher, educationist, b. Clarksburg, N. J., 1859; d. Belleplaine, N.J., March 25, 1946. [11]

Durfee, Job, jurist, b. Tiverton, R.I., 1790; d. Tiverton, R.I., July 26, 1847. [1; 3; 4; 7]

Durfee, Thomas, jurist, b. Tiverton, R.I., 1826; d. Providence, R.I., June 6, 1901. [1; 4; 10; 47]

Durfee, William Pitt, mathematician, b. Livonia, Mich., 1855; d. Geneva, N.Y., Dec. 17, 1941. [10]

Durham, Robert Lee, educationist, b. Shelby, N.C., 1870; d. Buena Vista, Va., Jan. 2, 1949. [10]

Durivage, Francis Alexander, journalist, b. Boston, Mass., 1814; d. New York, N.Y., Feb. 1, 1881. [1; 3; 4; 7]

Durland, Kellogg, sociologist, b. New York, N.Y., 1881; d. Middletown, N.Y., Nov. 22, 1911. [10]

Durrett, Reuben Thomas, lawyer and historian, b. Henry county, Ky., 1824; d. Louisville, Ky., Sept. 16, 1913. [4; 7; 10; 34; 74]

Durrie, Daniel Steele, librarian and genealogist, b. Albany, N.Y., 1819; d. Madison, Wis., Aug. 31, 1892. [1; 3; 4; 7]

Duryee, William Rankin, clergyman and poet, b. Newark, N.J., 1838; d. New Jersey, Jan. 20, 1907. [3]

Dussauce, Hippolyte, chemist, b. France; d. New Lebanon, N.Y., June 20, 1869. [3]

Dutcher, Addison Porter, physician, b. Durham, N.Y., 1818; d. Cleveland, O., Jan. 30, 1884. [3; 8]

Dutcher, Jacob Conkling, clergyman, b. 1820; d. 1888. [6]

Dutton, Clarence Edward, geologist, b. Wallingford, Conn., 1841; d. Englewood. N.J., Jan. 4, 1912. [1; 3; 4; 10]

Dutton, Emily Helen, educationist, b. Shirley, Mass., 1870; d. Lynchburg, Va., June 18, 1947.

Dutton, Samuel Train, educationist, b. Hillsboro Bridge, N.H., 1849; d. Atlantic City, N.J., March 28, 1919. [1; 4; 10]

Dutton, Samuel William Southmayd, clergyman, b. Guilford, Conn., 1814; d. Millbury, Mass., Jan. 26, 1866. [3; 62]

Duval, Delphine, educationist, b. France, 1837; d. Northampton, Mass., Oct. 22, 1906.

Duval, John Crittenden, surveyor and prospector, b. Florida, 1816; d. Jan. 15, 1897. [7]

Duyckinck, Evert Augustus, editor and biographer, b. New York, N.Y., 1816; d. New York, N.Y., Aug. 13, 1878. [1; 3; 4; 7; 8]

Duyckinck, George Long, editor and biographer, b. New York, N.Y., 1823; d. New York, N.Y., March 30, 1863. [1; 3; 4; 6; 7; 8]

Duyckinck, Whitehead Cornell, genealogist, b. Brooklyn, N.Y., 1843; d. Plainfield, N.J., Feb. 21, 1936. [62]

Dwight, Benjamin Woodbridge, clergyman and educationist, b. New Haven, Conn., 1816; d. Sept. 18, 1889. [1; 3; 4; 8]

Dwight, Edwin Welles, clergyman, b. Stockbridge, Mass., 1789; d. Stockbridge, Mass., Feb. 25, 1841. [8; 62]

Dwight, Harrison Gray Otis, missionary, b. Conway, Mass., 1803; d. near Bennington, Vt., Jan. 25, 1862. [1; 4; 8]

Dwight, Henry Edwin, educationist, b. New Haven, Conn., 1797; d. New Haven, Conn., Aug. 11, 1832. [3; 8; 62]

Dwight, Henry Otis, missionary, b. Constantinople, Turkey, 1843; d. Roselle, N.J., June 20, 1917. [1; 4; 7; 8]

Dwight, James McLaren Breed, lawyer and poet, b. Norwich, Conn., 1825; d. New Haven, Conn., June 28, 1897. [62]

Dwight John Sullivan, music critic, b. Boston, Mass., 1813; d. Boston, Mass., Sept. 5, 1893. [1; 3; 4; 7]

Dwight, Mrs. Margaret D., née **Brush,** poet, b. Brooklyn, N.Y., 1883; d. New York, N.Y., Feb. 24, 1946.

Dwight, Mary Ann, teacher of art, b. Northampton, Mass., 1806; d. Morrisania, N.Y., Nov. 4, 1858. [3; 8]

Dwight, Nathaniel, educationist, b. Northampton, Mass., 1770; d. Oswego, N.Y., June 11, 1831. [1; 3; 8]

Dwight, Sereno Edwards, clergyman and educationist, b. Fairfield, Conn., 1786; d. Philadelphia, Pa., Nov. 30, 1850. [1; 3; 4; 8]

Dwight, Theodore, lawyer, b. Northampton, Mass., 1764; d. New York, N.Y., June 12, 1846. [1; 3; 7; 8]

Dwight, Theodore, educationist, b. Hartford, Conn., 1796; d. Brooklyn, N.Y., Oct. 16, 1866. [1; 3; 4; 6; 7; 8]

Dwight, Theodore William, lawyer, b. Catskill, N.Y., 1822; d. Clinton, N.Y., June 29, 1892. [1; 3; 4; 8]

Dwight, Thomas, anatomist, b. Boston, Mass., 1843; d. Nahant, Mass., Sept. 9, 1911. [1; 3; 4; 7; 10]

Dwight, Tilton (pseud.). See Quint, Wilder Wright.

Dwight, Timothy, clergyman and educationist, b. Northampton, Mass., 1752; d. New Haven, Conn., Jan. 11, 1817. [1; 3; 4; 6; 7; 8]

Dwight, Timothy, clergyman and educationist, b. Norwich, Conn., 1828; d. New Haven, Conn., May 26, 1916. [1; 3; 4; 7; 10; 62]

Dwinell, Melvin, journalist, b. East Calais, Vt., 1825; d. Rome, Ga., Dec. 28, 1887. [43]

Dyar, Harrison Gray, entomologist, b. New York, N.Y., 1866; d. Washington, D.C., Jan. 21, 1929. [1; 4; 10]

Dyde, Samuel Walters, clergyman and educationist, b. Ottawa, Ont., 1862; d. Edmonton, Alta., Jan. 22, 1947. [30]

Dye, Charity, educationist, b. 1849; d. ?

Dye, Mrs. Eva, née **Emery,** novelist and historian, b. Prophetstown, Ill., 1855; d. Oregon City, Ore., Feb. 25, 1947. [4; 7; 1; 41]

Dye, William McEntyre, soldier, b. Pennsylvania, 1831; d. Muskegon, Mich., Nov. 13, 1899. [1; 3]

Dyer, Alexander Brydie, soldier, b. Fayetteville, N.C., 1852; d. San Francisco, Calif., July 9, 1920. [4; 10]

Dyer, Mrs. Catherine Cornelia, née **Joy,** clergyman's wife, b. Ludlowville, N.Y., 1817; d. 1903. [3; 7; 10]

Dyer, David Patterson, jurist, b. Henry county, Va., 1838; d. St. Louis, Mo., April 29, 1924. [10]

Dyer, Ebenezer Porter, clergyman, b. Abington, Mass., 1813; d. Abington, Mass., Aug. 22, 1882. [45]

Dyer, Edward Oscar, clergyman and poet, b. Whitman, Mass., 1853; d. Chester, Conn., Dec. 28, 1914. [45]

Dyer, Frank Lewis, inventor, b. Washington, D.C., 1870; d. Ventnor, N.J., June 4, 1941. [10]

Dyer, Heman, clergyman, b. Shaftesbury, Vt., 1810; d. New York, N.Y., 1900. [3; 4; 8; 10]

Dyer, Isaac Watson, lawyer, b. Baldwin, Me., 1855; d. Portland, Me., Feb. 13, 1937. [10; 11; 46]

Dyer, Isadore, physician, b. Galveston, Tex., 1865; d. New Orleans, La., Oct. 12, 1920. [1; 10]

Dyer, Louis, educationist, b. Chicago, Ill., 1854; d. London, England, July 20, 1908. [4; 7; 10; 51]

Dyer, Mrs. Mary, née **Marshall,** religious controversialist, b. 1780; d. ? [4]

Dyer, Oliver, journalist, b. Porter, N.Y., 1824; d. Beverly Farms, Mass., 1907. [4; 10]

Dyer, Sidney, clergyman, b. Cambridge, N.Y., 1814; d. 1898. [3; 6; 7; 8; 10; 34]

Dyer, Walter Alden, journalist and novelist, b. Roslindale, Mass., 1878; d. Pelham, Mass., June 20, 1943. [7; 10; 11]

Dyke, Cornelius Gysbert, radiologist, b. Orange City, Ia., 1900; d. New York, N.Y., April 23, 1943.

Dylander, John, clergyman, b. about 1709; d. Philadelphia, Pa., Nov. 3, 1741. [1]

Dyott, Thomas W., manufacturer, b. England, 1771; d. Philadelphia, Pa., Jan. 17, 1861. [1]

Dyson, Charles Wilson, naval officer, b Cambridge, Md., 1861; d. Washington, D.C., Oct. 25, 1930. [10]

E

Eaches, Owen Philips, clergyman, b. Phoenixville, Pa., 1840; d. Haddonfield, N.J., Jan. 10, 1930. [10]

Eads, James Buchanan, engineer, b. Lawrenceburg, Ind., 1820; d. Nassau, Bahamas, March 8, 1887. [4; 6]

Eakle, Arthur Starr, mineralogist, b. Washington, D.C., 1862; d. Honolulu, Hawaii, July 5, 1931. [10; 11]

Eames, Mrs. Jane, née Anthony, traveller, b. 1816; d. 1894.

Eames, Wilberforce, bibliographer, b. Newark, N.J., 1855; d. New York, N.Y., Dec. 6, 1937. [4; 7; 10]

Earhart, Amelia, aviatrix, b. Atchison, Kans., 1898; d. about July 2, 1937. [10]

Earl, Henry Hilliard, banker, b. 1842; d. Fall River, Mass., Oct. 22, 1927.

Earle, Mrs. Alice, née Morse, historian, b. Worcester, Mass., 1853; d. Hempstead, Long Island, N.Y., Feb. 16, 1911. [1; 4; 7; 10]

Earle, Franklin Sumner, botanist and agriculturist, b. Dwight, Ill., 1856; d. Cuba, Jan. 31, 1929. [4; 10]

Earle, Mortimer Lamson, educationist, b. New York, N.Y., 1864; d. Italy, Sept. 26, 1905. [1; 4; 10]

Earle, Pliny, physician and psychiatrist, b. Leicester, Mass., 1809; d. Northampton, Mass., May 17, 1892. [1; 3; 4; 6; 8]

Earle, Ralph, naval officer, b. Worcester, Mass., 1874; d. Worcester, Mass., Feb. 13, 1939. [10]

Earle, Swepson, hydrographic engineer, b. Queen Anne county, Md., 1879; d. Baltimore, Md., Nov. 14, 1943. [10]

Earle, Samuel T., physician, b. near Centreville, Md., 1849; d. Baltimore, Md., Feb. 19, 1931. [10]

Earle, Thomas, lawyer, b. Leicester, Mass., 1796; d. Philadelphia, Pa., July 14, 1849. [1; 3; 4; 8]

Earls, Michael, priest and poet, b. 1873; d. New York, N.Y., Jan. 31, 1937. [21; 22]

Early, Jubal Anderson, soldier, b. Franklin county, Va., 1816; d. Lynchburg, Va., March 2, 1894. [1; 3; 4; 8]

East, Edward Murray, biologist, b. Du Quoin, Ill., 1879; d. Boston, Mass., Nov. 9, 1938. [10]

Eastburn, James Wallis, clergyman, b. London, England, 1797; d. at sea, Dec. 2, 1819. [3; 4; 8]

Eastburn, Manton, bishop, b. Leeds, England, 1801; d. Boston, Mass., Sept. 11, 1872. [3; 4; 8]

Easter, Marguerite Elizabeth, poet, b. Leesburg, Va., 1839; d. Baltimore, Md., 1894. [7; 34]

Eastman, Charles Gamage, journalist and poet, b. Fryeburg, Me., 1816; d. Montpelier, Vt., Sept. 16, 1860. [1; 3; 4; 7]

Eastman, Francis Smith, educationist, b. Randolph, Vt., about 1800; d. Charlestown, Mass., about 1847. [43]

Eastman, Julia Arabella, writer of books for young people, b. Fulton, N.Y., 1837; d. Wellesley, Mass., Dec. 25, 1911. [3; 6; 7; 8; 10]

Eastman, Lucius Root, clergyman, b. Hadley, Mass., 1809; d. Framingham, Mass., March 29, 1892. [45]

Eastman, Mrs. Mary, née Henderson, soldier's wife, b. Warrenton, Va., 1818; d. 1890. [7; 34]

Eastman, Seth, soldier, b. Brunswick, Me., 1808; d. Washington, D.C., Aug. 31, 1875. [3; 4; 7; 8]

Eaton, Amasa Mason, lawyer, b. Providence, R.I., 1841; d. Providence, R.I., Oct. 3, 1914. [10; 47]

Eaton, Amos, educationist, b. Chatham, N.Y., 1776; d. Troy, N.Y., May 6, 1842. [1; 3; 4]

Eaton, Arthur Wentworth Hamilton, clergyman, poet, and historian, b. Kentville, N.S., 1849; d. Boston, Mass., July 11, 1937. [7; 10; 11; 27; 51]

Eaton, Asa, clergyman, b. Plaistow, N.H., 1778; d. Boston, Mass., March 24, 1858. [3; 51]

Eaton, Cyrus, educationist, b. Framingham, Mass., 1784; d. Warren, Me., Jan. 21, 1875. [3; 4]

Eaton, Daniel Cody, botanist, b. Fort Gratiot, Mich., 1834; d. New Haven, Conn,. June 29, 1895. [1; 3; 4]

Eaton, Daniel Cody, art historian, b. Johnstown, N.Y., 1837; d. New Haven, Conn., May 11, 1912. [10; 62]

Eaton, Dorman Bridgman, lawyer and reformer, b. Hardwick, Vt., 1823; d. New York, N.Y., Dec. 23, 1899. [1; 3; 4; 6; 43]

Eaton, Edith, novelist, b. 1867; d. Montreal, Que., April 7, 1914.

Eaton, Edward Dwight, clergyman and educationist b. Lancaster, Wis., 1851; d. Fairfield, Conn., June 18, 1942. [7; 10; 62]

Eaton, Elon Howard, ornithologist, b. Springville, N.Y., 1866; d. Geneva, N.Y., March 27, 1934. [10]

Eaton, Frank Herbert, educationist, b. Kentville, N.S., 1851; d. Victoria, B.C., Jan. 11, 1908. [33]

Eaton, James Webster, lawyer, b. Albany, N.Y., 1856; d. Albany, N.Y., 1901. [10]

Eaton, John, educationist, b. Sutton, N.H., 1829; d. Washington, D.C., Feb. 9, 1906. [10; 49]

132

Eaton, John Henry, lawyer and politician, b. Tennessee, 1790; d. Washington, D.C., Nov. 17, 1856. [4]

Eaton, Marquis, lawyer, b. Mattawan, Mich., 1876; d. Chicago, Ill., Sept. 19, 1925. [10; 53]

Eaton, Samuel John Mills, clergyman, b. Fairview, Pa., 1820; d. 1899. [3; 8]

Eaton, Seymour, journalist, b. Epping, Ont., 1859; d. Lansdowne, Pa., March 13, 1916. [2; 7; 10]

Eaton, Thomas Treadwell, clergyman, b. Murfreesborough, Tenn., 1845; d. 1907. [4; 10; 34]

Eayrs, Hugh Smithurst, publisher, b. Leeds, England, 1894; d. Toronto, Ont., April 29, 1940. [27]

Eberhart, Mrs. Nelle Richmond, née McCurdy, song-writer, b. Detroit, Mich.; d. Kansas City, Mo., Nov. 15, 1944. [7; 10]

Eberle, John, physician, b. Lancaster county, Pa., 1787; d. Lexington, Ky., Feb. 2, 1838. [1; 3; 4; 6]

Ebersole, Ezra Christian, lawyer, b. Mount Pleasant, Pa., 1840; d. Toledo, Ia., July 14, 1919. [10; 45]

Ebersole, John Franklin, educationist, b. North Tonawanda, N.Y., 1884; d. Belmont, Mass., June 24, 1945. [10]

Ebert, Justus, journalist, b. New York, N.Y., 1869; d. New York, N.Y, Dec. 25, 1946.

Eby, Louise Saxe, educationist, b. Hazleton, Pa., 1902; d. Milwaukee, Wis., May 14, 1948.

Eccles, Robert Gibson, physician, b. Scotland, 1848; d. Brooklyn, N.Y., June 9, 1934. [10]

Echols, William Holding, mathematician, b. San Antonio, Tex., 1858; d. University, Va., Sept. 25, 1934. [10]

Eckel, Mrs. Lizzie, née St. John. See Harper, Mrs. Lizzie, née St. John.

Eckerson, Theodore John, soldier and poet, fl. 1850-1891. [41]

Eckles, Clarence Henry, professor of dairy husbandry, b. Marshall county, Ia., 1875; d. St. Paul, Minn., Feb. 13, 1933. [10; 11]

Eckley, William Thomas, anatomist, b. Lancaster, Ia., 1855; d. near Grand Haven, Mich., Sept. 12, 1908. [10]

Eckman, George Peck, clergyman, b. Gouldsboro, Pa., 1860; d. Scranton, Pa., June 28, 1920. [4; 10; 60]

Eckoff, William Julius, educationist, b. Hamburg, Germany, 1853; d. Newark, N.J., 1908. [10]

Eckstorm, Fannie Hardy, naturalist and anthropoligist, b. Brewer, Me., 1865; d. Brewer, Me., Dec. 31, 1946. [7; 10; 11]

Eddy, Arthur Jerome, lawyer, b. Flint, Mich., 1859; d. Chicago Ill., July 21, 1920. [10]

Eddy, Clarence, organist, b. Greenfield, Mass., 1851; d. Winnetka, Ill., Jan. 10, 1937. [4; 10]

Eddy, Daniel Clarke, clergyman and traveller, b. Salem, Mass., 1823; d. Brooklyn, N.Y., July 26, 1896. [4; 7]

Eddy, David Brewer, clergyman, b. Leavenworth, Kans., 1877; d. Falmouth, Mass., June 1, 1946. [62]

Eddy, Harrison Prescott, civil engineer, b. Millbury, Mass., 1870; d. Newton Centre, Mass., June 15, 1937. [10]

Eddy, Henry Turner, mathematician and physicist, b. Stoughton, Mass., 1844; d. Minneapolis, Minn., Dec. 11, 1921. [1; 3; 4; 10]

Eddy, Mrs. Mary Morse, née Baker, founder of Christian Science, b. Bow, N.H., 1821; d. Chestnut Hill, Mass., Dec. 3, 1910. [1; 2; 3; 4; 5; 6; 7; 8; 10]

Eddy, Richard, clergyman, b. Providence, R.I., 1828; d. 1906. [10]

Eddy, Samuel, jurist, b. Johnston, R.I., 1769; d. Providence, R.I., Feb. 2, 1839. [3; 4]

Eddy, Sarah J., writer of books on animals, b. Boston, Mass., 1851; d. Portsmouth, R.I., March 29, 1945.

Eddy, Thomas, prison reformer, b. Philadelphia, Pa., 1758; d. New York, N.Y., Sept. 16, 1827. [1; 3; 4; 8]

Eddy, Thomas Mears, clergyman, b. Hamilton county, O., 1823; d. New York, N.Y., Oct. 7, 1874. [3; 4; 8]

Eddy, Zachary, clergyman, b. Stockbridge, Vt., 1815; d. Detroit, Mich., Nov. 15, 1891. [3; 4; 43]

Edes, Henry Herbert, genealogist and biographer, b. Charlestown, Mass., 1849; d. Cambridge, Mass., Oct. 13, 1922. [7; 10]

Edes, Robert Thaxter, physician, b. Eastport, Me., 1838; d. Springfield, Mass., Jan. 12, 1913. [7; 10]

Edgar, James Clifton, obstetrician, b. New York, N.Y., 1859; d. Greenwich, Conn., April 7, 1939. [10]

Edgar, Sir James David, lawyer and politician, b. Hatley, Que., 1841; d. Toronto, Ont., July 31, 1899. [27]

Edgar, Matilda, Lady, née Ridout, historian, b. Toronto, Ont., 1844; d. London, England, Sept. 29, 1910. [27]

Edgar, Pelham, educationist, b. Toronto, Ont., 1871; d. Canton, Ont., Oct. 7, 1948. [30]

Edgar, Randolph, journalist, b. Minneapolis, Minn., 1884; d. Boston, Mass., July 10, 1931. [10; 11; 70]

Edgar, William Crowell, journalist, b. La Crosse, Wis., 1856; d. Maxine-on-St. Croix, Minn., Dec. 2, 1932. [10; 70]

Edgerly, Webster, lawyer and philosopher, b. Salem, Mass., 1852; d. Trenton, N.J., Nov. 5, 1926. [4]

Edgerton, James Arthur, journalist, poet, and politician, b. Plantsville, O., 1869; d. Beverly Hills, Va., Dec. 3, 1938. [4; 10; 11]

Edgett, Edwin Francis, journalist, b. Boston, Mass., 1867; d. Arlington, Mass., March 12, 1946. [7; 10]

Edgington, Thomas Benton, lawyer, b. Ontario, O., 1837; d. Memphis, Tenn., Jan. 4, 1929. [10]

Edgren, August Hjalmar, educationist, b. Sweden, 1840; d. Lincoln, Neb., Dec. 9, 1903. [4; 7]

Edgren, John Alexis, clergyman, b. Sweden, 1839; d. Oakland, Calif., 1908. [10]

Edidin, Ben M., educationist, b. Russia, 1900; d. New York, N.Y., Aug. 6, 1948.

Edmands, John, librarian, b. Framingham, Mass., 1820; d. Philadelphia, Pa., Oct. 17, 1915. [1; 4; 7; 10]

Edmonds, George (pseud.). See Meriwether, Mrs. Elizabeth, née Avery.

Edmonds, John Worth, jurist, b. Hudson, N.Y., 1799; d. New York, N.Y., April 5, 1874. [1; 3; 4; 6; 8]

Edmonds, Richard Hathaway, journalist, b. Norfolk, Va., 1857; d. Baltimore, Md., Oct. 4, 1930. [4; 10]

Edmondson, Thomas William, mathematician, b. Yorkshire, England, 1859; d. Mount Vernon, N.Y., Nov. 4, 1938. [10]

Edmunds, Albert Joseph, librarian and poet, b. Tottenham, England, 1857; d. Cheltenham, Pa., Dec. 17, 1941. [7; 10]

Edmunds, Charles Wallis, medical educationist, b. Dorset, England, 1873; d. Ann Arbor, Mich., March 1, 1941. [10]

Edmunds, Sterling Edwin, lawyer, b. St. Louis, Mo., 1880; d. St. Louis, Mo., July 13, 1944. [10]

Edson, Obed, local historian, b. 1832; d. Falconer, N.Y., Nov. 22, 1919.

Edstrom, David, sculptor, b. Sweden, 1873; d. Los Angeles, Calif., Aug. 12, 1938. [10]

Edwards, Albert (pseud.). See Bullard, Arthur.

Edwards, Arthur Robin, physician, b. Chicago, Ill., 1867; d. Chicago, Ill., May 17, 1936. [10; 11]

Edwards, Bela Bates, clergyman, b. Southampton, Mass., 1802; d. Athens, Ga., April 20, 1852. [1; 4; 7]

Edwards, Boyd, clergyman and educationist, b. Lisle, N.Y., 1876; d. Arlington, Vt., Nov. 10, 1944. [10]

Edwards, Charles, lawyer, b. Norwich, England, 1797; d. New York, N.Y., May 30, 1868. [1; 3; 6; 8]

Edwards, Charles Lincoln, naturalist, b. Oquawka, Ill., 1863; d. Los Angeles, Calif., May 4, 1937. [4; 10]

Edwards, Edward Bartholomew, illustrator, b. Columbia, Pa., 1873; d. Hasbrouck Heights, N.J., Feb. 16, 1948. [7; 10]

Edwards, Elisha Jay, journalist, b. 1847; d. Greenwich, Conn., April 25, 1924. [26]

Edwards, Frederick, clergyman and poet, b. Cornwall, England, 1863; d. De Land, Fla., Oct. 5, 1948.

Edwards, George Cunningham, lawyer, b. 1787; d. 1837.

Edwards, George Cunningham, mathematician, b. 1852; d. 1930. [13]

Edwards, George Thornton, musician, b. Annapolis, Md., 1868; d. Portland, Me., March 21, 1932. [10]

Edwards, Harry Stillwell, novelist, b. Macon, Ga., 1855; d. Macon, Ga., Oct. 22, 1938. [4; 7; 10; 11]

Edwards, Isaac, lawyer, b. Saratoga county, N.Y., 1819; d. Albany, N.Y., March 26, 1879. [4]

Edwards, James Thomas, educationist, b. Barnegat, N.J., 1838; d. Randolph, N.Y., Aug. 20, 1914. [4; 10]

Edwards, John, poet, b. Wales, 1806; d. near Rome, N.Y., Jan. 20, 1887. [3; 8]

Edwards, John Ellis, clergyman, b. Guilford county, N.C., 1814; d. Lynchburg, Va., 1891. [3; 8; 34]

Edwards, John Milton (pseud.). See Cook, William Wallace,

Edwards, John Newman, historian, b. 1839; d. 1889. [34]

Edwards, Jonathan, theologian, b. East Windsor, Conn., 1703; d. Princeton, N.J., March 22, 1758. [1; 2; 3; 4; 5; 6; 7; 8]

Edwards, Jonathan, theologian, b. Northampton, Mass., 1745; d. Schenectady, N.Y., Aug. 1, 1801. [1; 4; 56]

Edwards, Jonathan, local historian, b. 1847; d. 1929.

Edwards, Joseph F., physician, b. 1853; d. Dec. 6, 1897. [55]

Edwards, Joseph Plimsoll, historian, b. 1857; d. Halifax, N.S., Feb. 3, 1930. [27]

Edwards, Justin, clergyman, b. Westhampton, Mass., 1787; d. Bath Alum, Va., July 23, 1853. [1; 4; 61]

Edwards, Loren McClain, clergyman, b. Rising Sun, Ind., 1877; d. Newton, Ia., 1945. [10; 11]

Edwards, Louise Betts, journalist and novelist, b. Philadelphia, Pa.; d. Philadelphia, Pa., Jan. 8, 1928. [10]

Edwards, Maurice Dwight, clergyman, b. Pittsburgh, Pa., 1847; d. St. Paul, Minn., Dec. 3, 1940. [4; 70]

Edwards, Morgan, clergyman, b. Monmouthshire, Wales, 1722; d. Pencador, Del., Jan. 28, 1795. [1; 3; 4; 8]

Edwards, Ninian Wirt, lawyer and historian, b. Frankfort, Ky., 1809; d. Springfield, Ill., Sept. 2, 1889. [1; 3; 4; 8; 36]

Edwards, Tryon, clergyman and compiler, b. Hartford, Conn., 1809; d. Detroit, Mich., Jan. 4, 1894. [4; 52]

Edwards, William Emory, novelist, b. Prince Edward county, Va., 1842; d. 1903. [3; 8; 34]

Edwards, William Henry, naturalist, b. Hunter, N.Y., 1822; d. Coalburg, W. Va., 1909. [10; 61]

Edwards, William Seymour, lawyer and traveller, b. New York, N.Y., 1856; d. Coalburg, W. Va., Dec. 26, 1915. [10]

Eells, Myron, clergyman, b. Walker's Prairie, Wash., 1843; d. Twana, Wash., 1907. [10]

Effington, C. (pseud.). See Cooke, John Esten.

Egan, Maurice Francis, diplomat and littérateur, b. Philadelphia, Pa., 1852; d. Brooklyn, N.Y., Jan. 15, 1924. [1; 4; 7; 10]

Egan, William Constantine, horticulturist, b. New York, N.Y., 1841; d. Highland Park, Ill., Jan. 10, 1930. [4]

Egar, John Hodson, clergyman, b. Cambridgeshire, England, 1832; d. 1942. [6]

Egbert, James Chidester, educationist, b. New York, N.Y., 1859; d. New York, N.Y., July 17, 1948. [10; 11; 68]

Egbert, Seneca, physician, b. Petroleum Centre, Pa., 1863; d. Wayne, Pa., Dec. 6, 1939. [10; 56]

Eggert, Charles Augustus, educationist, b. Magdeburg, Prussia, 1853; d. Rockford, Ill., Feb. 2, 1931. [10]

Eggleston, Edward, novelist and historian, b. Vevay, Ind., 1837; d. Joshua's Rock, Lake George, N.Y., Sept. 3, 1902. [1; 2; 3; 4; 5; 6; 7; 8; 71; 72]

Eggleston, George Cary, journalist and novelist, b. Vevay, Ind., 1839; d. New York, N.Y., April 14, 1911. [1; 2; 4; 7; 10; 34]

Egle, William Henry, librarian and historian, b. Lancaster county, Pa., 1830; d. Harrisburg, Pa., Feb. 19, 1901. [4; 7; 10]

Egleston, Thomas, mining engineer, b. New York, N.Y., 1832; d. New York, N.Y., Jan. 15, 1900. [4; 10; 62]

Ehrmann, Mary Bartholomew, poet and musician, b. Cincinnati, O.; d. Miami Beach, Fla., March 2, 1939. [10]

Ehrmann, Max, poet and playwright, b. Terre Haute, Ind., 1872; d. Indianapolis, Ind., Sept. 9, 1945. [7; 11]

Eidmann, Frank Lewis, mechanical engineer, b. Kingston, N.Y., 1887; d. New York, N.Y., Sept. 4, 1941. [10]

Eigenmann, Carl H., biologist, b. Germany, 1863; d. Bloomington, Ind., April 24, 1927. [4; 10]

Eilshemius, Louis Michel, painter, b. Arlington, N.J., 1864; d. New York, N.Y., Dec. 29, 1941. [7; 10]

Eiselen, Frederick Carl, educationist, b. Germany, 1872; d. Evanston, Ill., May 5, 1937. [10; 11]

Eisen, Gustavus Augustus, biologist and archaeologist, b. Stockholm, Sweden, 1847; d. New York, N.Y., Oct. 29, 1940. [7; 10; 11]

Eisendrath, Daniel Nathan, surgeon, b. Chicago, Ill., 1867; d. Paris, France, June 1, 1939. [10; 11]

Eitan, Israel, philologist, b. 1885; d. Pittsburgh, Pa., Oct. 11, 1935. [11]

Elbertus, Fra (pseud.). See Hubbard, Elbert.

Elder, Cyrus, lawyer and poet, b. Somerset, Pa., 1833; d. Philadelphia, Pa., Dec. 14, 1912. [10]

Elder, Mrs. Susan, née Blanchard, poet, b. 1835; d. 1923. [4; 34]

Elder, William, clergyman, b. Hants county, N.S., 1784; d. Cape Breton, N.S., 1848. [27]

Elder, William, physician and publicist, b. Somerset, Pa., 1806; d. Washington, D.C., April 5, 1885. [1; 3; 6; 8]

Elderhorst, William, mineralogist, b. 1828; d. 1861.

Eldon, Carl William, historian, b. 1901; d. Philadelphia, Pa., July 9, 1949.

Eldredge, Charles Q., collector, b. 1845; d. Old Mystic, Conn., Feb. 2, 1938.

Eldredge, Zoeth Skinner, banker and historian, b. Buffalo, N.Y., 1846; d. ? [10]

Eldridge, Frederick William, journalist and playwright, b. Alexandria, Va., 1877; d. Los Angeles, Calif., Aug. 9, 1937. [10; 35]

Eldridge, George Dyre, underwriter and novelist, b. 1848; d. ?

Eldridge, George Homans, geologist, b. Yarmouth, Mass., 1854; d. Chevy Chase, Md., 1905. [10]

Eleanore, Sister Mary, educationist, b. Pierceton, Ind., 1890; d. Holy Cross, Ind., Feb. 17, 1940. [21; 22]

Eliot, Annie (pseud.). See Trumbull, Annie Eliot.

Eliot, Charles William, educationist, b. Boston, Mass., 1834; d. Cambridge, Mass., Aug. 22, 1926. [1; 2; 3; 4; 5; 7; 8; 10; 51]

Eliot, Ellsworth, surgeon and historian, b. New York, N.Y., 1864; d. New York, N.Y., Nov. 2, 1945. [62]

Eliot, George Edwin, essayist, b. Clinton, Conn., 1864; d. Madison, Conn., Nov. 11, 1943. [62]

Eliot, Jared, clergyman, physician, and agriculturist, b. Guilford, Conn., 1685; d. Clinton, Conn., April 22, 1763. [1; 3; 6; 62]

Eliot, John, missionary to the Indians, b. Hertfordshire, England, 1604; d. Roxbury, Mass., May 21, 1690. [1; 2; 3; 4; 6]

Eliot, Samuel, historian and educationist, b. Boston, Mass., 1821; d. Beverly Farms, Mass., Sept. 14, 1898. [1; 3; 4; 6; 7]

Eliot, Samuel Atkins, politician and man of letters, b. Boston, Mass., 1798; d. Cambridge, Mass., Jan. 29, 1862. [1; 3; 4; 6; 7; 51]

Eliot, Walter Graeme, civil engineer, and genealogist, b. New York, N.Y., 1857; d. May 3, 1931. [10]

Eliot, William Greenleaf, clergyman and educationist, b. New Bedford, Mass., 1811; d. Pass Christian, Miss., Jan. 23, 1881. [1; 3; 4; 7; 8]

Eliot, William Horace, genealogist, b. 1824; d. 1852. [62]

Elkins, Felton Broomall, short-story writer, b. Philadelphia, Pa., 1889; d. near San Francisco, Calif., Jan. 6, 1944.

Eller, Homer C., lawyer, b. Mishawaka, Ind., 1845; d. St. Paul, Minn., Nov. 3, 1896. [70]

Ellerbe, Rose Lucille, journalist, b. New York, N.Y., 1861; d. Los Angeles, Calif., 1929. [35]

Ellet, Charles, engineer, b. Penn's Manor, Bucks county, Pa., 1810; d. Cairo, Ill., June 21, 1862. [1; 3; 4; 6; 8]

Ellet, Mrs. Elizabeth Fries, née Lummis, poet and historian, b. Sodus Point, N.Y., 1818; d. New York, N.Y., June 3, 1877. [1; 3; 4; 6; 7; 8]

Ellice, Edward, merchant, b. 1781; d. Ardochy, Glengarry, Scotland, Sept. 17, 1863. [27]

Ellicott, Andrew, surveyor, b. Bucks county, Pa., 1754; d. West Point, N.Y., Aug. 28, 1820. [1; 3; 4]

Ellingwood, Albert Russell, political scientist, b. Cedar Rapids, Ia., 1887; d. Evanston, Ill., May 12, 1934. [10; 11]

Ellingwood, Finley, physician, b. Manchester, Ind., 1852; d. Evanston, Ill., June 29, 1920. [10]

Ellinwood, Frank Field, clergyman, b. Clinton, N.Y., 1826; d. Cornwall, Conn., Sept. 30, 1908. [10; 63]

Ellinwood, Ralph Everett, journalist, b. Flagstaff, Ariz., 1893; d. Tucson, Ariz., Aug. 30, 1930. [10; 45]

Elliot, Daniel Giraud, zoologist, b. New York, N.Y., 1835; d. New York, N.Y., Dec. 22, 1915. [4; 10]

Elliot, George Henry, military engineer, b. Lowell, Mass., 1831; d. 1900. [3; 8]

Elliot, George Thomson, physician, b. 1827; d. 1871. [48]

Elliot, Henry Rutherford, novelist, b. Woodbridge, Conn., 1849; d. New York N.Y., April 18, 1906. [4; 7; 10; 62]

Elliot, James, politician, b. Gloucester, Mass., 1775; d. Newfane, Vt., Nov. 10, 1839. [10]

Elliot, Samuel, jurist, b. Gloucester Mass., 1777; d. Brattleboro, Vt., Dec. 10, 1845. [43]

Elliot, Samuel Hayes, clergyman, b. Brattleboro, Vt., 1809; d. New Haven, Conn., Sept. 11, 1869. [7; 43]

Elliott, Arthur Henry, chemist, d. Feb. 28, 1918. [48]

Elliott, Benjamin, lawyer, b. Charleston, S.C., 1787; d. 1836. [1; 34]

Elliott, Byron Kosciusko, lawyer, b. Hamilton, O., 1835; d. Indianapolis, Ind., April 19, 1913. [10]

Elliott, Charles, clergyman and historian, b. Donegal county, Ireland, 1792; d. Mount Pleasant, Ia., Jan. 8, 1869. [1; 3; 4; 6; 8]

Elliott, Charles, educationist, b. Castleton, Scotland, 1815; d. Easton, Pa., Feb. 14, 1892. [36]

Elliott, Charles Burke, jurist, b. Morgan county, O., 1861; d. Minneapolis, Minn., Sept. 18, 1935. [1a; 4; 10]

Elliott, Charles Gleason, drainage engineer, b. La Salle county, Ill.,1850; d. Washington, D.C., Sept. 14, 1926. [4; 10]

Elliott, Charles Wylys, miscellaneous writer, b. Guilford, Conn., 1817; d. Guilford, Conn., Aug. 23, 1883. [3; 4; 6; 8]

Elliott, Emilia (pseud.) See Jacobs, Caroline Emilia.

Elliott, Ernest Eugene, journalist, b. Indianapolis, Ind., 1878; d. Kansas City, Mo., 1941. [10; 11]

Elliott, Francis Perry, novelist, b. Nashville, Tenn., 1861; d. Nashville, Tenn., Aug. 13, 1924. [10]

Elliott, Franklin Reuben, horticulturist, b. Guilford, Conn., 1817; d. Cleveland, O., Jan. 10, 1878. [3; 6; 8]

Elliott, George, clergyman, b. Licking county, O., 1851; d. New York, N.Y., Nov. 2, 1930. [10]

Elliott, Henry Wood, naturalist, b. 1846; d. Earlington, Wash., May 25, 1930. [26]

Elliott, Howard, railway president, b. New York, N.Y., 1860; d. New York, N.Y., July 8, 1928. [4; 10]

Elliott, Mrs. Kathleen, née Morrow, writer of books for children, b. Illinois, 1897; d. New York, N.Y., March 3, 1940. [12]

Elliott, Mrs. Maud, née Howe, novelist, biographer, and traveller, b. Boston, Mass., 1854; d. Newport R.I. March 19, 1948. [7; 10; 11]

Elliott, Orrin Leslie, educationist, b. Centerville, N.Y., 1860; d. Stanford University, Calif., Aug. 28, 1940. [10]

Elliott, Robert G., official executioner, b. 1874; d. New York, N.Y., Oct. 10, 1939. (2b)

Elliott, Sarah Barnwell, novelist, b. Georgia, 1848; d. Sewanee, Tenn., Aug. 30, 1928. [1; 3; 4; 7; 8; 10; 34]

Elliott, Simon Bolivar, forester, b. 1830; d. 1917.

Elliott, Sophronia Maria, home economist, b. 1854; d. Boston, Mass., March 16, 1942. [47]

Elliott, Stephen, naturalist, b. Beaufort, S.C., 1771; d. Charleston, S.C., March 28, 1830. [1; 3; 4; 8; 34]

Elliott, Stephen, bishop, b. Beaufort, S.C., 1806; d. Savannah, Ga., Dec. 21, 1866. [4; 34]

Elliott, Walter Hackett Robert, priest, b. Detroit, Mich., 1842; d. Washington, D.C., April 18, 1928. [1; 7; 10; 21]

Elliott, William, agriculturist, b. Beaufort, S.C., 1788; d. Charleston, S.C., Feb. 3, 1863. [1; 3; 4; 6; 7; 8; 34]

Elliott, William Frederick, lawyer, b. Indianapolis, Ind., 1859; d. Indianapolis, Ind., June 5, 1927. [4]

Ellis, Mrs. Anne, pioneer, b. 1875; d. 1938. [7]

Ellis, Arthur Blake, lawyer, b. 1854; d. Boston, Mass., 1923. [51]

Ellis, Benjamin, physician, b. 1798; d. 1831. [55]

Ellis, Carleton, chemist, b. Keene, N.H., 1876; d. Miami Beach, Fla., Jan. 13, 1941. [10; 13]

Ellis, Charles Mayo, lawyer, b. Boston, Mass., 1818; d. Brookline, Mass., Jan. 26, 1878. [3; 8; 51]

Ellis, Edward Sylvester, historian and dime novelist, b. Gen va, O., 1840; d. Upper Montclair, N.J., June 20, 1916. [4; 7; 10]

Ellis, Erastus Ranney, physician, b. Pittstown, N.Y., 1832; d. Grand Rapids, Mich., 1914. [39]

Ellis, Franklin, local historian, b. 1828; d. 1885.

Ellis, George Edward, clergyman and historian, b. Boston, Mass., 1814; d. Boston, Mass., Dec. 20, 1894. [1; 3; 4; 6; 7]

Ellis, George Washington, lawyer and sociologist, b. Weston, Mo., 1875; d. Chicago, Ill., Nov. 26, 1919. [1; 4; 7; 10]

Ellis, Harold Milton. See Ellis, Milton.

Ellis, James Whitcomb, local historian, b. Danville, Ind., 1848; d. Maquoketa, Ia., April 9, 1929. [37]

Ellis, Job Bicknell, mycologist, b. Potsdam, N.Y., 1829; d. Newfield, N.J., 1905. [10]

Ellis, John, physician, b. Ashfield, Mass., 1815; d. 1896. [4]

Ellis, John Harvard, lawyer, b. Boston, Mass., 1841; d. May 3, 1870. [51]

Ellis, John William, clergyman, b. Carthage, Ill., 1839; d. Plattsburg, Mo., 1910. [10]

Ellis, Milton, educationist, b. Belfast, Me., 1885; d. Orono, Me., May 18, 1947. [7; 11; 14]

Ellis, Robert Walpole, geologist, b. Nevinville, Ia., 1868; d. Albuquerque, N.M., May 10, 1937. [10]

Ellis, Sumner, clergyman, b. North Orange, Mass., 1828; d. Chicago, Ill., Jan. 26, 1886. [3; 6; 8]

Ellis, William Hodgson, educationist and poet, b. Derbyshire, England, 1845; d. Toronto, Ont., Aug. 23, 1921. [27]

Ells, Robert Wheelock, geologist, b. Sheffield Mills, N.S., 1845; d. Ottawa, Ont., May 23, 1911. [27]

Ellsworth, Ephraim Elmer, soldier, b. Mechanicsville, N.Y., 1837; d. Alexandria, Va., May 24, 1861. [36]

Ellsworth, Erastus Wolcott, poet, b. Windsor, Conn., 1822; d. East Windsor Hill, Conn., Jan. 5, 1902. [45]

Ellsworth, Henry William, lawyer, b. Windsor, Conn., 1814; d. New Haven, Conn,. Aug. 14, 1864. [1; 3; 8]

Ellsworth, Henry William, educationist, b. Stockton, N.Y., 1837; d. Binghampton, N.Y., July 8, 1924. [4]

Ellsworth, Mrs. Mary Wolcott, née Janvrin, novelist, b. Exeter, N.H., 1830; d. Newton, Mass., Aug. 16, 1870. [4; 7]

Ellsworth, William Webster, publisher b. Hartford, Conn., 1855; d. Torrington, Conn., Dec. 18, 1936. [7; 10; 11]

Ellwanger, George Herman, horticulturist, and poet, b. Rochester, N.Y., 1848; d. 1906. [4; 7; 10]

Ellwanger, Henry Brooks, horticulturist, b. Rochester, N.Y., 1851; d. Aug. 7, 1883. [4]

Ellwanger, William De Lancey, poet and essayist, b. Rochester, N.Y., 1855; d. Rochester, N.Y., Feb. 16, 1913. [4; 7; 10; 62]

Ellwood, Charles Abram, sociologist, b. near Ogdensburg, N.Y., 1873; d. Durham, N.C., Sept. 25, 1946. [7; 10; 11]

Elmendorf, Dwight Lathrop, photographer and lecturer, b. Brooklyn, N.Y., 1859; d. New York, N.Y., May 7, 1929. [10]

Elmendorf, John Jay, philosopher, b. 1827; d. 1896. [44]

Elmendorf, Mrs. Theresa Hubbell, née West, librarian, b. Pardeeville, Wis., 1855; d. Buffalo, N.Y., Sept. 4, 1932. [4; 10]

Elmer, Herbert Charles, educationist, b. 1860; d. Ithaca, N.Y., Nov. 24, 1935. [11]

Elmer, Lucius Quintius Cincinnatus, jurist, b. Bridgeton, N.J., 1793; d. Bridgeton, N.J., March 11, 1883. [1; 3; 4; 8]

Elmore, Jefferson, educationist, b. Ashley, Mo., 1862; d. about 1935. [10; 11]

Elmore, Wilber Theodore, clergyman, b. St. Charles, Ill., 1871; d. Wayne, Pa., Nov. 27, 1935. [10]

Elmwood, Elnathan (pseud.). See Green, Asa.

Elser, Frank Ball, journalist, novelist and playwright, b. Fort Worth, Tex., 1885; d. British West Indies ,Jan.' 31, 1935. [7; 10]

Elshemus. Louis Michael. See Eilshemius, Louis Michel.

Elsner, Henry Leopold, physician, b. Syracuse, N.Y., 1855; d. Syracuse, N.Y., Feb. 17, 1916. [10]

Elson, Arthur, music critic, b. Boston, Mass., 1873; d. Boston, Mass., Feb. 24, 1940. [7; 10; 11]

Elson, Louis Charles, writer on music, b. Boston, Mass., 1848; d. Boston, Mass., Feb. 14, 1920. [1; 2; 3; 4; 7; 10]

Elson, William Harris, educationist, b. Carrollton, O., 1856; d. Chicago, Ill., Feb. 2, 1935. [10]

Eltinge, Le Roy, soldier, b. South Woodstock, N.Y., 1872; d. Washington, D.C., May 13, 1931. [10]

Eltzholtz, Carl Frederick, clergyman, b. Denmark, 1840; d. Los Angeles, Calif., April 17, 1929. [10]

Elwell, Edward Henry, journalist, b. Portland, Me., 1825; d. Bar Harbor, Me., July 14, 1890. [4; 38]

Elwell, John Johnson, physician and lawyer, b. near Warren, O., 1820; d. Cleveland O., March 13, 1900. [1]

Elwell, Joseph Bowne, bridge whist expert, b. 1874; d. New York, N.Y., June 10, 1920.

Elwell, Levi Henry, educationist, b. Northampton, Mass., 1854; d. Amherst, Mass., Dec. 27, 1916. [10; 45]

Elwyn, Alfred Langdon, physician and compiler, b. Portsmouth, N.H., 1804; d. March 15, 1884. [1; 4; 7; 51]

Ely, Alfred, lawyer and politician, b. Lyme, Conn., 1815; d. Rochester, N.Y., May 18, 1892.

Ely, Edward Talbot, humorist, b. 1850; d. 1885.

Ely, Ezra Stiles, clergyman, b. Lebanon, Conn., 1786; d. Philadelphia, Pa., June 18, 1861. [3; 62]

Ely, Helen Rutherford, horticulturist, d. 1920.

Ely, Richard Theodore, economist, b. Ripley, N.Y., 1854; d. Old Lyme, Conn., Oct. 4, 1943. [4; 10]

Elzas, Barnett Abraham, rabbi, b. Germany, 1867; d. New York, N.Y., Oct. 18, 1936. [10]

Emard, Joseph Médard, bishop, b. Laprairie, Que., 1853; d. Ottawa, Ont., March 28, 1927. [27]

Embree, Charles Fleming, novelist, b. Princeton, Ind., 1874; d. Santa Ana, Calif., 1905. [7; 10]

Embry, James Crawford, bishop, b. 1834; d. 1897.

Embury, Mrs. Emma Catherine, née Manley, poet and novelist, b. New York, N.Y., about 1806; d. Brooklyn, N.Y., Feb. 10, 1863. [1; 3; 4; 6; 7; 8]

Emerson, Mrs. Adaline, née Talcott, poet, b. 1837; d. 1915.

Emerson, Mrs. Alice, née Fernald, poet, b. Boston, Mass., d. Indianapolis, Ind., July 27, 1941.

Emerson, Benjamin Dudley, educationist, b. 1781; d. Jamaica Plain, Mass., Oct. 1, 1872. [49]

Emerson, Benjamin Kendall, geologist, b. Nashua, N.H., 1843; d. Amherst, Mass., April 7, 1932. [1a; 4; 13]

Emerson, Charles Noble, lawyer, b. Williamstown, Mass., 1821; d. New York, N.Y., April 15, 1869. [3; 8; 61]

Emerson, Charles Phillips, physician, b. Methuen, Mass., 1872; d. Indianapolis, Ind., Sept. 26, 1938. [10]

Emerson, Charles Wesley, lecturer, b. Pittsfield, Vt., 1837; d. 1908. [10]

Emerson, Edward Randolph, wine-grower, b. New York, N.Y., 1856; d. Washington-ville, N.Y., Dec. 27, 1924. [7; 10]

Emerson, Edward Waldo, biographer, b. Concord, Mass., 1844; d. Concord, Mass., Jan. 27, 1930. [1; 7; 8; 10]

Emerson, Edwin, educationist and poet, b. 1823; d. 1908. [4; 56]

Emerson, Mrs. Ellen, née Russell, ethnologist, b. New Sharon, Me., 1837; d. Boston, Mass., June 12, 1907. [1; 4; 7; 8; 10]

Emerson, Frederick educationist, b. Hampstead, N.H., 1788; d. Boston, Mass., 1857. [3; 8]

Emerson, George Barrell, educationist, b. Wells, Me., 1797; d. Newton, Mass., March 4, 1881. [1; 3; 4; 6; 7; 8]

Emerson, George Homer, clergyman, b. 1822; d. 1898.

Emerson, Harrington, efficiency expert, b. Trenton., NJ., 1853; d. New York, N.Y., May 23, 1931. [4; 10]

Emerson, Henry Poindexter, educationist, b. Lynnfield, Mass., 1846; d. Middleton, Mass., 1930. [10]

Emerson, Jesse Milton, publisher and traveller, b. 1818; d. 1898. [4]

Emerson, Joseph, clergyman, b. Hollis, N.H., 1777; d. Wethersfield, Conn., May 14, 1833. [3; 4]

Emerson, Mrs. Lucy, née Reed, writer on cooking, b. about 1769; d. Montpelier, Vt., Sept. 18, 1855. [43]

Emerson, Mrs. Nannette Snow, poet, b. 1840; d. 1884. [6]

Emerson, Nathaniel Bright, physician, b. Oahu, Hawaii, 1839; d. Honolulu, Hawaii, July 15, 1915. [10; 61]

Emerson, Nathaniel Waldo, surgeon, b. Boston, Mass., 1854; d. Jamaica Plain, Mass., Dec. 20, 1930. [10; 46]

Emerson, Oliver Farrar, philologist, b. near Wolf Creek, Ia., 1860; d. Ocala, Fla., March 13, 1927. [1; 4; 7; 10]

Emerson, Paul, soil bacteriologist, b. Wilmington, Del., 1887; d. Ames, Ia., Sept. 17, 1937. [10; 13]

Emerson, Ralph, clergyman, b. Hollis, N.H., 1787; d. Rockford, Ill., May 26, 1863. [3; 4; 8]

Emerson, Ralph Waldo, essayist, poet, and philosopher, b. Boston, Mass., 1803; d. Concord, Mass., April 27, 1882. [1; 2; 3; 4; 5; 6; 7; 8; 71; 72]

Emerson, Samuel Franklin, clergyman and educationist, b. Norwich, Vt., 1850; d. Orlando, Fla., April 5, 1939. [10; 62]

Emerson, Sara Anna, educationist, b. 1855; d. Roxbury, Mass., Nov. 1, 1939.

Emerson, Walter Crane, journalist and naturalist, b. 1863; d. Squirrel Island, Me., May 22, 1929. [2a]

Emerson, William, clergyman, b. Concord, Mass., 1769; d. Boston, Mass., May 12, 1811. [1; 3; 4; 6]

Emerson, William Andrew, local historian, b. 1851; d. ?

Emerson, William Dana, poet, b. 1813; d. 1891.

Emerson, Willis George, novelist, b. near Blakesbury, Ia., 1856; d. Los Angeles, Calif., Dec. 11, 1918. [10; 35]

Emerton, Ephraim, historian, b. Salem. Mass., 1851; d. Cambridge, Mass., March 3, 1935. [1a; 4; 7; 10]

Emerton, James Henry, naturalist, b. Salem, Mass., 1847; d. Boston, Mass., Dec. 5, 1930. [1a; 3; 4; 6; 7; 8; 10]

Emery, Fred Parker, educationist, b. Pembroke, N.H., 1865; d. Hanover, N.H., Jan. 16, 1927. [10; 49]

Emery, George Alexander, local historian, b. 1821; d. 1894. [38]

Emery, George Davis, lawyer, b. Northfield, Minn., 1855; d. ? [70]

Emery, Henry Crosby, economist, b. Ellsworth, Me., 1872; d. on board ship in the Pacific ocean, Feb. 6, 1924. [1; 4; 10]

Emery, Ina Capitola, instructor in short-story writing, b. Bethel, Vt., 1868; d. Washington, D.C., July 25, 1941. [10; 11; 16]

Emery, Lucilius Alonzo, jurist, b. Carmel, Me., 1840; d. Ellsworth, Me., Aug. 26, 1920. [4; 10; 46]

Emery, Mabel Sarah, traveller, b. 1859; d. ?

Emery, Philip Alfred, poet and working-man, b. 1830; d. ?

Emery, Rufus, clergyman and genealogist, b. 1827; d. ?

Emery, Samuel Hopkins, clergyman and local historian, b. 1815; d. 1901. [51]

Emery, Sarah Anna, novelist, b. Newburyport, Mass., 1821; d. Newburyport, Mass., 1907. [10]

Emery, Stephen Albert, musician, b. Paris, Me., 1841; d. Boston, Mass., April 15, 1891. [1; 4; 20]

Emery, Susan L., religious journalist, b. Dorchester, Mass., 1846; d. Boston, Mass., 1917. [10; 21]

Emmerton, James Arthur, physician and genealogist, b. Salem, Mass., 1834; d. 1888. [3; 6; 7; 51]

Emmet, Thomas Addis, Irish patriot, b. Cork, Ireland, 1764; d. New York, N.Y., Nov. 14, 1827. [1; 3; 4; 8]

Emmet, Thomas Addis, physician, b. near Charlottesville, Va., 1828; d. New York, N.Y., March 1, 1919. [1; 3; 4; 7; 10; 34]

Emmet, William Le Roy, electrical engineer, b. New Rochelle, N.Y., 1859; d. Erie, Pa., Sept. 26, 1941. [4; 10; 11]

Emmons, Ebenezer, geologist, b. Middlefield, Mass., 1799; d. Brunswick county, N.C., Oct. 1, 1863; [1; 3; 4; 8]

Emmons, George Foster, naval officer, b. Clarendon, Vt., 1811; d. Princeton, N.J., July 23, 1884. [1; 2; 4; 43]

Emmons, Nathanael, clergyman, b. East Haddam, Conn., 1775; d. Franklin, Mass., Sept. 23, 1840. [1; 3; 4; 8; 62]

Emmons, Richard, physician and poet, b. 1788; d. about 1837.

Emmons, Samuel Franklin, geologist, b. Boston, Mass., 1841; d. Washington, D.C., March 29, 1911. [1; 2; 3; 4; 8; 10]

Emory, Frederick, novelist, b. Centreville, Md., 1853; d. Queenstown, Md., 1908. [10]

Emory, John, bishop, b. Queen Anne county, Md., 1789; d. Reisterstown, Md., Dec. 17, 1835. [1; 4; 8; 34]

Emory, Robert, educationist, b. Philadelphia, Pa., 1814; d. Baltimore, Md., May 18, 1848. [3; 8; 34]

Emory, William Hemsley, soldier, b. Queen Anne county, Md., 1811; d. Washington, D.C., Dec. 1, 1887. [3; 4; 8; 34]

Emswiler, John Edward, educationist, b. Lebanon, Ill., 1880; d. Ann Arbor, Mich., Sept. 23, 1940. [13]

Enander, Johan Alfred, journalist, b. Sweden, 1842; d. Chicago, Ill., Sept. 9, 1910. [4; 10]

Endicott, Charles Moses, sea-captain and antiquary, b. Danvers, Mass., 1793; d. Salem, Mass., Dec. 14, 1863. [1; 3; 7; 8]

Endicott, William Crowninshield, lawyer, b. Salem, Mass., 1860; d. Boston Mass., Nov. 28, 1936. [10; 51]

Enelow, Hyman Gerson, rabbi, b. Russia, 1877; d. at sea, Feb. 6, 1934. [1a; 10; 11]

Engelbrecht, Helmuth Carol, educationist, b. Chicago, Ill., 1895; d. near Trenton, N.J., Oct. 8, 1939. [11]

Engelhardt, Charles Anthony, See Engelhardt, Zephyrin.

Engelhardt, Fred, educationist, b. Naugatuck, Conn., 1885; d. Durham, N.H., Feb. 3, 1944. [10; 62]

Engelhardt, Zephyrin, priest and historian, b. Hanover, Germany, 1851; d. Santa Barbara, Calif., April 27, 1934. [1a; 10; 21; 22]

Engelmann, George, physician and botanist, b. Germany, 1809; d. St. Louis, Mo., Feb. 4, 1884. [4]

Engelmann, George Julius, physician, b. St. Louis, Mo., 1847; d. Nashua, N.H., Nov. 16, 1903. [1; 4; 8; 10]

England, George Allan, explorer and novelist, b. Fort McPherson, Neb., 1877; d. Concord, N.H., June 27, 1936. [7; 10; 11]

England, John, bishop, b. Cork, Ireland, 1786; d. Charleston, S.C., April 11, 1842. [1; 3; 4; 6; 7; 8]

Engle, Washington Alvord, physician and poet, d. Hartford, Mich., Nov. 27, 1907. [53]

Engleman, James Ozro, educationist, b. Jeffersonville, Ind., 1873; d. near Middle Bass Island, Lake Erie, Sept. 15, 1943. [7; 10; 11]

Engles, William Morrison, clergyman and editor, b. Philadelphia, Pa., 1797; b. Philadelphia, Pa., Nov. 21, 1867. [3; 6; 8]

English, George Bethune, adventurer, b. Cambridge, Mass., 1787; d. Washington, D.C., Sept. 20, 1828. [1; 3; 4; 6; 8; 51]

English, John Mahan, theologian, b. Tullytown, Pa., 1845; d. Newton Centre, Mass., May 17, 1927. [10]

English, Thomas Dunn, journalist, politician, and poet, b. Philadelphia, Pa., 1819; d. Newark, N.J., April 1, 1902. [1; 3; 4; 6; 7; 8]

English, William Eastin, freemason, b. Englishton Park, Ind., 1852; d. Indianapolis, Ind., April 29, 1926. [10]

English, William Hayden, lawyer, politician, and historian, b. Lexington, Ind., 1822; d. Indianapolis, Ind., Feb. 7, 1896. [1; 3; 4]

Ennis, William Duane, educationist, b. Bergen county, N.J., 1877; d. Suffern, N.Y., Oct. 14, 1947. [10]

Eno, Henry Lane, poet, b. New York, N.Y., 1871; d. Somerset, England, Sept. 10, 1928. [4; 62]

Eno, Joel Nelson, librarian and genealogist, b. 1852; d. New York, N.Y., Feb. 7, 1937. [47]

Eno, William Phelps, traffic expert, b. New York, N.Y., 1858; d. Norwalk, Conn., Dec. 4, 1945. [62]

Ensley, Enoch, economist, b. near Nashville, Tenn., 1836; d. Nov. 18, 1891. [1]

Eppens, Edward Henry, clergyman, b. Henderson, Ky., 1873; d. Ann Arbor, Mich., Sept. 10, 1941. [62]

Epstein, Abraham, social reformer, b. Russia, 1892; d. New York, N.Y., May 2, 1942. [10; 11]

Erdman, William Jacob, clergyman, b. Allentown, Pa., 1834; d. Germantown, Pa., Oct. 31, 1923. [68]

Erickson, Carl Gustav, clergyman and educationist, b. Oslo, Norway, 1877; d. Lutherland, Pa., Oct. 20, 1936. [62]

Ericsson, Henry, contractor, b. Torp, Sweden, 1861; d. Miami, Fla., Feb. 19, 1947.

Erikssen, Erik McKinley, historian, b. Odebolt, Ia., 1896; d. Los Angeles, Calif., May 22, 1941. [10; 11]

Ermatinger, Charles Oakes Zaccheus, jurist and historian, b. St. Thomas, Ont., 1851; d. St. Thomas, Ont., Dec. 16, 1921. [31a]

Ermatinger, Edward, fur-trader, b. Elba, 1797; d. St. Thomas, Ont., 1876. [27]

Ernst, Bernard Morris Lee, lawyer, b. Uniontown, Ala., 1879; d. New York, N.Y., Nov. 28, 1938. [10]

Ernst, Carl Wilhelm, journalist, b. near Hanover, Germany, 1845; d. Boston, Mass., April 12, 1919. [4]

Ernst, George Alexander Otis, lawyer, b. Spring Garden, O., 1850; d. Batavia, N.Y., June 13, 1912. [10]

Ernst, Harold Clarence, bacteriologist, b. Cincinnati, O., 1856; d. Plymouth, Mass., Sept. 7, 1923. [4; 10]

Ernst, Oswald Herbert, military engineer, b. near Cincinnati, O., 1842; d. Washington, D.C., March 21, 1926. [1; 3; 4; 10]

Erratic Enrique (pseud.). See Lukens, Henry Clay.

Errett, Isaac, clergyman, b. New York, N.Y., 1820; d. Cincinnati, O., Dec. 19, 1888. [1; 3; 4; 6; 7; 8; 10]

Erskine, Albert Russel, motor-car manufacturer, b. Huntsville, Ala., 1871; d. South Bend, Ind., July 1, 1933. [10]

Erskine, Mrs. Emma, née Payne, novelist, b. Racine, Wis., 1854; d. Tryon, N.C., March 5, 1924. [10]

Erving, Henry Wood, banker, b. Westfield, Mass., 1851; d. West Hartford, Conn., Jan. 14, 1941.

Erwin, Frank Alexander, lawyer, b. 1860; d. New York, N.Y., July 19, 1930. [61]

Erwin, James Shrewsbury, lawyer, b. 1857; d. 1918.

Esarey, Logan, historian, b. Branchville, Ind., 1873; d. Bloomington, Ind., Sept. 24, 1942. [10]

Esenwein, Joseph Berg, editor, b. Philadelphia, Pa., 1867; d. Long Meadow, Mass., Nov. 1, 1946. [7; 10; 11]

Esling, Mrs. Catherine Harbeson, née Waterman, poet, b. 1812; d. ?

Esling, Charles Henry Augustus, lawyer, b. Philadelphia, Pa., 1845; d. Stuttgart, Germany, Feb. 1, 1907. [3; 8; 10]

Esmeralda, Aurora (pseud.). See Mighels, Mrs. Ella Sterling, née Clark.

Espy, James Pollard, meteorologist, b. Westmoreland county, Pa., 1785; d. Cincinnati, O., Jan. 24, 1860. [1; 3; 4; 8]

Essary, Jesse Frederick, journalist, b. Washburn, Tenn., 1881; d. Washington, D.C., March 11, 1942. [10]

Essig, Charles James, dentist, b. 1841; d. 1901.

Estabrook, Henry Dodge, lawyer, b. Alden, N.Y., 1854; d. Tarrytown, N.Y., Dec. 22, 1917. [4; 10]

Estee, Morris M., lawyer, d. San Francisco, Calif., 1903. [10]

Estes, Dana, publisher, b. Gorham, Me., 1840; d. Brookline, Mass., June 16, 1909. [4; 10; 46]

Estes, David Foster, clergyman, b. Auburn, Me., 1851; d. Los Angeles, Calif., Feb. 19, 1926. [10; 59]

Estes, William Lawrence, surgeon, b. near Brownsville, Tenn., 1855; d. Bethlehem, Pa., Oct. 20, 1940. [10]

Estey, Stephen Sewall, clergyman, b. Calais, Me., 1861; d. Topeka, Kans., April 28, 1932. [10]

Estimauville, Robert Anne d', Chevalier de Beaumouchel, soldier and civil servant, b. Louisbourg, Cape Breton Island, 1754; d. Quebec, Lower Canada, July 31, 1831. [27]

Esty, Mrs. Annette, novelist, b. 1879; d. Dayton Beach, Fla., Nov. 11, 1948.

Esty, Lucien Coy, journalist, b. Urbana, Ill., 1899; d. New Haven, Conn., March 19, 1929. [45]

Esty, William, electrical engineer, b. Amherst, Mass., 1868; d. Pocono Lake Reserve, Pa., July 6, 1928. [10]

Etter, John W., clergyman, b. 1846; d. 1895.

Etting, Frank Marx, historian, d. Philadelphia, Pa., June 4, 1890. [55]

Ettlinger, Harold, journalist, b. about 1910; d. Chicago, Ill., May 11, 1944.

Eubank, Earle Edward, sociologist, b. Columbia, Mo., 1887; d. Cincinnati, O., Dec. 18, 1945. [7; 10]

Eustis, Henry Lawrence, educationist and genealogist, b. Boston, Mass., 1819; d. Cambridge, Mass., Jan. 11, 1885. [1; 51]

Evans, Mrs. Alice, née Pickford, philanthropist, b. 1868; d. Newton, Mass., Dec. 25, 1946.

Evans, Anthony Walton White, civil engineer, b. New Brunswick, N.J., 1817; d. New York, N.Y., Nov. 28, 1886. [1; 3; 4]

Evans, Augusta Jane. See Wilson, Mrs. Augusta Jane, née Evans.

Evans, Charles, physician and historian, b. 1802; d. 1879. [6]

Evans, Charles, librarian and bibliographer, b. Boston, Mass., 1850; d. Chicago, Ill., Feb. 8, 1935. [1a; 7; 10]

Evans, Charles Worthington, genealogist, b. 1812; d. 1889.

Evans, Chris, labour official, d. Nov. 2, 1924. [2b]

Evans, Clement Anselm, soldier and historian, b. Stewart county, Ga., 1833; d. Atlanta, Ga., July 2, 1911. [1; 4; 7; 10; 34]

Evans, Donald, poet, b. Philadelphia, Pa., 1884; d. New York, N.Y., May 27, 1921. [7; 10]

Evans, Edward Payson, scholar, b. Remsen, N.Y., 1831; d. New York, N.Y., March 6, 1917. [1; 3; 4; 7; 8]

Evans, Mrs. Elizabeth Edson, née Gibson, novelist and poet, b. Newport, N.H., 1832; d. Bad Aibling, Bavaria, Germany, Sept. 9, 1911. [1; 3; 7; 8; 10]

Evans, Mrs. Elizabeth Hewling, née Stockton, poet, b. Philadelphia, Pa., 1818; d. Amelia county, Va., 1855. [3]

Evans, Frank Edgar, naval officer, b. Franklin, Pa., 1876; d. Honolulu, Hawaii, Nov. 25, 1941 .[10]

Evans, Frederick William, Shaker elder, b. Worcestershire, England, 1808; d. Mount Lebanon, N.Y., March 6, 1893. [1; 3; 4; 6; 7; 8]

Evans, George, dentist, b. Ireland, 1844; d. New York, N.Y., Jan. 13, 1942.

Evans, George Alfred, physician, b. Brooklyn, N.Y., 1850; d. Brooklyn, N.Y. July 14, 1925. [1; 6]

Evans, George Samuel, lawyer b. Visalia, Calif., 1876; d. Oakland, Calif., May 26, 1904. [35]

Evans, Harry Carroll, journalist, b. Bloomfield, Ia., 1858; d. Des Moines, Ia., April 13, 1932. [11]

Evans, Hugh Davey, lawyer, b. Baltimore, Md., 1792; d. Baltimore, Md., July 16, 1868. [1; 3; 4; 6; 7; 8]

Evans, Larry, novelist, d. Tucson, Ariz., April 30, 1925.

Evans, Lawrence Boyd, lawyer, b. Radnor, O., 1870; d. Washington, D.C., Oct. 30, 1928. [10]

Evans, Lawton Bryan, educationist, b. Lumpkin, Ga., 1862; d. Augusta, Ga., April 6, 1934. [4; 10; 34]

Evans, Lewis, geographer, b. about 1700; d. New York, N.Y., June 12, 1756. [1; 4; 8]

Evans, Mrs. Mary Anna, née Buck, poet, b. 1857; d. ?

Evans, Milton G., clergyman and educationist, b. near Ebensburg, Pa., 1862; d. Carbondale, Pa., Sept. 17, 1939. [10]

Evans, Nathaniel, clergyman and poet, b. Philadelphia, Pa., 1742; d. Haddonfield, N.J., Oct. 29, 1868. [1; 3; 7; 8]

Evans, Nelson Wiley, lawyer and local historian, b. Sardinia, O., 1842; d. Portsmouth, O., May 27, 1913. [10]

Evans, Nevil Norton, chemist, b. Montreal, Que., 1865; d. Westmount, Que., Sept. 9, 1948. [13]

Evans, Oliver, inventor, b. near Newport, Del., 1755; d. New York, N.Y., April 15, 1819. [1 ;3; 4; 8]

Evans, Robley Dunglison, naval officer, b. Floyd Court House, Va., 1846; d. Washington, D.C., Jan. 3, 1912. [1; 4; 7; 10]

Evans, Samuel B., local historian, b. 1837; d. ? [37]

Evans, Simeon Adams, genealogist, b. Fryeburg, Me., 1837; d. Conway, N.Y., June 24, 1895.

Evans, Taliesin, publicist, b. Manchester, England, 1843; d. Pasadena, Calif., Oct. 24, 1926. [35]

Evans, Thomas, Quaker minister, b. Philadelphia, Pa., 1798; d. Philadelphia, Pa., May 25, 1868. [1; 3; 4; 6; 8]

Evans, Thomas Wiltberger, dentist and philanthropist, b. Philadelphia, Pa., 1823; d. Paris, France, Nov. 14, 1897. [1; 3; 4; 8]

Evans, Warren Felt, clergyman and mental healer, b. Rockingham, Vt., 1817; d. Salisbury, Mass., Sept. 4, 1889. [1; 4; 49]

Evans, William, agricultural writer, b. Ireland, 1786; d. Montreal, Que., 1857. [27]

Evanturel, Joseph Eudore Alphonse, poet, b. Quebec, Que., 1852; d. Boston, Mass., May 16, 1919. [27]

Evarts, Hal George, novelist, b. Topeka, Kans., 1887; d. at sea, near Rio de Janeiro, Brazil, Oct. 18, 1934. [7; 10]

Evarts, Jeremiah, lawyer and journalist, b. Sunderland, Vt., 1781; d. Charleston, S.C., May 10, 1831. [1; 2; 4]

Evarts, William Maxwell, lawyer, b. Boston, Mass., 1818; d. New York, N.Y., Feb. 28, 1901. [2; 4; 10; 62]

Eve, Joseph, inventor and poet, b. Philadelphia, Pa., 1760; d. near Augusta, Ga., Nov. 14, 1835. [1; 7]

Eve, Paul Fitzsimons, surgeon, b. near Augusta, Ga., 1806; d. Nashville, Tenn., Nov. 3, 1877. [1; 3; 4; 8]

Eveleth, Ephraim, clergyman, b. Princeton, Mass., 1801; d. New York, N.Y., March 1, 1829. [45]

Evelyn, Chetwood (pseud.). See Pell, Roger Conger.

Everard, George, clergyman, b. 1828; d. 1901.

Everest, Charles William, clergyman and poet, b. Windsor, Conn., 1814; d. Waterbury, Conn., Jan. 11, 1877. [3; 7]

Everett, Alexander Hill, journalist and diplomat, b. Boston, Mass., 1790; d. Macao, China, June 29, 1847. [1; 3; 4; 6; 7; 8]

Everett, Mrs. Caroline Kane, née Mills,, essayist, d. Paris, France, July 14, 1921.

Everett, Charles Carroll, theologian, b. Brunswick, Me., 1829; d. Cambridge, Mass., Oct. 16, 1900. [1; 3; 4; 7; 8; 10]

Everett, David, lawyer and journalist, b. Princeton, Mass., 1770; d. Marietta, O., Dec. 21, 1813. [1; 3; 7; 8]

Everett, Edward, clergyman and orator, b. Dorchester, Mass., 1794; d. Boston, Mass., Jan. 15, 1865. [1; 3; 7; 71]

Everett, Erastus, educationist, b. Princeton, Mass., 1813; d. Brooklyn, N.Y., May 7, 1900. [3; 8]

Everett, Franklin, local historian, b. Worthington, Mass., 1812; d. 1887. [39]

Everett, George Thomas, soldier, b. 1886; d. Washington, D.C., April 1, 1934. [2a]

Everett, Walter Goodnow, educationist, b. Rowe, Mass., 1860; d. Berkeley, Calif., July 29, 1937. [10; 47]

Everett, William, educationist, b. Watertown, Mass., 1839; d. Quincy, Mass., Feb. 16, 1910. [3; 8; 10]

Everhart, Benjamin Matlack, mycologist, b. West Chester, Pa. 1818; d. West Chester, Pa., 1904. [3; 4; 8; 10]

Everhart, George Marlow, poet, b. 1826; d. 1891.

Everhart, James Bowen, poet and politician, b. near West Chester, Pa., 1831; d. West Chester, Pa., Aug. 23, 1888. [3; 4; 8]

Evermann, Barton Warren, ichthyologist, b. Monroe county, Ia., 1853; d. San Francisco, Calif., Sept. 27, 1932. [1a; 4; 10; 11]

Everpoint (pseud.). See Field, Joseph M.

Everts, Orpheus, physician and poet, b. Salem Settlement, Ind., 1826; d. Cincinnati, O., June 19, 1903. [10]

Everts, William Wallace, clergyman, b. Granville, N.Y., 1814; d. Chicago, Ill., Sept. 26, 1890. [3; 4; 6; 8]

Evjen, John Oluf, educationist, b. Ishpeming, Mich., 1874; d. Chicago, Ill., Jan. 4, 1942. [7; 10]

Ewart, Frank Carman, educationist, b. Marietta, O., 1871; d. Hamilton, N.Y., Sept. 29, 1942. [10]

Ewart, John Skirving, lawyer, b. Toronto, Ont., 1849; d. Ottawa, Ont., Feb. 21, 1933. [27]

Ewbank, Thomas, inventor and manufacturer, b. Durham, England, 1792; d. New York, N.Y., Sept. 16, 1870. [1; 3; 4; 6; 7; 8]

Ewell, Alice Maude, novelist, b. 1860; d. Richmond, Va., June 25, 1946. [34]

Ewell, James, physician, b. Prince William county, Va., 1773; d. Covington, La., Nov. 2, 1832. [1]

Ewell, John Louis, clergyman and educationist, b. Byfield, Rowley, Mass., 1840; d. Washington, D.C., March 16, 1910. [62]

Ewell, Marshall Davis, lawyer, b. Oxford, Mich., 1844; d. Oct. 4, 1928. [4; 8; 10]

Ewell, Thomas, physician, b. near Dumfries, Va., 1785; d. Centerville, Va., May 1, 1826. [1]

Ewer, Ferdinand Cartwright, clergyman, b. Nantucket, Mass., 1826; d. Montreal, Que., Oct. 10, 1883. [1; 3; 4; 6; 8]

Ewing, Elmore Ellis, soldier, b. 1840; d. 1900.

Ewing, Mrs. Emma, née Pike, writer on cooking, b. 1838; d. ?

Ewing, Finis, clergyman, b. Bedford county, Va., 1773; d. Lexington, Va., July 4, 1841. [1; 3; 4; 8; 34]

Ewing, Hugh Boyle, soldier, b. Lancaster, O., 1826; d. near Lancaster, O., June 30, 1905. [1; 3; 4; 7; 8; 10]

Ewing, James, pathologist, b. Pittsburg, Pa., 1866; d. New York, N.Y., May 16, 1943. [10]

Ewing, Sir James Caruthers Rhea, missionary, b. Armstrong county, Pa., 1854; d. Princeton, N.J., Aug. 20, 1925. [1; 10]

Ewing, John, clergyman and educationist, b. East Nottingham, Md., 1732; d. Norristown, Pa., Sept. 8, 1802. [1; 3; 8; 34]

Ewing, Joseph Grant, musketry expert and poet, b. Harrisburg, Pa., 1866; d. Washington, D.C., Aug. 23, 1938. [62]

Ewing, Presley Kittredge, lawyer and genealogist, b. La Fourche, La., 1860; d. Houston, Tex., Feb. 4, 1927. [4; 10]

Eycleshymer, Albert Chauncey, anatomist, b. Cambridge, N.Y., 1867; d. Oak Park, Ill., Dec. 30, 1925. [10]

Eyster, Mrs. Nellie, née Blessing, novelist, b. Frederick, Md., 1831; d. Berkeley, Calif., Feb. 21, 1922. [4; 34; 35]

Eytinge, Rose, actress, b. Philadelphia, Pa., 1835; d. Amityville, Long Island, N.Y., Dec. 20, 1911. [1; 10]

F

Fabbri, Cora, poet, b. 1871; d. 1892.

Fabens, Joseph Warren, diplomat, b. Salem, Mass., 1821; d. New York, N.Y., March 13, 1875. [2; 4; 8]

Faber, William Frederic, bishop, b. Buffalo, N.Y., 1860; d. Glacier Park, Mont., July 20, 1934. [10; 63]

Fabre, Hector, journalist, b. Montreal, Que., 1834; d. Paris, France, Sept. 2, 1910. [27]

Fadette (pseud.). See Reeves, Marian Calhoun Legaré.

Fagg, John Gerardus, clergyman, b. Bethlehem, Wis., 1860; d. New York, N.Y., May 3, 1917. [10]

Fagnani, Charles Prospero, theologian, b. New York, N.Y., 1854; d. Paris, France, Nov. 25, 1940. [10; 11; 68]

Faillon, Etienne Michel, priest and historian, b. Tarascon, France, 1799; d. Paris, France, Oct. 25, 1870. [27]

Fair, Eugene, educationist, b. near Gilman City, Mo., 1877; d. Kirksville, Mo., Oct. 13, 1937. [10; 11]

Fairall, Herbert S., journalist, b. 1858; d. 1907. [6; 37]

Fairbairn, Robert Brinckerhoff, clergyman, b. New York, N.Y., 1818; d. Brooklyn, N.Y., Jan. 27, 1899. [4; 6; 8]

Fairbank, Calvin, clergyman, b. Wyoming county, N.Y., 1816; d. Angelica, N.Y., Oct. 12, 1898. [1; 3b; 8]

Fairbanks, Arthur, educationist, b. Hanover, N.H., 1864; d. Cambridge, Mass., Jan. 13, 1944. [10; 49]

Fairbanks, Edward Taylor, clergyman, b. St. Johnsbury, Vt., 1836; d. St. Johnsbury, Vt., Jan. 12, 1919. [10; 62]

Fairbanks, George Rainsford, lawyer and historian, b. Watertown, N.Y., 1820; d. Aug., 1906. [4; 10; 34]

Fairbanks, Lorenzo Sayles, lawyer, b. Pepperell, Mass., 1825; d. Boston, Mass., May 22, 1897. [8; 49]

Fairchild, Ashbel Green, clergyman, b. Hanover, N.J., 1875; d. Smithfield, Pa., 1864. [3; 7; 8]

Fairchild, George Moore, sportsman, b. Quebec, Que., 1854; d. Quebec, Que., Sept. 18, 1924. [27]

Fairchild, George Thompson, educationist, b. Brownhelm, O., 1838; d. Columbus, O., March 16, 1901. [1; 10]

Fairchild, Mrs. Helen, née Lincklaen, historian, b. Cazenovia, N.Y., 1845; d. Cazenovia, N.Y., May 5, 1931.

Fairchild, Herman Le Roy, geologist, b. Montrose, Pa., 1850; d. Rochester, N.Y., Nov. 29, 1943. [4; 10; 11]

Fairchild, James Harris, educationist, b. Stockbridge, Mass., 1817; d. Oberlin, O., March 19, 1902. [1; 3; 4; 6; 10]

Fairchild, Mrs. Mary Salome, née Cutler, librarian, b. Dalton, Mass., 1855; d. Dec. 20, 1921. [4; 10]

Fairclough, Henry Rushton, educationist, b. near Barrie, Ont., 1862; d. Palo Alto, Calif., Feb. 12, 1938. [10; 11; 30]

Fairfax, Beatrice (pseud.). See Gasch, Mrs. Marie, née Manning.

Fairfax, L. (pseud.). See Connelly, Mrs. Celia.

Fairfield, Caroline E. See Corbin, Mrs. Caroline Elizabeth, née Fairfield.

Fairfield, Edmund Burke, educationist, b. Parkersburg, Va., 1821; d. Oberlin, O., Nov. 17, 1904. [1; 4]

Fairfield, Francis Gerry, journalist, b. Stafford, Conn., 1844; d. New York, N.Y., April 4, 1887. [3; 8]

Fairfield, Mrs. Jane, née Frazee, biographer, b. Rahway, N.J., about 1810; d. ? [3; 8]

Fairfield, Sumner Lincoln, poet, b. Warwick, Mass., 1803; d. New Orleans, La., March 6, 1844. [1; 3; 4; 7; 8; 71]

Fairley, Edwin, educationist, b. March, England, 1864; d. Barneveld, N.Y., May 16, 1941. [10; 45]

Fairlie, John Archibald, political scientist, b. Glasgow, Scotland, 1872; d. Atlanta, Ga., Jan. 23, 1947. [10; 11]

Falconer, Sir Robert Alexander, educationist, b. Charlottetown, P.E.I., 1867; d. Toronto, Ont., Nov. 4, 1943. [27]

Falk, Myron Samuel, civil engineer, b. New York, N.Y., 1878; d. New York, N.Y., Nov. 26, 1945.

Falkner, William C., poet and novelist, b. 1833; d. 1889. [6; 34]

Fall, Charles Gershom, lawyer and poet, b. Malden, Mass., 1845; d. Boston, Mass., Jan. 22, 1932. [4; 8; 10; 51]

Fall, Delos, chemist, b. Ann Arbor, Mich., 1848; d. Bradentown, Fla., Feb. 19, 1921. [4; 10; 53]

Fall, Henry Clinton, entomologist, b. Farmington, N.H., 1862; d. Tyngsboro, Mass., Nov. 14, 1939. [10; 11; 49]

Falloon, Daniel, clergyman, b. Ireland; d. Montreal, Que., Sept., 1862. [27; 29]

Fallows, Alice Katherine, biographer, b. Milwaukee, Wis., 1872; d. Jan. 9, 1932. [10; 11; 44]

Fallows, Edward Huntington, lawyer, b. Appleton, Wis., 1865; d. Norfolk, Conn., Jan. 12, 1940. [4; 10; 45; 62]

Fallows, Samuel, bishop, b. Lancashire, England, 1835; d. Chicago, Ill., Sept. 5, 1922. [1; 2; 4; 10; 44]

Falls, De Witt Clinton, soldier and artist, b. New York, N.Y., 1864; d. London, England, Sept. 7, 1937. [10]

Falstaff, Jake (pseud.). See Fetzer, Herman.

Fanning, Edmund, sea-captain and explorer, b. Stonington, Conn., 1769; d. New York, N.Y., April 23, 1841. [1; 4]

Fanning, John Thomas, hydraulic engineer, b. Norwich, Conn., 1837; d. Minneapolis, Minn., Feb. 6, 1911. [1; 3; 4; 10; 70]

Fanning, Nathaniel, naval officer, b. Stonington, Conn., 1755; d. Charleston, S.C., Sept. 30, 1805. [1]

Farabee, William Curtis, anthropologist, b. Washington county, Pa., 1865; d. Washington, Pa., June 24, 1925. [7; 10]

Farbrick, Jonathan (pseud.). See Holbrook, Silas Pinckney.

Faribault, Georges Barthélemi, bibliographer, b. Quebec, Canada, 1789; d. Quebec, Que., Dec. 21, 1866. [27]

Faris, John Thomson, clergyman and editor, b. Cape Girardeau, Mo., 1871; d. Nashville, Tenn., April 3, 1949. [10]

Farley, Frederick Augustus, clergyman, b. 1800; d. 1892. [8; 51]

Farley, Harriet. See Donlevy, Mrs. Harriet, née Farley.

Farley, John Murphy, cardinal, b. Armagh county, Ireland, 1842; d. New York, N.Y., Sept. 17, 1918. [1; 4; 10; 21]

Farlow, John Woodford, physician, b. 1853; d. Manchester, N.H., Sept. 23, 1937. [51]

Farlow, William Gilson, botanist, b. Boston, Mass., 1844; d. Cambridge, Mass., June 13, 1919. [1; 3; 4; 6; 8; 10; 51]

Farman, Elbert Eli, jurist and diplomat, b. Oswego county, N.Y., 1831; d. Warsaw, N.Y., Dec. 30, 1911. [1; 4; 10]

Farmer, A. W. (pseud.). See Seabury, Samuel.

Farmer, Elihu Jerome, journalist, b. 1836; d. ? [4; 8]

Farmer, Fannie Merritt, dietitian, b. Boston, Mass., 1857; d. Boston, Mass., Jan. 15, 1915. [1; 4; 7; 10]

Farmer, Henry Tudor, poet, b. England, 1782; d. Charleston, S.C., Jan., 1828. [3; 7; 8; 34]

Farmer, James Eugene, educationist, b. Cleveland, O., 1867; d. New York, N.Y., May, 1915. [7; 8; 62]

Farmer, John, antiquary and genealogist, b. Chelmsford, Mass., 1789; d. Concord, N.H., Aug. 13, 1838. [1; 3; 4; 6; 7; 8]

Farmer, John, cartographer, b. Saratoga county, N.Y., 1798; d. Detroit, Mich., March 24, 1859. [1; 3]

Farmer, Mrs. Lydia, née Hoyt, novelist and biographer, b. Cleveland, O., 1842; d. Dec. 27, 1903. [4; 6; 7; 8; 10]

Farmer, Silas, publisher and historian, b. Detroit, Mich., 1839; d. Detroit, Mich., Dec. 28, 1902. [3; 8; 10]

Farnam, Charles Henry, genealogist, b. New Haven, Conn., 1846; d. Denver, Col., Sept. 24, 1909. [3; 62]

Farnam, Henry Walcott, political economist, b. New Haven, Conn., 1853; d. New Haven, Conn., Sept. 5, 1933. [1a; 10; 62]

Farnham, Charles Haight, biographer, b. near Poughkeepsie, N.Y., 1841; d. Cocoanut Grove, Fla., Feb. 27, 1929. [10]

Farnham, Mrs. Eliza Woodson, née Burhans, philanthropist, b. Rensselaerville, N.Y., 1815; d. Milton-on-the-Hudson, N.Y., Dec. 15, 1864. [1; 3; 4; 6; 7; 8]

Farnham, Thomas Jefferson, lawyer and traveller, b. Vermont, 1804; d. San Francisco, Calif., Sept. 13, 1848. [1; 3; 4; 7; 8; 43]

Farnsworth, Charles Hubert, educationist, b. Cesarea, Turkey, 1859; d. Thetford, Vt., May 22, 1947. [7; 10; 20]

Farnum, Alexander, merchant, b. 1830; d. Providence, R.I.., May 11, 1884. [6; 47]

Farquhar, Arthur Briggs, manufacturer and economist, b. 1838; d. York, Pa., March 5, 1925. [4; 10]

Farquhar, Edward, librarian and poet, b. Sandy Spring, Md., 1843; d. 1905. [10]

Farquhar, Henry, economist, b. Sandy Spring, Md., 1851; d. Washington, D.C., Oct., 1925. [10]

Farquharson, Martha (pseud.). See Finley, Martha.

Farr, Frederic William, clergyman, b. Litchfield, Me., 1860; d. Los Angeles, Calif., June 24, 1939. [10]

Farrand, Elizabeth Martha, physician, d. Port Huron, Mich., Aug. 17, 1900. [53]

Farrand, Livingston, educationist, b. Newark, N.J., 1867; d. New York, N.Y., Nov. 8, 1939. [4; 7; 10; 13]

Farrand, Max, historian, b. Newark, N.J., 1869; d. Bar Harbor, Me., June 17, 1945. [7; 10; 11]

Farrar, Charles Alden John, writer on wilderness travel, d. Jamaica Plain, Mass., 1893. [6; 8; 38]

Farrar, Edgar Howard, lawyer, b. Concordia, La., 1849; d. Biloxi, Miss., Jan. 6, 1922. [1; 4; 10]

Farrar, Mrs. Eliza Ware, née Rotch, writer of books for young people, b. Belgium, 1791; d. Springfield, Mass., April 22, 1870. [3; 4; 6; 7]

Farrar, James McNall, clergyman, b. Candor, Pa., 1853; d. Brooklyn, N.Y., June 22, 1921. [10; 56]

Farrar, John, mathematician and astronomer, b. Lincoln, Mass., 1799; d. Cambridge, Mass., May 8, 1853. [1; 3; 6; 51]

Farrar, Timothy, lawyer, b. New Ipswich, N.H., 1788; d. Boston, Mass., Oct. 27, 1874. [1; 3; 4; 49]

Farrington, Edward Holyoke, educationist, b. Brewer, Me., 1860; d. Madison, Wis., March 22, 1934. [10; 11; 62]

Farrington, Frederic Ernest, educationist, b. Waltham, Mass., 1872; d. June 1, 1930. [10; 48; 51]

Farrington, Harry Webb, clergyman and poet, b. Nassau, B.W.I., 1880; d. Brooklyn, N.Y., Oct. 25, 1931. [4; 10]

Farrington, Oliver Cummings, geologist, b. Brewer, Me., 1864; d. Chicago, Ill., Nov. 3, 1933. [10; 11]

Farriss, Charles Sherwood, educationist, b. Warrenton, N.C., 1856; d. De Land, Fla., April 14, 1938. [10]

Farrow, Edward Samuel, soldier and engineer, b. Snow Hill, Md., 1855; d. New York, N.Y., Dec. 21, 1942. [7; 10]

Farwell, John Villiers, merchant, b. Painted Post, N.Y., 1825; d. Chicago, Ill., 1903. [4; 10]

Farwell, Parris Thaxter, clergyman, b. Pelham, N.H., 1856; d. Cochituate, Mass., Nov. 6, 1930. [45]

Fasquelle, Jean Louis, educationist, b. France, 1808; d. Ann Arbor, Mich., Oct. 1, 1862. [6; 53]

Fassett, James Hiram, educationist, b. Nashua, N.H., 1869; d. Orlando, Fla., Nov. 9, 1930. [10; 49]

Faucher de Saint-Maurice, Narcisse Henri Edouard, soldier and journalist, b. Quebec, Que., 1844; d. April, 1897. [27]

Fauley, Wilbur Finley, journalist and novelist, b. Fultonham, O., 1872; d. New York, N.Y., Dec. 21, 1942. [7; 10]

Faulkner, Herbert Waldron, artist, b. Stamford, Conn., 1860; d. Washington, Conn., March 27, 1940. [10; 11]

Faulkner, John Alfred, theologian, b. Grand Pré, N.S., 1857; d. Madison, N.J., Sept. 6, 1931. [4; 10; 11]

Faulks, Mrs. Theodosia, née **Pickering,** See Garrison, Mrs. Theodosia, née Pickering.

Faunce, Daniel Worcester, clergyman, b. Plymouth, Mass., 1829; d. Providence, R.I., Jan. 3, 1911. [3; 6; 8; 10]

Faunce, William Herbert Perry, clergyman and educationist, b. Worcester, Mass., 1859; d. Providence, R.I., Jan. 31, 1930. [1; 4; 7; 10]

Faust, Frederick, novelist, b. Seattle, Wash., 1892; d. on active service in Italy, May 11, 1944. [7; 9; 10]

Fauteux, Aegidius, librarian, b. Montreal, Que., 1876; d. Montreal, Que., April 22, 1941. [27]

Faverel, Arthur (pseud.). See Lespérance, John.

Faversham, Mrs. Julie, née **Opp,** actress, b. New York, N.Y., 1871; d. New York, N.Y., April 8, 1921. [10]

Favill, John, clergyman, b. Milford, Wis., 1847; d. Lake Mills, Wis., Sept. 6, 1927. [10; 44]

Favill, John, neurologist, b. 1886; d. Winnetka, Ill., Dec. 21, 1946. [62]

Fawcett, Edgar, novelist, poet, and essayist, b. New York, N.Y., 1847; d. London, England, May 2, 1904. [1; 3; 4; 7; 10; 71; 72]

Faxon, Frederick Winthrop, library agent and bibliographer, b. West Roxbury, Mass., 1866; d. Boston, Mass., Aug. 31, 1936. [7; 10; 11]

Faxon, Walter, naturalist, b. Jamaica Plain., Mass., 1848; d. Lexington, Mass., Aug. 10, 1920. [10; 51]

Fay, Albert Hill, mining engineer, b. Appleton City, Mo., 1871; d. Easton, Pa., Aug. 7, 1937. [10]

Fay, Amy, musician, b. Bayou Goula, La., 1844; d. 1928. [7; 10; 20]

Fay, Charles Norman, manufacturer and economist, b. Burlington, Vt., 1848; d. Cambridge, Mass., April 7, 1944. [11; 51]

Fay, Charles Rolph, educationist, b. Appleton, Wis., 1867; d. Brooklyn, N.Y., Sept. 11, 1934. [45]

Fay, Edward Allen, educationist, b. Morristown, N.J., 1843; d. Kendall Green, Mass., July 14, 1923. [1; 10]

Fay, Edwin Whitfield, educationist, b. Minden, La., 1865; d. Austin, Tex., Feb. 17, 1920. [1; 10]

Fay, Heman Allen, soldier, b. Bennington, Vt., 1779; d. Bennington, Vt., Aug. 20, 1865. [43]

Fay, Irving Wetherbee, chemist, b. Natick, Mass., 1861; d. Brooklyn, N.Y., Feb. 10, 1936. [10; 13]

Fay, Jonas, physician and politician, b. Westborough, Mass., 1737; d. Bennington, Vt., March 8, 1818. [1; 4]

Fay, Theodore Sedgwick, diplomat and novelist, b. New York, N.Y., 1807; d. Berling, Germany, Nov. 17, 1898. [1; 3; 4; 7; 8; 71]

Fearing, Lilian Blanche, poet and novelist, b. 1862; d. 1901. [8; 37]

Fearn, Mrs. Anne, née **Walter,** physician, b. Holly Springs, Miss., 1868; d. Berkeley, Calif., April 28, 1939.

Fedden, Mrs. Katherine Waldo, née **Douglas,** novelist, b. New York, N.Y.; d. near Tolosa, Spain, April 7, 1939. [7; 10; 11]

Fee, Harry Thomas, poet, b. Stockton, Calif., 1871; d. Stockton, Calif., about 1934. [35]

Fee, John Gregg, clergyman and educationist, b. Bracken county, Ky., 1816; d. Berea, Ky., Jan. 11, 1901. [1; 26]

Fehlandt, August Frederick, clergyman and educationist, b. Mazomanie, Wis., 1869; d. Chicago, Ill., Oct. 26, 1939. [10; 11; 44]

Feingold, Gustave Alexander, educationist, b. Kiev, Russia, 1880; d. Hartford, Conn., June 5, 1948. [51]

Felderman, Leo, physician, b. Rumania, 1890; d. Philadelphia, Pa., May 14, 1945.

Feldman, Herman, educationist, b. New York, N.Y., 1894; d. Hanover, N.H., Oct. 16, 1947. [10; 49]

Felix, Pastor (pseud.). See Lockhart, Arthur John.

Felland, Ole Gunderson, clergyman, b. Utica, Wis., 1853; d. near Coldwater, Mich., June 10, 1938. [10]

Fellowes, Edward Colton, clergyman, b. Hartford, Conn., 1864; d. Cambridge, Mass., April 23, 1928. [62]

Fellowes, Francis, lawyer, b. Montville, Conn., 1803; d. Hartford, Conn., April 25, 1888. [62]

Fellows, George Emery, educationist, b. Beaver Dam, Wis., 1858; d. Great Neck, N.Y., Jan. 14, 1942. [4; 10]

Fellows, Henry Parker, lawyer, b. Hudson, N.Y., 1848; d. Hudson, N.Y., Aug. 9, 1927. [62]

Fellows, John, miscellaneous writer, b. Sheffield, Mass., 1759; d. New York, N.Y., Jan. 3, 1844. [3; 4; 8; 62]

Felt, Ephraim Porter, entomologist, b. Salem, Mass., 1868; d. Stamford, Conn., Dec. 14, 1943. [4; 10; 11; 13]

Felt, Joseph Barlow, historian, b. Salem, Mass., 1789; d. Salem, Mass., Sept. 8, 1869. [1; 3; 4; 6; 7; 8]

Felter, Harvey Wickes, physician, b. Rensselaerville, N.Y., 1865; d. Cincinnati, O., Oct. 27, 1927. [10]

Felter, William Landon, educationist, b. Brooklyn, N.Y., 1862; d. Brooklyn, N.Y., March 19, 1933. [10]

Felton, Cornelius Conway, educationist, b. West Newbury, Mass., 1807; d. Chester, Pa., Feb. 26, 1862. [1; 3; 4; 7; 8; 51]

Felton, Cyrus, genealogist, b. 1815; d. 1890.

Felton, Mrs. Rebecca, née **Latimer,** journalist and politician, b. near Decatur, Ga., 1835; d. Cartersville, Ga., Jan. 24, 1930. [1; 4; 7; 34]

Fenety, George Edward, journalist, b. Halifax, N.S., 1812; d. Fredericton, N. B., Sept. 30, 1899. [27]

Fenn, William Wallace, theologian, b. Boston, Mass., 1862; d. Cambridge, Mass., March 6, 1932. [1a; 10; 51]

Fennell, James, actor and playwright, b. London, England, 1766; d. Philadelphia, Pa., June 14, 1816. [1; 3; 4; 7]

Fenneman, Nevin Melancthon, geologist, b. Lima, O., 1865; d. Cincinnati O., July 4, 1945. [10; 13]

Fenner, Christopher Smith, physician, b. 1823; d. 1879.

Fenner, Cornelius George, poet, b. Providence, R.I., 1822; d. Cincinnati, O., Jan. 4, 1847. [3; 4; 8; 47]

Fenner, Erasmus Darwin, physician, b. 1807; d. 1866.

Fenollosa, Ernest Francisco, poet and student of Oriental art, b. Salem, Mass., 1853; d. London, England, Sept. 21, 1908. [1; 7; 10]

Ferber, Nat Joseph, journalist and novelist, b. 1889; d. Santa Monica, Calif., June 21, 1945. [7]

Ferguson, Mrs. Emma, née **Henry,** musician and novelist, b. Charlotte county, Va., 1840; d. Balham, Gooch county, Va., 1905. [10; 34]

Ferguson, George Dalrymple, historian, b. Montreal, Lower Canada, 1829; d. Kingston, Ont., Aug. 21, 1926. [27]

Ferguson, Henry, clergyman and educationist, b. Stamford, Conn., 1848; d. Hartford, Conn., March 30, 1917. [8; 10]

Ferguson, Jesse Babcock, spiritualist, d. 1870. [6]

Ferguson, John, physician, b. Glasgow, Scotland, 1850; d. Toronto, Ont., Dec. 6, 1939. [30]

Ferguson, Thompson B., novelist, b. Polk county, Ia., 1857; d. Watonga, Okla., Feb. 14, 1921. [10; 75]

Ferguson, William Porter Frisbee, clergyman, b. Delhi, N.Y., 1861; d. Franklin, Pa., June 23, 1929. [1; 10]

Fergusson, Edmund Morris, clergyman, b. Philadelphia, Pa., 1864; d. Swarthmore, Pa., March 14, 1934. [1; 11]

Ferland, Jean Baptiste Antoine, priest and historian, b. Montreal, Lower Canada, 1805; d. Quebec, Que., Jan. 11, 1865. [27]

Fern, Fanny (pseud.). See Parton, Mrs. Sara Payson, née Willis.

Fernald, Charles Henry, biologist, b. Mount Desert, Me., 1838; d. Amherst, Mass,. Feb. 22, 1921. [1; 3; 4; 8; 10; 11]

Fernald, Chester Bailey, novelist and playwright, b. Boston, Mass., 1869; d. Dover, England, April 10, 1938. [7; 10; 11]

Fernald, James Champlin, clergyman and editor, b. Portland, Me., 1838; d. Upper Montclair, N.J., Nov. 10, 1918. [1; 7; 8; 10; 51]

Fernald, Merritt Caldwell, educationist, b. South Levant, Me., 1838; d. Orono, Me., Jan. 8, 1916. [3; 4; 10; 46]

Fernald, Robert Heywood, engineer, b. Orono Me., 1871; d. Haverford, Pa., April 24, 1937. [10]

Fernow, Bernhard Edouard, forester, b. Posen, Germany, 1851; d. Toronto, Ont., Feb. 6, 1923. [4; 10; 27]

Fernow, Berthold, historian and archivist, b. Posen, Germany, 1837; d. Togus, Me., March 3, 1908. [1; 3; 4; 8; 10]

Ferree, Barr, architect, b. Philadelphia, Pa., about 1864; d. Demarest, N.J., Oct. 14, 1924. [10]

Ferrel, William, meteorologist, b. Fulton county, Pa., 1817; d. Maywood, Kans., Sept. 18, 1891. [1; 4; 8]

Ferrie, William, clergyman, b. St. Andrews, Scotland, 1815; d. Monticello, O., Dec. 29, 1903. [27]

Ferrier, William Warren, educationist, b. Metz, Ind., 1855; d. Berkeley, Calif., Aug. 20, 1945. [10]

Ferrin, Clark Ela, clergyman, b. Holland, Vt., 1818; d. Plainfield, Vt., June 27, 1881. [43]

Ferris, Anita Brockway, writer on missions, .b. 1881; d. 1923.

Ferris, Benjamin, historian, d. Wilmington, Del., 1867. [3]

Ferris, George Hooper, clergyman, b. Lamartine, Wis., 1867; d. Philadelphia, Pa., Sept. 16, 1917. [10]

Ferris, George Titus, miscellaneous writer, b. 1840; d. ?

Fess, Simeon Davidson, educationist and politician, b. Allen county, O., 1861; d. Yellow Springs, O., Dec. 23, 1936. [10]

Fessenden, Francis, lawyer and soldier, b. Portland, Me., 1839; d. Portland, Me., Jan. 2, 1906. [1; 4; 10]

Fessenden, Mrs. Laura, née **Dayton,** novelist, b. New York, N.Y.; d. May 11, 1924. [7; 10]

Fessenden, Reginald Aubrey, scientist, b. Milton, Que., 1866; d. Bermuda, July 22, 1932. [1a; 4; 10; 13]

Fessenden, Thomas, clergyman, b. Cambridge, Mass., 1739; d. Walpole, N.H., 1813. [3; 43; 51]

Fessenden, Thomas Green, poet and journalist, b. Walpole, N.H., 1771; d. Boston, Mass., Nov. 11, 1837. [1; 4; 6; 7; 43; 49]

Fetherstonhaugh, Robert Collier, historian, b. Montreal, Que., 1892; d. Montreal, Que., Jan. 13, 1949.

Festetits, Mrs. Kate Neely, née **Hill,** writer of stories for children, b. Virginia, 1837; d. ? [34]

Fetter, Frank Albert, economist, b. Peru, Ind., 1863; d. Princeton, N.J., March 21, 1949. [10]

Fetzer, Herman, columnist, b. Akron, O., 1899; d. Cleveland, O., Jan. 17, 1935. [7]

Feuchtwanger, Lewis, chemist, b. Germany, 1805; d. New York, N.Y., June 25, 1876. [3; 6; 8]

Fewkes, Jesse Walter, ethnologist, b. Newton, Mass., 1850; d. Glen Forest, Md., May 31, 1930. [4; 7; 10; 51]

Fezandié, Hector, engineer and novelist, b. Paris, France, 1856; d. Summit, N.J., April 27, 1943.

Fibbleton, George (pseud.). See Green, Asa.

Fick, Henry H., educationist, b. Luebeck, Germany, 1849; d. Cincinnati, O., March 23, 1935. [10]

Ficke, Arthur Davidson, poet, b. Davenport, Ia., 1883; d. Hudson, N.Y., Nov. 30, 1945. [7; 10; 37; 51]

Ficklen, John Rose, historian, b. Falmouth, Va., 1858; d. Lake Chautauqua, N.Y., Aug. 4 ,1907. [7; 10; 34]

Ficklin, Joseph, mathematician, b. Winchester, Ky., 1833; d. 1887. [3; 8]

Fiebeger, Gustav Joseph, military engineer, b. Akron, O., 1858; d. Washington, D.C., Oct. 18, 1939. [10]

Field, Benjamin Rush, physician and Shakespearean scholar, b. Easton, Pa., 1861; d. Easton, Pa., May 1, 1935. [4; 10]

Field, Mrs. Caroline Leslie, née **Whitney,** novelist and poet, b. Milton, Mass., 1853; d. Milton, Mass., Dec. 1, 1902. [7; 8; 10]

Field, David Dudley, clergyman and historian, b. Madison, Conn., 1781; d. Stockbridge, Mass., April 15, 1867. [1; 3; 4; 6]

Field, David Dudley, lawyer, b. Haddam, Conn., 1805; d. New York, N.Y., April 13, 1894. [1; 3; 4; 6]

Field, Edward, antiquary, b. Providence, R.I., 1858; d. Sept., 1928. [7; 47]

Field, Edward Salisbury, playwright, b. 1878; d. Zaca, Calif., Sept. 20, 1936.

Field, Eugene, poet and humorist, b. St. Louis, Mo., 1850; d. Chicago, Ill., Nov. 4, 1895. [1; 7; 71; 72]

Field, George Washington, lawyer, d. 1889. [6; 37]

Field, Henry Martyn, clergyman, b. Stockbridge, Mass., 1822; d. Stockbridge, Mass., Jan. 26, 1907. [1; 3; 4; 6; 7; 10]

Field, Henry Martyn, physician, b. 1837; d. 1912.

Field, James Alfred, economist, b. Milton, Mass., 1880; d. Boston, Mass., July 15, 1927. [10; 51]

Field, Joseph M., actor and playwright, b. Ireland, 1810; d. Mobile, Ala., Jan. 28, 1836. [1; 3; 4; 7; 34]

Field, Kate. See Field, Mary Katherine Keemle.

Field, Mary Katherine Keemle, journalist, lecturer, and actress; b. St. Louis, Mo., 1838; d. Honolulu, Hawaii, May 19, 1896. [1; 3; 6; 7; 8]

Field, Maunsell Bradhurst, lawyer, b. New York, N.Y., 1822; d. New York, N.Y., Jan. 24, 1875. [1; 3; 4; 6; 8]

Field, Peter, mathematician, b. Mitchell county, Ia., 1876; d. Ann Arbor, Mich., Sept. 24, 1949. [13]

Field, Rachel Lyman, poet, novelist, and playwright, b. New York, N.Y., 1894; d. Beverly Hills, Calif., March 15, 1942. [7; 10]

Field, Richard Stockton, lawyer and politician, b. Burlington county, N.J., 1803; d. Princeton, N.J., May 25, 1870. [1; 3]

Field, Roswell Martin, journalist and novelist, b. St. Louis, Mo., 1851; d. Morristown, N.J., Jan. 10, 1919. [1; 4; 7; 10]

Field, Stephen Johnson, jurist, b. Haddam, Conn., 1816; d. Washington, D.C., April 9, 1899. [1; 4]

Field, Thomas Warren, historian and bibliographer, b. near Syracuse, N.Y., 1821; d. Brooklyn, N.Y., Nov. 25, 1881. [1; 3; 6; 7; 8]

Field, Walter Taylor, editor, b. Galesburg, Ill., 1861; d. Hinsdale, Ill., Aug. 18, 1939. [7; 10; 11; 45; 50]

Fielde, Adele Marion, missionary, b. East Rodman, N.Y., 1839; d. Seattle, Wash., Feb. 3, 1916. [10]

Fielding, Mantle, architect and biographer, b. New York, N.Y., 1865; d. Chestnut Hill, Pa., May 27, 1941. [10]

Fields, Mrs. Annie, née **Adams,** poet and biographer, b. Boston, Mass., 1834; d. Boston, Mass., Jan. 5, 1915. [1; 3; 4; 7; 8]

Fields, James Thomas, publisher and poet, Portsmouth, N.H., 1817; d. Boston, Mass., April 24, 1881. [1; 3; 4; 7; 71]

Fields, Maurice C., poet, b. 1915; d. 1938. [21]

Fields, William Claude, comedian, b. Philadelphia, Pa., 1880; d. Pasadena, Calif., Dec. 25, 1946. [10; 12]

Fiero, James Newton, lawyer, b. Saugerties, N.Y., 1847; d. Albany, N.Y., April 13, 1931. [10; 11]

Fife, George Buchanan, journalist, b. Charlestown, Mass., 1869; d. Flushing, N.Y., March., 12, 1939. [7; 10]

Fifield, Lawrence Wendell, clergyman, b. Berrien Springs, Mich., 1891; d. Seattle, Wash., March 10, 1935. [10]

Filene, Edward Albert, merchant, b. Salem, Mass., 1860; d. Paris, France, Sept. 26, 1937. [10; 11]

Fillebrown, Charles Bowdoin, economist and genealogist, b. Winthrop, Me., 1842; d. Dec., 1917. [4; 10]

Fillebrown, Thomas, dental surgeon, b. 1836; d. Boston, Mass., Jan. 22, 1908. [4]

Filley, Chauncey Ives, politician, b. Lansingburg, N.Y., 1829; d. St. Louis, Mo., Sept. 24, 1923. [10]

Filley, Mrs. Anna, née Adams, politician's wife, d. St. Louis, Mo., March 9, 1896. [6; 34]

Fillmore, John Comfort, musician, b. near Franklin, Conn., 1843; d. Taftville, Conn., Aug. 14, 1898. [1; 4; 8; 20]

Fillmore, Parker Hoysted, banker, b. Cincinnati, O., 1878; d. New York N.Y., June 6, 1944. [7; 10]

Filson, John, explorer and historian, b. Chester county, Pa., about 1747; d. on the Little Miami River, O., Oct., 1788. [1; 2; 3; 4; 7; 8; 34]

Finch, Francis Miles, jurist and poet, b. Ithaca, N.Y., 1827; d. Ithaca, N.Y., July 31, 1907. [1; 3; 4; 7; 8; 62]

Finch, John Bird, temperance orator, b. 1852; d. 1887. [8]

Finch, William Albert, lawyer, b. Newark, N.J., 1855; d. Brooklyn, N.Y., March 31, 1912. [10]

Finck, Edward Bertrand, lawyer, b. Louisville, Ky., 1870; d. Louisville, Ky., June 20, 1931. [7; 11; 74]

Finck, Henry Theophilus, music critic and traveller, b. Bethel, Mo., 1854; d. Rumford Falls, Me., Oct. 1, 1926. [1; 3; 4; 7; 8; 10]

Fincke, Charles Louis, physician, b. Brooklyn, N.Y., 1873; d. Brooklyn, N.Y., March 19, 1906. [62]

Findley, Samuel, clergyman, b. West Middletown, Pa., 1818; d. 1889. [3; 8]

Findley, Samuel, educationist, b. 1831; d. 1908.

Findley, William, politician, b. Ireland, 1741; d. Westmoreland county, Pa., April 5, 1821. [1; 3; 4; 8]

Fine, Henry Burchard, mathematician, b. Chambersburg, Pa., 1858; d. Princeton, N.J., Dec. 22, 1928. [1; 4; 10]

Fine, John, jurist, b. New York, N.Y., 1794; d. Ogdensburg, N.Y., Jan. 4, 1867. [3; 4]

Finegan, James Emmet, lawyer, b. Chico, Calif., 1876; d. Brooklyn, N.Y., Feb. 10, 1940. [10]

Finegan, Thomas Edward, educationist, b. West Fulton, N.Y., 1866; d. Rochester, N.Y., Nov. 25, 1932. [4; 10; 11; 49]

Finerty, John Frederick, journalist and historian, b. Galway, Ireland, 1846; d. Chicago, Ill., June 10, 1908. [4; 7; 8; 10]

Finger, Charles Joseph, adventurer and miscellaneous writer, b. Willesden, England, 1869; d. Fayetteville, Ark., Jan. 8, 1941. [7; 10; 11]

Fink, William Wescott, poet, b. 1844; d. ? [37]

Finkelnburg, Gustavus Adolphus, lawyer, b. near Cologne, Germany, 1837; d. St. Louis, Mo., 1908. [10]

Finley, James Bradley, clergyman, b. 1781; d. Cincinatti, O., Sept. 6, 1856. [1; 3; 4; 7; 8]

Finley, John, poet, b. Brownsburg, Va., 1797; d. Richmond, Ind., Dec. 23, 1866. [3; 7; 8]

Finley, John Huston, educationist and journalist, b. Grand Ridge, Ill., 1863; d. New York, N.Y., March 7, 1940. [4; 7; 10]

Finley, Martha, writer of books for girls, b. Chillicothe, O., 1828; d. Elkton, Md., Jan. 30, 1909. [1; 2; 3; 4; 5; 6; 7; 8; 10; 34]

Finley, Robert, clergyman, b. Princeton, N.J., 1772; d. Athens, Ga., Oct. 3, 1817. [1; 3]

Finley, Samuel, clergyman and educationist, b. Armagh county, Ireland, 1715; d. Philadelphia, Pa., July 17, 1766. [1; 3; 4]

Finn, Francis James, priest and writer of juvenile stories, b. St. Louis, Mo., 1859; d. Cincinnati, O., Nov. 2, 1928. [1; 4; 7; 8; 10; 21]

Finn, Henry James William, actor and playwright, b. Sydney, N.S., 1787; d. Long Island sound, N.Y., Jan. 13, 1840. [1; 4; 7]

Finn, Sister Mary Paulina, poet, b. 1842; d. Washington, D.C., Feb. 28, 1935. [21]

Finney, Charles Grandison, clergyman and educationist, b. Warren, Conn., 1792; d. Oberlin, O., Aug. 16, 1875. [1; 3; 4; 6; 7; 8]

Finney, Frederick Norton, traveller, b. Boston, Mass., 1832; d. San Francisco, Calif., March 18, 1916. [10]

Finney, Ross Lee, educationist. b. Postville, Ia., 1875; d. Minneapolis, Minn., Feb. 24, 1934. [10; 11]

Finotti, Joseph Maria, priest and bibliographer, b. Ferrara, Italy, 1817; d. Denver, Colo., Jan. 10, 1879. [1; 3; 4; 6; 7; 8]

Firestone, Harvey Samuel, manufacturer, b. Columbia county, O., 1868; d. Miami Beach, Fla., Feb. 7, 1938. [10]

Firestone, Mrs. May Elizabeth, née Costello, publicist, b. 1869; d. 1909.

Firkins, Chester, poet, b. Minneapolis, Minn., 1882; d. New York, N.Y., March 1, 1915.

Firkins, Ina Ten Eyck, librarian, b. Minneapolis, Minn., 1866; d. at sea, July 16, 1937.

Firkins, Oscar W., educationist, critic, and playwright, b. Minneapolis, Minn., 1864; d. Minneapolis, Minn., March 7, 1932. [7; 10]

Fischer, George Alexander, biographer, b. Troy, N.Y.; d. Los Angeles, Calif., May 17, 1922. [10]

Fischer, Louis Albert, physicist, b. Washington, D.C., 1865; d. Washington, D.C., July 25, 1921. [10]

Fischer, William Joseph, physician, poet, and novelist, b. Waterloo, Ont., 1879; d. 1912. [21; 29]

Fiset, Louis Joseph Cyprien, poet, b. Quebec, Lower Canada, 1825; d. 1898. [3a; 27]

Fisguill, Richard (pseud.). See Wilson, Richard Henry.

Fish, Asa Israel, lawyer, b. Trenton, N.J., 1820; d. Philadelphia, Pa., May 5, 1879. [4; 51]

Fish, Carl Russell, historian, b. Central Falls, R.I., 1876; d. Madison, Wis., July 10, 1932. [1a; 7; 10; 11; 47]

Fish, Daniel, lawyer and bibliographer, b. Cherry Valley, Ill., 1848; d. Minneapolis, Minn., Feb. 9, 1924. [10; 70]

Fish, Daniel W., mathematician, b. 1820; d. 1899.

Fish, Everett W., physician and journalist, b. Livingston county, N.Y., 1845; d. ? [70]

Fish, Ezra Job, clergyman, b. Macedon, N.Y., 1828; d. Bronson, Mich., Jan. 22, 1890. [62]

Fish, Frank Leslie, jurist, b. Newfane, Vt., 1863; d. Vergennes, Vt., Sept. 7, 1927. [4; 10]

Fish, Henry Clay, clergyman, b. Halifax, Vt., 1820; d. Newark, N.J., Oct. 2, 1877. [3; 4; 6; 8; 68]

Fish, Horace, journalist, novelist, and playwright, b. Richmond Hill, Long Island, N.Y., 1885; d. 1929. [10; 11]

Fish, Pierre Augustine, veterinary surgeon, b. Chatham, N.Y., 1865; d. Ithaca, N.Y., Feb. 19, 1931. [4; 8; 10]

Fish, Williston, lawyer and novelist, b. Berlin Heights, O., 1858; d. near Chicago, Ill., Dec. 19, 1939. [7; 10; 11]

Fisher, Benjamin Franklin, poet, b. 1873; d. Canton, O., 1914.

Fisher, Clarence Stanley, archaeologist, b. Philadelphia, Pa., 1876; d. Jerusalem, Palestine, July 20, 1941. [10]

Fisher, Daniel Webster, clergyman and educationist, b. Huntingdon county, Pa., 1838; d. Washington, D.C., Jan. 28, 1913. [1; 4]

Fisher, Ebenezer, clergyman, b. Charlotte, Me., 1815; d. Canton, N.Y., Feb. 21, 1879. [1; 3; 4; 8]

Fisher, Elizabeth Florette, geologist, b. Boston, Mass., 1873; d. Los Angeles, Calif., April 25, 1941. [10; 11]

Fisher, Frances Christine. See Tiernan, Mrs. Frances Christine, née Fisher.

Fisher, Frederick Bohn, bishop, b. Greencastle, Pa., 1882; d. Detroit, Mich., April 15, 1938. [10]

Fisher, George Egbert, mathematician, b. Westerloo, N.Y., 1863; d. Philadelphia, Pa., March 28, 1920. [10]

Fisher, George Jackson, physician, b. North Castle, N.Y.. 1825; d. Ossining, N.Y., Feb. 3, 1893. [1; 3]

Fisher, George Park, clergyman and historian, b. Wrentham, Mass., 1827; d. Litchfield, Conn., Dec. 20, 1909. [1; 3; 4; 6; 7; 10; 62]

Fisher, Harrison, illustrator, b. Brooklyn, N.Y., 1877; d. New York, N.Y., Jan. 19, 1934. [1a; 7; 10]

Fisher, Horace Newton, lawyer, b. Boston. Mass., 1836; d. March 12, 1916. [10; 51]

Fisher, Irving, economist, b. Saugerties, N.Y., 1867; d. New York, N.Y., April 29, 1947. [4; 7; 10; 11; 12; 62]

Fisher, John Dix, physician, b. Needham, Mass., 1797; d. Boston, Mass., March 3, 1850. [1; 3; 47; 51]

Fisher, Jonathan, clergyman, b. New Braintree, Mass., 1768; d. Blue Hill, Me., Sept. 22, 1847. [3; 38; 51]

Fisher, Joshua, physician, b. Dedham, Mass., 1748; d. Beverly, Mass., March 15, 1833. [3; 51]

Fisher, Joshua Francis, publicist, b. Philadelphia, Pa., 1807; d. Philadelphia, Pa., Jan. 21, 1873. [1; 3; 8]

Fisher, Lewis Beals, clergyman and educationist, b. Charlotte, Me., 1857; d. Chicago., Ill., March 22, 1936. [10]

Fisher, Mary, educationist, and novelist, b. La Prairie, Ill., 1858; d. ? [7; 8; 35]

Fisher, Mary Ann, novelist, b. 1839; d. ?

Fisher, Michael Montgomery, educationist, b. near Rockville, Ind., Oct. 8., 1834; d. Columbia, Mo., Feb. 20, 1891. [3; 4; 6; 8]

Fisher, Peter, historian, b. Staten Island, N.Y., 1782; d. New Brunswick, Aug. 15, 1848. [27]

Fisher, Redwood S., statistician, b. Philadelphia, Pa., 1782; d. Philadelphia, Pa., May 17, 1856. [3]

Fisher, Samuel Reed, clergyman, b. Norristown, Pa., 1810; d. Tiffin, O., June 5, 1881. [3; 8]

Fisher, Samuel Ware, clergyman, b. Morristown, N.J., 1814; d. near Cincinnati, O., Jan. 18, 1874. [3; 4; 8; 68]

Fisher, Sidney George, lawyer and poet, b. Philadelphia, Pa., 1809; d. Philadelphia, Pa., July 25, 1871. [1; 3b; 8]

Fisher, Stokely S., clergyman and poet, b. near Graysville, O., 1865 d. Kansas City, Kans., May 30, 1924. [10]

Fisher, Sydney George, lawyer and historian, b. Philadelphia, Pa., 1856; d. near Philadelphia, Pa., Feb. 22, 1927. [1; 3b; 4; 8; 10]

Fisher, Theodore Willis, psychiatrist, b. Westboro, Mass., 1837; d. Belmont, Mass., Oct. 10, 1914. [1; 3; 8; 10]

Fisher, Thomas, scientist and poet, b. Philadelphia, Pa., 1801; d. Philadelphia, Pa., Feb. 12, 1856. [3; 6; 8]

Fisher, William Albert, ophthalmologist, b. 1859; d. Chicago, Ill., July 3, 1944.

Fisher, William Arms, musician, b. San Francisco, Calif., 1861; d. Brookline, Mass., Dec. 18, 1948. [10; 20]

Fisher, William Hubbell, lawyer, b. 1843; d. 1909. [48]

Fisk, Archie Campbell, capitalist, b. Steuben county, N.Y., 1836; d. ? [4]

Fisk, Benjamin Franklin, educationist, d. 1832. [51]

Fisk, Callene (pseud.). See Crafts, Wilbur Fisk.

Fisk, Clinton Bowen, soldier, b. York, N.Y., 1828; d. New York, N.Y., July 9, 1890. [2; 4; 6]

Fisk, Eugene Lyman, physician, b. Brooklyn, N.Y., 1867; d. Dresden, Germany, July 5, 1931. [10; 11]

Fisk, Franklin Woodbury, clergyman, b. Hopkinton, N.H., 1820; d. Chicago, Ill., July 4, 1901. [8; 62]

Fisk, George Mygatt, economist, b. Canfield, O., 1864; d. Madison, Wis., April 29, 1910. [10]

Fisk, Otis Harrison, lawyer, b. Covington, Ky., 1870; d. Framingham, Mass., Jan. 10, 1944. [62]

Fisk, Wilbur, clergyman and educationist, b. Brattleboro, Vt., 1792; d. Middletown, Vt., Feb. 22, 1839. [1; 3; 6; 7; 8]

Fiske, Amos Kidder, journalist, b. Whitefield, N.H., 1842; d. Cambridge, Mass., Sept. 18, 1921. [1; 2; 4; 7; 10; 51]

Fiske, Asa Severance, clergyman, b. Strongsville, O., 1833; d. New Orleans La., July 30, 1925. [10]

Fiske, Bradley Allen, naval officer, b. Lyons, N.Y., 1854; d. New York, N.Y., April 7, 1942. [4; 10; 11]

Fiske, Charles, bishop, b. New Brunswick, N.J., 1868; d. Baltimore, Md., Jan. 8, 1942. [10; 11]

Fiske, Daniel Willard, librarian, b. Ellisburg, N.Y., 1831; d. Frankfort, Germany, Sept. 17, 1904. [1; 3]

Fiske, Fidelia, missionary, b. Shelburne, Mass., 1816; d. Shelburne, Mass., July 26, 1864. [1; 3; 4]

Fiske, George Converse, educationist, b. Roxbury Highlands, Mass., 1872; d. Madison, Wis., Jan. 8, 1927. [1; 10]

Fiske, George Walter, theologian, b. Holliston, Mass., 1872; d. Framingham, Mass., Oct. 10, 1945. [7; 10; 11]

Fiske, Horace Spencer, poet and educationist, b. Dexter, Mich., 1859; d. Chicago, Ill., June 2, 1940. [4; 7; 10; 11]

Fiske, John, philosopher and historian, b. Hartford, Conn., 1842; d. Gloucester, Mass., July 4, 1901. [1; 2; 3; 4; 5; 6; 7; 8; 10; 71]

Fiske, Lewis Ransom, clergyman and educationist, b. Penfield, N.Y., 1825; d. Denver, Colo., Feb. 14, 1901. [4; 10]

Fiske, Mrs. Mary H., née Farnham, journalist, d. 1889.

Fiske, Nathan, clergyman, b. Weston, Mass., 1733; d. Brookfield, Mass., Nov. 24, 1799. [3; 4; 7; 8]

Fiske, Nathan Welby, clergyman, b. Weston, Mass., 1798; d. Jerusalem, Palestine, May 27, 1847. [3; 4; 6; 8]

Fiske, Samuel Wheelock, humorist, b. Shelburne Falls, Mass., 1828; d. Fredericksburg, Va., May 22, 1864. [4; 7]

Fiske, Stephen Ryder, journalist, playwright, and short-story writer, b. New Brunswick, N.J., 1840; d. New York, N.Y., April 27, 1916. [1; 2; 7; 10]

Fiske, Willard. See Fiske, Daniel Willard.

Fitch, Albert Parker, clergyman and educationist, b. Boston, Mass., 1877; d. Englewood, N.J., May 22, 1944. [10; 11; 68]

Fitch, Asa, physician and naturalist, b. Fitch's Point, N.Y., 1809; d. Fitch's Point, N.Y., April 8, 1878. [3; 4]

Fitch, Asahel Norton, lawyer, b. 1847; d. 1915.

Fitch, Charles Elliott, journalist, b. Syracuse, N.Y., 1835; d. Skaneateles, N.Y., Jan. 16, 1918. [4; 10]

Fitch, Clyde, playwright, b. New York, N.Y., 1865; d. Chalons-sur-Marne, France, Sept. 4, 1909. [1; 4; 7; 8; 10]

Fitch, Eleazar Thompson, educationist, b. New Haven, Conn., 1791; d. Jan. 31, 1871. [62]

Fitch, Elijah, clergyman and poet, b. 1745; d. Hopkinton, Mass., Dec. 16, 1788. [3; 4; 8; 62]

Fitch, Ernest Robert, clergyman, b. Kingsville, Ont., 1878; d. Granville, O., Feb. 1935. [27]

Fitch, George Hamlin, journalist, b. Lancaster, N.Y., 1852; d. Arcadia, Calif., Feb. 24, 1925. [7; 10]

Fitch, George Helgeson, journalist, b. Galva, Ill., 1877; d. Berkeley, Calif., Aug. 9, 1915. [7; 10; 37]

Fitch, James, clergyman, b. Bocking, Essex, England, 1622; d. Lebanon, Conn., Nov. 18, 1702. [3]

Fitch, James Monroe, lawyer and novelist, b. 1878; d. New York, N.Y., Aug. 20, 1942.

Fitch, Simon, surgeon, b. Horton, N.S., 1820; d. Halifax, N.S., Sept. 13, 1905. [3; 6]

Fitch, Thomas, politician and jurist, b. Norwalk, Conn., 1700; d. Norwalk, Conn., July 18, 1774. [62]

Fitch, William Clyde. See Fitch, Clyde.

Fitton, James, missionary, b. Boston, Mass., 1805; d. Boston, Mass., Sept. 15, 1881. [1]

Fitts, Ada M., poet, b. 1869; d. Buffalo, N.Y., Nov. 29, 1943.

Fitts, James Franklin, journalist and novelist, b. 1840; d. 1890. [7; 8]

Fitzgerald, Desmond, civil engineer, b. Nassau, New Providence, 1846; d. Brookline, Mass., Jan. 12, 1928. [4; 10]

Fitzgerald, Edward, comedian, b. New York, N.Y., 1856; d. Kansas City, Kans., Feb. 16, 1928. [1]

Fitzgerald, Francis Scott Key, novelist, b. St. Paul, Minn., 1896; d. Hollywood, Cal., Dec. 21, 1940. [7; 10; 11]

Fitz-Gerald, John Driscoll, educationist, b. Newark, N.J., 1873; d. Urbana, Ill., June 8, 1946. [7; 13]

Fitzgerald, Maurice O'Regan, short-story writer, b. county Limerick, Ireland, 1881; d. New York, N.Y., Oct. 16. 1942.

Fitzgerald, Oscar Penn, bishop, b. Caswell county, N.C., 1829; d. Monteagle. Tenn., Aug. 5, 1911. [1; 3a; 4; 7; 8; 34]

Fitz Gibbon, Mary Agnes, historical writer, b. Belleville. Ont., 1851; d. Toronto, Ont., May 17, 1915. [27]

Fitzhugh, George, lawyer and sociologist, b. Prince William county, Va., 1806; d. Huntsville, Tex., 1881. [1; 3; 4; 7; 8; 34]

Fitzpatrick, Alfred, welfare-worker, b. Millsville, N.S., 1862; d. Toronto, Ont., June 16, 1936. [27]

Fitz-Patrick, Hugh Louis, journalist, b. Brooklyn, N.Y., 1861; d. Feb. 2, 1921. [10]

Fitzpatrick, John Clement, historian and archivist, b. Washington, D.C., 1876; d. Washington, D.C., Feb. 10, 1940. [7; 10; 21]

Fitzpatrick, John Tracy, lawyer, b. Washington, D.C., 1878; d. Albany, N.Y., May 16, 1933. [10; 11]

Fitzsimmons, Cortland, writer of mystery stories, b. Richmond Hill, Long Island, N.Y., 1893; d. Los Angeles, Calif., July 25, 1949. [10]

Fitzsimmons, Robert, pugilist, b. Cornwall, England, 1862; d. Chicago, Ill., Oct. 22, 1917. [1; 2]

Flaccus (pseud.). See Ward, Thomas.

Flaccus Horatius (pseud.). See Wright, Robert William.

Flagg, Charles Allcott, librarian, b. Sandwich, Mass., 1870; d. Bangor, Me., March 28, 1920. [4; 10]

Flagg, Charles Noël, artist, b. Brooklyn, N.Y., 1848; d. Hartford, Conn., Nov. 10, 1916. [4; 10]

Flagg, Edmund, journalist and diplomat, b. Wiscasset, Me., 1815; d. Fairfax county, Va., Nov. 1, 1890. [1; 3; 4; 6; 7; 8]

Flagg, Edward Octavius, clergyman and poet, b. Georgetown, S.C., 1824; d. 1911. [4; 8; 10]

Flagg, Ernest, architect, b. Brooklyn, N.Y., 1857; d. New York, N.Y., April 10, 1947. [10; 11]

Flagg, Isaac, educationist and poet, b. Beverly, Mass., 1843; d. Berkeley, Calif., Feb. 9, 1931. [7; 10; 35]

Flagg, Jared Bradley, clergyman, b. New Haven, Conn., 1820; d. New York, N.Y., Sept. 25, 1899. [1; 10]

Flagg, John Foster Brewster, physician, b. Boston, Mass., 1804; d. West Chester, Pa., Sept. 8, 1872. [3; 8]

Flagg, John Henry, poet, b. 1843; d. 1911.

Flagg, Josiah, musician, b. Woburn, Mass., 1737; d. about 1795. [1]

Flagg, Josiah Foster, dentist, b. 1789; d. 1853.

Flagg, Josiah Foster, civil engineer, b. Dedham, Mass., 1835; d. Santa Barbara, Calif., April 13, 1928. [10; 51]

Flagg, Thomas Wilson, naturalist, b. Beverly, Mass., 1805; d. Cambridge, Mass., May 6, 1884. [1; 3; 4; 7; 71]

Flagg, William Joseph, viticulturist, politician, and novelist, b. New Haven, Conn., 1818; d. New York, N.Y., April 15, 1898. [6; 8]

Flagg, Wilson. See Flagg, Thomas Wilson.

Flanders, Henry, lawyer, b. Plainfield, N.H., 1824; d. Philadelphia, Pa., April 3, 1911. [1; 3; 4; 10]

Flandrau, Charles Eugene, soldier and jurist, b. New York, N.Y., 1828; d. St Paul, Minn., Sept. 9, 1903. [1; 7; 10; 70]

Flandrau, Charles Macomb, essayist, b. St. Paul, Minn., 1871; d. St. Paul, Minn., March 27, 1938. [7; 10; 51; 70]

Flash, Henry Lynden, poet, b. Cincinnati, O., 1835; d. Los Angeles, Calif., 1914. [4; 10; 34]

Flather, John Joseph, mechanical engineer, b. Philadelphia, Pa., 1862; d. Minneapolis, Minn., May 14, 1926. [1; 4; 10]

Flattery, Maurice Douglas, playwright and novelist, b. Ireland, 1870; d. Boston, Mass., Nov. 25, 1925. [10]

Fleming, Mrs. Ann Cuthbert, schoolteacher, b. Scotland; d. Montreal, Que., 1860. [27]

Fleming, Archibald, clergyman, b. Paisley, Scotland, 1800; d. Malone, N.Y., June 3, 1875.

Fleming, Burton Percival, civil engineer, b. Valley, Neb., 1881; d. Las Cruces, N.M., May 26, 1936. [10]

Fleming, George (pseud.). See Benson, Eugene.

Fleming, George (pseud.). See Fletcher, Julia Constance.

Fleming, George Thornton, historian, b. 1855; d. 1928.

Fleming, John, merchant, b. Scotland, about 1786; d. Montreal, Lower Canada, July 30, 1932. [27]

Fleming, Mrs. May Agnes, née Early, novelist, b. near Saint John, N.B., 1840; d. Brooklyn, N.Y., March 24, 1880. [3; 6; 8; 27]

Fleming, Robins, engineer, b. Somerset county, N.J., 1856; d. New York, N.Y., Nov. 2, 1942.

Fleming, Sir Sandford, civil engineer, b. Kirkcaldy, Scotland, 1827; d. Halifax, N.S., July 22, 1915. [27]

Fleming, Walter Lynwood, historian, b. Brundige, Ala., 1874; d. Nashville, Tenn., Aug. 3, 1932. [1a; 10; 34]

Fleming, William Hansell, Shakespearian scholar, b. Philadelphia, Pa., 1844; d. Oct. 1, 1915. [7; 8; 10]

Fleming, Mrs. Williamina Paton, née Stevens, astronomer, b. Dundee, Scotland, 1857; d. Boston, Mass., May 21, 1911. [1; 4; 10]

Fleming, William Stuart, local historian, b. Maury county, Tenn., 1816; d. Columbia, Tenn., July 13, 1896. [62]

Flemming, Harford (pseud.). See McClellan, Mrs. Harriet, née Hare.

Fletcher, Alfred Charles Benson, traveller, b. 1885; d. 1928.

Fletcher, Alice Cunningham, ethnologist, b. Cuba, 1838; d. Washington, D.C., April 6, 1923. [1; 4; 7; 10]

Fletcher, Edward Taylor, surveyor and poet, b. Canterbury, England, about 1816; d. New Westminster, B.C., Jan. 30, 1897. [27]

Fletcher, Horace, nutritionist, b. Lawrence, Mass., 1849; d. Copenhagen, Denmark, Jan. 13, 1919. [1; 4; 8; 10]

Fletcher, James, naturalist, b. Kent, England, 1852; d. Montreal, Que., Nov. 8, 1908. [27]

Fletcher, James Cooley, missionary, b. Indianapolis, Ind., 1823; d. Los Angeles, Calif., April 23, 1901. [1; 4; 6; 8]

Fletcher, Jefferson Butler, educationist, b. Chicago, Ill., 1865; d. York Village, Me., Aug. 17, 1946. [7; 10; 37]

Fletcher, John, lawyer, b. Williamstown, Vt., 1791; d. Natchez, Miss., Aug., 1862. [43; 49]

Fletcher, John Madison, psychologist, b. near Murfreesboro, Tenn., 1873; d. New Orleans, La., Dec. 12, 1944. [10]

Fletcher, Julia Constance, novelist and playwright, b. 1858; d. Venice, Italy, June 9, 1938. [7]

Fletcher, Orlin Ottman, clergyman and educationist, b. Brant county, Ont., 1847; d. Brooklyn, N.Y., Oct. 20, 1937. [10; 11]

Fletcher, Robert Howe, soldier and novelist, b. Cincinnati, O., 1850; d. Washington, D.C., Oct. 29, 1936. [35]

Fletcher, Robert Huntington, educationist, b. Hanover, N.H., 1875; d. Brookline, Mass., June 26, 1919. [49]

Fletcher, William Baldwin, physician, b. Indianapolis, Ind., 1837; d. Orlando, Fla., April 25, 1907. [1; 10]

Fletcher, William Isaac, librarian, b. Burlington, Vt., 1844; d. Amherst, Mass., June 15, 1917. [4; 10]

Fletcher, William Meade, lawyer, b. Sperryville, Va., 1870; d. Richmond, Va., Dec. 19, 1943. [10; 11]

Flexner, Jennie Maas., librarian, b. Louisville, Ky., 1882; d. New York, N.Y., Nov. 18, 1944.

Flexner, Simon, physician, b. Louisville, Ky., 1863; d. New York, N.Y., May 2, 1946. [10]

Flick, Alexander Clarence, archivist and historian, b. Galion, O., 1869; d. Santa Rosa, Fla., July 30, 1942. [7; 10; 11]

Flick, Lawrence Francis, physician, b. Carrolltown, Pa., 1856; d. Philadelphia, Pa., July 7, 1938. [10; 11; 21]

Flickinger, Daniel Krumler, bishop, b. Butler county, O., 1824; d. Columbus, O., Aug. 29, 1911. [1; 4; 10]

Flickinger, Robert Elliott, local historian, b. 1848; d. ? [37]

Flickinger, Roy Caston, educationist, b. Seneca, Ill., 1876; d. Iowa City, Ia., July 6, 1942. [7; 10]

Fling, Fred Morrow, historian, b. Portland, Me., 1870; d. Lincoln, Neb., June 8, 1934. [4; 10; 46]

Flinn, John Joseph, journalist, b. Ireland, 1851; d. Glencoe, Ill., Nov. 27, 1929. [10]

Flint, Abel, clergyman, b. Windham, Conn., 1765; d. Hartford, Conn., March 7, 1825. [3; 8; 62]

Flint, Albert Stowell, astronomer, b. Salem, Mass., 1853; d. Madison, Wis., Feb. 22, 1923. [4; 10; 51]

Flint, Austin, physician, b. Petersham, Mass., 1812; d. New York, N.Y., March 13, 1886. [1; 3; 4; 6; 8; 51]

Flint, Austin, physiologist, b. Northampton, Mass., 1836; d. New York, N.Y., Sept. 22, 1915. [1; 4; 10; 51]

Flint, Charles Louis, agriculturist, b. Middleton, Mass., 1824; d. Hillman, Ga., Feb. 26, 1889. [1; 3; 6; 8]

Flint, Charles Ranlett, industrialist, b. Thomaston, Me., 1850; d. Washington, D.C., Feb. 12, 1934. [4; 10]

Flint, Grover, war correspondent, b. New York, N.Y., 1867; d. Newport News, Va., Jan. 31, 1909. [8]

Flint, Henry Martyn, journalist, b. Philadelphia, Pa., 1829; d. Camden, N.J., Dec. 12, 1868. [3; 4;' 6; 8]

Flint, Jacob, clergyman, b. Reading, Mass., 1767; d. Marshfield, Mass., Oct. 11, 1835. [3; 51]

Flint, Martha Bockée, local historian, d. Flushing, Long Island, N.Y., 1900. [8]

Flint, Micah P., lawyer and poet, b. Lunenburg, Mass., 1807; d. 1830. [3; 8]

Flint, Timothy, missionary and journalist, b. Reading, Mass., 1780; d. Salem, Mass., Aug. 16, 1840. [1; 3; 4; 71]

Flint, Wesley Pillsbury, entomologist, b. South Hampton, N.H., 1882; d. Urbana, Ill., June 3, 1943. [11; 13]

Flint, William Ruthven, chemist, b. McIndoo Falls, Vt., 1875; d. Pasadena, Calif., Sept. 23, 1933. [13; 62]

Florence, William Jermyn (pseud.). See Conlin, Bernard.

Flournoy, Parke Poindexter, clergyman, b. Chesterfield, Va., 1839; d. Washington, D.C., June 14, 1935. [10]

Flower, Benjamin Orange, editor and social reformer, b. Albion, Ill., 1858; d. Boston, Mass., Dec. 24, 1918. [1; 2; 4; 7; 10]

Flower, Elliott, journalist and novelist, b. Madison, Wis., 1863; d. July 3, 1920. [7; 8; 10; 44]

Flower, Frank Abial, journalist and historian, b. Cattaraugus county, N.Y., 1854; d. 1911. [7; 10; 44]

Flower, George, pioneer, b. Hertford, England, 1788; d. Grayville, Ill., Jan. 15, 1862. [1; 3; 4]

Flowers, Montaville, educationist, b. Cincinnati, O., 1868; d. Pasadena, Calif., Nov. 10, 1934. [10]

Floy, James, clergyman, b. New York, N.Y., 1806; d. New York, N.Y., Oct. 14, 1863. [1; 3; 4; 8]

Floyd, David Bittle, clergyman, b. Middletown, Md., 1846; d. Jan. 23, 1922. [10]

Floyd, Nicholas Jackson, genealogist, b. 1828; d. ? [34]

Floyd, Robert Mitchell, poet, b. New Orleans, La., 1849; d. ?

Floyd, William, journalist, b. Englewood, N.J., 1871; d. New York, N.Y., Nov. 26, 1943. [11; 56]

Floyd-Jones, De Lancey, soldier, b. Queens county, N.Y., 1826; d. 1902. [3b; 8; 10]

Flügel, Ewald, philologist, b. Leipzig, Germany, 1863; d. Stanford University, Calif., Nov. 14, 1914. [10]

Fluegel, Maurice, theologian, b. 1833; d. Baltimore, Md., Feb. 14, 1911.

Flynn, Joseph Michael, priest, b. Springfield, Mass., 1848; d. Morristown, N.J., Jan. 5, 1910. [10; 21]

Flynt, Josiah (pseud.). See Willard, Josiah Flynt.

Foerster, Robert Franz, economist, b. Pittsburg, Pa., 1883; d. Wolfeboro, N.H., July 30, 1941. [10; 11; 51]

Fogg, Lawrence Daniel, journalist, b. Sheffield, England, 1879; d. Springfield, Mass., Feb. 12, 1914. [10]

Fogie, Francis, sr. (pseud.). See Payson, George.

Foik, Paul Joseph, priest, b. Stratford, Ont., 1880; d. Austin, Tex., March 1, 1941.

Foley, George Cadwalader, theologian, b. Philadelphia, Pa., 1851; d. Philadelphia, Pa., May 8, 1935. [10; 11]

Foley, James William, poet and journalist, b. St. Louis, Mo., 1874; d. Pasadena, Calif., May 18, 1939. [10; 11]

Foley, Patrick Kevin, book-seller and bibliographer, b. Cork county, Ireland, 1856; d. Boston, Mass., April 13, 1937. [7]

Folger, Henry Clay, oil magnate, b. New York, N.Y., 1857; d. Brooklyn, N.Y., June 11, 1930. [7; 10; 45]

Folger, Peter, pioneer, b. Norwich, England, 1617; d. Nantucket, N.Y., 1690. [1; 3; 4; 7; 8]

Folin, Otto Knut Olof, biological chemist, b. Sweden, 1867; d. Brookline, Mass., Oct. 25, 1934. [1a; 10; 13]

Folk, Edgar Estes, clergyman, b. Haywood county, Tenn., 1856; d. Nashville, Tenn., Feb. 27, 1917. [8; 10]

Folkmar, Daniel, anthropologist, b. Roxbury, Wis., 1861; d. Washington, D.C., July 22, 1932. [10]

Follen, Charles Theodore Christian, educationist, b. Germany, 1796; d. Long Island sound, N.Y., Jan. 13, 1840. [1; 3; 4; 6; 8]

Follen, Mrs. Eliza Lee, née Cabot, writer of books for children, b. Boston, Mass., 1787; d. Brookline, Mass., Jan. 26, 1860. [1; 3; 6; 8]

Follett, Mary Parker, political scientist, b. Quincy, Mass., 1868; d. Boston, Mass., Dec. 18, 1933. [1a; 10]

Folsom, Benjamin, compiler, b. 1790; d. 1833.

Folsom, Charles Follen, physician, b. Haverhill, Mass., 1842; d. New York, N.Y., Aug. 20, 1907. [3; 10; 51]

Folsom, George, historian, b .Kennebunk, Me., 1802; d. Rome, Italy, March 27, 1869. [1; 3; 4; 7; 8]

Folsom, James Madison, historian, b. 1838; d. ? [34]

Folsom, John Dana, clergyman, b. Raymond, N.H., 1842; d. Raymond, N.H., June 4, 1912.

Folsom, Justus Watson, entomologist, b. Cambridge, Mass., 1871; d. Tallulah, La., Sept. 24, 1936. [10; 11; 51]

Folsom, Montgomery Morgan, journalist and poet, b. Lowndes county, Ga., 1857; d. Atlanta, Ga., July 2, 1898. [34]

Folsom, Nathaniel Smith, clergyman b. Portsmouth N.H., 1806; d. Asheville, N.C., Nov. 10, 1890. [3; 49]

Folsom, William Henry Carman, politician and historian, b. Saint John, N.B., 1817; d. Taylor's Falls, Minn., Dec. 15, 1900. [70]

Foltz, Charles Steinman, journalist, b. Philadelphia, Pa., 1859; d. Lancaster, Pa., Jan. 15, 1941. [7]

Foltz, Jonathan Messersmith, surgeon, b. Lancaster, Pa., 1810; d. Philadelphia, Pa., April 22, 1877. [3; 4]

Folwell, William Watts, educationist and historian, b. Romulus, N.Y., 1833; d. Minneapolis, Minn., Sept. 18, 1929. [1; 4; 7; 10; 70]

Fontaine, Arthur Benjamin, lawyer and politician, b. Green Bay, Wis., 1876; d. Green Bay, Wis., Dec. 30, 1940. [10; 44]

Fontaine, Edward, clergyman, b. Virginia, 1814; d. 1884. [8]

Fontaine, Francis, novelist, b. 1844; d. 1901. [8; 34]

Fontaine, Lamar, soldier and civil engineer, b. Laberde, Tex., 1829; d. ? [3a; 10; 34]

Fontaine, William Morris, scientist, b. Louisa county, Va., 1835; d. Charlottesville, Va., April 29, 1913. [4; 10]

Foord, John, journalist, b. Perthshire, Scotland, 1842; d. 1922. [4]

Foot, Joseph Ives, clergyman, b. Watertown, Conn., 1796; d. near Knoxville, Tenn., April 21, 1840. [3]

Foot, Samuel Alfred, jurist, b. Watertown, Conn., 1790; d. Geneva, N.Y., May 11, 1878. [3; 4]

Foote, Albert E., scientist, b. Hamilton, N.Y., 1846; d. Atlanta, Ga., Oct. 10, 1895.

Foote, Allen Ripley, economist, b. Olcott, N.Y., 1842; d. Columbus, O., 1921. [2; 10]

Foote, Andrew Hull, naval officer, b. New Haven, Conn., 1806; d. New York, N.Y., June 26, 1863. [1; 2; 3; 4]

Foote, Arthur William, musician, b. Salem, Mass., 1853; d. Boston, Mass., April 9, 1937. [10; 20; 51]

Foote, Edward Bliss, physician, b. Cleveland, O., 1829; d. Larchmont, N.Y., Oct. 5, 1906. [10]

Foote, Edward Bond, physician, b. Cleveland, O., 1854; d. New York, N.Y., Oct. 12, 1912. [10]

Foote, Henry Stuart, lawyer and politician, b. Fauquier county, Va., 1804; d. Nashville, Tenn., May 20, 1880. [1; 2; 3; 4; 7; 8]

Foote, Henry Wilder, clergyman, b. Salem, Mass., 1838; d. Boston, Mass., May 29, 1889. [3; 8; 11; 51]

Foote, James Stephen, physician, b. Colchester, Conn., 1851; d. Omaha, Neb., June 30, 1925. [62]

Foote, John Ambrose, pediatrician, b. Archbald, Pa., 1874; d. Washington, D.C., April 12, 1931. [1a; 10]

Foote, John Parsons, educationist, b. 1783; d. 1865. [6]

Foote, Lucius Harwood, lawyer and poet, b. Winfield, N.Y., 1826; d. San Francisco, Calif., June 4, 1913. [1; 10; 35]

Foote, Mrs. Mary, née Hallock, novelist, b. Milton, N.Y., 1847; d. Boston, Mass., June 25, 1938. [2; 4; 7; 10; 35]

Foote, Mary Selina, lawyer, b. Northford, Conn., 1887; d. New Haven, Conn., Sept. 30, 1924. [62]

Foote, William Henry, clergyman, b. Colchester, Conn., 1794; d. Romney, W. Va., Nov. 18, 1869. [1a; 3; 8]

Footner, Hulbert, novelist, playwright, and historian, b. Hamilton, Ont., 1879; d. Baltimore, Md. Nov. 25, 1944. [7; 10; 11]

Foraker, Joseph Benson, lawyer and politician, b. Highland county, O., 1846; d. Cincinnati, O., May 10, 1917. [1; 2; 10]

Foran, Joseph Kearney, poet and littérateur, b. Aylmer, Que., 1857; d. Mount Royal, Que., 1931. [27]

Forbes, Aleck (pseud.). See Rathborne, St. George Henry.

Forbes, Charles Henry, educationist, b. Providence, R.I., 1866; d. Andover, Mass., March 12, 1933. [10; 11; 51]

Forbes, Edwin, illustrator, b. New York, N.Y., 1839; d. Flatbush, N.Y., March 6, 1895. [1; 4; 7]

Forbes, Eli, clergyman, b. Westborough, Mass., 1726; d. Gloucester, Mass., Dec. 15, 1804. [3; 51]

Forbes, Henry Prentiss, theologian, b. Paris, Me., 1849; d. Oct. 2, 1913. [10]

Forbes, James, playwright, b. Salem, Ont., 1871; d. Frankfort-on-Main, Germany, May 26, 1938. [7; 10]

Forbes, John Murray, capitalist and politician, b. Bordeaux, France, 1813; d. Milton, Mass., Oct. 12, 1898. [1]

Forbes, Robert Bennet, merchant and mariner, b. Jamaica Plain, Mass., 1804; d. Boston, Mass., Nov. 23, 1889. [1; 6; 7; 8]

Forbes, Stephen Alfred, naturalist, b. Silver Creek, Ill., 1844; d. Urbana, Ill., March 13, 1930. [1; 4; 8; 10]

Forbush, Edward Howe, ornithologist, b. Quincy, Mass., 1858; d. Westboro, Mass., March 8, 1929. [1; 4; 10]

Force, Manning Ferguson, soldier and lawyer, b. Washington, D.C., 1824; d. Erie county, N.Y., May 8, 1899. [1; 3; 6; 8; 10]

Force, Peter, archivist and historian, b. near Passaic Falls, N.J., 1790; d. Washington, D.C., Jan. 23, 1868. [1; 3; 6; 8]

Force, William Quereau, scholar, b. Washington, D.C., 1820; d. Washington, D.C., Dec. 18, 1880. [3; 8]

Ford, Corydon La, physician, b. Lexington, N.Y., 1813; d. Ann Arbor, Mich., April 14, 1894. [3; 8; 53]

Ford, David Barnes, clergyman, b. Scituate, Mass., 1820; d. Hanover, N.H., May 3, 1903. [47]

Ford, Mrs. Elisabeth, née Smith, novelist, b. Mount Vernon, Ia., about 1895; d. New York, N.Y., May 24, 1944.

Ford, Mrs. Emily Ellsworth, née Fowler, poet, b. Durham, Conn., 1825; d. Brooklyn, N.Y., Nov. 24, 1893. [3; 8]

Ford, George Burdett, architect, b. Clinton, Mass., 1879; d. New York, N.Y., Aug. 14, 1930. [1a; 10]

Ford, Harriet. See Morgan, Mrs. Harriet French, née Ford.

Ford, Henry Allen, local historian, d. Detroit, Mich., 1894. [39]

Ford, Henry Jones, historian and political scientist, b. Baltimore, Md., 1851; d. Blue Ridge Summit, Pa., Aug. 29, 1925.

Ford, Isaac Nelson, journalist, b. Buffalo, N.Y., 1848; d. London, England, Aug. 7, 1912. [10]

Ford, James, educationist, b. Clinton, Mass., 1884; d. Stockbridge, Mass., May 12, 1944. [12; 51]

Ford, James Lauren, humorist, b. St. Louis, Mo., 1854; d. Bay Shore, Long Island, N.Y., Feb. 26, 1928. [2; 7; 8; 10]

Ford, John Donaldson, naval officer, b. Baltimore, Md., 1840; d. Baltimore, Md., April 8, 1918. [10]

Ford, Mrs. Mary Anne, née McMullen, poet, b. 1841; d. 1876.

Ford, Patrick, journalist, b. Galway, Ireland, 1835; d. Brooklyn, N.Y., Sept. 23, 1913. [1; 7; 10]

Ford, Paul Leicester, novelist, historian, and bibliographer, b. Brooklyn, N.Y., 1865; d. New York, N.Y., May 8, 1902. [1; 2; 4; 7; 10; 71; 72]

Ford, Mrs. Sallie, née Rochester, novelist, b. Boyle county, Ky., 1828; d. St. Louis, Mo., Feb., 1910. [3; 7; 8; 10; 34; 74]

Ford, Samuel Howard, historian, b. 1819; d. St. Louis, Mo., July 6, 1905. [8; 10; 34]

Ford, Sewell, novelist, b. South Levant, Me., 1868; d. Keene, N.H., Oct. 26, 1946. [4; 7; 10; 11]

Ford, Sheridan, journalist, b. Monroe county, Mich.; d. Detroit, Mich., April, 1922. [4; 39]

Ford, Stephen Van Rensselaer, journalist, b. Greenville, N.Y., 1836; d. New York, N.Y., June 7, 1910.

Ford, Thomas, politician and historian, b. Fayette county, Pa., 1800; d. Peoria, Ill., Nov. 3, 1850. [1]

Ford, Worthington Chauncey, historian. b. Brooklyn, N.Y., 1858; d. at sea, March 7, 1941. [4; 7; 10]

Foreman, Edward Reuben, local historian, b. Lima, N.Y., 1868; d. Rochester, N.Y., Feb. 22, 1936.

Forest, William Edward, physician, b. Winooski, Vt., 1850; d. Rockaway Park, N.Y., July 30, 1903. [59]

Forester, Fanny (pseud.). See Judson. Mrs. Emily, née Chubbuck.

Forestier, Auber (pseud.). See Moore, Mrs. Annie Aubertine, née Woodward.

Forgan, James Berwick, banker, b. St. Andrews, Scotland, 1852; d. Chicago, Ill., Oct. 28, 1924. [1; 4; 10]

Forman, Justus Miles, novelist, b. Le Roy, N.Y., 1875; d. at sea, May 7, 1915. [1; 4; 10; 62]

Formento, Felix, surgeon, b. New Orleans, La., 1837; d. New Orleans, La., June 4, 1907. [3b; 4; 8; 10; 34]

Fornaro, Carlo de, caricaturist, b. 1871; d. New York, N.Y., Aug. 25, 1949.

Forney John Wien, journalist, b. Lancaster, Pa., 1817; d. Philadelphia, Pa., Dec. 9, 1881. [1; 3; 4; 7; 8]

Forney, Matthias Nace, engineer and inventor, b. Hanover, Pa., 1835; d. New York, N.Y., Jan. 14, 1908. [1; 4]

Forrest, Edmund William, pioneer, b. London, England; d. Hull, Que., July 4, 1880. [27]

Forrest, Mary (pseud.). See Freeman, Mrs. Julia Deane.

Forrester, Dexter J. (pseud.) See Goldfrap, John Henry.

Forrester, Francis (pseud.). See Wise, Daniel.

Forry, Samuel, physician, b. Berlin, Pa., 1811; d. Nov. 8, 1944. [3; 8]

Forsander, Nils, theologian, b. Sweden, 1846; d. Rock Island, Ill., Aug. 21, 1926. [10]

Forsell, Knut Emil, clergyman, b. Sweden, 1864; d. Minneapolis, Minn., Jan. 28, 1916. [62]

Forsslund, Mary Louise, novelist, b. Sayville, N.Y., 1873; d. Sayville, N.Y., May, 1910. [10]

Forster, Frank Joseph, architect, b. New York, N.Y., 1886; d. Killingworth, Conn., March 4, 1948. [10]

Forsyth, Cecil, musician, b. Greenwich, England, 1870; d. New York, N.Y., Dec. 7, 1941. [20]

Forsyth, George Alexander, soldier, b. Muncy, Pa., 1837; d. Rockfort, Mass., Sept. 12, 1915. [10]

Forsyth, James Bell, merchant, b. Kingston, Upper Canada, 1803; d. Quebec, Que., 1869. [27]

Forsyth, John, clergyman, b. Newburgh, N.Y., 1810; d. Newburgh, N.Y., Oct. 17, 1886. [1; 3; 4]

Forsyth-Grant, Mrs. Minnie Caroline, née Robinson, traveller, b. Toronto, Ont.; d. Toronto, Ont., Nov. 2, 1923. [27]

Fort, Charles Hoy, writer on science, b. Albany, N.Y., 1874; d. Bronx, N.Y., May 3, 1932. [7]

Fort, George Franklin, physician and politician, b. Pemberton, N.J., 1809; d. New Egypt, Ocean county ,N.J., April 22, 1872. [3; 4; 8]

Fortier, Alcée, educationist and historian, b. St. James Parish, La., 1856; d. New Orleans, La., Feb. 14, 1914. [1; 4; 7; 8; 10; 34]

Fortune, Timothy Thomas, poet, b. Mariana, Fla., 1856; d. June 2, 1928. [7]

Forwood, William Stump, physician, b. near Darlington, Md., 1830; d. 1892. [3; 8]

Fosdick, Charles Austin, writer of books for boys, b. Randolph, N.Y., 1842; d. Hamburg, N.Y., Aug. 22, 1915. [1; 6; 7; 8; 10]

Fosdick, James William, artist, b. Charlestown, Mass., 1858; d. Boston, Mass., Sept. 14, 1937. [10]

Fosdick, William Whiteman, lawyer and littérateur, b. Cincinnati, O., 1825; d. Cincinnati, O., March 8, 1862. [1; 3; 4; 6; 7; 8]

Foss, Claude William, educationist, b. Geneva, Ill., 1855; d. Rock Island, Ill., Feb. 8, 1935. [10]

Foss, Cyrus David, bishop, b. Kingston, N.Y., 1834; d. Philadelphia, Pa., Jan. 29, 1910. [1; 3; 10; 60]

Foss, Sam Walter, poet, journalist, and librarian, b. Candia, N.H., 1858; d. Boston, Mass., Feb. 26, 1911. [1; 8; 10; 47]

Fossler, Laurence, educationist, b. Würtemberg, Germany, 1857; d. Lincoln, Neb., Jan. 7, 1933. [10]

Foster, Agness Greene, lecturer and poet, b. Athens, Ala., 1863; d. Washington, D.C., Sept. 12, 1933. [7; 10; 11]

Foster, Allyn King, clergyman, b. Baltimore, Md. 1868; d. Baltimore, Md., Nov. 10, 1934. [10; 62]

Foster, Benjamin, clergyman, b. Peabody, Mass., 1750; d. New York, N.Y., Aug. 26, 1798. [3;. 62]

Foster, Charles James, sporting journalist, b. Bicester, England, 1820; d. Astoria, N.Y., Sept. 12, 1883. [1; 7]

Foster, David Skaats, poet and novelist, b. Utica, N.Y., 1862; d. Syracuse, N.Y., June 23, 1920. [1; 7; 10]

Foster, Edna Abigail, writer of books for children, b. Sullivan, Me.; d. Boston, Mass., July 11, 1945. [7; 10]

Foster, Ellsworth Decatur, editor, b. Clayton, Mich., 1869; d. Chicago, Ill., Nov. 2, 1936. [10]

Foster, Eugene Clifford, welfare worker, b. Philadelphia, Pa., 1867; d. Springfield, Mass., Nov. 5, 1927. [10]

Foster, Frank Hugh, clergyman and educationist, b. Springfield, Mass., 1851; d. Oberlin, O., Oct. 20, 1935. [1a; 10; 11; 51]

Foster, Frank Keyes, printer, b. Palmer, Mass., 1854; d. 1909. [10]

Foster, Frank Pierce, physician, b. Concord, N.H., 1841; d. Chadwick, N.J., Aug. 13, 1911. [1; 10]

Foster, George Burman, clergyman and educationist, b. Alderson, W. Va., 1858; d. Chicago, Ill., Dec. 22, 1918. [1; 4; 10]

Foster, Sir George Eulas, politician, b. Carleton county, N.B., 1847; d. Ottawa, Ont., Dec. 30, 1931. [27]

Foster, George G., journalist, d. 1850. [7]

Foster, Mrs. Hannah, née Webster, novelist, b. 1759; d. Montreal, Lower Canada, April 17, 1840. 1; 3; 5; 7; 8]

Foster, Harry La Tourette, writer of adventure stories, b. Brooklyn, N.Y., 1894; d. New York, N.Y., March 15, 1932. [7; 10; 11]

Foster, Henry Albert, educationist, b. Maxwell, Tenn., 1874; d. Maryville, Mo., Aug. 7, 1944. [62]

Foster, Herbert Hamilton, educationist, b. Huron, N.Y., 1875; d. Beloit, Wis., Dec. 1, 1942. [10]

Foster, Horatio Alvah, electrical engineer, b. Philadelphia, Pa., 1858; d. Yonkers, N.Y., 1913. [10]

Foster, Isaac, clergyman, b. 1725; d. 1807. [62]

Foster, James S., printer, b. 1828; d. 1890.

Foster, John Gray, soldier, b. Whitefield, N.H., 1823; d. Nashua, N.H., Sept. 2, 1874. [1; 3; 4]

Foster, John McGaw, clergyman, b. Bangor, Me., 1860; d. Cambridge, Mass., Oct. 30, 1928. [10; 51]

Foster, John Watson, lawyer, politician, and diplomat, b. Pike county, Ind., 1836; d. Washington, D.C., Nov. 15, 1917. [1; 4; 7; 10]

Foster, John Wells, geologist, b. Brimfield, Mass., 1815; d. Chicago, Ill., June 29, 1873. [3; 4; 8]

Foster, Joseph, naval officer, b. 1841; d. Portsmouth, N.H., May 18, 1930. [10]

Foster, Mrs. Judith Ellen, née Horton, lecturer, b. Lowell, Mass., 1840; d. Washington, D.C., 1910. [4; 8; 10]

Foster, Mary Louise. See Forsslund, Mary Louise.

Foster, Maximilian, journalist and novelist, b. San Francisco, Calif., 1872; d. New York, N.Y., Sept. 22, 1943. [7; 10; 35]

Foster, Nathan Lanesford, poet, b. 1787; d. 1859.

Foster, Randolph Sinks, bishop, b. Williamsburg, O., 1820; d. Newton, Mass., May 2, 1903. [1; 3; 4; 6]

Foster, Robert Verrell, theologian, b. Wilson county, Tenn., 1845; d. Lebanon, Tenn., Jan. 27, 1914. [10; 34; 68]

Foster, Roger, lawyer, b. Worcester, Mass., 1857; d. New York, N.Y., Feb. 22, 1924. [1; 10; 62]

Foster, Stephen Collins, musical composer, b. Pittsburg, Pa., 1826; d. New York, N.Y., Jan. 13, 1864. [1; 2; 3; 4; 7; 20]

Foster, Stephen Symonds, abolitionist, b. Canterbury, N.H., 1809; d. near Worcester, Mass., Sept. 8, 1881. [1; 3; 4; 8]

Foster, Mrs. Theodosia Maria, née Toll, novelist, b. Verona, N.Y., 1838; d. Verona, N.Y., Oct. 24, 1923. [2; 6; 7; 10]

Foster, Walter Bertram, novelist, b. Providence, R.I., 1869; d. Fort Lee, N.J. April 26, 1929. [7]

Foster, William, chemist, b. Hartford, Ky., 1869; d. Princeton, N.J., May 24, 1937. [10; 11; 13]

Foster, William Eaton, librarian, b. Brattleboro, Vt., 1851; d. Providence, R.I., Sept. 10, 1930. [8; 10; 47]

Foster, William Silliman, psychologist, b. 1886; d. Minneapolis, Minn., Jan. 2, 1926.

Fougner, Gustav Selmer, journalist, b. Chicago, Ill., 1884; d. Washington, D.C., April 2, 1941. [7; 10; 11]

Foulke, William Dudley, lawyer, politician, and poet, b. New York, N.Y., 1848; d. Richmond, Ind., May 30, 1935. [1a; 4; 7; 10; 11]

Fournier, Jules, journalist, b. Coteau-du-Lac, Que., 1884; d. Ottawa, Ont., 1918. [27]

Fowke, Gerard, archaeologist, b. Maysville, Ky., 1855; d. Madison, Ind., March 5, 1933. [1a; 4; 10]

Fowle, Daniel, printer, b. Charlestown, Mass., 1715; d. Portsmouth, N.H., June 8, 1787. [1; 3; 4; 7]

Fowle, Otto, local historian, b. Moscow, Mich., 1852; d. Sault Ste. Marie, Mich., Aug. 21, 1920. [39]

Fowle, William Bentley, educationist, b. Boston, Mass., 1795; d. Medfield, Mass., Feb. 6, 1865. [1; 4]

Fowler, Charles Henry, bishop, b. Burford, Upper Canada, 1837; d. New York, N.Y., March 20, 1908. [1; 3; 4; 7; 10; 60]

Fowler, Charles Newell, banker and politician, b. Lena, Ill., 1852; d. Orange, N.J., March 27, 1932. [10; 62]

Fowler, Frank, painter, b. Brooklyn, N.Y., 1852; d. New York, N.Y., Aug. 18, 1910. [1; 10]

Fowler, George, novelist, fl. 1810-1835. [7]

Fowler, George Little, mechanical engineer, b. Cherry Valley, N.Y., 1855; d. Brooklyn, N.Y., July 2, 1926. [10; 45]

Fowler, George Ryerson, surgeon, b. Brooklyn, N.Y., 1843; d. Albany, N.Y., Feb. 6, 1906. [1; 10]

Fowler, Henry, clergyman, b. Stockbridge, Mass., 1824; d. Vineyard Haven, Mass., Aug. 4, 1872. [3; 8; 61]

Fowler, Henry Thatcher, educationist, b. Fishkill, N.Y., 1867; d. Harmony, R.I., Jan. 23, 1948. [7; 10; 11; 62]

Fowler, Jessie Allen, phrenologist, b. New York, N.Y., 1856; d. New York, N.Y., Oct. 15, 1932. [4; 10]

Fowler, John A., writer on insurance, d. 1911.

Fowler, Lorenzo Niles, phrenologist, b. Cohocton, N.Y., 1811; d. West Orange, N.J., Sept. 2, 1896. [3; 4; 8]

Fowler, Mrs. Lydia, née Folger, physician, b. Nantucket, Mass., 1823; d. London, England, Jan. 26, 1879. 3; 8]

Fowler, Nathaniel Clark, business expert, b. Yarmouth, Mass., 1858; d. Boston, Mass., Nov. 25, 1918. [10]

Fowler, Orin, clergyman, b. Lebanon, Conn., 1791; d. Washington, D.C., Sept. 3, 1852. [1; 3; 4; 6; 8; 62]

Fowler, Orson Squire, phrenologist, b. Cohocton, N.Y., 1809; d. near Sharon, Conn., Aug. 18, 1887, [2; 3; 4; 6; 8]

Fowler, Philemon Halstead, clergyman, b. Albany, N.Y., 1814; d. Utica, N.Y., Dec. 19, 1879. [3; 8]

Fowler, Robert Ludlow, lawyer, b. Newburgh, N.Y., 1849; d. New York, N.Y., July 13, 1936. [10; 47]

Fowler, Samuel Page, antiquary, b. Danvers, Mass., 1800; d. 1888. [3]

Fowler, William Chauncey, clergyman and educationist, b. Clinton, Conn., 1793; d. Durham, Conn., Jan. 15, 1881. [3; 8; 62]

Fowler, William Worthington, lawyer and stockbroker, b. Middlebury, Vt., 1833; d. Durham, Conn., Sept. 18, 1881. [3; 6; 43; 45]

Fowler, James H., clergyman, b. Nassau, Bahama, 1812; d. Philadelphia, Pa., 1854. [3; 62]

Fox, Charles, clergyman and agriculturist, b. Durham, England, 1815; d. Detroit, Mich., July 24, 1854. [39]

Fox, Charles James, lawyer and local hsitorian, b. Antrim, N. H., 1811; d. Nashua, N.H., Feb. 17, 1846. [49]

Fox, Charles Shattuck, educationist, b. Oil City, Pa., 1868; d. Bethlehem, Pa., July 5, 1939. [10; 51]

Fox, David (pseud.). See Ostrander, Isabel Egenton.

Fox, Dixon Ryan, historian, b. Potsdam, N.Y., 1887; d. Schenectady, N.Y., Jan. 30, 1945. [7; 10; 11]

Fox, Dorus Martin, soldier and politician, b. 1817; d. 1901. [37]

Fox, Ebenezer, revolutionist, b. East Roxbury, Mass., 1763; d. East Roxbury, Mass., 1843. [3; 8]

Fox, Mrs. Emma Augusta, née **Stowell,** club woman, b. Binghampton, N.Y., 1847; d. Detroit, Mich., Feb. 8, 1945. [10]

Fox, Florence Cordelia, educationist, b. 1861; d. 1933.

Fox, Fontaine Talbot, jurist and biographer, b. Pulaski county, Ky., 1836; d. Louisville, Ky., April 9, 1926. [4]

Fox, George Henry, dermatologist, b. Ballston Spa, N.Y., 1846; d. New York, N.Y., May 3, 1937. [10; 11]

Fox, George Levi, educationist, b. New Haven, Conn., 1852; d. New Haven, Conn., Aug. 6, 1931. [4; 10; 62]

Fox, Mrs. Gertrude Elizabeth, née **Wilbur,** writer on animal husbandry, b. Boston, Mass., 1878; d. Bradenton, Fla., May 19, 1947.

Fox, Henry John, clergyman and educationist, b. Kingston-upon-Hull, England, 1821; d. 1891. [48]

Fox, Herbert, pathologist, b. Atlantic City, N.J., 1880; d. Philadelphia, Pa., Feb. 27, 1942. [13; 55]

Fox, John William, novelist, b. Stony Point, Ky., 1863; d. Big Stone Gap, Va., July 8, 1919. [1; 2; 4; 7; 10; 51; 72]

Fox, Junius Bost, clergyman, b. 1860; d. 1900.

Fox, Lawrence Webster, opthalmologist, b. Hummelstown, Pa., 1853; d. Philadelphia, Pa., June 4, 1931. [4; 10]

Fox. Margaret, spiritualistic medium, b. Canada, 1833; d. Brooklyn, N.Y., March 8, 1893. [1]

Fox, Norman, clergyman, b. Glens Falls, N.Y., 1836; d. New York, N.Y., June 23, 1907. [8; 10]

Fox, Richard Kyle, journalist, b. 1846; d. Red Bank, N.J., Nov. 16, 1922.

Fox, Thomas Bayley, clergyman, b. Boston, Mass., 1808; d. Dorchester, Mass., 1876. [3; 51]

Fox, Walter Dennis, poet and playwright, b. Murfreesboro, Tenn., 1867; d. Dec. 8, 1912. [7; 10; 34]

Fox, William Freeman, soldier and forester, b. Ballston Spa, N.Y., 1840; d. Albany, N.Y., June 16, 1909. [10]

Foxcroft, Frank, journalist, b. Boston, Mass., 1850; d. Boston, Mass., Dec. 10, 1921. [4; 10; 11; 51]

Foxcroft, Thomas, clergyman, b. Cambridge, Mass., 1697; d. Boston, Mass., June 18, 1769. [3; 51]

Foy, Eddie (pseud.). See Fitzgerald, Edward.

Foye, James Clark, mineralogist, b. Great Falls, N.H., 1841; d. 1896. [3; 6; 8; 61]

Foye, Wilbur Garland, geologist, b. Brockton, Mass., 1886; d. Middletown, Conn., Jan. 9, 1935. [10; 51]

Frachtenberg, Leo Joachim, anthropologist, b. Austria, 1883; d. Chicago, Ill., Nov. 26, 1930. [10]

Fradenburgh, Adelbert Grant, educationist, b. Point Peninsula, N.Y., 1868; d. Brooklyn, N.Y., July 2, 1936. [10]

Fradenburgh, Jason Nelson, clergyman, b. Gouverneur, N.Y., 1843; d. ? [10]

Française (pseud.). See Barry, Robertine.

France, Lewis Browne, lawyer, b. Washington, D.C., 1833; d. Denver Colo., 1907. [7; 8; 10]

Franchère, Gabriel, fur-trader, b. Montreal, Canada, 1786; d. St. Paul, Minn., April 12, 1863. [27]

Franchot, Nicholas Van Vranken, banker, b. Morris, N.Y., 1855; d. Olean, N.Y., May 6, 1943.

Francis, Charles Spencer, diplomat, b. Troy,N .Y., 1853; d. Troy, N.Y., Dec. 1, 1911. [1; 4; 10]

Francis, Convers, clergyman and educationist, b. Cambridge, Mass., 1795; d. Cambridge, Mass., April 7, 1863. [1; 3; 4; 6; 7; 8; 51]

Francis, David Rowland, politician and diplomat, b. Richmond, Ky., 1850; d. St. Louis, Mo., Jan. 15, 1927. [1; 4; 10; 34]

Francis, James Allan, clergyman, b. Upper Stewiacke, N.S., 1864; d. Los Angeles, Calif., June 30, 1928. [4; 10]

Francis, James Bicheno, civil engineer, b. Oxfordshire, England, 1815; d. Lowell, Mass., Sept. 18, 1892. [1; 3; 4; 8]

Francis, John Wakefield, physician, b. New York, N.Y., 1789; d. New York, N.Y., Feb. 8, 1861. [1; 3; 4; 6; 7; 8]

Francis, Joseph, inventor, b. Boston, Mass., 1801; d. Cooperstown, N.Y., May 10, 1893. [1; 3]

Francis, Joseph Greene, artist, b. 1849; d. April 15, 1930. [7]

Francis, Samuel Ward, physician, b. New York, N.Y., 1835; d. Newport, R.I., March 25, 1886. [1; 3; 4; 6; 7; 8]

Francis, Valentine Mott, physician, b. 1834; d. West Roxbury, Mass., June 7, 1907. [3; 8]

Francke, Kuno, educatonist, b. Kiel, Germany, 1855; d. Cambridge, Mass., June 25, 1930. [1; 4; 7; 10]

François, Victor Emmanuel, educationist, b. Belgium, 1866; d. St. Petersburg, Fla., March 15, 1944. [10]

Frank, Dr. (pseud.). See Perry, Joseph Franklin.

Frank, Glenn, educationist and publicist, b. Queen City, Mo., 1887; d. near Green Bay, Wis., Sept. 15, 1940. [10; 44]

Frank, Henry, clergyman, b. Lafayette, Ind., 1854; d. San Diego, Calif., July 31, 1933. [4; 10; 11; 35]

Frank, Robert Tilden, gynaecologist, b. New York, N.Y., 1875; d. New York, N.Y., Oct. 15, 1949. [13]

Frank, Tenney, educationist, b. Clay Center, Kans., 1876; d. Oxford, England, April 3, 1939. [4; 7; 10; 11]

Franklin, Benjamin, printer, journalist, scientist, politician, and diplomat, b. Boston, Mass., 1706; d. Philadelphia, Pa., April 17, 1790. [1; 2; 3; 4; 5; 6;7; 8]

Franklin, Benjamin, minister of the Disciples of Christ, b. Belmont county, O., 1812; d. Anderson, Ind., Oct. 22, 1878. [10]

Franklin, Benjamin, clergyman, b. 1819; d. Nov. 2, 1898. [6; 7; 47]

Franklin, Mrs. Christine, née **Ladd.,** psychologist, b. Windsor, Conn., 1847; d. New York, N.Y., March 5, 1930. [1; 4; 10]

Franklin, Edward Carroll, physician and surgeon, b. 1822; d. St. Louis, Mo., Dec. 17, 1885. [6; 55]

Franklin, Edward Zeus (pseud.). See Wickes, Edward Zeus Franklin.

Franklin, Fabian, journalist and educationist, b. Hungary, 1853; d. New York, N.Y., Jan. 16, 1939. [10]

Franklin, Leo Morris, rabbi, b. Cambridge City, Ind., 1870; d. Detroit, Mich., Aug. 8, 1948. [10]

Franklin, Samuel Rhoades, naval officer, b. York, Pa., 1825; d. Washington, D.C., Feb. 24, 1909. [1; 4; 10]

Franklin, William, last royal governor of New Jersey, b. Philadelphia, Pa., 1731; d. England, Nov. 16, 1813. [1; 3; 4]

Franklin, William Suddards, physicist, b. Geary City, Kans., 1863; d. Wilmington, N.C., June 6, 1930. [4; 10; 13]

Franks, Mrs. Thetta, née **Quay,** home economist, b. 1867; d. Pasadena, Calif., April 14, 1947.

Franz, Shepherd Ivory, psychologist, b. Jersey City, N.J., 1874; d. Los Angeles, Calif., Oct. 14, 1933. [1a; 10]

Fraser, Alexander, historian and archivist, b. Inverness-shire, Scotland, 1860;, d. Toronto, Ont., Feb. 9, 1936. [27]

Fraser, Annie Ermatinger, novelist, b. Kingston, Ont.; d. Vancouver, B.C., 1930. [27]

Fraser, Cecil Eaton, educationist, b. Champaign, Ill., 1895; d. Cambridge, Mass., Feb. 23, 1947. [10; 51]

Fraser, Donald, clergyman, b. Inverness, Scotland, 1826; d. London, England, Feb. 13, 1892. [27]

Fraser, John, merchant, b. Lachine, Lower Canada, 1820; d. Lachine, Que., Oct. 12, 1899. [27]

Fraser, William Alexander, novelist, b. River John, N.S., 1859; d. Toronto, Ont., Nov. 9, 1933. [11; 27]

Fraser, William Henry, educationist, b. Bond Head, Ont., 1853; d. York Mills, near Toronto, Ont., Dec. 26, 1916. [27]

Fraser, William Kaspar, lawyer, b. Toronto, Ont., 1884; d. Toronto, Ont., Feb. 21, 1949.

Frazar, Douglas, soldier, b. Danbury, Mass., 1836; d. Somerville, Mass., Feb. 20, 1896. [8]

Frazee, George, lawyer, b. 1821; d. 1904. [37]

Frazee, Louis Jacob, physician, b. Germantown, Ky., 1819; d. Louisville, Ky., Aug. 12, 1905. [74]

Frazer, Perry D., sportsman and editor, b. 1866; d. Ridgewood, N.J., June 20, 1943.

Frazer, Persifor, scientist, b. Philadelphia, Pa., 1844; d. Philadelphia, Pa., April 19, 1909. [1; 4; 10; 55]

Frazier, Charles Harrison, surgeon, b. Germantown, Pa., 1870; d. Philadelphia, Pa., Aug. 26, 1936. [10; 55]

Fréchette, Louis Honoré, poet, b. Lévis, Lower Canada, 1839; d. Montreal, Que., May 31, 1908. [27]

Frederic, Harold, novelist, b. Utica, N.Y., 1856; d. Hornby, England, Oct. 19, 1898. [1; 2; 4; 7; 72]

Frédéric de Ghyvelde, Franciscan priest, b. Ghyvelde, France, 1838; d. Montreal, Que., Aug. 4, 1916. [27]

Fredericks, Arnold (pseud.). See Kummer, Frederic Arnold.

Frederiksen, Johan Ditlev, dairyman, b. 1848; d. St. Petersburg, Fla., Feb. 1926.

Fredet, Peter, educationist, b. France, 1801; d. Ellicott's Mills., Md., 1856. [3; 8]

Free, Edward Elway, chemist, b. Dagus Mines, Pa., 1883; d. New York, N.Y., Nov. 24, 1939. [10; 13]

Freedley, Angelo Tillinghast, lawyer, b. Cincinnati, O., 1850; d. Philadelphia, Pa., 1907. [10]

Freedley, Edwin Troxell, economist, b. Philadelphia, Pa., 1827; d. 1904. [3; 4; 6; 8; 10]

Freehoff, Joseph C., economist, b. La Crosse, Wis., 1864; d. Valhalla, N.Y., May 1, 1939.

Freeland, Daniel Niles, clergyman, b. 1825; d. Elizabeth, N.J., July 21, 1913. [55]

Freeman, Abraham Clark, lawyer, b. Hancock county, Ill., 1843; d. San Francisco, Calif., 1911. [10]

Freeman, Bernard, clergyman, b. Hanover, Germany, 1660; d. New Utrecht, Long Island, N.Y., Jan., 1743. [1; 3; 4; 8]

Freeman, Frederick, clergyman, b. Sandwich, Mass., 1799; d. Sandwich, Mass., 1883. [3; 6; 8]

Freeman, James Edward, bishop, b. New York, N.Y., 1866; d. Washington, D.C., June 7, 1943. [4; 10; 11]

Freeman, James Edwards, painter, b. Indian Island, N.B., 1808; d. Rome, Italy, Nov. 21, 1884. [1; 3; 4]

Freeman, James Midwinter, clergyman and writer of books for boys, b. New York, N.Y., 1827; d. Morristown, N.J., Feb. 27, 1900. [2; 8; 10; 60]

Freeman, Mrs. Julia Deane, bio-bibliographer, fl. 1861. [7]

Freeman, Mrs. Mary Eleanor, née Wilkins, novelist, poet, and short-story writer, b. Randolph, Mass., 1862; d. Metuchen, N.J., March 14, 1930. [1; 2; 3; 4; 5; 6; 7; 8; 10; 72]

Freeman, Robert, clergyman, b. Edinburgh, Scotland, 1878; d. Pasadena, Calif., June 28, 1940. [10; 35]

Freeman, Samuel, jurist, b. Portland, Me., 1743; d. Portland, Me., Sept. 2, 1831. [3; 8; 38]

Freeman, Ward, geologist, b. Yankton, S.D., 1879; d. Easton, Pa., Sept. 14, 1943.

Freeman, Winfield, lawyer and librarian, b. London, O.; 1848; d. July, 1926. [10]

Freer, Mrs. Martha Agnes, née Rand, poet, b. Chicago, Ill.; d. Chicago, Ill., July 23, 1939. [10]

Freer, Paul Caspar, chemist, b. Chicago, Ill., 1862; d. Manila, Philippines, April 17, 1912. [4; 10]

Freese, Jacob R., physician, b. 1826; d. 1885. [6]

Freese, John Wesley, antiquary, b. 1840; d. 1911.

Freeze, John Gosse, historian and poet, b. 1825; d. 1913.

Freligh, Martin, physician, b. Dutchess county, N.Y., 1813; d. Kingston, N.Y., Aug. 31, 1889. [3b]

Frémont, Mrs. Jessie, née Benton, traveller and story-writer, b. near Lexington, Va., 1824; d. Los Angeles, Calif., Dec. 27, 1902. [1; 3; 4; 7; 8]

Frémont, John Charles, explorer and politician, b. Savannah, Ga., 1813; d. New York, N.Y., July 13, 1890. [1; 2; 3; 4; 5; 6; 7; 8]

French, Alice, novelist and short-story writer, b. Andover, Mass., 1850 d. Davenport, Ia., Jan. 9, 1934. [1a; 2; 3a; 7; 8; 10; 34]

French, Alvah P., local historian, b. 1867; d. May 15, 1927.

French, Mrs. Anne, née Warner, novelist, b. St. Paul, Minn., 1869; d. England, Feb. 1, 1913. [4; 10; 70]

French, Mrs. Austa Malinda, née Winchell, abolitionist, b. Granville, O., 1810; d. New York, N.Y., Oct. 25, 1880.

French, Benjamin Franklin, historian, b. Richmond, Va., 1799; d. New York, N.Y., May 30, 1877. [3; 4; 6; 8]

French, Charles Sheldon, poet, b. about 1855; d. 1914.

French, Charles Wallace, educationist, b. Woodstock, Vt., 1858; d. Chicago, Ill., Nov. 11, 1920. [10; 49]

French, Ferdinand Courtney, educationist, b. Berkley, Mass., 1861; d. Hamilton, N.Y., March 15, 1927. [10; 47]

French, George, writer on advertising, b. North Clarendon, Vt., 1853; d. March 20, 1935. [10]

French, George Hazen, entomologist, b. Tully, N.Y., 1841; d. Herrin, Ill., 1935. [13]

French, Henry Flagg, agriculturist, b. 1813; d. 1885.

French, Henry Willard, journalist and novelist, b. Hartford, Conn., 1854; d. ? [7; 8; 10]

French, Hollis, engineer and collector, b. Boston, Mass., 1868; d. Boston, Mass., Nov. 21, 1940. [10]

French, James Strange, novelist, b. 1807; d. 1886.

French, John Homer, educationist, b. 1824; d. Dec. 23, 1888.

French, John McLean, novelist, b. Ottawa, Ont., 1863; d. Toronto, Ont., Dec. 19, 1940.

French, John William, clergyman, b. about 1810; d. 1871. [8]

French, Joseph Lewis, novelist and editor, b. New York, N.Y., 1858; d. Orangeburg, N.Y., Dec. 13, 1936. [7; 10]

French, Lillie Hamilton, journalist, b. Washington, D.C., 1854; d. Newport, R.I., June 3, 1939. [7; 10]

French, Mrs. Lucy Virginia, née Smith, poet and novelist, b. Accomac county, Va., 1825; d. McMinnville, Tenn., March 31, 1881. [1; 3; 4; 6; 7; 8; 34]

French, Nathaniel Stowers, educationist, b. Prospect, Me., 1854; d. 1905. [10]

French, Thomas Ewing, educationist, b. Mansfield, O., 1871; d. Columbus, O., Nov. 2, 1944. [10]

French, William Henry, soldier, b. Baltimore, Md., 1815; d. Baltimore, Md., May 20, 1881. [4; 6; 8]

Freneau, Philip Morin, poet, b. New York, N.Y., 1752; d. near Middletown Point, N.J., Dec. 19, 1832. [1; 2; 3; 4; 5; 6; 7; 8; 71; 72]

Freshman, Charles, clergyman, b. Hungary, 1819; d. Ingersoll, Ont., Jan. 4, 1875. [27]

Freund, Ernst, educationist, b. New York, N.Y., 1864; d. Chicago, Ill., Oct. 20, 1932. [1a; 10]

Frey, Albert Romer, librarian, b. 1858; d. New York, N.Y., Jan. 19, 1926. [6; 8]

Frey, Joseph Samuel Christian Frederick, clergyman, b. Germany, 1771; d. Pontiac, Mich., June 5, 1850. [1; 3; 6; 8]

Frick, Charles, physician, b. Baltimore, Md., 1823; d. Baltimore, Md., March 25, 1860. [3]

Frick, George, physician, b. 1793; d. Dresden, Germany, March 26, 1870. [55]

Frick, William Keller, clergyman, b. Lancaster, Pa., 1850; d. Milwaukee, Wis., Aug. 20, 1918. [4; 10]

Friday, David, economist, b. Coloma, Mich., 1876; d. Washington, D.C., March 16, 1945. [10; 11]

Friedlaender, Israel, educationist, b. Russia, 1876; d. New York, N.Y., July 5, 1920. [1; 7; 10]

Friedlander, Alfred, physician, b. Cincinnati, O., 1871; d. Cincinnati, O., May 28, 1939. [10; 51]

Friedman, Isaac Kahn, journalist and novelist, b. Chicago, Ill., 1870; d. Winnetka, Ill., Sept. 22, 1931. [8; 10; 53]

Fries, Adelaide Lisetta, archivist, b. Salem, N.C., 1871; d. Winston-Salem, N.C., N.C., Nov. 29, 1949. [10]

Friesner, Isidore, physician, b. New York, N.Y., 1874; d. Katonah, N.Y., Sept. 8, 1945.

Frieze, Henry Simmons, educationist, b. Boston, Mass., 1817; d. Detroit, Mich., Dec. 7, 1889. [1; 3; 4; 8; 47]

Frink, Henry Allyn, educationist, b. Amherst, Mass., 1844; d. Amherst, Mass., March 24, 1898. [45]

Frisbie, Alvah Lillie, clergyman and poet, b. Delaware county, N.Y., 1830; d. Des Moines, Ia., Dec. 17, 1917. [10; 37; 45; 62]

Frisbie, Levi, clergyman, b. Branford, Conn., 1748; d. Ipswich, Mass., 1806. [1; 3; 4; 6; 8]

Frisbie, Levi, educationist, b. Ipswich, Mass., 1783; d. Cambridge, Mass., July 9, 1822. [1; 3; 4; 6; 8]

Frisbie, Robert Dean, South Sea trader, b. Cincinnati, O., 1896; d. Rarotonga, Cook Islands, Nov. 19, 1948. [10]

Frisselle, Frank Monroe, poet, b. 1862; d. 1925.

Fritz, John, mechanical engineer, b. Chester county, Pa., 1822; d. Bethlehem, Pa., Feb. 13, 1913. [4; 10]

Frizell, Joseph Palmer, hydraulic engineer, b. Barford, Lower Canada, 1832; d. Dorchester, Mass., May 4, 1910. [1; 4; 10]

Frobisher, Joseph Edwin, elocutionist, fl. 1867-1882. [6]

Frost, Arthur Burdett, illustrator and humorist, b. Philadelphia, Pa., 1851; d. Pasadena, Calif., June 22, 1928. [1; 4; 7; 8; 10]

Frost, Charles Christopher, botanist, b. Brattleboro, Vt., 1806; d. Brattleboro, Vt., March 15, 1880. [3; 49]

Frost, Edwin Brant, astronomer, b. Brattleboro, Vt., 1866; d. Chicago, Ill., May 14, 1935. [1a; 10; 49]

Frost, Holloway Halstead, naval officer, b. Brooklyn, N.Y., 1889; d. Kansas City, Mo., Jan. 26, 1935. [1a]

Frost, James Marion, church official, b. 1849; d. Nashville, Tenn., Oct. 31, 1916. [10]

Frost, John, educationist and compiler, b. Kennebunk, Me., 1800; d. Philadelphia, Pa., Dec. 28, 1859. [3; 6; 7; 8; 51]

Frost, Mrs. Josephine C., née Stillman, genealogist, b. 1864; d. Brooklyn, N.Y., Dec. 31, 1942.

Frost, Mrs. Marguerite, née Scribner, poet, b. Yonkers, N.Y., 1876; d. Yonkers, N.Y., Feb. 28, 1944.

Frost, Sarah Annie, miscellaneous writer, fl. 1859-1889. [6]

Frost, Stanley, journalist, b. Oberlin, O., 1881; d. Richmond, Va., June 14, 1942. [10]

Frost, Thomas Gold, lawyer, b. Galesburg, Ill., 1866; d. Mount Vernon, N.Y., Feb. 13, 1948. [4; 10]

Frost, Timothy Prescott, clergyman, b. Mount Holly, Vt., 1850; d. Bradford, Vt., July 5, 1937. [10; 60]

Frost, William Goodell, educationist, b. Leroy, N.Y., 1854; d. Berea, Ky., Sept. 12, 1938. [11]

Frost, William Henry, journalist, b. North Providence, R.I., 1863; d. March 21, 1902. [10; 47]

Frothingham, Arthur Lincoln, archaeologist, b. Boston, Mass., 1859; d. New York, N.Y., July 28, 1923. [1; 4; 7; 8; 10]

Frothingham, Ellen, translator, b. Boston, Mass., March 25, 1935; d. 1902. [10]

Frothingham, Jessie Peabody, miscellaneous writer, b. Newton, Mass., 1862; d. Princeton, N.J., Jan. 17, 1949.

Frothingham, Louis Adams, lawyer, b. Jamaica Plain, Mass., 1871; d. Easton, Mass., Aug. 23, 1928. [10; 51]

Frothingham, Nathaniel Langdon, clergyman, b. Boston, Mass., 1793; d. Boston, Mass., April 4, 1870. [1; 3; 4; 6; 7; 8]

Frothingham, Octavius Brooks, clergyman, b. Boston, Mass., 1822; d. Boston, Mass., Nov. 27, 1895. [1; 3; 4; 6; 7; 8; 51]

Frothingham, Paul Revere, clergyman, b. Jamaica Plain, Mass., 1864; d. Boston, Mass., Nov. 27, 1926. [1; 7; 8; 10; 51

Frothingham, Richard, historian, b. Charlestown, Mass., 1812; d. Charlestown, Mass., Jan. 29, 1880. [1; 3; 4; 6; 7; 8; 51]

Frothingham, Robert, traveller and anthologist, b. Galesville, Wis., 1865; d. San Francisco, Calif., Dec. 7, 1937. [10; 11]

Frothingham, Washington, clergyman, b. Fonda, N.Y., 1822; d. ? [6; 10]

Fruit, John Phelps, educationist, b. Pembroke, Ky., 1855; d. Liberty, Mo., 1938. [7; 10; 34; 74]

Fry, Benjamin St. James, journalist and clergyman, b. Rutledge, Tenn., 1824; d. St. Louis, Mo., Feb. 5, 1892. [3; 4; 34]

Fry, Charles Luther, sociologist, b. Philadelphia, Pa., 1894; d. Rochester, N.Y., April 2, 1932. [10; 11]

Fry, Henry Davidson, physician, b. Richmond, Va., 1853; d. Washington, D.C., May 12, 1919. [10]

Fry, Jacob, clergyman, b. Trappe, Pa., 1834; d. Philadelphia, Pa., Feb. 19, 1920. [10]

Fry, James Barnet, soldier, b. Carrollton, Jll., 1827; d. Newport, R.I., July 11, 1894. [1; 3; 4; 6; 7; 8]

Fry, John Hemming, artist, b. Greene county, Ind., 1860; d. Greenwich, Conn., Feb. 24, 1946. [10]

Fry, Joseph Reese, banker, b. 1811; d. Philadelphia, Pa., June, 1865. [3; 6; 7]

Fry, William Henry, journalist, b. Philadelphia, Pa., 1815; d. Santa Cruz, West Indies, Dec. 21, 1864. [1; 3]

Frye, Alexis Everett, geographer, b. New Haven, Me., 1859; d. Loma Linda, Calif., July 1, 1936. [7; 10]

Frye, James Albert, soldier, b. Boston, Mass., 1863; d. Keene, N.Y., March 8, 1933. [10; 51]

Frye, Prosser Hall, educationist, b. New York, N.Y., 1866; d. Lincoln, N.B., June 3, 1934. [10]

Fryer, John, educationist, b. Hythe, England, 1839; d. Berkeley, Calif., July 2, 1928. [4]

Fuchs, Emil, painter and sculptor, b. Vienna, Austria, 1866; d. New York, N.Y., Jan. 13, 1929. [10]

Fuerbringer, Ludwig Ernest, theologian, b. Frankenmuth, Mich., 1874; d. St. Louis, Mo., May 6, 1947. [10; 11]

Fuertes, James Hillhouse, engineer, b. Ponce, Porto Rico, 1863; d. Brooklyn, N.Y., Jan. 30, 1932. [10]

Fuertes, Louis Agassiz, painter and naturalist, b. Ithaca, N.Y., 1874; d. Unadilla, N.Y., Aug. 22, 1927. [4; 10]

Fuessle, Newton Augustus, journalist and novelist, b. Chicago, Ill., 1883; d. Middleton, Mass., March 18, 1924. [10]

Fulkerson, Horace Smith, journalist, b. 1818; d. 1891. [34]

Fullam, William Freeland, naval officer, b. Monroe county, N.Y., 1855; d. Washington, D.C., Sept. 23, 1927. [4; 10]

Fuller, Andrew Samuel, horticulturist, b. Utica, N.Y., 1828; d. Ridgewood, N.J., May 4, 1896. [1; 8]

Fuller, Anna, novelist, b. Cambridge, Mass., 1853; d. New York, N.Y., July 11, 1916. [7; 10]

Fuller, Arthur Buckminster, clergyman, b. Cambridgeport, Mass., 1822; d. Fredericksburg, Va., Dec. 11, 1862. [3; 4; 51]

Fuller, Edward, journalist and novelist, b. Syracuse, N.Y., 1860; d. Philadelphia, Pa., April 29, 1938. [7; 10; 52]

Fuller, Edwin Wiley, poet and novelist, b. Louisburg, N.C., 1847; d. 1876. [7; 8; 34]

Fuller, Eugene, surgeon, b. Wayland, Mass., 1858; d. Seattle, Wash., June 4, 1930. [10; 51]

Fuller, Frances, See Victor, Mrs. Frances, née Fuller.

Fuller, George Warren, engineer, b. New York, N.Y., 1868; d. New York, N.Y., June 15, 1934. [1a; 10]

Fuller, George Washington, librarian and historian, b. Boston, Mass., 1876; d. Spokane, Wash., Oct. 23, 1940. [10]

Fuller, Harvey Austin, blind lecturer and poet, b. Mannsville, N.Y., 1834; d. Hillsdale, Mich., 1925. [39]

Fuller, Henry Blake, novelist, b. Chicago, Ill., 1857; d. Chicago, Ill., July 28, 1929. [1; 2; 4; 7; 10; 71; 72]

Fuller, Henry Starkey, journalist, b. New York, N.Y., 1852; d. ? [7]

Fuller, Hiram, journalist, b. Halifax, Mass., 1814; d. Paris, France, Nov. 19, 1880. [1; 3; 6; 7; 8]

Fuller, Hugh Nelson, educationist, b. Atlanta, Ga., 1890; d. Atlanta, Ga., Dec. 29, 1943.

Fuller, Joseph Vincent, historian, b. Knoxville, Tenn., 1890; d. Washington, D.C., April 1, 1932. [1a; 51]

Fuller, Metta Victoria. See Victor, Mrs. Metta Victoria, née Fuller.

Fuller, Osgood Eaton, clergyman, b. 1835; d. Caro, Mich., Oct. 5, 1900. [53]

Fuller, Richard, clergyman, b. Beaufort, S.C., 1804; d. Baltimore, Md., Oct. 19, 1896. [1; 3; 4; 8; 34]

Fuller, Richard Frederick, lawyer, b. Cambridge, Mass., 1821; d. Wayland, Mass., May 30, 1869. [3; 8; 51]

Fuller, Robert Higginson, journalist, b. Deerfield, Mass., 1864; d. New York, N.Y., Dec. 23, 1927. [10; 51]

Fuller, Samuel, clergyman and educationist, b. Rensselaerville, N.Y., 1802; d. Middletown, Conn., March 9, 1895. [6; 8]

Fuller, Sarah Margaret, Marchioness Ossoli, journalist, critic, and social reformer, b. Cambridgeport, Mass., 1810; d. near New York, N.Y., July 19, 1850. [1; 2; 3; 4; 5; 6; 7; 8]

Fuller, William Henry, art connoisseur, b. Barryville, N.Y., 1836; d. New York, N.Y., Nov. 26, 1902. [62]

Fuller, William Oliver, journalist, b. Rockland, Me., 1856; d. Rockland, Me., Sept. 21, 1941. [7; 10; 11]

Fullerton, Edith Loring, gardener, b. Brooklyn, N.Y., 1876; d. Aug. 9, 1931. [10; 11]

Fullerton, George Stuart, philosopher, b. Fategarh, India, 1859; d. Poughkeepsie, N.Y., March 23, 1925. [1; 4; 7; 8; 10]

Fullerton, Hugh Stuart, journalist, b. Hillsboro, O., 1873; d. Dunedin, Fla., Dec. 27, 1945. [7]

Fullerton, Kemper, educationist, b. Cincinnati, O., 1865; d. Oberlin, O., March 23, 1941. [10; 11; 68]

Fulmer, Clark Adelbert, educationist, b. Marcellus, N.Y., 1867; d. Lincoln, Neb., Sept. 1, 1940. [10; 11]

Fulmore, Zachary Taylor, lawyer, b. Robeson county, N.C., 1846; d. 1923. [4; 10; 34]

Fulton, Alexander R., pioneer, b. 1825; d. 1891. [37]

Fulton, Ambrose Cowperthwaite, sailor, b. 1811; d. 1903. [37]

Fulton, Chandos, novelist, playwright, and historian, b. Richmond, Va., 1839; d. New York, N.Y., Jan. 11, 1904.

Fulton, John, clergyman, b. Glasgow, Scotland, 1834; d. Philadelphia, Pa., 1907. [10]

Fulton, Justin Dewey, clergyman, b. Earlville, N.Y., 1828; d. Somerville, Mass., April 16, 1901. [1; 3; 4; 6; 10]

Fulton, Robert, inventor, b. Lancaster county, Pa., 1765; d. New York, N.Y., Feb. 24, 1815. [1; 2; 3; 4; 5; 6]

Fulton, Robert Irving, educationist, b. Leesburg, Va., 1855; d. Delaware, O., July 2, 1916. [10]

Funk, Henry Daniel, educationist, b. Schapsville, Ill., 1875; d. St. Paul, Minn., June 2, 1925. [10]

Funk, Isaac Kauffman, clergyman and publisher, b. Clifton, O., 1839; d. Montclair, N.J., April 4, 1912. [1; 4; 7; 8; 10]

Funk, William R., publishing agent, b. West Newton, Pa., 1861; d. Dayton, O., Nov. 2, 1935. [10]

Funston, Frederick, soldier, b. New Carlisle, O., Nov. 9, 1865; d. San Antonio, Tex. Feb. 19, 1917. [1; 2; 4; 10]

Fuqua, Stephen Ogden, soldier, b. Baton Rouge, La., 1874; d. New York, N.Y., May 11, 1943. [10]

Furman, Alfred Antoine, poet, b. 1856; d. Passaic, N.J., Aug. 14, 1940.

Furman, Charles Edwin, clergyman and poet, b. Clinton, N.Y., 1801; d. Rochester, N.Y., June 10, 1880. [6]

Furman, Franklin De Ronde, educationist, b. Ridgely, Md. 1870; d. Passaic, N.J., Nov. 20, 1943. [10; 11]

Furman, Gabriel, jurist, b. Brooklyn, N.Y., 1800; d. Brooklyn, N.Y., Nov. 11, 1854. [3]

Furman, Garrit, novelist and poet, b. 1782; d. 1848.

Furman, Howard Van Fleet, engineer, d. 1902. [48]

Furman, Richard, clergyman, b. Aesopus, N.Y., 1755; d. Charleston, S.C., 1825. [4; 34; 47]

Furman, Richard, clergyman and poet, b. 1816; d. 1886. [34]

Furness, Caroline Ellen, astronomer, b. Cleveland, O., 1869; d. New York, N.Y., Feb. 9, 1936. [10; 11; 13; 58]

Furness, Clifton Joseph, educationist, b. Sheridan, Ind., 1898; d. Cambridge, Mass., May 26, 1946. [7; 51]

Furness, Mrs. Helen Kate, née Rogers, compiler, b. Philadelphia, Pa., 1837; d. Oct. 30, 1883. [3; 8]

Furness, Horace Howard, Shakespearian scholar, b. Philadelphia, Pa., 1833; d. near Philadelphia, Pa., Aug. 13, 1912. [1; 2; 3; 4; 7; 8; 10]

Furness, Horace Howard, Shakespearian scholar, b. Philadelphia, Pa., 1865; d. Philadelphia, Pa., April 15, 1930. [1; 4; 7; 10]

Furness, William Henry, clergyman, b. Boston, Mass., 1802; d. Philadelphia, Pa., Jan. 30, 1896. [1; 3; 4; 6; 7; 8]

Furness, William Henry, physician, b. Wallingford, Pa., 1866; d. Wallingford, Pa., Aug. 11, 1920. [10]

Furniss, Grace Livingston, playwright, b. 1864; d. Rye, N.Y., April 20, 1938. [7]

Furniss, William, traveller, b. 1820; d. 1882.

Furst, Clyde Bowman, educationist, b. Williamsport, Pa., 1873; d. New York, N.Y., March 6, 1931. [1a; 10]

Furstenburg, Mrs. Gertrude, née Sanborn, novelist, b. 1881; d. Milwaukee, Wis., July 17, 1928.

Fussell, Milton Howard, physician, b. Chester county, Pa., 1855; d. near Williamsburg, Pa., Nov. 15, 1921. [10]

Futhey, John Smith, jurist, b. Chester county, Pa., 1820; d. Chester county, Pa., Nov. 26, 1888. [3; 4; 6; 8]

Futrelle, Jacques, novelist and short-story writer, b. Pike county, Ga., 1875; drowned in the *Titanic* disaster, April 15, 1912. [7; 10]

Fyfe, Robert Alexander, clergyman, b. near Montreal, Lower Canada, 1816; d. Woodstock, Ont., Sept. 4, 1878. [27]

Fyles, Franklin, drama critic, b. 1847; d. New York, N.Y., July 4, 1911. [7; 10]

Fynn, Arthur John, ethnologist, b. 1857; d. Denver, Colo., Dec. 30, 1930. [11]

Fyshe, Thomas, banker, b. East Lothian, Scotland, 1845; d. Montreal, Que., Nov. 26, 1911. [27]

G

Gabb, William More, palaeontologist, b. Philadelphia, Pa., 1839; d. Philadelphia, Pa., May 30, 1878. [3; 4; 6; 8]

Gabelle, James, journalist and poet, b. Kansas, 1874; d. Paterson, N.J., Nov. 13, 1940.

Gabriel, Charles Hutchinson, hymnwriter, b. 1856; d. Hollywood, Calif., Sept. 14, 1932.

Gabriels, Henry, bishop, b. Belgium, 1838; d. Ogdensburg, N.Y., April 23, 1921. [4; 10]

Gaddis, Maxwell Pierson, clergyman, b. 1811; d. 1888. [6]

Gadsden, Christopher Edwards, bishop, b. Charleston, S.C., 1785; d. Charleston, S.C., June 24, 1852. [3; 4; 34]

Gaebelein, Arno Clemens, clergyman, b. Germany, 1861; d. Mount Vernon, N.Y., Dec. 25, 1945. [7; 10; 11]

Gag, Wanda, writer and illustrator of children's books, b. New Ulm, Minn., 1893; d. New York, N.Y., June 27, 1946. [7]

Gage, Alfred Payson, educationist, b. Hopkinton, N.H., 1836; d. Arlington, Mass., Feb. 23, 1903. [10; 49]

Gage, Mrs. Emma, née Abbott, traveller, d. 1925.

Gage, Mrs. Frances Dana, née Barker, poet, novelist, and reformer, b. Marietta, O., 1808; d. Greenwich, Conn., Nov. 10, 1884. [1; 3; 4; 7; 8]

Gage, Mrs. Matilda, née Joslyn, female suffragist, b. Cicero, N.Y., 1826; d. Chicago, Ill., March 18, 1898. [1; 3; 4; 6]

Gage, Simon Henry, biologist, b. Otsego county, N.Y., 1851; d. Interlaken, N.Y., Oct. 20, 1944. [10; 11; 13]

Gage, William Leonard, clergyman, b. Loudon, N.H., 1832; d. Philadelphia, Pa., May 31, 1889. [6; 8; 51]

Gager, Charles Stuart, botanist, b. Norwich, N.Y., 1872; d. Waterville, Me., Aug. 9, 1943. [10, 11; 13]

Gagnon, Charles Alphonse Nathanael, journalist and civil servant, b. St. Jean Port Joli, Que., 1851; d. Quebec, Que., Oct. 4, 1932. [27]

Gagnon, Ernest, musician and historian, b. Louiseville, Lower Canada, 1834; d. Quebec, Que., Sept. 15, 1915. [27]

Gagnon, Philéas, bibliographer, b. Quebec, Que., 1854; d. Quebec, Que., March 25, 1915. [27]

Gaige, Crosby, theatrical producer and publisher, b. Nelson, N.Y., 1882; d. Peekskill, N.Y., March 8, 1949. [10]

Gailor, Thomas Frank, bishop, b. Jackson, Miss., 1856; d. Sewanee, Tenn., Oct. 3, 1935. [1a; 7; 10; 11; 34]

Gaines, Charles Kelsey, educationist, b. Royalton, N.Y., 1854; d. Canton, N.Y., Jan. 2, 1943. [7; 10; 11]

Gaines, Garry (pseud.) See Patterson, Mrs. Virginia, née Sharpe.

Gaines, Morrell Walker, financier, b. Litchfield, Conn., 1875; d. Tompkinsville, Staten Island, N.Y., Feb. 21, 1931. [62]

Gaines, Wesley John, bishop, b. Wilkes county, Ga., 1840; d. Atlanta, Ga., Jan. 12, 1912. [1; 4; 34]

Galbraith, Anna Mary, physician, b. Carlisle, Pa., 1859; d. Carlisle, Pa., Feb. 1923. [10]

Galbraith, Robert Christy, clergyman, b. Frankfort, O., 1833; d. Chillicothe, O., Nov. 18, 1916. [63]

Galbreath, Charles Burleigh, librarian, b. near Leetonia, O., 1858; d. Columbus, O., Feb. 23, 1934. [1a; 7; 10]

Galbreath, Thomas Crawford, invalid, b. b. 1876; d. 1916.

Gale, Amory, clergyman, b. Royalston, Mass., 1815; d. Jaffa, Syria, Nov. 26, 1874. [47]

Gale, Benjamin, physician, b. Jamaica, Long Island, N.Y., 1715; d. Killingworth, Conn., May 21, 1790. [1; 3; 4; 62]

Gale, George, lawyer, b. 1816; d. 1868. [6]

Gale, George, journalist, b. Quebec, Que., 1857; d. Montreal, Que., March 9, 1944. [27]

Gale, Henry Gordon, physicist, b. Aurora, Ill., 1874; d. Chicago, Ill., Nov. 16, 1942. [10; 11; 13]

Gale, Levin, lawyer, b. Cecil county, Md., 1824; d. Baltimore, Md., April 28, 1875. [3]

Gale, Nahum, clergyman, b. Auburn, Mass., 1812; d. Newburyport, Mass., Sept. 18, 1876. [45]

Gale, Samuel, lawyer, b. St. Augustine, Fla., 1783; d. Montreal, Que., June, 1865. [27]

Gale, Zona, novelist and playwright, b. Portage, Wis., 1874; d. Chicago, Ill., Dec. 27, 1938. [10; 11; 44]

Gallagher, Charles Wesley, educationist, b. Boston, Mass., 1846; d. Dec. 14, 1916. [10; 60]

Gallagher, James Thomas, physician and poet, b. Sligo county, Ireland, 1855; d. Boston, Mass., June 30, 1936. [21]

Gallagher, Mary Antonio. See Mercedes, Sister.

Gallagher, William Davis, journalist and poet, b. Philadelphia, Pa., 1808; d. Louisville, Ky., June 27, 1894. [1; 4; 7; 34; 74]

Gallaher, James, clergyman, b. 1792; d. 1853.

Galland, Joseph Stanislaus, educationist, b. Biddeford, Me., 1882; d. Chicago, Ill., Nov. 28, 1947. [14]

Gallatin, Albert, politician, b. Geneva, Switzerland, 1761; d. Astoria, Long Island, N.Y., Aug. 12, 1849. [1; 2; 3; 4; 5; 6; 7; 8]

Gallatin, James, banker, b. 1796; d. Paris, France, May 29, 1876.

Gallaudet, Edward Miner, educationist, b. Hartford, Conn., 1837; d. Washington, D.C., Sept. 26, 1917. [1; 4; 10]

Gallaudet, Herbert Draper, clergyman,, b. Washington, D.C., 1876; d. Pine Orchard, Conn., June 24, 1944. [62]

Gallaudet, Thomas Hopkins, clergyman and educationist, b. Philadelphia, Pa., 1787; d. Hartford, Conn., Sept. 10, 1851. [1; 4; 7; 62]

Gallaway, Edward, printer, b. 1869; d. 1930.

Gallier, James, architect, b. Ireland, 1798; d. at sea off Cape Hatteras, May 16, 1868. [1a]

Gallizier, Nathan, novelist, b. Germany, 1866; d. Cincinnati, O., Jan. 11, 1927. [10]

Galloway, Beverly Thomas, botanist, b. Millersbury, Mo., 1863; d. Takoma Park, D.C., June 13, 1939. [4; 10; 11; 13]

Galloway, Charles Betts, bishop, b. Kosciusko, Miss., 1849; d. Jackson, Miss., May 12, 1909. [1; 4; 10; 34]

Galloway, Joseph, lawyer and loyalist, b. Anne Arundel county, Md., 1731; d. Watford, Herts, England, Aug. 29, 1803. [1; 3; 4; 6

Galloway, Thomas Walton, biologist, b. Columbia, Tenn., 1866; d. New York, N.Y., July 16, 1929. [4; 10; 13]

Gallup, Mrs. Elizabeth, née Wells, Shakespearian student, b. 1846; d. Detroit, Mich., 1935.

Gallup, Joseph Adams, physician, b. Stonington, Conn., 1769; d. Woodstock, Vt., Oct. 12, 1849. [3; 4; 43]

Galt, Sir Alexander Tilloch, politician, b. London, England, 1817; d. Montreal, Que., Sept. 19, 1893. [27]

Galt, John Minson, alienist, b. Williamsburg, Va., 1819; d. Williamsburg, Va., May 12, 1862.

Gamble, Samuel Walter, clergyman, b. Worthington, Pa., 1852; d. Los Angeles, Calif., Dec. 29, 1932. [10; 11]

Gambrall, Theodore Charles, clergyman, b. about 1842; d. Baltimore, Md., May 19, 1897.

Gambrell, James Bruton, clergyman, b. Anderson, S.C., 1841; d. June 10, 1921. [1; 4; 10; 34]

Game, Josiah Bethea, educationist, b. Mullins, S.C., 1869; d. March 4, 1935. [10; 11]

Gamertsfelder, Solomon Jacob, theologian, b. Coshocton county, O., 1851; d. Cleveland, O., Aug. 6, 1925. [10]

Gammack, Arthur James, clergyman, b. Scotland, 1871; d. Greenwich, Conn., April 29, 1927. [4; 62]

Gammell, Isaac, educationist, b. about 1861; d. Morrin Heights, Que., May 24, 1932. [27]

Gammell, William, educationist, b. Medfield, Mass., 1812; d. Providence, R.I., April 3, 1889. [3; 6; 8; 47]

Gandier, Alfred, clergyman, b. Hastings county, Ont., 1861; d. Toronto, Ont., June 13, 1932. [27]

Gannet, Mrs. Deborah, née Sampson, heroine, b. Plymouth, Mass., 1760; d. Sharon, Mass., April 29, 1827.

Gannett, Henry, geographer, b. Bath, Me., 1846; d. Washington, D.C., Nov. 5, 1914. [4; 7; 10]

Gannett, Mabel Anstice, educationist, d. Medford, Mass., March 15, 1933. [11]

Gannett, William Channing, clergyman, b. Boston, Mass., 1840; d. Rochester, N.Y., Dec. 15, 1923. [1; 4; 7; 10; 51]

Gano, John, clergyman, b. Hopewell, N.J., 1727; d. near Lexington, Ky., 1804. [3; 34]

Ganong, William Francis, botanist and historian, b. Saint John, N.B., 1864; d. d. Saint John, N.B., Sept. 7, 1941. [4; 10; 27]

Ganse, Hervey Doddridge, clergyman, b. 1822; d. 1891.

Ganss, Henry George, priest, b. Darmstadt, Germany, 1855; d. Lancaster, Pa., Dec. 25, 1912. [1; 21]

Ganter, Franz S., poet, fl. 1871-1873. [34]

Gantt, Henry Laurence, engineer and industrialist, b. Calver county, Md., 1861; d. Montclair, N.J., Nov. 23, 1919. [1; 4; 10]

Gantvoort, Arnold Johan, musician, b. Amsterdam, Holland, 1857; d. Los Angeles, Calif., May 18, 1937. [10; 11; 20]

Garber, John Palmer, educationist, b. White House, Pa., 1858; d. Philadelphia, Pa., Dec. 16, 1936. [10; 11]

Garden, Alexander, clergyman, b. Scotland, about 1685; d. Charleston, S.C., Sept. 27, 1756. [3; 4; 8; 34]

Garden, Alexander, soldier, b. Charleston, S.C., 1757; d. Charleston, S.C., Feb. 29, 1829. [1; 3; 4; 6; 8; 34]

Gardener, Mrs. Helen Hamilton, née Chenoweth, essayist and novelist, b. Winchester, Va., 1853; d. Washington, D.C., July 26, 1925. [1; 4; 7; 10]

Gardenhire, Samuel Major, novelist, b. Fayette, Mo., 1855; d. Richmond Hill, N.Y., Feb. 28, 1923. [10]

Gardiner, Asa Bird, soldier, b. New York, N.Y., 1839; d. May 28, 1919. [4; 10]

Gardiner, Charles Alexander, lawyer, b. Canada, 1855; d. New York, N.Y., April 23, 1910. [10; 48]

Gardiner, Charles Fox, physician, b. 1857; d. Colorado Springs, Colo., July 31, 1947.

Gardiner, Frederic, clergyman and educationist, b. Gardiner, Me., 1822; d. Middletown, Conn., July 17, 1889. [4; 8; 38; 46]

Gardiner, Harry Norman, philosopher, b. Norwich, England, 1855; d. Norwich, England, Nov. 6, 1927. [1a; 4; 10; 45; 68]

Gardiner, Herbert Fairbairn, journalist, b. Brockville, Ont., 1849; d. Hamilton, Ont., Oct. 27, 1924. [27]

Gardiner, John Hays, educationist, b. Gardiner, Me., 1863; d. Boston, Mass., May 14, 1913. [10]

Gardiner, John Sylvester John, clergyman, b. Wales, 1765; d. Harrogate, England, July 29, 1830. [1; 2; 3; 4]

Gardner, Alexander, photographer, b. 1821; d. 1882.

Gardner, Augustus Kinsley, physician, b. Roxbury, Mass., 1812; d. New York, N.Y., April 7, 1876. [3; 6; 8; 51]

Gardner, Augustus Peabody, soldier and politician, b. Boston, Mass., 1865; d. Macon, Ga., Jan. 14, 1918. [10; 51]

Gardner, Celia Emmeline, poet and novelist, b. Sharon, Conn., 1884; d. ? [6; 10]

Gardner, Charles Kitchel, soldier, b. Morris county, N.J., 1787; d. Washington, D.C., Nov. 1, 1869. [1; 3; 4; 6; 8]

Gardner, Daniel Pereira, physician, d. 1853. [55]

Gardner, Dorsey, journalist, b. Philadelphia, Pa., 1842; d. Short Hilla, N.J., Nov. 30, 1894. [3; 6; 8; 62]

Gardner, Eugene Clarence, architect, b. Ashfield, Mass., 1836; d. Springfield, Mass., Feb. 7, 1915. [8; 10]

Gardner, Frank, clergyman, b. New York, N.Y., 1856; d. Phenix, R.I., March 22, 1922.

Gardner, Frank Augustine, physician and genealogist, b. 1861; d. Salem, Mass., Oct. 18, 1938.

Gardner, Gilson, journalist, b. Chicago, Ill., 1869; d. Washington, D.C., Aug. 16, 1935. [1a; 7; 10; 11]

Gardner, John Lane, soldier, b. Boston, Mass., 1793; d. Wilmington, Del., Feb. 19, 1869. [1; 4]

Gardner, Robert Waterman, architect, b. Jackson, Miss., 1866; d. Long Island, N.Y., Aug. 6, 1937. [10]

Gardner, Samuel Jackson, journalist, b. Brookline, Mass., 1788; d. White Mountains, N.H., July 14, 1864. [4; 51]

Gardner, Willam Henry, surgeon, b. Fayetteville, N.C., 1837; d. ? [10]

Gardner, William Henry, song-writer, b. Boston, Mass., 1865; d. Winthrop, Mass., March 12, 1932. [10]

Gardner-Sharp, Mrs. Abbie. See Sharp, Mrs. Abigail, née Gardner.

Gariépy, Charles Napoléon, priest and educationist, b. Château-Richer, Que., 1868; d. Quebec. Que., July 29, 1932. [27]

Garland, Augustus Hill, lawyer, b. Tipton county, Tenn., 1832; d. Washington, D.C., Jan. 26, 1899. [1; 3; 4]

Garland, George Minot, physician, b. Laconia, N.H., 1848; d. Wellesley Farms, Mass., March 2, 1926. [51]

Garland, Hannibal Hamlin, novelist, b. West Salem, Wis., 1860; d. Hollywood, Calif., March 4, 1940. [2; 4; 7; 10; 11; 12; 72]

Garland, Harry Parsons, manufacturer, b. Biddeford, Me., 1859; d. Weldon, N.C., April 10, 1935. [62]

Garland, Hugh A., lawyer, b. Nelson county, Va., 1805; d. St. Louis, Mo., Oct. 15, 1854. [3; 34]

Garland, James Albert, horseman, b. New York, N.Y., 1870; d. 1906. [10]

Garland, Landon Cabell, mathematician, b. Nelson county, Va., 1810; d. Nashville, Tenn., Feb. 12, 1895. [1; 3; 4; 8; 34]

Garlick, Theodatus, surgeon and pisciculturist. b. Middlebury, Vt., 1805; d. Cleveland, O., Dec. 9, 1884. [1]

Garman, Samuel, naturalist, b. Indiana county, Pa., 1843; d. Arlington Heights, Mass., Oct. 1, 1927. [4; 10]

Garneau, François Xavier, historian, b. Quebec, Lower Canada, 1809; d. Quebec, Que., Feb. 3, 1866. [27]

Garneau, St. Denys, poet, b. 1912; d. 1943.

Garner, James Wilford, political scientist, b. Pike county, Miss., 1871; d. Champaign, Ill., Dec. 9, 1938. [7; 10; 11]

Garner, Richard Lynch, naturalist, b. Abingdon, Va., 1848; d. Chattanooga, Tenn., Jan. 22, 1920. [4; 10]

Garnett, James Mercer, politician and educationist, b. Essex county, Va., 1770; d. Essex county, Va., April 23, 1843. [1; 4; 34]

Garnett, James Mercer, educationist, b. Loudoun county, Va., 1840; d. Baltimore, Md., Feb. 18, 1916. [1; 4; 7; 8; 10; 34]

Garnett, Louis Anacharsis, capitalist, b. 1821; d. 1901. [10]

Garnett, Mrs. Louise, née **Ayres,** musician, b. Plymouth, Ind., d. Evanston, Ill., Oct. 31, 1937. [7; 10; 11]

Garnett, Captain Mayn Clew (pseud.). See Hains, Thornton Jenkins.

Garnett, Muscoe Russell Hunter, politician, b. Essex county, Va., 1821; d. Essex county, Va., Feb. 14, 1864. [1; 3]

Garnier, John Hutchison, physician, b. Scotland, about 1810; d. Lucknow, Ont., Feb. 1, 1898. [27]

Garraghan, Gilbert Joseph, priest and historian, b. Chicago, Ill., 1872; d. Chicago, Ill., June 7, 1942. [21]

Garrard, Lewis Hector, agriculturist, b. Cincinnati, O., 1829; d. Lakewood, N.Y., July, 1887. [70]

Garratt, Alfred Charles, physician, b. about 1813; d. 1891. [6]

Garretson, Arthur Samuel, railway-builder, b. Morgan county, O., 1851; d. ? [10]

Garretson, Ferdinand Van Derveer, clergyman, b. New Brunswick, N.Y., 1839; d. New York, N.Y., Feb. 15, 1919. [62]

Garretson, James Edmund, dentist and philosopher, b. Wilmington, Del., 1828; d. Lansdowne, Pa., Oct. 26, 1895. [1; 3; 4; 6; 7; 8]

Garrett, Alexander Charles, bishop, b. Ballymore, Ireland, 1832; d. Dallas, Tex., Feb. 18, 1924. [4; 10; 34]

Garrett, Alfred Cope, educationist, b. Philadelphia, Pa., 1867; d. Philadelphia, Pa., Sept. 28, 1946. [10; 51]

Garrett, Edmund Henry, artist, b. Albany, N.Y., 1853; d. Needham, Mass., April 2, 1929. [1; 7; 8; 10]

Garrett, Lewis, clergyman, b. 1773; d. 1857. [34]

Garrett, Pat F., constable, b. 1850; d. 1908.

Garrett, William Robertson, historian, b. Williamsburg, Va., 1839; d. Nashville, Tenn., Feb. 12, 1904. [1; 4; 10; 34]

Garrettson, Freeborn, itinerant minister, b. Maryland, 1752; d. Rhinebeck, N.Y., Sept. 26, 1827. [1; 4]

Garrigues, Henri Jacques, physician, b. Copenhagen, Denmark, 1831; d. Tryon, N.C., July 7, 1913. [10]

Garrioch, Alfred Campbell, clergyman and historian, b. Kildonan, near Winnipeg, N.W.T., 1848; d. Winnipeg, Man., Dec. 3, 1934. [27]

Garrison, Edwin William, clergyman, b. 1805; d. 1840. [38]

Garrison, Elisha Ely, financier, b. Cincinnati, O., 1871; d. St. Petersburg, Fla., March 26, 1935. [62]

Garrison, Fielding Hudson, physician and librarian, b. Washington, D.C., 1870; d. Baltimore, Md., April 18, 1935. [1a; 7; 10; 11]

Garrison, George Pierce, historian, b. Carrollton, Ga., 1853; d. Austin, Tex., July 3, 1910. [10; 34]

Garrison, James Harney, clergyman, b. Ozark, Mo., 1842; d. Los Angeles, Calif., Jan. 14, 1931. [4; 10; 11]

Garrison, Joseph Fithian, clergyman, b. Fairton, N.J., 1823; d. Philadelphia, Pa., Jan. 20, 1892. [3; 8; 55]

Garrison, Lloyd McKim, lawyer, b. Orange, N.J., 1867; d. Lenox, Mass., Oct. 4, 1900. [51]

Garrison, Sidney Clarence, educationist, b. Lincolnton, N.C., 1887; d. Nashville, Tenn,. Jan. 18, 1945. [10]

Garrison, Stephen Olin, clergyman, b. Millville, N.J., 1853; d. Vineland, N.J., April 17, 1900. [6; 60]

Garrison, Mrs. Theodosia, née **Pickering,** poet, b. Newark, N.Y., 1874; d. Short Hills, N.J., Oct. 9, 1944. [7; 10]

Garrison, Wendell Phillips, literary journalist, b. Cambridgeport, Mass., 1840; d. South Orange, N.J., Feb. 27, 1907. [4; 6; 7; 8; 10; 51]

Garrison, William Lloyd, social reformer, b. Newburyport, Mass., 1805; d. New York, N.Y., May 24, 1879. [1; 2; 3; 4; 5; 6; 7; 8]

Garrison, William Lloyd, merchant and publicist, b. Boston, Mass., 1838; d. Lexington, Mass., Sept. 12, 1909. [10]

Garside, Alston Hill, economist, b. New Bedford, Mass., 1888; d. Tarrytown, N.Y., April 25, 1946. [51]

Garth, Thomas Russell, psychologist, b. Paducah, Ky., 1872; d. Denver, Colo., April 20, 1939. [10]

Garver, John Anson, lawyer, b. Scotland, Pa., 1854; d. Oyster Bay, N.Y., Oct. 23, 1936.

Garvie, Alexander Rae, poet, b. Demerara, British Guiana, 1839; d. Canada, 1875. [27]

Garvin, John William, editor, b. Lynden, Ont., 1859; d. Toronto, Ont., Aug. 19, 1935. [27]

Gasch, Mrs. Marie, née **Manning,** journalist and novelist, b. Washington, D.C., 1875; d. Washington, D.C., Nov. 28, 1945.

Gass, Patrick, explorer, b. Falling Springs, Pa., 1771; d. Wellsburg, O., April 30, 1870 [1; 7]

Gassaway, Franklin Harrison, poet, b. Maryland; d. Oakland, Calif., May 21, 1923. [35]

Gaston, James McFadden, surgeon, b. near Chester, S.C., 1824; d. Atlanta, Ga., Nov. 15, 1903. [1; 34]

Gaston, Joseph, industrialist and historian, b. Ohio, 1833; d. Portland, Ore., July 20, 1913. [41]

Gatchell, Charles, physician and novelist, b. Cincinnati, O., 1851; d. Los Angeles, Calif., Jan. 26, 1910. [10]

Gates, Caleb Frank, educationist, b. Chicago, Ill., 1857; d. Denver, Colo., April 9, 1946. [10; 11]

Gates, Mrs. Ellen Maria, née **Huntington,** poet, b. Torrington, Conn., 1835; d. New York, N.Y., Oct. 23, 1920. [8; 10]

Gates, Elmer, psychologist, b. Dayton, O., 1859; d. Philadelphia, Pa., Dec. 3, 1923. [4; 10]

Gates, George Augustus, educationist, b. Topsham, Vt., 1851; d. Winter Park, Fla., Nov. 20, 1912. [1; 4; 10; 49]

Gates, Isaac Edgar, clergyman, b. Mart, Tex., 1874; d. San Antonio, Tex., July 17, 1933. [10]

Gates, Mrs. Josephine, née **Scribner,** writer of books for children, b. Mount Vernon, O., 1859; d. Toledo, O., Aug. 21, 1930. [7; 10]

Gates, Lewis Edwards, educationist, b. Warsaw, N.Y., 1860; d. Albany, N.Y., Sept. 24, 1930. [8; 10; 51]

Gates, Mrs. Susa, née **Young,** Mormon writer, b. Salt Lake City, Utah, 1856; d. Salt Lake City, Utah, May 27, 1933. [10;; 11]

Gates, Theodore Burr., soldier, b. Oneonta, N.Y., 1824; d. Brooklyn, N.Y., July 11, 1911.

Gates, William Edmond, educationist, b. 1863; d. Baltimore, Md., April 24, 1940.

Gatien, Félix, priest, b. Quebec, Canada, 1776; d. Cap Santé, Que., July 19, 1844. [27]

Gatineau, Félix, merchant and historian, b. Ste. Victoire, Que., 1857; d. South Bridge, Mass., Dec. 31, 1927.

Gattinger, Augustin, physician, botanist, and librarian, b. Munich, Bavaria, 1825; d. Memphis, Tenn., July 18, 1903. [10]

Gaudet, Placide, historian, b. near Shediac, N.B., 1850; d. Shediac, N.B., Nov. 9, 1930. [27]

Gause, Harry Taylor, ship-builder, b. Wilmington, Del., 1853; d. Wilmington, Del., April 22, 1925. [52]

Gaut, John McReynolds, lawyer, b. Cleveland, Tenn., 1841; d. Nashville, Tenn., Dec. 19, 1918. [1; 4; 10]

Gauvreau, Charles Arthur, notary public, b. Isle Verte, Que., 1860; d. Rivière-du-Loup, Que., Oct. 9, 1924. [27]

Gavin, Frank Stanton Burns, clergyman, b. Cincinnati, O., 1890; d. New York, N.Y., March 20, 1938. [7; 10]

Gavitt, Elnathan Corrington, clergyman, b. 1808; d. 1896.

Gay, Ebenezer, clergyman, b. Dedham, Mass., 1696; d. Hingham, Mass., March 18, 1787. [1; 4; 51]

Gay, Frederick Parker, pathologist, b. Boston, Mass., 1874; d. New Hartford, Conn., July 14, 1939. [10; 51]

Gay, Harry Nelson, historian, b. Newton, Mass., 1870; d. Monte Carlo, Aug. 13, 1932. [10; 11; 45]

Gay, James, poetaster, b. Clovelly, England, 1810; d. Guelph, Ont., Feb. 23, 1891. [27]

Gay, Mary Ann Harris, novelist, b. Jones county, Ga., 1829; d. ? [34]

Gay, Sydney Howard, journalist and historian, b. Hingham, Mass., 1814; d. New Brighton, Staten Island, N.Y., June 25, 1888. [1; 3; 4; 6; 7;]

Gayarré, Charles Etienne Arthur, historián, b. New Orleans, La., 1805; d. New Orleans, La., Feb. 11, 1895. [1; 3; 4; 6; 7; 34]

Gayler, Charles, playwright and novelist, b. New York, N.Y., 1820; d. Brooklyn, N.Y., May 28, 1892. [1; 2; 3; 6; 7; 8]

Gayley, Charles Mills, educationist, b. Shanghai, China, 1858; d. Berkeley, Calif., July 26, 1932. [7; 8; 10; 11]

Gaylord, Franklin Augustus, clergyman and poet, b. Glenwood, N.Y., 1856; d. West Englewood, N.J., Aug. 14, 1943. [10; 62]

Gaylord, Glance (pseud.). See Bradley, Warren Ives.

Gaylord, Willis, agricultural journalist, b. Bristol, Conn., 1792; d. near Camillus, N.Y., March 27, 1844. [1; 4]

Gaynor, William Jay, politician, b. Oneida county, N.Y., 1851; d. New York, N.Y., Sept. 10, 1913. [10]

Gazzam, Audley William, lawyer, b. 1836; d. 1884.

Gebhard, Elizabeth Louisa, historian, b. 1859; d. 1924.

Geddes, James, educationist, b. Boston, Mass., 1858; d. Brookline, Mass., Sept. 20, 1948. [4; 10; 11]

Gee, John Archer, educationist, b. Fall River, Mass., 1894; d. New Haven, Conn., Aug. 4, 1944. [62]

Gee, Joshua, clergyman, b. Boston, Mass., 1698; d. Boston, Mass., May 22, 1748. [3]

Geer, Alpheus, humanitarian, b. New York, 1863; d. New York, N.Y., Aug. 17, 1941.

Geer, Curtis Manning, theologian, b. Hadlyme, Conn., 1864; d. West Hartford, Conn., Aug. 2, 1938. [10; 61]

Geer, George Jarvis, clergyman, b. Waterbury, Conn., 1821; d. New York, N.Y., March 16, 1885. [3; 4; 8]

Geer, Theodore Thurston, pioneer, b. near Silverthorn, Ore., 1851; d. Portland, Ore., Feb. 21, 1924. [4; 10; 41]

Geer, Walter, manufacturer and historian, b. Williamstown, Mass., 1857; d. Long Beach, Long Island, N.Y., Feb. 23, 1937. [4; 7; 10]

Gehring, Albert, musician, b. Cleveland, O., 1870; d. Cleveland, O., Feb. 25, 1926. [10; 51]

Gehring, John George, neurologist, b. Cleveland, O., 1857; d. Bethel, Me., Sept. 1, 1932. [10]

Geil, William Edgar, explorer, b. near Doylestown, Pa., 1865; d. Venice, Italy, April 12, 1925. [7; 10]

Geissinger, James Allen, clergyman, b. Burbank, O., 1873; d. Oct. 21, 1935. [10]

Geldert, Mrs. Grace, née Duffie. See Boylan, Mrs. Grace, née Duffie.

Gélinas, Joseph Gérin, priest, b. Louiseville, Que., 1874; d. Three Rivers, Que., Jan. 24, 1927. [27]

Gemmill, John Alexander, lawyer and genealogist, b. Lanark county, Ont., 1847; d. Ottawa, Ont., Nov. 7, 1905. [27]

Gemmill, William Nelson, jurist, b. Shannon, Ill., 1860; d. Chicago, Ill., March 31, 1930. [10; 11]

Gemünder, George, violin-maker, b. Württemberg, Germany, 1816; d. New York, N.Y., Jan. 15, 1899. [1; 3; 4; 8]

Genin, John Nicholas, hatter, b. New York, N.Y., 1819; d. New York, N.Y., April 30, 1878. [1; 3; 4; 8]

Genin, Thomas Hedges, lawyer and poet, b. Suffolk county, Long Island, N.Y., 1796; d. 1868. [7]

Genone, Hudor (pseud.). See Roe, William James.

Genthe, Arnold, photographer, b. Berlin, Germany, 1869; d. Milford, Conn., Aug. 9, 1942. [7; 10]

Gentry, Thomas George, educationist, b. Holmesburg, Pa., 1843; d. 1905. [8; 10]

Gentry, William Daniel, physician, b. 1836; d. ?

Genung, George Frederick, clergyman, b. Tioga county, N.Y., 1850; d. Greenfield, Mass., Jan. 6, 1935. [10; 11]

Genung, John Franklin, educationist, b. Tioga county, N.Y., 1850; d. Amherst, Mass., Oct. 1, 1919. [1; 7; 8; 10]

Geoffrion, Louis Philippe, lawyer and lexicographer, b. near Varennes, Que., 1875; d. Quebec, Que., Sept. 3, 1942. [27]

George, Andrew Jackson, educationist, b. Goffstown, N.H., 1854; d. Brookline, Mass., Dec. 27, 1907. [10; 45]

George, Arial Wellington, radiologist, b. Yonkers, N.Y., 1882; d. Brookline, Mass., Dec. 24, 1948.

George, Edward Augustus, clergyman, b. Providence, R.I., 1865; d. New Haven, Conn., Dec. 22, 1921. [62]

George, Harold Coulter, engineer, b. Oil City, Pa., 1881; d. Pittsburgh, Pa., Sept. 23, 1937. [10]

George, Henry, economist and social reformer, b. Philadelphia, Pa., 1839; d. New York, N.Y., Oct. 29, 1897. [1; 2; 3; 4; 5; 6; 7; 8]

George, Henry, journalist, b. Sacramento, Calif., 1862; d. Washington, D.C., Nov. 14, 1916. [1; 7; 10]

George, James, clergyman and educationist, b. Perthshire, Scotland, about 1801; d. Stratford, Ont., Aug. 26, 1870. [27]

George, James Zachariah, jurist and politician, b. Monroe county, Ga., 1826; d. Mississippi City, Miss., Aug. 14, 1897. [1; 3; 4]

George, Nathan Dow, clergyman, b. 1808; d. 1896. [8]

George, William Reuben, educationist, b. West Dryden, N.Y., 1866; d. Freeville, N.Y., April 25, 1936. [10; 11]

Georgie, Leyla, actress, playwright, and novelist, b. Budapest, Hungary, 1906; d. New York, N.Y., Sept. 23, 1945.

Gerard, James Watson, lawyer, b. New York, N.Y., 1823; d. New York, N.Y., Jan. 28, 1900. [3; 4; 8; 10]

Gerberding, George Henry, clergyman, b. Pittsburgh, Pa., 1847; d. Minneapolis, Minn., March 27, 1927. [10]

Gerfen, Ernest E., clergyman and educationist, d. Toledo, O., Dec. 13, 1944.

Gerhard, William Paul, sanitary engineer, b. Hamburg, Germany, 1854; d. Scarsdale, N.Y., July 8, 1927. [3; 10]

Gerhard, William Wood, physician, b. Philadelphia, Pa., 1809; d. Philadelphia, Pa., April 28, 1872. [1; 4; 8; 55]

Gerhart, Emanuel Vogel, theologian, b. Snyder county, Pa., 1817; d. Mercersburg, Pa., May 6, 1904. [1; 4; 8; 10]

Gérin-Lajoie, Antoine, journalist and novelist, b. Yamachiche, Lower Canada, 1824; d. Ottawa, Ont., Aug. 4, 1882. [27]

Gerould, Mrs. Katharine, née Fullerton, novelist and short-story writer, b. Brockton, Mass., 1879; d. Princeton, N.J., July 27, 1944. [7; 10]

Gerould, Samuel Lankton, clergyman, b. East Alstead, N.H., 1834; d. Hollis, N.H., May 22, 1906. [49; 68]

Gerrish, Frederic Henry, physician and educationist, b. Portland, Me., 1845; d. Portland, Me., Sept. 8, 1920. [1; 4; 10; 38; 46]

Gerrish, Theodore, clergyman, b. Houlton, Me., 1846; d. Summertown, Tenn., Feb. 9, 1923. [8; 10; 38]

Gerry, Charles Frederick, poet, b. Sudbury, Mass., 1823; d. Sudbury, Mass., Sept. 4, 1900.

Gersoni, Henry, rabbi, b. Wilna, Russia, 1844; d. New York, N.Y., June 29, 1897. [6]

Gerstenberg, Charles William, publisher and educationist, b. Brooklyn, N.Y., 1882; d. Setauket, Long Island, N.Y., Sept. 16, 1948. [10; 11]

Gerster, Arpad Geyza Charles, surgeon, b. Hungary, 1848; d. New York, N.Y., March 11, 1923. [1; 4; 10]

Gesner, Abraham, geologist, b. Cornwallis, N.H., 1797; d. Halifax, N.S., April 19, 1864. [27]

Gest, John Marshall, jurist, b. Philadelphia, Pa., 1859; d. Overbrook, Pa., Nov. 20, 1934. [10]

Gest, William Purves, banker, b. Philadelphia, Pa., 1861; d. Merion, Pa., Jan. 12, 1939. [10]

Gestefeld, Ursula Newell, expositor of "New Thought", b. Augusta, Me., 1845; d. Kenosha, Wis., Oct. 22, 1921. [10]

Gettemy, Charles Ferris, statistician, b. Chicago, Ill., 1868; d. Dorchester, Mass., 1939. [10; 11]

Gettemy, Mrs. Mary Ellen, née Ferris, educationist, b. 1839; d. Galesburg, Ill., Feb. 29, 1908.

Getty, Jennie Violet, naturalist, b. 1861; d. Seattle, Wash., 1913.

Giauque, Florien, lawyer, b. Holmes county, O., 1843; d. Cincinnati, O., May 8, 1921. [10]

Gibb, William Travis, surgeon, b. Bellefonte, Pa., 1862; d. New York, N.Y., July 6, 1939.

Gibbes, Robert Wilson, physician, b. Charleston, S.C., 1809; d. Columbia, S.C., Oct. 15, 1866. [1; 3; 4; 6; 7; 8; 34]

Gibbon, John, soldier, b. near Holmesburg, Pa., 1827; d. Baltimore, Md., Feb. 6, 1896. [1; 8]

Gibbon, Thomas Edward, lawyer, b. near Devall Bluff, Ark., 1860; d. Los Angeles, Calif., June 23, 1921. [10]

Gibbons, Floyd Phillips, war correspondent, b. Washington, D.C., 1887; d. Saylorsburg, Pa., Sept. 24, 1939. [7; 10]

Gibbons, Henry, physician b. Wilmington, Del., 1808; d. Wilmington, Del., Nov. 5, 1884. [3; 4; 6; 8]

Gibbons, Herbert Adams, journalist, b. Annapolis, Md., 1880; d. Grundslee, Austria, Aug. 7, 1934. [1a; 7; 10; 11]

Gibbons, James, cardinal, b. Baltimore, Md., 1834; d. Baltimore, Md., March 24, 1921. [1; 2; 3; 4; 5; 8; 10; 21; 34]

Gibbons, James Sloan, banker and abolitionist, b. Wilmington, Del., 1810; d. New York, N.Y., Oct. 17, 1892. [1; 3; 4; 6; 7; 8]

Gibbons, John, jurist, b. Donegal county, Ireland, 1848; d. Chicago, Ill., Feb. 11, 1917. [10]

Gibbons, Mrs. Phoebe H., née Earle, esayist, b. 1821; d. ? [6]

Gibbons, William, physician, b. Philadelphia, Pa., 1781; d. Wilmington, Del., July 25, 1845. [1; 4; 8]

Gibbs, George, historian and ethnologist, b. Astoria, Long Island, N.Y., 1815; d. New Haven, Conn., April 9, 1873. [1; 3; 6; 8]

Gibbs, George Fort, novelist and painter, b. New Orleans, La., 1870; d. Philadelphia, Pa., Oct. 10, 1942. [7; 10; 11]

Gibbs, Josiah Francis, historian, b. 1845; d. Marysvale, Utah, Aug. 5, 1932.

Gibbs, Josiah Willard, philologist, b. Salem, Mass., 1790; d. New Haven, Conn., March 25, 1861. [1; 3; 6; 8]

Gibbs, Josiah Willard, mathematician and physicist, b. New Haven, Conn., 1839; d. New Haven, Conn., April 28, 1903. [1; 7; 8; 62]

Gibbs, Winifred Stuart, home economist, b. New York, N.Y., 1871; d. New York, N.Y., Feb. 8, 1928. [10]

Gibier, Paul, biologist, b. France, 1851; d. New York, N.Y., 1900.

Gibney, Virgil Pendleton, surgeon, b. Jessamine county, Ky., 1847; d. Bridgeport, Conn., June 16, 1927. [4; 10]

Gibran, Kahlil, artist, b. Mount Lebanon, Syria, 1883; d. New York, N.Y., April 10, 1931.

Gibson, Charles Dana, illustrator, b. Roxbury, Mass., 1867; d. New York, N.Y., Dec. 23, 1944. [2; 4; 7; 10; 12]

Gibson, Mrs. Eva Katherine, née **Clapp,** novelist, b. Bradford, Ill., 1857; d. Chicago, Ill., 1916. [7; 8; 10]

Gibson, Frank Markey, clergyman, b. Bedford Springs, Pa., 1857; d. Baltimore, Md., Sept. 24, 1929. [10]

Gibson, George Herbert Rae, physician, b. Edinburgh, Scotland, 1881; d. Edinburgh, Scotland, July 10, 1932.

Gibson, George Miles, clergyman, b. Tazewell county, Va., 1860; d. Dallas, Tex., March 30, 1932. [10]

Gibson, Joseph Thompson, clergyman, b. Jefferson county, Va., 1844; d. Pittsburgh, Pa., July 17, 1922. [10]

Gibson, Louis Henry, architect, b. Aurora, Ind., 1854; d. 1908. [10]

Gibson, Preston, playwright, b. Washington, D.C., 1879; d. New York, N.Y., Feb. 15, 1937. [7; 10]

Gibson, Robert Edward Lee, poet, b. Steelville, Mo., 1864; d. St. Louis, Mo., Jan. 1, 1918. [34]

Gibson, Robert Williams, architect, b. Essex, England, 1854; d. Woodbury, N.Y., Aug. 17, 1927. [10]

Gibson, Walter Murray, adventurer and politician, b. at sea, 1823; d. San Francisco, Calif., Jan. 21, 1888. [1; 4]

Gibson, William, surgeon, b. Baltimore, Md., 1788; d. Savannah, Ga., March 2, 1868. [1; 3; 4; 8]

Gibson, William, naval officer and poet, b. Maryland, 1826; d. 1887. [6; 8]

Gibson, William Hamilton, artist and naturalist, b. Sandy Hook, Conn., 1850; d. Washington, Conn., July 16, 1896. [1; 3; 4; 7; 71]

Giddings, Franklin Henry, sociologist, b. Sherman, Conn., 1855; d. Scarsdale, N.Y., June 11, 1931. [1a; 4; 7; 8; 10]

Giddings, Howard Andrus, explorer, b. Hartford, Conn., 1868; d. Hartford, Conn., March 16, 1949. [10]

Giddings, Joshua Reed, politician, b. Athens, Pa., 1795; d. Montreal, Que., May 27, 1864. [1; 3; 4; 6; 7; 8]

Gielow, Mrs. Martha, née **Sawyer,** lecturer and novelist, b. Greensboro, Ala., d. Long Beach, Calif., Jan. 30, 1933. [10; 34]

Giesy, Samuel Hensel, clergyman, b. Lancaster, O., 1826; d. Washington, D.C., May 27, 1888. [3a]

Giffin, William Milford, educationist, b. Heuvelton, N.Y., 1850; d. Chicago, Ill., April 12, 1912. [10]

Gifford, Mrs. Augusta, née **Hale,** historian, b. Turner, Me., 1842; d. Portland, Me., Feb. 9, 1915. [8; 10]

Gifford, Franklin Kent, clergyman and novelist, b. Garrison, N.Y., 1861; d. Cambridge, Mass., Nov. 26, 1948. [51]

Gifford, John Clayton, forester, b. May's Landing, N.J., 1870; d. Miami, Fla., June 25, 1949. [10; 11]

Gifford, Miram Wentworth, clergyman, b. Newcastle, Ont., 1851; d. ? [10]

Gifford, Orrin Philip, clergyman, b. Montague, Mass., 1847; d. Pasadena, Calif., Feb. 1, 1932. [10; 47]

Gignac, Joseph Narcisse, priest, b. Deschambault, Que., 1864; d. Quebec, Que., April 18, 1939. [32]

Gigot, Francis Ernest Charles, priest, b. Lhuant, France, 1859; d. Yonkers, N.Y., 1920. [10; 21]

Gihon, Albert Leary, naval surgeon, b. Philadelphia, Pa., 1833; d. New York, Nov. 17, 1901. [1; 2; 3; 4; 6; 8]

Gilberg, Charles Alexander, chess expert, b. Camden, N.J., 1835; d. Brooklyn, N.Y., 1898. [3a; 4; 6; 10]

Gilbert, Mrs. Anne Jane, née **Hartley,** actress, b. Rochdale, England, 1821; d. Chicago, Ill., Dec. 2, 1904. [2; 8]

Gilbert, Arthur Witter, agricultural writer, b. West Brookfield, Mass., 1882; d. Belmont, Mass., Dec. 7, 1936. [10; 11]

Gilbert, Benjamin, miller, b. Philadelphia, Pa., 1711; d. on the St. Lawrence river, June 2, 1780. [3; 6; 8]

Gilbert, Benjamin Davis, journalist, b. Albany, N.Y., 1835; d. 1907. [10]

Gilbert, Charles Benajah, educationist, b. Wilton, Conn., 1855; d. New York, N.Y., Aug. 26, 1913. [10; 61; 70]

Gilbert, Clinton Wallace, journalist, b. Long Island, N.Y., 1871; d. Washington, D.C., May 17, 1933. [10]

Gilbert, Frank, journalist, b. Pittsford, Vt., 1839; d. Chicago, Ill., Nov. 4, 1899. [4]

Gilbert, Frank Bixby, lawyer, b. Bainbridge, N.Y., 1866; d. Schodack, N.Y., Aug. 28, 1927. [10]

Gilbert, Franklin Warner. See Gilbert, Frank.

Gilbert, George, journalist and novelist, b. 1874; d. Binghampton, N.Y., March 24, 1943.

Gilbert, George Abner, physician, b. 1859; d. Danbury, Conn., March 27, 1926. [48]

Gilbert, George Blodgett, clergyman, b. 1871; d. Middletown, Conn., Feb. 20, 1948. [10]

Gilbert, George Holley, theologian, b. Cavendish, Vt., 1854; d. Wellesley Hills, Mass., Feb. 11, 1930. [10; 49; 68]

Gilbert, Grove Karl, geologist, b. Rochester, N.Y., 1843; d. May 1, 1918. [4; 10]

Gilbert, Henry Franklin Belknap, musical composer, b. Somerville, Mass., 1868; d. Cambridge, Mass., May 19, 1928. [1; 10; 20]

Gilbert, Howard Worcester, poet, b. 1819; d. 1894. [8]

Gilbert, James Eleazer, clergyman, b. Alexander, N.Y., 1839; d. 1909. [10]

Gilbert, Levi, clergyman, b. Brooklyn, N.Y., 1852; d. Cincinnati, O., Dec. 24, 1917. [8; 10]

Gilbert, Linda, philanthropist, b. Rochester, N.Y., 1847; d. Mount Vernon, N.Y., Oct. 24, 1895. [1]

Gilbreth, Frank Bunker, engineer, b. Fairfield, Me., 1868; d. Montclair, N.J., June 14, 1924. [10]

Gilchrist, Mrs. Annie, née Somers, novelist and poet, fl. 1884-1906. [34]

Gilchrist, Mrs. Fredericka Raymond, née Beardsley, literary critic, b. Oswego, N.Y., 1845; d. ? [3a; 8]

Gilchrist, James Grant, surgeon, d. Iowa City, Ia., March 22, 1906. [37]

Gilchrist, Thomas Caspar, dermatologist, b. Crewe, England, 1862; d. Baltimore, Md., Nov. 14, 1927. [10]

Gilder, Jeannette Leonard, journalist and literary critic, b. Flushing, N.Y., 1849; d. New York, N.Y., Jan. 17, 1916. [1; 4; 7; 10]

Gilder, Joseph Benson, literary journalist, b. Flushing, N.Y., 1858; d. New York, N.Y., Dec. 9, 1936. [7; 10]

Gilder, Richard Watson, poet and journalist, b. Bordentown, N.J., 1844; d. New York, N.Y., Nov. 18, 1909. [1; 4; 7; 9; 10; 71]

Gilder, William Henry, journalist, b. Philadelphia, Pa., 1838; d. Newark, N.J., Feb. 5, 1900. [1; 3; 4; 8]

Gildersleeve, Basil Lanneau, educationist, b. Charleston, S.C., 1831; d. Baltimore, Md., Jan. 9, 1924. [1; 2; 3; 4; 7; 8; 10]

Gildersleeve, Mrs. C. H., née Buchanan. See Longstreet, Mrs. Rachel Abigail, née Buchanan.

Giles, Charles, clergyman and poet, b. 1783; d. 1867. [19]

Giles, Chauncey, clergyman, b. Charlemont, Mass., 1813; d. Philadelphia, Pa., Nov. 6, 1893. [1; 3; 4; 6; 7; 8; 61]

Giles, Ella Augusta. See Ruddy, Mrs. Ella Augusta, née Giles.

Giles, Frye Williams, local historian, b. 1819; d. 1898.

Giles, Henry, clergyman, b. Wexford county, Ireland, 1809; d. near Boston, Mass., July 10, 1892. [3; 4; 6; 7; 8]

Giles, William Branch, politician, b. Amelia county, Va., 1762; d. Albemarle county, Va., Dec. 4, 1830. [1; 3; 4; 7; 34]

Gilfillan, Joseph Alexander, clergyman and novelist, b. Londonderry, Ireland, 1838; d. New York, N.Y., Nov. 20, 1913.

Gilhooley, Lord (pseud.). See Seymour, Frederick Henri.

Gill, Augustus Herman, chemist, b. Canton, Mass., 1864; d. Belmont, Mass., Nov. 11, 1936. [10; 11; 13]

Gill, Charles Clifford, naval officer, b. Junction City, Kans., 1885; d. Pearl Harbor, Hawaii, Jan. 10, 1948. [11]

Gill, Charles Ignace Adélard, poet and artist, b. Sorel, Que., 1871; d. Montreal, Que., Oct. 16, 1918. [27]

Gill, Corrington, economist, b. Grand Rapids, Mich., 1898; d. Washington, D.C., July 12, 1946. [10]

Gill, Frances, poet, b. 1885; d. Portland, Ore., March 20, 1937. [10]

Gill, Theodore Nicholas, biologist, b. New York, N.Y., 1837; d. 1914. [4; 10]

Gill, William Fearing, journalist, b. Boston, Mass., 1844; d. Oct. 18, 1917. [6; 8; 10]

Gill, William Hugh, clergyman, b. Ireland, 1841; d. Philadelphia, Pa., 1904. [10]

Gill, William Icrin, clergyman, b. Bradford, England, 1831; d. Neuvitar, Cuba, March 4, 1902. [6; 8]

Gill, Wilson Lindsley, educationist, b. Columbus, O., 1851; d. Philadelphia, Pa., Sept. 12, 1941. [4; 10; 62]

Gillard, John Thomas, priest, b. Scranton, Pa., 1900; d. Jan. 13, 1942. [21]

Gillespie, Charles Bancroft, local historian, b. 1865; d. 1915.

Gillespie, Mrs. Elizabeth, née Duane, social leader, b. Philadelphia, Pa., 1821; d. Philadelphia, Pa., Oct. 13, 1901. [8]

Gillespie, Frances Elma, historian, b. 1895; d. Chicago, Ill., Nov. 29, 1948.

Gillespie, George, clergyman, b. Glasgow, Scotland, 1683; d. Delaware, Jan. 2, 1760. [3; 8]

Gillespie, Joseph H., clergyman and poet, b. 1861; d. 1889. [34]

Gillespie, Louis John, chemist, b. Hillsboro Bridge, N.H., 1886; d. Boston, Mass., Jan. 24, 1941. [13; 47]

Gillespie, Marian Evans, journalist, b. Muncie, Ind., 1884; d. New York, N.Y., Dec. 26, 1946.

Gillespie, William Mitchell, civil engineer, b. New York, N.Y., 1816; d. New York, N.Y., Jan. 1, 1868. [1; 3; 4; 6; 8]

Gillespy, George. See Gillespie, George.

Gillespy, William, poet and journalist, b. near Carlisle, England, 1824; d. Hamilton, Ont., April 19, 1886. [27]

Gillet, Eliphalet, clergyman, b. Colchester, Conn., 1768; d. Hallowell, Me., Oct. 19, 1848. [38; 49]

Gillet, Joseph Anthony, educationist, b. Lebanon Springs, N.Y., 1837; d. New York, N.Y., Jan. 28, 1908. [4]

Gillet, Ransom Hooker, politician, b. New Lebanon, N.Y., 1800; d. Washington, D.C., Oct. 24, 1876. [1; 3; 4; 6; 8]

Gillett, Charles Ripley, archaeologist, b. New York, N.Y., 1855; d. Norfolk, Conn., Sept. 3, 1948.

Gillett, Ezra Hall, clergyman, b. Colchester, Conn., 1823; d. Harlem, N.Y., Sept. 2, 1875. [1; 3; 4; 6; 7; 8; 62]

Gillett, Frederick Huntington, biographer, b. Westfield, Mass., 1851; d. Springfield, Mass., July 31, 1935. [1a; 10]

Gillett, Henry Webster, dentist, b. 1861; d. New York, N.Y., March 12, 1943.

Gillette, Abram Dunn, clergyman, b. Cambridge, N.Y., 1807; d. Bluff Point, Lake George, N.Y., Aug. 24, 1882. [3]

Gillette, Edward, civil engineer, b. New Haven, Conn., 1854; d. Sheridan, Wyo., Jan. 3, 1936. [62]

Gillette, Mrs. Fanny Lemira, née **Camp,** writer on cooking, b. 1828; d. Beverly Hills, Calif., Dec. 25, 1926. [10]

Gillette, John Morris, sociologist, b. Nodaway county, Mo., 1866; d. Grand Forks, N.D., Sept. 24, 1949. [10; 11]

Gillette, King Camp, manufacturer, b. Fond du Lac, Wis., 1855; d. near Los Angeles, Calif., July 9, 1932. [1a; 10]

Gillette, Mrs. Lucia Fidelia, née **Woolley,** poet, b. 1827; d. ? [8]

Gillette, William Hooker, actor and playwright, b. Hartford, Conn., 1855; d. Hartford, Conn., April 29, 1937. [7; 8; 10]

Gilliam, Charles Frederic, physician b. 1853; d. ?

Gilliam, David Tod, surgeon, b. Hebron, O., 1844; d. Columbus, O., Oct. 2, 1923. [1; 4; 10]

Gilliam, Edward Winslow, physician and novelist, b. Charleston, S.C., 1834; d. 1925. [21]

Gillies, Archibald C., clergyman, b. Lotbinière, Lower Canada, 1834; d. Dunedin, New Zealand, Oct., 1887. [27]

Gillis, James Andrew, lawyer, b. 1829; d. Salem, Mass., Oct. 8, 1914. [51]

Gillis, William Robert, pioneer, b. 1840; d. 1929.

Gilliss, James Melville, astronomer, b. Georgetown, D.C., 1811; d. Washington, D.C., Feb. 9, 1865. [1; 2; 4; 6]

Gilliss, Walter, printer, b. Lexington, Ky., 1855; d. New York, N.Y., Sept. 24, 1925. [1; 4; 7]

Gillman, Henry, poet and scientist, b. Kinsale, Ireland, 1833; d. Detroit, Mich., July 30, 1915. [1; 4; 8; 10]

Gillmore, Quincy Adams, military engineer, b. Lorain county, O., 1825; d. Brooklyn, N.Y., April 7, 1888. [1; 3; 6; 8]

Gillmore, Rufus Hamilton, novelist, b. Chelsea, Mass., 1879; d. New York, N.Y., Jan. 22, 1935. [7; 10; 11]

Gilman, Arthur, historian, b. Alton, Ill., 1837; d. Atlantic City, N.J., Dec. 28, 1909. [1; 3; 4; 7; 8; 10]

Gilman, Benjamin Ives, museum official, b. New York, N.Y., 1852; d. Boston, Mass., March 18, 1933. [10]

Gilman, Bradley, clergyman, b. Boston, Mass., 1857; d. Boston, Mass., June 19, 1932. [10; 51]

Gilman, Mrs. Caroline, nèe **Howard,** poet and writer for children, b. Boston, Mass., 1794; d. Washington, D.C., Sept. 15, 1888. [1; 3; 4; 6; 7; 8]

Gilman, Chandler Robbins, physician, b. Marietta, O., 1802; d. Middletown, Conn., Sept. 26, 1865. [3; 7; 8]

Gilman, Mrs. Charlotte, née **Perkins.** poet and novelist, b. Hartford, Conn., 1860; d. Pasadena, Calif., Aug. 17, 1935. [1a; 4; 10; 11; 35]

Gilman, Daniel Coit, educationist, b. Norwich, Conn., 1831; d. Norwich, Conn., Oct. 13, 1908. [1; 3; 4; 7; 8; 62]

Gilman, Lawrence, music critic, b. Flushing, N.Y., 1878; d. Franconia, N.Y., Sept. 8, 1939. [10; 20]

Gilman, Mrs. Maria (pseud.). See Barnard, Charles.

Gilman, Nicholas Paine, educationist, b. Quincy, Ill., 1849; d. Meadville, Pa., Jan. 23, 1912. [4; 7; 10]

Gilman, Samuel, clergyman, b. Gloucester, Mass., 1791; d. Kingston, Mass., Feb. 9, 1858. [1; 3; 4; 6; 7; 8]

Gilman, Theodore, banker, b. Alton, Ill., 1841; d. Yonkers, N.Y., Aug. 9, 1930. [8; 10; 61]

Gilman, Wenona (pseud.). See Schoeffel, Mrs. Florence Blackburn, née White.

Gilmer, Francis Walker, lawyer, b. Albemarle county, Va., 1790; d. Albemarle county, Va., Feb. 25, 1826. [1; 4]

Gilmer, George Rockingham, politician, b. Oglethorpe county, Va., 1790; d. Lexington, Ga., Nov. 16, 1859. [1; 3; 4; 8; 34]

Gilmor, Harry, soldier, b. Baltimore, Md., 1838; d. Baltimore, Md., March 4, 1883. [3; 4; 34]

Gilmore, George William, theologian, b. London, England, 1858; d. Brooklyn, N.Y., Aug. 22, 1933. [10; 11; 68]

Gilmore, James Roberts, novelist and historian, b. Boston, Mass., 1823; d. Glens Falls, N.Y., Nov. 16, 1903. [1; 3; 4; 6; 7; 8]

Gilmore, Joseph Henry, clergyman and educationist, b. Boston, Mass., 1834; d. Rochester, N.Y., July 23, 1918. [1; 3; 4; 7; 8; 47]

Gilmore, Melvin Randolph, ethnologist, b. Valley, Neb. 1868; d. Lincoln, Neb., July 25, 1940. [10; 11]

Gilmour, Richard, bishop, b. Glasgow, Scotland, 1824; d. St. Augustine, Fla., April 13, 1891. [1; 3; 4; 21]

Gilpin, Edwin, mining engineer, b. Halifax, N.S., 1851; d. 1907. [33]

Gilpin, Henry Dilworth, lawyer, b. Lancaster, England, 1801; d. Philadelphia, Pa., Jan. 29, 1860. [1; 3; 4; 6; 8]

Gilpin, Joshua, poet, b. Philadelphia, Pa., 1765; d. Philadelphia, Pa., 1840. [3; 6; 8]

Gilpin, Thomas, manufacturer, b. Philadelphia, Pa., 1776; d. Philadelphia, Pa., March 3, 1853. [3; 6]

Gilpin, William, adventurer and politician, b. Brandywine, Pa., 1813; d. Denver, Colo., Jan. 20, 1894. [1; 3a; 4]

Gilson, Jewett Castello, educationist, b. Rockingham, Vt., 1844; d. Oakland, Calif., Feb. 25, 1926. [45]

Gilson, Roy Rolfe, journalist, clergyman, and novelist, b. Clinton, Ia., 1875; d. Salisbury, Md., Aug. 12, 1933. [8; 10; 11]

172 DICTIONARY OF NORTH AMERICAN AUTHORS

Gingras, Joseph Apollinaire, priest and poet, b. St. Antoine de Tilly, Que., 1847; d. Chicoutimi, Que., 1935. [27]
Gingras, Jules Fabian, translator, b. about 1829; d. Ottawa, Ont., Feb. 6. 1884. [27]
Gingras, Léon, priest and educationist, b. Quebec, Lower Canada, 1808; d. Paris, France, Feb. 18, 1860. [27]
Girard, Charles Frédéric, naturalist, b. Mülhausen, France, 1822; d. near Paris, France, Jan. 29, 1895. [1; 3; 4;]
Girardeau, John Lafayette, clergyman, b. near Charleston, S.C., 1825; d. Columbia, S.C., June 23, 1898. [1; 4; 8; 34]
Girardey, Ferreol, priest, b. 1839; d. St. Louis, Mo., July 31, 1930. [21]
Girod, Amury, adventurer, b. France; d. near Pointe-aux-Trembles, Lower Canada, Dec., 1837. [27]
Girouard, Désiré, jurist and historian, b. St. Timothée, Lower Canada, 1836; d. Ottawa, Ont., March 22, 1911. [27]
Girty, George Herbert, palaeontologist, b. Cleveland, O., 1869; d. Washington, D.C., Jan. 27, 1939. [10; 62]
Given, Welker, journalist, b. Millersburg, O., 1853; d. Clinton, Ia., March 6, 1938. [37]
Givins, Robert Cartwright, novelist, b. near Kingston, Ont., 1845; d. San Francisco, Calif., April 14, 1915.
Gjerset, Knut, educationist, b. Romsdal, Norway, 1865; d. Decorah, Ia., Oct. 29, 1936. [7; 10; 11]
Glackemeyer, Charles, lawyer, b. Montreal, Lower Canada, 1820; d. Montreal, Que., April 9, 1892. [27]
Glackemeyer, Edward Claude, notary public, b. Quebec, Lower Canada, 1826; d. Quebec, Que., Feb. 5, 1910. [27]
Gladden, Washington, clergyman, b. Pottsgrove, Pa., 1836; d. Columbus, O., July 2, 1918. [2; 4; 7; 10]
Gladwin, Mary Elizabeth, nurse, b. Stoke-upon-Trent, England, 1862; d. Akron, O., Nov. 22, 1939. [10]
Gladwin, William Zachary (pseud.). See Zollinger, Gulielma.
Glaenzer, Richard Butler, editor, b. Paris, France, 1876; d. New York, N.Y., April 15, 1937. [7; 10]
Glasgow, Ellen Anderson Gholson, novelist, b. Richmond, Va., 1874; d. Richmond, Va., Nov. 21, 1945. [7; 10; 11; 12; 34]
Glaspell, Susan, playwright and novelist, b. Davenport, Ia., 1882; d. Provincetown, Mass., July 27, 1948. [10; 11]
Glass, Carter, politician, b. Lynchburg, Va., 1858; d. Washington, D.C., May 28, 1946. [7; 10; 12]
Glass, Chester, lawyer, b. London, Ont.; d. New York. N.Y., 1921. [31a]
Glass, Francis, classical scholar, b. Londonderry, Ireland, 1790; d. Dayton, O., 1825. [3; 7]
Glass, Montague Marsden, playwright and short-story writer, b. Manchester, England, 1877; d. Westport, Conn., Feb. 3, 1934. [1a; 2; 7; 10]

Glazier, Willard, soldier and explorer, b. Fowler, N.Y., 1841; d. Albany, N.Y., 1905. [3; 4; 8; 10; 70]
Glazier, William Belcher, lawyer and poet, b. Hallowell, Me., 1817; d. Cincinnati, O., Oct. 25, 1870. [38; 51]
Gleason, Arthur Huntington, journalist, b. Newark, N.J., 1878; d. Washington, D.C., Dec. 30, 1923. [10; 62]
Gleason, Edward Baldwin, physician, b. Philadelphia, Pa., 1854; d. Philadelphia, Pa., Nov. 30, 1934. [10; 11]
Gleason, Lafayette Blanchard, lawyer, b. Delhi, N.Y., 1863; d. Delhi, N.Y., Oct. 24, 1937. [10]
Gleason, Mrs. Rachel, née Brooks, physician, b. Vermont, 1820; d. ? [8]
Gleaves, Albert, naval officer, b. Nashville, Tenn., 1858; d. Haverford, Pa., Jan. 6, 1937. [10; 11]
Gleed, Charles Sumner, lawyer, .b. Morrisville, Vt., 1856; d. Topeka, Kans., July 25, 1920. [10]
Gleed, James Willis, lawyer, b. Morrisville, Vt., 1859; d. Topeka, Kans., Oct. 12, 1926. [10]
Glenn, Earl Rouse, educationist, b. Vevay, Ind., 1887; d. Atlanta, Ga., Jan. 24, 1939. [11]
Glenn, Edwin Forbes, soldier and lawyer, b. near Greensboro, N.C., 1857; d. Mentor, O., Aug. 5, 1926. [10]
Glenn, Garrard, lawyer and educationist, b. Atlanta, Ga., 1878; d. Charlottesville, Va., Jan. 25, 1949. [10]
Glenn, Mrs. Mary Willcox, née Brown, welfare worker, b. Baltimore, Md., 1869; d. New York, N.Y., Nov. 3, 1940. [10]
Glisan, Rodney, physician, b. Linganore, Md., 1827; d. Portland, Ore., June, 1890. [3; 4; 6; 8]
Globensky, Charles Auguste Maximilien, historian, b. St. Eustache, Lower Canada, 1830; d. St. Eustache, Que., Feb. 12, 1906. [27]
Glover, Robert Hall, missionary, b. Leeds, Que., 1871; d. Philadelphia, Pa., March 23, 1947. [10]
Gluck, James Fraser, lawyer, b. Niagara Falls, N.Y., 1852; d. New York, N.Y., Dec. 15, 1897. [3]
Glyndon, Howard (pseud.). See Searing, Mrs. Laura Catherine, née Redden.
Glynes, Mrs. Ella Maria, née Dietz. See Clymer, Mrs. Ella Maria, née Dietz.
Gmeiner, John, priest, b. Germany, 1847; d. Richfield, Minn., Nov. 11, 1913. [1; 3; 8; 10; 70]
Gobright, Lawrence Augustus, poet, b. Baltimore, Md., 1816; d. Washington, D.C., May 22, 1879. [4]
Godbey, John Emory, clergyman, b. Casey county, Ky., 1839; d. Kirkwood, Mo., Feb. 29, 1932. [10; 11]
Godbey, William B., clergyman, b. 1833; d. Zarepath, N.J., 1920.
Godchaux, Mrs. Elma, novelist, b. near Napoleonville, La.; d. New Orleans, La., April 3, 1941.

Goddard, Dwight, Buddhist missionary, b. Worcester, Mass., 1861; d. Thetford, Vt., July 5, 1939.

Goddard, Frederick Bartlett, advertiser, b. 1834; d. ?

Goddard, John Calvin, clergyman, b. New York, N.Y., 1852; d. Orlando, Fla., March 17, 1945. [10; 11; 62]

Goddard, Morrill, journalist, b. Portland, Me., 1866; d. New York, N.Y., July 1, 1937. [10]

Goddard, Paul Beck, physician, b. Baltimore, Md., 1811; d. Philadelphia, Pa., July 3, 1866. [1; 3; 4; 6; 34]

Goddard, Pliny Earle, ethnologist, b. Lewiston, Me., 1869; d. Newtown, Conn., July 12, 1928. [1; 4; 7; 10; 13]

Goddard, Ralph Willis, electrical engineer, b. Waltham, Mass., 1887; d. Mesilla Park, N.M., Dec. 31, 1929. [10]

Goddard, William, printer and journalist, b. New London, Conn., 1740; d. Providence, R.I., Dec. 23, 1817. [1; 3; 7]

Godding, William Whitney, physician, b. Winchester, Mass., 1831; d. Washington, D.C., May 6, 1899. [49]

Godfrey, Hollis, engineer, b. Lynn, Mass., 1874; d. Duxbury, Mass., Jan. 17, 1936. [10; 13]

Godfrey, Thomas, poet and playwright, b. Philadelphia, Pa., 1736; d. Wilmington, Del., Aug. 3, 1763. [1; 3; 7; 8; 34]

Goding, Frederic Webster, consul, b. Hyde Park, Mass., 1858; d. Livermore Falls, Me., May 5, 1933. [10]

Godkin, Edwin Lawrence, journalist, b. Moyne, Ireland, 1831; d. Brixham, England, May 21, 1902. [1; 2; 3; 4; 7; 10]

Godman, John Davidson, naturalist, b. Annapolis, Md., 1794; d. Germantown, Pa., April 17, 1830. [1; 3; 4; 6; 7; 8; 34]

Godoy, José Francisco, diplomat, b. Tampico, Mexico, 1851; d. Mexico City, Mexico, July 29, 1930. [35]

Godrycz, John A., priest, b. Chelm, Russian Poland, 1872; d. 1923. [21]

Godwin, Parke, journalist, b. Paterson, N.J., 1816; d. New York, N.Y., Jan. 7, 1904. [1; 3; 4; 6; 7; 8; 10]

Goelet, Augustin Hardin, gynaecologist, b. Wilmington, N.C., 1854; d. New York, N.Y., April 26, 1910. [10]

Goepp, Philip Henry, musician, b. New York, N.Y., 1864; d. Philadelphia, Pa., Aug. 26, 1936. [10; 11]

Goessmann, Charles Anthony, chemist, b. Germany, 1827; d. Amherst, Mass., Sept. 2, 1910. [1; 3; 4; 10]

Goethals, George Washington, military engineer, b. Brooklyn, N.Y., 1858; d. New York, N.Y., Jan. 21, 1928. [1; 4; 10]

Goetschius, Percy, musician, b. Paterson, N.J., 1853; d. Manchester, N.H., Oct. 29, 1943. [10; 11; 20]

Goff, Emmet Stull, horticulturist, b. Elmira, N.Y., 1852; d. Madison, Wis., June 6, 1902. [1; 4]

Goff, Henry Slade, poet, b. 1842; d. Minneapolis, Minn., June 19, 1917. [4]

Going, Ellen Maud, naturalist, b. West-

chester, N.Y., 1859; d. Montreal, Que., Feb. 17, 1925. [10]

Gold, Theodore Sedgwick, agriculturist, b. Madison, N.Y., 1818; d. West Cornwall, Conn., March 20, 1906. [62]

Gold, William Jason, clergyman, b. Washington, D.C., 1845; d. Chicago, Ill., Jan. 11, 1903. [10; 51]

Goldbeck, Robert, musician, b. Potsdam, Prussia, 1839; d. St. Louis, Mo., May 16, 1908. [4; 10; 20]

Goldberg, Isaac, literary critic, b. Boston, Mass., 1887; d. Brookline, Mass., July 14, 1938. [10; 11; 51]

Golden, Michael Joseph, mechanical engineer, b. Stratford, Ont., 1862; d. Lafayette, Ind., 1918. [10]

Goldenweiser, Alexander, anthropologist, b. Kiev, Russia, 1880; d. Portland, Ore:, July 6, 1940. [7; 10]

Golder, Frank Alfred, historian, b. near Odessa, Russia, 1877; d. Stanford University, Calif., Jan. 7, 1909. [1; 4; 7; 10]

Goldfrap, John Henry, journalist and writer of books for boys, b. 1879; d. New York, N.Y., Nov. 21, 1917.

Goldman, Emma, anarchist, b. Kovno, Russia, 1869; d. Toronto, Ont., May 14, 1940.

Goldsborough, Charles Washington, civil servant, b. Cambridge, Md.. 1779; d. Washington, D.C., Sept. 14, 1843. [3; 34]

Goldsborough, Edmund Kennedy, b. about 1844; d. Washington, D.C., March 14, 1912.

Goldsborough, William Worthington, soldier, b. 1831; d. 1901.

Goldsmith, Christabel (pseud.). See Smith, Fannie M.

Goldsmith, Glenn Warren, botanist, b. Hutcheson, Minn., 1886; d. Austin, Tex., Oct. 28, 1943. [13]

Goldsmith, Middleton, physician, b. Port Tobacco, Md., 1818; d. Rutland, Vt., Nov. 26, 1887. [1; 4]

Goldsmith, Oliver, poet, b. Annapolis, N.S., 1787; d. Liverpool, England, July, 1861. [27]

Goldsmith, Robert, journalist, b. Kingston, N.Y., 1882; d. Glenside, Pa., Feb. 24, 1924. [10]

Goldstein, Joseph M., economist, b. Russia, 1868; d. New York, N.Y., Oct. 31, 1939.

Goldstein, Max Aaron, physician, b. St. Louis, Mo., 1870; d. Clayton, Mo., July 27, 1941. [10]

Goldthwait, James Walter, geologist, b. Lynn, Mass., 1880; d. Hanover, N.H., Jan. 1, 1948. [13; 49]

Golobie, John, journalist, b. Jugoslavia; d. Oklahoma City, Okla., May 30, 1927. [75]

Gompers, Samuel, labour leader, b. London, England, 1850; d. San Antonio, Tex., Dec. 13, 1924. [1; 4; 10]

Gonthier, Pierre Théophile, priest, b. St. Gervais, Que., 1853; d. St. Hyacinthe, Que., June 16, 1917. [27]

Gonzales, Ambrose Elliott, journalist and writer of negro dialect stories, b. Colleton county, S.C., 1857; d. Columbia, S.C., July 11, 1926. [1; 7; 10]

Gooch, Mrs. Fanny, née **Chambers.** See Iglehart, Mrs. Fanny, née Chambers.

Gooch, Frank Austin, chemist, b. Watertown, Mass., 1852; d. New Haven, Conn., Aug. 12, 1929. [4; 10; 13; 51]

Good, James Isaac, clergyman and historian, b. York, Pa., Dec. 31, 1850; d. Philadelphia, Pa., Jan. 22, 1924. [1; 4; 7; 8; 10]

Good, Jeremiah Haak, clergyman, b. Rehrersburg, Pa., 1822; d. Tiffin, O., Jan. 25, 1888. [1; 6]

Goodale, George Lincoln, botanist, b. Saco, Me., 1839; d. Cambridge, Mass., April 12, 1923. [1; 3; 8; 10; 45]

Goodale, Stephen Lincoln, agriculturist, b. South Berwick, Me., 1815; d. Saco, Me., Nov. 5, 1897. [1; 38]

Goodchild, Frank Marsden, clergyman, b. Philadelphia, Pa., 1860; d. New York, N.Y., Feb. 18, 1928. [10]

Goode, George Brown, ichthyologist, b. New Albany, Ind., 1851; d. Washington, D.C., Sept. 6, 1896. [1; 3; 4; 6; 8; 34]

Goode, John, lawyer and politician, b. Bedford county, Va., 1829; d. Norfolk, Va., July 14, 1909. [1; 3; 4; 10; 34]

Goode, John Paul, educationist, b. Stewartville, Minn., 1862; d. Chicago, Ill., Aug. 5, 1932. [1a; 4; 10]

Goode, William Henry, clergyman, b. 1807; d. 1879.

Goodell, Charles Le Roy, clergyman, b. Dudley, Mass., 1854; d. New York, N.Y., April 27, 1937. [10; 11; 60]

Goodell, Constans Liberty, clergyman, b. Calais, Vt., 1830; d. St. Louis, Mo., Feb. 1, 1886. [3a; 59]

Goodell, Edwin Burpee, lawyer, b. Rockville, Conn., 1851; d. Montclair, N.J., Oct. 16, 1942. [62]

Goodell, Henry Hill, educationist, b. Constantinople, Turkey, 1839; d. at sea, April 23, 1905. [3; 4; 10]

Goodell, Thomas Dwight, educationist, b. Ellington, Conn., 1854; d. New Haven, Conn., July 7, 1920. [4; 8; 10; 62]

Goodell, William, missionary, b. Templeton, Mass., 1792; d. Philadelphia, Pa., Feb. 18, 1867. [1; 4; 6; 7; 8]

Goodell, William, reformer, b. Coventry, N.Y., 1792; d. Janesville, Wis., Feb. 14, 1878. [1]

Goodell, William, physician, b. Malta, 1829; d. Philadelphia, Pa., Oct. 27, 1894. [3; 6; 8; 61]

Goodenough, Arthur, clergyman, b. Jefferson, N.Y., 1838; d. Winchester, Conn., Feb. 9, 1921. [62]

Goodenough, George Alfred, educationist, b. Davidson, Mich.,, 1868; d. Urbana, Ill., Sept. 29, 1929. [10; 11]

Goodenow, John Milton, jurist, b. Westmoreland, N.H., 1782; d. New Orleans, La., July, 1838. [1; 49]

Goodenow, Smith Bartlett, clergyman, b. Damariscotta, Me., 1817; d. Battle Creek, Ia., March 26, 1897. [38; 46]

Goodhue, Bertram Grosvenor, architect, b. Pomfret, Conn., 1869; d. New York, N.Y., April 23, 1924. [1; 4; 8; 10]

Goodhue, Josiah Fletcher, clergyman, b. Westminster, Vt., 1791; d. Whitewater, Wis., May, 1863. [43]

Goodhue, Willis Maxwell, playwright, b. Akron, O., 1873; d. New York, N.Y., Nov. 22, 1938. [7]

Goodlander, Mabel Ray, educationist, b. Rockford, Ill., 1868; d. Rockford, Ill., Feb. 28, 1944.

Goodloe, Daniel Reaves, journalist and politician, b. Louisburg, N.C., 1814; d. Warrenton, N.C., Jan. 18, 1902. [1; 4; 7; 34]

Goodman, Kenneth Sawyer, playwright, b. Chicago, Ill., 1883; d. Great Lakes Station, Ill., Nov. 29, 1918. [1; 7]

Goodnow, Frank Johnson, educationist, b. Brooklyn, N.Y., 1859; d. Baltimore, Md., Nov. 15, 1939. [4; 10]

Goodrich, Aaron, jurist, b. Cayuga county, N.Y., 1807; d. St. Paul, Minn., June 23, 1887. [3; 4; 8; 70]

Goodrich, Alfred John, musician, b. Chilo, O., 1847; d. Paris, France, April 25, 1920. [1; 4; 8; 10; 20]

Goodrich, Arthur Frederick, novelist and playwright, b. New Britain, Conn., 1878; d. New York, N.Y., June 26, 1941. [7; 10]

Goodrich, Caspar Frederick, naval officer, b. Philadelphia, Pa., 1847; d. Princeton, N.J., Dec. 26, 1925. [4; 10]

Goodrich, Charles Augustus, clergyman, b. Ridgefield, Conn., 1790; d. Hartford, Conn., Jan. 4, 1862. [1; 3; 4; 6; 8; 62]

Goodrich, Chauncey, horticulturist, b. Hinsdale, Mass., 1798; d. Burlington, Vt., Sept. 11, 1858. [1; 43]

Goodrich, Chauncey, missionary, b. Hinsdale, Mass., 1836; d. Peking, China, Sept. 28, 1925. [1; 68]

Goodrich, Chauncey Allen, clergyman and lexicographer, b. New Haven, Conn., 1790; d. New Haven, Conn., Feb. 25, 1860. [1; 3; 4; 6; 7; 62]

Goodrich, Frank Boott, journalist and playwright, b. Boston, Mass., 1826; d. Morristown, N.Y., March 15, 1895. [1; 3; 4; 6; 7; 8; 51]

Goodrich, Frederick Elizur, journalist, b. Hartford, Conn., 1843; d. Jamaica Plain, Mass., Jan. 12, 1925. [62]

Goodrich, Joseph King, educationist, b. Philadelphia, Pa., 1850; d. Brooklyn, N.Y., Aug. 13, 1921. [10]

Goodrich, Massena, clergyman and local historian, b. 1819; d. 1900.

Goodrich, Samuel Griswold, publisher and writer of books for young people, b. Ridgefield, Conn., 1793; d. New York, N.Y., May 9, 1860. [1; 2; 3; 4; 6; 7; 61]

Goodsell, Charles True, educationist, b. Medina, N.Y., d. Kalamazoo, Mich., Nov. 25, 1941.

Goodsell, Daniel Ayres, bishop, b. Newburgh, N.Y., 1840; d. New York, N.Y., Dec. 5, 1909. [1; 4; 7; 8; 10]

Goodspeed, Calvin, clergyman and educationist, b. Nashwaak, N.B., 1842; d. Paradise, N.S., July 6, 1912. [27]

Goodspeed, Edgar Johnson, clergyman, b. Johnsburg, N.Y., 1833; d. Columbia, S.C., June 12, 1881. [6]

Goodspeed, George Stephen, educationist, b. Janesville, Wis., 1860; d. Chicago, Ill., Feb. 17, 1905. [8; 62]

Goodspeed, Thomas Wakefield, clergyman and educationist, b. Glens Falls, N.Y., 1842; d. Chicago, Ill., Dec. 16, 1927. [1; 4; 7; 10]

Goodspeed, Weston Arthur, poet and historian, b. 1852; d. 1926.

Goodwin, Charles Carroll, journalist, b. 1832; d. Marysville, Calif., 1917. [35]

Goodwin, Charles Jaques, educationist, b. Farmington, Me., 1866; d. Farmington, Me., Sept. 20, 1935. [10; 11]

Goodwin, Daniel, lawyer, b. New York, N.Y., 1832; d. Detroit, Mich., 1901. [5; 8; 10]

Goodwin, Daniel, clergyman, b. Sutton, Mass., 1835; d. East Greenwich, R.I., Aug. 28, 1922, [3; 10; 47]

Goodwin, Daniel Raynes, clergyman and educationist, b. North Berwick, Me., 1811; d. Philadelphia, Pa., March 15, 1890. [1; 3; 4; 6; 8; 46]

Goodwin, Elijah, clergyman, b. Champaign county, O., 1807; d. near Cleveland, O., Sept. 4, 1879. [1]

Goodwin, Frank, lawyer, b. 1841; d. 1912. [51]

Goodwin, Mrs. Hannah Elizabeth, née **Bradbury.** See Goodwin-Talcott, Mrs. Hannah Elizabeth, née Bradbury.

Goodwin, Henry Martyn, clergyman, b. Hartford, Conn., 1820; d. Williamstown, Mass., March 3, 1893. [62]

Goodwin, Hermon Camp, local historian, b. Ulysses, N.Y., 1813; d. Homer, N.Y., Dec. 31, 1891. [8]

Goodwin, Isaac, lawyer, b. Plymouth, Mass., 1786; d. Worcester, Mass., Sept. 16, 1832. [3a; 8]

Goodwin, John Abbot, politician and historian, b. Stirling, Mass., 1824; d. Lowell, Mass., Sept. 21, 1884. [3a; 8; 51]

Goodwin, Mrs. Lavinia Stella, née **Tyler,** novelist, b. St. Johnsbury, Vt., 1833; d. Boston, Mass., 1911. [8; 10]

Goodwin, Mrs. Maud, née **Wilder,** novelist, b. Ballston Spa, N.Y., 1856; d. Greenwich, Conn., Feb. 5, 1935. [7; 8; 10]

Goodwin, Nathaniel, genealogist, b. Hartford, Conn., 1782; d. Hartford, Conn., May 29, 1855. [3; 8]

Goodwin, William Archer Rutherford, clergyman, b. Richmond, Va., 1869; d. Williamsburg, Pa., Sept. 7, 1939. [10]

Goodwin, William Frederic, lawyer and historian, b. Limington, Me., 1823; d. Concord, N.H., March 12, 1872. [3; 38]

Goodwin, William Lawton, educationist, b. Baie Verte, N.B., 1856; d. Montreal, Que., Jan. 17, 1941. [11; 31a]

Goodwin, William Watson, educationist, b. Concord, Mass., 1831; d. Cambridge, Mass., June 16, 1912. [4; 10; 51]

Goodwin-Talcott, Mrs. Hannah Elizabeth, née **Bradbury,** writer of books for young people, b. Chesterville, Me., 1827; d. Boston, Mass., June 1, 1893. [3b; 6; 7; 8]

Goodyear, Watson Andrews, geologist, b. Hamden, Conn., 1838; d. San Francisco, Calif., April 10, 1891. [62]

Goodyear, William Henry, art museum curator, b. New Haven, Conn., 1846; d. Brooklyn, N.Y., Feb. 19, 1923. [1; 4; 7; 8; 10; 62]

Gookin, Daniel, pioneer, b. 1612; d. Cambridge, Mass., March 19, 1686-7. [1; 3; 4; 7; 8]

Gookin, Frederick William, orientalist; b. 1853; d. Winnetka, near Chicago, Ill., Jan. 18, 1936.

Gookin, Nathaniel, clergyman, b. Cambridge, Mass., 1687; d. Hampton, N.H., Aug. 25, 1734. [51]

Goold, Marshall Newton, essayist and playwright, b. Montrose, Scotland, 1881; d. Leicester, Mass., Oct. 25, 1935. [10]

Goold, Nathan, librarian and historian, b. 1846; d. Portland, Me., Feb. 27, 1914.

Goold, William, historian, b. 1809; d. 1890. [38]

Goolrick, John Tackett, jurist, b. 1844; d. Fredericksburg, Va., Sept. 16, 1925.

Gordin, Harry Mann, b. Russia, 1855; d. Chicago, Ill., July 5, 1923. [10]

Gordin, Jacob, playwright, b. Russia, 1853; d. Brooklyn, N.Y., June 11, 1909. [1; 4]

Gordon, Adoniram Judson, clergyman, b. New Hampton, N.H., 1836; d. Boston, Mass., Feb. 2, 1895. [3; 4; 6; 8; 47]

Gordon, Andrew, missionary, b. Putnam, N.Y., 1828; d. Philadelphia, Pa., Aug. 13, 1887. [1]

Gordon, Anna Adams, reformer, b. Boston, Mass., 1853; d. Castile, N.Y., June 15, 1931. [10]

Gordon, Armistead Churchill, lawyer and littérateur, b. Albemarle county, Va., 1855; d. Staunton, Va., Oct. 21, 1931. [4; 7; 8; 10; 11; 34]

Gordon, Charles William, novelist, b. Glengarry county, Ont., 1860; d. Winnipeg, Man., Oct. 31, 1937. [11; 27]

Gordon, Clarence, writer of books for boys, b. New York, N.Y., 1835; d. Manhattan, N.Y., Nov. 26, 1920. [3; 4; 6; 8]

Gordon, Daniel Miner, educationist, b. Pictou, N.S., 1845; d. Kingston, Ont., Sept. 1, 1925. [27]

Gordon, Mrs. Eleanor Lytle, née **Kinzie,** biographer, b. Chicago, Ill., 1835; d. Savannah, Ga., Feb. 22, 1917. [10]

Gordon, Elizabeth, writer of books for children, b. Winn, Me., 1865; d. Chicago, Ill., April 2, 1922. [10]

Gordon, Elizabeth Putnam, social worker, b. 1851; d. 1933.

Gordon, George Angier, clergyman, b. Aberdeenshire, Scotland, 1855; d. Boston, Mass., Oct. 25, 1929. [1; 4; 7; 10]

Gordon, George Byron, archaeologist, b. New Perth, P.E.I., 1870; d. Philadelphia, Pa., Jan. 30, 1927. [1; 7; 10]

Gordon, George Henry, soldier, b. Charlestown, Mass., 1823; d. Boston, Mass., Aug. 30, 1886. [1; 3; 4; 6; 8]

Gordon, Hanford Lennox, lawyer, poet, and politician, b. Andover, N.Y., 1836; d. Los Angeles, Calif., Nov. 13, 1920. [35; 70]

Gordon, Harry Allen, lawyer, b. New York, N.Y., 1883; d. New York, N.Y., May 16, 1947.

Gordon, James, poet, b. Monroe county, Miss., 1833; d. Okolona, Miss., Nov. 28, 1912. [1; 10]

Gordon, James D., missionary, b. Cascumpeque, P.E.I.; d. Erromanga, New Hebrides, 1872. [27]

Gordon, James Lindsay, poet, b. Louisa county, Va., 1850; d. New York, N.Y., Nov. 30, 1904.

Gordon, James Logan, clergyman, b. Philadelphia, Pa., 1858; d. San Francisco, Calif., Oct. 11, 1930. [10]

Gordon, John, clergyman and educationist, b. Pittsburgh, Pa., 1850; d. New York, N.Y., Feb. 9, 1923. [10; 62]

Gordon, John Brown, soldier and polititician, b. Upson county, Ga., 1832; d. Miami, Fla., Jan. 9, 1904. [1; 4; 10; 34]

Gordon, Joseph Claybaugh, educationist, b. Piqua, O., 1842; d. Jacksonville, Ill., 1903. [10]

Gordon, Julien (pseud.). See Cruger, Mrs. Julie Grinnell, née Storrow.

Gordon, Laura De Force, suffragist, b. Erie county, Pa., 1838; d. San Joaquin county, Calif., April 6, 1907. [1; 4]

Gordon, Marquis Lafayette, missionary, b. Waynesburg, Pa., 1843; d. Kyoto, Japan, 1900. [10]

Gordon, Neal MacDougal, poet, d. 1871.

Gordon, Patrick, soldier, b. 1644; d. Philadelphia, Pa., Aug. 5, 1736. [3]

Gordon, Thomas Francis, historian, b. Philadelphia, Pa., 1787; d. Beverly, N.J., Jan. 17, 1860. [3; 4; 6; 8]

Gordon, William, clergyman and historian, b. Hertfordshire, England, 1728; d. Ipswich, England, Oct. 19, 1807. [1; 3; 4; 6; 7; 8]

Gordon, William Clark, clergyman, b. Ware, Mass., 1865; d. Peekskill, N.Y., June 5, 1936. [62]

Gordon, William Robert, clergyman, b. New York, N.Y., 1811; d. 1897. [3; 6; 8; 48]

Gordon, William St. Clair, physician, b. Raleigh, N.C., 1858; d. Richmond, Va., April 24, 1924. [10]

Gordy, John Pancoast, historian and philosopher, b. near Salisbury, Md., 1851; d. New York, N.Y., Dec. 31, 1908. [1; 8; 10]

Gordy, Wilbur Fisk, educationist, b. near Salisbury, Md., 1854; d. Hartford, Conn., Dec. 23, 1929. [4; 7; 8; 10]

Gore, Christopher, lawyer and politician, b. Boston, Mass., 1758; d. Waltham, Mass., March 1, 1827. [3; 4]

Gore, James Howard, educationist, b. near Winchester, Va., 1856; d. Chevy Chase, Md., June 10, 1939. [10; 11]

Gorgas, Ferdinand James Samuel, dentist, b. Winchester, Va., 1835; d. Baltimore, Md., April 8, 1914. [10]

Gorgas, William Crawford, surgeon, b. near Mobile, Ala., 1854; d. London, England, July 3, 1920. [1; 4; 10]

Gorham, Frederick Poole, biologist, b. Providence, R.I., 1871; d. Gloucester, R.I., June 4, 1933. [10; 47]

Gorham, George Congdon, journalist, b. Greenport, N.Y., 1832; d. 1909. [10]

Gorman, John Berry, physician, b. Newberry district, S.C., 1793; d. Talbot county, Ga., Nov. 12, 1864. [3; 34]

Gorrie, John, physician, b. Charleston, S.C., 1803; d. Apalachicola, Fla., June 16, 1855. [1; 4]

Gorrie, Peter Douglas, clergyman, b. Glasgow, Scotland, 1813; d. Potsdam, N.Y., Sept. 12, 1884. [3; 4; 6; 8]

Gorringe, Henry Honeychurch, naval officer, b. Barbados, B.W.I., 1841; d. New York, N.Y., July 6, 1885. [1; 3; 4; 8]

Gorton, Benjamin, religious enthusiast, b. about 1757; d. 1836.

Gorton, David Allyn, physician, b. 1832; d. Brooklyn, N.Y., Feb. 22, 1916. [8]

Gorton, Samuel, religious heretic, b. Gorton, near Manchester, England, about 1592; d. Warwick, Mass., 1677. [1; 3; 4]

Goslin, Omar Pancoast, clergyman, b. Woodstown, N.J., 1899; d. Bronxville, N.Y., Dec. 18, 1942.

Gosnell, R. Edward, journalist, b. Lake Beauport, Que., 1860; d. Vancouver, B.C., Aug. 5, 1931. [27]

Goss, Charles Frederic, clergyman and novelist, b. Meridian, N.Y., 1852; d. Cincinnati, O., May 8, 1930. [7; 10; 63]

Goss, Dwight, local historian, b. Portage county, O., 1857; d. Alta Dena, Calif., March 29, 1909. [39]

Goss, Elbridge Henry, banker and historian, b. Boston, Mass., 1830; d. Melrose, Mass., Oct. 9, 1908. [8; 10]

Goss, Warren Lee, soldier and journalist, b. Brewster, Mass., 1835; d. Rutherford, N.J., Nov. 20, 1925. [7; 10]

Goss, William Freeman Myrick, mechanical engineer, b. Barnstable, Mass., 1859; d. New York, N.Y., March 23, 1928. [4; 10]

Gosselin, Amédée Edmond, priest and historian, b. St. Charles de Bellechasse, Que., 1863; d. Quebec, Que., Dec. 20, 1941. [27]

Gosselin, Auguste Honoré, priest and historian, b. St. Charles de Bellechasse, Que., 1843; d. Aug. 14, 1917. [27]

Gosselin, David, priest and historian, b. St. Laurent, Isle d'Orléans, Que., 1836; d. Quebec, Que., March 2, 1926. [27]

Gotshall, William Charles, engineer, b. St. Louis, Mo., 1870; d. New York, N.Y., Aug. 20, 1935. [1a; 10]

Gott, Charles, educationist, b. Arlington, Mass., 1887; d. West Medford, Mass., Feb. 18, 1938. [10]

Gottheil, Gustav, rabbi, b. Prussia, 1827; d. New York, N.Y., April 15, 1903. [1; 3a; 10]

Gottheil, Richard James Horatio, orientalist, b. Manchester, England, 1862; d. New York, N.Y., May 22, 1936. [4; 10]

Gottschalk, Alfred Louis Moreau, poet, b. New York, N.Y., 1873; d. Rio de Janiero, Brazil, March 1, 1918. [10]

Goucher, John Franklin, educationist, b. Waynesburg, Pa., 1847; d. near Baltimore, Md., July 19, 1922. [1; 4; 7; 10]

Goudy, Frederic William, type designer, b. Bloomington, Ill., 1865; d. Marlboro, N.Y., May 11, 1947. [7; 10; 11]

Gougar, Mrs. Helen Mar, née Jackson, traveller, b. Hillsdale, Mich., 1843; d. Lafayette, Ind., June 6, 1907. [10]

Gouge, William M., economist, b. Philadelphia, Pa., 1796; d. Trenton, N.J., July 14, 1863. [1; 3; 8]

Gough, John Bartholomew, temperance orator, b. Sandgate, England, 1817; d. Frankford, Pa., Feb. 18, 1886. [1; 3; 4; 6; 7; 8]

Gould, Augustus Addison, physician and naturalist, b. New Ipswich, N.H., April 23, 1805; d. Boston, Mass., Sept, 15, 1866. [4; 51]

Gould, Benjamin Apthorp, educationist, b. Lancaster, Mass., 1787; d. Boston, Mass., Oct. 24, 1859. [1; 3; 4; 8]

Gould, Benjamin Apthorp, astronomer, b. Boston, Mass., 1824; d. Cambridge, Mass., Nov. 26, 1896. [1; 3; 6; 8]

Gould, Benjamin Apthorp, manufacturer, b. Cambridge, Mass., 1870; d. Toronto, Ont., June 23, 1937. [51]

Gould, Charles Winthrop, lawyer, b. New York, N.Y., 1849; d. Santa Barbara, Calif., March 18, 1931. [62]

Gould, Mrs. Cora, née Smith, poet, b. Brooklyn, N.Y., 1855; d. Fort Lauderdale, Fla., April 3, 1945.

Gould, Daniel, clergyman, b. England, about 1625; d. Rhode Island, 1716.

Gould, Edward Sherman, novelist and critic, b. Litchfield, Conn., 1805; d; New York, N.Y., Feb. 21, 1885. [1; 3; 4; 6; 7; 8]

Gould, Edward Sherman, civil engineer, b. New York, N.Y., 1837; d. Yonkers, N.Y., 1905. [10]

Gould, Elgin Ralston Lovell, economist and reformer, b. Oshawa, Ont., 1860; d. near North Bay, Ont., Aug. 18, 1915. [1; 2; 4; 8]

Gould, Elizabeth Lincoln, writer of books for girls, b. Boston, Mass.; d. Boston, Mass., Dec. 12, 1914. [10]

Gould, Elizabeth Porter, poet and novelist, b. 1848; d. 1906.

Gould, Ezra Palmer, clergyman, b. Boston, Mass., 1841; d. Whitelake, Sullivan county, N.Y., Aug. 22, 1900. [8; 10; 51]

Gould, George Milbry, physician, b. Auburn, Me., 1848; d. Atlantic City, N.J., Aug. 2, 1922. [1; 2; 4; 8; 10]

Gould, Hannah Flagg, poet, b. Lancaster, Mass., 1789; d. Newburyport, Mass., Sept. 5, 1865. [1; 3; 4; 7; 8; 71]

Gould, James, jurist, b. Branford, Conn., 1770; d. Litchfield, Conn., May 11, 1838. [1; 3; 4; 6; 8; 62]

Gould, Jay, capitalist, b. Roxbury, N.Y., 1836; d. Philadelphia, Pa., Nov. 25, 1892. [1; 2; 4; 5; 6]

Gould, John Melville, lawyer, b. 1848; d. Boston, Mass., April, 1909. [47]

Gould, John W., sailor, b. Litchfield, Conn., 1814; d. at sea, Oct. 1, 1838. [3; 8]

Gould, Mark, clergyman and poet, b. Wilton, Me., 1811; d. Worcester, Mass., Aug. 7, 1896. [46]

Gould, Nathaniel Duren, musician, b. Bedford, Mass., 1781; d. Boston, Mass., May 28, 1864. [1; 3; 4; 6; 8; 20]

Gould, Sylvester Clark, journalist, b. Weare, N.H., 1840; d. Manchester, N.H., July 19, 1909.

Gould, Thomas Ridgeway, sculptor, b. Boston, Mass., 1818; d. Florence, Italy, Nov. 26, 1881. [1; 4]

Goulding, Francis Robert, clergyman and writer of books for children, b. Liberty county, Ga., 1810; d. Roswell, Ga., Aug. 22, 1881. [1; 3; 4; 6; 7; 8; 34]

Gouley, John William Severin, physician, b. New Orleans, La., 1832; d. Brooklyn, N.Y., April 26, 1920. [6]

Gouraud, Aimée Crocker, short-story writer, b. Sacramento, Calif., 1863; d. Sacramento, Calif., Feb. 7, 1941. [35]

Gourlay, John Edgar Reginald, journalist, b. Hamilton, Ont., 1854; d. Ottawa, Ont., Feb. 25, 1923. [27]

Gourlay, John Lowry, clergyman, b. Tyrone county, Ireland, 1821; d. Ottawa, Ont., 1904. [27]

Gourlay, Robert Fleming, land-agent, b. Fifeshire, Scotland, 1778; d. Edinburgh, Scotland, Aug. 1, 1863. [27]

Gouverneur, Mrs. Marion, née Campbell, writer of reminiscences, b. Jamaica, Long Island, N.Y.; d. Washington, D.C., March 12, 1913. [10]

Gove, Charles Augustus, naval officer, b. Concord, N.H., 1854; d. Mare Island, Calif., Sept. 11, 1910. [10]

Gove, Mrs. Mary Sargeant, née Neal. See Nichols, Mrs. Mary Sargeant, née Neal.

Gow, George Coleman, musician, b. Ayer Junction, Mass., 1860; d. Poughkeepsie, N.Y., Jan. 12, 1938. [20]

Gow, John Milne, educationist, b. Perth, Scotland, 1844; d. Lower La Have, N.S., 1898. [27]

Gowan, Ogle Robert, journalist and politician, b. Wexford county, Ireland, 1796; d. Toronto, Ont., Aug. 21, 1876. [27]

Gowans, William, bibliographer, b. Scotland, 1803; d. New York, N.Y., Nov. 27, 1870. [3]

Grabau, Amadeus William, palaeontologist, b. Cedarburg, Wis., 1870; d. Peiping, China, March 27, 1946. [10; 11]

Gracie, Archibald, soldier, b. 1858; d. New York, N.Y., Dec. 4, 1912, [4]

Gradle, Henry, opthalmologist, b. Frankfurt,· Germany, 1855; d. Santa Barbara, Calif., April 4,· 1911. [1; 10]

Grady, Benjamin Franklin, planter and politician, b. Duplin county, N.C., 1831; d. Clinton, N.C., March 6, 1914. [54]

Grady, Henry Woodfin, orator, b. Athens, Ga., 1851; d. Atlanta, Ga., Dec. 23, 1889. [4; 7; 34]

Graebner, Augustus Lawrence, theologian and historian, b. Frankentrost, Mich., 1849; d. St. Louis, Mo., Dec. 7, 1904. [1; 8; 10; 11]

Grafton, Charles Chapman, bishop, b. Boston, Mass., 1830; d. Fond du Lac, Wis., Aug. 30, 1912. [1; 4; 10;_44]

Graham, Andrew Jackson, teacher of stenography, b. Sandusky, O., 1830; d. Orange, N.J., May 19, 1894. [6]

Graham, Christopher Columbus, philosopher, b. 1784; d. 1884.

Graham, Daniel McBride, clergyman, b. 1817; d. Philadelphia, Pa., 1889.

Graham, David, lawyer, b. London, England, 1808; d. Nice, France, May 27, 1852. [1; 3; 8]

Graham, Edward Kidder, educationist, b. Charlotte, N.C., 1876; d. Chapel Hill, N.C., Oct. 26, 1918. [1; 4; 10]

Graham, Mrs. Emma, née **Jeffers,** journalist, b. Wilton, Ont.; d. Toronto, Ont., Aug. 20, 1922. [27]

Graham, Frank Dunstone, economist, b. Halifax, N.S., 1890; d. Princeton, N.J., Sept. 24, 1949. [10; 14]

Graham, George Washington, physician, b. Hillsboro, N.C., 1847; d. May 8, 1923. [34]

Graham, Mrs. Isabella, née **Marshall,** philanthropist, b. Scotland, 1742; d. New York, N.Y., July 27, 1814. [4]

Graham, John Andrew, lawyer, b. Southbury, Conn., 1764; d. New York, N.Y., Aug. 29, 1841. [1; 3; 6; 8; 43]

Graham, John Hamilton, educationist, b. Overton, Scotland, 1826; d. about 1900. [27]

Graham, Malcolm Kintner, financier, b. 1872; d. Graham, Tex., July 12, 1941.

Graham, Mrs. Margaret, née **Collier,** novelist, b. Van Buren county, Ia., 1850; d. Pasadena, Calif., Jan. 17, 1910. [8; 10; 35]

Graham, Sylvester, reformer, b. West Suffield, Conn., 1794; d. Northampton, Mass., Sept. 11, 1851. [1; 3; 4; 6; 8]

Graham, William Alexander, lawyer, b. Lincoln county, N.C., 1804; d. Saratoga Springs, N.Y., Aug. 11, 1875. [4; 34]

Gramm, Carl H., clergyman, b. Tiflin, O., 1879; d. New Brunswick, N.J., Oct. 7, 1945.

Granbery, John Cowper, bishop, b. Norfolk, Va., 1829; d. Ashland, Va., April 1, 1907. [3; 4; 6; 7; 10; 34]

Grandgent, Charles Hall, educationist, b. Dorchester, Mass., 1862; d. Cambridge, Mass., Sept. 11, 1939. [4; 7; 10; 11]

Granger, Alfred Hoyt, architect, b. Zanesville, O., 1867; d. Roxbury, Conn., Dec. 3, 1939. [10]

Granger, Frank Butler, physician, b. Belmont, Nev., 1875; d. Boston, Mass., Oct. 23, 1928. [10]

Granger, Gideon, lawyer and politician, b. Suffield, Conn., 1767; d. Canandaigua, N.Y., Dec. 31, 1822. [1; 4]

Granger, John Albert, lawyer, b. Canandaigua, N.Y., 1833; d. Canandaigua Lake, N.Y., Oct. 26, 1906. [62]

Granger, Moses Moorhead, jurist, b. Zanesville, O., 1831; d. Zanesville, O., April 29, 1913. [10]

Granger, William Alexander, clergyman, b. Cambridgeshire, England, 1850; d. Mount Vernon, N.Y., Sept. 10, 1922. [10]

Grannan, Charles P., priest, b. 1846; d. Pensacola, Fla., May 19, 1924. [21]

Granniss, Anna Jane, poet, b. Berlin, Conn., 1856; d. Plainville, Conn., July 1, 1947. [7; 10; 11]

Granrud, John Evenson, educationist, b. Norway, 1863; d. Minneapolis, Minn., 1920. [70]

Grant, Albert Weston, naval officer, b. East Benton, Me., 1856; d. Philadelphia, Pa., Sept. 30, 1930. [1; 10]

Grant, Allan (pseud.). See Wilson, James Grant.

Grant, Asahel, physician and missionary, b. Marshall, N.Y., 1807; d. Mosul, Asiatic Turkey, April 24, 1844. [1; 4; 8]

Grant, Douglas (pseud.). See Ostrander, Isabel Egenton.

Grant, Elihu, archaeologist, b. Stevensville, Pa., 1873; d. New York, N.Y., Nov. 2, 1942. [7; 10; 11]

Grant, Mrs. Ethel, née **Watts,** playwright, poet, and novelist, b. New York, N.Y.; d New York, N.Y., May 2, 1940. [10]

Grant, George Barnard, mechanical engineer, b. Farmington, Me., 1849; d. Pasadena, Calif., Aug. 1, 1917. [1; 49; 51]

Grant, George Monro, educationist, b. Albion Mines, N.S., 1835; d. Kingston, Ont., May 10, 1902. [27]

Grant, James Miller, poet and writer of books for children, b. Grantown, Scotland, 1853; d. Toronto, Ont., March, 1940. [11; 27]

Grant, Jesse Root, biographer, b. near St. Louis, Mo., 1858; d. Los Altos, Calif., June 8, 1934. [7; 10]

Grant, Madison, lawyer and zoologist, b. New York, N.Y., 1865; d. New York, N.Y., May 30, 1937. [10; 62]

Grant, Percy Stickney, clergyman and poet, b. Boston, Mass., 1860; d. Mount Kisco, N.Y., Feb. 13, 1927. [1; 4; 7; 10]

Grant, Robert, jurist and novelist, b. Boston, Mass., 1852; d. Boston, Mass., May 19, 1940. [7; 10; 11]

Grant, Ulysses Sherman, geologist, b. Moline, Ill., 1867; d. Evanston, Ill., Sept. 22, 1932. [10; 11; 13]

Grant, Ulysses Simpson, eighteenth president of the United States, b. Point Pleasant, O., 1822; d. near Saratoga, N.Y., July 23, 1885. [1; 2; 3; 4; 5; 6; 7; 8]

Grant, William Lawson, educationist and historian, b. Halifax, N.S., 1872; d. Toronto, Ont., Feb. 3, 1935. [27]

Granville, William Anthony, mathematician, b. White Rock, Minn., 1863; d. Chicago, Ill., Feb. 4, 1943. [11; 62]

Grapho (pseud.). See Adams, James Alonzo.

Grasty, Charles Henry, journalist, b. Fincastle, Va., 1863; d. Pikesville, Md., Jan. 19, 1924. [4; 7; 10]

Grasty, John Sharshall, geologist, b. Versailles, Ky., 1880; d. Charlottesville, Va., June 5, 1930. [10]

Gratacap, Louis Pope, geologist and littérateur, b. Brooklyn, N.Y., 1851; d. West New Brighton, Staten Island, N.Y., Dec. 19, 1917. [3; 8; 10]

Grattan, Lawrence, playwright, b. Concord, N.H., 1870; d. New York, N.Y., Dec. 9, 1941.

Gratz, Simon, collector of autographs, b. 1840; d. Philadelphia, Pa., Aug. 21, 1925. [7]

Grau, Robert, theatrical manager, b. 1858; d. Aug. 9, 1916.

Graustein, William Caspar, mathematician, b. Cambridge, Mass., 1888; d. Cambridge, Mass., Jan. 22, 1941. [10; 11; 51]

Graves, Mrs. Adelia Cleopatra, née Spencer, miscellaneous writer, b. Kingsville, O., 1821; d. Tennessee, 1895. [34]

Graves, Anson Rogers, bishop, b. Rutland county, Vt., 1842; d. La Mesa, Calif., Jan. 1, 1932. [4; 10]

Graves, Charles Alfred, lawyer and educationist, b. Albemarle county, Va., 1850; d. Charlottesville, Va., Nov. 10. 1928. [4; 10]

Graves, Henry Clinton, clergyman, b. Deerfield, Mass., 1830; d. Somerville, Mass., Sept. 14, 1917. [45]

Graves, Jackson Alpheus, pioneer, b. 1852; d. Alhambra, Calif., Feb. 13, 1933. [7; 10]

Graves, James Robinson, clergyman, b. Chester, Vt., 1820; d. Memphis, Tenn., June 26, 1893. [1; 3; 6; 8; 34]

Graves, John Temple, journalist, b. Abbeville county, S.C., 1856; d. Washington, D.C., Aug. 8, 1925. [1; 4; 10; 34]

Graves, Lulu Grace, nutritionist, b. Fairbury, Neb. 1874; d. Berkeley, Calif., July 31, 1949. [10]

Graves, Ralph Henry, journalist, b. Chapel Hill, N.C., 1878; d. New York, N.Y., Dec. 1, 1939. [7; 10; 11]

Graves, Rosewell Hobart, missionary, b. Baltimore, Md., 1833; d. Canton, China, June 3, 1912. [1]

Graves, William Phillips, gynaecologist, b. Andover, Mass., 1870; d. Boston, Mass., Jan. 25, 1933. [1a; 10; 11]

Graves, William Sidney, soldier, b, Mount Calm, Tex., 1865; d. Shrewsbury, N.J., Feb. 27, 1940. [10; 11]

Gray, Albert Zabriskie, clergyman, b. New York, N.Y., 1840; d. Chicago, Ill., Feb. 16, 1889. [3; 6; 8]

Gray, Alexander, electrical engineer, b. Edinburgh, Scotland, 1882; d. Ithaca, N.Y., Oct. 13, 1921. [10]

Gray, Alonzo, educationist, b. Townsend, Vt., 1868; d. Brooklyn, N.Y., March 10, 1860. [3; 6; 43; 45]

Gray, Asa, botanist, b. Oneida county, N.Y., 1810; d. Cambridge, Mass., Jan. 30, 1888. [1; 2; 3; 4; 6; 8]

Gray, Austin Kayingham, librarian, b. Cambridge, England, 1888; d. New York, N.Y., Dec. 4, 1945.

Gray, Barry (pseud.). See Coffin, Robert Barry.

Gray, Carl (pseud.). See Park, Charles Carroll.

Gray, Carolyn Elizabeth, hospital superintendent, b. 1873; d. Miami, Calif., Dec. 29, 1938.

Gray, Charlotte Elvira, religious writer, b. Reading, Mich., 1873; d. Coronado, Calif., Sept. 28, 1926. [10; 11]

Gray, Clifton Daggett, educationist, b. Somerville, Mass., 1874; d. Kennebunk, Me., Feb. 21, 1948. [10; 14; 51]

Gray, David, journalist, b. Edinburgh, Scotland, 1836; d. Binghampton, N.Y., March 18, 1888. [3; 4; 6; 8]

Gray, Edward Dundas McQueen, educationist, b. Lanarkshire, Scotland, 1854; d. Dorking, England, May 21, 1932.

Gray, Elisha, inventor, b. Belmont county, O., 1835; d. near Boston, Mass., Jan. 21, 1901. [1; 3; 4]

Gray Francis Calley, philanthropist, b. Salem, Mass., 1790; d. Boston, Mass., Dec. 29, 1856. [1; 3; 4; 8]

Gray, George Seaman, clergyman, b. New York, N.Y., 1835; d. Cincinnati, O., Aug. 26, 1885. [62]

Gray, George Zabriskie, clergyman, b. New York, N.Y., 1838; d. Sharon Springs, N.Y., Aug. 4, 1889. [3; 4; 6; 8]

Gray, Horatio, clergyman, b. 1828; d. Feb. 11, 1903. [47]

Gray, James, clergyman, b. Ireland, 1770; d. Gettysburg, Pa., Sept. 20, 1824. [3]

Gray, James Martin, clergyman, b. 1851; d. Chicago, Ill.. Sept. 21, 1935. [10]

Gray, John Chipman, lawyer, b. Boston, Mass., 1839; d. Boston, Mass., Feb. 25, 1915. [1; 8; 10; 51]

Gray John Hamilton, politician, b. St. George's, Bermuda, 1814; d. Victoria, B.C., June 5, 1889. [27]

Gray, John Henry, economist, b. Charleston, Ill., 1859; d. near Winter Park, Fla., April 4, 1946. [4; 10]

Gray, Landon Carter, physician, b. 1850; d. New York, N.Y., May 8, 1900. [4]

Gray, Morris lawyer and poet, b. Boston, Mass., 1856; d. Boston, Mass., Jan. 12, 1931. [8; 10; 51]

Gray, Robertson (pseud.). See Raymond, Rossiter Worthington.

Gray, Rosalie (pseud.). See Mann, Mrs. Delos H.

Gray, Thomas, physician and novelist, b. 1803; d. 1849. [51]

Gray, Walter T. (pseud.). See Victor, Mrs. Metta Victoria.

Gray, William Cunningham, journalist, b. Butler county, O., 1830; d. 1901. [10]

Gray, William Henry, historian, b. Fairfield, N.Y., 1810; d. Portland, Ore., 1889. [41]

Graydon, Alexander, soldier and politician, b. Bristol, Pa., 1752; d. Philadelphia, Pa., May 2, 1818. [1; 3; 4; 6; 7; 8]

Graydon, William, lawyer, b. near Bristol, Pa., 1759; d. Harrisburg, Pa., Oct. 13, 1840. [3; 4]

Grayson, Charles Prevost, physician, b. Philadelphia, Pa., 1859; d. Philadelphia, Pa., Aug. 16, 1939. [10]

Grayson, David (pseud.). See Baker, Ray Stannard.

Grayson, E. (pseud.). See Bixby, John Munson.

Grayson, Eldred (pseud.). See Hare, Robert.

Grayson, William John, politician and poet, b. Beaufort, S.C., 1788; d. Newbern, S.C., Oct. 4, 1863. [3; 4; 8; 34]

Greatorex, Henry Wellington, musician, b. Burton-on-Trent, England, 1816; d. Charleston, S.C., Sept. 1858. [3; 4]

Grece, Charles Frederick, agriculturist, b. about 1771; d. Ste. Thérèse de Blainville, Que., March 12, 1844. [27]

Greeley, Horace, journalist, b. Amherst, N.H., 1811; d. Pleasantville, near New York, N.Y., Nov. 29, 1872. [1; 2; 3; 4; 5; 6; 7; 8; 9]

Greely, Adolphus Washington, soldier and explorer, b. Newburyport, Mass., 1844; d. Washington, D.C., Oct. 20, 1935. [1a; 2; 3; 4; 5; 7; 8; 10]

Green, Alexander Little Page, clergyman, b. Sevier county, Tenn., 1806; d. Nashville, Tenn., July 15, 1874. [1; 3; 4; 8; 34]

Green, Anna Katharine, novelist, b. Brooklyn, N.Y., 1846; d. Buffalo, N.Y., April 11, 1935. [1a; 2; 3; 4; 5; 6; 7; 8; 9; 72.

Green, Anson, clergyman, b. Schoharie county, N.Y., 1801; d. Toronto, Ont., Feb. 19, 1879. [27]

Green, Asa, satirist, b. Ashby, Mass., 1789; d. about 1837. [1; 6]

Green, Ashbel, clergyman, b. Hanover, N.J., 1762; d. Philadelphia, Pa., May 19, 1848. [1; 4; 8]

Green, Benjamin Edwards, lawyer, politician, and promoter, b. Elkton, Ky., 1822; d. Dalton, Ga., May 12, 1907. [1; 4]

Green, Beriah, clergyman, b. Preston, Conn., 1795; d. Whitesboro, N.Y., May 4, 1874. [1; 3; 4; 8]

Green, Charles Montraville, obstetrician, b. Medford, Mass., 1850; d. Boston, Mass., Nov. 20, 1928. [10]

Green, Charles Ransley, historian, b. 1845; d. 1915.

Green, Duff, journalist and politician, b. Woodford county, Ky., 1791; d. Dayton, Ga., June 10, 1875. [1; 3; 4; 6; 7; 8; 34]

Green, Elmer S., lawyer and historian, b. Peoria, Ill., 1886; d. Yonkers, N.Y., Jan. 22, 1947.

Green, Fitzhugh, naval officer, b. St. Joseph, Mo., 1888; d. Danbury, Conn., Dec. 2, 1947. [10; 11]

Green, Mrs. Frances Harriet, née Whipple, reformer, b. Smithfield, R.I., 1805; d. Oakland, Calif., June 10, 1878. [1; 7]

Green, Francis, philanthropist, b. Boston, Mass., 1842; d. Medford, Mass., April 21, 1909. [1; 51]

Green, Francis Mathews, naval officer, b. Boston, Mass., 1835; d. Albany, N.Y., Dec. 19, 1902. [1; 3; 8; 10]

Green, Gabriel Marcus, mathematician, b. New York, N.Y., 1891; d. Cambridge, Mass., Jan. 24, 1919. [1; 48]

Green, George Walton, lawyer, b. New York, N.Y., 1854; d. Springfield, Mass., Dec. 13, 1903. [8; 51]

Green, Horace, physician, b. Chittenden, Vt., 1802; d. Sing Sing, N.Y., Nov. 29, 1866. [1; 43]

Green, Horace, journalist and publisher b. New York, N.Y., 1885; d. Great Neck, Long Island, N.Y., Nov. 14, 1943. [7; 10]

Green, Jacob, clergyman, b. Malden, Mass., 1722; d. Morristown, N.J., May 24, 1790. [1; 3]

Green, Jacob, naturalist and chemist, b. Philadelphia, Pa., 1790; d. Philadelphia, Pa., Feb. 1, 1841. [1; 3; 4; 6; 8]

Green, Joseph, poet and satirist, b. Boston, Mass., 1706; d. London, England, Dec. 11, 1780. [1; 3; 4; 7; 8]

Green, Levi Worthington, writer of books for boys, b. 1858; d. Dec. 19, 1932. [11]

Green, Mason Arnold, journalist, b. Dansville, N.Y., 1850; d. Boston, Mass., March 22, 1926. [45]

Green, Nathan, lawyer and educationist, b. Winchester, Tenn., 1827; d. Lebanon, Tenn., Feb. 17, 1919. [8; 10; 51]

Green, Nicholas St. John, lawyer, b. 1830; d. 1876. [4; 51]

Green, Olive (pseud.). See Reed, Myrtle.

Green, Rufus Smith, clergyman, b. Sidney Plains, N.Y., 1848; d. Redlands, Calif., June 3, 1925. [4; 8]

Green, Samuel Abbott, physician and historian, b. Groton, Mass., 1830; d. Boston, Mass., Dec. 5, 1918. [1; 2; 3; 4; 5; 6; 8; 10]

Green, Samuel Bowdlear, horticulturist, b. Chelsea, Mass., 1859; d. Minneapolis, Minn., July 11, 1910. [1; 10; 70]

Green, Samuel Swett, librarian, b. Worcester, Mass., 1837; d. Worcester, Mass., Dec. 8, 1918. [1; 7; 10; 51]

Green, Sanford Moon, lawyer, b. 1807; d. 1901.

Green, Seth, pisciculturist, b. Monroe county, N.Y., 1817; d. Rochester, N.Y., Aug. 20, 1888. [1; 4]

Green, Thomas Edward, clergyman, b. Harrisville, Pa., 1857; d. Jan. 20, 1940. [7; 10; 11]

Green, Thomas Jefferson, soldier, b. Warren county, N.C., 1801; d. Warren county, N.C., Dec. 13, 1863. [3; 34]

Green, Thomas Marshall, journalist and historian, b. near Danville, Ky., 1836; d. Danville, Ky., April, 1904. [34; 74]

Green, William Henry, theologian, b. Groveville, N.J., 1825; d. Princeton, N.J., Feb. 10, 1900. [1; 3; 4; 6; 10]

Green, William Mercer, bishop, b. Wilmington, N.C., 1798; d. Sewanee, Tenn., Feb. 13, 1887. [3; 8; 34]

Green, William Raymond, politician and jurist, b. Colchester, Conn., 1856; d. Bellport, Long Island, N.Y., June 11, 1947. [10]

Greene, Aella, journalist, poet, and novelist, b. Massachusetts, 1838; d. Springfield, Mass., 1903. [8; 10]

Greene, Albert Gorton, lawyer and poet, b. Providence, R.I., 1802; d. Cleveland, O., Jan. 4, 1868. [1; 2; 3; 4; 6; 7; 8; 47]

Greene, Asa. See Green, Asa.

Greene, Belle C. See Greene, Mrs. Isabel Catherine. née Colton.

Greene, Charles Ezra, civil engineer, b. Cambridge, Mass., 1842; d. Ann Arbor, Mich., Oct. 16, 1903. [1; 10]

Greene, Charles Lyman, physician, b. Gray, Me., 1862; d. St. Paul, Minn., Jan. 19, 1929. [10; 70]

Greene, Charles Samuel, librarian, b. Bridgeport, Conn., 1856; d. Oakland, Calif., May 7, 1930. [10; 11; 35]

Greene, Charles Warren, physician and naturalist, b. Belchertown, Mass., 1840; d. Merchantville, N.J., Jan. 3, 1920. [3; 6; 7; 8; 10; 49]

Greene, Clay Meredith, playwright, b. San Francisco, Calif., 1850; d. San Francisco, Calif., Sept. 5, 1933. [10; 35]

Greene, Daniel Howland, physician, b. 1807; d. 1886.

Greene, Dascom, mathematician, b. Richmond, N.Y., 1825; d. 1900. [4]

Greene, David Maxson, engineer, b. Brunswick, N.Y., 1832; d. Troy, N.Y., 1905. [10]

Greene, Edward Lee, botanist, b. Hopkinton, R.I., 1843; d. Washington, D.C., Nov. 10, 1915. [1; 4; 8; 10; 13]

Greene, Evarts Boutell, historian, b. Kobe, Japan, 1870; d. Croton-on-Hudson, N.Y., June 24 ,1947. [7; 10; 11; 51]

Greene, Francis Vinton, soldier and engineer, b. Providence, R.I., 1850; d. New York, N.Y., May 15, 1921. [1; 4; 10]

Greene, George Francis, clergyman, b. North Greenwich, N.Y., 1858; d. Cranford, N.J., Nov. 19, 1926. [10; 56]

Greene, George Washington, historian and biographer, b. East Greenwich, R.I., 1811; d. East Greenwich, R.I., Feb. 2, 1883. [1; 3; 4; 6; 7; 8]

Greene, Harris Ray, clergyman and educationist, b. 1829; d. Aug. 18, 1892. [6; 47]

Greene, Herbert Wilber, musician, b. Holyoke, Mass., 1851; d. Sept. 25, 1924. [10]

Greene, Homer, lawyer, novelist and poet, b. Ariel, Pa., 1853; d. Honesdale, Pa., Nov. 26, 1940. [4; 7; 10]

Greene, Mrs. Isabel Catherine, née Colton, novelist, b. Pittsfield, Vt., 1842; d. ? [8; 10]

Greene, John Priest, educationist, b. Scotland county, Mo., 1849; d. Santa Ana, Calif., March 10, 1933. [10; 11]

Greene, Nathaniel, journalist, politician, and translator, b. Boscawen, N.H., 1797; d. Boston, Mass., Nov. 29, 1877. [1; 3; 4; 8]

Greene, Richard Gleason, clergyman, b. East Haddam, Conn., 1829; d. New York, N.Y., July 7, 1914. [10; 62]

Greene, Richard Henry, lawyer, b. New York, N.Y., 1839; d. New York, N.Y., Feb. 13, 1926. [62]

Greene, Samuel Stillman, educationist, b. Belchertown, Mass., 1810; d. Providence, R.I., Jan. 24, 1883. [1; 3; 4; 6; 8]

Greene, Mrs. Sarah Pratt, née McLean, novelist, b. Simsbury, Conn., 1856; d. Lexington, Mass., Dec. 29, 1935. [7; 10]

Greene, Thomas Lyman, journalist, b. Albany, N.Y., 1851; d. New York, N.Y., 1904. [10]

Greene, Wesley, botanist, b. Yellow Springs, Pa., 1849; d. Cleveland, O., March 28, 1935. [37]

Greene, William Batchelder, soldier and clergyman, b. Haverhill, Mass., 1819; d. Weston-super-Mare, England, May 30, 1878. [3; 6; 8]

Greene, William Batchelder, poet, b. 1851; d. ?

Greene, William Houston, chemist, b. Columbia, Pa., 1853; d. Philadelphia Pa., Aug. 8, 1918. [3; 8; 10]

Greenfield, Abraham Lincoln, radiologist, b. New York, N.Y., 1898; d. Far Rockaway, N.Y., July 25, 1941.

Greenhow, Robert, physician and historian, b. Richmond, Va., 1800; d. San Francisco, Calif., March 27, 1854. [1; 3; 6; 8]

Greenlaw, Edwin Almiron, educationist, b. Flora, Ill., 1874; d. Chapel Hill, N.C., Sept. 11, 1931. [1a; 10]

Greenleaf, Benjamin, educationist, b. Haverhill, Mass., 1786; d Bradford, Mass., Oct. 29, 1864. [1; 3; 4; 6; 8]

Greenleaf, Charles Ravenscroft, medical officer, b. 1838; d. San José, Calif., Sept. 3, 1911. [10]

Greenleaf, Mrs. Georgie H., née Franck, philanthropist, b. Baltimore, Md., 1842; d. Feb. 17, 1913. [10]

Greenleaf, Jeremiah, educationist, b. 1791; d. Guilford, Vt., 1864. [4; 43]

Greenleaf, Jonathan, clergyman, b. Newburyport, Mass., 1785; d. Brooklyn, N.Y., April 24, 1865. [3; 4; 6; 8]

Greenleaf, Lawrence Nichols, poet, b. 1838; d. ?

Greenleaf, Moses, geographer and mapmaker, b. Newburyport, Mass., 1777; d. Williamsburg, Me., March 20, 1834. [1; 3; 8; 38]

Greenleaf, Simon, jurist, b. Newburyport, Mass., 1873; d. Cambridge, Mass., Oct. 6, 1853. [1; 3; 4; 6; 8]

Greenough, Chester Noyes, educationist, b. Wakefield, Mass., 1874; d. Boston, Mass., Feb. 26, 1938. [7; 10; 51]

Greenough, Henry, architect and novelist, b. Boston, Mass., 1807; d. Cambridge, Mass., Oct. 31, 1883. [1; 3; 4; 7; 8]

Greenough, Horatio, sculptor, b. Boston, Mass., 1805; d. Somerville, Mass,. Dec. 18, 1852. [1; 3; 4; 7]

Greenough, James Bradstreet, educationist, b. Portland, Me., 1833; d. Cambridge, Mass., Oct. 11, 1901. [1; 3; 4; 7; 8; 10; 51]

Greenough, James Carruthers, educationist, b. Wendell, Mass., 1829; d. Westfield, Mass., Dec. 5, 1924. [10]

Greenough, Mrs. Sarah Dana, née Loring, novelist and poet, b. Boston, Mass., 1827; d. Franzensbad, Austria, Aug. 9, 1885. [3; 8]

Greenwald, Emanuel, theologian, b. near Frederick, Md., 1811; d. Lancaster, Pa., Dec. 21, 1885. [1; 3; 6; 8]

Greenway, Walter Burton, clergyman, b. Broylesville, Tenn., 1876; d. Stanhope, N.J., Dec. 21, 1940. [10]

Greenwood, Allen, opthalmologist, b. Chelsea, Mass., 1866; d. Miami, Fla., Oct. 23, 1942. [10]

Greenwood, Francis William Pitt, clergyman, b. Boston, Mass., 1797; d. Dorchester, Mass., Aug. 2, 1843. [3; 6; 8]

Greenwood, Grace (pseud.). See Lippincott, Mrs. Sara Jane, née Clarke.

Greenwood, Isaac, mathematician, b. Boston, Mass., 1702; d. Charlestown, Mass., Oct. 22, 1745. [1; 51]

Greenwood, Isaac John, genealogist, b. 1833; d. 1911.

Greenwood, James Mickleborough, educationist, b. near Springfield, Ill., 1837; d. 1914. [3; 4; 8; 10]

Greenwood, William, clergyman and educationist, b. Boston, Mass., 1845; d. Washington, D.C., Feb. 19, 1931. [37; 62]

Greer, David Hummell, bishop, b. Wheeling, W. Va., 1844; d. New York, N.Y., May 19, 1919. [1; 4; 8; 10]

Greer, Hilton Ross, journalist and poet, b. Hawkins, Tenn., 1879; d. Dallas Tex., Nov. 27, 1949. [10; 11]

Greey, Edward, writer on Japan, b. Sandwich, England, 1835; d. New York, N.Y., Oct. 1, 1888. [3; 4; 6; 8]

Gregg, Alexander, bishop, b. Society Hill., S.C., 1819; d. Austin, Tex., July 10, 1893. [3; 4; 6; 8; 34]

Gregg, David, theologian, b. Pittsburg, Pa., 1845; d. Brooklyn, N.Y., Oct. 11, 1919. [8; 10]

Gregg, David McMurtrie, soldier, b. Huntingdon, Pa., 1833; d. Reading, Pa., Aug. 7, 1916. [1; 3; 4; 10]

Gregg, James Edgar, clergyman, b. Hartford, Conn., 1875; d. Pittsfield, Mass., Feb. 23, 1946. [10]

Gregg, Jarvis, educationist, b. 1808; d. 1836.

Gregg, John Robert, teacher of shorthand, b. Rockcorry, Ireland, 1867; d. New York, N.Y., Feb. 24, 1948. [10; 11]

Gregg, Josiah, trader, b. Overton county, Tenn., 1806; d. California, Feb. 25, 1850. [1; 4; 7]

Gregg, Rollin Robinson, physician, b. Palmyra, N.Y., 1828; d. Buffalo, N.Y., Aug. 4, 1886. [2b]

Gregg, William, church historian, b. county Donegal, Ireland, 1817; d. Toronto, Ont., May 26, 1909. [27]

Gregg, Willis Ray, meteorologist, b. Phoenix, N.Y., 1880; d. Takoma Park, Md., Sept. 14, 1938. [10; 11; 13]

Gregg, Wilson, biographer, d. 1899.

Grégoire, Georges Stanislas, physician and poet, b. Ristigouche, Que., 1845; d. Sherbrooke, Que., April 6, 1928. [27]

Gregory, Caspar René, theologian, b. Philadelphia, Pa., 1846; d. France, April 9, 1917. [2; 10]

Gregory, Charles Noble, lawyer and educationist, b. Otsego county, N.Y., 1851; d. Washington, D.C., July 10, 1932. [1a; 10; 11]

Gregory, Cladius Jabez, novelist, b. England, about 1879; d. Burlington, Ont., Oct. 1, 1944. [27]

Gregory, Daniel Seelye, clergyman, b. Carmel, N.Y., 1832; d. East Orange, N.J., April 14, 1915. [1; 3; 4; 7; 8]

Gregory, Edward S., clergyman and poet, b. Lynchburg, Va., 1843; d. 1884. [34]

Gregory, Eliot, painter and essayist, b. New York, N.Y., 1854; d. New York, N.Y., June 1, 1915. [1; 4; 7; 8; 10]

Gregory, Jackson, novelist, b. Salinas, Calif., 1882; d. Los Angeles, Calif., June 12, 1943. [10; 11; 35]

Gregory, John, politician and historian, b. Norwich, Conn., 1810; d. Northfield, Vt., Sept. 26, 1881. [43]

Gregory, John Goadby, journalist, b. 1856; d. Beaver Falls, Pa., April 12, 1947. [7; 44]

Gregory, John Milton, clergyman and educationist, b. Sand Lake, N.Y., 1822; d. Washington, D.C., Oct. 19, 1898. [1; 3; 4; 8; 36]

Gregory, John Uriah, civil servant, b. Troy, N.Y., 1830; d. Quebec, Que., May 30, 1913. [27]

Gregory, Samuel, reformer, b. Guilford, Vt., 1813; d. Boston, Mass., March 23, 1872. [1]

Grenell, Zelotes, clergyman, b. New York, N.Y., 1841; d. La Grange, Ill., April 28, 1918. [10]

Grenfell, Sir Wilfred Thomason, medical missionary, b. near Chester, England, 1865; d. Charlotte, Vt., Oct. 9, 1940. [10; 11]

Greve, Charles Theodore, lawyer, b. Cincinnati, O., 1863; d. Cincinnati, O., Sept. 4, 1930. [4; 10]

Grey, Barton (pseud.). See Sass, George Herbert.

Grey, Jane (pseud.). See Carpenter, Anna May.

Grey, Katharine (pseud.). See Smith, Mrs. Katharine Grey, née Hogg.

Grey, William (pseud.). See White, William Francis.

Grey, Zane, novelist, b. Zanesville, O., 1875; d. Altadena, Calif., Oct. 23, 1939. [7; 10; 11; 35]

Greylock, Godfrey (pseud.). See Smith, Joseph Edward Adams.

Grey Owl, naturalist, b. England, about 1890; d. Prince Albert, Sask., April 13, 1938. [27]

Gridley, Albert Leverett, clergyman, b. 1839; d. 1927.

Gridley, Amos Delos, clergyman, b. Clinton, N.Y., 1819; d. Clinton, N.Y., Oct. 23, 1876. [63]

Gridley, Selah, physician and poet, b. Farmington, Conn., 1767; d. Exeter, N.H., about 1826. [43]

Grier, James Alexander, clergyman, b. Waltz's Mills, Pa., 1846; d. Pittsburgh, Pa., Oct. 6, 1918. [10]

Grierson, Francis, musician and essayist, b. Birkenhead, England, 1848; d. Los Angeles, Calif., May 29, 1927. [1; 7]

Griesbach, William Antrobus, lawyer, soldier, and politician, b. Fort Qu'Appelle, Sask., 1878; d. Edmonton, Alta., Jan. 21, 1945. [27]

Grieve, Lucia Catherine Graeme, classical scholar, b. 1862; d. Asbury Park, N.J., Nov. 26, 1946.

Grieve, Robert, journalist, b. 1855; d. Providence, R.I., Oct. 15, 1924. [47]

Griffin, Appleton Prentiss Clark, librarian, b. Wilton, N.H., 1852; d. Washington, D.C., April 15, 1926. [1; 3a; 7; 10]

Griffin, Edmund Dorr, clergyman, b. Wyoming, Pa., 1804; d. New York, N.Y., Sept. 1, 1830. [3]

Griffin, Edmund Dorr, clergyman, b. East Haddam, Conn., 1770; d. Newark, N.J., Nov. 8, 1837. [1; 3; 4; 8]

Griffin, Eugene, soldier, b. Ellworth, Me., 1855; d. 1907. [4; 10]

Griffin, Frederick, lawyer, b. Montreal, Lower Canada, 1798; d. 1879. [27]

Griffin, Frederick, journalist, b. county Down, Ireland, 1889; d. Toronto, Ont., Jan. 15, 1946. [27]

Griffin, George lawyer, b. East Haddam, Conn., 1778; d. New York, N.Y., May 6, 1860. [3; 6; 8]

Giffin, George Hermon, clergyman, b. New York, N.Y., 1839; d. Springfield, Mass., Sept. 9, 1894. [62]

Griffin, Gilderoy Wells, journalist and consul, b. Louisville, Ky., 1840; d. Louisville, Ky., Oct. 21, 1891. [3; 6; 8; 74]

Griffin, La Roy Freese, clergyman, b. 1844; d. May 24, 1916. [47]

Griffin, Levi Thomas, lawyer and educationist, b. Clinton, N.Y., 1837; d. Detroit, Mich., March 17, 1906. [10; 53]

Griffin, Martin Ignatius Joseph, historian, b. Philadelphia, Pa., 1842; d. Philadelphia, Pa., Nov. 10, 1911. [1a; 10; 21]

Griffin, Nathaniel Edward, educationist, b. Williamstown, Mass., 1873; d. Springfield, Mass., Aug. 25, 1940. [10]

Griffin, Simon Goodell, soldier and politician, b. Nelson, N.H., 1824; d. Keene, N.H., Jan. 14, 1902. [1; 4; 49]

Griffin, Solomon Bulkley, journalist, b. Williamstown, Mass., 1852; d. Springfield, Mass., Dec. 11, 1925. [1; 4; 8; 10]

Griffis, William Elliot, clergyman, b. Philadelphia, Pa., 1843; d. Winter Park, Fla., Feb. 5, 1928. [1; 3; 4; 7; 8; 10; 11]

Griffith, Benjamin, clergyman, b. South Wales, 1688; d. Montgomery county, Pa., about Oct. 5, 1768. [1]

Griffith, Charles Thorpe, soldier, b. 1882; d. Philadelphia, Pa., Sept. 28, 1943.

Griffith, Elmer Cummings, educationist, b. Mount Carroll, Ill., 1869; d. Kalamazoo, Mich., Feb. 21, 1928. [10]

Griffith, Frank Carlos, theatrical manager, b. Dixfield, Me., 1851; d. Middleboro, Mass., May 8, 1939. [10; 11]

Griffith, Grace, educationist, b. Pennsburg, Pa., 1890; d. New Rochelle, N.Y., Dec. 4, 1949.

Griffith, Ira Samuel, educationist, b. 1874; d. 1924.

Griffith, John Price Crozer, pediatrician, b. Philadelphia, Pa., 1856; d. Devon, Pa., July 28, 1941. [10; 55]

Griffith, Robert Eglesfield, physician, b. Philadelphia, Pa., 1798; d. June 26, 1850. [3; 4; 8]

Griffith, Mrs. Susan M., novelist, b. 1851; d. ?

Griffith, Thomas Walters, historian, b. 1767; d. 1838. [34]

Griffith, William, lawyer, b. Boundbrook, N.J., 1766; d. Burlington, N.J., June 27, 1826. [1]

Griffith, William, poet and editor, b. Memphis, Mo., 1876; d. New York, N.Y., April 1, 1936. [7; 10]

Griffiths, Eliza, physician, d. Philadelphia, Pa., July 4, 1847. [55]

Griffiths, John Willis, naval architect, b. New York, N.Y., 1809; d. Brooklyn, N.Y., April 29, 1882. [1; 3; 4; 6; 8]

Griggs, Nathan Kirk, lawyer and poet, b. Frankfort, Ind., 1844; d. Lincoln, Neb., 1910. [10]

Grignon, Wilfrid, physician, b. Terrebonne, Que., 1854; d. Ste. Adèle, Que., June 23, 1915. [27]

Grigsby, Hugh Blair, historian, b. Norfolk, Va., 1806; d. Charlotte county, Va., April 28, 1881. [1; 3; 4; 34]

Grile, Dod (pseud.). See Bierce, Ambrose.

Grimes, James Stanley, philosophist, b. Boston, Mass., 1807; d. Evanston, Ill., Sept. 27, 1903.

Grimes, John Bryan, historian, b. Pitt county, N.C., 1868; d. Raleigh, N.C., Jan. 11, 1923. [10; 54]

Grimké, Angelina Emily, reformer, b. Charleston, S.C., 1805; d. Hyde Park, Mass., Oct. 26, 1879. [1; 4; 7]

Grimké, Archibald Henry, lawyer and publicist, b. near Charleston, S.C., 1849; d. Washington, D.C., Feb. 25, 1930. [1; 4; 7; 8; 10]

Grimké, Frederick, jurist, b. Charleston, S.C., 1791; d. Chillicothe, O., March 8, 1863. [3; 4; 8; 34; 62]

Grimké, John Faucheraud, jurist, b. Charleston, S.C., 1752; d. Charleston, S.C., Aug. 9, 1819. [1; 4; 8; 34]

Grimké, Sarah Moore, reformer, b. Charleston, S.C., 1792; d. Hyde Park, N.Y., Dec. 23, 1873. [1; 3; 4; 6; 8; 34]

Grimshaw, William, lexicographer and editor, b. Greencastle, Ireland, 1782; d. Philadelphia, Pa., 1852. [3; 8]

Gringo, Harry (pseud.). See Wise, Henry Augustus.

Grinnell, Charles Edward, lawyer, b. Baltimore, Md., 1841; d. Boston, Mass., Feb. 2, 1916. [8; 10; 51]

Grinnell, Mrs. Elizabeth, née **Pratt,** naturalist, b. Waldo county, Me., 1851; d. California, July 6, 1935. [10]

Grinnell, George Bird, naturalist, explorer, and historian, b. Brooklyn, N.Y., 1849; d. New York, N.Y., April 11, 1938. [4; 7; 8; 10]

Grinnell, Josiah Bushnell, politician and philanthropist, b. New Haven, Vt., 1821; d. Marshalltown, Ia., March 31, 1891. [1; 3; 4; 6; 8]

Grinnell, Morton, surgeon, b. New York, N.Y., 1855; d. Milford, Conn., Dec. 13, 1905. [10; 62]

Grinnell, William Morton, lawyer, b. New York, N.Y., 1857; d. New York, N.Y., 1906. [10]

Grinstead, Durward, diplomat and novelist, b. 1894; d. Los Angeles, Calif., Oct. 2, 1944.

Griscom, John, educationist, b. Hancock's Bridge, N.J., 1774; d. Burlington, N.J., Feb. 26, 1852. [1; 3; 4; 6; 8]

Griscom, John Hoskins, physician, b. New York, N.Y., 1809; d. New York, N.Y., April 28, 1874. [3; 6; 8]

Grissom, Arthur, poet b. Payson, Ill., 1869; d. New York, N.Y., Dec. 3, 1901. [3b]

Griswold, Alexander Viets, bishop, b. Simsbury, Conn., 1766; d. Boston, Mass., Feb. 15, 1843. [1; 3; 4; 8]

Griswold, Bert Joseph, artist and local historian, b. 1873; d. Fort Wayne, Ind., 1927.

Griswold, Mrs. Florence, née **Young,** poet, b. 1870; d. Hawthorne, N.Y., Aug. 22, 1943.

Griswold, Mrs. Frances Irene, née **Burge,** novelist, b. Wickford, R.I., 1826; d. 1900. [7; 8]

Griswold, Frank Gray, merchant and sportsman, b. New York, N.Y., 1854; d. New York, N.Y., March 30, 1937. [7; 10; 11]

Griswold, Mrs. Hattie, née **Tyng,** poet and literary critic, b. Boston, Mass., 1840; d. 1909. [3; 4; 8; 10]

Griswold, Jeremiah, insurance agent, b. about 1814; d. 1894.

Griswold, Latta, clergyman, b. Lancaster, O., 1876; d. Lenox, Mass., Aug. 16, 1931. [7; 10; 11]

Griswold, Lorenzo, novelist, b. Mystic Bridge, Conn., 1847; d. ? [6]

Griswold, Rufus Wilmot, editor and literary critic, b. Benson, Vt., 1815; d. New York, N.Y., Aug. 27, 1857. [1; 3; 4; 6; 7; 8]

Griswold, Stephen Morrell, clergyman, b. 1835; d. 1916.

Griswold, William McCrillis, bigliographer, b. Bangor, Me., 1853; d. Seal Harbor, Me., Aug. 3, 1899. [1; 4; 7; 8; 38; 51]

Groenings, James, priest, b. 1833; d. 1911. [21]

Groff, George G., physician, b. Chester Valley, Pa., 1851; d. Lewisburg, Pa., Feb. 19, 1910. [4; 10]

Groff, John Eldred, physician, b. 1854; d. ?

Gronlund, Laurence, socialist, b. Denmark, 1846; d. New York, N.Y., Oct. 15, 1899. [1; 4; 8; 10]

Grooch, William Stephen, aviator, b. 1889; d. Mexico, Nov. 13, 1939.

Groome, Harry Connelly, soldier, b. 1860; d. Warrenton, Va., May 20, 1941.

Gros, John Daniel, philosopher, b. Bavaria, 1738; d. Canajoharie, N.Y., May 25, 1812. [1; 3; 8]

Grose, Clyde Leclare, historian, b. Deweyville, O., 1809; d. Evanston, Ill., May 6, 1942. [10; 14]

Grose, Howard Benjamin, clergyman, b. Millerton, N.Y., 1851; d. Waltham, Mass., May 19, 1939. [10]

Grose, William, soldier and politician, b. near Dayton, O., 1812; d. Newcastle, Ind., July 30, 1900. [1]

Grosh, Aaron Burt, clergyman, b. 1803; d. 1884.

Gross, Albert Haller, lawyer, b. Louisville, Ky., 1844; d. Langhorne, Pa., Oct. 28, 1918. [10]

Gross, Charles, historian, b. Troy, N.Y., Feb. 10, 1857; d. Cambridge, Mass., Dec. 3, 1909. [1; 4; 7; 10]

Gross, Christian Channing, diplomat, b. Chicago, Ill., 1895; d. Fort Lauderdale, Fla., March 26, 1933. [10]

Gross, Fred Louis, lawyer, b. Brooklyn, N.Y., 1878; d. Brooklyn, N.Y., Jan. 16, 1947.

Gross, John Daniel. See Gros, John Daniel.

Gross, Samuel David, surgeon, b. near Easton, Pa., 1805; d. Philadelphia, Pa., May 6, 1884. [1; 3; 4; 6; 8; 74]

Gross, Samuel Eberly, playwright, b. Dauphin, Pa., 1843; d. 1913. [4]

Gross, Samuel Weissell, surgeon, b. Cincinnati, O., 1837; d. Philadelphia, Pa., April 16, 1889. [1; 3; 6; 8]

Grossmann, Georg Martin, clergyman, b. Germany, 1823; d. Waverly, Ia., Aug. 24, 1897. [1]

Grossmann, Louis, rabbi, b. Vienna, Austria, 1863; d. Detroit, Mich., Sept. 21, 1926. [1; 4; 10]

Grosvenor, Charles Henry, politician, b. Pomfret, Conn., 1833; d. Athens, O., Oct. 30, 1917. [1; 4; 10]

Grosvenor, Edwin Augustus, educationist, b. Newburyport, Mass., 1845; d. Amherst, Mass., Sept. 15, 1936. [2a; 4; 8; 10; 11]

Grosvenor, William Mason, journalist and publicist, b. Ashfield, Mass., 1835; d. New York, N.Y., July 20, 1900. [1; 4; 6]

Grossmann, Maximilian Paul Eugen, educationist, b. Germany, 1855; d. Plainfield, N.J., Oct. 2, 1922. [10]

Grote, Augustus Radcliffe, entomologist, b. Liverpool, England, 1841; d. Hildesheim, Germany, Sept. 12, 1903. [1; 4; 8]

Grotius (pseud.). See Clinton, De Witt.

Groton, William Mansfield, theologian, b. Waldsboro, Me., 1850; d. Philadelphia, Pa., May 25, 1915. [10]

Grouard, Emile Jean Baptiste, missionary, b. France, 1840; d. Grouard, Alta, March 7, 1931. [27; 32]

Grout, Josiah, soldier and politician, b. Compton, Que., 1841; d. Newport, Vt., July 19, 1925. [10]

Grout, Lewis, missionary, b. Newfane, Vt., 1815; d. West Brattleboro, Vt., March 12, 1905. [10; 62]

Groves, Mrs. **Edith,** née **Leleans,** educationist, b. Cornwall, England; d. Toronto, Ont., Oct. 17, 1931. [27]

Groves, Ernest Rutherford, sociologist, b. Framingham, Mass., 1877; d. Arlington, Mass., Aug. 28, 1946. [2a; 10; 11; 62]

Growoll, Adolf, bibliographer, b. New York, N.Y., 1850; d. New York, N.Y., Dec. 7, 1909. [10]

Grozier, Edwin Atkins, journalist, b. San Francisco, Calif., 1859; d. Cambridge, Mass., May 9, 1924. [4; 10]

Gruber, Levi Franklin, clergyman, b. near Reading, Pa., 1871; d. Chicago, Ill., Dec. 5, 1941. [7; 10; 11]

Gruelle, John Barton, cartoonist, b. 1870; d. Miami Springs, Fla., Jan. 9, 1938. [7]

Grumbine, Ezra Light, physician and poet, b. 1845; d. Lebanon, Pa., Feb. 16, 1923. [55]

Grumbler, Anthony (pseud.). See Hoffman, David.

Grund, Francis Joseph, journalist, b. Bohemia, 1805; d. Philadelphia, Pa., Sept. 29, 1863. [1a; 3; 4; 6; 8]

Grunsky, Carl Ewald, civil engineer, b. San Joaquin county, Calif., 1855; d. San Francisco, Calif., Jan. 9, 1934. [4; 10; 11]

Guay, Charles, priest, b. Lévis, Que., 1845; d. Lévis, Que., Dec. 2, 1922. [27]

Gue, Benjamin F., journalist and historian, b. Greene county, N.Y., 1828; d. Des Moines, Ia., June 1, 1904. [1; 7; 37]

Guerber, Hélène Adeline, educationist, b. Mount Clemens, Mich., 1859; d. Montclair, N.J., June 3, 1929. [8; 10]

Guerlac, Othon Goepp, educationist, b. St. Louis, Mo., 1870; d. Ithaca, N.Y., Jan. 16, 1933. [10]

Guernsey, Alfred Hudson, editor, b. Brandon, Vt., 1818; d. New York, N.Y., Jan. 17, 1902. [3; 4; 6; 7; 8]

Guernsey, Alice Margaret, educationist, b. Rindge, N.H., 1850; d. Sept., 1924. [10]

Guernsey, Clara Florida, writer of books for young people, b. Pittsford, N.Y., 1839; d. ? [4; 6; 8]

Guernsey, Egbert, physician, b. Litchfield, Conn., 1823; d. New York, N.Y., Sept. 19, 1903. [1; 4; 6; 8; 10]

Guernsey, Henry Newell, physician, b. 1817; d. Philadelphia, Pa., 1885. [8]

Guernsey, Lucy Ellen, writer of books for young people, b. Pittsford, N.Y., 1826; d. Rochester, N.Y., Nov. 3, 1899. [4; 6; 7; 8; 10]

Guernsey, Rocellus Sheridan, lawyer, b. Otsego county, N..Y, 1836; d. New York, N.Y., Dec. 9, 1918. [3a; 4; 8; 10]

Guernsey, Samuel James, anthropologist, b. Dover, Me., 1868; d. Arlington, Mass., May 22, 1936. [10]

Guerrant, Edward Owings, clergyman, b. Sharpsburg, Ky., 1838; d. Wilmore, Ky., April 26, 1916. [4; 10]

Guerrier, George Pearce, poet, b. London, England, 1836; d. Boston, Mass., July 13, 1911.

Guest, Moses, poet, fl. 1784-1824.

Guggenheim, William, industrialist, b. Philadelphia, Pa., 1868; d. New York, N.Y., June 28, 1941. [4; 10]

Guild, Calvin, genealogist, b. 1808; d. 1897.

Guild, Mrs. **Caroline Snowden,** née **Whitmarsh,** religious writer, b. Boston, Mass., 1827; d. 1898. [6; 8]

Guild, Courtenay, editor, b. Boston, Mass., 1863; d. Boston, Mass., April 24, 1946. [10; 11; 51]

Guild, Curtis, journalist, b. Boston, Mass., 1827; d. Boston, Mass., March 12, 1911. [1; 3; 4; 7; 8; 10]

Guild, Josephus Conn, lawyer, b. 1802; d. 1883. [34]

Guild, Reuben Aldridge, librarian, b. West Dedham, Mass., 1822; d. Providence, R.I., May 13, 1899. [1; 3; 4; 6; 7; 8; 47]

Guild, Thacher Howland, playwright, b. Providence, R.I., 1879; d. Urbana, Ill., July 21, 1914. [47]

Guilday, Peter Keenan, priest and historian, b. Chester, Pa., 1884; d. Washington, D.C., July 31, 1947. [7; 10; 21]

Guilford, Linda Thayer, educationist, fl. 1848-1899.

Guilford, Nathan, educationist, b. Spencer, Mass., 1786; d. Cincinnati, O., Dec. 18, 1854. [1; 4; 7; 62]

Guilford, Simeon Hayden, dentist, b. Lebanon, Pa., 1841; d. Philadelphia, Pa., Jan. 18, 1919. [10]

Guiney, Louise Imogen, poet, b. Boston, Mass., 1861; d. Chipping Camden, England, Nov. 2, 1920. [1; 4; 7; 10; 72]

Guiterman, Arthur, poet and playwright, b. Vienna, Austria, 1871; d. Pittsburgh, Pa., Jan. 11, 1943. [7; 10; 11]

Gulick, Edward Leeds, clergyman, b. Honululu, Hawaii, 1862; d. Brookline, Mass., April 27, 1931. [10; 49; 68]

Gulick, John Thomas, missionary, b. Kauai, Hawaii, 1832; d. April 16, 1923. [4; 10; 61]

Gulick, Luther Halsey, missionary, b. Honolulu, Hawaii, 1828; d. Springfield, Mass., April 8, 1891. [1]

Gulick, Luther Halsey, educationist, b. Honolulu, Hawaii, 1865; d. at his camp in the Maine woods, Aug. 13, 1918. [1; 7; 10]

Gulick, Sidney Lewis, missionary, b. Marshall Islands, 1860; d. Boise, Ida., Dec. 20, 1945. [7; 11; 49]

Gummere, Mrs. Amelia, née **Mott,** historian, N.J., 1859; d. Haverford, Pa., Oct. 7, 1937. [7; 11]

Gummere, Francis Barton, philologist, b. Burlington, N.J., 1855; d. Haverford, Pa., May 30, 1919. [1; 4; 7; 8; 10]

Gummere, John, educationist, b. Willow Grove, Pa., 1784; d. Burlington, N.J., May 31, 1845. [1; 3; 4; 8]

Gummere, Samuel René, educationist, b. Horsham, Pa., 1789; d. Burlington, N.J., Sept. 13, 1866. [1; 3; 4; 8]

Gunckel, John Elstner, philanthropist and historian, b. Germantown, O., 1846; d. Toledo, O., Aug. 16, 1915. [10]

Gunn, Donald, historian, b. Caithness, Scotland, 1797; d. St. Andrews, Man., Nov. 30, 1878. [27]

Gunn, Otis Berthoude, soldier, b. 1828; d. 1901.

Gunn, Robert Alexander, physician and novelist, b. 1844; d. ?

Gunning, William D., educationist, b. Bloomingburg, O., 1830; d. Greeley, Colo., March 8, 1888. [3b]

Gunnison, Almon, educationist, b. Hallowell, Me., 1844; d. Brooklyn, N.Y., June 30, 1917. [4; 8; 10]

Gunnison, Elisha Norman, poet and journalist, b. 1837; d. 1880. [8]

Gunnison, Herbert Foster, journalist, b. Halifax, N.S., 1858; d. Brooklyn, N.Y., Nov. 25, 1932. [10]

Gunnison, John Williams, soldier, b. New Hampshire, 1812; d. near Sevier Lake, Utah, Oct. 26, 1853. [1; 3; 4; 8]

Gunnison, Lynn (pseud.). See Ames, Joseph Bushnell.

Gunsaulus, Frank Wakeley, clergyman, b. Chesterville, O., 1856; d. Chicago, Ill., March 17, 1921. [1; 3; 4; 7; 8; 10]

Gunter, Archibald Clavering, novelist and playwright, b. Liverpool, England, 1847; d. New York, N.Y., Feb. 24, 1907. [1; 4; 7; 8; 10]

Gunther, Charles Godfrey, geologist, b. 1880; d. Dec. 26, 1929. [48]

Gunton, George, economist, b. Cambridgeshire, England, 1845; d. New York, N.Y., Sept. 11, 1919. [1; 4; 8; 10]

Gurd, Fraser Baillie, surgeon, b. Montreal, Que., 1883; d. Chicago, Ill., Feb. 22, 1948. [30]

Gurd, Norman St. Clair, lawyer, b. Sarnia, Ont., 1870; d. Sarnia, Ont., July 16, 1943. [27; 30]

Gurler, Henry Benjamin, dairy farmer, b. Chesterfield, N.H., 1840; d. April 2, 1928. [10]

Gurley, Ralph Randolph, clergyman, b. Lebanon, Conn., 1797; d. Washington, D.C., July 30, 1872. [1; 3; 4]

Gurowski, Count Adam, Polish exile, b. Kalisz, Poland, 1805; d. Washington, D.C., May 4, 1866. [1a; 4; 7; 8]

Gurteen, Stephen Humphreys Villier, clergyman, b. near Canterbury, England, 1840; d. Jamestown, R.I., Aug. 10, 1908. [4]

Gustafson, Mrs. Zadel, née **Barnes,** journalist, b. Middletown, Conn., 1841; d. 1917. [3; 6; 8; 10]

Guth, William Westley, clergyman, b. Nashville, Tenn., 1871; d. Baltimore, Md., April 19, 1929. [10; 57]

Guthe, Karl Eugen, physicist, b. Hanover, Germany, 1866; d. Ashland, Ore., Sept. 10, 1915. [1; 4; 10]

Gutheim, James Koppel, rabbi, b. Westphalia, Germany, 1815; d. New Orleans, La., July, 1886. [8; 34]

Guthrie, Anna Lorraine, editor, b. York, N.Y.; d. Seattle, Wash., Jan. 2, 1936. [10]

Guthrie, Joseph Edward, biologist, b. York, N.Y., 1871; d. Ames, Ia., April 16, 1935. [10; 11]

Guthrie, Kenneth Sylvan, clergyman, b. Dundee, Scotland, 1871; d. Yonkers, N.Y., April, 1940. [10; 11]

Guthrie, Norman Gregor, poet, b. Guelph, Ont., 1877; d. Ottawa, Ont., Dec. 1, 1929. [27]

Guthrie, Samuel, chemist and physician, b. Brimfield, Mass., 1782; d. Sacketts Harbor, N.Y., Oct. 19, 1848. [1; 4]

Guthrie, William Buck, educationist, b. Sand Spring, Ia., 1869; d. Tuckahoe, N.Y., Nov. 6, 1940. [10]

Guthrie, William Dameron, lawyer, b. San Francisco, Calif., 1859; d. Lattingtown, Long Island, N.Y., Dec. 8, 1935. [1a; 10]

Guyot, Arnold Henry, geographer, b. Switzerland, 1807; d. Princeton, N.J., Feb. 8, 1884. [1; 3; 4; 6; 8]

Gwathmey, James Tayloe, physician, b. Roanoke, Va., 1865; d. Fayetteville, Ark., Feb. 11, 1944. [10]

Gwyn, Mrs. Laura, poet and novelist, b. 1833; d. ? [34; 42]

Gwynne, Erskine, journalist, b. 1899; d. New York, N.Y., May 6, 1948.

Gwynne, Walker, clergyman, b. Strabane, Ireland, 1845; d. Summit, N.J., Feb. 19, 1931. [10]

Gyles, John, soldier, b. about 1678; d. 1755.

H

Haanel, Eugene Emil Felix Richard, geologist, b. Breslau, Germany, 1841; d. Ottawa, Ont., June 26, 1927. [27]

Haardt, Sara. See Mencken, Mrs. Sara Powell, née Haardt.

Haaren, John Henry, educationist, b. 1855; d. 1916.

Haas, Carl de, journalist, b. Germany, 1817; d. Fond du Lac, Wis., 1875. [4]

Haas, John Augustus William, educationist, b. Philadelphia, Pa., 1862; d. Allentown, Pa., July 22, 1937. [4; 10; 11]

Habberton, John, novelist, b. Brooklyn, N.Y., 1842; d. Glen Ridge, N.J., Feb. 24, 1921. [1; 2; 3; 4; 5; 6; 7; 8; 10]

Habersham, Alexander Wylly, naval officer, b. New York, N.Y., 1826; d. Annapolis, Md., March 26, 1883. [1; 4; 34]

Hackett, Frank Warren, lawyer and politician, b. Portsmouth, N.H., 1841; d. Portsmouth, N.H., Aug. 10, 1926. [1; 10; 51]

Hackett, Horatio Balch, theologian, b. Salisbury, Mass., 1808; d. Rochester, N.Y., Nov. 2, 1875. [1; 3; 5; 6]

Hackett, James Dominick, labour expert, b. Kilkenny, Ireland, 1877; d. Flushing, N.Y., Feb. 11, 1936.

Hackett, James Henry, actor, b. New York, N.Y., 1800; d. Jamaica, Long Island, N.Y., Dec. 28, 1871. [1; 3; 4; 7]

Hackett, Walter, playwright, b. 1876; d. New York, N.Y., Jan. 20, 1944. [12]

Hackh, Ingo Waldemar Dagobert, chemist, b. Stuttgart, Germany, 1890; d. San Francisco, Calif., Oct. 19, 1938. [10]

Hackley, Charles William, mathematician, b. Herkimer county, N.Y., 1809; d. New York, N.Y., Jan. 10, 1861. [3]

Hackney, Louise Wallace, lecturer and novelist, b. Chicago, Ill.; d. New York, N.Y., March 27, 1945.

Hadden, James, historian, b. 1845; d. Uniontown, Pa., June, 1923.

Haddock, Charles Brickett, educationist, b. Franklin, N.H., 1796; d. West Lebanon, N.H., Jan. 15, 1861. [1; 3; 4]

Haddock, Frank Channing, lawyer and psychologist, b. Watertown, N.Y., 1853; d. Boston, Mass., Feb. 9, 1915. [10]

Haddock, John A., local historian, b. Jefferson county, N.Y., 1823; d. ?

Hadermann, Jeannette Ritchie. See Walworth, Mrs. Jeannette Ritchie, née Hadermann.

Hadley, Arthur Twining, educationist, b. New Haven, Conn., 1856; d. Kobe, Japan, March 6, 1930. [1; 2; 3; 4; 7; 10; 11; 62]

Hadley, Herbert Spencer, lawyer and politician, b. Olathe, Kans., 1872; d. St. Louis, Mo., Dec. 1, 1927. [4; 10]

Hadley, Hiram, educationist, b. near Wilmington, O., 1833; d. Mesilla Park, N.M., Dec. 3, 1922. [4; 10]

Hadley, James, educationist, b. Fairfield, N.Y., 1821; d. New Haven, Conn., Nov. 14, 1872. [1; 3; 4; 6; 62]

Hadley, John Vestal, jurist, b. Hendricks county, Ind., 1842; d. Danville, Ind., Nov. 17, 1915. [4; 10]

Hadley, Samuel Hopkins, missionary, b. 1842; d. 1906.

Hadra, Berthold Ernest, physician, b. Germany, 1842; d. Dallas, Tex., July 12, 1903.

Haferkorn, Henry Ernest, bibliographer, b. 1859; d. 1933.

Hagan, Horace Henry, lawyer, b. St. Marys, Kans., 1891; d. Tulsa, Okla., Nov. 3, 1936. [10; 11]

Hagan, James, playwright, b. Richmond, Va., about 1887; d. Cincinnatti, O., Sept. 1, 1947.

Hagar, Daniel Barnard, mathematician, b. Middlesex county, Mass., 1820; d. Sharon, Mass., Aug. 4, 1896. [4]

Hagar, George Jotham, editor, b. Newark, N.J., 1847; d. Newark, N.J., June 25, 1921. [10]

Hagboldt, Peter, educationist, b. Germany, 1886; d. Chicago, Ill., Aug. 3, 1943. [14]

Hage, Hyacinth, priest, b. 1851; d. 1900. [21]

Hageman, John Frelinghuysen, lawyer, b. 1816; d. 1892. [8; 56]

Hageman, Samuel Miller, clergyman and poet, b. 1848; d. Brooklyn, N.Y., April 2, 1905. [6; 8]

Hagen, Hermann August, entomologist, b. Königsberg, Prussia, 1817; d. Cambridge, Mass., Nov. 9, 1893. [1; 4; 8]

Hagen, John Cole, poet, fl. 1853-1866.

Hager, Albert David, geologist, b. Chester, Vt., 1817; d. Chicago, Ill., July 29, 1888. [3; 4; 43]

Hager, Levi Lewis, clergyman and poet, d. 1919.

Hagerman, Herbert James, diplomat and politician, b. Milwaukee, Mich., 1871; d. Santa Fé., N.M., Jan. 28, 1935. [10]

Hagert, Henry Schell, lawyer and poet, b. Philadelphia, Pa., 1826; d. Philadelphia, Pa., Dec. 18, 1885. [3]

Haggard, William David, surgeon, b. Nashville, Tenn., 1872; d. Palm Beach, Fla., Jan. 28, 1940. [10]

Haggerty, Melvin Everett, psychologist, b. Bunker Hill, Ind., 1875; d. Minneapolis, Minn., Oct. 6, 1937. [10]

Hagner, Alexander Burton, jurist, b. Washington, D.C., 1826; d. Washington, D.C., June 30, 1915. [10]

Hagood, Johnson, soldier, b. Orangeburg, S.C., 1873; d. Charleston, S.C., Dec. 22, 1948. [10]

Hagood, Lewis Marshall, clergyman, b. 1853; d. 1936.

Hague, Arnold, geologist, b. Boston, Mass., 1840; d. Washington, D.C., May 14, 1917. [4; 10; 62]

Hague, Charles Arthur, civil engineer, b. Newton, Mass., 1849; d. New York, N.Y., June 24, 1911.

Hague, Dyson, clergyman, b. Toronto, Ont., 1857; d. Galt, Ont., May 6, 1935. [27]

Hague, George, banker, b. Rotherham, England, 1825; d. Montreal, Que., Aug. 26, 1915.. [27]

Hague, James Duncan, mining engineer, b. Boston, Mass., 1836; d. Stockbridge, Mass., Aug. 4, 1908. [1; 3; 4; 8; 10]

Hague, John, journalist, b. Rotherham, England, 1829; d. Montreal, Que., Aug. 19, 1906. [27]

Hague, Mrs. Parthenia Antoinette, née Vardaman, writer of reminiscences, b. Harris county, Ga., 1838; d. ? [3; 10; 34]

Hague, William, clergyman, b. Pelham, N.Y., 1808; d. Boston, Mass., Aug. 1, 1887. [3; 4]

Hahn, Benjamin Davies, clergyman, b. Todd township, O., 1859; d. Greenville, S.C., May 5, 1938. [10; 11]

Haight, Canniff, historian, b. Adolphustown, Upper Canada, 1825; d. Toronto, Ont. June 25, 1901. [27]

Hailey, John, historian, b. 1835; d. 1921.

Hailey, Orren Luico, clergyman, b. Fayette county, Tenn., 1852; d. Nashville, Tenn., Feb. 10, 1934. [10]

Hailmann, William Nicholas, educationist, b. Switzerland, 1836; d. Pasadena, Calif., 1920. [3; 7; 10]

Haines, Alanson Austin, clergyman, b. Hamburg, N.J., 1830; d. Hamburg, N.J., Dec. 11, 1891. [3; 6]

Haines, Charles Glidden, lawyer and politician, b. Canterbury, N.H., 1792; d. New York, N.Y., July 3, 1825. [1; 4]

Haines, Charles Grove, political scientist, b. Lineboro, Md., 1879; d. Laguna Beach, Calif., Dec. 27, 1948. [10]

Haines, Elijah Middlebrook, lawyer, b. Oneida county, N.Y., 1822; d. Waukegan, Ill., April 25, 1889. [36]

Haines, Elwood Lindsay, bishop, b. Philadelphia, Pa., 1893; d. Los Angeles,, Calif., Oct. 28, 1949. [10]

Haines, Henry Stevens, lawyer, b. 1836; b. Lenox, Mass., Nov. 3, 1923. [2a]

Haines, Lynn, journalist, b. Waseca, Minn., 1876; d. Washington, D.C., Oct. 9, 1929. [1]

Haines, Walter Stanley, toxicologist, b. Chicago, Ill., 1850; d. Chicago, Ill., Jan. 27, 1923. [10]

Hains, Thornton Jenkins, sailor and novelist, b. Washington, D.C., 1866; d. ? [8; 10]

Halbert, Henry Sale, historian, b. Pickens county, Ala., 1837; d. Montgomery, Ala., May 9, 1916. [10; 34]

Halbert, Homer Valmore, physician, b. Otsego, N.Y., 1858; d. Chicago, Ill., May 29, 1927. [10; 61]

Haldeman, Isaac Massey, clergyman, b. Concordville, Pa., 1845; d. New York, N.Y., Sept. 27, 1933. [10]

Haldeman, Samuel Stehman, naturalist, b. Locust Grove, Pa., 1812; d. Chickies, Pa., Sept. 10, 1880. [1; 3; 4; 6; 7; 8]

Hale, Albert Barlow, physician and educationist, b. Jonesville, Mich., 1860; d. San Juan, Porto Rico, April 30, 1929. [10]

Hale, Anne Gardner, poet and novelist, b. Newburyport, Mass., 1823; d. Newburyport, Mass., Nov. 1914. [8; 10]

Hale, Mrs. Annie Riley, miscellaneous writer, b. 1859; d. Altadena, Calif., Dec. 26, 1944.

Hale, Benjamin, educationist, b. Newburyport, Mass., 1797; d. Newburyport, Mass., July 15, 1863. [1; 3; 4;]

Hale, Charles, journalist, b. Boston, Mass., 1831; d. Boston, Mass., March 1, 1882. [1; 3]

Hale, Charles Reuben, bishop, b. Lewiston, Pa., 1837; d. Cairo, Ill., Dec. 25, 1900. [1; 4; 10]

Hale, Edward, clergyman, b. Northampton, Mass., 1858; d. Chestnut Hill, Mass., March 27, 1918. [51]

Hale, Edward Everett, clergyman, b. Boston, Mass., 1822; d. Boston, Mass., June 10, 1909. [1; 2; 3; 4; 5; 6; 7; 8; 9; 10]

Hale, Edward Everett, educationist, b. Boston, Mass., 1863; d. Schenectady, N.Y., Aug. 19, 1932. [7; 10; 51]

Hale, Edwin Moses, physician, b. Newport, N.H., 1829; d. Chicago, Ill., Jan. 15, 1899. [1; 4; 6]

Hale, Enoch, physician, b. Westhampton, Mass., 1790; d. Boston, Mass., Nov. 12, 1848. [1; 4; 51]

Hale, Franklin Darius, poet, b. Barnet, Vt., 1854; d. Lyndon Center, Vt., April 21, 1940. [10]

Hale, George Ellery, astronomer, b. Chicago, Ill., 1868; d. Pasadena, Calif., Feb. 21, 1938. [10; 11]

Hale, Harris Grafton, clergyman, b. Salem, Mass., 1865; d. Marblehead, Mass., Oct. 7, 1945. [51]

Hale, Horatio, ethnologist, b. Newport, N.H., 1817; d. Clinton, Ont., Dec. 28, 1896. [1; 3; 27]

Hale, John, clergyman, b. Charlestown, Mass., 1636; d. Beverly, Mass., May 15, 1700. [51]

Hale, John Peter, historian, b. 1824; d. 1902.

Hale, Mrs. Louise, née Closser, actress and novelist, b. Chicago, Ill., 1872; d. Hollywood, Calif., July 26, 1933. [1a; 7; 10]

Hale, Lucretia Peabody, writer of books for young people, b. Boston, Mass., 1820; d. Boston, Mass., June 12, 1900. [1; 3; 4; 6;. 7; 10]

Hale, Mary Whitwell, poet, b. 1810; d. 1862.

Hale, Nathan, journalist, b. Westhampton, Mass., 1784; d. Brookline, Mass., Feb. 9, 1863. [1; 3; 4; 61]

Hale, Philip, music critic, b. Norwich, Vt., 1854; d. Boston, Mass., Nov. 30, 1934. [1a; 10; 20; 62]

Hale, Philip Leslie, artist, b. Boston, Mass., 1865; d. Boston, Mass., Feb. 2, 1931. [1; 10]

Hale, Philip Thomas, clergyman, b. New Market, Ala., 1857; d. Louisville, Ky., Dec. 23, 1926. [10; 34]

Hale, Richard Walden, lawyer, b. Milton, Mass., 1871; d. Dover, Mass., March 5, 1943. [51]

Hale, Robert Beverly, poet, b. Milton, Mass., 1869; d. Roxbury, Mass., Oct. 6, 1895. [8; 51]

Hale, Salma, historian, b. Cheshire county, N.H., 1787; d. Somerville, Mass., Nov. 19, 1866. [3; 4]

Hale, Mrs. Sarah Josepha, née Buell, poet, novelist, and editor, b. Newport, N.H., 1788; d. Philadelphia, Pa., April 30, 1879. [1; 3; 4; 6; 7; 8]

Hale, Susan, artist, b. Boston, Mass., 1833; d. Matunuck, R.I., Sept 3, 1910. [6; 8; 10]

Hale, Walter, artist, b. Chicago, Ill., 1869; d. New York, N.Y., Dec. 4, 1917. [10]

Hale, William, physician, b. 1856; d. Wakefield, R.I., March 30, 1938. [47]

Hale, William Bayard, journalist, b. Richmond, Ind., 1869; d. Munich, Germany, April 10, 1924. [1; 4; 10]

Hale, William Benjamin, lawyer, b. St. Louis, Mo., 1871; d. Brooklyn, N.Y., March, 1924. [10]

Hale, William Gardner, educationist, b. Savannah, Ga., 1849; d. Shippan Point, Conn., June 23, 1928. [1; 4; 10]

Hale, William Thomas, journalist, b. Liberty, Tenn., 1857; d. Nashville, Tenn., July 12, 1926. [3a; 7; 8; 10; 34]

Hales, Benjamin Jones, naturalist, b. 1868; d. Brandon, Man., Dec. 23, 1945.

Haley, Jesse James, clergyman, b. Rockcastle county, Ky., 1851; d. Haines City, Fla., April 8, 1924. [10]

Haley, Thomas Preston, clergyman, b. near Lexington, Mo., 1832; d. Kansas City, Mo., 1913. [4]

Haley, William D'Arcy, clergyman, b. 1828; d. 1890.

Haliburton, Robert Grant, lawyer, b. Windsor, N.S., 1831; d. Pass Christian, Mo., March 7, 1901. [27]

Haliburton, Thomas Chandler, jurist and humorist, b. Windsor, N.S., 1796; d. Islesworth, England, Aug. 27, 1865. [4; 27]

Halkett, Mrs. Sarah Phelps Stokes, writer of verse for children, b. 1869; d. Washington, D.C., Feb. 7, 1943.

Hall, Abraham Okey, lawyer and politician, b. Albany, N.Y., 1826; d. New York, N.Y., Oct. 7, 1898. [1; 3a; 4; 6; 7]

Hall, Alexander Wilford, evangelist, b. Bath, N.Y., 1819; d. 1902. [4; 8; 10]

Hall, Alfred Bates, educationist, b. Plainville, Conn., 1875; d. Lakeville, Conn., Jan. 3, 1936. [62]

Hall, Arethusa, educationist, b. Huntington, Mass., 1802; d. Northampton, Mass., May 24, 1891. [1; 3; 4; 6; 7]

Hall, Arnold Bennett, political scientist, b. Franklin, Ind., 1881; d. Washington, D.C., June 1, 1936. [10; 11]

Hall, Arthur Cleveland, educationist, b. New York, N.Y., 1865; d. Gambier, O., 1910. [10]

Hall, Arthur Crawshay Alliston, bishop, b. Berkshire, England, 1847; d. Burlington, Vt., Feb. 26, 1930. [10]

Hall, Arthur Dudley, actor, novelist, and journalist, b. Concord, Mass., 1852; d. New York, N.Y., Nov. 22, 1912. [51]

Hall, Arthur Graham, mathematician, b. Memphis, Mich., 1865; d. Ann Arbor, Mich., Jan. 10, 1925. [10]

Hall, Asaph, astronomer, b. Goshen, Conn., 1829; d. Annapolis, Md., Nov. 22, 1907. [4; 10]

Hall, Baynard Rush, clergyman and educationist, b. Philadelphia, Pa., 1798; d. Brooklyn, N.Y., Jan. 23, 1863. [1; 3; 4; 7]

Hall, Benjamin Franklin, jurist, b. Whitehall, N.Y., 1814; d. Auburn, N.Y., Sept. 6, 1891. [3; 4; 8]

Hall, Benjamin Homer, lawyer, b. Troy, N.Y., 1830; d. Troy, N.Y., April 6, 1893. [3; 43; 51]

Hall, Bert. See Hall, Weston B.

Hall, Bolton, lawyer, b. Ireland, 1854: d. Thomasville, Ga., Dec. 10, 1938. [10; 11]

Hall, Charles Cuthbert, clergyman, b. New York, N.Y., 1852; d. New York, N.Y., March 25, 1908. [1; 4; 10]

Hall, Charles Francis, explorer, b. Rochester, N.H., 1821; d. Arctic Circle, Nov. 8, 1871. [1; 3; 4; 7]

Hall, Charles Gilbert, writer of books for children, b. Amelia, O., 1866; d. New York, N.Y., Nov. 4, 1947.

Hall, Charles Henry, clergyman, b. Augusta, Ga., 1820; d. Brooklyn, N.Y., Sept. 12, 1895. [1; 3; 4; 6; 62]

Hall, Charles Mercer, clergyman, b. New York, N.Y., 1864; d. Bridgeport, Conn., Nov. 28, 1929. [10; 11]

Hall, Charles Roswell, lawyer, b. 1853; d. 1931.

Hall, Charles Samuel, lawyer, b. Middletown, Conn., 1827; d. Binghampton, N.Y., March 15 ,1910. [62]

Hall, Charles Winslow, writer of books for boys, b. Chelsea, Mass., 1843; d. 1916. [6; 8; 10; 51]

Hall, Christopher Webber, geologist, b. Wardsboro, Vt., 1845; d. Minneapolis, Minn., May 10, 1911. [4; 8; 10; 70]

Hall, Clayton Colman, historian, b. 1847; d. Baltimore, Md., 1916.

Hall, Clifton Rumery, educationist, b. Danvers, Mass., 1884; d. Princeton, N.J., April 19, 1945.

Hall, Edward Brooks, clergyman, b. Medford, Mass., 1800; d. Providence, R.I., March 3, 1866. [3; 4]

Hall, Edward Hagaman, journalist, b. Auburn, N.Y., 1858; d. Laramie, Wyo., May 4, 1936. [10]

Hall, Edward Henry, clergyman, b. Cincinnati, O., 1831; d. Cambridge, Mass., 1912. [10; 51]

Hall, Edward Winslow, educationist, b. 1840; d. 1910. [38]

Hall, Edwin, clergyman, b. Granville, N.Y., 1802; d. Auburn, N.Y., Sept. 8, 1877. [3]

Hall, Edwin Herbert, physicist, b. Gorham, Me., 1855; d. Cambridge, Mass., Nov. 20, 1938. [10]

Hall, Eliza Calvert (pseud.). See Obenchain, Mrs. Eliza Caroline, née Calvert.

Hall, Eugene J., poet, b. 1845; d. ? [6]

Hall, Fanny W., traveller, b. Grafton, Vt., about 1796; d. ? [43]

Hall, Fitzedward, philologist, b. Troy, N.H., 1825; d. Marlesford, England, Feb. 1, 1901. [1; 4; 7]

Hall, Mrs. Florence Marion, née Howe, miscellaneous writer, b. Boston, Mass., 1845; d. High Bridge, N.J., April 10, 1922. [1; 4; 7; 8; 10]

Hall, Francis Joseph, theologian, b. Ashtabula, O., 1857; d. Baldwinsville, N.Y., March 12, 1932. [10; 11]

Hall, Frank, historian, b. 1836; d. 1918.

Hall, Frank Oliver, clergyman, b. New Haven, Conn., 1860; d. New York, N.Y., Oct. 18, 1941. [10; 11]

Hall, Frederic, lawyer, b. 1825; d. 1898.

Hall, Frederic Aldin, educationist, b. Brunswick, Me., 1854; d. St. Louis, Mo., March 24, 1925. [4; 10]

Hall, Frederick, educationist, b. Grafton, Vt., 1780; d. Peru, Ill., July 27, 1843. [3; 8]

Hall, Granville Stanley, psychologist, b. Ashfield, Mass., 1844; d. Worcester, Mass., April 24, 1924. [1; 4; 7; 10; 13]

Hall, Guillermo Franklin, educationist, b. Grand Rapids, Mich., 1866; d. Boston, Mass., June 1, 1940. [14]

Hall, Harlan Page, journalist, b. Ravenna, O., 1838; d. St. Paul, Minn., April 9, 1907. [70]

Hall, Harrison, scientist, b. Cecil county, Md., 1785; d. Cincinnati, O., March 9. 1866. [3]

Hall, Harvey Monroe, botanist, b. Lee county, Ill., 1874; d. Berkeley, Calif., 1932. [10; 13]

Hall, Hazel, poet, b. St. Paul, Minn., 1886; d. Portland, Ore. May 11, 1924. [1; 7; 41]

Hall, Henry, lawyer, b. Rutland, Vt., 1814; d. Rutland, Vt., April 3, 1889. [43]

Hall, Henry, journalist b. Auburn, N.Y., 1845; d. Bronxville, N.Y., Feb. 6, 1920. [10]

Hall, Herbert James, physician, b. Manchester, N.H., 1870; d. Marblehead, Mass., Feb. 19, 1923. [4; 10]

Hall, Hiland, historian, b. Bennington, Vt., 1795; d. Springfield, Mass., Dec. 18, 1885. [1; 3; 4; 7; 43]

Hall, Holworthy (pseud.). See Porter, Harold Everett.

Hall, Howard, playwright and novelist, d. 1921. [7]

Hall, Isaac Freeman, educationist, b. Dennis, Mass., 1847; d. North Adams, Mass.. May 27, 1928. [49]

Hall, Isaac Hollister, orientalist, b. Norwalk, Conn., 1837; d. New York, N.Y., July 2, 1896. [1; 4]

Hall, James, clergyman, b. Carlisle, Pa., 1744; d. Bethany, N.C., July 25, 1826. [1; 3; 4; 34]

Hall, James, soldier, jurist, and banker, b. Philadelphia, Pa., 1793; d. near Cincinnati, O., July 5, 1868. [1; 3; 4; 6; 7; 8]

Hall, James, geologist, b. Hingham, Mass., 1811; d. Echo Hill, N.H., Aug. 7, 1898. [3; 4; 6; 8]

Hall, James, artist, b. Boston, Mass., 1869; d. North Scituate, Mass., Feb. 14, 1917. [10]

Hall, James Parker, lawyer, b. Frewsburg, N.Y., 1871; d. Chicago, Ill., March 13, 1928. [10]

Hall, Jennie, educationist, b. Grand Rapids,, Mich., 1875; d. Chicago, Ill., June 12, 1921. [10]

Hall, John, educationist, b. 1783; d. 1847.

Hall, John, clergyman, b. Philadelphia, Pa., 1806; d. Trenton, N.J., May 10, 1894. [3; 8]

Hall, John, clergyman, b. county Armagh, Ireland, 1829; d. Bangor, county Down, Ireland, Sept. 17, 1898. [1; 3; 4; 6; 8]

Hall, John Elihu, lawyer, b. Philadelphia, Pa., 1783; d. Philadelphia, Pa., June 12, 1829. [1; 3; 4; 6; 7]

Hall, John Lesslie, educationist, b. Richmond, Vt., 1856; d. Williamsburg, Va., Feb. 23, 1928. [10; 34]

Hall, Josiah Newhall, physician, b. North Chelsea, Mass., 1859; d. Denver, Colo., Dec. 17, 1939. [10; 11]

Hall, Mrs. Louisa Jane, née Park, poet, b, Newburyport, Mass., 1802; d. Cambridge, Mass., Sept. 8, 1892. [3; 4; 6; 7; 8]

Hall, Lyman, mathematician, b. Americus, Ga., 1859; d. Atlanta, Ga., 1905. [10]

Hall, Maurice Crowther, biologist, b. Golden, Colo., 1881; d. Chevy Chase, D.C., 1938. [10]

Hall, Newton Marshall, clergyman, b. Manchester, N.H., 1865; d. Springfield, Mass., Jan. 25, 1926. [10]

Hall, Prescott Farnsworth, lawyer, b. Boston, Mass., 1868; d. Brookline, Mass., May 28, 1921. [10; 51]

Hall, Randall Cooke, theologian, b. Wallingford, Conn., 1842; d. New York, N.Y., July 27, 1921. [10]

Hall, Robert Pleasants, lawyer and poet, b. Chester district, S.C., 1825; d. Macon, Ga., Dec. 4, 1854. [3; 34]

Hall, Ruth, novelist, b. Schoharie, N.Y., 1858; d. Catskill, N.Y., Nov. 2, 1934. [7; 8; 10; 11]

Hall Samuel Read, educationist, b. Croydon, N.H., 1795; d. Bennington, Vt., June 24, 1877. [1; 3; 4; 43]

Hall, Mrs. **Sarah,** née **Ewing,** religious writer, b. Philadelphia, Pa., 1761; d. Philadelphia, Pa., April 8, 1830. [1; 3; 4; 7]

Hall, Theodore Parsons, genealogist, b. 1835; d. Detroit, Mich., 1909.

Hall, Thomas Bartlett, lawyer, b. Springfield, Mass., 1824; d. Boston, Mass., 1903. [10; 51]

Hall, Thomas Cuming, theologian, b. county Armagh, Ireland, 1858; d. Goettingen, Germany, May 27, 1936. [3; 10; 11; 68]

Hall, Thomas Proctor, physician, b. Hornby, Ont., 1858; d. Vancouver, B.C., March 25, 1931. [8; 10]

Hall, Thomas Winthrop, poet and novelist, b. Ogdensburg, N.Y., 1862; d. Hannibal, Mo., Aug. 21, 1900. [8; 10]

Hall, Walter Henry, musician, b. London, England, 1862; d. New York, N.Y., Dec. 11, 1935. [10; 20]

Hall, Weston B., aviator, b. 1886; d. Fremont, O., Dec. 6, 1948.

Hall, William Shafer, mathematician, b. Chester, Pa., 1861; d. Easton, Pa., Dec. 17, 1948. [10; 13]

Hall, William Whitty, physician, b. Paris, Ky., 1810; d. New York, N.Y., May 10, 1876. [1; 3; 4; 6; 34]

Hall, Winfield Scott, physician, b. Batavia, Ill., 1861; d. near Chicago, Ill., Oct. 2, 1942. [4; 10; 11]

Hallam, Douglas, aviator and novelist, d. Toronto, Ont., Dec. 14, 1948. [30]

Hallam, Mrs. **Julia Kirkland,** née **Clark,** feminist, b. Portage, Wiss., 1860; d. Aug. 10, 1927. [8; 10]

Halleck, Fitz-Greene, poet, b. Guilford, Conn., 1790; d. Guilford, Conn., Nov. 19, 1867. [1; 3; 4; 6; 7; 8; 72]

Halleck, Henry Wager, soldier, lawyer, and capitalist, b. Oneida county, N.Y., 1815; d. Louisville, Ky., Jan. 9, 1872. [1; 3; 4; 6]

Halleck, Reuben Post, educationist, b. Rocky Point, N.Y., 1859; d. Louisville, Ky., Dec. 24, 1936. [7; 10; 11; 34; 62]

Hallett, Benjamin Franklin, journalist and politician, b. Osterville, Mass., 1797; d. Boston, Mass., Sept. 30, 1862. [1; 3; 4]

Halliburton, Sir **Brenton,** jurist, b. Rhode Island, 1775; d. near Halifax, N.S., July 15, 1860. [27]

Halliburton, Richard, traveller, b. Brownsville, Tenn., 1900; d. Pacific Ocean, about March 21, 1939. [2a; 7; 10; 11]

Halliday, Samuel Byram, clergyman, b. Morristown, N.J., 1812; d. Orange, N.J., July 9, 1897. [3b; 8]

Hallimond, John Greener, missionary, b. 1852; d. Belmar, N.J., Nov. 21, 1924.

Hallner, Andrew, clergyman, b. 1846; d. Turlock, Calif., July 31, 1930.

Hallock, Charles, journalist and sportsman, b. New York, N.Y., 1834; d. Washington, D.C., Dec. 2, 1917. [1; 3a; 4; 7; 10; 70]

Hallock, Mrs. **Ella,** née **Boldry,** educationist, b. Jonesville, N.Y., 1861; d. Southold, N.Y., Aug. 18, 1934.

Hallock, Joseph Newton, clergyman and journalist, b. Franklinville, N.Y., 1832; d. Brooklyn, N.Y., March 24, 1913. [4; 10; 62]

Hallock, Leavitt Homan, clergyman, b. Plainfield, Mass., 1842; d. Portland, Me., Sept. 23, 1921. [45]

Hallock, Mrs. **Mary Angeline,** née **Ray,** writer of books for children, b. Rowe, Franklin county, Mass., 1810; d. ? [3; 6; 8]

Hallock, Robert Crawford, clergyman, b. Holliday's Cove, W. Va., 1857; d. Valatie, N.Y., June 24, 1932. [10]

Hallock, William, physicist, b. Milton, N.Y., 1857; d. New York, N.Y., May 20, 1913. [10]

Hallock, Willam Allen, journalist, b. Plainfield, Mass., 1794; d. New York, N.Y., Oct. 2, 1880. [1; 3; 4; 6]

Hallowell, Mrs. **Anna,** née **Davis,** biographer, b. Philadelphia, Pa., 1838; d. ? [7; 8; 10]

Hallowell, Benjamin, educationist, b. Montgomery county, Pa., 1799; d. Sandy Spring, Md., Sept. 7, 1877. [1; 4]

Hallowell, Richard Price, Quaker historian, b. Philadelphia, Pa., 1835; d. West Medford, Mass., Jan. 5, 1905. [1; 3; 4; 6]

Hallowell, Mrs. **Sara Catherine,** née **Fraley,** journalist, b. Philadelphia, Pa., 1833; d. ? [8; 10]

Hallum, John, lawyer, b. 1833; d. ? [8; 34]

Halpin, Patrick Albert, priest, b. 1847; d. 1920. [21]

Halpine, Charles Grahame, poet, soldier, and journalist, b. county Meath, Ireland, 1829; d. New York, N.Y., Aug. 3, 1868. [1; 3; 4; 6; 7; 71]

Halsey, Charles Storrs, educationist, b. 1834; d. San Diego, Calif., Dec. 18, 1933. [4; 61]

Halsey, Edmund Drake, historian, b. 1840; d. 1896. [4; 56]

Halsey, Francis Whiting, journalist, b. Unadilla, N.Y., 1851; d. New York, N.Y., Nov. 24, 1919. [4; 7; 8; 10]

Halsey, Frank Davis, editor, b. Elizabeth, N.J., 1891; d. Princeton, N.J., April 8, 1941. [7; 56]

Halsey, Frederick Arthur, engineer, b. Unadilla, N.Y., 1856; d. New York, N.Y., Oct. 20, 1935. [1a; 8; 10]

Halsey, Harlan Page, novelist, b. New York, N.Y., 1837; d. Brooklyn, N.Y., Dec. 16, 1898. [3b; 4; 8]

Halsey, Leroy Jones, clergyman, b. Goochland county, Va., 1812; d. Chicago, Ill., June 18, 1896. [3; 4; 6; 8]

Halsey, Lewis, clergyman, b. Trumansburg, N.Y., 1843; d. Wyoming, O., Dec. 25, 1914. [67]

Halsey, Rena Isabella, writer of books for girls, b. New York, N.Y., 1860; d. New York, N.Y., Oct. 24, 1932. [10; 11]

Halsey, Richard Townley Haines, art. critic and antiquary, b. Elizabeth, N.J., 1865; d. New Haven, Conn., Feb. 7, 1942. [10; 56]

Halsey, William Donaldson, banker, b. 1860; d. Bridgehampton, N.Y., April 28, 1939.

Halstead, Ada L. (pseud.). See Newhall, Mrs. Laura Eugenia.

Halstead, Murat, journalist, b. Butler county, O., 1829; d. Cincinnati, O., July 2, 1908. [1; 4; 7; 8; 10]

Halstead, Oliver Spencer, lawyer, b. Elizabeth, N.J., 1792; d. Lyons Farms, N.J., Aug. 29, 1877. [3; 4; 6]

Halstead, William Riley, clergyman, b. Vigo county, Ind., 1848; d. Terre Haute, Ind., Dec. 19, 1931. [10; 11]

Halsted, Byron David, botanist, b. Venice, N.Y., 1852; d. Terre Haute, Ind., Aug. 28, 1919. [3; 4; 10]

Halsted, George Bruce, mathematician, b. Newark, N.J., 1853; d. New York, N.Y., March 16, 1922. [1; 3; 4; 10]

Halsted, William Stewart, surgeon, b. New York, N.Y., 1852; d. Baltimore, Md., Sept. 7, 1922. [1; 4; 10; 62]

Ham, Charles Henry, lawyer, b. Canterbury, N.H., 1831; d. Paterson, N.J., Oct. 16, 1902. [3b]

Ham, George Henry, journalist, b. Trenton, Ont., 1847; d. Montreal, Que., April 16, 1926. [27]

Hambidge, Jay, artist, b. Simcoe, Ont., 1867; d. New York, N.Y., Jan. 20, 1924. [1]

Hamblen, Herbert Elliott, novelist, b. Ossippee, N.H., 1849; d. ? [7; 8; 10]

Hamby, William Henry, journalist and novelist, b. Wright county, Mo., 1875; d. San Diego, Calif., Jan. 25, 1928. [10]

Hamel, Thomas Etienne, priest, b. Quebec, Lower Canada, 1830; d. Quebec, Que., July 16, 1913. [27]

Hamersley, James Hooker, poet, b. New York, N.Y., 1844; d. Garrisons-on-Hudson, N.Y., Sept. 14, 1901. [4; 8; 10]

Hamersley, Lewis Randolph, naval officer, b. 1847; d. 1910. [6; 8]

Hamersley, William, jurist, b. Hartford, Conn., 1835; d. Hartford, Conn., Sept. 17, 1920. [4; 10]

Hamill, Howard Melanchthon, clergyman, b. Lowndesboro, Ala., 1849; d. Tate Springs, Tenn., Jan. 22, 1915. [4; 10; 34]

Hamilton, Alexander, physician, b. Edinburgh, Scotland, 1712; d. Annapolis, Md., May 11, 1756. [1]

Hamilton, Alexander, politician, b. Nevis, Leeward Islands, 1757; d. New York, N.Y., July 12, 1804. [1; 2; 3; 4; 5; 6; 7; 8]

Hamilton, Alexander, soldier and poet, b. New York, N.Y., 1815; d. Tarrytown, N.Y., Dec. 10, 1907. [10]

Hamilton, Alice King, novelist, fl. 1881-1889. [6; 8]

Hamilton, Allan McLane, physician and biographer, b. Brooklyn, N.Y., 1848; d. Great Barrington, Mass., Nov. 23, 1919. [1; 4; 10]

Hamilton, Betsy (pseud) See Moore, Mrs. Idora, née McClellan.

Hamilton, Charles Frederick, journalist, b. Roslin, Ont., 1869; d. Ottawa, Ont., Dec. 4, 1933. [27]

Hamilton, Clarence Grant, musician, b. Providence, R.I., 1865; d. Wellesley, Mass., Feb. 14, 1935. [10; 11; 20]

Hamilton, Clayton, playwright and drama critic, b. Brooklyn, N.Y., 1881; d. New York, N.Y., Sept. 17, 1946. [4; 10; 11; 12]

Hamilton, David Henry, clergyman, b. Canajoharie, N.Y., 1813; d. Kingsboro, N.J., July 4, 1879. [63]

Hamilton, Edward John, clergyman and philosopher, b. Belfast, Ireland, 1834; d. Buffalo, N.Y., Nov. 21, 1918. [1; 3a; 10; 37; 56]

Hamilton, Mrs. Flora, née Brent, essayist and poet, d. 1933.

Hamilton, Frank Hastings, surgeon, b. Wilmington, Vt., 1813; d. New York, N.Y., Aug. 11, 1886. [1; 3; 4; 6; 8; 10]

Hamilton, Franklin Elmer Ellsworth, bishop, b. Pleasant Valley, O., 1866; d. Pittsburgh, Pa., May 4, 1918. [10; 51]

Hamilton, Frederick William, clergyman, b. Portland, Me., 1860; d. Boston, Mass., May 22, 1940. [10]

Hamilton, Gail (pseud.). See Dodge, Mary Abigail.

Hamilton, George Livingstone, educationist, b. Boston, Mass., 1874; d. Ithaca, N.Y., Sept. 25, 1940. [10; 12]

Hamilton, Henry (pseud.). See Cox, Henry Hamilton.

Hamilton, Henry (pseud.). See Spalding, John Lancaster.

Hamilton, Henry Raymond, historian, b. 1861; d. Chicago, Ill., June 17, 1940.

Hamilton, James Alexander, lawyer and politician, b. New York, N.Y., 1788; d. New York, N.Y., Sept. 24, 1878. [1; 3; 7]

Hamilton, James Cleland, lawyer, b. Belfast. Ireland, 1836; d. Toronto, Ont., Feb., 1907. [27]

Hamilton, John Brown, surgeon, b. Jersey county, Ill., 1847; d. Elgin, Ill., Dec. 24, 1898. [3b; 4]

Hamilton, John Church, lawyer, b. Philadelphia, Pa., 1792; d. Long Branch, N.J., July 25, 1882. [3; 7; 8]

Hamilton, John McLure, artist, b. Philadelphia, Pa., 1853; d. Mandeville, Jamaica, Sept. 11, 1936. [10; 11]

Hamilton, John William, bishop, b. Weston, Va., 1845; d. Boston, Mass., July 24, 1934. [1a; 3; 4; 10; 11]

Hamilton, Kate Waterman, novelist and poet, b. Schenectady, N.Y., 1841; d. Bloomington, Ill., Nov. 28, 1934. [3; 4; 7; 10]

Hamilton, Laurentine, clergyman, b. Dix, N.Y., 1826; d. Oakland, Calif., April 9, 1882.

Hamilton, Peter Joseph, lawyer, b. Mobile, Ala., 1859; d. San Juan, Porto Rico, July 13, 1927. [4; 10]

Hamilton, Pierce Stevens, journalist, b. Brookfield, N.S., 1826; d. Halifax, N.S., Feb. 22, 1893. [27]

Hamilton, Rufus (pseud.). See Gillmore, Rufus Hamilton.

Hamilton, Samuel King, lawyer, b. Waterboro, Me., 1837; d. Wakefield, Mass., May 8, 1922. [4; 10]

Hamilton, Schuyler, soldier, b. New York, N.Y., 1822; d. New York, N.Y., March 18, 1903. [4; 10]

Hamilton, Stanislaus Murray, archivist, b. Washington, D.C., 1855; d. Washington, D.C., May 10, 1909. [10]

Hamilton, William Peter, journalist, b. England, 1867; d. Brooklyn, N.Y., Dec. 9, 1929. [10]

Hamilton, William Reeve, soldier, b. Fond du Lac, Wis., 1855; d. Milwaukee, Wis., Sept. 16, 1914. [4; 10; 44]

Hamilton, William Thomas, frontiersman, b. England, 1822; d. Columbus, Mont., May 24, 1908. [1]

Hamlin, Alfred Dwight Foster, architect, b. Constantinople, Turkey, 1855; d. New York, N.Y., March 21, 1926. [1; 4; 7; 10]

Hamlin, Augustus Choate, surgeon, b. Columbia, Me., 1829; d. Bangor, Me., Nov. 19, 1905. [3; 6; 10; 38]

Hamlin, Charles, lawyer, b. Hampden, Me., 1837; d. Bangor, Me., May 15, 1911. [10; 38; 46]

Hamlin, Charles Eugene, journalist, b. Orland, Me., 1861; d. New York, N.Y., June 27, 1921. [51]

Hamlin, Cyrus, missionary, b. near Waterford, Me., 1811; d. Lexington, Mass., Aug. 8, 1900. [1; 3; 4; 6]

Hamlin, Mrs. Myra Louise, née Sawyer, writer of books for children, b. 1856; d. New York, N.Y., Oct. 30, 1927.

Hamlin, Teunis Slingerland, clergyman, b. Glenville, N.Y., 1847; d. 1907. [4; 8; 10]

Hamline, Leonidas Lent, bishop, b. 1847; d. Mount Pleasant, Ia., March 23, 1865. [1; 4]

Hamm, Margherita Arlina, journalist, b. St. Stephens, N.B., 1871; d. 1907. [4; 7; 10]

Hammer, Bonaventure, priest, b. 1842; d. 1917. [21]

Hammer, William Joseph, electrical engineer, b. Cressona, Pa., 1858; d. New York, N.Y., March 24, 1934. [1a; 4; 10; 11]

Hammett, Samuel Adams, journalist, b. Jewett City, Conn., 1816; d. Brooklyn, N.Y., Dec. 24, 1865. [1; 3; 4; 6; 7]

Hammon, Jupiter, negro slave, b. about 1720; d. about 1800. [1]

Hammond, Charles, clergyman, b. Union, Conn., 1813; d. Monson, Mass., Nov. 7, 1878. [62]

Hammond, Edward Payson, evangelist, b. Ellington, Conn., 1831; d. Hartford, Conn., July 18, 1910. [1; 3; 4; 6; 10]

Hammond, Eleanor Prescott, educationist, b. Worcester, Mass., 1866; d. Chicago, Ill., Feb. 23, 1934. [10]

Hammond, Harriot Milton, biographer, b. 1838; d. 1903.

Hammond, Mrs. Henrietta, née Hardy, novelist, b. Virginia, 1854; d. 1883. [7; 8; 34]

Hammond, Jabez Delano, historian and politician, b. New Bedford, Mass., 1778; d. Cherry Valley, N.Y., Aug. 18, 1855. [1; 3; 4; 6]

Hammond, James Henry, politician, b. Newberry county, S.C., 1807; d. Aiken county, S.C., Nov. 13, 1864. [3; 8; 34]

Hammond, John Hays, mining engineer, b. San Francisco, Calif., 1855; d. Gloucester, Mass., June 8, 1936. [4; 10; 62]

Hammond, John Henry, lawyer, b. Louisville, Ky., 1871; d. Rye, N.Y., June 28, 1949. [10]

Hammond, John Winthrop, journalist, b. Lynn, Mass., 1887; d. Schenectady, N.Y., Dec. 27, 1934. [10]

Hammond, Mrs. Lily, née Hardy, novelist, b. Newark, N.J., 1859; d. Islip, N.Y., Jan. 24, 1925. [10]

Hammond, Matthew Brown, economist, b. South Bend, Ind., 1868; d. Columbus, O., Sept. 28, 1933. [10; 11]

Hammond, Melvin Ormond, journalist, b. Clarkson, Ont., 1876; d. Toronto, Ont., Oct. 7, 1934. [27]

Hammond, Mrs. Natalie, née Harris, historian, d. Washington, D.C., June 18, 1931.

Hammond, Nathaniel Job, lawyer, b. Elbert county, Ga., 1833; d. Atlanta, Ga., April 20, 1899.

Hammond, Otis Grant, historian, b. Manchester, N.H., 1867; d. Concord, N.H., Oct. 2, 1944. [11]

Hammond, Percy, drama critic, b. Cadiz, O., 1873; d. New York, N.Y., April 25, 1936. [7; 10]

Hammond, Samuel H., journalist, b. 1809; d. 1878.

Hammond, Stephen Tillinghast, sporting writer, b. 1831; d. ?

Hammond, William Alexander, physician and novelist, b. Annapolis, Md., 1828; d. Washington, D.C., Jan. 5, 1900. [1; 3; 4; 6; 7; 10]

Hammond, William Alexander, educationist, b. New Athens, O., 1861; d. Washington, D.C., May 7, 1938. [11]

Hammond, William Gardiner, lawyer, b. Newport, R.I., 1829; d. St. Louis, Mo., April 12, 1894. [1; 4; 37]

Hamon, Edouard, priest, b. Vitré, France, 1841; d. Leeds, Que., June, 1904. [32]

Hamp, Sidford Frederick, writer of books for boys, b. Liverpool, England, 1855; d. Colorado Springs, Colo., Sept. 3, 1919. [7; 10]

Hampton, Benjamin Bowles, journalist, b. Macomb, Ill., 1875; d. New York, N.Y., Jan. 31, 1932. [10]

Hampton, Isabel Adams. See Robb, Mrs. Isabel Adams, née Hampton.

Hanaford, Mrs. Jennie Estelle, poet, d. Stamford, Conn., July 30, 1924.

Hanaford, Mrs. Phoebe Ann, née Coffin, poet, novelist, and biographer, b. Nantucket Island, Mass., 1829; d. Rochester, N.Y., June 2, 1921. [1; 3; 4; 7; 10]

Hanchett, Henry Granger, physician and musician, b. Syracuse, N.Y., 1853; d. Siasconset, Mass., Aug. 19, 1918. [1; 7; 10; 20]

Hancock, Albert Elmer, educationist, b. Philadelphia, Pa., 1870; d. Haverford, Pa., 1915. [10]

Hancock, Edward Lee, engineer, b. 1873; d. 1911.

Hancock, Elizabeth Hazlewood, journalist, b. near Charlottesville, Va., 1871; d. 1915. [10]

Hancock, Harrie Irving, journalist and writer of books for boys, b. Waltham, Mass., 1868; d. March 12, 1922. [10]

Hancock, Harris, mathematician, b. Albemarle county, Va., 1867; d. Charlottesville, Va., March 19, 1944. [4; 10; 13]

Hancock, Joseph Lane, naturalist, b. 1864; d. 1922.

Hancock, Samuel Farwell, clergyman, b. Maulmain, Burma, 1836; d. Cleveland, O., Feb. 11, 1905.

Handerson, Henry Ebenezer, medical historian, b. Orange, O., 1837; d. Cleveland, O., April 23, 1918. [1; 10]

Handford, Thomas W., editor and compiler, b. England; d. Chicago, Ill., 1904. [6]

Handlin, William Wallace, educationist, b. New Orleans, La., 1830; d. ? [34]

Handy, Isaac William Ker, clergyman, b. 1815; d. 1878.

Hanes, Edward L., physician, b. Chenango Falls, N.Y., 1871; d. Altadena, Calif., 1941.

Haney, James Parton, art director, b. New York, N.Y., 1869; d. New York, N.Y., March 3, 1923. [10]

Hanford, Cornelius Holgate, jurist and novelist, b. Van Buren county, Ia., 1849; d. Honolulu, Hawaii, Feb. 28, 1926. [10; 11]

Hanford, Mrs. Helen Margaret, née **Ellwanger,** sociologist, b. Rochester, N.Y., 1882; d. Cleveland, O., Jan. 9, 1944.

Hanifan, Lyda Judson, educationist, b. Elkins, W. Va., 1879; d. Paducah, Ky., Dec. 12, 1932. [10; 11]

Hankins, Arthur Preston, novelist, b. Sac City, Ia., 1880; d. San José, Calif., Jan. 12, 1932. [11]

Hanks, Charles Stedman, lawyer, b. Lowell, Mass., 1856; d. Boston, Mass., March 23, 1908. [4; 10; 51]

Hanly, James Franks, lawyer, b. St. Joseph, Ill., 1863; d. Indianapolis, Ind., Aug. 1, 1920. [4; 10]

Hanna, David Blythe, railway-builder, b. Thornliebank, Scotland, 1858; d. Toronto, Ont., Dec. 1, 1938. [27]

Hanna, Matthew Elting, diplomat, b. Gillespieville, O., 1873; d. Tucson, Ariz., Feb. 19, 1936. [10]

Hannan, Frederick Watson, clergyman, b. Cochecton, N.Y., 1866; d. Brooklyn, N.Y., Feb. 11, 1929. [10]

Hannay, James, historian, b. Richibucto, N.B., 1842; d. Saint John, N.B., Jan. 12, 1910. [27]

Hannibal, Professor Julius Caesar (pseud.) See Levinson, William H.

Hansbrough, Henry Clay, journalist and politician, b. Prairie du Rocher, Ill., 1848; d. Washington, D.C., Nov. 16, 1933. [4; 10]

Hansell, Howard Forde, opthalmologist, b. Philadelphia, Pa., 1855; d. Philadelphia, Pa., Nov. 5, 1934. [10]

Hansen, Allen Oscar, educationist, b. Bagbo, Sweden, 1881; d. New York, N.Y., Jan. 19, 1944.

Hansen, George, landscape architect, b. Hildesheim, Germany, 1863; d. Berkeley, Calif., March 31, 1908. [1; 4; 10]

Hansen, Marcus Lee, historian, b. Neenah, Wis., 1892; d. Urbana, Ill., May 11, 1938.

Hanshew, Thomas W., actor and novelist, b. 1857; d. London, England, March 3, 1914.

Hanson, Alexander Contee, jurist, b. Annapolis, Md., 1749; d. Annapolis, Md., Jan. 16, 1806. [1; 4]

Hanson, Edgar Filmore, religious writer, b. Lincoln, Me., 1853; d. ? [8; 39]

Hanson, James Christian Meinich, librarian, b. Norway, 1864; d. Green Bay, Wis., Nov. 8, 1943. [10; 11]

Hanson, James Hobbs, educationist, b. China, Me., 1816; d. Waterville, Me., 1894. [4; 39]

Hanson, John Halloway, clergyman and poet, b. 1815; d. 1854. [6]

Hanson, John Wesley, clergyman, b. Boston, Mass., 1823; d. 1901. [3; 8]

Hanson, Ole, politician, b. Racine county, Wis., 1874; d. Los Angeles, Calif., July 6, 1940. [10]

Hanus, Paul Henry, educationist, b. Germany, 1855; d. Cambridge, Mass., Dec. 14, 1941. [10; 11]

Hapgood, Hutchins, journalist, b. Chicago, Ill., 1869; d. Provincetown, Mass., Nov. 18, 1944. [7; 10; 11]

Hapgood, Isabel Florence, translator and journalist, b. Boston, Mass., 1850; d. New York, N.Y., June 26, 1928. [1; 4; 7; 10]

Hapgood, Norman, editor, b. Chicago, Ill., 1868; d. New York, N.Y., April 29, 1937. [2a; 7; 10]

Haraszthy de Mokcsa, Agostin, viticulturist, b. Hungary, 1812; d. near Leon, Nicaragua, Aug. 10, 1869. [3]

Harbaugh, Henry, clergyman, b. Franklin county, Pa., 1817; d. Mercersburg, Pa., Dec. 28, 1867. [1; 3; 4; 6; 7]

Harbaugh, James Fleming Linn, biographer, b. Lancaster, Pa., 1860; d. 1916. [10]

Harbaugh, Thomas Chalmers, poet and novelist, b. Middletown, Md., 1849; d. Piqua, O., Oct. 28, 1924. [4; 7; 8; 10]

Harben, William Nathaniel, novelist, b. Dalton, Ga., 1858; d. New York, N.Y., Aug. 7, 1919. [1; 4; 7; 10; 34]

Harbert, Mrs. Elizabeth Morrison, née **Boynton,** journalist, b. Crawfordsville, Ind., 1845; d. Pasadena, Calif., Jan. 19, 1925. [10]

Harbord, James Guthrie, soldier, b. Bloomington, Ill., 1866; d. Aug. 20, 1947. [10; 12]

Harbour, Jefferson Lee, short-story writer, b. Oskaloosa, Ill., 1857; d. Fall River, Mass., Feb. 25, 1931. [10]

Harby, Isaac, journalist and playwright, b. Charleston, S.C., 1788; d. New York, N.Y., Nov. 14, 1828. [1; 3; 4; 6; 7; 34]

Harcourt, Helen (pseud.). See Warner, Helen Garnie.

Harcourt, Richard, clergyman, b. Ireland, 1840; d. 1911.

Hardaway, William Augustus, physician, b. Mobile, Ala., 1850; d. St. Louis, Mo., March 3, 1923. [10]

Hardee, William Joseph, soldier, b. Camden county, Ga., 1815; d. Wytheville, Va., Nov. 6, 1873. [1; 3; 4; 34]

Harden, Edward Jenkins, lawyer, b. Bryan county, Ga., 1813; d. Indian Springs, Ga., April 19, 1873. [34]

Harden, William, librarian, b. Savannah, Ga., 1844; d. Savannah, Ga., Jan. 4, 1936. [10]

Hardie, Alexander, clergyman, b. 1841; d. Los Angeles, Calif., June 25, 1936.

Hardie, James, educationist, b. Scotland, about 1760; d. 1832. [3]

Hardin, George Anson, local historian, b. b. 1832; d. 1900. [10]

Harding, Mrs. Alice, née Howard, horticulturist, b. Keene, N.H.; d. Plainfield, N.J., April 17, 1938. [10]

Harding, Arthur McCracken, educationist, b. Pine Bluff, Ark, 1884; d. Fayetteville, Ark., Dec. 24, 1947. [10; 11]

Harding, Benjamin Fosdick, educationist, b. New York, N.Y., 1857; d. Milton, Mass., Sept. 22, 1923. [51]

Harding, Mrs. Edward. See Harding, Mrs. Alice, née Howard.

Harding, Gardner Ludwig, journalist, b. Boston, Mass., 1887; d. New York, N.Y., March 20, 1940. [51]

Harding, Samuel Bannister, educationist, b. Indianapolis, Ind., 1866; d. Minneapolis, Minn., Jan. 29, 1927. [10]

Harding, Warren Gamaliel, twenty-ninth president of the United States, b. Corsica, O., 1865; d. San Francisco, Calif., Aug. 2, 1923. [1; 2; 4; 10]

Harding, William Procter Gould, banker, b. Greene county, Ala., 1864; d. Boston, Mass., April 7, 1930. [1; 10; 11]

Hardinge, E. M. (pseud.). See Going, Ellen Maud.

Hardman, Frederick (pseud.). See Sealsfield, Charles.

Hard Pan (pseud.). See Bonner, Geraldine.

Hardwicke, Henry, lawyer, b. 1861; d. 1909.

Hardy, Arthur Sherburne, educationist, novelist, and diplomat, b. Andover, Mass., 1847; d. Woodstock, Conn., March 13, 1930. [1; 4; 7; 10]

Hardy, Charles Oscar, economist, b. Island City, Mo., 1884; d. Washington, D.C., Nov. 30, 1940.

Hardy, Marjorie, educationist, b. Adrian, Mich. 1888; d. Adrian, Mich., June 17, 1948.

Hardy, Mrs. Mary, née Earle, poet and writer of books for children, b. New Haven, Conn., 1846; d. Grand Rapids, Mich., Sept. 29, 1928. [10; 11; 39]

Hare, Mrs. Emily (pseud.). See Johnson, Mrs. Laura, née Winthrop.

Hare, George Emlen, clergyman, b. Philadelphia, Pa., 1808; d. Philadelphia, Pa., Feb. 15, 1892. [1; 4]

Hare, Hobart Amory, physician, b. Philadelphia, Pa., 1862; d. Philadelphia, Pa., June 15, 1931. [4; 10; 11]

Hare, John Innes Clark, jurist, b. Philadelphia, Pa., 1816; d. Radnor, Pa., Dec. 29, 1905. [1; 3]

Hare, Mrs. Maud, née Cuney, musician, b. 1874; d. 1936.

Hare, Robert, scientist, b. Philadelphia, Pa., 1781; d. Philadelphia, Pa., May 15, 1858. [1; 3; 4; 6; 7; 8]

Hare, William Hobart, bishop, b. Princeton, N.J., 1838; d. Atlantic City, N.J., Oct. 23, 1909. [1; 4; 10]

Harger, Oscar, palaeontologist, b. Oxford, Conn., 1843; d. New Haven, Conn., Nov. 6, 1887. [62]

Hargis, Robert Bell Smith, physician, b. 1818; d. 1893.

Hargitt, Charles Wesley, biologist, b. near Lawrenceburg, Ind., 1852; d. Syracuse, N.Y., June 11, 1927. [4; 10]

Hargrave, Joseph James, fur-trader, b. York Factory, Hudson's Bay Territories, 1841; d. Edinburgh, Scotland, Feb. 22, 1894. [27]

Hark, Joseph Maxmilian, clergyman, b. Philadelphia, Pa., 1849; d. St. Croix, Virgin Islands, July 24, 1930. [8; 10]

Harkavy, Alexander, lexicographer, b. Lithuania, 1863; d. New York, N.Y., Nov. 27, 1939.

Harker, Oliver, lawyer, b. Fountain City, Ind., 1846; d. Carbondale, Ill., Dec. 3, 1936. [10]

Harker, Samuel, clergyman, fl. 1752-1763. [3]

Harkey, Simeon Walcher, clergyman, b. Iredell county, N.C., 1811; d. Knoxville, Ill., March 1, 1889. [4; 8; 34]

Harkness, Albert, educationist, b. Mendon, Mass., 1822; d. Providence, R.I., May 27, 1907. [1; 3; 4; 10]

Harkness, James, clergyman, b. Scotland, 1803; d. Jersey City, N.J., July 4, 1878. [3; 8]

Harkness, Mrs. Ruth, née McCoombs, explorer, b. 1901; d. Pittsburgh, Pa., July 19, 1947.

Harlan, Caleb, physician and poet, b. 1814; d. Farmhurst, Del., June 12, 1902. [6]

Harlan, Edgar Rubey, historian, b. Spartansburg, Ind., 1869; d. Des Moines, Ia., July 13, 1941. [10]

Harlan, George Cuvier, physician, b. 1835; d. Philadelphia, Pa., Sept. 25, 1909. [8]

Harlan, John Marshall, jurist, b. Boyle county, Ky., 1833; d. Washington, D.C., Oct. 14, 1911. [1; 4; 10; 34]

Harlan, John Maynard, lawyer, b. Frankfort, Ky., 1864; d. May 23, 1934. [10]

Harlan, Josiah, traveller, b. 1799; d. 1871.

Harlan, Richard, naturalist, b. Philadelphia, Pa., 1796; d. New Orleans, La., Sept. 30, 1843. [1; 3; 6]

Harland, Henry, novelist, b. New York, N.Y., 1861; d. San Remo, Italy, Dec. 20, 1905. [1; 3; 4; 10]

Harland, Marion (pseud.). See Terhune, Mrs. Mary Virginia, née Hawes.

Harlow, Henry Addison, clergyman, b. Plumb Island, N.Y., 1830; d. Nyack, N.Y., June 27, 1913. [56]

Harlow, William Burt, educationist, b. Portland, Me., 1856; d. Bermuda, Feb. 23, 1928. [8; 51]

Harman, Henry Elliott, poet and publisher, b. Lexington, S.C., 1866; d. 1927. [10; 11; 34]

Harman, Henry Martyn, clergyman, b. 1822; d. 1897. [6; 8]

Harmer, Bertha, nurse, d. Toronto, Ont., Dec. 14, 1934.

Harmon, Daniel Williams, fur-trader, b. Bennington, Vt., 1778; d. Montreal, Que., March 26, 1845. [1; 27]

Harnden, Henry, soldier, b. 1823; d. Madison, Wis., March 17, 1900. [3b]

Harney, George Edward, architect, b. Lynn, Mass., 1840; d. New York, N.Y., Nov. 12, 1924. [4; 10]

Harney, John Milton, poet, b. Sussex county, Del., 1789; d. Bardstown, Ky., Jan. 15, 1825. [3; 7; 34; 74]

Harney, William Wallace, journalist, b. Bloomington, Ind., 1831; d. Jacksonville, Fla., March 28, 1912. [10; 74]

Harold, Childe (pseud.). See Field, Edward Salisbury.

Harper, Carrie Anna, educationist, b. Boston, Mass.; d. Sunderland, Mass., Dec. 13, 1918. [10]

Harper, Mrs. Frances Ellen, née **Watkins,** poet and journalist, b. 1825; d. ?

Harper, George Andrew, mathematician, b. Jamestown, O., 1879; d. Tucson, Ariz., July 7, 1939. [10; 11]

Harper, George McLean, educationist, b. Shippensburg, Pa., 1863; d. Princeton, N.J., July 14, 1947. [7; 10; 11]

Harper, Mrs. Ida, née **Husted,** journalist, b. Fairfield, Ind., 1851; d. Washington, D.C., March 14, 1931. [1; 7; 10]

Harper, Jacob Chandler, lawyer, b. Strickersville, Pa., 1858; d. La Jolla, Calif., May 17, 1939. [10]

Harper, John Lyell, engineer, b. Harpersfield, N.Y., 1873; d. Niagara Falls, N.Y., Nov. 28, 1924. [1; 4]

Harper, John Murdoch, educationist, b. Johnstone, Scotland, 1845; d. Quebec, Que., March 1, 1919. [27]

Harper, Joseph Henry, publisher, b. 1850; d. Paris, France, Jan. 25, 1938. [2a]

Harper, Mrs. Lizzie, née **St. John,** autobiographer, b. 1837; d. about 1916.

Harper, Merritt Wesley, educationist, b. Grove City, O., 1877; d. Ithaca, N.Y., May 9, 1938. [10; 11]

Harper, Olive (pseud.). See D'Apery, Mrs. Ellen, née Burrell.

Harper, Paul Tompkins, physician, b. Schenevus, N.Y., 1881; d. Philadelphia, Pa., July 11, 1931. [10]

Harper, Robert Francis, Assyriologist, b. New Concord, O., 1864; d. London, England, Aug. 5, 1914. [1; 4; 10]

Harper, Robert Goodloe, politician, b. near Fredericksburg, Va., 1765; d. Baltimore, Md., Jan. 14, 1825. [1; 3; 4; 34]

Harper, Samuel Northrup, educationist, b. Morgan Park, Ill., 1882; d. Chicago, Ill., Jan. 18, 1943. [10; 14]

Harper, Theodore Acland, writer of books for children, b. Christ Church, New Zealand, 1871; d. Portland, Ore., May 6, 1942. [7; 10; 11]

Harper, William, jurist and politician, b. Antigua, 1790; d. South Carolina, Oct. 10, 1847. [1; 4; 34]

Harper, William Allen, educationist, b. Berkley, Va., 1880; d. Black Mountain, N.C., May 11, 1942. [7; 10; 11]

Harper, William Hudson, journalist, b. New York, N.Y., 1857; d. Santa Barbara, Calif., Oct. 24, 1946. [62]

Harper, William Rainey, educationist, b. New Concord, O., 1856; d. Chicago, Ill., Jan. 10, 1906. [1; 2; 4; 10]

Harrell, John Mortimer, soldier and lawyer, fl. 1850-1899. [34]

Harrer, Gustave Adolphus, educationist, b. Brooklyn, N.Y., 1886; d. Chapel Hill, N.C., Nov. 26, 1943. [10; 11]

Harrigan, Edward, playwright, b. New York, N.Y., 1843; d. New York, N.Y., June 6, 1911. [1; 4]

Harriman, Alice, journalist, b. Newport, Me., 1861; d. Hollywood, Calif., Dec. 24, 1925. [10; 35]

Harriman, Karl Edwin, editor and novelist, b. Ann Arbor, Mich., 1875; d. near Philadelphia, Pa., Oct. 1, 1935. [4; 7; 10]

Harriman, Walter, soldier and politician, b. Warner, N.H., 1817; d. Concord, N.H., July 25, 1884. [1; 3; 4]

Harrington, Bernard James, educationist, b. St. Andrews, Que., 1848; d. Montreal, Que., Nov. 29, 1907. [27]

Harrington, Charles, physician, b. Salem, Mass., 1856; d. Lynton, Devonshire, England, Sept. 11, 1908. [1]

Harrington, Charles Kendall, missionary, b. Sydney, N.S., 1858; d. Albany, N.Y., May 12, 1920.

Harrington, Charles Loammi, educationist, b. Paxton, Mass., 1847; d. New York, N.Y., June 7, 1927. [45]

Harrington, George (pseud.). See Baker, William Mumford.

Harrington, Harry Franklin, educationist, b. Logan, O., 1882; d. Evanston, Ill., Sept. 2, 1935. [10; 11]

Harrington, Jeremiah C., priest, b. 1882; d. 1926. [21]

Harrington, Mark Walrod, meteorologist, b. Sycamore, Ill., 1848; d. Oct. 9, 1926. [1; 4]

Harrington, Milton Alexander, psychiatrist, b. Walkerton, Ont., 1884; d. Martha's Vineyard, Mass., May 27, 1942.

Harrington, Thomas Francis, physician, b. Lowell, Mass., 1866; d. Boston, Mass., Jan. 19, 1919. [1; 4; 10]

Harriott, Mrs. Clara, née Morris. See Morris, Clara.

Harris, Albert Mason, educationist, b. Old Mystic, Conn., 1868; d. Nashville, Tenn., Aug. 6, 1945. [10]

Harris, Alexander, historian, b. 1827; d. ? [6]

Harris, Amanda Bartlett, writer of books for young people, b. Warner, N.H., 1824; d. Warner, N.H., Jan. 13, 1917. [6; 8; 10]

Harris, Carlton Danner, clergyman, b. Wardensville, W. Va., 1864; d. Baltimore, Md., Sept. 28, 1928. [10]

Harris, Chapin Aaron, dentist, b. Pompey, N.Y., 1806; d. Baltimore, Md., Sept. 29, 1860. [1; 3; 4]

Harris, Charles, educationist, b. Albion, Ill., 1859; d. Cleveland, O., Sept. 3, 1943. [10]

Harris, Charles Kassell, song-writer, b. Poughkeepsie, N.Y., 1865; d. New York, N.Y., Dec. 22, 1930. [1; 4; 10]

Harris, Mrs. Cora May, née White, novelist, b. Farm Hill, Ga., 1869; d. Atlanta, Ga., Feb. 9, 1935. [7; 10; 11; 34]

Harris, Edward William, lawyer, b. Norfolk county, Upper Canada, 1832; d. London, Ont., Oct. 1, 1925. [27]

Harris, Elijah Paddock, chemist, b. Leroy, N.Y., 1832; d. Warsaw, N.Y., Dec. 10, 1920. [10]

Harris, Ella Isabel, educationist, b. New York, N.Y., 1859; d. Clifton Springs, N.Y., May 1, 1923. [62]

Harris, Emerson Pitt, journalist, b. Kennedy, N.Y., 1853; d. Franklinville, N.Y., Feb. 17, 1937. [10; 11]

Harris, Garrard, journalist, b. Columbus, Ga., 1875; d. Birmingham, Ala., March 19, 1927. [10]

Harris, George, clergyman, b. East Machias, Me., 1844; d. New York, N.Y., March 1, 1922. [1; 4; 10; 49]

Harris, George Washington, humorist, b. Allegheny City, Pa., 1814; d. near Knoxville, Tenn., Dec. 11, 1869; [1; 3; 4; 7]

Harris, Hunter Lee, poet, b. Granville county, N.C., 1866; d. Raleigh, N.C., July 13, 1893. [34]

Harris, James Arthur, biologist, b. Plantsville, O., 1880; d. Minneapolis, Minn., April 26, 1930. [4; 10; 13]

Harris, Joel Chandler, writer of negro dialect stories and verse, b. Eatonton, Ga., 1848; d. Atlanta, Ga., July 3, 1908. [1; 2; 3; 4; 5; 7; 10; 71; 72]

Harris, John Andrews, clergyman, b. Philadelphia, Pa., 1834; d. Philadelphia, Pa., 1922. [10]

Harris, John Howard, educationist, b. Indiana, Pa., 1847; d. Scranton, Pa., April 4, 1925. [10]

Harris, Joseph, agricultural writer, b. Shrewsbury, England, 1828; d. near Rochester, N.Y., Nov. 18, 1892. [1; 6]

Harris, Lee O., poet, b. 1839; d. Indiana, 1909. [8]

Harris, Maurice Henry, rabbi, b. London, England, 1859; d. New York, N.Y., June 23, 1930. [1; 10]

Harris, Merriman Colbert, missionary, b. Beallsville, O., 1846; d. Tokyo, Japan, May 10, 1921. [1; 4; 10]

Harris, Mrs. Miriam, née Coles, novelist, b. near Glen Cove, N.Y., 1834; d. Pau, France, Jan. 23, 1925. [1; 3; 6; 7; 10]

Harris, Nathaniel Edwin, politician and jurist, b. Junesboro, Tenn., 1846; d. Macon, Ga., Sept. 21, 1929. [4; 10]

Harris, Rollin Arthur, mathematician, b. Randolph, N.Y., 1863; d. Washington, D.C., Jan, 20, 1918. [1; 4; 10]

Harris, Samuel, theologian, b. East Machias, Me., 1814; d. Litchfield, Conn., June 25, 1899. [1; 3; 4; 10]

Harris, Samuel Smith, bishop, b. Autauga county, Ga., 1841; d. London, England, Aug. 21, 1888. [4; 6; 8; 34]

Harris, Thaddeus Mason, clergyman, b. Charlestown, Mass., 1768; d. Dorchester, Mass., April 3, 1842. [1; 3; 4; 6; 7; 8]

Harris, Thaddeus William, entomologist, b. Dorchester, Mass., 1795; d. Cambridge, Mass., Jan. 16, 1856. [1; 3; 6]

Harris, Thomas, naval surgeon, b. 1784; d. 1861. [6]

Harris, Thomas Lake, poet and mystic, b. Fenny Stratford, England, 1823; d. New York, N.Y., March 23, 1906. [1; 3; 4; 6; 7; 8; 10]

Harris, Thomas Le Grand, historian, b. Hamilton county, Ind., 1863; d. Greencastle, Ind., Aug. 23, 1941. [10]

Harris, William Charles, journalist and sportsman, b. Baltimore, Md., 1830; d. New York, N.Y., May 18, 1905. [10]

Harris, William Logan, bishop, b. near Mansfield, O., 1817; d. Brooklyn, N.Y., Sept. 2, 1887. [1; 3; 6]

Harris, William Richard, priest and historian, b. Cork, Ireland, 1847; d. Toronto, Ont., March 5, 1923. [27]

Harris, William Torrey, philosopher, b. near North Killingly, Conn., 1835; d. Providence, R.I., Nov. 5, 1909. [1; 3; 4; 7; 10]

Harrison, Mrs. Amelia, née Williams, writer of books for children, b. 1852; d. 1903.

Harrison, Benjamin, twenty-third president of the United States, b. North Bend, O., 1833; d. Indianapolis, Ind., March 13, 1901. [1; 2; 3; 4; 5; 6; 7; 10]

Harrison, Birge. See Harrison, Lovell Birge.

Harrison, Mrs. Burton. See Harrison, Mrs. Constance, née Cary.

Harrison, Carter Henry, politician, b. near Lexington, Ky., 1825; d. Chicago, Ill., Oct. 28, 1893. [1; 3; 4]

Harrison, Mrs. Constance, née Cary, novelist, b. Fairfax county, Va., 1843; d. Washington, D.C., Nov. 21, 1920. [1; 2; 3; 5; 6; 7; 8; 10; 71]

Harrison, Elizabeth, educationist, b. Athens, Ky., 1849 d. San Antonio, Tex., Oct. 31, 1927. [1; 4; 7; 10; 37]

Harrison, Fairfax, railway executive, historian, and agriculturist, b. New York, N.Y., 1869; d. Baltimore, Md., Feb. 2, 1938. [10; 62]

Harrison, Gabriel, playwright and artist, b. Philadelphia, Pa., 1818; d. Brooklyn, N.Y., Dec. 15, 1902. [1; 3; 4; 6; 7; 10; 71]

Harrison, George Leib, philanthropist, b. Philadelphia, Pa., 1811; d. Philadelphia, Pa., Sept. 9, 1885. [3; 8]

Harrison, Gessner, educationist, b. Harrisonburg, Va., 1807; d. Nelson county, Va., April 7, 1862. [1; 3; 6; 34]

Harrison, Hall, clergyman, b. Howard county, Md., 1837; d. 1900. [3; 10; 34]

Harrison, Henry Sydnor, journalist and novelist, b. Sewanee, Tenn., 1880; d. Atlantic City, N.J., July 14, 1930. [1; 4; 7; 10; 34]

Harrison, Mrs. Ida, née **Withers,** social worker, b. Grand Gulf, Miss., 1851; d. Lexington, Ky., 1927. [10]

Harrison, James Albert, educationist, b. Pass Christian, Miss., 1848; d. Charlottesville, Va., Jan. 31, 1911. [1; 3; 5; 7; 10; 34]

Harrison, Jennie (pseud.). See Tomkins, Jane Harrison.

Harrison, John Hoffman, physician, b. Washington, D.C., 1808; d. New Orleans, La., March 19, 1849. [3; 34]

Harrison, John Pollard, physician, b. 1796; d. Cincinnati, O., 1849;

Harrison, Jonathan Baxter, clergyman, b. Ohio, 1835; d. 1907. [6; 8; 10]

Harrison, Joseph, mechanical engineer, b. Philadelphia, Pa., 1810; d. Philadelphia, Pa., March 27, 1874. [1; 3; 4; 6]

Harrison, Leon, rabbi, b. Liverpool, England, 1866; d. St. Louis, Mo., Sept. 1, 1928.

Harrison, Lovell Birge, landscape painter, b. Philadelphia, Pa., 1854; d. Woodstock, N.Y., May 11, 1929. [1; 10]

Harrison, Robert Alexander, jurist, b. Montreal, Lower Canada, 1833; d. Toronto, Ont., Nov. 1, 1878. [6; 27]

Harrison, Mrs. Susie Frances, née **Riley,** poet and novelist, b. Toronto, Ont., 1859; d. Toronto, Ont., May 6, 1935. [27]

Harrison, Thomas Skelton, diplomat, b. Philadelphia, Pa., 1837; d. Philadelphia, Pa., May 3, 1919. [10]

Harrison, Thomas Walter, jurist, b. Leesburg, Va., 1856; d. Winchester, Va., May 9, 1935. [10]

Harrison, William Pope, clergyman, t. Savannah, Ga., 1830; d. Columbus, Ga., Feb. 7, 1895. [1; 4; 34]

Harrison, William Samuel, poet, b. 1834; d. 1917.

Harrison, William Welsh, genealogist, b. 1850; d. near Glenside, Pa., March 4, 1927.

Harrop, George Argale, physician, b. Peru, Ill., 1890; d. New York, N.Y., Aug. 4, 1945. [10]

Harry, Joseph Edward, educationist, b. Harford county, Md., 1863; d. New York, N.Y., Aug. 7, 1949.

Harsha, David Addison, miscellaneous writer, b. Argyle, N.Y., 1827; d. 1895. [3; 7; 8]

Harshberger, John William, botanist, b. Philadelphia, Pa., 1869; d. Philadelphia, Pa., April 27, 1929. [1; 4; 10]

Harshman, Samuel Rufus, clergyman, b. 1841; d. 1912.

Hart, Adolphus Mordecai, historian, b. Three Rivers, Lower Canada, 1816; d. Montreal, Que., March 23, 1879. [7; 27]

Hart, Albert Bushnell, historian, b. Clarksville, Pa., 1854; d. Boston, Mass., June 16, 1943. [4; 7; 10; 11; 14]

Hart, Burdett, clergyman, b. New Britain, Conn., 1821; d. Philadelphia, Pa., May 24, 1906. [4; 8; 10; 62]

Hart, Charles Henry, art expert, b. Philadelphia, Pa., 1847; d. New York, N.Y., July 29, 1918. [1; 3; 4; 6; 7; 10]

Hart, Charles Porter, physician, b. 1827; d. about 1902.

Hart, Edward, chemist, b. Doylestown, Pa., 1854; d. Easton, Pa., June 6, 1931. [1a; 10; 11; 13]

Hart, Mrs. Frances, née **Noyes,** novelist, b. Silver Springs, Md., 1890; d. New Canaan, Conn., Oct. 25, 1943. [7; 10; 11]

Hart, Gerald Ephraim, historian, b. Montreal, Que., 1849; d. Montreal, Que., July 13, 1936. [27]

Hart, Hastings Hornell, clergyman and social worker, b. Brookfield, O., 1851; d. White Plains, N.Y., May 9, 1932. [1a; 4; 10; 11]

Hart, Henry Martyn, clergyman, b. Otley, England, 1838; d. Denver, Colo., March 24, 1920. [8; 10]

Hart, James Morgan, philologist, b. Princeton, N.J., 1839; d. Washington, D.C., April 18, 1916. [1; 4; 7; 10]

Hart, Jerome Alfred, journalist, b. San Francisco, Calif., 1854; d. San Francisco, Calif., Jan. 3, 1937. [10; 11; 35]

Hart, John Seely, educationist, b. Stockbridge, Mass., 1810; d. Philadelphia, Pa., March 26, 1877. [1; 3; 4; 6]

Hart, Joseph C., educationist, d. New York, N.Y., 1855. [7]

Hart, Joseph Kinmont, educationist, b. near Columbia City, Ind., 1876; d. Hudson, N.Y., March 10, 1949. [7; 10; 11]

Hart, Mrs. Julia Catherine, née **Beckwith,** novelist, b. Fredericton, N.B., 1796; d. Fredericton, N.B., Nov. 28, 1867. [7; 27]

Hart, Luther, clergyman, b. Goshen, Conn., 1783; d. Plymouth, Conn., April 24, 1834. [3; 62]

Hart, Samuel, clergyman, b. Saybrook, Conn., 1845; d. Hartford, Conn., Feb. 25, 1917. [1; 4; 10]

Hart, Stephen, poet, b. 1782; d. 1857.

Hart, Virgil Chittenden, missionary, b. Lorraine, N.Y., 1840; d. Burlington, Ont., Feb. 24, 1904. [4; 6]

Hart, William Octave, lawyer, b. New Orleans, La., 1857; d. New Orleans, La., Oct. 19, 1929. [10]

Harte, Bret, poet and story-teller, b. Albany, N.Y., 1839; d. London, England, May 5, 1902. [1; 2; 3; 4; 5; 6; 7; 8; 10; 71; 72]

Harte, Richard Hickman, surgeon, b. Rock Island, Ill., 1855; d. Philadelphia, Pa., Nov. 14, 1925. [4; 10]

Harte, Walter Blackburn, essayist, b. 1867; d. 1898. [8]

Hartley, Cecil B., biographer, fl. 1860-1869. [6; 8]

Hartley, George Inness, ornithologist, b. Montclair, N.J., 1887; d. Southampton, Long Island, N.Y., Feb. 11, 1949. [7]

Hartley, Isaac Smithson, clergyman, b. New York, N.Y., 1830; d. Great Barrington, Mass., July 2, 1899. [3b; 6]

Hartley, Jonathan Scott, sculptor, b. Albany, N.Y., 1845; d. New York, N.Y., Dec. 6, 1912. [1; 2; 4; 10]

Hartley, Oliver Cromwell, lawyer, b. 1823; d. 1850.

Hartley, Robert Milham, social reformer, b. Cockermouth, England, 1796; d. New York, N.Y., 1881. [6; 8]

Hartman, Mrs. Blanche, née Taggart, poet and genealogist, b. 1863; d. Pittsburgh, Pa., Sept. 22, 1946.

Hartman, Herbert Weidler, educationist, b. Lancaster, Pa., 1901; d. Brunswick, Me., Oct. 2, 1945. [62]

Hartman, John Clark, journalist, b. Waterloo, Ia., 1861; d. Waterloo, Ia., Jan. 3, 1941. [10]

Hartman, Lee Foster, editor and novelist, b. Fort Wayne, Ind., 1879; d. New York, N.Y., Sept. 23, 1941. [10]

Hartman, Leon Wilson, educationist, b. Downsville, N.Y., 1876; d. Palo Alto, Calif., Aug. 27, 1943. [10]

Hartman, Levi Balmer, clergyman, b. 1838; d. Trenton, N.J., Nov. 2, 1907.

Hartman, William Dell, physician, b. 1817; d. West Chester, Pa., Aug. 16, 1899. [55]

Hartmann, Francis M., electrical engineer, b. Cochecton, N.Y., 1870; d. New York, N.Y., March 28, 1932. [10]

Hartmann, Sadakichi, artist, b. Nagasaki, Japan, 1867; d. St. Petersburg, Fla., Nov. 21, 1944. [7]

Hartness, James, manufacturer, b. Schenectady, N.Y., 1861; d. Springfield, Vt., Feb. 2, 1934. [10]

Hartridge, Clifford Wayne, novelist, b. Savannah, Ga., 1866; d. New York, N.Y., April 10, 1937. [62]

Hartshorn, Charles Warren, lawyer, b. 1814; d. 1893. [51]

Hartshorn, Edwin Alonzo, economist, fl. 1874-88.

Hartshorn, William Newton, publisher, b. Greenville, N.H., 1843; d. Cambridge, Mass., Sept., 1920. [10]

Hartshorne, Charles Hopkins, lawyer, b. Jersey City, N.J., 1851; d. 1918. [10]

Hartshorne, Henry, physician, b. Philadelphia, Pa., 1823; d. Tokvo, Japan, Feb. 10, 1897. [1; 3; 4; 6; 7; 8]

Hartsock, Ernest Abner, poet and musician, b. Atlanta, Ga., 1903; d. Dec. 14, 1930. [7; 11]

Hartt, Charles Frederick, naturalist, b. Fredericton, N.B., 1840; d. Rio de Janeiro, Brazil, March 18, 1878. [3; 4; 6]

Hartt, Rollin Lynde, clergyman, b. Ithaca, N.Y., 1869; d. New York, N.Y., June 17, 1946. [7]

Hartwell, Charles Stearns, educationist, b. Foochow, China, 1855; d. Shanghai, China, March 6, 1931. [45]

Hartwell, Edward Mussey, statistician, b. Exeter, N.H., 1850; d. Jamaica Plain, Mass., Feb. 19, 1922. [10; 45]

Hartwell, Mary. See Catherwood, Mrs. Mary, née Hartwell.

Hartzell, Jonas Hazard, clergyman, b. Washington county, Pa., 1830; d. Waverly, N.Y., June 9, 1890. [3; 8]

Hartzell, Josiah, lawyer and journalist, b. Deerfield, O., 1833; d. Canton, O., Nov. 11, 1914.

Hartzler, Henry Burns, bishop, b. York county, Pa., 1840; d. Harrisburg, Pa., Sept. 3, 1920. [10]

Harvard, Senior (pseud.). See Ward, Henry Dana.

Harvard, William Martin, clergyman, b. 1790; d. Richmond, England, Dec. 15, 1857. [27]

Harvey, Alexander, journalist, b. Brussels, Belgium, 1868; d. Dumont, N.J., Nov. 20, 1949. [7; 10; 11]

Harvey, George Brinton McClellan, editor and diplomat, b. Peacham, Vt., 1864; d. Dublin, N.H., Aug. 20, 1928. [1; 4; 7; 10]

Harvey, George Cockburn, editor and playwright, b. Thornby, England, 1858; d. New York, N.Y., May 25, 1935. [7; 10]

Harvey, Hezekiah, clergyman, b. England, 1821; d. Hamilton, N.Y., June 28, 1893. [3a]

Harvey, James Clarence, elocutionist, b. 1859; d. New York, N.Y., Sept. 29, 1917.

Harvey, Lorenzo Dow, mathematician, b. Deerfield, N.H., 1848; d. Menomie, Wis., June 1, 1922. [4; 10]

Harvey, Margaret Boyle, poet and musician, d. 1912.

Harvey, Moses, clergyman, b. county Armagh, Ireland, 1820; d. St. John's Newfoundland, Sept. 3, 1901. [3; 31]

Harvey, Oscar Jewell, historian, b. Wilkesbarre, Pa., 1851; d. Kingston, Pa., March 26, 1922.

Harvey, Peter, politician, b. Barnet, Vt., 1810; d. Boston, Mass., June 27, 1877. [3; 43]

Harvey, Rowland Hill, educationist, b. Battle Creek, Ia., 1889; d. Los Angeles, Calif., March 11, 1943. [10]

Harvey, Thomas W., educationist, b. 1821; d. 1892.

Harvey, William Hope, lawyer and economist, b. Buffalo, W. Va., 1851; d. Monte Ne, Ark., Feb. 11, 1936. [4; 8; 10; 11]

Harwood, Andrew Allen, naval officer, b. Settle, Pa., 1802; d. Marion, Mass., Aug. 28, 1884. [3; 6]

Harwood, John Edmund, actor and poet, b. England, 1771; d. Germantown, Pa., Sept. 21, 1809. [3]

Harwood, William Sumner, journalist, b. Charles City, Ia., 1857; d. Los Gatos, Calif., 1908. [10; 70]

Hasbrouck, Joseph, lawyer, b. 1840; d. ?

Hascall, Daniel, clergyman, b. Bennington, Vt., 1782; d. Hamilton, N.Y., June 28, 1852. [3; 43]

Haskel, Daniel, clergyman, b. Preston, Conn., 1784; d. Brooklyn, N.Y., Aug. 9, 1848. |3; 4; 6; 7]

Haskell, Thomas Hawes, jurist, b. New Gloucester, Me., 1842; d. Portland, Me., Sept. 24, 1900. [10; 38]

Haskell, Thomas Nelson, clergyman, b. 1826; d. 1906.

Haskin, Frederic Jennings, journalist, b. Shelbina, Mo., 1872; d. Washington, D.C., April 24, 1944. [10; 11]

Haskin, William Lawrence, soldier, b. Houlton, Me., 1841; d. New London, Conn., Sept. 24, 1931. [10; 38]

Haskins, Caryl Davis, electrical engineer, b. Waltham, Mass., 1867; d. Schenectady, N.Y., 1911. [10]

Haskins, Charles Homer, historian, b. Meadville, Pa., 1870; d. Cambridge, Mass., May 14, 1937. [7; 10; 11]

Haskins, Charles Nelson, mathematician, b. New Bedford, Mass., 1874; d. Hanover, N.H., Nov. 14, 1942. [10; 49]

Haskins, Charles Waldo, accountant, b. Brooklyn, N.Y., 1852; d. New York, N.Y., 1903. [4; 10]

Haskins, David Greene, clergyman, b. 1818; d. 1896. [6; 8; 51]

Haskins, George Foxcroft, clergyman, b. 1806; d. 1872. [51]

Haskins, Howard Davis, biochemist, b. Springfield. Mass., 1871; d. Portland, Ore., Nov. 20, 1933. [10; 13]

Haskins, Robert Willson, phrenologist, b. 1796; d. 1870.

Hassam, John Tyler, genealogist, b. Boston, Mass., 1841; d. Boston, Mass., April 22, 1903. [10; 51]

Hassard, Albert Richard, lawyer, b. Petigo, Ireland, 1873; d. Toronto, Ont., June 26, 1940. [27]

Hassard, John Rose Greene, journalist, b. New York, N.Y., 1836; d. New York, N.Y., April 18, 1888. [1; 3; 4; 6]

Hassaurek, Friedrich, journalist, b. Vienna, Austria, 1832; d. Paris, France, Oct. 3, 1885. [3]

Hassell, Cushing Biggs, clergyman, b. Martin county, N.C., 1808; d. Williamston, N.C., April 11, 1880. [4; 34]

Hasskarl, Gottlieb Christopher Henry, clergyman, b. 1855; d. 1929.

Hassler, Charles William, lawyer, d. 1888. [48]

Hassler, Edgar Wakefield, local historian, b. 1859; d. 1905.

Hassler, Ferdinand Rudolph, surveyor, b. Switzerland, 1770; d. Philadelphia, Pa., Nov. 20, 1843. [1; 3; 4; 6]

Hastings, Charles Sheldon, physicist, b. Clinton, N.Y., 1848; d. Greenwich, Conn., Jan. 31, 1932. [1a; 8; 10; 62]

Hastings, Ernest Clement, merchandizing expert, b. about 1887; d. New York, N.Y., March 1, 1942.

Hastings, Frank Warren, agriculturist, b. Waterford, Vt., 1856; d. Feb. 3, 1925. [10; 11]

Hastings, Horace Lorenzo, religious journalist, b. Watertown, Mass., 1831; d. Goshen, Mass., Oct. 21, 1899. [3b; 6; 8]

Hastings, Lansford Warren, pioneer, b. 1819; d. about 1870. [41]

Hastings, Mrs. Sarah, née Anderson, poet, b. 1773; d. 1812.

Hastings, Thomas, musician, b. Washington, Conn., 1784; d. New York, N.Y., May 15, 1872. [1; 3; 4; 6; 7; 20]

Hastings, Thomas Samuel, theologian, b. Utica, N.Y., 1827; d. New York, N.Y., April 2, 1911. [4; 10; 68]

Hastings, Wells Southworth, novelist, b. New Haven, Conn., 1878; d. Los Angeles, Calif., May 8, 1923. [10; 62]

Haswell, Alanson Mason, poet, b. Burma, 1847; d. ? [7; 11]

Haswell, Anthony, printer, b. Portsmouth, England, 1756; d. Bennington, Vt., May 22, 1816. [1; 4; 7; 43]

Haswell, Charles Haynes, engineer, b. New York, N.Y., 1809; d. New York, N.Y., May 12, 1907. [1; 3; 4; 6; 10]

Hatch, David Patterson, philosopher, b. Dresden, Me., 1846; d. Los Angeles, Calif., 1912. [35]

Hatch, Louis Clinton, historian, b. Bangor, Me., 1872; d. Bangor, Me., Dec. 2, 1931. [4; 10]

Hatch, Mrs. Mary R., née Platt, novelist, b. 1848; d. Santa Monica, Calif., Nov. 28, 1935. [7; 11]

Hatcher, Eldridge Burwell, clergyman, b. Fork Union, Va., 1865; d. Bryn Mawr, Pa., July 21, 1943. [10]

Hatcher, John Bell, palaeontologist, b. Cooperstown, Ill., 1861; d. Pittsburgh, Pa., July 3, 1904. [4; 10]

Hatcher, Orie Latham, educationist, b. Petersburg, Va.; d. Richmond, Va., April 1, 1946. [11]

Hatcher, William Bass, educationist, b. Ripley, Miss., 1888; d. Baton Rouge, La.. April 3, 1947.

Hatcher, William Eldridge, clergyman, b. Bedford county, Va., 1834; d. Fort Union, Va., Aug. 24, 1912. [1; 4; 10; 34]

Hatfield, Edwin Francis, clergyman, b. Elizabeth-town, N.J., 1807; d. Summit, N.J., Sept. 22, 1883. [1; 3; 4; 7]

Hatfield, James Taft, educationist, b. Brooklyn, N.Y., 1862; d. Evanston, Ill., Oct. 3, 1945. [7; 10; 11]

Hatfield, Marcus Patten, physician, b. New York, N.Y., 1849; d. Chicago, Ill., Nov.. 11, 1909. [10]

Hatfield, Robert Griffith, architect, b. 1815; d. 1879.

Hathaway, Arthur Stafford, mathematician, b. Keeler, Mich., 1855; d. Houston, Tex., March 11, 1934. [10; 11; 13]

Hathaway, Benjamin, poet, b. Cayuga county, N.Y., 1822; d. ? [7; 39]

Hathaway, Ernest Jackson, biographer, b. Toronto, Ont., 1871; d. Toronto, Ont., March 3, 1930. [27]

Hathaway, Warren, clergyman, b. Milton, N.J., 1828; d. 1909. [10]

Hatheway, Calvin, historian, b. Burton, N.B., 1796; d. Saint John, N.B., Aug. 20, 1866. [27]

Hatheway, Warren Franklin, merchant and politician, b. Saint John, N.B., 1850; d. Saint John, N.B., Oct. 29, 1923. [27]

Hatton, Frederic, playwright, b. Peru, Ill., 1879; d. Rutland, Ill., April 13, 1946.

Haubold, Herman Arthur, surgeon and novelist, b. New York, N.Y., 1867; d. New York, N.Y., May 5, 1931. [10; 11]

Hauck, Mrs. Louise, née Platt, novelist, b. Argentina, Kans. 1883; d. St. Joseph, Mo., Dec. 10, 1943. [10; 11]

Haugen, Nils Pederson, politician, b. Norway, 1849; d. Madison, Wis., April 23, 1931. [10; 44]

Haughton, Percy Duncan, football coach, b. Staten Island, N.Y., 1876; d. New York, N.Y., Oct. 27, 1924. [1]

Haultain, Theodore Arnold, littérateur, b. Cannanore, India, 1857; d. England, June 11, 1941. [27]

Haupt, Alexander James Derbyshire, clergyman, b. Greenfield, Mass., 1859; d. Horicon, Wis., Sept. 29, 1934.

Haupt, Charles Elvin, clergyman, b. Harrisburg, Pa., 1852; d. Lancaster, Pa., Oct. 14, 1920. [10]

Haupt, Herman, civil engineer, b. Philadelphia, Pa., 1817; d. Jersey City, N.J., Dec. 14, 1905. [1; 3; 4; 6; 10; 70]

Haupt, Lewis Muhlenberg, civil engineer, b. Gettysburg, Pa., 1844; d. Cynwyd, Pa., March 10, 1937. [3; 4; 10]

Hauser, Conrad Augustine, clergyman, b. Frederick, Md., 1872; d. Philadelphia, Pa., March 13, 1943. [10]

Hauser, James Joseph, local historian, b. 1854; d. ?

Havard, Valery, military surgeon, b. Compiègne, France, 1846; d. at sea, Nov. 6, 1927. [10]

Havemeyer, John Craig, manufacturer, b. New York, N.Y., 1833; d. Yonkers, N.Y., June 8, 1922. [10]

Haven, Mrs. Alice, née Bradley, novelist, b. Hudson, N.Y., 1828; d. Mamaroneck, N.Y., Aug. 23, 1863. [1; 3; 4; 6; 7; 8]

Haven, Charles Chauncy, historian, d. 1874. [51]

Haven, Mrs. Emily, née Bradley, See Haven, Mrs. Alice, née Bradley.

Haven, Erastus Otis, educationist and bishop, b. Boston, Mass., 1820; d. Salem, Ore., Aug. 2, 1881. [1; 3; 4; 6]

Haven, Gilbert, bishop, b. Malden, Mass., 1821; d. Malden, Mass., Jan. 3, 1880. [1; 3; 4; 6]

Haven, Joseph, philosopher, b. Dennis, Mass., 1816; d. Chicago, Ill., May 23, 1874. [1; 3; 4; 6]

Haven, Samuel Foster, librarian, b. Dedham, Mass., 1806; d. Worcester, Mass., Sept. 5, 1881. [3; 6; 8; 45]

Haven, Samuel Foster, physician and bibliographer, b. 1831; d. 1862. [51]

Havens, Catherine Elizabeth, music teacher, b. New York, N.Y., 1839; d. Stamford, Conn., Feb. 19, 1939.

Haverly, Christopher, theatrical manager, b. 1837; d. Salt Lake City, Utah, Sept. 28, 1901. [1]

Haviland, C. Augustus, lawyer and poet, b. 1832; d. Brooklyn, N.Y., Sept. 20, 1918.

Haviland, Clarence Floyd, psychiatrist, b. Spencertown, N.Y., 1875; d. Cairo, Egypt, Jan. 1, 1930. [4; 10]

Haviland, John, architect, b. near Taunton, England, 1792; d. Philadelphia, Pa., March 28, 1852. [1; 3; 4]

Haviland, Mrs. Laura, née Smith, social worker, b. Leeds county, Upper Canada, 1808; d. Grand Rapids, Mich., April 20, 1898. [39]

Hawes, Charles Boardman, writer of books for boys, b. Clifton Springs, N.Y., 1889; d. Gloucester, Mass., July 15, 1923. [1; 7]

Hawes, Charles Henry, anthropologist, b. New Southgate, England, 1867; d. near Alexandria, Va., Dec. 13, 1943. [7; 10; 11]

Hawes, Harry Bartow, politician, b. Covington, Ky., 1869; d. Washington, D.C., July 31, 1947. [10]

Hawes, James Anderson, lawyer, b. New York, N.Y., 1873; d. Mount Kisco, N.Y., Feb. 28, 1936. [62]

Hawes, James William, lawyer and genealogist, b. Chatham, Mass., 1844; d. Aug. 31, 1918. [10; 51]

Hawes, Joel, clergyman, b. Medway, Mass., 1789; d. Gilead, Conn., June 5, 1867. [3; 4; 6; 8]

Hawes, John Bromham, physician, b. Montclair, N.J., 1877; d. Brookline, Mass., July 20, 1938. [10; 11; 51]

Hawes, William Post, lawyer and essayist, b. New York, N.Y., 1803; d. New York, N.Y., 1842. [3; 4; 7; 8]

Hawkes, Arthur, journalist, b. Aylesford, England, 1871; d. Toronto, Ont., Oct. 12, 1933. [27]

Hawkes, Herbert Edwin, educationist, b. Templeton, Mass., 1872; d. New York, N.Y., May 4, 1943. [10; 11]

Hawkes, Nathan Mortimer, local historian, b. 1843; d. North Saugus, Mass., Feb. 7, 1919.

Hawkins, Alfred, historian, b. Bridgeport, England, about 1802; d. Quebec, Que., June 30, 1854. [27]

Hawkins, Benjamin, Indian agent, b. Warren county, N.C., 1754; d. Hawkinsville, Ga., June 6, 1816. [3; 4; 34]

Hawkins, Chauncey Jeddie, clergyman, b. Vacaville, Calif., 1876; d. Badger, Calif., Aug. 9, 1930. [10; 62]

Hawkins, John Parker, soldier, b. Indianapolis, Ind., 1830; d. Indianapolis, Ind., Feb. 7, 1914. [10]

Hawkins, Nehemiah, mechanical engineer, b. 1833; d. Jan. 16, 1928.

Hawkins, Rush Christopher, soldier and book-collector, b. Pomfret, Vt., 1831; d. New York, N.Y., Oct. 25, 1920. [1; 3; 4; 7; 10; 43]

Hawkins, William George, clergyman, b. Baltimore, Md., 1823; d. Denver, Colo., July 18, 1909. [3; 6; 10; 34]

Hawkridge, Emma. See Loomis, Mrs. Emma, née Hawkridge.

Hawks, Francis Lister, bishop, b. New Bern, N.C., 1798; d. New York, N.Y., Sept. 27, 1866. [1; 3; 4; 6; 7; 8]

Hawks, Wells, press agent, b. Charleston, W.Va., 1870; d. Pomona, N.Y., Dec. 5, 1941.

Hawksworth, Hallam (pseud.). See Atkinson, Francis Blake.

Hawley, Bostwick, clergyman, b. Camillies, N.Y., 1814; d. Saratoga Springs, N.Y., July 29, 1910. [3; 6; 10]

Hawley, Charles, clergyman, b. Catskill, N.Y., 1819; d. Auburn, N.Y., Nov. 26, 1885. [3; 6]

Hawley, Frederick Barnard, economist, b. Albany, N.Y., 1843; d. May 31, 1929.

Hawley, Gideon, lawyer, b. Huntington, Conn., 1785; d. Albany, N.Y., July 17, 1870. [1; 3; 4; 6; 8]

Hawley, Hattie Louise, educationist, b. 1890; d. July 4, 1934.

Hawley, James H., politician and local historian, b. Dubuque, Ia., 1847; d. Boise, Ida., Aug. 3, 1929. [4; 10]

Hawley, John Gardner, lawyer, b. Detroit, Mich., 1845; d. Detroit, Mich., 1900. [39]

Hawley, Walter Augustus, traveller, b. 1863; d. Santa Barbara, Calif., March, 1920.

Hawley, William Fitz, poet, b. 1804; d. Laprairie, Que., Jan., 1855. [27]

Hawley, Zerah, traveller, b. 1781; d. 1856. [62]

Hawley, Zerah Kent, clergyman, b. Avon, Conn., 1806; d. Memphis, Tenn., Dec. 28, 1869. [62]

Hawn, Henry Gaines, elocutionist, b. Richmond, Va., 1864; d. ? [4; 10]

Haworth, Paul Leland, historian and explorer, b. West Newton, Ind., 1876; d. Indianapolis, Ind., March 24, 1938. [7; 10]

Hawthorne, Emily (pseud.). See Charles, Mrs. Emily, née Thornton.

Hawthorne, Julian, novelist and man of letters, b. Boston, Mass., 1846; d. San Francisco, Calif., July 14, 1934. [1a; 2; 3; 4; 5; 6; 7; 8; 10]

Hawthorne, Nathaniel, novelist, b. Salem, Mass., 1804 d. Plymouth, N.H., May 18, 1864. [1; 2; 3; 4; 5; 6; 7; 8; 71: 72]

Hay, Charles Augustus, clergyman and educationist, b. York, Pa., 1821; d. Gettysburg, Pa., June 26, 1893. [1; 3]

Hay, Elzey (pseud.). See Andrews, Eliza Frances.

Hay, George, jurist, b. Williamsburg, Va., 1765; d. Richmond, Va., Sept. 21, 1830. [1; 3; 4; 34]

Hay, Gustavus, lawyer, b. Boston, Mass.. 1866; d. Avon, Mass., Sept. 18, 1901. [51]

Hay, James, journalist and novelist, b. Harrisonburg, Va., 1881; d. Washington, D.C., May 7, 1936. [7; 10; 11]

Hay, John Milton, poet, journalist, historian, and diplomat, b. Salem, Ind., 1838; d. Newbury, N.H., July 1, 1905. [1; 2; 3; 4; 5; 7; 10; 71, 72]

Hay, Oliver Perry, palaeontologist, b. Jefferson county, Ind., 1846; d. Washington, D.C., Nov. 2, 1930. [4; 10; 13]

Hay, Richard Carman, sales manager, b. Fort Chester, Mont., 1893; d. Charlemont, Mass., Sept. 16, 1930. [62]

Hay, Timothy (pseud.). See Rollins, Montgomery.

Hayden, Edward Everett, naval officer, b. Boston, Mass., 1858; d. Baltimore, Md., Nov. 7, 1932. 1a; 4; 10]

Hayden, Ferdinand Vandiveer, geologist, b. Westfield, Mass., 1829; d. Philadelphia, Pa., Dec. 22, 1887. [1; 3; 4; 6; 8]

Hayden, Horace Edwin, clergyman and genealogist, b. Catonville, Md., 1837; d. Aug. 22, 1917. [4; 7; 10; 34]

Hayden, Horace H., geologist, b. Windsor, Conn., 1769; d. Baltimore, Md., Jan. 26, 1844. [1; 3; 34]

Hayden, Jabez Haskell, genealogist, b. 1811; d. 1902.

Hayden, William Benjamin, clergyman, b. 1816; d. 1893. [6; 8]

Haydn, Hiram Collins, clergyman, b. Pompey, N.Y., 1831; d. Cleveland, O., July 31, 1913. [3a; 4; 7; 8; 10; 68]

Haydon, Andrew, politician and historian, b. Pakenham, Ont., 1867; d. Ottawa, Ont., Nov. 10, 1932. [27]

Hayes, Abner Pierce, jurist, b. Bethlehem, Conn., 1876; d. Milford, Conn., July 26, 1929. [62]

Hayes, Augustus Allen, historian and novelist, b. Roxbury, Mass., 1837; d. Paris, France, April 18, 1892. [3b;. 4; 7; 8]

Hayes, Charles Harris, clergyman, b. Newark, N.J., 1868; d. Madison, N.J., July 18, 1910. [10]

Hayes, Charles Wells, clergyman, b. 1828; d. Nov. 29, 1908. [47]

Hayes, Charles Willard, geologist, b. Granville, O., 1859; d. Washington, D.C., Feb. 8, 1916. [10]

Hayes, Doremus Almy, theologian, b. Russelville, O., 1863; d. Evanston, Ill., May, 1936. [10; 11]

Hayes, Edward Cary, sociologist, b. Lewiston, Me., 1868; d. Urbana, Ill., Aug. 7, 1928. [1a; 10]

Hayes, Ellen, mathematician, b. Granville, O., 1851; d. West Park, N.Y., Oct. 27, 1930. [10]

Hayes, Henry (pseud.). See Kirk, Mrs. Ellen Warner, née Olney.

Hayes, Isaac Israel, physician and explorer, b. Chester county, Pa., 1832; d. New York, N.Y., Dec. 17, 1881. [1; 3; 4; 6; 7]

Hayes, Jeff W., miscellaneous writer, b. Cleveland, O., 1858; d. Portland, Ore., 1917. [41]

Hayes, John, poet, d. 1815. [7]

Hayes, John Lord, lawyer, b. South Berwick, Me., 1812; d. Cambridge, Mass., April 18, 1887. [1; 3; 4; 6]

Hayes, John Russell, poet and librarian, b. West Chester, Pa., 1866; d. West Chester, Pa., Dec. 29, 1945. [11]

Hayes, Lyman Simpson, local historian, b. 1850; d. Bellows Falls, Vt., 1935.

Hayes, Philip Cornelius, soldier and politician, b. Granby, Conn., 1833; d. Joliet, Ill., July 13, 1916. [3; 10]

Hayes, Stephen Quentin, electrical engineer, b. Washington, D.C., 1873; d. Pittsburgh, Pa., April 4, 1936. [10]

Hayes, William Allen, lawyer, b. Portsmouth, N.H., 1843; d. Cambridge, Mass., April 1, 1924. [51]

Hayford, John Fillmore, civil engineer, b. Rouse Point, N.Y., 1868; d. Chicago, Ill., March 10, 1925. [1; 4; 10]

Haygood, Atticus Green, bishop, b. Watkinsville, Ga., 1839; d. Oxford, Ga., Jan. 19, 1896. [1; 3; 4; 6; 7; 34]

Hayley, Herman Wadsworth, educationist, b. Somerset, Mass., 1867; d. Boston, Mass., Sept. 4, 1899. [3b]

Hayley, John William, clergyman, b. Tuftonboro, N.H., 1834; d. Wolfeboro, N. H., Oct. 3, 1927. [10; 49]

Hayne, Joseph E., clergyman, b. Charleston, S.C., 1849; d. Brooklyn, N.Y., Jan. 17, 1911.

Hayne, Paul Hamilton, poet, b. Charleston, S.C., 1830; d. near Augusta, Ga., July 6, 1886. [1; 2; 3; 4; 6; 7; 34; 71]

Hayne, Robert Young, lawyer, b. 1853; d. 1903.

Hayne, William Hamilton, poet, b. Charleston, S.C., 1856; d. Augusta, Ga., Jan. 7, 1929. [8; .10; 34]

Hayner, Rutherford, local historian, b. Clarendon, N.Y., 1877; d. West Sand Lake, N.Y., March 14, 1939. [10]

Haynes, Dudley Cammet, clergyman, b. Portland, Me., 1809; d. Binghampton, N.Y., Feb. 21, 1888. [26]

Haynes, Edwin Mortimer, clergyman, b. Concord, Mass., 1836; d. Rutland, Vt., Dec. 15, 1910. [49]

Haynes, Emory James, clergyman and novelist, b. Cabot, Vt., 1847; d. Poughkeepsie, N.Y., Dec. 31, 1914. [8; 10; 49]

Haynes, George Henry, descriptive writer, b. 1855; d. 1912. [38]

Haynes, Irving Samuel, physician, b. Saranac, N.Y., 1851; d. Oct. 9, 1946. [10; 13]

Haynes, Lemuel, clergyman, b. West Hartford, Conn., 1753; d. Granville, N.Y., Sept. 28, 1834. [4]

Haynes, Nathaniel Smith, clergyman, b. Washington, Ky., 1844; d. Jan. 12, 1925. [10]

Haynes, Roy Asa, prohibitionist, b. Hillsboro, O., 1881; d. Hillsboro, O., Oct. 20, 1940. [10; 11]

Haynie, James Henry, journalist, b. Winchester, Ill., 1841; d. Newton Centre, Mass., May 15, 1912. [7; 10]

Hays, Calvin Cornwell, clergyman, b. Cumberland county, Pa., 1861; d. Johnstown, Pa., Feb. 4, 1935. [10]

Hays, George Peirce, clergyman, b. 1838; d. Kansas City, Mo., 1897. [8]

Hays, Harold Melvin, physician, b. Rochester, N.Y., 1880; d. Scarsdale, N.Y., Aug. 20, 1940.

Hays, Isaac, physician, b. Philadelphia, Pa., 1796; d. Philadelphia, Pa., April 13, 1879. [1; 3; 4; 6]

Hays, Isaac Minis, physician, b. Philadelphia, Pa., 1847; d. Philadelphia, Pa., June 5, 1925. [10]

Hays, Mrs. Margaret Parker, née Gebbie, writer of books for children, b. Philadelphia, Pa., 1874; d. Sept. 13, 1925. [10]

Hays, Willet Martin, agriculturist, b. Hardin county, Ia., 1859; d. 1928. [2; 10; 37; 70]

Hays, William Shakespeare, song-writer, b. Louisville, Ky., 1837; d. Louisville, Ky., July 24, 1907. [1; 3; 4; 7; 10; 74]

Hayward, Edward Farwell, clergyman and poet, b. Lowell, Mass., 1851; d. Chicopee, Mass., Dec. 23, 1923. [8; 10]

Hayward, George, physician, b. Boston, Mass., 1791; d. Boston, Mass., Oct. 7, 1863. [3; 4]

Hayward, Harrison Washburn, mathematician, b. 1873; d. Cambridge, Mass., Oct. 18, 1932.

Hayward, James, civil engineer, b. Concord, Mass., 1786; d. Boston, Mass., July 27, 1866. [3]

Hayward, John, compiler of gazetteers, b. Boston, Mass., 1781; d. Boston, Mass., Oct. 13, 1862. [3; 4; 6]

Hayward, Silvanus, local historian, b. Gilsum, N.H., 1828; d. Southbridge, Mass., Sept. 1, 1908. [49]

Hayward, William C., local historian, b. 1847; d. 1917. [37]

Hayward, William H., soldier and poet, b. 1813; d. 1876.

Haywarde, Richard (pseud.). See Cozzens, Frederick Swartwout.

Haywood, John, jurist and historian, b. Halifax county, N.C., 1762; d. Nashville, Tenn., Dec. 22, 1826. [1; 3; 4; 34]

Haywood, Marshall De Lancey, historian, b. 1871; d. 1933.

Haywood, William Dudley, labour agitator, b. Salt Lake City, Utah, 1869; d. Moscow, Russia, March 18, 1928. [1]

Hazard, Caroline, educationist, b. Peacedale, R.I., 1856; d. Santa Barbara, Calif., March 19, 1945. [4; 7; 10]

Hazard, Ebenezer, historian, b. Philadelphia, Pa., 1744; d. Philadelphia, Pa., June 13, 1817. [1; 3]

Hazard, Elizabeth, poet, b. 1799; d. 1882.

Hazard, Joseph, poet, b. 1757; d. 1817.

Hazard, Marshall Custiss, religious journalist, b. Tioga county, Pa., 1839; d. Dorchester Center, Mass., Feb. 14, 1929. [8; 10]

Hazard, Rowland Gibson, philosopher, b. South Kingstown, R.I., 1801; d. Peacedale, R.I., June 24, 1888. [1; 3; 4; 6; 8]

Hazard, Samuel, archaeologist, b. Philadelphia, Pa., 1784; d. Philadelphia, Pa., May 22, 1870. [1; 3; 4; 7]

Hazard, Samuel, historian, b. 1834; d. 1876. [6]

Hazard, Thomas Robinson, social reformer, b. South Kingstown, R.I., 1797; d. New York, N.Y., March 26, 1886. [1; 3; 6; 7]

Hazard, Willis Pope, miscellaneous writer, b. 1825; d. Philadelphia, Pa., Feb. 18, 1913. [6; 8; 55]

Hazelius, Ernest Lewis, clergyman, b. Prussia, 1777; d. South Carolina, Feb. 20, 1853. [1; 3; 6; 34]

Hazeltine, Horace (pseud.). See Wayne, Charles Stokes.

Hazeltine, Mary Emogene, librarian, b. Jamestown, N.Y., 1868; d. Jamestown, N.Y., June 17, 1949. [10]

Hazeltine, Mayo Williamson, journalist, b. Boston, Mass., 1841; d. Atlantic City, N.J., Sept. 14, 1909. [7; 10; 51]

Hazeltine, Miron James, chess-player, b. 1824; d. about 1907.

Hazelton, George Cochrane, lawyer and playwright, b. Boscobel, Wis., 1868; d. New York, N.Y., June 24, 1921. [7; 10]

Hazelton, John Morton, journalist, b. near Shawnee, O., 1867; d. Kansas City, Mo., July 15, 1940.

Hazen, Allen, civil engineer, b. Hartford, Vt., 1869; d. Miles City, Mont., July 26, 1930. [1a; 10]

Hazen, Charles Downer, historian, b. Barnet, Vt., 1868; d. New York, N.Y., Sept. 18, 1941. [7; 10; 14]

Hazen, Henry Allen, clergyman, b. Hartford, Vt., 1832; d. Hartford, Vt., Aug. 4, 1900. [10; 49]

Hazen, Henry Allen, meteorologist, b. India, 1849; d. Washington, D.C., Jan. 23, 1900. [3b; 4; 10]

Hazen, Jasper, clergyman, b. about 1790; d. Woodstock, Vt., March 30, 1882. [43]

Hazen, John Munger, railway contractor, b. Troy, N.Y., 1838; d. ? [70]

Hazen, Marshman Williams, lawyer, b. Beverly, Mass., 1845; d. New York, N.Y., July 22, 1911. [10; 49]

Hazen, William Babcock, soldier, b. West Hartford, Vt., 1830; d. Washington, D.C., Jan. 16, 1887. [1; 3; 4; 6; 43]

Hazzard, Charles, osteopath, b. Peoria, Ill., 1871; d. Stinson Lake, N.H., Aug. 24, 1938. [10]

Hazzard, John Edward, playwright and poet, b. New York, N.Y., 1881; d. Great Neck, Long Island, N.Y., Dec. 2, 1935. [10]

Head, Franklin Harvey, banker and littérateur, b. Paris, N.Y., 1835; d. Chicago, Ill., June 28, 1914. [10]

Headland, Isaac Taylor, missionary, b. Freedom, Pa., 1859; d. Alliance, O., Aug. 2, 1942. [7; 10; 11]

Headley, Joel Tyler, journalist and biographer, b. Walton, N.Y., 1813; d. Newburgh, N.Y., Jan. 16, 1897. [1; 3; 4; 6; 7; 9]

Headley, Phineas Camp, clergyman, historian, and biographer, b. Walton, N.Y., 1819; d. Lexington, Mass., Jan. 4, 1903. [1; 2; 3; 4; 6; 7; 9]

Heady, Morrison, deaf and blind poet, b. Spencer county, Ky., 1829; d. 1915. [4; 34]

Heagerty, John Joseph, physician, b. Montreal, Que., 1879; d. Ottawa, Ont., Feb. 7, 1946. [30]

Heagle, David, clergyman, b. Montgomery county, N.Y., 1836; d. Chicago, Ill., Feb. 13, 1922. [67]

Healy, George Peter Alexander, portrait painter, b. Boston, Mass., 1813; d. Chicago, Ill., June 24, 1894. [1; 4]

Healy, Patrick Joseph, priest, b. Waterford, Ireland, 1871; d. Washington, D.C., May 19, 1937. [10; 21]

Healy, Tim, soldier, b. Sydney, Australia, 1893; d. Fort Worth, Tex., Oct. 13, 1947.

Heap, David Porter, soldier, b. San Stefano, Turkey, 1843; d. Pasadena, Calif., Oct. 25, 1910. [3; 8; 10]

Heap, Gwynn Harris, diplomat, b. Chester, Pa., 1817; d. Constantinople, Turkey, March 6, 1887. [3; 6; 8]

Heard, Franklin Fiske, lawyer, b. Wayland, Mass., 1825; d. Boston, Mass., Sept. 29, 1889. [1; 3; 4; 6; 7; 8]

Heard, Isaac V.D., lawyer, b. Goshen, N.Y., 1834; d. 1913. [70]

Heard, William H., bishop, b. Elbert county, Ga., 1850; d. Philadelphia, Pa., Sept. 3, 1937. [4; 10]

Hearn, Lafcadio, prose stylist and writer on Japan, b. Smyrna, Asia Minor, 1850; d. Tokyo, Japan, Sept. 26, 1904. [1; 2; 3; 4; 5; 6; 7; 8; 9; 10; 71; 72]

Heath, Herbert Milton, lawyer, b. Gardiner, Me., 1853; d. Augusta, Me., Aug. 18, 1912. [38]

Heath, James Ewell, novelist and playwright, b. Virginia, 1792; d. June 28, 1862. [1; 7]

Heath, Mrs. Mary, née Hubbard, biographer, b. 1864; d. Buffalo, N.Y., May 24, 1942.

Heath, S. Burton, journalist, b. Lynn, Mass., 1898; d. India, July 12, 1949. [10]

Heath, William, soldier, b. Roxbury, Mass., 1737; d. Roxbury, Mass., Jan. 24, 1814. [1; 3; 4]

Heatherington, Alexander, geologist, d. 1878. [33]

Heaton, Augustus Goodyear, artist, b. Philadelphia, Pa., 1844; d. Washington, D.C., Oct. 11, 1930. [4; 10]

Heaton, John Langdon, journalist, b. Canton, N.Y., 1860; d. Brooklyn, N.Y., Feb. 21, 1935. [1a; 4; 7; 10; 11]

Heatwole, Lewis James, bishop, b. Dale Enterprise, Va., 1852; d. Dec. 26, 1932. [10; 11]

Hebard, Grace Raymond, educationist, b. Clinton, Ia., 1861; d. Laramie, Wyo., Oct. 11, 1936. [10; 11]

Hebberd, Stephen Southric, clergyman, b. Jefferson, N.Y., 1841; d. Spokane, Wash., Oct. 3, 1922. [60]

Hebel, John William, educationist, b. Auburn, Ind., 1891; d. Ithaca, N.Y., Feb. 7, 1934. [10]

Hebron, Mrs. Ellen, née Ellington, poet, b. 1839; d. 1904. [34]

Hecht, Selig, educationist, b. Austria, 1892; d. New York, N.Y., Sept. 18, 1947. [10]

Heck, Fannie Exile Scudder, poet, b. 1862; d. 1915.

Heck, William Harry, educationist, b. Raleigh, N.C., 1879; d. University, Va., Jan. 4, 1919. [10; 34]

Hecker, Isaac Thomas, priest, b. New York, N.Y., 1819; d. New York, N.Y., Dec. 22, 1888. [1; 3; 4; 6; 7]

Heckewelder, John Gottlieb Ernestus, missionary, b. Bedford, England, 1743; d. Bethlehem, Pa., Jan. 31, 1823. [1; 3; 4]

Hedge, Frederic Henry, clergyman and educationist, b. Cambridge, Mass., 1805; d. Cambridge, Mass., Aug. 21, 1890. [1; 3; 4; 6; 7]

Hedge, Levi, philosopher, b. Warwick, Mass., 1766; d. Cambridge, Mass., Jan. 3, 1844. [1; 3]

Hedges, Gilbert Lawrence, lawyer, b. Canemah, Ore., 1874; d. Oregon City, Ore., Jan. 23, 1929. [62]

Hedges, Henry Parsons, lawyer, b. East Hampton, N.Y., 1817; d. Bridgehampton, N.Y., Sept. 26, 1911. [62]

Hedges, Job Elmer, lawyer, b. Elizabeth, N.J., 1862; d. Atlantic City, N.J., Feb. 22, 1925. [10]

Hedges, Samuel, priest, b. 1854; d. 1916. [21]

Hedley, James Alexander, journalist, b. Prestonpans, Scotland, 1844; d. Toronto, Ont., Dec. 23, 1916. [27]

Hedrick, Earle Raymond, mathematician, b. Union City, Ind., 1876; d. Providence, R.I., Feb. 3, 1943. [10; 13]

Heermans, Forbes, journalist, b. Syracuse, N.Y., 1856; d. Syracuse, N.Y., Sept. 18, 1928. [7; 10]

Heggen, Thomas O., novelist and playwright, b. Fort Dodge, Ia., 1919; d. New York, N.Y., May 19, 1949.

Heidel, William Arthur, educationist, b. Burlington, Ia., 1868; d. Middletown, Conn., Jan. 15, 1941. [7; 10; 11]

Heilprin, Angelo, geologist and explorer, b. Hungary, 1853; d. New York, N.Y., July 17, 1907. [1; 3; 4; 6; 7; 10]

Heilprin, Louis, educationist, b. Hungary, 1851; d. 1914. [3; 8; 10]

Heilprin, Michael, scholar and journalist, b. Poland, 1823; d. New York, N.Y., May 10, 1888. [1; 3; 4]

Heindel, Max, Rosicrucian, b. 1865; d. 1919.

Heinrich, Max, concert-singer, b. Chemnitz, Saxony, 1853; d. New York, N.Y., Aug. 9, 1916. [1; 4; 20]

Heiskell, Samuel Gordon, lawyer and historian, b. Monroe county, Tenn., 1858; d. Knoxville, Tenn., Sept. 17, 1923. [10]

Heisler, Charles Washington, educationist, b. Minersville, Pa., 1857; d. ? [4]

Heisler, Daniel Yost, clergyman, b. 1820; d. 1888.

Heiss, Michael, archbishop, b. Bavaria, 1818; d. Milwaukee, Wis., March 26; 1890. [1; 3; 4]

Heistand, Henry Olcot Sheldon, soldier, b. near Richwood, O., 1856; d. Richwood, O., Aug. 8, 1924. [10]

Heitman, Francis Bernard, historian, b. 1838; d. 1926.

Heitzman, Charles, physician, b. Hungary, 1836; d. New York, N.Y., 1896. [3; 6; 8]

Held, Isidore William, physician, b. Austria, 1876; d. New York, N.Y., March 3, 1947.

Haller, Albert Henry, engineer, b. 1866; d. 1906.

Heller, Edmund, naturalist, b. Freeport, Ill., 1875; d. San Francisco, Calif., July 19, 1939. [7; 10]

Heller, Maximilian, rabbi, b. Prague, Bohemia, 1860; d. New Orleans, La., March 30, 1929. [1; 10]

Heller, Otto, educationist, b. Saxony, 1863; d. Torch Lake, Mich., July 29, 1941. [7; 10; 11]

Heller, William Jacob, genealogist and local historian, b. 1857; d. Easton, Pa., 1920.

Hellinger, Mark, journalist, b. New York, N.Y., 1903; d. Hollywood, Calif., Dec. 21, 1947. [7; 10]

Helm, Mary, social worker, b. 1845; d. 1913.

Helms, William Thomas, clergyman, d. 1900. [34]

Helmuth, William Tod, surgeon, b. Philadelphia, Pa., 1833; d. New York, N.Y., May 15, 1902. [1; 4; 7; 8; 10]

Helper, Hinton Rowan, reformer, b. Davie county, N.C., 1829; d. Washington, D.C., March 9, 1909. [1; 3; 6; 7; 34]

Hemans, Lawton Thomas, lawyer and historian, b. Collamer, N.Y., 1864; d. Mason, Mich., Nov. 17, 1916. [10; 39]

Hembdt, Phil Harold, educationist, b. Jeffersonville, N.Y., 1875; d. Albion, Mich., Oct. 12, 1927. [10]

Hemenway, Abby Maria, poet and historian, b. Ludlow, Vt., 1828; d. Chicago, Ill., Feb. 24, 1890. [6; 8; 43]

Hemenway, Asa, genealogist, b. Shoreman, Vt., 1810; d. Manchester, Vt., Feb. 26, 1892. [43]

Hemenway, Henry Bixby, physician, b. Montpelier, Vt., 1856; d. Springfield, Ill., Jan. 1, 1931. [10]

Heming, Arthur, artist, b. Paris, Ont., 1870; d. Hamilton, Ont., Oct. 26, 1940. [10; 27]

Hemmenway, Moses, clergyman, b. Framingham, Mass., 1735; d. Wells, Mass., Aug. 5, 1811. [3; 6]

Hemmeon, Morley De Wolfe, historian, b. Saint John, N.B., 1868; d. Wolfville N.S., Aug. 22, 1919. [27]

Hemmeter, John Conrad, physiologist, b. Baltimore, Md., 1863; d. Baltimore, Md., Feb. 25, 1931. [1; 4; 10]

Hempel, Charles Julius, physician, b. Germany, 1811; d. Grand Rapids, Mich., Sept. 24, 1879. [1; 3; 6]

Hemphill, James Calvin, journalist, b. Due West, S.C., 1850; d. Abbeville, S.C., Nov. 20, 1927. [4; 34]

Hemphill, Vivia, journalist, b. Auburn, Calif., 1889; d. Berkeley, Calif., Oct. 20, 1934. [35]

Hempl, George, philologist, b. Whitewater, Wis., 1859; d. Palo Alto, Calif., Aug. 14, 1921. [1; 4; 10]

Hempstead, Fay, poet, b. Little Rock, Ark., 1847; d. Little Rock, Ark., April 24, 1934. [7; 10]

Hempstead, Junius Lackland, poet, b. 1842; d. ? [34]

Hempstead, Thomas, clergyman and poet, b. 1822; d. 1886.

Hemstreet, Charles, journalist, b. New York, N.Y., 1866; d. ? [2; 7]

Henck, John Benjamin, civil engineer, b. Philadelphia, Pa., 1815; d. Montecito, Calif., Jan. 3, 1903. [1; 3; 10]

Henderson, Mrs. Alice, née **Corbin,** poet, b. St. Louis, Mo., 1881; d. Santa Fé, N.M., July 18, 1949. [10]

Henderson, Charles Hanford, educationist, b. Philadelphia, Pa., 1861; d. Daytona Beach, Fla., Jan. 9, 1941. [7; 10; 14]

Henderson, Charles Richmond, sociologist, b. Covington, Ind., 1848; d. Charleston, S.C., March 29, 1915. [1; 4; 7; 8; 10]

Henderson, Daniel McIntyre, poet, b. Glasgow, Scotland, 1851; d. Baltimore, Md., Sept. 8, 1906. [1; 7]

Henderson, Ernest Flagg, historian, b. New Brighton, N.Y., 1861; d. Cambridge, Mass., Dec. 30, 1928. [8; 10; 51]

Henderson, Ernest Norton, educationist, b. La Salle county, Ill., 1869; d. Brooklyn, N.Y., March 4, 1938. [10]

Henderson, Gerard Carl, lawyer, b. Williamstown, Mass., 1891; d. New York, N.Y., Aug. 31, 1927. [10; 51]

Henderson, Howard Andrew Millet, clergyman, b. Paris, Ky., 1836; d. Hartwell, O., 1912. [10]

Henderson, Isaac, journalist, b. Brooklyn, N.Y., 1850; d. Rome, Italy, March 31, 1909. [4; 7; 8; 10]

Henderson, John Brooks, lawyer, b. Louisiana, Mo., 1870; d. Washington, D.C., Jan. 4, 1923. [8; 10; 34]

Henderson, Junius, naturalist, b. Marshalltown, Ia., 1865; d. Boulder, Colo., Nov. 4, 1937. [10; 13]

Henderson, Lawrence Joseph, biochemist, b. Lynn, Mass., 1878; d. Boston, Mass., Feb. 10, 1942. [10; 13; 51]

Henderson, Marc Antony (pseud.). See Strong, George Augustus.

Henderson, Mrs. Mary Newton, née **Foote,** dietician, b. New York, N.Y., 1844; d. Bar Harbor, Me., July 16, 1931. [3; 8; 10]

Henderson, Peter, horticulturist, b. near Edinburgh, Scotland, 1822; d. Jersey City, N.J., Jan. 17, 1890. [1; 3; 4; 6]

Henderson, Robert, actuary, b. Russell, Ont., 1871; d. Crown Point, N.Y., Feb. 16, 1942. [10]

Henderson, Thomas, surgeon, b. 1789; d. Lexington, Va., Aug. 11, 1854. [55]

Henderson, Velyien Ewart, pharmacologist, b. Cobourg, Ont., 1877; d. Go Home, Georgian Bay, Ont., Aug. 6, 1945. [30]

Henderson, Walter Brooks Drayton, educationist, b. Jamaica, B.W.I., 1887; d. Montreal, Que., July 10, 1939. [7; 10]

Henderson, William James, journalist and music critic, b. Newark, N.J., 1855; d. New York, N.Y., June 5, 1937. [4; 7; 10; 11; 20]

Henderson, Yandell, physiologist, b. Louisville, Ky., 1873; d. La Jolla, Calif., Feb. 18, 1944. [13; 62]

Hendrick, Burton Jesse, biographer and historian, b. New Haven, Conn., 1871; d. New York, N.Y., March 24, 1949. [10; 11; 62]

Hendrick, Ellwood, chemist, b. Albany, N.Y., 1861; d. New York, N.Y., Oct. 29, 1930. [1; 4; 10; 13]

Hendricks, Eldo Lewis, educationist, b. Rossville, Ind., 1866; d. Warrensburg, Mo., Nov. 22, 1938. [10]

Hendrix, Eugene Russell, bishop, b. Fayette, Mo., 1847; d. Kansas City, Mo., Nov. 11, 1927. [1; 3a; 4; 10; 34]

Heney, Hughes, lawyer, b. 1789; d. Three Rivers, Que., Jan. 15, 1844. [27]

Hening, William Waller, lawyer, b. Virginia, about 1767; d. Richmond, Va., April 1, 1828. [1; 3; 6; 34]

Henius, Max, chemist, b. Denmark, 1859; d. Chicago, Ill., Nov. 15, 1935. [10]

Henkle, Moses Montgomery, clergyman, b. Pendleton county, Va., 1798; d. Richmond, Va., 1864. [3; 34]

Henneman, John Bell, educationist, b. Spartansburg, S.C., 1864; d. Richmond, Va., Nov. 26, 1908. [7; 10; 34]

Hennequin, Alfred, educationist, b. France, 1846; d. 1914. [7; 10]

Hennessy, Roland Burke, editor and poet, b. Milford, Mass., 1870; d. Larchmont, N.Y., Feb. 1, 1939. [7]

Hennessy, William B., historian, b. England; d. St. Paul, Minn., March 4, 1921. [70]

Henney, William Franklin, lawyer, b. Enfield, Conn., 1852; d. Hartford, Conn., Feb. 7, 1928. [10; 11; 56]

Hennrich, Kilian Joseph, priest, b. Holland, 1880; d. New York, N.Y., Nov. 23, 1946. [21]

Henri, Robert, artist, b. Cincinnati, O., 1865; d. New York, N.Y., July 12, 1929. [1; 4; 10; 11]

Henrotin, Mrs. Ellen M., née **Martin,** feminist, b. Portland, Me., 1847; d. South Berlin, N.Y., June 29, 1922. [10]

Henry, Alexander, fur-trader, b. New Brunswick, N.J., 1739; d. Montreal, Lower Canada, April 4, 1824. [1a; 27]

Henry, Alfred Judson, meteorologist, b. New Bethlehem, Pa., 1858; d. Washington, D.C., Oct. 5, 1931. [4; 10]

Henry, Arthur, journalist, novelist, and playwright, b. 1867; d. Narragansett Pier, Long Island, N.Y., June 2, 1934. [7; 10]

Henry, Caleb Sprague, clergyman and educationist, b. Rutland, Mass., 1804; d. New York, N.Y., March 9, 1884. [1; 3; 4; 6; 7]

Henry, Hugh Thomas, priest, b. Philadelphia, Pa., 1862; d. Jessup, Pa., March 12, 1946. [22]

Henry, James, historian, b. Philadelphia, Pa., 1809; d. Boulton, Pa., June 14, 1895. [3; 8]

Henry, John Flournoy, physician, b. Henry's Mills, Ky., 1793; d. Burlington, Ia., Nov. 12, 1873. [8; 34]

Henry, John Joseph, soldier, b. 1758; d. 1881. [3; 8; 27]

Henry, Joseph, physicist, b. Albany, N.Y., 1799; d. Washington, D.C., May 13, 1878. [1; 3; 4; 6; 8]

Henry, Mrs. Mary H., writer of books for girls, fl. 1871-1899. [6]

Henry, Mathew Schropp, local historian, b. 1790; d. 1862.

Henry, Mellinger Edward, educationist, b. Mount Pleasant, Pa., 1873; d. Englewood, N.J., Jan. 31, 1946.

Henry, O. (pseud.). See Porter, William Sydney.

Henry, Mrs. Sarepta Myrenda, née Irish, poet and novelist, b. Albion, Pa., 1839; d. Jan. 16, 1900. [4; 6; 7; 8]

Henry, Thomas Charlton, clergyman, b. Philadelphia, Pa., 1790; d. Charleston, S.C., Oct. 4, 1827. [3; 6; 8]

Henry, Walter, army surgeon, b. Donegal, Ireland, 1791; d. Belleville, Ont., June 27, 1860. [27]

Henry, William Arnon, agriculturist, b. Norwalk, O., 1850; d. San Diego, Calif., Nov. 25, 1932. [1a; 10]

Henry, William Elmer, librarian, b. near Connersville, Ind., 1857; d. Seattle, Wash., March 20, 1936. [10]

Henry, William Seaton, soldier, b. Albany, N.Y., 1816; d. New York, N.Y., March 5, 1851. [3; 8]

Henry, William Wirt, biographer, b. Charlotte county, Va., 1831; d. Richmond, Va., Dec. 5, 1900. [1; 3; 4; 7; 10]

Henry-Ruffin, M. E., See Ruffin, Mrs. Margaret Ellen, née Henry.

Hensel, Octavia (pseud.). See Seymour, Mrs. Mary Alice, née Ives.

Hensel, William Uhler, lawyer, b. Baltimore, Md., 1836; d. Lancaster, Pa., Feb. 27, 1915. [8; 10]

Henshall, James Alexander, physician and naturalist, b. Baltimore, Md., 1836; d. Cincinnati, O., April 4, 1925. [1; 8; 10]

Henshaw, David, politician, b. Leicester, Mass., 1791; d. Leicester, Mass., Nov. 11, 1852. [1; 4; 6; 8]

Henshaw, Helen Manville, welfare worker, b. 1876; d. 1908. [37]

Henshaw, Henry Wetherbee, naturalist, b. Cambridge, Mass., 1850; d. Washington, D.C., Aug. 1, 1930. [1; 10]

Henshaw, John Prentiss Kewley, bishop, b. Middletown, Conn., 1792; d. Providence, R.I., July 20, 1852. [3; 4; 6; 8]

Henshaw, Joshua Sidney, sailor and lawyer, b. Boston, Mass., 1811; d. Utica, N.Y., April 29, 1859. [3; 6; 8]

Henshaw, Mrs. Julia Wilmotte, née Henderson, journalist, novelist, and botanist, b. Durham, England, 1869; d. Vancouver, B.C., Nov. 18, 1937. [11; 27]

Henshaw, Marshall, educationist, b. Bethany, Pa., 1820; d. Amherst, Mass., Dec. 12, 1900. [45]

Henshaw, Nevil Gratiot, novelist, b. St. Louis, Mo., 1880; d. Charlottesville, Va., 1938. [11; 34]

Henson, Josiah, escaped negro slave, b. Charles county, Md., 1789; d. Dresden, Ont., May 5, 1883. [1; 3; 4; 7]

Henson, Poindexter Smith, clergyman, b. Fluvanna county, Va., 1831; d. Chicago, Ill., April 24, 1914. [4; 10]

Hentz, Mrs. Caroline Lee, née **Whiting,** playwright and novelist, b. Lancaster, Mass., 1800; d. Marianna, Fla., Feb. 11, 1856. [1; 3; 4; 6; 7]

Hentz, Nicholas Marcellus, educationist, b. Versailles, France, 1797; d. Marianna, Fla., Nov. 4, 1856. [3; 4; 8]

Hepburn, Alonzo Barton, banker and philanthropist, b. Colton, N.Y., 1846; d. New York, N.Y., Jan. 25, 1922. [1; 4; 10; 37]

Hepburn, Andrew Dousa, educationist, b. Williamsport, Pa., 1830; d. Oxford, O., Feb. 14, 1921. [10]

Hepburn, James Curtis, medical missionary, b. Milton, Pa., 1815; d. East Orange, N.J., Sept. 21, 1911. [1; 8; 10]

Hepworth, George Hughes, clergyman, b. Boston, Mass., 1833; d. New York, N.Y., June 7, 1902. [1; 3; 4; 7; 10]

Herbermann, Charles George, educationist and editor, b. Westphalia, Germany, 1840; d. New York, N.Y., Aug. 24, 1916. [1; 3; 4; 7; 10]

Herbert, Henry William, novelist, historian, and writer on sport, b. London, England, 1807; d. New York, N.Y., May 17, 1858. [1; 2; 3; 4; 5; 6; 7; 8; 72]

Herbert, Hilary Abner, lawyer and politician, b. Laurensville, S.C., 1834; d. Tampa, Fla., March 6, 1919. [1; 3a; 4; 10; 34]

Herbert, Leila, social historian, b. Greenville, Ala., 1868; d. Washington, D.C., 1897. [34]

Herbert, Mary E., journalist, fl. 1859-1865. [27]

Herbert, Sarah, poet, b. Ireland, 1824; d. Halifax, N.S., 1844. [29; 33]

Herbert, William (pseud.). See Croly, Herbert David.

Herbin, John Frederic, historian, b. Windsor, N.S., 1860; d. Wolfville, N.S., Dec. 29, 1923. [27]

Hereford, William Richard, journalist, b. St. Joseph, Mo., 1871; d. Paris, France, Sept. 21, 1928. [10]

Herford, Oliver Brook, humorist, artist, and playwright, b. Sheffield, England, 1863; d. New York, N.Y., July 5, 1935. [1a; 2; 7; 10; 72]

Hering, Carl, electrical engineer, b. Philadelphia, Pa., 1860; d. Philadelphia, Pa., May 10, 1926. [1; 4; 10]

Hering, Constantine, physician, b. Saxony, 1800; d. Philadelphia, Pa., July 23, 1880. [4]

Hering, Daniel Webster, physicist, b. Smithsburg, Md., 1850; d. New York, N.Y., March 24, 1938. [10; 11; 13]

Hering, Oswald Constantin, architect, b. Philadelphia, Pa., 1874; d. Falls Village, Conn., March 6, 1941. [10]

Hering, Rudolph, sanitary engineer, b. Philadelphia, Pa., 1847; d. New York, N.Y., May 30, 1923. [1; 4]

Hermance, William Ellsworth, philosopher, b. Cuba, N.Y., 1862; d. Norfolk, Va., Sept. 27, 1927. [10]

Herndon, Mrs. Mary Eliza, née Hicks, novelist, b. Fayette county, Ky., 1820; d. ? [3; 8; 34]

Herndon, William Henry, biographer, b. Greensburg, Ky., 1818; d. March 18, 1891. [1; 4; 7]

Herndon, William Lewis, naval officer, b. Fredericksburg, Va., 1813; d. at sea, Sept. 12, 1857. [1; 3; 4; 8]

Herold, Justin, physician, b. New York, N.Y., 1861; d. Scarsdale, N.Y., Feb. 3, 1942.

Herr, John, bishop, b. Lancaster county, Pa., 1781; d. Humberstone, Ont., May 3, 1850. [1; 4]

Herrick, Mrs. Christine, née Terhune, writer on domestic science, b. Newark, N.J., 1859; d. Washington, D.C., Dec. 2, 1944. [4; 10]

Herrick, Clarence Luther, educationist, b. Minneapolis, Minn., 1858; d. Socorro, N.M., Sept. 15, 1904. [8; 10; 70]

Herrick, Francis Hobart, biologist, b. Woodstock, Vt., 1858; d. Cleveland, O., Sept. 11, 1940. [4; 7; 10; 13]

Herrick, George Frederick, missionary, b. Milton, Vt., 1834; d. Bristol, R.I., Feb. 15, 1926. [10]

Herrick, Henry Martyn, clergyman, b. Rockford, Ill., 1861; d. Rockford, Ill., Feb. 24, 1945. [62]

Herrick, Henry Walker, artist, b. Hopkinton, N.H., 1824; d. 1906. [10]

Herrick, Huldah (pseud.). See Ober, Sarah Endicott.

Herrick, John Russell, clergyman, b. Milton, Vt., 1822; d. Chicago, Ill., July 26, 1912. [3; 6; 8; 38]

Herrick, Lucius Carroll, genealogist, b. Randolph, Vt., 1840; d. Columbus, O., 1903. [10]

Herrick, Myron Timothy, politician, b. Huntington, O., 1854; d. Paris, France, March 31, 1929. [1; 4; 10]

Herrick, Robert, novelist, b. Cambridge, Mass., 1868; d. Virgin Islands, Dec. 23, 1938. [4; 7; 10; 11; 51]

Herick, Samuel Edward, clergyman, b. Southampton, N.Y., 1841; d. Boston, Mass., Dec. 4, 1904. [3; 8; 10]

Herrick, Mrs. Sophia McIlvaine, née Bledsoe, journalist, b. Gambier, O., 1837; d. Oct. 9, 1919. [1; 3; 7; 10]

Herrick, William Augustus, lawyer, b. Boxford, Mass., 1831; d. Boxford, Mass., Aug. 24, 1885. [49]

Herrick, William Dodge, clergyman, b. Methuen, Mass., 1831; d. Amherst, Mass., Dec. 10, 1903. [45]

Herridge, William Thomas, clergyman, b. Reading, England, 1857; d. Ottawa, Ont., Nov. 17, 1929. [27]

Herring, Needham Bryan, physician, b. 1839; d. Wilson, N.C., May 27, 1923.

Herrington, Walter Stevens, lawyer and historian, b. Prince Edward county, Ont., 1860; d. Napanee, Ont., July 16, 1947. [30]

Herrmann, Alexander, magician, b. Paris, France, 1844; d. near Great Valley, N.Y., Dec. 17, 1896. [3b; 4]

Herron, George Davis, clergyman and socialist, b. Montezuma, Ind., 1862; d. Munich, Germany, Oct. 9, 1925. [1; 4; 10]

Herschel, Clemens, hydraulic engineer, b. Boston, Mass., 1842; d. Glen Ridge, N.J., March 1, 1930. [1; 4; 10]

Herschell, William, poet and journalist, b. Spencer, Ind., 1873; d. Indianapolis, Ind., Dec. 2, 1939. [10]

Hersey, Heloise Edwina, educationist, b. Oxford, Me., 1855; d. Boston, Mass., Feb. 3, 1933. [8; 10; 11]

Hershey, Amos Shartle, educationist, b. Hershey, Pa., 1867; d. Madison, Ind., June 12, 1933. [10; 11]

Hershey, Scott Funk, clergyman, b. Colburn, Ind., 1852; d. Lake Helen, Fla., Jan. 10, 1931. [10]

Herter, Christian Archibald, physician and biochemist, b. Glenville, Conn., 1865; d. New York, N.Y., Dec. 5, 1910. [1; 10]

Herty, Charles Holmes, chemist, b. Milledgeville, Ga., 1867; d. Savannah, Ga., July 27, 1938. [4; 10; 13]

Hertz, Emanuel, lawyer, b. Austria, 1870; d. New York, N.Y., May 23, 1940. [7; 10]

Hertzberg, Hans Rudolph Reinhart, poet, b. San Antonio Tex. 1871; d. Chicago, Ill., March 18, 1920. [10]

Hertzler, Arthur Emanuel, surgeon, b. West Point, Ia., 1870; d. Halstead, Kans., Sept. 12, 1946. [2a; 4; 7]

Hervey, Alpheus Baker, clergyman, b. Triangle, N.Y., 1839; d. Baldwin, N.Y., March 10, 1931. [4; 10]

Hervey, John Lewis, writer on horseracing, b. 1870; d. Chicago, Ill., Dec. 31, 1947.

Hess, Alfred Fabian, physician, b. New York, N.Y., 1875; d. New York, N.Y., Dec. 5, 1933. [1a; 10; 51]

Hess, Herbert William, educationist, b. St. Louis, Mo., 1880; d. Germantown, Pa., Feb. 20, 1949. [10]

Hessler, John Charles, educationist, b. Syracuse, N.Y., 1869; d. Decatur, Ill., July 29, 1944. [10]

Heth, Henry, soldier, b. Chesterfield county, Va., 1825; d. Washington, D.C., Sept. 27, 1899. [1; 3; 4]

Heuser, Herman Joseph, priest, b. 1851; d. Philadelphia, Pa., Aug. 22, 1933. [21]

Heustis, Jabez Wiggins, physician, b. Saint John, N.B., 1784; d. Talladega Springs, Ala., 1841. [3; 34]

Heuston, Benjamin Franklin, lawyer, b. 1859; d. 1907.

Hewes, Fletcher Willis, statistician and historian, b. Le Roy, N.Y., 1838; d. 1910. [10]

Hewes, George Robert Twelves, revolutionist, b. Boston, Mass., 1731; d. Richfield, Oswego county, N.Y., Nov. 5, 1840. [3; 4]

Hewes, Robert, fencing master, b. Boston, Mass., 1751; d. Boston, Mass., July, 1830. [1; 4]

Hewett, Edgar Lee, archaeologist, b. Warren county, Ill., 1865; d. Albuquerque, N.M., Dec. 31, 1946. [7; 10]

Hewett, Edwin Crawford, educationist, b. Sutton, Mass., 1828; d. Normal, Ill., 1905. [3; 8; 10]

Hewett, Waterman Thomas, educationist, b. Miami, Mo., 1846; d. London, England, Sept, 17, 1921. [1; 3; 4; 7; 10]

Hewins, Caroline Maria, librarian, b. Roxbury, Mass., 1846; d. Hartford, Conn., Nov. 4, 1926. [4; 8; 10]

Hewit, Augustine Francis, priest, b. Fairfield, Conn., 1820; d. New York, N.Y., July 3, 1897. 1; 3; 4; 21]

Hewit, Nathaniel Augustus. See Hewit, Augustus Francis.

Hewitt, Charles Gordon, biologist, b. England, 1885; d. Ottawa, Ont., Feb. 29, 1920. [27]

Hewitt, John Haskell, educationist, b. Preston, Conn., 1835; d. Williamstown, Mass., Oct. 6, 1920. [10; 62]

Hewitt, John Hill, poet, musician, and journalist, b. New York, N.Y., 1801; d. Baltimore, Md., Oct. 7, 1890. [1; 4; 7]

Hewitt, Mrs. Mary Elizabeth, née **Moore,** poet, b. Malden, Mass., 1818; d. ? [3; 7; 8]

Hewitt, Walter Charles, educationist, b. 1859; d. Oshkosh, Wis., Jan. 17, 1940. [44]

Hewlett, Albion Walter, physician, b. Petaluma, Calif., 1874; d. San Francisco, Calif., Nov. 10, 1925. [10]

Hewson, Addinell, physician, b. Philadelphia, Pa., 1828; d. Philadelphia, Pa., Sept. 11, 1889. [3; 55]

Hexamer, Charles John, civil engineer, b. Philadelphia, Pa., 1862; d. Philadelphia, Pa., Oct. 15, 1921. [10]

Heydt, Herman August, lawyer and poet, b. New York, N.Y., 1868; d. New York, N.Y., Aug. 4, 1941. [10]

Heymann, Hans, economist, b. Koenigsberg, Germany, 1885; d. Champaign, Ill., Oct. 1, 1949. [10]

Heysham, Theodore, clergyman, b. Montgomery county, Pa., 1864; d. Norristown, Pa., Sept. 25, 1935. [10; 11]

Heysinger, Isaac Winter, physician, b. Fayetteville, Pa., 1842; d. Philadelphia, Pa., May 18, 1917. [10]

Heyward, Du Bose, poet and novelist, b. Charleston, S.C., 1885; d. Tryon, N.C., June 16, 1940. [7; 10; 11]

Heyward, Mrs. Janie, née **Screven,** poet, b. 1865; d. Tryon, N.C., June 11, 1939. [34]

Heywood, John Healy, clergyman, b. 1818; d. 1880.

Heywood, Joseph Converse, poet, d. 1900. [6; 51]

Heywood, William Sweetzer, local historian, b. 1824; d. 1905.

Hibbard, Augustine George, clergyman, b. 1833; d. ?

Hibbard, Freeborn Garrettson, clergyman, b. New Rochelle, N.Y., 1811; d. Clifton Springs, N.Y., Jan. 27, 1895. [1; 3; 6]

Hibbard, George Abiah, librarian and short-story writer, b. Buffalo, N.Y., 1858; d. Buffalo, N.Y., July 3, 1928. [1; 4; 7; 10; 51; 71]

Hibben, John Grier, educationist, b. Peoria, Ill., 1861; d. Woodbridge, N.J., May 16, 1933. [1a; 5; 7; 10]

Hibben, Paxton Pattison, diplomat, b. Indianapolis, Ind., 1880; d. New York, N.Y., Dec. 5, 1928. [1; 4; 7; 10]

Hibernicus (pseud.). See Clinton, De Witt.

Hichborn, Philip, naval officer, b. Charlestown, Mass., 1839; d. Washington D.C., May 1, 1910. [1; 10]

Hichborn, Philip, short-story writer, b. 1882; d. 1912.

Hickcox, John Howard, librarian, b. Albany, N.Y., 1832; d. Washington, D. C., Jan. 30, 1897. [3; 8]

Hickenlooper, Andrew, engineer, b. Hudson, O., 1837; d. Cincinnati, O., May 12, 1904. [1; 3]

Hickey, John J., policeman, b. Ireland, 1860; d. New York, N.Y., March 4, 1938.

Hickey, William, civil servant, b. about 1790; d. ?

Hickok, Laurens Perseus, philosopher, b. Bethel, Conn., 1798; d. Amherst, Mass., May 6, 1888. [1; 3; 4; 6; 8]

Hicks, Elias, Quaker minister, b. Hempstead, N.Y., 1748; d. Jericho, N.Y., Feb. 27, 1830. [1; 3; 4; 6; 7; 8]

Hicks, Frederick Cocks, politician, b. Westbury, Long Island, N.Y., 1872; d. Washington, D.C., Dec. 14, 1925. [10]

Hicks, John, journalist and diplomat, b. Auburn, N.Y., 1847; d. San Antonio, Tex., Dec. 20, 1917. [1; 4; 10]

Hicks, Lewis Wilder, clergyman, b. Charlton, Mass., 1845; d. Wellesley, Mass., Dec. 23, 1933. [62]

Hicks, Mrs. Mary Amelia, née **Dana.** See Prang, Mrs. Mary Amelia, née Dana.

Hicks, Ratcliffe, lawyer, b. 1843; d. New York, N.Y., Sept. 19, 1906. [47]

Hicks, William Watkin, publisher, b. 1837; d. about 1915.

Higgins, Alvin McCaslin, lawyer, b. Superior, Wis., 1866; d. Croton-on-the-Hudson, N.Y., April 6, 1938. [10; 11]

Higgins, David William, journalist, b. Halifax, N.S., 1834; d. Victoria, B.C., Nov. 30, 1917. [27]

Higgins, Mrs. Katharine Elizabeth, née **Chapin,** genealogist, b. Manchester, N.H., 1847; d. Worcester, Mass., Jan. 9, 1925. [10]

Higgins, Thomas Alfred, clergyman, b. Rawdon, N.S., 1823; d. Wolfville, N.S., May 9, 1905. [27]

Higginson, Mrs. Ella, née **Rhoades,** poet and novelist, b. Council Grove, Kans., 1862; d. Bellingham, Wash., Dec. 29, 1940. [7; 10]

Higginson, Francis John, physician, b. Boston, Mass., 1806; d. Brookline, Mass., March 9, 1872. [51]

Higginson, Henry Lee, banker, b. New York, N.Y., 1834; d. Boston, Mass., Nov. 15, 1919. [1; 10; 11]

Higginson, Mrs. Mary Potter, née **Thatcher,** poet, b. Machias, Me., 1844; d. Cambridge, Mass., Jan. 9, 1941. [7; 10; 11]

Higginson, Mrs. Sarah Jane, nee **Hatfield,** novelist, b. 1840; d. 1916. [8]

Higginson, Stephen, merchant, b. Salem, Mass., 1743; d. Boston, Mass., Nov. 22, 1828. [3; 4; 8]

Higginson, Thomas Wentworth, clergyman, man of letters, and reformer, b. Cambridge, Mass., 1823; d. Cambridge, Mass., May 9, 1911. [1; 2; 3, 4; 5; 6; 7; 8; 9, 10; 71]

High, James Lambert, lawyer, b. 1844; d. Chicago, Ill., Oct. 3, 1898.

Higinbotham, Harlow Niles, merchant, b. near Joliet, Ill., 1838; d. New York, N.Y., April 18, 1919. [1; 4; 10]

Higley, Charles, lawyer, b. South Bend, Ind., 1866; d. Cleveland, O., Aug. 2, 1943.

Hildebrand, Arthur Sturges, adventurer, b. Hartford, Conn., 1887; d. between Greenland and Labrador, about 1925. [62]

Hildeburn, Charles Swift Riché, bibliographer, b. Philadelphia, Pa., 1855; d. Bologna, Italy, May 2, 1901. [3; 8; 10]

Hildeburn, Mrs. Mary Jane, née **Reed,** writer of books for children, b. Philadelphia, Pa., 1821; d. Philadelphia, Pa., Sept. 18, 1882. [3; 6; 8]

Hildreth, Azro Benjamin Franklin, pioneer. b. 1816; d. 1909. [37]

Hildreth, Charles Lotin, poet and novelist, b. New York, N.Y., 1856; d. New York, N.Y., Aug. 19, 1896. [7]

Hildreth, Ezekiel, educationist, b.[1] Westford, Mass., 1784; d. Wheeling, Va., March 15, 1856. [3; 8]

Hildreth, Hosea, clergyman, b. Chelmsford, Mass., 1782; d. Sterling, Vt., July 10, 1835. [3; 4]

Hildreth, Richard, journalist, b. Deerfield, Mass., 1807; d. Florence, Italy, July 11, 1865. [1; 3; 4; 6; 7; 8]

Hildreth, Samuel Prescott, physician and historian, b. Methuen, Mass., 1783; d. Marietta, O., July 24, 1863. [1; 3; 4; 7]

Hildt, John Coffey, educationist, b. Baltimore, Md., 1882; d. Northampton, Mass., Feb. 4, 1938. [10]

Hilgard, Eugene Woldemar, educationist, b. Bavaria, 1833; d. Berkeley, Calif., Jan. 8, 1916. [1; 3; 4; 10]

Hilgard-Villard, Heinrich, See Villard, Henry.

Hill, Adams Sherman, educationist, b. Boston, Mass., 1833; d. Boston, Mass., Dec. 25, 1910. [7; 8; 10; 51]

Hill, Mrs. Agnes, née **Leonard,** journalist and evangelist, b. Louisville, Ky., 1842; d. Chicago, Ill., Jan. 20, 1917. [4; 10; 34]

Hill, Albert Ross, educationist, b. Five Islands, N.S., 1869; d. Kansas City, Mo., May 6, 1943. [4]

Hill, Allan Massie, clergyman, b. Halifax, N.S., 1875; d. Montreal, Que., Oct. 9, 1943. [27]

Hill, Arthur Edward, chemist, b. Newark, N.J., 1880; d. New York, N.Y., March 16, 1939. [10; 11; 13]

Hill, Benjamin Dionysius, priest, b. Buckinghamshire, England, 1842; d. England, Aug. 21, 1916. [21]

Hill, Benjamin Harvey, politician, b. Jasper county, Ga., 1823; d. Atlanta, Ga., Aug. 19, 1882. [1; 3; 4; 8; 34]

Hill, Britton Armstrong, lawyer, b. Milford, N.J., 1816; d. St. Louis, Mo., Oct. 21, 1888. [3a; 6; 8; 23]

Hill, Charles Edward, educationist, b. Rochelle, Ill., 1881; d. Washington, D.C., May 10, 1936. [10; 11]

Hill, Daniel Harvey, soldier, b. York district, S.C., 1821; d. Charlotte, N.C., Sept. 24, 1889. [1; 3; 4; 34]

Hill, Daniel Harvey, educationist, b. Davidson College, N.C., 1859; d. Raleigh, N.C., July 31, 1924. [4; 10; 34]

Hill, David Jane, diplomat and historian, b. Plainfield, N.J., 1850; d. Washington, D.C., March 2, 1932. [1a; 4; 7; 8; 10; 11]

Hill, Edward Judson, lawyer, b. 1833; d. 1908. [6]

Hill, Frank Alpine, educationist, b. Biddeford, Me., 1841; d. Boston, Mass., Sept. 12, 1903. [1; 4; 46]

Hill, Frank Pierce, librarian, b. Concord, N.H., 1855; d. Hartford, Conn., Aug. 24, 1941. [4; 7; 10]

Hill, Frederic Stanhope, poet and playwright, b. Boston, Mass., 1805; d. Boston, Mass., April 7, 1851. [1; 7; 8; 9]

Hill, Frederic Stanhope, naval officer and journalist, b. Boston, Mass., 1829; d. 1913. [7; 10]

Hill, Frederick Trevor, lawyer, novelist, and historian, b. Brooklyn, N.Y., 1866; d. Yonkers, N.Y., March 17, 1930. [1; 7; 10; 11; 62]

Hill, George, poet, b. Guilford, Conn., 1796; d. New York, N.Y., Dec. 15, 1871. [3; 6; 7; 8]

Hill, George Anthony, physicist, b. Sherborn, Mass., 1842; d. Cambridge, Mass., Aug. 17, 1916. [10; 51]

Hill, George Canning, journalist, b. Norwich, Conn., 1835; d. Boston, Mass., Nov. 14, 1898. [62]

Hill, George William, clergyman, b. Halifax, N.S., 1824; d. England, 1906. [27]

Hill, George William, mathematician, b. New York, N.Y., 1838; d. April 16, 1914. [1; 4; 10]

Hill, Mrs. Grace, née **Livingston,** novelist, b. Wellsville, N.Y., 1865; d. Swarthmore, Pa., Feb. 23, 1947. [7; 10; 11]

Hill, Hamilton Andrews, merchant, b. 1827; d. 1895. [8]

Hill, Helen, writer of books for children, d. New York, N.Y., Feb. 23, 1942.

Hill, Henry, traveller b. 1895; d. ? [8]

Hill, Henry Barker, chemist, b. Waltham, Mass., 1849; d. Cambridge, Mass., April 6, 1903. [1; 3; 51]

Hill, Henry Wayland, lawyer and politician, b. Isle La Motte, Vt., 1853; d. Buffalo, N.Y., Dec. 6, 1929. [4]

Hill, Howard Copeland, educationist, b. St. Louis, Mo., 1878; d. Chicago, Ill., June 25, 1940. [7; 10; 11]

Hill, Ira, educationist, b. Maryland, about 1783; d. Hagerstown, Md., May 5, 1838.

Hill, James Jerome, railway-builder, b. near Guelph, Upper Canada, 1838; d. St. Paul, Minn., May 29, 1916. [1; 4; 10; 70]

Hill, James Langdon, clergyman, b. Garnaville, Ia., 1848; d. Salem, Mass., March 5, 1931. [10]

Hill, Mrs. Janet, née **McKenzie,** writer on domestic science, b. Westfield, Mass., 1852; d. Needham, Mass., Sept., 1933. [10]

Hill, John Alexander, publisher, b. near Bennington, Vt., 1858; d. New York, N.Y., Jan. 24, 1916. [10]

Hill, John Boynton, lawyer and historian, b. Mason, N.H., 1796; d. Temple, N.H., May 3, 1886. [3b]

Hill, John Edward, civil engineer, b. New York, N.Y., 1864; d. Providence, R.I., Nov. 2, 1934. [10; 47]

Hill, John Wesley, clergyman, b. Kalida, O., 1863; d. New York, N.Y., Oct. 12, 1936. [4; 10]

Hill, Kate Neely. See Festitits, Mrs. Kate Neely, née Hill.

Hill, Laurance Landreth, publicist, b. Denison, Tex., 1887; d. Hollywood, Calif., May 13, 1932. [10]

Hill, Lysander, lawyer, b. Union, Me., 1834; d. Chicago, Ill., Oct. 30, 1914. [4; 10]

Hill, Mrs. Marion, novelist, b. Vicksburg, Miss., 1870; d. Wilkes-Barré, Pa., Jan. 2, 1918. [10]

Hill, Nathaniel Peter, politician, b. Montgomery, N.Y., 1832; d. Denver, Colo., May 22, 1900. [1; 4; 10]

Hill, Patty Smith, educationist, b. Louisville, Ky., 1868; d. New York, N.Y., May 25, 1946.

Hill, Theophilus Hunter, poet, b. near Raleigh, N.C., 1836; d. Raleigh, N.C., June 29, 1901. [3; 7; 8; 10; 34]

Hill, Thomas, clergyman, b. New Brunswick, N.J., 1818; d. Waltham, Mass., Nov. 21, 1891. [1; 3 ;4; 6; 7; 8]

Hill, Thomas, poet, d. Fredericton, N.B., Oct., 1860. [27]

Hill, Thomas Edie, compiler, b. Sandgate, Vt., 1832; d. Glen Ellyn, Ill., July 13, 1915. [10]

Hill, Walter Barnard, lawyer, b. Talbot county, Ga., 1851; d. Atlanta, Ga., Dec. 28, 1905. [1; 4; 34]

Hill, Walter Henry, priest and educationist, b. near Lebanon, Ky., 1822; d. St. Louis, Mo., 1907. [3; 6; 8; 10; 34]

Hill, William, clergyman, b. Cumberland county, Va., 1769; d. Winchester, Va., Nov. 16, 1852. [3; 34]

Hill, William Bancroft, clergyman and educationist, b. Colebrook, N.H., 1857; d. Poughkeepsie, N.Y., Jan. 23, 1945. [7; 10]

Hillard, George Stillman, lawyer and biographer, b. Machias, Me., 1808; d. near Boston, Mass., Jan. 21, 1879. [1; 3; 4; 6; 7; 8; 9]

Hillebrand, William Francis, chemist, b. Honolulu, Hawaii, 1853; d. Washington, D.C., Feb. 7, 1925. [1; 3b; 4; 10; 13]

Hillegas, Howard Clemens, war correspondent, b. Pennsburg, Pa., 1872; d. New Brighton, N.Y., Jan. 29, 1918. [8; 10]

Hillhouse, James Abraham, poet, b. New Haven, Conn., 1789; d. New Haven, Conn., Jan. 5, 1841. [1; 3; 4; 6; 7; 71]

Hillhouse, Mansfield Lovell, novelist, b. Watervliet, N.Y., 1858; d. New York, N.Y., Feb. 6, 1908.

Hilliard, Francis, jurist, b. Cambridge, Mass., 1806; d. Worcester, Mass., Oct. 9, 1878. [1; 3; 4; 6; 51]

Hilliard, Henry Washington, lawyer and politician, b. Fayetteville, N.C., 1808; d. Atlanta, Ga., Dec. 17, 1892. [1; 3; 4; 7]

Hilliard, John Northern, journalist, b. Palmyra, N.Y., 1872; d. March 14, 1935. [10; 11; 35]

Hillis, Mrs. Annie Louise, née **Patrick,** sociologist, b. Marengo, Ill., 1862; d. Bronxville, N.Y., Nov. 13, 1930. [10]

Hillis, Newell Dwight, clergyman, b. Magnolia, Ia., 1857; d. Bronxville, N.Y., Feb. 29, 1929. [1; 4; 7; 8; 10]

Hillquit, Morris, lawyer and socialist, b. Riga, Latvia, 1869; d. New York, N.Y., Oct. 7, 1933. [1a; 10]

Hills, Aaron Merritt, clergyman and educationist, b. Dowagiac, Mich., 1848; d. Altadena, Calif., Sept. 11, 1935. [62]

Hills, Elijah Clarence, educationist, b. Arlington, Ill., 1867; d. Berkeley, Calif., April 21, 1932. [1a; 4; 10; 11]

Hilla, George Morgan, clergyman, b. Auburn, N.Y., 1825; d. Tacoma, Wash., Oct. 15, 1890. [3; 6; 8]

Hills, Lucius Perry, poet, b. 1844; d. Atlanta, Ga., Aug. 9, 1914. [34]

Hills, Oscar Armstrong, clergyman, b. 1837; d. Wooster, O., Jan. 9, 1919.

Hill-Tout, Charles, anthropologist, b. Buckland, England, 1858; d. Vancouver, B.C., June 30, 1944. [27]

Hillyer, Shaler Granby, clergyman, b. Wilkes county, Ga., 1809; d. Feb. 19, 1900. [34]

Hillyer, Virgil Mores, educationist, b. Weymouth, Mass., 1875; d. Baltimore, Md., Dec. 21, 1931. [7; 10; 51]

Hilprecht, Hermann Volrath, Assyriologist, b. Germany, 1859; d. Philadelphia, Pa., March 19, 1925. [1; 3; 4; 10]

Hilton, David (pseud.). See Wheeler, David Hilton.

Hiltz, Joseph Henry, clergyman, b. near Niagara, Upper Canada, 1819; d. Dundas, Ont., 1903. [27]

Himes, Charles Francis, educationist, b. Lancaster county, Pa., 1838; d. Baltimore, Md., Dec. 6, 1918. [1; 3; 4]

Himes, George Henry, pioneer, b. Troy, Pa., 1844; d. Portland, Ore., Jan. 6, 1940. [4; 41]

Himes, John Andrew, educationist, b. McAllisterville, Pa., 1848; d. Gettysburg, Pa., Aug. 11, 1923. [10; 62]

Himes, Norman Edwin, sociologist, b. 1899; d. Venice, Italy, June 6, 1949.

Hinchman, Mrs. Lydia Swain, née **Mitchell,** historian, b. Nantucket Island, N.Y., 1845; d. Philadelphia, Pa., Dec. 3, 1938.

Hinchman, Theodore H., merchant, b. Morris county, N.J., 1818; d. Detroit, Mich., May 12, 1895. [39]

Hinckley, George Walter, clergyman, b. Guilford, Conn., 1853; d. ? [7; 11]

Hincks, Sir Francis, journalist and polician, b. Cork, Ireland, 1807; d. Montreal, Que., Aug. 18, 1885. [27]

Hind, Henry Youle, geologist and explorer, b. Nottingham, England, 1823; d. Windsor, N.S., Aug. 9, 1908. [27]

Hinds, Asher Crosby, politician, b. Benton, Me., 1863; d. Washington, D.C., May 1, 1919. [1; 4; 10]

Hinds, John Iredelle Dillard, chemist, b. Guilford county, N.C., 1847; d. March 4, 1921. [4; 10]

Hinds, William Alfred, socialist, b. Enfield, Mass., 1833; d. Kenwood, N.Y., May 28, 1910. [10; 62]

Hine, Charles De Lano, railway executive, b. Fairfax county, Va., 1867; d. New York, N.Y., Feb. 13, 1927. [1; 4; 10]

Hine, Frank Elijah, engineer, b. Milford, Conn., 1869; d. New London, Conn., Nov. 25, 1922. [62]

Hine, Orlo Daniel, clergyman, b. New Milford, Conn., 1815; d. Mamaroneck, N.Y., Aug. 9, 1890. [62]

Hines, Gustavus, clergyman, b. 1809; d. 1873. [41]

Hines, Harvey Kimball, clergyman, b. 1828; d. 1902. [41]

Hines, Linnaeus Neal, educationist, b. Carthage, Mo., 1871; d. Terre Haute, Ind., July 14, 1936. [10; 11]

Hines, Walker Downer, lawyer, b. Russellville, Ky., 1870; d. Merano, Italy, Jan. 14, 1934. [1a; 10]

Hingeley, Joseph Beaumont, clergyman, b. Carmichaels, Pa., 1856; d. Pasadena, Calif., July 25, 1929. [10; 45]

Hingston, James, journalist, b. Ireland, 1856; d. Ellenville, N.Y., March 18, 1911.

Hingston, William Edward, detective, b. 1851; d. ?

Hingston, Sir William Hales, surgeon, b. Hinchinbrook, Lower Canada, 1829; d. Montreal, Que., Feb. 19, 1907. [27]

Hinke, William John, clergyman and educationist, b. Germany, 1871; d. Auburn, N.Y., Jan. 1, 1946. [7; 10; 11]

Hinkle, Thomas Clark, writer of books about animals, b. Laclede, Ill., 1876; d. Little River, Kans., May 13, 1949. [7; 10]

Hinman, Royal Ralph, lawyer and politician, b. Southbury, Conn., 1785; d. New York, N.Y., Oct. 16, 1868. [3; 4; 8; 62]

Hinman, Russell, geographer, b. Cincinnati, O., 1853; d. New York, N.Y., April 28, 1912. [10]

Hinman, Wilbur F., soldier fl. 1861-1898. [7]

Hinrichs, Gustavus Detlef, chemist, b. Germany, 1836; d. St Louis, Mo., Feb. 14, 1923. [3; 4; 6; 8; 10; 37]

Hinsdale, Burke Aaron, educationist, b. Wadsworth, O., 1837; d. Atlanta, Ga., Nov. 29, 1900. [1; 3; 4; 7; 10]

Hinsdale, Wilbert B., anthropologist, b. Wadsworth, O., 1851; d. Ann Arbor, Mich., July 25, 1944. [10]

Hinson, Walter Benwell, clergyman, b. England, 1862; d. Portland, Ore., Aug. 8, 1926. [10]

Hinton, Edward Wilcox, lawyer, b. Rochester, Me., 1868; d. Chicago, Ill., Jan. 2, 1936. [10; 11]

Hinton, Howard, novelist, b. New York, N.Y., 1834; d. New York, N.Y., March 21, 1920.

Hinton, Isaac Taylor, clergyman, b. Oxford, England, 1799; d. New Orleans, La., Aug. 28, 1847. [3; 8; 47]

Hinton, Richard Josiah, journalist, b. London, England, 1830; d. London, England, Dec. 20, 1901. [3b; 8; 10]

Hipsher, Edward, Ellsworth, music critic, b. 1872; d. Marion, O., March 7, 1948.

Hirsch, Alcan, chemical engineer, b. Corpus Christi, Tex., 1885; d. New Rochelle, N.Y., Nov. 24, 1938. [10]

Hirsch, Emil Gustav, rabbi, b. Luxembourg, 1852; d. Chicago, Ill., Jan. 7, 1923. [4; 10]

Hirschfelder, Jacob Maier, educationist, b. Baden-Baden, Germany, 1819; d. Toronto, Ont., Aug. 2, 1902. [27]

Hirschl, Andrew Jackson, lawyer, b. 1852; d. 1908. [37]

Hirst, Barton Cooke, physician, b. Philadelphia, Pa., 1861; d. Philadelphia, Pa., Sept. 2, 1935. [1a; 10]

Hirst, Henry Beck, poet, b. Philadelphia, Pa., 1813; d. Philadelphia, Pa., March 30, 1874. [1; 3; 4; 6; 7; 9; 71]

Hiscox, Edward Thurston, clergyman, b. Westerly, R.I., 1814; d. Mount Vernon, N.Y., Dec. 12, 1901.

Hiscox, Gardner Dexter, engineer, b. Elizabethtown, N.Y., 1822; d. East Orange, N.J., Sept. 13, 1908. [4]

Historicus (pseud.). See Burr, William Henry.

Hitchcock, Albert Spear, botanist, b. Owosso, Mich., 1865; d. at sea, Dec. 15, 1935. [10]

Hitchcock, Albert Wellman, clergyman, b. Kalamazoo, Mich., 1861; d. Worcester, Mass., April 10, 1907. [45]

Hitchcock, Alfred, surgeon, b. Westminster, Vt., 1813; d. Fitchburg, Mass., March 30, 1874. [3; 4; 8]

Hitchcock, Alfred Marshall, educationist, b. Troy, N.Y., 1868; d. Augusta, Ga., April 14, 1941. [7; 10; 11]

Hitchcock, Charles Henry, geologist, b. Amherst, Mass., 1836; d. Honolulu, Hawaii, Nov. 5, 1919. [1; 3; 4; 6; 10]

Hitchcock, David, poet, b. Bethlehem, Conn., 1773; d.,? [3]

Hitchcock, Edward, educationist, b. Deerfield, Mass., 1793; d. Amherst, Mass., Feb. 27, 1864. [1; 3; 4; 6]

Hitchcock, Edward, physician, b. Amherst, Mass., 1828; d. Amherst, Mass., Feb. 15, 1911. [1; 3; 4; 10; 45]

Hitchcock, Edward, educationist, b. Strafford, Conn., 1854; d. Northampton, Mass., Dec. 24, 1925. [4; 45]

Hitchcock, Enos, clergyman, b. Springfield, Mass., 1844; d. Providence, R.I., Feb. 27, 1803. [1; 3; 4; 6; 7]

Hitchcock, Ethan Allen, soldier, b. Vergennes, Vt., 1798; d. Sparta, Ga., Aug. 5, 1870. [1; 3; 4; 6; 7; 43]

Hitchcock, Frederic Hills, publisher, b. Boston, Mass., 1867; d. New York, N.Y., July 10, 1928. [7; 10; 45]

Hitchcock, Frederick Lyman, lawyer, b. Waterbury, Conn., 1837; d. Scranton, Pa., Oct. 9, 1924. [4]

Hitchcock, Henry, lawyer, b. near Mobile, Ala., 1829; d. St. Louis, Mo., March 18, 1902. [4; 10; 34; 62]

Hitchcock, Loranus Eaton, lawyer, b. Rochester, Vt., 1851; d. Cambridge, Mass., March 15, 1920. [45]

Hitchcock, James Ripley Wellman, art critic and literary adviser, b. Fitchburg, Mass., 1857; d. New York, N.Y., May 4, 1918. [1; 3; 7; 10]

Hitchcock, Roswell Dwight, clergyman and educationist, b. East Machias, Me., 1817; d. Somerset, Mass., June 16, 1887. [1; 3; 4; 6; 7]

Hitchcock, Thomas, lawyer, b. New York, N.Y., 1831; d. New York, N.Y., June 23, 1910. [4]

Hitchcock, Velma. See Seeley, Mrs. Velma, née Hitchcock.

Hite, Lewis Field, clergyman, b. near Middletown, Va., 1852; d. Cambridge, Mass., April 26, 1945. [10]

Hittell, John Shertzer, journalist and statistician, b. Jonestown, Pa., 1825; d. San Francisco, Calif., March 8, 1901. [1; 4; 7; 8; 10; 35]

Hittell, Theodore Henry, lawyer, b. Marietta, Pa., 1830; d. San Francisco, Calif., Feb. 23, 1917. [1; 4; 8; 10; 62]

Hoadley, George Arthur, physicist, b. Sheffield, Mass., 1848; d. Philadelphia, Pa., May 18, 1936. [10]

Hoadley, James Hart, clergyman, b. 1847; d. New York, N.Y., April 12, 1924.

Hoadley, John Chipman, civil engineer, b. Turin, N.Y., 1818; d. Boston, Mass., Oct. 21, 1886 .[3; 4]

Hoadly, Charles Jeremy, librarian, b. Hartford, Conn., 1828; d. Hartford, Conn., Oct. 21, 1900. [3]

Hoag, Ernest Bryant, physician, b. Evanston, Ill., 1868; d. Los Angeles, Calif., June 12, 1924. [4; 10]

Hoagland, Dennis Robert, botanist, b. Golden, Colo., 1884; d. Berkeley, Calif., Sept. 5, 1949. [10; 13]

Hoar, George Frisbie, lawyer and politician, b. Concord, Mass., 1826; d. Worcester, Mass., Sept. 30, 1904. [1; 4; 7; 10]

Hoar, Leonard, educationist, b. England, about 1630; d. Braintree, Mass., Nov. 28, 1675. [1; 3; 4; 51]

Hobart, Aaron, lawyer, b. 1787; d. Sept. 19, 1858. [47]

Hobart, Alvah Sabin, clergyman, b. Whitby, Ont., 1847; d. Yonkers, N.Y., May 7, 1930. [10]

Hobart, Benjamin, lawyer, b. 1781; d. Jan. 25, 1877. [47]

Hobart, Chauncey, clergyman, b. St. Albans, Vt., 1811; d. Red Wing, Minn., Jan. 3, 1904. [70]

Hobart, George Vere, humorist and playwright, b. Cape Breton, N.S., 1867; d. Cumberland, Md., Jan. 31, 1926. [7; 10]

Hobart, Henry Metcalf, engineer, b. Boston, Mass., 1868; d. Schenectady, N.Y., Oct. 11, 1946. [10]

Hobart, John Henry, bishop, b. Philadelphia, Pa., 1775; d. Auburn, N.Y., Sept. 12, 1830. [1; 3; 4; 6]

Hobart, John Henry, clergyman, b. New York, N.Y., 1817; d. Fishkill, N.Y., Aug. 31, 1889. [3]

Hobart, Mrs. Marie Elizabeth, née Jefferys, playwright, b. Liège, Beljium, 1860; d. East Hampton, N.Y., Sept. 18, 1928. [10]

Hobart, Nehemiah, clergyman, b. Hingham, Mass., 1648; d. Newton, Mass., Aug. 25, 1712. [51]

Hobart, Noah, clergyman, b. Hingham, Mass., 1705; d. Fairfield, Conn., Dec. 6, 1773. [3]

Hobbie, Alfred M., poet, d. Texas, 1881. [7]

Hobbs, Aspasia (pseud.). See Hubbard, Elbert.

Hobbs, Roe Raymond, novelist, b. 1871; d. Louisville, Ky., March 21, 1933. [10; 34]

Hoben, Allan, educationist, b. Devon, N.B., 1874; d. Kalamazoo, Mich., April 29, 1935. [10]

Hobson, John Peyton, jurist, b. Powhatan county, Va., 1850; d. Frankfort, Ky., June 3, 1934. [10; 11]

Hobson, Richmond Pearson, naval officer, b. Greensboro, Ala., 1870; d. New York, N.Y., March 16, 1937. [4; 7; 10; 34]

Hoch, August, psychiatrist, b. Basel, Switzerland, 1868; d. Montecito, Calif., Sept. 22, 1919. [4; 10]

Hochwalt, Albert Frederick, publisher, b. Dayton, O., 1869; d. Dayton, O., July 24, 1938. [7; 10; 11]

Hochwalt, Albert G., bird-fancier, b. 1893; d. 1920.

Hodder, Alfred, educationist, b. Celina, O., 1866; d. New York, N.Y., March 4, 1907. [4; 10]

Hodder, Edward Mulberry, surgeon, b. Sandgate, England, 1810; d. Toronto, Ont., Feb. 20, 1878. [27]

Hodder, Frank Heywood, educationist, b. Aurora, Ill., 1860; d. Lawrence, Kans., Dec. 27, 1935. [10]

Hodge, Archibald Alexander, clergyman, b. Princeton, N.J., 1823; d. Princeton, N.J., Nov. 11, 1886 [1; 3; 4; 6; 7]

Hodge, Charles, theologian, b. Philadelphia, Pa., 1797; d. Princeton, N.J., June 19, 1878. [1; 3; 4; 6; 7]

Hodge, Hugh Lenox, physician, b. Philadelphia, Pa., 1796; d. Philadelphia, Pa., Feb. 26, 1873. [1; 3; 4; 8]

Hodge, John Aspinwall, clergyman, b. Philadelphia, Pa., 1831; d. Lincoln University, Chester county, Pa., June 23, 1901. [3b; 8; 10]

Hodges, Arthur, novelist, b. Detroit, Mich., 1868; d. London, England, Sept. 21, 1949. [11]

Hodges, George, clergyman, b. Rome, N.Y., 1856; d. Boston, Mass., May 27, 1919. [1; 4; 7; 8; 10]

Hodges, Harry Foot, military engineer, b. Boston, Mass., 1860; d. Chicago, Ill., Sept. 24, 1929. [1; 10]

Hodges, Richard Manning, surgeon, b. 1827; d. 1896. [51]

Hodgin, Cyrus Wilburn, educationist, b. near Farmland, Ind., 1842; d. 1908. [10]

Hodgins, John George, educationist, and historian, b. Dublin, Ireland, 1821; d. Toronto, Ont., Dec. 23, 1912. [27]

Hodgins, Thomas, lawyer, b. Dublin, Ireland, 1828; d. Toronto, Ont., Jan. 14, 1910.

Hodgkin, Henry Theodore, educationist, b. Darlington, England, 1877; d. Dublin, Ireland, March 26, 1933. [10; 11]

Hodgkins, Louise Manning, educationist, b. Ipswich, Mass., 1846; d. Nov. 29, 1935. [7; 10]

Hodgkinson, John, actor and playwright, b. England, 1766; d. near Bladensburg, Md., Sept. 12, 1805. [1; 3; 4]

Hodgman, Edwin Ruthven, clergyman, b. Camden, Me., 1819; d. Townsend, Mass., June 1, 1900. [45; 49]

Hodgson, Francis, clergyman, b. Duffield, England, 1805; d. April 16, 1877. [3; 8]

Hodgson, Frederick Thomas, architect, b. 1836; d. ?

Hodgson, Joseph, soldier and lawyer, b. Fluvanna county, Va., 1838; d. Mobile, Ala., April 24, 1913. [34; 69]

Hodgson, Laurence Curran, journalist, b. Hastings, Minn., 1874; d. St. Paul, Minn., March 25, 1937. [10]

Hodgson, William Brown, orientalist, b. Georgetown, D.C., 1801; d. New York, N.Y., June 26, 1871. [1a]

Hoe, Robert, printer and book-collector, b. New York, N.Y., 1839; d. London, England, Sept. 22, 1909. [1; 2; 4; 7; 10]

Hoeber, Arthur, painter, b. New York, N.Y., 1854; d. Nutley, N.J., April 29, 1915. [10]

Hoff, Emanuel Buechley, theologian, b. Wooster, O., 1860; d. Maywood, Ill., Dec. 28, 1928. [10]

Hoff, William Bainbridge, See Bainbridge-Hoff, William.

Hoffenstein, Samuel, journalist and poet, b. Lithuania, 1890; d. Los Angeles, Calif., Oct. 6, 1947. [7]

Hoffman, Aaron, playwright, b. 1880; d. New York, N.Y., May 29, 1924.

Hoffman, Charles Fenno, journalist, b. New York, N.Y., 1806; d. Harrisburg, Pa., June 7, 1884. [1; 3; 4; 6; 7; 71]

Hoffman, Charles Frederick, clergyman, b. New York, N.Y., 1843; d. Jekyll Island, near Brunswick, Ga., March 4, 1897. [3a; 4; 8]

Hoffman, David, lawyer, b. Baltimore, Md., 1784; d. New York, N.Y., Nov. 11, 1854. [1; 3; 4; 5; 6; 7; 8; 34]

Hoffman, David Murray, jurist, b. New York, N.Y., 1791; d. Flushing, N. Y., May 7, 1878. [1; 3; 6]

Hoffman, Eugene Augustus, clergyman, b. New York, N.Y., 1829; d. New York, N.Y., June 17, 1902. [1; 3a; 4]

Hoffman, Frank Sargent, educationist, b. Sheboygan Falls, Wis., 1852; d. Schenectady, N.Y., Dec. 21, 1928. [4; 10; 62]

Hoffman, Frederick Ludwig, statistician, b. Varel, Germany, 1865; d. San Diego, Calif., Feb. 23, 1946. [10]

Hoffman, John N., clergyman, b. Adams county, Pa., 1804; d. Reading, Pa., July 26, 1857. [3; 6; 8]

Hoffman, Murray. See Hoffman, David Murray.

Hoffman, Richard, musician, b. Manchester, England, 1831; d. Mount Kisco, N.Y., Aug. 17, 1909. [1; 10; 20]

Hoffman, Wickham, soldier and diplomat, b. New York, N.Y., 1821; d. Atlantic City, N.J., May 21, 1900. [1; 4]

Hoffmann, Alexius, priest, b. St. Paul, Minn., 1863; d. Collegeville, Minn., July 6, 1940. [21]

Hoffmann, Frederick, chemist, b. 1832; d. 1904.

Hoffmann, Ralph, ornithologist, b. Cambridge, Mass., 1870; d. Santa Barbara, Cal., July 21, 1932. [10; 51]

Hofman, Heinrich Oscar, metallurgist, b. Heidelberg, Germany, 1852; d. Boston, Mass., April 28, 1924. [1; 4; 10; 13]

Hofmann, Julius, clergyman, b. Friedberg, Germany. 1865; d. Baltimore, Md., May 19, 1928. [10]

Hogan, John, politician, b. Mallow, county Cork, Ireland, 1805; d. St Louis, Mo., Feb. 5, 1892. [1; 3; 6; 8; 9]

Hogan, John Baptist, priest, b. county Clare, Ireland, 1839; d. Paris, France, Sept. 30, 1901. [3b; 21]

Hogan, John Joseph, bishop, b. county Limerick, Ireland, 1829; d. Kansas City, Mo., Feb. 21, 1913. [4; 10]

Hogan, John Sheridan, journalist, b. near Dublin, Ireland, about 1815; d. Toronto, Ont., 1859. [27]

Hogan, Mrs. Louise E., née **Shimer,** dietician, b. Shimersville, Pa., 1855; d. New York, N.Y., Jan. 10, 1929. [8; 10]

Hogan, Walter, poultry breeder, d. Kansas City, Mo., 1921.

Hogan, William, excommunicated priest, d. 1848. [6]

Hoge, Peyton Harrison, clergyman, b. Hampden Sydney, Va., 1858; d. Oct. 12, 1940. [7; 11; 34]

Hoge, William James, clergyman, b. Hampden Sydney, Va., 1821; d. Petersburg, Va., July 5, 1864. [3; 4; 8; 34]

Hogg, Charles Edgar, lawyer, b. Mason county, Va., 1852; d. Point Pleasant, W.Va., June 15, 1935. [4]

Hogg, James, poet, b. Leitrim, Ireland, 1800; d. Fredericton, N.B., June 12, 1866. [27]

Hogue, Wilson Thomas, clergyman, b. Lynden, N.Y., 1852; d. Michigan City, Ind., Feb. 13, 1920. [1; 10]

Hohfeld, Wesley Newcomb, lawyer, b. Oakland, Calif., 1879; d. Alameda, Calif., Oct. 21, 1918. [1]

Hohman, Arthur Joseph, priest and chemist, b. Buffalo, N.Y., 1886; d. Jersey City, N.J., Aug. 3, 1943.

Hoisington, Henry Richard, missionary, b. Vergennes, Vt., 1801; d. Centerbrook, Conn., May 16, 1858. [1]

Hoke, Jacob, soldier, b. 1825; d. 1893. [6; 8]

Holbrook, Alfred, educationist, b. Derby, Conn., 1816; d. Lebanon, O., April 16, 1909. [1; 3; 10]

Holbrook, Evans, lawyer, b. Onawa, Ia., 1875; d. Ann Arbor, Mich., June 6, 1932. [10; 11]

Holbrook, Florence, educationist, b. Peru, Ill., 1860; d. Chicago, Ill., Sept. 29, 1932. [8; 10]

Holbrook, James, journalist and detective, b. 1812; d. Brooklyn, Conn., April 28, 1864. [3]

Holbrook, John C., clergyman, fl. 1807-1897.

Holbrook, John Edwards, naturalist, b. Beaufort, S.C., 1794; d. Norfolk, Mass., Sept. 8, 1871. [1; 3; 4; 6; 8; 34]

Holbrook, Josiah, educationist, b. 1788; d. 1854.

Holbrook, Martin Luther, physician, b. Mantua, O., 1831; d. New York, N.Y., Aug. 12, 1902. [3a; 4; 6; 8; 10]

Holbrook, Richard Thayer, educationist, b. Windsor Locks, Conn., 1870; d. San Francisco, Calif., July 31, 1934. [7; 10; 11; 62]

Holbrook, Silas Pinckney, lawyer, b. Beaufort, S.C., 1796; d. Pineville, S.C., May 26, 1835. [3; 4; 7; 34]

Holbrook, Zephaniah Swift, clergyman, b. Berea, O., 1847; d. Brookline, Mass., Oct. 23, 1901. [3b]

Holcomb, Walter, lawyer, b. New Hartford, Conn., 1853; d. Torrington, Conn., Aug. 17, 1938. [62]

Holcombe, Chester, missionary and diplomat, b. Winfield, N.Y., 1844; d. Rochester, N.Y., April 25, 1912. [1; 4; 10]

Holcombe, Henry, clergyman, b. Prince Edward county, Va., 1762; d. Philadelphia, Pa., May 22, 1824. [1; 3; 4; 6; 34]

Holcombe, Hosea, clergyman, b. Union district, S.C., 1780; d. Jefferson county, Ala., 1841. [3; 4; 8; 34]

Holcombe, James Philemon, lawyer, b. Lynchburg, Va., 1820; d. Capon Springs, Va., Aug. 26, 1873. [1; 3; 4; 8; 34]

Holcombe, Return Ira, journalist, b. Gallia county, O., 1845; d. 1916. [70]

Holcombe, William Frederic, physician, b. Sterling, Mass., 1827; d. 1904. [3; 8; 10]

Holcombe, William Henry, physician, b. Lynchburg, Va., 1825; d. New Orleans, La., Nov. 28, 1893. [1; 3; 4; 6; 7; 34]

Holden, Edgar, physician, b. Hingham, Mass., 1838; d. Chatham, N.Y., July 18, 1909. [10]

Holden, Edward Goodman, journalist, b. Cincinnati, O., 1839; d. Tryon, N.C., Dec. 24, 1927. [62]

Holden, Edward Singleton, astronomer and librarian, b. St. Louis, Mo., 1846; d. West Point, N.Y., March 16, 1914. [1; 3; 4; 10]

Holden, George Henry, bird-fancier, b. 1848; d. 1914. [8]

Holden, George Parker, surgeon and angler, b. Yonkers, N.Y., 1869; d. Yonkers, N.Y., July 15, 1935. [10; 11]

Holden, James D., economist, b. Pontiac, Mich., 1846; d. New York, N.Y., June 13, 1925. [10]

Holden, John A., publisher, b. New York, N.Y., 1855; d. Mount Vernon, N.Y., Feb. 12, 1941.

Holden, Mrs. Martha Everts, journalist and novelist, b. Hartford, Conn., 1844; d. Chicago, Ill., Jan. 16, 1896. [3b; 7]

Holden, Warren, poet, b. 1817; d. 1903.

Holder, Charles Frederick, naturalist, b. Lynn, Mass., 1851; d. Pasadena, Calif., Oct. 10, 1915. [1; 3; 6; 7; 10]

Holder, Joseph Bassett, physician, b. Lynn, Mass., 1824; d. New York, N.Y., Feb. 27, 1888. [1; 3; 4]

Holdich, Joseph, clergyman, b. England, 1804; d. Morristown, N.J., April 10, 1893. [3; 8]

Holeman, Francis Rader, clergyman and poet, d. 1913.

Holgate, Jerome Bonaparte, historical writer, fl. 1838-1864. [6]

Holgate, Thomas Franklin, mathematician, b. Hastings county, Ont., 1859; d. Evanston, Ill., April 11, 1945. [10; 11]

Holland, Edwin Clifford, poet, b. Charleston, S.C., 1794; d. Charleston, S.C., Sept. 11, 1824. [1; 3; 6; 7; 9; 34]

Holland, Elihu Goodwin, essayist and poet, b. Solon, N.Y., 1817; d. 1878. [6]

Holland, Frederic May, clergyman, b. Boston, Mass., 1836; d. Concord, Mass., May 20, 1908. [3; 6; 8; 10; 51]

Holland, Frederick West, clergyman, b. Boston, Mass., 1811; d. Cambridge, Mass., March 26, 1895. [3; 6; 8]

Holland, James William, physician, b. Nashville, Tenn., 1849; d. Philadelphia, Pa., Feb. 10, 1922. [4; 10]

Holland, Josiah Gilbert, journalist, poet, and novelist, b. Belchertown, Mass., 1819; d. New York, N.Y., Oct. 12, 1881. [1; 2; 3; 4; 5; 6; 7; 71]

Holland, Norah Mary, poet, b. Collingwood, Ont.; d. Toronto, Ont., April 27, 1925. [27]

Holland, Robert Afton, clergyman, b. Nashville, Tenn., 1844; d. 1909. [10; 34]

Holland, Robert Emmett, priest, b. Olympia, Wash., 1892; d. New York, N.Y., Aug. 2, 1941. [21; 22]

Holland, William Jacob, naturalist, b. Bethany, Jamaica, 1848; d. Pittsburgh, Pa., Dec. 13, 1932. [1a; 7; 10]

Hollander, Jacob Harry, political economist, b. Baltimore, Md., 1871; d. Baltimore, Md., July 9, 1940. [4; 10; 12]

Hollands, Mrs. Hulda Theodate, née St. Bernard, miscellaneous writer, b. near St. Clair, Mich., 1837; d. 1910. [39]

Holley, Alexander Lyman, mechanical engineer, b. Lakeville, Conn., 1832; d. Brooklyn, N.Y., Jan. 29, 1882. [1; 3; 4; 6; 47]

Holley, George Washington, politician, b. Salisbury, Conn., 1810; d. Ithaca, N.Y., June 12, 1897. [3b]

Holley, Henry Whitcomb, poet and essayist, b. 1828; d. 1897.

Holley, Marietta, humorist, poet, essayist and novelist, b. Jefferson county, N.Y., 1836; d. Pierrepont Manor, N.Y., March 1, 1926. [1; 2; 3; 4; 6; 8; 10]

Holley, Mrs. Mary, née **Austin,** historian, b. New Haven, Conn., 1784; d. New Orleans, La., Aug. 2, 1846. [3; 6; 8; 9]

Holley, Orville Luther, journalist, b. Salisbury, Conn., 1791; d. Albany, N.Y., March 25, 1861. [3; 8]

Holliday, Carl, educationist, b. Hanging Rock, O., 1879; d. Aug. 16, 1936. [10; 11]

Holliday, Robert Cortes, journalist, b. Indianapolis, Ind., 1880; d. New York, N.Y., Dec. 1, 1946. [7; 10; 11]

Hollingworth, Mrs. Leta, née **Stetter,** psychologist, b. Chadron, Neb., 1886; d. New York, N.Y., Nov. 27, 1939. [10]

Hollis, Ira Nelson, naval engineer, b. Mooresville, Ind., 1856; d. Cambridge, Mass., Aug. 14, 1930. [1; 4; 10]

Hollister, Gideon Hiram, historian and novelist, b. Washington, Conn., 1817; d. Litchfield, Conn., March 24, 1881. [1; 3; 4; 6; 7; 9]

Hollister, Horace, physician, b. Salem, Pa., 1822; d. Scranton, Pa., Dec. 29, 1893. [8]

Hollister, Horace Adelbert, educationist, b. Manchester, Ia., 1857; d. Chicago, Ill., July 26, 1931. [37]

Hollister, John Fletcher, poet, b. 1811; d. 1882.

Hollister, Ned, naturalist, b. Delavan, Wis., 1876; d. Washington, D.C., Nov. 3, 1924. [4; 10]

Hollister, Ovando James, business man, b. 1834; d. 1892.

Hollopeter, William Clarence, physician, b. Muncy, Pa., 1858; d. Philadelphia, Pa., Dec. 16, 1927. [10]

Holloway, Edward Stratton, art director, b. Ashland, N.Y., 1859; d. Philadelphia, Pa., Nov. 3, 1939. [10; 11]

Holls, George Frederick William, lawyer and publicist, b. Zelienople, Pa., 1857; d. Yonkers, N.Y., July 23, 1903. [1; 2; 10]

Holly, Henry Hudson, architect, b. New York, N.Y., 1834; d. New York, N.Y., Sept. 4, 1892. [3b; 8]

Holm, Saxe (pseud.). See Jackson, Mrs. Helen Maria, née Fiske.

Holman, Frederick Van Voorhies, lawyer, b. Baker's Bay, Ore., 1852; d. Portland, Ore., July 6, 1927. [10; 11]

Holman, Louis Arthur, antiquary and illustrator, b. Summerside, P.E.I., 1866; d. Boston, Mass., Dec. 14, 1939. [7; 10]

Holman, Richard Morris, botanist, b. Pittsburgh, Pa., 1886; d. Berkeley, Calif., 1935. [11; 13]

Holman, Silas Whitcomb, educationist, b. 1856; d. 1900.

Holmberg, Gustav Fredrik, musician, b. 1872; d. Norman, Okla., Jan. 1, 1936. [10; 11]

Holme, John Gunnlaugur, biographer, b. 1878; d. 1922.

Holmes, Abiel, clergyman, b. Woodstock, Conn., 1763; d. Cambridge, Mass., June 4, 1837. [; 3; 4; 5; 7; 62]

Holmes, Alice A., poet, b. England, 1821; d. ? [19]

Holmes, Bayard Taylor, surgeon, b. North Hero, Vt., 1852; d. Fairhope, Ala., April 3, 1924. [1; 4; 10]

Holmes, Calvin Pratt, lawyer, b. 1839; d. 1902. [37]

Holmes, Clarence, economist, b. Lansing, Ia., 1879; d. Alexandria, Va., Dec. 16, 1938. [10; 13]

Holmes, Daniel Henry, lawyer and poet, b. New York, N.Y., 1851; d. Hot Springs, Va., Dec. 15, 1908. [1; 4; 7]

Holmes, David, clergyman, b. Newburg, N.Y., 1810; d. Battle Ground, Mich., 1873. [3; 6]

Holmes, Francis Simmons, geologist, b. 1815; d. Charleston, S.C., 1882.

Holmes, George Frederick, educationist, b. Demerara, British Guiana, 1820; d. Richmond, Va., Nov. 4, 1897. [1; 3b; 4; 34]

Holmes, Isaac Edward, politician, b. Charleston, S.C., 1796; d. Charleston, S.C., Feb. 24, 1867. [1; 3; 4; 34]

Holmes, Jean, priest and educationist, b. Windsor, Vt., 1799; d. Lorette, Que., 1852. [27]

Holmes, John, politician, b. Kingston, Mass., 1773; d. Portland, Me., July 7, 1843. [1; 3; 4; 38]

Holmes, Ludvig, clergyman and poet, b. Sweden, 1858; d. Evanston, Ill., 1910. [10]

Holmes, Mary Caroline, missionary, b. Deposit, N.Y., 1859; d. New York, N.Y., March 3, 1927. [10]

Holmes, Mrs. Mary Jane, née Hawes, novelist, b. Brookfield, Mass., 1825; d. Brockport, N.Y., Oct. 6, 1907. [1; 3; 4; 7; 10; 34]

Holmes, Nathaniel, jurist, b. Peterborough, N.H., 1814; d. Cambridge, Mass., Feb. 26, 1901. [3; 4; 8; 10]

Holmes, Oliver Wendell, physician and man of letters, b. Cambridge, Mass., 1809; d. Boston, Mass., Oct. 8, 1899. [1; 2; 3; 4; 5; 6; 7; 8; 9; 71; 72]

Holmes, Oliver Wendell, jurist, b. Boston, Mass., 1841; d. Washington, D.C., March 6, 1935. [1a; 3; 4; 7; 10]

Holmes, Richard Sill, clergyman, b. Brooklyn, N.Y., 1841; d. Philadelphia, Pa., Sept. 6, 1912. [10]

Holmes, Robert Shailor, poet, b. Unadilla, Mich., 1870; d. Daytona Beach, Fla., July 24, 1939. [7; 10; 11]

Holmes, Samuel, lawyer, b. 1839; d. ? [37]

Holmes, William Henry, archaeologist, b. Harrison county, O., 1846; d. Royal Oak, Mich., April 20, 1933. [4; 10]

Holmes, William Henry, educationist, b. Augusta, Me., 1874; d. Portland, Me., Jan. 6, 1948.

Holmested, George Smith, lawyer, b. London, England, 1841; d. Toronto, Ont., Jan. 25, 1928. [27]

Holst, Hermann Eduard von, historian, b. Fellin, Esthonia, 1841; d. Freiburg, Baden, Germany, Jan. 20, 1904. [1; 3; 4; 7; 10]

Holstein, H. Lafayette Villaume. See Ducoudray-Holstein, H. Lafayette Villaume.

Holt, Adoniram Judson, clergyman, b. Somerset, Ky., 1847; d. Arcadia, Fla., May 15, 1933. [10]

Holt, Arthur Erastus, theologian, b. Longmont, Colo., 1876; d. Chicago, Ill., Jan. 13, 1942. [10]

Holt, Byron Webber, economist, b. Rutland, O., 1857; d. Maplewood, N.J., Dec. 11, 1933. [10; 11]

Holt, George Chandler, jurist, b. Mexico, N.Y., 1843; d. France, Jan. 26, 1931. [10]

Holt, Guy, publisher, b. Boston, Mass., 1892; d. Montville, Conn., April 21, 1934. [7; 10]

Holt, Henry, publisher, b. Baltimore, Md., 1840; d. New York, N.Y., Feb. 13, 1926. [1; 4; 7; 10; 62]

Holt, John Saunders, novelist, b. Mobile, Ala., 1826; d. Natchez, Miss., Feb. 27, 1886. [3; 4]

Holt, Luther Emmett, pediatrician, b. Webster, N.Y., 1855; d. Pekin, China, Jan. 14, 1924. [1; 4; 10]

Holt, Martin (pseud.). See Ross, Henry Martin.

Holt, Roland, drama critic, b. New York, N.Y., 1867; d. New Canaan, Conn., July 8, 1931. [4; 10]

Holton, David Parsons, genealogist, b. 1812; d. 1883. [48]

Holton, Isaac Farwell, educationist, b. Westminster, Vt., 1812; d. Everett, Mass., Jan. 25, 1874. [45]

Holway, Mrs. Mary Gordon, historian, d. July 18, 1922.

Holyoke, Edward Augustus, physician, b. Marblehead, Mass., 1728; d. Salem, Mass., March 31, 1829. [1; 4]

Holyoke, Hetty (pseud.). See Guild, Mrs. Caroline Snowden, née Whitmarsh.

Holyoke, Samuel, musician, b. Boxford, Mass., 1762; d. Concord, N.H., Feb. 21, 1820. [1; 4; 7]

Homans, Isaac Smith, editor, 1807; d. 1879. [6]

Homer, Joy, relief worker, b. Rye, N.Y., 1915; d. New York, N.Y., Oct. 23, 1946.

Homes, Mrs. Mary Sophie, née Shaw, poet, b. Frederick county, Md., 1830; d. ? [3; 7; 8; 34]

Homes, William, clergyman, b. Ireland, 1663; d. Martha's Vineyard, Mass., June 20, 1746. [3]

Honan, James Henry, physician, b. Delphi, Ind., 1859; d. Augusta, Ga., Nov. 11, 1917. [10]

Honeyman, Abraham Van Doren, lawyer and historian, b. 1849; d. Plainfield, N.J., Sept. 4, 1936.

Honeyman, David, geologist, b. 1814; d. Halifax, N.S., Oct. 17, 1889. [27]

Honline, Moses Alfred, clergyman, b. Hillsboro, O., 1873; d. Pasadena, Calif., March 14, 1932. [10]

Hood, Edmund Lyman, theologian, b. Ravenna, O., 1858; d. Oakland, Calif., Aug. 14, 1931. [10; 11; 62]

Hood, Frazer, educationist, b. Tupelo, Miss., 1875; d. Charlotte, N.C., June 19, 1944. [11; 62]

Hood, George, musician, b. about 1815; d. Philadelphia, Pa., May 18, 1869. [3]

Hood, James Walker, bishop, b. Chester county, Pa., 1831; d. Fayetteville, N.C., Oct. 30, 1918. [1; 3; 10]

Hood, John Bell, soldier, b. Bath county, Ky., 1831; d. New Orleans, La., Aug. 30, 1879. [1; 3; 4; 34]

Hood, Samuel, lawyer, b. Ireland, about 1800; d. Philadelphia, Pa., 1875. [3]

Hooker, Brian, poet, playwright, and novelist, b. New York. N.Y., 1880; d. New London, Conn., Dec. 28, 1946. [7; 10; 62]

Hooker, Charles Edward, soldier and politician, b. Union, S.C., 1825; d. Jackson, Miss., Jan. 8, 1914. [4; 10]

Hooker, Edward William, clergyman, b. Goshen, Conn., 1794; d. Fort Atkinson, Wis., March 31, 1875. [3]

Hooker, Mrs. Forrestine, née **Cooper,** novelist, b. Philadelphia Pa. 1867; d. Washington, D.C., March 21, 1932. [7; 10]

Hooker, Herman, clergyman, b. Poultney, Vt., 1804; d. Philadelphia, Pa., July 25, 1865. [3; 4; 8]

Hooker, Horace, clergyman, b. Berlin, Conn., 1793; d. Hartford, Conn., Dec. 17, 1864. [3; 8; 62]

Hooker, Mrs. Isabella, née **Beecher,** reformer, b. Litchfield, Conn., 1822; d. Hartford, Conn., Jan. 26, 1907. [1; 3; 6; 7]

Hooker, John, lawyer and politician, b. Farmington, Conn., 1816; d. Hartford, Conn., Feb. 12, 1901. [3; 62]

Hooker, Le Roy, clergyman, b. Canada, about 1840; d. Chicago, Ill., July 6, 1906.

Hooker, William Francis, journalist, b. Fond du Lac, Wis., 1856; d. Bartow, Fla., Dec. 24, 1938. [44]

Hooker, Worthington, physician, b. Springfield, Mass., 1806; d. New Haven, Conn., Nov. 6, 1867. [1; 3; 4; 5; 7; 51; 62]

Hooper, Charles Edward, designer, b. Medford, Mass., 1867; d. Middle Haddam, Conn., May 16, 1920. [10]

Hooper, Edward James, agriculturist, b. England, 1803; d. 1882. [8]

Hooper, Johnson Jones, humorist, b. Wilmington, N.C., 1815; d. Richmond, Va., June 7, 1862. [1; 3; 4; 7; 34]

Hooper, Lucy, poet, b. Newburyport, Mass., Feb. 4, 1816; d. Brooklyn, N.Y., Aug. 1, 1841. [3; 7; 8]

Hooper, Mrs. Lucy, née **Hamilton,** poet and novelist, b. Philadelphia, Pa., 1835; d. Paris, France, Aug. 31, 1893. [1; 3; 4; 6; 7]

Hooper, Osman Castle, educationist, b. Alexandria, O., 1858; d. Columbus, O., May 11, 1941. [7; 10]

Hooper, Samuel, merchant and politician, b. Marblehead, Mass., 1808; d. Washington, D.C., Feb. 14, 1875. [1; 4]

Hooper, William Leslie, electrical engineer, b. Halifax, N.S., 1855; d. Tufts College, Mass., Oct. 3, 1918. [10]

Hoopes, Josiah, nurseryman, b. West Chester, Pa., 1832; d. 1904. [3; 8; 10]

Hoose, James Harmon, educationist, b. Cobleskill, N.Y., 1835; d. West Chester, Pa., Aug. 31, 1915. [10]

Hoover, Francis Trout, clergyman, b. 1841; d. 1921.

Hoover, Irwin Hood, usher, b. 1871; d. Washington, D.C., Sept. 14, 1933.

Hoover, Simon Robert, educationist, b. Bedford county, Pa., 1867; d. Cleveland, O., June 28, 1936. [10]

Hope, James Barron, poet, b. Norfolk, Va., 1829; d. Norfolk, Va., Sept. 15, 1887. [1; 3; 4; 6; 7; 34]

Hopkins, Albert Allis, editor, b. Albion, N.Y., 1869; d. New York, N.Y., June 11, 1939.

Hopkins, Alfred, architect, b. 1870; d. Princeton, N.J., May 5, 1941.

Hopkins, Alphonso Alvah, journalist, b. Burlington Flats, N.Y., 1843; d. Sept. 25, 1918. [7; 8; 10]

Hopkins, Archibald, lawyer, b. Williamstown, Mass., 1842; d. Washington, D.C., June 18, 1926. [4; 10]

Hopkins, Arthur John, chemist, b. Bridge-

Hopkins, Caspar Thomas, journalist, b. Alleghany City, Pa., 1826; d. San Francisco, Calif., Oct. 4, 1893. [3]

Hopkins, Charles Wyman, genealogist, b. Exeter, R.I., 1839; d. Providence, R.I., June, 1910.

Hopkins, Cyril George, agricultural chemist, b. near Chatfield, Minn., 1866; d. Gibraltar, Oct. 6, 1919. [1; 10]

Hopkins, Edward Washburn, educationist, b. Northampton, Mass., 1857; d. Madison, Conn., July 16, 1932. [1a; 4; 8; 10]

Hopkins, Erastus, clergyman, b. Hadley, Mass., 1810; d. Northampton, Mass., Jan. 24, 1872. [3; 8]

Hopkins, George Milton, inventor, b. Oakfield, N.Y., 1842; d. Cheshire, Mass., Aug. 17, 1902. [3a]

Hopkins, Herbert Müller, clergyman and poet, b. Hannibal, Mo., 1870; d. 1910. [8; 10]

Hopkins, Isabel Thompson, novelist, fl. 1869-1894. [6]

Hopkins, James Frederick, educationist, b. Newton, Mass., 1868; d. near Monterey, Calif., Nov. 11, 1931. [10]

Hopkins, James Herron, politician, b. Washington, Pa., 1832; d. North Hatley, Que., June 17, 1904.

Hopkins, James Love, lawyer, b. St. Louis, Mo., 1868; d. St. Louis, Mo., Aug. 30, 1931. [10]

Hopkins, John Castell, publicist, b. Dyersville, Ia., 1864; d. Toronto, Ont., Nov. 5, 1923. [27]

Hopkins, John Henry, bishop, b. Dublin, Ireland, 1792; d. Rock Point, Vt., Jan. 9, 1868. [1; 3; 4; 6; 7; 43]

Hopkins, John Henry, clergyman, b. Pittsburgh, Pa., 1820; d. near Hudson, N.Y., Aug. 13, 1891. [3; 6; 43]

Hopkins, Josiah, clergyman, b. Pittsford, Vt., 1786; d. Geneva, N.Y., 1862. [43]

Hopkins, Lemuel, poet, b. Waterbury, Conn., 1750; d. Hartford, Conn., April 14, 1801. [1; 3; 4; 6; 7]

Hopkins, Linton Cooke, lawyer and novelist, b. 1872; d. Atlanta, Ga., June 29, 1943.

Hopkins, Livingston, illustrator, b. 1846; d. 1927. [7]

Hopkins, Mrs. Louisa, née **Payson,** writer of books for children, b. Portland, Me., 1812; d. Jan. 24, 1862. [3; 4; 6; 8]

Hopkins, Mrs. Louisa Parsons, née **Stone,** poet and educationist, b. 1834; d. 1895. [8]

Hopkins, Mark, educationist, b. Stockbridge, Mass., 1802; d. Williamstown, Mass., June 17, 1887. [1; 3; 4; 6; 7; 8]

Hopkins, Mark, novelist, b. 1851; d. Pau, France, June 22, 1935.

Hopkins, Nevil Monroe, engineer and novelist, b. Portland, Me., 1873; d. New York, N.Y., March 25, 1945. [10]

Hopkins, Rufus Clement, poet, b. 1816; d. ?

Hopkins, Samuel, clergyman, b. Waterbury, Conn., 1693; d. Springfield, Mass., Oct. 6, 1755. [4; 62]

Hopkins, Samuel, clergyman, b. Waterbury, Conn., 1721; d. Newport, R.I., Dec. 20, 1803. [1; 3; 4; 6; 7; 43; 62]

Hopkins, Samuel, clergyman, b. Northampton, Mass., 1807; d. Springfield, Mass., Feb. 10, 1887. [3; 4; 6; 7; 43]

Hopkins, Samuel Augustus, dentist, b. Jersey City, N.J., 1858; d. Boston, Mass., March 14, 1921. [10]

Hopkins, Samuel Miles, jurist, b. Salem, Conn., 1772; d. Geneva, N.Y., March 9, 1837. [3]

Hopkins, Samuel Miles, clergyman, b. Geneseo, N.Y., 1814; d. Auburn, N.Y., Oct. 29, 1901. [3; 8; 10]

Hopkins, Stephen, politician, b. Providence, R.I., 1707; d. Providence, R.I., July 13, 1785. [1; 3; 4; 6]

Hopkins, Thomas Cramer, geologist, b. Center county, Pa., 1861; d. 1935. [11; 13]

Hopkins, William Barton, physician, b. 1853; d. Philadelphia, Pa., May 5, 1904. [55]

Hopkins, William John, novelist, b. New Bedford, Mass., 1863; d. Wellesley Hills, Mass., Nov. 24, 1926. [7; 10]

Hopkinson, Francis, politician and miscellaneous writer, b. Philadelphia, Pa., 1737; d. Philadelphia, Pa., May 9, 1791. [1; 2; 3; 4; 5; 6; 7; 9]

Hopley, John Edward, local historian, b. Elkton, Ky., 1850; d. Bucyrus, O., July 10, 1927. [10]

Hopper, De Wolf, comedian, b. New York, N.Y., 1858; d. Kansas City, Mo., Sept. 23, 1935. [1a; 4; 7; 10]

Hopper, Edward, clergyman and poet, b. New York, N.Y., 1818; d. New York, N.Y., April 23, 1888. [3a; 6; 8]

Hopper, Mrs. Jane, née Agar, historian, d. Toronto, Ont., April 4, 1922. [27]

Hopper, William De Wolf. See Hopper, De Wolf.

Hoppin, Augustus, artist, b. Providence, R.I., 1828; d. Flushing, N.Y., April 1, 1896. [1; 3; 4; 6; 7; 8]

Hoppin, Benjamin, educationist, b. Salem, Mass., 1851; d. Baddeck, N.S., June 2, 1923. [62]

Hoppin, Frederick Street, publisher, b. Providence, R.I., 1876; d. Englewood, N.J., Feb. 12, 1946.

Hoppin, James Mason, clergyman and educationist, b. Providence, R.I., 1820; d. New Haven, Conn., Nov. 15, 1906. [1; 3; 4; 6; 7; 10; 62]

Hoppin, Joseph Clark, archaeologist, b. Providence, R.I., 1870; d. Boston, Mass., Jan. 31, 1925. [1; 10; 51]

Hopson, George Bailey, educationist, b. Naugatuck, Conn., 1838; d. Annandale, N.Y., Aug., 1916. [10]

Hopwood, Avery, playwright, b. Cleveland, O., 1884; d. Juan-les-Pins, France, July 1, 1928. [1; 7; 10]

Hopwood, Josephus, educationist, b. Montgomery county, Ky., 1843; d. Johnson City, Tenn., Jan. 27, 1935. [10]

Horgan, Stephen Henry, printer and inventor, b. near Norfolk, Va., 1854; d. Orange, N.J., Aug. 30, 1941.

Horn, Edward Traill, clergyman, b. Easton, Pa., 1850; d. Philadelphia, Pa., March 4, 1915. [1; 3; 10]

Horn, Paul Whitfield, educationist, b. Booneville, Mo., 1870; d. Lubbock, Tex., April 13, 1932. [10; 11]

Hornaday, William Temple, naturalist, b. Plainfield, Ind., 1854; d. Stamford, Conn., March 6, 1937. [3; 4; 7; 10; 11; 37]

Hornblow, Arthur, novelist and playwright, b. Manchester, England, 1865; d. Asbury Park, N.J., May 6, 1942. [7; 10]

Horne, Abraham Reeser, clergyman, b. 1834; d. 1902.

Horne, Charles Francis, educationist, b. Jersey City, N.J., 1870; d. Annapolis, Md., Sept. 15, 1942. [7; 10; 11]

Horne, Herman Harrell, educationist, b. Clayton, N.C., 1874; d. Leonia, N.J., Aug. 16, 1946. [10; 11]

Horner, John B., educationist, b. near La Grange, Tex., 1856; d. Corvallis, Ore., Sept. 14, 1933. [10; 11; 41]

Horner, William Edmonds, anatomist, b. Warrenton, Va., 1793; d. Philadelphia, Pa., March 13, 1853. [1; 3; 4; 6]

Hornsby, John Allan, physician, b. St. Louis, Mo., 1859; d. Washington, D.C., June 4, 1939. [10]

Horr, George Edwin, clergyman, b. Boston, Mass., 1856; d. Newton, Mass., Jan. 22, 1927. [1; 10; 68]

Horsford, Eben Norton, chemist and archaeologist, b. Moscow, N.Y., 1818; d. Cambridge, Mass., Jan. 1, 1893. [1; 3; 4; 51]

Horsford, Mrs. Mary L'Hommedieu, née Gardiner, poet, b. New York, N.Y., 1824; d. Cambridge, Mass., Nov. 25, 1855. [3]

Horsmanden, Daniel, jurist, b. England, 1694; d. Flatbush, N.Y., Sept. 28, 1778. [1; 3; 4]

Horstmann, Ignatius Frederick, bishop, b. Philadelphia, Pa., 1840; d. Cleveland, O., May 13, 1908. [4; 10]

Horton, Edward Augustus, clergyman, b. Springfield, Mass., 1843; d. Boston, Mass., April 15, 1931. [4; 10]

Horton, George, diplomat, poet, and novelist, b. Fairville, N.Y., 1859; d. Staten Island, N.Y., June 5, 1942. [7; 10]

Horton, George Firman, genealogist, b. Terrytown, Pa., 1806; d. Terrytown, Pa., Dec. 20, 1886. [3; 8]

Horton, Robert Elmer, hydraulic engineer, b. Parma, Mich., 1875; d. Vorheesville, N.Y., April 22, 1945. [10; 11]

Horton, Rushmore G., journalist, b. Fishkill, N.Y., 1826; d. ? [6]

Horton, Samuel Dana, economist, b. Pomeroy, O., 1844; d. Washington, D.C., Feb. 23, 1895. [1; 3b; 4; 8]

Horton, Thomas Corwin, clergyman, b. Cincinnati, O., 1848; d. Los Angeles, Calif., Feb. 27, 1932. [10; 11]

Hosack, David, physician, b. New York, N.Y., 1769; d. New York, N.Y., Dec. 22, 1835. [1; 3; 4; 6]

Hosford, Benjamin Franklin, clergyman, b. Thetford, Vt., 1817; d. Haverhill, Mass., Aug. 10, 1864. [43; 49]

Hosford, Frances Juliette, educationist, b. 1853; d. 1937.

Hosford, Oramel, educationist, b. Thetford, Vt., 1820; d. Olivet, Mich., Dec. 9, 1893. [3]

Hoshour, Samuel Klinefelter, clergyman, b. York county, Pa., 1803; d. Indianapolis, Ind., Nov. 29, 1883. [1; 4; 7]

Hoskins, Franklin Evans, missionary, b. Rockdale, Pa., 1858; d. Beirut, Syria, Nov. 12, 1920. [10; 68]

Hoskins, Leander Miller, educationist, b. Evansville, Wis., 1860; d. Palo Alto, Calif., Sept. 8, 1937. [10]

Hoskins, Nathan, lawyer and historian, b. Wethersfield, Vt., 1795; d. Williamstown, Mass., April 21, 1869. [3; 8]

Hosmat, Hyton (pseud.). See Baker, William Deal.

Hosmer, Frederick Lucian, clergyman, b. Framingham, Mass., 1840; d. Berkeley, Calif., June 7, 1929. [1; 4; 7; 8; 51]

Hosmer, George Leonard, geologist, b. Lynn, Mass., 1874; d. Woburn, Mass., Jan. 10, 1935. [11; 13]

Hosmer, George Washington, physician and journalist, b. 1830; d. Summit, N.J., June 2, 1914. [7; 10]

Hosmer, Hezekiah Lord, jurist, b. Hudson, N.Y., 1814; d. San Francisco, Calif., Oct. 31, 1893. [1; 4; 7]

Hosmer, James Kendall, librarian and historian, b. Northfield, Mass., 1834; d. Minneapolis, Minn., May 11, 1927. [1; 3; 4; 6; 7; 8; 10]

Hosmer, John Allen, traveller, b. Toledo, O., 1850; d. 1907. [7]

Hosmer, Mrs. Margaret, née Kerr, journalist and novelist, b. Philadelphia, Pa., 1830; d. Philadelphia, Pa., Feb. 3, 1897. [3; 7; 8; 35]

Hosmer, William, clergyman, fl. 1851-53. [6]

Hosmer, William Henry Cuyler, poet, b. Avon, N.Y., 1814; d. Avon, N.Y., May 23, 1877. [1; 3; 4; 6; 7; 71]

Hoss, Elijah Embree, bishop, b. Washington county, Tenn., 1849; d. Muskogee, Okla., April 23, 1919. [4; 10]

Hoss, George Washington, educationist, b. Brown county, O., 1824; d. 1906. [10]

Hotchkin, James Harvey, clergyman, b. Prattsburg, N.Y., 1781; d. 1851. [6]

Hotchkin, Samuel Fitch, clergyman, b. Sauquoit, N.Y., 1833; d. Philadelphia, Pa., Aug. 1, 1912. [3b; 4; 10]

Hotchkiss, Chauncey Crafts, novelist, b. New York, N.Y., 1852; d. Brooklyn, N.Y., Dec. 15, 1920. [7; 8; 10]

Hotchkiss, George Woodward, lumberman, b. New Haven, Conn., 1831; d. Evanston, Ill., March 1, 1926. [10]

Hotchkiss, James Harvey, clergyman, b. Cornwall, Conn., 1781; d. Prattsburg, N.Y., Sept. 21, 1851. [3; 8]

Hotchkiss, Jedidiah, topographical engineer, b. 1827; d. 1899. [6; 34]

Hott, James William, clergyman, b. 1844; d. 1902. [8]

Houck, Louis, historian, b. St. Clair county, Ill., 1840; d. Cape Girardeau, Mo., Feb. 17, 1925. [10]

Houdini, Harry, magician, b. Appleton, Wis., 1874; d. Detroit, Mich., Oct. 31, 1926. [1; 4; 10]

Hough, Alfred J., poet, b. 1848; d. 1922.

Hough, Emerson, journalist and novelist, b. Newton, Ia., 1857; d. Evanston, Ill., April 30, 1923. [1; 4; 7; 10; 72]

Hough, Franklin Benjamin, physician and historian, b. Martinsburg, N.Y., 1820; d. Lowville, N.Y., June 6, 1885. [1; 3; 4; 6]

Hough, George Washington, astronomer, b. Montgomery county, N.Y., d. Evanston, Ind., Jan. 1, 1909. [1; 2; 3; 4; 10]

Hough, Lewis Sylvester, poet and publicist, b. Martinsburg, N.Y., 1819; d. Media, Pa., Feb. 18, 1903. [45]

Hough, Mrs. Mary Paul, née Hallowell, genealogist, b. 1858; d. Philadelphia, Pa., July 25, 1941.

Hough, Romeyn Beck, forestry expert, b. Albany, N.Y., 1857; d. Utica, N.Y., Sept. 2, 1924. [4; 10]

Hough, Theodore, physiologist, b. Front Royal, Va., 1865; d. University, Va., Nov. 30, 1924. [4; 10]

Hough, Walter, anthropologist, b. Morgantown, W. Va., 1859; d. Washington, D.C., Sept. 20, 1935. [1a; 10]

Hough, William Samuel, educationist, b. Williston, Vt., 1860; d. Sept. 18, 1912. [10]

Houghton, Frederick Lowell, cattle-breeder, b. Brookline, Mass., 1859; d. Putney, Vt., Dec. 19, 1927.

Houghton, George Washington Wright, poet, b. Cambridge, Mass., 1850; d. Yonkers, N.Y., April 1, 1891. [3; 4; 7; 8]

Houghton, Henry Clarke, physician, b. Roxbury, Mass., 1837; d. New York, N.Y., Dec. 1, 1901. [3b; 10]

Houghton, Mrs. Louise, née Seymour, editor, b. Piermont, N.Y., 1838; d. Huntington, Long Island, N.Y., Aug. 22, 1920. [8; 10]

Houghton, Walter Raleigh, politician, fl. 1880-1898.

Houghton, William Addison, educationist, b. Holliston, Mass., 1852; d. Plainfield, N.J., Oct. 22, 1917. [10; 62]

Houk, Mrs. Eliza Phillips, née Thruston, poet and novelist, b. Dayton, O., 1833; d. near Dayton, O., 1914. [10]

Hourwich, Isaac Aaronovich, lawyer and economist, b. Vilna, Russia, 1860; d. New York, N.Y., July 9, 1924. [1; 10]

House, Edward Howard, journalist, b. Boston, Mass., 1836; d. Tokyo, Japan, Dec. 17, 1901. [1; 3; 4; 7; 10]

House, Edward Mandell, politician and diplomat, b. Houston, Tex., 1858; d. Austin, Tex., March 28, 1938. [2; 7; 10]

House, Elwin Lincoln, clergyman, b. Lebanon, N.H., 1861; d. Hood River, Ore., Jan. 19, 1932,. [10; 11; 51]

House, Homer Clyde, educationist, b. Manson, Ia., 1871; d. College Park, Md., Aug. 28, 1939. [7; 10; 11]

House, Jay Elmer, journalist, b. Plymouth, Ill., 1870; d. Topeka, Kans., Jan. 5, 1936. [10]

House, Ralph Emerson, educationist, b. Delhi, Ia., 1873; d. Iowa City, Ia., April 4, 1940. [10]

Houser, John David, psychologist, b. Meadville, Pa., 1888; d. Darien, Conn., May 11, 1938.

Housser, Frederick Broughton, journalist, b. Winnipeg, Man., 1889; d. Toronto, Ont., Dec. 28, 1936. [27]

Houston, David Franklin, politician, b. Monroe, N.C., 1866; d. New York, N.Y., Sept. 2, 1940. [7; 10]

Houston, Edwin James, educationist, b. Alexandria, Va., 1847; d. Philadelphia, Pa., March 1, 1914. [1; 4; 10]

Houston, William, journalist, b. Lanark, Ont., 1844; d. Hamilton, Ont., Oct. 16, 1931. [27]

Hovey, Alvah, clergyman, b. Chenango county, N.Y., 1820; d. Boston, Mass., Sept. 6, 1903. [1; 3; 4]

Hovey, Charles Mason, horticulturist, b. Cambridge, Mass., 1810; d. Cambridge, Mass., Sept. 2, 1887. [1; 3; 8]

Hovey, Horace Carter, clergyman, b. Rob Roy, Ind., 1833; d. Newburyport, Mass., July 27, 1914. [4; 8; 10; 70]

Hovey,' Otis Ellis, civil engineer, b. East Hardwick, Vt., 1864; d. New York, N.Y., April 16, 1941. [10]

Hovey, Richard, poet, b. Normal, Ill., 1864; d. New York, N.Y., Feb. 24, 1900. [1; 4; 7; 10; 72]

Hovey, Sylvester, educationist, b. 1797; d. 1840. [62]

Hovey, William Alfred, journalist, b. 1841; d. 1906, [6]

How, Henry, scientist, d. Sept. 27, 1879. [27]

How, Louis, novelist and poet, b. St. Louis, Mo., 1873; d. Gloucester, Mass., Oct. 3, 1947. [10; 51]

How, Samuel Blanchard, b. Burlington, N.J., 1790; d. New Brunswick, N.J., Feb. 29, 1868. [3; 4; 8]

Howard, Alice Gertrude, poet, b. Chelsea, Mass., 1850; d. Berkeley, Calif., June 4, 1925. [35]

Howard, Blanche Willis, novelist, b. Bangor, Me., 1847; d. Munich, Germany, Oct. 7, 1898. [1; 3; 4; 6; 7; 9]

Howard, Bronson Crocker, playwright, b. Detroit, Mich., 1842; d. Avon-by-the-sea, N.J., Aug. 4, 1908. [1; 3; 4; 7; 9; 10]

Howard, Burt Estes, clergyman and educationist, b. Clayton, N.Y., 1862; d. Stanford University, Calif., July 10, 1913. [10]

Howard, Ernest, journalist, b. Windsor, Vt., 1860; d. Springfield, Mass., July 20, 1939. [10]

Howard, Frank Key, soldier, b. 1826; d. 1872.

Howard, George Elliott, educationist, b. Saratoga, N.Y., 1849; d. June 9, 1928. [1; 4; 7; 8; 10]

Howard, George Fitzalan Bronson, journalist, novelist, and playwright, b. Howard county, Md., 1884; d. Hollywood, Calif., Nov. 20, 1922. [7; 10]

Howard, George Henry, musician, b. Norton, Mass., 1843; d. Boston, Mass., Feb. 27, 1917. [20]

Howard, George Henry, lawyer, b. Yorkshire, England, 1844; d. Norwich, Conn., Jan. 15, 1925. [10]

Howard, Harry Clay, clergyman, b. Monroe county, Ala., 1866; d. Emory University, Ga., Dec. 28, 1930. [10]

Howard, Henry, clergyman, b. Melbourne, Australia, 1859; d. London, England, June 29, 1933. [10; 11]

Howard, James Quay, librarian, b. Newark, O., 1836; d. Washington, D.C., Nov. 15, 1912. [7; 10]

Howard, John, musician, b. Boston, Mass., 1838; d. New York, N.Y., Oct. 3, 1904. [62]

Howard, John Galen, architect and poet, b. Chelmsford, Mass., 1864; d. San Francisco, Calif., July 18, 1931. [4; 10; 35]

Howard, John Raymond, publisher, b. Brooklyn, N.Y., 1837; d. Stafford Springs, Conn., Dec. 29, 1926. [7; 10]

Howard, Joseph, journalist, b. Brooklyn, N.Y., 1833; d. New York, N.Y., March 31, 1908. [4; 10]

Howard, Oliver Otis, soldier, b. Leeds, Me., 1830; d. Burlington, Vt., Oct. 26, 1909. [1; 3; 4; 7; 10]

Howard, Philip Eugene, publisher, b. Lynn, Mass., 1870; d. Morristown, N.J., June 22, 1946. [7; 10]

Howard, Sidney Coe, playwright, b. Oakland, Calif., 1891; d. near Tyringham, Mass., Aug. 23, 1939. [7 ;10; 35]

Howard, Timothy Edward, jurist, b. near Ann Arbor, Mich., 1837; d. South Bend, Ind., July 9, 1916. [1; 4; 10]

Howard, William Lee, physician, b. Hartford, Conn., 1860; d. Boston, Mass., March 11, 1918. [4; 10]

Howarth, Mrs. Ellen Clementine, née Doran, poet, b. Cooperstown, N.Y., May 20, 1827; d. Trenton, N.J., Dec. 23, 1899. [3a; 4; 8; 10]

Howay, Frederick William, jurist and historian, b. near London, Ont., 1867; d. New Westminster, B.C., Oct. 4, 1943. [30]

Howe, Andrew Jackson, surgeon, b. Paxton, Mass., 1825; d. Cincinnati, O., Jan. 16, 1892. [1; 4; 51]

Howe, Mrs. Caroline, née Dana, poet, d. 1907. [8; 38]

Howe, Daniel Wait, lawyer and historian, b. Patriot, Ind., 1839; d. Indianapolis, Ind., Oct. 28, 1921. [4; 8; 10]

Howe, Edgar Watson, journalist and novelist, b. Treaty, Ind., 1853; d. Atchison, Kans., Oct. 3, 1937. [3; 4; 7; 10]

Howe, Edward Everett, chronicler, b. 1862; d. 1913. [39]

Howe, Fisher, merchant and traveller, b. Rochester, Vt., 1798; d. Brooklyn, N.Y., Oct. 7, 1871. [3; 6; 8]

Howe, Frederic Clemson, lawyer and economist, b. Meadville, Pa., 1867; d. Martha's Vineyard, Mass., Aug. 3, 1940. [10; 11]

Howe, George, clergyman, b. Dedham, Mass., 1802; d. Columbia, S.C., April 15, 1883. [1; 8; 34]

Howe, George, educationist, b. Wilmington, N.C., 1876; d. Richmond, Va., June 22, 1936. [10; 11]

Howe, Harrison Estell, chemist, b. Georgetown, Ky., 1881; d. Washington, D.C., Dec. 10, 1942. [10; 11]

Howe, Henry, historian, b. New Haven, Conn., 1816; d. Cincinnati, O., Oct. 14, 1893. [1; 3; 4; 6; 7]

Howe, Henry Marion, metallurgist, b. Boston, Mass., 1848; d. Bedford Hills, N.Y., May 14, 1922. [10]

Howe, Herbert Alonzo, astronomer, b. Brockport, N.Y., 1858; d. Denver, Colo., Nov. 2, 1926. [1; 4; 8; 10]

Howe, John Badlam, politician and economist, b. Boston, Mass., 1813; d. Lima, Ind., Jan. 22, 1882. [3; 6; 8]

Howe, John Benedict, journalist, b. Utica, N.Y., 1859; d. Syracuse, N.Y., May 16, 1943. [10]

Howe, Joseph William, physician, b. Chatham, N.B., 1843; d. at sea, June 7, 1890. [3b]

Howe, Julia Romana, poet, b. Rome, Italy, 1844; d. Boston, Mass., March 10, 1886. [3]

Howe, Mrs. Julia, née Ward, poet and feminist, b. New York, N.Y., 1819; d. Middletown, R.I., Oct. 17, 1910. [1; 2; 3; 4; 5; 6; 7; 71]

Howe, Lucien, ophthalmologist, b. Standish, Me., 1848; d. Belmont, Mass., Dec. 27, 1928. [1; 4; 10]

Howe, Mrs. Marie, née Jeremy, biographer, d. Feb., 1934. [11]

Howe, Mark Anthony De Wolfe, bishop, b. Bristol, R.I., 1808; d. near Bristol, R.I., July 31, 1895. [1; 3; 4]

Howe, Marshall Avery, botanist, b. Newfane, Vt., 1867; d. Pleasantville, N.Y., Dec. 24, 1936. [10; 11]

Howe, Reginald Heber, naturalist, b. Quincy, Mass., 1875; d. Belmont, Mass., Jan. 28, 1932. [10; 11]

Howe, Samuel Burnett, educationist, b. Groton, N.Y., 1879; d. Cranberry Lake, N.J., Feb. 16, 1941. [10; 11]

Howe, Samuel Gridley, philanthropist, b. Boston, Mass., 1801; d. Boston, Mass., Jan. 9, 1876. [1; 3; 4; 6; 7; 8]

Howe, Walter, lawyer, b. New York, N.Y., 1849; d. off Newport, R.I., Aug. 22, 1890. [3b]

Howe, Will David, educationist, b. Charlestown, Md., 1873; d. Athens, Ga., Dec. 6, 1946. [7]

Howe, William F., lawyer, b. Boston, Mass., 1828; d. New York, N.Y., Sept. 1, 1902. [1; 4]

Howe, William Wirt, jurist, b. Canandaigua, N.Y., 1833; d. New Orleans, La., March 17, 1909. [1; 4; 7; 8; 34]

Howell, Alfred, lawyer, b. near Toronto, Ont., 1836; d. Toronto, Ont., July 10, 1911. [27]

Howell, Charles Boynton, lawyer, b. Chautauqua county, N.Y., 1840; d. Detroit, Mich., Oct. 2, 1888. [39]

Howell, Charles Fish, journalist, b. South Amboy, N.J., 1868; d. Brooklyn, N.Y., June 5, 1943. [10]

Howell, Clark, journalist and historian, b. Barnwell county, S.C., 1863; d. Atlanta, Ga., Nov. 14, 1936. [4; 7; 10; 34]

Howell, Fleming, surgeon, b. 1849; d. Buckhannon, W. Wa., Jan. 8, 1941.

Howell, George Rogers, clergyman and librarian, b. Southampton, Long Island, N.Y., 1833; d. Albany N.Y., April 5, 1899. [3; 4; 8; 62]

Howell, Henry Spencer, traveller, b. Galt, Ont., 1857; d. Galt, Ont., Aug. 6, 1912. [27]

Howell, Robert Boyté Crawford, clergyman, b. Wayne county, N.C., 1801; d. Nashville, Tenn., April 5, 1868. [1; 3; 6; 34]

Howell, Thomas Jefferson, botanist, b. Pisgah, Mo., 1842; d. Portland, Ore., Dec. 3, 1912. [1; 41]

Howell, William Henry, physiologist, b. Baltimore, Md., 1860; d. Baltimore, Md., Feb. 6, 1945. [10; 11; 13]

Howells, William Cooper, journalist, b. 1807; d. 1894. [8]

Howells, William Dean, novelist and playwright, b. Martin's Ferry, O., 1837; d. New York, N.Y., May 11, 1920. [1; 2; 3; 4; 5; 6; 7; 8; 9 72]

Howerth, Ira Woods, educationist, b. Brown county, Ind., 1860; d. Greeley, Colo., July 4, 1938. [10; 11]

Howerton, James Robert, educationist, b. Lafayette, Ky., 1861; d. Lexington, Va., June 14, 1924. [10]

Howison, George Holmes, philosopher, b. Montgomery county, Md., 1834; d. San Francisco, Calif., Dec. 31, 1916. [1; 4; 7; 10]

Howison, Robert Reid, clergyman and historian, b. Fredericksburg, Va., 1820; d. Fredericksburg, Va., Nov. 1, 1906. [4; 8; 10; 34]

Howland, Edward, socialist, b. Charleston, S.C., 1832; d. Sinaloa, Mexico, Dec. 25, 1890. [51]

Howland, Mrs. Frances Louise, née Morse, novelist, b. Lockport, N.Y., 1855; d. New Haven, Conn., Feb. 27, 1944. [9; 11]

Howland, Franklyn, genealogist, b. 1843; d. 1907.

Howland, George, educationist, b. Conway, Mass., 1824; d. Chicago, Ill., Oct. 22, 1892. [3; 4; 8]

Howland, Henry Raymond, educationist, b. Springfield, Mass., 1844; d. Buffalo, N.Y., Feb. 4, 1930. [4; 10]

Howland, Hewitt Hanson, editor, b. Indianapolis, Ind., 1863; d. New York, N.Y., May 10, 1944. [7; 10]

Howland, Louis, journalist, b. Indianapolis, Ind., 1857; d. Indianapolis, Ind., March 26, 1934. [7; 10; 62]

Howland, Oliver Aiken, politician, b. Lambton Mills, Ont., 1847; d. Toronto, Ont., March 9, 1905. [27]

Howlett, Thomas Rosling, clergyman, b. England, 1827; d. Philadelphia, Pa., Feb. 22, 1898. [3b; 8]

Howley, Michael Francis, archbishop, b. Ireland, 1843; d. St. John's, Newfoundland, Oct. 15, 1914. [27]

Hows, John William Stanhope, elocutionist, b. London, England, 1797; d. New York, N.Y., 1871. [6; 8]

Hoxie, Robert Franklin, economist, b. Edmeston, N.Y., 1868; d. Chicago, Ill., June 22, 1916. [1; 4; 10]

Hoyt, Arthur Stephen, clergyman and educationist, b. Meridian, N.Y., 1851; d. Auburn, N.Y., March 16, 1924. [10; 63]

Hoyt, Charles Hale, playwright, b. Concord, N.H., 1860; d. Charlestown, N.Y., Nov. 20, 1900. [7; 10]

Hoyt, Charles Oliver, educationist, b. Middlesex, N.Y., 1856; d. Ypsilanti, Mich., April 14, 1927. [10; 39]

Hoyt, Charles Wilson, advertising agent, b. New Haven, Conn., 1872; d. Mineola, N.Y., Sept. 16, 1928. [4; 62]

Hoyt, David Webster, genealogist, b. Amesbury, Mass., 1833; d. Providence, R.I., May 8, 1921. [10; 47]

Hoyt, Deristhe Levinte, art teacher, b. Wentworth, N.H., about 1844; d. ? [10]

Hoyt, Epaphras, soldier and historian, b. Deerfield, Mass., 1765; d. Deerfield, Mass., Feb. 8, 1850. [3; 8]

Hoyt, Francis Deming, lawyer, b. 1843; d. Lakewood, N.J., July 21, 1922.

Hoyt, Franklin Chase, jurist, b. Pelham, N.Y., 1876; d. New York, N.Y., Nov. 13, 1937. [10; 11]

Hoyt, Henry Franklin, physician, b. 1854; d. Yokohama, Japan, Jan. 21, 1930.

Hoyt, Henry Martyn, lawyer and politician, b. Kingston, Pa., 1830; d. Philadelphia, Pa., Dec. 1, 1892. [1; 3; 4]

Hoyt, Henry Martyn, artist and poet, b. Rosemont, Pa., 1887; d. New York, N.Y., Aug. 24, 1920. [62]

Hoyt, James Philip, clergyman, b. Coventry, N.Y., 1844; d. West Newton, Mass., Aug. 4, 1925. [62]

Hoyt, Jehiel Keeler, compiler, b. New York, N.Y., 1820; d. Plainfield, N.J., Feb. 9, 1895. [3b]

Hoyt, John Wesley, educationist, b. Franklin county, O., 1831; d. Washington, D.C., May 23, 1912. [1; 3; 4; 10]

Hoyt, John William, clergyman and poet, b. 1903; d. 1937.

Hoyt, Joseph Gibson, educationist, b. Dumbarton, N.H., 1815; d. St. Louis, Mo., Nov. 26, 1862. [3; 62]

Hoyt, Mrs. Juliet, née Alves, poet and novelist, b. Henderson, Ky., 1887; d. New York, N.Y., July 16, 1947.

Hoyt, Ralph, poet, b. New York, N.Y., 1806; d. New York, N.Y., Oct. 11, 1878. [3; 4; 6; 7; 8]

Hoyt, Wayland, clergyman, b. Cleveland, O., 1838; d. Salem, Mass., Sept. 27, 1910. [8; 10; 47; 70]

Hoyt, Wilbur Franklin, chemist, b. Reedsville, O., 1864; d. Peru, Neb., June 25, 1930. [10; 13]

Hrbek, Jeffrey Dolezal, poet, b. 1882; d. 1907. [27]

Hrdlicka, Ales, anthropologist, b. Hobemia, 1869; d. Washington, D.C., Sept. 5, 1943. [7; 10; 11; 13]

Huard, Victor Alphonse, priest, b. St. Roch, Que., 1853; d. Oct. 15, 1929. [13; 27]

Hubbard, Mrs. Alice, née Moore, educationist, b. Wales, N.Y., 1861; d. at sea, May 7, 1915. [10]

Hubbard, Bela, geologist, b. Utica, N.Y., 1814; d. Detroit, Mich., June 13, 1896. [3; 8; 39]

Hubbard, Elbert, journalist and masterprinter, b. Bloomington, Ill., 1856; d. at sea, May 7, 1915. [1; 2; 4; 7; 10]

Hubbard, Frank McKinney, caricaturist, b. Bellefontaine, O., 1868; d. Indianapolis, Ind., Dec. 26, 1930. [1; 7; 10]

Hubbard, Gardiner Greene, philanthropist, b. Boston, Mass., Aug. 25, 1822; d. Washington, D.C., Dec. 11, 1897. [3b; 4]

Hubbard, Harvey, poet, d. 1862.

Hubbard, Henry Vincent, landscape architect, b. Taunton, Mass., 1875; d. Milton, Mass., Oct. 6, 1947. [10; 11]

Hubbard, John, educationist, b. Townsend, Mass., 1859; d. Hanover, N.H., Aug. 14, 1810. [3; 43; 49]

Hubbard, John Niles, clergyman, b. Angelica, N.Y., 1815; d. Tracy, Calif., Oct. 16, 1897. [62]

Hubbard, Kin. See Hubbard, Frank McKinney.

Hubbard, Lucius Lee, geologist, b. Cincinnati, O., 1849; d. Hough*on, Mich., Aug. 3, 1933. [7; 10; 11; 51]

Hubbard, Oliver Payson, physician, b. Pomfret, Conn., 1809; d. New York, N.Y., March 9, 1900. [3b; 4; 10; 62]

Hubbard, Richard Bennett, politician and diplomat, b. Walton county, Ga., 1832; d. Tyler, Tex., July 12, 1901. [1; 4; 34]

Hubbard, Mrs. Sara Anderson, née Blakely, teacher and journalist, b. East Berkshire, Vt., 1832; d. July 31, 1918. [10]

Hubbard, Stephen Grosvenor, physician, b. Rome, N.Y., 1816; d. New Haven, Conn., June 30, 1905. [49; 62]

Hubbard, Mrs. Theodora, née **Kimball,** librarian, b. Newton, Mass., 1887; d. Milton, Mass., Nov. 7, 1935. [10; 11]

Hubbard, William, clergyman and historian, b. England, about 1621; d. Ipswich, Mass., Sept. 14, 1704. [1; 3; 4; 6; 7; 51]

Hubbard-Kernan, Will. See Kerman, Will Hubbard.

Hubbell, Alvin Allace, ophthalmologist, b. Conewango, N.Y., 1846; d. Buffalo, N.Y., 1911. [10]

Hubbell, Mrs. Martha, née **Stone,** clergyman's wife, b. Oxford, Conn., 1814; d. North Stonington, Conn., 1856. [3; 7; 8]

Hubbell, Walter, poet, novelist, and genealogist, b. 1851; d. ?

Huber, John Bessner, physician, b. New York, N.Y., 1864; d. Pomfret, Conn., Feb. 16, 1924. [10]

Huberich, Charles Henry, lawyer, b. Toledo, O., 1877; d. Cambridge, Mass., June 18, 1945. [10; 62]

Hubert, Petrus, notary public, b. Yamachiche, Lower Canada, 1810; d. Three Rivers, Que., April 1, 1882. [27]

Hubert, Philip Gengembre, journalist, b. Cincinnati, O., 1852; d. Bellport, N.Y., Jan. 3, 1925. [4; 10]

Hubner, Charles William, poet and librarian, b. Baltimore, Md., 1835; d. Atlanta, Ga., Jan. 3, 1929. [1; 4; 7; 10; 34]

Huckel, Oliver, clergyman, b. Philadelphia, Pa., 1864; d. Orlando, Fla., Feb. 3, 1940. [7; 10; 11]

Huddy, Xenophon Pearce, lawyer, b. Newport, R.I., 1878; d. Milford, Pa., April 8, 1943. [62]

Hudon, Maxime, priest and poet, b. St. Denis, Que., 1841; d. Berthier-en-bas, Que., Oct. 6, 1914. [27]

Hudson, Alfred Sereno, local historian and poet, b. 1839; d. 1907.

Hudson, Charles, historian, b. Marlborough, Mass., 1795; d. Lexington, Mass., May 4, 1881. [1; 3; 7]

Hudson, Erasmus Darwin, surgeon, b. Torringford, Conn., 1805; d. Greenwich, Conn., Dec. 31, 1880. [3; 4; 8]

Hudson, Erasmus Darwin, physician, b. Northampton, Mass., 1843; d. May 9, 1887. [3; 6; 8]

Hudson, Frederic, journalist, b. Quincy, Mass., 1819; d. Concord, Mass., Oct. 21, 1875. [1a; 3; 4]

Hudson, Henry Norman, clergyman and Shakespearian scholar, b. Cornwall, Vt., 1814; d. Cambridge, Mass., Jan. 16, 1886. [1; 3; 4; 6; 7; 8]

Hudson, Horace Bushnell, publisher, b. Cincinnati, O., 1861; d. Minneapolis, Minn., 1920. [70]

Hudson, Hoyt Hopewell, educationist, b. Norfolk, Neb., 1893; d. ·Palo Alto, Calif., June 13, 1944. [10]

Hudson, James Fairchild, journalist, b. Oberlin, O., 1846; d. Ben Avon, Pa., May 2, 1915. [8; 10]

Hudson, Joseph Kennedy, journalist, b. Carrollton, O., 1840; d. 1907. [4; 10]

Hudson, Mrs. Mary, née **Clemmer.** See Ames, Mrs. Mary, née Clemmer.

Hudson, Robert Paine, poet, fl. 1887 1907. [34]

Hudson, Thomas Jay, journalist, b.Windham, O., 1834; d. Detroit, Mich., May 26, 1903. [1; 4; 8; 10]

Hudson, William Cadwalader, journalist and novelist, b. New Brunswick, N.J., 1843; d. Pearl River, N.Y., Oct. 16, 1915. [7; 10]

Hudson, William Sloane, clergyman, b. Muncy, Pa., 1822; d. Cincinnati, O., July 30, 1861. [3]

Hudson, William Sloane, biographer and littérateur, b. Brecksville, O., 1850; d. West Yarmouth, Mass., Aug. 4, 1929. [1; 10; 62]

Hudson, William Smith, mechanical engineer, b. near Derby, England, 1810; d. Newark, N.J., July 20, 1881. [1]

Hütten, Ulric von (pseud.). See David, Henry Winter.

Huey, Edmund Burke, psychologist, b. 1870; d. 1913.

Hufeland, Otto, local historian, b. New York, N.Y., 1855; d. Mount Vernon, N.Y., Oct. 14, 1940.

Huff, Jacob K., poet and journalist, b. 1851; d. 1910.

Huffcut, Ernest Wilson, lawyer, b. Kent. Conn., 1860; d. Ithaca, N.Y., May 4, 1907. [10]

Huggins, Eli Lundy, soldier and poet, b. Schuyler county, Ill., 1842; d. San Diego, Calif., Oct. 22, 1929. [10]

Hughes, Mrs. Adelaide Manola, née **Mould,** poet, b. 1884; d. 1923.

Hughes, Charles Evans, politician and jurist, b. Glens Falls, N.Y., 1862; d. Osterville, Mass., Aug. 27, 1948. [7; 10; 12]

Hughes, Daniel E., physician, b. 1851; d. Philadelphia, Pa., Oct. 28, 1892.

Hughes, David John, jurist, b. Kingsbridge, Devon, England, 1820; d. St Thomas, Ont., April 14, 1915. [31a]

Hughes, George, clergyman, b. 1828; d. 1904.

Hughes, Hatcher, playwright, b. Polkville, N.C., 1881; d. New York, N.Y., Oct. 19, 1945. [7; 12]

Hughes, Henry, lawyer, b. about 1826; d. Port Gibson, Miss., Oct. 3, 1862. [1]

Hughes, James Laughlin, educationist, b. near Bowmanville, Ont., 1846; d. Toronto, Ont., Jan. 3, 1935. [27]

Hughes, John Joseph, archbishop, b. county Tyrone, Ireland, 1797; d. New York, N.Y., Jan. 3, 1864. [1; 3; 4; 6; 7]

Hughes, Katherine, biographer, b. Melbourne, P.E.I.; d. New York, N.Y., April 27, 1925. [27]

Hughes, Matthew Simpson, bishop, b. Doddridge county, Va., 1863; d. Portland, Ore., April 4, 1920. [4; 10]

Hughes, Nicholas Collin, clergyman, b. 1822; d. 1893. [8]

Hughes, Robert Morton, lawyer, b. Abingdon, Va., 1855; d. Norfolk, Va., Jan. 15, 1940. [7; 10; 11]

Hughes, Robert William, jurist, b. Powhatan county, Va., 1821; d. near Abingdon, Va., Dec. 10, 1901. [1; 3; 4; 10; 34]

Hughes, Thomas, journalist, b. Minersville, O., 1854; d. Mankato, Minn., 1934. [70]

Hughes, Thomas Aloysius, priest and historian, b. Liverpool, England, 1849; d. 1929. [7; 21]

Hughes, Thomas Houghton, educationist, b. Manhattan, N.Y., 1884; d. New York, N.Y., May 25, 1944.

Hughes, Thomas Patrick, Orientalist, b. Ludlow, England, 1838; d. King's Park, N.Y., Aug. 8, 1911. [8; 10]

Hughes, William Joseph, lawyer, b. Upland, Pa., 1863; d. Washington, D.C., Jan. 28, 1939. [10; 21]

Hughes, William Taylor, lawyer, b. 1850; d. Bath, N.Y., Dec. 14, 1925.

Hughs, Mrs. Mary, née Robson, b. England, prior to 1800; d. ? [6]

Hughson, Shirley Carter, clergyman, b. Camden, S.C., 1867; d. West Park, N.Y., Nov. 16, 1949.

Hugolin, Rev. Père. See Lemay, Hugolin Marie.

Huguet-Latour, Louis A., historian, b. about 1824; d. Montreal, Que., May 2, 1924. [3; 27]

Huhner, Max, physician, b. Berlin, Germany, 1873; d. New York, N.Y., Nov. 8, 1947. [10; 11]

Huidekoper, Frederic, theologian, b. Meadville, Pa., 1817; d. Meadville, Pa., May 16, 1892. [1; 3; 4; 6]

Huidekoper Frederic Louis, soldier, b. Meadville, Pa., 1874; d. Washington, D.C., March 7, 1940. [10; 11]

Huidekoper, Henry Shippen, soldier, b. Meadville, Pa., 1839; d. Philadelphia, Pa., Nov. 9, 1918. [3; 10]

Huidekoper, Rush Shippen, physician, b. Meadville, Pa., 1854; d. Philadelphia, Pa., Dec. 17, 1901. [3b; 8]

Huiginn, Eugene Joseph Vincent, clergyman and poet, b. Dublin, Ireland, 1860; d. Beverly, Mass., Nov. 30, 1927. [4]

Huizinga, Henry, educationist, b. New Groningen, Mich., 1873; d. Dec. 3, 1945. [7; 10]

Hulbert, Archer Butler, historian, b. Bennington, Vt., 1873; d. Colorado Springs, Colo., Dec. 24, 1933. [1a; 7; 10; 11]

Hulbert, Edwin James, mining engineer, b. Sault Ste. Marie, Mich., 1829; d. Rome, Italy, Oct. 20, 1910. [1]

Hulbert, Henry Woodward, clergyman, b. Sheldon, Vt., 1858; d. Framingham, Mass., Oct. 31, 1937. [10]

Hulbert, Homer Bezaleel, educationist, b. New Haven, Vt., 1863; d. Seoul, Korea, Aug. 5, 1949. [49]

Hulbert, Mrs. Mary, née Allen, writer on cooking, b. Grand Rapids, Mich., 1863; d. Norwalk, Conn., Dec. 17, 1939.

Hulbert, William Davenport, naturalist, b. Mackinac Island, Mich., 1868; d. Seattle, Wash., Nov. 2, 1913. [10]

Huling, Caroline Alden, journalist, b. Saratoga Springs, N.Y., 1857; d. Maywood, Ill., March 11, 1941.

Hulit, Leonard, angler, b. 1856; d. 1924.

Hull, Augustus Longstreet, historian, b. Athens, Ga., 1847; d. 1909. [34]

Hull, Amos Girard, lawyer, b. Paris, N.Y., 1815; d. Brooklyn, N.Y., May 7, 1898.

Hull, Charles Henry, educationist, b. Ithaca, N.Y., 1864; d. Ithaca, N.Y., July 15, 1936. [10]

Hull, George Huntington, economist, b. Dansville, N.Y., 1840; d. Los Angeles, Calif., March 12, 1921. [4; 10]

Hull, Moses, spiritualist, b. 1835; d. ? [37]

Hull, William, soldier, b. Derby, Conn., 1753; d. Newton, Mass., Nov. 29, 1825. [1; 3; 4; 8]

Hull, William Isaac, educationist, b. Baltimore, Md., 1868; d. Swarthmore, Pa., Nov. 14, 1939. [7; 10]

Hulley, Lincoln, educationist, and poet, b. Camden, N.J., 1865; d. Deland, Fla., Jan. 20, 1934. [10; 11]

Hult, Adolph, clergyman, b. Moline, Ill., 1869; d. Moline, Ill., March 6, 1943. [10]

Humbert, Stephen, loyalist, b. New Jersey, about 1767; d. New Brunswick, Jan. 16, 1849. [27]

Humble, Henry Wilbur, lawyer, b. 1883; d. Brooklyn, N.Y., Jan. 11, 1941.

Humboldt, Gay (pseud.). See Naramore, Gay Humboldt.

Hume, John Ferguson, broker, b. 1830; d. ? [6]

Hume, Robert Allen, missionary, b. Bombay, India, 1847; d. Brookline, Mass., June 24, 1929. [1; 10; 62]

Hume, Robert Ernest, clergyman, b. India, 1877; d. New York, N.Y., Jan. 4, 1948. [10; 62]

Humes, Thomas William, clergyman ,b. Knoxville, Tenn., 1815; d. Knoxville, Tenn., Jan. 16, 1892. [1; 6; 34]

Humphrey, Edward Porter, clergyman, b. Fairfield, Conn., 1809; d. Louisville, Ky., Dec. 9, 1887. [6; 8]

Humphrey, Mrs. Frances A., writer of books for children, fl. 1882-1890. [6]

Humphrey, Heman, clergyman and educationist, b. Hartford county, Conn., 1779; d. Pittsfield, Mass., April 3, 1861. [1; 3; 4; 6]

Humphrey, Lucy H., See Smith, Mrs. Lucy, née Humphrey.

Humphrey, Seth King, capitalist, b. Fairbault, Minn., 1864; d. Boston, Mass., May 23, 1932. [4; 10; 11]

Humphrey, Willis C., soldier and historian, b. Lima, N.Y., 1839; d. Detroit, Mich., April 13, 1888. [39]

Humphrey, Zephaniah Moore, clergyman, b. Amherst, Mass., 1824; d. Cincinnati, O., Nov. 13, 1881. [45]

Humphreys, Alexander Crombie, mechanical engineer, b. Edinburgh, Scotland, 1851; d. New York, N.Y., Aug. 14, 1927. [1; 4; 10]

Humphreys, Andrew Atkinson, soldier, b. Philadelphia, Pa., 1810; d. Washington, D.C., Dec. 27, 1883. [1; 3; 4]

Humphreys, David, poet, b. Derby, Conn.. 1752; d. New Haven, Conn., Feb. 21, 1818. [1; 3; 6; 7]

Humphreys, Edward Rupert, educationist, b. England, 1820; d. Boston, Mass., March 20, 1893. [3; 6; 8]

Humphreys, Francis Landon, clergyman, b. Auburn, N.Y., 1858; d. New Canaan, Conn., July 18, 1937. [10]

Humphreys, Frederick, physician, b. Marcellus, N.Y., 1816; d. Monmouth Beach, N.J., July 8, 1900. [3b; 4]

Humphreys, George W., clergyman, b. 1875; d. Pottsville, Pa., Nov. 5, 1949.

Humphreys, Ida Frances, novelist, b. Cato, N.Y., 1852; d. ? [11]

Humphreys, Mary Gay, writer of books for young people, b. Ripley, O.; d. New York, N.Y., Oct. 10, 1915. [10]

Humphreys, Mrs. Phebe Westcott, miscellaneous writer, b. 1868; d. Philadelphia, Pa., June 17, 1939.

Humphreys, West Hughes, jurist, b. Montgomery county, Tenn., 1806; d. near Nashville, Tenn., Oct. 16, 1882. [1; 4; 34]

Humphreys, Willard Cunningham, educationist, b. New York, N.Y., 1867; d. Princeton, N.J., Sept. 26, 1902. [3b; 10]

Hun, Henry, physician, b. Albany, N.Y., 1854; d. Albany, N.Y., March 14, 1924. [4; 10; 62]

Hun, John Gale, mathematician, b. Albany, N.Y., 1877; d. Princeton, N. J., Sept. 15, 1945. [10]

Hundley, Daniel Robinson, soldier, b. Alabama, 1832; d. 1899. [34]

Huneker, James Gibbons, music critic, b. Philadelphia, Pa., 1860; d. Brooklyn, N.Y., Feb. 9, 1921. [1; 4; 7; 10; 20; 72]

Hungerford, Edward, writer on transportation, b. Dexter, N.Y., 1875; d. New York, N.Y., July 29, 1948. [7; 10]

Hungerford, Mrs. Mary, née **Churchill,** writer of books for young people, b. Staffordshire, England, 1832; d. Paris, France, Sept. 18, 1901. [3b]

Hunnewell, James Frothingham, historian, b. Charlestown, Mass., 1832; d. 1910. [4; 8; 10]

Hunnicutt, James W., clergyman, b. Pendleton district, S.C., 1814; d. ? [6; 8]

Hunnicutt, William Littleton Clark, education, b. 1834; d. 1910.

Hunt, Arthur Prince, clergyman, b. Springfield, Mass., 1874; d. New York, N.Y., July 3, 1925. [10]

Hunt, Caroline Louisa, home economist, b. Chicago, Ill., 1865; d. Washington, D.C., 1927. [10]

Hunt, Charles Warren, civil engineer, b. New York, N.Y., 1858; d. New York, N.Y., July 23, 1932. [10]

Hunt, Ezra Mundy, physician, b. Middlesex county, N.J., 1830; d. Trenton, N.Y., July 1, 1894. [3; 4; 6]

Hunt, Freeman, publisher, b. Quincy, Mass., 1804; d. Brooklyn, N.Y., March 2, 1858. [1; 3; 6; 7]

Hunt, Gaillard, historian, b. New Orleans, La., 1862; d. Washington, D.C., March 20, 1924. [1; 4; 7; 10]

Hunt, Harriot Kezia, physician and reformer, b. Boston, Mass., 1805; d. Boston, Mass., Jan. 2, 1875. [1; 3; 4]

Hunt, Mrs. Helen Maria, née **Fiske.** See Jackson, Mrs. Helen Maria, née Fiske.

Hunt, Henry Jackson, soldier, b. Detroit, Mich., 1819; d. Washington, D.C., Feb. 11, 1889. [1; 3; 4; 8]

Hunt, Isaac, lawyer and clergyman, b. Barbados, about 1742; d. London, England, 1809. [1; 3; 47]

Hunt, Mrs. Mary Hannah, née **Hanchett,** educationist, b. Canaan, Conn., 1830; d. New York, N.Y., April 24, 1906. [1; 4; 10]

Hunt, Sandford, clergyman, b. Eden, N.Y., 1825; d. Cincinnati, O., Feb. 10, 1896. [3b; 4]

Hunt, Theodore Whitefield, educationist, b. Metuchen, N.J., 1844; d. Princeton, N.J., April 12, 1930. [1; 3; 4; 7; 10]

Hunt, Thomas, lawyer, b. New Orleans, La., 1855; d. New York, N.Y., Oct. 19, 1933. [62]

Hunt, Thomas Forsyth, agriculturist, b. Stephenson county, Ill., 1862; d. Berkeley, Calif., April 26, 1927. [10]

Hunt, Thomas Poage, clergyman, b. Charlotte county, Va., 1794; d. Wyoming Valley, Pa., Dec. 5, 1876. [3; 6; 8]

Hunt, Thomas Sterry, chemist and geologist, b. Norwich, Conn., 1826; d. New York, N.Y., Feb. 12, 1892. [1; 3; 4; 27]

Hunt, Timothy Dwight, clergyman, b. Rochester, N.Y., 1821; d. Whitesboro, N.Y., Feb. 7, 1895. [62]

Hunt, William Morris, painter, b. Brattleboro, Vt., 1842; d. Isles of Shoals, N.H., Sept. 8, 1879. [1; 4; 43]

Hunt, William Southworth, journalist, b. Newark, N.J., 1879; d. South Orange, N.J., Jan. 26, 1940. [7; 10]

Hunter, Alexander, civil war veteran, b. 1843; d. ? [34]

Hunter, Alexander Stuart, educationist, b. Bavington, Pa., 1857; d. Pittsburgh, Pa., July 31, 1926. [10; 11]

Hunter, Andrew Frederick, archaeologist, b. Innisfil, Ont., 1863; d. Toronto, Ont., Oct. 19, 1940. [27]

Hunter, Clingham (pseud.). See Adams, William Taylor.

Hunter, George Leland, art editor, b. Bellingham, Mass., 1867; d. New York, N.Y., Oct. 30, 1927. [10; 51]

Hunter, George William, educationist, b. Mamaroneck, N.Y., 1873; d. Claremont, Calif., Feb. 4, 1948. [10; 11; 13]

Hunter, John Dunn, adventurer, b. about 1798; d. near Nagogdoches, Tex., early in 1827. [3; 7; 34]

Hunter, John Howard, educationist, b. Bandon, Ireland, 1839; d. Toronto, Ont., Nov. 1911. [3; 27]

Hunter, Merlin Harold, economist, b. Chandlersville, O., 1887; d. Chicago, Ill., May 31, 1948. [10; 11]

Hunter, Robert, sociologist, b. Terre Haute, Ind., 1874; d. Santa Barbara, Calif., May 15, 1942. [4; 10]

Hunter, Samuel John, entomologist, b. Bandon, Ireland, 1866; d. Lawrence, Kans., July 10, 1946. [10; 11]

Hunter, Stephen Alexander, clergyman, b. Christiana, Pa., 1851; d. Pittsburgh, Pa., Oct. 13, 1925. [10]

Hunter, Thomas, educationist, b. Ardglass, Ireland, 1831; d. New York, N.Y., Oct. 14, 1915. [1; 4]

Hunter, Wiles Robert. See Hunter, Robert.

Hunter, William Armstrong, clergyman, b. Peterborough, Ont., 1855; d. Riverside, Calif., Feb. 21, 1920. [10]

Hunter, William C., merchant, b. Kentucky, 1812; d. Nice, France, June 25, 1891. [1; 7]

Hunter-Duvar, John, poet, b. Scotland, 1830; d. Alberton, P.E.I., Jan. 25, 1899. [27]

Huntington, Arria Sargent, educationist, b. Roxbury, Mass., 1848; d. ? [7; 10]

Huntington, Charles Andrew, clergyman, b. Vergennes, Vt., 1822; d. Portland, Ore., Sept. 24, 1904. [59]

Huntington, Dan, clergyman, b. Lebanon, Conn., 1774; d. Hadley, Mass., Oct. 31, 1864. [62]

Huntington, Daniel, clergyman, b. Norwich, Conn., 1788; d. New London, Conn., May 21, 1858. [3; 47]

Huntington, David Lynde, electrical engineer, b. New London, Conn., 1870; d. Spokane, Wash., Sept. 27, 1929. [62]

Huntington, De Witt Clinton, clergyman, b. Townsend, Vt., 1830; d. 1912. [10]

Huntington, Dwight Williams, naturalist, b. 1851; d. Oceanside, Long Island, N.Y., Nov. 26, 1939.

Huntington, Elijah Baldwin, clergyman, b. Bozrah, Conn., 1816; d. South Coventry, Conn., Dec. 27, 1877. [62]

Huntington, Ellsworth, geographer, b. Galesburg, Ill., 1876; d. New Haven, Conn., Oct. 17, 1947. [7; 10; 11; 13]

Huntington, Emily, kitchen gardener, b. Lebanon, Conn.. 1841; d. Windham. Conn.. Dec. 5, 1909. [10]

Huntington, Faye (pseud.). See Foster, Mrs. Theodosia Maria, née Toll.

Huntington, Frederic Dan, bishop, b. Hadley, Mass., 1819; d. Hadley, Mass., July 11, 1904. [1; 3; 4; 6; 7; 8; 10]

Huntington, George, clergyman and educationist, b. Brooklyn, Conn., 1835; d. Rochester, N.Y., Jan. 2, 1916. [10; 70]

Huntington, Gurdon, clergyman and poet, b. 1818; d. 1875. [4]

Huntington, H. S. (pseud.). See Smith, Henry Huntington.

Huntington, Harwood, clergyman, b. New Haven, Conn., 1861; d. Los Angeles, Calif., Jan. 4, 1923. [10; 48]

Huntington, Henry Strong, clergyman, b. New York, N.Y., 1836; d. Roselle, N.J., Jan. 8, 1920. [62]

Huntington, James Otis Sargent, clergyman, b. Boston, Mass., 1854; d. New York, N.Y., June 29, 1938. [10]

Huntington, Jedidiah Vincent, novelist and man of letters, b. New York, N.Y., 1815; d. Pau, France, March 10, 1862. [1; 3; 4; 7]

Huntington, Joseph, clergyman, b. Windham, Conn., 1835; d. Coventry, Conn., Dec. 25, 1794. [3; 62]

Huntington, Joshua, clergyman, b. Norwich, Conn., 1786; d. Groton, Mass., Sept. 11, 1819. [3]

Huntington, Joshua, physician, b. Boston, Mass., 1812; d. Washington, D.C., March 23, 1900. [62]

Huntington, Lucius Seth, politician and novelist, b. Compton, Lower Canada, 1827; d. New York, N.Y., May 19, 1886. [27]

Huntington, Tuley Francis, educationist and printer, b. near Barrington, Ill., 1870; d. Palo Alto, Calif., May 4, 1938. [7; 10]

Huntington, Willard Vincent, poet, b. Oneonta, N.Y., 1856; d. 1915. [35]

Huntington, William Reed, clergyman, b. Lowell, Mass., 1838; d. Nahant, Mass., July 26, 1909. [1; 3; 4; 7; 10]

Huntington-Wilson, Francis Mairs. See Wilson, Francis Mairs Huntington.

Huntley, Mrs. Florence, née **Chance,** journalist, b. Alliance, O.; d. Chicago, Ill., Feb. 1, 1912. [10]

Huntley, Lydia Howard. See Sigourney, Mrs. Lydia Howard, née Huntley.

Huntley, Stanley, humorist, d. 1885.

Hunton, William Lee, clergyman, b. Morrisburg, Ont., 1864; d. Philadelphia, Pa., Oct. 12, 1930. [1; 7; 10]

Huot, Antonio, priest, b. Quebec, Que., 1877; d. Quebec, Que., April 7, 1929. [27]

Hurd, Charles Edwin, journalist, b. Croydon, N.H., 1833; d. Boston, Mass., April 22, 1910. [10]

Hurd, Edward Payson, physician, b. Compton, Lower Canada, 1838; d. Newburyport, Mass., Feb. 24, 1899. [10; 76]

Hurd, Henry Mills, physician, b. Union City, Mich., 1843; d. Ventnor, N.J., July 19, 1927. [4; 10]

Hurd, John Codman, lawyer, b. Boston, Mass., 1816; d. Boston, Mass., June 25, 1892. [1; 3; 4; 62]

Hurd, Marian Kent. See McNeely, Mrs. Marian, née Hurd.

Hurd, Richard Melancthon, financier, b. New York, N.Y., 1865; d. New York, N.Y., June 6, 1941. [10; 62]

Hurd, Samuel, clergyman and educationist, b. Corinth, Vt., 1804; d. Troy, Miss., June 28, 1846. [43; 49]

Hurlbert, William Henry, journalist, b. Charleston, S. C., 1827; d. Cadenabbia, Italy, Sept. 4, 1895. [1; 3; 4; 7; 8; 34]

Hurlburt, Jesse Beaufort, clergyman, educationist, and civil servant, b. about 1812; d. Ottawa, Ont., May 12, 1891. [27]

Hurlbut, Henry Higgins, merchant, b. 1813; d. 1890.

Hurlbut, Jesse Lyman, clergyman, b. New York, N.Y., 1843; d. Bloomfield, N.J., Aug. 2, 1930. [1; 4; 10]

Hurlbut, William Henry. See Hurlbert, William Henry.

Hurley, Edward Nash, financier, b. Galesburg, Ill., 1864; d. Chicago, Ill., Nov. 14, 1933. [1a; 10; 21]

Hurll, Estelle May, educationist, b. New Bedford, Mass., 1863; d. Wellesley, Mass., May 8, 1924. [10]

Hurst, John Fletcher, bishop, b. near Salem, Md., 1834; d. Washington, D.C., May 4, 1903. [1; 3; 4; 10]

Husband, Joseph, advertising agent, b. Rochester, N.Y., 1885; d. New York, N.Y., Sept. 19, 1938. [7; 10]

Husband, Richard Wellington, educationist, b. Milton, Ont., 1869; d. Hanover, N.H., April 9, 1939. [10]

Husbands, Herman, patriot, b. probably in Cecil county, Md., 1694; d. near Philadelphia, Pa., 1795. [1; 3; 4]

Husik, Isaac, educationist, b. Russia, 1876; d. Philadelphia, Pa., March 22, 1939. [10; 11]

Husmann, George, viticulturist, b. Prussia, Germany, 1827; d. Napa, Calif., Nov. 5, 1902. [1]

Hussey, Tacitus, printer, b. Terre Haute, Ind., 1833; d. ? [10; 37]

Hussey, William Joseph, astronomer, b. Mendon, O., 1862; d. London, England, Oct. 28, 1926. [4; 10]

Huston, Charles, lawyer, d. 1849.

Huston, James, journalist, b. Lower Canada, 1820; d. Quebec, Que., Sept. 21, 1854. [27]

Hutchings, James Mason, pioneer, b. 1820; d. 1902.

Hutchins, Harry Burns, educationist, b. Lisbon, N.H., 1847; d. Ann Arbor, Mich., Jan. 25, 1930. [1; 4; 10]

Hutchins, Stilson, capitalist, b. Whitefield, N.H., 1838; d. Washington, D.C., April 22, 1912. [4; 10]

Hutchins, Thomas, geographer, b. Monmouth, N.J., 1730; d. Pittsburgh, Pa., April 28, 1789. [1; 3; 4; 34]

Hutchinson, Ellen Mackay. See Cortissoz, Mrs. Ellen Mackay, née Hutchinson.

Hutchinson, Emilie Josephine, economist, b. 1877; d. New York, N.Y., Jan. 12, 1938.

Hutchinson, Mrs. Frances, née Kinsley, writer on country life, b. Baltimore, Md., 1857; d. ? [7; 44]

Hutchinson, John Alexander, lawyer, b. 1840; d. 1896.

Hutchinson, John Russell, educationist, b. Columbia county, Pa., 1807; d. Feb. 24, 1878. [3]

Hutchinson, John Wallace, singer and musician, b. Milford, N.H., 1821; d. 1908. [3; 4; 8; 10]

Hutchinson, Thomas, historian, b. Boston, Mass., 1711; d. London, England, June 3, 1780. [1; 2; 3; 4; 5; 6; 7; 8]

Hutchinson, Woods, physician, b. Selby, England, 1862; d. Brookline, Mass., April 26, 1930. [1; 4; 10]

Hutchison, Joseph Chrisman, physician, b. Howard county, Mo., 1822; d. Brooklyn, N.Y., July 16, 1887. [3; 6; 8]

Hutchison, Robert Allen, clergyman, b. Claysville, Pa., 1862; d. Pittsburgh, Pa., Dec. 11, 1937. [10; 11]

Hutson, Charles Woodward, educationist, b. McPhersonville, S.C., 1840; d. New Orleans, La., June, 1936. [7; 10; 11]

Hutton, Frederick Remsen, mechanical engineer, b. New York, N.Y., 1853; d. New York, N.Y., May 14, 1918. [1; 4; 10]

Hutton, Joseph, playwright and poet, b. Philadelphia, Pa., 1787; d. 1828. [7]

Hutton, Laurence, literary critic, b. New York, N.Y., 1843; d. Princeton, N.J., June 10, 1904. [1; 3; 4; 7; 10]

Hutton, Maurice, educationist, b. Manchester, England, 1856; d. Toronto, Ont., April 5, 1940. [11; 27]

Hutton, William, agricultural writer, d. July 19, 1861. [27]

Hutton, William Rich, civil engineer, b. Washington, D.C., 1826; d. Cloppers, Md., Dec. 11, 1901. [3b]

Hyamson, Moses, rabbi, b. Suwalki, Poland, 1862; d. New York, N.Y., June 9, 1949. [10; 11]

Hyatt, Alpheus, naturalist, b. Washington, D.C., 1838; d. Cambridge, Mass., Jan. 15, 1902. [1; 3b; 4; 10]

Hyde, Alexander, writer on exploration, b. 1814; d. 1881.

Hyde, Ammi Bradford, educationist, b. Oxford, N.Y., 1824; d. near Denver, Colo., March 23, 1921. [10]

Hyde, Cornelius Willet Gillam, educationist, b. Franklinville, N.Y., 1838; d. 1920. [10; 70]

Hyde, Edward Wyllys, mathematician, b. Saginaw, Mich., 1843; d. Cincinnati, O., Nov. 4, 1930. [3; 8; 10; 13]

Hyde, James Nevins, physician, b. Norwich, Conn., 1840; d. Prouts Neck, Me., Sept. 6, 1910. [1; 10; 62]

Hyde, James Thomas, clergyman, b. Norwich, Conn., 1827; d. Chicago, Ill., March 21, 1886. [8; 62]

Hyde, Mary Caroline, novelist, b. Plainfield, Vt.; d. Pottsville, Pa., 1904. [10]

Hyde, Mary Kendall, religious journalist, b. Winchendon, Mass., 1858; d. Cambridge, Mass., Aug., 1940. [10]

Hyde, Miles Goodyear, physician, b. Cortland, N.Y., 1841; d. Brooklyn, N.Y., May 24, 1928. [7; 10; 62]

Hyde, Thomas Alexander, clergyman, b. Glasgow, Scotland, about 1859; d. Weymouth, Mass., Feb. 21, 1925. [51]

Hyde, Thomas Worcester, soldier, b. Florence, Italy, 1841; d. Old Point Comfort, Va., Nov. 14, 1899. [3b; 8; 10]

Hyde, William De Witt, educationist, b. Winchendon, Mass., 1858; d. Brunswick, Me., June 29, 1917. [1; 4; 10; 51]

Hyla (pseud.). See Chaplin, Mrs. Jane, née Dunbar.

Hylton, John Dunbar, physician and poet, b. 1837; d. Palmyra, N.J., Oct. 25, 1893. [4; 6; 8]

Hyneman, Leon, editor, b. Montgomery county, Pa., 1805; d. New York, N.Y., 1879. [3; 6; 8]

Hyslop, James Hervey, philosopher and psychologist, b. Xenia, O., 1854; d. Upper Montclair, N.J., June 17, 1920. [1; 4; 7; 10]

I

Idamore (pseud.). See Cutts, Mary.
Iddings, Joseph Paxson, geologist, b. Baltimore, Md., 1857; d. Olney, Md., Sept. 8, 1920. [1; 3; 4; 10; 62]
Ide, Mrs. **Frances Otis,** née **Ogden,** writer of books for children, b. Brooklyn, N.Y., 1853; d. Brooklyn N.Y., July 2, 1927. [7; 8; 10]
Ide, George Barton, clergyman, b. Coventry, Vt., 1804; d. Springfield, Mass., April 16, 1872. [3; 6; 8]
Ide, George Edward, insurance expert, b. Brooklyn, N.Y., 1860; d. Locust Valley, N.Y., July 9, 1919. [62]
Idleman, Finis Schuyler, clergyman, b. Vandalia, Ill., 1875; d. New York, N.Y., March 22, 1941. [10]
Iglehart, Asa, lawyer, b. 1817; d. 1887.
Iglehart, Mrs. **Fanny,** née **Chambers,** descriptive writer, b. Mississippi, 1851; d. ? [8; 10]
Iglehart, Ferdinand Cowle, clergyman, b. Warrick county, Ind., 1845; d. July 21, 1922. [10]
Iblseng, Magnus Colbjorn, mechanical engineer, b. Norway, 1852; d. New York, N.Y., July 12, 1930. [10]
Iles, George, writer on popular science, b. Gibraltar, 1852; d. New York, N.Y., Oct. 3, 1942. [7; 10]
Iliowizi, Henry, rabbi, b. Russia, 1850; d. 1911. [70]
Ill, Edward Joseph, surgeon, b. Newark, N.J., 1854; d. Island Heights, N.J., June 9, 1942. [4; 10]
Illoway, Henry, physician, b. Bohemia, 1848; d. New York, N.Y., Jan. 15, 1932. [10]
Ilsley, Charles Parker, poet and historian, b. Portland, Me., 1807; d. 1887. [7; 8; 38]
Imboden, John Daniel, mining promoter, b. Augusta county, Va., 1823; d. Damascus, Va., Aug. 15, 1895. [1]
Imbrie, Robert Whitney, diplomat, b. Washington, D.C., 1883; d. Teheran, Persia, July 18, 1924. [62]
Imbrie, William, clergyman and educationist, b. 1845; d. Evanston, Ill., Aug. 4, 1928.
Imlay, Gilbert, political adventurer, b. Monmouth county, N.J., about 1754; d. probably on the island of Jersey, Nov. 20, 1828. [1; 3; 6; 7; 74]
Imlay, Lorin Everett, electrical engineer, b. Guernsey county, O., 1864; d. Niagara Falls, N.Y., June 6, 1941. [10; 13]
Immel, Ray Keesler, educationist, b. West Gilead, Mich., 1885; d. Inglewood, Calif., April 11, 1945. [10; 11]

Imrie, John, poet, b. Glasgow, Scotland, 1846; d. Toronto, Ont., 1902. [27]
Ingalesa, Mrs. **Isabella,** née **Weller,** miscellaneous writer, b. Jamestown, N.Y., 1855; d. ? [11]
Ingalesa, Richard, lawyer, b. Savannah, Ga., 1863; d. ? [11]
Ingall, Oswald Drew, forester, b. Sault Ste. Marie, Ont., 1884; d. Altadena, Calif., March 17, 1938. [62]
Ingalls, James Monroe, soldier, b. Sutton, Vt., 1837; d. Providence, R.I., May 1, 1927. [10]
Ingalls, John James, journalist and politician, b. Middleton, Mass., 1833; d. East Las Vegas, N.M., Aug. 16, 1900. [1; 4; 7; 10]
Ingalls, Jeremiah, musician, b. Andover, Mass., 1764; d. Rochester, Vt., 1838. [43]
Ingalls, Joshua King, social reformer, b. 1816; d. ? [8]
Ingalls, William, physician, b. Newburyport, Mass., 1769; d. Wrentham, Mass., Sept. 8, 1851. [3]
Ingals, Ephraim Fletcher, physician, b. Lee Center, Ill., 1848; d. Chicago, Ill., April 30, 1918. [1; 10]
Ingersoll, Charles, lawyer, b. 1805; d. 1882. [55]
Ingersoll, Charles Jared, lawyer and politician, b. Philadelphia, Pa., 1782; d. Philadelphia, Pa., May 1, 1862. [1; 3; 4; 7; 8]
Ingersoll, Edward, lawyer, b. 1790; d. Florence, Italy, July 7, 1841. [3]
Ingersoll, Edward, lawyer, b. Philadelphia, Pa., 1817; d. Germantown, Pa., Feb. 19, 1893. [1; 3; 8]
Ingersoll, Elihu Parsons, clergyman, b. Lee, Mass., 1804; d. Rosevale, Clay county, Kans., March 29, 1887. [3b. 62]
Ingersoll, Ernest, naturalist, b. Monroe, Mich., 1852; d. Brattleboro, Vt., Nov. 13, 1946. [4; 7; 10; 11]
Ingersoll, Henry Hulbert, jurist, b. Oberlin, O., 1844; d. Knoxville, Tenn., March 12, 1915. [4; 10; 34]
Ingersoll, Joseph Reed, lawyer, b. Philadelphia, Pa., Feb. 20, 1868. [3; 4; 8]
Ingersoll, Lurton Dunham, librarian, fl. 1866-1879. [6; 8; 37]
Ingersoll, Robert Green, lecturer, b. Dresden, N.Y., 1833; d. Dobbs Ferry, N.Y., July 21, 1899. [1; 2; 3; 4; 5; 6; 7; 8]
Ingersoll, Royal Rodney, naval officer, b. Niles, Mich., 1847; d. La Porte, Ind., April 21, 1931. [1; 10]
Ingham, Ellery Percy, lawyer, b. 1856; d. Sept., 1926. [8]
Ingham, Col. Frederic (pseud.). See Hale, Edward Everett.

Ingle, Edward, journalist, b. Baltimore, Md., 1861; d. Baltimore, Md., Jan. 6, 1924. [6; 8; 10; 34]

Inglis, Alexander James, educationist, b. Middletown, Conn., 1879; d. Boston, Mass., April 12, 1924. [1; 4; 7; 10]

Inglis, Charles, bishop, b. Ireland, 1734; d. Halifax, N.S., Feb. 24, 1816. [1; 3; 8; 27]

Inglis, William, journalist, b. Brooklyn, N.Y., 1872; d. New York, N.Y., Sept. 22, 1949.

Ingraham, Charles Anson, physician, b. Cambridge, N.Y., 1852; d. Nov. 24, 1935. [11]

Ingraham, Edward Duffield, lawyer, b. Philadelphia, Pa., 1793; d. Philadelphia, Pa., Nov. 5, 1854. [1; 3; 4]

Ingraham, John Phillips Thurston, clergyman, b. Hallowell, Me., 1817; d. 1906. [10]

Ingraham, Joseph Holt, clergyman and novelist, b. Portland, Me., 1809; d. Holly Springs, Miss., Dec. 18, 1860. [1; 3; 4; 6; 7; 9; 34]

Ingraham, Prentiss, soldier and novelist, b. Natchez, Tenn., 1843; d. Beauvoir, Miss., Aug. 17, 1904. [1; 7; 8; 10]

Ingram, Edward Lovering, educationist, b. Philadelphia, Pa., 1862; d. Grand View, N.Y., July 25, 1938. [10; 11]

Ingram, Eleanor Marie, novelist, b. New York, N.Y., 1886; d. New York, N.Y., March 22, 1921. [10]

Ingram, Henry Atlee, lawyer, b. 1858; d. Philadelphia, Pa., Aug. 20, 1927. [55]

Inkster, John Gibson, clergyman, b. Orkney Islands, Scotland, 1867; d. Toronto, Ont., Dec. 19, 1946. [30]

Inman, Henry, soldier and journalist, b. New York, N.Y., 1837; d. Topeka, Kans., Nov. 13, 1899. [1; 4; 7; 8; 10]

Inness, George, artist, b. Paris, France, 1854; d. Cragsmoor, N.Y., July 27, 1926. [4; 10]

Innsley, Owen (pseud.). See Jennison, Lucy White.

Inskip, John Swanel, clergyman, b. Huntingdon, England, 1816; d. Ocean Grove, N.J., March 7, 1884. [1; 3; 6; 8]

Ioor, William, playwright, b. Dorchester, S.C., about 1780; d. 1830. [1; 7]

Irby, Richard, educationist, b. 1825; d. 1902. [8; 34]

Ireland, John, archbishop, b. Ireland, 1828; d. St. Paul, Minn., Sept. 25, 1918. [1; 3; 4; 10]

Ireland, Joseph Norton, historian of the theatre, b. New York, N.Y., 1817; d. Bridgeport, Conn., Dec. 29, 1898. [1; 7; 8]

Ireland, Mrs. Mary Eliza, née Haines, writer and translator of books for children, b. Calvert, Md., 1834; d. ? [8; 10]

Irvine, Alexander Fitzgerald, clergyman, b. county Antrim, Ireland, 1863; d. Hollywood, Calif., March 15, 1941. [10]

Irving, John Beaufain, physician and sportsman, b. 1800; d. 1881.

Irving John Beaufain, artist, b. Charleston, S.C., 1825; d. New York, N.Y., April 20, 1877. [34]

Irving, John Treat, novelist, b. New York, N.Y., 1812; d. New York, N.Y., Feb. 27, 1906. [1; 3; 4; 6; 7; 8; 10]

Irving, Lukin Homfray, civil servant, b. Galt, Ont., 1855; d. Toronto, Ont., Dec. 22, 1942. [27]

Irving, Minna (pseud.). See Odell, Minna.

Irving, Peter, novelist, b. New York, N.Y., 1771; d. New York, N.Y., June 27, 1838. [1; 3; 7; 8]

Irving, Pierre Munro, lawyer, b. 1803; d. New York, N.Y., Feb. 11, 1876. [1; 3; 8]

Irving, Roland Duer, geologist, b. New York, N.Y., 1847; d. Madison, Wis., May 27, 1888. [1; 8; 44]

Irving, Theodore, educationist, b. New York, N.Y., 1809; d. New York, N.Y., Dec. 20, 1880. [3; 6; 8]

Irving, Washington, man of letters, b. New York, N.Y., 1783; d. Irvington, N.Y., Nov. 28, 1859. [1; 2; 3; 4; 5; 6; 7; 8; 9; 71; 72]

Irwin, Elisabeth Antoinette, educationist, b. Brooklyn, N.Y.; d. New York, N.Y., Oct. 16, 1942.

Irwin, John Arthur, physician, b. Ireland, 1853; d. New York, N.Y., June 1, 1912. [4; 10]

Irwin, William Henry, journalist and novelist, b. Oneida, N.Y., 1873; d. New York, N.Y., Feb. 24, 1948. [7; 10; 11]

Isaacs, Abraham Samuel, educationist, b. New York, N.Y., 1851; d. Paterson, N.J., Dec. 22, 1920. [1; 4; 8; 10]

Isaacs, Nathan, educationist, b. Cincinnati, O., 1886; d. Cambridge, Mass., Dec. 18, 1941. [10]

Isaacson, Charles David, musician, b. 1891; d. New York, N.Y., Feb. 15, 1936. [10; 11]

Isabel (pseud.). See Ritchie, Mrs. Anna Cora, née Ogden.

Isham, Asa Brainerd, physician, b. 1844; d. 1912. [8]

Isham, Charles, lawyer, b. New York, N.Y., 1853; d. New York, N.Y., June 9, 1919. [51]

Isham, Frederic Stewart, journalist, novelist, and playwright, b. Detroit, Mich., 1866; d. New York, N.Y., Sept. 7, 1922. [4; 7; 8; 10]

Isham, Mary Keyt, psychiatrist, b. 1871; d. Cincinnati, O., Sept. 28, 1947. [10]

Isham, Norman Morrison, architect, b. Hartford, Conn., 1864; d. Wickford, R.I., Jan. 1, 1943. [10]

Isham, Samuel, artist, b. New York, N.Y., 1855; d. Easthampton, Long Island, N.Y., June 12, 1914. [1; 7; 10; 62]

Isham, Warren, clergyman, b. Massachusetts, 1800; d. Marquette, Mich., May 18, 1863. [39]

Isherwood, Benjamin Franklin, mechanical engineer, b. New York, N.Y., 1822; d. New York, N.Y., June 19, 1915. [1; 4; 6; 10]

Ives, Charles, poet, b. 1815; d. 1880.

Ives, Charles Linnaeus, physician, b. New Haven, Conn., 1831; d. Burlington, N.J., March 21, 1879. [8; 62]

Ives, Ella Gilbert, educationist, b. 1847; d. 1913.

Ives, Frederic Eugene, inventor, b. Litchfield, Conn., 1856; d. Philadelphia, Pa., May 27, 1937. [4; 10]

Ives, George Burnham, editor, b. Salem, Mass., 1856; d. Salem, Mass., Aug. 21, 1930. [10; 51]

Ives, Howard Chapin, civil engineer, b. Cheshire, Conn., 1878; d. Waterbury, Conn., Oct. 6, 1944. [11; 62]

Ives, Joseph Christmas, soldier and explorer, b. New York, N.Y., 1828; d. New York, N.Y., Nov. 12, 1868. [1]

Ives, Joseph Moss., lawyer, b. Danbury, Conn., 1876; d. Danbury, Conn., April 8, 1939. [10; 62]

Ives, Levi Silliman, bishop, b. Meriden, Conn., 1797; d. New York, N.Y., Oct. 13, 1867. [1; 3; 4; 6; 8]

Ivey, Thomas Neal, clergyman, b. Marion, S.C., 1860; d. Nashville, Tenn., May 14, 1923. [10]

Ivins, Anthony Woodward, farmer and merchant, b. Toms River, N.J., 1852; d. Salt Lake City, Utah, Sept. 23, 1934. [10]

Ivins, William Mills, lawyer, b. Monmouth county, N.J., 1851; d. New York, N.Y., July 23, 1915. [1; 4; 10]

Ivory, Bertha May, poet, fl. 1891-1895. [34]

Izard, George, soldier, b. Richmond, England, 1776; d. Iittle Rock, Ark., Nov. 22, 1828. [1; 3; 4]

Izax, Ikabod (pseud.). See Stebbins, George Stanford.

J

J. S. of Dale (pseud.). See Stimson, Frederic Jesup.

Jack, Mrs. Annie L., miscellaneous writer, b. England, 1839; d. Châteauguay, Que., Feb. 15, 1912. [27]

Jack, David Russell, historian, b. Saint John, N.B., d. Clifton Springs, N.Y., Dec. 2, 1913. [27]

Jack, Isaac Allen, lawyer, b. Saint John, N.B., 1843; d. April 5, 1903. [27]

Jackman, Alonzo, mathematician, b. Thetford, Vt., 1809; d. Northfield, Vt., Feb. 24, 1879. [4; 43]

Jackman, Wilbur Samuel, educationist, b. Mechanicstown, O., 1855; d. Chicago, Ill., Jan. 28, 1907. [1; 8; 10]

Jackson, Abraham Valentine Williams, educationist, b. New York, N.Y., 1862; d. New York, N.Y., Aug. 8, 1937. [4; 7; 10]

Jackson, Abraham Willard, clergyman, b. Portland, Me., 1843; d. Melrose, Mass., April 25, 1911. [1; 8; 10]

Jackson, Charles Davis, clergyman, b. Salem, Mass., 1811; d. Westchester, N.Y., June 28, 1871. [3; 8]

Jackson, Charles Ross, novelist, d. Lake Placid, N.Y., Jan. 4, 1915.

Jackson, Charles Thomas, physician, b. Plymouth, Mass., 1805; d. Somerville, Mass., Aug. 28, 1880. [1; 3; 4; 8]

Jackson, Dunham, mathematician, b. Bridgewater, Mass., 1888; d. Minneapolis, Minn., Nov. 6, 1946. [10; 51]

Jackson, Edward, ophthalmologist, b. West Goshen, Pa., 1856; d. Denver, Colo., Oct. 29, 1942. [4; 10]

Jackson, Edward Payson, educationist, b. Erzroom, Turkey, 1840; d. Dorchester, Mass., Oct. 12, 1905. [1; 3; 4; 6; 10]

Jackson, Francis, local historian, b. Newton, Mass., 1789; d. Boston, Mass., Nov. 14, 1861. [3; 8]

Jackson, George Anson, clergyman, b. North Adams, Mass., 1846; d. Swampscott, Mass., May 8, 1907. [4; 8; 10; 62]

Jackson, George Thomas, dermatologist, b. New York, N.Y., 1852; d. New York, N.Y., Jan. 3, 1916. [1; 4; 8; 10]

Jackson, Mrs. Helen Maria, née Fiske, poet and novelist, b. Amherst, Mass., 1831; d. San Francisco, Calif., Aug. 12, 1885. [1; 3; 4; 6; 7; 8; 72]

Jackson, Henry, clergyman, b. Providence, R.I., 1798; d. East Greenwich, R.I., March 2, 1863. [3]

Jackson, Henry Ezekiel, clergyman, b. Coatesville, Pa., 1869; d. New York, N.Y., April 20, 1939. [10]

Jackson, Henry Rootes, poet, b. Athens, Ga., 1820; d. Savannah, Ga., May 23, 1898. [1; 3; 4; 7; 8; 34; 62]

Jackson, Holmes Condict, physiologist, b. New York, N.Y., 1875; d. New York, N.Y., Oct. 25, 1927. [10]

Jackson, Isaac Rand, politician, d. 1845.

Jackson, Isaac Wilber, educationist, b. Cornwall, N.Y., 1804; d. Schenectady, N.Y., July 28, 1877. [3; 8]

Jackson, James, physician, b. Newburyport, Mass., 1777; d. Boston, Mass., Aug. 27, 1867. [1; 3; 4; 6; 8]

Jackson, James, physician, b. 1810; d. 1834.

Jackson, James Caleb, physician, b. Manlius, N.Y., 1811; d. Dansville, N.Y., July 11, 1895. [1; 3; 4; 6; 8]

Jackson, John Davies, physician, b. Danville, Ky., 1834; d. Dec. 8, 1875. [1; 6]

Jackson, Jonathan, politician, b. Boston, Mass., 1743; d. Boston, Mass., March 5, 1810. [3; 8]

Jackson, Joseph, botanist, b. 1847; d. Jan. 9, 1924. [47]

Jackson, Joseph, journalist, b. Philadelphia, Pa., 1867; d. Philadelphi, Pa., March 4, 1946. [7; 10; 11]

Jackson, Joseph Cooke, lawyer, b. Newark, N.J., 1835; d. New York, N.Y., May 22, 1913. [10; 62]

Jackson, Margaret Hastings, educationist, b. Florence, Italy, 1861; d. Wellesley, Mass., Sept. 25, 1939.

Jackson, Mrs. Mary Anna, née Morrison, biographer, b. Mecklenburgh county, N.C., d. Charlotte, N.C., March 24, 1915. [10; 34]

Jackson, Robert Montgomery Smith, physician, b. Alexandria, Pa., 1815; d. Chattanooga, Tenn., Jan. 28, 1865. [3]

Jackson, Robert Tracy, palaeontologist, b. Dorchester, Mass., 1861; d. New York, N.Y., Oct. 28, 1948. [10; 11]

Jackson, Samuel, physician, b. Philadelphia, Pa., 1787; d. Philadelphia, Pa., April 5, 1872. [1; 4; 8]

Jackson, Samuel Macauley, clergyman, b. New York, N.Y., 1851; d. New York, N.Y., Aug. 2, 1912. [1; 4; 7; 8; 10]

Jackson, Sheldon, clergyman, b. Minaville, N.Y., 1834; d. Asheville, N.C., May 2, 1909. [1; 3; 4; 10]

Jackson, Tatlow, lawyer, fl. 1862-1885. [6]

Jackson, Thomas William, humorist, b. 1867; d. 1934.

Jackson, Thomas Wright, army surgeon, b. Akron, O., 1869; d. Lake City, Fla., April 25, 1925. [10]

Jackson, William Henry, explorer and photographer, b. Keeseville, N.Y., 1843; d. New York, N.Y., June 30, 1942. [7; 10]

Jacob, Edward Frederick Fulford, journalist and novelist, b. Elora, Ont., 1882; d. Toronto, Ont., June 3, 1928. [27]

Jacob, John G., biographer, fl. 1859-1882.

Jacobi, Abraham, physician, b. Germany, 1830; d. Lake George, N.Y., July 10, 1919. [1; 3; 4; 6; 8; 10]

Jacobi, Mrs. Mary, née **Putnam,** physician, b. London, England, 1842; d. New York, N.Y., June 10, 1906. [1; 4; 6; 8; 10]

Jacobs, Albert Poole, lawyer, b. 1853; d. Detroit, Mich., Jan. 30, 1909. [53]

Jacobs, Mrs. Caroline Elliott, née **Hoogs,** writer of books for girls, b. 1835; d. 1916.

Jacobs, Caroline Emilia, writer of books for girls, b. 1872; d. 1909.

Jacobs, Charles Michael, clergyman, b. Gettysburg, Pa., 1875; d. Philadelphia, Pa., March 30, 1938. [7; 10]

Jacobs, Henry Eyster, theologian, b. Gettysburg, Pa., 1844; d. Mount Airey, Pa., July 7, 1932. [1a; 3; 4; 8; 10]

Jacobs, John Adamson, educationist, b. Leesburg, Va., 1806; d. Danville, Ky., Nov. 27, 1869. [3; 8]

Jacobs, Joseph, educationist and editor, b. Sydney, New South Wales, 1854; d. Yonkers, N.Y., Jan. 27, 1916. [1; 7; 10; 15]

Jacobs, Orange, politician and jurist, b. near Genesee, N.Y., 1827; d. Seattle, Wash., May 21, 1914. [41]

Jacobs, Philip Peter, sociologist, b. Syracuse, N.Y., 1879; d. Morristown, N.J., June 12, 1940.

Jacobs, Samuel William, lawyer and politician, b. Lancaster, Ont., 1871; d. Montreal, Que., Aug. 21, 1938. [27]

Jacobs, Sarah Sprague, writer of books for children, b. Pawtuxet, R.I., 1813; d. ? [3; 6; 8]

Jacobsen, Gertrude Ann, educationist, b. Hillsboro, N.D., 1895; d. Minneapolis, Minn., March 3, 1942. [62]

Jacobson, Jacob Mark, lawyer, b. New York, N.Y., 1905; d. Washington, D.C., March 26, 1938. [62]

Jacobus, Melancthon Williams, clergyman, b. Newark, N.J., 1816; d. Allegheny City, Pa., Oct. 28, 1876. [3; 4; 6; 8]

Jacoby, George W., neurologist, b. St. Louis, Mo., 1856; d. New York, N.Y., Sept. 11, 1940. [10]

Jacoby, Harold, astronomer, b. New York, N.Y., 1865; d. Westport, Conn., July 20, 1932. [4; 8; 10; 13]

Jacques, Daniel Harrison, physician and horticulturist, b. about 1825; d. Fernandina, Fla., Aug. 28, 1877. [3; 6; 8]

Jaeger, Benedict, biologist, d. 1869.

Jaffray, Robert, merchant, b. New Rochelle, N.Y., 1854; d. New York, N.Y., Oct. 15, 1926. [62]

Jaggar, Thomas Augustus, bishop, b. New York, N.Y., 1839; d. Dec. 13, 1912. [4; 8; 10]

Jahnsenykes, William (pseud.). See Jenks, William.

Jakeway, Charles Edwin, physician and poet, b. Holland Landing, Ont., 1847; d. Stayner, Ont., 1906. [27]

James, Benjamin, lawyer, b. Stafford county, Va., 1768; d. Laurens district, S.C., Nov. 15, 1825. [34]

James, Bushrod Washington, physician, b. Philadelphia, Pa., 1836; d. 1903. [4; 8; 10]

James, Charles Canniff, civil servant and bibliographer, b. Napanee, Ont., 1863; d. St. Catherines, Ont., June 23, 1916. [27]

James, Charles Fenton, educationist, b. 1844; d. 1902. [8]

James, Charles Pinckney, jurist, b. Cincinnati, O., 1818; d. near Leesburg, Va., Aug. 9, 1899. [3b]

James, Edmund Janes, educationist, b. Jacksonville, Ill., 1855; d. Covina, Calif., June 17, 1925. [1; 3; 4; 8; 10; 37]

James, Edwin, naturalist, b. Weybridge, Vt., 1787; d. Burlington, Ia., Oct. 28, 1861. [1; 3; 7; 8]

James, George Francis, educationist, b. Normal, Ill., 1867; d. Chicago, Ill., Aug. 29, 1932. [8; 10; 11]

James, George Oscar, mathematician, b. Bowers Hill, Va., 1873; d. St. Louis, Mo., Nov. 24, 1931. [10]

James, George Wharton, ethnologist and explorer, b. Gainsborough, England, 1858; d. St. Helena, Calif., Nov. 8, 1923. [1; 4; 7; 10; 35]

James, Henry, theologian, b. Albany, N.Y., 1811; d. Cambridge, Mass., Dec. 18, 1882. [1; 3; 4; 6; 7; 8]

James, Henry, novelist, b. New York, N.Y., 1843; d. London, England, Feb. 28, 1916. [1; 2; 3; 4; 5; 6; 7; 8, 9; 10, 72]

James, Henry, lawyer and biographer, b. Boston, Mass., 1879; d. New York, N.Y., Dec. 13, 1947. [7; 10; 11; 51]

James, Henry Ammon, lawyer, b. Baltimore, Md., 1854; d. East Hampton, N.Y., Aug. 1, 1929. [62]

James, Maria, poet, b. Wales, 1793; d. Rhinebeck, N.Y., Sept. 11, 1868. [3]

James, Mrs. Mary Dagworthy, née **Yard,** biographer, b. 1810; d. 1883.

James, Police Captain (pseud.). See Van Orden, William H.

James, Samuel Humphreys, novelist, b. Cottage Oaks, La., 1857; d. ? [7; 34]

James, Thomas, Indian trader, b. Maryland, 1782; d. Monroe City, Ill., Dec., 1847. [1]

James, Thomas Potts, botanist, b. Radnor, Pa., 1808; d. Cambridge, Mass., Feb. 22, 1882. [1; 3; 8]

James, Will. See James, William Roderick.

James, William, philosopher and psychologist, b. New York, N.Y., 1842; d. Chocorua, N.H., Aug. 26, 1910. [1; 2; 4; 7; 8; 10]

James, William Roderick, novelist and artist, b. near Great Falls, Mont., 1892; d. Hollywood, Calif., Sept. 3, 1942. [7; 10; 11]

Jameson, Ephraim Orcutt, clergyman, b. 1832; d. 1902. [8]

Jameson, Horatio Gates, physician, b. York, Pa., 1778; d. New York, N.Y., Aug. 26, 1855. [1; 4]

Jameson, John Alexander, jurist, b. Irasburg, Vt., 1824; d. Hyde Park, Ill., June 16, 1890. [1; 3; 8]

Jameson, John Franklin, historian, b. near Boston, Mass., 1859; d. Washington, D.C., Sept. 28, 1937. [4; 7; 10]

Jamet, Albert, Benedictine monk, b. Tours, France, 1883; d. Quebec, Que., Aug. 23, 1948.

Jamieson, Leland Shattuck, novelist and airman, b. Stillwater, Okla, 1904; d. Jacksonville, Fla., July 9, 1941. [11; 75]

Jamieson, Mrs. Nina, née **Moore,** journalist, d. St. George, Ont., Nov. 6, 1932. [11; 27]

Jamison, Mrs. Cecilia Viets, née **Dakin,** artist and novelist, b. Yarmouth, N.S., about 1837; d. Roxbury, Mass., April 11, 1909. [1; 3; 7; 8;. 9; 34]

Jamison, David Flavel, historian, b. Orangeburg district, S.C., 1810; d. Charleston, S.C., Sept. 14, 1864. [6; 9; 34]

Janes, Edwin Lines, clergyman, b. Sheffield, Mass., 1807; d. Flushing, N.Y., Jan. 10, 1875. [3; 6; 8]

Janes, Lewis George, educationist, b. Providence, R.I., 1844; d. Eliot, Me., Sept. 4, 1901. [1; 3b; 4; 9; 10]

Janeway, Theodore Caldwell, physician, b. New York, N.Y., 1872; d. Baltimore, Md., Dec. 27, 1917. [1; 4; 10]

Janeway, Thomas Leiper, biographer, b. 1805; d. 1895.

Janney, Oliver Edward, physician, b. Washington, D.C., 1856; d. Baltimore Md., Nov. 17, 1930. [1; 10]

Janney, Samuel Macpherson, Quaker minister, b. Loudoun county, Va., 1801; d. Loudoun county, Va., April 30, 1880. [1; 3; 4; 6; 7; 9; 34]

Janvier, Caesar Augustus Rodney, educationist, b. Abington, Pa., 1861; d. Allahabad, India, Nov. 3, 1928. [10]

Janvier, Mrs. Catherine Ann, née **Drinker,** artist, b. Philadelphia, Pa., 1841; d. Merion, Pa., July 19, 1922. [1; 4; 7; 10]

Janvier, Francis de Haes, poet, b. 1817; d. 1885. [7; 8]

Janvier, Margaret Thomson, poet and novelist, b. New Orleans, La., 1844; d. Moorestown, N.J., Feb. 1913. [1; 3; 4; 7; 9; 10]

Janvier, Meredith, journalist, b. 1872; d. 1936. [7]

Janvier, Thomas Alibone, novelist and man of letters, b. Philadelphia, Pa., 1849; d. New York, N.Y., June 18, 1913. [1; 4; 7; 10; 72]

Jaques, George, pomologist, b. 1816; d. 1872.

Jaques, William Henry, naval architect, b. Philadelphia, 1848; d. Nov. 23, 1916. [8; 10]

Jarchow, Henry Nicholas, forester, b. Rostock, Germany, 1819; d. New York, N.Y., Feb. 24, 1899. [3b]

Jarratt, Devereux, clergyman, b. Richmond, Va., 1733; d. Virginia, Jan. 29, 1801. [1; 3; 4; 34]

Jarrold, Ernest, journalist, b. Brentwood, England, 1850; d. Amityville, N.Y., 1912. [8; 10]

Jarves, Deming, chemist, b. Boston, Mass., 1790; d. Boston, Mass., April 15, 1869. [1]

Jarves, James Jackson, diplomat and traveller, b. Boston, Mass., 1820; d. Tarasp, Switzerland, June 28, 1888. [1; 3; 4; 6; 7; 8]

Jarvis, Edward, physician, b. Concord, Mass., 1803; d. Dorchester, Mass., Oct. 31, 1884. [1; 3; 4]

Jarvis, Samuel Farmar, clergyman, b. Middletown, Conn., 1786; d. Middletown, Conn., March 26, 1851. [3; 4; 6; 8]

Jarvis, Thomas Stinson, lawyer and novelist, b. Toronto, Ont., 1854; d. Los Angeles, Calif., Jan. 1, 1926. [27]

Jarvis, William Henry Pope, journalist, b. Summerside, P.E.I., 1876; d. Canton, Ont., Dec. 14, 1944. [30]

Jastrow, Joseph, psychologist, b. Warsaw, Poland, 1863; d. Stockbridge, Mass., Jan. 8, 1944. [4; 7; 10; 11]

Jastrow, Marcus, orientalist, b. Posen, Germany, 1829; d. Germantown, Pa., Oct. 13, 1903. [1; 4]

Jastrow, Morris, educationist, b. 1861; d. Ogontz, Pa., June 22, 1921. [1; 4; 8; 10]

Jay, John, politician and diplomat, b. New York, N.Y., 1745; d. Bedford, N.Y., May 17, 1829. [1; 2; 3; 4; 5; 6; 7]

Jay, John, lawyer and diplomat, b. New York, N.Y., 1817; d. New York, N.Y., May 5, 1894. [1; 2; 3; 6; 8]

Jay, John, stock-broker, b. New York, N.Y., 1875; d. Hyannis, Mass., July 23, 1928. [62]

Jay, John Clarkson, physician and conchologist, b. New York, N.Y., 1808; d. Rye, N.Y., Nov. 15, 1891. [3b; 4; 6; 8]

Jay, William, jurist, b. New York, N.Y., 1789; d. Bedford, N.Y., Oct. 14, 1858. [1; 3; 4; 6; 7; 8; 9]

Jayne, Anselm Helm, lawyer and historian, b. Jackson, Miss., 1856; d. Houston, Tex., Aug. 26, 1915. [8; 10; 34; 51]

Jayne, Horace, biologist, b. Philadelphia, Pa., 1859; d. Wallingford, Pa., July 8, 1913. [1; 3; 4; 8; 10]

Jeffers, Eliakim Tupper, educationist, b. Upper Stewiacke, N.S., 1841; d. York, Pa., Nov. 18, 1915. [10]

Jeffers, James Frith, educationist, b. Belleville, Ont., 1842; d. Toronto, Ont., Feb. 24, 1917. [27]

Jeffers, Le Roy, librarian and explorer, b. Ipswich, Mass., 1878; d. Wawona, Calif., July 25, 1926. [7; 10]

Jeffers, William Nicholson, naval officer, b. Swedesboro, N.J., 1824; d. Washington, D.C., July 23, 1883. [1; 3; 4; 6]

Jefferson, Charles Edward, clergyman, b. Cambridge, O., 1860; d. Fitzwilliam Depot, N.H., Sept. 12, 1937. [10]

Jefferson, Joseph, actor, b. Philadelphia, Pa., 1829; d. Palm Beach, Fla., April 23, 1905. [1; 4; 7; 10]

Jefferson, Thomas, third president of the United States, b. Shadwell, Va., 1743; d. Monticello, Va., July 4, 1826. [1; 2; 3; 4; 5; 6; 7; 8]

Jeffery, Reuben, clergyman, b. Leicester, England, 1827; d. Brooklyn, N.Y., Dec. 15, 1889.

Jeffrey, Mrs. Rosa, née Griffith, poet and novelist, b. Natchez, Miss., 1828; d. Lexington, Ky., Oct. 6, 1894. [1; 3; 4; 6; 7; 34]

Jeffries, Benjamin Joy, physician, b. Boston, Mass., 1833; d. Boston, Mass., Nov. 21, 1915. [1; 10; 51]

Jeffries, James Graydon, poet, b. 1901; d. Brazil, Ind., Aug. 4, 1936.

Jelliffe, Smith Ely, neurologist, b. New York, N.Y., 1866; d. Lake George, N.Y., Sept. 25, 1945. [10; 11]

Jenkins, Burris Atkins, clergyman, b. Kansas, City, Mo., 1869; d. El Centro, Calif., March 13, 1945. [4; 7; 10; 11]

Jenkins, Charles Christopher, journalist and novelist, b. Hamilton, Ont., 1882; d. d. Toronto, Ont., Nov. 22, 1943. [27]

Jenkins, Charles Francis, physicist and inventor, b. near Dayton, O., 1867; d. Washington, D.C., June 6, 1934. [10; 13]

Jenkins, Frances, educationist, b. Oswego, N.Y., 1872; d. Cincinnati, O., Dec. 26, 1942. [10; 11]

Jenkins, Hester Donaldson, educationist, b. 1869; d. New York, N.Y., April 24, 1941.

Jenkins, Howard Malcolm, journalist and historian, b. Montgomery county, Pa., 1842; d. Philadelphia, Pa., Oct. 11, 1902. [1; 7; 8; 10]

Jenkins, John, clergyman, b. Exeter, England, 1813; d. 1898. [27]

Jenkins, John Stilwell, lawyer, journalist, and historian, b. Albany, N.Y., 1818; d. Syracuse, N.Y., Sept. 20, 1852. [1; 3; 6; 7; 9]

Jenkins, MacGregor, publisher and miscellaneous writer, b. Amherst, Mass., 1869; d. Williamstown, Mass., March 6, 1940. [7; 10; 11]

Jenkins, Oliver Louis, educationist, d. 1869. [6; 21]

Jenkins, Oliver Peebles, educationist, b. Bantam, O., 1850; d. Stanford University, Calif., Jan. 9, 1935. [10]

Jenkins, Paul Burrill, clergyman, b. Joliet, Ill., 1872; d. Williams Bay, Wis., Aug. 4, 1936. [10; 11; 44]

Jenkins, Ralph Carlton, educationist, b. Springfield, Vt., 1391; d. Danbury Conn., Oct. 2, 1946. [10]

Jenkins, Robert Smith, educationist and poet, b. Rosemont, Ont., 1870; d. Toronto, Ont., Nov. 12, 1931. [27]

Jenkins, Stephen, naval officer, b. Mount Vernon, N.Y., 1857; d. Lakewood, N.J., Oct. 10, 1913. [10]

Jenkins, Thomas Atkinson, educationist, b. Wilmington, Del., 1868; d. San Francisco, Calif., March 24, 1935. [10]

Jenks, Arthur Whipple, clergyman, b. Concord, N.H., 1863; d. New York N Y., April 19, 1923. [10]

Jenks, Edward Augustus, poet, b. 1830; d. 1908.

Jenks, Edward Watrous, physician, b. Victor, N.Y., 1833; d. on a train between Chicago, Ill., and Detroit, Mich., March 19, 1903. [4; 10]

Jenks, George Charles, journalist and novelist, b. London, England, 1850; d. Owasco, N.Y., Sept. 13, 1929. [1; 7; 10]

Jenks, Henry Fitch, clergyman, b. Boston, Mass., 1842; d. Waverly, Mass., Jan. 29, 1920. [3; 10; 51]

Jenks, Jeremiah Whipple, political economist, b. St. Clair, Mich., 1856; d. New York, N.Y., Aug. 24, 1929. [1; 4; 10]

Jenks, John Whipple Porter, clergyman and zoologist, b. West Boylston, Mass., 1819; d. Providence, R.I., Sept. 26, 1894. [3; 4; 8]

Jenks, Joseph William, educationist, b. Bath, Me., 1808; d. Newtonville, Mass., June 7, 1884. [3]

Jenks, Tudor, lawyer and writer of books for children, b. Brooklyn, N.Y., 1857; d. Bronxville, N.Y., Feb. 11, 1922. [1; 7; 8; 10; 62]

Jenks, William, clergyman, b. Newton, Mass., 1778; d. Boston, Mass., Nov. 13, 1866. [1; 3]

Jenks, William Lee, banker and historian, b. St. Clair, Mich., 1856; d. Port Huron, Mich., Dec. 4, 1936. [39]

Jenness, John Scribner, lawyer, b. 1827; d. 1879. [8; 51]

Jenness, Mary, educationist, d. New York, N.Y., Feb. 20, 1947.

Jenness, Mrs. Theodora, née Robinson, novelist, b. Greenwood, Me., 1847; d. ? [10]

Jenney, Charles Elmer, poet, b. Mattapoisett, Mass., 1872; d. Fresno, Calif., April 8, 1919. [35]

Jenny, Charles Francis, jurist, b. Middleborough, Mass., 1860; d. Boston, Mass., Nov. 29, 1923. [4; 10]

Jenney, William Le Baron, architect, b. Fairhaven, Mass., 1832; d. Los Angeles, Calif., June 15, 1907. [1; 4; 10]

Jennings, Clotilda, poet, b. Nova Scotia; d. Montreal, Que., 1895. [27]

Jennings, Francis, hymnologist, b. Wiltshire, England, 1808; d. Philadelphia, Pa., June 8, 1891. [3a]

Jennings, Henry C., publishing agent, b. Fremont, Ill., 1850; d. Chicago, Ill., Dec. 9, 1927. [10]

Jennings, Herbert Spencer, zoologist, b. Tonica, Ill., 1868; d. Santa Monica, Calif., April 14, 1947. [7; 10; 11; 13]

Jennings, Isaac, clergyman, b. Trumbull, Conn., 1816; d. Bennington, Vt., Aug. 25, 1887. [62]

Jennings, Isaac, physician, d. Oberlin, O., March 14, 1874.

Jennings, James Hennen, mining engineer, b. Hawesville, Ky., 1854; d. Washington, D.C., March 5, 1920. [1; 4; 10]

Jennings, John Joseph, journalist, b. St. Louis, Mo., 1853; d. New York, N.Y., June 30, 1909. [10; 34]

Jennings, Napoleon Augustus, journalist, b. 1856; d. New York, N.Y., Dec. 15, 1918. [8]

Jennings, Samuel Kennedy, physician and clergyman, b. Essex county, N.J., 1771; d. Baltimore, Md., Oct. 19, 1854. [3]

Jennison, Lucy White, poet, b. 1850; d. ? [8]

Jerauld, Mrs. Charlotte Ann, née Fillebrown, poet, b. Cambridge, Mass., 1820; d. Aug. 2, 1845. [7]

Jernegan, Marcus Wilson, historian, b. Edgartown, Mass., 1872; d. Edgartown, Mass., Feb. 19, 1949. [7; 10; 47]

Jerome, Chauncey, clock-maker, b. Canaan, Conn., 1793; d. New Haven, Conn., April 20, 1868. [1]

Jerome, Thomas Spencer, consular agent, b. Michigan, 1864; d. Capri, Italy, April 12, 1914. [39]

Jerome, William Travers, lawyer, b. New York, N.Y., 1850; d. New York, N.Y., Feb. 13, 1934. [1a; 2; 4; 10]

Jervey, Mrs. Caroline Howard, née Gilman, novelist, b. Charleston, S.C., 1823; d. Charleston, S.C., Jan. 29, 1877. [7; 8; 34]

Jervey, Henry, soldier, b. Virginia, 1866; d. Charleston, S.C., Sept. 30, 1942. [10]

Jervis, John Bloomfield, engineer, b. Huntington, N.Y., 1795; d. Rome, N.Y., Jan. 12, 1885. [1; 3; 4; 6]

Jervis, William Percival, writer on ceramics, b. 1850; d. Newark, N.J., Sept. 12, 1925.

Jessup, Henry Harris, missionary, b. Montrose, Pa., 1832; d. Beirut, Syria, April 28, 1910. [1; 3; 4; 62]

Jessup, Henry Wynans, lawyer, b. Beirut, Syria, 1864; d. New York, N.Y., Dec. 9, 1934. [11]

Jessup, Walter Abbott, educationist, b. Richmond, Ind., 1877; d. New York, N.Y., July 7, 1944. [7; 10]

Jesup, Henry Griswold, clergyman and botanist, b. Westport, Conn., 1826; d. Hanover, N.H., June 15, 1903. [10; 62]

Jeter, Jeremiah Bell, clergyman, b. Bedford county, Va., 1802; d. Richmond, Va., Feb. 25, 1880. [1; 3; 6; 34]

Jewell, Edward Alden, art critic and novelist, b. Grand Rapids, Mich., 1888; d. New York, N.Y., Oct. 11, 1947. [7; 10]

Jewell, Frederick Swartz, clergyman and educationist, b. Eliot Misson Station, Mo., 1821; d. Fond du Lac, Wis., Dec. 27, 1903. [6; 8; 10]

Jewell, Harvey, lawyer and genealogist, b. Winchester, N.H., 1820; d. Boston, Mass., Dec. 8, 1881. [1]

Jewell, Mrs. Louise, née Pond, novelist, b. Oberlin O.; d. Moorhead, Miss., Dec. 26, 1943. [7; 10]

Jewett, Charles, physician, b. 1807; d. 1879.

Jewett, Charles, physician, b. Bath, Me., 1839; d. Aug. 6, 1910. [4; 8; 10]

Jewett, Charles Coffin, librarian, b. Lebanon, Me., 1816; d. Braintree, Mass., Jan. 9, 1868. [1; 3; 4; 7]

Jewett, Edward Hurtt, clergyman, b. Nottingham, England, 1830; d. 1907. [8; 10]

Jewett, Frances Guilick, writer on hygiene, b. Micronesian Islands, 1854; d. Honolulu, Hawaii, Aug. 31, 1937. [11]

Jewett, Frank Fanning, chemist, b. Newton, Mass., 1844; d. Honolulu, Hawaii, July 1, 1926. [4; 10; 62]

Jewett, George Baker, educationist, b. Lebanon, Me., 1818; d. Salem, Mass., June 9, 1886. [3]

Jewett, Isaac Appleton, lawyer, b. Burlington, Vt., 1808; d. Keene, N.H., Jan. 14, 1853. [3; 6; 43]

Jewett, John Howard, journalist and writer of books for children, b. Hadley, Mass., 1843; d. Syracuse, N.Y., Sept. 18, 1925. [4; 7; 8; 10]

Jewett, Louise Rogers, educationist, d. 1914.

Jewett, Samuel A., lumberman, b. Gardiner, Me., 1816; d. Jewett Mills, Wis., Dec. 27, 1893. [70]

Jewett, Sarah Orne, novelist and short-story writer, b. South Berwick, Me., 1849; d. June 24, 1909. [1; 2; 3; 4; 5; 6; 7; 8; 9; 10; 71; 72]

Jewett, Sophie, educationist, b. Moravia, N.Y., 1861; d. 1909. [4; 7; 8; 10]

Jewett, Mrs. Susan W., poet, fl. 1840-1856. [3]

Jewitt, John Rogers, fur-trader, b. 1783; d. 1821. [27]

Jillson, Clark, lawyer, b. Whitingham, Vt., 1825; d. Worcester, Mass., 1894. [8; 43]

Job, Herbert Keightley, naturalist, b. Boston, Mass., 1864; d. Delmar, N.Y., June 17, 1933. [10; 51]

Jocelyn, Lydia A. See Smith, Mrs. Lydia Annie, née Jocelyn.

Jodoin, Alexandre, local historian, d. Longueuil, Que., Jan., 1915. [27]

John, John Price Durbin, educationist, b. Brookville, Ind., 1843; d. Aug. 7, 1916. [4; 10]

Johnes, Edward Rodolph, lawyer, b. Whitesboro, N.Y., 1852; d. New York, N.Y., March 28, 1903. [4; 8; 10; 62]

Johns, Clayton, pianist, b. New Castle, Del., 1857; d. Boston, Mass., March 5, 1932. [1a; 3; 4; 10; 20]

Johns, John, bishop, b. New Castle, Del., 1796; d. Fairfax county, Va., April 4, 1876. [1; 3; 4; 34]

Johnsen, Erik Kristian, theologian, b. Stavanger, Norway, 1863; d. St. Paul, Minn., Jan. 21, 1923. [10]

Johnson, Alexander, social worker, b. Ashton-under-Lyne, England, 1847; d. Atlanta, Ga., May 17, 1941. [10]

Johnson, Alexander Bryan, banker, b. Gosport, England, 1786; d. Utica, N.Y., Sept. 9, 1867. [1; 3; 6; 7]

Johnson, Alexander Bryan, surgeon, b. Albany, N.Y., 1860; d. East Hampton, N.Y., Sept. 4, 1917. [62]

Johnson, Allen, historian, b. Lowell, Mass., 1870; d. Washington, D.C., Jan. 18, 1931. [1; 4; 7; 10]

Johnson, Andrew, seventeenth president of the United States, b. Raleigh, N.C., 1808; d. near Carter's Station, Tenn., July 31, 1875. [1; 2; 3; 4; 5; 6; 7; 34]

Johnson, Anna C. See Miller, Mrs. Anna C., née Johnson.

Johnson, Artemas Nixon, musician, b. Middlebury, Vt., 1817; d. ? [43]

Johnson, Barton W., clergyman, b. 1833; d. 1894. [8; 37]

Johnson, Benjamin F. (pseud.). See Riley, James Whitcomb.

Johnson, Benjamin Franklin, publisher, b. Fauquier county, Va., 1856; d. Washington, D.C., June 11, 1921. [4; 10]

Johnson, Benjamin Pierce, agriculturist, b. Canaan, N.Y., 1793; d. Albany, N.Y., April 12, 1869. [1; 3; 6; 8]

Johnson, Bradley Tyler, soldier, lawyer, and politician, b. Frederick, Md., 1829; d. Amelia, Va., Oct. 5, 1903. [1; 3; 4; 8; 34]

Johnson, Charles Beneulyn, physician, b. 1843; d. Champaign, Ill., May 31, 1928.

Johnson, Charles Earl, lawyer, b. 1812; d. 1876.

Johnson, Charles Frederick, educationist, b. New York, N.Y., 1838; d. Hartford, Conn., Jan. 9, 1931. [7; 8; 10; 62]

Johnson, Charles Henry, welfare worker, b. Brooklyn, N.Y., 1870; d. New York, N.Y,. Oct. 28, 1948. [10]

Johnson, Charles W., journalist, b. Belleville, Ill., 1843; d. Minneapolis, Minn., Dec. 21, 1905. [70]

Johnson, Claude Ellsworth, musician, b. Erie, Pa., 1867; d. New York, N.Y., March 3, 1943.

Johnson, Clifton, illustrator and miscellaneous writer, b. Hadley, Mass., 1865; d. Jan. 22, 1940. [4; 7; 10; 11]

Johnson, David Newhall, merchant, b. 1824; d. 1906.

Johnson, Douglas Wilson, geologist, b. Parkersburg, W. Va., 1878; d. New York, N.Y., Feb. 24, 1944. [10; 11; 13]

Johnson, Duncan Starr, botanist, b. Cromwell, Conn., 1867; d. Baltimore, Md., Feb. 16, 1937. [10; 13]

Johnson, Edward Augustus, lawyer, b. Raleigh, N.C., 1860; d. New York, N.Y., July 25, 1944.

Johnson, Edwin A., clergyman, b. Gowanda, N.Y., 1829; d. ? [6; 8]

Johnson, Edwin Ferry, civil engineer, b. Essex, Vt., 1803; d. New York, N.Y., April 12, 1872. [1; 4]

Johnson, Effie (pseud.). See Richmond, Mrs. Euphemia Johnson, née Guernsey,

Johnson, Elias Finley, jurist, b. Van Wert, O., 1861; d. Palo Alto, Calif., July 31, 1933. 10]

Johnson, Elias Henry, theologian, b. Troy, N.Y., 1841; d. Upland, Pa., March 10, 1906. [1; 3; 10; 47]

Johnson, Mrs. Elizabeth, née Winthrop, novelist, b. Gramercy Park, N.Y., 1850; d. ? [6; 7; 10]

Johnson, Elwin Bird, educationist, b. Sugar Grove, Pa., 1865; d. 1928. [70]

Johnson, Emily Pauline, poet, b. near Brantford, Ont., 1862; d. Vancouver, B.C., March 7, 1913. [27]

Johnson, Ernest Clifton, life insurance agent, b. Washington, D.C., 1851; d. New Haven, Conn., July 12, 1933. [62]

Johnson, Francis Howe, clergyman, b. Boston, Mass., 1835; d. Oct. 27, 1920. [8; 10; 51]

Johnson, Frank Grant, physician and inventor, b. East Windsor, Conn., 1825; d. ? [3; 6; 8]

Johnson, Franklin, theologian, b. Frankfort, O., 1836; d. Brookline, Mass., Oct. 9, 1916. [1; 4; 10]

Johnson, Frederick Charles, physician, b. 1853; d. Wilkesbarre, Pa., March 5, 1913.

Johnson, George, statistician, b. Annapolis Royal, N.S., 1837; d. Grand Pré, N.S., Jan. 17, 1911. [27]

Johnson, George, priest and educationist, b. Toledo, O., 1889; d. Washington, D.C., June 5, 1944. [21]

Johnson, George Ellsworth, educationist, b. Springfield, Vt., 1862; d. Boston, Mass., Aug. 26, 1931. [10; 49]

Johnson, George Washington, poet and novelist, b. Binbrook, Upper Canada, 1839; d. Pasadena, Calif., Jan. 4, 1917. [27]

Johnson, Harriet Merrill, educationist, b. 1867; d. New York, N.Y., Feb. 22, 1934.

Johnson, Mrs. Helen Lossing, artist and writer of books for children, b. 1865; d. Yonkers, N.Y., Jan. 4, 1946.

Johnson, Mrs. Helen Louise, née Kendrick, novelist and editor, b. Hamilton, N.Y., 1844; d. New York, N.Y., Jan. 3, 1917. [1; 6; 7; 8; 10]

Johnson, Helen Mar, poet, b. Magog, Lower Canada, 1835; d. Magog, Que., March 3, 1863. [27]

Johnson, Henry, poet and translator, b. Gardiner, Me., 1855; d. Brunswick, Me., Feb. 7, 1918. [1; 4; 7; 10]

Johnson, Herrick, clergyman, b. Kaughnewaga, N.Y., 1832; d. Germantown, Pa., Nov. 20, 1913. [3; 4; 8; 10]

Johnson, Homer Uri, poet and historian, b. Ohio, about 1840; d. ?

Johnson, Hugh Samuel, soldier, b. Fort Scott, Kans., 1882; d. Washington, D.C., April 15, 1942. [7; 10]

Johnson, James Bowen, genealogist, b. 1830; d. 1899.

Johnson, James Weldon, poet and novelist, b. Jacksonville, Fla., 1871; d. Wiscasset, Me., June 26, 1938. [7; 10; 11]

Johnson, Jesse, lawyer, b. Bradford, Vt., 1842; d. Brooklyn, N.Y., Oct. 31, 1918. [10]

Johnson, John, clergyman, b. Charleston, S.C., Dec. 25, 1829; d. 1907. [4; 8; 10; 34]

Johnson, John Butler, civil engineer, b. Stark county, O., 1850; d. Pier Cove, Mich., June 23, 1902. [1; 3b; 4; 8]

Johnson, Joseph, physician and historian, b. near Charleston, S.C., 1776; d. Pineville, S.C., Oct. 6, 1862. [1; 3; 4; 8; 34]

Johnson, Joseph French, economist, b. Hardwick, Mass., 1853; d. Newfoundland, N.J., Jan. 22, 1925. [1; 7; 8; 10; 51]

Johnson, Mrs. Laura, née **Winthrop,** poet, b. New Haven, Conn., 1825; d. 1889. [6; 8]

Johnson, Laurence, pharmacologist, b. Wayne county, Pa., 1845; d. New York, N.Y., March 18, 1893. [4]

Johnson, Lewis Franklin, lawyer, b. 1859; d. 1931.

Johnson, Lorenzo Dow, miscellaneous writer, b. 1805; d. 1867.

Johnson, Luther Appeles, educationist, b. Tishomingo county, Miss., 1858; d. 1900. [10; 34]

Johnson, Martin Elmer, motion-picture explorer, b. Rockford, Ill., 1884; d. Los Angeles, Calif., Jan. 13, 1937. [7; 10]

Johnson, Merle De Vore, illustrator and bibliographer, b. Oregon City, Ore., 1874; d. New York, N.Y., Sept. 1, 1935. [7; 10]

Johnson, Nathaniel Emmons, clergyman, d. Jan. 15, 1847. [47]

Johnson, Oliver, journalist, b. Peacham, Vt., 1809; d. Brooklyn, N.Y., Dec. 10, 1889. [1; 3; 4; 7]

Johnson, Otis Coe, chemist, b. Kishwaukee, Ill., 1839; d. Ann Arbor, Mich., June 6, 1912. [4; 10]

Johnson, Philander Chase, journalist, b. Wheeling, W. Va., 1866; d. Rockville, Md., May 18, 1939. [7; 10]

Johnson, Richard W., soldier, b. Livingston county, Ky., 1827; d. St. Paul, Minn., April 21, 1897. [1; 3; 4; 70]

Johnson, Robert Gibbon, jurist, d. Salem, N.J., 1850.

Johnson, Robert Underwood, poet, b. Washington, D.C. 1853; d. New York, N.Y., Oct. 14, 1937. [2; 4; 7; 10; 11]

Johnson, Mrs. Rose, née **Griffith.** See Jeffreys, Mrs. Rose, née Griffith.

Johnson, Rossiter, editor and man of letters, b. Rochester, N.Y., 1840; d. Amagansett, Long Island, N.Y., Oct. 3, 1931. [4; 7; 8; 10; 11]

Johnson, Samuel, educationist, b. Guilford, Conn., 1696; d. Stratford, Conn., Jan. 6, 1772. [1; 3; 4; 6; 7; 8; 62]

Johnson, Samuel, lexicographer, b. Guilford, Conn., 1757; d. Guilford, Conn., Aug. 20, 1836. [3a]

Johnson, Samuel, poet, b. 1763; d. about 1843.

Johnson, Samuel, clergyman, b. Salem, Mass., 1822; d. North Andover, Mass., Feb. 19, 1882. [1; 3; 4; 6]

Johnson, Samuel William, agricultural chemist, b. Kingsboro, N.Y., 1830; d. New Haven, Conn., July 21, 1909. [1; 3; 4; 6]

Johnson, Mrs. Sarah, née **Barclay,** consul's wife b. Albemarle county, Va., 1837; d. Greenwich, Conn., April 21, 1885. [3; 4; 8]

Johnson, Theodore Taylor, pioneer, b. 1818; d. ?

Johnson, Thomas, poet, b. Virginia, about 1760; d. Danville, Ky., about 1830. [74]

Johnson, Thomas Cary, theologian, b. Fishbok Hill, Va., 1859; d. Richmond, Va., Feb. 15, 1936. [10; 11]

Johnson, Virginia Wales, novelist, b. Brooklyn, N.Y., 1849; d. Jan. 16, 1916. [1; 2; 3; 4; 6; 7; 8; 10]

Johnson, Walter Rogers, chemist, b. Leominster, Mass., 1794; d. Washington, D.C., April 26, 1852. [3; 4; 6; 8]

Johnson, William, jurist, b. Charleston, S.C., 1771; d. Brooklyn, N.Y., Aug. 11, 1834. [1; 3; 4; 6; 34]

Johnson, William Henry, physician, b. 1833; d. 1901.

Johnson, William Henry, clergyman, b. Beaufort, S.C., 1845; d. 1907. [8; 10; 34]

Johnson, William Samuel, lawyer and poet, b. Ellicottville, N.Y., 1859; d. New York, N.Y., March 2, 1937. [7; 10]

Johnson, William Savage, educationist, b. Portsmouth, O., 1877; d. Lawrence, Kans. Dec. 15, 1942. [11; 62]

Johnson, William Woolsey, mathematician, b. Tioga county, N.Y., 1841; d. Baltimore, Md. May 14, 1927. [1; 4; 7; 10; 62]

Johnson, Willis Fletcher, journalist, b New York, N.Y., 1857; d. Summit, N.J., March 28, 1931. [1; 7; 10; 11]

Johnson, Willis Grant, agricultural expert, b. New Albany, O., 1866; d. 1908. [10]

Johnston, Alexander, historian, b. Brooklyn, N.Y., 1849; d. Princeton, N.J., July 20, 1889. [1; 3; 9]

Johnston, Mrs. Annie, née **Fellows,** writer of books for boys and girls, b. Evansville, Ind., 1863; d. near Louisville, Ky., Oct. 5, 1931. [1; 4; 7; 8; 10; 15]

Johnston, Arthur, historian, b. England, 1841; d. Asheville, N.C., Nov. 20, 1919.

Johnston, Charles, miscellaneous writer, b. county Down, Ireland, 1867; d. New York, Oct. 16, 1931. [8; 10; 11]

Johnston, Charles Hughes, educationist, b. near Chapel Hill, N.C., 1877; d. Urbana, Ill., Sept. 4, 1917. [10]

Johnston, Christopher, educationist, b. Baltimore, Md., 1856; d. Baltimore, Md., June 26, 1914. [10]

Johnston, David Emmons, lawyer and politician, b. Giles county, Va., 1845; d. Portland, Ore., July 7, 1917.

Johnston, Donald Kent, clergyman, b. New York, N.Y., 1881; d. Uniontown, Pa., Sept. 8, 1944. [62]

Johnston, Elizabeth Bryant, historical writer, b. Mason county, Ky., 1833; d. Washington, D.C., 1907. [10; 34]

Johnston, Frederick, lawyer, b. 1811; d. 1894. [34]

Johnston, George, historian, b. 1829; d. 1891.

Johnston, Harold Whetstone, educationist, b. Rushville, Ill., 1859; d. Bloomington, Ind., 1912. [8; 10]

Johnston, Henry Phelps, historian, b. Trebizond, Turkey, 1842; d. Middletown, Conn., Feb. 28, 1923. [1; 4; 7; 8; 10; 62]

Johnston, Howard Angus, clergyman, b. Greene county, O., 1860; d. Milwaukee, Wis., April 15, 1936. [10]

Johnston, Hugh, clergyman, b. Elgin county, Ont., 1840; d. Baltimore, Md., Sept. 24, 1922. [3; 8; 10]

Johnston, James Wesley, clergyman, b. Ireland, 1847; d. Marion, Mass., July 22, 1936. [7; 10]

Johnston, John, educationist, b. Bristol, Me., 1806; d. Clifton, N.Y., Dec. 7, 1879. [3; 8; 38]

Johnston, John Black, educationist, b. Belle Center, O., 1868; d. Palo Alto, Calif., Nov. 19, 1939. [10]

Johnston, John Thomas Morris, banker, b. Ashland, Mo., 1856; d. Washington, D.C., Nov. 9, 1930. [10]

Johnston, Joseph Eggleston, soldier, b. Prince Edward county, Va., 1807; d. Washington, D.C., March 21, 1891. [1; 3; 4; 6; 34]

Johnston, Josiah Stoddard, politician, b. Salisbury, Conn., 1784; d. on the Red River, La., May 19, 1833.

Johnston, Josiah Stoddard, lawyer and journalist, b. New Orleans, La., 1833; d. Clayton, Mo., Oct. 4, 1913. [8; 10; 34; 62; 74]

Johnston, Julia Harriette, religious writer, b. Salineville, O., 1849; d. Peoria, Ill., March 6, 1919. [10]

Johnston, Mrs. Mabel A., née Stevenson, artist, d. Toronto, Ont., April 1, 1945.

Johnston, Mrs. Maria Isabella, née Barnett, novelist, b. Fredericksburg, Va., 1835; d. ? [10]

Johnston, Mary, novelist, b. Buchanan, Va., 1870; d. Warm Springs, Va., May 9, 1936. [4; 7; 10; 34; 72]

Johnston, Richard Malcolm, novelist, b. Powelton, Ga., 1822; d. Baltimore, Md., Sept. 23, 1898. [1; 3b; 4; 7; 9; 34]

Johnston, Robert Matteson, historian, b. Paris, France, 1867; d. Cambridge, Mass., Jan. 28, 1920. [1; 4; 7; 10]

Johnston, William, jurist, b. 1804; d. 1892.

Johnston, William, local historian and poet, b. Scotland, 1840; d. St. Mary's Ont., Jan. 13, 1917. [27]

Johnston, William Andrew, journalist and novelist, b. Pittsburgh, Pa., 1871; d. Chicago, Ill., Feb. 16, 1929. [1; 4; 10]

Johnston, William Atkinson, educationist, b. Boston, Mass., 1868; d. Belmont, Mass., Aug. 5, 1937. [10]

Johnston William Dawson, librarian, b. Essex Centre, A., 1871; d. Washington, D.C., Nov. 28, 1928. [10]

Johnston, William Preston, soldier, educationist, and poet, b. Louisville, Ky., 1831; d. Lexington, Va., July 16, 1899. [1; 3; 4; 8; 10; 34; 62]

Johnstone, Arthur Edward, musician, b. London, England, 1860; d. Wilkesbarre, Pa., Jan. 23, 1944. [10; 20]

Johnstone, William Jackson, clergyman, b. Daviess county, Ind., 1867; d. Billings, Mont., Jan. 21, 1938. [10; 11]

Johonnot, James, educationist, b. Bethel, Vt., 1823; d. Tarpon Springs, Fla., June 18, 1888. [3; 6; 8]

Joline, Adrian Hoffman, lawyer and book-collector, b. Sing Sing, N.Y., 1850; d. New York, N.Y., Oct. 15, 1912. [1; 4; 10]

Jolliffe, John, lawyer, b. 1804; d. 1868.

Jolys, Jean Marie Arthur, priest, d. St. Pierre-Jolys, Man., June 14, 1926. [32]

Jonas, Alberto, musician, b. Madrid, Spain, 1868; d. Philadelphia, Pa., Nov. 9, 1943.

Joncas, Louis Zephirin, sportsman, b. Gaspé, Que., 1846; d. March 28, 1903. [27]

Jones, Abner, religious reformer, b. Royalston, Mass., 1772; d. Exeter, N.H., May 29, 1841. [1]

Jones, Abner Dumont, biographer, b. 1807; d. 1872.

Jones, Adam Leroy, philosopher, b. Dunlap, Ill., 1873; d. Montclair, N.J., March 2, 1934. [7; 10]

Jones, Alexander, physician and journalist, b. North Carolina, about 1802; d. New York, N.Y., Aug. 22, 1863. [1; 3; 6; 34]

Jones, Alice, novelist, b. Halifax, N.S., 1855; d. Mentone, France, Feb. 27, 1933. [27]

Jones, Alice Ilgenfritz, novelist, d. 1906. [34]

Jones, Amanda Theodocia, poet, b. East Bloomfield, N.Y., 1835; d. Junction City, Kans., March 31, 1914. [1; 3; 4; 7; 10]

Jones, Anson, president of the republic of Texas, b. Great Barrington, Mass., 1798; d. Houston, Tex., Jan. 9, 1858. [1; 3; 4]

Jones, Arthur Edward, priest and historian, b. Brockville, Upper Canada, 1838; d. Montreal, Que., Jan. 19, 1918. [27]

Jones, Augustine, educationist, b. South China, Me., 1835; d. Newton, Mass., Sept. 10, 1925. [8; 10]

Jones, Burr W., jurist, b. Evansville, Wis., 1846; d. Madison, Wis., Jan. 7, 1935. [4; 10]

Jones, Carter Helm, clergyman, b. Nelson county, Va., 1861; d. Lynchburg, Va., May 6, 1946. [10]

Jones, Cave, clergyman, b. 1869; d. 1929.

Jones, Charles A., poet, b. Philadelphia, Pa., about 1815; d. Mill Creek, Hamilton county, O., July 4, 1851. [3]

Jones, Charles Colcock, clergyman, b. Liberty county, Ga., 1804; d. Liberty county, Ga., March 16, 1863. [3; 8; 34]

Jones, Charles Colcock, historian, b. Savannah, Ga., 1831; d. Augusta, Ga., July 19, 1893. [1; 3; 8; 34]

Jones, Charles Edward, educationist, b. Richland, N.Y., 1867; d. Albany, N.Y., Jan. 10, 1941. [10]

Jones, Charles Henry, lawyer, b. Reading, Pa., 1837; d. 1911. [3b; 4; 8; 10]

Jones, Chester Lloyd, educationist, b. Hillside, Wis., 1881; d. Madison, Wis., Jan. 13, 1941. [10; 44]

Jones, Clara Augusta, poet and novelist, fl. 1873-1892.

Jones, David, clergyman, b. Newcastle county, Del., 1736; d. Chester county, Pa., Feb. 5, 1820. [1; 3; 4]

Jones, David Morgan, poet, b. 1843; d. 1915.

Jones, Dwight Arven, lawyer, b. Utica, N.Y., 1854; d. St. Louis, Mo., Dec. 7, 1913. [62]

Jones, Easley Stephen, educationist, b. Nebraska, 1884; d. Santa Barbara, Calif., Feb. 18, 1947.

Jones, Edward Conway, clergyman and poet, b. 1820; d. Philadelphia, Pa., March 2, 1865. [55]

Jones, Edward Groves, surgeon, b. Chattooga county, Ga., 1874; d. Atlanta, Ga., Oct. 6, 1921. [10]

Jones, Elisha, educationist, b. Cayuga county, N.Y., 1832; d. Denver, Colo., Aug. 16, 1888. [39]

Jones, Erasmus W., clergyman, b. 1817; d ?

Jones, Franklin Daniel, lawyer, b. Webster, Neb., 1887; d. Washington, D.C., April 19, 1929. [10]

Jones, Frederick Robertson, educationist, b. Wicomico county, Md., 1872; d. Winter Park, Fla., Dec. 26, 1941. [10]

Jones, George, naval chaplain, b. York, Pa., 1800; d. Philadelphia, Pa., Jan. 22, 1870. [1; 3; 7; 62]

Jones, George Heber, missionary, b. Mohawk, N.Y., 1867; d. Miami, Fla., May 11, 1919. [1; 4; 10]

Jones, George Mallory, educationist, b. Port Perry, Ont., 1873; d. Toronto, Ont., Jan. 4, 1940. [11; 27]

Jones, George William, mathematician, b. East Corinth, Me., 1837; d. Ithaca, N.Y., Oct. 29, 1911. [10]

Jones, Guernsey, historian, b. Foreston, Ia., 1868; d. Lincoln, Neb., May 5, 1929. [10]

Jones, Harry Clary, physical chemist, b. New London, Md., 1865; d. Baltimore, Md., April 9, 1916. [1; 10; 13]

Jones, Harry Stuart Vedder, educationist, b. Charleston, S.C., 1878; d. Champaign, Ill., Jan. 10, 1942. [10; 11]

Jones, Horatio Gates, clergyman, b. Chester county, Pa., 1777; d. Philadelphia, Pa., Dec. 12, 1853. [3]

Jones, Horatio Gates, lawyer and historian, b. near Philadelphia, Pa., 1822; d. Philadelphia, Pa., March 14, 1893. [3; 6; 8]

Jones, Ignatius (pseud.). See Worth, Gorham A.

Jones, Mrs. Inis, née **Weed,** journalist, b. Kalamazoo county, Mich., 1878; d. Spokane, Wash., Nov. 27, 1938.

Jones, James Athearn, journalist, b. Tisbury, Mass., 1790; d. Brooklyn, N.Y., Aug., 1853. [3; 7; 8; 71]

Jones, James Edmund, lawyer and naturalist, b. Belleville, Ont., 1866; d. Toronto, Ont., June 13, 1939. [27]

Jones, James Thomas (pseud.). See Leslie, Mary.

Jones, Jenkin Lloyd, clergyman, b. Wales, 1843; d. Chicago, Ill., Sept. 12, 1918. [1; 4; 7; 8; 10]

Jones, Jesse Henry, clergyman, b. Belleville, Upper Canada, 1836; d. Halifax, Mass., April 19, 1904. [51]

Jones, Joel, jurist, b. Coventry, Conn., 1795; d. Philadelphia, Pa., Feb. 3, 1860. [1; 3; 4]

Jones, John, surgeon, b. Jamaica, N.Y., 1729; d. Philadelphia, Pa., June 23, 1791. [1; 3; 4]

Jones, John Beauchamp, journalist, b. Baltimore, Md., 1810; d. Burlington, N.J., Feb. 4, 1866. [1; 3; 6; 7; 71]

Jones, John Catron, educationist, b. Barbourville, Ky., 1889; d. Lexington, Ky., Dec., 1934. [10]

Jones, John G., clergyman, fl. 1866-1882. [34]

Jones, John Peter, missionary, b. Wales, 1847; d. Hartford, Conn., Oct. 3, 1916. [1; 4]

Jones, John Richter, lawyer and soldier, b. Salem, N.J., 1803; d. near New Berne, N.C., May 23, 1863. [3; 4; 7]

Jones, John Sparhawk, clergyman, b. Philadelphia, Pa., 1841; d. Bread Loaf, Vt., Aug. 20, 1910. [10]

Jones, John William, soldier and clergyman, b. Louisa, Va., 1836; d. Columbus, Ga., March 17, 1909. [1; 4; 6; 10; 34]

Jones, Joseph, physician, b. Liberty county, Ga., 1833; d. New Orleans, La., Feb. 17, 1896. [1; 3; 4; 6; 34]

Jones, Major Joseph (pseud.). See Thompson, William Tappan.

Jones, Joseph Huntington, clergyman, b. Coventry, Conn., 1797; d. Dec. 22, 1868. [3; 6; 8]

Jones, Joseph Seawell, lawyer and historian, b. Warren county, N.C., about 1811; d. Mississippi, Feb. 20, 1855. [4; 34]

Jones, Joseph Stevens, actor and playwright, b. Boston, Mass., 1809; d. Boston, Mass., Dec. 30, 1877. [1; 3; 7; 8]

Jones, Justin, novelist, fl. 1844-1869. [6; 7]

Jones, Laban, clergyman, b. 1796; d. 1848.

Jones, Leonard Augustus, jurist, b. Templeton, Mass., 1832; d. Boston, Mass., Dec. 9, 1909. [1; 3; 4; 10; 51]

Jones, Lewis Henry, educationist, b. Noblesville, Ind., 1844; d. Ypsilanti, Mich., Aug. 11, 1917. [10; 39]

Jones, Livingston French, missionary, b. Tuckerton, N.J., 1865; d. Fresno, Calif., Aug. 27, 1928. [10]

Jones, Mrs. Mabel, née **Cronise,** journalist and novelist, b. Tiffin, O., 1860; d. 1920. [10]

Jones, Marcus Eugene, botanist, b. Jefferson, O., 1852; d. Claremont, Calif., June 3, 1934. [10; 11]

Jones, Mrs. Mary Cadwalader, née **Rawle,** traveller, b. 1850; d. London, England, Sept. 22, 1935.

Jones, Matt Bushnell, lawyer and historian, b. Waitsfield, Vt., 1871; d. Newton Centre, Mass., July 1, 1940. [10]

Jones, Nelson Edwards, physician, b. Ross county, O., 1821; d. Circleville, O., 1901. [10]

Jones, Peter, Indian missionary, b. Burlington Heights, Upper Canada, 1802; d. Brantford, Ont., 1856. [27]

Jones, Philip Lovering, clergyman, b. Devonshire, England, 1838; d. Philadelphia, Pa., Aug. 26, 1913. [10]

Jones, Dr. Pleasant (pseud.). See Starnes, Ebenezer.

Jones, Richard, educationist, b. Berlin, Wis., 1855; d. Cambridge, Mass., Oct. 21, 1923. [8; 10]

Jones, Richard Uriah, chemist, b. Ottawa, Minn., 1877; d. St. Paul, Minn., July 9, 1941. [10; 13]

Jones, Rufus Matthew, educationist, b. South China, Me., 1863; d. Haverford, Pa., June 16, 1948. [7; 10; 11]

Jones, Samuel, clergyman, b. Wales, 1735; d. Philadelphia, Pa., Feb. 7, 1814. [3a]

Jones, Samuel, lawyer, b. Hebron, Me., 1778; d. Bangor, Me., Oct. 29, 1862. [38; 62]

Jones, Samuel Arthur, physician, b. 1834; d. Ann Arbor, Mich., March 9, 1912. [53]

Jones, Samuel Milton, social reformer, b. Wales, 1846; d. Toledo, O., July 12, 1904. [1a; 10]

Jones, Samuel Porter, evangelist, b. Chambers county, Ala., 1847; d. Raleigh, N.C., Oct. 15, 1906. [1; 3; 4; 8; 10]

Jones, Thomas Samuel, journalist and poet, b. Boonville, N.Y., 1882; d. New York, N.Y., Oct. 16, 1932. [7; 10; 11]

Jones, Uriah James, historian, b. 1818; d. 1864.

Jones, Walter, chemist, b. Baltimore, Md., 1865; d. Baltimore, Md., Feb. 28, 1935. [10; 13]

Jones, Walter Clyde, lawyer, b. Pilot Grove, Ia., 1870; d. Evanston, Ill., March 28, 1928. [10]

Jones, Wharton Stewart, educationist, b. Nashville, Tenn., 1849; d. Memphis, Tenn., Oct. 28, 1936. [10]

Jones, William, politician, b. Philadelphia, Pa., 1760; d. Bethlehem, Pa., 1831. [1; 3; 4]

Jones, William Alfred, librarian, b. New York, N.Y., 1817; d. Norwich Town, Conn., May 6, 1900. [1; 3; 4; 7; 10]

Jones, William Carey, educationist, b. Washington, D.C., 1854; d. Pekin, China, Oct. 2, 1923. [10]

Jones, William Caswell, lawyer, b. 1848; d. Robinson, Ill., Oct. 8, 1915. [53]

Jones, William Patterson, educationist, b. Philadelphia, Pa., 1831; d. Fullerton, Neb., Aug. 3, 1886. [1]

Jordan, Charles Bernard, educationist, b. Morrice, Mich., 1878; d. Lafayette, Ind., April 22, 1941. [10; 21]

Jordan, Mrs. Cordelia Jane, née Matthews, poet, b. Lynchburg, Va., 1830; d. 1898. [3; 7; 8; 34]

Jordan, David Francis, economist, b. Watervliet, N.Y., 1890; d. New York, N.Y., Aug. 20, 1942. [10]

Jordan, David Starr, educationist, b. Gainesville, N.Y., 1851; d. Stamford University, Calif., Sept. 19, 1931. [1; 2; 3; 4; 5; 7; 10; 11]

Jordan, Mrs. Dulcina, née Mason, poet, b. 1833; d. 1895. [8]

Jordan, Edwin Oakes, bacteriologist, b. Thomaston, Me., 1866; d. Lewiston, Me., Sept. 2, 1936. [10; 11]

Jordan, Elizabeth, journalist and novelist, b. Milwaukee, Wis., 1867; d. New York, N.Y., Feb. 24, 1947. [7; 10; 11; 22]

Jordan, Francis, merchant, b. Philadelphia, Pa., 1843; d. 1911. [10]

Jordan, John A., journalist, b. Quebec, Que., 1843; d. Quebec, Que., Oct. 13, 1917. [27]

Jordan, John Packard, accountant, b. 1877; d. 1932.

Jordan, John Woolf, librarian, b. Philadelphia, Pa., 1840; d. Philadelphia, Pa., June 11, 1921. [1; 3; 4; 7; 8; 10]

Jordan, Jules, musician, b. Willimantic, Conn., 1850; d. Providence, R.I., March 5, 1927. [4; 10; 20]

Jordan, Kate, novelist and playwright, b. Dublin, Ireland, 1862; d. Mountain Lakes, N.J., June 20, 1926. [1; 7; 10]

Jordan, Louis Henry, clergyman, b. Halifax, N.S., 1855; d. Oct. 4, 1923. [27]

Jordan, Mary Augusta, educationist, b. Ironton, O., 1855; d. New Haven, Conn., April 14, 1941. [7; 10]

Jordan, Richard, Quaker preacher, b. Norfolk county, Va., 1756; d. Newton, N.J., Oct. 14, 1826. [3; 34]

Jordan, Thomas, soldier, b. Paris, Tenn., 1832; d. West Meade, Tenn., Aug. 8, 1895. [3; 6; 8; 34]

Jordan, Whitman Howard, agricultural scientist, b. Raymond, Me., 1851; d. May 8, 1931. [10; 13]

Jordan, William Frederick, missionary, b. Compton, Que., 1867; d. Washington, D.C., Aug. 7, 1926. [10]

Jordan, William George, clergyman and educationist, b. Whitby, England, 1852; d. Toronto, Ont., May 31, 1939. [27]

Jordan, William George, editor, b. New York, N.Y., 1864; d. New York, N.Y. April 20, 1928. [1; 4; 7; 10]

Josephson, Aksel Gustav Salomon, librarian, b. Upsala, Sweden, 1860; d. Mobile, Ala., Dec. 13, 1944. [4; 7; 10; 11]

Joslin, Benjamin Franklin, physician, b. 1796; d. New York, N.Y., 1861. [6]

Joslin, Theodore Goldsmith, journalist, b. Leominster, Mass., 1890; d. Wilmington, Del., April 12, 1944. [10]

Josselyn, Charles, historian, b. 1847; d. San Francisco, Calif., Oct. 17, 1925. [8]

Josselyn, Freeman Marshall, educationist, b. Boston, Mass., 1866; d. 1916. [10]

Josselyn, Robert, poet, b. Massachusetts, 1810; d. Texas, 1884. [34]

Jouin, Louis, priest, b. Berlin, Germany, 1818; d. New York, N.Y., June 10, 1899. [3; 8; 10; 21]

Joyce, John Alexander, soldier, lawyer, poet, and biographer, b. Ireland, 1842; d. Washington, D.C., Jan. 18, 1915. [7; 10]

Joyce, Robert Dwyer, physician and poet, b. county Limerick, Ireland, 1836; d. Dublin, Ireland, Oct. 23, 1883. [3; 6; 7; 8]

Joynes, Edward Southey, educationist, b. Accomack county, Va., 1834; d. Columbia, S.C., June 18, 1917. [4; 10; 34]

Judah, Samuel Benjamin Helbert, playwright and satirist, b. New York, N.Y., about 1799; d. New York, N.Y., July 21, 1876. [1; 7; 9]

Judd, Charles Hubbard, psychologist, b. Bareilly, India, 1873; d. Santa Barbara, Calif., July 18, 1946. [7; 10; 11]

Judd, David Wright, publisher, b. Lockport, N.Y., 1838; d. New York, N.Y., Feb. 6, 1888. [3; 6; 8]

Judd, James Robert, surgeon, b. Honolulu, Hawaii, 1876; d. San Francisco, Calif., June 2, 1947. [62]

Judd, Mrs. Laura, née Fish, historian, d. 1873. [6]

Judd, Orrin Bishop, clergyman, b. Southington, Conn., 1816; d. Brooklyn, N.Y., Jan. 12, 1892. [3b]

Judd, Sylvester, antiquary, b. Westhampton, Mass., 1789; d. Northampton, Mass., April 18, 1860. [3]

Judd, Sylvester, clergyman, novelist, and poet, b. Westhampton, Mass., 1813; d. Augusta, Me., Jan. 26, 1853. [1; 3; 4; 6; 7; 9; 71]

Judd, Sylvester Dwight, ornithologist, b. West Orange, N.J., 1871; d. Oct. 22, 1905. [10; 51]

Judge, William Quan, theosophist, b. Dublin, Ireland, 1851; d. New York, N.Y., March 21, 1896. [1; 4; 7]

Judson, Abby Ann, spiritualist, b. Maulmain, Burma, 1835; d. Arlington, N.J., Dec. 1902. [70]

Judson, Adoniram, missionary, b. Malden, Mass., 1788; d. at sea, April 12, 1850. [1; 3; 4; 7]

Judson, Adoniram Brown, surgeon, b. Maulmain, Burma, 1837; d. New York, N.Y., Sept. 20, 1916. [4; 10]

Judson, Mrs. Ann, née Hasseltine, missionary, b. Bradford, Mass., 1789; d. Amherst, Burma, Oct. 24, 1826. [1; 3; 4]

Judson, Edward, clergyman, b. Maulmain, Burma, 1844; d. New York, N.Y., Oct. 23, 1914. [1; 3; 4; 10; 47]

Judson, Edward Zane Carroll, dime novelist, b. Philadelphia, Pa., 1822; d. Stamford, N.Y., July 16, 1886. [1; 3; 4; 6; 7; 8]

Judson, Mrs. Emily, née Chubbuck, missionary, b. near Hamilton, N.Y., 1817; d. Hamilton, N.Y., 1854. [1; 3; 4; 6; 7]

Judson, Frederick Newton, lawyer, b. St. Mary's, Ga., 1845; d. St. Louis, Mo., Oct. 18, 1919. [1; 4; 10; 62]

Judson, Harry Pratt, educationist, b. Jamestown, N.Y., 1849; d. Chicago, Ill., March 4, 1927. [1; 4; 7; 8; 10; 70]

Judson, Levi Carroll, historian, fl. 1839-1872. [8]

Judson, Mrs. Phoebe Newton, née Goodell, pioneer, b. 1832; d. 1926.

Judson, William Pierson, civil engineer, b. Oswego, N.Y., 1849; d. Broadalbin, N.Y., Feb. 12, 1925. [4; 10]

Juettner, Otto, physician, b. near Breslau, Germany, 1865; d. Cincinnati, O., Aug. 23, 1922. [10]

Julian, George Washington, abolitionist, b. 1817; d. near Indianapolis, Ind., July 7, 1899. [1; 3; 4; 6]

Julian, Isaac Hoover, journalist and poet, b. Wayne county, Ind., 1823; d. about 1911. [3; 4; 10]

Jump, Herbert Atchinson, clergyman, b. Albany, N.Y., 1875; d. Nantucket, Mass., Aug. 12, 1934. [10; 62]

June, Caroline Silver (pseud.). See Smith, Laura Rountree.

June, Jennie (pseud.). See Croly, Mrs. Jane, née Cunningham.

Juneau, Félix Emmanuel, educationist, b. near Quebec, Lower Canada, 1816; d. Quebec, Que., Feb. 16, 1886. [27]

Junius (pseud.). See Colton, Calvin.

Junkin, David Xavier, clergyman, b. Mercer, Pa., 1808; d. Martinsburg, Pa., April 22, 1880. [3; 4; 8]

Junkin, George, clergyman, b. near Carlisle, Pa., 1790; d. Philadelphia, Pa., May 20, 1868. [1; 3; 4; 6; 8]

Juriscola (pseud.). See Coxe, Tench.

Just, Ernest Everett, biologist, b. Charleston, S.C., 1883; d. Washington, D.C., Oct. 27, 1941. [10; 31; 49]

K

Kadmus, G. (pseud.). See Rawson, Albert Leighton.

Kagey, Rudolf, educationist and novelist, b. Tuscola, Ill., 1904; d. New York, N.Y., May 13, 1946. [7]

Kahlenberg, Louis Albert, chemist, b. Two Rivers, Wis., 1870; d. Sarasota, Fla., March 18, 1941. [10; 11; 13]

Kahn, Joseph, lawyer, b. Riga, Latvia; d. New York, N.Y., July 28, 1940.

Kahn, Max, b. 1887; d. April 8, 1926. [13]

Kahn, Otto Hermann, banker, b. Mannheim, Germany, 1867; d. New York, N.Y., March 29, 1934. [1a; 4; 10]

Kain, William Claiborne, lawyer, b. Knox county, Tenn., 1824; d. Knoxville, Tenn., Oct. 29, 1894. [62]

Kains, Maurice Grenville, horticulturist, b. St. Thomas, Ont., 1868; d. Livingston Manor, N.Y., Feb. 25, 1946. [10; 11]

Kaiser, Thomas Erlin, physician, b. 1863; d. Oshawa, Ont., Feb. 29, 1940. [27]

Kaler, James Otis, writer of books for boys, b. Winterport, Me., 1848; d. Portland, Me., Dec. 11, 1912. [3; 4; 7; 10; 15]

Kales, Albert Martin, lawyer, b. Chicago, Ill., 1875; d. Winnetka, Ill., July 26, 1922. [10]

Kalisch, Isidor, rabbi, b. Posen, Germany, 1816; d. Newark, N.J., May 11, 1886. [3b; 4; 8]

Kammeyer, Julius Ernest, educationist, b. Washington, Mo., 1867; d. Manhattan, Kans., Jan. 11, 1936. [10; 11]

Kanavel, Allen Buckner, surgeon, b. Sedgwick, Kans., 1874; d. Chicago, Ill., May 27, 1938. [10; 13]

Kander, Mrs. Lizzie, née Black, writer on cooking, b. 1858; d. Milwaukee, Wis., July 25, 1940. [11]

Kander, Mrs. Simon. See Kander, Mrs. Lizzie, née Black.

Kane, Elisha Kent, explorer, b. Philadelphia, Pa., 1820; d. Havana, Cuba, Feb. 16, 1857. [1; 2; 3; 4; 5; 6; 7]

Kane, Harry Hubbell, physician, b. 1854; d. ?

Kane, James Johnson, naval chaplain, b. Ottawa, Upper Canada, 1837; d. Philadelphia, Pa., March 9, 1921. [10]

Kane, John Kintzing, jurist, b. Albany, N.Y., 1795; d. Philadelphia, Pa., Feb. 21, 1858. [1; 3; 4]

Kane, Paul, painter, b. county Cork, Ireland, 1810; d. Toronto, Ont., Feb. 20, 1871. [27]

Kane, Thomas Leiper, soldier, b. Philadelphia, Pa., 1822; d. Philadelphia, Pa., Dec. 26, 1883. [1; 3; 8]

Kane, Thomas P., civil servant, b. 1848; d. Washington, D.C., March 1, 1923.

Karelitz, George Boris, educationist, b. Russia, 1895; d. New York, N.Y., Jan. 19, 1943. [13]

Karishka, Paul (pseud.). See Hatch, David Patterson.

Karsner, David, biographer, b. 1889; d. New York, N.Y., Feb. 20, 1941. [7]

Kasson, John Adam, lawyer and politician, b. Charlotte, Vt., 1822; d. Washington, D.C., May 19, 1910. [1; 4; 8; 10]

Kastle, Joseph Hoeing, chemist, b. Lexington, Ky., 1864; d. Lexington, Ky., Sept. 24, 1916. [10]

Katharine (pseud.). See Stephens, Louise G.

Kauffman, Calvin Henry, botanist, b. Lebanon, Pa., 1869; d. Ann Arbor, Mich., June 14, 1931. [1; 4; 10; 11; 13]

Kaufman, Herbert, journalist, b. Washington, D.C., 1878; d. Tarrytown, N.Y., Sept. 6, 1947. [7]

Kaun, Alexander Samuel, educationist, b. Russia, 1889; d. Berkeley, Calif., June 23, 1944.

Kautz, August Valentine, soldier, b. Germany, 1828; d. Seattle, Wash., Sept. 4, 1895. [1; 3; 4; 8]

Kavanagh, Marcus A., jurist, b. Des Moines, Ia., 1859; d. Chicago, Ill., Dec. 31, 1937. [10]

Kavanaugh, Benjamin Taylor, clergyman, b. Jefferson county, Ky., 1805; d. Boonsborough. Ky., July 3, 1888. [3; 34]

Kay, Gertrude Alice, illustrator and writer of books for children, b. Alliance. O., 1884; d. Youngstown, O., Dec. 17, 1939. [7; 10; 11]

Kaye, Frederick Benjamin, educationist, b. New York, N.Y., 1892; d. Boston, Mass., Feb. 28, 1930. [1; 7; 62]

Keagy, John Milton, physician and educationist, b. Lancaster county, Pa., 1795; d. Philadelphia, Pa., Jan. 30, 1837. [1; 3]

Keane, John Joseph, archbishop, b. Ballyshannon, Ireland, 1839; d. Dubuque, Ia., June 22, 1918. [1; 4; 10; 37]

Kearny, Thomas, biographer, b. Louisville, Ky., 1878; d. New York, N.Y., July 14, 1942.

Keasbey, Edward Quinton, lawyer, b. Salem, N.J., 1849; d. Newark, N.J., June 7, 1925. [4; 10]

Keating, John McLeod, journalist, b. Ireland, 1830; d. Gloucester, Mass., Aug. 15, 1906. [1; 3; 4; 7; 10]

Keating, John Marie, physician, b. Philadelphia, Pa., 1852; d. Colorado Springs, Colo., Nov. 17, 1893. [1; 3; 8]

Keating, Mrs. Sally Sayward, née Barrell.
See Wood, Mrs. Sally Sayward, née Barrell.
Keating, William Hypolitus, mineralogist, b. Wilmington, Del., 1799; d. London, England, May 17, 1840. [1; 3; 70]
Keays, Mrs. Hersilia A. Mitchell, née Copp, novelist, b. Woodstock, Ont., 1861; d. 1910. [10]
Keckley, Mrs. Elizabeth, née Hobbs, biographer, b. 1824; d. 1907.
Keddie, James, publisher, b. Scotland, 1883; d. New York, N.Y., Oct. 7, 1942.
Kedney, John Steinfort, theologian, b. Essex county, N.J., 1819; d. Salem, N.J., 1911. [3; 4; 8; 10; 70]
Kedzie, John Hume, educationist, b. 1815; d. Evanston, Ill., April 9, 1903.
Keedy, Charles Cochran, lawyer, b. Baltimore, Md., 1891; d. Wilmington, Del., May 15, 1934. [10]
Keedy, Edward Everett, clergyman, b. Rohrersville, Md., 1869; d. Minot, N.D., April 16, 1931. [62]
Keefer, Thomas Coltrin, civil engineer, b. Thorold, Upper Canada, 1821; d. Ottawa, Ont., Jan. 7, 1915. [27]
Keele, William Conway, lawyer, b. England, 1798; d. Toronto, Ont., July 11, 1872. [27]
Keeler, Bronson C., journalist, d. Los Angeles, Calif., Aug. 11, 1909.
Keeler, Charles Augustus, poet and naturalist, b. Milwaukee, Wis., 1871; d. Berkeley, Calif., July 31, 1937. [7; 10 11; 35]
Keeler, Harriet Louise, educationist, b. Delaware county, N.Y., 1846; d. Clifton Springs, N Y., Feb. 12, 1921. [10]
Keeler, Ralph Olmstead, journalist, b. Ohio, 1840; d. at sea, Dec. 17, 1873. [1; 3; 6; 7; 8]
Keeley, Leslie E., physician, b. St. Lawrence county, N.Y., 1832; d. Los Angeles, Calif., Feb. 21, 1900. [1; 10]
Keen, Samuel Ashton, clergyman, b. 1842; d. 1895.
Keen, William Williams, surgeon, b. Philadelphia, Pa., 1837; d. Philadelphia, Pa., June 7, 1932. [1a; 3; 4; 8; 10; 11]
Keenan, Henry Francis, journalist and novelist, b. Rochester, N.Y., 1847; d. ? [3; 7; 8; 10]
Keene, Edward Spencer, educationist, b. Rock Island, Ill., Oct. 8, 1864; d. North Fargo, N.D., Aug. 1928. [10]
Keene, Foxhall Parker, sportsman, d. Ayres Cliff, Que., Sept. 26, 1941.
Keener, John Christian, bishop, b. Baltimort, Md., 1819; d. New Orleans, La., Jan. 19, 1906. [3; 4; 10; 34]
Keener, William Albert, lawyer, b. Augusta, Ga., 1856; d. April 18, 1913. [1; 4; 8; 10]
Keep, Austin Baxter, educationist, b. Bloomfield, N.J., 1875; d. Asheville, N.C., Aug. 19, 1932.
Keep, Josiah, conchologist, b. Paxton, Mass., 1849; d. Pacific Grove, Calif., July 27, 1911. [8]

Keep, Robert Porter, educationist, b. Farmington, Conn., 1844; d. Farmington, Conn., June 3, 1904. [1; 8; 62]
Keese, John, bookseller, b. New York, N.Y., 1805; d. Brooklyn, N.Y., May 20, 1856. [3; 7]
Keese, William Linn, merchant, b. New York, N.Y., 1835; d. Brooklyn, N.Y., 1904. [3; 4; 6; 8; 10]
Keffer. Charles Albert, horticulturist, b. Des Moines, Ia., 1861; d. Knoxville, Tenn., Dec. 31, 1935. [10]
Keifer, Joseph Warren, soldier and lawyer, b. Clark county, O., 1836; d. Springfield, O., April 22, 1932. [1a; 4; 8; 10]
Keigwin, Albert Edwin, clergyman, b. Clinton, Ia., 1861; d. New York, N.Y., April 25, 1937. [10]
Keiller, William, physician, b. Midlothian, Scotland, 1861; d. Galveston, Tex., Feb. 22, 1931. [10; 11]
Keim, De Benneville Randolph, civil servant, b. 1841; d. 1914.
Keith, Alyn Yates (pseud.). See Morris, Mrs. Eugenia Laura, née Tuttle.
Keith, Charles Penrose, lawyer, b. Philadelphia, Pa., 1854; d. Philadelphia, Pa., April 23, 1939. [10; 11]
Keith, Edson, manufacturer, b. 1863; d. Sarasota, Fla., Feb. 4, 1939.
Keith, John Alexander Hull., educationist, b. Homer, Ill., 1869; d. Harrisburg, Pa., Feb. 22, 1931. [10; 11]
Keith, Melville Cox, physician, b. 1835; d. 1903.
Keith, Merton Spencer, educationist, b. Brockton, Mass., 1851; d. Cambridge, Mass., Nov. 15, 1920. [51]
Kell, John McIntosh, sailor, b. McIntosh county, Ga., 1823; d. 1900. [4; 34]
Kellar, Harry, magician, b. Erie, Pa., 1849; d. Los Angeles, Calif., March 10, 1922. [4; 10]
Keller, Matthias, poet, b. Ulm, Germany, 1813; d. Boston, Mass., Oct. 12, 1875. [1]
Kellerman, William Ashbrook, botanist, b. Asheville, O., 1850; d. Guatemala, March 8, 1908. [8; 10]
Kelley, Mrs. Adelaide, née Skeel, writer of fiction, b. Newburgh, N.Y., 1852; d. 1928.
Kelley, Edgar Stillman, musician, b. Sparta, Wis., 1857; d. New York, N.Y., Nov. 12, 1944. [4; 10; 20]
Kelley, Florence, humanitarian, b. Philadelphia, Pa., 1859; d. Philadelphia, Pa., Feb. 17, 1932. [1a; 4; 10]
Kelley, Hall Jackson, educationist and colonizer, b. Northwood, N.H., 1790; d. Palmer, Mass., Jan. 17, 1874. [1; 4; 6; 8]
Kelley, Henry Smith, lawyer, b. 1832; d. 1911. [6]
Kelley, James Douglas Jerrold, naval officer, b. New York, N.Y., 1847; d. New York, N.Y., April 30, 1922. 1; 7; 8; 10]
Kelley, Jay George, mining engineer, b. Worcester, Mass., 1838; d. Denver, Colo., 1899. [8; 10]

Kelley, Oliver Hudson, agriculturist, b. Boston, Mass., 1826; d. Washington, D.C., Jan. 20, 1913. [1; 4]

Kelley, Samuel Walter, surgeon and poet, b. Adamsville, O., 1855; d. Cleveland, O., April 20, 1929. [10]

Kelley, William Darrah, politician, b. Philadelphia, Pa., 1814; d. Washington, D.C., Jan. 9, 1890. [1; 3; 4; 6; 8]

Kelley, William Valentine, clergyman, b. Plainfield, N.J., 1843; d. Maplewood, N.J., Dec. 14, 1927. [4; 10]

Kellicott, William Erskine, biologist, b. Buffalo, N.Y., 1878; d. Hastings, N.Y., Jan. 29, 1919. [10; 13]

Kellner, Mrs. Elisabeth Willard, née Brooks, widow, b. Williamsport Pa.; d. Cambridge, Mass., April 16, 1916. [10]

Kellner, Max, theologian, b. Detroit, Mich., 1861; d. Cambridge, Mass., Aug. 5, 1935. [10]

Kellogg, Abner Otis, physician, b. 1818; d. 1888.

Kellogg, Albert, surgeon and botanist, b. New Hartford, Conn., 1813; d. Alameda, Calif., March 31, 1887. [1]

Kellogg, Alfred Hosea, clergyman, b. 1837; d. 1906. [8]

Kellogg, Alice Maud, educationist, b. Monroe, Mich., 1862; d. New Rochelle, N.Y., June 16, 1911.

Kellogg, Amos Markham, educationist, b. Utica, N.Y., 1832; d. New Rochelle, N.Y., Oct. 3, 1914. [8; 10]

Kellogg, Brainerd, educationist, d. Morristown, N.J., Jan. 9, 1930.

Kellogg, Mrs. Celia, née **Logan.** See Connelly, Mrs. Celia, née Logan.

Kellogg, Clara Louise, singer, b. Sumterville, S.C., 1842; d. Hartford, Conn., May 13, 1916. [1; 2; 4; 10]

Kellogg, Edward, economist, b. Norwalk, Conn., 1790; d. New York, N.Y., April 29, 1858. [1; 3; 7; 8]

Kellogg, Elijah, clergyman and writer of books for boys, b. Portland, Me., 1813; d. Harpswell, Me., March 18, 1901. [1; 3; 4; 6; 7]

Kellogg, Frank Eugene, writer of books for boys, b. 1854; d. ?

Kellogg, James Lawrence, biologist, b. Kewanee, Ill., 1866; d. Williamstown, Mass., July 8, 1938. [10; 13]

Kellogg, John Harvey, surgeon, b. Tyrone, Mich., 1852; d. Battle Creek, Mich., Dec. 14, 1943. [10]

Kellogg, Louise Phelps, historian, b. Milwaukee, Wis., about 1872; d. Madison, Wis., July 12, 1942. [7; 10; 11; 44]

Kellogg, Samuel Henry, clergyman, b. Quogue, Long Island, N.Y., 1839; d. Landour, India, May 2, 1899. [1; 3; 8]

Kellogg, Sanford Cobb, soldier, b. 1842; d. ? [34]

Kellogg, Sarah Prescott, poet, b. 1829; d. 1895.

Kellogg, Theodore H., physician, fl. 1865-1908. [10]

Kellogg, Vernon Lyman, biologist, b. Emporia, Kans., 1867; d. Hartford, Conn., Aug. 8, 1937. [4; 10; 11]

Kelly, Allen, humorist, b. New York, N.Y., 1852; d. Los Angeles, Calif., May 16, 1916. [35]

Kelly, Aloysius Oliver Joseph, physician, b. Philadelphia, Pa., 1870; d. Philadelphia, Pa., Feb. 23, 1911. [1; 10]

Kelly, Clyde. See Kelly, Melville Clyde.

Kelly, Edmond, lawyer and sociologist, b. near Toulouse, France, 1851; d. near Nyack, N.Y., Oct. 4, 1909. [1; 4; 8; 10]

Kelly, Mrs. Florence, née **Finch,** journalist and novelist, b. Girard, Ill., 1858; d. New Hartford, Conn., Dec. 17, 1939. [7; 10; 11]

Kelly, George C., novelist, b. 1858; d. Brooklyn, N.Y., July 24, 1895.

Kelly, Harry Eugene, lawyer, b. Des Moines, Ia., 1870; d. Evanston, Ill., Jan. 14, 1936. [4; 10]

Kelly, Howard Atwood, surgeon, b. Camden, N.J., 1858; d. Baltimore, Md., Jan. 12, 1943. [4; 10; 11]

Kelly, James, bibliographer, b. Ireland, 1829; d. East Orange, N.J., May 16, 1907. [4]

Kelly, John Frederick, architect, b. Lowville, N.Y., 1888; d. Hamden, Conn., Sept. 1, 1947.

Kelly, Jonathan Falconbridge, humorist, b. Philadelphia, 1818; d. Cincinnati, O., 1854. [3; 7]

Kelly, Luther Sage, army scout, b. Geneva, N.Y., 1849; d. Paradise, Calif., Dec. 17, 1928. [1; 7]

Kelly, Melville Clyde, politician, b. Bloomfield, O., 1883; d. Pittsburgh, Pa., April 29, 1935. [10]

Kelly, Michael J., baseball player, b. Troy, N.Y., 1857; d. Boston, Mass., Nov. 8, 1894. [1]

Kelly, Myra, educationist and writer of fiction, b. Dublin, Ireland, 1875; d. Torquay, England, March 30, 1910. [1; 7; 10]

Kelman, John, clergyman, b. Dundonald, Scotland, 1864; d. New York, N.Y., May 3, 1929. [10]

Kelsey, Charles Boyd, physician, b. Farmington, Conn., 1850; d. New York, N.Y., Aug. 4, 1917. [10]

Kelsey, Francis Willey, educationist, b. Ogden, N.Y., 1858; d. Ann Arbor, Mich., May 11, 1927. [1; 4; 7; 10]

Kelsey, Frederick Wallace, nurseryman, b. Ogden, N.Y., 1850; d. South Orange, N.J., Oct. 20, 1935. [10]

Kelsey, Mrs. Jeannette Garr, née **Washburn,** novelist, b. 1850; d. ?

Kelsey, Rayner Wickersham, historian, b. Western Springs, Ill., 1879; d. Haverford, Pa., Oct. 29, 1934. [1a; 10]

Keiso, John Russell, spiritualist, b. 1831; d. 1891.

Kelton, Dwight H., soldier, b. Montpelier, Vt., 1843; d. Montpelier, Vt., Aug. 9, 1906.

Kelton, John Cunningham, soldier, b. Delaware county, Pa., 1828; d. near Washington, D.C., July 15, 1893. [1; 3; 4; 6; 8]

Kemble, Edward Cleveland, journalist, b. Troy, N.Y., about 1827; d. Mott Haven, N.Y., Feb. 10, 1886. [35]

Kemble, Edward Windsor, illustrator and cartoonist, b. Sacramento, Calif., 1861; d. Ridgefield, Conn., Sept. 19, 1933. [7; 10; 34]

Kemmerer, Edwin Walter, economist, b. Scranton, Pa., 1875; d. Princeton, N.J., Dec. 16, 1945. [10; 11; 14]

Kemp, Alexander Ferrie, clergyman, b. Greenock, Scotland, 1822; d. Hamilton, Ont., May 4, 1884. [27]

Kemp, James Furman, geologist, b. New York, N.Y., 1859; d. Great Neck, N.Y., Nov. 17, 1926. [1; 4; 8; 10; 13]

Kemp, Robert H., concert-leader, b. Wellfleet, Mass., 1820; d. Charlestown, Mass., May 15, 1897. [1]

Kemp, William Webb, educationist, b. Placerville, Calif., 1873; d. San Francisco, Calif., May 14, 1946. [11]

Kemper, William Harrison, surgeon, b. Rush county, Ind., 1839; d. Muncie, Ind., Sept. 26, 1927. [10]

Kendall, Amos, journalist, b. Dunstable, Mass., 1789; d. Washington, D.C., Nov. 11, 1869. [1; 3; 4; 6; 7; 8]

Kendall, Calvin Noyes, educationist, b. Augusta, N.Y., 1858; d. Knoxboro, N.Y., Sept. 2, 1921. [10]

Kendall, Elizabeth Kimball, historian, b. Middlebury, Vt., 1855; d. ?

Kendall, Ezra Fremont, comedian, b. Alleghany county, N.Y., 1861; d. Martinsville, Ind., Jan. 24, 1910.

Kendall, Ezra Otis, astronomer, b. Wilmington, Mass., 1818; d. Philadelphia, Pa., 1899. [3b; 4]

Kendall, George Wilkins, journalist, b. Mount Vernon, N.H., 1809; d. near Bowie, Tex., Oct. 22, 1867. [1; 3; 4; 7; 8]

Kenderdine, Thaddeus S., pioneer, b. Lumberton, Pa., 1836; d. Newtown, Pa., Feb. 22, 1922.

Kendrick, Asahel Clark, educationist, b. Poultney, Vt., 1809; d. Rochester, N.Y., Oct. 21, 1895. [1; 3; 4; 6; 43]

Kendrick, Benjamin Burks, educationist, b. 1884; d. West Dresden, Me., Oct. 27, 1946. [10]

Kendrick, Eliza Hall, educationist, b. 1863; d. Coconut Grove, Fla., April 11, 1940. [10]

Kendrick, John B., auditor, b. Wallingford, Conn., 1851; d. Wallingford, Conn., Oct. 9, 1931. [62]

Kendrick, John William, railway executive, b. Worcester, Mass., 1853; d. Chicago, Ill., Feb. 16, 1924. [10]

Kenison, Ervin M., educationist, b. Charlestown, Mass., 1869; d. Huntington, W. Va., May 12, 1942.

Keniston, James Mortimer, physician, b. Newburyport, Mass., 1848; d. Portland, Me., July 13, 1927. [10]

Kenlon, John, sailor and fireman, b. Dundalk, Ireland, 1859; d. New York, N.Y., May 30, 1940.

Kenly, John Reese, lawyer, b. Baltimore, Md., 1822; d. Baltimore, Md., Dec. 20, 1891. [3; 4; 8; 34]

Kennan, George, explorer and war correspondent, b. Norwalk, O., 1845; d. Medina, N.Y., May 10, 1924. [1; 3; 4; 7; 8; 10; 11]

Kennard, Joseph Spencer, lawyer and littérateur, b. Bridgeton, N.J., 1859; d. Coral Gables, Fla., Aug. 15, 1944. [7; 10]

Kennedy, Archibald, pamphleteer, b. Scotland, 1685; d. New York, N.Y., June 14, 1763. [1; 3]

Kennedy, Crammond, lawyer, b. North Berwick, Scotland, 1842; d. Feb. 20, 1918. [3; 4; 7; 8; 10]

Kennedy, Daniel Joseph, priest, Knox county, Tenn., 1862; d. Washington, D.C., 1930. [10; 11]

Kennedy, Elijah Robinson, financier and historian, b. Hartford, Conn., 1846; d. Brooklyn, N.Y., April 25, 1926. [10]

Kennedy, Henry Dawson, evangelist, b. 1869; d. Peterborough, Ont., Oct. 9, 1925. [27]

Kennedy, Howard Angus, journalist, b. London, England, 1861; d. Montreal, Que., Feb. 15, 1938. [11; 27]

Kennedy, James, poet, b. Scotland, 1850; d. New York, N.Y., Aug. 14, 1922. [10]

Kennedy, James Henry, journalist, b. Farmington, O., 1849; d. Altadena, Calif., Jan. 22, 1934. [10]

Kennedy, John Pendleton, politician and littérateur, b. Baltimore, Md., 1795; d. Newport, R.I., Aug. 18, 1870. [1; 2; 3; 4; 5; 6; 7; 34; 71; 72]

Kennedy, Joseph, educationist, b. Oshawa, Minn., 1858; d. Grand Forks, N.D., April 1, 1937. [10; 11]

Kennedy, Joseph Camp Griffith, statistician, b. Meadville, Pa., 1813; d. Washington, D.C., July 13, 1887. [3; 4]

Kennedy, Philip Pendleton, historian, b. about 1808; d. 1864. [6]

Kennedy, Robert Emmet, musician, b. Gretna, La., 1877; d. New Orleans, La., Nov. 21, 1941. [7]

Kennedy, Robert Patterson, local historian, b. Bellefontaine, O., 1840; d. Columbus, O., May 6, 1918. [1; 4; 10]

Kennedy, Mrs. Sara Beaumont, née Cannon, poet and novelist, b. Somerville, Tenn.; d. Memphis, Tenn., March 12, 1921. [7; 8; 10; 34]

Kennedy, Sinclair, lawyer, b. Boston, Mass., 1875; d. Canaan, Conn., Aug. 3, 1947.

Kennedy, Thomas, poet, b. 1776; d. 1832.

Kennedy, Walker, journalist, b. Louisville, Ky., 1857; d. Memphis, Tenn., Nov. 12, 1909. [7; 10; 34]

Kennedy, William G., poet, b. 1829; d. 1893.

Kennedy, William Henry John, educationist, b. Boston, Mass., 1888; d. Boston, Mass., Aug. 23, 1948. [10]

Kennedy, William Sloane, journalist, b. Brecksville, O., 1850; d. West Yarmouth, Mass., Aug. 3, 1929. [7; 10; 11; 62]

Kennelly, Arthur Edwin, electrical engineer, b. Bombay, India, 1861; d. Boston, Mass., June 18, 1939. [7; 10; 11]

Kenney, James Francis, archivist, b. Marysville, Ont., 1884; d. Ottawa, Ont., June 4, 1946. [11; 30]

Kenny, Michael, priest, b. Tipperary, Ireland, 1863; d. Spring Hill, Ala., Nov. 22, 1946. [10]

Kenrick, Francis Patrick, archbishop, b. Dublin, Ireland, 1797; d. Baltimore, Md., July 6, 1863. [1; 3; 4; 6; 7; 8]

Kenrick, William, nurseryman, b. Newton, Mass., 1789; d. Newton, Mass., Feb. 14, 1872. [1]

Kent, Charles Foster, theologian, b. Palmyra, N.Y., 1867; d. Mount Carmel, Conn., May 2, 1925. [1; 7; 10; 62]

Kent, Charles William, educationist, b. Louisa Court House, Va., 1860; d. Charlottesville, Va., Oct. 5, 1917. [4; 7; 10; 34]

Kent, Edwin Newell, dentist, b. Newburyport, Mass., 1875; d. Rockport, Mass., June 8, 1947.

Kent, James, jurist, b. Putnam county, N.Y., 1763; d. New York, N.Y., Dec. 12, 1847. [1; 3; 4; 6; 7; 8]

Kent, James, novelist, fl. 1877-1878. [6]

Kent, James Tyler, physician, b. Woodhull, N.Y., 1849; d. Stevensville, Mich., June 5, 1916. [10]

Kent, Karlene (pseud.). See Norton, Mrs. Edith Eliza, née Ames.

Kent, Lucien Hervey, poet, b. 1816; d. 1900.

Kent, Raymond Asa, educationist, b. Plymouth, Ia., 1883; d. near Louisville, Ky., Feb. 28, 1943. [10; 11]

Kent, Robert Thurston, mechanical engineer, b. Jersey City, N.J., 1860; d. Montclair, N.J., May 23, 1947.

Kent, William, engineer, b. Philadelphia, Pa., 1851; d. Montclair, N.J., Sept. 18, 1918. [1; 8; 10]

Kent, William, politician, b. Chicago, Ill., 1864; d. San Rafael, Calif., March 13, 1928. [10]

Kent, William H. B., novelist, b. 1878; d. Glendora, Calif., Dec. 24, 1947.

Kent, Willis (pseud.). See Collison, Wilson.

Kenyon, Alfred Monroe, mathematician, b. Medina, O., 1869; d. Lafayette, Ind., July 27, 1921. [10]

Kenyon, James Benjamin, poet, b. Frankfort, N.Y., 1858; d. New York, N.Y., May 11, 1924. [2; 3; 4; 7; 8; 10]

Kenyon, Orr (pseud.) See Carter, Russell Kelso.

Kenyon, William Asbury, poet, b. Hingham, Mass., 1817; d. Hingham, Mass., Jan. 25, 1862. [3]

Kenzel, Francis La Fayette, priest and dramatist, b. 1863; d. Saratoga Springs, N.Y., Dec. 23, 1943. [21]

Kephart, Cyrus Jeffries, bishop, b. Clearfield county, Pa., 1852; d. Shelby, Neb., July 21, 1932. [8; 10; 11; 37]

Kephart, Ezekiel Boring, bishop, b. Clearfield county, Pa., 1834; d. Indianapolis, Ind., Jan. 24, 1906. [1; 8; 10]

Kephart, Horace, librarian, b. East Salem, Pa., 1862; d. near Bryson City, N.C., April 2, 1931. [4; 7; 10]

Kephart, Isaiah Lafayette, clergyman, b. Clearfield county, Pa., 1832; d. Dayton, O., Oct. 28, 1908. [1; 4; 10]

Keppel, Frederick, art critic, b. Ireland, 1845; d. New York, N.Y., March 7, 1912. [1; 4; 7; 10]

Keppel, Frederick Paul, educationist, b. Staten Island, N.Y., 1875; d. New York, N.Y., Sept. 8, 1943. [7; 10]

Ker, David, writer of books for boys, b. 1842; d. 1914. [6]

Ker, Henry, traveller, b. Boston, Mass., about 1785; d. ? [3]

Kerbey, Joseph Orton, soldier and journalist, d. 1913.

Kerby, George William, clergyman and educationist, b. Lambton county, Ont., 1860; d. Calgary, Alta., Feb. 9, 1944. [11; 27]

Kerby, William Joseph, priest, b. Lawler, Ia., 1870; d. Washington, D.C., July 27, 1936. [10; 21; 22]

Kercheval, Albert Fenner, poet, b. Preble county, O., 1829; d. Los Angeles, Calif., Jan. 24, 1893. [35]

Kercheval, Samuel, historian, b. 1786; d. about 1845. [34]

Kerfoot, John Barrett, editor, b. Chicago, Ill., 1865; d. London, England, April 19, 1927. [4; 10; 11]

Kerl, Simon, educationist, fl. 1858-1870.

Kerley, Charles Gilmore, pediatrician, b. Red Hook, N.Y., 1863; d. New York, N.Y., Sept. 7, 1945. [10; 11]

Kerlin, Isaac Newton, psychiatrist, b. Burlington, N.J., 1834; d. Elwyn, Pa., Oct. 25, 1893. [1; 4]

Kern, John Adam, clergyman, b. Frederick county, Va., 1846; d. Dallas, Tex., March 24, 1926. [4; 8; 10; 34]

Kern, John Dwight, educationist, b. Germantown, O., 1900; d. Philadelphia, Pa., Nov. 24, 1948. [10]

Kernan, Will Hubbard, poet, b. Bellefontaine, O., 1845; d. Memphis, Tenn., Jan. 28, 1905. [34]

Kerney, James, journalist, b. Trenton, N.J., 1873; d. Baltimore., April 8, 1934. [1a; 10]

Kerney, Martin Joseph, educationist, b. Lewiston, Md., 1819; d. Baltimore, Md., March 16, 1861. [3; 34]

Kernighan, Robert Kirkland, poet and journalist, b. near Hamilton, Ont., 1857; d. Rockton, Ont., Nov. 3, 1926. [27]

Kernot, Henry, bibliographer, b. London, England, 1806; d. New York, N.Y., Oct. 25, 1874. [3]

Kerr (pseud.). See Pinnix, Mrs. Hannah Courtney, née Baxter.

Kerr, Albert Boardman, lawyer, b. Clearfield, Pa., 1875; d. Charlottesville, Va., June 20, 1945. [10; 62]

Kerr, Alva Martin, editor, d. Nov. 1, 1928. [11]

Kerr, Alvah Milton, journalist and novelist, b. Athens, O., 1858; d. Hollywood, Cal., Sept. 26, 1924. [7; 10]

Kerr, Hugh, poet, b. Ireland; d. Texas, 1843. [34]

Kerr, James Manford, lawyer, b. near Tippecanoe City, O., 1851; d. Pasadena, Calif., 1929. [10; 11]

Kerr, John Henry, clergyman, b. Monongahela City, Va., 1858; d. Berkeley, Calif., June 3, 1936. [10]

Kerr, Orpheus C. (pseud.). See Newell, Henry Robert.

Kerr, Robert Pollok, clergyman, b. Greensboro, Ala., 1850; d. Baltimore, Md., March 25, 1923. [8; 10; 34]

Kerrick, Harrison Summers, soldier, b. 1873; d. Hot Springs, Ark., May 15, 1939. [10]

Kester, Paul, playwright, b. Delaware, O., 1870; d. Lake Mohegan, N.Y., June 20, 1933. [1a; 7; 10]

Kester, Vaughan, novelist, b. New Brunswick, N.J., 1869; d. Fairfax county, Va., July 5, 1911. [1; 7; 10; 34]

Ketcham, Victor Alvin, educationist, b. Perry county, O., 1883; d. Columbus, O., July 20, 1947. [10]

Ketcham, William Ezra, clergyman, b. New York, N.Y., 1837; d. 1903. [10]

Ketchum, Mrs. Annie, née Chambers, novelist and poet, b. Scott county, Ky., 1824; d. Jan. 27, 1904. [3; 7; 8; 34; 74]

Ketchum, John Buckhout, journalist, b. New York, N.Y., 1837; d. Brooklyn, N.Y., Dec. 8, 1914. [10]

Ketchum, Milo Smith, civil engineer, b. Burns, Ill., 1872; d. Champaign, Ill., Dec. 19, 1934. [10; 11]

Ketchum, Silas, clergyman, b. Barre, Vt., 1835; d. Dorchester, Mass., April 24, 1880. [43]

Ketchum, Thomas Carleton Lee, journalist, b. about 1862; d. Woodstock, N.B., Feb. 27, 1927. [27]

Ketchum, William, historian, b. Bloomfield, N.Y., 1798; d. Buffalo, N.Y., Oct. 1, 1876.

Ketchum, William Quintard, clergyman, b. Woodstock, N.B., 1818; d. St. Andrews, N.B., Aug. 9, 1901. [27; 33]

Ketler, Isaac Conrad, educationist, b. Northumberland, Pa., 1853; d. Grove City, Pa., July 2, 1913. [10]

Kettell, Samuel, editor, b. Newburyport, Mass., 1800; d. Malden, Mass., Dec. 3, 1855. [1; 3; 6; 7; 8]

Kewen, Edward John Cage, poet and politician, b. Columbus, Miss., 1825; d. Los Angeles, Calif., Nov. 25, 1879. [35]

Key, Francis Scott, poet, b. Frederick county, Md., 1780; d. Baltimore, Md., Jan. 11, 1843. [1; 2; 3; 4; 5; 7; 71]

Key, Pierre Van Rensselaer, music critic, b. Grand Haven, Mich., 1872; d. New York, N.Y., Nov. 28, 1945. [7; 10; 11]

Keyes, Asa, jurist and genealogist, b. Putney, Vt., 1787; d. Brattleboro, Vt., 1880. [43]

Keyes, Charles Henry, educationist, b. Banfield, Wis., 1858; d. Jan. 17, 1925. [10]

Keyes, Clinton Walker, educationist, b. 1888; d. Monterey, Mass., Aug. 5, 1943. [14]

Keyes, Edward Lawrence, physician, b. Fort Moultrie, S.C., 1843; d. New York, N.Y., Jan. 24, 1924. [1; 3; 4; 7; 8; 10; 62]

Keyes, Edward Loughborough, urologist, b. Elizabeth, N.J., 1874; d. New York, N.Y., March 17, 1949. [10; 11]

Keyes, Emerson Willard, educationist, b. Jamestown, N.Y., 1828; d. Brooklyn, N.Y., Oct. 17, 1897. [3 8]

Keyes, Erasmus Darwin, soldier, b. Brimfield, Mass., 1810; d. Nice, France, Oct. 14, 1895. [1; 3; 4; 8]

Keyes, Rowena Keith, educationist, b. Brooklyn, N.Y., 1880; d. Danbury, Conn., Nov. 9, 1948. [11]

Keyes, Thomas Bassett, physician, b. Oneonta, N.Y., 1874; d. Butternut, Wis., Oct. 2, 1938. [10]

Keyes, Wade, lawyer, b. 1821; d. 1879. [34]

Keyser, Cassius Jackson, mathematician, b. 1862; d. New York, N.Y., May 8, 1947. [11]

Keyser, Charles Shearer, lawyer, b. Philadelphia, Pa., 1825; d. Brooklyn, N.Y., Sept. 25, 1904. [10]

Keyser, Leander Sylvester, clergyman, b. Tuscarawas county, O., 1856; d. Springfield, O., Oct. 18, 1937. [10; 11]

Keyser, Peter Dirck, physician, b. Philadelphia, Pa., 1835; d. 1897. [3]

Keyt, Alonzo Thrasher, physiologist, b. Higginsport, O., 1827; d. Cincinnati, O., Nov. 9, 1885. [1; 4]

Keyworth, Maurice Reed, educationist, b. Shabbona, Mich., 1884; d. Hamtranck, Mich., June 22, 1935. [10]

Kidd, Adam, poet, b. Ireland, 1802; d. Quebec, Lower Canada, July 5, 1831. [27]

Kidd, Howard Carson, economist, b. 1892; d. Pittsburgh, Pa., Jan. 27, 1933.

Kidd, James Harvey, soldier, b. Ionia, Mich., 1840; d. Ionia, Mich., March 19, 1913. [39]

Kidder, Daniel Parish, clergyman, b. Darien, N.Y., 1815; d. Evanston, Ill., July 29, 1891. [1; 3; 4; 6; 7; 8]

Kidder, Frank Eugene, architect, b. Bangor, Me., 1859; d. 1905. [8; 10]

Kidder, Frederic, antiquary, b. New Ipswich, N.H., 1804; d. Melrose, Mass., Dec. 19, 1885. [1; 3; 6; 7; 8; 9]

Kidder, Samuel Theodore, poet, b. 1848; d. 1919.

Kiddle, Henry, educationist, b. Bath, England, 1824; d. New York, N.Y., Sept. 25, 1891. [3; 4; 6; 8]

Kieffer, Aldine Silliman, poet, b. 1840; d. 1904. [8]

Kieffer, Henry Martyn, clergyman, b. Mifflinburg, Pa., 1845; d. Atlantic City, N.J., April 22, 1930. [8; 10; 11]

Kieffer, Joseph Spangler, clergyman, b. Mifflinburg, Pa., 1842; d. May 16, 1919. [10]

Kiehle, David Litchard, educationist, b. Dansville, N.Y., 1837; d. 1918. [10; 70]

Kies, Marietta, philosopher, d. Pueblo, Colo., July 20, 1899.

Kiester, Jacob Armel, local historian, b. Mount Pleasant, Pa., 1832; d. Blue Earth City, Minn., Dec. 13, 1904. [70]

Kilborne, Russell Donald, economist, b. Ralston, Pa., 1892; d. Hanover, N.H., Nov. 12, 1932. [49]

Kilbourn, Dwight C., lawyer, b. 1837; d. Litchfield, Conn., Oct. 28, 1914.

Kilbourn, John, educationist, b. Berlin, Conn., 1787; d. 1831. [3; 6]

Kilbourne, Payne Kenyon, poet, historian, and genealogist, b. Litchfield, Conn., 1815; d. Litchfield, Conn., July 19, 1859. [3; 7; 8]

Kilby, Cyrus Hamlin, journalist, b. Maine, 1828; d. ? [38]

Kilby, William Henry, local historian, b. Eastport, Me., 1820; d. ? [38]

Kildare, Owen Frawley, journalist and novelist, b. New York, N.Y., 1864; d. New York, N.Y., Feb. 4, 1911. [7; 10]

Kilduffe, Robert Anthony, physician, b. 1884; d. White Sulphur Springs, W. Va., April 5, 1943.

Kilgo, John Carlisle, bishop, b. Laurens, S.C., 1861; d. Charlotte, N.C., Aug. 10, 1922. [4; 10]

Killebrew, Joseph Buckner, agriculturist and journalist, b. Montgomery county, Tenn., 1831; d. Nashville, Tenn., March 17, 1906. [10; 34]

Killikelly, Sarah Hutchins, historian, b. Vincennes, Ind., 1840; d. Pittsburgh, Pa., May 4, 1912. [10]

Kilmer, Alfred Joyce. See Kilmer, Joyce.

Kilmer, Mrs. Aline, née **Murray,** poet and essayist, b. Norfolk, Va., 1888; d. Stillwater, N.J., Oct. 1, 1941. [7; 10; 11; 22]

Kilmer, Mrs. Annie, née **Kilburn,** biographer, b. Albany, N.Y.; d. Jan. 1, 1932. [7]

Kilmer, Joyce, poet and journalist, b. New Brunswick, N.J., 1886; d. on active service in France, July 30, 1918. [1; 4; 7; 10; 72]

Kilmer, Theron Wendell, physician, b. Chicago, Ill., 1872; d. Hempstead, Long Island, N.Y., July 31, 1946. [10; 11]

Kilpatrick, Thomas Buchanan, clergyman and educationist, b. Glasgow, Scotland, 1857; d. Toronto, Ont., March 20, 1930. [27]

Kilty, William, jurist and poet, b. London, England, 1757; d. Annapolis, Md., Oct. 10, 1821. [1; 9]

Kilvert, Mrs. M. A. See Cameron, Margaret.

Kimball, Arthur Lalanne, physicist, b. Succasunna Plains, N.J., 1856; d. Amherst, Mass., Oct. 22, 1922. [7; 10]

Kimball, Arthur Livingstone, physicist, b. Baltimore, Md., 1886; d. Schenectady, N.Y., March 20, 1943. [13]

Kimball, Arthur Reed, journalist, b. New York, N.Y., 1855; d. Waterbury, Conn., Jan. 27, 1933. [10; 62]

Kimball, George Selwyn, novelist, b. Hampden, Me., 1846; d. Bangor, Me., 1909. [10]

Kimball, Gertrude Selwyn, historian, b. 1863; d. Providence, R.I., June 20, 1910. [47]

Kimball, Gustavus Sylvester, educationist, b. Yale, Mich., 1860; d. New York, N.Y., April 22, 1937. [10; 11]

Kimball, Harriet McEwen, poet, b. Portsmouth, N.H., 1834; d. Portsmouth, N.H., Sept. 3, 1917. [3; 4; 7; 8; 10]

Kimball, Henry Dox, educationist, b. Raymertown, N.Y., 1841; d. Salem, Ore., May 31, 1915. [10]

Kimball, James William, religious writer, b. Salem, Mass., 1812; d. Newton, Mass., March 28, 1885. [3; 8]

Kimball, John Calvin, clergyman, b. Ipswich, Mass., 1832; d. Greenfield, Mass., Feb. 16, 1910. [10; 45]

Kimball, Kate Fisher, traveller, b. Orange, N.J., 1860; d. New York, N.Y., Jan. 17, 1917. [10]

Kimball, Mrs. Maria Porter, née **Brace,** elocutionist, b. 1852; d. March 31, 1933.

Kimball, Richard Burleigh, lawyer and littérateur, b. Plainfield, N.H., 1816; d. New York, N.Y., Dec. 28, 1892. [1; 3; 4; 6; 9]

Kimball, Sumner Increase, biographer, b. Lebanon, Me., 1834; d. Washington, D.C., June 21, 1923. [1; 4; 10]

Kimball, William Wirt, naval officer, b Paris, Me., 1848; d. Washington, D.C., Jan. 26, 1930. [10; 11]

Kinealy, John Henry, engineer, b. Hannibal, Mo., 1864; d. Ferguson, Mo., May 6, 1928. [10]

King, Albert Barnes, clergyman, b. Morristown, N.J., 1828; d. Brooklyn, N.Y., Dec. 18, 1914. [56]

King, Albert Freeman Africanus, physician, b. England, 1841; d. Washington, D.C., Dec. 13, 1914. [10]

King, Alonzo, clergyman, b. Wilbraham, Mass., 1796; d. Westborough, Mass., Nov. 29, 1835. [3]

King, Basil. See King, William Benjamin Basil.

King, Benjamin Franklin, poet, b. St. Joseph, Mich., 1857; d. St. Joseph, Mich., March 7, 1894. [7]

King, Mrs. Caroline Blanche, née **Campion,** dietitian, b. Chicago, Ill., 1871; d. Philadelphia, Pa., Dec. 2, 1947.

King, Charles, educationist, b. New York, N.Y., 1789; d. Frascati, Italy, Sept. 27, 1867. [1; 3; 4; 6]

King, Charles, soldier and novelist, b. Albany, N.Y., 1844; d. Milwaukee, Wis., March 17, 1933. [3; 4; 6; 7; 8; 10; 11]

King, Charles Francis, educationist, b. Wilton, N.H., 1843; d. Boston, Mass., May 22, 1924. [10]

King, Clarence, geologist, b. Newport, R.I., 1842; d. Phoenix, Ariz., Dec. 24, 1901. [1; 3; 4; 7; 8; 10]

King, Clyde Lyndon, educationist, b. Burlington, Kans, 1879; d. West Town, Pa., June 21, 1937. [10; 11]

King, Dan, physician, b. Mansfield, Conn., 1791; d. Smithfield, R.I., Nov. 13, 1864. [1; 3; 6; 7; 8]

King, David Bennett, lawyer, b. Westmoreland county, Pa., 1848; d. Ridgefield, Conn., April 1, 1926. [3; 8; 10]

King, Dougall Macdougall, physician, b. Berlin, Ont., 1878; d. Denver, Colo., March 18, 1922. [10; 11]

King, Edward Skinner, astronomer, b. Liverpool, N.Y., 1861; d. Cambridge, Mass., Sept. 10, 1931. [1; 10]

King, Edward Smith, journalist and novelist, b. Middlefield, Mass., 1848; d. Brooklyn, N.Y., March 27, 1896. [1; 3; 6; 7; 8]

King, Mrs. Eleanor, née Anthony, naturalist, d. New York, N.Y., July 6, 1949.

King, Mrs. Francis. See King, Mrs. Louisa, née Yeomans.

King, Franklin Hiram, agricultural scientist, b. Whitewater, Wis., 1848; d. Madison, Wis., Aug. 4, 1911. [1; 8; 10]

King, Georgiana Goddard, educationist, b. West Columbia, Va., 1871; d. Hollywood, Calif., May 4, 1939. [7; 11]

King, Gordon Congdon, educationist, b. New York, N.Y., 1893; d. New York, N.Y., July 11, 1930. [7; 51]

King, Grace Elizabeth, novelist and historian, b. New Orleans, La., 1851; d. New Orleans, La., Jan. 12, 1932. [1; 4; 7; 8; 10; 34]

King, Henry Churchill, clergyman and educationist, b. Hillsdale, Mich., 1858; d. Oberlin, O., Feb. 27, 1934. [1a; 7; 8; 10; 11]

King, Henry Melville, clergyman, b. Oxford, Me., 1838; d. Providence, R.I., June 16, 1919. [1; 8; 10]

King, Horatio, lawyer and politician, b. Paris, Me., 1811; d. Washington, D.C., May 20, 1897. [1; 3; 4; 7; 8]

King, Horatio Collins, soldier and lawyer, b. Portland, Me., 1837; d. Brooklyn, N.Y., Nov. 15, 1918. [3; 4; 8]

King, Hoyt, reformer, b. Danville, Ind., 1870; d. Wilmette, Ill., Dec. 27, 1946.

King, James Joseph, physician, b. Columbia, Tenn., 1882; d. New York, N.Y., Nov. 29, 1935. [10; 11]

King, James Marcus, clergyman, b. Girard, Pa., 1839; d. Philadelphia, Pa., Oct. 3, 1907. [10]

King, James Wilson, naval officer, b. Baltimore, Md., 1818; d. 1905. [8; 10]

King, John, physician, b. New York, N.Y., 1813; d. North Bend, O., June 19, 1893. [1; 4; 6]

King, John, lawyer, b. Toronto, Ont., 1843; d. Toronto, Ont., Aug. 30, 1916. [27]

King, John Henry, physician, b. 1843; d. ?

King, John Mark, clergyman, b. Roxburghshire, Scotland. 1829; d. Winnipeg, Man., March 5, 1899. [27]

King, Julia Anne, educationist, b. Milan, Mich.; d. Ypsilanti, Mich., 1919. [39]

King, Katherine Douglas. See Burr, Mrs. Katherine Douglas, née King.

King, Mrs. Louisa, née Yeomans, writer on gardening, b. Washington, N.J., 1863; d. Milton, Mass., Jan. 16, 1948. [11]

King, Marquis Fayette, local historian, b. Oxford, Me., 1835; d. 1904.

King, Moses, publisher, b. London, England, 1853; d. New York, N.Y., June 12, 1909. [51]

King, Rufus, lawyer, b. 1817; d. 1891. [8]

King, Stoddard, journalist and poet, b. Jackson, Wis., 1889; d. Spokane, Wash., June 13, 1933. [7; 10; 62]

King, Mrs. Susan, née Petigru, novelist, b. Charleston, S.C., 1826; d. Charleston, S.C., 1875. [34]

King, Thomas Davies, littérateur, b. Bristol, England, 1819; d. Montreal, Que., Nov. 8, 1884. [27]

King, Thomas Starr, clergyman, b. New York, N.Y., 1824; d. San Francisco, Calif., March 4, 1863. [1; 31; 41; 61; 71; 8]

King, Thorold (pseud.). See Gatchell, Charles.

King, Toler (pseud.). See Fox, Mrs. Emily, née Toye.

King, William, physician, b. 1830; d. Augusta, Ga., July, 1917. [34]

King, William Benjamin Basil, novelist, b. Charlottetown, P.E.I., 1859; d. Cambridge, Mass., June 22, 1928. [27]

King, William Fletcher, educationist, b. near Zanesville, O., 1830; d. Mount Vernon, Ia., Oct. 23, 1921. [10; 11]

King, William Rufus, soldier, b. New York, N.Y., 1839; d. Rock Island, Ill., May 18, 1898. [4; 6; 8]

King, Willis Percival, physician, b. 1839; d. Kansas City, Mo., July 12, 1909.

Kingman, Bradford, historian and genealogist, b. 1831; d. 1903.

Kingman, Henry, clergyman, b. 1863; d. 1921.

Kingsbury, Benjamin, lawyer, b. Boston, Mass., 1813; d. Portland, Me., May 13, 1886. [3b]

Kingsbury, Benjamin Freeman, histologist, b. St. Charles, Mo., 1872; d. Chapel Hill, N.C., July 8, 1946. [10; 13]

Kingsbury, Charles P., soldier, b. New York, N.Y., 1818; d. Brooklyn, N.Y., Dec. 25, 1879. [3; 8]

Kingsbury, Harmon, clergyman, d. 1868. [6]

Kingsbury, Oliver Addison, clergyman, b. 1839; d. 1914.

Kingsbury, Susan Myra, social economist, b. San Pablo, Calif., 1870; d. Bryn Mawr, Va., Nov. 26, 1949. [14]

Kingsford, Jane (pseud.). See Barnard, Charles.

Kingsford, Rupert Etherege, lawyer, b. 1849; d. Toronto, Ont., Oct. 6, 1920. [27]

Kingsford, William, engineer and historian, b. London, England, 1819; d. Toronto, Ont., Sept. 28, 1898. [27]

Kingsley, Calvin, bishop, b. Oneida county, N.Y., 1812; d. Beirut, Syria, April 6, 1870. [1; 3; 4; 6; 8]

Kingsley, Charlotte May (pseud.). See Hanshew, Thomas W.

Kingsley, Mrs. Florence, née Morse, novelist, b. near Medina, O., 1859; d. New York, N.Y., Oct. 27, 1937. [7; 10; 11]

Kingsley, Howard L., educationist, b. Shelby, Mich., 1892; d. Boston, Mass., April 7, 1948. [10]

Kingsley, James Luce, educationist, b. Windham, Conn., 1778; d. New Haven, Conn., Aug. 31, 1852. [1; 3; 4; 62]

Kingsley, John Sterling, biologist, b. Cincinnatus, N.Y., 1853; d. at sea, Aug. 29, 1929. [7; 10; 11; 13]

Kingsley, Norman William, dentist, b. St. Lawrence county, Ky., 1829; d. Warren Point, N.J., Feb. 20, 1913. [1; 10]

Kingsley, Sherman Colver, sociologist, b. 1866; d. Narberth, Pa., Feb. 27, 1946.

Kingsley, William Lathrop, editor, b. New Haven, Conn., 1824; d. New Haven, Conn., Feb. 14, 1896. [3b; 62]

Kingsmill, William, soldier, b. England, about 1794; d. Toronto, Ont., May 6, 1876. [27]

Kingston, George Templeman, meteorologist, b. Oporto, Portugal, 1817; d. Toronto, Ont., Jan. 21, 1886. [27]

Kingston, John, biographer, fl. 1809-1817.

Kingston, May (pseud.). See Lane, Sarah.

Kinley, David, educationist, b. Dundee, Scotland, 1861; d. Urbana, Ill., Dec. 3, 1944. [10; 11]

Kinloch, Francis, politician, b. Charleston, S.C., 1755; d. Charleston, S.C., Feb. 8, 1826. [3; 34]

Kinne, Helen, educationist, b. Norwich, Conn., 1861; d. Woodbury, Conn., Dec. 29, 1917. [10]

Kinney, Abbot, publisher, b. Brookside, N.J., 1850; d. Venice, Calif., Nov. 4, 1920. [8; 10]

Kinney, Coates, poet, b. Kinney's Corners, N.Y., 1826; d. 1904. [3; 4; 7; 8; 10]

Kinney, Mrs. Elizabeth Clementine, née Dodge, poet, b. New York, 1810; d. Summit, N.J., Nov. 19, 1889. [1; 3; 7; 8; 9]

Kinney, Jonathan Kendrick, lawyer, b. 1843; d. 1917. [51]

Kinney, Troy, artist, b. Kansas City, Mo., 1871; d. Canaan, Conn., Jan. 29, 1938. [7; 10; 11]

Kinnicutt, Leonard Parker, educationist, b. Worcester, Mass., 1854; d. Worcester, Mass., Feb. 6, 1911. [1; 10]

Kinnicutt, Lincoln Newton, banker, b. Worcester, Mass., 1849; d. Worcester, Mass., Dec. 1921. [10]

Kinsley, William Wirt, miscellaneous writer, b. Buffalo, N.Y., 1837; d. July 12, 1923. [10; 11]

Kinsman, Josiah Burnham, lawyer, d. 1912. [51]

Kintzing, Pearce, physician, b. Liberty, Pa., 1861; d. Baltimore, Md., Jan. 30, 1917. [10]

Kinzie, Mrs. Juliette Augusta, née Magill, novelist, b. 1806; d. Chicago, Ill., 1870. [8]

Kip, Leonard, lawyer and novelist, b. New York, N.Y., 1826; d. Albany, N.Y., Feb. 15, 1906. [3; 4; 7; 8; 10]

Kip, William Ingraham, bishop, b. New York, N.Y., 1811; d. San Francisco, Calif., April 7, 1893. [1; 3; 4; 6; 7; 8; 62]

Kippax, John Robert, physician, b. Brantford, Ont., 1849; d. Olean, N.Y., June 27, 1922. [10]

Kirby, Clarence Valentine, educationist, b. Canajoharie, N.Y., 1875; d. near Harrisburg, Pa., Sept. 27, 1947. [10]

Kirby, Mrs. Georgiana, née Bruce, reformer, b. Bristol, England, 1818; d. ? [6; 8]

Kirby, William, poet and novelist, b. England, 1817; d. Niagara, Ont., June 23, 1906. [27]

Kirchhoff, Charles William Henry, editor, b. San Francisco, Calif., 1853; d. New York, N.Y., July 22, 1916. [10]

Kirchwey, George Washington, lawyer, b. Detroit, Mich., 1855; d. New York, N.Y., March 3, 1942. [10]

Kirk, Edward, metallurgist, b. 1846; d. ?

Kirk, Edward Norris, clergyman, b. New York, N.Y., 1802; d. Boston, Mass., March 27, 1874. [1; 3; 4; 6; 8]

Kirk, Eleanor (pseud.). See Ames, Mrs. Eleanor Maria, née Easterbrook.

Kirk, Mrs. Ellen Warner, née Olney, novelist, b. Southington, Conn., 1842; d. 1928. [3; 4; 6; 7; 8; 10; 11]

Kirk, Hyland Clare, educationist, b. Phelps, N.Y., 1846; d. Washington, D.C., May 6, 1917.

Kirk, John Foster, historian and bibliographer, b. Fredericton, N.B., 1824; d. Philadelphia, Pa., Sept. 21, 1904. [1; 3; 4; 6; 7; 8; 10]

Kirk, William Frederick, journalist and poet, b. Mankato, Minn., 1877; d. Chippawa Falls, Wis., March 25, 1927. [10]

Kirkbride, Thomas Story, physician, b. near Morrisville, Pa., 1809; d. Philadelphia, Pa., Dec. 16, 1883. [1; 3; 4; 8]

Kirke, Edmund (pseud.). See Gilmore, James Roberts.

Kirkham, Samuel, educationist, fl. 1823-1857. [6]

Kirkham, Stanton Davis, traveller and writer of books for children, b. Nice, France, 1868; d. Canandaigua, N.Y., Jan. 6, 1944. [7; 10; 11]

Kirkland, Mrs. Caroline Matilda, née Stansbury, miscellaneous writer, b. New York, N.Y., 1801; d. New York, N.Y., April 6, 1864. [1; 3; 4; 6; 7; 8]

Kirkland, Elizabeth Stansbury, educationist, b. Geneva, N.Y., 1828; d. Chicago, Ill., July 30, 1896. [3; 6; 8]

Kirkland, Joseph, lawyer and novelist, b. Geneva, N.Y., 1830; d. Chicago, Ill., April 29, 1894. [1; 3; 4; 6; 7; 8 71]

Kirkland, Thomas, educationist, b. Ireland, 1835; d. Toronto, Ont., Dec. 31, 1898. [27]

Kirkland, Winifred Margaretta, novelist and religious writer, b. Columbia, Pa., 1872; d. Sewanee, Tenn., May 14, 1943. [7; 10; 11]

Kirkman, Marshall Monroe, raliwayman, b. Morgan county, Ill., 1842; d. Chicago, Ill., April 18, 1921. [1; 3; 4; 6; 7; 10]

Kirkpatrick, Edwin Asbury, psychologist, b. Peoria, Ia., 1862; d. Deland, Fla., Jan. 4, 1937. [10; 11]

Kirkpatrick, Frank Home, educationist, b. Gwillimbury township, Ont., 1874; d. Toronto, Ont., April 4, 1940. [27]

Kirkpatrick, Mrs. Jane, née **Bayard,** historian, b. Philadelphia, Pa., 1772; d. New Brunswick, N.J., Feb. 16, 1850. [3]

Kirkpatrick, John Ervin, clergyman and educationist, b. Chenoa, Ill., 1869; d. Topeka, Kans., Jan. 31, 1931. [62]

Kirkwood, Daniel, mathematician, b. Bladensburg, Md., 1814; d. Riverside, Calif., June 11, 1895. [1; 3; 4; 6; 8]

Kirkwood, Joseph Edward, botanist, b. Cedar Rapids, Ia., 1872; d. Flathead Lake, Mont., Aug. 16, 1928. [10; 13]

Kirlin, Joseph Louis Jerome, priest, b. Philadelphia, Pa., 1868; d. Philadelphia, Pa., Nov. 26, 1926. [1; 21]

Kirsch, Felix Marie, priest, b. Wheeling, W. Va., 1884; d. Washington, D.C., March 22, 1945. [22]

Kirschbaum, Richard Warren, writer on aviation, b. Newark, N.J., 1894; d. Newark, N.J., Nov. 20, 1948.

Kirwan (pseud.). See Murray, Nicholas.

Kirwan, Thomas, soldier, b. 1829; d. 1911.

Kiser, Samuel Ellsworth, journalist and poet, b. Shippensville, Pa., 1862; d. New Rochelle, N.Y., Jan. 30, 1942. [7; 10; 11]

Kissam, Richard Sharpe, physician, b. 1806; d. 1861. [48]

Kissam, Samuel, clergyman and poet, b. 1796; d. 1868.

Kitchel, Courtney Smith, insurance executive, b. Thomaston, Conn., 1843; d. Toledo, O., June 4, 1931. [62]

Kitchen, Joseph Moses Ward, physician, b. 1846; d. Feb. 3, 1931.

Kitchen, Karl Kingsley, journalist, b. Cleveland, O., 1885; d. New York, N.Y., June 21, 1935. [7]

Kitchin, William Copeman, educationist, b. St. George, Ont., 1855; d. Scotia, N.Y., Jan. 8, 1920. [10]

Kittredge, George Lyman, educationist, b. Boston, Mass., 1860; d. Barnstable, Mass., July 23, 1941. [4; 7; 10]

Kittredge, Henry Grattan, textile manufacturer, b. Claremont, N.H., 1845; d. Reading , Mass., 1909. [10]

Kittredge, Walter, song composer, b. Merrimac, N.H., 1834; d. Reed's Ferry, N.H., July 8, 1905. [7; 10]

Kittrell, Norman Goree, jurist, b. Greensboro, Ala., 1849; d. Houston, Tex., Jan. 24, 1927. [10; 34]

KixMiller, William, lawyer, b. Vincennes, Ind., 1885; d. Chicago, Ill., April 13, 1945. [10]

Klaer, Fred Harlen, physician, b. Milford, Pa., 1878; d. Philadelphia, Pa., Feb. 27, 1915.

Klarmann, Andrew Francis, priest, b. near Bamberg, Bavaria, 1866; d. Brooklyn, N.Y., March 24, 1931. [22]

Klauser, Julius, musician, b. New York, N.Y., 1854; d. 1907.

Kleeberg, Mrs. Minna, née **Cohen,** poet, b. Germany, 1841; d. New Haven, Conn., Dec. 31, 1878. [3]

Klein, Charles, playwright, b. London, England, 1867; d. at sea, May 7, 1915. [1; 7; 10]

Klein, Joseph Frederic, mechanical engineer, b. Paris, France, 1849; d. Bethlehem, Pa., Feb. 11, 1918. [1; 10; 62]

Klein, Norman, journalist and novelist, b. Kansas City, Mo., 1897; d. New York, N.Y., Oct. 27, 1948. [11]

Klein, William Livingston, journalist, b. Barry, Ill., 1851; d. Minneapolis, Minn., Aug. 20, 1931. [70]

Klemm, Louis Richard, educationist, b. Düsseldorf, Germany, 1845; d. Washington, D.C., 1916. [8; 10]

Kline, Marion Justus, clergyman, b. Frederick, Md., 1871; d. Sept. 29, 1934. [10]

Kline, Otis Adelbert, novelist, b. 1891; d. New York, N.Y., Oct. 26, 1946.

Klippart, John Hancock, agricultural writer, b. near Canton, O., 1823; d. Oct. 24, 1878. [1; 4]

Klipstein, Louis Frederick, philologist, b. Winchester, Va., 1813; d. Florida, Aug. 20, 1878. [1]

Kloss, Charles Luther, clergyman, b. New Berlin, O., 1862; d. San Mateo, Calif., Oct. 28, 1931. [10]

Kloss, Phillips Wray, poet, b. Webster Groves, Mo., 1902; d. 1933. [35]

Klotz, Oscar, pathologist, b. Preston, Ont., 1878; d. Toronto, Ont., Nov. 3, 1936. [10; 27]

Klyce, Scudder, scientist, b. Friendship, Tenn., 1879; d. Jan. 28, 1933. [10]

Knab, Frederick, entomologist, b. Würzburg, Germany, 1865; d. Washington, D.C., Nov. 2, 1918. [1]

Knapp, Adeline, journalist, b. Buffalo, N.Y., 1860; d. Hill Valley, Calif., June 6, 1909. [10; 35]

Knapp, Arthur May, clergyman, b. Charlestown, Mass., 1841; d. Boston, Mass., 1921. [7; 10; 51]

Knapp, Charles, philologist, b. New York, N.Y., 1868; d. New York, N.Y., Sept. 17, 1936. [10]

Knapp, Horace S., local historian, fl. 1863-1872.

Knapp, Jacob, clergyman, b. Otsego county, N.Y., 1799; d. 1874. [6]

Knapp, Martin Wells, clergyman, b. 1853; d. 1901.

Knapp, Moses L., physician, b. 1799; d. 1879.

Knapp, Samuel Lorenzo, miscellaneous writer, b. Newburyport, Mass., 1783; d. Hopkinton, Mass., July 8, 1838. [1; 3; 4; 6; 7; 8]

Knapp, Shepherd, clergyman, b. New York, N.Y., 1873; d. Worcester, Mass., Jan. 11, 1946. [10; 62]

Knapp, Thad Johnson, educationist, b. Northville, Mich., 1876; d. Northville, Mich., April 21, 1933. [10]

Knapp, William Ireland, educationist, b. Greenport, N.Y., 1835; d. Paris, France, Dec. 6, 1908. [1; 7; 10]

Kneass, Strickland Landis, mechanical engineer, b. Philadelphia, Pa., 1861; d. Philadeplhia, Pa., Nov. 24, 1928. [10; 13]

Kneeland, Abner, editor, b. Gardner, Mass., 1774; d. Farmington, Ia., Aug. 27, 1844. [1; 3; 6]

Kneeland, Samuel, naturalist, b. Boston, Mass., 1821; d. Hamburg, Germany, Sept. 27, 1888. [1; 3; 6; 7; 8]

Kneeland, Stillman Foster, lawyer, b. South Stukely, Que., 1845; d. New York, N.Y., Aug. 30, 1926; [1; 4; 7; 10]

Knibbs, Henry Herbert, poet and novelist, b. Clifton, Ont., 1874; d. La Jolla, Calif., May 17, 1945. [7; 10; 11]

Knickerbacker, Joseph Foster, poet, b. 1824; d. 1882.

Knickerbocker, Diedrich (pseud.). See Irving, Washington.

Knickerbocker, Hubert Renfro, journalist, b. Yoakum, Tex., 1898; d. India, July 12, 1948. [10]

Knickerbocker, Jr. (pseud.). See Suydam, John Howard.

Knight, Archibald Patterson, biologist, b. near Renfrew, Ont., 1849; d. Kingston, Ont., Oct. 19, 1935. [27]

Knight, Austin Melvin, naval officer, b. Ware, Mass., 1854; d. Washington, D.C., Feb. 26, 1927. [4; 10]

Knight, Edward Henry, mechanical expert, b. London, England, 1824; d. Bellefontaine, O., Jan. 22, 1883. [1; 3; 6; 8]

Knight, Frederic Butterfield, educationist, b. Springfield. Mass., 1891; d. Lafayette, Ind., June 19, 1948. [11]

Knight, Frederick, poet, b. Hampton, N.H., 1791; d. Rowley, Mass., Nov. 20, 1849. [3; 8]

Knight, George Thomson, theologian, b. South Windham, Me., 1850; d. 1911. [10]

Knight, George Wells, educationist, b. Ann Arbor. Mich., 1858; d. Columbus, O., Feb. 10, 1932. [4; 10]

Knight, Mrs. Helen, née **Cross,** religious writer, fl. 1845-1872. [7]

Knight, Henry Cogswell, poet, b. Newburyport, Mass.. 1788; d. Rowley, Mass., Jan. 10, 1835. [1; 3; 6; 7; 8]

Knight, James, physician, b. Taneytown, Md.. 1810; d. New York, N.Y., Oct. 24, 1887. [3; 6; 8]

Knight, Lewis Washington. physician. b. 1816; d. Nashville, Tenn., Nov. 2, 1904.

Knight, Lucian Lamar, journalist and historian, b. Atlanta, Ga., 1868; d. Atlanta, Ga., Nov. 19, 1933. [1a; 7; 10; 11; 34]

Knight. Ora Willis, naturalist, b. Bangor, Me., 1874; d. Portland, Me., Nov. 11, 1913. [10]

Knister, Raymond, novelist, b. Essex county, Ont., 1900; d. by drowning in Lake St. Clair, Aug. 30, 1932. [27]

Knoeppel, Charles Edward, industrial engineer, b. Milwaukee, Wis., 1881; d. Philadelphia, Pa., Nov. 29, 1936.

Knopf, Carl Sumner, clergyman and educationist, b. Columbus, O., 1889; d. Salem, Ore., June 23,1942. [10; 62]

Knopf, Sigard Adolphus, physician, b. Germany, 1857; d. New York, N.Y., July 16, 1940. [10]

Knowles, Daniel Clark, clergyman, b. Yardville, N.J., 1836; d. Tilton, N.H., Feb. 13, 1913. [10; 60]

Knowles, Mrs. Ellin J., née **Toy,** religious writer, b. Camden, N.J., 1834; d. April 10, 1929. [10]

Knowles, Frederic Lawrence, editor and anthologist, b. Lawrence, Mass., 1869; d. Roxbury, Mass., Sept. 20, 1905. [7; 8; 10]

Knowles, James Davis, clergyman, b. Providence, R.I., 1798; d. Newton Centre, Mass., May 9, 1838. [3; 8]

Knowles, John Harris, clergyman, b. 1832; d. 1908.

Knowles, Robert Edward, novelist, b. Maxville, Ont., 1868; d. Galt, Ont., Nov. 15, 1946. [11; 27]

Knowlton, Charles, physician, b. Templeton, Mass., 1800; d. Feb. 20, 1850. [1]

Knowlton, Frank Hall, palaeontologist, b. near Brandon, Vt., 1860; d. Ballston, Va., Nov. 22, 1926. [1; 4; 8; 10]

Knowlton, Helen Mary, artist, b. Littleton, Mass., 1832; d. Needham, Mass., May 5, 1918. [8; 10]

Knowlton, Isaac Case, clergyman, b. 1820; d. 1894. [38]

Knowlton, Miles Justin, missionary, b. West Wardsborough, Vt., 1825; d. Ningpo, China, Sept. 10, 1874. [3; 8]

Knox, Mrs. Adeline, née **Trafton,** novelist, b. Saccarrappa, Me., 1845; d. ? [8; 10]

Knox, Charles Eugene, clergyman, b. Knoxboro, N.Y., 1833; d. Point Pleasant, N.J., April 30, 1900. [3b; 8]

Knox, George William, missionary, b. Rome. N.Y., 1853; d. Seoul, Korea, April 25, 1912. [1; 4; 8; 10]

Knox, John Armoy, journalist, b. Armoy, Ireland. 1850; d. New York, N.Y., Dec. 18, 1906. [6]

Knox, John Jay, financier, b. Knoxboro, N.Y., 1828; d. New York, N.Y., Feb. 9, 1892. [1; 3; 4; 6; 8]

Knox, Martin Van Buren, clergyman, b. 1841; d. ? [8]

Knox, Samuel, clergyman and educationist, b. Armagh county, Ireland, 1756; d. Virginia, Aug. 31, 1832. [1]

Knox, Thomas Wallace, journalist and writer of books for boys, b. Pembroke, N.H., 1835; d. New York, N.Y., Jan. 6, 1896. [1; 3; 4; 6; 7; 8; 9]

Knubel, Frederick Hermann, clergyman, b. New York. N.Y., 1870; d. New Rochelle, N.Y., Oct. 16, 1945. [10]

Knudsen, Carl Wilhelm, educationist, b. Copenhagen, Denmark, 1818; d. South Norwalk, Conn., Feb. 26, 1896. [3b]

Kobbé, Gustav, journalist and music critic, b. New York, N.Y., 1857; d. near Bayshore, Long Island, N.Y., July 27, 1918. [1; 4; 7; 8; 10]

Kober, George Martin, physician, b. Germany, 1850; d. Washington, D.C., April 24, 1931. [1; 10]

Koch, Felix John, traveller and photographer, b. Cincinnati, O., 1882; d. Cincinnati, O., Dec. 27, 1933. [10]

Koch, Frederick Conrad, biochemist, b. Chicago, Ill., 1876; d. Chicago, Ill., Jan. 26, 1948. [11; 13]

Koch, Frederick Henry, educationist, b. Covington,Ky., 1877; d. Miami, Fla., Aug. 16, 1944. [7; 10]

Koch, Theodore Wesley, librarian, b. Philadelphia, Pa., 1871; d. Evanston, Ill., March 23, 1941. [7; 10]

Koehler, Sylvester Rosa, art critic, b. Leipzig, Germany, 1837; d. Littleton, N.H., Sept. 15, 1900. [1; 3; 6; 7; 8; 10]

Koenig, George Augustus, chemist, b. Baden, Germany, 1844; d. Houghton, Mich., Jan. 15, 1913. [10]

Koenigsberg, Moses, journalist, b. New Orleans, La., 1878; d. New York, N.Y., Sept. 21, 1945. [7; 10; 11]

Koeppen, Adolphus Louis, historian, b. Copenhagen, Denmark, 1804; d. Athens, Greece, April 14, 1873. [3]

Koerner, Gustav Philipp, lawyer, b. Frankfort, Germany, 1809; d. Belleville, Ill., April 9, 1896. [4; 36]

Koester, Frank, engineer, b. Germany, 1876; d. New York, N.Y., Oct. 6, 1927. [10; 11]

Koffka, Kurt, psychologist, b. Berlin, Germany, 1886; d. Northampton, Mass., Nov. 22, 1941. [10]

Kohler, Kaufmann, rabbi, b. Germany, 1843; d. New York, N.Y., Jan. 28, 1926. [1; 4; 7; 10; 11]

Kohler, Max James, lawyer, b. Detroit, Mich., 1871; d. Long Lake, N.Y., July 24, 1934. [1a; 10; 11]

Kohlmann, Anthony, priest, b. Kaisersberg, France, 1771; d. Rome, Italy, April, 1838. [1; 3; 8]

Kohlsaat, Herman Henry, politician, b. Albion, Ill., 1853; d. Washington, D.C., Oct. 17, 1924. [4; 7; 10]

Kohn, August, journalist, b. Orangeburg, S.C., 1868; d. Columbia, S.C., May 29, 1930. [10; 11]

Kohon, Mrs. Ethel, née Chadowski, writer of books for children, b. Sheffield, England, 1890; d. New York, N.Y., Nov. 22, 1946.

Kohut, George Alexander, poet and editor, b. 1874; d. New York, N.Y., Dec. 31, 1933. [1a]

Kolle, Frederick Strange, plastic surgeon, b. Hanover, Germany, 1872; d. New York, N.Y., May 10, 1929. [1; 8; 10]

Kollock, Shepard Kosciuszko, clergyman, b. Elizabethtown, N.J., 1895; d. Philadelphia, Pa., April 7, 1865. [3; 6; 8]

Konkle, Burton Alva, historian, b. Albion, Ind., 1861; d. Philadelphia, Pa., Oct. 24, 1944. [7; 10]

Koopman, Harry Lyman, librarian and poet. b. Freeport, Me., 1860; d. Providence, R.I., Jan., 1938. [7; 10]

Koren, John, statistician, b. Decora, Ia., 1861; d. at sea, Nov. 9, 1923. [7; 10]

Koresh (pseud.). See Teed, Cyrus Reed.

Korff, Sergius Alexander, historian, b. Russia, 1876; d. Washington, D.C., March 7, 1924. [10]

Kost, John, physician, b. Carlisle, Pa., 1819; d. Adrian, Mich., 1904. [8; 10]

Kouns, Nathan Chapman, lawyer and librarian, b. Fulton, Mo., 1833; d. Jefferson City, Mo., Sept. 2, 1890. [3; 8]

Kraemer, Henry, pharmacist, b. Philadelphia, Pa., 1868; d. Detroit, Mich., Sept. 9, 1924. [1; 10]

Kraetzer, Arthur Furman, physician, b. Brooklyn, N.Y., 1891; d. New York, N.Y., March 2, 1940. [10]

Krafka, Joseph, histologist, b. Ottumwa, Ia., 1890; d. Augusta, Ga., Nov. 5, 1946. [10; 13]

Krag, Mary Miller (pseud.). See Wight, Mrs. Emily, née Carter.

Kraitsir, Charles V., philologist, b. Hungary, 1804; d. Morrisania, N.Y., May 7, 1860; [3; 8]

Kramer, Harold Morton, novelist, b. Frankfort, Ind., 1873; d. Frankfort, Ind., March 20, 1930. [10; 11]

Kramer, John Wesley, clergyman, b. Baltimore, Md., 1832; d. Brooklyn, N.Y., Dec. 22, 1898. [3b]

Krantz, Philip (pseud.). See Rombro, Jacob.

Krapp, George Philip, educationist, b. Cincinnati, O., 1872; d. New York, N.Y., April 22, 1934. [1a; 7; 10; 11]

Kratz, Henry Elton, educationist, b. Sterling, O., 1849; d. Chicago, Ill., Aug. 5, 1929. [10; 11]

Kraus, Adolph, lawyer, b. Bohemia, 1850; d. Chicago, Ill., Oct. 22, 1928. [10]

Kraus, John, educationist, b. Nassau, Germany, 1815; d. New York, N.Y., March 4, 1896. [1; 3; 4]

Kraus, René journalist, b. Austria, 1902; d. New York, N.Y., July 16, 1947. [10]

Krause, Allen Kramer, physician, b. Lebanon, Pa., 1881; d. Providence, R.I., May 12, 1941. [10; 11]

Krause, Carl Albert, educationist, b. Germany, 1872; d. Brooklyn, N.Y., June 15, 1929. [10; 11]

Krausé, Lyda Farrington, novelist, b. St. Croix, Danish West Indies, 1864; d. Princeton, N.J., Oct. 31, 1939. [7; 10]

Krauskopf, Joseph, rabbi, b. Germany; 1858; d. Atlantic City, N.J., June 12, 1923. [1; 4; 8; 10]

Krauth, Charles Porterfield, clergyman, b. Martinsburg, Va., 1823; d. Philadelphia, Pa., Jan. 2, 1883. [1; 3; 4; 6; 8]

Krebs, John Michael, clergyman, b. Hagerstown, Md., 1804; d. New York, N.Y., Sept. 30, 1867. [34]

Krebs, Stanley Le Fevre, clergyman, b. Waynesboro, Pa., 1864; d. New York, N.Y., Sept. 26, 1935. [10]

Krehbiel, Henry Edward, music critic, b. Ann Arbor, Mich., 1854; d. New York, N.Y., March 20, 1923. [1; 2; 3; 4; 7; 8; 10; 20]

Kriebel, Oscar Schultz, clergyman, b. Hereford, Pa., 1863; d. Pennsburg, Pa., Feb. 6, 1932. [10; 11]

Kroeger, Adolph Ernest, journalist, b. Schleswig, 1837; d. St. Louis, Mo., March 8, 1882. [1; 3; 4; 6; 8]

Kroeger, Alice Bertha, librarian, d. Philadelphia, Pa., Oct. 31, 1909.

Krohn, William Otterbein, psychiatrist, b. Galion, O., 1868; d. Chicago, Ill., July 17, 1927. [10; 62]

Kron, Karl (pseud.). See Bagg, Lyman Hotchkiss.

Krout, Caroline Virginia, novelist, b. Crawfordsville, Ind., 1853; d. Oct. 3, 1931. [7]

Krout, Mary Hannah, journalist, b. Crawfordsville, Ind., 1857; d. May 31, 1927. [10]

Krueger, Ernest Theodore, sociologist, b. Blue Island, Ill., 1885; d. Nashville, Tenn., June 19, 1945. [10]

Krüsi, Johann Heinrich Hermann, educationist, b. Switzerland, 1817; d. Alameda, Calif., Jan. 28, 1903. [1]

Kruhm, Adolph, gardener, b. Germany, 1884; d. Amityville, Long Island, N.Y., June 5, 1940.

Kuegele, Frederick, clergyman, b. 1846; d. 1916.

Kümmel, Henry Barnard, geologist, b. 1867; d. Trenton, N.J., Oct. 23, 1945. [13]

Kuhns, Luther Melancthon, clergyman, b. Omaha, Neb., 1861; d. Omaha, Neb., March 18, 1939. [10; 11]

Kuhns, Oscar, educationist, b. Columbia, Pa., 1856; d. Middletown, Conn., Aug. 20, 1929. [4; 7; 8; 10]

Kumm, Hermann Karl Wilhelm, explorer, b. Hanover, Germany, 1874; d. San Diego, Calif., Aug. 23, 1930. [4; 10]

Kummer, Frederic Arnold, novelist and playwright, b. Catonsville, Md., 1873; d. Baltimore, Md., Nov. 22, 1943. [7; 10; 11]

Kunhardt, Charles P., yachtsman, b. 1849; d. about 1892.

Kunz, George Frederick, jewel expert, b. New York, N.Y., 1856; d. New York, N.Y., June 29, 1932. [1a; 3; 8; 10; 11]

Kunze, Johann Christoph, clergyman, b. Saxony, 1744; d. New York, N.Y., July 24, 1807. [1; 3; 4; 6; 8]

Kurtz, Benjamin, clergyman, b. Harrisburg, Pa., 1795; d. Baltimore, Md., Dec. 29, 1865. [1; 3; 8]

Kutchin, Victor, clergyman, b. 1851; d. Green Lake, Wis., Nov. 22, 1939.

Kyle, David Braden, laryngologist, b. Cadiz, O., 1863; d. Philadelphia, Pa., Oct. 23, 1916. [1; 10]

Kyle, John Johnson, physician, b. Aurora, Ind., 1869; d. Los Angeles, Calif., Aug. 29, 1920. [10]

Kyle, Melvin Grove, clergyman, b. near Cadiz, O., 1858; d. Pittsburgh, Pa., May 25, 1933. [10; 11]

Kynett, Alpha Jefferson, clergyman, b. Adams county, Pa., 1829; d. Harrisburg, Pa., Feb. 23, 1899. [3b; 4]

L

Labagh, Isaac P., clergyman, b. Leeds, N.Y., Aug. 14, 1804; d. Fairfield, Ia., Dec. 29, 1879. [3]

Labat, Gaston P., journalist, b. France, 1843; d. Montreal, Que., Feb. 9, 1908. [27]

Labberton, Robert Henlopen, educationist, b. Marseilles, France, 1812; d. New York, N.Y., Oct. 13, 1898. [3b; 8]

La Borde, Maximilian, educationist, b. Edgefield, S.C., 1804; d. Columbia, S.C., Nov. 6, 1873. [1; 3; 4; 7; 34]

Labrie, Jacques, physician and politician, b. St. Charles de Bellechasse, Que., 1784; d. Oct. 6, 1831. [27]

La Bruère, Pierre Boucher de. See Boucher de la Bruère, Pierre.

Lacasse, Pierre Zacharie, missionary, b. St. Jacques de l'Achigan, Que., 1845; d. Gravelbourg, Sask., Feb. 28, 1921. [27]

Lacert, Mme. Adéle, née Bourgeois, novelist, b. St. Hyacinthe, Que., 1870; d. Ottawa, Ont., May 21, 1935. [11]

Lacey, Alexander, educationist, b. Exploits, Newfoundland, 1887; d. Toronto, Ont., Feb. 26, 1949. [30]

Lacey, John Fletcher, lawyer, b. New Martinsville, W. Va., 1841; d. Oskaloosa, Ia., Sept. 29, 1913. [10; 37]

Lacey, Thomas James, clergyman, b. Cincinnati, O., 1870; d. Brooklyn, N.Y., Feb. 5, 1944.

Lacey, William Brittingham, clergyman, b. Wilmington, Del., 1781; d. Okolona, Miss., Oct. 31, 1866. [3]

Lackland, Thomas (pseud.). See Hill, George Canning.

Lacombe, Albert, missionary, b. St. Sulpice, Lower Canada, 1827; d. near Calgary, Alta., Dec. 11, 1916. [27]

Lacorne, St. Luc de, soldier, b. 1712; d. 1784. [27]

Lacroix, Henri Olivier, civil servant, b. Monroe, Mich., 1826; d. Montreal, Que., Feb. 26, 1897. [27]

Lacy, Ernest, poet and playwright, b. Warren, Pa., 1863; d. Philadelphia, Pa., June 17, 1916. [1; 4; 7; 9; 10]

Lacy, William M., lawyer, d. 1912.

Ladd, Mrs. Anna Coleman, née Watts, sculptor and novelist, b. Philadelphia, Pa., 1878; d. Santa Barbara, Calif., June 3, 1939. [7; 10; 11]

Ladd, Carl Edwin, educationist, b. McLean, N.Y., 1888; d. Ithaca, N.Y., July 23, 1943. [10]

Ladd, Edwin Fremont, chemist, b. Starks, Me., 1859; d. Baltimore, Md., June 22, 1925. [1; 10; 13]

Ladd, Frederic Pierpont, journalist and novelist, b. Tolland, Conn., 1870; d. Staunton, Va., March 13, 1947.

Ladd, George Trumbull, educationist, b. Painesville, O., 1842; d. New Haven, Conn., Aug. 8, 1921. [1; 2; 3; 4; 5; 6; 7; 10]

Ladd, Henry Andrews, educationist, b. Portland, Ore., 1895; d. Bronxville, N.Y., June 27, 1941.

Ladd, Horatio Oliver, clergyman, b. Hallowell, Me., 1839; d. Brookline, Mass., Feb. 16, 1932. [8; 10; 11]

Ladd, Joseph Brown, poet, b. Newport, R.I., 1764; d. Charleston, S.C., Nov. 2, 1786. [1; 3; 4; 7; 9]

Ladd, William, philanthropist, b. Exeter, N.H., 1778; d. Portsmouth, N.H., April 9, 1841. [3; 4]

Ladd, William Palmer, clergyman, b. Lancaster, N.H., 1870; d. New Haven, Conn., July 1, 1941. [10; 49]

Ladd-Franklin, Mrs. Christine. See Franklin, Mrs. Christine, née Ladd.

La Farge, John, artist, b. New York, N.Y., 1835; d. Providence, R.I., Nov. 14, 1910. [1; 4; 7; 8; 9; 10]

Lafever, Minard, architect, b. Morristown, N.J., 1798; d. Williamsburg, Long Island, N.Y., Sept. 26, 1854. [1a; 6]

Laffan, William Mackay, art connoisseur, b. Dublin, Ireland, 1848; d. Lawrence, Long Island, N.Y., Nov. 19, 1909. [1; 7; 10]

Lafferty, John James, clergyman, b. on the Roanoke, Va., 1837; d. Richmond, Va., 1909. [10; 34]

Laflamme, Joseph Clovis Kemner, priest and geologist, b. St. Anselme, Que., 1849; d. Quebec, Que., July 6, 1910. [27]

Laflèche, Louis François Richer, bishop, b. Ste. Anne de la Pérade, Lower Canada, 1818; d. Three Rivers, Que., July 14, 1898. [27]

La Flesche, Francis, ethnologist, b. Omaha Reservation, Neb., about 1860; d. near Macy, Neb., Sept. 5, 1932. [7; 10]

Lafleur, Eugène, lawyer, b. Longueuil, Que., 1856; d. Ottawa, Ont., April 29, 1930. [27]

Lafleur, Paul Theodore, educationist, b. Montreal, Que.; d. Luxor, Egypt, Feb. 9, 1924. [27]

La Follette, Robert Marion, politician, b. Primrose, Wis., 1855; d. Washington, D.C., June 18, 1925. [1; 4; 10]

Lafontaine, Sir Louis Hippolyte, Bart., politician and jurist, b. near Boucherville, Lower Canada, 1807; d. Montreal, Que., Feb. 26, 1864. [27]

Lafrance, Charles Joseph Lévesque dit, educationist, b. Quebec, Lower Canada, 1833; d. Quebec, Que., Dec. 12, 1921. [27]

Lagacé, Pierre Minier, priest, b. Ste. Anne de la Pocatière, Lower Canada, 1830; d. Quebec, Que., Dec. 6, 1884. [27; 32]

Lagerquist, Walter Edwards, economist, b. Essex, Ia., 1881; d. Boston, Mass., Feb. 22, 1944. [62]

Laguna, Theodore de Leo de. See De Laguna, Theodore de Leo.

Laidlaw, Alexander Hamilton, physician, lexicographer, and poet, b. near Lanark, Scotland, 1828; d. New York, N.Y., July 29, 1908. [4; 8; 10]

Laidlaw, Alexander Hamilton, short-story writer and playwright, b. Jersey City, N.J., 1869; d. New York, N.Y., July 11, 1908. [8; 10]

Laidlaw, George, railway-builder, b. Scotland, about 1828; d. near Coboconk, Ont., Aug. 6, 1889. [27]

Laidlaw, Walter, clergyman, b. Norval, Ont., 1861; d. New York, N.Y., May 20, 1936. [10]

Laidley, Theodore Thaddeus Sobieski, soldier, b. Guyandotte, Va., 1822; d. Palatka, Fla., April 4, 1886. [3; 6; 34]

Laighton, Albert, poet, b. Portsmouth, N.H., 1829; d. Portsmouth, N.H., Feb. 6, 1887. [3; 71]

Laighton, Oscar, poet, b. Portsmouth, N.H., 1839; d. Portsmouth, N.H., April 4, 1939.

Laing, Mrs. Caroline H., née **Butler,** miscellaneous writer, fl. 1855-1875.

Laing, Gordon Jennings, educationist, b. London, Ont., 1869; d. near Lake Zurich, Ill., Sept. 1, 1945. [10; 14]

Laing, Mary Elizabeth, educationist, b. North Hebron, N.Y., 1854; d. London, England, Nov. 1, 1931. [11]

Lajoie, Henri Gérin. See Gérin-Lajoie, Henri.

Lake, Kirsopp, historian, b. Southampton, England, 1872; d. Pasadena, Calif., Nov. 10, 1946. [7; 10]

Lake, Mrs. Laura Spofford, née **Wiltsie,** poet, b. Newburgh, N.Y., 1859; d. Brooklyn, N.Y., Aug. 13, 1949.

Lakes, Arthur, mining engineer, b. Somersetshire, England, 1844; d. near Nelson, B.C., Nov., 1917. [10]

Lalande, Louis, priest, b. St. Hermas, Que., 1869; d. Montreal, Que., Oct. 20, 1944. [32]

Lally, John Patrick, novelist, b. Sharpsville, Pa., 1892; d. Chicago, Ill., Aug. 11, 1942.

Lalor, John Joseph, publisher, d. Washington, D.C., June 10, 1899. [3b]

Lamar, Ashton (pseud.). See Sayler, Harry Lincoln.

Lamar, Mrs. Clarinda Huntington, née **Pendleton,** historian, b. Bethany, W. Va., 1856; d. Atlanta, Ga., April 27, 1943. [10; 11]

Lamar, James Sanford, clergyman, b. Gwinett county, Ga., 1829; d. 1908. [8; 10; 34]

Lamar, Mrs. Joseph Rucker. See Lamar, Mrs. Clarinda Huntington, née Pendleton.

Lamar, Mirabeau Buonaparte, soldier, politician, and poet, b. Louisville, Ga., 1798; d. Richmond, Tex., Dec. 19, 1859. [1; 3; 4; 7; 8; 34]

Lamb, Mrs. Martha Joanna Reade, née **Nash,** historian, b. Plainfield, Mass., 1829; d. New York, N.Y., Jan. 2, 1893. [1; 3; 4; 6; 7; 8]

Lamb, Martin Thomas, clergyman, b. 1838; d. 1912.

Lamb, Mrs. Mary Elizabeth, née **Jordan,** novelist, b. 1839; d. ?

Lamb, Osborn Rennie, playwright and essayist, b. New York, N.Y., 1858; d. Englewood, N.J., June 27, 1928.

Lamb, Peter Oswald, soldier and journalist, b. Kandy, Ceylon, 1890; d. Bedminster, N.J., Nov. 29, 1935. [10]

Lambert, Edward Rodolphus, historian, b. Milford, Conn., 1808; d. ?

Lambert, Louis Aloisius, priest, b. Charleroy, Pa., 1835; d. Newfoundland, N.J., Sept. 25, 1910. [1; 8; 10]

Lambert, Samuel Waldron, physician, b. New York, N.Y., 1859; d. New York, N.Y., Feb. 9, 1942. [10; 62]

Lambert, Thomas Scott, physician, b. near Boston, Mass., 1819; d. Stamford, Conn., March 21, 1897. [3b; 6; 8]

Lamberton, John Porter, editor, b. Philadelphia, Pa., 1839; d. Philadelphia, Pa., July 26, 1917. [7; 10]

Lambeth, William Alexander, educationist, b. Thomasville, N.C., 1867; d. Charlottesville, Va., June 24, 1944. [10; 11]

Lambing, Andrew Arnold, priest and historian, b. Manorville, Pa., 1842; d. Wilkinsburg, Pa., Dec. 24, 1918. [1; 4; 21]

Lambourne, Alfred, poet and pioneer, b. about 1850; d. Salt Lake City, Utah, June 6, 1926.

Lambuth, Walter Russell, missionary, b. Shanghai, China, 1854; d. Yokohama, Japan, Sept. 26, 1921. [1; 4; 10]

Lamme, Benjamin Garver, engineer, b. near Springfield, O., 1864; d. Pittsburgh, Pa., July 8, 1924. [1; 4; 10]

Lamon, Ward Hill, lawyer, b. Frederick county, Pa., 1828; d. near Martinsburg, W. Va., May 7, 1893. [1; 3b; 6; 7; 8]

Lamont, Hammond, educationist, b. Monticello, N.Y., 1864; d. New York, N.Y., May 6, 1909. [1; 7; 10; 51]

Lamont, Thomas William, financier, b. Claverack, N.Y., 1870; d. Boca Grande, Fla., Feb. 2, 1948. [10; 12; 51]

La Monte, John Life, historian, b. Columbus, O., 1902; d. Philadelphia, Pa., Oct. 2, 1949. [14]

Lamphere, George N., journalist, b. Mystic, Conn., 1845; d. ? [70]

Lampman, Archibald, poet, b. Morpeth, Ont., 1861; d. Ottawa, Ont., Feb. 10, 1899. [27]

Lampton, William James, journalist, b. Lawrence county, O., about 1860; d. New York, N.Y., May 30, 1917. [10]

Lamson, Alvan, clergyman, b. Weston, Mass., 1792; d. Dedham, Mass., July 17, 1864. [3; 52]

Lamson, Daniel Lowell, physician, b. Hopkinton, N.H., 1834; d. 1894. [3; 8]

Lamson, Darius Franklin, clergyman, b. Weston, Mass., 1832; d. Newton, Mass., July 14, 1914.

Lamson, Joseph, sailor, b. 1801; d. 1894. [38]

Lamson, Mrs. Mary, née **Swift,** educationist, b. 1822; d. ? [8]

Lamson, William Judson, physician, b. Orange, N.J., 1871; d. Summit, N.J., Nov. 28, 1931. [62]

Lamson-Scribner, Frank, botanist, b. Cambridgeport, Mass., 1851; d. Washington, D.C., Feb. 22, 1938. [10]

Lancaster, Ellsworth Gage, educationist, b. Dixfield, Me., 1861; d. Gainesville, Fla., Nov. 11, 1934. [10]

Lancaster, F. Hewes, novelist, b. Lancaster Lodge, Miss., 1871; d. Cuevas, Miss., May 1, 1933. [10; 11]

Lancaster, Joseph, educationist, b. London, England, Nov. 25, 1778; d. New York, N.Y., Oct. 24, 1838. [1; 3; 6; 8]

Lance, William, lawyer and politician, b. Charleston, S.C., 1791; d. Texas, 1840. [3; 8; 34]

Lancefield, Richard Thomas, librarian, b. London, England, 1854; d. Toronto, Ont., Sept. 21, 1911. [27]

Lancewood, Lawrence (pseud.). See Wise, Daniel.

Land, Charles Henry, dentist, b. Simcoe, Ont., 1847; d. Detroit, Mich., Aug. 3, 1922. [4; 10]

Land, Robert Ernest Augustus, lawyer, b. 1847; d. Santa Monica, Calif., Jan. 31, 1927. [27]

Landacre, Francis Le Roy, anatomist, b. Hilliards, O., 1867; d. Columbus, O., Aug. 23, 1933. [10]

Lander, Meta (pseud.). See Lawrence, Mrs. Margaret Oliver, née Woods.

Lander, Sarah West, writer of books for children, b. Salem, Mass., 1819; d. Salem, Mass., Nov. 15, 1872. [3; 6; 8]

Landes, Margaret Winifred, educationist, b. Brazil, 1887; d. Istanbul, Turkey, June 28, 1932. [62]

Landi, Elissa, actress and novelist, b. Venice, Italy, 1904; d. Kingston, N.Y., Oct. 21, 1948. [7; 35]

Landis, Carole, movie actress, b. 1919; d. Hollywood, Calif., July 5, 1948. [12]

Landis, Frederick, journalist and politician, b. Butler county, O., 1872; d. Logansport, Ind., Nov. 25, 1934. [7; 10; 11]

Landis, Henry Gardner, physician, b. 1848; d. 1886. [3]

Landis, John Herr, politician, b. 1853; d. 1923.

Landis, Robert Wharton, poet, d. 1883.

Landis, Simon Mohler, physician, fl. 1857-1888.

Landman, Isaac, rabbi, b. Russia, 1880; d. Starlake, N.Y., Sept. 3, 1946. [7; 10; 11]

Landon, Judson Stuart, jurist, b. Salisbury, Conn., 1832; d. Schenectady, N.Y., Sept. 6, 1905. [8; 10]

Landon, Louise (pseud.). See Hauck, Mrs. Louise, née Platt.

Landon, Melville De Lancey, humorist, b. Eaton, N.Y., 1839; d. Yonkers, N.Y., Dec. 16, 1910. [1; 4; 8; 10]

Landreth, Burnet, agriculturist, b. Philadelphia, Pa., 1842; d. Bristol, Pa., Dec. 2, 1928. [10]

Landry, Auguste Charles Philippe Robert, farmer and politician, b. Quebec, Que., 1846; d. Dec. 20, 1919. [3; 27]

Lane, Alfred Church, geologist, b. Boston, Mass., 1863; d. Cambridge, Mass., April 15, 1948. [4; 13]

Lane, Benjamin Ingersol, clergyman, b. 1797; d. 1875.

Lane, Clarence Bronson, civil servant, b. 1870; d. 1929.

Lane, Mrs. Elinor, née **Macartney,** novelist, b. Maryland, about 1864; d. Lynchburg, Va., March 15, 1909. [7; 10; 34]

Lane, Franklin Knight, lawyer and politician, b. near Charlottetown, P.E.I., 1864; d. Rochester, Minn., May 18, 1921. [1; 2; 4; 10]

Lane, George Martin, educationist, b. Charlestown, Mass., 1823; d. Cambridge, Mass., June 30, 1897. [1; 3b; 8]

Lane, Isaac, bishop, b. Jackson, Tenn., 1834; d. Jackson, Tenn., Dec. 6, 1937. [10]

Lane, James Pillsbury, clergyman, b. 1832; d. 1889.

Lane, John Jay, educationist, b. Vicksburg, Miss., 1833; d. Austin, Tex., July 17, 1899. [34]

Lane, Levi Cooper, surgeon, b. near Somerville, O., 1830; d. San Francisco, Calif., Feb. 18, 1902. [1; 10]

Lane, Samuel Alanson, local historian, b. 1815; d. Akron, O., 1905.

Lane, Sarah, novelist, fl. 1883-1888.

Lane, Walter Paye, soldier, b. 1817; d. 1892.

Laney, Francis Baker, geologist, b. Greene county, Mo., 1874; d. Moscow, Ida., April 24, 1938. [10; 621]

Lang, William, local historian, b. 1815; d. ?

Langdale, John William, clergyman, b. Newcastle, England, 1874; d. Brooklyn, N.Y., Dec. 10, 1940. [10]

Langdell, Christopher Columbus, lawyer, b. Hillsborough county, N.H., 1826; d. Cambridge, Mass., July 6, 1906. [1; 4; 6; 8; 10]

Langdon, Courtney, educationist and poet, b. Rome Italy, 1861; d. Providence, R.I., Nov. 19, 1924. [1; 4; 7; 10]

Langdon, Mary (pseud.). See Pike, Mrs. Mary Hayden, née Green.

Langdon, Samuel, clergyman, b. Boston, Mass., 1723; d. Hampton Falls, N.H., Nov. 29, 1797. [1; 3; 4; 8]

Langdon, Stephen Herbert, Assyriologist, b. Monroe, Mich., 1876; d. Oxford, England, May 19, 1937. [10; 11]

Langdon, William Chauncy, antiquary, b. Florence, Italy, 1871; d. Westport, Conn., April 11, 1947. [7; 10]

Lange, Dietrich, writer of books for boys, b. Germany, 1863; d. St. Paul, Minn., Nov. 18, 1940. [7; 10; 11]

Langelier, Charles, politician and jurist, b. Ste. Rosalie, Que., 1851; d. Quebec, Que., Feb. 7, 1920. [27]

Langelier, Sir François Charles Stanislas, jurist, b. Ste. Rosalie, Lower Canada, 1838; d. Quebec, Que., Feb. 8, 1915. [27]

Langelier, Jean Chrysostome, civil servant, d. Quebec, Que., May 7, 1910. [27]

Langevin, Edmond Charles Hippolyte, priest, b. Quebec, Lower Canada, 1824; d. Rimouski, Que., June 2, 1889. [3; 27]

Langevin, Sir Hector Louis, lawyer and politician, b. Quebec, Lower Canada, 1826; d. Quebec, Que., June 11, 1906. [3; 27]

Langevin, Jean Pierre François La Force, bishop, b. Quebec, Lower Canada, 1821; d. Jan. 26, 1892. [27]

Langford, Nathaniel Pitt, banker, b. Westmoreland, N.Y., 1832; d. St. Paul, Minn., Oct. 18, 1911. [7; 10; 70]

Langford, Renwick Harcourt, poet, b. 1852; d. Kansas City, Mo., Sept. 18, 1933.

Langille, James Hibbard, clergyman, b. Mahone Bay, N.S., 1841; d. Forest Glen, N.Y., April 9, 1923. [6]

Langley, Samuel Pierpont, mathematician and astronomer, b. Roxbury, Mass., 1834; d. Aiken, S.C., Feb. 27, 1906. [1; 4; 8; 10]

Langlois, Joseph Godefroy, journalist, b. St. Scholastique, Que., 1866; d. Brussels, Belgium, April 6, 1928. [27]

Langston, John Mercer, lawyer and politician, b. Louisa county, Va., 1829; d. Washington, D.C., Nov. 15, 1897. [1; 3; 4; 8]

Langstroth, Lorenzo Lorraine, apiarist, b. Philadelphia, Pa., 1810; d. Dayton, O., Oct. 6, 1895. [1; 3b; 62]

Langton, William Alexander, architect, b. Peterborough, Ont., 1854; d. Toronto, Ont., April 3, 1933. [27]

Langtry, Albert Perkins, publisher, b. Wakefield, Mass., 1860; d. Waltham, Mass., Aug. 27, 1939. [10; 11]

Langtry, John, clergyman, b. near Burlington, Upper Canada, 1834; d. Toronto, Ont., Aug. 22, 1906. [27]

Langworthy, Edward, revolutionary patriot, b. Savannah, Ga., about 1738; d. Baltimore, Md., Nov. 1, 1802. [1; 3; 4]

Langworthy, Franklin, pioneer, b. 1798; d. about 1855.

Langworthy, William Franklin, genealogist, b. near West Edmeston, N.Y., 1864; d. Hamilton, N.Y., July 23, 1947.

Lanier, Clifford Anderson, poet and novelist, b. Griffin, Ga., 1844; d. Montgomery, Ala., Nov. 3, 1908. [3; 4; 7; 8; 10; 34]

Lanier, Sidney, poet, b. Macon, Ga., 1842; d. Lynn, N.C., Sept. 7, 1881. [1; 2; 3; 4; 5; 6; 7; 8; 9; 71; 72]

Lanigan, George Thomas, journalist and humorist, b. St. Charles, Que., 1845; d. Philadelphia, Pa., Feb. 5, 1886. [1; 3; 4; 7; 27; 71]

Lanigan, John Alphonsus, poet, b. 1854; d. 1919.

Lanman, Charles, librarian, b. Monroe, Mich., 1819; d. Washington, D.C., March 5, 1895. [1; 2; 3; 4; 5; 6; 7; 8]

Lanman, Charles Rockwell, orientalist, b. Norwich, Conn., 1850; d. Boston, Mass., Feb. 20, 1941. [10; 62]

Lanman, James Henry, lawyer, b. Norwich, Conn., 1812; d. Middletown, Conn., Jan. 10, 1887. [3]

Lanning, William Mershon, jurist, b. Mercer county, N.J., 1849; d. Trenton, N.J., 1912. [10]

Lanphier, Robert Carr, manufacturer, b. Springfield, Ill., 1878; d. Springfield, Ill., Jan. 29, 1939. [62]

Lansing, Dirck Cornelius, clergyman, b. Lansingburg, N.Y., 1785; d. Walnut Hills, O., March 19, 1857. [3]

Lansing, Gulian, missionary, b. Albany county, N.Y., 1825; d. Cairo, Egypt, Sept. 12, 1892. [1]

Lansing, Isaac J., clergyman, b. Watervliet, N.Y., 1846; d. Ridgewood, N.J., Aug. 1, 1920. [60]

Lansing, John Gulian, clergyman, b. 1851; d. 1906.

Lansing, Robert, diplomat, b. Watertown, N.Y., 1864; d. Washington, D.C., Oct. 30, 1928. [2; 4; 7; 10; 11]

Lansing, William, lawyer, b. 1837; d. 1908.

Lanz, Henry, educationist, b. Moscow, Russia, 1886; d. Palo Alto, Calif., Nov. 1, 1945.

Lanza, Gaetano, mechanical engineer, b. Boston, Mass., 1848; d. Philadelphia, Pa., March 22, 1928. [8; 10]

Lapham, Increase Allen, naturalist, b. Palmyra, N.Y., 1811; d. Oconomewec, Wis., Sept. 14, 1875. [1; 3; 4; 6]

Lapham, William Berry, genealogist, b. Bethel, Me., 1828; d. Togus, Me., Feb. 22, 1894. [1; 3; 6; 38]

Larcom, Lucy, poet, b. Beverly, Mass., 1824; d. Boston, Mass., April 17, 1893. [1; 3; 4; 6; 7; 8; 9; 71]

Lard, Mrs. Rebecca, née **Hammond,** poet, b. New Bedford, Mass., 1772; d. Paris, Ind., Sept. 28, 1855. [43]

Lardner, Mrs. Lena Bogardus, née **Phillips,** poet, b. Catskill, N.Y., 1843; d. 1919. [10]

Lardner, Ringold Wilmer, humorist, b. Niles, Mich., 1885; d. East Hampton, Long Island, N.Y., Sept. 25, 1933. [1a; 2; 7; 10; 72]

Lareau, Edmond, journalist and historian, b. St. Grégoire, Que., 1848; d. Montreal, Que., April 22, 1890. [27]

Larison, Cornelius Wilson, physician and spelling reformer, b. 1837; d. Ringoes, N.J., Jan. 10, 1910.

Larkin, Clarence, clergyman, b. 1850; d. 1924.

Larkin, Edgar Lucien, astronomer, b. La Salle county, Ill., 1847; d. Uplands, Calif., Oct. 11, 1924. [4; 10]

Larkin, John, priest and educationist, b. Newcastle-on-Tyne, England, 1801; d. Canada, Dec. 11, 1858. [27]

Larned, Augusta, journalist, b. Rutland, N.Y., 1835; d. Summit, N.J., 1924. [3; 4; 6; 7; 8; 10]

Larned, Charles William, soldier, b. New York, N.Y., 1850; d. Dansville, N.Y., June 19, 1911. [10]

Larned, Ellen Douglas, local historian, b. Thompson, Conn., 1825; d. 1912. [3; 10]

Larned, Josephus Nelson, librarian, b. Chatham, Ont., 1836; d. Buffalo, N.Y., Aug. 15, 1913. [1; 4; 7; 8; 10]

Larned, Mrs. Linda, née Hull, household economist, b. Little Falls, N.Y., 1853; d. Syracuse, N.Y., June 24, 1939. [10; 11]

Larned, Walter Cranston, lawyer, b. Chicago, Ill., 1850; d. Lake Forest, Ill., June 19, 1914. [7; 10; 51]

Larned, William, Trowbridge, journalist, b. St. Louis, Mo., d. St. Louis, Mo., Feb. 9, 1928. [10]

La Roche, René, physician, b. Philadelphia, Pa., 1795; d. Philadelphia, Pa., Dec., 1872. [3; 7]

Larose, Wilfrid, lawyer, b. 1863; d. Ottawa, Ont., Aug. 24, 1936. [27]

Larpenteur, Charles, fur-trader, b. near Fontainebleau, France, 1807; d. Harrison county, Ia., Nov. 15, 1872. [1]

Larrabee, Edward Allan, clergyman, b. Chicago, Ill., 1852; d. Chicago Ill., June 13, 1924. [10]

Larrabee, William, politician, b. Ledyard, Conn., 1832; d. Clermont, Ia., Nov. 16, 1912. [1; 4; 10; 37]

Larrabee, William Clark, educationist, b. Cape Elizabeth, Me., 1802; d. Greencastle, Ind., May 4, 1859. [1; 3; 8; 38]

Larrabee, William Henry, editor, b. Alfred, Me., 1829; d. Plainfield, N.J., May 13, 1913. [10]

Larremore, Wilbur, lawyer and poet, b. New York, N.Y., 1855; d. New York, N.Y., Aug. 11, 1918. [10]

Larric, Jack, journalist and playwright, b. 1888; d. New York, N.Y., Aug. 18, 1941.

Larrowe, Marcus Dwight, lecturer, b. 1832; d. ? [8]

Larsen, Hanna Astrup, journalist, b. Decorah, Ia., 1873; d. Elmsford, N.Y., Dec. 3, 1945. [7; 10]

Larson, Laurence Marcellus, historian, b. near Bergen, Norway, 1868; d. Urbana, Ill., March 9, 1938. [10; 11]

La Rue, François Alexandre Hubert, historian, b. Isle d'Orléans, Lower Canada, 1833; d. Quebec, Que., Sept. 25, 1881. [27]

Lasance, Francis Xavier, priest, b. Cincinnati, O., 1860; d. Cincinnati, O., Dec. 12, 1946. [21]

Lasher, George William, clergyman, b. Duanesburg, N.Y., 1851; d. Feb., 1920. [10]

Latané, John Holliday, historian, b. Staunton, Va., 1869; d. Baltimore, Md., Jan. 1, 1932. [1a; 4; 10; 11]

Latch, Edward Biddle, Biblical student, b. Montgomery county, Pa., 1833; d. Philadelphia, Pa., April 13, 1911. [8; 10]

Laterrière, Pierre de Sales, physician, b. St. Salvy, France, 1747; d. Quebec, Lower Canada, June 8, 1815. [27]

Laterrière, Pierre de Sales, physician, b. 1785; d. Les Eboulements, Lower Canada, Dec. 15, 1834. [27]

Lathbury, Albert Augustus, clergyman, b. Manchester, N.Y., 1849; d. Ridgewood, N.J., Feb. 28, 1937. [10]

Lathbury, Mary Artemisia, religious writer, b. Manchester, N.Y., 1841; d. East Orange, N.J., Oct. 20, 1913. [1; 4; 8; 10]

Lathe, Herbert William, clergyman, b. Worcester, Mass., 1851; d. Brookline, Mass., Aug. 24, 1932. [8; 10; 11; 62]

Lathern, John, clergyman, b. England, 1831; d. Halifax, N.S., Jan. 8, 1905. [27]

Lathers, Richard, merchant, b. Georgetown, S.C., 1820; d. 1903. [34]

Lathrop, Clarissa Caldwell, autobiographer, d. 1892.

Lathrop, Mrs. Cordelia, née Penfield, novelist, b. 1892; d. Bridgeport, Conn., Jan. 15, 1938.

Lathrop, George Parsons, poet, novelist, and critic, b. Honolulu, Hawaii, 1851; d. New York, N.Y., April 19, 1898. [1; 2; 3; 4; 5; 6; 7; 9; 71]

Lathrop, Henry Burrowes, educationist, b. Gold Hill, Nev., 1867; d. Madison, Wis., Nov. 6, 1936. [10]

Lathrop, Henry Warren, biographer, b. 1819; d. 1902. [37]

Lathrop, John, poet, b. Boston, Mass., 1772; d. Georgetown, D.C., Jan. 30, 1820. [1; 3; 4; 7; 9]

Lathrop, Joseph, clergyman, b. Norwich, Conn., 1831; d. West Springfield, Mass., Dec. 31, 1820. [3; 8]

Lathrop, Mrs. Rose, née Hawthorne, daughter of Nathaniel Hawthorne (q.v.), b. Lenox, Mass., 1851; d. Hawthorne, N.Y., July 9, 1926. [1; 4; 7]

Lathrop, William Gilbert, clergyman, b. Providence, R.I., 1865; d. New Haven, Conn., Jan. 12, 1948. [62]

Latil, Alexandre, poet, b. New Orleans, La., 1816; d. New Orleans, La., March, 1851. [1; 34]

Latimer, Charles, engineer, b. Washington, D.C., 1827; d. Cleveland, O., March 25, 1888. [3; 8]

Latimer, Mrs. Elizabeth, née Wormeley, historian and novelist, b. London, England, 1822; d. Baltimore, Md., Jan. 4, 1904. [1; 3; 4; 6; 7; 8; 9]

Latimer, Faith (pseud.). See Miller, Mrs. John A.

Latimer, Margery. See Toomer, Mrs. Margery Bodine, née Latimer.

Latrobe, John Hazelhurst Boneval, lawyer, b. Philadelphia, Pa., 1803; d. Baltimore, Md., Sept. 11, 1891. [1; 3; 4; 5; 7; 8; 9]

Latta, James, clergyman, b. Ireland, 1732; d. Lancaster county, Pa., Jan. 29, 1801. [3]

Latta, Robert Ray, pioneer, b. 1836; d. ?

Latta, Samuel Arminius, physician, b. Muskingum county, O., 1804; d. Cincinnati, O., June 28, 1852. [3; 8]

Latta, Thomas Albert, journalist, b. Park Hill Mission, Indian Territory, 1872; d. Tulsa, Okla., April 11, 1931. [10; 11]

Lau, Robert Frederick, clergyman, b. Jersey City, N.J., 1885; d. New York, N.Y., Oct. 5, 1943. [10]

Lauck, William Jett, economist, b. Keyser, W. Va., 1879; d. Port Royal, Va., June 14, 1949. [10]

Laughlin, Clara Elizabeth, novelist and writer of travel books, b. New York, N.Y., 1873; d. Chicago, Ill., March 3, 1941. [7; 10; 11]

Loughlin, James Laurence, political economist, b. Deerfield, O., 1850; d. Jaffrey, N.H., Nov. 28, 1933. [1a; 3; 4; 6; 7; 10]

Launt, Francis Albemarle Delbretons, clergyman, b. Hamilton, N.Y., 1864; d. Philadelphia, Pa., Jan. 19, 1928. [10]

Laurie, Thomas, clergyman, b. Edinburgh, Scotland, 1821; d. Providence, R.I., Oct. 10, 1897. [3b; 8]

Laussat, Antony, lawyer, b. Philadelphia, Pa., 1806; d. Philadelphia, Pa., Nov. 2, 1833. [3]

Laut, Agnes Christina, journalist, novelist, and historian, b. Stanley, Ont., 1871; d. Wassaic, N.Y., Nov. 15, 1936. [7; 10; 27]

Lautman, Maurice Farvish, physician, b. Meriden, Conn., 1890; d. Hot Springs, Ark., Sept. 23, 1938. [62]

Laux, John Joseph, priest and historian, b. Germany, 1878; d. Cincinnati, O., Feb. 8, 1939. [21]

La Valinière, Pierre Huet de, priest, b. Varade, France, 1732; d. L'Assomption, Lower Canada, June 29, 1806. [3; 32]

Lavell, Cecil Fairfield, educationist, b. Kingston, Ont., 1872; d. Toronto, Ont., May 1, 1948. [7; 10]

Lavely, Henry Alexander, poet, b. Pittsburgh, Pa., 1831; d. ? [10]

Laverdière, Charles Honoré, priest and historian, b. Château-Richer, Lower Canada, 1826; d. Quebec, Que., March 27, 1873. [27; 32]

Lavergne, Armand Renaud, politician, b. Arthabaskaville, Que., 1880; d. Ottawa, Ont., March 6, 1935. [27]

Law, Andrew, psalmodist, b. Milford, Conn., 1749; d. Cheshire, Conn., July 13, 1821. [1; 3]

Law, James, veterinary surgeon, b. Edinburgh, Scotland, 1838; d. Springfield, Mass., May 10, 1921. [8; 10]

Law, John, jurist, b. New London, Conn., 1796; d. Evansville, Ind., Oct. 7, 1873. [1; 3; 4]

Law, Marion, clergyman, b. Coleta, Ill., 1867; d. San Diego, Calif., Nov. 10, 1930. [4]

Law, Robert, clergyman, b. Scotland, 1860; d. Toronto, Ont., April 7, 1919. [27]

Law, Mrs. Sallie Chapman, née Gordon, patriot, b. Wilkes county, N.C., 1805; d. Memphis, Tenn., June 28, 1894. [1]

Law, Sidney Gibbs, clergyman and poet, b. 1831; d. 1899.

Law, Stephen Dodd, lawyer, b. Meredith, N.Y., 1820; d. Tarrytown, N.Y., Oct. 22, 1886. [62]

Law, Thomas, capitalist and economist, b. 1759; d. Washington, D.C., Oct. 1834.

Lawes, Lewis Edward, penologist, b. Elmira, N.Y., 1883; d. Garrison, N.Y., April 23, 1947. [7; 10]

Lawrance, Uriah Marion, Sunday school worker, b. Winchester, O., 1850; d. Portland, Ore., May 1, 1924. [1; 10]

Lawrance, William Irvin, clergyman, b. Winchester, O., 1853; d. Berkeley, Calif., March, 1935. [10]

Lawrance, William Vickers, poet, b. 1834; d. 1905.

Lawrence, Benjamin Franklin, clergyman, b. Jay, Me., 1835; d. Marlboro, Mass., Jan. 5, 1917. [11]

Lawrence, Byrem, clergyman and educationist, b. Monkton, Vt., 1802; d. Brazil, Ind., Oct. 13, 1854.

Lawrence, E. Addison, educationist, b. Groton, Mass., 1823; d. Orange, N.J., Feb. 2, 1911.

Lawrence, Edward Alexander, clergyman, b. St. Johnsbury, Vt., 1808; d. Marblehead, Mass., Sept. 4, 1883. [43; 49]

Lawrence, Edward Alexander, clergyman, b. Marblehead, Mass., 1847; d. Baltimore, Md., Nov. 10, 1893. [49; 51]

Lawrence, Egbert Charles, clergyman, b. Borodine, N.Y., 1845; d. Schenectady, N.Y., June 10, 1916. [10; 56]

Lawrence, Eugene, historian, b. New York, N.Y. 1823; d. New York, N.Y., Aug. 17, 1894. [3; 6; 8]

Lawrence, Henry Wells, historian, b. Nyack, N.Y., 1879; d. New London, Conn., Jan. 3, 1942. [10]

Lawrence, James Cooper, educationist, b. Columbus, O., 1890; d. Minneapolis, Minn., Aug. 14, 1932. [10]

Lawrence, Joseph Wilson, historian, b. Saint John, N.B., 1818; d. Saint John, N.B., Nov. 6, 1892. [27]

Lawrence, Mrs. Margaret Oliver, née Woods, miscellaneous writer, b. 1813; d. 1901. [6; 8]

Lawrence, Robert Fowler, clergyman, b. Moira, N.Y., 1810; d. Albany, N.Y., Oct. 20, 1886.

Lawrence, Robert Means, physician, b. Boston, Mass., 1847; d. Boston, Mass., March 7, 1935. [8; 10; 11; 51]

Lawrence, Vincent, playwright, b. Boston, Mass., 1890; d. Corpus Christi, Tex., Nov. 25, 1946.

Lawrence, William, bishop, b. Boston, Mass., 1850; d. Readville, Mass., Nov. 6, 1941. [7; 10]

Lawrence, William Beach, jurist, b. New York, N.Y., 1800; d. New York, N.Y., March 26, 1881. [1; 3; 4; 6; 8]

Lawrence, William Richards, philanthropist, b. Boston, Mass., 1812; d. Swampscott, Mass., Sept. 20, 1885. [3]

Laws, Frank Arthur, electrical engineer, b. Brockton, Mass., 1867; d. 1936. [10]

Laws, Samuel Spahr, clergyman, b. Ohio county, Va., 1824; d. Washington, D.C., Jan. 9, 1921. [1; 4; 10]

Lawson, Albert Gallatin, clergyman, b. Poughkeepsie, N.Y., 1842; d. Danbury, N.H., March 8, 1929. [10]

Lawson, George, botanist, b. Newport, Fifeshire, Scotland, 1827; d. Halifax, N.S., Nov. 10, 1895. [3; 27]

Lawson, J. Murray, journalist, b. Yarmouth, N.S., 1848; d. Yarmouth, N.S., May 27, 1925. [27]

Lawson, James, poet and editor, b. Glasgow, Scotland, 1799; d. Yonkers, N.Y., March 20, 1880. [1; 3; 7; 9]

Lawson, Mrs. Jessie Kerr, journalist, b. Fifeshire, Scotland, about 1839; d. Toronto, Ont., July 30, 1917. [27]

Lawson, John, historian, d. North Carolina, 1711. [1; 4]

Lawson, John Davison, jurist, b. Hamilton, Ont., 1852; d. Columbia, Mo., Oct. 28, 1921. [4; 8; 10; 11]

Lawson, Leonidas Moreau, physician, b. Nicholas county, O., 1812; d. 1864. [6; 8]

Lawson, Mrs. Mary Jane, née **Katzmann,** poet, b. near Dartmouth, N.S., 1828; d. Halifax, N.S., 1890. [27]

Lawson, Publius Virgilius, manufacturer, b. Corning, N.Y., 1853; d. Menasha, Wis., Dec. 1, 1920. [4; 10; 11]

Lawson, Thomas William, financier, b. Charlestown, Mass., 1857; d. Boston, Mass., Feb. 8, 1925. [1; 7; 10]

Lawton, Captain Wilbur (pseud.). See Goldfrap, John Henry.

Lawton, William Cranston, educationist, b. New Bedford, Mass., 1853; d. near Philadelphia, Pa., April 18, 1941. [7; 10]

Lay, Benjamin, Quaker reformer, b. Colchester, England, 1677; d. Abington, Pa., Feb. 3, 1759. [1; 3; 6]

Lay, Henry Champlin, bishop, b. Richmond, Va., 1823; d. Easton, Md., Sept. 17, 1885. [1; 3; 4; 6; 8; 34]

Laycock, Craven, educationist, b. Bradford, England, 1866; d. Hanover, N.H., April 4, 1940. [10]

Lazarus, Emma, poet, b. New York, N.Y., 1849; d. New York, N.Y., Nov. 19, 1887. [1; 3; 4; 6; 7; 8; 9; 71]

Lazarus, Josephine, essayist, b. New York, N.Y., 1846; d. ? [8]

Lazell, Frederick John, journalist, b. 1868; d. Des Moines, Ia., Sept. 23, 1940. [37]

Lazelle, Henry Martyn, soldier, b. Enfield, Mass., 1832; d. Washington, D.C., July 21, 1917. [3; 8; 10]

Lea, Albert Miller, soldier, b. 1807; d. 1890.

Lea, Henry Charles, historian, b. Philadelphia, Pa., 1825; d. Philadelphia, Pa., Oct. 24, 1909. [1; 3; 4; 6; 7; 8; 10]

Lea, Homer, soldier, b. Denver, Colo., 1876; d. Los Angeles, Calif., Nov. 1, 1912. [1; 4; 7; 10]

Lea, Isaac, naturalist, b. Wilmington, Del., 1792; d. Philadelphia, Pa., Dec. 8, 1886. [3b; 4; 6; 8]

Lea, James Henry, genealogist, b. 1846; d. 1914.

Lea, Mathew Carey, chemist, b. Philadelphia, Pa., 1823; d. Philadelphia, Pa., March 15, 1897. [1; 3; 4; 6]

Leach, Albert Ernest, chemist, b. Boston, Mass., 1864; d. Denver, Colo., 1910. [10]

Leach, Clifford (pseud.) See Clark, Kenneth Sherman.

Leach, Daniel Dyer, educationist, b. Bridgewater, Mass., 1806; d. May 16, 1891. [10]

Leach, Josiah Granville, lawyer and genealogist, b. Cape May, N.J., 1842; d. Philadelphia, Pa., May 27, 1922. [4; 10]

Leacock, Stephen Butler, economist and humorist, b. Hampshire, England, 1869; d. Toronto, Ont., March 28, 1944. [10; 11; 12; 27]

Leahy, William Augustus, journalist, b. Boston, Mass., 1867; d. Boston, Mass., June 4, 1941. [7; 10]

Leakin, George Armistead, clergyman, b. 1818; d. near Baltimore, Md., July 10, 1912. [8]

Leaming, James Rosebrugh, physician, b. Groveland, N.Y., 1820; d. New York, N.Y., Dec. 5, 1892. [36]

Leaming, Jeremiah, clergyman, b. Middletown, Conn., 1717; d. New Haven, Conn., Sept., 1804. [3; 6; 8]

Leamy, Hugh Anthony, editor, b. Dublin, Ireland, 1899; d. New York, N.Y., Feb. 9, 1935. [10]

Leamy, Mrs. Margaret, née **Hanly,** historian, b. 1869; d. New York, N.Y., April 25, 1939.

Lean, John Udy, arithmetician, d. 1913.

Learned, Mrs. Ellin, née **Craven,** writer on etiquette, b. New Jersey; d. New York, N.Y., Jan. 8, 1940. [10; 11]

Learned, Henry Barrett, educationist, b. Exeter, N.H., 1868; d. Stanford University, Calif., Oct. 12, 1931. [10; 62]

Learned, Marion Dexter, educationist, b. near Dover, Del., 1857; d. Philadelphia, Pa., Aug. 2, 1917. [1; 4; 10]

Learned, Walter, poet and anthologist, b. New London, Conn., 1847; d. New London, Conn., Dec. 11, 1915. [4; 7; 8; 10]

Learned, William Law, jurist, b. New London, Conn., 1821; d. Albany, N.Y., Sept. 20, 1904. [3; 8; 62]

Leary, Daniel Bell, psychologist, b. New York, N.Y., 1886; d. Buffalo, N.Y., April 30, 1946. [7; 10; 11]

Leary, John Joseph, journalist, b. Lynn, Mass., 1874; d. Lynn, Mass., Jan. 4, 1944. [10; 11]

Lease, Emory Bair, educationist, b. New Berlin, Pa., 1863; d. New York, N.Y., May 19, 1931. [10; 11]

Lease, Mrs. Mary Elizabeth, née **Clyens,** lawyer and politician, b. Ridgway, Pa., 1853; d. Callicoon, N.Y., Oct. 29, 1933. [1a; 10]

Leavell, Landrum Pinson, religious worker, b. Oxford, Miss., 1874; d. Oxford, Miss., June 4, 1929. [10]

Leavenworth, Charles Samuel, historian, b. 1874; d. New Haven, Conn., Oct. 2, 1949.

Leavenworth, Elias Warner, lawyer, b. Canaan, N.Y., 1803; d. Syracuse, N.Y., Nov. 25, 1887. [3]

Leavitt, John McDowell, educationist, b. Steubenville, O., 1824; d. Annapolis, Md., Dec., 1909. [3; 4; 5; 6; 8]

Leavitt, Joshua, reformer, b. Heath, Mass., 1894; d. Brooklyn, N.Y., Jan. 16, 1873. [1; 3; 4; 6]

Leavitt, Mrs. Martha Cornelia, poet, b. Turner, Me., 1841; d. ?

Leavitt, Michael Bennett, theatre manager, b. 1843; d. Miami Beach, Fla., June 27, 1935.

Leavitt, Robert Greenleaf, botanist, b. 1865; d. North Parsonfield, Me., Oct. 2, 1942. [13]

Leavitt, Sheldon, physician, b. Grand Rapids, Mich., April 9, 1848; d. Chicago, Ill., Feb. 2, 1933. [10]

Leavitt, Thaddeus W.H., journalist and local historian, b. Leeds county, Ont., about 1844; d. Bancroft, Ont., June 21, 1909. [27]

Le Baron, Grace (pseud.). See Upham, Mrs. Grace Le Baron, née Locke.

Le Baron, Marie (pseud.). See Urie, Mrs. Mary Le Baron, née Andrews.

Leblond de Brumath, Adrien, educationist, b. Alsace, 1854; d. Montreal, Que., May 3, 1939. [27]

Le Cato, Nathaniel James Walter, novelist, b. 1835; d. ?

Lecky, Walter (pseud.). See McDermott, William A.

Lecompte, Edouard, priest, b. near Montreal, Que., 1856; d. Montreal, Que., Dec. 30, 1929. [27]

Le Conte, Joseph, geologist, b. Liberty county, Ga., 1823; d. Yosemite valley, July 6, 1901. [1; 3; 4; 6; 8]

Lednum, John, clergyman, b. Sussex county, Del., 1797; d. Philadelphia, Pa., Nov. 18, 1863.

Ledoux, Louis Vernon, poet and industrialist, b. New York, N.Y., 1880; d. New York, N.Y., Feb. 25, 1948. [7; 10]

Le Duc, William Gates, soldier, b. Wilkesville, O., 1823; d. Hastings, Minn., Oct. 30, 1917. [10; 70]

Lee, Agnes (pseud.). See Freer, Mrs. Martha Agnes, née Rand.

Lee, Albert, editor, b. New Orleans, La., 1868; d. Norwalk, Conn., Dec. 10, 1946. [4; 7; 62]

Lee, Alfred, bishop, b. Cambridge, Mass., 1807; d. Wilmington, Del., April 12, 1887. [1; 3; 4; 6]

Lee, Alfred Emory, historian, b. Ohio, 1838; d. California, about 1928.. [4; 8]

Lee, Andrew, clergyman, b. Lyme, Conn., 1745; d. Lisbon, Conn., Aug. 25, 1832. [3]

Lee, Arthur Tracy, soldier and poet, d. 1879.

Lee, Benjamin, physician, b. Norwich, Conn., 1833; d. Point Pleasant, N.Y., July 11, 1913. [3; 4; 6; 8; 10]

Lee, Charles Alfred, physician, b. Salisbury, Conn., 1801; d. Peekskill, N.Y., Feb. 14, 1872. [1; 3; 4; 6]

Lee, Charles C. (pseud.). See Rose, Mrs. Martha Emily, née Parmelee.

Lee, Charles Henry, lawyer, b. 1818; d. 1900.

Lee, Chauncey, clergyman, b. Salisbury, Conn., 1763; d. Hartwick, N.Y., Nov. 5, 1842. [3; 62]

Lee, David Russell, educationist, b. Hamilton, Ont., 1869; d. Knoxville, Tenn., Oct. 19, 1933. [10]

Lee, Day Kellogg, clergyman, b. Sempronius, N.Y., 1816; d. New York, N.Y., June 2, 1869. [3; 6; 8;]

Lee, Mrs. Eliza, née Buckminster, miscellaneous writer, b. Portsmouth, N.H., 1794; d. Brookline, Mass., June 22, 1864. [1; 3; 6; 7]

Lee, Fitzhugh, soldier, b. Clermont, Va., 1835; d. Washington, D.C., April 28, 1905. [4; 10]

Lee, Mrs. Frank. See Lee, Mrs. Mary, née Chappell.

Lee, Frank Theodosius, clergyman, b. Kenosha, Wis., 1847; d. Claremont, Calif., June 11, 1934. [10; 62]

Lee, Franklyn Warner, journalist, b. New York, N.Y., 1864; d. Rush City, Minn., March 18, 1898. [70]

Lee, Frederic Schiller, physiologist, b. Canton, N.Y., 1859; d. Waverly, S.C., Dec. 14, 1939. [10]

Lee, George Herbert, lawyer, b. Springhill, N.B., 1854; d. Boston, Mass., Aug. 25, 1905. [27]

Lee, George Hyde, physician, b. Hudson, O., 1848; d. Miami, Fla., April 1, 1920. [10]

Lee, Gerald Stanley, clergyman, b. Brockton, Mass., Oct. 4, 1862; d. Northampton, Mass., April 3, 1944. [7; 10]

Lee, Guy Carleton, publicist, b. 1862; d. Green Village, near Carlisle, Pa., Dec. 26, 1936. [7; 10; 11; 34]

Lee, Mrs. Hannah Farnum, née Sawyer, miscellaneous writer, b. Newburyport, Mass., 1780; d. Boston, Mass., Dec. 27, 1865. [1; 3; 6; 7; 8]

Lee, Henry, soldier, b. Westmoreland county, Va., 1756; d. Cumberland Island, Ga., March 25, 1818. [1; 3; 4; 6; 7]

Lee, Henry, soldier, b. Westmoreland county, Va., 1787; d. Paris, France, Jan. 30, 1837. [1; 3; 4; 6; 7]

Lee, Isaac Lawrence, educationist, b. Denver, Colo., 1892; d. Syracuse, N.Y., Oct. 22, 1942.

Lee, Ivy Ledbetter, journalist and publicist, b. Cedartown, Ga., 1877; d. New York, N.Y., Nov. 9, 1934. [1a; 10; 34]

Lee, James Kendall, soldier, b. 1829; d. 1861.

Lee, James Melvin, journalist, b. Port Crane, N.Y., 1878; d. New York, N.Y., Nov. 17, 1929. [1; 4; 7; 10]

Lee, James Wideman, clergyman, b. Rockbridge, Ga., 1849; d. St. Louis, Mo., Oct. 4, 1919. [1; 4; 8; 10; 11; 34]

Lee, Jesse, missionary, b. Prince George county, Va., 1758; d. Baltimore, Md., Sept. 12, 1816. [3; 4; 8; 34]

Lee, John Doyle, Mormon elder, b. Kaskaskia, Ill., 1812; d. Mountain Meadows, Utah, March 23, 1877. [1]

Lee, John Stebbins, clergyman, b. Vernon, Vt., 1820; d. Canton, N.Y., Sept 10, 1902. [4; 8; 10; 43]

Lee, Leroy Madison, clergyman, b. Petersburg, Va., 1808; d. Ashland, Va., April 20, 1882. [3; 8; 34]

Lee, Joseph, clergyman, b. 1847; d. ?

Lee, Luther, clergyman, b. Schoharie, N.Y., 1800; d. Flint, Mich., Dec. 13, 1889. [1; 3; 6; 8]

Lee, Margaret, novelist, b. New York, N.Y., 1841; d. Brooklyn, N.Y., Dec. 24, 1914. [4; 7; 8; 10]

Lee, Mrs. Mary, née Chappell, novelist, b. 1849; d. ?

Lee, Mrs. Mary Catherine, née Jenkins, novelist, b. New Bedford, Mass.; d. Springfield, Mass., Oct. 9, 1927. [8; 11]

Lee, Mary Elizabeth, poet, b. Charleston, S.C., 1813; d. Charleston, S.C., Sept. 23, 1849. [3; 4; 8; 34]

Lee, Mrs. Melicent, née Humason, writer of books for children, b. 1889; d. Oct. 4, 1943. [10]

Lee, Minnie Mary (pseud.). See Wood, Mrs. Julia Amanda, née Sargent.

Lee, Nelson, ranger, b. 1807; d. ?

Lee, Patty (pseud.). See Cary, Alice.

Lee, Porter Raymond, social worker, b. Buffalo, N.Y., 1879; d. Englewood, N.J., March 8, 1939. [10]

Lee, Richard Henry, biographer, b. Westmoreland county, Va., 1794; d. Washington, Pa., Jan. 3, 1865. [3; 6; 34]

Lee, Robert Edward, agriculturist, b. Arlington House, Va., 1843; d. Upperville, Va., Oct. 20, 1914. [4; 10; 34]

Lee, Samuel, clergyman b. Berlin, Conn., 1803; d. New Ipswich, N.H., Aug. 27, 1881. [62]

Lee, William George, physician, b. 1873; d. Chicago, Ill., Feb. 10, 1927.

Lee, Willis Thomas, geologist, b. Brooklyn, Pa., 1864; d. June 16, 1926. [10]

Leech, Mrs. Lucille, née Pittman, poet, b. Vicksburg, Miss.; d. Evanston, Ill., Dec. 4, 1946.

Leech, Samuel Vanderlip, clergyman and poet, b. Albany, N.Y., 1837; d. 1916. [3; 8]

Leeds, Daniel, religious writer, b. England, 1652; d. Burlington, N.J., Sept. 28, 1720. [1; 3; 4; 6; 7]

Leeds, Samuel Penniman, clergyman, b. New York. N.Y., 1824; d. Hanover, N.H., June 25, 1910. [10; 49]

Leeper, David Rohrer, pioneer, b. 1832; d. 1900.

Leeser, Isaac, rabbi, b. Prussia, 1806; d. Philadelphia, Pa., Feb. 1, 1868. [1; 3; 4; 6]

Lefevre, Arthur, educationist, b. Baltimore, Md., 1863; d. Houston, Tex., March 4, 1929. [10; 11]

Lefevre, Edwin, journalist and novelist, b. Colon, Colombia, 1871; d. New York, N.Y., Feb. 22, 1943. [7; 10; 11]

Lefevre, Egbert, physician, b. Raritan, N.J., 1858; d. New York, N.Y., March 30, 1914. [10]

Lefevre, Mrs. Lily Alice, poet, d. Vancouver, B.C., Oct. 17, 1938. [27]

Lefferts, George Morewood, physician, b. Brooklyn, N.Y., 1846; d. Katonah, N.Y., Sept. 21, 1920. [3; 4; 8; 10]

Lefferts, Walter, educationist, b. Philadelphia, Pa., 1877; d. Philadelphia, Pa., Nov. 7, 1948. [11]

Leffingwell, Albert, physician, b. Aurora, N.Y., 1845; d. Aurora, N.Y., Sept. 1, 1917. [8; 10]

Leffingwell, Charles Wesley, clergyman, b. Ellington, Conn., 1840; d. Pasadena, Calif., Oct. 9, 1928. [10]

Leffingwell, William Bruce, sportsman, fl. 1888-1895.

Leffingwell, William Henry, management engineer, b. Woodstock, Ont., 1876; d. Westfield, N.J., Dec. 19, 1934. [10]

Leffler, Ray Victor, economist, b. Leipsic, O., 1892; d. Toledo, O., April 10, 1941. [10]

Leffmann, Henry, chemist, b. Philadelphia, Pa., 1847; d. Philadelphia, Pa., Dec. 25, 1930. [1; 10; 13]

Lefroy, Augustus Henry Frazer, lawyer, b. Toronto, Ont., 1852; d. Ottawa, Ont., March 7, 1919. [27]

Légal, Emile Joseph, archbishop, b. France, 1849; d. Edmonton, Alta., March 10, 1920. [27]

Legaré, Hugh Swinton, lawyer and politician, b. Charleston, S.C., 1797; d. Boston, Mass., June 20, 1843. [3; 4; 7; 8]

Legaré, James Matthews, lawyer and poet, b. Charleston, S.C., 1823; d. Aiken, S.C., March 30, 1859. [4; 8; 42]

Legendre, Napoléon, poet, b. Nicolet, Lower Canada, 1841; d. Quebec, Que., Dec. 16, 1907. [27]

Legendre, Sidney Jennings, explorer, b. 1903; d. Mount Holly, S.C., March 8, 1948.

Legge, Charles, civil engineer, b. Gananoque, Upper Canada, 1829; d. Toronto, Ont., April 12, 1881. [27]

Leggett, Benjamin Franklin, educationist, b. Chestertown, N.Y., 1834; d. Chestertown, N.Y., July 18, 1924. [10; 60]

Leggett, William, poet and journalist, b. New York, N.Y., 1802; d. New Rochelle, N.Y., May 29, 1839. [1; 3; 4; 6; 7; 71]

Leggett, William Martin, clergyman and poet, b. Sussex Vale, N.B., 1813; d. ? [27]

Leggo, William, lawyer, b. Perth, Upper Canada, 1822; d. Winnipeg, Man., March 31, 1888. [27]

Legion (pseud.). See Sullivan, Robert Baldwin.

Legler, Henry Eduard, librarian, b. Palermo, Italy, 1861; d. Chicago, Ill., Sept. 13, 1917. [1; 7; 10]

Lehmer, Derrick Norman, educationist and poet, b. Somerset, Ind., 1867; d. Berkeley, Calif., Sept. 8, 1938. [10; 11; 35]

Lehr, Mrs. Elizabeth, née Drexel. See Decies, Elizabeth Wharton, Baroness, née Drexel.

Leidy, Joseph, naturalist, b. Philadelphia, Pa., 1823; d. Philadelphia, Pa., April 30, 1891. [1; 3; 4; 6]

Leigh, Edwin, educationist, b. South Berwick, Me., 1815; d. Kerr county, Tex., April 9, 1890. [4]

Leigh, Stuart (pseud.). See Clarke, Mrs. Mary Bayard, née Devereux.

Leighton, Frederick, educationist, b. South Avon, N.Y., 1874; d. Oswego, N.Y., June 2, 1942.

Leighton, William, poet, b. Cambridge, Mass., 1833; d. 1911. [3; 4; 6; 8; 34; 51]

Leiper, Macon Anderson, educationist, b. Malvern, Ark., 1879; d. Bowling Green, Ky., June 17, 1936. [10; 11]

Leitch, William, clergyman, b. Rothesay, Scotland, 1814; d. Kingston, Ont., May 9, 1864. (27)

Le Jeune, Louis Marie, priest, b. Brittany, France, 1857; d. Ottawa, Ont., Feb. 4, 1935. [27]

Leland, Charles Godfrey, poet, essayist, and humorist, b. Philadelphia, Pa., 1824; d. Florence, Italy, March 20, 1903. [1; 2; 3; 4; 5; 6; 7; 8; 9; 71]

Leland, Henry Perry, humorist, b. Philadelphia, Pa., 1828; d. Philadelphia, Pa., Sept. 22, 1868. (3; 6; 8]

Leland, John, clergyman, b. Grafton, Mass., 1754; d. North Adams, Mass., Jan. 14, 1841. [1; 3; 4]

Leland, Samuel Phelps, lecturer, b. Huntsburg, O., 1837; d. ? [10]

Leland, Sherman, genealogist, b. 1783; d. 1853.

Lemay, Georges, journalist, b. St. Paul, Minn., 1857; d. New York, N.Y., April 17, 1902. [27]

Lemay, Hugolin Marie, priest and bibliographer, b. 1877; d. Montreal, Que., June 25, 1938. [27]

Lemay, Léon Pamphile, poet and novelist, b. Lotbinière, Lower Canada, 1837; d. St. Jean-Deschaillons, Que., June 11, 1918. [27]

Lemcke, Mrs. Gesine, née Knubel, writer on cooking, b. Bremen, Germany, 1841; d. New York, N.Y., 1904. [8; 10]

Le Mercier, Andrew, clergyman, b. Caën, France, 1692; d. Boston, Mass., March 31, 1763. [3]

Lemieux, Rodolphe, lawyer and politician, b, Montreal, Que., 1866; d. Montreal, Que., Sept. 29, 1937. [27]

Lemly, Henry Rowan, soldier, b. near Bethania, N.C., 1851; d. Washington, D.C., Oct. 12, 1925. [10]

Le Moine, Sir James MacPherson, historian, b. Quebec, Lower Canada, 1825; d. Quebec, Que., Feb. 5, 1912. [27]

Lemon, Joel Bunyan, clergyman, b. Nace, Va., 1862; d. Providence, R.I., Jan. 4, 1936.

Lemore, Clara. See Roberts, Mrs. Clara, née Lemore.

Le Moyne, Louis Valcoulon, landscape architect, b. Chicago, Ill., 1860; d. Kenilworth, Ill., July 28, 1928. [10]

Lendrum, John, historian, fl. 1795-1836.

Lenker, John Nicholas, clergyman, b. Sunbury, Pa., 1858; d. Minneapolis, Minn., May 16, 1929. [4; 10]

Lennox, Mrs. Charlotte, née Ramsay, novelist and poet, b. New York, N.Y., 1720; d. Westminster, England, Jan. 4, 1804. [4; 7]

Lenoir, Joseph, poet, b. near Montreal, Lower Canada, 1822; d. April 3, 1861. [27]

Lenski, Richard Charles Henry, clergyman, b. Prussia, 1864; d. Columbus, O., 1936. [10; 11]

Lent, William Bement, traveller, b. 1842; d. Norfolk, Conn., June 23, 1902. [8]

Lentilhon, Eugène, engineer, b. New York, N.Y., 1869; d. Paris, France, Jan. 25, 1932. [62]

Lenygon, Francis Henry, interior decorator, b. Lincoln, England, 1877; d. New York, N.Y., June 12, 1943. [10]

Leonard, Agnes. See Hill, Mrs. Agnes, née Leonard.

Leonard, Baird, See Zogbaum, Mrs. Baird Leonard.

Leonard, Charles Hall, clergyman, b. Northwood, N.H., 1822; d. 1918. [10]

Leonard, Charles Henri, physician, b. Akron, O., 1850; d. Detroit, Mich., July 31, 1925. [10]

Leonard, Daniel, jurist, b. Norton, Mass., 1740; d. London, England, June 27, 1829. [3; 7; 8]

Leonard, Delavan Levant, clergyman, b. Pendleton, N.Y., 1834; d. Oberlin, O., Jan. 26, 1917. [10; 70]

Leonard, Eddie, actor, b. 1875; d. New York, N.Y., July 29, 1941.

Leonard, Fred Eugene, educationist. b. Darlington, Wis., 1866; d. Oberlin, O., Dec. 10, 1922. [10]

Leonard, Gardner Cotrell, manufacturer, b. West Springfield, Mass., 1865; d. Albany, N.Y., April 15, 1921. [61]

Leonard, Jacob Calvin, clergyman, b. Lexington, N.C., 1867; d. Lexington, N.C., March 15, 1943.

Leonard, John William, editor, b. London, England, 1849; d. Brooklyn, N.Y., June 30, 1932. [8; 10]

Leonard, Joseph Alexander, local historian, b. Cambridge, Md., 1830; d. Rochester, Minn., Dec. 28, 1908. [70]

Leonard, Levi Washburn, clergyman and educationist. b. Bridgewater, Mass., 1790; d. Exeter, N.H., Dec. 12, 1864. [1; 3]

Leonard, Lewis Alexander, historical writer, b. 1845; d. 1926.

Leonard, Mary Hall, educationist, b. Bridgewater, Mass., 1847; d. Rochester, Mass., Nov., 1921. [4; 10]

Leonard, Robert Josselyn, educationist, b. San José, Calif., 1885; d. New York, N.Y., Feb. 9, 1929. [1; 10; 11]

Leonard, Sterling Andrus, educationist, b. National City, Calif., 1888; d. Lake Mendota, Wis., May 15, 1931. [1; 10; 11]

Leonard, William Andrew, bishop, b. Southport, Conn., 1848; d. Gambier, O., Sept. 21, 1930. [1; 3; 4; 10]

Leonard, William Edwin, physician, b. 1855; d. Minneapolis, Minn., Aug. 28, 1935.

Leonard, William Ellery, educationist, b. Plainfield, N.J., 1876; d. Madison, Wis., May 2, 1944. [7; 10; 11]

Leonard, Zenas, trapper, b. near Clearfield, Pa., 1809; d. Sibley, Mo., July 14, 1857. [1; 7; 9]

Leonowens, Mrs. Annie Harriette, née **Crawford,** educationist, b. Caernarvon, Wales, 1834; d. Montreal, Que., Jan. 19, 1915. [3; 8; 10]

Le Plongeon, Mrs. Alice, née **Dixon,** explorer, b. 1851; d. ?

Leprohon, Mrs. Rosanna Eleanor, née **Mullins,** novelist and poet, b. Montreal, Lower Canada, 1832; d. Montreal, Que., Sept. 20, 1879. [27]

Lerner, Eugene, psychologist, b. Budapest, Hungary, 1901; d. New York, N.Y., Sept. 21, 1944.

Le Roux, Mrs. Hugues. See Van Vorst, Mrs. Bessie, née McGinnis.

Le Row, Caroline Bigelow, educationist, b. New Brighton, N.Y., 1843; d. ? [10]

Le Roy, James Alfred, historian, b. 1875; d. Fort Bayard, N.M., Feb. 26, 1909. [39]

Leroy, Louis, pathologist, b. Chelsea, Mass., 1874; d. Memphis, Tenn., May 9, 1944. [10]

Lesley, J. Peter, geologist, b. Philadelphia, Pa., 1819; d. Philadelphia, Pa., June 1, 1903. [1; 3; 4; 6; 7; 8; 9]

Lesley, Mrs. Susan Inches, née **Lyman,** biographer, b. Northampton, Mass., 1823; d. 1904. [3; 8; 10]

Leslie, Amy (pseud.). See Brown-Buck, Mrs. Lillie, née West.

Leslie, Eliza, home economist, b. Philadelphia, Pa., 1878; d. Gloucester, N.J., Jan. 1, 1858. [1; 3; 4; 6; 7; 9]

Leslie, Mrs. Madeline (pseud.). See Baker, Mrs. Harriette Newell, née Woods.

Leslie, Mary, novelist and versifier, b. Wellington county, Ont., 1842; d. Toronto, Ont., March 1, 1920. [27]

Leslie, Mrs. Miriam Florence, née **Follin,** editor and publisher, b. New Orleans, La., about 1836; d. New York, N.Y., Sept. 18, 1914. [1; 3; 7; 10]

Lesperance, Jean Talon, journalist, b. St. Louis, Mo., 1838; d. Montreal, Que., March 10, 1891. [27]

Lesquereux, Leo, palaeobotanist, b. near Neuchâtel, Switzerland, 1806; d. Columbus, O., Oct. 25, 1889. [1; 3; 4; 8]

Lessing, Bruno (pseud.). See Block, Rudolph.

Lester, Charles Edwards, clergyman and journalist, b. Griswold, Conn., 1815; d. Detroit, Mich., Jan. 29, 1890. [1; 3; 4; 6; 7; 8; 9]

L'Estrange, Corinne (pseud.). See Hartshorne, Henry.

Le Sueur, William Dawson, biographer, b. Quebec, Lower Canada, 1840; d. Ottawa, Ont., Sept. 28, 1917. [27]

Letchworth, William Pryor, philanthropist, b. Brownville, N.H., 1823; d. Castile, N.Y., Dec. 1, 1910. [1; 4; 10]

Lett, William Pittman, journalist, b. Wexford county, Ireland, 1819; d. Ottawa, Ont., Aug. 15, 1892. [27]

Letterman, Jonathan, army surgeon, b. Canonsburg, Pa., 1824; d. San Francisco, Calif., March 15, 1872. [1; 4]

Leuba, James Henry, psychologist, b. Neuchâtel, Switzerland, 1868; d. Winter Park, Fla., Dec. 8, 1946. [7; 10; 11]

Leupp, Francis Ellington, journalist, b. New York, N.Y., 1849; d. Washington, D.C., Nov. 19, 1918. [1; 4; 7; 10]

Le Van, William Barnet, engineer, b. Easton, Pa., 1829; d. ? [6]

Levasseur, Nazaire, journalist, b. Quebec, Que., 1848; d. Quebec, Que., Nov. 8, 1927. [27]

Levere, William Collin, miscellaneous writer, b. New Haven, Conn., 1872; d. Evanston, Ill., Feb. 22, 1927. [10; 11]

Leverett, Charles Edward, genealogist, d. 1868. [51]

Leverett, Frederick Percival, educationist, b. Portsmouth, N.H., 1803; d. Boston, Mass., Oct. 6, 1836. [3; 8; 51]

Levering, Joseph Mortimer, bishop, b. Hardin county, Tenn., 1849; d. Bethlehem, Pa., April 4, 1908. [1]

Levering, Mrs. Julia, née **Henderson,** historian, b. Covington, Ind., 1851; d. Feb. 19, 1922.

Levermore, Charles Herbert, educationist, b. Mansfield, Conn., 1856; d. Berkeley, Calif., Oct. 20, 1927. [1; 4; 10; 11; 62]

Leverson, Montague Richard, physician, b. London, England, 1830; d. ? [10]

Le Vert, Mrs. Octavia, née **Walton,** traveller, b. near Augusta, Ga., about 1810; d. Augusta, Ga., March 13, 1877. [3; 4; 8; 34]

Leverton, Garrett Hasty, editor, b. 1896; d. New York, N.Y., Nov. 11, 1949.

Levi, Harry, rabbi, b. Cincinnati, O., 1875; d. Brookline, Mass., June 13, 1944. [7; 10]

Levison, William H., humorist, b. 1822; d. 1857.

Levitas, Arnold, typographer, b. Libau, Latvia, 1883; d. East Orange, N.J., Aug. 1934. [10]

Levy, Florence Nightingale, educationist, b. New York, N.Y., 1870; d. New York, N.Y., Nov. 15, 1947.

Levy, John, psychiatrist, b. London, England, 1897; d. Boston, Mass., July 11, 1938. [13]

Lewin, Raphael De Cordova, rabbi, b. West Indies, 1844; d. New York, N.Y., June 26, 1886. [3; 8]

Lewis, Abram Herbert, clergyman, b. Scott, N.Y., 1836; d. Plainfield, N.J., Nov., 1908. [8; 10]

Lewis, Alexander, clergyman, b. Hudson, Wis., 1864; d. Kansas City, Mo., May 7, 1912. [10]

Lewis, Alfred Henry, journalist and novelist, b. Cleveland, O., about 1858; d. New York, N.Y., Dec. 23, 1914. [1; 7; 10]

Lewis, Alonzo, poet, b. Lynn, Mass., 1794; d. Lynn, Mass., Jan. 21, 1861. [3; 6; 7; 71]

Lewis, Caleb (pseud.). See Lewis, Edwin Herbert.

Lewis, Calvin Leslie, educationist, b. Nineveh, N.Y., 1868; d. Oquaga Lake, N.Y., June 13, 1935. [10]

Lewis, Charles Bertrand, humorist, b. Liverpool, O., 1842; d. Brooklyn, N.Y., Aug. 21, 1924. [1; 4; 7; 8; 9; 10]

Lewis, Charlton Miner, educationist, b. Brooklyn, N.Y., 1866; d. New Haven, Conn., March 12, 1923. [7; 8; 10; 62]

Lewis, Charlton Thomas, educationist, b. West Chester, Pa., 1834; d. Morristown, N.J., May 26, 1904. [1; 3; 4; 6; 10; 62]

Lewis, Mrs. Constance, née **Deming,** poet, b. New York, N.Y.; d. Augusta, Ga., Jan. 28, 1940.

Lewis, Dean De Witt, surgeon, b. Kewanee, Ill., 1874; d. Baltimore, Md., Oct. 9, 1941. [10]

Lewis, Dio, physician, b. Auburn, N.Y., 1823; d. Yonkers, N.Y., May 21, 1886. [3; 4; 6; 8]

Lewis, Ebenezer Ellesville, lawyer, b. Bishop Stortford, England, 1841; d. Sioux City, Ia., Sept. 6, 1919. [10]

Lewis, Edward Samuel, clergyman, b. Natick, Mass., 1855; d. Cincinnati, O., Oct. 14, 1934. [10]

Lewis, Edwin Herbert, educationist, b. Westerly, R.I., 1866; d. Palo Alto, Calif., June 6, 1938. [7; 10]

Lewis, Elisha Jarrett, physician, b. Baltimore, Md., 1820; d. Philadelphia, Pa., Feb. 10, 1877. [3; 8]

Lewis, Ellis, jurist, b. Lewisberry, Pa., 1798; d. Philadelphia, Pa., March 19, 1871. [1; 3; 4]

Lewis, Enoch, mathematician and publicist, b. Radnor, Pa., 1776; d. Philadelphia, Pa., June 14, 1856. [1; 3; 4; 8]

Lewis, Mrs. Estelle Anna Blanche, née **Robinson,** poet and dramatist, b. near Baltimore, Md., 1824; d. London, England, Nov. 24, 1880. [1; 3; 4; 6; 7; 8; 34; 71]

Lewis, Ethel, interior decorator, b. 1896; d. Balboa, C.Z., in the spring of 1944.

Lewis, Francis Albert, lawyer, b. 1857; d. Springfield, Mass., Nov. 25, 1917. [8; 10]

Lewis, Frank Grant, librarian, b. Gang Mills, N.Y., 1865; d. Penn Yann, N.Y., Nov. 19, 1945. [7; 10; 11]

Lewis, George Andrew, writer on stammering, b. 1870; d. 1915.

Lewis, George Henry, lawyer and stockbroker, b. New Britain, Conn., 1842; d. Des Moines, Ia., March 16, 1913. [62]

Lewis, Gilbert Newton, chemist, b. Weymouth, Mass., 1875; d. Berkeley, Calif., March 23, 1946. [10; 13; 51]

Lewis, Mrs. H.C. See Cameron, Margaret.

Lewis, Mrs. Harriet, novelist, b. Penn Yann, N.Y., 1841; d. Rochester, N.Y., May 20, 1878. [3b; 8]

Lewis, Henry Clay, humorist, fl. 1850-1858.

Lewis, Henry Harrison, writer of books for boys, b. Anderson, Ind., 1863; d. ? [10]

Lewis, Isaac Newton, lawyer, b. 1848; d. Walpole, Mass., 1937. [4; 8; 51]

Lewis, James Hamilton, lawyer and politician, b. Danville, Va., 1863; d. Washington, D.C., April 9, 1939. [4; 10]

Lewis, John, lawyer, b. Suffield, Conn., 1842; d. Lawrence, Kans., June 26, 1921. [62]

Lewis, John, journalist, b. Toronto, Ont., 1858; d. Toronto, Ont., May 18, 1935. [27]

Lewis, John Frederick, lawyer, b. Philadelphia, Pa., 1860; d. Philadelphia, Pa., Dec. 24, 1932. [10]

Lewis, Judd Mortimer, poet, b. Fulton, N.Y., 1867; d. Houston, Tex., July 25, 1945. [7; 10; 11]

Lewis, Lawrence, lawyer, b. Philadelphia, Pa., 1856; d. near West Chester, Pa., Sept. 2, 1890. [1; 3; 6; 8]

Lewis, Leo Rich, musician, b. South Woodstock, Vt., 1865; d. Medford, Mass., Sept. 8, 1945. [10; 11; 20]

Lewis, Leon (pseud.), novelist, fl. 1888-1899.

Lewis, Lloyd Downs, journalist, b. Pendleton, Ind., 1891; d. Libertyville, Ill., April 21, 1949. [7; 10]

Lewis, Lowery Laymon, educationist, b. Newport, Tenn., 1869; d. Stillwater, Okla., Sept. 26, 1922. [10]

Lewis, Nelson Peter, civil engineer, b. Red Hook, N.Y., 1856; d. Brooklyn, N.Y., March 30, 1924. [10]

Lewis, Orlando Faulkland, penologist, b. Boston, Mass., 1873; d. New Rochelle, N.Y., Feb. 24, 1922. [1; 10; 11]

Lewis, Mrs. Sarah Anna, née **Robinson.** See Lewis, Mrs. Estelle Anna Blanche, née Robinson.

Lewis, Tayler, educationist, b. Northumberland, N.Y., 1802; d. Schenectady, N.Y., May 11, 1877. [1; 3; 4; 6; 8]

Lewis, Terrell, genealogist, b. 1811; d. 1893. [34]

Lewis, Thomas Hamilton, clergyman, b. Dover, Del., 1852; d. Washington, D.C., June 14, 1929. [10]

Lewis, Virgil Anson, historian, b. Mason county, W. Va., 1848; d. Mason, W. Va., Dec. 5, 1912. [10]

Lewis, Wells, soldier, b. 1917; d. on active service in France, Oct. 29, 1944.

Lewis, William Draper, lawyer, b. Philadelphia, Pa., 1867; d. Northeast Harbor, Me., Sept. 2, 1949. [10; 11]

Lewis, William Henry, clergyman, b. Litchfield, Conn., 1803; d. 1877. [6]

Lewisohn, Mrs. Mary Arnold, née **Crocker,** playwright, b. Surrey, England; d. Brooklyn, N.Y., April 8, 1946. [11]

Ley, John Cole, clergyman, b. 1822; d. Jacksonville, Fla., Aug. 19, 1907. [34]

Leyburn, John, clergyman, b. Lexington, Va., 1814; d. 1894. [3; 6; 34]

Leypoldt, Frederick, bibliographer, b. Stuttgart, Germany, 1835; d. New York, N.Y., March 31, 1884. [1; 3; 4; 6; 7]

Liautard, Alexandre François Augustin, physician and veterinary surgeon, b. 1835; d. 1918.

Libbey, Laura Jean, novelist, b. New York, N.Y., 1862; d. Brooklyn, N.Y., Oct. 25, 1924. [4; 7; 10]

Libbey, William, educationist, b. Jersey City, N.J., 1855; d. Princeton, N.J., Sept. 6, 1927. [10]

Libby, Melanchthon Fennessy, educationist, b. Port Hope, Ont., 1864; d. Boulder, Colo., May 2, 1921. [10]

Liberman, Simon Isaevich, historian, b. Russia, 1881; d. New York, N.Y., Jan. 5, 1946.

Lichtwitz, Leopold, physician, b. Germany, 1876; d. New Rochelle, N.Y., March 18, 1943.

Licks, H.E. (pseud.). See Merriman, Mansfield.

Liddell, Mark Harvey, educationist, b. Clearfield, Pa., 1866; d. Orleans, Mass., July 28, 1936. [7; 10]

Lieber, Francis, educationist, b. Berlin, Germany, 1800; d. New York, N.Y., Oct. 2, 1872. [1; 3; 4; 6; 8; 34]

Lieber, Guido Norman, soldier, b. Columbia, S.C., 1837; d. Washington, D.C., April 25, 1923. [8; 10]

Lieber, Oscar Montgomery, geologist, b. Boston, Mass., 1830; d. Richmond, Va., June 27, 1862. [3; 4; 8]

Liebman, Joshua Loth, rabbi, b. Hamilton, O., 1907; d. Brookline, Mass., June 9, 1948.

Liefeld, Ernest Theophilus, educationist, b. New Haven, Conn., 1860; d. Berne, Switzerland, June 10, 1930. [62]

Liggett, Hunter, soldier, b. Reading, Pa., 1857; d. San Francisco, Calif., Dec. 30, 1935. [1a; 10; 11]

Liggett, Walter William, journalist, b. Benson, Minn., 1886; d. Minneapolis, Minn., Dec. 9, 1935. [1a; 7; 10]

Liggins, John, missionary, b. Nuneaton, England, May 11, 1829; d. Ocean City, N.J., Jan. 8, 1912. [8; 10]

Light, George Washington, journalist, b. Portland, Me., 1809; d. Somerville, Mass., Jan. 27, 1868. [3; 8]

Light, Golden (pseud.). See Hicks, William Watkins.

Lighton, William Beebey, clergyman, b. 1805; d. ?

Lighton, William Rheem, novelist, b. Lycoming county, Pa., 1866; d. Los Angeles, Calif., Jan. 25, 1923. [7; 10]

Lile, William Minor, lawyer and educationist, b. Trinity, Ala., 1859; d. University, Va., Dec. 13, 1935. [1a; 10]

Lilienthal, Howard, surgeon, b. Albany, N.Y., 1861; d. New York, N.Y., April 30, 1946. [10; 11]

Lilienthal, Samuel, physician, b. 1815; d. 1891. [6]

Liljencrantz, Ottilie Adaline, novelist, b. Chicago, Ill., 1876; d. Chicago, Ill., 1910. [7; 10]

Lilley, George, mathematician, b. Kewanee, Ill., 1854; d. Eugene, Ore., 1904. [10]

Lillibridge, William ʳ Otis, novelist, b. Union county, S.D., 1877; d. 1909. [10]

Lillie, Adam, clergyman, b. Glasgow, Scotland, 1803; d. Montreal, Que., Oct., 1869. [27]

Lillie, Mrs. Lucy Cecil, née **White,** writer of books for boys and girls, b. New York, N.Y., 1855; d. about 1908. [6; 7; 8; 10]

Lilly, David Clay, clergyman, b. Irvine, Ky., 1870; d. Reynolds, N.C., May 28, 1939. [10]

Lincoln, Abraham, sixteenth president of the United States, b. Hardin county, Ky., 1809; d. Washington, D.C., 1865. [1; 2; 3; 4; 5; 6; 7; 8]

Lincoln, Charles Henry, archivist and historian, b. Milbury, Mass., 1869; d. Worcester, Mass., Jan. 31, 1938. [51]

Lincoln, Charles Zebina, lawyer, b. 1848; d. July 27, 1925.

Lincoln, David Francis, physician, b. Boston, Mass., 1841; d. Boston, Mass., Oct. 15, 1916. [3; 8; 10; 51]

Lincoln, Enoch, poet, b. Worcester, Mass., 1788; d. Augusta, Me., Oct. 8, 1829. [3]

Lincoln, Heman, clergyman, b. Boston, Mass., 1821; d. Newton Centre, Mass., Oct. 18, 1887. [3; 6; 8]

Lincoln, Mrs. Jeanie Thomas, née **Gould,** novelist, b. Troy, N.Y., 1846; d. Aug. 8, 1921. [3; 7; 10]

Lincoln, Joseph Crosby, novelist, b. Brewster, Mass., 1870; d. Winter Park, Fla., March 10, 1944. [4; 7; 10; 11]

Lincoln, Levi, politician, b. Hingham, Mass., 1749; d. Worcester, Mass., April 14, 1820. [3; 4]

Lincoln, Mrs. Mary Johnson, née **Bailey,** writer on cooking, b. South Attleboro, Mass., 1844; d. Boston, Mass., Dec. 2, 1921. [1; 3; 4; 10]

Lincoln, Natalie Sumner, novelist, b. Washington, D.C., 1822; d. Washington, D.C., Aug. 31, 1935. [7; 10; 11]

Lincoln, Solomon, historian and genealogist, b. 1804; d. 1881.

Lincoln, Varnum, poet, b. 1819; d. 1907.

Lincoln, Waldo, genealogist, b. Worcester, Mass., 1849; d. Worcester, Mass., April 7, 1933. [4; 10; 11; 51]

Lincoln, William, antiquary, b. Worcester, Mass., 1801; d. Worcester, Mass., Oct. 5, 1843. [3]

Lind, George Dallas, educationist, b. 1847; d. ?

Lindberg, Conrad Emil, clergyman, b. Sweden, 1852; d. Rock Island, Ill., Aug. 2, 1930. [1; 10]

Lindbergh, Charles Augustus, lawyer and politician, b. Stockholm, Sweden, 1859; d. Crookston, Minn., May 24, 1924. [1; 10]

Lindemann, Paul, clergyman, b. Pittsburgh, Pa., 1881; d. St. Paul, Minn., Dec. 13, 1938.

Linderman, Frank Bird, trapper and journalist, b. Cleveland, O., 1869; d. Somers, Mont., May 12, 1938. [7; 10; 11]

Linderman, Henry Richard, economist, b. Pike county, Pa., 1825; d. Washington, D.C., Jan. 27, 1879. [1; 3; 4]

Lindgren, Waldemar, geologist, b. Sweden, 1860; d. Brookline, Mass., Nov. 3, 1939. [10; 13]

Lindley, Curtis Holbrook, lawyer, b. Marysville, Calif., 1850; d. San Francisco, Calif., Nov. 20, 1920. [1; 10]

Lindley, Jacob, educationist, b. Washington county, Pa., 1774; d. Connellsville, Pa., Jan. 29, 1857. [1; 4]

Lindley, Walter, physician, b. Monrovia, Ind., 1852; d. Los Angeles, Calif., Jan. 24, 1922. [4; 10]

Lindsay, Mrs. Anna Robertson, née **Brown,** religious writer, b. Washington, D.C., 1864; d. New York, N.Y., Feb. 28, 1948. [10]

Lindsay, Clara A., poet, b. 1844; d. 1909.

Lindsay, Frederic Nye, clergyman, b. Troy, N.Y., 1866; d. Rochester, N.Y., Feb. 26, 1939. [62]

Lindsay, James Hubert, newspaper publisher, b. Casanova, Va., 1862; d. Charlottesville, Va., Feb. 7, 1933. [10]

Lindsay, Lionel St. Georges, priest, b. Montreal, Que., 1849; d. Quebec, Que., Feb. 10, 1921. [27; 32]

Lindsay, Nicholas Vachell, poet, b. Springfield, Ill., 1879; d. Springfield, Ill., Dec. 5, 1931. [1; 4; 7; 10; 11; 72]

Lindsay, Thomas Bond, educationist, b. New York, N.Y., 1853; d. Glenview, Ky., July 22, 1909. [10; 60]

Lindsay, Vachell. See Lindsay, Nicholas Vachell.

Lindsay, Walter Manville, lawyer, b. 1867; d. 1907.

Lindsey, Benjamin Barr, jurist and reformer, b. Jackson, Tenn., 1869; d. Los Angeles, Calif., March 26, 1943. [4; 7; 10; 12]

Lindsey, Charles, journalist, b. Lincolnshire, England, 1820; d. Toronto, Ont., April 12, 1908. [27]

Lindsey, George Goldwin Smith, lawyer, b. Toronto, Ont., 1860; d. Toronto, Ont., May 27, 1920. [27]

Lindsey, William, poet and novelist, b. Fall River, Mass., 1858; d. Boston, Mass., Nov. 25, 1922. [1; 7; 8; 10]

Lindsley, David Philip, teacher of stenography, b. 1834; d. 1897.

Lindsley, John Berrien, physician, b. Princeton, N.J., 1822; d. Nashville, Tenn., Dec. 7, 1897. [1; 3; 4; 6; 34]

Lindsley, Philip, educationist, b. Morristown, N.J., 1786; d. Nashville, Tenn., May 25, 1855. [1; 3; 4; 6; 34]

Lindsley, Philip, lawyer, b. Nashville, Tenn., 1842; d. ? [34]

Linebarger, Paul Myron Wentworth, lawyer, b. Warren, Ill., 1871; d. Washington, D.C., Feb. 20, 1939. [7; 10; 11]

Linen, James, poet, b. Scotland, 1808; d. New York, N.Y., Nov. 20, 1873. [3; 8; 35]

Ling, George Herbert, mathematician, b. Wallacetown, Ont., 1874; d. Toronto, Ont., Oct. 21, 1942. [11; 27]

Lingley, Charles Ramsdell, historian, b. Worcester, Mass., 1877; d. Hanover, N.H., Jan. 30, 1934. [10; 11]

Lining, John, physician, b. Scotland, 1708; d. Charleston, S.C., 1760. [3; 8]

Link, Samuel Albert, educationist, b. near Lebanon, Tenn., 1848; d. ? [10; 34]

Linkinwater, Tim (pseud.). See Waldo, James Curtis.

Linn, James Weber, educationist and novelist, b. Winnebago, Ill., 1876; d. Lakeside, Mich., July 16, 1939. [7; 10]

Linn, John Blair, clergyman and poet, b. Shippensburg, Pa., 1777; d. Philadelphia, Pa., Aug. 30, 1804. [1; 3; 4; 6; 7; 8]

Linn, John Blair, historian, b. Lewisburg, Pa., 1831; d. 1899. [3; 8]

Linn, John Joseph, pioneer, b. Ireland, 1798; d. Texas, 1885. [34]

Linn, William, clergyman, b. Shippensburg, Pa., 1752; d. Albany, N.Y., Jan. 8, 1808. [3; 4; 8]

Linn, William, lawyer, b. New York, N.Y., 1790; d. Ithaca, N.Y., Jan. 14, 1867. [3; 8]

Linn, William Alexander, journalist, b. Sussex, N.J., 1846; d. Hackensack, N.J., Feb. 23, 1917. [1; 8; 10; 62]

Linnell, Gertrude Baldwin, advertising manager, d. New York, N.Y., March 18, 1933.

Linscott, Thomas S., clergyman, b. Devonshire, England, 1846; d. Quebec, Que., March 1, 1919. [27]

Linsley, George Thomas, clergyman, b. New Haven, Conn., 1864; d. Farmington, Conn., Aug. 6, 1937. [62]

Linthicum, Richard, journalist, b. Libertytown, Md., 1859; d. Washington, D.C., Jan. 20, 1934. [7; 8; 10]

Linton, John James Edmonstoune, pioneer, b. Rothesay, Scotland, 1804; d. Stratford, Ont., Jan. 23, 1869. [27]

Linton, Moses L., physician, b. 1808; d. 1872.

Lipari, Angelo, educationist, b. Palermo, Sicily, 1887; d. New York, N.Y., Nov. 4, 1947.

Lipman, Jacob Goodale, agricultural chemist, b. Latvia, 1874; d. New Brunswick, N.J., April 19, 1939. [10; 11; 13]

Lippard, George, novelist, b. near Yellow Springs, Pa., 1822; d. Philadelphia, Pa., Feb. 9, 1854. [1; 3; 6; 7; 8; 9]

Lippe, Adolph, physician, b. Berlin, Germany, 1812; d. Philadelphia, Pa., Jan. 23, 1888. [3b]

Lippé, Joseph Alfred, priest, b. Lanoraie, Que., 1865; d. Côteau Station, Que., Jan. 26, 1915. [32]

Lippincott, Mrs. Esther J., née **Trimble,** educationist, b. 1838; d. 1888. [8]

Lippincott, James Starr, genealogist, b. Philadelphia, Pa., 1819; d. Haddonfield, N.J., March 17, 1885. [3]

Lippincott, Mrs. Sara Jane, née Clarke, poet and miscellaneous writer, b. Pompey, N.Y., 1823; d. New Rochelle, N.Y., April 20, 1904. [1; 3; 4; 6; 7; 8; 9; 10]

Lippincott, William Adams, poultryman, b. Jacksonville, Ill., 1882; d. Beverley, Calif., Jan. 5, 1931. [10]

Lippitt, Francis James, lawyer, b. Providence, R.I., 1812; d. Washington, D.C., Dept. 27, 1902. [3b]

Lipscomb, Andrew Adgate, clergyman, b. Georgetown, D.C., 1816; d. Athens, Ga., Nov. 23, 1890. [1; 3; 4; 6; 8; 34]

Lipscomb, David, clergyman, b. Franklin county, Tenn., 1831; d. Nashville, Tenn., 1918. [10]

Lipsky, Abraham, educationist, b. Germany, 1872; d. Washington, D.C., May 2, 1946.

Lisle, William McIntire, clergyman, b. New Haven, O., 1842; d. Boston, Mass., Oct. 25, 1910.

Listemann, Bernhard, violinist, b. Germany, 1841; d. Boston, Mass., Feb. 11, 1917. [1; 10]

Litchfield, Grace Denio, poet and novelist, b. New York, N.Y., 1849; d. Goshen, N.Y., Dec. 4, 1944. [7; 11]

Litere (pseud.). See Sommers, Lillian E.

Littell, John Stockton, biographer, b. Burlington, N.J., 1806; d. Philadelphia, Pa., July 11, 1875. [3; 4; 6]

Littell, Philip, journalist, b. Brookline, Mass., 1868; d. Oct. 31, 1943. [10]

Littell, Squire, physician, b. Burlington, N.J., 1803; d. Philadelphia, Pa., July 4, 1886. [3; 6; 8]

Littell, William, lawyer, b. New Jersey, 1768; d. Frankfort, Ky., Sept. 26, 1824. [1; 3; 4; 6; 7; 8; 9; 34]

Little, Arthur West, soldier, b. New York, N.Y., 1873; d. New York, N.Y., July 18, 1943. [10]

Little, Arthur Wilde, clergyman, b. Brooklyn, N.Y., 1856; d. Evanston, Ill., 1910. [8; 10]

Little, Charles Eugene, clergyman, b. Waterbury, Vt., 1838; d. April 15, 1918. [8; 10]

Little, Charles Joseph, educationist, b. Philadelphia, Pa., 1840; d. Chicago, Ill., March 11, 1911. [1; 10]

Little, Frances (pseud.). See Macaulay, Mrs. Fannie, née Caldwell.

Little, George Obadiah, clergyman, b. Madison, Ind., 1839; d. Washington, D.C., Nov. 4, 1925. [10; 11]

Little, George Thomas, librarian, b. Auburn, Me., 1857; d. Brunswick, Me., Aug. 5, 1915. [10]

Little, Henry Gilman, writer of reminiscences, b. 1813; d. 1900.

Little, John Andrew, autobiographer, b. 1796; d. Delaware, O., Jan. 13, 1877.

Little, John Peyton, physician and local historian, b. 1818; d. 1873.

Little, Lucius Powhattan, biographer, b. 1836; d. ?

Little, Seelye William, physician, b. Rochester, N.Y., 1867; d. Rochester, N.Y., Feb. 27, 1937. [69]

Little, Mrs. Sophia Louise, née Robbins, poet, b. Newport, R.I., 1799; d. about 1890. [3; 8]

Little, William, local historian, b. Warren, N.H., 1833; d. Manchester, N.H., Dec. 19, 1893. [49]

Littlefield, George Emery, bookseller, b. Boston, Mass., 1844; d. Hamilton, Mass., Sept. 4, 1915. [7; 10; 51]

Littlefield, Milton Smith, clergyman, b. New York, N.Y., 1864; d. Corona, Long Island, N.Y., June 11, 1934. [10; 11]

Littlefield, Walter, editor and translator, b. Boston, Mass., 1867; d. New Canaan, Conn., March 25, 1948. [7; 10]

Littlejohn, Abram Newkirk, bishop, b. Florida, N.Y., 1824; d. Williamstown, Mass., Aug. 3, 1901. [1; 3; 4; 10]

Littlejohn, Flavius Josephus, lawyer, b. Herkimer county, N.Y., 1804; d. Allegan, Mich., April 28, 1880. [39]

Littleton, Jesse Talbot, educationist, b. Portsmouth, Va., 1856; d. Fort Pierce, Fla., Jan. 26, 1929. [10]

Littleton, Mark (pseud.). See Kennedy, John Pendleton.

Livermore, Abiel Abbot, clergyman, b. Wilton, N.H., 1811; d. Wilton, N.H., Nov. 28, 1892. [1; 3; 4; 6; 8; 51]

Livermore, Daniel Parker, clergyman, b. Worcester, Mass., 1819; d. Melrose, Mass., July 5, 1899. [3b]

Livermore, George, antiquary, b. Cambridge, Mass., 1809; d. Cambridge, Mass., Aug. 30, 1865. [1; 3; 4]

Livermore, Harriet, poet and religious enthusiast, b. 1788; d. 1868.

Livermore, Mrs. Mary Ashton, née Rice, female suffragist, b. Boston, Mass., 1820; d. Melrose, Mass., May 23, 1905. [1; 3; 4; 6; 7; 8; 9; 10]

Livermore, Samuel, lawyer, b. Concord, N.H., 1786; d. Florence, Ala., July 11, 1833. [1; 3; 4; 6; 8; 34]

Livermore, Samuel Truesdale, clergyman, b. 1824; d. 1892.

Livermore, Thomas Leonard, financier, b. b. 1844; d. Boston, Mass., Jan. 9, 1918. [10]

Livermore, William Roscoe, soldier, b. Cambridge, Mass., 1843; d. Washington, D.C., Sept. 26, 1919. [10]

Livesay, John Frederick Bligh, journalist, b. Isle of Wight, England, 1875; d. Clarkson, Ont., June 15, 1944. [27]

Livingston, Alfred Tennyson, poet, b. 1849; d. 1923.

Livingston, Edward, lawyer, b. Clermont, N.Y., 1764; d. Rhinebeck, N.Y., May 23, 1836. [1; 3; 4; 6; 7; 8]

Livingston, John Henry, clergyman, b. Poughkeepsie, N.Y., 1746; d. New Brunswick, N.J., Jan. 20, 1825. [1; 3; 4; 6]

Livingston, Luther Samuel, bibliographer, b. Grand Rapids, Mich., 1864; d. Cambridge, Mass., Dec. 24, 1914. [7]

Livingston, Mrs. Ophelia, née **Mead,** poet, b. 1807; d. 1873.

Livingston, Robert R., jurist, b. New York, N.Y., 1746; d. Clermont, N.Y., Feb. 26, 1813. [3; 4; 6; 8]

Livingston, Stuart, poet, b. Hamilton, Ont., 1865; d. Vancouver, B.C., Nov. 13, 1923. [27]

Livingston, William, historian, b. Albany, N.Y., 1723; d. Elizabethtown, N.J., July 25, 1790. [3; 4; 6; 7; 8; 9]

Livingstone, William, banker, b. Dundas, Ont., 1844; d. Detroit, Mich., Oct. 17, 1925. [10]

Lizars, Kathleen Macfarlane, historian, b. Stratford, Ont.; d. Toronto Ont., April 20, 1931. [27]

Lizars, Robina, historian, d. Toronto, Ont., Aug. 26, 1918. [27]

Lloyd, Alfred Henry, philosopher, b. Montclair, N.J., 1864; d. Detroit, Mich., May 11, 1927. [1; 4; 7; 10; 11; 51]

Lloyd, Arthur Selden, bishop, b. Alexandria county, Va., 1857; d. Darien, Conn., July 22, 1936. [10]

Lloyd, Cecil Francis, poet, b. Herefordshire, England, 1884; d. Winnipeg, Man., July 13, 1938. [27]

Lloyd, Curtis Gates, mycologist, b. Florence, Ky., 1859; d. Cincinnati, O., Nov. 11, 1926. [10; 13]

Lloyd, Frederick Ebenezer John, archbishop, b. Milford Haven, Wales, 1859; d. Chicago, Ill., 1933. [10; 11]

Lloyd, Henry Demarest, economist, b. New York, N.Y., 1847; d. Winnetka, Ill., Sept. 28, 1903. [1; 4; 7; 8; 10]

Lloyd, John Uri, pharmacist, b. West Bloomfield, N.Y., 1849; d. Los Angeles, Calif., April 9, 1936. [4; 7; 8; 10; 11]

Lloyd, Nelson McAllister, journalist and novelist, b. Philadelphia, Pa., 1872; d. Lawrenceville, N.J., Feb. 8, 1933. [7; 8; 10]

Lloyd, Rees, clergyman, b. 1759; d. 1838.

Lloyd, Robert, novelist, b. Birkenhead, England, 1864; d. Alameda, Calif., March 12, 1930. [35]

Lloyd, Wallace (pseud.). See Algie, James.

Lloyd, Warren Estelle, lawyer, b. Nebraska City, Neb., 1869; d. Los Angeles, Calif., Aug. 5, 1922. [62]

Llwyd, John Plummer Derwent, clergyman, b. Manchester, England, 1861; d. Halifax, N.S., Feb. 22, 1933. [11; 27]

Lobstein, Johann Friedrich Daniel, physician, b. 1777; d. 1840.

Lochhead, William, biologist, b. Perth county, Ont., 1864; d. Ste. Anne de Bellevue, Que., March 26, 1927. [27]

Locke, Charles Edward, bishop, b. Pittsburgh, Pa., 1858; d. Santa Monica, Calif., March 4, 1940. [7; 10; 11]

Locke, Clinton, See Locke, James Dewitt Clinton.

Locke, David Ross, journalist, b. Vestal, N.Y., 1833; d. Toledo, O., Feb. 15, 1888. [1; 3; 4; 6; 7; 71]

Locke, George Herbert, librarian, b. Beamsville, Ont., 1870; d. Toronto, Ont., Jan. 28, 1937. [10; 11; 27]

Locke, James, journalist and novelist, b. Buffalo, N.Y., 1869; d. New Haven, Conn., Feb. 11, 1928. [10; 62]

Locke, James Dewitt Clinton, clergyman, b. New York, N.Y., 1829; d. 1904. [8; 10]

Locke, Mrs. Jane Ermina, née **Starkweather,** poet, b. Worthington, Mass., 1805; d. Ashburnham, Mass., March 8, 1859. [3; 6; 7; 8]

Locke, John, educationist, b. Fryeburg, Me., 1792; d. Cincinnati, O., July 10, 1856. [1; 3; 4]

Locke, John Lymburner, clergyman, b. 1832; d. 1876. [38]

Locke, John Staples, educationist, b. Biddeford, Me., 1836; d. Saco, Me., 1906. [7; 8; 10; 38]

Locke, Leslie Leland, educationist, b Grove City, Pa., 1875; d. Brooklyn, N.Y., Aug. 28, 1943.

Locke, Richard Adams, journalist, b. New York, N.Y., 1800; d. Staten Island, N.Y., Feb. 16, 1871. [3; 4; 7; 8]

Locke, Una (pseud.). See Bailey, Mrs. Urania Locke, née Stoughton.

Lockhart, Arthur John, clergyman, b. King's county, N.S., 1850; d. Springfield, Mass., June 29, 1926. [7; 10; 27]

Lockhart, Walter Samuel, lawyer, b. Orange county, N.C., 1874; d. Durham, N.C., 1937. [10]

Lockridge, Ross Franklin, novelist, b. 1914; d. Bloomington, Ind., March 6, 1948. [10; 12]

Lockwood, Charles Daniel, surgeon, b. Effingham, Ill., 1868; d. Pasadena, Calif., June 11, 1932. [10]

Lockwood, George Browning, journalist and politician, b. Forest, Ill., 1872; d. Muncie, Ind., Feb. 12, 1932. [10; 11]

Lockwood, George Roe, physician, b. New York, N.Y., 1861; d. Washington, D.C., March 6, 1931. [10]

Lockwood, Henry Clay, lawyer, b. 1839; d. New York, N.Y., Dec. 24, 1902. [3b]

Lockwood, Ingersoll, lawyer and editor, b. Ossining, N.Y., 1841; d. Sept. 30, 1918. [7; 8]

Lockwood, John Hoyt, clergyman, b. Troy, N.Y., 1848; d. Springfield, Mass., Oct. 20, 1928. [69]

Lockwood, Mrs. Mary, née **Smith,** historical writer, b. 1831; d. Plymouth, Mass., Nov. 10, 1922. [4; 8]

Lockwood, Ralph Ingersoll, lawyer and novelist, b. Greenwich, Conn., 1798; d. April 12, 1858. [1; 7; 8; 9]

Lockwood, Samuel, clergyman, b. Nottinghamshire, England, 1819; d. Freehold, N.J., Jan. 9, 1894. [3b]

Lockwood, Thomas Dixon, electrical engineer, b. Staffordshire, England, 1848; d. Melrose, Mass., April 5, 1927. [10]

Locy, William Albert, biologist, b. Troy, Mich., 1857; d. Evanston, Ill., Oct. 9, 1924. [1; 4; 10]

Lodge, George Cabot, poet, b. Boston, Mass., 1873; d. Tuckemuck Island, Mass., Aug. 22, 1909. [1; 7; 8; 10]

Lodge, Gonzalez, educationist, b. Fort Littleton, Pa., 1863; d. New Canaan, Conn., Dec. 23, 1942. [10; 11]

Lodge, Henry Cabot, historian and politician, b. Boston, Mass., 1850; d. Cambridge, Mass., Dec. 9, 1924. [1; 4; 7; 9; 10; 11]

Loeb, Jacques, physiologist, b. Germany, 1859; d. Hamilton, Bermuda, Feb. 11, 1924. [1; 4; 8; 10]

Loeb, Mrs. Sophie Irene, née **Simon,** journalist and sociologist, b. Russia, 1876; d. New York, N.Y., Jan. 18, 1929. [1; 10]

Loeffler, Charles Martin, violinist, b. Mülhausen, Alsace, 1861; d. Medfield, Mass, May 19, 1935. [1a; 10; 20]

Loesch, Frank Joseph, lawyer, b. Buffalo, N.Y., 1852; d. Cooperstown, N.Y., July 31, 1944. [10]

Lofland, John, physician and poet, b. Milford, Del., 1798; d. Milford, Del., Jan. 22, 1849. [7]

Lofthouse, Joseph, missionary bishop, b. Yorkshire, England, 1855; d. Dawlish, England, Dec. 16, 1933. [27]

Lofting, Hugh, writer of books for children, b. Maidenhead, Berkshire, England, 1886; d. Los Angeles, Calif., Sept. 26, 1947. [7; 10; 11]

Lofton, George Augustus, clergyman, b. Panola county, Miss., 1839; d. Nashville, Tenn., Dec. 11, 1914. [4; 10]

Logan, Algernon Sydney, poet and novelist, b. Philadelphia, Pa., 1849; d. Dec. 11, 1925. [7]

Logan, Cornelius Ambrose, physician, b. Deerneld, Mass., 1832; d. Los Angeles, Calif., Jan. 30, 1899. [1; 4; 8]

Logan, Cornelius Ambrosius, actor and playwright, b. near Baltimore, Md., 1806; d. near Marietta, O., Feb. 23, 1853. [1; 4; 7; 8; 34]

Logan, George, physician, b. Charleston, S.C., 1778; d. New Orleans, La., Feb. 13, 1861. [34]

Logan, George Wood, naval officer, b. 1868; d. Portsmouth, N.H., April 22, 1915.

Logan, John Alexander, soldier and politician, b. Jackson county, Ill., 1826; d. Washington, D.C., Dec. 26, 1886. [1; 3; 4; 6; 7; 8]

Logan, John Alexander, soldier, b. Illinois, 1865; d. in action in the Philippines, Nov. 12, 1899. [8; 10]

Logan, John Daniel, journalist and educationist, b. Antigonish, N.S., 1869; d. Milwaukee, Ill., Jan. 24, 1929. [27]

Logan, John Henry, physician and hisorian, b. Abbeville district, S.C., 1822; d. Atlanta, Ga., March 28, 1885. [3; 4; 6; 8; 34]

Logan, Mrs. Josephine, née **Hancock,** poet, b. 1862; d. Chicago, Ill., Nov. 1, 1943. [7; 10]

Logan, Margaret Ann, poet, b. 1840; d. 1919.

Logan, Mrs. Mary Simmerson, née **Cunningham,** editor, b. Petersburg, Mo., 1838; d. Washington, D.C., Feb. 22, 1923. [4; 10]

Logan, Mrs. Olive, née **Logan,** actress and journalist, b. Elmira, N.Y., 1839; d. Bunstead, England, April 27, 1909. [1; 4; 6; 7; 9; 10]

Logan, Samuel Crothers, clergyman, b. 1823; d. 1907.

Logan, Sir William Edmond, geologist, b. Montreal, Lower Canada, 1798; d. Wales, June 22, 1875, [27]

Logan, William Newton, geologist, b. Barboursville, Ky., 1869; d. Bloomington, Ind., Aug. 28, 1941. [10; 13]

Loguen, Jermain Wesley, clergyman, b. 1814; d. 1872.

Loiseaux, Louis Marie Auguste, educationist, b. France, 1870; d. Poughkeepsie,, N.Y., Jan. 27, 1947.

Loisette, Alphonso (pseud.). See Larrowe, Marcus Dwight.

Lomax, John Avery, anthologist, b. Goodman, Miss., 1872; d. Greenville, Miss., Jan. 26, 1948. [7; 11]

Lomax, John Tayloe, jurist, b. Port Tobago, Va., 1781; d. Fredericksburg, Va., Oct. 10, 1862. [3; 4; 8; 34]

Lombard, Warren Plimpton, physiologist, b. Newton, Mass., 1855; d. Ann Arbor, Mich., July 13, 1939. [10]

Lombardi, Mrs. Cynthia, née **Richmond,** novelist, b. New York, N.Y.; d. New York, N.Y., Jan. 9, 1942. [10; 21]

London, Jack, novelist, b. San Francisco, Calif., 1876; d. Glen Ellen, Calif., Nov. 22, 1916. [1; 4; 7; 9; 10; 35; 72]

London, John Griffith. See London, Jack.

Lonergan, William Ignatius, priest and educationist, b. San Francisco, Calif., 1884; d. Danbury, Conn., March 13, 1936. [10; 21]

Long, Armistead Lindsay, soldier, b. Campbell county, Va., 1827; d. Charlottesville, Va., April 29, 1891. [1; 3; 7; 34]

Long, Charles Chaillé. See Chaillé-Long, Charles.

Long, Edwin McKean, clergyman, b. 1827; d. 1894. [8]

Long, Mrs. Ellen, née **Call,** historian, b. Tallahassee, Fla., 1825; d. Tallahassee, Fla., Dec. 18, 1905, [34]

Long, Huey Pierce, politician, b. Winnfield, La., 1893; d. Baton Rouge, La., Sept. 10, 1935. [1a; 2a; 10]

Long, John Davis, lawyer and politician, b. Buckfield, Me., 1838; d. Hingham, Mass., Aug. 28, 1915. [1; 3; 4; 6; 7; 10]

Long, John Dixon, clergyman, b. 1817; d. 1894.

Long, John Harper, chemist, b. Steubenville, O., 1856; d. Chicago, Ill., June 14, 1918. [1; 4; 10]

Long, John Luther, playwright and short-story writer, b. Hanover, Pa., 1861; d. Clifton Springs, N.Y., Oct. 31, 1927. [1; 7; 8; 10]

Long, Joseph Ragland, lawyer and educationist, b. Charlottesville, Va., 1870; d. Boulder, Colo., March 15, 1932. [1a; 10; 11]

Long, Joseph Schuyler, educationist, b. Marshalltown, Ia., 1869; d. Council Bluffs, Ia., Oct. 30, 1933. [37]

Long, Lily Augusta, poet and short-story writer, b. St. Paul, Minn.; d. St. Paul, Minn., Sept. 9, 1927. [10]

Long, Ray, editor, b. Lebanon, Ind., 1878; d. Beverly Hills, Calif., July 9, 1935. [7; 10]

Long, Robert James, bibliographer, b. Liverpool, N.S., 1849; d. Boston, Mass., Nov. 3, 1933. [27]

Long, Simon Peter, clergyman, b. Mc-Zena, O., 1860; d. Chicago, Ill., Jan. 3, 1929. [10]

Long, Stephen Harriman, engineer and explorer, b. Hopkinton, N.H., 1784; d. Alton, Ill., Sept. 4, 1864. [1; 3; 4; 7; 70]

Longacre, John, insurance broker, b. Philadelphia, Pa., 1873; d. Philadelphia, Pa., April 22, 1939. [62]

Longan, Mrs. Emma, née **Lard,** political scientist, b. 1854; d. Kansas City, Mo., May 1, 1924.

Longfellow, Henry Wadsworth, poet, b. Portland, Me., 1807; d. Cambridge, Mass., March 24, 1882. [1; 2; 3; 4; 5; 6; 7; 8; 9; 71; 72].

Longfellow, Marion, See Morris, Mrs. Marion, née Longfellow.

Longfellow, Samuel, clergyman, b. Portland, Me., 1819 d. Portland, Me., Oct. 3, 1892. [1; 3; 4; 6; 7; 8; 9]

Longfellow, William Pitt Preble, architect, b. Portland, Me., 1836; d. East Gloucester, Mass., Aug. 3, 1915. [1; 4; 8; 10]

Longley, Alcander, publisher and social reformer, b. Oxford, O., 1832; d. Chicago, Ill., April 17, 1918. [1]

Longley, James Wilberforce, biographer, b. Paradise, N.S., 1849; d. Halifax, N.S., March 16, 1922. [27]

Longman, Irwin (pseud.). See Lockwood, Ingersoll.

Longshore, Joseph Skelton, physician, b. Bucks county, Pa., 1809; d. Dec., 1879. [4]

Longstreet, Mrs. Abby, née **Buchanan,** See Longstreet, Mrs. Rachel Abigail, née Buchanan.

Longstreet, Augustus Baldwin, clergyman and humorist, b. Augusta, Ga., 1790; d. Oxford, Miss., Sept. 9, 1870. [1; 3; 4; 6; 7; 8; 9; 42]

Longstreet, James, soldier, b. Edgefield district, S.C., 1821; d. near Gainesville, Ga., Jan. 2, 1904. [1; 3; 4; 7; 8; 10; 34]

Longstreet, Mrs. Rachel Abigail, née **Buchanan,** writer on social usages, fl. 1866-1896.

Lonsdale, Herman Lilienthal, clergyman, b. 1858; d. Colchester, Conn., Aug. 16, 1940.

Looker, O. N. (pseud.). See Urner, Nathan D.,

Loomis, Alfred Lebbeus, physician, b. Bennington, Vt., 1831; d. New York, N.Y., Jan. 23, 1895. [3b; 4]

Loomis, Augustus Ward, missionary, b. Andover, Conn., 1816; d. 1891. [6; 8]

Loomis, Charles Battell, novelist and humorist, b. Brooklyn, N.Y., 1871; d. Hartford, Conn., Sept. 23, 1911. [1; 2; 4; 7; 10]

Loomis, Dwight, jurist, b. Columbia, Conn., 1821; d. near Waterbury, Conn., Sept. 17, 1903. [1; 4; 10; 62]

Loomis, Eben Jenks, astronomer, b. Oppenheim, N.Y., 1828; d. Amherst, Mass., Dec. 2, 1912. [8; 10]

Loomis, Elias, educationist, b. Willington, Conn., 1811; d. New Haven, Conn., Aug. 15, 1889. [1; 3; 4; 6; 8]

Loomis, Elisha Scott, mathematician, b. 1852; d. Cleveland, O., Dec. 11, 1940. [4]

Loomis, Mrs. Emma, née **Hawkridge,** poet, b. Malden, Mass., 1888; d. Boston, Mass., Feb. 27, 1948.

Loomis, Frederic Brewster, geologist and palaeontologist, b. Brooklyn, N.Y., 1873; d. Sitka, Alaska, July 28, 1937. [10; 11]

Loomis, Frederic Morris, gynaecologist, b. Ann Arbor, Mich., 1877; d. Piedmont, Calif., Feb. 9, 1949. [10]

Loomis, Harmon, clergyman, b. Georgia, Vt., 1805; d. Brooklyn, N.Y., Jan. 19, 1880. [43]

Loomis, Justin Rudolph, educationist, b. Bennington, Vt., 1810; d. Lewisburg, N.Y., June 22, 1898. [3; 6; 8]

Loomis, Lafayette Charles, educationist, b. Coventry, Conn., 1824; d. Washington, D.C., Oct. 17, 1905. [3; 6; 8]

Loomis, Leverett Mills, ornithologist, b. Roseville, O., 1857; d. San Francisco, Calif., Jan. 12, 1928. [10]

Loomis, Samuel Lane, clergyman, b. Littleton, Mass., 1856; d. Orlando, Fla., Jan. 11, 1938. [10; 11]

Loomis, Silas Laurence, physician and educationist, b. Coventry, Conn., 1822; d. Fernandina, Fla., June 22, 1896. [3; 8]

Looms, George, journalist and novelist, b. Louisville, Ky., 1886; d. Denver, Colo., Dec. 24, 1926. [10]

Loos, Isaac Althaus, educationist, b. Upper Bern, Pa., 1856; d. Iowa City, Ia., March 24, 1919. [10; 37; 62]

Loper, Samuel Ward, poet, b. Guilford, Conn., 1835; d. Middletown, Conn., March 31, 1910. [60]

Lopp, William Thomas, educationist and explorer, b. Valley City, Ind., 1864; d. Seattle, Wash., April 10, 1939. [10]

Loram, Charles Templeman, educationist, b. Pietermaritzburg, Natal, 1879; d. Ithaca, N.Y., July 8, 1940. [10]

Loranger, Thomas Jean Jacques, jurist, b. Ste. Anne d'Yamachiche, Lower Canada, 1823; d. Isle d'Orleans, Que., Aug. 18, 1885. [27]

Lord, Arthur, lawyer, b. Port Washington, Wis., 1850; d. Boston, Mass., April 10, 1925. [10; 51]

Lord, Augustus Mendon, clergyman, b. San Francisco, Calif., 1861; d. Providence, R.I., Sept. 14, 1941. [10; 51]

Lord, Benjamin, clergyman, b. Saybrook, Conn., 1694; d. Norwich, Conn., March 31, 1784. [3; 62]

Lord, Charles Chase, poet and historian, b. 1841; d. Hopkinton, N.H., Jan. 7, 1910.

Lord, Charles Eliphalet, clergyman, b. Portsmouth, N.H., 1817; d. Newburyport, Mass., Feb. 19, 1902. [49]

Lord, Chester Sanders, journalist, b. Romulus, N.Y., 1850; d. Garden City, N.Y., Aug. 1, 1933. [1a; 4; 10]

Lord, Daniel, lawyer, b. Stonington, Conn., 1795; d. New York, N.Y., March 4, 1868. [1; 3; 62]

Lord, David Nevins, merchant, b. Franklin, Conn., 1792; d. New York, N.Y., July 14, 1880. [1; 3; 6; 62]

Lord, Eleazar, financier, b. Franklin, Conn., 1788; d. Piermont, N.Y., June 3, 1871. [1; 3; 6; 7]

Lord, Elizabeth Evans, psychologist, b. Plymouth, Mass., 1890; d. Boston, Mass., Jan. 10, 1943. [62]

Lord, Frances Ellen, educationist, b. Maine, 1837; d. Wakefield, Mass., Aug. 1, 1920.

Lord, Franklin Atkins, lawyer, b. Winnebago, Minn., 1876; d. New York, N.Y., Jan. 16, 1945. [62]

Lord, Frederick Taylor, physician, b. Bangor, Me., 1875; d. Boston, Mass., Nov. 4, 1941. [10; 11]

Lord, Grace Virginia, novelist, d. 1885.

Lord, Herbert Gardiner, educationist, b. West Newton, Mass., 1849; d. New York, N.Y., March 12, 1930. [4; 10]

Lord, John, historical lecturer, b. Portsmouth, Me., 1810; d. Stamford, Conn., Dec. 15, 1894. [1; 3b; 7; 8; 9]

Lord, John Chase, clergyman, b. Buffalo, N.Y., 1805; d. Buffalo, N.Y., Jan. 21, 1877. [3; 8]

Lord, John King, educationist, b. Cincinnati, O., 1848; d. Wonalancet, N.H., June 26, 1926. [4; 10; 49]

Lord, Nathaniel Wright, educationist, b. Cincinnati, O., 1854; d. Columbus, O., May 23, 1911. [10]

Lord, William Rogers, clergyman, b. Boston, Mass., 1848; d. Dover, Mass., Feb. 1, 1916. [41]

Lord, William Sinclair, merchant and poet, b. Sycamore, Ill., 1863; d. Sept. 24, 1925. [7; 10]

Lord, William Wilberforce, clergyman and poet, b. Madison county, N.Y., 1819; d. New York, N.Y., April 22, 1907. [1; 3; 4; 6; 7; 8; 9; 10]

Lord, Willis, clergyman, b. Bridgeport, Conn., 1809; d. Guilford, Conn., Oct. 28, 1888. [3; 5; 8]

Lorenz, Daniel Edward, clergyman, b. Canal Fulton, O., 1862; d. New York, N.Y., Feb. 27, 1941. [10]

Lorenz, Edmund Simon, music publisher, b. Canal Fulton, O., 1854; d. Dayton, O., July 10, 1942. [62]

Lorimer, George Claude, clergyman, b. Edinburgh, Scotland, 1838; d. Aix-les-Bains, France, Sept. 7, 1904. [1; 3; 4; 6; 10]

Lorimer, George Horace, editor, b. Louisville, Ky., 1868; d. Wyncote, Pa., Oct. 22, 1937. [4; 7; 10]

Loring, Amasa, clergyman, b. North Yarmouth, Me., 1813; d. Dover, Me., 1890. [38]

Loring, Charles Greely, lawyer, b. Boston, Mass., 1794; d. Beverly, Mass., Oct. 8, 1868. [3; 4; 6; 8]

Loring, Edward Greely, physician, b. Boston, Mass., 1837; d. New York, N.Y., April 23, 1888. [1; 3b; 8]

Loring, Frederic Wadsworth, poet, b. Fall River, Mass., 1848; d. near Wickenburg, Ariz., Nov. 5, 1871. [1; 3; 4; 7; 9]

Loring, George Bailey, agriculturist, b. North Andover, Me., 1817; d. Salem, Mass., Sept. 14, 1891. [1; 3; 4]

Loring, James Spear, bookseller, b. Boston, Mass., 1799; d. Brooklyn, N.Y., April 12, 1884. [3; 6]

Loring, John Alden, naturalist, b. Cleveland, O., 1871; d. Owego, N.Y., May 8, 1947. [7; 10]

Loring, William Wing, soldier, b. Wilmington, N.C., 1818; d. New York, N.Y., Dec. 30, 1886 [1; 3; 4; 6]

Lorrain, Léon, poet, b. about 1852; d. by drowning in the Richelieu river, Que., Jan. 29, 1892. [27]

Lorraine, Madison Johnson, civil engineer, b. 1853; d. ?

Lortie, Stanislas Alfred, priest, b. Quebec, Que., 1869; d. Curran, Ont., Aug. 19, 1912. [27]

Losch, Henry, clergyman, b. 1823; d. ?

Lossing, Benson John, historian, b. Dutchess county, N.Y., 1813; d. Dutchess county, N.Y., June 3, 1891. [1; 2; 3; 4; 5; 6; 7; 8; 9]

Loth, Moritz, merchant, b. Moravia, Austria, 1832 d. Cincinnati, O., Feb. 18, 1913.

Lothrop, Amy (pseud.). See Warner, Anna Bartlett.

Lothrop, Daniel, publisher, b. Rochester, N.H., 1831; d. Boston, Mass., March 19, 1892. [3b; 4; 7]

Lothrop, Mrs. Harriett Mulford, née Stone, writer of books for children, b. New Haven, Conn., 1844; d. San Francisco, Cal., Aug. 2, 1924. [1; 3; 4; 7; 9; 10]

Lothrop, Samuel Kirkland, clergyman, b. Utica, N.Y., 1804; d. Boston, Mass., June 12, 1886. [3; 4; 7]

Lothrop, Thornton Kirkland, lawyer, b. Dover, N.H., 1830; d. Boston, Mass., Nov. 2, 1913. [4; 8; 10; 51]

Lotka, Alfred James, statistician, b. Poland, 1880; d. Red Bank, N.J., Dec. 5, 1949.

Lott, Noah (pseud.). See Hobart, George Vere.

Lottridge, Silas Alpha, naturalist, b. New York, N.Y., 1863; d. East Orange, N. J., Feb. 12, 1940. [10]

Loucks, Henry Langford, politician, b. Hull, Lower Canada, 1840; d. Clearlake, S.D., Dec. 29, 1928. [1]

Loud, Frank Herbert, mathematician, b. Weymouth, Mass., 1852; d. St. Petersburg, Fla., March 3, 1927. [10]

Loud, Mrs. Marguerite St. Leon, née Barstow, poet, b. about 1812; d. 1889. [3; 8]

Louden, Thomas, playwright, b. Belfast, Ireland, 1875; d. Santa Monica, Calif., March 15, 1948.

Loughborough, Mrs. Mary Ann, née Webster, journalist, b. New York, N.Y., 1836; d. Little Rock, Ark., Aug. 27, 1887. [3; 7; 8; 34]

Lounsberry, Clement Augustine, historian, b. De Kalb county, Ind., 1843; d. Washington, D.C., Oct. 3, 1926. [70]

Lounsbury, Thomas Rainesford, educationist, b. Ovid, N.Y., 1838; d. New Haven, Conn., April 9, 1915. [1; 2; 4; 7; 8; 9; 10]

Love, Emanuel King, clergyman, b. Perry county, Ala., 1850; d. Savannah, Ga., April 24, 1900. [1; 4]

Love, Robertus Donnell, journalist, b. near Irondale, Mo., 1867; d. St. Louis, Mo., May 7, 1930. [1; 7; 10; 11]

Love, Samuel Gurley, educationist, b. New York, N.Y., 1821; d. Jamestown, N.Y., 1893. [4; 6]

Love, William De Loss, clergyman, b. Barre, N.Y., 1819; d. St. Paul, Minn., Sept. 6, 1898. [3b; 4]

Love, William De Loss, clergyman, b. New Haven, Conn., 1851; d. Hartford, Conn,. April 8, 1918. [8; 10]

Lovejoy, Benjamin G., lawyer, d. 1889. [6]

Lovejoy, Joseph Cammet, clergyman, b. Albion, Me., 1805; d. Cambridge, Mass., Oct., 19, 1871. [38]

Lovejoy, Mrs. Mary Evelyn, née Wood, local historian, b. 1847; d. Royalton, Vt., June 4, 1928.

Lovejoy, Owen, politician, b. Albion, Me., 1811; d. Brooklyn, N.Y., March 25, 1864. [3; 4]

Loveland, Franklin Olds, lawyer, b. 1861; d. 1915.

Lovell, Albert Alonzo, historian, b. 1842; d. Sept. 3, 1890.

Lovell, John Epy, educationist, b. Colne, England, 1795; d. Milwaukee, Wis., May 3, 1892. [1]

Lovell, John Harvey, botanist, b. Waldoboro, Me., 1860; d. Sanford, Me., Aug. 2, 1939. [10; 11; 13; 45]

Loveman, Robert, poet, b. Cleveland, O., 1864; d. Hot Springs, Ark., July 10, 1923. [4; 7; 8; 10; 34]

Loverling, Anna Temple, physician, d. Boston, Mass., Feb. 22, 1914.

Lovett, Henry Almon, lawyer, b. Brooklyn, N.S., 1866; d. Winnipeg, Man., June 29, 1944. [27]

Lovett, Robert Williamson, physician, b. Beverly, Mass., 1859; d. Boston, Mass., July 2, 1924. [1; 10; 51]

Low, Benjamin Robbins Curtis, lawyer and poet, b. Fair Haven, Mass., 1880; d. Bridgewater, Vt., June 22, 1941. [7; 10; 11; 62]

Low, Mrs. Berthe, née Julienne, writer on cooking, b. Caën, France, 1853; d. 1909. [10]

Low, Frederick Rollins, mechanical engineer, b. Chelsea, Mass., 1860; d. Jan. 22, 1936. [10; 11]

Low, George Jacobs, clergyman, b. Calcutta, India, 1836; d. Ottawa, Ont., Dec. 14, 1906. [27]

Low, Samuel, poet, b. 1865; d. ? [3; 4]

Low, Will Hicok, artist, b. Albany, N.Y., 1853; d. Bronxville, N.Y., Nov. 27, 1932. [1a; 4; 7; 10]

Low, William Gilman, lawyer, b. Brooklyn, N.Y., 1844; d. Bristol, R.I., June 28, 1936. [10; 48]

Lowber, James William, clergyman, b. Chaplin, Ky., 1847; d. Austin, Tex., Dec. 5, 1930. [8; 10; 11]

Lowe, Mrs. Martha Ann, née Perry, poet, b. Keene, N.H., 1829; d. Somerville, Mass., 1902. [3; 4; 7; 8; 10]

Lowe, Percival Green, soldier, b. 1828; d. ?

Lowe, Walter Irenaeus, historian, b. Ilion, N.Y., 1867; d. Winter Park, Fla., Feb. 21, 1929. [10; 62]

Lowell, Abbott Lawrence, educationist, b. Boston, Mass., 1856; d. Boston, Mass., Jan. 6, 1943. [4; 7; 10; 51]

Lowell, Amy, poet, b. Brookline, Mass., 1874; d. Brookline, Mass., May 12, 1925. [1; 2; 3; 4; 7; 10; 11; 72]

Lowell, Mrs. Anna Cabot, née Jackson, educationist, b. Boston, Mass., 1819; d. Cambridge, Mass., Jan. 7, 1874. [3; 8]

Lowell, Charles, clergyman, b. Boston, Mass., 1782; d. Cambridge, Mass., Jan. 20, 1861. [3; 4; 8]

Lowell, Daniel Ozro Smith, educationist, b. Denmark, Me., 1851; d. Malden, Mass., March 12, 1928. [10; 11; 46]

Lowell, Delmar Rial, clergyman, b. South Valley, N.Y., 1844; d. Washington, D.C., Feb. 1, 1912. [10]

Lowell, Edward Jackson, historian, b. Boston, Mass., 1845; d. Cotuit, Mass., May 11, 1894. [1; 3; 7; 8; 9; 51]

Lowell, Francis Cabot, jurist, b. Boston, Mass., 1855; d. Boston, Mass., March 7, 1911. [4; 8; 10; 51]

Lowell, Guy, architect, b. Boston, Mass., 1870; d. Madeira, Feb. 4, 1927. [1; 10; 51]

Lowell, James Russell, poet and essayist, b. Cambridge, Mass., 1819; d. Cambridge, Mass., Aug. 12, 1891. [1; 2; 3; 4; 5; 6; 7; 8; 9; 71; 72]

Lowell, John, political writer, b. Newburyport, Mass., 1769; d. Boston, Mass., March 12, 1840. [1; 3; 4; 6]

Lowell, John, jurist, b. Boston, Mass., 1824; d. Boston, Mass., May 14, 1897. [1]

Lowell, Mrs. Josephine, née **Shaw,** philanthropist and reformer, b. Roxbury, Mass., 1843; d. New York, N.Y., Oct. 12, 1905. [1; 2; 3; 4; 8; 10]

Lowell, Mrs. Maria, née **White,** poet, b. Watertown, Mass., 1821; d. Cambridge, Mass., Oct. 27, 1853. [3; 4; 7; 8]

Lowell, Mary Chandler, genealogist, b. 1863; d. Bangor, Me., June 26, 1949.

Lowell, Percival, astronomer, b. Boston, Mass., 1855; d. Flagstaff, Ariz., Nov. 12, 1916. [1; 4; 7; 8; 10; 51]

Lowell, Robert Traill Spence, clergyman, b. Boston, Mass., 1816; d. Schenectady, N.Y., Sept. 12, 1891. [1; 3; 4; 6; 7; 8; 9; 51]

Lowery, Woodbury, lawyer and historian, b. New York, N.Y., 1853 d. Taormina, Sicily, April 11, 1906. [1; 4; 7; 10; 51]

Lowndes, Arthur Edward Gilbert, clergyman, b. London, England, 1858; d. New York, N.Y., Jan. 2, 1917. [10]

Lowndes, Mary Elizabeth, educationist, b. Wallasey, England, 1857; d. Greenwich, Conn., March 19, 1947. [7]

Lowrey, Charles Emmet, educationist, d. Boulder, Colo., Aug. 19, 1894.

Lowrie, John Cameron, clergyman, b. Butler, Pa., 1808; d. East Orange N.J., May 31, 1900. [3b; 4; 10]

Lowrie, John Marshall, clergyman, b. Pittsburgh, Pa., 1817; d. Fort Wayne, Ind., Sept. 26, 1867. [3; 6; 8]

Lowrie, Samuel Thompson, clergyman, b. Pittsburgh, Pa., 1835; d. Philadelphia, Pa., Sept. 22, 1924. [6; 10]

Lowrie, Walter Macon, missionary, b. Butler, Pa., 1819; d. China, Aug. 19, 1847. [3]

Lowry, Edith Belle, physician, b. Austin, Minn., 1878; d. St. Charles, Ill., March 8, 1945. [10]

Lowry, Edward George, journalist, b. Atlanta, Ga., 1876; d. New York, N.Y., July 21, 1943. [10]

Lowry, Robert, clergyman, b. Philadelphia, Pa., 1826; d. Plainfield, N.J., Nov. 23, 1899. [7; 10]

Lowry, Robert, lawyer, b. Chesterfield district, S.C., 1830; d. Jackson, Miss., Jan. 19, 1910. [1; 4; 10; 34]

Lowry, Thomas, lawyer and financier, b. Logan county, Ill., 1843; d. Minneapolis, Minn., Feb. 4, 1909. [1; 10; 70]

Lowther, Granville, horticulturist, b. Doddridge county, W. Va., 1848; d. Seattle, Wash., Sept. 9, 1933. [10]

Lowy, Alexander, chemist, b. New York, N.Y., 1889; d. Pittsburgh, Pa., Dec. 25, 1941. [10; 11; 13]

Loy, Matthias, clergyman, b. Cumberland county, Pa., 1828; d. Columbus, O., Jan. 26, 1915. [1; 3; 4; 6; 7; 8; 10]

Loyd, Samuel, chess-player, b. Philadelphia, Pa., 1841; d. Brooklyn, N.Y., April 10, 1911. [1]

Lozeau, Albert, poet, b. Montreal, Que., 1878; d. Montreal, Que., March 24, 1924. [27]

Lubbock, Francis Richard, politician, b. Beaufort, S.C., 1815; d. Austin, Tex., June 22, 1905. [1; 4; 10]

Lubin, David, merchant and reformer, b. 1849; d. Rome, Italy, Jan. 1. 1919. [4; 10]

Luby, James Patrick Kenyon, journalist, b. Dublin, Ireland, 1856; d. Brooklyn, N.Y., May 30, 1925. [4; 10]

Luby, Thomas Clarke, journalist, b. Dublin, Ireland, 1722; d. Jersey City, N.J., Nov. 28, 1901. [3b; 8]

Lucas, Daniel Bedinger, jurist and poet, b. near Charlestown, Va., 1836; d. near Charleston, W. Va., July 28, 1909. [1; 3; 4; 6; 7; 8; 9; 10; 34]

Lucas, Daniel Vannorman, clergyman, b. near Niagara Falls, N.Y., 1834; d. Hamilton, Ont., June 10, 1911. [27]

Lucas, Frederic Augustus, naturalist, b. Plymouth, Mass., 1852; d. Flushing, N.Y., Feb. 9, 1929. [1; 4; 8; 10; 13]

Luccock, Naphtali, bishop, b. Guernsey county, O., 1853; d. Helena, Mont., April 1, 1916. [10]

Luce, Stephen Bleecker, naval officer, b. Albany, N.Y., 1827; d. Newport, R.I., July 28, 1917. [1; 3; 4; 6; 10]

Luckenbach, William Henry, clergyman, b. 1828; d. 1896.

Luckenbill, Daniel David, educationist, b. near Hamburg, Pa., 1881; d. London, England, June 5, 1927. [4; 10]

Luckey, George Washington Andrew, educationist, b. near Decatur, Ind., 1855; d. Lincoln, Neb., March 30, 1933. [8; 10; 11]

Luckey, Samuel, clergyman, b. Rensselaerville, N.Y., 1791; d. Rochester, N.Y., Oct. 11, 1869. [3]

Ludden, William, musician, b. Williamsburg, Mass., 1823; d. Brooklyn, N.Y., Jan. 2, 1912. [62]

Ludewig, Hermann Ernst, lawyer, b. Dresden, Saxony, 1809; d. Brooklyn, N.Y., Dec. 12, 1856. [3]

Ludington, Arthur Crosby, educationist, b. New York, N.Y., 1880; d. New York, N.Y., Nov. 4, 1914. [10]

Ludlam, Reuben, physician, b. Camden, N.J., 1831; d. Chicago, Ill., 1899. [4; 10]

Ludlow, Arthur Clyde, clergyman, b. Chardon, O., 1861; d. Cleveland, O., April 16, 1927. [10]

Ludlow, FitzHugh, journalist, b. New York, N.Y., 1836; d. Geneva, Swtizerland, Sept. 12, 1870. [1; 3; 4; 6; 7; 9; 71]

Ludlow, Henry Hunt, soldier, b. Easton, Pa., 1854; d. Washington, D.C., 1926. [10]

Ludlow, James Meeker, clergyman, and novelist, b. Elizabeth, N.J., 1841; d. Norfolk, Conn., Oct. 4, 1932. [4; 7; 8; 10; 11]

Ludlow, John Livingston, physician, b. 1819; d. Philadelphia, Pa., June 21, 1888. [4]

Ludlow, Noah Miller, actor, b. New York,, N.Y., 1795; d. St. Louis, Mo., Jan. 9, 1886. [1; 3; 7; 8]

Ludlum, Jean Kate, novelist, fl. 1887-1905.

Lüders, Charles Henry, poet, b. 1858; d. Philadelphia, Pa., Jan. 21, 1891. [7; 8]

Lugrin, Charles Henry, journalist, b. Fredericton, N.B., 1846; d. Victoria, B.C., June 14, 1917. [27]

Luigi (pseud.). See Pelletier, Alexis.

Lukens, Henry Clay, journalist, b. Philadelphia, Pa., 1838; d. Jersey City, N.J., about 1900. [3; 4; 6; 7; 8; 9]

Lull, Edward Phelps, naval officer, b. Windsor, Vt., 1836; d. Pensacola, Fla., March 5, 1887. [1; 3]

Lum, Dyer Daniel, social philosopher, fl. 1872-1882.

Lummis, Charles Fletcher, journalist and librarian, b. Lynn, Mass., 1859; d. Los Angeles, Calif., Nov. 25, 1928. [1; 4; 7; 8; 10; 51]

Lundy, John Patterson, clergyman, b. Danville, Pa., 1820; d. Philadelphia, Pa., Dec. 12, 1892. [3; 8]

Lunettes, Henry (pseud.). See Conkling, Margaret Cockburn.

Lunt, George, poet and politician, b. Newburyport, Mass., 1803; d. Boston, Mass., May 17, 1885. [1; 3; 4; 6; 7; 9; 71]

Lunt, William Parsons, clergyman, b. Newburyport, Mass., 1805; d. Akabah, Arabia Petraea, March 20, 1857. [3; 6; 8]

Lupton, Frank M., publisher and compiler, b. 1854; d. Brooklyn, N.Y., Oct. 5, 1910.

Lupton, Nathaniel Thomas, chemist, b. Frederick county, Va., 1830; d. Auburn, Ala., June 12, 1893. [3; 4; 6; 8; 34]

Luquiens, Jules, educationist, b. Lausanne, Switzerland, 1845; d. Salem, O., Aug. 23, 1899. [62]

Lush, Charles Keeler, journalist and novelist, b. La Crosse, Wis., 1861; d. ? [10; 11]

Lusignan, Alphonse, miscellaneous writer, b. 1843; d. Ottawa, Ont., Jan. 5, 1892. [27]

Lusk, Graham, physiologist, b. Bridgeport, Conn., 1866; d. New York, N.Y., July 18, 1932. [1a; 4; 10; 11]

Lusk, William Thompson, obstetrician, b. Norwich, Conn., 1838; d. New York, N.Y., June 12, 1897. [1; 3; 4; 8]

Luska, Sidney (pseud.). See Harland, Henry.

Lust, Benedict, physician, b. Germany, 1872; d. Butler, N.J., Sept. 4, 1945.

Lust, Herbert Confield, lawyer, b. New York, N.Y., 1885; d. Lafayette, Ind., July 22, 1936. [62]

Lutes, Mrs. Della, née Thompson, novelist and editor, b. Jackson, Mich.; d. Cooperstown, N.Y., July 13, 1942. [7; 10; 11]

Luther, Clair Franklin, clergyman, b. Burton, O., 1866; d. Amherst, Mass., Sept. 11, 1938. [62]

Lutkin, Peter Christian, musician, b. Thompsonville, Wis., 1858; d. Evanston, Ill., Dec. 27, 1931. [1; 10; 11]

Lutton, Anne, poet, b. 1791; d. 1881.

Lutz, Frank Eugene, entomologist, b. Bloomsburg, Pa., 1879; d. New York, N.Y., Nov. 27, 1943. [10; 13]

Lydig, Mrs. Rita, née de Acosta, social leader, b. 1879; d. New York, N.Y., Oct. 19, 1929.

Lydston, George Frank, physician, b. Jacksonville, Calif., 1857; d. Los Angeles, Calif., March 14, 1923. [1; 10; 35]

Lyford, James Otis, lawyer, b. Boston, Mass., 1853; d. Concord, N.H., Sept 19, 1924. [10]

Lyle, William, poet, b. Edinburgh, Scotland, 1822; d. ? [3]

Lyle, William Thomas, civil engineer, b. Utica, N.Y., 1875; d. Lexington, Va., Oct. 31, 1933. [10; 11]

Lyman, Albert Josiah, clergyman, b. Williston, Vt., 1845; d. Brooklyn, N.Y., Aug. 22, 1915. [1; 10]

Lyman, Benjamin Smith, geologist, b. Northampton, Mass., Dec. 11, 1835; d. Philadelphia, Pa., Aug. 30, 1920. [1; 3; 4; 10]

Lyman, Edward Branch, publicist, b. Greenfield, Mass., 1872; d. New York, N.Y., Jan. 12, 1943. [11; 62]

Lyman, Elmer Adelbert, mathematician, b. Manchester, Vt., 1861; d. Ypsilanti, Mich., Oct. 9, 1934. [10; 13]

Lyman, Henry Munson, physician, b. Hilo, Hawaiian Islands, 1835; d. Evanston, Ill., Nov. 21, 1904. [3; 4; 10]

Lyman, Horace Sumner, historian, b. Polk county, Ore. 1855; d. Portland, Ore., Dec. 22, 1904. [41]

Lyman, Joseph Bardwell, agriculturist, b. Chester, Mass., 1829; d. Richmond Hill, Long Island, N.Y., Jan. 28, 1872. [1; 3; 4; 6; 8]

Lyman, Payson Williston, clergyman, b. Easthampton, Mass., 1842; d. Brookline, Mass., April 15, 1924.

Lyman, Rollo La Verne, educationist, b. Windsor, Wis., 1878; d. Chicago, Ill., Dec. 22, 1937. [7]

Lyman, Samuel P., biographer, b. 1804; d. 1869.

Lyman, Theodore, philanthropist, b. Boston, Mass., 1792; d. Brookline, Mass., July 18, 1849. [1; 3; 6; 7]

Lyman, Theodore, naturalist, b. Waltham, Mass., 1833; d. Nahant, Mass., Sept. 9, 1897. [1; 3; 6; 51]

Lyman, William Denison, historian, b. Portland, Ore., 1852; d. Walla Walia, Wash., June 21, 1920. [10]

Lyman, Wyllys, lawyer, b. 1830; d. 1900. [51]

Lynch, Ella Frances, educationist, b. 1882; d. Minerva, N.Y., Aug. 31, 1945.

Lynch, Frederick Henry, clergyman, b. Peace Dale, R.I., 1867; d. New York, N.Y., Dec. 19, 1934. [10; 62]

Lynch, Mrs. Harriet Louise, née Husted, novelist, b. Boston, Mass., 1864; d. New York, N.Y., Sept. 17, 1943. [11]

Lynch, James Daniel, lawyer, b. Mecklenburg county, Va., 1836; d. Sulphur Springs, Tex., July 19, 1903. [1; 3; 7; 8; 34]

Lynch, Jeremiah, capitalist and reformer, b. Fall River, Mass., 1849; d. San Francisco, Calif., 1917. [10]

Lynch, John Fairfield, lawyer, b. Harrington, Me., 1845; d. Machias, Me., May 1, 1923. [10]

Lynch, John Roy, politician, b. near Vidalia, La., 1847; d. Chicago, Ill., Nov. 2, 1939. [10]

Lynch, Lawrence L. (pseud.). See Van Deventer, Emma Murdoch.

Lynch, William Francis, naval officer, b. Norfolk, Va., 1801; d. Baltimore, Md., Oct. 17, 1865. [1; 3; 4; 6; 7; 8]

Lynd, Samuel W., clergyman, b. Philadelphia, Pa., 1796; d. Lockport, Ill., June 17, 1876.

Lynde, Francis, novelist, b. Lewiston, N.Y., 1856; d. near Chattanooga, Tenn., May 16, 1930. [1; 4; 7; 8; 10; 11; 34]

Lyndon, Barry (pseud.). See Austin, George Lowell.

Lynn, Ethel (pseud.). See Beers, Mrs. Ethelinda, née Eliot.

Lyon, Amos Maynard, poet, b. Brandon, Vt., 1818; d. New York, N.Y., Oct. 14, 1916. [10]

Lyon, David Gordon, educationist, b. Benton, Ala., 1852; d. Boston, Mass., Dec. 4, 1935. [1a; 8; 10; 11]

Lyon, Edmund, humanitarian, d. Rochester, N.Y., April 24, 1920. [10]

Lyon, George William Amos, educationist, b. Boston, Mass., 1854; d. New York, N.Y., Aug. 14, 1919. [62]

Lyon, Harris Merton, journalist, b. Santa Fé, N.M., 1883; d. New York, N.Y., June 2, 1916. [1; 7; 10]

Lyon, Irving Whitall, physician, b. Bedford, N.Y., 1840; d. Hartford, Conn., March 4, 1896. [3b]

Lyon, James, clergyman, b. Newark, N.J., 1735; d. Machias, Me., Oct. 12, 1794. [1]

Lyon, Thomas Lyttleton, educationist, b. Pittsburgh, Pa., 1869; d. Ithaca, N.Y., Oct. 7, 1938. [10; 11; 13]

Lyon, William Henry, clergyman, b. Fall River, Mass., 1846; d. Brookline, Mass., Dec. 20, 1915. [8; 10]

Lyon, William Scrugham, botanist, b. 1852; d. ?

Lyons, Albert Brown, chemist, b. Hawaiian Islands, 1841; d. Detroit, Mich., April 13, 1926. [3; 4; 8; 10; 39]

Lyons, James Gilborne, poet, b. England; d. Haverford, Pa., Jan. 2, 1808. [3]

Lyons, Timothy Augustine, naval officer, b. Ireland, 1845; d. New York, N.Y., 1919. [8; 10]

Lyte, Eliphalet Oram, educationist, b. 1842; d. Millersville, Pa., Jan. 3, 1913. [4; 8; 10]

M

Maas, Anthony John, priest and educationist, b. Germany, 1858; d. Poughkeepsie, N.Y., Feb. 20, 1927. [1; 10; 21]

Mabie, Hamilton Wright, editor and essayist, b. Coldspring, N.Y., 1845; d. Summit, N.J., Dec. 31, 1916. [1; 2; 3; 4; 7; 10]

Mabie, Henry Clay, clergyman, b. Belvedere, Ill., 1847; d. Boston, Mass., April 30, 1918. [10; 70]

McAdam, David, jurist, b. New York, N.Y., 1838; d. New York, N.Y., Dec. 22, 1901. [3b; 4; 10]

McAdam, Dunlap Jamison, educationist, b. Moorefield, O., 1843; d. Washington, Pa., Feb. 15, 1925. [10]

McAdie, Alexander George, meteorologist, b. New York, N.Y., 1863; d. Hampton, Va., Nov. 1, 1943. [10; 51]

McAdoo, Eva T., guide-book writer, b. Lynchburg, Va.; d. New York, N.Y., May 13, 1942.

McAdoo, William, lawyer and politician, b. county Donegal, Ireland, 1853; d. New York, N.Y., June 7, 1930. [10]

McAdoo, William Gibbs, jurist, b. near Knoxville, Tenn., 1820; d. 1894. [8; 34]

McAdoo, William Gibbs, politician, b. near Marietta, Ga., 1863; d. Washington, D.C., Feb. 1, 1941. [4; 10]

McAfee, Cleland Boyd, clergyman, b. Ashley, Mo., 1866; d. Asheville, N. C., Feb. 4, 1944. [10]

McAfee, Robert Breckinridge, lawyer, b. Mercer county, Ky., 1784; d. Mercer county, Ky., March 12, 1849. [1; 4; 6; 8; 34]

MacAlarney, Robert Emmet, journalist and novelist, b. Harrisburg, Pa., 1873; d. New York, N.Y., Nov. 15, 1945. [10]

McAleer, George, physician, b. Eastern Townships, Que., 1845; d. Worcester, Mass., Sept. 19, 1923. [31a]

MacAlister, James, educationist, b. Glasgow, Scotland, 1840; d. Philadelphia, Pa., Dec. 11, 1913. [1; 3; 4]

McAllister, Charles Albert, naval engineer, b. Dorchester, N.J., 1867; d. New York, N.Y., Jan. 26, 1932. [10]

McAllister, David, clergyman, b. New York, N.Y., 1835; d. Allegheny, Pa., 1907. [10]

McAllister, Samuel Ward, society leader, b. Savannah, Ga., 1827; d. New York, N.Y., Jan. 31, 1895. [1; 4]

McAllister, Ward. See McAllister, Samuel Ward.

McAlpine, Charles Alonzo, clergyman, b. Mansfield, Mass., 1874; d. New York, N.Y., Aug. 5, 1945. [10]

McAlpine, William Jarvis, civil engineer, b. New York, N.Y., 1812; d. New Brighton, N.Y., Feb. 16, 1890. [1; 3; 4]

McAnally, David Rice, clergyman, b. Granger county, Tenn., 1810; d. St. Louis, Mo., July 11, 1895. [1; 3; 34]

Macara, John, lawyer, b. Edinburgh, Scotland, 1813; d. Goderich, Ont., Feb. 20, 1882. [27]

MacArthur, Arthur, jurist, b. Glasgow, Scotland, 1815; d. Atlantic City, N.J., Aug. 24, 1896. [3; 4; 8]

McArthur, Peter, journalist, b. Middlesex county, Ont., 1866; d. London, Ont., Oct. 28, 1924. [27]

MacArthur, Robert Stuart, clergyman, b. Dalesville, Que., 1841; d. Daytona Beach, Fla., Feb. 23, 1923. [1; 4; 10]

Macartney, William Napier, physician, b. Fort Covington, N.Y., 1862; d. Fort Covington, N.Y., June 15, 1940. [7]

McAtamney, Hugh Entwistle, journalist, b. 1860; d. Scarsdale, N.Y., Feb. 20, 1929.

Macaulay, Mrs. Fannie, née Caldwell, novelist, b. Shelbyville, Ky., 1863; d. Louisville, Ky., Jan. 6, 1941. [7; 10; 74]

McBain, Howard Lee, educationist, b. Toronto, Ont., 1880; d. New York, N.Y., May 7, 1936. [10]

MacBean, William Munro, biographer, b. 1852; d. 1924.

McBee, Silas, editor, b. Lincolnton, N.C., 1853; d. Charleston, S.C., Sept. 3, 1924. [10]

MacBeth, Roderick George, clergyman, b. Kildonan, Man., 1858; d. Vancouver, B.C., Feb. 28, 1934. [27]

McBride, Isaac, journalist, d. Washington, D.C., Aug. 3, 1941.

McBride, James, local historian, b. 1788; d. 1859. [8]

McBride, James Harvey, physician, b. La Fayette, Ore., 1849; d. Pasadena, Calif., Sept. 1, 1928. [10; 13]

Macbride, Thomas Huston, botanist, b. Rogersville, Tenn., 1848; d. Seattle, Wash., March 27, 1934. [10; 13; 37]

McCabe, James Dabney, novelist and historian, b. Richmond, Va., 1842; d. Germantown, Pa., Jan. 27, 1883. [3; 4; 6; 7; 8; 34]

McCabe, John Collins, clergyman and poet, b. Richmond, Va., 1810; d. Chambersburg, Pa., Feb. 26, 1875. [1; 3; 4; 34]

McCabe, Lida Rose, journalist, b. Columbus, O., 1865; d. New York, N.Y., Dec. 9, 1938. [7; 10]

McCabe, William Gordon, educationist, b. Richmond, Va., 1821; d. Richmond, Va., June 1, 1920. [1; 3; 4; 6; 7; 34]

McCaig, Donald, poet, b. Cape Breton, N.S., 1832; d. Collingwood, Ont., July 28, 1905. [27]

McCain, Charles Curtice, railway executive, b. Minneapolis, Minn., Sept. 18, 1856; d. East Orange, N.Y., July 14, 1942. [10]

McCain, George Nox, journalist, b. Pittsburg, Pa., 1856; d. near Philadelphia, Pa., Dec. 11, 1934. [10]

McCaine, Alexander, clergyman, b. Tipperary, Ireland, about 1768; d. Montgomery, Ala., June 1, 1856. [1; 3]

McCall, George Archibald, soldier, b. Philadelphia, Pa., 1802; d. West Chester, Pa., Feb. 26, 1868. [3; 8]

McCall, Henry Strong, lawyer, b. about 1819; d. 1893. [6]

McCall, Hugh, soldier and historian, b. South Carolina, 1767; d. Savannah, Ga., July 9, 1824. [3; 8; 34]

McCall, John Cadwalader, poet, b. Philadelphia, Pa., 1793; d. Philadelphia, Pa., Oct. 3, 1846. [3]

McCall, Peter, lawyer, b. Trenton, N.J., 1809; d. Philadelphia, Pa., Oct. 30, 1880. [3; 4; 8]

McCall, Samuel Walker, lawyer and politician, b. East Providence, Pa., 1851; d. Winchester, Mass., Nov. 4, 1923. [1; 4; 8; 10]

McCalla, Daniel, clergyman, b. Neshaminy, Pa., 1748; d. Wappetaw, S.C., April 6, 1809. [3]

McCalla, William Latta, clergyman, b. near Lexington, Ky., d. near Bayou Bidal, La., Oct. 12, 1859. [1; 3; 34]

McCallum, Daniel Craig, engineer, b. Renfrewshire, Scotland, 1815; d. Brooklyn, N.Y., Dec. 27, 1878. [1; 3]

McCallum, John Archibald, clergyman, b. Gananoque, Ont., 1874; d. Philadelphia, Pa., Dec. 31, 1945. [10; 11]

McCandlish, Edward Gerstell, writer and illustrator of books for children, b. Piedmont, W. Va., 1887; d. North Brookfield, Mass., Dec. 6, 1946.

McCann, Alfred Watterson, journalist, b. Pittsburgh, Pa., 1879; d. New York, N.Y., Jan. 19, 1931. [1; 10]

McCann, Sister Mary Agnes, historian, b. 1851; d. Cincinnati, O., Oct. 12, 1931. [21]

McCann, Rebecca, illustrator, b. Quincy, Ill.; d. New York, N.Y., Dec. 22, 1927. [10]

McCarroll, James, poet and humorist, b. county Longford, Ireland, 1814; d. New York, N.Y., April 11, 1892. [1; 3; 7; 9]

McCarter, Mrs. Margaret, née **Hill,** novelist, b. Charlottesville, Ind.; d. Topeka, Kans., Aug. 31, 1938. [2; 7; 10; 11]

McCarty, Carlton, miscellaneous writer, b. Richmond, Va., 1847; d. Richmond, Va., April 16, 1936. [34]

McCarthy, Charles, political scientist, b. Brockton, Mass., 1873; d. Prescott, Ariz., March 26, 1921. [1; 4; 10; 47]

McCarthy, Charles Hallan, historian, b. Franklin, N.J., 1860; d. Washington, D.C., Dec. 22, 1941. [21]

McCarthy, Denis Aloysius, poet and journalist, b. Tipperary county, Ireland, 1870; d. Arlington, Mass., Aug. 18, 1931. [10; 11; 21]

McCarthy, Eugene, angler, b. 1857; d. 1903.

MacCarthy, James Philip, journalist, b. 1869; d. 1920.

McCarthy, Justin, lawyer, b. 1786; d. Quebec, Lower Canada, July, 1832. [27]

M'Cartney, Washington, educationist and jurist, b. Westmoreland county, Pa., 1812; d. Philadelphia, Pa., July, 1856. [3; 8]

McCarty, Joseph Hendrickson, clergyman, b. Berlin, Pa., 1830; d. 1897. [6; 8]

McCarty, Justin Richard, railway executive, b. Clarksburg, Va., 1851; d. Kansas City, Mo., June 16, 1934. [10]

McCaul, John, educationist, b. Dublin, Ireland, 1807; d. Toronto, Ont., April 16, 1886. [27]

MacCauley, Clay, clergyman, b. Chambersburg, Pa., 1843; d. Berkeley, Calif., Nov. 15, 1925. [1; 7; 8; 10]

McCauley, William Fletcher, clergyman, b. near West Salem, O., 1858; d. McKeesport, Pa., March 13, 1915. [10]

McCharles, Aeneas, mining pioneer, b. Middle River, Cape Breton, N.S., 1844; d. Sudbury, Ont., Aug. 5, 1906. [27]

McChesney, Dora Greenwell, novelist, b. Chicago, Ill., 1871; d. Chicago, Ill., July 5, 1912. [7; 10]

Maccheta, Mrs. Blanche Roosevelt, née **Tucker,** opera singer, b. Sandusky, O., 1853; d. London, England, Sept. 15, 1898. [3b; 8]

McClain, Emlin, jurist, b. Salem, O., 1851; d. Des Moines, Ia., May 25, 1915. [1; 4; 10]

McCleary, James Thompson, politician, b. Ingersoll, Ont., 1853; d. La Crosse, Wis., Dec. 17, 1924. [8; 10; 70]

McClellan, Carswell, civil engineer, b. Philadelphia, Pa., 1835; d. St. Paul, Minn., March 6, 1892. [3; 4; 5; 8]

McClellan, Elisabeth, writer on costume, b. Philadelphia, Pa., 1851; d. Germantown, Pa., Dec. 3, 1920. [10]

McClellan, Ely, army surgeon, b. Philadelphia, Pa., 1834; d. Chicago, Ill., May 8, 1893. [3a; 5; 8]

McClellan, George, surgeon, b. Woodstock, Conn., 1796; d. Philadelphia, Pa., May 9, 1847. [3; 4; 5]

McClellan, George, anatomist and physician, b. Philadelphia, Pa., 1849; d. Philadelphia, Pa., March 29, 1913. [1; 4]

McClellan, Mrs. George. See McClellan, Mrs. Harriet, née Hare.

McClellan, George Brinton, soldier, b. Philadelphia, Pa., 1826; d. Orange, N.J., Oct. 29, 1885. [1; 2; 3; 4; 5; 6; 7]

McClellan, George Brinton, politician and publicist, b. Dresden, Germany, 1865; d. Washington, D.C., Nov. 30, 1940. [7; 10]

McClellan, Mrs. Harriet, née **Hare,** novelist, fl. 1873-1913.

McClellan, Henry Brainerd, soldier, b. Philadelphia, Pa., 1840; d. Lexington, Ky., Oct. 1, 1904. [1; 3; 4; 5]

McClelland, Alexander, clergyman, b. Schenectady, N.Y., 1796; d. New Brunswick, N.J., Dec. 19, 1864. [3; 4; 5; 6]

McClelland, Mary Greenway, novelist, b. Norwood, Va., 1853; d. Norwood, Va., Aug. 2, 1895. [4; 8; 34]

McClelland, Milo Adams, physician, b. Sharon, Pa., 1837; d. Knoxville, Ill., Nov. 26, 1898. [3; 8]

McClelland, Thomas Calvin, clergyman, b. New York, N.Y., 1869; d. Brooklyn, N.Y., Oct. 24, 1917. [10; 68]

McClenachan, Charles Thompson, freemason, b. Washington, D.C., 1829; d. ? [6; 8]

McClintock, Alexander, soldier, d. New York, N.Y., June 27, 1918.

McClintock, James Harvey, historian, b. Sacramento, Calif., 1864; d. Phoenix, Ariz., May 10, 1934. [1a; 10; 11]

McClintock, John, educationist, b. Philadelphia, Pa., 1814; d. Madison, N.J., March 4, 1870. [1; 3; 4; 5; 6; 8]

McClintock, John Norris, historian, b. 1846; d. Dorchester, Mass., Aug. 13, 1914.

McClintock, Walter, ethnologist, b. Pittsburgh, Pa., 1870; d. Pittsburgh, Pa., March 24, 1949. [10; 11; 62]

McCloskey, George Victor Andronicus, lawyer and poet, b. New York, N.Y., 1883; d. New York, N.Y., March 29, 1933. [10]

McClumpha, Charles Flint, merchant and scholar, b. Amsterdam, N.Y., 1863; d. Amsterdam, N.Y., Jan. 7, 1933. [70]

McClung, Clarence Erwin, zoologist, b. Clayton, Calif., 1870; d. Swarthmore, Pa., Jan. 17, 1946. [10; 11; 13]

McClung, John Alexander, clergyman, b. Washington, Mason county, Ky., 1804; drowned in the Niagara river, Aug. 7, 1859. [3; 4; 6; 7; 34; 74]

McClung, John W., lawyer, b. near Maysville, Ky., 1826; d. St. Paul, Minn., May 27, 1888. [70]

McClure, Alexander Kelly, journalist and politician, b. Sherman's Valley, Pa., 1828; d. Wallingford, Pa., June 6, 1909. [1; 4; 10]

McClure, Alexander Wilson, clergyman, b. Boston, Mass., 1808; d. Canonsburg, Pa., Sept. 20, 1865. [1; 3; 4; 6; 7]

McClure, Alfred James Pollock, clergyman, b. Pennsylvania, 1854; d ? [56]

McClure, Mrs. Anne, née **Dinsmore,** poet, b. Austin, Tex., 1865; d. Oklahoma City, Okla., Sept., 1938. [75]

McClure, Archibald, clergyman, b. Lake Forest, Ill., 1890; d. South Bend, Ind., April 8, 1931. [62]

McClure, David, clergyman, b. Newport, R.I., 1748; d. East Windsor, Conn., June 25, 1820. [3; 62]

McClure, James Baird, editor, b. 1832; d. 1895. [7]

McClure, James Gore King, clergyman and educationist, b. Albany, N.Y., 1848; d. Lake Forest, Ill., Jan. 18, 1932. [5; 7; 8; 10; 62]

McClure, Samuel Sidney, editor, b. county Antrim, Ireland, 1857; d. New York, N.Y., March 21, 1949. [7; 10; 11]

McCole, Camille John, educationist, b. Sagola, Wis., 1905; d. New York, N.Y., Jan. 14, 1939. [22]

MacColl, Evan, poet, b. Kenmore, Scotland, 1808; d. Toronto, Ont., July 25, 1898. [27]

MacColl, Mary Jemima. See Schulte, Mrs. Mary Jemima, née MacColl.

McCollester, Sullivan Holman, clergyman, b. Marlboro, N.H., 1826; d. Stamford, Conn., May 20, 1921. [3; 10]

McCombs, William Frank, politician, b. Hamburg, Ark., 1875; d. New York, N.Y., Feb. 22, 1921. [10]

McConaughy, David, clergyman, b. Menallen, Pa., 1775; d. Washington, Pa., Jan. 29, 1852. [3]

McConaughy, James, editor, b. Gettysburg, Pa., 1857; d. Philadelphia, Pa., Dec. 6, 1934. [10; 11; 68]

McConaughy, John, journalist, b. 1884; d. 1933.

McConaughy, Mrs. Julia E., née **Loomis,** writer of juvenile fiction, b. 1834; d. ? [8]

McConkey, Mrs. Harriet E., née **Bishop.** See Bishop, Harriet E.

McConnel, John Ludlum, novelist, b. Scott county, Ill., 1826; d. Jacksonville, Ill., Jan. 17, 1862. [1; 3; 4; 6; 7; 9]

McConnell, James Rogers, aviator, b. 1887; d. 1917.

McConnell, Joseph Moore, educationist, b. McConnellsville, S.C., 1875; d. Davidson, N.C., May 16, 1935. [10]

McConnell, Lincoln, evangelist, b. Maryville, Tenn., 1867; d. St. Petersburg, Fla., May 6, 1930. [10]

McConnell, William John, politician, b. Oakland county, Mich., 1839; d. Moscow, Idaho, March 30, 1925. [4; 10]

McCook, Henry Christopher, clergyman and naturalist, b. New Lisbon, O., 1837; d. Philadelphia, Pa., Oct. 31, 1911. [1; 3; 4; 6; 7; 10]

MacCord, Charles William, educationist, b. Dutchess county, N.Y., 1836; d. Hoboken, N.Y., April 13, 1915. [10]

McCord, Frederick Augustus, historian, b. b. Aylmer, Que., 1856; d. Ottawa, Ont., July 23, 1908. [27]

McCord, Joseph, novelist, b. Moline, Ill., 1880; d. Los Angeles, Calif., Jan. 27, 1943. [7; 10]

McCord, Mrs. Louisa Susanna, née **Cheves,** poet and essayist, b. Charleston, S.C., 1810; d. Charleston, S.C., Nov. 23, 1879. [1; 3; 4; 6; 7; 8; 9; 34]

McCord, Peter B., cartoonist, d. Newark, N.J., Nov. 10, 1908.

McCord, Thomas, jurist, b. Montreal, Lower Canada, 1828; d. Quebec, Que., Feb. 19, 1886. [27]

MacCorkle, William Alexander, politician, b. Lexington, Ga., 1857; d. Charleston, W. Va., Sept. 24, 1930. [10]

McCormick, Brooks (pseud.). See Adams, William Taylor.

McCormick, Mrs. Harriet, née Hammond, art connoisseur, b. Monmouth, England, 1862; d. Chicago, Ill., Jan. 17, 1921. [4; 10]

McCormick, Henry, educationist, b. Ireland, 1837; d. Normal, Ill., July 18, 1918.

McCormick, John Francis, priest, b. Chicago, Ill., 1874; d. Chicago, Ill., July 15, 1943. [10; 21]

McCormick, John Newton, bishop, b. Richmond, Va., 1863; d. Grand Rapids, Mich., Nov. 26, 1939. [10]

McCormick, Leander Hamilton, lawyer, b. Chicago, Ill., 1859; d. Miami, Fla., Feb. 2, 1934. [10]

McCormick, Leander James, manufacturer, b. Rockbridge county, Va., 1819; d. Chicago, Ill., Feb. 20, 1900. [1; 4; 10]

McCormick, Richard Cunningham, journalist, b. New York, N.Y., May 23, 1832; d. Jamaica, Long Island, N.Y., June 2, 1901. [1; 3; 6; 8]

McCormick, William, journalist, b. Harrisburgh, Pa., 1866; d. Reading, Pa., Feb. 11, 1923. [10; 62]

McCorvey, Thomas Chalmers, educationist, b. Monroe county, Ala., 1851; d. Tuscaloosa, Ala., April 2, 1932. [8; 10; 34]

McCosh, James, clergyman and educationist, b. Ayrshire, Scotland, 1811; d. Princeton, N.J., Nov. 16, 1894. [1; 2; 3; 4; 5; 6; 7; 8; 9]

MacCoun, Townsend, cartographer, b. Troy, N.Y., 1845; d. New York, N.Y., Sept. 10, 1932. [10]

McCoy, Herbert Newby, chemist, b. Richmond, Ind., 1870; d. Los Angeles, Calif May 7, 1945. [10; 13]

McCoy, Isaac, clergyman, b. Fayette county, Pa., 1781; d. Louisville, Ky., June 21, 1846. [1; 3; 4]

McCoy, Joseph Geating, cattleman, b. Sangamon county, Ill., 1837; d. Kansas City, Mo., Oct. 19, 1915. [1]

McCoy, William Johnston, musician, b. Crestline, O., 1848; d. Oakland, Calif., Oct. 15, 1926. [20]

McCrackan, William Denison, historian, b. Munich, Germany, 1864; d. New York, N.Y., June 12, 1923. [4; 8; 10]

MacCracken, Henry Mitchell, clergyman and educationist, b. Oxford, O., 1840; d. Orlando, Fla., Dec. 24, 1918. [1; 4; 5; 10]

MacCracken, John Henry, educationist, b. Rochester, Vt., 1875; d. New York, N.Y., Feb. 1, 1948. [4; 10]

McCrady, Edward, lawyer and historian, b. Charleston, S.C., 1833; d. Charleston, S.C., Nov. 1, 1903. [1; 4; 7; 8; 10; 34]

McCrae, John, physician and poet, b. Guelph, Ont., 1872; d. Boulogne, France, Jan. 28, 1918. [27]

McCrary, George Washington, politician, b. near Evansville, Ind., 1835; d. St. Joseph, Mo., June 23, 1890. [3; 4; 5; 8]

McCrea, Mrs. Anna T., née Lincoln, educationist, d. Wilmington, Del., July 14, 1942.

McCrea, Nelson Glenn, educationist, b. Brooklyn, N.Y., 1863; d. New York, N.Y., May 31, 1944. [10]

McCready, Harold, engineer, b. Milford, Ont., 1885; d. East Orange, N.J., Aug. 2, 1945.

McCreery, John Luckey, poet, d. 1906. [37]

McCrimmon, Abraham Lincoln, educationist, b. Delhi, Ont., 1865; d. Hamilton, Ont., April 16, 1935. [27]

McCulloch, Mrs. Catherine, née Waugh, lawyer, b. Ransomville, N.Y., 1862; d. Evanston, Ill., April 20, 1945. [10]

McCulloch, Hugh, civil servant, b. Kennebunk, Me., 1808; d. Prince George's county, Ind., May 24, 1895. [1; 3; 4; 5; 7]

McCulloch, Hugh, poet, b. Fort Wayne, Ind., 1869; d. Florence, Italy, March 27, 1902. [3b; 7; 8]

MacCulloch, Hunter, poet, b. 1847; d. ? [8]

M'Culloch, John, printer, fl. 1787-1798.

McCulloch, Robert Osborne, lawyer, b. Galt, Ont., 1864; d. Galt, Ont., May 5, 1943. [27]

McCulloch, Robert W., novelist, b. Terre Haute, Ind., 1867; d. New York, N.Y., Feb. 4, 1946.

McCulloch, Thomas, clergyman and educationist, b. Renfrewshire, Scotland, 1777; d. Halifax, N.S., 1843. [27]

McCulloh, James Haines, archaeologist, b. about 1793; d. 1870. [3; 34]

McCullough, Ernest, structural engineer, b. Staten Island, N.Y., 1867; d. Long Island City, N.Y., Oct. 1, 1931. [1; 10]

McCullough, Mrs. Myrtle, née Reed. See Reed, Myrtle.

McCully, Laura Elizabeth, poet, b. Toronto, Ont., 1886; d. Toronto, Ont., July 8, 1924. [27]

McCune, George McAfee, educationist, b. Korea, 1908; d. Berkeley, Calif., Nov. 5, 1948.

MacCurdy, George Grant, anthropologist, b. Warrensburg, Mo., 1863; d. Plainfield, N.J., Nov. 15, 1947. [4; 10; 11]

McCurdy, Irwin Pounds, educationist, b. Westmoreland county, Pa., 1856; d. Lansford, Pa., 1916. [7; 10]

McCurdy, James Frederick, orientalist, b. Chatham, N.B., 1847; d. Toronto, Ont., March 31, 1935. [11; 27]

McCurdy, Stewart LeRoy, surgeon, b. Bowerston, O., 1859; d. Pittsburgh, Pa., Sept. 8, 1931. [4; 10; 11]

McCutcheon, Ben Frederick, journalist, b. Lafayette, Ind., 1875; d. Chicago, Ill., Aug. 27, 1934. [7; 10]

McCutcheon, George Barr, novelist, b. near Lafayette, Ind., 1866; d. New York, N.Y., Oct. 23, 1928. [1; 4; 7; 10; 72]

McDermott, Hugh Farrar, journalist, b. 1833; d. 1890. [8]

McDermott, William A., priest, b. 1863; d. 1913. [21]

McDill, John Rich, surgeon, b. Plover, Wis., 1862; d. Cornwall-on-Hudson, N.Y., Sept. 15, 1934. [10]

MacDonald, Alexander, bishop, b. Cape Breton, N.S., 1858; d. Antigonish, N.S., Feb. 24, 1941. [21; 22]

McDonald, Archibald, fur-trader, b. Argyllshire, Scotland, 1790; d. St. Andrew's, Que., Jan. 15, 1853. [27]

MacDonald, Arthur, anthropologist, b. Caledonia, N.Y., 1856; d. Washington, D.C., Jan. 17, 1936. [7; 10]

McDonald, Daniel, historian, b. 1833; d. Chicago, Ill., Jan. 10, 1916.

McDonald, David, jurist, b. near Millersburg, Ky., 1803; d. Indianapolis, Ind., Aug. 26, 1869. [5]

Macdonald, Duncan Black, theologian, b. Glasgow, Scotland, 1863; d. Hartford, Conn., Sept. 6, 1943. [10]

Macdonald, Edward Mortimer, politician, b. Pictou, N.S., 1865; d. Pictou, N.S., May 25, 1940. [27]

Macdonald, Mrs. Elizabeth, née Roberts. See Macdonald, Mrs. Jane Elizabeth Gostwycke, née Roberts.

MacDonald, Mrs. Ewan. See Montgomery, Lucy Maud.

MacDonald, George Alexander, lawyer, b. New York, N.Y., 1869; d. Brooklyn, N.Y., July 5, 1936. [10]

MacDonald, George Everett Hussey, journalist, b. Gardiner, Me., 1857; d. Upper Montclair, N.J., July 21, 1944. [10]

Macdonald, James Alexander, clergyman and journalist, b. Middlesex county, Ont., 1862; d. Toronto, Ont., May 13, 1923. [27]

Macdonald, James Edward Harvey, painter and poet, b. Durham, England, 1874; d. Toronto, Ont., Nov. 26, 1932. [27]

Macdonald, James Madison, clergyman, b. Limerick, Me., 1812; d. Princeton, N.J., April 19, 1876. [3; 5; 8]

Macdonald, Mrs. Jane Elizabeth Gostwycke, née Roberts, poet, b. Westcock, N.B., 1864; d. Ottawa, Ont., Nov. 8, 1922. [27]

McDonald, John, biographer, b. 1775; d. 1853.

MacDonald, John, educationist, b. 1843; d. 1916.

MacDonald, John Alexander, historian, b. 1846; d. Toronto, Ont., April, 1922. [27]

Macdonald, John William, surgeon, b. Antigonish, N.S., 1844;* d. Minneapolis, Minn., March 4, 1913. [10]

Macdonald, Loren Benjamin, clergyman, b. Newport, N.S., 1858; d. Minneapolis, Minn., Nov. 22, 1924. [51]

Macdonald, Marcia (pseud.). See Hill, Mrs. Grace, née Livingston.

MacDonald, Robert Gear, poet, b. St. Johns, Newfoundland, 1874; d. St Johns, Newfoundland, 1943. [30]

McDonald, William, clergyman, b. Belmont, Me., 1820; d. West Somerville, Mass., Sept. 11, 1901. [3b]

MacDonald, William, historian, b. Providence, R.I., 1863; d. New York, N.Y., Dec. 15, 1938. [10]

McDonald, William Naylor, soldier, b. 1834; d. 1898.

Macdonell, Blanche Lucile, novelist, b. 1853; d. Montreal, Que., Nov. 24, 1924. [27]

Macdonell, John Alexander, lawyer, b. Kingston, Ont., 1851; d. Alexandria, Ont., April 25, 1930. [27]

MacDonnell, James Francis Carlin, poet, b. Bay Shore, Long Island, N.Y., 1882; d. New York, N.Y., March 11, 1945. [10; 21]

McDonnell, William, poet and novelist, b. Cork, Ireland, 1814; d. Lindsay, Ont., June 20, 1900. [27]

McDonnold, Benjamin Wilburn, educationist, b. Overton county, Tenn., 1827; d. Lebanon, Tenn., Feb. 27, 1889. [5; 34]

McDougall, Donald, clergyman, b. about 1856; d. April 2, 1920.

McDougall, Mrs. Frances Harriet, née Whipple. See Green, Mrs. Frances Harriet, née Whipple.

McDougall, John, missionary, b. Owen Sound, Ont., 1842; d. Calgary, Alta., Jan. 15, 1917. [27]

McDougall, Mrs. Margaret, poet and novelist, b. about 1826; d. 1898. [39]

Macdougall, Robert, psychologist, b. Dewittville, Que., 1866; d. Montclair, N.J., Oct. 31, 1939. [10; 13]

McDougall, William, politician, b. York (Toronto), Upper Canada, 1822; d. Ottawa, Ont., May 29, 1905. [27]

McDougall, William, psychologist, b. Lancashire, England, 1871; d. Durham, N.C., Nov. 28, 1938. [7; 10; 11]

McDowall, Robert, clergyman, b. 1769; d. Fredericksburgh, Ont., Aug. 3, 1841. [27]

MacDowell, Edward Alexander, musical composer, b. New York, N.Y., 1861; d. New York, N.Y., Jan. 23, 1908. [1; 10; 20]

McDowell, John, clergyman, b. Dalry, Scotland, 1870; d. New York, N.Y., Nov. 13, 1937. [10]

McDowell, Mrs. Katherine Sherwood, née Bonner, novelist and short-story writer, b. Holly Springs, Miss., 1849; d. Holly Springs, Miss., July 22, 1883. [1; 3; 4; 6; 7; 8; 9; 34]

M'Dowell, William Adair, physician, b. 1795; d. 1853.

McDowell, William Fraser, bishop, b. Millersburg, O., 1858; d. Washington, D.C., April 26, 1937. [10; 11]

McDuffie, George, politician, b. Columbia county, Ga., 1790; d. Charleston, S.C., March 11, 1851. [1; 2; 3; 4; 34]

Mace, Aurelia Gay, religious writer, b. 1835; d. 1910.

Mace, Fayette, religious writer, fl. 1837-1838. [38]

Mace, Mrs. Frances Parker, née Laughton, poet, b. Orono, Me., 1836; d. Los Gatos, Calif., July 20, 1899. [3b; 4; 7; 8; 35]

Mace, William Harrison, historian, b. Lexington, Ind., 1852; d. Gananoque, Ont., Aug. 10, 1938. [7; 10; 11]

McElligott, James Napoleon, educationist, b. Richmond, Va., 1812; d. New York, N.Y., Oct. 22, 1866. [3; 4; 34]

McElrath, Thomas, lawyer, b. Williamsport, Pa., 1807; d. New York, N.Y., June 6, 1888. [1; 3; 4]

McElroy, John, soldier and journalist, b. Greenup county, Ky., 1846; d. Washington, D.C., Oct. 12, 1929. [1; 4; 7; 10]

McElroy, John George Repplier, educationist, b. Philadelphia, Pa., 1842; d. Philadelphia, Pa., Nov. 26, 1890. [5]

McElroy, John McConnell, clergyman, b. 1830; d. 1908.

McElroy, Mrs. Lucy, née **Cleaver,** novelist, b. Lebanon, Ky., 1860; d. 1901. [8; 34]

McElroy, William Henry, journalist, b. 1838; d. New York, N.Y., Nov. 7, 1918. [10]

MacElwee, Roy Samuel, engineer, b. Parkville, Mich., 1883; d. Arlington, Va., Feb. 6, 1944. [10]

McEvoy, Bernard, poet and journalist, b. Birmingham, England, 1842; d. Vancouver, B.C., Feb. 16, 1932. [11; 27]

McEvoy, John Millar, jurist, b. Caradoc, Ont., 1864; d. Toronto, Ont., April 16, 1935. [27]

McEvoy, Thomas Jefferson, educationist, b. Cortland, N.Y., 1859; d. Syracuse, N.Y., Nov. 7, 1942.

McFarland, Boynton Wells, chemist, b. Erie, Pa., 1868; d. New Haven, Conn., March 13, 1922, [62]

McFarland, John Thomas, clergyman, b. Mount Vernon, Ind., 1851; d. Maplewood, N.J., Dec. 22, 1913. [1; 10]

McFarland, Raymond, educationist, b. Lamoine, Me., 1872; d. East Aurora, N.Y., Sept. 6, 1944. [7; 10; 11; 62]

McFarland, Samuel Gamble, missionary, b. Washington county, Pa., 1830; d. Canonsburg, Pa., April 25, 1897. [1]

Macfarlane, Alexander, mathematician, b. Blairgowrie, Scotland, 1851; d. Chatham, Ont., Aug. 28, 1913. [10]

McFarlane, Arthur Emerson, novelist, b. Islington, Ont., 1876; d. New York, N.Y., April 11, 1945. [7; 10]

Macfarlane, Charles William, economist, b. Philadelphia, Pa., 1850; d. Philadelphia, Pa., May 15, 1931. [1; 4; 10]

Macfarlane, James, geologist, b. 1819; d. 1885.

MacFarlane, Janet, novelist, b. 1912; d. Oct. 31, 1949.

Macfarlane, John, poet, b. Lanarkshire, Scotland, 1857; d. Montreal, Que., Sept. 7, 1914. [27]

Macfarlane, John James, librarian and statistician, b. 1846; d. Philadelphia, Pa., Jan. 7, 1930.

Macfarlane, John Muirhead, botanist, b. Kirkaldy, Scotland, 1855; d. Lancaster, N.H., Sept. 16, 1943. [10; 13]

MacFarlane, Peter Clark, novelist, b. St. Clair county, Mo., 1871; d. San Francisco, Calif., June 9, 1924. [10; 35]

Macfarlane, Robert, editor, b. near Glasgow, Scotland, 1815; d. Brooklyn, N.Y., Dec. 21, 1883. [1; 3]

Macfarlane, Thomas, mining engineer, b. Renfrewshire, Scotland, 1834; d. Ottawa, Ont., June 10, 1907. [27]

McFaul, James Augustine, bishop, b. Larne, Ireland, 1850; d. Trenton, N.J., June 16, 1917. [10; 21]

McFerrin, John Berry, clergyman, b. Rutherford county, Tenn., 1807; d. Nashville, Tenn., May 10, 1887. [1; 3; 4; 6; 8; 34]

MacFetridge, Nathaniel S., clergyman, b. 1842; d. 1886.

MacGahan, Januarius Aloysius, journalist, b. Perry county, O., 1844; d. Constantinople, Turkey, June 9, 1878. [1; 3; 4; 6; 9]

McGarrity, Joseph, poet, b. Carrickmore, Ireland, 1874; d. Wynnefield, Pa., Aug. 5, 1940. [21]

McGarry, William James, priest and educationist, b. Hamilton, Mass., 1894; d. New York, N.Y., Sept. 23, 1941. [21; 22]

McGarvey, John William, theologian, b. Hopkinsville, Ky., 1829; d. Lexington, Ky., Oct. 6, 1911. [1; 3; 4; 6; 7; 10; 34]

McGee, Gentry Richard, historian, b. 1840; d. 1922.

McGee, Thomas D'Arcy, politician, b. county Louth, Ireland, 1825; d. Ottawa, Ont., April 7, 1868. [27]

McGeoch, John Alexander, psychologist, b. Argyle, N.Y., 1898; d. Iowa City, Ia., March 3, 1942. [13]

MacGeorge, Robert Jackson, clergyman, b. near Glasgow, Scotland, about 1811; d. Rothesay, Scotland, May 14, 1884. [27]

McGibbon, Robert Davidson, lawyer, b. 1857; d. Montreal, Que., April 18, 1906. [27]

McGiffert, Arthur Cushman, theologian, b. Sauquoit, N.Y., 1861; d. Dobbs Ferry, N.Y., Feb. 23, 1933. [1a; 7; 8; 10; 11; 68]

McGiffert, James, mathematician, b. Stockport, N.Y., 1868; d. Los Angeles, Calif., June 18, 1943. [10]

McGill, Alexander Taggart, clergyman, b. Canonsburg, Pa., 1807; d. Princeton, N.J., Jan. 13, 1889. [3; 4; 5; 8]

McGill, John, bishop, b. Philadelphia, Pa., 1809; d. Richmond, Va., Jan. 14, 1872. [1; 3; 4; 34]

McGill, Robert, clergyman, b. Ayrshire, Scotland, 1798; d. Montreal, Que., Feb. 4, 1856. [27]

McGillicuddy, Paul Clark, aviator, b. Toronto, Ont., 1918; d. Littlehampton, England, Aug. 21, 1942. [27]

MacGillivray, Alexander Dyer, entomologist, b. Inverness, O., 1868; d. Urbana, Ill., March 24, 1924. [10]

MacGillivray, Carrie Holmes, novelist, b. near Williamstown, Ont.; d. Toronto, Ont., May 16, 1949.

McGilvary, Daniel, missionary, b. Moore county, N.C., 1828; d. Cheing-Mai, Siam, Aug. 22, 1911. [1]

McGlannan, Alexius, surgeon, b. Baltimore, Md., 1872; d. Baltimore, Md., Feb. 25, 1940. [10; 11; 21]

McGlashan, Charles Fayette, pioneer, b. 1847; d. 1931.

McGlauflin, William Henry, clergyman, b. Charlotte, Me., 1856; d. Scranton, Pa., March 8, 1927. [10; 11]

McGloin, Frank, jurist, b. Ireland, 1846; d. near Baton Rouge, La., Aug. 30, 1921. [21; 34]

McGlothlin, William Joseph, educationist, b. near Gallatin, Tex., 1867; d. Gastonia, N.C., May 28, 1933. [1a; 10; 11]

McGoldrick, Mrs. Rita, née **Connell,** novelist, b. Brooklyn, N.Y., 1890; d. Brooklyn, N.Y., May 12, 1949. [21]

McGoun, Archibald, lawyer, b. Montreal, Que., 1853; d. Montreal, Que., June 5, 1921. [27]

McGovern, James Joseph, priest, b. 1839; d. 1914. [21]

McGovern, John, journalist, b. Troy, N.Y., 1850; d. Chicago, Ill., Dec. 17, 1917. [1; 7; 10]

MacGowan, Alice, novelist, b. Perrysburg, O., 1858; d. Los Gatos, Calif., March 10, 1947. [35]

McGowan, Francis Xavier, priest, b. 1854; d. 1903. [21]

McGowan, Jonas Hartzell, lawyer, b Columbiana county, O., 1837; d. Washington, D.C., July 5, 1909.

MacGrath, Harold, novelist, b. Syracuse, N.Y., 1871; d. Syracuse, N.Y., Oct. 30, 1932. [4; 7; 10; 11]

McGraw, John Joseph, baseball player, b. Truxton, N.Y., 1873; d. New Rochelle, N.Y., Feb. 25, 1934. [1a]

McGregor, James, clergyman, b. Perthshire, Scotland, 1759; d. Pictou, N.S., 1830. [27]

McGregor, James Clyde, educationist, b. Wheeling, W. Va., 1883; d. Washington, Pa., Feb. 15, 1940. [10]

McGregor, James Gordon, physicist, b. Halifax, N.S., 1852; d. Edinburgh, Scotland, May 21, 1913. [27]

MacGregor, Patrick, lawyer, b. Perthshire, Scotland, 1816; d. Toronto, Ont., Jan. 25, 1882. [27]

McGregory, Joseph Frank, chemist, b. Wilbraham, Mass., 1855; d. Hamilton, N.Y., Oct. 14, 1934. [10; 11]

McGrew, Thomas Fletcher, poultryman, b. 1850; d. 1930.

McGroarty, John Steven, politician and poet, b. Luzerne county, Pa., 1862; d. Los Angeles, Calif., Aug. 7, 1944. [10. 11; 21; 22; 35]

McGuffey, Alexander Hamilton, educationist, b. Youngstown, O., 1816; d. Cincinnati, O., June 4, 1896. [3b]

McGuffey, William Holmes, educationist, b. Washington county, Pa., 1800; d. Charlottesville, Va., May 4, 1873. [1; 4; 7; 9]

McGuire, Hunter Holmes, surgeon, b. Winchester, Va., 1835; d. Richmond, Va., 1900. [10; 34]

McGuire, Mrs. Judith White, née **Brockenbrough,** diarist, b. Richmond, Va., 1813; d. ? [34]

McGuire, William Anthony, playwright, b. Chicago, Ill., 1887; d. Beverley Hills, Calif., Sept. 16, 1940. [7; 10]

Machar, Agnes Maule, poet and novelist, b. Kingston, Upper Canada, 1837; d. Kingston, Ont., Jan. 24, 1927. [27]

McHatton-Ripley, Mrs. Eliza. See Ripley, Mrs. Eliza Moore, née Chinn.

Machen, John Gresham, theologian, b. Baltimore, Md., 1881; d. Philadelphia, Pa., Jan. 1, 1937. [10; 11]

McHenry, James, soldier and politician, b. Ballymena, Ireland, 1753; d. near Baltimore, Md., May 3, 1816. [1; 3; 4]

McHenry, James, poet and novelist, b. Larne, Ireland, 1775; d. Larne, Ireland, July 21, 1845. [1; 3; 6; 7; 9]

MacHugh, Augustin, playwright, b. 1877; d. New York, N.Y., Aug. 24, 1928. [7]

McHugh, Hugh (pseud.). See Hobart, George Vere.

McIlhenny, Edward Avery, artist and naturalist, b. 1872; d. Avery Island, La., Aug. 8, 1949.

McIlvaine, Charles, naturalist, b. Chester county, Pa., 1840; d. Cambridge, Md., 1909. [8; 10]

McIlvaine, Charles Pettit, bishop, b. Burlington, Vt., 1799; d. Florence, Italy, March 13, 1873. [1; 3; 4; 5; 6]

McIlvaine, James Hall, clergyman, b. Utica, N.Y., 1846; d. Pittsburgh, Pa., March 14, 1921. [10]

McIlvaine, Joshua Hall, clergyman and educationist, b. Lewis, Del., 1815; d. Princeton, N.J., Jan. 30, 1897. [3; 4; 8]

McIlwaine, Richard, clergyman and educationist, b. Petersburg, Va., 1834; d. Richmond, Va., Aug. 10, 1913. [1; 3; 5; 10; 34]

McIlwraith, Jean Newton, novelist and biographer, b. Hamilton, Ont., 1859; d. Burlington, Ont., Nov. 17, 1938. [11; 27]

McIlwraith, Thomas, ornithologist, b. Ayrshire, Scotland, 1824; d. Hamilton, Ont., Jan. 31, 1903. [27]

McInnes, James Campbell, singer and elocutionist, b. Lancashire, England, 1874; d. Toronto, Ont., Feb. 8, 1945. [27]

McIntosh, Atwell Campbell, lawyer, b. Fayetteville, N.C., 1859; d. Durham, N.C., Jan. 27, 1939. [11; 34]

McIntosh, Burr, actor, b. Wellsville, O., 1862; d. Los Angeles, Calif., April 28, 1942. [10]

McIntosh, John, ethnologist, fl. 1836-1859.

McIntosh, Maria Jane, novelist, b. Sunbury, Ga., 1803; d. Morristown, N.J., Feb. 25, 1878. [3; 4; 6; 8]

McIntyre, James, poetaster, b. Forres, Scotland, 1827; d. Ingersoll, Ont., March 5, 1906. [27]

McIntyre, Oscar Odd, journalist, b. Plattsburg, Mo., 1884; d. New York, N.Y., Feb. 14, 1938. [7; 10; 11]

McIntyre, Robert, bishop and poet, b. Selkirk, Scotland, 1851; d. Chicago, Ill., Aug. 30, 1914. [4; 10]

McIntyre, Willard Ezra, clergyman, b. Cumberland Point, N.B., 1852; d. Saint John, N.B., Sept. 28, 1915. [27]

MacIsaac, Frederick John, novelist, b. Cambridge, Mass., 1886; d. Hollywood, Calif., Aug. 5, 1940. [7; 10; 35]

McIvor, Ivor Ben (pseud.). See Welsh, Charles.

McJilton, John Nelson, clergyman, b. Baltimore, Md., 1805; d. New York, N.Y., April 13, 1875. [3b]

McJimsey, William, clergyman and poet, b. 1797; d. 1881.

Mack, Ebenezer, printer, fl. 1813-1848.

Mack, William, law editor, b. Sumter county, S.C., 1865; d. Brooklyn, N.Y., Dec. 10, 1941. [10]

Mackall, Louis, physician, b. 1801; d. 1876.

McKay, Claude, poet and novelist, b. Jamaica, 1890; d. Chicago, Ill., May 22, 1948. [7; 10]

Mackay, Douglas, journalist, b. Woodstock, Ont., Dec. 6, 1900; d. Jan. 10, 1938. [27]

McKay, Frederic Edward, drama critic, d. Brooklyn, N.Y., 1870; d. Port Washington, Long Island, N.Y., Feb. 29, 1944.

Mackay, George Leslie, missionary, b. Zorra, Ont., 1844; d. Formosa, China, June 2, 1901. [27]

MacKay, Mrs. Isabel Ecclestone, née Macpherson, poet and novelist, b. Woodstock, Ont., 1875; d. Vancouver, B.C., Aug. 15, 1928. [27]

MacKay, John, clergyman and educationist, b. Kintore, Ont., 1870; d. Winnipeg, Man., May 16, 1938. [27]

McKay, John George, poet, b. Little Branch, N.B., 1886; d. Montreal, Que., Aug. 7, 1923. [27]

Mackay, Robert Walter Stuart, publisher, b. Scotland, about 1809; d. Montreal, Que., Oct. 9, 1854. [27]

MacKay, William Alexander, clergyman, b. Zorra, Ont., 1842; d. Woodstock, Ont., Nov. 28, 1905. [27]

MacKaye, Harold Steele, lawyer and novelist, b. Paris, France, 1866; d. Yonkers, N.Y., June 22, 1928. [10]

Mackaye, Hazel, dramatist, b. New York, N.Y., 1882; d. Westport, Conn., Aug. 11, 1944. [10]

MacKaye, James, educationist, b. New York, N.Y., 1872; d. Hanover, N.H., Jan. 22, 1935. [4; 10]

MacKaye, James Morrison Steele, dramatist, b. Buffalo, N.Y., 1842; d. Timpas, Colo., Feb. 25, 1894. [1; 3; 4; 6; 7]

MacKaye, Mrs. Maria Ellery, née Goodwin, essayist, b. 1830; d. ? [8]

MacKaye, Mrs. Mary Keith, née Medbery, playwright, b. 1845; d. 1924.

MacKaye, Steele. See MacKaye, James Morrison Steele.

MacKay, Mrs. Steele. See MacKaye, Mrs. Mary Keith, née Medbery.

McKeag, Anna Jane, educationist, b. 1864; d. Wellesley, Mass., Nov. 23, 1947.

McKean, Thomas, lawyer and politician, b. New London, Pa., 1734; d. Philadelphia, Pa., June 24, 1817. [1; 2; 3; 4; 6]

McKean, Thomas, novelist and playwright, b. Philadelphia, Pa., 1869; d. Villanova, Pa., Feb. 7, 1942. [7; 10]

McKee, James Harvey, soldier, b. 1840; d. 1918.

McKeen, Phebe F., novelist, b. Bradford, Vt.; d. on the train from New York to Boston, June 1, 1880. [43]

McKeen, Silas, clergyman, b. Corinth, Va., 1791; d. Bradford, Vt., Dec. 10, 1877. [43]

McKeever, Harriet Burn, novelist, b. Philadelphia, Pa., 1807; d. Chester, Pa., Feb. 7, 1886. [3; 6; 7; 8]

McKeever, William Arch, educationist, b. Jackson county, Kans., 1868; d. Oklahoma City, Okla., July 8, 1940. [10; 11; 75]

McKellar, Thomas, printer and poet, b. New York, N.Y., 1812; d. Philadelphia, Pa., Dec. 29, 1899. [1; 3; 4; 6; 7; 8; 9; 10]

McKelvey, John Jay, lawyer, b. Sandusky, O., 1863 d. Mount Kisco, N.Y., Oct. 19, 1947. [10; 11]

McKenna, Charles Hyacinth, missionary, b. county Derry, Ireland, 1835; d. Jacksonville, Fla., Feb. 21, 1917.

McKenna, Maurice, poet, b. 1846; d. Fond du Lac, Wis., Aug. 23, 1927.

McKenny, Thomas Loraine, administrator, b. Hopewell, Md., 1785; d. New York, N.Y., Feb. 19, 1859. [1; 3; 6]

McKenny, Arthur Frank, clergyman, b. Cleveland, O., 1894; d. New Haven, Conn., Dec. 13, 1945. [62]

McKenny, Charles, educationist, b. Dimondale, Mich., Sept. 5, 1860; d. Ypsilanti, Mich., Sept. 24, 1933. [10; 11]

Mackenzie, Alexander, politician, b. Perthshire, Scotland, 1822; d. Toronto, Ont., April 17, 1892. [27]

McKenzie, Alexander, clergyman, b. New Bedford, Mass., 1830; d. Cambridge, Mass., Aug. 6, 1914. [1; 3; 5; 6; 10]

Mackenzie, Alexander Slidell, naval officer, b. New York, N.Y., 1803; d. Tarrytown, N.Y., Sept. 13, 1848. [1; 3; 4; 5; 6; 7; 8]

Mackenzie, Arthur Stanley, educationist, b. Pictou, N.S., 1865; d. Halifax, N.S., Oct. 2, 1938. [11; 27]

Mackenzie, Cameron, novelist, b. Wilkesbarre, Pa., 1882; d. at sea, March 18, 1921. [10]

Mackenzie, Catherine, journalist, b. Baddeck, Cape Breton, N.S., 1894; d. New York, N.Y., Oct. 24, 1949.

Mackenzie, Donald, theologian, b. Isle of Lewis, Scotland, 1882; d. Princeton, N.J., Oct. 19, 1941.

Mackenzie, Frederick Arthur, war correspondent, b. Quebec., Que., 1869; d. Ziest, Holland, July 31, 1931. [27]

Mackenzie, James Bovell, poet, b. 1851; d. Toronto, Ont., Jan. 7, 1919. [27]

Mackenzie, Jean Kenyon, missionary, b. Elgin, Ill., 1874; d. New York, N.Y., Sept. 2, 1936. [10; 11]

McKenzie, Kenneth, educationist, b. Cambridge, Mass., 1870; d. New Haven, Conn., Nov. 3, 1949. [10; 51]

McKenzie, Nathaniel Murdoch William John, fur-trader, b. near Stromness, Orkneys, Scotland, 1856; d. Winnipeg, Man., Feb. 15, 1943. [27]

Mackenzie, Robert Shelton, journalist, b. county Limerick, Ireland, 1809; d. Philadelphia, Pa., Nov. 21, 1881. [1; 3; 6; 7; 9]

McKenzie, Robert Tait, physician and sculptor, b. Almonte, Ont., 1867; d. Philadelphia, Pa., April 28, 1938. [10]

McKenzie, Roderick Duncan, sociologist, b. Carman, Man., 1885; d. Ann Arbor, Mich., May 6, 1940. [10]

Mackenzie, William Douglas, theologian, b. South Africa, 1859; d. Hartford, Conn., March 29, 1936. [10]

Mackenzie, William Lyon, politician and rebel, b. Dundee, Scotland, 1795; d. Toronto, Ont., Aug. 28, 1861. [27]

McKenzie, William Patrick, poet and religious teacher, b. Almonte, Ont., 1861; d. Cambridge, Mass., Sept. 8, 1942. [10; 12]

McKeown, Hugh Charles, lawyer, d. St. Catherines, Ont., March 24, 1889. [27]

MacKeracher, William Mackay, poet and journalist, b. Châteauguay, Que., 1871; d. Montreal, Que., April 6, 1913. [27]

Mackey, Albert Gallatin, freemason, b. Charleston, S.C., 1807; d. Fortress Monroe, Va., June 20, 1881. [1; 3; 5; 6]

Mackey, John, educationist, b. Charleston, S.C., 1765; d. Charleston, S.C., Dec. 14, 1831. [3; 8]

Mackey, Thomas Jefferson, lawyer, b. 1830; d. 1909.

McKibbin, Archibald, clergyman, b. Huron county, Ont., 1863; d. London, Ont., Nov. 18, 1925. [27]

MacKie, Charles Paul, historian, fl. 1887-1892.

Mackie, John Milton, educationist, b. Wareham, Mass., 1813; d. Great Barrington, Mass., July 27, 1894. [3; 4; 6; 7; 8]

McKim, Randolph Harrison, clergyman, b. Baltimore, Md., 1842; d. Washington, D.C., July 15, 1921. [8; 10]

McKim, William Duncan, physician, b. Baltimore, Md., 1855; d. Washington, D.C., April 10, 1935. [10; 11]

McKinley, Albert Edward, educationist, b. Philadelphia, Pa., 1870; d. Philadelphia, Pa., Feb. 26, 1936. [10]

McKinley, Carlyle, journalist, essayist, and poet, b. Newnan, Ga., 1847; d. Charleston. S.C., Aug. 24, 1904. [1; 9; 10; 34]

McKinley, Earl Baldwin, bacteriologist, b. Emporia, Kans., 1894; d. Washington, D.C., July 29, 1938. [10; 13]

McKinley, William, clergyman, b. Glasgow, Scotland, 1834; d. Winona, Minn., 1918. [70]

McKinney, Alexander Harris, clergyman, b. New York, N.Y., 1858; d. Jamaica, N.Y., April 22, 1941. [10; 68]

McKinney, Edward Pascal, soldier, b. Cooperstown, N.Y., 1838; d. Binghampton, N.Y., Oct. 18, 1925. [62]

McKinney, Mordecai, lawyer, b. near Carlisle, Pa., 1796; d. Harrisburg, Pa., Dec. 17, 1867. [3; 5; 6; 8]

McKinney, Thomas Emery, educationist, b. Hebron, W. Va., 1864; d. Marietta, O., April 12, 1930. [10; 11; 13]

Mackinnon, Clarence, clergyman and educationist, b. Hopewell, N.S., 1868; d. Halifax, N.S., Oct. 9, 1937. [27]

McKinnon, William Charles, clergyman, b. Cape Breton, N.S.; d. Nova Scotia, March 26, 1862. [27]

McKishnie, Archie P., novelist, b. New Scotland, Ont., 1876; d. Toronto, Ont., July 7, 1946. [11; 30]

McKnight, Charles, novelist and historian, b. Pittsburgh, Pa., 1826; d. Philadelphia, Pa., Jan. 22, 1881. [4; 8]

McKnight, George, poet, b. Sterling, N.Y., 1840; d. 1897. [3; 8]

McKnight, William James, historian, b. 1836; d. 1918.

Mackubin, Ellen, writer of fiction, b. Chicago, Ill.; d. 1915. [8]

McLachlan, Alexander, poet, b. Renfrewshire, Scotland, 1818; d. Orangeville, Ont., March 30, 1896. [27]

McLachlan, Robert Wallace, numismatist, b. Montreal, Que., 1845; d. Montreal, Que., May 10, 1926. [27]

MacLafferty, James Henry, poet, b. San Diego, Calif., 1871; d. June 9, 1937. [35]

McLain, John Scudder, journalist, b. Brown county, O., 1853; d. Nov. 17, 1931. [10]

MacLane, Mary, journalist and motion-picture actress, b. Winnipeg, Man., 1883; d. Chicago, Ill., Aug. 7, 1929. [7; 10]

McLane, William Ward, clergyman, b. Lewisville, Pa., 1846; d. Lynn, Mass., June 14, 1931. [62]

MacLaren, James Henry, miscellaneous writer, b. 1864; d. 1928.

Maclaren, John James, jurist, b. Lachute, Que., 1842; d. Toronto, Ont., July 8, 1926. [27]

MacLaren, Malcolm, educationist, b. Annapalis, Md., 1869; d. Princeton, N.J., Sept. 24, 1945. [10]

McLaren, William Edward, bishop, b. Geneva, N.Y., 1831; d. Chicago, Ill., Feb. 19, 1905. [1; 3; 4; 6; 10]

McLaughlin, Andrew Cunningham, historian, b. Beardstown, Ill., 1861; d. Chicago, Ill., Sept. 24, 1947. [4; 7; 10; 11; 14]

McLaughlin, Edward Augustus, poet, b. North Stamford, Conn., 1798; d. New York, N.Y., Nov. 15, 1861. [3]

McLaughlin, Edward Tompkins, educationist, b. Sharon, Conn., 1860; d. New Haven, Conn., July 25, 1893. [62]

McLaughlin, George Asbury, clergyman, b. Nashua, N.H., 1851; d. Walnut Park, Calif., March 10, 1933. [10; 11]

McLaughlin, James, civil servant, b. Avonmore, Ont., 1842; d. Washington, D.C., July 28, 1923. [1; 10]

McLaughlin, James Fairfax, lawyer, b. Alexandria, Va., 1839; d. Dec., 1903. [7; 34]

McLaughlin, Mrs. Marie Louise, née Buisson, half-breed, b. 1842; d. ?

McLaughlin, Robert William, clergyman, b. New Haven, Conn., 1866; d. Newagen, Me., March 20, 1936. [10; 11]

McLaurin, Colin Campbell, clergyman, b. Clarence, Ont., 1853; d. Calgary, Alta., Feb. 20, 1941. [30]

McLaws, Emily Lafayette, novelist, b. Augusta, Ga., 1874; d. ? [7; 34]

Maclay, Arthur Collins, lawyer, b. 1853; d. Nov. 11, 1930.

Maclay, Edgar Stanton, historian, b. Foochow, China, 1863; d. Washington, D.C., Nov. 2, 1919. [1; 4; 7; 9; 10]

Maclay, Robert Samuel, missionary, b. Concord, Pa., 1824; d. San Fernando, Calif., Aug. 18, 1907. [1; 10]

McLean, Alexander, clergyman, b. North Uist, Scotland, 1827; d. Morriston, Ont., May 24, 1864. [27]

Maclean, Alexander, clergyman, b. near Hopewell, N.S., 1822; d. Eureka, N.S., Aug. 17, 1916. [27]

MacLean, Annie Marion, sociologist, b. St. Peter's Bay, P.E.I.; d. Pasadena, Calif., May 1, 1934. [10; 11]

McLean, Archibald, clergyman, b. Prince Edward Island, 1850; d. Cincinnati, O., Dec. 15, 1920. [1; 10]

MacLean, Charles Thomas Agnew, editor and novelist, b. Ballymena, Ireland, 1880; d. Brooklyn, N.Y., June 17, 1928. [10]

Maclean, Mrs. Clara Victoria, née Dargan, novelist, b. South Carolina, 1840; d. ? [8]

MacLean, George Edwin, educationist, b. Rockville, Conn., 1850; d. Washington, D.C., May 3, 1938. [10; 11; 62; 70]

Maclean, John, educationist, b. Glasgow, Scotland, 1771; d. Princeton, N.J., Feb. 17, 1814. [1; 3; 6]

Maclean, John, educationist, b. Princeton, N.J., 1800; d. Princeton, N.J., Aug. 10, 1886. [1; 3; 4]

McLean, John, physician, b. 1837; d. Chicago, Ill., April 25, 1921.

Maclean, John, missionary, b. Kilmarnock, Scotland, 1851; d. Winnipeg, Man., March 7, 1928. [27]

MacLean, John Patterson, clergyman, b. Franklin, O., 1848; d. Greenville, O., Aug. 12, 1939.

McLean, McDugald Keener, physician, b. 1886; d. Asheville, N.C., Sept. 8, 1922.

McLean, Ridley, naval officer, b. Pulaski, Tenn., 1872; d. San Francisco, Calif., Nov. 12, 1933. [10]

McLean, Sarah Pratt. See Greene, Mrs. Sarah Pratt, née McLean.

McLean, Simon James, economist, b. Brooklyn, N.Y., 1871; d. Ottawa, Ont., Oct. 5, 1946. [30]

MacLear, Anne Bush, educationist, b. Wilmington, Del., about 1873; d. Mount Vernon, N.Y., April 26, 1938. [10; 11]

McLellan, Isaac, sportsman and poet, b. Portland, Me., 1806; d. Greenport, Long Island, N.Y., Aug. 20, 1899. [1; 3b; 4; 7; 9]

McLellan, James Alexander, educationist, b. Shubenacadie, N.S., 1832; d. Toronto, Ont., Aug. 11, 1907. [27]

McLennan, John Stewart, historian, b. Montreal, Que., 1853; d. Ottawa, Ont., Sept. 15, 1939. [27]

MacLennan, Simon Fraser, educationist, b. Harriston, Ont., 1870; d. Oberlin, O., May 17, 1938. [10; 11]

McLennan, William, novelist, b. Montreal, Que., 1856; d. Vallombrosa, Italy, Aug. 12, 1904. [27]

McLeod, Alexander, clergyman, b. Island of Mull, Scotland, 1774; d. New York, N.Y., Feb. 17, 1833. [1; 3; 4; 6]

McLeod, Clement Henry, educationist, b. Cape Breton, N.S., 1851; d. Montreal, Que., Dec. 26, 1917. [27]

McLeod, Donald, rebel and historian, b. Aberdeen, Scotland, 1779; d. Cleveland, O., July 22, 1879. [27]

MacLeod, Donald. See MacLeod, Xavier Donald.

MacLeod, Mrs. Elizabeth Susan, née MacQueen, poet, b. Edinburgh, Scotland, 1842; d. Charlottetown, P.E.I.. Jan. 14, 1939. [27]

McLeod, Mrs. Georgiana A., née Hulse, educationist, d. 1890. [6; 8; 34]

MacLeod, John M., clergyman, b. West River, N.S., 1825; d. ? [27]

McLeod, Malcolm, publicist, b. Green lake, Beaver river, N.W.T., 1821; d. Ottawa, Ont., 1899. [27]

McLeod, Malcolm James, clergyman, b. Prince Edward Island, 1867; d. Bronxville, N.Y., Oct. 5, 1940. [10; 11]

McLeod, Robert Randall, clergyman, b. Brookfield, Queens county, N.S., 1839; d. Brookfield, N.S., Feb. 12, 1909. [27; 51]

MacLeod, Xavier Donald, clergyman, b. New York, N.Y., 1821; d. near Cincinnati, O., July 20, 1865. [3; 4; 6; 8]

Macloskie, George, educationist, b. Castledown, Ireland, 1834; d. Princeton, N.J., Jan. 4, 1920.

Maclure, William, geologist, b. Ayr, Scotland, 1763; d. San Angel, Mexico, March 23, 1840. [1; 3; 4; 5; 6]

MacMahan, Mrs. Anna, née Benneson, journalist, b. Quincy, Ill., 1846; d. Bryn Mawr, Pa., Nov. 1919. [7; 10]

MacMahon, Bernard, horticulturist, b. Ireland, about 1775; d. Philadelphia, Pa., Sept. 16, 1816. [1; 3; 6]

McMahon, James, mathematician, b. Armagh county, Ireland, 1856; d. Ithaca, N.Y., June 1, 1922. [10]

MacMahon, John Van Lear, lawyer and historian, b. Cumberland, Md., 1800; d. Cumberland, Md., June 15, 1871. [1; 3; 4; 6; 9]

MacManus, Theodore Francis, publicist, b. Buffalo, N.Y., 1873; d. Sudbury, Ont., Sept. 12, 1940. [21]

McMaster, Gilbert, clergyman, b. Ireland, 1778; d. New Albany, Ind., March 15, 1854. [3; 6; 8]

McMaster, Guy Humphrey, jurist, b. Wayne county, N.Y., 1829; d. Bath, N.Y., Sept. 13, 1887. [1 ;3; 4; 7]

McMaster, John Bach, historian, b. Winnsboro, S.C., 1867; d. Darien, Conn., May 24, 1932. [1; 4; 7; 10]

MacMechan, Archibald McKellar, educationist, b. Kitchener, Ont., 1862; d. Halifax, N.S., Aug. 7, 1933. [27]

McMichael, William, lawyer, b. Philadelphia, Pa., 1841; d. New York, N.Y., April 20, 1893. [3b]

MacMillan, Conway, botanist, b. Hillsdale, Mich., 1867; d. June 24, 1929. [70]

McMillan, Duncan Cameron, court reporter, b. Rondout, N.Y., 1848; d. Closter, N.J., March 22, 1899. [3b]

McMillin, Hamilton, lawyer, b. Fayetteville, N.C., 1837; d. Feb., 1916. [34]

Macmillan, John C., priest, b. Dundas, P.E.I., 1862; d. Charlottetown, P.E.I., April 18, 1926. [27]

Macmillan, John Walker, clergyman, b. Mount Forest, Ont., 1868; d. Toronto, Ont., April 16, 1932. [27]

Macmillan, Kerr Duncan, educationist, b. Mount Forest, Ont., 1871; d. Aurora-on-Cayuga, N.Y., March 13, 1939. [10; 56]

McMillan, William Franklin, novelist and genealogist, b. 1843; d. ?

MacMinn, Edwin, clergyman, b. 1851; d. 1923.

McMullen, John Mercier, historian, b. Ireland, 1820; d. Brockville, Ont., Feb. 9, 1907. [27]

McMullen, Mary Anne. See Ford, Mrs. Mary Anne, née McMullen.

MacMurchy, Angus, lawyer, b. Toronto, Ont., 1860; d. en route from Montreal, Que., to Toronto, Ont., May 3, 1931. [31a]

MacMurchy, Archibald, educationist, b. Argyllshire, Scotland, 1832; d. Toronto, Ont., April 27, 1912. [27]

MacMurchy, Marjory, See Willison, Marjory, Lady, née MacMurchy.

Macmurray, Thomas James, clergyman and poet, b. 1852; d. ?

McMurray, William Josiah, physician, b. Williamson county, Tenn., 1842; d. Nashville, Tenn., Dec. 4, 1905. [4; 10] ¹

McMurrich, James Playfair, educationist, b. Toronto, Ont., 1859; d. Toronto, Ont., Feb. 9, 1939. [27]

McMurry, Charles Alexander, educationist, b. Crawfordsville, Ind., 1857; d. Nashville, Tenn., March 24, 1929. [10; 11]

McMurry, Frank Morton, educationist, b. Crawfordsville, Ind., 1862; d. Pawling, N.Y., Aug. 1, 1936. [10]

McMurry, Lida Brown, writer of books for children, b. Kiantone, N.Y., 1853; d. ? [7; 11]

McMurtrie, Douglas Crawford, writer on typography, b. Belmar, N.J., 1888; d. Evanston, Ill., Sept. 29, 1944. [7; 10]

McMurtrie, Henry, physician and educationist, b. Philadelphia, Pa., 1793; d. Philadelphia, Pa., May 26, 1865. [3; 8]

MacNair, Harley Farnsworth, educationist, b. Greenfield, Pa., 1891; d. Chicago, Ill., June 23, 1947. [10; 11]

McNamara, John, clergyman, b. Dromore, Ireland, 1824; d. North Platte, Neb., Oct. 24, 1885. [3; 8]

McNaugher, John, clergyman, b. Allegheny, Pa., 1857; d. Pittsburgh, Pa., Dec. 11, 1947. [10]

Macnaughton, John, educationist, b. Perthshire, Scotland, 1858; d. Montreal, Que., Feb. 5, 1943. [27]

Macnaughton, John Hugh, poet, b. Caledonia, N.Y., 1829; d. 1891. [6; 8]

McNeal, Thomas Allen, journalist, b. Marion county, O., 1853; d. ? [4; 7]

McNeely, Mrs. Marian, née Hurd, writer of books for girls, b. Dubuque, Ia., 1877; d. Dubuque, Ia., Dec. 18, 1930. [11; 15]

McNeil, Henry Everett, writer of books for boys, b. near Stoughton, Wis., 1862; d. Tacoma, Wash., Dec. 14, 1929. [10; 11]

McNeill, George Edwin, labour organizer, b. Amesbury, Mass., 1837; d. Somerville, Mass., May 19, 1906. [1; 8; 10]

MacNeill, John, clergyman, b. Bruce county, Ont., 1874; d. Hamilton, Ont., Feb. 10, 1937. [27]

McNeill, John Charles, journalist and poet, b. 1874; d. Charlotte, N.C., Oct. 17, 1907. [10; 34]

McNemar, Richard, religious enthusiast, b. 1770; d. 1839.

Macneven, William James, physician, b. county Galway, Ireland, 1763; d. New York, N.Y., July 12, 1841. [1; 3; 4; 6]

McNichols, John Patrick, priest and educationist, b. St. Louis, Mo., 1875; d. Detroit, Mich., April 26, 1932. [10; 11]

Macnie, John, educationist, b. Stirling, Scotland, 1836; d. Minneapolis, Minn., Oct. 30, 1909.

McNutt, William Fletcher, physician, b. b. Lower Truro, N.S., 1839; d. San Francisco, Calif., Jan. 29, 1924. [33]

Macomb, Alexander, soldier, b. Detroit, Mich., 1782; d. Washington, D.C., June 25, 1841. [1; 3; 4; 6]

Macomber, William, lawyer, b. Oakfield, N.Y., 1857; d. Buffalo, N.Y., Feb., 1920. [10]

Macon, John Alfred, journalist, b. Alabama, 1851; d. Richmond, Va., 1891. [4; 8; 34]

Macoun, John, botanist, b. county Down, Ireland, 1832; d. Ottawa, Ont., July 18, 1920. [27]

Macoy, Robert, writer on freemasonry, b. 1806; d. Brooklyn, N.Y., Jan. 9, 1895. [6]

Macphail, Sir Andrew, physician and littérateur, b. Orwell, P.E.I., 1864; d. Montreal, Que., Sept. 23, 1938. [11; 27]

DICTIONARY OF NORTH AMERICAN AUTHORS

McPharlin, Paul, designer and illustrator, b. 1903; d. Birmingham, Mich., Sept. 28, 1948. [12]

Macpherson, Mrs. Charlotte Holt, née Gethings, writer of reminiscences, fl. 1828-1890. [27]

Macpherson, Mrs. Daniel. See Macpherson, Mrs. Charlotte Holt, née Gethings.

McPherson, Edward, journalist and politician, b. Gettysburg, Pa., 1830; d. Gettysburg, Pa., Dec. 14, 1895. [1; 3; 4; 6; 9]

Macpherson, James Pennington, biographer, b. Kingston, Upper Canada, 1839; d. Ottawa, Ont., Feb. 9, 1916. [27]

McPherson, John, poet, b. Liverpool, N.S., 1817; d. Brookfield, N.S., July 26, 1845. [27]

McPherson, Logan Grant, economist, b. Circleville, O., 1863; d. New York, N.Y., March 23, 1925. [1; 8; 10]

McPherson, William David, lawyer, b. Lambton county, Ont., 1863; d. Toronto, Ont. May 2, 1929. [27]

McPherson, William Lenhart, journalist, b. Gettysburg, Pa., 1865; d. New York, N.Y., Nov. 8, 1930. [10; 11]

MacPhie, John Peter, clergyman, b. Pictou county, N.S., 1854; d. Pasadena, Calif., Nov. 24, 1931. [33]

MacQueary, Thomas Howard, clergyman, b. near Charlottesville, Va., 1861; d. St. Louis, Mo., July, 1930. [10]

MacQueen, Peter, explorer, b. Wigtonshire, Scotland, 1865; d. Boothbay Harbor, Me., Jan. 11, 1924. [10; 68]

McQuill, Thursty (pseud.). See Bruce, Wallace.

McRae, Milton Alexander, newspaper publisher, b. Detroit, Mich., 1858; d. La Jolla, Calif., Oct. 11, 1930. [1; 4; 7; 10]

McRaye, Walter Jackson, lecturer, b. 1877; d. Grimsby, Ont., Aug. 7, 1946.

McRee, Griffith John, lawyer, b. Wilmington, N.C., 1820; d. Wilmington, N.C., April 29, 1872. [3; 4]

McReynolds, Robert, soldier, d. Colorado Springs, Colo., Dec. 29, 1928.

McRoberts, Mrs. Harriet Pearl, née Skinner, miscellaneous writer, b. Creston, Ia., 1874; d. White Plains, N.Y., Jan. 22, 1946. [10]

McRoskey, Mrs. Racine, née McCoy, journalist, b. Portland, Ore., 1873; d. San Mateo, Calif., April 5, 1915. [35]

McShane, Charles, railwayman, b. 1867; d. 1902.

McSherry, James, lawyer, b. Frederick county, Md., 1819; d. Frederick county, Md., July 13, 1869. [3; 4; 5; 6; 34]

McSherry, Richard, physician, b. Martinsburg, W. Va., 1817; d. Baltimore, Md., Oct. 7, 1885. [3; 4; 8; 34]

McSherry, Richary Meredith, historian, b. 1842; d. 1898.

McTavish, Newton McFaul, journalist, b. Staffa, Ont., 1877; d. Toronto, Ont., Aug. 17, 1941. [27]

McTyeire, Holland Nimmons, bishop, b. Barnwell county, S.C., 1824; d. Nashville, Tenn., Feb. 15, 1889. [1; 3; 4; 5; 6; 8; 34]

Macurdy, Grace Harriet, educationist, b. Robbinstown, Me.; d. Poughkeepsie, N.Y., Oct. 23, 1946. [14]

Macvane, Silas Marcus, educationist, b. Bothwell, P.E.I., 1842; d. Rome, Italy, Jan. 19, 1914. [8; 10]

MacVannel, John Angus, educationist, b. St. Mary's Ont., 1871; d. St. Mary's, Ont., Nov. 10, 1915. [27]

MacVeagh, Rogers, lawyer, b. Narragansett, R. I., 1888; d. Portland, Ore., Sept. 19, 1943. [51]

McVey, William E., physician, b. Waverly, Ill., 1864; d. Topeka, Kans., Oct. 21, 1931. [10]

MacVicar, Malcolm, educationist, b. Argyleshire, Scotland, 1829; d. Cato, N.Y., May 18, 1904. [1; 3; 4; 27]

MacVicar, William Mortimer, educationist, b. Port Medway, N.S., 1851; d. Watertown, Mass., 1928. [27]

McVickar, John, clergyman and economist, b. New York, N.Y., 1787; d. New York, N.Y., Oct. 29, 1868. [1; 3; 4; 6; 9]

McVickar, William Augustus, clergyman, b. New York, N.Y., 1827; d. New York, N.Y., Sept. 24, 1877. [3; 8]

McVickar, William Bard, lawyer, b. Irvington-on-Hudson, N.Y., 1858; d. Morristown, N.J., March 30, 1901. [3b]

McWatters, George, police detective, fl. 1871-1892.

McWhinney, Thomas Martin, clergyman, b. Ohio, 1823; d. Yellow Springs, O., 1909. [10]

MacWhorter, Alexander, clergyman, b. New Castle county, Del., 1734; d. Newark, N.J., July 20, 1807. [1]

MacWhorter, Alexander, clergyman, b. Newark, N.J., 1822; d. New Haven, Conn., June 24, 1880. [62]

Macy, James Cartwright, musician, b. 1845; d. 1918.

Macy, Jesse, educationist, b. Henry county, Ind., 1842; d. Grinnell, Ia., Nov. 2, 1919. [1; 4; 5; 9; 10]

Macy, John Albert, journalist, b. Detroit, Mich., 1877; d. Stroudsburg, Pa., Aug. 26, 1932. [1; 4; 7; 10]

Macy, Obed, local historian, b. Nantucket, Mass., 1762; d. Nantucket, Mass., Dec. 24, 1844.

Macy, William Francis, local historian, b. Nantucket, Mass., 1867; d. Aug. 27, 1935.

Macy, William Hussey, sailor, b. 1826; d. March 11, 1891.

Madden, John, physician, b. 1860; d. Mankato, Minn., 1928.

Maddox, William Arthur, educationist, b. Richmond, Va., 1883; d. Rockford, Ill., Aug. 10, 1933. [10; 11]

Madeira, Louis Cephas, merchant and musician, b. Doylestown, Pa., 1819; d. Philadelphia, Pa., April 3, 1896.

Madigan, Thomas F., dealer in autographs, b. 1891; d. Pelham Manor, N.Y., April 19, 1936.

Madison, James, fourth president of the United States, b. Port Conway, Va., 1751; d. Montpelier, Orange county, Va., June 28, 1836. [1; 2; 3; 4; 5; 6]

Madison, Mrs. Lucy, née **Foster,** writer of books for young people, b. Kirksville, Mo., 1865; d. Hudson Falls, N.Y., March 16, 1932.. [10]

Maery, Helen (pseud.). See Mug, Sister Mary Theodosia.

Maes, Camillus Paul, bishop, b. Courtrai, Belgium, 1846; d. Covington, Ky., May 10, 1915. [1; 4; 10]

Maeser, Karl Gottfried, educationist, b. 1828; d. Provo, Utah, 1901.

Maffitt, John Newland, clergyman, b. Dublin, Ireland, 1795; d. near Mobile, Ala., May 28, 1850. [1; 3; 6]

Maffitt, John Newland, naval officer, b. at sea, 1819; d. Wilmington, N.C., May 15, 1886. [3]

Magee, Harvey White, lawyer, b. 1847; d. ?

Magee, James Dysart, educationist, b. Morrisdale Mines, Pa., 1881; d. Cleveland, O., April 7, 1948. [10; 11]

Magee, John Benjamin, clergyman and educationist, b. Albion, Ia., 1887; d. Mount Vernon, Ia., April 6, 1943. [7; 10]

Magee, Knox, journalist and novelist, b. South Gower, Ont., 1877; d. Winnipeg, Man., May 9, 1934. [27]

Magee, Louis Jones, poet, b. 1862; d. 1907.

Magie, David, clergyman, b. Elizabeth, N.J., 1795; d. Elizabeth, N.J., May 10, 1865. [3]

Magill, Edward Hicks, educationist, b. Solebury , Pa., 1825; d. New York, N.Y., Dec. 5, 1907. [1; 3; 4; 10]

Magill, Mary Tucker, educationist, b. Jefferson county, Va., 1830; d. near Richmond, Va., April 29, 1899. [3b; 8; 34]

Maglathlin, Henry Bartlett, educationist, b. 1819; d. 1910.

Magnan, Aristide, priest, b. Ste. Ursule de Maskinongé, Que., 1863; d. St. Désiré du Lac-Noir, Que., Feb. 22, 1929. [27]

Magnan, Joseph Roch, priest, b. L'Assomption, Que., 1857; d. Rome, Italy, June 12, 1904. [27]

Magner, Dennis, horse-tamer, fl. 1863-1903.

Magoffin, Ralph Van Deman, educationist, b. Rice county, Kans., 1874; d. Columbia, S.C., May 15, 1942. [7; 10; 11]

Magonigle, Harold Van Buren, architect, b. Bergen Heights, N.J., 1867; d. Bain Harbor, Vt., Aug. 29, 1935. [1a; 4; 10; 11]

Magoon, Charles Edward, lawyer and administrator, b. Steele county, Minn., 1861; d. Washington, D.C., Jan. 14, 1920. [1; 4; 10]

Magoon, Elias Lyman, clergyman, b. Lebanon, N.H., 1810; d. Philadelphia, Pa., Nov. 25, 1886. [3; 4; 6; 7; 8]

Magoun, George Frederic, clergyman, b. Bath, Me., 1821; d. Grinnell, Ia., Jan. 30, 1896. [1; 37]

Magruder, Allan Bowie, politician, b. Kentucky, about 1775; d. Opelousas, La., April 16, 1822. [3; 4; 5; 8; 34; 74]

Magruder, Allan Bowie, biographer, b. 1812; d. 1885. [34]

Magruder, Julia, novelist and short-story writer, b. Charlottesville, Va., 1854; d. Richmond, Va., June 9, 1907. [1; 3; 4; 7; 8; 9; 34]

Magruder, Thomas Pickett, naval officer, b. Yazoo county, Miss., 1867; d. Jamestown, R.I., May 26, 1938. [10]

Magruder, William H. N., biographer, b. 1815; d. 1899.

Maguire, Edward, soldier, d. 1892.

Maguire, James George, politician, b. Boston, Mass., 1853; d. San Francisco, Calif., June 20, 1920. [5]

Maguire, Thomas, priest, b. Philadelphia, Pa., 1776; d. Quebec, Que., July 17, 1854. [3; 27]

Mahan, Alfred Thayer, naval officer and historian, b. West Point, N.Y., Sept. 27, 1840; d. Washington, D.C., Dec. 1, 1914. [1 2; 4; 7; 9; 10]

Mahan, Asa, educationist, b. Vernon, N.Y., 1800; d. Eastbourne, England, April 4, 1889. [1; 3; 4; 5; 6; 7; 8]

Mahan, Dennis Hart, engineer, b. New York, N.Y., 1802; d. near Stony Point, N.Y., Sept. 16, 1871. [1; 3; 4; 5; 6; 8]

Mahan, Milo, educationist, b. Suffolk, Va., 1819; d. Baltimore, Md., Sept. 3, 1870. [1; 3; 4; 5; 6; 34]

Maher, Stephen John, physician, b. New Haven, Conn., 1860; d. New Haven, Conn., June 6, 1939. [10; 62]

Maher, William H., commercial traveller, fl. 1878-1893.

Mahin, John Lee, advertising expert, b. Muscatine, Ia., 1869; d. New York, N.Y., Nov. 9, 1930. [10; 11]

Mahon, John Coleman, lawyer, b. Hartford, Conn., Jan. 3, 1884; d. Brooklyn, N.Y., Jan. 27, 1939. [62]

Mahony, Michael Joseph, priest, b. county Tipperary, Ireland, 1860; d. Fordham, N.Y., March 13, 1936. [10; 21; 35]

Mailloux, Alexis, priest, b. Ile aux Coudres, Lower Canada, 1801; d. Ile aux Coudres, Que., Aug. 4, 1877. [27]

Main, Arthur Elwin, theologian, b. Adams Centre, N.Y., 1846; d. Alfred, N.Y., Jan. 29, 1933. [10]

Main, John (pseud.). See Parsons, Mrs. Elsie Worthington, née Clews.

Main, William Holloway, clergyman, b. Adams Centre, N.Y., 1862; d. Wyncote, Pa., Jan. 4, 1933. [10]

Mains, George Preston, clergyman and publishing agent, b. Newport, N.Y., 1844; d. Altadena, Calif., Sept. 6, 1930. [4; 10]

Mair, Charles, poet, b. Lanark, Upper Canada, 1838; d. Victoria, B.C., July 7, 1927. [27]

Mair, George Macdonald. See Major, George Macdonald.

Maisch, John Michael, pharmacist, b. Germany, 1831; d. Philadelphia, Pa., Sept. 10, 1893. [1; 3; 4]

Maitland, James A., journalist and novelist, fl. 1855-1860. [6; 7]

Major, Charles, novelist, b. Indianapolis, Ind., 1856; d. Shelbyville, Ind., Feb. 13, 1913. [1; 2; 4; 7; 10]

Major, George Macdonald, poet, fl. 1882-1903.

Majors, Alexander, pioneer, b. near Franklin, Ky., 1814; d. Chicago, Ill., Jan. 12, 1900. [1; 34]

Makemie, Francis, clergyman, b. county Donegal, Ireland, about 1658; d. Accomac county, Va., 1708. [1; 3; 4; 6]

Malcom, Howard, clergyman and educationist, b. Philadelphia, Pa., 1799; d. Philadelphia, Pa., March 25, 1879. [1; 3; 4; 6; 8]

Maldclewith, Ronsby (pseud.). See Smith, Byron, Caldwell.

Malinowski, Bronislaw Kasper, anthropologist, b. Cracow, Poland, 1884 d. New Haven, Conn., May 16, 1942. [10; 12; 13]

Malisoff, William Marias, biochemist, b. Russia, 1895; d. New York, N.Y., Nov. 16, 1947. [13]

Malkiel, Theresa Serber, social worker, b. 1873; d. New York, N.Y., Nov. 17, 1949.

Mallalieu, Willard Francis, bishop, b. Sutton, Mass., 1828; d. Auburndale, Mass., Aug. 1, 1911. [4; 5; 10]

Mallard, Robert Quarterman, clergyman, b. Liberty county, Ga., 1830; d. ? [34]

Mallary, Charles Dutton, clergyman, b. Poultney, Vt., 1801; d. near Albany, Ga., July 31, 1864. [3; 5; 34]

Mallary, Mrs. Mary Jeanie, née **Dagg,** novelist, fl. 1868-1892. [34]

Mallary, Raymond De Witt, clergyman, b. Fulton, N.Y., 1851; d. Springfield, Mass., Jan. 29, 1911. [45]

Mallery, Garrick, ethnologist, b. Wilkesbarre, Pa., 1831; d. Washington, D.C., Oct. 24, 1894. [1; 3; 4; 62]

Mallett, Daniel Trowbridge, publisher, b. New Haven, Conn., 1862; d. Hackensack, N.J., Oct. 11, 1944. [10]

Mallett, Frank James, clergyman, b. King's Lynn, England, 1858; d. May 27, 1944. [4]

Malloch, Douglas, journalist, poet, and novelist, b. Muskegon, Mich., 1877; d. Muskegon, Mich., July 2, 1938. [7; 10; 11; 39]

Mallon, Guy Ward, lawyer and capitalist, b. Cincinnati, O., 1864; d. Cincinnati, O., Dec. 23, 1933. [62]

Mallon, Mrs. Isabel Allderdice, née **Sloan,** journalist, b. Baltimore, Md., 1857; d. New York, N.Y., Dec. 27, 1898. [3b; 8]

Mallory, Frank Burr, pathologist, b. Cleveland, O., 1862; d. Brookline, Mass., Sept. 27, 1941. [10; 51]

Mallory, Herbert Samuel, educationist, b. Akron, O., 1872; d. Ypsilanti, Mich., Dec. 30, 1927. [62]

Malone, James Henry, historian, b. 1851; d. Memphis, Tenn., June 23, 1929.

Malone, Walter, jurist and poet, b. near Pleasant Hill, Miss., 1866; d. Memphis, Tenn,. May 18, 1915. [1; 4; 7; 9; 10; 34]

Maloney, Russell, journalist, b. 1910; d. New York, N.Y., Sept. 4, 1948.

Maltbie, William Henry, lawyer, b. Toledo, O., 1867; d. Baltimore, Md., Jan. 23, 1926. [10]

Maltby, Albert Elias, educationist, b. 1850; d. 1924.

Maltby, Isaac, soldier, b. Northfield, Conn., 1767; d. Waterloo, N.Y., Sept. 9, 1819. [3; 6; 8]

Malter, Henry, rabbi, b. Galicia, Austria, 1864; d. Philadelphia, Pa., April 4, 1925. [1; 10]

Manahan, Ambrose, priest, b. New York, N.Y., 1814; d. Troy, N.Y., Dec. 7, 1867. [3b]

Manahan, James, lawyer, b. Chatfield, Minn., 1866; d. St. Paul, Minn., Jan. 9, 1932. [4; 10]

Manatt, James Irving, educationist, b. Millersburg, O., 1854; d. Providence, R.I., Feb. 13, 1915. [1; 4; 7; 10; 62]

Mancur, John Henry, novelist, fl. 1834-1846. [6; 7]

Mandel, Edward, lawyer, b. New York, N.Y., 1873; d. Forest Hills, N.Y., May 25, 1942.

Manderson, Charles Frederick, lawyer, soldier, and politician, b. Philadelphia, Pa., 1837; d. at sea, Sept. 28, 1911. [1; 4; 5; 10]

Mandeville, Giles Henry, clergyman, b. New York, N.Y., 1825; d. New York, N.Y., 1904. [5; 10]

Mandeville, Henry, clergyman and educationist, b. Kinderhook, N.Y., 1804; d. Mobile, Ala., Oct. 2, 1858. [3; 6]

Mangan, John Joseph, physician, b. 1857; d. Lynn, Mass., March 29, 1935.

Mangum, Adolphus Williamson, clergyman and poet, b. 1834; d. 1890. [34]

Manhart, Franklin Pierce, theologian, b. Catawissa, Pa., 1852; d. Selingsgrove, Pa., Sept. 13, 1933. [10]

Manhattan (pseud.). See Scoville, Joseph Alfred.

Maniates, Belle Kanaris, novelist, b. Marshall, Mich.; d. Lansing, Mich., about 1925. [7; 10; 39]

Manigault, Gabriel, miscellaneous writer, b. Charleston, S.C., 1809; d. London, Ont., Jan. 20, 1888. [27]

Manion, Robert James, physician and politician, b. Pembroke, Ont., 1881; d. Ottawa, Ont., July 2, 1943. [27]

Manley, Frederick, poet, d. Madison, N.H., Dec., 1914.

Manley, Thomas Henry, physician, b. Tewksbury, Mass., 1851; d. New York, N.Y., Jan. 13, 1905. [10]

Manly, Basil, clergyman, b. Edgefield district, S.C., 1825; d. Louisville, Ky., Jan. 31, 1892. [1; 3; 4; 5; 6; 34]

Manly, John G., clergyman, b. 1841; d. Toronto, Ont., 1908. [27]

Manly, John Matthews, educationist, b. Sumter county, Ala., 1865; d. Tucson, Ariz., April 2, 1940. [7; 10]

Manly, Louise, educationist, b. Richmond, Va., 1857; d. Greenville, S.C., Jan. 2, 1936. [34]

Manly, Marline (pseud.). See Rathbone, St. George Henry.

Manly, William Lewis, pioneer, b. 1820; d ?

Mann, A. Chester (pseud.). See Roberts, Philip Hott.

Mann, Albert Russell, economist, b. Hawkins, Pa., 1880; d. New York, N.Y., Feb. 21, 1947. [10]

Mann, Arthur Sitgreaves, missionary, b. New York, N.Y., 1878; d. near Kuling, China, July 29, 1907. [62]

Mann, Cameron, bishop, b. New York, N.Y., April 3, 1851; d. Winter Park, Fla., Feb. 8, 1932. [4; 8; 10; 11]

Mann, Charles Addison, lawyer, b. Utica, N.Y., 1835; d. St. Paul, Minn., March 12, 1896. [62]

Mann, Charles Holbrook, clergyman, b. Syracuse, N.Y., 1839; d. New York, N.Y., April 10, 1918. [7; 10]

Mann, Charles Wesley, educationist, b. 1862; d. 1909.

Mann, Cyrus, clergyman, b. Orford, N.H., 1785; d. Stoughton, Mass., Feb. 9, 1859. [3; 8; 49]

Mann, Delos H., physician, b. 1824; d. Brooklyn, N.Y., May 2, 1906.

Mann, Mrs. Delos H., novelist, fl. 1880-1882.

Mann, Edward Cox, alienist, b. Braintree, Mass., 1850; d. Hubbardston, Mass., Jan., 1908.

Mann, Henry, journalist, b. Glasgow, Scotland, 1828; d. New York, N.Y., Nov. 16, 1915. [10]

Mann, Herman, biographer, b. 1772; d. 1833.

Mann, Herman, local historian, b. 1795; d. Dedham, Mass., 1851. [6]

Mann, Horace, educationist, b. Franklin, Mass., 1796; d. Yellow Springs, O., Aug. 2, 1859. [1; 3; 4; 6; 7; 9]

Mann, James, physician, b. Wrentham, Mass., 1759; d. Governor's Island, N.Y., Nov. 7, 1832. [1; 3; 6]

Mann, John Henry, lawyer, b. Utica, N.Y., 1863; d. San Antonio, Tex., Dec. 29, 1942. [62]

Mann, Jonathan B., politician, fl. 1840-1888.

Mann, Mrs. Mary Tyler, née Peabody, miscellaneous writer, b. Cambridgeport, Mass., 1806; d. Jamaica Plain, Mass., Feb. 11, 1887. [1; 3; 6; 7; 9]

Mann, Matthew Derbyshire, gynaecologist, b. Utica, N.Y., 1845; d. Buffalo, N.Y., March 2, 1921. [4; 10; 62]

Mann, Newton, clergyman, b. Cazenovia, N.Y., 1836; d. Chicago, Ill., July 25, 1926. [1; 4; 10]

Mann, William D'Alton, publisher and editor, b. 1839; d. Morristown, N.J., May 17, 1920. [10]

Mann, William Julius, clergyman, b. Stuttgart, Germany, 1819; d. Boston, Mass., June 20, 1892. [1; 3; 5; 6]

Mann, William Justin, historian, b. 1852; d. 1931.

Manner, Jane, elocutionist, b. New York, N.Y.; d. New York, N.Y., May 26, 1943. [10]

Mannering, May (pseud.). See Nowell, Mrs. Harriet P. H.

Manners, Mrs. (pseud.). See Richards, Mrs. Cornelia Holroyd, née Bradley.

Manners, John Hartley, actor and playwright, b. London, England, 1870; d. New York, N.Y., Dec. 19, 1928. [1; 7; 10]

Mannheimer, Jenny. See Manner, Jane.

Manning, Jacob Merrill, clergyman, b. Greenwood, N.Y., 1824; d. Portland, Me., Nov. 29, 1882. [3; 5; 8]

Manning, James Hilton, capitalist, b. Albany, N.Y., 1854; d. Albany, N.Y., July 4, 1925. [10]

Manning, Joseph Bolles, lawyer, b. Rockport, Mass., 1787; d. Ipswich, Mass., May 22, 1854. [51]

Manning, Marie. See Gasch, Mrs. Marie, née Manning.

Manning, Robert, pomologist, b. Salem, Mass., 1784; d. Salem, Mass., Oct. 10, 1842. [1; 3; 6]

Manning, William Ray, civil servant, b. Home. Kans., 1871; d. Washington, D.C., Oct. 28, 1942. [10]

Manning, William Thomas, bishop, b. Northampton, England, 1866; d. New York, N.Y., Nov. 18, 1949. [10]

Mannix, Mary Ellen, novelist, b. 1846; d. San Diego, Calif., 1939. [21; 23]

Manola, Adelaide (pseud.). See Hughes, Mrs. Adelaide Manola, née Mould.

Manseau, Joseph, teacher of stenography, b. St. Polycarpe, Lower Canada, 1837; d. Montreal, Que., Oct. 31, 1887. [27]

Mansfield, Daniel H., clergyman, b. 1810; d. 1855.

Mansfield, Edward Deering, lawyer and journalist, b. New Haven, Conn., 1801; d. Morrow, O., Oct. 27, 1880. [1; 3; 4; 5; 6; 7; 8; 9]

Mansfield, Francis, clergyman, b. Carlisle, Mass., 1834; d. Brooklyn, N.Y., July 1, 1911.

Mansfield, George Campbell, local historian, b. Canada, 1880; d. San Francisco, Calif., Jan. 28, 1936. [35]

Mansfield, Howard, lawyer, b. Hamden, Conn., 1849; d. Seal Harbor, Me., Aug. 14, 1938. [10; 62]

Mansfield, Jared, mathematician, b. New Haven, Conn., 1759; d. New Haven, Conn., Feb. 3 1830. [1; 3; 4; 5; 6]

Mansfield, John Brainard, historian, b. Andover, Vt., 1826; d. Effingham, Kans., Oct. 29, 1886. [3]

Mansfield, Lewis William, miscellaneous writer, b. 1816; d ? [8]

Mansfield, Richard, actor, b. Berlin, Germany, 1854; d. New London, Conn., Aug. 30, 1907. [1; 3; 4; 10]

Manship, Andrew, clergyman, b. Caroline county, Md., 1824; d. ? [3; 6; 8; 34]
Manson, Marsden, civil engineer, b. Campbell county, Va., 1850; d. San Francisco, Calif., Feb. 21, 1931. [10; 11]
Manson, Otis Frederick, physician, b. Richmond, Va., Jan. 25, 1888. [1; 4]
Mantle, Burns, journalist, b. Watertown, N.Y., 1873; d. New York, N.Y., Feb. 9, 1948. [7; 10; 11]
Manton, Walter Porter, physician, b. Providence, R.I., 1858; d. Pasadena, Calif., Sept. 24, 1925. [10]
Manville, Mrs. Helen Adelia, née **Wood,** poet, b. 1839; d. ? [8]
Manwaring, Christopher, essayist, b. 1774; d. 1832.
Manwaring, Elizabeth Wheeler, educationist, b. Bridgeport, Conn., 1879; d. Wellesley, Mass., Feb. 12, 1949. [10; 14]
Mapes, Victor, novelist and playwright, b. New York, N.Y., 1870; d. Cannes, France, Sept. 27, 1943. [7; 10; 11]
Maple, Joseph Cowgill, biographer, b. 1833; d. 1917.
Maple Knot (pseud.). See Clemo, Ebenezer.
Mapleton, Mark (pseud.). See Wilson, Robert.
Marble, Albert Prescott, educationist, b. Vassalboro, Me., 1836; d. New York, N.Y., March 25, 1906. [1; 3; 4; 10]
Marble, Mrs. Annie, née **Russell,** literary critic, b. Worcester, Mass., 1864; d. Worcester, Mass., Nov. 23, 1936. [7; 10; 11]
Marburg, Edgar, civil engineer, b. 1864; d. Philadelphia, Pa., June 27, 1918. [10]
Marburg, Theodore, publicist, b. Baltimore, Md., 1862; d. Vancouver, B.C., March 3, 1946. [4; 10]
Marbury, Elisabeth, literary agent, b. New York, N.Y., 1856; d. New York, N.Y., Jan. 22, 1933. [1a; 7; 10]
March, Alden, journalist, b. Easton, Pa., 1869; d. New York, N.Y., Sept. 14, 1942. [10]
March, Anne (pseud.). See Woolson, Constance Fenimore.
March, Benjamin, lecturer on Oriental art, b. 1899; d. Ann Arbor, Mich., Dec. 14, 1934.
March, Charles Wainwright, journalist, b. Portsmouth, N.H., 1815; d. Alexandria, Egypt, Jan. 24, 1864. [3; 7; 8]
March, Daniel, clergyman, b. Millbury, Mass., 1816; d. Woburn, Mass., March 2, 1909. [3; 5; 8; 10; 62]
March, Francis Andrew, philologist, b. Millbury, Mass., 1825; d. Easton, Pa., Sept. 9, 1911. [1; 3; 4; 6; 7; 8; 10]
March, Francis Andrew, lexicographer, b. Easton, Pa., 1863; d. Easton, Pa., Feb. 28, 1929. [1; 7; 10]
March, Thomas Stone, educationist, b. Easton, Pa., 1868; d. Chevy Chase, Md., Jan. 13, 1939. [10; 11]
March, Walter (pseud.). See Willcox, Orlando Bolivar.

Marchand, Félix Gabriel, journalist and politician, b. St. John's, Lower Canada, 1832; d. St. John's, Que., Sept. 16, 1900. [27]
Marcin, Max, playwright, b. Posen, Germany, 1879; d. Tucson, Ariz., March 30, 1948. [7]
Marcou, Jules, geologist, b. Salins, France, 1824; d. Cambridge, Mass., April 17, 1898. [1; 3; 5; 6; 8]
Marcus (pseud.). See Blunt, Joseph.
Marcy, Erastus Edgerton, physician, b. Greenwich, Mass., 1815; d. New York, N.Y., Dec. 27, 1900. [6; 8]
Marcy, Henry Orlando, surgeon, b. Otis, Mass., 1837; d. Cambridge, Mass., Jan. 1, 1924. [1; 4; 8; 10]
Marcy, Randolph Barnes, soldier, b. Greenwich, Mass., 1812; d. West Orange, N.J., Nov. 22, 1887. [1; 3; 4; 5; 6; 7] '
Marden, Charles Carroll, philologist, b. Baltimore, Md., 1867; d. Princeton, N.J., May 11, 1932. [1; 10]
Marden, Orison Swett, journalist, b. near Thornton, N.H., 1850; d. Los Angeles, Calif., March 10, 1924. [1; 4; 7; 10]
Marean, Mrs. Emma, née **Endicott,** poet, b. Boston, Mass., 1854; d. Cambridge, Mass., Oct. 17, 1936. [7; 10]
Maretzek, Max, opera impresario, b. Brünn, Moravia, 1821; d. Pleasant Plains, Staten Island, N.Y., May 14, 1897. [1; 3; 4; 8; 20]
Margolis, Max Leopold, educationist, b. Vilna, Russia, 1866; d. Philadelphia, Pa., April 2, 1932. [1; 4; 10]
Marguerittes, Julie, Contesse de, née **Granville,** journalist, b. London, England, 1814; d. Philadelphia, Pa., June 21, 1866. [3b]
Marie Paula, Sister, educationist, b. New York, N.Y., 1867; d. New York, N.Y., 1940. [21; 22]
Marigny, Bernard, politician, b. New Orleans, La., 1785; d. New Orleans, La., Feb. 3, 1868. [1; 34]
Marinoni, Antonio, educationist, b. Pozzolengo, Italy, 1879; d. New Brunswick, N.J., Aug. 6, 1944. [62]
Marion, Albert Marie Philippe, priest and educationist, b. L'Assomption county, Que., 1876; d. Ottawa, Ont., May 23, 1925. [27]
Marion, Henri, educationist, b. 1857; d. Culver, Ind., Aug. 14, 1913.
Maris, George Lewis, educationist, b. 1842; d. San Francisco, Calif., Jan. 10, 1890.
Markell, Charles Frederick, lawyer and politician, b. Frederick, Md., 1855; d. Birmingham, Ala., July 5, 1941. [10; 34]
Markens, Isaac, journalist, b. New York, N.Y., 1846; d. Newark, N.J., Aug. 14, 1928. [10]
Markham, Edwin, poet, b. Oregon City, Ore., 1852; d. Westerleigh, N.Y., March 7, 1940. [4; 7; 10; 11; 72]
Markham, Reuben Henry, journalist, b. Twelve Mile, Kans., 1887; d. Washington, D.C., Dec. 29, 1949. [10]

Markoe, Peter, poet and dramatist, b. Santa Cruz, West Indies, about 1752; d. Philadelphia, Pa., Jan. 30, 1792. [1; 3; 4; 6; 7; 9]

Markoe, Ralston Joshua, lawyer, b. Waukesha county, Wis., 1854; d. St. Paul, Minn., 1927. [70]

Markoe, Thomas Masters, physician, b. Philadelphia, Pa., 1813; d. East Hampton, Long Island, N.Y., Aug. 26, 1901. [8; 10]

Marks, Elias, physician and educationist, b. Charleston, S.C., 1790; d. Washington, D.C., June 22, 1886. [1; 3; 34]

Marks, George Edwin, manufacturer, b. 1853; d. Oct. 9, 1932.

Marks, Henry Kingdom, physician, b. San Francisco, Calif., 1883; d. Lyons, France, Sept. 1, 1942. [7; 10]

Marks, Mrs. Lionel Simeon. See Peabody, Josephine Preston.

Marks, William Dennis, civil engineer, b. St. Louis, Mo., 1849; d. Plattsburg, N.Y., Jan. 7, 1915. [7; 10; 62]

Marlow, Sidney (pseud.). See Coggins, Paschal Heston.

Marlowe, Alexander, poet, b. Denmark, 1880; d. Londonderry, N.H., Nov. 29, 1938.

Marmette, Joseph Etienne Eugène, novelist, b. Montmagny, Que., 1844; d. Ottawa, Ont., May 7, 1895. [27]

Marny, Suzanne (pseud.). See Johnston, Mrs. Mabel A., née Sullivan.

Marot, Helen, economist, b. Philadelphia, Pa., 1865; d. New York, N.Y., June 4, 1940. [10]

Marquand, Allan, educationist, b. New York, N.Y., 1853; d. New York, N.Y., Sept. 24, 1924. [1; 7; 10]

Marquis, Don, poet, humorist, journalist, and playwright, b. Walnut, Ill., 1878; d. Forest Hills, N.Y., Dec. 29, 1937. [7; 10; 11]

Marquis, John Abner, clergyman and educationist, b. Dinsmore, Pa., 1861; d. New York, N.Y., July 5, 1931. [1; 4; 10]

Marquis, Thomas Bailey, physician, b. 1869; d. Hardin, Mont., 1935.

Marquis, Thomas Guthrie, miscellaneous writer, b. Chatham, N.B., 1864; d. Toronto, Ont., April 1, 1936. [27]

Marr, Frances Harrison, poet, b. Warrenton, Va., 1835; d. ? [34]

Marr, Kate Thyson, novelist, d. 1907.

Marriner, Harry Lee, poet and journalist, b. 1872; d. Dallas, Tex., 1914.

Marriott, Crittenden, journalist, b. Baltimore, Md., 1867; d. Washington, 'D.C., March 28, 1932. [7; 10]

Marsden, Joshua, missionary, b. near Liverpool, England, 1777; d. England. 1837. [27]

Marsh, Alfred Henry, lawyer, b. near Brighton, Ont., 1851; d. Toronto, Ont., Sept. 6, 1909. [27]

Marsh, Mrs. Caroline, née Crane, poet, b. Berkley, Mass., 1816; d. Scarsdale, N.Y., Oct. 27, 1901. [3b]

Marsh, Charles, lawyer, b. Lebanon, Conn., 1765; d. Woodstock, Vt., Jan. 11, 1849. [43]

Marsh, Christopher Columbus, accountant, b. Boston, Mass., 1806; d. ? [6]

Marsh, Edward Clark, publisher, b. Portland, Mich., 1875; d. Pawling, N.Y., Sept. 24, 1922. [10]

Marsh, Frank Burr, historian, b. Big Rapids, Mich., 1880; d. Dallas, Tex., June 1, 1940. [10]

Marsh, George Perkins, diplomat and scholar, b. Woodstock, Vt., 1801; d. Vallombrosa, Italy, July 23, 1882. [1; 3; 4; 6; 7; 9; 43]

Marsh, George Tracy, lawyer and novelist, b. Lansingburgh, N.Y., 1876; d. Providence, R.I., Aug. 10, 1945. [7; 10; 62]

Marsh, Howard Daniel, educationist, b. Bloomington, Ill., 1871; d. St. Petersburg, Fla., Aug. 26, 1945. [14]

Marsh, James, educationist, b. Hartford, Vt., 1794; d. Burlington, Vt., July 3, 1842. [1; 3; 4; 5; 6; 43]

Marsh, John, clergyman, b. Wethersfield, Conn., 1788; d. Brooklyn, N.Y., Aug. 4, 1868. [1; 3; 5; 6; 62]

Marsh, Leonard, physician, b. Hartford, Vt., 1800; d. Burlington, Vt., Aug. 16, 1870. [3b; 43; 49]

Marsh, Luther Rawson, lawyer and spiritualist b. Pompey Hill, N.Y., 1813; d. Middletown, N.Y., Aug. 15, 1902. [3b; 4]

Marsh, Othniel Charles, palaeontologist, b. Lockport, N.Y., 1831; d. New Haven, Conn., March 18, 1899. [1; 3; 4; 6; 62]

Marsh, Samuel, clergyman, b. Danville, Vt., 1796; d. Underhill, Vt., April 1, 1874. [43]

Marsh, Walter Randall, mathematician, b. Boston, Mass., 1867; d. Garden City, N.Y., Feb. 23, 1947. [10]

Marshall, Albert Brainerd, clergyman, b. Bryan, Pa., 1849; d. Bellevue, Neb., Oct. 29, 1931. [10; 70]

Marshall, Benjamin Tinkham, clergyman and educationist, b. Boston, Mass., 1872, d. Haverhill, Mass., June 30, 1946.

Marshall, Edward, journalist and novelist, b. Enfield Center, N.Y., 1869; d. New Brunswick, N.J., Feb. 24, 1933. [2a; 10]

Marshall, Edward Chauncey, journalist, b. Herkimer county, N.Y., 1824; d. New York, N.Y., Nov. 5, 1898. [3; 5; 8]

Marshall, Henry Rutgers, architect and psychologist, b. New York, N.Y., 1852; d. New York, N.Y., May 3, 1927. [1; 4; 7; 10; 11]

Marshall, Humphrey, historian, b. Fauquier county, Va., 1760; d. Lexington, Ky., July 9, 1841. [1; 3; 4; 5; 34; 74]

Marshall, Humphry, botanist, b. West Bradford, Pa., 1722; d. West Bradford, Pa., Nov. 5, 1801. [3]

Marshall, John, jurist and biographer, b. near Midland, Va., 1755; d. Philadelphia, Pa., July 6, 1835. [1; 2; 3; 4; 5; 6; 7; 9]

Marshall, John George, jurist, b. Country Harbour, N.S., 1786; d. Halifax, N.S., April 7, 1880. [27]

Marshall, John Patten, musician, b. Rockport, Mass., 1877; d. Boston, Mass., Jan. 17, 1921. [10; 20]

Marshall, Mary. See Dyer, Mrs. Mary, née Marshall.

Marshall, Nelly Nichol, novelist, b. Louisville, Ky., 1845; d. Washington, D.C., April 19, 1898. [3; 4; 34]

Marshall, Orsamus Holmes, historian, b. Franklin, Conn., 1813; d. Buffalo, N.Y., July 9, 1884. [3]

Marshall, Thomas Francis, lawyer, b. Frankfort, Ky., 1801; d. near Versailles, Ky., Sept. 22, 1864. [3; 34]

Marshall, Thomas Maitland, historian, b. Lansing, Mich., 1876; d. Campbell, Calif., April 12, 1936. [10]

Marshall, Thomas Riley, politician, b. North Manchester, Ind., 1854; d. Washington, D.C., June 1, 1925. [1; 4; 7; 10]

Marshall, William Isaac, educationist, b. Fitchburg, Mass., 1840; d. Chicago, Ill., Oct. 30, 1906.

Marshall, William Vickroy, economist, b. 1847; d. ?

Marsten, Francis Edward, clergyman, b. Jersey City, N.J., 1855; d. Boston, Mass., Aug. 22, 1915. [10; 45]

Marston, Mrs. Mildred (pseud.). See Scott, Mrs. Anna, née Kay.

Marston, William Moulton, psychologist, b. Cliftondale, Mass., 1893; d. Rye, N.Y., May 2, 1947. [10; 13]

Martens, Frederick Herman, writer on music, b. New York, N.Y., 1874; d. Mountain·Lake, N.J., Dec. 18, 1932. [10; 20]

Martin, Alexander, jurist, b. 1833; d. 1902.

Martin, Alfred Wilhelm, clergyman, b. Cologne, Germany, 1862; d. New York, N.Y., Oct. 15, 1932. [10; 11]

Martin, Archer, jurist, b. Hamilton, Ont., 1865; d. Victoria, B.C., Sept. 1, 1941. [27]

Martin, Arthur Theodore, lawyer and educationist, b. Hadjin, Turkey, 1902; d. Columbus, O., Feb. 7, 1946.

Martin, Aurelius, poet, b. 1869; d. 1922. [35]

Martin, Benjamin Ellis, traveller, b. New York. N.Y.; d. New York, N.Y., 1909. [10]

Martin, Chalmers, clergyman, b. Ashland, Ky., 1859; d. Princeton, N.J., Feb. 28, 1934. [10; 56]

Martin, Deborah Beaumont, librarian, b. Green Bay, Wis.; d. Green Bay, Wis., Oct. 1, 1931. [44]

Martin, Edward, surgeon, b. Philadelphia, Pa., 1859; d. Philadelphia, Pa., March 17, 1938. [10]

Martin, Edward Sandford, poet and essayist, b. Willowbrook, N.Y., 1856; d. New York, N.Y., June 13, 1939. [4; 7; 10; 11]

Martin, Edward Winslow (pseud.). See McCabe, James Dabney.

Martin, Edwin Campbell, meteorologist, b. Hamilton, O., 1850; d. Watchung, N.J., July 23, 1915.

Martin, Edwin Moore, clergyman, b. Tiffin, O., 1872; d. Cincinnati, O., Oct. 12, 1935. [10]

Martin, Mrs. Elizabeth Gilbert, née Davis, novelist, b. 1837; d. ?

Martin, Ernest Gale, physiologist, b. Minneapolis, Minn., 1876; d. Stanford University, Calif., Oct. 17, 1934. [10; 11]

Martin, Everett Dean, sociologist, b. Jacksonville, Ill., 1880; d. Claremont, Calif., May 10, 1941. [7; 10]

Martin, Fernando Wood, chemist, b. Volga, W. Va., 1863; d. Lynchburg, Va., March 22, 1933. [10; 13]

Martin, François Xavier, jurist and historian, b. Marseilles, France, 1762; d. New Orleans, La., Dec. 10, 1846. [1; 3; 4; 5; 6; 9; 34]

Martin, Frank Lee, journalist and educationist, b. Benedict, Neb., 1881; d. Columbia, Mo., July 18, 1941. [7; 10; 11]

Martin, Franklin Henry, surgeon, b. Ixonia, Wis., 1857; d. Phoenix, Ariz., March 7, 1935. [1a; 10; 11]

Martin, Frederick Townsend, philanthropist, b. Albany, N.Y., 1849; d. London, England, March 8, 1914. [1; 7; 10]

Martin, George, poet, b. county Derry, Ireland, 1822; d. Montreal, Que., 1900. [27]

Martin, Mrs. George, née **Madden,** novelist, b. Louisville, Ky., 1866; d. Louisville, Ky., Nov. 30, 1946. [10; 11; 34]

Martin, George A., agriculturist, d. 1904.

Martin, George Curtis, geologist, b. Cheshire, Mass., 1875; d. Washington, D.C., June 23, 1943. [10; 13]

Martin, George Edward, clergyman, b. Norwich, Conn., 1851; d. Fairhaven, Mass., Nov. 15, 1920. [62]

Martin, George Henry, educationist, b. Lynn, Mass., 1841; d. West Lynn, Mass., March 25, 1917. [10]

Martin, Mrs. Helen, née **Riemensnyder,** novelist, b. Lancaster, Pa., 1868; d, New Canaan, Conn., June 29, 1939. [7; 10; 11]

Martin, Henry Newell, physiologist, b. Newry, Ireland, 1848; d. Burley, Yorkshire, England Oct. 27, 1896. [1; 3; 4; 5]

Martin, John (pseud.). See Shepard, Morgan.

Martin, Mrs. John. See Martin, Mrs. Prestonia, née Mann.

Martin, John Alexander, journalist, soldier, and politician, b. Brownsville, Pa., 1839; d. Atchison, Kans., Oct. 2, 1889. [1; 3; 4; 5]

Martin, John Hill, lawyer and historian, b. Philadelphia, Pa., 1823; d. Philadelphia, Pa., April 7, 1906. [1; 3]

Martin, Joseph Hamilton, clergyman and poet, b. Jefferson county, Tenn., 1825; d. Georgetown, Ky., Feb. 7, 1887. [3; 34]

Martin, Lillien Jane, psychologist, b. Olean, N.Y., 1851; d. San Francisco, Calif., March 26, 1943. [4; 10; 13]

Martin, Louis Adolphe, mechanical engineer, b. Hoboken, N.J., 1880; d. Newton, Mass., Aug. 16, 1938. [10]

Martin, Luther, politician, b. near New Brunswick, N.J., about 1748; d. New York, N.Y., July 10, 1826. [1; 3; 4; 34]

Martin, Mrs. Margaret, née **Maxwell,** poet, b. Dumfries, Scotland, 1807; d. 1869. [3; 8; 34]

Martin, Mrs. Martha, née **Evans,** journalist, b. Terre Haute, Ind.; d. near Watchung, N.J., Jan. 5, 1925. [10]

Martin, Percy Alvin, educationist, b. Jamestown, N.Y., 1879; d. Laguna Beach, Calif., March 8, 1942. [7; 10; 11]

Martin, Mrs. Prestonia, née **Mann,** economist, b. 1861; d. near Winter Park, Fla., April 1, 1945.

Martin, Samuel Albert, educationist, b. Canonsburg, Pa., 1853; d. Easton Pa., March 26, 1921. [8; 10]

Martin, Thomas Commerford, editor, b. London, England, 1856; d. Pittsfield, Mass., May 17, 1924. [1; 4; 10]

Martin, Mrs. Victoria, née **Claflin.** See Woodhull, Mrs. Victoria, née Claflin.

Martin, William Alexander Parsons, missionary, b. Livonia, Ind., 1827; d. Pekin, China, Dec. 17, 1916. [1; 3; 7; 10]

Martin, William Maxwell, poet, b. Columbia, S.C., 1837; d. Columbia, S.C., Feb. 21, 1861. [34; 42]

Martindale, Joseph Comly, physician, d. Philadelphia, Pa., Dec. 4, 1872. [6]

Martindale, Thomas, merchant and sportsman, b. Weardale, England, 1845; d. Yukon, Canada, Sept. 20, 1916. [4; 10]

Martingale, Hawser (pseud.). See Sleeper, John Sherburne.

Marty, Martin, bishop, b. Schwyz, Switzerland, 1834; d. St. Cloud, Minn., Sept. 19, 1896. [4; 10]

Martyn, Carlos, clergyman, b. New York, N.Y., 1841; d. Noroton, Conn., Aug. 4, 1917. [5; 10; 68]

Martyn, Mrs. Sarah Towne, née **Smith,** journalist, novelist, and historian, b. Hopkinton, N.H., 1805; d. New York, N.Y., Nov. 22, 1879. [1; 3; 5; 6; 7; 9]

Martyn, William Carlos. See Martyn, Carlos.

Martzolff, Clement Luther, educationist, b. Perry county, O., 1869; d. Athens, O., Aug. 5, 1922.

Marvel, Ik (pseud.). See Mitchell, Donald Grant.

Marvin, Abijah Perkins, clergyman, b. Lyme, Conn., 1813; d. Lancaster, Mass., Oct. 19, 1889. [6]

Marvin, Dwight Edwards, clergyman, b. Greenwich, N.Y., 1851; d. Summit, N.J., Feb. 28, 1940. [7; 10; 11; 68]

Marvin, Enoch Mather, bishop, b. Great Bentley, England 1825; d. St. Louis, Mo., Dec. 3, 1877. [1; 3; 4; 5; 6; 34]

Marvin, Fred Richard, journalist, b. Garden City, Minn., 1868; d. Westminster West, Vt., July 14, 1939. [7; 10]

Marvin, Frederick Rowland, clergyman, b. Troy, N.Y., 1847; d. Albany, N.Y., July 22, 1919. [4; 10]

Marvin, John Gage, lawyer, d. 1855.

Marvin, Walter Taylor, philosopher, b. New Brunswick, N.J., 1872; d. New Brunswick, N.J., May 26, 1944. [7; 10; 11]

Marvin, Winthrop Lippitt, journalist, b. Newcastle, N.H., 1863; d. New York, N.Y., Feb. 3, 1926. [10]

Marwedel, Emma Jacobina Christiana, kindergartner, b. near Göttingen, Germany, 1818; d. San Francisco, Calif., Nov. 17, 1893. [1]

Mary Angelita, Sister, poet and educationist, b. Vincennes, Ind., 1878; d. April 3, 1934. [21; 22]

Maryott, Erastus Edgar, physician, b. 1845; d. 1904.

Mary Theodosia, Sister. See Mug, Sister Mary Theodosia.

Mason, Alfred Bishop, lawyer and miscellaneous writer, b. Bridgeport, Conn., 1851; d. Florence, Italy, Jan. 26, 1933. [10; 11; 62]

Mason, Alfred De Witt, clergyman, b. Brooklyn, N.Y., 1855; d. Brooklyn, N.Y., Jan. 26, 1923. [10]

Mason, Mrs. Amelia Ruth, née **Gere,** historian, b. Northampton, Mass., 1831; d. Chicago, Ill., Aug. 11, 1923. [10]

Mason, Mrs. Caroline, née **Atwater,** novelist, b. Providence, R.I., 1853; d. Danvers, Mass., May 2, 1939. [4; 5; 7; 10; 11]

Mason, Mrs. Caroline Atherton, née **Briggs,** poet, b. Marblehead, Mass., 1823; d. Fitchburg, Mass., 1890. [3; 7; 8]

Mason, Charles Field, medical officer, b. 1864; d. 1922.

Mason, Mrs. Clara Stevens Arthur, poet, b. 1844; d. 1884.

Mason, David Hastings, journalist, b. Philadelphia, Pa., 1829; d. 1903. [3; 4; 5; 10]

Mason, Edward Gay, historian, b. 1839; d. Chicago, Ill., Dec. 18, 1898.

Mason, Edward Tuckerman, editor, b. New York, N.Y., 1847; d. Ossining, N.Y., 1911. .[6; 10]

Mason, Emily Virginia, educationist, b. Lexington, Ky., 1815; d. Georgetown, D.C., 1909. [3; 4; 7; 8; 10; 34; 74]

Mason, George Champlin, architect, b. Newport, R.I., 1820; d. Philadelphia, Pa., Feb. 1, 1894. [3; 5; 6; 7; 8]

Mason, Henry Burrall, lawyer, b. Bridgeport, Conn., 1848; d. Chicago Ill., Feb. 20, 1932. [62]

Mason, John Leonard, physical instructor, b. 1880; d. Philadelphia, Pa., Aug. 10, 1942.

Mason, John Mitchell, clergyman, b. New York, N.Y., 1770; d. New York, N.Y., Dec. 26, 1829. [1; 3; 4; 5; 6]

Mason, Joseph Warren Teets, journalist, b. Newburgh, N.Y., 1879; d. New York, N.Y., May 13, 1941. [7; 10; 12]

Mason, Louise Emily, journalist, b. Waterloo, Ont.; d. Toronto Ont., Dec. 18, 1946.

Mason, Lowell, hymn-writer, b. Medfield, Mass., 1792; d. Orange, N.J., Aug. 11, 1872. [4; 7; 20]

Mason, Otis Tufton, ethnologist, b. Eastport, Me., 1838; d. Washington, D.C., Nov. 5, 1908. [1; 3; 4; 5; 10]

Mason, Redfern, music critic, d. Yuba City, Calif., April 16, 1941. [35]

Mason, Rufus Osgood, physician and psychologist, b. Sullivan, N.H., 1830; d. New York, N.Y., May 12, 1903. [5; 8; 10]

Mason, Walt, poet and humorist, b. Columbus, Ont., 1862; d. La Jolla, Calif., June 22, 1939. [2a; 7; 10]

Mason, William, musician, b. Boston, Mass., 1829; d. New York, N.Y., July 14, 1908. [1; 4; 5; 10; 20]

Mason, William Ernest, politician, b. Franklinville, N.Y., 1850; d. Washington, D.C., June 16, 1921. [1; 4; 5; 10]

Mason, William Pitt, sanitary engineer, b. New York, N.Y., 1853; d. Little Boar's Head, N.H., Jan. 25, 1937. [10]

Masquerier, Lewis, sociologist, b. Paris, Ky., 1802; d. ? [1; 9]

Massett, Stephen, actor, b. London, England, 1820; d. New York, N.Y., Aug. 22, 1898. [3b]

Massey, George Betton, physician, b. Kent county, Md., 1856; d. Philadelphia, Pa., March 29, 1927. [1; 10]

Massey, Wilbur Fisk, horticulturist, b. Accomac county, Va., 1839; d. Salisbury, Md., March 30, 1923. [10]

Massicotte, Edouard Zotique, archivist, b. Montreal, Que., 1867; d. Montreal, Que., Nov. 7, 1947. [30]

Massie, David Meade, lawyer, b. Chillicothe, O., 1859; d. Chillicothe, O., Dec. 3, 1927. [10]

Massie, Eugene Carter, lawyer, b. Orange county, Va., 1861; d. Richmond, Va., April 14, 1924. [10]

Massingham, William Jeremiah, poet, b. Kane county, Ill., 1849; d. ? [70]

Masson, Louis François Rodrigue, politician and historian, b. Terrebonne, Lower Canada, 1833; d. Montreal, Que., Nov. 8, 1903. [27]

Masson, Thomas Lansing, humorist, b. Essex, Conn., 1866; d. Glen Ridge, N.J., June 18, 1934. [1a; 4; 7; 10]

Mast, Samuel Ottmar, biologist, b. Washenaw county, Mich., 1871; d. Baltimore, Md., Feb. 3, 1947. [10; 11; 13]

Masten, Cornelius Arthur, jurist, b. La Colle, Que., 1857; d. Toronto, Ont., Aug. 29, 1942. [27]

Masters, Charles Harding, lawyer, b. Amherst, N.S., 1852; d. Ottawa, Ont., Feb. 10, 1931. [27]

Masury, John Wesley, manufacturer, b. Salem, Mass., 1820; d. New York, N.Y., May 14, 1895. [1; 4]

Mather, Cotton, clergyman, b. Boston, Mass., 1663; d. Boston, Mass., Feb. 13, 1728. [1; 2; 3; 4; 5; 6; 7; 9; 51]

Mather, Fred, pisciculturist, b. Greenbush, N.Y., 1833 d. near Lake Nebagomain, Wis., Feb. 16, 1900. [1; 3; 4; 7; 10]

Mather, Frederic Gregory, journalist, b. Cleveland, O., 1844; d. Stamford, Conn., Aug. 31, 1925. [10; 49]

Mather, Increase, clergyman and educationist, b. Dorchester, Mass., 1639; d. Boston, Mass., Aug. 23, 1723. [1; 2; 3; 4; 5; 6; 7; 9; 51]

Mather, Moses, clergyman, b. Lyme, Conn., 1719; d. Darien, Conn., Sept. 21, 1906. [3; 8; 62]

Mather, Richard, clergyman, b. Lancashire, England, 1596; d. Dorchester, Mass., April 22, 1669. [1; 3; 4; 7; 9]

Mather, Samuel, clergyman, b. Boston, Mass., 1706; d. Boston, Mass., June 27, 1785. [1; 3; 4; 6; 7]

Mather, Thomas William, mechanical engineer, b. Cromwell, Conn., 1850; d. Cocoanut Grove, Fla., July 3, 1917. [62]

Mather, William Williams, geologist, b. Brooklyn, Conn., 1804; d. Columbus, O., Feb. 26, 1859. [1; 3; 4]

Mathews, Albert, miscellaneous writer, b. New York, N.Y., 1820; d. Lake Mohawk, N.Y., Sept. 9, 1903. [1; 3; 4; 5; 7; 9; 62]

Mathews, Alfred, editor, b. Painesville, O., 1852; d. Philadelphia, Pa., 1904. [8; 10]

Mathews, Charles Thompson, architect, b. Paris, France, 1863; d. New York, N.Y., Jan. 11, 1934. [7; 10; 11; 62]

Mathews, Cornelius, poet, playwright, and journalist, b. Port Chester, N.Y., 1817; d. New York, N.Y., March 25, 1889. [1; 2; 3; 4; 5; 6; 7; 9; 71]

Mathews, Ferdinand Schuyler, illustrator, b. New Brighton, N.Y., 1854; d. Plymouth, N.H., Aug. 20, 1938. [10; 11]

Mathews, Frances Aymar, novelist and playwright, b. New York, N.Y., about 1865; d. New York, N.Y., Sept. 11, 1925. [7; 10]

Mathews, Mrs. Gertrude, née Singleton. See Shelby, Mrs. Gertrude Mathews, née Singleton.

Mathews, James McFarlane, clergyman, b. Salem, N.Y., 1785; d. New York, N.Y., Jan. 28, 1870. [3; 4; 6; 8]

Mathews, Joanna Hooe, writer of books for girls, b. New York, N.Y., 1849; d. Summit, N.J., April 28, 1901. [6; 8]

Mathews, Joseph McDowell, clergyman, b. 1804; d. 1879.

Mathews, Joseph McDowell, physician, b. New Castle, Ky., 1847; d. Los Angeles, Calif., Dec. 2, 1928. [4; 10]

Mathews, Shailer, theologian, b. Portland, Me., 1863; d. Chicago, Ill., Oct. 23, 1941. [4; 7; 10; 11]

Mathews, William, educationist, b. Waterville, Me., 1818; d. Boston, Mass., Feb. 14, 1909. [1; 3; 4; 6; 7; 9; 10]

Mathews, William Smythe Babcock, musician, b. Loudon, N.H., 1837; d. Denver, Colo., April 1, 1912. [1; 6; 7; 10; 20]

Mathewson, Christopher, baseball-player, b. 1880; d. Saranac Lake, N.Y., Oct. 7, 1925. [1]

Mathis, Juliette Estelle, poet, b. Glens Falls, N.Y., 1893; d. ? [35]

Matignon, Francis, priest, b. Paris, France, 1753; d. Boston, Mass., Sept. 19, 1818. [1; 3]

Matlack, Lucius Columbus, clergyman, b. 1816; d. June 24, 1883.

Matsell, George Washington, police commissioner, b. England, 1811; d. New York, N.Y., July 25, 1877. [3b]

Matson, Henry, clergyman and librarian, b. Ellsworth, O., 1829; d. Oberlin, O., May 21, 1901. [8; 10]

Matson, Nehemiah, historian, b. 1816; d. 1883.

Matson, William A., clergyman, d. Richmond Hill, N.Y., March 18, 1904.

Matthewman, Lisle de Vaux, journalist, b. Yorkshire, England, 1867; d. New York, N.Y., 1904. [8; 10]

Matthews, Brander. See Matthews, James Brander.

Matthews, Franklin, journalist, b. St. Joseph, Mich., 1858; d. New York, N.Y., Nov. 26, 1917. [1; 10]

Matthews, James Brander, educationist, b. New Orleans, La., 1852; d. New York, N.Y., March 31, 1929. [1; 2; 3; 4; 5; 7; 9; 10; 71]

Matthews, James Newson, journalist, b. Bungay, England, 1828; d. Buffalo, N.Y., Dec. 20, 1888. [3b; 4]

Matthews, James Newton, physician and poet, b. 1852; d. near Mason, Ill., March 7, 1910. [8]

Matthews, John, clergyman, b. Guilford county, N.C., 1772; d. New Albany, Ind., May 19, 1848. [3; 34]

Matthews, Joseph Merritt, chemist, b. Philadelphia, Pa., 1874; d. San Diego, Calif., Oct. 11, 1931. [1; 10; 11]

Matthews, Lyman, clergyman, b. Middlebury, Vt., 1801; d. Cornwall, Vt., Aug. 17, 1866. [43]

Matthews, Nathan, lawyer and politician, b. Boston, Mass., 1854; d. Boston, Mass., Dec. 11, 1927. [1; 10; 51]

Matthews, Stanley, jurist, b. Cincinnati, O., 1824; d. Washington, D.C., March 22, 1889. [3; 4]

Matthews, Washington, ethnologist, b. county Dublin, Ireland, 1843; d. Washington, D.C., April 29, 1905. [4; 7; 10]

Matthews, William Baynham, lawyer, b. Lynchburg, Va., 1850; d. 1914. [8; 10]

Matthews, William Henry, social worker, b. England, 1873; d. Yonkers, N.Y., June 18, 1946. [10; 61]

Mattison, Hiram, clergyman, b. Norway, N.Y., 1811; d. Jersey City, N.J., Nov. 24, 1868. [1; 3; 4; 6]

Mattison, Seth, clergyman and poet, b. 1788; d. 1843.

Mattocks, Brewer, physician, b. Keeseville, N.Y., 1841; d. ? [70]

Mattoon, Arthur Martyn, astronomer, b. Maxtown, O., 1855; d. Albany, Ore., Jan. 7, 1924. [10]

Mattson, Hans, journalist, b. Sweden, 1832; d. Minneapolis, Minn., March 5, 1893. [1; 7; 70]

Mattson, Morris, manufacturer, b. about 1809; d. 1885. [6; 7]

Matulka, Barbara, educationist, b. 1903; d. New York, N.Y., July 5, 1936. [11]

Maturin, Edward, educationist, novelist, and poet, b. Dublin, Ireland, 1812; d. New York, N.Y., May 25, 1881. [3; 7; 8]

Maude, John Edward, clergyman, b. Lancashire, England, 1855; d. Fall River, Mass., June 26, 1885. [51]

Maurault, Joseph Pierre Anselme, priest and historian, b. Kamouraska, Lower Canada, 1819; d. July 5, 1871. [27]

Maurer, James Hudson, socialist, b. Reading, Pa., 1864; d. Reading, Pa., March 16, 1944. [10]

Maurice, Arthur Bartlett, literary critic, b. Rahway, N.J., 1873; d. Stamford, Conn., May 31, 1946. [7; 10; 11]

Maury, Ann, editor, b. Liverpool, England, 1803; d. New York, N.Y., Jan., 1876. [3; 6; 8]

Maury, Dabney Herndon, soldier, b. Fredericksburg, Va., 1822; d. Peoria, Ill., Jan. 11, 1900. [1; 3; 4; 5; 7; 34]

Maury, Magruder Gordon, journalist, b. Philadelphia, Pa., 1878; d. Bethesda, Md., Nov. 22, 1948. [10]

Maury, Matthew Fontaine, naval officer and oceanographer, b. near Fredericksburg, Va., 1806; d. Lexington, Va., Feb. 1, 1873. [1; 3; 4; 5; 6; 7; 34]

Maury, Mrs. Sarah Mytton, née Hughes, humanitarian, b. Liverpool, England, Nov 1, 1803; d. Virginia, Oct., 1849. [3; 6; 8; 34]

Maus, Louis Mervin, soldier, b. Silver Springs, Md., 1851; d. New Windsor, Md., Feb. 9, 1930. [10]

Maver, William, electrical engineer, b. Forfar, Scotland, 1851; d. New York, N.Y., Aug. 8, 1928. [10]

Mavor, James, economist, b. Stranraer, Scotland, 1854; d. Glasgow, Scotland, Oct. 31, 1925. [27]

Maxcy, Carroll Lewis, educationist, b. Norristown, Pa., 1865; d. Williamstown, Mass., Aug. 18, 1936. [10; 11; 61]

Maxim, Hiram Percy, inventor, b. Brooklyn, N.Y., 1869; d. La Junta, Calif., Feb. 17, 1936. [4; 10]

Maxim, Hudson, inventor, b. Orneville, Me., 1853; d. Lake Hopatcong, N.J., May 6, 1927. [1; 4; 10]

Maxson, Edwin R., physician, fl. 1861-1895. [6]

Maxwell, Charles Robert, educationist, b. Fayston, Vt., 1878; d. Laramie, Wyo., Sept. 14, 1939. [10; 11]

Maxwell, Mrs. Ellen, née Blackmar, novelist, b. West Springfield, Pa.; d. Bethlehem, N.Y., Dec. 21, 1938. [4; 10]

Maxwell, Hu, forestry expert, b. 1860; d. Aug. 20, 1927.

Maxwell, Mrs. Sadie B., local historian, b. 1837; d. 1904. [37]

Maxwell, Samuel, jurist, b. Lodi, N.Y., 1825; d. Fremont, Neb., Feb. 11, 1901. [1; 4; 10]

Maxwell, Sidney Denise, statistician, b. Centreville, O., 1831; d. Cincinnati, O., Nov. 13, 1913. [5]

Maxwell, William, educationist, b. Norfolk, Va., 1874; d. near Williamsburg, Va., Jan. 10, 1857. [1; 3; 4; 5]

Maxwell, William Henry, educationist, b. county Tyrone, Ireland, 1852; d. Flushing, New York, May 3, 1920. [1; 3; 5; 10]

May, Caroline, poet and anthologist, b. England, about 1820; d. ? [3; 7; 8]

May, Charles Henry, ophthalmologist, b. Baltimore, Md., 1861; d. New York, N.Y., Dec. 7, 1943. [4; 10; 11]

May, Edith (pseud.). See Drinker, Anna.

May, Heber J., lawyer, b. 1848; d. 1915.

May, John Walker, poet, b. 1828; d. 1899. [38]

May, John Wilder, lawyer, b. Attleboro, Mass., 1819; d. Boston, Mass., Jan. 11, 1883. [3; 8]

May, Julia Harris, poet, b. Strong, Me., 1833; d. Auburn, Me., May 6, 1912. [10]

May, Reginald (pseud.). See Stokes, J. Lemacks.

May, Samuel, clergyman, b. Boston, Mass., 1810; d. Leicester, Mass., Nov. 24, 1899. [3b; 4; 8]

May, Samuel Joseph, clergyman and reformer, b. Boston, Mass., 1797; d. Syracuse, N.Y., July 1, 1871. [1; 3; 4; 5; 6; 7]

May, Sophie (pseud.). See Clarke, Rebecca Sophia.

May, Thomas P., novelist, fl. 1879-1882. [6]

Mayer, Alfred Goldsborough. See Mayor, Alfred Goldsborough.

Mayer, Alfred Marshall, physicist, b. Baltimore, Md., 1836; d. Maplewood, N.J., July 13, 1897. [1; 3b; 4; 5; 8; 34]

Mayer, Brantz, lawyer, diplomat, and historian, b. Baltimore, Md., 1809; d. Baltimore, Md., March 21, 1879. [4; 7; 9; 34]

Mayer, Lewis, clergyman, b. Lancaster, Pa., 1783; d. York, Pa., Aug. 25, 1849. [1]

Mayer, Lewis, lawyer, b. 1836; d. 1886.

Mayes, Edward, lawyer and educationist, b. near Jackson, Miss., 1846; d. Jackson, Miss., Aug. 9, 1917. [1; 4; 5; 10; 34]

Mayfield, Millie (pseud.). See Homes, Mrs. Mary Sophie, née Shaw.

Mayhew, Experience, missionary, b. Martha's Vineyard, Mass., 1673; d. Martha's Vineyard, Mass., Nov. 29, 1758. [1; 3; 4; 7; 9]

Mayhew, Ira, educationist, b. Ellisburg, N.Y., 1814; d. Detroit, Mich., April 7, 1894. [4; 39]

Mayhew, Jonathan, clergyman, b. Martha's Vineyard, Mass., 1720; d. Boston, Mass., July 9, 1766. [1; 3; 4; 5; 6; 7; 9]

Mayhew, Matthew, missionary to the Indians, b. England; d. Martha's Vineyard, Mass., 1710. [3]

Mayhew, Thomas, missionary to the Indians, b. Southampton, England, about 1621; d. at sea, 1657. [1; 3; 4]

Maynard, Charles Johnson, naturalist, b. West Newton, Mass., 1845; d. West Newton, Mass., Oct. 15, 1929. [1; 6; 7; 10; 11]

Maynard, Mrs. Henrietta Sturdevant, née **Colburn,** spiritualist, b. Bolton, Conn., 1841; d. White Plains, N.Y., June 27, 1892.

Maynard, Laurens, poet and publisher, b. Boston, Mass., 1866; d. 1917. [10]

Maynard, Mrs. Lucy, née **Warner,** ornithologist, b. 1852; d. ?

Maynard, Mrs. Nettie Colburn. See Maynard, Mrs. Henrietta Sturdevant, née Colburn.

Maynard, Samuel Taylor, horticulturist, b. Hardwick, Mass., 1844; d. Northboro, Mass., 1923. [10]

Maynard, Mrs. Sara Katherine, née **Casey,** writer of books for children, b. South Africa; d. Westminster, Md., Nov. 26, 1945. [21]

Mayne, Dexter Dwight, educationist, b. Beetown, Wis., 1863; d. St. Paul, Minn., 1929. [10; 11; 70]

Mayo, Amory Dwight, clergyman, b. Warwick, Mass., 1823; d. Washington, D.C., April 8, 1907. [1; 3; 4; 5; 7; 10]

Mayo, Joseph, lawyer, b. Fine Creek Mills, Va., 1795; d. Richmond, Va., Aug. 9, 1872. [3]

Mayo, Katherine, publicist, b. Ridgeway, Pa., 1867; d. Bedford Hills, N.Y., Oct. 9, 1940. [7; 10; 11]

Mayo, Robert, civil servant, b. Powhatan county, Va., 1784; d. Washington, D.C., Oct. 31, 1864. [3; 4; 8; 34]

Mayo, Thomas Jefferson, physician, b. 1846; d. Philadelphia, Pa., Feb. 14, 1918. [6]

Mayo, William Starbuck, physician and novelist, b. Ogdensburg, N.Y., 1811; d. New York, N.Y., Nov. 22, 1895. [1; 3; 4; 5; 6; 7; 9]

Mayor, Alfred Goldsborough, biologist, b. near Frederick, Md., 1868; d. Tortugas, Fla., June 24, 1922. [1; 4; 10]

Mayo-Smith, Richmond, economist, b. Troy, O., 1854; d. New York, N.Y., Nov. 11, 1901. [1; 3b; 9; 10]   !

Meacham, Alfred Benjamin, ethnologist, b. Orange county, Ind., 1826; d. Washington, D.C., Feb. 16, 1882.

Mead, Asa, clergyman, b. 1792; d. 1831. [6]

Mead, Charles, poet and educationist, fl. 1819-1828.

Mead, Charles Marsh, clergyman, b. Cornwall, Vt., 1836; d. Hartford, Conn., Feb. 15, 1911. [1; 3; 4; 5; 10]

Mead, Daniel M., local historian, b. Greenwich, Conn., 1834; d. Greenwich, Conn., Sept. 19, 1862.

Mead, Edward Campbell, genealogist, b. Newton, Mass., 1837; d. Keswick, Va., 1908. [8; 10; 34]

Mead, Edwin Doak, editor and lecturer, b. Chesterfield, N.H., 1849; d. Boston, Mass., Aug. 17, 1937. [3; 4; 7; 8; 10, 11]

Mead, Elwood, engineer, b. Patriot, Ind., 1858; d. Washington, D.C., Jan. 28, 1936. [4; 10; 11]

Mead, George Herbert, philosopher, b. South Hadley, Mass., 1863; d. Chicago, Ill., April 25, 1931. [1a; 10]

Mead, George Whitfield, clergyman, b. Norwalk, O., 1865; d. Asheville, N.C., Dec. 18, 1946. [10; 11]

Mead, Mrs. Kate Campbell, née Hurd, physician, b. 1867; d. Middletown, Conn., Jan. 1, 1941. [10; 12]

Mead, Mrs. Lucia True, née Ames, pacifist, b. Boscawen, N.H., 1856; d. Brookline, Mass., Nov. 1, 1936. [10; 11]

Mead, Theodore Hoe, manufacturer, b. New York, N.Y., 1837; d. ? [4]

Mead, Whitman, traveller, b. 1792; d. 1833. [62]

Mead, William Edward, educationist, b. Gallupville, N.Y., 1866; d. Middletown, Conn., July 12, 1949. [10; 11]

Meade, George Gordon, historian, b. Philadelphia, Pa., 1877; d. Philadelphia, Pa., Sept. 24, 1947.

Meade, Julian Rutherford, educationist, b. 1909; d. Danville, Va., July 9, 1940.

Meade, Richard Kidder, chemical engineer, b. Charlottesville, Va., 1874; d. Oct. 13, 1930. [4; 10]

Meade, Richard Worsam, naval officer, b. New York, N.Y., 1837; d. Washington, D.C., May 4, 1897. [1; 3b; 4; 5]

Meade, William, bishop, b. Frederick county, Va., 1789; d. Richmond, Va., March 14, 1862. [1; 3; 4; 5; 6; 34]

Meadowcroft, William Henry, inventor, b. Manchester, England, 1853; d. Boonton, N.J., Oct. 14, 1937. [7; 10; 11]

Meagher, James Luke, priest, b. county Tipperary, Ireland, 1848; d. Long Island, N.Y., May 8, 1920. [10; 21]

Meagher, Nicholas Hogan, jurist, b. Mabou, N.S., 1842; d. Halifax, N.S., Aug. 26, 1932. [27]

Meagher, Thomas Francis, soldier, b. Waterford, Ireland, 1823; d. near Fort Benton, Mont., July 1, 1867. [1; 3; 4; 6]

Meakin, Frederick, philosopher, b. 1848; d. 1923. [51]

Meanes, Lenna Leota, physician, b. Prairie City, Ia., 1871; d. New York, N.Y., Dec. 4, 1942.

Means, Alexander, clergyman, b. Statesville, N.C., 1801; d. Oxford, Ga., June 5, 1883. [3; 4; 34]

Means, Mrs. Celina Eliza, educationist, b. 1840; d. Columbia, S.C., 1909. [34]

Means, David McGregor, lawyer, b. Groton, Mass., 1847; d. New York, N.Y., April 24, 1931. [8; 10; 62]

Means, Stewart, clergyman, b. Steubenville, O., 1852; d. New Haven, Conn., March 11, 1940. [11; 68]

Meany, Edmond Stephen, historian, b. East Saginaw, Mich., 1862; d. Seattle, Wash., April 22, 1935. [1a; 10]

Mearns, Edgar Alexander, soldier and naturalist, b. Highland Falls, N.Y., 1856; d. Washington, D.C., Nov. 1, 1916. [1; 10]

Mears, David Otis, clergyman, b. Essex, Mass., 1842; d. Williamstown, Mass., April 29, 1915. [1; 4; 8; 10]

Mears, Eliot Grinnell, educationist, b. Worcester, Mass., 1889; d. Middlebury, Vt., May 27, 1946. [10; 11; 51]

Mears, Frederick, aviator, b. Anchorage, Alaska; d. near San Diego, Calif., June 26, 1943. [62]

Mears, James Ewing, surgeon, b. Indianapolis, Ind., 1838; d. Philadelphia, Pa., 1918. [10]

Mears, John William, clergyman, b. Reading, Pa., 1825; d. Clinton, N.Y., Nov. 10, 1881. [1; 3; 4; 7]

Mease, James, physician and scientist, b. Philadelphia, Pa., 1771; d. Philadelphia, Pa., May 14, 1846. [1; 3; 6]

Mechem, Floyd Russell, lawyer, b. Nunda, N.Y., 1858; d. Chicago, Ill., Dec. 11, 1928. [1; 4; 10]

Medbery, James Knowles, journalist, b. 1838; d. New York, N.Y., Aug. 31, 1873. [47]

Medbery, Mrs. Rebecca B., née Stetson, biographer, b. Roxbury, Mass., 1808; d. Lynn, Mass., 1868. [3]

Medbury, Charles Sanderson, clergyman, b. Warren, O., 1865; d. Des Moines, Ia., April 24, 1932. [10; 37]

Medicus (pseud.). See Slade, Daniel Denison.

Meehan, Mrs. Jeanette Porter. See Porter, Mrs. Gene, née Stratton.

Meehan, Thomas, horticulturist, b. Middlesex, England, 1826; d. Philadelphia, Pa., Nov. 19, 1901. [1; 3b; 4; 5; 7]

Meehan, Thomas Francis, journalist, b. Brooklyn, N.Y., 1854; d. Brooklyn, N.Y., July 7, 1942. [21]

Meek, Alexander Beaufort, miscellaneous writer, b. Columbia, S.C., 1814; d. Columbus, Miss., Nov. 1, 1865. [1; 3; 4; 5; 7; 9; 34]

Meek, Basil, local historian, b. New Castle, Ind., 1829; d. Fremont, O., April 16, 1922.

Meek, Edward, lawyer, b. Port Stanley, Ont., 1845; d. Toronto, Ont., Dec. 31, 1925. [27]

Meek, Fielding Bradford, palaeontologist, b. Madison, Ind., 1817; d. Washington, D.C., Dec. 21, 1876. [1; 3; 4]

Meek, Seth Eugene, biologist, b. Hicksville, O., 1859; d. Chicago, Ill., July 5, 1914. [10]

Meeker, Ezra, pioneer, b. near Huntsville, O., 1830; d. Seattle, Wash., Dec. 3, 1928. [1; 4; 7; 10]

Meeker, James Edward, economist, b. Bridgeport, Conn., 1890; d. New York, N.Y., July 26, 1934. [62]

Meeker, Nathan Cook, journalist and Indian agent, b. Euclid, O., 1817; d. White River Reservation, Colo., Sept. 29, 1879. [1; 4; 7]

Meeker, Mrs. Nellie J., novelist, fl. 1883-1902.

Meekins, Lynn Roby, journalist, b. Salem, Md., 1862; d. Baltimore, Md., Nov. 8, 1933. [10]

Meeks, Leslie Howard, educationist, b. Thorntown, Ind., 1895; d. Lake Independence, Mich., July 23, 1938. [62]

Mees, Arthur, musician, b. Columbus, O., 1850; d. New York, N.Y., April 26, 1923. [1; 10; 20]

Mees, Theophilus, educationist, b. Columbus, O., 1848; d. New York, N.Y., July 25, 1923. [10]

Meginnis, John Franklin, journalist and historian, b. Colerain, Pa., 1827; d. Williamsport, Pa., Nov. 11, 1899. [4]

Megrue, Roi Cooper, playwright, b. New York, N.Y., 1883; d. New York, N.Y., Sept. 27, 1927. [1; 4; 7; 10]

Meigs, Arthur Vincent, physician, b. Philadelphia, Pa., 1850; d. Philadlephia, Pa., Jan. 1, 1912. [1; 4; 10]

Meigs, Charles Delucena, physician, b. St. George, Bermuda, 1792; d. Hamanassett, Pa., June 22, 1869. [1; 3; 4; 6]

Meigs, John Forsyth, physician, b. Philadelphia, Pa., 1818; d. Philadelphia, Pa., Dec. 16, 1882. [1; 3; 6]

Meigs, John Forsyth, naval officer, b. 1848; d. 1924.

Meigs, Return Jonathan, lawyer, b. Clark county, Ky., 1801; d. Washington, D.C., Oct. 19, 1891. [1; 4; 34]

Meigs, William Montgomery, lawyer and historian, b. Philadelphia, Pa., 1852; d. Philadelphia, Pa., Dec. 30, 1929. [1; 7; 10; 11]

Meilleur, Jean Baptiste, educationist, b. St. Laurent, Lower Canada, 1796; d. Montreal, Que., Dec. 6, 1878. [27]

Meinzer, Oscar Edward, geologist, b. near Davis, Ill., 1876; d. Washington, D.C., June 15, 1948. [10; 11; 13]

Meissner, Mme. Sophie de, née **Radford,** novelist, b. Morristown, N.J., 1854; d. ? [7]

Melamed, Samuel Max, scholar, b. Russia, 1885; d. New York, N.Y., June 19, 1938. [11]

Melden, Charles Manly, clergyman, b. Salem, Mass., 1853; d. ? [11]

Melendy, Mrs. Mary, née **Ries,** writer on popular medicine, b. 1841; d. ?

Melendy, Peter, local historian, b. 1823; d. 1901. [37]

Meleney, Clarence Edmund, educationist, b. Salem, Mass., 1853; d. Brooklyn, N.Y., March 26, 1938. [10]

Meline, James Florant, soldier and journalist, b. Sackett's Harbor, N.Y., 1811; d. Brooklyn, N.Y., Aug. 14, 1873. [3; 4; 5; 6; 7; 8]

Meline, Mary Miller, novelist, fl. 1869-1874. [6]

Melish, John, geographer and traveller, b. Perthshire, Scotland, 1771; d. Philadelphia, Pa., Dec. 30, 1822. [1; 4; 6; 7]

Mell, Clayton Dissinger, forester, b. Wernersville, Pa., 1875; d. Merida, Mexico, Feb. 25, 1945. [62]

Mell, Patrick Hues, clergyman, b. Liberty county, Ga., 1814; d. Athens, Ga., Jan. 26, 1888. [1; 3; 4; 5; 6; 34]

Mell, Patrick Hues, scientist, b. Penfield, Ga., 1850; d. Fredericksburg, Va., Oct. 12, 1918. [1; 3; 4; 5; 10; 34]

Mellen, Grenville, poet, b. Biddeford, Me., 1799; d. New York, N.Y., Sept. 5, 1841. [1; 3; 4; 6; 7; 9; 71]

Mellen, John, clergyman, b. Hopkinton, Mass., 1722; d. Reading, Mass., 1807. [3; 6]

Mellen, John, clergyman, b. 1752; d. 1828. [6]

Mellick, Andrew D., genealogist, b. 1844; d. Plainfield, N.J., Nov. 6, 1895.

Mellish, Mrs. Maud, née **Headline,** librarian, b. 1862; d. 1933.

Mellon, Andrew William, industrialist and politician, b. Pittsburgh, Pa., 1855; d. Southampton, Long Island, N.Y., Aug. 26, 1937. [10]

Meloney, William Brown, journalist, b. San Francisco, Calif., 1878; d. Pawling, N.Y., Sept. 7, 1925. [4; 7; 10; 11]

Melton, Wightman Fletcher, poet and journalist, b. Ripley, Tenn., 1867; d. Atlanta, Ga., Nov. 13, 1944. [7; 10; 11; 34]

Melville, George Wallace, naval officer, b. New York, N.Y., 1841; d. Philadelphia, Pa., March 17, 1912. [1; 3; 4; 10]

Melville, Henry, lawyer, b. Nelson, N.H., 1858; d. New York, N.Y., Oct. 21, 1930. [10]

Melville, Henry Reed, surgeon, d. London, England, March 25, 1868. [27]

Melville, Herman, adventurer, novelist, and poet, b. New York, N.Y., 1819; d. New York. N.Y., Sept. 28, 1891. [1; 2; 3; 4; 6; 7; 8; 71; 72]

Memminger, Allard, physician, b. Charleston, S.C., 1854; d. Charleston, S.C., Jan. 16, 1936. [10]

Menand, Louis, horticulturist, b. 1807; d. 1900.

Mencken, Mrs. Sara Powell, née **Haardt,** miscellaneous writer, b. Montgomery, Ala., 1898; d. Baltimore, Md., May 31, 1935. [7; 10]

Mendel, Lafayette Benedict, biochemist, b. Delhi, N.Y., 1872; d. New Haven, Conn., Dec. 9, 1935. [1a; 10; 11; 62]

Mendell, George Henry, engineer, b. 1831; d. 1902.

Mendelsohn, Charles Jastrow, educationist, b. Wilmington, N.C., 1880; d. New York, N.Y., Sept. 27, 1939. [10]

Mendenhall, Charles Elwood, physicist, b. Columbus, O., 1872; d. Madison, Wis., Aug. 18, 1935. [1a; 10]

Mendenhall, George, physician, b. Sharon, Pa., 1814; d. Cincinnati, O., June 4, 1874. [3; 4]

Mendenhall, Harlan George, clergyman, b. Coatesville, Pa., 1851; d. Litchfield, Conn., May 15, 1940. [10; 11]

Mendenhall, James W., clergyman, b. Ohio, 1844; d. Colorado Springs, Colo., June 18, 1892. [3b; 8]

Mendenhall, Thomas Corwin, physicist, b. near Hanoverton, O.; d. Ravenna, O., March 23, 1924. [1; 3; 4; 5; 10]

Mendes, Henry Pereira, rabbi, b. Birmingham, England, 1852; d. New York, N.Y., Oct. 21, 1937. [10; 11]

Menge, Edward John von Komorowski, psychobiologist, b. Fond du Lac, Wis., 1882; d. Joliet, Ill., Jan. 9, 1941. [10; 11; 21]

Menken, Adah Isaacs, actress and poet, b. probably near New Orleans, La., about 1835; d. Paris, France, Aug. 10, 1868. [1; 3; 4; 7; 9]

Mentor (pseud.). See Urner, Nathan D.

Méras, Albert Amédée, educationist, b. New York, N.Y., 1880; d. New York, N.Y., March 1, 1926. [10]

Méras, Baptiste, educationist, b. France, 1850; d. near Oak Bluffs, Mass., July 26, 1944.

Mercedes, Sister, poet, b. Philadelphia, Pa., 1846; d. ? [21]

Mercein, Thomas FitzRandolph, clergyman, b. New York, N.Y., 1825; d. Sheffield, Mass., Sept. 15, 1856. [3; 8]

Mercer, Asa Shinn, pioneer, b. 1839; d. Buffalo, Wyo., Aug. 10, 1917.

Mercer, Charles Fenton, politician, b. Fredericksburg, Va., 1778; d. Howard, Fairfax county, Va., May 4, 1858. [1; 3; 4; 5; 8]

Mercer, Henry Chapman, archaeologist, b. Doylestown, Pa., 1856; d. Doylestown, Pa., March 9, 1930. [1; 4; 5; 10; 11; 51]

Mercer, Lewis Pyle, clergyman, b. Chester county, Pa., 1847; d. Urbana, O., July 6, 1906. [1; 4]

Mercer, Margaret, reformer, b. Annapolis, Md., July 1, 1791; d. Belmont, Va., Sept. 17, 1846. [1; 4; 34]

Merchant, Francis Walter, educationist, b. Oil Springs, Ont., 1855; d. Toronto, Ont., Jan. 29, 1937. [27]

Mercier, Charles Albert, physician and littérateur, b. New Orleans, La., 1816; d. New Orleans, La., May 12, 1894. [1; 7; 34]

Mercier, Honoré, politician, b. St. Athanase, Lower Canada, 1840; d. Montreal, Que., Oct. 30, 1894. [27]

Mercur, James, soldier, b. Towanda, Pa., 1842; d. West Point, N.Y., April 22, 1896. [3b; 5; 8]

Meredith, Albert Barrett, educationist, b. Gorham, N.H., 1871; d. Wakefield, N.H., April 12, 1946. [11]

Meredith, William Henry, clergyman, b. Bristol, England, 1844; d. Framingham, Mass., 1911. [10]

Meredith, William Tuckey, novelist, b. Philadelphia, Pa., 1839; d. ? [8]

Meriwether, Colyer, educationist, b. Clark's Hill, S.C.; d. Washington, D.C., Aug. 26, 1920. [10]

Meriwether, Mrs. Elizabeth, née Avery, novelist and playwright, b. Bolivar, Tenn., 1832; d. St. Louis, Mo., Nov. 4, 1917. [7; 8; 10]

Merrell, Edward Huntington, clergyman, b. New Hartford, N.Y., 1835; d. Ripon, Wis., Feb. 18, 1910. [5]

Merrell, Mrs. Nellie Dryden, horticulturist, b. 1864; d. New Canaan, Conn., July 4, 1940.

Merriam, Augustus Chapman, archaeologist, b. Leyden, N.Y., 1843; d. Athens, Greece, Jan. 20, 1895. [1; 3b; 4; 5]

Merriam, Charles, sporstman, b. Fort Spokane, Wash., 1885; d. New York, N.Y., Dec. 31, 1946.

Merriam, Clinton Hart, naturalist, b. New York, N.Y., 1855; d. Berkeley, Calif., March 19, 1942. [4; 7; 10]

Merriam, Edmund Franklin, clergyman, b. Winthrop, Me., 1847; d. Boston, Mass., Nov. 1, 1930. [4; 10; 11]

Merriam, George, publisher, b. Worcester, Mass., 1803; d. Springfield, Mass., June 22, 1880. [3]

Merriam, George Ernest, clergyman, b. Greenville, N.H., 1873; d. Cortland, N.Y., March 10, 1941.

Merriam, George Spring, publisher, b. Springfield, Mass., 1843; d. Springfield, Mass., Jan. 22, 1914. [7; 10; 62]

Merriam, John Campbell, palaeontologist, b. Hopkinton, Ia., 1869; d. Oakland, Calif., Oct. 30, 1945. [7; 10; 11]

Merrick, Mrs. Caroline Elizabeth, née Thomas, historian, b. New Orleans, La., 1825; d. ? [4; 8; 34]

Merrick, Edwin Thomas, jurist, b. Wilbraham, Mass., 1808; d. New Orleans, La., Jan. 12, 1897. [1; 3b; 4]

Merrick, Edwin Thomas, lawyer, b. Point Coupée Parish, La., 1859; d. New Orleans, La., June 21, 1935. [4; 10]

Merrick, Frederick, clergyman, b. Wilbraham, Mass., 1810; d. Delaware, O., Jan. 12, 1897. [1; 4]

Merrick, George Byron, steamboat pilot, b. 1841; d. Madison, Wis., April 21, 1931. [44]

Merrick, Mrs. Henrietta, née Sands, traveller, b. 1886; d. New York, N.Y., June 18, 1944.

Merrick, James Lyman, missionary, b. Monson, Mass., 1803; d. South Amherst, Mass., June 18, 1866. [3]

Merrifield, Fred, clergyman, b. Amboy, Ill., 1874; d. Chicago, Ill., Feb. 6, 1935. [10; 11]

Merrill, Allyne Litchfield, educationist, b. Malden, Mass., 1864; d. Harrison, Me., Feb. 26, 1941. [10]

Merrill, Arthur Truman, educationist and poet, b. Quebec, Vt., 1874; d. Glendale, Calif., Jan. 31, 1935. [11; 35]

Merrill, Ayres Phillips, physician, b. Pittsfield, Mass., 1793; d. New York, N.Y., Nov. 3, 1873. [3; 4; 6]

Merrill, Catharine, educationist, b. Corydon, Ind., 1824; d. Indianapolis, Ind., May 30, 1900. [4]

Merrill, Daniel, clergyman, b. Essex county, Mass., 1765; d. Sedgwick, Me., June 3, 1833. [1; 3 ;6]

Merrill, Elmer Truesdell, educationist, b. Millville, Mass., 1860; d. Santa Barbara, Calif., April 20, 1936. [4; 10; 11]

Merrill, George, lawyer, b. New Hampshire, 1831; d. ?

Merrill, George Edmands, clergyman and educationist, b. Charlestown, Mass., Dec. 19, 1846; d. Hamilton, N.Y., June 11, 1908. [1; 4; 5; 10; 51]

Merrill, George Perkins, geologist, b. Auburn, Me., 1854; d. Auburn, Me., Aug. 15, 1929. [1; 4; 5; 10; 11]

Merrill, Helen Abbot, mathematician, b. Orange, N.J., 1864; d. Wellesley, Mass., May 1, 1949. [13]

Merrill, James Andrew, geologist, b. Rockcastle county, Ky., 1861; d. Superior, Wis., June 23, 1938. [10; 11; 44]

Merrill, James Milford, novelist, b. Muskegon, Mich., 1847; d. Grandville, Mich., about 1930. [10; 39]

Merrill, James Warren, local historian, b. 1833; d. 1908. [37]

Merrill, John Leverett, local historian, b. 1833; d. Boston, Mass., Jan. 30, 1913.

Merrill, Joseph, local historian, b. Amesbury, Mass., 1814; d. Amesbury, Mass., Feb. 9, 1898. [3b]

Merrill, Samuel, publisher, b. Indianapolis, Ind., 1831; d. Long Beach, Calif., Sept. 3, 1924. [10]

Merrill, Samuel, journalist, b. Charlestown, N.H., 1855; d. Cambridge, Mass., Jan. 12, 1932. [10; 49]

Merrill, Selah, clergyman, b. Canton Center, Conn., 1837; d. near Oakland, Calif., Jan. 22, 1909. [1; 3; 4; 5; 10]

Merrill, Stephen Mason, bishop, b. Jefferson county, O., 1825; d. Keyport, N.J., Nov. 12, 1905. [1; 3; 4; 5; 6; 10]

Merrill, Stuart FitzRandolph, poet, b. Hempstead, N.Y., 1863; d. Paris, France, Dec. 1, 1915. [7; 1]

Merrill, Thomas Abbot, clergyman, b. Andover, Mass., 1780; d. Middlebury, Vt., April 25, 1855. [43]

Merrill, William Augustus, educationist, b. Newburyport, Mass., 1860; d. Berkeley, Calif., Dec. 21, 1930. [10]

Merrill, William Bradford, journalist, b. Salisbury, N.H., 1861; d. New York, N.Y., Nov. 26, 1928. [1; 4; 10]

Merrill, William Emery, soldier and engineer, b. Fort Howard, Wis., 1837; d. near Edgefield, Ill., Dec. 14, 1891. [1; 3; 4; 6]

Merriman, Mrs. Effie, née Woodward, novelist, b. 1857; d. ?

Merriman, Mrs. Helen, née Bigelow, miscellaneous writer, b. Boston, Mass., 1844; d. July 25, 1933. [10]

Merriman, Mansfield, civil engineer, b. Southington, Conn., 1848; d. New York, N.Y., June 7, 1925. [3; 4; 5; 6; 8; 10; 62]

Merriman, Roger Bigelow, historian, b. Boston, Mass., 1876; d. St. Andrews-by-the-sea, N.B., Sept. 7, 1945. [7; 10; 51]

Merriman, Titus Mooney, clergyman, b. East Hatley, Lower Canada, 1822; d. Cambridge, Mass., 1912. [8; 10]

Merritt, Abraham, journalist and novelist, b. Beverly, N.J., 1884; d. Indian Rocks Beach, Fla., Aug. 21, 1943. [7; 10]

Merritt, Mrs. Anna, née Lea, painter, b. Philadelphia, Pa., 1844; d. London, England, April 7, 1930. [1; 10; 11]

Merritt, Edward Percival, banker, b. Boston, Mass., 1860; d. Monte Carlo, April 16, 1932. [10; 51]

Merritt, Edwin Atkins, politician, b. Sudbury, Vt., 1828; d. Potsdam, N.Y., Dec. 26, 1916. [10]

Merritt, Jedediah Prendergast, biographer, b. 1830; d. St. Catharines, Ont., Nov. 18, 1901. [27]

Merritt, Timothy, clergyman, b. Barkhamsted, Conn., 1775; d. Lynn, Mass., May 2, 1845. [3; 8]

Merritt, William Hamilton, mining engineer, b. St. Catharines, Ont., 1855; d. Toronto, Ont., Oct. 26, 1918. [27]

Merriweather, Magnus (pseud.). See Talbot, Charles Remington.

Mershon, Stephen Lyon, historian, b. East Hampton, N.Y., 1859; d. Montclair, N.J., Jan. 24, 1938.

Mershon, William Butts, lumberman, b. Saginaw, Mich., 1856; d. Saginaw, Mich., July 12, 1943. [10; 11; 39]

Merwin, Henry Childs, lawyer, b. Pittsfield, Mass., 1853; d. Brookline, Mass., Jan. 21, 1929. [8; 10; 51]

Merwin, Samuel, novelist, b. Evanston, Ill., 1874; d. New York, N.Y., Oct. 17, 1936. [7; 10; 11]

Merwin, Samuel John Mills, clergyman, b. New Haven, Conn., 1819; d. New Haven, Conn., Sept. 12, 1888. [62]

Merz, Charles Hope, freemason, b. Oxford, O., 1861; d. Sandusky, O., Oct. 14, 1947.

Merz, Karl, musician, b. Bensheim, Germany, 1836; d. Wooster, O., Jan. 30, 1890. [1; 20]

Meserve, Charles Francis, educationist, b. North Abington, Mass., 1850; d. Raleigh, N.C., April 20, 1936. [5; 10]

Meserve, Harry Chamberlain, clergyman, b. Quincy, Ill., 1868; d. Boston, Mass., Oct. 22, 1925. [62]

Meservey, Atwood Bond, educationist, b. 1831; d. 1901.

Messenger, Mrs. Lillian, née Rozell, poet and journalist, b. Ballard county, Ky., 1843; d. 1921. [5; 7; 8; 10; 34]

Messinger, Rosewell, clergyman, b. 1776; d. 1844. [51]

Messiter, Arthur Henry, organist, b. Somersetshire, England, 1834; d. New York, N.Y., July 2, 1916. [10; 20]

Messler, Abraham, clergyman, b. Whitehouse, N.J., 1800; d. Somerville, N.J., June 12, 1882. [3; 6]

Metcalf, Clell Lee, entomologist, b. Lakeville, O., 1888; d. New Britain, Pa., Aug. 8, 1948. [10; 13]

Metcalf, Frank Johnson, hymnologist, b. Ashland, Mass., 1865; d. Washington, D.C., Feb. 25, 1945.

Metcalf, Henry Harrison, journalist, b. Newport, N.H., 1841; d. Concord, N.Y., Feb. 5, 1932. [1; 4; 10; 11]

Metcalf, Leonard, civil engineer, b. Galveston, Tex., 1870; d. Concord, Mass., Jan. 29, 1926. [10]

Metcalf, Richard, clergyman, b. Providence, R.I., 1829; d. Winchester, Mass., June 30, 1881. [3; 8; 47]

Metcalf, Theron, jurist, b. Franklin, Mass., 1784; d. Boston, Mass., Nov. 12, 1875. [1; 3; 4; 6]

Metcalf, William, manufacturer, b. Pittsburgh, Pa., 1838; d. Pittsburgh, Pa., Dec. 2, 1909. [1; 4; 10]

Metcalfe, Henry, soldier, b. New York, N.Y., 1847; d. 1927. [10]

Metcalfe, James Stetson, drama critic, b. Buffalo, N.Y., 1858; d. New York, N.Y., May 26, 1927. [1; 7; 62]

Metcalfe, Samuel Lytler, chemist and physician, b. near Winchester, Va., 1798; d. Cape May, N.J., July 17, 1856. [1; 3; 4; 34]

Mettler, Lee Harrison, physician, b. New York, N.Y., 1863; d. Hgihland Park, Ill., March 20, 1939. [11]

Metzelthin, Mrs. Pearl Violette, née Newfield, dietician, b. 1894; d. Nassau, Long Island, N.Y., Jan. 1, 1948.

Metzler, William Henry, mathematician, b. Odessa, Ont., 1863; d. Lockport, N.Y., April 18, 1943. [10]

Mevis, Daniel Stafford, pioneer, b. Royalton, N.Y., 1837; d. Lansing, Mich., Dec. 11, 1930. [39]

Meyer, Edward Bernard, engineer, b. Newark, N.J., 1882; d. South Orange, N.J., Jan. 30, 1937. [10]

Meyer, Fulgence, priest, b. Remich, Luxembourg, 1876; d. Mount Clemens, Mich., Nov. 14, 1938. [21]

Meyer, George Homer, journalist, b. San Francisco, Calif., 1858; d. Burlingame, Calif., Feb., 1926. [10; 35]

Meyer, Henry Coddington, sanitary engineer, b. Hamburg, Germany, 1844; d. Montclair, N.J., March 27; 1935. [1a; 4]

Meyer, Jacob G. Arnold, engineer, d. 1900.

Meyer, Mrs. Lucy Jane, née Rider, educationist, b. New Haven, Vt., 1849; d. Chicago, Ill., March 16, 1922. [10]

Meyer, Martin Abraham, rabbi, b. San Francisco, Calif., 1879; d. San Francisco, Calif., June 27, 1923. [1; 10]

Meyer, Rudolph J., priest, b. St Louis, Mo., 1841; d. St Louis, Mo., Dec. 1, 1912. [21]

Meyers, George Julian, naval officer, b. Council Bluffs, Ia., 1881; d. at sea, off San Pedro, Calif., Dec. 7, 1939. [10]

Meyers, Robert Cornelius V., miscellaneous writer, b. Philadelphia, Pa., May 1, 1858; d. 1915. [7; 10]

Mezes, Sidney Edward, educationist, b. Belmont, Calif., 1863; d. Altadena, Calif., Sept. 10, 1931. [1; 4; 10; 34]

Michael, Mrs. Helen Cecilia De Silver, née Abbott, chemist, b. Philadelphia, Pa., 1857; d. 1904. [10]

Michael, William Henry, civil servant, b. Marysville, O., 1845; d. Washington, D.C., May 16, 1916. [10]

Michaelis, Richard C., journalist, b. Germany, 1839; d. 1909. [10]

Michaud, Régis, educationist, b. France, 1880; d. California, Feb. 7, 1939. [7; 10]

Michel, Arthur Eugene, advertising agent, b. St. Louis, Mo., 1880; d. New York, N.Y., Nov. 9, 1939.

Michel, Virgil George, priest, b. St. Paul, Minn., 1890; d. Collegeville, Minn., Nov. 26, 1938. [21; 22]

Michel, William Middleton, physician, b. Charleston, S.C., 1822; d. June 4, 1894. [1; 5; 34]

Michelson, Albert Abraham, physicist, b. Prussia, 1852; d. Pasadena, Calif., May 9, 1931. [1; 3; 4; 5; 10; 13]

Michelson, Miriam, novelist, b. Calaveras, Calif., 1870; d. San Francisco, Calif., May 28, 1942. [7; 10; 35]

Michelson, Truman, ethnologist, b. New Rochelle, N.J., 1879; d. Washington, D.C., July 26, 1938. [7; 10; 11; 13; 51]

Michener, Ezra, physician and botanist, b. Chester county, Pa., 1794; d. near Toughkenamon, Pa., June 24, 1887. [1; 4; 6]

Michie, Peter Smith, soldier, b. Brechin, Scotland, 1839; d. West Point, N.Y., Feb. 16, 1901. [1; 3; 4; 5; 10]

Micou, Richard Wilde, clergyman, b. New Orleans, La., 1848; d. Oxford, England, June 4, 1912. [4; 10]

Middlebrook, Louis Frank, historian, b. Trumbull, Conn., 1866; d. Hartford, Conn., Feb. 1, 1937. [10]

Middlemiss, James, clergyman, b. Berwickshire, Scotland, 1823; d. Guelph, Ont., March 10, 1907. [27]

Middleton, Arthur Renwick, chemist, b. Webster, N.Y., 1869; d. West Lafayette, Ind., Feb. 6, 1944. [13]

Middleton, Henry, political economist, b. Paris, France, 1797; d. Washington, D.C., March 15, 1876. [3; 4; 5]

Middling, Theophilus (pseud.). See Snider, Denton Jacques.

Mielziner, Moses, rabbi, b. Germany, 1828; d. Cincinnati, O., Feb. 18, 1903. [1; 4; 5; 10]

Mifflin, Lloyd, poet, b. Columbia, Pa., 1846; d. Columbia, Pa., July 16, 1921. [1; 4; 7; 10]

Mighels, Mrs. Ella Sterling, née Clark, miscellaneous writer, b. near Folsom, Calif., 1853; d. San Francisco, Calif., Dec. 10, 1934. [7; 10; 35]

Mighels, Philip Verrill, poet, novelist, and playwright, b. Carson City, Nev., 1869; d. Bliss Ranch, Nev., Oct. 13, 1911. [7; 10]

Mignault, Pierre Basil, jurist, b. Worcester, Mass., 1854; d. Montreal, Que., Oct. 15, 1945. [30]

Mikell, William Ephraim, lawyer and educationist, b. Sumter, S.C., 1868; d. Charleston, S.C., Jan. 20, 1944. [10; 11]

Mikesh, James Stephen, mathematician, b. Spillville, Ia., 1881; d. Trenton, N.J., Jan. 29, 1949.

Milans, Henry Fetter, journalist, b. New Bloomfield, Pa., 1861; d. Chicago, Ill., Sept. 25, 1946.

Milburn, William Henry, clergyman, b. Philadelphia, Pa., 1823; d. Santa Barbara, Calif., April 10, 1903. [1; 3; 4; 5; 6; 7; 34]

Miles, Austin, hymn-writer and novelist, b. Lakehurst, N.J., 1868; d. Philadelphia, Pa., March 10, 1946.

Miles, Mrs. Emma, née **Bell,** naturalist, b. Evansville, Ind., 1879; d. 1919. [10]

Miles, George Henry, poet and dramatist, b. Baltimore, Md., 1824; d. Thornbrook, near Emmettsburg, Md., July 23, 1871. [1; 3; 4; 7; 9; 34; 71]

Miles, Henry Adolphus, clergyman, b. Grafton, Mass., 1809; d. Hingham, Mass., May 31, 1895. [1; 3b]

Miles, Henry Hopper, educationist, b. London, England, 1818; d. Quebec, Que., Aug. 4, 1895. [27]

Miles, James Warley, clergyman, b. Charleston, S.C., 1818; d. Charleston, S.C., Aug., 1875. [3; 6; 34]

Miles, Louis Wardlaw, soldier and educationist, b. Baltimore, Md., 1873; d. Baltimore, Md., Jane 27, 1944. [10]

Miles, Manly, physician and agriculturist, b. Homer, N.Y., 1826; d. Lansing, Mich., Feb. 15, 1898. [1; 4]

Miles, Nelson Appleton, soldier, b. near Westminster, Mass., 1839; d. Washington, D.C., May 15, 1925. [1; 4; 5; 7; 10]

Miles, Pliny, traveller, b. Watertown, N.Y., 1818; d. Malta, April 7, 1865. [3; 4; 6; 8]

Miles, Robert Parker, clergyman and lecturer, b. Lancashire, England, 1866; d. Cleveland, O., Dec. 28, 1940. [10]

Miley, John, clergyman and educationist, b. Butler county, O., 1813; d. Madison, N.J., 1895. [8]

Miley, John David, soldier, b. 1862; d. Manila, Philippine Islands, Sept. 19, 1899. [3b]

Militz, Mrs. Annie, née **Rix,** religious writer, d. 1924.

Millar, Alexander Copeland, clergyman and educationist, b. McKeesport, Pa., May 17, 1861; d. Little Rock, Ark., Nov. 9, 1940. [10; 11]

Millar, John, educationist, b. Ireland; d. Toronto, Ont., Oct. 3, 1905. [27]

Millard, Bailey. See Millard, Frank Bailey.

Millard, David, clergyman, b. Ballston, N.Y., 1794; d. Jackson, Mich., Aug. 3, 1873. [3]

Millard, Edward Eames, angler, b. 1843; d. ?

Millard, Frank Bailey, journalist, b. Markesan, Wis., 1859; d. Los Angeles, Calif., March 20, 1941. [4; 7; 10; 35]

Millard, Henry B., physician, b. near Utica, N.Y., 1832; d. Paris, France, Sept. 14, 1893. [3b]

Millard, Thomas Franklin Fairfax, journalist, b. Phelps county, O., 1868; d. Seattle, Wash., Sept. 8, 1942. [10]

Millay, Kathleen, poet, novelist, and playwright, b. Union, Me., 1897; d. New York, N.Y., Sept. 21, 1943. [7; 10]

Miller, Adam, clergyman and physician, b. Maryland, 1810; d. Chicago, Ill., July 29, 1901. [3b]

Miller, Alfred Brashear, educationist, b. Brownsville, Pa., 1829; d. Waynesburg, Pa., Jan. 30, 1902. [3b; 10]

Miller, Alfred Stanley, mining engineer, b. Normal, Pa., 1856; d. Moscow, Ida., Aug. 23, 1928. [10]

Miller, Mrs. Alice, née **Duer,** poet and novelist, b. New York, N.Y., 1874; d. New York, N.Y., Aug. 22, 1942. [7; 10; 11; 12]

Miller, Mrs. Anna C., née **Johnson,** miscellaneous writer, b. 1832; d. 1883. [6]

Miller, Arthur McQuiston, geologist, b. Eaton, O., 1861; d. near Palatka, Fla., Oct. 28, 1929. [10; 13]

Miller, Benjamin Kurtz, lawyer, b. Milwaukee, Wis., 1857; d. Milwaukee, Wis., March 17, 1929. [10]

Miller, Charles Armand, clergyman, b. Shepherdstown, W. Va., 1864; d. Philadelphia, Pa., Sept. 10, 1917. [8; 10]

Miller, Charles C., apiarist, b. Ligonier, Pa., 1831; d. Marengo, Ill., Sept. 4, 1920. [10]

Miller, Charles Grant, journalist, b. 1866; d. Forest Hills, Long Island, N.Y., Oct. 13, 1928.

Miller, Charles Henry, painter, b. New York, N.Y., 1842; d. New York, N.Y., Jan. 21, 1922. [1; 3; 4; 10]

Miller, Charles Jefferson, surgeon, b. Winchester, Tenn., 1874; d. New Orleans, La., March 21, 1936. [10]

Miller, Charles Russel, lawyer, b. Canton, O., 1858; d. Cleveland, O., Dec. 18, 1916. [10]

Miller, Cincinnatus Heine. See Miller, Joaquin.

Miller, Daniel Long, bishop, b. near Hagerstown, Md., 1841; d. Mount Morris, Ill., June 8, 1921. [10; 11]

Miller, David Hunter, lawyer, b. New York,, N.Y., 1875; d. New York, N.Y., June 22, 1934. [10; 11]

Miller, Dayton Clarence, physicist, b. Strongsville, O., 1866; d. Cleveland, O., Feb. 22, 1941. [4; 10; 13]

Miller, Edmund Howd, chemist, b. Fairfield, Conn., 1869; d. Nyack, N.Y., Nov. 9, 1906. [4; 10]

Miller, Edward Furber, mechanical engineer, b. Somerville, Mass., 1866; d. Newton Centre, Mass., June 12, 1934. [10]

Miller, Edwin Lillie, educationist, b. Aurora, Ill., 1868; d. Detroit, Mich., Aug. 21, 1934. [10; 11; 39]

Miller, Elihu Spencer, lawyer, b. Princeton, N.J., 1817; d. Philadelphia, Pa., March 6, 1879. [3; 4; 6; 8]

Miller, Elizabeth Smith, home economist, b. Hampton, N.Y., 1822; d. Rochester, N.Y., May 23, 1911.

Miller, Elva E., agriculturist, b. 1879; d. 1927.

Miller, Elvira Sydnor, poet and short-story writer, fl. 1864-1889. [34]

Miller, Emile, geographer, b. St Placide, Que., 1885; d. Contrecoeur, Que., Aug. 3, 1922. [27]

Miller, Mrs. Emily Clark, née **Huntington,** poet, novelist, and educationist, b. Brooklyn, Conn., 1833; d. Northfield, Minn., Nov. 2, 1913. [1; 4; 5; 6; 7; 9; 10; 70]

Miller, Emory, clergyman, b. 1834; d. ?

Miller, Ephraim, mathematician, b. near Carrollton, O., 1833; d. Pasadena, Calif., Nov. 20, 1930. [10]

Miller, Frank Justus, educationist, b. Clinton, Tenn., 1858; d. Norwalk, Conn., April 23, 1938. [7; 10; 11; 62]

Miller, George Morey, educationist, b. Cope, Ind., 1868; d. Moscow, Ida., Jan. 16, 1937. [10]

Miller, George Noyes, novelist, b. Putney, Vt., 1845; d. Short Beach, Conn., July 11, 1904. [10; 62]

Miller, Grace Moncrieff, educationist, b. St. Louis, Mo., 1875; d. Brookline, Mass., Nov. 6, 1933. [10; 11]

Miller, Gustavus Hindman, miscellaneous writer, b. near Coryell, Tex., 1857; d. Chattanooga, Tenn., Dec. 12, 1929. [10; 34]

Miller, Mrs. Harriet, née **Mann,** naturalist and writer of books for children, b. Auburn, N.Y., 1831; d. Los Angeles, Calif., Dec. 25, 1918. [1; 3; 4; 5; 7; 9; 10]

Miller, Harry Edward, political economist, b. Boston, Mass., 1897; d. Brookline, Mass., Nov. 13, 1937. [10]

Miller, Henry, physician, b. Glasgow, Ky., 1800; d. Louisville, Ky., Feb. 8, 1874. [1; 3; 4; 6]

Miller, Isaiah Leslie, mathematician, b. Campbellsville, Ky., 1889; d. 1936. [13]

Miller, James Collins, educationist, b. Wellington county, Ont., 1880; d. Philadelphia, Pa., Sept. 30, 1940. [10]

Miller, James Martin, journalist, b. St. Mary's, W. Va., 1859; d. Los Angeles, Calif., Aug. 18, 1939. [10]

Miller, James Russell, clergyman, b. Harshaville, Pa., 1840; d. Philadelphia, Pa., July 2, 1912. [1; 4; 5; 10]

Miller, Joaquin, poet, journalist, and dramatist, b. Liberty, Ind., 1839; d. San Francisco, Calif., Feb. 17, 1913. [1; 2; 3; 4; 6; 7; 8; 9; 10; 35]

Miller, John, clergyman, b. Princeton, N.J., 1819; d. Princeton, N.J., April 14, 1895. [1; 3; 4; 6]

Miller, Mrs. John A., religious writer, fl. 1868-1887. [6]

Miller, John Bleecker, lawyer, b. New York, N.Y., 1856; d. New York, N.Y., June 11, 1922. [8]

Miller, John Ormsby, clergyman and educationist, b. Liverpool, England, 1861; d. Toronto, Ont., Nov. 17, 1936. [27]

Miller, Jonathan Peckham, soldier, b. Randolph, Vt., 1796; d. Montpelier, Vt., Feb. 17, 1847. [1; 43]

Miller, Joseph Dana, economist and poet, b. New York, N.Y., 1864; d. Jersey City, N.J., May 8, 1939. [7; 10; 11]

Miller, Kelly, educationist, b. Winnsboro, S.C., 1863; d. Washington, D.C., Dec. 29, 1939. [10]

Miller, Kempster Blanchard, engineer, b. Boston, Mass., 1870; d. Pasadena, Calif., Nov. 23, 1933. [1a; 10; 11]

Miller, Leslie William, artist, b. Brattleboro, Vt., 1848; d. Oak Bluffs, Mass., March 7, 1931. [1; 10; 11]

Miller, Lewis Bennett, novelist, b. Cooke county, Tex., 1861; d. ? [7]

Miller, Louise Klein, gardener, b. near Centerville, O., 1854; d. Cleveland, O., Oct. 24, 1943. [10; 11]

Miller, Mrs. Maria, née **Morris,** botanist, b. Halifax, N.S., 1813; d. Halifax, N.S., Oct. 28, 1875. [27]

Miller, Mrs. Mary Esther, writer of books for children, b. 1826; d. Springfield, Mass., Jan. 5, 1896. [6]

Miller, Maurice Norton, physician, b. 1838; d. 1888.

Miller, Mrs. Minnie, née **Willis,** religious writer, b. Lebanon, N.H., 1845; d. ? [7; 8]

Miller, Olive Thorne (pseud.). See Miller, Mrs. Harriet, née Mann.

Miller, Peyton Farrell, lawyer, b. 1846; d. ?

Miller, Robert Johnson, clergyman, b. Hanover, Pa., Feb. 1, 1853; d. Pittsburgh, Pa., 1934. [10; 11]

Miller, Rufus Wilder, editor, b. Easton, Pa., 1862; d. Philadelphia, Pa., Oct. 11, 1925. [10; 11]

Miller, Samuel, clergyman, b. near Dover, Del., 1769; d. Princeton, N.J., Jan. 7, 1850. [1; 3; 4; 5; 6]

Miller, Samuel, lawyer, b. Princeton, N.J., 1816; d. Mount Holly, N.J., Oct. 12, 1883. [4]

Miller, Samuel Almond, lawyer and geologist, b. Coolville, O., 1836; d. Cincinnati, O., Dec. 19, 1897. [3b]

Miller, Samuel Freeman, jurist, b. Richmond, Ky., 1816; d. Washington, D.C., Oct. 13, 1890. [1; 3b; 4; 5]

Miller, Stephen Franks, lawyer, b. near Trenton, N.C., 1810; d. Oglethorpe, Ga., 1867. [3; 4; 34]

Miller, Walter, educationist, b. Ashland county, O., 1864; d. Columbia, Mo., July 28, 1949. [10; 11]

Miller, Webb, journalist, b. Pokagon, Mich., 1892; d. near London, England, May 8, 1940. [10]

Miller, Wesson Gage, clergyman, b. 1822; d. 1894. [44]

Miller, Willet Green, geologist, b. Norfolk county, Ont., 1868; d. Toronto, Ont., Feb. 4, 1925. [27]

Miller, William, religious leader, b. Pittsfield, Mass., 1782; d. Hampton, N.Y., Dec. 20, 1849. [1; 3; 4; 7]

Miller, William Edward, lawyer b. Mount Pleasant, Pa., 1823; d. Des Moines, Ia., Nov. 7, 1896. [4; 37]

Miller, William Snow, anatomist, b. Stirling, Mass., 1858; d. Madison, Wis., Dec. 27, 1939. [10; 62]

Miller, Willoughby Dayton, dentist, b. Licking county, O., 1853; d. Newark, O., July 27, 1907. [1]

Millet, Francis Davis, painter, b. Mattapoisett, Mass., 1846; d. at sea, in the *Titanic* disaster, April 15, 1912. [1; 4; 5; 7; 10]

Millet, Joshua, clergyman, b. 1803; d. 1848. [38]

Milligan, Ezra McLeod, clergyman, b. New York, N.Y., 1858; d. Pittsburgh, Pa., May 27, 1935. [10]

Milligan, Robert, educationist, b. county Tyrone, Ireland, 1814; d. Lexington, Ky., March 20, 1875. [3; 4; 6; 34]

Milliken, Charles Francis, local historian, b. Canandaigua, N.Y., 1854; d. Canandaigua, N.Y., July 12, 1933.

Millikin, Vergil Stanley, poet, b. 1879; d. 1907. [47]

Millington, John, engineer, b. London, England, 1779; d. Richmond, Va., July 10, 1868. [1; 6]

Millis, Harry Alvin, economist, b. Paoli, Ind., 1873; d. Chicago, Illl., June 25, 1948. [10]

Mills, Abraham, educationist, b. Dutchess county, N.Y., 1796; d. New York, N.Y., July 8, 1867. [3; 6; 8]

Mills, Adelbert Philo, educationist, d. 1918.

Mills, Anson, soldier, b. Boone county, Ind., 1834; d. Washington, D.C., Nov. 5, 1924. [1; 4; 10]

Mills, Benjamin Fay, evangelist, b. Rahway, N.J., 1857; d. Grand Rapids, Mich., May 1, 1916. [1; 10]

Mills, Charles De Berard, miscellaneous writer, b. 1821; d. 1900. [4; 6]

Mills, Charles Karsner, neurologist, b. Philadelphia, Pa., 1845; d. Philadelphia, Pa., May 28, 1931. [1; 5; 10; 11]

Mills, Enos Abijah, naturalist, b. near Kansas City, Kans., 1870; d. Long's Peak, Colo., Sept. 21, 1922. [1a; 4; 7; 10]

Mills, Frank Moody, industrialist, b. Ladoga, Ind., 1831. d. Sioux Falls, S.D., 1930. [10; 11]

Mills, Harlow Spencer, clergyman, b. 1846; d. Feb. 1, 1931.

Mills, Harriette Melissa, educationist, b. Burlington, Conn.; d. New York, N.Y., July 23, 1929. [4; 10]

Mills, Henry, clergyman, b. Morristown, N.J., 1786; d. Auburn, N.Y., June 10, 1867.

Mills, Henry Edmund, lawyer, b. Montrose, Pa., 1850; d. San Diego, Calif., 1918. [4; 10]

Mills, Herbert Elmer, economist, b. Salem N.H., 1861; d. Poughkeepsie, N.Y., March 9, 1946. [14]

Mills, Jared Warner, lawyer, b. Lancaster, Wis., 1852; d. Denver, Colo., 1907. [10]

Mills, Job Smith, bishop, b. near Plymouth, O., 1848; d. Annville, Pa., 1909. [10]

Mills, John, radio engineer, b. Morgan Park, Ill., 1880; d. Rochester, N.Y., June 14, 1948. [10]

Mills, Lawrence Heyworth, orientalist, b. New York, N.Y., 1837; d. Oxford, England, Jan. 29, 1918. [7]

Mills, Lewis Este, lawyer, b. Morristown, N.J., 1836; d. Florence, Italy, April 10, 1878. [62]

Mills, Ogden Livingston, lawyer and politician, b. Newport, R.I., 1884; d. New York, N.Y., Oct. 11, 1937. [10]

Mills, Robert, architect, b. Charleston, S.C., 1781; d. Washington, D.C., March 3, 1855. [1; 3; 4; 5; 6; 34]

Mills, Samuel John, clergyman, b. Torrington, Conn., 1783; d. at sea, June 16, 1818. [1; 3; 4]

Mills, Thomas Wesley, physiologist, b. Brockville, Ont., 1847; d. London, England, Feb. 13, 1915. [27]

Mills, Walter Sands, physician, b. 1865; d. New York, N.Y., Jan. 2, 1934.

Mills, Walter Thomas, political economist, b. 1856; d. Los Angeles, Calif., May 7, 1942.

Mills, William Corless, archaeologist, b. Montgomery county, O., 1860; d. Columbus, O., Jan. 27, 1928. [4; 10]

Mills, William Hathorn, poet, b. Wakeville, England, 1848; d. ? [35]

Mills, William Stowell, lawyer and historian, d. Nov. 4, 1929.

Millspaugh, Charles Frederick, botanist, b. Ithaca, N.Y., 1854; d. Chicago, Ill., Feb. 15, 1923. [1; 8; 10; 11]

Miln, Mrs. Louise, née **Jordan,** novelist, b. Macomb, Ill., 1864; d. near Calais, France, Sept. 22, 1933.

Milne, Mrs. Frances Margaret, née **Tener,** poet, b. county Tyrone, Ireland, 1846; d. San Luis Obispo, Calif. April 20, 1910. [35]

Milne, James Mollison, educationist, b. Scotland, 1850; d. New York, N.Y., 1904. [10]

Milne, William James, educationist, b. Scotland, 1843; d. Bethlehem, N.H., Sept. 4, 1914. [10]

Milner, Duncan Chambers, clergyman, b. Mount Pleasant, O., 1841; d. Chicago, Ill., March 18, 1928. [10]

Milner, John Turner, civil engineer, b. Pike county, Ga., 1826; d. Newcastle, Ala., Aug. 18, 1898. [1; 4; 34]

Milnor, William, merchant and sportsman, b. Philadelphia, Pa., 1769; d. Burlington, N.J., Dec. 13, 1848.

Mims, Edwin, educationist, b. Durham, N.C., 1800; d. New York, N.Y., Jan. 1, 1945. [7; 10; 11; 62]

Miner, Alonzo Ames, clergyman, b. Lempster, N.H., 1814; d. Boston, Mass., June 14, 1895. [1; 3b; 4; 6; 8]

Miner, Charles, journalist and politician, b. Norwich, Conn., 1870; d. near Wilkesbarre, Pa., Oct. 26, 1865. [1; 3; 4; 5; 6; 7]

Miner, Enoch Newton, stenographer, d. 1923.

Miner, George Washington, accountant, b. 1860; d. 1935.

Miner, Jack, naturalist, b. Dover Centre, O., 1865; d. Kingsville, Ont., Nov. 3, 1944. [27]

Miner, Luella, missionary, b. Oberlin, O., 1861; d. Tsinan, China, Dec. 3, 1935. [10]

Miner, Thomas, physician, b. Middletown, Conn., 1777; d. Worcester, Mass., April 23, 1841. [3; 4]

Miner, William Harvey, journalist, b. New Haven, Conn., 1877; d. St. Louis, Mo., Feb. 10, 1934. [10]

Mines, Flavel Scott, clergyman, b. Leesburg, Va., 1811; d. San Francisco, Calif., 1852. [3]

Mines, John, clergyman and poet, d. about 1850.

Mines, John Flavel, journalist, b. Paris, France, 1835; d. New York, N.Y., Nov. 5, 1891. [3b; 8]

Ming, John Joseph, priest, b. Unterwalden, Switzerland, 1838; d. Parma, O., June 17, 1910. [1; 21]

Minifie, William, architect, b. Devonshire, England, 1805; d. Baltimore, Md., Oct. 24, 1880. [3; 8]

Minor, George Henry, lawyer, b. Deposit, N.Y., 1866; d. Cleveland, O., March 21, 1937. [10]

Minor, John Barbee, lawyer, b. Louisa county, Va., 1813; d. Richmond, Va., July 29, 1895. [1; 3b; 4; 8; 34]

Minor, Raleigh Colston, lawyer and educationist, b. University, Va., 1869; d. Richmond, Va., June 14, 1923. [1; 10]

Minot, Charles Sedgwick, biologist, b. Boston, Mass., 1852; d. Boston, Mass., Nov. 19, 1914. [1; 2; 4; 5; 10]

Minot, George Richards, jurist and historian, b. Boston, Mass., 1758; d. Boston, Mass., Jan. 2, 1802. [1; 3; 4; 5; 9]

Minot, Henry Davis, naturalist, b. 1859; d. 1890. [8]

Minot, William, lawyer, b. 1849; d. 1900. [8; 51]

Minto, John, poet, b. England, 1822; d. Salem, Ore., 1915. [4]

Minton, Henry Collin, clergyman, b. Prosperity, Pa., 1855; d. San Rafael, Calif., June 14, 1924. [10]

Minturn, Robert Bowne, traveller, b. New York, N.Y., 1836; d. 1889. [3; 8]

Mirick, George Alonzo, educationist, b. Sterling, Mass., 1863; d. Brookline, Mass., Jan. 20, 1938. [10; 11]

Mirza, Youel Benjamin, writer of books for children, b. Persia, 1888; d. Dayton, O., Sept. 29, 1947. [11]

Mitchel, Frederick Augustus, journalist, b. Cincinnati, O., 1839; d. East Orange, N.J., Aug. 19, 1918. [7; 8; 10; 47]

Mitchel, John, journalist and historian, b. county Derry, Ireland, 1815; d. Cork, Ireland, March 20, 1875. [1; 3; 6]

Mitchel, Ormsby MacKnight, astronomer, b. Morganfield, Ky., 1809; d. Beaufort, S.C., Oct. 30, 1862. [1; 3; 4; 6]

Mitchell, Charles Bayard, bishop, b. Allegheny City, Pa., 1857; d. Pasadena, Calif., Feb. 23, 1942. [4; 10; 11]

Mitchell, Mrs. Clara, née **Goodell,** compiler, b. 1865; d. Denver, Colo., June 3, 1944.

Mitchell, Clifford, physician, b. Nantucket, Mass., 1854; d. Chicago, Ill., Oct. 19, 1939. [10; 11; 51]

Mitchell, Donald Grant, littérateur, b. Norwich, Conn., 1822; d. Edgewood, Conn., Dec. 15, 1908. [1; 2; 3; 4, 5; 6; 7; 8, 9; 71; 72]

Mitchell, Edmund, journalist and novelist, b. Glasgow, Scotland, 1861; d. New York, N.Y., March 31, 1917. [7; 10; 35]

Mitchell, Edward Coppée, lawyer, b. Savannah, Ga., 1836; d. Philadelphia, Pa., Jan. 25, 1887. [3; 34]

Mitchell, Edward Craig, clergyman, b. St. Louis, Mo., 1836; d. St Paul, Minn., Dec. 8, 1911. [70]

Mitchell, Edward Cushing, educationist, b. East Bridgewater, Mass., 1829; d. New Orleans, La., Feb. 27, 1900. [1; 3; 5; 6; 10]

Mitchell, Edward Page, journalist, b. Bath, Me., 1852; d. New London, Conn., Jan. 22, 1927. [1; 4; 10; 11]

Mitchell, Edwin Knox, clergyman, b. Locke, O., 1853; d. Hartford, Conn., Oct. 5, 1934. [1a; 10; 11]

Mitchell, Elisha, geologist, b. Washington, Conn., 1793; d. near Mitchell's Peak, N.C., June 27, 1857. [1; 3; 4; 34]

Mitchell, Henry, hydrographer, b. Nantucket, Mass., 1830; d. New York, N.Y., Dec. 1, 1902. [1; 3; 4; 10]

Mitchell, Hinckley Gilbert Thomas, clergyman, b. Lee, N.Y., 1846; d. Boston, Mass., May 19, 1920. [1; 3; 4; 5; 10]

Mitchell, Isaac, novelist, b. near Albany, N.Y., about 1759; d. Poughkeepsie, N.Y., Nov. 26, 1812. [1; 7; 9]

Mitchell, James Coffield, lawyer, b. Mecklenburg county, N.C., 1786; d. near Jackson, Miss., Aug. 7, 1843. [34]

Mitchell, James Tyndale, jurist, b. near Belleville, Ill., 1834; d. Philadelphia, Pa., July 4, 1915. [1; 4; 6; 10]

Mitchell, James W. S., writer on freemasonry, b. 1800; d. 1873.

Mitchell, John, clergyman, b. Chester, Conn., 1794; d. Stratford, Conn., April 28, 1870. [3; 4; 8; 62]

Mitchell, John, physician and poet, d. 1885.

Mitchell, John, labour leader, b. Braidwood, Ill., 1870; d. New York, N.Y., Sept. 9, 1919. [1; 4; 10]

Mitchell, John Ames, artist and novelist, b. New York, N.Y., 1845; d. Ridgefield, Conn., June 29, 1918. [1; 4; 7; 9; 10]

Mitchell, John Kearsley, physician, b. Shepherdstown, W. Va., 1793; d. Philadelphia, Pa., April 4 ,1858. [1; 3; 4; 5; 6; 7]

Mitchell, John Kearsley, physician, b. Philadelphia, Pa., 1859; d. Philadelphia, Pa., April 10, 1917. [10]

Mitchell, Langdon Elwyn, playwright, b. Philadelphia, Pa., 1862; d. Philadelphia, Pa., Oct. 21, 1935. [1a; 4; 7; 10; 11]

Mitchell, Mrs. Lucy Myers, née **Wright,** archaeologist, b. Persia, 1845; d. Lausanne, Switzerland, March 10, 1888. [1; 3a; 4; 5; 6; 8]

Mitchell, Margaret, novelist, b. Atlanta, Ga., 1900; d. Atlanta, Ga., Aug. 16, 1949. [7; 10; 12]

Mitchell, Nahum, jurist, historian, and musician, b. East Bridgewater, Mass., 1769; d. Plymouth, Mass., Aug. 1, 1853. [1; 3; 6]

Mitchell, Peter, politician, b. Newcastle, N.B., 1824; d. Montreal, Que., Oct. 25, 1899. [27]

Mitchell, Roy, theatrical director, b. Fort Gratiot, Mich., 1884; d. New Canaan, Conn., July 27, 1944. [27]

Mitchell, Samuel Augustus, geographer, b. Bristol, England, 1792; d. Philadelphia, Pa., Dec. 18, 1868. [1; 3; 6; 7]

Mitchell, Silas Weir, physician, poet, and novelist, b. Philadelphia, Pa., 1829; d. Philadelphia, Pa., Jan. 4, 1914. [1; 2; 3; 4; 5; 6; 7; 8; 9; 10; 71; 72]

Mitchell, Sydney Knox, educationist, b. Lakeville, N.Y., 1874; d. New Haven, Conn., Jan. 23, 1948. [62]

Mitchell, Thomas Duché, physician, b. Philadelphia, Pa., 1791; d. Philadelphia, Pa., May 13, 1865. [1]

Mitchell, Thomas Henry, clergyman, b. Markham, Ont., 1865; d. London, Ont., Sept. 6, 1945. [30]

Mitchell, Walter, clergyman, b. Nantucket, Mass., 1826; d. New York, N.Y., April 15, 1908. [6; 7; 8; 10; 51]

Mitchell, Wesley Clair, economist, b. Rushville, Ill., 1874; d. New York, N.Y., Oct. 29, 1948. [10; 11]

Mitchell, William, clergyman, b. Chester, Conn., 1793; d. Corpus Christi, Tex., Aug. 1, 1867. [3; 62]

Mitchell, William, soldier, b. Nice, France, 1879; d. New York, N.Y., Feb. 19, 1936. [10]

Mitchell, William Samuel, clergyman, b. Bloomfield, Ia., 1877; d. Malden, Mass., Sept. 17, 1936. [10; 11]

Mitchill, Samuel Latham, physician, b. North Hempstead, Long Island, N.Y., 1764; d. New York, N.Y., Sept. 7, 1831. [1; 3; 4; 5; 6]

Mittelman, Edward Becker, economist b. Poland, 1889; d. New York, N.Y., Sept. 26, 1949. [14]

Mixer, Albert Harrison, educationist, b. Forestville, N.Y., 1822; d. Rochester, N.Y., Feb. 8, 1908. [10]

Mixer, Knowlton, philanthropist, b. Buffalo, N.Y., 1869; d. Los Gatos, Calif., Feb. 19, 1939. [62]

Mixter, George Webber, engineer, b. Rock Island, Ill., 1876; d. New York, N.Y., Jan. 29, 1947. [62]

Mizner, Addison, architect, b. Benicia, Calif., 1872; d. Palm Beach, Fla., Feb. 5, 1933. [1a]

Moberly, Henry John, fur-trader, b. Penetanguishene, Upper Canada, 1835; d. Duck Lake, Sask., July 9, 1931. [27]

Moberly, Walter, civil engineer, b. Oxfordshire, England, 1832; d. Vancouver, B.C., May 14, 1915. [27]

Mockridge, Charles Henry, church historian, b. Brantford, Ont., 1844; d. Louisville, Ky., Feb. 25, 1913. [27]

Mörck, Paal (pseud.) See Rölvaag, Ole Edvart.

Moffat, James Clement, clergyman and educationist, b. Glencree, Scotland, 1811; d. Princeton, N.J., June 7, 1890. [1; 3b; 5; 6; 7]

Moffat, John Little, ophthalmologist, b. Brooklyn, N.Y., 1853; d. Ithaca, N.Y., Feb. 18, 1917. [10]

Moffat, William David, publisher and editor, b. Princeton, N.J., 1866; d. New York, N.Y., Sept. 29, 1946. [7; 10; 11]

Moffett, Cleveland, journalist, novelist, and playwright, b. Boonville, N.Y., 1863; d. Paris, France, Oct. 14, 1926. [1; 4; 7; 10; 62]

Moffet, Samuel Erasmus, journalist, b. St. Louis, Mo., 1860; d. Normandie-sur-Mer, France, Aug. 1, 1908. [8; 10]

Moffet, Thomas Clinton, clergyman, b. Madison, Ind., 1869; d. Long Island, N.Y., Nov. 14, 1945. [10]

Mohldehnke, Edward Frederick, clergyman, b. East Prussia, 1836; d. Watchung, N.J., June 25, 1904. [1; 5; 10]

Mohr, Charles Theodore, botanist, b. Germany, 1824; d. Asheville, N.C., July 17, 1901. [1; 5; 34]

Moïse, Penina, poet, b. Charleston, S.C., 1797; d. Charleston, S.C., Sept. 13, 1880. [1; 3; 7; 9; 34]

Moldenke, Charles Edward, clergyman, b. East Prussia, 1860; d. Watchung, N.J., Jan. 18, 1935. [3; 8; 10]

Moldenke, Richard George Gottlob, metallurgist, b. Watertown, Wis., 1864; d. Plainfield, N.J., Nov. 17, 1930. [1; 4; 10; 11]

Mombert, Jacob Isidor, clergyman, b. Cassel, Germany, 1829; d. Paterson, N.J., Oct. 7, 1913. [1; 3; 5; 6; 7; 10]

Monaghan, James, lawyer, b. St. Louis, Mo., 1854; d. Buck Hill Falls, Pa., April 3, 1949. [10; 11]

Monahan, Michael, journalist, and critic, b. county Cork, Ireland, 1865; d. New York, N.Y., Nov. 22, 1933. [7; 10; 11]

Moncrief, John Wildman, educationist, b. Wirt, Ind., 1850; d. Chicago, Ill., March 29, 1936. [10]

Mondelet, Charles Joseph Elzéar, jurist, b. St. Charles, Lower Canada, 1801; d. Montreal, Que., Dec. 31, 1876. [27]

Monell, Claudius L., jurist, b. Hudson, N.Y., 1815; d. Narragansett Pier, R.I., Aug. 1, 1876. [3]

Monell, Gilbert Chichester, physician, b. 1816; d. 1881.

Monell, Samuel Howard, physician, b. 1857; d. New York, N.Y., Dec. 3, 1918.

Monette, John Wesley, physician and historian, b. near Staunton, Va., 1803; d. Madison parish, La., March 1, 1851. [1; 3a; 4; 7; 9; 34]

Monfort, Francis Cassatte, clergyman, b. Greensburg, Ind., 1844; d. Cincinnati, O., Sept. 30, 1928. [10]

Monis, Judah, educationist, b. Italy or Algiers, 1683; d. Northborough, Mass., April 25, 1764. [1; 3]

Monk, Maria, impostor, b. about 1817; d. New York, N.Y., about 1850; [3; 7]

Monnette, Orra Eugene, banker and lawyer, b. near Bucyrus, O., 1873; d. Los Angeles, Calif., Feb. 24, 1936. [10; 11; 35]

Monro, Alexander, civil engineer, b. Banff, Scotland, 1813; d. Baie Verte, N.B., Dec. 26, 1896. [27]

Monroe, Anne Shannon, essayist and novelist, b. Bloomington, Mo., 1877; d. Lake Grove, Ore., Oct. 18, 1942. [7; 10; 41]

Monroe, Forest (pseud.). See Wiechmann, Ferdinand Gerhard.

Monroe, Harriet, poet, b. Chicago, Ill., 1860; d. Peru, South America, Sept. 26, 1936. [7; 8; 10; 11]

Monroe, Mrs. Harriet, née **Earhart,** educationist, b. Indiana, Pa., 1842; d. Washington, D.C., July 16, 1926. [10]

Monroe, James, fifth president of the United States, b. Westmoreland county, Va., 1758; d. New York, N.Y., July 4, 1831. [1; 2; 3; 4; 5; 6; 7]

Monroe, James, soldier, b. Albemarle county, Va., 1799; d. Orange, N.J., Sept. 7, 1870.

Monroe, James, educationist and politician, b. Plainfield, Conn., 1821; d. Oberlin, O., July 6, 1898.

Monroe, Lewis Baxter, educationist, b. about 1825; d. 1879.

Monroe, Paul, educationist, b. Madison, Ind., 1869; d. Garrison, N.Y., Dec. 6, 1947. [7; 10; 11]

Monroe, Will Seymour, educationist, b. Hunlock, Pa., 1863; d. Burlington, Vt., Jan. 29, 1939. [10]

Montague, Charles Howard, journalist and novelist, b. Greenfield, Mass., 1858; d. Boston, Mass., Nov. 19, 1889. [3b; 7]

Montague, James Jackson, journalist and poet, b. Mason City, Ia., 1873; d. Belmont, Mass., Dec. 16, 1941. [10]

Montague, William Lewis, educationist, b. Belchertown, Mass., 1831; d. Amherst, Mass., July 27, 1908. [3; 4; 6; 8; 10]

Montani, Nicola Aloysius, musician, b. Utica, N.Y., 1880; d. Philadelphia, Pa., Jan. 10, 1948.

Montclair, J. W. (pseud.). See Weidemeyer, John William.

Montefiore, Joshua, journalist, b. London, England, 1762; d. St. Albans, Vt., June 26, 1843. [1; 3; 6]

Monteith, James, geographer, b. county Tyrone, Ireland, 1831; d. New York, N.Y., Sept. 11, 1890. [3b]

Monteith, John, educationist, b. Elyria, O., 1833; d. South Orange, N.J., May 4, 1918. [4; 62]

Montez, Lola, adventuress, b. Ireland, about 1818; d. Astoria, Long Island, N.Y., June 30, 1861. [3; 7]

Montgomery, David Henry, historian, b. Syracuse, N.Y., 1837; d. Cambridge, Mass., May 28, 1928. [1; 7; 9; 10]

Montgomery, Edmund Duncan, philosopher, b. Edinburgh, Scotland, 1835; d. near Hempstead, Tex., April 17, 1911. [1; 10]

Montgomery, Edward Emmet, physician, b. Newark, O., 1849; d. Philadelphia, Pa., April 17, 1927. [4; 10; 11]

Montgomery, George Redington, educationist, b. Turkey, 1870; d. Stamford, Conn., Nov. 29, 1945. [62]

Montgomery, Mrs. Helen, née **Barrett,** religious leader, b. Kingsville, O., 1861; d. Rochester, N.Y., Oct. 18, 1934. [10; 11]

Montgomery, Henry, biographer, fl. 1840-1860.

Montgomery, James Eglinton, chronicler, d. Pasadena, Calif., April 17, 1909.

Montgomery, John Harold, educationist, b. Woodstock, Ont., 1874; d. Los Angeles, Calif., Jan. 9, 1929. [10]

Montgomery, Lucy Maud, novelist, b. Clifton, P.E.I., 1874; d. Toronto, Ont., April 24, 1942. [27]

Montgomery, Marcus Whitman, clergyman, b. 1839; d. 1894. [8]

Montgomery, Morton Luther, local historian, b. 1846; d. Allentown, Pa., Dec. 14, 1933.

Montgomery, Mrs. Roselle, née **Mercier,** poet, b. Crawfordville, Ga.; d. Riverside, Conn., Sept. 16, 1933. [10; 11]

Montgomery, Thomas Harrison, financier, b. 1830; d. 1905.

Montgomery, Thomas Harrison, biologist, b. New York, N.Y., 1873; d. Philadelphia, Pa., March 19, 1912. [1; 4; 10]

Montgomery, Zachariah, politician, b. 1825; d. 1900.

Monti, Luigi, educationist, b. Palermo, Sicily, 1830; d. New York, N.Y., 1912. [3; 6; 7; 8]

Montigny, Benjamin Antoine Testard de, jurist, b. St. Jérôme, Lower Canada, 1838; d. Montreal, Que., Aug. 15, 1899. [27]

Montigny, Henri Gaston Testard de, journalist, b. St. Jérôme, Que., 1870; d. Montreal, Que., Oct. 30, 1914. [27]

Montminy, Théophile, priest, b. St. Jean Chrysostome, Que., 1842; d. Quebec, Que., Dec. 17, 1899. [27; 32]

Montpetit, André Napoleon, journalist, b. Beauharnois, Lower Canada, 1840; d. Montreal, Que., May 26, 1898. [27]

Mooar, George, theologian, b. Andover, Mass., 1830; d. Oakland, Calif., 1904. [3; 8; 10; 61]

Mood, Francis Asbury, clergyman, b. Charleston, S.C., 1830; d. Waco, Tex., Nov. 12, 1884. [1]

Moodie, Roy Lee, palaeontologist, b. Bowling Green, Ky., 1880; d. Los Angeles, Calif., Feb. 16, 1934. [10; 13]

Moodie, Mrs. Susanna, née **Strickland,** poet and novelist, b. Suffolk, England, 1803; d. Toronto, Ont., April 8, 1885. [27]

Moody, Dwight Lyman, evangelist, b. Northfield, Mass., 1837; d. Northfield, Mass., Dec. 22, 1899. [1; 2; 3b; 4; 7; 10]

Moody, Mrs. Helen, née **Watterson,** feminist, b. Cleveland, O., 1859; d. New York, N.Y., Dec. 13, 1928. [4]

Moody, Herbert Raymond, chemist, b. Chelsea, Mass., 1869; d. Vienna, Va., Oct. 20, 1947. [10; 11; 13]

Moody, Joel, poet, b. 1834; d. 1914.

Moody, Paul Dwight, clergyman and educationist, b. Baltimore, Md., 1879; d. Middlebury, Vt., Aug. 18, 1947. [10]

Moody, Walter Dwight, business organizer, b. Detroit, Mich., 1874; d. Chicago, Ill., Nov. 21, 1920. [10]

Moody, William Godwin, economist, fl. 1879-1883.

Moody, William Revell, educationist, b. Chicago, Ill., 1869; d. East Northfield, Mass., Oct. 12, 1933. [10; 62]

Moody, William Vaughn, poet and playwright, b. Spencer, Ind., 1869; d. Colorado Springs, Colo., Oct. 17, 1910. [1; 4; 7; 10; 51; 72]

Moon, Carl, artist, b. Wilmington, O., 1879; d. San Francisco, Calif., June 24, 1948. [7; 10; 11]

Moon, Frederick Franklin, forester, b. Easton, Pa., 1880; d. Syracuse, N.Y., Sept. 3, 1929. [10; 62]

Moon, Mrs. Grace, née **Purdie,** writer of books for children, b. Indianapolis, Ind., 1877; d. Pasadena, Calif., Sept. 7, 1947. [7; 10; 11]

Moon, Lorna, novelist and short-story writer, b. Scotland, 1899; d. Albuquerque, N.M., May 1, 1930.

Moon, Parker Thomas, educationist, b. New York, N.Y., 1892; d. New York, N.Y., June 11, 1936. [10; 11; 21]

Mooney, Charles Patrick Joseph, journalist, b. Bardstown Junction, Ky., 1865; d. Memphis, Tenn., Nov. 22, 1926. [7; 10]

Mooney, James, ethnologist, b. Richmond, Ind., 1861; d. Washington, D.C., Dec. 22, 1921. [1; 8; 10]

Moorad, George, journalist, b. Indianapolis, Ind., 1908; d. near Bombay, India, July 12, 1949.

Moore, Addison Webster, philosopher, b. Plainfield, Ind., 1866; d. London, England, Aug. 25, 1930. [1; 10; 11]

Moore, Albert Weston, clergyman, b. 1842; d. Cliftondale, Mass., Dec. 12, 1924. [8]

Moore, Mrs. Alice Medora, née **Rogers,** miscellaneous writer, b. Quincy, Ill., 1857; d. Watertown, Mass., Jan. 16, 1928. [4; 10]

Moore, Ambrose Yoemans, clergyman, d. 1904.

Moore, Mrs. Annie Aubertine, née **Woodward,** musician, b. Montgomery county, Pa., 1841; d. Madison, Wis., Sept. 22, 1929. [1; 10]

Moore, Benjamin Burges, architect and traveller, b. New York, N.Y., 1878; d. Cap Ferrat, France, Nov. 22, 1934. [62]

Moore, Mrs. Bertha, née **Pearl,** novelist, b. 1894; d. Baltimore, Md., May 1, 1925.

Moore, Blaine Free, political scientist, b. Republic, O., 1879; d. Washington, D.C., June 15, 1941. [10]

Moore, Charles, librarian and historian, b. Ypsilanti, Mich., 1855; d. Sept. 25, 1942. [7; 10; 39]

Moore, Charles Herbert, artist, b. New York, N.Y., 1840; d. Winchfield, Hampshire, England, Feb. 15, 1930. [1; 7; 10]

Moore, Charles Leonard, poet, b. Philadelphia, Pa., 1854; d. 1925. [3; 4; 7; 8; 10]

Moore, Mrs. Clara Sophia, née **Jessup.** See Bloomfield-Moore, Mrs. Clara Sophia, née Jessup.

Moore, Clement Clarke, educationist and poet, b. New York, N.Y., July 15, 1779; d. Newport, R.I., July 10, 1863. [1; 3; 4; 6; 7; 8; 9]

Moore, Clifford Herschel, educationist, b. Sudbury, Mass., 1866; d. Cambridge, Mass., Aug. 31, 1931. [1; 7; 10; 51]

Moore, Cornelius, freemason, b. 1806; d. ?

Moore, David Albert, physician, b. Lansing, N.Y., 1814; d. ? [3; 6; 8]

Moore, David Hastings, bishop, b. Athens, O., 1838; d. Cincinnati, O., Nov. 23, 1915. [4; 10]

Moore, Dewitt Clinton, lawyer, b. 1856; d. 1916.

Moore, Edward Alexander, soldier, b. 1842; d. ? [34]

Moore, Edward Caldwell, theologian, b. West Chester, Pa., 1857; d. Cambridge, Mass., March 27, 1943. [7; 10; 68]

Moore, Edward Colman, music critic, b. Fond du Lac, Wis., 1877; d. Highland Park, Ill., Oct. 6, 1935. [10; 20; 62]

Moore, Mrs. Ella Maude, née **Smith,** poet, b. Warren, Me., 1849; d. Thomaston, Me., May, 1922. [10; 38]

Moore, Ellen Whitley, educationist, b. Coldwater, Mich., 1889; d. St. Petersburg, Fla., Feb. 1, 1941.

Moore, Erasmus Darwin, clergyman, b. Winsted, Conn., 1802; d. 1889. [3; 8]

Moore, Forris Jewett, chemist, b. Pittsfield, Mass., 1867; d. Cambridge, Mass., Nov. 20, 1926. [10; 11]

Moore, Francis Cruger, insurance agent, b. Houston, Tex., 1842; d. ? [10]

Moore, Frank, editor, b. Concord, N.H., 1828; d. Waverly, Mass., Aug. 10, 1904. [1; 3; 6; 7; 9]

Moore, George Foot, theologian and historian, b. West Chester, Pa., 1851; d. Cambridge, Mass., May 16, 1931. [1; 4; 7; 10; 62]

Moore, George Henry, librarian, b. Concord, N.H., 1823; d. New York, N.Y., May 5, 1892. [1; 3; 4; 6; 7; 8; 9]

Moore, Mrs. Hannah, née **Hudson,** journalist, b. New York, N.Y., 1857; d. Rochester, N.Y., Oct. 1, 1927.

Moore, Horatio Newton, miscellaneous writer, b. New Jersey, 1814; d. Philadelphia, Pa., Aug. 26, 1859; d. ? [3; 7; 8]

Moore, Humphrey, clergyman, b. Princeton, Mass., 1778; d. April 8, 1871. [51]

Moore, Mrs. Idora, née **McClellan,** writer of stories and sketches, b. near Talladega, Ala., 1843; d. Richmond, Va., Feb., 1929. [7; 34]

Moore, Ira M., lawyer, b. 1837; d. Chicago, Ill., April 6, 1905.

Moore, Jacob Bailey, printer and journalist, b. Andover, N.H., 1797; d. Bellows Falls, Vt., Sept. 1, 1853. [1; 3; 4; 6; 7]

Moore, Jacob Bailey, local historian, b. 1815; d. 1893.

Moore, James, army surgeon and poet, fl. 1858-1883.

Moore, James Edward, surgeon, b. Clarksville, Pa., 1852; d. Minneapolis, Minn., Nov. 2, 1918. [1; 4; 10]

Moore, James Solomon, economist, b. Königsberg, Germany, 1821; d. New York, N.Y., March 4, 1892. [3b]

Moore, James Wamsley, physicist, b. Easton, Pa., 1844; d. Easton, Pa., Feb. 28, 1909. [4; 8; 10]

Moore, John Bassett, jurist, b. Smyrna, Del., 1860; d. New York, N.Y., Nov. 13, 1947. [4; 7; 10; 11]

Moore, John Henry, educationist, b. 1874; d. 1909.

Moore, John Howard, educationist, b. Linden, Mo., 1862; d. Chicago, Ill., June 17, 1916. [10]

Moore, John Milton, clergyman, b. Butler county, Pa., 1871; d. Winter Park, Fla., Feb. 10, 1947. [10]

Moore, John Stethem, poet, fl. 1844-1847.

Moore, John Trotwood, journalist, novelist, and historian, b. Marion, Ala., 1858; d. Nashville, Tenn., May 10, 1929. [1; 4; 7; 10; 34]

Moore, John Weeks, printer and musician, b. Andover, N.H., 1807; d. Manchester, N.H., March 23, 1889. [1; 3; 4; 6; 7]

Moore, John Wheeler, historian, b. 1833; d. 1906. [34]

Moore, Joseph West, journalist, fl. 1884-1895. [8]

Moore, Josiah Staunton, b. Richmond, Va., 1843; d. Richmond, Va., May 3, 1913. [10; 34]

Moore, Mrs. Julia A., née **Davis,** poet, b. 1847; d. near Manton, Mich., June, 1920. [39]

Moore, Martin, clergyman, b. Sterling, Mass., 1790; d. Cambridge, Mass., March 12, 1866. [3]

Moore, Matthew Henry, clergyman, b. 1857; d. ? [34]

Moore, N. Hudson (pseud..). See Moore, Mrs. Hannah, née Hudson.

Moore, Nathaniel Fish, educationist, b. Newton, Long Island, N.Y., 1782; d. in the highlands of the Hudson River, N.Y., April 27, 1872. [1; 3; 4; 5; 6]

Moore, Rebecca Deming, journalist, b. St. Stephen, N.B., 1877; d. New York, N.Y., Oct. 18, 1935.

Moore, Richard Bishop, chemist, b. Cincinnati, O., 1871; d. Lafayette, Ind., Jan. 20, 1931. [1; 10; 13]

Moore, Robert Braden, clergyman, b. 1835; d. 1906.

Moore, Robert Webber, educationist, b. Delphi, Ind., 1862; d. Philadelphia, Pa., Nov. 21, 1942. [10; 11]

Moore, Samuel, educationist, b. Lancaster, Pa., 1877; d. Ann Arbor, Mich., Sept. 26, 1934. [10]

Moore, Theophilus Wilson, clergyman, b. Mount Tirza, N.C., 1832; d. 1908.

Moore, Thomas Verner, priest, b. Louisville, Ky., 1877; d. Brookland, D.C., May 22, 1926. [10; 11; 21]

Moore, Thomas Vernon, clergyman, b. Newville, Pa., Feb. 1, 1818; d. Nashville, Tenn., Aug. 5, 1871. [3; 8; 34]

Moore, Veranus Alva, bacteriologist, b. Hounsfield, N.Y., 1859; d. Ithaca, N.Y., Feb. 11, 1931. [1; 4; 10]

Moore, Vida Frank, educationist, b. Steuben, Me., 1867; d. Elmira, N.Y., June 11, 1915. [10]

Moore, Walter William, clergyman and educationist, b. Charlotte, N.C., 1857; d. Richmond, Va., June 14, 1926. [10; 11; 34]

Moore, William Emmet, journalist, b. La Grange, Mo., 1878; d. Miami Beach, Fla., Dec. 27, 1941. [10]

Moore, William Eves, clergyman, b. Strasburg, Pa., 1823; d. Columbus, O., June 5, 1899. [3; 8; 10; 62]

Moore, William Francis, educationist, b. Durham county, Ont., 1851; d. Hamilton, Ont., Aug. 29, 1935. [27]

Moore, William Thomas, clergyman, b. Henry county, Ky., 1832; d. Orlanda, Fla., Sept. 7, 1926. [1; 10; 34]

Moore, Willis Luther, meteorologist, b. Scranton, Pa., 1856; d. Pasadena, Calif., Dec. 18, 1927. [4; 10; 11]

Moorehead, Warren King, archaeologist, b. Siena, Italy, 1866; d. Boston, Mass., Jan. 5, 1939. [4; 10; 11]

Moorehead, William Gallogly, clergyman, b. Muskingum county, O., 1836; d. Xenia, O., March 1, 1914. [1; 10]

Moores, Charles Washington, lawyer, b. Indianapolis, Ind., 1862; d. Indianapolis, Ind., Dec. 7, 1923. [10]

Moorman, John Jennings, physician, b. Bedford county, Va., 1802; d. 1885. [6]

Moos, Herman M., novelist, b. 1836; d. 1894. [6]

Mootz, Herman Edwin, novelist, d. Los Angeles, Calif., March 2, 1949.

Moqué, Mrs. Alice Lee, née **Horner,** journalist, b. New Orleans, La., 1865; d. Washington, D.C., July 16, 1919. [10]

Mora, Joseph Jacinto, sculptor, b. Montevideo, Uruguay, 1876; d. Monterey, Calif., Oct. 10, 1947.

Moran, Benjamin, diplomat, b. Lancaster county, Pa., 1820; d. London, England, June 20, 1886. [1; 3; 4; 7]

Moran, Frank E., soldier, d. Baltimore, Md., Dec. 9, 1892.

Moran, Mrs. Jeannie Wormley, née **Blackburn,** novelist, b. Virginia, 1842; d. Nov. 13, 1929. [34]

Moran, Thomas Francis, educationist, b. Columbia, Mich., 1860; d. Lafayette, Ind., Oct. 1928. [10]

Moravsky, Maria. See Coughlan, Mrs. Maria, née Moravsky.

Morawetz, Victor, lawyer, b. Baltimore, Md., 1859; d. Charleston, S.C., May 18, 1938. [10]

Mordecai, Alfred, soldier, b. Warrenton, N.C., 1804; d. Philadelphia, Pa., Oct. 23, 1887. [1; 3; 4; 6; 34]

Mordecai, Samuel Fox, lawyer and educationist, b. Richmond, Va., 1852; d. Durham, N.C., Dec. 29, 1927. [10]

More, Enoch Anson, novelist, b. Dayton, O., 1854; d. Denver, Colo., June 2, 1932. [10]

More, Paul Elmer, scholar and literary critic, b. St. Louis, Mo., 1864; d. Princeton, N.J., March 9, 1937. [7; 10; 11; 51]

Moreau, Louis Edmond, priest, b. Repentigny, Lower Canada, 1834; d. St. Barthélemi, Que., April 28, 1895. [27; 32]

Morecamp, Arthur (pseud.). See Pilgrim, Thomas,

Morecroft, John Harold, electrical engineer, b. 1881; d. Pasadena, Calif., Jan. 26, 1934.

Morehead, Charles Slaughter, lawyer and politician, b. Nelson county, Ky., 1802; d. near Greenville, Miss., Dec. 21, 1868. [1; 3; 4; 34]

Morehead, James Turner, lawyer and politician, b. Bullitt county, Ky., 1797; d. Covington, Ky., Dec. 28, 1854. [1; 3; 4; 34]

Morehouse, Frances Milton Irene, educationist, b. Annawan, Ill., 1881; d. Montevideo, Minn., March 21, 1945. [10; 11]

Morehouse, Frederic Cook, editor, b. Milwaukee, Wis., 1868; d. Milwaukee, Wis., June 25, 1932. [10; 11; 44]

Morehouse, Henry Lyman, clergyman, b. Stanford, N.Y., 1834; d. Brooklyn, N.Y., May 5, 1917. [10]

Morehouse, William Russell, banker, b. Bay City, Mich., 1879; d. Los Angeles, Calif., Dec. 7, 1937. [10; 35]

Morell, Parker, biographer, b. 1906; d. Philadelphia, Pa., March 17, 1943.

Moresby, L. (pseud.). See Beck, Mrs. Lily Adams, née Moresby.

Moreton, Mrs. Clara (pseud.). See Bloomfield-Moore, Mrs. Clara Sophia, née Jessup.

Moretti, Onorio, soldier, b. 1881; d. San Diego, Calif., Oct. 23, 1939.

Morey, William Carey, educationist, b. North Attleboro, Mass., 1843; d. Rochester, N.Y., Jan. 21, 1925. [10]

Morfit, Campbell, chemist, b. Herculaneum, Mo., 1820; d. London, England, Dec. 8, 1897. [1; 3; 5; 6]

Morford, Henry, journalist, poet, novelist, and playwright, b. New Monmouth, N.J., 1823; d. New York, N.Y., May 5, 1881. [1; 3; 7; 9; 71]

Morgan, Abel, clergyman, b. Welsh Tract, Del., 1713; d. Middletown, N.J., Nov. 24, 1785. [3]

Morgan, Anna, educationist, b. Auburn, N.Y., d. Chicago, Ill., Aug. 25, 1936. [10]

Morgan, Appleton. See Morgan, James Appleton.

Morgan, Mrs. Caroline, née Starr, writer of books for children, fl. 1870-1910. [8; 10]

Morgan, Charles Carroll, lawyer, b. Meredith Bridge, N.H., 1832; d. Nashua, N.H., Oct. 23, 1918. [10; 49]

Morgan, Charles Herbert, clergyman, b. Oakland county, Mich., 1852; d. Detroit, Mich., Oct. 30, 1939. [10; 39]

Morgan, Dick Thompson, lawyer and politician, b. Prairie Creek, Ind., 1853; d. Danville, Ill., July 4, 1920. [4; 10]

Morgan, Forrest, librarian, b. Rockville, Conn., 1852; d. Hartford, Conn., Feb. 24, 1924. [7; 10]

Morgan, George, journalist, novelist, and biographer, b. Concord, Del., 1854; d. West Philadelphia, Pa., Jan. 8, 1936. [7; 10; 11]

Morgan, Mrs. Harriet French, née Ford, playwright, b. Seymour, Conn., 1868; d. New York, N.Y., Dec. 12, 1949. [10]

Morgan, Henry, clergyman, b. Newton, Conn., 1825; d. Boston, Mass., March 23, 1884. [3; 6; 8]

Morgan, Henry James, biographer and bibliographer, b. Quebec, Que., 1842; d. Brockville, Ont., Dec. 27, 1913. [27]

Morgan, James Appleton, Shakespearian scholar, b. Portland, Me., 1845; d. New York, N.Y., Aug. 15, 1928. [3; 4; 6; 7; 8; 10]

Morgan, James Henry, educationist, b. Concord, Del., 1857; d. Carlisle, Pa., Oct. 17, 1939. [10]

Morgan, James Morris, naval officer, b. New Orleans, La., 1845; d. Washington, D.C., April 21, 1928. [1; 5; 7]

Morgan, Jane (pseud.). See Cooper, James Fenimore.

Morgan, John, physician, b. Philadelphia, Pa., 1735; d. Philadelphia, Pa., Oct. 15, 1789. [1; 3; 4; 6]

Morgan, John Hill, lawyer, b. New York, N.Y., 1870; d. Farmington, Conn., July 16, 1945. [10; 11; 62]

Morgan, John Jacob Brooke, psychologist, b. Norristown, Pa., 1888; d. Evanston, Ill., Aug. 16, 1945. [10; 13]

Morgan, John Livingston Rutgers, chemist, b. New Brunswick, N.J., 1872; d. New York, N.Y., April 13, 1935. [10; 13]

Morgan, Jonathan, educationist, b. 1778; d. 1871. [38]

Morgan, Lewis Henry, ethnologist, b. near Aurora, N.Y., Dec. 17, 1881. [1; 3; 4; 5; 6; 7; 9]

Morgan, Matthew Somerville, cartoonist and painter, b. London, England, 1839; d. New York, N.Y., June 2, 1890. [1; 3; 4; 5]

Morgan, Morris Hicky, educationist, b. Providence, R.I., 1859; d. Newport, R.I., March 16, 1910. [1; 7; 10; 51]

Morgan, Thomas Jefferson, soldier and clergyman, b. Franklin, Ind., 1839; d. Ossining, N.Y., July 13, 1902. [1; 3b; 4; 5; 10]

Morgan, William, freemason, b. Virginia, 1777; d. perhaps about 1826. [1; 3; 6; 34]

Morgan, William Thomas, historian, b. Dell Roy, O., 1883; d. Bloomington, Ind., June 9, 1946. [7; 10; 11; 62]

Morgan, William Yoast, journalist, b. Cincinnati, O., 1866; d. Hutchinson, Kans., Feb. 17, 1932. [4; 10; 11]

Morgenthau, Henry, diplomat, b. Mannheim, Germany, 1856; d. New York, N.Y., Nov. 25, 1946. [4; 7; 10; 11; 12]

Moriarty, Helen Louise, poet and short-story writer, d. Nov. 11, 1928.

Moriarty, James Joseph, priest, b. county Kerry, Ireland, 1843; d. Utica, N.Y., Dec. 4, 1887. [3; 6]

Moriarty, Patrick Eugene, priest, b. Dublin, Ireland, 1804; d. Villanova, Pa., July 10, 1875. [1; 3; 21]

Moriarty, William Daniel, economist, b. Oil City, Pa., 1877; d. Los Angeles, Calif., April 14, 1936. [10; 11]

Morice, Adrian Gabriel, missionary, b. France, 1859; d. St. Boniface, Man., April 21, 1938. [27]

Morison, George Shattuck, engineer, b. New Bedford, Mass., 1842; d. July 1, 1903. [1; 4; 5; 10; 51]

Morison, Horace, educationist, b. Peterboro, N.H., 1810; d. Peterboro, N.H., Aug. 5, 1870. [51]

Morison, John Hopkins, clergyman, b. Peterboro, N.H., 1808; d. Boston, Mass., April 26, 1896. [3b; 6; 8; 51]

Morley, Frank, mathematician, b. Woodbridge, England, 1860; d. Baltimore, Md., Oct. 17, 1937. [4; 10]

Morley, Margaret Warner, naturalist, b. Montrose, Ia., 1858; d. Washington, D.C., Dec. 12, 1923. [1; 7; 10; 37]

Morley, Percival Fellman, civil servant, b. about 1884; d. near Montreal, Que., 1936. [27]

Morley, Ralph (pseud.). See Hinton, Howard.

Morley, Sylvanus Griswold, archaeologist, b. Chester, Pa., 1883; d. Santa Fé, N.M., Sept. 2, 1948. [10]

Morman, James Bale, economist, b. Ilfracombe, England, 1866; d. De Land, Fla., Nov. 15, 1930. [10; 11]

Morphis, James M., historian, b. 1826; d. Austin, Tex., Dec. 17, 1900. [6]

Morrell, Benjamin, sea-captain, b. Worcester county, Mass., 1795; d. Mozambique, 1839. [1; 3; 6]

Morrill, Arthur Boothby, educationist, b. Portland, Me., 1853; d. New Haven, Conn., March 18, 1926. [62]

Morrill, Charles Henry, banker, b. Concord, N.H., 1843; d. Stromsburg, Neb., Dec. 11, 1928. [10]

Morrill, Donald Littlefield, jurist, b. 1860; d. Chicago, Ill., March 26, 1923.

Morrill, Golightly (pseud.). See Morrill, Gulian Lansing.

Morrill, Gulian Lansing, clergyman, b. Newark, N.J., 1857; d. 1928. [70]

Morrill, Justin Smith, politician, b. Strafford, Vt., 1810; d. Washington, D.C., Dec. 28, 1898. [1; 3b; 4; 5]

Morris, Alexander, politician, b. Perth, Upper Canada, 1826; d. Toronto, Ont., Oct. 28, 1889. [27]

Morris, Benjamin Franklin, clergyman, b. 1810; d. 1867.

Morris, Caspar, physician, b. Philadelphia, Pa., 1805; d. Philadelphia, Pa., March 17, 1884. [1; 3; 6]

Morris, Charles, miscellaneous writer and compiler, b. Chester, Pa., 1833; d. Philadelphia, Pa., Sept. 6, 1922. [7; 10]

Morris, Clara, actress, b. Toronto, Ont., 1848; d. New Canaan, Conn., Nov. 20, 1925. [1; 2; 3; 4; 5; 7; 10]

Morris, Edmund, journalist, b. Burlington, N.J., 1804; d. Burlington, N.J., May 4, 1874. [1; 3]

Morris, Edward Dafydd, clergyman, b. Utica, N.Y., 1825; d. Columbus, O., Nov. 21, 1915. [1; 3; 6; 10; 62]

Morris, Edward Joy, politician and diplomat, b. Philadelphia, Pa., 1815; d. Philadelphia, Pa., Dec. 31, 1881. [1; 3; 4; 7]

Morris, Edward Parmelee, educationist, b. Auburn, N.Y., 1853; d. New York, N.Y., Nov. 16, 1938. [1; 10; 11; 62]

Morris, Mrs. Eugenia Laura, née Tuttle, novelist, b. 1833; d. ? [8]

Morris, George Pope, journalist and poet, b. Philadelphia, Pa., 1802; d. New York, N.Y., July 6, 1864. [1; 3; 4; 5; 6; 7; 9; 71]

Morris, George Sylvester, philosopher, b. Norwich, Vt., 1840; d. Ann Arbor, Mich., March 23, 1889. [1; 3; 7]

Morris, George Van Derveer, clergyman, b. Bridgeton, N.J., 1867; d. St. Petersburg, Fla., Aug. 3, 1928. [10; 11; 34]

Morris, Gouverneur, politician and diplomat, b. Morrisania, N.Y., 1752; d. Morrisania, N.Y., Nov. 6, 1816. [1; 2; 3; 4; 5; 6; 7]

Morris, Harrison Smith, art director, b. 1856; d. Philadelphia, Pa., April 12, 1948. [4; 7; 10; 11]

Morris, Herbert William, clergyman, b. Wales, 1818; d. Rochester, N.Y., May 15, 1897. [3; 5; 6; 8]

Morris, Hilda, poet and novelist, b. Ithaca, N.Y., 1888; d. Larchmont, N.Y., June 12, 1947.

Morris, Ira Nelson, diplomat, b. Chicago, Ill., 1875; d. Chicago, Ill., Jan. 15, 1942. [10]

Morris, John Emery, genealogist, b. Springfield, Mass., 1843; d. Hartford, Conn., May 30, 1911.

Morris, John Gottlieb, clergyman, b. York, Pa., 1803; d. Lutherville, Pa., Oct. 10, 1895. [1; 3b; 4; 5; 6; 7]

Morris, John Seybold, educationist, b. 1902; d. East Orange, N.J., May 7, 1938.

Morris, Mrs. Marian, née Longfellow, poet, b. 1849; d. Shawmut, Calif., Jan. 23, 1924.

Morris, Martin Ferdinand, jurist, b. Washington, D.C., 1834; d. Washington, D.C., 1909. [8; 10]

Morris, Phineas Pemberton, lawyer, b. Bucks county, Pa., 1817; d. Philadelphia, Pa., March 1, 1888. [3; 5; 8]

Morris, Robert, writer on freemasonry, b. near Boston, Mass., 1818; d. La Grange, Ky., July 31, 1888. [1; 3; 6]

Morris, Robert (pseud.). See Gibbons, James Sloan.

Morris, Robert Clark, lawyer, b. Bridgeport, Conn., 1869; d. New York, N.Y., Oct. 13, 1938. [7; 10; 62]

Morris, Robert Tuttle, surgeon, b. Seymour, Conn., 1857; d. Stamford, Conn., Jan. 9, 1945. [4; 10; 11]

Morris, Roger Sylvester, physician, b. Ann Arbor, Mich., 1877; d. Cincinnati, O., March 2, 1934. [10]

Morris, Samuel Leslie, clergyman, b. Abbeville, S.C., 1854; d. Atlanta, Ga., May 10, 1937. [10; 11]

Morris, Thomas Asbury, bishop, b. near Charlestown, Va., 1794; d. Springfield, O., Sept. 2, 1874. [3; 4; 5; 8]

Morris, William Alfred, historian, b. near Dallas, Ore., 1875; d. Berkeley, Calif., Feb. 20, 1946. [10; 14]

Morris, William Clarke, cartoonist, b. Salt Lake City, Utah, 1874; d. Grand View, N.Y., April 5, 1940. [10]

Morris, William Hopkins, soldier, b. New York, N.Y., 1826; d. Long Branch, N.J., Aug. 26, 1900. [1; 3; 4; 5; 6; 8]

Morrison, Charles Robert, jurist, b. Bath, N.H., 1819; d. Concord, N.H., Sept. 15, 1893. [3; 5; 6; 8]

Morrison, George Austin, genealogist, b. New York, N.Y., 1864; d. New York, N.Y., Nov. 29, 1916. [10]

Morrison, Henry Clay, bishop, b. Montgomery county, Tenn., 1842; d. Leesburg, Fla., Dec. 20, 1921. [4; 10; 34]

Morrison, Henry Clinton, educationist, b. Oldtown, Me., 1871; d. Chicago, Ill., March 19, 1945. [10; 11]

Morrison, John Frank, soldier, b. Charlotteville, N.Y., 1857; d. Washington, D.C., Oct. 23, 1932. [4; 10]

Morrison, John Harrison, mariner, b. 1841; d. 1917.

Morrison, Leonard Allison, historian and genealogist, b. Windham, N.H., 1843; d. Derry, N.H., Dec. 14, 1902. [3; 8; 49]

Morrison, Mrs. Mary Jane, née **Whitney,** writer of books for children, b. Saccarappa, Me., 1832; d. Waltham, Mass., 1904.

Morrison, Robert, lawyer, b. 1843; d. 1920.

Morrison, Sarah Elizabeth, writer of books for children, fl. 1893-1898. [7]

Morrison, Sarah Parke, genealogist, b. 1833; d. ? [7]

Morrow, Dwight Whitney, banker and diplomat, b. Huntington, W. Va., 1873; d. Englewood, N.J., Oct. 5, 1931. [1; 2; 4; 10]

Morrow, Gilbert (pseud.). See Gibbs, George.

Morrow, Mrs. Honoré Willsie, née McCue, novelist, b. Ottumwa, Ia., about 1880; d. New Haven, Conn., April 12, 1940. [7; 10; 12]

Morrow, Lester William Wallace, electrical engineer, b. Hammond, W. Va., 1888; d. near New Brunswick, N.J., Nov. 16, 1942. [10]

Morrow, May (pseud.). See Carpenter, Anna May.

Morrow, Prince Albert, physician and sociologist, b. Mount Vernon, Ky., 1846; d. New York, N.Y., March 17, 1913. [1; 4; 10]

Morrow, William Chambers, miscellaneous writer, b. Selma, Ala., 1853; d. San Francisco, Calif., April 3, 1923. [7; 10; 35]

Morse, Abner, genealogist, b. Medway, Mass., 1893; d. Sharon, Mass., May 16, 1865. [3; 8]

Morse, Alexander Porter, lawyer, b. Martinville, La., 1842; d. Washington, D.C., July 2, 1921. [10]

Morse, Anson Daniel, historian, b. Cambridge, Vt., 1846; d. Amherst, Mass., March 13, 1916. [1; 4; 10]

Morse, Mrs. Charlotte Dunning, née Wood. See Wood, Charlotte Dunning.

Morse, Edward Lind, painter, b. Poughkeepsie, N.Y., 1857; d. Pittsfield, Mass., June 9, 1923. [62]

Morse, Edward Sylvester, biologist, b. Portland, Me., 1838; d. Salem, Mass., Dec. 20, 1925. [1; 3; 4; 6; 10]

Morse, Edwin Wilson, journalist, b. Natick, Mass., 1855; d. New York, N.Y., Oct. 5, 1924. [10; 51]

Morse, Harmon Northrop, chemist, b. Cambridge, Vt., 1848; d. Chebeague, Cumberland county, Me., Sept. 8, 1920. [1; 4; 10]

Morse, Harry Wheeler, physicist, b. San Diego, Calif., 1873; d. Stanford University, Calif., March 12, 1936. [10]

Morse, Horace Webster, clergyman, b. 1810; d. 1903.

Morse, Hosea Ballou, sinologist, b. Brookfield, N.S., 1855; d. England, Feb. 13, 1934. [10; 11; 51]

Morse, Howard Holdridge, lawyer and historian, b. Rhinebeck, N.Y., 1842; d. New York, N.Y., Dec. 31, 1911.

Morse, James Herbert, poet, b. Hubbardston, Mass., 1841; d. 1923. [4; 10; 51]

Morse, Jedidiah, clergyman and geographer, b. Woodstock, Conn., 1761; d. New Haven, Conn., June 9, 1826. [1; 2; 3; 4; 5; 6; 7; 9]

Morse, John Lovett, pediatrician, b. Taunton, Mass., 1865; d. Newton, Mass., April 3, 1940. [10; 11]

Morse, John Torrey, lawyer and historian, b. Boston, Mass., 1840; d. Boston, Mass., March 27, 1937. [1; 3; 5; 7; 10]

Morse, Mrs. Lucy, née **Gibbons,** novelist and illustrator, b. 1839; d. New York, N.Y., July 13, 1936. [7; 8; 10]

Morse, Nathan Clark, physician, b. 1856; d. Eldora, Ia., Jan. 18, 1919.

Morse, Richard Cary, clergyman, b. Hudson, N.Y., 1841; d. Brooklyn, N.Y., Dec. 25, 1926. [10; 11; 62]

Morse, Samuel, journalist and novelist, b. Omaha, Neb., 1888; d. New York, N.Y., June 21, 1946.

Morse, Samuel Finley Breese, inventor, b. Charlestown, Mass., 1791; d. New York, N.Y., April 2, 1872. [1; 2; 3; 4; 6]

Morse, Sidney Edwards, inventor, b. Charlestown, Mass., 1794; d. New York, N.Y., Dec. 23, 1871. [1; 2; 3; 4; 5; 6; 7; 9]

Morse, Verranus, physician, b. 1818; d. Brooklyn, N.Y., March 9, 1904.

Mortimer, Charlotte B., novelist, fl. 1850-1868. [6]

Mortimer, Frederick Edward, clergyman, b. London, England, 1854; d. Jersey City, N.J., May 29, 1944.

Mortimer, Lillian, actress and playwright, d. Petersburg, Mich., Dec. 18, 1946.

Morton, Arthur Silver, historian, b. Trinidad, B.W.I., 1870; d. Saskatoon, Sask., Jan. 26, 1945. [27]

Morton, Bowditch, physician, b. 1857; d. Long Beach, Calif., July 19, 1909.

Morton, Charles, clergyman, b. Cornwall, England, about 1627; d. Boston, Mass., April 11, 1698. [1; 3; 7]

Morton, Daniel Oliver, clergyman, b. Winthrop, Me., 1788; d. Bristol, N.H., March 25, 1852.

Morton, Eliza Happy, educationist, b. near Portland, Me.; d. near Portland, Me., July 31, 1916. [10; 38]

Morton, Guy Eugene, novelist, b. North Gwillimbury, Ont., 1884; d. Toronto, Ont., Feb. 26, 1948.

Morton, Henry, physicist, b. New York, N.Y., 1836; d. New York, N.Y., May 8, 1902. [1; 3b; 5]

Morton, Henry Holdich, surgeon, b. Hoboken, N.J., 1861; d. Brooklyn, N.Y., May 3, 1940. [10; 11]

Morton, James Ferdinand, museum curator, b. Littleton, Mass., 1870; d. Paterson, N.J., Oct. 7, 1941. [10; 11]

Morton, James St. Clair, soldier and engineer, b. Philadelphia, Pa., 1829; d. Petersburg, Va., June 17, 1864. [1; 3; 6]

Morton, Julius Sterling, historian, b. Adams, N.Y., 1832; d. Lake Forest, Ill., April 27, 1902. [1; 3b; 4]

Morton, Martha, playwright, b. 1865; d. New York, N.Y., Feb. 18, 1925.

Morton, Nathaniel, pioneer, b. Leyden, Holland, 1613; d. Plymouth, Mass., June 16, 1685. [1; 3; 4; 5; 6; 7; 9]

Morton, Oliver Throck, lawyer, b. 1860; d. Nov., 1898. [8]

Morton, Oren Frederic, journalist and historian, b. Fryeburg, Me., 1857; d. Winchester, Va., May, 1926. [10; 11]

Morton, Samuel George, physician and naturalist, b. Philadelphia, Pa., 1799; d. Philadelphia, Pa., May 15, 1851. [1; 3; 4; 5; 6]

Morton, Mrs. Sarah Wentworth, née **Apthorp,** poet, b. Boston, Mass., 1759; d. Quincy, Mass., May 14, 1846. [1; 3; 4; 6; 7; 9]

Morton, Thomas George, physician, b. Philadelphia, Pa., 1835; d. Cape May, N.J., May 20, 1903. [3; 6; 8]

Morton, William James, neurologist, b. Boston, Mass., 1845; d. Miami, Fla., March 26, 1920. [1; 4; 10; 51]

Morton, William Thomas Green, dentist and anaesthetist, b. Charlton, Mass., 1819; d. New York, N.Y., July 15, 1868. [1; 3; 4; 6]

Mosby, John Singleton, soldier, b. Edgemont, Va., 1833; d. Washington, D.C., May 30, 1916. [1; 3; 4; 5; 10; 34]

Mosby, Mrs. Mary Webster, née **Pleasants,** miscellaneous writer, b. Henrico county, Va., 1791; d. Richmond, Va., Nov. 19, 1844. [3; 34]

Moses, Adolph, rabbi, b. Posen, Germany, about 1840; d. Louisville, Ky., Jan. 8, 1902. [3b; 4]

Moses, Alfred Joseph, mineralogist, b. Brooklyn, N.Y., 1859; d. New York, N.Y., Feb. 27, 1920. [8; 10]

Moses, Bernard, political scientist and historian, b. Burlington, Conn., 1846; d. Walnut Creek, Calif., March 5, 1930. [1; 5; 7; 10]

Moses, Faraway (pseud.). See Huff, Jacob K.

Moses, John, historian, b. Niagara Falls, Upper Canada, 1825; d. Chicago, Ill., July 3, 1898. [36]

Moses, Montrose Jonas, drama critic and editor, b. New York, N.Y., 1878; d. New York, N.Y., March 29, 1934. [1a; 7; 10]

Moses, Thomas P., poet, b. 1808; d. 1881.

Mosher, Clelia Duer, physician, b. Albany, N.Y., 1853; d. Palo Alto, Calif., Dec. 21, 1940. [10; 11]

Mosher, Eliza Maria, physician, b. Cayuga county, N.Y., Oct. 2, 1846; d. New York, Oct. 16, 1928. [1; 4; 10; 11]

Mosher, John Chapin, short-story writer, b. 1892; d. New York, N.Y., Sept. 3, 1942.

Mosher, Thomas Bird, publisher, b. Biddeford, Me., 1852; d. Portland, Me., Aug. 31, 1923. [4; 7; 10]

Mosher, William Eugene, educationist, b. Syracuse, N.Y., 1877; d. Alexandria, Va., June 1, 1945. [10; 11]

Mosier, Jeremiah George, educationist, b. Pike county, O., 1862; d. Urbana, Ill., 1922. [10]

Moss, Frank, reformer, b. Coldspring, N.Y., 1860; d. Manhattan, N.Y., June 5, 1920. [1; 4; 10]

Moss, James Alfred, soldier, b. Lafayette, La., 1872; d. New York, N.Y., April 23, 1941. [10]

Moss, Lemuel, clergyman, b. Boone county, Ky., 1829; d. New York, N.Y., July 12, 1904. [1; 3; 4; 6; 10]

Moss, Leslie Bates, clergyman, b. Minneapolis, Minn., 1889; d. Gibbon, Neb., April 2, 1949. [10]

Moss, Mary, novelist, b. Philadelphia, Pa., 1864; d. Philadelphia, Pa., 1914. [10]

Moss, Sidney Walter, novelist, b. Kentucky, 1810; d. Oregon City, Ore., 1901. [41]

Most, Johann Joseph, anarchist, b. Augsburg, Germany, 1846; d. Cincinnati, O., March 17, 1906. [1]

Moth, Axel, librarian, b. 1867; d. New York, N.Y., June 12, 1932.

Motherwell, Hiram, journalist, b. Fort Wayne, Ind., 1888; d. New York, N.Y., Dec. 1, 1945. [12; 51]

Motley, John Lothrop, historian, b. Boston, Mass., 1814; d. near Dorchester, England, May 29, 1877. [1; 2; 3; 4; 5; 6; 7; 8; 9; 71]

Moton, Robert Russa, educationist, b. Amelia county, Va., 1867; d. Capahosic, Va., May 31, 1940. [7; 10; 11]

Mott, Mrs. Abigail, née **Field,** miscellaneous writer, b. 1766; d. 1851.

Mott, Edward Harold, journalist, b. 1845; d. Goshen, N.Y., April 7, 1920. [4]

Mott, George Scudder, clergyman, b. New York, N.Y., 1829; d. East Orange, N.J., Oct. 12, 1901. [3b; 4; 8; 10]

Mott, Henry Augustus, chemist, b. Clifton, N.Y., 1852; d. New York, N.Y., Nov. 8, 1896. [3b; 4; 8]

Mott, Hopper Striker, historian, b. 1854; d. New York, N.Y., June 16, 1924.

Mott, James, reformer, b. North Hempstead, N.Y., 1788; d. Brooklyn, N.Y., Jan. 26, 1868. [1]

Mott, Lawrence, novelist, b. Cleveland, O., 1881; d. Roseburg, Ore., June 3, 1931. [1; 51]

Mott, Lewis Freeman, educationist, b. New York, N.Y., 1863; d. New York, N.Y., Nov. 20, 1941. [4; 10; 11]

Mott, Valentine, surgeon, b. Glen Cove, Long Island, N.Y., 1785; d. New York, N.Y., April 26, 1865. [1; 3; 4; 5; 6]

Mottier, David Myers, botanist, b. Switzerland county, Ind., 1864; d. Bloomington, Ind., March 25, 1940. [4; 10; 11; 13]

Mott-Smith, Morton Churchill, physicist, b. Honolulu, Hawaii, 1877; d. Baltimore, Md., June 9, 1944. [13]

Moulton, Augustus Freedom, historian, b. 1848; d. Portland, Me., March 16, 1933. [4; 38]

Moulton, Charles Wells, publisher and editor, b. Alexander, N.Y., 1859; d. Buffalo N,Y., March 17, 1913. [4; 7; 10]

Moulton, Joseph White, lawyer, b. Stratford, Conn., 1789; d. Roslyn, Long Island, N.Y., April 20, 1875. [3; 6; 8]

Moulton, Mrs. Ellen Louise, née **Chandler,** poet and writer of books for children, b. Pomfret, Conn., 1835; d. Boston, Mass., Aug. 10, 1908. [1; 2; 3; 4; 5; 7; 9; 10; 71]

Moulton, Luther Vanhorn, lawyer, b. Howard, Mich., 1843;. d. Grand Rapids, Mich., Sept. 9, 1919.

Moulton, Richard Green, educationist, b. Preston, England. 1849; d. Tunbridge Wells, England, Aug. 15, 1924. [1; 7; 10]

Moultrie, William, soldier, b. Charleston, S.C., 1730; d. Charleston, S.C., Sept. 27, 1805. [1; 3; 4; 5; 6]

Mountain, George Jehoshaphat, bishop, b. Norwich, England, 1789; d. Quebec, Que., Jan. 6, 1863. [27]

Mountain, Jacob, bishop, b. Norfolk, England, 1749; d. Quebec, Lower Canada, June 16, 1825.· [27]

Mountford, Mrs. Lydia Mary Olive, née **Mamreoff von Finkelstein,** lecturer, b. 1855; d. 1917.

Mountford, William, clergyman and spiritualist, b. Kidderminster, England 1816; d. Boston, Mass., April 20, 1885. [3; 6; 8]

Mouzon, Edwin Du Bose, bishop, b. Spartanburg, S.C., 1869; d. Charlotte, N.C., Feb. 10, 1937. [10]

Mowatt, Mrs. Anna Cora, née **Ogden.** See Ritchie, Mrs. Anna Cora, née Ogden.

Mowbray, J. P. (pseud.). See Wheeler Andrew Carpenter.

Mowry, Sylvester, explorer, b. Providence, R.I., 1830; d. London, England, Oct. 16, 1871.' [3; 8]

Mowry, William Augustus, historian, b. Uxbridge, Mass., 1829; d. Hyde Park, Mass., May 22, 1917. [1; 5; 7; 8; 10]

Moxey, Edward Preston, educationist, b. 1881; d. Philadelphia, Pa., April 6, 1943.

Moxom, Philip Stafford, clergyman, b. Markham, Ont., 1848; d. Springfield, Mass., Aug. 13, 1923. [1; 4; 5; 7; 10]

Moyen, Jean, priest, b. France, 1828; d. Alix, France, Jan. 8, 1899. [27]

Moyer, Lycurgus R., historian, b. Niagara county, N.Y., 1848; d. Minnesota, 1917. [70]

Mozans, H. J. (pseud.). See Zahm, John Augustine.

Muckey, Floyd Summer, physician, b. Medford, Minn., 1858; d. New York, N.Y., Feb. 22, 1930. [10]

Mudge, Alfred, genealogist, b. Almouth, N.H., 1809; d. Hull, Mass., Aug. 14, 1882. [3]

Mudge, James, clergyman, b. West Springfield, Mass., 1844; d. Malden, Mass., May 7, 1918. [1; 5; 7; 10]

Mudge, Zachariah Atwell, clergyman, b. Orrington, Me., 1813; d. Newton Upper Falls, Mass., June 15, 1888. [1; 3; 6; 7; 8]

Mühlenberg, Henry. See Muhlenberg, Henry.

Müller, Margarethe, educationist, b. Hanover, Germany, 1862; d. Munich, Germany, Jan. 8, 1934. [10]

Müller, Richard William, physician, b. 1850; d. New York, N.Y., June 3, 1920.

Münsterberg, Hugo, psychologist, b. Danzig, Germany, 1863; d. Cambridge, Mass., Dec. 16, 1916. [1; 4; 7; 10]

Mug, Sister Mary Theodosia, religious writer, b. Attica, Ind., 1860; d. St. Mary-of-the-Woods, Ind., March 23, 1943. [21]

Muhleman, Maurice Louis, economist, b. near Alton, Ill., 1852; d. Bronxville, N.Y., June 12, 1913. [8; 10]

Muhlenberg, Henry, clergyman and botanist, b. Montgomery county, Pa., 1753; d. Lancaster, Pa., May 23, 1815. [1; 3; 5; 6]

Muhlenberg, Henry Augustus, biographer, b. 1823; d. 1854.

Muhlenberg, William Augustus, clergyman, b. Philadelphia, Pa., 1796; d. New York, N.Y., April 8, 1877. [1; 3; 4; 5; 6; 7]

Muir, James, clergyman, b. Cumnock, Scotland, 1757; d. Alexandria, Va., Aug. 8, 1820. [3; 34]

Muir, John, naturalist, b. Dunbar. Scotland, 1838; d. Los Angeles, Calif., Dec. 24, 1914. [1; 2; 4; 7; 10; 35; 72]

Muir, Robert Cuthbertson, local historian, b. Burford, Ont., 1856; d. Burford, Ont., June 19, 1935. [27]

Mulchahey, James, clergyman, fl. 1888.

Muldrew, William Hawthorne, educationist, b. 1867; d. Guelph, Ont., Oct. 7, 1904. [27]

Mulford, Elisha, clergyman, b. Montrose, Pa., 1833; d. Cambridge, Mass., Dec. 9, 1885. [1; 3; 5; 7; 62]

Mulford, Isaac S., physician, fl. 1822-1851.

Mulford, Prentice, journalist and philosopher, b. Sag Harbor, Long Island, N.Y., 1834; d. Sheepshead Bay, Long Island, N.Y., May 27, 1891. [1; 3b; 4; 7; 9; 35]

Mulford, Uri, journalist, b. Richmond, Pa., 1852; d. Corning, N.Y., Sept., 1931.

Mulholland, St. Clair Augustin, soldier, b. county Antrim, Ireland, 1839; d. Philadelphia, Pa., Feb. 17, 1910. [1; 10]

Mullaly, John, journalist, b. Belfast, Ireland, 1835; d. New York, N.Y., Jan. 4, 1915. [10]

Mullan, John, explorer and road-builder, b. Norfolk, Va., 1830; d. Washington, D.C., Dec. 28, 1909. [1]

Mullaney, Thomas W., priest, b. Elizabethport, N.Y., 1866; d. Saratoga Springs, N.Y., May 26, 1948. [21]

Mullany, John Francis, priest, b. Utica, N.Y., 1853; d. 1916. [10; 21]

Mullany, Patrick Francis, educationist, essayist, and philosopher, b. county Tipperary, Ireland, 1849; d. Plattsburg, N.Y., Aug. 20, 1893. [1; 3b; 4; 5]

Muller, Albert Arney, clergyman, b. Charleston, S.C., about 1800; d. ? [3; 34]

Muller, Joseph, librarian, d. Closter, N.J., May 9, 1939.

Mulligan, John, educationist, b. Ireland, 1793; d. 1864. [6]

Mulliken, Samuel Parsons, chemist, b. Newburyport, Mass., 1864; d. Newburyport, Mass., Oct. 24, 1934. [1a; 10; 13]

Mullins, Edgar Young, clergyman, b. Franklin county, Miss., 1860; d. Louisville, Ky., Nov. 23, 1928. [1; 4; 7; 10; 11]

Mullins, Mrs. Isla May, née Hawley, writer of books for children, b. Summerfield, Ala., 1859; d. Louisville, Ky., Feb. 6, 1936. [7; 10; 11]

Mulvany, Charles Pelham, clergyman, b. Dublin, Ireland, 1835; d. Toronto, Ont., May 31, 1885. [27]

Mulvey, Thomas, lawyer, b. Toronto, Ont., 1863; d. Ottawa, Ont., Dec. 1, 1935. [27]

Mumford, Eben, sociologist, d. Lansing, Mich., Oct. 18, 1942.

Mumford, Mrs. Ethel, née Watts. See Grant, Mrs. Ethel, née Watts.

Mumford, James Gregory, surgeon, b. Rochester, N.Y., 1863; d. Clifton Springs, N.Y., Oct. 18, 1914. [1; 7; 10]

Mumford, John Kimberly, dealer in Oriental rugs, b. Watkins, N.Y., 1863; d. April 17, 1926. [10]

Munday, John William, writer of books for boys, b. 1844; d. ? [8]

Mundé, Paul Fortunatus, physician, b. Dresden, Germany, 1846; d. New York, N.Y., Feb. 2, 1902. [1; 3b; 4; 6;]

Mundy, Talbot Chetwynd, novelist, b. London, England, 1879; d. Bradenton Beach, Fla., Aug. 5, 1940. [7; 10; 35]

Munford, Robert, soldier and dramatist, b. Prince George county, Va.; d. Mecklenburg county, Va., 1784. [1; 7; 9; 34]

Munford, William, lawyer and poet, b. Mecklenburg county, Va., 1775; d. Richmond, Va., June 21, 1825. [1; 4; 34]

Munger, George Goundry, lawyer, b. Morrisville, N.Y., 1828; d. New York, N.Y., March 14, 1895. [3b]

Munger, Theodore Thornton, clergyman, b. Bainbridge, N.Y., 1830; d. New Haven, Conn., Jan. 11, 1910. [1; 3; 4; 5; 6; 7; 9; 10; 62]

Munk, Joseph Amasa, physician and educationist, b. Columbiana county, O., 1847; d. Los Angeles, Calif., Dec. 4, 1927. [10; 11]

Munkittrick, Richard Kendall, poet and humorist, b. Manchester, England, 1853; d. Summit, N.J., Oct. 17, 1911. [4; 7; 10]

Munn, Charles Clark, novelist, b. Southington, Conn., 1848; d. Springfield, Mass., July 8, 1917. [7; 8; 10]

Munro, Bruce Weston, humorist, b. near Newcastle, Ont., 1860; d. about 1900. [27]

Munro, Dana Carleton, historian, b. Bristol, R.I., 1866; d. New York, N.Y., Jan. 13, 1933. [1; 4; 7; 10; 11]

Munro, David Ransom, forester, b. Saint John, N.B., 1828; d. Roanoke, Va., July 9, 1890. [27]

Munro, Wilfred Harold, educationist, b. Bristol, R.I., 1849; d. Providence, R.I., Aug. 9, 1934. [7; 10; 11; 47]

Munroe, Charles Edward, chemist and inventor, b. Cambridge, Mass., 1849; d. Forest Glen, Md., Dec. 7, 1938. [3; 4; 5; 10]

Munroe, Henry Smith, geologist, b. Brooklyn, N.Y., 1850; d. Litchfield, Conn., May 4, 1933. [10]

Munroe, James Phinney, manufacturer, b. Lexington, Mass., 1862; d. Boston, Mass., Feb, 2. 1929. [4; 8; 10; 11]

Munroe, Kirk, writer of books for boys, b. near Prairie-du-Chien, Wis., 1850; d. Orlando, Fla., June 16, 1930. [4; 5; 7; 8; 10; 15]

Munsell, Albert Henry, portrait painter, b. Boston, Mass., 1858; d. Chestnut Hill, Mass., June 28, 1918. [4; 10]

Munsell, Joel, printer and antiquary, b. Northfield, Mass., 1808; d. Albany, N.Y., Jan. 15, 1880. [1; 3; 5; 6; 7]

Munsey, Frank Andrew, publisher, b. Mercer, Me., 1854; d. New York, N.Y., Dec. 22, 1925. [1; 4; 7; 10]

Munson, Cyrus La Rue, lawyer, b. Bradford, N.Y., 1854; d. Pekin, China, Dec. 8, 1922. [4; 62]

Munson, Edward Lyman, medical officer, b. New Haven, Conn., 1868; d. New Haven, Conn., July 7, 1947. [10; 11]

Munson, James Eugene, stenographer, b. Paris, N.Y., 1835; d. New York, N.Y., 1906. [8; 10]

Munson, John P., biologist, b. Norway, 1860; d. Ellensburg, Wash., Feb. 27, 1928. [10; 13; 62]

Munson, John William, soldier, b. 1845; d. ? [34]

Munson, Myron Andrews, clergyman, b. Chester, Mass., 1835; d. New Haven, Conn., Oct. 30, 1922. [10; 51]

Munson, Thomas Volney, viticulturiest, b. near Astoria, Ill., 1843; d. Denison, Tex., Jan. 21, 1913. [1]

Murch, Artemas Allerton, clergyman, b. Corinna, Me., 1848; d. Warsaw, N.Y., Jan. 12, 1915. [62]

Murdoch, Beamish, historian, b. Halifax, N.S., about 1800; d. Lunenburg, N.S., Feb. 9, 1876. [27]

Murdoch, David, clergyman, b. 1823; d. 1899.

Murdoch, James Edward, actor and elocutionist, b. Philadelphia, Pa., 1811; d. near Cincinnati, O., May 19, 1893. [1; 3; 4; 5; 6]

Murdoch, John Gormley, educationist, b. Pittsburgh, Pa., 1861; d. Troy, N.Y., March 15, 1917. [10]

Murdoch, William, poet, b. Paisley, Scotland, 1823; d. Saint John, N.B., May 4, 1887. [27]

Murdock, Charles Albert, publisher, b. Leominster, Mass., 1841; d. Piedmont, Calif., Jan. 11, 1928. [10; 11]

Murdock, Harold, banker, b. Boston, Mass., 1862; d. Chestnut Hill, Mass., April 5, 1934. [7; 8; 10]

Murdock, James, clergyman, b. Westbrook, Conn., 1776; d. Columbus, Miss., Aug. 10, 1856. [1; 3; 4;6]

Murdock, Joseph Ballard, naval officer, b. Hartford, Conn., 1851; d. Manchester, N.H., March 20, 1931. [1; 10]

Murfree, Mary Noailles, novelist and short-story writer, b. near Murfreesboro, Tenn., 1850; d. Murfreesboro, Tenn., July 31, 1922. [1; 2; 3; 4; 5; 6; 7; 8; 9; 10; 34; 72]

Murfree, William Law, lawyer, b. Murfreesboro, N.C., 1817; d. Murfreesboro, Tenn., Aug. 23, 1892. [4; 8]

Murphey, Archibald De Bow, jurist, b. Caswell county, N.C., about 1777; d. Hillsborough, N.C., Feb. 1, 1832. [1; 3; 4; 34]

Murphy, Lady Blanche Elizabeth Mary Annunciata, née **Noel,** miscellaneous writer, b. Exton Hall, England, 1845; d. North Conway, N.H., March 22, 1881. [3; 4; 6; 8]

Murphy, Mrs. Claudia, née **Quigley,** home economist, b. Toledo, O., 1867; d. Grand Rapids, Mich., Oct. 2, 1941.

Murphy, Clyde F., novelist, b. 1899; d. North Hollywood, Calif., June 5, 1946.

Murphy, Edward Gardner, clergyman, b. Forth Smith, Ark., 1869; d. New York, N.Y., June 23, 1913. [1; 10; 34]

Murphy, Mrs. Emily Gowan, née **Ferguson,** novelist, b. Cookstown, Ont., 1868; d. Edmonton, Alta., Oct. 27, 1933. [11; 27]

Murphy, Henry Cruse, lawyer, politician, and historian, b. Brooklyn, N.Y., 1810; d. Brooklyn, N.Y., Dec. 1, 1882. [1; 3; 4; 5; 6; 7; 8; 9]

Murphy, John Benjamin, surgeon, b. near Appleton, Wis., 1857 d. Mackinac Island, Mich., Aug. 11, 1916. [1; 4; 10]

Murphy, John McLeod, civil engineer, b. Northcastle, N.Y., 1827; d. New York, N.Y., June 1, 1871. [3]

Murphy, Michael Charles, athletic coach, b. Westboro, Mass., 1861; d. Philadelphia, Pa., June 4, 1913. [10]

Murphy, Robert Wilson, physician, b. 1821; d. 1901.

Murphy, Thomas, clergyman, b. county Antrim, Ireland, 1823; d. Philadelphia, Pa., Dec. 26, 1900. [3; 5; 6; 8]

Murphy, Thomas Dowler, art publisher, b. Monroe, Ia., 1866; d. Red Oak, Ia., Sept. 15, 1928. [4; 10; 11; 37]

Murphy, Walter, lawyer, d. Salt Lake City, Utah, Feb. 5, 1897.

Murray, Lieut. (pseud.). See Ballou, Maturin Murray.

Murray, Amy, poet, b. Goshen, N.Y., 1865; d. Philadelphia, Pa., Jan. 13, 1947.

Murray, Arthur, soldier, b. Bowling Green, Mo., 1851; d. Washington, D.C., May 12, 1925. [10]

Murray, Augustus Taber, educationist, b. New York, N.Y., 1866; d. Palo Alto, Calif., March 8, 1940. [7; 10; 35]

Murray, Benjamin Lindley, chemist, d. Dec. 13, 1930.

Murray, Charles Theodore, journalist and novelist, b. Goshen, Ind., 1843; d. Wardensville, W. Va., Nov. 20, 1924. [7; 10; 34]

Murray, Clay Ray, surgeon, b. New York, N.Y., 1890; d. New York, N.Y., June 14, 1947.

Murray, Daniel Alexander, mathematician, b. Scotsburn, N.S., 1862; d. Montreal, Que., Oct. 19, 1934. [13; 31a]

Murray, David, educationist, b. Delaware county, N.Y., 1830; d. New Brunswick, N.J., March 7, 1905. [1; 3; 5; 6; 10]

Murray, George, poet, b. London, England, 1830. d. Montreal, Que., March 13, 1910. [27]

Murray, George Washington, politician, b. Sumter county, S.C., 1853; d. Chicago, Ill., April 21, 1926.

Murray, James Ormsbee, clergyman, b. Camden, S.C., 1827; d. Princeton, N.J., March 27, 1899. [1; 3b; 34]

Murray, John, clergyman, b. Hampshire, England, 1741; d. Boston, Mass., Sept. 3, 1815. [1; 3; 4; 7]

Murray, John Clark, philosopher, b. Paisley, Scotland, 1836; d. Montreal, Que., Nov. 20, 1917. [27]

Murray, John Ogden, soldier, b. 1840; d. ?

Murray, John O'Kane, historian, b. county Antrim, Ireland, 1847; d. Chicago, Ill., July 30, 1885. [3; 6; 7; 8]

Murray, Mrs. Judith, née Sargent, poet and essayist, b. Gloucester, Mass., 1751; d. Natchez, Miss., June 6, 1820. [1; 3; 6; 7]

Murray, Lindley, grammarian, b. Dauphin county, Pa., 1745; d. Holgate, England, Jan. 16, 1826. [1; 4; 7; 9]

Murray, Mrs. Louise Shipman, née Welles, archaeologist and historian, d. Athens, Pa., 1854; d. April 22, 1931. [1]

Murray, Nicholas, clergyman, b. Ireland, 1802; d. Elizabethtown, N.J., Feb. 4, 1861. [3; 4; 6; 8]

Murray, Sinclair (pseud.). See Sullivan, Alan.

Murray, Thomas Edward, engineer and inventor, b. Albany, N.Y., 1860; d. Southampton, Long Island, N.Y., July 21, 1929. [1]

Murray, Thomas Hamilton, historian, b. 1857; d. Providence, R.I., June 5, 1908. [10]

Murray, Wendell Phillips, lawyer, b. Boston, Mass., 1876; d. Boston, Mass., Feb. 28, 1946.

Murray, William D., lawyer and philanthropist, b. New York, N.Y., 1858; d. Plainfield, N.J., Nov. 20, 1939. [10]

Murray, William Henry Harrison, clergyman, b. Guilford, Conn., 1840; d. Guilford. Conn., March 3, 1904. [3; 4; 5; 6; 7; 8; 62]

Murray, William Spencer, engineer, b. Annapolis, Md., 1873; d. New York, N.Y., Jan. 9, 1942. [10]

Murray, William Vans, diplomat, b. Cambridge, Md., 1760; d. Cambridge, Md., Dec. 11, 1803. [1; 3; 4; 5; 8]

Murray-Aaron, Eugene, naturalist, geographer, and editor, b. Norristown, Pa., 1852; d. ?

Muschamp, Edward A., biographer, b. 1884; d. South Waterford, Me., May 8, 1942.

Musgrave, Wayne Montgomery, lawyer, b. near Kenton, O., 1870; d. New York, N.Y., July 22, 1941. [62]

Musick, John Roy, novelist, b. St. Louis, Mo., 1849; d. Omaha, Neb. April 14, 1901. [3b; 5; 7; 8; 10; 34]

Musidora (pseud.). See Converse, Mrs. Harriet, née Maxwell.

Musin, Ovide, musician, b. Liège, Belgium, 1854; d. Brooklyn, N.Y., Nov. 24, 1929. [1; 10; 20]

Musser, John, historian, b. Huntingdon, Pa., 1887; d. Seaside Park, N.J., March 21, 1949. [10]

Musser, John Herr, physician, b. Strasburg, Pa., 1856; d. Philadelphia, Pa., April 3, 1912. [4; 10]

Musser, John Herr, physician, b. Philadelphia, Pa., 1883; d. New Orleans, La., Sept. 6, 1947. [10; 11]

Mussey, Henry Raymond, economist, b. 1875; d. Wellesley, Mass., Feb. 10, 1940.

Mussey, Reuben Dimond, surgeon, b. Pelham, N.H., 1780; d. Boston, Mass., June 21, 1866. [1; 3; 4; 5]

Mustard, Wilfred Pirt, educationist, b. Uxbridge, Ont., 1864; d. Toronto, Ont., July 30, 1932. [10; 11]

Mutch, William James, clergyman, b. Hillsboro, Wis., 1858; d. Nov. 24, 1947. [10; 44]

Muttkowski, Richard Anthony, biologist, b. 1887; d. Detroit, Mich., April 15, 1943. [13]

Muybridge, Eadward, inventor, b. Kingston-on-Thames, England, 1830; d. near Woking, England, May 8, 1904. [1; 4]

Muzzarelli, Antoine, educationist, b. Angoulême, France, 1847; d. New York, N.Y., 1908. [10]

Muzzey, Artemas Bowers, clergyman, b. Lexington, Mass., 1802; d. Cambridge, Mass., April 21, 1892. [3; 5; 7; 8; 51]

Myer, Albert James, soldier, b. Newburgh, N.Y., 1829; d. Buffalo, N.Y., Aug. 24, 1880. [1; 4; 5]

Myer, Edmund John, music teacher, b. York Springs, Pa., 1846; d. Los Angeles, Calif., Jan. 25. 1934. [7; 10; 20]

Myer, Isaac, lawyer, b. 1836; d. Narragansett Pier, R.I., Aug. 2, 1902. [5; 8; 10]

Myers, Cortland, clergyman, b. Kingston, N.Y., 1864; d. Los Angeles, Calif., Dec. 26, 1941. [10; 11]

Myers, Frank A., journalist, b. 1848; d. Evansville, Ind., Aug. 4, 1930.

Myers, George William, mathematician, b. Champaign county, Ill., 1864; d. Chicago, Ill., Nov. 23, 1931. [10; 11]

Myers, Gustavus, historian, b. Trenton, N.J., 1872; d. New York, N.Y., Dec. 7, 1942. [7; 10; 11]

Myers, Jerome, painter, b. Petersburg, Va., 1867; d. New York, N.Y., June 19, 1940. [7; 10]

Myers, Mrs. Minnie, née Walter, descriptive writer, b. 1852; d. ? [8; 10; 34]

Myers, Peter Hamilton, poet and novelist, b. Herkimer, N.Y., 1812; d. Brooklyn, N.Y., Oct. 30, 1878. [3; 4; 5; 7; 71]

Myers, Philip Van Ness, historian, b. Tribes Hill, N.Y., 1846; d. Cincinnati, O., Sept. 20, 1937. [4; 7; 8; 10; 62]

Myers, Mrs. Sarah Ann, née Irwin, writer of books for children, b. Wilmington, Del., 1800; d. Carlisle, Pa., Dec. 11, 1876. [3; 6; 8]

Myerson, Abraham, psychiatrist, b. Russia, 1881; d. Boston, Mass., Sept. 3, 1948. [10; 11]

Myrand, Ernest, historian, b. Quebec, Que., 1854; d. Quebec, Que., May 21, 1921. [27]

Myrick, Herbert, agricultural editor, b. Arlington, Mass., 1860; d. Bad Nauheim, Germany, July 6, 1927. [1; 7; 10]

Myrick, Mrs. Lucy Caroline, née **Whittemore,** poet, b. 1832; d. 1879.

Myron, Paul (pseud.). See Linebarger, Paul Myron Wentworth.

Myrtle, Lewis (pseud.). See Hill, George Canning.

Myrtle, Molly (pseud.). See Hill, Mrs. Agnes, née Leonard.

Myth, M. Y. T. H. (pseud.). See Nicolovius, Ludwig.

N

Nack, James, poet, b. New York, N.Y., 1809; d. New York, N.Y., Sept. 3, 1879. [1; 3; 4; 6; 7; 9; 71]

Nadal, Bernard Harrison, clergyman, b. Maryland, 1812; d. Madison, N.J., June 20, 1870. [3b; 4; 34]

Nadal, Bernard Harrison, poet and playwright, b. 1850; d. 1929.

Nadal, Ehrman Syme, essayist, b. Greenbrier county, Va., 1843; d. Princeton, N.J., July 26, 1922. [1; 3; 4 ;7; 9; 34; 62]

Nadir, Isaac Moishe, journalist and humorist, b. Galicia, 1885; d. Woodstock, N.Y., June 8, 1943.

Nagle, James C., civil engineer, b. Richmond, Va., 1865; d. Dallas Tex., April 6, 1927. [10; 11]

Naglee, Henry Morris, soldier, b. Philadelphia, Pa., 1815; d. Santa Clara, Calif., March 5, 1886. [3b; 4]

Nairn, Robert, poet, b. Ayrshire, Scotland, 1853; d. Kenora, Ont., April 21, 1937.

Nairne, Charles Murray, psychologist, b. Perth, Scotland, 1808; d. Warrenton, Va., May 28, 1882. [3]

Nakashian, Avedis, physician, b. Armenia, about 1868; d. New York, N.Y., March 29, 1943.

Nancrède, Charles Beylard Guérard de, surgeon, b. Philadelphia, Pa., 1847; d. Ann Arbor, Mich., April 12, 1921. [1; 4; 10]

Nantel, Antonin, priest and educationist, b. St. Jérôme, Lower Canada, 1839; d. Ste. Thérèse de Blainville, Que., July 30, 1929. [3; 27]

Naphegyi, Gabor, physician, b. Hungary, 1824; d. 1884. [6]

Napheys, George Henry, physician, b. 1842; d. Philadelphia, Pa., 1876. 6; 8]

Napton, William Barclay, local historian, b. 1839; d. ?

Naramore, Gay Humboldt, poet, fl. 1857-1873. [43]

Nasby, Petroleum Vesuvious (pseud.). See Locke, David Ross,

Nash, Arthur, manufacturer, b. Topton county, Ind., 1870; d. Cincinnati, O., Oct. 30, 1927. [1; 10]

Nash, Charles Ellwood clergyman, b. Allamuchey, N.J., 1855; d. Los Angeles, Calif., March 4, 1932. [10]

Nash, Charles Sumner, clergyman and educationist, b. Granby, Mass., 1856; d. Berkeley, Calif., Nov. 22, 1926. [1; 10; 11]

Nash, Charles William, naturalist, b. Bognor, England, 1848; d. Toronto, Ont., Feb. 12, 1926. [27]

Nash, Eugene Beauharnais, physician, b. 1838; d. Cortland, N.Y., 1917.

Nash, Gilbert, poet, b. 1825; d. 1888. [6]

Nash, Henry Sylvester, theologian, b. Newark, O., 1854; d. Cambridge, Mass., Nov. 6, 1912. [1; 10; 51]

Nash, John Adams, agriculturist, b. Conway, Mass., 1798; d. 1877.

Nash, Leonidas Lydwell, clergyman, b. Mecklenburg county, Va., 1846; d. July 11, 1917. [10]

Nash, Philip Curtis, educationist, b. Hingham Mass. 1890; d. Toledo, O., May 6, 1947. [10]

Nash, Simeon, lawyer, b. South Hadley, Mass., 1804; d. Gallipolis, O., Jan. 19, 1879. [3]

Nash, Sylvester, clergyman, b. 1795; d. 1862.

Nash, Wallis, lawyer, b. England, about 1836; d. Portland, Ore., March 13, 1926.

Nasmyth, George William, sociologist, b. Cleveland, O., 1882; d. Geneva, Switzerland, Sept, 20, 1920. [4; 10]

Nason, Arthur Huntington, educationist, b. Augusta, Me., 1877; d. Gardiner, Me., April 22, 1944. [7; 10; 11]

Nason, Elias, clergyman and educationist, b. Wrentham, Mass., 1811; d. near Billerica, Mass., June 17, 1887. [1; 3; 5; 6; 7; 8]

Nason, Mrs. Emma, née Huntington, poet and historian, b. Hallowell, Me., 1845; d. Gardiner, Me., Jan. 11, 1921. [10; 38]

Nason, Frank Lewis, mining engineer, b. New London, Wis., 1856; d. Glens Falls, N.Y., Sept. 12, 1928. [10; 11]

Nason, Henry Bradford, chemist, b. Foxboro, Mass., 1831; d. Troy, N.Y., Jan. 18, 1895. [1; 3b; 4; 5]

Nassau, Robert Hamill, missionary, b. near Norristown, Pa., 1835; d. Ambler, Pa. May 6, 1921. [1; 7; 10; 11]

Nast, William, clergyman, b. Stuttgart, Germany, 1807; d. Cincinnati, O., May 16, 1899. [1; 3; 4; 5; 6]

Nation, Mrs. Carry Amelia, née Moore, temperance agitator, b. Garrard county, Ky., 1846; d. Leavenworth, Kans., June 9, 1911. [1; 7]

Nauman, Mary Dummett. See Robinson, Mrs. Mary Dummett, née Nauman.

Nave, Orville James, army chaplain, b. Galion, O., 1841; d. Los Angeles, Calif., June 24, 1917. [10]

Naylor, Emmett Hay, lawyer, b. St. Paul, Minn., 1885; d. Cummington, Mass., July, 1938. [10]

Naylor, James Ball, physician, poet, and novelist, b. Pennsville, O., 1860; d. Connellsville, O., April 1, 1945. [7; 10; 11]

Naylor, William Keith, soldier, b. Bloomington, Ill., 1874; d. Uniontown, Pa., Aug. 3, 1942. [10]

Nead, Benjamin Matthias, lawyer, b. Antrim township, Pa., 1847; d. Chambersburg, Pa., March 31, 1923. [3; 10; 62]

Neal, Mrs. Alice, née **Bradley.** See Haven, Mrs. Alice, née Bradley.

Neal, Austin E., journalist, b. 1869; d. Kansas City, Mo., March 15, 1941.

Neal, Ernest, poet, b. Sparta, Ga., 1858; d. Atlanta, Ga., Jan. 23, 1943.

Neal, Herbert Vincent, biologist, b. Lewiston, Me., 1869; d. near Pecos, Tex., Feb. 21, 1940. [10; 13]

Neal, John, poet and novelist, b. Portland, Me., 1793; d. Portland, Me., June 20, 1876. [1; 2; 3; 4; 5; 6; 7; 8, 9; 71]

Neal, Joseph Clay, humorist, b. Greenland, N.H., 1807; d. Philadelphia, Pa., July 18, 1847. [1; 3; 4; 7; 9; 71]

Neal, Robert Wilson, journalist, b. Murrayville Ill., 1871; d. Springfield, Mass., May 6, 1939. [10; 62]

Neale, Rollin Heber, clergyman, b. Southington, Conn., 1808; d. Boston, Mass., Sept. 19, 1879. [3; 4]

Neale, Walter, publisher, b. Eastville, Va., 1873; d. New York, N.Y., Sept. 28, 1933. [7; 10; 34]

Near, Irvin W., local historian, b. 1835; d. 1911.

Needham, George Carter, evangelist, b. Ireland, 1846; d. Philadelphia, Pa., Feb. 16, 1902. [3b]

Needham, Henry Beach, journalist, b. Castile, N.Y., 1871; d. Wyncote, Pa., June 17, 1915. [10]

Neef, Francis Joseph Nicholas, educationist, b. Alsace, 1770; d. New Harmony, Ind., April 6, 1854. [1; 7]

Neely, Thomas Benjamin, bishop, b. Philadelphia, Pa., 1841; d. Philadelphia, Pa., Sept. 4, 1925. [1; 10]

Neff, Elizabeth Clifford, genealogist, b. Paris, Ill., 1851; d. North Canton, O., March 21, 1933.

Neff, Silas Shoemaker, educationist, b. West Overton, Pa., 1853; d. Philadelphia, Pa., Oct. 20, 1937. [10]

Neftel, William Basil, physician, b. Riga, Russia, 1830; d. New York, N.Y., 1906. [10]

Nehrling, Henry, ornithologist, b. Herman, Wis., 1853; d. Orlando, Fla., Nov 22, 1839. [1; 10; 13]

Neidhard, Charles, physician, b. Bremen, Germany, 1809; d. Philadelphia, Pa., April 17, 1895. [1; 4]

Neil, Charles Edmund, educationist, b. Illinois, 1871; d. Boston, Mass., Nov. 5, 1930. [11]

Neil, Stephen, novelist, b. 1877; d. near Markham, Ont., May 29, 1947.

Neill, Edward Duffield, clergyman and educationist, b. Philadelphia, Pa., 1823; d. St. Paul, Minn., Sept. 26, 1893. [1; 3; 4; 5; 6; 7; 8; 9; 70]

Neill, John, surgeon, b. Philadelphia, Pa., 1819; d. Philadelphia, Pa., Feb. 11, 1880. [1; 3; 6]

Neill, John Rea, illustrator, b. Philadelphia, Pa., 1878; d. near Flanders, N.J., Sept. 19, 1943.

Neill, William, clergyman, b. Alleghany county, Pa., 1778; d. Philadelphia, Pa., Aug. 8, 1860. [3; 4]

Neilson, Joseph, lawyer, b. Argyle, N.Y., 1813; d. Brooklyn, N.Y., Jan. 26, 1888. [3b]

Neilson, Nellie, historian, b. Philadelphia, Pa., 1873; d. South Hadley, Mass., May 26, 1947. [10]

Neilson, William Allan, educationist, b. Doune, Scotland, 1869; d. Northampton, Mass., Feb. 13, 1946. [7; 10; 11; 14]

Neligan, William Hayes, priest, b. Ireland, 1814; d. New York, N.Y., Jan. 30, 1880. [3]

Nell, William Cooper, journalist and civil servant, b. Boston, Mass., 1816; d. Boston, Mass., May 25, 1874. [1; 3; 4; 7; 9]

Nelles, Samuel Sobieski, educationist, b. Mount Pleasant, Upper Canada, 1823; d. Cobourg, Ont., Oct. 17, 1887. [27]

Nelles, Walter, lawyer and educationist, b. Leavenworth, Kans., 1883; d. New Haven, Conn., March 31, 1937. [10]

Nelson, Charles Alexander, local historian, b. Calais, Me., 1839; d. Philadelphia, Pa., Jan. 12, 1933. [1; 5; 7; 10; 11]

Nelson, David, clergyman, b. near Jonesboro, Tenn., 1793; d. Oakland, Ill., Oct. 17, 1844. [1; 3]

Nelson, Edward William, naturalist, b. Manchester, N.H., 1855; d. Washington, D.C., May 19, 1934. [1a; 10; 11; 13]

Nelson, Harry Leverett, lawyer, b. Mendon, Mass., 1858; d. Worcester, Mass., Aug. 16, 1889. [51]

Nelson, Henry Addison, clergyman, b. Amherst, Mass., 1820; d. St. Louis, Mo., Dec. 31, 1906. [10]

Nelson, Henry Loomis, educationist, b. New York, N.Y., 1846; d. New York, N.Y., Feb. 29, 1908. [1; 4; 7; 10; 11]

Nelson, Horatio, physician, d. Montreal, Que., Jan., 1863. [27]

Nelson, John, journalist, b. Paisley, Ont., 1873; d. Chicago, Ill., Jan. 24, 1936. [27]

Nelson, Richard, educationist, b. 1822; d. 1900.

Nelson, Richard Henry, bishop, b. New York, N.Y., 1859; d. Albany, N.Y., April 25, 1931. [4; 10]

Nelson, Robert, physician, b. Montreal, Lower Canada, 1794; d. Staten Island, N.Y., March 1, 1873. [27]

Nelson, William, lawyer and historian, b. Newark, N.J., 1847; d. Matamoras, Pa., Aug. 10, 1914. [1; 5; 10]

Nelson, Wolfred, physician, b. Montreal, Que., 1846; d. New York, N.Y., Jan. 15, 1913. [10]

Nemo (pseud.). See Coffin, Roland Folger.

Nesbit, Charles Francis, genealogist, b. Akron, O., 1867; d. Washington, D.C., April 25, 1934.

Nesbit, Wilbur Dick, poet and journalist, b. Xenia, O., 1871; d. Chicago, Ill., Aug. 20, 1927. [7; 10]

Nesmith, James Ernest, poet, b. 1856; d. Lowell, Mass., July 26, 1898. [4; 7]

Nessmuk (pseud.). See Sears, George W.

Nettle, Richard, pisciculturist, d. Ottawa, Ont., 1905. [27]

Nettleton, Alvred Bayard, journalist, b. Berlin, O., 1838; d. Chicago, Ill., Aug. 14, 1911. [1; 4; 10]

Nettleton, Asahel, clergyman, b. North Killingworth, Conn., 1783; d. East Windsor, Conn., May 16, 1844. [1; 3]

Neumann, George Bradford, sociologist, b. 1882; d. Buffalo, N.Y., Dec. 23, 1936.

Neumark, David, philosopher, b. Galicia, 1866; d. Cincinnati, O., Dec. 15, 1924. [1; 10]

Neve, Frederick William, clergyman, b. England, 1855; d. Ivy Depot, Va., Nov. 16, 1948.

Nevers, C. O. (pseud.). See Converse, Charles Crozat.

Nevin, Alfred, clergyman, b. Shippensburg, Pa., 1816; d. Lancaster, Pa., Sept. 2, 1890. [1; 3; 5; 6]

Nevin, Edwin Henry, clergyman, b. Shippensburg, Pa., 1814; d. Philadelphia, Pa., June 2, 1889. [1; 3; 5; 6]

Nevin, John Williamson, clergyman and educationist, b. near Strasburg, Pa., 1803; d. Lancaster, Pa., June 6, 1886. [1; 3; 6]

Nevin, Robert Jenkins, clergyman, b. Allegheny, Pa., 1839; d. Mexico City, Mexico, Sept. 20, 1906. [3; 5; 10]

Nevin, Robert Peebles, journalist, b. Shippensburg, Pa., 1820; d. near Pittsburgh, Pa., June 28, 1908. [1; 7; 10]

Nevin, Theodore Williamson, journalist, b. Sewickley, Pa., 1854; d. Sewickley, Pa., Nov. 2, 1918. [10]

Nevin, William Marvel, educationist, b. Shippensburg, Pa., 1806; d. Lancaster, Pa., Feb. 11, 1892. [5]

Nevin, William Wilberforce, journalist, b. Allegheny, Pa., 1836; d. 1899. [3]

Nevins, William, clergyman, b. Norwich, Conn., 1797; d. Baltimore, Md., Sept. 14, 1835. [3]

Nevins, Winfield Scott, historian, d. Salem, Mass., Oct. 23, 1921. [4]

Nevius, Mrs. Helen Sanford, née **Coan,** missionary, b. 1833; d. 1910.

Nevius, John Livingston, missionary, b. Ovid, N.Y., 1829; d. Cheefoo, China, Oct. 18, 1893. [1; 4; 69]

New, Clarence Herbert, journalist and novelist, b. New York, N.Y., 1862; d. Brooklyn, N.Y., Jan. 8, 1933. [10; 11]

Newberry, Mrs. Fannie E., née **Stone,** novelist, b. Monroe, Mich., 1848; d. Coldwater, Mich., Jan. 24, 1942. [39]

Newberry, John Stoughton, lawyer, b. Waterville, N.Y., 1826; d. Detroit, Mich., Jan. 2, 1887. [4; 39]

Newberry, Perry, novelist and playwright, b. Union City, Mich., 1870; d. Carmel, Calif., Dec. 6, 1938. [7; 10; 11; 35]

Newbold, William Romaine, educationist, b. Wilmington, Del., 1865; d. Philadelphia, Pa., Sept. 26, 1926. [1; 4; 7; 10]

Newbrough, John Ballou, religious leader, b. Springfield, O., 1828; d. Las Cruces, N.M., April 22, 1891. [10]

Newburger, Gabriel F., poet, b. Rock Island, Ill.; d. Coral Gables, Calif., July 31, 1939. [7]

Newcomb, Charles Benjamin, philosopher, b. Boston, Mass., 1845; d. Brookline, Mass., March 8, 1922. [10; 11]

Newcomb, Harvey, clergyman, b. Thetford, Vt., 1803; d. Brooklyn, N.Y., Aug. 30, 1863. [7; 3; 5; 6]

Newcomb, John Bearss, genealogist, b. 1824; d. 1897.

Newcomb, Mrs. Katherine, née **Hinchman,** healer, b. Brooklyn, N.Y., 1852; d. Brookline, Mass., July 25, 1920. [10]

Newcomb, Simon, astronomer, b. Wallace, N.S., 1835; d. Washington, D.C., July 11, 1909. [1; 2; 3; 4, 5; 6, 7, 8; 9; 10]

Newcomer, Alphonso Gerard, educationist, b. Mount Morris, Ill., 1864; d. Stanford University, Calif., Sept. 16, 1913. [10; 35]

Newcomer, Mrs. Marion Anastasia, née **Staats,** physician b. 1889; d. New York, N.Y., Dec. 29, 1949.

Newell, Charles Martin, sailor and physician, b. Concord, N.H., 1823; d. Watertown, Mass., May 24, 1900. [3b; 6; 7]

Newell, Chester, clergyman, b. Belchertown, Mass., 1803; d. Savannah, Ga., June 24, 1892. [62]

Newell, Cicero, soldier and Indian agent, b. Ypsilanti, Mich., 1840; d. 1914. [10]

Newell, Ebenezer Francis, clergyman, b. 1775; d. 1867.

Newell, Edward Theodore, numismatist, b. Kenosha, Wis., 1886; d. Manhattan, Long Island, N.Y., Feb. 18, 1941. [10; 11]

Newell, Franklin Spilman, gynaecologist, b. Roxbury, Mass., 1871; d. Boston, Mass., March 3, 1949.

Newell, Frederick Haynes, civil engineer, b. Bradford, Pa., 1862; d. Washington, D.C., July 5, 1932. [1; 4; 10]

Newell, John Robert, clergyman and poet, b. Springfield, Ont., 1853; d. Sarnia, Ont., Oct. 14, 1912. [27]

Newell, Lyman Churchill, chemist, b. Pawtucket, R.I., 1867; d. Brookline, Mass., Dec. 13, 1933. [10; 13]

Newell, Martin L., lawyer, b. 1838; d. 1906.

Newell, Peter, cartoonist and illustrator, b. McDonough county, Ill., 1862; d. Little Neck, N.Y., Jan. 15, 1924. [1; 4; 5; 7; 10; 11]

Newell, Robert Henry, poet, journalist, and humorist, b. New York, N.Y., 1836; d. Brooklyn, N.Y., July 11, 1901. [1; 3b; 4; 7; 9]

Newell, William Wells, literary scholar, b. Cambridge, Mass., 1839; d. Cambridge, Mass., Jan. 21, 1907. [1; 4; 7; 9; 10]

Newell, William Whiting, evangelist, b. 1807; d. 1891.

Newfang, Oscar, economist, b. Columbus, O., 1875; d. New York, N.Y., Feb. 14, 1943. [10]

Newhall, Charles Stedman, educationist, b. Boston, Mass., 1842; d. Berkeley, Calif., April 11, 1935. [10; 35; 45; 68]

Newhall, James Robinson, local historian, b. 1809; d. Lynn, Mass., Oct. 24, 1893.

Newhall, John B., pioneer, d. 1849. [37]

Newhall, Mrs. Laura Eugenia, novelist, b. Dutch Flat, Calif., 1861; d. ? [35]

Newkirk, Garrett, dentist, b. Calhoun county, Mich., 1847; d. Pasadena, Calif., April 7, 1921. [10]

Newkirk, Newton, journalist, b. Bentleyville, Va., 1870; d. Brookline, Mass., May 15, 1938. [7; 10]

Newlon, Jesse Homer, educationist, b. Salem, Ind., 1882; d. New Hope, Pa., Sept. 1, 1941. [10; 11]

Newman, Albert Henry, clergyman, b. Edgefield county, S.C., 1852; d. Austin, Tex., June 4, 1933. [1a; 10; 34]

Newman, Mrs. Angelia French, née Thurston, social worker, b. Montpelier, Vt., 1837; d. Lincoln, Neb., 1910. [10]

Newman, Arthur, clergyman, b. 1853; d. Bridgehampton, N.Y., Dec. 28, 1924.

Newman, Eugene William, journalist, b. Barren county, Ky., 1845; d. ? [34]

Newman, Frances, novelist, b. Atlanta, Ga.; d. New York, N.Y., Oct. 22, 1928. [7; 10; 11]

Newman, John B., physician, fl. 1846-1875.

Newman, John E., lawyer, b. 1819; d. 1873.

Newman, John Philip, bishop, b. New York, N.Y., 1826; d. Saratoga, N.Y., July 5, 1899. [1; 3b; 4; 7; 10]

Newman, Richard Brinsley (pseud.). See Gifford, Franklin Kent.

Newman, Samuel Phillips, educationist, b. Andover, Mass., 1797; d. Andover, Mass., Feb. 10, 1842. [1; 3; 4; 6; 7]

Newman, Sylvanus Chace, antiquary, b. 1802; d. ?

Newman, Thomas Gabriel, apiarist, b. 1833; d. 1903.

Newmark, Harris, merchant, b. Neumark, West Prussia, 1834; d. Los Angeles, Calif., April 4, 1916. [4; 10]

Newport, David, poet, b. 1822; d. 1911.

Newsom, William Monypeny, naturalist, b. Columbus, O., 1887; d. Jamaica, N.Y., Feb. 1, 1942. [10; 62]

Newson, Henry Byron, educationist, b. Mount Gilead, O., 1860; d. Lawrence, Kans., 1910. [10]

Newson, Thomas McLean, journalist, b. New York, N.Y., 1827; d. Malaga, Spain, March 30, 1893. [3b; 70]

Newton, Alfred Edward, bibliophile, b. 1863; d. Philadelphia, Pa., Sept. 29, 1940. [7; 10; 72]

Newton, Alonzo Eliot, spiritualist, b. 1821; d. 1889.

Newton, David F., clergyman, b. 1796; d. ?

Newton, Mrs. Emma, née Mersereau, novelist, fl. 1881-1926.

Newton, Richard, clergyman, b. Liverpool, England, 1812; d. Philadelphia, Pa., May 25, 1887. [1; 3; 4; 6]

Newton, Richard Heber, clergyman, b. Philadelphia, Pa., 1840; d. East Hampton, Long Island, N.Y., Dec. 19, 1914. [1; 3; 4; 5; 6; 7; 9; 10]

Newton, Robert Safford, surgeon, b. near Gallipolis, O., 1818; d. New York, N.Y., Oct. 9, 1881. [1; 3; 4; 5]

Newton, Watson James, novelist, b. England, 1846; d. Washington, D.C., Jan. 16, 1,913. [10]

Newton, William, clergyman, b. about 1820; d. West Chester, Pa., 1893. [6]

Newton, William, clergyman, d. Victoria, B.C., Feb. 11, 1910. [27]

Newton, William Wilberforce, clergyman, b. Philadelphia, Pa., 1843; d. Brookline, Mass., June 25, 1914. [1; 3; 4; 7; 9; 10]

Niblack, Albert Parker, naval officer, b. Vincennes, Ind., 1859; d. Nice, France, Aug. 20, 1929. [1; 10]

Niblack, William Caldwell, lawyer and banker, b. 1854; d. Chicago, Ill., May 6, 1920.

Niccolls, Samuel Jack, clergyman, b. Westmoreland county, Pa., 1838; d. Aug. 19, 1915. [4; 10]

Nicholas, Anna, journalist, b. Meadville, Pa., 1849; d. Indianapolis, Ind., Jan. 29, 1929. [10]

Nicholas, Samuel Smith, jurist, b. Lexington, Ky., 1796; d. Louisville, Ky., Nov. 27, 1869. [5; 34]

Nicholls, Charles Wilbur de Lyon, clergyman, b. Nichols, Conn., 1854; d. Bridgeport, Conn., May 29, 1923. [10]

Nichols, Charles Lemuel, bibliophile, b. Worcester, Mass., 1851; d. Worcester, Mass., Feb. 19, 1929. [1; 7; 10]

Nichols, Charles Wilbur de Lyon. See Nicholls, Charles Wilbur de Lyon.

Nichols, Edward Leamington, physicist, b. Leamington, England, 1854; d. Palm Beach, Fla., Nov. 10, 1937. [10; 11; 13]

Nichols, Edward West, mathematician, b. Petersburg, Va., 1858; d. Lexington, Va., July 1, 1927. [10]

Nichols, Francis Henry, journalist, b. Brooklyn, N.Y., 1868; d. 1904. [10]

Nichols, George Ward, soldier and art connoisseur, b. Mount Desert, Me., 1831; d. Cincinnati, O., Sept. 15, 1885. [1; 3; 4; 6; 7; 9]

Nichols, George Warner, clergyman, b. Fairfield, N.Y., 1817; d. Norwalk, Conn., Feb. 16, 1900. [62]

Nichols, Harry Peirce, clergyman, b. Salem, Mass., 1850; d. North Conway, N.H., Nov. 15, 1940. [10; 51]

Nichols, Henry Wyman, manufacturer, b. Waterville, Me., 1872; d. Fall River, Mass., July 2, 1945.

328   DICTIONARY OF NORTH AMERICAN AUTHORS

Nichols, Herbert, educationist, b. Walpole, N.H., 1852; d. Brookline, Mass., Dec.
6, 1936. [10; 11]

Nichols, Ichabod, clergyman, b. Portsmouth, N.H., 1784; d. Cambridge, Mass.,
Jan. 2, 1859. [3; 4; 6]

Nichols, Isaac T., local historian, b. 1848;
d. Bridgeton, N.J., Feb. 10, 1915.

Nichols, James Lawrence, publisher, d.
1895.

Nichols, James Robinson, chemist, b.
Merrimac, Mass., 1819; d. Haverhill, Mass.,
Jan. 2, 1888. [1; 3; 4 ;6]

Nichols, Mrs. Mary Sargeant, née Neal,
physician and reformer, b. Goffstown, N.H.,
1810; d. London, England, May 30, 1884.
[1; 3; 4; 6; 7; 9]

Nichols, Nicholas (pseud.). See Lathe,
Herbert William.

Nichols, Mrs. Rebecca Shepard, née Reed,
poet, b. Greenwich, N.J., 1819; d. 1903.
[3]

Nichols, Spencer Van Bokkelen, publicist,
b. New York, N.Y., 1882; d. New York,
N.Y., July 1, 1947. [10]

Nichols, Starr Hoyt, clergyman and poet,
b. Bethel, Conn., 1834; d. Honolulu,
Hawaii, May 30, 1909. [62]

Nichols, Thomas Low, dietician and
hydrotherapist, b. Orford, N.H., 1815; d.
Chaumont-en-Vezin, France, 1901. [1; 6;
7; 9]

Nichols, Walter Hammond, educationist,
and writer of books for boys, b. Chicago,
Ill., 1866; d. Palo Alto, Calif., Oct. 10,
1935. [10; 11; 35]

Nichols, Wilbur Fisk, mathematician, b.
Stillwater, Minn., 1857; d. Springfield,
Mass., Jan. 19, 1926.

Nichols, William Ford, bishop, b. Lloyd,
N.Y., 1849; d. San Francisco, Calif., June
5, 1924. [1; 4; 10]

Nichols, William Ripley, chemist, b. Boston, Mass., 1847; d. Hamburg, Germany,
July 14, 1886. [3; 6; 51]

Nichols, William Theophilus, journalist
and writer of books for boys, b. Cincinnati,
O., 1863; d. Manchester, N.H., Jan. 26,
1931. [10; 11; 62]

Nicholson, Mrs. Asenath, née Hatch,
social reformer, fl. 1800-1853.

Nicholson, Byron, journalist, b. Hamilton,
Ont., 1857; d. Ottawa, Ont., June, 1916.
[27]

Nicholson, Mrs. Eliza Jane, née Poitevant, poet, b. Hancock county, Miss.,
1849; d. New Orleans, La., Feb. 15, 1896.
[1; 4; 7; 9; 34]

Nicholson, Mrs. Florence Van Lear, née
Earle. See Coates, Mrs. Florence Van
Lear, née Earle.

Nicholson, James Bartram, book-binder,
b. St. Louis, Mo., 1820; d. Philadelphia,
Pa., March 4, 1901. [1; 3; 7; 10]

Nicholson, James William, mathematician, b. Tuskegee, Ala., 1844; d. Baton
Rouge, La., 1917. [4; 10]

Nicholson, John, agriculturist, fl. 1814-
1820.

Nicholson, Joseph J., clergyman, fl. 1852-
1856.

Nicholson, Meredith, journalist and novelist, b. Crawfordsville, Ind., 1866; d. Indianapolis, Ind., Dec. 21, 1947. [7; 10; 11]

Nicholson, William Rufus, bishop, b.
Greene county, Miss., 1822; d. Philadelphia,
Pa., 1901. [3; 10; 34]

Nicklin, Philip Holbrook, bookseller, b.
Philadelphia, Pa., 1786; d. Philadelphia, Pa.,
March 2, 1842. [3; 4; 5]

Nicola, Lewis, soldier, b. France, 1717;
d. Alexandria, Va., Aug. 9, 1807. [1]

Nicolar, Joseph, Indian chief, b. Penob-
scot reservation, Me., about 1827; d. Indian
Island, Me., Feb. 14, 1894. [3b]

Nicolas, Jean Henri, horticulturist, b.
1875; d. Albany, N.Y., Sept. 25, 1937.

Nicolay, John George, biographer, b.
Bavaria, 1832; d. Washington, D.C., Sept.
26, 1901. [1; 3; 4; 5; 7; 9; 10]

Nicolet, Charles Cathcart, novelist, b.
Kansas City, Mo., 1900; d. Jan. 22, 1943.

Nicolls, William Jasper, civil engineer and
novelist, b. Camden, N.J., 1854; d. Philadelphia, Pa., Feb. 14, 1916. [10]

Nicolovius, Ludwig, short-story writer, b.
1837; d. ?

Nicolson, Alexander Wylie, clergyman,
d. Halifax, N.S., June 8, 1903. [27]

Nicolson, Frank Walter, educationist, b.
Sackville, N.B., 1864; d. Middletown, Conn.,
Dec. 21, 1946. [14; 51]

Nicum, John, clergyman, b. Germany,
1851; d. Rochester, N.Y., 1901. [3; 6; 10]

Nield, Thomas, clergyman and poet, b.
1834; d. 1913.

Nieriker, Mrs. Abigail May, née Alcott,
artist, b. Concord, Mass., 1840; d. 1879.
[2; 3]

Nies, James Buchanan, archaeologist, b.
Newark, N.J., 1856; d. Palestine, June 18,
1922. [1; 4; 10]

Nightingale, Augustus Frederick, educationist, b. Quincy, Mass., 1843; d. Evanston,
Ill., Dec. 4, 1925. [10; 11]

Nil Admirari, Esq. (pseud.). See Shelton, Frederick William.

Niles, Alfred Salem, jurist, b. St. Louis,
Mo., 1860; d. Baltimore, Md., Nov. 2,
1926. [10]

Niles, George McCallum, physician, b.
Marshallville, Ga., 1864; d. Atlanta, Ga.,
June 5, 1932. [10; 11]

Niles, Hezekiah, journalist, b. Chester
county, Pa., 1777; d. Wilmington, Del.,
April 2, 1839. [1; 3; 4; 5; 6; 7; 9]

Niles, John Milton, journalist and politician, b. Windsor, Conn., 1787; d. Hartford, Conn., May 31, 1856. [1; 3; 4; 5; 6;
7; 9]

Niles, Samuel, clergyman, b. Block Island, N.Y., 1674; d. Braintree, Mass., May
1, 1762. [1; 3; 4; 5; 6; 51]

Niles, Willys (pseud.). See Hume, John
Ferguson.

Nilsson, Hjalmar, journalist and musician,
b. Nora, Sweden, 1860; d. St. Paul, Minn.,
Dec. 24, 1936. [10]

Ninde, Edward Summerfield, clergyman, b. Cincinnati, O., 1866; d. Philadelphia, Pa., Aug. 15, 1935. [10; 11]

Nipgen, Alvin Probasco, lawyer, b. Chillicothe, O., 1871; d. Chillicothe, O., Jan. 30, 1936. [62]

Nipher, Francis Eugene, physicist, b. Byron, N.Y., 1847; d. Kirkwood, Mo., Oct. 6, 1926. [1; 3; 4; 10; 13]

Nirdlinger, Charles Frederic, playwright, b. Fort Wayne, Ind., about 1863; d. Atlantic City, N.J., May 13, 1940. [7]

Nisbet, Charles, clergyman and educationist, b. Haddington, Scotland, 1736; d. Carlisle, Pa., Jan. 18, 1804. [1; 4]

Nisbet, Ebenezer, clergyman, b. Edinburgh, Scotland, 1826; d. Westchester, N.Y., July 20, 1893.

Nisbet, James Douglas, physician, b. Waxhaw, S.C., 1861; d. Van Wyck, S.C., July 27, 1913. [10]

Nissen, Hartvig, physical instructor, b. Norway, 1855; d. Boston, Mass., April 22, 1924. [10]

Nitchie, Edward Bartlett, educationist, b. Brooklyn, N.Y., 1876; d. New York, N.Y., Oct. 5, 1917. [1]

Nitram, Notca W. (pseud.). See Acton, Martin William.

Nitsch, Mrs. Helen Alice, née **Matthews,** home economist, d. Plainfield, N.J., 1889. [6]

Niven, Frederick, novelis,t b. Valparaiso, Chile, 1878; d. Vancouver, B.C., Jan. 30, 1944. [11; 27]

Nixdorff, George Augustus, clergyman, b. 1823; d. 1907.

Nixdorff, Henry Morris, biographer and short-story writer, b. 1830; d. ?

Nixon, John Thompson, jurist, b. Cumberland county, N.J., 1820; d. Stockbridge, Mass., Sept. 28, 1889. [1; 3; 4]

Nixon, Oliver Woodson, journalist, b. Guilford county, N.C., 1825; d. Chicago, Ill., 1905. [4; 10]

Nixon-Roulet, Mrs. Mary F. See Roulet, Mrs. Mary F., née Nixon.

Noah, Mordecai Manuel, journalist and dramatist, b. Philadelphia, Pa., 1785; d. New York, N.Y., May 22, 1851. [1; 3; 4; 5; 7; 9; 72]

Nobile, Achilles Alexander, educationist, b. 1833; d. ?

Noble, Annette Lucile, novelist, b. Albion, N.Y., 1844; d. Albion, N.Y., Nov. 27, 1932. [3; 5; 6; 7; 10; 11]

Noble, Charles, educationist, b. New York, N.Y., 1847; d. Washington, D.C., Oct. 5, 1938. [7; 10; 11]

Noble, Charles P., physician, b. Federalsburg, Md., 1863; d. Radnor, Pa., Nov. 21, 1935. [10]

Noble, Edmund, journalist, b. Glasgow, Scotland, 1853; d. Malden, Mass., Jan. 8, 1937. [10; 11]

Noble, Franklin, clergyman, b. Washington, D.C., 1837; d. Washington, D.C., April 25, 1922. [69]

Noble, Frederick Alphonso, clergyman, b. Baldwin, Me., 1832; d. Evanston, Ill., Dec. 31, 1917. [1; 4; 10; 62; 70]

Noble, Gladwyn Kingsley, biologist, b. Yonkers, N.Y., 1894; d. Englewood, N.J., Dec. 9, 1940. [10; 11]

Noble, Louis Legrand, clergyman, b. Lisbon, N.Y., 1813; d. Ionia, Mich., Feb. 6, 1882. [3; 5; 6; 7]

Noble, Marcus Cicero Stephens, educationist, b. Louisburg, N.C., 1855; d. Chapel Hill, N.C., June 1, 1942. [10]

Noble, William Francis Pringle, clergyman, b. 1827; d. 1882. [6]

Noble, William Nelson, lawyer, d. May 29, 1919.

Nobles, Milton, actor and playwright, b. Almont, Mich., 1847; d. Brooklyn, N.Y., June 14, 1924. [10]

Nobody, Nathan (pseud.). See Yellott, George.

Nock, Albert Jay, journalist, b. 1873; d. Wakefield, R.I., Aug. 19, 1945. [7]

Noel, Mrs. John Vavasour, novelist, b. Ireland, 1815; d. Kingston, Ont., June 21, 1873. [27]

Noel, Joseph, playwright, b. Philadelphia, Pa., 1881; d. New York, N.Y., Aug. 6, 1946.

Nolan, Preston Meredith, financial counsel, b. Uhrichsville, O., 1875; d. Chicago, Ill., Jan. 9, 1931. [10]

Nolen, John, city-planner and landscape architect, b. Philadelphia, Pa., 1869; d. Cambridge, Mass., Feb. 18, 1937. [10; 11]

Noll, Arthur Howard, clergyman, b. Caldwell, N.J., 1855; d. Memphis, Tenn., July 17, 1930. [10]

Noon, Alfred, clergyman, b. Elstead, Surrey, England, 1845; d. Brookline, Mass., March 7, 1926.

Noonan, Margaret Eleanor, educationist, b. St. Louis, Mo., 1884; d. ? [10]

Nordegg, Martin, mining engineer, b. Germany, 1868; d. New York, N.Y., Sept. 13, 1948.

Nordheimer, Isaac, orientalist, b. Memelsdorf, Bavaria, 1809; d. New York, N.Y., Nov. 3, 1842. [1; 3; 6]

Nordhoff, Charles, traveller and journalist, b. Westphalia, Germany, 1830; d. San Francisco, Calif., July 14, 1901. [1; 3; 4; 5; 6; 7; 9; 10]

Nordhoff, Charles Bernard, novelist, b. London, England, 1887; d. Santa Barbara, Calif., April 11, 1947. [7; 10; 35]

Norelius, Eric, clergyman, b. Sweden, 1833; d. Rock Island, Ill., March 15, 1916. [1; 10; 70]

Norlin, George, educationist, b. Concordia, Kans., 1871; d. Boulder, Colo., March 30, 1942. [10]

Norman, Benjamin Moore, bookseller, b. Hudson, N.Y., 1809; d. near Summit, Miss., Feb. 1, 1900. [6; 34]

Normano, Joao Frederico, economist, b. Kiev, Russia, 1870; d. New York, N.Y., April 25, 1945.

Norris, Benjamin Franklin, novelist, b. Chicago, Ill., 1870; d. San Francisco, Calif., Oct. 25, 1902. [1; 4; 7; 10; 35; 72]

Norris, Charles Gilman, novelist, b. Chicago, Ill., 1881; d. Palo Alto, Calif., July 25, 1945. [7; 10; 11; 35]

Norris, Frank. See Norris, Benjamin Franklin.

Norris, George Washington, surgeon, b. Philadelphia, Pa., 1808; d. Philadelphia, Pa., March 4, 1875. [1; 3; 6]

Norris, Henry Hutchinson, electrical engineer, b. Philadelphia, Pa., 1873; d. Winchester, Mass., April 14, 1940. [10]

Norris, Henry McCoy, genealogist, b. Trenton, N.J., 1686; d. Cincinnati, O., Dec. 27, 1925. [10; 11]

Norris, Homer Albert, musician, b. Wayne, Me., 1860; d. Lakewood, N.J., Aug. 14, 1920. [10; 20]

Norris, James Flack, chemist, b. Baltimore, Md., 1871; d. Boston, Mass., Aug. 4, 1940. [10; 11; 13]

Norris, Joseph Parker, Shakespearian student, b. 1847; d. Philadelphia, Pa., March 17, 1916.

Norris, Mary Harriott, educationist and novelist, b. Boonton, N.J., 1848; d. Morristown, N.J., Sept. 14, 1919. [1; 5; 7; 9; 10]

Norris, Philetus W., anthropologist, b. 1821; d. 1885.

Norris, Thaddeus, sportsman, b. Warrenton, Va., 1811; d. Philadelphia, Pa., April 10, 1877. [3; 6; 34]

Norris, William Fisher, ophthalmologist, b. Philadelphia, Pa., 1839; d. Philadelphia, Pa., Nov. 18, 1901. [1; 4; 10]

Norsworthy, Naomi, psychologist, b. New York, N.Y., 1877; d. New York, N.Y., Dec. 25, 1916. [1; 10]

North, Barclay (pseud.). See Hudson, William Cadwalader.

North, Elisha, physician, b. Goshen, Conn., 1771; d. New London, Conn., Dec. 29, 1843. [1; 3; 4; 6;]

North, Erasmus Darwin, educationist, b. Connecticut, 1806; d. 1858. [62]

North, F. H., (pseud.). See Pratt, Jacob Loring.

North, James William, local historian, b. 1810; d. 1882. [38]

North, Leigh (pseud.). See Phelps, Mrs. Elizabeth Steward, née Natt.

North, Levi, lawyer, b. 1821; d. 1901.

North, Nelson Luther, physician, b. 1830; d. Brooklyn, N.Y., Nov. 23, 1904.

North, Ralph, lawyer, b. 1814; d. 1883.

North, Simeon, educationist, b. Berlin, Conn., 1802; d. near Clinton, N.Y., Feb. 9, 1884. [4; 7]

North, Simon Newton Dexter, editor, b. Clinton, N.Y., 1848; d. Wilton, Conn., Aug. 3, 1924. [1; 4; 10]

Northen, William Jonathan, politician, b. 1835; d. Atlanta, Ga., March 25, 1913. [1; 4; 10]

Northend, Charles, educationist, b. Kent, Conn., 1817; d. New Britain, Conn., Aug. 7, 1895. [1; 3b; 5; 6]

Northend, Mary Harrod, miscellaneous writer, b. Salem, Mass., 1850; d. Salem, Mass., Dec., 1925. [10; 11]

Northend, William Dummer, lawyer and historian, b. Byfield, Mass., 1823; d. Salem, Mass., Oct. 29, 1902. [3; 10; 46]

Northrop, Mrs. Alice, née **Rich,** naturalist, b. 1864; d. Mount Riga, N.Y., May 6, 1922.

Northrop, Birdsey Grant, educationist, b. Kent, Conn., 1817; d. Clinton, Conn., April 27, 1898. [1; 3b; 4]

Northrop, Cyrus, educationist, b. near Ridgefield, Conn., 1834; d. Minneapolis, Minn., April 3, 1922. [1; 4; 10; 62; 70]

Northrop, Henry Davenport, clergyman, b. Poultney, N.Y., 1836; d. Yonkers, N.Y., Aug. 28, 1909. [10]

Northrop, Nira B., local historian, b. 1791; d. 1878.

Northrup, Ansel Judd, lawyer, b. Madison county, N.Y., 1833; d. Syracuse, N.Y., Nov. 23, 1919. [3; 4; 5; 10]

Northrup, Edwin Fitch, electrical engineer, b. Syracuse, N.Y., 1866; d. Princeton, N.J., April 29, 1940. [10]

Norton, Andrews, theologian, b. Hingham, Mass., 1786; d. Newport, R.I., Sept. 18, 1852. [1; 3; 4; 5; 6; 7; 9]

Norton, Anthony Banning, local historian, d. Mount Vernon, O., 1890.

Norton, Arthur Brigham, oculist, b. New Marlborough, Mass., 1856; d. New York, N.Y., June 18, 1919. [4; 10]

Norton, Augustus Theodore, clergyman, b. Cornwall, Conn., 1808; d. Alton, Ill., April 29, 1884. [3; 62]

Norton, Charles Benjamin, journalist, b. Hartford, Conn., 1825; d. Chicago, Ill., Jan. 29, 1891. [3b; 6]

Norton, Charles Eliot, educationist and man of letters, b. Cambridge, Mass., 1827; d. Cambridge, Mass., Oct. 21, 1908. [1; 2; 3; 4; 5; 6; 7; 8; 9; 10; 71]

Norton, Charles Ledyard, novelist and editor, b. Farmington, Conn., 1837; d. Sandwich, Mass., Dec. 14, 1909. [3; 10; 62]

Norton, Charles Phelps, lawyer, b. Buffalo, N.Y., 1858; d. Buffalo, N.Y., July 11, 1922. [10; 11]

Norton, David, local historian, b. 1812; d. ? [38]

Norton, Mrs. Edith Eliza, née **Ames,** traveller, b. Lockport, N.Y., 1864; d. New Haven, Conn., Oct. 30, 1929. [10; 11]

Norton, Eliot, lawyer, b. Cambridge, Mass., 1863; d. London, England, Oct. 18, 1932. [10; 51]

Norton, Frank Henry, librarian and journalist, b. Hingham, Mass., 1836; d. Brooklyn, N.Y., Feb. 19, 1921. [2; 3; 4; 5; 6]

Norton, Mrs. Frances Marie, née **Guiteau,** novelist, fl. 1888-1898.

Norton, Frank Louis, clergyman, b. 1845; d. 1891.

Norton, Franklin Pierce, playwright, b. 1852; d. ?

Norton, Frederick Owen, educationist, b. Brudenell, P.E.I., 1869; d. Chester, Pa., Feb. 29, 1924. [10; 11]

Norton, George Hatley, clergyman, b. Ontario county, N.Y., 1824; d. 1893. [3]

Norton, Grace, essayist, b. Cambridge, Mass., 1834; d. Cambridge, Mass., May 5, 1926. [7; 10]

Norton, Herman, clergyman, b. New Hartford, N.Y., 1799; d. New York, N.Y., Nov. 20, 1850. [3]

Norton, John, clergyman, b. Bishop's Stortford, England, 1606; d. Boston, Mass., April 5, 1663. [1; 3; 4; 5; 6; 7; 9]

Norton, John Nicholas, clergyman, b. Waterloo, N.Y., 1820; d. Louisville, Ky., Jan. 18, 1881. [1; 3; 4; 5; 6; 34]

Norton, John Pitkin, agricultural chemist, b. Albany, N.Y., 1822; d. Farmington, Conn., Sept. 5, 1852. [1; 3; 4; 6]

Norton, Lemuel, sailor and clergyman, b. 1785; d. ?

Norton, Lewis Adelbert, lawyer and adventurer, b. Chautauqua, N.Y., 1819; d. Healdsburg, Calif., Aug. 16, 1891. [35]

Norton, Mrs. Mary Alice, née Peloubet, home economist, b. 1860; d. Northampton, Mass., Feb. 23, 1928. [1; 11]

Norton, Richard, archaeologist, b. Dresden, Germany, 1872; d. Paris, France, Aug. 2, 1918. [10; 51]

Norton, Roy, explorer and novelist, b. Kewanee, Ill., 1869; d. Freeport, Long Island, N.Y., June 28, 1942. [7; 10; 11]

Norton, Sidney Augustus, chemist, b. Bloomfield, O., 1835; d. Aug. 30, 1918. [3; 4; 10]

Norton, Stephen Alison, clergyman, b. Bradford, Pa., 1854; d. Claremont, Calif., Jan. 1, 1930. [10; 45]

Norton, Thomas Herbert, chemist, b. Rushford, N.Y., 1851; d. White Plains, N.Y., Dec. 2, 1941. [4; 10; 11]

Norton, Wilbur Theodore, historian, b. 1844; d. Jan. 8, 1925.

Norton, William Augustus, civil engineer, b. East Bloomfield, N.Y., 1810; d. New Haven, Conn., Sept. 21, 1883. [3; 4; 6]

Norton, William Bernard, religious editor, b. Freeport, Ill., 1857; d. Portland, Ore., Aug. 31, 1936. [10; 11]

Norton, William Harmon, geologist, b. Willoughby, O., 1856; d. Mount Vernon, Ia., Dec. 11, 1946. [10; 11; 13]

Norwood, Robert Winkworth, clergyman, poet, and novelist, b. Lunenburg county, N.S., 1874; d. New York, N.Y., Sept. 28, 1932. [1; 7; 10; 11; 27]

Norwood, Thomas Manson, politician, b. Talbot county, Ga., 1830; d. near Savannah, Ga., June 19, 1913. [4; 10; 34]

Noss, Theodore Bland, educationist, b. near Waterloo, Pa., 1852; d. Chicago, Ill., Feb. 28, 1909. [1; 10]

Nott, Charles Cooper, jurist, b. Schenectady, N.Y., 1827; d. New York, N.Y., March 6, 1916. [1; 4; 5; 10]

Nott, Eliphalet, clergyman and educationist, b. Ashford, Conn., 1773; d. Schenectady, N.Y., Jan. 29, 1866. [1; 3; 4; 5; 6; 7; 9]

Nott, Henry Junius, educationist, b. Union district, S.C., 1797; d. off the coast of North Carolina, Oct. 9, 1837. [1; 3; 4; 5; 6; 7; 9]

Nott, Josiah Clark, physician and ethnologist, b. Columbia, S.C., 1804; d. Mobile, Ala., March 31, 1873. [1; 3; 4; 5; 6; 34]

Nott, Richard Means, clergyman, b. Boston, Mass., 1831; d. Wakefield, Mass., Dec. 21, 1880. [3]

Nott, Samuel, missionary, b. Franklin, Conn., 1788; d. Hartford, Conn., June 1, 1869. [3; 5]

Notz, William Frederick, economist, b. Watertown, Wis., 1879; d. Chevy Chase, Md., June 4, 1935. [10; 11]

Nourse, Charles Clinton, lawyer, b. 1829; d. ¹1916. [37]

Nourse, Edward Everett, theologian, b. Bayfield, Wis., 1863; d. Hartford, Conn., April 29, 1929. [10]

Nourse, Henry Stedman, civil engineer, b. Lancaster, Mass., 1831; d. South Lancaster, Mass., Nov. 14, 1903. [4; 10; 51]

Nourse, James Duncan, novelist, b. Bardstown, Ky., 1817; d. St. Louis, Mo., June 1, 1854. [3; 6; 7; 34]

Nourse, Joseph Everett, clergyman and educationist, b. Washington, D.C., 1819; d. Washington, D.C., Oct. 8, 1889. [3; 4; 5; 34]

Nourse, Mrs. Laura A., née Sunderlin, medium and clairvoyant, b. 1836; d. ? [37]

Nowell, Mrs. Harriet P. H., novelist, fl. 1868-1871. [6]

Nowlin, William, pioneer, b. Putnam county, N.Y., 1821; d. near Grand Rapids, Mich., 1884. [39]

Nox, Owen (pseud.). See Cory, Charles Barney.

Noxon, Frank Wright, economist, b. Syracuse, N.Y., 1873; d. Alexandria, Va., March 20, 1945. [10]

Noyce, Elisha, writer of books for boys, fl. 1858-59.

Noyes, Alexander Dana, journalist, b. Montclair, N.J., 1862; d. New York, N.Y., April 22, 1945. [10; 11]

Noyes, Alva Josiah, pioneer, b. 1855; d. near Harlem, Mont., Aug. 25, 1917.

Noyes, Arthur Amos, chemist, b. Newburyport, Mass., 1866; d. Pasadena, Calif., June 3, 1936. [4; 10; 11]

Noyes, Charles, poet and dramatist, b. about 1849; d. St. Louis, Mo., Aug. 4, 1909.

Noyes, Clara Dutton, nursing sister, b. Port Deposit, Md.; d. Washington, D.C., June 3, 1936. [10; 11]

Noyes, David, local historian, b. 1788; d. Norway, Me., 1881. [38]

Noyes, Eli, missionary, b. Jefferson, Me., 1814; d. Lafayette, Ind., Sept. 10, 1854. [3; 6]

Noyes, George Rapall, clergyman, b. Newburyport, Mass., 1798; d. Cambridge, Mass., June 3, 1868. [1; 3; 4; 6]

Noyes, Henry Drury, ophthalmologist, b. New York, N.Y., 1832; d. Mount Washington, Mass., Nov. 12, 1900. [1; 10]

Noyes, James Oscar, physician, b. Cayuga county, N.Y., 1829; d. New Orleans, La. Sept. 11, 1872. [3 ;6; 34]

Noyes, John Humphrey, religious enthusiast and social reformer b. Brattleboro, Vt., 1811; d. Niagara Falls, Ont., April 13, 1886. [1; 3; 4; 6; 7; 9]

Noyes, Newbold, poet, b. Washington, D.C., 1892; d. Washington, D.C., Apirl 16, 1942. [10; 62]

Noyes, Nicholas, clergyman, b. Newbury, Mass., 1647; d. Salem, Mass.. Dec. 13, 1717. [3; 4; 7; 51]

Noyes, Theodore Williams, journalist, b. Washington, D.C., 1858; d. Washington, D.C., July 4, 1946. [10]

Noyes, Walter Chadwick, jurist, b. Lyme, Conn., 1865; d. New York, N.Y., June 12, 1926. [1; 4; 10; 11]

Noyes, William Horace, educationist, b. Madura, India, 1862; d. Albany, N.Y., July 8, 1928. [45]

Nugent, George, philanthropist, b. Philadelphia, Pa., 1809; d. Atlantic City, N.J., June 21, 1883. [3; 6]

Nugent, Homer Heath, educationist, b. Waterbury, Conn., 1893; d. Troy, N.Y., May 28, 1945.

Nugent, John Charles, actor and playwright, b. 1878; d. New York, N.Y., April 21, 1947.

Nugent, Paul Cook, civil engineer, b. New Orleans, La., 1871; d. Tucson, Ariz., July 15, 1924. [10]

Nursey, Walter R., journalist, b. Norfolk, England, 1847; d. Toronto, Ont., March 14, 1927. [27]

Nutt, Charles, genealogist and historian, b. Natick, Mass., 1868; d. Wareham, Mass., Aug. 27, 1918. [51]

Nuttall, George Henry Falkiner, biologist, b. San Francisco, Calif., 1862; d. Cambridge, England, Dec. 16, 1937. [10; 11; 13]

Nuttall, Thomas, botanist and ornithologist, b. Yorkshire, England, 1786; d. near Liverpool, England, Sept. 10, 1859. [1; 2; 3; 4; 5; 6; 7; 9]

Nuttall, Mrs. Zelia, archaeologist, b. San Francisco, Calif., 1858; d. April 12, 1933. [10]

Nutter, William Herbert, journalist, b. 1874; d. Dedham, Mass., March 19, 1941.

Nutting, Charles Cleveland, biologist, b. Jacksonville, Ill., 1858; d. Iowa City, Ia., Jan. 25, 1927. [1; 4; 10; 11; 13]

Nutting, Herbert Chester, educationist, b. New York, N.Y., 1872; d. San Francisco, Calif., Sept. 23, 1934. [10; 11; 62]

Nutting, John Keep, clergyman, b. Groton, Mass., 1832; d. Crystal Springs, Fla., Sept. 17, 1917.

Nutting, Mary Adelaide, nurse, b. Quebec, Que., 1859; d. New York, N.Y., Oct. 3, 1948.

Nutting, Mary Olivia, novelist, b. Randolph Center, Vt., 1831; d. 1910. [10]

Nutting, Rufus, educationist, b. 1793; d. Detroit, Mich., July 12, 1878. [43]

Nutting, Wallace, clergyman, antiquary, and photographer, b. Marlboro, Mass., 1861; d. Framingham, Mass., July 19, 1941. [7; 10; 11; 51]

Nydegger, James Archibald, physician, b. Fort Pendleton, Md., 1864; d. Baltimore, Md., Feb. 18, 1934. [10]

Nye, Bill (pseud.). See Nye, Edgar Wilson.

Nye, Edgar Wilson, humorist, b. Shirley, Me., 1850; d. Asheville, N.C., Feb. 22, 1896. [1; 2; 3b; 4; 5]

Nye, Joseph Warren, poet, b. 1816; d. 1901.

Nystrom, John William, civil engineer, b. 1824; d. 1885. [6]

O

Oak, Lyndon, local historian, b. 1816; d. 1902.

Oakes, Urian, clergyman, educationist, and poet, b. London, England, about 1631; d. Cambridge, Mass., July 25, 1681. [1; 2; 3; 4; 7; 8; 10]

Oakey, Charles Cochran, local historian, b. 1845; d. 1908.

Oakey, Emily Sullivan, educationist, b. Albany, N.Y., 1829; d. Albany, N.Y., May 11, 1883. [3]

Oakey, Maria Richards. See Dewing, Mrs. Maria Richards, née Oakey.

Oakleaf, Joseph Benjamin, lawyer, b. Moline, Ill., 1858; d. Moline, Ill., June 2, 1930. [10]

Oakley, Henry Augustus, financier, b. New York, N.Y., 1827; d. 1907. [3; 6; 10]

Oakley, Mrs. Imogen, née **Brashear,** miscellaneous writer, b. Dover, O., 1854; d. Philadelphia, Pa., Sept. 14, 1933. [10]

Oakley, Thomas Pollock, educationist, b. Port Jefferson, N.Y., 1884; d. White Plains, N.Y., Jan. 9, 1943.

Oakum, John (pseud.). See Phillips, Walter Polk.

Oakwood, Oliver (pseud.). See Potts, Stacy Gardner.

Oates, William Calvin, soldier and politician, b. Bullock county, Ala., 1835; d. Montgomery, Ala., Sept. 9, 1910. [1; 4; 5; 10; 34]

Obenchain, Mrs. Eliza Caroline, née **Calvert,** novelist, b. Bowling Green, Ky., 1856; d. ? [7; 10; 11]

Ober, Charles Kellogg, Y.M.C.A. secretary, b. Beverly, Mass., 1856; d. White Plains, N.Y., July 13, 1948. [10]

Ober, Frederick Albion, ornithologist and explorer, b. Beverly, Mass., 1849; d. Hackensack, N.J., June 1, 1913. [1; 3; 4; 7; 10]

Ober, Sarah Endicott, missionary, b. 1854; d. ? [10]

Oberholtzer, Ellis Paxson, historian, b. Philadelphia, Pa., 1868; d. Philadelphia, Pa., Dec. 8, 1936. [7; 10; 11]

Oberholtzer, Mrs. Sara Louise, née **Vickers,** poet and philanthropist, b. Chester county, Pa., 1841; d. Philadelphia, Pa., Feb. 2, 1930. [1; 3; 4; 7; 9; 10; 11]

O'Brien, Cornelius, archbishop, b. Prince Edward Island, 1843; d. Halifax, N.S., March 9, 1906. [27]

O'Brien, Dillon, journalist and novelist, b. Kilmore, Ireland, 1817; d. St. Paul, Minn., Feb. 12, 1882. [70]

O'Brien, Edward Joseph Harrington, literary critic, b. Boston, Mass., 1890; d. Gerrards Cross, Buckinghamshire, England, Feb. 25, 1941. [7; 10; 11]

O'Brien, Fitz-James, poet and story-writer, b. county Limerick, Ireland, about 1828; d. Cumberland, Va., April 6, 1862. [1; 3; 4; 5; 7; 9]

O'Brien, Frank George, journalist, b. Calais, Me., 1843; d. Minneapolis, Minn., 1920. [70]

O'Brien, Frank Michael, journalist, b. Dunkirk, N.Y., 1875; d. New York, N.Y., Sept. 22, 1943. [7; 10]

O'Brien, Frederick, journalist, b. Baltimore, Md., 1869; d. Sausalito, Calif., Jan. 9, 1932. [1; 7; 10; 11]

O'Brien, Howard Vincent, journalist and novelist, b. Chicago, Ill., 1888; d. Evanston, Ill., Sept. 30, 1947. [10; 62]

O'Brien, John, priest, b. 1841; d. Emmetsburg, Md., 1879. [34]

O'Brien, John Paul Jones, soldier, b. Philadelphia, Pa., 1817; d. Indianola, Tex., March 31, 1850. [3]

O'Brien, John Sherman, writer of books of adventure, b. 1898; d. New York, N.Y., Dec. 6, 1938.

O'Brien, Patrick Joseph, journalist, b. 1892; d. Penfield, Pa., June 10, 1938. [7]

O'Brien, Thomas Dillon, lawyer, b. La Point, Wis., 1859; d. St. Paul, Minn., Sept. 3, 1935. [4; 10; 70]

O'Callaghan, Edmund Bailey, journalist and historian, b. Mallow, Ireland, 1797; d. New York, N.Y., May 27, 1880. [1; 3; 4; 7; 9; 27]

O'Callaghan, Jeremiah, priest, b. county Cork, Ireland, 1780; d. Holyoke, Mass., Feb. 23, 1861. [1]

Occom, Samson, Indian missionary, b. near New London, Conn., 1723; d. New Stockbridge, N.Y., July 14, 1792. [1; 3; 7]

Ochsenford, Solomon Erb, clergyman, b. 1855; d. 1932.

Ochsner, Albert John, surgeon, b. Baraboo, Wis., 1858; d. Chicago, Ill., July 25, 1925. [1; 4; 10; 11]

Ocker, William C., soldier and aviator, b. Philadelphia, Pa., 1876; d. Washington, D.C., Sept. 15, 1942.

Ockside, Knight Russ (pseud.). See Underhill, Edward Fitch.

O'Connell, Cornelius Joseph, priest, b. Frankfort, Ky., 1853; d. Louisville, Ky., April 2, 1920. [21]

O'Connell, Daniel, poet, b. county Clare, Ireland, 1849; d. Sausalito, Calif., Feb. 23, 1899. [35]

O'Connell, Jeremiah Joseph, clergyman, b. county Cork, Ireland, 1821; d. Charleston, S.C., 1894. [3; 4; 34]

O'Connor, John, politician and jurist, b. Boston, Mass., 1824; d. Cobourg, Ont., Nov. 3, 1887. [27]

O'Connor, Joseph, journalist and poet, b. Tribes Hill, N.Y., 1841; d. 1908. [4; 5; 10]

O'Connor, William Douglas, journalist, b. Boston, Mass., 1833; d. Washington, D.C., May 9, 1889. [1; 3; 4; 7; 9; 71]

O'Conor, Charles, lawyer, b. New York, N.Y., 1804; d. New York, N.Y., May 12, 1884. [1; 3; 4]

O'Conor, John Francis Xavier, priest, b. New York, N.Y., 1852; d. ? [21]

O'Dav, John Christopher, physician, b. 1867; d. Honolulu, Hawaii, July 2, 1945.

O'Dea, James, song-writer, b. Hamilton, Ont., 1871; d. New York, N.Y., April 12, 1914. [7; 10]

Odell, Benjamin Barker, politician, b. Newburgh, N.Y., 1854; d. Newburgh, N.Y., May 9, 1926. [1; 4; 10]

Odell, George Clinton Densmore, educationist, b. Newburgh, N.Y., 1866; d. New York, N.Y., Oct. 17, 1949. [7; 10]

Odell, Jonathan, clergyman and poet, b. Newark, N.J., 1737; d. Fredericton, N.B., Nov. 25, 1818. [1; 3; 7; 9]

Odell, Joseph Henry, clergyman, b. London, England, 1871; d. Wilmington, Del., Aug. 29, 1929. [10]

Odell, Minna, poet, b. Tarrytown, N.Y., about 1857; d. Wyckoff, N.Y., July 23, 1940. [10]

Odell, Samuel W., lawyer and novelist, b. 1865; d. Culver City, Calif., Oct. 9, 1948.

Odenheimer, William Henry, bishop, b. Philadelphia, Pa., 1817; d. Burlington, N.J., Aug. 14, 1879. [1; 3; 4; 5; 6]

Odiorne, James Creighton, freemason and genealogist, b. London, England, 1802; d. Wellesley, Mass., Feb. 5, 1879. [62]

Odiorne, Thomas, poet, b. Exeter, N.H., 1769; d. Malden, Mass., May 18, 1851. [3]

O'Donnell, Charles Lee, clergyman, b. Greenfield, Ind., 1884; d. Notre Dame, Ind., June 4, 1934. [7; 10; 11; 22]

O'Donnell, Daniel Kane, journalist and poet, b. Philadelphia, Pa., 1838; d. Philadelphia, Pa., Sept. 8, 1871. [3; 7]

O'Donnell, Edwin Patrick, novelist, b. New Orleans, La., 1895; d. New Orleans, La., April 19, 1943.

O'Donnell, James, lawyer, b. 1816; d. 1886. [39]

O'Donnell, Jessie Fremont, poet, b. 1860; d. 1897.

O'Donnell, John Harrison, physician, b. Simcoe, Ont., 1844; d. Winnipeg, Man., Oct. 26, 1912. [27]

O'Donnell, John Hugh, priest and educationist, b. Grand Rapids, Mich., 1895; d. South Bend, Ind., June 12, 1947. [10; 21]

Oemler, Arminius, physician and agriculturist, b. Savannah, Ga., 1827; d. Savannah, Ga., Aug. 8, 1897. [1]

Oemler, Mrs. Marie, née Conway, novelist, b. Savannah, Ga., 1879; d. Charleston, S.C., June 7, 1932. [7; 10; 11]

Oerter, John Henry, clergyman, b. 1831; d. 1915.

O'Ferrall, Charles Triplett, politician, b. Frederick county, Va., 1840; d. Richmond, Va., Sept. 22, 1905. [1; 4; 5; 10; 34]

Officer, Morris, missionary, b. Holmes county, O., 1823; d. Topeka, Kans., Nov. 1, 1874. [3]

Ogden, George W., merchant, fl. 1823.

Ogden, Henry Alexander, artist, b. Philadelphia, Pa., 1856; d. Englewood, N.J., June 15, 1936. [10]

Ogden, Henry Neely, civil engineer, b. Dexter, Me., 1868; d. Ithaca, N.Y., Sept. 29, 1947. [10]

Ogden, John, educationist, b. Crestline, O., 1824; d. Seattle, Wash., Aug. 10, 1910.

Ogden, John Cosens, clergyman, b. 1751; d. Chestertown, Md., 1800. [3]

Ogden, Robert Curtis, merchant, b. Philadelphia, Pa., 1836; d. New York, N.Y., Aug. 6, 1913. [10]

Ogden, Rollo, journalist, b. Sand Lake, N.Y., 1856; d. New York, N.Y., Feb. 22, 1937. [7; 10]

Ogden, Ruth (pseud.). See Ide, Mrs. Frances Otis, née Ogden.

Ogden, Uzal, clergyman, b. Newark, N.J., 1744; d. Newark, N.J., Nov. 4, 1822. [1; 3; 5]

Ogilby, John David, clergyman, b. Dublin, Ireland, 1870; d. Paris, France, Feb. 2, 1851. [3; 6]

Ogilvie, James, educationist, b. 1760; d. Aberdeen, Scotland, 1820. [6]

Ogilvie, John Stuart, publisher, b. 1843; d. Brooklyn, N.Y., Feb. 10, 1910. [4; 7]

Ogilvie, William, administrator, b. Ottawa, Ont., 1846; d. Winnipeg, Man., Nov. 13, 1912. [27]

Oglesby, Thaddeus Kosciusko, lawyer, b. Boonerville, Mo., 1847; d. ? [34]

O'Gorman, Thomas, bishop, b. Boston, Mass., 1843; d. Sioux Falls, N.D., Sept. 18, 1921. [1; 4; 5; 10]

O'Hagan, Thomas, poet, educationist, and journalist, b. near Toronto, Ont., 1855; d. Toronto, Ont., March 2, 1939. [27]

O'Hanly, John Lawrence Power, civil engineer, b. Waterford, Ireland, 1829; d. Ottawa, Ont., March 22, 1912. [27]

O'Hara, Edward H., publisher, b. Skaneateles, N.Y., 1853; d. Syracuse, N.Y., Feb. 10, 1936. [10]

O'Hara, Frank, economist, b. Lanesboro, Minn., 1876; d. Washington, D.C., July 30, 1938. [10]

O'Hara, John Myers, stockbroker and poet, b. Cedar Rapids, Ia., 1874; d. New York, N.Y., Nov. 17, 1944.

O'Harra, Cleophas Cisney, geologist, b. Bentley, Ill., 1866; d. Rapid City, S.D., Feb. 21, 1935. [10]

O'Higgins, Harvey, novelist and playwright, b. London, Ont., 1876; d. Martinstown, N.J., Feb. 28, 1929. [1; 10; 27]

Ohl, Jeremiah Franklin, clergyman, b. Cherryville, Pa., 1850; d. Philadelphia, Pa., Jan. 21, 1941. [10; 11]

Ohl, Mrs. Maude Annulet, née Andrews, novelist, b. 1862; d. Bronxville, N.Y., Jan. 7, 1943. [34]

Okakura, Kakuzo, museum curator, b. Japan, 1862; d. Tokyo, Japan, Sept. 4, 1913. [10]

O'Kelly, James, clergyman, b. about 1735; d. Raleigh, N.C., Oct. 16, 1826. [1]

Olcott, Charles Sumner, publisher, b. Terre Haute, Ind., 1864; d. Cambridge, Mass., May 3, 1935. [7; 10; 11]

Olcott, George N., educationist, b. Brooklyn, N.Y., 1869; d. Rome Italy, March 2, 1912. [4; 10]

Olcott, Henry Steel, theosophist, b. Orange, N.J., 1832; d. Adyar, India, Feb. 17, 1907. [1; 4; 7; 10]

Olcott, William Tyler, astronomer, b. Chicago, Ill., 1873; d. July, 1936. [7; 10; 11]

Oldberg, Oscar, pharmacist, b. Sweden, 1846; d. Chicago, Ill., Feb. 27, 1913. [4; 10]

Older, Fremont, journalist, b. Appleton, Wis., 1856; d. Stockton, Calif., March 3, 1935. [1a; 7; 10; 11]

Oldham, William Fitzjames, bishop, b. Bangalore, India, 1854; d. Glendale, Calif., March 27, 1937. [4; 10; 11]

Old Harlo (pseud.). See Abbott, Charles Edwards.

Oldpath, Obadiah (pseud.). See Newhall, James Robinson.

Oldroyd, Osborn Hamline, biographer, b. 1842; d. Oct. 8, 1930.

Oldschool, Oliver (pseud.). See Sargent, Nathan.

Old Sleuth (pseud.). See Halsey, Harlan Page.

Old Stager (pseud.). See Adams, William Taylor.

Olerich, Henry, miscellaneous writer, b. 1852; d. 1926.

Oleson, Charles Wilmot, physician, b. 1840; d. Lombard, Ill., Dec. 1, 1906.

Olin, Arvin Solomon, educationist, b. Low Moor, Ia., 1855; d. March 25, 1935. [10]

Olin, Mrs. Helen Maria, née Remington, educationist, b. 1854; d. Madison, Wis., Jan. 14, 1922.

Olin, John Myers, lawyer, b. Lexington, O., 1851; d. Madison, Wis., Dec. 7, 1924. [10]

Olin, Mrs. Julia Matilda, née Lynch, religious writer, b. New York, N.Y., 1814; d. New York, N.Y., May 1, 1879. [3]

Olin, Stephen, clergyman and educationist, b. Leicester, Vt., 1797; d. Middletown, Conn., Aug. 16, 1851. [1; 3; 4; 5; 6; 7]

Olin, Walter Herbert, agriculturist, b. Walnut Grove, Calif., 1862; d. Denver, Colo., June 21, 1933. [10]

O'Lincoln, Robert (pseud.). See Mason, George Champlin.

Oliphant, Samuel Grant, educationist, b. 1864; d. April 13, 1936.

Oliver, Andrew, jurist and scientist, b. Boston, Mass., 1731; d. Salem, Mass., Dec. 6, 1799. [1; 3; 4]

Oliver, Benjamin Lynde, physician, b. 1760; d. 1835.

Oliver, Benjamin Lynde, lawyer, b. Marblehead, Mass., 1788; d. 1843. [3]

Oliver, Charles Augustus, ophthalmologist, b. Cincinnati, O., 1853; d. Philadelphia, Pa., April 8, 1911. [1; 10]

Oliver, Daniel, physician, b. Marblehead, Mass., 1787; d. Cambridge, Mass., June 1, 1842. [3; 4]

Oliver, Edmund Henry, educationist and historian, b. Kent county, Ont., 1882; d. Round Lake, Sask., July 11, 1935. [27]

Oliver, Edwin Austin, journalist, b. New York, N.Y., 1855; d. Yonkers, N.Y., April 22, 1924. [10]

Oliver, Fitch Edward, physician and historian, b. Cambridge, Mass., 1819; d. Boston, Mass., Dec. 8, 1892. [1; 3]

Oliver, George Fletcher, clergyman, b. 1853; d. Cleveland, O., Jan. 13, 1924.

Oliver, George Watson, botanist, b. 1858; d. 1923.

Oliver, Mrs. Grace Atkinson, née Little, biographer, b. Boston, Mass., 1844; d. Marblehead, Mass., May 21, 1899. [3; 5; 7; 10]

Oliver, James, physician, b. 1836; d. Athol, Mass., Feb. 8, 1918.

Oliver, James Edward, mathematician, b. Portland, Me., 1829; d. Ithaca, N.Y., March 27, 1895. [4]

Oliver, John Rathbone, clergyman, psychiatrist, and novelist, b. Albany, N.Y., 1872; d. Waverley, Mass., Jan. 22, 1943. [7; 10; 51]

Oliver, Mrs. Martha, née Capps, poet and journalist, b. Jacksonville, Ill., 1845; d. 1916. [10]

Oliver, Peter, jurist, b. Boston, Mass., 1713; d. Birmingham, England, Oct., 1791. [1; 3; 4; 7; 9]

Oliver, Peter, lawyer and historian, b. Hanover, N.H., 1822; d. at sea, 1855. [3]

Oliver, Temple (pseud.). See Smith, Mrs. Jeanie Oliver, née Davidson.

Olivia (pseud.). See Briggs, Mrs. Emily, née Edson.

Olmstead, Albert Ten Eyck, orientalist, b. Troy, N.Y., 1880. d. Chicago, Ill., April 11, 1945. [7; 10; 11]

Olmstead, Dwight Hinckley, lawyer, b. about 1827; d. 1901.

Olmstead, Frederick Law. See Olmsted, Frederick Law.

Olmstead, James Munson, clergyman, b. Stillwater, N.Y., 1794; d. Philadelphia, Pa., Oct. 16, 1870. [3; 6]

Olmsted, Alexander Fisher, chemist, b. Chapel Hill, N.C., 1822; d. New Haven, Conn., 1853. [6; 34]

Olmsted, Charles Sanford, bishop, b. Olmstedville, N.Y., 1853; d. Denver, Colo., Oct. 21, 1918. [4; 10]

Olmsted, Denison, educationist, b. near East Hartford, Conn., 1791; d. New Haven, Conn., May 13, 1859. [1; 3; 4; 5; 6; 62]

Olmsted, Mrs. Elizabeth Martha, née Allen, poet, b. 1825; d. 1910.

Olmsted, Francis Allyn, physician, b. Chapel Hill, N.C., 1819; d. New Haven, Conn., July 19, 1844. [34]

Olmsted, Frederick Law, landscape architect, b. Hartford, Conn., 1822; d. Waverly, Mass., Aug. 28, 1903. [1; 3; 4; 5; 6; 7; 9; 10]

Olmsted, Miles Newell, clergyman, b. 1811; d. 1885.

Olmsted, Millicent, writer of books for children, b. Cleveland, O.; d. Cleveland, O., June 3, 1939. [7; 10]

Olney, Edward, mathematician, b. Moreau, N.Y., 1827; d. Ann Arbor, Mich., Jan. 16, 1887. [3b]

Olney, George Washington, journalist, b. Charleston, S.C., 1835; d. New York, N.Y., June 20, 1916. [10]

Olney, Jesse, educationist, b. Union, Conn., 1798; d. Stratford, Conn., July 30, 1872.

Olney, Oliver (pseud.). See Des Voignes, Jules Verne.

Olssen, William Whittingham, clergyman, b. New York, N.Y., 1827; d. June 21, 1917. [3; 4]

O'Mahoney, Mrs. Katharine A., née O'Keeffe, religious writer, d. 1918. [21]

O'Malley, Andrew, priest, d. Toronto, Ont., Nov. 8, 1921. [27]

O'Malley, Austin, oculist, b. Pittston, Pa., 1858; d. Philadelphia, Pa., Feb. 25, 1932. [7; 10; 11]

O'Malley, Frank Ward, journalist, b. Pittston, Pa., 1875; d. Tours, France, Oct. 19, 1932. [1; 7; 10; 11]

O'Meara, Henry, poet, b. 1850; d. ?

Omwake, George Leslie, educationist, b. Greencastle, Pa., 1871; d. Collegeville, Pa., Feb. 3, 1937. [11; 62]

Onderdonk, Henry, local historian, b. North Hempstead, N.Y., 1804; d. Jamaica, N.Y., June 22, 1886. [1; 3; 5; 6; 7; 9]

Onderdonk, Henry Ustick, bishop, b. New York, N.Y., 1789; d. Philadelphia, Pa., Dec. 6, 1858. [1; 3; 4; 5; 6; 7]

Onderdonk, James Lawrence, administrator, b. 1854; d. 1899.

O'Neall, John Belton, jurist, b. Bush River, S.C., 1793; d. near Newberry, S.C., Sept. 27, 1863. [1; 3; 4; 5; 34]

O'Neil, Charles Augustine, lawyer, d. Sept. 5, 1930.

O'Neil, George, poet and playwright, b. 1898; d. Hollywood, Calif., May 24, 1940.

O'Neil, James Louis, priest, b. Brooklyn, N.Y., Aug. 7, 1858; d. San Francisco, Calif.. Jan. 28, 1904. [21]

O'Neil, Jerold, educationist, b. New Britain, Conn., 1882; d. Stamford, Conn., Dec. 20, 1942.

O'Neill, Harold Edgar, journalist, b. 1888; d. New Brunswick, N.J., May 23, 1942.

O'Neill, Rose Cecil, artist and novelist, b. Wilkesbarre, Pa., 1874; d. Springfield, Mo., April 6, 1944. [7; 10]

Opdyke, George, merchant, b. Hunterdon county, N.J., 1805; d. New York, N.Y., June 12, 1880. [1; 3; 4; 6]

Opie, John Newton, soldier and lawyer, b. 1845; d. ? [34]

Opp, Julie. See Faversham, Mrs. Julie, née Opp.

Oppenheim, James, poet and novelist, b. St. Paul, Minn. 1882; d. New York, N.Y., Aug. 4, 1932. 1; 7; 10; 11; 70]

Oppenheim, Nathan, physician, b. Albany, N.Y., 1865; d. New York, N.Y., April 5, 1916. [10; 51]

Oppenheim, Samuel, lawyer, b. New York, N.Y., 1859; d. New York, N.Y., Aug. 11, 1928. [10]

Opper, Frederick Burr., artist, b. Madison, O., 1857; d. New Rochelle, N.Y., Aug. 27, 1937. [4; 10; 11]

Optic, Oliver (pseud.). See Adams, William Taylor.

Orbison, Thomas James, physician, b. India, 1866; d. Los Angeles, Calif., March 26, 1938. [10]

Orcutt, Hiram, educationist, b. Acworth, N.H., 1815; d. Brookline, Mass., April 17, 1899. [1; 49]

Orcutt, Samuel, clergyman, b. Albany county, N.Y., 1824; d. Bridgeport, Conn., Jan. 14, 1893. [5]

Ord, George, naturalist, b. Philadelphia, Pa., 1871; d. Philadelphia, Pa., Jan. 24, 1866. [1; 3; 4; 5]

Ordronaux, John, lawyer and physician, b. New York, N.Y., 1830; d. Glen Head, Long Island, N.Y., Jan. 20, 1908. [1; 4; 10]

Ordway, Albert, soldier, b. Boston, Mass., 1843; d. New York, N.Y., Nov. 21, 1897. [3b].

O'Reilly, Augustine J., priest, fl. 1872-1908. [21]

O'Reilly, Bernard, bishop, b. Ireland, 1818; d. Mount St. Vincent, N.Y., May, 1907. [1; 3; 4; 6; 32]

O'Reilly, Edward S., soldier of fortune, b. Texas, 1880; d. Sunmount, N.Y., Dec. 8, 1946.

O'Reilly, Henry. See O'Rielly, Henry.

O'Reilly, John Boyle, journalist and poet, b. county Meath, Ireland, 1844; d. Hull, Mass., Aug. 10, 1890. [1; 2; 3; 4; 6; 7; 9; 71]

O'Reilly, Mary Boyle, journalist, b. Boston, Mass., 1873 d. Auburndale, Mass., Oct. 28, 1937. [10]

O'Reilly, Michael Francis. See Potamian, Brother.

O'Reilly, Miles (pseud.). See Halpine, Charles Grahame.

Orem, Preston Ware, musician, b. 1865; d. Philadelphia, Pa., May 26, 1938. [10; 20]

Organ, Mrs. Margaret, née Stephenson, physician, b. 1840; d. ?

O'Rielly, Henry, journalist, b. Ireland, 1806; d. Rochester, N.Y., Aug. 17, 1886. [1; 3]

Orleanian (pseud.). See Wharton, Edward Clifton.

Ormond, Alexander Thomas, philosopher, b. Punxsutawney, Pa., 1847; d. near Grove City, Pa., Dec. 18, 1915. [10; 70]

Ormond, Frederic (pseud.). See Dey, Frederick Van Rensselaer.

Ormsby, Robert McKinley, educationist, b. Corinth, Vt., 1814; d. Mount Vernon, N.Y., Feb. 20, 1881. [43]

Ormsby, Waterman Lilly, engraver, b. Hampton, Conn., 1809; d. Brooklyn, N.Y., Nov. 1, 1883. [1; 3; 5]

Orne, Caroline Frances, poet, b. Cambridge, Mass., 1818; d. Cambridge, Mass., Feb. 8, 1905. [4; 10]

Orne, Philip (pseud.). See Lowell, Francis Cabot.

Ornstein, Martha. See Bronfenbrenner, Mrs. Martha, née Ornstein.

Oronhyatekha, insurance executive, b. near Brantford, Ont., 1841; d. Savannah, Ga., March 3, 1907. [27]

O'Rourke, Charles Edward, engineer, b. New York, N.Y., 1896; d. Ithaca, N.Y., Jan. 10, 1946. [10]

Orr, Hector, physician, b. 1770; d. East Bridgewater, Mass., 1855. [6]

Orr, William, educationist, b. Philadelphia, Pa., 1860; d. Fairhaven, Mass., July 21, 1939. [7; 10; 11]

Orth, Samuel Peter, educationist, b. Capac, Mich., 1873; d. Nice, France, Feb. 26, 1922. [10]

Ortmann, Arnold Edward, naturalist, b. Magdeburg, Germany, 1863; d. Pittsburgh, Pa., Jan. 3, 1927. [10; 11]

Orton, Edward Francis Baxter, educationist, b. Deposit, N.Y., 1829; d. Columbus O., Oct. 16, 1899. [1; 3; 4]

Orton, James, educationist and explorer, b. Seneca Falls, N.Y., 1830; d. Lake Titicaca, Peru, Sept. 25, 1877. [1; 3; 4; 5; 6; 7]

Orton, Jason Rockwood, physician and poet, b. Hamilton, N.Y., 1806; d. Brooklyn, N.Y., Feb. 13, 1867. [3; 6; 7]

Orton, Samuel Torrey, psychiatrist, b. Columbus, O., 1879; d. Poughkeepsie, N.Y., Nov. 17, 1948. [10]

Orvis, Julia Swift, historian, b. Dixon, Ill., 1873; d. Boston, Mass., March 16, 1949. [58]

Orwig, Wilhelm W., clergyman, b. 1810; d. 1889.

Osander (pseud.). See Allen, Benjamin.

Osbon, Bradley Sillick, naval officer, b. Rye, N.Y., 1828; d. New York, N.Y., May 6, 1912. [7; 10]

Osborn, Albert Sherman, handwriting expert, b. Sharon, Mich., 1858; d. Montclair, N.J., Dec. 14, 1946. [10]

Osborn, Benjamin, clergyman, b. Litchfield, Conn., 1751; d. Wallingford, Vt., July 7, 1818. [43]

Osborn, Chase Salmon, publisher and politican, b. Huntington county, Ind., 1860; d. Poulan, Ga., April 11, 1949. [4; 10; 11]

Osborn, Edwin Faxon, clergyman, b. Climax, Mich., 1859; d. Kalamazoo, Mich., July 29, 1937. [10; 11]

Osborn, Elbert, clergyman, b. 1800; d. 1881.

Osborn, Frank Chittenden, civil engineer, b. Greenland, Mich. 1857; d. Cleveland, O., Jan. 31, 1922. [4; 10; 11]

Osborn, Henry Fairfield, palaeontologist, b. Fairfield, Conn., 1857; d. Garrison, N.Y., Nov. 6, 1935. [1a; 7; 10; 11]

Osborn, Henry Leslie, educationist, b. Newark, N.J., 1857; d. St. Paul, Minn., Jan. 3, 1940. [10]

Osborn, Henry Stafford, clergyman and educationist, b. Philadelphia, Pa., 1823; d. New York, N.Y., Feb. 2, 1894. [1; 3; 4; 5; 6]

Osborn, Laughton, poet and dramatist, b. New York, N.Y., 1809; d. New York, N.Y., Dec. 12, 1878. [1; 3; 7; 9; 71]

Osborn, Mrs. Lucretia Thatcher, née Perry, scientist's wife, b. about 1858; d. Aug. 26, 1930.

Osborn, Norris Galpin, journalist, b. New Haven, Conn., 1858; d. New Haven, Conn., May 6, 1932. [1; 7; 10; 62]

Osborn, Selleck, journalist and poet, b. Trumbull, Conn., 1783; d. Philadelphia, Pa., Oct. 1, 1826. [1; 3; 7; 9]

Osborne, Albert B., traveller, b. 1866; d. 1913.

Osborne, Charles Francis, architect, b. Burlington, N.J., 1855; d. Philadelphia, Pa., Dec. 23, 1914.

Osborne, Duffield, lawyer and novelist, b. Brooklyn, N.Y., 1858; d. New York, N.Y., Nov. 20, 1917. [7; 10]

Osborne, Edward William, bishop, b. Calcutta, India, 1845; d. San Diego, Calif., July 5, 1926. [4; 10]

Osborne, George Abbott, mathematician, b. Danvers, Mass., 1839; d. Boston, Mass., Nov. 12, 1927. [10; 13]

Osborne, Mrs. Marian, née Francis, poet, b. Montreal, Que., 1871; d. Ottawa, Ont., Sept. 5, 1931. [27]

Osborne, Samuel Duffield. See Osborne, Duffield.

Osborne, Thomas Burr, biochemist, b. New Haven, Conn., 1859; d. New Haven, Conn., Jan. 29, 1929. [1; 4; 10; 13; 62]

Osborne, Thomas Mott, penologist, b. Auburn, N.Y., 1859; d. Auburn, N.Y., Oct. 20, 1926. [1; 4; 10; 11]

Osborne, William Hamilton, lawyer and novelist, b. Newark, N.J., 1873; d. Newark, N.J., Dec. 25, 1942. [10]

Osbourne, Lloyd, novelist, b. San Francisco, Calif., 1868; d. Glendale, Calif., May 22, 1947. [4; 7; 9; 10; 35]

Osgood, Charles Stuart, local historian, b. 1839; d. 1897.

Osgood, Mrs. Frances Sargent, née Locke, poet, b. Boston, Mass., 1811; d. Hingham, Mass., May 12, 1850. [1; 3; 4; 5; 6; 7; 9; 71]

Osgood, Hamilton, physician, b. 1838; d. 1908. [6]

Osgood, Henry Osborne, music critic, b. Peabody, Mass., 1879; d. New York, N.Y., May 9, 1927. [10; 20]

Osgood, Herbert Levi, historian, b. Canton, Me., 1855; d. Brentwood, N.Y., Sept. 11, 1918. [1; 7; 10; 45]

Osgood, Mrs. Irene, née **De Bellot,** novelist, b. Virginia, 1875; d. Northampton, England, Dec. 12, 1922. [7; 10]

Osgood, Samuel, clergyman, b. Charlestown, Mass., 1812; d. New York, N.Y., April 14, 1880. [3; 4; 5; 6; 7]

Osgood, Wilfred Hudson, biologist, b. Rochester, N.H., 1875; d. Chicago, Ill., June 20, 1947. [10; 11; 13]

Osgoodby, William Wesley, teacher of stenography, b. 1839; d. 1916.

O'Shaughnessy, Mrs. Edith Louise, née **Coues,** miscellaneous writer, b. Columbia, S.C., 1870; d. New York, N.Y., Feb. 18, 1939. [7; 10; 11; 21; 22]

O'Shea, Michael Vincent, educationist, b. Le Roy, N.Y., 1866; d. Madison, Wis., Jan. 14, 1932. [1; 10]

O'Shea, William James, educationist, b. New York, N.Y., 1864; d. New York, N.Y., Jan. 16, 1939. [10]

Oskison, John Milton, novelist and historian, b. Vinita, Okla., 1874; d. Tulsa, Okla., Feb. 26, 1947. [7; 10; 75]

Osler, Sir William, Bart., physician, b. Bond Head, Ont., 1849; d. Oxford, England, Dec. 29, 1919. [1; 2; 4; 7; 27]

Osman, Eaton Goodell, historian, b. 1853; d. Pasadena, Calif., Oct. 15, 1929.

Osmond, Alfred, poet, b. 1861; d. Salt Lake City, Utah, April 1, 1938.

Osmond, Samuel McClurg, clergyman, b. 1825; d. 1907.

Osmun, Thomas Embley, elocutionist and drama critic, b. Montrose, O., 1828; d. New York, N.Y., Oct. 26, 1902. [3b; 4; 5; 10]

Ossoli, Marchioness. See Fuller, Sarah Margaret, Marchioness Ossoli.

Osterberg, Max, consulting engineer, b. Frankfort, Germany, 1869; d. New York, N.Y., 1905. [10]

Ostrander, Alson Bowles, soldier, b. 1849; d. Seattle, Wash., July 9, 1934.

Ostrander, Dempster, lawyer, b. Clay, N.Y., 1834; d. Chicago, Ill., 1907. [4; 10]

Ostrander, Fannie Eliza, writer of books for children, b. North Haven, Conn.; d. New Haven, Conn., May 4, 1921. [10; 11]

Ostrander, Isabel Egenton, novelist, b. New York, N.Y., 1885; d. Long Beach, Long Island, N.Y., April 26, 1924. [7; 10; 11]

Ostrander, Russell Cowles, jurist, b. Ypsilanti, Mich., 1851; d. Lansing, Mich., Sept. 11, 1919. [4; 10; 39]

Ostrolenk, Bernhard, economist, b. Warsaw, Poland, 1887; d. near Doylestown, Pa., Nov. 26, 1944. [10]

Ostrom, Henry, evangelist, b. Belleville, Ont., 1862; d. Greencastle, Ind., Dec. 20, 1941. [10]

Ostrom, Homer Irvin, physician, b. 1852; d. Boston, Mass., April 5, 1925. [4]

O'Sullivan, Dennis Ambrose, lawyer, b. Northumberland county, Ont., 1848; d Toronto, Ont., 1892. [27]

Oswald, Felix Leopold, naturalist, b. Namur, Belgium, 1845; d. Grand Rapids, Mich., 1906. [3; 10]

Oswald, John Clyde, publisher, b. Fort Recovery, O., 1872; d. New York, N.Y., June 22, 1938. [7; 10; 11]

Otero, Miguel Antonio, politician, b. St. Louis, Mo., 1859; d. Santa Fé, N.M., Aug. 7, 1944. [7; 10]

Otey, James Hervey, bishop, b. Bedford county, Va., 1800; d. Memphis, Tenn., April 23, 1863. [1; 3; 4; 5; 34]

Otheman, Edward, clergyman, fl. 1843-1845.

Otis, Alexander, lawyer and novelist, b. Charles River, Mass., 1867; d. New York, N.Y., Oct. 15, 1939.

Otis, Edward Osgood, physician, b. Rye, N.H., 1848; d. Exeter, N.H., May 28, 1933. [7; 10; 11]

Otis, Mrs. Eliza Henderson, née **Bordman,** novelist, b. Boston, Mass., 1796; d. Boston, Mass., Jan. 21, 1873. [3; 4]

Otis, Elwell Stephen, soldier, b. Frederick, Md., 1838; d. Rochester, N.Y., Oct. 21, 1909. [1; 3; 4; 5; 6]

Otis, Fessenden Nott, physician, b. Ballston Springs, N.Y., 1825; d. New Orleans, La., May 24, 1900. [1; 3; 4; 5; 6]

Otis, George Edmund, lawyer and poet, b. 1846; d. 1906.

Otis, Harrison Gray, politician, b. Boston, Mass., 1765; d. Boston, Mass., Oct. 28, 1848. [1; 3; 4; 5; 6; 7; 9]

Otis, Harrison Gray, soldier and journalist, b. Marietta, O., 1837; d. Hollywood, Calif., July 30, 1917. [1; 3; 7; 10]

Otis, Mrs. Harrison Gray. See Otis, Mrs. Eliza Henderson, née Bordman.

Otis, James, politician and publicist, b. West Barnstable, Mass., 1725; d. Andover, Mass., May 3, 1783. [1; 2; 3; 4; 5; 7; 9]

Otis, James (pseud.). See Kaler, James Otis.

Otis, Philo Adams, realtor, b. Berlin Heights, O., 1846; d. Chicago, Ill., Sept. 23, 1930. [10]

Otis, Raymond, novelist, b. Evanston, Ill., 1900; d. Santa Fé, N.M., July 13, 1938. [7; 62]

Otis, William Augustus, architect, b. Almond, N.Y., 1855; d. Winnetka, Ill., June 9, 1929. [10]

O'Toole, George Barry, priest and educationist, b. Toledo, O., 1886; d. Washington, D.C., March 26, 1944. [21; 22]

Ott, Isaac, physician, b. Northampton county, Pa., 1847; d. Philadelphia, Pa., Jan. 1, 1916. [1; 3; 4; 10]

Otten, Bernard John, priest, b. 1862; d. St. Louis, Mo., May 22, 1930. [21]

Otter, William, labourer, b. 1789; d. ?

Otter, Sir William Dillon, soldier, b. near Clinton, Ont., 1843; d. Toronto, Ont., May 6, 1929. [27]

Ottman, Ford Cyrinde, clergyman, b. Seward, N.Y., 1859; d. Dec. 15, 1929. [4; 10]

Ottolengui, Rodrigues, dentist and novelist, b. Charleston, S.C., 1861; d. New York, N.Y., July 11, 1937.

Otts, John Martin Philip, clergyman, b. Union, S.C., 1838; d. Knoxville, Tenn., 1901. [3; 6; 10; 34]

Ouimet, Adolphe, journalist, b. near Montreal, Lower Canada, 1840; d. Montreal, Que., March 13, 1910. [27]

Outcault, Richard Felton, cartoonist, b. Lancaster, O., 1863; d. Flushing, N.Y., Sept. 25, 1928. [1; 4; 7; 10]

Overall, John Wilford, journalist, b. Shenandoah Valley, Pa., 1823; d. New York, N.Y., May 20, 1899. [34]

Overman, Frederick, metallurgist, b. Germany, about 1803; d. Philadelphia, Pa., Jan. 7, 1852. [1; 3; 6]

Overs, Walter Henry, bishop, b. Harbury, England, 1870; d. Jamestown, N.Y., June 17, 1934. [10]

Overton, Grant Martin, journalist, literary critic, and novelist, b. Patchogue, N.Y., 1887; d. Patchogue, N.Y., July 4, 1930. [10]

Ovington, Irene Helen, nurse, b. New York, N.Y., 1836; d. Brooklyn, N.Y., 1905. [10]

Owen, Catherine (pseud.). See Nitsch, Mrs. Helen Alice, née Matthews.

Owen, Charles Hunter, lawyer, b. Hartford, Conn., 1838; d. Hartford, Conn., April 21, 1922. [62]

Owen, Egbert Americus, local historian, d. Hamilton, Ont., May 2, 1908. [27]

Owen, Epenetus, clergyman, b. 1815; d ?

Owen, Eric Trevor, educationist, b. England, 1882; d. Toronto, Ont., March 2, 1948- [30]

Owen, Frank Allen, chemist, b. 1854; d. 1921.

Owen, George Washington, novelist, d. 1916.

Owen, James J., miscellaneous writer, fl. 1881-1893.

Owen, John Jason, clergyman, b. Colebrook, Conn., 1803; d. New York, N.Y., April 18, 1869. [3; 4; 6]

Owen, Luella Agnes, geologist, d. St. Joseph, Mo., 1932. [13]

Owen, Mary Alicia, anthropologist, b. St. Joseph, Mo., 1858; d. St. Joseph, Mo., Jan. 5, 1935. [4; 7; 10]

Owen, Olin Marvin, clergyman, b. 1847; d. 1918.

Owen, Orville Ward, physician, b. Marine City, Mich., 1854; d. Detroit, Mich., Mar. 31, 1924. [39]

Owen, Richard, geologist, b. near New Lanark, Scotland, 1810; d. New Harmony, Ind., March 25, 1890. [3; 4; 5; 6]

Owen, Robert Dale, social reformer, b. Glasgow, Scotland, 1801; d. Lake George, N.Y., June 24, 1877. [1; 2; 3; 4; 5; 6; 7; 9]

Owen, Thomas McAdory, lawyer and archivist, b. Jonesboro, Ala., 1866; d. Montgomery, Ala., March 25, 1920. [1a; 4; 10; 34]

Owen, Tom (pseud.). See Thorpe, Thomas Bangs.

Owen, William Baxter, educationist, b. Wysox, Pa., 1843; d. Easton, Pa., Dec. 4, 1917. [4; 10]

Owen, William Otway, medical officer, b. Nollichucky River, Tenn., 1854; d. Washington, D.C., Dec. 25, 1924. [10]

Owens-Adair, Mrs. Bethenia Angelina. See Adair, Mrs. Bethenia Angelina, née Owens.

Owl, Eugene (pseud.). See Pilgrim, Thomas.

Owre, Alfred, educationist, b. Norway, 1870; d. New York, N.Y., Jan. 2, 1935. [1a; 10; 11]

Oxley, James Macdonald, writer of books for boys, b. Halifax, N.S., 1855; d. Toronto, Ont., Sept. 9, 1907. [27]

Oxtoby, Frederic Breading, educationist, b. Saginaw, Mich., 1881; d. Jacksonville, Ill., Oct. 19, 1941. [10]

Oyen, Henry, journalist and novelist, b. Norway, 1883; d. Forest Hills, Long Island, N.Y., Oct. 23, 1921. [10]

Oyster, John Houck, physician, b. 1849; d. ?

P

Pabodie, William Jewett, lawyer and poet, b. Providence, R.I., about 1815; d. 1870. [19]

Pabor, William Edgar, agriculturist, b. 1834; d. Denver, Colo., Aug. 29, 1911.

Pace, Homer St. Clair, educationist, b. Rehoboth, O., 1879; d. New York, N.Y., May 22, 1942. [10]

Pace, Roy Bennett, educationist, d. 1918. [51]

Pacifique Rév. Père, missionary, b. Poitiers, France, 1863; d. 1943. [11; 32]

Pack, Charles Lathrop, banker and economist, b. Lexington, Mich., 1857; d. New York, N.Y., June 14, 1937. [10]

Pack, Frederick James, geologist, b. Bountiful, Utah, 1875; d. Salt Lake City, Utah, Dec. 2, 1938. [10; 11; 13]

Packard, Alpheus Spring, clergyman, b. Chelmsford, Mass., 1798; d. Squirrel Island, Me., July 13, 1884. [7; 46]

Packard, Alpheus Spring, entomologist, b. Brunswick, Me., 1839; d. Providence, R.I., Feb. 14, 1905. [1; 2; 3; 4; 5; 6; 7; 10; 46]

Packard, Mrs. Clarissa (pseud.). See Gilman, Mrs. Caroline, née Howard.

Packard, Mrs. Elizabeth Parsons, née Ware, asylum inmate, b. 1816; d. 1895.

Packard, Frank Lucius, novelist, b. Montreal, Que., 1877; d. Lachine, Que., Feb. 17, 1942. [7; 10; 27]

Packard, Frederick Adolphus, clergyman, b. Marlboro, Mass., 1794; d. Philadelphia, Pa., Nov. 11, 1867. [1; 3; 6; 7]

Packard, Hannah James, poet, b. Duxbury, Mass., 1815; d. Aug. 10, 1831. [7; 10]

Packard, Jasper, politician, b. Austintown, O., 1832; d. Lafayette, Ind., Dec. 13, 1899. [3; 5]

Packard, John Hooker, surgeon, b. Philadelphia, Pa., 1832; d. Philadelphia, Pa., May 21, 1907. [1; 3; 4; 6; 10]

Packard, Joseph, clergyman, b. Wiscasset, Me., 1812; d. Seminary Hill, Va., May 3, 1902. [1; 3; 4; 5; 10]

Packard, Lewis Richard, educationist, b. Philadelphia, Pa., 1836; d. New Haven, Conn., Oct. 26, 1884. [3; 4]

Packard, Silas Sadler, pioneer in business education, b. Cummington, Mass., 1826; d. New York, N.Y., Oct. 27, 1898. [1; 3; 4]

Packard, Theophilus, clergyman, b. Shelburne, Mass., 1802; d. Manteno, Ill., Dec. 8, 1885. [45]

Packard, Winthrop, naturalist, b. Boston, Mass., 1862; d. Canton, Mass., April 2, 1943. [7; 10]

Paddack, William C., sailor, b. 1831; d. ?

Paddock, Buckley B., soldier and historian, b. Cleveland, O., 1844; d. Fort Worth, Tex., Jan. 9, 1922. [10]

Paddock, Mrs. Cornelia, novelist, fl. 1879-1881. [6]

Paddock, John Robert, educationist, b. Cheshire, Conn., 1851; d. East Orange, N.J., Oct. 23, 1920. [62]

Paddock, Miner Hamlin, educationist, b. Syracuse, N.Y., 1846; d. Providence, R.I., Sept. 30, 1928. [10]

Paddock, Zachariah, clergyman, b. 1798; d. 1879.

Padelford, Frank William, clergyman, b. Haverhill, Mass., 1872; d. Claremont, Calif., Feb. 18, 1944. [10]

Padelford, Frederick Morgan, educationist, b. Haverhill, Mass., 1875; d. Los Angeles, Calif., Dec. 3, 1942. [7; 10; 11]

Paetow, Louis John, historian, b. Milwaukee, Wis., 1880; d. Berkeley, Calif., Dec. 22, 1928. [4; 10]

Pagan, Oliver Elwood, b. Toledo, O., 1858; d. Washington, D.C., April 2, 1932. [10]

Page, Abraham (pseud.). See Holt, John Saunders.

Page, Charles Edward, physician, b. Norridgewock, Me., 1840; d. Melrose, Mass., Nov. 23, 1925. [4; 10]

Page, Charles Grafton, physicist, b. Salem, Mass., 1812; d. Washington, D.C., May 5, 1868. [1; 3; 4]

Page, Charles Whitney, physician, b. 1845; d. Feb. 16, 1932.

Page, Curtis Hidden, educationist, b. Greenwood, Me., 1870; d. Laconia, N.H., Dec. 12, 1946. [7; 10; 11]

Page, David Perkins, educationist, b. Epping, N.H., 1810; d. Albany, N.Y., Jan. 1, 1848. [1; 3; 7; 9]

Page, Edward Day, merchant, b. Haverhill, Mass., 1856; d. Oakland, N.J., Dec. 25, 1918. [10; 62]

Page, James Augustus, poet, b. 1821; d. 1880.

Page, James Madison, soldier, b. 1839; d. ? [34]

Page, James Morris, mathematician, b. Sylvania, Va., 1864; d. University, Va., March 18, 1936. [10]

Page, Logan Waller, engineer, b. Richmond, Va., 1870; d. Washington, D.C., Dec. 9, 1918. [10]

Page, Rhoda Ann, poet, b. Hackney, England, 1826; d. near Rice Lake, Ont., 1863. [27]

Page, Richard Channing Moore, physician, b. Turkey Hill, Va., 1841; d. New York, N.Y., June 19, 1898. [4; 5; 34]

Page, Rosewell, politician, b. 1858; d. near Richmond, Va., Jan. 1, 1939. [7; 34]

Page, Thomas Jefferson, naval officer and explorer, b. Matthews county, Va., 1808; d. Rome, Italy, Oct. 26, 1899. [1; 3; 4; 5; 6; 34]

Page, Thomas Nelson, novelist and short-story writer, b. Hanover county, Va., 1853, d. Hanover county, Va., Nov. 1, 1922. [1; 2; 4; 7; 9; 71; 72]

Pagé, Thomas Walker, economist, b. Cobham, Va., 1866; d. Charlottesville, Va., Jan. 13, 1937. [10]

Page, Victor Wilfred, mechanical engineer, b. 1885; d. Middleboro, Mass., April 2, 1947.

Page, Walter Gilman, artist, b. Boston, Mass., 1862; d. Nantucket, Mass., March 24, 1934. [10; 11]

Page, Walter Hines, journalist and diplomat, b. Cary, N.C., 1855; d. Pinehurst, N.C., Dec. 21, 1918. [1; 2; 4; 7; 10; 34]

Page, William Nelson, civil engineer, b. Campbell county, Va., 1854; d. Washington, D.C., March 7, 1932. [10]

Page, William Tyler, civil servant, b. Frederick, Md., 1868; d. Washington, D.C., Oct. 20, 1942. [10]

Paget, Mrs. Amelia M., anthropologist, b. Fort Simpson, N.W.T., 1867; d. July 10, 1922. [27]

Paget, Edward Clarence, bishop, b. Leicestershire, England, 1851; d. Calgary, Alta., March 26, 1927. [27]

Paget, R. L. (pseud.). See Knowles, Frederick Lawrence.

Pagnuelo, Siméon, jurist, b. Laprairie, Lower Canada, 1840; d. Montreal, Que., May 14, 1915. [27]

Pahlow, Mrs. Gertrude Curtis, née Brown, novelist, b. Reading, Mass., 1881; d. Columbus, O., Jan. 29, 1937. [7; 10; 11]

Paige, Elbridge Gerry, journalist, b. 1816; d. 1859.

Paige, James, lawyer and educationist, b. St. Louis, Mo., 1863; d. Minneapolis, Minn., Feb. 4, 1940. [70]

Paige, Lucius Robinson, clergyman, b. Hardwick, Mass., 1802; d. Cambridge, Mass., Sept. 2, 1896. [3b; 4]

Paine, Albert Bigelow, editor and littérateur, b. New Bedford, Mass., 1861; d. New Smyrna, Fla., April 9, 1937. [2; 4; 7; 10; 11; 15]

Paine, Albert Ware, lawyer, b. Winslow, Me., 1812; d. 1907. [38]

Paine, Halbert Eleazer, lawyer and politician, b. Chardon, O., 1824; d. Washington, D.C., Dec. 26, 1893. [1; 3; 4]

Paine, Harriet Eliza, educationist, b. Rehoboth, Mass., 1845; d. Groveland, Mass., 1910. [5; 10]

Paine, John Alsop, botanist, b. Newark, N.J., 1840; d. Tarrytown, N.Y., July 24, 1912. [1; 10]

Paine, John Knowles, musician, b. Portland, Me., 1839; d. Boston, Mass., April 25, 1906. [1; 3; 4; 5; 7; 10; 20]

Paine, Josiah, local historian, b. 1836; d. 1917.

Paine, Levi Leonard, clergyman and educationist, b. Holbrook, Mass., 1832; d. Bangor, Me., May 10, 1902. [3b; 62]

Paine, Martyn, physician, b. Williamstown, Vt., 1794; d. New York, N.Y., Nov. 10, 1877. [1; 3; 4; 6]

Paine, Nathaniel, banker, b. Worcester, Mass., 1832; d. Worcester, Mass., Jan. 14, 1917. [10]

Paine, Nathaniel Emmons, physician, b. New Hartford, N.Y., 1853; d. Newton, Mass., Nov. 30, 1948. [11]

Paine, Ralph Delahaye, journalist, historian, and novelist, b. Lemont, Ill., 1871; d. Concord, N.H., April 29, 1925. [1; 7; 10; 15; 62]

Paine, Robert, bishop, b. Person county, N.C., 1799; d. Aberdeen, Miss., Oct. 20, 1882. [1; 3; 4; 34]

Paine, Robert Treat, poet, b. Taunton, Mass., 1773; d. Boston, Mass., Nov. 13, 1811. [1; 3; 4; 7; 9]

Paine, Thomas, political reformer, b. Thetford, England, 1737; d. New York, N.Y., June 8, 1809. [1; 2; 3; 4; 5; 6; 7; 9]

Paine, Timothy Otis, clergyman, b. Winslow, Me., 1834; d. Boston, Mass., Dec. 6, 1895. [3]

Paine, William, physician, b. Chesterfield, Mass., 1821; d. ? [3]

Paine, Willis Seaver, banker, b. Rochester, N.Y., 1848; d. New York, N.Y., April 13, 1927. [10; 11]

Painter, Franklin Verzelius Newton, educationist, b. Hampshire county, Va., 1852; d. Marion, Va., Jan. 18, 1931. [10; 11; 34]

Pai Ta-Shun (pseud.). See Peterson, Frederick.

Palfrey, Francis Winthrop, lawyer, b. Boston, Mass., 1831; d. Cannes, France, Dec. 5, 1889. [3; 6]

Palfrey, John Gorham, clergyman and historian, b. Boston, Mass., 1796; d. Cambridge, Mass., April 26, 1881. [1; 3; 4; 5; 6; 7; 7]

Palfrey, Sara Hammond, poet and novelist, b. Boston, Mass., 1823; d. 1914. [3; 4; 10]

Palladino, Lawrence Benedict, missionary, b. Italy, 1837; d. Helena, Mont., Aug. 19, 1927. [1]

Pallen, Condé Benoist, editor and publicist, b. St. Louis, Mo., 1858; d. New York, N.Y., May 26, 1929. [1; 7; 10]

Palliser, George, architect, b. 1849; d. 1903.

Palm, Andrew J., publicist, b. 1847; d. Meadville, Pa., Jan. 5, 1934.

Palmer, Albert de Forest, physicist, b. Tewksbury, Mass., 1869; d. Pasadena, Calif., Jan. 13, 1940. [10; 13]

Palmer, Albert Gallatin, clergyman, b. North Stonington, Conn., 1813; d. June 30, 1891. [3]

Palmer, Mrs. Alice Elvira, née Freeman, educationist, b. Colesville, N.Y., 1855; d. Paris, France, Dec. 6, 1902. [1; 4; 7]

Palmer, Alonzo Benjamin, physician, b. Richfield, N.Y., 1815; d. Ann Arbor, Mich., Dec. 23, 1887. [1; 3; 6]

Palmer, Mrs. Anna, née **Campbell,** journalist, b. Elmira, N.Y., 1854; d. Elmira, N.Y., June 18, 1928. [4; 7; 10; 11]

Palmer, Archie Emerson, journalist, b. Winterton, N.Y., 1853; d. at sea, April 28, 1925. [10; 11]

Palmer, Asa C., clergyman, b. Gorham, Me.; d. ? [38]

Palmer, Benjamin Morgan, clergyman, b. Philadelphia, Pa., 1781; d. Charleston, S.C., Oct. 9, 1847. [3; 34]

Palmer, Benjamin Morgan, clergyman, b. Charleston, S.C., 1818; d. New Orleans, La., May 28, 1902. [1; 3; 4; 5; 6; 34]

Palmer, Charles Skeele, chemist, b. Danville, Ill., 1858; d. Pittsburgh, Pa., Dec. 1, 1939. [10; 11]

Palmer, Mrs. Clarissa Elizabeth, née **Skeele,** local historian, b. about 1830; d. 1911.

Palmer, Claude Irwin, mathematician, b. Barry county, Mich., 1871; d. Chicago, Ill., April 8, 1931. [10; 11]

Palmer, Daniel David, chiropractor, b. near Toronto, Ont., 1845; d. Los Angeles, Calif., Oct. 20, 1913. [1; 4]

Palmer, Edwin Franklin, soldier and lawyer, b. Waitsfield, Vt., 1836; d. Waterbury, Vt., Oct. 8, 1914. [43; 49]

Palmer, Elihu, religious writer, b. Canterbury, Conn., 1764; d. Philadelphia, Pa., April 7, 1806. [1; 3; 9]

Palmer, Mrs. Fanny, née **Purdy,** poet, b. New York, N.Y., 1839; d. 1923. [7; 35]

Palmer, Francis Bolles, clergyman and educationist, b. Parma, N.Y., 1834; d. Fredonia, N.Y., March 4, 1923. [67]

Palmer, Frederic, clergyman, b. Boston, Mass., 1848; d. Cambridge, Mass., July 4, 1932. [10; 11; 51]

Palmer, George Herbert, philosopher, b. Boston, Mass., 1842; d. Cambridge, Mass., May 7, 1933. [1; 4; 5; 7; 10; 51]

Palmer, Mrs. Henrietta, née **Lee,** miscellaneous writer, b. Baltimore, Md., 1834; d. 1908. [3; 10; 34]

Palmer, Henry Robinson, journalist, b. 1867; d. Stonington, Conn., March 7, 1943.

Palmer, Henry Wilbur, lawyer and politician, b. Clifford, Pa., 1839; d. Wilkesbarre, Pa., Feb. 15, 1913. [1; 4; 10]

Palmer, Horatio Richmond, musician, b. Sherburne, N.Y., 1834; d. Yonkers, N.Y., Nov. 15, 1907. [1; 3; 4; 7; 10; 20]

Palmer, Howard, mountaineer, b. Norwich, Conn., 1883 d. Westerly, R.I., Oct. 24, 1944. [7; 10; 11; 62]

Palmer, James Croxall, naval surgeon, b. Baltimore. Md., 1811; d. Washington, D.C., April 24, 1883. [1; 4; 5]

Palmer, Joel, pioneer, b. Upper Canada. 1810; d. Wayton, Ore., June 9, 1881. [1; 7; 9]

Palmer, John McAuley, politician, b. Scott county, Ky., 1817; d. Springfield, Ill., Sept. 25, 1900. [1; 3; 4; 5; 10]

Palmer, John Williamson, physician and littérateur, b. Baltimore, Md., 1825; d. Baltimore, Md., Feb. 26, 1906. [1; 3; 4; 5; 6; 7; 9; 10]

Palmer, Julius Auboineau, sailor and journalist, b. Boston, Mass., 1840; d. 1899. [10]

Palmer, Mrs. Lucia A., née **Chapman,** artist, b. Dryden, N.Y., d. ? [10]

Palmer, Lynde (pseud.). See Peebles, Mrs. Mary Louise, née Parmalee.

Palmer, Margaretta, educationist, b. Branford, Conn., 1862; d. New Haven, Conn., Jan. 30, 1924 .[62]

Palmer, Peter Sailly, lawyer, b. Hampton, N.Y., 1814; d. Plattsburg, N.Y., Aug. 15, 1890. [3b]

Palmer, Mrs. Phoebe, née **Worrell,** religious writer, b. 1807; d. New York, N.Y., Nov. 2, 1874. [3b; 6]

Palmer, Ray, clergyman and poet, b. Little Compton, R.I., 1808; d. Newark, N.J., March 29, 1887. [1; 2; 3; 4; 5; 6; 7; 9; 62]

Palmer, Reginald Heber, foundryman, b. 1853; d. April 3, 1930.

Palmer, Silas Wheelock. See Arvine, Kazlitt.

Palmer, Thomas H., printer, b. Kelso, Scotland, 1782; d. Pittsford, Vt., July 20, 1861. [43]

Palmer, Truman Garrett, statistician, b. West Walworth, N.Y., 1858; d. Washington, D.C., May 29, 1925. [4; 10]

Palmer, Walter Clark, physician, b. 1804; d. 1883.

Palmer, William Pitt., poet, b. Stockbridge, Mass., 1805; d. Brooklyn, N.Y., May 2, 1884. [3; 7]

Pammel, Louis Hermann, botanist, b. La Crosse, Wis., 1862; d. on a train between San Francisco, Calif., and Salt City, Utah, March 23, 1931. [1; 4; 10; 11; 13]

Pampalon, Pierre, priest, b. Lévis, Que., 1861; d. Montreal, Que., Jan. 22, 1921. [27]

Panbourne, Oliver (pseud.). See Rockey, Howard.

Pancoast, Henry Khunrath, physician, b. Philadelphia, Pa., 1875; d. Merion, Pa., May 20, 1939. [10]

Pancoast, Henry Spackman, educationist, b. Germantown, Pa., 1858; d. Philadelphia, Pa., March 25, 1928. [7; 10; 11]

Pancoast, Joseph, surgeon, b. near Burlington, N.J., 1805; d. Philadelphia, Pa., March 7, 1882. [1; 3; 4; 5]

Pancoast, Seth, physician, b. Darby, Pa., 1823; d. Philadelphia, Pa., Dec. 16, 1889. [1; 3; 5; 6]

Pangborn, Frederic Werden, journalist, b. St. Albans, Vt., 1855; d. New York, N.Y., Dec. 31, 1934. [7; 10; 62]

Pangborn, Joseph Gladding, railway official, b. Albany, N.Y., 1844; d. Baltimore, Md., Aug. 15, 1914. [4]

Panin, Ivan Nikolayevitsh, Biblical scholar, b. Russia. 1855; d. near Aldershot, Ont., Oct. 30, 1942. [51]

Panneton, Joseph Elie, priest, b. Three Rivers, Lower Canada, 1835; d. Montreal, Que., Dec. 1, 1910. [27]

Pansy (pseud.). See Alden, Mrs. Isabella, née Macdonald.

Pâquet, Benjamin, priest and educationist, b. St. Nicolas, Lower Canada, 1832; d. Quebec, Que., Feb. 25, 1900. [27]

Pâquet, Etienne Théodore, local historian, b. St. Nicolas, Que., 1850; d. Quebec, Que., May 23, 1916. [27]

Pâquet, Louis Adolphe, priest and educationist, b. St. Nicolas, Que., 1859; d. Quebec, Que., Feb. 24, 1942. [27]

Paquin, Elzéar, physician, b. 1850; d. Montreal, Que., Jan. 16, 1947.

Paquin, Julien, priest, b. St. André, Que., 1858; d. Wikwemikong, Manitoulin Island, Ont., May 11, 1938. [27]

Paradis, J. Gaudiose, physician, b. 1860; d. Quebec, Que., Dec. 1, 1924. [27]

Paradis, Louis Laurent, priest, b. Quebec, Que., 1859; d. Quebec, Que., May 26, 1938. [27]

Paradis, Odilon, priest, b. Quebec, Lower Canada, 1829; d. Quebec, Que., March 1, 1889. [27]

Paradise, Frank Ilsley, clergyman, b. Boston, Mass., 1859; d. Vevey, Switzerland, Feb. 24, 1926. [10; 62]

Paradise, Nathaniel Burton, educationist, b. New Orleans, La., 1895; d. New Haven, Conn., April 24, 1942. [62]

Pardee, Richard Gay, horticulturist, b. Sharon, N.Y., 1811; d. New York, N.Y., Feb. 4, 1869. [3b]

Pardoe, Hiles C., clergyman, b. Lewisburg, Pa., 1839; d. Altoona, Pa., Sept. 14, 1919.

Parent, Amand, clergyman, b. Quebec, Lower Canada, 1818; d. Waterloo, Que., Feb. 18, 1907. [27]

Paret, William, bishop, b. New York, N.Y,. 1826; d. Baltimore, Md., Jan. 18, 1911. [4; 10]

Paris, Firmin (pseud.). See Hudon, Maxime.

Parish, Elijah, clergyman, b. Lebanon, Conn., 1762; d. Byfield, Mass., Oct. 15, 1825. [1; 3; 4; 6]

Parish, John Carl, historian, b. Des Moines, Ia., 1881; d. Los Angeles, Calif., Jan. 13, 1939. [10]

Parish, Julia Royce, novelist, b. Moravia, N.Y., 1844; d. 1918. [39]

Parish, Leonard Woods, educationist, b. 1850; d. 1910. [37]

Park, Charles Carroll, novelist, b. Allegheny City, Pa., 1860; d. Santa Barbara, Calif., Aug. 14, 1931. [35]

Park, Edwards Amasa, clergyman, b. Providence, R.I., 1808; d. Andover, Mass., June 4, 1900. [1; 3; 4; 5; 6; 9; 10]

Park, Robert Ezra, sociologist, b. Luzerne county, Pa., 1864; d. Nashville, Tenn., Feb. 7, 1944. [10; 11]

Park, Roswell, educationist, b. Lebanon, Conn., 1807; d. Chicago, Ill., July 16, 1869. [1; 3; 4; 5; 6; 7]

Park, Roswell, surgeon, b. Pomfret, Conn., 1852; d. Buffalo, N.Y., Feb. 15, 1914. [1; 4; 7; 10]

Park, William Hallock, bacteriologist, b. New York, N.Y., 1863; d. New York, N.Y., April 6, 1939. [10; 11]

Parke, John, soldier and poet, b. Dover, Del., 1754; d. near Dover, Del., Dec. 11, 1789. [1; 3; 4; 7; 9]

Parke, John Grubb, soldier, b. near Coatesville, Pa., 1827; d. Washington, D.C., Dec. 16, 1900. [1; 3; 4; 6; 10]

Parke, Joseph Richardson, physician, b. 1854; d. Philadelphia, Pa., March 8, 1938.

Parke, Uriah, mathematician, fl. 1839-1849.

Parker, Alvin Pierson, missionary, b. near Austin, Tex., 1850; d. Oakland, Calif., Sept. 10, 1924. [1]

Parker, Amasa Junius, lawyer, b. Delhi, N.Y., 1843; d. Albany, N.Y., May 2, 1938. [4; 10]

Parker, Amos Andrew, lawyer and politician, b. Fitzwilliam, N.H., 1791; d. Fitzwilliam, N.H., May 12, 1893. [59]

Parker, Austin, journalist and aviator, b. 1893; d. Los Angeles, Calif., March 20, 1938.

Parker, Benjamin Strattan, poet, b. 1833; d. New Castle, Ind., 1911.

Parker, Carleton Hubbell, economist, b. Red Bluff, Calif., 1878; d. Seattle, Wash., March 17, 1918. [1]

Parker, Edward Frost, physician, b. Charleston, S.C., 1867; d. Charleston, S.C., March 28, 1938. [10; 11; 34]

Parker, Edward Griffin, lawyer, b. Boston, Mass., 1825; d. New York, N.Y., March 30, 1868. [3; 62]

Parker, Edwin Pond, clergyman, b. Castine, Me., 1836; d. Hartford, Conn., May 28, 1920. [1; 10]

Parker, Fitzgerald Sale, clergyman, b. Caddo parish, La., 1863; d. Nashville, Tenn., 1937. [11]

Parker, Foxhall Alexander, naval officer, b. New York, N.Y., 1821; d. Annapolis, Md., June 10, 1879. [1; 3; 4; 6]

Parker, Francis Jewett, miscellaneous writer, b. 1825; d. 1909.

Parker, Francis Wayland, educationist, b. Bedford, N.H., 1837; d. Chicago, Ill., March 2, 1902. [1; 3; 5; 7; 10]

Parker, George Frederick, journalist, b. Lafayette, Ind., 1847; d. New York, N.Y., May 31, 1928. [10; 11]

Parker, Sir Gilbert, Bart. See Parker, Sir Horatio Gilbert, Bart.

Parker, Mrs. Helen, née Fitch, miscellaneous writer, b. Auburn, N.Y., 1827; d. Amherst, Mass., Dec. 4, 1874. [3; 6; 7]

Parker, Henry Taylor, journalist, b. Boston, Mass., 1867; d. Boston, Mass., March 30, 1934. [1a; 7; 10; 20]

Parker, Henry Webster, clergyman, b. Danby, N.Y., 1824; d. Flushing, N.Y., Nov. 21, 1903. [3; 37]

Parker, Sir Horatio Gilbert, Bart, novelist, b. Camden East, Ont., 1862; d. London, England, Sept. 6, 1932. [27]

Parker, Horatio William, musician, b. Auburndale, Mass., 1863; d. Cedarhurst, N.Y., Dec. 18, 1919. [1; 4; 5; 7; 10; 20]

Parker, James, naval officer, b. 1832; d. ?
Parker, James, soldier, b. Newark, N.J.,
1854; d. New York, N.Y., June 2, 1934.
[10]
Parker, James Cutler Dunn, musician, b.
Boston, Mass., 1828; d. Brookline, Mass.,
Nov. 27, 1916. [1; 5; 10; 20]
Parker, Mrs. Jane, née Marsh, novelist,
b. Milan, N.Y., 1836; d. Los Angeles,
Calif., March 13, 1913. [1; 4; 5; 6; 7; 9; 10]
Parker, Joel, jurist, b. Jaffrey, N.H., 1795;
d. Cambridge, Mass., Aug. 17, 1875. [1;
3; 4; 5; 6; 7]
Parker, Joel, clergyman, b. Bethel, Vt.,
1799; d. New York, N.Y., May 2, 1873.
[1; 3; 4; 5; 6]
Parker, Johns Dempster, clergyman, b.
Homer, N.Y., 1831; d. San Francisco, Cal.,
March 8, 1909. [10]
Parker, Leonard Fletcher, educationist, b.
Arcade, N.Y., 1825; d. 1911. [10; 37]
Parker, Lottie Blair, novelist and play-
wright, b. Oswego, N.Y., 1859; d. Great
Neck, Long Island, N.Y., Jan. 5, 1937. [4;
7; 10]
Parker, Mrs. Mary Moncure, née Payn-
ter, actress and playwright, b. Missouri,
1862; d. Cleveland, O., April 13, 1941. [11]
Parker, Orson, clergyman, b. 1800; d.
1876.
Parker, Mrs. Permelia Jane, née Marsh.
See Parker, Mrs. Jane. née Marsh.
Parker, Peter, medical missionary, b.
Framingham, Mass., 1804; d. Washington,
D.C., Jan. 10, 1888. [3; 4; 62]
Parker, Richard Green, educationist, b.
Boston, Mass., 1799; d. Boston, Mass., Sept.
26, 1869. [1; 3; 6; 7]
Parker, Mrs. Rosa, née Abbott, writer
of books for young people, fl. 1868-1871.
Parker, Samuel, clergyman, b. Ashfield,
Mass., 1879; d. Ithaca, N.Y., March 24,
1866. [1; 3; 4; 9]
Parker, Samuel Chester, educationist, b.
Cincinnati, O., 1880; d. Chicago, Ill., July
21, 1924. [1; 10]
Parker, Theodore, clergyman, b. Lexing-
ton, Mass., 1810; d. Florence, Italy, May
10, 1860. [1; 2; 3; 4; 5; 6; 7; 8; 9]
Parker, Thomas, jurist and local historian,
b. 1783 d. 1860. [38]
Parker, Willard, surgeon, b. Hillsborough,
N.H., 1800; d. New York, N.Y., April 25,
1884. [1; 3; 4; 5]
Parker, William Belmont, editor and
literary adviser, b. Hasbury, England, 1871;
d. Boston, Mass., Oct. 6, 1934. [7; 10]
Parker, William Frederick, lawyer, b.
Halifax, N.S., 1860; d. Wolfville, N.S.,
March 10, 1918. [27]
Parker, William Harwar, naval officer, b.
New York, N.Y., 1826; d. Washington,
D.C., Dec. 30, 1896. [1; 3; 7; 34]
Parker, William Ruston Percvial, lawyer,
b. Brantford, Ont., 1872; d. Toronto, Ont.,
April 21, 1936. [27]
Parker, William Thornton, physician, b.
1849; d. Northampton, Mass., 1925.

Parkhurst, Charles Henry, clergyman, b.
Framingham, Mass., 1842; d. Atlantic City,
N.J., Sept. 8, 1933. [1; 2; 3; 4; 5; 7; 10]
Parkhurst, Howard Elmore, musician, b.
Ashland, Mass., 1848; d. Lavallette, N.J.,
Aug. 18, 1916. [10; 20]
Parkhurst, John Adelbert, astronomer, b.
Dixon, Ill., 1861; d. Williams Bay, Wis.,
March 1, 1925. [1; 4; 10]
Parkin, Sir George Robert, educationist,
b. Salisbury, N.B., 1846; d. London, Eng-
land, June 25, 1922. [27]
Parkins, Almon Ernest, geographer, b.
Marysville, Mich., 1879; d. Nashville, Tenn.,
Jan. 3, 1940. [10; 11]
Parkinson, Daniel Baldwin, educationist,
b. Madison county, Ill., 1845; d. Carbon-
dale, Ill., Oct. 8, 1923. [4; 10]
Parkinson, Mrs. Sarah Woods, blind his-
torian, d. Carlisle, Pa., Aug. 15, 1933.
Parkinson, William, clergyman, b. Fred-
erick county, Md., 1774; d. New York, N.Y.,
March 10, 1848. [3]
Parkman, Francis, clergyman, b. Boston,
Mass., 1788; d. Boston, Mass., Nov. 12,
1852. [3; 6]
Parkman, Francis, historian, b. Boston,
Mass., 1823; d. Boston, Mass., Nov. 8,
1893. [1; 2; 3; 4; 5; 6; 7; 8; 9; 71; 72]
Parks, James Lewis, lawyer, b. Middle-
town, Conn., 1886; d. Columbia, Mo.,
March 6, 1934. [10]
Parks, Leighton, clergyman, b. New York,
N.Y., 1852; d. London, England, March 21,
1938. [5; 7; 10; 11]
Parks, William Arthur, geologist, b. Ham-
ilton, Ont., 1868; d. Toronto, Ont., Oct.
3, 1936. [27]
Parkyns, Mansfield, traveller, b. 1823; d.
1894.
Parlette, Ralph Albert, lecturer and pub-
lisher, b. near Delaware, O., 1870; d. Chic-
ago, Ill., Nov. 19, 1930. [10; 11]
Parley, Peter (pseud.). See Goodrich,
Samuel Griswold.
Parlin, Frank Edson, educationist, b.
Leeds, Me., 1860; d. Hampstead, N.H.,
March 28, 1939. [10]
Parloa, Maria, home economist, b. 1843;
d. Bethel, Conn., Aug. 21, 1909. [10]
Parmele, Mrs. Mary, née Platt, historian,
b. Albany, N.Y., 1843; d. New York, N.Y.,
May 26, 1911. [10]
Parmelee, George William, educationist,
b. Waterloo, Que., 1860; d. Quebec, Que.,
Sept. 9, 1941. [27]
Parmelee, Moses Payson, missionary, b.
Westford, Vt., 1834; d. 1902. [43]
Parmly, Eleazar, dentist and poet, b.
Braintree, Vt., 1797; d. New York, N.Y.,
Dec. 13, 1874. [1]
Parmly, Levi Spear, dentist, b. 1790; d.
1859.
Parr, Samuel Wilson, chemist, b. Gran-
ville, Ill., 1857; d. Urbana, Ill., May 16,
1931. [10; 11]
Parrington, Vernon Lewis, educationist,
b. Aurora, Ill., 1871; d. Winchcomb, Eng-
land, June 16, 1929. [1; 7; 10]

Parrish, Edward, pharmacist, b. Philadelphia, Pa., 1822; d. Fort Sill, Indian Territory, Sept. 9, 1872. [1; 3; 5; 6]

Parrish, Emma Kenyon, poet, b. Calhoun county, Mich., 1849; d. ? [11]

Parrish, Joseph, physician, b. Philadelphia, Pa., 1779; d. Philadelphia, Pa., March 18, 1840. [1; 3; 4; 5]

Parrish, Joseph, physician, b. Philadelphia, Pa., 1818; d. Burlington, N.J., Jan. 15, 1891. [3b; 4]

Parrish, Morris Longstreth, bibliographer, b. Philadelphia, Pa., 1867; d. Pine Valley, N.J., July 8, 1944.

Parrish, Randall, journalist and novelist, b. Henry county Ill., 1858; d. Kewanee, Ill., Aug. 9, 1923. [7; 10]

Parrish, Rob Roy McGregor, poet, b. Ohio, 1846; d. Schulavista, Calif., March 11, 1924. [41]

Parrish, Samuel Longstreth, lawyer and art patron, b. 1849; d. New York, N.Y., April 22, 1932.

Parry, David Maclean, manufacturer, b. near Pittsburgh, Pa., 1852; d. Indianapolis, Ind., May 12, 1915. [4; 10]

Parry, Edwin Satterthwaite, advertising executive, b. Beverly, N.J., 1879; d. Riverton, N.J., Dec. 9, 1936. [45]

Parry, John Stubbs, obstetrician, b. Lancaster county, Pa., 1843; d. Jacksonville, Fla., March 11, 1876. [1]

Parsons, Albert Richard, anarchist, b. Montgomery, Ala., 1848; d. Chicago, Ill., Sept. 14, 1887. [1]

Parsons, Albert Ross, musician, b. Sandusky, O., 1847; d. Mount Kisco, N.Y., June 14, 1933. [1; 4; 5; 7; 10; 20]

Parsons, Charles Grandison, physician, b. 1807; d. 1864.

Parsons, Edward Smith, educationist, b. Brooklyn, N.Y., 1863; d. Cambridge, Mass., April 22, 1943. [10; 11]

Parsons, Mrs. Elsie Worthington, née Clews, anthropologist, b. 1875; d. New York, N.Y., Dec. 19, 1941. [7; 10]

Parsons, Eugene, editor, b. Henderson, N.Y., 1855; d. Denver, Colo., June 22, 1933. [7; 10; 11]

Parsons, Floyd William, editor and engineer, b. Keyser, W. Va., 1880; d. New York, N.Y., Aug. 6, 1941. [10; 11]

Parsons, Francis, lawyer and banker, b. Hartford, Conn., 1871; d. Hartford, Conn., Dec. 30, 1937. [62]

Parsons, Frank, politicial scientist, b. Mount Holly, N.J., 1854; d. Boston, Mass., Sept. 26, 1908. [1; 4; 5; 10]

Parsons, George Frederic, journalist, b. Brighton, England, 1840; d. New York, N.Y., July 10, 1893. [3b; 4; 7]

Parsons, Harry de Berkeley, consulting engineer, b. New York, N.Y., 1862; d. New York, N.Y., Jan. 26, 1935. [10; 11]

Parsons, James, lawyer and educationist, b. 1834; d. 1900.

Parsons, James Challis, clergyman, b. Gloucester, Mass., 1833; d. West Bridgewater, Mass., June 30, 1897. [45]

Parsons, James Russell, educationist, b. Hoosick Falls, N.Y., 1861; d. Mexico, Dec. 5, 1905. [10]

Parsons, John Usher, educationist, b. 1761; d. 1838.

Parsons, Jonathan, clergyman, b. Springfield, Mass., 1705; d. Newburyport, Mass., July 19, 1776. [3; 62]

Parsons, Julia Stoddard, social historian, b. 1855; d. Santa Barbara, Calif., March 7, 1946.

Parsons, Reuben, priest, b. 1851; d. 1906. [21]

Parsons, Samuel Bowne, horticulturist, b. Flushing, N.Y., 1819; d. Flushing, N.Y., Jan. 4, 1906. [1]

Parsons, Samuel Bowne, landscape architect, b. Bedford, Mass., 1844; d. New York, N.Y., Feb. 3, 1923. [4; 5; 10; 62]

Parsons, Theophilus, jurist, b. Byfield, Mass., 1750; d. Boston, Mass., Oct. 30, 1813. [1; 3]

Parsons, Theophilus, lawyer and educationist, b. Newburyport, Mass., 1797; d. Cambridge, Mass., Jan. 26, 1882. [1; 3; 4; 5; 6]

Parsons, Thomas William, poet, b. Boston, Mass., 1819; d. Scituate, Mass., Sept. 3, 1892. [1; 3; 4; 6; 7; 9; 71]

Parsons, Usher, physician and surgeon, b. Alfred, Me., 1788; d. Providence, R.I., Dec. 19, 1868. [1; 3; 4; 6]

Parsons, William Barclay, engineer, b. New York, N.Y., 1859; d. New York, N.Y., May 9, 1932. [1; 4; 5; 10]

Parsons, William Leonard, clergyman, b. Fair Haven, Vt., 1811; d. Leroy, N.Y., Dec. 23, 1877.

Particular, Pertinax (pseud.). See Watkins, Tobias.

Partington, Frederick Eugene, educationist, b. 1854; d. Sept. 22, 1924.

Partington, Ruth (pseud.). See Shillaber, Benjamin Penhallow.

Parton, Ethel, writer of books for children, b. New York, N.Y., 1862; d. Newburyport, Mass., Feb. 27, 1944. [7]

Parton, James, biographer and littérateur, b. Canterbury, England, 1822; d. Newburyport, Mass., Oct. 17, 1891. [1; 2; 3; 4; 5; 6; 7; 8; 9; 71]

Parton, Mrs. Sara Payson, née Willis, essayist and novelist, b. Portland, Me., 1811; d. Brooklyn, N.Y., Oct. 10, 1872. [1; 2; 3; 4; 5; 6; 7; 9]

Partridge, Charles S., printer, b. 1856; d. Chicago, Ill., Nov. 8, 1916. [4]

Partridge, Edward Lasell, physician, b. Newton, Mass., 1853; d. May 2, 1930. [4; 10]

Partridge, William Ordway, sculptor, b. Paris, France, 1861; d. New York, N.Y., May 22, 1930. [1; 4; 5; 7; 10]

Partsch, Herman, physician, b. 1849; d. Berkeley, Calif., Sept. 6, 1934.

Parvin, Theodore Sutton, lawyer, educationist, and librarian, b. Cedarville, N.J., 1817; d. Cedar Rapids, Ia., June 28, 1901. [1; 3; 4; 37]

Parvin, Theophilus, obstetrician, b. Buenos Aires, Argentine, 1829; d. Philadelphia, Pa., Jan. 29, 1898. [1; 3; 4]

Pascalis-Ouvrière, Félix, physician, b. France, about 1750; d. New York, N.Y., July 29, 1833. [1; 3]

Paschal, George Washington, jurist, b. Skull Shoals, Ga., 1812; d. Washington, D.C., Feb. 16, 1878. [1; 3; 5]

Paschall, Edwin, journalist, b. Mecklenburgh county, Va., 1799; d. near Nolensville, Tenn., June 5, 1869. [3; 34]

Pasquin, Anthony (pseud.). See Williams, John (1761-1818).

Passano, Leonard Magruder, educationist, b. Baltimore, Md., 1866; d. Laguna Beach, Calif., Jan. 30, 1943.

Passmore, Joseph Clarkson, clergyman, b. Lancaster, Pa., 1818; d. Racine, Wis., Aug. 12, 1866. [3; 6]

Pastor, Tony (pseud.). See Halsey, Harlan Page.

Patch, John, poet, b. Ipswich, Mass., 1807; d. 1887. [19]

Patch, Mrs. Kate, née **Whiting,** writer of books for children, b. Elizabeth, N.J., 1870; d. 1909. [7; 10]

Patchin, Frank Glines, journalist and writer of books for boys, b. Wayland, N.Y., 1861; d. Jacksonville, Fla., March 22, 1925. [7; 10]

Paterson, Stephen Van Rensselaer, engineer and poet, b. Perth Amboy, N.J., 1817; d. 1872. [19]

Paterson, William, jurist and poet, b. Perth Amboy, N.J., 1817; d. Perth Amboy, N.J., Jan. 1, 1899. [3b; 4; 19]

Patillo, Henry, clergyman, b. Scotland, 1726; d. Dinwiddie county, Va., 1801. [1]

Patillo, Thomas Richard, sportsman, b. Liverpool, N.S., 1833; d. Halifax, N.S., July 8, 1910. [27]

Paton, David, archaeologist, d. Nov. 27, 1925.

Paton, James Morton, archaeologist, b. New York, N.Y., 1863; d. Boston, Mass., Nov. 23, 1944. [10]

Paton, Lewis Bayles, orientalist, b. New York, N.Y., 1864; d. Hartford, Conn., Jan. 24, 1932. [1; 10]

Paton, Stewart, psychiatrist, b. New York, N.Y., 1865; d. St. James, Long Island, N.Y., Jan. 7, 1942. [10; 13]

Paton, William Agnew, traveller, b. New York, N.Y., 1848; d. New York, N.Y., Dec. 11, 1918. [10]

Patrick, Alfred, civil servant, b. Kingston, Upper Canada, 1811; d. Niagara-on-the-Lake, Ont., July 18, 1892. [27]

Patrick, George Thomas White, psychologist, b. North Boscawen, N.H., 1857; d. Palo Alto, Calif., May 21, 1949. [10; 11; 62]

Patrick, James Newton, educationist, fl. 1891-1903.

Patrick, Mary Mills, educationist, b. Canterbury, N.H., 1850; d. Palo Alto, Calif., Feb. 25, 1940. [10; 11]

Pattee, William Samuel, physician and local historian, d. 1881.

Pattee, William Sullivan, lawyer, b. Jackson, Me., 1846; d. Minneapolis, Minn., April 4, 1911. [10; 46]

Patten, Claudius Buchanan, banker, b. 1835; d. 1886.

Patten, George Washington, soldier and poet, b. Newport, R.I., 1808; d. Houlton, Me., April 28, 1882. [3; 4; 7]

Patten, Gilbert, writer of books for boys, b. Corinna, Me., 1866; d. near San Diego, Calif., Jan. 16, 1945. [7; 10]

Patten, Simon Nelson, political economist, b. De Kalb county, Ill., 1852; d. Brown's-Mills-in-the-Pines, N.J., July 24, 1922. [1; 4; 7; 9; 10]

Patten, William, clergyman, b. Halifax, Mass., 1763; d. Hartford, Conn., March 9, 1839. [3; 5; 7]

Patten, William, biologist, b. Watertown, Mass., 1861; d. Hanover, N.H., Oct. 27, 1932. [1; 10; 13]

Pattengill, Henry Romaine, educationist, b. Mount Vision, N.Y., 1852; d. Lansing, Mich., Nov. 26, 1918. [39]

Patterson, Mrs. Antoinette de Coursey, poet, b. Philadelphia, Pa., 1866; d. April 30, 1925. [10]

Patterson, Burd Shippen, journalist, b. Pottsville, Pa., 1859; d. Pittsburgh, Pa., June 19, 1924. [10]

Patterson, Calvin, educationist, fl. 1873-1903.

Patterson, Charles Brodie, lecturer and editor, b. Nova Scotia, 1854; d. New York, N.Y., June 23, 1917. [10]

Patterson, Christopher Stuart, lawyer and banker, b. Philadelphia, Pa., 1842; d. Philadelphia, Pa., Nov. 6, 1924. [3; 4; 10]

Patterson, Edward Lloyd Stewart, banker, b. Strathroy, Ont., 1869; d. Toronto, Ont., Sept. 4, 1932. [27]

Patterson, Frank Allen, educationist, b. Allen's Hill, N.Y., 1878; d. Palisades Park, N.J., Aug. 4, 1944. [7; 10]

Patterson, George, clergyman and historian, b. Pictou, N.S., 1824; d. New Glasgow, N.S., Oct. 26, 1897. [27]

Patterson, George Washington, mathematician, b. Corning, N.Y., 1864; d. Ann Arbor, Mich., May 22, 1930. [10; 62]

Patterson, Henry Stuart, physician, b. 1815; d. Philadelphia, Pa., 1854. [6]

Patterson, Howard, naval officer, b. 1856; d. 1916.

Patterson, Mrs. Jane, née **Lippitt,** religious journalist, b. Otsego, N.Y., 1829; d. ? [10]

Patterson, Marjorie, actress and novelist, b. Baltimore, Md.; d. New York, N.Y., March 11, 1948. [7; 11]

Patterson, Raymond Albert, journalist, b. Chicago, Ill., 1856; d. 1909. [10]

Patterson, Robert, soldier, b. county Tyrone, Ireland, 1792; d. Philadelphia, Pa., Aug. 7, 1881. [1; 3; 4; 5; 6]

Patterson, Robert, clergyman, b. Ireland, 1829; d. Brooklyn, Calif., 1885. [3]

Patterson, Robert, mathematician, b. Ireland, 1843; d. Philadelphia, Pa., July 22, 1924. [1; 3; 4; 5; 6]

Patterson, Robert Mayne, clergyman, b. Philadelphia, Pa., 1832; d. Philadelphia, Pa., April 6, 1911. [1; 3; 4; 5; 6; 7; 10]

Patterson, Sterling, gardener, b. Nashville, Tenn., 1893; d. Indianapolis, Ind., Oct. 26, 1943. [62]

Patterson, Mrs. Virginia, née Sharpe, journalist, b. Delaware, O., 1841; d. May 30, 1913. [10]

Patterson, William Brown, sociologist, b. Brownsville, Pa., 1873; d. 1925. [10]

Patterson, William John, economist, b. Glasgow, Scotland, 1815; d. Montreal, Que., June 12, 1886. [27]

Patteson, Mrs. Susanna Louise, née Griesser, writer of books for children, b. Zürich, Switzerland, 1853; d. Gary, Ind., Jan. 11, 1922. [10; 11]

Pattie, James Ohio, explorer, b. Bracken county, Ky., about 1804; d. California, about 1850. [1; 3; 7; 9; 34; 74]

Pattison, Everett Wilson, lawyer, b. Waterville, Me., 1839; d. St. Louis, Mo., Nov. 14, 1919. [10]

Pattison, James William, painter, b. Boston, Mass., 1844; d. Asheville, N.C., May 29, 1915. [1; 10]

Pattison, Robert Everett, clergyman, b. Benson, Vt., 1800; d. St. Louis, Mo., Nov. 21, 1874. [3; 4; 5]

Pattison, Thomas Harwood, clergyman, b. Cornwall, England, 1838; d. Rochester, N.Y., Feb. 13, 1904. [10]

Patton, Mrs. Abby, née Hutchinson, singer, b. New Hampshire, 1829; d. New York, N.Y., Nov. 24, 1892. [3b; 4]

Patton, Carl Safford, clergyman, b. Greenville, Mich., 1866; d. Berkeley, Calif., Oct. 16, 1939. [10; 11]

Patton, Cornelius Howard, clergyman, b. Chicago, Ill., 1860; d. Waterville Valley, N.H., Aug. 17, 1939. [7; 10; 11]

Patton, Francis Landey, educationist, b. Warwick, Bermuda, 1843; d. Hamilton, Bermuda, Nov. 25, 1932. [1; 3; 4; 5; 6; 7; 10]

Patton, Harald Smith, economist, b. Minnedosa, Man., 1889; d. Washington, D.C., Sept. 1, 1945. [14]

Patton, Jacob Harris, educationist, b. Fayette county, Pa., 1812; d. New York, N.Y., Nov. 24, 1903. [3; 5; 7; 10]

Patton, John Shelton, librarian, b. near Staunton, Va., 1857; d. Charlottesville, Va., Oct. 1, 1932. [7; 10; 11; 34]

Patton, John Woodbridge, lawyer, b. 1843; d. Philadelphia, Pa., April 21, 1921. [4]

Patton, Joseph McIntyre, physician, b. Ralston, Pa., 1860; d. Chicago, Ill., April 16, 1930. [10]

Patton, Walter Melville, educationist, b. Montreal, Que., 1863; d. Montreal, Que., Aug. 5, 1928. [10; 11; 62]

Patton, William, clergyman, b. Philadelphia, Pa., 1798; d. New Haven, Conn., Sept. 9, 1879. [1; 3; 4; 5; 6; 7]

Patton, William Macfarland, civil engineer, b. Richmond, Va., 1845; d. 1905. [10]

Patton, William Weston, educationist, b. New York, N.Y., 1821; d. Westfield, N.J., Dec. 31, 1889. [3; 4; 5; 6]

Paul, Howard, actor, b. Philadelpha, Pa., 1835; d. England, 1905. [3; 7]

Paul, John (pseud.). See Webb, Charles Henry.

Paul, Joshua Hughes, educationist, b. Salt Lake City, Utah, 1863; d. March 6, 1939. [7; 10]

Paul, Mrs. Katherine S., née Green, bibliographer, d. 1927.

Paul, Mrs. Nanette, née Baker, lawyer, b. Delaware county, O., 1866; d. Washington, D.C., April 10, 1928. [10]

Paul, Willard Augustus, physician, b. Parkman, Me., 1855; d. Weston, Mass., Dec. 2, 1926. [10; 11]

Paulding, Frederick, actor and playwright, b. 1859; d. Rutherford, N.J., Sept. 7, 1937. [21]

Paulding, Hiram, naval officer, b. near Peekskill, N.Y., 1797; d. Huntington, N.Y., Oct. 20, 1878. [3; 4; 5; 6; 7]

Paulding, James Kirke, poet, novelist, and littérateur, b. Dutchess county, N.Y., 1779; d. Hyde Park, N.Y., April 6, 1860. [1; 2; 3; 4; 5; 6; 7; 8; 9; 71; 72]

Paulding, William Irving, biographer, b. about 1825; d. 1890.

Paull, Mrs. George A. See Paull, Mrs. Minnie E., née Kenney.

Paull, Mrs. Minnie E., née Kenney, writer of books for young people, b. 1859; d. 1895.

Paulton, Edward Antonio, playwright, b. Glasgow, Scotland, 1868; d. Hollywood, Calif., March 20, 1939.

Paxson, Frederic Logan, historian, b. Philadelphia, Pa., 1877; d. Berkeley, Calif., Oct. 24, 1948. [7; 10; 11]

Paxson, Ruth, missionary, b. 1876; d. Westfield, Mass., Oct. 1, 1949.

Paxson, William Alpha, lawyer, b. Green county, O., 1850; d. ? [10]

Paxton, Alexander Sterret, writer of reminiscences, b. Virginia, 1840; d. ? [34]

Paxton, John D., clergyman, b. 1784; d. Princeton, Ind., 1868.

Paxton, John Gallatin, lawyer, b. Lexington, Va., 1859; d. Independence, Mo., Sept. 24, 1928. [10; 34]

Paxton, Joseph Rupert, lawyer, b. Columbia county, Pa., 1827; d. Houston, Tex., Aug. 20, 1867. [3]

Paxton, Philip (pseud.). See Hammett, Samuel Adams.

Paxton, William McClung, poet and genealogist, b. Washington, Ky., 1819; d. Platte City, Mo., July 21, 1916. [4]

Paxton, William Miller, clergyman, b. Adams county, Pa., 1824; d. Princeton, N.J., Nov. 28, 1904. [4]

Payne, Abraham, lawyer, b. 1818; d. Providence, R.I., May 22, 1886. [47]

Payne, Arthur Frank, educationist, b. 1876; d. Andover, N.J., May 20, 1939.

Payne, Charles Henry, educationist, b. Taunton, Mass., 1830, d. Clifton Springs, May 5, 1899. [3b; 4; 10]

Payne, Daniel Alexander, bishop, b. Charleston, S.C., 1811; d. Xenia, O., Nov. 29, 1893. [1; 3; 4; 5; 6]

Payne, David Wells, foundryman, b. 1843; d. 1927.

Payne, Mrs. Elizabeth Stancy, née Magovern, novelist, b. Brooklyn, N.Y.; d. East Orange, N.J., Jan. 10, 1944. [7; 10; 11]

Payne, F. M. (pseud.). See Carey, Thomas Joseph.

Payne, Frank Owen, educationist, fl. 1898-1913.

Payne, George Henry, journalist and politician, b. New York, N.Y., 1876; d. Hollis, N.Y., March 3, 1945. [7; 10; 11]

Payne, Harold (pseud.). See Kelly, George C.,

Payne, Harry Thom, naturalist, b. 1844; d. ?

Payne, Henry Mace, mining engineer, b. New York, N.Y., 1868; d. Los Angeles, Calif., Jan. 7, 1943. [13]

Payne, John, bishop, b. Westmoreland county, Va., 1815; d. Westmoreland county, Va., Oct. 23, 1874. [3; 4]

Payne, John Howard, poet, actor, and dramatist, b. New York, N.Y., 1792; d. Tunis, North Africa, April 10, 1852. [1; 2; 3; 4; 5; 6; 7; 9; 71]

Payne, William Harold, educationist, b. Ontario county, N.Y., 1836; d. Detroit, Mich., June 18, 1907. [1; 3; 4; 6; 10]

Payne, William Morton, educationist and literary critic, b. Newburyport, Mass., 1858; d. Chicago, Ill., July 11, 1919. [1; 4; 5; 7; 10]

Paynter, Henry Martyn, clergyman, b. 1827; d. 1893.

Payson, Edward, clergyman, b. Rindge, N.H., 1783; d. Portland, Me., Oct. 22, 1827. [1; 3; 4; 6]

Payson, Edward, lawyer, b. Portland, Me., 1813; d. July 21, 1890. [4; 46]

Payson, Edward Payson, lawyer, b. Westbrook, Me., 1849; d. Boston, Mass., March 28, 1914. [46]

Payson, George, lawyer, b. Portland, Me., 1824; d. Chicago, Ill., Dec. 1, 1893. [46]

Payson, George Shipman, clergyman, b. Harpersfield, N.Y., 1845; d. New York, N.Y., Feb. 20, 1923. [10; 62]

Payson, Lieut. Howard (pseud.). See Goldfrap, John Henry.

Payson, Seth, clergyman, b. Walpole, Mass., 1758; d. Rindge, N.H., Feb. 26, 1820. [1; 3; 6]

Payson, William Farquhar, publisher and novelist, b. New York, N.Y., 1876; d. New York, N.Y., April 15, 1939. [5; 7; 10]

Peabody, Andrew Preston, clergymar and educationist, b. Beverly, Mass., 1811, d. Boston, Mass., March 10, 1893. [1; 3; 4; 5; 6; 7; 9]

Peabody, Cecil Hobart, engineer, b. Burlington, Vt., 1855; d. Boston, Mass., May 4, 1934. [1a; 10; 11]

Peabody, David, clergyman, b. Topsfield, Mass., 1805; d. Hanover, N.H., Oct. 17, 1839. [6; 49]

Peabody, Mrs. Elizabeth, née Palmer, educationist, b. 1778; d. 1853.

Peabody, Elizabeth Palmer, educationist, d. Billerica, Mass., 1804; d. Jamaica Plain, Mass., Jan. 3, 1894. [1; 2; 3; 4; 5; 6; 7; 9]

Peabody, Francis Greenwood, theologian, b. Boston, Mass., 1847; d. Cambridge, Mass., Dec. 28, 1936. [7; 10; 11; 51]

Peabody, Francis Weld, physician, b. Cambridge, Mass., 1881; d. Cambridge, Mass., Oct. 13, 1927. [10; 51]

Peabody, Frederick William, lawyer, b. Brooklyn, N.Y., 1862; d. New York, N.Y., Aug. 15, 1938. [10]

Peabody, James, railwayman, b. 1845; d. 1916.

Peabody, Josephine Preston, poet and playwright, b. Brooklyn, N.Y., 1874; d. Dec. 4, 1922. [1; 2; 4; 7; 10]

Peabody, Mrs. Mark (pseud.). See Victor, Mrs. Metta Victoria, née Fuller.

Peabody, Mary Tyler. See Mann, Mrs. Mary Tyler, née Peabody.

Peabody, Oliver William Bourn, biographer, b. Exeter, N.H., 1799; d. Burlington, Vt., July 5, 1848. [1; 3; 4; 7]

Peabody, Robert Swain, architect, b. New Bedford, Mass., 1845; d. Marblehead, Mass., Sept. 23, 1917. [1; 4; 10]

Peabody, Selim Hobart, educationist, b. Burlington, Vt., 1829; d. St. Louis, Mo., May 26, 1903. [1; 4; 5; 10]

Peabody, William Bourn Oliver, clergyman, b. Exeter, N.H., 1799; d. Springfield, Mass., May 28, 1847. [1; 3; 4; 6; 7]

Peacock, Thomas Brower, poet, b. Cambridge, O., 1852; d. ? [3; 6; 10; 34]

•Peacocke, James S., physician, fl. 1856-1890. [34]

Peale, Arthur Lincoln, local historian, b. Norwich, Conn., 1870; d. Norwich, Conn., March 1, 1947.

Peale, Charles Willson, naturalist and painter, b. Queen Anne county, Md.,'1741; d. Philadelphia, Pa., Feb. 22, 1827. [1; 2; 3; 4; 5; 6]

Peale, Rembrandt, painter, b. Bucks county, Pa., 1778; d. Philadelphia, Pa., Oct. 3, 1860. [1; 3; 4; 5; 6; 7]

Peale, Titian Ramsay, naturalist and painter, b. Philadelphia, Pa., 1799; d. Philadelphia, Pa., March 13, 1885. [1; 3; 4]

Pearce, Haywood Jefferson, educationist, b. Columbus, Ga., 1871; d. Gainesville, Ga., May 1, 1943. [10; 11]

Pearce, Liston Houston, clergyman, b. near Springfield, O., 1838; d. Clifton Springs, N.Y., Feb. 24, 1924. [10]

Pearce, Richard Mills, pathologist, b. Montreal, Que., 1874; d. New York, N.Y., Feb. 16, 1930. [1; 4; 10; 11]

Pearce, Stewart, local historian, b. 1820; d. 1882. [6]

Pearl, Bertha. See Moore, Mrs. Bertha, née Pearl.

Pearl, Cyril, clergyman, b. 1805; d. Freeport, Me., 1865. [38]

Pearl, Raymond, biologist, b. Farmington, N.H., 1879; d. Hershey, Pa., Nov. 17, 1940. [4; 7; 10; 11]

Pearman, Mrs. Mabel, née Capelle, poet, d. Berkeley, Calif., Dec. 18, 1940.

Pearse, John Barnard, metallurgist, b. Philadelphia, Pa., 1842; d. Georgeville, Que., Aug. 24, 1914. [1; 10; 62]

Pearson, Alfred John, educationist, b. Sweden, 1869; d. Des Moines, Ia., Aug. 10, 1939. [7; 10; 11]

Pearson, Charles H., clergyman, fl. 1869-1896.

Pearson, Mrs. Charles H. See Pearson, Mrs. Emily, née Clemens.

Pearson, Charles William, clergyman and educationist, b. Selby, England, 1846; d. Quincy, Ill., 1905. [10]

Pearson, Edmund Lester, librarian, b. Newburyport, Mass., 1880; d. New York, N.Y., Aug. 8, 1937. [7; 10; 11]

Pearson, Mrs. Emily, née Clemens, novelist, fl. 1853-1890.

Pearson, Francis Bail, educationist, b. Clark county, O., 1853; d. Columbus, O., Sept. 26, 1938. [10; 11]

Pearson, Francis Calhoun, clergyman and poet, fl. 1873-1887.

Pearson, Henry Clemens, editor, b. Le Roy, Minn., 1858; d. Pasadena, Calif., June 10, 1936. [10]

Pearson, Henry Greenleaf, educationist, b. Portland, Me., 1870; d. Newton Centre, Mass., Dec. 28, 1939. [7; 10; 11]

Pearson, Jonathan, educationist, b. Chichester, N.H., 1813; d. Schenectady, N.Y., June 20, 1887. [3; 5]

Pearson, Peter Henry, educationist, b. Sweden, 1864; d. McPherson, Kans., July 3, 1940. [7; 10; 11]

Pearson, Thomas Gilbert, ornithologist, b. Tuscola, Ill., 1873; d. New York, N.Y., Sept. 3, 1943. [7; 10; 11]

Pearson, William Henry, local historian, b. 1832; d. Toronto, Ont., April 5, 1920. [27]

Peary, Robert Edwin, Arctic explorer, b. Cresson, Pa., 1856; d. Washington, D.C., Feb. 20, 1920. [1; 2; 4; 5; 7; 10]

Pease, Aaron Gaylord, clergyman, b. Canaan, Conn., 1811; d. Rutland, Vt., Aug. 7, 1877. [43; 59]

Pease, Abraham Per Lee, physician, b. 1847; d. Massillon, O., June 26, 1926.

Pease, Charles Giffin, physician and reformer, b. New York, N.Y., 1854; d. New York, N.Y., Oct. 7, 1941. [10]

Pease, John Chauncey, geographer, b. 1782; d. 1859.

Pease, Theodore Calvin, historian, b. Cassopolis, Mich., 1887; d. Urbana, Ill., Aug. 11, 1948. [10; 11]

Pease, Theodore Claudius, clergyman, b. Poughkeepsie, N.Y., 1853; d. Andover, Mass., Nov. 19, 1893. [51]

Pease, Thomas Huntington, lawyer, b. Albany, N.Y., 1837; d. Chicago, Ill., Dec. 15, 1900.

Pease, Zephaniah Walter, journalist, b. New Bedford, Mass., 1861; d. June 24, 1933. [10]

Peaslee, Edmund Randolph, physician, b. Newton, N.H., 1814; d. New York, N.Y., Jan. 21, 1878. [1; 4]

Peaslee, John Bradley, educationist, b. Plaistow, N.H., 1842; d. 1912. [4; 5; 10]

Peattie, Mrs. Elia, née Wilkinson, journalist, b. Kalamazoo, Mich., 1862; d. Wallingford, Vt., July 12, 1935. [7; 10]

Peck, Annie Smith, mountaineer, b. Providence, R.I., 1850; d. New York, N.Y., July 18, 1935. [4; 7; 10; 11]

Peck, Charles Horton, botanist, b. Sand Lake, N.Y., 1833; d. 1917. [4; 10]

Peck, Edmund James, missionary, b. near Manchester, England, 1850; d. Toronto, Ont., Sept. 10, 1924. [27]

Peck, Ellen, novelist, fl. 1867-1875. [7]

Peck, Epaphroditus, jurist, b. Bristol, Conn., 1860; d. Bristol, Conn., Oct. 29, 1938. [7; 10; 11; 62]

Peck, George, clergyman, b. Middlefield, N.Y., 1797; d. Scranton, Pa., May 20, 1876. [1; 3; 5; 6; 7]

Peck, George Bacheler, physician and clergyman, b. Cincinnati, O., 1833; d. Boston, Mass., Jan. 22, 1906. [4; 63]

Peck, George Clarke, clergyman, b. Lowell, Mass., 1867; d. Baltimore, Md., Jan. 27, 1927. [7; 10; 11; 62]

Peck, George Washington, journalist, b. Rehoboth, Mass., 1817; d. Boston, Mass., June 6, 1859. [1; 3; 6; 7; 9]

Peck, George Wilbur, humorist, b. Henderson, N.Y., 1840; d. Milwaukee, Wis., April 16, 1916. [1; 2; 4; 5; 7; 9; 10]

Peck, Harry Thurston, educationist, b. Stamford, Conn., 1856; d. Stamford, Conn., March 23, 1914. [1; 4; 5; 7; 9; 10]

Peck, Hiram David, lawyer, b. Harrison county, Ky., 1844; d. Oct. 11, 1914. [10]

Peck, Ira Ballou, genealogist, b. Wrentham, Mass., 1805; d. 1888. [4]

Peck, Jesse Truesdell, bishop, b. Middlefield, N.Y., 1811; d. Syracuse, N.Y., May 17, 1883. [1; 3; 4; 5; 6]

Peck, John Lord, philosopher, fl. 1871-1889. [6]

Peck, John Mason, clergyman, b. Litchfield, Conn., 1789; d. Rock Spring, Ill., March 14, 1858. [1; 3; 5; 6; 7; 9]

Peck, Luther Wesley, clergyman and poet, b. Kingston, Pa., 1825; d. Scranton, Pa., March 31, 1900. [3; 5; 6]

Peck, Paul Frederick, educationist, b. Grinnell, Ia., 1873; d. Evanston, Ill., Nov. 20, 1925. [10]

Peck, Samuel Minturn, poet, b. Tuscaloosa, Ala., 1854; d. Tuscaloosa, Ala., May 3, 1938. [4; 7; 10; 11; 34]

Peck, Thomas Bellows, genealogist, b. 1842; d. Walpole, N.H., 1915. [51]

Peck, Thomas Ephraim, clergyman, b. Columbia, S.C., 1822; d. Richmond, Va., Oct. 2, 1893. [1]

Peck, William Farley, journalist, b. Rochester, N.Y., 1840; d. Rochester, N.Y., 1908. [3; 10]

Peck, William Guy, mathematician, b. Litchfield, Conn., 1820; d. Greenwich, Conn., Jan. 7, 1892. [3b; 4]

Peck, William Henry, novelist, b. Augusta, Ga., 1830; d. South Jacksonville, Fla., Feb. 4, 1892. [3; 4; 7; 34; 51]

Peckham, George Williams, entomologist, b. Albany, N.Y., 1845; d. Milwaukee, Wis., Jan. 10, 1914. [1; 4; 10]

Peckham, James, historian, b. 1828; d. 1869.

Peckham, Le Roy Bliss, lawyer and educationist, b. Windham, Conn., 1853; d. Yreka, Calif., Jan. 19, 1928. [62]

Peckham, Mrs. Mary Chace, née **Peck,** poet, b. Nantucket, Mass., 1839; d. Ann Arbor, Mich., March 20, 1892. [4]

Peckham, Stephen Farnum, chemist, b. near Providence, R.I., 1839; d. July 11, 1918. [1; 3; 4; 5; 10]

Pedder, James, agriculturist, b. Isle of Wight, England, 1775; d. near Boston, Mass., Aug. 27, 1859. [1; 3; 6; 7]

Peddle, John Bailey, educationist, b. Terre Haute, Ind., 1868; d. Terre Haute, Ind., April 6, 1933. [10]

Pederson, Mrs. **Rachel Lyman,** née **Field.** See Field, Rachel Lyman.

Pedley, Charles, clergyman, b. Hanley, England, 1821; d. Coldsprings, Ont., Feb. 17, 1872. [27]

Pedley, Hugh, clergyman, b. Durham, England, 1852; d. Knowlton, Que., July 26, 1923. [27]

Pedley, James Henry, soldier and lawyer, b. Vancouver, B.C., 1892; d. Toronto, Ont., Dec. 26, 1945. [27]

Pedley, James William, clergyman, b. Durham, England, 1856; d. Toronto, Ont., May 24, 1933. [27]

Peebles, James Martin, physician, b. Whitingham, Vt., 1822; d. Los Angeles, Calif., Feb. 15, 1922. [4; 10]

Peebles, Mrs. **Mary Louise,** née **Parmelee,** writer of books for boys and girls, b. near Troy, N.Y., 1833; d. Troy, N.Y., April 25, 1915. [3; 4; 7; 10]

Peek, Comer Leonard, novelist, b. Georgia, 1851; d. ? [34]

Peek, Frank William, electrical engineer, b. Calaveras county, Calif., 1881; d. Port Daniels, Que., July 26, 1933. [1; 10]

Peeke, George Hewson, clergyman, b. Rotterdam, N.Y., 1833; d. Sandusky, O., Dec. 26, 1915. [10]

Peeke, Mrs. **Margaret Bloodgood,** née **Peck,** teacher of occult philosophy, b. Mechanicsville, N.Y., 1838; d. Nov. 2, 1908. [10]

Peele, Robert, educationist, b. New York, N.Y., 1858; d. New York, N.Y., Dec. 8, 1942. [10; 11]

Peers, Benjamin Orrs, clergyman and educationist, b. Loudoun county, Va., 1800; d. Louisville, Ky., Aug. 20, 1842. [1; 3; 4; 5; 6; 34]

Peet, Dudley, physician, b. Hartford, Conn., 1830; d. New York, N.Y., April 18, 1862. [3]

Peet, Harvey Prindle, educationist, b. Bethlehem, Conn., 1794; d. New York, N.Y., Jan. 1, 1873. [1; 3; 4; 5]

Peet, Isaac Lewis, educationist, b. Hartford, Conn., 1824; d. New York, N.Y., Dec. 27, 1898. [1; 3; 4; 5; 62]

Peet, Louis Harman, journalist, b. Brooklyn, N.Y., 1863; d. Brooklyn, N.Y., Oct. 18, 1905. [10; 62]

Peet, Stephen, missionary, b. Sandgate, Va., 1795; d. Chicago, Ill., March 21, 1855. [43]

Peet, Stephen Denison, clergyman and archaeologist, b. Euclid, O., 1831; d. Salem, Mass., May 24, 1914. [1; 3; 5; 7; 10]

Peffer, William Alfred, journalist and politician, b. Cumberland county, Pa., 1831; d. Grenola, Kans., Oct. 6, 1912. [1; 4; 5; 7; 9; 10]

Peirce, Benjamin, librarian, b. Salem, Mass., 1778; d. Cambridge, Mass., July 26, 1831. [3; 7; 51]

Peirce, Benjamin, mathematician, b. Salem, Mass., 1809; d. Cambridge, Mass., Oct. 6, 1880. [1; 3; 4; 6; 9]

Peirce, Benjamin Osgood, physicist, b. Beverly, Mass., 1854; d. Cambridge, Mass., Jan. 14, 1914. [1; 3; 4; 5; 10; 51]

Peirce, Bradford Kinney, clergyman, b. Royalton, Vt., 1819; d. Newton Center, Mass., April 19, 1889. [1; 3; 5; 7]

Peirce, Charles Henry, physician, b. Salem, Mass., 1814; d. Cambridge, Mass., June 16, 1855. [3; 51]

Peirce, Charles Sanders, philosopher and scientist, b. Cambridge, Mass., 1839; d. Milford, Pa., April 19, 1914. [1; 2; 3; 4; 5; 7; 9; 10; 51]

Peirce, Ebenezer Weaver, historian and genealogist, b. Freetown, Mass., 1822; d. Freetown, Mass., 1903. [3; 4; 5]

Peirce, Hayford, archaeologist, b. Bangor, Me., 1883; d. Bangor, Me., March 4, 1946.

Peirce, James Mills, mathematician, b. Cambridge, Mass., 1834; d. Cambridge, Mass., March 21, 1906. [1; 3; 4; 5; 6; 10; 51]

Peirce, Mrs. **Melusina,** née **Fay,** reformer, b. Burlington, Vt., 1836; d. ? [10]

Peirce, Oliver Beale, educationist, b. Massachusetts, 1808; d. ? [6]

Peirce, Thomas, poet, b. Chester county, Pa., 1786; d. Cincinnati, O., 1850. [3; 7]

Peirce, Thomas May, educationist, b. Chester, Pa., 1837; d. 1896. [4]

Peirson, Mrs. **Lydia Jane,** née **Wheeler,** poet, b. Middletown, Conn., 1802; d. Adrian, Mich., 1862. [3]

Peissner, Elias, educationist, b. Bavaria, 1826; d. Chancellorsville, Va., May, 1863. [6]

Peixotto, Ernest Clifford, painter and illustrator, b. San Francisco, Calif., 1869; d. New York, N.Y., Dec. 6, 1940. [4; 7; 10; 11]

Peixotto, Jessica Blanche, economist, b. New York, N.Y., 1864; d. San Francisco, Calif., Oct. 19, 1941. [10; 11]

Pelican, A. (pseud.). See Gerard, James Watson.

Pell, Edward Leigh, clergyman, b. Raleigh, N.C., 1861; d. Greensboro, N.C., June 11, 1943. [10; 34]

Pell, Ferris, publicist, fl. 1806-1833.

Pell, George Pierce, lawyer, b. Raleigh, N.C., 1870; d. Raleigh, N.C., May 11, 1938. [10; 11]

Pell, Robert Conger, compiler, b. 1825; d. Interlachen, Switzerland, 1868. [6]

Pelland, Alfred, civil servant, b. Chambly, Que., 1873; d. Quebec, Que., Jan. 27, 1915. [27]

Pelland, Joseph Octave, lawyer, b. 1861; d. Montreal, Que., Sept. 16, 1924. [27]

Pelletier, Alexis, priest, b. St. Arsène de Témiscouata, Lower Canada, 1837; d. Montreal, Que., June 25, 1910. [27]

Pelletreau, William Smith, historian and genealogist, b. 1840; d. 1918.

Pellew, George, journalist, b. Isle of Wight, England, 1861; d. New York, N.Y., Feb. 19, 1892. [3b; 4; 51]

Peloubet, Francis Nathan, clergyman, b. New York, N.Y., 1831; d. Auburndale, March 29, 1920. [1; 3; 5; 10]

Peloubet, Seymour S., publisher, b. 1844; d. March 7, 1914.

Pelouze, Percy Starr, physician, b. Camden, N.J., 1876; d. Philadelphia, Pa., March 12, 1947.

Pelton, Frank Curtis, historian, b. 1874; d. Monticello, N.Y., June 7, 1943.

Pelzer, Louis, historian, b. Griswold, Ia., 1879; d. Iowa City, Ia., June 28, 1946. [7; 10; 11]

Pember, Mrs. Phoebe Yates, née Levy, nurse, b. 1823; d. 1913. [6]

Pemberton, Henry, chemist, b. Philadelphia, Pa., 1826; d. 1911. [10]

Pemberton, Henry, Shakespearian scholar, b. Philadelphia, Pa., 1855; d. Philadelphia, Pa., Oct. 25, 1913. [4]

Pemberton, Ralph, physician, b. Philadelphia, Pa., 1877; d. Philadelphia, Pa., June 17, 1949. [10]

Pénard, Jean Marie, missionary, b. Brittany, France, 1864; d. The Pas, Man., Nov. 13, 1939. [27]

Pendleton, Edmund, novelist, b. Cincinnati, O., 1845; d. Washington, D.C., March 14, 1910. [4; 10]

Pendleton, Edmund Monroe, physician and chemist, b. Eatonton, Ga., 1815; d. Atlanta, Ga., Jan. 26, 1884. [1; 3; 6]

Pendleton, James Madison, clergyman, b. Spotsylvania county, Pa., 1811; d. Bowling Green, Ky., March 4, 1891. [1; 3; 34]

Pendleton, Louis Beauregard, journalist and novelist, b. Waycross, Ga., 1861; d. Bryn Athyn, Pa., May 13, 1939. [4; 5; 7; 10; 11; 34]

Pendleton, William Nelson, clergyman, b. Richmond, Va., 1809; d. Lexington, Va., Jan. 15, 1883. [1; 3; 4; 5; 34]

Pène du Bois, Henri, bibliophile, b. 1858; d. 1906.

Penfield, Edward, painter and illustrator, b. Brooklyn, N.Y., 1866; d. Beacon, N.Y., Feb. 8, 1925. [1; 5; 7; 10]

Penfield, Frederic Courtland, journalist and diplomat, b. East Haddam, Conn., 1855; d. New York, N.Y., June 19, 1922. [1; 4; 5; 10]

Penfield, Samuel Lewis, mineralogist, b. Catskill, N.Y., 1856; d. South Woodstock, Conn., Aug. 12, 1906. [10; 62]

Penhallow, David Pearce, botanist, b. Kittery Point, Me., 1854; d. at sea, Oct. 20, 1910. [4; 10]

Penhallow, Samuel, jurist and historian, b. Cornwall, England, 1665; d. Portsmouth, N.H., Dec. 2, 1726. [1; 3; 4; 7; 9]

Penick, Charles Clifton, bishop, b. Charlotte county, Va., 1843; d. Baltimore, Md., April 13, 1914. [1; 3; 4; 10; 34]

Penn, Arthur (pseud.). See Matthews, James Brander.

Penn, Irvine Garland, educationist, b. New Glasgow, Va., 1867; d. Cincinnati, O., July 22, 1930. [10]

Penn, Mr. (pseud.). See Colwell, Stephen.

Penn, Rachel (pseud.). See Willard, Mrs. Caroline McCay, née White.

Pennell, Mrs. Elizabeth, née Robins, miscellaneous writer, b. Philadelphia, Pa., 1855; d. New York, N.Y., Feb. 8, 1836. [4; 7; 10]

Pennell, Joseph, etcher and illustrator, b. Philadelphia, Pa., 1857; d. Brooklyn, N.Y., April 23, 1926. [1; 4; 5; 7; 10]

Pennell, Robert Franklin, educationist, b. Freeport, Me., 1850; d. San Francisco, Calif., Oct. 22, 1905. [51]

Pennell, William Wesley, physician, b. 1853; d. Cincinnati, O., Sept. 30, 1930. [4]

Penniman, Alford Brown, clergyman, d. Calumet, Mich., Oct. 1, 1915.

Penniman, James Hosmer, educationist, b. Alexandria, Va., 1860; d. Philadelphia, Pa., April 6, 1931. [1; 4; 7; 10; 11; 62]

Penniman, Josiah Harmar, educationist, b. Concord, Mass., 1868; d. Philadelphia, Pa., April 10, 1941. [10]

Pennington, James W. C., preacher, b. Maryland, 1809; d. Jacksonville, Fla., Oct. 20, 1870. [1; 4; 7]

Pennington, John Rawson, surgeon, b. Corydon, Ind., 1858; d. Chicago, Ill., Feb. 3, 1927. [4; 10]

Pennington, Myles, railwayman, b. Lancashire, England, 1814; d. Toronto, Ont., 1898. [27]

Pennington, Patience (pseud.). See Pringle, Mrs. Elizabeth Waties, née Allston.

Pennington, William Sandford, jurist, b. Newark, N.J., 1757; d. Newark, N.J., Sept. 17, 1826. [1; 3; 4]

Pennot, Rev. Peter (pseud.). See Round, William Marshall Fitts.

Penny, Virginia, feminist, b. Louisville, Ky., 1826; d. ? [3; 34]

Pennybacker, Mrs. Anna J., née Hardwicke, educationist, b. Petersburg, Va., 1861; d. Austin, Tex., Feb. 4, 1938. [7; 10; 11]

Pennypacker, Isaac Rusling, poet and historian, b. Phoenixville, Pa., 1852; d. Ardmore, Pa., Sept. 23, 1935. [4; 7; 10]

Pennypacker, Samuel Whitaker, lawyer and politician, b. Phoenixville, Pa., 1843; d. near Schwenksville, Pa., Sept. 2, 1916. [1; 3; 4; 5; 6; 7; 10]

Penrose, Charles Bingham, physician, b. Philadelphia, Pa., 1862; d. on a raliway train near Washington, D.C., Feb. 27, 1925. [4; 10]

Penrose, Charles William, Mormon high priest, b. Camberwell, England, 1832; d. Salt Lake City, Utah, May 16, 1925. [10]

Penrose, Richard Alexander Fullerton, geologist, b. Philadelphia, Pa., 1863; d. Philadelphia, Pa., July 31, 1931. [4; 10]

Penrose, Stephen Beasley Linnard, educationist, b. Germantown, Pa., 1864; d. Walla Walla, Wash., April 29, 1947. [4; 10; 11; 62]

Pentecost, George Frederick, clergyman, b. Albion, Ill., 1842; d. New York, N.Y., Aug. 7, 1921. [1; 3; 4; 5; 6; 10]

Peple, Edward Henry, novelist and playwright, b. Richmond, Va., 1869; d. New York, N.Y., July 28, 1924. [7; 10]

Pepoon, Herman Silas, botanist, b. Warren, O., 1860; d. Chicago, Ill., Dec. 26, 1941.

Pepper, Charles Melville, journalist, b. Bloomfield, O., 1859; d. New York, N.Y., Nov. 4, 1930. [4; 10]

Pepper, George Whitfield, clergyman, b. Ireland, 1833; d. Cleveland, O., Aug. 6, 1899. [3b]

Pepper, John Robinson, merchant, b. Montgomery county, Va., 1850; d. Memphis, Tenn., March 31, 1931. [11]

Pepper, Mary Sifton, historian, d. 1908.

Pepper, William, physician, b. Philadelphia, Pa., 1843; d. Pleasanton, Calif., July 28, 1898. [1; 3; 5; 6]

Pepperbox, Peter (pseud.). See Fessenden, Thomas Green.

Pepperpod, Pip (pseud.). See Stoddard, Charles Warren.

Perce, Elbert, miscellaneous writer, b. New York, N.Y., 1831; d. Brooklyn, N.Y., Jan. 18, 1869. [3b; 6; 7]

Perch, Philemon (pseud.). See Johnston, Richard Malcolm.

Percival, Henry Robert, clergyman, b. Philadelphia, Pa., 1854; d. Devon, Pa., Sept. 22, 1903. 10]

Percival, James Gates, poet, b. Kensington, Conn., 1795; d. Hazel Green, Wis., May 2, 1856. [1; 3; 4; 5; 6; 7; 9; 71]

Percy, Florence (pseud.). See Akers, Mrs. Elizabeth, née Chase.

Percy, William Alexander, poet, b. Greenville, Miss., 1885; d. Greenville, Miss., Jan. 21, 1942. [7; 10; 11; 62]

Perdue, Virginia, novelist, b. 1899; d. Los Angeles, Calif., Feb. 24, 1945.

Periam, Jonathan, agriculturist, b. Newark, N.J., 1823; d. Chicago, Ill., Dec. 9, 1911. [1]

Perin, George Landor, clergyman, b. Jasper county, Ia., 1854; d. Brookline, Mass., Dec., 1921. [10]

Perkins, Alice Jane Gray, educationist, b. Schenectady, N.Y., 1866; d. New York, N.Y., Feb. 14, 1948.

Perkins, Mrs. Angie Villette, née **Warren,** educationist, b. Danielson, Conn., 1858; d. Knoxville, Tenn., Jan. 29, 1921. [4; 10; 11]

Perkins, Augustus Thorndike, art connoisseur, b. 1827; d. 1891. [51]

Perkins, Charles Callahan, art critic, b. Boston, Mass., March 1, 1823; d. near Windsor, Vt., Aug. 25, 1886. [1; 3; 4; 5; 6; 7]

Perkins, Mrs. Edna, née **Brush,** social worker, b. Cleveland, O., 1880; d. Cleveland, O., Oct. 11, 1930. [4]

Perkins, Frederic Beecher, librarian, b. Hartford, Conn., 1828; d. Morristown, N.J., Jan. 27, 1899. [1; 3; 5; 7; 9]

Perkins, George Gilpin, jurist, b. 1839; d. Lake Mohonk, N.Y., Aug. 17, 1933.

Perkins, George Henry, botanist and zoologist, b. Cambridge, Mass., 1844; d. Burlington, Vt., Sept. 12, 1933. [4; 10; 11; 43; 62]

Perkins, George Roberts, mathematician, b. Otsego county, N.Y., 1812; d. New Hartford, Conn., Aug. 22, 1876. [3; 6]

Perkins, James Breck, historian, b. St. Croix Falls, Wis., 1847; d. Rochester, N.Y., March 11, 1910. [1; 3; 4; 5; 7; 10]

Perkins, James Handasyd, social worker and historian, b. Boston, Mass., 1810; d. near Cincinnati, O., Dec. 14, 1849. [1; 3; 7]

Perkins, Jane Gray. See Perkins, Alice Jane Gray.

Perkins, Justin, missionary, b. Holyoke, Mass., 1805; d. Chicopee, Mass., Dec. 31, 1869. [1; 3; 4; 6]

Perkins, Mrs. Lucy, née **Fitch,** writer of books for children, b. Maples, Ind., 1865; d. Evanston, Ill., March 20, 1937. [7; 10; 11; 15]

Perkins, Maurice B., chemist, b. New London, Conn., 1836; d. Schenectady, N.Y., June 18, 1901. [3; 10]

Perkins, Samuel, lawyer, b. Lisbon, Conn., 1767; d. Windham, Conn., Sept., 1850. [3; 6]

Perkins, Samuel Elliott, jurist, b. Brattleboro, Vt., 1811; d. Indianapolis, Ind., Dec. 17, 1879. [1; 3; 5; 43]

Perkins, William Rufus, poet, b. Erie, Pa., 1847; d. Erie, Pa., Jan. 28, 1895. [3b]

Perley, Jeremiah, lawyer, b. 1784; d. 1834. [38]

Perley, Martin Van Buren, educationist and journalist, b. Ipswich, Mass., 1835; d. Danvers, Mass., Sept. 3, 1926. [4]

Perley, Moses Henry, naturalist, b. Maugerville, N.B., 1804; d. Forteau, Labrador, Aug. 17, 1862. [27]

Perley, Sidney, lawyer and antiquary, b. Boxford, Mass., 1858; d. Salem, Mass., June 9, 1928. [7; 10; 11]

Pernet, Emile, educationist, b. France; d. Philadelphia, Pa., Oct., 1916. [27]

Perrault, Joseph François, educationist, b. Quebec, Canada, 1753; d. Quebec, Que., April 4, 1844. [27]

Perrault, Joseph François, agriculturist, b. Quebec, Lower Canada, 1838; d. April 7, 1905. [27]

Perret, Frank Alvord, volcanologist, b. Hartford, Conn., 1867; d. New York, N.Y., Jan. 12, 1943. [4]

Perrin, Bernadotte, educationist, b. Goshen, Conn., 1847; d. Saratoga, N.Y., Aug. 31, 1920. [1; 4; 10; 62]

Perrin, Harold Livingston, lawyer, b. Wellesley, Mass., 1889; d. ? [11]

Perrin, Marshall Livingston, educationist, b. Wellesley Hills, Mass., 1855; d. Wellesley, Mass., Dec. 2, 1935. [10]

Perrin, Raymond St. James, manufacturer, b. New York, N.Y., 1849; d. New York, N.Y., Aug. 30, 1915. [10]

Perrin, William, clergyman and poet, b. Berlin, Vt., 1792; d. Berlin, Vt., Feb., 1824. [43]

Perrin, William Henry, journalist and historian, b. Breckenridge county, Ky., 1834; d. Parkland, Ky., Sept. 14, 1891. [34; 74]

Perrine, Frederic Auten Combs, electrical engineer, b. Manalapan, N.J., 1862; d. Plainfield, N.J., Oct. 21, 1908. [1; 4; 10]

Perry, Albert, poet, b. 1820; d. 1862.

Perry, Alice, novelist, b. 1854; d. 1883. [6]

Perry, Amos, historian, b. South Natick, Mass., 1812; d. New London, Conn., Aug. 10, 1899. [3b; 4]

Perry, Arthur Latham, economist, b. Lyme, N.H., 1830; d. Williamstown, Mass., July 9, 1905. [1; 3; 4; 7; 9; 10]

Perry, Bela C., dermatologist, fl. 1859-1865. [6]

Perry, Benjamin Franklin, politician, b. Pendleton district, S.C., 1805; d. Greenville, S.C., Dec. 3, 1886. [1; 3; 4; 5; 9; 34]

Perry, Calbraith Bourn, clergyman, b. 1846; d. Dec. 6, 1914. [47]

Perry, Carroll, clergyman. b. Williamstown, Mass., 1869; d. Los Angeles, Calif., Oct. 2, 1937. [7; 10; 62]

Perry, Charles Ebenezer, clergyman, b. Clarke township, Upper Canada, 1835; d. Toronto, Ont., Feb. 20, 1917. [27]

Perry, Clarence Arthur, educationist and social worker, b. Truxton, N.Y., 1872; d. New Rochelle, N.Y., Sept. 5, 1944. [10; 11]

Perry, David, soldier, b. Rehoboth, Mass., 1741; d. ? [43]

Perry, Edward Baxter, pianist, b. Haverhill, Mass., 1855; d. Camden, Me., June 13, 1924. [1; 10; 20]

Perry, Edward Delavan, educationist, b. Troy, N.Y., 1854; d. New York, N.Y., March 28, 1938. [10]

Perry, George Bone, novelist, b. 1845; d. 1906.

Perry, Jairus Ware, lawyer, b. 1821; d. 1877.

Perry, James De Wolf, clergyman, b. Bristol, R.I., 1839; d. Philadelphia, Pa., April 11, 1927. [10; 47]

Perry, James De Wolf, bishop, b. Germantown, Pa., 1871; d. Summerville, S.C., March 20, 1947. [10]

Perry, Joseph Franklin, physician, b. Biddeford, Me., 1846; d. 1909. [10]

Perry, Mrs. Lilla, née **Cabot,** painter and poet, b. Boston, Mass., 1848; d. Feb. 28, 1933. [7; 10]

Perry, Matthew Calbraith, naval officer, b. Newport, R.I., 1794; d. New York, N.Y., March 4, 1858. [1; 2; 3; 4; 5; 6]

Perry, Nelson William, engineer, b. 1853; d. 1900.

Perry, Nora, poet, journalist, and writer of books for girls; b. Webster, Mass., 1831; d. Dudley, Mass., May 13, 1896. [1; 3; 4; 5; 7; 9; 10]

Perry, Richard Ross, lawyer, b. Washington, D.C., 1846; d. Washington, D.C., July 17, 1915. [10]

Perry, Rufus Lewis, clergyman, b. Smith county, Tenn., 1834; d. Brooklyn, N.Y., June 18, 1895. [1; 3b]

Perry, Thomas Sergeant, educationist, b. Newport, R.I., 1845; d. Boston, Mass., May 7, 1928. [1; 3; 4; 5; 6; 9; 10]

Perry, Walter Scott, art director, b. Stoneham, Mass., 1855; d. Stoneham, Mass., Aug. 23, 1934. [1a; 10; 11]

Perry, William Armstrong, publicist, b. Williamsport, Pa., 1877; d. Westport, Conn., July 5, 1938. [11]

Perry, William B. (pseud.) See Brown, William Perry.

Perry, William Stevens, bishop, b. Providence, R.I., 1832; d. Dubuque, Ia., May 13, 1898. [1; 3; 4; 5; 6; 7; 51]

Pershing, Howell Terry, physician, b. Johnstown, Pa., 1858; d. Denver, Colo., Nov. 29, 1935. [10; 11]

Pershing, John Joseph, soldier, b. Linn county, Mo., 1860; d. Washington, D.C., July 15, 1949. [2; 4; 10; 12]

Persons, Warren Milton, economist, b. West De Pere, Wis., 1878; d. Cambridge, Mass., Oct. 11, 1937. [10]

Peter, Luther Crouse, ophthalmologist, b. St. Clairsville, Pa., 1869; d. Philadelphia, Pa., Nov. 12, 1942. [10; 11]

Peter, Philip Adam, clergyman, b. Germany, 1832; d. Verona, O., 1919. [10]

Peter, Robert, physician and chemist, b. Cornwall, England, 1805; d. Winton, Ky., April 26, 1894. [1; 3; 4; 34]

Peterkin, George William, bishop, b. Washington county, Md., 1841; d. Richmond, Va., Sept. 22, 1916. [1; 3; 4; 5; 10; 34]

Peters, Absalom, clergyman, b. Wentworth, N.H., 1793; d. New York, N.Y., May 18, 1869. [1; 3; 6]

Peters, Dewitt Clinton, physician, d. 1876. [6; 7]

Peters, Edward Dyer, mining engineer, b. Dorchester, Mass., 1849; d. Dorchester, Mass., Feb. 17, 1917. [1; 3; 10]

Peters, George Nathaniel Henry, clergyman, b. New Berlin, Pa., 1825; d. ? [3]

Peters, Harry Twyford, merchant, b. Greenwich, Conn., 1881; d. New York, N.Y., June 1, 1948. [7; 10]

Peters, Jeremy (pseud.). See Smith, Thomas Lacey.

Peters, John Charles, physician, b. New York, N.Y., 1819; d. Williston, Long Island, N.Y., Oct. 21, 1893. [1; 3; 6]

Peters, John Punnett, clergyman, b. New York, N.Y., 1852; d. New York, N.Y., Nov. 10, 1921. [1; 4; 7; 10; 62]

Peters, Mrs. Lulu, née Hunt, physician, b. Milford, Me., 1873; d. London, England, June 28, 1930. [10; 11]

Peters, Madison Clinton, clergyman, b. Lehigh county Pa., 1859; d. New York, N.Y., Oct. 12, 1918. [1; 4; 7; 10]

Peters, Richard, agriculturist and jurist, b. Philadelphia, Pa., 1744; d. Philadelphia, Pa., Aug. 22, 1828. [1; 3; 5; 9]

Peters, Richard, lawyer, b. Philadelphia, Pa., 1779; d. Philadelphia, Pa., May 2, 1848. [1; 3; 5]

Peters, Samuel Andrew, clergyman, b. Hebron, Conn., 1735; d. New York, N.Y., April 19, 1826. [1; 3; 4; 6; 7; 9; 62]

Peters, Thomas McClure, clergyman, d. Nov. 12, 1926.

Peters, Thomas Pollock, lawyer, b. Hartford, Conn., 1868; d. Brooklyn, N.Y., Dec. 3, 1936. [10]

Peters, William Cumming, musician, b. Devonshire, England, 1805; d. Cincinnati, O., April 20, 1866. [1; 3]

Peters, William Elisha, educationist, b. Bedford county, Va., 1829; d. Charlottesville, Va., 1906. [10]

Petersilea, Carlyle, spiritualist, b. Boston, Mass., 1844; d. 1903. [3]

Peterson, Arthur, poet, b. Philadelphia, Pa., 1851; d. Overbrook, Pa., Feb. 18, 1932. [3; 10]

Peterson, Arthur Everett, local historian, b. Weymouth, Mass., 1871; d. New York, N.Y., March 27, 1943.

Peterson, Charles Jacob, publisher and novelist, b. Philadelphia, Pa., 1819; d. Philadelphia, Pa., March 4, 1887. [1; 3; 5; 6; 7; 9]

Peterson, Edward, clergyman, b. Newport, R.I., 1796; d. Newport, R.I., 1855. [6]

Peterson, Frederick, physician and poet, b. Faribault, Minn., 1859; d. New York, N.Y., July 9, 1938. [4; 7; 10; 11]

Peterson, Mrs. Hannah Mary, née Bouvier, astronomer, b. Philadelphia, Pa., 1811; d. Long Branch, N.J., Sept. 4, 1870. [3]

Peterson, Henry, poet and novelist, b. Philadelphia, Pa., 1818; d. Germantown, Pa., Oct. 10, 1891. [1; 3; 5; 6; 7; 9]

Peterson, Joseph, psychologist, b. Huntsville, Utah, 1878; d. Nashville, Tenn., Sept. 20, 1935. [10; 11; 13]

Peterson, Otto Peter, educationist, b. Russia, 1879; d. New York, N.Y., Feb. 27, 1946.

Peterson, Robert Evans, lawyer and physician, b. Philadelphia, Pa., 1812; d. Asbury Park, N.J., Oct. 30, 1894. [3b; 4]

Peterson, Sir William, educationist, b. Edinburgh, Scotland, 1856; d. London, England, Jan. 4, 1921. [27]

Petitclair, Pierre, poet and dramatist, b. Quebec, Lower Canada, 1813; d. Pointe-au-Pot, Labrador, Aug. 15, 1860. [27]

Petrie, George Laurens, clergyman, b. Cheraw, S.C., 1840; d. Charlottesville, Va., March, 1931. [10]

Pettengill, Samuel Barrett, clergyman, b. Grafton, Vt., 1839; d. Saxton's River, Vt., Oct. 22, 1909. [43]

Pettibone, Chauncey John Vallette, biochemist, b. 1884; d. 1929. [13]

Pettigrew, James Johnston, lawyer and soldier, b. Tyrrell county, N.C., 1828; d. near Bunker Hill, Va., July 14, 1863. [1; 3; 4; 5; 34]

Pettigrew, Richard Franklin, politician, b. Ludlow, Vt., 1848; d. Sioux Falls, S.D., Oct. 5, 1926. [1; 4; 5 10]

Pettingell, John Hancock, clergyman, b. Manchester, Vt., 1815; d. New Haven, Conn., Feb. 27, 1887. [3b]

Pettit, Henry, civil engineer, b. Philadelphia, Pa., 1842; d. Island Heights, N.J., Aug. 11, 1921. [10]

Petty, Alonzo Ray, clergyman and poet, b. Santa Ana, Calif., 1887; d. Philadelphia, Pa., Oct. 25, 1932. [10]

Petty, Carl Wallace, clergyman, b. Topeka, Kans., 1884; d. Pittsburg, Pa., Sept. 9, 1932. [10]

Petty, Orlando Henderson, physician, b. Cadiz, O., 1874; d. Philadelpiha, Pa., June 2, 1932. [10]

Petty, Orville Anderson, clergyman, b. Cadiz, O., 1874; d. New Haven, Conn., Aug. 12, 1942. [10; 62]

Pew, William Andrews, soldier, b. 1858; d. Feb. 25, 1933.

Peyton, Jesse Enlows, publicist, b. Maysville, Ky., 1815; d. Haddonsfield, N.J., April 28, 1897. [3b; 34]

Peyton, John Howe, railway president, b. Howard county, Mo., 1864; d. Nashville, Tenn., Sept. 14, 1918. [10]

Peyton, John Lewis, miscellaneous writer, b. near Staunton, Va., 1824; d. near Staunton, Va., May 21, 1896. [1; 3; 4; 5; 6; 7; 34]

Pfanstiehl, Carl, engineer and inventor, b. Columbia, Mo., 1888; d. Chicago, Ill., March 1, 1942. [10]

Phaneuf, Elie, religious brother, b. near St. Hyacinthe, Que., 1875; d. Aug. 31, 1922. [27]

Phares, David Lewis, agriculturist, b. 1817; d. 1892.

Phelan, David Samuel, priest and journalist, b. Sydney, N.S., 1841; d. St. Louis, Mo., Sept. 21, 1915. [1; 21]

Phelan, James, historian, b. Aberdeen, Miss., 1856; d. Nassau, Bahamas, Jan. 30, 1891. [1; 3; 7]

Phelan, James Duval, politician, b. San Francisco, Calif., 1861; d. near San José, Calif., Aug. 7, 1930. [1; 4; 10]

Phelan, Michael, billiards-player, b. Ireland, 1816; d. New York, N.Y., Oct. 21, 1871. [3]

Phelon, William Arlie, journalist, b. 1871; d. Chicago, Ill., Aug. 19, 1925.

Phelps, Abner, physician, b. Belchertown, Mass., 1779; d. Boston, Mass., Feb. 24, 1873. [3]

Phelps, Mrs. Adaliza, née **Cutter,** poet, b. Jaffrey, N.H., 1823; d. June 3, 1852. [19]

Phelps, Mrs. Almira, née **Hart,** educationist, b. Berlin, Conn., 1793; d. Baltimore, Md., July 15, 1884. [1; 3; 4; 5; 6; 7]

Phelps, Amos Augustus, clergyman, b. Farmington, Conn., 1805; d. Roxbury, Mass., Sept. 12, 1847. [3; 4]

Phelps, Mrs. Anna, née **Olson,** poet, b. Peru, Ill., 1870; d. Berkeley, Calif., April 5, 1946.

Phelps, Austin, clergyman, b. West Brookfield, Mass., 1820; d. Bar Harbor, Me., Oct. 13, 1890. [4; 7]

Phelps, Charles, surgeon, b. Milford, Mass., 1834; d. New York, N.Y., Dec. 30, 1913. [10]

Phelps, Charles Abner, biographer, b. Boston, Mass., 1820; d. Boston, Mass., April 27, 1902. [69]

Phelps, Charles Edward, jurist, b. Guilford, Vt., 1833; d. Baltimore, Md., Dec. 27, 1908. [1; 4; 5; 10]

Phelps, Charles Edward Davis, novelist and agriculturist, b. Homer, N.Y., 1851; d. New Brunswick, N.J., May 5, 1934. [7; 10]

Phelps, Edward Bunnell, journalist, b. New Haven, Conn., 1863; d. New York, N.Y., July 24, 1915. [10; 62]

Phelps, Edward John, lawyer and diplomat, b. Middlebury, Vt., 1822; d. New Haven, Conn., March 9, 1900. [1; 3; 4; 5]

Phelps, Mrs. Elizabeth Steward, née **Natt,** novelist, d. Atlantic City, N.J., Feb. 11, 1920. [7]

Phelps, Elizabeth Stuart. See Ward, Mrs. Elizabeth Stuart, née Phelps.

Phelps, Mrs. Elizabeth, née **Stuart,** novelist, b. Andover, Mass., 1815; d. Boston, Mass., Nov. 30, 1852. [3; 4; 5; 7; 9]

Phelps, Guy Fitch, clergyman and novelist, b. Coyville, Kans., 1872; d. Salem, Ore., Dec. 15, 1933. [10; 11]

Phelps, Henry Pitt, journalist, b. 1844; d. ?

Phelps, John Wolcott, soldier, b. Guilford, Vt., 1813; d. Guilford, Vt., Feb. 2, 1885. [6; 7; 43]

Phelps, Myron Henry, lawyer, b. Lewiston, Ill., 1856; d. Bombay, India, Dec. 29, 1916. [62]

Phelps, Noah Amherst, local historian, b. 1788; d. 1872.

Phelps, Richard Harvey, local historian, fl. 1844-1876.

Phelps, Mrs. S. B. (pseud.). See Griswold, Mrs. Frances Irene, née Burge.

Phelps, Samuel Merrick, clergyman, b. Suffield, Conn., 1770; d. Bridgeport, Conn., Dec. 26, 1841. [62]

Phelps, Sylvanus Dryden, clergyman, b. Suffield, Conn., 1816; d. New Haven, Conn., Nov. 23, 1895. [3; 6]

Phelps, William Franklin, educationist, b. Auburn, N.Y., 1822; d. St. Paul, Minn., Aug. 15, 1907. [3; 4; 10; 70]

Phelps, William Lyon, educationist, b. New Haven, Conn., 1865; d. New Haven, Conn., Aug. 21, 1943. [2a; 7; 10; 12; 14]

Phelps, Willis Burton, clergyman, b. Syracuse, N.Y., 1836; d. Independence, Ia., Sept. 30, 1918.

Phifer, Charles Lincoln, journalist, b. Vandalia, Ill., 1860; d. Sept. 30, 1931.

Philbrick, Edward Southwick, engineer, b. Boston, Mass., 1827; d. 1889. [6]

Philbrick, John Dudley, educationist, b. Deerfield, N.H., 1818; d. Danvers, Mass., Feb. 2, 1896. [3; 4; 6]

Philipp, Emanuel Lorenz, politician, b. Sauk county, Wis., 1861; d. Milwaukee, Wis., June 15, 1925. [1; 4; 10]

Philips, Albert Edwin, novelist, b. 1845; d. ?

Philips, George Morris, educationist, b. Atglen, Pa., 1851; d. March 11, 1920. [5; 10]

Philips, Melville, journalist and novelist, fl. 1881-1900.

Philips, Samuel, clergyman, b. near Hagerstown, Md., 1823; d. 1892. [3; 34]

Philipson, David, rabbi, b. Wabash, Ind., 1862; d. Boston, Mass., June 29, 1949. [10; 11]

Phillippi. Joseph Martin, clergyman, b. Fulton county, Ill., 1869; d. Dayton, O., Sept. 27, 1926. [10]

Phillipps-Wolley, Sir Clive Oldnall Long, poet, b. Dorsetshire, England, 1854; d. Somenos, B.C., July 8, 1913. [27]

Phillips, Alexander Lacy, clergyman, b. Chapel Hill, N.C., 1859; d. Richmond, Va., May 2, 1915. [10]

Phillips, Andrew Wheeler, mathematician, b. Griswold, Conn., 1844; d. New Haven, Conn., Jan. 20, 1915. [10; 62]

Phillips, Arthur Edward, educationist, b. Sheerness-on-Sea, England, 1867; d. Port Washington, Wis., July 18, 1932. [4]

Phillips, Barnet, journalist, b. Philadelphia, Pa., 1828; d. Brooklyn, N.Y., April 8, 1905. [3; 10]

Phillips, Charles James, philatelist, b. Birmingham, England, 1863; d. New York, N.Y., June 2, 1940.

Phillips, Charles Joseph MacConaghy, educationist, b. New Richmond, Wis., 1880; d. Minneapolis, Minn., Dec. 29, 1933. [10; 21; 44]

Phillips, Daniel Lyon, local historian, b. 1852; d. Jewett City, Conn., March 27, 1940.

Phillips, Daniel T., clergyman, b. 1842; d. 1905.

Phillips, David Graham, novelist, b. Madison, Ind., 1867; d. New York, N.Y., Jan. 24, 1911. [1; 4; 7; 10; 72]

Phillips, Ethel Calvert, writer of books for children, b. Jersey City, N.J.; d. Nutley, N.J., Feb. 6, 1947. [7; 10; 11]

Phillips, Francis Clifford, chemist, b. Philadelphia, Pa., 1850; d. Ben Avon, Pa., Feb. 16, 1920. [4; 10]

Phillips, George Searle, journalist, b. Peterborough, England, 1816; d. Morristown, N.J., Jan. 14, 1889. [3b; 6]

Phillips, Henry, numismatist and translator, b. Philadelphia, Pa., 1838; d. Philadelphia, Pa., June 6, 1895. [1; 3; 6]

Phillips, Henry Wallace, novelist, b. New York, N.Y., 1869; d. New York, N.Y., May 24, 1930. [7; 10]

Phillips, John Arthur, journalist, b. Liverpool, England, 1842; d. Ottawa, Ont., Jan. 8, 1907. [27]

Phillips, John Burton, educationist, b. Holt, Mich., 1866; d. Bloomington, Ind., Oct. 9, 1923. [10]

Phillips, John Charles, naturalist and sportsman, b. Boston, Mass., 1876; d. Dover, N.H., Nov. 14, 1938. [7; 10]

Phillips, John Herbert, educationist, b. Covington, Ky., 1853; d. Birmingham, Ala., July 21, 1921. [10; 34]

Phillips, Ludern Merriss, physician, b. 1858; d. Penn Yan, N.Y., Nov. 10, 1902.

Phillips, Morris, journalist, b. London, England, 1834; d. Huntington, Long Island, N.Y., Aug. 30, 1904. [3; 4; 5; 10]

Phillips, Philip, lawyer, b. Charleston, S.C., 1807; d. Washington, D.C., Jan. 14, 1884. [4]

Phillips, Philip, singing evangelist, b. Cassadaga, N.Y., 1834; d. Delaware, O., June 25, 1895. [1; 3b; 4; 7]

Phillips, Philip Lee, librarian and cartographer, b. Washington, D.C., 1857; d. Washington, D.C., Jan. 4, 1924. [10]

Phillips, Richard Jones, physician, b. Chester county, Pa., 1861; d. Upper Darby, Pa., 1925. [10]

Phillips, Samuel, clergyman, b. near Hagerstown, Md., 1823; d. ? [34]

Phillips, Samuel G., clergyman, b. 1831; d. Brockville, Ont., March 3, 1892. [27]

Phillips, Samuel Louis, lawyer, b. 1838; d. Sept. 11, 1924.

Phillips, Thomas Wharton, philanthropist, b. Lawrence county, Pa., 1835; d. New Castle, Pa., July 21, 1912. [1; 10]

Phillips, Ulrich Bonnell, historian, b. La Grange, Ga., 1877; d. New Haven, Conn., Jan. 21, 1934. [1a; 7; 10; 11]

Phillips, Waldorf Henry, lawyer, b. New York, N.Y., 1853; d. Baltimore, Md., Oct. 2, 1915.

Phillips, Walter Polk, journalist, b. Grafton, Mass., 1846; d. Vineyard Haven, Mass., Jan. 31, 1920. [1; 4; 7]

Phillips, Walter Shelley, artist, b. 1867; d. Seattle, Wash., Sept. 1, 1940. [7]

Phillips, Wendell, orator and reformer, b. Boston, Mass., 1811; d. Boston, Mass., Feb. 2, 1884. [1; 2; 3; 4; 5; 6; 7; 9]

Phillips, Wendell Christopher, surgeon, b. Hammond, N.Y., 1857; d. New York, N.Y., Nov. 16, 1934. [10]

Phillips, Willard, lawyer, b. Bridgewater, Mass., 1784; d. Cambridge, Mass., Sept. 9, 1873. [1; 3; 4; 5; 6; 7]

Phillips, William, clergyman, b. Kentucky, 1797; d. 1836. [6]

Phillips, William Addison, soldier and politician, b. Paisley, Scotland, 1824; d. Fort Gibson, Indian Territories, Nov. 30, 1893. [1; 4; 5; 9]

Phillips, William Hallett, lawyer, b. 1853; d. 1897.

Phillips, William Hamilton, journalist, b. 1830; d. Aug. 26, 1916.

Phin, John, publisher, b. near Melrose, Scotland, 1830; d. Paterson, N.J., Dec. 29, 1913. [10]

Phipps, Isaac Newton, poet and novelist, b. 1850; d. ?

Phipps, William Henry, clergyman and poet, b. Shropshire, England, 1825; d. Miami, Fla., Nov. 28, 1903.

Phisterer, Frederick, soldier, b. Stuttgart, Germany, 1836; d. Albany, N.Y., July 13, 1909. [1; 4; 10]

Phoebus, William, clergyman, b. Somerset county, Md., 1754; d. New York, N.Y., Nov. 9, 1831. [3]

Phoenix, John (pseud.). See Derby, George Martin.

Phoenix, Stephen Whitney, genealogist, b. New York, N.Y., 1839; d. New York, N.Y., Nov. 3, 1881. [3; 5]

Phucher, Itothe (pseud.). See Chittenden, Hiram Martin.

Phyfe, William Henry Pinkney, compiler, b. New York, N.Y., 1855; d. New York, N.Y., March 7, 1915. [4; 7; 10]

Piatt, Donn., journalist, b. Cincinnati, O., 1819; d. near West Liberty, O., Nov. 12, 1891. [1; 3b; 4; 7]

Piatt, John James, poet and journalist, b. Milton, Ind., 1835; d. Cincinnati, O., Feb. 16, 1917. [1; 3; 4; 5; 6; 7; 9; 10]

Piatt, Mrs. Sarah Morgan, née **Bryan,** poet, b. Lexington, Ky., 1836; d. Caldwell, N.J., Dec. 22, 1919. [1; 3; 4; 5; 6; 7; 9; 10]

Picard, George Henry, novelist, b. Berea, O., 1850; d. New York, N.Y., Oct. 7, 1916. [7; 10]

Pick, Bernard, clergyman, b. Prussia, 1842; d. Newark, N.J., April 10, ·1917. [3; 4; 6; 10]

Pickard, Mrs. Florence née **Willingham,** artist, b. Smyrna, S.C., 1862; d. Tifton, Ga., Dec. 2, 1930. [10; 11]

Pickard, Josiah Little, educationist, b. Rowley, Mass., 1824; d. Cupertino, Calif., March 27, 1914. [4; 10; 37]

Pickard, Samuel Thomas, printer and biographer, b. Rowley, Mass., 1828; d. Amesbury, Mass., Feb. 12, 1915. [1; 5; 7; 10]

Pickard, William Lowndes, clergyman, b. Upson county, Ga., 1861; d. Albany, Ga., Sept. 4, 1935. [10; 11; 34]

Pickell, John, biographer, b. about 1802; d. 1865.

Pickering, Charles, physician and naturalist, b. Susquehanna county, Pa., 1805; d. Boston, Mass., March 17, 1878. [1; 3; 4; 5; 6]

Pickering, Edward Charles, astronomer, b. Boston, Mass., 1846; d. Boston, Mass., Feb. 3, 1919. [1; 3; 4; 5; 10]

Pickering, Henry, poet, b. Newburg, N.Y., 1781; d. New York, N.Y., May 8, 1831. [3; 6; 7; 71]

Pickering, Henry Goddard, lawyer, b. Boston, Mass., 1846; d. Boston, Mass., 1926. [51]

Pickering, John, lawyer and philologist, b. Salem, Mass., 1777; d. Boston, Mass., May 5, 1846. [1; 3; 4; 5; 6; 7; 9]

Pickering, Octavius, biographer, b. Wyoming, Pa., 1791; d. Boston, Mass., Oct. 29, 1868. [3]

Pickering, Timothy, soldier and politician, b. Salem, Mass., 1745; d. Salem, Mass., Jan. 29, 1829. [1; 3; 4; 5; 6; 7]

Pickering, William Henry, astronomer, b. Boston, Mass., 1858; d. Mandeville, Jamaica, Jan. 16, 1938. [3; 5; 10; 11]

Picket, Albert, educationist, b. 1771; d. Delaware, O., Aug. 3, 1850. [1]

Pickett, Albert James, historian, b. Anson county, N.C., 1810; d. Montgomery, Ala., Oct. 28, 1858. [1; 3; 4; 6; 7; 9; 34]

Pickett, James Chamberlayne, diplomat, b. Fauquier county, Va., 1793; d. Washington, D.C., July 10, 1872. [3; 4; 5]

Pickett, Mrs. La Salle, née **Corbell,** miscellaneous writer, b. Nansemond county, Va., 1848; d. Rockville, Md., March 22, 1931. [5; 10; 34]

Pickett, Leander Lycurgus, clergyman, b. Burnsville, Ky., 1859; d. May 8, 1928. [11; 34]

Pickett, Thomas Edward, physician, b. Mason county, Ky., 1841; d. Sept. 3, 1913. [10; 34]

Pickett, William Passmore, lawyer, b. 1855; d. New York, N.Y., Oct. 27, 1936.

Pickthall, Marjorie Lowry Christie, poet and novelist, b. near London, England, 1883; d. Vancouver, B.C., April 19, 1922. [27]

Picton, Thomas, soldier and journalist, b. New York, N.Y., 1822; d. New York, N.Y., Feb. 20, 1891. [1; 3; 4; 7; 9]

Pidge, John Bartholomew Gough, clergyman, b. Providence, R.I., 1844; d. Philadelphia, Pa., April 8, 1932. [4; 10]

Pidgeon, William, archaeologist, b. near James River, Va., 1796; d. Sept. 15, 1866.

Pidgin, Charles Felton, statistician and novelist, b. Roxbury, Mass., 1844; d. Melrose, Mass., June 3, 1923. [1; 4; 7; 10; 11]

Pieper, Franz August Otto, theologian, b. Germany, 1852; d. St. Louis, Mo., June 3, 1931. [1; 3; 10]

Pier, Garrett Chatfield, archaeologist, b. London, England, 1875; d. St. Petersburg, Fla., Dec. 30, 1943.

Pierce, Arthur Henry, psychologist, b. Westboro, Mass., 1867; d. Northampton, Mass., Feb. 20, 1914. [10]

Pierce, Edward Lillie, lawyer and biographer, b. Stoughton, Mass., 1829; d. Paris, France, Sept. 5, 1897. [1; 3b; 4; 5; 6; 7]

Pierce, Edward Wallace, chemist, b. Washington, D.C., 1875; d. Paterson, N.J., Feb. 8, 1941.

Pierce, Emmons Sylvester, poet, b. 1831; d. 1901.

Pierce, Frank Cushman, historian, b. 1858; d. 1918.

Pierce, Franklin, economist, b. 1853; d. New Haven, Conn., March 26, 1935. [62]

Pierce, Frederick Clifton, journalist and genealogist, b. Worcester, Mass., 1856; d. 1904. [3; 4; 5; 10]

Pierce, Frederick Erastus, educationist, b. South Britain, Conn., 1878; d. New Haven, Conn., March 26, 1935. [62]

Pierce, George Foster, bishop, b. Greene county, Ga., 1811; d. near Sparta, Ga., Sept. 3, 1884. [1; 3; 4; 5; 34]

Pierce, George Winslow, lawyer, b. Boston, Mass., 1841; d. Nov. 8, 1917. [51]

Pierce, Gilbert Ashville, journalist and politician, b. East Otto, N.Y., 1839; d. Chicago, Ill., Feb. 15, 1901. [1; 4; 5; 7; 9; 10; 70]

Pierce, Grace Adele, journalist, b. Randolph, N.Y.; d. Santa Monica, Calif., Dec. 8, 1923. [10; 35]

Pierce, Henry Niles, bishop, b. Pawtucket, R.I., 1820; d. Fayetteville, Ark., Sept. 5, 1899. [3b; 4; 10]

Pierce, James Oscar, lawyer, b. Syracuse, N.Y., 1836; d. Mound, Minn., April 12, 1907. [5; 70]

Pierce, Josiah, local historian, b. 1792; d. 1866. [38]

Pierce, Lyman B., soldier, b. 1834; d. ? [37]

Pierce, Newton Barris, vegetable pathologist, b. Brockport, N.Y., 1856; d. Santa Ana, Calif., 1917. [10]

Pierce, Ray Vaughn, physician, b. 1840; d. Buffalo, N.Y., Feb. 4, 1914.

Pierce, Squier Littell, novelist, b. Butler county, O., 1832; d. ? [70]

Pierce, William Henry, Indian missionary, b. Fort Rupert, B.C., 1856; d. Prince Rupert, B.C., April 10, 1948.

Pierce, William Leigh, poet, fl. 1808-1813. [56]

Pierpont, James, mathematician, b. 1866; d. San Mateo, Calif., Dec. 9, 1938. [4; 10]

Pierpont, John, clergyman and poet, b. Litchfield, Conn., 1785; d. Medford, Mass., Aug. 27, 1866. [1; 3; 4; 5; 7; 9; 62; 71]

Pierrepont, Edward Willoughby, diplomat, b. New York, N.Y., 1860; d. Rome, Italy, April 16, 1885. [3]

Piers, Harry, librarian, b. Halifax, N.S., 1870; d. Halifax, N.S., Jan. 24, 1940. [11; 27]

Piersel, Alba Chambers, educationist, b. Kentucky, 1867; d. Bloomington, Ill., March 27, 1934. [10]

Piersol, George Arthur, anatomist, b. Philadelphia, Pa., 1856; d. Philadelphia, Pa., Aug. 7, 1924. [10]

Pierson, Arthur Tappan, clergyman, b. New York, N.Y., 1837; d. Brooklyn, N.Y., June 3, 1911. [1; 4; 10]

Pierson, Azariah Theodore Crane, physician, b. Morris Plains, N.J., 1815; d. St. Paul, Minn., Nov. 26, 1889. [70]

Pierson, Charles Wheeler, lawyer, b. Florida, N.Y., 1864; d. New York, N.Y., May 4, 1934. [10; 62]

Pierson, David Lawrence, local historian, b. 1865; d. East Orange, N.J., July 11, 1938. [7]

Pierson, Delavan Leonard, biographer and editor, b. Waterford, N.Y., 1867; d. Oct. 9, 1935. 10; 11]

Pierson, Ernest De Lancey, novelist, fl. 1887-1897.

Pierson, Hamilton Wilcox, clergyman, b. Bergen, N.Y., 1817; d. Bergen, N.Y., Sept. 7, 1888. [1; 3; 5; 7]

Pierson, Ward Wright, lawyer, b. 1879; killed in action, France, Nov. 9, 1918.

Pieters, Adrian John, agronomist, b. Alto, Wis., 1866; d. Takoma Park, D.C., April 26, 1940. [10]

Pieters, Aleida Johanna, educationist, b. Holland, Mich., 1876; d. Milwaukee, Wis., April 6, 1936. [10; 11]

Piette, Eugene Constantine, pathologist, b. Russian Crimea, 1892; d. Chicago, Ill., Dec. 5, 1946. [13]

Piette, Maximin Charles, priest, b. Belgium, 1885; d. Montreal, Que., Nov. 6, 1948.

Piffard, Henry Granger, physician, b. Piffard, N.Y., 1842; d. New York, N.Y., June 8, 1910. [10]

Piggott, Aaron Snowden, physician, b. Philadelphia, Pa., 1822; d. 1869. [6]

Pike, Albert, lawyer, soldier, and freemason, b. Boston, Mass., 1809; d. Washington, D.C., April 2, 1891. [1; 3; 4; 5; 6; 7; 9; 34]

Pike, Mrs. Frances West, née **Atherton,** novelist, b. Prospect, Me., 1819; d. ? [3; 6]

Pike, James Shepherd, journalist, b. Calais, Me., 1811; d. Calais, Me., Nov. 24, 1882. [1; 3; 4; 5; 6; 7; 9]

Pike, John, clergyman, b. 1813; d. 1899.

Pike, Joseph Brown, educationist, b. Chicago, Ill., 1866; d. Palo Alto, Calif., Nov. 1, 1938. [10]

Pike, Mrs. Mary Hayden, née **Green,** novelist, b. Eastport, Me., 1824; d. Baltimore, Md., Jan. 15, 1908. [1; 3; 6; 7; 9]

Pike, Nicholas, arithmetician, b. Somersworth, N.H., 1743; d. Dec. 9, 1819. [1; 4]

Pike, Zebulon Montgomery, soldier and explorer, b. Trenton, N.J., 1779; d. near York [now Toronto], Upper Canada, April 27, 1813. [1; 2; 3; 4; 5; 6; 7; 9; 70]

Pilch, Frederick Henry, poet, b. Newark, N.J., 1842; d. Dec. 3, 1889. [7]

Pilcher, James Evelyn, military surgeon, b. Adrian, Mich., 1857; d. Savannah, Ga., April 8, 1911. [10]

Pilcher, Lewis Stephen, surgeon, b. Adrian, Mich., 1845; d. Montclair, N.J., Dec. 24, 1934. [1a; 10; 11]

Pilcher, Paul Monroe, surgeon and urologist, b. Brooklyn, N.Y., 1876; d. Jan. 4, 1917. [1]

Pilgrim, Thomas, writer of books for boys, d. 1882. [6]

Pilling, James Constantine, ethnologist, b. Washington, D.C., 1846; d. Olney, Md., July 27, 1895. [1; 3; 4; 5]

Pillsbury, Albert Enoch, lawyer, b. Milford, N.H., 1849; d. West Newton, Mass., Dec. 23, 1930. [4; 10; 11]

Pillsbury, Arthur Judson, journalist, b. Londonderry, N.H., 1854; d. Berkeley, Calif., April 1, 1937. [10]

Pillsbury, John Henry, biologist, b. Limington, Me., 1846; d. Waban, Mass., Dec. 20, 1910. [10]

Pillsbury, Parker, reformer, b. Hamilton, Mass., 1809; d. Concord, N.H., July 7, 1898. [1; 3; 4; 5]

Pilote, François, priest, b. St. Antoine de Tilly, Lower Canada, 1811; d. Portneuf, Que., April 5, 1886. [27; 32]

Pinchot, Gifford, politician and reformer, b. Simsbury, Conn., 1865; d. New York, N.Y., Oct. 4, 1946. [4; 7; 10; 11]

Pinckney, Charles Cotesworth, clergyman, b. Charleston, S.C., 1812; d. Flat Rock, N.C., Aug. 12, 1898. [5; 10; 34]

Pindar, Susan, poet, b. near Tarrytown, N.Y., about 1820; d. near Tarrytown, N.Y., 1892. [3; 6; 7]

Pine, Cuyler (pseud.). See Peck, Ellen.

Pine, John Buckley, lawyer, b. Dubuque, Ia., 1857; d. New York, N.Y., Oct. 28, 1922. [10]

Pine, M. S. (pseud.). See Finn, Sister Mary Paulina.

Pingree, Hazen Stuart, politician, b. Denmark, Me., 1840; d. London, England, June 18, 1901. [1; 4; 5; 10]

Pingrey, Darius Harlan, lawyer, b. 1841; d. Highland Park, Ill., August 9, 1918.

Pinkerton, Allan, detective, b. Glasgow, Scotland, 1819; d. Chicago, Ill., July 1, 1884. [1; 2; 3; 4; 5; 6; 7]

Pinkham, Edwin George, journalist, b. 1876; d. Atherton, Calif., Sept. 12, 1948.

Pinkham, Mrs. Rebekah, née **Porter,** biographer, b. 1892; d. 1839.

Pinkney, Edward Coote, poet, b. London, England, 1802; d. Baltimore, Md., April 11, 1828. [1; 3; 4; 5; 6; 7; 9; 71]

Pinkney, Ninian, soldier, b. Baltimore, Md., 1776; d. Baltimore, Md., Dec. 16, 1825. [3; 4]

Pinkney, William, bishop, b. Annapolis, Md., 1810; d. Cockeysville, Md., July 4, 1883. [3; 4; 5; 34]

Pinneo, Timothy Stone, grammarian, b. Milford, Conn., 1804; d. Norwalk, Conn., Aug. 2, 1893. [3b; 62]

Pinner, Max, physician, b. Berlin, Germany, 1891; d. Berkeley, Calif., Jan. 7, 1948.

Pinney, Norman, clergyman and educationist, b. Simsbury, Mass., 1804; d. New Orleans, La., Oct. 1, 1862. [1; 3; 4; 6]

Pinnix, Mrs. Hannah Courtney, née **Baxter,** novelist, b. 1851; d. Dec. 29, 1931.

Pinson, William Washington, clergyman, b. Cheatham county, Tenn., 1854; d. Nashville, Tenn., Oct. 7, 1930. [10; 11; 34]

Piper, Charles Vancouver, agronomist, b. Victoria, B.C., 1867; d. Washington, D.C., Feb. 11, 1926. [1; 10; 11]

Piper, Edwin Ford, educationist and poet, b. Auburn, Neb. 1871; d. Iowa City, Ia., May 17, 1939. [7; 10; 11]

Piper, Richard Upton, physician, b. Stratham, N.H., 1818; d. 1897. [3]

Pipkin, Charles Wooten, political scientist, b. Little Rock, Ark., 1899; d. New Orleans, La., Aug. 4, 1941. [10]

Piquefort, Jean (pseud.). See Routhier, Sir Adolphe Basile.

Pirazzini, Agide, educationist, b. Cotignola, Italy, 1875; d. New York, N.Y., Feb. 1, 1934. [10]

Pirsson, Louis Valentine, geologist, b. Fordham, N.Y., 1860; d. New Haven, Conn., Dec. 8, 1919. [1; 4; 10; 62]

Pise, Charles Constantine, priest, b. Annapolis, Md., 1801; d. Brooklyn, N.Y., May 26, 1866. [1; 3; 5; 6; 7; 21; 34]

Pitezel, John H., clergyman, b. 1814; d. 1906.

Pitkin, Timothy, lawyer, b. Farmington, Conn., 1766; d. New Haven, Conn., Dec. 18, 1847. [1; 3; 4; 5; 6; 9]

Pitman, Benn, stenographer, b. Trowbridge, England, 1822; d. Cincinnati, O., Dec. 28, 1910. [1; 3; 4; 5; 6]

Pitman, Frank Wesley, historian, b. New Haven, Conn., 1882; d. Claremont, Calif., April 11, 1849. [10; 62]

Pitman, Mrs. Marie J., née Davis, traveller, b. Hartwick, N.Y., 1850; d. 1888. [3]

Pitman, Norman Hinsdale, sinologist, b. Lamont, Mich., 1876; d. Tientsin, China, March 6, 1925. [10; 11]

Pittenger, William, clergyman, b. Jefferson county, O., 1840; d. Burbank, Calif., 1904. [3; 4; 5; 6; 10]

Pittman, Mrs. Hannah, née Daviess, novelist, b. Harrodsburgh, Ky., 1840; d. St. Louis, Mo., March 22, 1919. [7; 10; 34]

Pitzer, Alexander White, clergyman, b. Salem, Va., 1834; d. July 22, 1927. [3; 6; 10; 34]

Plant, James Stuart, psychiatrist, b. Minneapolis, Minn., 1890; d. South Orange, N.J., Sept. 7, 1947. [13]

Plantz, Mrs. Myra, née Goodwin, writer of books for young people, b. Brookville, Ind., 1856; d. 1914. [10]

Plantz, Samuel, educationist, b. Johnstown, N.Y., 1859; d. Sturgeon Bay, Wis., Nov. 13, 1924. [10; 11]

Platner, Samuel Ball, educationist, b. Unionville, Conn., 1863; d. at sea, Aug. 20, 1921. [1; 4; 10; 62]

Platt, Charles, physician, b. Montclair, N.J., 1869; d. Ardmore, Pa., June 13, 1928. [10; 11]

Platt, Charles Adams, architect and painter, b. New York, N.Y., 1861; d. Cornish, N.Y., Sept. 12, 1933. [1; 4; 10]

Platt, Charles Davis, local historian, b. 1856; d. 1923.

Platt, Dan Fellows, traveller, d. Englewood, N.J., May 6, 1938.

Platt, Edmund, local historian, b. Poughkeepsie, N.Y., 1865; d. near Chazy, N.Y., Aug. 27, 1939. [10; 11]

Platt, Horace Garvin, lawyer, b. 1856; d. 1910.

Platt, Isaac Hull, physician, b. Brooklyn, N.Y., 1853; d. Wallingford, Pa., Aug. 16, 1912. [4; 10]

Platt, Smith H., clergyman, fl. 1859-1900.

Platt, Thomas Collier, politician, b. Owego, N.Y., 1833; d. New York, N.Y., March 6, 1910. [1; 2; 3; 4; 5; 10]

Platt, William Henry, lawyer and clergyman, b. Amenia, N.Y., 1821 d. Petersburg, Va., Dec. 18, 1898. [3; 5; 6;]

Playter, George Frederick, clergyman, b. about 1811; d. Frankford, Ont., Oct. 24, 1866. [27]

Pleasants, Julia, novelist and poet, b about 1827; d. 1886.

Pleasonton, Augustus James, soldier, b. Washington, D.C., 1808; d. Philadelphia, Pa., July 26, 1894. [3b; 4]

Plimpton, Florus Beardsley, poet, b. 1830; d. 1886. [4]

Plimpton, George Arthur, publisher, b. Walpole, Mass., 1855; d. Walpole, Mass., July 1, 1936. [4; 7; 10]

Plowman, George Taylor, etcher, b. Le Sueur, Minn., 1869; d. Cambridge, Mass., March 26, 1932. [1; 4; 10; 11]

Plum, William Rattle, lawyer, b. Massilon, O., 1845; d. Chicago, Ill., April 28, 1927. [62]

Plumb, Charles Sumner, educationist, b. Westfield, Mass., 1860; d. Columbus, O., March 4, 1939. [5; 10; 11]

Plumb, Glenn Edward, lawyer, b. Washington county, Ia., 1866; d. Washington, D.C., Aug. 1, 1922. [1; 10]

Plumbe, George Edward, statistician, b. Pawlet, Vt., 1837; d. Chicago, Ill., April 24, 1912. [10]

Plumbe, John, railwayman and photographer, b. Wales, 1809; d. Dubuque, Ia., July. 1857. [1]

Plumer, William, poet and politician, b. Epping, N.H., 1789; d. Epping, N.H., Sept. 18, 1854. [3; 4]

Plumer, William Swan, clergyman, b. Darlington, Pa., 1802; d. Baltimore, Md., Oct. 22, 1880. [1; 3; 4; 5; 6; 34]

Plummer, Edward Clarence, lawyer, b. Freeport, Me., 1863; d. Washington, D.C., March 20, 1932. [4; 10; 11]

Plummer, Mary Wright, librarian, b. Richmond, Ind., 1856; d. New York, N.Y., Sept. 21, 1916. [1; 5; 7; 10]

Plunkett, Mrs. Harriette Merrick, née Hodge, miscellaneous writer, b. 1826; d. ?

Plympton, Almira George, writer of books for children, b. Boston, Mass; d. Dover, Mass., 1939. [7; 10]

Plympton, George Washington, engineer, b. Waltham, Mass., 1827; d. 1907. [3; 4; 5; 10]

Pocahontas (pseud.). See Pearson, Mrs. Emily Clemens.

Pockman, Philetus Theodore, clergyman, b. East Greenbush, N.Y., 1853; d. Nov. 17, 1919. [10]

Poe, Edgar Allan, poet and story-teller, b. Boston, Mass., 1809; d. Baltimore, Md., Oct. 7, 1849. [1, 2; 3; 4; 5; 6; 7; 8; 9, 71; 72]

Poe, John Prentiss, lawyer, b. Baltimore, Md., 1836; d. Baltimore, Md., Oct. 14, 1909. [10]

Poffenbarger, Mrs. Livia Nye, née **Simpson,** historian, b. Pomeroy, O., 1862; d. Charleston, W. Va., Oct. 27, 1937. [7; 10]

Poinsett, Joel Roberts, politician and diplomat, b. Charleston, S.C., 1779; d. near Statesburg, S.C., Dec. 12, 1851. [1; 3; 4; 5; 6; 34]

Poirier, Pascal, politician, b. Shediac, N.B., 1852; d. Shediac, N.B., Sept. 25, 1933. [27]

Poisson, Adolphe, poet, b. Gentilly, Que., 1849; d. Arthabaska, Que., April 22, 1922. [27]

Polak, John Osborn, gynaecologist and obstetrician, b. Brooklyn, N.Y., 1870; d. Brooklyn, N.Y., June 29, 1931. [1; 10]

Poland, John Scroggs, soldier, b. Princeton, Ind., 1836; d. Asheville, N.C., Aug. 8, 1898. [3]

Poland, William, priest, b. 1848; d. Chicago, Ill., Jan. 14, 1923. [21]

Poland, William Carey, educationist, b. Gofftown, N.H., 1846; d. Providence, R.I., March 19, 1929. [4; 10]

Polinto (pseud.). See Wilkie, Franc Bangs.

Polk, Mrs. Cynthia Brown, née **Martin,** genealogist, b. 1848; d. June 15, 1921.

Polk, Jefferson J., physician, b. near Georgetown, Ky., 1802; d. Perryville, Ky., May 23, 1881. [74]

Polk, William Mecklenburg, physician, b. Ashwood, Tenn., 1844; d. Atlantic City, N.J., June 23, 1918. [1; 3; 4; 5; 34]

Pollak, Gustav, editor and literary critic, b. Vienna, Austria, 1849; d. Cambridge, Mass., Nov. 1, 1919. [1; 7; 10]

Pollard, Edward Albert, journalist, b. Albemarle county, Va., 1831; d. Lynchburg, Va., Dec. 16, 1872. [1; 3; 4; 6; 7; 9; 34]

Pollard, Edward Bagby, clergyman and educationist, b. Stevensville, Va., 1864; d. Chester, Pa., July 12, 1927. [10; 62]

Pollard, Joseph Percival, critic and novelist, b. Germany, 1869; d. Baltimore, Md., Dec. 17, 1911. [1; 7; 10]

Pollard, Josephine, poet and writer of books for children, b. New York, N.Y., 1843; d. New York, N.Y., Aug. 15, 1892. [3; 6; 7]

Pollard, Mrs. Rebecca, née **Smith,** poet and educationist, b. 1831; d. 1917.

Pollard, Robert Thomas, educationist, b. Chambersburg, Pa., 1897; d. Seattle, Wash., April 12, 1939.

Polley, Joseph Benjamin, soldier, b. 1840: d. ? [34]

Pollock, Channing, playwright, b. Washington, D.C., 1880; d. Shoreham, Long Island, N.Y., Aug. 17, 1946. [7; 10; 11]

Pollock, James Barkley, botanist, b. Orangeville, Ill., 1863; d. Ann Arbor, Mich., June 29, 1934. [13]

Pollok, Allan, clergyman, b. Scotland, 1829; d. Halifax, N.S., July 7, 1918. [27]

Pomeroy, "Brick." See Pomeroy, Marcus Mills.

Pomeroy, Hiram Sterling, physician, b. Somers, Conn., 1848; d. Auburndale, Mass., April 20, 1917. [62]

Pomeroy, John Norton, lawyer, b. Rochester, N.Y., 1828; d. San Francisco, Calif., Feb. 15, 1885. [1; 3]

Pomeroy, Marcus Mills, journalist, b. Elmira, N.Y., 1833; d. Brooklyn, N.Y., May 30, 1896. [1; 3; 4; 5; 6; 7; 9]

Pomeroy, Oren Day, physician, b. Somers, Conn., 1834; d. Whitestone, Long Island, N.Y., March, 1902. [4]

Pond, Enoch, clergyman, b. Wrentham, Mass., 1791; d. Bangor, Me., Jan. 21, 1882. [1; 3; 5; 6; 7]

Pond, Frederick Eugene, writer on field sports, b. Marquette county, Wis., 1856; d. Brooklyn, N.Y., Nov. 1, 1925. [1; 3; 4; 6; 7; 10]

Pond, George Edward, journalist, b. Boston, Mass., 1837; d. Spring Lake, N.J., Sept. 22, 1899. [1; 3; 4; 5; 7; 10]

Pond, George Gilbert, chemist, b. Holliston, Mass., 1861; d. State College, Pa., May 20, 1920. [10; 13]

Pond, Irving Kane, architect, b. Ann Arbor, Mich., 1857; d. Washington, D.C., Sept. 29, 1939. [4; 10; 11]

Pond, James Burton, lecture manager, b. Cuba, N.Y., 1838; d. Jersey City, N.Y., June 21, 1903. [1; 4; 5; 7; 10]

Pond, Samuel William, missionary, b. New Preston, Conn., 1808; d. Shakopee, Minn., Dec. 12, 1891. [1; 7; 70]

Pond, Samuel William, biographer, b. Shakopee, Minn., 1850; d. Minneapolis, Minn., Oct. 21, 1916.

Pond, William Chauncey, clergyman, b. 1830; d. San Francisco, Calif., Oct. 21, 1925.

Pool, Maria Louise, novelist, b. Abington, Mass., 1841; d. Rockland, Mass., May 19, 1898. [1; 3; 4; 5; 7; 9]

Pool, William, local historian, b. 1825; d. 1912.

Poole, Cecil Percy, electrical engineer, b. Elizabeth City, N.C., 1865; d. Atlanta, Ga., Feb. 23, 1921. [10]

Poole, De Witt Clinton, soldier, b. Amsterdam, N.Y., 1828; d. Madison, Wis., Nov. 30, 1917. [6]

Poole, Herman, chemist, b. Boston, Mass., 1849; d. 1906. [10]

Poole, Mrs. Hester Martha, née **Hunt,** housekeeper, b. 1843; d. 1932.

Poole, Murray Edward, genealogist, b. Centre Moreland, Pa., 1857; d. Ithaca, N.Y., April 10, 1925. [10]

Poole, Thomas W., physician, b. 1831; d. Lindsay, Ont., Aug. 27, 1905. [27]

Poole, William Frederick, historian and bibliographer, b. Salem, Mass., 1821; d. Evanston, Ill., March 1, 1894. [1; 3; 4; 5; 6; 7; 9]

Poole, William Henry, clergyman, b. Ireland, 1820; d. Detroit, Mich., Aug. 7, 1896. [27]

Poor, Agnes Blake, writer of fiction, b. 1842; d. Brookline, Mass., Feb. 28, 1922. [4; 7; 10]

Poor, Henry Varnum, journalist and economist, b. Andover, Me., 1812; d. Brookline, Mass., Jan. 4, 1905. [1; 6; 7]

Poor, John Alfred, lawyer, b. Andover, Me., 1808; d. Portland, Me., Sept. 5, 1871. [1; 3]

Poor, Laura Elizabeth, linguist, b. 1834; d. 1896.

Poor, Lucy Tappan, novelist, b. New York, N.Y., 1855; d. Brookline, Mass., Dec. 23, 1946.

Poor, Walter Stone, lawyer, b. Andover, Me., 1836; d. Morristown, N.J., June 21, 1906.

Poore, Benjamin Perley, journalist, b. near Newburyport, Mass., 1820; d. Washington, D.C., May 29, 1887. [1; 3; 4; 5; 6; 7; 9]

Poore, Henry Rankin, artist, b. Newark, N.J., 1859; d. Orange, N.J., Aug. 15, 1940. [7; 10; 11]

Pope, Alexander, artist, b. Boston, Mass., 1849; d. Hingham, Mass., Sept. 9, 1924. [4; 10]

Pope, Charles Henry, clergyman and genealogist, b. Machias, Me., 1841; d. Cambridge, Mass., Feb. 19. 1918. [46]

Pope, Curran, physician, b. Louisville, Ky., 1866; d. Louisville, Ky., Sept. 21, 1934. [10; 11]

Pope, Franklin Leonard, electrical engineer, b. Great Barrington, Mass., 1840; d. Great Barrington, Mass., Oct. 13, 1895. [1; 3; 4; 5; 6]

Pope, John, soldier, b. Louisville, Ky., 1822; d. Sandusky, O., Sept. 23, 1892. [1; 3; 4; 5; 6; 34]

Pope, Sir Joseph, civil servant, b. Charlottetown, P.E.I., 1854; d. Ottawa, Ont., Dec. 2, 1925. [27]

Pope, William Cox, clergyman, b. Philadelphia, Pa., 1841; d. 1917. [70]

Pope, William F., jurist, b. 1814; d. 1895. [34]

Pope, William Henry, politician, b. Bedeque, P.E.I., 1825; d. Summerside, P.E.I., Oct. 7, 1879. [27]

Popkin, John Snelling, clergyman and educationist, b. Boston, Mass., 1771; d. Cambridge, Mass., March 2, 1852. [3; 51]

Popkin, Martin E., engineer, b. Havre, France, 1897; d. New York, N.Y., Jan. 29, 1940.

Porcher, Francis Peyre, physician and botanist, b. Berkeley county, S.C., 1825; d. Charleston, S.C., Nov. 19, 1895. [1; 3; 5; 6; 34]

Porter, Mrs. Alice, née **Downey,** educationist, b. Greencastle, Ind., 1856; d. Providence, R.I., Nov. 19, 1947.

Porter, Anthony Toomer, clergyman, b. 1828; d. 1902. [34]

Porter, Arthur Kingsley, architect, b. Stamford, Conn., 1883; d. off the cost of county Donegal, Ireland, July 8, 1933. [1a; 10; 11; 62]

Porter, Benjamin Faneuil, lawyer, b. Charleston, S.C., 1808; d. 1868. [3; 34]

Porter, Charles Leland, poet, b. Plattsburg, N.Y., 1830; d. Colona, Ill., Dec. 24, 1896. [45]

Porter, Charles T., political writer, fl. 1849.

Porter, Charles Talbot, engineer, b. Auburn, N.Y., 1826; d. New York, N.Y., Aug. 28, 1910. [4]

Porter, Charlotte Endymion, literary critic, b. Towanda, Pa., 1859; d. Boston, Mass., Jan. 16, 1942. [7; 11]

Porter, David, naval officer, b. Boston, Mass., 1780; d. San Stefano, Turkey, March 3, 1843. [1; 3; 4; 5; 6; 7]

Porter, David Dixon, naval officer and novelist, b. Chester, Pa., 1813; d. Washington, D.C., Feb. 13, 1891. [1; 3; 4; 5; 6; 7]

Porter, Mrs. Delia, née **Lyman,** compiler, b. New Haven, Conn.; d. New Haven, Conn., Jan. 16, 1933. [10; 11]

Porter, Dick (pseud.). See Porter, Napoleon Bonaparte.

Porter, Duval, poet, b. 1844; d. Richmond, Va., April 9, 1925. [34]

Porter, Dwight, educationist, b. Hartford, Conn., 1855; d. Malden, Mass., Feb. 26, 1935. [10]

Porter, Ebenezer, clergyman and educationist, b. Cornwall, Conn., 1772; d. Andover, Mass., April 8, 1834. [1; 3; 4; 5; 6]

Porter, Edward, Griffin, clergyman, b. Boston, Mass., 1837; d. 1900. [51]

Porter, Mrs. Eleanor, née **Hodgman,** novelist, b. Littleton, N.H., 1868; d. Cambridge, Mass., May 21, 1920. [4; 7; 10]

Porter, Frank Chamberlin, theologian, b. Beloit, Wis., 1859; d. New Haven, Conn., Jan. 24, 1946. [10; 62]

Porter, Mrs. Gene, née **Stratton,** novelist and illustrator, b. Wabash county, Ind., 1868; d. Los Angeles, Calif., Dec. 6, 1924. [1a; 4; 7; 10]

Porter, Harold Everett, novelist, b. Hyde Park, Mass., 1887; d. Torrington, Conn., June 21, 1936. [2a; 7; 10; 11; 51]

Porter, Henry Dwight, missionary, b. Green Bay, Wis., 1845; d. La Mesa, Calif., Oct. 23, 1916. [10]

Porter, Horace, soldier, b. Huntingdon, Pa., 1837; d. New York, N.Y., May 29, 1921. [1; 3; 4; 5; 7]

Porter, James, clergyman, b. Middleborough, Mass., 1808; d. Brooklyn, N.Y., April 16, 1888. [3b; 6]

Porter, Jermain Gildersleeve, astronomer, b. Buffalo, N.Y., 1852; d. Cincinnati, O., April 14, 1933. [1; 4; 10]

Porter, John Addison, chemist, b. Catskill, N.Y., 1822; d. New Haven, Conn., Aug. 25, 1866. [1; 3; 5]

Porter, John Addison, journalist, b. New Haven, Conn., 1856; d. Pomfret, Conn., Dec. 15, 1900. [3; 4; 10; 62]

Porter, John William, clergyman, b. 1863; d. Lexington, Ky., Sept. 8, 1937. [10; 11]

Porter, Joseph Whitcomb, genealogist and historian, b. Milton, Mass., 1824; d. 1901. [38]

Porter, Linn Boyd, novelist, b. Westfield, Mass., 1851; d. Brookline, Mass., June 29, 1916. [7; 10]

Porter, Mrs. Lydia Ann, née **Emerson,** novelist, b. Newburyport, Mass., 1816; d. 1898. [3]

Porter, Mrs. M. É., miscellaneous writer, fl. 1871-1909.

Porter, Mrs. Mary W., novelist, fl. 1879-1881. [6]

Porter, Mrs. Mel-Inda Jennie, poet and novelist, fl. 1881-1887.

Porter, Napoleon Bonaparte, railwayman, b. 1853; d. ?

Porter, Noah, educationist, b. Farmington, Conn., 1811; d. New Haven, Conn., March 4, 1892. [1; 2; 3; 4; 5; 6; 7; 8; 9; 62]

Porter, Robert Percival, journalist, b. Norwich, England, 1852; d. Feb. 28, 1917. [1; 4; 7; 10]

Porter, Rose, novelist and compiler, b. New York, N.Y., 1845; d. New Haven, Conn., Sept. 10, 1906. [4; 6; 7; 10]

Porter, Roy P., journalist, b. Chicago, Ill., 1907; d. Fairfield, Ia., Dec. 26, 1947.

Porter, Rufus, inventor, b. Boxford, Mass., 1792; d. New Haven, Conn., Aug. 13, 1884. [1; 3; 4; 5; 7]

Porter, Will, local historian, b. 1833; d. 1913. [37]

Porter, William Augustus, jurist, b. Huntingdon county, Pa., 1821; d. Philadelphia, Pa., June 28, 1886. [3]

Porter, William Henry, clergyman, b. Rye, N.H., 1817; d. Roxbury, Mass., May 26, 1861. [6; 62]

Porter, William Henry, clergyman, b. Port Medway, N.S., 1840; d. New Westminster, B.C., June 1, 1928. [27]

Porter, William Henry, physician, b. New York, N.Y., 1853; d. Norfolk, Conn., March 27, 1933. [10; 11]

Porter, William Smith, historian, b. 1799; d. 1866.

Porter, William Sydney, short-story writer, b. Greenboro, N.C., 1862; d. New York, N.Y., June 5, 1910. [1; 4; 7; 10; 72]

Porter, William Trotter, journalist, b. Newbury, Vt., 1809; d. New York, N.Y., July 19, 1858. [1; 3; 5; 7]

Porter, William Wagener, jurist, b. Philadelphia, Pa., 1856; d. Valley Forge, Pa., Nov. 16, 1928. [10]

Posey, Alexander Lawrence, journalist and poet, b. near Eufala, Indian Territory, 1873; d. North Canadian River, Okla., May 27, 1908. [1; 4; 7; 75]

Posey, William Campbell, ophthalmologist, b. Philadelphia, Pa., 1866; d. Sept. 5, 1934. [10; 11]

Post, Alfred Charles, surgeon, b. New York, N.Y., 1806; d. New York, N.Y., Feb. 7, 1886. [3; 4]

Post, Charles Asa, historian, b. 1848; d. Cleveland, O., May 2, 1943.

Post, Charles Cyrel, journalist, b. Shiawassee, Mich., 1846; d. ? [10]

Post, Edwin, educationist, b. Woodbury, N.J., 1851; d. Greencastle, Ind., Oct. 9, 1932. [10]

Post, George Edward, missionary and physician, b. New York, N.Y., 1838; d. Beirut, Syria, Sept. 29, 1909. [1; 5; 10]

Post, Mrs. Helen, née **Wilmans,** mental healer, fl. 1890-1900.

Post, Henry Albertson Van Zo, humanitarian, d. 1932.

Post, Isaac, spiritualist, b. Westbury, N.Y., 1897; d. Rochester, N.Y., May 9, 1872. [1; 3; 6]

Post, Louis Freeland, reformer, b. near Danville, N.J., 1849; d. Washington, D.C., Jan. 10, 1928. [1; 4; 5; 10; 11]

Post, Mrs. Lydia, née **Minturn,** soldier's wife, fl. 1780-1865.

Post, Mrs. Marie Caroline, née de Trobriand, biographer, b. Venice, Italy, 1845; d New York, N.Y., March 5, 1926.

Post, Melville Davisson, lawyer, novelist, and short-story writer, b. Romines Mills, W. Va., 1871; d. Clarksburg, W. Va., June 23, 1930. [1; 7; 10; 34]

Post, Truman Marcellus, clergyman, b. Middlebury, Vt., 1810; d. St. Louis, Mo., Dec. 31, 1886. [1; 3]

Post, Wiley, aviator, b. Grand Plain, Tex., 1899; d. near Point Barrow, Alaska, Aug. 15, 1935. [10]

Postgate, John William, journalist, b. 1851; d. ?

Postl, Karl Anton. See Sealsfield, Charles.

Poston, Charles Debrill, explorer and poet, b. Hardin county, Ky., 1825; d. Phoenix, Ariz., June 24, 1902. [1; 7]

Potamian, Brother, educationist, b. county Cavan, Ireland, 1847; d. New York, N.Y., Jan. 20, 1917. [1; 21]

Poteat, Edwin McNeill, clergyman, b. Caswell county, N.C., 1861; d. Greenville, S.C., June 26, 1937. [4; 7; 10; 11]

Poteat, William Louis, educationist, b. Caswell county, N.C., 1856; d. Wake Forest, N.C., March 12, 1978. [7; 10; 11]

Pott, Francis Lister Hawks, missionary, b. New York, N.Y., 1864; d. Shanghai, China, March 7, 1947. [10]

Potter, Alfred Claghorn, librarian, b. New Bedford, Mass., 1867; d. San Clemente, Calif., Nov. 1, 1940. [7; 10]

Potter, Alonzo, bishop, b. Dutchess county, N.Y., 1800; d. San Francisco, Calif., July 4, 1865. [1; 3; 4; 5; 6; 7]

Potter, Burton Willis, lawyer, b. Colesville, N.Y., 1843; d. Dec. 8, 1927. [10]

Potter, Chandler Eastman, jurist and historian, b. Concord, N.H., 1807; d. Flint, Mich., Aug. 3, 1868. [3; 4; 6]

Potter, Mrs. Cora, née **Urquhart,** actress, b. New Orleans, La., 1859; d. Beaulieu-sur-Mer, France, Feb. 12, 1936. [10]

Potter, Eliphalet Nott, clergyman and educationist, b. Schenectady, N.Y., 1836; d. Mexico City, Mexico, Feb. 6, 1901. [1; 4; 5; 7; 10]

Potter, Elisha Reynolds, jurist and historian, b. South Kingston, R.I., 1811; d. South Kingston, R.I., April 10, 1882. [1; 3; 4; 5; 6]

Potter, Mrs. Frances Boardman, née **Squire,** educationist, b. Elmira, N.Y., 1867; d. March 25, 1914. [4; 10; 70]

Potter, Frank Hunter, journalist, b. Philadelphia, Pa., 1851; d. Katonah, N.Y., Sept. 19, 1932. [69]

Potter, Henry Codman, bishop, b. Schenectady, N.Y., 1835; d. Cooperstown, N.Y., July 21, 1908. [1; 3; 4; 5; 7]

Potter, Homer Dexter, industrial engineer, b. Johnstown, N.Y., 1878; d. Louisville, Ky., Nov. 24, 1924. [10]

Potter, Israel Ralph, soldier, b. Cranston, R.I., 1744; d. Cranston, R.I., about 1826. [3; 4]

Potter, Jeffery Watson, poet, d. Wakefield, R.I., 1925.

Potter, Margaret Horton, novelist, b. Chicago, Ill., 1881; d. Chicago, Ill., 1911. [7; 10]

Potter, Mary Knight, artist, b. Boston, Mass.; d. Boston, Mass., Oct. 5, 1915. [7; 10]

Potter, Murray Anthony, educationist, b. 1871; d. 1915. [51]

Potter, Nathaniel, physician, b. Easton, Md., 1770; d. Baltimore, Md., Jan. 2, 1843. [1; 3; 4; 34]

Potter, Paul (pseud.). See Congdon, Charles Taber.

Potter, Platt, jurist, b. Galway, N.Y., 1800; d. Schenectady, N.Y., Aug. 11, 1891. [1; 3; 4; 5]

Potter, Ray, clergyman, b. 1795; d. 1858.

Potter, Samuel Otway Lewis, physician, b. county Antrim, Ireland, 1846; d. San Francisco, Calif., April 21, 1914. [10]

Potter, William James, clergyman, b. North Dartmouth, Mass., 1829; d. Boston, Mass., Dec. 21, 1893. [1; 5; 10; 51]

Potter, Woodburne, soldier, fl. 1836-1854.

Potterton, Thomas Edward, clergyman, b. Clarksburg, Mass., 1868; d. Brooklyn, N.Y., Dec. 8, 1933. [10]

Potts, Charles Sower, physician, b. Philadelphia, Pa., 1864; d. Philadelphia, Pa., Feb. 16, 1930. [1; 10; 11]

Potts, James Henry, clergyman, b. Woodhouse. Ont., 1848; d. Algonac, Mich., March 11, 1942. [4; 10; 11]

Potts, Stacy Gardner, jurist, b. Harrisburg, Pa., 1799; d. Trenton, N.J., April 9, 1865. [3; 6]

Potts, William, sociologist, b. Philadelphia, Pa., 1838; d. Philadelphia, Pa., July 29, 1908. [7; 10]

Potwin, Lemuel Stoughton, clergyman and educationist, b. East Windsor, Conn., 1832; d. Cleveland, O., Jan. 9, 1907. [62]

Potwin, Thomas Stoughton, clergyman, b. East Windsor, Conn., 1829; d. Hartford, Conn., Oct. 22, 1896. [62]

Pouliot, Joseph Elzéar, lawyer, b. Rimouski, Lower Canada, 1838; d. Rivière-du-Loup, Que., July 3, 1906. [27]

Poulsson, Anne Emilie, writer of books for children, b. Cedar Grove, N.J., 1853; d. Brookline, Mass., March 18, 1939. [4; 7; 10; 11]

Poutré, Félix, patriot, b. St. Jean d'Iberville, Lower Canada, 1816; d. Montreal, Que., Feb. 22, 1885. [27]

Powderly, Terence Vincent, labour leader, b. Carbondale, Pa., 1849; d. Washington, D.C., June 24, 1924. [1; 5; 10]

Powell, Aaron Macy, temperance advocate, b. Clinton, N.Y., 1832; d. Philadelphia, Pa., May 13, 1899. [3b; 4; 10]

Powell, Mrs. Alma Webster, née **Hall,** singer, b. Elgin, Ill., 1874; d. Mahwah, N.J., March 11, 1930. [1; 4; 10; 20]

Powell, Chilton Latham, educationist, b. 1885; d. Baltimore, Md., May 24, 1928.

Powell, Edward Payson, clergyman, b. Clinton, N.Y., 1833; d. Sorrento, Fla., May 14, 1915. [1; 4; 5; 7; 10]

Powell, Elmer Ellsworth, educationist, b. Clayton, Ill., 1861; d. Oxford, O., July 7, 1947. [10; 14]

Powell, George Harold, horticulturist, b. Ghent, N.Y., 1872; d. Pasadena, Calif., Feb. 18, 1922. [1; 4; 10; 11]

Powell, John Benjamin, journalist, b. Marion county, Mo., 1890; d. Washington, D.C., Feb. 28, 1947. [10; 11]

Powell, John J., descriptive writer, fl. 1874-1881.

Powell, John Wesley, geologist and anthropologist, b. Mount Morris, N.Y., 1834; d. Haven, Me., Sept. 23, 1902. [1; 3; 4; 5; 7; 10]

Powell, Lyman Pierson, clergyman and educationist, b. Farmington, Del.. 1866; d. Morristown, N.J., Feb. 10, 1946. [4; 10; 11]

Powell, Richard Stillman (pseud.). See Barbour, Ralph Henry.

Powell, Talcott Williams, journalist, b. Lansdowne, Pa., 1901; d. Greenwich, Conn., April 4, 1937. [7; 10]

Powell, Thomas, poet and journalist, b. England, 1809; d. Newark, N.J., Jan. 14, 1887. [1; 3; 5; 7; 9]

Powell, Thomas, physician, b. Montgomery county, Tenn., 1837; d. Aug. 17, 1916. [10]

Powell, Thomas Watkins, lawyer, b. 1797; d. 1882.

Powell, Walter Anderson, lawyer and historian, b. Kent county, Del., 1855; d. ? [11]

Powell, William Bramwell, educationist, b. Castile, N.Y., 1836; d. Washington, D.C., Feb. 6, 1904. [1; 3; 4; 7; 10]

Powell, William Byrd, physician, b. Bourbon county, Ky., 1799; d. Covington, Ky., May 13, 1866. [1; 3; 34]

Powell, William David, clergyman, b. Madison, Miss., 1854; d. Opelika, Ala., May 15, 1934. [10]

Powell, William Henry, soldier and historian, b. Washington, D.C., 1838; d. Sackett's Harbor, N.Y., Nov. 16, 1901. [3b]

Powelson, John Abraham, accountant, b. Middletown, N.Y., 1883; d. Syracuse, N.Y., Aug. 6, 1933. [11; 51]

Power, Frederick Belding, chemist, b. Hudson, N.Y., 1853; d. Washington, D.C., March 26, 1927. [1; 3; 10; 13]

Power, Frederick Dunglison, minister, b. Yorktown, Va., 1851; d. Washington, D.C., June 14, 1911. [1; 10; 34]

Power, John Carroll, historian and biographer, b. Kentucky, 1819; d. 1894. [6]

Power, John Hamilton, clergyman, b. 1798; d. 1873.

Power, John Hatch, physician, b. 1806; d. 1863. [6]

Power, Mrs. Susan C., née Dunning, journalist, fl. 1875-1899.

Power, Thomas, poet, b. 1786; d. 1868.

Powers, Caleb, politician, b. Whitley county, Ky., 1869; d. Baltimore, Md., July 25, 1932. [10; 11]

Powers, George Whitefield, compiler, b. 1834; d. 1903.

Powers, Grant, clergyman, b. Hollis, N.H., 1784; d. Goshen, Conn., April 10, 1841. [3; 6]

Powers, Harry Huntington, educationist, b. Hebron, Wis., 1859; d. Newton, Mass., Dec. 8, 1936. [10; 11]

Powers, Horatio Nelson, clergyman, b. Amenia, N.Y., 1826; d. Piermont, N.Y., Sept. 6, 1890. [3; 4; 6; 7]

Powers, James T., actor, b. New York, N.Y., 1862; d. New York, N.Y., Feb. 11, 1943. [10]

Powers, Julius Henry, local historian, b. 1830; d. 1907. [37]

Powers, Le Grand, statistician, b. Preston, N.Y., 1847; d. 1933. [10; 70]

Powers, Leland Todd, elocutionist, b. Pultneyville, N.Y., 1857; d. Nov. 27, 1920. [10]

Powers, Orlando Woodworth, lawyer, b. 1851; d. Jan. 2, 1914. [10]

Powers, Samuel Leland, politician, b. Cornish, N.H., 1848; d. Newton, Mass., Nov. 30, 1929. [4; 10]

Powers, Stephen, anthropologist, b. Waterford, O., 1840; d. Jacksonville, Fla., April 2, 1904. [7]

Powers, William Dudley, clergyman, b. Richmond, Va., 1849; d. Richmond, Va., March 24, 1924. [10; 34]

Poyas, Catherine Gendron, poet, b. Charleston, S.C., 1813; d. Charleston, S.C., Feb. 7, 1882. [3; 34; 42]

Poyas, Mrs. Elizabeth Anne, historian, fl. 1853-1870. [34]

Prall, David Wight, educationist, b. 1886; d. San Francisco, Calif., Oct. 21, 1940. [10]

Prall, William, clergyman, b. Paterson, N.J., 1853; d. New York, N.Y., March 22, 1933. [4; 10]

Prang, Mrs. Mary Amelia, née Dana, art teacher, b. Syracuse, N.Y., 1836; d. Melrose, Mass., Nov. 7, 1927. [1; 10; 11]

Prang, Louis, art publisher, b. Breslau, Germany, 1824; d. Los Angeles, Calif., June 15, 1909. [1; 2; 7; 10]

Pratt, Charles Stuart, writer of books for children, b. South Weymouth, Mass., 1854; d. Warner, N.H., April 3, 1921. [7; 11]

Pratt, Cornelia Atwood. See Comer, Mrs. Cornelia Atwood, née Pratt.

Pratt, Dwight Mallory, clergyman, b. West Cornwall, Conn., 1852; d. Cleveland, O., April 12, 1922. [10; 11]

Pratt, Edwin Hartley, surgeon, b. Towanda, Pa., 1849; d. Chicago, Ill., March 6, 1930. [4; 10]

Pratt, Mrs. Ella Ann, née Farman, writer of books for girls, b. Augusta, N.Y., 1837; d. Warner, N.H., May 22, 1907. [1; 6; 7; 10]

Pratt, Enoch, clergyman, b. Middleborough, Mass., 1781; d. Brewster, Mass., Feb. 2, 1860. [3; 4; 7]

Pratt, Henry Sherring, zoologist, b. Toledo, O., 1859; d. Orlando, Fla., Oct. 5, 1946. [10; 11; 13]

Pratt, Jacob Loring, clergyman, b. South Weymouth, Me., 1835; d. Strong, Me., Nov. 15, 1891. [38; 45]

Pratt, James Bissett, philosopher, b. Elmira, N.Y., 1875; d. Williamstown, Mass., Jan. 15, 1944. [7; 10; 11]

Pratt, John Barnes, publisher, b. 1865; d. Montclair, N.J., Oct. 1, 1943.

Pratt, Joseph Hyde, engineer and geologist, b. Hartford, Conn., 1870; d. Chapel Hill, N.C., June 2, 1942. [10; 13]

Pratt, Luther, educationist, fl. 1824-1828.

Pratt, Orson, Mormon apostle, b. Hartford, N.Y., 1811; d. Salt Lake City, Utah, Oct. 3, 1881. [1a; 3; 4; 5]

Pratt, Parley Parker, Mormon apostle, b. Burlington, N.Y., 1807; d. near Van Buren, Ark., May 13, 1857. [1; 3; 4; 5]

Pratt, Samuel Wheeler, clergyman, b. Livonia, N.Y., 1838; d. Campbell, N.Y., June 17, 1910. [3; 4; 5; 10]

Pratt, Sereno Stansbury, journalist, b. Westmoreland, N.Y., 1858; d. Troy, N.Y., Sept. 14, 1915. [1; 10]

Pratt, Silas Gamaliel, musician, b. Addison, Vt., 1846; d. Pittsburgh, Pa., Oct. 30, 1916. [1; 4; 20]

Pratt, Waldo Selden, musician, b. Philadelphia, Pa., 1857; d. Hartford, Conn., July 29, 1939. [4; 7; 10; 11; 20]

Pray, Isaac Clark, journalist, b. Boston, Mass., 1813; d. New York, N.Y., Nov. 28, 1869. [1; 3; 4; 5; 6; 7; 51]

Pray, James Sturgis, landscape architect, b. Boston, Mass., 1871; d. Cambridge, Mass., Feb. 22, 1929. [10; 11]

Pray, Kenneth Louis Moffatt, educationist, b. Whitewater, Wis., 1881; d. Philadelphia, Pa., March 2, 1948.

Pray, Lewis Glover, philanthropist, b. Quincy, Mass., 1793; d. Roxbury, Mass., Oct. 7, 1882. [3]

Preble, George Henry, naval officer, b. Portland, Me., 1816; d. Boston, Mass., March 1, 1885. [1; 2; 3; 4; 5; 6; 7]

Preble, Jedidiah, autobiographer, b. 1765; d. 1847.

Preble, Robert Bruce, physician, b. Chicago, Ill., 1866; d. Chicago, Ill., July 26, 1948. [11]

Preble, William Pitt, jurist, b. York, Me., 1783; d. Portland, Me., Oct. 11, 1857. [1; 3; 4; 38]

Prentice, George, clergyman and educationist, b. Grafton, Mass., 1834; d. Pasadena, Calif., Oct. 10, 1893. [60]

Prentice, George Dennison, journalist, b. New London county, Conn., 1802; d. Louisville, Ky., Jan. 22, 1870. [1; 3; 4; 5; 6; 7; 9; 34]

Prentice, William Packer, lawyer, b. Albany, N.Y., 1834; d. New York, N.Y., Dec. 22, 1915. [10]

Prentis, Noble Lovely, historian, b. 1839; d. 1900.

Prentiss, Albert Nelson, agriculturist, b. Cazenovia, N.Y., 1836; d. 1896. [4]

Prentiss, Mrs. Caroline, née **Edwards,** poet, b. Brooklyn, N.Y., 1852; d. Brooklyn, N.Y., March 27, 1940.

Prentiss, Charles, journalist, b. Reading, Mass., 1774; d. Brimfield, Mass., Oct. 20, 1820. [3; 5; 6]

Prentiss, Charles William, biologist, b. 1874; d. 1915.

Prentiss, Mrs. Elizabeth, née **Payson,** writer of religious and juvenile fiction, b. Portland, Me., 1818; d. Dorset, Vt., Aug. 13, 1878. [1; 3; 4; 5; 7]

Prentiss, George Lewis, clergyman, b. Gorham, Me., 1816; d. New York, N.Y., March 19, 1903. [1; 3; 4; 5; 6; 7; 10]

Presbrey, Eugene Wiley, playwright, b. Williamsburg, Mass., 1853; d. Hollywood, Calif., Sept. 9, 1931. [7; 10]

Presbrey, Frank Spencer, advertising agent, b. Buffalo, N.Y., 1855; d. Greenwich, Conn., Oct. 10, 1936. [10]

Prescott, Albert Benjamin, chemist, b. Hastings, N.Y., 1832; d. Ann Arbor, Mich., Feb. 25, 1905. [1; 2; 4; 5; 6; 10]

Prescott, Dorothy (pseud.). See Poor, Agnes Blake.

Prescott, George Bartlett, electrical engineer, b. Kingston, N.H., 1830; d. New York, N.Y., Jan. 18, 1894. [1; 3; 4; 5; 6]

Prescott, Harriet Elizabeth. See Spofford, Mrs. Harriet Elizabeth, née Prescott.

Prescott, Mary Newmarch, poet and story-writer, b. Calais, Me., 1849; d. Amesbury, Mass., June 14, 1888. [3; 4]

Prescott, Thomas H. (pseud.). See Blake, William O.,

Prescott, William, physician, b. Gilmanton, N.H., 1788; d. Gilmanton, N.H., Oct. 18, 1875. [3; 49]

Prescott, William Hickling, historian, b. Salem, Mass., 1796; d. Boston, Mass., Jan. 28, 1859. [1; 2; 3; 4; 5; 6; 7; 8; 9, 71]

Prescott, Winward, collector of bookplates, b. 1886; d. March 2, 1932.

Presser, Theodore, music publisher, b. Pittsburgh, Pa., 1848; d. Philadelphia, Pa., Oct. 28, 1925. [1; 4; 10]

Preston, Ann., physician, b. Westgrove, Pa., 1813; d. Philadelphia, Pa., April 18, 1872. [1; 3; 4; 5; 6]

Preston, Daniel Swan, poet, b. Boston, Mass., 1838; d. Meran, Austria, June 11, 1893. [51]

Preston, George Junkin, physician, b. Lexington, Va., 1858; d. Baltimore, Md., June 17, 1908. [10]

Preston, Harriet Waters, miscellaneous writer, b. Danvers, Mass., 1836; d. Cambridge, Mass., June 3, 1911. [1; 2; 3; 4; 5; 6; 7; 9; 10]

Preston, Howard Willis, historian, b. Providence, R.I., 1859; d. Providence, R.I., Feb. 1, 1936. [10; 11]

Preston, John, educationist, b. 1755; d. ?

Preston, Keith, educationist and journalist, b. Chicago, Ill., 1884; d. Chicago, Ill., July 7, 1927. [4; 10; 11]

Preston, Mrs. Margaret, née **Junkin,** poet and novelist, b. Philadelphia, Pa., 1820; d. Baltimore, Md., March 27, 1897. [1; 3; 4; 5; 6; 7; 9; 34]

Preston, Paul (pseud.). See Picton, Thomas.

Preston, Sydney Herman, humorist, b. Ottawa, Ont., 1858; d. Clarkson, Ont., Jan. 6, 1931. [27]

Preston, Thomas Lewis, planter, b. Botetourt county, Va., 1812; d. 1903. [4; 34]

Preston, Thomas Scott, priest, b. Hartford, Conn., 1824; d. New York, N.Y., Nov. 4, 1891. [1; 3; 4; 5; 6; 21]

Preston, William Thomas Rochester, politician and civil servant, b. Ottawa, Ont., 1851; d. Croydon, England, Nov. 2, 1942. [27]

Preuss, Arthur, journalist, b. St. Louis, Me., 1871; d. St. Louis, Mo., Dec. 16, 1934. [10; 22]

Price, Carl Fowler, insurance broker, b. New Brunswick, N.J., 1881; d. New York, N.Y., April 12, 1948. [7; 10]

Price, Ebenezer, clergyman, b. Newburyport, Mass., 1771; d. Boston, Mass., Feb. 19, 1864. [49]

Price, Eldridge Cowman, physician, b. Priceville, Md., 1854; d. ? [11]

Price, Eli Kirk, lawyer, b. East Bradford, Pa., 1797; d. Philadelphia, Pa., Nov. 15, 1884. [1; 3; 4; 6]

Price, George Frederic, soldier, d. 1888.

Price, George Moses, physician, b. Poltava, Russia, 1864; d. New York, N.Y., July 30, 1942. [10]

Price, Ira Maurice, Orientalist, b. near Newark, O., 1856; d. Olympia, Wash., Sept. 18, 1939. [4; 10]

Price, Overton Westfeldt, forester, b. Liverpool, England, 1873; d. Rugby Grange, N.C., June 11, 1914. [10]

Price, Samuel Woodson, soldier and artist, b. 1828; d. St. Louis, Mo., Jan. 22, 1918. [34]

Price, Theodore Hazeltine, manufacturer, b. New York, N.Y., 1861; d. May 4, 1935. [1a; 10]

Price, Warwick James, journalist, b. Cleveland, O., 1870; d. Philadelphia, Pa., April 6, 1934. [7; 10; 11; 62]

Price, William, novelist, b. about 1794; d. 1868.

Price, William Raleigh, educationist, b. Belington, W. Va., 1875; d. New York, N.Y., March 17, 1936. [10; 11]

Price, William Thompson, drama critic, b. Jefferson county, Ky., 1846; d. New York, N.Y., May 3, 1920. [1; 7; 9; 10]

Price-Brown, John. See Brown, John Price.

Priceman, James (pseud.). See Kirkland, Winifred Margaretta.

Prichard, Harold Adye, clergyman, b. Bristol, England, 1882; d. Mount Kisco, N.Y., May 7, 1944. [7; 10; 11]

Prichard, Sarah Johnson, novelist, b. Waterbury, Conn., 1830; d. 1909. [5; 7; 10]

Priddy, Al (pseud.). See Brown, Frederic Kenyon.

Pridgeon, Charles Hamilton, clergyman, b. Baltimore, Md., June 7, 1863; d. Pittsburgh, Pa., July 21, 1932. [10]

Priest, George Madison, educationist, b. Hendersen, Ky., 1873; d. Princeton, N.J., Feb. 18, 1947. [7; 10; 11]

Priest, Josiah, miscellaneous writer, b. 1788; d. Western New York, 1851. [3; 7]

Priestley, Herbert Ingram, historian, b. Fairfield, Mich., 1875; d. Berkeley, Calif., Feb. 10, 1944. [10; 11]

Priestley, Joseph, scientist and philosopher, b. near Leeds, Yorkshire, England, 1733; d. Northumberland, Pa., Feb. 6, 1804. [1; 2; 3; 4; 5; 6; 7]

Prieur, François Xavier, rebel, b. Soulanges country, Lower Canada, 1814; d. Montreal, Que., Feb. 1, 1891. [27]

Prime, Benjamin Young, physician and poet, b. Huntington, Long Island, N.Y., 1733; d. Huntington, Long Island, N.Y., Oct. 31, 1791. [1; 3; 4; 5; 6; 7]

Prime, Daniel Noyes, genealogist, b. 1790; d. 1881.

Prime, Edward Dorr Griffin, clergyman, b. Cambridge, N.Y., 1814; d. New York, N.Y., April 7, 1891. [1; 3; 4; 5; 6]

Prime, George Wendell, clergyman, b. 1837; d. 1907.

Prime, Nathaniel Scudder, clergyman, b. Huntington, Long Island, N.Y., 1785; d. Mamaroneck, N.Y., March 27, 1856. [3; 4; 5; 6]

Prime, Samuel Irenaeus, clergyman, b. Ballston, N.Y., 1812; d. Manchester, Vt., July 18, 1885. [1; 3; 4; 5; 6; 7]

Prime, Temple, genealogist, b. 1832; d. 1903. [51]

Prime, William Cowper, journalist, b. Cambridge, N.Y., 1825; d. New York, N.Y., Feb. 13, 1905. [1; 3; 4; 5; 6; 7; 10]

Prime-Stevenson, Edward Irenaeus, music critic, b. Madison, N.J., 1868; d. Lausanne, Switzerland, July 23, 1942. [10; 20]

Prince, Benjamin F., local historian, b. Westville, O., 1840; d. Springfield, O., Sept. 11, 1933. [10]

Prince, David, physician, b. 1816; d. 1890.

Prince, Mrs. Helen Choate, née Pratt, novelist, b. Dorchester, Mass., 1857; d. ? [7; 10]

Prince, John Dynely, educationist, b. New York, N.Y., 1868; d. New York, N.Y., Oct. 11, 1945. [10; 11]

Prince, John Tilden, educationist, b. Kingston, Mass., 1844; d. West Newton, Mass., Aug. 5, 1916. [10]

Prince, Le Baron Bradford, jurist and historian, b. Flushing, N.Y., 1840; d. Flushing, N.Y., Dec. 8, 1922. [1; 3; 4; 5; 6; 7; 9; 10; 11]

Prince, Leon Cushing, educationist, b. Concord, N.H., 1875; d. Carlisle, Pa., Jan. 31, 1937. [10]

Prince, Morton, physician, b. Boston, Mass., 1854; d. Brookline, Mass., Aug. 31, 1929. [1; 7; 10; 11; 51]

Prince, Thomas, clergyman and historian, b. Sandwich, Mass., 1687; d. Boston, Mass., Oct. 22, 1758. [1; 2; 3; 4; 5; 6; 7; 9; 51]

Prince, Walter Franklin, clergyman, b. Detroit, Me., 1863; d. Boston, Mass., Aug. 7, 1934. [10; 11; 62]

Prince, William, horticulturist, b. Flushing, N.Y., 1766; d. Flushing, N.Y., April 9, 1842. [1; 3; 5; 6]

Prince, William Robert, horticulturist, b. Flushing, N.Y., 1795; d. Flushing, N.Y., March 28, 1869. [1; 3; 4; 5; 6]

Prindle, Mrs. Frances Weston, née Carruth, novelist and poet, b. Newton, Mass., 1867; d. April 9, 1934. [7; 10]

Prindle, Franklin Cogswell, naval officer, b. Sandgate, Va., 1841; d. Washington, D.C., March 7, 1923. [10]

Pringle, Mrs. Elizabeth Waties, née Allston, historian, b. 1845; d. 1921.

Pringle, Jacob Farrand, jurist and historian, b. Valenciennes, France, 1816; d. Cornwall, Ont., Feb. 1, 1901. [27]

Pritchard, John Wagner, journalist, b. Pittsburgh, Pa., 1851; d. Montclair, N.J., March 1, 1924. [10; 11]

Pritchard, Myron Thomas, educationist, b. North Adams, Mass., 1853; d. Daytona Beach, Fla., Jan. 23, 1935. [10; 11]

Pritchard, Sara Johnson, See Prichard, Sarah Johnson.

Pritchett, Henry Smith, educationist, b. Fayette county, Mo., 1857; d. Santa Barbara, Calif., Aug. 28, 1939. [4; 10]

Pritts, Joseph, historian, fl. 1839-1849.

Proctor, Edna Dean, poet, b. Henniker, N.H., 1829; d. Framingham. Mass., Dec. 18, 1923. [3; 4; 5; 6; 7; 10]

Proctor, Harry George, journalist, b. Pittsburgh, Pa., 1882; d. Haddon Heights, N.J., July 20, 1946.

Proctor, Henry Hugh, clergyman, b. near Fayetteville, Tenn., 1868; d. Brooklyn, N.Y., May 12, 1933. [1; 10; 11; 62]

Proctor, John James, journalist, b. Liverpool, England, 1838; d. Dec. 17, 1909. [27]

Proctor, Lucien Brock, lawyer, b. Hanover, N.H., 1823; d. Albany, N.Y., April 1, 1900. [1; 3; 4; 5; 6]

Proffatt, John, lawyer, b. 1845; d. 1879.

Prokosch, Eduard, educationist, b. Austria, 1876; d. New Haven, Conn., Aug. 11, 1938. [10]

Prolix, Peregrine (pseud.). See Nicklin, Philip Holbrook.

Prosch, Thomas Wickham, historian, b. Brooklyn, N.Y., 1850; d. near Allentown, Wash., March 30, 1915.

Proud, Robert, historian, b. Yorkshire, England, 1728; d. Philadelphia, Pa., July 5, 1813. [1; 7; 9]

Proudfit, Alexander Moncrief, clergyman, b. Pequea, Pa., 1770; d. New Brunswick, N.Y., Nov. 23, 1843. [3; 6]

Proudfit, David Law, poet and novelist, b. Newburgh, N.Y., 1842; d. New York, N.Y., Feb. 22, 1897. [3; 4; 5; 7]

Proudfoot, John James Aitchison, clergyman, b. Scotland, 1821; d. Toronto, Ont., Jan. 14, 1903. [27]

Proulx, Jean Baptiste, priest, b. Ste. Anne, Que., 1846; d. Ottawa, Ont., March 1, 1904. [27]

Provancher, Léon, priest and naturalist, b. Courtnoyer, Lower Canada, 1820; d. Cap Rouge, near Quebec, Que., March 23, 1892. [27]

Provost, Théophile Stanislas, priest, b. Varennes, Lower Canada, 1835; d. Joliette, Que., May 23, 1904. [27]

Prowell, George R., historian, b. near York, Pa., 1849; d. Feb. 23, 1928. [10]

Prowse, Daniel Woodley, jurist and historian, b. Newfoundland, 1834; d. St. John's, Newfoundland, March 14, 1914. [27]

Prudden, Lillian Eliza, social worker, b. 1852; d. New Haven, Conn., March 22, 1937.

Prudden, Theodore Philander, clergyman, b. Middlebury, Conn., 1847; d. Brookline, Mass., Nov. 9, 1915. [62]

Prudden, Theophil Mitchell, pathologist, b. Middlebury, Conn., 1849; d. New York, N.Y., April 10, 1924. [1; 4; 5; 10; 62]

Prussing, Eugene Ernst, lawyer, b. Chicago, Ill., 1855; d. Hollywood, Calif., 1928. [10]

Pryer, Charles, historian, b. New Rochelle, N.Y., 1851; d. New York, N.Y., June 8, 1916.

Pryor, James Chambers, naval surgeon, b. Winchester, Tenn., 1871; d. Brooklyn, N.Y., Sept. 8, 1947. [10]

Pryor, Roger Atkinson, politician, b. near Petersburg, Va., 1828; d. New York, N.Y., March 14, 1919. [1; 4; 5; 10]

Pryor, Mrs. Sara Agnes, née Rice, miscellaneous writer, b. Halifax county, Va., 1830; d. New York, N.Y., Feb. 15, 1912. [7; 10; 34]

Pryor, William Clayton, writer of books for children, b. 1895; d. Paris, France, March 30, 1949.

Pryor, William Rice, gynaecologist, b. about 1857; d. New York, N.Y., Aug. 26, 1904. [10]

Puddefoot, William George, clergyman, b. Westerham, Kent, England, 1842; d. Brighton, Mass., Dec. 8, 1925. [10]

Pugh, Edward Fox, lawyer, b. 1847; d. Philadelphia, Pa., Dec. 13, 1915.

Pugh, Mrs. Eliza Lofton, née **Phillips,** novelist, b. Bayou Lafourche, La., 1841; d. ? [3; 34]

Pugh, Ellis, Quaker preacher, b. Merionethshire, Wales, 1656; d. Gwynned, Pa., Oct. 3, 1718. [1; 3; 7]

Pugley, Richard Marriotte, mariner, b. 1866; d. New York, N.Y., March 22, 1918.

Pulitzer, Ralph, publisher and poet, b. St. Louis, Mo., 1879; d. New York, N.Y., June 14, 1939. [7; 10; 11]

Pulitzer, Walter, publisher, b. New York, N.Y., 1878; d. Buffalo, N.Y., Sept. 5, 1926. [7; 10]

Pulliam, Roscoe, educationist, b. Millstadt, Ill., 1897; d. Carbondale, Ill., March 27, 1944. [10]

Pulsifer, David, historian, b. Ipswich, Mass., 1802; d. Augusta, Me., Aug. 9, 1894. [3; 5]

Pulsifer, William Henry, manufacturer, d. St. Louis, Mo., 1905. [6]

Pulte, Joseph Hippolyt, physician, b. Westphalia, Germany, 1811; d. Cincinnati, O., Feb. 25, 1884. [1; 3; 6]

Pummill, James, poet, b. 1828; d. ?

Pumpelly, Josiah Collins, lawyer, b. Owego, N.Y., 1839; d. New York, N.Y., Jan. 5, 1920. [10]

Pumpelly, Mrs. Mary Hollenback, née **Welles,** poet, b. Athens, Pa., 1803; d. Paris, France, Dec. 4, 1879. [3]

Pumpelly, Raphael, geologist and explorer, b. Owego, N.Y., 1837; d. Newport, R.I., Aug. 10, 1923. [1; 2; 3; 4; 5; 6; 7; 10]

Punchard, George, clergyman, b. Salem, Mass., 1806; d. Boston, Mass., April 2, 1880. [3; 6]

Pupin, Michael Idvorsky, educationist, b. Hungary, 1858; d. New York, N.Y., March 12, 1935. [1a; 4; 7; 10]

Purdy, Charles Wesley, physician, b. 1846; d. 1901.

Purdy, Richard Augustus, playwright, b. New York, N.Y., 1863; d. New York, N.Y., April 18, 1925. [10]

Purdy, Truman Harvey, poet, b. 1830; d. 1898.

Purington, George Colby, educationist, b. Embden, Me., 1848; d. Farmington, Me., 1909. [10]

Purinton, Daniel Boardman, educationist, b. Preston county, Va., 1850; d. Morgantown, W. Va., Nov. 27, 1933. [4; 5; 10; 34]

Purinton, Herbert Ronelle, educationist, b. Bowdoinham, Me., 1867; d. Lewiston, Me., Nov. 5, 1934. [10; 11]

Purnell, Benjamin, religious leader, b. Mayville, Ky., 1861; d. Benton Harbor, Mich., Dec. 16, 1927. [1a]

Purple, Edwin Ruthven, genealogist, b. Sherburne, N.Y., 1831; d. New York, N.Y., Jan. 20, 1879. [3]

Purrington, William Archer, lawyer, b. Washington, D.C., 1852; d. New York, N.Y., Oct. 26, 1926. [10; 51]

Purves, George Tybout, educationist, b. Philadelphia, Pa., 1852; d. New York, N.Y., Sept. 12, 1901. [5; 10]

Purviance, Robert, historian, b. Baltimore, Md., 1779; d. Baltimore Md., April 3, 1858.

Pusey, William Allen, physician, b. Elizabethtown, Ky., 1865; d. Chicago, Ill., Aug. 29, 1940. [10; 11]

Puterbaugh, Sabin Don, lawyer, b. 1834; d. 1892.

Putman, John Harold, educationist, b. Lincoln county, Ont., 1866; d. Ottawa, Ont., Sept. 11, 1940. [27]

Putnam, Albigence Waldo, historian, b. Marietta, O., 1799; d. Nashville, Tenn., Jan. 20, 1869. [3; 34]

Putnam, Alfred Porter, clergyman, b. Danvers, Mass., 1827; d. Salem, Mass., April 15, 1906. [4; 10]

Putnam, Allen, clergyman, b. Danvers, Mass., 1802; d. 1887. [6]

Putnam, Mrs. Catherine Hunt, née **Palmer,** religious worker, b. Framingham, Mass., 1792; d. New York, N.Y., Jan. 8, 1869. [3]

Putnam, Daniel, educationist, b. 1824; d. Ypsilanti, Mich., July 29, 1906.

Putnam, Eben, historian and genealogist, b. Salem, Mass., 1868; d. Wellesley Farms, Mass., Jan. 22, 1933. [1; 4; 7; 10; 11]

Putnam, Eleanor (pseud.). See Bates, Mrs. Harriet Leonora, née Vose.

Putnam, Mrs. Elizabeth, née **Lowell,** poet and essayist, b. Boston, Mass., 1862; d. Boston, Mass., June 5, 1935. [11]

Putnam, Mrs. Emily James, née **Smith,** educationist, b. Canandaigua, N.Y., 1865; d. Sept. 5, 1944. [7; 10; 11]

Putnam, Frederic Ward, archaeologist and naturalist, b. Salem, Mass., 1839; d. Cambridge, Mass., Aug. 14, 1915. [1; 3; 4; 5; 7; 10]

Putnam, George Ellsworth, economist, b. Richmond, Kans., 1887; d. Chicago, Ill., June 24, 1939. [10; 11]

Putnam, George Haven, publisher, b. London, England, 1844; d. New York, N.Y., Feb. 27, 1930. [1; 2; 3; 4; 5; 7; 10; 11]

Putnam, George Israel, journalist, b. 1860; d. San Diego, Calif., May 4, 1937. [7]

Putnam, George Palmer, publisher, b. Brunswick, Me., 1814; d. New York, N.Y., Dec. 20, 1872. [1; 2; 3; 4; 5; 6; 7]

Putnam, James Jackson, neurologist, b. Boston, Mass., 1846; d. Boston, Mass., Nov. 4, 1918. [1; 10]

Putnam, James Osborne, lawyer and diplomat, b. Attica, N.Y., 1818; d. Bulfalo, N.Y., April 24, 1903. [1; 3; 10]

Putnam, James William, economist, b. Hersman, Ill., 1865; d. Indianapolis, Ind., Jan. 23, 1940. [10; 11]

Putnam, John Bishop, publisher, b. Staten Island, N.Y., 1849; d. Rye, N.Y., Oct. 7, 1915. [7; 10]

Putnam, John Pickering, architect, b. Boston, Mass., 1847; d. Boston, Mass., Feb. 23, 1917. [10; 51]

Putnam, Mrs. Mary Traill Spence, née **Lowell,** miscellaneous writer, b. Boston, Mass., 1810; d. Boston, Mass., June 1, 1898. [3; 4; 5; 6; 7]

Putnam, Ruth, historian, b. Yonkers, N.Y., 1856; d. Geneva, Switzerland, Feb. 12, 1931. [1; 7; 10]

Putnam, Mrs. Sallie A., née **Brock,** miscellaneous writer, b. Madison Court House, Va., 1845; d. ? [3; 4; 6; 7; 34]

Putnam, Samuel Porter, miscellaneous writer, b. 1838; d. 1896.

Putnam, Thomas Milton, educationist, b. Petaluma, Calif., 1875; d. Berkeley, Calif., Sept. 22, 1942. [10; 11]

Putnam, Mrs. William Lowell. See Putnam, Mrs. Elizabeth, née Lowell.

Putney, Albert Hutchinson, lawyer and educationist, b. Boston, Mass., 1872; d. Washington, D.C., Oct. 22, 1928. [10; 62]

Puyjalon, Henry de, recluse, b. France, 1839; d. Ile-à-la-Chasse, Que., Aug. 17, 1905. [27]

Pyle, Ernest Taylor, war correspondent, b. Dana, Ind., 1900; d. Ie Jima, near Okinawa, Pacific Ocean, April 18, 1945. [10; 12]

Pyle, Howard, artist and littérateur, b. Wilmington, Del., 1853; d. Florence, Italy, Nov. 9, 1911. [1; 2; 4; 7; 10; 72]

Pyle, Joseph Gilpin, biographer, b. Calvert, Md., 1853; d. St. Paul, Minn., July 27, 1930. [62]

Pyle, Katharine, artist, b. Wilmington, Del.; d. Wilmington, Del., Feb. 19, 1938. [7; 10; 11]

Pyle, Walter Lytle, ophthalmologist, b. Philadelphia, Pa., 1871; d. Philadelphia, Pa., Oct. 8, 1921. [1; 4; 10]

Pydolet, F. (pseud.). See Leypoldt, Frederick.

Pynchon, Thomas Ruggles, clergyman and educationist, b. New Haven, Conn., 1823; d. New Haven, Conn., Oct. 6, 1904. [1; 3; 5; 6; 10]

Pyrnelle, Louisa Clarke, writer of books for children, b. near Uniontown, Ala., 1852; d. ? [7; 34]

Pyre, James Francis Augustin, educationist, b. 1871; d. Madison, Wis., May 28, 1934. [10]

Q

Quackenbos, George Payn, educationist, b. New York, N.Y., 1826; d. New London, N.H., July 24, 1881. [3; 4; 5; 6]

Quackenbos, John Duncan, educationist and physician, b. New York, N.Y., 1848; d. Lake Sunapee, N.H., Aug. 1, 1926. [3; 4; 5; 6; 10; 11]

Quad, M. (pseud.). See Lewis, Charles Bertrand.

Qualtrough, Edward Francis, naval officer, b. Rochester, N.Y., 1850; d. Nov. 18, 1913. [10]

Quarles, Edwin Latham, poet, b. Clarksburg, W.Va., 1880; d. New York, N.Y., March 29, 1932. [10]

Quayle, William Alfred, bishop, b. Parkville, Mo., 1860; d. Baldwin, Kans., March 9, 1925. [1; 4; 5; 7; 10; 34]

Quick, John Herbert, lawyer, politician, and novelist, b. Grundy county, Ia., 1861; d. Columbia, Mo., May 10, 1925. [1; 7; 10]

Quigg, Lemuel Ely, journalist and politician, b. near Chestertown, Md., 1863; d. New York, N.Y., July 1, 1919. [1; 4]

Quillem, Harry (pseud.). See Kewen, Edward John Cage.

Quin, Dan (pseud.). See Lewis, Alfred Henry.

Quinan, John Russell, physician, b. Lancaster, Pa., 1822; d. Baltimore, Md., Nov. 11, 1890. [1]

Quinby, George Washington, clergyman, b. Westbrook, Me., 1810; d. Augusta, Me., Jan. 10, 1884. [3; 6; 38]

Quinby, Henry Cole, lawyer, b. Lake Village, N.H., 1892; d. New York, N.Y., Oct. 23, 1922. [51]

Quinby, Isaac Ferdinand, soldier, b. Morristown, N.J., 1821; d. Rochester, N.Y., Sept. 18, 1891. [3; 5]

Quinby, Moses, apiarist, b. 1810; d. 1875.

Quince, Peter (pseud.). See Story, Isaac.

Quincy, Edmund, merchant, b. Braintree, Mass., 1703; d. Braintree, Mass., 1788. [3]

Quincy, Edmund, miscellaneous writer, b. Boston, Mass., 1808; d. Dedham, Mass., May 17, 1877. [1; 3; 4; 7; 9]

Quincy, Josiah, jurist, b. Boston, Mass., 1744; d. at sea, April 26, 1775. [1; 3; 4; 5; 9]

Quincy, Josiah, historian and biographer, b. Braintree, Mass., 1772; d. Quincy, Mass., July 1, 1864. [1; 3; 4; 5; 6; 7; 9; 51]

Quincy, Josiah, historian, b. Boston, Mass., 1802; d. Quincy, Mass., Nov. 2, 1882. [3; 4]

Quincy, Josiah Phillips, historian and poet, b. Boston, Mass., 1829; d. Boston, Mass., Oct. 31, 1910. [1; 3; 4; 7; 9; 10]

Quiner, Edwin Bentlee, historian, d. 1868.

Quinn, Daniel, priest, b. Yellow Springs, O., 1861; d. Cincinnati, O., March 3, 1918. [4; 10; 21]

Quinn, John Philip, reformer, b. 1846; d. ?

Quinn, Silvanus Jackson, local historian, b. 1837; d. Fredericksburg, Va., Sept. 6, 1910.

Quint, Alonzo Hall, clergyman, b. Barnstead, N.H., 1828; d. Boston, Mass., Nov. 4, 1896. [3]

Quint, Wilder Dwight, journalist, b. Salem, Mass., 1863; d. Boston, Mass., Jan. 4, 1936. [7; 10]

Quintard, Edward, physician and poet, b. Stamford, Conn., 1867; d. Chattanooga, Tenn., Feb. 12, 1936. [10]

Quisenberry, Anderson Chenault, historian and genealogist, b. near Winchester, Ky., 1850; d. Lexington, Ky., Dec. 4, 1921. [4; 7; 10; 74]

Quitman, Frederick Henry, clergyman, b. Westphalia, Germany, 1760; d. Rhinebeck, N.Y., June 26, 1832. [3; 4]

R

Rabb, Mrs. Kate, née Milner, miscellaneous writer, b. Rockport, Ind.; d. Indianapolis, Ind., July 3, 1937. [10; 11]

Rachford, Benjamin Knox, physician, b. Alexandria, Ky., 1857; d. Cincinnati, O., May 4, 1929. [10; 11]

Radasch, Henry Erdmann, histologist, b. Keokuk, Ia., 1874; d. Philadelphia, Pa., Nov. 30, 1942. [13]

Radcliffe, Alida Graveraet, writer on art, fl. 1876-1894.

Rader, Paul, evangelist, b. Denver, Colo., 1879; d. Hollywood, Calif., July 19, 1938. [10]

Rader, William, clergyman and journalist, b. Cedarville, Pa., 1862; d. San Francisco, Calif., April 9, 1930. [10; 11]

Radford, Benjamin Johnson, clergyman, b. Eureka, Ill., 1838; d. April 27, 1933. [10]

Rae, Herbert (pseud.). See Gibson, George Herbert Rae.

Rae, John, economist, b. near Aberdeen, Scotland, 1796; d. Staten Island, N.Y., July 14, 1872. [1; 9; 27]

Rae, Luzerne, educationist and poet, b. New Haven, Conn., 1811; d. Hartford, Conn., Sept. 16, 1854. [3]

Raff, George Wertz, jurist, b. Stark county, O., 1825; d. Canton, O., April 14, 1888. [3; 6]

Raffensperger, Mrs. Anna Frances, writer of books for children, fl. 1876-1888. [6]

Raffety, William Edward, clergyman, b. Roodhouse, Ill., 1876; d. Redlands, Calif., Sept. 28, 1937. [10; 11]

Rafinesque, Constantine Samuel, botanist, b. near Constantinople, Turkey, 1784; d. Philadelphia, Pa., Sept. 18, 1842. [1; 2; 3; 4; 5; 6; 7; 74]

Rafter, George W., civil engineer, b. Orleans, N.Y., 1851; d. Karlsbad, Austria, Dec. 29, 1907. [1; 4]

Ragozin, Mme. Zénaïde Alexeïevna, historian, b. Russia, 1835; d. 1924. [10]

Raguet, Condy, economist, b. Philadelphia, Pa., 1784; d. Philadelphia, Pa., March 21, 1842. [1; 3; 6]

Rainer, Joseph, priest, b. Kaltern, Tyrol, Austria, 1845; d. 1927. [4; 10; 21]

Rainey, Thomas, mathematician, fl. 1850-1858.

Rainsford, William Stephen, clergyman, b. Dublin, Ireland, 1850; d. New York, N.Y., Dec. 16, 1933. [1; 2a; 10; 11]

Rainwater, Clarence Elmer, educationist, b. near New Canton, Ill., 1884; d. Pasadena, Calif., July 22, 1925. [4; 10]

Ralph, Julian, journalist, b. New York, N.Y., 1853; d. New York, N.Y., Jan. 20, 1903. [1; 4; 5; 7; 10]

Ralphson, George Harvey, writer of books for boys, b. 1879; d. 1940.

Ralston, Jackson Harvey, lawyer, b. Sacramento, Calif., 1857; d. Palo Alto, Calif., Oct. 13, 1945. [10]

Ralston, Robert, lawyer, b. 1863; d. Philadelphia, Pa., Jan. 22, 1916.

Ralston, Thomas Neely, clergyman, b. Bourbon county, Ky., 1806; d. Newport, Ky., Nov. 25, 1891. [3; 6]

Ramaker, Albert John, clergyman and educationist, b. Milwaukee, Wis., 1860; d. Rochester, N.Y., Feb. 12, 1946. [10]

Ramble, Robert (pseud.). See Frost, John.

Ramsay, Andrew John, poet, d. 1907. [27]

Ramsay, David, physician and historian, b. Lancaster county, Pa., 1749; d. Charleston, S.C., May 8, 1815. [1; 3; 4; 5; 6; 7; 9; 34]

Ramsay, Franklin Pierce, clergyman, b. Pike county, Ala., 1856; d. Staten Island, N.Y., Sept. 30, 1926. [4; 34]

Ramsay, J. R. (pseud.). See Ramsay, Andrew John.

Ramsay, Thomas Kennedy, jurist, b. Ayr, Scotland, 1826; d. St. Hugues, Que., Dec. 22, 1886. [27]

Ramsey, James Gettys McGready, physician and historian, b. near Knoxville, Tenn., 1797; d. Knoxville, Tenn., April 11, 1884. [1; 3; 5; 6; 34]

Ramsey, Milton Worth, carpenter, b. Frankfort, Ala., about 1848; d. Minneapolis, Minn., Oct. 28, 1906.

Ramskill, Jerome Hinds, educationist, b. Evanston, Ill., 1880; d. Missoula, Mont., March 31, 1942. [62]

Ranck, George Washington, historian, b. Louisville, Ky., Feb. 13, 1841; d. Lexington, Ky., Aug. 2, 1901. [3b; 10; 34]

Ranck, Henry Haverstick, clergyman, b. Lancaster, Pa., 1868; d. Lancaster, Pa., Aug. 19, 1948. [10]

Rand, Addison Crittenden, manufacturer, b. Westfield, Mass., 1841; d. New York, N.Y., March 9, 1900. [1; 4]

Rand, Asa, clergyman, b. Rindge, N.H., 1783; d. Ashburnham, Mass., Aug. 24, 1871. [3]

Rand, Benjamin, educationist, b. Canning, N.S., 1856; d. Canning, N.S., Nov. 9, 1934. [1a; 7; 10; 11; 51]

Rand, Benjamin Howard, teacher of penmanship, b. Charlestown, Mass., 1792; d. Philadelphia, Pa., June 9, 1862. [3; 6]

Rand, Benjamin Howard, physician b. Philadelphia, Pa., 1827; d. Philadelphia, Pa., Feb. 14, 1883. [3; 6]

Rand, Edward Augustus, clergyman and novelist, b. Portsmouth, N.H., 1837; d. Watertown, Mass., Oct. 5, 1903. [4; 6; 7; 10]

Rand, Edward Lothrop, lawyer, b. 1859; d. Cambridge, Mass., Oct. 9, 1924. [51]

Rand, Edward Sprague, horticulturist, b. Boston, Mass., 1834; d. Para, Brazil, Sept. 28, 1897. [3; 5; 51]

Rand, Kenneth, poet, b. Minneapolis, Minn., 1891; d. Washington, D.C., Oct. 15, 1918. [62]

Rand, Mrs. Mary Frances, née Abbott, miscellaneous writer, b. Thomaston, Me., 1840; d. ? [6; 10]

Rand, Silas Tertius, clergyman and philologist, b. Cornwallis, N.S., 1810; d. Hantsport, N.S., Oct. 4, 1889. [27]

Rand, Theodore Harding, educationist and poet, b. Cornwallis, N.S., 1835; d. Fredericton, N.B., May 29, 1900. [27]

Rand, William Wilberforce, clergyman, b. Gorham, Me., 1816; d. Yonkers, N.Y., March 3, 1909. [3; 10]

Randall, Mrs. Alice Elizabeth, née Sawtelle, educationist, b. San Francisco, Calif., 1865; d. Hartford, Conn., Dec. 9, 1909. [62]

Randall, Burton Alexander, physician, b. Annapolis, Md., 1858; d. Philadelphia, Pa., Jan. 4, 1932. [10]

Randall, Daniel Boody, clergyman, b. 1807; d. 1899. [38]

Randall, David Austin, clergyman, b. Colchester, Conn., 1813; d. Columbus, O., June 27, 1884. [3b; 4; 6]

Randall, Dexter, lawyer, b. 1788; d. Providence, R.I., April 23, 1867. [47]

Randall, Edward Caleb, lawyer, b. Ripley, N.Y., 1860; d. Buffalo, N.Y., July 3, 1935. [10; 11]

Randall, Emilius Oviatt, lawyer and historian, b. Richfield, O., 1850; d. Columbus, O., Dec. 18, 1919. [4; 10]

Randall, George Maxwell, bishop, b. Warren, R.I., 1810; d. Denver, Colo., Sept. 28, 1873. [3; 4]

Randall, Gurdon P., architect, b. Northfield, Vt., about 1821; d. Northfield, Vt., Sept. 20, 1884. [43]

Randall, Henry Stephens, agriculturist, b. Brookfield, N.Y., 1811; d. Cortland, N.Y., Aug. 14, 1876. [1; 3; 6; 7]

Randall, James Ryder, poet, b. Baltimore, Md., 1839; d. Augusta, Ga., Jan. 14, 1908. [1; 3; 4; 5; 7; 9; 21; 34]

Randall, Jean (pseud.). See Hauck, Mrs. Louise, née Platt.

Randall, John Witt, naturalist and poet, b. Boston, Mass., 1813; d. Boston, Mass., Jan. 27, 1892. [3b; 7; 51]

Randall, Otis Everett, educationist, b. North Stonington, Conn., 1860; d. Providence, R.I., Aug. 11, 1946. [10; 11; 47]

Randall, Samuel Bond, clergyman, b. Adams, N.Y., 1860; d. Oakland, Calif., 1904. [10]

Randall, Samuel Sidwell, educationist, b. Norwich, N.Y., 1809; d. New York, N.Y., June 3, 1881. [1; 3; 4; 6]

Randall, Thomas, poet, b. 1778; d. Eaton, N.H., 1859. [38]

Randall, Wyatt William, chemist, b. Annapolis, Md., 1867; d. Baltimore, Md., July 22, 1930. [1; 10; 13]

Randolph, Alfred Magill, bishop, b. near Winchester, Va., 1836; d. April 6, 1918. [1; 3; 4; 5; 10]

Randolph, Anson Davies Fitz, publisher and poet, b. Woodbridge, N.J., 1820; d. West Hampton, Long Island, N.Y., July 6, 1896. [3; 4; 6]

Randolph, Carman Fitz, lawyer, b. Jersey City, N.J., 1856; d. Oct. 12, 1920. [10]

Randolph, Coleman. See Randolph, Carman Fitz.

Randolph, Edwin Archer, lawyer, b. Richmond, Va., 1850; d. Danville, Va., Dec. 24, 1919. [62]

Randolph, Henry Fitz, lawyer and littérateur, b. New York, N.Y., 1856; d. New York, N.Y., May 10, 1892. [45]

Randolph, J. Thornton (pseud.). See Peterson, Charles Jacob.

Randolph, Jacob, surgeon, b. Philadelphia, Pa., 1796; d. Philadelphia, Pa., Feb. 29, 1848. [1; 3; 4; 6]

Randolph, John, politician and orator, b. Prince George county, Va., 1773; d. Philadelphia, Pa., May 24, 1833. [1; 2; 3; 4; 5; 6; 7; 34]

Randolph, Joseph Fitz, lawyer, b. New Brunswick, N.J., 1843; d. Morristown, N.J., Feb. 16, 1932. [10; 11; 62]

Randolph, Lewis Van Syckle Fitz, financier and poet, b. Somerville, N.J., 1838; d. Plainfield, N.J., Jan. 1, 1921. [4; 10]

Randolph, Paschal Beverly, physician and spiritualist, b. New York, N.Y., 1825; d. 1874. [6]

Randolph, Peter, clergyman, fl. 1855-1893.

Randolph, Richard, physician, d. Philadelphia, Pa., Jan. 10, 1906.

Randolph, Sarah Nicholas, educationist, b. Albemarle county, Va., 1839; d. Baltimore, Md., April 25, 1892. [1; 3; 5; 6; 7; 34]

Randolph, Thomas Jefferson, financier, b. Monticello, Va., 1792; d. Edge Hill, Albemarle county, Va., Oct. 7, 1875. [1; 3; 4; 5; 6; 34]

Ranger, Roger (pseud.). See Freeman, James Midwinter.

Rank, Otto, psychologist, b. Vienna, Austria, 1884; d. New York, N.Y., Oct. 31, 1939.

Rankin, Adam, clergyman, b. Pennsylvania, 1755; d. Philadelphia, Pa., Nov. 25, 1827. [74]

Rankin, George Cameron, novelist, d. Jan. 6, 1903. [27]

Rankin, George Clark, clergyman, b. Jefferson county, Tenn., 1849; d. Dallas, Tex., Feb. 2, 1915. [10]

Rankin, Henry Bascom, biographer, b. Sangamon county, Ill., 1837; d. Springfield, Ill., Aug. 15, 1927. [10; 11]

Rankin, Isaac Ogden, clergyman, b. New York, N.Y., 1852; d. Brookline, Mass., June 15, 1936. [10; 11; 68]

Rankin, Jeremiah Eames, clergyman, educationist, and poet, b. Thornton, N. H., 1828; d. Cleveland, O., Nov. 28, 1904. [1; 3; 4; 5; 6; 7; 9; 10]

Rankin, John, clergyman, b. Jefferson county, Tenn., 1793; d. Ironton, O., March 18, 1886. [3; 34]

Rankin, John Chambers, clergyman, b. Guilford county, N.C., 1816; d. Baskingridge, N.J., April 24, 1900. [3; 10]

Ranney, Ambrose Lewis, physician, b. Hardwick, Mass., 1848; d. New York, N.Y., Dec. 1, 1905. [1; 10]

Ranney, Darwin H., clergyman, b. Chester, Vt., 1812; d. West Brattleboro, Vt., Sept. 27, 1870. [43]

Ranous, Mrs. Dora Knowlton, née Thompson, editor, b. Ashfield, Mass., 1859; d. New York, N.Y., Jan. 19, 1916. [4; 7; 10]

Ransohoff, Joseph, surgeon, b. Cincinnati, O., 1853; d. Cincinnati, O., March 10, 1921. [1; 10]

Ransom, James Harvey, chemist, b. 1861; d. Decatur, Ill., May 30, 1940. [13]

Ransom, Truman Bishop, soldier, b. Woodstock, Vt., 1802; d. near Mexico City, Mexico, Sept. 13, 1847. [3]

Rantoul, Robert, reformer, b. Beverly, Mass., Aug. 13, 1805; d. Washington, D.C., Aug. 7, 1852. [1; 3; 4; 5]

Rantoul, Robert Samuel, lawyer, b. Beverly, Mass., 1832; d. 1922. [4; 10; 51]

Rapalje, Stewart, lawyer, b. 1843; d. Northport, N.Y., Oct. 8, 1896. [5]

Raphall, Morris Jacob, rabbi, b. Stockholm, Sweden, 1798; d. New York, N.Y., June 23, 1868. [1; 3; 5; 6; 7]

Rapp, William Jourdan, playwright, b. New York, N.Y., 1895; d. Lake Mohonk, N.Y., Aug. 12, 1942. [7; 10]

Rarey, John Solomon, horse-tamer, b. Groveport, O., 1827; d. Cleveland, O., Oct. 4, 1866. [1; 3]

Rast, Jeremiah, clergyman, b. 1828; d. ?

Rathbone, Charles Horace, artist, b. 1902; d. Miami Beach, Fla., Feb. 22, 1936.

Rathbone, Josephine Adams, librarian, b. Jamestown, N.Y.; d. Augusta, Ga., May 17, 1941. [7; 10; 11]

Rathborne, St. George Henry, novelist and writer of books for boys, b. Covington, Ky., 1854; d. Newark, N.J., Dec. 16, 1938. [7; 10; 11; 34]

Rattermann, Heinrich Armin, historian, b. Germany, 1832; d. Cincinnati, O., Jan. 6, 1923. [1]

Rattray, William Jordan, journalist, b. London, England, 1835; d. Toronto, Ont., Sept. 19, 1883. [27]

Rau, Charles, archaeologist, b. Verviers, Belgium, 1826; d. Washington, D.C., July 25, 1887. [1; 3; 4; 5; 6]

Raub, Albert Newton, educationist, b. 1840; d. ?

Rauch, Edward H., lexicographer, b. 1826; d. 1902.

Rauch, Frederick Augustus, educationist, b. Germany, 1806; d. Mercersburg, Pa., March 2, 1841. [1; 3; 4; 5; 6; 9]

Rauch, John Henry, physician, b. Lebanon, Pa., 1828; d. Lebanon, Pa., March 24, 1894. [1; 3; 4; 5]

Raue, Charles Gottlieb, physician, b. Germany, 1820; d. Philadelphia, Pa., Aug. 21, 1896. [1; 3; 4]

Raum, Green Berry, soldier and politician, b. Golconda, Ill., 1829; d. Chicago, Ill., Dec. 18, 1909. [1; 3; 4; 5; 6; 10]

Raum, John O., local historian, b. Trenton, N.J., 1824; d. Trenton, N.J., June 9, 1893.

Rauschenbusch, Walter, clergyman, b. Rochester, N.Y., 1861; d. Rochester, N.Y., July 25, 1918. [1; 4; 7; 10]

Raven, John Howard, theologian, b. Brooklyn, N.Y., 1870, d. New Brunswick, N.J., Feb. 25, 1949. [10]

Raven, Ralph (pseud.). See Payson, George.

Ravenel, Mrs. Harriott Horry, née Rutledge, historian, b. Charleston, S.C., 1832; d. Charleston, S.C., July 2, 1912. [1; 7; 10; 34]

Ravenel, Henry William, botanist, b. Berkeley, S.C., 1814; d. Aiken, S.C., July 17, 1887. [1; 3; 4; 5; 6]

Ravenel, Mrs. St. Julien. See Ravenel, Mrs. Harriott Horry, née Rutledge.

Ravenscroft, John Stark, bishop, b. near Petersburg, Va., 1772; d. Raleigh, N.C., March 5, 1830. [1; 3; 4; 5; 34]

Ravogli, Augustus, physician, b. Rome, Italy, 1851; d. Cincinnati, O., July 25, 1934. [10]

Ravoux, Augustin, missionary, b. Langeac, France, 1815; d. St. Paul, Minn., Jan. 17, 1906. [1; 21; 70]

Rawie, Henry Christian, economist, b. 1860; d. 1938.

Rawle, Francis, merchant and politician, b. Plymouth, England, about 1662; d. Philadelphia, Pa., March 5, 1726. [1; 4]

Rawle, William, lawyer, b. Philadelphia, Pa. 1759; d. Philadelphia, Pa., April 12, 1836. [1; 3; 4; 5; 6]

Rawle, William Henry, lawyer, b. Philadelphia, Pa., 1823; d. Philadelphia, Pa., April 19, 1889. [1; 3; 4; 5; 6]

Rawles, William A., educationist, b. Remington, Ind., 1863; d. Bloomington, Ind., May 17, 1936. [10; 11]

Rawson, Albert Leighton, artist, b. Chester, Vt., 1829; d. New York, N.Y., Nov., 1902. [3; 10]

Rawson, Edward Kirk, naval chaplain, b. Albany, N.Y., 1846; d. Brookline, Mass., Feb. 1, 1934. [10; 62]

Rawson, Grindall, clergyman, b. Boston, Mass., 1659; d. Mendon, Mass., Aug. 27, 1715. [3; 51]

Rawson, James, clergyman, fl. 1847-1850.

Rawson, Jonathan, soldier, b. 1759; d. 1794.

Rawson, Sullivan Sumner, genealogist, b. 1806; d. 1866.

Ray, Agnes (pseud.). See Benjamin, Mrs. Elizabeth Dundas, née Bedell.

Ray, Charles Andrew, lawyer, b. 1829; d. ?

Ray, Charles Walker, clergyman, b. 1832; d. Germantown, Pa., 1917.

Ray, Charles Wayne, clergyman, b. Riley, Ind., 1872; d. Platte, Neb., April, 1928. [10]

Ray, David Burcham, clergyman, b. 1830; d. Bolivar, Mo., 1922.

Ray, Edward Chittenden, clergyman, b. Rochester, N.Y., 1849; d. Santa Barbara, Calif., March 15, 1923. [10]

Ray, George R., fur-trader, d. Edmonton, Alta., Oct. 13, 1935. [27]

Ray, Henriette Cordelia, poet, d. 1916.

Ray, Isaac, physician, b. Beverly, Mass., 1807; d. Philadelphia, Pa., March 31, 1881. [1; 3; 6]

Ray, John, lawyer, b. Washington county, Mo., 1816; d. New Orleans, La., March 4, 1888. [3; 34]

Ray, Joseph, physician and mathematician, b. Virginia, 1807; d. Cincinnati, O., 1855. [4; 6]

Ray, T. Bronson, clergyman, b. Buckeye, Ind., 1868; d. Richmond, Va., Jan. 17, 1934. [10]

Ray, William, sailor, b. Salisbury, Conn., 1771; d. Auburn, N.Y., 1827. [4; 6]

Raymond, Andrew Van Vranken, educationist, b. Visscher's Ferry, N.Y., 1854; d. April 7, 1918. [4; 10]

Raymond, Bradford Paul, clergyman, b. Stamford, Conn., 1846; d. Middletown, Conn., Feb. 27, 1916. [4; 10]

Raymond, Daniel, lawyer and economist, b. New Haven, Conn., 1786; d. about 1849. [1; 4; 9]

Raymond, Mrs. Evelyn, née Hunt, novelist, b. Watertown, N.Y., 1843; d. April 18, 1910. [7; 10]

Raymond, George Lansing, educationist, b. Chicago, Ill., 1839; d. Washington, D.C., July 11, 1929. [1; 3; 4; 5; 7; 9; 10; 11]

Raymond, Grace (pseud.). See Stillman, Annie Raymond.

Raymond, Henry Jarvis, journalist and politician, b. Lima, N.Y., 1820; d. New York, N.Y., June 18, 1869. [1; 3; 4; 5; 7; 9]

Raymond, Henry Warren, journalist, b. New York, N.Y., 1847; d. Germantown, Pa., Feb. 18, 1925. [10; 62]

Raymond, Ida (pseud.). See Tardy, Mrs. Mary T.

Raymond, James, lawyer, b. Connecticut, 1796; d. Westminster, Md., Jan., 1858. [3; 6]

Raymond, James F., novelist, b. 1826; d. ?

Raymond, Joseph Howard, physiologist, b. 1845; d. Brooklyn, N.Y., March 7, 1915. [10]

Raymond, Miner, theologian, b. New York, N.Y., 1811; d. Evanston, Ill., Nov. 25, 1897. [1; 3b]

Raymond, Robert Raikes, educationist, b. New York, N.Y., 1817; d. Brooklyn, N.Y., Nov. 16, 1888. [3; 6]

Raymond, Rossiter Worthington, mining engineer and littérateur, b. Cincinnati, O., 1840; d. Brooklyn, N.Y., Dec. 31, 1918. [1; 3; 4; 5; 6; 7; 10]

Raymond, Thomas Lynch, lawyer, b. East Orange, N.J., 1875; d. Oct. 7, 1928. [10]

Raymond, William Galt, engineer, b. Princeton, Ia., 1859; d. Iowa City, Ia., June 17, 1926. [4; 10; 11; 37]

Raymond, William Gould, religious leader, b. 1819; d. 1893.

Raymond, William Lee, investment banker and poet, b. Cambridge, Mass., 1877; d. Waltham, Mass., March 19, 1942. [7; 10; 11; 51]

Raymond, William Odber, clergyman and historian, b. Woodstock, N.B., 1853; d. Toronto, Ont., Nov. 23, 1923. [27]

Rayne, Mrs. Martha Louise, novelist, fl. 1879-1893.

Rayner, Emma, novelist, b. Cambridge, England; d. Goshen, N.H., Nov. 20, 1926. [7; 10]

Rayner, Isidor, lawyer and politician, b. Baltimore, Md., 1850; d. Washington, D.C., Nov. 25, 1912. [1; 4; 5; 10]

Rayner, Kenneth, politician, b. Bertie county, N.C., about 1810; d. Washington, D.C., March 4, 1884. [1; 3; 5]

Rayner, Menzies, clergyman, b. 1770; d. 1850.

Read, Benjamin Maurice, historian, b. 1853; d. Santa Fé, N.M., Sept. 14, 1927.

Read, Collinson, lawyer, b. Philadelphia, Pa., 1751; d. Reading, Pa., March 1, 1815. [3; 6]

Read, Daniel, musician, b. Rehoboth, Mass., 1757; d. New Haven, Conn., Dec. 4, 1836. [1; 3; 4; 7; 20]

Read, David, biographer, b. Warren, Mass., 1799; d. Burlington, Vt., Oct. 1, 1881. [43]

Read, David Breakenridge, lawyer and historian, b. Augusta, Upper Canada, 1823; d. Toronto, Ont., May 11, 1904. [27]

Read, Elizabeth Fisher, lawyer, b. Westport, Conn., Dec. 13, 1943.

Read, George Henry, naval officer, b. 1843; d. 1924.

Read, Harriette Fanning, actress, fl. 1848-1860. [6]

Read, Hollis, missionary, b. Newfane, Vt., 1802; d. Somerville, N.J., April 7, 1887. [3; 5; 6; 43]

Read, John Meredith, diplomat, b. Philadelphia, Pa., 1837; d. Paris, France, Dec. 27, 1896. [1; 2; 3; 5]

Read, Melbourne Stuart, educationist, b. Berwick, N.S., 1869; d. Hamilton, N.Y., April 4, 1927. [10]

Read, Opie Percival, novelist and humorist, b. Nashville, Tenn., 1852; d. Chicago, Ill., Nov. 2, 1939. [2; 4; 5; 7; 10; 11; 34]

Read, Thomas Buchanan, painter and poet, b. Chester county, Pa., 1822; d. New York, N.Y., May 11, 1872. [1; 2; 3; 4; 5; 6; 7; 9; 71]

Read, Thomas Thornton, metallurgist, b. Monmouth county, N.J., 1880; d. White Plains, N.Y., May 29, 1947. [10]

Read, William, physician, b. about 1820; d. 1889.

Read, William, clergyman and poet, b. 1825; d. 1900.

Read, William Thompson, biographer, d. 1873. [56]

Reade, John, journalist and poet, b. county Donegal, Ireland, 1837; d. Montreal, Que., March 20, 1919. [27]

Reade, Philip Hildreth, soldier, b. Lowell, Mass., 1844; d. Boston, Mass., Oct. 21, 1919. [10]

Reader, Francis Smith, journalist, b. Coal Centre, Pa., 1842; d. New Brighton, Pa., Dec. 31, 1928. [4; 10]

Reading, Joseph Hankinson, missionary, b. 1849; d. Woodstown, N.J., July 14, 1920.

Reagan, Albert B., archaeologist, b. Maxwell, Ia., 1871; d. 1936. [13]

Reagan, John Henninger, politician, b. Sevierville, Tenn., 1818; d. Palestine, Tex., March 6, 1905. [1; 4; 5; 10; 34]

Realf, Richard, poet, b. Sussex, England, 1834; d. Oakland, Calif., Oct. 28, 1878. [1; 3; 7; 9]

Rearden, Timothy Henry, essayist, b. 1839; d. 1892.

Reavis, Logan Uriah, journalist, b. Sangamon Bottom, Ill., 1831; d. St. Louis, Mo., April 25, 1889. [3]

Reber, Samuel, soldier, b. St. Louis, Mo., 1864; d. New York, N.Y., April 16, 1933. [10]

Reccord, Augustus Phineas, clergyman, b. Achusnet, Mass., 1870; d. Detroit, Mich., Oct. 4, 1946. [10; 11]

Record, Samuel James, educationist, b. Crawfordsville, Ind., 1881; d. New Haven, Conn., Feb. 3, 1945. [10; 62]

Rector, George, restaurant proprietor, b. Chicago, Ill., 1878; d. New York, N.Y., Nov. 27, 1947. [10]

Red, William Stuart, clergyman, b. 1857; d. 1933.

Reddale, Frederic (pseud.). See Reddall, Henry Frederic.

Reddall, Henry Frederick, musician and journalist, b. London, England, 1856; d. 1921. [3; 10]

Redden, Laura Catherine. See Searing, Mrs. Laura Catherine, née Redden.

Redding, Moses Wolcott, freemason, fl. 1876-1903.

Reden, Karl (pseud.). See Converse, Charles Crozat.

Redfield, Amasa Angell, lawyer, b. Clyde, N.Y., 1837; d. Farmington, Conn., Oct. 19, 1902. [1; 3; 10]

Redfield, Mrs. Anna Maria, née Treadwell, naturalist, b. L'Orignal, Upper Canada, 1800; d. Syracuse, N.Y., June 15, 1888. [4; 5]

Redfield, Isaac Fletcher, jurist, b. Weathersfield, Vt., 1804; d. Charlestown, Mass., March 23, 1876. [1; 3; 4; 5; 6]

Redfield, James W., physician, fl. 1849-1863. [6]

Redfield, John Howard, naturalist, b. Cromwell, Conn., 1815; d. Philadelphia, Pa., Feb. 27, 1895. [3]

Redfield, William C., meteorologist, b. Middletown, Conn., 1789; d. New York, N.Y., Feb. 12, 1857. [1; 3; 4; 5; 6]

Redfield, William Cox, politician, b. Albany, N.Y., 1858; d. Brooklyn, N.Y., June 13, 1932. [1; 10; 11]

Redivivus, Quevedo, jr. (pseud.). See Wright, Robert William.

Redlich, Marcellus Donald Alexander von, lawyer, b. Austria, 1893; d. Chicago, Ill., June 24, 1946. [11]

Redman, George A., physician, b. 1835; d. ?

Redmond, Daniel Webster, educationist, b. Oxford, N.Y., 1876; d. New York, N.Y., Nov. 13, 1934. [10]

Redmond, Nicolaus M., priest, d. 1915. [21]

Redpath, James, journalist and lecture promoter, b. Berwick-on-Tweed, Scotland, 1833; d. New York, N.Y., Feb. 10, 1891. [1; 3; 4; 5; 6; 7; 9]

Redway, Jacques Wardlaw, geographer, b. near Murfreesboro, Tenn., 1849; d. Mount Vernon, N.Y., Nov. 6, 1942. [4; 10; 11]

Reed, Albert Granberry, educationist, b. near Paducah, Ky., 1870; d. Baton Rouge, La., May 18, 1932. [7; 10; 11; 62]

Reed, Alfred Zantzinger, educationist, b. Colorado Springs, Colo., 1875; d. Colorado Springs, Colo., March 11, 1949. [10; 51]

Reed, Alonzo, educationist, d. Remsenburg, N.Y., Aug. 19, 1899. [3b]

Reed, Anna Stevens, novelist, b. 1849; d. June 11, 1932.

Reed, Boardman, physician, b. Scottsville, N.Y., 1842; d. Alhambra, Calif., Oct. 31, 1917. [10]

Reed, Caleb, journalist, b. West Bridgewater, Mass., 1797; d. Boston, Mass., Oct. 14, 1854. [3]

Reed, Charles Alfred Lee, physician, b. Wolf Lake, Ind., 1856; d. Gloucester, Mass., Aug. 28, 1928. [4; 10]

Reed, Charles Bert, surgeon, b. Harvard, Ill., 1866; d. Chicago, Ill., Sept. 5, 1940. [10; 11]

Reed, Charles K., taxidermist, b. Cummington, Mass., 1851; d. Worcester, Mass., March 11, 1921.

Reed, Chester Albert, naturalist, b. Worcester, Mass., 1876; d. Worcester, Mass., Dec. 16, 1912.

Reed, Earl Howell, etcher, b. Geneva, Ill., 1863; d. Chicago, Ill., July 9, 1931. [1; 7; 10; 11]

Reed, Edward Bliss, educationist, b. Lansingburgh, N.Y., 1872; d. Springfield, Mass., Feb. 16, 1940. [7; 10; 62]

Reed, Edwin, Shakespearian scholar, b. Phippburg, Me., 1835; d. Boston, Mass., Oct. 15, 1908. [10]

Reed, Mrs. Elizabeth, née **Armstrong,** orientalist, b. Winthrop, Me., 1842; d. Chicago, Ill., June 16, 1915. [1; 2; 4; 5; 7; 10]

Reed, Frank Fremont, lawyer, b. Monmouth, Ill., 1857; d. Chicago, Ill., Jan. 15, 1926. [10]

Reed, Frederic Alonzo, clergyman, b. 1821; d. 1883.

Reed, Mrs. H. V. See Reed, Mrs. Elizabeth, née Armstrong.

Reed, Helen Leah, writer of books for girls, b. Saint John, N.B., about 1860; d. July, 1926. [7; 10]

Reed, Henry, lawyer, b. Philadelphia, Pa., 1846; d. New York, N.Y., Feb. 23, 1896. [3]

Reed, Henry Albert, soldier, b. Plattsburg, N.Y., 1844; d. San Juan, Porto Rico, Nov. 21, 1930. [10; 11]

Reed, Henry Hope, educationist, b. Philadelphia, Pa., 1808; d. at sea, Sept. 27, 1854. [1; 3; 4; 5; 6]

Reed, Hugh Daniel, biologist, b. Hartsville, N.Y., 1875; d. Ithaca, N.Y., Aug. 23, 1937. [10; 13]

Reed, Hugh T., soldier, b. Richmond, Ind., 1850; d. Richmond, Ind., Nov. 30, 1934. [3]

Reed, Isaac George, poet and novelist, b. Philadelphia, Pa., 1836; d. New York, N.Y., Jan. 22, 1903. [6]

Reed, Isaac N., physician, fl. 1880-1888.

Reed, Jacob Whittemore, genealogist, b. 1805; d. 1869.

Reed, James, clergyman, b. Boston, Mass., 1834; d. Boston, Mass., May 21, 1921. [1; 4; 5; 6; 10; 51]

Reed, John, lawyer, b. 1786; d. 1850.

Reed, John, journalist, poet and revolutionist, b. Portland, Ore., 1887; d. Moscow, Russia, Oct. 19, 1920. [1; 4; 7; 10; 51]

Reed, John Calvin, jurist, b. Appling, Ga., 1836; d. Montgomery, Ala., Jan. 12, 1910. [10; 34]

Reed, John Eugene, clergyman, b. Philadelphia, Pa., 1843; d. Philadelphia, Pa., Jan. 24, 1931. [64]

Reed, John Oren, physicist, b. New Castle, Ind., 1856; d. Ann Arbor, Mich., Jan. 22, 1916. [10]

Reed, John Sanders, clergyman, b. 1844; d. Philadelphia, Pa., Jan. 30, 1910.

Reed, Jonas, local historian, b. 1759; d. Rutland, Mass., 1839.

Reed, Milton, lawyer, b. Haverhill, Mass., 1848; d. Fall River, Mass., Sept. 18, 1932. [10; 51]

Reed, Myron Winslow, clergyman, b. Brookfield, Vt., 1836; d. Denver, Colo., Jan. 30, 1899. [3b; 4]

Reed, Myrtle, poet and novelist, b. Chicago, Ill., 1874; d. Chicago, Ill., Aug. 17, 1911. [1; 4; 7; 10]

Reed, Newton, local historian, b. Amenia, N.Y., 1805; d. near Amenia, N.Y., March 19, 1896. [63]

Reed, Orville, clergyman, b. Lansingburgh, N.Y., 1854; d. New York, N.Y., Nov. 3, 1927. [62]

Reed, Parker McCobb, lawyer and historian, b. 1813; d. ? [38; 44]

Reed, Peter Fishe, artist, fl. 1862-1869. [6]

Reed, Rebecca Perley, religious writer, fl. 1873-1874. [6; 38]

Reed, Rebecca Theresa, proselyte, b. East Cambridge, Mass., about 1813; d. ? [3]

Reed, Richard Clark, clergyman, b. Hamilton county, Tenn., 1851; d. Columbia, S.C., July 9, 1925. [1; 10; 34]

Reed, Sampson, religious writer, b. West Bridgewater, Mass., 1800; d. Boston, Mass., July 8, 1880. [1; 3; 9]

Reed, Samuel Burrage, architect, fl. 1878-1900.

Reed, Samuel Rockwell, soldier, d. 1889. [6]

Reed, Sarah Ann, philanthropist, b. Ashtabula, O., 1838; d. Erie, Pa., Jan. 27, 1934. [7; 10; 11]

Reed, Thomas Brackett, lawyer and politician, b. Portland, Me., 1839; d. Washington, D.C., Dec. 7, 1902. [1; 3; 4; 5; 10; 38]

Reed, Thomas E., physician, b. 1844; d. Middletown, O., Aug. 15, 1931.

Reed, Verner Zevola, miscellaneous writer, b. Richland county, O., 1863; d. Coronado, Calif., April 20, 1919. [4; 7; 10]

Reed, Wallace Putnam, journalist, b. 1849; d. 1903. [34]

Reed, William Bradford, lawyer and diplomat, b. 1806; d. New York, N.Y., Feb. 18, 1876. [1; 3; 4; 5; 6]

Reed, William Howell, soldier, b. Boston, Mass., 1837; d. Belmont, Mass., Oct. 26, 1914.

Reeder, Charles, manufacturer, b. Baltimore, Md., 1817; d. Baltimore, Md., Dec. 1900. [3; 4]

Reedy, William Marion, journalist, b. St. Louis, Mo., 1862; d. San Francisco, Calif., July 28, 1920. [1; 4; 7; 10]

Reemelin, Charles, viticulturist, b. Germany, 1814; d. ? [6]

Rees, Byron Johnson, educationist, b. Westfield, Ind., 1877; d. Williamstown, Mass., Feb. 18, 1920. [10]

Rees, James, journalist and playwright, b. Norristown, Pa., 1802; d. 1885. [6]

Rees, Robert Irwin, business executive, b. Houghton, Mich., 1871; d. Detroit, Mich., Nov. 23, 1936. [10]

Rees, Thomas, newspaper publisher, b. Pittsburgh, Pa., 1850; d. Springfield, Ill., Sept. 9, 1933. [10; 11]

Reese, David Meredith, physician, b. 1800; d. New York, N.Y., Aug. 12, 1861. [3; 6]

Reese, John James, toxicologist, b. Philadelphia, Pa., 1818; d. Atlantic City, N.J., Sept. 4, 1892. [1; 3; 4; 6]

Reese, Lizette Woodworth, poet, b. Baltimore county, Md., 1856; d. Baltimore Md., Dec. 17, 1935. [1a; 4; 7; 10; 34]

Reese, Thomas, clergyman, b. 1742; d. near Pendleton, S.C., 1794. [3; 34]

Reeve, Arthur Benjamin, novelist, b. Patchogue, N.Y., 1880; d. Trenton, N.J., Aug. 9, 1936. [7; 10; 11; 21]

Reeve, Charles McCormick, soldier, b. Dansville, N.Y., 1847; d. Minnetonka Beach, Minn., June 24, 1947. [62; 70]

Reeve, James Knapp, journalist, b. Hancock, N.Y., 1856; d. Franklin, O., Oct. 25, 1933. [10]

Reeve, Sidney Armor, engineer, b. Dayton, O., 1866; d. Nyack, N.Y., June 13, 1941. [10; 11]

Reeve, Tapping, jurist, b. Brookhaven, Long Island, N.Y., 1744; d. Litchfield, Conn., Dec. 13, 1823. [1; 3; 4; 5; 6]

Reeves, Alfred Gandy, lawyer, b. Millville, N.J., 1859; d. Brooklyn, N.Y., Jan. 10, 1927. [10]

Reeves, Arthur Middleton, historian, b. Cincinnati, O., 1856; d. near Hagerstown, Ind., Feb. 25, 1891. [1]

Reeves, Francis Brewster, merchant, b. Bridgeton, N.J., 1836; d. Germantown, Pa., May 6, 1923. [4; 10]

Reeves, Ira Lewis, soldier and educationist, b. Jefferson City, Mo., 1872; d. Eldon, Mo., Oct. 23, 1939. [4; 10]

Reeves, James Edmund, physician, b. 1829; d. Chattanooga, Tenn., Jan. 4, 1896. [6]

Reeves, Jeremiah Bascom, educationist, b. Siloam, N.C., 1884; d. Fulton, Mo., Nov. 7, 1946. [62]

Reeves, Jesse Siddall, lawyer and educationist, b. Richmond, Ind., 1872; d. Ann Arbor, Mich., July 7, 1942. [10]

Reeves, Marian Calhoun Legaré, novelist, b. Charleston, S.C., 1854; d. ? [3; 7; 34]

Regan, James, soldier, b. 1844; d. 1906. [6]

Regan, Mary Jane, librarian, b. 1842; d. 1925. [21]

Regester, Seeley (pseud.). See Victor, Mrs. Metta Victoria, née Fuller.

Register, Edward Chauncey, physician, b. Rose Hill, N.C., 1860; d. Charlotte, N.C., Feb. 18, 1920. [4; 10]

Reich, Max Isaac, clergyman, b. Berlin, Germany, 1867; d. Bryn Mawr, Pa., Aug. 11, 1945. [10]

Reichel, George Valentine, clergyman, b. Brooklyn, N.Y., 1863; d. Columbus, O., May 14, 1914. [4; 63]

Reichel, Levin Theodore, bishop, b. Bethlehem, Pa., 1812; d. Hernhut, Saxony, Germany, May 23, 1878. [4; 34]

Reichel, William Cornelius, clergyman, b. Salem, N.C., 1824; d. Bethlehem, Pa., Oct. 25, 1876. [1; 3; 4; 5; 6]

Reichert, Edward Tyson, physiologist, b. Philadelphia, Pa., 1855; d. St. Petersburg, Fla., Dec. 25, 1931. [4; 10]

Reid, Mrs. Bertha, née Westbrook, biographer, d. Newark, N.J., July 28, 1939.

Reid, Christian (pseud.). See Tiernan, Mrs. Frances Christine, née Fisher.

Reid, Gilbert, missionary, b. Laurel, Long Island, N.Y., 1857; d. Shanghai, China, Sept. 30, 1927. [1; 10; 68]

Reid, Hal. See Reid, James Halleck.

Reid, Harvey, biographer, b. 1842; d. 1910. [37]

Reid, Hiram Alvin, journalist, b. Lisbon, O., 1834; d. Pasadena, Calif., 1906.

Reid, James Halleck, playwright, d. 1920.

Reid, John Morrison, clergyman, b. New York, N.Y., 1820; d. New York, N.Y., May 16, 1896. [1; 3; 4; 5; 6]

Reid, P. Fish. See Reed, Peter Fishe.

Reid, Robie Lewis, historian, b. Cornwallis, N.S., 1866; d. Vancouver, B.C., Feb. 6, 1945. [27]

Reid, Samuel Chester, lawyer, soldier and journalist, b. New York, N.Y., 1818; d. Washington, D.C., Aug. 13, 1897. [3; 5; 6; 7]

Reid, Sydney Robert Charles Forneri, journalist, b. Toronto, Ont., 1857; d. Brooklyn, N.Y., July 20, 1936. [31a]

Reid, Whitelaw, journalist and diplomat, b. near Xenia, O., 1837; d. London, England, Dec. 15, 1912. [1; 2; 3; 4; 5; 6; 7; 9; 10]

Reid, William Duncan, physician, b. Newton, Mass., 1885; d. Parsons Field, Me., Sept. 29, 1929. [10; 11; 51]

Reid, William Maxwell, historian, b. Amsterdam, N.Y., 1839; d. Amsterdam, N.Y., Nov. 27, 1911. [10]

Reifsnider, Mrs. Anna Cyrene, née Porter, miscellaneous writer, b. near Troy, Mo., 1850; d. Cincinnati, O., Feb. 24, 1932. [4]

Reigert, John Franklin, soldier, fl. 1844-1878. [6]

Reigert, John Franklin, educationist, b. Lancaster, Pa., 1863; d. Yonkers, N.Y., April 22, 1946.

Reighard, Jacob Ellsworth, biologist, b. Laporte, Ind., 1861; d. Ann Arbor, Mich., Feb. 14, 1942. [4; 10]

Reik, Henry Ottridge, physician, b. Baltimore, Md., 1868; d. New York, N.Y., June 2, 1938. [10]

Reilly, Bernard James, priest, b. 1865; d. 1930. [21]

Reily, William McClellan, clergyman, b. 1837; d. Wyoming, Del., Nov. 21, 1892.

Reimensnyder, Junius Benjamin. See Remensnyder, Junius Benjamin.

Reinhard, George Louis, lawyer, b. 1843; d. 1906.

Reinsch, Paul Samuel, educationist and diplomat, b. Milwaukee, Wis., 1869; d. Shanghai, China, Jan. 24, 1923. [1; 2; 4; 7; 10]

Reischauer, Robert Karl, historian, b. 1907; d. Shanghai, China, Aug. 14, 1937.

Reisner, Christian Fichthorne, clergyman, b. Atchison, Kans., 1872; d. New York, N.Y., July 18, 1940. [10; 11]

Reiss, Isaac. See Nadir, Isaac Moishe.

Reist, Henry Gerber, engineer, b. Mount Joy, Pa., 1862; d. Schenectady, N.Y., July 5, 1942. [10]

Relf, Samuel, journalist and novelist, b. Virginia, 1776; d. Virginia, Feb. 14, 1823. [3]

Remensnyder, Junius Benjamin, clergyman, b. Staunton, Va., 1843; d. New York, N.Y., Jan. 2, 1927. [3; 4; 6; 10; 11]

Remick, Martha, novelist, fl. 1862-1865. [6]

Remick, Oliver Philbrick, genealogist, b. 1853; d. 1913.

Remington, Frederic, painter and illustrator, b. Canton, N.Y., 1861; d. Ridgefield, Conn., Dec. 26, 1909. [1; 2; 4; 7; 10; 72]

Remington, Harold, lawyer, b. Quincy, Ill., 1865; d. New York, N.Y., Dec. 15, 1937. [10; 11]

Remington, Joseph Price, pharmacist, b. Philadelphia, Pa., 1847; d. Philadelphia, Pa., Jan. 1, 1918. [1; 3; 4; 10]

Remington, Stephen, clergyman, b. Bedford, N.Y., 1803; d. Brooklyn, N.Y., March 23, 1869. [3]

Reminisco, Don Pedro Quaerendo (pseud.). See Tousey, Sinclair.

Remondino, Peter Charles, physician, b. Turin, Italy, 1846; d. San Diego, Calif., Dec. 11, 1926. [4; 10]

Remsburg, John Eleazer, lecturer, b. Fremont, O., 1848; d. Sept. 23, 1919. [10]

Remsen, Daniel Smith, lawyer, b. Tecumseh, Mich., 1853; d. Bound Brook, N.J., April 25, 1935. [10]

Remsen, Ira, chemist, b. New York, N.Y., 1846; d. Carmel, Calif., March 4, 1927. [1; 2; 3; 4; 5; 6; 7; 10; 11. 13]

Rémy, Henri, lawyer and journalist, b. Agen, France, about 1811; d. New Orleans, La., Feb. 21, 1867. [1; 34]

Rennelson, Mrs. Clara H., née **Morse,** novelist, b. Norwalk, O., 1845; d. ? [10]

Rennert, Hugo Albert, educationist, b. Philadelphia, Pa., 1858; d. Washington, D.C,. Dec. 31, 1927. [4; 10; 11]

Reno, Conrad, lawyer, b. Mount Vernon, Ala., 1859; d. May 7, 1933. [10]

Renwick, Edward Sabine, inventor, b. New York, N.Y., 1823; d. Short Hills, N.J., March 19, 1912. [1; 3; 4; 10]

Renwick, Henry Brevoort, engineer, b. New York, N.Y., 1817; d. New York, N.Y., Jan. 27, 1895. [1; 3; 4]

Renwick, James, engineer, b. Liverpool, England, 1792; d. New York, N.Y., Jan. 12, 1863. [1; 3; 4; 5; 6]

Requa, Mark Lawrence, mining engineer, b. Virginia City, Nev., 1866; d. Santa Barbara, Calif., March 6, 1937. [10; 35]

Requier, Augustus Julian, poet and jurist, b. Charleston, S.C., 1825; d. New York, N.Y., March 19, 1887. [1; 3; 7; 9; 34]

Restarick, Henry Bond, bishop, b. Somerset, England, 1854; d. Honolulu, Hawaii, Dec. 8, 1933. [1a; 4; 10]

Retort, Jack (pseud.). See Hunt, Isaac.

Reu, Johann Michael, theologian, b. Bavaria, Germany, 1869; d. Dubuque, Ia., Oct. 15, 1943. [10; 11]

Reuter, Edward Byron, sociologist, b. Holden, Mo., 1880; d. Nashville, Tenn., May 28, 1946. [10; 11]

Reuterdahl, Arvid, educationist, b. Sweden, 1876; d. St. Paul, Minn., Jan. 13, 1933. [10; 11]

Revell, Alexander Hamilton, golfer, b. Chicago, Ill., 1858; d. Chicago, Ill., March 13, 1931. [4; 10]

Revere, Joseph Warren, naval and military officer, b. Boston, Mass., 1812; d. Hoboken, N.J., April 20, 1880. [1; 3; 4; 5; 6; 7]

Reverie, Reginald (pseud.). See Mellen, Grenville.

Revusky, Abraham, journalist, b. Haifa, Palestine, 1889; d. New York, N.Y., Feb. 8, 1946.

Reville, Frederick Douglas, local historian, b. Witney, England, 1866; d. Brantford, Ont., Aug. 11, 1944. [27]

Reville, John Clement, priest, b. 1867; d. 1929. [21]

Revons, E. C. (pseud.). See Converse, Charles Crozat.

Rexdale, Robert, journalist, b. 1859; d. Rock Island, Ill., Oct. 28, 1929. [10]

Rexford, Eben Eugene, poet and horticulturist, b. Johnsburgh, N.Y., 1848; d. Green Bay, Wis., Oct. 19, 1916. [3; 4; 7; 10]

Rexford, Elson Irving, clergyman, b. South Bolton, Que., 1850; d. Montreal, Que., Oct. 21, 1936. [30]

Reynolds, Charles Bingham, travel bureau executive, b. Morrisania, N.Y., 1856; d. Mountain Lakes, N.J., Nov. 10, 1940. [10]

Reynolds, Cuyler, historian, b. Albany, N.Y., 1866; d. May 24, 1934. [7]

Reynolds, Dexter, lawyer, b. 1828; d. Albany, N.Y., Aug. 26, 1906.

Reynolds, Elhanan Winchester, clergyman, b. 1827; d. 1867.

Reynolds, George, Mormon elder, b. London, England, 1842; d. Salt Lake City, Utah, Aug. 9, 1909.

Reynolds, Helen Wilkinson, historian, b. 1875; d. Poughkeepsie, N.Y., Jan. 3, 1943.

Reynolds, Henry Dunbar, clergyman, b. Dublin, Ireland, 1820; d. Greenock, Scotland, July 23, 1864. [27]

Reynolds, James Joseph, educationist, b. New York, N.Y., 1874; d. Brooklyn, N.Y., May 26, 1945.

Reynolds, Jeremiah N., explorer, b. 1799; d. 1858.

Reynolds, John, clergyman, fl. 1828-1839. [43]

Reynolds, John, politician and historian, b. Montgomery county, Pa., 1788; d. Belleville, Ill., May 8, 1865. [1; 3; 4; 5; 6; 9]

Reynolds, Joseph, physician, b. Wilmington, Mass., about 1796; d. 1872. [6]

Reynolds, Myra, educationist, b. Troupsburg, N.Y., 1852; d. Los Angeles, Calif., Aug. 2, 1936. [7; 10]

Reynolds, Myron Herbert, veterinarian, b. Wheaton, Ill., 1865; d. St. Paul, Minn., Jan. 15, 1929. [10; 11]

Reynolds, William, lawyer, fl. 1883-1912.

Reynolds, William Kilby, journalist, b. Saint John, N.B., 1848; d. Saint John, N.B., Dec. 2, 1902. [27]

Reynolds, William Morton, clergyman, b. Fayette county, Pa., 1812; d. Oak Park, Ill., Sept. 5, 1876. [3; 6]

Reywas, Mot (pseud.). See Spivey, Thomas Sawyer.

Rhead, Frederick Hurten, potter, b. Staffordshire, England, 1881; d. New York, N.Y., Nov. 2, 1942. [10]

Rhead, Louis John, artist and angler, b. Staffordshire, England, 1857; d. Amityville, N.Y., July 29, 1926. [10]

Rhees, Rush, educationist, b. Chicago, Ill., 1860; d. Rochester, N.Y., Jan. 5, 1939. [4; 10; 11]

Rhees, William Jones, bibliographer, b. Philadelphia, Pa., 1830; d. Washington, D.C., March 18, 1907. [1; 3; 4; 5; 6; 7; 10]

Rhine, Abraham Benedict, rabbi, b. Lithuania, 1877; d. Hot Springs, Ark., Aug. 8, 1941. [10]

Rhinelander, Philip Mercer, bishop, b. Newport, R.I., 1869; d. near Gloucester, Mass., Sept. 21, 1939. [10]

Rhinewine, Abraham, journalist, b. Poland, 1887; d. Toronto, Ont., 1932. [11; 27]

Rhoades, Cornelia Harsen, writer of books for children, b. New York, N.Y., 1863; d. New York, N.Y., Nov. 28, 1940. [7; 10]

Rhoades, Nina (pseud.). See Rhoades Cornelia Harsen.

Rhoads, Thomas Jefferson Boyer, physician, b. Boyertown, Pa., 1837; d. Boyertown, Pa., Dec. 23, 1919. [4]

Rhoads, Thomas Y., historian, fl. 1856-1857.

Rhode, William, caterer, b. Germany, 1902; d. New York, N.Y., Nov. 26, 1946.

Rhodes, Albert, consul, b. Pittsburgh, Pa., 1840; d. ? [3; 6; 7]

Rhodes, Eugene Manlove, novelist, b. Tecumseh, Neb., 1869; d. near San Diego, Calif., June 27, 1934. [1a; 7; 10; 11]

Rhodes, Frederick Leland, electrical engineer, b. Boston, Mass., 1870; d. March 18, 1933. [10]

Rhodes, Harrison Garfield, novelist and playwright, b. Cleveland, O., 1871; d. Hereford, England, Sept. 20, 1929. [7; 10; 51]

Rhodes, James Ford, historian, b. Cleveland, O., 1848; d. Brookline, Mass., Jan. 22, 1927. [1; 2; 4; 5; 7; 10; 11]

Rhodes, Mosheim, clergyman, b. Williamsburg, Pa., 1837; d. 1924. [3; 6]

Rhodes, William Henry, lawyer and poet, b. North Carolina, 1822; d. California, about 1875. [34]

Rhone, Daniel Laporte, jurist, d. March 29, 1908.

Rice, Mrs. Alice Caldwell, née Hegan, novelist, b. Shelbyville, Ky., 1870; d. Louisville, Ky., Feb. 10, 1942. [4; 7; 10; 11; 74]

Rice, Allen Thorndike. See Rice, Charles Allen Thorndike.

Rice, Benjamin Franklin, lawyer, b. Washington, D.C., 1875; d. Tulsa, Okla., July 27, 1924. [4; 10]

Rice, Cale Young, poet, playwright, and novelist, b. Dixon, Ky., 1872; d. Louisville, Ky., Jan. 23, 1943. [4; 7; 10; 11; 34; 74]

Rice, Charles Allen Thorndike, editor, b. Boston, Mass., 1851; d. New York, N.Y., May 16, 1889. [1; 3; 4; 5; 6; 7]

Rice, David, clergyman, b. Hanover county, Va., 1753; d. Green county, Ky., June 18, 1816. [1; 3; 6]

Rice, Edward Irving, industrialist, b. Syracuse, N.Y., 1868; d. Oct. 8, 1927. [10]

Rice, Edwin Wilbur, clergyman, b. Kingsborough, N.Y., 1831; d. Philadelphia, Pa., Dec. 3, 1929. [1a; 3; 5; 6; 7; 10; 11]

Rice, Frank Sumner, lawyer, b. Elmira, N.Y., 1850; d. Springfield, Mass., Nov. 5, 1898. [4]

Rice, Franklin Pierce, historian, b. Marlborough, Mass., 1852; d. Worcester, Mass., Jan. 4, 1919. [10]

Rice, George Edward, poet, b. Boston, Mass., 1822; d. Roxbury, Mass., Aug. 10, 1861. [3; 6; 7]

Rice, Harvey, lawyer, b. Conway, Mass., 1800; d. Cleveland, O., Nov. 7, 1891. [3; 4; 6; 7]

Rice, Isaac Leopold, lawyer, b. Bavaria, Germany, 1850; d. New York, N.Y., Nov. 2, 1915. [1; 3; 4; 10]

Rice, James Henry, naturalist, b. Abbeville county, S.C., 1868; d. Wiggins, S.C., March 23, 1935. [10; 11]

Rice, James Montgomery, soldier, b. 1842; d. 1912.

Rice, John Holt, clergyman, b. Bedford county, Va., 1777; d. Hampden-Sidney, Va., Sept. 3, 1831. [1; 3; 4; 5; 34]

Rice, John Minot, mathematician, b. 1833; d. 1901. [6]

Rice, Joseph Mayer, educationist, b. Philadelphia, Pa., 1857; d. Philadelphia, Pa., June 24, 1934. [4; 10]

Rice, Martin, clergyman and poet, b. 1814; d. ? [34]

Rice, Nathan Lewis, clergyman, b. Garrard county, Ky., 1807; d. Chatham, Ky., June 11, 1877. [1; 3; 4; 5; 6; 34]

Rice, Rosella, novelist, b. Perrysville, O., 1827; d. ? [3; 7]

Rice, Roswell, poet, b. 1803; d. ?

Rice, Mrs. Ruth Little, née Mason, novelist and poet, b. Brockport, N.Y., 1884; d. 1927. [11]

Rice, Wallace de Groot Cecil, journalist, b. Hamilton, Ont., 1859; d. Chicago, Ill., Dec. 15, 1939. [4; 7; 10; 11]

Rice, William, clergyman, b. Springfield, Mass., 1821; d. Springfield, Mass., Aug. 17, 1897. [3b]

Rice, William Gorham, publicist, b. Albany, N.Y., 1856; d. Albany, N.Y., Sept. 12, 1945. [11]

Rice, William Henry, clergyman, b. Bethlehem, Pa., 1840; d. South Bethlehem, Pa., Jan. 10, 1911. [62]

Rice, William North, geologist, b. Marblehead, Mass., 1845; d. Delaware, O., Nov. 13, 1928. [1; 3; 4; 5; 10; 62]

Rich, Edwin Gile, literary agent, b. Farmington, Me., 1879; d. Burford, England, Nov., 1939. [10]

Rich, Joseph Warford, historian, b. Marcellus, N.Y., 1838; d. Iowa City, Ia., June 12, 1920. [37]

Rich, Obadiah, bibliographer, b. Truro, Mass., about 1783; d. London, England, Jan. 20, 1850. [1; 3; 6]

Rich, Shebnah, local historian, b. Truro, Mass., 1824; d. Waltham, Mass., July 1, 1907.

Rich, Thomas Hill, educationist, b. Bangor, Me., 1822; d. July 6, 1893. [46]

Rich, Wesley Everett, educationist, b. Chelsea, Mass., 1889; d. Camp Devens, Sept. 25, 1918. [51]

Richard, Edouard, historian, b. Princeville, Que., 1844; d. Battleford, N.W.T., March 27, 1904. [27]

Richard, Ernst, educationist, b. Bonn., Germany, 1859; d. New York, N.Y., Nov. 20, 1914. [10]

Richard, James William, clergyman, b. near Winchester, Va., 1843; d. Philadelphia, Pa., March 7, 1909. [1; 7; 10]

Richard, Louis, priest, b. Nicolet, Lower Canada, 1838; d. Three Rivers, Que., Jan. 6, 1908. [27]

Richards, Charles Herbert, clergyman, b. Meriden, N.H., 1839; d. New York, N.Y., Feb. 16, 1925. [1; 3; 10; 62]

Richards, Charles Russell, educationist, b. Boston, Mass., 1865; d. New York, N.Y., Feb. 21, 1936. [10]

Richards, Mrs. Cornelia Holroyd, née **Bradley,** miscellaneous writer, b. Hudson, N.Y., 1822; d. Detroit, Mich., May 1, 1892. [3; 5]

Richards, Cyrus Smith, educationist, b. Hartford, Vt., 1808; d. Madison, Wis., July 19, 1885. [3]

Richards, Elias Jones, clergyman, b. 1813; d. 1872.

Richards, Mrs. Ellen Henrietta, née **Swallow,** home economist, b. Dunstable, Mass., 1842; d. Jamaica Plain, Mass., March 30, 1911. [1; 3; 4; 5; 10]

Richards, Eugene Lamb, educationist, b. Brooklyn, N.Y., 1838; d. Beach Haven, N.J., Aug. 5, 1912. [10; 62]

Richards, Frank, engineer, b. Taunton, England, 1839; d. North Plainfield, N.J., May 21, 1933.

Richards, George, lawyer, b. Boston, Mass., March 23, 1849; d. New York, N.Y., May 24, 1930. [10; 62]

Richards, Mrs. Gertrude Moore, anthologist, d. 1927.

Richards, Harry Sanger, lawyer, b. Osceola, Ia., 1868; d. April 21, 1929. [10]

Richards, Herbert Maule, botanist, b. Germantown, Pa., 1871; d. New York, N.Y., Jan. 9, 1928. [10; 13]

Richards, Jarrett Thomas, lawyer, b. Chambersburg, Pa., 1843; d. May 21, 1920. [21; 35]

Richards, John, mechanical engineer, b. 1834; d. ? [6]

Richards, John Evan, jurist, b. San Jose, Calif., 1856; d. San Jose, Calif., June 25, 1932. [4; 10; 35]

Richards, John Thomas, lawyer, b. Ironton, O., 1851; d. ? [11]

Richards, Joseph Havens Cowles, priest, b. Columbus, O., 1851; d. Worcester, Mass., June 9, 1923. [5; 10; 21]

Richards, Joseph William, metallurgist, b. Worcestershire, England, 1864; d. Philadelphia, Pa., Oct. 12, 1921. [1; 4; 10]

Richards, Mrs. Laura Elizabeth, née **Howe,** novelist, biographer, and poet, b. Boston, Mass., 1850; d. Gardiner, Me., Jan. 14, 1943. [4; 7; 10; 11; 15]

Richards, Louis, lawyer, b. 1842; d. 1924.

Richards, Lysander Salmon, historian, b. 1835; d. near Marshfield, Mass., Nov. 12, 1926.

Richards, Mrs. Maria, née **Tolman,** religious writer, b. Dorchester, Mass., 1821; d. ? [3; 6]

Richards, Ralph Reed, bridge expert, b. Chicago, Ill., 1876; d. Detroit, Mich., June 9, 1943.

Richards, Robert Hallowell, metallurgist, b. Gardiner, Me., 1844; d. South Natick, Mass., March 27, 1945. [10; 13]

Richards, Thomas Addison, painter and illustrator, b. London, England, 1820; d. Annapolis, Md., June 28, 1900. [1; 3; 4; 5; 6; 7; 9; 10]

Richards, Mrs. Waldo. See Richards, Mrs. Gertrude Moore.

Richards, William, missionary, b. Plainfield, Mass., 1793; d. Honolulu, Hawaii, Nov. 7, 1847. [1; 3; 4]

Richards, William, convert, b. 1819; d. 1899. [21]

Richards, William Carey, clergyman, b. London, England, 1818; d. Chicago, Ill., May 19, 1892. [3; 5; 6]

Richards, William Rogers, clergyman, b. Boston, Mass., 1853; d. New York, N.Y., Jan. 8, 1910. [10; 62]

Richards, Zalmon, educationist, b. Cummington, Mass., 1811; d. Washington, D.C., Nov. 1, 1899. [1; 4]

Richardson, Mrs. Abby, née **Sage,** actress, b. Lowell, Mass., 1837; d. Rome, Italy, Dec. 5, 1900. [3; 4; 5; 6; 7; 10]

Richardson, Albert Deane, journalist, b. Franklin, Mass., 1833; d. New York, N.Y., Dec. 2, 1869. [1; 3; 4; 5; 6; 7; 9]

Richardson, Mrs. Anna Steese, née **Sausser,** journalist and writer on etiquette, b. Massillon, O., 1865; d. New York, N.Y., May 10, 1949.

Richardson, Charles, soldier, fl. 1862-1907. [34]

Richardson, Charles, financier, b. Philadelphia, Pa., 1841; d. Philadelphia, Pa., Nov. 19, 1922. [10]

Richardson, Charles Francis, educationist, b. Hallowell, Me., 1851; d. Sugar Hill, N.H., Oct. 8, 1913. [1; 3; 4; 5; 6; 7; 9; 10]

Richardson, Charles Henry, geologist, b. Topsham, Vt., 1862; d. Syracuse, N.Y., Sept. 19, 1935. [10; 13]

Richardson, Mrs. Charlotte, née **Smith,** poet, b. 1775; d. about 1850.

Richardson, Clifford, chemical engineer, b. Worcester, Mass., 1856; d. Nice, France, Feb. 27, 1932. [10; 51]

Richardson, Daniel Sidney, poet, b. West Acton, Mass., 1851; d. Berkeley, Calif., Sept. 11, 1922. [35]

Richardson, David Nelson, journalist, b. 1832; d. 1898. [6; 27]

Richardson, Dennett Leroy, physician, b. Newport, Me., 1879; d. Providence, R.I., Sept. 6, 1946.

Richardson, Erastus, local historian, b. 1837; d. Woonsocket, R.I., Sept. 28, 1911. [47]

Richardson, Ernest Cushing, librarian, b. Woburn, Mass., 1860; d. Washington, D.C., June 3, 1939. [4; 7; 10]

Richardson, George Lynde, clergyman, b. Troy, N.Y., 1867; d. Peterborough, N.H., Jan. 24, 1935. [10]

Richardson, George Tilton, journalist, b. Boston, Mass.; d. Worcester, Mass., Sept. 11, 1938. [7; 10]

Richardson, Mrs. Hester, née **Dorsey,** historian, b. Baltimore, Md., 1867; d. Baltimore, Md., Dec. 10, 1933. [10]

Richardson, Hobart Wood, journalist, b. 1831; d. 1889. [38]

Richardson, Jabez (pseud.). See Day, Benjamin Henry.

Richardson, James Bailey, jurist, b. Oxford, N.H., 1832; d. Boston, Mass., 1911. [10]

Richardson, James Daniel, politician, b. Rutherford county, Tenn., 1843; d. Murfreesboro, Tenn., July 24, 1914. [1; 4; 5; 10; 34]

Richardson, James Perkins, novelist, b. Aurora, Ill., 1868; d. Houston, Tex., April 8, 1922. [62]

Richardson, John, soldier and novelist, b. Queenston, Upper Canada, 1796; d. near New York, N.Y., May 12, 1852. [27]

Richardson, John Fram, educationist, b. Vernon, N.Y., 1808; d. Rochester, N.Y., Feb. 10, 1868. [3; 6]

Richardson, Joseph, clergyman, b. Billerica, Mass., 1778; d. Hingham, Mass., Sept. 25, 1871. [3]

Richardson, Joseph, dental surgeon, fl. 1860-1886. [6]

Richardson, Joseph Gibbons, physician, b. 1836; d. Philadelphia, Pa., Nov. 13, 1886.

Richardson, Leander Pease, journalist, b. Cincinnati, O., 1856; d. Feb. 2, 1918. [7; 10]

Richardson, Nathaniel Smith, clergyman, b. Middlebury, Conn., 1810; d. Bridgeport, Conn., Aug. 7, 1883. [3; 62]

Richardson, Noble Asa, economist, d. San Bernardino, Calif., May 20, 1931.

Richardson, Norman Egbert, educationist, b. Bethany, Ont., 1878; d. Evanston, Ill., Oct. 25, 1945. [10; 11]

Richardson, Norval, diplomat and novelist, b. Vicksburg, Miss., 1877; d. Hamilton, Bermuda, Oct. 22, 1940. [7; 10; 11]

Richardson, Oliver Huntington, educationist, b. Providence, R.I., 1867; d. Seattle, Wash., Sept. 22, 1936. [10; 62]

Richardson, Robert, physician and educationist, b. Pittsburgh, Pa., 1806; d. Bethany, W. Va., Oct. 22, 1876. [1]

Richardson, Robert Lorne, journalist, b. Lanark county, Ont., 1860; d. Winnipeg, Man., Nov. 6, 1921. [27]

Richardson, Rufus Byam, educationist, b. Westford, Mass., 1845; d. Clifton Springs, N.Y., March 10, 1914. [1; 7; 10; 62]

Richardson, Warfield Creath, educationist and poet, ᵇb. Maysville, Ky., 1823; d. Tuscaloosa, Ala., March 13, 1914. [10; 34]

Richardson, William Adams, jurist, b. Tyngsborough, Mass., 1821; d. Washington, D.C., Oct. 9, 1896. [1; 3; 4; 5; 6]

Richardson, William Lambert, obstetrician, b. Boston, Mass., 1842; d. Boston, Mass., Oct. 20, 1932. [1; 10; 51]

Richardson, William Merchant, jurist, b. Pelham, N.H., 1774; d. Chester, N.H., March 23, 1838. [1; 3; 4; 5; 6]

Richardson, William Payson, lawyer and educationist, b. Farm Center, O., 1864; d. Morristown, N.J., Aug. 29, 1945. [10]

Richey, Matthew, clergyman, b. Ramelton, Ireland, 1803; d. Halifax, N.S., Oct. 24, 1883. [27]

Richey, Thomas, theologian, d. New York, N.Y., June 2, 1905. [6]

Richman, Arthur, playwright, b. New York N.Y., 1886; d. New York, N.Y., Sept. 10, 1944. [7; 10]

Richman, Irving Berdine, historian, b. Muscatine, Ia., 1861; d. Muscatine, Ia., Dec. 6, 1938. [5; 10; 11; 37]

Richmond, Almon Benson, lawyer, b. Switzerland county, Ind., 1825; d. Meadville, Pa., July 18, 1906.

Richmond, Charles Alexander, clergyman and educationist, b. New York, N.Y., Jan. 7, 1862; d. Washington, D.C., July 12, 1940. [4; 10]

Richmond, Mrs. Cora Linn Victoria, née **Scott,** spiritualist, b. 1840; d. 1923.

Richmond, Mrs. Euphemia Johnson, née **Guernsey,** novelist, b. near Mount Upton, N.Y., 1825; d. ? [4; 7; 10]

Richmond, James Cook, clergyman, b. Providence, R.I., 1808; d. Poughkeepsie, N.Y., July 20, 1866. [3; 6]

Richmond, John Francis, clergyman, d. McConnellsville, O., Dec. 29, 1929.

Richmond, John Wilkes, physician and publicist, b. 1775; d. Philadelphia, Pa., March 4, 1857. [1]

Richmond, Mary Ellen, social worker, b. Belleville, Ill., 1861; d. New York, N.Y., Sept. 12, 1928. [1; 4; 7; 10]

Richmond, Winifred Vanderbilt, psychologist, b. Elizabeth, W. Va., 1876; d. Santa Fé, N.M., July 6, 1945.

Richter, George Martin, writer on art, b. San Francisco, Calif., 1875; d. Norwalk, Conn., June 9, 1942.

Richtmyer, Floyd Karker, physicist, b. Cobleskill, N.Y., Oct. 12, 1881; d. Ithaca, N.Y., Nov. 7, 1939. [10; 11]

Ricker, Joseph, clergyman, b. 1814; d. 1897. [38]

Ricker, Mrs. Marilla M., lawyer and freethinker, b. Durham, N.H., 1840; d. Dover, N.H., Nov. 12, 1920. [4; 10]

Ricker, Nathan Clifford, educationist, b. Acton, Me., 1843; d. Urbana, Ill., March 19, 1924. [10]

Rickert, Martha Edith, educationist, b. Dover, O., 1871; d. Chicago, Ill., May 23, 1938. [7; 10]

Ricketson, Daniel, historian and poet, b. New Bedford, Mass., 1813; d. New Bedford, Mass., July 16, 1898. [1; 7; 9]

Ricketts, Howard Taylor, pathologist, b. Findlay, O., 1871; d. Mexico City, Mexico, May 3, 1910. [1a]

Ricketts, Palmer Chamberlain, engineer, b. Elkton, Md., 1856; d. Baltimore, Md., Dec. 10, 1934. [1a; 10]

Ricketts, Pierre de Peyster, mining engineer, d. Nov. 20, 1918.

Rickoff, Andrew Jackson, educationist, b. near Newhope, N.J., 1824; d. San Francisco, Calif., March 29, 1899. [3b; 4]

Ricord, Mrs. Elizabeth, née Stryker, educationist, b. Utrecht, Long Island, N.Y., 1788; d. Newark, N.J., Oct. 10, 1865. [3]

Ricord, Frederick William, librarian, b. Guadeloupe, 1819; d. Newark, N.J., Aug. 12, 1897. [1; 3; 4; 5; 6]

Riddell, John Leonard, botanist and inventor, b. Leyden, Mass., 1807; d. New Orleans, La., Oct. 7, 1865. [1; 3; 4; 6]

Riddell, William Renwick, jurist, b. Hamilton township, Ont., 1852; d. Toronto, Ont., Feb. 18, 1945. [27]

Riddle, Albert Gallatin, lawyer, politician, and novelist, b. Monson, Mass., 1816; d. Washington, D.C., May 15, 1902. [1; 2; 3; 4; 5; 6; 7; 10]

Riddle, George Peabody, actor and elocutionist, b. Charlestown, Mass., 1851; d. Boston, Mass., Nov. 26, 1910. [1; 3; 4; 5; 10]

Riddle, Griffith Hatton, nutritionist, b. Washington, D.C., 1892; d. New York, N.Y., Nov. 27, 1949.

Riddle, James Whitford, clergyman, b. Scotland, 1844; d. Valley Forge, Pa., Feb. 25, 1917.

Riddle, Matthew Brown, theologian, b. Pittsburgh, Pa., 1836; d. Edgeworth, Pa., Sept. 1, 1916. [4; 10]

Riddle, William, historian, b. 1837; d. Lancaster, Pa., June 3, 1926.

Rideing, William Henry, journalist, b. Liverpool, England, 1853; d. Brookline, Mass., Aug. 22, 1918. [1; 3; 4; 5; 6; 7; 8; 9; 10]

Ridenour, Peter Darcuss, genealogist, b. 1831; d. 1909.

Rideout, Henry Milner, novelist, b. Calais, Me., 1877; d. at sea, Sept. 17, 1927. [4; 7; 10; 11; 35]

Rider, George Thomas, clergyman, b. Rice City, R.I., 1829; d. New York, N.Y., Aug. 14, 1892. [3; 6; 7]

Rider, Sidney Smith, bookseller and historian, b. 1833; d. Providence, R.I., Jan. 31, 1917.

Ridgaway, Henry Bascom, clergyman, b. Talbot county, Md., 1830; d. Evanston, Ill., March 30, 1895. [1; 3; 4; 6]

Ridge, John Rollin, poet and journalist, b. near Rome, Ga., 1827; d. Grass Valley, Nevada county, Calif., Oct. 5, 1867. [3; 7; 35; 75]

Ridge, Lola, poet, b. Dublin, Ireland, 1883; d. Brooklyn, N.Y., May 19, 1941. [2b; 7]

Ridgely, Benjamin H., consular official, b. Ridgely, Carolina county, Md., 1861; d. 1908. [10]

Ridgely, David, librarian and local historian, b. about 1790; d. about 1841. [6]

Ridgely, James Lot, Oddfellow, b. Baltimore, 1807; d. Baltimore, Md., Nov. 16, 1881. [3]

Ridgeway, Algernon (pseud.). See Wood, Anna Cogswell.

Ridgway, Robert, ornithologist, b. Mount Carmel, Ill., 1850; d. Olney, Ill., March 25, 1929. [1; 2; 3; 4; 5; 6; 10; 11; 13]

Ridlon, Gideon Tibbetts, clergyman and genealogist, b. 1841; d. ? [38]

Ridout, John Gibbs, lawyer, b. Toronto, Ont., 1840; d. Toronto, Ont., Aug. 22, 1911. [27]

Ridpath, John Clark, historian, b. Putnam county, Ind., 1841; d. New York, N.Y., July 31, 1900. [1; 3; 4; 5; 6; 7; 9; 10]

Riel, Louis David, poet and rebel, b. St. Boniface, Rupertsland, 1844; d. Regina, N.W.T., Nov. 16, 1885. [27]

Ries, William Frederick, lecturer, b. Weston, O., 1855; d. Toledo, O., Jan. 30, 1944.

Riesenberg, Mrs. Emily, née Schorb, home economist, b. 1855; d. Yonkers, N.Y., May 4, 1936.

Riesenberg, Felix, sea-captain and novelist, b. Milwaukee, Wis., 1879; d. Bronxville, N.Y., Nov. 19, 1939. [7; 10; 11]

Riesman, David, physician, b. near Eisenach, Germany, 1867; d. Philadelphia, Pa., June 3, 1940. [10]

Rigdon, Jonathan, educationist, b. Rigdon, Ind., 1858; d. Danville, Ind., Dec. 30, 1933. [10; 11]

Rigge, William Francis, priest and astronomer, b. Cincinnati, O., 1857; d. Omaha, Neb., March 31, 1927. [10; 11; 21]

Riggs, Austen Fox, psychiatrist, b. Germany, 1876; d. Stockbridge, Mass., March 5, 1940. [10]

Riggs, Elias, missionary and linguist, b. New Providence, N.J., 1810; d. Constantinople, Turkey, Jan. 17, 1901. [1; 3; 4; 5; 6]

Riggs, James Gilbert, educationist, b. Dexter, N.Y., 1861; d. Oswego, N.Y., Feb. 20, 1936. [10]

Riggs, James Stevenson, clergyman, b. New York, N.Y., 1853; d. April 16, 1936.

Riggs, Mrs. Kate Douglas, née Smith. See Wiggins, Mrs. Kate Douglas, née Smith

Riggs, Mrs. Mary Ann Clark, née Longley, missionary, d. Beloit, Wis., 1869.

Riggs, Norman Colman, mathematician, b. Bowling Green, Mo., 1870; d. Pittsburgh, Pa., July 18, 1942. [10]

Riggs, Stephen Return, missionary, b. Steubenville, O., 1812; d. Beloit, Wis., Aug. 24, 1883. [1; 3; 4; 5; 6; 7; 70]

Riggs, Thomas Lawrason, priest, b. New London, Conn., 1888; d. New Haven, Conn., April 26, 1943. [22; 62]

Rightor, Henry, journalist and poet, b. New Orleans, La., 1870; d. June 23, 1922. [10; 34]

Rigmarole, Crayon (pseud.). See Sims Alexander Dromgoole.

Rihani, Ameen Fares, poet and translator, b. Mount Lebanon, 1876; d. Freike, Mount Lebanon, Sept. 14, 1940. [10]

Rihbany, Abraham Mitrie, clergyman, b. Lebanon, Syria, 1869; d. Stamford, Conn., July 5, 1944. [10]

Riis, Jacob August, journalist and reformer, b. Ribe, Denmark, 1849; d. Barre, Tex., May 26, 1914. [1; 2; 4; 5; 7; 10]

Riker, Carroll Livingston, mechanical engineer, b. Staten Island, N.Y., 1854; d. May 7, 1931. [10]

Riker, James, historian, b. New York, N.Y., May 11, 1822; d. Waverly, N.H., July 15, 1889. [3; 6]

Riley, Benjamin Franklin, clergyman and educationist, b. near Pineville, Ala., 1849; d. Birmingham, Ala., Dec. 14, 1925. [1; 4; 5; 7; 10; 11; 34]

Riley, Cassius Marcellus, physician, b. Delaware county, O., 1844; d. St. Louis, Mo., Oct. 18, 1925. [10]

Riley, Charles Valentine, entomologist, b. London, England, 1843; d. Washington, D.C., Sept. 14, 1895. [1; 3; 4; 5; 6]

Riley, Elihu Samuel, lawyer and journalist, b. Annapolis, Md., 1845; d. ? [78]

Riley, Francis Lawrence, physician and lecturer, b. 1870; d. Los Angeles, Calif., Oct. 17, 1940.

Riley, Franklin Lafayette, historian, b. near Hebron, Miss., 1868; d. Lexington, Va., Nov. 10, 1929. [10; 11; 34]

Riley, Henry Hiram, lawyer, b. Great Barrington, Mass., 1813; d. Constantine, Mich., Feb. 8, 1888. [3; 7]

Riley, Isaac Woodbridge, philosopher, b. New York, N.Y., 1869; d. Cape May, N.J., Sept. 2, 1933. [1; 7; 10; 62]

Riley, James, mariner, b. Middletown, Conn., 1777; d. at sea, March 15, 1840. [3]

Riley, James, journalist, b. county Longford, Ireland, 1848; d. Boston, Mass., Jan. 28, 1930. [7; 10]

Riley, James Whitcomb, poet and humorist, b. Greenfield, Ind., 1849; d. Indianapolis, Ind., July 22, 1916. [1; 2; 4; 7; 9; 10; 71; 72]

Riley, John Campbell, physician, b. Georgetown, D.C., 1828; d. Washington, D.C., Feb. 22, 1879. [3; 6]

Riley, Phil Madison, editor, b. Belmont, N.H., 1882; d. Brooklyn, N.Y., Feb. 21, 1926. [10; 11]

Riley, Thomas James, sociologist, b. Johnson county, Kans., 1870; d. New York, N.Y., Oct. 10, 1931. [10]

Riley, Woodbridge. See Riley, Isaac Woodbridge.

Rindge, Frederick Hastings, philanthropist, b. Cambridge, Mass., 1857; d. Yreka, Calif., Aug. 29, 1905. [1; 4; 51]

Rinehart, Stanley Marshall, physician, b. 1867; d. Washington, D.C., Oct. 28, 1932.

Rinfret, Fernand, journalist and politician, b. Montreal, Que., 1883; d. Los Angeles, Calif., July 12, 1939. [27]

Ring, Mrs. Lina Barbara, née Taylor, physician and playwright, b. Scotland; d. Arlington Heights, Mass., Aug. 31, 1941.

Ringbolt, Captain (pseud.). See Codman, John.

Ringgold, George Hay, soldier, b. Hagerstown, Md., 1814; d. San Francisco, Calif., April 4, 1864. [3]

Ringgold, James Trapier, lawyer, b. 1852; d. 1898.

Ringrose, Hyacinthe, lawyer, b. London, England, 1874; d. Yonkers, N.Y., June 19, 1946. [62]

Ringwalt, John Luther, miscellaneous writer, fl. 1871-1888. [6]

Rion, Hanna. See Ver Beck, Mrs. Hanna, née Rion.

Riordan, Roger, artist, b. Ireland, 1848; d. New York, N.Y., Nov. 26, 1904. [10]

Ripley, Mrs. Eliza Moore, née Chinn, writer of reminiscences, b. 1832; d. 1912.

Ripley, Ezra, clergyman, b. Woodstock, Conn., 1751; d. Concord, Mass., Sept. 21, 1841. [1; 3; 4; 9]

Ripley, George, reformer, literary critic, and encyclopaedist, b. Greenfield, Mass., 1802; d. New York, N.Y., July 4, 1880. [1; 2; 3; 4; 5; 6; 7; 9]

Ripley, Henry Jones, clergyman, b. Boston, Mass., 1798; d. Newton Centre, Mass., May 21, 1875. [3; 4; 6]

Ripley, Mary A., poet, b. 1831; d. 1893.

Ripley, Roswell Sabine, soldier, b. Franklin county, O., 1823; d. New York, N.Y., March 26, 1887. [1; 3; 4; 6]

Ripley, William Zebina, economist, b. Medford, Mass., 1867; d. East Edgecomb, Me., Aug. 16, 1941. [10; 51]

Rishell, Charles Wesley, clergyman, b. near Williamsport, Pa., 1850; d. 1908. [10]

Risley, Richard Voorhees, novelist, b. New York, N.Y., 1874; d. New York, N.Y., March 30, 1904. [10]

Risteen, Allan Douglas, physicist, b. Amesbury, Mass., 1866; d. Hartford, Conn., Dec. 30, 1932. [13; 62]

Ritchie, Albert Cabell, lawyer and politician, b. Richmond, Va., 1876; d. Baltimore, Md., Feb. 24, 1936. [10]

Ritchie, Andrew, clergyman, b. 1827; d. 1897.

Ritchie, Mrs. Anna Cora, née Ogden, actress, playwright, and novelist, b. Bordeaux, France, 1819; d. Twickenham, England, July 21, 1870. [1; 2; 3; 4; 6]

Ritchie, Arthur, clergyman, b. Philadelphia, Pa., 1849; d. New York, N.Y., July 9, 1921. [10]

Ritchie, Frank Herbert Thomas, philanthropist, b. Montreal, Que., 1878; d. New York, N.Y., Sept. 6, 1940.

Ritchie, James S., pioneer, fl. 1857-1862. [44]

Ritchie, John Woodside, biologist, b. near Sparta, Ill., 1871; d. Flemington, N.J., May 29, 1943. [10; 13]

Ritchie, Robert Welles, journalist and novelist, b. Quincy, Ill., 1879; d. Carmel, Calif., Aug. 2, 1942. [7; 10; 35]

Ritchie, Sir William Johnstone, jurist, b. Annapolis, N.S., 1813; d. Ottawa, Ont., Sept. 25, 1892. [27]

Ritter, Abraham, merchant, b. Philadelphia, Pa., 1792; d. Philadelphia, Pa., Oct. 8, 1860. [3]

Ritter, Fanny Raymond. See Ritter, Mrs. Frances Malone, née Raymond.

Ritter, Mrs. Frances Malone, née **Raymond,** vocalist and poet, b. Leeds, England, 1830; d. Poughkeepsie, N.Y., Oct. 26, 1890. [3; 5]

Ritter, Frédéric Louis, musician, b. Strasbourg, Alsace, 1834; d. Antwerp, Belgium, July 6, 1891. [1; 3; 4; 5; 6; 7; 20]

Ritter, John P., novelist, fl. 1886-1901.

Ritter, Thomas, physician, d .1876.

Ritter, William Emerson, zoologist, b. near Hampden, Wis., 1856; d. Berkeley, Calif., Jan. 10, 1944.. [4; 10; 11; 13]

Rivers, George Robert Russell, lawyer, politician, and novelist, b. Providence, R.I., 1853; d. Milton, Mass., Feb. 11, 1900. [51]

Rivers, Pearl (pseud.). See Nicholson, Mrs. Eliza, Jane, née Poitevant.

Rivers, Richard Henderson, clergyman and educationist, b. Montgomery county, Tenn., 1814; d. Louisville, Ky., June 21, 1894. [3; 5; 6; 34]

Rivers, William James, educationist, b. Charleston, S.C., 1822; d. Baltimore, Md., June 22, 1909. [1; 3; 7; 34]

Rives, Amélie, novelist and playwright, b. Richmond, Va., 1863; d. Charlottesville, Va., June 15, 1945. [4; 10; 12; 34]

Rives, George Lockhart, lawyer and historian, b. New York, N.Y., 1849; d. Newport, R.I., Aug. 18, 1917. [1; 4; 7; 10]

Rives, Mrs. Judith Page, née **Walker,** miscellaneous writer, b. Castle Hill, Va., 1802; d. Castle Hill, Va., Jan. 23, 1882. [3]

Rives, William Cabell, politician and diplomat, b. Amherst county, Va., 1793; d. Castle Hill, Va., April 25, 1868. [1; 3; 4; 5; 6; 34]

Rix, Frank Reader, educationist, b. Lowell, Mass., 1853; d. New York, N.Y., March 16, 1919. [51]

Rix, Guy Scoby, genealogist, b. 1828; d. 1917.

Rixford, Emmet Hawkins, lawyer, b. East Highgate, Que.; d. San Francisco, Calif., Aug. 19, 1928.

Roads, Charles, clergyman, b. Hamburg, Pa., 1855; d. Philadelphia, Pa., July 31, 1937. [7; 10; 11]

Roads, Samuel, local historian, b. Marblehead, Mass., 1853; d. Marblehead, Mass., Jan. 28, 1904.

Roark, Ruric Nevel, educationist, b. Greenville, Ky., 1859; d. Richmond, Ky., April 14, 1909. [1; 10; 34]

Robb, Mrs. Isabel Adams, née **Hampton,** nurse, b. 1859; d. 1910.

Robb, Hunter, physician, b. Burlington, N.J., 1863; d. Burlington, N.J., May 15, 1940. [10]

Robb, James Burch, lawyer, b. Baltimore, Md., 1817; d. Boston, Mass., Nov. 3, 1876. [3]

Robb, John S., humorist, fl. 1847-1858. [6; 7]

Robb, Russell, electrical engineer, b. Dubuque, Ia., 1864; d. Concord, Mass., Feb. 15, 1927. [10]

Robbins, Alexander Henry, lawyer, b. St. Louis, Mo., 1875; d. St. Louis, Mo., Jan. 24, 1922. [10]

Robbins, Archibald, mariner, b. 1792; d. 1865.

Robbins, Chandler, physician, b. Hallowell, Me., 1796; d. Cheraw, S.C., May 24, 1836. [46]

Robbins, Chandler, clergyman, b. Lynn, Mass., 1810; d. Weston, Mass., Sept. 11, 1882. [1; 3; 4; 6]

Robbins, Clarence Aaron, novelist, b. Brooklyn, N.Y., 1888; d. St. Jean, Cap Ferrat, France, May 10, 1949.

Robbins, Eliza, educationist, b. 1786; d. 1853. [6]

Robbins, Hayes, economist, b. Angelica, N.Y., 1873; d. Newton Highlands, Mass., April 8, 1941. [10]

Robbins, Leonard Harman, journalist, b. Lincoln, Neb., 1877; d. Wolfeboro, N.H., June 24, 1947. [10]

Robbins, Mrs. Mary Caroline, née **Pike,** writer on art and landscape-gardening, b. Calais, Me., 1841; d. Hingham, Mass., Nov. 5, 1912. [7; 10]

Robbins, Royal, clergyman, b. Connecticut, 1878; d. Berlin, Conn., March 26, 1861. [3b; 4]

Robbins, Mrs. Sarah, née **Stuart,** writer of books for young people, b. 1817; d. Andover, Mass., Aug. 16, 1910.

Robbins, Thomas, clergyman and antiquary, b. Norfolk, Conn., 1777; d. Colebrook, Conn., Sept. 13, 1856. [1; 3; 4; 6]

Robbins, Wilford Lash, clergyman, b. Boston, Mass., 1859; d. Bethel, Me., Sept. 5, 1927. [10]

Robert, Arthur. See Robert, Joseph Arthur.

Robert, Henry Martyn, soldier, b. Robertville, S.C., 1837; d. Hornell, N.Y., May 11, 1923. [1a; 4; 10]

Robert, Joseph Arthur, priest and educationist, b. Beauport, Que., 1876; d. Quebec, March 21, 1939. [27]

Roberton, Thomas Beattie, journalist, b. Glasgow, Scotland, 1879; d. Winnipeg, Man., Jan. 13, 1936. [27]

Roberts, Mrs. Anna Smith, née **Rickey,** poet, b. Philadelphia, Pa., 1827; d. Philadelphia, Pa., Aug. 10, 1858. [3; 7]

Roberts, Benjamin Titus, clergyman, b. Gowanda, N.Y., 1823; d. Cattaraugus, N.Y., Feb. 27, 1893. [1]

Roberts, Benson Howard, clergyman, b. Brockport, N.Y., 1853; d. Catonsville, Md., March 2, 1930. [10; 11]

Roberts, Brigham Henry, Mormon elder, b. Lancashire, England, 1857; d. Salt Lake City, Utah, Sept. 27, 1933. [7; 10]

Roberts, Sir Charles George Douglas, poet and novelist, b. Douglas, N.B., 1860; d. Toronto, Ont., Nov. 26, 1943. [27]

Roberts, Charles Humphrey, lawyer and novelist, b. Mount Pleasant, O., 1847; d. Hot Springs, Ark., Nov. 30, 1911. [10]

Roberts, Charlotte Fitch, chemist, b. New York, N.Y., 1859; d. Wellesley, Mass., Dec. 5, 1917. [4; 10]

Roberts, Mrs. Clara, née Lemore, novelist, d. 1898.

Roberts, Clarence, agriculturist, b. Clarksville, Tenn., 1890; d. Oklahoma City, Okla., Dec. 4, 1942. [10]

Roberts, Daniel, lawyer, b. Wallingford, Vt., 1811; d. 1899. [43]

Roberts, David, lawyer, b. 1804; d. 1879. [51]

Roberts, Edmund Quincy, diplomat, b. Portsmouth, N.H., 1784; d. Macao, China, June 12, 1836. [1; 2; 3]

Roberts, Edwards, traveller, b. 1855; d. Concord, Mass., July 6, 1926. [51]

Roberts, Elizabeth Madox, poet and novelist, b. near Springfield, Ky., 1886; d. Orlando, Fla., March 13, 1941. [7; 10; 12]

Roberts, Ellis Henry, journalist and historian, b. Utica, N.Y., 1827; d. Utica, N.Y., Jan. 8, 1918. [1; 3; 4; 5; 62]

Roberts, Ellwood, poet and historian, b. Wilmington, Del., 1846; d. Swarthmore, Pa., Jan. 30, 1921.

Roberts, Elmer, journalist, b. Wabash county, Ind., 1863; d. Jacksonville, Fla., Nov. 17, 1937. [10; 11]

Roberts, George Evan, economist, b. Delaware county, Ia., 1857; d. Larchmont, N.Y., June 6, 1948. [4; 10; 11]

Roberts, George Litch, lawyer, b. Boston, Mass., 1836; d. Brookline, Mass., April 29, 1929. [10; 60]

Roberts, George Simon, journalist, b. New York, N.Y., 1860; d. Enfield, N.H., Jan. 19, 1940.

Roberts, Isaac Phillips, educationist, b. Seneca county, N.Y., 1833; d. Palo Alto, Calif., March 17, 1928. [10; 37]

Roberts, James Hudson, missionary, b. Hartford, Conn., 1851; d. Wethersfield, Conn., May 15, 1945. [62]

Roberts, Job, agriculturist, b. near Gwynedd,, Pa., 1757; d. near Gwynedd, Pa., Aug. 20, 1851. [1; 3]

Roberts, John Bingham, surgeon, b. Philadelphia, Pa., 1852; d. Philadelphia, Pa., Nov. 28, 1924. [4; 10]

Roberts, John Hawley, educationist, b. Peoria, Ill., 1897; d. Boston, Mass., Dec. 8, 1949. [14]

Roberts, Jonathan Manning, lawyer and spiritualist, b. Montgomery county, Pa., 1821; d. Burlington, N.J., Feb. 28, 1888. [3]

Roberts, Joseph, soldier, b. near Middletown, Del., 1814; d. Philadelphia, Pa., Oct. 19, 1898. [3]

Roberts, Lewis Niles, playwright, b. Boston, Mass., 1870; d. Hyères, France, March 31, 1929. [51]

Roberts, Maggie, miscellaneous writer, fl. 1875-1876.

Roberts, Oliver Ayer, librarian, b. Haverhill, Mass., 1838; d. Dec. 4, 1922.

Roberts, Oran Milo, jurist and politician, b. Laurens district, S.C., 1815; d. Austin, Tex., May 19, 1898. [1; 2; 3; 4; 5; 6]

Roberts, Peter, clergyman, b. South Wales, 1859; d. Mount Vernon, N.Y., Dec. 2, 1932. [10; 11; 62]

Roberts, Philip Ilott, evangelist, b. 1872; d. 1938.

Roberts, Richard, clergyman, b. North Wales, 1874; d. New York, N.Y., April 11, 1945. [10]

Roberts, Robert Ellis, historian, b. Utica, N.Y., 1809; d. Detroit, Mich., Feb. 18, 1888. [3]

Roberts, Seldon Low, clergyman, b. Monroeville, Ind., 1871; d. Philadelphia, Pa., June 11, 1930. [10]

Roberts, Stewart Ralph, physician, b. Oxford, Ga., 1878; d. Atlanta, Ga., April 14, 1941. [10; 11]

Roberts, Thomas Paschall, engineer, b. Carlisle, Pa., 1843; d. Pittsburgh, Pa., Feb. 25, 1924. [5; 10]

Roberts, Thomas Sadler, physician and ornithologist, b. Philadelphia, Pa., 1858; d. Minneapolis, Minn., April 19, 1946. [10]

Roberts, Vasco Harold, lawyer, b. St. Joseph, Mich., 1874; d. St. Louis, Mo., 1910. [10]

Roberts, Walter Coe, clergyman, b. Milwaukee, Wis., 1855; d. Mauch Chunk, Pa., Oct. 28, 1930. [62]

Roberts, William, historian, b. Haddonfield, N.J., 1798; d. ? [6]

Roberts, William Henry, clergyman, b. Holyhead, Wales, 1844; d. Philadelphia, Pa., June 26, 1920. [1; 2; 3; 5; 10]

Robertson, Archibald Thomas, theologian, b. near Chatham, Va., 1863; d. Louisville, Ky., Sept. 24, 1934. [7; 10; 11; 34]

Robertson, Ben, journalist, b. South Carolina, 1905; d. Lisbon, Portugal, Feb. 22, 1943.

Robertson, Charles, physician and local historian, b. 1799; d. ?

Robertson, Donald, actor, b. Edinburgh, Scotland, 1860; d. Chicago, Ill., May 20, 1926.

Robertson, Mrs. Ella, née Broadus, religious writer, b. Greenville, S.C., 1872; d. Louisville, Ky., Dec. 5, 1945. [10; 11]

Robertson, George, jurist, b. Mercer county, Ky., 1790; d. Lexington, Ky., May 16, 1874. [1; 4; 5; 34; 74]

Robertson, Harrison, journalist and novelist, b. Murfreesboro, Tenn., 1856; d. Louisville, Ky., Nov. 11, 1939. [7; 10; 11; 34; 74]

Robertson, Ignatius Loyola (pseud.). See Knapp, Samuel Lorenzo.

Robertson, James, clergyman, b. Scotland, 1802; d. Middleton, N.S., Jan. 19, 1878. [27]

Robertson, James Alexander, historian, b. Corry, Pa., 1873; d. Takoma Park, Md., March 20, 1939. [7; 10; 11]

Robertson, James Rood, historian, b. Rockford, Ill., 1864; d. Berea, Ky., April 15, 1932. [10]

Robertson, John, jurist and poet, b. near Petersburg, Va., 1787; d. Mount Athos, Campbell county, Va., July 5, 1873. [1; 3; 4; 5; 7; 34]

Robertson, John Palmerston, librarian, b. Fortingal, Scotland, 1841; d. Los Angeles, Calif., April 11, 1919. [27]

Robertson, John Ross, journalist and historian, b. Toronto, Ont., 1841; d. Toronto, Ont., May 30, 1918. [27]

Robertson, Louis Alexander, poet, b. Saint John, N.B., 1856; d. San Francisco, Calif., June 22, 1910. [35]

Robertson, Morgan Andrew, novelist and short-story writer, b. Oswego, N.Y., 1861; d. Atlantic City, N.J., March 24, 1915. [1; 7; 10; 72]

Robertson, Norman, local historian, b. 1845; d. Walkerton, Ont., June 21, 1936. [27]

Robertson, Peter, drama critic, b. Scotland, 1847; d. Boyes Springs, Calif., Aug. 9, 1911. [10; 35]

Robertson, Samuel Lowrie, educationist and poet, b. Jackson county, Ala., 1838; d. Birmingham, Ala., Sept. 2, 1909. [34]

Robertson, Mrs. Sarah Franklin, née Davis, novelist, b. 1845; d. 1889.

Robertson, Stuart, educationist, b. Newark, N.J., 1892; d. Philadelphia, Pa., May 1, 1940. [10]

Robertson, Thomas Bolling, politician and jurist, b. near Petersburg, Va., 1779; d. White Sulphur Springs, Va., Nov. 5, 1828. [1; 3; 4; 5; 34]

Robertson, Wyndham, politician, b. Manchester, Va., 1803; d. Washington county, Va., Feb. 11, 1888. [1; 3; 4; 6; 34]

Robie, Thomas, educationist, b. Boston, Mass., 1688; d. Saiem, Mass., Aug. 28, 1729. [3; 51]

Robie, Walter Franklin, physician, b. Bradford, Vt., 1866; d. Winchendon, Mass., Aug. 29, 1928. [10]

Robins, Edward, journalist, b. Pau, France, 1862; d. Philadelphia, Pa., April 21, 1943. [4; 7; 10]

Robins, Henry Ephriam, clergyman, b. Hartford, Conn., 1827; d. Greenfield, Mass., April 23, 1917. [1; 4; 5; 10]

Robins, John Bradley, clergyman, b. Putnam county, Ga., 1851; d. Elberton, Ga., Nov. 23, 1913. [34]

Robins, Kingman Nott, economist, b. Waterville, Me., 1881; d. Rochester, N.Y., Feb. 5, 1923. [4]

Robins, Mrs. Sally, née Nelson, novelist, b. Gloucester county, Va.; d. Richmond, Va., Feb. 4, 1925. [10; 11]

Robinson, Albert Gardner, journalist, b. Winchester, Mass., 1855; d. New York, N.Y., Aug. 30, 1932. [10]

Robinson, Alfred, pioneer, b. Massachusetts, 1806; d. San Francisco, Calif., 1895. [35]

Robinson, Andrew Rose, physician, b. Claude, Ont., 1845; d. Caledonia, Ont., July 8, 1924. [31a]

Robinson, Mrs. Annie Douglas, née Green, writer of books for children, b. Plymouth, N.H., 1842; d. ? [3; 4; 10]

Robinson, Beverley, physician, b. Philadelphia, Pa., 1844; d. New York, N.Y., June 21, 1924. [4; 10; 11]

Robinson, Byron. See Robinson, Frederick Byron.

Robinson, Mrs. Caroline, née Hadley, scientist, b. 1885; d. Philadelphia, Pa., Dec. 13, 1946.

Robinson, Mrs. Caroline Elizabeth, née Rodman, genealogist, b. 1833; d. 1906.

Robinson, Chalfant, historian, b. Cincinnati, O., 1871; d. Princeton, N.J., Jan. 1, 1947. [7; 10]

Robinson, Charles, politician, b. Hardwick, Mass., 1818; d. near Lawrence, Kans., Aug. 17, 1894. [1; 3; 4; 5]

Robinson, Charles Edward, clergyman, b. Ludlowville, N.Y., 1835; d. March 20, 1920. [63]

Robinson, Charles Henry, soldier, b. 1843; d. Nov. 26, 1930.

Robinson, Charles Leonard Frost, yachtsman, b. Sayville, N.Y., 1874; d. Woods Hole, Mass., July 6, 1916. [10; 62]

Robinson, Charles Mulford, journalist, and city-planner, b. Ramapo, N.Y., 1869; d. Albany, N.Y., Dec. 30, 1917. [1; 7; 10]

Robinson, Charles Seymour, clergyman, b. Bennington, Vt., 1829; d. New York, N.Y., Feb. 1, 1899. [1; 2; 3; 4; 5; 6; 7]

Robinson, Conway, lawyer, b. Richmond, Va., 1805 d. Philadelphia, Pa., Jan. 30, 1884. [1; 3; 4; 5; 6; 34]

Robinson, Mrs. Corinne, née Roosevelt, poet, b. New York, N.Y., 1861; d. New York, N.Y., Feb. 17, 1933. [10; 11]

Robinson, Dwight Nelson, educationist, b. Winchester, Mass., 1886; d. Delaware, O., Oct. 30, 1941. [10]

Robinson, Edith, writer of books for girls, b. Boston, Mass., 1858; d. ? [7]

Robinson, Edward, Biblical scholar, b. Southington, Conn., 1794; d. New York, N.Y., Jan. 27, 1863. [1; 3; 5; 6; 7; 9]

Robinson, Edward Van Dyke, economist, b. Bloomington, Ill., 1867; d. New York, N.Y., Dec. 10, 1915. [1; 10; 70]

Robinson, Edwin Arlington, poet, b. Head Tide, Me., 1869; d. New York, N.Y., April 6, 1935. [1a; 2; 7; 10; 11; 72]

Robinson, Edwin Meade, journalist, b. Howe, Ind., 1878; d. Provincetown, Mass., Sept. 20, 1946. [11]

Robinson, Eliot Harlow, novelist, b. Middleboro, Mass., 1884; d. Boston, Mass., Nov. 21, 1942. [51]

Robinson, Ezekiel Gilman, clergyman and educationist, b. near South Attleboro, Mass., 1815; d. Boston, Mass., June 13, 1894. [1; 3; 4; 5]

Robinson, Fayette, miscellaneous writer, b. Virginia; d. New York, N.Y., March 26, 1859. [3; 6; 34]

Robinson, Frank Torrey, journalist and art critic, b. Salem, Mass., 1845; d. Roxbury, Mass., June 3, 1898. [3b]

Robinson, Franklin Clement, educationist, b. East Orrington, Me., 1852; d. Portland, Me., May 25, 1910. [10]

Robinson, Frederick Bertrand, educationist, b. Brooklyn, N.Y., 1883; d. New York, N.Y., 1941. [10; 11]

Robinson, Frederick Byron, physician, b. near Mineral Point, Wis., 1855; d. Chicago, Ill., March 23, 1910. [1; 10]

Robinson, George F., local historian, b. 1838; d. 1901.

Robinson, Gil, circus performer, b. 1844; d. Cincinnati, O., Aug. 17, 1928.

Robinson, Harold McAfee, clergyman, b. Shelbyville, Mo., 1881; d. Germantown, Pa., March 4, 1939. [10; 11]

Robinson, Mrs. Harriet Jane, née Hanson, female suffragist, b. Boston, Mass., 1825; d. Malden, Mass., Dec. 22, 1911. [1; 3; 4; 6; 7; 10]

Robinson, Mrs. Helen, née Ring journalist and politician, b. Eastport, Me., 1878; d. Denver, Colo., July 10, 1923. [10]

Robinson, Henry Pynchon, educationist, b. Putnam, Conn., 1840; d. Guilford, Conn., June 5, 1913. [4; 62]

Robinson, Horatio Nelson, mathematician, b. Hartwick, N.Y., 1806; d. Elbridge, N.Y., Jan. 19, 1867. [3; 4; 6]

Robinson, James Harvey, historian, b. Bloomington, Ill., 1863; d. New York, N.Y., Feb. 16, 1936. [7; 10]

Robinson, Mrs. Jane Marie, née Bancroft, philanthropist, b. West Stockbridge, Mass., 1847; d. Pasadena, Calif., May 29, 1932. [10]

Robinson, John, botanist, b. Salem, Mass., 1846; d. Salem, Mass., April 9, 1925. [10; 13]

Robinson, John Beverley, architect, b. New York, N.Y., 1853; d. St. Louis, Mo., Nov. 12, 1923. [4; 10]

Robinson, John Bunyan, clergyman, b. 1834; d. 1912.

Robinson, John Henry, aviculturist, b. 1863; d. March 30, 1935.

Robinson, John Hovey, physician and dime novelist. b. Lubec, Me., 1835; d. ? [6; 7]

Robinson, Lelia Josephine, lawyer, b. 1850; d. 1891.

Robinson, Leonard George, banker and lawyer, b. Russia, 1875; d. Long Island, N.Y., Dec. 8, 1947. [10]

Robinson, Mrs. Mary Dummett, née Nauman, novelist. fl. 1869-1918. [10]

Robinson, Mrs. Mary Stephens, novelist, d. Mamaroneck, N.Y., Oct. 16, 1909.

Robinson, Maurice Henry, economist, b. New Hampshire, 1867; d. Winter Park, Fla., Feb. 28, 1946. [10; 62]

Robinson, Phinehas, clergyman and poet, b. 1799; d. Franklinville, N.Y., April 30, 1871. [56]

Robinson, Reuel, local historian, b. 1858; d. Camden, Me., June 19, 1927.

Robinson, Rowland Evans, novelist, b. Ferrisburg, Vt., 1833; d. Ferrisburg, Vt., Oct. 15, 1900. [1; 3; 4; 7; 10; 72]

Robinson, Samuel, physician, fl. 1825-1835.

Robinson, Mrs. Sara Tappan Doolittle, née Lawrence, historian, b. Belchertown, Mass., 1827; d. 1911. [3; 5; 10]

Robinson, Solon, pioneer and agriculturist, b. Tolland, Conn., 1803; d. Jacksonville, Fla., Nov. 3, 1880. [1; 3; 4; 5; 6; 7; 9]

Robinson, Stillman Williams, engineer and inventor, b. near South Reading, Vt., 1838; d. Columbus, O., Oct. 31, 1910. [1; 3; 4; 5; 6; 10]

Robinson, Stuart, clergyman, b. Strabane, Ireland, 1814; d. Louisville, Ky., Oct. 5, 1881. [1; 3; 4; 5; 6]

Robinson, Mrs. Therese Albertine Louise, née von Jakob, miscellaneous writer, b. Halle, Germany, 1797; d. Hamburg, Germany, April 13, 1870. [1; 3; 4; 6; 7]

Robinson, Tracy, consular official, b. Clarendon, N.Y., 1833; d. 1915. [7; 10]

Robinson, Victor, medical historian, b. Ukraine, Russia, 1886; d. Philadelphia, Pa., Jan. 8, 1947. [10; 11]

Robinson, William Callyhan, lawyer and educationist, b. Norwich, Conn., 1834; d. Washington, D.C., Nov. 6, 1911. [1; 4; 5; 10; 21]

Robinson, William Davis, merchant, b. Georgetown, D.C., about 1775; d. about 1821. [4; 6]

Robinson, William Erigena, journalist and politician, b. county Tyrone, Ireland, 1814; d. Brooklyn, N.Y., Jan. 23, 1892. [1; 3; 5; 7]

Robinson, William Henry, anthropologist, b. Lexington, Ill., 1867; d. Chandler, Ariz., April 5, 1938. [7; 10; 11]

Robinson, William Josephus, physician, b. Russia, 1867; d. New York, N.Y., Jan. 6, 1936. [10]

Robinson, William Stevens, journalist, b. Concord, Mass., 1818; d. Malden, Mass., March 11, 1876. [1; 3; 4; 5; 6; 7]

Robinson, Wirt, soldier, b. Buckingham county, Va., 1864; d. Washington, D.C., Jan. 19, 1929. [10; 11]

Robson, Albert Henry, art connoisseur, b. Lindsay, Ont., 1882; d. Toronto, Ont., March 6, 1939. [27; 30]

Roche, Arthur Somers, novelist, b. Somerville, Mass., 1883; d. Palm Beach, Fla., Feb. 17, 1935. [1a; 7; 10]

Roche, James Jeffrey, journalist and poet, b. Queen's county, Ireland, 1847; d. Berne, Switzerland, April 3, 1908. [1; 3; 4; 5; 7; 9; 10; 21]

Roche, John Alexander, clergyman, b. Stillpond, Md., 1813; d. New York, N.Y., Feb. 15, 1898. [3b]

Roche, Olin Scott, clergyman, b. 1852; d. New York, N.Y., Aug. 29, 1935.

Roche, Spencer Summerfield, clergyman, b. 1849; d. Garden City, N.Y., March 6, 1916.

Rochelle, James Henry, naval officer, b. 1826; d. 1889. [34]

Rockefeller, John Davidson, capitalist, b. Richford, N.Y., July 8, 1839; d. Ormond, Fla., May 23, 1937. [4; 10]

Rockey, Howard, novelist, b. Philadelphia, Pa., 1886; d. New York, N.Y., May 27, 1934. [7; 10]

Rockhill, William Woodville, orientalist and diplomat, b. Philadelphia, Pa., 1854; d. Honolulu, Hawaii, Dec. 8, 1914. [1; 4; 7; 10]

Rockne, Knut Kenneth, football coach, b. Voss, Norway, 1888; d. in an airplane crash in southeastern Kansas, March 31, 1931. [1; 10; 21]

Rockwell, Alfred Perkins, engineer, b. Norwich, Conn., 1834; d. New Haven, Conn., Dec. 24, 1903. [4; 10; 62]

Rockwell, Alphonso David, physician, b. New Canaan, Conn., 1840; d. New York, N.Y., April 12, 1933. [1; 3; 5; 10; 11]

Rockwell, Charles, clergyman, b. Colebrook, Conn., 1806; d. Albany, N.Y., April 15, 1882. [3; 62]

Rockwell, Francis Williams, lawyer, b. Pittsfield, Mass., 1844; d. Pittsfield, Mass., June 26, 1929. [45]

Rockwell, George Lounsbury, genealogist, b. 1869; d. Ridgefield, Conn., May 28, 1947.

Rockwell, Joel Edson, clergyman, b. Salisbury, Vt., 1816; d. Brooklyn, N.Y., July 29, 1882. [3; 4]

Rockwell, John Arnold, jurist and politician, b. Norwich, Conn., 1803; d. Washington, D.C., Feb. 10, 1861. [3; 62]

Rockwell, Julius Ensign, editor, b. Millbury, Mass., 1860; d. 1926. [10; 11]

Rockwell, Reese, novelist, fl. 1883-1890.

Rockwell, William Hayden, physician, b. Brattleboro, Vt., 1867; d. Paris, France, Sept. 21, 1930. [10; 62]

Rockwood, Caroline Washburn, novelist, fl. 1889-1897.

Rockwood, Elbert William, chemist, b. Franklin, Mass., July 4, 1860; d. Iowa City, Ia., July 17, 1935. [10; 11; 13; 62]

Rockwood, Harry (pseud.). See Young, Ernest A.

Roddy, Harry Justin, educationist, b. Landisburg, Pa., 1856; d. Pittsburgh, Pa., Sept. 4, 1943. [10]

Rodenbough, Theophilus Francis, soldier, b. Easton, Pa., 1838; d. New York, N.Y., Dec. 19, 1912. [1; 3; 4; 5; 6; 10]

Rodger, James George, clergyman, b. Hammond, N.Y., 1852; d. ? [68]

Rodgers, Curtis Charles, artist, b. Chicago, Ill., 1913; d. Cairo, Egypt, May 1, 1943. [62]

Rodgers, Miles M., physician, fl. 1846-1848.

Rodman, Ella (pseud.). See Church, Mrs. Ella Rodman, née MacIlvane.

Rodman, Thomas Jackson, soldier and inventor, b. near Salem, Ind., 1815; d. Rock Island, Ill., June 7, 1871. [1; 3; 4; 5]

Rodman, Warren Anson, architect, b. Boston, Mass., 1855; d. ? [10]

Rodman, William Louis, surgeon, b. Frankfort, Ky., 1858; d. March 8, 1916. [10]

Rodney, Mrs. Marian Calhoun Legaré, née Reeves. See Reeves, Marian Calhoun Legaré.

Roe, Alfred Seelye, soldier, b. 1844; d. Jan. 7, 1917.

Roe, Azel Stevens, novelist, b. New York, N.Y., 1798; d. East Windsor Hill, Conn., Jan. 1, 1886. [3; 4; 6; 7]

Roe, Clifford Griffith, lawyer, b. Rolling Prairie, Ind., 1875; d. Chicago, Ill., June 28, 1934. [10]

Roe, Edward Payson, clergyman, horticulturist, and novelist, b. New Windsor, N.Y., 1838; d. Cornwall, N.Y., July 19, 1888. [1; 3; 4; 5; 6; 7; 9]

Roe, Edward Reynolds, physician, soldier, and novelist, b. Lebanon, O., 1813; d. Chicago, Ill., Nov. 6, 1893. [36]

Roe, Francis Asbury, naval officer, b. Elmira, N.Y., 1823; d. Washington, D.C., Dec. 28, 1901. [1; 3; 4; 5; 10]

Roe, Gilbert Ernstein, lawyer, b. Oregon, Wis., 1865; d. New York, N.Y., Dec. 22, 1929. [1; 4; 10]

Roe, Henry, clergyman, b. Henryville, Lower Canada, 1829; d. Richmond, Que., Aug. 3, 1909. [27]

Roe, John Elisha, writer on the Shakespeare-Bacon controversy, b. 1840; d. Genesee, N.Y., June, 1927.

Roe, Mary Abigail, novelist, b. about 1840; d. ? [7]

Roe, Mrs. Nora Ardelia, née Metcalf, soldier's wife, b. Franklin, Mass., 1856; d. ? [10]

Roe, William James, novelist and poet, b. 1843; d. ?

Roebling, John Augustus, engineer, b. Germany, 1806; d. Brooklyn, N.Y., July 22, 1869. [1; 3; 4; 5]

Roeding, George Christian, horticulturist, b. San Francisco, Calif., 1868; d. July 23, 1928. [1]

Roehrig, Frederic Louis Otto, linguist, b. Halle, Prussia, 1819; d. Pasadena, Calif., 1908. [10]

Roelker, Bernard, lawyer, b. Hanover, Germany, 1816; d. New York, N.Y., March 5, 1888. [3; 6]

Rölvaag, Ole Edvart, educationist and novelist, b. Helgeland, Norway, 1876; d. Northfield, Minn., Nov. 5, 1931. [1; 10]

Roemer, Jean, soldier and educationist, b. England, 1812; d. Lenox, Mass., Aug. 31, 1892. [3; 6]

Rogé, Mrs. Charlotte Fiske, née Bates. See Bates, Charlotte Fiske.

Roger, Charles, journalist, b. Dundee, Scotland, 1819; d. Ottawa, Ont., 1878. [27]

Rogers, Agnes Low, educationist, b. Dundee, Scotland, 1884; d. Bryn Mawr, Pa., July 16, 1943. [10]

Rogers, Allen, chemist, b. Hampden, Me., 1876; d. Hampden, Me., Nov. 4, 1938. [10; 11; 13]

Rogers, Ammi, clergyman, b. Branford, Conn., 1770; d. Milton, N.Y., April 10, 1852. [62]

Rogers, Mrs. Anna, née **Alexander,** essayist, d. 1908.

Rogers, Arthur, clergyman, b. Providence, R.I., 1864; d. Newport, R.I., June 10, 1938. [10]

Rogers, Arthur Kenyon, educationist, b. Dunellen, N.J., 1868; d. Rockport, Mass., Nov. 1, 1936. [7; 10; 11]

Rogers, Mrs. Clara Kathleen, née **Barnett,** singer, b. Cheltenham, England, 1844; d. Boston, Mass., March 8, 1931. [1; 10; 11]

Rogers, David L., surgeon, b. 1799; d. New York, N.Y., Nov. 10, 1877. [3b]

Rogers, Ebenezer Platt, clergyman, b. New York, N.Y., 1817; d. Montclair, N.J., Oct. 23, 1881. [3]

Rogers, Edward Coit, spiritualist and abolitionist, fl. 1835-1856.

Rogers, Edward Sidney, lawyer, b. Castine, Me., 1875; d. Greenwich, Conn., May 22, 1949. [10]

Rogers, Fairman, civil engineer, b. Philadelphia, Pa., 1833; d. Vienna, Austria, Aug. 23, 1900. [3; 4; 10]

Rogers, George, clergyman, fl. 1838-1851.

Rogers, George Adelmer, optometrist, b. 1852; d. ?

Rogers, Henry Darwin, geologist, b. Philadelphia, Pa., 1808; d. Glasgow, Scotland, May 29, 1866. [1; 3; 4; 5; 6]

Rogers, Henry J., inventor, b. Baltimore, Md., 1811; d. Baltimore, Md., Aug. 20, 1879. [1; 3; 4]

Rogers, Henry Munroe, lawyer, b. Boston, Mass., 1839; d. Boston, Mass., March 29, 1937. [7; 10; 51]

Rogers, Henry Wade, jurist, b. Holland Patent, N.Y., 1853; d. near Trenton, N.J., Aug. 16, 1926. [1; 5; 10]

Rogers, Horatio, lawyer, b. Providence, R.I., 1836; d. Nov. 12, 1904. [3; 4; 6; 10]

Rogers, James Harvey, economist, b. Society Hill, S.C., 1886; d. Rio de Janeiro, Brazil, Aug. 13, 1939. [10; 62]

Rogers, James Richard, press agent, b. 1840; d. New York, N.Y., Oct. 7, 1932.

Rogers, James Swift, genealogist, b. Danby, Vt., 1840; d. Boston, Mass., April 9, 1905. [51]

Rogers, James Webb, poet and dramatist, b. Hillsborough, N.C., 1822; d. Bladensburg, Md., Jan. 2, 1896. [3; 6; 34]

Rogers, Janet Pierpont, social worker, d. San Mateo, Calif., April 14, 1940.

Rogers, Jason, journalist, b. New York, N.Y., 1868; d. Falmouth, Mass., April 26, 1932. [10]

Rogers, Jesse La Fayette, lawyer, b. 1855; d. 1911.

Rogers, Mrs. Jessie, poet, b. 1874; d. Chicago, Ill., Oct. 11, 1949.

Rogers, John, religious leader, b. Milford, Conn., 1648; d. New London, Conn., Oct. 17, 1721. [1; 3; 6; 9]

Rogers, John Almanza Rowley, clergyman and educationist, b. Cromwell, Conn., 1828; d. Woodstock, Ill., July 22, 1906. [1]

Rogers, John Rankin, politician, b. Brunswick, Me., 1838; d. Olympia, Wash., Dec. 26, 1901. [1; 3b; 4; 7]

Rogers, John Raphael, inventor, b. Roseville, Ill., 1856; d. Brooklyn, N.Y., Feb. 18, 1934. [1; 10]

Rogers, Joseph Morgan, journalist, b. Decatur, O., 1861; d. Philadelphia, Pa., May 16, 1922. [10;]

Rogers, Lebbeus Harding, inventor, b. 1847; d. Portland, Ore., Dec. 16, 1932.

Rogers, Lester Courtland, poet, b. 1829; d. 1900.

Rogers, Loyal Dexter, physician, b. 1856; d. Chicago, Ill., July 25, 1935.

Rogers, Nathaniel Peabody, journalist, b. Portsmouth, N.H., 1794; d. Concord, N.H., Oct. 16, 1846. [3; 4]

Rogers, Norman McLeod, educationist and politician, b. Amherst, N.S., 1894; d. near Newtonville, Ont., June 10, 1940. [2a; 27; 30]

Rogers, Robert, soldier, b. Methuen, Mass., 1731; d. London, England, May 18, 1795. [1; 3; 9; 27]

Rogers, Robert Cameron, journalist and poet, b. Buffalo, N.Y., 1862; d. Santa Barbara, Calif., April 20, 1912. [4; 7; 10; 35; 62]

Rogers, Robert Emmons, educationist, b. Haddonfield, N.J., 1888; d. Cambridge, Mass., May 13, 1941. [7; 11]

Rogers, Robert Vashon, lawyer, b. Kingston, Ont., 1843; d. Kingston, Ont., May 2, 1911. [27]

Rogers, Robert William, orientalist, b. Philadelphia, Pa., 1864; d. near Chadds Ford, Pa., Dec. 12, 1930. [1; 4; 5; 7; 10]

Rogers, Sara Bulkley, scholar, b. Waterbury, Conn., 1864; d. Bridgeport, Conn., Feb. 3, 1907. [62]

Rogers, Thomas Jones, politician, b. Waterford, Ireland, 1871; d. New York, N.Y., Dec. 7, 1832. [3; 5]

Rogers, Timothy, clergyman, b. 1589; d. about 1650.

Rogers, Walter Forwood, lawyer, d. 1925.

Rogers, Walter Pingrey, historian, b. Randolph, N.Y., 1903; d. Potsdam, N.Y., Oct. 10, 1948.

Rogers, Will. See Rogers, William Penn Adair.

Rogers, William (pseud.). See Hawkins, Nehemiah.

Rogers, William Allen, cartoonist, b. Springfield, O., 1854; d. Washington, D.C., Oct. 20, 1931. [1; 7; 10]

Rogers, William Barton, geologist, b. Philadelphia, Pa., 1804; d. Boston, Mass., May 30, 1882. [1; 3; 4; 5]

Rogers, William Penn Adair, philosopher and comedian, b. Oolagah, Okla., 1879; d. Alaska, Aug. 15, 1935. [1a; 2; 7; 10; 75]

Rogin, Leo, economist, b. 1893; d. Oakland, Calif., July 21, 1947.

Rohe, Charles Henry, clergyman, b. Syracuse, N.Y., 1846; d. 1903. [10]

Rohé, George Henry, physician, b. Baltimore, Md., 1851; d. New Orleans, La., Feb. 6, 1899. [1; 4; 10]

Rohlfs, Mrs. Anna Katharine, née **Green,** See Green, Anna Katharine.

Roland, John (pseud.). See Oliver, John Rathbone.

Roland, Walpole, civil engineer, d. Detroit, Mich., March 30, 1931. [27]

Rolapp, Henry Hermann, lawyer, b. Germany, 1860; d. Salt Lake City, Utah, Jan. 8, 1936. [4; 10]

Rolfe, George William, chemist, b. Cambridge, Mass., 1864; d. Oak Bluffs, Mass., June 21, 1942. [10; 13]

Rolfe, John Carew, educationist, b. Lawrence, Mass., 1859; d. Alexandria, Va., March 26, 1943. [7; 10; 51]

Rolfe, William James, educationist, b. Newburyport, Mass., 1827; d. Tisbury, Martha's Vineyard, Mass., July 7, 1910. [1; 2; 3; 4; 5; 6; 7; 8; 9; 10]

Rollins, Mrs. Alice Marland, née **Wellington,** poet and novelist, b. Boston, Mass., 1847; d. Bronxville, N.Y., Dec. 5, 1897. [1; 3; 4; 5; 6; 7]

Rollins, Mrs. Ellen Chapman, née **Hobbs,** historian, b. Wakefield, N.H., 1831; d. Philadelphia, Pa., May 29, 1881. [3; 6]

Rollins, Frank, educationist, b. 1860; d. May 12, 1920.

Rollins, Frank West, banker, politician, and novelist, b. Concord, N.H., 1860; d. Boston, Mass., Oct. 27, 1915. [1; 4; 5; 10]

Rollins, John Rodman, genealogist, b. 1817; d. 1892.

Rollins, Montgomery, banker, b. Concord, N.H., 1867; d. Brookline, Mass., April 18, 1918. [10]

Rollins, William, physician, b. 1852; d. 1929.

Rolph, Thomas, physician, b. about 1800; d. Portsmouth, England, 1883. [3; 27]

Romaine, Robert Dexter (pseud.). See Payson, George.

Roman, Alfred, jurist, b. St. James Parish, La., 1824; d. New Orleans, La., Sept. 20, 1892. [34]

Roman, Frederick William, educationist, b. Sidney, O., 1876; d. Hollywood, Calif., April 9, 1948. [10]

Romans, Bernard, civil engineer, soldier, and naturalist, b. Netherlands about 1720; d. at sea about 1784. [1; 3; 4; 6; 7]

Rombauer, Robert Julius, soldier, b. Hungary, 1830; d. St. Louis, Mo., Sept. 26, 1925.

Rombauer, Roderick Emile, lawyer, b. Hungary, 1833; d. St. Louis, Mo., March 27, 1924. [10]

Rombro, Jacob, labour leader, b. Russia, 1858; d. New York, N.Y., Nov. 28, 1922. [1; 10]

Ronald, Mary (pseud.). See Arnold, Mrs. Augusta, née Foote.

Ronayne, Maurice, priest, b. Castlemartyr, Ireland, 1828; d. New York, N.Y., 1903. [3; 6; 21]

Rondthaler, Edward, clergyman and educationist, b. 1817; d. 1855. [6]

Rondthaler, Edward, bishop, b. near Nazareth, Pa., 1842; d. Winston-Salem, N.C., Jan. 31, 1931. [1; 4; 10]

Rongy, Abraham Jacob, gynaecologist, b. Russia, 1878; d. New York, N.Y., Oct. 11, 1949. [10]

Rood, Anson, clergyman, d. 1887. [43]

Rood, Henry Harrison, soldier, b. 1841; d. 1915. [37]

Rood, Ogden Nicholas, physicist, b. Danbury, Conn., 1831; d. New York, N.Y., Nov. 12, 1902. [1; 3; 4; 5; 6; 10]

Roode, Charles Lambert de, poet, b. St. Pol, France, 1859; d. Montreal, Que., June 24, 1925. [27]

Rooney, John Jerome, jurist and poet, b. Binghampton, N.Y., 1866; d. New York, N.Y., Nov. 27, 1934. [10; 21]

Roorbach, George Byron, economist, b. Herkimer county, N.Y., 1878; d. Washington, D.C., May 23, 1934. [10]

Roorbach, Orville Augustus, publisher and bibliographer, b. Red Hook, Dutchess county, N.Y., 1803; d. Schenectady, N.Y., June 21, 1861. [3; 6]

Roorbach, Orville Augustus, publisher, b. 1833; d. 1893.

Roosa, Daniel Bennett St. John, physician, b. Bethel, N.Y., 1838; d. New York, N.Y., March 7, 1908. [1; 3; 4; 5; 6; 10]

Roosevelt, Blanche (pseud.). Se Maccheta, Mrs. Blanche Roosevelt, née Tucker.

Roosevelt, Clinton, political scientist, b. 1804; d. 1898.

Roosevelt, Franklin Delano, thirty-first president of the United States, b. Hyde Park, N.Y., 1882; d. Warm Springs, Ga., April 12, 1945. [2a; 10; 12]

Roosevelt, Kermit, soldier and adventurer, b. Oyster Bay, Long Island, N.Y., 1889; d. Alaska, June 4, 1943. [10; 11; 12]

Roosevelt, Robert Barnwell, lawyer, b. New York, N.Y., 1829; d. Sayville, Long Island, N.Y., June 14, 1906. [1; 3; 4; 5; 6; 7; 10]

Roosevelt, Silas Weir, poet, b. 1823; d. 1870.

Roosevelt, Theodore, twenty-sixth president of the United States, b. New York, N.Y., Oct. 27, 1858; d. Oyster Bay, Long Island, N.Y., Jan. 6, 1919. [1; 2; 3; 4; 5; 6; 7; 8; 10; 72]

Roosevelt, Theodore, soldier and publisher, b. Oyster Bay, Long Island, N.Y., 1887; d. Normandy, France, July 12, 1944. [7; 10; 12]

Root, Amos Ives, apiarist, b. near Medina, O., 1839; d. April 30, 1923. [1; 10; 11]

Root, Elihu, lawyer, politician, and diplomat, b. Clinton, N.Y., 1845; d. New York, N.Y., Feb. 7, 1937. [2; 4; 7; 10]

Root, Erastus, lawyer and politician, b. Hebron, Conn., 1773; d. New York, N.Y., Dec. 24, 1846. [1; 3; 5; 6]

Root, Frank Albert, journalist, b. Binghampton, N.Y., 1837; d. Topeka, Kans., June 21, 1926. [1; 7; 10]

Root, Frederick Stanley, clergyman, b. New Haven, Conn., 1853; d. New Haven, Conn., Jan. 18, 1906. [10; 62]

Root, George Frederick, musician, b. Sheffield, Mass., 1820; d. Bailey's Island, Me., Aug. 6, 1895. [3; 5; 7; 20]

Root, Harmon Knox, physician, fl. 1853-1858.

Root, James Pierce, genealogist, b. 1829; d. 1887.

Root, Joseph Pomeroy, physician and diplomat, b. Greenwich, Mass., 1826; d. Wyandotte, Kans., July 20, 1885. [1; 4]

Root, Nathaniel William Taylor, clergyman, b. New Haven, Conn., 1829; d. Portland, Me., Dec. 14, 1872. [62]

Root, Oren, educationist, b. Syracuse, N.Y., 1838; d. Clinton, N.Y., Aug. 26, 1907. [5; 10]

Root, Paul Adelbert, educationist, b. Seattle, Wash., 1903; d. Dallas, Tex., May 12, 1947.

Root, William Thomas, psychologist, b. Concordia, Kans., 1882; d. Pittsburgh, Pa., Jan. 24, 1945. [10; 13]

Roper, Stephen, mechanical engineer, b. New Hampshire, 1823; d. Cambridge, Mass., June 1, 1896. [3b]

Roper, William Winston, football coach, b. Philadelphia, Pa., 1880; d. Germantown, Pa., Dec. 10, 1933. [10]

Ropes, Charles Joseph Hardy, clergyman, b. St. Petersburg, Russia, 1851; d. Bangor, Me., Jan. 5, 1915. [10; 62]

Ropes, James Hardy, theologian, b. Salem, Mass., 1866; d. Cambridge, Mass., Jan. 7, 1933. [1; 10; 11; 51]

Ropes, John Codman, historian, b. St. Petersburg, Russia, 1836; d. Boston, Mass., Oct. 27, 1899. [1; 3; 4; 5; 6; 7; 8; 9; 10; 51]

Rorer, David, lawyer, b. Pittsylvania county, Va., 1806; d. Burlington, Ia., July 7, 1884. [1; 37]

Rorer, Jonathan Taylor, mathematician, b. West Chester, Pa., 1871; d. Croton Falls, N.Y., Aug. 13, 1948. [13]

Rorer, Mrs. Sarah Tyson, née **Heston,** domestic scientist, b. Richboro, Pa., 1849; d. Colebrook, Pa., Dec. 27, 1937. [4; 10]

Rorke, Louise Richardson, writer of books for children, b. Thornbury, Ont.; d. Pickering, Ont., July 23, 1949.

Rorty, Malcolm Churchill, engineer, b. Paterson, N.J., 1875; d. New York, N.Y., Jan. 18, 1936. [10; 11]

Rosa (pseud.). See Jeffrey, Mrs. Rosa, née Griffith.

Rosa, Narcisse, ship-builder, b. 1823; d. Quebec, Que., Nov. 3, 1907. [27]

Rosanoff, Aaron Joshua, psychiatrist, b. Pinsk, Russia, 1878; d. Los Angeles, Calif., Jan. 7, 1943. [10; 13]

Roscoe, William E., local historian, b. 1837; d. Cobleskill, N.Y., Feb. 13, 1929.

Rose, Achilles, physician, b. 1839; d. New York, N.Y., Jan. 10, 1916.

Rose, Aquila, poet, b. England, about 1695; d. Philadelphia, Pa., Aug. 22, 1723. [1; 3; 4; 7; 9]

Rose, Augustus Foster, art teacher, b. Hebron, N.S., 1873; d. Providence, R.I., July 20, 1946.

Rose, Edward Everley, playwright, b. Stanstead, Que., 1862; d. Fremont, Wis., April 2, 1939. [7; 10]

Rose, George MacLean, publisher, b. Caithness-shire, Scotland, 1829; d. Toronto, Ont., Feb. 10, 1898. [27]

Rose, Jacob Servoss, physician, b. about 1797; d. Philadelphia, Pa., 1865. [6]

Rose, John Carter, jurist, b. Baltimore, Md., 1861; d. Atlantic City, N.J., March 26, 1927. [1; 10]

Rose, Joseph Nelson, botanist, b. near Liberty, Ind., 1862; d. Washington, D.C., May 4, 1928. [1; 10; 13]

Rose, Mrs. Martha Emily, née **Parmelee,** miscellaneous writer, b. Norton, O., 1834; d. Cleveland, O., May 5, 1923. [4; 10; 11]

Rose, Mrs. Mary Davies, née **Swartz,** nutritionist, b. Newark, O., 1874; d. Edgewater, N.J., Feb. 1, 1941. [10; 11]

Rose, Robert Hutchinson, poet, b. 1776; d. 1842.

Rose, Uriah Milton, jurist, b. Bradfordsville, Ky., 1834; d. Little Rock, Ark., Aug. 12, 1913. [1; 4; 10; 34]

Rose, Victor M., miscellaneous writer, d. 1893. [34]

Rose, Mrs. W. G. See Rose, Mrs. Martha Emily, née Parmelee.

Rose, Wallace Dickinson, physician, b. Little Rock, Ark., 1887; d. Little Rock, Ark., Aug. 17, 1928. [10; 11]

Rose, Walter Malins, lawyer, b. Toronto, Ont., 1872; d. Los Angeles, Calif., Feb. 12, 1908. [1; 4; 10]

Roseboro', Viola, editor and novelist, b. Pulaski, Tenn., 1857; d. Huguenot, Staten Island, N.Y., Jan. 29, 1945. [7; 10; 34]

Rosebrugh, Abner Mulholland, physician, b. near Galt, Upper Canada, 1835; d. Toronto, Ont., Nov. 6, 1914. [27]

Rosecrans, Sylvester Horton, bishop, b. Homer, O., 1827; d. Columbus, O., Oct. 21, 1878. [1; 3; 4; 5]

Rosen, Lew (pseud.). See Rosenthal, Lewis.

Rosen, Peter, priest, b. Germany, 1850; d. ? [10; 70]

Rosenau, Milton Joseph, sanitarian, b. Philadelphia, Pa., 1869; d. Chapel Hill., N.C., April 9, 1946. [10; 11; 13]

Rosenberg, Solomon Leopold Millard, educationist, b. Germany, 1869; d. Los Angeles, Calif., July 10, 1934. [10; 11]

Rosenblatt, Frank Ferdinand, educationist, b. 1882; d. Nov. 7, 1927.

Rosenfeld, Morris, poet, b. Russian Poland, 1862; d. New York, N.Y., June 22, 1923. [1; 7; 10]

Rosenfeld, Paul, music and art critic, b. 1890; d. New York, N.Y., July 21, 1946. [7; 12; 62]

Rosenfeld, Sydney, playwright, b. Richmond, Va., 1855; d. New York, N.Y., June 13, 1931. [10; 34]

Rosengarten, Joseph George, lawyer and historian, b. Philadelphia, Pa., 1835; d. Philadelphia, Pa., Jan. 14, 1921. [3; 6; 10]

Rosenthal, Lewis, journalist, b. Baltimore, Md., 1856; d. Washington, D.C., May 26, 1909. [3]

Roset, Hipponax (pseud.). See Paxton, Joseph Rupert.

Rosewater, Victor, journalist, b. Omaha, Neb., 1871; d. Philadelphia, Pa., July 12, 1940. [2a; 4; 7; 10; 11]

Ross, Abel Hastings, clergyman, b. Winchendon, Mass., 1831; d. Port Huron, Mich., May 13, 1893. [1]

Ross, Albert (pseud.). See Porter, Linn Boyd.

Ross, Alexander, fur-trader, b. Nairnshire, Scotland, 1783; d. Red River Settlement, Hudson's Bay Territories, Oct. 23, 1856. [1; 7; 9; 27]

Ross, Mrs. Alexander. See Ross, Mrs. Ellen, née McGregor.

Ross, Alexander Milton, naturalist, b. Belleville, Upper Canada, 1832; d. Montreal, Que., Oct. 27, 1897. [27]

Ross, Arthur Amasa, clergyman, b. Thompson, Conn., 1791; d. Pawtucket, R.I., June 16, 1864. [4]

Ross, Clinton, novelist and short-story writer, b. Binghampton, N.Y., 1861; d. Owego, N.Y., March 26, 1920. [7; 10; 62]

Ross, Denman Waldo, educationist, b. Cincinnati, O., 1853; d. London, England, Sept. 12, 1935. [1a; 10; 51]

Ross, Dunbar, politician, b. Clonakilty, Ireland, about 1800; d. Quebec, Que., May 16, 1865. [27]

Ross, Edmund Gibson, journalist and politician, b. Ashland, O., 1826; d. Albuquerque, N.M., May 8, 1907. [1; 3; 4; 5]

Ross, François Xavier, bishop, b. Grosses Roches, Matane county, Que., 1869; d. Quebec, Que., July 5, 1945.

Ross, Mrs. Elizabeth, née Williams, poet, b. 1852; d. 1926.

Ross, Mrs. Ellen, née McGregor, novelist, b. Banff, Scotland; d. Montreal, Que., 1892. [27]

Ross, Frederick Augustus, clergyman, b. Cobham, Va., 1796; d. Huntsville, Ala., April 13, 1883. [3; 34]

Ross, George Alexander Johnston, theologian, b. Inverness, Scotland, 1865; d. Honolulu, Hawaii, Jan. 22, 1937. [10; 11]

Ross, Sir George William, politician, b. near Nairn, Middlesex county, Ont., 1841; d. Toronto, Ont., March 7, 1914. [27]

Ross, Harvey Lee, pioneer, b. Seneca county, N.Y., 1817; d. Oakland, Calif., 1907.

Ross, Henry Martin, novelist, fl. 1905-1908. [21]

Ross, James, educationist, b. 1744; d. 1827. [4; 6]

Ross, Joel Horton, physician, fl. 1844-1852. [6]

Ross, John Dawson, librarian, b. Edinburgh, Scotland, 1853; d. New York, N.Y., Oct. 29, 1939. [7; 10]

Ross, John Elliot, priest, b. Baltimore, Md., 1884; d. New York, N.Y., Sept. 19, 1946. [7; 10; 11; 21; 22]

Ross, Patrick Hore Warriner, banker, b. Bombay, India, 1858; d. near Newark, N.J., April 13, 1928. [4; 10]

Ross, Peter, historian, b. 1847; d. 1902.

Ross, Philip Dansken, journalist, b. Montreal, Que., 1858; d. Ottawa, Ont., July 5, 1949. [30]

Ross, Robert, educationist, b. 1726; d. 1799. [56; 62]

Ross, Victor Harold, journalist and industrialist, b. Walkerton, Ont., 1878; d. Toronto, Ont., Feb. 23, 1934. [27]

Ross, William Wilson, clergyman, b. 1838; d. Ingersoll, Ont., March 28, 1884. [27]

Rosser, Leonidas, clergyman, b. Petersburg,, Va., 1815; d. Ashland, Va., Jan. 25, 1892. [3; 34]

Rossiter, Stealy Bales, clergyman, b. Berne, N.Y., 1842; d. Newark, N.J., June 24, 1914. [10]

Rossiter, William Sidney, statistician, b. Westfield, Mass., 1861; d. Concord, N.H., Jan. 23, 1929. [1; 4; 7; 10]

Rotch, Abbott Lawrence, meteorologist, b. Boston, Mass., 1861; d. Boston, Mass., April 7, 1912. [1; 4; 5; 10]

Rotch, Thomas Morgan, physician, b. Philadelphia, Pa., 1849; d. Boston, Mass., March 9, 1914. [1; 4; 10; 51]

Roth, Edward, educationist, b. Kilkenny, Ireland, 1826; d. Philadelphia, Pa., 1911. [6; 21]

Roth, Filibert, forester, b. Würtemberg, Germany, 1858; d. Ann Arbor, Mich., Dec. 4, 1925. [4; 10]

Rothensteiner, John Ernest, priest, b. St. Louis, Mo., 1860; d. St. Louis, Mo., Sept. 26, 1936. [21]

Rothrock, Joseph Trimble, physician and botanist, b. McVeytown, Pa., 1839; d. West Chester, Pa., June 2, 1922. [1; 4; 5; 10]

Rothschild, Alonzo, journalist, b. New York, N.Y., 1862; d. East Foxboro, Mass., Sept. 29, 1915. [10]

Rothwell, Richard Pennefather, mining engineer, b. Ingersoll, Upper Canada, 1836; d. New York, N.Y., April 17, 1901. [1; 3; 4; 10]

Rotzell, Willett Enos, physician and naturalist, b. Philadelphia, Pa., 1871; d. Philadelphia, Pa., July, 1913. [4; 10]

Rouillard, Eugène, geographer, b. Quebec, Que., 1851; d. Quebec, Que., Oct. 16, 1926. [27]

Rouleau, Charles Edmond, soldier, b. Ste. Anne de la Pocatière, Que., 1841; d. Quebec, Que., Dec. 24, 1926. [27]

Roulet, Mrs. Mary F., née Nixon, novelist, d. Chicago, Ill., 1930. [21]

Round, William Marshall Pitts, journalist and novelist, b. Pawtucket, R.I., 1845; d. Acushnet, Mass., Jan. 3, 1906. [1; 3; 5; 6; 7; 10]

Rouquette, Adrien Emmanuel, priest and poet, b. New Orleans, La., 1813; d. New Orleans, La., July 15, 1887. [1; 3; 7; 34; 74]

Rouquette, François Dominique, poet, b. Bayou Lacombe, La., 1810; d. Bonfouca, La., May, 1890. [1; 3; 7; 34]

Rourke, Constance Mayfield, literary critic, b. Cleveland, O., 1885; d. Grand Rapids, Mich., March 23, 1941. [7; 10]

Rouse, Adelaide Louise, novelist, b. Athens, N.Y.; d. New York, N.Y., 1912. [7; 10]

Rouse, Mrs. Lydia L., novelist, fl. 1881-1894. [6]

Rouse, Michael Francis. See Bede, Brother.

Rousseau, Edmond, archivist and miscellaneous writer, d. Quebec, Que., March 8, 1909. [27]

Rousseau, Pierre, priest, b. Nantes, France, 1827; d. Montreal, Que., Feb. 8, 1912. [27]

Roussy de Sales, Raoul Jean Jacques François. See De Roussy de Sales, Raoul Jean Jacques François.

Routhier, Sir Adolphe Basile, jurist, b. St. Placide, Lower Canada, 1839; d. St. Irénée-les-Bains, Que., June 27, 1920. [27]

Routzahn, Evart Grant, social worker, b. Dayton, O., 1869; d. New York, N.Y., April 24, 1939. [10; 11]

Row, Robert Keable, publisher, b. Woodstock, Ont., 1858; d. Evanston, Ill., Dec. 22, 1932. [10; 11]

Rowan, Andrew Summers, soldier, b. 1857; d. San Francisco, Calif., Jan. 11, 1943. [7; 11]

Rowe, George Clinton, poet, b. 1853; d. 1903.

Rowe, Harry Marc, accountant, b. 1860; d. 1926.

Rowe, Mrs. Henrietta, née **Gould** novelist, b. East Corinth, Me., 1835; d. 1910. [7; 10]

Rowe, Horace, poet, b. 1852; d. 1884. [34]

Rowe, Joseph Eugene, educationist, b. Emmitsburg, Md., 1883; d. Baltimore, Md., Oct. 2, 1939. [10]

Rowe, Leo Stanton, publicist, b. McGregor, Ia., 1871; d. Washington, D.C., Dec. 5, 1946. [4; 10; 11]

Rowe, Stuart Henry, educationist, b. New Haven, Conn., 1869; d. Yonkers, N.Y., June 5, 1945. [62]

Rowell, George Presbury, publisher, b. Concord, Vt., 1838; d. Poland Springs, Me., Aug. 28, 1908. [1; 4; 7; 10]

Rowell, Newton Wesley, jurist and politician, b. near London, Ont., 1867; d. Toronto, Ont., Nov. 22, 1941. [11; 27; 30]

Rowland, Adoniram Judson, clergyman, b. Valley Forge, Pa., 1840; d. Philadelphia, Pa., Jan. 31, 1917. [10]

Rowland, Dunbar, historian, b. Oakland, Miss., 1864; d. Jackson, Miss., Nov. 1, 1937. [7; 10; 11]

Rowland, Henry Augustus, physicist, b. Honesdale, Pa., 1848; d. Baltimore, Md., April 16, 1901. [1; 3; 4; 5; 10]

Rowland, Henry Cottrell, physician, novelist and traveller, b. New York, N.Y., 1874; d. Washington, D.C., June 6, 1933. [7; 10]

Rowland, Kate Mason, biographer, b. Virginia; d. Baltimore, Md., June 28, 1916. [5; 7; 10]

Rowlandson, Mrs. Mary, née **White,** Indian captive, b. probably in England, about 1635; d. Wethersfield, Conn., after 1678. [1; 3; 4; 9]

Rowlee, Willard Winfield, educationist, b. Fulton, N.Y., 1861; d. Ithaca, N.Y., Aug. 8, 1923. [10]

Rowley, John, taxidermist, b. Hastings-on-Hudson, N.Y., 1866; d. Alhambra, Calif., Jan. 2, 1928. [10]

Rowley, Owsley Robert, church historian, b. Yarmouth, N.S., 1866; d. Toronto, Ont., Nov. 24, 1949. [30]

Rowson, Mrs. Susanna, née **Haswell,** novelist and playwright, b. Portsmouth, England, 1762; d. Boston, Mass., March 2, 1824. [1; 2; 3; 4; 6; 7; 9; 72]

Roy, Andrew, economist, b. 1834; d. ?

Roy, Camille. See Roy, Joseph Camille.

Roy, Ferdinand, jurist, b. Ancienne Lorette, Que., 1873; d. Quebec, Que., June 22, 1948. [11; 30]

Roy, James, clergyman, b. Montreal, Lower Canada, 1834; d. Montreal, Que., May 25, 1922. [27]

Roy, Mrs. Jennet, schoolmistress, fl. 1847-1864. [29]

Roy, Joseph Camille, priest and educationist, b. Berthier-en-bas, Que., 1870; d. Quebec, Que., June 24, 1943. [27]

Roy, Joseph Edmond, historian, b. Lévis, Que., 1858; d. Quebec, Que., May 8, 1913. [27]

Roy, Joseph Edwin, clergyman, b. 1827; d. Chicago, Ill., March 4, 1908.

Roy, Mrs. Lillian Elizabeth, née **Becker,** writer of books for young people, b. Morristown, N.J., 1868; d. Mountain Lakes, N.J., June 12, 1932. [10

Roy, William L., educationist, fl. 1817-1848. [6]

Royal, George, physician, b. Alford, Mass., 1853; d. Des Moines, Ia., Dec. 31, 1931. [10; 11]

Royal, Joseph, journalist and historian, b. Repentigny, Lower Canada, 1837; d. Montreal, Que., Aug. 23, 1902. [27]

Royal, Ralph (pseud.). See Abarbanell, Joseph Ralph.

Royall, Mrs. Anne, née **Newport,** traveller, b. Maryland, 1769; d. Washington, D.C., Oct. 1, 1854. [1; 3; 6; 7; 9; 34]

Royall, William Lawrence, lawyer, b. Fauquier county, Va., 1844; d. Avon, N.J., Aug. 24, 1911. [4; 34]

Royce, Andrew, clergyman, b. Marlow, N.H., 1805; d. Waterbury, Vt., Oct. 15, 1864. [43]

Royce, Charles C., ethnologist, b. Defiance, O., 1845; d. 1923. [2]

Royce, George Monroe, clergyman, b. Richmond, Va., 1850; d. London, England, March 25, 1928. [10]

Royce, Josiah, philosopher, b. Grass Valley, Nevada county, Calif., 1855; d. Cambridge, Mass., Sept. 14, 1916. [1; 2; 3; 4; 5; 6; 7; 10; 35]

Royce, Moses S., clergyman, d. 1873.

Royle, Edwin Milton, actor, playwright, and novelist, b. Lexington, Mo., 1862; d. New York, N.Y., Feb. 16, 1942. [7; 10]

Royse, Noble Kilby, educationist, fl. 1872-1891. [6]

Royster, James Finch, educationist, b. Raleigh, N.C., 1880; d. Richmond, Va., March 21, 1930. [1; 10]

Rozier, Firmin A., historian, b. 1820; d. Ste. Geneviève, Mo., Feb. 11, 1897. [34]

Rubek, Sennoia (pseud.). See Burke, John.

Rubens, Horatio Seymour, lawyer, b. New York, N.Y., 1869; d. Garrison, N.Y., April 8, 1941. [10]

Rubinow, Isaac Max, social worker, b. Russia, 1875; d. Cincinnati, O., Sept. 1, 1936. [10; 11]

Rucker, William Colby, sanitarian, b. Kenney, Ill., 1875; d. New Orleans, La., May 22, 1930. [10]

Ruskstull, Frederic Wellington, sculptor and art critic, b. Alsace, France, 1853; d. New York, N.Y., Feb. 16, 1942. [11; 12]

Rud, Anthony Melville, novelist, b. Chicago, Ill., 1893; d. New York, N.Y., Nov. 31, 1942. [11]

Rudd, Edward Huntting, clergyman, b. Sag Harbor, Long Island, N.Y., 1860; d. Dedham, Mass., July 8, 1909.

Rudd, John Churchill, clergyman, b. Norwich, Conn., 1779; d. 1848. [6]

Ruddock, Edward Harris, physician, b. 1822; d. 1875.

Ruddy, Mrs. Ella Augusta, née **Giles,** poet and novelist, b. 1851; d. Madison, Wis., 1917.

Ruddy, Howard Shaw, journalist, b. Bridgeport, Ill., 1856; d. Rochester, N.Y., Dec. 13, 1922. [10]

Ruediger, William Carl, educationist, b. Fountain City, Wis., 1874; d. Washington, D.C., July 4, 1947. [10]

Ruffin, Edmund, agriculturist and publisher, b. Prince George county, Va., 1794; d. Amelia county, Va., June 18, 1865. [1; 3; 4; 7; 34]

Ruffin, Mrs. Margaret Ellen, née **Henry,** poet and novelist, b. Daphne, Ala., 1857; d. 1941. [7; 21]

Ruffner, Henry, clergyman, b. Shenandoah county, Va., 1790; d. Malden, W. Va., Dec. 17, 1861. [1; 3; 4; 34]

Ruffner, William Henry, clergyman and educationist, b. Lexington, Va., 1824; d. Ashville, N.C., Nov. 24, 1908. [1; 10; 34]

Rugg, Henry Warren, clergyman, b. Framingham, Mass., 1833; d. 1910. [10]

Ruggles, Colden L'Hommedieu, soldier, b. Omaha, Neb., 1869; d. Charleston, S.C., April 2, 1933. [10]

Ruggles, Henry Joseph, lawyer, b. Poughkeepsie, N.Y., 1813; d. New York, N.Y., March 6, 1906. [10]

Rugh, Charles Edward, educationist, b. Lamartine, Pa., 1867; d. Berkeley, Calif., Sept. 30, 1938. [10; 11]

Ruhl, Arthur Brown, journalist, b. Rockford, Ill., 1876; d. Queens, Long Island, N.Y., June 7, 1935. [1a; 7; 10; 51]

Ruhrüh, John, physician, b. Chillicothe, O., 1872; d. Baltimore, Md., March 10, 1935. [1a; 10; 11]

Rulison, Nelson Somerville, bishop, b. Carthage, N.Y., 1842; d. Bad Nauheim, Germany, Sept. 1, 1897. [3; 4; 5; 6]

Rumbold, Thomas Frazier, physician, b. Aberdeen, Scotland, 1830; d. St. Louis, Mo., 1901. [10]

Rumple, Jethro, clergyman, b. Cabarrus county, N.C., 1827; d. 1906. [3; 34]

Rumsey, William, jurist, b. Bath, N.Y., 1841; d. Bath, N.Y., Jan. 16, 1903. [1; 4; 10]

Runcie, Mrs. Constance, née **Faunt Le Roy,** poet, b. Indianapolis, Ind., 1836; d. Winnetka, Ill., May 17, 1911. [1; 4; 7; 10]

Runkle, John Daniel, mathematician, b. Root, Montgomery county, N.Y., 1822; d. Southwest Harbor, Me., July 8, 1902. [1; 3; 4; 10]

Runnells, Moses Thurston, clergyman, b. Cambridge, Vt., 1830; d. Charlestown, N.H., May 17, 1902. [49]

Runyon, Damon, poet, columnist, and story-writer, b. Manhattan, Kans., 1884; d. New York, N.Y., Dec. 10, 1946. [7; 10; 12]

Ruoff, Henry Woldmar, editor and publisher, b. Brünn, Austria, 1865; d. Atlanta, Ga., July 2, 1935. [10; 11]

Rupert, William Whitehead, educationist, b. 1852; d. Pottstown, Pa., Jan. 6, 1929.

Rupp, Frederick Augustine, physician, b. 1876; d. Lewistown, Pa., July 23, 1934.

Rupp, Israel Daniel, historian, b. Cumberland county, Pa., 1803; d. Philadelphia, Pa., May 31, 1878. [1; 3; 5; 6; 7]

Ruschenberger, William Samuel Waithman, naval surgeon, b. Cumberland county, N.J., 1807; d. Philadelphia, Pa., March 24, 1895. [3; 4; 5; 6]

Rush, Benjamin, physician, b. near Philadelphia, Pa., 1745; d. Philadelphia, Pa., April 19, 1813. [1; 2; 3; 4; 5; 6; 7; 8; 9]

Rush, Christopher, bishop, b. Craven county, N.C., 1777; d. New York, N.Y., July 16, 1873. [3; 5]

Rush, Jacob, jurist, b. near Philadelphia, Pa., 1746; d. Philadelphia, Pa., Jan. 5, 1820. [3; 4; 5; 6]

Rush, James, physician and psychologist, b. Philadelphia, Pa., 1786; d. Philadelphia, Pa., May 26, 1869. [1; 3; 4; 5; 6; 9]

Rush, Richard, lawyer, politician, and diplomat, b. Philadelphia, Pa., 1780; d. Philadelphia, Pa., July 30, 1859. [1; 3; 4; 5; 6]

Rush, Sylvester R., lawyer, b. Greene county, Pa., 1860; d. Omaha, Neb., March, 1932. [10]

Rush, Thomas Edward, lawyer, b. New York, N.Y., 1867; d. New York, N.Y., June 3, 1927. [10]

Rusk, John, clergyman, b. Ashton-under-Lyne, England, 1849; d. Chicago, Ill., 1910. [10]

Rusling, James Fowler, lawyer, b. Washington, N.J., 1834; d. Trenton, N.J., April 1, 1918. [4; 10]

Rusling, Joseph, clergyman, b. Lincolnshire, England, 1788; d. 1839. [6]

Russell, Addison Peale, printer and politician, b. Wilmington, O., 1826; d. 1912. [4; 7; 10]

Russell, Alexander Jamieson, civil servant, b. Glasgow, Scotland, 1807; d. Ottawa, Ont., 1887. [3; 27]

Russell, Alfred, lawyer, b. Plymouth, N.H., 1830; d. Detroit, Mich., May 8, 1906. [10; 49]

Russell, Archibald, philanthropist, b. Edinburgh, Scotland, 1811; d. New York, N.Y., April 12, 1871. [3]

Russell, Benjamin, jurist, b. Dartmouth, N.S., 1849; d. Halifax, N.S., Sept. 21, 1935. [11; 27]

Russell, Charles Edward, journalist, b. Davenport, Ia., 1860; d. Washington, D.C., April 23, 1941. [7; 10; 11]

Russell, Charles Marion, artist, b. St. Louis, Mo., 1865; d. Great Falls, Mont., Oct. 24, 1927. [7; 10]

Russell, Charles Taze, religious leader, b. Pittsburgh, Pa., 1852; d. on a train in Texas, Oct. 31, 1916. [1; 2; 4; 7; 10]

Russell, Charles Wells, lawyer and novelist, b. 1824; d. 1867. [4]

Russell, Charles Wells, lawyer, diplomat, and poet, b. Wheeling, W. Va., 1856; d. Washington, April 5, 1927. [1; 4; 10]

Russell, Mrs. Frances Theresa, née Peet, educationist, b. Anamosa, Ia., 1873; d. Stanford University, Calif., Feb. 15, 1936. [7; 11]

Russell, Francis Thayer, clergyman, b. Boston, Mass., 1828; d. 1910. [3; 10]

Russell, Frank, clergyman, b. 1840; d. Meadville, Pa., July 22, 1905.

Russell, Frank, educationist, b. Fort Dodge, Ia., 1868; d. Kingman, Ariz., Nov. 7. 1903. [4; 10; 51]

Russell, George Besore, clergyman, b. 1824; d. 1908.

Russell, Gurdon Wadsworth, physician, b. Hartford, Conn., 1815; d. Hartford, Conn., Feb. 3, 1909. [62]

Russell, Henry Benajah, journalist, b. Russell, Mass., 1859; d. Suffield, Conn., Nov. 25, 1945. [7; 10; 11]

Russell, Howard Hyde, clergyman, b. Stillwater, Minn., 1855; d. Westerville, O.; June 30, 1946. [4; 10; 11]

Russell, Irwin, poet, b. Port Gibson, Miss., 1853; d. New Orleans, La., Dec. 23, 1879. [1; 4; 7; 9; 34]

Russell, Issac Franklin, jurist, b. Hamden, Conn., 1857; d. Brooklyn, N.Y., Nov. 20, 1931. [10; 11]

Russell, Israel Cook, geologist, b. Garrattsville, N.Y., 1852; d. Ann Arbor, Mich., May 1, 1906. [1; 3; 4; 5; 10; 44]

Russell, James Earl, educationist, b. Hamden, N.Y., 1864; d. Trenton, N.J., Nov. 4, 1945. [10]

Russell, James Solomon, clergyman, b. Palmer's Springs, Va., 1857; d. March 28, 1935. [1a; 10]

Russell, John, educationist, fl. 1837-1854.

Russell, John, historian, b. Cavendish, Vt., 1793; d. Bluffdale, Green county, Ill., Jan. 21, 1863. [43]

Russell, John Andrew, journalist, b. Sheboygan, Wis., 1865; d. Detroit, Mich., April 6, 1936. [10; 11; 21; 44]

Russell, John Edward, clergyman and educationist, b. Walpole, N.H., 1848; d. Williamstown, Mass., Feb. 25, 1917. [10; 62]

Russell, Lucy May (pseud.). See Coryell, John Russell.

Russell, Martha, story-writer, fl. 1856-1859. [6]

Russell, Morris Craw, journalist, b. Venago county, Pa., 1840; d. 1913. [70]

Russell, Thomas Herbert, compiler, b. England, 1862; d. Chicago, Ill., Sept. 7, 1947. [7]

Russell, William, educationist, b. Glasgow, Scotland, 1798; d. Lancaster, Mass., Aug. 16, 1873. [1; 3; 6].

Russell, William Eustis, politician, b. Cambridge, Mass., 1857; d. St. Adelaide de Pabos, Que., July 16, 1896. [1; 5; 10]

Russell, William Hepburn, lawyer, b. Hannibal, Mo., 1857; d. New York, N.Y., Nov. 21, 1911. [4; 10]

Russell, William Shaw, historian, b. 1792; d. 1863. [6]

Russell, William Thomas, bishop, b. Baltimore, Md., 1863; d. Charleston, S.C., March 18, 1927.

Russell, Willis, hotel proprietor, b. 1814; d. 1887. [27]

Rust, Richard Sutton, clergyman, b. Ipswich, Mass., 1815; d. Cincinnati, O., Dec. 22, 1906. [1; 4]

Rusticus, gent. (pseud.). See Furman, Garrit.

Rustler, Robin (pseud.). See Maclean, John (1851-1928).

Ruter, Martin, clergyman, b. Charlton, Mass., 1785; d. Washington, Tex., May 16, 1838. [1; 3; 5; 6]

Rutgers, Lispenard (pseud.). See Smith, Henry Erskine.

Rutherford, Joseph Franklin, lawyer and religious leader, b. Versailles, Mo., 1869; d. San Diego, Calif., Jan. 8, 1942. [11]

Rutherford, Mildred Lewis, historian, b. Athens, Ga., 1851; d. Athens, Ga., Aug. 15, 1928. [4; 7; 10; 11; 34]

Rutledge, Edward, clergyman, b. Charleston, S.C., 1797; d. Savannah, Ga., March 13, 1832. [3; 4; 6; 34]

Rutledge, Samuel Albert, educationist, b. Pikeville, Tenn., 1888; d. Brooklyn, N.Y., Aug. 15, 1941. [62]

Rutt, Christian Ludwig, journalist, b. Milwaukee, Wis., 1859; d. St. Joseph, Mo., 1937. [21]

Ruttan, Henry, inventor, b. Adolphustown, Upper Canada, 1792; d. Cobourg, Ont., July 31, 1871. [27]

Ruttenber, Edward Manning, historian, b. Bennington, Vt., 1825; d. Newburgh, N.Y., Dec. 5, 1907. [10]

Ruud, Martin Brown, educationist, b. Fergus Falls, Minn., 1885; d. Minneapolis, Minn., Feb. 8, 1941. [7; 10]

Ryan, Abram Joseph, priest and poet, b. Hagerstown, Md., 1838; d. Louisville, Ky., April 22, 1886. [1; 3; 4; 5; 6; 9; 21; 34]

Ryan, Carroll. See Ryan, William Thomas Carroll.

Ryan, Daniel Joseph, lawyer, b. Cincinnati, O., 1855; d. Columbus, O., June 15, 1923. [10]

Ryan, Harris Joseph, electrical engineer, b. Powells Valley, Pa., 1866; d. Palo Alto, Calif., July 3, 1934. [1a; 10]

Ryan, James, educationist, fl. 1824-1847. [6]

Ryan, James Hugh, archbishop, b. Indianapolis, Ind., 1886; d. Omaha, Neb., Nov. 23, 1947. [7; 10; 21]

Ryan, John Augustine, priest and economist, b. Dakota county, Minn., 1869; d. St. Paul, Minn., Sept. 16, 1945. [7; 10; 11; 21; 22; 70]

Ryan, Mrs. Marah Ellis, née **Martin,** b. Butler county, Pa., 1860; d. July 11, 1934. [7; 10]

Ryan, Stephen Vincent, bishop, b. near Almonte, Upper Canada, Jan. 1, 1825; d. Buffalo, N.Y., April 10, 1896. [1; 3; 4; 5; 21]

Ryan, Thomas, musician, b. Ireland, 1827; d. New Bedford, Mass., 1903. [4]

Ryan, Thomas Curran, lawyer, b. Utica, N.Y., 1841; d. Wasan, Wis., Dec. 10, 1911. [10]

Ryan, William Thomas Carroll, poet, b. Toronto, Upper Canada, 1839; d. Montreal, Que., March 24, 1910. [27]

Rydberg, Per Axel, botanist, b. Sweden, 1860; d. New York, N.Y., July 25, 1931. [1; 10; 13]

Ryden, George Herbert, archivist, b. Kansas City, Mo., 1884; d. Chicago, Ill., Oct. 11, 1941. [10; 62]

Ryder, Arthur William, educationist, b. Oberlin, O., 1877; d. Berkeley, Calif., March 21, 1938. [7; 10; 11; 35; 51]

Ryder, George Hope, obstetrician, b. Plainfield, N.J., 1872; d. Babylon, N.Y., Aug. 27, 1946. [10; 62]

Ryder, Robert Oliver, journalist, b. Oberlin, O., 1875; d. Berkeley, Calif., March 16, 1936. [10]

Ryder, William Henry, clergyman, b. Provincetown, Mass., 1822; d. Chicago, Ill., March 8, 1888. [3; 4]

Ryerson, Adolphus Egerton, clergyman and educationist, b. Charlotteville, Norfolk county, Upper Canada, 1803; d. Toronto, Ont., Feb. 19, 1882. [27]

Ryerson, George Ansel Sterling, physician, b. Toronto, Ont., 1854; d. Toronto, Ont., May 20, 1925. [27]

Ryerson, John, clergyman, b. Charlottesville, Norfolk county, Upper Canada, 1800; d. Simcoe, Ont., Oct. 4, 1878. [27]

Ryerson, Martin, philanthropist, b. Paterson, N.J., 1818; d. Boston, Mass., Sept. 6, 1887. [3]

Rylance, Joseph Hine, clergyman, b. near Manchester, England, 1826; d. New York, N.Y., Sept. 24, 1907. [3; 6; 10]

Ryland, Robert, clergyman, b. King and Queen county, Va., 1805; d. Lexington, Ky., April 23, 1899. [1; 3; 4; 5]

Ryland, William James, historian, b. Amsterdam, N.Y., 1885; d. Jenkintown, Pa., Nov. 16, 1946. [62]

Ryley, Mrs. Madeline Lucette, novelist and playwright, b. London, England, 1868; d. Feb. 21, 1934. [10]

S

Sabin, Alvah Horton, chemist, b. Norfolk, N.Y., 1857; d. Flushing, N.Y., July 11, 1940. [10; 11]

Sabin, Elbridge Hosmer, lawyer and soldier, b. Middletownpoint, N.J., 1865; d. Chula Vista, Calif., Jan. 30, 1934. [10]

Sabin, Elijah Robinson, clergyman, b. Tolland, Conn., 1776; d. Augusta, Ga., May 4, 1818. [3]

Sabin, Frances Ellis, educationist, b. Naperville, Ill., 1870; d. Jonesboro, Tenn., Jan. 10, 1943. [10; 11]

Sabin, Henry, educationist, b. Pomfret, Conn., 1829; d. Chula Vista, Calif., March 22, 1918. [10; 37]

Sabin, Joseph, bibliographer, b. England, 1821; d. Brooklyn, N.Y., June 5, 1881. [1; 2; 3; 4; 6; 7; 9]

Sabin, Oliver Corwin, Christian scientist, b. 1840; d. 1914.

Sabine, Lorenzo, historian, b. Lisbon, N.H., 1803; d. Boston, Mass., April 14, 1877. [1; 2; 3; 4; 5; 6; 7; 9]

Sabine, Wallace Clement, physicist, b. Richwood, O., 1868; d. Boston, Mass., Jan. 10, 1919. [1; 4; 10; 51]

Sabrevois de Bleury, Clément Charles, lawyer, b. Sorel, Lower Canada, 1798; d. St. Vincent de Paul, Que., Sept. 15, 1862. [27]

Sachs, Bernard, neurologist, b. Baltimore, Md., 1858; d. New York, N.Y., Feb. 8, 1944. [10; 11]

Sachs, Hanns, psychoanalyst, b. Vienna, Austria, 1881; d. Boston, Mass., Jan. 10, 1947.

Sachs, Julius, educationist, b. Baltimore, Md., 1849; d. New York, N.Y., Feb. 2, 1934. [1; 4; 10]

Sachse, Julius Friedrich, antiquary, b. Philadelphia, Pa., 1842; d. Philadelphia, Pa., Nov. 14, 1919. [1; 10]

Sackett, Milton Bert, writer of books for young people, b. 1891; d. Sept. 6, 1947.

Sackett, Robert Samuel, engineer, b. Mount Clemens, Mich., 1867; d. New York, N.Y., Oct. 6, 1946. [10]

Sackett, William Edgar, journalist, b. New York, N.Y., 1848; d. East Orange, N.J., Nov. 18, 1926. [10]

Sadler, Mrs. Lena, née Kellogg, physician, b. Abscota, Mich., 1875; d. Chicago, Ill., Aug. 8, 1939. [10; 11]

Sadler, Sylvester Baker, jurist, b. Carlisle, Pa., 1876; d. Carlisle, Pa., March 1, 1931. [10]

Sadlier, Anna Theresa, novelist, b. Montreal, Que., 1854; d. Ottawa, Ont., April 16, 1932. [6; 21; 22]

Sadlier, Frank X., publisher, b. New York, N.Y., 1873; d. June 2, 1939. [21]

Sadlier, Mrs. James. See Sadlier, Mrs. Mary Anne, née Madden.

Sadlier, Mrs. Mary Anne, née Madden, novelist, b. county Cavan, Ireland, 1820; d. Montreal, Que., April 5, 1903. [1; 3; 7; 21; 27]

Sadtler, Samuel Philip, chemist, b. Pine Grove, Pa., 1847; d. Philadelphia, Pa., Dec. 20, 1923. [1; 3; 4; 10]

Saffell, William Thomas Roberts, historian, b. 1820; d. 1891. [6]

Safford, James Merrill, geologist, b. Zanesville, O., 1822; d. Dallas, Tex., July 3, 1907. [1; 3; 4; 5; 6; 10]

Safford, Mary Joanna, translator, b. Salem, Mass.; d. Washington, D.C., 1916.

Safford, Oscar Fitzalan, biographer, b. 1837; d. 1907.

Safford, Truman Henry, astronomer, b. Royalton, Vt., 1836; d. Williamstown, Mass., June 13, 1901. [1; 3; 4; 5; 10; 43]

Safford, William Edwin, botanist, b. Chillicothe, O., 1859; d. Washington, D.C., Jan. 10, 1926. [1; 4; 10]

Safford, William Harrison, jurist, b. Parkersburg, Va., 1821; d. April 20, 1903. [3; 6; 34]

Sage, Agnes Carolyn, writer of books for children, b. Brooklyn, N.Y., 1854; d. Hackensack, N.J., Nov. 12, 1928. [7; 11]

Sage, Agnes Carr (pseud.). See Sage, Agnes Carolyn.

Sage, Bernard Janin, lawyer, b. near New Haven, Conn., 1821; d. New Orleans, La., Sept. 2, 1902. [1]

Sage, Rufus B., pioneer, b. New England, 1817; d. ? [7]

Sage, William Francis, playwright, b. Manchester, N.H., 1849; d. New York, N.Y., Dec. 24, 1900.

Sahler, Charles Oliver, physician, b. Ulster Park, N.Y., 1854; d. Kingston-on-Hudson, N.Y., Sept. 17, 1917. [10]

St. Aimé, Georges (pseud.). See Pelletier, Alexis.

St. Clair, Arthur, soldier, b. Thurso, Scotland, 1736; d. Chestnut Ridge, Pa., Aug. 31, 1818. [1; 2; 3; 4; 5; 6]

St. Clair, Victor (pseud.). See Browne, George Waldo.

Saint-Cyr, Joseph Fortunat, lawyer, b. 1875; d. Montreal, Que., Jan. 29, 1934.

Saint-Cyr, Napoléon Dominique, naturalist, b. Nicolet, Lower Canada, 1826; d. Quebec, Que., March 3, 1889. [27]

Saint-Denis, Joseph, priest, b. Montreal, Que., 1857; d. Montreal, Que., April 10, 1927. [27]

St. George, Armin Von, pathologist, b. Jersey City, N.J., 1892; d. New York, N.Y., Nov. 20, 1943.

St. Germain, Hyacinthe, agriculturist, b. Repentigny, Lower Canada, 1838; d. Danville, Que., Dec. 8, 1909. [27]

St. Ignatius, Mother. See Wheaton, Louisa

St. Ignatius, Sister, historian, b. 1856; d. ? [21]

Saint-Jacques, Mme. Henriette, née Dessaulles, journalist, b. 1860; d. St. Hyacinthe, Que., Nov. 17, 1946.

St. John, Charles Elliott, clergyman, b. Prairie du Chien, Wis., 1856; d. Feb. 25, 1916. [1a; 10; 11; 51]

St. John, Mrs. Cynthia, née Morgan, educationist, b. Ithaca, N.Y., 1852; d. Aug., 1919. [10]

St. John, Samuel, geologist, b. New Canaan, Conn., 1813; d. New Canaan, Conn., Sept. 9, 1876. [62]

Saint Maur, Mrs. Kate, née Vandenhof, actress, b. Seneca Falls, N.Y., 1866; d. Danbury, Conn., Sept. 27, 1942.

St. Pierre, Télesphore, journalist, b. Lavaltrie, Que., 1869; d. St. Boniface, Man., Oct. 25, 1912. [27]

Sait, Edward McChesney, educationist, b. Montreal, Que., 1881; d. Claremont, Calif., Oct. 27, 1943. [10; 11; 27]

Sajous, Charles Euchariste de Médicis, physician, b. at sea, 1852; d. Philadelphia, Pa., April 27, 1929. [1; 4; 10; 11]

Sale, Charles Partlow, humorist, b. Huron, S.D., 1885; d. Hollywood, Calif., Nov. 7, 1936. [7; 10]

Sales, Francis, educationist, b. Roussillon, France, 1771; d. Cambridge, Mass., Feb. 16, 1854. [3]

Salisbury, Albert, educationist, b. Lima, Wis., 1843; d. Whitewater, Wis., June 2, 1911. [1; 4; 10]

Salisbury, Edward Elbridge, educationist, b. Boston, Mass., 1814; d. New Haven, Conn., Feb. 5, 1901. [1; 3; 4; 5; 62]

Salisbury, James Henry, physician, b. Scott, N.Y., 1823; d. Dobbs Ferry, N.Y., Aug. 23, 1905. [1; 3; 4; 10]

Salisbury, Rollin D., educationist, b. Spring Prairie, Wis., 1858; d. Chicago, Ill., Aug. 15, 1922. [4; 10]

Salisbury, Stephen, lawyer and archaeologist, b. Worcester, Mass., 1835; d. Worcester, Mass., Nov. 19, 1905. [51]

Sallmon, William Henry, clergyman, b. London, Ont., 1866; d. National City, Calif., Feb. 4, 1938. [10; 62]

Salmon, Daniel Elmer, civil servant, b. Mount Olive, N.J., 1850; d. Aug. 30, 1914. [1; 10]

Salmon, Lucy Maynard, historian, b. Fulton, N.Y., 1853; d. Poughkeepsie, N.J., Feb. 14, 1927. [1; 7; 10]

Salmon, Thomas William, physician, b. Lansingburg, N.Y., 1876; d. Long Island Sound, N.Y., Aug. 13, 1927. [1; 4; 10]

Salome (pseud.). See Converse, Mrs. Harriet, née Maxwell.

Salpointe, Jean Baptiste, archbishop, b. France, 1825; d. Tuscon, Ariz., July 16, 1898. [3; 4]

Salter, William, clergyman, b. Brooklyn, N.Y., 1821; d. Burlington, Ia., Aug. 15, 1910. [1; 4; 7; 10; 37]

Salter, William Mackintire, philosopher, b. Burlington, Ia., 1853; d. Silver Lake, N.H., July 18, 1931. [1; 10; 11; 37]

Saltus, Edgar Evertson, novelist and humorist, b. New York, N.Y., 1855; d. New York, N.Y., July 31, 1921. [1; 4; 7; 10; 71; 72]

Saltus, Francis Saltus, poet, b. New York, N.Y., 1849; d. Tarrytown, N.Y., June 24, 1889. [3b; 4]

Salyards, Joseph, poet, b. near Front Royal, Va., 1808; d. Aug. 10, 1885. [34]

Samaroff Stokowski, Mrs. Olga, née Hickenlooper, musician, b. San Antonio, Tex., 1882; d. New York, N.Y., May 17, 1948. [10]

Saminsky, Mrs. Lillian Morgan, née Buck, poet and novelist, b. 1893; d. Rye, N.Y., May 26, 1945.

Sampey, John Richard, theologian, b. Fort Deposit, Ala., 1863; d. Louisville, Ky., Aug. 18, 1946. [10]

Sample, Robert Fleming, clergyman, b. Corning, N.Y., 1829; d. New York, N.Y., Aug. 12, 1905. [2; 5; 10]

Sampson, Alden, littérateur, b. Manchester, Me., 1853; d. New York, N.Y., Jan. 5, 1925. [51]

Sampson, Deborah. See Gannett, Mrs. Deborah, née Sampson.

Sampson, Mrs. Emma, née Speed, novelist, b. Louisville, Ky., 1868; d. Richmond, Va., May 7, 1947. [7; 10; 11]

Sampson, Ezra, clergyman, b. Middleborough, Mass., 1749; d. New York, N.Y., Dec. 12, 1823. [3; 6]

Sampson, Martin Wright, educationist, b. Cincinnati, O., 1866; d. Pittsburgh, Pa., Aug. 22, 1930. [1; 10]

Sampson, William, lawyer, b. Londonderry, Ireland, 1764; d. New York, N.Y., Dec. 28, 1836. [1; 3; 4; 6]

Sams, Conway Whittle, lawyer and historian, b. McPhersonville, S.C., 1864; d. Norfolk, Va., May 11, 1935.

Samson, George Whitefield, educationist, b. Harvard, Mass., 1819; d. New York, N.Y., Aug. 8, 1896. [3; 4; 5; 6]

Samuel, Elizabeth Ida, educationist, b. Bennington, Ill., 1860; d. Jan. 6, 1937. [11]

Samuel, William Henry, educationist, b. 1840; d. Feb. 27, 1931.

Samuels, Adelaide Florence. See Bassett, Mrs. Adelaide Florence, née Samuels.

Samuels, Edward Augustus, naturalist, b. Boston, Mass., 1836; d. Fitchburg, Mass., May 27, 1908. [1; 3; 4; 5; 10]

Samuels, Samuel, mariner, b. Philadelphia, Pa., 1823; d. Brooklyn, N.Y., May 18, 1908. [1; 3; 4; 7; 10]

Samuels, Mrs. Susan Blagge, née Caldwell, writer of stories for children, b. Dedham, Mass., 1848; d. ? [3]

Sanborn, Edwin David, educationist, b. Gilmanton, N.H., 1808; d. New York, N.Y., Dec. 29, 1885. [1; 3; 4; 5; 6]

Sanborn, Edwin Webster, social scientist, b. 1857; d. March, 1928.

Sanborn, Franklin Benjamin, journalist, b. Hampton Falls, N.H., 1831; d. Plainfield, N.J., Feb. 24, 1917. [1; 2; 3; 4; 5; 6; 7; 9; 10]

Sanborn, Gertrude. See Furstenburg, Mrs. Gertrude, née Sanborn.

Sanborn, Helen Josephine, biographer, b. Greene, Me., 1857; d. Somerville, Mass., April 26, 1917. [10]

Sanborn, John Benjamin, lawyer and soldier, b. Epsom, N.H., 1826; d. St. Paul, Minn., May 16, 1904. [3; 4; 5; 10; 70]

Sanborn, John Pitts, music critic, b. Port Huron, Mich., 1879; d. New York, N.Y., March 8, 1914. [10; 20; 51]

Sanborn, John Wentworth, educationist, b. 1848; d. 1922.

Sanborn, Joseph Brown, soldier, b. Chester, N.H., 1855; d. Chicago, Ill., Dec. 22, 1934. [10]

Sanborn, Katharine Abbott, educationist, b. Hanover, N.H., 1839; d. Holliston, Mass., July 9, 1917. [1; 3; 4; 5; 6; 7; 10]

Sanborn, Mrs. Mary Farley, née **Sanborn,** poet and novelist, b. Manchester, N.H., 1853; d. ? [7]

Sanborn, Pitts. See Sanborn, John Pitts.

Sanborn, Ruth Burr, novelist, b. Framingham, Mass., 1895; d. Southern Pines, N.C., June 29, 1942. [11]

Sanborn, Victor Channing, genealogist, b. 1867; d. 1921.

Sanchez, Mrs. Nellie, née **Van der Grift,** historian, b. Indianapolis, Ind., 1856; d. Oakland, Calif., Jan. 4, 1935. [7; 10; 11]

Sanders, Charles Walton, educationist. b. Newport, N.Y., 1805; d. New York, N.Y., July 5, 1889. [1; 4; 6]

Sanders, Daniel Clarke, clergyman, b. Sturbridge, Mass., 1768; d. Medfield, Mass., Oct. 18, 1850. [1; 3; 4; 5; 6; 43]

Sanders, Mrs. Elizabeth, née **Elkins,** reformer, b. Salem, Mass., 1762; d. Salem, Mass., Feb. 19, 1851. [1; 3; 6]

Sanders, Frank Knight, . clergyman and educationist, b. Ceylon, 1861; d. Rockport, Mass., Feb. 20, 1933. [1; 5; 7; 10; 11; 62]

Sanders, Frederic William, educationist, b. Westchester county, N.Y., 1864; d. 1920. [10]

Sanders, James Harvey, agricultural journalist, b. Union county, O., 1832; d. Memphis, Tenn., Dec. 22, 1899. [1]

Sanders, Mrs. Sue A., née **Pike,** traveller, b. 1842; d. 1931.

Sanders, Thomas Jefferson, educationist, b. near Burbank, O., 1855; d. Westerville, O., Dec. 26, 1946. [7; 10]

Sanderson, John, educationist, b. near Carlisle, Pa., 1783; d. Philadelphia, Pa., April 5, 1844. [1; 3; 4; 6; 7; 9]

Sanderson, John Philip, soldier, b. Lebanon, Pa., 1818; d. St. Louis, Mo., Oct 14, 1864. [3; 4; 6]

Sanderson, Joseph, clergyman, b. county Monaghan, Ireland, 1823; d. 1915. [3; 10]

Sanderson, Joseph Edward, clergyman, b. York [Toronto], Upper Canada, 1830; d. Sault Ste. Marie, Ont., Aug. 3, 1913. [27]

Sanderson, Robert Louis, educationist, b. Laon, France, 1851; d. Duxbury, Mass., Nov. 6, 1922. [10; 11]

Sandette (pseud.). See Walsh, Marie A.

Sandham, Alfred, historian and numismatist. b. Montreal, Lower Canada, 1838; d. Toronto, Ont., Dec. 25, 1910. [27]

Sandiford, Peter, educationist, b. Derbyshire, England, 1882; d. Toronto, Ont., Oct. 12, 1941. [11; 27]

Sands, Alexander Hamilton, lawyer, b. Williamsburg, Va., 1828; d. Richmond, Va., Dec. 22, 1887. [3; 6; 34]

Sands, George W., poet, b. about 1824; d. 1874.

Sands, Robert Charles, journalist, b. New York, N.Y., 1799; d. Hoboken, N.J., Dec. 16, 1832. [1; 3; 4; 5; 6; 7]

Sands, William Franklin, diplomat, b. Washington, D.C., 1874; d. Washington, D.C., June 18, 1946. [10; 22]

Sandt, George Washington, clergyman, b. Belfast, Pa., 1854; d. 1930. [10; 11]

Sandwell, Arnold Hugh, aviator, b. New Britain, Conn., 1892; d. Montreal, Que., March 10, 1940. [27]

Sandys, Edwyn, journalist, b. Chatham, Ont., 1860; d. 1909. [10]

Sanford, Mrs. D. P., writer of books for children, fl. 1872-1899. [7]

Sanford, Edmund Clark, psychologist, b. Oakland, Calif., 1859; d. Boston, Mass., Nov. 22, 1924. [1; 4; 10]

Sanford, Elias Benjamin, clergyman, b. Westbrook, Conn., 1843; d. Middlefield, Conn., July 3, 1932. [1; 10]

Sanford, Enoch, clergyman, b. 1795; d. Nov. 30, 1890. [47]

Sanford, Ezekiel, historian, b. Ridgefield, Conn., 1796; d. Columbia, S.C., 1822. [3]

Sanford, Fernando, physicist, b. Taylor, Ill., 1854; d. Stanford, Calif., May 21, 1948. [10; 11; 13]

Sanford, Mrs. Nettie, local historian, b. 1830; d. 1901. [37]

Sanford, Rufus Bishop, novelist, b. 1820; d. 1889.

Sanford, Shelton Palmer, educationist, b. Greensboro, Ga., 1816; d. ? [34]

Sandford, Steadman Vincent, educationist, b. Covington, Ga., 1871; d. Athens, Ga., Sept. 15, 1945. [10; 11]

Sanger, William Wallace, physician, d. 1872. [6]

Sangster, Charles, poet, b. Kingston, Upper Canada, 1822; d. Kingston, Ont., Dec. 19, 1893. [27]

Sangster, John Herbert, educationist and physician, b. London, Upper Canada, 1831; d. Port Perry, Ont., Jan. 27, 1904. [3; 27]

Sangster, Mrs. Margaret Elizabeth, née **Munson,** writer of books for girls, b. New Rochelle, N.Y., 1838; d. Maplewood, N.J., June 4, 1912. [1; 2; 3; 4; 5; 6; 7; 9; 10]

Sanial, Lucien, socialist, b. 1836; d. Northport, N.Y., Jan. 7, 1927.

Sankey, Ira Allen, music publisher, b. Edinburgh, Scotland, 1874; d. Brooklyn, N.Y., Dec. 30, 1915. [10]

Sankey, Ira David, singing evangelist, b. Edinburgh, Pa., 1840; d. Brooklyn, N.Y., Aug. 13, 1908. [1; 4; 5; 7; 10]

Sansom, Joseph, traveller, fl. 1801-1820. [6]

Santee, Ellis Monroe, physician, b. Hughesville, Pa., 1862; d. Dec. 22, 1931. [10; 11]

Santee, Harris Ellett, anatomist, b. Snodes, O., 1864; d. Chicago, Ill., Feb. 28, 1936. [10]

Sapir, Edward, anthropologist, b. Germany, 1884; d. New Haven, Conn., Feb. 4, 1939. [10; 13]

Sappington, Clarence Olds, physician, b. Kansas City, Mo., 1889; d. Chicago, Ill., Nov. 6, 1949. [10]

Sappington, John, physician, b. Maryland, 1776; d. near Arrow Rock, Mo., Sept. 7, 1856. [1]

Sarg, Anthony Frederick, artist, b. Guatemala, Central America, 1882; d. New York, N.Y., March 7, 1947. [7; 10]

Sarg, Tony. See Sarg, Anthony Frederick.

Sargent, Charles Edward, religious writer, b. 1854; d. June 16, 1935.

Sargent, Charles Sprague, botanist, b. Boston, Mass., 1841; d. Brookline, Mass., March 22, 1927. [1; 3; 4; 5; 10; 13; 51]

Sargent, Dudley Allen, physician, b. Belfast, Me., 1849; d. Peterboro, N.H., July 21, 1924. [1; 4; 10; 46; 62]

Sargent, Epes, journalist, poet, novelist, and playwright, b. Gloucester, Mass., 1813; d. Boston, Mass., Dec. 30, 1880. [1; 3; 4; 5; 6; 7; 9]

Sargent, Epes Winthrop, drama critic, b. Nassau, Bahamas, 1872; d. Brooklyn, N.Y., Dec. 6, 1938.

Sargent, FitzWilliam, physician, b. Gloucester, Mass., 1820; d. Bournemouth, England, April 25, 1889. [1; 3; 6]

Sargent, Frederick Leroy, botanist, b. Boston, Mass., 1863; d. Cambridge, Mass., Jan. 16, 1928. [10; 11; 13]

Sargent, George Henry, journalist and bibliographer, b. Warner, N.H., 1867; d. Warner, N.H., Jan. 14, 1931. [1; 7; 10; 11]

Sargent, Henry Jackson, poet, b. Boston, Mass., 1808; d. 1867. [6]

Sargent, Henry, Winthrop, horticulturist, b. Boston, Mass., 1810; d. Fishkill, N.Y., Nov. 11, 1882. [1; 5]

Sargent, Herbert Howland, soldier, b. Carlinville, Ill., 1858; d. Jacksonville, Ore., Sept. 16, 1921. [4; 5; 10; 11]

Sargent, John Osborne, lawyer and journalist, b. Gloucester, Mass., 1811; d. Dec. 28, 1891. [1; 3; 4; 6]

Sargent, Mrs. John T. See Sargent, Mrs. Mary Elizabeth, née Fiske.

Sargent, Joseph, physician, d. 1888. [51]

Sargent, Lucius Manlius, miscellaneous writer, b. Boston, Mass., 1796; d. West Roxbury, Mass., June 2, 1867. [1; 3; 4; 5; 6; 7; 9]

Sargent, Mrs. Mary Elizabeth, née Fiske, literary historian, b. 1827; d. New York, N.Y., May 31, 1904.

Sargent, Nathan, journalist, b. Putney, Vt., 1794; d. Washington, D.C., Feb. 2, 1875. [1; 3; 4; 6; 7; 9]

Sargent, Walter, educationist, b. Worcester, Mass., 1868; d. North Scituate, Mass., Sept. 19, 1927. [10; 11]

Sargent, William Mitchell, historian, b. El Dorado, Ark., 1848; d. 1891.

Sargent, Winthrop, soldier and administrator, b. Gloucester, Mass., 1753; d. near New Orleans, La., Jan. 3, 1820. [1; 3; 5; 6]

Sargent, Winthrop, historian, b. Philadelphia, Pa., 1825; d. Paris, France, May 18, 1870. [1; 3; 4; 5; 6; 7]

Sarles, John Wesley, clergyman, b. Bedford, N.Y., 1817; d. Stelton, N.J., Aug. 24, 1903. [67]

Sartain, John, engraver and publisher, b. London, England, 1808; d. Philadelphia, Pa., Oct. 25, 1897. [1; 3; 4; 5; 6; 7]

Sasia, Joseph Casimir, priest, b. 1843; d. 1928. [21]

Sasnett, William Jacob, clergyman, b. Hancock county, Ga., 1820; d. Montgomery, Ala., Nov. 3, 1865. [3]

Sass, George Herbert, poet and journalist, b. Charleston, S.C., 1845; d. Charleston, S.C., Feb. 10, 1908. [7; 10; 34]

Satterlee, Mrs. Anna Eliza, née Hickox, novelist, b. Rockville, Conn., 1851; d. ? [11; 35]

Satterlee, Francis Le Roy, physician, b. New York, N.Y., 1847; d. 1917. [4]

Satterlee, Francis Le Roy, radiologist, b. 1881; d. Montauk, Long Island, N.Y., Dec. 3, 1935.

Satterlee, George Reese, physician, b. Dobbs Ferry, N.Y., 1873; d. New York, N.Y., Feb. 8, 1928. [10; 13]

Satterlee, Henry Yates, bishop, b. New York, N.Y., 1843; d. Washington, D.C., Feb. 22, 1908. [1; 3; 4; 5; 10]

Satterlee, William Wilson, clergyman, b. Laporte, Ind., 1837; d. Minneapolis, Minn., May 27, 1893. [70]

Satterthwaite, Thomas Edward, physician, b. New York, N.Y., 1843; d. New York, N.Y., Sept. 19, 1934. [4; 10; 62]

Sattler, Eric Ericson, physician, b. Cincinnati, O., 1859; d. Cincinnati, O., July 26, 1926. [10]

Saunby, John William, missionary, b. Manotick. Ont., 1858; d. Victoria, B.C., June 22, 1925. [27]

Saunders, Sir Charles Edward, scientist, b. London, Ont., 1867; d. Toronto, Ont., July 25, 1937. [27]

Saunders, Charles Francis, naturalist, b. Bucks county, Pa., 1859; d. Pasadena, Calif., May 1, 1941. [7; 10; 11; 35]

Saunders, Edward Manning, clergyman and historian, b. Aylsford, N.S., 1829; d. Toronto, Ont., March 15, 1916. [27]

Saunders, Eugene Davis, jurist, b. Campbell county, Va., 1853; d. New Orleans, La., 1914. [10; 34]

Saunders, Frederick, librarian, b. London, England, 1807; d. New York, N.Y., Dec. 12, 1902. [1; 3; 4; 5; 6; 7; 10]

Saunders, John Monk, journalist and scenario-writer, b. Hinckley, Minn., 1897; d. Fort Myers, Fla., March 11, 1940. [7; 10]

Saunders, Margaret Marshall, novelist, b. Milton, N.S., 1861; d. Toronto, Ont., Feb. 15, 1947. [11; 30]

Saunders, Marshall. See Saunders, Margaret Marshall.

Saunders, Prince, reformer, b. Lebanon, Conn., or Thetford, Vt., about 1775; d. Port-au-Prince, Hayti, Feb., 1839. [1; 3; 6]

Saunders, Ripley Dunlap, journalist, b. Ripley, Miss., 1856; d. St. Louis, Mo., March 16, 1915. [10]

Saunders, William, agricultural scientist, b. Devonshire, England, 1836; d. London, Ont., Sept. 13, 1914. [27]

Saunders, William Laurence, journalist and historian, b. Raleigh, N.C., 1835; d. Raleigh, N.C., April 2, 1891. [1; 4; 7; 9]

Saunders, William Lawrence, engineer and inventor, b. Columbus, Ga., 1856; d. Teneriffe, Canary Islands, June 25, 1931. [1; 4; 10; 11]

Saunders, William Trebell, clergyman, d. 1889.

Sauveur, Albert, metallurgist, b. Louvain, Belgium, 1863; d. Boston, Mass., Jan. 26, 1939. [10; 11; 13]

Sauzade, John S., novelist, b. New York, N.Y., 1828; d. ? [6]

Savage, Courtenay, playwright, b. New York, N.Y., 1890; d. Rome, Italy, Aug. 23, 1946. [7; 10; 22]

Savage, Edward Hartwell, police officer, b. Alstead, N.H., 1812; d. Boston, Mass., 1893. [3]

Savage, Giles Christopher, ophthalmologist, b. near Rienzi, Miss., 1854; d. Nashville, Tenn., April 8, 1930. [10]

Savage, James, antiquary, b. Boston, Mass., 1784; d. Boston, Mass., March 8, 1873. [1; 3; 4; 5; 6; 7]

Savage, John, journalist, b. Dublin, Ireland, 1828; d. near Spragueville, Pa., Oct. 9, 1888. [1; 3; 4; 5; 6; 7; 9]

Savage, John Houston, soldier, lawyer, and politician, b. McMinnville, Tenn., 1815; d. McMinnville, Tenn., April 5, 1904. [10]

Savage, Minot Judson, clergyman, b. Norridgewock, Me., 1841; d. Boston, Mass., May 22, 1918. [1; 3; 4; 5; 6; 7; 10]

Savage, Philip Henry, poet, b. North Brookfield, Mass., 1868; d. Boston, Mass., June 4, 1899. [1; 3b; 4; 7; 10; 51]

Savage, Richard Henry, soldier and novelist, b. Utica, N.Y., 1846; d. New York, N.Y., Oct. 11, 1903. [7; 10; 35]

Savage, Sarah, novelist, b. 1785; d. Salem, Mass., 1837. [6; 7]

Savary, Alfred William, jurist and historian, b. Plympton, N.S., 1831; d. Annapolis Royal, N.S., 1920. [27]

Savary, Charles, journalist, b. Coutances, France, 1845; d. Ottawa, Ont., Sept. 9, 1889. [27]

Savary, John, poet, b. 1832; d. 1910.

Savidge, Eugene Coleman, physician, b. Allegany county, Md., 1863; d. New York, N.Y., Oct. 10, 1924. [10]

Savigny, Mrs. Annie, née **Gregg,** novelist, d. Toronto, Ont., July 10, 1901. [27]

Saville, Marshall Howard, archaeologist, b. Rockport, Mass., 1867; d. New York, N.Y., May 7, 1935. [1a; 10; 13]

Sawin, Theophilus Parsons, clergyman, b. Lynn, Mass., 1841; d. Troy, N.Y., 1906. [10]

Sawitzky, William, art historian, b. Riga, Russia, 1879; d. Stamford, Conn., Feb. 2, 1947.

Sawtelle, Alice Elizabeth. See Randall, Mrs. Alice Elizabeth, née Sawtelle.

Sawtelle, Henry Allen, clergyman, b. Sidney, Me., 1832; d. Waterville, Me., Nov. 22, 1885. [3; 6]

Sawtelle, Ithamar Bard, local historian, b. Brookline, N.H., 1814; d. West Townsend, Mass., Nov. 1, 1905.

Sawyer, Alvah Littlefield, lawyer, b. Burnett, Wis., 1854; d. Menominee, Mich., Feb. 5, 1925. [39]

Sawyer, Mrs. Caroline Mehetabel, née **Fisher,** miscellaneous writer, b. Newton, Mass., 1812; d. College Hill, Mass., May 19, 1894. [3b; 6; 7]

Sawyer, Eugene Taylor, novelist, b. 1846; d. San Jose, Calif., Oct. 29, 1924. [7]

Sawyer, Frederick William, lawyer, b. Saco, Me., 1810; d. Boston, Mass., 1875. [3; 6]

Sawyer, George S., lawyer, fl. 1858. [34]

Sawyer, Joseph Dillaway, merchant and historian, b. Boston, Mass., 1849; d. New York, N.Y., May 20, 1933. [10; 11]

Sawyer, Leicester Ambrose, clergyman, b. Pinckney, N.Y., 1807; d. Whitesboro, N.Y., Dec. 29, 1898. [1; 3; 5; 6]

Sawyer, Lemuel, politician and littérateur, b. Camden county, N.C., 1777; d. Washington, D.C., Jan. 9, 1852. [1; 3; 5; 6; 7; 9; 34]

Sawyer, Matthias Enoch, physician, fl. 1793-1831.

Sawyer, Thomas Jefferson, clergyman, b. Reading, Vt., 1804; d. Somerville, Mass., July 24, 1899. [1; 3; 5; 6; 10]

Sawyer, Walter Leon, journalist and writer of books for boys, b. Cumberland, Me., 1862; d. Brookline, Mass., Jan. 30, 1915. [10]

Sawyer, Wesley Caleb, educationist, b. Harvard, Mass., 1839; d. 1921. [10; 51]

Saxe, George Alexander De Santos, physician, b. St. Petersburg, Russia, 1876; d. New York, N.Y., 1911. [10]

Saxe, John Godfrey, poet, b. Highgate, Vt., 1816; d. Albany, N.Y., March 31, 1887. [1; 2; 3; 4; 5; 6; 7; 9; 71]

Saxe, Mary Solace, librarian, b. St. Albans, Vt., about 1868; d. Montreal, Que., May 27, 1942. [27]

Saxon, John A., novelist, b. 1886; d. Alhambra, Calif., Feb. 17, 1947.

Saxon, Lyle, journalist, novelist, and historian, b. Baton Rouge, La., 1891; d. New Orleans, La., April 9, 1946. [2a; 7; 11; 12]

Saxton, Luther Calvin, historian, b. 1806; d. ? [3]

Say, Benjamin, physician, b. Philadelphia, Pa., 1755; d. Philadelphia, Pa., April 23, 1813. [1; 3; 5; 6]

Say, Thomas, naturalist, b. Philadelphia, Pa., 1787; d. New Harmony, Ind., Oct. 10, 1834. [1; 3; 4; 5; 6; 7]

Sayford, Samuel M., social worker, d. 1921.

Sayler, Harry Lincoln, writer of books for boys, b. Little York, O., 1863; d. May 31, 1913. [7]

Sayler, John Riner, lawyer, b. 1841; d. 1914.

Sayles, John, lawyer, b. Ithaca, N.Y., 1825; d. Waco, Tex., May 22, 1897. [1; 3; 5; 6]

Sayre, Lewis Albert, surgeon, b. Madison, N.J., 1820; d. New York, N.Y., Sept. 21, 1900. [1; 3; 4; 5; 6; 10]

Sayre, Lucius Elmer, pharmacist, b. Bridgeton, N.J., 1847; d. Lawrence, Kans., July 21, 1925. [4; 10]

Scacheri, Mario, camera editor, b. Milan, Italy, 1899; d. New York, N.Y., July 31, 1940.

Scadding, Henry, clergyman, b. Devonshire, England, 1813; d. Toronto, Ont., May 6, 1901. [27]

Scaeva (pseud.). See Stuart, Isaac William.

Scales, John, local historian, b. 1835; d. Dover, N.H., July 6, 1928.

Scammon, Charles Melville, naval officer, b. Pittston, Me., 1825; d. 1911. [3]

Scanlan, Charles Martin, lawyer, b. 1854; d. Milwaukee, Wis., Feb. 15, 1940.

Scanlan, John Francis, economist, b. 1839; d. 1920.

Scanlan, Michael, poet, b. 1836; d. 1917.

Scanland, Mrs. Agnes, née Leonard. See Hill, Mrs. Agnes, née Leonard.

Scarborough, Dorothy, educationist, b. Mount Carmel, Tex., 1877; d. New York, N.Y., Nov. 7, 1935. [1a; 7; 10; 11]

Scarborough, Harold Ellicott, journalist, b. Bel Air, Md., 1897; d. at sea, April 7, 1935. [10]

Scarborough, Lee Rutland, clergyman, b. Colfax, La., 1870; d. Amarillo, Tex., April 10, 1945. [10; 62]

Scarborough, Mildred, novelist, fl. 1886-1907.

Scarborough, William Saunders, educationist, b. Macon, Ga., 1852; d. Wilberforce, O., Sept. 9, 1926. [1; 3; 4; 10]

Scarlett, John, itinerant preacher, b. 1803; d. 1889.

Schaad, John Christian, poet, fl. 1856-1866.

Schack, Albert Peter, b. 1847; d. ?

Schaeffer, Charles William, clergyman, b. Hagerstown, Md., 1813; d. Philadelphia, Pa., March 15, 1896. [1; 3; 4; 6]

Schaeffer, Luther Melanchthon, traveller, b. Frederick, Md., 1821; d. ? [6]

Schaeffer, Mrs. Mary Townsend, née Sharples, explorer, b. West Chester, Pa., 1861; d. Banff, Alta, Jan. 23, 1939. [10]

Schaeffer, Nathan Christ, educationist, b. near Kutztown, Pa., 1849; d. Philadelphia, Pa., March 15, 1919. [1; 3; 4; 10]

Schaeffer, William Christ, clergyman, b. Maxatawny, Pa., 1851; d. Lancaster, Pa., April 16, 1921. [4; 10]

Schaff, David Schley, clergyman, b. Mercersburg, Pa., 1852; d. Winter Park, Fla., Oct. 7, 1941. [7; 10; 62]

Schaff, Morris, historian, b. Kirkersville, O., 1840; d. Cambridge, Mass., Oct. 19, 1929. [10; 11]

Schaff, Philip, ecclesiastical historian, b. Switzerland, 1819; d. New York, N.Y., Oct. 20, 1893. [1; 2; 3; 4; 5; 6; 7; 9]

Schaffner, John Henry, botanist, b. Marion county, O., 1866; d. Columbus, O., Jan. 27, 1939. [10; 13]

Schamberg, Jay Frank, dermatologist, b. Philadelphia, Pa., 1870; d. Philadelphia, Pa., March 30, 1934. [1; 10; 11; 13]

Scharf, John Thomas, soldier and historian, b. Baltimore, Md., 1843; d. New York, N.Y., Feb. 28, 1898. [1; 2; 3; 4; 5; 6; 7; 9; 34]

Schauffler, Adolphus Frederick, clergyman, b. Constantinople, Turkey, 1845; d. New York, N.Y., Feb. 18, 1919. [4; 10]

Schauffler, William Gottlieb, missionary, b. Stuttgart, Germany, 1798; d. New York, N.Y., Jan. 26, 1883. [1; 3; 4; 5]

Schayer, Mrs. Julia, née **Thompson,** short-story writer, b. Deering, Me., 1840; d. ? [6]

Schechter, Solomon, educationist, b. Roumania, 1850; d. New York, N.Y., Nov. 15, 1915. [1; 4; 7; 10]

Scheffauer, Herman George, artist and poet, b. San Francisco, Calif., 1878; d. Berlin, Germany, Oct. 7, 1927. [10; 35]

Schele de Vere, Maximilian, educationist, b. Sweden, 1820; d. Washington, D.C., May 12, 1898. [1; 7; 8; 34]

Schell, Edwin Allison, clergyman, b. Deer Creek, Ind., 1859; d. Glendale, Calif., 1937. [10]

Schell, Henry Sayler, physician, d. San Diego, Calif., March 15, 1890.

Schelling, Felix Emanuel, educationist, b. New Albany, Ind., 1858; d. Mount Vernon, N.Y., Dec. 15, 1945. [7; 10; 11]

Schem, Alexander Jacob, journalist, b. Germany, 1826; d. Hoboken, N.J., May 21, 1881. [1; 3; 4; 5; 7]

Schem, Lida Clara, novelist, b. 1875; d. Hoboken, N.J., Feb. 13, 1923.

Schenck, Ferdinand Schureman, clergyman, b. Plattekill, N.Y., 1845; d. White Plains, N.Y., April 6, 1925. [1; 10]

Scheppegrell, William, physician, b. Hanover, Germany, 1860; d. New Orleans, La., July 9, 1928. [7; 10; 11]

Scherer, Melanchthon Gideon Groseclose, clergyman, b. Catawba county, N.C., 1861; d. New York, N.Y., March 9, 1932. [10]

Schereschewsky, Joseph William, physician, b. Pekin, China, 1873; d. Belmont, Mass., July 9, 1940. [10]

Scherger, George Lawrence, clergyman, b. Lawrenceburg, Ind., 1874; d. Chicago, Ill., March 31, 1941. [10]

Schermerhorn, Holden Bovee, lawyer, b. 1868; d. 1935.

Schermerhorn, Martin Kellogg, clergyman, b. Durham, N.Y., 1841; d. Cambridge, Mass., Dec. 13, 1923. [4; 10]

Schick, John Michael, clergyman, b. Richmond, Va., 1848; d. Washington, D.C., July 22, 1913. [10]

Schieferdecker, Christian Charles, physician, fl. 1843-1870.

Schieffelin, Samuel Bradhurst, druggist, b. New York, N.Y., 1811; d. New York, N.Y., Sept. 13, 1900. [3; 4; 6; 10]

Schierbrand, Wolf von. See Von Schierbrand, Wolf.

Schiff, Jacob Henry, financier and philanthropist, b. Germany, 1847; d. New York, N.Y., Sept. 25, 1920. [1; 4; 10]

Schilder, Paul Ferdinand, psychiatrist, b. Vienna, Austria, 1886; d. New York, N.Y., Nov. 8, 1940.

Schimmelpfennig, Alexander, soldier, b. Germany, 1824; d. Minersville, Pa., Sept. 7, 1865. [3; 5]

Schindler, Kurt, musician, b. Berlin, Germany, 1882; d. New York, N.Y., Nov. 16, 1935. [1a; 10; 20]

Schindler, Solomon, rabbi, b. Germany, 1842; d. Boston, Mass., May 5, 1915. [1; 2; 4; 10]

Schinz, Albert, educationist, b. Neuchâtel, Switzerland, 1870; d. Iowa City, Ia., Dec. 19, 1943. [7; 10; 11]

Schley, Winfield Scott, naval officer, b. Frederick county, Md., 1839; d. New York, N.Y., Oct. 2, 1909. [1; 2; 3; 4; 5; 10]

Schlosser, Alexander L., lawyer, b. 1888; d. Hoboken, N.J., Feb. 10, 1943.

Schluter, William Charles, economist, b. Lowden, Ia., 1890; d. 1932. [11]

Schmauk, Theodore Emanuel, clergyman, b. Lancaster, Pa., 1860; d. Philadelphia, Pa., March 23, 1920. [1; 4; 10]

Schmid, Placid, priest, b. 1856; d. 1932. [21]

Schmidt, Carl Louis August, chemist, b. Brown county, S.D., 1885; d. Berkeley, Calif., Feb. 23, 1946. [10]

Schmidt, Henry Immanuel, clergyman, b. Nazareth, Pa., 1806; d. New York, N.Y., Feb. 11, 1889. [3; 6]

Schmidt, Nathaniel, orientalist, b. Sweden, 1862; d. Ithaca, N.Y., June 30, 1939. [10]

Schmucker, John George, clergyman, b. Germany, 1771; d. Williamsburg, Pa., Oct. 7, 1854. [1; 3; 4; 6]

Schmucker, Samuel Christian, biologist, b. Allentown, Pa., 1860; d. West Chester, Pa., Dec. 28, 1943. [7; 10; 13]

Schmucker, Samuel Mosheim, lawyer, b. New Market, Va., 1823; d. Philadelphia, Pa., May 12, 1863. [3; 4; 5; 6]

Schmucker, Samuel Simon, theologian, b. Hagerstown, Md., 1799; d. Gettysburg, Pa., July 26, 1873. [1; 3; 4; 5; 6]

Schneider, Albert, bacteriologist, b. Granville, Ill., 1863; d. Portland, Ore., Oct. 27, 1928. [1; 4; 5; 10]

Schneider, Frederick William, clergyman, b. Boonville, Ind., 1862; d. East Lansing, Mich., Dec. 18, 1941. [10]

Schneider, Herman, educationist, b. Summit Hill, Pa., 1872; d. Cincinnati, O., March 28, 1939. [10]

Schodde, George Henry, clergyman, b. Allegheny, Pa., 1854; d. Sept. 15, 1917. [1; 3; 10]

Schoeffel, Mrs. Florence Blackburn, née White, novelist, b. 1860; d. New York, N.Y., April 16, 1900.

Schoenhof, Jacob, economist, b. Germany, 1839; d. New York, N.Y., March 14, 1903. [1]

Schoen-René, Anna Eugénie, musician, b. Coblenz, Germany, 1864; d. New York, N.Y., Nov. 13, 1942.

Schofield, Frank Howard, historian, b. Black River, N.S., 1859; d. Victoria, B.C., Dec. 10, 1929. [27]

Schofield, Henry, lawyer, b. Dudley, Mass., 1866; d. Chicago, Ill., Aug. 15, 1918. [1; 10]

Schofield, John McAllister, soldier, b. Gerry, N.Y., 1831; d. St. Augustine, Fla., March 4, 1906. [1; 3; 4; 5; 10]

Schofield, William Henry, educationist, b. Brockville, Ont., 1870; d. Peterboro, N.H., June 24, 1920. [1; 7; 10]

Scholefield, Ethelbert Olaf Stuart, librarian and historian, b. Ryde, Isle of Wight, England, 1874; d. Victoria, B.C., Dec. 24, 1919. [27]

Scholes, Adam, poet, b. about 1830; d. 1900.

Scholz, Richard Frederick, educationist, b. Milwaukee, Wis., 1880; d. Portland, Ore., July 23, 1924. [10]

Schoolcraft, Henry Rowe, explorer and ethnologist, b. Albany county, N.Y., 1793; d. Washington, D.C., Dec. 10, 1864. [1; 2; 3; 4; 5; 6; 7; 9]

Schoolcraft, Mrs. Mary, née Howard, novelist, fl. 1847-1867. [34]

Schoonmaker, Edwin Davies, educationist, b. Scranton, Pa., 1873; d. Woodstock, N.Y., May 4, 1940. [10; 11]

Schoonmaker, Marius, local historian, b. 1811; d. 1894.

Schott, Charles Anthony, geodesist, b. Mannheim, Germany, 1826; d. Washington, D.C., July 31, 1901. [1; 3; 5]

Schouler, James, lawyer and historian, b. Arlington, Mass., 1839; d. Intervale, N.H., April 16, 1920. [1; 3; 4; 5; 6; 7; 10; 51]

Schouler, William, historian, b. near Glasgow, Scotland, 1814; d. West Roxbury, Mass., Oct. 24, 1872. [1; 3; 6; 7]

Schroeder, Henry Joseph, priest and educationist, b. Detroit, Mich., 1876; d. Columbus, O., May 7, 1942. [21]

Schroeder, John Frederick, clergyman, b. Baltimore, Md., 1800; d. Brooklyn, N.Y., Feb. 26, 1857. [1; 3; 4; 6; 34]

Schroeder, Seaton, naval officer, b. Washington, D.C., 1849; d. Washington, D.C., Oct. 19, 1922. [1; 5; 10]

Schuchert, Charles, geologist, b. Cincinnati, O., 1858; d. New Haven, Conn., Nov. 20, 1942. [4; 10; 11]

Schuckers, Jacob W., economist, fl. 1874-1894.

Schuette, Conrad Herman Louis, clergyman, b. Hanover, Germany, 1843; d. Columbus, O., Aug. 11, 1926. [3; 6; 10]

Schuh, Henry Jacob, clergyman, b. 1851; d. 1934.

Schuh, Louis Herman, clergyman, b. 1858; d. Sept. 29, 1936.

Schulte, Mrs. Mary Jemima, née Mac-Coll, poet, b. Liverpool, England, 1847; d. ? [6]

Schultz, Charles Henry, educationist, b. Philadelphia, Pa., 1856; d. 1932. [21]

Schultz, Frederick Walter, miscellaneous writer, b. 1840; d. Baltimore, Md., Jan. 24, 1917.

Schultze, Augustus, clergyman, b. Potsdam, Germany, 1840; d. Bethlehem, Pa., Nov. 12, 1918. [1; 4; 10]

Schultze, Carl Emil, cartoonist, b. Lexington, Ky., 1866; d. New York, N.Y., Jan. 18, 1939. [7; 10]

Schultze, Frederick, priest, b. 1855; d. 1930. [21]

Schurman, Jacob Gould, educationist and diplomat, b. Freetown, P.E.I., 1854; d. New York, N.Y., Aug. 12, 1942. [4; 7; 10]

Schurz, Carl, journalist, politician, and diplomat, b. near Cologne, Germany, 1829; d. New York, N.Y., May 14, 1906. [1; 2; 3; 4; 5; 7; 9; 10]

Schuyler, Aaron, educationist, b. Seneca county, N.Y., 1828; d. Feb. 1, 1913. [5; 6; 10]

Schuyler, Eugene, diplomat, b. Ithaca, N.Y., 1840; d. Venice, Italy, July 16, 1890. [1; 3; 4; 5; 6; 7; 9; 62]

Schuyler, George Lee, yachtsman, b. Rhinebeck, N.Y., 1811; d. New London, Conn., July 31, 1890. [3; 4]

Schuyler, George Washington, politician, historian, and genealogist, b. Stillwater, N.Y., 1810; d. Ithaca, N.Y., Feb. 1, 1888. [1; 3; 6; 7]

Schuyler, Hamilton, clergyman, b. Oswego, N.Y., 1862; d. Trenton, N.J., Jan. 23, 1933. [10]

Schuyler, James Dix, engineer, b. Ithaca, N.Y., 1848; d. Ocean Park, Fla., Sept. 13, 1912. [1; 4; 10]

Schuyler, Livingston Rowe, clergyman, b. New York, N.Y., 1868; d. New York, N.Y., Jan. 1, 1931. [10]

Schuyler, Montgomery, clergyman, b. New York, N.Y., 1814; d. St. Louis, Mo., March 19, 1896. [3; 5]

Schuyler, Montgomery, journalist, b. Ithaca, N.Y., 1843; d. New Rochelle, N.Y., July 16, 1914. [1; 4; 5; 7; 10]

Schuyler, William, educationist, b. St. Louis, Mo., 1855; d. St. Louis, Mo., July 7, 1914. [10]

Schwab, John Christopher, educationist, b. New York, N.Y., 1865; d. New Haven, Conn., Jan. 12, 1916. [1; 7; 10; 62]

Schwab, Laurence Henry, clergyman, b. New York, N.Y., 1857; d. Sharon, Conn., May 28, 1911. [62]

Schwab, Sidney Isaac, neurologist, b. Memphis, Tenn., 1871; d. Boston, Mass., Nov. 12, 1947. [10]

Schwamb, Peter, engineer, b. Arlington, Mass., 1858; d. 1928. [10]

Schwarze, William Nathaniel, clergyman, b. Chaska, Minn., 1875; d. Bethlehem, Pa., March 14, 1948.

Schwatka, Frederick, explorer, b. Galena, Ill., 1849; d. Portland, Ore., Nov. 2, 1892. [4; 7; 9]

Schwatt, Isaac Joachim, educationist, b. Russia, 1867; d. Philadelphia, Pa., April 18, 1934. [10]

Schweinitz, Edmund Alexander de. See De Schweinitz, Edmund Alexander.

Schweinitz, Lewis David von. See Von Schweinitz, Lewis David.

Schwertner, Thomas Maria, priest, b. Canton, O., 1888; d. Feb. 17, 1933. [21]

Scidmore, Eliza Ruhamah, traveller, b. Madison, Wis., 1856; d. Geneva, Switzerland, Nov. 3, 1928. [1; 5; 7; 9; 10]

Scipio (pseud.). See Tracy, Uriah.

Sclater, John Robert Paterson, clergyman, b. Manchester, England, 1876; d. Edinburgh, Scotland, Aug. 23, 1949. [30]

Scofield, Cyrus Ingerson, clergyman, b. Lenawee county, Mich., 1843; d. Douglastown, Long Island, N.Y., July 24, 1921. [10]

Scofield, William Bacon, poet, b. Hartford, Conn., 1864; d. Worcester, Mass., Jan. 22, 1930. [10; 11]

Scollard, Clinton, poet and novelist, b. Clinton, N.Y., 1860; d. Kent, Conn., Nov. 19, 1932. [1; 2; 3; 4; 5; 7; 10; 11; 71]

Scotson-Clark, George Frederick, art director, b. Brighton, England, 1872; d. Norwalk, Conn., Dec. 21, 1927. [4; 10]

Scott, Mrs. Anna, née **Kay,** missionary, b. 1838; d. 1923.

Scott, Mrs. Anna M., née **Steele,** missionary, fl. 1858-1874. [6]

Scott, Charles, lawyer, b. Knoxville, Tenn., 1811; d. Jackson, Miss., May 30, 1861. [34]

Scott, Charlotte Angas, mathematician, b. Lincoln, England, 1858; d. London, England, Nov. 8, 1931. [10]

Scott, Colin Alexander, psychologist, b. Ottawa, Ont., 1861; d. 1925. [10]

Scott, David, clergyman, fl. 1832-1863.

Scott, Duncan Campbell, poet, b. Ottawa, Ont., 1862; d. Ottawa, Ont., Dec. 19, 1947. [30]

Scott, Eben Greenough, lawyer, b. Wilkesbarre, Pa., 1836; d. Wilkesbarre, Pa., July 5, 1919. [10; 62]

Scott, Mrs. Ellen, née **Corrigan,** novelist, b. Kensington, Conn., 1862; d. Milford, Del., June 18, 1936. [7; 10; 11; 21]

Scott, Frank Jesup, architect, b. Columbia, S.C., 1828; d. Toledo, O., 1919. [10]

Scott, Fred Newton, educationist, b. Terre Haute, Ind., 1860; d. San Diego, Calif., May 29, 1931. [1; 4; 7; 10]

Scott, Frederick George, clergyman and poet, b. Montreal, Que., 1861; d. Quebec, Que., Jan.19, 1944. [27]

Scott, Hamilton Percy, lawyer, b. Windsor, N.S., 1856; d. Windsor, N.S., Dec. 11, 1937. [11; 27]

Scott, Harriet Maria, educationist, d. Pasadena, Calif., 1906. [10]

Scott, Harvey Whitefield, journalist, b. Tazewell county, Ill., 1838; d. Baltimore, Md., Aug. 7, 1910. [1; 4; 7; 10]

Scott, Henri Arthur, priest and historian, b. St. Nicholas, Que., 1858; d. Quebec, Que., Jan. 23, 1931. [27]

Scott, Henry Lee, soldier, b. New Berne, N.C., 1814; d. New York, N.Y., Jan. 6, 1886. [3b; 34]

Scott, Hugh Lenox, soldier, b. Danville, Ky., 1853; d. Washington, D.C., April 30, 1934. [1a; 4; 10]

Scott, Hugh McDonald, clergyman, b. Guysborough, N.S., 1848; d. Chicago, Ill., 1909. [10]

Scott, Mrs. Hugh Roy. See Scott, Mrs. Anna M., née Steele.

Scott, James, clergyman, b. Langside, Scotland, 1806; d. 1858. [3; 6]

Scott, James Brown, authority on international law, b. Kincardine, Ont., 1866; d. Annapolis, Md., June 25, 1943. [7; 10; 11]

Scott, James Foster, physician, b. India, 1863; d. Washington, D.C., Feb. 20, 1946. [62]

Scott, Job, Quaker preacher, b. Providence, R.I., 1751; d. Ballitore, Ireland, Nov. 22, 1793. [1; 4; 6]

Scott, John, soldier, b. Virginia, 1820; d. 1907. [4; 5; 34]

Scott, John, clergyman, b. Washington county, Pa., 1820; d. ? [3; 6]

Scott, John, agriculturist, b. Jefferson county, O., 1824; d. Des Moines, Ia., 1903. [4; 5; 10; 37]

Scott, John Adams, educationist, b. Fletcher, Ill., 1867; d. Augusta, Mich., Oct. 26, 1947. [10]

Scott, John Rutledge, educationist, b. McConnelsville, O., 1843; d. Columbia, Mo., Jan. 3, 1936.

Scott, Jonathan French, historian, b. Newark, N.J., 1882; d. Yonkers, N.Y., May 30, 1942. [7; 10; 11]

Scott, Joseph, geographer, fl. 1795-1807. [6]

Scott, Lawrence Winfield, clergyman, b. 1846; d. ?

Scott, Mrs. Lena Becker, social service worker, b. Maytown, Ill., 1875; d. 1935. [75]

Scott, Leroy, novelist, b. Fairmount, Ind., 1875; d. Chateaugay Lake, N.Y., July 21, 1929. [1; 7; 10]

Scott, Mrs. Lucy, née **Jameson,** writer of books for children, b. Irasburg, Vt., 1843; d. Brooklyn, N.Y., Feb. 2, 1920. [10]

Scott, Mary Augusta, educationist, b. Dayton, O., 1851; d. Baltimore, Md., March 28, 1918. [10; 62]

Scott, Milton Robinson, journalist, b. Jacksontown, O., 1841; d. Newark, O., June 9, 1921.

Scott, Orange, clergyman, b. Brookfield, Vt., 1800; d. Newark, N.J., July 31, 1847. [1; 3; 4; 5]

Scott, Richard John Ernst, physician, b. Whitchurch, England, 1863; d. Brooklyn, N.Y., Oct. 24, 1932. [10]

Scott, Robert, clergyman, b. about 1761; d. 1834.

Scott, Robert Graham, soldier, b. 1845; d. ?

Scott, Robert Nicholson, soldier, b. Winchester, Tenn., 1838; d. Washington, D.C., March 5, 1887. [3; 4; 5; 34]

Scott, Samuel Parsons, lawyer and historian, b. Hillsboro, O., 1846; d. Hillsboro, O., May 30, 1929. [1; 4; 7; 10; 11]

Scott, Sutton Selwyn, lawyer and planter, b. Huntsville, Ala., 1829; d. 1907. [5; 10; 34]

Scott, Temple, bibliophile and editor, b. Hull, England, 1864; d. Edinburgh, Scotland, Sept. 30, 1939.

Scott, Walter, religious reformer, b. Moffat, Scotland, 1796; d. Mayslick, Ky., April 23, 1861. [1; 3; 4; 34]

Scott, Wilfred Welday, chemist, b. Zanesville, O., 1876; d. Los Angeles, Calif., May 3, 1932. [10; 11; 13]

Scott, William, clergyman, b. about 1812; d. Ottawa, Ont., Oct. 5, 1891. [27]

Scott, William Anderson, clergyman, b. Bedford county, Tenn., 1813; d. San Francisco, Calif., Jan. 14, 1885. [1; 3; 4; 5; 6; 34]

Scott, William Berryman, geologist, b. Cincinnati, O., 1858; d. Princeton, N.J., March 29, 1947. [10, 11; 13]

Scott, William Cowper, clergyman, b. Martinsburg, Va., 1817; d. Bethesda, Va., Oct. 23, 1854. [3; 34]

Scott, William Earl Dodge, ornithologist, b. Brooklyn, N.Y., 1852; d. Saranac Lake, N.Y., Feb. 6, 1910. [4; 10]

Scott, William Forse, soldier and lawyer, b. Dayton, O., 1844; d. ? [10]

Scott, William J., clergyman, b. Clarke county, Ga., 1826; d. Atlanta, Ga., 1899. [34]

Scott, William Wallace, local historian, b. Orange county, Va., 1845; d. Gordonsville, Va., Jan. 16, 1929.

Scott, William Walter, journalist, b. Woodville, N.C., 1853; d. Adako, N.C., May 3, 1931.

Scott, William Winfield, local historian, b. 1855; d. Passaic, N.J., Sept. 30, 1935.

Scott, Winfield, soldier, b. near Petersburg, Va., 1786; d. West Point, N.Y., May 29, 1866. [1; 2; 3; 4; 5; 6; 7]

Scott, Winfield Gemain, chemist, b. Emerald Grove, Wis., 1854; d. Long Beach, Calif., Aug. 21, 1919. [4]

Scottow, Joshua, merchant and historian, b. England, 1615; d. Boston, Mass., Jan. 20, 1698. [3; 6]

Scovil, Elisabeth Robinson, nurse, b. 1849; d. 1934.

Scovil, William Elias, clergyman, b. 1810; d. 1876.

Scoville, Joseph Alfred, journalist and novelist, b. Woodbury, Conn., 1815; d. New York, N.Y., June 25, 1864. [1; 3; 4; 6; 7; 9]

Scranton, Erastus, clergyman, b. Madison, Conn., 1777; d. Burlington, Conn., Oct. 5, 1861. [62]

Scribner, Benjamin Franklin, soldier, b. 1825; d. 1900. [7]

Scribner, Charles Harvey, lawyer, b. near Norwalk, Conn., 1826; d. 1897. [6]

Scribner, Frank Kimball, novelist, b. New York, N.Y., 1867; d. Cornwall-on-Hudson, N.Y., Nov. 10, 1935. [7; 10]

Scribner, Frank Lamson. See Lamson-Scribner, Frank.

Scribner, Gilbert Hilton, lawyer, b. Monroe county, N.Y., 1831; d. Yonkers, N.Y., Jan. 5, 1910. [10]

Scribner, Harvey, lawyer, b. Mount Vernon, O., 1850; d. Toledo, O., Jan. 21, 1913. [10]

Scribner, Isaac W., physician, d. Lowell, Mass., 1864. [6]

Scribner, William, clergyman, b. New York, N.Y., 1820; d. Plainfield, N.J., March 3, 1884. [6]

Scripps, James Edmund, journalist, b. London, England, 1835; d. Detroit, Mich., May 29, 1906. [1; 4; 7; 9; 10]

Scriven, George Percival, soldier, b. Philadelphia, Pa., ·1854; d. Southern Pines, N.C., March 7, 1940. [4; 10; 21]

Scriven, Joseph Medlicott, hymn-writer, b. county Down, Ireland, 1819; d. near Bewdley, Ont., Aug. 10, 1886. [27]

Scruggs, William Lindsay, diplomat, b. near Knoxville, Tenn., 1836; d. Atlanta, Ga., July 18, 1912. [1; 4; 10; 34]

Scudder, Charles Locke, surgeon, b. Kent, Conn., 1860; d. Boston, Mass., Aug. 19, 1949. [10; 62]

Scudder, Doremus, clergyman, b. New York, N.Y., 1858; d. Puente, Calif., July 23, 1942. [62]

Scudder, Horace Elisha, editor, biographer, and writer of books for children, b. Boston, Mass., 1838; d. Cambridge, Mass., Jan. 11, 1902. [1; 2; 3; 4; 5; 6; 7; 8; 9; 10; 71]

Scudder, Janet, sculptor, b. Terre Haute, Ind., 1873; d. Rockport, Mass., June 9, 1940. [4; 7; 10; 11]

Scudder, John Milton, physician, b. Harrison, O., 1829; d. Daytona, Fla., Feb. 17, 1894. [1; 3; 6]

Scudder, Moses Lewis, clergyman, b. Charlestown, Mass., 1843; d. Oct. 29, 1917. [10]

Scudder, Myron Tracy, educationist, b. India, 1860; d. New York, N.Y., Dec. 28, 1935. [10; 11]

Scudder, Samuel Hubbard, entomologist, b. Boston, Mass., 1837; d. Cambridge, Mass., May 25, 1911. [1; 2; 3; 4; 5; 6; 10]

Scull, Guy Hamilton, journalist and adventurer, b. Boston, Mass., 1876; d. New York, N.Y., Oct. 20, 1920. [51]

Seabrook, William Buehler, journalist, b. Westminster, Md., 1886; d. Rhinebeck, N.Y., Sept. 30, 1945. [7; 10]

Seabury, George John, pharmacist, b. New York, N.Y., 1844; d. New York, N.Y., Feb. 13, 1909. [1]

Seabury, Joseph Bartlett, clergyman, b. New Bedford, Mass., 1846; d. Natick, Mass., July 5, 1923. [45]

Seabury. Samuel, bishop, b. Groton, Conn., 1729; d. New London, Conn., Feb. 25, 1796. [1; 2; 3; 4; 5; 6; 7]

Seabury, Samuel, clergyman, b. New London, Conn., 1801; d. New York, N.Y., Oct. 10, 1872. [1; 3; 5; 6; 9]

Seabury, William Jones, clergyman, b. New York, N.Y., 1837; d. New York, N.Y., Aug. 30, 1916. [10; 48]

Seabury, William Marston, lawyer, b. New York, N.Y., 1878; d. New York, N.Y., Nov. 8, 1949. [10]

Seager, Charles, lawyer, b. Wellington, England, 1844; d. Goderich, Ont., Jan. 1939. [27]

Seager, Charles Allen, archbishop, b. Goderich, Ont., 1872; d. London, Ont., Sept. 9, 1948. [30]

Seager, Henry Rogers, economist, b. Lansing, Mich., 1870; d. Kiev, Russia, Aug. 23, 1930. [1; 4; 10; 11]

Sealsfield, Charles, novelist, b. Poppitz, Moravia, 1793; d. Solothurn, Switzerland, May 26, 1864. [1; 3; 4; 5; 7; 9]

Seaman, Abel (pseud.). See Chase, Frank Eugene.

Seaman, Mrs. Elizabeth, née Cochrane, journalist, b. Cochran Mills, Pa., 1867; d. New York, N.Y., Jan. 27, 1922. [1; 7; 9]

Seaman, Ezra Chapman, civil servant, b. Chatham, N.Y., 1805; d. Ann Arbor, Mich., July 1, 1880. [1; 3; 39]

Seaman, James N., clergyman and poet, d. Hampden, Me., 1831.

Seaman, Louis Livingston, physician, b. Newburgh, N.Y., 1851; d. New York, N.Y., Jan. 31, 1932. [4; 10; 11]

Seaman, Valentine, physician, b. Hempstead, Long Island, N.Y., 1770; d. New York, N.Y., July 3, 1817. [3; 6]

Search, Preston Willis, educationist, b. Marion, O., 1853; d. Carmel-by-the-Sea, Calif., Dec. 12, 1932. [10; 11]

Searing, Mrs. Annie Eliza, née **Pidgeon,** writer ot books for children, b. Brooklyn, N.Y., 1857; d. Kingston, N.Y., April 22, 1942.

Searing, Mrs. Laura Catherine, née **Redden,** poet, b. Somerset county, Md., 1840; d. San Mateo, Calif., Aug. 10, 1923. [1; 3; 4; 6; 7; 10; 34]

Searle, Arthur, astronomer, b. London, England, 1837; d. Cambridge, Mass., Oct. 23, 1920. [1; 3; 4; 5; 10; 51]

Searle, George Mary, priest and astronomer, b. London, England, 1839; d. New York, N.Y., July 7, 1918. [3; 10; 21; 51]

Searle, January (pseud.). See Phillips, George Searle.

Searle, William Smith, physician, b. 1833; d. Brooklyn, N.Y., Oct. 30, 1910.

Searles, William Henry, engineer, b. Cincinnati, O., 1837; d. Elyria, O., April 25, 1921. [10]

Sears, Barnas, clergyman and educationist, b. Berkshire county, Mass., 1802; d. Saratoga Springs, N.Y., July 6, 1880. [1; 3; 4; 5; 6]

Sears, Charles Hatch, clergyman, b. Preble, N.Y., 1870; d. Yonkers, N.Y., May 3, 1943. [10]

Sears, Edmund Hamilton, clergyman, b. Berkshire county, Mass., 1810; d. Weston, Mass., Jan. 16, 1876. [1; 3; 4; 5; 6; 7; 9]

Sears, Edward Isidore, editor, b. county Mayo, Ireland, 1819; d. New York, N.Y., Dec. 7, 1876. [3; 6; 7]

Sears, Fred Coleman, pomologist, b. Lexington, Mass., 1866; d. Northampton, Mass., Oct. 9, 1949. [10; 11]

Sears, George W., woodsman, b. Douglas Woods, Mass., 1821; d. ? [6]

Sears, John Harold, lawyer, b. Knoxville, Ia., 1882; d. Ridgefield, Conn., Oct. 21, 1929. [62]

Sears, John Van der Zee, journalist, b. Albany, N.Y., 1835; d. ? [10]

Sears, Joseph Hamblen, publisher, b. Boston, Mass., 1865; d. Kingsport, Tenn., Feb. 15, 1946. [10]

Sears, Lorenzo, clergyman and educationist, b. Searsville, Mass:, 1838; d. Providence, R.I., March 1, 1916. [7; 10; 62]

Sears, Minnie Earl, librarian, b. Lafayette, Ind., 1873; d. New York, N.Y., Nov. 28, 1933. [7]

Sears, Robert, publisher and compiler, b. Saint John, N.B., 1810; d. Toronto, Ont., Feb. 17, 1892. [1; 3; 4; 5; 6; 7]

Searson, John, merchant and poetaster, b. Ireland, about 1750; d. ? [7; 19]

Seashore, Carl Emil, psychologist, b. Sweden, 1866; d. Lewiston, Idaho, Oct. 16, 1949. [7; 10; 11]

Seath, John, educationist, b. Auchtermuchty, Scotland, 1844; d. Toronto, Ont., March 17, 1919. [27]

Seaton, George Whiting, writer of travel books, d. Aug. 27, 1944.

Seatsfield, Charles. See Sealsfield, Charles.

Seaver, Edwin Pliny, mathematician, b. Northborough, Mass., 1838; d. Cambridge, Mass., Dec. 7, 1917. [10; 51]

Seaver, Emily, poet, b. Charlestown, Mass., 1835; d. ? [43]

Seaver, Horace Holley, journalist, b. 1810; d. 1889.

Seaver, James Everett, biographer, b. 1787; d. 1827. [6]

Seaver, Jay Webber, physician, b. Craftsbury, Vt., 1855; d. Berkeley, Calif., May 5, 1915. [62]

Seavey, William Munro, lawyer, b. Fairmount, Mass., 1862; d. Boston, Mass., July 22, 1902. [51]

Seawell, Molly Elliot, novelist, b. Gloucester county, Va., 1860; d. Washington, D.C., Nov. 15, 1916. [1; 2; 4; 5; 7; 10; 21; 34]

Seay, Frank, clergyman, b. New Orleans, La., 1881; d. Dallas, Tex., Feb. 14, 1920. [10]

Secomb, Daniel Franklin, local historian, b. 1820; d. 1895.

Second, Henry (pseud.). See Harrison, Henry Sydnor.

Secondsight, Solomon (pseud.). See McHenry, James.

Secretan, James Henry Edward, civil engineer, b. 1854; d. Ottawa, Ont., Dec. 22, 1926. [27]

Secrist, Horace, economist, b. Farmington, Utah, 1881; d. Evanston, Ill., March 5, 1943. [10]

Sedgewick, Garnet Gladman, educationist, b. Musquodoboit, N.S., 1882; d. Vancouver, B.C., Sept. 5, 1949. [14; 30]

Sedgwick, Anne Douglas, novelist, b. Englewood, N.J., 1873; d. Hampstead, England, July 19, 1935. [1a; 7; 10; 11]

Sedgwick, Arthur George, lawyer and journalist, b. New York, N.Y., 1844; d. Stockbridge, Mass., July 14, 1915. [1; 2; 7; 10; 51]

Sedgwick, Catherine Maria, novelist, b. Stockbridge, Mass., 1789; d. West Roxbury, Mass., July 31, 1867. [1; 2; 3; 4; 5; 6; 7; 8; 9]

Sedgwick, Mrs. Charles. See Sedgwick, Mrs. Elizabeth Buckminster, née Dwight.

Sedgwick, Charles Frederick, local historian, b. 1795; d. 1882.

Sedgwick, Mrs. Elizabeth Buckminster, née **Dwight,** educationist, b. 1791; d. 1864. [3]

Sedgwick, Henry Dwight, lawyer, b. Sheffield, Mass., ˙1785; d. Stockbridge, Mass., Dec. 23, 1831. [3; 5; 6]

Sedgwick, Henry Dwight, lawyer, b. Stockbridge, Mass., 1824; d. 1903. [5; 10]

Sedgwick, Mrs. Susan Ann Livingston, née **Ridley,** novelist, b. 1788; d. Stockbridge, Mass., Jan. 20, 1867. [3; 4; 5; 6; 7]

Sedgwick, Theodore, lawyer, b. Sheffield, Mass., 1780; d. Pittsfield, Mass., Nov. 7, 1839. [1; 3; 4; 5; 7]

Sedgwick, Theodore, lawyer and diplomat, b. Albany, N.Y., 1811; d. Stockbridge, Mass., Dec. 8, 1859. [1; 3; 4; 5; 6; 7]

Sedgwick, Mrs. Theodore. See Sedgwick, Mrs. Susan Ann Livingston, née Ridley.

Sedgwick, William Thompson, biologist, b. West Hartford, Conn., 1855; d. Boston, Mass., Jan. 25, 1921. [1; 4; 5; 10; 62]

Sedley, Henry, novelist, b. Boston, Mass., 1831; d. New York, N.Y., Jan. 25, 1899. [3; 6; 7; 10]

See, James Waring, mechanical engineer, b. 1850; d. Hamilton, O., 1920.

See, T. J. (pseud.). See Carey, Thomas Joseph.

Seeger, Alan, soldier and poet, b. New York, N.Y., 1888; d. near Belloy-en-Santerre, France, July 4, 1916. [1; 4; 7; 51]

Seegmiller, Wilhelmina, art director and poet, b. Fairview, Ont., 1866; d. Indianapolis, Ind., May 24, 1913. [10]

Seeley, C. Sumner (pseud.). See Munday, John William.

Seeley, Levi, educationist, b. North Harpersfield, N.Y., 1847; d. Trenton, N.J., Dec. 23, 1928. [10; 11]

Seeley, Mrs. Velma, née Hitchcock, poet, b. 1900; d. 1938.

Seely, Amos Warren, clergyman, b. New York, N.Y.; d. Brooklyn, N.Y., Sept. 12, 1865. [56]

Seely, Edward Howard, novelist, b. New York, N.Y., 1856; d. Brooklyn, N.Y., June 22, 1894. [3b; 62]

Seely, Grace Hart, educationist, b. 1882; d. Ithaca, N.Y., May 23, 1948.

Seely, Howard. See Seely, Edward Howard.

Seelye, Mrs. Elizabeth, née Eggleston, historian, b. St. Paul, Minn., 1858; d. Philadelphia, Pa., Nov. 13, 1923. [7; 70]

Seelye, Julius Hawley, clergyman, b. Bethel, Conn., 1824; d. Amherst, Mass., May 12, 1895. [1; 3; 4; 5; 6; 7]

Seelye, Laurenus Clark, educationist, b. Bethel, Conn., 1837; d. Northampton, Mass., Oct. 12, 1924. [4; 7; 10]

Seelye, William James, educationist, b. Schenectady, N.Y., 1857; d. Woodbridge, D.C., March 28, 1931. [4]

Seemüller, Mrs. Anne Moncure, née Crane, novelist, b. Baltimore, Md., 1838; d. Stuttgart, Germany, 1872. [6; 7]

Seerley, Homer Horatio, educationist, b. 1848; d. Cedar Falls, Ia., Dec. 22, 1932. [37]

Segale, Sister Blandina, educationist, b. Italy, 1850; d. Mount St. Joseph, O., Jan., 1941. [21]

Segar, Elzie Crisler, cartoonist, b. 1894; d. Santa Monica, Calif., Oct. 13, 1938.

Seguin, Edward, psychiatrist, b. Clamecy, France, 1812; d. New York, N.Y., Oct. 28, 1880. [1; 3; 4; 5; 6]

Seguin, Edward Constant, neurologist, b. Paris, France, 1843; d. New York, N.Y., Feb. 19, 1898. [1; 3b; 5]

Seibert, George C., clergyman, b. Germany, 1828; d. at sea, Sept. 9, 1902. [3b]

Seibold, Louis, journalist, b. Washington, D.C., 1866; d. Washington, D.C., 1945. [10]

Seidensticker, Oswald, historian, b. Göttingen, Germany, 1825; d. Philadelphia, Pa., Jan. 10, 1894. [1]

Seifert, Mathias Joseph, physician, b. 1866; d. Chicago, Ill., Feb. 1, 1947. [10]

Seiler, Carl, physician, b. Switzerland, 1849; d. Reading, Pa., Oct. 11, 1905. [1]

Seilhamer, George Overcash, historian and genealogist, b. 1839; d. ?

Seiss, Joseph Augustus, clergyman, b. Frederick county, Md., 1823; d. Philadelphia, Pa., June 21, 1904. [1; 3; 4; 5; 6; 7]

Seitz, Don Carlos, journalist, b. Portage, O., 1862; d. Brooklyn, N.Y., Dec. 4, 1935. [1a; 7; 10]

Selby, Julian A., historian, b. 1833; d. 1907. [34]

Selby, Paul, compiler, b. 1825; d. 1913.

Selden, Edward Griffin, clergyman, b. Hadlyme, Conn., 1847; d. Saratoga Springs, N.Y., June 3, 1904. [62]

Selden, Samuel, physician and poet, b. 1834; d. 1880. [34]

Selfridge, Thomas, naval officer, b. Charlestown, Mass., 1836; d. Washington, D.C., Feb. 4, 1924. [1; 4; 5; 10]

Seligman, Edwin Robert Anderson, economist, b. New York, N.Y., 1861; d. Lake Placid, N.Y., July 18, 1939. [3; 5; 10; 11]

Selim (pseud.). See Woodworth, Samuel.

Sell, Henry Thorne, clergyman, b. Brooklyn, N.Y., 1854; d. New York, N.Y., July 20, 1928. [10; 62]

Sellar, Robert, journalist, b. Glasgow, Scotland, 1841; d. Huntingdon, Que., Nov. 30, 1919. [27]

Sellew, Walter Ashbel, bishop, b. Gowanda, N.Y., 1844; d. Jamestown, N.Y., Jan. 16, 1929. [10]

Sells, Elijah Watt, accountant, b. Muscatine, Ia., 1858; d. New York, N.Y., March 19, 1924.

Sellstedt, Lars Gustaf, painter, b. Sweden, 1819; d. Buffalo, N.Y., June 4, 1911. [1; 4; 5; 10]

Seltzer, Charles Alden, novelist, b. Janesville, Wis., 1875; d. North Olmsted, O., Feb. 9, 1942. [7; 10]

Seltzer, Thomas, publisher and translator, b. Poltava, Russia; d. New York, N.Y., Sept. 11, 1943.

Semmes, John Edward, lawyer, b. near Cumberland, Md., 1851; d. Baltimore, Md., May 17, 1925. [4]

Semmes, Raphael, naval officer, b. Charles county, Md., 1809; d. Mobile, Ala., Aug. 30, 1877. [1; 2; 3; 4; 5; 6; 7; 21; 34]

Semmes, Raphael Thomas, genealogist, b. 1857; d. 1916.

Semple, Ellen Semple, geographer, b. Louisville, Ky., 1863; d. West Palm Beach, Fla., May 8, 1932. [1; 10; 34]

Semple, Henry Churchill, priest, b. Montgomery, Ala., 1853; d. New Orleans, La., June 27, 1925. [10; 21]

Semple, Robert Baylor, clergyman, b. King and Queen county, Ga., 1769; d. Fredericksburg, Va., Dec. 25, 1831. [3; 4; 34]

Senarens, Luis Philip, dime novelist, b. 1863; d. New York, N.Y., Dec. 26, 1939. [7]

Senn, Nicholas, surgeon, b. Switzerland, 1866; d. Chicago, Ill., Jan. 2, 1908. [1; 4; 10]

Senour, Faunt Le Roy, clergyman, b. Madison, Ind., 1824; d. Titusville, Pa., April 23, 1910. [56]

Sensenig, David Martin, mathematician, b. Lancaster county, Pa., 1840; d. 1907. [10]

Sentinel (pseud.). See Bogart, William Henry.

Sergeant, Henry Jonathan, lawyer, b. about 1815; d. Philadelphia, Pa., April 30, 1858.

Sergeant, John, lawyer and politician, b. Philadelphia, Pa., 1779; d. Philadelphia, Pa., Nov. 23, 1852. [1; 3; 4; 5; 6]

Sergeant, Thomas, jurist, b. Philadelphia, Pa., 1782; d. Philadelphia, Pa., May 5, 1860. [1; 3; 4; 5; 6]

Sergel, Charles Hubbard, publisher, b. Muscatine, Ia., 1861; d. Chicago, Ill., Jan. 7, 1926. [10]

Serly, Ludovicus Textoris, musician, b. 1855; d. New York, N.Y., Feb. 1, 1939.

Serrano, Mrs. Mary Jane, née **Christie,** poet and translator, d. New York, N.Y., July 1, 1923.

Serviss, Garrett Putnam, journalist, novelist, and astronomer, b. Sharon Springs, N.Y., 1851; d. Englewood, N.J., May 24, 1929. [4; 5; 10; 11]

Sessions, Alexander Joseph, clergyman, b. 1809; d. 1892.

Sessions, Francis Charles, merchant and traveller, b. 1820; d. 1892.

Sessions, Henry Clay, lawyer, b. 1844; d. 1934.

Sessions, Mrs. Ruth, née **Huntington,** miscellaneous writer, b. 1859; d. Syracuse, N.Y., Dec. 2, 1946.

Sestini, Benedict, priest, mathematician, and astronomer, b. Florence, Italy, 1816; d. Frederick, Md., Jan. 17, 1890. [1]

Setchell, William Albert, botanist, b. Norwich, Conn., 1864; d. Berkeley, Calif., April 5, 1943. [62]

Seton, Ernest Thompson, artist, naturalist, and writer of stories about animals, b. South Shields, England,, 1860; d. near Santa Fé, N. M., Oct. 23, 1946. [4; 7; 10; 11; 12]

Seton, Robert, archbishop, b. Pisa, Italy, 1839; d. Convent, N.J., March 22, 1927. [1; 3; 4; 5; 6; 10; 21]

Seton, William, novelist, b. New York, N.Y., 1835; d. New York, N.Y., March 15, 1905. [1; 3; 5; 6; 7; 21]

Severance, Frank Hayward, historian, b. Manchester, Mass., 1856; d. Buffalo, N.Y., Jan. 26, 1931. [1; 7; 10; 11]

Severance, John Franklin, clergyman, b. Shelburne, Mass., 1817; d. Chicago, Ill., Jan. 19, 1898.

Severance, Mark Sibley, real estate operator, b. Cleveland, O., 1846; d. Princeton, N.J., Jan. 20, 1931. [51]

Sewall, Albert Cole, clergyman, b. Blue Hill, Me., 1845; d. Canandaigua, N.Y., Oct. 5, 1928. [63]

Sewall, Frank, clergyman, b. Bath, Me., 1837; d. Washington, D.C., Dec. 7, 1915. [1; 5; 10]

Sewall, Henry, physician, b. Winchester, Va., 1855; d. Denver, Colo., July 8, 1936. [10]

Sewall, John Smith, clergyman and educationist, b. New Castle, Me., 1830; d. Bangor, Me., Oct. 11, 1911. [10]

Sewall, Jonathan Mitchell, lawyer and poet, b. Salem, Mass., 1748; d. Portsmouth, N.H., March 29, 1808. [1; 3; 4; 6; 7; 9]

Sewall, Jotham, clergyman, b. 1791; d. 1884. [38]

Sewall, Jotham Bradbury, clergyman and educationist, b. New Castle, Me., 1825; d. Brookline, Mass., June 16, 1913. [4; 46]

Sewall, Mrs. May Eliza, née **Wright,** feminist, b. Milwaukee, Wis., 1844; d. Indianapolis, Ind., July 22, 1920. [1; 4; 5; 10]

Sewall, Oliver, local historian, d. 1861. [38]

Sewall, Rufus King, lawyer and historian, b. Edgecombe, Me., 1814; d. Wiscasset, Me., April 16, 1903. [3; 6; 10; 38]

Sewall, Samuel, clergyman, b. Marblehead, Mass., 1785; d. Burlington, Mass., Feb. 18, 1868. [3]

Sewall, Stephen, educationist, b. York, Me., 1734; d. Boston, Mass., July 23, 1804. [1; 3; 4; 5]

Sewall, Thomas, physician, b. Augusta, Me., 1786; d. Washington, D.C., April 10, 1845. [3; 6]

Seward, Frederick William, journalist and diplomat, b. Auburn, N.Y., 1830; d. April 25, 1915. [1; 3; 4; 5; 6; 10]

Seward, George Frederick, diplomat, b. Florida, N.Y., 1840; d. New York, N.Y., Nov. 28, 1910. [1; 10]

Seward, Josiah Lafayette, clergyman, b. Sullivan, N.H., 1845; d. 1917. [51]

Seward, Samuel Swayze, educationist, b. Wilmington, Del., 1876; d. Palo Alto, Calif., Aug. 27, 1932. [4; 10; 11]

Seward, Theodore Frelinghuysen, musician, b. Florida, N.Y., 1835; d. Orange, N.J., Aug. 30, 1902. [1; 3; 4; 5; 10]

Seward, William Foote, local historian, b. Yonkers, N.Y., 1853; d. Binghampton, N.Y., Aug. 28, 1928. [69]

Seward, William Henry, politician, b. Florida, N.Y., 1801; d. Auburn, N.Y., Oct. 10, 1872. [1; 2; 3; 4; 5; 6; 7]

Sewell, Cornelius Van Vorst, miscellaneous writer, d. Nov. 17, 1927. [48]

Sewell, Henry Fane, banker and poet, b. India; d. Vancouver, B.C., Oct. 5, 1944. [27]

Sewell, Jonathan, lawyer, b. Cambridge, Mass., 1766; d. Quebec, Lower Canada, Nov. 12, 1839. [27]

Sewell, William George Grant, journalist, b. Quebec, Lower Canada, 1829; d. Quebec, Que., 1862. [27]

Sexton, Samuel, physician, b. Xenia, O., 1833; d. New York, N.Y., July 11, 1896. [3]

Seybert, Adam, physician, b. Philadelphia, Pa., 1773; d. Paris, France, May 2, 1825. [1; 3; 4; 5; 6]

Seyffarth, Gustavus, archaeologist and theologian, b. Germany, 1796; d. New York, N.Y., Nov. 17, 1885. [1; 3; 6]

Seymour, Augustus Sherrill, jurist, b. Ithaca, N.Y., 1836; d. New York, N.Y., Feb. 19, 1897. [3]

Seymour, Charles C. B., journalist, b. London, England, 1829; d. New York, N.Y., May 2, 1869. [3; 6]

Seymour, E. Sandford, traveller, fl. 1849-1850.

Seymour, Frederick Henri, humorist, b. Waterbury, Conn., 1850; d. Detroit, Mich., July 28, 1913. [4]

Seymour, George Franklin, bishop, b. New York, N.Y., 1829; d. Springfield, Ill., Dec. 8, 1906. [1; 3; 4; 5; 10]

Seymour, Horatio, politician, b. Pompey Hill, N.Y., 1810; d. Utica, N.Y., Feb. 12, 1886. [1; 3; 4; 5; 6]

Seymour, Horatio Winslow, journalist, b. Cayuga county, N.Y., 1854; d. New York, N.Y., Dec. 17, 1920. [1; 4; 7; 10]

Seymour, James Cooke, clergyman, b. Ulster, Ireland, 1839; d. Paisley, Ont., Sept. 1, 1902. [27]

Seymour, Mrs. Mary Alice, née **Ives,** novelist. fl. 1857-1892. [6]

Seymour, Mrs. Mary Harrison, née **Browne,** writer of books for children, b. Oxford, Conn., 1835; d. Litchfield, Conn., June 26, 1913. [3; 4; 5; 6; 10]

Seymour, Robert Gillin, clergyman, b. New York, N.Y., 1841; d. 1913. [10]

Seymour, Silas, engineer, b. Stillwater, N.Y., 1817; d. New York, N.Y., July 15, 1890.

Seymour, Thomas Day, educationist, b. Hudson, O., 1848; d. New Haven, Conn., Dec. 31, 1907. [1; 4; 5; 7; 10]

Shackelford, John Cockrill, clergyman, b. 1829; d. 1918.

Shackleford, Thomas Mitchell, jurist, b. Fayetteville, Tenn., 1859; d. Tampa, Fla., Sept. 21, 1927. [4; 10; 34]

Shackleton, Robert, miscellaneous writer, b. Mazomanie, Wis., 1860; d. Hyères, France, Feb. 24, 1923. [4; 7; 10]

Shafer, Mrs. Sara, née **Andrew,** novelist, b. La Porte, Ind.; d. La Porte, Ind., Oct. 18, 1913. [7; 10]

Shaffer, Newton Melman, surgeon, b. Kinderhook, N.Y., 1846; d. New York, N.Y., Jan. 2, 1928. [4; 10]

Shaffner, Taliaferro Preston, inventor, b. Smithfield, Va., 1818; d. Troy, N.Y., Dec. 11, 1881. [3; 4; 6]

Shahan, Thomas Joseph, bishop, b. Manchester, N.H., 1857; d. Washington, D.C., March 9, 1932. [1; 4; 10; 21]

Shaler, Nathaniel Southgate, educationist, b. Newport, Ky., 1841; d. Cambridge, Mass., April 10, 1906. [1; 3; 4; 5; 6; 7; 10; 34; 74]

Shaler, William, sea-captain and consular agent, b. Bridgeport, Conn., 1773; d. Havana, Cuba, March 29, 1833. [1; 3; 4; 6]

Shambaugh, Benjamin Franklin, historian, b. Elvira, Ia., 1871; d. Iowa City, Ia., April 7, 1940. [7; 10; 11; 37]

Shane, Nevis (pseud.). See Shearer, Sonia M.

Shane, Susannah (pseud.). See Ashbrook, Harriette.

Shanks, David Carey, soldier, b. Salem, Va., 1861; d. Washington, D.C., April 10, 1940. [2a; 10]

Shanks, Lewis Piaget, educationist, b. Albany, N.Y., 1878; d. Baltimore, Md., Jan. 28, 1935. [10; 11]

Shanks, William Franklin Gore, journalist, b. Shelbyville, Ky., 1837; d. Brooklyn, N.Y., 1905. [3; 4; 5; 7; 34]

Shannon, Martha A., lecturer, b. 1848; d. New Haven, Conn., Oct. 24, 1938.

Shannon, Robert Thomas, lawyer, b. near Lobelville, Tenn., 1860; d. Nashville, Tenn., Sept. 6, 1931. [10; 11]

Shannon, William, anthologist, fl. 1852-1876. [27]

Shapley, Rufus Edmonds, lawyer, b. Carlisle, Pa., 1840; d. Philadelphia, Pa., 1906. [4; 10]

Sharkey, Mary Agnes, nun, b. Mauch Chunk, Pa., 1866; d. Elizabeth, N.J., Jan. 1, 1940. [21]

Sharp, Mrs. Abigail, née **Gardner,** frontierswoman, b. Seneca county, N.Y., 1843; d. 1921. [37; 70]

Sharp, Dallas Lore, naturalist, b. Haleyville, N.J., 1870; d. Hingham, Mass., Nov. 29, 1929. [1; 7; 10; 11; 15]

Sharp, Frank Chapman, educationist, b West Hoboken, N.J., 1866; d. Madison, Wis., May 4, 1943. [7; 10; 11; 14]

Sharp, Katharine Lucinda, librarian, b. Elgin, Ill., 1865; d. June 1, 1914. [1; 10]

Sharp, William Graves, diplomat, b. Mount Gilead, O., 1859; d. Elyria, O., Nov. 17, 1922. [1; 4; 10]

Sharpe, Henry Granville, soldier, b. Kingston, N.Y., 1858; d. Providence, R.I., July 13, 1947. [10]

Sharpe, William Carvosso, local historian and genealogist, b. 1839; d. Seymour, Conn., 1924.

Sharpe-Patterson, Mrs. Virginia. See Patterson, Mrs. Virginia, née Sharpe.

Sharples, Stephen Paschall, chemist, b. West Chester, Pa., 1842; d. Aug. 21, 1923. [10]

Sharpless, Isaac, educationist, b. Chester county, Pa., 1848; d. Haverford, Pa., Jan. 16, 1920. [1; 2; 4; 5; 7; 10]

Sharswood, George, jurist, b. Philadelphia, Pa., 1810; d. Philadelphia, Pa., May 28, 1883. [1; 3; 4; 5; 6]

Sharswood, William, educationist, b. 1836; d. Feb. 17, 1905.

Shastid, Thomas Hall, ophthalmologist and novelist, b. Pittsfield, Ill., 1866; d. Duluth, Minn., Feb. 15, 1947. [7; 10; 11]

Shatford, Allan Pearson, clergyman, b. St. Margaret's Bay, N.S., 1873; d. Nova Scotia, Aug. 16, 1935. [27]

Shattuck, Frederick Cheever, physician, b. Boston, Mass., 1847; d. Boston, Mass., Jan. 11, 1929. [1; 4; 10; 51]

Shattuck, George Burbank, geologist, b. Lowell, Mass., 1869; d. Glen Cove, Long Island, N.Y., July 7, 1934. [10; 13]

Shattuck, George Cheyne, physician, b. Templeton, Mass., 1783; d. Boston, Mass., March 18, 1854. [1; 3; 4; 5; 6]

Shattuck, Mrs. Harriette Lucy, née Robinson, law clerk, b. Lowell, Mass., 1850; d. March 22, 1937. [10; 11]

Shattuck, Lemuel, genealogist, b. Ashby, Mass., 1793; d. Boston, Mass., Jan. 17, 1859. [1; 3; 6]

Shaw, Adèle Marie, educationist, b. Concord, N.H., about 1865; d. Andover, Mass., Dec. 4, 1941. [11]

Shaw, Albert, journalist, b. Shandon, O., 1857; d. New York, N.Y., June 25, 1947. [4; 7; 10; 11]

Shaw, Anna Howard, reformer, b. Newcastle-upon-Tyne, England, 1847; d. Moylan, Pa., July 2, 1919. [1; 10]

Shaw, Avery Albert, educationist, b. South Berwick, N.S., 1870; d. Claremont, Calif., March 17, 1949. [10]

Shaw, Charles, lawyer, b. Bath, Me., 1782; d. Montgomery, Ala., 1828. [3; 6]

Shaw, Charles Gray, philosopher, b. Elizabeth, N.J., 1871; d. Spring Lake, N.J., July 28, 1949. [10]

Shaw, Cornelia Rebekah, librarian, b. 1869; d. Davidson, N.C., 1936. [11]

Shaw, Edward Richard, educationist, b. Bellport, N.Y., 1850; d. Yonkers, N.Y., Feb. 11, 1903. [1; 10]

Shaw, Henry Wheeler, humorist, b. Lanesboro, Mass., 1818; d. Monterey, Calif., Oct. 14, 1885. [1; 2; 3; 4; 5; 6; 7; 9]

Shaw, Howard Burton, electrical engineer, b. Winslow, Me., 1869; d. Raleigh, N.C., Dec. 15, 1943. [10]

Shaw, John Balcom, clergyman and educationist, b. Bellport, N.Y., 1860; d. Keene Valley, N.Y., Aug. 28, 1935. [10]

Shaw, Leslie Mortier, banker and politician, b. Morristown, Vt., 1848; d. Washington, D.C., March 28, 1932. [1; 4; 5; 10; 11; 37]

Shaw, Marloy Alexander, educationist, b. 1867; d. Iowa City, Ia., Dec. 1, 1929. [27]

Shaw, Ralph Henry, poet, b. 1860; d. Lowell, Mass., June 15, 1937.

Shaw, Stephen Chester, local historian, b. 1808; d. 1891.

Shaw, Thomas, agricultural expert, b. Niagara, Ont., 1843; d. St. Paul, Minn., 1918. [1; 31a; 70]

Shaw, William, social worker, b. 1860; d. Santa Monica, Calif., Dec. 4, 1941.

Shawkey, Morris Purdy, educationist, b. Sigel, Pa., 1868; d. Charleston, W. Va., Feb. 6, 1941. [7; 10; 11]

Shea, George, jurist, b. Cork, Ireland, 1826; d. New York, N.Y., Jan. 15, 1895. [3]

Shea, John Augustus, journalist and poet, b. Cork, Ireland, 1802; d. New York, N.Y., Aug. 15, 1845. [3; 6; 7]

Shea, John Dawson Gilmary, historian, b. New York, N.Y., 1824; d. Elizabeth, N.J., Feb. 22, 1892. [1; 2; 3; 4; 5; 6; 7; 9; 21]

Sheahan, James Washington, journalist, b. 1824; d. 1883. [6]

Sheard, Mrs. Virginia, née Stanton, novelist and poet, b. Cobourg, Ont.; d. Toronto, Ont., Feb. 22, 1943. [27]

Sheard, Virna (pseud.). See Sheard, Mrs. Virginia, née Stanton.

Shearer, James William, clergyman, b. 1840; d. 1941.

Shearer, John Bunyan, educationist, b. Appomattox county, Va., 1832; d. Davidson, N.C., June 14, 1918. [10; 34]

Shearer, John Sanford, physicist, b. New York, N.Y., 1865; d. Ithaca, N.Y., May, 1922. [10; 13]

Shearer, Sonia M., novelist, d. Oct. 9, 1934.

Shearin, Hubert Gibson, educationist, b. near Danville, Ky., 1878; d. Eagle Rock City, Calif., Aug. 11, 1919. [10; 62]

Shearman, Thomas Gaskell, lawyer and economist, b. Birmingham, England, 1834; d. Brooklyn, N.Y., Sept. 29, 1900. [1; 3; 4; 5; 6; 10]

Sheatsley, Clarence Valentine, clergyman, b. Paris, O., 1873; d. Columbus, O., Jan. 19, 1943. [10]

Shecut, John Linnaeus Edward Whitridge, physician, botanist, and novelist, b. Beaufort, S.C., 1770; d. Charleston, S.C., June 1, 1836. [1; 3; 7; 34]

Shedd, George Clifford, novelist, b. Ashland, Neb., 1877; d. Los Angeles, Calif., Jan. 8, 1937. [7; 10; 59]

Shedd, Mrs. Julia Ann, née Clark, writer on art, b. Newport, Me., 1834; d. April 7, 1897. [3; 4; 6]

Shedd, Solon, geologist, b. Illinois, 1860, d. Stanford University, Calif., March 4, 1941. [10; 11; 13]

Shedd, William Ambrose, missionary, b. Persia, 1865; d. Sain Kala, Persian Kurdistan, Aug. 7, 1918. [1]

Shedd, William Greenough Thayer, theologian, b. Acton, Mass., 1820; d. New York, N.Y., Nov. 17, 1894. [1; 3; 4; 5; 6; 7; 9]

Sheedy, Morgan Madden, priest, b. Ireland, 1853; d. Altoona, Pa., Oct. 25, 1939. [4; 11; 21]

Sheehan, Perley Poore, journalist, novelist, and playwright, b. Cincinnati, O., 1875; d. Sierra Madre, Calif., Oct. 1, 1943. [7; 10; 11]

Sheerin, James, clergyman, b. Scotland, 1865; d. Bucyrus, O., Dec. 24, 1933. [10]

Shelby, Mrs. Gertrude Mathews, née Singleton, journalist and novelist, b. Momence, Ill., 1881; d. Venice, Fla., Nov. 1, 1936. [7; 10]

Sheldon, Addison Erwin, historian, b. Sheldon, Minn., 1861; d. Lincoln, Neb., Nov. 24, 1943. [7; 10; 11]

Sheldon, Arthur Frederick, educationist, b. Vernon, Mich., 1868; d. Dec. 21, 1935. [10]

DICTIONARY OF NORTH AMERICAN AUTHORS

411

Sheldon, Caroline, educationist, b. Potsdam, N.Y., 1860; d. Grinnell, Ia., June 16, 1929. [10; 11]

Sheldon, Charles, explorer and hunter, b. Rutland, Vt., 1867; d. Kedgemakooge, N.S., Sept. 21, 1928. [10; 62]

Sheldon, Charles Monroe, clergyman and novelist, b. Wellsville, N.Y., 1857; d. Topeka, Kans., Feb. 24, 1946. [7; 10]

Sheldon, David Newton, clergyman, b. Suffield, Conn., 1807; d. Waterville, Me., Oct. 4, 1889. [4]

Sheldon, Edward Austin, educationist, b. near Perry Center, N.Y., 1823; d. Oswego, N.Y., Aug. 26, 1897. [1; 3; 4; 6]

Sheldon, Edward Brewster, playwright, b. Chicago, Ill., 1886; d. New York, N.Y., April 1, 1946. [7]

Sheldon, Edward Stevens, philologist, b. Waterville, Me., 1851; d. Cambridge, Mass., Oct. 16, 1925. [1; 4; 5; 7; 10]

Sheldon, Mrs. Electa Maria, née Bronson, historian, b. Genessee county, N.Y., 1817; d. Detroit, Mich., 1902. [39]

Sheldon, George, local historian, b. Deerfield, Mass., 1818; d. Deerfield, Mass., Dec. 23, 1916. [4]

Sheldon, George William, writer of books on art, b. Summerville, S.C., 1843; d. Summit, N.J., Jan. 29, 1914. [3; 6; 10; 34]

Sheldon, Mrs. Georgie (pseud.). See Downs, Mrs. Sarah Elizabeth, née Forbush.

Sheldon, Grace Carew, journalist, b. Buffalo, N.Y., 1855; d. ? [5; 10]

Sheldon, Henry Clay, clergyman, b. Martinsburg, N.Y., 1845; d. West Newton, Mass., Aug. 4, 1928. [3; 5; 10; 11; 62]

Sheldon, Henry Newton, jurist, b. Waterville, Me., 1843; d. Boston, Mass., Jan. 14, 1926. [1; 4; 10; 51]

Sheldon, Mary Downing. See Barnes, Mrs. Mary Downing, née Sheldon.

Sheldon, Samuel, electrical engineer, b. Middlebury, Vt., 1862; d. Brooklyn, N.Y., Sept. 4, 1920. [4; 10]

Sheldon, Stewart, clergyman, b. 1823; d. 1912.

Sheldon, Theodore, lawyer, b. Plainfield, N.J., 1853; d. Chicago, Ill., May 25, 1905. [4]

Sheldon, Walter Lorenzo, religious teacher, b. West Rutland, N.Y., 1858; d. St. Louis, Mo., June 5, 1907. [1; 5; 7; 10]

Sheldon, Winthrop Dudley, educationist, b. Raymond, N.H., 1839; d. Germantown, Pa., Jan. 19, 1931. [10; 62]

Shelford, Melvia Thomas, clergyman, b. Chemung county, N.Y., 1873; d. Westfield, N.J., Sept. 15, 1941.

Shelley, A. Fishe (pseud.). See Gerard, James Watson.

Shelly, Percy Van Dyke, educationist, b. Philadelphia, Pa., 1883; d. Philadelphia, Pa., June 26, 1943. [14]

Shelton, Albert Leroy, missionary, b. Indianapolis, Ind., 1875; d. near Batang, Tibet, Feb. 17, 1922. [1]

Shelton, Don Odell, evangelist, b. Odessa, N.Y., 1868; d. Briarcliffe Manor, N.Y., Jan. 29, 1941. [7; 10]

Shelton, Frederick William, clergyman, b. Jamaica, Long Island, N.Y., 1815; d. Carthage Landing, N.Y., June 20, 1881. [1; 3; 4; 6; 7; 9]

Shelton, Jane de Forest, historian, b. Derby, Conn.; d. Derby, Conn., 1914. [10]

Shelton, Louise, horticulturist, d. Morristown, N.J., March 26, 1934. [10]

Shelton, Mason Bradford, pioneer, b. 1838; d. Larkinsville, Ala., ?

Shelton, William Henry, painter, b. Ontario county, N.Y., 1840; d. Morristown, N.J., March 15, 1912. [5; 7; 10]

Shenton, Herbert Newhard, sociologist, b. Pottstown, Pa., 1884; d. New York, N.Y., Jan. 7, 1937. [10]

Shepard, Charles Edward, lawyer, b. Dansville, N.Y., 1848; d. Spokane, Wash., March 31, 1928. [10; 62]

Shepard, Charles Upham, mineralogist, b. Little Compton, R.I., 1804; d. Charleston, S.C., May 1, 1886. [1; 3; 4; 6]

Shepard, Edward Martin, geologist, b. West Winsted, Conn., 1854; d. Springfield, Mo., April 28, 1934. [4; 10; 11]

Shepard, Edward Morse, lawyer, b. New York, N.Y., 1850; d. Lake George, N.Y., July 28, 1911. [1; 4; 10]

Shepard, Elihu Hotchkiss, educationist, b. 1795; d. 1876.

Shepard, Elizabeth G., journalist, b. Boston, Mass.; d. Reservoir, Mass., April 4, 1899. [3b]

Shepard, Frank Hartson, musician, b. Bethel, Conn., 1863; d. Orange, N.J., 1913.

Shepard, George, clergyman, b. 1801; d. Amherst, Mass., Dec. 12, 1868. [4; 6]

Shepard, Isaac Fitzgerald, soldier and poet, b. South Natick, Mass., 1816; d. Bellingham, Mass., Aug. 25, 1889. [3; 5; 7]

Shepard, James, historian, b. 1838; d. Feb. 15, 1926.

Shepard, James Henry, chemist, b. Lyons, Mich., 1850; d. St. Petersburg, Fla., Feb. 21, 1918. [1; 4; 10]

Shepard, Morgan, writer of books for children, b. Brooklyn, N.Y., 1865; d. New York, N.Y., May 16, 1947. [11]

Shepard, Seth, jurist, b. Washington county, Tex., 1847; d. Washington, D.C., Dec. 3, 1917. [4; 10]

Shepard, Thomas Griffin, musician, b. Madison, Conn., 1848; d. Brooklyn, N.Y., 1905.

Shepardson, Daniel, clergyman, b. Granville, O., 1868; d. Honolulu, Hawaii, Nov. 5, 1905. [62]

Shepardson, Francis Wayland, educationist, b. Cincinnati, O., 1862; d. Pataskala, O., Aug. 9, 1937. [10; 62]

Shepardson, George Defrees, engineer, b. Cheviot, O., 1864; d. Minneapolis, Minn., May 26, 1926. [4; 10; 11]

Shepherd, Dorothea Alice (pseud.). See Pratt, Mrs. Ella Ann, née Farman.

Shepherd, Henry Elliot, educationist, b. Fayetteville, N.C., 1844; d. Baltimore, Md., May 29, 1929. [5; 10; 11; 34]

Shepherd, Thomas James, clergyman, d. Glenwood, Md., Dec. 1, 1898. [6]

Shepherd, William Gunn, journalist, b. Springfield, O., 1878; d. Washington, D.C., Nov. 4, 1933. [10]

Shepherd, William Robert, educationist, b. Charleston, S.C., 1871; d. Berlin, Germany, June 7, 1934. [1a; 10]

Sheppard, Edmund Ernest, journalist, b. Elgin county, Ont., 1855; d. California, Nov. 6, 1924. [27]

Sheppard, Furman, lawyer, b. Bridgeton, N.J., 1823; d. Philadelphia, Pa., Nov. 3, 1893. [3; 6]

Sheppard, George, journalist, b. Newark-on-Trent, England, 1819; d. Jamaica Plain, Mass., 1912. [27]

Sheppard, John Hannibal, lawyer and biographer, b. Cirencester, England, 1789; d. Boston, Mass., June 25, 1873.

Sheppard, Nathan, journalist and lecturer, b. Baltimore, Md., 1834; d. New York, N.Y., Jan. 24, 1888. [3; 6; 7]

Sheppard, Robert Dickinson, clergyman, b. Chicago, Ill., 1846; d. Spokane, Wash., May 15, 1933. [4]

Shepperson, Alfred, merchant, b. Virginia, 1837; d. New York, N.Y., Nov. 20, 1911.

Sheran, William Henry, priest and educationist, d. Chicago, Ill., 1923. [21]

Sheraton, James Paterson, clergyman and educationist, b. Saint John, N.B., 1841; d. Toronto, Ont., Jan. 24, 1906. [27]

Sherburne, Andrew, sailor, b. Rye, N.H., 1765; d. Augusta, Oneida county, N.Y., 1831. [3; 6]

Sherburne, John Henry, miscellaneous writer, b. Portsmouth, N.H., 1794; d. Europe, about 1850. [3; 6; 7]

Sheridan, Philip Henry, soldier, b. Albany, N.Y., 1831; d. Nonquitt, Mass., Aug. 5, 1888. [1; 2; 3; 4; 5; 7; 21]

Sheridan, Wilbur Fletcher, clergyman, b. Rossville, Ind., 1863; d. Evanston, Ill., March 10, 1920. [10]

Sherlock (pseud.). See Southwick, Solomon.

Sherlock, Chesla Clella, journalist, b. Keswick, Ia., 1895; d. near Cortland, N.Y., July 1, 1938. [10; 11]

Sherman, Andrew Magoun, clergyman, b. Marshfield, Mass., 1844; d. Morristown, N.J., Dec. 28, 1921. [10]

Sherman, Charles Pomeroy, lawyer, b. Brooklyn, N.Y., 1847; d. Atlantic City, N.J., Jan. 21, 1944.

Sherman, David, clergyman, b. New Lebanon, N.Y., 1822; d. Brooklyn, Mass., Aug. 14, 1897. [60]

Sherman, Edgar Jay, lawyer and politician, b. 1834; d. 1914.

Sherman, Edwin Allen, soldier, b. 1829; d. 1914.

Sherman, Eleazer, minister, b. 1795; d. ?

Sherman, Francis Joseph, poet, b. Fredericton, N.B., 1871; d. Atlantic City. N.J., June 15, 1926. [27]

Sherman, Frank Dempster, poet, genealogist, and educationist, b. Peekskill, N.Y., 1860; d. New York, N.Y., Sept. 19, 1916. [1; 4; 5; 7; 9; 10]

Sherman, Frederic Fairchild, art connoisseur, b. 1874; d. Westport, Conn., Oct. 23, 1940. [7]

Sherman, George Henry, physician, b. Napoleon, O., 1858; d. Melbourne, Fla., April 19, 1932. [39]

Sherman, Henry, lawyer, b. Albany, N.Y., 1808; d. Washington, D.C., March 28, 1879. [3; 6; 62]

Sherman, John, clergyman, b. New Haven, Conn., 1772; d. Trenton Falls, N.Y., Aug. 2, 1828. [3; 6]

Sherman, John, politician, b. Lancaster, O., 1823; d. Washington, D.C., Oct. 22, 1900. [1; 2; 3; 4; 5; 10]

Sherman, Lewis, physician, b. 1844; d. Milwaukee, Wis., July 2, 1915.

Sherman, Lucius Adelno, educationist, b. Douglas, Mass., 1847; d. Lincoln, Neb., Feb. 13, 1933. [4; 7; 10; 11; 62]

Sherman, Mrs. Mary Belle, née King, club woman, b. Albion, N.Y.; d. Washington, D.C., Jan. 15, 1935. [10]

Sherman, Merritt Masters, stockman, b. Salem, N.Y., 1854; d. Crawford, Kans., June 12, 1937. [10]

Sherman, Philemon Tecumseh, lawyer, b. St. Louis, Mo., 1867; d. New York, N.Y., Dec. 6, 1941. [10; 62]

Sherman, Samuel Sterling, nonagenarian, b. 1815; d. 1914.

Sherman, Stuart Pratt, literary critic, b. Anita, Ia., 1881; d. Dunewood, Mich., Aug. 21, 1926. [1; 4; 7; 10; 11]

Sherman, Thomas Townsend, genealogist, b. London, England, 1853; d. London, England, Aug. 27, 1931. [62]

Sherman, William Tecumseh, soldier, b. Lancaster, O., 1820; d. New York, N.Y., Feb. 14, 1891. [1; 2; 3; 4; 5; 6; 7]

Shero, William Francis, clergyman, b. Fredonia, N.Y., 1863; d. Greensburg, Pa., May 12, 1943. [10; 11]

Sherrill, Charles Hitchcock, diplomat, b. Washington, D.C., 1867; d. Paris, France, June 25, 1936. [4; 7; 10; 11; 62]

Sherrill, Hunting, physician, b. 1783; d. 1866.

Sherwell, Guillermo Antonio, educationist, b. Mexico, 1878; d. Washington, D.C., July 7, 1926. [10]

Sherwell, Samuel, physician, b. 1841; d. Brooklyn, N.Y., Dec. 21, 1927.

Sherwin, Thomas, educationist, b. Westmoreland, N.H., 1799; d. Boston, Mass., July 23, 1869. [1; 3; 4; 6]

Sherwood, Adiel, clergyman, b. Fort Edward, N.Y., 1791; d. St. Louis, Mo., Aug. 18, 1879. [1; 3; 4; 5; 7; 34]

Sherwood, Andrew, geologist, b. Mansfield, Pa., 1848; d. Portland, Ore., Oct. 31, 1933. [10]

Sherwood, Elisha Barber, clergyman, b. 1810; d. St. Joseph, Mo., Aug. 19, 1905.

Sherwood, Frederick Augustus, business agent, b. Ottawa, Ill., 1881; d. Guatemala City, Guatemala, Sept. 29, 1938. [62]

Sherwood, Henry Hall, physician, d. 1847. [6]

Sherwood, Isaac Ruth, soldier and politician, b. Stanford, N.Y., 1835; d. Toledo, O., Oct. 15, 1935. [1; 4; 5; 7; 10]

Sherwood, James Manning, clergyman, b. Fishkill, N.Y., 1814; d. Brooklyn, N.Y., Oct. 22, 1890. [3; 6]

Sherwood, John D., lawyer, b. Fishkill, N.Y., 1818; d. Englewood, N.J., April 30, 1891. [3; 62]

Sherwood, Mrs. Katharine Margaret, née **Brownlee,** reformer, b. Poland, O., 1841; d. Washington, D.C., Feb. 15, 1914. [1; 4; 5; 7; 10]

Sherwood, Mrs. Mary Elizabeth, née **Wilson,** miscellaneous writer, b. Keene, N.H., 1826; d. New York, N.Y., Sept. 12, 1903. [1; 3; 4; 5; 6; 7; 9; 10]

Sherwood, Robert Edmund, publisher, b. St. Clairsville, O., 1864; d. Brooklyn, N.Y., March 9, 1946.

Sherwood, Sidney, educationist, b. Saratoga county, N.Y., 1860; d. Ballston, N.Y., Aug. 6, 1901. [10]

Sherwood, Thomas Adiel, jurist, b. Eatonton, Ga., 1834; d. California, Nov. 11, 1918. [1; 4; 5; 10]

Shetter, Mrs. Stella, née **Cross,** writer of books for children, b. Butler county, Pa., 1880; d. Clarksburg, W. Va., Dec. 31, 1936. [10; 11]

Shew, Joel, physician, b. Saratoga county, N.Y., 1816; d. Oyster Bay, N.Y., Oct. 6, 1855. [3; 6]

Shibley, Fred Warner, industrialist, b. Canada, 1864; d. New York, N.Y., March 1, 1944.

Shields, Charles Woodruff, clergyman and educationist, b. New Albany, Ind., 1825; d. Newport, R.I., Aug. 26, 1904. [1; 3; 4; 5; 6; 7; 10]

Shields, George Oliver, naturalist, b. Batavia, O., 1846; d. New York, N.Y., Nov. 11, 1925. [7; 9; 10; 11]

Shields, Joseph Dunbar, historian, b. 1820; d. 1886. [34]

Shields, Mrs. Sarah Annie, née **Frost.** See Frost, Sarah Annie.

Shields, Thomas Edward, priest and educationist, b. near Mendota, Minn., 1862; d. Washington, D.C., Feb. 15, 1921. [1; 10; 21]

Shiells, Robert, clergyman, b. 1825; d. 1908.

Shillaber, Benjamin Penhallow, journalist, poet, and humorist, b. Portsmouth, N.H., 1814; d. Chelsea, Mass., Nov. 25, 1890. [1; 3; 4; 7; 9]

Shimmeal, Richard Cunningham, clergyman, b. New York, N.Y., 1803; d. New York, N.Y., March 19, 1874. [3; 6]

Shimmell, Lewis Slifer, educationist, b. 1852; d. Harrisburg, Pa., March 9, 1914.

Shindler, Mrs. Mary Stanley Bunce, née **Palmer,** poet, b. Beaufort, S.C., 1810; d. Shelbyville, Ky., 1883. [3; 6; 7; 42; 74]

Shinn, Asa, clergyman, b. 1781; d. Brattleboro, Vt., Feb. 11, 1853. [1; 3; 6; 7]

Shinn, Charles Howard, forester, b. Austin, Tex., 1852; d. Ukiah, Calif., Dec. 2, 1924. [4; 10]

Shinn, Earl, art critic, b. Philadelphia, Pa., 1837; d. 1886. [6]

Shinn, Mrs. Florence, née **Scovel,** illustrator and lecturer, b. Camden, N.J.; d. New York, N.Y., Oct. 17, 1940. [7; 10]

Shinn, George Wolfe, clergyman, b. Philadelphia, Pa., 1839; d. 1910. [3; 4; 5; 6; 10]

Shinn, Josiah Hazen, educationist, b. 1849; d. 1917. [34]

Shinn, Milicent Washburn, psychologist, b. Niles, Calif., 1858; d. Alameda county, Calif., Aug. 13, 1940. [10; 11; 35]

Shipley, Frederick William, educationist, b. Cheltenham, Ont., 1871; d. St. Louis, Mo., Feb. 11, 1945. [4; 10; 11]

Shipley, Mrs. Marie Adelaide, née **Brown,** historian, b. 1843; d. 1900.

Shipley, Maynard, scientist, b. Baltimore, Md., 1872; d. California, June 18, 1934. [10]

Shipman, Benjamin Jonson, lawyer, b. East Haddam, Conn., 1853; d. Seattle, Wash., Sept. 3, 1915. [10; 62; 70]

Shipman, George Elias, physician, b. New York, N.Y, 1820; d. Chicago, Ill., 1893. [3]

Shipman, Louis Evan, playwright, b. Brooklyn, N.Y., 1869; d. France, Aug. 2, 1933. [7; 10]

Shipman, Samuel, playwright, b. New York, N.Y., 1883; d. New York, N.Y., Feb. 9, 1937. [7; 10]

Shipp, Albert Micajah, clergyman, b. Stokes county, N.C., 1819; d. Cleveland Springs, N.C., June 27, 1887. [1; 3; 4; 5; 34]

Shipp, Bernard, poet and historian, b. near Natchez, Miss., 1813; d. ? [3; 5; 6; 10; 34]

Shippee, Lester Burrell, historian, b. East Greenwich, R.I., 1879; d. Palm Beach, Fla., Feb. 9, 1944. [7; 10]

Shippen, Edward, naval surgeon, b. New Jersey, 1826; d. Philadelphia, Pa., June 16, 1911. [3; 4; 6; 10]

Shippey, Josiah, poet, b. near New Brunswick, N.J., 1778; d. ? [19]

Shiras, Alexander, clergyman, b. 1813; d. 1894. [6]

Shiras, George, naturalist, b. Allegheny, Pa., 1859; d. Marquette, Mich., March 24, 1942. [10; 62]

Shiras, Oliver Perry, jurist, b. Pittsburgh, Pa., 1833; d. Dubuque, Ia., Jan. 7, 1916. [1; 5; 10]

Shirley, John Major, lawyer, b. Sanbornton, N.H., 1831; d. Andover, N.H., May 21, 1887. [3]

Shirley, Penn (pseud.). See Clarke, Sarah J.

Shock, William Henry, naval engineer, b. Baltimore, Md., 1821; d. ? [3; 4; 10]

Shoemaker, Jacob W., educationist, b. 1842; d. 1880.

Shoemaker, Mrs. J. W. See Shoemaker, Mrs. Rachel Walter, née Hinkle.

Shoemaker, John Vietch, physician, b. Chambersburg, Pa., 1852; d. Philadelphia, Pa., Oct. 11, 1910. [4; 10]

Shoemaker, Michael Myers, traveller, b. Covington, Ky., 1853; d. Paris, France, Aug. 11, 1924. [10]

Shoemaker, Mrs. Rachel Walter, née Hinkle, elocutionist, b. Plumstead, Pa., 1838; d. Wayne, Pa., Feb. 1, 1915. [10]

Shorey, Paul, educationist, b. Davenport, Ia., 1857; d. April 24, 1934. [1; 4; 7; 10; 11]

Shorey, Samuel Fernald, bookseller, d. Seattle, Wash., Feb. 19, 1932.

Short, Edward Lyman, lawyer, d. July 30, 1905.

Short, John Thomas, educationist, b. Galin, O., 1850; d. Columbus, O., Nov. 11, 1883. [5; 6]

Short, Josephine Helena, traveller, b. Urbana, Ill.; d. ? [10]

Short-and-Fat, Sampson (pseud.). See Kettell, Samuel.

Shortfield, Luke (pseud.). See Jones, John Beauchamp.

Shortt, Adam, economist and historian, b. near London, Ont., 1859; d. Ottawa, Ont., Jan. 14, 1931. [27]

Shotwell, Walter Gaston, jurist and historian, b. Cadiz, O., 1856; d. Cadiz, O., March 11, 1938. [62]

Shoup, Francis Asbury, soldier, educationist, and clergyman, b. Laurel, Ind., 1834; d. Columbia, Tenn., Sept. 4, 1896. [1; 3; 5; 6; 34]

Showalter, Anthony Johnson, musician, b. Rockingham county, Va., 1858; d. Chattanooga, Tenn., Sept. 15, 1924. [10]

Showalter, Noah David, educationist, b. Cass county, Neb., 1869; d. Olympia, Wash., Aug. 4, 1937. [10]

Showerman, Grant, educationist. b. Brookfield, Wis., 1870; d. Madison, Wis., Nov. 13, 1935. [1a; 7; 10; 11; 44]

Shrady, George Frederick, physician, b. New York, N.Y., 1837; d. New. York, N.Y., Nov. 30, 1907. [1; 4; 5; 10]

Shrady, John, physician, b. 1830; d. Nov. 16, 1914. [4]

Shreve, Charles J., clergyman, b. Lunenburg, N.S., 1808; d. Halifax, N.S., 1878. [27]

Shreve, Samuel Henry, engineer, b. Trenton, N.J., 1829; d. New York, N.Y., Nov. 27, 1884. [3; 6]

Shreve, Thomas Hopkins, journalist, b. Alexandria, Va., 1808; d. Louisville, Ky., Dec. 23, 1853; [1; 3; 6; 7; 34]

Shriner, Charles Anthony, journalist, b. Cincinnati, O., 1853; d. Paterson, N.J., March 26, 1945. [11]

Shriver, John Shultz, journalist, b. Baltimore, Md., 1857; d. Washington, D.C., April 11, 1915. [10]

Shuck, Henrietta Hall, missionary, b. Kilmarnock, Va., 1817; d. Hong Kong, China, Nov. 27, 1844. [3; 34]

Shuck, John Lewis, missionary, b. Alexandria, Va., 1812; d. Barnwell, S.C., Aug. 20, 1863. [1; 3; 34]

Shuck, Oscar Tully, lawyer, b. Hong Kong, China, 1843; d. 1905. [35]

Shuey, Edwin Longstreet, welfare worker, b. Cincinnati, O., 1857; d. Dayton, O., Sept. 27, 1924. [1; 4; 10]

Shuey, Mrs. Lillian, née Hinman, poet and novelist, b. Toulon, Ill., 1853; d. July 18, 1921. [35]

Shufeldt, Robert Wilson, army surgeon and naturalist, b. New York, N.Y., 1850; d. 1934. [10; 11]

Shuffle, Rube (pseud.). See Heaton, Augustus Goodyear.

Shumaker, Elmer Ellsworth, clergyman, b. Muncy, Pa., 1862; d. Blakely, Pa., Nov. 21, 1936. [10; 62]

Shuman, Edwin Llewellyn, journalist, b. Lancaster county, Pa., 1863; d. Yonkers, N.Y., Dec. 13, 1941. [4; 7; 10; 11]

Shumway, Edgar Solomon, educationist, b. Belchertown, Mass., 1856; d. Brooklyn, N.Y., April 18, 1928. [10; 11; 45]

Shunk, William Findlay, civil engineer, b. Harrisburg, Pa., 1830; d. 1907. [10]

Shupe, Henry Fox, clergyman, b. near Scottdale, Pa., 1860; d. Oct. 13, 1926. [10; 11]

Shurly, Ernest Alonzo, physician, b. Buffalo, N.Y., 1845; d. 1913. [39]

Shurtleff, Ernest Warburton, clergyman and poet, b. Boston, Mass., 1862; d. Paris, France, Aug., 1917. [10]

Shurtleff, Harold Robert, historian, b. Concord, N.H., 1883; d. Dec. 6, 1938. [51]

Shurtleff, Nathaniel Bradstreet, antiquary, b. Boston, Mass., 1810; d. Boston, Mass., Oct. 17, 1874. [1; 3; 4; 5; 6; 7]

Shute, Daniel Kerfoot, physician, b. Alexandria, Va., 1858; d. Washington, D.C., Oct. 21, 1935. [10]

Shute, Henry Augustus, jurist and writer of books for boys, b. Exeter, N.H., 1856; d. Exeter, N.H., Jan. 25, 1943. [7; 10; 11]

Shute, Samuel Moore, educationist, b. Philadelphia, Pa., 1823; d. Kerfoot, Va., April 15, 1902. [3; 6; 10]

Shutter, Marion Daniel, clergyman, b. New Philadelphia, Pa., 1853; d. Minneapolis, Minn., Aug. 31, 1939. [10; 70]

Sibert, William Luther, military engineer, b. Gadsden, Ala., 1860; d. Bowling Green, Ky., Oct. 16, 1942. [1a; 4; 10]

Sibley, Edwin Day, lawyer, b. Boston, Mass., 1857; d. Somerville, Mass., March 1, 1927. [51]

Sibley, Frederick Hubbard, educationist, b. Oxford, Mass., 1872; d. Reno, Nev., April 2, 1941. [10; 11]

Sbiley, Hiram Luther, lawyer, b. Trumbull county, O., 1836; d. Marietta, O., Nov. 5, 1920. [10]

Sibley, John Langdon, librarian, b. Union, Me., 1804; d. Cambridge, Mass., Dec. 9, 1885. [1; 3; 4; 5; 6; 7; 51]

Sibley, William Giddings, journalist, b. Racine, O., 1860; d. Jan. 30, 1935. [10; 11]

Sickels, Daniel Edgar, freemason, b. New York, N.Y., 1825; d. May 2, 1914. [1; 5; 6; 10]

Sickels, David Banks, diplomat and poet, b. New York, N.Y., 1837; d. Paterson, N.J., July 19, 1918. [4; 10]

Sickels, Ivin, educationist, b. Nyack, N.Y., 1853; d. Nyack, N.Y., Aug. 5, 1943. [10; 13]

Siddall, John MacAlpine, journalist, b. Oberlin, O., 1874; d. Ardsley, N.Y., July 16, 1923. [4; 10]

Sidis, Boris, pyschophathologist, b. Kiev, Russia, 1867; d. Portsmouth, N.H., Oct. 24, 1923. [1; 10; 51]

Sidney, Algernon (pseud.). See Granger, Gideon.

Sidney, Margaret (pseud.). See Lothrop, Mrs. Harriett Mulford, née Stone.

Siebel, John Ewald, chemist, b. Germany, 1845; d. Chicago, Ill., Dec. 20, 1919. [10]

Siegvolk, Paul (pseud.). See Mathews, Albert.

Siff, Henry, physician, b. Kovno, Russia, 1863; d. New York, N.Y., June 19, 1939.

Sigma (pseud.). See Sargent, Lucius Manlius.

Sigman, James Garfield, educationist, b. Elverson, Pa., 1881; d. Philadelphia, Pa., Sept. 14, 1940.

Sigmund, Jay G., poet, b. Waubeck, Ia., 1885; d. Waubeck, Ia., Oct. 19, 1937. [7; 10; 11]

Sigourney, Mrs. Lydia Howard, née Huntley, poet and miscellaneous writer, b. Norwich, Conn., 1791; d. Hartford, Conn., June 10, 1865. [1; 2; 3; 4; 5; 6; 7; 8; 9; 71]

Sigsbee, Charles Dwight, naval officer, b. Albany, N.Y., 1845; d. New York, N.Y., July 19, 1923. [1; 4; 5; 10]

Sihler, Ernest Gottlieb, educationist, b. Fort Wayne, Ind., 1853; d. Mount Vernon, N.Y., Jan. 7, 1942. [7; 10; 11]

Sikes, Enoch Walter, educationist, b. Union county, N.C., 1868; d. Clemson, S.C., Jan. 8, 1941. [7; 10; 34]

Sikes, Mrs. Olive, née **Logan.** See Logan, Mrs. Olive, née Logan.

Sikes, William Wirt, journalist, b. Watertown, N.Y., 1836; d. Cardiff, Wales, Aug. 18, 1883. [1; 3; 5; 6; 7]

Silber, William Beinhauer, educationist, b. New York, N.Y., 1826; d. New York, N.Y., May 5, 1906. [4; 60]

Sill, Edward Rowland, poet, b. Windsor, Conn., 1841; d. Cleveland, O., Feb. 27, 1887. [1; 3; 4; 5; 6; 7; 9; 34; 71]

Sill, Frederick Schroeder, clergyman, d. 1919.

Sill, John Mahelm Berry, educationist, b. Black Rock, N.Y., 1831; d. Detroit, Mich., April 6, 1901. [3; 4; 6; 10]

Silliman, Augustus Ely, banker, b. Newport, R.I., 1807; d. Brooklyn, N.Y., May 30, 1884. [3; 4; 5; 6]

Silliman, Benjamin, educationist, b. Trumbull, Conn., 1779; d. New Haven, Conn., Nov. 24, 1864. [1; 2; 3; 4; 5; 6; 9; 62]

Silliman, Benjamin, chemist, b. New Haven, Conn., 1816; d. New Haven, Conn., Jan. 14, 1885. [1; 3; 4; 5; 6; 62]

Silloway, Thomas William, architect, b. Newburyport, Mass., 1828; d. 1910. [3; 6; 10]

Sills, Milton, actor, b. Chicago, Ill., 1882; d. Santa Monica, Calif., Sept. 15, 1930. [1; 10]

Silsbee, Mrs. Marianne Cabot, née Devereux, anthologist, b. 1812; d. 1889. [6]

Silver, John Arthur, historian, b. Harford county, Md., 1863; d. Geneva, N.Y., Feb. 5, 1916. [69]

Silvernail, William Henry, lawyer, d. 1901.

Silvers, Earl Reed, educationist and writer of books for boys, b. Jersey City, N.J., 1891; d. Sarasota, Fla., March 25, 1948. [7; 10; 11]

Silzer, George S., lawyer and politician, b. New Brunswick, N.J., 1870; d. Newark, N.J., Oct. 16, 1940. [10]

Simard, Henri, priest and educationist, b. Quebec, Que., 1869; d. Quebec, Que., Nov. 7, 1927. [27; 32]

Simkins, William Stewart, lawyer and educationist, b. Edgefield, S.C., 1842; d. Austin, Tex., Feb. 22, 1929. [10; 11]

Simmons, Charles, clergyman, b. about 1789; d. North Wrentham, Mass., 1856. [6]

Simmons, Edward, painter, b. Concord, Mass., 1852; d. Baltimore, Md., Nov. 17, 1931. [1; 4; 10]

Simmons, Enoch Spencer, lawyer, d. March 29, 1904. [54]

Simmons, George Frederick, clergyman, b. Boston, Mass., 1814; d. Concord, Mass., Sept. 5, 1855. [3; 4; 5; 6]

Simmons, Henry Martyn, clergyman, b. Paris Hill, N.Y., 1841; d. Minneapolis, Minn., May 26, 1905. [10; 70]

Simmons, J. F., jurist and poet, fl. 1881-1885. [6]

Simmons, James, lawyer, b. Middlebury, Vt., 1821; d. Geneva, Wis., 1899. [3]

Simmons, James P., clergyman, fl. 1871-1878. [34]

Simmons, James Wright, poet, b. Charleston, S.C., about 1800; d. Memphis, Tenn., about 1867. [3; 6; 34; 42]

Simmons, William Hayne, physician and poet, b. Charleston, S.C., 1784; d. Charleston, S.C., June 14, 1870. [3; 6; 34; 52]

Simmons, William Johnson, clergyman and educationist, b. Charleston, S.C., 1849; d. ? [34]

Simms, Jephtha Root, historian, b. Canterbury, Conn., 1807; d. Fort Plain, N.Y., May 31, 1883. [3; 4; 6; 7]

Simms, Joseph, physician, b. Plainfield Centre, N.Y., 1833; d. New York, N.Y., April 11, 1920. [3; 4; 6; 10]

Simms, William Gilmore, poet and novelist, b. Charleston, S.C., 1806; d. Charleston, S.C., June 11, 1870. [1; 2; 3; 4; 5; 6; 7; 8; 9; 71; 72]

Simon, Charles Edmund, physician, b. Baltimore, Md., 1866; d. Nov. 8, 1927. [10; 11]

Simon, William, chemist, b. Germany, 1844; d. Catonville, Md., July 19, 1916. [4; 10]

Simonds, Frank Herbert, journalist, b. Concord, Mass., 1878; d. Washington, D.C., Jan. 23, 1936. [7; 10; 51]

Simonds, Frederic William, educationist, b. Charlestown, Mass., 1853; d. Austin, Tex., March 27, 1941. [10]

Simonds, Gifford Kingsbury, industrialist, b. Fitchburg, Mass., 1880; d. Brookline, Mass., March 20, 1941. [10]

Simonds, John Cameron, historian, d. 1896.

Simonds, Ossian Cole, landscape gardener, b. Grand Rapids, Mich., 1855; d. Chicago, Ill., Nov. 20, 1931. [10]

Simonds, Thomas C., local historian, b. about 1833; d. 1857.

Simonds, William, journalist, b. Charlestown, Mass., 1822; d. Winchester, Mass., July 7, 1859. [3; 4; 6; 7]

Simonds, William Edgar, lawyer and politician, b. Canton, Conn., 1841; d. Hartford, Conn., March 14, 1903. [4; 5; 10; 62]

Simonds, William Edward, educationist, b. Peabody, Mass., 1860; d. Ithaca, N.Y., June 24, 1947. [7; 10; 11]

Simons, Ezra De Freest, clergyman, b. 1840; d. 1888.

Simons, Michael Laird, journalist, b. Philadelphia, Pa., 1843; d. Philadelphia, Pa., Nov. 17, 1880. [3; 6]

Simons, Minot, clergyman, b. Manchester, N.H., 1868; d. New York, N.Y., May 25, 1941. [10]

Simonton, Charles Henry, soldier and jurist, b. Charleston, S.C., 1829; d. Philadelphia, Pa., April 25, 1904. [1; 4; 5; 10; 34]

Simonton, Ida Vera, novelist, b. Pittsburgh, Pa.; d. New York, N.Y., July 5, 1931. [10]

Simpson, Albert Benjamin, clergyman, b. Bayview, P.E.I., 1843; d. Nyack, N.Y., Oct. 29, 1919. [1; 10]

Simpson, Alexander, jurist, b. Philadelphia, Pa., 1855; d. Philadelphia, Pa., July 24, 1935. [10]

Simpson, Charles Torrey, naturalist, b. Tiskilwa, Ill., 1846; d. Miami, Fla., Dec. 17, 1932. [1a; 4; 7; 10; 11]

Simpson, Edward, naval officer, b. New York, N.Y., 1824; d. Washington, D.C., Dec. 1, 1888. [1; 3; 4; 5; 6]

Simpson, Edward, naval officer, b. Annapolis, Md., 1860; d. Ruxton, Md., Sept. 6, 1930. [10]

Simpson, Eyler Newton, educationist, b. 1901; d. Princeton, N.J., July 1, 1938.

Simpson, Henry, biographer, b. 1790; d. Philadelphia, Pa., March 25, 1868. [3]

Simpson, James Hervey, soldier, b. New Brunswick, N.J., 1813; d. St. Paul, Minn., March 2, 1883. [1; 3; 6; 70]

Simpson, John Andrew, agriculturist, b. near Salem, Neb., 1871; d. Washington, D.C., March 15, 1934. [1; 10]

Simpson, Lola Jean, novelist, b. 1884; d. New York, N.Y., Feb. 26, 1934. [10]

Simpson, Matthew, bishop. b. Cadiz, O., 1811; d. Philadelphia, Pa., March 15, 1884. [1; 3; 4; 5; 6]

Simpson, Robert, novelist, b. Strathy, Scotland, 1886; d. New York, N.Y., Jan. 7, 1934. [7; 10]

Simpson, Samuel L., journalist and poet, b. 1845; d. Portland, Ore., June 14, 1899. [41]

Simpson, Stephen, miscellaneous writer, b. Philadelphia, Pa., 1789; d. Philadelphia, Pa., Aug. 17, 1854. [1; 3; 4; 5; 6; 7; 9]

Sims, Alexander Dromgoole, novelist, b. Brunswick county, Va., 1803; d. Kingstree, S.C., Nov. 11, 1848. [3; 4; 34]

Sims, Charles N., clergyman, b. Fairfield, Ind., 1835; d. Liberty, Ind., March 27, 1908. [1; 3; 4; 5; 6]

Sims, Clifford Stanley, jurist, b. near Harrisburg, Pa., 1839; d. Trenton, N.J., March 3, 1896. [3; 5]

Sims, James Marion, physician, b. Lancaster county, S.C., 1813; d. New York, N.Y., Nov. 13, 1883. [1; 3; 4; 5; 6]

Sims, Philip Hal, bridge expert, b. Selma, Ala., 1886; d. Havana, Cuba, Feb. 26, 1949.

Sims, William Sowden, naval officer, b. Port Hope, Ont., 1858; d. Boston, Mass., Sept. 26, 1936. [2a; 10; 11]

Sinclair, Alexander Maclean, clergyman, b. near Antigonish, N.S., 1840; d. Feb. 14, 1924. [27]

Sinclair, Angus, engineer, b. Scotland, 1841; d. Milburn, N.J., Jan. 2, 1919. [10]

Sinclair, Mrs. Bertha, née Muzzy, novelist, b. Cleveland, Minn., 1875; d. Hollywood, Calif., July 23, 1940. [10; 35]

Sinclair, Carrie Bell, poet, b. Milledgeville, Ga., 1839; d. ? [3; 34]

Sinclair, Samuel Bower, educationist, b. Ridgetown, Ont., 1855; d. Toronto, Ont., Dec. 20, 1933. [27]

Singer, Daniel Jasper, big game hunter, b. 1875; d. New York, N.Y., Sept. 28, 1924.

Singer, Edgar Arthur, educationist, d. Philadelphia, Pa., Jan. 28, 1909.

Singer, Isidore, editor, b. Austria, 1859; d. New York, N.Y., Feb. 20, 1939. [4; 7; 10]

Singer, Israel Joshua, novelist, b. Russian Poland, 1893; d. New York, N.Y., Feb. 10, 1944.

Singleton, Arthur (pseud.). See Knight, Henry Cogswell.

Singleton, Esther, writer on music and the arts, b. Baltimore, Md., 1865; d. Stonington, Conn., July 2, 1930. [1; 5; 7; 10; 11]

Singmaster, John Alden, clergyman, b. Lehigh county, Pa., 1852; d. Gettysburg, Pa., Feb. 27, 1926. [10]

Singularity, Thomas (pseud.). See Nott, Henry Junius.

Siogvolk, Paul (pseud.). See Mathews, Albert.

Sioussat, Mrs. Annie Middleton, née Leakin historian, b. Georgetown, D.C., 1850; d. Baltimore, Md., March 15, 1942. [78]

Sipes, William B., soldier and politician, d. 1905.

Siringo, Charles A., cowboy and detective, b. Matagorda county, Tex., 1855; d. Hollywood, Calif., Oct. 19, 1928. [1; 7]

Sirois, Joseph, notary, b. Quebec, Que., 1881; d. Quebec, Que., Jan. 17, 1941. [27]

Sirois, Napoléon Joseph Théodule, priest, b. 1835; d. Cap St. Ignace, Que., Oct. 20, 1911. [27; 32]

Sisson, Edgar Grant, journalist, b. Alto, Wis., 1875; d. New York, N.Y., March 12, 1948. [10]

Sisson, Edward Octavius, educationist, b. Gateshead, England, 1859; d. Monterey, Calif., Jan. 24, 1949. [10]

Sisson, Septimus, anatomist, b. Gateshead, England, 1865; d. Columbus, O., 1924. [10]

Sites, Mrs. Sarah, née **Moore,** biographer, b. 1838; d. 1912.

Sitgreaves, Charles, politician, b. Easton, Pa., 1803; d. Phillipsburg, N.J., March 17, 1878.

Sitterly, Charles Fremont, theologian, b. Liverpool, N.Y., 1861; d. Madison, N.J., Nov. 8, 1945. [7; 10; 11]

Siu Sin Far (pseud.). See Eaton, Edith.

Siviter, Mrs. Anne, née **Pierpont,** miscellaneous writer, b. Fairmont, Va., 1859; d. March 12, 1932. [10; 11]

Sizer, Nelson, phrenologist, b. Chester, Mass., 1812; d. Brooklyn, N.Y., Oct. 18, 1897. [1; 4; 6]

Sjolander, John Peter, poet, b. Sweden, 1851; d. Cedar Bayou, Tex., June, 1939. [4; 10; 34; 77]

Skeel, Adelaide. See Kelley, Mrs. Adelaide, née Skeel.

Skelly, Andrew Maria, priest, b. Ireland, 1855; d. Ross., Calif., 1938. [21]

Skelton, Oscar Douglas, economist and biographer, b. Orangeville, Ont., 1878; d. Ottawa, Ont., Jan. 28, 1941. [27]

Skene, Alexander Johnston Chalmers, gynaecologist, b. Fyvie, Scotland, 1837; d. Highmount, Ulster county, N.Y., July 4, 1900. [1; 3; 4; 6; 10]

Skene, Don, journalist, b. Brooklyn, N.Y., 1897; d. New York, N.Y., May 16, 1938.

Skene, Norman Locke, boat-designer, b. 1878; d. near Marblehead, Mass., June, 1932.

Skeyhill, Thomas John, poet and biographer, b. 1896; d. May 22, 1932.

Skidmore, Harriet Marie, poet, b. New York, N.Y., 1837; d. San Francisco, Calif., March 16, 1904. [21; 35]

Skidmore, Hubert Standish, novelist, b. Webster Springs, W. Va., 1911; d. near Reading, Pa., Feb. 2, 1946. [10]

Skidmore, Sydney Tuthill, educationist, b. Wading River, N.Y., 1844; d. Bailey Island, Me., Aug. 22, 1928. [11; 45]

Skiff, Frederick Woodward, book-collector, b. Kent, Conn., 1868; d. Tillamook, Ore., March 15, 1947.

Skillern, Ross Hall, laryngologist, b. Philadelphia, Pa., 1875; d. Philadelphia, Pa., Sept. 20, 1930. [1; 10; 11]

Skilton, Charles Sanford, musician, b. Northampton, Mass., 1868; d. Lawrence, Kans., March 12, 1941. [10; 11; 62]

Skinflint, Obediah (pseud.). See Harris, Joel Chandler.

Skinner, Alanson Buck, anthropologist, b. Buffalo, N.Y., 1886; d. near Tokio, N.D., Aug. 17, 1925. [1; 10]

Skinner, Avery Warner, educationist, b. Mexico, N.Y., 1870; d. Albany, N.Y., Dec. 13, 1937. [10]

Skinner, Charles Montgomery, journalist, b. Victor, N.Y., 1852; d. 1907. [5; 7; 10]

Skinner, Charles Rufus, politician and educationist, b. Oswego county, N.Y., 1844; d. Pelham Manor, N.Y., June 30, 1928. [1; 4; 5; 10; 11]

Skinner, Clarence Russell, clergyman, b. Brooklyn, N.Y., 1881; d. Long Ridge, Conn., Aug. 27, 1949. [10; 11]

Skinner, Constance Lindsay, novelist and historian, b. British Columbia, 1879; d. New York, N.Y., March 27, 1939. [2a; 7; 10; 11]

Skinner, Davis Nevens, physician, b. Lewiston, Me., 1841; d. Auburn, Me., June 18, 1892. [46]

Skinner, Ernest Brown, educationist, b. Redfield, Perry county, O., 1863; d. Madison, Wis., April 3, 1935. [10]

Skinner, Harriet Pearl. See McRoberts, Mrs. Harriet Pearl, née Skinner.

Skinner, Mrs. Henrietta Channing, née **Dana,** novelist, b. Cambridge, Mass., 1857; d. New York, N.Y., Jan. 29, 1928. [5; 10; 11; 21]

Skinner, Hubert Marshall, educationist, b. Valparaiso, Ind., 1855; d. Morgan Park, Ill., June 4, 1916. [7; 10]

Skinner, Ichabod, clergyman, b. Colchester, Conn., 1767; d. Brooklyn, N.Y., Jan. 29, 1852. [62]

Skinner, John Stuart, writer on agriculture, b. Calvert county, Md., 1788; d. Baltimore, Md., March 21, 1851. [1; 3; 4; 6; 7]

Skinner, Joseph John, educationist, b. Putney, Vt., 1842; d. Oneida, N.Y., Nov. 12, 1919. [62]

Skinner, Joseph Osmun, lawyer, b. 1875; d. Oct. 19, 1933.

Skinner, Otis, actor, b. Cambridge, Mass., 1858; d. New York, N.Y., Jan. 4, 1942. [4; 7; 10]

Skinner, Otis Ainsworth, clergyman, b. Royalton, Vt., 1807; d. Napierville, Ill., Sept. 18, 1861. [3; 6; 7; 43]

Skinner, Richard Dana, economist, b. Detroit, Mich., 1893; d. Norwalk, Conn., Nov. 6, 1941. [21; 51]

Skinner, Thomas Harvey, clergyman, b. Harvey's Neck, N.C., 1791; d. New York, N.Y., Feb. 1, 1871. [1; 3; 4; 5; 6; 34]

Skipton, Mrs. Amy, née **Connelly,** local historian, b. Cornwall, N.Y., 1882; d. New Rochelle, N.Y., Oct. 29, 1945.

Skitt (pseud.). See Taliaferro, Hardan E.

Slack, David B., physician, b. 1798; d. Providence, R.I., Oct. 6, 1871. [47]

Slack, John Hamilton, physician, d. Aug. 27, 1874.

Slade, Daniel Denison, physician, b. Boston, Mass., 1823; d. Chestnut Hill, Mass., Feb. 11, 1896. [3; 6]

Slade, William, lawyer and politician, b. Cornwall, Vt., 1786; d. Middlebury, Vt., Jan. 16, 1859. [1; 3; 4; 5; 6; 43]

Slafter, Carlos, clergyman, b. 1825; d. Dedham, Mass., July 18, 1909.

Slafter, Edmund Farwell, clergyman and historian, b. Norwich, Vt., 1816; d. Hampton, N.H., Sept. 22, 1906. [1; 3; 5; 6; 7; 10]

Slaght, William Ernest Andrew, educationist, b. Woodstock, Ont., 1875; d. Mount Vernon, Ia., March 26, 1932. [10]

Slate, Frederick, physicist, b. London, England, 1852; d. Berkeley, Calif., Feb. 26, 1930. [10; 11; 13]

Slater, Nelson, clergyman, b. Champlain, N.Y., 1805; d. Sacramento, Calif., May 2, 1886. [63]

Slattery, Charles Lewis, bishop, b. Pittsburgh, Pa., 1867; d. Boston, Mass., March 12, 1930. [1; 4; 10; 11; 70]

Slattery, Harry, lawyer, b. Greenville, S.C., 1887; d. Washington, D.C., Sept. 2, 1949. [10]

Slattery, John Richard, priest, b. 1851; d. 1926. [21]

Slattery, John Theodore, priest, b. Albany, N.Y., 1866; d. Troy, N.Y., March 27, 1938. [10; 11; 21]

Slaughter, Mrs. Linda, née **Warfel,** social worker, b. Cadiz, O.; d. St. Cloud, Minn., July 5, 1911.

Slaughter, Moses Stephen, educationist, b. Brooklyn, Ind., 1860; d. Madison, Wis., Dec. 29, 1923. [10]

Slaughter, Philip, clergyman and historian, b. Culpeper county, Va., 1808; d. Richmond, Va., June 12, 1890. [1; 3; 5; 6; 7; 34]

Slaughter, William Bank, politician, b. Culpeper county, Va., 1798; d. Madison, Wis., July 21, 1879. [3; 6; 34]

Sledd, Andrew, educationist, b. Lynchburg, Va., 1870; d. Decatur, Ga., March 16, 1939. [10; 11; 34; 62]

Sledd, Benjamin, poet and educationist, b. Bedford county, Va., 1864; d. Wake Forest, N.C., Jan. 4, 1940. [7; 10; 34]

Sleeper, John Sherburne, novelist, b. Tyngsboro, Mass., 1794; d. Boston Highlands, Mass., Nov. 14, 1878. [3; 4; 6; 7]

Sleeper, William True, clergyman and poet, b. Danbury, N.H., 1819; d. Sept. 24, 1904. [59]

Sleigh, William Willcocks, miscellaneous writer, b. 1796; d. ?

Sleight, Henry Dering, historian, b. 1875; d. Sag Harbor, Long Island, N.Y., Nov. 4, 1933.

Sleight, Mary Breck, novelist, b. New York, N.Y.; d. Slide Harbor, Long Island, N.Y., 1928. [7; 10]

Slemons, Josiah Morris, obstetrician, b. Salisbury, Md., 1876; d. Los Angeles, Calif., April 30, 1948. [10; 11]

Slenker, Mrs. Elmina, née **Drake,** writer of books for children, b. La Grange, N.Y., 1827; d. about 1909. [3; 4; 6; 34]

Slesinger, Tess, novelist, b. 1905; d. Los Angeles, Calif., Feb. 21, 1945. [7]

Slicer, Henry, clergyman, b. Annapolis, Md., 1801; d. Baltimore, Md., April 23, 1874. [3; 6]

Slicer, Thomas Roberts, clergyman, b. Washington, D.C., 1847; d. New York, N.Y., May 29, 1916. [1; 5; 10]

Slick, Jonathan (pseud.). See Stephens, Mrs. Ann Sophia, née Winterbotham.

Slick, Sam (pseud.). See Haliburton, Thomas Chandler.

Slick, Sam, Jr. (pseud.). See Avery, Samuel Putnam.

Slight, Benjamin, clergyman, b. about 1798; d. Napanee, Ont., Jan. 16, 1858. [27]

Slingerland, Mark Vernon, entomologist, b. Otto, N.Y., 1864; d. Ithaca, N.Y., 1909. [4; 10]

Slingerland, William Henry, social worker, b. 1854; d. Denver, Colo., Dec. 21, 1924.

Sloan, George White, pharmacist, b. 1835; d. 1903.

Sloan, James Forman, jockey, b. near Kokomo, Ind., 1874; d. Los Angeles, Calif., Dec. 21, 1933. [1; 2b; 10]

Sloan, John Alexander, soldier, b. Greensboro, N.C., 1839; d. Baltimore, Md., Nov., 1886. [4]

Sloan, Laurence Henry, economist, b. Spencer, Ind., 1889; d. New Haven, Conn., May 6, 1949. [10]

Sloan, Richard Elihu, jurist, b. Preble county, O., 1857; d. Phoenix, Ariz., Dec. 14, 1933. [1; 10]

Sloan, Samuel, architect, b. Chester, county, Pa., 1815; d. Raleigh, N.C., July 19, 1884. [3; 6]

Sloan, Tod. See Sloan, James Forman.

Sloan, William Hill, missionary, b. Fort Washita, I.T., 1843; d. Leavenworth, Kans., April 27, 1917. [67]

Sloan, William Niccolls, clergyman, b. 1849; d. Mountainview, Calif., Nov. 18, 1919.

Sloane, Charles William, lawyer, d. July 26, 1929.

Sloane, Thomas O'Conor, scientist, b. New York, N.Y., 1851; d. South Orange, N.J., Aug. 7, 1940. [10; 21]

Sloane, William Milligan, historian, b. Richmond, O., 1850; d. Princeton, N.J., Sept. 11, 1928. [1; 2; 3; 4; 5; 7; 10]

Slocum, Charles Elihu, physician and historian, b. Northville, N.Y., 1841; d. Aug. 7, 1916. [4; 10]

Slocum, Joshua, mariner, b. Wilmot township, N.S., 1814; d. at sea, about 1910. [1; 7; 10]

Slosson, Mrs. Annie, née **Trumbull,** novelist, b. Stonington, Conn., 1838; d. New York, N.Y., Oct. 4, 1926. [7; 10]

Slosson, Edwin Emery, educationist, b. Albany, Kans., 1865; d. Washington, D.C., Oct. 15, 1929. [1; 4; 7; 10; 11]

Sluter, George, clergyman, b. St. Louis, Mo., 1837; d. Stirling, N.J., Aug. 24, 1908. [3; 6; 10]

Sly, William James, clergyman, b. London, England, 1867; d. Washington, D.C., Jan. 24, 1940. [10]

Small, Abner Ralph, soldier, b. 1836; d. 1910. [38]

Small, Albion Woodbury, educationist, b. Buckfield, Me., 1854; d. Chicago, Ill., March 24, 1926. [1; 4; 5; 7; 10]

Small, Alvan Edmond, physician, b. Wales, Me., 1811; d. Chicago, Ill., Dec. 31, 1886. [1; 3; 4; 6]

Small, Elden, journalist, b. Marshall, Mich., 1876; d. Detroit, Mich., Aug. 29, 1934. [7; 10]

Small, George G., entertainer, fl. 1871-1894.

Small, Henry Beaumont, civil servant, b. Leicestershire, England, 1832; d. Bermuda, Feb. 8, 1919. [27]

Small, John Bryan, bishop, b. St. Joseph's parish, Barbados, 1845; d. ? [5]

Small, John Kunkel, botanist, b. Harrisburg, Pa., 1869; d. New York, N.Y., Jan. 20, 1938. [10; 13]

Small, John Turnbull, lawyer, b. Toronto, Ont.; d. Pinehurst, N.C., Jan. 30, 1919.

Small, Samuel White, evangelist, b. Knoxville, Tenn., 1851; d. Atlanta, Ga., Nov. 21, 1931. [10]

Smalley, Eugene Virgil, journalist, b. Portage county, O., 1841; d. St. Paul, Minn., Dec. 30, 1899. [1; 3; 6; 7; 10; 70]

Smalley, Frank, educationist, b. Towanda, Pa., 1846; d. Syracuse, N.Y., April 3, 1931. [4; 10; 11]

Smalley, George Washburn, journalist, b. Franklin, Mass., 1833; d. London, England, April 4, 1916. [1; 4; 5; 7; 10; 62]

Smalley, Harrison Standish, economist, b. Chicago, Ill., 1878; d. Charlevoix, Mich., Sept. 23, 1912. [10; 39]

Smalley, John, clergyman, b. Lebanon, Conn., 1734; d. New Britain, Conn., June 1, 1820. [3; 6]

Smarius, Cornelius Francis, priest, b. Holland, 1823; d. Detroit, Mich., March 2, 1870. [3; 21]

Smart, Charles, soldier and physician, b. Aberdeen, Scotland, 1841; d. Washington, D.C., 1905. [10]

Smart, George Thomas, clergyman, b. Leicester, England, 1863; d. Norton, Conn., March 13, 1928. [10]

Smart, James Henry, educationist, b. Center Harbor, N.H., 1841; d. Lafayette, Ind., Feb. 21, 1900. [1; 3; 10; 49]

Smead, Wesley, physician, b. Westchester county, N.Y., 1800; d. Poughkeepsie, N.Y., Jan. 6, 1871. [3]

Smedes, Mrs. Susan, née **Dabney,** biographer, b. Raymond, Miss., 1840; d. Sewanee, Tenn., 1913. [3; 6; 7; 34]

Smedley, Robert C., physician, d. 1883.

Smedley, William Thomas, artist, b. Chester county, Pa., 1858; d. New York, N.Y., March 26, 1920. [4; 7; 10]

Smet, Pierre Jean de. See De Smet, Pierre Jean.

Smiley, Joseph Bert, poet, b. Anoke, Minn., 1864; d. Galesburg, Mich., 1903. [39]

Smiley, Sarah Frances, religious writer, b. Vassalboro, Me., 1830; d. Saratoga Springs, N.Y., 1917. [10]

Smiley, Thomas Ewing, poet, b. 1866; d. 1910.

Smiley, Thomas Tucker, educationist, d. Philadelphia, Pa., Dec. 17, 1879. [6]

Smith, Abner Comstock, lawyer, b. Randolph, Vt., 1814; d. Litchfield, Minn., Sept. 20, 1880. [43; 70]

Smith, Albert, physician, b. Peterborough, N.H., 1801; d. Peterborough, N.H., Feb. 22, 1878. [3b]

Smith, Albert Edwin, educationist, b. New Richmond, O., 1860; d. Lakeside, O., Aug. 26, 1941. [10]

Smith, Albert Hatcher, clergyman, b. Hamilton, Va.; d. Pasadena, Calif., Dec. 16, 1932. [11]

Smith, Albert William, engineer and educationist, b. Westmoreland, N.Y., 1856; d. Ithaca, N.Y., Aug. 16, 1942. [10]

Smith, Alexander, chemist, b. Edinburgh, Scotland, 1865; d. Edinburgh, Scotland, Sept. 8, 1922. [1; 4; 10]

Smith, Alfred Emanuel, politician, b. New York, N.Y., 1873; d. New York, N.Y., Oct. 4, 1944. [2; 7; 10; 12]

Smith, Mrs. Alfred Franklin. See Smith, Mrs. Lucy Hahn King, née Cunningham.

Smith, Allen John, physician, b. York, Pa., 1863; d. St. Davids, Pa., Aug. 19, 1926. [4; 10]

Smith, Almiron, clergyman, b. 1841; d. 1919.

Smith, Mrs. Amanda, née **Berry,** evangelist, b. 1837; d. ?

Smith, Andrew Heermance, physician, b. Charlton, N.Y., 1837; d. New York, N.Y., 1910. [4; 10]

Smith, Andrew Madsen, numismatist, b. 1841; d. 1915.

Smith, Andrew Thomas, educationist, b. near Norristown, Pa., 1862; d. West Chester, Pa., Feb. 8, 1928. [10; 11]

Smith, Mrs. Ann Eliza, née **Brainerd,** novelist and poet, b. St. Alban's, Vt., 1818; d. 1905. [43]

Smith, Anna Tolman, educationist, b. Boston, Mass., 1840; d. Washington, D.C., Aug. 28, 1917. [10]

Smith, Mrs. Annie H., novelist, b. Columbia, S.C., 1850; d. Atlanta, Ga., Aug. 31, 1909. [34]

Smith, Arthur Cosslett, lawyer, b. Lyons, N.Y., 1852; d. Rochester, N.Y., May 22, 1906. [7; 10]

Smith, Arthur Donaldson, physician and explorer, b. Andalusia, Pa., 1864; d. Philadelphia, Pa., Feb. 18, 1939. [4; 10]

Smith, Arthur Douglas Howden, journalist, b. New York, N.Y., 1887; d. New York, N.Y., Dec. 18, 1945.

Smith, Arthur Henderson, missionary, b. Vernon, Conn., 1845; d. Claremont, Calif., Aug. 31, 1932. [1; 7; 10; 11]

Smith, Asa Dodge, clergyman and educationist, b. Amherst, N.H., 1804; d. Hanover, N.H., Aug. 16, 1877. [1; 3; 4; 5; 6]

Smith, Augustus William, educationist, b. Newport, N.Y., 1802; d. Annapolis, Md., March 26, 1866. [3; 4; 6]

Smith, Baker, physician, b. 1850; d. Camden, N.Y., April 23, 1922.

Smith, Baxter Perry, historian, b. Lyme, N.H., 1829; d. Washington, D.C., Feb. 6, 1884. [49]

Smith, Benjamin Mosby, clergyman, b. Powhatan county, Va., 1811; d. March 14, 1893. [1; 3; 34]

Smith, Boston W., evangelist, b. England, 1863; d. Minneapolis, Minn., Sept. 9, 1908. [70]

Smith, Buckingham, lawyer and antiquary, b. Cumberland Island, Ga., 1810; d. New York, N.Y., Jan. 5, 1871. [1; 3; 6; 7; 34]

Smith, Byron Caldwell, educationist, b. Jefferson county, O., 1849; d. Boulder, Colo., May 4, 1877. [1]

Smith, C. Harold, adventurer, b. London, England, 1860; d. New York, N.Y., 1933.

Smith, Mrs. Caroline L., journalist, fl. 1867-1873. [6]

Smith, Charles, bookseller, b. New York, N.Y., 1768; d. New York, N.Y., 1808. [3; 6]

Smith, Charles Adam, clergyman, b. New York, N.Y., 1809; d. Philadelphia, Pa., Feb. 15, 1879. [3; 6]

Smith, Charles Alphonso, educationist, b. Greensboro, N.C., 1864; d. Annapolis, Md., June 13, 1924. [1; 7; 10; 34]

Smith, Charles Billings, clergyman, b. Paris, N.Y., 1814; d. Grand Rapids, Mich., Sept. 17, 1890. [62]

Smith, Charles Edward, clergyman, b. Fall River, Mass., 1835; d. Fredonia, N.Y., Sept. 9, 1929. [67]

Smith, Charles Ernest, clergyman, b. Cheshire, England, 1855; d. Washington, D.C., June 2, 1939. [10]

Smith, Charles Forster, educationist, b. Abbeville county, S.C., 1852; d. Racine, Wis., Aug. 3, 1931. [1; 4; 5; 7; 10; 11]

Smith, Charles Henry, journalist and humorist, b. Lawrenceville, Ga., 1826; d. Atlanta, Ga., Aug. 24, 1903. [1; 2; 3; 4; 5; 6; 7; 9; 10; 34]

Smith, Charles Spencer, bishop, b. Colborne, Ont., 1852; d. Detroit, Mich., Feb. 1, 1923. [10]

Smith, Charles Sprague, educationist, b. Andover, Mass., 1853; d. Montclair, N.J., March 29, 1910. [1; 7; 10]

Smith, Clyde (pseud.). See Smith, George.

Smith, Daniel, soldier and politician, b. Stafford county, Va., 1748; d. Sumner county, Tenn., June 16, 1818. [1; 3; 4; 5; 6]

Smith, Daniel, clergyman, b. Salisbury, Conn., 1806; d. Kingston, N.Y., June 23, 1852. [3; 6]

Smith, Daniel B., pharmacist, b. Philadelphia, Pa., 1792; d. Germantown, Pa., March 29, 1883. [1; 3; 4; 6]

Smith, Daniel D., clergyman, fl. 1836-1847. [38]

Smith, David Eugene, mathematician, b. Cortland, N.Y., 1860; d. New York, N.Y., July 29, 1944. [7; 10; 11]

Smith, David Thomas, lawyer and physician, b. Hardin county, Ky., 1840; d. Louisville, Ky., Oct. 1, 1914. [10; 34]

Smith, Dean Tyler, surgeon, b. Portland, Mich., 1860; d. Ann Arbor, Mich., Jan. 30, 1933. [10]

Smith, Dexter, poet, b. 1842; d. ?

Smith, E. Fitch, lawyer, fl. 1848-1876.

Smith, Edgar Fahs, educationist, b. York, Pa., 1854; d. Philadelphia, Pa., May 3, 1928. [1; 4; 10]

Smith, Edmund Munroe, historian, b. Brooklyn, N.Y., 1854; d. New York, N.Y., April 13, 1926. [1; 10]

Smith, Edward M., local historian, b. Red Hook, N.Y., 1817; d. Rhinebeck, N.Y., Jan. 28, 1901.

Smith, Edward Parmelee, clergyman, b. South Britain, Conn., 1827; d. Accra, West Africa, June 15, 1876. [3; 6; 62]

Smith, Edwin Dudley, physician, b. 1833; d. 1906.

Smith, Egbert Watson, clergyman, b. Greensboro, N.C., 1862; d. Greensboro, N.C., Aug. 25, 1944. [10; 11]

Smith, Elbert H., poet, fl. 1846-1849.

Smith, Elbert Sidney, jurist, b. Twinsburg, O., 1847; d. Springfield, Ill., Feb. 18, 1934. [10]

Smith, Eli, missionary, b. Northford, Conn., 1801; d. Beirut, Syria, Jan. 11, 1857. [1; 3; 4; 5; 6; 62]

Smith, Elias, clergyman, b. Lyme, Conn., 1769; d. Lynn, Conn., June 29, 1846. [1; 3; 6]

Smith, Elihu Hubbard, physician, b. Litchfield, Conn., 1771; d. New York, N.Y., Sept. 19, 1798. [1; 3; 4; 6; 7; 9]

Smith, Mrs. Eliza Roxey, née Snow, poet, b. Becket, Mass., 1804; d. Salt Lake City, Utah, Dec. 5, 1887. [1]

Smith, Mrs. Elizabeth Oakes, née Prince, novelist and writer of books for children, b. North Yarmouth, Me., 1806; d. Hollywood, N.C., Nov. 15, 1893. [1; 3; 4; 5; 6; 7; 9]

Smith, Mrs. Ellen M., née Cyr, educationist, b. Montreal, Que.; d. Flatbush, N.Y. July 25, 1920. [10]

Smith, Mrs. Emeline Sherman, poet, b. New Baltimore, N.Y., 1823; d. ?

Smith, Mrs. Emily Ann, née Jones, biographer, b. 1840; d. ?

Smith, Mrs. Emma Pow, née Bander, clergyman's wife, b. Adams, Mich., 1848; d. Pacific Grove, Calif., 1901. [35]

Smith, Erasmus Peshine, jurist, b. New York, N.Y., 1814; d. Rochester, N.Y., Oct. 21, 1882. [3; 6]

Smith, Ernest Ashton, educationist, b. Fletcher, O., 1868; d. Piqua, O., Dec. 28, 1926. [10]

Smith, Erwin Frink, botanist, b. Oswego county, N.Y., 1854; d. Washington, D.C., April 6, 1927. [1; 4; 10; 13]

Smith, Ethan, clergyman, b. Belchertown, Mass., 1762; d. Pompey, N.Y., Aug. 29, 1849. [3; 6; 43]

Smith, Eugene, engineer and zoologist, b. New York, N.Y., 1860; d. Dec. 25, 1912. [10]

Smith, Eugene, lawyer, b. New York, N.Y., 1839; d. New York, N.Y., April 5, 1928. [10; 62]

Smith, Eugene Allen, geologist, b. Washington, Ala., 1841; d. Tuscaloosa, Ala., Sept. 7, 1927. [1; 3; 4; 5; 10]

Smith, Mrs. Euphemia, née **Vale.** See Blake, Mrs. Euphemia, née Vale.

Smith, Fannie M., novelist, fl. 1872-1881. [6]

Smith, Floyd Robinson, educationist, b. Piermont, N.Y., 1866; d. Maplewood, N.J., Jan. 3, 1942. [62]

Smith, Mrs. Frances Irene, née **Burge.** See Griswold, Mrs. Frances Irene, née Burge.

Smith, Francis Asbury, lawyer, b. Salisbury, Mass., 1837; d. 1915. [10]

Smith, Francis Gurney, physician, b. Philadelphia, Pa., 1818; d. Philadelphia, Pa., April 6, 1878. [3b; 4]

Smith, Francis Henney, educationist, b. Norfolk, Va., 1812; d. Lexington, Va., March 21, 1890. [1; 3; 5; 6; 34]

Smith, Francis Henry, educationist, b. Leesburg, Va., 1829; d. University, Va., July 5, 1928. [7; 10; 34]

Smith, Francis Hopkinson, novelist, b. Baltimore, Md., 1838; d. New York, N.Y., April 7, 1915. [1; 2; 3; 4; 5; 7; 9; 10; 71; 72]

Smith, Francis Ormand Jonathan, lawyer and politician, b. Brentwood, N.H., 1806; d. Woodford, Me., Oct. 14, 1876. [3]

Smith, Francis Shubael, journalist and poet, b. New York, N.Y., 1819; d. New York, N.Y., Feb. 1, 1887. [4; 6; 7]

Smith, Frank Clifford, journalist and novelist, b. Kendal, England, 1865; d. Montreal, Que., July 1, 1937. [27]

Smith, Frank Webster, educationist, b. Lincoln, Mass., 1854; d. Paterson, N.J., Feb. 11, 1943. [10; 11]

Smith, Fred Burton, religious leader, b. Lone Tree, Ia., 1865; d. White Plains, N.Y., Sept. 4, 1936. [10; 11]

Smith, George, physician, b. Delaware county, Pa., 1804; d. Upper Darby, Pa., March 10, 1882. [3]

Smith, George, jurist, b. Cambuslang, Scotland, 1852; d. Windsor, Ont., July 28, 1930. [27]

Smith, George Albert, Mormon leader, b. Potsdam, N.Y., 1817; d. Salt Lake City, Utah, Sept. 1, 1875. [4]

Smith, George Carroll, physician, b. 1853; d. Boston, Mass., Feb. 8, 1936.

Smith, George Gilman, clergyman, b. Newton county, Ga., 1836; d. Macon, Ga., May 7, 1913. [34]

Smith, George Henry, journalist, b. Knoxville, Tenn., 1873; d. Maplewood, N.J., Jan. 9, 1931. [1; 7; 62]

Smith, George Hugh, lawyer, b. Philadelphia, Pa., 1834; d. Los Angeles, Calif., Feb. 7, 1915.

Smith, George Jay, educationist, b. Lebanon, O., 1866; d. New York, N.Y., Jan. 2, 1937. [7; 10; 11]

Smith, George Martin, educationist, b. Belgrade, Me., 1847; d. Sioux City, Ia., June 25, 1920. [10]

Smith, George Washington, lawyer, b. Philadelphia, Pa., 1800; d. Philadelphia, Pa. April 22, 1876. [3; 6]

Smith, George Washington, educationist, b. 1855; d. Carbondale, Ill., Nov. 20, 1945.

Smith, George Williamson, clergyman and educationist, b. Catskill, N.Y., 1836; d. Washington, D.C., Dec. 27, 1925. [10]

Smith, Gerald Birney, theologian, b. Middlefield, Mass., 1868; d. Dayton, O., April 2, 1929. [1; 7; 10; 11]

Smith, Gerrit, reformer, b. Utica, N.Y., 1797; d. New York, N.Y., Dec. 28, 1874. [1; 2; 3; 4; 5; 6]

Smith, Gertrude, writer of books for children, b. Coloma, Eldorado county, Calif., 1860; d. 1917. [7; 10]

Smith, Goldwin, journalist and historian, b. Reading, England, 1823; d. Toronto, Ont., June 7, 1910. [27]

Smith, Gordon Arthur, novelist, b. Rochester, N.Y., 1886; d. Wakefield, R.I., May 7, 1944. [7; 10; 51]

Smith, Grant F. O., biographer, b. 1877; d. Toronto, Ont., Feb. 3, 1949.

Smith, Gustavus Woodson, civil and military engineer, b. Georgetown, Ky., 1822; d. New York, N.Y., June 24, 1896. [1; 3; 5; 6; 34]

Smith, Hamilton, mining engineer, b. near Louisville, Ky., 1840; d. Durham, N.H., July 4, 1900. [1]

Smith, Hamilton Jewett, educationist, b. Detroit, Mich., 1890; d. Port Washington, N.Y., Dec. 11, 1937. [62]

Smith, Hamilton Lanphere, educationist, b. New London, Conn., 1818; d. New London, Conn., Aug. 1, 1903. [4; 5; 10; 62]

Smith, Mrs. Hannah, née **Whitall,** religious writer, b. Philadelphia, Pa., 1832; d. near Oxford, England, May 1, 1911. [1]

Smith, Harlan Ingersoll, archaeologist, b. East Saginaw, Mich., 1872; d. Ottawa, Ont., June 28, 1940. [10; 11]

Smith, Mrs. Harriet, née **Lummis,** writer of books for girls, b. Auburndale, Mass.; d. Philadelphia, Pa., May 9, 1947. [7; 10]

Smith, Harry Bache, poet and playwright, b. Buffalo, N.Y., 1860; d. Atlantic City, N.J., Jan. 1, 1936. [7; 10]

Smith, Harry Eaton, naval officer, b. Fremont, O., 1869; d. March 26, 1931. [10]

Smith, Harry James, playwright and novelist, b. New Britain, Conn., 1880; d. near Murrayville, B.C., March 16, 1918. [1; 10]

Smith, Harry Worcester, sportsman, b. Worcester, Mass., 1865; d. Worcester, Mass., April 5, 1945. [10]

Smith, Hay Watson, clergyman, b. Greensboro, N.C., 1868; d. Little Rock, Ark., Jan. 20, 1940. [10]

Smith, Helen Evertson, historian, b. Sharon, Conn., 1839; d. ? [7; 10]

Smith, Henry, clergyman, b. 1769; d. ?

Smith, Henry Boynton, theologian, b. Portland, Me., 1815; d. New York, N.Y., Feb. 7, 1877. [1; 3; 4; 5; 6; 7]

Smith, Henry Bradford, philosopher, b. Philadelphia, Pa., 1882; d. Philadelphia, Pa. Nov. 17, 1938. [10]

Smith, Henry Erskine, playwright, b. New York, N.Y., about 1842; d. New York, N.Y., March 8, 1932. [7; 11]

Smith, Henry Hollingsworth, physician, b. Philadelphia, Pa., 1815; d. Philadelphia, Pa., April 11, 1890. [3; 6]

Smith, Henry I., soldier, d. 1910. [37]

Smith, Henry Justin, journalist, b. Chicago, Ill., 1875; d. Evanston, Ill., Feb. 9, 1936. [7; 10; 11]

Smith, Henry Perry, local historian, b. 1839; d. Syracuse, N.Y., May 22, 1925.

Smith, Henry Preserved, theologian, b. Troy, O., 1847; d. Poughkeepsie, N.Y., Feb. 26, 1927. [1; 4; 7; 10; 11]

Smith, Herbert Huntington, naturalist, b. Manlius, N.Y., 1851; d. University, Ala., March 22, 1919. [10]

Smith, Hildegarde Angell, biographer, d. Kansas City, Mo., July 23, 1933.

Smith, Homer Erastus, physician, b. 1856; d. Norwich, Conn., Oct. 5, 1928.

Smith, Horace Edwin, lawyer, b. 1817; d. 1902.

Smith, Horace Wemyss, journalist, b. Philadelphia county, Pa., 1825; d. Philadelphia, Pa., Dec. 9, 1891. [3; 6]

Smith, Horatio Elwin, educationist, b. Cambridge, Mass., 1886; d. New York, N.Y., Sept. 9, 1946. [7; 10]

Smith, Hubbard Madison, physician, b. 1820; d. Vincennes, Ind., Dec. 23, 1907.

Smith, Huron Herbert, botanist, b. Danville, Ind., 1883; d. Feb. 25, 1933. [10]

Smith, Mrs. J. Gregory. See Smith, Mrs. Ann Eliza, née Brainerd.

Smith, Jabez Burritt, lawyer, b. Sherburn, N.Y., 1852; d. Madison, Wis., Dec. 31, 1914. [10; 44]

Smith, James, soldier and pioneer, b. Franklin county, Pa., about 1737; d. Washington county, Ky., about 1814. [1; 3; 6; 7; 34]

Smith, James, agriculturist, b. Caraquet, N.B., 1821; d. St. Laurent de Matapédia, N.B., May 18, 1888. [27]

Smith, James Allen, political scientist, b. Pleasant Hill, Mo., 1860; d. Seattle, Wash., Jan. 30, 1924. [1; 10]

Smith, James Franklin, clergyman, b. Gadsden, Tenn., 1868; d. Dallas, Tex., April 28, 1920. [10]

Smith, James Frazer, medical missionary, b. Dornoch, Ont., 1858; d. Edmonton, Alta., April 26, 1948. [30]

Smith, James Gerald, economist, b. Denver, Colo., 1897; d. Princeton, N.J., Nov. 28, 1946. [10]

Smith, James Henry Oliver, clergyman, b. Warren county, O., 1857; d. Oklahoma City, Okla., Dec. 27, 1935. [10]

Smith, James Perrin, palaeontologist, b. near Cokesbury, S.C., 1864; d. Stanford University, Calif., Jan. 1, 1931. [1; 10; 11]

Smith, James Reuel, historian, b. Skaneateles, N.Y., 1852; d. Yonkers, N.Y., Nov. 12, 1935.

Smith, James Thorne. See Smith, Thorne.

Smith, James Tinker, poet, b. St. Mary's parish, La., 1816; d. Franklin, La., Aug. 10, 1854. [34]

Smith, James Wheaton, clergyman, b. Providence, R.I., 1823; d. May 5, 1900. [3]

Smith, Mrs. Jane Luella, née **Dowd,** poet, b. Sheffield, Mass., 1847; d. Hudson, N.Y., July 4, 1941. [4; 10; 11]

Smith, Mrs. Jeanie Oliver, née **Davidson,** poet and novelist, b. Troy, N.Y., 1836; d. Johnstown, N.Y., Nov. 16, 1925. [10]

Smith, Jennie, religious writer, b. 1842; d. ?

Smith, Jeremiah, jurist, b. Exeter, N.H., 1837; d. St. Andrews, N.B., Sept. 3, 1921. [1; 4; 10]

Smith, Jerome van Crowninshield, physician, b. Conway, N.H., 1800; d. New York, N.Y., Aug. 21, 1879. [3; 6; 7]

Smith, Jessie Willcox, artist, b. Philadelphia, Pa.; d. Philadelphia, Pa., May 3, 1935. [7; 10]

Smith, Job Lewis, physician, b. Spafford, N.Y., 1827; d. New York, N.Y., June 9, 1897. [1; 3]

Smith, John, clergyman and educationist, b. Newbury, Mass., 1752; d. Hanover, N.H., April 30, 1809. [3; 6]

Smith, John Augustine, physician, b. Westmoreland county, Va., 1782; d. New York, N.Y., Feb. 9, 1865. [1; 3; 5; 6; 34]

Smith, John Bernhard, entomologist, b. New York, N.Y., 1858; d. New Brunswick, N.J., March 12, 1912. [1; 5; 10]

Smith, John Byington, clergyman, b. Schroon Lake, N.Y., 1830; d. Fayetteville, N.Y., Aug. 5, 1911. [67]

Smith, John C. clergyman, b. 1809; d. 1883.

Smith, John Carpenter, clergyman, b. 1816; d. 1901.

Smith, John Corson, freemason, b. Philadelphia, Pa., 1832; d. 1910. [10]

Smith, John Cotton, clergyman, b. Andover, Mass., 1826; d. New York, N.Y., Jan. 9, 1882. [1; 3; 4; 5; 6; 7]

Smith, John Day, jurist, b. Litchfield, Me., 1845; d. Minneapolis, Minn., March 5, 1933. [10; 70]

Smith, John Hyatt, clergyman, b. Saratoga, N.Y., 1824; d. Brooklyn, N.Y., Dec. 7, 1886. [3; 6]

Smith, John Jay, librarian, b. Burlington county, N.J., 1798; d. Germantown, Pa., Sept. 23, 1881. [1; 3; 6; 7]

Smith, John Lawrence, mineralogist, b. near Charleston, S.C., 1818; d. Louisville, Ky., Oct. 12, 1883. [1; 3; 4; 5; 34]

Smith, John Merlin Powis, educationist, b. London, England, 1866; d. New York, N.Y., Sept. 26, 1932. [1; 7; 10; 11]

Smith, John Talbot, priest, b. Saratoga, N.Y., 1855; d. Dobbs Ferry, N.Y., Sept. 24, 1923. [3; 10; 21]

Smith, John Warren, meteorologist, b. Grafton, N.H., 1863; d. Jan. 21, 1940. [10]

Smith, Johnston (pseud.). See Crane, Stephen.

Smith, Jonathan, historian, b. Peterborough, N.H., 1842; d. Clinton, Mass., Feb. 28, 1930. [4]

Smith, Jonathan Ritchie, clergyman, b. Baltimore, Md., 1852; d. Englewood, N.J., Feb. 23, 1936. [10; 11]

Smith, Joseph, clergyman, b. Westmoreland county, Pa., 1796. d. Greenburg, Pa., Dec. 4, 1868. [3; 6]

Smith, Joseph, Mormon leader, b. Sharon, Vt., 1805; d. Carthage, Ill., June 27, 1844. [1; 2; 3; 4; 5; 6; 7]

Smith, Joseph, Mormon leader, b. Kirtland, O., 1832; d. Independence, Mo., Dec. 10, 1914. [1; 2; 10]

Smith, Joseph Aubin, local historian, b. 1832; d. ?

Smith, Joseph Edward Adams, journalist, b. Portsmouth, N.H., 1822; d. Pittsfield, Mass., Oct. 29, 1896. [3b; 6]

Smith, Joseph Emerson, lawyer, b. Wiscasset, Me., 1835; d. Chicago, Ill., June 16, 1881.

Smith, Joseph Fielding, Mormon leader, b. Far West, Mo., 1838; d. Salt Lake City, Utah, Nov. 19, 1918. [1; 4; 10]

Smith, Joseph H., local historian, b. 1833; d. ? [37]

Smith, Joseph Henry, local historian, b. West Flamboro, Upper Canada, 1839; d. Hamilton, Ont., 1917. [27]

Smith, Joseph Mather, physician, b. New Rochelle, N.Y., 1789; d. New York, N.Y., April 22, 1866. [3; 4; 6]

Smith, Joseph Tate, clergyman, b. about 1819; d. 1906.

Smith, Joshua, preacher, d. 1795.

Smith, Joshua Hett, politician, b. New York, N.Y., 1749; d. New York, N.Y., 1818. [3]

Smith, Judson, educationist, b. Middlefield, Mass, 1837; d. Roxbury, Mass., June 29, 1906. [1; 3; 4; 5; 10]

Smith, Mrs. Julie P., novelist, d. 1883. [6; 7]

Smith, Julius, missionary, b. 1857; d. ?

Smith, Junius, lawyer and promoter, b. Plymouth, Conn., 1780; d. Bloomingdale, N.Y., Jan. 22, 1852. [1; 3; 4; 6]

Smith, Justin Almerin, clergyman, b. Ticonderoga, N.Y., 1819; d. Chicago, Ill., Feb. 4, 1896. [3; 6]

Smith, Justin Harvey, historian, b. Boscawen, N.H., 1857; d. New York, N.Y., March 21, 1930. [1; 7; 10]

Smith, Katharine. See Dos Passos, Mrs. Katharine, née Smith.

Smith, Mrs. Katharine Grey, née **Hogg,** novelist, b. Booneville, Ky., 1876; d. Beverly Hills, Calif., Jan. 6, 1933. [35]

Smith, Kirby Flower, educationist, b. Pawlet, Vt., 1862; d. Baltimore, Md., Dec. 6, 1918. [10]

Smith, Langdon, journalist, b. Kentucky, 1858; d. 1908. [10; 34]

Smith, Laura Rountree, writer of books for children, b. Chicago, Ill., 1876; d. Feb. 22, 1924. [7; 10; 11]

Smith, Lloyd Pearsall, librarian, b. Philadelphia, Pa., 1822; d. Germantown, Pa., July 2, 1886. [1; 3; 6]

Smith, Logan Pearsall, essayist and literary critic, b. Millville, N.J., 1865; d. London, England, March 2, 1946. [7; 10]

Smith, Lucio C., educationist, b. about 1853; d. 1896.

Smith, Lucius Edwin, journalist, b. Williamstown, Mass., 1822; d. 1900. [3; 6]

Smith, Mrs. Lucy, née **Humphrey,** poet and anthologist, b. 1869; d. Ithaca, N.Y., Nov. 18, 1939. [7]

Smith, Mrs. Lucy Hahn King, née **Cunningham,** poet, b. Columbus, O., 1871; d. Nashville, Tenn., June 23, 1940. [16]

Smith, Mrs. Lydia Adeline, née **Jackson,** mental patient, b. 1835; d ?

Smith, Mrs. Lydia Annie, née **Jocelyn,** novelist, b. 1836; d. ?

Smith, Lyman Cyrus, poet, b. Wentworth county, Ont., 1850; d. Oshawa, Ont., Jan. 30, 1928. [27]

Smith, Mrs. M. B., novelist, fl. 1860-1897.

Smith, Mabell Shippie Clarke, miscellaneous writer, b. Boston, Mass., 1864; d. New York, N.Y., May 25, 1942. [7; 10; 11]

Smith, Mrs. Margaret, née **Bayard,** social leader, 1778; d. Washington, D.C., June 7, 1844. [1; 3; 6; 7]

Smith, Margaret Vowell, historian, b. Louisville, Ky., 1839; d. Alexandria, Va., March, 1926. [34]

Smith, Marion Couthouy, novelist and poet, b. Philadelphia, Pa.; d. New York, N.Y., Nov. 19, 1931. [10; 11]

Smith, Mary Elizabeth, deaconess, b. Dawson county, Ga., 1880; d. Belton, S.C., March 31, 1915. [10]

Smith, Mrs. Mary Louise, née **Riley.** See Smith, Mrs. May, née Riley.

Smith, Mrs. Mary Prudence, née **Wells,** writer of books for children, b. Attica, N.Y., 1840; d. Greenfield, Mass., Dec. 17, 1930. [3; 5; 7; 10; 11]

Smith, Mrs. Mary Stuart, née **Harrison,** miscellaneous writer, b. University, Va., 1834; d. 1917. [7; 34]

Smith, Matthew Hale, clergyman, b. Portland, Me., 1816; d. Brooklyn, N.Y., Nov. 7, 1879. [3; 4; 5; 6]

Smith, Mrs. May, née **Riley,** poet, b. Rochester, N.Y., 1842; d. New York, N.Y., Jan. 14, 1927. [7; 10]

Smith, Michael, clergyman and topographer, fl. 1808-1814. [27]

Smith, Minna Caroline, novelist and translator, b. Monterey, Calif., 1860; d. Feb. 26, 1929. [10]

Smith, Moses, sailor, b. Huntington, N.Y., 1785; d. ?

Smith, Moses, clergyman, b. 1817; d. 1869.

Smith, Moses, clergyman, b. Hebron, Conn., 1830; d. Chicago, Ill., Nov. 30, 1904. [62]

Smith, Munroe. See Smith, Edmund Munroe.

Smith, Mrs. Nancy W., née Paine, historian, b. 1859; d. Sept. 2, 1940.

Smith, Nathan, physician, b. Rehoboth, Mass., 1762; d. New Haven, Conn., Jan. 26, 1829. [1; 3; 4; 5; 6]

Smith, Nathan Ryno, surgeon, b. Cornish, N.H., 1797; d. Baltimore, Md., July 3, 1877. [1; 3; 4; 6; 34]

Smith, Nelson Foot, local historian, b. 1813; d. 1861. [34]

Smith, Nicholas, soldier and journalist, b. Blackburn, England, 1836; d. Milwaukee, Wis., 1911. [7; 10]

Smith, Nora Archibald, educationist and writer of books for children, b. Philadelphia, Pa., about 1857; d. Portland, Me., Feb. 1, 1934. [7; 10; 15]

Smith, Oberlin, engineer, b. Cincinnati, O., 1840; d. Bridgeton, N.J., July 18, 1926. [4; 10; 11]

Smith, Oliver Hampton, lawyer, b. Bucks county, Pa., 1794; d. Indianapolis, Ind., March 19, 1859. [1; 3; 4; 5; 6]

Smith, Onnie Warren, angler, b. Weyauwega, Wis., 1872; d. Mondovi, Wis., Sept. 22, 1941. [10; 11; 44]

Smith, Orlando Jay, journalist, b. near Terre Haute, Ind., 1842; d. Dobbs Ferry, N.Y., Dec. 20, 1908. [10]

Smith, Paul Ernest, civil servant, d. Quebec, Que., Sept. 4, 1914. [27]

Smith, Penn. See Smith, Richard Penn.

Smith, Percy Frazer, biographer, b. 1848; d. St. Louis, Mo., Jan. 10, 1937.

Smith, Persifor Frazer, lawyer, b. 1808; d. 1882.

Smith, Peter Francisco, lawyer, b. about 1841; d. 1913.

Smith, Philip Henry, historian, b. 1842; d. ? [6]

Smith, Preserved, historian, b. Cincinnati, O., 1880; d. Louisville, Ky., May 15, 1941. [7; 10; 11]

Smith, Ralph Dunning, local historian, b. 1804; d. 1874.

Smith, Reed, educationist, b. Washington, D.C., 1881; d. Pawley's Island, S.C., July 24, 1943. [7; 10]

Smith, Reuben, clergyman, b. South Hadley, Mass., 1789; d. Beaver Dam, Wis., Nov. 7, 1860. [56]

Smith, Richard McAllister, educationist, b. 1819; d. 1870.

Smith, Richard Morris, genealogist, b. 1827; d. 1896.

Smith, Richard Penn, lawyer and playwright, b. Philadelphia, Pa., 1799; d. near Philadelphia, Pa., Aug. 12, 1854. [1; 3; 6; 7; 9]

Smith, Richard Somers, merchant, b. 1789; d. 1884.

Smith, Richard Somers, soldier and educationist, b. Philadelphia, Pa., 1813; d. Annapolis, Md., Jan. 23, 1877. [1; 3; 4; 6]

Smith, Richmond Mayo. See Mayo-Smith, Richmond.

Smith, Robert Henry, educationist, b. Cowansville, Que., 1862; d. Watertown, Mass., Dec. 11, 1933.

Smith, Robert Seneca, clergyman, b. Clarendon, Vt., 1880; d. Hamden, Conn., Jan. 14, 1939. [10; 62]

Smith, Robert Walter, local historian, b. 1816; d. 1881.

Smith, Mrs. Robina, née Lizars. See Lizars, Robina.

Smith, Roderick A., local historian, b. 1831; d. 1918. [37]

Smith, Roland Cotton, clergyman, b. New York, N.Y., 1860; d. Ipswich, Mass., Aug. 30, 1934. [10; 45]

Smith, Roswell Chamberlain, educationist, b. Franklin, Conn., 1797; d. Hartford, Conn., April 20, 1875. [6]

Smith, Ruel Perley, journalist and novelist, b. Bangor, Me., 1869; d. Brooklyn, N.Y., July 30, 1937. [7; 10]

Smith, Samuel, historian, b. Burlington, N.J., 1720; d. Burlington, N.J., 1776. [3; 6]

Smith, Samuel Calvin, physician, b. Hollidaysburg, Pa., 1881; d. East Stroudsberg, Pa., July 31, 1939. [10]

Smith, Samuel Francis, clergyman and poet, b. Boston, Mass., 1808; d. Boston, Mass., Nov. 16, 1895. [1; 2; 3; 4; 5; 6; 7; 9]

Smith, Samuel George, clergyman, b. Birmingham, England, 1852; d. St. Paul Minn., March 25, 1915. [10]

Smith, Samuel Harrison, journalist, b. Philadelphia, Pa., 1772; d. Washington, D.C., Nov. 1, 1845. [1; 3; 4; 6]

Smith, Mrs. Samuel Harrison. See Smith, Mrs. Margaret, née Bayard.

Smith, Samuel Stanhope, clergyman and educationist, b. Pequea, Pa., 1750; d. Princeton, N.J., Aug. 21, 1819. [1; 3; 4; 5; 6]

Smith, Saqui, journalist, b. 1860; d. New York, N.Y., April 19, 1924.

Smith, Mrs. Sara, née Henderson, poet, d. 1884.

Smith, Sara Trainer, writer of books for children, d. 1899. [21]

Smith, Mrs. Sarah Hathaway, née Bixby, poet, b. San Juan Bautista, Calif., 1871; d. Long Beach, Calif., Sept. 13, 1935. [11; 35]

Smith, Mrs. Sarah Louise, née Hickman, poet, b. Detroit, Mich., 1811; d. New York, N.Y., Feb. 12, 1832. [3; 7]

Smith, Seba, political satirist, journalist, and poet, b. Buckfield, Me., 1792; d. Patchogue, Long Island, N.Y., July 28, 1868. [1; 2; 3; 4; 5; 6; 7; 8; 9; 71]

Smith, Sebastian Bach, priest, b. Germany, 1845; d. Havana, Cuba, March 2, 1895. [3b; 21]

Smith, Seymour Wemyss, journalist, b. Cleveland, O., 1896. d. New York, N.Y., Jan. 4, 1932. [10; 11]

Smith, Sidney, cartoonist, b. Bloomington, Ill., 1877; d. Chicago, Ill., Oct. 20, 1935. [7; 10]

Smith, Solomon Franklin, comedian and theatrical manager, b. Norwich, N.Y., 1801; d. St. Louis, Mo., Feb. 14, 1869. [1; 3; 4; 6]

Smith, Stephe R., journalist, fl. 1871-1895.

Smith, Stephen, surgeon, b. near Skaneateles, N.Y., 1823; d. Montour Falls., N.Y., Aug. 26, 1922. [1; 3; 4; 10]

Smith, Stephen Rensselaer, clergyman, b. 1788; d. 1850.

Smith, Mrs. Susan E., née Drake, hospital matron, b. 1817; d. ? [34]

Smith, Sylvanus, fisherman, b. 1829; d. Gloucester, Mass., 1917.

Smith, Theobald, pathologist, b. Albany, N.Y., 1859; d. Princeton, N.J., Dec. 10, 1934. [1a; 10]

Smith, Theodate Louise, psychologist, b. Hallowell, Me., 1859; d. Worcester, Mass., Feb. 16, 1914. [1; 62]

Smith, Thomas Barlow, novelist, b. Windsor, N.S., 1839; d. Windsor, N.S., July 22, 1933. [27]

Smith, Thomas Berry, poet and educationist, b. Bowling Green, Mo., 1850; d. May 8, 1933. [10; 11]

Smith, Thomas Buckingham. See Smith, Buckingham.

Smith, Thomas Edward Vermilye, lawyer, b. 1857; d. March 3, 1922.

Smith, Thomas Lacey, lawyer, b. 1805; d. 1875.

Smith, Thomas Laurens, local historian, b. 1797; d. 1882. [38]

Smith, Thomas Marshall, historian, d. about 1859.

Smith, Thomas Robert, literary editor, b. Phillipsburg, N.J., 1880; d. New York, N.Y., April 11, 1942. [7; 10]

Smith, Thomas Watson, clergyman, b. about 1835; d. March 8, 1902. [27]

Smith, Thorne, novelist, b. 1893; d. Sarasota, Fla., June 20, 1934. [7]

Smith, Truman, lawyer and politician, b. Roxbury, Conn., 1791; d. Stamford, Conn., May 3, 1884. [1; 3; 4; 5; 6]

Smith, Uriah, religious leader, b. West Wilton, N.H., 1832; d. Battle Creek, Mich., March 6, 1903. [1; 10]

Smith, Wallace, novelist, b. 1895; d. Hollywood, Calif., Jan. 31, 1937.

Smith, Walter, art teacher, b. 1836; d. 1886.

Smith, Walter, educationist, b. England, 1859; d. Charlottesville, Va., Jan. 10, 1907.

Smith, Walter Denton, lawyer, b. Jackson, Mich., 1871; d. Ann Arbor, Mich., Sept. 20, 1896. [3b]

Smith, Walter George, lawyer, b. Logan county, O., 1854; d. Torresdale, Pa., April 4, 1924. [4; 10; 21]

Smith, Walter Robinson, sociologist, b. Excelsior Springs, Mo., 1875; d. Lawrence, Kans., Jan. 7, 1937. [10; 11]

Smith, Wesley, clergyman, b. 1815; d. 1902.

Smith, Wilder, clergyman, b. Boston, Mass., 1835; d. Hartford, Conn., Sept. 1, 1891. [62]

Smith, William, clergyman and educationist, b. Aberdeen, Scotland, 1727; d. Philadelphia, Pa., May 14, 1803. [1; 2; 3; 4; 5; 6; 7; 8; 9]

Smith, William, jurist, b. New York, N.Y, 1728; d. Quebec, Lower Canada, Dec. 6, 1793. [1; 3; 7; 27]

Smith, William, clergyman, b. Scotland, about 1754; d. New York, N.Y., April 6, 1821. [1; 3; 6]

Smith, William, historian, b. New York, N.Y., 1769; d. Quebec, Que., Dec. 16, 1847. [9; 27]

Smith, William, historian, b. Hamilton, Ont., 1859; d. Ottawa, Ont., Jan. 28, 1932. [11; 27]

Smith, William Andrew, clergyman and educationist, b. Fredericksburg, Va., 1802; d. Richmond, Va., March 1, 1870. [1; 3; 6; 34]

Smith, William Benjamin, educationist, b. Stamford, Ky., 1850; d. Columbia, Mo., Aug. 6, 1934. [4; 7; 10; 11; 34]

Smith, William C., clergyman, b. 1809; d. 1886.

Smith, William C., clergyman, b. Blenheim, N.Y., 1818; d. 1891. [6]

Smith, William Farrar, soldier, b. St. Albans, Vt., 1824; d. Philadelphia, Pa., Feb. 28, 1903. [1; 3; 4; 5; 10]

Smith, William Griswold, engineer, b. Toledo, O., 1870; d. Paterson, N.J., Dec. 25, 1943. [10]

Smith, William Hawley, educationist, b. Franklin county, Mass., 1845; d. May 9, 1922. [10]

Smith, William Henry, compiler, fl. 1846-73. [27]

Smith, William Henry, journalist, b. Austerlitz, N.Y., 1833; d. Lake Forest, Ill., July 27, 1896. [1; 3; 4; 5; 6; 7]

Smith, William Henry, journalist, b. Noblesville, Ind., 1839; d. Washington, D.C., Feb. 12, 1935.

Smith, William Henry, physician, b. Three Rivers, Mich., 1846; d. St. Clair, Mich., Nov. 2, 1925. [53]

Smith, William L. G., consular agent, b. West Haven, Vt., 1814; d. 1878. [6; 43]

Smith, William Loughton, politician, b. Charleston, S.C., 1758; d. Charleston, S.C., Dec. 19, 1812. [1; 3; 6]

Smith, William Moore, lawyer and poet, b. 1859; d. Philadelphia, Pa., March 12, 1921. [19]

Smith, William Pitt, physician, b. 1760; d. 1795. [6]

Smith, William Prescott, railwayman, b. about 1822; d. Baltimore, Md., Oct. 1, 1872.

Smith, William Richmond, journalist, b. Ottawa, Ont., 1868; d. New York, N.Y., Feb. 19, 1934. [27]

Smith, William Robert Lee, clergyman, b. 1846; d. Norfolk, Va., Nov. 12, 1935.

Smith, William Roy, historian, b. Bluff Springs, Tex., 1876; d. Bryn Mawr, Pa., Feb. 13, 1938. [7; 10]

Smith, William Rudolph, soldier and historian, b. 1787; d. Aug. 29, 1868. [3b; 44]

Smith, William Russell, lawyer and politician, b. Russellville, Ky., 1815; d. Washington, D.C., Feb. 26, 1896. [1; 3; 4; 5; 6; 7]

Smith, William Spooner, clergyman, b. Leverett, Mass., 1821; d. Auburndale, Mass., Jan. 11, 1916.

Smith, William Thayer, physician, b. New York, N.Y., 1839; d. Hanover, N.H., Sept. 17, 1909. [10; 62]

Smith, William Walter, clergyman, b. New York, N.Y., 1868; d. New York, N.Y., March 2, 1942. [10; 11]

Smith, William Waugh, educationist, b. Warrenton, Va., 1845; d. Lynchburg, Va., Nov. 29, 1912. [1; 3; 4; 10]

Smith, William Wye, clergyman and poet, b. Jedburgh, Scotland, 1827; d. Burford, Ont., Jan. 6, 1917. [27]

Smith, Winchell, playwright, b. Hartford, Conn., 1871; d. Farmington, Conn., June 10, 1933. [7; 10]

Smith, Zachariah Frederick, historian, b. Henry county, Ky., 1827; d. Louisville, Ky., July 4, 1911. [3; 4; 34; 74]

Smithers, William West, lawyer, b. Philadelphia, Pa., 1864; d. Philadelphia, Pa., March 18, 1947. [7; 10]

Smithey, Royall Bascom, educationist, b. Amelia county, Va., 1851; d. July 18, 1925. [10]

Smithson, Noble, lawyer, b. Nolensville, Tenn., 1841; d. 1919. [10]

Smithwick, Noah, pioneer, b. Kentucky, 1808; d. 1899.

Smock, John Conover, geologist, b. Monmouth county, N.J., 1842; d. Hudson, N.Y., April 21, 1926. [4; 10]

Smoot, Richmond Kelley, clergyman, b. 1836; d. about 1904.

Smoote, George Parker, poet, b. 1828; d. 1891.

Smucker, Samuel Mosheim. See Schmucker, Samuel Mosheim.

Smylie, Charles Albert, soldier, b. 1858; d. 1902.

Smyser, William Emory, educationist, b. Baltimore county, Md., 1866; d. Delaware, O., May 24, 1935. [10; 11]

Smyth, Albert Henry, educationist, b. Philadelphia, Pa., 1863; d. Philadelphia, Pa., May 4, 1907. [1; 5; 7; 9; 10]

Smyth, Alexander, soldier and politician, b. Rathlin, Ireland, 1765; d. Washington, D.C., April 17, 1830. [1; 3; 6]

Smyth, Clifford, journalist and biographer, b. New York, N.Y., 1866; d. Armonk, N.Y., Nov. 30, 1943. [10; 11]

Smyth, Egbert Coffin, theologian, b. Brunswick, Me., 1829; d. Andover, Mass., April 12, 1904. [1; 3; 4; 5; 6; 10]

Smyth, George Hutchinson, clergyman, b. county Antrim, Ireland, 1839; d. Holyoke, Mass., May 4, 1911. [56]

Smyth, Herbert Weir, educationist, b. Wilmington, Del., 1857; d. Bar Harbor, Me., July 16, 1937. [4; 7; 10; 11; 51]

Smyth, Hugh Patrick, priest, b. 1855; d. Evanston, Ill., Nov. 6, 1927. [4; 21]

Smyth, John Paterson, clergyman, b. Ireland, 1852; d. Montreal, Que., Feb. 14, 1932. [11; 27]

Smyth, Julian Kennedy, clergyman, b. New York, N.Y., 1856; d. White Sulphur Springs, Va., April 4, 1921. [1; 10]

Smyth, Newman. See Smyth, Samuel Phillips Newman.

Smyth, Samuel Phillips Newman, theologian, b. Brunswick, Me., 1843; d. New Haven, Conn., Jan. 6, 1925. [1; 5; 7; 10]

Smyth, Thomas, clergyman, b. Belfast, Ireland, 1808; d. Charleston, S.C., Aug. 20, 1873. [1; 3; 4; 5; 6]

Smyth, William, mathematician, b. Pittston, Me., 1797; d. Brunswick, Me., April 4, 1868. [1; 3; 4; 5; 6; 38]

Smythe, Albert Ernest Stafford, journalist and poet, b. county Antrim, Ireland, 1861; d. Hamilton, Ont., Oct. 2, 1947. [30]

Smythe, Charles Winslow, educationist, b. 1829; d. 1865.

Smythe, George Franklin, clergyman, b. Toledo, O., 1852; d. Aug. 25, 1934. [10]

Smythe, William Ellsworth, journalist, b. Worcester, Mass., 1861; d. New York, N.Y., Oct. 6, 1922. [4; 10; 11]

Snead, Littleton Upshur, clergyman, b. Freedom, Pa., 1840; d. near Mayfield, N.Y., Aug. 24, 1924.

Snead, Thomas Lowndes, soldier, b. Henrico county, Va., 1828; d. New York, N.Y., Oct. 17, 1890. [1; 3; 4; 34]

Sneath, Elias Hershey, educationist, b. Mountville, Pa., 1857; d. New Haven, Conn., Dec. 20, 1935. [10; 11; 62]

Sneddon, Robert William, novelist, b. Beith, Scotland, 1880; d. New York, N.Y., March 8, 1944. [7; 11]

Snell, Thomas, clergyman, b. Cummington, Mass., 1774; d. North Brookfield, Mass., May 4, 1862. [3]

Snelling, Mrs. Anna L., née **Putnam,** novelist, d. New York, N.Y., about 1859.

Snelling, Henry Hunt, photographer, b. Plattsburg, N.Y., 1817; d. St. Louis, Mo., June 24, 1897. [1; 3; 6]

Snelling, Richard, lawyer, b. about 1828; d. Toronto, Ont., July 26, 1893. [27]

Snelling, William Joseph, journalist, b. Boston, Mass., 1804; d. Chelsea, Mass., Dec. 24, 1848. [1; 3; 4; 6; 7; 9; 70]

Snethen, Nicholas, clergyman, b. Glen Cove, Long Island, N.Y., 1769; d. Princeton, Ind., May 30, 1845. [1; 3; 4]

Snider, Benjamin S., itinerant preacher, b. Rushville, N.Y., 1821; d. ?

Snider, Denton Jacques, educationist, poet, and lecturer, b. near Mount Gilead, O., 1841; d. St. Louis, Mo., Nov. 25, 1925. [1; 3; 5; 7; 10]

Snider, Guy Edward, economist, b. Cambridge, Ia., 1876; d. New York, N.Y., Jan. 10, 1940.

Snively, William Andrew, clergyman, b. Greencastle, Pa., 1833; d. Louisville, Ky., March 2, 1901. [3b; 10]

Snoddy, James Samuel, educationist, d. 1922.

Snodgrass, Joseph Evans, physician, b. 1813; d. 1880.

Snodgrass, William Davis, clergyman, b. West Hanover, Pa., 1796; d. Goshen, N.Y., May 28, 1886.

Snow, Alpheus Henry, lawyer, b. Claremont, N.H., 1859; d. New York, N.Y., Aug. 19, 1920. [10; 62]

Snow, Caleb Hopkins, physician, b. Boston, Mass., 1796; d. Boston, Mass., July 6, 1836. [3; 6]

Snow, Eliza Roxey. See Smith, Mrs. Eliza Roxey, née Snow.

Snow, Elliot, naval officer, b. 1866; d. Bryn Mawr, Pa., Nov. 27, 1939.

Snow, Francis Woolson, journalist, b. Boston, Mass., 1877; d. New York, N.Y., Feb. 6, 1949. [11; 51]

Snow Freeman, educationist, b. Palmyra, N.Y., 1841; d. Nelson, Pa., Sept. 12, 1894. [3b; 51]

Snow, George Washington, poet, b. Bangor, Me., 1809; d. 1900. [38]

Snow, Herman, spiritualist, b. 1812; d. 1905.

Snow, Marshall Solomon, educationist, b. Hyannis, Mass., 1842; d. Taunton, Mass., May 28, 1916. [4; 10; 51]

Snow, Samuel Sheffield, journalist and clergyman, fl. 1848-1863.

Snow, Walter Bradlee, advertising agent, b. 1860; d. Aug. 9, 1929. [11]

Snow, William Joseph, soldier, b. Brooklyn, N.Y., 1868; d. Washington, D.C., Feb. 27, 1947.

Snowden, James Henry, theologian, b. Hookstown, Pa., 1852; d. Pittsburgh, Pa., Dec. 18, 1936. [10; 11]

Snowden, James Ross, numismatist, b. Chester, Pa., 1809; d. Hulmeville, Bucks county, Pa., March 21, 1878. [1; 3; 4; 5; 6]

Snowden, Richard, educationist, d. Philadelphia, Pa., March 30, 1825. [7]

Snowden, Yates, historian, b. Charleston, S.C., 1858; d. Columbia, S.C., Feb. 22, 1933. [10]

Snyder, Albert Whitcomb, clergyman, b. Lisbon, N.Y., 1842; d. Elmhurst, N.Y., Feb. 23, 1914. [10]

Snyder, Carl, economist, b. Cedar Falls, Ia., 1869; d. Santa Barbara, Calif., Feb. 15, 1946.

Snyder, Harry, chemist, b. Cherry Valley, N.Y., 1867; d. Minneapolis, Minn., Oct. 11, 1927. [10; 11; 70]

Snyder, Henry Nelson, educationist, b. Macon, Ga., 1865; d. Spartanburg, S.C., Sept. 18, 1949. [10]

Snyder, John Francis, historian, b. Prairie du Pont, Ill., 1830; d. Virginia, April 30, 1921. [7]

Snyder, William Lamartine, lawyer, b. Hollidaysburg, Pa., 1848; d. Dec. 2, 1916. [10]

Sohier, Elizabeth Putnam, local historian, d. 1926.

Solberg, Thorvald, writer on copyright, b. Manitowoc, Wis., 1852; d. Bethesda, Md., June 15, 1949. [7; 10]

Soldan, Frank Louis, educationist, b. Frankfort-on-the-Main, Germany, 1842; d. St. Louis, Mo., March 27, 1908. [1]

Soley, James Russell, educationist, b. Roxbury, Mass., 1850; d. New York, N.Y., Sept. 11, 1911. [1; 3; 4; 5; 6; 7; 9; 10; 51]

Solis-Cohen, Solomon, physician, b. 1857; d. Philadelphia, Pa., July 12, 1948. [10]

Solly, Samuel Edwin, physician, b. London, England, 1845; d. Colorado Springs, Colo., 1906. [10]

Sombre, Samuel (pseud.). See Gerard, James Watson.

Somerby, Frederic Thomas, journalist, b. Newburyport, Mass., 1814; d. Worcester, Mass., Jan. 18, 1871. [3; 7]

Somerville, Alexander, soldier and journalist, b. East Lothian, Scotland, 1811; d. Toronto, Ont., June 17, 1885. [27]

Somerville, William Clarke, diplomat, b. St. Mary's county, Md., 1790; d. Auxerre, France, Jan. 5, 1826. [3; 4]

Sommers, Charles George, clergyman, b. London, England, 1793; d. New York, N.Y., Dec. 19, 1868. [3; 4]

Sommers, Lillian E., novelist, fl. 1887-1890.

Sommerville, Maxwell, archaeologist, b. Philadelphia, Pa., 1829; d. 1904. [4; 5; 10]

Sommerville, William, clergyman, b. Ireland, 1800; d. Nova Scotia, 1878. [27]

Sonneck, Oscar George Theodore, musician, b. Jersey City, N.J., 1873; d. New York, N.Y., Oct. 30, 1928. [7; 10; 11]

Sonnichsen, Albert, journalist, b. San Francisco, Calif., 1878; d. Willimantic, Conn., Aug. 15, 1931. [1; 7; 10]

Sooy, Josephus Leander, clergyman, b. 1849; d. 1915.

Sophocles, Evangelinus Apostolides, educationist, b. near Mount Pelion, Greece, 1807; d. Cambridge, Mass., Dec. 17, 1883. [1; 3; 4; 6; 9]

Soran, Charles, poet, b. 1807; d. 1857.

SoRelle, Rupert Pitt, business college executive, b. Lexington, Tex., 1871; d. New York, N.Y., Dec. 14, 1937. [11]

Sorenson, Alfred Rasmus, local historian, b. 1850; d. Omaha, Neb., Oct. 31, 1939.

Sotheran, Charles, bibliographer, b. Newington, Surrey, England, 1847; d. New York, N.Y., June 27, 1902. [3; 6; 10]

Sothern, Edward Hugh, actor, b. New Orleans, La., 1859; d. New York, N.Y., Oct. 28, 1933. [1; 2; 4; 5; 7; 10]

Soule, Mrs. Caroline Augusta, née White, religious worker, b. Albany, N.Y., 1824; d. 1903. [3; 6; 10]

Soule, Charles Carroll, publisher, b. Boston, Mass., 1842; d. Brookline, Mass., Jan. 7, 1913. [10; 51]

Soulé, Franklin, journalist, b. Freeport, Me., 1810; d. San Francisco, Calif., July 3, 1882. [35; 60]

Soulé, George, mathematician, b. Barrington, N.Y., 1834; d. New Orleans, La., Jan. 26, 1926. [1; 3; 4; 6]

Soule, Henry Birdsall, clergyman, d. 1852.

Soule, Richard, lexicographer, b. Duxbury, Mass., 1812; d. St. Louis, Mo., Dec. 25, 1877. [3; 4; 6]

Sousa, John Philip, bandmaster and novelist, b. Washington, D.C., 1854; d. Reading, Pa., March 6, 1932. [1; 2; 3; 4; 5; 7; 10; 20]

Souter, William Norwood, physician, b. 1861; d. New Castle, N.H., Nov. 24, 1935.

Southall, James Cocke, journalist, b. Charlottesville, Va., 1828; d. Norfolk, Va., Sept. 13, 1897. [1; 4; 6]

Southard, Elmer Ernest, physician, b. Boston, Mass., 1876; d. New York, N.Y., Feb. 8, 1920. [4; 10; 51]

Southard, Samuel Lewis, jurist and politician, b. Basking Ridge, N.J., 1787; d. Fredericksburg, Va., June 26, 1842. [1; 3; 4; 5; 6]

Southard, Samuel Lewis, clergyman, b. 1819; d. 1859. [3]

Southgate, Horatio, bishop, b. Portland, Me., 1812; d. Astoria, Long Island, N.Y., April 13, 1894. [1a; 3; 4; 5; 6]

Southwick, Albert Plympton, educationist, b. Charlestown, Mass., 1855; d. ? [7; 10]

Southwick, George Rinaldo, gynaecologist, b. Sangersfield, N.Y., 1859; d. Boston, Mass., Jan. 7, 1930. [4; 10; 11]

Southwick, Solomon, journalist, b. Newport, R.I., 1773; d. Albany, N.Y., Nov. 18, 1839. [1; 3; 4; 6; 7]

Southworth, Alvan S., explorer, b. 1846; d. New York, N.Y., Jan. 7, 1901. [6]

Southworth, Mrs. Emma Dorothy Eliza, née Nevitte, novelist, b. Washington, D.C., 1819; d. Washington, D.C., June 30, 1899. [1; 2; 3; 4; 5; 6; 7; 9; 10]

Southworth, George Champlin Shepard, educationist, b. West Springfield, Mass., Feb. 19, 1918. [7; 10; 62]

Southworth, Mrs. S. A., novelist, fl. 1854-1900. [6]

Sowell, Andrew Jackson, historian, b. 1848; d. 1921.

Sozinskey, Thomas S., physician, b. about 1852; d. 1889. [6]

Spaeth, Phillip Friedrich Adolph Theodor, clergyman, b. Esslingen, Germany, 1839; d. Philadelphia, Pa., July 2, 1910. [1; 3; 10]

Spafford, Horatio Gates, educationist, b. 1778; d. 1832. [6]

Spahr, Charles Barzillai, economist, b. Columbus, Ohio, 1860; d. by drowning in the English channel, Aug. 30, 1904. [1; 5; 10]

Spalding, Albert Goodwill, merchant, b. Byron, Ill., 1850; d. Point Loma, Calif., Sept. 9, 1915. [10]

Spalding, Charles Carroll, local historian, b. Montpelier, Vt., 1826; d. Boston, Mass., Jan. 19, 1877.

Spalding, Frederick Putnam, educationist, b. Wysox, Pa., 1857; d. Columbia, Mo., Sept. 4, 1923. [10]

Spalding, Henry Stanislaus, priest, b. Bardstown, Ky., 1865; d. Dec. 27, 1934. [21]

Spalding, Hugh Mortimer, lawyer, fl. 1877-1903.

Spalding, J. Willett, sailor, b. Richmond, Va., 1827; d. ? [6]

Spalding, James Alfred, physician, b. 1846; d. Portland, Me., Feb. 27, 1938.

Spalding, James Field, clergyman and educationist, b. Enfield, Conn., 1839; d. Cambridge, Mass., Aug. 12, 1921. [10]

Spalding, John Franklin, bishop, b. Belgrade, Me., 1828; d. Erie, Pa., March 9, 1902. [3; 4; 6; 10]

Spalding, John Lancaster, bishop, b. Lebanon, Ky., 1840; d. Chicago, Ill., Aug. 25, 1916. [1; 3; 4; 5; 6; 10; 21]

Spalding, Joshua, clergyman, b. 1760; d. 1825. [6]

Spalding, Josiah, clergyman, b. Plainfield, Conn., 1751; d. Buckland, Mass., May 8, 1823. [62]

Spalding, Martin John, archbishop, b. Rolling Fork, Ky., 1810; d. Baltimore, Md., Feb. 7, 1872. [1; 3; 4; 5; 6; 7; 21; 34]

Spalding, Phebe Estelle, educationist, b. Westfield, Vt., 1859; d. Claremont, Calif., March 12, 1937. [35]

Spalding, Samuel Jones, genealogist, b. 1820; d. 1892.

Spalding, Volney Morgan, botanist, b. East Bloomfield, N.Y., 1849; d. Loma Linda, Calif.; Nov. 12, 1918. [1; 10]

Spalding, William Andrew, miscellaneous writer, b. Ann Arbor, Mich. 1852; d. Los Angeles, Calif., Sept. 7, 1941. [10; 35]

Spangenberg, Mrs. Fanny, née Ilgenfritz, poet, b. York, Pa., 1838; d. Prescott, Wash., July 20, 1930.

Spangler, Andrew M., journalist, b. York, Pa., 1818; d. Philadelphia, Pa., Nov. 2, 1897. [3b]

Spangler, Henry Wilson, engineer and educationist, b. Carlisle, Pa., 1858; d. Philadelphia, Pa., March 17, 1912. [1; 10]

Spare, John, physician, b. Canton, Mass., 1816; d. New Bedford, Mass., May 22, 1901. [45]

Sparhawk, Frances Campbell, novelist, b. Amesbury, Mass., 1847; d. Brookline, Mass., Jan. 9, 1930. [4; 7; 10; 11]

Sparks, Edwin Earle, educationist, b. Licking county, O., 1860; d. State College, Pa., June 15, 1924. [4; 7; 10; 11]

Sparks, Jared, clergyman, biographer, and historian, b. Willington, Conn., 1789; d. Cambridge, Mass., March 14, 1866. [1; 2; 3; 4; 5; 6; 7; 9]

Sparks, William Henry, lawyer, b. St. Simon's Island, Ga., 1800; d. Marietta, Ga., Jan. 13, 1882. [3; 4; 34]

Sparrow, William, clergyman, b. Charlestown, Mass., 1801; d. Alexandria, Va., Jan. 17, 1874. [1; 3; 4; 6; 34]

Spaulding, Edward Gleason, educationist, b. Burlington, Vt., 1873; d. Princeton, N.J., Jan. 31, 1940. [7; 10; 11]

Spaulding, Elbridge Gerry, banker, b. Cayuga county, N.Y., 1809; d. Buffalo, N.Y., May 5, 1897. [1; 3; 4; 5; 6]

Spaulding, Henry George, clergyman, b. Spencer, Mass., 1837; d. Brookline, Mass., Sept. 13, 1920. [4; 10; 51]

Spaulding, John, clergyman, b. 1800; d. 1889.

Spaulding, Jonah, historian, fl. 1819-1837. [38]

Spaulding, Oliver Lyman, soldier, b. Michigan, 1875; d. Washington, D.C., March 27, 1947. [10]

Spayth, Henry, draught-player, b. Pennsylvania, 1825; d. ? [6]

Spear, Charles, philanthropist, b. Boston, Mass., 1801; d. Washington, D.C., April 18, 1863. [1; 3; 6]

Spear, John Murray, clergyman, b. 1804; d. ? [6]

Spear, John W., novelist, fl. 1883-1897. [6]

Spear, Samuel Thayer, clergyman, b. Ballston Spa, N.Y., 1812; d. Brooklyn, N.Y., April 1, 1891. [3; 4; 6]

Spearman, Frank Hamilton, novelist, b. Buffalo, N.Y., 1859; d. Hollywood, Calif., Dec. 29, 1937. [7; 10; 11; 21; 35]

Spears, John Randolph, journalist and historian, b. Ohio, 1850; d. Utica, N.Y., Jan. 25, 1936. [4; 7; 10]

Spedon, Andrew Learmont, journalist, b. Edinburgh, Scotland, 1831; d. Bermuda, Sept. 26, 1884. [27]

Speece, Conrad, clergyman, b. New London, Va., 1776; d. Staunton, Va., Feb. 15, 1836. [3; 34]

Speed, John Gilmer, journalist, b. Louisville, Ky., 1853; d. Mendham, N.J., Feb. 2, 1909. [3; 4; 7; 10; 34]

Speed, Nell (pseud.). See Sampson, Mrs. Emma, née Speed.

Speed, Thomas, lawyer, b. Bardstown, Ky., 1841; d. Louisville, Ky., Dec. 20, 1904. [10; 34; 74]

Speer, Emory, jurist, b. Culloden, Ga., 1848; d. Macon, Ga., Dec. 13, 1918. [1; 5; 10; 34]

Speer, John, biographer, b. Kittanning, Pa., 1817; d. 1906. [4]

Speer, Robert Elliott, foreign mission secretary, b. Huntingdon, Pa., 1867; d. Bryn Mawr, Pa., Nov. 23, 1947. [7; 10; 11; 12]

Speer, William, missionary, b. New Alexandria, Pa., 1822; d. Washington, Pa., Feb. 15, 1904. [1; 3; 5; 6; 10]

Speicher, Jacob, missionary, b. Brooklyn, N.Y., 1866; d. Swatow, China, July 17, 1930. [67]

Speirs, Frederic William, economist, b. 1867; d. 1905.

Spence, Irving, church historian, b. 1799; d. Snowhill, Md., Jan. 11, 1836. [34]

Spence, John David Macdonald, lawyer, b. Mount Forest, Ont., 1867; d. Toronto, Ont., April 19, 1943. [30]

Spencer, Mrs. Anna, née Garlin, reformer, b. Attleboro, Mass., 1851; d. New York, N.Y., Feb. 12, 1931. [1; 4; 10; 11]

Spencer, Armon, clergyman and poet, b. Huron, N.Y., 1818; d. Newark, N.Y., June 1, 1898. [63]

Spencer, Mrs. Bella Zilfa, novelist, b. London, England, 1840; d. Tuscaloosa, Ala., Aug. 1, 1867. [3]

Spencer, Claudius Buchanan, clergyman and editor, b. Fowlerville, Mich., 1856; d. July 14, 1934. [10]

Spencer, Mrs. Cornelia, née Phillips, historian, b. Harlem, N.Y., 1825; d. Cambridge, Mass., March 11, 1908. [1; 3; 5; 7; 34]

Spencer, Mrs. George E. See Spencer, Mrs. William Loring, née Nunez.

Spencer, Guilford Lawson, chemist, b. Lafayette, Ind., 1858; d. Herricks, Me., March 23, 1925. [10]

Spencer, Hazelton, educationist, b. Methuen, Mass., 1893; d. Baltimore, Md., July 28, 1944. [7; 10]

Spencer, Hiram Ladd, journalist and poet, b. Castleton, Vt., 1829; d. Saint John, N.B., Oct. 15, 1915. [4; 27]

Spencer, Ichabod Smith, clergyman, b. Rupert, Vt., 1798; d. Brooklyn, N.Y., Nov. 23, 1854. [3; 4; 6; 43]

Spencer, Jesse Ames, clergyman, b. Hyde Park, Dutchess county, N.Y., 1816; d. New York, N.Y., Sept. 2, 1898. [1; 3; 5; 6; 7]

Spencer, John Canfield, lawyer and politician, b. Hudson, N.Y., 1788; d. Albany, N.Y., May 17, 1855. [1; 3; 4; 5; 6]

Spencer, John Henderson, clergyman, fl. 1866-1886. [34]

Spencer, Joseph William Winthrop, geologist, b. Dundas, Ont., 1851; d. Toronto, Ont., Oct. 9, 1921. [4]

Spencer, Lillian, novelist, fl. 1885-1888. [6]

Spencer, Maja (pseud.). See Spencer, Mrs. William Loring, née Nunez.

Spencer, Morton W., poet and clergyman, b. 1836; d. ?

Spencer, Oliver M., clergyman, b. about 1781; d. ?

Spencer, Richard Henry, genealogist, b. 1833; d. ?

Spencer, Mrs. Sara Jane, née Andrews, educationist, b. Savona, N.Y., 1837; d. New York, N.Y., 1909. [3; 10]

Spencer, Theodore, clergyman, b. Hudson, N.Y., 1800; d. Utica, N.Y., June 14, 1870. [3; 4]

Spencer, Theodore, educationist and poet, b. Villanova, Pa., 1902; d. Cambridge, Mass., Jan. 18, 1949. [10]

Spencer, Thomas, physician, b. Great Barrington, Mass., 1793; d. Philadelphia, Pa., May 30, 1857. [3; 4; 6]

Spencer, Thomas, clergyman, b. London, England, 1851; d. Petersburg, Va., Oct. 23, 1904.

Spencer, Mrs. William Loring, née Nuñez, novelist, fl. 1877-1902. [3; 10; 34]

Spenzer, John George, physician and chemist, b. Cleveland, O., 1864; d. Cleveland, O., July 26, 1932. [10; 11; 13]

Speranza, Gino Charles, lawyer, b. Connecticut, 1872; d. July 12, 1927. [10]

Sperry, Andrew F., soldier, b. 1839; d. ? [37]

Sperry, Lyman Beecher, physician and lecturer, b. Sherman, N.Y., 1841; d. Los Angeles, Calif., July 1, 1923. [10; 11; 70]

Sperry, Philip, photographer, b. 1901; d. Brooklyn, N.Y., Jan. 24, 1949.

Spicer, Mrs. Anne, née Higginson, poet, b. Burlington, Ia.; d. Kenilworth, Ill., Sept. 9, 1935. [7; 10; 11]

Spicer, Tobias, clergyman, b. 1788; d. ?

Spicer, William Arnold, military historian, b. 1845; d. 1913.

Spicker, Max, musician, b. Königsberg, Germany, 1858; d. New York, N.Y., Oct. 15, 1912. [1; 20]

Spiegelberg, Mrs. Flora, née Langerman, writer of books for children, b. 1859; d. New York, N.Y., Dec. 9, 1943.

Spies, August Vincent Theodore, anarchist, b. Landeck, Germany, 1855; d. Chicago, Ill., Nov. 11, 1887. [3]

Spillane, Daniel, musician, b. 1861; d. 1893.

Spillman, William Jasper, agricultural economist, b. Lawrence county, Mo., 1863; d. Washington, D.C., July 11, 1931. [10; 11]

Spingarn, Joel Elias, educationist, journalist, soldier, and poet, b. New York, N.Y., 1875; d. New York, N.Y., July 26, 1939. [4; 7; 10; 11]

Spinney, William Anthony, educationist, b. Meadowvale, N.S., 1847; d. Boston, Mass., Jan. 1, 1911. [51]

Spitzka, Edward Charles, neurologist, b. New York, N.Y., 1852; d. New York, N.Y., Jan. 13, 1914. [1; 4; 10]

Spivak, Charles David, physician and editor, b. Poltava, Russia, 1861; d. Denver, Colo., Oct. 16, 1927. [1; 10]

Spivey, Thomas Sawyer, manufacturer and novelist, b. Gallatin county, Ill., 1856; d. Cincinnati, O., Nov. 7, 1938. [10]

Splawn, Andrew Jackson, stockman, b. Holt county, Mo., 1845; d. North Yakima, Wash., March 2, 1917. [4]

Spofford, Ainsworth Rand, librarian, b. Gilmanton, N.H., 1825; d. Holderness, N.H., Aug. 11, 1908. [1; 3; 4; 5; 6; 7; 10]

Spofford, Mrs. Harriet Elizabeth, née Prescott, novelist, b. Calais, Me., 1835; d. Deer Island, near Newburyport, Mass., Aug. 14, 1921. [1; 2; 3; 4; 5; 6; 7; 10; 71; 72]

Spofford, Jeremiah, physician, b. 1787; d. 1880.

Spoolman, Jacob, clergyman, b. East Clinton, Ill., 1874; d. Ashland, Wis., Oct. 30, 1946. [62]

Spooner, Alden Jeremiah, lawyer, b. Sag Harbor, Long Island, N.Y., 1810; d. Hempstead, Long Island, N.Y., Aug. 2, 1881. [3; 7]

Spooner, Lysander, lawyer, b. Athol, Mass., 1808; d. Boston, Mass., May 14, 1887. [1; 3; 4; 6]

Spooner, Shearjashub, dentist, b. Brandon, Vt., 1809; d. Plainfield, N.J., March 14, 1859. [1; 3; 6; 7]

Spotton, Henry Byron, botanist, b. Port Hope, Ont., 1844; d. Galt, Ont., Feb. 24, 1933. [27]

Spottswood, Mrs. Lucy A., novelist, fl. 1873-1885. [6]

Spottswood, Wilson Lee, clergyman, b. 1822; d. 1892.

Spragge, Mrs. Arthur, née Cameron, traveller, b. Toronto, Ont, 1854; d. Toronto, Ont., May 2, 1932. [27]

Sprague, Achsa W., poet, b. about 1828; d. Plymouth Notch, Vt., July 6, 1862. [1; 7; 9; 43]

Sprague, Alfred White, educationist, b. Oahu, Hawaii, 1821; d. Wollaston, Mass., Dec. 7, 1891. [3; 6]

Sprague, Carleton, manufacturer and poet, b. Buffalo, N.Y., 1858; d. New York, N.Y., Nov. 19, 1916. [10; 51]

Sprague, Charles, poet, b. Boston, Mass., 1791; d. Boston, Mass., Jan. 22, 1875. [1; 3; 4; 6; 7; 9]

Sprague, Charles Ezra, banker, b. Nassau, N.Y., 1842; d. New York, N.Y. March 21, 1912. [1; 3; 6; 10]

Sprague, Delos E., clergyman, b. Milo, N.Y., 1867; d. Dec. 5, 1937.

Sprague, Franklin Monroe, clergyman, b. East Douglas, Mass., 1841; d. Tampa, Fla., Dec. 30, 1926. [10; 11; 62]

Sprague, Henry Harrison, lawyer, b. Athol, Mass., 1841; d. Boston, Mass., July 28, 1920. [4; 10]

Sprague, Homer Baxter, educationist, b. Sutton, Mass., 1829; d. Newton, Mass., March 23, 1918. [1; 7; 10; 62]

Sprague, Horace, poet, b. 1798; d. ?

Sprague, Jesse Rainsford, merchant, b. Le Roy, N.Y., 1872; d. New York, N.Y., Sept. 4, 1946. [7; 10; 11]

Sprague, John Francis, lawyer and historian, b. 1848; d. Dover, Me., Nov. 25, 1931. [38]

Sprague, John Titcomb, soldier, b. Newburyport, Mass., 1810; d. New York, N.Y., Sept. 6, 1878. [3; 6]

Sprague, Levi L., educationist, b. Beekman, N.Y., 1844; d. Kingston, Pa., March 6, 1936. [10]

Sprague, Peleg, jurist, b. Duxbury, Mass., 1793; d. Boston, Mass., Oct. 13, 1880. [1; 3; 4; 5; 6; 38]

Sprague, Philo Woodruff, clergyman, b. 1852; d. 1927.

Sprague, Roger, novelist, b. 1869; d. Napa, Calif., about 1935. [35]

Sprague, William Buell, clergyman, b. Andover, Conn., 1795; d. Flushing, Long Island, N.Y., May 7, 1876. [1; 3; 4; 5; 6; 7; 62]

Sprague, William Cyrus, lawyer and miscellaneous writer, b. Malta, O., 1860; d. Chicago, Ill., Nov. 29, 1922. [4; 10; 39]

Sprecher, Samuel, theologian, b. Washington county, 1810; d. San Diego, Calif., Jan. 10, 1906. [1; 3; 6]

Spreng, Samuel Peter, bishop, b. Big Prairie, O., 1853; d. Naperville, Ill., April 18, 1946. [10; 11]

Spring, Gardiner, clergyman, b. Newburyport, Mass., 1785; d. New York, N.Y., Aug. 18, 1873. [1; 3; 4; 5; 6; 62]

Spring, La Verne Ward, metallurgist, b. Coldwater, Mich., 1876; d. Chicago, Ill., March 23, 1932. [11]

Spring, Leverett Wilson, clergyman and educationist, b. Grafton, Vt., 1840; d. Boston, Mass., Dec. 23, 1917. [1; 5; 7; 10]

Spring, Lindley, reformer, fl. 1861-1868.

Spring, Samuel, clergyman, b. Uxbridge, Mass., 1746; d. Newburyport, Mass., March 4, 1817. [1; 3; 4; 6]

Spring, Samuel, clergyman and novelist, b. Newburyport, Mass., 1792; d. East Hartford, Conn., Dec. 13, 1877. [7; 62]

Springer, Arthur, local historian, b. Louisa county, Ia., 1855; d. Wapello, Ia., Dec. 9, 1936. [37]

Springer, Frank, lawyer and palaeontologist, b. Wapella, Ia., 1848; d. Philadelphia, Pa., Sept. 22, 1927. [1; 4; 10]

Springer, Mrs. Helen Emily, née **Chapman,** missionary, b. New Sharon, Me., 1868; d. Belgian Congo, Aug. 23, 1949.

Springer, John S., lumberman, b. Augusta, Me., 1799; d. Weston, Me., July 29, 1883. [38]

Springer, Moses, clergyman, b. 1796; d. about 1870. [38]

Springer, Mrs. Rebecca, née **Ruter,** poet and novelist, b. Indianapolis, Ind., 1832; d. 1904. [3; 5; 7; 10]

Sproat, Mrs. Nancy, poet, fl. 1830-1867.

Sproull, Thomas, clergyman, b. Westmoreland county, Pa., 1803; d. Pittsburgh, Pa., March 21, 1892. [1; 3; 4; 6]

Sprunt, James, merchant and historian, b. Glasgow, Scotland, 1846; d. Wilmington, N.C., July 9, 1924. [1; 4; 7; 34]

Spurlock, James Aquila, lawyer, b. 1825; d. ?

Spykman, Nicholas John, educationist, b. Amsterdam, Holland, 1893; d. New Haven, Conn., June 26, 1943. [10]

Squair, John, educationist, b. Bowmanville, Ont., 1850; d. Toronto, Ont., Feb. 15, 1928. [27]

Squibb, Edward Robinson, chemist, b. Wilmington, Del., 1819; d. Brooklyn, N.Y., Oct. 26, 1900. [1; 3b; 4]

Squibb, Robert, nurseryman, fl. 1787-1827.

Squibob (pseud.). See Derby, George Martin.

Squier, Ephraim George, journalist, diplomat, and archaeologist, b. Bethlehem, N.Y., 1821; d. Brooklyn, N.Y., April 17, 1888. [1; 3; 4; 5; 6; 7; 9]

Squier, George Owen, soldier and electrical engineer, b. Dryden, Mich., 1865; d. Washington, D.C., March 24, 1934. [1; 10]

Squier, John Bentley, surgeon, b. New York, N.Y., 1873; d. New York, N.Y., March 1, 1948. [10]

Squier, Miles Powell, clergyman, b. Cornwall, Vt., 1792; d. Geneva, N.Y., June 22, 1866. [3; 4; 6]

Squire, Frances. See Potter, Mrs. Frances Boardman, née Squire.

Squires, Mrs. Edith, née **Lombard,** poet, b. New York, N.Y., 1884; d. Richmond, Ind., June 2, 1939.

Squires, William Henry Tappey, clergyman, b. Petersburg, Va., 1875; d. Norfolk, Va., April 20, 1948. [7; 10; 11]

Srygley, Fletcher Douglas, clergyman, fl. 1879-1900. [34]

Stabler, Edward, farmer and machinist, b. 1794; d. 1883. [6]

Stabler, Mrs. Jamie Latham, novelist, d. 1882. [34]

Stabler, William, biographer, b. 1895; d. 1852.

Stace, Francis Augustine, lawyer, b. 1834; d. 1922.

Stacey, Arthur Merrill, poet, b. '1857; d. 1882. [38]

Stackpole, Edward James, journalist, b. McVeytown, Pa., 1861; d. Harrisburg, Pa., Jan. 2, 1936. [7; 10; 11]

Stackpole, Everett Schermerhorn, clergyman, b. Durham, Me., 1850; d. Bath, Me., July 28, 1927. [10]

Stacy, James, clergyman, b. Liberty county, Ga., 1830; d. 1912. [34]

Stacy, Nathaniel, clergyman, fl. 1828-1850.

Stacy, Thomas Hobbs, clergyman, b. North Berwick, Me., 1850; d. May 14, 1927. [10; 11]

Stadelman, William Francis Xavier, priest, b. Pittsburgh, Pa., 1869; d. Pittsburgh, Pa., Nov. 6, 1928. [10; 21]

Stafford, Ezra Adams, clergyman, b. Elgin county, Upper Canada, 1839; d. Hamilton, Ont., Dec. 21, 1891. [27]

Stafford, Orin Fletcher, chemist, b. Hillsboro, O., 1873; d. Eugene, Ore., Sept. 17, 1941. [10; 13]

Stafford, Ward, clergyman, b. Washington, N.H., 1788; d. Bloomfield, N.J., March 26, 1851. [62]

Stager, Walter, lawyer, d. Lititz, Pa., July 25, 1940.

Stagg, Clinton Holland, novelist, b. 1890; d. 1916.

Stagg, Edward, poet, fl. 1847-1852.

Stagg, John Weldon, educationist, b. Richmond, Va., 1864; d. Anniston, Ala., Dec. 24, 1915. [10]

Stahl, John Meloy, journalist, b. Mendon, Ill., 1860; d. Asheville, N.C., Oct. 18, 1944. [7; 11]

Stainton, Schuyler (pseud.). See Baum, Lyman Frank.

Staley, Cady, civil engineer, b. Montgomery county, N.Y., 1840; d. Minaville, N.Y., June 27, 1928. [1; 4; 10]

Stall, Sylvanus, clergyman, b. Elizaville, Columbus county, N.Y., 1847; d. Atlantic City, N.J., Nov. 6, 1915. [3; 10]

Stallo, Johann Bernhard, diplomat, b. Oldenberg, Germany, 1823; d. Florence, Italy, Jan. 6, 1900. [1; 3; 4; 5; 6; 10]

Stanard, Mrs. Mary Mann Page, née **Newton,** historian, b. Westmoreland county, Va., 1865; d. Richmond, Va., June 5, 1929. [1; 7; 10; 34]

Stanard, William Glover, editor and antiquary, b. Richmond, Va., 1858; d. Richmond, Va., May 6, 1933. [1; 7; 10; 34]

Stander, Henricus Johannes, gynaecologist, b. Georgetown, South Africa, 1894; d. Scarsdale, N.Y., May 2, 1948. [10]

Standing Bear, Luther, Indian chief, b. Sioux Pine Ridge Reservation, S.D., 1865; d. Huntington Park, Calif., Feb. 19, 1939. [7]

Standish, Burt (pseud.). See Cook, William Wallace.

Standish, Burt L. (pseud.) See Patten, Gilbert.

Standish, Myles, physician, b. Boston, Mass., 1851; d. Boston, Mass., June 26, 1928. [4; 10; 51]

Standish, Winn (pseud.). See Sawyer, Walter Leon.

Stanford, Arthur Willis, missionary, b. Lowell, Mass., 1859; d. Auburndale, Mass., July 8, 1921. [4; 62]

Stanford, John, clergyman, b. Wandsworth, Surrey, England, 1754; d. New York, N.Y., Jan. 14, 1834. [1]

Stang, William, bishop, b .Baden, Germany, 1854; d. Rochester, Minn., Feb. 2, 1907. [1; 10; 21]

Staniford, Daniel, educationist, b. 1753; d. 1830.

Stanley, Albert Augustus, musician, b. Manville, R.I., 1851; d. Ann Arbor, Mich., May 19, 1932. [1; 10; 20]

Stanley, Anthony Dumond, mathematician, b. East Hartford, Conn., 1810; d. East Hartford, Conn., March 16, 1853. [3]

Stanley, Mrs. Caroline Hart, née Abbot, educationist and novelist, b. Callaway county, Mo., 1849; d. Washington, D.C., Jan. 13, 1919. [10; 39]

Stanley, Edwin James, clergyman, b. Buffalo, Mo., 1848; d. Whitehall, Mont., April 17, 1919. [10]

Stanley, Hiram Alonzo, journalist and novelist, b. Vestal, N.Y., 1849; d. ? [4; 7]

Stanley, Marie (pseud.). See Buck, Mrs. Lillie, née West.

Stanley, T. Lloyd (pseud.). See Smith, Richard Morris.

Stansbury, Charles Frederick, economist, d. 1882. [56]

Stansbury, Charles Frederick, journalist, b. London, England, 1854; d. New York, N.Y., May 14, 1922. [10]

Stansbury, Howard, soldier and explorer, b. New York, N.Y., 1806; d. Madison, Wis., April 17, 1863. [1; 3; 6]

Stansbury, Philip, traveller, b. New York, N.Y., about 1802; d. about 1870. [3]

Stanser, Robert, bishop, b. Yorkshire, England, 1760; d. Hampton, Middlesex, England, 1828. [27]

Stanton, Mrs. Elizabeth, née **Cady,** female suffragist and reformer, b. Johnstown, N.Y., 1815; d. New York, N.Y., Oct. 25, 1902. [1; 2; 3; 4; 5; 6; 7; 8; 9; 10]

Stanton, Frank Lebby, poet and journalist, b. Charleston, S.C., 1857; d. Atlanta, Ga., Jan. 7, 1927. [1; 4; 7; 10; 34]

Stanton, Gerrit Smith, journalist, b. 1845; d. April 24, 1927.

Stanton, Henry Brewster, reformer, b. Griswold, Conn., 1805; d. New York, N.Y., Jan. 14, 1887. [1; 3; 4; 5; 6]

Stanton, Henry Thompson, poet, b. Alexandria, Va., 1834; d. Frankfort, Ky., May 7, 1899. [3; 6; 34]

Stanton, Horace Coffin, clergyman, b. Wolfboro, N.H., 1849; d. Philadelphia, Pa., Nov. 15, 1925. [10; 11]

Stanton, Richard Henry, jurist, b. Alexandria, Va., 1812; d. Maysville, Ky., Nov., 1891. [3; 4; 5; 34]

Stanton, Robert Livingston, clergyman and educationist, b. Griswold, Conn., 1810; d. at sea, May 23, 1885. [3; 5; 6]

Stanton, Theodore, publisher's agent, b. Seneca Falls, N.Y., 1851; d. New Brunswich, N.J., March 1, 1925. [4; 10; 11]

Stanton, William Alonzo, clergyman, b. Lawrenceville, Pa., 1854; d. Pasadena, Calif., Sept. 18, 1929. [67]

Stanwood, Edward, historian, b. Augusta, Me., 1841; d. Brookline, Mass., Oct. 11, 1923. [1; 4; 7; 10]

Stanyan, John Minot, soldier, b. 1828; d. d. 1905.

Staples, Abram Penn, lawyer, b. Patrick county, Va., 1858; d. Sept., 1913. [10]

Staples, Arthur Gray, journalist, b. Bowdoinham, Me., 1861; d. Auburn, Me., April 2, 1940. [10]

Staples, William Read, historian, b. Providence, R.I., 1798; d. Providence, R.I., Oct. 19, 1868. [1; 3; 4; 5; 6; 7]

Stapleton, Ammon, clergyman, b. Earl, Berks county, Pa., 1850; d. Sept. 18, 1916. [10]

Stapleton, Mrs. Patience, née **Tucker,** novelist, b. Wiscasset, Me., about 1863; d. New York, N.Y., Nov. 25, 1893. [4; 8]

Stapley, Mildred. See Byne, Mrs. Mildred, née Stapley.

Starbuck, Alexander, journalist and historian, b. Nantucket, Mass., 1841; d. Waltham, Mass., May 6, 1925. [4]

Starbuck, Edwin Diller, educationist, b. Bridgeport, Ind., 1866; d. Rio del Marz, Calif., Nov. 18, 1947. [10]

Starbuck, Mary Eliza, poet, b. 1858; d. Nantucket, Mass., June 4, 1938.

Starbuck, Robert Macy, sanitary engineer, b. 1844; d. Hartford, Conn., 1927.

Starbuck, Roger, dime novelist, fl. 1865-1890. [7]

Starbuck, Victor Stanley, poet, b. Chuluota, Fla., 1887; d. March 31, 1935. [11]

Starcross, Roger (pseud.). See Pope, Charles Henry.

Stark, Caleb, lawyer and historian, b. Dunbarton, N.H., 1804; d. Dunbarton, N.H., Feb. 1, 1864. [3; 6]

Stark, James Henry, historian, b. 1847; d. Boston, Mass., Aug. 30, 1919.

Starke, Richard, lawyer, d. July 30, 1772.

Starke, Richard Griffin, printer and poet, b. 1831; d. Montreal, Que., Dec. 16, 1909. [27]

Starnes, Ebenezer, controversialist, d. about 1870.

Starr, Burgis Pratt, genealogist, b. 1822; d. 1883.

Starr, Edward Comfort, clergyman, b. 1844; d. Cornwall, Conn., Jan. 16, 1941. [62]

Starr, Eliza Allen, poet and writer on art, b. Deerfield, Mass., 1824; d. Durand, Ill., Sept. 7, 1901. [1; 3; 4; 5; 6; 7; 10; 21]

Starr, Emmet, physician and historian, b. Adair county, Okla., 1870; d. St. Louis, Mo., Jan. 30, 1930. [75]

Starr, Frederic Ratchford, farmer, b. Halifax, N.S., 1821; d. 1889. [6]

Starr, Frederick, anthropologist, b. Auburn, N.Y., 1858; d. Tokio, Japan, Aug. 14, 1933. [7; 10; 11]

Starr, Mrs. Ida May Hill, novelist, b. 1859; d. Easton, Pa., Feb. 3, 1938.

Starr, Louis, physician, b. Philadelphia, Pa., 1849; d. Dinard, France, Sept. 12, 1925. [1; 10]

Starr, Moses Allen, neurologist, b. Brooklyn, N.Y., 1854; d. New York, N.Y., Sept. 4, 1932. [1; 4; 10; 11]

Starrett, Francis Marion, local historian, b. 1845; d. Troy, O., Dec. 26, 1925.

Starrett, Mrs. Helen, née Ekin, educationist, b. Allegheny county, Pa., 1840; d. Portland, Ore., Dec. 16, 1920. [10]

Starrett, Lewis Frederick, lawyer, b. Warren, Me., 1844; d. ? [10]

Starrett, William Aiken, architect, b. Lawrence, Kans., 1877; d. Madison, N.J., March 26, 1932. [1; 10]

Staton, Frances Maria, librarian, d. Toronto, Ont., March 27, 1947.

Staton, Mrs. Kate Elony, née Baker, anthologist, b. 1850; d. 1924.

Staub, Walter Adolph, accountant, b. Philadelphia, Pa., 1864; d. Philadelphia, Pa., Nov. 4, 1945. [10]

Stauffer, David McNeely, civil engineer, b. Lancaster county, Pa., 1845; d. Yonkers, N.Y., Feb. 5, 1913. [1; 4; 7; 10]

Stauffer, Francis Henry, miscellaneous writer, b. 1832; d. 1895.

Stauffer, Vernon, educationist, b. New London, O., 1875; d. Lexington, Ky., July 15, 1925. [10]

Staunton, William, clergyman, b. Chester, England, 1803; d. New York, N.Y., Sept. 29, 1889. [3; 4; 6]

Steadman, John Marcellus, educationist, b. Greenwood, S.C., 1889; d. Atlanta, Ga., Dec. 20, 1945. [10]

Stearly, Wilson Reiff, bishop, b. Philadelphia, Pa., 1869; d. Montclair, N.J., Nov. 8, 1941. [10]

Stearns, Albert, soldier, fl. 1862-1896.

Stearns, Arthur Adelbert, lawyer, b. 1858; d. Jan. 25, 1932.

Stearns, Asahel, lawyer, b. Lunenburg, Mass., 1774; d. Cambridge, Mass., Feb. 5, 1839. [1; 3]

Stearns, Charles, clergyman, b. Leominster, Mass., 1753; d. Lincoln, Mass., July 26, 1826. [3; 6]

Stearns, Charles Woodward, physician, b. Springfield, Mass., 1817; d. Longmeadow, Mass., Sept. 8, 1887. [3; 6; 62]

Stearns, Daniel Miner, clergyman, b. 1844; d. 1920.

Stearns, Edward Josiah, clergyman and educationist, b. Bedford, Mass., 1810; d. 1890. [3; 51]

Stearns, Ezra Scollay, historian and genealogist, b. Rindge, N.H., 1838; d. Fitchburg, Mass., March 9, 1915. [4]

Stearns, Frank Preston, writer on literature and art, b. Medford, Mass., 1846; d. Jan., 1917. [4; 7; 10; 51]

Stearns, Harold Edmund, journalist, b. Barre, Mass., 1891; d. Hempstead, Long Island, N.Y., Aug. 13, 1943. [7; 10]

Stearns, Henry Putnam, physician, b. Sutton, Mass., 1828; d. Hartford, Conn., May 27, 1905. [1; 4; 10; 62]

Stearns, Jesse George Davis, clergyman, b. Ashburnham, Mass., 1812; d. Zumbrota, Minn., Nov. 1, 1882. [45]

Stearns, John Glazier, clergyman, b. Ackworth, N.H., 1795; d. Clinton, N.Y., Jan. 16, 1874. [3; 6]

Stearns, John Newton, temperance reformer, b. New Ipswich, N.H., 1829; d. Brooklyn, N.Y., April 21, 1895. [1; 3; 4; 5; 6; 7]

Stearns, Jonathan French, clergyman, b. Bedford, Mass., 1808; d. New Brunswick, N.J., Nov. 11, 1889. [3; 6]

Stearns, Lewis French, theologian, b. 1847; d. Bangor, Me., Feb. 9, 1892.

Stearns, Marshal, lawyer, b. Brookline, Mass., 1877; d. Montreal, Que., Jan. 21, 1943. [51]

Stearns, Oakman Sprague, clergyman and educationist, b. Bath, Me., 1817; d. Newton Centre, Mass., April 20, 1893. [3; 6]

Stearns, Samuel, physician and astronomer, b. Bolton, Mass., 1747; d. Brattleboro, Vt., Aug. 8, 1819. [3; 6; 43]

Stearns, Wallace Nelson, educationist, b. Chagrin Falls, O., 1866; d. Jacksonville, Ill., Feb. 3, 1934. [10; 11; 51]

Stearns, William Augustus, clergyman and educationist, b. Bedford, Mass., 1805; d. Amherst, Mass., June 8, 1876. [1; 3; 4; 5; 6; 7]

Stearns, Winfred Alden, explorer and ornithologist, b. Cambridgeport, Mass., 1852; d. Worcester, Mass., May 10, 1909. [45]

Stebbins, Emma, biographer, b. New York, N.Y., 1815; d. New York, N.Y., Oct. 25, 1882. [4; 5]

Stebbins, George Stanford, physician, fl. 1873.

Stebbins, Giles Badger, economist and reformer, b. 1817; d. 1900. [6]

Stebbins, Horatio Ward, engineer, b. 1878; d. Feb. 2, 1933.

Stebbins, Mrs. Mary Elizabeth, née Moore. See Hewitt, Mrs. Mary Elizabeth, née Moore.

Stebbins, Nathaniel Livermore, sailor, b. 1847; d. ?

Stebbins, Roderick, clergyman, b. Portland, Me., 1859; d. Milton, Mass., Jan. 29, 1928. [51]

Stebbins, Rufus Phineas, clergyman, b. South Wilbraham, Mass., 1810; d. Cambridge, Mass., Aug. 13, 1885. [1; 3; 4; 6]
Stebbins, Mrs. Sarah, née **Bridges,** poet and novelist, fl. 1877-1890. [6]
Stedman, Edmund Clarence, poet, critic, and journalist, b. Hartford, Conn., 1833; d. New York, N.Y., Jan. 18, 1908. [1; 2; 3; 4; 5; 6; 7; 8; 9; 10; 71]
Stedman, Thomas Lathrop, physician, b. Cincinnati, O., 1853; d. New York, N.Y., May 26, 1938. [10]
Steel, John Honeywood, physician, b. 1780; d. 1838.
Steel, Kurt (pseud.). See Kagey, Rudolf.
Steel, Samuel Augustus, clergyman, b. 1849; d. Feb. 19, 1934.
Steele, Mrs. Albert. See Conkling, Margaret Cockburn.
Steele, Ashbel, clergyman, b. 1796; d. ? [6]
Steele, Daniel, clergyman, b. Windham, N.Y., 1824; d. Milton, Mass., Sept. 2, 1914. [1; 4; 5; 10]
Steele, David, clergyman, b. near Londonderry, Ireland, 1827; d. Philadelphia, Pa., 1906. [5; 10]
Steele, Eliphalet, clergyman, b. Hartford, Conn., 1762; d. Paris, N.Y., Oct. 7, 1817. [62]
Steele Mrs. **Eliza R.,** miscellaneous writer, fl. 1841-1852. [6]
Steele, Mrs. Esther, née **Baker,** historian, b Lysander, N.Y., 1835; d. Nov. 23, 1911. [10]
Steele, George McKendree, clergyman and educationist, b. Strafford, Vt., 1823; d. Kenilworth, Ill., Jan. 14, 1902. [5; 6]
Steele, James, novelist, fl. 1873-1892. [7]
Steele, James King, traveller, b. Keokuk, Ia., 1875; d. Reno, Nev., Dec. 25, 1937. [7; 10; 11; 35]
Steele, James William, consular agent, b. 1840; d. 1906. [6]
Steele, Joel Dorman, educationist, b. Lima, N.Y., 1836; d. Elmira, N.Y., May 25, 1886. [1; 3; 4; 5; 6]
Steele, John, clergyman and pioneer, b. 1832; d. Lodi, Wis., 1905.
Steele, John Beatty, clergyman and poet, b. 1796; d. 1884.
Steele, John Washington, oil operator, b. near Sheakleyville, Pa., 1843; d. Fort Crook, Neb., Dec. 31, 1920.
Steele, Mrs. Margaret Cockburn, née **Conkling,** See Conkling, Margaret Cockburn.
Steele, Oliver Gray, publisher, b. 1805; d. Buffalo, N.Y., 1879.
Steele, Rufus Mills, journalist, b. Hope, Ark., 1877; d. Boston, Mass., Dec. 25, 1935. [7; 10; 35]
Steele, Sir Samuel Benfield, soldier, b. Purbrook, Ont., 1849; d. London, England, Jan. 30, 1919. [27]
Steele, Sherman, lawyer and educationist, b. 1876; d. Chicago, Ill., April 18, 1945.
Steele, Thomas Sedgwick, artist, b. Hartford, Conn., 1845; d. 1903. [4; 7; 10]

Steele, Zadock, Indian captive, b. 1758; d. 1845.
Steell, Willis, journalist, novelist, and playwright, b. Detroit, Mich., 1866; d. New York, N.Y., Feb. 1, 1941. [7; 10]
Steen, Moses Duncan Alexander, clergyman, b. near Blue Creek, O., 1841; d. Worthington, O., June 22, 1924. [56]
Steen, Robert Service, clergyman, b. 1880; d. Orange, N.J., April 18, 1908.
Steenstra, Peter Henry, theologian, b. Holland, 1833; d. Robbinston, Me., 1911. [10]
Steffens, Cornelius Martin, educationist, b. Germany, 1866; d. Chicago, Ill., Jan. 17, 1933. [10]
Steffens, Joseph Lincoln, journalist, b. San Francisco, Calif., 1866; d. Carmel, Calif., Aug. 9, 1936. [4; 7; 10]
Steiger, Ernest, publisher, b. Germany, 1832; d. New York, N.Y., Aug. 2, 1917. [10]
Stein, Evaleen, artist, poet, and writer of books for children, b. Lafayette, Ind., 1863; d. Lafayette, Ind., Dec. 11, 1923. [1; 7; 10; 15]
Stein, Gertrude, literary experimenter, b. Allegheny, Pa., 1874; d. Paris, France, July 27, 1946. [7; 10; 11; 12]
Stein, Leo, art critic, b. 1872; d. near Florence, Italy, July 29, 1947.
Steiner, Bernard Christian, librarian and historian, b. Guilford, Conn., 1867; d. Baltimore, Md., Jan. 12, 1926. [1; 4; 7; 10; 11; 62]
Steiner, Florence B., school-teacher and poet, b. 1877; d. Toronto, Ont., Sept. 26, 1946.
Steinitz, William, chess-player, b. Prague, Bohemia, 1836; d. New York, N.Y., Aug. 12, 1900. [1; 3; 4; 10]
Steinmetz, Charles Proteus, electrical engineer, b. Breslau, Germany, 1865; d. Schenectady, N.Y., Oct. 26, 1923. [1; 4; 10]
Stella (pseud.). See Lewis, Mrs. Estelle Anna Blanche, née Robinson.
Stella, Antonio, physician, b. Muro Lucano, Italy, 1868; d. New York, N.Y., July 3, 1927. [4; 10]
Stelle, James Parish, technician, fl. 1868-1885.
Stelwagon, Henry Weightman, physician, b. Philadelphia, Pa., 1853; d. Philadelphia, Pa., Oct. 18, 1919. [4; 10]
Stelzle, Charles, clergyman, b. New York, N.Y., 1869; d. New York, N.Y., Feb. 27, 1941. [7; 10; 11]
Stengel, Alfred, pathologist, b. Pittsburgh, Pa., 1868; d. Philadelphia, Pa., April 10, 1939. [10; 13]
Stephen, Alexander Maitland, poet and novelist, b. near Hanover, Ont., 1882; d. Vancouver, B.C., July 1, 1942. [11; 27]
Stephens, Alexander Hamilton, politician, b. Wilkes county, Ga., 1812; d. Atlanta, Ga., March 4, 1883. [1; 2; 3; 4; 5; 6; 7]
Stephens, Mrs. Ann Sophia, née **Winterbotham,** novelist, b. Derby, Conn., 1813; d. Newport, R.I., Aug. 20, 1886. [1; 3; 4; 5; 6; 7; 8]

Stephens, Charles Asbury, scientist and writer of books for boys, b. Norway Lake, Me., 1844; d. Norway, Me., Sept. 22, 1931. [1; 4; 5; 7; 10]

Stephens, Charles Henry, lawyer, b. Montreal, Que.; d. Montreal, Que., May 2, 1914. [27]

Stephens, Edwin William, journalist, b. Columbia, Mo., 1849; d. Columbia, Mo., May 22, 1931. [1; 7; 10]

Stephens, George Washington, soldier and public offical, b. Montreal, Que., 1866; d. Los Angeles, Calif., Feb. 6, 1942. [27]

Stephens, Mrs. Harriet Marion, née **Ward,** novelist, b. 1823; d. East Hampden, Me., 1858. [3; 6]

Stephens, Henry, banker and traveller, b. Detroit, Mich., 1883; d. Prides Crossing, Mass., Aug. 20, 1932. [51]

Stephens, Henry Morse, historian, b. Edinburgh, Scotland, 1857; d. San Francisco, Calif., April 16, 1919. [1; 4; 7; 10; 35]

Stephens, Henry Louis, painter and illustrator, b. Philadelphia, Pa., 1824; d. Bayonne, N.Y., Dec. 13, 1882. [4; 6]

Stephens, John Lloyd, archaeologist, b. Shrewsbury, N.J., 1805; d. New York, N.Y., Oct. 10, 1852. [1; 3; 4; 5; 6; 7]

Stephens, Kate, educationist, b. Moravia, N.Y., 1853; d. Concordia, Kans., May 10, 1938. [7; 10; 11]

Stephens, Kit (pseud.). See Stephens, Charles Asbury.

Stephens, Louise G., descriptive writer, b. 1843; d. ?

Stephens, Robert Neilson, journalist, novelist, and playwright, b. New Bloomfield, Pa., 1867; d. 1906. [5; 7; 10]

Stephens, William A., poet, b. Belfast, Ireland, 1809; d. Owen Sound, Ont., March 21, 1891. [27]

Stephens, William Picard, yachtsman, b. Philadelphia, Pa., 1856; d. New York, N.Y., May 10, 1946.

Stephenson, Edward Morris, clergyman, b. Carnforth, England, 1853; d. Camp Hill, Pa., Feb. 18, 1926. [10]

Stephenson, Harold Edward, advertising expert, b. 1874; d. 1940.

Stephenson, Isaac, politician, b. Fredericton, N.B., 1829; d. Marinette, Wis., March 15, 1918. [1; 4; 10]

Stephenson, Matthew F., geologist, fl. 1870-1878.

Stephenson, Nathaniel Wright, novelist and historian, b. Cincinnati, O., 1867; d. Claremont, Calif., Jan. 17, 1935. [1a; 7; 10]

Sterling, Ada, miscellaneous writer, b. Holyoke, Mass., 1870; d. New York, N.Y., Sept. 1, 1939. [7]

Sterling, Charles F., novelist, fl. 1847-1848. [7]

Sterling, George, poet, b. Sag Harbor, N.Y., 1869; d. San Francisco, Calif., Nov. 17, 1926. [1; 7; 10; 11; 35; 72]

Sterling, Richard, educationist, b. 1812; d. 1883.

Stern, Frances, nutritionist, b. Boston, Mass., 1873; d. Newton, Mass., Dec. 23, 1947.

Stern, Herman Isidore, clergyman, b. Galion, O., 1854; d. Berkeley, Calif., July 3, 1926.

Stern, Louis William, psychologist, b. Germany, 1871; d. Durham, N.C., March 27, 1938.

Stern, Renée Bernd, journalist, b. Philadelphia, Pa., 1875; d. Philadelphia, Pa., May 19, 1940. [7; 11]

Stern, Simon Adler, banker, b. Philadelphia, Pa., 1838; d. Philadelphia, Pa., 1904. [10]

Sternberg, Constantin Ivanovitch von, musician, b. St. Petersburg, Russia, 1852; d. Philadelphia, Pa., March 3, 1924. [20]

Sternberg, George Miller, bacteriologist and soldier, b. Otsego county, N.Y., 1838; d. Washington, D.C., Nov. 3, 1915. [1; 3; 4; 5; 6; 10]

Sterne, Simon, lawyer and civic reformer, b. Philadelphia, Pa., 1839; d. New York, N.Y., Sept. 22, 1901. [1; 3; 6; 10]

Sterne, Stuart (pseud.). See Bloede, Gertrude.

Sterrett, James Macbride, clergyman, b. Howard, Pa., 1847; d. Washington, D.C., May 31, 1923. [1; 10]

Sterrett, John Robert Sitlington, archaeologist, b. Rockbridge Baths, Va., 1851; d. Ithaca, N.Y., June 15, 1914. [1; 3; 5; 7; 10]

Stetson, Mrs. Augusta Emma, née **Simmons,** religious leader, b. Waldoboro, Me., about 1842; d. Rochester, N.Y., Oct. 12, 1928. [1; 4; 10]

Stetson, Mrs. Charlotte, née **Perkins.** See Gilman, Mrs. Charlotte, née Perkins.

Stetson, Mrs. Grace Ellery, née **Channing.** See Channing, Grace Ellery.

Stetson, William Wallace, educationist, b. Greene, Me., 1849; d. Auburn, Me., July 1, 1910. [1; 4; 10]

Stettinius, Edward Reilly, diplomat, b. Chicago, Ill., 1900; d. Greenwich, Conn., Oct. 31, 1949. [10; 12]

Steuben, Friedrich Wilhelm Ludolf Gerhard Augustin, Baron **von,** soldier, b. Madgeburg, Germany, 1730; d. Steubenville, N.Y., Nov. 28, 1794. [1; 2; 3; 4; 5; 6]

Stevens, Abel, clergyman and historian, b. Philadelphia, Pa., 1815; d. San José, Calif., Sept. 13, 1897. [1; 4; 5; 7]

Stevens, Albert Clark, journalist, b. Buffalo, N.Y., 1854; d. East Orange, N.J., Aug., 1919. [10]

Stevens, Alexander Hodgdon, surgeon, b. New York, N.Y., 1789; d. New York, N.Y., March 30, 1869. [1; 3; 4; 5; 6; 62]

Stevens, Alviso Burdett, pharmacist, b. Tyrone, Mich., 1853; d. Escondido, Calif., Jan. 24, 1940. [4; 10; 11]

Stevens, Bertha, educationist, b. Jersey City, N.J., about 1881; d. Downers Grove, Ill., April 9, 1947.

Stevens, Charles Ellis, clergyman, b. Boston, Mass., 1853; d. Lake George, N.Y., Aug. 28, 1906. [10]

Stevens, Charles Emery, lawyer, b. 1815; d. 1893.

Stevens, Charles McClellan, miscellaneous writer, b. 1861; d. ?

Stevens, Charles Wistar, physician, b. 1835; d. Charlestown, Mass., Jan. 25, 1901. [51]

Stevens, Charles Woodbury, angler, b. 1831; d. ?

Stevens, Daniel Gurden, clergyman, b. Baltimore, Md., 1869; d. Lansdowne, Pa., May 11, 1931. [10]

Stevens, David Kilburn, editor and versifier, b. Fitchburg, Mass., 1860; d. Boston, Mass., June 29, 1946. [10; 11]

Stevens, Edward Fletcher, architect, b. Dunstable, Mass., 1850; d. Newton, Mass., Feb. 28, 1946. [10; 11]

Stevens, Elbert Marcus, educationist, b. Ringwood, Ill., 1867; d. Rochester, Minn., Jan. 28, 1937. [11; 62]

Stevens, Frank Everett, historian, b. 1856; d. Springfield, Ill., Oct. 16, 1939.

Stevens, Frank Lincoln, botanist, b. near Syracuse, N.Y., 1871; d. Aug. 18, 1934. [10; 11; 13]

Stevens, Frank Walker, lawyer, b. Leon, N.Y., 1847; d. Covina, Calif., Nov. 8, 1928. [10]

Stevens, George Barker, theologian, b. Spencer, N.Y., 1854; d. New Haven, Conn., June 22, 1906. [1; 5; 10; 62]

Stevens, George Thomas, physician, b. Essex county, N.Y., 1832; d. New York, N.Y., Jan. 30, 1921. [4; 10]

Stevens, George Washington, museum director and poet, b. Utica, N.Y., 1866; d. Toledo, O., Oct. 29, 1926. [1; 7; 10]

Stevens, Hazard, lawyer, b. Newport, R.I., 1842; d. Boston, Mass., Oct. 11, 1918. [10; 51]

Stevens, Henry Davis, clergyman, b. Calais, Vt., 1846; d. Whitman, Mass., March 22, 1918. [10]

Stevens, Hiram Fairchild, lawyer, b. St. Albans, Vt., 1852; d. St. Paul, Minn., March 9, 1904. [1; 4; 10; 70]

Stevens, Isaac Ingalls, soldier, b. Andover, Mass., 1818; d. Chantilly, Va., Sept. 1, 1862. [1; 3; 4; 5; 6]

Stevens, Isaac Newton, lawyer and novelist, b. Newark, O., 1858; d. Philadelphia, Pa., Feb. 11, 1920. [4; 10]

Stevens, James Stacy, educationist, b. Lima, N.Y., 1864; d. Winter Park, Fla., March 24, 1940. [10; 11]

Stevens, James Wilson, historian, fl. 1797-1800.

Stevens, John Austin, financier and historian, b. New York, N.Y., 1827; d. Newport, R.I., June 16, 1910. [1; 3; 4; 5; 6; 7; 10]

Stevens, John Harrington, pioneer and historian, b. Brompton Falls, Lower Canada, June 13, 1820; d. Minneapolis, Minn., May 28, 1900. [1; 4; 70]

Stevens, John Leavitt, journalist, diplomat, and historian, b. Mount Vernon, Me., 1820; d. Augusta, Me., Feb. 8, 1895. [1; 3; 4; 5]

Stevens, Lorenzo Gorham, clergyman, b. Bedford, Mass., 1846; d. 1927. [51]

Stevens, Nettie Maria, biologist, b. 1861; d. 1912.

Stevens, Paul, b. Belgium, 1830; d. Coteau du Lac, Que., 1882. [27]

Stevens, Samuel Eugene, physician, b. 1839; d. Dec., 1933.

Stevens, Mrs. Susan Sheppard, née **Pierce,** novelist, b. Mobile, Ala., 1862; d. 1909. [10; 34]

Stevens, Thomas, journalist and traveller, b. England, 1855; d. ? [7]

Stevens, Thomas Wood, playwright and educationist, b. Daysville, Ill., 1880; d. Tucson, Ariz., Jan. 29, 1842. [7; 10]

Stevens, Walter Barlow, historian, b. Meriden, Conn., 1848; d. St. Louis, Mo., Aug. 28, 1939. [4; 7; 10; 34]

Stevens, William Arnold, theologian, b. Granville, O., 1839; d. Rochester, N.Y., Jan. 2, 1910. [1; 10]

Stevens, William Bacon, bishop and historian, b. Bath, Me., 1815; d. Philadelphia, Pa., June 11, 1887. [1; 3; 4; 5; 6; 7; 34]

Stevens, William Burnham, lawyer, b. Stoneham, Mass., 1843; d. Stoneham, Mass., July 15, 1931. [10]

Stevens, William Chase, botanist, b. Princeton, Ill., 1861; d. Lawrence, Kans., Jan. 2, 1943. [11; 13]

Stevenson, Adlai Ewing, politician, b. Christian county, Ky., 1835; d. Chicago, Ill., June 14, 1914. [1; 4; 5; 10; 34]

Stevenson, Edward Irenaeus. See Prime-Stevenson, Edward Irenaeus.

Stevenson, Edward Luther, cartographer, b. Rozetta, Ill., 1860; d. Yonkers, N.Y., July 16, 1944. [10; 11]

Stevenson, George Edward, engineer, b. 1860; d. 1931.

Stevenson, James Henry, Assyriologist, b. Peterborough, Ont., 1860; d. Nashville, Tenn., Dec. 20, 1919. [10]

Stevenson, John Alford, insurance executive, b. Cobden, Ill., 1886; d. Philadelphia, Pa., Aug. 31, 1949. [10; 11]

Stevenson, John James, geologist, b. New York, N.Y., 1841; d. New Canaan, Conn., Aug. 10, 1924. [1; 4; 10]

Stevenson, John McMillan, clergyman, b. 1812; d. 1896.

Stevenson, John Rudderow, physician, b. 1834; d. Haddonfield, N.J., Dec. 20, 1917.

Stevenson, Mrs. Katharine Adelia, née **Lent,** temperance advocate, b. Copake, N.Y., 1853; d. March 28, 1919. [10]

Stevenson, Mark Delimon, oculist, b. Trafalgar, Ont., 1876; d. Akron, O., May 21, 1915. [10]

Stevenson, Paul Eve, yachtsman, b. New York, N.Y., 1868; d. New York, N.Y., Dec. 20, 1910. [10]

Stevenson, Richard Randolph, physician, fl. 1860-1876. [6]

Stevenson, Richard Taylor, historian, b. Taylorsville, Ky., 1853; d. Delaware, O., 1919. [4; 10]

Stevenson, Mrs. Sara, née Yorke, archaeologist, b. Paris, France, 1847; d. Philadelphia, Pa., Nov. 14, 1921. [1; 3; 4; 5; 10]

Stevenson, Sarah Hackett, physician, b. Buffalo Grove, Ill., 1843; d. Chicago, Ill., Aug. 14, 1909. [10]

Stevenson, William G., physician, b. Troy, N.Y., 1843; d. ? [6]

Stevenson, William Wesley, educationist, b. 1875; d. Philadelphia, Pa., July 23, 1941.

Steventon, John (pseud.). See Tarkington, John Stevenson.

Steward, Austin, escaped negro slave, b. Prince William county, Va., 1793; d. 1860. [34]

Steward, John Fletcher, historian, b. 1841; d. 1915.

Steward, Theophilus Gould, clergyman, b. Gouldtown, N.J., April 17, 1843; d. ? [3]

Stewardson, Langdon Cheeves, educationist, b. Marietta, Ga., 1850; d. 1930. [4; 10]

Stewart, Alexander Morrison, clergyman, b. 1814; d. 1875.

Stewart, Alvan, reformer, b. South Granville, N.Y., 1790; d. New York, N.Y., May 1, 1849. [1; 3; 4; 6]

Stewart, Andrew, politician, b. Fayette county, Pa., 1791; d. Uniontown, Pa., July 16, 1872. [1; 5]

Stewart, Charles Samuel, clergyman, b. Flemington, N.J., 1795; d. Cooperstown, N.Y., Dec. 15, 1870. [3; 6]

Stewart, Charles West, librarian and historian, b. Champaign, Ill., 1859; d. Washington, D.C., Oct. 3, 1929. [10]

Stewart, David Denison, physician, b. Philadelphia, Pa., 1858; d. Philadelphia, Pa., 1905. [10]

Stewart, De Lisle, astronomer, b. Wabasha, Minn., 1870; d. Cleves, O., Feb. 9, 1941. [10]

Stewart, Mrs. Electa Maria, née Bronson. See Sheldon, Mrs. Electa Maria, née Bronson.

Stewart, Mrs. Eliza, née Daniel, temperance advocate, b. Piketon, O., 1816; d. Hicksville, O., Aug. 6, 1908. [1; 4; 10]

Stewart, Elliott W., writer on agriculture, fl. 1866-1890.

Stewart, Ferdinand Campbell, physician, b. 1815; d. 1899. [6]

Stewart, Francis Edward, physician, b. Albion, N.Y., 1853; d. Germantown, Pa., Feb. 20, 1941.

Stewart, Francis Torrens, surgeon, b. Philadelphia, Pa., 1877; d. Philadelphia, Pa., Feb. 4, 1920. [10]

Stewart, George, journalist, b. New York, N.Y., 1848; d. Quebec, Que., Feb. 26, 1906. [27]

Stewart, George Black, theologian, b. Columbus, O., 1854; d. Auburn, N.Y., June 23, 1932. [10]

Stewart, George Craig, bishop, b. Saginaw, Mich., 1878; d. Chicago, Ill., May 2, 1940. [10; 11]

Stewart, Gilbert Holland, jurist, b. 1847; d. 1913.

Stewart, Henry, agricultural writer, fl. 1876-1900.

Stewart, James, physician, b. New York, N.Y., 1799; d. Rye, N.Y., Sept. 12, 1864. [3]

Stewart, James Hervey, physician, b. 1809; d. 1879.

Stewart, John, clergyman, b. 1795; d. 1876.

Stewart, John Hoff, lawyer, d. 1890.

Stewart, Joseph Spencer, educationist, b. Oxford, Ga., 1863; d. March 25, 1934. [10]

Stewart, McLeod, lawyer, b. Bytown [now Ottawa], Ont., 1847; d. Ottawa, Ont., Oct. 9, 1926. [27]

Stewart, Merch Bradt, soldier, b. Mitchell Station, Va., 1875; d. St. Augustine, Fla., July 3, 1934. [10]

Stewart, Morse, physician, b. 1818; d. 1906.

Stewart, Oscar Milton, educationist, b. Neosho, Mo., 1869; d. Columbia, Mo., May 17, 1944. [10]

Stewart, Robert, missionary, b. Sidney, O., 1839; d. Sialkot, Punjab, India, Oct. 23, 1915. [1; 10]

Stewart, Robert Laird, educationist, b. Murrayville, Pa., 1840; d. Alhambra, Calif., July 28, 1916. [10]

Stewart, Samuel J., clergyman, fl. 1881-82. [38]

Stewart, Seth Thayer, educationist, b. 1850; d. 1913.

Stewart, Thomas Brown Phillips, poet, b. 1864; d. Toronto, Ont., Feb. 2, 1892. [27]

Stewart, Thomas McCants, clergyman and lawyer, b. Charleston, S.C., 1853; d. Monrovia, Liberia, 1932. [3; 10]

Stewart, William Blair, physician, b. 1867; d. Atlantic City, N.J., July 11, 1933.

Stewart, William Henry, soldier and orator, b. 1838; d. 1912. [34]

Stewart, William Morris, lawyer and politician, b. Galen, N.Y., 1827; d. Washington, D.C., April 23, 1909. [1; 4; 5; 10; 62]

Stewart, William Peter, insurance actuary, b. Bath, Me., 1840; d. ? [10]

Stewart, William Rhinelander, philanthropist, b. New York, N.Y., 1852; d. New York, N.Y., Sept. 4, 1929. [1; 10]

Stibitz, George, clergyman and educationist, b. Schuylkill county, Pa., 1856; d. Dayton, O., March 11, 1944. [62]

Stickney, Albert, lawyer, b. Boston, Mass., 1839; d. Greenwich, Conn., 1908. [10]

Stickney, Alpheus Beede, railway president, b. Wilton, Me., 1840; d. St. Paul, Minn., Aug. 9, 1916. [1; 4; 10; 70]

Stickney, Charles E., local historian, b. about 1840; d. Sussex, N.J., Aug., 1930.

Stickney, John, musician, b. Stoughton, Mass., 1742; d. South Hadley, Mass., 1826. [3]

Stickney, Mrs. Mary Etta, née Smith, novelist and short-story writer, b. 1853; d. ?

Stickney, Matthew Adams, genealogist, b. 1805; d. Salem, Mass., Aug. 12, 1894.

Stickney, Joseph Trumbull, poet, b. Geneva, Switzerland, 1874; d. Cambridge, Mass., Oct. 11, 1904. [51]

Stidger, William Le Roy, clergyman, b. Moundsville, W. Va., 1885; d. Newton Center, Mass., Aug. 7, 1949. [7; 10]

Stiff, Edward, soldier, fl. 1840-1847. [7]

Stifler, James Madison, theologian, b. Altoona, Pa., 1839; d. Roxbury, Mass., Dec. 15, 1902. [10; 64]

Stiles, Edward Holcomb, lawyer, b. Granby, Conn., 1836; d. 1927. [4; 37]

Stiles, Ezra, clergyman and educationist, b. North Haven, Conn., 1727; d. New Haven, Conn., May 12, 1795. [1; 2; 3; 4; 5; 6; 7; 8; 9; 62]

Stiles, Henry Reed, physician, historian, and genealogist, b. New York, N.Y., 1832; d. Hill View, Lake George, N.Y., Jan. 8, 1909. [1; 3; 4; 5; 6; 7]

Stiles, Joseph Clay, clergyman, b. Savannah, Ga., 1795; d. Savannah, Ga., March 27, 1875. [3; 34; 62]

Stiles, Meredith Newcomb, journalist, b. New Bedford, Mass., 1880; d. Rochester, N.Y., June 26, 1937. [10]

Stiles, Percy Goldthwait, physiologist, b. Newtonville, Mass., 1875; d. Newtonville, Mass., 1936.

Stiles, Robert, soldier and lawyer, b. Woodford, Ky., 1836; d. near Richmond, Va., Oct. 5, 1905. [34; 62]

Stiles, William Curtis, clergyman, b. Stoneham, Me., 1851; d. Brooklyn, N.Y., Aug. 15, 1911. [10]

Stiles, William Henry, lawyer and politician, b. Savannah, Ga., 1808; d. Savannah, Ga., Dec. 20, 1865. [3; 4; 6; 34]

Still, Andrew Taylor, founder of osteopathy, b. Jonesboro, Va., 1828; d. Kirksville, Mo., Dec. 12, 1917. [1; 2; 4]

Still, Charles Edwin, journalist, b. Willington, Conn., 1872; d. Ticonderoga, N.Y., June 21, 1949.

Still, William, reformer, b. Burlington county, N.J., 1821; d. Philadelphia, Pa., July 14, 1902. [1; 3; 4; 6; 7]

Stillé, Alfred, physician, b. Philadelphia, Pa., 1813; d. Philadelphia, Pa., Sept. 24, 1900. [1; 3; 4; 5; 6; 10; 62]

Stillé, Charles Janeway, historian, b. Philadelphia, Pa., 1819; d. Atlantic City, N.J., Aug. 11, 1899. [1; 3; 4; 5; 6; 7; 10; 62]

Stillman, Annie Raymond, novelist, b. Charleston, S.C., 1855; d. ? [34]

Stillman, Jacob Davis Babcock, physician, b. 1819; d. 1888. [6]

Stillman, John Maxson, chemist, b. New York, N.Y., 1852; d. Stanford University, Calif., Dec. 13, 1923. [4; 10]

Stillman, Samuel, clergyman, b. Philadelphia, Pa., 1737; d. Boston, Mass., March 12, 1807. [1; 3; 6]

Stillman, Thomas Bliss, chemist, b. Plainfield, N.J., 1852; d. Jersey City, N.J., Aug. 10, 1915. [1; 4; 10]

Stillman, William, miscellaneous writer, b. 1767; d. 1858.

Stillman, William James, artist and journalist, b. Schenectady, N.Y., 1828; d. Frimley Green, Surrey, England, July 6, 1901. [1; 3; 4; 6; 7; 9; 10]

Stillman, William Olin, physician, b. Normansville, N.Y., 1856; d. March 15, 1924. [4; 10]

Stillwell, John Edwin, physician, historian, and genealogist, b. New York, N.Y., 1853; d. New York, N.Y., Oct. 6, 1930.

Stillwell, John R., missionary, b. Cheapside, Ont., 1855; d. Ramachandropuram, India, Oct. 21, 1924. [67]

Stillwell, Leander, soldier, b. 1843; d. Erie, Kans., Aug. 10, 1934.

Stilwell, Arthur Edward, financier, b. Rochester, N.Y., 1859; d. New York, N.Y., Sept. 26, 1928. [4; 10; 11]

Stimpson, Mrs. Mary, née **Stoyell,** journalist, b. Farmington, Me., 1857; d. Montclair, N.J., Nov. 6, 1939.

Stimson, Alexander Lovett, expressman and novelist, b. Boston, Mass., 1816; d. Glens Falls, N.Y., Jan. 2, 1906. [1; 3; 6; 7]

Stimson, Elam, physician, b. Tolland, Conn., 1792; d. St. George, Ont., Jan. 1, 1869. [27]

Stimson, Frederic Jesup, lawyer and diplomat, b. Dedham, Mass., 1855; d. Dedham, Mass., Nov. 19, 1943. [4; 7; 10; 11; 51]

Stimson, Henry Albert, clergyman, b. New York, N.Y., 1842; d. New York, N.Y., July 18, 1936. [4; 10; 11; 62]

Stimson, John Ward, artist, b. Paterson, N.J., 1850; d. Corona, Calif., June 13, 1930. [3; 10; 11; 62]

Stimson, Julia Catherine, nurse, b. Worcester, Mass., 1881; d. Poughkeepsie, N.Y., Sept. 30, 1948.

Stimson, Lewis Atterbury, surgeon, b. Paterson, N.J., 1844; d. Shinnecock Hills, Long Island, N.Y., Sept. 17, 1917. [1; 10; 62]

Stinchfield, Ephraim, clergyman, b. 1761; d. 1837. [38]

Stine, James Henry, historian, d. 1906.

Stine, Milton Henry, clergyman, b. East Prospect, Pa., 1853; d. Los Angeles, Calif., March 27, 1940. [10; 11]

Stine, Wilbur Morris, educationist and poet, b. Tyrone, Pa., 1863; d. Penfield, Pa., July 4, 1934. [10]

Stinson, John Harrison, philosopher, b. 1830; d. 1880.

Stirling, Yates, naval officer, b. Vallejo, Calif., 1872; d. Baltimore, Md., Jan. 27, 1948. [7; 10; 11]

Stith, William, clergyman and educationist, b. Virginia, 1707; d. Williamsburg, Va., Sept. 19, 1755. [1; 3; 4; 5; 6; 7; 9; 34]

Stitt, Edward Walmsley, educationist, b. New York, N.Y., 1862; d. July 14, 1927. [10]

Stobo, Robert, soldier, b. Glasgow, Scotland, 1727; d. about 1772. [1; 27]

Stock, Mrs. Etta Florence, née **Nightingale,** novelist, b. Dorchester, Mass., 1858; d. ? [11]

Stockard, Charles Rupert, biologist, b. Washington county, Miss., 1879; d. New York, N.Y., April 7, 1939. [10]

Stockard, Henry Jerome, poet, b. Chatham county, N.C., 1858; d. Raleigh, N.C., Sept. 5, 1914. [10; 34]

Stockbridge, Frank Parker, journalist, b. Gardiner, Me., 1870; d. Stockbridge, Mass., Dec. 7, 1940. [7; 10; 11]

Stockbridge, George Herbert, poet, b. 1852; d. 1916.

Stockbridge, Henry Smith, lawyer, b. North Hadley, Mass., 1822; d. Baltimore, Md., March 11, 1895. [1; 3]

Stockbridge, Horace Edward, educationist, b. near Hadley, Mass., 1857; d. Atlanta, Ga., Oct. 30, 1930. [1; 4; 10]

Stockbridge, John Calvin, clergyman, b. Yarmouth, Me., 1818; d. Providence, R.I., April 2, 1896.

Stocker, Harry Emilius, clergyman, b. Nazareth, Pa., 1876; d. New York, N.Y., Dec. 26, 1929. [10; 11]

Stockett, Maria Letitia, poet and historian, b. 1884; d. Boston, Mass., March 13, 1949.

Stockham, Mrs. Alice, née **Bunker,** physician, b. Cardington, O., 1833; d. Dec. 3, 1912. [10]

Stocking, Jay Thomas, clergyman, b. Lisbon, N.Y., 1870; d. Newton Center, Mass., Jan. 27, 1936. [10; 11; 62]

Stocking, William, journalist, b. Waterbury, Conn., 1840; d. Detroit, Mich., Jan. 26, 1930. [39; 62]

Stockton, Alfred Augustus, lawyer and politician, b. Studholm, N.B., 1842; d. Ottawa, Ont., March 15, 1907. [27]

Stockton, Charles G., physician, b. Madison, O., 1853; d. Buffalo, N.Y., Jan. 5, 1931. [1; 10; 11]

Stockton, Charles Herbert, naval officer, b. Philadelphia, Pa., 1845; d. Washington, D.C., May 31, 1924. [1; 10]

Stockton, Francis Richard, novelist and humorist, b. Philadelphia, Pa., 1834; d. Washington, D.C., April 20, 1902. [1; 2; 3; 4; 5; 6; 7; 8; 9; 71; 72]

Stockton, Louise, novelist, b. Philadelphia, Pa., 1838; d. 1914. [4; 7; 10]

Stockton, Thomas Hewlings, clergyman, b. Mount Holly, N.J., 1808; d. Philadelphia, Pa., Oct. 9, 1868. [1; 3; 5; 6]

Stockwell, Chester Twitchell, dental surgeon, b. Royalston, Mass., 1841; d. 1911. [10]

Stockwell, John Nelson, astronomer and mathematician, b. near Northampton, Mass., 1832; d. Cleveland, O., May 18, 1920. [1; 10]

Stockwell, Thomas Blanchard, educationist, b. 1839; d. Providence, R.I., Feb. 9, 1906. [47]

Stoddard, Amos, soldier and lawyer, b. Woodbury, Conn., 1762; d. Fort Meigs, O., May 11, 1813. [1; 4]

Stoddard, Asa H., poet, b. 1814; d. 1906. [39]

Stoddard, Charles Augustus, clergyman, b. Boston, Mass., 1833; d. New York, N.Y., June 5, 1920. [4; 7; 10]

Stoddard, Charles Warren, journalist and educationist, b. Rochester, N.Y., 1843; d. Monterey, Calif., April 24, 1909. [1; 3; 4; 5; 6; 7; 8; 9; 10; 21; 35; 71]

Stoddard, Elijah Woodward, clergyman, b. Coventryville, N.Y., 1820; d. Succasunna, N.J., Oct. 13, 1913. [45]

Stoddard, Mrs. Elizabeth Drew, née **Barstow,** novelist and poet, b. Mattapoisett, Mass., 1823; d. New York, N.Y., Aug. 1, 1902. [1; 3; 4; 5; 6; 7; 9; 71]

Stoddard, Elliott Joseph, lawyer, b. Seymour, Conn., 1859; d. Detroit, Mich., May 19, 1939. [62]

Stoddard, Enoch Vine, physician, b. New London, Conn., 1840; d. Rochester, N.Y., June 6, 1908. [4; 10]

Stoddard, Francis Hovey, educationist, b. Middlebury, Vt., 1847; d. New York, N.Y., Feb. 26, 1936. [4; 7; 10]

Stoddard, Henry Luther, journalist, b. 1861; d. New York, N.Y., Dec. 13, 1947. [10]

Stoddard, John Fair, educationist, b. Greenfield, N.Y., 1825; d. Kearny, N.J., Aug. 6, 1873. [1; 3; 6]

Stoddard, John Lawson, lecturer, b. Brookline, Mass., 1850; d. near Merano, Italy, June 5, 1931. [1; 5; 7; 10; 11; 21]

Stoddard, John Tappan, chemist, b. Northampton, Mass., 1852; d. Northampton, Mass., Dec. 9, 1919. [1; 10; 13]

Stoddard, Richard Henry, poet and literary critic, b. Hingham, Mass., 1825; d. New York, N.Y., May 12, 1903. [1; 2; 3; 4; 5; 6; 7; 9; 71]

Stoddard, Seneca Roy, writer of guidebooks, d. Glens Falls, N.Y., April 27, 1917. [7]

Stoddard, Soloman, clergyman, b. Boston, Mass., 1643; d. Northampton, Mass., Feb. 11, 1728-29. [1; 4; 7; 51]

Stoddard, William Osborn, journalist, inventor, and writer of books for boys, b. Homer, N.Y., 1835; d. Madison, N.J., Aug. 29, 1925. [1; 4; 7; 9; 10; 11]

Stoddart, James Henry, actor, b. Yorkshire, England, 1827; d. Sewaren, N.J., Dec. 9, 1907. [1; 4; 10]

Stoek, Harry Harkness, mining engineer, b. Washington, D.C., 1866; d. Urbana, Ill., March 1, 1923. [10]

Stoever, Martin Luther, educationist, b. Germantown, Pa., 1820; d. Philadelphia, Pa., July 22, 1870. [1; 3; 6]

Stokely, Mrs. Edith, née **Keeley,** writer of books for children, b. Janesville, Wis., 1862; d. Scarsdale, N.Y., Sept. 1, 1943.

Stokes, Alfred Cheatham, physician, b. about 1847; d. Trenton, N.J., April 15, 1926.

Stokes, Anson Phelps, banker, b. New York, N.Y., 1838; d. New York, N.Y., June 28, 1913. [1; 4; 5; 10]

Stokes, Caroline Phelps, novelist, b. New York, N.Y., 1854; d. Redlands, Calif., April 26, 1909. [1]

Stokes, Ellwood Haines, clergyman, b. Medford, N.J., 1815; d. Ocean Grove, N.J., July 16, 1897. [3b]

Stokes, Frederick Abbot, publisher, b. Brooklyn, N.Y., 1857; d. New York, N.Y., Nov. 15, 1939. [7; 10]

Stokes, J. Lemacks, clergyman, fl. 1886. [34]

Stokes, Olivia Egleston Phelps, philanthropist, b. New York, N.Y., 1847; d. Washington, D.C., Dec. 14, 1927. [1]

Stokes, Mrs. Rose Harriet Pastor, née **Wieslander,** socialist, b. Russian Poland, 1879; d. Frankfurt-am-Main, Germany, June 20, 1933. [1; 10]

Stokes, William Earl Dodge, capitalist, b. New York, N.Y., 1852; d. New York, N.Y., May 19, 1926. [1; 62]

Stokowski, Mrs. Olga Samaroff, née **Hickenlooper.** See Samaroff Stokowski, Mrs. Olga, née Hickenlooper.

Stoller, Hugh Montgomery, engineer, b. Schenectady, N.Y., 1891; d. Hoboken, N.J., Nov. 17, 1947.

Stolper, Gustav, economist, b. Vienna, Austria, 1888; d. New York, N.Y., Dec. 28, 1947. [10]

Stolz, Karl Ruf, educationist, b. Traverse City, Mich., 1884; d. Hartford, Conn., March 30, 1943. [10]

Stomberg, Andrew Adin, educationist, b. Carver, Minn., 1871 d. Minneapolis, Minn., Nov. 6, 1943. [10; 11; 70]

Stone, Arthur Fairbanks, journalist, b. St. Johnsbury, Vt., 1863; d. St. Johnsbury, Vt., Sept. 3, 1944. [10]

Stone, Barton Warren, evangelist, b. near Port Tobacco, Md., 1772; d. Hannibal, Mo., Nov. 9, 1844. [1; 3; 6]

Stone, Charles Arthur, educationist, b. Chicago, Ill., 1893; d. Chicago, Ill., Aug. 14, 1944. [10]

Stone, David Marvin, editor and publisher, b. Oxford, Conn., 1817; d. Brooklyn, N.Y., April 2, 1895. [1; 3; 4; 7]

Stone, Ebenezer Whitten, soldier, b. Boston, Mass., 1801; d. Roxbury, Mass., April 8, 1880. [3; 6]

Stone, Edwin Martin, clergyman, b. Framingham, Mass., 1805; d. Providence, R.I., Dec. 15, 1883. [3; 6]

Stone, Eliot Kays, poet, b. Scranton, Pa., 1880; d. Philadelphia, Pa., March 24, 1944.

Stone, George Hapgood, mining geologist, b. New York, N.Y., 1841; d. Colorado Springs, Colo., Feb. 20, 1917. [10; 13]

Stone, Mrs. Hannah Mayer, physician, b. New York, N.Y., 1894; d. New York, N.Y., July 10, 1941. [10]

Stone, Herbert Stuart, publisher, b. Chicago, Ill., 1871; d. 1915. [51]

Stone, James Bennett, civil engineer, b. Boonton, N.J., 1844; d. Berkeley, Calif., Aug. 9, 1921. [62]

Stone, James Kent, priest and educationist, b. Boston, Mass., 1840; d. San Mateo, Calif., Oct. 14, 1921. [1; 3; 4; 7; 21 51]

Stone, James Samuel, clergyman, b. Shipston-on-Stour, England, 1852; d. Evanston, Ill., May 8, 1928. [4; 10]

Stone, John Charles, mathematician, b. Albion, Ill., 1867; d. St. Petersburg, Fla., May 20, 1940. [10; 11]

Stone, John Seely, clergyman, b. West Stockbridge, Mass., 1795; d. Cambridge, Mass., Jan. 13, 1882. [1; 3; 6]

Stone, Julius Frederick, manufacturer, b. Lenawee county, Mich., 1855; d. Santa Monica, Calif., July 25, 1947. [10]

Stone, Livingston, pisciculturist, b. Cambridge, Mass., 1835; d. Edgewood Park, Pa., Dec. 24, 1912. [10; 51]

Stone, Mrs. Margaret Manson née **Barbour,** psychical researcher, b. St. Louis, Mo., 1841; d. ? [10]

Stone, Mrs. Mary Amelia, née **Boomer,** miscellaneous writer, b. 1823; d. ?

Stone, Mary E. See Bassett, Mrs. Mary E., née Stone.

Stone, Melville Elijah, journalist, b. Hudson, Ill., 1848; d. New York, N.Y., Feb. 15, 1929. [1; 4; 7; 10]

Stone, Melvin Ticknor, physician, b. 1854; d. Troy, N.Y., Nov. 23, 1934.

Stone, Richard Cecil, genealogist, b. 1798; d. ?

Stone, Richard French, physician, b. near Sharpsburg, Ky., 1844; d. Indianapolis, Ind., Oct. 3, 1913. [1]

Stone, Richard Henry, missionary, b. 1837; d. ?

Stone, Rufus Barrett, lawyer, b. Groton, Mass, 1847; d. Bradford, Pa., March 19, 1929. [10; 11]

Stone, Thomas Newcomb, poet, b. Wellfleet, Mass., 1818; d. May 15, 1876. [46]

Stone, Thomas Treadwell, clergyman, b. Waterford, Me., 1801; d. Bolton, Mass., Nov. 13, 1895. [3; 46]

Stone, Timothy Dwight Porter, educationist, b. Cornwall, Conn., 1811; d. Albany, N.Y., April 11, 1887. [45]

Stone, Wilbur Fisk, lawyer, b. Litchfield, Conn., 1833; d. Denver, Colo., Dec. 27, 1920. [1; 4; 10]

Stone, Wilbur Macey, bibliophile, b. 1862; d. East Orange, N.J., Dec. 21, 1942.

Stone, William Alexis, lawyer, b. Tioga county, Pa., 1846; d. Philadelphia, Pa., March 1, 1920. [4; 10]

Stone, William Leete, journalist and historian, b. Guilford, Conn., 1792; d. Saratoga Springs, N.Y., Aug. 15, 1844. [1; 2; 3; 4; 5; 6; 7; 9]

Stone, William Leete, journalist and historian, b. New York, N.Y., 1835; d. Mount Vernon, N.Y., June 11, 1908. [1; 2; 3; 4; 5; 6; 7; 10]

Stone, Witmer, naturalist, b. Philadelphia, Pa., 1866; d. Philadelphia, Pa., May 23, 1939. [7; 10; 11; 13]

Stoner, Dayton, zoologist, b. North Liberty, Ia., 1883; d. Albany, N.Y., May 8, 1944.

Stoner, Mrs. Winifred d'Estcourte, née **Sackville,** educationist, b. 1883; d. New York, N.Y., Nov. 10, 1931. [7; 10; 11]

Stoney, Emily Marjory Armstrong, nurse, fl. 1895-1916.

Storer, David Humphreys, physician and naturalist, b. Portland, Me., 1804; d. Boston, Mass., Sept. 10, 1891. [1; 3; 4; 5; 6]

Storer, Francis Humphreys, chemist, b. Boston, Mass., 1832; d. Boston, Mass., July 30, 1914. [1; 3; 4; 5; 6; 10]

Storer, Horatio Robinson, physician, b. Boston, Mass., 1830; d. Newport, R.I., Sept. 18, 1922. [1; 3; 4; 5; 6; 10]

Storer, Malcolm, physician, b. Milton, Mass., 1862; d. Boston, Mass., Jan. 2, 1935. [51]

Storer, Mrs. Maria, née **Longworth,** novelist, b. Cincinnati, O., 1849; d. Paris, France, April 30, 1932. [4; 10]

Storey, Moorfield, lawyer and publicist, b. Roxbury, Mass., 1845; d. Lincoln, Mass., Oct. 24, 1929. [1; 4; 7; 10; 11]

Stork, Charles Augustus, clergyman, b. near Jefferson, Md., 1838; d. Philadelphia, Pa., Dec. 7, 1883. [3]

Stork, Theophilus, clergyman, b. near Salisbury, N.C., 1814; d. Philadelphia, Pa., March 28, 1874. [3; 6]

Stork, Theophilus Baker, lawyer, b. Philadelphia, Pa., 1854; d. Newport, R.I., Oct. 13, 1937.

Storke, Charles Albert, journalist, b. Branchport, N.Y., 1847; d. Santa Barbara, Calif., Dec. 6, 1936.

Storke, Elliot G., historian, b. 1811; d. about 1880.

Storm, Ashley Van, educationist, b. Walnut, Ill., 1861; d. San Diego, Calif., Oct. 27, 1943. [11]

Storms, Albert Boynton, clergyman, b. Lima, Mich., 1860; d. July 1, 1933. [10; 11]

Storrow, Charles Storer, engineer, b. Montreal, Lower Canada, March 25, 1809; d. Boston, Mass., April 30, 1904. [1; 4]

Storrs, Caryl B., physician and journalist, b. Saginaw, Mich., 1870; d. Minneapolis, Minn., Jan. 18, 1920. [10]

Storrs, Charles, genealogist, b. 1822; d. 1884.

Storrs, George, clergyman, b. 1796; d. about 1879. [6]

Storrs, Lewis Austin, lawyer, b. Hartford, Conn., 1866; d. Hartford, Conn., July 4, 1945. [10]

Storrs, Richard Salter, clergyman, b. Longmeadow, Mass., 1787; d. Braintree, Mass., Aug. 11, 1873. [1; 3; 4; 6; 7]

Storrs, Richard Salter, clergyman, b. Braintree, Mass., 1821; d. Brooklyn, N.Y., June 5, 1900. [1; 3; 4; 5; 6; 7; 10]

Story, Isaac, poet, b. Marblehead, Mass., 1774; d. Marblehead, Mass., July 19, 1803. [1; 3; 4; 6; 7; 9]

Story, Joseph, jurist, b. Marblehead, Mass., 1779; d. Cambridge, Mass., Sept. 10, 1845. [1; 2; 3; 4; 5; 6; 7; 8; 9]

Story, Mrs. Margaret, née **McElroy-Frost,** writer on clothes, b. Athens county, O., 1879; d. 1936. [11]

Story, Russell McCulloch, educationist, b. Washburn, Ill., 1883; d. Pomona, Calif., March 26, 1942. [11]

Story, William Wetmore, lawyer, poet, and essayist, b. Salem, Mass., 1819; d. Vallombroso, Italy, Oct. 8, 1895. [1; 2; 3; 4; 5; 6; 7; 8; 9]

Stotsenburg, John Hawley, lawyer, b. Wilmington, Del., 1830; d. New Albany, Ind., about 1910.

Stott, William Taylor, educationist, b. near Vernon, Ind., 1836; d. Franklin, Ind., Nov. 2, 1918. [4; 10]

Stoudt, John Baer, clergyman and historian, b. Topton, Pa., 1878; d. Allentown, Pa., April 8, 1944.

Stough, Henry Wellington, evangelist, b. Pulaski, O., 1870; d. Knoxville, Tenn., Oct. 27, 1939. [10]

Stoughton, John Alden, lawyer, b. East Windsor, Conn., 1848; d. East Hartford, Conn., March 14, 1915. [62]

Stout, Andrew P., clergyman, fl. 1885-1895.

Stout, Charles Bartelotte, educationist, b. Flemington, N.J., 1824; d. ? [6]

Stoutenburgh, Henry Augustus, local historian, b. 1842; d. Long Island, N.Y., Feb. 13, 1919.

Stovall, Denis H., writer of books for boys, b. Texas; d. South Pasadena, Calif., Dec. 5, 1941. [41]

Stovall, Pleasant Alexander, journalist and diplomat, b. Augusta, Ga., 1857; d. Savannah, Ga., May 14, 1935. [1a 10; 34]

Stover, Wesley Maier, missionary, b. 1850; d. 1922.

Stow, Baron, clergyman, b. Croydon, N.H., 1801; d. Boston, Mass., Dec. 27, 1869. [1; 3; 6]

Stow, Mrs. Joseph W. See Stow, Mrs. Marietta Lois, née Beers.

Stow, Mrs. Marietta Lois, née **Beers,** feminist, d. 1902.

Stowe, Calvin Ellis, educationist, b. Natick, Mass., 1802; d. Hartford, Conn., Aug. 22, 1886. [1; 3; 4; 5; 6; 7; 9]

Stowe, Charles Edward, clergyman, b. Brunswick, Me., 1850; d. Santa Barbara, Calif., July 24, 1934. [7; 10; 35]

Stowe, Mrs. Harriet Elizabeth, née **Beecher,** novelist, b. Litchfield, Conn., 1811; d. Hartford, Conn., July 1, 1896. [1; 2; 3; 4; 5; 6; 7; 8; 9; 71; 72]

Stowe, John M., clergyman and local historian, b. Hubbardston, Mass., 1824; d. Hubbardston, Mass., May 9, 1877.

Stowe, Lyman E., palmist and astrologer, b. 1843; d. Detroit, Mich., Aug. 4, 1919.

Stowell, Calvin Llewellyn, financier, b. Ansonia, Pa., 1854; d. Rochester, N.Y., about 1920. [4; 10]

Stowell, Charles Henry, physician and educationist, b. Perry, N.Y., 1850; d. Lowell, Mass., 1932. [10]

Stowell, Theodore Barrows, educationist, b. 1847; d. Providence, R.I., May 29, 1916.

Stowell, Thomas Blanchard, educationist, b. Perry, N.Y., 1846; d. Los Angeles, Calif., July 29, 1927. [4; 10]

Stowell, William Henry Harrison, manufacturer, b. Windsor, Vt., 1840; d. Amherst, Mass., April 27, 1922. [10]

Stowell, William Leland, physician, b. 1859; d. Bronxville, N.Y., Sept. 30, 1931.

Strahan, Edward (pseud.). See Shinn, Earl.

Strahan, Mrs. Kay, née **Cleaver,** novelist, b. La Grande, Ore., 1888; d. Portland, Ore., Aug. 14, 1941. [7; 10; 11]

Strain, Isaac G., naval officer and explorer, b. Roxbury, Pa., 1821; d. Colon, Panama, May 14, 1857. [1; 3; 6]

Strait, Newton Allen, civil servant, d. 1922.

Straith, John, clergyman, b. Aberdeenshire, Scotland, 1826; d. Sherburne, Ont., Jan. 10, 1885. [27]

Straker, David Augustus, lawyer, d. Detroit, Mich., 1908.

Strang, Hugh Innes, educationist, b. Galt, Ont., 1841; d. Goderich, Ont., April 4, 1919. [27]

Strang, James Jesse, Mormon leader, b. Scipio, N.Y., 1813; d. Voree, Mich., July 9, 1856. [1; 4; 7]

Strang, Lewis Clinton, journalist, b. Westfield, Mass., 1869; d. Boston, Mass., Jan. 14, 1935. [7; 10]

Strange, Robert, politician and novelist, b. Manchester, Va., 1796; d. Fayetteville, N.C., Feb. 19, 1854. [3; 4; 5; 34]

Stratemeyer, Edward, writer of books for boys, b. Elizabeth, N.J., 1862; d. Newark, N.Y., May 10, 1930. [1; 4; 5; 7; 10]

Straton, Barry, poet, b. Fredericton, N.B., 1854; d. Fredericton, N.B., 1906. [27]

Straton, John Roach, clergyman and reformer, b. Evansville, Ind., 1875; d. Clifton Springs, N.Y., Oct. 29, 1929. [1; 10; 11]

Stratton, Ezra M., historian, b. 1809; d. 1883.

Stratton, Joseph Buck, clergyman, b. 1815; d. 1903. [34]

Stratton, Royal B., chronicler, d. 1875.

Stratton-Porter, Mrs. Gene. See Porter, Mrs. Gene, née Stratton.

Straus, Nathan, philanthropist, b. Germany, 1848; d. New York, N.Y., Jan. 11, 1931. [1; 4; 10]

Straus, Oscar Solomon, lawyer and diplomat, b. Germany, 1850; d. New York, N.Y., May 3, 1926. [1; 4; 5; 7; 10]

Straus, Simon William, banker and financier, b. Ligonier, Ind., 1866; d. New York, N.Y., Sept. 7, 1930. [1; 10]

Strawbridge, Anne West, aviatrix, b. 1883; d. Philadelphia, Pa., Sept. 9, 1941.

Strayer, Paul Moore, clergyman, b. Edesville, Md., 1871; d. Rochester, N.Y., April 3, 1929. [4; 10; 11; 62]

Streamer, Volney, editor and librarian, b. Magnolia, Ill., 1850; d. New York, N.Y., April 14, 1915. [10]

Strebor, Eiggam (pseud.). See Roberts, Maggie.

Strecker, Herman, naturalist, b. Philadelphia, Pa., 1836; d. Reading, Pa., Nov. 30, 1901. [3; 4; 10]

Street, Alfred Billings, lawyer, librarian, and poet, b. Poughkeepsie, N.Y., 1811; d. Albany, N.Y., June 2, 1881. [1; 3; 4; 5; 6; 7; 9; 71]

Street, Charles Stuart, bridge expert, b. 1864; d. Southampton, Long Island, N.Y., Aug. 15, 1939.

Street, George Edward, clergyman, b. Cheshire, Conn., 1835; d. Hartford, Conn., Dec. 26, 1903. [62]

Street, Ida Maria, educationist, b. Oskaloosa, Ia., 1856; d. 1933. [10]

Street, J. Fletcher, architect and naturalist, b. Beverly, N.J., 1880; d. Beverly, N.J., Sept. 18, 1944. [10]

Street, Julian Leonard, novelist and littérateur, b. Chicago, Ill., 1879; d. Lakeville, Conn., Feb. 19, 1947. [7; 10; 11; 12]

Street, Lottie E., librarian, b. 1859; d. New Haven, Conn., Jan. 20, 1942.

Street, Mrs. Mary Evarts, née **Anderson,** traveller and genealogist, b. 1838; d. 1905.

Street, Robert Gould, lawyer, b. Greensboro, Ala., 1843; d. Galveston, Tex., 1925. [10]

Street, Thomas Atkins, jurist, b. Marshall county, Ala., 1872; d. Montgomery, Ala., March 17, 1936. [10; 11]

Streeter, Oscar Willard, poet, b. about 1821; d. 1902.

Streeter, Russell, priest, b. Chesterfield, N.H., 1791; d. Woodstock, Vt., Feb. 15, 1880. [43]

Streets, Thomas Hale, physician, b. 1847; d. Wyncote, Pa., March 3, 1925.

Streighthoff, Frank Hatch, economist, b. Brooklyn, N.Y., 1886; d. Indianapolis, Ind., Jan. 13, 1935. [10]

Strelsky, Nikander, educationist, b. Russia, 1893; d. Saranac Lake, N.Y., June 20, 1946.

Strickland, Samuel, b. Reydon Hall, Suffolk, England, 1804; d. Lakefield, Ont., 1867. [27]

Strickland, William, architect and engineer, b. Philadelphia, Pa., about 1787; d. Nashville, Tenn., April 6, 1854. [1; 3; 4; 6]

Strickland, William Peter, clergyman, b. Pittsburgh, Pa., 1809; d. Ocean Grove, N.J., July 15, 1884. [3; 6]

Strickler, Givens Brown, clergyman, b. Strickler's Springs, Va., 1840; d. Richmond, Va., 1914. [10; 34]

Strickler, William Maberry, physician, b. 1838; d. ?

Stringer, George Alfred, miscellaneous writer, b. Hartford, Conn., 1845; d. Buffalo, N.Y., Nov. 9, 1922. [4]

Stringham, Washington Irving, mathematician, b. Delavan, N.Y., 1847; d. Berkeley, Calif., Oct. 5, 1909. [1; 10]

Strobel, B. B., physician, fl. 1826-1840.

Strobel, Edward Henry, diplomat, b. Charleston, S.C., 1855; d. Bangkok, Siam, Jan. 15, 1908. [1; 4; 5; 10]

Strobel, Philip A., clergyman, d. Dansville, N.Y., Nov. 26, 1882.

Strobridge, George Egerton, clergyman, b. 1839; d. 1910.

Strobridge, Mrs. Idah, née **Meacham,** bookbinder, b. Contra Costa county, Calif., 1855; d. Los Angeles, Calif., Feb. 8, 1932. [10; 11; 35]

Strodach, Paul Zeller, clergyman, b. Norristown, Pa., 1876; d. Easton, Pa., May 30, 1947. [10]

Stroh, Grant, clergyman, b. 1863; d. Bradenton, Fla., July 25, 1949.

Strohm, Gertrude, compiler, b. Greene county, O., 1843; d. ? [10]

Stromme, Peer Olsen, journalist, b. Winchester, Wis., 1856; d. Madison, Wis., Sept. 15, 1921. [1; 4; 10]

Strong, Augustus Hopkins, theologian, b. Rochester, N.Y., 1836; d. Pasadena, Calif., Nov. 29, 1921. [1; 3; 4; 5; 6; 7; 10; 62]

Strong, Caleb, lawyer and politician, b. Northampton, Mass., 1745; d. Northampton, Mass., Nov. 7, 1819. [1; 3; 4; 5; 6]

Strong, Charles Augustus, psychologist, b. Haverhill, Mass., 1862; d. Fiesole, Italy, Jan. 23, 1940. [7; 10]

Strong, Charles Hall, clergyman, b. New Orleans, La., 1850; d. Milledgeville, Ga., Jan. 21, 1914. [10; 62]

Strong, Elnathan Ellsworth, clergyman, b. Hardwick, Vt., 1832; d. Boston, Mass., April 2, 1914. [10]

Strong, Frank, educationist, b. Venice, N.Y., 1859; d. Lawrence, Kans., Aug. 6, 1934. [4; 10; 62]

Strong, George Augustus, poet, b. 1832; d. 1912.

Strong, George Crockett, soldier, b. Stockbridge, Vt., 1832; d. New York, N.Y., July 30, 1863. [3; 4; 6]

Strong, George Vaughn, poet and jurist, b. 1827; d. Oct. 10, 1897. [34]

Strong, Grace, novelist, d. 1887.

Strong, Hero (pseud.). See Jones, Clara Augusta.

Strong, James, educationist, b. New York, N.Y., 1822; d. Round Lake, N.Y., Aug. 7, 1894. [1; 3; 4; 5; 6; 7]

Strong, John Ruggles, lawyer and poet, b. 1851; d. New York, N.Y., Feb. 6, 1941.

Strong, Joseph Dwight, clergyman, fl. 1859-1869.

Strong, Josiah, clergyman, b. Naperville, Ill., 1847; d. New York, N.Y., April 29, 1916. [1; 3; 4; 5; 6; 7]

Strong, Latham Cornell, poet, b. Troy, N.Y., 1845; d. Tarrytown, N.Y., Dec. 17, 1879. [3; 6; 7; 43]

Strong, Moses McCure, historian, b. Rutland. Vt., 1810; d. Mineral Point, Wis., July 20, 1894. [1; 44]

Strong, Nathan, clergyman, b. Coventry, Conn., 1748; d. Hartford, Conn., Dec. 25, 1816. [3; 6]

Strong, Nehemiah, educationist, b. Northampton, Mass., 1730; d. Bridgeport, Conn., Aug. 12, 1807. [3; 6; 62]

Strong, Sydney Dix, clergyman, b. Seville, O., 1860; d. Seattle, Wash., Dec. 30, 1938.

Strong, Theodore, mathematician, b. South Hadley, Mass., 1790; d. New Brunswick, N.J., Feb. 1, 1869. [1; 3; 4; 5; 6; 62]

Strong, Theron George, lawyer, b. Palmyra, N.Y., 1846; d. New York, N.Y., Dec. 6, 1924. [10]

Strong, Thomas Morris, clergyman, b. Cooperstown, N.Y., 1797; d. Flatbush, Long Island, N.Y., June 14, 1861. [3; 6]

Strong, Thomas Nelson, historian, b. Cathlamet, Ore., 1853; d. Portland, Ore., April 15, 1927. [41]

Strong, Titus, clergyman, b. Brighton, Mass., 1787; d. Greenfield, Mass., June, 1855.

Strong, William, jurist, b. Somers, Conn., 1808; d. Lake Minnewaska, Ulster county, N.Y., Aug. 19, 1895. [1; 3; 4; 5; 6; 62]

Strong, William Chamberlain, agriculturist, b. 1823; d. 1913.

Strong, William Ellsworth, clergyman, b. South Natick, Mass., 1860; d. Newtonville, Mass., March 7, 1934. [10]

Strong, William McCreery, advertising expert, b. New Britain, Conn., 1899; d. Pasadena, Calif., March 23, 1941.

Strother, David Hunter, soldier and illustrator, b. Martinsburg, W. Va., 1816; d. Charles Town, W. Va., March 8, 1888. [1; 3; 4; 5; 6; 7; 34]

Strother, French, journalist, b. Marshall, Mo., 1883; d. Washington, D.C., March 12, 1933. [10; 11]

Stroud, George McDowell, jurist, b. Stroudsburg, Pa., 1795; d. Germantown, Pa., June 29, 1875. [3; 6]

Strover, Carl Bernhard Wittekind, lawyer, b. Prussia, 1865; d. Chicago, Ill., April 19, 1941. [10; 11]

Strunk, William, educationist, b. Cincinnati, O., 1869; d. Ithaca, N.Y., Sept. 26, 1946. [10]

Strunsky, Simeon, journalist, b. Vitebsk, Russia, 1879; d. Princeton, N.J., Feb. 5, 1948. 7; 10]

Struve, Gustav, revolutionist, b. Munich, Bavaria, Oct. 11, 1805; d. Vienna, Austria, Aug. 21, 1870. [1; 3]

Stryker, Melancthon Woolsey, educationist, b. Vernon, N.Y., 1851; d. Rome, N.Y., Dec. 6, 1929. [1; 4; 5; 7; 10]

Stryker, William Scudder, lawyer and historian, b. Trenton, N.J., 1838; d. Trenton, N.J., Oct. 29, 1900. [3; 4; 5; 10]

Stuart, Addison A., soldier, b. Massachusetts, 1832; d. March 10, 1910. [37]

Stuart, Alexander Hugh Holmes, politician, b. Staunton, Va., 1807; d. Staunton, Va., Feb. 13, 1891. [1; 3; 4; 5; 6; 34]

Stuart, Andrew, lawyer and politician, b. Kingston, Canada, 1785; d. Quebec, Lower Canada, Feb. 21, 1840. [27]

Stuart, Carlos D., poet, b. Berlin, Vt., 1820; d. Northampton, Mass., Jan. 23, 1862. [6; 43]

Stuart, Charles, reformer, b. Jamaica, 1783; d. near Thornbury, Ont., 1865. [1; 3; 6]

Stuart, Charles Beebe, engineer, b. Madison county, N.Y., 1814; d. Cleveland, O., Jan. 4 ,1881. [1; 3; 6]

Stuart, Charles Duff, lawyer, b. San Francisco, Calif., 1854; d. Dec., 1929. [10] 35]

Stuart, Charles Macaulay, clergyman, b. Glasgow, Scotland, 1853; d. La Jolla, Calif., Jan. 26, 1932. [1; 4; 10; 11]

Stuart, Donald Clive, educationist, b. Battle Creek, Mich., 1881; d. Trenton, N.J., June 2, 1943. [10; 11]

Stuart, Duane Reed, educationist, b. Oneida, Ill., 1873; d. Greensboro, Vt., Aug. 30, 1941. [10]

Stuart, Edwin Roy, military engineer, b. Arnettsville, W. Va., 1874; d. West Point, N.Y., March 6, 1920. [10]

Stuart, Eleanor (pseud.). See Porter, Mrs. Eleanor, née Hodgman,

Stuart, George, educationist, b. 1831; d. 1897.

Stuart, George Hay, banker and philanthropist, b. county Down, Ireland, 1816; d. Philadelphia, Pa., April 11, 1890. [3b]

Stuart, George Rutledge, clergyman, b. Talbott, Tenn., 1857; d. Birmingham, Ala., May 11, 1926. [10]

Stuart, Gordon (pseud.).   See Sayler, Harry Lincoln.

Stuart, Granville, pioneer, b. Clarksburg, Va., 1834; d. Missoula, Mont., Oct. 2, 1918. [1; 4; 7]

Stuart, Henry Longan, novelist and literary critic, b. London, England, 1874; d. New York, N.Y., Aug. 26, 1928. [4]

Stuart, Isaac William, educationist, b. New Haven, Conn., 1809; d. Hartford, Conn., Oct. 2, 1861. [1; 3; 6; 7; 62]

Stuart, Joseph Alonzo, genealogist, b. 1825; d. Palo Alto, Calif., Jan. 22, 1910.

Stuart, Milo H., educationist, b. Sheridan, Ind., 1871; d. July 24, 1933. [10]

Stuart, Moses, theologian, b. Wilton, Conn., 1780; d. Andover, Mass., Jan. 4, 1852. [1; 3; 4; 5; 6; 9; 62]

Stuart, Mrs. Ruth, née **McEnery,** writer of short stories, b. Marksville, La., 1849; d. New York, N.Y., May 6, 1917. [1; 4; 5; 7; 9; 10; 34

Stubbs, William Carter, genealogist, b. Gloucester county, Va., 1846; d. July 7, 1924. [10]

Stuck, Hudson, missionary, b. London, England, 1863; d. Fort Yukon, Alaska, Oct. 10, 1920. [1; 4; 7; 10]

Stuckenberg, John Henry Wilbrandt, theologian and sociologist, b. Hanover, Germany, 1835; d. London, England, May 28, 1903. [1; 3; 6; 10]

Studer, Jacob Henry, ornithologist, b. Columbus, O., 1840; d. New York, N.Y., Aug. 2, 1904. [10]

Stump, Joseph, theologian, b. Marietta, Pa., 1866; d. May 24, 1935. [10; 11]

Stuntz, Homer Clyde, bishop, b. Albion, Pa., 1858; d. Omaha, Neb., June 3, 1924. [4; 10]

Stuntz, Stephen Conrad, librarian and botanist, b. Clarno, Wis., 1875; d. Vienna, Va., Feb. 2, 1918. [10]

Sturdy, William Allen, educationist, b. 1840; d. ?

Sturgis, Frederic Russell, physician, b. Manila, Philippine Islands, 1844; d. New York, N.Y., May 6, 1919. [4; 10]

Sturgis, Russell, architect, b. Baltimore, Md., 1836; d. New York, N.Y., Feb. 11, 1909. [1; 4; 5; 7; 10]

Sturtevant, Edward Lewis, agricultural scientist, b. Boston, Mass., 1842; d. Framingham, Mass., July 30, 1898. [1; 3; 6]

Sturtevant, Julian Monson, clergyman and educationist, b. Warren, Conn., 1805; d. Jacksonville, Ill., Feb. 11, 1886. [1; 3; 4; 6; 62]

Stutsman, Jesse Orila, criminologist, b. Philadelphia, Pa., 1871; d. Lewisburg, Pa., April 25, 1933. [10; 11]

Suares, M. R., clergyman, b. South Carolina, 1812; d. 1884. [34]

Suddoth, Mrs. Harriet Almaria, née **Baker,** miscellaneous writer, fl. 1873-1883. [6]

Sudworth, George Bishop, forester, b. Kingston, Wis., 1864; d. Washington, D.C., May 10, 1927. [4; 10; 11]

Sullivan, Alan, novelist, b. Montreal, Que., 1868; d. Tilford, England, Aug. 6, 1947. [30]

Sullivan, Edward Dean, journalist, b. New Haven, Conn., 1888; d. Hollywood, Calif., April 4, 1938. [7; 10]

Sullivan, Harry Stack, psychiatrist, b. New York, N.Y., 1892; d. Paris, France, Jan. 15, 1949. [13]

Sullivan, James, lawyer and politician, b. Berwick, Me., 1744; d. Boston, Mass., Dec. 10, 1808. [1; 3; 4; 5; 6]

Sullivan, James, educationist, b. Baltimore, Md., 1873; d. Albany, N.Y., Oct. 8, 1931. [10]

Sullivan, James Edward, writer on athletic sports, b. New York, N.Y., 1860; d. New York, N.Y., Sept. 16, 1914. [1; 4; 10]

Sullivan, James William, printer and sociologist, b. Carlisle, Pa., 1848; d. Carlisle, Pa., Sept. 28, 1938. [10]

Sullivan, John Lawrence, pugilist, b. Boston, Mass., 1858; d. West Abingdon, Mass., Feb. 2, 1918. [1; 2; 5; 10]

Sullivan, Joseph, clergyman, b. county Derry, Ireland, 1864; d. Chicopee, Mass., Jan. 11, 1929.

Sullivan, Louis Henri, architect, b. Boston, Mass., 1856; d. Chicago, Ill., April 14, 1924. [1; 7; 10]

Sullivan, Louis Robert, anthropologist, b. Houlton, Me., 1892; d. Tucson, Ariz., April 23, 1925. [1; 4]

Sullivan, Mrs. Margaret Frances, née **Buchanan,** journalist, b. Tyrone, Ireland; d. Chicago, Ill., 1903. [10]

Sullivan, Peter Marcus, publicist, b. 1843; d. Oklahoma City, Okla., 1928.

Sullivan, Robert, lawyer, b. 1837; d. Toronto, Ont., July 3, 1870. [29]

Sullivan, Robert Baldwin, politician and jurist, b. near Cork, Ireland, 1802; d. Toronto, Ont., April 14, 1853. [27]

Sullivan, Thomas Russell, novelist, b. Boston, Mass., 1849; d. Boston, Mass., June 28, 1916. [3; 4; 7; 10]

Sullivan, William, lawyer and politician, b. Biddeford, Me., 1774; d. Boston, Mass., Sept. 3, 1839. [1; 3; 4; 6; 7]

Sullivan, William Laurence, clergyman, b. East Braintree, Mass., 1872; d. Oct. 5, 1935. [10]

Sullivant, William Starling, botanist, b. Franklinton, O., 1803; d. Columbus, O., April 30, 1873. [1; 3; 4; 5; 6]

Sulte, Benjamin, historian, b. Three Rivers, Que., 1841; d. Ottawa, Ont., Aug. 6, 1923. [27]

Sulzberger, Mayer, jurist and Biblical scholar, b. Germany, 1843; d. Philadelphia, Pa., April 20, 1923. [1; 4; 10]

Sulzer, Robert Frederick, missionary, b. 1845; d. July 1, 1925.

Sulzer, William, politician, b. Elizabeth, N.J., 1863; d. New York, N.Y., Nov. 6, 1941. [4; 10]

Summerbell, Carlyle, clergyman, b. Springboro, Pa., 1873; d. Boston, Mass., May 21, 1935. [10]

Summerbell, Joseph James, clergyman, d. 1916.

Summerbell, Martyn, educationist, b. Naples, N.Y., 1847; d. Lakemont, N.Y., Sept. 12, 1939. [10; 11]

Summerdale (pseud.). See Young, Alexander (1836-1891).

Summerfield, Charles (pseud.). See Arrington, Alfred W.

Summerfield, John, clergyman, b. Preston, Lancashire, England, 1798; d. New York, N.Y., June 13, 1825. [6]

Summerhayes, Mrs. Martha, née **Dunham,** soldier's wife, b. Nantucket, Mass., 1846; d. Schenectady, N.Y., May 12, 1911.

Summers, John Edward, surgeon, b. Fort Kearney, Neb., 1858; d. Omaha, Neb., Feb. 7, 1935. [4; 10]

Summers, Thomas Osmond, clergyman, b. Dorsetshire, England, 1812; d. Nashville, Tenn., May 6, 1882. [1; 3; 6; 34]

Sumner, Charles, politician and abolitionist, b. Boston, Mass., 1811; d. Washington, D.C., March 11, 1874. [1; 2; 3; 4; 5; 6; 7; 8; 9]

Sumner, Charles Allen, journalist and court reporter, b. Great Barrington, Mass., 1835; d. 1903. [3; 6; 10; 35]

Sumner, George, physician and botanist, b. Pomfret, Conn., 1793; d. Hartford, Conn., Feb. 20, 1855. [3; 6; 62]

Sumner, Samuel Barstow, poet, b. 1830; d. 1891.

Sumner, William Graham, social scientist, b. Paterson, N.J., 1840; d. Englewood, N.J., April 2, 1910. [1; 4; 7; 9; 10; 62]

Sumner, William Hyslop, soldier, b. Roxbury, Mass., 1780; d. Jamaica Plain, Mass., Oct. 24, 1861. [3; 5; 6]

Sunday, William Ashley, evangelist, b. Ames, Ia., 1863; d. Chicago, Ill., Nov. 6, 1935. [1a; 2a; 10]

Sunderland, Jabez Thomas, clergyman, b. Yorkshire, England, 1842; d. Ann Arbor, Mich., Aug. 13, 1936. [10; 11]

Sunderland, James, clergyman. b. 1834; d. Oakland, Calif., April 23, 1924.

Sunderland, La Roy, abolitionist, b. Exeter, R.I., 1804; d. Quincy, Mass., May 15, 1885. [1; 3; 4; 6]

Super, Charles William, educationist, b. Pottsville, Pa., 1842; d. Athens, O., Oct. 9, 1939. [4; 10]

Suplée, Thomas Danly, educationist, b. Philadelphia, Pa., 1846; d. Philadelphia, Pa., May 2, 1928. [3; 56]

Surdez, Georges, novelist, b. Switzerland, 1900; d. Brooklyn, N.Y., Nov. 5, 1949.

Surette, Louis A., freemason, b. Nova Scotia, 1818; d. ? [6]

Surette, Thomas Whitney, musician, b. Concord, Mass., 1862; d. Concord, Mass., May 19, 1941. [10; 11]

Surface, Andrew Jay, educationist, b. 1843; d. 1919.

Surratt, John Harrison, conspirator, b. 1844; d. April 21, 1916. [1]

Suter, John Wallace, clergyman, b. Boston, Mass., 1859; d. Boston, Mass., April 11, 1942. [10; 11; 51]

Sutherland, Alexander, clergyman, b. near Guelph, Upper Canada, 1833; d. Toronto, Ont., June 30, 1910. [27]

Sutherland, Mrs. Evelyn Greenleaf, née **Baker,** journalist and playwright, b. Cambridge, Mass., 1855; d. Boston, Mass., 1908. [7; 10]

Sutherland, George, clergyman, b. New Glasgow, N.S., 1830; d. Sydney, New South Wales, 1893. [27]

Sutherland, Jabez Gridley, lawyer, b. Van Buren, N.Y., 1825; d. 1902. [4]

Sutherland, Joel Barlow, jurist, b. Philadelphia, Pa., 1792; d. Philadelphia, Pa., Nov. 15, 1861. [1; 3; 4; 5; 6]

Sutherland, John Campbell, educationist, b. Galt, Ont., 1860; d. Quebec, Que., April 10, 1936. [27]

Sutherland, John Preston, physician, b. Charlestown, Mass., 1854; d. Boston, Mass., Feb. 21, 1941. [10]

Sutherland, Thomas Jefferson, filibuster-er, fl. 1837-1841. [27]

Sutherland, William Andrew, lawyer and freemason, b. Hopewell, N.Y., 1849; d. Rochester, N.Y., 1908. [4; 10]

Sutherland, William James, educationist, b. 1865; d. 1914.

Sutliffe, Albert, poet, b. 1830; d. ? [3]

Sutphen, William Gilbert Van Tassel, clergyman and golfer, b. Philadelphia, Pa., 1861; d. Morristown, N.J., Sept. 20, 1945. [7; 10; 11]

Sutro, Adolph Heinrich Joseph, mining engineer, b. Aix-la-Chapelle, Prussia, 1830; d. San Francisco, Calif., Aug. 8, 1898. [1; 3; 4; 5; 6; 7]

Sutro, Theodore, lawyer, b. Aix-la-Chapelle, Prussia, 1845; d. New York, N.Y., Aug. 28, 1927. [4; 10; 51]

Sutton, Clarence Wesley, educationist, b. 1870; d. 1936.

Sutton, Frederick Ellsworth, journalist, d. Kansas City, Mo., Sept., 1937. [75]

Sutton, Katherine Augusta, educationist, b. New Canaan, Conn., 1888; d. Danbury, Conn., Feb. 10, 1949.

Sutton, Ransom, journalist, b. Greeley, Kans., 1869; d. Los Angeles, Calif., Oct. 14, 1934. [10]

Sutton, William Seneca, educationist, b. Fayetteville, Ark., 1860; d. Austin, Tex., Nov. 26, 1928. [1; 4; 10]

Sutton, Xavier, priest, b. 1852; d. Chicago, Ill., July 28, 1926. [21]

Suydam, John Howard, clergyman, b. Brooklyn, N.Y., 1832; d. 1909. [3; 10]

Suzor, Louis Théodore, soldier, b. Lower Canada, 1834; d. Quebec, Que., Aug. 18, 1866. [27]

Suzzallo, Henry, educationist, b. San José, Calif., Aug. 22, 1875; d. Seattle, Wash., Sept. 25, 1933. [1; 7; 10; 11]

Swaim, Samuel Budd, clergyman, b. Pemberton, N.J., 1809; d. Cambridge, Mass., Feb. 3, 1865.

Swain, Clara A., medical missionary, b. Elmira, N.Y., 1834; d. Castile, N.Y., Dec. 25, 1910. [1]

Swain, David Lowry, educationist, b. Buncombe county, N.C., 1801; d. Chapel Hill, N.C., Sept. 3, 1868. [1; 3; 4; 5; 6; 34]

Swain, George Fillmore, educationist, b. San Francisco, Calif., 1857; d. Squam Lake, N.H., July 1, 1931. [1a; 4; 10; 11]

Swain, Henry Huntington, educationist, b. Providence, R.I., 1863; d. Helena, Mont., Jan. 13, 1941. [10]

Swain, James Barrett, journalist, b. New York, N.Y., 1820; d. Sing Sing, N.Y., May 27, 1895. [1; 3; 4; 6]

Swales, Mrs. Susan Matilda, née Bradshaw, novelist, b. 1843; d. ?

Swallow, Silas Comfort, clergyman, b. near Wilkesbarre, Pa., 1839; d. Harrisburg, Pa., Aug. 13, 1930. [1; 10]

Swan, Alonzo M., local historian, b. 1830; d. Albuquerque, N.M., Sept. 19, 1902.

Swan, James, financier, b. Fifeshire, Scotland, 1754; d. Paris, France, July 31, 1830. [1; 3; 6]

Swan, James Gilchrist, ethnologist, b. Medford, Mass., 1818; d. Port Townsend, Wash., 1900.

Swan, Joseph Rockwell, jurist, b. Oneida county, N.Y., 1802; d. Columbus, O., Dec. 18, 1884. [1; 3; 4; 6]

Swan, Joshua Augustus, poet, b. 1823; d. 1871. [51]

Swan, William Draper, educationist, b. Dorchester, Mass., 1809; d. Dorchester, Mass., Nov. 2, 1864. [3; 6]

Swander, John I., theologian, b. Warren county, N.J., 1833; d. Tiffin, O., 1925. [10]

Swaney, William Bentley, lawyer, b. Sumner county, Tenn., 1858; d. near Chattanooga, Tenn., July 28, 1945. [10]

Swank, James Moore, historian and statistician, b. Westmoreland county, Pa., 1832; d. Philadelphia, Pa., June 21, 1914. [1; 3; 4; 6; 10]

Swartz, Joel, clergyman and poet, b. Shenandoah county, Va., 1827; d. 1914. [3; 10]

Swasey, John B., miscellaneous writer, fl. 1876-1886.

Swayze, George Banghart Henry, physician, b. Hope, N.J., 1833; d. Philadelphia, Pa., Aug. 22, 1914. [10]

Swazey, Arthur, novelist, b. 1824; d. 1887.

Sweat, Mrs. Margaret Jane, née Mussey, miscellaneous writer, b. Portland, Me., 1823; d. ? [3; 38]

Sweeney, Zachary Taylor, clergyman, b. Liberty, Ky., 1849; d. Columbus, Ind., Feb. 4, 1926. [4; 10; 11]

Sweeny, Robert, poet, d. Montreal, Lower Canada, 1840. [27]

Sweet, Alexander Edwin, humorist, b. Saint John, N.B., March 28, 1841; d. New York, N.Y., May 20, 1901. [3; 4; 6; 10]

Sweet, Caroline C., educationist, d. 1901.

Sweet, Charles Filkins, missionary, b about 1854; d. 1927.

Sweet, Frank Herbert, writer of books for boys and girls, b. West Greenwich, R.I., 1856; d. Feb. 3, 1920. [7; 10; 11]

Sweet, Homer De Lois, engineer, b. Pompey, N.Y., 1826; d. 1893. [3; 6]

Sweet, James Sylvester, educationist, b. 1853; d. Santa Rosa, Calif., Nov. 10, 1930.

Sweet, John Edson, mechanical engineer, b. near Pompey, N.Y., 1832; d. Syracuse, N.Y., May 8, 1916. [1; 4; 10]

Sweet, Samuel Niles, educationist, b. Jefferson county, N.Y., 1805; d. ? [6]

Sweetser, Charles Humphreys, journalist, b. Athol, Mass., 1841; d. Palatka, Fla., Jan. 1, 1871. [3]

Sweetser, Delight, journalist, b. Hartford City, Ind., 1873; d. 1903. [10]

Sweetser, Edwin Chapin, clergyman, b. Wakefield, Mass., 1847; d. Philadelphia, Pa., Oct. 22, 1929. [10]

Sweetser, Kate Dickinson, writer of books for children, b. New York, N.Y.; d. New York, N.Y., March 22, 1939. [7; 10; 11]

Sweetser, Lewis Hobart, spiritualist, b. San Francisco, Calif., 1868; d. Los Angeles, Calif., June 5, 1944. [62]

Sweetser, Moses Foster, writer of guidebooks, b. Newburyport, Mass., 1848; d. Dorchester, Mass., July, 1897. [3; 6]

Sweetser, Seth, clergyman, b. 1807; d. 1878. [51]

Sweetser, William, physician, b. Boston, Mass., 1797; d. New York, N.Y., Oct. 14, 1875. [3; 6; 51]

Swensson, Carl Aaron, clergyman, b. Sugargrove, Pa., 1857; d. Los Angeles, Calif., Feb. 16, 1904. [1; 4; 10]

Swett, John, educationist, b. near Pittsfield, N.H., 1830; d. near Martinez, Calif., Aug. 22, 1913. [1; 4; 10]

Swett, John Appleton, physician, b. Boston, Mass., 1808; d. New York, N.Y., Sept. 17, 1854. [3; 6]

Swett, Josiah, clergyman and educationist, b. Claremont, N.H., 1814; d. Highgate, Vt., Jan. 4, 1890. [3; 4; 6]

Swett, Samuel, military historian, b. Newburyport, Mass., 1782; d. Boston, Mass., Oct. 28, 1866. [3; 4; 6]

Swett, Sophia Miriam, writer of books for young people, b. Brewer, Me., 1858; d. Nov. 12, 1912. [7; 10]

Swett, Susan Hartley, short-story writer, b. Brewer, Me.; d. Arlington Heights, Mass., 1907. [10]

Swett, William, educationist, b. Henniker, N.H., 1825; d. Beverly, Mass., March 25, 1884. [3; 6]

Swezey, Goodwin Deloss, astronomer, b. Rockford, Ill., 1851; d. Lincoln, Neb., July 10, 1934. [10; 11]

Swift, Augustus, M., novelist, d. 1884.

Swift, Charles Francis, local historian, b. 1825; d. Yarmouth, Mass., April 29, 1903.

Swift, Clarence Franklin, clergyman, b. Oberlin, O., 1861; d. Denver, Colo., March 25, 1919. [4; 10]

Swift, Edgar James, educationist, b. Ravenna, O., 1860; d. Salmon Falls, Hollis, Me., Aug. 30, 1932. [10; 11]

Swift, Elisha Pope, clergyman, b. Williamstown, Mass., 1792; d. Alleghany, Pa., April 3, 1865. [3; 6]

Swift, Fletcher Harper, educationist, b. New York, N.Y., 1876; d. Berkeley, Calif., May 28, 1947. [7; 10; 11]

Swift, Job, clergyman, b. Sandwich, Mass., 1743; d. Enosburgh, Vt., Oct. 20, 1804. [6; 62]

Swift, John Franklin, lawyer and diplomat, b. Bowling Green, Mo., 1829; d. Tokyo, Japan, March 10, 1891. [1; 3; 4; 5; 7; 35]

Swift, John Lindsay, soldier, b. 1828; d. 1895.

Swift, Judson, clergyman, d. New York, N.Y., Aug. 19, 1921.

Swift, Julia M., poet, fl. 1872-1877.

Swift, Lindsay, librarian, b. Boston, Mass., 1856; d. Cambridge, Mass., Sept. 11, 1921. [10; 11; 51]

Swift, Lucius Burrie, lawyer, b. Orleans county, N.Y., 1844; d. Indianapolis, Ind., July 3, 1929. [1]

Swift, Polemus Hamilton, clergyman, b. Palmyra, Wis., 1855; d. Oak Park, Ill., April 14, 1935. [10; 11]

Swift, Samuel, jurist, b. Amenia, N.Y., 1782; d. Middlebury, Vt., July 7, 1875. [3; 6; 43]

Swift, Walter Babcock, physician, b. Geneva, Switzerland, 1868; d. Boston, Mass., May 3, 1942.

Swift, Zephaniah, jurist, b. Wareham, Mass., 1759; d. Warren, O., Sept. 27, 1823. [1; 3; 4; 5; 6]

Swigert, Jacob, lawyer, b. 1793; d. 1869.

Swinburne, Louis Judson, littérateur, b. Albany, N.Y., 1855; d. Colorado Springs, Colo., Dec. 9, 1887. [3; 62]

Swineford, Alfred P., journalist and politician, b. Ashland, O., 1836; d. Alaska, 1909. [4]

Swing, Albert Temple, clergyman, b. Bethel, O., 1849; d. Chicago, Ill., Sept. 21, 1925. [10; 62]

Swing, David, clergyman, b. Cincinnati, O., 1830; d. Chicago, Ill., Oct. 3, 1894. [1; 3; 4; 5; 6]

Swingle, Calvin Franklin, locomotive engineer, b. 1846; d. Chicago, Ill., July 4, 1930.

Swinton, John, journalist and social reformer, b. Salton, Scotland, 1829; d. Brooklyn, N.Y., Dec. 15, 1901. [1; 3; 4; 5; 7; 10]

Swinton, William, journalist, b. Salton, Scotland, 1833; d. Brooklyn, N.Y., Oct. 25, 1892. [1; 3; 4; 5; 6; 7]

Swisher, Mrs. Bella French, poet and novelist, b. 1837; d. 1894.

Swisher, Charles Clinton, educationist, b. Muncy, Pa., 1846; d. Tacoma Park, Md., Feb. 4, 1940. [10]

Swisshelm, Mrs. Jane Grey, née Cannon, reformer, b. near Pittsburgh, Pa., 1815; d. Swissvale, Pa., July 22, 1884. [1; 3; 4; 6; 7; 70]'

Switzer, Maurice, advertising manager, b. New Orleans, La., 1870; d. April 6, 1929. [10]

Switzler, William Franklin, journalist, politician, and historian, b. Fayette county, Ky., 1819; d. Columbia, Mo., May 24, 1906. [1; 7; 9; 34]

Swope, Gilbert Ernest, genealogist, b. 1860; d. 1899.

Sydenstricker, Edgar, statistician, b. Shanghai, China, 1881; d. New York, N.Y., March 19, 1936. [10; 11]

Sykes, Frederick Henry, educationist, b. Queensville, Ont., 1863; d. Cambridge, Mass., Oct. 14, 1917. [27]

Sykes, Godfrey, scientist, b. London, England, 1861; d. Tucson, Ariz., Dec. 22, 1948. [13]

Syle, Louis Du Pont, educationist, b. Shanghai, China, 1857; d. Oakland, Calif., Nov. 14, 1903. [10; 62]

Sylvester, Frederick Oakes, painter and poet, b. Brockton, Mass., 1869; d. St. Louis, Mo., March 2, 1915. [1; 7; 10]

Sylvester, Herbert Milton, lawyer and historian, b. Lowell, Mass., 1849; d. Brooklyn, N.Y., about April 19, 1923. [7; 10]

Sylvester, Nathaniel Bartlett, historian, b. Denmark, N.Y., 1825; d. Argyle, N.Y., July 13, 1894. [3; 6]

Symmes, Francis Edward. See Clark, Francis Edward.

Symmes, Frank Rosebrook, clergyman, b. Madison, Ind., Oct. 24, 1856; d. Freehold, N.J., March 22, 1928.

Symmes, Harold, poet, b. San Francisco, Calif., 1877; d. Feb. 7, 1910. [35]

Symmes, John Cleves, soldier, b. New Jersey, 1780; d. Hamilton, O., May 28, 1829. [3; 4; 6]

Symonds, Brandreth, physician, b. 1863; d. New York, N.Y., Aug. 10, 1924.

Symonds, Henry Clay, soldier and writer of text-books, d. 1900. [6]

Sypher, Josiah Rhinehart, lawyer, b. Liverpool, Pa., 1832; d. ? [3; 6; 10]

Szinnyey, Stephen Ivor, journalist, b. Hungary, 1863; d. New York, N.Y., March 16, 1919. [10]

Szold, Benjamin, rabbi, b. Hungary, 1829; d. Baltimore, Md., July 31, 1902. [1; 4]

T

Taaffe, Thomas Gaffney, educationist, b. 1869; d. Yonkers, N.Y., April 29, 1936. [21]

Tabb, John Bannister, priest and poet, b. Amelia county, Va., 1845; d. Baltimore, Md., Nov. 19, 1909. [1; 4; 5; 7; 9; 10; 34]

Taber, Charles Austin Mendell, scientist, b. 1824; d. 1911.

Taber, Clarence Wilbur, editor and miscellaneous writer, b. Jersey City, N.J., 1870; d. ? [11]

Taber, Henry Morehouse, freethinker, b. 1825; d. 1897.

Taber, Mrs. Mary Jane, née Howland, miscellaneous writer, b. Aurora, N.Y., 1834; d. New Bedford, Mass., Jan. 10, 1923. [10]

Tabor, Edward A., clergyman, b. 1857; d. ?

Taché, Alexandre Antonin, archbishop, b. Rivière-du-Loup, Lower Canada, 1823; d. Winnipeg, Man., June 22, 1894. [27]

Taché, Sir Etienne Paschal, politician, b. St. Thomas, Lower Canada, 1795; d. St. Thomas, Que., July 30, 1865. [27]

Taché, Joseph Charles, journalist, b. Kamouraska, Lower Canada, 1820; d. Ottawa, Ont., April 16, 1894. [27]

Taché, Louis Hyppolite, lawyer b. St. Hyacinthe, Que., 1859; d. Montreal, Que., May 22, 1927. [27]

Tadd, James Liberty, educationist, b. England, 1854; d. Philadelphia, Pa., June 9, 1917. [10]

Taft, Mrs. Helen, née Herron, writer of reminiscences, b. 1861; d. May 22, 1943. [4; 12]

Taft, Horace Dutton, educationist, b. Cincinnati, O., 1861; d. Watertown, Conn., Jan. 28, 1943. [10; 12]

Taft, Henry Waters, lawyer, b. Cincinnati, O., 1859; d. New York, N.Y., Aug. 12, 1945. [10; 62]

Taft, Jonathan, educationist, b. Russellville, O., 1820; d. Ann Arbor, Mich., Oct. 16, 1903. [6; 39]

Taft, Lorado, sculptor, b. Elmwood, Ill., 1860; d. Chicago, Ill., Oct. 30, 1936. [4; 10; 11]

Taft, Marcus Lorenzo, missionary, b. Brooklyn, N.Y., 1850; d. Pasadena, Calif., Oct. 18, 1936. [60]

Taft, Oren Byron, financier, b. Medina, N.Y., 1846; d. Chicago, Ill., Oct. 23, 1924. [4]

Taft, William Howard, twenty-seventh president of the United States, b. Cincinnati, Ohio, 1857; d. Washington, D.C., March 8, 1930. [1; 4; 5; 7; 10; 62]

Taggard, Geneviève, poet, b. Waitsburg, Wash., 1895; d. New York, N.Y., Nov. 8, 1948.

Taggart, Cynthia, poet, b. 1801; d. near Newport, R.I., 1849. [6]

Taggart, Marion Ames, writer of books for girls, b. Haverhill, Mass., 1861; d. Harrisburg, Pa., Jan. 19, 1945. [5; 10; 22]

Tailfer, Patrick, physician, fl. 1740-1741. [3; 9; 34]

Taintor, Charles Newhall, writer of guidebooks, b. 1840; d. 1920.

Tait, James, clergyman, b. Scotland, 1829; Montreal, Que., Dec. 22, 1899. [27; 31]

Tait, James Selwin, miscellaneous writer, b. 1846; d. 1917.

Tait, John Robinson, artist and poet, b. Cincinnati, O., 1834; d. Baltimore, Md., July 29, 1909. [3; 4; 5]

Talbot, Arthur Newell, engineer, b. Cortland, Ill., 1857; d. Chicago, Ill., April 2, 1942. [10]

Talbot, Charles Remington, clergyman and novelist, b. 1849; d. Wrentham, Mass., Aug. 15, 1892. [7; 47]

Talbot, Edward Allen, journalist, b. Tipperary county, Ireland, 1801; d. Lockport, N.Y., Jan. 9, 1839. [27]

Talbot, Ethelbert, bishop, b. Fayette, Mo., 1848; d. Tuckahoe, N.Y., Feb. 27, 1928. [1; 4; 5; 10]

Talbot, Eugene Solomon, dentist, b. Sharon, Mass., 1847; d. Chicago, Ill., Dec. 20, 1924. [4; 10]

Talbot, George Foster, lawyer, b. East Machias, Me., 1819; d. Aug. 17, 1907.

Talbot, Henry Paul, chemist, b. Boston, Mass., 1864; d. Boston, Mass., June 18, 1927. [1; 10]

Talbot, Thomas Hammond, publicist, b. 1823; d. 1907.

Talbott, Everett Guy, clergyman and social service worker, b. Tuscola, Ill., 1883; d. San Francisco, Calif., Feb. 5, 1945. [10]

Talcott, Alvan, physician, b. North Bolton, Conn., 1804; d. Guilford, Conn., Jan. 17, 1891. [3b; 62]

Talcott, Daniel Smith, clergyman, b. Newburyport, Mass., 1813; d. Bangor, Me., Jan. 19, 1896. [3b]

Talcott, Mrs. Hannah Elizabeth, née Bradbury. See Goodwin-Talcott, Mrs. Hannah Elizabeth, née Bradbury.

Talcott, Sebastian Visscher, genealogist, b. New York, N.Y., 1812; d. ?

Taliaferro, Harden E., humorist, b. about 1818; d. 1875. [7]

Tall, Lida Lee, educationist, b. Dorchester county, Md.; d. Baltimore, Md., Feb. 21, 1942. [10]

Talley, Susan Archer. See Weiss, Mrs. Susan Archer, née Talley.

Talling, Marshall P., clergyman, b. Bowmanville, Ont., 1857; d. Toronto, Ont., Dec. 13, 1921. [27; 31a]

Tallmadge, Benjamin, soldier, b. Brookhaven, N.Y., 1754; d. Litchfield, Conn., March 7, 1835. [3; 4; 6]

Tallmadge, Thomas Eddy, architect, b. Washington, D.C., 1876; d. in train wreck near Arcola, Ill., Jan. 1, 1940. [10; 11]

Tallman, George Douglas, humorist, fl. 1877-1895.

Talmage, Frank De Witt, clergyman, d. Philadelphia, Pa., Feb. 9, 1912.

Talmage, James Edward, Mormon leader, b. Hungerford, Berkshire, England, 1862; d. Salt Lake City, Utah, July 27, 1933. [1; 10]

Talmage, John Van Nest, missionary, b. Somerville, N.J., 1819; d. Boundbrook, N.J., Aug. 19, 1892. [1; 3; 6]

Talmage, Thomas DeWitt, clergyman b. Boundbrook, N.J., 1832; d. Boundbrook, N.J., April 12, 1902. [1; 2a; 3; 4; 5; 6; 7; 9; 10]

Talman, Charles Fitzhugh, meteorologist, b. Detroit, Mich., 1874; d. Washington, D.C,. July 24, 1936. [10; 13]

Talmey, Bernard Simon, physician, b. 1862; d. New York, N.Y., June 30, 1926.

Talvi (pseud.). See Robinson, Mrs. Therese Albertine Louise, née von Jakob.

Taneyhill, Richard Henry, local historian, b. 1822; d. 1898.

Tanguay, Cyprien, priest and genealogist, b. Quebec, Lower Canada, 1819; d. Ottawa, Ont., April 28, 1902. [27]

Tannehill, Wilkins, journalist, b. Pittsburgh, Pa., 1787; d. Nashville, Tenn., June 2, 1858. [3; 6; 34]

Tannenbaum, Samuel Aaron, psychoanalyst and bibliographer, b. Hungary, 1874; d. New York, N.Y., Oct. 31, 1948. [10]

Tanner, Benjamin Tucker, negro bishop, b. Pittsburgh, Pa., 1835; d. Philadelphia, Pa., Jan. 15, 1923. [3; 4; 6; 10]

Tanner, Edwin Platt, educationist, b. Paterson, N.J., 1874; d. Syracuse, N.Y., July, 1936. [10; 11]

Tanner, Elias Fitch, clergyman, b. 1833; d. 1894.

Tanner, George Clinton, clergyman, b. West Greenwich, R.I., 1834; d. Faribault, Minn., Feb. 12, 1923. [10; 11; 70]

Tanner, Henry Schenk, geographer, b. New York, N.Y., 1786; d. New York, N.Y., 1858. [1; 3; 6; 7]

Tanner, John Henry, educationist, b. Fort Plain, Montgomery county, N.Y., 1861; d. Ithaca, N.Y., March 11, 1940. [10; 11]

Tappan, David, clergyman, b. Manchester, Mass., 1752; d. Cambridge, Mass., April 27, 1803. [3; 5; 6]

Tappan, Eli Todd, educationist, b. Steubenville, O., 1824; d. Columbus, O., Oct. 23, 1888. [1; 3; 5; 6]

Tappan, Eva March, writer of books for children, b. Blackstone, Mass., 1854; d. Worcester, Mass., Jan. 30, 1930. [4; 7; 10; 11; 15] .

Tappan, Henry Philip, clergyman and educationist, b. Rhinebeck, N.Y., 1805; d. Vevey, Switzerland, Nov. 15, 1881. [1; 3; 5; 6; 9; 39]

Tappan, Lewis, merchant, b. Northampton, Mass., 1788; d. Brooklyn, N.Y., June 21, 1873. [1; 3; 4; 5; 6; 7]

Tappan, William Bingham, poet, b. Beverly, Mass., 1794; d. West Needham, Mass., June 18, 1849. [3; 4; 6; 7; 71]

Tarbell, Arthur Wilson, educationist, b. Boston, Mass., 1872; d. Hyannis, Mass., Nov. 25, 1946.

Tarbell, Frank Bigelow, educationist, b. West Groton, Mass., 1853; d. New Haven, Conn., Dec. 4, 1920. [1; 9; 10; 62]

Tarbell, Horace Sumner, educationist, b. Chelsea, Vt., 1838; d. 1904. [10]

Tarbell, Ida Minerva, biographer and social worker, b. Erie county, Pa., 1857; d. Bridgeport, Conn., Jan. 6, 1943. [4; 7; 10; 11]

Tarbell, John Adams, physician, b. Boston, Mass., 1810; d. Boston, Mass., Jan. 21, 1864. [3; 6]

Tarbox, Increase Niles, clergyman, b. East Windsor, Conn., 1815; d. West Newton, Mass., May 3, 1888. [1; 3; 6; 7; 62]

Tardivel, Jules Paul, journalist, b. Covington, Ky., 1851; d. Quebec, Que., April 24, 1905. [27]

Tardy, Mrs. Mary T., literary historian, fl. 1870-1872. [34]

Tardy, William Thomas, clergyman, b. 1874; d. 1919.

Tarkington, Booth, novelist, b. Indianapolis, Ind., 1869; d. Indianapolis, Ind., May 19, 1946. [4; 7; 10; 11; 12]

Tarkington, John Stevenson, lawyer, b. Centreville, Ind., 1832; d. Indianapolis, Ind., Jan. 30, 1923. [10]

Tarleton, Fiswoode, novelist, b. 1890; d. near Bryson City, N.C., April 2, 1931. [7]

Tarr, Frederick Courtney, educationist, b. Baltimore, Md., 1896; d. Princeton, N.J., Aug. 31, 1939. [10]

Tarr, Ralph Stockman, educationist, b. Gloucester, Mass., 1864; d. Ithaca, N.Y., March 21, 1912. [4; 10]

Tarr, William Arthur, geologist, b. New Cambria, Mo., 1881; d. Columbia, Mo., July 28, 1939. [10]

Tarte, Joseph Israel, journalist and politician, b. Lanoraie, Que., 1848; d. Montreal, Que., Dec. 18, 1907. [27]

Taschereau, Elzéar Alexandre, cardinal archbishop, b. Ste. Marie de la Beauce, Lower Canada, 1820; d. Quebec, Que., April 12, 1898. [27]

Tasistro, Louis Fitzgerald, journalist and lecturer, b. Ireland, about 1808; d. about 1868. [3]

Tassé, Joseph, politician and historian, b. Montreal, Que., 1848; d. Montreal, Que., Jan. 18, 1895. [27]

Tassin, Algernon de Vivier, educationist, b. Fort Halleck, Nev., 1869; d. Montclair, N.J., Nov. 3, 1941. [7; 10; 11; 51]

Tate, Alfred O., private secretary, b. Peterborough, Ont., 1863; d. Brooklyn, N.Y. April 6, 1945.

Tate, Benjamin, lawyer, fl. 1845-1860. [6]

Tate, Joseph, lawyer, fl. 1823-1841.

Tate, William Knox, educationist, b. near Tate Springs, Tenn., 1870; d. Nashville, Tenn., Feb. 7, 1917. [10]

Tatlock, John Strong Perry, educationist, b. Stamford, Conn., 1876; d. Northampton, Mass., June 24, 1948. [7; 10; 11]

Tatman, Charles Taylor, numismatist, b. Worcester, Mass., 1871; d. Worcester, Mass., Dec. 23, 1945.

Tatsch, Jacob Hugo, freemason, b. Milwaukee, Wis., 1888; d. London, England, July 18, 1939. [10; 11]

Tatum, Richard Parry, genealogist, b. 1859; d. 1925.

Taussig, Charles William, industrialist, b. New York, N.Y., 1896; d. Bay Shore, Long Island, N.Y., May 10, 1948. [7; 10]

Taussig, Frank William, economist, b. St. Louis, Mo., 1859; d. Cambridge, Mass., Nov. 11, 1940. [4; 7; 10; 11]

Taussig, Frederick Joseph, physician, b. Brooklyn, N.Y., 1872; d. Bar Harbor, Me., Aug. 21, 1943. [10; 51]

Taverner, Percy Algernon, ornithologist, b. Guelph, Ont., 1875; d. Ottawa, Ont., May 10, 1947. [30]

Tawney, Guy Allan, educationist, b. Tippecanoe City, O., 1870; d. Urbana, Ill., Jan. 6, 1947. [10]

Taylor, Albert Reynolds, educationist, b. Magnolia, Ill., 1846; d. Decatur, Ill., Aug. 12, 1929 [4; 10]

Taylor, Archibald McAlpine, lawyer, fl. 1881-1890.

Taylor, Asher, soldier, b. 1880; d. 1878.

Taylor, Barnard Cook, clergyman, b. Holmdel, N.J., 1850; d. Red Bank, N.J., Sept. 24, 1937. [10; 11]

Taylor, Bayard, poet, novelist, and traveller, b. Chester county, Pa., 1825; d. Berlin, Germany, Dec. 19, 1878. [1; 2; 3; 4; 5; 6; 7; 9; 71]

Taylor, Benjamin Cook, clergyman, b. Philadelphia, Pa., 1801; d. Bergen, N.J., Feb. 2, 1881. [3; 6]

Taylor, Benjamin Franklin, poet and journalist, b. Lowville, N.Y., 1819; d. Cleveland, Ohio, Feb. 24, 1887. [1; 3; 4; 5; 6; 7; 9; 39]

Taylor, Bert Leston, journalist, b. Goshen, Mass., 1866; d. Chicago, Ill., March 19, 1921. [1; 7; 10]

Taylor, Bushrod Shedden, clergyman, b. Poultney, Vt., 1849; d. Marcy, N.Y., Oct. 8, 1935.

Taylor, C. B., historian, fl. 1828-1880. [6]

Taylor, Charles, missionary, b. Boston, Mass., 1819; d. ? [3]

Taylor, Charles Alonzo, playwright, b. 1863; d. Glendale, Calif., March 20, 1942.

Taylor, Charles Elisha, educationist, b. Richmond, Va., 1842; d. Wake Forest, N.C., Nov. 5, 1916. [10; 34]

Taylor, Charles Fayette, surgeon, b. Williston, Vt., 1827; d. Los Angeles, Calif., Jan. 25, 1899. [1; 3; 4; 6; 10; 43]

Taylor, Charles Fremont, editor, b. Attica, Ind., 1856; d. Philadelphia Pa., Nov. 4, 1919. [10]

Taylor, Charles James, local historian, b. 1824; d. 1904.

Taylor, Charles Jay, illustrator, b. New York, N.Y., 1855; d. Pittsburgh, Pa., Jan. 18, 1929. [7; 10]

Taylor, Charles Maus, traveller and photographer, b. 1849; d. ?

Taylor, Charles Vincent, biologist, b. Whitesville, Mo., 1895; d. Palo Alto, Calif., Feb. 22, 1946. [10; 13]

Taylor, Conyngham Crawford, merchant, b. county Leitrim, Ireland, 1823; d. Toronto, Ont., about 1898. [27; 31]

Taylor, David Henry, clergyman, b. French Lake, N.B., 1847; d. Newtonville, Mass., Dec. 10, 1890. [67]

Taylor, David Watson, naval officer, b. Louisa county, Va., 1864; d. Washington, D.C., July 29, 1940. [4; 10; 11]

Taylor, David Wooster, biographer, b. San Francisco, Calif., 1884; d. San Francisco, Calif., Nov. 25, 1937. [35]

Taylor, Edward, educationist, fl. 1878-1897.

Taylor, Edward Robeson, lawyer and poet, b. Springfield, Ill., 1838; d. San Francisco, Calif., July 5, 1923. [5; 10; 35]

Taylor, Mrs. Elkanah, née East, poet, b. 1888; d. Norfolk, Va., Aug. 7, 1945. [10]

Taylor, Emerson Gifford, educationist and littérateur, b. Pittsfield, Mass., 1874; d. Hartford, Conn., June 25, 1932. [7; 62]

Taylor, Ernest Manly, clergyman, b. Potton, Que., 1848; d. Knowlton, Que. March 27, 1941. [27; 31a]

Taylor, Fennings. See Taylor, John Fennings.

Taylor, Fitch Waterman, naval chaplain, b. Middle Haddam, Conn., 1803; d. Brooklyn, N.Y., July 23, 1865. [3; 6; 7]

Taylor, Francis Richards, biographer, b. Philadelphia, Pa., 1884; d. Philadelphia, Pa., March 12, 1947.

Taylor, Frank Hamilton, historian and writer of guide-books, b. 1846; d. Philadelphia, Pa., May 24, 1927.

Taylor, Frederick Manville, educationist, b. Northville, Mich., 1855; d. South Pasadena, Calif., Aug. 6, 1932. [1; 10]

Taylor, Frederick Winslow, efficiency engineer, b. Germantown, Pa., 1856; d. Philadelphia, Pa., March 21, 1915. [1; 4; 10]

Taylor, George, lawyer and politician, b. Wheeling, W. Va., 1820; d. Washington, D.C., Jan. 18, 1894.

Taylor, George, poet, b. 1834; d. ?

Taylor, George Boardman, missionary, b. Richmond, Va., 1832; d. Rome, Italy, Sept. 28, 1907. [1; 3; 4; 10; 34]

Taylor, George Braxton, clergyman, b. Staunton, Va., 1860; d. Roanoke, Va., March 9, 1942. [10; 11]

Taylor, George Henry, physician, b. Williston, Vt., 1821; d. 1896. [3; 4; 6; 43]

Taylor, George Lansing, clergyman and poet, b. Skaneateles, N.Y., 1835; d. Brooklyn, N.Y., July 26, 1903. [3; 6]

Taylor, Mrs. Gertrude, nèe Bartlett, poet, b. Newhaven, N.Y., 1876; d. Montreal, Que., Sept. 27, 1942.

Taylor, Graham, sociologist, b. Schenectady, N.Y., 1851; d. Chicago, Ill., Sept. 26, 1938. [10]

Taylor, Hannis, lawyer and diplomat, b. New Bern, N.C., 1851; d. Washington, D.C., Dec. 26, 1922. [1; 4; 5; 10; 34]

Taylor, Henry, book-agent, b. probably England; d. Canada between 1860 and 1866. [27]

Taylor, Henry Ling, surgeon, b. New York, N.Y., 1857; d. Montclair, N.J., June 9, 1923. [10]

Taylor, Henry Osborn, historian, b. New York, N.Y., 1856; d. New York, N.Y., April 13, 1941. [7; 10; 51]

Taylor, Henry William, physician, b. 1841; d. 1901.

Taylor, Irwin, lawyer, b. Maysville, Mason county, Ky., 1845; d. ?

Taylor, James Barnett, clergyman, b. Barton-on-Humber, England, 1804; d. Richmond, Va., Dec. 22, 1871. [3; 6; 34]

Taylor, James Monroe, soldier and sportsman, b. Lexington, Ky., 1838; d. Rutherford, N.J., Sept. 1, 1910.

Taylor, James Monroe, clergyman and educationist, b. Brooklyn, N.Y., 1848; d. New York, N.Y., Dec. 19, 1916. [1; 2; 4; 5; 7; 10]

Taylor, James Morford, educationist, b. Holmdel, N.J., 1843; d. Greenwich, Conn., July 31, 1930. [10; 11]

Taylor, James Wickes, consular officer, b. Penn Yan, N.Y., 1819; d. Winnipeg, Man., April 28, 1893. [1; 3; 5; 6]

Taylor, Jeremiah, biographer, b. 1817; d. 1898.

Taylor, Jeremiah Humphre, religious writer, b. 1797; d. 1882.

Taylor, John, political writer and agriculturist, b. Virginia, 1753; d. Caroline county, Va., Aug. 21, 1824. [1; 2; 3; 5; 6; 7; 9; 34]

Taylor, John, itinerant preacher, b. Fauquier county, Va., 1752; d. Franklin county, Ky., 1833. [3; 4]

Taylor, John, Mormon leader, b. Milnthorpe, Westmoreland county, England, 1808; d. Kaysville, Utah, July 25, 1887. [1; 3; 4]

Taylor, John Fennings, civil servant, b. London, England, 1817; d. Old Point Comfort, Va., May 4, 1882. [27]

Taylor, John Jay, physician, b. 1853; d. South Ocean City, N.J., Aug. 1, 1912.

Taylor, John Lord, educationist, b. Warren, Conn., 1811; d. Andover, Mass., Sept. 23, 1884. [62]

Taylor, John Louis, jurist, b. London, England, 1769; d. Raleigh, N.C., Jan. 29, 1829. [1; 3; 4; 5; 6; 34]

Taylor, John Madison, physician, b. Lancaster county, Pa., 1855; d. Philadelphia, Pa., Oct. 3, 1931. [4; 11]

Taylor, John Metcalf, insurance executive, b. 1845; d. Hartford, Conn., Nov. 6, 1918. [10]

Taylor, John Neilson, lawyer, b. New Brunswick, N.J., 1805; d. New Brunswick, N.J., Feb. 6, 1878. [3; 6]

Taylor, John Orville, educationist, b. Charlton, N.Y., 1808; d. New Brunswick, N.J., Jan. 18, 1890. [3]

Taylor, Joseph Judson, clergyman, b. Henry county, Va., 1855; d. Lexington, Ky., 1930. [10; 34]

Taylor, Joseph Marion, educationist, b. 1854; d. ?

Taylor, Joseph Russell, educationist and poet, b. Circleville, O., 1868; d. Columbus, O., March 30, 1933. [10; 11]

Taylor, Joseph Schimmel, educationist, b. Passer, Pa., 1856; d. July 3, 1932. [10]

Taylor, Justus Hurd, biographer, b. 1834; d. ?

Taylor, Katharine Haviland, novelist, playwright, and poet, b. Mankato, Minn., 1888; d. St. Cloud, Fla., Nov. 28, 1941. [7; 10; 11]

Taylor, Landon, clergyman, b. 1813; d. 1885.

Taylor, Lewis Leroy, local historian, b. 1838; d. ?

Taylor, Mrs. Marie, née Hansen, miscellaneous writer, b. Gotha, Germany, 1829; d. Bavaria, Germany, July 9, 1925. [3; 6; 7; 10]

Taylor, Marshall W., showman, b. 1878; d. Philadelphia, Pa., May 30, 1937.

Taylor, Marshall William, negro clergyman, b. Lexington, Ky., 1846; d. Louisville, Ky., Sept. 11, 1887. [1; 3; 6; 34]

Taylor, Mrs. Mary Atwater, née Mason, poet, d. New York, N.Y., June 1, 1949. [58]

Taylor, Mary Imlay, novelist, b. Washington, D.C.; d. Miami, Fla., Aug. 28, 1938. [7; 10; 11]

Taylor, Nathaniel William, clergyman, b. New Milford, Conn., 1786; d. New Haven, Conn., March 10, 1858. [1; 3; 4; 6; 62]

Taylor, Oliver Alden, clergyman, b. Yarmouth, Mass., 1801; d. Manchester, Mass., Dec. 18, 1851. [3; 6]

Taylor, Richard, soldier, b. New Orleans, La., 1826; d. New York, N.Y., April 12, 1879. [1; 3; 4; 5; 6; 34; 62]

Taylor, Robert Longley, educationist, b. New Rochelle, N.Y., 1861; d. Williamstown, Mass., May 27, 1923. [10; 62]

Taylor, Robert Love, politician and lecturer, b. Happy Valley, Carter county, Tenn., 1850; d. Nashville, Tenn., March 31, 1912. [1; 4; 5; 7; 10; 34]

Taylor, Robert Tunstall, physician, b. Norfolk, Va., 1867; d. Baltimore, Md., Feb. 21, 1929. [1; 10]

Taylor, Robert William, physician, b. London, England, 1842; d. New York, N.Y., Jan. 5, 1908. [10]

Taylor, Samuel Harvey, educationist, b. Londonderry, N.H., 1807; d. Andover, Mass., Jan. 29, 1871. [1; 3; 4; 5; 6]

Taylor, Thomas, chemist, b. Perth, Scotland, 1820; d. Washington, D.C., 1910. [10]

Taylor, Thomas House, clergyman, b. Georgetown, S.C., 1799; d. West Park, N.Y., Sept. 9, 1867. [3; 6; 34]

Taylor, Thomas Ulvan, engineer, b. Parker county, Tex., 1858; d. Austin, Tex., May 28, 1941. [10]

Taylor, Sir Thomas Wardlaw, jurist, b. Auchtermuchty, Scotland, 1833; d. Hamilton, Ont., March 2, 1917. [27]

Taylor, Timothy Alden, clergyman, b. Hawley, Mass., 1809; d. Slatersville, R.I., March 2, 1858.

Taylor, Walter C., physician, fl. 1871-1872.

Taylor, Walter Herron, banker, b. Norfolk, Va., 1838; d. Norfolk, Va., March 1, 1916. [4; 10; 34]

Taylor, William, clergyman, b. parish of Dennie, Scotland, 1803; d. Montreal, Que., Sept. 4, 1876. [27]

Taylor, William, missionary bishop, b. Rockbridge county, Va., 1821; d. Palo Alto, Calif., May 18, 1902. [1; 3; 4; 5; 6; 7; 10; 34]

Taylor, William Alexander, journalist, b. Perry county, O., 1937; d. 1912. [10]

Taylor, William George Langworthy, educationist, b. New York, N.Y., 1859; d. San Diego, Calif., July 5, 1941. [10; 51]

Taylor, William Henry, physician and chemist, b. Richmond, Va., 1835; d. Richmond, Va., April 14, 1917. [4; 10]

Taylor, William James Romeyn, clergyman, b. Schodack, N.Y., 1823; d. 1891. [3]

Taylor, William Mackergo, clergyman, b. Kilmarnock, Scotland, 1829; d. New York, N.Y., Feb. 8, 1895. [1; 3; 4; 5; 6; 7]

Tazewell, Littleton Waller, lawyer and politician, b. Williamsburg, Va., 1774; d. Norfolk, Va., May 6, 1860. [1; 3; 4; 5; 6]

Teagar, Michael Moores, poet, b. 1833; d. ?

Teal, Angeline, novelist, fl. 1884-1897.

Teale, Oscar Schutte, draftsman, b. 1848; d. ?

Teall, Edward Nelson, journalist, b. Brooklyn, N.Y., 1880; d. Matawan, N.J., Feb. 17, 1947. [10]

Teall, Francis Horace, editor, b. Brooklyn, N.Y., 1850; d. ? [10]

Teasdale, Sara, poet, b. St. Louis, Mo., 1884; d. New York, N.Y., Jan. 29, 1933. [1; 7; 10; 11; 72]

Teasdale, Thomas Cox, clergyman, b. 1808; d. 1891. [34]

Teed, Cyrus Reed, religious leader, b. 1839; d. 1908.

Teele, Albert Kendall, clergyman, b. Somerville, Mass., 1823; d. Milton, Mass., March 11, 1901. [62]

Teele, Ray Palmer, economist, b. Fillmore county, Minn., 1868; d. Silver Springs, Md., Aug. 27, 1927. [4; 10; 11]

Tefft, Benjamin Franklin, clergyman, b. Floyd, N.Y., 1813; d. Brewer, Me., Sept. 16, 1885. [3; 4; 6]

Tefft, Lyman Beecher, clergyman, b. Exeter, R.I., 1833; d. Cranston, R.I., Nov. 29, 1926. [4; 10; 11]

Tefft, Thomas Alexander, architect, b. Richmond, R.I., 1826; d. Florence, Italy, Dec. 12, 1859. [3; 6]

Teller, Daniel Webster, clergyman, d. Fredonia, N.Y., March 23, 1894.

Teller, Thomas (pseud.). See Tuttle, George.

Tello, Manly, lawyer, b. Brooklyn, N.Y., 1842; d. 1905. [21]

Temple, Edward Lowe, miscellaneous writer, b. Fort Winnebago, Wis., 1844; d. Wellesley, Mass., Oct. 9, 1928. [4; 5; 10; 11]

Temple, Mrs. Jean, née Barnum, educatoinist and novelist, b. Sturgis, Mich., 1894; d. Far Rockaway, N.Y., Jan. 13, 1945.

Temple, Josiah Howard, clergyman, b. 1815; d. Framingham, Mass., April, 1893.

Temple, Oliver Perry, lawyer, b. Green county, Tenn., 1820; d. 1907. [1; 5; 10; 34]

Ten Broeke, James, educationist, b. Panton, Vt., 1859; d. Middlebury, Vt., Oct. 23, 1937. [62]

Ten Brook, Andrew, educationist, b. 1814; d. Detroit, Mich., Nov. 5, 1899. [39]

Tenella (pseud.). See Clarke, Mrs. Mary Bayard, née Devereux.

Tennent, Gilbert, clergyman, b. county Armagh, Ireland, 1703; d. Philadelphia, Pa., July 23, 1764. [1; 3; 4; 5; 6; 9]

Tennent, John, physician, b. England, about 1700; d. about 1760. [1; 9]

Tenner, Armin, advertising agent, fl. 1871-1894.

Tenney, Mrs. Abby Amy, née Gore, writer of books for children, b. 1836; d. ? [3]

Tenney, Edward Payson, clergyman and educationist, b. Concord, N.H., 1835; d. Lynn, Mass., July 24, 1916. [1; 4; 5; 7; 10]

Tenney, Henry Martyn, clergyman, b. Hanover, N.H., 1841; d. Webster Groves, Mo., Feb. 22, 1932. [10]

Tenney, Horace Addison, genealogist, b. 1820; d. Madison, Wis., March 13, 1906. [44]

Tenney, Jonathan, biographical writer, b. Corinth, Vt., 1817; d. Albany, N.Y., Feb. 24, 1888. [43; 49]

Tenney, Martha Jane, genealogist, b. 1832; d. ?

Tenney, Sanborn, naturalist, b. Stoddard, N.H., 1827; d. Buchanan, Mich., July 9, 1877. [3; 6]

Tenney, Mrs. Sarah M., née Brownson, novelist and biographer, b. Chelsea, Mass., 1839; d. Elizabeth, N.J., Oct. 30, 1876. [3; 6; 7]

Tenney, Mrs. Tabitha, née Gilman, novelist and compiler, b. Exeter, N.H., 1762; d. Exeter, N.H., May 2, 1837. [1; 3; 6; 7; 9]

Tenney, William Jewett, journalist and editor, b. Newport, R.I., 1811; d. Newark, N.J., Sept. 20, 1883. [1; 3; 5; 6]

Terhune, Albert Payson, journalist and novelist, b. Newark, N.J., 1872; d. Pompton Lakes, N.J., Feb. 18, 1942. [4; 7; 10; 11; 12]

Terhune, Mrs. Mary Virginia, née Hawes, novelist and writer on domestic science, b. Amelia county, Va., 1830; d. New York, N.Y., June 4, 1922. [1; 3; 4; 5; 6; 7; 9; 10; 34]

Terhune, William Lewis, publisher, b. Newark, N.J., 1850; d. Pasadena, Calif., Feb. 22, 1936. [10]

Terrill, Frederick William, lawyer, b. Stanstead Plain, Lower Canada, 1836; d. Bury, Que., March, 1902.

Terry, Adrian Russell, physician b. 1808; d. Chicago, Ill., Dec. 4, 1864. [62]

Terry, Benjamin Stites, historian, b. St. Paul, Minn., 1857; d. Chicago, Ill., Oct. 31, 1931. [4; 10; 11]

Terry, Earle Melvin, physicist, b. 1879; d. Madison, Wis., 1929. [13]

Terry, Edmund Roderick, lawyer, b. Brooklyn, N.Y., 1856; d. Brooklyn, N.Y., April 5, 1932. [62]

Terry, Ezekiel, printer, b. 1775; d. 1829.

Terry, Henry Taylor, lawyer and educationist, b. Hartford, Conn., 1847; d. New York, N.Y., Dec. 26, 1936. [10; 11; 62]

Terry, John Orville, poet, b. Orient, N.Y., 1796; d. Greenport, N.Y., April 7, 1869. [3; 4]

Terry, Marshall Orlando, physician, b. Watervliet Center, N.Y., 1848; d. Coronado, Calif., Oct. 11, 1933. [1; 4; 10]

Terry, Milton Spenser, theologian, b. Coeymans, N.Y., 1840; d. Los Angeles, Calif., July 13, 1914. [1; 3; 10]

Terry, Samuel Hough, merchant, fl. 1839-1917. [6]

Terry, Theodore Brainard, agriculturist, b. Lafayette, N.Y., 1843; d. Jan. 1, 1916. [10]

Teschemacher, James Englebert, merchant and naturalist, b. Nottingham, England, 1790; d. near Boston, Mass., Nov. 9, 1853. [3; 6]

Teskey, Adeline Margaret, novelist, b. Appleton, Ont.; d. Toronto, Ont., March 21, 1924. [27]

Tesla, Nikola, inventor, b. Jugoslavia, 1856; d. New York, N.Y., Jan. 8, 1943. [4; 10; 12]

Tessier, François Xavier, physician, b. Quebec, Lower Canada, 1800; d. Quebec, Lower Canada, Dec. 24, 1835. [27]

Test, Louis Agassiz, chemist, b. Dundee, Ill., 1874; d. Ann Arbor, Mich., April 22, 1943. [13]

Testut, Charles, journalist, poet, and physician, b. France, about 1818; d. New Orleans, La., July 1, 1892. [1; 7; 34]

Tetlow, John, educationist, b. Providence, R.I., 1843; d. Brookline, Mass., Dec. 9, 1911. [10]

Têtu, Charles, notary public, b. Montmagny, Lower Canada, 1796; d. Laprairie, Que., Dec. 12, 1864. [27]

Têtu, Henri, historian, b. Rivière Ouelle, Que., 1849; d. Quebec, Que., June 15, 1915. [27]

Têtu, Horace, journalist, b. Quebec, Que., 1842; d. Quebec, Que., March 31, 1915, [27]

Teuffel, Mrs. Blanche Willis von, nèe Howard. See Howard, Blanche Willis.

Tevis, Mrs. Julia Ann, née Hieronymous, school-teacher, b. near Winchester, Ky., 1799; d. Shelbyville, Ky., April 21, 1880. [74]

Thacher, Amos Bateman, authority on oriental rugs, b. Albany, N.Y., 1882; d. Garden City, N.Y., Jan. 13, 1946. [62]

Thacher, James, physician and historian, b. Barnstable, Mass., 1754; d. Plymouth, Mass., May 23, 1844. [1; 2; 3; 4; 5; 6; 7; 9]

Thacher, John Boyd, historian, b. Ballston Spa., N.Y., 1847; d. Albany, N.Y., Feb. 25, 1909. [1; 4; 7; 10]

Thacher, Samuel Cooper, clergyman, b. Boston, Mass., 1785; d. Moulins, France, Jan. 2, 1818. [1; 3; 4; 6]

Thacher, Thomas, clergyman, b. Salisbury, England, 1620; d. Boston, Mass., Oct. 15, 1678. [3; 4; 6]

Thalheimer, Mary Elsie, educationist, d. Cincinnati, O., 1917.

Thames, Travis Butler, clergyman, b. Monroe county, Ala., 1856; d. Newman, Ga., Feb. 26, 1914. [10]

Thanet, Octave (pseud.) See French, Alice.

Tharin, Robert Seymour Symmes, lawyer, b. near Charleston, S.C., 1830; d. ? [3; 6; 10; 34]

Thatcher, Benjamin Bussey, lawyer and littérateur, b. Warren, Me., 1809; d. Boston, Mass., July 14, 1840. [1; 3; 4; 6; 7]

Thatcher, Erastus, lawyer, b. about 1825; d. ? [45]

Thatcher, Marshall P., soldier, b. Orleans county, N.Y., 1840; d. ?

Thatcher, Oliver Joseph, historian, b. Wilmington, O., 1857; d. Aug. 19, 1937. [4; 10; 11; 68]

Thatcher, Roscoe Wilfred, educationist, b. Chatham Centre, O., 1872; d. Amherst, Mass., Dec. 6, 1933. [1; 10; 13]

Thaxter, Adam Wallace, journalist, b. Boston, Mass., 1832; d. Boston, Mass., June 8, 1864. [3]

Thaxter, Mrs. Celia, née Laighton, poet, b. Portsmouth, N.H., 1835; d. Isle of Shoals, N.H., Aug. 26, 1894. [1; 2; 3; 4; 5; 6; 7; 8; 9; 71]

Thayer, Alexander Wheelock, biographer, b. South Natick, Mass., 1817; d. Trieste, Austria-Hungary, July 15, 1897. [4; 51]

Thayer, Amos Madden, jurist, b. Mina, N.Y., 1841; d. St. Louis, Mo., 1905. [4; 10]

Thayer, Mrs. Caroline Matilda, née Warren, novelist and school teacher, b. New England, about 1787; d. Louisana, 1844. [6; 9]

Thayer, Claudius, poet, b. Tonawanda, N.Y., 1854; d. Berkeley, Calif., May 7, 1923. [35]

Thayer, Edward H., local historian, b. 1832; d. 1904. [37]

Thayer, Eli, educationist and politician, b. Mendon, Mass., 1819; d. Worcester, Mass., April 15, 1899. [1; 3; 4; 5; 6]

Thayer, Elihu, clergyman, b. Braintree, Mass., 1747; d. Kingston, N.H., April 3, 1812. [3; 6]

Thayer, Mrs. Emma, née Homan, painter, b. New York, N.Y., 1842; d. Denver, Colo., 1908. [10]

Thayer, Erastus William, clergyman, b. Barre, Mass., 1812; d. Springfield, Ill., May 3, 1902. [45]

Thayer, George Burton, lawyer, b. Rockville, Conn., 1853; d. Manchester, Conn., June 28, 1928. [62]

Thayer, Gerald Handerson, artist and naturalist, b. Cornwall-on-Hudson, N.Y., 1883; d. Keene, N.H., June 5, 1939.

Thayer, Henry Otis, clergyman, b. Paris, Me., 1832; d. Jackson Heights, N.Y., March 28, 1927. [46]

Thayer, James Bradley, lawyer and educationist, b. Haverhill, Mass., 1823; d. Cambridge, Mass., Feb. 14, 1902. [1; 2; 3; 4; 5; 6; 10; 51]

Thayer, John Adams, publisher, b. Boston, Mass., 1861; d. Westport, Conn., Feb. 21, 1936. [1; 7]

Thayer, Joseph Henry, clergyman, b. Boston, Mass., 1828; d. Cambridge, Mass., Nov. 26, 1901. [1; 3; 4; 5; 6; 7; 10]

Thayer, Stephen Henry, banker and poet, b. New Ipswich, N.H., 1839; d. Dec. 16, 1919. [4; 7; 10]

Thayer, Sylvanus, soldier, b. Braintree, Mass., 1785; d. South Braintree, Mass., Sept. 7, 1872. [1; 2; 3; 4; 5; 6]

Thayer, Thomas Baldwin, clergyman, b. Boston, Mass., 1812; d. Roxbury, Mass., Feb. 12, 1886. [1; 3; 6]

Thayer, Wildie, poet, b. 1872; d. 1912.

Thayer, William Makepeace, clergyman, b. Franklin, Mass., 1820; d. Franklin, Mass., April 7, 1898. [1; 2; 3; 5; 6; 7]

Thayer, William Roscoe, historian and biographer, b. Boston, Mass., 1859; d. Cambridge. Mass., Sept. 7, 1923. [1; 2; 4; 5; 7; 10; 51]

Thayer, William Sydney, physician, b. Milton, Mass., 1864; d. Washington, D.C., Dec. 10, 1932. [1; 10; 51]

Thébaud, Augustus J., priest, b. Nantes, France, 1807; d. Fordham, N.Y., Dec. 17, 1885. [1; 3; 4; 6; 7; 21]

Thein, John, priest, d. 1912. [21]

Theller, Edward Alexander, filibusterer, b. Lower Canada, about 1810; d. Honitas, Calif., 1859. [27]

Theobald, Samuel, ophthalmologist, b. Baltimore, Md., 1846; d. Baltimore, Md., Dec. 20, 1930. [1; 10]

Thibault, Benoit Clovis, priest, b. St. Benoit des Deux Montagnes, Que., 1854; d. ? [32]

Thibault, Charles, lawyer, b. St. Athanase, Que., 1840; d. Sutton, Que., Jan. 2, 1905. [27]

Thieblin, Nicholas Léon, journalist, b. St. Petersburg, Russia, 1834; d. New York, N.Y., Nov. 1, 1888. [3b]

Thieme, Hugo Paul, educationist, b. Fort Wayne, Ind., 1870; d. Ann Arbor, Mich., June 2, 1940. [7; 10; 11]

Thierry, Camille, poet, b. New Orleans, La., 1814; d. April, 1875. [7; 34]

Thilly, Frank, philosopher, b. Cincinnati, O., 1865; d. Ithaca, N.Y., Dec. 28, 1934. [1a; 7; 10; 11]

Thinker, Theodore (pseud.). See Woodworth, Francis Channing.

Thirkield, Wilbur Patterson, bishop, b. Franklin, O., 1854; d. Brooklyn, N.Y., Nov. 7, 1936. [10]

Thiusen, Ismar (pseud.). See Macnie, John.

Thoburn, James Mills, bishop. b. Clairsville, O., 1836; d. Meadville, Pa., Nov. 28, 1922. [1; 3; 4; 7; 10]

Thom, Adam, jurist, b. Scotland, 1802; d. London, England, Feb. 21, 1890. [27]

Thom, Alfred Pembroke, lawyer, b. Northampton county, Va., 1854; d. Washington, D.C., Feb. 15, 1935. [10]

Thom, Burton Peter, physician, b. Baltimore, Md., 1874; d. Long Island, N.Y., May 3, 1933. [10]

Thom, De Courcy Wright, industrialist, b. Baltimore, Md., 1858; d. Baltimore, Md., Aug. 6, 1932. [10; 11]

Thom, William Taylor, educationist, b. 1849; d. ? [34]

Thomas, Abel Charles, clergyman, b. Exeter, Pa., 1807; d. Philadelphia, Pa., Sept. 28, 1880. [3; 6; 7]

Thomas, Albert Ellsworth, novelist and playwright, b. Chester, Mass., 1872; d. Wakefield, R.I., June 18, 1947. [10]

Thomas, Alexander, educationist, b. 1775; d. 1809.

Thomas, Allen Clapp, educationist, b. Baltimore, Md., 1846; d. Haverford, Pa., Dec. 15, 1920. [4; 10; 34]

Thomas, Amos Russell, physician, b. Watertown, N.Y., 1826; d. Chicago, Ill., Oct. 31, 1895. [1; 3; 4]

Thomas, Arad, local historian, fl. 1853-1871.

Thomas, Augustus, playwright, b. St. Louis, Mo., 1857; d. Nyack, N.Y., Aug. 12, 1934. [1; 4; 5; 7; 10]

Thomas, Augustus Orloff, educationist, b. Mercer county, Ill., 1863; d. Augusta, Me., Jan. 30, 1935. [10]

Thomas, Benjamin Franklin, jurist, b. Boston, Mass., 1813; d. Salem, Mass., Sept. 27, 1878. [3; 4; 6]

Thomas, Calvin, educationist, b. Lapeer, Mich., 1854; d. New York, N.Y., Nov. 4, 1919. [1; 4; 5; 7; 10]

Thomas, Charles Swain, educationist, b. Pendleton, Ind., 1868; d. West Newton, Mass., June 26, 1943. [7; 10]

Thomas, Cyrus, ethnologist, b. Kingsport, Tenn., 1825; d. Washington, D.C., June 26, 1910. [1; 3; 4; 5; 6; 7; 10; 34]

Thomas, Cyrus, educationist and historian, b. Troy, N.Y., 1836; d. Richford, Vt., Feb. 14, 1908. [27]

Thomas, David, engineer, b. Montgomery county, Pa., 1776; d. Cayuga county, N.Y., 1859. [3]

Thomas, Ebenezer Smith, journalist, b. Lancaster, Mass., 1780; d. Cincinnati, O., Aug. 1844. [3; 4; 6; 7; 9; 34]

Thomas, Edith Matilda, poet, b. Chatham, O., 1854; d. New York, N.Y., Sept. 13, 1925. [1; 4; 5; 7; 9; 10]

Thomas, Edward Beers, jurist, b. Cortland, N.Y., 1848; d. Brooklyn, N.Y., March 27, 1929. [10; 62]

Thomas, Elmer Erwin, hunter, b. 1860; d. 1923.

Thomas, Ernest, clergyman, b. England, 1865; d. Toronto, Ont., Feb. 19, 1940. [27]

Thomas, Flavel Shurtleff, physician, b. Hanson, Mass., 1852; d. South Hanson, Mass., Nov. 26, 1922. [10]

Thomas, Frank Morehead, clergyman, b. Bowling Green, Ky., 1868; d. Nashville, May 9, 1921. [10]

Thomas, Frederick William, journalist, poet, and novelist, b. Charleston, S.C., 1806; d. Washington, D.C., Aug. 27, 1866. [1; 3; 6; 7; 9; 34; 71]

Thomas, Henry Franklin, physician, b. 1843; d. Allegan, Mich., April 17, 1912.

Thomas, Henry Walter, civil servant, b. 1842; d. ?

Thomas, Hiram Washington, clergyman, b. Hampshire county, Va., 1832; d. Chicago, Ill., 1909. [4; 6; 10]

Thomas, Hugh Evan, clergyman, b. 1830; d. 1889.

Thomas, Isaiah, printer, b. Boston, Mass., 1749; d. Worcester, Mass., April 4, 1831. [1; 2; 3; 4; 5; 6; 7; 8; 9]

Thomas, James Augustus, merchant, b. Lawsonville, N.C., 1862; d. White Plains, N.Y., Sept. 10, 1940. [7; 10]

Thomas, Mrs. Jane, née Hamilton, compiler, fl. 1867-1881. [6]

Thomas, Jesse Burgess, clergyman, b. Edwardsville, Ill., 1832; d. Brooklyn, N.Y., June 6, 1915. [1; 3; 4; 5; 6; 10]

Thomas, John, religious leader, b. London, England, 1805; d. Jersey City, N.J., March 5, 1871. [3; 6]

Thomas, John Allen Miner, novelist, b. New York, N.Y., 1900; d. New York, N.Y., March 12, 1932. [62]

Thomas, John Daniel, educationist, b. 1853; d. 1930.

Thomas, John Jacob, pomologist, b. Cayuga county, N.Y., 1810; d. Union Springs, Feb. 22, 1895. [1; 3; 6]

Thomas, John Jenks, neurologist, b. Columbus, O., 1861; d. Boston, Mass., July 17, 1935. [10; 11]

Thomas, John Lilburn, lawyer, b. 1833; d. ?

Thomas, John Peyre, soldier, b. 1833; d. Columbia, S.C., Feb. 11, 1912. [34]

Thomas, Joseph, poet, b. Virginia, 1791; d. 1835. [34]

Thomas, Joseph, physician, educationist, and lexicographer, b. Cayuga county, N.Y., 1811; d. Philadelphia, Pa., Dec. 25, 1891. [1; 3; 4; 6; 7]

Thomas, Lawrence Buckley, clergyman, b. 1848; d. 1914. [6]

Thomas, Lewis Foulk, poet, b. Baltimore county, Md., 1815; d. Washington, D.C., May 26, 1868. [3; 7; 9]

Thomas, Martha Carey, educationist, b. Baltimore, Md., 1857; d. Bryn Mawr, Pa., Dec. 2, 1935. [1a; 4; 7; 10]

Thomas, Martha McCannon, novelist, b. Baltimore, Md., 1823; d. about 1897. [3; 6; 34]

Thomas, Mary von Erden, novelist, b. Charleston, S.C., 1825; d. ? [3; 6; 34]

Thomas, Moses Bross, clergyman, b. Barryville, N.Y., 1845; d. 1925. [68]

Thomas, R., historian, fl. 1834-1848. [6]

Thomas, Reuen, clergyman, b. near Birmingham, England, 1840; d. Brookline, Mass., Nov. 9, 1907. [4; 10]

Thomas, Richard Henry, physician, b. Baltimore, Md., 1854; d. Baltimore, Md., 1904. [7; 10; 34]

Thomas, Rolla L., physician, b. Harrison, O., 1857; d. Cincinnati, O., Dec. 28, 1932. [10]

Thomas, Theodore, musician, b. Hanover, Germany, 1835; d. Chicago, Ill., Jan. 4, 1905. [1; 10; 20]

Thomas, Theodore Gaillard, physician, b. Edisto Island, S.C., 1831; d. Thomasville, Ga., Feb. 28, 1903. [1; 3; 4; 6; 10; 34]

Thomas, William, abolitionist, d. about 1836.

Thomas, William Henry Griffith, clergyman, b. Oswestry, England, 1861; d. Germantown, Pa., June 2, 1924. [10]

Thomas, William Isaac, sociologist, b. Virginia, 1863; d. Berkeley, Calif., Dec. 5, 1947. [10]

Thomas, William Lyman, local historian, b. St. Louis, Mo., 1846; d. Maplewood, Mo., July 19, 1918.

Thomas, William Sturgis, physician, b. Poughkeepsie, N.Y., 1871; d. New York, N.Y., Dec. 21, 1941.

Thomas, William Widgery, lawyer, politician, and diplomat, b. Portland, Me., 1839; d. Portland, Me., April 25, 1927. [1; 3; 4; 5; 10]

Thomason, Denny R, clergyman, fl. 1831-1867. [6]

Thomason, John William, soldier, b. Huntsville, Tex., 1893; d. San Diego, Calif., March 12, 1944. [7; 10]

Thomen, August Astor, physician, b. New York, N.Y., 1892; d. New York, N.Y., Sept. 12, 1943.

Thomes, William Henry, novelist, b. Portland, Me., 1824; d. Boston, Mass., March 6, 1895. [1; 3; 6; 7; 9]

Thompson, Abram Warren, lawyer, b. 1830; d. ?

Thompson, Adele Eugenia, novelist, b. Mansfield, O., 1849; d. Middlefield, O., April 4, 1929. [7; 10; 11]

Thompson, Alton Howard, dentist, b. 1849; d. 1914.

Thompson, Augustus Charles, clergyman, b. Goshen, Conn., 1812; d. Boston, Mass., 1901. [2; 3; 6; 7; 10]

Thompson, Basil, poet, b. New Orleans, La., 1892; d. New Orleans, La., April 6, 1924. [10]

Thompson, Benjamin Franklin, lawyer and local historian, b. 1784; d. 1849.

Thompson, Bradley Martin, lawyer, b. Milford, Mich., 1835; d. Ann Arbor, Mich., Sept. 30, 1917. [39]

Thompson, Carl Dean, economist, b. Berlin, Mich., 1870; d. Lincoln, Neb., July 3, 1949. [10; 11]

Thompson, Charles Lemuel, clergyman, b. Allentown, Pa., 1839; d. Atlantic City, N.J., April 14, 1924. [3; 4; 10]

Thompson, Charles Miner, editor, b. Montpelier, Vt., 1864; d. Cambridge, Mass., Dec. 19, 1941. [7; 10; 51]

Thompson, Charles Willis, journalist, b. Kalamazoo, Mich., 1871; d. New York, N.Y., Sept. 8, 1946. [7; 10; 22]

Thompson, Mrs. Clara M., novelist, fl. 1860-1873. [6]

Thompson, Daniel Greenleaf, philosopher, b. Montpelier, Vt., 1850; d. New York, N.Y., July 10, 1897. [3b; 4; 43]

Thompson, Daniel Pierce, lawyer and novelist, b. Boston, Mass., 1793; d. Montpelier, Vt., June 6, 1868. [1; 3; 4; 5; 6; 7; 8; 9; 71]

Thompson, David, school-teacher and historian, b. Scotland, about 1796; d. Niagara, Ont., 1868. [27]

Thompson, David Decamp, journalist, b. Cincinnati, O., 1852; d. St. Louis, Mo., Nov. 10, 1908. [4; 10]

Thompson, Denman, actor and playwright, b. near Girard, Pa., 1833; d. West Swanzey, N.H., April 14, 1911. [1; 4; 7; 9; 10]

Thompson, Edward Herbert, archaeologist, b. Worcester county, Mass., 1860; d. Plainfield, N.J., May 11, 1935. [1a; 7; 10]

Thompson, Edwin Porter, historian, b. 1834; d. Louisville, Ky., March 3, 1903. [34]

Thompson, Mrs. Eliza Jane, née Trimble, temperance advocate, b. Hillsboro, O., 1816; d. Hillsboro, O., 1905. [10]

Thompson, Mrs. Elizabeth, née Rowell, philanthropist, b. Lyndon, Vt., 1821; d. Littleton, N.H., July 20, 1899. [3; 6]

Thompson, Francis McGee, local historian, b. 1833; d. 1916.

Thompson, Frank Charles, clergyman, b. 1858; d. Santa Monica, Calif., May 3, 1940.

Thompson, Frederick Diodati, traveller, b. New York, N.Y., 1850; d. New York, N.Y., Oct. 9, 1906. [4; 10]

Thompson, George, abolitionist and missionary, d. 1893.

Thompson, George B., clergyman, b. Aurora, Ind., 1862; d. Washington, D.C., June 21, 1930. [10; 11]

Thompson, George Fayette, writer on animal industry, b. 1860; d. 1906.

Thompson, George Western, jurist, b. St. Clairsville, O., 1806; d. near Wheeling, W. Va., Feb. 24, 1888. [3; 6; 34]

Thompson, Henry Adams, clergyman, b. Stormstown, Pa., 1837; d. Dayton, O., July 8, 1920. [10]

Thompson, Henry Dallas, mathematician, b. Metuchen, N.J., 1864; d. Santa Barbara, Calif., Aug. 31, 1927. [10]

Thompson, Henry Tazewell, soldier, b. Columbia, S.C., 1859; d. Columbia, S.C., Jan. 27, 1932. [11]

Thompson, Holland, historian, b. Randolph county, N.C., 1873; d. New York, N.Y., Oct. 21, 1940. [7; 10]

Thompson, Hugh Miller, bishop, b. Londonderry, Ireland, 1830; d. Jackson, Miss., Nov. 18, 1902. [1; 3; 4; 5; 6; 7; 9; 34]

Thompson, Isaac Grant, lawyer, b. 1840; d. 1879. [6]

Thompson, James Marshall, clergyman, b. Carlisle, Ind., 1845; d. Berkeley, Calif., Nov. 19, 1931. [68]

Thompson, James Maurice, poet and novelist, b. Fairfield, Md., 1844; d. Crawfordsville, Ind., Feb. 15, 1901. [1; 5; 9; 10; 34; 71; 72]

Thompson, James Westfall, historian, b. Pella, Ia., 1869; d. Berkeley, Calif., Sept. 30, 1941. [7; 10]

Thompson, Mrs. Jeannette May, writer of books for children, b. Guilford, Conn., 1865; d. Yonkers, N.Y., March 4, 1944. [7]

Thompson, John. See Thomson, John [1776-1799].

Thompson, John, publisher and banker, b. Berkshire county, Mass., 1802; d. New York, N.Y., April 19, 1891. [1; 3; 4; 6]

Thompson, John, escaped slave, b. Maryland, 1812; d. ?

Thompson, John, clergyman, b. Norham, England, 1834; d. Sarnia, Ont., May 12, 1903. [27]

Thompson, John Gilbert, educationist, b. 1862; d. Fitchburg, Mass., Oct. 31, 1940. [10]

Thompson, John Reuben, editor and poet, b. Richmond, Va., 1823; d. New York, N.Y., April 30, 1873. [1; 3; 4; 5; 6; 7; 9; 34]

Thompson, John Samuel, clergyman, b. Ireland, 1787; d. ? [6]

Thompson, John Wallace, horse-breeder, b. Canton, Me., 1844; d. ? [38]

Thompson, Joseph Frank, clergyman, b. 1850; d. ?

Thompson, Joseph Parrish, clergyman, b. Philadelphia, Pa., 1819; d. Berlin, Germany, Sept. 20, 1879. [1; 3; 4; 5; 6; 7; 62]

Thompson, Julia Carrie, novelist, fl. 1870-1872. [6]

Thompson, Langdon Shook, educationist, b. 1838; d. ?

Thompson, Leander, clergyman, b. Woburn, Mass., 1812; d. Woburn, Mass., Oct. 18, 1896. [45]

Thompson, Lewis Olson, clergyman, b. Bergen, Norway, 1839; d. Henry, Ill., July 16, 1887. [3; 5; 6]

Thompson, Marcellus M., lawyer, b. 1859; d. 1902.

Thompson, Mary Pickering, local historian, b. Durham, N.H., 1825; d. Durham, N.H., June 6, 1894.

Thompson, Matthew La Rue Perrine, clergyman, b. Fulton county, N.Y., 1809; d. ? [6]

Thompson, Maurice. See Thompson, James Maurice.

Thompson, Mortimer Neal. See Thomson, Mortimer Neal.

Thompson, Oscar, music critic, b. Crawfordsville, Ind., 1887; d. New York, N.Y., July 3, 1945. [10; 12; 20]

Thompson, Rezin, physician, fl. 1860-1870.

Thompson, Richard Wigginton, lawyer and politician, b. Culpeper county, Va., 1809; d. Indianapolis, Ind., Feb. 9, 1900. [1; 3; 4; 5; 6; 7; 10; 34]

Thompson, Robert Ellis, educationist, b. near Lurgan, Ireland, 1844; d. Philadelphia, Pa., Oct. 19, 1924. [1; 3; 4; 5; 6; 7; 9; 10]

Thompson, Robert John, consular agent, b. La Porte City, Ia., 1865; d. Montreux, Switzerland, Aug. 24, 1931. [10; 11]

Thompson, Robert Thomas, educationist, b. Davidson, N.C., 1896; d. New Brunswick, N.J., April 1, 1945.

Thompson, Samuel, journalist, b. London, England, 1810; d. Toronto, Ont., July 8, 1886. [27]

Thompson, Seymour Dwight, jurist, b. Will county, Ill., 1842; d. East Orange, N.J., Aug. 11, 1904. [1; 4; 10]

Thompson, Slason, journalist, b. Fredericton, N.B., 1849; d. Lake Forest, Ill., Dec. 22, 1935. [1a; 7; 10; 11]

Thompson, Thomas Payne, insurance underwriter, b. Montgomery, Ala., 1860; d. New Orleans, La., Nov. 5, 1924. [10]

Thompson, Thomas Phillips, journalist, b. Newcastle-on-Tyne, England, 1843; d. Oakville, Ont., May 22, 1933. [27]

Thompson, Vance, playwright, novelist, and miscellaneous writer, b. 1863; d. Nice, France, June 5, 1925. [4; 7; 10]

Thompson, Waddy, lawyer and diplomat, b. Pickensville, S.C., 1798; d. Tallahasssee, Fla., Nov. 23, 1868. [1; 3; 4; 5; 6; 7; 34]

Thompson, Waddy, historian, b. Columbia, S.C., 1867; d. Atlanta, Ga., March 19, 1939. [7; 10]

Thompson, Wallace, editor, b. Topeka, Kans., 1883; d. New York, N.Y., Jan. 7, 1936. [10]

Thompson, Will Henry, lawyer and poet, b. Calhoun, Ga., 1848; d. 1918. [4; 7; 34]

Thompson, William Gilman, physician, b. New York, N.Y., 1856; d. New York, N.Y., Oct. 27, 1927. [1; 10; 11; 62]

Thompson, William Tappan, humorist, b. Ravenna, O., 1812; d. Savannah, Ga., March 24, 1882. [1; 3; 4; 5; 7; 9; 34]

Thompson, Zadock, educationist, b. Bridgewater, Vt., 1796; d. Burlington, Vt., Jan. 19, 1856. [1; 3; 4; 6; 9]

Thoms, Craig Sharpe, clergyman, b. Elgin, Ill., 1860; d. Vermilion, S.D., Sept. 27, 1945. [10; 11]

Thomson, Alexander McDonald, journalist and historian, b. 1822; d. 1898. [44]

Thomson, Charles, secretary of the Continental Congress, b. county Derry, Ireland, 1729; d. near Philadelphia, Pa., Aug. 16, 1824. [1; 2; 3; 4; 5; 6; 9]

Thomson, Charles Goff, novelist, b. Little Falls, N.Y., 1883; d. San Francisco, Calif., March 23, 1937. [10; 11; 35]

Thomson, Charles West, poet, b. Philadelphia, Pa., 1798; d. York, Pa., April 17, 1879. [3; 6; 7; 71]

Thomson, Edward, bishop, b. Portsmouth, England, 1810; d. Wheeling, W.Va., March 21, 1870. [1; 3; 6]

Thomson, Edward William, journalist, b. Toronto township, Peel county, Ont., 1849; d. Boston, Mass., March 5, 1924. [1; 7; 10; 27]

Thomson, Estelle, journalist, b. Meadville, Pa., 1846; d. ? [35]

Thomson, Hugh Christopher, journalist, b. Scotland, about 1791; d. Kingston, Upper Canada, April 23, 1834. [27]

Thomson, Ignatius, clergyman, b. 1774; d. 1848. [43]

Thomson, James Bates, educationist, b. Springfield, Vt., 1808; d. Brooklyn, N.Y., June 22, 1883. [3; 6; 43]

Thomson, John, clergyman, d. 1753.

Thomson, John, political writer, b. Petersburg, Va., 1776; d. Petersburg, Va., Jan. 25, 1799. [1]

Thomson, John, librarian, b. England, 1835; d. Philadelphia, Pa., Feb. 23, 1916. [10]

Thomson, John Lewis, historian, fl. 1816-1873. [6]

Thomson, Mortimer Neal, humorist, b. Riga, Monroe county ,N.Y., 1831; d. New York, N.Y., June 25, 1875. [1; 5; 9]

Thomson, Peter Gibson, bibliographer, b. Cincinnati, O., 1851; d. Cincinnati, O., July 10, 1931.

Thomson, Robert Boyd, botanist, b. Prescott, Ont., 1870; d. Agincourt, Ont., July 31, 1947. [13; 30]

Thomson, Samuel, physician, b. Alstead, N.H., 1769; d. Boston, Mass., Oct. 4, 1843. [1; 3; 4; 6]

Thomson, William de Forest, poet, b. New York, N.Y., 1873; d. Nice, France, Dec. 29, 1944. [62]

Thomson, William Hanna, physician, b. 1833; d. New York, N.Y., Jan. 18, 1918. [4; 10]

Thomson, William McClure, clergyman, b. Spring Dale, O., 1806; d. Denver, Colo., April 8, 1894. [1; 3b; 4; 6]

Thone, Frank Ernest Aloysius, biologist, b. Davenport, Ia., 1891; d. Washington, D.C., Aug. 25, 1949. [13]

Thorburn, Grant, merchant, b. Dalkeith, Scotland, 1773; d. New Haven, Conn., Jan. 21, 1863. [1; 3; 4; 5; 6; 7]

Thorburn, James, physician, b. Queenston, Upper Canada, 1830; d. Toronto, Ont., May 26, 1905. [3; 31]

Thoreau, Henry David, naturalist, b. Concord, Mass., 1817; d. Concord, Mass., May 6, 1862. [1; 2; 3; 4; 5; 6; 7; 8; 9; 71; 72]

Thorington, James, surgeon, b. Davenport, Ia., 1858; d. Philadelphia, Pa., Oct. 29, 1944. [10]

Thorn, Alice Green, educationist, b. 1890; d. New York, N.Y., Oct. 1, 1942.

Thornburgh, George, freemason, b. Havana, Ill., 1847; d. Little Rock, Ark., March 9, 1923. [10]

Thorndike, Ashley Horace, educationist, b. Houlton, Me., 1871; d. New York, N.Y., April 17, 1933. [1; 7; 10; 11]

Thorndike, Edward Lee, psychologist, b. Williamsburg, Mass., 1874; d. Montrose, N.Y., Aug. 9, 1949. [4; 7; 10; 11]

Thorne, Charles Embree, agriculturist, b. Greene county, O., 1846; d. Wooster, O., Feb. 29, 1936. [10]

Thorne, Marion (pseud.). See Thurston, Mrs. Ida, née Treadwell.

Thorne, P. (pseud.). See Smith, Mrs. Mary Prudence, née Wells.

Thorne, William Henry, poet, b. Stokesub-Hampden, England, 1839; d. 1907. [10]

Thornton, Augustus Willoughby, physician, b. 1833; d. San Diego, Calif., Oct. 27, 1924.

Thornton, Edward Quin, physician and educationist, b. Marion, Ala., 1866; d. Philadelphia, Pa., Jan. 17, 1945. [10]

Thornton, James Bankhead, lawyer, b. Mount Zephyr, Va., 1806; d. Memphis, Tenn., Oct. 12, 1867. [4; 34]

Thornton, Jessy Quinn, pioneer, b. near Point Pleasant, W.Va., 1810; d. Salem, Ore., Feb. 5, 1888. [1; 3a; 6]

Thornton, John Wingate, historian, b. Saco, Me., 1818; d. Scarboro, Me., June 6, 1878. [1; 3; 4; 5; 6; 7; 38]

Thornton, Richard Hopwood, lawyer, b. 1845; d. March, 1925. [7]

Thornton, Thomas C., clergyman, b. Dumfries, Va., 1794; d. Mississippi, March 23, 1860. [3; 6; 34]

Thornton, William, civil servant, b. Virgin Islands, May 20, 1759; d. Washington, D.C., March 28, 1828. [1; 3; 6]

Thornton, William Wheeler, lawyer, b. near Logansport, Ind., 1851; d. Indianapolis, Ind., Jan. 21 1932. [10; 11]

Thornwell, James Henley, clergyman and educationist, b. Marlboro district, S.C., 1812; d. Charlotte, N.C., Aug. 1, 1862. [1; 3; 4; 5; 6; 34]

Thorpe, Campa (pseud.). See Bellamy, Mrs. Elizabeth Whitfield, née Croom.

Thorpe, Francis Newton, educationist, b. Swampscott, Mass., 1857; d. May 8, 1926. [4; 7; 10; 11]

Thorpe, Mrs. Rose, née **Hartwick,** novelist and poet, b. Mishawaka, Ind., 1850; d. San Diego, Calif., July 20, 1939. [4; 7; 10; 11; 35]

Thorpe, Sheldon Brainerd, historian, b. 1838; d. 1924.

Thorpe, Thomas Bangs, journalist, b. Westfield, Mass., 1815; d. New York, N.Y., Oct., 1878. [1; 2; 3; 4 ;5; 6; 7; 8; 9; 71]

Thorpe, William (pseud.). See Vreeland, Frank.

Thrall, Homer S., clergyman, d. 1894. [34]

Thrasher, John S., journalist, b. Portland, Me., 1817; d. Galveston, Tex., Nov. 10, 1879. [3; 34]

Thrasher, Max Bennett, journalist, b. Westmoreland, N.H., 1860; d. New York, N.Y., 1903. [10]

Thresher, Leonard, physician, fl. 1871-1875. [43]

Throckmorton, Archibald Hall, lawyer, b. Loudoun county, Va., 1876; d. Cleveland, O., May 20, 1938. [10; 11]

Throop, Benjamin Henry, physician, b. Oxford, N.Y., 1811; d. Scranton, Pa., June 26, 1897. [4]

Throop, Montgomery Hunt, jurist, b. Auburn, N.Y., 1827; d. Albany, N.Y., Sept. 11, 1892. [1; 3; 5; 6]

Thrum, Thomas George, anthropologist, b. 1843; d. ?

Thruston, Gates Phillips, soldier, lawyer, and archaeologist, b. Dayton, O., 1835; d. Nashville, Tenn., 1912. [10; 34]

Thruston, Mrs. Lucy Meacham, née **Kidd,** novelist, b. King and Queen county, Va., 1862; d. ? [7; 11; 34]

Thurber, Charles Herbert, editor and publisher, b. Oswego, N.Y., 1864; d. Boston, Mass., Dec. 8, 1938. [10]

Thurber, Francis Beatty, merchant and lawyer, b. Delhi, N.Y., 1842; d. New York, N.Y., July 4, 1907. [4; 10]

Thurber, Samuel, educationist, b. Worcester, Mass., 1879; d. Boston, Mass., June 13, 1943.

Thurston, Brown, publisher, b. Winthrop, Me.; d. 1900. [38]

Thurston, Carl Hammond Philander, art critic, b. Sutton, Mass., 1887; d. Pasadena, Calif., Jan. 26, 1947. [62]

Thurston, David, clergyman, b. 1779; d. Winthrop, Me., 1865. [38]

Thurston, Mrs. Elizabeth A., miscellaneous writer, fl. 1866-1881. [6]

Thurston, George Henry, local historian b. 1822; d. Atlantic City, N.J., April 11, 1895.

Thurston, Henry Winfred, social worker, b. Barré, Vt., 1861; d. Montclair, N.J., Sept. 19, 1946. [10; 11; 49]

Thurston, Howard, magician, b. Columbus, O., 1869; d. Miami, Fla., April 13, 1936. [4; 10]

Thurston, Mrs. Ida, née **Treadwell,** novelist, b. 1848; d. Washington, D.C., June 3, 1918. [7; 10]

Thurston, John Henry, pioneer, b. 1824; d. Forest City, Ia., Sept. 19, 1896.

Thurston, Lorrin Andrews, lawyer, b. Honolulu, Hawaii, 1858; d. Honolulu, Hawaii, May 11, 1931. [1; 7; 10]

Thurston, Louise M., writer of books for children, fl. 1868-1873. [6]

Thurston, Oliver (pseud.). See Flanders, Henry.

Thurston, Robert Henry, educationist, b. Providence, R.I., 1839; d. Ithaca, N.Y., Oct. 25, 1903. [1; 3; 4; 5; 6; 10]

Thwaites, Reuben Gold, historian, b. Dorchester, Mass., 1853; d. Madison, Wis., Oct. 22, 1913. [1; 2; 4; 5; 7; 10]

Thwing, Annie Haven, historian, b. 1851 d. Roxbury, Mass., June 5, 1940.

Thwing, Charles Burton, physicist, b. Theresa, N.Y., 1860; d. Philadelphia, Pa., Dec. 12, 1946. [11; 13]

Thwing, Charles Franklin, educationist, b. New Sharon, Me., 1853; d. Cleveland, O., Aug. 29, 1937. [3; 4; 5; 7; 10; 11; 51]

Thwing, Edward Payson, clergyman, b. Ware, Mass., 1830; d. Canton, China, May 9, 1893. [3b; 51]

Thwing, Eugene, editor, b. Quincy, Mass., 1866; d. Ridgwood, N.J., May 29, 1936. [7; 10; 11]

Thwing, Walter Eliot, genealogist, b. 1848; d. Roxbury, Mass., July 25, 1935.

Tibbles, Thomas Henry, journalist, b. Washington county, O., 1838; d. Omaha, Neb., May 14, 1928. [1; 4; 7; 10]

Tichenor, Henry Mulford, editor, b. Orange, N.J., 1858; d. Los Angeles, Calif., Dec. 4, 1922. [4]

Ticknor, Almon, educationist, b. Salisbury, Conn., 1796; d. ? [6]

Ticknor, Caleb Bingham, physician, b. Salisbury, Conn., 1804; d. New York, N.Y., Sept. 19, 1840. [3; 6]

Ticknor, Caroline, miscellaneous writer, b. Boston, Mass., 1866; d. Jamaica Plain, Mass., May 11, 1937. [7; 10]

Ticknor, Francis Orray, physician and poet, b. Fortville, Ga., 1822; d. near Columbus, Ga., Dec. 18, 1874. [1; 4; 7; 34; 77]

Ticknor, George, educationist, b. Boston, Mass., 1791; d. Boston, Mass., Jan. 26, 1871. [1; 2; 3; 4; 5; 6; 7; 8; 9; 71]

Tidball, John Caldwell, soldier, b. Ohio county, W.Va., 1825; d. Newark, N.J., May 15, 1906. [1; 3; 5; 6; 10]

Tidball, Thomas Allen, clergyman, b. Winchester, Va., 1847; d. 1925. [10; 34]

Tidwell, Josiah Blake, clergyman, b. Alabama, 1870; d. Waco, Tex., March 17, 1946. [11]

Tiedeman, Christopher Gustavus, lawyer and educationist, b. Charleston, S.C., 1867; d. New York, N.Y., Aug. 25, 1903. [1; 5; 10]

Tiernan, Charles Bernard, lawyer, b. Baltimore, Md., Sept. 4, 1840; d. ? [34]

Tiernan, Mrs. Frances Christine, née Fisher, novelist, b. Salisbury, N.C., 1846; d. Salisbury, N.C., March 24, 1920. [1; 4; 5; 6; 7; 10; 21; 34]

Tiernan, Mrs. Mary Spear, née Nicholas, novelist, b. 1836; d. 1891. [6; 34]

Tierney, Richard Henry, priest and journalist, b. Spuyten Duyvil, N.Y., 1870; d. New York, N.Y., Feb. 10, 1928. [1; 10; 21]

Tietjens, Mrs. Eunice, née **Hammond,** poet, lecturer, and writer of books for young people, b. Chicago, Ill., 1884; d. Chicago, Ill., Sept. 6, 1944. [7; 10]

Tiffany, Alexander Ralston, jurist, b. Niagara, Upper Canada, 1796; d. Palmyra, Mich., Jan. 14, 1868. [3; 4; 6]

Tiffany, Charles Comfort, clergyman, b. Baltimore, Md., 1829; d. Northeast Harbor, Me., Aug. 20, 1907. [10]

Tiffany, Edward Herbert, lawyer, b Hamilton, Ont., 1842; d. Alexandria, Ont., 1916.

' **Tiffany, Francis,** clergyman, b. 1827; d. Cambridge, Mass., Sept. 3, 1908. [10]

Tiffany, Francis Buchanan, lawyer, b. Springfield, Mass., 1855; d. St. Paul, Minn., Oct. 25, 1936. [10; 51]

Tiffany, Henry Stanton, publisher, b. 1845; d. 1914.

Tiffany, Joel, lawyer, b. 1811; d. 1893. [6]

Tiffany, John Kerr, philatelist, b. 1843; d. 1897.

Tiffany, Osmond, miscellaneous writer, b. Baltimore, Md., 1823; d. Nov. 18, 1895. [3; 7]

Tiger Lily (pseud.). See Blake, Mrs. Lillie Umstead, née Devereux.

Tigert, John James, clergyman, b. Louisville, Ky., 1856; d. Tulsa, Indian Territories, Nov. 21, 1906. [1; 5; 7; 10; 11; 34]

Tighe, Ambrose, lawyer, b. Brooklyn, N.Y., 1859; d. St. Paul, Minn., Nov. 11, 1928. [10; 62]

Tilden, Frank William, educationist, b. Knowlesville, N.Y., 1868; d. Black Mountain, N.C., March 28, 1940. [11]

Tilden, John Henry, physician, b. Montgomery county, Ill., 1851; d. Denver, Colo., Sept. 1, 1940. [10]

Tilden, John Newel, educationist, b. 1842; d. 1902

Tilden, Samuel Jones, lawyer and politician, b. New Lebanon, N.Y., 1814; d. Winchester county, N.Y., Aug. 4, 1886. [1; 2; 3; 4; 5; 6; 7]

Tilden, William Phillips, clergyman, b. 1811; d. 1890.

Tilden, William Smith, local historian, b. 1830; d. 1912.

Tildsley, John Lee, educationist, b. Pittsburg, Pa., 1867; d. New York, N.Y., Nov. 21, 1948. [10]

Tileston, Mrs. Mary Wilder, née Foote, anthologist, b. Salem, Mass., 1843; d. Brookline, Mass., July 3, 1934. [7; 10]

Tillett, Wilbur Fisk, clergyman, b. Henderson, N.C., 1854; d. Nashville, Tenn., June 4, 1936. [7; 10; 11; 34]

Tillinghast, Benjamin Franklin, descriptive writer, b. 1849; d. ? [37]

Tillinghast, John L., lawyer, b. about 1786; d. ? [48]

Tillinghast, Nicholas, educationist, b. Taunton, Mass., 1804; d. Bridgewater, Mass., April 10, 1856. [3]

Tillitt, Malvern Hall, lawyer and journalist, b. Elizabeth City, N.C., 1881; d. New York, N.Y., April 4, 1945.

Tillman, Charlie Davis, clergyman and hymn-writer, b. 1861; d. Atlanta, Ga., Sept. 2, 1943.

Tillman, Samuel Dyer, lawyer and musician, b. Utica, N.Y., 1815; d. New York, N.Y., Sept. 4, 1875. [3; 6]

Tillman, Samuel Escue, soldier, b. near Shelbyville, Tenn., 1847; d. Southampton, Long Island, N.Y., June 24, 1942. [10; 11]

Tillotson, Mrs. Mary Ella, née **Tillotson,** poet, b. 1816; d. ? [6]

Tillson, George William, engineer, b. Thomaston, Me., 1852; d. La Grange, Ill., May 12, 1940. [10; 11]

Tilney, Frederick, neurologist, b. Brooklyn, N.Y., 1875; d. Centre Island, N.Y., Aug. 7, 1938. [10; 62]

Tilney, Robert, soldier and poet, fl. 1862-1912.

Tilton, Dwight (pseud.). See Richardson, George Tilton, and Quint, Wilder Dwight.

Tilton, George Henry, clergyman, b. Nashua, N.H., 1845; d. Melrose, Mass., Jan. 8, 1926. [10]

Tilton, Howard Winslow, journalist, b. Frankfort, Me., 1849; d. Council Bluffs, Ia., 1902. [10]

Tilton, James, army surgeon, b. Kent county, Del., 1745; d. near Wilmington Del., May 14, 1822. [1; 3; 6]

Tilton, Theodore, journalist, poet, and novelist, b. New York, N.Y., 1835; d. Paris, France, May 25, 1907. [1; 3; 4; 6; 7; 9; 10]

Timayenis, Telemachus Thomas, educationist, b. Greece, 1853; d. ? [6]

Timby, Theodore Ruggles, inventor, b. Dover, N.Y., 1819; d. Brooklyn, N.Y., Nov. 9, 1909. [1; 3; 4; 5; 10]

Timlow, Elizabeth Westyn, educationist and writer of books for girls, b. Rhinebeck, N.Y., 1861; d. Fitzwilliam, N.H., Jan. 17, 1931. [10; 11]

Timlow, Heman Rowlee, clergyman, b. 1831; d. 1892.

Timoleon (pseud.). See Tilton, James.

Timon, John, bishop, b. Conewago, Pa., 1797; d. Buffalo, N.Y., April 16, 1867. [1; 3; 4; 5; 6; 21]

Timon, John (pseud.). See Mitchell, Donald Grant.

Timperlake, James, insurance agent, b. Bolton, Lancashire, England, 1841; d. ?

Timrod, Henry, poet, b. Charleston, S.C., 1828; d. Columbia, S. C., Oct. 6, 1867. [1; 3; 4; 5; 6; 7; 9; 34; 71]

Timsol, Robert (pseud.). See Bird, Frederic Mayer.

Tincker, Mary Agnes, novelist, b. Ellsworth, Me., 1831; d. Dorchester, Mass., Nov. 27, 1907. [1; 3; 4; 5; 6; 7; 10]

Tindall, William, historian, b. 1844; d. Washington, D.C., May 2, 1932.

Tingley, Mrs. Katherine A., née **Westcott,** theosophist, b. Newburyport, Mass., 1852; d. Visingsoe, Sweden, July 11, 1929. [1; 4; 10]

Tippett, Edward D., school-teacher, b. 1789; d. ?

Tipple, Ezra Squier, clergyman and educationist, b. Camden, N.Y., 1861; d. New York, N.Y., Oct. 17, 1936. [4; 10; 11]

Tipton, Thomas Weston, politician, b. Cadiz, O., 1817; d. Washington, D.C., Nov. 26, 1899. [4]

Tirrell, Norton Quincy, physician, b. 1817; d. 1878.

Titchener, Edward Bradford, psychologist, b. Chichester, England, 1867; d. Ithaca, N.Y., Aug. 3, 1927. [1; 4; 7; 10]

Titcomb, Sarah Elizabeth, miscellaneous writer, b. 1841; d. 1895.

Titcomb, Timothy (pseud.). See Holland, Josiah Gilbert.

Titherington, Richard Handfield, editor, b. Chester, England, 1861; d. New York, N.Y., Dec. 5, 1935. [10]

Titsworth, Alfred Alexander, educationist, b. Plainfield, N.J., 1852; d. New Brunswick, N.J., Aug. 15, 1936. [10]

Titterington, Mrs. Sophie, née **Bronson,** writer of books for children, b. Assam, India, 1846; d. ? [7]

Titterwell, Timothy (pseud.). See Kettell, Samuel.

Titus, John Henry, poet, b. Ohio, 1846; d. New York, N.Y., Oct. 20, 1947.

Titus, Timothy Tilghman, clergyman, b. 1829; d. 1873. [6]

Titus, William P., local historian, b. 1852; d. May 12, 1928.

Titzell, Josiah Carlton, journalist, b. 1905; d. Danbury, Conn., May 15, 1943.

Tjader, Charles Richard, big-game hunter, b. Karlskrona, Sweden, 1869; d. New York, N.Y., Dec. 27, 1916. [4; 10]

Tobie, Edward Parsons, historian, b. 1838; d. ? [38]

Toch, Maxmilian, chemist and art expert, b. New York, N.Y., 1864; d. New York, N.Y., May 28, 1946. [10; 11]

Tocque, Philip, clergyman, b. Newfoundland, 1814; d. Toronto, Ont., Oct. 22, 1899. [27]

Todd, Albert May, political economist, b. St. Joseph county, Mich., 1850; d. Kalamazoo, Mich., Oct., 1931. [10; 39]

Todd, Alfred, civil servant, b. England, 1819; d. Ottawa, Ont., June 6, 1874. [3; 27]

Todd, Alpheus, librarian, b. London, England, 1821; d. Ottawa, Ont., Jan. 22, 1884. [3; 27]

Todd, Charles Burr, historian, b. Redding, Conn., 1849; d. ? [3; 27]

Todd, Charles Stewart, lawyer, soldier, and diplomat, b. near Danville, Ky., 1791; d. Baton Rouge, La., May 17, 1871. [1; 34]

Todd, David Peck, astronomer, b. Lake Ridge, N.Y., 1855; d. Madison Heights, Va., June 1, 1939. [4; 7; 10]

Todd, Henry Cook, traveller, b. England; d. Canada, 1862. [27]

Todd, James Campbell, pathologist, b. Shreve, O., 1874; d. Jan. 6, 1928. [11]

Todd, John, clergyman, b. Rutland, Vt., Oct. 9, 1800; d. Pittsfield, Mass., Aug. 24, 1873. [1; 3; 4; 6; 7; 62]

Todd, John Adams, clergyman, b. 1822; d. 1900.

Todd, John Edwards, clergyman, b. Northampton, Mass., 1833; d. Riverside, Calif., Aug. 3, 1907. [62]

Todd, Lawrie (pseud.). See Thorburn, Grant.

Todd, Luther Edward, clergyman, b. New Franklin, Mo., 1874; d. St. Louis, Mo., Nov. 25, 1937. [10]

Todd, Mrs. Mabel, née **Loomis,** miscellaneous writer, b. Cambridge, Mass., 1856; d. Hog Island, Me., Oct. 14, 1932. [1; 4; 5; 7; 10; 11]

Todd, Mrs. Marion, née **Marsh,** lawyer, b. Plymouth, N.Y., 1841; d. ? [7; 10]

Todd, Mrs. Mary Van Lennup, née **Ives,** novelist, b. 1849; d. ? [8]

Todd, Sereno Edwards, agriculturist and journalist, b. Tompkins county, N.J., 1820; d. near Orange, N.J., Dec. 26, 1898. [1; 3b; 4]

Todd, Thomas Wingate, anatomist, b. Sheffield, England, 1885; d. Cleveland, O., Dec. 28, 1938. [10]

Todd, William Cleaves, educationist, b. Atkinson, N.H., 1823; d. Atkinson, N.H., June 26, 1903.

Todkill, Anas (pseud.). See Cooke, John Esten.

Toland, Hugh Hughes, surgeon, b. 1806; d. 1880.

Toland, Mrs. Mary Bertha, née **McKenzie,** poet, b. Maine, about 1825; d. San Francisco, Calif., Nov., 1895. [35]

Toler, Sidney, actor and playwright, b. Warrensburg, Mo.; d. Hollywood, Calif., Feb. 11, 1947.

Tolman, Albert Harris, educationist, b. Lanesboro, Mass., 1856; d. Chicago, Ill., Dec. 25, 1928. [10; 11]

Tolman, Cyrus Fisher, geologist, b. Chicago, Ill., 1873; d. Spokane, Wash., Oct. 13, 1942. [10; 11]

Tolman, Herbert Cushing, educationist, b. South Scituate, Mass., 1865; d. Nashville, Tenn., Nov. 24, 1923. [1; 4; 7; 10; 34; 62]

Tolman, Judson Allen, educationist, b. Sandwich, Ill., 1879; d. Georgetown, Ky., Jan. 30, 1949. [10]

Tolman, Richard Chace, physician, b. West Newton, Mass., 1881; d. Pasadena, Calif., Sept. 5, 1948. [10; 11]

Tome, Philip, hunter, b. Dauphin county, Pa., 1782; d. April 30, 1855. [7]

Tomes, Robert, physician, b. New York, N.Y., 1817; d. Brooklyn, N.Y., Aug. 28, 1882. [3; 4; 6; 7]

Tomkins, David Beveridge, clergyman, b. Scotland, 1872; d. East Northfield, Mass., July 12, 1941.

Tomkins, Floyd Williams, clergyman, b. New York, N.Y., 1850; d. Philadelphia, Pa., March 24, 1932. [10; 11; 51]

Tomkins, Jane Harrison, novelist and poet, b. 1841; d. 1912.

Tomlinson, Everett Titsworth, writer of books for boys, b. Shiloh, N.J., 1859; d. Elizabeth, N.J., Oct. 30, 1931. [1; 5; 7; 10; 11]

Tomlinson, William P., poet, fl. 1859-1866.

Tompkins, Arnold, educationist, b. near Paris, Ill., 1859; d. Menlo, Ga., Aug. 12, 1905. [1; 10]

Tompkins, Daniel Augustus, engineer and manufacturer, b. Edgefield county, S.C., 1851; d: Montreat, N.C., Oct. 18. 1914. [1; 10;, 34]

Tompkins, Edward Staats De Grote, clergyman, b. Chatham, N.Y., 1858; d. Coxsackie, N.Y., Dec. 21, 1932. [62]

Tompkins, Hamilton Bullock, bibliographer, b. 1843; d. Newport, R.I., Dec. 23, 1921.

Tompson, Benjamin, poet, b. Quincy, Mass., 1642; d. Roxbury, Mass., April 13, 1714. [1; 3; 4; 6; 7; 9; 34]

Tone, William Theobald Wolfe, soldier, b. Dublin, Ireland, 1791; d. New York, N.Y., Oct. 10, 1828. [3; 6]

Toner, Joseph Meredith, physician, b. Pittsburgh, Pa., 1825; d. Cresson, Pa., July 30, 1896. [1; 3; 4; 6; 7]

Toohey, John Peter, journalist, b. Binghampton, N.Y., 1880; d. Manhattan, N.Y., Nov. 8, 1946. [10]

Tooker, Lewis Frank, editor, b. Port Jefferson, N.Y., 1854; d. Greenwich, Conn., Sept. 17, 1925. [4; 7; 10; 62]

Tooker, Robert Newton, physician, b. 1841; d. 1902.

Tooker, William Wallace, anthropologist, b. 1847; d. 1917.

Toomer, Mrs. Margery Bodine, née **Latimer,** novelist and short-story writer, b. 1899; d. Chicago, Ill., Aug. 17, 1932. [10]

Toppan, Robert Noxon, lawyer, b. Philadelphia, Pa., 1836; d. 1901. [10; 51]

Torchiana, Henry Albert Willem van Coenen, consul-general, b. Java, Dutch East Indies, 1867; d. San Francisco, Calif., March 1, 1940. [10; 11; 35]

Torrey, Bradford, ornithologist, b. Weymouth, Mass., 1843; d. Santa Barbara, Calif., Oct. 7, 1912. [1; 3; 4; 5; 9; 10]

Torrey, Charles Turner, reformer, b. Scituate, Mass., 1813; d. Baltimore, Md., May 9, 1846. [1; 3; 4; 6]

Torrey, David, clergyman, b. 1818; d. Cazenovia, N.Y., Sept. 29, 1894.

Torrey, George Arnold, lawyer, b. 1838; d. 1911. [51]

Torrey, Henry Augustus Pearson, philosopher, b. Beverly, Mass., 1837; d. Beverly, Mass., Sept. 20, 1902. [3b; 43]

Torrey, Jesse, physician and educationist, b. 1787; d. ? [6]

Torrey, John, botanist, b. New York, N.Y., 1796; d. New York, N.Y., March 10, 1873. [1; 2; 3; 4; 5; 6; 7; 9]

Torrey, Joseph, educationist, b. Rowley, Mass., 1797; d. Burlington, Vt., Nov. 26, 1867. [3; 4; 6; 43]

Torrey, Mrs. Marian, née **Richards,** novelist, d. New Haven, Conn., Oct. 5, 1946.

Torrey, Mary Cutler, poet, b. Burlington, Vt., 1831; d. ? [3; 43]

Torrey, Mrs. Mary, née Ide, miscellaneous writer, b. 1817; d. 1869. [8]

Torrey, Raymond Hezekiah, conservationist, b. Georgetown, Mass., 1880; d. Hollis, Long Island, N.Y., July 15, 1938. [10]

Torrey, Reuben Archer, evangelist, b. Hoboken, N.J., 1856; d. Asheville, N.C., Oct. 26, 1928. [4; 10; 11; 62]

Torrey, Rufus Campbell, local historian, b. about 1813; d. 1882.

Torrey, William, sailor, b. 1814; d. ?

Torrey, William Turner, clergyman, b. Kingston, Mass., 1786; d. Madison, O., Oct. 29, 1861. [51]

Torry, Alvin, missionary, b. Stafford, Conn., 1797; d. Homer, N.Y., 1874.

Tory, Henry Marshall, educationist, b. Guysboro, N.S., 1864; d. Ottawa, Ont., Feb. 6, 1947. [30]

Totten, Benjamin J., naval officer, b. West Indies, 1806; d. New Bedford, Mass., May 9, 1877. [3]

Totten, Charles Adiel Lewis, soldier and British-Israelite, b. New London, Conn., 1851; d. Milford, Conn., April 12, 1908. [3; 6; 10]

Totten, George Oakley, architect, b. New York, N.Y., 1866; d. Washington, D.C., Feb. 1, 1939. [10; 11]

Totten, Silas, clergyman, b. Schoharie county, N.Y., 1804; d. Lexington, Ky., Oct. 7, 1873. [4; 6]

Toulmin, Harry, jurist, b. Taunton, England, 1766; d. Washington county, Ala., Nov. 11, 1823. [1; 3; 4; 5; 6; 34]

Toumey, James William, forester, b. Lawrence, Mich., 1865; d. New Haven, Conn., May 6, 1932. [1; 10; 11]

Tourgée, Albion Winegar, jurist, journalist, and novelist, b. Williamsfield, O., 1838; d. Bordeaux, France, May 21, 1905. [1; 3; 4; 5; 6; 7; 9; 10]

Tourscher, Francis Edward, priest, b. Dushore, Pa., 1870; d. Villanova, Pa., Jan. 30, 1939. [7; 10; 21]

Tousey, Sinclair, publisher, b. New Haven, Conn., 1818; d. New York, N.Y., June 16, 1887. [1; 3; 6; 7]

Toussaint, François Xavier, educationist, b. St. Jean, Island of Orleans, Lower Canada, 1821; d. Quebec, Que., Dec. 2, 1895. [27]

Towart, William George, clergyman, b. Scotland, 1880; d. Bennington, Vt., Dec. 6, 1949.

Tower, Charlemagne, diplomat, b. Philadelphia, Pa., 1848; d. Philadelphia, Pa., Feb. 24, 1923. [1; 4; 5; 10; 51]

Tower, David Bates, educationist, b. 1808; d. 1868. [6]

Tower, Francis Emory, clergyman, b. Petersham, Mass., 1836; d. Auburn, R.I., Feb. 13, 1916.

Tower, George Bates Nichols, engineer, fl. 1874-1889.

Tower, Henry Mendell, local historian, b. 1847; d. 1904.

Tower, Philo, clergyman, fl. 1854-1856.

Tower, Ralph Winfred, physiologist, b. Amherst, Mass., 1870; d. Jan. 26, 1926. [10; 11]

Towle, George Makepeace, journalist and historian, b. Washington, D.C., 1841; d. Brookline, Mass., Aug. 9, 1893. [1; 3; 4; 5; 7;]

Towle, Nancy, evangelist, b. 1796; d. ?

Towle, Nathaniel Carter, civil servant, b. Alton, N.H., 1805; d. Andover, Mass., April 25, 1898. [3; 6]

Towler, John, educationist, b. Yorkshire, England, 1811; d. Orange, N.J., April 2, 1889. [1; 3; 6]

Town, Ithiel, architect, b. Thompson, Conn., 1784; d. New Haven, Conn., June 13, 1844. [1; 3; 6]

Town, Salem, educationist, b. Belchertown, Mass., 1779; d. Greencastle, Ind., Feb. 24, 1864. [3; 6]

Towndrow, Thomas, stenographer, b. 1810; d. 1898. [6]

Towne, Charles Hanson, editor, b. Louisville, Ky., 1877; d. New York, N.Y., Feb. 28, 1949. [10]

Towne, Edward Cornelius, clergyman and journalist, b. Goshen, Mass., 1834; d. Brooklyn, N.Y., June 20, 1911. [62]

Towne, Henry Robinson, manufacturer, b. Philadelphia, Pa., 1844; d. New York, N.Y., Oct. 15, 1924. [1; 4; 10]

Towne, Paul Allen, educationist, b. Hardwick, Mass., 1823; d. ? [6]

Towner, Ausburn, miscellaneous writer, b. 1836; d. 1909.

Towner, James William, genealogist, b. 1823; d. 1913.

Townes, John Charles, lawyer, b. Tuscumbia, Ala., 1852; d. Dec. 18, 1923. [10]

Townley, Adam, clergyman, b. England, 1808; d. Paris, Ont., Feb. 11, 1887. [27]

Townsend, Calvin, lawyer, d. 1881. [6]

Townsend, Charles, clergyman, b. Buffalo, N.Y., July 15, 1857; d. Orange, N.J., 1914.

Townsend, Charles, journalist and playwright, b. near Troy, N.Y., 1859; d. May 24, 1917.

Townsend, Charles Wendell, naturalist, b. Boston, Mass., 1859; d. Boston, Mass., April 3, 1934. [7; 10; 11; 51]

Townsend, Clara Virginia, journalist, b. 1858; d. Fulton, Mo., July 8, 1939.

Townsend, Edward Davis, soldier, b. Boston, Mass., 1817; d. Washington, D.C., May 10, 1893. [1; 3; 4; 5; 6]

Townsend, Edward Waterman, journalist, b. Cleveland, O., 1855; d. New York, N.Y., March 16, 1942. [4; 7; 10; 35]

Townsend, Frederic, essayist, fl. 1851-1857.

Townsend, George Alfred, journalist, b. Georgetown, Del., 1841; d. New York, N.Y., April 15, 1914. [1; 3; 4; 5; 6; 7; 8; 9; 10]

Townsend, George Washington, lawyer and merchant, b. West Chester, Pa., 1839; d. Philadelphia, Pa., 1905. [10]

Townsend, Horace, journalist, b. Cheshire, England, 1859; d. New York, N.Y., May 9, 1922. [10]

Townsend, James Bliss, editor, b. New York, N.Y., 1855; d. New York, N.Y., March 10, 1921. [7; 10]

Townsend, John Kirk, naturalist, b. Philadelphia, Pa., 1809; d. Washington, D.C., Feb. 16, 1851. [1; 3; 5; 6]

Townsend, Luther Tracy, clergyman and educationist, b. Orono, Me., 1838; d. Brookline, Mass., Aug. 2, 1922 .[1; 3; 4; 5; 6; 10]

Townsend, Mrs. Mary Ashley, née **Van Voorhis,** poet, b. Lyons, N.Y., 1832; d. Galveston, Tex., June 7, 1901. [1; 3; 4; 5; 6; 7; 8; 9; 10]

Townsend, Peter Solomon, physician, d. 1849. [6; 48]

Townsend, Shippie, pamphleteer, fl. 1783-1794.

Townsend, Thomas C., church elder, b. 1799; d. ? [37]

Townsend, Thomas Seaman, historical writer, b. New York, N.Y., 1829; d. 1908. [3]

Townsend, Virginia Frances, writer of books for girls, b. New Haven, Conn., 1836; d. Arlington, Mass., Aug. 11, 1920. [1; 3; 4; 5; 6; 7; 10]

Townsend, William Kneeland, jurist, b. New Haven, Conn., 1848; d. New Haven, Conn., June 1, 1907. [10; 62]

Townshend, Charles Hervey, sea-captain, b. 1833; d. 1904.

Townshend, Sir **Charles James,** jurist, b. Amherst, N.S., 1844; d. Wolfville, N.S., June 16, 1924. [27]

Townshend, John, lawyer, b. 1819; d. ?

Toy, Crawford Howell, educationist, b. Norfolk, Va., March 23, 1836; d. Cambridge, Mass., May 12, 1919. [1; 3; 4; 5; 6; 7; 10]

Trabert, George Henry, clergyman, b. Lancaster county, Pa., 1843; d. Minneapolis, Minn., Sept. 16, 1931. [4]

Trabue, Isaac Hodgen, novelist and chess-player, b. Russell county, Ky., 1829; d. 1907. [10; 34]

Tracy, Charles Chapin, missionary, b. East Smithfield, Pa., 1838; d. Los Angeles, Calif., April 20, 1917. [1; 3; 4; 6; 10]

Tracy, Ebenezer Carter, journalist, b. Hartford, Vt., 1796; d. Windsor, Vt., May 15, 1862. [3; 6; 43]

Tracy, Edward Aloysius, physician, b. 1863; d. Boston, Mass., Jan. 12, 1935.

Tracy, Frank Basil, journalist and historian, b. Brighton, Ia., 1866; d. 1912. [10]

Tracy, Ira, missionary, b. Hartford, Vt., 1806; d. Bloomington, Wis., Nov. 10, 1875. [3; 6; 43]

Tracy, James Madsion, musician, b. Bath, N.H., 1837; d. Denver, Colo., Sept. 3, 1928. [10]

Tracy, Joseph, clergyman, b. Hartford, Vt., 1793; d. Beverly, Mass., March 24, 1874. [1; 3; 4; 6; 43]

Tracy, Joshua L., miscellaneous writer, fl. 1857-1870.

Tracy, Roger Sherman, physician, b. Windsor, Vt., 1841; d. Ballardvale, Mass., March 6, 1926. [3; 10; 11; 62]

Tracy, Samuel Mills, botanist, b. Hartford, Vt., 1847; d. Biloxi, Mass., Sept. 5, 1920. [4; 10]

Tracy, Stephen, medical missionary, fl. 1830-1853. [6]

Tracy, Uriah, politician, b. Franklin, Conn., 1755; d. Washington, D.C., July 19, 1807. [1; 3; 4; 5]

Tracy, Vera Marie, poet and short-story writer, b. Denison, Tex.; d. Colorado Springs, Colo., Sept. 24, 1940. [21]

Tracy, William, lawyer, b. 1805; d. 1881.

Tracy, William Warner, writer on agriculture, b. 1845; d. 1922.

Trafton, Adeline. See Knox, Mrs. Adeline, née Trafton.

Trafton, Mark, clergyman, b. Bangor, Me., 1810; d. West Somerville, Mass., 1901. [10]

Trahey, James Joseph, priest, b. 1875; d. 1906.

Trail, Florence, literary critic, b. 1854; d. Frederick, Md., April, 1944. [78]

Traill, Mrs. Catherine Parr, née **Strickland,** b. London, England, 1802; d. Lakefield, Ont., Aug. 29, 1899. [27]

Train, Arthur Cheney, lawyer and novelist, b. Boston, Mass., 1875; d. New York, N.Y., Dec. 22, 1945. [4; 7; 10; 12]

Train, Charles Russell, lawyer, b. Framingham, Mass., 1817; d. July 29, 1885.

Train, Elizabeth Phipps, novelist, b. Dorchester, Mass., 1856; d. ? [7; 10]

Train, Mrs. Ethel, née **Kissam,** short-story writer, b. New York, N.Y., 1875; d. New York, N.Y., May 15, 1923. [7; 10]

Train, George Francis, merchant and politician, b. Boston, Mass., 1829; d. New York, N.Y., Jan. 19, 1904. [1; 3; 4; 5; 6; 7; 10]

Traine, Gypsey (pseud.). See Lovejoy, Mrs. Mary Evelyn, née Wood.

Trainer, John, educationist, b. near Wilkesville, O., 1844; d. Mena, Ark., Oct. 8, 1913.

Trajetta, Philip, musician, b. Venice, Italy, about 1776; d. Philadelphia, Pa., Jan. 9, 1854. [1]

Trall, Russell Thacher, physician, b. Vernon, Conn., 1812; d. Florence, N.J., Sept. 23, 1877. [3; 6]

Trammell, William Dugas, novelist, b. Georgia, 1850; d. Texas, 1884. [34]

Traprock, Dr. Walter E., (pseud.). See Chappell, George Shepard.

Trask, Albert, lawyer, d. Saginaw, Mich., Dec 27, 1913.

Trask, George, clergyman, b. Beverly, Mass., 1798; d. Fitchburg, Mass., Jan. 25, 1875. [3]

Trask, Mrs. Kate, née **Nichols,** poet, playwright, and novelist, b. Brooklyn, N.Y., 1853; d. Saratoga Springs, N.Y., Jan. 7, 1922. [4; 7; 10]

Trask, Katrina (pseud.). See Trask, Mrs. Kate, née Nichols.

Trask, Robert Dana, philosopher, b. 1852; d. Haverhill, Mass., Oct. 27, 1932.

Trask, Spencer, banker, b. New York, N.Y., 1844; d. 1909. [4; 10]

Trask, William Blake, antiquary and genealogist, b. Dorchester, Mass., Nov. 25, 1812; d. 1906. [3; 6; 10]

Traubel, Horace L., journalist, b. Camden, N.J., 1858; d. Bon Echo, Ont., Sept. 8, 1919. [1; 7; 10]

Trautwine, John Cresson, civil engineer, b. Philadelphia, Pa., 1810; d. Philadelphia, Pa., Sept. 14, 1883. [1; 3; 4; 6]

Travis, Mrs. Elma, née **Allen,** physician and novelist, b. 1861; d. Winston-Salem, N.C., Aug., 1917.

Travis, Jeremiah, lawyer, d. 1911.

Travis, Joseph, clergyman, b. Maryland, 1786; d. Mississippi, Sept. 16, 1858. [3; 6]

Travis, Walter John, golfer, b. Victoria, Australia, 1862; d. Denver, Colo., July 31, 1927. [1]

Travis, William, educationist, b. 1838; d. ?

Treacy, William P., priest, b. Ireland; d. East Millstone, N.J., March 29, 1906. [21]

Treadwell, Augustus, poet, b. 1841; d. ?

Treadwell, John H., miscellaneous writer, fl. 1872-1881.

Treadwell, Seymour Boughton, politician, b. Bridgeport, Conn., 1795; d. Jackson, Mich., June 9, 1867. [3]

Treanor, Thomas Coghill, journalist, b. California, 1908; d. France, Aug. 19, 1944.

Treat, John Harvey, genealogist, b. Pittsfield, N.H., 1839; d. Pittsfield, N.H., Nov. 8, 1908. [3; 6; 10]

Treat, Mrs. Mary Adelia, née **Davis,** naturalist, b. 1830; d. Newstead, N.Y., April 11, 1923. [6; 7]

Treat, William, compiler, b. 1814; d. 1861.

Trebor, Snivig C. (pseud.). See Givins, Robert Cartwright.

Tredwell, Daniel M., lawyer, b. Hempstead, Long Island, N.Y., 1826; d. Brooklyn, N.Y., Nov. 10, 1921. [10]

Trego, Benjamin Brooke Thomas, clergyman, b. 1861; d. July 7, 1933.

Trego, Brooke. See Trego, Benjamin Brooke Thomas.

Trego, Charles B., geographer, b. 1794; d. 1874. [6]

Tregoe, James Harry, economist, b. Baltimore, Md., 1865; d. Chicago, Ill., Oct. 5, 1935. [10]

Tremain, Henry Edwin, lawyer, b. New York, N.Y., 1840; d. 1910. [10]

Trémaudan, Auguste Henri de, historian and playwright, b. Châteauguay, Que., 1874; d. Los Angeles, Calif., Oct. 29, 1929. [27]

Tremblay, Jules, poet, b. Montreal, Que., 1879; d. Ottawa, Ont., Nov. 28, 1927. [27]

Tremblay, Rémi, poet, b. St. Barnabé, Que., April 2, 1847; d. Guadeloupe, Jan. 31, 1926. [27]

Tremeear, William James, lawyer, b. Bowmanville, Ont., 1864; d. Pasadena, Calif., Sept. 26, 1927. [27]

Trenholm, William Lee, banker, b. Charleston, S.C., 1836; d. New York, N.Y., Jan. 11, 1901. [3b; 10; 34]

Trenholme, Norman Maclaren, historian, b. Montreal, Que., 1874; d. Columbia, Mo., June 11, 1925. [4; 10]

Trent, William Peterfield, educationist, b. Richmond, Va., 1862; d. Hopewell Junction, N.Y., Dec. 7, 1939. [7; 10; 11; 34]

Trepoff, Ivan (pseud.). See Haubold, Herman Arthur.

Trescot, William Henry, historian and diplomat, b. Charleston, S.C., 1822; d. Pendleton, S.C., May 4, 1898. [1; 3; 4; 5; 6; 7; 34]

Trestrail, Burdick A., industrial counselor, b. Kansas City, Mo.; d. Toronto, Ont., Dec. 10, 1949.

Trever, Albert Augustus, historian, b. Calumet county, Wis., 1874; d. Appleton, Wis., April 25, 1940. [10; 11]

Trever, George Henry, educationist, b. Newcastle, England, 1856; d. Atlanta, Ga., 1941. [10; 11]

Trevert, Edward (pseud.). See Bubier, Edward Trevert.

Trevor, Joseph Ellis, educationist, b. Lockport, N.Y., 1864; d. Ithaca, N.Y., May 4, 1941. [10; 11]

Trexler, Samuel Geiss, clergyman, b. Bernville, Pa., 1877; d. New York, N.Y., May 30, 1949. [10; 11]

Trezevant, Mrs. Eva, née **Whitthorne,** essayist, b. Arkansas, 1865; d. 1905. [34]

Trickett, William, lawyer and educationist, b. Leicester, England, 1840; d. Carlisle,, Pa., Aug. 1, 1928. [10; 11]

Tridon, André, psychoanalyst, b. 1877; d. New York, N.Y., Nov. 21, 1922.

Triggs, Oscar Lovell, educationist, b. Greenwood, Ill., 1865; d. Nov. 1930. [4; 10]

Trimble, Harvey Marion, jurist, b. near Wilmington, O., 1842; d. Princeton, Ill., Jan. 10, 1918. [10]

Trimble, Henry, pharmacist, b. 1853; d. St. David's, Pa., Aug. 24, 1898. [4]

Tripler, Charles Stuart, military surgeon, b. 1806; d. 1866. [6]

Triplett, Frank, soldier, fl. 1882-1884.

Triplett, Henry Franklin, educationist, b. 1854; d. Beaumont, Tex., Dec. 14, 1928.

Tripp, Alonzo, educationist, b. Harwick, Mass., 1818; d. Newton, Mass., Dec. 20, 1891. [3b]

Tripp, Bartlett, jurist, b. Harmony, Me., 1842; d. Yankton, S.D., Dec. 8, 1911. [1; 4; 5; 10]

Tripp, George Henry, lawyer, b. South Yarmouth, Mass., 1844; d. Washington, D.C., April 8, 1880. [51]

Tripp, John, clergyman, b. Dartmouth, Mass., 1761; d. 1847. [38]

Trivanovitch, Vaso, educationist, b. Yugoslavia, 1900; d. Agawam, Mass., Nov. 5, 1949.

Troland, Leonard Thompson, research engineer, b. Norwich, Conn., 1889; d. May 27, 1932. [10]

Troop, James, entomologist, b. 1853; d. Champaign, Ill., Oct. 14, 1941.

Trotter, Bernard Freeman, poet, b. Toronto, Ont., 1890; killed in action, France, May 7, 1917. [27]

Trotter, Spencer, educationist, b. Philadelphia, Pa., 1860; d. West Chester, Pa., April 10, 1931. [10]

Trotter, Thomas, clergyman, b. Berwickshire, Scotland, about 1781; d. Antigonish, N.S., 1855. [27]

Troubat, Francis Joseph, lawyer, b. Philadelphia, Pa., 1802; d. near Paris, France, Oct. 8, 1868. [3; 6]

Troubetzkoy, Princess **Amélie,** née **Rives.** See Rives, Amélie.

Trout, Ethel Wendell, editor, b. Philadelphia, Pa., 1878; d. Atlantic City, N.J., Jan. 16, 1935. [10; 11]

Trow, James, politician, b. Montgomeryshire, Wales, 1827; d. Toronto, Ont., Sept. 10, 1892. [3; 27]

Trow, John Fowler, printer, b. Andover, Mass., 1810; d. Orange, N.J., Aug. 8, 1886. [1; 3; 6; 7]

Trowbridge, Catherine Maria, writer of books for children, b. Mansfield, Conn., 1818; d. ? [6]

Trowbridge, Edward Dwight, engineer, b. Turkey, 1870; d. Detroit, Mich., Nov. 24, 1929. [10; 11]

Trowbridge, Francis Bacon, genealogist, b. New Haven, Conn., 1866; d. New Haven, Conn., Dec. 27, 1943. [62]

Trowbridge, John, physicist, b. Boston, Mass., 1843; d. Cambridge, Mass., Feb. 18, 1923. [1; 3; 4; 5; 6; 10]

Trowbridge, John Townsend, journalist and novelist, b. Ogden, N.Y., 1827; d. Arlington, Mass., Feb. 12, 1916. [1; 3; 4; 5; 6; 7; 9; 10; 72]

Trowbridge, Mrs. Mary Elizabeth, née **Day,** historian, b. Sturgis, Mich., 1840; d. New York, N.Y., Oct. 1, 1918. [10; 39]

Trowbridge, Oliver R., lawyer and educationist, d. Bloomington, Ill., April 30, 1937.

Trowbridge, William Petit, engineer, b. Troy, N.Y., 1828; d. New Haven, Conn., Aug. 12, 1892. [1; 3; 4; 6]

Trudeau, Edward Livingston, physician, b. New York, N.Y., 1848; d. Saranac Lake, N.Y., Nov. 15, 1915. [1; 4; 7; 10]

Trudel, François Xavier Anselme, lawyer and politician, b. Ste. Anne de la Pérade, Lower Canada, 1838; d. Jan. 17, 1890. [27]

Trudelle, Charles, priest, b. Charlesbourg, Lower Canada, 1822; d. Quebec, Que., July 14, 1904. [27]

Trudelle, Joseph, librarian, d. Quebec, Que., July 2, 1921. [27]

True, Alfred Charles, civil servant, b. Middletown, Conn., 1853; d. Washington, D.C., April 23, 1929. [1; 10]

True, Charles Kittridge, educationist, b. Portland, Me., 1809; d. Brooklyn, N.Y., June 20, 1878. [3; 6; 7]

True, Eliza S., poet, b. Portland, Me., about 1750; d. ? [38]

True, Hiram L., physician, b. Athens, O., 1845; d. McConnelsville, O., Oct. 22, 1912. [10]

True, John Preston, writer of books for boys, b. Bethel, Me., 1859; d. Waban, Mass., Jan. 14, 1933. [7; 10; 11]

Trueblood, Benjamin Franklin, publicist, b. Salem, Ind., 1847; d. Newton Highlands, Mass., Oct. 26, 1916. [4; 10]

Trueman, George Johnstone, educationist, b. Pointe de Bute, N.B., 1872; d. Sackville, N.B., Feb. 18, 1949. [31a]

Trueman, Howard, historian, b. Pointe de ¡Bute, N.B., 1837; d. Pointe de Bute, N.B., March 22, 1908. [27]

Truesdell, Mrs. Amelia, née **Woodward,** poet, b. Lowell, Mass., 1839; d. Dec. 19, 1912. [35]

Truesdell, Mrs. Helen, poet, fl. 1852-1859. [19]

Truesdell, Seneca Ellis, journalist, b. Geneseo, N.Y., 1852; d. La Crosse, Wis., Dec. 27, 1899. [70]

Truette, Everett Ellsworth, organist, b. Rockland, Mass., 1861; d. Brookline, Mass., Dec. 16, 1933. [10; 11]

Truman, Benjamin Cummings, journalist, b. Providence, R.I., 1835; d. Los Angeles, Calif., July 18, 1916. [1; 3; 6; 7; 10; 35]

Truman, Howard James, poet, d. Philadelphia, Pa., Dec. 11, 1897. [55]

Trumble, Alfred, journalist, fl. 1881-1896.

Trumbull, Annie Eliot, novelist, poet, and playwright, b. Hartford, Conn., 1857; d. Hartford, Conn., Dec. 22, 1949. [2; 7; 8]

Trumbull, Benjamin, clergyman and historian, b. Hebron, Conn., 1735; d. North Haven, Conn., Feb. 2, 1820. [1; 3; 5; 6; 9; 62]

Trumbull, Charles Gallaudet, religious journalist, b. Hartford, Conn., 1872; d. Pasadena, Calif., Jan. 13, 1941. [7; 10; 11]

Trumbull, Gurdon, artist and ornithologist, b. Stonington, Conn., 1841; d. Hartford, Conn., Dec. 28, 1903. [2; 3; 10]

Trumbull, Henry, historian, b. about 1793; d. ? [6; 7]

Trumbull, Henry Clay, clergyman, b. Stonington, Conn., 1830; d. Philadelphia, Pa., Dec. 8, 1903. [1; 3; 4; 5; 6; 7; 10]

Trumbull, James Hammond, historian and philologist, b. Stonington, Conn., 1821; d. Hartford, Conn., Aug. 5, 1897. [1; 3; 4; 5; 6; 7; 9; 62]

Trumbull, James Russell, local historian, b. 1825; d. 1899.

Trumbull, John, poet and jurist, b. Westbury, Conn., 1750; d. Detroit, Mich., May 11, 1831. [1; 3; 5; 6; 7; 9]

Trumbull, John, painter, b. Lebanon, Conn., 1756; d. New York, N.Y., Nov. 10, 1843. [1; 2; 3; 4; 5; 6; 7]

Trumbull, Levi R., journalist, b. Montgomery, N.Y., 1834; d. Paterson, N.J., Oct. 23, 1918. [10]

Trumbull, Matthew Mark, economist, b. London, England, 1826; d. Chicago, Ill., June 11, 1894. [3; 6]

Trumbull, William, lawyer, b. Valparaiso, Chile, 1861; d. New York, N.Y., Jan. 11, 1933. [62]

Trunk, Joseph V., priest and educationist, d. Sioux City, Ia., July, 1940. [21]

Trusta, H. (pseud.). See Phelps, Mrs. Elizabeth, née Stuart.

Tryon, Frederick Gale, economist, b. Minneapolis, Minn., 1892; d. Feb. 15, 1940. [10]

Tryon, George Washington, conchologist, b. Philadelphia, Pa., 1838; d. Philadelphia, Pa., Feb. 5, 1888. [1; 3; 5; 6]

Tubbs, Arthur Lewis, playwright, b. Glens Falls, N.Y., 1867; d. Philadelphia, Pa., Jan. 28, 1946. [7; 10; 11]

Tucker, Benjamin Ricketson, journalist, b. Massachusetts, 1854; d. Monaco, June 22, 1939. [4]

Tucker, Beverley Dandridge, bishop, b. Richmond, Va., 1846; d. Norfolk, Va., Jan. 17, 1930. [10; 11]

Tucker, Beverley Randolph, physician, b. Richmond, Va., 1874; d. Richmond, Va., June 19, 1945. [10]

Tucker, David Hunter, physician, fl. 1837-1848.

Tucker, Ephraim W., traveller, fl. 1839-1844.

Tucker, George, educationist, b. St. George's, Bermuda, 1775; d. Albemarle county, Va., April 10, 1861. [1; 3; 4; 5; 6; 7; 8; 9; 34]

Tucker, George Fox, lawyer and novelist, b. New Bedford, Mass., 1852; d. Feb. 14, 1929. [4; 7; 10]

Tucker, Gideon John, lawyer, journalist and poet, b. New York, N.Y., 1826; d. New York, N.Y., July 7, 1899. [3b]

Tucker, Gilbert Milligan, journalist, b. Albany, N.Y., 1847; d. Albany, N.Y., Jan. 13, 1932. [1; 7; 10; 11]

Tucker, Henry Holcombe, clergyman, b. Warren county, Ga., 1819; d. Atlanta, Ga., Sept. 9, 1889. [1; 3; 4; 5; 34]

Tucker, Henry St. George, jurist, b. Chesterfield county, Va., 1780; d. Winchester, Va., Aug. 28, 1848. [1; 3; 4; 5; 6; 34]

Tucker, Henry St. George, lawyer and politician, b. Winchester, Va., 1853; d. Lexington, Va., July 23, 1932. [1; 4; 5; 10; 11]

Tucker, John Randolph, lawyer, b. Winchester, Va., 1823; d. Lexington, Va., Feb. 13, 1897. [1; 3; 4; 5]

Tucker, Joshua Thomas, clergyman, b. Milton, Mass., 1812; d. Boston, Mass., June 11, 1897. [3; 6; 62]

Tucker, Mrs. Mary Eliza, née **Perine,** poet and journalist, b. Cahawba, Ala., 1838; d. ? [3; 6]

Tucker, Nathaniel Beverley, lawyer and novelist, b. Chesterfield county, Va., 1784; d. Winchester, Va., Aug. 26, 1851. [1; 3; 4; 5; 6; 7; 34]

Tucker, Pomeroy, journalist, b. Palmyra, N.Y., 1802; d. June 30, 1870. [3; 6]

Tucker, St. George, jurist, b. Port Royal, Bermuda, 1752; d. Warminster, Va., Nov. 10, 1827. [1; 3; 4; 5; 6; 7; 34]

Tucker, St. George, lawyer and novelist, b. Winchester, Va., 1828; d. 1863. [34]

Tucker, Mrs. Sarah, née **Fish,** Quaker preacher, b. Portsmouth, R.I., 1779; d. 1840. [3; 6]

Tucker, Walter Leon, clergyman, b. 1871; d. June 8, 1934.

Tucker, Willard Davis, local historian, b. 1841; d. 1927.

Tucker, William Bowman, clergyman, b. London, England, 1859; d. Bristol, England, Aug. 11, 1934. [11; 27]

Tucker, William Howard, local historian, b. Sharon, Vt., 1826; d. Hartford, Vt., Nov. 12, 1895.

Tucker, William Jewett, educationist, b. Griswold, Conn., 1839; d. Hanover, N.H., Sept. 29, 1926. [1; 4; 5; 10]

Tuckerman, Alfred, bibliographer, b. New York, N.Y., 1848; d. Newport, R.I., May 25, 1925. [10]

Tuckerman, Arthur Lyman, architect, b. New York, N.Y., 1861; d. New York, N.Y., 1892. [3]

Tuckerman, Bayard, biographer and genealogist, b. New York, N.Y., 1855; d. Ipswich, Mass., Oct. 20, 1923. [1; 4; 5; 7; 10; 51]

Tuckerman, Charles Keating, diplomat, b. Boston, Mass., 1821; d. Florence, Italy, Feb. 26, 1896. [3; 4; 5; 6]

Tuckerman, Edward, botanist, b. Boston, Mass., 1817; d. Amherst, Mass., March 15, 1886. [1; 3; 4; 5; 6]

Tuckerman, Frederick, naturalist, b. Greenfield, Mass., 1857; d. Amherst, Mass., Nov. 8, 1929. [1; 10]

Tuckerman, Frederick Goddard, poet, b. Boston, Mass., 1821; d. Greenfield, Mass., May 14, 1877. [1; 3; 7; 51]

Tuckerman, Henry Theodore, littérateur, b. Boston, Mass., 1813; d. New York, N.Y., Dec. 17, 1871. [1; 3 ;4; 5; 6; 7; 9; 71]

Tuckerman, Joseph, clergyman, b. Boston, Mass., 1778; d. Havana, Cuba, April 20, 1840. [1; 3; 4; 5; 6]

Tuckley, Henry, clergyman, d. Aug. 23, 1909.

Tudor, William, merchant, diplomat, and littérateur, b. Boston, Mass., 1779; d. Rio de Janeiro, Brazil, March 9, 1830. [1; 3; 4; 5; 6; 7; 71]

Tuel, John E., miscellaneous writer, fl. 1843-1867. [7]

Tufts, James Hayden, educationist, b. Monson, Mass., 1862; d. Berkeley, Calif., Aug. 5, 1942. [4; 7; 10; 11; 62]

Tufts, Marshall, clergyman, b. Lexington, Mass., 1802; d. Lexington, Mass., May 18, 1855. [51]

Tufts, William Whittemore, novelist, b. 1832; d. 1901.

Tuley, Henry Enos, physician, b. Louisville, Ky., 1870; d. Louisville, Ky., Oct. 22, 1923. [4; 10; 11]

Tuley, William Floyd, genealogist, b. 1836; d. New Albany, Ind., Oct. 4, 1914.

Tullidge, Edward Wheelock, historian and biographer, b. 1829; d. Salt Lake City, Utah, May 21, 1894.

Tully, Jim, novelist, b. near St. Marys, O., 1891; d. Canoga Park, Calif., June 22, 1947. [7; 10; 11; 35]

Tully, William, physician, b. Saybrook Point, Conn., 1785; d. Springfield, Mass., Feb. 28, 1859. [1; 3; 6]

Tunell, George Gerard, economist, b. Chicago, Ill.; d. Chicago, Ill., April 29, 1942.

Tunison, Joseph Salathiel, journalist, b. near Bucyrus, O., 1849; d. 1916. [7; 10]

Tunstall, Robert Williamson, educationist, b. Norfolk, Va., 1851; d. Nov., 1917. [10]

Tuomey, Michael, geologist, b. Cork, Ireland, 1805; d. Tuscaloosa, Ala., March 30, 1857. [3; 4; 6; 34]

Tupper, Mrs. Edith Sessions, novelist, d. Aug. 3, 1927. [7]

Tupper, Henry Allen, clergyman, b. Charleston, S.C., 1828; d. Richmond, Va., March 27, 1902. [1; 3; 4; 6; 10; 34]

Tupper, Henry Allen, clergyman, b. Washington, Ga., 1856; d. Baltimore, Md., Sept. 29, 1927. [10]

Turchin, John Basil, soldier, b. Russia, 1822; d. Anna, Ill., June 19, 1901. [3; 4; 10]

Turcotte, Louis Philippe, historian, b. St. Jean, Isle d'Orléans, Que., 1842; d. Quebec, Que., April 3, 1878. [27]

Turell, Ebenezer, clergyman, b. Boston, Mass., 1702; d. Medford, Mass., Dec. 8, 1778. [3; 4; 6]

Turk, Morris Howland, clergyman, b. Greenwood, Ind., 1867; d. Los Angeles, Calif., March 2, 1939. [10]

Turnbull, Mrs. Francese Hubbard, née Litchfield, novelist, b. New York, N.Y.; d. Baltimore, Md., Feb. 28, 1927. [10]

Turnbull, Laurence, physician b. Lanarkshire, Scotland, 1821; d. Philadelphia, Pa., Oct. 22, 1900. [3; 6; 10]

Turnbull, Mrs. Lawrence. See Turnbull, Mrs. Francese Hubbard, née Litchfield.

Turnbull, Robert, clergyman, b. Linlithgowshire, Scotland, 1809; d. Hartford, Conn., Nov. 20, 1877. [3; 4; 6]

Turnbull, Robert James, political writer, b. New Smyrna, Fla., 1775; d. Charleston, S.C., June 15, 1833. [1; 3; 5; 6; 34]

Turnbull, Stephen Hague, lawyer, d. 1886.

Turnbull, William Paterson, ornithologist, b. Scotland, 1830; d. Philadelphia, Pa., July 5, 1871. [3; 6]

Turner, Bessie A., novelist, fl. 1875-1884.

Turner, Douglas Kellogg, clergyman, b. Stockbridge, Mass., 1823; d. Hartsville, Pa., March 8, 1902. [10; 62]

Turner, Edward Raymond, educationist, b. Baltimore, Md., 1881; d. Baltimore, Md., Dec. 31, 1929. [1; 7; 10]

Turner, Mrs. Eliza, née Sproat, poet, b. 1826; d. 1903.

Turner, Frederick Jackson, historian, b. Portage, Wis., 1861; d. Pasadena, Calif., March 14, 1932. [1; 4; 7; 10]

Turner, George, jurist, fl. 1790-1836.

Turner, Herbert Barclay, clergyman, b. Brooklyn, N.Y., 1852; d. Washington, Conn., May 1, 1927. [4; 45]

Turner, Herbert Bryant, traveller, b. 1871; d. Genoa, Italy, Oct. 27, 1937.

Turner, James William, educationist, b. 1848; d. Evansville, Ind., May 13, 1932.

Turner, Jonathan Baldwin, publicist, b. Templeton, Mass., 1805; d. Jacksonville, Ill., Jan. 10, 1899. [1; 62]

Turner, Orsamus, local historian, b. Ontario county, N.Y., 1801; d. near Lockport, N.Y., March 21, 1855.

Turner, Samuel Epes, lawyer, b. Baltimore, Md., 1846; d. Cambridge, Mass., May 15, 1896. [51]

Turner, Samuel Hulbeart, clergyman, b. Philadelphia, Pa., 1790; d. New York, N.Y., Dec. 21, 1861. [1; 3; 5; 6]

Turner, Thomas Sloss, journalist and poet, b. Kentucky, 1860; d. ? [8; 34]

Turner, Walter Victor, engineer, b. Essex, England, 1866; d. Wilkinsburg, Pa., Jan. 9, 1919. [1; 10]

Turner, William, bishop, b. Ireland, 1871; d. Buffalo, N.Y., July 10, 1936. [10; 21]

Turner, William Smith, clergyman, b. 1826; d. Spokane, Wash, Nov. 11, 1920.

Turner, William Wilberforce, novelist, b. Georgia, 1830; d. ? [34]

Turney, Edmund, clergyman, b. Easton, Conn., 1816; d. Washington, D.C., Sept. 28, 1872. [67]

Turnley, Parmenas Taylor, soldier, b. Dandridge, Tenn., 1821; d. Highland Park, Ill., 1911. [10]

Tuthill, Franklin, journalist, b. Greenport, Long Island, N.Y., 1822; d. Brooklyn, N.Y., Aug. 27, 1865. [45]

Tuthill, Mrs. Louisa Caroline, née Huggins, miscellaneous writer, b. New Haven, Conn., 1798; d. Princeton, N.J., June 1, 1879. [3; 6; 7]

Tuthill, William Burnet, architect, b. New York, N.Y., 1855; d. New York, N.Y., Aug. 25, 1929. [1; 10]

Tuttle, Albert Henry, biologist, b. Cuyahoga Falls, 1844; d. Berkeley, Calif., Jan. 23, 1927. [10; 13]

Tuttle, Albert Henry, surgeon, d. Brookline, Mass., March 1, 1926.

Tuttle, Alexander Harrison, clergyman, b. Bordentown, N.J., 1844; d. East Orange, N.J., Dec. 4, 1932. [10; 11]

Tuttle, Charles Herbert, journalist and educationist, b. Bennington, Vt., 1846; d. Binghampton, N.Y., June 21, 1894. [1; 3; 5; 6]

Tuttle, Charles Richard, historian and publicist, b. 1848; d. ? [27]

Tuttle, Charles Wesley, historian, b. Newfield, Me., 1829; d. Boston, Mass., July 17, 1881. [1; 3]

Tuttle, Daniel Sylvester, bishop, b. Windham, N.Y., 1837; d. St. Louis, Mo., April 17, 1923. [1; 4; 5; 10]

Tuttle, Edmund Bostwick, army chaplain, b. 1815; d. 1881.

Tuttle, Edwin Hotchkiss, editor, b. New Haven, Conn., 1879; d. Washington, D. C., Jan. 25, 1939. [62]

Tuttle, Mrs. Emma, née Rood, poet, b. Braceville, O , 1839; d. ? [7; 10]

Tuttle, George, story-writer, b. 1804; d. 1872.

Tuttle, George Marvine, physician, b. Morris, N.Y., 1866; d. St. Louis, Mo., Sept. 2, 1926. [10]

Tuttle, Herbert. See Tuttle, Charles Herbert.

Tuttle, Hudson, spiritualist, b. Berlin Heights, O., 1836; d. 1910. [3; 6; 10]

Tuttle, James Harvey, clergyman, b. Salisbury, N.Y., 1824; d. New York, N.Y., Dec. 8, 1903. [70]

Tuttle, James Percival, physician, b. 1857; d. Jan. 31, 1913.

Tuttle, Joseph Farrand, educationist, b. Bloomfield, N.J., 1818; d. Indiana, June, 1901. [3; 6; 10]

Tuttle, Mrs. Maria Jeannette, née Brookings, historian, b. Athol, Mass., 1864; d. Scarsdale, N.Y., Jan. 22, 1938.

Tuttle, Mrs. Mary McArthur, née Thompson, artist and novelist, b. Hillsboro, O., 1849; d. Hillsboro, O., Sept. 1, 1916. [4; 10]

Tuttle, Samuel Lawrence, clergyman, d. 1866. [56]

Tuttle, Romulus Morrison, poet, b. 1842; d. 1904. [34]

Tuttle, Sarah, writer on missions, fl. 1830-1842.

Twain, Mark (pseud.). See Clemens, Samuel Langhorne.

Tweed, Benjamin Franklin, educationist, b. 1811; d. 1896.

Tweedy, Frank, short-story writer, b. New York, N.Y., 1854; d. July 1, 1937. 10]

Twells, Mrs. Julia Helen, née Watts, novelist, fl. 1875-1878. [6]

Twells, Julia Helen, novelist, fl. 1896-1919.

Twichell, Joseph Hopkins, clergyman, b. Southington, Conn., 1838; d. Hartford, Conn., Dec. 20, 1918. [1; 7; 10; 62]

Twing, Mrs. Carolinn Edna Skinner, spiritualistic medium, b. 1844; d. ?

Twiss, George Ransom, educationist, b. Columbus, O., 1863; d. Fort Myers, Fla., Feb. 16, 1944. [10; 11]

Twitchell, Mrs. Hannah, née Stackpole, biographer, b. 1851; d. ?

Twitchell, Ralph Emerson, lawyer, b. Ann Arbor, Mich., 1859; d. Los Angeles, Calif., Aug. 26, 1925. [10; 11]

Twombly, Alexander Stevenson, clergyman, b. Boston, Mass., 1832; d. Newton, Mass., Nov. 19, 1907. [10; 62]

Tydings, Richard, clergyman, b. Anne Arundel county, Md., 1783; d. Bullitt county, Ky., Oct. 3, 1865. [34]

Tygel, Zelig, Zionist, b. Warsaw, Poland, 1890; d. New York, N.Y., March 12, 1937.

Tyler, Albert Franklin, radiologist, b. Logan county, Ill., 1881; d. Omaha, Neb., Feb. 25, 1944. [11]

Tyler, Bennet, clergyman, b. Middlebury, Conn., 1783; d. South Windsor, Conn., May 14, 1858. [1; 3; 4; 5; 6; 62]

Tyler, Charles Mellen, clergyman, b. Limington, Me., 1832; d. Scranton, Pa., May 15, 1918. [1; 10; 62]

Tyler, Charles Waller, jurist and novelist, b. 1841; d. Clarksville, Tenn., May 27, 1920.

Tyler, Harry Walter, educationist, b. Ipswich, Mass., 1863; d. Washington, D.C., Feb. 3, 1938. [10]

Tyler, Henry Mather, educationist, b. Amherst, Mass., 1843; d. Northampton, Mass., Nov. 3, 1931. [10]

Tyler, John Mason, biologist, b. Amherst, Mass., 1851; d. Amherst, Mass., April 12, 1929. [4; 10; 11]

Tyler, Josiah, missionary, b. Hanover, N.H., 1823; d. Asheville, N.C., Dec. 20, 1895. [45]

Tyler, Lyon Gardiner, educationist, b. Charles City county, Va., 1853; d. Feb. 12, 1935. [1a; 3; 7; 10; 11]

Tyler, Mrs. Mary, née Palmer, "American matron", b. Watertown, Mass., 1775; d. 1866. [43]

Tyler, Mason Whiting, lawyer, b. Amherst, Mass., 1840; d. New York, N.Y., July 2, 1907. [4; 10]

Tyler, Mason Whiting, educationist, b. Amherst, Mass., 1884; d. Minneapolis, Minn., March 15, 1923. [45]

Tyler, Moses Coit, educationist, b. Griswold, Conn., 1835; d. Ithaca, N.Y., Dec. 28, 1900. [1; 2; 3; 4; 5; 6; 7; 9; 10]

Tyler, Ransom Hubert, jurist, b. Franklin county, Mass., 1815; d. Fulton, N.Y., Nov. 21, 1881. [1; 3; 4; 6]

Tyler, Robert, lawyer, politician, and poet, b. Charles City county, Va., 1816; d. Montgomery, Ala., Dec. 3, 1877. [1; 3; 4; 6; 7; 34]

Tyler, Royall, jurist, novelist, and playwright, b. Boston, Mass., 1757; d. Brattleboro, Vt., Aug. 26, 1826. [1; 3; 4; 5; 6; 7; 8; 9; 43; 51]

Tyler, Royall, jurist, b. Brattleboro, Vt., 1812; d. Brattleboro, Vt., Oct. 27, 1896. [43]

Tyler, Samuel, lawyer, b. Prince George's county, Md., 1809; d. Georgetown, D.C., Dec. 15, 1877. [1; 3; 4; 5; 6; 34]

Tyler, William Seymour, educationist, b. Harford, Pa., 1810; d. Amherst, Mass., Nov. 19, 1897. [1; 3 4; 6]

Tyndale, Julius Hilgard, physician, b. 1843; d. Lincoln, Neb., June 7, 1929.

Tyndall, Charles Herbert, clergyman, b. Alton, N.Y., 1857; d. Mount Vernon, N.Y., Feb. 22, 1935. [10; 11]

Tyng, Dudley Atkins, clergyman, b. Prince George county, Md., 1825; d near Philadelphia, Pa., April 19, 1858. [3; 6]

Tyng, Stephen Higginson, clergyman, b. Newburyport, Mass., 1800; d. Irvington, N.Y., Sept. 4, 1885. [1; 3; 4; 5; 6; 7]

Tyng, Stephen Higginson, clergyman, b. Philadelphia, Pa., 1839; d. Paris, France, Nov. 17, 1898. [3; 6]

Typist, Topsy (pseud.). See Miner, Enoch N.

Tyrer, Alfred Henry, clergyman, b. 1870; d. Toronto, Ont., April 28, 1942. [27]

Tyrrell, Charles Alfred, physician, b. 1846; d. ?

Tyrrell, Henry, journalist, b. 1865; d. New York, N.Y., Jan. 13, 1933. [10]

Tyrrell, James Williams, explorer, b. Weston, Ont., 1863; d. near Hamilton, Ont., Jan. 16, 1945. [27]

Tyson, James, physician, b. Philadelphia, Pa., 1841; d. Philadelphia, Pa., Feb. 21, 1919. [1; 3; 5; 6]

Tyson, Job Roberts, lawyer and politician, b. Philadelphia, Pa., 1803; d. Philadelphia, Pa., June 27, 1858. [1; 3; 6]

Tyson, John Shoemaker, biographer, b. 1797; d. 1864.

Tyson, Philip Thomas, chemist, b. Baltimore, Md., 1799; d. Baltimore, Md., Dec. 16, 1877. [3; 4; 6]

Tyson, Stuart Lawrence, clergyman, b. Penllyn, Pa., 1873; d. New York, N.Y., Sept. 16, 1932. [10; 11]

Tytler, James, miscellaneous writer, b. Brechin, Scotland, about 1747; d. near Salem, Mass., 1805. [3; 6]

U

Udden, Johan August, geologist, b. Sweden, 1859; d. Austin, Tex., Jan. 5, 1932. [10; 11]

Udell, John, pioneer, b. 1795; d ?

Ufford, Walter Shepard, social worker, b. Cambridge, Mass., 1859; d. Washington, D.C., 1940. [10]

Uhl, Willis Lemon, educationist, b. Angola, Ind., 1885; d. Seattle, Wash., Feb. 28, 1940. [10; 11]

Ulman, Joseph Nathan, jurist, b. Baltimore, Md., 1878; d. Baltimore, Md., April 18, 1943. [10]

Ulmann, Albert, historian, b. New York, N.Y., 1861; d. New York, N.Y., Oct. 8, 1948. [7]

Ulrich, Bessie Kenyon, writer of books for children, b. 1859; d. Philadelphia, Pa., Sept. 29, 1927.

Ulrich, Charles Kenmore, journalist and novelist, b. 1859; d. Long Island City, N.Y., July 5, 1941. [7]

Ulyat, William Clarke, clergyman, b. 1823; d. Princeton, N.J., Dec. 19, 1905.

Umbstaetter, Herman Daniel, journalist and writer of short stories, b. Parma, O., 1851; d. Lovell, Me., Nov. 25, 1913. [10]

Umphraville, Angus, poet, b. 1798; d. ?

Uncle Dudley (pseud.). See Russell, Morris Craw.

Uncle Jesse (pseud.). See Babb, Clement Edwin.

Uncle Remus (pseud.). See Harris, Joel Chandler.

Uncle Toby (pseud.). See North, Elisha.

Underhill, Andrew Findlay, clergyman, b. Brooklyn, N.Y., 1859; d. Brookline, Mass., May 16, 1931.

Underhill, Edward Fitch, stenographer, b. Wolcott, N.Y., 1830; d. New York, N.Y., June 18, 1898. [3]

Underhill, Frank Pell, educationist, b. Brooklyn, N.Y., 1877; d. New Haven, Conn., June 28, 1932. [1; 10; 11; 62]

Underhill, Harry Clay, lawyer, b. 1858; d. Brooklyn, N.Y., May 1, 1918.

Underhill, Mrs. Lora Altine, née Woodbury, genealogist, b. 1844; d. Brighton, Mass., April 18, 1938.

Underhill, Mrs. Zoe, née Dana, compiler and translator, b. West Roxbury, Mass., 1847; d. Dec. 5, 1934. [7]

Underwood, Adin Baliou, soldier, b. Milford. Mass., 1828; d. Boston, Mass., Jan. 14, 1888. [3; 4]

Underwood, Almon, clergyman, b. Monson, Mass., 1809; d. Irvington, N.J., June 10, 1887. [6]

Underwood, Benjamin Franklin, journalist, b. New York, N.Y., 1839; d. Westerly, R.I., Nov. 10, 1914. [1; 10]

Underwood, Bert Elias, photographer, b. Oxford, Ill., 1862; d. Tucson, Ariz., Dec. 27, 1943.

Underwood, Francis Henry, lawyer, novelist, and biographer, b. Enfield, Mass., 1825; d. Edinburgh, Scotland, Aug. 7, 1894. [1; 3; 4; 5; 6; 7; 8; 9]

Underwood, Horace Grant, missionary, b. London, England, 1859; d. Atlantic City, N.J., Oct. 12, 1916. [1; 10]

Underwood, John, poet, b. 1818; d. ?

Underwood, John Curtis, poet, b. Rockford, Ill., 1874; d. near Santa Cruz, N.M., Jan. 14, 1949. [10]

Underwood, Mrs. Lillias Stirling, née Horton, physician, b. 1851; d. Seoul, Korea, Oct. 20, 1921.

Underwood, Loring, landscape architect, b. Belmont, Mass., 1874; d. Boston, Mass., Jan. 13, 1930. [1; 10]

Underwood, Lucien Marcus, botanist, b. New Woodstock, N.Y., 1853; d. Redding, Conn., Nov. 16, 1907. [1; 3; 4; 5; 6; 10]

Underwood, Oscar Wilder, politician, b. Louisville, Ky., 1862; d. Woodlawn, Va., Jan. 25, 1929. [1; 5; 10]

Underwood, Mrs. Sara A., née Francis, suffragist, b. Penrith, England, 1838; d. Quincy, Ill., 1911. [10]

Underwood, William Lyman, naturalist, b. Belmont, Mass., 1864; d. Belmont, Mass., Jan. 28, 1929. [10; 11]

Unger, Gladys Buchanan, playwright, b. 1885; d. New York, N.Y., May 25, 1940. [7; 35]

Uniacke, Richard John, politician, b. Castletown, county Cork, Ireland, 1753; d. Mount Uniacke, N.S., Oct. 11, 1830. [27]

Uno (pseud.). See Baker, George Melville.

Upchurch, John Jordan, labour organizer, b. Franklin county, N.C., 1820; d. Steelville, Mo., Jan. 18, 1887. [1; 3]

Updike, Daniel Berkeley, printer, b. Providence, R.I., 1860; d. Boston, Mass., Dec. 28, 1941. [7; 10]

Updike, Wilkins, lawyer, b. Kingston, R.I., 1874; d. Kingston, R.I., Jan. 14, 1867. [3; 4; 6]

Updyke, Frank Arthur, educationist, b. Tioga county, Pa., 1866; d. Sept. 20, 1918. [10]

Upham, Albert Gookin, physician, b. Rochester, N.H., 1819; d. Boston, Mass., June 16, 1847. [3]

470

Upham, Alfred Horatio, educationist, b. Eaton, O., 1877; d. Oxford, O., Feb. 17, 1945. [10; 11]

Upham, Arthur Aquila, educationist, b. 1853; d. 1929.

Upham, Charles Wentworth, clergyman and historian, b. Saint John, N.B., 1802; d. Salem, Mass., June 15, 1875. [1; 3; 4; 6; 7]

Upham, Francis Bourne, clergyman, b. Bristol, R.I., 1862; d. Mamaroneck, N.Y., March 19, 1941. [10; 11]

Upham, Francis William, educationist, b. Rochester, N.H., 1817; d. New York, N.Y., Oct. 17, 1895. [3; 6]

Upham, Frank Kidder, soldier and genealogist, b. 1841; d. ?

Upham, Mrs. Grace Le Baron, née **Locke,** writer of books for boys and girls, b. Lowell, Mass., 1845; d. 1916. [7; 10]

Upham, Samuel Curtis, traveller, b. Montpelier, Vt., 1819; d. Philadelphia, Pa., June 29, 1885. [3; 43]

Upham, Thomas Cogswell, philosopher, b. Deerfield, N.H., 1799; d. New York, N.Y., April 2, 1872. [1; 3; 4; 6]

Upham, Warren, geologist and archaeologist, b. Amherst, N.H., 1850; d. St. Paul, Minn., Jan. 29, 1934. [1; 4; 5; 10; 11; 70]

Upham, William Phineas, archivist, b. Salem, Mass., 1836; d. Newtonville, Mass., Nov. 23, 1905. [51]

Upjohn, James Atchison, clergyman, b. about 1838; d. 1908.

Upright, Mrs. Blanche, née **Caro,** novelist, b. San Francisco, Calif., Feb. 22, 1880; d. Palm Springs, Calif., April 3, 1948. [35]

Upshur, Abel Parker, politician, b. Northampton county, Va., 1790; d. near Washington, D.C., Feb. 28, 1844. [1; 3; 5; 6; 34]

Upshur, John Nottingham, physician, b. Norfolk, Va., 1848; d. Richmond, Va., Dec. 10, 1924. [10; 11]

Upson, Arthur Wheelock, poet, b. Camden, N.Y., 1877; d. Bemidji, Minn., Aug. 14, 1908. [7; 10; 70]

Upson, Henry Swift, physician, b. 1859; d. 1914.

Upton, Emory, soldier, b. Batavia, N.Y., 1839; d. San Francisco, Calif., March 14, 1881. [1; 3; 4; 5; 6]

Upton, Francis Henry, lawyer, b. Salem, Mass., 1814; d. New York, N.Y., June 25, 1876. [3; 6]

Upton, George Putnam, journalist and music critic, b. Roxbury, Mass., 1834; d. Chicago, Ill., May 19, 1919. [1; 3; 4; 5; 6; 7; 10]

Upton, Mrs. Harriet, née **Taylor,** historian, b. Ravenna, O.; d. Pasadena, Calif., Nov. 2, 1945. [10; 11]

Upton, Jacob Kenrick, lawyer and civil servant, b. Wilmot, N.H., 1837; d. 1902. [3; 10]

Upton, Ralph Richard, educationist, b. Portland, Ore., 1869; d. near Wanatah, Ind., Aug. 5, 1935. [62]

Upton, Mrs. Susan Condé, née **Osgood,** poet, b. Verona, N.Y., 1845; d. ?. [35]

Upton, Wheelock Samuel, lawyer, b. Salem, Mass., 1811; d. Carrollton, La., Oct. 18, 1860. [3]

Upton, Winslow, astronomer and meteorologist, b. Salem, Mass., 1853; d. Providence, R.I., Jan. 8, 1914. [1; 3; 4; 10]

Urban, John W., soldier, fl. 1860-1892.

Urbino, Mrs. Levina, née **Buoncuore,** educationist, fl. 1854-1884. [6]

Ure, George P., journalist, b. Scotland; d. Montreal, Canada, Aug. 22, 1860. [27]

Urie, Mrs. Mary Le Baron, née **Andrews,** novelist, b. 1842; d. 1894.

Urmy, Clarence Thomas, poet and musician, b. San Francisco, Calif., 1858; d. San José, Calif., June 2, 1923. [10; 35]

Urmy, William Smith, clergyman, b. Ossining, N.Y., 1830; d. Berkeley, Calif., June 7, 1907.

Urner, Nathan D., novelist, fl. 1882-1891.

Usher, Edward Preston, lawyer and railway official, b. Lynn, Mass., 1851; d. Dec. 26, 1923. [4; 10; 51]

Usher, Ellis Baker, historian, b. 1852; d. Milwaukee, Wis., April 21, 1931.

Utley, Henry Munson, librarian, b. Plymouth, Mich., 1836; d. Detroit, Mich., Feb. 16, 1917. [4; 10]

Utley, George Burwell, librarian, b. Hartford, Conn., 1876; d. Winsted, Conn., Oct. 4, 1946. [7; 10]

Utter, Mrs. Rebecca, née **Palfrey,** poet, b. Barnstable, Mass., 1844; d. 1905. [7; 10]

Utter, Robert Palfrey, educationist, b. Olympia, Wash., 1875; d. Berkeley, Calif., Feb. 17, 1936. [7; 10; 11]

V

Vaché, Alexander F., physician, b. 1800; d. 1857.

Vahey, John W., priest, fl. 1875-1890. [21]

Vail, Albert Lenox, clergyman, b. La Grange, Tex., 1844; d. Philadelphia, Pa., March 5, 1935.

Vail, Alfred, inventor, b. Morristown, N.J., 1807; d. Morristown, N.J., Jan. 18, 1859. [1; 3; 4; 5; 6]

Vail, Charles Henry, clergyman, b. Tully, N.Y., 1866; d. Auburn, N.Y., June 15, 1924. [4; 10]

Vail, Henry Hobart, publisher, b. Pomfret, Vt., 1839; d. Woodstock, Vt., Sept. 2, 1925. [7; 10]

Vail, Isaac Newton, geologist, b. 1840; d. 1912.

Vail, Stephen Montford, clergyman, b. Union Vale, N.Y., 1816; d. Jersey City, N.J., Nov. 26, 1880. [1; 3; 6]

Vail, Theodore Newton, telephone executive, b. near Minerva, O., 1845; d. Baltimore, Md., April 16, 1920. [1; 10]

Vail, Thomas Hubbard, bishop, b. Richmond, Va., 1812; d. Bryn Mawr, Pa., Oct. 6, 1889. [3; 4; 5; 6; 34]

Vaile, Mrs. Charlotte Marion, née White, writer of books for girls, b. Brookfield, Mass., 1854; d. Denver, Colo., July 10, 1902. [8]

Vaile, William Newell, lawyer, b. Kokomo, Ind., 1876; d. Rocky Mountain National Park, Colo., July 2, 1927. [10; 62]

Vaill, Theodore Frelinghuysen, soldier, b. 1832; d. 1875.

Vaka, Demetra. See Brown, Mrs. Demetra, née Vaka.

Vale, Euphemia. See Blake, Mrs. Euphemia née Vale.

Vale, Gilbert, educationist and journalist, b. London, England, 1788; d. Brooklyn, N.Y., Aug. 17, 1866. [3; 7]

Valentine, David Thomas, historian, b. East Chester, N.Y., 1801; d. New York, N.Y., Feb. 25, 1869. [1; 3; 4; 6; 7]

Valentine, Ferdinand Charles, physician, b. 1851; d. 1910. [6]

Valentine, Jane (pseud.). See Meeker, Mrs. Nellie J.

Valentine, Milton, theologian, b. near Uniontown, Md., 1825; d. Gettysburg, Pa., Feb. 7, 1906. [3; 5; 10]

Valentine, Thomas Weston, genealogist, b. 1818; d. 1879.

Valentine, William, lecturer and entertainer, fl. 1849-1859.

Valentino, Rudolph, motion picture actor, b. Italy, 1895; d. New York, N.Y., Aug. 23, 1926. [2a; 10]

Vallandigham, Clement Laird, politician, b. New Lisbon, O., 1820; d. Lebanon, O., June 17, 1871. [1; 3; 4; 5; 6]

Vallandigham, Edward Noble, educationist, b. 1885; d. Seville, Spain, 1930.

Vallandigham, James Laird, clergyman, b. New Lisbon, O., 1812; d. ? [5]

Vallée, Arthur, physician, b. Quebec, Que., 1882; d. Quebec, Que., Jan. 8, 1939. [27]

Van Alstyne, Mrs. Frances Jane, née Crosby. See Crosby, Fanny.

Van Alstyne, Lawrence, genealogist, b. 1839; d. Sharon, Conn., Nov. 30, 1923.

Van Amburgh, Fred De Witt, journalist, b. Newburgh, N.Y., 1866; d. Binghampton, N.Y., Oct. 23, 1934. [7; 10]

Van Amringe, John Howard, educationist, b. Philadelphia, Pa., 1835; d. New York, N.Y., Sept. 10, 1915. [1; 4; 10]

Van Antwerp, David Davis, clergyman, b. Rensselaer county, N.Y., 1822; d. Idaho Springs, Colo., Dec. 20, 1887.

Van Antwerp, William Clarkson, banker, b. Omaha, Neb., 1867; d. California, Feb. 17, 1938. [10]

Vanardy, Varick (pseud.). See Dey, Frederick Van Rensselaer.

Van Arkel, Garret (pseud.). See Buffett, Edward Payson.

Van Arsdale, Henry, physician, d. 1864.

Van Bibber, Thomas Emory, poet, b. 1812; d. 1881.

Van Brunt, Henry, architect, b. Boston, Mass., 1932; d. Kansas City, Mo., April 8, 1903. [1; 4; 10; 51]

Van Buren, Mrs. Alicia, née Keisker, poet, b. Louisville, Ky., 1860; d. Louisville, Ky., April 11, 1922. [10]

Van Buren, James Heartt, bishop, b. Watertown, N.Y., 1850; d. Easton, Pa., July 9, 1917. [4; 10; 62]

Van Buren, John Dash, civil engineer, b. New York, N.Y., 1838; d. 1905. [3]

Van Buren, Martin, eighth president of the United States, b. Kinderhook, N.Y., 1782; d. Kinderhook, N.Y., July 24, 1862. [1; 2; 3; 4; 5; 6; 7]

Van Buren, William Holme, surgeon, b. Philadelphia, Pa., 1819; d. New York, N.Y., March 25, 1883. [1; 3; 4; 6; 62]

Vance, Arthur Turner, editor, b. Scranton, Pa., 1872; d. New York, N.Y., Sept. 8, 1930. [7; 10]

Vance, Hiram Albert, educationist, b. Frankfort, N.Y., 1860; d. 1906. [10]

Vance, James Isaac, clergyman, b. Arcadia, Tenn., 1862; d. Blowing Rock, N.C., Nov. 24, 1939. [7; 10; 11; 34]

Vance, John Thomas, law librarian, b. Lexington, Ky., 1884; d. Lexington, Ky., April 12, 1943. [10]

Vance, Joseph Hardcastle, lawyer, d. Ann Arbor, Mich., Dec. 23, 1900.

Vance, Louis Joseph, novelist, b. Washington, D.C., 1879; d. New York, N.Y., Dec. 16, 1933. [1a; 2a; 7; 10; 11]

Vance, Robert Brank, soldier, politician, and poet, b. near Asheville, N.C., 1828; d. Alexander, near Asheville, N.C., Nov. 28, 1899. [34]

Vance, William Reynolds, lawyer and educationist, b. Middletown, Ky., 1870; d. New Haven, Conn., Oct. 23, 1940. [10]

Vance, Wilson, journalist and novelist, b. Findlay, O., 1846; d. Chattanooga, Tenn., Nov. 10, 1911. [10]

Van Cleef, Frank Louis, educationist, b. Wellington, O., 1863; d. Brooklyn, N.Y., March 19, 1942.

Van Cleve, Mrs. Charlotte Ouisconsin, née Clark, pioneer, b. Prairie du Chien, Wis., 1819; d. Minneapolis, Minn., April 1, 1907. [70]

Van Cortlandt, Edward, physician, b. Newfoundland, 1805; d. Ottawa, Ont., March 25, 1875. [27]

Van Cott, Mrs. Maggie, née Newton, revivalist, b. 1830; d. ?

Vandegrift, Margaret (pseud.). See Janvier, Margaret Thomson.

Van Deman, Esther Boise, archaeologist, b. South Salem, O., 1862; d. Rome, Italy, May 3, 1937. [10; 11]

Van Denburg, Marvin W., physician, b. 1843; d. Mount Vernon, N.Y., Dec. 8, 1921.

Van Denburgh, Mary Turrill, short-story writer, b. San Francisco, Calif., 1865; d. March 8, 1907. [35]

Vandenhoff, George, actor, b. Liverpool, England, 1813; d. Brighton, England, June 16, 1885. [1; 3; 4; 6; 9]

Vanderbilt, Mrs. Gertrude L., née Lefferts, local historian, b. 1824; d. Brooklyn, N.Y., Jan. 5, 1902.

Vanderburgh, Frederick Augustus, clergyman, b. Thornhill, N.Y., 1847; d. New York, N.Y., Oct. 29, 1923.

Vanderlip, Frank Arthur, banker, b. Aurora, Ill., 1864; d. New York, N.Y., June 29, 1937. [4; 10]

Vander Meulen, John Marinus, clergyman, b. Milwaukee, Wis., 1870; d. Chicago, Ill., June 7, 1936. [10]

Van der Naillen, Albert, engineer, b. Belgium, 1830; d. Oakland, Calif., Oct. 27, 1928. [10; 35]

Vanderpoel, Mrs. Emily, née Noyes, artist, b. New York, N.Y., 1842; d. New York, N.Y., Feb. 20, 1939. [7; 10; 11]

Vanderpoel, John Henry, artist, b. Holland, 1857; d. St. Louis, Mo., May 2, 1911. [10]

Vanderslice, John Mitchell, historian, b. 1846; d. Philadelphia, Pa., March 12, 1915.

Vandersloot, Jacob Samuel, clergyman, b. 1834; d. 1882.

VanderSmissen, William Henry, educationist, b. Toronto, Ont., Aug. 18, 1844; d. Toronto, Ont., Jan. 3, 1929. [27]

Van Dervoort, William Humphrey, manufacturer, b. Ypsilanti, Mich., 1869; d. Moline, Ill., Feb. 25, 1921. [10]

Van der Vries, John Nicholas, mathematician, b. Kalamazoo, Mich., 1876; d. Wilmette, Ill., Feb. 14, 1936. [10]

Van Deventer, Emma Murdoch, novelist, fl. 1879-1912.

Vandewalker, Nina Catherine, educationist, b. 1857; d. Nov. 22, 1934.

Van de Warker, Edward Ely, physician, b. West Troy, N.Y., 1841; d. Syracuse, N.Y., Sept. 5, 1910. [1; 4]

Van de Water, George Roe, clergyman, b. Flushing, N.Y., 1854; d. New York, N.Y., March 15, 1925. [3; 10]

Vandewater, Robert J., writer of guide books, fl. 1830-1841.

Van de Water, Mrs. Virginia, née Terhune, novelist, b. Newark, N.J., 1865; d. Pompton Lakes, N.J., Oct. 18, 1945. [10]

Van Dine, S. S. (pseud.). See Wright, Willard Huntington.

Van Doren, Dirck (pseud.). See Dey, Frederick Van Rensselaer.

Van Doren, William Howard, clergyman, b. 1810; d. 1882.

Van Dusen, Conrad, clergyman, b. 1800; d. Whitby, Ont., Aug. 19, 1878. [27]

Van Duzee, Ira Damon, poet, b. 1829; d. 1909.

Van Dyke, Henry, clergyman, educationist, and diplomat, b. Germantown, Pa., 1852; d. Princeton, N.J., April 10, 1933. [1; 2a; 3; 4; 5; 6; 7; 8; 10; 11]

Van Dyke, Henry Jackson, clergyman, b. Abington, Pa., 1822; d. Brooklyn, N.Y., May 25, 1891. [3; 4; 5]

Van Dyke, John Charles, art critic and librarian, b. New Brunswick, N.J., 1856; d. New York, N.Y., Dec. 5, 1932. [1; 3; 5; 6; 7; 10; 11]

Van Dyke, Joseph Smith, clergyman, b. Bound Brook, N.J., 1832; d. Hightstown, N.J., Nov. 1, 1915. [3; 6; 10]

Van Dyke, Paul, educationist, b. Brooklyn, N.Y., 1859; d. Washington, Conn., Aug. 30, 1933. [1; 7; 10; 11]

Van Dyke, Theodore Strong, lawyer and naturalist, b. New Brunswick, N.J., 1842; d. Daggett, Calif., June 28, 1923. [3; 10; 35]

Van Dyke, Woodbridge Strong, soldier and producer of moving pictures, b. San Diego, Calif., 1890; d. Hollywood, Calif., Feb. 4, 1943. [35]

Van Dyne, Edith (pseud.). See Baum, Lyman Frank.

Van Dyne, Frederick, lawyer and consular agent, b. Palmyra, N.Y., 1861; d. Chevy Chase, Md., April 21, 1915. [10]

Van Epps, Howard, jurist, b. Eufaula, Ala., 1847; d. Florida, Dec. 25, 1909. [4; 34]

Van Eps, Frank Stanley, clergyman, b. near Schenectady, N.Y., 1859; d. 1921.

Van Evrie, John H., physician, b. 1814; d. 1896. [6]

Van Fleet, James Alvin, clergyman, b. New Jersey, 1839; d. New York, N.Y., June 22, 1924. [53]

Van Fleet, John McKee, jurist, b. 1842; d. Elkhart, Ind., Dec. 23, 1907.

Van Fleet, Walter, naturalist, b. Piermont, N.Y., 1857; d. Miami, Fla., Jan. 26, 1922. [1; 10]

Van Harlingen, Arthur, physician, b. Philadelphia, Pa., 1845; d. Bryn Mawr, Pa., Sept. 26, 1936. [10; 11]

Van Hise, Charles Richard, educationist, b. Fulton, Wis., 1857; d. Milwaukee, Wis., Nov. 19, 1918. [1; 4; 10]

Van Hook, Weller, surgeon, b. Greenville, Ind., 1862; d. Coopersville, Mich., July 1, 1933. [1; 10]

Van Horne, David, clergyman, b. Glen, N.Y., 1837; d. Amsterdam, N.Y., April 12, 1930. [10; 11]

Van Horne, Thomas Budd, clergyman, b. Ohio; d. 1895. [6]

Van Lennep, Henry John, missionary, b. Smyrna, Asia Minor, 1815; d. Great Barrington, Mass., Jan. 11, 1889. [1; 3; 6]

Van Loan, Charles Emmett, journalist and short-story writer, b. San José, Calif., 1879; d. Arlington, Pa., Feb. 2, 1919. [10]

Van Loon, Mrs. Elizabeth, novelist, fl. 1878-1880. [6]

Van Loon, Hendrik Willem, journalist and historian, b. Rotterdam, Holland, 1882; d. Greenwich, Conn., March 11, 1944. [7; 10; 11; 12]

Van Marter, Martha, editor, b. Lyons, N.Y., 1839; d. ? [10]

Vannah, Kate, poet, b. Gardiner, Me., 1855; d. Boston, Mass., Oct. 11, 1933. [21]

Vannah, Letitia Katherine. See Vannah. Kate.

Van Ness, Thomas, clergyman, b. Baltimore, Md., 1859; d. Boston, Mass., March 14, 1931. [10; 11]

Van Ness, William Peter, politician and jurist, b. Columbia county, N.Y., about 1778; d. New York, N.Y., Sept. 6, 1826. [1; 3; 4; 5; 6]

Van Nest, Abraham Rynier, clergyman, b. New York, N.Y., 1823; d. New York, N.Y., June 1, 1892. [1; 3; 5; 6]

Van Noppen, Leonard Charles, lecturer and poet, b. Holland, 1868; d. Glen Cove, Long Island, N.Y., July 21, 1935. [10]

Van Norden, Charles clergyman, b. New York, N.Y., 1843; d. East Auburn, Calif., May 12, 1913. [10; 11; 35]

Van Norman, Hubert Everett, dairy husbandman, b. Tillsonburg, Ont., 1872; d. Chicago, Ill., July 28, 1938. [10]

Van Orden, William H., miscellaneous writer, fl. 1884-1896.

Van Rensselaer, Cortlandt, clergyman, b. Albany, N.Y., 1808; d. Burlington, N.J., July 25, 1860. [1; 3; 4; 5; 6]

Van Rensselaer, Jeremiah, geologist, d. 1828. [51]

Van Rensselaer, Mrs. John King. See Van Rensselaer, Mrs. May, née King.

Van Rensselaer, Mrs. Mariana, née Griswold, art critic, b. New York, N.Y., 1851; d. New York, N.Y., Jan. 20, 1934. [1; 4; 7; 10]

Van Rensselaer, Martha, home economist, b. Randolph, N.Y., 1864; d. Ithaca, N.Y., May 26, 1932. [1; 4; 10]

Van Rensselaer, Maunsell, clergyman, b. Albany, N.Y., 1819; d. Lakewood, N.J., Feb. 17, 1900. [3; 5; 6; 10]

Van Rensselaer, Mrs. May, née King, miscellaneous writer, b. New York, N.Y., 1848; d. New York, N.Y., May 11, 1925. [7; 10]

Van Rensselaer, Mrs. Schuyler. See Van Rensselaer, Mrs. Mariana, née Griswold.

Van Rensselaer, Solomon, soldier and politician, b. Rensselaer county, N.Y., 1774; d. Albany, N.Y., April 23, 1852. [1; 3; 4; 5; 6]

Van Rensselaer, Stephen, antiquary, b. West Orange, N.J., 1871; d. Morristown, N.J., Dec. 17, 1945.

Vansant, Nicholas, clergyman, b. 1823; d. ?

Van Santvoord, Cornelius, clergyman, b. Belleville, N.J., 1816; d. Kingston, N.Y., Oct. 31, 1901. [3; 6]

Van Santvoord, George, jurist, b. Belleville, N.J., 1819; d. East Albany, N.Y., March 6, 1863. [1; 3; 5; 6]

Van Santvoord, Seymour, lawyer, b. Troy, N.Y., 1858; d. Troy, N.Y. Nov. 15, 1938. [10; 11]

Van Schaack, Henry Cruger, historian, b. Kinderhook, N.Y., 1802; d. Manlius, N.Y., Dec. 16, 1887. [1; 3; 5; 6; 7]

Van Schaack, Henry Cruger, lawyer, b. 1861; d. 1900.

Van Schaick, George Gray, surgeon and novelist, b. 1861; d. New York, N.Y., Feb. 17, 1924.

Van Sickle, James Hixon, educationist, b. South Livonia, N.Y., 1852; d. Feb. 12, 1926. [10]

Van Slingerland, Mrs. Nellie Bingham, novelist and playwright, b. Oakland county, Mich., 1850; d. ? [10]

Van Slyke, Lucius Lincoln, chemist, b. Centerville, N.Y., 1859; d. Geneva, N.Y., Sept. 30, 1931. [1; 10; 11; 13]

Van Tramp, John C., pioneer, fl. 1860-1870.

Van Tyne, Claude Halstead, historian, b. Tecumseh, Mich., 1869; d. Ann Arbor, Mich., March 21, 1930. [1; 7; 10; 11; 39]

Van Valkenburg, John, historian, b. 1832; d. 1890.

Van Valzah, William Ward, physician, b. 1849; d. Atlantic City, N.J., July 22, 1929.

Van Vechten, Jacob, clergyman, b. Catskill, N.Y., 1788; d. Auburn, N.Y., Sept. 15, 1871. [3]

Van Voorhis, Elias William, genealogist, b. 1844; d. 1892.

Van Vorhis, Flavius Josephus, lawyer, b. Marion county, Ind., 1840; d. 1913. [10]

Van Vorst, Mrs. Bessie, née McGinnis, novelist, b. New York, N.Y., 1873; d. Paris, France, May 18, 1928. [7; 10]

Van Vorst, Mrs. John. See Van Vorst, Mrs. Bessie, née McGinnis.

Van Vorst, Marie, novelist and poet, b. New York, N.Y. 1867; d. Florence, Italy, Dec. 16, 1936. [7; 10]

Van Wagenen, Anthony, lawyer, b. Brighton, Ia., 1852; d. Casa Grande, Ariz., Sept. 8, 1937. [10; 11]

Van Wagenen, Theodore Francis, engineer, d. Los Angeles, Calif., Jan. 6, 1936. [48]

Van Waters, George, poet, fl. 1841-1859.

Van Wert, Leland Russell, metallurgist, b. Raymertown, N.Y., 1892; d. Philadelphia, Pa., March 26, 1945. [13]

Van Winkle, Daniel, genealogist and historian, b. 1839; d. Jersey City, N.J., March 21, 1935.

Van Wyck, Frederick, historian, b. New York, N.Y., 1853; d. New York, N.Y., Feb. 16, 1936.

Van Zandt, Abraham Brooks, clergyman, b. Albany county, N.Y., Nov. 17, 1816; d. New Brunswick, N.J., July 21, 1881.

Van Zile, Edward Sims, journalist, poet, and novelist, b. Troy, N.Y., 1863; d. New York, N.Y., May 29, 1931. [4; 7; 10; 11]

Van Zile, Philip Taylor, jurist, b. Osceola, Pa., 1843; d. Detroit, Mich., Oct. 26, 1917. [10]

Varney, Almond Clother, interior decorator, b. Luzerne, N.Y., 1849; d. ? [39]

Varney, George Jones, historian, b. Brunswick, Me., 1836; d. Boston, Mass., Feb. 9, 1901. [38]

Varney, George Reuben, clergyman, b. East Sumner, Me., 1865; d. McMinnville, Ore., June 21, 1924. [67]

Varnum, Joseph Bradley, lawyer, b. Washington, D.C., 1818; d. Astoria, Long Island, N.Y., Dec. 31, 1874. [3; 6; 62]

Varnum, William Harrison, educationist, b. Cambridge, Mass., 1878; d. Madison, Wis., July 4, 1946. [11]

Vartooguian, Armayis P., historian, b. Constantinople, Turkey, 1874; d. New York, N.Y., Aug. 20, 1897.

Vasey, George, botanist, b. near Scarborough, England, 1822; d. Washington, D.C., March 4, 1893. [1; 3]

Vass, Lachlan Cumming, clergyman, b. 1831; d. 1896. [34]

Vassar, John Guy, philanthropist, b. Poughkeepsie, N.Y., 1811; d. Poughkeepsie, N.Y., Oct. 27, 1888. [3; 4; 5; 6]

Vassar, Thomas Edwin, clergyman, b. Poughkeepsie, N.Y., 1834; d. Elizabeth, N.J., July 3, 1918. [3; 4]

Vauclain, Samuel Matthews, manufacturer, b. Philadelphia, Pa., 1856; d. Philadelphia, Pa., Feb. 4, 1940. [10]

Vaughan, Benjamin, political economist, diplomat, and agriculturist, b. Jamaica, B.W.I. 1751; d. Hallowell, Me., Dec. 8, 1835. [1; 3; 6]

Vaughan, Clement Read, clergyman, b. 1827; d. ?

Vaughan, Daniel, astronomer, b. county Clare, Ireland, about 1818; d. Cincinnati, O., April, 1879. [1; 3; 4]

Vaughan, Herbert Hunter, educationist, b. Ann Arbor, Mich., 1884; d. Oakland, Calif., Jan. 4, 1948. [10]

Vaughan, John Colin, surgeon, b. Calais, Me., 1875; d. New York, N.Y., Jan. 12, 1940. [10]

Vaughan, John Gaines, clergyman, b. Arcadia, Tenn., 1858; d. Appleton, Wis., May 11, 1921. [10]

Vaughan, John Henry, educationist, b. Dobson, N.C., 1880; d. State College, N.M., Oct. 26, 1924. [10]

Vaughan, Lawrence James, priest, b. Newark, N.J., 1864; d. Janesville, Wis., May 10, 1909. [10]

Vaughan, Victor Clarence, biochemist, b. Randolph county, Mo., 1851; d. Richmond, Va., Nov. 21, 1929. [1; 4; 10]

Vaughan, Walter, biographer, b. Monmouth, Wales, 1865; d. Montreal, Que., June, 1922. [27]

Vaughan, William Warren, genealogist, b. 1848; d. Hallowell, Me., Sept. 4, 1939.

Vaughn, Mrs. Kate. née Brew, dietitian, b. Nashville, Tenn., 1874; d. May 21, 1933. [10; 11]

Vaughn, Robert, pioneer and stockraiser, b. Montgomeryshire, Wales, 1837; d ?

Vaux, Calvert, landscape architect, b. London, England, 1824; d. Bensonhurst, Long Island, N.Y., Nov. 19, 1895. [1; 3; 4; 5; 6]

Vaux, Richard, penologist, b. Philadelphia, Pa., 1816; d. Philadelphia, Pa., March 22, 1895. [1; 3; 4; 5; 6]

Vaux, Roberts, philanthropist, b. Philadelphia, Pa., 1786; d. Philadelphia, Pa., Jan. 7, 1836. [1; 3; 4; 6]

Vawter, Clara, poet and short-story writer, d. 1900.

Veatch, Arthur Clifford, geologist, b. Evansville, Ind., 1878; d. Port Washington, Long Island, N.Y., Dec. 24, 1938. [10; 13]

Veatch, Byron Elbert, merchant, b. Springfield, Ill., 1858; d. Chicago, Ill., Jan. 23, 1930. [10]

Veblen, Andrew Anderson, educationist, b. Ozaukee county, Wis., 1848; d. 1932. [10; 11]

Veblen, Mrs. Ellen May, née Rolfe, writer of a book for children, d. near Palo Alto, Calif., May, 1926.

Veblen, Thorstein, economist and sociologist, b. Manitowoc county, Wis., 1857; d. Palo Alto, Calif., Aug. 3, 1929. [1; 4; 7; 10; 11; 62]

Vecki, Victor G., surgeon, b. Zagreb, Yugoslavia, 1857; d. San Francisco, Calif., Nov. 16, 1938. [10; 11]

Vedder, Elihu, painter and illustrator, b. New York, N.Y., 1836; d. Rome, Italy, Jan. 29, 1923. [1; 3; 4; 5; 10]

Vedder, Henry Clay, clergyman and educationist, b. De Ruyter, N.Y., 1853; d. Chester, Pa., Oct. 13, 1935. [1a; 7; 10]

Veditz, Charles William August, educationist, b. 1872; d. Washington, D.C., Feb. 20, 1926. [4; 10; 11]

Veeder, Mrs. Emily Elizabeth, née Ferris, novelist and poet, b. 1841; d. ?

Veiller, Bayard, playwright, b. Brooklyn, N.Y., 1869; d. New York, N.Y., June 16, 1943. [7; 10]

Velvin, Ellen, journalist, b. Southampton, England; d. New York, N.Y., 1918. [10]

Venable, Charles Scott, soldier and educationist, b. Prince Edward county, Va., 1827; d. Richmond, Va., Aug. 11, 1900. [1; 3; 4; 34]

Venable, Edward Carrington, novelist, b. Petersburg, Va., 1884; d. St. Servan, France, May 17, 1936. [7; 56]

Venable, Francis Preston, chemist, b. Prince Edward county, Va., 1856; d. Richmond, Va., March 17, 1934. [1; 3; 4; 5; 6; 7; 10; 11; 34]

Venable, Matthew Walton, octogenarian, b. 1847; d. Charleston, W. Va., May 21, 1930.

Venable, Richard Morton, lawyer, b. Charlotte county, Va., 1839; d. Baltimore, Md., 1910. [10]

Venable, William Henry, educationist, b. near Waynesville, O., 1836; d. Cincinnati, O., July 6, 1920. [1; 3; 4; 5; 6; 7; 10]

Venner, Orlin Hale, educationist, b. Corydon, Ind., 1873; d. Hastings, Neb., June 22, 1920. [62]

Vennor, Henry George, ornithologist, b. Montreal, Lower Canada, 1841; d. Montreal,, Que., June 8, 1884. [27]

Ver Beck, Frank. See Ver Beck, William Francis.

Ver Beck, Mrs. Hanna, née Rion, miscellaneous writer, b. Winnsboro, S.C., 1875; d. Bermuda, B.W.I., May 5, 1924. [10]

Ver Beck, William Francis, illustrator, b. Belmont county, O., 1858; d. England, July 13, 1933. [7; 10; 11]

Verelart, Myndart (pseud.). See Saltus, Edgar Everston.

Ver Mehr, Jean Leonard Henri Corneille, clergyman, fl. 1864-1877.

Vermilye, Ashbel Green, clergyman, b. 1822; d. 1905.

Vermilye, Mrs. Kate, née Jordan. See Jordan, Kate.

Vernon, Charles William, clergyman, b. London England, 1871; d. Toronto, Ont., Jan. 30, 1934. [11; 27]

Vernon, Grenville, drama critic, b. Providence, R.I., 1883; d. New York, N.Y., Nov. 30, 1941. [10; 22]

Vernon, Max (pseud.). See Kellogg, Vernon Lyman.

Vernon, Samuel Milton, clergyman, b. near Crawfordsville, Ind., 1841; d. Philadelphia, Pa., May 27, 1920. [10]

Verplanck, Gulian Crommelin, lawyer and politician, b. New York, N.Y., 1786; d. New York, N.Y., March 18, 1870. [1; 3; 4; 5; 6; 7; 8; 9]

Verplanck, William Edward, lawyer, b. 1856; d. Dec. 18, 1928. [48]

Verreau, Hospice Anthelme Jean Baptiste, priest and historian, b. L'Islet, Lower Canada, 1828; d. Montreal, Que., May 15, 1901. [27]

Verrill, Addison Emory, zoologist, b. Greenwood, Me., 1839; d. Santa Barbara, Calif., Dec. 10, 1926. [1; 4; 5; 10]

Versteeg, Dingman, historian, d. Holland, July 16, 1936.

Verwyst, Chrysostom Adrian, missionary, b. Uden, North Brabant, Holland, 1841; d. Bayfield, Wis., June 23, 1925. [1; 21]

Very, Edward Wilson, naval officer, b. 1847; d. 1910. [3]

Very, Frank Washington, astronomer, b. Salem, Mass., 1852; d. Westwood, Mass., Nov. 24, 1927. [4; 10; 11]

Very, Jones, poet, b. Salem, Mass., 1813; d. Salem, Mass., May 8, 1880. [1; 3; 4; 6; 7; 9]

Very, Lydia Louisa Ann, poet and novelist, b. Salem, Mass., 1823; d. Salem, Mass., Sept. 10, 1901. [1; 3; 4; 6; 7; 9; 10]

Vethake, Henry, economist, b. Essequibo county, British Guiana, 1792; d. Philadelphia, Pa., Dec. 16, 1866. [1; 3; 4; 5; 6]

Vetromile, Eugène, missionary, b. Gallipoli, Italy, 1819; d. Gallipoli, Italy, Aug. 21, 1881. [3; 6]

Vézina, François, banker, b. Quebec, Lower Canada, Aug. 30, 1818; d. Quebec, Que., Jan. 25, 1882. [27]

Viator (pseud.). See Varnum, Joseph Bradley.

Vibbert, William Henry, clergyman, b. New Haven, Conn., 1839; d. Aug. 27, 1918. [10]

Vickers, George Morley, poet and entertainer, b. 1841; d. ?

Vickers, Robert Henry, lawyer, b. Dublin, Ireland, about 1830; d. Chicago, Ill., April 3, 1897.

Victor, Mrs. Frances, née Fuller, poet and historian, b. Oneida county, N.Y., 1826; d. Portland, Ore., Nov. 14, 1902. [1; 3; 4; 5; 6; 7; 9; 35; 41]

Victor, Mrs. Metta Victoria, née Fuller, novelist, b. near Erie, Pa., 1831; d. Hohokus, N.J., June 26, 1886. [3; 4; 5; 6; 7; 9]

Victor, Orville James, publisher, b. Sandusky, O., 1827; d. Hohokus, N.J., March 14, 1910. [1; 3; 4; 5; 6; 7; 9; 10]

Victor, William B., journalist, fl. 1859-1861.

Vielé, Egbert Ludovickus, engineer, b. Waterford, N.Y., 1825; d. New York, N.Y., April 22, 1902. [1; 3; 4; 5; 6; 7; 10]

Vielé, Herman Knickerbocker, journalist and novelist, b. New York, N.Y., 1856; d. New York, N.Y., Dec. 14, 1908. [4; 7; 10]

Vielé, Mrs. Teresa, née Griffin, army officer's wife, b. 1832; d. ?

Viesselman, Percival William, lawyer and educationist, b. Fairmont, Minn., 1890; d. Lawrence, Kans., Aug. 11, 1945. [10]

Viger, Denis Benjamin, politician, b. Montreal, Canada, 1774; d. Montreal, Que., Feb. 13, 1861. [27]

Viger, Jacques, antiquary, b. Montreal, Canada, 1787; d. Montreal, Que., Dec. 12, 1858. [27]

Vilas, Charles Harrison, surgeon, b. Chelsea, Vt., 1846; d. Madison, Wis., Nov. 22, 1920. [10]

Vilas, William Freeman, lawyer and politician, b. Chelsea, Vt., 1840; d. Madison, Wis., Aug. 27, 1908. [1; 3; 4; 5; 10]

Viles, Jonas, historian, b. 1875; d. Columbia, Mo., Feb. 6, 1948. [51]

Villard, Mrs. Fanny, née Garrison. See Villard, Mrs. Helen Frances, née Garrison.

Villard, Mrs. Helen Frances, née Garrison, reformer, b. Boston, Mass., 1844; d. Dobbs Ferry, N.J., July 5, 1928. [1]

Villard, Henry, journalist and financier, b. Speyer, Bavaria, 1835; d. Dobbs Ferry, N.Y., Nov. 12, 1900. [1; 3; 4; 5; 6; 7; 10]

Villard, Oswald Garrison, journalist, b. Wiesbaden, Germany, 1872; d. New York, N.Y., Oct. 1, 1949. [4; 7; 10; 11]

Villers, Thomas Jefferson, clergyman, b. Centerville, Va., 1861; d. Detroit, Mich., March 16, 1935.

Vincent, Boyd, bishop, b. Erie, Pa., 1845; d. Cincinnati, O., 1935. [4; 10; 62]

Vincent, Edgar La Verne, journalist, b. farmer and novelist, b. Persia, N.Y., 1851; d. Binghampton, N.Y., July 3, 1936. [10]

Vincent, Francis, journalist, b. Bristol, England, 1822; d. Wilmington, Del., June 23, 1884. [3; 6; 7]

Vincent, Frank, traveller, b. Brooklyn, N.Y., 1848; d. Woodstock, N.Y., June 19, 1916. [1; 3; 5; 6; 7; 10; 62]

Vincent, George Edgar, educationist, b. Rockford, Ill., 1864; d. New York, N.Y., Feb. 1, 1941. [2a; 4; 10]

Vincent, Henry Bethuel, musician, b. Denver, Colo., 1872; d. Erie, Pa., Jan. 7, 1941. [10]

Vincent, John Heyl, bishop, b. Tuscaloosa, Ala., 1832; d. Chicago, Ill., May 9, 1920. [1; 3; 4; 5; 10; 34]

Vincent, John Martin, historian, b. Elyria, O., 1857; d. La Jolla, Calif., Sept. 22, 1939. [4; 10; 11]

Vincent, Leon Henry, educationist, b. Chicago, Ill., 1859; d. Boston, Mass., Feb. 12, 1941. [7; 10]

Vincent, Marvin Richardson, theologian, b. Poughkeepsie, N.Y., 1834; d. Forest Hills, Long Island, N.Y., Aug. 18, 1922. [1; 3; 4; 5; 6; 7; 10]

Vincent, Thomas MacCurdy, soldier, b. near Cadiz, O., 1832; d. 1909. [3; 6; 10]

Vincent, Walter Borodell, lawyer, b. Mystic, Conn., 1845; d. Providence, R.I., Nov. 14, 1931. [10]

Vingut, Francisco Javier, educationist, b. Cuba, 1823; d. ? [3; 6]

Vingut, Mrs. Gertrude, née Fairfield, novelist, b. Philadelphia, Pa., about 1830; d. ? [6; 7]

Vining, Edward Payson, railway executive, b. Belchertown, Mass., 1847; d. Brookline, Mass., Dec. 31, 1920. [10]

Vinson, Taylor, lawyer, b. Wayne county, W. Va., 1857; d. Jan. 31, 1929. [10]

Vinton, Alexander Hamilton, clergyman, b. Providence, R.I., 1807; d. Philadelphia, Pa., April 26, 1881. [1; 3; 4; 6]

Vinton, Arthur Dudley, lawyer and novelist, b. Brooklyn, N.Y., 1853; d. Brooklyn, N.Y., Sept. 13, 1906; [10]

Vinton, Francis, clergyman, b. Providence, R.I., 1809; d. Brooklyn, N.Y., Sept. 29, 1872. [1; 3; 4; 5; 6]

Vinton, Francis Laurens, soldier, engineer, and poet, b. Portland, Me., 1835; d. Leadville, Colo., Oct. 6, 1879. [1; 3; 4]

Vinton, Frederic, librarian, b. Boston, Mass., 1817; d. Princeton, N.J., Jan. 1, 1890. [4; 7]

Vinton, John Adams, genealogist, b. Boston, Mass., 1801; d. Winchester, Mass., Nov. 13, 1877. [3; 4; 5; 6]

Vinton, Jonathan Dwight, physician and poet, b. 1831; d. West Chester, Pa., June 14, 1903.

Vinton, Stallo, lawyer, b. Indianapolis, Ind., 1876; d. Hackensack, N.J., Nov. 5, 1946.

Violette, Eugene Morrow, historian, b. Pittsville, Mo., 1873; d. Baton Rouge, La., March 26, 1940.

Virgil, Mrs. Antha Minerva, née Patchen, musician, b. Elmira, N.Y., d. Bergenfield, N.J., Feb. 9, 1939. [10]

Virgin, William Wirt, jurist, b. 1823; d. 1893. [38]

Visscher, William Lightfoot, journalist and poet, b. Owingsville, Ky., 1842; d. Chicago, Ill., Feb. 10, 1924. [7; 10]

Vittum, Edmund March, clergyman and educationist, b. Sandwich, N.H., 1855; d. Grinnell, Ia., Jan. 19, 1938. [10; 11; 62]

Vittum, Willis Hall, physician and poet, b. Baraboo, Wis., 1855; d. St. Paul, Minn., Dec. 29, 1910. [70]

Vivian, Harold Acton, journalist, b. near Kandy, Ceylon, 1875; d. Albany, N.Y., Oct. 15, 1929. [10]

Vivian, Thomas Jondrie, journalist, b. Cornwall, England, 1858; d. New York, N.Y., Dec. 14, 1925. [10; 35]

Vizetelly, Francis Horace, lexicographer and editor, b. London, England, 1864; d. New York, N.Y., Dec. 20, 1938. [7; 10; 11]

Vlachos, Nicholas Panagis, educationist, b. Amsterdam, Holland, 1875; d. Merchantsville, N.J., April 15, 1943.

Vogdes, William, lawyer and mathematician, b. Philadelphia, Pa., 1802; d. Philadelphia, Pa., Dec. 29, 1886. [3]

Vogt, Augustus Stephen, musician, b. Washington, Ont., 1861; d. Toronto, Ont., Sept. 17, 1926. [20; 27]

Voigt, Andrew George, clergyman, b. Philadelphia, Pa., 1859; d. Columbia, S.C., Jan. 2, 1933. [10]

Voldo, Venier, poet, fl. 1876-1890.

Volk, Leonard Wells, sculptor, b. Wells, N.Y., 1828; d. Osceola, Wis., Aug. 19, 1895. [1; 3; 5]

Vollmer, Philip, theologian, b. Germany, 1860; d. Palmyra, N.J., Dec. 10, 1929. [4; 10]

Vondenvelden, William, surveyor, d. St. Henri, Lower Canada, June 20, 1809. [27]

Von Holst, Hermann Eduard. See Holst, Hermann Edward von.

Von Ruck, Karl, physician, b. Stuttgart, Germany, 1849; d. Asheville, N.C., 1922. [1; 4; 10]

Von Schierbrand, Wolf, historian, b. 1851; d. Manhattan, N.Y., Dec. 1, 1920.

Von Schweinitz, Lewis David, clergyman, and botanist, b. Bethlehem, Pa., 1780; d. Bethlehem, Pa., Feb. 8, 1834. [1; 3; 4; 5; 6]

Von Sternberg, Constantin Ivanovitch. See Sternberg, Constantin Ivanovitch von.

Von Teuffel, Mrs. Blanche Willis, née **Howard.** See Howard, Blanche Willis.

Voorhees, Daniel Wolsey, lawyer and politician, b. Liberty, O., 1827; d. Washington, D.C., April 10, 1897. [1; 3; 4; 5]

Voorhees, Edward Burnett, agricultural chemist, b. Pine Brook, N.J., 1856; d. New Brunswick, N.J., June 6, 1911. [1; 4; 10]

Voorhies, Felix, lawyer, b. parish of St. Martin, La., 1839; d. 1919. [34]

Voorsanger, Jacob, rabbi, b. Amsterdam, Holland, 1852; d. San Francisco, Calif., April 27, 1908. [1; 10]

Vopicka, Charles Joseph, diplomat, b. Bohemia, 1857; d. Chicago, Ill., Sept. 4, 1935. [1a; 10]

Vorse, Albert White, journalist, b. Littleton, Mass., 1866; d. New York, N.Y., June 15, 1910. [7; 10]

Vos, Geerhardus, clergyman, b. Netherlands, 1862; d. Grand Rapids, Mich., Aug. 13, 1949.

Vosburg, John Henry, poet, fl. 1865-1874.

Vosburgh, Royden Woodward, genealogist, b. Buffalo, N.Y., 1875; d. New Brighton, N.Y., May 18, 1931.

Vose, George Leonard, engineer and educationist, b. Augusta, Me., 1831; d. Brunswick, Me., March 30, 1910. [1; 3; 6]

Vose, Harriet Leonora. See Bates, Mrs. Harriet Leonora, née Vose.

Vose, James Gardiner, clergyman, b. Boston, Mass., 1830; d. Providence, R.I., March 13, 1908. [62]

Vose, John, educationist, b. Bedford, N.H., 1766; d. Atkinson, N.H., 1840. [6; 43]

Vose, Reuben, publisher, fl. 1856-1860.

Voss, Louis, clergyman, b. 1856; d. New Orleans, La., 1936.

Votaw, Clyde Weber, educationist, b. Wheaton, Ill., 1864; d. Pasadena, Calif., March 24, 1946. [62]

Vought, John G., vendor of patent medicines, fl. 1821-1828.

Vought, Walter Joy, physician, b. Buffalo, N.Y., 1862; d. New York, N.Y., Sept. 24, 1893. [62]

Voyer, Ludger Napoléon, soldier, b. Quebec, Que., 1842; d. Quebec, Que., Feb. 22, 1876. [27]

Vreeland, Frank, playwright, b. 1891; d. Norwich, Conn., Jan. 6, 1946.

Vreeland, Williamson Updike, educationist, b. Rocky Hill, N.J., 1870; d. Princeton, N.J., Nov. 6, 1942. [7; 10; 11]

Vroom, Fenwick Williams, clergyman and educationist, b. St. Stephen, N.B., 1856; d. Halifax, N.S., Jan. 8, 1944. [11; 27]

Vroom, Garret Dorset Wall, jurist, b. Trenton, N.J., 1843; d. Trenton, N.J., March 4, 1914. [10]

Vye, John Alexander, educationist, b. Fair Haven, Minn., 1867; d. May 11, 1942. [70]

W

Wachenheim, Frederick Leopold, physician, b. 1870; d. New Rochelle, N.Y., March 4, 1926.

Wachsman, Zvi H., journalist, b. Palestine; d. Montreal, Que., Sept. 13, 1948.

Wachsmuth, Charles, palaeontologist, b. Hanover, Germany, 1829; d. Burlington, Ia., Feb. 7, 1896. [1; 4; 37]

Wackerhagen, Augustus, clergyman, b. Hanover, Germany, 1774; d. Clermont, N.Y., Nov. 1, 1865. [3]

Wackernagel William, educationist, b. Basel, Switzerland, 1838; d. Allentown, Pa., May 21, 1926. [10]

Waddel, Charles Carey. See Waddell, Charles Carey.

Waddel, Moses, clergyman, b. Iredell county, N.C., 1770; d. Athens, Ga., July 21, 1840. [1; 3; 5; 6]

Waddell, Alfred Moore, lawyer and historian, b. Hillsboro, N.C., 1834; d. Wilmington, N.C., March 17, 1912. [1; 4; 10]

Waddell, Charles Carey, journalist, b. Chillicothe, O., 1868; d. New York, N.Y., June 11, 1930. [10]

Waddell, Mrs. Charles Carey. See Forsslund, Mary Louise.

Waddell, John, chemist, b. Pictou, N.S., 1858; d. Kingston, Ont., June 4, 1923.

Waddell, John Alexander Low, engineer, b. Port Hope, Ont., 1854; d. New York N.Y., March 3, 1938. [4; 10; 11]

Waddell, Joseph Addison, historian, b. Staunton, Va., 1823; d. Staunton, Va., Feb. 17, 1914. [4; 10; 34]

Waddell, William Henry, educationist, d. Milford, Va., 1878. [4; 34]

Waddington, Alfred, pioneer, b. England, about 1800; d. Ottawa, Ont., Feb. 26, 1872. [27]

Waddy, Mrs. Virginia, née **Waddey,** educationist, b. 1850; d. 1911.

Wade, Blanche Elizabeth, novelist, b. Buffalo, N.Y.; d. Norwalk, Conn., 1928. [10; 11]

Wade, Decius Spear, jurist and novelist, b. near Andover, O., 1835; d. near Andover, O., Aug. 3, 1905. [1; 4; 7]

Wade, Edward, lawyer, b. 1829; d. 1890.

Wade, Frederick Coate, lawyer, b. Bowmanville, Ont., 1860; d. London, England, Nov. 9, 1924. [27]

Wade, Mark Sweeten, physician and historian, b. Sunderland, England, 1858; d. Vancouver, B.C., April 19, 1929. [11]

Wade, Martin Joseph, jurist, b. Burlington, Vt., 1861; d. Los Angeles, Calif., April 16, 1931. [1; 10]

Wade, Mrs. Mary Hazelton, née **Blanchard,** writer of books for young people, b. Charlestown, Mass., 1860; d. Windsor, Conn., March 5, 1936. [7; 10; 11]

Wade, Reuben Alexander Slaven, poet, b. Mill Gap, Va., 1848; d. ? [35]

Wade, William Pratt, lawyer, b. 1839; d. 1894. [6]

Wadleigh, George, local historian, d. Dover, N.H., Aug. 12, 1884.

Wadlin, Horace Greeley, librarian, b. Wakefield, Mass., 1851; d. Winchester, Mass., Nov. 5, 1925. [4; 10]

Wadsworth, Benjamin, clergyman and educationist, b. Milton, Mass., 1669; d. Cambridge, Mass., March 16, 1737. [3; 4; 5; 6; 51]

Wadsworth, Horace Andrew, historian and genealogist, b. 1837; d. 1890.

Wadsworth, Marshman Edward, geologist and mineralogist, b. Livermore Falls, Me., 1847; d. Pittsburgh, Pa., April 21, 1921. [3; 4; 10]

Waffle, Albert Edward, clergyman, b. Steuben county, N.Y., 1846; d. Oct. 26, 1927. [10; 11]

Wager, Charles Henry Adams, educationist, b. Cohoes, N.Y., 1869; d. Oberlin, O., July 1, 1939. [10]

Wager, Daniel Elbridge, historian, b. 1828; d. Rome, N.Y., 1896.

Waggaman, Mrs. Mary Teresa, née McKee, writer of books for children, b. Baltimore, Md., 1846; d. Washington, D.C., July 31, 1931. [1; 7; 21; 22]

Waggaman, Samuel, physician and pharmacist, b. about 1844; d. Washington, D.C., May 30, 1913.

Waggoner, Clark, historian, b. 1820; d. Toledo, O., July 2, 1903. [4]

Waggoner, George Andrew, pioneer, b. Iowa, 1842; d. Lebanon, Ore., Oct. 7, 1916. [41]

Wagner, Arthur Lockwood, soldier, b. Ottawa, Ill., 1853; d. June 17, 1905. [10]

Wagner, Clinton, physician, b. Baltimore, Md., 1837; d. Geneva, Switzerland, Nov. 25, 1914. [1; 4; 10]

Wagner, Frank, miscellaneous writer, b. 1853; d. Vancouver, Wash., July 13, 1938.

Wagner, Harr. See Wagner, James Harrison.

Wagner, Hugh Kiernan, lawyer, b. 1870; d. St. Louis, Mo., 1941. [10; 11]

Wagner, James Harrison, miscellaneous writer, b. Pennsylvania, 1857; d. San Francisco, Calif., June 20, 1936. [10]

Wagner, Mrs. Madge, née **Morris,** poet, d. San Francisco, Calif., Feb. 28, 1924. [35]

Wagner, Philip Matthew, poet, b. 1868; d. 1914.

Wahl, William Henry, metallurgist, b. Philadelphia, Pa., 1848; d. Philadelphia, Pa., March 23, 1909. [1; 4; 10]

Wahlstad, Peter P., educationist, b. Oslo, Norway, 1865; d. Madison, N.J., July 9, 1943.

Wailes, Benjamin Leonard Covington, planter, b. Columbia county, Ga., 1797; d. Nov. 16, 1862. [1]

Wainwright, John William, physician, b. 1850; d. ?

Wainwright, Jonathan Mayhew, bishop, b. Liverpool, England, 1792; d. New York, N.Y., Sept. 21, 1854. [1; 3; 4; 5; 6; 7]

Waisbrooker, Mrs. Lois, née **Nichols,** novelist, b. 1826; d. ? [3]

Wait, Benjamin, rebel, b. Markham township, Upper Canada, 1813; d. Grand Rapids, Mich., 1895. [3; 27]

Wait, John Cassan, lawyer and civil engineer, b. Norwich, N.Y., 1860; d. New York, N.Y., Oct. 4, 1936. [4; 10; 11]

Wait, William, lawyer, b. Ephratah, N.Y., 1821; d. Johnstown, N.Y., Dec. 29, 1880. [1; 3; 6]

Waite, Alice Vinton, educationist, b. Brattleboro, Vt., 1864; d. Wellesley, Mass., April 6, 1943. [10; 11]

Waite, Benjamin Franklin, printer, b. 1844; d. Dunmore, Pa., Nov. 10, 1941.

Waite, Mrs. Catherine, née **Van Valkenburg,** lawyer and editor, b. Dumfries, Upper Canada, 1829; d. Chicago, Ill., Nov. 9, 1913. [3; 6; 10]

Waite, Charles Burlingame, jurist, b. Wayne county, N.Y., 1824; d. March 26, 1909. [3; 6; 10]

Waite, Henry Randall, clergyman and editor, b. Copenhagen, N.Y., 1846; d. East Orange, N.J., May 5, 1909. [3; 6; 10]

Waite, Mrs. Marjorie Peabody, philanthropist, b. Minneapolis, Minn.; d. Saratoga Springs, N.Y., Dec. 6, 1944.

Waite, Merton Benway, botanist, b. Oregon, Ill., 1865; d. Washington, D.C., June 5, 1945. [13]

Waite, Otis Frederick Reed, local historian, b. 1818; d. 1895. [43]

Waitt, David M., accountant, fl. 1872-1883. [38]

Wakefield, Homer, physician, b. Bloomington, Ill., 1865; d. New York, N.Y., Sept. 1, 1946.

Wakefield, John Allen, historian, b. 1797; d. 1873.

Wakefield, Mrs. Nancy Amelia Woodbury, née **Priest,** poet, b. Royalton, Mass., 1836; d. Winchendon, Mass., Sept. 21, 1870. [3]

Wakefield, Samuel, clergyman, b. 1799; d. 1895.

Wakeham, Frederick Leopold. See Wachenheim, Frederick Leopold.

Wakeley, Joseph Beaumont, clergyman, b. Danbury, Conn., 1809; d. New York, N.Y., April 27, 1875. [1; 3; 6]

Wakeman, Abram, historian, b. Troy, N.Y., 1850; d. New York, N.Y., Jan. 30, 1928.

Wakeman, Joel, clergyman, b. Rhinebeck, N.Y., 1809; d. May 24, 1898. [63]

Walbran, John T., master mariner, b. England; d. Victoria, B.C., March 31, 1913. [27]

Walcot, Charles Melton, playwright, b. London, England, about 1816; d. May 15, 1868. [7]

Walcott, Arthur Stuart, lawyer, b. New York, N.Y., 1869; d. New York, N.Y., Feb. 18, 1923. [51]

Walcott, Charles Doolittle, geologist, b. New York Mills, N.Y., 1850; d. Washington, D.C., Feb. 9, 1927. [1; 4; 5; 10; 11]

Walcott, Charles Folsom, lawyer, b. Hopkinton, Mass., 1836; d. Gooseberry Island, Salem Harbor, Mass., June 11, 1887. [51]

Walcott, Charles Hosmer, lawyer, b. Concord, Mass., 1848; d. Concord, Mass., April 25, 1901. [51]

Walcott, Earle Ashley, journalist, b. Magnolia, Ill., 1859; d. San Francisco, Calif., Jan. 1, 1931. [10; 11; 35]

Walcott, Mrs. Mary Morris, née **Vaux,** botanist, b. Philadelphia, Pa., 1860; d. Nova Scotia, Aug. 22, 1940.

Wald, Lillian D., sociologist and welfare worker, b. Ohio, 1867; d. Westport, Conn., Sept. 1, 1940. [7; 10; 11]

Waldack, Charles, photographer, fl. 1860-1865.

Walden, Jacob Treadwell, clergyman, b. Walden, N.Y., 1830; d. Boston, Mass., May 21, 1918. [1; 6; 10]

Waldo, Clarence Abiathar, educationist, b. Hammond, N.Y., 1852; d. New York, N.Y., Oct. 1, 1926. [4; 10]

Waldo, Frank, meteorologist, b. Cincinnati, O., 1857; d. May 7, 1920. [10]

Waldo, Fullerton Leonard, journalist, b. Cambridge, Mass., 1877; d. Philadelphia, Pa., Oct. 24, 1933. [7; 10; 11]

Waldo, Howard Lansing, physician, b. Centerville, N.Y., 1852; d. Flushing, N.Y., May 7, 1936. [11]

Waldo, James Curtis, novelist, b. 1835; d. 1901. [34]

Waldo, Samuel Putnam, biographer, b. Pomfret, Conn., 1779; d. Hartford, Conn., Feb. 23, 1826. [1; 3; 6; 7]

Waldron, Frederick A., consulting engineer, b. Windsor, Vt., 1864; d. Westfield, N.J., July 13, 1939.

Waldron, Malcolm Thomas, miscellaneous writer, b. 1903; d. 1931.

Waldron, Webb, journalist, b. Vergennes, Mich., 1882; d. Bridgeport, Conn., Aug. 5, 1945. [7; 10; 11; 39]

Waldstein, Abraham Solomon, educationist. b. 1874; d. Tel-Aviv, Palestine, June, 1932.

Waldstein, Louis, physician, b. New York, N.Y., 1853; d. London, England, April 12, 1915. [10]

Wales, Philip Skinner, naval surgeon, b. Annapolis, Md., 1837; d. 1906. [3; 4; 6; 10]

Walke, Henry, naval officer, b. Princess Anne county, Va., 1808; d. Brooklyn, N.Y., March 8, 1896. [1; 3; 4; 5; 6]

Walkem, William Wymond, physician, b. Montreal, Que., 1850; d. Vancouver, B.C., Sept. 29, 1919. [27]

Walker, Albert Henry, lawyer, b. Fairfax, Vt., 1844; d. New York, N.Y., Sept. 1, 1915. [4; 10]

Walker, Albert Perry, educationist, b. Alton Bay, N.H., 1862; d. Newtonville, Mass., March 28, 1911. [7; 10]

Walker, Aldace Freeman, soldier and lawyer, b. Rutland, Vt., 1842; d. 1901. [4; 10; 43]

Walker, Alexander, soldier and poet, fl. 1848-1867. [27]

Walker, Alexander, journalist, b. Fredericksburg, Va., 1818; d. Fort Smith, Ark., Jan. 24, 1893. [1; 3; 6; 7; 34]

Walker, Amasa, political economist, b. Woodstock, Conn., 1799; d. Brookfield, Mass., Oct. 29, 1875. [1; 3; 4; 5; 6; 7]

Walker, Asa, naval officer, b. Portsmouth, N.H., 1845; d. Annapolis, Md., March 7, 1916. [1; 10]

Walker, Bryant, lawyer and naturalist, b. Detroit, Mich., 1856; d. Detroit, Mich., May 26, 1936. [10]

Walker, Sir Byron Edmund, banker, b. Seneca township, Haldimand county, Ont., 1848; d. Toronto, Ont., March 27, 1924. [27]

Walker, Charles Howard, architect, b. Boston, Mass., 1857; d. Boston, Mass., April 12, 1936. [4; 10; 11]

Walker, Charles Manning, journalist, b. Athens, O., 1834; d. Jan. 25, 1920. [3; 6; 10]

Walker, Charles Swan, clergyman, b. Cincinnati, O., 1846; d. Stamford, Conn., Jan. 14, 1933. [62]

Walker, Cornelius, clergyman, b. near Richmond, Va., 1819; d. 1907. [3; 5; 6; 10; 34]

Walker, Cornelius Irvine, historian, b. 1842; d. Charleston, S.C., Nov. 6, 1927.

Walker, David, negro leader, b. Wilmington, N.C., 1785; d. Richmond, Va., June 28, 1830. [1]

Walker, Dugald Stewart, illustrator and writer of books for children, b. Richmond, Va., 1888; d. Richmond, Va., Feb. 26, 1937. [10]

Walker, Mrs. Edward Ashley. See Walker, Mrs. Katharine Kent, née Child.

Walker, Edward Dwight, editor, b. 1859; d. 1890. [6]

Walker, Edwin C., bookseller, b. 1849; d. New York, N.Y., Feb. 4, 1931.

Walker, Edwin Sawyer, clergyman, b. Whiting, Vt., 1828; d. Springfield, Ill., Aug. 15, 1912. [43; 67]

Walker, Francis Amasa, economist, b. Boston, Mass., 1840; d. Boston, Mass., Jan. 5, 1897. [1; 3 ;4; 5; 6; 7; 45]

Walker, George Leon, clergyman, b. Rutland, Vt., 1830; d. 1900. [10; 43]

Walker, Harvey Day, educationist, b. Princeton, Mass., 1817; d. Aug. 27, 1912. [6]

Walker, Horace Eaton, poet, b. 1852; d. ?

Walker, James, clergyman, b. Woburn, Mass., 1794; d. Cambridge, Mass., Dec. 23, 1874. [1; 3; 4; 5; 6; 7]

Walker, James Barr, clergyman, b. Philadelphia, Pa., 1805; d. Wheaton, Ill., March 6, 1887. [1; 3; 6; 7]

Walker, James Bradford Richmond, clergyman, b. Taunton, Mass., 1821; d. Jan. 24, 1885. [3; 6]

Walker, James Perkins, publisher, b. Portsmouth, N.H., 1829; d. Boston, Mass., May 10, 1868. [3; 6; 7]

Walker, Jerome, physician, b. 1845; d. Brooklyn, N.Y., June 19, 1924. [6]

Walker, Joseph Burbeen, historian and genealogist, b. Concord, N.H., 1822; d. Concord, N.H., Jan. 8, 1913. [3; 62]

Walker, Mrs. Katharine, Kent, née Child, writer of books for children, b. Pittsford, Vt., 1833; d. ? [3]

Walker, Mary Edwards, physician, b. 1832; d. Oswego, N.Y., Feb. 21, 1919. [1; 4; 10]

Walker, Mrs. Mary, née Spring, temperance novelist, fl. 1868-1876. [6]

Walker, Perley Francis, mechanical engineer, b. Embden, Me., 1875; d. Lawrence, Kans., Oct. 16, 1927. [10; 11]

Walker, S. F., historian, b. 1831; d. ? [37]

Walker, Stuart, playwright, b. Augusta, Ky., 1888; d. Beverly Hills, Calif., March 13, 1941. [7; 10; 11]

Walker, Thomas Leonard, mineralogist, b. Peel county, Ont., 1867; d. Toronto, Ont., Aug. 7, 1942. [27; 30]

Walker, Timothy, jurist, b. Wilmington, Mass., 1802; d. Cincinnati, O., Jan. 15, 1856. [1; 3; 4; 6]

Walker, William, adventurer, b. Nashville, Tenn., 1824; d. Trujillo, Honduras, Sept. 12, 1860. [1; 3; 4; 6; 7; 34]

Walker, William David, bishop, b. New York, N.Y., 1839; d. Buffalo, N.Y., May 2, 1917. [4; 10]

Walker, William Hultz, chemical engineer, b. Pittsburgh, Pa., 1869; d. Seabrook, N.H., July 9, 1934. [10]

Walker, Williston, church historian, b. Portland, Me., 1860; d. New Haven, Conn., March 9, 1922. [1; 4; 7; 10]

Wall, Alexander James, librarian, b. New York, N.Y., 1884; d. New York, N.Y., April 15, 1944. [7; 10]

Wall, Caleb Arnold, local historian, b. about 1821; d. 1898.

Wall, Edward John, writer on photography, b. England, 1860; d. Wollaston, Mass., Oct. 13, 1928. [10]

Wall, Evander Berry, autobiographer, b. New York, N.Y., 1860; d. Monte Carlo, Monaco, May 5, 1940. [2a; 7]

Wall, James Walter, politician, b. Trenton, N.J., 1820; d. Elizabeth, N.J., June 9, 1872. [3; 4; 6]

Wall, Oscar Garrett, journalist, b. near Logansport, Ind., 1844; d. Friday Harbor, Wash., Aug. 11, 1911. [70]

Wall, Otto Augustus, chemist, b. 1846; d. 1922. [13]

Wall, William Edmund, house decorator, b. 1858; d. May 8, 1934.

Wallace, Adam, clergyman, b. 1825; d. 1903. [6]

Wallace, Benjamin Bruce, tariff expert, b. Wooster, 1882; d. Washington, D.C., Jan. 5, 1946.

Wallace, Charles William, educationist, b. Hopkins, Mo., 1865; d. Wichita Falls, Aug. 7, 1932. [1; 4; 7; 10]

Wallace, David Alexander, clergyman, b. 1826; d. 1883.

Wallace, Dillon, explorer and writer of books for boys, b. Craigsville, N.Y., 1863; d. Beacon, N.Y., Sept. 28, 1939. [7; 10; 11]

Wallace, Edward Wilson, clergyman and educationist, b. Metuchen, N.J., 1880; d. Toronto, Ont., June 20, 1941. [11; 27; 30]

Wallace, Ellerslie, physician, b. 1819; d. 1885.

Wallace, Francis Huston, theologian, b. Ingersoll, Ont., 1851; d. Toronto, Ont., June 2, 1930. [27]

Wallace, Henry, clergyman and journalist, b. West Newton, Pa., 1836; d. 1916. [1; 7; 9; 10]

Wallace, Henry Cantwell, journalist, b. Rock Island, Ill., 1866; d. Washington, D.C., Oct. 25, 1924. [1; 4; 10]

Wallace, Horace Binney, miscellaneous writer, b. Philadelphia, Pa., 1817; d. Paris, France, Dec. 16, 1852. [1; 3; 4; 6; 7]

Wallace, Hugh Campbell, diplomat, b. Lexington, Mo., 1863; d. Washington, D.C., Jan. 1, 1931. [1; 10]

Wallace, Isaiah, clergyman, b. Coverdale, N.B., 1826; d. Aylesford, N.S., Dec. 24, 1907. [27]

Wallace, James, mathematician, d. South Carolina, 1851. [6]

Wallace, James, educationist, b. near Wooster, O., 1849; d. St. Paul, Minn., Aug. 23, 1939. [10]

Wallace, James Nevin, surveyor and historian, b. Ireland; d. Spring Banks, Alta., Jan. 12, 1941. [27]

Wallace, John, politician, fl. 1862-1888.

Wallace, John Hankins, horse-breeder, b. Allegheny county, Pa., 1822; d. New York, N.Y., May 2, 1903. [1]

Wallace, John Sherman, clergyman, b. Linn county, Ore., 1877; d. Rochester, N.Y., May 24, 1934. [10; 11]

Wallace, John William, lawyer, b. Philadelphia, Pa., 1815; d. Philadelphia, Pa., Jan. 12, 1884. [1; 3; 6]

Wallace, Joseph, lawyer and historian, b. Carroll county, Ky., 1834; d. Springfield, Ill., 1904. [10]

Wallace, Lewis, soldier and novelist, b. Brookville, Ind., 1827; d. Crawfordsville, Ind., Feb. 15, 1905. [1; 3; 4; 6; 8; 71; 72]

Wallace, Michael A., clergyman, d. 1892.

Wallace, Oates Charles Symonds, clergyman, b. Canaan, N.S., 1856; d. Baltimore, Md., Aug. 29, 1947. [10; 11]

Wallace, Mrs. Susan Arnold, née **Elston,** miscellaneous writer, b. Crawfordsville, Ind., 1830; d. Oct. 1, 1907. [3; 4; 5; 7; 10]

Wallace, William Allen, local historian, b. 1815; d. 1893.

Wallace, William Clay, oculist, d. 1898. [6]

Wallace, William De Witt, miscellaneous writer, b. 1838; d. ?

Wallace, William George, clergyman, b. Galt, Ont., 1858; d. Toronto, Ont., Dec. 22, 1949. [30]

Wallace, William H., lawyer, b. Clark county, Ky., 1848; d. Kansas City, Mo., Oct. 22, 1937. [10]

Wallace, William Ross, lawyer and poet, b. Lexington, Ky., 1819; d. New York, N.Y., May 5, 1881. [1; 3; 4; 5; 6; 7; 9; 34; 71]

Wallack, John Lester, actor and playwright, b. New York., N.Y., 1820; d. Stamford, Conn., Sept. 6, 1888. [1; 3; 4; 5; 71]

Waller, Henry Davey, clergyman, d. Amagansett, Long Island, N.Y., Sept. 13, 1925.

Waller, John Lightfoot, clergyman, b. Woodford county, Ky., 1809; d. Louisville, Ky., Oct. 10, 1854. [1; 4; 6]

Waller, Mary Ella, novelist and essayist, b. Boston, Mass., 1855; d. Wellesley, Mass., June 14, 1938. [7; 9; 10]

Waller, Willard Walter, sociologist, b. Murphysboro, Ill., 1899; d. El Paso, Tex., July 26, 1945. [10; 13]

Walling, George Washington, police officer, b. Monmouth county, N.J., 1823; d. Holmdel, Monmouth county, N.J., Dec. 31, 1891. [3b]

Walling, William English, social reformer, b. Louisville, Ky., 1877; d. Amsterdam, Holland, Sept. 12, 1936. [10]

Wallington, Mrs. Nellie, née **Urner,** journalist, b. Cincinnati, O., 1847; d. Parkerford, Pa., Jan. 12, 1933. [10]

Wallis, Frank Edwin, architect, b. Eastport, Me., 1862; d. Paris, France, March 21, 1929. [4]

Wallis, Jenny (pseud.). See Morrison, Mrs. Mary Jane, née Whitney.

Wallis, Severn Teackle, lawyer, b. Baltimore, Md., 1816; d. Baltimore, Md., April 11, 1894. [1; 3; 4]

Walmsley, William Henry, merchant, b. 1830; d. ?

Waln, Robert, merchant, b. Philadelphia, Pa., 1765; d. Philadelphia, Pa., Jan. 24, 1836. [1; 3; 4; 6]

Waln, Robert, satirist, b. Philadelphia, Pa., 1794; d. Providence, R.I., July 4, 1825. [1; 3; 6; 7; 9]

Walser, George Henry, poet, b. 1834; d. 1910.

Walsh, Alexander Stewart, clergyman, b. New York, N.Y., 1841; d. Brooklyn, N.Y., Sept. 17, 1918. [26]

Walsh, Francis Augustine, priest and educationist, b. Cincinnati, O., 1884; d. Washington, D.C., Aug. 13, 1938. [21]

Walsh, Henry Collins, journalist, b. Florence, Italy, 1863; d. Philadelphia, Pa., April 29, 1927. [1; 7; 10]

Walsh, James Anthony, bishop, b. Cambridge, Mass., 1867; d. Ossining, N.Y., April 14, 1936. [10; 21]

Walsh, John, priest, b. Ireland, 1847; d. Troy, N.Y., Nov. 19, 1919. [21]

Walsh, John Henry, educationist, b. Brooklyn, N.Y., 1853; d. Brooklyn, N.Y., Dec. 13, 1924. [10]

Walsh, John Johnston, missionary, b. Newburgh N.Y., 1830; d. Amenia, N.Y., Feb. 7, 1844. [3; 6]

Walsh, Joseph M., merchant, fl. 1884-1896.

Walsh, Marie A., novelist, fl. 1878-1898.

Walsh, Michael, educationist, b. Ireland, 1763; d. Amesbury, Mass., Aug. 20, 1840. [3; 6]

Walsh, Michael, politician, b. Youghall, Ireland, 1810; d. New York, N.Y., March 17, 1859. [1; 3; 6]

Walsh, Ralph, physician, b. 1841; d. Jerusalem, Md., Jan. 15, 1915.

Walsh, Robert, journalist, b. Baltimore, Md., 1784; d. Paris, France, Feb. 7, 1859. [1; 3; 4; 6; 7]

Walsh, Robert F., miscellaneous writer, b. Kinsale, Ireland, 1858; d. New York, N.Y., Dec. 28, 1895. [3b]

Walsh, Thomas, poet and critic, b. Brooklyn, N.Y., 1871; d. Brooklyn, N.Y., Oct. 29, 1928. [1; 7; 10; 11; 21]

Walsh, William Francis, lawyer and educationist, b. Hancock, Mass., 1875; d. Bridgeport, Mass., Sept. 15, 1946. [10]

Walsh, William Shepard, editor, b. Paris, France, 1854; d. Dec. 8, 1919. [3; 6; 7]

Walsh, William Thomas, biographer, novelist, and poet, b. Waterbury, Conn., 1891; d. White Plains, N.Y., Feb. 22, 1949. [10; 21; 62]

Walshe, John D., clergyman and poet, b. 1850; d. San José, Calif., 1930. [35]

Walter, Mrs. Carrie, née Stevens, b. Savannah, Mo., 1846; d. San José, Calif., April 26, 1907. [35]

Walter, Edward Lorraine, educationist, b. 1845; d. at sea, July 4, 1898. [53]

Walter, Ellery, traveller and journalist, b. Philadelphia, Pa., 1906; d. St. Petersburg, Fla., April 2, 1935. [7; 10]

Walter, Eugene, playwright, b. Cleveland, O., 1874; d. Hollywood, Calif., Sept. 26, 1941. [7; 10]

Walter, Frank Keller, librarian, b. Point Pleasant, Pa., 1874; d. Minneapolis, Minn., Oct 28, 1945. [7; 10]

Walter, Frederick (pseud.). See Schultz, Frederick Walter.

Walter, Howard Arnold, missionary, b. New Britain, Conn., 1883; d. Nov. 11, 1918. [10]

Walter, Johnston Estep, clergyman and educationist, b. Saltsburg, Pa., 1843; d. West Newton, Pa., July 17, 1924. [67]

Walter, Nehemiah, clergyman, b. Youghall, Ireland, 1663; d. Roxbury, Mass., Sept. 17, 1750. [3; 6; 51]

Walter, Robert, physician, b. Acton, Ont., 1841; d. Reading, Pa., Oct. 26, 1921. [10]

Walter, Thomas, clergyman, b. Roxbury, Mass., 1696; d. Roxbury, Mass., Jan. 10, 1725. [1; 3; 6; 7]

Walter, Thomas Ustick, architect, b. Philadelphia, Pa., 1804; d. Philadelphia, Pa., Oct. 30, 1887. [1; 3; 4; 6]

Walter, William Bicker, poet, b. Boston, Mass., 1796; d. Charleston, S.C., April 23, 1822. [3; 6]

Walter, William Henry, musician, b. Newark, N.J., 1825; d. 1893. [3; 6]

Walter, William Joseph, educationist, b. England; d. Philadelphia, Pa., Oct. 9, 1846.

Waltermire, Beecher Wesley, poet, b. 1858; d. Columbus, O., 1932.

Walters, Alexander, bishop, b. Bardstown, Ky., 1858; d. Feb. 2, 1917. [1; 10]

Walters, John Daniel, educationist, b. 1847; d. 1929.

Walther, Carl Ferdinand Wilhelm, theologian, b. near Waldenburg, Saxony, 1811; d. St. Louis, Mo., May 7, 1887. [1; 3; 6]

Walton, Clifford Stevens, lawyer, b. Chardon, O., 1861; d. Washington, D.C., May 15, 1912. [4; 10]

Walton, George Augustus, educationist, b. South Reading, Mass., 1822; d. 1908. [10]

Walton, George Edward, physician, b. Cincinnati, O., 1839; d. Terre Haute, Ind., June 26, 1917. [3; 6]

Walton, George Lincoln, neurologist, b. Lawrence, Mass., 1854; d. Boston, Mass., Jan. 18, 1841. [10; 11; 51]

Walton, Joseph Solomon, historian, d. Newtown, Pa., Jan. 22, 1912.

Walton, Josiah Proctor, genealogist and local historian, b. 1826; d. Muscatine, Ia., 1899. [37]

Walton, Mason Augustus, backwoodsman, b. Oldtown, Me., 1838; d. 1917. [10]

Walton, William, painter, b. Philadelphia, Pa., 1843; d. Nov. 3, 1915. [10]

Walton, William Claiborne, clergyman, b. Hanover county, Va., 1793; d. Hartford, Conn., Feb. 18, 1834. [3; 34]

Waltz, Mrs. Elizabeth, née Cherry, novelist, b. Columbus, O., 1866; d. Louisville, Ky., Sept. 19, 1903. [7; 10]

Walworth, Clarence Augustus, priest, b. Plattsburg, N.Y., 1820; d. Albany, N.Y., Sept. 19, 1900. [1; 3; 4; 5; 6; 7; 21]

Walworth, Mrs. Ellen, née Hardin, historian and biographer, b. Jacksonville, Ill., 1832; d. Washington, D.C., June 22, 1915. [3; 7; 10; 21]

Walworth, Mrs. Jeannette Ritchie, née Hadermann, novelist, b. Philadelphia, Pa., 1837; d. New Orleans, La., Feb. 4, 1918. [1; 3; 4; 6; 7; 10; 34]

Walworth, Mansfield Tracy, novelist, b. Albany, N.Y., 1830; d. New York, N.Y., June 3, 1873. [3; 4; 6; 7]

Walworth, Reuben Hyde, jurist, b. Bozrah, Conn., 1788; d. Saratoga Springs, N.Y., Nov. 27, 1867. [1; 3; 4; 5; 6]

Wambaugh, Eugene, lawyer and educationist, b. near Brookville, O., 1856; d. Dublin, N.H., Aug. 6, 1940. [10; 51]

Wanamaker, John, merchant, b. Philadelphia, Pa., 1838; d. near Philadelphia, Pa., Dec. 12, 1922. [1; 2; 4; 5; 10]

Wanamaker, Reuben Melville, jurist, b. North Jackson, O., 1866; d. Columbus, O., June 18, 1924. [1]

Wandell, Samuel Henry, lawyer, b. Oswego county, N.Y., 1860; d. Mexico, N.Y., Sept. 25, 1943. [10]

Wanger, Ruth, educationist, b. 1897; d. Norristown, Pa., Aug. 18, 1943.

Wanless, Andrew, poet, b. Berwickshire, England; d. Detroit, Mich., 1898. [39]

Wanless, Sir **William James,** medical missionary, b. Charleston, Ont., 1865; d. Glendale, Calif., March 3, 1933. [1]

Wanner, Aaron, clergyman, fl. 1853-1888.

Waples, Dorothy, educationist, b. China, 1896. d. Appleton, Wis., June 11, 1948. [62]

Waples, Rufus, lawyer, b. Millsboro, Del., 1825; d. 1902. [10]

Warburg, Paul Moritz, banker, b. Hamburg, Germany, 1868; d. New York, N.Y., Jan. 24, 1932. [1; 10]

Warburton, Alexander Bannerman, politician, b. Charlottetown, P.E.I., 1852; d. Charlottetown, P.E.I., Jan. 14, 1929. [27]

Warburton, George Augustus, biographer, b. 1859; d. Toronto, Ont., Feb. 21, 1929.

Ward, Aaron, soldier and politician, b. Sing Sing, N.Y., 1790; d. Georgetown, D.C., March 2, 1867. [3; 4; 6]

Ward, Andrew Henshaw, antiquary, b. Shrewsbury, Mass., 1784; d. Newtonville, Mass., Feb. 18, 1864. [3; 6]

Ward, Anna Lydia, compiler, b. Bloomfield, N.J., about 1850; d. Waterbury, Conn., Feb. 2, 1933. [7; 10; 11]

Ward, Artemas, advertising agent, b. 1848; d. New York, N.Y., March 14, 1925. [4]

Ward, Artemus (pseud.). See Browne, Charles Farrar.

Ward, Caleb Theophilus, clergyman, b. 1843; d. Feb. 18, 1918.

Ward, Mrs. **Catherine Weed,** née **Barnes,** journalist, b. Albany, N.Y., 1851; d. July 31, 1913. [7; 10]

Ward, Charles Henshaw, educationist, b. Norfolk, Neb., 1872; d. New Haven, Conn., Oct. 8, 1935. [1a; 10; 62]

Ward, Christopher Longstreth, lawyer and historian, b. Wilmington, Del., 1868; d. Wilmington, Del., Feb. 20, 1943. [7; 10; 11]

Ward, Cyrenus Osborne, labour leader, b. western New York, 1831; d. Yuma, Ariz., March 19, 1902. [1; 4]

Ward, Delancey Walton, chemist, b. 1866; d. March 16, 1930. [48]

Ward, Durbin, lawyer, b. Augusta, Ky., 1819; d. Lebanon, O., May 22, 1886. [3; 4; 6]

Ward, Duren James Henderson, clergyman and educationist, b. Dorchester, Ont., 1851; d. Denver, Colo., Jan. 23, 1942. [10; 11]

Ward, Elijah, politician, b. Sing Sing, N.Y., 1816; d. Roslyn, Long Island, N.Y., Feb. 7, 1882. [3; 4; 5; 6]

Ward, Mrs. **Elizabeth Stuart,** née **Phelps,** novelist, b. Boston, Mass., 1844; d. Newton Centre, Mass., Jan. 28, 1911. [1; 2; 3; 4; 5; 6; 7; 8; 9; 10]

Ward, Estelle Frances, historian, b. Chicago, Ill.; d. Lake Forest, Ill., April 20, 1941. [11]

Ward, Ferdinand De Wilton, missionary, b. Bergen, N.Y., 1812; d. Clarens, Switzerland, Aug. 11, 1891. [3; 6]

Ward, Florence Elizabeth, educationist, b. Mauston, Wis.; d. Washington, D.C., Feb., 1934. [10; 11]

Ward, Franklin Wilmer, soldier, b. Philadelphia, Pa., 1870; d. Albany, N.Y., March 17, 1938. [10]

Ward, Genevieve, actress, b. New York, N.Y., 1838; d. London, England, Aug. 18, 1922. [1; 4; 10]

Ward, Mrs. **H. O.** (pseud.). See Bloomfield-Moore, Mrs. Clara Sophia, née Jessup.

Ward, Harry Parker, publisher and genealogist, b. 1865; d. Columbus, O., Oct. 3, 1926.

Ward, Henry Alson, physician, b. 1853; d. Richfield, N.Y., June 30, 1928.

Ward, Henry Augustus, naturalist, b. Rochester, N.Y., 1834; d. Buffalo, N.Y., July 4, 1906. [1; 3; 4; 5; 10]

Ward, Henry Baldwin, zoologist, b. Troy, N.Y., 1865; d. Urbana, Ill., Nov. 30, 1945. [4; 10; 13]

Ward, Henry Dana, clergyman, b. Shrewsbury, Mass., 1797; d. Philadelphia, Pa., Feb. 29, 1884. [1; 3]

Ward, Henshaw. See Ward, Charles Henshaw.

Ward, Herbert Dickinson, publicist and novelist, b. Waltham, Mass., 1861; d. Portsmouth, N.H., June 18, 1932. [1; 3; 4; 5; 6; 7; 10; 11]

Ward, James Harman, naval officer, b. Hartford, Conn., 1806; d. near Matthias Point, Potomac river, June 27, 1861. [1; 3; 5; 6]

Ward, James Warner, librarian and poet, b. Newark, N.J., 1816; d. Buffalo, N.Y., June 28, 1897. [1; 3; 4; 6; 7; 19]

Ward, John, soldier and physician, b. New York, N.Y., 1838; d. 1896. [3; 6]

Ward, John William George, clergyman, b. Liverpool, England, 1879; d. Chicago, Ill., Sept. 29, 1945. [10]

Ward, Julius Hammond, clergyman, b. Charlton, Mass., 1837; d. Worcester, Mass., May 30, 1897. [3; 62]

Ward, Lester Frank, sociologist, b. Joliet, Ill., 1841; d. Washington, D.C., April 18, 1913. [1; 2; 3; 4; 5; 9; 10]

Ward, Louis B., business counsellor, b. Watertown, N.Y., 1891; d. Detroit, Mich., April 20, 1942. [21]

Ward, Mrs. Lydia, née **Avery,** poet, b. Lynchburg, Va., 1845; d. Chicago, Ill., Feb. 26, 1924. [1; 7; 10]

Ward, Matthew Flournoy, cotton-planter, b. Scott county, Ky., 1826; d. Helena, Ark., Sept. 30, 1862. [3; 6; 34]

Ward, Mrs. May, née **Alden,** biographer, b. Ohio, 1853; d. Cambridge, Mass., Jan. 15, 1918. [7; 10]

Ward, Osborne. See Ward, Cyrenus Osborne.

Ward, Richard Halsted, physician, b. Bloomfield, N.J., 1837; d. Troy, N.Y., Oct. 28, 1917. [1; 3; 4; 5; 10]

Ward, Robert De Courcy, climatologist, b. Boston, Mass., 1867; d. Cambridge, Mass., Nov. 12, 1931. [1; 10; 51]

Ward, Samuel, diplomat and poet, b. New York, N.Y., 1814; d. Pegli, Italy, May 19, 1884. [1; 3; 4; 5; 6; 7]

Ward, Susan Hayes, religious writer, b. Abington, Mass., 1838; d. South Berwick, Me., 1924. [10]

Ward, Thomas, poet, b. Newark, N.J., 1807; d. New York, N.Y., April 13, 1873. [1; 3; 4; 6; 7; 9]

Ward, William Godman, educationist, b. Sandusky, O., 1848; d. Nov. 3, 1923. [5; 7; 10]

Ward, William Hayes, archaeologist and journalist, b. Abington, Mass., 1835; d. South Berwick, Me., Aug. 28, 1916. [1; 3; 7; 10]

Wardall, Ruth Aimée, home economist, b. Tolono, Ill., 1877; d. Urbana, Ill., July 15, 1936. [10; 11]

Warde, Frederic, printer, b. Wells, Minn., 1894; d. July 31, 1939. [7]

Warde, Frederick Barkham, actor, b. Oxfordshire, England, 1851; d. Brooklyn, N.Y., Feb. 7, 1935. [1a; 4; 10; 11]

Warden, Robert Bruce, jurist, b. Bardstown, Ky., 1824; d. Washington, D.C., Dec. 3, 1888. [1; 3; 6]

Warder, George Woodward, lawyer, poet, and novelist, b. Richmond, Mo., 1848; d. Kansas City, Mo., Jan., 1907. [10; 34]

Warder, John Aston, physician, forester, and horticulturist, b. Philadelphia, Pa., 1812; d. North Bend, O., July 14, 1883. [1; 3; 4; 6]

Wardman, Ervin, journalist, b. Salt Lake City, Utah, 1865; d. New York, N.Y., Jan. 13, 1923. [1; 7; 10]

Wardner, Henry Steele, local historian, b. Windsor, Vt., 1867; d. Windsor, Vt., March 5, 1935. [7]

Ware, Eugene Fitch, lawyer and poet, b. Hartford, Conn., 1841; d. Cascade, Colo., July 1, 1911. [4; 7; 10]

Ware, Francis Morgan, horseman, b. Cambridge, Mass., 1857; d. Arlington, Mass., Oct. 24, 1926. [10; 51]

Ware, George Frederick, poet, b. 1820; d. 1849. [51]

Ware, Henry, clergyman, b. Sherborn, Mass., 1764; d. Cambridge, Mass., July 12, 1845. [1; 3; 4; 6; 7; 9]

Ware, Henry, clergyman, b. Hingham, Mass., 1794; d. Framingham, Mass., Sept. 22, 1843. [1; 3; 4; 5; 6; 7; 8; 9; 51]

Ware, John, physician, b. Hingham, Mass., 1795; d. Boston, Mass., April 29, 1864. [1; 3; 5; 6]

Ware, John Fothergill Waterhouse, clergyman, b. Boston, Mass., 1818; d. Milton, Mass., Feb. 26, 1881. [1; 3; 6]

Ware, Jonathan, lawyer and economist, b. Wrentham, Mass., 1767; d. Andover, N.H., Feb. 1, 1838. [43]

Ware, Joseph, poet, b. 1841; d. Mechanicsburg, O., Sept. 1, 1922.

Ware, Lewis Sharpe, engineer, b. Philadelphia, Pa., 1851; d. Nov. 20, 1918. [4; 10]

Ware, Mrs. Mary Greene, née **Chandler,** religious writer, b. Petersham, Mass., 1818; d. ? [3; 6]

Ware, Mrs. Mary Smith, née **Dabney,** traveller, b. Raymond, Miss., 1842; d. ? [11]

Ware, Nathaniel A., public official, b. about 1780; d. near Galveston, Tex., 1854. [1; 3; 4; 34]

Ware, William, clergyman, b. Hingham, Mass., 1797; d. Cambridge, Mass., Feb. 19, 1852. [1; 3; 4; 5; 6; 7; 8; 9; 71]

Ware, William Robert, architect, b. Cambridge, Mass., 1832; d. Milton, Mass., June 9, 1915. [1; 3; 4; 10; 51]

Wareing, Ernest Clyde, clergyman, b. Volga, Ind., 1872; d. Lakeside, O., Feb. 4, 1944. [10]

Warfel, Linda. See Slaughter, Mrs. Linda, née Warfel.

Warfield, Benjamin Breckinridge, theologian, b. near Lexington, Ky., 1851; d. Princeton, N.J., Feb. 16, 1921. [1; 4; 5; 10]

Warfield, Mrs. Catherine Anne, née **Ware,** novelist, b. Natchez, Miss., 1816; d. Pewee Valley, Ky., May 21, 1877. [1; 3; 4; 5; 6; 7; 34; 71]

Warfield, Ethelbert Dudley, educationist, b. Lexington, Ky., 1861; d. Chambersburg, Pa., July 6, 1943. [4; 10; 34]

Warfield, Joshua Dorsey, educationist, b. Maryland, 1838; d. ? [78]

Warfield, Perry Snowden, lawyer, d. 1853. [56]

Warfield, William, explorer and engineer, b. Easton, Pa., 1891; d. Ridgefield Park, N.J., March 16, 1947. [11]

Waring, George Edwin, sanitary engineer and agriculturist, b. Poundridge, N.Y., 1833; d. New York, N.Y., Oct. 28, 1898. [1; 3; 4; 6; 7]

Waring, George J., priest, b. Blackburn, England, 1872; d. New York, N.Y., Feb. 13, 1943. [21]

Waring, Guy, pioneer, b. about 1859; d. March 28, 1936.

Waring, Henry Fish, clergyman and educationist, b. Saint John, N.B., 1870; d. Boston, Mass., July 10, 1936.

Waring, Janet, decorator, b. 1870; d. Yonkers, N.Y., Jan. 18, 1941.

Waring, Luther Hess, clergyman, b. Tyrone, Pa., 1865; d. Washington, D.C., Feb. 3, 1941.

Waring, Mrs. Malvina Sarah, née Black, novelist, b. Newberry, S.C., 1842; d. Columbia, S.C., Dec. 6, 1930. [10; 34]

Wark, David, physician, fl. 1868-1912.

Warman, Cy, poet and short-story writer, b. Greenup, Ill., 1855; d. Chicago, Ill., April 7, 1914. [1; 4; 7; 10; 27]

Warman, Edward Barrett, lecturer, b. Scotts Mountain, Warren county, N.J., 1847; d. Nov. 26, 1931. [10; 11; 37]

Warmoth, Henry Clay, soldier, lawyer, and politician, b. MacLeansboro, Ill., 1842; d. New Orleans, La., Sept. 30, 1931. [1; 4; 5; 10]

Warne, Francis Wesley, bishop, b. Erin, Ont., 1854; d. Brooklyn, N.Y., March 1, 1932. [10]

Warne, Joseph Andrews, clergyman, b. 1795; d. 1881.

Warner, Adoniram Judson, politician, b. Wales, Erie county, N.Y., 1834; d. Marietta, O., Aug. 12, 1910. [1; 3; 4; 5; 6; 10]

Warner, Amos Griswold, sociologist, b. Elkader, Ala., 1861; d. Las Cruces, N.M., Jan. 17, 1900. [1; 4; 10]

Warner, Anna Bartlett, novelist and writer of books for children, b. New York, N.Y., 1827; d. Highland Falls, N.Y., Jan. 22, 1915. [1; 3; 4; 6; 7; 9; 10]

Warner, Anne. See French, Mrs. Anne, née Warner.

Warner, Beverley Ellison, clergyman, b. Jersey City, N.J., 1855; d. 1910. [10; 34]

Warner, Charles Dudley, essayist, novelist, and editor, b. Plainfield, Mass., 1829; d. Hartford, Conn., Oct. 20, 1900. [1; 2; 3; 4; 5; 6; 7; 8; 9; 10; 71]

Warner, Daniel Sidney, clergyman, b. 1842; d. 1895.

Warner, Mrs. Ellen E., née Kenyon, educationist, fl. 1889-1912.

Warner, George Henry, editor, b. Plainfield, Mass., 1833; d. Tryon, N.C., May 29, 1919. [10]

Warner, Helen Garnie, miscellaneous writer, b. 1846; d. ?

Warner, Mrs. Helen P., compiler, fl. 1871-1875. [6]

Warner, Henry Edward, journalist and poet, b. Elyria, O., 1876; d. Baltimore, Md., April 11, 1941. [7; 10]

Warner, Henry Whiting, lawyer, d. 1875. [6]

Warner, Horace Emory, clergyman, b. Castleton, N.Y., 1855; d. Dec. 15, 1911.

Warner, Horace Everett, lawyer and civil servant, b. Lake county, O., 1839; d. Oct. 29, 1930. [10]

Warner, Ira de Ver, physician, b. Lincklaen, N.Y., 1840; d. Jan. 11, 1913.

Warner, James Franklin, musician, b. 1802; d. 1864. [6]

Warner, John De Witt, lawyer and politician, b. Reading, N.Y., 1851; d. New York, N.Y., May 27, 1925. [4; 10]

Warner, Jonathan Trumbull, pioneer, b. Hadlyme, Conn., 1807; d. Los Angeles, Calif., April 22, 1895. [1]

Warner, Juan José. See Warner, Jonathan Trumbull.

Warner, Lucien Calvin, physician and capitalist, b. Cuyler, N.Y., 1841; d. New York, N.Y., July 30, 1925. [4; 10]

Warner, Moses Melborn, local historian, b. Iowa, 1855; d. Lyons, Neb., Nov. 17, 1921.

Warner, Susan Bogert, novelist, b. New York, N.Y., 1819; d. Highland Falls, N.Y., March 17, 1885. [1; 2; 3; 4; 5; 6; 7; 8; 9; 71]

Warr, John W., accountant, b. Cleveland, O., 1844; d. ?

Warren, Arthur, journalist, b. Dorchester, Mass., 1860; d. Bermuda, B.W.I., April 16, 1924. [7; 10]

Warren, Caroline Matilda, See Thayer, Mrs. Caroline Matilda, née Warren.

Warren, Cornelia, novelist, b. Waltham, Mass., 1857; d. Waltham, Mass., June 5, 1921.

Warren, David M., publisher, b. Worcester, Mass., 1820; d. Baltimore, Md., 1861. [6]

Warren, Ebenezer W., clergyman, b. 1820; d. ? [34]

Warren, Edward, physician, b. Boston, Mass., 1804; d. 1878. [3; 6]

Warren, Edward, physician, b. Tyrrell county, N.C., 1828; d. Paris, France, Sept. 16, 1893. [9]

Warren, Edward Henry, lawyer and educationist, b. Worcester, Mass., 1873; d. Boston, Mass., July 24, 1945. [10]

Warren, Edward Royal, naturalist, b. Waltham, Mass., 1860; d. Colorado Springs, Colo., April 20, 1942. [10]

Warren, Mrs. Eliza, née Spalding, pioneer, b. Oregon Territory, 1837; d. Coeur d'Alène, Ore., June 21, 1919.

Warren, Frederick Morris, educationist, b. Durham, Me., 1859; d. New Haven, Conn., Dec. 6, 1931. [4; 7; 10; 11]

Warren, George Frederick, educationist, b. Harvard, Neb., 1874; d. Ithaca, N.Y., May 24, 1938. [10; 11]

Warren, George Henry, surveyor, b. Oakfield, N.Y., 1845; d. Minneapolis, Minn., Jan. 23, 1927. [70]

Warren, George Washington, dentist, b. Ocean county, N.J., 1863; d. May 29, 1934. [10; 11]

Warren, George William, organist and composer, b. Albany, N.Y., 1828; d. New York, N.Y., March 17, 1902. [3; 4; 20]

Warren, Henry Clarke, Orientalist, b. Cambridge, Mass., 1854; d. Cambridge, Mass., Jan. 4, 1899. [1]

Warren, Henry Pitt, educationist, b. Windham, Me., 1846; d. Albany, N.Y., May 27, 1919. [10; 62]

Warren, Henry Vallette, clergyman, d. 1906.

Warren, Henry Waterman, politician, b. 1838; d. Holden, Mass., Feb. 21, 1919.

Warren, Henry White, bishop, b. Williamsburg, Mass., 1831; d. University Park, near Denver, Colo., July 22, 1912. [1; 3; 4; 5; 6; 10]

Warren, Herbert Langford, architect, b. Manchester, England, 1857; d. Cambridge, Mass., June 27, 1917. [1a; 10]

Warren, Howard Crosby, psychologist, b. Montclair, N.J., 1867; d. New York, N.Y., Jan. 4, 1934. [1; 7; 10; 11]

Warren, Ira, physician, b. Hawkesbury, Upper Canada, 1806; d. 1864. [3]

Warren, Israel Perkins, clergyman, b. Woodbridge, Conn., 1814; d. Portland, Me., Oct. 9, 1892. [1; 3; 4; 6; 7; 62]

Warren, John, surgeon, b. Roxbury, Mass., 1753; d. Boston, Mass., April 4, 1815. [1; 3; 4; 6; 9]

Warren, John, naturalist, fl. 1834.

Warren, John, anatomist, b. Beverley, Mass., 1874; d. July 17, 1928. [51]

Warren, John Collins, surgeon, b. Boston, Mass., 1778; d. Boston, Mass., May 4, 1856. [1; 3; 6]

Warren, John Collins, surgeon, b. Boston, Mass., 1842; d. Boston, Mass., Nov. 3, 1927. [1; 3; 5; 6; 10; 51]

Warren, John Esaias, traveller, b. Troy, N.Y.; d. Brussels, Belgium, July 6, 1896. [6; 70]

Warren, Jonathan Mason, surgeon, b. Boston, Mass., 1811; d. Boston, Mass., Aug. 19, 1867. [3; 6]

Warren, Joseph, missionary, fl. 1841-1873.

Warren, Joseph, lawyer, b. Boston, Mass., 1876; d. Boston, Mass., Sept. 19. 1942.

Warren, Josiah, reformer, b. Boston, Mass., 1798; d. Charlestown, Mass., April 14, 1874. [1; 3; 4; 9]

Warren, Marvin, lawyer, fl. 1854-1896.

Warren, Mrs. Maude Lavinia, née **Radford,** novelist and writer of books for children, b. Wolfe Island, Ont., 1875; d. Ithaca, N.Y., July 6, 1934. [7; 10]

Warren, Mrs. Mercy, née **Otis,** poet, playwright, and historian, b. Barnstable, Mass., 1728; d. Plymouth, Mass., Oct. 19, 1814. [1; 3; 4; 6; 7; 9]

Warren, Nathan Boughton, musician, b. Troy, N.Y., 1815; d. Troy, N.Y., Sept. 3, 1898. [3b; 4]

Warren, Patience (pseud.). See Kelsey, Mrs. Jeannette Garr, née Washburn.

Warren, Samuel Edward, mathematician, b. West Newton, Mass., 1831; d. 1909. [1; 3; 4; 6; 10]

Warren, Thomas Robinson, mariner, b. New York, N.Y., 1828; d. ? [6; 8]

Warren, Walter (pseud.). See Raymond, George Lansing.

Warren, William, clergyman, b. Waterford, Me., 1806; d. Gorham, Me., Jan. 28, 1879. [3; 6: 38]

Warren, William Fairfield, clergyman and educationst, b. Williamsburg, Mass., 1833; d. Brookline, Mass., Dec. 6, 1929. [1; 3; 4; 5; 6; 10]

Warren, William Henry, clergyman, b. North River, P.E.I. 1845; d. Bridgetown, N.S., March 11, 1911. [33]

Warren, William Wilkins, traveller, b. 1814; d. 1890.

Warriner, Edward Augustus, clergyman b. Agawam, Mass., 1829; d. 1908. [4; 10]

Warriner, Edwin, clergyman, b. 1839; d. 1898.

Warriner, Francis, clergyman, b. Springfield, Mass., 1804; d. Chester, Mass., April 22, 1866. [3; 6; 45]

Warring, Charles Bartlett, educationist, b. Charlton, N.Y., 1825; d. 1907. [10]

Warrington, Joseph, physician, fl. 1828-1846. [6]

Warshow, Robert Irving, biographer and financial writer, b. 1898; d. New York, N.Y., Nov. 6, 1938.

Warthin, Aldred Scott, physician and educationist, b. Greensburg, Ind., 1866; d. Ann Arbor, Mich., May 23, 1931. [1; 10; 11]

Warvelle, George William, lawyer, b. 1852; d. Chicago, Ill., Nov. 11, 1940. [10]

Warwick, Charles Franklin, lawyer and historian, b. Philadelphia, Pa., 1852; d. Philadelphia, Pa., April 4, 1913. [10]

Washburn, Cephas, missionary, b. 1793; d. 1860.

Washburn, Charles Ames, journalist and diplomat, b. South Livermore, Me., 1822; d. New York, N.Y., Jan. 26, 1889. [3; 4; 5; 6; 7]

Washburn, Charles Grenfill, politician and manufacturer, b. Worcester, Mass., 1857; d. Lenox, Mass., May 25, 1928. [1; 10; 51]

Washburn, Claude Carlos, novelist and playwright, b. Mankato, Minn., 1883; d. Duluth, Minn., Aug. 11, 1926. [10; 11]

Washburn, Edward Abiel, clergyman, b. Boston, Mass., 1819; d. New York, N.Y., Feb. 2, 1881. [1; 3; 4; 6; 7]

Washburn, Edward Wight, chemist, b. Beatrice, Neb., 1881; d. Washington, D.C., Feb. 6, 1934. [1; 10; 11]

Washburn, Edwin Chapin, railway executive, b. Minneapolis, Minn., 1870; d. Englewood, N.J., Aug. 10, 1937. [11]

Washburn, Elihu Benjamin. See Washburne, Elihu Benjamin.

Washburn, Emory, lawyer and politician, b. Leicester, Mass., 1800; d. Cambridge, Mass., March 18, 1877. [1; 3; 4; 5; 6]

Washburn, Francis clergyman, b. New York, 1843; d. Newburgh, N.Y., Dec. 5, 1914. [10]

Washburn, Frederic Leonard, entomologist, b. Brookline, Mass., 1860; d. Minneapolis, Minn., Oct. 15, 1927. [4; 10; 11; 51]

Washburn, George, missionary, b. Middleboro, Mass., 1833; d. Boston, Mass., Feb. 15, 1915. [1; 4; 10]

Washburn, George H., soldier, b. 1843; d. 1905.

Washburn, Henry Stevenson, manufacturer and poet, b. Providence, R.I., 1813; d. Boston, Mass., Oct. 1, 1903. [10]

Washburn, Israel, lawyer and politician, b. Livermore, Me., 1813; d. Philadelphia, Pa., May 12, 1883. [1; 3; 4; 6; 38]

Washburn, Mrs. Katharine, née **Sedgwick,** novelist, fl. 1871-1875.

Washburn, Margaret Floy, psychologist, b. New York, N.Y., 1871; d. Poughkeepsie, N.Y., Oct. 29, 1939. [10]

Washburn, Peter Thatcher, lawyer, b. Lynn, Mass., 1814; d. Woodstock, Vt., Feb. 7, 1870. [4; 43]

Washburn, Robert Morris, journalist, b. Worcester, Mass., 1868; d. Boston, Mass., Feb. 26, 1946. [10; 51]

Washburn, Slater, soldier, b. Princeton, Mass., 1896; d. Washington, D.C., July 12, 1941. [51]

Washburn, William Ives, lawyer, b. Bridgeport, Conn., 1854; d. Spring Lake Beach, N.J., July 30, 1933. [45]

Washburn, William Tucker, lawyer, b. Boston, Mass., 1841; d. New York, N.Y., Oct. 22, 1916. [10]

Washburne, Elihu Benjamin, politician and diplomat, b. Livermore, Me., 1816; d. Chicago, Ill., Oct. 23, 1887. [1; 3; 4; 5; 6; 7]

Washburne, Israel Albert, lawyer and educationist, b. 1862; d. New York, N.Y., June 30, 1938.

Washington, Booker Taliaferro, educationist, b. Franklin county, Va., 1856; d. Tuskegee, Ala., Nov. 14, 1915. [1; 2; 4; 5; 7; 10]

Washington, George, first president of the United States, b. Westmoreland county, Va., 1732; d. Mount Vernon, Va., Dec. 14, 1799. [1; 2; 3; 4; 5; 6]

Washington, Henry Stephens, petrologist, b. Newark, N.J., 1867; d. Washington, D.C., Jan. 7, 1934. [1; 10; 62]

Washington, Mrs. Lucy Hall, née **Walker,** poet, b. 1835; d. ? [43]

Washington, William D'Hertburn, economist, b. 1863; d. 1914.

Wason, Mrs. Harriet L., née **Castle,** poet, d. 1904.

Wasson, David Atwood, clergyman, b. West Brooksville, Me., 1823; d. West Medford, Mass., Jan. 21, 1887. [3; 4; 7; 38]

Wasson, George Savery, marine artist, b. Groveland, Mass., 1855; d. Bangor, Me., April 28, 1932. [10]

Waterbury, Jared Bell, clergyman, b. New York, N.Y., 1799; d. Brooklyn, N.Y., Dec. 31, 1876. [3; 6; 62]

Waterbury, Leslie Abram, civil engineer, b. 1880; d. 1918.

Waterhouse, Alfred James, poet, b. Columbia county, Wis., 1855; d. Oakland, Calif., Sept. 6, 1928. [11; 35]

Waterhouse, Benjamin, physician, b. Newport, R.I., 1754; d. Cambridge, Mass., Oct. 2, 1846. [1; 3; 4; 5; 6]

Waterhouse, Sylvester, educationist, b. Barrington, N.H., 1830; d. St. Louis, Mo., Feb. 12, 1902. [1; 4; 51]

Waterloo, Stanley, journalist and novelist, b. St. Clair county, Mich., 1846; d. Chicago, Ill., Oct. 11, 1913. [5; 7; 10]

Waterman, Arba Nelson, jurist and historian, b. Greensboro, Vt., 1836; d. Chicago, Ill., March 16, 1917. [10]

Waterman, Harrison Lyman, local historian, b. 1840; d. 1918.

Waterman, John Henry, local historian, b. 1846; d. Beaver Crossing, Neb., Aug. 3, 1927.

Waterman, Joshua, lawyer, b. 1824; d. 1892.

Waterman, Lucius, clergyman, b. Providence, R.I., 1851; d. July 26, 1923. [10]

Waterman, Luther Dana, poet, b. 1830; d. 1918.

Waterman, Mrs. Mary, née **Bissell,** poet and novelist, b. 1836; d. 1889.

Waterman, Moses W., physician, b. 1849; d. Chicago, Ill., Jan. 25, 1907.

Waterman, Nixon, poet, b. Newark, Ill., 1859; d. Canton, Mass., Sept. 1, 1944. [7; 10; 11]

Waterman, Thomas Glasby, lawyer, b. New York, N.Y., 1788; d. Binghampton, N.Y., Jan. 7, 1862. [3; 6]

Waterman, Thomas Whitney, lawyer, b. Binghampton, N.Y., 1821; d. Binghampton, N.Y., Dec. 7, 1898. [1; 3; 4; 6]

Waters, Mrs. Clara, née **Erskine.** See Clement, Mrs. Clara, née Erskine.

Waters, Henry Fitz-Gilbert, genealogist, b. 1833; d. 1913. [51]

Waters, Henry Jackson, educationist, b. Center, Ralls county, Mo., 1856; d. Kansas City, Mo., Oct. 26, 1925. [10; 11]

Waters, Nacy McGee, clergyman, b. Independence, W. Va., 1866; d. May 12, 1916. [10]

Waters, Robert, educationist, b. Thurso, Scotland, 1835; d. Hoboken, N.J., Nov. 28, 1910. [3; 7; 10]

Waters, Russell Judson, lawyer, banker, and novelist, b. Halifax, Windham county, Vt., 1843; d. Los Angeles, Calif., Sept. 25, 1911. [10; 35]

Waters, Thomas Franklin, clergyman, b. Salem, Mass., 1851; d. Ipswich, Mass., Nov. 23, 1919. [51]

Waters, William Everett, educationist, b. Winthrop, Me., 1856; d. New York, N.Y., Aug. 3, 1924. [1; 5; 10; 62]

Waters, Wilson, clergyman, b. 1855; d. Chelmsford, Mass., June 13, 1933.

Waterston, Mrs. Anne Cabot Lowell, née **Quincy,** poet and biographer, b. Boston, Mass., 1812; d. Boston, Mass., Oct. 14, 1899. [3b]

Waterston, Robert Cassie, clergyman, b. Kennebunk, Me., 1812; d. Boston, Mass., Feb. 21, 1893. [3b]

Wathen, John Roach, surgeon, b. Louisville, Ky., 1872; d. Louisville, Ky., May 25, 1935. [10]

Watkins, Albert, historian, b. Worcester, England, 1848; d. Lincoln, Neb., Nov. 19, 1923. [10]

Watkins, Edgar, lawyer, b. Campbell county, Ga., 1868; d. Atlanta, Ga., Aug. 22, 1945. [10]

Watkins, Frances Ellen. See Harper, Mrs. Frances Ellen, née Watkins.

Watkins, George Pendleton, economist, b. 1876; d. Washington, D.C., Oct. 24, 1933.

Watkins, James Lawrence, civil servant, b. 1850; d. Dec. 28, 1930.

Watkins, John Elfrith, engineer, b. Ben Lomond, Va., 1852; d. New York, N.Y., Aug. 11, 1903. [1; 10]

Watkins, Lyman, physician, b. 1854; d. Cincinnati, O., Jan. 21, 1912.

Watkins, Robert Lincoln, physician, b. 1863; d. New York, N.Y., Oct. 26, 1934.

Watkins, Samuel R., soldier, b. Tennesee, 1838; d. ? [34]

Watkins, Tobias, physician, b. Maryland, 1780; d. Washington, D.C., Nov. 14, 1855. [3; 5; 7; 34]

Watlington, Francis, mariner, b. 1833; d. ?

Watmough, Edmund Carmick, angler, b. 1796; d. Philadelphia, Pa., July 14, 1848.

Watrous, Andrew Edward, poet and short story writer, d. 1902.

Watrous, Mrs. Elizabeth Snowden, née **Nichols,** artist, b. New York, N.Y., 1858; d. Oct. 4, 1921.

Watrous, George Ansel, educationist, b. Binghampton, N.Y., 1872; d. 1904. [10]

Watrous, Jerome Anthony, soldier and historian, b. 1840; d. Milwaukee, Wis., June 5, 1922. [4]

Watrous, Sophia, poet, fl. 1841. [43]

Watson, Albert Durrant, poet and physician, b. Dixie, Ont., 1859; d. Toronto, Ont., May 3, 1926. [11; 27]

Watson, Andrew, missionary, b. Perthshire, Scotland, 1834; d. Cairo, Egypt, Dec. 9, 1916. [1; 10]

Watson, Mrs. Annah Walker, née **Robinson,** poet and genealogist, b. 1848; d. Memphis, Tenn., May 1, 1930. [34]

Watson, Mrs. Augusta, née **Campbell,** novelist, b. New York, N.Y., 1862; d. Eastern Point, Groton, Conn., Aug. 11, 1936. [8]

Watson, Benjamin Frank, lawyer and soldier, b. Warner, N.H., 1826; d. 1905. [10]

Watson, Beriah André, physician, b. Lake George, N.Y., 1836; d. Jersey City, N.J., Dec. 22, 1892. [3; 6]

Watson, Bruce Mervellon, educationist, b. Windsor, N.Y., 1860; d. Philadelphia, Pa., Jan. 26, 1943. [10; 11]

Watson, Charles Roger, educationist, b. Cairo, Egypt, 1873; d. Bryn Mawr, Pa., Jan. 11, 1948. [10]

Watson, David Kemper, lawyer and politician, b. near London, Madison county, O., 1849; d. Columbus, O., Sept. 28, 1918. [10]

Watson, Edward Willard, physician and poet, b. Newport, R.I., 1843; d. Philadelphia, Pa., Nov. 20, 1925. [7; 10; 11]

Watson, Egbert Pomeroy, engineer, fl. 1867-1899.

Watson, Elkanah, merchant and promoter, b. Plymouth, Mass., 1758; d. Port Kent, N.Y., Dec. 5, 1842. [1; 3; 4; 6]

Watson, Emily H., miscellaneous writer, fl. 1866-1882. [6]

Watson, Emory Olin, clergyman, b. Newberry county, S.C., 1865; d. Beaufort, S.C., Oct. 30, 1935. [10]

Watson, George, navigator, b. 1771; d. 1860. [38]

Watson, George Douglas, evangelist, b. Accomac county, Va., 1845; d. 1924. [10]

Watson, Henry Clay, journalist and historian, b. Baltimore, Md., 1831; d. Sacramento, Calif., June 24, 1867. [1; 3; 4; 5; 6]

Watson, Irving Allison, physician, b. Salisbury, N.H., 1849; d. Concord, N.H., April 3, 1918. [4; 10]

Watson, James, editor, b. Edinburgh, Scotland, 1845; d. 1914. [10]

Watson, James Craig, astronomer, b. near Fingal, Upper Canada, 1838; d. Madison, Wis., Nov. 22, 1880. [1; 3; 4; 5; 6]

Watson, James Madison, writer of textbooks, b. Onondaga Hill, N.Y., 1827; d. Elizabeth, N.J., Sept. 29, 1900. [1; 3; 6]

Watson, James V., clergyman, b. London, England, 1814; d. Chicago, Ill., Oct. 17, 1856. [3; 6]

Watson, John, physician, b. Londonderry, Ireland, 1807; d. New York, N.Y., June 3, 1863. [3; 6]

Watson, John, philosopher, b. Glasgow, Scotland, 1847; d. Kingston, Ont., Jan. 27, 1939. [11; 27; 30]

Watson, John Fanning, historian, b. Burlington county, N.J., 1779; d. Philadelphia, Pa., Dec. 23, 1860. [1; 3; 4; 6; 7]

Watson, John Thomas, physician, fl. 1847-1879.

Watson, John Whittaker, poet, b. New York, N.Y., 1824; d. New York, N.Y., July 19, 1890. [3; 6; 7]

Watson, Mrs. Mary, née **Devereux.** See Devereux, Mary.

Watson, Paul Barron, lawyer and historian, b. Morristown, N.J., 1861; d. Boston, Mass., March 19, 1948. [7; 10; 11]

Watson, Robert, novelist, b. Glasgow, Scotland, 1882; d. Laguna Beach, Calif., Jan. 15, 1948. [11]

Watson, Samuel, clergyman, b. 1813; d. ? [6]

Watson, Samuel James, librarian, b. Armagh, Ireland, 1837; d. Toronto, Ont., Oct. 31, 1881. [27]

Watson, Samuel Newell, clergyman, b. Lyons, Ia., 1861; d. Santa Barbara, Calif., March 27, 1942. [10]

Watson, Sereno, botanist, b. East Windsor Hill, Conn., 1826; d. Cambridge, Mass., March 9, 1892. [1; 3; 4; 6]

Watson, Thomas, clergyman and poet, b. Yorkshire, England, 1857; d. Toronto, Ont., Feb. 16, 1937.

Watson, Thomas Augustus, ship-builder, b. Salem, Mass., 1854; d. Passagrille Key, Fla., Dec. 13, 1934. [1; 10]

Watson, Thomas Edward, politician, b. Columbia county, Ga., 1856; d. Washington, D.C., Sept. 26, 1922. [1; 4; 5; 7; 10]

Watson, Thomas Leonard, geologist, b. Chatham, Va., 1871; d. University, Va., Nov. 10, 1924. [10; 13]

Watson, William, engineer, b. Nantucket, Mass.. 1834; d. Sept. 30, 1915. [1; 3; 4; 5; 6; 10]

Watson, William, engineer, b. Nantucket, Mass., 1834; d. Sept. 30, 1915. [1; 3; 4; 5; 6; 10]

Watson, Winslow Cossoul, agriculturist and historian, b. Albany, N.Y., 1803; d. ? [3; 6]

Watt, Homer Andrew, educationist, b. Wilkesbarre, Pa., 1884; d. New York, N.Y., Oct. 4, 1948. [10]

Watters, Dennis Alonzo, clergyman, b. 1849; d. ?

Watters, George Manker, playwright, b. Rochester, N.Y., 1892; d. Los Angeles, Calif., March 14, 1943.

Watters, Philip Melancthon, clergyman, b. Brooklyn, N.Y., 1860; d. New York, N.Y., March 30, 1926. [10]

Watterson, Henry, journalist, b. Washington, D.C., 1840; d Jacksonville, Fla., Dec. 22, 1921. [1; 2; 4; 5; 7; 10]

Watterston, George, librarian, b. New York, N.Y., 1783; d. Washington, D.C., Feb. 4, 1854. [1 ;3; 5; 6; 7]

Wattles, Gurdon Wallace, banker, b. Richford, N.Y., 1855; d. Jan. 31, 1932. [4; 10]

Watts, Harvey Maitland, journalist and poet, b. Philadelphia, Pa., 1864; d. Blue Hill, Me., Aug. 11, 1939. [10]

Watts, Ralph Levi, horticulturist, b. near Clearfield, Pa., 1869; d. State College, Pa., July 2, 1949. [10]

Wauchope, George Armstrong, educationist, b. Natural Bridge, Va., 1862; d. Columbia, S.C., June 9, 1943. [7; 10; 11]

Waugh, Mrs. Elizabeth Dey, née Jenkinson, biographer, b. Newark, N.J., 1903; d. Newburgh, N.Y., March 20, 1944.

Waugh, Lorenzo, pioneer, b. 1808; d. ?

Waugh, William Francis, physician, b. Greenville, Pa., 1849; d. Muskegon, Mich., Sept. 5, 1918. [10]

Waugh, William Templeton, historian, b. Manchester, England, 1884; d. Montreal Que., Oct. 17, 1932. [27]

Waxham, Frank Endoras, physician, b. Laporte, Ind., 1852; d. Sugar City, Colo., Sept. 4, 1911.

Waxman, Percy, journalist, b. Australia, 1885; d. New York, N.Y., Jan. 13, 1948. [7; 10]

Wayland, Francis, clergyman and educationist, b. New York, N.Y., 1796; d. Providence, R.I., Sept. 30, 1865. [1; 3; 4; 5; 6; 7]

Wayland, Francis, lawyer, b. Boston, Mass., 1826; d. New Haven, Conn., Jan. 9, 1904. [1; 3; 5; 6; 10]

Wayland, Heman Lincoln, clergyman and educationist, b. Providence, R.I., 1830; d. Wernersville, Pa., Nov. 7, 1898. [3; 4; 6]

Wayland, Julius Augustus, socialist, b. Versailles, Ind., 1854; d. Girard, Kans., Nov. 11, 1912. [10]

Wayman, Alexander Walker, bishop, b. Caroline county, Md., 1821; d. Baltimore, Md., Nov. 30, 1895. [1; 3; 4; 6]

Wayne, Arthur Trezevant, ornithologist, b. Blackville, S.C., 1863; d. Charleston, S.C., May 5, 1930. [1; 10]

Wayne, Charles Stokes, novelist and playwright, b. Philadelphia, Pa., 1858; d. ?

Wayne, Henry Constantine, soldier, b. Savannah, Ga., 1815; d. Savannah, Ga., March 15, 1883. [3; 6; 34]

Wead, Charles Kasson, physicist, b. Malone, N.Y., 1848; d. Ann Arbor, Mich., April 2, 1925. [10; 39]

Wead, Frank Wilber, aviator and playwright, b. Peoria, Ill., 1895; d. Santa Monica, Calif., Nov. 15, 1947.

Wear, George Wallace, miscellaneous writer, b. Black Hawk, Miss., 1852; d. ?

Weatherly, Ulysses Grant, educationist, b. West Newton, Ind., 1865; d. Cortland, N.Y., July 18, 1940. [10; 11]

Weaver, Benjamin Franklin, physician, b. 1839; d. ?

Weaver, Edward Ebenezer, clergyman, b. Canton, O., 1864; d. Watertown, Mass., June 24, 1931. [10; 11]

Weaver, Eli Witwer, social worker, b. 1862; d. 1922.

Weaver, Emily Poynton, novelist and historian, b. near Manchester, England, 1865; d. Toronto, Ont., March 11, 1943. [27]

Weaver, Erasmus Morgan, soldier, b. Lafayette, Ind., 1854; d. Nov. 13, 1920. [10]

Weaver, George Sumner, clergyman, b. Rockingham, Vt., 1818; d. 1908. [3; 6; 43]

Weaver, James Baird, politician, b. Dayton, O., 1833; d. Des Moines, Ia., Feb. 6, 1912. [1; 3; 4; 5; 10; 37]

Weaver, John Van Alstyne, poet, novelist, and playwright, b. Charlotte, N.C., 1893; d. Colorado Springs, Colo., June 15, 1938. [7; 10]

Weaver, Jonathan, bishop, b. Carroll county, O., 1824; d. Dayton, O., Feb. 6, 1901. [3; 4; 6; 10]

Weaver, Raymond Melbourne, educationist, b. Baltimore, Md., 1888; d. New York, N.Y., April 4, 1948. [10]

Weaver, Rufus Washington, clergyman, b. Greensboro, N.C., 1870; d. Washington, D.C., Jan. 31, 1947. [10]

Weaver, Silas Matteson, jurist, b. Chautauqua county, N.Y., 1845; d. Iowa Falls, Ia., Nov. 6, 1923. [4; 10; 37]

Weaver, W. T. G., poet, b. Missouri, 1834; d. Texas, 1877. [34]

Weaver, William Augustus, naval officer, b. Dumfries, Va., 1797; d. Dumfries, Va., 1846. [3]

Weaver, William Lawton, local historian, b. 1816; d. 1867.

Webb, Alexander Stewart, soldier and educationist, b. New York, N.Y., 1835; d. Riverdale, N.Y., Feb. 12, 1911. [1; 3; 4; 5; 6; 10]

Webb, Anne C., educationist, fl. 1857-1879. [6]

Webb, Benedict Joseph, journalist, b. Bardstown, Ky., 1814; d. Louisville, Ky., Aug. 2, 1897. [21]

Webb, Charles Henry, journalist, poet, and humorist, b. Rouse's Point, N.Y., 1834; d. New York, N.Y., May 24, 1905. [1; 3; 4; 5; 6; 7; 9; 10; 35]

Webb, Ezekiel, physician, fl. 1833-1834.

Webb, Edmund Fuller, lawyer, b. 1835; d. Waterville, Me., 1898. [38]

Webb, Mrs. Frances Isabel, née Currie, novelist, b. Springfield, N.J., 1857; d. New York, N.Y., Dec. 20, 1895. [8]

Webb, Frank Rush, musician and woodsman, b. Covington, Ind., 1851; d. Ruxton, Md., Oct. 20, 1934. [10]

Webb, George, magistrate, d. New Kent county, Va., 1758.

Webb, George James, musician, b. near Salisbury, England, 1803; d. New York, N.Y., Oct. 7, 1887. [1; 3; 6; 20]

Webb, James Henry, jurist, b. Santa Fé, N.M., 1854; d. Hamden, Conn., April 19, 1924. [10; 62]

Webb, James Watson, journalist and diplomat, b. Claverack, N.Y., 1802; d. New York, N.Y., June 7, 1884. [1; 3; 4; 6; 7; 9]

Webb, John Russell, educationist, b. Jefferson county, N.Y., 1824; d. Benton Harbor, Mich., Sept. 10, 1887. [3; 6]

Webb, Robert Alexander, clergyman, b. Oxford, Miss., 1856; d. Louisville, Ky., May 23, 1919. [10 34]

Webb, Thomas Smith, freemason, b. Boston, Mass., 1771; d. Providence, R.I., July 6, 1819. [1; 3; 6]

Webb, Walter Loring, engineer, b. Rye, N.Y., 1863; d. Philadelphia, Pa., Jan. 24. 1941. [10; 11]

Webb, William Benning, lawyer, b. Washington, D.C., 1825; d. 1896. [3; 4]

Webb, William Henry, ship-builder, b. New York, N.Y., 1816; d. New York, N.Y., Oct. 30, 1899. [36; 4; 10]

Webb, William Seward, capitalist, b. New York, N.Y., 1851; d. Shelburne, Vt., Oct. 29, 1926. [4; 10]

Webb, William Walter, bishop, b. Germantown, Pa., 1857; d. Milwaukee, Wis., Jan. 15, 1933. [4; 10]

Webber, Charles Wilkins, journalist, explorer, naturalist, and soldier, b. Russellville, Ky., 1819; d. Nicaragua, Central America, April 11, 1856. [1; 3; 4; 6; 7; 9; 34]

Webber, Henry William, lawyer, b. New York, N.Y., 1869; d. New York, N.Y., May 20, 1935. [10]

Webber, James Plaisted, educationist, b. 1878; d. Bathe, Me., Dec. 7, 1930. [11]

Webber, Samuel, educationist, b. Byfield, Mass., 1759; d. Cambridge, Mass., July 17, 1810. [3; 4; 6]

Webber, Samuel, physician, b. Cambridge, Mass., 1797; d. Charlestown, N.H., Dec. 5, 1880. [3; 6]

Webber, Samuel Gilbert, physician, b. Boston, Mass., 1838; d. Newton, Mass., 1926. [10; 51]

Webber, Winfield Paul, mathematician, b. 1874; d. Baton Rouge, La., 1935. [13]

Weber, Gustavus Adolphus, economist, b. St. Louis, Mo. 1863; d. Washington, D.C., Dec. 7, 1942. [4; 10; 11]

Weber, Herman Carl, clergyman, b. Chautauqua county, N.Y., 1873; d. East Orange, N.J., July 25, 1939. [10]

Weber, John Langdon, clergyman, b. Union, S.C., 1862; d. March 19, 1923. [10; 34]

Weber, William Lander, educationist, b. Lenoir, N.C., 1866; d. Shreveport, La., 1910. [10; 34]

Webster, Albert Lowry, engineer, b. Orange, N.J., 1859; d. New York, N.Y., March 24, 1930. [62]

Webster, Alice Jane Chandler, novelist, b. Fredonia, N.Y., 1876; d. New York, N.Y., June 11, 1916. [1; 9; 10]

Webster, Arthur Gordon, physicist, b. Brookline, Mass., 1863; d. Worcester, Mass., May 15, 1923. [1; 4; 10]

Webster, Daniel, lawyer and politician, b. Salisbury, N.H., 1782; d. Marshfield, Mass., Oct. 24, 1852. [1; 2; 3; 4; 5; 6; 7; 8; 9]

Webster, Edward, miscellaneous writer, b. 1818; d. 1890.

Webster, Edward Harlan, educationist, b. Westfield, Pa., 1876; d. Upper Montclair, N.J., Nov. 14, 1937. [10]

Webster, Epinetus, stenographer, fl. 1852-1854.

Webster, Fletcher, lawyer, b. Portsmouth, N.H., 1813; d. near Bull Run, Va., Aug. 30, 1862. [3; 4; 6]

Webster, George Sidney, clergyman, b. Meredith, N.Y., 1853; d. Brooklyn, N.Y., Oct. 27, 1937. [10; 11]

Webster, George Van O'Linda, osteopath, b. Rossie, N.Y., 1880; d. 1937. [10; 11]

Webster, Hanson Hart, editor, b. Lewiston, Me., 1877; d. Swampscott, Mass., May 9, 1940. [7; 11]

Webster, Henry Kitchell, novelist, b. Evanston, Ill., 1875; d. Evanston, Ill., Dec. 8, 1932. [7; 9; 10]

Webster, Herbert Tracy, physician, b. 1836; d. Los Angeles, Calif., Sept. 25, 1931.

Webster, James Benjamin, missionary, b. Barnet, Vt., 1879; d. Stockholm, Calif., Dec. 8, 1929. [64]

Webster, Jean. See Webster, Alice Jane Chandler.

Webster, John Calvin, biographer, b. 1810; d. 1884.

Webster, John Calvin, physician, b. 1843; d. 1915.

Webster, John White, educationist, b. Boston, Mass., 1793; d. Boston, Mass., Aug. 30, 1850. [1; 3; 5; 6]

Webster, Jonathan Vinton, poet and playwright, fl. 1883-1904. [35]

Webster, Kimball, pioneer, b. 1828; d. 1916.

Webster, Leslie Tillotson, physician, b. New York, N.Y., 1894; d. Scarsdale, N.Y., July 12, 1943. [10]

Webster, Lorin, educationist, b. Claremont, N.H., 1857; d. Pekin, China, July 5, 1923. [10]

Webster, Mrs. M. M. (pseud.). See Mosby, Mrs. Mary Webster, née Pleasants.

Webster, Nathan Burnham, chemist, b. Unity, N.H., 1821; d. 1900. [3; 6; 10]

Webster, Noah, lexicographer, b. West Hartford, Conn., 1758; d. New Haven, Conn., May 28, 1843. [1; 2; 3; 4; 5; 6; 7; 8; 9]

Webster, Pelatiah, economist, b. Lebanon, Conn., 1726; d. Philadelphia, Pa., Sept. 2, 1795. [1; 3; 4; 5; 6]

Webster, Prentiss, lawyer, b. Lowell, Mass., 1851; d. Lowell, Mass., Oct. 28, 1898. [49]

Webster, Ralph Waldo, physician, b. Monmouth,, Ill., 1873; d. Chicago, Ill., July 2, 1930. [10]

Webster, Richard, clergyman, b. Albany, N.Y., 1811; d. Mauch Chunk, Pa., June 19, 1856. [3; 6]

Webster, Samuel, clergyman, b. Bradford, Mass., 1719; d. Salisbury, Mass., 1796. [6]

Webster, Sidney, lawyer, b. Gilmanton, N.H., 1828; d. Newport, R.I., May 30, 1910. [10; 62]

Webster, Thomas, clergyman, b. Ireland, 1809; d. Newbury, Ont., May 2, 1901. [27]

Webster, William, anaesthetist, b. Manchester, England, 1865; d. Winnipeg, Man., Oct. 23, 1934. [11]

Webster, William Franklin, educationist, b. Clearwater, Minn., 1862; d. Minneapolis, Minn., Oct. 20, 1936. [70]

Webster, William Greenleaf, lexicographer, b. New Haven, Conn., 1805; d. 1869. [6]

Wedderburn, Alexander, emigration officer, b. Aberdeen, Scotland, about 1796; d. Saint John, N.B., about June 19, 1843. [27]

Wedgwood, William B., lawyer, d. New York, N.Y., 1888. [38]

Weed, Alonzo Rogers, jurist, b. Bangor, Me., 1867; d. Newton, Mass., Dec. 29, 1937. [10]

Weed, Clarence Moores, naturalist, b. Toledo, O., 1864; d. Plymouth, N.H., July 18, 1947. [7; 10]

Weed, George Ludington, educationist, b. Union Mission, Arkansas Territory, 1828; d. Philadelphia, Pa., 1904. [10]

Weed, Samuel Richards, fire underwriter, b. New York, N.Y., 1837; d. Feb. 5, 1918. [10]

Weed, Thurlow, politician and journalist, b. Greene county, N.Y., 1797; d. Albany, N.Y., Nov. 22, 1882. [1; 2; 3; 4; 5; 6; 7; 8; 9]

Weed, Truman Andrew Wellington, clergyman, b. 1841; d. Concord, N.H., Aug. 13, 1927.

Weed, Walter Harvey, geologist, b. St. Louis, Mo., 1862; d. Sept. 7, 1944. [11; 13]

Weed, William Xenophon, lawyer, b. 1867; d. Dec. 4, 1934.

Weeden, Howard, poetess, b. Huntsville, Ala., 1847; d. Huntsville, Ala., April 11, 1905. [7; 10; 34]

Weeden, William Babcock, manufacturer and historian, b. Bristol, R.I., 1834; d. Providence, R.I., March 28, 1912. [1; 6; 7; 10]

Weekes, Refine, poet, b. 1759; d. ? [19]

Weekes, Robert Dodd., educationist, b. Clinton, N.Y., 1819; d. East Orange, N.J., Feb. 23, 1898. [3b]

Weekley, William Marion, bishop, b. Tyler county, Va., 1851; d. Parkersburg, W.Va., Jan. 8, 1926. [10]

Weeks, Arland Deyett, educationist, b. McLean, N.Y., 1871; d. Fargo, N.D., Nov. 13, 1936. [7; 10; 11]

Weeks, Edward P., lawyer, fl. 1877-1880.

Weeks, Edwin Lord, artist and traveller, b. Boston, Mass., 1849; d. Paris, France, Nov. 17, 1903. [1; 4; 5; 7; 10]

Weeks, Helen C. See Campbell, Mrs. Helen, née Stuart.

Weeks, John Moseley, agriculturist, b. Litchfield, Conn., 1788; d. Salisbury, Vt., Sept. 1, 1858. [43]

Weeks, Joseph Dame, statistician, b. Massachusetts, 1841; d. Pittsburgh, Pa., Dec. 26, 1896. [1; 3b]

Weeks, Leroy Titus, educationist and poet, b. Mount Vernon, Ia., 1854; d. Council Bluffs, Ia., March 4, 1927.

Weeks, Lyman Horace, historian and genealogist, fl. 1882-1916.

Weeks, Mrs. Mary Hezlep, née **Harmon,** educationist, b. Warren, O., 1851; d. Kansas City, Mo., May 24, 1940. [10; 11]

Weeks, Robert Kelley, poet, b. New York, N.Y., 1840; d. Harlem, N.Y., April 13, 1876. [4; 6; 7; 62]

Weeks, Stephen Beauregard, historian, b. Pasquotank county, N.C., 1865; d. Washington, D.C., May 3, 1918. [1; 4; 5; 7; 10]

Weeks, William Raymond, clergyman and educationist, b. Brooklyn, Conn., 1783; d. Oneida, N.Y., June 27, 1848. [3; 6]

Weems, Mason Locke, clergyman and biographer, b. Anne Arundel county, Md., 1759; d. Beaufort, S.C., May 23, 1825. [1; 2; 3; 4; 5; 6; 7; 34]

Weger, George Stephen, surgeon, b. Baltimore, Md., 1874; d. Redlands, Calif., Jan. 16, 1935. [10]

Wegmann, Edward, engineer, b. Rio de Janiero, Brazil, 1850; d. Yonkers, N.Y., Jan. 3, 1935. [1a; 4; 10; 11]

Weidemeyer, John William, music publisher, b. Fredericksburg, Va., 1819; d. Amityville, Long Island, N.Y., Jan. 19, 1896. [3; 4; 34]

Weidenmann, Jacob, landscape architect, b. Switzerland, 1829; d. Hartford, Conn., Feb. 6, 1893. [1]

Weidenreich, Franz, anthropologist, b. Germany, 1873; d. New York, N.Y., July 11, 1948.

Weidig, Adolph, musician, b. Hamburg, Germany, 1867; d. Hinsdale, Ill., Sept. 23, 1931. [10; 11; 20]

Weidner, Revere Franklin, theologian, b. Centre Valley, Pa., 1851; d. Tangerine, Fla., Jan. 6, 1915. [1; 3; 4; 10]

Weik, Jesse William, biographer, b. Greencastle, Ind., 1857; d. 1930. [7]

Weil, Arthur William, lawyer, b. 1881; d. April 29, 1940.

Weill, Felix, educationist, b. Versailles, France, 1871; d. New York, N.Y., Dec. 20, 1948. [14]

Weimer, Albert Barnes, lawyer, b. Philadelphia, Pa., 1857; d. Philadelphia, Pa., Nov. 13, 1938. [10; 51]

Weinbaum, Stanley Grauman, novelist, d. 1935.

Weir, Archibald, lawyer, b. 1855; d. Sarnia, Ont., Sept. 1, 1930. [31a]

Weir, Arthur, poet, b. Montreal, Que., 1864; d. 1902. [27]

Weir, Mrs. Florence, née **Roney,** novelist, b. Waupun, Wis., 1861; d. Seattle, Wash., Nov. 13, 1932. [10; 11]

Weir, Frank, lawyer, b. Montreal, Que., 1860; d. ? [27]

Weir, George Moir, educationist and politician, b. Miami, Man., 1885; d. Vancouver, B.C., Dec. 4, 1949. [30]

Weir, Hugh C., editor, b. Virginia, Ill., 1884; d. New York, N.Y., March 16, 1934. [7; 10]

Weir, Irene, artist, b. St. Louis, Mo., 1863; d. Yorktown Heights, N.Y., March 22, 1944. [62]

Weir, James, banker and novelist, b. Greenville, Ky., 1821; d. Owensboro, Ky., Jan. 31, 1906. [7; 74]

Weir, James, physician, b. Owensboro, Ky., 1856; d. Virginia Beach, Va., Aug. 9, 1906. [7; 10]

Weir, John Ferguson, artist and educationist, b. West Point, N.Y., 1841; d. Providence, R.I., April 8, 1926. [1; 4; 10]

Weir, Lebert Howard, authority on recreation, b. Scottsburg, Ind., 1878; d. Indianapolis, Ind., Nov. 13, 1949.

Weir, Robert Stanley, jurist, b. Hamilton, Ont., Nov. 15, 1856; d. near Lake Memphramagog, Que., Aug. 20, 1926. [27]

Weir, William, banker, b. near Brechin, Scotland, 1823; d. Montreal, Que., March 25, 1905. [27]

Weir, William Alexander, jurist, b. Montreal, Que., Oct. 15, 1858; d. London, England, Oct. 21, 1929. [27]

Weir, William John, poet and playwright, b. New York, N.Y., 1856; d ? [35]

Weise, Arthur James, local historian, b. Shepherdstown, Va., 1838; d. Bernardsville, N.J., Jan. 7, 1921. [10]

Weisenburg, Theodore Herman, neurologist, b. Budapesth, Hungary, 1876; d. Philadelphia, Pa., Aug. 3, 1934. [1; 10]

Weiser, Clement Zwingli, clergyman, b. 1830; d. 1898.

Weiss, Albert Paul, psychologist, b. Germany, 1879; d. Columbus, O., April 3, 1931. [10]

Weiss, Ehrich. See Houdini, Harry.

Weiss, Howard Frederick, forester, b. 1883; d. Wisconsin Dells, Wis., July 7, 1940. [62]

Weiss, John, clergyman, b. Boston, Mass., 1818; d. Boston, Mass., March 9, 1879. [1; 3; 4; 6; 7]

Weiss, Mrs. Susan Archer, née **Talley,** poet, b. Hanover county, Vt., 1835; d. ? [3; 8]

Weiss, William Stix, lawyer, b. New York, N.Y., 1888; d. New York, N.Y., Sept. 23, 1946. [62]

Weisse, Faneuil Dunkin, surgeon, b. Watertown, Mass., 1842; d. New York, N.Y., June 22, 1915. [4; 10]

Weisse, John Adam, philologist, b. France, 1810; d. New York, N.Y., Jan. 12, 1888. [3; 6]

Weitzel, Mrs. Sophie, née **Winthrop,** poet and novelist, b. 1840; d. 1892. [6; 8]

Welburn, Drummond, poet, b. 1818; d. ? [34]

Welby, Mrs. Amelia Ball, née **Coppuck,** poet, b. Saint Michaels, Md., 1819; d. Louisville, Ky., May 3, 1852. [1; 3; 4; 5; 7; 34]

Welch, Adonijah Strong, educationist and politician, b. East Hampton, Conn., 1821; d. Pasadena, Calif., March 14, 1889. [1; 3; 4; 5; 6]

Welch, Anthony Cummings, clergyman, b. Harrison county, O., 1859; d. July 25, 1930. [10]

Welch, Deshler, journalist, b. Buffalo, N.Y., 1854; d. Jan. 7, 1920. [10]

Welch, Follansbee Goodrich, educationist, b. Concord, N.H., 1843; d. ? [6]

Welch, George Theodore, physician, b. 1845; d. Passaic, N.J., Aug. 27, 1924.

Welch, John, jurist and politician, b. Harrison county, O., 1805; d. Athens, O., Aug. 5, 1891. [1; 3; 4; 6]

Welch, Lewis Sheldon, journalist, b. Hartford, Conn., 1867; d. New Haven, Conn., March 29, 1940. [62]

Welch, Mrs. Mary, née **Beaumont,** writer on cookery, b. 1840; d. 1923.

Welch, Philip Henry, humorist, b. Angelica, N.Y., 1849; d. Brooklyn, N.Y., Feb. 24, 1889. [4; 7]

Welch, Ransom Bethune, clergyman, b. Greenville, N.Y., 1824; d. Healing Springs, Va., June 29, 1890. [3; 6]

Welch, Samuel Manning, local historian, d. Buffalo, N.Y., Nov. 12, 1902.

Welch, William Henry, pathologist, b. Norfolk, Conn., 1850; d. Baltimore, Md., April 30, 1934. [1; 4; 7; 10; 62]

Welcker, Adair, poet and miscellaneous writer, b. Troy, N.Y., 1858; d. Oakland, Calif., Feb. 14, 1926. [35]

Weld, Allen Hayden, educationist, b. Braintree, Vt., 1812; d. Troy, Wis., Oct. 18, 1882. [38; 49; 62]

Weld, Mrs. Angelina Emily, née **Grimké.** See Grimké, Angelina Emily.

Weld, Horatio Hastings, clergyman, b. Boston, Mass., 1811; d. Riverton, N.J., Aug. 27, 1888. [3; 6; 7]

Weld, Laenas Gifford, educationist, b. Sherwood, Mich., 1862; d. Pullman, Ill., Nov. 28, 1919. [4; 10]

Weld, Mason Cogswell, agriculturist, b. Philadelphia, Pa., 1829; d. near Closter, N.J., Sept. 25, 1887. [3b]

Weld, Theodore Dwight, abolitionist, b. Hampton, Conn., 1803; d. Hyde Park, Mass., Feb. 3, 1895. [1; 3; 4; 5; 6]

Weldon, Richard E., lawyer, b. Bedford, Mass., 1872; d. Flushing, N.Y., Aug. 22, 1947.

Weller, Charles Heald, archaeologist, b. Tyrone, N.Y., 1870; d. Iowa City, Ia., March 2, 1927. [10; 62]

Weller, Stuart, geologist, b. Maine, N.Y., 1870; d. Chicago, Ill., Aug. 5, 1927. [10]

Welles, Albert, genealogist, b. New York, N.Y., 1810; d. New York, N.Y., 1881.

Welles, C. M., adventurer, fl. 1859-1864.

Welles, Elijah Gardiner, clergyman, d. 1855. [62]

Welles, Gideon, politician, b. Glastonbury, Conn., 1802; d. Hartford, Conn., Feb. 11, 1878. [1; 2; 3; 4; 5; 6; 7]

Welles, Henry Titus, lumberman, b. Glastonbury, Conn., 1821; d. Minneapolis, Minn., March 4, 1898. [4; 70]

Welles, Noah, clergyman, b. Colchester, Conn., 1718; d. Stamford, Conn., Dec. 31, 1778. [1; 3; 6; 62]

Welles, Roger, lawyer, b. Newington, Conn., 1829; d. Newington, Conn., May 15, 1904. [62]

Welling, James Clarke, journalist and educationist, b. Trenton, N.J., 1825; d. Hartford, Conn., Sept. 4, 1894. [1; 4]

Welling, Richard Ward Greene, lawyer, b. North Kingston, R.I., 1858; d. New York, N.Y., Dec. 17, 1946. [4; 11]

Wellington, Alice. See Rollins, Mrs. Alice, née Wellington.

Wellington, Andrew (pseud.). See Weed, Truman Andrew Wellington.

Wellington, Arthur Mellen, civil engineer and journalist, b. Waltham, Mass., 1847; d. New York, N.Y., May 16, 1895. [1; 3; 4; 6]

Wellman, Francis Lewis, lawyer, b. Brookline, Mass., 1854; d. New York, N.Y., June 7, 1942. [10; 51]

Wellman, Joshua Wyman, clergyman, b. Cornish, N.H., 1821; d. Malden, Mass., Sept. 28, 1915. [4, 49]

Wellman, Thomas B., local historian, b. 1838; d. Lynnfield, Mass., Aug. 14, 1907.

Wellman, Walter, journalist, explorer and aeronaut, b. Mentor, O., 1858; d. New York, N.Y., Jan. 31, 1934. [1; 10]

Wellner, George Christian, physician, b. 1849; d. Minneapolis, Minn., March 3, 1933.

Wells, Amos Russel, religious journalist, b. Glen Falls, N.Y., 1862; d. Boston, Mass., March 6, 1933. [7; 10]

Wells, Mrs. Anna Maria, née **Foster,** poet, b. Gloucester, Mass., 1797; d. 1868. [6; 19]

Wells, Benjamin Willis, educationist, b. Walpole, N.H., 1856; d. Dec. 19, 1923. [7; 10; 51]

Wells, Carolyn, novelist, b. Rahway, N.J., d. New York, N.Y., March 27, 1942. [4; 7; 10; 11; 12]

Wells, Mrs. Catherine Boott, née **Gannett,** novelist, b. England, 1838; d. Boston, Mass., Dec. 13, 1911. [7; 10]

Wells, Charles Luke, clergyman, b. Boston, Mass., 1858; d. Sewanee, Tenn., April 18, 1938. [10; 11; 51]

Wells, Chauncey Wetmore, educationist, b. Baltimore, Md., 1872; d. Berkeley, Calif., Aug. 31, 1933. [62]

Wells, David Ames, economist, b. Springfield, Mass., 1828; d. Norwich, Conn., Nov. 5, 1898. [1; 3; 4; 5; 6; 7; 8; 9]

Wells, David Dwight, novelist, b. Norwich, Conn., 1868; d. Norwich, Conn., June 15, 1900. [7; 10; 51]

Wells, Edmund Williams, pioneer, b. Lancaster, O., 1846; d. ? [7]

Wells, Edward Laight, lawyer, b. New York, N.Y., 1839; d. ? [10; 34]

Wells, Mrs. Emmeline Blanche, née **Woodward,** poet, b. 1828; d. 1921.

Wells, Ernest Alden, surgeon, b. Rocky Hill, Conn., 1875; d. Hartford, Conn., April 15, 1927. [62]

Wells, Frank, physician, b. Boston, Mass., 1842; d. March 4, 1919. [51]

Wells, Frederic De Witt, lawyer, b. Brooklyn, N.Y., 1874; d. New York, N.Y., Dec. 19, 1929. [10]

Wells, Frederic Palmer, local historian, b. 1850; d. Newbury, Vt., March 31, 1934.

Wells, Frederick Howard, genealogist, b. Whitehall, N.Y., 1870; d. White Plains, N.Y., July 30, 1932.

Wells, Harry Gideon, pathologist, b. New Haven, Conn., 1875; d. Chicago, Ill., April 26, 1943. [11; 62]

Wells, Henry Parkhurst, lawyer, b. Providence, R.I., 1842; d. Brooklyn, N.Y., Nov. 23, 1904. [10]

Wells, Henry Ward, lawyer, b. 1833; d. ?

Wells, Horace, dentist, b. Hartford, Vt., 1815; d. New York, N.Y., Jan. 24, 1848. [1; 3; 5; 6; 43]

Wells, Horace Lemuel, chemist, b. New Britain, Conn., 1855; d. New Haven, Conn., Dec. 19, 1924. [10; 62]

Wells, James Edward, educationist, b. Harvey, N.B., 1836; d. Toronto, Ont., Sept. 18, 1898. [27]

Wells, James Monroe, lawyer, b. 1838; d. ? [34]

Wells, James Simpson Chester, engineer, b. Brooklyn, N.Y., 1851; d. Dobbs Ferry, N.Y., Oct. 29, 1931. [10]

Wells, John Cleland, lawyer, fl. 1870-1883.

Wells, John Daniel, journalist, b. Erie county, Pa., 1878; d. Buffalo, N.Y., April 2, 1932. [10; 11]

Wells, John Dunlap, clergyman, b. Whitesboro, N.Y., 1815; d. Brooklyn, N.Y., Oct. 31, 1903.

Wells, John Edwin, educationist, b. Philadelphia, Pa., 1875; d. New London, Conn., June 22, 1943. [7; 10; 11; 62]

Wells, John G., lawyer, fl. 1856-1874. [6]

Wells, Mrs. Kate, née **Gannett.** See Wells, Mrs. Catherine Boott, née Gannett.

Wells, Lemuel Henry, bishop, b. Yonkers, N.Y., 1841; d. Tacoma, Wash., March 27, 1936. [4; 10]

Wells, Reuben Field, agriculturist and journalist, b. Hatfield, Mass., 1880; d. Montpelier, Vt., April 11, 1938. [45]

Wells, Robert William, jurist, b. Winchester, Va., 1795; d. Bowling Green, Ky., Sept. 22, 1864. [1]

Wells, Rollin John, poet, b. 1848; d. ?

Wells, Samuel Roberts, phrenologist, b. West Hartford, Conn., 1820; d. New York, N.Y., April 13, 1875. [1; 3; 6]

Wells, Walter, educationist, b. Salisbury, N.H., 1830; d. Portland, Me., April 21, 1881. [3; 6; 38]

Wells, Webster, mathematician, b. Boston, Mass., 1851; d. near Boston, Mass., May 23, 1916. [4; 10]

Wells, William Benjamin, jurist, b. Augusta, Upper Canada, 1809; d. Toronto, Ont., April 8, 1881. [27]

Wells, William Harvey, educationist, b. Tolland, Conn., 1812; d. Chicago, Ill., Jan. 21, 1885. [1; 3; 4; 6]

Wells, William Hughes, physician, b. Philadelphia, Pa., 1859; d. Feb. 24, 1919. [10]

Wells, William Vincent, journalist and adventurer, b. Boston, Mass., 1826; d. Napa, Calif., June 1, 1876. [1; 3; 4; 6]

Welsh, Alfred Hix, educationist, b. Fostoria, O., 1850; d. 1889. [3; 6]

Welsh, Charles, editor, b. Ramsgate, England, 1850; d. Yonkers, N.Y., Sept. 12, 1914. [7; 10]

Welsh, Herbert, artist and publicist, b. Philadelphia, Pa., 1851; d. Montpelier, Vt., June 28, 1941. [10; 11]

Welsh, Lilian, physician, b. Columbia, Pa., 1858; d. Columbia, Pa., Feb. 23, 1938. [10]

Welsh, William, philanthropist, b. Philadelphia, Pa., 1807; d. Philadelphia, Pa., Feb. 11, 1878.

Weltmer, Sidney Abram, mental healer, b. Wooster, O., 1858; d. Nevada, Mo., Dec. 5, 1930. [10]

Welton, Arthur Dorman, novelist, b. 1867; d. Chicago, Ill., Oct. 28, 1940.

Welty, Edwin Arthur, poet, b. Canal Dover, O., 1853; d. St. Joseph, Mo., Sept. 18, 1928.

Wemyss, Francis Courtney, actor and manager, b. London, England, 1797; d. New York, N.Y., Jan. 5, 1859. [1; 3; 6; 7]

Wenckebach, Carla, educationist, b. Hildesheim, Germany, 1853; d. Boston, Mass., Dec. 29, 1902. [3; 10]

Wendel, Hugo Christian Martin, historian, b. Philadelphia, Pa., 1884; d. Radburn, N.J., Jan. 16, 1949. [10]

Wendell, Barrett, educationist and littérateur, b. Boston, Mass., 1855; d. Boston, Mass., Feb. 8, 1891. [1; 2; 3; 4; 5; 6; 7; 8; 9; 10]

Wendling, George Reuben, lawyer and lecturer, b. Shelbyville, Ill., 1845; d. Sept. 14, 1915. [10; 34]

Wendte, Charles William, clergyman, b. Boston, Mass., 1844; d. Berkeley, Calif., Sept. 9, 1931. [1; 4; 10]

Weninger, Franz Xaver, priest, b. Austria, 1805; d. Cincinnati, O., 1888. [6; 21]

Wenley, Robert Mark, philosopher, b. Edinburgh, Scotland, 1861; d. Ann Arbor, Mich., March 29, 1929. [1; 7; 10; 11]

Wenner, George Unangst, clergyman, b. Bethlehem, Pa., 1844; d. New York, N.Y., Nov. 1, 1934. [1; 10; 11; 62]

Wenstrom, William Holmes, soldier and meteorologist, b. Sweden, 1898; d. Santa Barbara, Calif., April 2, 1942. [62]

Wentworth, George Albert, educationist, b. Wakefield, N.H., 1835; d. Dover, N.H., May 24, 1906. [1; 4; 7; 10; 51]

Wentworth, John, journalist and politician, b. Sandwich, N.H., 1815; d. Chicago, Ill., Oct. 16, 1888. [1; 3; 4; 5; 6; 7; 36; 49]

Wentworth, John Brodhead, clergyman, b. Bristol, N.H., 1823; d. Buffalo, N.Y., Aug. 6, 1893. [59]

Wentworth, John Theodore, lawyer, b. Saratoga Springs, N.Y., 1854; d. Racine, Wis., Sept. 19, 1916. [62]

Wentworth, Walter (pseud.). See Gilman, Bradley.

Wenzlaff, Gustav Gottlieb, educationist, b. Ukraine, Russia, 1865; d. Yankton, S.C., 1939. [10; 11]

Werfel, Franz, novelist and playwright, b. Prague, Austria-Hungary, 1890; d. Hollywood, Calif., Aug. 26, 1945. [10; 12]

Wergeland, Agnes Mathilde, historian, b. 1857; d. March 6, 1914.

Werner, Carl Avery, poet and novelist, b. Watertown, N.Y., 1873; d. Brooklyn, N.Y., Feb. 18, 1945.

Wert, J. Howard, poet, fl. 1886-1891.

Wertheimer, Mildred Salz, historian, b. 1896; d. San Diego, Calif., May 6, 1937.

Werthner, William Benjamin, geographer, b. 1855; d. Dayton, O., 1929.

Weseen, Maurice Harley, educationist, b. Oakland, Neb., 1890; d. Lincoln, Neb., April 14, 1941. [7; 10; 11]

Wesselhoeft, Conrad, physician, b. Germany, 1834; d. Boston, Mass., Dec. 17, 1904. [1; 4; 10]

Wesselhoeft, Mrs. Elizabeth Foster, née **Pope,** writer of books for children, b. Dorchester, Mass., 1840; d. Boston, Mass., Jan. 31, 1919. [7; 10]

Wesselhoeft, Mrs. Lily F. See Wesselhoeft, Mrs. Elizabeth Foster, née Pope.

Wesson, William H., student, b. 1813; d. ?

West, Andrew Fleming, educationist, b. Allegheny, Pa., 1853; d. Princeton, N.J., Dec. 27, 1943. [4; 7; 10]

West, Anson, clergyman, b. Robertson county, N.C., 1823; d. 1907. [10; 34]

West, Mrs. Florence, née **Duval,** poet, b. Florida; d. Texas, 1881. [34]

West, Henry Litchfield, journalist, b. Staten Island, N.Y., 1859; d. Washington, D.C., Sept. 3, 1940. [10]

West, James Hadley, historian, b. 1873; d. Williamstown, Mass., Feb. 2, 1942.

West, James Harcourt, publisher and poet, b. Melrose, Mass., 1856; d. ? [7; 8]

West, Judson S., lawyer, b. 1855; d. ?

West, Kenyon (pseud.). See Howland, Mrs. Frances Louise, née Morse.

West, Leoti L., school-teacher, b. 1851; d. ?

West, Lillie. See Buck, Mrs. Lillie, née West.

West, Marvin (pseud.). See Goldfrap, John Henry.

West, Mary Allen, educationist, b. Galesburg, Ill., 1837; d. Tokyo, Japan, Dec. 1, 1892. [3]

West, Max, economist, b. St. Cloud, Minn., 1870; d. Washington, D.C., Jan. 7, 1909. [10]

West, Nathanael, novelist, d. near El Centro, Calif., Dec. 21, 1940.

West, Nathaniel, clergyman, b. Ulster, Ireland, 1794; d. Philadelphia, Pa., Sept. 2, 1864. [3; 6]

West, Nathaniel, clergyman, b. about 1824; d. Washington, D.C., July 7, 1906.

West, Paul Clarendon, journalist, b. Boston, Mass., 1871; d. New York, N.Y., Oct. 30, 1918. [7; 10]

West, Robert Athow, journalist b. Yorkshire, England, 1808; d. Georgetown, D.C., 1865. [60]

West, Samuel, clergyman, b. Yarmouth, Mass., 1730; d. Tiverton, R.I., Sept. 24, 1807. [1; 3; 6]

West, Simeon Henry, farmer and politician, b. Bourbon county, Ky., 1827; d. McLean county, Ill., April 2, 1920.

West, Stephen, clergyman, b. Tolland, Conn., 1735; d. Stockbridge, Mass., May 15, 1819. [3; 6; 62]

West, Thomas Dyson, foundryman, b. Manchester, England, 1851; d. Cleveland, O., June 18, 1915. [10]

West, Victor J., educationist, b. Bushnell, Ill., 1880; d. Palo Alto, Calif., Feb. 26, 1927. [10; 11]

West, Willis Mason, historian, b. St. Cloud, Minn., 1857; d. Minneapolis, Minn., May 2, 1931. [4; 10; 70]

Westbrook, Richard Brodhead, clergyman, fl. 1882-1892.

Westcott, Edward Noyes, banker and novelist, b Syracuse, N.Y., 1846; d. Syracuse, N.Y., March 31, 1898. [1; 2; 3b; 9; 72]

Westcott, Frank Nash, clergyman, b. Syracuse, N.Y., 1858; d. June 27, 1915. [10]

Westcott, James Horatio, chemist, b. 1872; d. Larchmont, N.Y., May 1, 1938.

Westcott, Thompson, lawyer, journalist, and historian, b. Philadelphia, Pa., 1820; d. Philadelphia, Pa., May 8, 1888. [1; 3; 6; 7]

Westervelt, Mrs. Frances A., née Johnson, local historian, b. Nyack, N.Y., 1858; d. Hackensack, N.J., May 4, 1942.

Westlake, James Willis, educationist, b. Devonshire, England, 1830; d. Lake Helen, Fla., Oct. 18, 1912. [10]

Westley, George Hembert, journalist, b. Newfoundland. 1865; d. Boston, Mass., Sept. 25, 1936. [7; 10]

Westman, Habbakuk O. (pseud.). See Ewbank, Thomas.

Westmoreland, John G., physician, b. 1816; d. ?

Westmoreland, Mrs. Maria Elizabeth, née Jourdan, novelist, b. 1815; d. ? [34]

Weston, Edmund Brownell, engineer, b. Duxbury, Mass., 1850; d. Providence, R.I., Dec. 9, 1916. [10]

Weston, Edward Payson, educationist, b. Cumberland, Me., 1819; d. Oct. 13, 1879. [46]

Weston, Edward Payson, long-distance walker, b. Providence, R.I., 1839; d. Brooklyn, N.Y., May 12, 1929. [1; 10]

Weston, George Melville, lawyer, b. 1816; d. 1887. [38]

Weston, Henry Griggs, clergyman and educationist, b. Lynn, Mass., 1820; d. Chester, Pa., Feb. 6, 1909. [3; 4; 10]

Weston, Isaac, clergyman, b. 1787; d. 1870. [38]

Weston, James Augustus, clergyman, b. Hyde county, N.C., 1838; d. 1905. [10]

Weston, Mrs. Maria, née **Gaines,** novelist, fl. 1847-1866.

Weston, Mrs. Mary Catherine, née **North,** religious writer, b. Albany, N.Y., 1822; d. Greenwich, Conn., Aug. 4, 1882. [3; 6]

Weston, Stephen Francis, educationist, b. Madison, Me., 1855; d. March 7, 1935. [10]

Weston, Thomas, local historian, b. 1834; d. Newton, Mass., April 19, 1920.

Weston, Thomas Alfred, horticulturist, b. London, England, 1878; d. New York, N.Y., May 6, 1946.

Weston, Thomas Chesmer, geologist, b. Birmingham, England, 1832; d. Quebec, Ont., Oct. 20, 1940. [27]

Westrup, Alfred B., economist, fl. 1879-1915.

Wetherald, Agnes Ethelwyn, poet, b. Rockwood, Ont., 1857; d. Fenwick, Ont., March 9, 1940. [27]

Wetherell, James Elgin, educationist, b. Port Dalhousie, Ont., 1851; d. Toronto, Ont. Oct., 20, 1940. [27]

Wetherell, Mrs. Margaret Hubner, née **Smith,** historian, d. 1933. [27]

Wetherill, Charles Mayer, chemist, b. Philadelphia, Pa., 1825; d. Bethlehem, Pa., March 5, 1871. [1; 3; 4; 6]

Wetjen, Albert Richard, novelist, b. London, England, 1900; d. San Francisco, Calif., March 8, 1948. [7; 10]

Wetmore, Claude Hazeltine, traveller, b. Cuyahoga Falls, O., 1862; d. ? [7; 10]

Wetmore, Mrs. Elizabeth, née **Bisland,** novelist, b. Fairfax Plantation, La., 1861; d. near Charlottesville, Va., Jan. 6, 1929. [10; 11]

Wetmore, James Carnahan, genealogist, b. Columbus, O., 1813; d. ? [6]

Wetmore, Prosper Montgomery, poet, b. Stratford, Conn., 1798; d. Great Neck, Long Island, N.Y., March 16, 1876. [3; 6]

Weyburn, Samuel Fletcher, journalist, b. New York, N.Y., 1853; d. Paterson, N.J., Feb. 21, 1941.

Weygant, Charles H., soldier and genealogist, b. 1839; d. Newburgh, N.Y., 1909.
Weyl, Walter Edward, economist, b. Philadelphia, Pa., 1873; d. New York, N.Y., Nov. 9, 1919. [10]
Whacker, John Bouche (pseud.). See Dabney, Virginius.
Whaley, Samuel, clergyman, b. 1812; d. 1899.
Whallon, Edward Payson, clergyman, b. Putnamville, Ind., 1849; d. Richmond, Ind., June 3, 1939. [10; 11]
Wharey, James, clergyman, b. Rutherford county, N.C., 1789; d. Goochland county, Va., April 29, 1842. [3; 6; 34]
Wharton, Anne Hollingsworth, historian, b. Southampton Furnace, Pa., 1845; d. Philadelphia, Pa., July 29, 1928. [1; 3; 4; 7; 10]
Wharton, Charles Henry, clergyman, b. St. Mary's county, Md., 1748; d. Burlington, N.J., July 22, 1833. [1; 3; 4; 5; 6; 34]
Wharton, Mrs. Edith Newbold, née **Jones,** novelist, b. New York, N.Y., 1862; d. near Saint Brice, France, Aug. 11, 1937. [1; 2; 4; 7; 10; 11; 72]
Wharton, Edward Clifton, novelist, b. 1827; d. Louisiana, 1891. [34]
Wharton, Francis, lawyer, clergyman, and educationist, b. Philadelphia, Pa., 1820; d. Washington, D.C., Feb. 21, 1889. [1; 3; 4; 5; 6; 62]
Wharton, Henry, lawyer, b. Philadelphia, Pa., 1827; d. Philadelphia, Pa., Nov. 11, 1880. [3; 6]
Wharton, Henry Marvin, clergyman, b. Culpeper county, Va., 1848; d. June 23, 1928. [7; 10; 34]
Wharton, Henry Redwood, surgeon, b. Philadelphia, Pa., 1853; d. Philadelphia, Pa., Dec. 3, 1925. [10]
Wharton, John, physician and poet, fl. 1814. [34]
Wharton, Morton Bryan, clergyman, b. Orange county, Va., 1839; d. 1908. [10; 34]
Wharton, Thomas Isaac, lawyer, b. Philadelphia, Pa., 1791; d. Philadelphia, Pa., April 7, 1856. [1; 3; 5; 6]
Yharton, Thomas Isaac, lawyer, b. Philadelphia, Pa., 1859; d. Philadelphia, Pa., April 3, 1896. [3; 7]
Wheat, John Thomas, clergyman, b. Washington, D.C., 1800; d. Salisbury, N.C., Feb. 2, 1888. [3]
Wheat, Marvin, traveller, fl. 1857-1865.
Wheatley, Charles Moore, mineralogist, b. Essex, England, 1822; d. Phoenixville, Pa., May 6, 1882. [3]
Wheatley, Richard, clergyman, b. near York, England, 1831; d. Hancock, N.Y., June, 1909. [6; 10]
Wheaton, Campbell (pseud.). See Campbell, Mrs. Helen, née Stuart.
Wheaton, Henry, jurist and diplomat, b. Providence, R.I., 1785; d. Dorchester, Mass., March 11, 1848. [1; 3; 4; 5; 6; 7; 8; 9]
Wheaton, Louisa, nun, b. Poughkeepsie, N.Y., 1863; d. New York, N.Y., 1927. [21]

Wheaton, Nathaniel Sheldon, clergyman and educationist, b. Washington, Conn., 1792; d. Washington, Conn., March 18, 1862. [1; 3; 4; 5; 6; 62]
Whedon, Daniel Denison, clergyman, b. Onondaga, N.Y., 1808; d. Atlantic City, N.J., June 8, 1885. [1; 3; 5; 6]
Wheelbarrow (pseud.). See Trumbull, Matthew Mark.
Wheeler, Andrew Carpenter, journalist, b. New York, N.Y., 1835; d. Monsey, Rockland county, N.Y., March 10, 1903. [1; 3; 6; 7; 10]
Wheeler, Arthur Leslie, educationist, b. Hartford, Conn., 1871; d. Princeton, N.J., May 22, 1932. [1a; 10; 11; 62]
Wheeler, Arthur Stanley, poultry farmer, b. New Haven, Conn., 1881; d. New York, N.Y., Oct. 26, 1926. [62]
Wheeler, Benjamin Ide, educationist, b. Randolph, Mass., 1854; d. Vienna, Austria, May 2, 1927. [1; 4; 5; 7; 10; 11]
Wheeler, Mrs. Candace, née **Thurber,** decorative artist, b. Delbi, N.Y., 1827; d. Aug. 5, 1923. [10]
Wheeler, Charles Gilbert, chemist, b. London, Upper Canada, 1836; d. Chicago, Ill., 1912. [6; 10]
Wheeler, Charles Henry, clergyman, b. Salem, Mass., 1831; d. Winchendon, Mass., June 30, 1888. [6; 51]
Wheeler, Charles Kirkland, physician, d. 1912. [51]
Wheeler, Chris. (pseud.). See MacOwen, Arthur H.
Wheeler, Crosby Howard, missionary, b. Hampden, Me., 1823; d. Auburndale, Mass., Oct. 11, 1896. [6; 46]
Wheeler, Mrs. Crosby Howard. See Wheeler, Mrs. Susan Anna, née Brookings.
Wheeler, Curtis. See Wheeler, Edward Curtis.
Wheeler, David Hilton, clergyman and educationist, b. Ithaca, N.Y., 1829; d. 1902. [3; 4; 6; 10]
Wheeler, Edmund, local historian, b. 1814; d. 1897.
Wheeler, Edward Curtis, soldier, b. Philadelphia, Pa., 1889; d. Great Bend, N.Y., July 6, 1927. [62]
Wheeler, Edward Jewitt, journalist, b. Cleveland, O., 1859; d. Lake Placid, N.Y., July 15, 1922. [4; 10]
Wheeler, Edward Smith, historian, b. 1834; d. 1883.
Wheeler, Ella. See Wilcox, Mrs. Ella, née Wheeler.
Wheeler, Mrs. Esther Gracie, née **Lawrence,** miscellaneous writer, fl. 1883-1893.
Wheeler, Everett Pepperell, lawyer, b. New York, N.Y., 1840; d. New York, N.Y., Feb. 8, 1925. [1; 4; 10; 11]
Wheeler, George Augustus, physician and local historian, b. 1837; d. Castine, Me., Jan. 14, 1923. [38]
Wheeler, Gervase, architect, fl. 1851-1872. [6]
Wheeler, Henry, clergyman, b. Somersetshire, England, 1835; d. Ocean Grove, N.J., April 25, 1925. [10; 11]

Wheeler, Henry Nathan, mathematician, b. Concord, Mass., 1850; d. Cambridge, Mass., July 7, 1905. [10]

Wheeler, Henry Warren, genealogist, b. 1849; d. 1894. [38]

Wheeler, Hial A., pharmacist, b. 1854; d. ? [37]

Wheeler, Homer Jay, agricultural chemist, b. Bolton, Mass., 1861; d. Montclair, N.J., Nov. 18, 1945. [10; 11]

Wheeler, Homer Webster, soldier, b. Montgomery, Vt., 1848; d. Los Angeles, Calif., April 11, 1930. [10]

Wheeler, Jacob D., lawyer, fl. 1823-1841. [6]

Wheeler, James Cooper, journalist, b. Brooklyn, N.Y., 1849; d. ? [10]

Wheeler, James Rignall, archaeologist, b. Burlington, Vt., 1859; d. Feb. 9, 1918. [1; 10]

Wheeler, Jessie L., educationist, b. 1811; d. Haverstraw, N.Y., March 1, 1949.

Wheeler, John Brooks, surgeon, b. Stowe, Vt., 1853; d. Burlington, Vt., May 1, 1942. [10]

Wheeler, John Hill, lawyer and historian, b. Murfreesboro, N.C., 1806; d. Washington, D.C., Dec. 7, 1882. [1; 3; 4; 5; 6; 34]

Wheeler, Joseph, soldier and politician, b. near Augusta, Ga., 1836; d. Brooklyn, N.Y., Jan. 25, 1906. [1; 3; 4; 5; 6; 10; 34]

Wheeler, Joseph Trank, editor, b. Philadelphia, Pa., 1868; d. Philadelphia, Pa., Dec. 25, 1919. [10]

Wheeler, Junius Brutus, soldier, b. Murfreesboro, N.C., 1830; d. Lenoir, N.C., July 15, 1886. [3; 6]

Wheeler, Marianna, nurse, b. Brooklyn, N.J., 1856; d. about 1939. [10]

Wheeler, Mrs. Mary, née **Sparkes,** evangelist, b. Tintern Abbey, England, 1835; d. Ocean Grove, N.J., Jan. 21, 1919. [10]

Wheeler, Olin Dunbar, advertising agent, b. Mansfield, O., 1852; d. St. Paul, Minn., Sept. 10, 1925. [7; 10; 70]

Wheeler, Orville Gould, clergyman and poet, b. Charlotte, Vt., 1817; d. Burlington, Vt., Feb. 1, 1892. [43]

Wheeler, Mrs. Susan Anna, née **Brookings,** missionary, fl. 1856-1899.

Wheeler, Wayne Bidwell, prohibitionist, b. Brookfield, O., 1869; d. Washington, D.C., Sept. 5, 1927. [4; 10; 11]

Wheeler, William Adolphus, librarian, b. Leicester, Mass., 1833; d. Boston, Mass., Oct. 28, 1874. [1; 3; 4; 6; 7]

Wheeler, Mrs. William Lamont. See Wheeler, Mrs. Esther Gracie, née Lawrence.

Wheeler, William Morton, biologist, b. Milwaukee, Wis., 1865; d. Boston, Mass., April 19, 1937. [10]

Wheeler, William Ogden, genealogist, b. 1837; d. 1900.

Wheeler, William Wallace, merchant and novelist, b. East Haddam, Conn., Jan. 11, 1853; d. Meriden, Conn., Dec. 27, 1916.

Wheeler, William Webb, traveller, b. Ashtabula county, O., 1845; d. St. Joseph, Mo., June 7, 1925. [4; 10]

Wheeler, Wilmot Henry, clergyman, b. Turkey, 1858; d. Los Angeles, Calif., March 21, 1929. [45]

Wheelock, Eleazar, educationist, b. Windham, Conn., 1711; d. Hanover, N.H., April 24, 1779. [1; 2; 3; 4; 5; 6; 7]

Wheelock, Mrs. Elizabeth Marian, writer of a book for children, b. 1859; d. 1917.

Wheelock, Mrs. Irene, née **Grosvenor,** naturalist, b. Monroe, Mich., 1867; d. Oct. 24, 1927. [10; 39]

Wheelock, John, educationist, b. Lebanon, Conn., 1754; d. Hanover, N.H., April 4, 1817. [1; 3; 4; 5; 6]

Wheelock, Julia Susan, hospital nurse, b. Avon, O., 1833; d. ? [3]

Wheelwright, Edmund March, architect, b. Roxbury, Mass., 1854; d. Boston, Mass., Aug. 14, 1912. [1; 10; 51]

Wheelwright, John, poet, b. Milton, Mass., 1897; d. Boston, Mass., Sept. 15, 1940.

Wheelwright, John Tyler, lawyer, b. Roxbury, Mass., 1856; d. Boston, Mass., Dec. 23, 1925. [10; 51]

Wheildon, William Wilder, journalist and historian, b. Boston, Mass., 1806; d. Concord, Mass., Jan. 7, 1892. [3; 6; 7]

Whelan, Charles Elbert, lawyer and miscellaneous writer, b. Mazomanie, Wis., 1862; d. Madison, Wis., Nov. 30, 1928. [10; 11]

Whelan, Edward, politician, b. county Mayo, Ireland, 1824; d. Charlottetown, P.E.I., Dec. 10, 1867. [27]

Whelan, Russell, journalist, b. 1901; d. New York, N.Y., Sept. 14, 1946.

Whelpley, Henry Milton, pharmacist, b. Battle Creek, Mich., 1861; d. Argentine, Kans., June 26, 1926. [1; 4; 10]

Whelpley, Samuel, clergyman, b. Stockdale, Mass., 1766; d. New York, N.Y., July 14, 1817. [3; 6]

Wherry, Elwood Morris, missionary, b. South Bend, Pa., 1843; d. Cincinnati, O., Oct. 5, 1927. [1; 10; 11]

Whicher, George Meason, educaitonist and poet, b. Muscatine, Ia., 1860; d. Amherst, Mass., Nov. 2, 1937. [7; 10; 11]

Whidden, David Graham, local historian, b. 1857; d. Wolfville, N.S., July 10, 1941. [27]

Whidden, John D., mariner, b. 1832; d. ?

Whiffen, Mrs. Blanche, née **Galton,** actress, b. England, 1844; d. near Montvale, Va., Nov. 25, 1936.

Whinery, Samuel, engineer, b. near Salem, O., 1845; d. East Orange, N.J., Jan. 14, 1925. [4; 10]

Whipple, Edwin Percy, lecturer and littérateur, b. Gloucester, Mass., 1819; d. Boston, Mass., June 16, 1886. [1; 3; 4; 5; 6; 7; 9; 71]

Whipple, George Chandler, engineer, b. New Boston, N.H., 1866; d. Cambridge, Mass., Nov. 27, 1924. [10]

Whipple, Guy Montrose, psychologist, b. Danvers, Mass., 1876; d. Salem, Mass., Aug. 1, 1941. [7; 10]

Whipple, Henry Benjamin, bishop, b. Adams, N.Y., 1822; d. Faribault, Minn., Sept. 16, 1901. [1; 3; 4; 5; 10; 70]

Whipple, Leander Edmund, mental healer, fl. 1888-1914.

Whipple, Squire, engineer, b. Hardwick, Mass., 1804; d. Albany, N.Y., March 15, 1888. [1; 3; 4; 6]

Whipple, Thomas King, educationist, b. 1890; d. Berkeley, Calif., June 3, 1939.

Whipple, Wayne, editor, b. near Meadville, Pa., 1856; d. New York, N.Y., Oct. 22, 1942. [7; 10; 11]

Whistler, James Abbott McNeill, painter, b. Lowell, Mass., 1834; d. London, England, July 17, 1903. [1; 2; 4; 7; 72]

Whitaker, Charles Harris, architect, b. Rhode Island, 1872; d. Drovers Rest, Va., Aug. 10, 1938. [7; 10; 11]

Whitaker, Epher, clergyman, b. Fairfield, N.J., 1820; d. Southold, Long Island, N.Y., Sept. 1, 1916. [4; 10]

Whitaker, Evelyn, novelist, fl. 1891-1903.

Whitaker, Herbert Coleman, mathematician, b. Cape May, N.J., 1862; d. Philadelphia, Pa., Nov. 17, 1921. [10]

Whitaker, Herman, novelist, b. Huddersfield, England, 1867; d. New York, N.Y., Jan. 20, 1919. [10; 35]

Whitaker, John Thompson, journalist, b. Chattanooga, Tenn., 1906; d. Washington, D.C., Sept. 11, 1946. [10]

Whitaker, Lily C., poet, b. Charleston, S.C., 1850; d. ? [3]

Whitaker, Mrs. Mary Scrimzeour, née **Furman,** poet and novelist, b. Beaufort district, S.C., Feb. 22, 1820; d. 1906. [3; 4; 6; 34]

Whitaker, Nicholas Tillinghast, clergyman, b. Boston, Mass., 1840; d. Dec. 28, 1923. [10]

Whitaker, Robert, clergyman and poet, b. Lancashire, England, 1863; d. Los Angeles, Calif., June 30, 1944. [10; 11; 35]

Whitaker, Walter Claiborne, clergyman, b. Lenoir, N.C., 1867; d. Knoxville, Tenn., Sept. 2, 1938. [7; 10; 34]

Whitbeck, Ray Hughes, educationist, b. Rochester, N.Y., 1871; d. Madison, Wis., July 27, 1939. [10; 11]

Whitcher, Mrs. Frances Miriam, née **Berry,** humorist, b. Whitesboro, N.Y., 1814; d. Whitesboro, N.Y., Jan. 4, 1852. [1; 3; 4; 5; 7; 9]

Whitcher, William Frederick, clergyman and journalist, b. Benton, N.H., 1845; d. 1918. [60]

Whitcomb, Ida Prentice, educationist and writer of books for children, b. Brooklyn, N.Y., 1843; d. Brooklyn, N.Y., June 16, 1931. [10; 11]

Whitcomb, Merrick, educationist, b. Nunda, N.Y., 1859; d. Shawanee-on-Delaware, Pa., Oct. 12, 1923. [10; 51]

Whitcomb, Russell, writer of books for boys, d. Feb. 9, 1931.

Whitcomb, Selden Lincoln, educationist, b. Grinnell, Ia., 1866; d. Lawrence, Kans., April 22, 1930. [1; 7; 10; 37]

White, Mrs. Alma, née **Bridwell,** bishop, b. Lewis county, Ky., 1862; d. Zarephath, N.J., June 26, 1946. [7; 10; 11]

White, Andrew Dickson, educationist and diplomat, b. Homer, N.Y., 1832; d. Ithaca, N.Y., Nov. 4, 1918. [1; 2; 4; 5; 6; 7; 8; 9; 10]

White, Anna, religious writer, b. 1831; d. 1910.

White, Benjamin, bacteriologist, b. Cooperstown, N.Y., 1879; d. Southern Pines, N.C., March 28, 1938. [62]

White, Carlos, bookseller, b. Topsham, Vt., 1842; d. ? [6; 43]

White, Caroline Earl, novelist, b. Philadelphia, Pa., 1833; d. Philadelphia, Pa.. Sept. 7, 1916. [7; 10]

White, Caroline Louisa, educationist, b. Roxbury, Mass., 1849; d. Brookline, Mass., Feb. 23, 1905. [62]

White, Catherine Ann, mother superior, b. 1825; d. 1878. [6]

White, Charles, clergyman, b. Randolph, Vt., 1795; d. Crawfordsville, Ind., Oct. 29, 1861. [3; 6]

White, Charles Edward, educationist, b. Ohio, 1848; d. Syracuse, N.Y., March 18, 1923.

White, Charles Ignatius, priest, b. Baltimore, Md., 1807; d. Washington, D.C., April 1, 1878. [1; 3; 6; 21]

White, Charles Joyce, mathematician, b. Cambridge, Mass., 1839; d. Cambridge, Mass., Feb. 12, 1917. [10; 51]

White, Charles Lincoln, clergyman, b. Nashua, N.H., 1863; d. New York, N.Y., April 21, 1941. [7; 10; 11]

White, Daniel Appleton, jurist, b. Lawrence, Mass., 1776; d. Salem, Mass., March 30, 1861. [3; 6]

White, Edward Albert, floriculturist, b. West Townsend, Mass., 1872; d. Ithaca, N.Y., May 13, 1943. [10; 11]

White, Edward Joseph, lawyer, b. St. Louis, Mo., 1869; d. Indianapolis, Ind., Dec. 30, 1935. [10; 11]

White, Edward Lucas, educationist and novelist, b. Bergen, N.J., 1868; d. Baltimore, Md., March 30, 1934. [4; 7; 10; 11; 15]

White, Edwin Augustine, clergyman, b. Cornwall, Conn., 1854; d. July 6, 1925. [10]

White, Eliza Orne, novelist, b. Keene, N.H., 1856; d. Brookline, Mass., Jan. 23, 1947. [4; 7; 10]

White, Mrs. Ellen Gould, née **Harmon,** religious leader, b. Gorham, Me., 1827; d. St. Helena, Calif., July 16, 1915. [1]

White, Emerson Elbridge, educationist, b. Mantua, O., 1829; d. Columbus, O., Oct. 21, 1902. [1; 4; 10]

White, Erskine Norman, clergyman, b. New York, N.Y., 1833; d. New York, N.Y., Feb. 13, 1911. [10; 62]

White, Eugene Richard, journalist, b. 1872; d. Buffalo, N.Y., March 16, 1906.

White, Frank, lawyer, b. Deposit, N.Y., 1858; d. New York, N.Y., Nov. 28, 1927. [10]

White, George, clergyman and historian, b. Charleston, S.C., 1802; d. Memphis, Tenn., April 30, 1887. [1; 34]

White, George Frederic, chemist, b. Melrose, Mass., 1885; d. Evanston, Ill., Sept., 1929. [10; 13]

White, George Savage, clergyman, b. Bath, England, 1784; d. March 3, 1850. [3; 4]

White, Greenough, clergyman and educationist, b. Cambridge, Mass., 1863; d. Sewanee, Tenn., July 3, 1901. [3b; 4; 10; 34]

White, Henry, clergyman, b. Wilbraham, Mass., 1790; d. Garland, Me., Dec. 8, 1858. [3; 4; 6]

White, Henry Alexander, educationist, b. Virginia, 1861; d. Columbus, S.C., Oct. 8, 1926. [7; 10; 34]

White, Henry Clay, educationist, b. Baltimore, Md., 1848; d. Athens, Ga., Dec. 1, 1927. [1; 3; 5; 6; 10]

White, Henry Seely, mathematician, b. Cazenovia, N.Y., 1861; d. Poughkeepsie, N.Y., May 20, 1943. [4; 10]

White, Hervey, novelist and poet, b. New London, Ia., 1866; d. Kingston, N.Y., Oct. 19, 1944. [7; 10]

White, Homer, clergyman, b. Weathersfield, Vt., 1837; d. Randolph, Vt., Jan. 19, 1926. [43]

White, Horace, journalist and economist, b. Colebrook, N.Y., 1834; d. New York, N.Y., Sept. 16, 1916. [1; 3; 4; 5; 7; 9; 10]

White, Horatio Stevens, educationist, b. Syracuse, N.Y., 1852; d. Cambridge, Mass., Dec. 12, 1934. [4; 10; 51]

White, James, clergyman, b. Palmyra, Me., 1821; d. Battle Creek, Mich., Aug. 6, 1881.

White, James, geographer, b. Ingersoll, Ont., 1863; d. Ottawa, Ont., Feb. 26, 1928. [27]

White, James Clarke, dermatologist, b. Belfast, Me., 1833; d. Boston, Mass., Jan. 5, 1916. [1; 4; 10; 51]

White, James Terry, publisher and poet, b. Newburyport, Mass., 1845; d. New York, N.Y., April 5, 1920. [4; 10]

White, James William, dentist, b. 1826; d. 1891.

White, James William, surgeon, b. Philadelphia, Pa., 1850; d. Paris, France, April 24, 1916. [1; 4; 10]

White, John, clergyman, b. Watertown, Mass., 1677; d. Gloucester, Mass., Jan. 17, 1760. [3; 4; 6; 51]

White, John, naval officer, d. 1840.

White, John Blake, artist and dramatist, b. near Eutaw Springs, S.C., 1871; d. Charleston, S.C., Aug. 24, 1859. [1; 3; 4; 6; 7; 34]

White, John Ellington, clergyman, b. Clayton, N.C., 1868; d. July 21, 1931. [10]

White, John Josiah, physician and poet, d. Philadelphia, Pa., 1878.

White, John Silas. See White, John Stuart.

White, John Stuart, educationist, b. Wrentham, Mass., 1847; d. Oct. 5, 1922. [10; 51]

White, John Williams, educationist, b. Cincinnati, O., 1849; d. Cambridge, Mass., May 9, 1917. [1; 3; 4; 6; 7; 10]

White, Joseph M., lawyer and politician, b. Franklin county, Ky., 1781; d. St. Louis, Mo., Oct. 19, 1839. [34]

White, Joshua E., physician, b. Pennsylvania; d. Savannah, Ga., Aug. 25, 1820. [6]

White, Mrs. Margaret Eliot, née Harding, compiler, b. 1823; d. 1903.

White, Matthew, editor and novelist, b. New York, N.Y., 1857; d. Westport, Conn., Sept. 17, 1940. [7; 10]

White, Newman Ivey, educationist, b. Statesville, N.C., 1892; d. Cambridge, Mass., Dec. 5, 1948. [7; 10]

White, Owen Payne, journalist, b. El Paso, Tex., 1879; d. New York, N.Y., Dec. 7, 1946. [10; 11]

White, Pliny Holton, clergyman, b. Springfield, Conn., 1822; d. Coventry, Vt., April 24, 1869. [3; 6; 43]

White, Mrs. Rhoda Elizabeth, née Waterman, miscellaneous writer, fl. 1858-1886. [6]

White, Richard Edward, poet, b. Dublin, Ireland, 1843; d. San Francisco, Calif., March 14, 1918. [35]

White, Richard Grant, journalist and littérateur, b. New York, N.Y., 1821; d. New York, N.Y., April 8, 1885. [1; 2; 3; 4; 5; 6; 7; 8; 9; 71]

White, Rufus Austin, clergyman, b. Bradford county, Pa.; d. Chicago, Ill., July 25, 1937. [10]

White, Sally Joy (pseud.). See White, Mrs. Sarah Elizabeth, née Joy.

White, Samuel, soldier, fl. 1812-1830.

White, Mrs. Sarah Elizabeth, née Joy, domestic scientist, b. Winchester, N.H., 1845; d. Dedham, Mass., March 25, 1909. [10]

White, Stewart Edward, novelist, b. Grand Rapids, Mich., 1872; d. San Francisco, Calif., Sept. 18, 1946. [4; 7; 10; 11; 12; 35]

White, Ten Eyck, journalist, b. 1854; d. Chicago, Ill., Aug. 31, 1942.

White, Trumbull, editor and explorer, b. Winterset, Ia., 1868; d. New York, N.Y., Dec. 14, 1941. [7; 10]

White, Wilbert Webster, clergyman, b. Ashland, O., 1863; d. New York, N.Y., Aug. 13, 1944. [10; 62]

White, William, bishop, b. Philadelphia, Pa., 1748; d. Philadelphia, Pa., July 17, 1836. [1; 3; 4; 6]

White, William, lawyer, b. 1783; d. 1831. [38]

White, William, educationist, b. 1815; d. ?

White, William, civil servant, b. London, England, 1830; d. Ottawa, Ont., Oct. 3, 1912. [27]

White, William Alanson, psychiatrist, b. Brooklyn, N.Y., 1870; d. Washington, D.C., March 7, 1937. [10; 11]

White, William Allen, journalist, b. Emporia, Kans., 1868; d. Emporia, Kans., Jan. 29, 1944. [4; 7; 10; 11; 12]

White, William Charles, lawyer and playwright, b. Boston, Mass., 1777; d. Worcester, Mass., May 2, 1818. [3; 4; 7]

White, William Charles, physician, b. Woodstock, Ont., 1874; d. Washington, D.C., Aug. 11, 1947.

White, William Francis, pioneer, b. 1829; d. California, 1891. [35]

White, William John, lawyer, b. Peterborough, Ont., 1861; d. Montreal, Que., Jan. 22, 1934. [27]

White, William Nathaniel, horticulturist, b. Longridge, Conn., 1819; d. Athens, Ga., July 14, 1867. [1; 3; 6]

White, William Prescott, clergyman, b. Honey Brook, Pa., 1840; d. Philadelphia, Pa., Feb. 22, 1929.

White, William Spottswood, clergyman, b. 1800; d. 1873.

Whiteaves, Joseph Frederick, palaeontologist, b. Oxford, England, 1835; d. Ottawa, Ont., Aug. 8, 1909. [27]

Whitehair, Charles Wesley, banker, b. Selma, Ind., 1887; d. Cleveland, O., June 12, 1933. [10]

Whitehead, Alfred North, philosopher, b. England, 1861; d. Cambridge, Mass., Dec. 30, 1947. [7]

Whitehead, Edward Jenkins, lawyer, b. 1838; d. Plainfield, N.J., March 24, 1924.

Whitehead, John, lawyer and historian, b. Licking county, O., 1819; d. 1905. [4]

Whitehead, John, theologian, b. England, 1850; d. Cambridge, Mass., Nov. 30, 1930. [10]

Whitehead, Richard Henry, anatomist, b. Salisbury, N.C., 1865; d. Feb. 6, 1916. [10]

Whitehead, Wilbur Cherrier, bridge expert, b. Cleveland, O., 1866; d. at sea, June 27, 1931. [1]

Whitehead, William, poet, b. 1807; d. 1886.

Whitehead, William Adee, historian, b. Newark, N. J., 1810; d. Perth Amboy, N.J., Aug. 8, 1884. [1; 3; 6; 7]

Whitehorne, Earl, editor, b. Verona, N.J., 1881; d. Caldwell, N.J., Oct. 23, 1941. [10]

Whitehouse, Henry Remsen, diplomat and historian, b. New York, 1857; d. Genoa, Italy, March 19, 1935. [10]

Whitehouse, Robert Treat, lawyer, b. Augusta, Me., 1869; d. Falmouth Foreside, Me., Feb. 15, 1924. [4; 10; 51]

Whiteley, Mrs. **Isabel,** née **Nixon,** novelist, b. Cambridge, N.Y., 1859; d. 1935. [10; 21]

Whitelock, Mrs. **Louise,** née **Clarkson,** poet and novelist, b. Baltimore, Md., 1865; d. Baltimore, Md., about April 7, 1928. [7; 10]

Whitelock, William Wallace, educationist, b. near Baltimore, Md., 1869; d. New York, N.Y., Jan. 29, 1940. [7; 10]

Whitford, William Clarke, educationist, b. Edmeston, N.Y., 1828; d. Milton, Wis., May 20, 1902. [4; 10]

Whitham, Jay Manuel, engineer, b. 1853; d. ?

Whitin, Ernest Stagg, sociologist, b. Morristown, N.J., 1881; d. New York, N.Y., Feb. 11, 1946. [10]

Whiting, Albert Bennet, spiritualist, b. 1835; d. 1871.

Whiting, Charles Goodrich, editor, critic, and poet, b. St. Albans, Vt., 1842; d. Springfield, Mass., June 21, 1922. [4; 7; 10; 11]

Whitting, George Elbridge, musician, b. Holliston, Mass., 1840; d. Cambridge, Mass., Oct. 14, 1923. [1; 4; 10; 20]

Whiting, Harold, educationist, b. Roxbury, Mass., 1855; drowned in the Pacific Ocean, off the coast of Mexico, May 27, 1895. [51]

Whiting, Henry, soldier and poet, b. Lancaster, Mass., 1788; d. St. Louis, Mo., Sept. 16, 1851. [3; 4; 6; 7]

Whiting, Lilian, journalist, b. Niagara Falls, N.Y., 1859; d. Boston, Mass., April 30, 1942. [4; 7; 10; 11]

Whiting, Mrs. **Meredith,** née **Gooch,** poet, b. Marblehead, Mass.; d. New Haven, Conn., Aug. 26, 1946.

Whiting, Robert Rudd, journalist, b. New York, N.Y., 1877; d. Darien, Conn., Oct. 15, 1918. [10]

Whiting, Sarah Frances, educationist, b. Wyoming, N.Y., 1847; d. Wilbraham, Mass., Sept. 13, 1927. [10]

Whiting, William, lawyer, b. Concord, Mass., 1813; d. Boston, Mass., June 29, 1873. [1a; 3; 4; 6]

Whitley, Hiram C., secret service agent, fl. 1874-1894.

Whitlock, Brand, politician, diplomat, and novelist, b. Urbana, O., 1869; d. Cannes, France, May 24, 1934. [1; 2; 4; 7; 10]

Whitlock, George Clinton, clergyman and educationist, b. Hubbardton, Vt., 1808; d. 1864. [6; 43]

Whitlock, Herbert Percy, mineralogist, b. New York, N.Y., 1868; d. New York, N.Y., Feb. 22, 1948. [7; 10; 13]

Whitlock, William Francis, clergyman, b. near Dayton, O., 1833; d. 1909. [10]

Whitman, Albery Allson, clergyman and poet, b. Hart county, Ky., 1851; d. Atlanta, Ga., June 29, 1901. [1; 7]

Whitman, Alonzo Garcelon, educationist, b. 1842; d. ? [38]

Whitman, Benaiah Longley, clergyman, b. Wilmot, N.S., 1862; d. Seattle, Wash., Nov. 27, 1911. [4; 10]

Whitman, Bernard, clergyman, b. East Bridgewater, Mass., 1796; d. Waltham, Mass., Nov. 5, 1834. [3; 6]

Whitman, Charles Huntington, educationist, b. Abbott, Me., 1873; d. Highland Park, N.J., Dec. 27, 1937. [10; 11; 62]

Whitman, Charles Otis, biologist, b. North Woodstock, Me., 1842; d. Chicago, Ill., Dec. 6, 1910. [1; 4; 10]

Whitman, Charles Sidney, lawyer, b. 1840; d. ? [6]

Whitman, Mrs. Eleanor, née **Wood,** educationist, b. Hanover, Mich., 1873; d. Cambridge, Mass., Dec. 25, 1948. [16]

Whitman, James L., librarian, b. Northampton, Mass., 1835; d. Cambridge, Mass., Sept. 26, 1910.

Whitman, Jason, clergyman, b. Bridgewater, Mass., 1799; d. Lexington, Mass., Jan. 25, 1848. [3; 6; 38]

Whitman, Peleg Spencer, clergyman, b. 1815; d. 1900.

Whitman, Mrs. Sarah Helen, née **Power,** poet, b. Providence, R.I., 1803; d. Providence, R.I., June 27, 1878. [1; 3; 4; 6; 7; 9; 71]

Whitman, Walt, poet, b. Huntington, Long Island, N.Y., 1819; d. Camden, N.J., March 26, 1892. [1; 2; 3; 4; 5; 6; 7; 8; 9; 71; 72]

Whitman, William Edward Seaver, journalist, b. Boston, Mass., 1832; d. Augusta, Me., 1901. [4; 10; 38]

Whitmarsh, Caroline Snowden. See Guild, Mrs. Caroline Snowden, née Whitmarsh.

Whitmer, David, Mormon leader, b. near Harrisburg, Pa., 1805; d. Richmond, Mo., Jan. 25, 1888. [1; 3; 6]

Whitmore, Frank Clifford, chemist, b. North Attleboro, Mass., 1887; d. State College, Pa., June 24, 1947. [10; 11; 13]

Whitmore, Laura Ann, poet, b. 1855; d. ?

Whitmore, William Henry, genealogist, b. Dorchester, Mass., 1836; d. Boston Mass., June 14, 1900. [1; 7; 10]

Whitnall, Harold Orville, geologist, b. Morristown, N.Y., 1877; d. Hamilton, N.Y., May 18, 1945. [10; 13]

Whitney, Mrs. Adeline Dutton, née **Train,** writer of books for girls, b. Boston, Mass., 1824; d. Boston, Mass., March 21, 1906. [1; 3; 4; 6; 7; 10]

Whitney, Albert Wurts, educationist, b. Geneva, Ill., 1870; d. New York, N.Y., July 27, 1943.

Whitney, Anne, poet and sculptor, b. Watertown, Mass., 1821; d. Boston, Mass., Jan. 23, 1915. [1; 4; 10]

Whitney, Asa, merchant, b. North Groton, Conn., 1797; d. Washington, D.C., Sept. 17, 1872. [1; 3; 4; 6]

Whitney, Caroline, sociologist, b. 1901; d. New York, N.Y., Nov. 19, 1938.

Whitney, Mrs. Carrie, née **Westlake,** librarian, b. Virginia; d. Kansas City, Mo., April 8, 1934. [10]

Whitney, Caspar, explorer, b. Boston, Mass., 1864; d. New York, N.Y., Jan. 18, 1929. [1a; 7; 10]

Whitney, Elliott (pseud.). See Sayler, Harry Lincoln.

Whitney, George, clergyman, b. Quincy, Mass., 1804; d. Jamaica Plain, Mass., April 2, 1842. [3; 6]

Whitney, George Washington Tapley, educationist, b. Bethel, Vt., 1871; d. Essex Junction, Vt., May 28, 1938.

Whitney, Mrs. Gertrude, née **Capen,** novelist, b. Canton, Mass., 1861; d. Augusta, Ga., May 22, 1941. [7; 10; 11]

Whitney, Harry, explorer, b. New Haven, Conn., 1873; d. Kennet Square, Pa., May 20, 1936. [10]

Whitney, Henry Clay, lawyer, b. Detroit, Me., 1831; d. 1905. [10]

Whitney, James Amaziah, lawyer and poet, b. Rochester, N.Y., 1839; d. 1909. [3; 6; 7; 10]

Whitney, James Lyman, librarian, b. Northampton, Mass., 1835; d. Boston, Mass., Sept. 25, 1910. [1; 7; 10; 62]

Whitney, James Parker, sportsman, b. 1835; d. 1913.

Whitney, Josiah Dwight, geologist, b. Northampton, Mass., 1819; d. Lake Sunapee, N.H., Aug. 19, 1896. [1; 3; 4; 5; 6; 62]

Whitney, Loren Harper, lawyer, b. Erie county, O., 1834; d. 1912. [10]

Whitney, Mrs. Louisa, née **Goddard,** chronicler, b. Manchester, England, 1819; d. Cambridge, Mass., May 13, 1882. [3; 6]

Whitney, Milton, agricultural chemist, b. Baltimore, Md., 1860; d. Washington, D.C., Nov. 11, 1927. [10]

Whitney, Orson Ferguson, historian, b. 1855; d. Salt Lake City, Utah, May 16, 1931.

Whitney, Peter, clergyman, b. Northampton, Mass., 1744; d. Northampton, Mass., Feb. 29, 1816. [3; 6]

Whitney, Samuel Worcester, clergyman, b. Hawaii, 1822; d. Germantown, Pa., July 13, 1905. [45]

Whitney, Thomas Richard, journalist and politician, b. New York, N.Y., 1807; d. New York, N.Y., April 12, 1858. [3; 6]

Whitney, William Collins, lawyer, politician, and financier, b. Conway, Mass., 1841; d. New York, N.Y., Feb. 2, 1904. [1; 4; 10; 62]

Whitney, William Dwight, educationist, b. Northampton, Mass., 1827; d. New Haven, Conn., June 7, 1894. [1; 2; 3; 4; 5; 6; 7; 8; 9]

Whiton, James Morris, clergyman and educationist, b. Boston, Mass., 1833; d. New York, N.Y., Jan. 25, 1920. [1; 3; 4; 5; 6; 10; 62]

Whiton, John Milton, clergyman, b. Winchendon, Mass., 1785; d. Antrim, N.H., Sept. 28, 1856. [3; 6; 62]

Whiton-Stone, Mrs. Cara Elizabeth, née **Hanscom,** poet, b. 1831; d. ?

Whitridge, Frederick Wallingford, lawyer, b. New Bedford, Mass., 1852; d. New York, N.Y., Dec. 30, 1916. [4; 10]

Whitsett, William Thornton, educationist, b. Whitsett, N.C., 1866; d. March 22, 1934. [10]

Whitsitt, William Heth, clergyman, b. Nashville, Tenn., 1841; d. 1911. [1; 3; 4; 6; 10]

Whitson, John Harvey, novelist, b. Seymour, Ind., 1854; d. Rowley, Mass., May 2, 1936. [7; 10; 11]

Whittaker, Frederick, journalist and novelist, b. London, England, 1838; d. ? [3; 6; 7; 8]

Whittaker, Henry, law clergk, b. Radnorshire, Wales, 1808; d. New York, N.Y., Feb. 9, 1881. [3; 6]

Whittaker, James Thomas, physician, b. Cincinnati, O., 1843; d. Cincinnati, O., June 5, 1900. [10]

Whitteker, John Edwin, clergyman, b. North Williamsburg, O., 1851; d. Maywood, Ill., April 13, 1925. [10]

Whittemore, Edwin Cary, educationist, b. 1858; d. Waterville, Me., Nov. 1, 1932.

Whittemore, Mrs. Emma, née Mott, religious writer, b. 1850; d. New York, N.Y., Jan. 2, 1931.

Whittemore, Henry, genealogist, b. 1833; d. ?

Whittemore, Thomas, clergyman, b. Boston, Mass., 1800; d. Cambridge, Mass., March 21, 1861. [1; 3; 4; 6; 7]

Whittemore, William Lewis, educationist, b. Francestown, N.H., 1824; d. Milford, N.J., July 2, 1911.

Whittet, Robert, poet, b. Scotland, 1829; d. ? [34]

Whittier, John Greenleaf, poet, b. Haverhill, Mass., 1807; d. Hampton Falls, N.H., Sept. 7, 1892. [1; 2; 3; 4; 5; 6; 7; 8; 9; 71; 72]

Whittingham, William Rollinson, bishop, b. New York, N.Y., 1805; d. Orange, N.J., Oct. 17, 1879. [1; 3; 4; 6]

Whittle, Walter Andrew, clergyman, b. Alabama; d. ? [34]

Whittlesey, Charles, geologist, b. Southington, Conn., 1808; d. Cleveland, O., Oct. 18, 1886. [3]

Whittlesey, Elsie Leigh, novelist, fl. 1872-1877. [6]

Whittlesey, Sarah Johnson Cogswell, poet and novelist, b. Williamstown, N.C., 1825; d. 1896. [3; 6; 34]

Whitty, James Howard, editor, b. Baltimore, Md., 1859; d. Richmond, Va., June 2, 1937. [7; 10]

Whitworth, John Ford, lawyer, b. 1854; d. ?

Wiborg, Frank Bestow, manufacturer, b. Cleveland, O., 1855; d. New York, N.Y., May 12, 1930. [10; 11]

Wick, William Watson, lawyer and politician, b. Canonsburg, Pa., 1796; d. Franklin, Ind., May 19, 1868. [4]

Wickersham, George Woodward, lawyer and politician, b. Pittsburgh, Pa., 1858; d. New York, N.Y., Jan. 25, 1936. [4; 7; 10]

Wickersham, James, jurist, b. Patoka, Ill., 1857; d. Juneau, Alaska, Oct. 24, 1939. [7; 10]

Wickersham, James Alexander, poet and novelist, b. 1851; d. ?

Wickersham, James Pyle, educationist, b. Chester county, Pa., 1825; d. Lancaster, Pa., March 25, 1891. [3; 4; 5; 6]

Wickes, Edward Zeus Franklin, physician, fl. 1865-1884.

Wickes, Stephen, physician, b. Jamaica, Long Island, N.Y., 1813; d. Orange, N.J., July 8, 1889. [1; 3; 6]

Wickes, Thomas, clergyman, b. Jamaica, Long Island, N.Y., 1814; d. Orange, N.J., Nov. 10, 1870. [3]

Wickett, Samuel Morley, political economist, b. Brooklin, Ont., 1872; d. Dec. 7, 1915. [27]

Wickham, Mrs. Gertrude, née Van Rensselaer, genealogist, b. 1844; d. Cleveland, O., May 20, 1930.

Wickham, Harvey, novelist and essayist, b. Middletown, N.Y., 1872; d. Rome, Italy, Nov. 15, 1930. [7]

Wickson, Edward James, educationist, b. Rochester, N.Y., 1848; d. Berkeley, Calif., July 16, 1923. [1; 4; 10]

Wicksteed, Gustavus William, poet, b. Liverpool, England, 1799; d. Ottawa, Ont., Aug. 18, 1898. [27]

Widdifield, Charles Howard, jurist, b. Uxbridge, Ont., 1859; d. Toronto, Ont., June 10, 1937. [11; 27; 30]

Widener, Peter Arrell Brown, philanthropist, b. Long Branch, N.J., 1895; d. Philadelphia, Pa., April 20, 1948. [4; 7; 10]

Widney, Joseph Pomeroy, educationist, b. Miami county, O., 1841; d. Los Angeles, Calif., July 4, 1938. [35]

Widtsoe, Osborne John Peter, educationist, b. 1877; d. Salt Lake City, Utah, 1920.

Wiechmann, Ferdinand Gerhard, chemist, b. Brooklyn, N.Y., 1858; d. Edgewater, N.J., April 24, 1919. [1; 4; 10]

Wiener, Leo, educationist, b. Bialystok, Poland, 1862; d. Belmont, Mass., Dec. 12, 1939. [7; 10; 11]

Wiener, Mrs. Renée, née von Eulenberg, physician, b. Austria, 1882; d. New York, N.Y., Feb. 15, 1942.

Wier, Albert Ernest, musician, b. Chelsea, Mass., 1879; d. Brooklyn, N.Y., Sept. 8, 1945. [20]

Wierzbicki, Felix Paul, physician, b. Poland, 1815; d. California, 1860. [3; 6]

Wiggin, Edward, local historian, b. 1837; d. Presque Isle, Me., 1912.

Wiggin, Frederick Alonzo, spiritualist, b. Tuftonboro, N.H., 1858; d. Brookline, Mass., July 26, 1940. [10]

Wiggin, James Henry, clergyman, b. Boston, Mass., 1836; d. Boston, Mass., Nov. 3, 1900. [1]

Wiggin, Mrs. Kate Douglas, née Smith, novelist, b. Philadelphia, Pa., 1856; d. Harrow, England, Aug. 24, 1923. [1; 4; 7; 10]

Wiggins, Ezekiel Stone, civil servant, b. Queen's county, N.B., 1839; d. Ottawa, Ont., Aug. 14, 1910. [27]

Wigglesworth, Edward, clergyman and educationist, b. Malden, Mass., about 1693; d. Cambridge, Mass., Jan. 16, 1765. [1; 3; 4; 5; 6; 51]

Wigglesworth, Edward, lawyer and merchant, b. Boston, Mass., 1804; d. Boston, Mass., Oct. 15, 1876. [3]

Wigglesworth, Michael, clergyman, educationist, and poet, b. England, 1631; d. Malden, Mass., June 10, 1705. [1; 3; 4; 6; 7; 51]

Wight, Charles Albert, clergyman, b. Ashfield, Mass., 1856; d. Chicopee Falls, Mass., April 15, 1915. [62]

Wight, Danforth Phipps, physician, b. 1791; d. 1874.

Wight, Mrs. Emily, née Carter, playwright, b. 1871; d. 1939.

Wight, Jarvis Sherman, physician, b. 1834; d. Brooklyn, N.Y., Nov. 16, 1901.

Wight, John Green, educationist, b. Gilead, Me., 1842; d. Clinton, N.Y., Nov. 23, 1913. [10]

Wight, Orlando Williams, physician, b. Centreville, N.Y., 1824; d. Detroit, Mich., Oct. 19, 1888. [3; 4; 6; 7]

Wight, William Ward, lawyer, b. Troy, N.Y., 1849; d. Milwaukee, Wis., Jan. 2, 1931. [4; 10; 11]

Wightman, Frederick Arnold, clergyman, b. Bayswater, N.B., 1860; d. Fredericton, N.B., Aug. 2, 1939. [27]

Wightman, Henry, humorist, fl. 1833-1835.

Wightman, William May, bishop, b. Charleston, S.C., 1808; d. Charleston, S.C., Feb. 15, 1882. [3; 4; 6; 34]

Wigle, Hamilton, clergyman and poet, b. Essex county, Ont., 1858; d. Sault Ste. Marie, Ont., Jan. 7, 1934. [27]

Wigmore, John Henry, lawyer and educationist, b. San Francisco, Calif., 1863; d. Chicago, Ill., April 20, 1943. [10]

Wikoff, Henry, adventurer, b. Philadelphia, Pa., about 1813; d. Brighton, England, May 2, 1884. [1; 3; 4; 6; 7]

Wilber, Charles Dana, writer on mining, b. 1831; d. about 1893.

Wilbour, Charles Edwin, Egyptologist, b. Little Compton, R.I., 1833; d. Paris, France, Dec. 17, 1896. [3; 6]

Wilbur, Henry Watson, editor, b. Easton, N.Y., 1851; d. Swarthmore, Pa., Sept. 5, 1914. [10]

Wilbur, James Benjamin, historian, b. Cleveland, O., 1856; d. Manchester, Vt., April 28, 1929. [10]

Wilbur, La Fayette, local historian, b. 1834; d. Portland, Ore., Aug., 1918.

Wilbur, Mrs. R. M., novelist, fl. 1882-1895. [6]

Wilbur, Ray Lyman, politician and educationist, b. Boonsboro, Ia., 1875; d. Palo Alto, Calif., June 26, 1949. [4; 7; 10]

Wilbur, Russell Ignatius Jones, priest, b. Omaha, Neb., 1876; d. Aug. 24, 1940. [21]

Wilcocke, Samuel Hull, hack-writer, b. Reigate, Surrey, England, about 1766; d. Quebec, Lower Canada, July 3, 1833. [27]

Wilcox, Alvin H., local historian, b. Cattaraugus county, N.Y., 1834; d. near Brainerd, Minn., June 29, 1908. [70]

Wilcox, Cadmus Marcellus, soldier, b. Wayne county, N.C., 1824; d. Washington, D.C., Dec. 2, 1890. [1; 3; 4; 5; 6; 34]

Wilcox, Carlos, clergyman, b. Newport, N.H., 1794; d. Danbury, Conn., May 29, 1827. [3; 6]

Wilcox, Delos Franklin, economist, b. near Ida, Mich., 1873; d. New York, N.Y., April 4, 1928. [1; 10; 11]

Wilcox, Mrs. Ella, née Wheeler, poet, b. Johnstown Center, Wis., 1850; d. Short Beach, Conn., Oct. 30, 1919. [1; 2; 3; 4; 5; 6; 7; 8; 9; 10]

Wilcox, Lucius Merle, agriculturist, b. 1858; d. ?

Wilcox, Marrion, lawyer and editor, b. Augusta, Ga., 1858; d. New York, N.Y., Dec. 26, 1926. [7; 10; 11; 62]

Wilcox, Milton Charles, Seventh Day adventist, b. 1853; d. 1935.

Wilcox, Phineas Bacon, lawyer, b. Middletown, Conn., 1798; d. Columbus, O., March 25, 1863. [3; 6; 62]

Wilcox, Ralph McIntosh, civil engineer, b. Portland, Conn., 1860; d. Long Beach, Calif., March 19, 1932. [62]

Wilcox, Reynold Webb, physician, b. Madison, Conn., 1856; d. Princeton, N.J., June 6, 1931. [1; 4; 10; 11; 62]

Wilcox, Sidney Freeman, surgeon, b. Fort Atkinson, Wis., 1855; d. Middletown, N.Y., April 20, 1920. [10]

Wild, Joseph, clergyman, b. Lancashire, England, 1834; d. Brooklyn, N.Y., Aug. 18, 1908. [27]

Wilde, Arthur Herbert, educationist, b. Framingham, Mass., 1865; d. Needham, Mass., Jan. 4, 1944.

Wilde, Richard Henry, poet, scholar, and politician, b. Dublin, Ireland, 1789; d. New Orleans, La., Sept. 10, 1847. [1; 3; 4; 5; 6; 7; 8; 9; 34]

Wilder, Alexander, physician, b. Verona, N.Y., 1823; d. Newark, N.J., Sept. 18, 1908. [1; 3; 4; 10]

Wilder, Burt Green, physician and educationist, b. Boston, Mass., 1841; d. Newton Centre, Mass., Jan. 21, 1925. [3; 4; 6; 10]

Wilder, Mrs. Charlotte Frances, née Felt, writer of books for children, b. Templeton, Mass.; d. Manhattan, Kans., Dec., 1916. [10]

Wilder, Daniel Webster, journalist and politician, b. Blackstone, Mass., 1832; d. Kansas City, Mo., 1911. [3; 4; 6; 7; 10; 51]

Wilder, David, local historian, b. 1778; d. 1866.

Wilder, Fred William, industrialist, b. 1853; d. 1906.

Wilder, Gerrit Parmile, horticulturist, b. Honolulu, Hawaii, 1863; d. Honolulu, Hawaii, Sept. 29, 1935. [10]

Wilder, Harris Hawthorne, zoölogist, b. Bangor, Me., 1864; d. Northampton, Mass., Feb. 27, 1928. [1; 10; 11]

Wilder, Mrs. Inez, née Whipple, zoölogist, b. Diamond Hill, R.I., 1871; d. Northampton, Mass., April 29, 1929. [10; 13]

Wilder, Mrs. Louise, née Beebe, horticulturist, b. Baltimore, Md., 1878; d. New York, N.Y., April 21, 1938. [10; 13]

Wilder, Marshall Pinckney, merchant and agriculturist, b. Rindge, N.H., 1798; d. Boston, Mass., Dec. 16, 1886. [1; 3; 4; 5; 6]

Wilder, Marshall Pinckney, entertainer, b. Geneva, N.Y., 1859; d. Jan. 10, 1915. [4; 10]

Wilder, Mrs. Martha L., née **Thornton,** novelist, b. 1843; d. ?

Wilder, Moses Hale, genealogist, b. 1798; d. 1879.

Wilder, Robert Parmalee, religious worker, b. Kolhapur, India, 1863; d. Oslo, Norway, March 27, 1938. [10]

Wilder, Royal Gould, clergyman, b. Bridgeport, Vt., 1816; d. New York, N.Y., Oct. 10, 1887. [3b]

Wildman, Edwin, journalist, b. Corning, N.Y., 1867; d. New York, N.Y., Nov. 3, 1932. [10; 11]

Wildman, Murray Shipley, economist, b. Selma, O., 1868; d. Stanford University, Calif., Dec. 24, 1930. [1; 10]

Wildman, Rounsevelle, consular agent, b. Batavia, N.Y., 1864; d. San Francisco, Calif., Feb. 22, 1901. [10]

Wildwood, Will (pseud.). See Pond, Frederick Eugene.

Wile, Frederic William, journalist, b. La Porte, Ind., 1873; d. Washington, D.C., April 7, 1941. [7; 10]

Wile, Ira Solomon, psychiatrist, b. Rochester, N.Y., 1877; d. New York, N.Y., Oct. 11, 1943. [10; 11]

Wiley, Calvin Henderson, educationist, b. Guilford county, N.C., 1819; d. Winston, N.C., Jan. 11, 1887. [1; 3; 6; 7; 34]

Wiley, Edwin, librarian, b. Coal Creek, Tenn., 1872; d. Peoria, Ill., Oct. 20, 1924. [4; 10; 11]

Wiley, Franklin Baldwin, journalist, b. New York, N.Y., 1861; d. Wayne, Pa., Aug. 6, 1930. [7; 10; 51]

Wiley, Frederick Levi, clergyman, b. Maryland, N.Y., 1836; d. Laconia, N.H., April 11, 1926.

Wiley, Harvey Washington, chemist, b. Kent, Ind., 1844; d. Washington, D.C., June 30, 1920. [1; 4; 10; 11; 12]

Wiley, Isaac William, bishop, b. Lewiston, Pa., 1825; d. Foochow, China, Nov. 22, 1884. [3; 4; 6]

Wiley, Sara King. See Drummond, Mrs. Sara King, née Wiley.

Wiley, William Halsted, publisher and politician, b. New York, N.Y., 1842; d. East Orange, N.J., May 2, 1925. [4; 7; 10]

Wilfley, Xenophon Pierce, lawyer and politician, b. Andrain county, Mo., 1871; d. St. Louis, Mo., May 4, 1931. [10]

Wilgus, Horace La Fayette, lawyer and educationist, b. near Conover, O.; d. Ann Arbor, Mich., Oct. 8, 1935. [10]

Wilgus, James Alva, educationist, b. 1866; d. Platteville, Wis., July 24, 1939. [44]

Wilhelm, Donald George, journalist, b. Defiance, O., 1887; d. Brooklyn, N.Y., Feb. 25, 1945. [7]

Wilhelm, Thomas, soldier, fl. 1871-1881.

Wilkes, Charles, naval officer and explorer, b. New York, N.Y., 1798; d. Washington, D.C., Feb. 8, 1877. [1; 2; 3; 4; 5; 6; 7]

Wilkes, George, journalist, b. New York, N.Y., 1817; d. New York, N.Y., Sept. 23, 1885. [1; 3; 5; 6; 9]

Wilkeson, Frank, soldier, b. 1845; d. ? [3]

Wilkeson, Samuel, abolitionist, b. Carlisle, Pa., 1781; d. Kingston, Tenn., July 7, 1848. [1; 3; 4; 6]

Wilkie, Franc Bangs, journalist, b. West Charlton, N.Y., 1832; d. Norwood Park, Ill., April 12, 1892. [1; 3; 4; 6; 7]

Wilkie, Daniel, educationist, b. Tollcross, Scotland, 1777; d. Quebec, Que., May 10, 1851. [27]

Wilkie, Daniel Robert, banker, b. Quebec, Que., 1846; d. Toronto, Ont., Nov. 19, 1914. [27]

Wilkin, George Francis, clergyman, b. Warsaw, N.Y., 1848; d. Minneapolis, Minn., July 6, 1924. [67]

Wilkins, Harriet Annie, poetess, b. England, 1829; d. Hamilton, Ont., Jan. 7, 1888. [27]

Wilkins, Henry, physician, b. 1767; d. Baltimore county, Md., 1847.

Wilkins, John Hubbard, astronomer, b. Amherst, N.H., 1794; d. Boston, Mass., Dec. 31, 1861. [6; 51]

Wilkins, Lawrence Augustus, educationist, b. Des Moines, Ia., 1878; d. New York, N.Y., Dec. 24, 1945. [11]

Wilkins, Mary Eleanor. See Freeman, Mrs. Mary Eleanor, née Wilkins.

Wilkins, William Glyde, engineer, b. Pittsburgh, Pa., 1854; d. Pittsburgh, Pa., April 12, 1921. [10]

Wilkinson, Alfred Ernest, lawyer, b. Skaneateles, N.Y., 1846; d. Austin, Tex., July 15, 1932. [10]

Wilkinson, Andrews, journalist, b. Plaquemines parish, La.; d. New Orleans, La., May 16, 1921. [10; 34]

Wilkinson, James, soldier, b. Calvert county, Md., 1757; d. near Mexico City, Mexico, Dec. 28, 1825. [1; 2; 3; 4; 5; 6; 7; 34]

Wilkinson, John, naval officer, b. Norfolk, Va., 1821; d. Annapolis, Md., Dec. 29, 1891. [1; 3; 4; 5; 34]

Wilkinson, Mrs. Marguerite Ogden, née **Bigelow,** poet and playwright, b. Halifax, N.S., 1883; d. Coney Island, N.Y., Jan. 11, 1928. [4; 10; 11]

Wilkinson, William Cleaver, clergyman and educationist, b. Westford, Vt., 1833; d. Chicago, Ill., April 25, 1920. [3; 4; 6; 7; 10]

Will, Allen Sinclair, educationist, b. Antioch, Va., 1868; d. New York, N.Y., March 10, 1934. [1; 7; 10; 11]

Willard, Ammiel Jenkins, lawyer, b. 1822; d. 1900.

Willard, Ashton Rollins, writer on art, b. Montpelier, Vt., 1858; d. Boston, Mass., Oct. 3, 1918. [7; 10; 49]

Willard, Mrs. Caroline McCoy White, missionary, b. New Castle, Pa., 1853; d. ?

Willard, Charles Dwight, miscellaneous writer, b. 1860; d. 1914.

Willard, Charles E., insurance agent, b. 1846; d. 1898.

Willard, Mrs. Clara A., novelist, fl. 1869-1872. [6]

Willard, David, local historian, b. 1790; d. 1855.

Willard, De Forest, surgeon, b. Newington, Conn., 1846; d. Lansdowne, Pa., Oct. 14, 1910. [1; 4; 10]

Willard, Mrs. Emma, née **Hart,** educationist, b. Berlin, Conn., 1787; d. Troy, N.Y., April 15, 1870. [1; 3; 4; 5; 6; 7; 8; 9]

Willard, Frances Elizabeth, reformer, b. Churchville, N.Y., 1839; d. New York, N.Y., Feb. 18, 1898. [1; 2; 3; 4; 5; 6; 7]

Willard, Henry Kellogg, financier, b. Washington, D.C., 1856; d. Pasadena, Calif., May 17, 1926. [4; 62]

Willard, James Field, historian, b. Philadelphia, Pa., 1876; d. Boulder, Colo., Nov. 21, 1935. [1a; 10; 11]

Willard, John, jurist, b. Guilford, Conn., 1792; d. Saratoga Springs, N.Y., Aug. 31, 1862. [3; 4; 6]

Willard, John (pseud.). See Bolte, John Willard.

Willard, Joseph, lawyer and historian, b. Cambridge, Mass., 1798; d. Boston, Mass., May 12, 1865. [1; 3; 4; 6]

Willard, Joseph Augustus, law clerk, b. Cambridge, Mass., 1816; d. Boston, Mass., Aug. 14. 1904. [10]

Willard, Josiah Flint, sociologist, b. Appleton, Wis., 1869; d. Chicago, Ill., Jan. 21, 1907. [1a; 4; 7; 10]

Willard, Samuel, clergyman and educationist, b. Concord, Mass., 1640; d. Boston, Mass., Sept. 12, 1707. [1; 3; 4; 5; 6; 51]

Willard, Samuel, clergyman, educationist, and hymn-writer, b. Petersham, Mass., 1775; d. Deerfield, Mass., Oct. 8, 1859. [1; 3; 6; 51]

Willard, Samuel, educationist, b. Lunenburg, Vt., Dec. 30, 1821; d. ? [6; 36; 43]

Willard, Sidney, educationist, b. Beverly, Mass., 1780; d. Cambridge, Mass., Dec. 6, 1856. [1; 3; 4; 6; 7; 51]

Willard, Theodore Arthur, inventor and explorer, b. Castle Rock, Minn., 1862; d. Beverly Hills, Calif., Feb. 3, 1943. [10]

Willard, Xerxes Addison, dairyman, b. 1820; d. 1882. [6]

Willcox, Cornélis de Witt, soldier, b. Geneva, Switzerland, 1861; d. Naples, Italy, Jan. 19, 1938. [10]

Willcox, Giles Buckingham, clergyman, b. New York, N.Y., 1826; d. Chicago, Ill., July 22, 1922. [62]

Willcox, James Mark, philosopher, fl. 1860-1875. [6]

Willcox, James Mark, financier, b. Philadelphia, Pa., 1861; d. Berwyn, Pa., Dec. 26, 1935. [10]

Willcox, Mrs. Louise, née **Collier,** essayist and anthologist, b. Chicago, Ill., 1865; d. Paris, France, Sept. 13, 1929. [1; 7; 10; 11]

Willcox, Orlando Bolivar, soldier, b. Detroit, Mich., 1823; d. Cobourg, Ont., May 10, 1907. [1; 3; 4; 5; 6; 10]

Willemse, Cornelius William, detective, b. Holland, 1871; d. New York, N.Y., July 12, 1942.

Willers, Diedrich, local historian, b. 1833; d. 1908.

Willet, Joseph Edgerton, educationist, b. Macon, Ga., 1826; d. 1897. [3; 6; 34]

Willet, Nathaniel Louis, local historian, b. 1851; d. Warrenton, Va., May 14, 1933.

Willett, Herbert Lockwood, clergyman and educationist, b. Ionia, Mich., 1864; d. Winter Park, Fla., March 27, 1944. [7; 10; 11]

Willett, William Marinus, clergyman and educationist, b. New York, N.Y., 1803; d. Jersey City, N.J., Dec. 8, 1895. [3b; 6]

Willetts, Jacob, educationist, b. Fishkill; N.Y., 1785; d. near Mechanic, Dutchess county, N.Y., Sept. 12, 1860. [3]

Willey, Arthur, zoologist, b. Scarborough, England, 1867; d. Montreal, Que., Dec. 26, 1942. [27]

Willey, Austin, clergyman, b. Campton, N.H., 1806; d. Northfield, Minn., March 28, 1896. [3b]

Willey, Benjamin Glazier, clergyman, b. Conway, N.H., 1796; d. East Sumner, Me., April 17, 1867. [3; 6]

Willey, Freeman Otis, economist, fl. 1883-1900.

Willey, Henry, botanist, b. Genesee, N.Y., 1824; d. Weymouth, Mass., 1907. [3; 4; 10]

Willey, John Heston, clergyman, b. Maryland, 1854; d. Montclair, N.J., Nov. 8, 1942. [4; 11]

Willey, Nathan, actuary, fl. 1870-1891. [6]

Willey, Samuel Hopkins, clergyman and educationist, b. Campton, N.H., 1821; d. Berkeley, Calif., Jan. 21, 1914. [1; 10]

Willey, William Patrick, educationist, b. Morgantown, W. Va., 1840; d. Morgantown, W. Va., May 3, 1900.

Williams, Albert, clergyman, b. Orange, N.J., 1809; d. West Orange, N.J., June 4, 1893.

Williams, Alfred Mason, journalist, b. Taunton, Mass., 1840; d. St. Kitts, West Indies, March 9, 1896. [4; 6; 7]

Williams, Allen Samuel, sociologist, b. 1858; d. New York, N.Y., Feb. 5, 1922.

Williams, Alonzo, educationist, b. Foster, R.I., 1842; d. Providence, R.I., March 16, 1901. [3b]

Williams, Mrs. Anna Vernon, née **Dorsey,** novelist, fl. 1889-1924.

Williams, Augustus Warner, clergyman, b. 1844; d. 1920.

Williams, B. Brown, physician, fl. 1848-1887.

Williams, Blanche Colton, educationist, b. Attala county, Miss., 1879; d. Jackson, Miss., Aug. 9, 1944. [7; 10]

Williams, Byron, local historian, b. 1843; d. Williamsburg, O., Feb. 15, 1915.

Williams, Mrs. Catharine Read, née **Arnold,** poet, novelist, and biographer, b. Providence, R.I., 1787; d. Providence, R.I., Oct. 11, 1872. [1; 3; 6; 7; 9]

Williams, Charles Ashley, clergyman and educationist, b. Salem, N.Y., 1814; d. Geneva, Wis., Aug. 18, 1885. [69]

Williams, Charles David, bishop, b. Belle-vue, O., 1860; d. Detroit, Mich., Feb. 14, 1923. [1; 4; 10]

Williams, Charles Evarts, novelist and biographer, b. Virginia, 1839; d. ? [38]

Williams, Charles Frederic, lawyer, b. 1842; d. 1895. [6; 8]

Williams, Charles Richard, journalist and poet, b. Prattsburg, N.Y., 1853; d. Princeton, N.J., May 6, 1927. [1; 4; 7; 10]

Williams, Chauncey Pratt, soldier, b. Albany, N.Y., 1860; d. Albany, N.Y., Dec. 25, 1936. [62]

Williams, Chauncy Kilborn, lawyer, b. Rutland, Vt., 1832; d. Rutland, Vt., Jan. 7, 1879. [43]

Williams, Clement Clarence, educationist, b. Bryant, Ill., 1882; d. Madison, Wis., Feb. 20, 1947. [10; 11]

Williams, Cora May, poet, b. 1862; d. Los Angeles, Calif., March 1, 1946.

Williams, Daniel Roderick, lawyer, b. Dawn, Mo., 1871; d. Manila, Philippine Islands, 1931. [10]

Williams, Dwight, clergyman and poet, b. 1824; d. 1898.

Williams, Edward Franklin, clergyman, b. Uxbridge, Mass., 1832; d. Winnetka, Ill., May 26, 1919. [10; 62]

Williams, Edward Higginson, educationist, b. Proctorsville, Vt., 1849; d. Woodstock, Vt., Nov. 2, 1933. [62]

Williams, Edward Huntington, physician, b. Durand, Ill., 1868; d. Santa Monica, Calif., June 24, 1944. [7; 10; 11; 35]

Williams, Edward Thomas, diplomat and orientalist, b. Columbus, O., 1854; d. Berkeley, Calif., Jan. 27, 1944. [7; 10; 11]

Williams, Edwin, journalist, b. Norwich, Conn., 1797; d. New York, N.Y., Oct. 21, 1854. [1; 3; 6; 7; 10]

Williams, Eleazar, missionary, b. Caughnawaga, Canada, about 1789; d. Hogansburg, N.Y., Aug. 28, 1858. [1; 3; 4; 6; 7]

Williams, Ephie Augustus, educationist, b. Erwinton, S.C., 1864; d. Atlanta, Ga., July 22, 1940.

Williams, Espy William Hendricks, poet and playwright, b. Carrollton, La., 1852; d. New Orleans, La., 1908. [7; 10; 34]

Williams, Mrs. Flora, née **McDonald,** novelist, b. 1842; d. ? [34]

Williams, Francis Churchill, editor and novelist, b. Philadelphia, Pa., 1869; d. Plumstead township, Pa., April 11, 1945. [4; 10]

Williams, Francis Henry, physician, b. Uxbridge, Mass., 1852; d. Boston, Mass., June 22, 1926. [4; 10]

Williams, Francis Howard, poet and playwright, b. Philadelphia, Pa., 1844; d. Germantown, Pa., June 18, 1922. [7; 10]

Williams, Francis Stanton, educationist, b. Boston, Mass., 1817; d. 1889. [6; 51]

Williams, Frankwood Earl, physician, b. Cardington, O., 1883; d. New York, N.Y., Sept. 24, 1936. [10]

Williams, Frederick Wells, educationist, b. Macao, China, 1857; d. New Haven, Conn., Jan. 22, 1928. [1; 10; 62]

Williams, Gardner Fred, mining engineer, b. Saginaw, Mich., 1842; d. San Francisco, Calif., Jan. 22, 1922. [4; 10]

Williams, Gardner Stewart, engineer, b. Saginaw, Mich., 1866; d. Ann Arbor, Mich., Dec. 12, 1931. [10; 11]

Williams, Gatenby (pseud.). See Guggenheim, William.

Williams, George Alfred, illustrator, b. Newark, N.J., 1875; d. Kennebunkport, Me., Feb. 29, 1932. [10; 11]

Williams, George Forrester, journalist, b. Gibraltar, 1837; d. New York, N.Y., Dec. 30, 1920. [7; 10]

Williams, George Henry, politician, b. New Lebanon, N.Y., 1820; d. Portland, Ore., April 4, 1910. [1; 4; 10]

Williams, George Huntington, mineralogist, b. Utica, N.Y., 1856; d. Utica, N.Y., July 12, 1894. [1; 5]

Williams, George S., educationist, fl. 1861-1872. [6]

Williams, George Walton, banker, b. Burke county, N.C., 1820; d. Charleston, S.C., 1903. [4; 10]

Williams, George Washington, soldier and politician, b. Bedford Springs, Pa., 1849; d. Blackpool, England, Aug. 4, 1891. [1; 3; 4; 6; 7]

Williams, Gershom Mott, bishop, b. Fort Hamilton, N.Y., 1857; d. Paris, France, April 14, 1923. [4; 10]

Williams, Gorham Deane, lawyer, b. East Bridgewater, Mass., 1842; d. 1907. [10; 51]

Williams, Harold, physician and novelist, b. Brookline, Mass., Dec. 5, 1853; d. Boston, Mass., April 3, 1926. [10; 11; 51]

Williams, Henry Francis, clergyman, b. Hannibal, Mo., 1847; d. Nashville, Tenn., Feb. 11, 1933. [10; 11]

Williams, Henry Horace, educationist, b. Sunbury, N.C., 1858; d. Chapel Hill, N.C., Dec. 26, 1940. [10; 11]

Williams, Henry Shaler, palaeontologist, b. Ithaca, N.Y., 1847; d. Havana, Cuba, July 30, 1918. [1; 4; 10; 62]

Williams, Henry Smith, physician, b. Durand, Ill., 1863; d. Los Angeles, Calif., July 4, 1943. [7; 10]

Williams, Henry T., publisher, fl. 1867-1885. [6]

Williams, Henry Willard, opthalmologist, b. Boston, Mass., 1821; d. Boston, Mass., June 13, 1895. [1; 3; 4; 6]

Williams, Herbert Upham, pathologist, b. Buffalo, N.Y., 1866; d. Buffalo, N.Y., Dec. 8, 1938. [10; 11]

Williams, Herschel. See Williams, Wilbur Herschel.

Williams, Isabel Cecilia, short-story writer, b. Boston, Mass., 1875; d. Boston, Mass., 1911. [21]

Williams, James, journalist and diplomat, b. Grainger county, Tenn., 1796; d. Gratz, Austria, April 10, 1869. [1; 4; 6; 7]

Williams, Jesse Lynch, novelist and playwright, b. Sterling, Ill., 1871; d. Herkimer county, N.Y., Sept. 14, 1929. [1; 4; 7; 10; 11]

Wliliams, John, clergyman, b. Roxbury, Mass., 1664; d. Deerfield, Mass., June 12, 1729. [1; 2; 3; 4; 5; 6; 7; 51]

Williams, John, poet, satirist, and critic, b. London, England, 1761; d. Brooklyn, N.Y., Oct. 12, 1818. [4; 7]

Williams, John, bishop, b. Old Deerfield, Mass., 1817; d. Middletown, Conn., Feb. 7, 1899. [1; 3; 4; 5; 6]

Williams, John C., soldier and local historian, b. Danby, Vt., 1843; d. ? [43]

Williams, John Camp, bibliographer, b. about 1859; d. Morristown, N.J., 1929.

Williams, John Fletcher, librarian, b. Cincinnati, O., 1834; d. Rochester, Minn., April 28, 1895. [1; 4; 70]

Williams, John Lee, civil engineer and lawyer, b. Salem, Mass., 1775; d. Picoloto, Fla., 1856. [34]

Williams, John Milton, theologian, b. 1817; d. 1900.

Williams, John Sharp, politician, b. Memphis, Tenn.,1854; d near Yazoo City, Tenn., Sept. 27, 1932. [1; 4; 5; 10; 11]

William, John Whitridge, physician, b. Baltimore, Md., 1866; d. Baltimore, Md., Oct. 21, 1931. [1; 10; 11]

Williams, Jonathan, merchant, soldier, and scientist, b. Boston, Mass., 1750; d. Philadelphia, Pa., May 16, 1815. [1; 3; 4; 6]

Williams, Joseph, pioneer, b. about 1778; d. ?

Williams, Joseph John, priest and educationist, b. Boston, Mass., 1875; d. Lenox, Mass., Oct. 28, 1940. [7; 10; 21]

Williams, Linsly Rudd, physician, b. New York, N.Y., 1875; d. New York, N.Y., Jan. 8, 1934. [1; 10]

Williams, Louis Lafayette, educationist, b. 1841; d. 1919.

Williams Mary Wilhelmine, educationist, b. Stanislaus county, Calif., 1878; d. Palo Alto, Calif., March 10, 1944. [7; 10; 11]

Williams, Meade Creighton, historian, b. 1840; d. Michilimackinac, Mich., 1906.

Williams, Milan Bertrand, evangelist, fl. 1896-1910.

Williams, Nathan Winslow, lawyer, b. Cleveland, O., 1860; d. Baltimore, Md., 1925. [4; 10]

Williams, Nathaniel Marshman, clergyman, b. Salem, Mass., 1813; d. Newton, Mass., Feb. 10, 1895. [6]

Williams, Ralph Olmsted, educationist and lexicographer, b. Palmyra, N.Y., 1838; d. New Haven, Conn., July 17, 1908. [7; 10; 62]

Williams, Richard Jordan, lawyer, b. 1830; d. Philadelphia, Pa., Sept. 16, 1915.

Williams, Richard Richardson, editor, b. Waterford, Ireland, 1843; d. Glen Ridge, N.J., Sept. 30, 1915. [10]

Williams, Roger, clergyman, b. London, England, about 1603; d. Rhode Island, early in 1682-83. [1; 2; 3; 4; 5; 7]

Williams, Roger D., soldier, b. Lexington, Ky., 1856; d. Lexington, Ky., Dec. 12, 1925. [10]

Williams, Rufus Phillips, chemist, b. Ashfield, Mass., 1851; d. Cambridge, Mass., August 23, 1911. [10]

Williams, Samuel, clergyman, b. Waltham, Mass., 1743; d. Rutland, Vt., Jan. 2, 1817. [3; 6]

Williams, Samuel Gardner, educationist, b. Herkimer county, N.Y., 1827; d. 1900. [4]

Williams, Samuel Wells, missionary and diplomat, b. Utica, N.Y., 1812; d. New Haven, Conn., Feb. 16, 1884. [1; 3; 4; 5; 6; 7; 8; 9]

Williams, Samuel Wesley, editor, b. Chillicothe, O., 1827; d. Wyoming, O., Feb. 14, 1928.

Williams, Sherman, educationist, b. Cooperstown, N.Y., 1846; d. Glens Falls, N.Y., Dec. 12, 1923. [10]

Williams, Sidney Clark, novelist, b. Wells, Md., 1878; d. Norristown, Pa., May 24, 1949. [7; 10; 11]

Williams, Stephen West, physician, b. Deerfield, Mass., 1790; d. Laona, Ill., July 6, 1855. [1; 3; 4; 6]

Williams, Talcott, journalist, b. Abeih, Turkey, 1849; d. New York, N.Y., Jan. 24, 1928. [1; 4; 7; 10]

Williams, Theodore Chickering, clergyman, b. Brookline, Mass., 1855; d. 1915. [10; 51]

Williams, Thomas, clergyman, b. Pomfret, Conn., 1779; d. Providence, R.I., Sept. 29, 1876. [3; 4; 6; 62]

Williams, Tudor, poet, fl. 1879-1895.

Williams, Walter, educationist, b. Boonville, Mo., 1864; d. Columbia, Mo., July 29, 1935. [1a; 10; 11]

Williams, Walter Erskine, lawyer, b. Collierville, Tenn., 1860; d. Fort Worth, Tex., Aug. 29, 1938. [10]

Williams, Wayland Wells, artist, novelist, and poet, b. New Haven, Conn., 1888; d. New Haven, Conn., May 6, 1945. [7; 10; 11; 62]

Williams, Wilbur Herschel, journalist, b. North Manchester, Ind., 1874; d. Boston, Mass., Sept. 15, 1935. [10]

Williams, William Asbury, clergyman, b. 1854; d. Camden, N.J., May 6, 1938.

Williams, William George, clergyman and educationist, b. Chillicothe, O., 1822; d. Delaware, O., 1902. [10]

Williams, William Huntsman, lawyer, b. Stroudsburg, Pa., 1873; d. Verona, N.J., Feb. 14, 1943.

Williams, William R., clergyman, b. New York, N.Y., 1804; d. New York, N.Y., April 1, 1885. [1; 3; 4; 6]

Williams, William Robert, physician, b. Watertown, Wis., 1867; d. New York, N.Y., Nov. 17, 1940. [10]

Williams, William Stoddard, physician and clergyman, b. 1850; d. ?

Williams, William W., local historian, fl. 1878-1879.

Williamson, Alexander Johnston, poet, b. about 1796; d. Toronto, Ont., Oct. 13, 1870. [27]

Williamson, Edward Hand, lawyer and novelist, fl. 1869-1893. [6]

Williamson, Ernest Jefferson, hotelman, b. 1885; d. May 18, 1930.

Williamson, Hugh, physician, historian, scientist, and politician, b. West Nottingham, Pa., 1735; d. New York, N.Y., May 22, 1819. [1; 2; 3; 4; 5; 6; 34]

Williamson, Isaac Dowd, clergyman, b. Pomfret, Vt., 1807; d. Cincinnati, O., Nov. 26, 1876. [3; 6; 43]

Williamson, James, astronomer, b. Edinburgh, Scotland, 1806; d. Kingston, Ont., Sept. 25, 1895. [27]

Williamson, James Joseph, soldier, b. 1834; d. 1915. [34]

Williamson, Jefferson. See Williamson, Ernest Jefferson.

Williamson, John, soldier, d. Edinburgh, Scotland, 1840. [27]

Williamson, John, naturalist, b. 1857; d. 1884.

Williamson, John Poage, clergyman, b. Lac Qui Parle, Minn., 1835; d. Greenwood, S.D., Oct. 3, 1917. [10]

Williamson, Joseph, lawyer, historian, and bibliographer, b. Belfast, Me., 1828; d. Belfast, Me., 1902. [4; 10]

Williamson, Julia May, poet, b. New Sharon, Me., 1859; d. 1909. [7; 10]

Williamson, Mrs. Mary Lynn, née Harrison, writer of books for children, b. near Charlottesville, Va., 1850; d. ? [10; 34]

Williamson, Robert Stockton, soldier, b. New York, N.Y., 1824; d. San Francisco, Calif., Nov. 10, 1882. [3; 6]

Williamson, Scott Graham, novelist, b. 1899; d. Dec. 10, 1948.

Williamson, Walter, physician, b. Newton, Delaware county, Pa., 1811; d. Philadelphia, Pa., Dec. 19, 1870. [3; 4; 6]

Williamson, William Durkee, historian and politician, b. Canterbury, Conn., 1779; d. Bangor, Me., May 27, 1846. [1; 3; 4; 5; 6; 38]

Williard, George Washington, clergyman, b. 1818; d. 1900.

Willing, Mrs. Jennie, née **Fowler,** writer of books for young people, b. 1834; d. ?

Willis, Anson, lawyer, b. Ulster county, N.Y., 1802; d. Portchester, N.Y., Dec. 14, 1874. [3]

Willis, Bailey, geologist, b. Idlewild-on-Hudson, N.Y., 1857; d. Palo Alto, Calif., Feb. 20, 1949. [10; 13]

Willis, Frederick Milton, theosophist, b. San Francisco, Calif., 1868; d. Brooklyn, N.Y., Sept. 10, 1942. [35]

Willis, Henry Augustus, soldier, b. 1830; d. 1918.

Willis, Henry Parker, economist, b. Weymouth, Mass., 1874; d. New Brighton, N.Y., Aug. 14, 1874. [10; 11]

Willis, Michael, clergyman and educationist, b. Greenock, Scotland, 1799; d. Aberdour, Scotland, Aug. 19, 1879. [27]

Willis, Nathaniel Parker, poet and littérateur, b. Portland, Me., 1806; d. near Cornwall-on-the-Hudson, N.Y., Jan. 20, 1867. [1; 3; 4; 7; 62]

Willis, Oliver Rivington, botanist, b. 1815; d. 1902.

Willis, Mrs. Olympia, née **Brown,** suffragist, b. Prairie Ronde, Mich., 1835; d. Oct. 23, 1926. [10]

Willis, Richard Storrs, musician and poet, b. Boston, Mass., 1819; d. Detroit, Mich., May 7, 1900. [1; 3; 6; 20; 62]

Willis, William, lawyer, b. Haverhill, Mass., 1794; d. Portland, Me., Feb. 17, 1870. [1; 3; 6; 7; 51]

Willison, Sir John Stephen, journalist, b. Huron county, Ont., 1856; d. Toronto, Ont., May 27, 1927. [27]

Willison, Marjorie, Lady, née **Mac-Murchy,** journalist, d. Toronto, Ont., Dec. 15, 1938. [27]

Williston, Ebenezer Bancroft, educationist, b. Turnbridge, Vt., 1801; d. Norwich, Vt., Dec. 27, 1837. [3; 6]

Williston, Samuel Wendell, palaeontologist, b. Boston, Mass., 1852; d. Chicago, Ill., Aug. 30, 1918. [1; 10; 62]

Williston, Seth, clergyman, b. Suffield. Conn., 1770; d. Guilford Center, N.Y., March 2, 1851. [1; 3; 6]

Willkie, Wendell Lewis, lawyer and politician, b. Elwood, Ind., 1892; d. New York, N.Y., Oct. 8, 1944. [7; 10; 12]

Willman, Rheinhold, physician, b. 1855; d. Kansas City, Mo., June 14, 1837.

Willmott, Arthur Brown, geologist, b. Nanticoke, Ont., 1867; d. Toronto, Ont., May 8, 1914. [27]

Willoughby, Hugh Laussat, explorer, b. Solitude, Delaware county, N.Y., 1856; d. Port Sewall, Fla., April 4, 1939. [4; 10]

Willoughby, Westel Woodbury, educationist, b. Alexandria, Va., July 20, 1867; d. Washington, D.C., March 26, 1945. [4; 7; 10; 11]

Wills, Joshua Edwin, clergyman, b. 1854; d. Mullica Hill, N.J., July 30, 1932. [6]

Wills, Samuel, clergyman, fl. 1850-1852 [6]

Willsie, Mrs. Honoré. See Morrow, Mrs. Honoré Willsie, née McCue.

Willson, Mrs. Araballa M., née **Stuart,** miscellaneous writer, fl. 1851-1870. [7]

Willson, David, religious enthusiast, b. Dutchess county, N.Y., about 1778; d. Sharon, Ont., Jan. 19, 1866. [27]

Willson, Forceythe, poet, b. Little Genesee, N.Y., April 10, 1837; d. Alfred, N.Y., Feb. 2, 1867. [3; 4; 6; 34]

Willson, Frederick Newton, educationist, b. Brooklyn, N.Y., 1855; d. Princeton, N.J., Nov. 15, 1939. [10]

Willson, Hugh Bowlby, lawyer and journalist, b. Winona, Upper Canada, 1813; d. New York, N.Y., April 29, 1880. [27]

Willson, James Renwick, clergyman, b. near Pittsburgh, Pa., 1780; d. Coldenham, N.Y., Sept. 29, 1853. [3; 6]

Willson, Marcius, educationist, b. West Stockbridge, Mass., 1813; d. Vineland, N.J., July 2, 1905. [3; 4; 6; 10]

Willson, Robert Newton, physician, b. Philadelphia, Pa., 1873; d. Philadelphia, Pa., Jan. 1, 1916. [10]

Willson, Robert Wheeler, astronomer, b. Roxbury, Mass., 1853; d. Cambridge, Mass., Nov. 1, 1922. [10]

Wilmer, James Jones, clergyman, b. Maryland, 1749; d. Detroit, Mich., April 14, 1814. [1]

Wilmer, Lambert A., journalist, b. about 1805; d. Brooklyn, N.Y., Dec. 21, 1863. [3; 7]

Wilmer, Richard Hooker, bishop, b. Alexandria, Va., 1816; d. Mobile, Ala., June 14, 1900. [1; 3; 4; 62]

Wilmshurst, Zavarr, journalist and poet, b. Tunbridge Wells, England, 1824; d. Brooklyn, N.Y., Jan. 27, 1887. [3; 6; 7]

Wilner, Merton Merriman, journalist and historian, b. Portage, N.Y., 1867; d. Buffalo, N.Y., Dec. 20, 1933.

Wilson, Sir Adam, jurist, b. Edinburgh, Scotland, 1814; d. Toronto, Ont., Dec. 28, 1891. [27]

Wilson, Albert Frederick, journalist, b. Greenfield Hill, Conn., 1883; d. Rogers Rock Club, Lake George, N.Y., June 25, 1940. [7; 10]

Wilson, Alexander, ornithologist, b. Renfrewshire, Scotland, 1766; d. Philadelphia, Pa., Aug. 23, 1813. [1; 3; 4; 6; 7]

Wilson, Alpheus Waters, bishop, b. Baltimore, Md., 1834; d. Baltimore, Md., Nov. 21, 1916. [3; 10]

Wilson, Anne Elizabeth. See Blochin, Mrs. Anne Elizabeth, née Wilson.

Wilson, Anneliza Caruthers, teacher, b. Salem, Va.; d. Lexington, Va., 1924.

Wilson, Mrs. Augusta Jane, née Evans, novelist, b. Columbus, Ga., 1835; d. Mobile, Ala., May 9, 1909. [1; 4; 7; 10]

Wilson, Bingham Thoburn, poet, b. Grafton, W. Va., 1867; d. Hollywood, Calif., Sept. 24, 1937. [11; 35]

Wilson, Bird, jurist and clergyman, b. Carlisle, Pa., 1777; d. New York, N.Y., April 14, 1859. [1; 3; 4; 6]

Wilson, Calvin Dill, clergyman, b. Baltimore, Md., 1857; d. Glendale, O., April 28, 1946. [7; 10; 11]

Wilson, Charles Branch, biologist, b. Exeter, Me., 1861; d. Westfield, Mass., Aug. 18, 1941. [10; 11; 13]

Wilson, Clarence True, clergyman, b. Milton, Del., 1872; d. Portland, Ore., Feb. 16, 1939. [4; 10]

Wilson, Sir Daniel, educationist, b. Edinburgh, Scotland, 1816; d. Toronto, Ont., Aug. 6, 1892. [27]

Wilson, Daniel Munro, clergyman, b. 1848; d. Quincy, Mass., Oct. 11, 1935.

Wilson, David, lawyer, b. West Hebron, Washington county, N.Y., 1818; d. Albany, N.Y., June 9, 1887. [3; 6; 7]

Wilson, Edmund Beecher, biologist, b. Geneva, Ill., 1856; d. New York, N.Y., March 3, 1939. [4; 10; 62]

Wilson, Edward Livingston, photographer, b. Flemington, N.J., 1838; d. 1903. [10]

Wilson, Edward Stanbury, journalist, b. Newark, O., 1841; d. Columbus O., Dec. 18, 1919. [10]

Wilson, Elijah Nicholas, frontiersman, b. 1842; d. 1915.

Wilson, Mrs. Ella Calista, née **Handy,** educationist, b. 1851; d. ?

Wilson, Epiphanius, clergyman, b. 1845; d. New York, N.Y., May 16, 1916. [8]

Wilson, Erasmus, journalist, b. Belmont county, O., 1842; d. Pittsburgh, Pa., Jan. 14, 1922. [10]

Wilson, Ernest Henry, botanist and traveller, b. Chipping Camden, England, 1876; d. near Worcester, Mass., Oct. 15, 1930. [1; 7; 10]

Wilson, Eugene Benjamin, engineer, b. New Haven, Conn., 1857; d. Scranton, Pa., June 16, 1929. [10]

Wilson, Floyd Baker, lawyer, b. Watervliet, N.Y., 1845; d. New York, N.Y., March 28, 1934. [4; 10; 11]

Wilson, Forrest. See Wilson, Robert Forrest.

Wilson, Francis, actor, b. Philadelphia, Pa., 1854; d. New York, N.Y., Oct. 7, 1935. [1a; 4; 7; 10; 11]

Wilson, Francis Mairs Huntington, diplomat, b. Chicago, Ill., 1875; d. New Haven, Conn., Dec. 31, 1946. [10]

Wilson, George, banker, b. Sac and Fox Agency, Ia., 1842; d. Lexington, Mo., 1906. [10]

Wilson, George Arthur, educationist, b. Wabash, Ind., 1864; d. Cambridge, Mass., Oct. 4, 1941. [10; 11]

Wilson, George Henry, dentist, b. Painesville, O., 1855; d. Lakewood, O., April 12, 1922. [10; 11]

Wilson, George Washington, religious writer, b. 1853; d. ?

Wilson, Gilbert Livingston, anthropologist, b. Clifton, O., 1868; d. St. Paul, Minn., June 9, 1930. [11; 56]

Wilson, Harry Bruce, educationist, b. Frankfort, Ind., 1874; d. Berkeley, Calif., Aug. 9, 1932. [10; 11]

Wilson, Harry Leon, novelist and playwright, b. Oregon, Ill., 1867; d. Monterey, Calif., June 28, 1939. [7; 10; 11; 35; 72]

Wilson, Henry, politician, b. Farmington, N.H., 1812; d. Washington, D.C., Nov. 22, 1875. [1; 3; 4; 6; 7]

Wilson, Henry, clergyman, b. 1841; d. 1908.

Wilson, Henry Blauvelt, clergyman, b. 1870; d. 1923.

Wilson, Henry H., lawyer, b. Sandusky county, O., 1854; d. Lincoln, Neb., June 28, 1941. [4; 10; 11]

Wilson, Henry Lane, diplomat, b. Crawfordsville, Ind., 1857; d. Indianapolis, Ind., Dec. 22, 1932. [1; 4; 10]

Wilson, Herbert Michael, engineer, b. Glasgow, Scotland, 1860; d. Sewickley, Pa., Nov. 25, 1920. [10]

Wilson, Hill Peebles, biographer, b. 1840; d. ?

Wilson, Hugh Blair, lawyer, b. 1827; d. ?

Wilson, Hugh Robert, diplomat, b. Evanston, Ill., 1885; d. Old Bennington, Vt., Dec. 28, 1946. [4; 10; 62]

Wilson, Mrs. Ibbie McColm, poet, b. Baltimore, Md., 1834; d. Iowa, 1908. [78]

Wilson, Jacob, lawyer, b. St. Johnsville, N.Y., 1831; d. Newark, N.Y., March 16, 1914. [4]

Wilson, James, politician and jurist, b. near St. Andrews, Scotland, 1742; d. Edenton, N.C., Aug. 21, 1798. [1; 3; 4; 6; 7]

Wilson, James, clergyman, b. 1760; d. Providence, R.I., Sept. 14, 1839.

Wilson, James Cornelius, physician, b. Philadelphia, Pa., 1847; d. Philadelphia, Pa., Oct. 28, 1934. [10]

Wilson, James Grant, soldier, publisher, and editor, b. Edinburgh, Scotland, 1832; d. New York, N.Y., Feb. 1, 1914. [1; 3; 4; 5; 6; 7; 10]

Wilson, James Harrison, soldier and engineer, b. Shawneetown, Ill., 1837; d. Wilmington, Del., Feb. 23, 1925. [1; 3; 4; 5; 6; 7; 10; 11]

Wilson, James Patriot, clergyman, b. Lewes, Sussex county, Del., 1769; d. Bucks county, Pa., Dec. 9, 1830. [3; 6]

Wilson, Jennie Lansley, feminist, b. 1847; d. about 1934. [37]

Wilson, John, printer, b. Glasgow, Scotland, 1802; d. Cambridge, Mass., Aug. 3, 1868. [3; 4; 6; 7]

Wilson, John Eastman, physician, b. 1857; d. New York, N.Y., Dec. 19, 1929.

Wilson, John Fleming, novelist, b. Erie, Pa., 1877; d. Santa Monica, Calif., March 5, 1922. [1; 7; 10; 35]

Wilson, John Grover, clergyman, b. Middletown, Del., 1810; d. Philadelphia, Pa., Feb. 20, 1885. [3; 6]

Wilson, John Laird, journalist, b. Renfrewshire, Scotland, 1832; d. Brooklyn, N.Y., May 22, 1896. [3; 6; 7]

Wilson, John Leighton, missionary, b. near Salem, S.C., 1809; d. near Mayesville, S.C., July 13, 1886. [1; 3; 4; 6; 34]

Wilson, John Lyde, lawyer, b. Marlborough district, S.C., 1784; d. Charleston, S.C., Feb. 12, 1849. [3; 34]

Wilson, John Stainback, physician, b. 1821; d. 1892. [6; 34]

Wilson, Joseph, clergyman, b. 1797; d. 1878.

Wilson, Joseph, naval surgeon, d. 1887.

Wilson, Joseph Miller, engineer, b. Phoenixville, Pa., 1838; d. Philadelphia, Pa., Nov. 24, 1902. [3b; 4]

Wilson, Joseph Thomas, historian, b. 1836; d. 1891.

Wilson, Lewis Gilbert, clergyman, b. Southboro, Mass., 1858; d. 1928. [10]

Wilson, Louis N., librarian, b. Yorkshire, England, 1857; d. Worcester, Mass., Sept. 12, 1937. [10]

Wilson, Mrs. Lucy Langdon, née **Williams,** educationist, b. St. Albans, Vt., 1864; d. Philadelphia, Pa., Sept. 3, 1937. [10]

Wilson, Luther Barton, bishop, b. Baltimore, Md., 1856; d. Baltimore, Md., June 4, 1928. [4; 10]

Wilson, Mortimer, musician, b. Chariton, Ia., 1876; d. New York, N.Y., Jan. 27, 1932. [1; 4; 10; 20]

Wilson, Oliver Morris, lawyer, b. Logansport, Ind., 1836; d. Kansas City, Mo., July 19, 1907. [3; 4]

Wilson, Peter, educationist, b. Banff, Scotland, 1746; d. New Barbadoes, N.J., Aug. 1, 1825. [1; 3; 4; 6]

Wilson, Peter Mitchel, civil servant, b. 1848; d. Washington, D.C., June 24, 1939.

Wilson, Richard Albert, educationist, b. Renfrew, Ont., 1874; d. Vancouver, B.C., Jan. 2, 1949. [30]

Wilson, Richard Henry, educationist, b. Christian county, Ky., 1870; d. Charlottesville, Va., May 21, 1948. [34]

Wilson, Robert, clergyman, b. Fort George, Scotland, 1833; d. Saint John, N.B., June 24, 1912. [27]

Wilson, Robert Anderson, lawyer, b. Cooperstown, N.Y., 1803; d. Washington, D.C., Jan. 15, 1872. [4; 59]

Wilson, Robert Burns, painter, poet, and novelist, b. near Washington, Pa., 1850; d. Brooklyn, N.Y., March 31, 1916. [1; 4; 7; 10]

Wilson, Robert Dick, clergyman and educationist, b. 1856; d. Philadelphia, Pa., Oct. 11, 1930. [56]

Wilson, Robert Forrest, journalist, b. Warren, O., 1883; d. Weston, Conn., May 9, 1942. [10]

Wilson, Rufus Rockwell, writer on Abraham Lincoln, b. Troy, Pa., 1865; d. Elmira, N.Y., Dec. 14, 1949. [10; 11]

Wilson, Samuel Farmer, journalist, b. Connecticut, 1805; d. New Orleans, La., March 11, 1870. [3]

Wilson, Samuel Graham, missionary, b. Indiana, Pa., 1858; d. Tabriz, Persia,, July 2, 1916. [1; 7; 10]

Wilson, Samuel Jerome, physician, b. 1850; d. about 1918.

Wilson, Stanley Kidder, novelist and poet, b. Madison, N.J., 1879; d. New York, N.Y., Nov. 15, 1944. [7]

Wilson, Theodore Delavan, ship-builder, b. Brooklyn, N.Y., May 11, 1840; d. Boston, Mass., June 29, 1896. [1 3; 4; 6]

Wilson, Thomas, journalist, b. Philadelphia, Pa., 1768; d. Philadelphia, Pa., about 1828. [3; 6]

Wilson, Thomas, museum curator, b. New Brighton, Pa., 1832; d. 1902. [4]

Wilson, Thomas Woodrow. See Wilson, Woodrow.

Wilson, Victor Tyson, educationist, b. Philadelphia, Pa., 1864; d. Detroit, Mich., Aug. 4, 1937. [10; 39]

Wilson, Warren Hugh, clergyman, b. Tidioute, Pa., 1867; d. New York, N.Y., March 2, 1937. [10]

Wilson, William, clergyman, b. Lincolnshire, England, 1798; d. Point de Bute, N.S., 1869. [27]

Wilson, William, publisher and poet, b. Crieff, Scotland, 1801; d. Poughkeepsie, N.Y., Aug. 25, 1860. [1; 3; 6; 7]

Wilson, William Bender, telegraph executive, b. 1839; d. Holmesburg, Pa., Feb. 27, 1919. [4]

Wilson, William Dexter, clergyman and educationist, b. Stoddard, N.H., 1816; d. Syracuse, N.Y., July 30, 1900. [1; 3; 4; 6; 10]

Wilson, William Lyne, politician, b. Jefferson county, Va., 1843; d. Lexington, Ga., Oct. 17, 1900. [1; 3; 4; 5; 10]

Wilson, William Robert Anthony, novelist, b. Washington, Ill., 1870; d. Pittsfield, Mass., May 14, 1911. [10]

Wilson, Woodrow, twenty-eight president of the United States, b. Staunton, Va., 1856; d. Washington, D.C., Feb. 3, 1924. [1; 2b; 4. 5; 7; 10; 72]

Wilstach, Frank Jenners, theatrical manager, b. Lafayette, Ind., 1865; d. New York, N.Y., Nov. 28, 1933. [7; 10]

Wilstach, John Augustine, lawyer and translator, b. Washington, D.C., 1824; d. Lafayette, Ind., July 24, 1897. [3; 7]

Wilstach, Joseph Walter, lawyer, b. Lafayette, Ind., 1857; d. Lafayette, Ind., Oct. 15, 1921. [3]

Wiltse, Henry Martin, historian, b. 1852; d. Chattanooga, Tenn., May 11, 1929.

Wiltse, Sara Eliza, educationist, b. Burns, Mich., 1849; d. ? [7]

Wiltsie, Charles Hastings, lawyer, b. Pittsford, N.Y., 1859; d. Rochester, N.Y., May 9, 1935. [10; 11]

Wiman, Erastus, financier, b. Churchville, Upper Canada, 1834; d. New York, N.Y., Feb. 9, 1904. [27]

Wimberley, Charles Franklin, clergyman, b. Jefferson county, Ill., 1866; d. Columbia, S.C., July 10, 1946. [10; 11]

Winans, Ross, engineer and inventor, b. Sussex County, N.J., 1796; d. Baltimore, Md., April 11, 1877. [1; 3; 4; 5; 6]

Winans, Samuel Rose, educationist, b. Lyons Farms, N.J., 1855; d. Princeton, N.J., July 25, 1910. [10]

Winans, Walter, sportsman, b. 1852; d. London, England, Aug. 12, 1920.

Winans, William, clergyman, b. Pennsylvania, 1788; d. Amite county, Miss., Aug. 31, 1857. [1; 3; 6]

Winans, William H., journalist, b. Kinderhook, N.Y., about 1820; d. Newark, N.J., Aug. 10, 1886.

Winant, John Gilbert, diplomat, b. New York, N.Y., 1889; d. Concord, N.Y., Nov. 3, 1947. [10; 12]

Winants, Garret E., capitalist, b. Staten Island, N.Y., 1813; d. Bayonne, N.J., Aug. 11, 1890. [3b]

Winbigler, Charles Fremont, clergyman, b. Middletown, Md., 1857; d. Los Angeles, Calif., Jan. 6, 1925. [10]

Winborne, Benjamin Brodie, jurist, b. 1854; d. Raleigh, N.C., Feb. 24, 1919.

Winburn, Hardy Lathan, clergyman, b. Bells, Tenn., 1877; d. Arkadelphia, Ark., Sept. 3, 1937. [10; 11]

Winchell, Alexander, geologist, b. Northeast, N.Y., 1824; d. Ann Arbor, Mich., Feb. 19, 1891. [1; 3; 4; 5; 6; 7]

Winchell, Horace Vaughn, geologist and mining engineer, b. Galesburg, Mich., 1865; d. Minneapolis, Minn., July 28, 1923. [1; 4; 10]

Winchell, Newton Horace, geologist and archaeologist, b. Northeast, N.Y., 1839; d. Minneapolis, Minn., May 2, 1914. [4; 10]

Winchell, Samuel Robertson, educationist, b. Northeast, N.Y., 1843; d. Chicago, Ill., July 14, 1925. [10]

Winchester, Boyd, politician and diplomat, b. Ascension parish, La., 1836; d. Louisville, Ky., May 18, 1923. [4]

Winchester, Caleb Thomas, educationist, b. Montville, Conn., 1847; d. Middletown, Conn., March 24, 1920. [1; 4; 7; 10]

Winchester, Carroll (pseud.). See Curtis, Mrs. Caroline Gardiner, née Cary.

Winchester, Charles Wesley, clergyman, b. Westminster, Vt., 1843; d. 1917. [10]

Winchester, Elhanan, clergyman, b. Brookline, Mass., 1751; d. Hartford, Conn., April 18, 1797. [1; 3; 6]

Winchester, James, soldier, b. Carroll county, Md., 1752; d. near Gallatin, Tenn., July 26, 1826. [1; 3; 5]

Winchester, Paul, journalist, b. 1851; d. Baltimore, Md., Feb. 5, 1932.

Winchester, Samuel Gover, clergyman, b. Rock Run, Hartford county, Md. ,1805; d. New York, N.Y., Aug. 31, 1841. [3; 6]

Winchester, William Eugene, textile expert, b. Providence, R.I., 1877; d. New York, N.Y., Jan. 14, 1943. [10]

Winchevsky, Morris, poet and journalist, b. Lithuania, 1856; d. New York, N.Y., March 18, 1932. [1; 7]

Windle, Mary Jane, miscellaneous writer, b. Wilmington, Del., 1825; d. ? [6; 7]

Wineberger, James Albert, historian, b. Washington, D.C., 1821; d. Washington, D.C., Feb. 1, 1906.

Winebrenner, John, clergyman, b. Frederick county, Md., 1797; d. Harrisburg, Pa., Sept. 12, 1860. [1; 3; 4; 6]

Wines, Abijah, clergyman, b. 1768; d. Charlestown, Mass., Feb. 11, 1833. [38; 49]

Wines, Enoch Cobb, clergyman and educationist, b. Hanover, N.J., 1806; d. Cambridge, Mass., Dec. 10, 1879. [1; 3; 4; 5; 6; 7]

Wines, Frederick Howard, social reformer, b. Philadelphia, Pa., 1838; d. Springfield, Ill., Jan. 31, 1912. [1; 3; 4; 10]

Winfield, Arthur M. (pseud.). See Stratemeyer, Edward.

Winfield, Charles Hardenburg, lawyer, b. Port Jervis, N.Y., 1829; d. Jersey City, N.J., March 9, 1898. [3b]

Wing, Charles Benjamin, civil engineer, b. Clinton Corners, N.Y., 1864; d. Palo Alto, Calif., Aug. 22, 1945. [10; 11]

Wing, Conway Phelps, clergyman, b. Marietta, O., 1809; d. Carlisle, Pa., May 7, 1889. [3b]

Wing, Henry Hiram, educationist, b. New York, N.Y., 1859; d. Little Falls, N.Y., Nov. 21, 1936. [10; 11]

Wing, Joseph Addison, lawyer and poet, b. East Montpelier, Vt., 1810; d. Montpelier, Vt., 1894. [43]

Wing, Joseph Elwyn, agriculturist, b. Hinsdale, N.Y., 1861; d. Marion, O., Sept. 10, 1915. [1]

Wing, Talcott Enoch, local historian, b. 1819; d. 1890.

Wingate, Charles Edgar Lewis, editor, b. Exeter, N.H., 1861; d. Winchester, Mass., May 15, 1944. [7; 10; 11]

Wingate, Charles Frederick, journalist and engineer, b. New York, N.Y., 1847; d. Twilight Park, Greene county, N.Y., Aug. 31, 1909. [3; 6; 10]

Wingate, George Wood, lawyer and soldier, b. New York, N.Y., 1840; d. Brooklyn, N.Y., March 22, 1928. [3; 10]

Wingfield, Alexander Hamilton, poet, b. Blantyre, Lanarkshire, Scotland, 1828; d. Hamilton, Ont., 1896. [27]

Winkler, Mrs. Angelina Virginia, née **Walton,** historian, b. Virginia, 1842; d. ? [34]

Winkler, Edwin Theodore, clergyman, b. Savannah, Ga., 1823; d. Marion, Ala., Nov. 10, 1883. [1; 3]

Winn, Edith Lynwood, musician, b. 1868; d. 1933.

Winn, Henry, lawyer, b. Whitingham, Vt., 1837; d. Malden, Mass., Jan. 24, 1916. [62]

Winner, Septimus, composer and publisher of music, b. Philadelphia, Pa., 1827; d. Philadelphia, Pa., Nov. 23, 1902. [3b; 4; 7; 10]

Winser, Henry Jacob, journalist, b. Bermuda, 1833; d. Newark, N.J., Aug. 23, 1896. [3b; 4]

Winship, Albert Edward, educationist, b. West Bridgewater, Mass., 1845; d. Cambridge, Mass., Feb. 17, 1933. [1; 4; 7; 10; 11]

Winslow, Arthur, mining engineer, b. Salem, N.C., 1860; d. Boston, Mass., March 28, 1938. [4; 10]

Winslow, Carroll Dana, aviator, b. New York, N.Y., 1889; d. New York, N.Y., Dec. 27, 1932. [62]

Winslow, Mrs. Catherine Mary, née **Reignolds,** actress, b. England; d. Concord, Mass., July 11, 1911. [4; 10]

Winslow, Charles Frederick, physician, b. Nantucket, Mass., 1811; d. 1877. [3; 6]

Winslow, Eben Eveleth, soldier, b. 1866; d. Raleigh, N.C., June 28, 1928. [4; 10]

Winslow, Helen Maria, journalist, b. Westfield, Vt., 1851; d. Shirley, Mass., March 27, 1938. [7; 10; 11]

Winslow, Hubbard, clergyman, b. Williston, Vt., 1799; d. Williston, Vt., Aug. 13, 1864. [1; 3; 4; 6; 7; 62]

Winslow, Isaac Oscar, educationist, b. Maine, 1856; d. Providence, R.I., Jan. 16, 1949. [11]

Winslow, John Bradley, jurist, b. Livingston county, N.Y., 1851; d. Madison, Wis., July 13, 1920. [1; 10]

Winslow, Margaret E., writer of books for young people, fl. 1875-1912. [6]

Winslow, Miron, missionary, b. Williston, Vt., 1789; d. Cape Town, South Africa, Oct. 22, 1864. [1; 3; 4; 6]

Winslow, William Copley, archaeologist, b. Boston, Mass., 1840; d. Boston, Mass., Feb. 2, 1925. [4; 7; 10]

Winslow, William Henry, physician, b. 1840; d. Roxbury, Mass., April 8, 1917.

Winsor, Frederick, educationist, b. Winchester, Mass., 1872; d. Boston, Mass., Nov. 26, 1940. [10]

Winsor, Henry, merchant, b. Duxbury, Mass., Dec. 31, 1803. d. Philadelphia, Pa., Oct. 28, 1889.

Winsor, Justin, historian and librarian, b. Boston, Mass., 1831; d. Cambridge, Mass., Oct. 22, 1897. [1; 3; 4; 5; 6; 7; 9; 51]

Winston, Annie Steger, journalist, b. Richmond, Va.; d. Richmond, Va., May 12, 1927. [10; 34]

Winston, Robert Watson, jurist and biographer, b. Windsor, N.C., 1860; d. Chapel Hill, N.C., Oct. 14, 1944. [7; 10; 11]

Winter, Mrs. Alice, née **Ames,** feminist, b. Albany, N.Y., 1865; d. Pasadena, Calif., April 5, 1944. [7; 10; 11]

Winter, Charles Francis, soldier and biographer, b. Montreal, Que., 1863; d. Ottawa, Ont., Oct. 20, 1946. [27]

Winter, Mrs. Elizabeth, née **Campbell,** novelist, b. Ederline, Loch Awe, Scotland, 1841; d. Los Angeles, Calif., April 7, 1922. [7; 10]

Winter, Irvah Lester, educationist, b. New Braintree, Mass., 1857; d. Cambridge, Mass., May 30, 1934. [10]

Winter, Lee, dental surgeon, b. New York, N.Y., 1890; d. Lawrence, Long Island, N.Y., July 6, 1948.

Winter, Nevin Otto, lawyer and traveller, b. Benton, O., 1869; d. Toledo, O., Sept. 2, 1936. [4; 7; 10; 11]

Winter, William, drama critic, poet, and essayist, b. Gloucester, Mass., July 15, 1836; d. Staten Island, N.Y., June 30, 1917. [1; 2; 3; 4; 5; 6; 7; 8; 9; 10; 71]

Winter, William West, novelist, b. Indianapolis, Ind., 1881; d. Rutland, Mass., May 17, 1940.

Winterburn, George William, physician, b. New York, N.Y., 1845; d. New York, N.Y., Nov. 19, 1911. [6; 10]

Winters, Cecil Marks, priest, b. near Lansing, Mich., 1895; d. 1943. [21]

Winterton, Gayle (pseud.). See Adams, William Taylor.

Winthrop, Edward, clergyman, b. New York, N.Y., 1811; d. Highgate, Vt., Oct. 21, 1865. [62]

Winthrop, James, jurist, b. Cambridge, Mass., 1752; d. Cambridge, Mass., Sept. 26, 1821. [1; 3; 6]

Winthrop, John, first governor of Massachusetts Bay, b. Edwardstone, Suffolk, England, 1587; d. Boston, Mass., March 26, 1649. [1; 2; 3; 4; 5; 6; 7]

Winthrop, John, astronomer, b. Boston, Mass., 1714; d. Cambridge, Mass., May 3, 1779. [1; 3; 4; 6]

Winthrop, Laura. See Johnson, Mrs. Laura, née Winthrop.

Winthrop, Robert Charles, politician and historian, b. Boston, Mass., 1809; d. Boston, Mass., Nov. 16, 1894. [1; 2; 3; 4; 5; 6; 7]

Winthrop, Robert Charles, biographer, b. Boston, Mass., 1834; d. 1905. [51]

Winthrop, Theodore, soldier and novelist, b. New Haven, Conn., 1828; d. near Great Bethel, Va., June 10, 1861. [1; 2; 3; 4; 7; 71]

Winthrop, William Woolsey, soldier, b. New Haven, Conn., 1831; d. Atlantic City, N.J., April 8, 1899. [3; 62]

Winton, Andrew Lincoln, chemist, b. Westport, Conn., 1864; d. Wilton, Conn., Oct. 17, 1946. [10; 62]

Winton, George Beverly, clergyman, b. Springfield, Mo., 1861; d. Nashville, Tenn., March 1, 1938. [10; 11]

Wirt, Mrs. Elizabeth Washington, née **Gamble,** botanist, b. Richmond, Va., 1784; d. Annapolis, Md., Jan. 24, 1857. [3; 4]

Wirt, William, lawyer, b. Bladensburg, Md., 1772; d. Washington, D.C., Feb. 18, 1834. [1; 3; 4; 5; 6; 7]

Wirt, William Albert, educationist, b. Markle. Ind., 1874; d. Gary, Ind., March 11, 1938. [10]

Wise, Aaron, rabbi, b. Hungary, 1845; d. New York, N.Y., March, 1896.

Wise, Daniel, clergyman, b. Portsmouth, England, Jan. 10, 1813; d. Engelwood, N.J., Dec. 19, 1898. [1; 3; 4; 6; 7]

Wise, George, soldier, fl. 1870-1916. [34]

Wise, Henry Alexander, soldier and politician, b. Drummondtown, Va., 1806; d. Richmond, Va., Sept. 12, 1876. [1; 3; 4; 6]

Wise, Henry Augustus, naval officer, b. Brooklyn, N.Y., 1819; d. Naples, Italy, April 2, 1869. [3; 4; 7; 71]

Wise, Isaac Mayer, rabbi, b. Steingrub, Bohemia, 1819; d. Cincinnati, O., March 26, 1900. [1; 3; 4; 6; 7]

Wise, John, clergyman, b. Roxbury, Mass., 1652; d. Ipswich, Mass., April 8, 1725. [1; 3; 4; 6; 7]

Wise, John, aeronaut, b. Lancaster, Pa., 1808; d. Lake Michigan, Sept. 29, 1879. [1; 3; 4; 6]

Wise, John Sergeant, lawyer and politician, b. Rio de Janeiro, Brazil, 1846; d. near Princess Anne, Md., May 12, 1913. [1; 3; 4; 7; 10]

Wise, Jonathan B. (pseud.). See Colwell, Stephen.

Wise, Peter Manuel, physician, b. Clarence, N.Y., 1851; d. New York, N.Y., Sept. 22, 1907. [10]

Wishard, John G., medical missionary, b. Danville, Ind., 1863; d. Wooster, O., July 15, 1940. [10; 11]

Wishard, Samuel Ellis, clergyman, b. Johnson county, O., 1825; d. Nov. 11, 1915. [10]

Wishart, Alfred Wesley, clergyman, b. New York, N.Y., 1865; d. Grand Rapids, Mich., April 25, 1933. [10; 11; 39]

Wishart, John Elliott, clergyman, b. New Athens, O., 1866; d. Pasadena, Calif., Dec. 23, 1940. [10]

Wishart, William Thomas, clergyman, b. Scotland; d. Saint John, N.B., 1853. [27]

Wismer, David Cassel, numismatist, b. 1857; d. Hatfield, Pa., May 31, 1949.

Wisner, Benjamin Blydenburg, clergyman, b. Goshen, Orange county, N.Y., 1794; d. Boston, Mass., Feb. 9, 1835. [3; 4; 6]

Wisner, Oscar Fitzallan, poet, d. 1900.

Wisner, William, clergyman, b. Warwick, N.Y., 1782; d. Cedar Rapids, Ia., Jan. 7, 1871. [3; 6]

Wisser, John Philip, soldier, b. St. Louis, Mo., 1852; d. Berkeley, Calif., Jan. 19, 1927. [3; 4; 10; 11]

Wissler, Clark, anthropologist, b. Wayne county, Ind., 1870; d. New York, N.Y., Aug. 25, 1947. [7; 10; 11]

Wistar, Caspar, physician, b. Philadelphia, Pa., 1761; d. Philadelphia, Pa., Jan. 22, 1818. [1; 3; 4; 5; 6]

Wistar, Isaac Jones, penologist, b. Philadelphia, Pa., 1827; d. Claymont, Del., Sept. 18, 1905. [2; 10]

Wister, Mrs. Annis Lee, née **Furniss,** translator, b. Philadelphia, Pa., 1830; d. Philadelphia, Pa., Nov. 15, 1908. [10]

Wister, Owen, novelist, b. Philadelphia, Pa., 1860; d. North Kingstown, R.I., July 21, 1938. [2; 4; 7; 9; 10; 11; 51; 72]

Witham, George Strong, manufacturer, b. 1860; d. Hudson Falls, N.Y., June 8, 1939.

Withers, Alexander Scott, lawyer, b. Virginia, 1792; d. 1865. [34]

Withers, Frederick Clarke, architect, b. Somersetshire, England, 1828; d. Yonkers, N.Y., Jan. 7, 1901. [1; 3; 6]

Withers, Robert Enoch, politician, b. Campbell county, Va., 1821; d. 1907. [3; 5; 10]

Witherspoon, John, clergyman, educationist, and politician, b. Haddingtonshire, Scotland, 1722; d. near Princeton, N.J., Sept. 15, 1794. [1; 3; 4; 5; 6; 7]

Witherspoon, Thomas Dwight, clergyman, b. Greensborough, A a., 1836; d. Louisville, Ky., Nov. 3, 1898. [3; 6]

Withington, Leonard, clergyman, b. Dorchester, Mass., 1789; d. Newbury, Mass., April 22, 1885. [3; 4; 6; 62]

Withrow, Oswald Charles Joseph, physician, b. Oxford county, Ont., 1878; d. Toronto, Ont., Feb. 5, 1946. [27]

Withrow, William Henry, clergyman, b. Toronto, Upper Canada, 1839; d. Toronto, Ont., Nov. 12, 1908. [27]

Wittenmyer, Mrs. Annie, née **Turner,** reformer, b. Sandy Springs, O., 1827; d. Sanatoga, Pa., Feb. 2, 1900. [3b; 4]

Witthaus, Rudolph August, chemist and toxicologist, b. New York, N.Y., 1846; d. New York, N.Y., Dec. 19, 1915. [1; 10]

Witwer, Harry Charles, humorist, b. Athens, Pa., 1890; d. Los Angeles, Calif., Aug. 9, 1929. [1a; 4; 7; 10]

Wodell, Frederick William, musician, b. London, England, 1859; d. St. Petersburg, Fla., Feb. 13, 1938. [20]

Woelfkin, Cornelius, clergyman, b. New York, N.Y., 1859; d. New York, N.Y., Jan. 6, 1928. [4; 10]

Woerner, John Gabriel, jurist, b. Würtemberg, Germany, 1826; d. St. Louis, Mo., Jan. 20, 1900. [4; 10]

Woerner, William F., lawyer, b. St. Louis, Mo., 1864; d. St. Louis, Mo., June 27, 1932. [10]

Woglom, Charlotte Rebecca. See Bangs, Mrs. Charlotte Rebecca, née Woglom.

Wohlfarth, Julia Helen, educationist, b. Norwich, Conn., 1861; d. Yonkers, N.Y., March 19, 1945.

Wolcott, Laura, short-story writer, d. 1916.

Wolcott, Robert Henry, biologist, b. Alton, Ill., 1868; d. Lincoln, Neb., Jan. 23, 1934. [10; 13]

Wolcott, Roger, poet, b. Windsor, Conn., 1679; d. Windsor, Conn., May 17, 1767. [1; 3; 4; 6; 7]

Wolcott, Samuel, clergyman, b. East Windsor, Conn., 1813; d. Longmeadow, Mass., Feb. 24, 1886. [62]

Wolcott, Townsend, engineer, b. 1857; d. 1910.

Wolf, Edmund Jacob, educationist, b. Rebersburg, Pa., 1840; d. 1905. [10]

Wolf, Emma, novelist, b. San Francisco, Calif., 1865; d. San Francisco, Calif., Aug. 30, 1932. [7; 11; 35]

Wolf, Luther Benaiah, clergyman, b. Abbottstown, Pa., 1857; d. Baltimore, Md., Nov. 25, 1939. [7; 10]

Wolf, Simon, lawyer, b. Bavaria, Germany, 1836; d. Washington, D.C., June 4, 1923. [1; 10]

Wolfe, Mrs. Linnie, née **Marsh,** biographer, b. Michigan, 1881; d. Berkeley, Calif., Sept. 15, 1945. [7]

Wolfe, Napoleon Bonaparte, physician, fl. 1859-1875.

Wolfe, Samuel Herbert, actuary, b. Baltimore, Md., 1874; d. New York, N.Y., Dec. 31, 1927. [10]

Wolfe, Theodore Frelinghuysen, physician, b. Kenvil, N.J., 1847; d. Succasumna, N.J., June 14, 1915. [4; 10]

Wolfe, Thomas, novelist, b. Asheville, N.C., 1900; d. Baltimore, Md., Sept. 15, 1938. [7; 9; 10; 72]

Wolfe, Walter Béran, psychiatrist, b. 1900; d. Martigny, Switzerland, Aug. 15, 1935.

Wolff, Lawrence, physician, d. about 1895.

Wolff, William Almon, journalist and novelist, b. Brooklyn, N.Y., 1885; d. July 15, 1933. [10; 11]

Woll, Fritz Wilhelm, agricultural chemist, b. Bergen, Norway, 1865; d. Berkeley, Calif., 1922. [10; 11]

Wolle, Francis, clergyman and biologist, b. Jacobsburg, Pa., 1817; d. Bethlehem, Pa., Feb. 10, 1893. [3b; 4]

Wood, Alphonso, botanist, b. Chesterfield, N.H., 1810; d. West Farms, N.Y., Jan. 4, 1881. [3; 4; 6]

Wood, Anna Cogswell, novelist, fl. 1891-1904. [34]

Wood, Arnold, publisher, b. New York, N.Y., 1872; d. June 21, 1942.

Wood, Benjamin, journalist and novelist, b. Shelbyville, Ky., 1820; d. New York, N.Y., Feb. 21, 1900. [3b]

Wood, Casey Albert, physician, b. Wellington, Ont., 1856; d. La Jolla, Calif., Jan. 26, 1942. [4; 10; 11; 31a]

Wood, Charles, clergyman, b. Brooklyn, N.Y., 1851; d. Overbrook, Pa., July 30, 1936. [3; 4; 11]

Wood, Charles Erskine Scott, soldier, lawyer, and poet, b. Erie, Pa., 1852; d. near Los Gatos, Calif., Jan. 22, 1944. [7; 10; 11; 35]

Wood, Charles James, clergyman, b. Cleveland, O., 1852; d. York, Pa., May 9, 1906.

Wood, Charles Seely, clergyman and novelist, b. Cincinnati, O., 1845; d. Urbana, O., Nov. 20, 1912. [4; 10]

Wood, Charlotte Dunning, novelist, b. 1858; d. ? [8]

Wood, Chester, clergyman, b. Lansing, Mich., 1863; d. Lansing, Mich., 1925. [39]

Wood, De Volson, engineer, b. Smyrna, N.Y., 1832; d. Hoboken, N.J., June 27, 1897. [3b; 4]

Wood, Edward Jenner, physician, b. Wilmington, N.C., 1878; d. Wilmington, N.C., Sept. 16, 1928. [10; 11]

Wood, Edwin Orin, historian, b. Goodrich, Mich., 1861; d. New York, N.Y., April 23, 1918. [10]

Wood, Eugene, humorist, b. near Bellefontaine, O., 1860; d. New York, N.Y., Feb. 25, 1923. [10]

Wood, Ezra Morgan, clergyman, b. 1838; d. 1912.

Wood, Mrs. Frances, née **Gilchrist,** novelist, b. Keokuk, Ia., 1859; d. West Englewood, N.J., Dec. 20, 1944. [7]

Wood, Frederic, political scientist, d. 1902.

Wood, George, lawyer, b. Chesterfield, N.J., 1789; d. New York, N.Y., March 17, 1860. [1; 3; 4; 6]

Wood, George, civil servant, b. Newburyport, Mass., 1799; d. Saratoga Springs, N.Y., Aug. 24, 1870. [3; 6; 7]

Wood, George Bacon, physician and educationist, b. Greenwich, Cumberland county N.J., 1797; d. Philadelphia, Pa., March 30, 1879. [1; 3; 4; 6]

Wood, Hazel (pseud.). See Smith, Mrs. M. B.

Wood, Henry, miscellaneous writer, b. Barre, Vt., 1834; d. Brookline, Mass., March 28, 1909. [4; 10]

Wood, Henry Alexander Wise, inventor, b. New York, N.Y., 1866; d. New York, N.Y., April 9, 1939. [4; 7; 10; 11]

Wood, Horace Gay, lawyer, b. Woodstock, Vt., 1831; d. Dublin, N.H., Jan. 8, 1893. [3b]

Wood, Horatio Charles, physician, b. Philadelphia, Pa., 1841; d. Philadelphia, Pa., Jan. 3, 1920. [1; 3; 4; 6; 10]

Wood, Irving Francis, educationist, b. Walton, N.Y., 1861; d. Washington, D.C., Aug. 29, 1934. [10; 11; 62]

Wood, James, clergyman, b. Greenfield, N.Y., 1799; d. Hightstown, N.J., April 7, 1867. [1; 3; 6]

Wood, Jeremiah, clergyman, b. Greenfield, N.Y., 1801; d. Mayfield, N.Y., June 6, 1876.

Wood, Jerome James, novelist, b. near Hudson, Mich., 1846; d. Hudson, Mich., 1903. [39]

Wood, Joanna E., novelist, b. Lanarkshire, Scotland; d. Detroit, Mich., 1919. [27]

Wood, John, pamphleteer and mapmaker, b. Scotland, about 1775; d. Richmond, Va., May 15, 1822. [1; 3; 6; 7]

Wood, John Allen, clergyman, b. 1828; d. ?

Wood, John Seymour, lawyer and novelist, b. Utica, N.Y., 1853; d. New York, N.Y., June 15, 1934. [4; 7; 10; 62]

Wood, Mrs. Julia Amanda, née **Sargent,** novelist, b. New London, N.H., 1825; d. St. Cloud, Minn., 1903. [6; 70]

Wood, Leonard, soldier, b. Winchester, N.H., 1860; d. Boston, Mass., Aug. 7, 1927. [1; 4; 10]

Wood, Mrs. Lydia Cope, née **Collins,** novelist, b. Philadelphia, Pa., 1845; d. ? [10]

Wood, Mrs. Mary Camilla, née **Foster,** poet, b. 1840; d. ? [35]

Wood, Mrs. Mary I., née **Stevens,** feminist, b. Woodstock, Vt., 1866; d. Portsmouth N.H., April 24, 1945. [10]

Wood, Matthew Patterson, engineer, b. 1835; d. New York, N.Y., Dec. 24, 1905.

Wood, Nathan Eusebius, clergyman, b. Forrestville, N.Y., 1849; d. Arlington, Mass., July 8, 1937. [10; 11]

Wood, Oliver Ellsworth, soldier, b. Hartford, Conn., 1844; d. Baltimore, Md., Sept 4, 1910.

Wood, Philip, actor and playwright, b. 1895; d. Hollywood, Calif., March 3, 1940.

Wood, Mrs. Sally Sayward, née **Barrell,** novelist, b. York, Me., 1759; d. Kennebunk, Me., 1855. [1; 38]

Wood, Samuel Thomas, journalist, b. Hastings county, Ont., Jan. 16, 1860; d. Toronto, Ont., Nov. 6, 1917. [27]

Wood, Silas, lawyer, b. Suffolk county, N.Y., 1769; d. Huntington, N.Y., March 2, 1847. [3; 4; 6]

Wood, William Burke, actor, b. Montreal, Que., 1779; d. Philadelphia, Pa., Sept. 23, 1861. [1; 3; 6]

Wood, William Charles Henry, historian, b. Quebec, Que., 1864; d. Quebec, Que., Sept. 2, 1947. [11; 30]

Wood, William H. S., publisher, b. New York, N.Y., 1840; d. 1907. [10]

Wood, William Maxwell, surgeon, b. Baltimore, Md., 1809; d. Owing's Mills, Baltimore county, Md., March 1, 1880. [3; 6]

Wood-Allen, Mrs. Mary. See Allen, Mrs. Mary, née Wood.

Woodberry, George Edward, poet, critic, and educationist, b. Beverly, Mass., 1855; d. Beverly, Mass., Jan. 2, 1930. [1; 3; 4; 7; 10; 11; 51]

Woodbridge, Frederick James Eugene, educationist, b. Windsor, Ont., 1867; d. New York, N.Y., June 1, 1940. [7; 10; 12]

Woodbridge, Samuel Merrill, clergyman, b. Greenfield, Mass., 1819; d. New Brunswick, N.J., June 24, 1905. [1; 3; 4; 6]

Woodbridge, Timothy, clergyman, b. Stockbridge, Mass., 1784; d. Spencertown, N.Y., Dec. 7, 1862. [3]

Woodbridge, William Channing, educationist, b. Medford, Mass., 1794; d. Boston, Mass., Nov. 9, 1845. [1; 3; 4; 6]

Woodburn, James Albert, historian, b. Bloomington, Ind., 1856; d. Madison, Wis., Dec. 22, 1943. [4; 7; 10; 11]

Woodburne, Angus Stewart, clergyman and educationist, b. London, Ont., 1881; d. Chester, Pa., Feb. 13, 1938. [10]

Woodbury, Augustus, clergyman, b. Beverly, Mass., 1825; d. Nov. 19, 1895. [3; 6]

Woodbury, Charles Herbert, artist, b. Lynn, Mass., 1864; d. Boston, Mass., Jan. 21, 1940. [10; 12]

Woodbury, Charles Jeptha Hill, engineer, b. Lynn, Mass., 1851; d. Lynn, Mass., March 20, 1916. [1; 4; 10]

Woodbury, Charles Johnson, industrialist, b. 1844; d. Oakland, Calif., May 11, 1927. [45]

Woodbury, Charles Levi, jurist, b. Portsmouth, N.H., 1820; d. Boston, Mass., July 1, 1898. [3b]

Woodbury, Daniel Phineas, soldier and engineer, b. New London, N.H., 1812; d. Key West, Fla., Aug. 15, 1864. [1; 3; 4; 6]

Woodbury, Ellen Carolina De Quincy, biographer, b. Portsmouth, N.H.; d. 1909. [10]

Woodbury, Mrs. Helen Laura, née **Sumner,** social economist, b. Sheboygan, Wis., 1876; d. New York, N.Y., March 10, 1933. [1; 10; 11]

Woodbury, Isaac Baker, musician, b. Beverly, Mass., 1819; d. Charleston, S.C., Oct. 26, 1858. [1; 3; 4; 6]

Woodbury, Mrs. Josephine Curtis, née **Battles,** poet, d. 1930.

Woodbury, Levi, jurist and politician, b. Francestown, N.H., 1789; d. Portsmouth, N.H., Sept. 4, 1851. [1; 3; 4; 6]

Woodbury, Louis Augustus, physician, b. 1844; d. Groveland, Mass., July 17, 1916. [4]

Woodbury, Mrs. Lucia Prudence, née **Hall,** short-story writer, b. 1848; d. Oakland, Calif., Feb. 15, 1927.

Woodford, Arthur Burnham, economist, b. Winsted, Conn., 1861; d. New Haven, Conn., Nov. 3, 1946. [11; 62]

Woodhouse, James, physician and chemist, b. Philadelphia, Pa., 1770; d. Philadelphia, Pa., June 4, 1809. [1; 3]

Woodhull, Alfred Alexander, military surgeon, b. Princeton, N.J., 1837; d. Princeton, N.J., Oct. 18, 1921. [1; 10]

Woodhull, George Heber, clergyman, b. Commack, N.Y., 1860; d. Emporia, Kans., May 25, 1942. [62]

Woodhull, John Francis, educationist, b. Westport, N.Y., 1851; d. San Diego, Calif., July 27, 1941. [10; 11]

Woodhull, Maxwell Van Zandt, soldier, b. Washington, D.C., 1843; d. Watkins, N.Y., July 25, 1921. [10]

Woodhull, Mrs. Victoria, née **Claflin,** reformer, b. Homer, O., 1838; d. Tewkesbury, England, June 10, 1927. [1; 7; 10]

Woodley, Oscar Israel, educationist, b. Canada, 1861; d. Clermont, Fla., Nov. 25, 1931. [10]

Woodlock, Thomas Francis, journalist, b. Dublin, Ireland, 1866; d. New York, N.Y., Aug. 25, 1945. [12; 21]

Woodman, Mrs. Abby, née **Johnson,** traveller, b. 1828; d. ? [10]

Woodman, Henry, historian, b. 1795; d. 1879.

Woodman, James Monroe, clergyman, b. Sanbornton, N.H., 1824; d. San Leandro, Calif., Dec. 27, 1903. [35]

Woodman, John Smith, educationist, b. Durham, N.H., 1819; d. Durham, N.H., May 5, 1871. [3]

Woodmansee, James, poet, b. 1814; d. 1887.

Woodrow, Mrs. Constance, née **Davies,** poet, d. Whitby, Ont., Aug. 1, 1937. [11; 27]

Woodrow, Mrs. Nancy Mann, née **Waddel,** novelist, b. Chillicothe, O., 1870; d. New York, N.Y., Sept. 7, 1935. [7]

Woodrow, Mrs. Wilson. See Woodrow, Mrs. Nancy Mann, née Waddel.

Woodruff, Anne Helena, novelist, b. St. David's Ont., 1850; d. ? [4; 7]

Woodruff, Charles Edward, military surgeon, b. Philadelphia, Pa., 1860; d. New Rochelle, N.Y., June 13, 1915. [1; 10]

Woodruff, Edwin Hamlin, lawyer and educationist, b. Ithaca, N.Y., 1862; d. Ithaca, N.Y., July 8, 1941. [10]

Woodruff, Mrs. Elizabeth, née **Webb,** journalist, d. White Plains, N.Y., Feb. 22, 1933.

Woodruff, Francis Eben, genealogist, b. New York, N.Y., 1844; d. Morristown, N.J., June 3, 1914. [10]

Woodruff, Frank Edward, educationist, b. Eden, Vt., 1855; d. Brunswick, Me., Nov. 19, 1922. [4]

Woodruff, George Catlin, lawyer, b. Litchfield, Conn., 1805; d. Litchfield, Conn., Nov. 21, 1885. [62]

Woodruff, Mrs. Helen, née **Smith,** novelist and playwright, b. Selma, Ala., 1888; d. New York, N.Y., Oct. 14, 1924. [10; 11]

Woodruff, Mrs. Julia Louisa Matilda, née **Curtiss,** poet and novelist, b. Newtown, Conn., 1833; d. 1909. [7; 10]

Woodruff, Stanley Rogers, physician, b. Orange, Conn., 1875; d. Bayonne, N.J., Oct. 13, 1945. [62]

Woodruff, Thomas Adams, ophthalmologist, b. St. Catharines, Ont., 1865; d. New London, Conn., April 15, 1941. [10; 11]

Woods, Alva, educationist, b. Shoreham, Vt., 1794; d. Providence, R.I., Sept. 6, 1887. [1; 4]

Woods, Edward Augustus, life-underwriter, b. Pittsburgh, Pa., 1865; d. Sewickley, Pa., Nov. 30, 1927. [10]

Woods, Frederick Adams, biologist, b. Boston, Mass., 1873; d. Rome, Italy, Nov. 5, 1939. [10; 11; 13]

Woods, Harriet F., local historian, b. Brookline, Mass., 1828; d. Brooklyn, Mass., Oct. 15, 1879.

Woods, James Haughton, educationist, b. Boston, Mass., 1864; d. Cambridge, Mass., Jan. 14, 1935. [1a; 10; 51]

Woods, Joseph Thatcher, soldier, b. 1828; d. ?

Woods, Mrs. Kate, née **Tannatt,** novelist, b. Peekskill, N.Y., 1838; d. Buffalo, N.Y., July 11, 1910. [3; 7; 8; 10]

Woods, Katharine Pearson, novelist, b. Wheeling, W. Va., 1853; d. Baltimore, Md., Feb. 19, 1932. [7; 10]

Woods, Leonard, theologian, b. Princeton, Mass., 1774; d. Andover, Mass., Aug. 24, 1854. [1; 3; 4; 5; 6]

Woods, Matthew, physician, b. Ireland, 1849; d. Philadelphia, Oct. 13, 1916. [10]

Woods, Patrick, clergyman, d. 1902.

Woods, Robert Archey, sociologist b. Pittsburgh, Pa., 1865; d. Boston, Mass., Feb. 18, 1925. [1; 10]

Woods, Robert Stuart, jurist and historian, b. Sandwich, Upper Canada, 1819; d. Chatham, Ont., Nov. 20, 1906. [27]

Woods, Virna, poet and novelist, b. Wilmington, O., 1864; d. Sacramento, Calif., March 6, 1903. [10; 35]

Woods, William Carson, historian, b. Quebec, Que., 1860; d. July, 1902. [27]

Wood-Seys, Roland Alexander, novelist, b. Stourbridge, England, 1854; d. California, 1919. [10]

Woodson, Marion Marle, journalist, b. 1879; d. Oklahoma City, Okla., Oct. 6, 1933. [75]

Woodson, Urey, journalist, b. Madisonville, Ky., 1859; d. Owensboro, Ky., Aug. 7, 1939. [10]

Woodsworth, James, clergyman, b. Toronto, Ont.; d. Winnipeg, Man., Jan. 26, 1917. [27]

Woodsworth, James Shaver, clergyman and politician, b. near Toronto, Ont., 1874; d. Vancouver, B.C., March 21, 1942. [12; 27]

Woodville, Jennie (pseud.). See Stabler, Mrs. Jennie Latham.

Woodward, Annie Aubertine. See Moore, Mrs. Annie Aubertine, née Woodward.

Woodruff, Hiram, horse-trainer, b. Flemington, N.J., 1817; d. Long Island, N.Y., March 13, 1867. [3; 6]

Woodward, Ashbel, physician, b. Wellington, Conn., 1804; d. Franklin, Conn., Nov. 20, 1885.

Woodward, Augustus Brevoort, jurist, b. New York, N.Y., 1774; d. Tallahassee, Fla., June 12, 1827. [1; 3; 6]

Woodward, Calvin Milton, educationist, b. near Fitchburg, Mass., 1837; d. St. Louis, Mo., Jan. 12, 1914. [1; 3; 4; 10; 34]

Woodward, Evan Morrison, soldier, fl. 1865-1884. [6]

Woodward, Henry H., poet, fl. 1867-1889.

Woodward, Hugh McCurdy, educationist, b. Huntington, Utah, 1881; d. San Francisco, Calif., Aug. 11, 1940. [10]

Woodward, Joseph Janvier, military surgeon, b. Philadelphia, Pa., 1833; d. Wawa, Pa., Aug. 17, 1884. [1; 3; 4; 6]

Woodward, Patrick Henry, banker, b. Franklin, Conn., 1833; d. Hartford, Conn., Sept. 4, 1917. [10; 62]

Woodward, Thomas Simpson, soldier, b. 1797; d. 1861. [34]

Woodward, William Elliot, antiquary, b. 1831; d. Roxbury, Mass., Jan. 5, 1892.

Woodworth, Francis Channing, writer of books for young people, b. Colchester, Conn., 1812; d. at sea, June 5, 1859. [4; 6; 7]

Woodworth, Herbert Grafton, novelist, b. Boston, Mass., 1860; d. Haverhill, Mass., Aug. 11, 1949. [51]

Woodworth, John, jurist, b. Schodack, N.Y., 1768; d. Albany, N.Y., June 1, 1858. [3]

Woodworth, Samuel, journalist, poet, and playwright, b. Scituate, Mass., 1785; d. New York, N.Y., Dec. 9, 1842. [1; 3; 4; 6; 7; 71]

Woody, Clifford, educationist, b. Thorntown, Ind., 1884; d. Ann Arbor, Mich., Nov. 19, 1948. [1; 10]

Woody, John Warren, educationist, b. Saxapahaw, N.C., 1841; d. Aug. 6, 1920.

Woofter, Thomas Jackson, educationist, b. Spencer, Va., 1862; d. Athens, Ga., Aug. 8, 1938. [10]

Woolbert, Charles Henry, educationist, b. Ottawa, Ill., 1877; d. Iowa City, Ia., June 9, 1929. [10; 11]

Wooldridge, Charles William, physician, b. Hull, England, 1847; d. Helena, Mont., Oct. 16, 1908. [10]

Wooldridge, Clifton Rodman, detective, b. 1854; d. Chicago, Ill., Aug. 15, 1933.

Woolf, Philip, physician and novelist, b. New York, N.Y., 1848; d. New York, N.Y., 1903. [10]

Woolf, Samuel Johnson, artist and journalist, b. New York, N.Y., 1880; d. New York, N.Y., Dec. 3, 1948. [7; 10; 11]

Woollcott, Alexander, journalist, b. Phalanx, N.J., 1887; d. New York N.Y., Jan. 23, 1943. [7; 10; 12]

Woollen, William Watson, lawyer, b. Indianapolis, Ind., 1838; d. Indianapolis, Ind., March 26, 1921.

Woollen, William Wesley, historian, b. Dorchester county, Md., 1828; d. Indianapolis, Ind., Sept. 24, 1902.

Woolley, Mrs. Celia, née **Parker,** minister and novelist, b. Toledo, O., 1848; d. Chicago, Ill., March 9, 1918. [1; 7; 10]

Woolley, Edward Mott, journalist, b. Milwaukee, Wis., 1867; d. Passaic, N.J., March 31, 1947. [7; 10]

Woolley, Edwin Campbell, educationist, b. Paris, Ill., 1878; d. Madison, Wis., Jan. 26, 1916. [10]

Woolley, John Granville, prohibitionist, b. Collinsville, O., 1850; d. Granada, Spain, Aug. 13, 1922. [1; 4; 10]

Woolley, Paul Gerhardt, pathologist, b. Paris, Ill., 1875; d. Pasadena, Calif., 1932. [10]

Woolman, Mrs. Mary, née **Schenk,** educationist, b. Camden, N.J., 1860; d. Aug. 1, 1940. [10; 11]

Woolsey, Abby Howland, philanthropist, d. April 7, 1893. [3b]

Woolsey, Sarah Chauncey, writer of books for children, b. Cleveland, O., 1845; d. Newport, R.I., April 9, 1905. [1; 3; 4; 6; 7; 10; 15]

Woolsey, Theodore Dwight, educationist, b. New York, N.Y., 1801; d. New Haven, Conn., July 1, 1889. [1; 3; 4; 5; 6; 7; 62]

Woolsey, Theodore Salisbury, jurist and educationist, b. New Haven, Conn., 1852; d. New Haven, Conn., April 24, 1929. [1; 10; 62]

Woolson, Mrs. Abba Louisa, née **Gould,** poet and essayist, b. Windham, Me., 1838; d. Maine, Feb. 6, 1921. [1; 4; 7; 10]

Woolson, Constance Fenimore, novelist, b. Claremont, N.H., 1848; d. Venice, Italy, Jan. 23, 1894. [1; 3; 4; 7; 71]

Woolson, Grace A., gardener, b. 1856; d. 1911.

Woolwine, Thomas Lee, lawyer, b. near Nashville, Tenn., 1874; d. Los Angeles, Calif., July 8, 1925. [10]

Worcester, Benjamin, biographer, b. 1824; d. 1911.

Worcester, David, educationist, b. Boston, Mass., 1907; d. Montreal, Que., June 20, 1947. [14]

Worcester, Dean Conant, educationist and civil servant, b. Thetford, Vt., 1866; d. Manila, Philippine Islands, May 2, 1924. [4; 10]

Worcester, Elwood, clergyman, b. Massillon, O., 1863; d. Kennebunkport, Me., July 19, 1940. [4; 7; 10]

Worcester, John, religious leader, b. 1834; d. 1900.

Worcester, Joseph Emerson, lexicographer and historian, b. Bedford, N.H., 1784; d. Cambridge, Mass., Oct. 27, 1865. [1; 3; 4; 5; 6; 7; 8; 9; 62]

Worcester, Noah, clergyman, b. Hollis, N.H.,1758; d. Brighton, Mass., Oct. 31, 1837. [1; 3; 4; 6]

Worcester, Samuel, clergyman, b. Hollis, N.H., 1770; d. Brainerd, Tenn., June 7, 1821. [1; 3; 4; 6]

Worcester, Samuel, educationist, b. 1793; d. 1844.

Worcester, Samuel, physician, b. 1847; d. 1918. [51]

Worcester, Samuel Melanchthon, clergyman, b. Fitchburg, Mass., 1801; d. Boston, Mass., Aug. 16, 1866. [3; 6]

Worcester, Samuel Thomas, educationist, b. 1804; d. 1882. [51]

Worcester, William Loring, clergyman, b. Waltham, Mass., 1859; d. Cambridge, Mass., Sept. 29, 1939. [10; 51]

Worden, Edward Chauncey, chemist, b Ypsilanti, Mich., 1875; d. Milburn, N.J., Sept. 22, 1940. [10; 11; 12]

Worden, James Avery, clergyman, b. Oxford, O., 1841; d. Philadelphia, Pa., Oct. 24, 1917. [4; 10]

Worden, Mrs. Wilbertine, née Teters, novelist, b. Caldwell, O.; d. New York, N.Y., April 27, 1949.

Work, Edgar Whitaker, clergyman, b. Logan, O., 1862; d. Fryeburg, Me., April 17, 1934. [10]

Work, Henry Clay, composer, b. Middletown, Conn., 1832; d. Hartford, Conn., June 8, 1884. [2; 3; 4; 7]

Work, Milton Cooper, lawyer and bridge expert, b. Philadelphia, Pa., 1864; d. Philadelphia, Pa., June 27, 1934. [1; 10]

Workman, Benjamin, writer of school-books, fl. 1788-1816. [6]

Workman, Mrs. Fanny, née Bullock, explorer, b. Worcester, Mass., 1859; d. Cannes, France, Jan. 22, 1925. [1; 7; 10]

Workman, George Coulson, clergyman, b. Grafton, Ont., 1848; d. Toronto, Ont., April 22, 1936. [27]

Workman, James, lawyer, d. New Orleans, La., 1832.

Workman, William Hunter, surgeon and explorer, b. Worcester, Mass., 1847; d. Newton, Mass., Oct. 7, 1937. [4; 7; 10; 62]

Works, John Downey, jurist and politician, b. Ohio county, Ind., 1847; d. Los Angeles, Calif., June 6, 1928. [4; 10; 11]

Worman, James Henry, educationist, b. Berlin, Germany, 1845; d. Plattsburg, N.Y., Jan. 24, 1930. [10; 11]

Wormeley, Katharine Prescott, philanthropist, b. Ipswich, England, 1830; d. Jackson, N.H., Aug. 4, 1908. [1; 4; 7; 10]

Wormley, Theodore George, physician and toxicologist, b. Wormleysburg, Pa., 1826; d. Philadelphia, Pa., Jan. 3, 1897. [1; 4]

Worth, Gorham A., journalist, d. 1856. [6]

Worthen, Mrs. Augusta née Harvey, local historian, b. Sutton, N.H., 1823; d. Sutton, N.H., April 4, 1910.

Worthen, William Ezra, civil engineer, b. Amesbury, Mass., 1819; d. New York, N.Y., April 2, 1897. [1; 3; 4; 6]

Worthing, Archie Garfield, physicist, b. Le Roy, Wis., 1881; d. Pittsburgh, Pa., July 30, 1949. [10; 13]

Worthington, Edward William, clergyman, b. Batavia, N.Y., 1854; d. Cleveland, O., 1906. [4; 10]

Worthington, Erastus, lawyer, b. Belchertown, Mass., 1779; d. Dedham, Mass., June 27, 1842. [3; 6]

Worthington, George Fitzhugh, clergyman and poet, d. 1887. [6]

Worthington, Henry Slack, economist, b. 1856; d. ?

Worthington, Thomas, soldier, b. 1807; d. 1884.

Wortman, Denis, clergyman, b. East Fishkill, N.Y., 1835; d. East Orange, N.J., Aug. 28, 1922. [45]

Wortman, Tunis, lawyer, d. New York, N.Y., 1822. [6]

Woywod, Stanislaus, priest, b. Germany, 1880; d. New York, N.Y., Sept. 19. 1941. [21]

Wray, Newton, clergyman and educationist, b. Shelby county, Ind., 1854; d. Upland, Ind., April 18, 1933. [10]

Wren, Christopher, librarian, b. Pottsville, Pa., 1853; d. Wilkesbarre, Pa., 1921. [4; 10]

Wren, Thomas, lawyer and politician, b. McArthurstown, O., 1826; d. Reno, Nev., Feb. 5, 1904.

Wright, Adam Henry, obstetrician, b. Brampton, Ont., 1846; d. Toronto, Ont., Aug. 20, 1930. [27]

Wright, Albert Jay, broker and novelist, b. Oswego, N.Y., 1858; d. Cazenovia, N.Y., July 2, 1940.

Wright, Albert Orville, educationist, b. 1842; d. Madison, Wis., June 19, 1905.

Wright, Arthur Silas, educationist, b. Decatur, N.Y., 1858; d. Chevy Chase, Md., Dec. 2, 1928. [10]

Wright, Asher, missionary, b. Hanover, N.H., 1803; d. Cattaraugus, N.Y., April 13, 1875. [3; 6]

Wright, Augustine Washington, civil engineer, b. Chicago, Ill., 1847; d. Los Angeles, Calif., Feb. 3, 1918. [4; 10]

Wright, Austin Tappan, educationist, b. Hanover, N.H., 1883; d. New Mexico, Sept. 17, 1931. [10]

Wright, Benjamin Cooper, journalist, b. Troy, N.Y., 1834; d. San Francisco, Calif., Jan. 29, 1922.

Wright, Caleb, traveller, d. 1869. [6]

Wright, Carroll Davidson, educationist, b. Dunbarton, N.H., 1840; d. Worcester, Mass., Feb. 20, 1909. [1; 4; 7; 10]

Wright, Charles Baker, educationist, b. Cleveland, O., 1859; d. Middlebury, Vt., April 24, 1942. [10; 11]

Wright, Chauncey, philosopher, b. Northampton, Mass., 1830; d. Cambridge, Mass., Sept. 12, 1875. [1; 3; 4; 6; 51]

Wright, Cuthbert, educationist, b. Elmira, N.Y., 1899; d. Worcester, Mass., Nov. 28. 1948. [22; 51]

Wright, Daniel Thew, lawyer and novelist, b. Cincinnati, O., 1825; d. Cincinnati, O., Sept. 11, 1912. [62]

Wright, David, lawyer, b. 1806; d. 1877.

Wright, David Sands, educationist, b. 1847; d. Cedar Falls, Ia., Oct. 30, 1931. [37]

Wright, Elizur, reformer, b. South Canaan, Conn., 1804; d. Medford, Mass., Nov. 22, 1885. [1; 3; 4; 6; 62]

Wright, George Edward, historian, b. 1853; d. Hartford, Conn., 1926.

Wright, George Frederick, educationist, b. Whitehall, N.Y., 1838; d. Oberlin, O., April 20, 1921. [1; 3; 4; 5; 6; 7; 10; 11]

Wright, Grant, illustrator, b. Decatur, Mich., 1865; d. Weehawken, N.J., Oct. 20, 1935. [7; 9]

Wright, Harold Bell, novelist, b. Rome, N.Y., 1872; d. La Jolla, Calif., May 24, 1944. [7; 10; 11; 12; 35]

Wright, Hartley Hezekiah, traveller, d. 1840. [51]

Wright, Hendrick Bradley, politician, b. Plymouth, Pa., 1808; d. Wilkesbarre, Pa., Sept. 2, 1881. [1; 3; 4; 6]

Wright, Henrietta Christian, writer of books for children, d. 1899. [7]

Wright, Henry Burt, educationist, b. New Haven, Conn., 1877; d. Oakham, Mass., Dec. 27 ,1923. [10; 62]

Wright, Henry Clarke, reformer, b. Sharon, Conn., 1797; d. Pawtucket, R.I., Aug. 16, 1870. [3; 4; 6]

Wright, Henry Collier, sociologist, b. Le Roy, O., 1868; d. New York, N.Y., Oct. 24, 1935. [10 ;11]

Wright, Henry Parks, educationist, b. Winchester, N.H., 1839; d. New Haven, Conn., March 17, 1918. [4; 10; 62]

Wright, Horace Winslow, ornithologist, b. Dorchester, Mass., 1848; d. Boston, Mass., 1920. [51]

Wright, James A., local historian, b. Moravia, N.Y., 1838; d. Auburn, N.Y., March 9, 1923.

Wright, James Homer, pathologist, b. Pittsburgh, Pa., 1869; d. Boston, Mass., Jan. 3, 1928. [10]

Wright, James North, novelist, b. Middletown, Conn., 1838; d. 1910. [39]

Wright, John, clergyman, b. Wilmington, Del., 1836; d. St. Paul, Minn., Dec. 24, 1919. [4; 10; 70]

Wright, John Henry, educationist, b. Urmia, Persia, 1852; d. Cambridge, Mass., Nov. 25, 1908. [1; 4; 7; 10]

Wright, John Stephen, journalist, b. Sheffield, Mass., 1815; d. Philadelphia, Pa., Sept. 26, 1874. [1; 3; 6]

Wright, John Westley, opthalmologist, b. Freeport, O., 1842; d. Columbus, O., May 23, 1935. [4; 10]

Wright, Joseph W., civil engineer and grammarian, fl. 1838-1844.

Wright, Mrs. Julia, née **MacNair,** novelist, b. Oswego, N.Y., 1840; d. Fulton, Mo., Sept. 2, 1903. [6; 7; 10]

Wright, Mrs. Louise Sophie, née **Wigfall,** writer of reminiscences, b. Providence, R.I., 1846; d. Baltimore, Md., March 7, 1915. [10]

Wright, Mrs. Mabel, née **Osgood,** novelist and naturalist, b. New York, N.Y., 1859; d. Fairfield, Conn., July 21, 1934. [4; 7; 10]

Wright, Marcus Joseph, soldier and historian, b. Purdy, Tenn., 1831; d. Washington, D.C., Dec. 27, 1922. [1; 4; 7; 10; 34]

Wright, Mrs. Marie, née **Robinson,** traveller, b. Newnan, Ga., 1866; d. Liberty, Sullivan county, N.Y., Feb. 1, 1914. [7; 10]

Wright, Mrs. Mary, née **Tappan,** novelist, b. Steubenville, O., 1851; d. Cambridge, Mass., Aug. 28, 1916. [7; 10]

Wright, Merle St. Croix, clergyman, b. East Boston, Mass., 1859; d. New York, N.Y., April 26, 1925. [51]

Wright, Nathaniel Hill, poet, b. 1787; d. 1824. [43]

Wright, Philip Green, economist and poet, b. Boston, Mass., 1861; d. Washington, D.C., Sept. 4, 1934. [1; 7; 10]

Wright, Robert Creighton, poet, b. 1852; d. 1897.

Wright, Robert Emmet, lawyer, b. Allentown, Pa., 1810; d. 1886. [3; 6]

Wright, Robert Joseph, social scientist, fl. 1866-1881.

Wright, Robert Ramsay, biologist, b. Alloa, Scotland, 1852; d. Droitwich, Worcestershire, England, Sept. 6, 1933. [27]

Wright, Robert William, lawyer, b. Ludlow, Vt., 1816; d. Cleveland, O., Jan. 9, 1885. [1; 3; 7; 62]

Wright, Rowland (pseud.). See Wells, Carolyn.

Wright, Mrs. Sarah Ann, novelist, fl. 1859-1871. [3]

Wright, Theodore Francis, clergyman, b. Dorchester, Mass., 1845; d. at sea, Nov. 13, 1907. [10; 51]

Wright, Theodore Lyman, educationist, b. Beloit, Wis., 1858; d. Beloit, Wis., Oct. 4, 1926. [10; 11; 44]

Wright, Thomas Lee, physician, b. Windham, O., 1825; d. 1893. [3]

Wright, Thomas Wallace, educationist, b. Galloway, Scotland, 1842; d. Schenectady, N.Y., Sept. 13, 1908. [62]

Wright, Willard Huntington, art critic and writer of detective stories, b. Charlottesville, Va., 1888; d. New York, N.Y., April 11, 1939. [4; 7; 9; 10; 11]

Wright, William, journalist, b. Ireland, 1824; d. Paterson, N.J., March 13, 1866. [3; 6]

Wright, William, journalist, b. Ohio, May 9, 1829; d. West Lafayette, Ia., March 16, 1898. [1a]

Wright, William Bull, poet, b. Orange county, N.Y., 1840; d. Atlanta, Ga., March 29, 1880. [3; 6]

Wright, William Burnet, clergyman, b. Cincinnati, O., 1838; d. Buffalo, N.Y., Aug. 2, 1924. [4; 10; 49]

Wright, William Henry, engineer, b. Wilmington, N.C., 1814; d. Wilmington, N.C., Dec. 29, 1845. [3; 6; 34]

Wright, William Henry, naturalist, b. 1856; d. 1934.

Wrong, George McKinnon, historian, b. Grovesend, Ont., 1860; d. Toronto, Ont., June 29, 1948. [11; 30]

Wroth, Peregrine, physician, b. 1786; d. 1879.

Wyatt, Francis, chemist, b. England, about 1855; d. Forest Hills, Long Island, N.Y., Feb. 27, 1916.

Wyatt, Thomas, compiler, fl. 1838-1852. [6]

Wyche, Richard Thomas, lecturer, b. Granville county, N.C., 1867; d. Washington, D.C., May 5, 1930. [10; 11]

Wyche, William, lawyer, fl. 1794.

Wyckoff, Walter Augustus, educationist, b. Mainpuri, India, 1865; d. Princeton, N.J., May 15, 1908. [1; 10]

Wyckoff, William Cornelius, journalist, b. New York, N.Y., 1832; d. Brooklyn, N.Y., May 2, 1888. [3]

Wyckoff, William Henry, educationist, b. New York, N.Y., 1807; d. Brooklyn, N.Y., Nov. 2, 1877. [3; 6]

Wyer, Henry Sherman, photographer and artist, b. 1847; d. Nantucket, Mass., Jan. 31, 1920.

Wyeth, John, publisher, b. Cambridge, Mass., 1770; d. Harrisburg, Pa., Jan. 23, 1858. [1; 6]

Wyeth, John Allan, surgeon, b. Missionary Station, Marshall county, Ala., 1845; d. New York, N.Y., May 28, 1922. [1; 3; 6; 10; 34]

Wyeth, John B., pioneer, b. about 1805; d. ?

Wyeth, Newton, lawyer, b. 1854; d. ?

Wyeth, Samuel Douglas, writer of guidebooks, fl. 1865-1893.

Wyeth, Walter Newton, clergyman, b. Wendell, Mass., 1833; d. Philadelphia, Pa., Oct. 20, 1899. [67]

Wylie, Andrew, educationist, b. Washington, Pa., 1789; d. Indianapolis, Ind., Nov. 11, 1851. [1; 3; 4; 6; 7]

Wylie, David, journalist and poet, b. Renfrewshire, Scotland, 1811; d. Brockville, Ont., Dec. 21, 1891. [27]

Wylie, Edmund Kiskaddon, editor, b. Delaware, O., 1913; d. Warsaw, Poland, July 27, 1936. [45]

Wylie, Mrs Edna, née **Edwards,** novelist, b. Sibley, Ia., 1876; d. 1907. [10]

Wylie, Mrs. Elinor, née **Hoyt,** poet, b. Somerville, N.J., 1885; d. New York, N.Y., Dec. 16, 1928. [1; 4; 7; 10; 72]

Wylie, Laura Johnson, educationist, b. Milton, Pa., 1855; d. Poughkeepsie, N.Y., April 2, 1932. [10; 11; 62]

Wylie, Richard Cameron, theologian, b. near Zanesville, O., 1846; d. Pittsburgh, Pa., 1928. [10]

Wylie, Samuel Brown, clergyman, b. county Antrim, Ireland, 1772; d. Philadelphia, Pa., Oct. 13, 1852. [1; 3; 4; 6]

Wylie, Theodore William John, clergyman, b. Philadelphia, Pa., 1818; d. Philadelphia, Pa., June 11, 1898. [3; 4; 6]

Wylie, Walker Gill, physician, b. Chester, S.C., 1848; d. New York, N.Y., March 13, 1923. [10]

Wyman, Bruce, lawyer, b. Boston, Mass., 1876; d. Waban, Mass., June 21, 1926. [10; 51]

Wyman, Edwin Allen, clergyman, b. Skowhegan, Me., 1834; d. Malden, Mass., May 30, 1900. [67]

Wyman, Hal C., physician, b. Anderson, Ind., 1852; d. Detroit, Mich., March 9, 1908. [10]

Wyman, Jeffries, anatomist, b. Chelmsford, Mass., 1814; d. Bethlehem, N.H., Sept. 4, 1874. [1; 3; 5; 6]

Wyman, Mrs. Lillie Buffum, née **Chace,** poet and biographer, b. Valley Falls, R.I., 1847; d. Newtonville, Mass., Jan. 10, 1929. [10; 11]

Wyman, Morrill, physician, b. Chelmsford, Mass., 1812; d. Boston, Mass., Jan. 30, 1903. [1; 3; 6; 51]

Wyman, Seth, burglar, b. Goffstown, N.H., 1784; d. Goffstown, N.H., April 2, 1843. [1; 7]

Wyman, Thomas Bellows, genealogist, b. 1817; d. 1878.

Wyman, Walter, surgeon, b. St. Louis, Mo., 1848; d. Washington, D.C., Nov. 21, 1911. [7; 10]

Wyman, Walter Forestus, business executive, b. Boston, Mass., 1881; d. Arlington, Mass., Nov. 21, 1940. [10; 11]

Wynkoop, Matthew Bennett, poet and printer, fl. 1852. [19]

Wynkoop, Richard, civil servant and genealogist, b. 1829; d. 1913. [6]

Wynne, James, physician, b. Utica, N.Y., 1814; d. Guatemala, Central America, Feb. 11, 1871. [3; 6]

Wynne, John Joseph, priest and historian, b. New York, N.Y., 1859; d. New York, N.Y., Nov. 31, 1948. [10; 21; 22]

Wynne, Mrs. Madeline, née **Yale,** short-story writer, b. Newport, N.Y., 1847; d. 1918. [10]

Wythe, Joseph Henry, clergyman and physician, b. Manchester, England, 1822; d. Oakland, Calif., Oct. 11, 1901. [3; 35]

Wythes, Joseph Henry. See Wythe, Joseph Henry.

X

X. (pseud.). See Raymond, William Lee.

Xariffa (pseud.). See Townsend, Mrs. Mary Ashley, née Van Voorhis.

Y

Yaggy, Levi W., compiler, fl. 1873-1921.

Yale, Caroline Ardelia, educationist, b. Charlotte, Vt., 1848; d. Northampton, Mass., July 2, 1933. [1; 10]

Yale, Mrs. Catherine, née Brooks, historian, b. Vermont, 1818; d. 1900. [8]

Yale, Cyrus, clergyman, b. Lee, Mass., 1786; d. New Hartford, Conn., May 21, 1854. [3]

Yale, Elisha, clergyman, b. Lee, Mass., 1780; d. Kingsborough, N.Y., Jan. 9, 1853. [3]

Yale, Gregory, lawyer, b. 1816; d. 1871.

Yale, Leroy Milton, physician, b. Martha's Vineyard, Mass., 1841; d. Quisset, Mass., Sept. 12, 1906. [3; 10]

Yancey, Lewis Alonzo, aviator, b. Chicago, Ill., 1895; d. Yonkers, N.Y., March 2, 1940.

Yarborough, Minnie Clare, educationist, b. 1889; d. New York, N.Y., March 2, 1941.

Yard, Robert Sterling, journalist and editor, b. Haverstraw, N.Y., 1861; d. Washington, D.C., May 17, 1945. [7; 10; 11]

Yarrow, Henry Crécy, physician and naturalist, b. Philadelphia, Pa., 1840; d. Washington, D.C., 1929. [3]

Yates, John Van Ness, lawyer, b. Albany, N.Y., 1779; d. St. Louis, Mo., Nov. 27, 1873. [1; 3; 5]

Yates, Lorenzo Gordin, naturalist, b. England, 1837; d. 1909. [10]

Yates, William, abolitionist, b. England, 1767; d. Norris, Otsego county, N.Y., March 7, 1857. [3]

Yeager, George, physician, d. Merces, Pa., April 22, 1898.

Yeaman, George Helm, lawyer and politician, b. Hardin county, Ky., 1829; d. Jersey City, N.J., Feb. 23, 1908. [3; 4; 10]

Yechton, Barbara (pseud.). See Krausé, Lyda Farrington.

Yehoash (pseud.). See Bloomgarden, Solomon.

Yeigh, Frank, civil servant and journalist, b. Burford, Ont., 1861; d. Toronto, Ont., Oct. 26, 1935. [27]

Yeigh, Mrs. Kate Westlake, novelist, b. London, Ont., 1856; d. Toronto, Ont., March 4, 1906. [27]

Yeiser, John Otto, lawyer, b. Danville, Ky., 1866; d. Omaha, Neb., March, 1928. [10; 11]

Yellott, George, satirist, b. 1819; d. ?

Yendes, Lucy A., educationist and journalist, b. Champion, Jefferson county, N.Y., 1851; d. ? [7; 10]

Yeo, Gerald Francis, physician, b. 1845; d. 1909.

Yeoman, Eric McKay, poet, b. Newcastle, N.B., 1885; d. February, 1909. [27]

Yingling, William A., physician, b. 1851; d. ?

Yoakum, Clarence Stone, psychologist, b. Leavenworth county, Kans., 1879; d. Ann Arbor, Mich., Nov. 20, 1945. [10]

Yoakum, Henderson, historian, b. Claiborne county, Tenn., 1810; d. Houston, Tex., Nov. 30, 1856. [1; 3; 5; 7; 9]

Yocum, Albert Duncan, educationist, b. York, Pa., 1869; d. Ridley Park, Pa., June 8, 1936. [10]

Yocum, Wilbur Fisk, educationist, b. Salem, O., 1840; d. ? [10]

Yohannan, Abraham, clergyman, b. 1853; d. Nov. 9, 1925. [48]

Yore, Clement, journalist and novelist, b. St. Louis, Mo., 1875; d. Estes Park, Colo., Oct. 24, 1936. [7; 10; 11]

York, Brantley, clergyman and educationist, b. Randolph county, N.C., 1805; d. Forest City, N.C., Oct. 7, 1891. [4]

York, Samuel Albert, banker, b. New Haven, Conn., 1868; d. New Haven, Conn., March 7, 1931. [10; 62]

York, Thomas, financial editor, b. Mount Carmel, Pa., 1883; d. New York, N.Y., Jan. 12, 1941.

Yorke, Anthony (pseud.). See Reilly, Bernard James.

Yorke, Peter Christopher, clergyman, b. Galway City, Ireland, 1864; d. San Francisco,. Calif., April 5, 1925. [1; 10]

Yorkel, Hans (pseud.). See Hall, Abraham Oakey.

Yost, Casper Salathiel, journalist, b. Sedalia, Mo., 1864; d. St. Louis, Mo., May 30, 1941. [7; 10]

Youmans, Edward Livingston, scientist, b. Albany county, N.Y., 1821; d. New York, N.Y., Jan. 18, 1887. [1; 3; 4; 5; 6; 7]

Youmans, Eliza Ann, botanist, b. Saratoga, N.Y., 1826; d. ? [3; 4]

Youmans, Mrs. Letitia, née Creighton, temperance reformer, b. Cobourg, Upper Canada, 1827; d. Toronto, Ont., July 19, 1891. [27]

Youmans, William Jay, editor, b. Saratoga, N.Y., 1838; d. Mount Vernon, N.Y., April 10, 1901. [1; 3; 4; 5; 7; 10]

Young, Abraham Van Eps, chemist, b. Sheboygan, Wis., 1853; d. Hendersonville, N.C., Dec. 23, 1921. [10; 11]

Young, Alexander, clergyman and historian, b. Boston, Mass., 1800; d. Boston, Mass., March 16, 1854. [1; 3; 5; 6; 7]

Young, Alexander, journalist and historian, b. Boston, Mass., 1836; d. Boston, Mass., March 19, 1891. [3b]

Young, Alfred, priest, b. Bristol, England, 1831; d. New York, N.Y., April 4, 1900. [1; 3b; 4; 7]

Young, Allyn Abbott, economist, b. Kenton, O., 1876; d. London, England, March 7, 1929. [1; 10]

Young, Andrew White, journalist and politician, b. Carlisle, N.Y., 1802; d. Warsaw, N.Y., Feb. 17, 1877.

Young, Mrs. Ann Eliza, née **Webb,** Mormon wife, b. 1844; d. ?

Young, Archibald Hope, historian, b. Sarnia, Ont., 1863; d. Toronto., Ont., April 6, 1935. [27]

Young, Arthur Henry, cartoonist and editor, b. near Orangeville, Ill., 1866; d. New York, N.Y., Dec. 29, 1943. [7]

Young, Augustus, lawyer and naturalist, b. Arlington, Vt., 1785; d. St. Alban's, Vt., June 17, 1857. [3; 4]

Young, Bennett Henderson, lawyer and historian, b. Nicholasville, Ky., 1843; d. Louisville, Ky., Feb. 23, 1919. [4; 10]

Young, Charles Augustus, astronomer, b. Hanover, N.H., 1834; d. Hanover, N.H., Jan. 4, 1908. [1; 3; 4; 5; 6; 10]

Young, Charles Lowell, educationist, b. Somerville, Mass., 1865; d. Wellesley, Mass., Oct. 10, 1937. [51]

Young, Claiborne Addison, poet, b. 1843; d. Lafayette, Ind., Nov. 3, 1912. [68]

Young, Clark Montgomery, educationist, b. Hiram, O., 1856; d. Vermillion, S.D., Feb. 28, 1908. [1; 10]

Young, David, poet and astronomer, b. Morris county, N.J., 1781; d. Hanover Neck, N.J., Feb. 13, 1852. [1; 4; 7]

Young, Egerton Ryerson, missionary, b. Crosby, Upper Canada, 1840; d. Bradford, Ont., Oct. 5, 1909. [27]

Young, Mrs. Ella, née **Flagg,** educationist, b. Buffalo, N.Y., 1845; d. Chicago, Ill., Oct. 26, 1918. [1; 4; 10]

Young, Ernest A., novelist, fl. 1883-1902.

Young, Ernest William, lawyer, b. 1860; d. ?

Young, Eugene Jared, journalist, b. Richfield, Utah, 1874; d. New York, N.Y., Feb. 22, 1939.

Young, Francis Crissey, pioneer, b. New York, N.Y., 1844; d. 1919. [7]

Young, Frederic George, historian, b. Burnett, Wis., 1858; d. Eugene, Ore., Jan. 4, 1929. [4; 10; 41]

Young, George, clergyman, b. Prince Edward county, Upper Canada, 1821; d. Toronto, Ont., Aug. 1, 1910. [27]

Young, George Paxton, educationist, b. Berwick-on-Tweed, England, 1819; d. Toronto, Ont., Feb. 26, 1889. [27]

Young, George Renny, journalist, b. Falkirk, Scotland, 1802; d. Halifax, N.S., June 30, 1853. [27]

Young, Gilbert Amos, educationist, b. Owosso, Mich., 1872; d. Lafayette, Ind., June 28, 1943. [10]

Young, Gordon Ray, novelist, b. Ray county, Mo., 1886; d. Los Angeles, Calif., Feb. 10, 1948. [7; 10; 35]

Young, Harry, pioneer, b. 1849; d. ? [41]

Young, Harry H., journalist, b. Virginia, 1825; d. St. Paul, Minn., Feb. 10, 1896. [70]

Young, Henry McClure, surgeon, b. St. Louis, Mo., 1877; d. Columbia, Mo., Aug. 12, 1946. [62]

Young, Hugh Hampton, surgeon, b. San Antonio, Tex., 1870; d. Baltimore, Md., Aug. 23, 1945. [10]

Young, Israel Gilbert, physician, b. 1840; d. Philadelphia, Pa., 1899. [55]

Young, Jacob, clergyman, b. Alleghany county, Pa., 1776; d. Harrisburg, O., Sept. 15, 1859. [3]

Young, James, politician, b. Galt, Upper Canada, 1835; d. Galt, Ont., Jan. 29, 1913. [27]

Young, James Capers, journalist, b. Atlanta, Ga., 1888; d. New York, N.Y., Oct. 27, 1945. [7]

Young, James Kelly, surgeon, b. Trenton, N.J., 1862; d. Philadelphia, Pa., Aug. 28, 1923. [4; 10]

Young, James Rankin, soldier and politician, b. Philadelphia, Pa., 1847; d. Washington, D.C., Dec. 18, 1924. [4; 10]

Young, Jesse Bowman, soldier and clergyman, b. Berwick, Pa., 1844; d. Chicago, Ill., July 30, 1914. [1; 4; 10]

Young, John, writer on agriculture, b. near Falkirk, Scotland, 1773; d. Halifax, N.S., Oct. 26, 1837. [27]

Young, John Freeman, bishop, b. Pittston, Me., 1820; d. New York, N.Y., Nov. 15, 1885. [3; 4]

Young, John Philip, journalist, b. Philadelphia, Pa., 1849; d. San Francisco, Calif., April 23, 1921. [4; 10]

Young, John Russell, journalist, b. Downington, Pa., 1841; d. Washington, D.C., Jan. 17, 1899. [1; 3; 4; 6; 7]

Young, John Wesley, mathematician, b. Columbus, O., 1879; d. Hanover, N.H., Feb. 17, 1932. [4; 10; 11]

Young, Mrs. Julia Evelyn, née **Ditto,** poet and novelist, b. Buffalo, N.Y., 1857; d. Buffalo, N.Y., April 19, 1915. [7; 10]

Young, Karl, educationist, b. Clinton, Ia., 1879; d. New Haven, Conn., Nov. 17, 1943. [7; 10; 11]

Young, Mrs. Kathleen, née **Millay,** See Millay, Kathleen.

Young, Lafayette, journalist and politician, b. Iowa, 1848; d. Des Moines, Ia., Nov. 15, 1926. [1; 10; 37]

Young, Loyal, clergyman, b. Charlemont, Mass., 1806; d. about 1890. [3]

Young, Lucien, naval officer, b. Lexington, Ky., 1852; d. New York, N.Y., Oct. 2, 1912. [4; 10]

Young, Mrs. Maude Jeannie, née **Fuller,** botanist, b. 1826; d. 1882.

Young, Richard Whitehead, lawyer, b. Salt Lake City, Utah, 1858; d. Salt Lake City, Utah, Dec. 27, 1919. [10]

Young, Mrs. Rida, née **Johnson,** playwright, b. Baltimore, Md., 1875; d. Southfield, Conn., May 8, 1926. [10]

Young, Robert Anderson, clergyman, b. Knox county, Tenn., 1824; d. Nashville, Tenn., 1902. [4; 10; 34]

Young, Rose Emmet, novelist, b. Lafayette county, Mo., 1869; d. Mount Kisco, N.Y., July 6, 1941. [7; 10; 11]

Young, Samuel, "the literary drayman", b. Pittsburgh, Pa., 1821; d. Butler county, Pa., March 27, 1891. [7]

Young, Samuel Hall, missionary, b. Butler, Pa., 1847; d. near Clarksburg, W.Va., Sept. 2, 1927. [1; 7; 10]

Young, Samuel Oliver, local historian, b. 1847; d. Houston, Tex., Feb. 16, 1926.

Young, Thomas Shields, clergyman, b. Davenport, Ia., 1863; d. 1928. [10]

Young, Mrs. Virginia, née **Durant,** novelist, b. Marion, S.C.; d. Fairfax, S.C., Nov. 2, 1906. [34]

Young, Walter Jorgensen, educationist, b. Owensboro, Ky., 1883; d. Fredericksburg, Va., Nov. 23, 1940. [10; 11]

Young, William, journalist, b. Deptford, England, 1809; d. Paris, France, April 15, 1888. [3]

Young, William, playwright, b. Illinois, 1847; d. Oct. 5, 1920. [10]

Young, William Henry, clergyman, b. Philadelphia, Pa., 1853; d. Mount Vernon, N.Y., March 14, 1937. [62]

Young, William Playford, entertainer, b. 1898; d. 1936.

Young, William T., lawyer, fl. 1852-1856.

Younger, Cole, bandit, b. 1844; d. March 21, 1916.

Youngman, Elmer Haskell, economist, b. New Lebanon, Ind., 1861; d. Brooklyn, N.Y., Oct. 13, 1948.

Youngs, Benjamin Seth, shaker, b. about 1773; d. ?

Youngs, James, clergyman, fl. 1820-1831.

Youtz, Herbert Alden, clergyman, b. Des Moines, Ia., 1867; d. Springfield, Mass., March 20, 1943. [10]

Yule, Mrs. Pamelia S., née **Vining,** poet, b. New York; d. Ingersoll, Ont., March 6, 1897. [27]

Yung Wing, educationist, b. near Macao, China, 1828; d. Hartford, Conn., April 21, 1912. [10; 62]

Z

Zabriskie, Francis Nicoll, clergyman, b. Hackensack, N.J., 1832; d. Princeton, N.J., May 31, 1891. [3b]

Zabriskie, Luther Kimbell, consul, b. Preston, Conn., 1879; d. Aguascalientes, Mexico, Jan. 17, 1921. [62]

Zachos, John Celivergos, educationist, b. Constantinople, Turkey, 1820; d. New York, N.Y., March 20, 1898. [3; 6]

Zahm, John Augustine, priest and educationist, b. New Lexington, O., 1851; d. Washington, D.C., Nov. 11, 1921. [4; 7; 10; 21]

Zane, John Maxcy, lawyer, b. Springfield, Ill., 1863; d. Chicago, Ill., Dec. 6, 1937. [10]

Zartman, Lester William, economist, b. Kankakee, Ill., 1878; d. Savoy Centre, Mass., Oct. 19, 1909. [62]

Zeigen, Frederic, clergyman, b. Saginaw, Mich., 1874; d. Detroit, Mich., May 20, 1942. [4; 7; 10; 11]

Zeigler, Wilbur Gleason, lawyer, b. Fremont, O., Sept. 29, 1857; d. ? [35]

Zeisberger, David, missionary, b. Moravia, 1721; d. Goshen, O., Nov. 17, 1808. [1; 3; 4; 27]

Zeitlin, Jacob, educationist, b. Gorky, Russia, 1883; d. Urbana, Ill., Dec. 8, 1937. [7; 10; 11]

Zelie, John Sheridan, clergyman, b. Princeton, Mass., 1866; d. Daytona Beach, Fla., Nov. 9, 1942. [7; 62]

Zema, Demetrius, priest, b. Reggio Calabria, Italy, 1886; d. New York, N.Y., Feb. 1, 1948. [21]

Zeno (pseud.). See Ross, Dunbar.

Zenos, Andrew Constantinides, clergyman, b. Constantinople, Turkey, 1855; d. Chicago, Ill., Jan. 25, 1942. [7; 10]

Zerbe, Alvin Sylvester, clergyman, b. Reading, Pa., 1847; d. Dayton, O., March 21, 1935. [10; 11]

Zerbe, James Slough, engineer, b. Womelsdorf, Pa., 1849; d. ? [7; 10]

Zeuner, Charles, musician, b. Eisleben, Germany, 1795; d. near Philadelphia, Pa., Nov. 7, 1857. [3; 4]

Ziegler, George Jacob, physician, b. 1821; d. Philadelphia, Pa., Feb. 20, 1895.

Ziegler, Henry, clergyman, b. near Old Fort, Centre county, Pa., 1816; d. Selinsgrove, Pa., Nov. 25, 1898. [3b]

Ziegler, Jesse A., bookseller, b. Galveston, Tex., 1857; d. Austin, Tex., Nov. 15, 1947.

Zigler, David Howard, clergyman, b. near Broadway, Va., 1857; d. Oct. 28, 1930. [10]

Zim (pseud.). See Zimmerman, Eugene.

Zimmerman, Eugene, cartoonist, b. Basel, Switzerland, 1862; d. near Elmira, N.Y., March 26, 1935. [1a; 7; 10]

Zimmerman, James Fulton, educationist, b. Glen Allen, Mo., 1887; d. Albuquerque, N.M., Oct. 21, 1944. [10]

Zimmerman, Jeremiah, clergyman, b. Snydersburg, Md., 1848; d. Syracuse, N.Y., Feb. 19, 1937. [10; 11]

Zimmerman, Thomas Cadwallader, journalist, b. Lebanon, Pa., 1838; d. Reading, Pa., Nov. 9, 1914. [10]

Zinsser, Hans, physician, b. New York, N.Y., 1878; d. New York, N.Y., Sept. 4, 1940. [7; 10]

Ziska (pseud.). See Cummings, Amos Jay.

Ziwet, Alexander, educationist, b. Breslau, Germany, 1853; d. Ann Arbor, Mich., Nov. 18, 1928. [10]

Zogbaum, Mrs. Baird Leonard, poet and journalist, b. 1889; d. New York, N.Y., Jan. 23, 1941. [7]

Zogbaum, Rufus Fairchild, artist, b. Charleston, S.C., 1849; d. New York, N.Y., Oct. 22, 1925. [7; 10]

Zollars, Ely Vaughan, clergyman and educationist, b. Salem, O., 1847; d. Warren, O., Feb. 10, 1916. [1; 4; 10]

Zollinger, Gulielma, writer of books for young people, b. Illinois, 1856; d. Newton, Ia., Aug. 24, 1917. [10; 15]

Zorbaugh, Charles Louis, clergyman, poet, and genealogist, b. Northfield, Ia., 1867; d. Toledo, O., Aug. 18, 1943.

Zucrow, Solomon, rabbi, b. 1870; d. 1932.

Zueblin, Charles, educationist, b. Pendleton, Ind., 1866; d. Corsier-Port, Switzerland, Sept. 15, 1924. [4; 10; 62]

Zundel, John, musician, b. Germany, 1815; d. Cannstadt, Germany, July, 1882. [4; 6]

Zunder, Theodore Albert, educationist, b. New Haven. Conn., 1901; d. Brooklyn, N.Y., Dec. 20, 1945. [62]

Zurcher, George, clergyman, b. Alsace, France, 1852; d. North Evans, N.Y., Sept. 10, 1931. [10]

Zybura, John Stanislaus, priest, b. Cleveland, O.; d. Colorado, Oct., 1934. [21; 22]

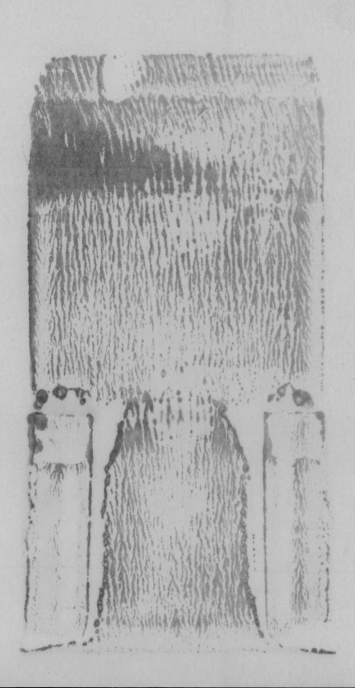